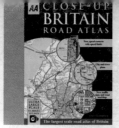

GW00360396

Atlas content

Map pages south	inside front cover

Route planning	**2–23**
Route planner	2–7
Speed cameras	8–17
Satnav friendly places to visit with postcodes	18–19
Traffic signs and road markings	20–23

Atlas symbols	**1**

Road maps	**2–609**

Britain at 1:100,000 scale

2–475, 480–503, 510–515, 526–529, 538–541, 554–561

Isles of Scilly 1:150,000 scale	3
Channel Islands 1:150,000 scale	34–35
Isle of Man 1:190,000 scale	322
Islay & Jura 1:150,000 scale	476–479
Mull, Tiree & Coll 1:150,000 scale	504–505, 516–518
Scottish Highlands 1:150,000 scale	
	506–509, 518–525, 531–537, 546–553, 562–589
Skye & Small Isles 1:150,000 scale	530, 542–545
Western Isles 1:150,000 scale	590–599
Orkney & Shetland Islands 1:150,000 scale	600–609

Ferry Ports		**11–561**

Aberdeen Harbour	561	Heysham Harbour	350	Port of Southampton	36
Calais/Coquelles Terminal	83	Holyhead Harbour	302	Port of Tyne	407
		Hull Port	349	Stranraer Ferry Port	414
Dover Port	83	Newhaven Harbour	56	Swansea Harbour	103
Fishguard Harbour	150	Plymouth Ferry Port	11	Weymouth Harbour	33
Folkestone Terminal	82	Poole Harbour	35		
Harwich Int. Port	177	Portsmouth Harbour	37		

Restricted junctions	**610–611**

Central London	**612–624**
Central London 1:10,000 scale	612–619

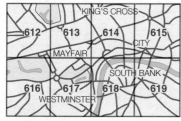

Central London street index	620–624

Town and airport plans	**625–651**

Aberdeen	625
Aberystwyth	204
Bath	625
Birmingham	627
Birmingham Airport	651
Blackpool	336
Bournemouth	626
Bradford	626
Brighton	55
Bristol	628
Brixham	13
Cambridge	629
Cardiff	628
Cheltenham	630
Coventry	630
Derby	631
Dover	631
Dundee	515
Durham	632
Edinburgh	633
Gatwick Airport	650
Glasgow	634
Glasgow Airport	651
Heathrow Airport	650
Inverness	632
Kingston upon Hull	635
Lancaster	350
Leeds	636
Leeds Bradford Airport	651
Leicester	635
Liverpool	637
Llandudno	306
London Central	612–619
Luton Airport	650
Manchester	638
Manchester Airport	651
Middlesbrough	397
Milton Keynes	639
Newcastle upon Tyne	640
Newquay	6
Norwich	641
Nottingham	641
Oxford	642
Paignton	21
Plymouth	10
Portsmouth	643
St Andrews	503
Scarborough	375
Sheffield	645
Southend-on-Sea	123
Southampton	644
Stansted Airport	650
Stockton-on-Tees	645
Stoke-on-Trent (Hanley)	646
Stratford-upon-Avon	646
Sunderland	407
Swansea	647
Swindon	647
Torquay	21
Tunbridge Wells	648
Wolverhampton	648
Worcester	649
York	649

Gazetteer of map entries & Distance chart	**652–728**
Using the National Grid	652
County, administrative area map	653
Recreation and leisure index	654–668
City, town and village index	669–727
Distance chart	728

Map pages north	inside back cover

2nd edition October 2008

© Automobile Association Developments Limited 2008

Original edition published 2006

Cartography:
All cartography in this atlas edited, designed and produced by the Mapping Services Department of AA Publishing (A03737b).

This product includes mapping data licensed from Ordnance Survey® with the permission of the Controller of Her Majesty's Stationery Office. © Crown copyright and database rights 2008. All rights reserved. Licence number 100021153.

Publisher's Notes:
Published by AA Publishing (a trading name of Automobile Association Developments Limited, whose registered office is Fanum House, Basing View, Basingstoke, Hampshire RG21 4EA, UK. Registered number 1878835).

ISBN: 978 0 7495 5806 2

A CIP catalogue record for this book is available from The British Library.

Disclaimer:
The contents of this atlas are believed to be correct at the time of the latest revision, it will not contain any subsequent amended, new or temporary information including diversions and traffic control or enforcement systems. The publishers cannot be held responsible or liable for any loss or damage occasioned to any person acting or refraining from action as a result of any use or reliance on material in this atlas, nor for any errors, omissions or changes in such material. This does not affect your statutory rights.

The publishers would welcome information to correct any errors or omissions and to keep this atlas up to date. Please write to the Atlas Editor, AA Publishing, The Automobile Association, Fanum House, Basing View, Basingstoke, Hampshire RG21 4EA, UK. E-mail: roadatlasfeedback@theaa.com

Acknowledgements:
AA Publishing would like to thank the following for their cooperation in producing this atlas:

RoadPilot® Information on fixed speed camera locations provided by RoadPilot © 2008 RoadPilot Driving Technology. Information on truckstops and transport cafés provided by John Eden (www.transportcafe.co.uk). A&E hospitals derived from data supplied by Johnsons. Filling station information supplied by Johnsons. Channel Islands updates provided by David Moran. Marina information supplied by Noble Marine (Insurance Brokers) Ltd (www.noblemarine.co.uk). National Cycle Network information supplied by Sustrans Limited (www.sustrans.org.uk) 0845 113 0065. Crematoria data provided by The Cremation Society of Great Britain. Cadw, English Heritage, English Nature, Forestry Commission, Historic Scotland, National Trust and National Trust for Scotland, Natural England, RSPB, Scottish Natural Heritage, The Countryside Council for Wales (road maps).

Crown copyright material (pages 10, 20–23) reproduced under licence from the Controller of HMSO and the Driving Standards Agency.

Schools address data provided by Education Direct. One-way street data provided by © Tele Atlas N.V. The copyright in all Postal Address Files (London postcodes) is owned by Royal Mail Group plc. The boundary of the London Congestion Charging Zone supplied by Transport for London (Central London mapping).

Tram and Metro system logos used by kind permission of Nottingham Express Transit, Subway (Glasgow) and Tyne & Wear Metro (town plans).

Printer:
Printed in Italy by Canale & C. S.p.A., Torino on paper produced from environmentally sustainable sources.

Paper:
80gsm Matt coated paper.

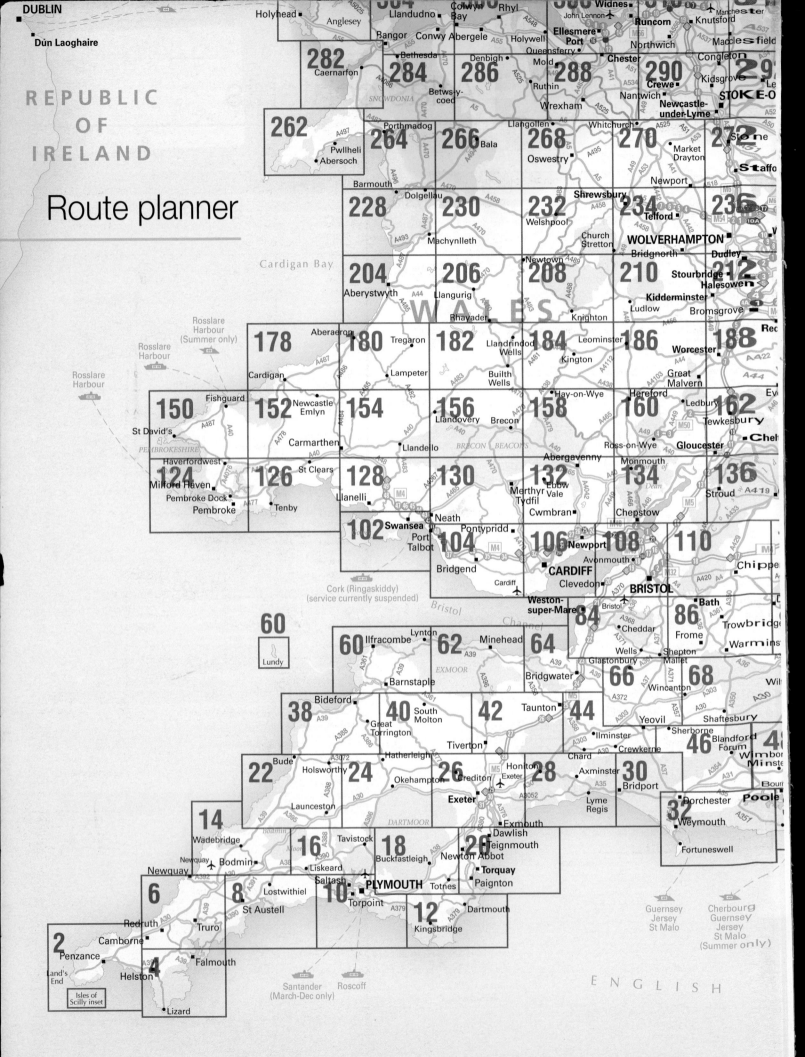

DUBLIN
Dún Laoghaire

REPUBLIC
OF
IRELAND

Route planner

Holyhead
Anglesey
Bangor
Bethesda
Caernarfon
Betws-y-coed

282
284
286
288
290

Llandudno
Colwyn Bay
Rhyl
Abergele
Conwy
Denbigh
Holywell
Queensferry
Mold
Ruthin
Wrexham
Whitchurch

Widnes
John Lennon
Runcorn
Ellesmere Port
Northwich
Chester
Crewe
Nantwich
Newcastle-under-Lyme

Knutsford
Macclesfield
Congleton
Kidsgrove
STOKE-O

SNOWDONIA

262
264
266
268
270
272

Porthmadog
Pwllheli
Abersoch
Bala
Llangollen
Oswestry
Market Drayton
Newport
Stone
Staffo

Cardigan Bay

228
230
232
234
236

Barmouth
Dolgellau
Machynlleth
Welshpool
Shrewsbury
Church Stretton
Telford
WOLVERHAMPTON
Bridgnorth
Dudley
Stourbridge
Halesowen

204
206
208
210
212

Aberystwyth
Llangurig
Newtown
Rhayader
Knighton
Ludlow
Kidderminster
Bromsgrove
Red

W A L E S

178
180
182
184
186
188

Aberaeron
Tregaron
Llandrindod Wells
Leominster
Worcester
Cardigan
Lampeter
Builth Wells
Kington
Great Malvern

Rosslare Harbour (Summer only)
Rosslare Harbour
Rosslare Harbour

150
152
154
156
158
160
162

Fishguard
St David's
Newcastle Emlyn
Carmarthen
Llandovery
Brecon
Hay-on-Wye
Hereford
Ledbury
Tewkesbury
Chel

PEMBROKESHIRE
Llandello
BRECON BEACONS
Ross-on-Wye
Gloucester

124
126
128
130
132
134
136

Haverfordwest
Milford Haven
St Clears
Llanelli
Merthyr Tydfil
Ebbw Vale
Monmouth
Stroud
Pembroke Dock
Pembroke
Tenby
Neath
Cwmbran
Chepstow

102
104
106
108
110

Swansea
Port Talbot
Pontypridd
Newport
Avonmouth
Chippe
Bridgend
Cardiff
CARDIFF
Clevedon
BRISTOL

Cork (Ringaskiddy) (service currently suspended)

Bristol Channel

Weston-super-Mare
Bristol
Bath
Cheddar
Frome
Trowbridge
Wells
Shepton Mallet
Warmins

84
86

60
Lundy

60
62
64
66
68

Ilfracombe
Lynton
Minehead
Barnstaple
Bridgwater
Glastonbury
Wincanton
EXMOOR
Wells

38
40
42
44

Bideford
South Molton
Taunton
Yeovil
Shaftesbury
Great Torrington
Tiverton
Ilminster
Sherborne

46
48

Blandford Forum
Wimbor
Minste

22
24
26
28
30

Bude
Holsworthy
Hatherleigh
Okehampton
Crediton
Exeter
Honiton
Chard
Axminster
Crewkerne
Bridport
Lyme Regis

14

Launceston
Exeter
Exmouth
DARTMOOR

32

Dorchester
Weymouth
Fortuneswell
Poole
Bourn

Wadebridge
Bodmin
Newquay
Tavistock
Buckfastleigh
Newton Abbot
Dawlish
Teignmouth

16
18
20

Liskeard
Saltash
PLYMOUTH
Torquay
Paignton

6
8
10
12

Newquay
Lostwithiel
St Austell
Torpoint
Totnes
Kingsbridge
Dartmouth

Redruth
Truro

Guernsey
Jersey
St Malo
Cherbourg
Guernsey
Jersey
St Malo
(Summer only)

2
Penzance
Camborne
Land's End
Isles of Scilly inset

4
Falmouth
Helston
Lizard

Santander (March-Dec only)
Roscoff

E N G L I S H

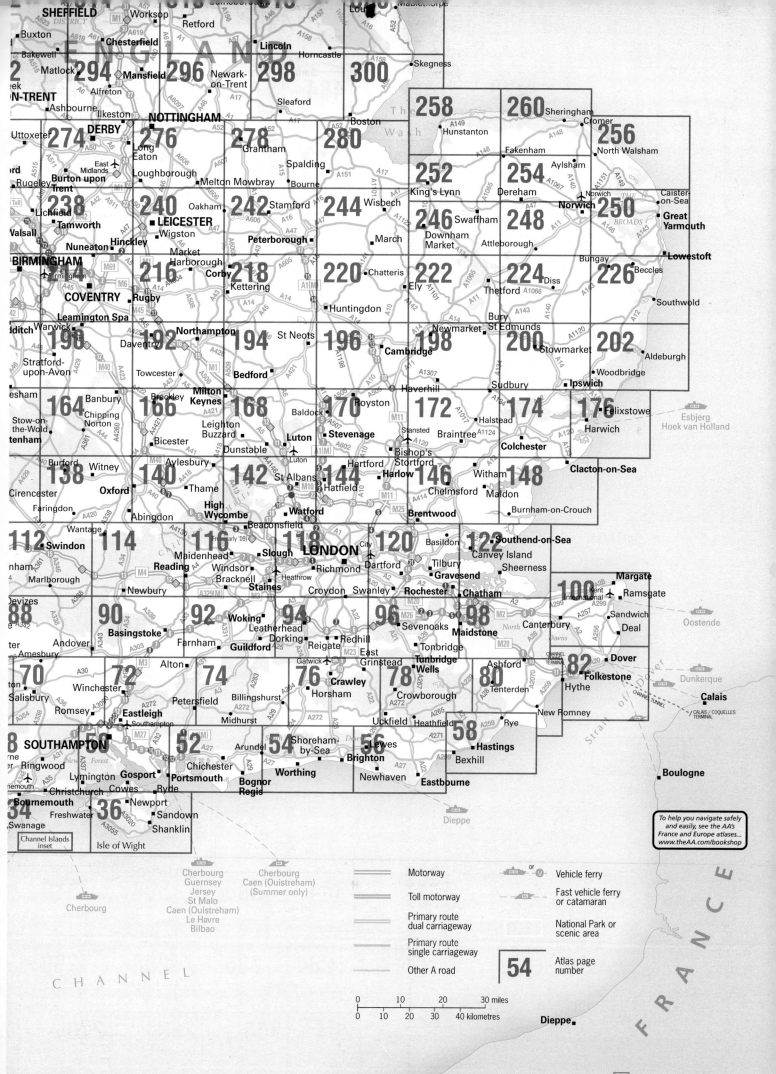

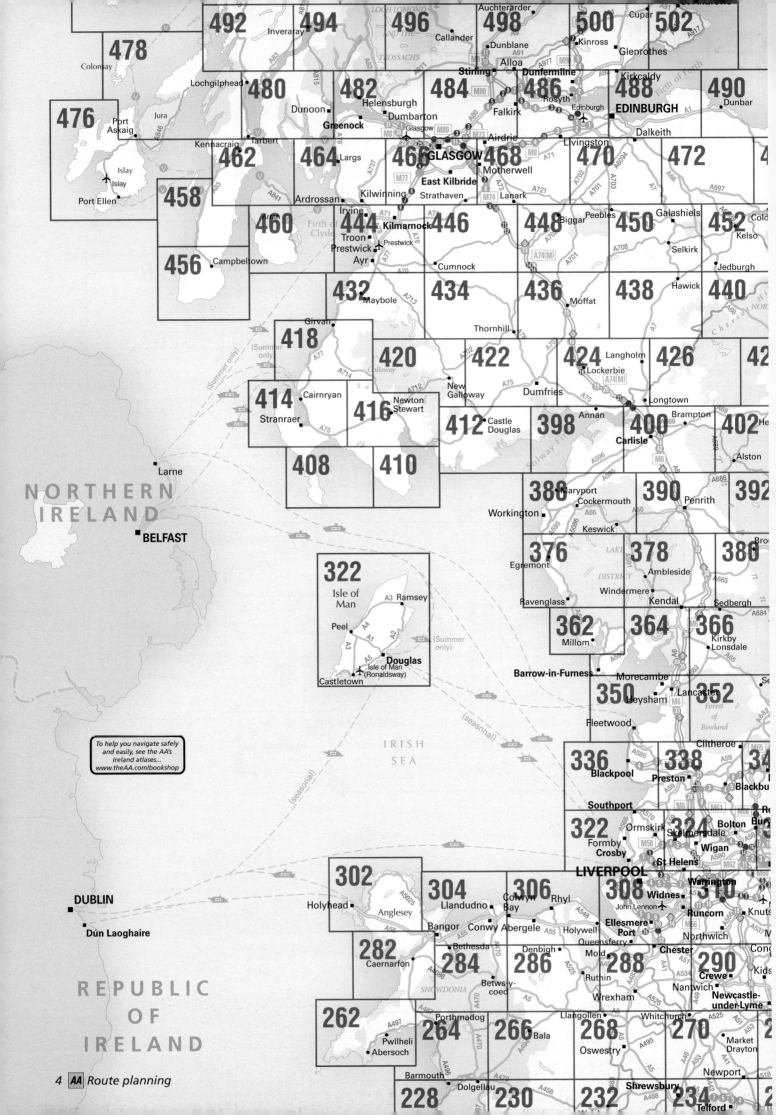

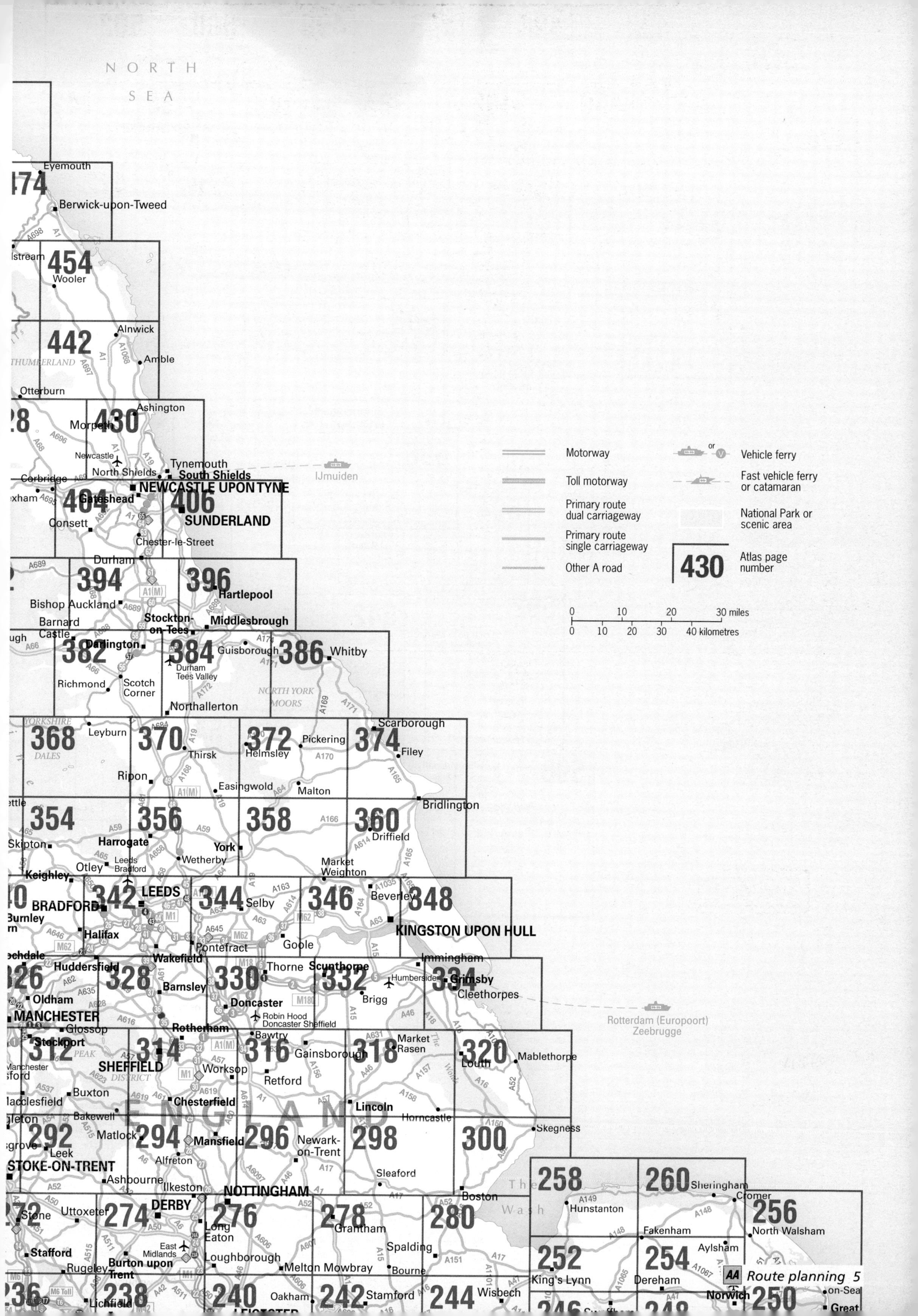

NORTH

SEA

Eyemouth

Berwick-upon-Tweed

474

lstream

454
Wooler

442 Alnwick

Amble

THUMBERLAND

28 Otterburn

430 Ashington
Morpeth

Newcastle
North Shields **Tynemouth**
Corbridge **South Shields** IJmuiden

xham **NEWCASTLE UPON TYNE**
404 **Gateshead**
Consett **406**
SUNDERLAND
Chester-le-Street

Durham
394 **396** **Hartlepool**
Bishop Auckland
Barnard **Stockton-on-Tees** **Middlesbrough**
Castle **382** **Darlington** **384** Guisborough **386** Whitby
Richmond Scotch Durham
Corner Tees Valley
Northallerton NORTH YORK
MOORS

YORKSHIRE Scarborough
368 Leyburn **370** **372** Pickering **374**
DALES Thirsk Helmsley Filey
Ripon Easingwold Malton
Bridlington
354 **356** **358** **360**
Skipton **Harrogate** **York** Driffield
Keighley Otley Leeds Wetherby Market
Bradford Weighton
BRADFORD **342** **LEEDS** **344** Selby **346** Beverley **348**
Burnley Halifax Goole **KINGSTON UPON HULL**
rn Wakefield Pontefract
chdale Huddersfield **328** Immingham
26 Barnsley Thorne **Scunthorpe** **334** **Grimsby**
Oldham **330** **332** Humberside Cleethorpes
MANCHESTER Doncaster Brigg Rotterdam (Europoort)
Glossop Rotherham Robin Hood Zeebrugge
Stockport **314** Doncaster Sheffield
312 Bawtry **631** Market
SHEFFIELD Worksop **316** Gainsborough **318** Rasen **320**
Buxton DISTRICT Retford Louth Mablethorpe
Macclesfield PEAK **Chesterfield** Lincoln
Bakewell Horncastle Skegness
292 Matlock **294** **Mansfield** **296** Newark-on-Trent **298** **300**
STOKE-ON-TRENT Alfreton Sleaford
Leek Ashbourne Ilkeston **NOTTINGHAM** Boston
Stone Uttoxeter **274** **DERBY** **276** **278** **280** **258** **260** Sheringham
Long Grantham Hunstanton Cromer
Stafford East Eaton Spalding **256**
Rugeley **Burton upon** Midlands Loughborough Bourne Fakenham North Walsham
Trent Melton Mowbray **252** **254** Aylsham
36 **238** **240** **242** Stamford **244** Wisbech King's Lynn Dereham
Lichfield **Norwich**

Motorway
Toll motorway
Primary route dual carriageway
Primary route single carriageway
Other A road

Vehicle ferry
Fast vehicle ferry or catamaran
National Park or scenic area

430 *Atlas page number*

0   10   20   30 miles
0 10 20 30 40 kilometres

AA *Route planning* **5**

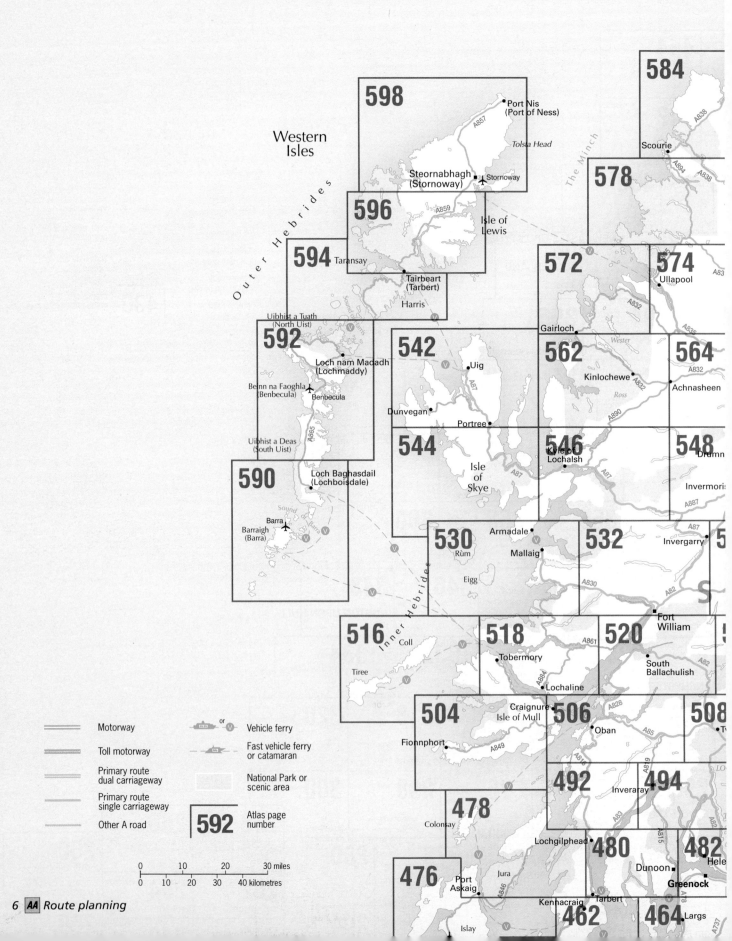

Western Isles

Outer Hebrides

598

Port Nis
(Port of Ness)

A857

Tolsta Head

Steornabhagh
(Stornoway)

Stornoway

596

A859

Isle of
Lewis

594 Taransay

Tairbeart
(Tarbert)

Harris

Uibhist a Tuath
(North Uist)

592

Sound of Harris

Loch nam Madadh
(Lochmaddy)

Beinn na Faoghla
(Benbecula)

Benbecula

Uibhist a Deas
(South Uist)

A865

590

Loch Baghasdail
(Lochboisdale)

Barra

Barraigh
(Barra)

Sound of Barra

The Minch

584

A838

Scourie

A894

A838

578

572

574

Ullapool

A835

A83

A832

Gairloch

Wester

562

564

Kinlochewe

A832

Achnasheen

A832

Ross

A890

542

Uig

A87

Dunvegan

Portree

546

Kyle of
Lochalsh

548

Drumn

A87

Invermoris

A887

544

Isle of
Skye

A87

Inner Hebrides

530

Armadale

Rùm

Mallaig

Eigg

532

Invergarry

A87

A82

S

A830

Fort
William

520

A82

South
Ballachulish

A82

516

Coll

Tiree

518

Tobermory

Lochaline

A861

A884

Craignure
Isle of Mull

506

A828

Oban

A85

508

Tv

504

Fionnphort

A849

A819

A816

492

Inveraray

494

LO

478

Colonsay

Lochgilphead

480

482

Hele

Dunoon

Greenock

476

Port
Askaig

Jura

A846

Kennacraig

Tarbert

462

464 Largs

Islay

Motorway

Toll motorway

Primary route
dual carriageway

Primary route
single carriageway

Other A road

or   Vehicle ferry

Fast vehicle ferry
or catamaran

National Park or
scenic area

592 Atlas page
number

0   10   20   30 miles
0   10   20   30   40 kilometres

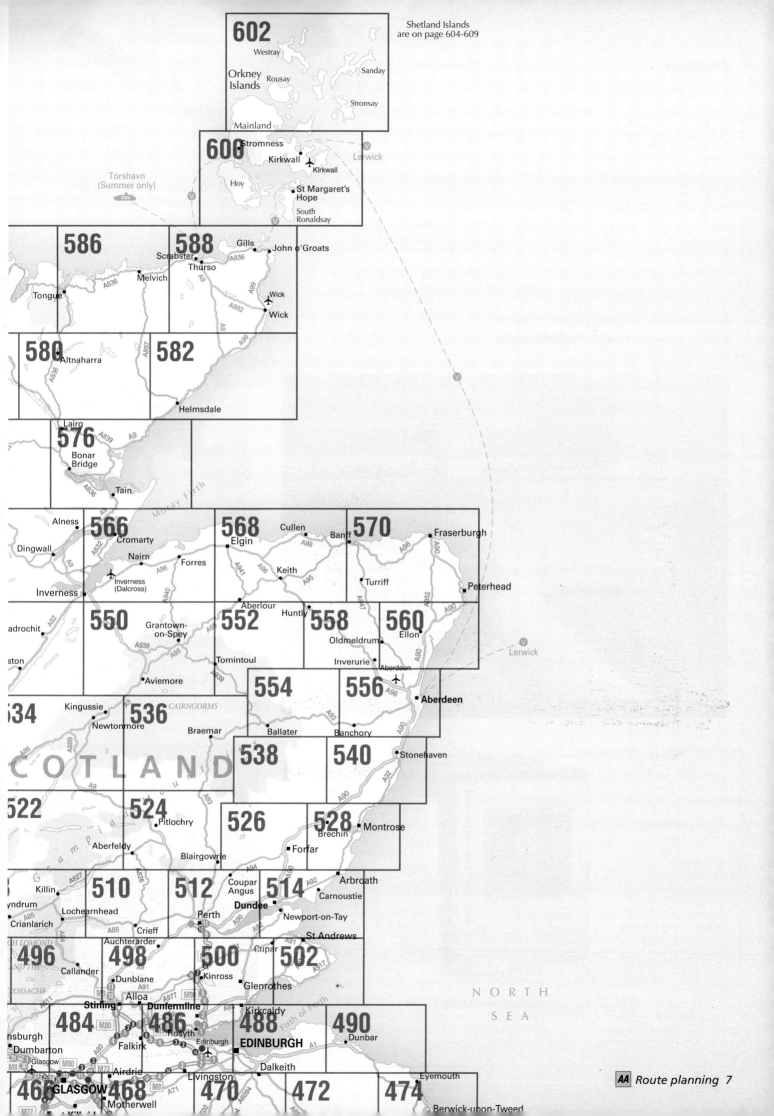

602

Orkney Islands

Westray
Rousay
Sanday
Stronsay

Mainland

Shetland Islands
are on page 604-609

600
Stromness
Kirkwall
Kirkwall
Hoy
St Margaret's Hope
South Ronaldsay
Lerwick

Tórshavn
(Summer only)

586
Tongue
Melvich
Scrabster
Thurso
A836

588
Gills
John o'Groats
A836
A9
A99
A882
Wick
Wick

580
Altnaharra
A836

582
A897
A9
A99
Helmsdale

576
Lairg
Bonar Bridge
A839
A9
Tain
A836
Moray Firth

566
Alness
Dingwall
Cromarty
Nairn
Forres
Inverness (Dalcross)
Inverness
A832
A9
A96

568
Cullen
Elgin
Keith
A98
A941
A96
A95

570
Banff
Fraserburgh
A98
A90
Turriff
A952
Peterhead
A947

550
adrochit
ston
Grantown-on-Spey
A82
A938
A95

552
Aberlour
Huntly
Tomintoul
A939

558
Oldmeldrum
Inverurie

560
Ellon
Lerwick
A90

534
Kingussie
Newtonmore

536
CAIRNGORMS
Braemar

554
Ballater

556
Aberdeen
A96

538
540
Banchory
Stonehaven
A93
A90
A32

S C O T L A N D

522
524
Pitlochry
Aberfeldy
Blairgowrie
A63
A9

526
Forfar
A94

528
Brechin
Montrose
A90

510
Killin
Lochearnhead
Crianlarich
Crieff
A85
A84
A827
A826

512
Perth
Dundee
A9

514
Coupar Angus
Newport-on-Tay
Carnoustie
Arbroath
A92
A90

496
Callander
LOCH LOMOND
AND THE
ROSSACHS

498
Auchterarder
Dunblane
Alloa
A91
A977
Stirling

500
Kinross
Glenrothes
A977
A90

502
Cupar
St Andrews
A91
A917

NORTH
SEA

484
nsburgh
Dumbarton
Glasgow
Falkirk
M80
M8
M73
M9

486
Dunfermline
Rosyth
Edinburgh

488
EDINBURGH
Kirkcaldy
Firth of Forth
A1

490
Dunbar

466
GLASGOW
M77
M8

468
Motherwell
Airdrie
M80
M73
M8

470
Livingston
Dalkeith
A71
A6094
A702

472
Eyemouth

474
Berwick-upon-Tweed

RoadPilot

RoadPilot is the developer of one of the largest and most accurate databases of speed camera locations in the UK and Europe. It has provided the speed camera information in this atlas. RoadPilot is the UK's pioneer and market leader in GPS (Global Positioning System) road safety technologies.

microGo (pictured below) is RoadPilot's latest in-car speed camera location system. It improves road safety by alerting you to the location of accident black spots, fixed and mobile camera sites.

RoadPilot's microGo does not jam police lasers and is therefore completely legal.

RoadPilot's database of fixed camera locations has been compiled with the full co-operation of regional police forces and the Safety Camera Partnerships.

For more information on RoadPilot's GPS road safety products, please visit **www.roadpilot.com** or telephone 0870 240 1701.

Global Positioning System (GPS)

Relaying information from a series of 24 satellites orbiting the earth, a GPS device listens for the signals of four or more satellites at a time in order to work out an accurate location.

RoadPilot is dedicated to creating and maintaining the most accurate database of safety cameras in Europe.

A team of surveyors visit and accurately record the exact position and attributes of each and every camera in the RoadPilot database. On average 400 new locations/modifications are added every month.

SPEED READING

■ Countries currently included

■ Planned / In progress

GPS Antena
microGo is directional, it only alerts you to cameras on your side of the road

Visual Countdown
To camera location

Your Speed
The speed you are travelling when approaching camera

Camera Types Located
Gatso, Specs, Truvelo, TSS/DSS, Traffipax, mobile camera sites, accident black spots, congestion charges, tolls

Voice Warnings
Only if you are exceeding the speed limit at the camera

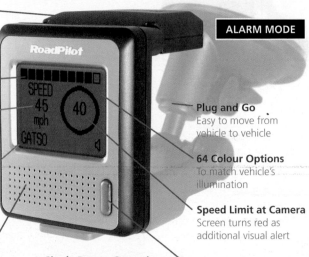

ALARM MODE

Plug and Go
Easy to move from vehicle to vehicle

64 Colour Options
To match vehicle's illumination

Speed Limit at Camera
Screen turns red as additional visual alert

Single Button Operation
For easy access to speed display, camera warning, rescue me location, trip computer, congestion charge, max speed alarm, date and time

RoadPilot®
RoadPilot Surveyors add approximately 400 new locations every month

Road safety and fixed speed cameras

First, the advice you would expect from the AA – **breaking the speed limit is illegal and can cost lives.**

Keeping to the speed limit is not always easy and it only takes one momentary lapse of concentration to break the law. The AA estimate that in 2007 more than 2 million drivers in the UK were fined for doing just that and that 20% of all households in Britain have received a speeding ticket.

Most fixed speed cameras are installed at accident 'black spots' where four or more fatal or serious road collisions have occurred over the previous three years. It is the policy of both the police and the Department for Transport to make the location of cameras as well known as possible. By showing speed camera locations in this atlas the AA is identifying the places where extra care should be taken while driving. Speeding is illegal and dangerous and you MUST keep within the speed limit at all times.

Gatso™

Truvelo™

SPECS™

Traffipax™

There are currently more than 3,000 fixed speed cameras in Britain. The map on this page gives an overview of where speed cameras occur in Britain and the road mapping in this atlas identifies their on-the-road locations.

Camera locations – read this before you use the atlas

1 The speed camera locations were correct at the time of finalising the information to go to press.

2 Camera locations are approximate due to limitations in the scale of road mapping used in this atlas.

3 In towns and urban areas speed camera locations are shown only on roads that appear on the road maps in this atlas.

4 Where two or more cameras occur close together a special symbol is used to indicate multiple cameras on the same stretch of road.

5 Our symbols do not indicate the direction in which speed cameras point.

6 On the mapping we symbolise more than 3,000 fixed camera locations. Mobile laser device locations and fixed 'red light' speed cameras cannot be shown.

Traffic signs giving orders

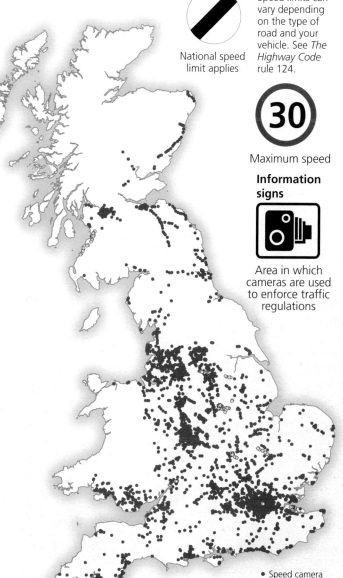

National speed limit applies

Speed limits can vary depending on the type of road and your vehicle. See *The Highway Code* rule 124.

30

Maximum speed

Information signs

Area in which cameras are used to enforce traffic regulations

- Speed camera
- ○ Average speed camera (SPECS™)

60 This symbol is used on the mapping to identify **individual** camera locations - with speed limits (mph)

40 This symbol is used on the mapping to identify **multiple** cameras on the same stretch of road - with speed limits (mph)

50 This symbol is used on the mapping to highlight SPECS™ camera systems which calculate your **average speed** along a stretch of road between two or more sets of cameras - with speed limits (mph)

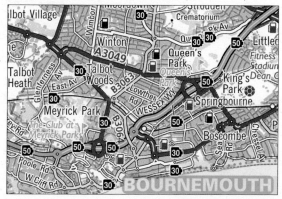

Road safety and mobile speed cameras

Breaking the speed limit is illegal and can cost lives. The AA advises drivers to follow the legal speed limit at all times.

Both the AA and the Government believe that speed cameras should be operated within a transparent system. By providing information relating to road safety and speed hotspots, the AA believes that the driver is better placed to be aware of speed limits and can ensure adherence to them, thus making the roads safer for all users. For this reason the AA has compiled a list of more than 3,000 regularly policed mobile camera sites, based on official regional Safety Camera and Casualty Reduction Partnership sources.

Mobile cameras are also deployed, generally on a temporary basis, at other sites and at roadworks. Due to the nature and purpose of mobile speed control devices the list cannot be exhaustive or completely accurate all of the time and **we advise drivers to always follow the signed speed limits.**

Speed Limits

Types of vehicle	Built up areas* MPH (km/h)	Single carriageways MPH (km/h)	Dual carriageways MPH (km/h)	Motorways MPH (km/h)
 **Cars & motorcycles** (including car derived vans up to 2 tonnes maximum laden weight)	30 (48)	60 (96)	70 (112)	70 (112)
 **Cars towing caravans or trailers** (including car derived vans and motorcycles)	30 (48)	50 (80)	60 (96)	60 (96)
Buses, coaches and minibuses (not exceeding 12 metres (39 feet) in overall length)	30 (48)	50 (80)	60 (96)	70 (112)
 **Goods vehicles** (not exceeding 7.5 tonnes maximum laden weight)	30 (48)	50 (80)	60 (96)	70† (112)
 **Goods vehicles** (exceeding 7.5 tonnes maximum laden weight)	30 (48)	40 (64)	50 (80)	60 (96)

* The 30mph (48km/h) limit usually applies to all traffic on all roads with street lighting unless signs show otherwise.
† 60mph (96km/h) if articulated or towing a trailer.

Britain's speed camera regions

(Map of Britain's speed camera regions, showing: NORTHERN SCOTLAND, NORTH EAST SCOTLAND, TAYSIDE, CENTRAL SCOTLAND, FIFE, STRATHCLYDE, LOTHIAN & BORDERS, DUMFRIES & GALLOWAY, NORTHUMBRIA, DURHAM CONSTABULARY, CLEVELAND, CUMBRIA, NORTH YORKSHIRE, LANCASHIRE, WEST YORKSHIRE, HUMBERSIDE, MERSEYSIDE, GT MAN, SOUTH YORKSHIRE, NORTH WALES, CHESHIRE, DERBYS, NOTTS, LINCOLNSHIRE, STAFFS, LEICESTER, LEICS & RUTLAND, NORFOLK, WEST MIDS, WARWKS, NHANTS, CAMBS, SUFFOLK, MID & SOUTH WALES, WEST MERCIA, BEDS & LUTON, ESSEX, GLOUCESTERSHIRE, THAMES VALLEY, HERTS, LONDON, WILTSHIRE & SWINDON, AVON & SOMERSET, HAMPSHIRE, SURREY, KENT & MEDWAY, ISLE OF WIGHT, SUSSEX, DEVON & CORNWALL, DORSET)

Region-by-region list of mobile camera sites

Road number	Location	Speed limit (mph)
ENGLAND		
Avon and Somerset		
A4	Newbridge Rd, Bath	30
A4	Anchor Rd, Bristol	30
A4	Bath Rd, Bristol (at Totterdown Bridge)	30
A4	Portway, Bristol (near Sea Mills)	50
A4	Portway, Bristol (near A4176 Bridge Valley Rd)	30
A4	Keynsham Bypass (at A4174 jct)	50
A30	Cricket St Thomas	50
A30	East Chinnock	30
A30	Roundham	40
A30	Sherborne Rd, Yeovil	30
A30	Hospital Roundabout, Yeovil	30
A37	Wells Rd, Bristol (near A4174 Airport Rd)	30
A37	Wells Rd, Totterdown, Bristol (near St John's La)	30
A37	Chilthorne Domer	60
A37	Emborough (south of B3139)	50
A37	Fosse Way (north of Podimore Roundabout)	60
A37	Gurney Slade	30
A37	Lydford, near Hornblotton (northbound)	60
A37	Lydford (southbound)	40
A37	Shepton Mallet	30
A38	Bathpool	30
A38	Heatherton Grange, Bradford-on-Tone	50
A38	Taunton Rd, Bridgwater	30
A38	Bedminster Down Rd/West St, Bedminster, Bristol	30
A38	Bedminster Down Rd, Bristol (near Bishopsworth Rd)	40
A38	Bridgwater Rd, Bedminster Down, Bristol	40
A38	Cheltenham Rd/Gloucester Rd, Bristol (near B4054 Cranbrook Rd)	30
A38	Gloucester Rd, Bristol (near B4052 Ashley Down Rd)	30
A38	Stokes Croft, Bristol	30
A38	Churchill to Lower Langford	40
A38	Cross	40
A38	North Petherton	30/40
A38	Aztec West, Patchway (near Bradley Stoke Way)	40
A38	Gloucester Rd, Patchway (near Highwood Rd)	40
A38	Gloucester Rd North, Patchway (near B4057 Gypsy Patch La)	40
A38	Pawlett	50
A38	Redhill	50
A38	Rooks Bridge	30
A38	Sidcot (near A371 jct)	30
A38	East Reach/Toneway, Taunton	30
A38	Wellington Rd, Taunton	30
A38	West Huntspill	30
A39	Ashcott	30
A39	Bilbrook	30
A39	Bath Rd, Bridgwater	30
A39	North Broadway, Bridgwater (near A38, Taunton Rd)	30
A39	Quantock Rd, Bridgwater	30
A39	North Broadway/Broadway/ Monmouth St, Bridgwater	30
A39	Chewton Mendip	30
A39	Coxley	40
A39	Green Ore	50
A39	Bath Rd, Horsey	40
A39	Walton	30
A46	Tormarton	60
A46	Dunkirk	40
A303	Buckland St Mary	50
A303	Downhead (near Ilchester)	50
A303/A358	Southfields Roundabout (near Ilminster)	60
A303/A3088	Cartgate Roundabout (near Martock)	70
A357	Templecombe	30
A358	Ashill	60
A358	Donyatt	30
A358	Henlade (near M5, jct 25)	30
A358	Hornsbury Mill	40
A358	Pen Elm (3km west of Taunton)	40
A358	Greenway Rd, Taunton	30
A358	Priorswood Rd, Taunton	30
A358	Staplegrove Rd, Taunton (near A3065)	30
A359	Mudford	30
A361	Doulting	30
A361	Durston	40
A361	Frome Bypass	60
A361	Othery	30
A361	Pilton	30
A361	West Pennard	30
A362	Terry Hill (near A366 jct)	40
A367	Bear Flat, Bath	30
A367	Green Park Rd, Bath	30
A367	Wells Rd, Radstock	30
A369	Abbots Leigh	40
A369	Martcombe Rd, Easton-in-Gordano	60
A370	Backwell	30

Road number	Location	Speed limit (mph)
A370	Cleeve Village	30
A370	Station Rd/Bristol Rd, Congresbury	30
A370	Flax Bourton (near B3130)	30
A370	Long Ashton Bypass, Bristol end	40
A370	Beach Rd, Weston-super-Mare	30
A370	Herluin Way, Weston-super-Mare (near Winterstoke Rd)	50
A370	Somerset Ave, Weston-super-Mare (M5 to A371)	50
A370	Winterstoke Rd, Weston-super-Mare	30
A371	Draycott	30
A371	Priestleigh	40
A372	Aller	30
A372	Red Post (at B3151, Kingsdon)	50
A378	Curry Rivel	30
A378	Wrantage	40
A403	Avonmouth Docks	40
A420	Clouds Hill Rd/Bell Hill Rd, St George, Bristol	30
A420	High St/London Rd, Warmley, Bristol (near A4175)	30
A420	Lawrence Hill, Bristol	30
A420	Old Market, Bristol (near Temple Way/ Bond St)	30
A420	Wick/Tog Hill	60
A431	Bath Rd, Longwell Green, Bristol (near Willsbridge)	30
A432	Badminton Rd, Bristol (near A4174 Avon Ring Rd)	40
A432	Fishponds Rd, Bristol (near B4048 Lodge Causeway)	30
A432	Fishponds Rd, Bristol (at B4469 Muller Rd)	30
A432	Fishponds Rd, Bristol (near B4469 Royate Hill)	30
A432	Stapleton Rd, Bristol (near A4320 Easton Way)	30
A432	Kendleshire	40
A432	Station Rd/B4059 Stover Rd, Yate	30
A3033	Devonshire Rd, Weston-super-Mare	30
A3088	Lysander Rd, Yeovil	30
A3259	Monkton Heathfield	30
A4018	Black Boy Hill/Whiteladies Rd, Bristol	30
A4018	Falcondale Rd, Westbury-on-Trym, Bristol	30
A4018	Park Row/Perry Rd, Bristol	30
A4018	Westbury Rd, Bristol (near B4054 North View)	30
A4018	Whiteladies Rd into Queens Rd, Bristol	30
A4018	Catbrain (near Cribbs Causeway)	40
A4018	Cribbs Causeway (at jct 17 M5)	30
A4044	Temple Way, Bristol	30
A4162	Sylvan Way/Dingle Rd/Canford La, Westbury-on-Trym, Bristol	30
A4174	Avon Ring Rd (near M32 jct 1)	50
A4174	Avon Ring Rd, Bromley Heath (west of A432)	50
A4174	Filton Rd/Avon Ring Rd (near Coldharbour La)	50
A4174	Hartcliffe Way, Bristol	30
A4174	Hengrove Way/Airport Rd, Bristol (near Creswicke Rd)	40
A4174	Station Rd, Filton (near Great Stoke Way)	40
A4320	St Philips Causeway, Bristol (near A4 Bath Rd)	30
B3124	Walton Rd, Clevedon	30
B3130	Stockway North/Chapel Ave, Nailsea	30
B3130	Wraxall	30/40
B3139	Chilcompton	30
B3139	Mark Causeway	30
B3141	East Huntspill	30
B3151	Compton Dundon	30
B3151	Ilchester	30
B3151	Somerton Rd, Street	30
B3153	Keinton Mandeville	30
B3170	Shoreditch Rd, Taunton	30
B3440	Locking Rd, Weston-super-Mare	30
B4054	Avonmouth Rd, Shirehampton, Bristol	30
B4054	Linden Rd, Westbury Park, Bristol	30
B4054	Shirehampton Rd, Sea Mills, Bristol	30
B4056	Southmead Rd, Bristol	30
B4057	Crow La, Henbury, Bristol (near Passage Rd)	30
B4057	Winterbourne Rd, Great Stoke (near B4427)	40
B4057	Gypsy Patch La, Stoke Gifford (near Hatchet Rd)	30
B4058	Frenchay Park Rd, Bristol	30
B4058	Winterbourne Hill/High St, Winterbourne	30
B4059	Goose Green Way, Yate	30
B4060	Station Rd/Bowling Hill/Rounceval St, Yate/ Chipping Sodbury	30
B4061	Bristol Rd, Thornbury	30
B4061	Gloucester Rd, Thornbury (near Morton Way)	30
B4465	Staplehill Rd/High St, Fishponds, Bristol	30
B4465	Broad St, Mangotsfield, Bristol	30
-	Berrow; Coast Rd	30
-	Bristol; Bishport Ave, Hartcliffe	30
-	Bristol; Broadwalk, Knowle	30
-	Bristol; Hawkfield Rd, Hartcliffe (near A4174 Hengrove Way)	30
-	Bristol; Kingsway, St George	30
-	Bristol; Long Cross, Lawrence Weston	30
-	Bristol; Northumbria Dr, Westbury Park	30
-	Bristol; Redcliffe Way	30
-	Bristol; Stoke Hill/Stoke Rd, Clifton (near Saville Rd)	30
-	Bristol; Sturminster Rd, Stockwood	30
-	Bristol; Whitchurch La/Hareclive Rd, Bishopsworth	30
-	Clevedon; Central Way	30
-	Taunton; Cheddon Rd	30
-	Taunton; Chestnut Dr	30
-	Taunton; Lisieux Way	30
-	Taunton; Trull Rd	30
-	Watergore; Harp Rd (near Over Stratton)	50
-	Weston-super-Mare; Locking Rd/Alexandra Pde/Regent St	30
-	Yeovil; Combe St	30

Bedfordshire and Luton

Road number	Location	Speed limit (mph)
A1	Sandy	50
A5	Battlesden	60
A5	Hockliffe	40
A5	Kensworth (near B4540)	60
A6	New Bedford Rd, Luton	30
A6	Pulloxhill	60
A6	near Silsoe	60
A421	Brogborough/Aspley Guise	50
A421	Wootton	60
A428	Bromham Rd, Bedford	30
A428	Goldington Rd, Bedford	30
A505	Luton Rd, Dunstable	30
A505	Leighton Buzzard Bypass	60
A505	Park Viaduct, Luton	30
A507	near Clifton	60
A507	Ridgmont	30
A603	Cardington Rd, Bedford	30
A603	Willington	40
A1081	Airport Way, Luton	30
A4146	Billington Rd, Leighton Buzzard	30
A5120	High St, Flitwick	30
A5120	Harlington	40
A5120	Bedford Rd, Houghton Regis	40
A5120	Station Rd, Toddington	30
A5134	High St, Kempston	30
B531	Bedford Rd, Kempston	30
B1040	Potton Rd, Biggleswade	30
B1042	Wrestlingworth	30
B4540	Markyate Rd, Slip End, Luton	30
-	Arlesey; Hitchin Rd	30
-	Aspley Guise; Bedford Rd/West Hill	30
-	Bedford; Park Ave	30
-	Bedford; Roff Ave	30
-	Bedford; Wentworth Dr	30
-	Bromham; Stagsden Rd	30
-	Bromham; Village Rd	30
-	Caddington; Dunstable Rd	30
-	Clapham; High St	30
-	Cranfield; High St	30
-	Eaton Bray; The Rye	30
-	Harlington; Barton Rd	30
-	Heath and Reach; Woburn Rd	30
-	Leighton Buzzard; Heath Rd	30
-	Luton; Crawley Green Rd	30
-	Luton; Dunstable Rd	40
-	Luton; Leagrave High St	30
-	Luton; Waller Ave	30
-	Luton; Whitehorse Vale	30
-	Upper Caldecote; Hitchin Rd	30
-	Wrestlingworth; High St	30

Cambridgeshire

Road number	Location	Speed limit (mph)
A1	Little Paxton to Southoe (northbound)	NSL
A1	south of Carpenter's Lodge Roundabout (B1081, south of Stamford)(northbound)	NSL
A10	Melbourn Bypass	NSL
A14	Jct 15 to 17 (eastbound)	NSL
A14	Jct 18 to 19 (westbound)	NSL
A14	Jct 20 (eastbound)	NSL
A14	West of jct 21 (A1) (eastbound)	NSL
A14	Jct 23 (eastbound)	NSL
A14	Girton to jct 31 (A1307) (westbound)	NSL
A14	Fen Ditton	NSL
A14	east of jct 35 (A1303) (westbound)	NSL
A14	Bottisham (westbound)	NSL
A14	north-east of jct 36 (A11) (eastbound)	NSL
A15	London Rd, Peterborough (New Rd to Rivergate)	30
A15	Paston Pkwy, Peterborough (northbound)	NSL
A47	Soke Pkwy, Peterborough (eastbound)	NSL
A47	west of Thorney Toll	NSL
A141	Huntingdon Northern Bypass	NSL
A141	at B1040 jct, south of Warboys (southbound)	NSL
A141	north-east of Warboys	NSL
A141	Clews Corner (south-west of Chatteris)	NSL
A141	Wimblington/Doddington Bypass	NSL
A142	Soham Bypass (southbound)	NSL
A142	Witchford Bypass (eastbound)	NSL
A428	St Neots Bypass	NSL
A505	east of Royston	NSL
A505	Thriplow	NSL
A603	Little Eversden	NSL
A605	Elton	NSL
A605	Oundle Rd, Peterborough (near Nene Pkwy jct)	30
A605	Kings Dyke (west of Whittlesey)	40
A605	Coates Rd, Eastrea	30
A1073	Masons Bridge/Steam House Farm (north of Eye)	NSL
A1101	Mildenhall Rd, Littleport	NSL
A1123	Houghton Hill, St Ives, east of B1090 (eastbound)	40
A1123	St Audrey La, St Ives	30
A1123	Needingworth Bypass	NSL
A1123	Wilburton bends to east of village	40
A1134	Trumpington Rd, Cambridge	30
A1198	Graveley/Hilton jcts	NSL
A1198	south of B1046 jct	NSL
A1303	near A1304 jct, Newmarket	NSL
A1307	Huntingdon Rd, Cambridge	40
A1307	Hills Rd, Cambridge (Gonville Pl to Worts' Cswy)(southbound)	30
A1307	Linton Bypass (westbound)	NSL
A1307	Bartlow Crossroads (dual carriageway)	NSL
A1309	Milton Rd, Chesterton, Cambridge	30
B198	Lynn Rd, Wisbech (north-east end)	40
B645	Tilbrook bends	40
B1061	Dullingham Rd, Newmarket	NSL
B1099	Wisbech Rd, March	30
-	Cambridge; Cherry Hinton Rd (at Cherry Hinton Hall)	30
-	Cambridge; Coldham's Lane (by airport)	40
-	Chatteris; Doddington Rd	40
-	Ramsey Forty Foot; Forty Foot Bank (2.5km east of village)	50

Cheshire

Road number	Location	Speed limit (mph)
A50	Manchester Rd/Toft Rd, Knutsford (Woodvale Rd to Garden Rd)	30
A50	Knutsford Rd, Grappenhall, Warrington (Heath Field Park to Cliff La)	30
A50	Long La, Warrington (Fisher Ave to Longfield Rd)	30
A54	Kelsall Rd, Ashton (west of B5393 Ashton La to Hollands La overbridge)	60/70
A56	Camsley La, Lymm (Deans La to M6 overbridge)	40
A57	New Manchester Rd, Paddington, Warrington (Larkfield Ave to Greymist Ave)	40
A523	London Rd, Poynton (South Park Dr to Clifford Rd)	30
A532	Coppenhall La/West St, Crewe (Marshfield Ave to Peel St)	30
A533	Booth La, Middlewich (Long La South to 320m south-east of Cledford La)	40
A533	Northwich Rd, Runcorn (A56 Chester Rd to Rivington Rd)	30
A537	Buxton New Rd, near Cat and Fiddle (100m north-west of Buxton Old Rd to A54)	50
A5019	Mill St/Vernon Way, Crewe (A532 Earle St to A534 Nantwich Rd)	30
A5032	Chester Rd, Whitby, Ellesmere Port (A5117 to 130m south of Dunkirk La)	30
A5034	Mereside Rd, Mere	60
A5104	Hough Green, Chester (A483 to Cliveden Rd)	30
B5071	Gresty Rd, Crewe (South St to 500m south of Davenport Ave)	30
B5078	Sandbach Rd North, Alsager (The Avenue to Leicester Ave)	30
B5082	Middlewich Rd, Northwich (East Ave to Pullman Dr)	30
B5132	Overpool Rd/Rivacre Rd, Ellesmere Port (B5132 Sutton Way to Netherpool Rd)	30
B5155	Runcorn, Heath Rd (Halton Rd to Boston Ave)	30
B5419	Widnes, Birchfield Rd (Pit La to Rose View Ave)	30
B5463	Station Rd, Little Sutton	30
B5470	Hurdsfield Rd/Rainow Rd, Macclesfield (Fence Ave to Well La)	30
-	Burtonwood; Lumber La (Green La to Melrose Ave)	30
-	Ellesmere Port; Overpool Rd (Wycliffe Rd to Fairview Rd)	30
-	Runcorn; Astmoor Rd (Lister Rd to Chadwick Rd)	40
-	Runcorn; Boston Ave (Morval Cres to Heath Rd)	30
-	Runcorn; Halton Rd (Daresbury Expressway overbridge to Boston Ave)	30
-	Runcorn; Heath Rd (Halton Rd to Boston Ave)	30
-	Runcorn; Moughland La/Clifton Rd (Greenway Rd to Beaufort Close)	30
-	Runcorn; Warrington Rd (Manor Park to Eastgate Rd)	30
-	Warrington; Battersby La, Howley	30
-	Warrington; Harpers Rd, Fearnhead (Pasture La to Freshfield Dr)	30
-	Warrington; Lovely La, Whitecross (Monks St to Clap Gates Rd)	30
-	Widnes; Hough Green Rd (B5178 Liverpool Rd to Arley Dr)	30
-	Widnes; Prescot Rd, Hough Green (Hough Green Rd to borough boundary)	30
-	Wilmslow; Hough La (northern end)	30
-	Winsford; Bradford La (either side of School Rd)	40
-	Winsford; St John's Dr (Brunner Pl to Forest Rd)	30
-	Winsford; Woodford Lane/Delamere St (southern end)	30

Cleveland

Road number	Location	Speed limit (mph)
A135	Yarm Rd, Eaglescliffe	30
A171	Charltons (near Margrove Park)	50
A171	Ormesby Bank, Ormesby	30
A172	Marton Rd, Middlesbrough (Longlands to St Lukes Hosp)	30
A172	Marton Rd, Middlesbrough (St Lukes to Marton crossroads)	40
A172	Dixons Bank, Nunthorpe (Guisborough Rd to Captain Cook's Cres)	40
A174	Carlin How (near Loftus)	30
A177	Durham Rd, Stockton-on-Tees (from Savacentre to county boundary)	50/60
A178	Coronation Drive, Hartlepool	40/30
A178	The Front, Seaton Carew	30
A179	Easington Rd/Powlett Rd, Hartlepool	30/40/50
A689	Stockton Rd, Hartlepool (from Sappers Corner)	50/40
A1027	Bishopton Ave, Stockton-on-Tees	30
A1032	Acklam Rd, Brookfield (Blue Bell to Crematorium)	40
A1032	Acklam Rd, Linthorpe	30
A1042	Kirkleatham La, Redcar	30/40
A1085	High St, Marske-by-the-Sea	30
A1130	Acklam Rd, Thornaby-on-Tees	30
A1130	Mandale Rd, Acklam	30
B1269	Redcar La, Redcar	30
B1274	Junction Rd, Stockton-on-Tees	30
B1276	Seaton La, Hartlepool	30
B1276	Station La, Seaton Carew	30
B1380	High St, Eston	30
B1380	Ladgate La, Marton (Marton crossroads to Ormesby Rd)	40
B1380	Normanby Rd, Ormesby	30
-	Acklam; Trimdon Ave	30
-	Billingham; Thames Rd	30
-	Billingham; White House Rd	30
-	Eston; Church La	30
-	Eston; Normanby Rd	30
-	Hartlepool; Catcote Rd	30
-	Hartlepool; Elwick Rd (York Rd to Elwick Rise)	30
-	Hartlepool; King Oswy Dr	30
-	Hartlepool; Owton Manor La	30
-	Hartlepool; Oxford Rd	30
-	Hartlepool; Raby Rd	30
-	Hartlepool; Throston Grange La	30
-	Hartlepool; Winterbottom Ave	30
-	Hartlepool; Wynyard Rd	30
-	Middlesbrough; Ormesby Rd	30
-	Normanby; Bankfields Rd	30
-	Normanby; Flatts La	30
-	Redcar; Broadway, Dormanstown	30
-	Redcar; Greenstones Rd	30
-	Redcar; Redcar Rd	30
-	Redcar; West Dyke Rd	30
-	Stanghow; Stanghow Rd	30
-	Stockton-on-Tees; Bishopton Rd West	30
-	Stockton-on-Tees; Darlington La	30
-	Stockton-on-Tees; Harrowgate La	30
-	Thornaby-on-Tees; Cunningham Ave	30
-	Thornaby-on-Tees; Thornaby Rd	30

Cumbria

Cumbria Safety Cameras no longer publish the locations of mobile safety camera sites and are developing new sites.

Road number	Location	Speed limit (mph)
M6	Jct 36 to 40	70
A6	London Rd, Carlisle	30
A6	Garnett Bridge north to Hollowgate	60
A6	Milnthorpe Rd, Kendal	30
A6	Shap Rd, Kendal	30
A6	Scotland Rd, Penrith	30
A6	Thiefside (south of High Hesket)	60
A7	Westlinton crossroads	60
A65	Burton Rd/Lound Rd/Kendal Lound Rd/ Oxenholme Rd, Kendal	30
A65	Devil's Bridge, Kirkby Lonsdale	40
A65	Hollin Hall to Hornsbarrow, Kirkby Lonsdale (north-west of town)	60
A66	Brough Hill, Warcop	60
A66	Brigham/Broughton to Bridgefoot	60
A66	Crackenthorpe	60
A66	Dubwath/Bassenthwaite Lake	60
A66	Sandford (either side of B6259 jct)	60
A66	Troutbeck (either side of A5091 jct)	60
A69	Aglionby (west of Warwick, single carr)	60
A69	Scarrow Hill (near Lanercost)	60
A74	Floriston (Todhills to River Esk)	70
A590	Bouth road ends (north of A5092 jct)	60
A590	Haverthwaite/Backbarrow	60
A590	Levens (A6 jct to west of A5074 jct)	70
A590	Newland, Ulverston	60
A592	Rayrigg Rd, Bowness	30/40
A595	Wigton Rd, Carlisle	30
A595	Greenhill Hotel, Red Dial	60
A595	West Woodside/Curthwaite jct	60
A595	Loop Rd, Whitehaven	40
A595	Wreaks End, Broughton-in-Furness	60
A596	Micklethwaite	60
A683	Cautley to Middleton	60
A685	Appleby Rd, Kendal	30
A686	Penrith to Gilderdale Forest	60
A5087	Ulverston	30
A6071	Smallstown Farm (near Longtown)	n/a
B5277	Lindale Rd, Grange-over-Sands	30
B5299	Dalston Rd, Carlisle	40
B5305	Sowerby Row	n/a
-	Barrow-in-Furness; Abbey Rd	30
-	Barrow-in-Furness; Michelson Rd	30
-	Carlisle; Blackwell Rd/Durdar Rd	30

Derbyshire

Road number	Location	Speed limit (mph)
A6	Duffield Rd, Allestree, Derby	30
A6	Allestree to Duffield	50
A6	Duffield	30/40
A6	Milford to Belper	40
A6	Belper	30
A6	Belper to Ambergate	50
A6	north of Crich to Cromford	50
A6	Cromford	40
A6	Matlock Bath	30
A6	Matlock Bath to Matlock	40
A6	Matlock (town centre)	30
A6	Dimple, Matlock	40
A6	Northwood	40
A6	Rowsley to Bakewell	50
A6	Bakewell	30
A6	Ashford in the Water	50
A6	Taddington to Buxton	50
A6	Buxton	30
A6	Buxton to Dove Holes	50
A6	Dove Holes	30
A6	Dove Holes to Chapel-en-le-Frith Bypass	50
A6	Furness Vale	40
A6	Furness Vale to Newtown	40
A6	London Rd, Derby (A5111 to Ascot Dr)	30
A52	Ashbourne Rd, Derby	30
A52	Mackworth, Derby	40
A52	east of Brailsford	50
A52	Shirley Hollow (5km south-east of Ashbourne)	50
A57	Snake Rd (at Ladybower Resr)	60
A514	Swadlincote (Darklands Rd to A511)	30
A514	Swadlincote to Hartshorne	40
A514	Hartshorne	30
A514	Ticknall	30
A514	Stanton by Bridge	40
A515	Alsop en le Dale	60
A515	north of A50 jct (for 2.5km)	50
A516	Uttoxeter New Rd, Derby	30/40
A601	Abbey St, Derby	30
A608	Smalley	30
A609	Kilburn to Horsley Woodhouse	30
A609	Stanley Common	40
A610	Bullbridge/Ridgeway to B6013	40
A610	Codnor	30
A615	Matlock Green, Matlock	30
A615	Tansley	30
A615	Tansley to Wessington	60
A616	Clowne	30
A616	Cresswell	30
A617	Bramley Vale (1km east of M1 jct 29)	40
A617	Glapwell to Pleasley	NSL
A619	west of Wadshelf	60
A623	Calver	40
A623	Stoney Middleton	30
A623	Stoney Middleton to Peak Forest	NSL
A623	Peak Forest	40
A623	Peak Forest to A6 jct	NSL
A624	Glossop (A57 to A6106)	30
A624	Chunal to Little Hayfield	50
A624	Hayfield to Chinley	50
A628	Tintwistle to county bdy	NSL
A632	Station Rd, Bolsover	30
A632	Hady to Calow (east of Chesterfield)	40
A632	Matlock	30
A5111	Warwick Ave, Derby	40
A6005	Draycott to Breaston	30
A6005	Breaston to Long Eaton (B6002 jct)	40
A6007	Codnor to Heanor	30
A6175	Holmewood	30
A6175	North Wingfield	30
B600	Somercotes	30
B5010	London Rd, Shardlow	30
B5010	Shardlow to Thulston (A6 jct)	60
B5020	Station Rd, Mickleover	30
B5353	Park Rd, Newhall, Swadlincote	30
B6051	Newbold Rd, Chesterfield (town centre to B6150)	30
B6052	Old Whittington, Chesterfield	30
B6057	Sheffield Rd, Stonegravels, Chesterfield	30
B6062	Buxton Rd, Chinley	30
B6179	Little Eaton	30
B6179	Little Eaton to Lower Kilburn	50
B6179	Lower Kilburn	40
B6179	Denby	40
B6179	Marehay to Ripley	30
-	Charlesworth; Long La	30
-	Chesterfield; Boythorpe Rd	30
-	Chesterfield; Old Rd	30
-	Derby; Shardlow Rd, Alvaston	30/40
-	Derby; Blagreaves La	30
-	Derby; Burton Rd, Littleover (Hillsway to A5111)	30
-	Derby; Kedleston Rd (A6 to A38)	30
-	Derby; London Rd (Litchurch La to A6)	30
-	Derby; Stenson Rd, Normanton (Village St to Sunnyhill Ave)	30
-	Derby; Stenson Rd, Stenson Fields (Wragley Way to Grampian Way)	40
-	Swadlincote; Hearthcote Rd	30

Devon and Cornwall

Road number	Location	Speed limit (mph)
A30	Chiverton Cross (A390/A3075 jct)	60
A30	Highgate	70
A30	Highgate Hill (A39 jct at Indian Queens)	70
A30	Monkton	40
A30	Sowton, Exeter	40
A30	Temple	60
A38	Lee Mill	70
A38	near Lower Clicker (B3251 jct, south-east of Liskeard)	70
A38	Deep Lane jct, Plympton	70
A38	Smithaleigh (4km west of Ivybridge)	70
A38	Smithaleigh (overbridge) (4km west of Ivybridge)	70
A38	Wrangaton-Bittaford straight	70
A39	Barras Moor (near Perranarworthal)	60
A39	Valley Truckle, Camelford	30
A39	Perranarworthal	40
A361	Ashford	50
A361	Eastern Ave, Barnstaple	30
A361	Knowle	40
A361	Knowle (Westerland)	30
A361	Wrafton	30
A374	Plymouth Rd, Plymouth	40
A374	Antony Rd, Torpoint	30
A376	Ebford	30
A376	Exeter Rd, Exmouth	30

Road number	Location	Speed limit (mph)
A377	Copplestone	30
A377	Western Rd, Crediton	30
A377	Alphington Rd, Exeter	30
A379	Brixton	30
A379	Dartmouth Rd, Paignton	30
A379	Starcross	30
A379	Teignmouth Rd, Teignmouth	30
A379	Babbacombe Rd, Torquay	30
A379	Yealmpton	30
A380	Newton Rd, Kingskerswell	40
A381	East St, Newton Abbot	30
A385	Totnes Rd, Collaton St Mary	30
A385	Ashburton Rd, Totnes	30
A386	Chub Tor (2km south of Yelverton)	60
A386	Outland Rd, Plymouth	30
A386	Roborough Down, Plymouth	60
A386	Tavistock Rd, Plymouth	40
A388	Kelly Bray (north of Callington)	30
A390	Penstraze (1.5km east of A30)	60
A390	Sticker Bypass	60
A394	Kenneggy Downs (near Praa Sands)	40
A396	Rewe	30
A396	Exeter Rd, Stoke Canon	30
A3015	Topsham Rd, Exeter	30
A3047	Trevenson Rd, Pool, Camborne	30
A3047	Tuckingmill, Camborne	30
A3058	Trewoon, St Austell	30
A3064	St Budeaux Bypass, Plymouth	30
A3074	Carbis Bay, St Ives	30
A3075	Rosecliston, near Newquay	60
B3165	Crewkerne Rd, Raymonds Hill (near A35)	30
B3174	Barrack Rd, Ottery St Mary	30
B3183	Heavitree Rd, Exeter	30
B3183	New North Rd, Exeter	30
B3212	Dunsford Rd, Exeter	30
B3212	Pinhoe Rd, Exeter	30
B3213	Wrangaton village	30
B3233	Bickington Rd, Barnstaple	30
B3250	North Hill, Plymouth	30
B3284	Liskey, Perranporth	30/60
B3344	Station Hill, Chudleigh	30
B3396	Milehouse Rd, Plymouth	30
B3416	Glen Rd, Plympton	30
B3432	Novorossisk Rd, Plymouth	40
-	Avonwick village	30
-	Castle-an-Dinas (4km east of St Columb Major)	60
-	Exeter; Buddle La	30
-	Exeter; Exwick La	30
-	Fraddon village	30
-	Ivybridge; Exeter Rd	30
-	Paignton; Colley End Rd	30
-	Paignton; Preston Down Rd	30
-	Plymouth; Beacon Park Rd	30
-	Plymouth; Church Hill, Eggbuckland	30
-	Plymouth; Devonport Rd, Stoke	30
-	Plymouth; Eggbuckland Rd	30
-	Plymouth; Glen Rd	30
-	Plymouth; Grenville Rd, St Judes	30
-	Plymouth; Haye Rd, Elburton	30
-	Plymouth; Honicknowle La	30
-	Plymouth; Lipson Rd	30
-	Plymouth; Mannamead Rd	30
-	Plymouth; Molesworth Rd	30
-	Plymouth; North Prospect Rd	30
-	Plymouth; Pomphlett Rd	30
-	Plymouth; Shakespeare Rd, Honicknowle	30
-	Plymouth; Southway Dr	30
-	Plymouth; St Levan Rd	30
-	Plymouth; Tamerton Foliot Rd	30
-	Plymouth; Union St	30
-	Plymouth; Weston Park Rd	30
-	Plymouth; Wolseley Rd	30
-	Saltash; Callington Rd	30

Dorset

Road number	Location	Speed limit (mph)
A30	Babylon Hill (1.5 km east of Yeovil)	70
A30	Long Cross, Shaftesbury	40
A31	Winterbourne Zelston	40
A35	Sea Rd South, Bridport	50
A35	Christchurch Bypass	70
A35	Lyndhurst Rd, Christchurch (near A337 jct)	60
A35	Friary Press, west of Dorchester	60
A35	Kingston Russell	60
A35	Baker's Arms Roundabout, Lytchett Minster, to roundabout with A350	70
A35	Upton Rd, Poole	30
A35	near Sherford/Slepe	60
A35	Vinney Cross (near Uploders)	60
A35	Whiteway Cross (2.5km west of Kingston Russell)	60
A37	Long Ash La, Frampton	60
A37	Holywell Cross, Holywell	60
A37	Staggs Folly (near Chalmington)	60
A338	Spur Rd (north of Hurn)	70
A338	Wessex Way, Bournemouth (near A3060 jct)	50
A348	Ringwood Rd, Bear Cross, Bournemouth (near A341 jct)	40
A349	Gravel Hill, Poole	40
A350	Holes Bay Rd, Poole	50
A350	Poole Rd (A31 to A35)	60
A350	Shaston Rd, Stourpaine	30
A350	Upton Country Park (east of Upton)	70
A352	Dorchester Rd, Wool	30
A354	Dorchester Rd, Ridgeway Hill (3km south of A35)	60
A354	Dorchester Rd, Upwey	30
A354	Dorchester Rd (Manor Roundabout to Weymouth Hospital)	30
A354	Dorchester Rd, Redlands, Weymouth	40
A354	Buxton Rd, Weymouth	30
A354	Winterbourne Whitechurch	30
B3065	Pinecliff Rd, Poole	30
B3065	The Avenue, Poole	30
B3073	Christchurch Rd, West Parley	30
B3073	Oakley Hill, Wimborne Minster	30
B3074	Higher Blandford Rd, Broadstone, Poole	30
B3081	Ringwood Rd, Ebblake, Verwood	30
B3082	Blandford Rd (near Badbury Rings)	60
B3092	Colesbrook, Gillingham	40
B3157	Portesham	30
B3157	Limekiln Hill, West Bexington (east of Clay La)	50
B3157	Chickerell Rd, Weymouth	30
B3157	Lanehouse Rocks Rd, Weymouth	30
B3369	Sandbanks Rd, Poole	30
B3369	Shore Rd, Poole	30
-	Blandford Forum; Salisbury Rd	30
-	Bournemouth; Branksome Wood Rd	30
-	Bournemouth; Carbery Ave	30
-	Bournemouth; Littledown Ave	30
-	Bournemouth; Southbourne Overcliff Dr	30
-	Ferndown; Wimborne Rd East, Stapehill	40
-	Poole; Constitution Hill Rd	30
-	Poole; Old Wareham Rd	30
-	Portland; Weston Rd	30
-	Upton; Poole Rd	30

Durham Constabulary area

Road number	Location	Speed limit (mph)
A66	Bowes Moor/Galley Bank/Greta Bridge	n/a
A167	North Rd, Darlington	n/a
A167	Durham (Merryoaks to Sniperley)	n/a
A690	Willington	n/a
A690	West Rainton, Durham	n/a
A693	Chester Rd, Stanley	n/a
A1086	Horden to Blackhall	n/a
B6168	Annfield Plain (to A692 jct)	n/a
B6280	Yarm Rd, Darlington	n/a
B6282	Woodhouse La, Bishop Auckland	n/a
B6284	Etherley La, Bishop Auckland	n/a
-	Darlington; McMullen Rd	n/a
-	Durham; Finchale Rd/Pit La	n/a
-	Peterlee; Essington Way	n/a

Essex

Road number	Location	Speed limit (mph)
A12	Overbridge, near Kelvedon interchange	70
A13	High St, Hadleigh (towards London)	30
A13	North Shoebury	n/a
A13	Ness Rd, Shoeburyness	30
A13	Bournes Green Chase, Southend-on-Sea	n/a
A13	Southchurch Blvd, Southend-on-Sea	n/a
A113	High Rd, Chigwell	30
A120	Harwich Rd, (Wix Arch Cottages to Cansey La, Goose Green)	n/a
A120	Horsley Cross (south-west to Park Rd)	n/a
A121	Goldings Hill, Loughton (at Monkchester Cl)	30
A121	High Rd, Loughton	30
A123	Fenpiece Rd, Grange Hill	30
A126	London Rd, Grays	30
A126	Montreal Rd, Tilbury	30
A128	High St, Chipping Ongar	30
A128	Brentwood Rd, Ingrave/Herongate	30
A128	Ongar Rd, Kelvedon Hatch	40
A129	Crays Hill, Basildon	30
A129	Southend Rd, Billericay	30
A129	London Rd, Rayleigh	30
A129	London Rd, Wickford	30
A129	Southend Rd, Wickford	30
A130	Long Rd, Canvey Island	30
A130	Canvey Way, South Benfleet	60
A131	Bournebridge Hill (near Halstead)	n/a
A133	Clacton Rd, Elmstead Market	30
A133	Colchester Rd (near Weeley)	n/a
A134	Nayland Rd, Great Horkesley	40
A137	Wignall St, Lawford	30
A414	Malden Rd, Danbury	30
A1016	Waterhouse La, Chelmsford	30
A1023	London Rd, Brentwood	30
A1023	Shenfield Rd/Chelmsford Rd, Brentwood	30
A1025	Second Ave, Harlow	40
A1025	Third Ave, Harlow	40
A1060	Lower Rd, Little Hallingbury	30
A1090	London Rd, Purfleet	30
A1090	Tank Hill Rd, Purfleet	30
A1124	Lexden Rd, Colchester	30
A1124	Hedingham Rd, Halstead	n/a
A1158	Southbourne Grove, Westcliff-on-Sea, Southend-on-Sea	30
A1168	Rectory La, Loughton	30
A1169	Southern Way, Harlow	40
A1232	Ipswich Rd, Colchester	30
A1235	Cranes Farm Rd, Basildon (at Honywood Rd)	40
B170	Chigwell Rise, Chigwell	30
B170	Roding La, Loughton	n/a
B172	Coppice Row, Theydon Bois	30
B173	Lambourne Rd, Chigwell	30
B184	Snow Hill, Great Easton	40
B186	South Rd, South Ockendon	30
B1002	High St, Ingatestone	30
B1007	Laindon Rd/High St/Stock Rd, Billericay	30
B1007	Galleywood Rd/Stock Rd, Chelmsford	n/a
B1008	Broomfield Rd, Chelmsford	30
B1013	Main Rd, Hawkwell	30
B1013	High Rd, Hockley	30
B1013	Southend Rd, Hockley/Hawkwell	30
B1013	High Rd, Rayleigh	30
B1014	Benfleet Rd, South Benfleet	30
B1016	Ness Rd, Shoeburyness	30
B1018	The Street, Latchingdon	30
B1018	The Causeway, Maldon	30
B1019	Maldon Rd, Hatfield Peveral	30
B1021	Church Rd, Burnham-on-Crouch	30
B1022	Maldon Rd, Colchester	30
B1022	Shrub End Rd, Colchester	30
B1022	Maldon Rd, Heckfordbridge	30
B1022	Colchester Rd, Maldon	30
B1027	St Osyth Rd, Alresford	40
B1027	St John's Rd, Clacton-on-Sea	30
B1027	Valley Rd/Old Rd, Clacton-on-Sea	30
B1027	Pump Hill, St Osyth	30
B1027	Brightlingsea Rd, (near Wivenhoe)	40
B1028	Colchester Rd, Wivenhoe	30
B1028	The Avenue, Wivenhoe	30
B1033	Frinton Rd, Kirby Cross	30
B1335	Stifford Rd, South Ockendon	40
B1352	Main Rd, Harwich	n/a
B1383	London Rd, Newport	30
B1383	Cambridge Rd, Stansted Mountfitchet	30
B1389	Hatfield Rd, Witham	30
B1393	High Rd, Epping	30
B1393	Palmers Hill, Epping	30
B1441	London Rd, Clacton-on-Sea	30
B1441	Clacton Rd, Weeley Heath	n/a
B1442	Thorpe Rd, Clacton-on-Sea	30
B1464	Clay Hill Rd, Basildon	30
B1464	London Rd, Bowers Gifford	30
-	Aveley; Purfleet Rd	30
-	Basildon; Ashlyns	30
-	Basildon; Clay Hill Rd	30
-	Basildon; Felmores	30
-	Basildon; Rectory Rd, Pitsea	30
-	Basildon; Sandon Rd, Barstable	30
-	Basildon; Vange Hill Dr	30
-	Basildon; Wash Rd, Laindon	30
-	Basildon; Whitmore Way	30
-	Basildon; Wickford Ave	30
-	Billericay; Mountnessing Rd	30
-	Braintree; Coldnailhurst Ave (Alexander Rd towards Church La)	30
-	Brentwood; Eagle Way (Clive Rd to Warley Rd)	30
-	Buckhurst Hill; Buckhurst Way/Albert Rd	30
-	Canvey Island; Dovervelt Rd	30
-	Canvey Island; Link Rd	30
-	Canvey Island; Thorney Bay Rd	30
-	Chadwell St Mary; Brentwood Rd	30
-	Chadwell St Mary; Linford Rd	30
-	Chadwell St Mary; River View	30
-	Chelmsford; Baddow Rd	30
-	Chelmsford; Chignall Rd	30
-	Chelmsford; Copperfield Rd	30
-	Chelmsford; Longstomps Ave	30
-	Chelmsford; New Bowers Way, Springfield	30
-	Clacton-on-Sea; Burrs Rd	30
-	Clacton-on-Sea; Kings Parade	30
-	Clacton-on-Sea; Marine Parade East	30
-	Clacton-on-Sea; St Osyth Rd, Rush Green	n/a
-	Colchester; Abbot's Rd	30
-	Colchester; Avon Way	30
-	Colchester; Bromley Rd	30
-	Colchester; Old Heath Rd	30
-	Daws Heath; Daws Heath Rd	30
-	Grays; Blackshots La	30
-	Grays; Lodge La	30
-	Harlow; Abercrombie Way (towards Southern Way)	40
-	Harlow; Howard Way	40
-	Hawkwell; Rectory Rd	30
-	Hullbridge; Coventry Hill	30
-	Leigh-on-Sea; Belton Way East (Marine Parade to Belton Gdns)	30
-	Leigh-on-Sea; Belton Way West	30
-	Leigh-on-Sea; Blenheim Chase	30
-	Leigh-on-Sea; Grand Parade/Cliff Parade	30
-	Leigh-on-Sea; Hadleigh Rd	30
-	Leigh-on-Sea; Highlands Blvd	30
-	Leigh-on-Sea; Manchester Dr	30
-	Leigh-on-Sea; Mountdale Gdns	30
-	Leigh-on-Sea; Western Rd	30
-	Loughton; Alderton Hill	30
-	Loughton; Loughton Way	30
-	Loughton; Valley Hill	30
-	Maldon; Fambridge Rd	30
-	Maldon; Holloway Rd	30
-	Maldon; Mundon Rd	30
-	North Benfleet; Pound Lane	n/a
-	Rayleigh; Bull La	30
-	Rayleigh; Down Hall Rd	30
-	Rayleigh; Trinity Rd (near Church Rd)	30
-	Rochford; Ashingdon Rd	30
-	Southend-on-Sea; Barnstaple Rd, Thorpe Bay	30
-	Southend-on-Sea; Bournemouth Park Rd	n/a
-	Southend-on-Sea; Chalkwell Ave, Westcliff-on-Sea	30
-	Southend-on-Sea; Green La (at Kendal Way), Eastwood	30
-	Southend-on-Sea; Hamstel Rd	30
-	Southend-on-Sea; Kenilworth Gdns, Prittlewell	30
-	Southend-on-Sea; Kings Rd, Westcliff-on-Sea	30
-	Southend-on-Sea; Lifstan Way	30
-	Southend-on-Sea; Prittlewell Chase, Prittlewell	30
-	Southend-on-Sea; Thorpe Hall Ave, Thorpe Bay	30
-	Southend-on-Sea; Western Approaches (at Rockall), Eastwood	30
-	Southend-on-Sea; Western Esplanade	30
-	South Woodham Ferrers; Hullbridge Rd	30
-	South Woodham Ferrers; Inchbonnie Rd	30
-	Stanford le Hope; London Rd	30
-	Stanford le Hope; Southend Rd, Corringham	30
-	Stanford le Hope; Springhouse Rd, Corringham	30
-	Theydon Bois; Piercing Hill	30
-	Waltham Abbey; Farm Hill Rd	30
-	Waltham Abbey; Paternoster Hill	30
-	Waltham Abbey; Sewardstone Rd	30
-	West Thurrock; London Road West Thurrock	30
-	Witham; Powers Hall End	30

Gloucestershire

Road number	Location	Speed limit (mph)
A38	Twigworth	40
A40	Andoversford (between A436 jcts)	60
A40	Gloucester Rd, St Marks, Cheltenham	40
A40	Churcham	50
A40	Farmington	60
A40	Hampnett	60
A40	Hazleton	60
A40	Little Barrington	60
A40	Northleach	60
A40	Whittington	60
A46	Ashchurch	40
A46	north of Nailsworth	40
A48	Stroat	60
A417	Burford Junction, Cirencester (north of A429 jct)	70
A417	Gloucester Rd, Corse	30
A417	Dartley Bottom (north-west of Cirencester)	70
A417	Lechlade on Thames	40
A417	Maisemore	30
A417	north of Hartpury	40
A419	Oldends La to Stonehouse Court, Stonehouse	40
A429	south-west of Bourton-on-the-Water	60
A429	Fossebridge	60
A430	Hempstead Bypass, Gloucester	40
A435	Colesbourne	60
A436	at jct with B4068	60
A4013	Princess Elizabeth Way, Arle, Cheltenham	30
A4013	Princess Elizabeth Way, Hester's Way, Cheltenham	30
A4019	Uckington	50
A4136	Brierley	40
A4136	Lower La, Coleford	40
A4136	Harrow Hill (near Nailbridge)	40
A4136	Little London	40
A4151	Steam Mills (north of Cinderford)	40
A4173	near St Peter's School, Tuffley, Gloucester	30
B4008	Bristol Rd, Olympus Park area, Quedgeley	30
B4008	Bristol Rd, Quedgeley (south of Tesco roundabout)	30
B4008	Gloucester Rd, Stonehouse	30
B4060	Kingswood (near B4058 jct)	30
B4215	south-east of Rudford	50
B4215	south of Newent Bypass	50
B4221	Kilcot Village	40
B4221	Picklenash School, Newent	30
B4226	Speech House (Forest of Dean)	60
B4228	Old Station Way, Coleford	30
B4228	Perrygrove, south of Coleford	40
B4231	Coleford Rd, Bream	30
B4633	Gloucester Rd, Cheltenham (near train station)	30
-	Cheltenham; St Georges Rd	30
-	Cheltenham; Swindon La	30
-	Cheltenham; Wyman's Lane	30
-	Cirencester; Chesterton La	30
-	Gloucester; Abbeymead Ave	30
-	Gloucester; Barrow Hill; Churchdown	30
-	Lydney; Highfield Rd	30
-	Minchinhampton Common	40
-	Parkend; Fancy Rd	30
-	Siddington	30
-	Tewkesbury; Gloucester Rd	40

Greater Manchester

Greater Manchester Casualty Reduction Partnership no longer make mobile safety camera sites freely available and are developing new sites.

Road number	Location	Speed limit (mph)
A6	Buxton Rd, Hazel Grove	30
A6	Buxton Rd, High Lane	30
A6	Stockport Rd, Manchester	30
A6	Wellington Rd North, Stockport	30
A6	Manchester Rd, Swinton	30
A34	Kingsway, Cheadle	40
A34	Birchfields Rd, Rusholme, Manchester	30
A34	Kingsway, Didsbury, Manchester	40
A49	Wigan Rd, Standish	30
A49	Warrington Rd, Marus Bridge, Wigan	30
A56	Jubilee Way, Bury	30
A56	Manchester Rd, Bury	30
A56	Walmersley Rd, Bury	30
A56	Bury New Rd, Manchester	30
A56	Chester Rd, Old Trafford (at White City Way)	30
A56	Bury New Rd, Prestwich	30
A56	Whalley Rd, Shuttleworth	30
A56	Manchester Rd, Whitefield	30
A57	Liverpool Rd, Eccles	30
A57	Manchester Rd, Hyde	30
A57	Mottram Rd, Hyde	30
A57	Hyde Rd/Manchester Rd, Manchester	30
A58	Lily La, Bamfurlong, Abram	30
A58	Liverpool Rd, Ashton-In-Makerfield	30
A58	Bury Rd, Bolton	30
A58	Wigan Rd, Deane, Bolton	30
A58	Wigan Rd, Hunger Hill, Bolton	40
A58	Angouleme Way, Bury	30
A58	Bolton Rd, Bury	30
A58	Rochdale Rd, Bury	30
A58	Bury and Bolton Rd, Radcliffe	40
A58	Halifax Rd, Rochdale	30
A62	Oldham Rd, Failsworth	30
A62	Oldham Rd, Manchester	30
A62	Manchester Rd, Werneth, Oldham	30
A62	Oldham Way, Oldham	40
A560	Shaftesbury Avenue,Timperley, Altrincham	30
A560	Mottram Old Rd, Hyde	30
A560	Crookilley Way, Stockport	50
A560	Wood St, Stockport	30
A571	Pemberton Rd, Winstanley, Wigan	30
A571	Victoria St, Newtown, Wigan	30
A572	Chaddock La, Astley, Tyldesley	30
A572	Newton Rd, Lowton (near Leigh)	30/40
A573	Wigan Rd, Golborne	30
A574	Warrington Rd, Leigh	30
A575	Walkden Rd, Worsley	30
A576	Middleton Rd, Crumpsall	30
A579	Atherleigh Way, Leigh	50
A580	East Lancashire Rd, Leigh	70
A580	East Lancashire Rd, Swinton/Worsley	50
A626	Marple Rd, Offerton, Stockport	30
A627	Oldham Rd, Ashton-under-Lyne	30
A627	Ashton Rd, Oldham	30
A627	Chadderton Way, Oldham	40
A635	Mancunian Way, Ardwick, Manchester	40
A635	Ashton Old Rd, Openshaw, Manchester	30
A635/ A6018	Stamford St, Stalybridge	30
A662	Ashton New Rd, Manchester	30
A663	Broadway, Failsworth	40
A664	Rochdale Rd, Manchester	30
A664	Manchester Rd, Castleton, Rochdale	30
A665	Bury Old Rd, Prestwich	30
A665	Cheetham Hill Rd, Manchester	30
A665	Water St/Blackburn St/Pilkington Way, Radcliffe	30
A665	New Rd, Radcliffe	30
A665	Higher La, Whitefield	30
A665	Radcliffe New Rd, Whitefield	30
A666	Blackburn Rd, Bolton	30
A666	St Peter's Way, Bolton	50
A666	Manchester Rd, Swinton	30
A667	Ringley Rd West, Whitefield	30
A670	Mossley Rd, Ashton-under-Lyne	30
A673	Chorley New Rd, Bolton	40
A676	Bolton Rd, Hawkshaw	30
A676	Bolton Rd West, Holcombe Brook, Ramsbottom	30
A676	Stubbins La, Ramsbottom	30
A680	Edenfield Rd, Rochdale	30
A5014	Talbot Rd, Stretford	30
A5079	Slade La, Levenshulme, Manchester	30
A5103	Princess Pkwy (M60 to M56)	40/50
A5103	Princess Rd, Manchester	30/40
A5106	Chorley Rd, Standish	30
A5143	Bridge La, Bramhall	30
A5143	Jacksons La, Hazel Grove	30
A5145	Edge La, Stretford	30
A5181	Mosley Rd, Trafford Park	30
A5209	Crow Orchard Rd, Shevington Moor	30
A5209	Almond Brook Rd, Standish	30
A6010	Alan Turing Way, Manchester	30
A6010	Pottery La, Manchester	30
A6017	Ashton Rd, Bredbury, Stockport	40
A6018	Mottram Rd, Stalybridge	30
A6033	Todmorden Rd, Littleborough	30
A6044	Hilton La, Prestwich	30
A6044	Sheepfoot La, Prestwich	30
A6045	Manchester Rd, Heywood	30
A6045	Heywood Old Rd, Middleton	30
A6046	Hollin La, Middleton	30
A6053	Dumers La, Radcliffe	30
A6104	Victoria Ave, Blackley, Manchester	30
A6144	Warburton La, Partington	30
A6144	Harboro Rd, Sale	30
A6144	Old Hall Rd, Sale Moor	30
A6145	Hulton La, Bolton	30
B5158	Lostock Rd, Urmston	30
B5160	Park Rd, Bowdon	30
B5165	Park Rd, Timperley, Altrincham	30
B5166	Ashton La, Ashton upon Mersey	30
B5166	Styal Rd, Heald Green, Gatley	30
B5206	Upholland Rd, Billinge	30
B5213	Church Rd, Flixton, Urmston	30
B5217	Seymour Grove, Old Trafford	30
B5218	Upper Chorlton Rd, Chorlton cum Hardy	30
B5237	Bickershaw La, Bickershaw, Abram	30
B5238	Scot La, Aspull	30
B5239	Bolton Rd, Aspull	30
B5239	Haigh Rd, Aspull	30
B5239	Dicconson La, Cooper Turning, Bolton	30
B5375	Miles La, Shevington	30
B5397	Dane Rd, Sale	30

Road number	Location	Speed limit (mph)
B6101	Strines Rd, Marple	30
B6167	Gorton Rd, Reddish	30
B6177	Stamford Rd, Mossley	30
B6194	Abbey Hills Rd, Oldham	30
B6194	Broad La, Rochdale	30
B6196	Ainsworth Rd, Bury	30
B6196	Church St, Ainsworth, Bury	30
B6196	Cockey Moor Rd, Ainsworth, Bury	30
B6196	Hardy Mill Rd, Harwood, Bolton	30
B6199	Plodder La, Farnworth	30
B6213	Bury Rd, Tottington	30
B6213	Turton Rd, Tottington	30
B6214	Brandlesholme Rd, Bury	30
B6214	Helmshore Rd, Holcombe, Ramsbottom	30
B6214	Longsight Rd, Holcombe Brook, Ramsbottom	30
B6215	Brandlesholme Rd, Greenmount, Ramsbottom	30
B6222	Bury Rd, Rochdale	30
B6225	Milnrow Rd, Littleborough	30
B6225	Wildhouse La, Milnrow	50
B6226	Chorley Old Rd, Bolton	30
B6226	Chorley Old Rd, Horwich	30
B6292	Ainsworth Rd, Radcliffe	30
B6292	Starling Rd, Radcliffe	30
B6377	Shawclough Rd, Rochdale	30
-	Bolton; Stitch-Mi-La	30
-	Bolton; Tottington Rd, Harwood	30
-	Bury; Croft La, Hollins	30
-	Bury; Radcliffe Rd	30
-	Bury; Walshaw Rd	30
-	Cheadle; Bird Hall La	30
-	Cheadle; Councillor La	30
-	Cheadle; Schools Hill	30
-	Cheadle Hulme; Carr Wood Rd	30
-	Hazel Grove; Chester Rd	30
-	Heywood; Bury Old Rd	30
-	Heywood; Queens Park Rd	30
-	Horwich; Lever Park Ave	30
-	Leigh; Queensway	30
-	Manchester; Blackley New Rd, Crumpsall	30
-	Manchester; Hazelbottom Rd/Waterloo St, Crumpsall	30
-	Mellor; Longhurst La	30
-	Pendlebury; Langley Rd	30
-	Radcliffe; Stand La	30
-	Rochdale; Bagslate Moor Rd	30
-	Rochdale; Caldershaw Rd	30
-	Rochdale; Smithybridge Rd, Smithy Bridge	30
-	Romiley; Sandy La	30
-	Sale; Glebelands Rd	30
-	Sale; Hope Rd	30
-	Sale; Norris Rd	30
-	Salford; Belvedere Rd	30
-	Stockport; Dialstone La, Offerton	30
-	Stockport; Harrytown, Bredbury	30
-	Stretford; Kings Rd	30
-	Trafford Park; Westinghouse Rd	30
-	Westhoughton; The Hoskers	30

Hampshire and the Isle of Wight

Road number	Location	Speed limit (mph)
A27	Portchester to Titchfield	30/40
A27	Parkgate to A3024	30/40
A30	Blackwater	30/40
A30	Hook	30/40
A33	Riseley to Basingstoke	50
A33	Millbrook Rd, Southampton	50
A33	The Avenue, Southampton	30
A325	Farnborough/Aldershot, Hawley La (B3272) to Cranmore La (B3008)	30/40/60/70
A325	Whitehill to county boundary near Farnham	30/40/60
A334	Wickham, A32 to B2177	n/a
A335	Eastleigh	30/40
A337	Lymington Rd/Christchurch Rd, New Milton	30/40
A337	Pennington, Lymington to Balmerlawn, Brockenhurst	30/40/50/60
A338	Fordingbridge to county boundary	40/60
A338	Ringwood to Ibsley	40/60
A339	Lasham	60
A340	Pamber End to Tadley	30/60
A2047	Fratton Rd, Portsmouth	30
A3020	Blackwater (IOW)	n/a
A3020	Blackwater Rd, Newport (IOW)	40
A3021	York Ave, East Cowes (IOW)	30
A3024	Bursledon Rd, Southampton	30/40
A3024	Northam Rd/Bitterne Rd West, Southampton	30
A3054	Binstead Hill, Binstead (IOW)	30
A3054	Fairlee Rd, Newport (IOW)	30/40
A3054	High St/Lushington Hill, Wootton Bridge (IOW)	30/40
A3055	High St/New Rd, Brading (IOW)	30
A3056	Blackwater (IOW)	n/a
B2149	New Rd, Havant	30
B2149	Petersfield Rd, Havant	40
B2177	A334 to Winchester Rd, Bishop's Waltham	30/40/60
B3037	Fair Oak to Eastleigh	30/40
B3055	Brockenhurst to A35	30/40
B3272	Yateley	30/40
B3321	Victoria Gr, East Cowes (IOW)	30
B3323	Carisbrooke Rd, Newport (IOW)	30
B3395	Sandown to Yaverland (IOW)	30
-	Basingstoke; Tobago Close	30
-	East Cowes; Adelaide Gr (IOW)	30
-	Gosport; Grange Rd	40
-	Newport; Long La (IOW)	30
-	Newport; Staplers Rd (IOW)	30
-	Portsmouth; Clarence Esplanade	30

Hertfordshire

Road number	Location	Speed limit (mph)
A119	North Rd, Hertford (at St Josephs School)	30
A409	Heathbourne Road, Bushey (at Bupa Hospital)	30
A411	London Rd, Bushey (east of Grange Rd)	30
A411	Barnet La, Elstree (at Edgwarebury La)	30
A411	Hempstead Rd, Watford (at Glen Way)	30
A414	St Albans Rd, Hemel Hempstead (at Longlands)	40
A414	St Albans Rd, Hemel Hempstead (near Rant Meadow)	40
A414	Hertingfordbury Rd, Hertford (at Valeside)	40
A505	Cambridge Rd, Hitchin (100m south-west of Queenswood Dr)	30
A505	Royston Rd, Baldock (at Slip End Farm)	70
A600	Bedford Rd, Hitchin (at Times Close)	30
A600	Bedford Rd, Hitchin (75m south of north jct of Wellingham Ave)	30
A602	Stevenage Rd, Hitchin	40
A602	Broadhall Way, Stevenage (A1072 to Shephalbury Park)	40
A602	Monkswood Way, Stevenage (100m north of Broadhall Way)	40
A1000	Barnet Rd, Ganwick Corner, Potters Bar (at Wagon Rd)	40
A1057	Hatfield Rd, St Albans (near Beechwood Ave)	30
A1057	St Albans Rd West, Hatfield (near Poplar Ave)	40
A1170	High Rd Wormley, Wormley	30
A4125	Sandy La, South Oxhey (180m south of Batchworth La)	40
A4147	Leverstock Green Rd, Hemel Hempstead (west of Bartel Cl)	30
A4251	London Rd, Bourne End	30
A5183	Elstree Hill South, Elstree	30
A5183	Park Street	30
A6141	Letchworth Gate, Letchworth (250m north-west of Baldock La)	40
B156	Goffs La, Cheshunt (at Goffs School)	30
B176	High St, Cheshunt (near Warwick Dr)	30
B197	London Rd, Baldock (at Hillcrest)	30
B197	North Rd, Stevenage (south of Rectory La)	30
B462	Aldenham Rd, Watford (at Met Police Club)	30
B487	Redbourn La, Hatching Green, Harpenden (at Oakfield Rd)	30
B487	Queensway, Hemel Hempstead (near Highfield La)	40
B488	Icknield Way, Tring (at Little Tring Rd)	40
B556	Mutton La, Potters Bar (near Albermarle Ave)	30
B1004	Windhill, Bishop's Stortford (west of Windhill Old Rd)	30
B1197	London Rd, Hertford Heath (north of Woodland Rd)	30
B1502	Stanstead Rd, Hertford (east of Foxholes Ave)	30
B4505	Chesham Rd, Bovingdon (near Hyde La)	30
B4630	Watford Rd, Chiswell Green, St Albans	30
B5378	Allum La, Borehamwood (at Lodge Ave)	30
B6426	Cavendish Way, Hatfield	30
-	Cheshunt; Hammondstreet Rd (west of Peakes La)	30
-	Hemel Hempstead; Bennetts End Rd (near Reddings)	30
-	Hemel Hempstead; High St Green	30
-	Hemel Hempstead; Long Chaulden	30
-	Hoddesdon; Essex Rd (at Pindar Rd)	30
-	Letchworth; Pixmore Way (at Shott La)	30
-	Royston; Old North Rd (York Way to Orchard Rd)	30
-	South Oxhey; Hayling Rd (Gosforth La to Arbroath Green)	30
-	St Albans; Sandpit La (at Gurney Court Rd)	30
-	Stevenage; Clovelly Way (Scarborough Ave to Eastbourne Ave)	30
-	Stevenage; Grace Way	30
-	Stevenage; Gresley Way, Poplars	30
-	Watford; Radlett Rd (north of Colonial Way)	30
-	Watford; Tolpits La (at Scammell Way)	30
-	Welwyn Garden City; Heronswood Rd (south of Linces Way)	30
-	Welwyn Garden City; Howlands (at garages at entrance to hospice)	30

Humberside

Road number	Location	Speed limit (mph)
M180	West of River Trent	70
A18	Barton Street (near Grimsby)	NSL
A18	Doncaster Rd, Scunthorpe	40
A18	Queensway, Scunthorpe	40
A46	Clee Rd, Cleethorpes	30
A46	Laceby Rd, Grimsby	30
A46	Weelsby Rd, Grimsby	30
A63	Castle St, Kingston upon Hull	40
A63	Daltry Street Flyover, Kingston upon Hull	40
A159	Ashby Rd, Scunthorpe	30
A159	Messingham Rd, Scunthorpe	30
A161	High Street, Belton	30
A163	Holme upon Spalding Moor	30
A164	Leconfield	30
A165	Beeford	30
A165	Kingsgate, Bridlington	30
A165	Coniston	40
A165	Freetown Way, Kingston upon Hull	30
A165	Holderness Rd, Kingston upon Hull	40
A165	Skirlaugh	30
A180	Great Coates junction	70
A614	Airmyn Rd, Goole	30
A614	Holme upon Spalding Moor	40
A614	Thorpe Rd, Howden	30
A614	Middleton on the Wolds	30
A614	Shiptonthorpe (both sides of roundabout)	60
A1031	Tetney Rd, Humberston	30
A1033	Thomas Clarkson Way, Kingston upon Hull	40
A1033	Thorngumbald	30
A1033	Withernsea	30
A1035	Hull Bridge Rd, Beverley	30
A1038	Quay Rd/St John's St, Bridlington	30
A1077	Barrow Rd, Barton-upon-Humber	30
A1079	Barmby Moor	50
A1079	Beverley Bypass (A1039 to Dunswell)	NSL
A1079	Beverley Rd, Kingston upon Hull (Desmond Ave to Riverdale Rd)	30
A1079	Beverley Rd, Kingston upon Hull (Sutton Rd to Mizzen Rd)	40
A1079	Beverley Rd, Kingston upon Hull (near Mizzen Rd)	40
A1079	Bishop Burton	30
A1079	Market Weighton Bypass	NSL
A1084	Bigby High Rd, Brigg	30
A1105	Boothferry Rd, Kingston upon Hull	40
A1136	Cromwell Rd, Grimsby	40
A1136	Great Coates Rd, Grimsby	30
A1174	Beverley Rd, Dunswell	30
A1174	Woodmansey	30
A1243	Louth Rd, Grimsby	30
B1203	Waltham Rd, Grimsby	30
B1206	Wold Rd, Barrow-upon-Humber	30
B1207	High St, Broughton	30
B1230	Gilberdyke	40
B1230	Newport	40
B1231	Anlaby Rd, Kingston upon Hull	30
B1232	Beverley Rd, Hessle	30
B1237	Leads Rd, Kingston upon Hull	30
B1237	Saltshouse Rd, Kingston upon Hull	30
B1238	Main Rd, Bilton, Kingston upon Hull	30
B1242	Rolston Rd, Hornsea	30
B1398	Greetwell	40
B1501	Grange La South, Ashby, Scunthorpe	30
-	Belton; Westgate Rd	30
-	East Halton; College Rd	30
-	Grimsby; Cromwell Rd	30
-	Immingham; Pelham Rd	30
-	Kingston upon Hull; Bricknell Ave	30
-	Kingston upon Hull; Bude Rd	30
-	Kingston upon Hull; Greenwood Ave	30
-	Kingston upon Hull; Hall Rd	30
-	Kingston upon Hull; John Newton Way	30
-	Kingston upon Hull; Marfleet La	30
-	Kingston upon Hull; Marfleet Ave	30
-	Kingston upon Hull; Priory Rd	30
-	Kingston upon Hull; Spring Bank West	40
-	Kingston upon Hull; Wawne Rd	30
-	Scunthorpe; Ashby Rd (near Pittwood House)	30
-	Scunthorpe; Cambridge Ave	30
-	Scunthorpe; Cottage Beck Rd	30
-	Scunthorpe; Doncaster Rd	40
-	Scunthorpe; Luneburg Way	30
-	Scunthorpe; Moorwell Rd, Yaddlethorpe	30
-	Scunthorpe; Rowland Rd	30
-	South Killingholme; Top Rd	30

Kent and Medway

Road number	Location	Speed limit (mph)
A2	Dunkirk to Upper Harbledown (eastbound)	70
A2	Guston (A256 to A258)	60
A2	Lydden (Wick La to Coxhill Rd, coastbound)	70
A2	London Rd, Strood, Rochester (opposite Lancelot Ave)	40
A21	Kipping's Cross	60
A21	Sevenoaks Bypass	70
A21	Castle Hill, Tonbridge	60
A25	Seal Rd, Sevenoaks (near Mill Pond)	30
A26	Maidstone Rd, Hadlow (Great Elms to Lonewood Way)	40
A28	Ashford Rd, Bethersden (near Kiln La)	40
A224	London Rd/Tubs Hill, Sevenoaks (Argyle Rd to Shoreham La)	30
A225	Sevenoaks Rd, Otford (Warham Rd to Old Otford Rd)	30
A226	Chalk, Gravesend	50
A226	Higham	40
A226	Shorne	50
A227	Culverstone Green	30
A227	Istead Rise	40
A227	Meopham Green	30
A228	Sundridge Hill, Cuxton	40
A228	Ratcliffe Highway, Chattenden	40
A228	Seven Mile Lane (A26 jct to south of Martin's La)	30
A229	Hartley Rd/Angley Rd, Cranbrook (Turnden Rd to High St)	40
A229	Blue Bell Hill, Maidstone (Tyland La to Chatham Rd)	50
A229	Linton Rd/Loose Rd, Loose, Maidstone (Linton Rd to Lancet La)	40/30
A229	City Way, Rochester	30
A249	South Street (Chalky Rd to Rumstead La)	70
A249	Chestnut Street (northbound, near slip rd to A2 Key St roundabout)	70
A256	Betteshanger	70
A256	Tilmanstone	70
A258	Dover Rd, Ringwould (north of Church La)	50
A259	Guldeford La (south-west of Brookland)	60
A259	High St, New Romney (near West St)	30
A259	St Mary's Bay (near Jefferstone La)	40
A260	Dover Rd, Folkestone (Wear Bay Rd to Southern Way)	30
A262	High St, Biddenden	30
A268	Queen St, Sandhurst	30
A289	Medway Tunnel, Chatham (near Vanguard Way)	50
A289	Wainscott Bypass (A228 to B2000)	70
A290	Blean	30
A291	Canterbury Rd, Herne (Lower Herne Rd to A299)	30
A299	Canterbury Road West, Cliffsend	30
A2990	Thanet Way, Swalecliffe, Whitstable (east of Chestfield roundabout)	60
B258	Barn End La, Wilmington, Dartford	30
B2000	Lower Rochester Rd, Rochester (north of A289)	40
B2005	Mill Way, Sittingbourne (Tribune Dr to Cooks La)	30
B2015	Maidstone Rd, Nettlestead Green (near Station Rd)	40
B2017	Badsell Rd, Five Oak Green (Whetstead Rd to Capel Grange Farm)	30
B2019	Seal Hollow Rd, Sevenoaks (A25 to Bayham Rd)	30
B2097	Maidstone Rd, Rochester (Horwood Close to Valley View)	30
-	Chatham; Street End Rd	30
-	Chatham; Walderslade Rd (Snodhurst Ave to Chestnut Ave)	30
-	Gillingham; Beechings Way (Bradbourne Ave to Beechings Green)	30
-	Herne Bay; Mickleburgh Hill	30
-	Longfield; Hartley Rd/Ash Rd (Castle Hill to Station Rd)	30
-	Margate; Shottendane Rd	30
-	Rainham; Maidstone Rd (Drury Dr to Thames Rd)	30
-	Rochester; Esplanade (Shorts Way to Hathaway Ct)	30
-	Sheerness; Marine Parade	30/40
-	Sole Street; Sole St (near Scratton Fields)	30
-	Teynham; Lower Rd (Station Rd to New Cottages)	30

Lancashire

Road number	Location	Speed limit (mph)
A6	Bolton Rd, Chorley	30/40
A6	Garstang Rd, Broughton (north of M55)	40
A6	Garstang Rd, Fulwood, Preston (north of Blackpool Rd)	30
A6	Garstang Rd, Fulwood, Preston (south of M55)	30
A6	Greaves Rd, Lancaster	30
A6	Scotforth Rd, Bailrigg, Lancaster (near Burrow La)	50
A6	North Rd, Preston	30
A6	Ringway, Preston	30
A56	Albert Rd, Colne	30
A56	Burnley Rd, Colne	30
A56	Leeds Rd, Nelson	30
A59	Gisburn Rd, Gisburn	60
A59	Liverpool Rd, Hutton	50
A59	New Hall La, Preston	30
A65	Cowan Bridge	40/60
A570	Southport Rd, Scarisbrick (at Brook House Farm)	40
A581	Southport Rd, Newtown	40
A583	Church St, Blackpool	30
A583	Whitegate Dr, Blackpool	30
A584	Promenade, Blackpool	30
A584	West/Central Beach, Lytham	30
A584	Lytham Rd, Warton	30/50
A587	East/North Park Dr, Blackpool	30
A587	Fleetwood Rd, Blackpool	30
A587	Rossall Rd/Crescent East, Cleveleys	30
A588	Lancaster Rd, Cockerham (at Gulf La)	60
A588	Head Dyke La, Preesall/Pilling	60
A666	Blackburn Rd, Earcroft, Darwen	30
A666	Blackburn Rd (Gr Manchester bdy to Bull Hill, Darwen)	50
A666	Bolton Rd, Darwen (near Cross St)	30
A666	Duckworth St, Darwen	30
A671	Whalley Rd, Read	30
A674	Preston Old Rd, Cherry Tree, Blackburn	30
A675	Belmont Rd (north of Belmont village)	50
A675	Belmont Rd (south of Belmont village)	50
A675	Bolton Rd, Abbey Village, Chorley (Dole La to Calf Hey Bridge)	30/60
A680	Rochdale Rd, Edenfield	40/60
A682	Gisburn Rd, Barrowford (near Moorcock Inn)	60
A682	Colne Rd, Brierfield	30
A682	Burnley Rd, Crawshawbooth	40
A682	Gisburn Rd, Gisburn	60
A682	Long Preston Rd, north of Gisburn	60
A683	Morecambe Rd, Lancaster	30
A5073	Waterloo Rd, Blackpool	30
A5085	Blackpool Rd, Lane Ends, Preston	30
A5209	Course La/Ash Brow, Newburgh	30
A6062	Livesey Branch Rd, Blackburn (near Green La)	30
A6068	Barrowford Rd, Barrowford	50
A6114	Casterton Ave, Burnley	30
B5192	Preston St, Kirkham	30
B5242	Bescar Brow La/Hall Rd, Scarisbrick	30
B5251	Pall Mall, Chorley	30
B5254	Leyland Rd/Watkin La, Lostock Hall	30
B5254	Leyland Rd, Penwortham, Preston (Talbot Rd to A59)	30
B5256	Turpin Green La, Leyland	30
B5266	Newton Dr, Blackpool	30
B5269	Whittingham La, Goosnargh	40
B6231	Union Rd, Oswaldtwistle	30
B6232	Haslingden Rd/Elton Rd (Belthorn to Grey Mare Inn, Blackburn)	40/50
B6232	Grane Rd, Haslingden (west of B6235)	50
B6243	Preston Rd, Longridge	50
-	Belmont; Egerton Rd	60
-	Blackburn; East Park Rd	30
-	Blackburn; Revidge Rd (near Pleckgate)	30
-	Blackburn; Whalley Old Rd, Sunny Bower (near A6119)	30
-	Blackpool; Dickson Rd (Queen St to Pleasant St)	30
-	Burnley; Burnley Rd, Harle Syke, Brierfield	30
-	Darwen; Lower Eccleshill Rd	30
-	Galgate; Bay Horse Rd	60
-	Nelson; Netherfield Rd	30
-	Preston; Lytham Rd	30
-	Preston; St George's Rd	30
-	St Annes; Church Rd/Albany Rd (near High School)	30

Leicester, Leicestershire and Rutland

Road number	Location	Speed limit (mph)
A1	Empingham	70
A1	Stretton	70
A5	Watling St, Hinckley (M69 to A47)	n/a
A5	Watling St, Hinckley (B578 to M69)	60
A5	Watling St, Sharnford (B4455 to B4114)	70
A6	Loughborough Rd, Birstall	40
A6	Abbey La, Leicester	40
A6	London Rd, Leicester (near A6030 jct)	30
A6	Derby Rd, Loughborough	30
A6	Glen Rd/Harborough Rd, Oadby	40
A47	Peterborough Rd, Barrowden	60
A47	Bisbrooke/Glaston	60
A47	Hinckley Rd, Earl Shilton	30
A47	1km west of Billesdon	50
A47	Uppingham Rd, Houghton on the Hill	40
A47	Hinckley Rd, Leicester	30
A47	Humberstone Rd, Leicester	30
A47	Glaston Rd, Morcott	50
A47	Uppingham Rd, Leicester	30
A50	Groby Rd/Leicester Rd, Glenfield, Leicester	40
A50	Woodgate/Frog Island, Leicester	30
A426	Lutterworth Rd, Dunton Bassett	50
A426	Leicester Rd, Lutterworth	60
A426	Leicester Rd, Glen Parva, Leicester	40
A426	Lutterworth Rd, Whetstone	60
A444	Atherstone Rd, Fenny Drayton	50
A444	Norton Juxta Twycross	50
A444	Main Rd, Twycross village	30
A447	Hinckley Rd, Cadeby	60
A447	Wash La/Melbourne Rd, Ravenstone	40
A512	Ashby Rd, Loughborough	30
A512	Ashby Rd Central, Shepshed	40
A563	Asquith Way, Leicester	30
A563	Attlee Way, Leicester	30
A563	Colchester Rd/Hungarton Blvd, Leicester	30
A563	Krefeld Way, Leicester	40
A563	New Parks Way, Leicester	30
A563	Glenhills Way, Leicester	30
A594	St Georges Way, Leicester	30
A606	Stamford Rd, Barnsdale (east of Oakham)	60
A606	Broughton	60
A606	Stamford Rd, Tinwell (west of A1)	60
A607	Melton Rd, Leicester	30
A607	Newark Rd, Thurmaston, Leicester	50
A607	Melton Rd, Waltham on the Wolds	60
A4304	Lubbenham Hill, Market Harborough	30
A5199	Welford Rd, Leicester	30
A5199	Bull Head St, Wigston	30
A5199	Leicester Rd, Wigston	30
A5460	Narborough Rd, Leicester	40
A6004	Alan Moss Rd, Loughborough	30
A6030	Wakerley Rd/Broad Ave, Leicester	30
A6121	Stamford Rd, Ketton	30
B568	Victoria Park Rd, Leicester	30
B581	Broughton Way/Station Rd, Broughton Astley	30
B582	Little Glen Rd, Blaby	30
B590	Rugby Rd, Hinckley	30
B591	Loughborough Rd, Charley (3km south-east of Shepshed)	60
B4114	Leicester Rd/King Edward Ave, Enderby/Narborough	40
B4114	Sharnford	30
B4666	Coventry Rd, Hinckley	30
B5366	Saffron La, Leicester	30
B6416	East Park Rd, Leicester	30
-	Ashby-de-la-Zouch; Tamworth Rd	30
-	Barrow-upon-Soar; Sileby Rd	30
-	Blaby; Lutterworth Rd	30
-	Ibstock; Leicester Rd	30
-	Leicester; Beaumont Leys La	30
-	Leicester; Fosse Rd South	30
-	Leicester; Station Rd, Glenfield	30
-	Loughborough; Forest Rd	30
-	Loughborough; Nanpantan Rd	30
-	Norris Hill; Ashby Rd (west of Ashby de la Zouch)	40
-	Shepshed; Leicester Rd	30

Lincolnshire

Road number	Location	Speed limit (mph)
A15	Ashby Lodge (2km north of B1191)	60
A15	Aswarby	60
A15	B1191 to Dunsby Hollow	60
A16	Tytton La, Boston	60
A16	Burwell	40
A16	Grainsby to Holton le Clay	60
A16	Market Deeping Bypass	50/60
A16	North Thoresby	60

Road number	Location	Speed limit (mph)
A16	Stickney (north of village)	60
A17	Fleet Hargate	60
A17	Hoffleet Stow (north of B1181)	60
A17	Moulton Common (south of B1357)	60
A52	Bridge End	60
A52	Swaton (west of B1394)	60
A52	Ropsley	60
A153	Billinghay	40
A153	Tattershall	50
A158	Scremby to Candlesby	40/50
A631	Dale Bridge near West Rasen	60
A631	Hemswell Cliff	50/60
B1188	Branston	30
B1188	Canwick (at Highfield House)	60
B1188	Potterhanworth (near B1178 jct)	60
B1191	Martin Dales	60

London

Road number	Location	Speed limit (mph)
M11	Woodford (near jct4)	n/a
M25	Jct 10 - 16	n/a
A1	Upper St, Islington	n/a
A1	Holloway Rd, Upper Holloway	n/a
A2	East Rochester Way, Bexley	n/a
A2	Old Kent Rd	n/a
A3	Clapham High St, Clapham	n/a
A3	Kennington Park Rd, Kennington	n/a
A3	Kingston Bypass	n/a
A3	Malden Way, New Malden	n/a
A3	Kingston Rd, Roehampton	n/a
A3	Clapham Rd, South Lambeth	n/a
A4	Great West Rd, Chiswick/Brentford/ Hounslow	n/a
A5	Edgware Rd, Cricklewood/Hendon	n/a
A5	Maida Vale, Maida Vale	n/a
A5	The Broadway, West Hendon	n/a
A10	Great Cambridge Rd, Edmonton	n/a
A10	Stamford Hill, Stoke Newington	n/a
A11	Bow Rd, Bow	n/a
A11	Mile End Rd, Stepney	n/a
A12	Colchester Rd, Romford	n/a
A12	Eastern Ave, Romford	n/a
A13	Alfred's Way, Barking	n/a
A13	Ripple Rd, Barking/Dagenham	n/a
A20	Sidcup Rd, Eltham/New Eltham	n/a
A20	Lee High Rd, Lewisham	n/a
A20	Lewisham Way, New Cross	n/a
A20	Sidcup Bypass, Sidcup	n/a
A21	Bromley Common	n/a
A21	Bromley Rd, Catford	n/a
A21	Rushey Green, Catford	n/a
A21	Bromley Rd, Downham	n/a
A22	Godstone Rd, Purley/Kenley	n/a
A23	Brixton Rd, Brixton	n/a
A23	Brixton Hill, Brixton	n/a
A23	Streatham High Road, Streatham	n/a
A23	Thornton Rd, Croydon	n/a
A24	Morden Rd, Merton	n/a
A24	High St Colliers Wood, Tooting	n/a
A40	Westway, Paddington/Shepherd's Bush	n/a
A40	Western Ave, Perivale	n/a
A40	Western Ave, Greenford	n/a
A40	Western Ave, Northolt	n/a
A40	Western Ave, Ruislip	n/a
A41	Gloucester Pl, Marylebone	n/a
A41	Park Rd, St John's Wood	n/a
A102	Homerton High St, Hackney	n/a
A105	Green La, Finsbury Park	n/a
A107	Cambridge Heath Rd, Bethnal Green	n/a
A107	Upper Clapton Rd, Clapton	n/a
A107	Clapton Common, Stamford Hill	n/a
A109	Bounds Green Rd, Bowes Park	n/a
A109	Oakleigh Rd South, Friern Barnet	n/a
A110	Enfield Rd, Enfield	n/a
A112	Chingford Rd, Walthamstow	n/a
A112	Hoe St, Walthamstow	n/a
A118	Romford Rd, Forest Gate	n/a
A118	London Rd, Romford	n/a
A124	Barking Rd, East Ham	n/a
A124	Barking Rd, Plaistow	n/a
A124	Rush Green Rd, Romford	n/a
A200	Creek Rd, Greenwich	n/a
A202	Camberwell New Rd, Camberwell	n/a
A202	Vauxhall Bridge Rd, Westminster	n/a
A205	Brownhill Rd, Catford	n/a
A205	Stanstead Rd, Catford	n/a
A205	Well Hall Rd, Eltham	n/a
A205	Upper Richmond Rd, Putney/Roehampton	n/a
A205	Upper Richmond Rd West, Richmond/Sheen	n/a
A206	Erith Rd, Belvedere	n/a
A206	Woolwich Rd, Belvedere	n/a
A206	Thames Rd, Crayford	n/a
A206	Woolwich Church St, Woolwich	n/a
A206	Beresford St, Woolwich	n/a
A207	Bellegrove Rd, Welling	n/a
A207	Great Western Rd, Westbourne Park	n/a
A208	Court Rd, Eltham	n/a
A208	Well Hall Rd, Eltham	n/a
A212	Gravel Hill, Croydon	n/a
A212	Grange Rd, South Norwood	n/a
A212	Westwood Hill, Sydenham	n/a
A213	Croydon Rd, Penge	n/a
A214	Elmers End Rd, Beckenham	n/a
A214	Trinity Rd, Wandsworth	n/a
A215	Denmark Hill, Camberwell	n/a
A215	Beulah Hill, Upper Norwood	n/a
A217	London Rd, Mitcham	n/a
A217	St Dunstan's Hill, Sutton	n/a
A217	Garratt La, Wandsworth	n/a
A218	Haydon's Rd, Wimbledon	n/a
A219	Fulham Palace Rd, Fulham	n/a
A219	Scrubs La, Willesden	n/a
A219	Parkside, Wimbledon	n/a
A221	Penhill Rd, Blackfen	n/a
A222	Long La, Addiscombe	n/a
A222	Bromley Rd, Beckenham	n/a
A223	North Cray Rd, Sidcup	n/a
A224	Sevenoaks Way, St Paul's Cray	n/a
A232	Croydon Rd, Wallington	n/a
A232	Cheam Rd, Sutton	n/a
A233	Main Rd, Biggin Hill	n/a
A234	Beckenham Rd, Beckenham/Penge	n/a
A234	Crystal Palace Park Rd, Sydenham	n/a
A236	Croydon Rd, Mitcham	n/a
A237	Smitham Bottom La, Purley	n/a
A238	Coombe La, Coombe	n/a
A239	Central Rd, Morden	n/a
A240	Kingston Rd, Tolworth/Stoneleigh	n/a
A298	Bushey Rd, Raynes Park	n/a
A307	Kew Rd, Kew	n/a
A307	Portsmouth Rd, Kingston upon Thames	n/a
A307	Richmond Rd, Kingston upon Thames	n/a
A308	Hampton Court Rd/Upper Sunbury Rd, Hampton	n/a
A311	High St, Teddington	n/a
A312	Harlington Rd West, Feltham	n/a

Road number	Location	Speed limit (mph)
A312	Uxbridge Rd, Hampton	n/a
A312	near Southall	n/a
A313	Park Rd/Hampton Rd, Teddington	n/a
A314	Hanworth Rd, Hounslow	n/a
A315	High St, Brentford	n/a
A315	Staines Rd, Feltham	n/a
A315	Hammersmith Rd, Hammersmith	n/a
A315	Kensington Rd, Kensington	n/a
A316	Lower Richmond Rd, North Sheen	n/a
A400	Junction Rd, Holloway	n/a
A400	Fortress Rd, Kentish Town	n/a
A400	Kentish Town Rd, Kentish Town	n/a
A402	Bayswater Rd, Bayswater	n/a
A402	Holland Park Ave, Notting Hill	n/a
A404	Hillside, Harlesden	n/a
A404	Watford Rd, Harrow	n/a
A404	Harrow Rd, Kensal Green	n/a
A404	Rickmansworth Rd, Northwood	n/a
A404	George V Ave, Pinner	n/a
A404	Watford Rd, Wembley	n/a
A406	Barking Relief Rd, Barking	n/a
A406	Southend Rd (North Circular), South Woodford	n/a
A406	North Circular Rd, Finchley	n/a
A406	North Circular Rd, Dollis Hill	n/a
A406	North Circular Rd, Neasden/Stonebridge	n/a
A408	Cowley Rd, Uxbridge	n/a
A408	High Rd, Cowley	n/a
A408	Stockley Rd, West Drayton	n/a
A410	Uxbridge Rd, Harrow Weald	n/a
A410	Fryent Way, Kingsbury	n/a
A501	Euston Rd, St Pancras	n/a
A501	Pentonville Rd, Pentonville	n/a
A503	Seven Sisters Rd, Finsbury Park/ South Tottenham	n/a
A1000	High Rd, Totteridge	n/a
A1010	Fore St, Edmonton	n/a
A1020	Royal Docks Rd, Beckton	n/a
A1020	North Woolwich Rd, Silvertown	n/a
A1055	Watermead Way, Tottenham	n/a
A1112	Rainham Rd North, Dagenham	n/a
A1112	Romford Rd, Hainault	n/a
A1112	Dagenham Rd, South Hornchurch	n/a
A1153	Porters Ave, Becontree	n/a
A1199	St Paul's Rd, Islington	n/a
A1199	Woodford Rd, South Woodford	n/a
A1206	Manchester Rd, Isle of Dogs	n/a
A1206	Westferry Rd, Poplar/Isle of Dogs	n/a
A1261	Aspen Wall, Poplar	n/a
A1400	Woodford Ave, Gants Hill	n/a
A2000	Perry St, Crayford	n/a
A2022	Foxley La, Purley	n/a
A2043	Cheam Common Rd, North Cheam	n/a
A2043	Malden Rd, Cheam	n/a
A2043	Cambridge Rd/Kingston Rd, Kingston upon Thames	n/a
A2206	Southwark Park Rd, Bermondsey	n/a
A2212	Burnt Ash La, Plaistow, Bromley	n/a
A2215	Peckham Rye	n/a
A3002	Boston Rd, West Ealing	n/a
A3205	Battersea Park Rd, Battersea	n/a
A3212	Chelsea Embankment, Chelsea	n/a
A3212	Millbank, Westminster	n/a
A3216	Sloane St, Belgravia	n/a
A3220	Latchmere Rd, Battersea	n/a
A4000	Horn La, Acton	n/a
A4006	Kenton Rd, Harrow/Kenton	n/a
A4006	Kingsbury Rd, Kingsbury	n/a
A4020	Uxbridge Rd, Shepherd's Bush	n/a
A4020	Uxbridge Rd, Southall	n/a
A4020	Uxbridge Rd, Hayes	n/a
A4020	Hillingdon Hill, Uxbridge	n/a
A4090	Imperial Dr, Harrow	n/a
A4090	Alexandra Ave, South Harrow	n/a
A4090	Whitton Ave East, Sudbury	n/a
A4127	Greenford Rd, Greenford	n/a
A4127	Greenford Rd, Southall	n/a
A4140	Honeypot La, Queensbury	n/a
A4180	Ducks Hill Rd, Northwood	n/a
A4180	West End Rd, South Ruislip	n/a
A4180	Ruislip Rd, Yeading	n/a
A5109	Totteridge Common, Totteridge	n/a
B112	Homerton Rd, Hackney	n/a
B155	Belmont Rd, Harringay	n/a
B160	Larkshall Rd, Chingford	n/a
B175	Orange Tree Hill, Havering-atte-Bower	n/a
B175	Havering Rd, Collier Row, Romford	n/a
B178	Ballards Rd, Dagenham	n/a
B187	St Mary's La, Upminster	n/a
B205	Salter Rd, Rotherhithe	n/a
B210	Hillreach, Greenwich	n/a
B213	Abbey Rd, Abbey Wood	n/a
B213	Lower Rd, Belvedere	n/a
B214	Albany Rd, Walworth	n/a
B218	Brockley Rd, Brockley/Crofton Park	n/a
B218	Brockley Rise, Forest Hill	n/a
B221	Kings Ave, Clapham Park	n/a
B229	Bolingbroke Grove, Balham	n/a
B238	Peckham Rye	n/a
B243	Park Hill Rd, Croydon	n/a
B266	Brigstock Rd, Thornton Heath	n/a
B272	Beddington La, Croydon	n/a
B272	Foresters Dr, South Beddington	n/a
B275	Upper Selsdon Rd, Croydon	n/a
B276	Marlpit La, Coulsdon	n/a
B278	Green La, Morden	n/a
B279	Tudor Dr, Morden Park	n/a
B282	West Barnes La, Raynes Park	n/a
B286	Martin Way, Morden	n/a
B302	Royal Hospital Rd, Chelsea	n/a
B349	Mill Hill Rd, Barnes	n/a
B353	Sandycombe Rd, Kew	n/a
B358	Church Gr, Hampton Wick	n/a
B358	Sixth Cross Rd, Strawberry Hill	n/a
B358	Nelson Rd/Hospital Bridge Rd, Whitton	n/a
B415	Kensington Park Rd, Notting Hill	n/a
B450	Ladbroke Gr, Notting Hill	n/a
B454	Church La, Kingsbury	n/a
B455	Ealing Rd, Brentford	n/a
B461	Whitchurch La, Stanmore	n/a
B466	Eastcote Rd, Ruislip	n/a
B472	Joel St, Northwood Hills/Eastcote	n/a
B483	Park Rd, Uxbridge	n/a
B550	Friern Barnet La, Friern Barnet	n/a
B1335	Wennington Rd, Rainham	n/a
B1421	Ockendon Rd, Upminster	n/a
B1459	Chase Cross Rd, Collier Row	n/a
B2030	Coulsdon Rd, Coulsdon	n/a
B2230	Brighton Rd, Sutton	n/a
B2230	Rose Hill, Sutton	n/a
-	Balham; Atkins Rd	n/a
-	Beckenham; Wickham Way	n/a
-	Bedfont; Hatton Rd	n/a
-	Bexleyheath; Pickford La	n/a
-	Brixton; Herne Hill Rd	n/a

Road number	Location	Speed limit (mph)
-	Brondesbury Park; The Avenue	n/a
-	Bushy Park; Chestnut Ave	n/a
-	Caterham; Coulsdon Rd	n/a
-	Catford; Whitefoot La	n/a
-	Collier Row; Pettits La North	n/a
-	Coulsdon; Chaldon Way	n/a
-	Coulsdon; Portnalls Rd	n/a
-	Coulsdon; St Andrew's Rd	n/a
-	Coulsdon; Woodplace La	n/a
-	Cricklewood; Crest Rd	n/a
-	Croydon; Farley Rd	n/a
-	Croydon; Shirley Hills Rd	n/a
-	Eastcote; Eastern Ave	n/a
-	East Wickham; King Harolds Way	n/a
-	Elmer's End; The Glade	n/a
-	Eltham; Glenesk Rd	n/a
-	Eltham; Rochester Way	n/a
-	Enfield; Lincoln Rd	n/a
-	Gidea Park; Heath Dr	n/a
-	Golders Green; Hampstead Way	n/a
-	Grove Park/Lee; Burnt Ash Hill	n/a
-	Hainault; Manford Way	n/a
-	Ham; Dukes Ave/Riverside Dr	n/a
-	Hampton; Broad La	n/a
-	Hanworth; Castle Way	n/a
-	Hanworth; Oak Ave	n/a
-	Hanworth; Swan Rd	n/a
-	Harefield; Church Hill	n/a
-	Harefield; Northwood Rd	n/a
-	Harrow; Harrow View	n/a
-	Harrow; Porlock Ave	n/a
-	Harrow Weald; Courtenay Ave	n/a
-	Harrow Weald; Long Elmes	n/a
-	Hayes; Kingshill Ave	n/a
-	Herne Hill; Sunray Ave	n/a
-	Heston; North Hyde La	n/a
-	Hillingdon; Charville La	n/a
-	Honor Oak; Brenchley Gdns	n/a
-	Hornchurch; Minster Way	n/a
-	Hornchurch; Parkstone Ave	n/a
-	Hornchurch; Wingletye La	n/a
-	Kenton; Woodcock Hill	n/a
-	Kilburn; Christchurch Ave	n/a
-	Morden; Buckfast Rd	n/a
-	Morden Park; Hillcross Ave	n/a
-	New Addington; Featherbed La	n/a
-	New Addington; King Henry's Dr	n/a
-	New Beckenham; Worsley Bridge Rd	n/a
-	North Harrow; Whittington Way	n/a
-	North Kensington; Barlby Rd	n/a
-	North Kensington; Chesterton Rd	n/a
-	North Kensington; Latimer Rd	n/a
-	North Kensington; St Helen's Gardens	n/a
-	Old Malden; Manor Dr North	n/a
-	Peckham Rye	n/a
-	Peckham; Linden Gr	n/a
-	Pinner; Bridle Rd	n/a
-	Pinner; The Ridgeway	n/a
-	Purley; Pampisford Rd	n/a
-	Purley; Woodcote Valley Rd	n/a
-	Queensbury; Camrose Ave	n/a
-	Rainham; Lamb's La South	n/a
-	Romford; Balgores La	n/a
-	Romford; Brentwood Rd	n/a
-	Romford; Crow La	n/a
-	Romford; Mashiters Hill	n/a
-	Romford; Slewins La	n/a
-	Ruislip; King's College Rd	n/a
-	Ruislip; Park Ave	n/a
-	Ruislip; Southbourne Gardens	n/a
-	Shirley; Orchard Ave	n/a
-	Shirley; Upper Shirley Rd	n/a
-	Sidcup; Faraday Ave	n/a
-	South Ruislip/Eastcote; Field End Rd	n/a
-	Southall; Lady Margaret Rd	n/a
-	Southall; Park Ave	n/a
-	St Helier, Morden; Middleton Rd	n/a
-	Twickenham; Waldegrave Pk	n/a
-	Upminster; Hall La	n/a
-	Upminster; Ingrebourne Gdns	n/a
-	Wallington; Parkgate Rd	n/a
-	Wallington; Sandy La	n/a
-	Wandsworth; Bolingbroke Grove	n/a
-	West Dulwich; Alleyn Park	n/a
-	West Kensington; Holland Villas Rd	n/a
-	Willesden Green; Mount Pleasant Rd	n/a
-	Wimbledon; Church Rd	n/a
-	Wimbledon; Ridgeway Pl	n/a
-	Wood Green; White Hart La	n/a

Merseyside

Road number	Location	Speed limit (mph)
A57	East Prescot Rd, Knotty Ash, Liverpool	40
A58	Prescot Rd, St Helens	30
A506	Longmoor La, Fazakerley, Liverpool	30
A551	Leasowe Rd, Wallasey	40
A553	Laird St, Birkenhead	30
A561	Speke Rd/Speke Blvd, Speke, Liverpool	40
A562	Parliament St/Upper Parliament St, Toxteth, Liverpool	30
A572	Common Rd, Newton-le-Willows	30
A580	East Lancashire Rd (near A57 jct), St Helens	60
A580	Townsend Ave, Norris Green, Liverpool	30
A5038	Southport Rd, Bootle	30
A5080	Bowring Park Rd/Roby Rd, Court Hey, Liverpool	30
A5098	Hornby Rd, Walton, Liverpool	30
B5136	New Chester Rd, Bebington	30
B5189	Green La, Tuebrook, Liverpool	30
-	Liverpool; Great Homer St, Everton	30
-	Liverpool; Lower House La/Dwerryhouse La, Dog & Gun	30
-	Liverpool; Muirhead Ave, West Derby	30
-	Liverpool; Netherfield Rd North, Everton	30
-	Liverpool; Park La, Aintree	30
-	Liverpool; Utting Ave East, Norris Green	30

Norfolk

Road number	Location	Speed limit (mph)
A10	Downham Market to Setchey	n/a
A11	Ketteringham	70
A11	Roudham Heath (A1075/B1111)	70
A11	Spooner Row (near B1172 jct)	70
A12	Hopton on Sea	70
A17	Terrington St Clement	60
A47	Wisbech to King's Lynn	n/a
A47	East Winch	60
A47	Narborough	60
A47	Swaffham to Dereham	n/a
A47	Tuddenham to Easton	n/a
A47	Postwick	70
A47	Burlingham to Great Yarmouth	60
A134	Mundford to Whittington	n/a
A134	Thetford (south)	30
A140	Scole to Long Stratton	n/a
A140	Saxlingham Thorpe	40
A140	Aylsham Road, Norwich	30
A140	Norwich (Ring Road) to A149 jct	n/a
A143	Scole to Harleston	n/a
A143	B1062 jct to Earsham	60
A143	Broome Bypass	60
A143	Gillingham to Toft Monks	60
A143	Haddiscoe (bends)	30
A146	Hales	60
A146	Stockton	60
A147	Riverside Rd/Bishop Bridge Rd, Norwich	30
A148	Grimston Rd, King's Lynn	40
A148	Wootton Rd, King's Lynn	30
A148	West Rudham	30
A148	Sculthorpe to Bale	n/a
A148	Sharrington to Letheringsett	60
A148	Bodham	60
A148	Pretty Corner (near A1082/Sheringham)	60
A149	Kings Lynn (A10/A47 to B1145)	60
A149	Knights Hill (King's Lynn) to Hunstanton	n/a
A149	Sheringham	30
A149	Cromer to A140 jct	n/a
A149	A140 jct to B1436 jct	60
A149	A1151 jct to Great Yarmouth	n/a
A1065	Weeting	60
A1065	Hilborough	60
A1065	South Acre	60
A1066	Mundford Rd, Thetford	40
A1066	Rushford	60
A1066	South Lopham	60
A1066	Roydon & Diss	30
A1067	Drayton to Foxley	n/a
A1075	East Wretham (heath)	60
A1078	Edward Benefer Way, South Wootton, King's Lynn	40
A1122	Swaffham/Beachamwell	60
A1151	near A149 jct	n/a
B1108	Earlham Rd, Norwich	30
B1140	Plumstead Rd, Norwich	30
B1149	Horsford Woods (north of Horsford)	60
B1150	Scottow	40
B1150	Westwick	50
B1332	Ditchingham	50
-	Caister-on-Sea; Ormesby Rd	30
-	Drayton/Thorpe Marriot; Reepham Rd	50
-	Harleston	30
-	Norwich; Fifers La	30
-	Norwich; Hall Rd (near A146 jct)	30/40
-	Norwich; Plumstead Rd East	30
-	Norwich; Salhouse Rd, Sprowston	n/a
-	Norwich; Spixworth Rd, Old Catton	30
-	Wymondham (A11) to B1113 (Wreningham/Bracon Ash)	50

Northamptonshire

Road number	Location	Speed limit (mph)
A5	Towcester	30
A5	Long Buckby to Watford	60
A5	Kilsby	30
A5	near M1, jct 18	60
A5	Lilbourne	60
A6	Burton Latimer Bypass	60
A43	Broughton to Kettering	60
A43	Weldon (near Corby)	50
A43	Duddington	60
A43	Main Rd, Collyweston	30
A43	Collyweston to Easton on the Hill	40
A43	Easton on the Hill	40
A45	Flore	30
A361	Daventry Rd, Kilsby	30
A361	Welton	60
A422	Brackley Bypass	60
A422	Brackley (west)	60
A427	Oakley Rd/Weldon Rd, Corby	40
A427	Oundle Rd, Upper Benefield	60
A428	East Haddon	60
A428	Harlestone Rd, Northampton	30
A428	Little Houghton	60
A428	Brafield on the Green	30
A508	Broad St, Northampton	30
A508	Harborough Rd, Northampton	30
A508	Grafton Regis	30
A508	Stoke Bruerne to Yardley Gobion	60
A509	Kettering Rd, Isham	30
A605	Thrapston	40
A605	Thorpe Waterville	60
A605	Barnwell	60
A605	Oundle Bypass	60
A605	Tansor	40
A4256	Eastern Way, Daventry	40
A4500	Ecton Brook	40
A5028	Northampton Rd, Rushden	30
A5076	Redhouse Rd, Moulton Park, Northampton	40
A5095	Kingsley Rd/Kingsthorpe Gr, Northampton	30
A5095	St Andrew's Rd, Northampton	30
A5193	Harrowden Rd, Wellingborough	30
A5193	London Rd, Wellingborough	40
A6003	Kettering to Great Oakley	50
A6014	Oakley Rd, Corby	40
A6116	Brigstock	60
A6116	Geddington Rd, Corby	40
A6116	Steel Rd, Corby	40
B526	Horton	30
B569	Station Rd/Wollaston Rd, Irchester	30
B569	Knuston Vale, Rushden	50
B570	Gipsy La, Irchester	30
B576	Harborough Rd, Desborough	30
B576	Rothwell Rd, Desborough	60
B4036	Eastern Way, Daventry	40
B4100	Croughton Rd, Aynho	30
B4525	Helmdon	60
B4525	Thorpe Mandeville	40
B5385	Main St, Watford	30
-	Boughton; Moulton La	30
-	Barton Seagrave; Cranford Rd	40
-	Cranford St John; High St	30
-	Daventry; Royal Oak Way South	30
-	Islip; Kettering Rd	30
-	Northampton; Rowtree Rd, East Hunsbury	30
-	Overstone; Sywell Rd	30
-	Wellingborough; Doddington Rd	30
-	Yarwell; Nassington Rd/Wansford Rd	30

Northumbria

Road number	Location	Speed limit (mph)
A1	Berwick Bypass near Dunns jct	60
A68	Colt Crag (reservoir)	60
A69	Haltwhistle Bypass	60
A69	Nafferton (near B6309)	70
A69	Two Mile Cottage, Hexham	70
A182	Houghton Rd, Houghton-le-Spring	30
A183	Chester Rd/The Broadway, Sunderland	30
A184	Western Terrace, West Boldon	30
A186	City Rd, Newcastle	30
A186	West Rd, Denton Burn, Newcastle (A1 to A191)	40
A186	Westgate Rd, Newcastle (west of Elswick Rd jct)	30
A189	Haddricks Mill Rd, South Gosforth	30

Road number	Location	Speed limit (mph)
A189	Cramlington	70
A190	Seghill	n/a
A191	Whitley Rd, Longbenton	30
A191	Springfield Rd, Blakelaw, Newcastle	30
A192	near Plessey Woods Country Park, Cramlington	30
A193	Shields Road Bypass, Byker	40
A193	Beresford Rd, Seaton Sluice	30
A193	Church Bank, Wallsend	30
A194	Newcastle Rd, Simonside (north-east of A1300 jct)	40
A194	Western Approach, South Shields (at Laygate)	30
A196	Blackclose Bank, Ashington	30
A690	Durham Rd, Houghton-le-Spring (at Stony Gate)	50
A690	Durham Rd, Sunderland	30
A692	Church St, Marley Hill (near Sunniside)	30
A694	Station Rd, Rowlands Gill	30
A694	Winlaton Mill	40
A695	Crawcrook Bypass	60
A695	Prudhoe Bypass (east)	40
A696	Belsay village	30
A696	Kirkwhelpington	60
A696	West Rd, Ponteland	30
A696	south-east of Otterburn	60
A697	Morpeth (1km north of A1 jct)	60
A697	Wooperton	60
A698	at B6470 jct	60
A1018	Ryhope Rd, Grangetown, Sunderland	30
A1052	Dairy La, Houghton-le-Spring	30
A1058	Jesmond Rd, Jesmond, Newcastle	30
A1068	Amble Industrial Estate	30
A1068	The Wynd, Amble	30
A1147	Gordon Terr, Stakeford (near Ashington)	30
A1171	Dudley La, Cramlington	30
A1290	Vermont, Washington	30
A1300	Prince Edward Rd, South Shields	30
A6085	Lemington Rd, Lemington, Newcastle	40
A6127	Durham Rd, Barley Mow, Birtley	30
B1288	Leam Lane, Gateshead (near A195)	40
B1296	Old Durham Rd (Sheriffs Hwy), Gateshead	30
B1297	Blackett St/Western Rd, Jarrow	30
B1298	New Rd, Boldon Colliery	30
B1301	Dean Rd/Laygate, South Shields	30
B1316	Lynn Rd, North Shields	30
B1318	Bridge St, Seaton Burn	30
B1404	Seaham Rd, Houghton-le-Spring	30
B1426	Sunderland Rd, Felling	30
B1505	Great Lime Rd, West Moor, Longbenton	30
B1523	Plessey Rd, Blyth	30
B6315	Hookergate La, High Spen	30
B6317	Main Rd, Ryton	30
B6317	Whickham Highway, Whickham	30
B6318	Military Rd, Whitchester (east of Harlow Hill)	60
B6318	Military Rd, Whittington Fell (west of A68)	60
B6322	Haltwhistle	60
B6324	Stamfordham Rd, Westerhope, Newcastle	40
B6918	Woolsington Village	30
-	Ashington; College Rd	30
-	Ashington; Station Rd	30
-	Bedlington; Barrington Rd	30
-	Blaydon; Shibdon Bank	30
-	Blyth; Amersham Rd	30
-	Boldon Colliery; Hedworth La/ Abingdon Way	40
-	Chopwell; Mill Rd	30
-	Crawcrook; Greenside Rd	30
-	Dinnington; Dinnington Rd (north of Brunton La)	60
-	Gateshead; Askew Rd West	30
-	Gateshead; Saltwell Rd South	30
-	Gateshead; Split Crow Rd	30
-	Hebburn; Campbell Park Rd	30
-	Longbenton; Coach La	30
-	Newcastle; West Denton Way, West Denton (east of Linhope Rd)	40
-	North Shields; Norham Rd	30
-	Shiney Row; Success Rd	40
-	South Shields; Harton La, Harton	30
-	South Shields; Nevinson Ave, Whiteleas	30
-	Sunderland; North Hylton Rd, Southwick (near Castletown Way)	40
-	Sunderland; North Moor La, Farringdon	40
-	Sunderland; St Luke's Rd, Pallion/ South Hylton	30
-	Sunderland; Silksworth Rd, New Silksworth (near Rutland Ave)	30
-	Sunderland; Springwell Rd	30
-	Sunderland; Warwick Ter, New Silksworth	30
-	Wallsend; Battle Hill Dr	30
-	Whickham; Fellside Rd	30

North Yorkshire

There is currently no safety camera partnership.

Nottinghamshire

Road number	Location	Speed limit (mph)
A52	Clifton Blvd, Nottingham (at Nottingham Univ Hospital)	40
A52	Derby Rd, Nottingham (A6514 to A6464)	30
A60	Carlton in Lindrick	30
A60	Cuckney to Market Warsop	60
A60	Nottingham Rd, Mansfield	30
A60	Nottingham (Mapperley to Trent Bridge)	30
A60	Ravenshead	50
A609	Ilkeston Rd/Wollaton Rd/Russel Dr/ Trowell Rd, Nottingham	30
A610	at Bobber's Mill, Nottingham	30
A611	Derby Rd, Annesley	30
A611	Hucknall Rd, Nottingham (A60 to A6002)	30
A612	Nottingham Rd, Southwell (Halloughton to Westgate)	30
A614	Ollerton Rd, Burntstump, Arnold (north of A60 jct)	60
A616	Ollerton Rd, Caunton	60
A620	Welham Rd, Retford	30
A631	Beckingham Bypass	50
A631	west of Beckingham	50
A631	Flood Plain Rd, west of Gainsborough	50
A6002	Bilborough Road, Nottingham	60
A6005	Castle Blvd/Abbey Bridge/Abbey St/ Beeston Rd, Nottingham	30
A6008	Canal St, Nottingham	30
A6130	Gregory Blvd, Nottingham	30
A6130	Radford Blvd/Lenton Blvd, Nottingham	30
A6191	Chesterfield Rd South, Mansfield	30
A6200	Derby Rd, Nottingham	30
B679	Wilford La, West Bridgford	30
B682	Sherwood Rise/Nottingham Rd/Vernon Rd, Basford, Nottingham	30
B6004	Strelley Rd/Broxtowe La, Broxtowe	30
B6004	Oxclose La, Arnold, Nottingham	30
B6010	Nottingham Rd, Giltbrook, Eastwood	30
B6020	Kirklington Rd, Rainworth	30
B6040	Retford Rd, Worksop	30
B6033	Bath La/Ravensdale Rd, Mansfield	30
B6166	Lincoln Rd/Northgate, Newark	30
B6326	London Rd, Newark	40
-	Hucknall; Nottingham Rd/Portland Rd/ Annesley Rd	30
-	Newark; Hawton La, Balderton	30
-	Nottingham; Beechdale Rd	30
-	Nottingham; Bestwood Park Drive	30
-	Nottingham; Ridge Way/Top Valley Drive	30
-	Nottingham; Wigman Rd	30

South Yorkshire

Road number	Location	Speed limit (mph)
A18	Carr House Rd, Doncaster (east of A6182)	40
A18	Tudworth Rd (near Hatfield)	60
A57	Mosborough Parkway, Sheffield (B6053 to B6064)	60
A57	Worksop Rd, South Anston	40
A60	Worksop Rd, Tickhill (near Friars Lane)	30
A61	Park Rd, Worsbrough Bridge, Barnsley	30
A61	Chesterfield Rd, Sheffield (near Tadcaster Way)	30
A61	Chesterfield Rd South, Sheffield (near Lowedges Rd)	40
A61	Halifax Rd, Sheffield	30
A61	Meadowhead, Norton, Sheffield	30
A628	Pontefract Rd, Lundwood/Cudworth	40
A628	Barnsley Rd, Penistone (at Nether Mill)	40
A629	Burncross Rd, Burncross, Chapeltown	30
A629	Wortley Rd, Kimberworth, Rotherham	30
A629	Upper Wortley Rd, Thorpe Hesley (near M1 jct 35)	40
A629	Halifax Rd, Wortley (at A616 overbridge)	40
A630	High Rd, Balby, Doncaster	40
A630	Wheatley Hall Rd, Doncaster	40
A630	Centenary Way, Rotherham (near Ickles Roundabout)	50
A630	Doncaster Rd, Thrybergh	40
A630	Sheffield Rd, Warmsworth	40
A631	Rotherham Rd, Maltby	30
A631	Bawtry Rd, Wickersley (west to A6021 jct)	40
A633	Rotherham Rd, Athersley South, Barnsley (near A61 jct)	30
A633	Rotherham Rd, Monk Bretton, Barnsley	40
A633	Barnsley Rd, Wombwell (near Aldham House La)	40
A635	Doncaster Rd, Ardsley, Barnsley	40
A638	Bawtry Rd, Doncaster (at racecourse)	40
A638	Great North Rd, Scawthorpe/Adwick-Le-Street	50
A638	York Rd, Scawthorpe/Sunnyfields, Doncaster	40
A6022	Rowns La, Swinton	30
A6023	Doncaster Rd, Mexborough	30
A6023	Mexborough Relief Rd (dual carr section)	40
A6101	Rivelin Valley Rd, Sheffield	30/40
A6102	Oughtibridge	30
A6102	Middlewood Rd, Sheffield (at ambulance station)	30
A6109	Meadow Bank Rd, Rotherham (near Oakdale Rd)	40
A6123	Herringthorpe Valley Rd, Rotherham (near Far La)	40
A6135	Ecclesfield Rd, Chapeltown	40
B6059	Kiveton Park/Wales	30
B6066	Whitehill La, Brinsworth, Rotherham	30
B6082	Carlisle St East, Sheffield	30
B6090	Wentworth Rd, Kilnhurst, Swinton	30
B6096	Station Rd, Wombwell	30
B6100	Hunningley La, Barnsley	30
B6200	Handsworth Rd/Retford Rd, Handsworth/ Orgreave, Sheffield	30
B6411	Houghton Rd, Thurnscoe	30
B6463	Stripe Rd (south of New Rossington)	60
-	Armthorpe; Hatfield La	30
-	Armthorpe; Nutwell La, Nutwell	30
-	Auckley; Hurst La (near Hayfield La)	40
-	Barnsley; Fish Dam La, Carlton	30
-	Barnsley; Pogmoor Rd	30
-	Chapeltown; Park View Rd	30
-	Conisbrough; Old Rd (Chestnut Gr to Gardens La)	30
-	Doncaster; Thorne Rd (near St Mary's Rd)	30
-	Doncaster; Urban Rd, Hexthorpe	30
-	Grimethorpe; Brierley Rd	30
-	New Edlington; Broomhouse La	30
-	Sheffield; Shirecliffe Rd, Shirecliffe	30
-	Sheffield; Wordsworth Ave (near Buchanan Rd)	30
-	Sprotbrough; Melton Rd	30
-	Stainforth; Station Rd/Church Rd	30
-	Thorne; Marshland Rd, Moorends	30
-	Wath upon Dearne; Doncaster Rd	30

Staffordshire

Road number	Location	Speed limit (mph)
A5	Weston-under-Lizard	40
A5	from M6 jct 12 to A460/A4601	50
A5	South Cannock, from A460/A4601 to A34 (Churchbridge)	30/50
A5	South Cannock, from A34 (Churchbridge) to B4154 (Turf Pub island)	30/ 60/70
A5	Brownhills, from Hanney Hay/Barracks La island to A461	60/70
A5	from A461 to A5127/A5148	70
A5	from A5127/A5148 to A38	60
A5	from A38 to B5404 Tamworth	40/50
A34	Talke, from A5011 to A500	30/60
A34	Newcastle-under-Lyme to Talke, from B5369 to A500	40/70
A34	Newcastle-under-Lyme (north), from B5369 to B5368	30/70
A34	Newcastle-under-Lyme (south), from Barracks Rd (A527) to Stoke City boundary (signed)	40
A34	Trent Vale, from A500 to London Rd Bowling Club	30/40
A34	Stone Rd, Hanford, from A5035 to A500	30/40
A34	north of Stafford, from A513 to Lloyds island/Eccleshall Rd	n/a
A34	Stafford (south), from A449 to Acton Hill Rd	30/40
A34	Cannock (north), from north of Holly La to A34/B5012 roundabout	30
A34	Cannock (south), through Great Wyrley from A5 to Jones La	30
A34	Cannock (south), from Jones La to county boundary	30/50
A50	Kidsgrove, from city boundary to Oldcott Dr	30
A51	Weston, from New Rd to 500m north-west of Sandy La	40/ 50/60
A51	Pasturefields, from Amerton La to Hoomill La	50
A51	Rugeley (north), from A460 (Sandy La) to Bower La	30/40
A51	Rugeley (south), from A460 (Sandy La) to Brereton island (A513)	30/40
A51	Longdon	60/70
A51	from A5127 (Birmingham Rd) to Heath Rd, Lichfield	30/40
A51	Tamworth Rd/Dosthill Rd, Tamworth, from Peelers Way to Ascot Dr	30
A52	Stoke-on-Trent (east), from A5272 to A520	30/40
A53	Baldwin's Gate	30
A53	Blackshaw Moor (north of Leek)	50
A53	Leek New Rd, Endon, from Nursery Ave to Dunwood La jct	30/ 40/60
A53	Longsden, from Dunwood La jct to Wallbridge Dr, Leek	60/ 40/30
A53	Leek New Rd, from A5272 (Hanley Rd) to B5051 at Endon	30/40
A444	Stanton Rd, Burton on Trent, from St Peters Bridge to Derbyshire boundary	30
A449	Stafford (south) from A34 to Gravel La	30
A449	Penkridge, from Lynehill La to half mile north of Goods Station La	40
A449	Gailey, from Rodbaston Dr to Station Dr (Four Ashes)	60/70
A449	Coven, from Station Dr (Four Ashes) to M54	40/70
A449	Stourton (Dunsley Rd to Ashwood Lower La)	40/ 50/60
A454	Bridgnorth Rd, Trescott, from Brantley La to Shop La	50
A460	Rugeley Rd/Uxbridge St, Hednesford	n/a
A460	Sandy La/Hednesford Rd, Rugeley, from A51 to south of Stile Cop Rd	30
A511	Burton upon Trent (north), from A5121 to Anslow La	30/40
A511	Burton upon Trent (south), from A5121 to Derbyshire boundary	30
A513	Weeping Cross (A34 jct) to Milford	30
A518	Stafford (west), from M6 to Bridge St	30
A518	Stafford (east), from Riverway to Blackheath La	30/40
A519	Clayton Rd, Newcastle-under-Lyme	40
A520	Weston Rd, Longton, from A50 north to city boundary	30
A520	Sandon Rd, Meir, Stoke-on-Trent, from Grange Rd to A50	30
A521	Cheadle Rd, Forsbrook	30
A4601	Avon Rd, Cannock, from A34 (Walsall Rd) to Longford island	30
A4601	Wolverhampton Rd, Cannock, from Longford island toward jct 11 to Saredon Rd	30/40
A4601	Old Hednesford Rd, Cannock, from A5190 (Lichfield Rd) to A460 (Eastern Way)	30
A5005	Lightwood Rd, Stoke-on-Trent, from A50 to A520	30/40
A5035	from A34 (Trentham) to A50 (Longton)	30
A5121	Burton upon Trent, from Borough Rd to B5108, Branston	30/ 40/50
A5121	Burton upon Trent, from Byrkley St, Horninglow, to Hillfield La, Stretton	30
A5127	Lichfield, from Upper St John St to Burton Rd	30
A5189	Burton upon Trent, from Wellington Rd (A5121) to Stapenhill Rd (A444)	30/40
A5190	Cannock Rd/Bridge Cross Rd, Burntwood, from Attwood Rd to Stockhay La	30
A5190	Cannock, from Five Ways island to Hednesford Rd	n/a
A5272	Dividy Rd from A52 to B5039	30
B5044	Silverdale, Newcastle-under-Lyme, from Sneyd Terrace to B5368	30
B5051	Stoke-on-Trent, from Smallthorne to Brown Edge	30
B5080	Pennine Way, Tamworth, from B5000 to Pennymoor Rd	30/40
B5404	Lichfield St, Tamworth, from A4091 to A453	30/40
B5404	Watling St, Tamworth, from A51 to A5	30
-	Burton upon Trent; Rosliston Rd, Stapenhill, from A5189 to county boundary	30
-	Cannock; Pye Green Rd, from A34 (Stafford Rd) to Brindley Rd	30
-	Crackley; Cedar Rd, from Crackley Bank to B5500 (Audley Rd)	30
-	Stoke-on-Trent; Oxford Rd/Chell Heath Rd, from A527 to B5051	30

Suffolk

Road number	Location	Speed limit (mph)
A11	Red Lodge to Elveden	n/a
A12	Stratford St Mary to Copdock (A14)	n/a
A12	Lound to Nacton (A14)	n/a
A14	Newmarket to Felixstowe	n/a
A134	Barnham to Nayland	n/a
A137	Brantham	30
A140	A14 jct to A143 jct	n/a
A143	Bury St Edmunds (near B1066)	30
A143	Chedburgh	30
A143	Stanton Bypass	40
A143	Highpoint Prison, Stradishall	40
A144	Ilketshall St Lawrence	40
A146	Beccles to Lowestoft	n/a
A1065	Eriswell	40
A1071	A134 jct to Ipswich	n/a
A1092	Stoke by Clare to Long Melford	n/a
A1101	Flempton	30
A1156	Foxhall, Ipswich (Felixstowe Rd)	40/ NSL
A1156	Norwich Rd, Ipswich	30
A1214	London Rd, Ipswich	40
A1302	Bury St Edmunds	30
A1304	Golf Club, Newmarket	NSL
B1078	Barking	30
B1078	Needham Market	30
B1106	Fornham	30
B1113	Bramford	40
B1115	Chilton	40
B1375	Corton (A12 jct) to Lowestoft	n/a
B1438	Melton Hill, Woodbridge	30
B1506	Kentford	40
-	Carlton Colville	30
-	Felixstowe; Grange Farm Ave	30
-	Felixstowe; Trinity Ave	30
-	Ipswich; Ellenbrook Rd	30
-	Ipswich; Foxhall Rd	30
-	Ipswich; Landseer Rd	30
-	Ipswich; Nacton Rd	30
-	Ipswich; Ropes Dr, Kesgrave	30

Surrey

Road number	Location	Speed limit (mph)
A23	Brighton Rd, Horley	30
A23	Brighton Rd, Salfords	40
A31	Hogs Back, Guildford (central and eastern sections)	60
A244	Copsem La, Esher	n/a
A307	Portsmouth Rd, Thames Ditton	n/a
A308	Staines Bypass, Staines	50
A318	Byfleet Rd/Oyster La, New Haw	n/a
-	Staines; Kingston Rd	30

Sussex

Road number	Location	Speed limit (mph)
A22	High St, Nutley	30
A27	Hammerpot, Angmering (east of Dapper's La)	70
A27	Upper Brighton Rd, Lancing (near Grand Ave)	40
A27	Holmbush, Shoreham (near A270 jct)	70
A29	Shripney Rd, Bognor Regis	40
A29	Westergate St, Westergate/Woodgate	30
A259	Marine Dr, Black Rock, Brighton	30
A259	Brighton Rd, Lancing	30
A259	Hotham Way, Bognor Regis	30
A259	Main Rd, Fishbourne	30
A259	Marine Dr, Saltdean	30
A271	North Trade Rd, Battle	30
A271	Hailsham Rd, Herstmonceux	30
A280	Patching	40
A281	Guildford Rd, Horsham	30
A283	Northchapel	30
A283	Lower St (east), Pulborough	30
A285	Stane St, Halnaker	40
A285	Station Rd, Petworth	30
A2032	Littlehampton Rd/Poulter's La, Worthing	30
A2038	Hangleton Rd, Hove	30
A2270	Eastbourne Rd, Willingdon	40
B2066	New Church Rd, Hove	30
B2070	London Rd, Rake (near Petersfield)	40
B2093	The Ridge, Hastings	30
B2100	Crowborough Hill, Crowborough	30
B2104	Ersham Rd, Hailsham	30
B2111	Lewes Rd, Lindfield, Haywards Heath	30
B2123	Falmer Rd, Woodingdean, Brighton	30
B2138	Lower St, Fittleworth	30
B2166	Aldwick Rd, Bognor Regis	30
B2203	Hailsham Rd, Heathfield	30
-	Bognor Regis; Chalcraft La	30
-	Brighton; Carden Ave	30
-	Crawley; Gatwick Rd (near Hazlewick Flyover)	30
-	Crawley; Gossops Dr	30
-	Crawley; Manor Royal	30
-	Eastbourne; Brodrick Rd, Hampden Park	30
-	Horsham; Pondtail Rd	30
-	Hove; Shirley Dr	30
-	Worthing; Marine Pde	30
-	Worthing; The Boulevard	30

Thames Valley

Road number	Location	Speed limit (mph)
A4	Bath Rd, Calcot, Reading	40
A4	Bath Rd, Maidenhead (near All Saints Ave)	30
A4	Bath Rd, Speen, Newbury	30
A4	Berkeley Ave, Reading	30
A4	London Rd, Slough	40
A4	Sussex Pl, Slough	30
A4	Bath Rd, Thatcham	30
A4	Bath Rd, Woolhampton	30
A30	London Rd, Sunningdale	30
A34	Chieveley	70
A34	Kennington	70
A34	Radley	70
A40	Cassington	60
A40	Forest Hill	70
A40	Oxford Rd, Denham	30
A40	West Wycombe Rd, High Wycombe	30
A41	Gatehouse Rd, Aylesbury	30
A44	Over Kiddington	50
A44	London Rd, Chipping Norton	40/60
A308	Braywick Rd, Maidenhead	40
A322	Bagshot Rd, Bracknell (near A332 jct)	70
A329	Shooters Hill, Pangbourne	30
A329	Kings Rd, Reading	30
A329	Vastern Rd, Reading	30
A329	Wokingham Rd, Reading	30
A329	London Rd, Wokingham	30
A330	Brockenhurst Rd, Sunninghill	40
A355	Farnham Rd, Slough	30
A361	Burford Rd, Chipping Norton	30
A404	Marlow Bypass (near A4155 jct)	70
A404	Marlow Hill, High Wycombe	30/40
A412	North Orbital Rd, Denham	40
A412	Uxbridge Rd, Slough	40
A413	Buckingham Rd, Aylesbury	30
A413	Gravel Hill, Chalfont St Peter	30
A413	Walton St, Aylesbury	30
A413	Wendover Rd, Aylesbury	30
A413	Wendover Bypass, Wendover	60
A417	Charlton Rd, Wantage	30
A417	Faringdon Rd, Stanford in the Vale	30
A418	Oxford Rd, Tiddington	30
A420	Headington Rd, Oxford	30
A420	London Rd, Oxford	30
A421	Standing Way, Woughton on the Green, Milton Keynes	70
A421	Tingewick Bypass, Tingewick	70
A422	Newport Rd, Hardmead	60
A422	Stratford Rd, Buckingham	30/40
A509	Emberton Bypass	60
A4010	Aylesbury Rd, Monks Risborough	30
A4010	New Rd, High Wycombe	30
A4074	Woodcote Rd, Caversham, Reading	30
A4074	Nuneham Courteney	50
A4095	Bampton Rd, Curbridge	40
A4095	Witney Rd, Freeland	40
A4130	Nuffield	60
A4130	Remenham Hill	40
A4155	Henley Rd, Reading	30
A4157	Oakfield Rd, Aylesbury	30
A4183	Oxford Rd, Abingdon	30
A4260	Banbury Rd, Rousham	60
A4260	Banbury Rd, Shipton-on-Cherwell	50
A4260	Oxford Rd, Kidlington	30
A4260	Steeple Aston	60
B480	Watlington Rd, Blackbird Leys, Oxford	30
B481	Peppard Rd, Sonning Common	30
B3018	Binfield Rd, Bracknell	30
B3349	Barkham Rd, Barkham	30
B3350	Wilderness Rd, Earley	30
B3430	Nine Mile Ride, Bracknell	50
B4009	Ewelme	50
B4011	Bicester Rd, Long Crendon	30
B4017	Drayton Rd, Abingdon	30
B4034	Buckingham Rd, Bletchley	30
B4044	Oxford Rd, Farmoor	40
B4447	Cookham Rd, Maidenhead	30
B4495	Windmill Rd, Oxford	30
-	Bracknell; Opladen Way	30
-	High Wycombe; Sawpit Hill, Hazlemere	30
-	High Wycombe; Holmers Farm Way	30
-	Maidenhead; Greenways Dr	30
-	Milton Keynes; Avebury Blvd	30
-	Milton Keynes; Midsummer Blvd	30
-	Milton Keynes; Silbury Blvd	30
-	Reading; Park La	30
-	Reading; Kentwood Hill, Tilehurst	30
-	Reading; Overdown Rd, Tilehurst	30
-	Reading; The Meadway, Tilehurst	30
-	Slough; Cippenham La	30
-	Slough; Buckingham Ave	30
-	Slough; Parlaunt Rd	30
-	Witney; Corn St	30
-	Woodley; Loddon Bridge Rd	30

Warwickshire

Road number	Location	Speed limit (mph)
A5	Churchover (north-west of A426)	NSL
A5	Grendon to Hinckley	50
A45	near Ryton-on-Dunsmore	50
A46	Stratford northern Bypass, near Snitterfield	60
A46	Kenilworth Bypass at Stoneleigh	70
A47	Hinckley Rd, Nuneaton	30
A47	The Long Shoot, Nuneaton	40
A422	Alcester Rd, Stratford-upon-Avon	30
A423	near Fenny Compton	60
A423	Marton village	30
A423	near Marton	60
A423	south of Southam	60
A425	Radford Semele	30
A425	Ufton	30
A426	Dunchurch Rd, Rugby	30
A426	near Stockton	60
A428	Rugby Rd, Binley Woods	30
A428	Church Lawford	60
A428	Long Lawford	40
A429	Stretton on Fosse	60
A429	south of Wellesbourne	60
A435	Mappleborough Green, Redditch	40
A439	Stratford-upon-Avon to A46	50
A446	Allen End	60
A452	Greys Mallory, near Bishop's Tachbrook	60
A452	Europa Way, Royal Leamington Spa	60
A3400	Alderminster	30
A3400	Little Wolford	60
A3400	north of Henley in Arden	40
A3400	Pathlow	50
A4091	Middleton	NSL
A4189	Outhill to Lower Norton	60
B4089	Arden Rd, Alcester	30
B4098	Tamworth Rd, Corley	40
B4100	near jct 13, M40	60
B4100	Gaydon	60
B4102	Arbury Rd, Nuneaton	30
B4112	Ansley Rd, Nuneaton	40
B4113	Coventry Rd, Hill Top, Nuneaton	30
B4114	Lutterworth Rd, Burton Hastings	60
B4114	Church End	60
B4114	Coleshill Rd, Ansley Common (near Chapel End)	30
B4114	Tuttle Hill, Nuneaton	30
B4429	Ashlawn Rd, Rugby	40
B4455	Fosse Way, south of Princethorpe	60
B5414	Clifton Rd, Rugby	30
-	Nuneaton; Donnithorne Ave	30
-	Warwick; Primrose Hill	30

West Mercia

Road number	Location	Speed limit (mph)
A5	Aston (2km south-east of A483 jct)	60
A5	Montford Bridge	60
A5	Moreton Bridge (1.5km south of Chirk)	60
A5	West Felton	60
A40	Pencraig	50
A41	Albrighton Bypass	40/60
A41	Chetwynd	60
A41	Ternhill	40
A41	Whitchurch Bypass	60
A44	Bromyard Rd, Worcester	30
A44	Wickhamford	40
A46	Beckford	50
A46	Evesham Bypass	60
A49	Ashton	60
A49	Dorrington	30
A49	Harewood End	40
A417	Parkway (1km south of Ledbury)	40
A438	Staunton-on-Wye	60
A441	Evesham Rd, Astwood Bank	30
A442	Crudgington	40
A448	Kidderminster Rd, Bromsgrove	30
A456	Blakedown	30
A456	Newnham Bridge	30
A458	Morville	40
A458	Much Wenlock	30
A465	Allensmore	60
A491	Sandy La (west of M5, jct 4)	60
A491	Stourbridge Rd (both sides of B4188 jct)	50
A528	Ellesmere Rd, Shrewsbury	30
A4103	Lumber La to Lugg Bridge, Hereford (at and east of A465 jct)	60
A4103	Newtown Cross	40
A4103	Stifford's Bridge to Storridge	50
A4104	Drake St, Welland	30
A4104	Marlbank Rd, Welland	30
A4110	Three Elms Rd, Hereford	30
A5064	London Rd, Shrewsbury	30
B4084	Cropthorne	40
B4096	Old Birmingham Rd, Marlbrook	30
B4190	Habberley La, Kidderminster	30
B4208	Welland	30
B4211	Church St/Barnard's Green Rd, Great Malvern	30
B4373	Castlefields Way, Telford	40
B4373	Wrockwardine Wood Way, Oakengates, Telford	40
B4368	Hungerford (near Broadstone)	40
B4638	Woodgreen Dr, Worcester	30
B5060	Castle Farm Way, St George's, Telford	40
B5062	Edgmond Rd, Newport	60
B5062	Sundorne Rd, Shrewsbury	30
-	Hereford; Yazor Rd	30
-	Newport; Wellington Rd	30
-	Redditch; Alders Dr, Winyates	40
-	Redditch; Bromsgrove Rd	30
-	Redditch; Coldfield Dr	40
-	Redditch; Studley Rd	30
-	Shrewsbury; Longden Rd (rural)	30
-	Shrewsbury; Monkmoor Rd	30
-	Telford; Britannia Way, Hadley	40
-	Telford; Stafford Park 1	40

West Midlands

Road number	Location	Speed limit (mph)
A41	Warwick Rd, Solihull	30
A452	Collector Rd, Castle Bromwich/Kingshurst	50
A4034	Oldbury Rd, Blackheath	30
A4036	Pedmore Rd, Dudley	40
A4040	Bromford La, Hodgehill	30
A4123	Birmingham New Rd, Tipton Green (near A457)	40
A4600	Ansty Rd, Wyken, Coventry	40
B425	Lode La, Solihull	30
B4114	Washwood Heath Rd, Ward End	30
B4121	Barnes Hill, Selly Oak	40
B4121	Shenley La, Selly Oak	40
B4135	Heath St, Smethwick	30
-	Solihull; Widney Manor Rd	30
-	Wolverhampton; The Droveway	30

West Yorkshire

Road number	Location	Speed limit (mph)
M606	At jct 1/26	50
A58	Easterly Rd, Leeds (east of B6159 Harehills La)	40
A61	Harrogate Rd, Alwoodley	40
A61	Scott Hall Rd, Leeds	40
A61	Wakefield Rd, Leeds (M621 to A654)	40
A62	Gelderd Rd, Birstall (A643 to M62)	30
A62	Linthwaite to Marsden	30
A62	Manchester Rd, Huddersfield	30
A64	York Rd, Leeds (A64(M) to B6159)	40
A65	Ilkley Rd (north-west of Burley in Wharfedale)	40
A65	Otley Rd, Guiseley	30
A616	Armitage Bridge to Brockholes	40/30
A629	Halifax Rd, Cullingworth	30
A629	Halifax Rd, Keighley (Dorothy St to Victoria Rd)	30
A629	Ovenden Rd, Ovenden, Halifax (Ovenden Way to Shay La)	30
A629	Skircoat Rd, Halifax	30
A635	Holmfirth Rd, New Mill	30
A638	Ossett Bypass (B6128 to M1)	50
A640	Westbourne Rd, Huddersfield	30
A642	Northfield La, Horbury	30
A644	Huddersfield Rd, Dewsbury	30
A644	Keelham (A629 to Deep la)	30
A645	Pontefract Rd, Featherstone	30
A645	Wakefield Rd, Featherstone	30
A646	Burnley Rd, Cornholme	30
A646	Halifax Rd, Todmorden	30
A646	Luddenden Foot	30
A647	Bradford Rd, Pudsey	40
A647	Great Horton Rd, Bradford (Moore Ave to B6147 Cooper La)	30
A650	Bradford Rd, Frizinghall, Bradford (Emm La to A6038)	30
A650/ A6037	Shipley Airedale Rd, Bradford	40
A651	Bradford Rd, Birkenshaw	30
A653	Leeds Rd, (Chidswell to M62)	40
A657	Leeds Rd, Thackley, Shipley	30
A6025	Elland Rd, (Brighouse to Elland)	40/50
A6036	Bradford Rd, Northowram	30
A6037/ A650	Shipley Airedale Rd, Bradford	40
A6038	Otley Rd, Baildon, Shipley	40
A6038	Otley Rd, Esholt (near Guiseley)	40
A6120	Station Rd, Cross Gates, Leeds	30
A6177	Ingleby Rd, Bradford	30
A6177	Rooley La, Bradford (east of M606 jct)	40
A6186	Asdale Rd, Durkar	30
B6144	Haworth Rd, Daisy Hill, Bradford (west of B6269 jct)	30
B6144	Toller La, Bradford (near A6177)	30
B6145	Thornton Rd, Bradford	30
B6265	Bradford Rd, Stockbridge, Keighley (A650 to Kingsway)	30
B6273	Wakefield Rd, Kinsley	30
B6380	Beacon Rd, Bradford (Stephen Rd to Wibsey rbt)	30
-	Bradford; Cutler Heights La	30
-	Bradford; Dick La	30
-	Bradford; Gain La	30
-	Bradford; Moore Ave	30
-	Halifax; Crag La, Ovenden	30
-	Huddersfield; Long La, Dalton	30
-	Leeds; Broad La, Moorside	30
-	Leeds; Low La, Horsforth	30
-	Leeds; Otley Old Rd, Lawnswood/Holt Park	30
-	Leeds; Willow Rd/Cardigan Rd, Headingley	30
-	Wakefield; Balne La/Batley Rd	30

Wiltshire and Swindon

Road number	Location	Speed limit (mph)
M4	approx 7km east of jct 15	70
M4	both sides of jct 15	70
M4	approx 1.8km west of jct 15	70
M4	approx 3km east of jct 16	70
M4	approx 8.5km west of jct 16	70
M4	approx 8.5km east of jct 17	70
M4	approx 2.5km east of jct 17	70
A4	Froxfield	40
A4	West Overton	60
A30	Fovant	40
A30	The Pheasant Hotel (1km west of A343 jct)	60
A36	Brickworth (at A27 jct)	60
A36	Hanging Langford	60
A36	Knook	50
A36	Wilton Rd, Salisbury	30
A36	Thoulstone (south of A3098 jct)	60
A36	south of Whaddon	60
A303	Chicklade	50
A303	near Cholderton	70
A303	Folly Bottom (2km east of A345 jct)	70
A303	Mere Bypass	70
A303	west of Winterbourne Stoke	60
A303	Willoughby Hedge (1.5km west of A350 jct)	60
A303	Wylye Bypass	70
A338	Boscombe	40
A338	Downton Rd, Salisbury	30
A338	Little Woodbury (Britford) (1.5km south of Salisbury)	30
A338	near Southgrove Copse (1.5km south of Burbage)	60
A342	Ludgershall	30
A344	Airmans Cross (at A360 jct)	60
A345	Salisbury Clumps (south of Amesbury)	60
A345	south of Highpost	60
A346	Chiseldon Firs (3.5km south of M4)	60
A346	Whitefield (4.5km south of M4)	60
A350	Chippenham Bypass (south of A4)	60
A350	near Hart Hill Farm (2.5km north of Shaftesbury)	50
A350	Heywood	60
A350	Pretty Chimneys (2km south of M4)	70
A354	Coombe Bissett	30
A360	Airmans Cross (at A344 jct)	60
A361	Devizes to Beckhampton	60
A361	Inglesham	60
A361	near jct with B3101, west of Devizes	70
A361	Southwick	30
A361	Frome Rd, Trowbridge	30
A363	Trowbridge Rd, Bradford-on-Avon	30
A363	Trowle Common (north of Trowbridge)	40
A419	near Covingham, Swindon (south of A420 jct)	70
A419	near Broad Blunsdon	70
A420	Ford	40
A420	Giddeahall to Ford	60
A420	The Shoe (3km east of Marshfield)	50
A3026	Tidworth Rd, Ludgershall	40
A3028	Larkhill Rd, Durrington	30
A3102	south of Hilmarton	50/60
A3102	Lyneham	30
A3102	Sandridge Rd, Melksham	30
A3102	Tockenham (north of Lyneham)	60
A3102	High St, Wootton Bassett	30
A4259	near Coate, Swindon	50
A4259	Queens Dr, Swindon (at Rushton Rd)	40
A4361	Broad Hinton	60
A4361	Swindon Rd, Wroughton	30
A4361	Uffcott crossroads	60
B390	Maddington Farm (2km west of Shrewton)	60
B3098	Bratton	30
B3105	Hill St/Marsh Rd, Hilperton	30
B3106	Hammond Way, Hilperton	30
B3107	Holt Rd, Bradford-on-Avon	30
B4006	Marlborough Rd, Swindon	40
B4006	Swindon Rd, Stratton St Margaret	30
B4006	Ermin St/Hyde Rd, Swindon	30
B4006	Whitworth Rd, Swindon	30
B4040	Leigh (near Cricklade)	50
B4041	Station Rd, Wootton Bassett	30
B4141	Hyde Rd, Swindon	30
B4143	Bridge End Rd, Swindon	30
B4289	Great Western Way, Swindon (near Bruce St Bridges)	40
B4528	Hungerdown La, Chippenham	30
B4553	Tewkesbury Way, Swindon	40
B4587	Akers Way, Swindon	30
-	Bulford Camp; Bulford Rd	30
-	Bulford Camp; Marlborough Rd	30
-	Calne; Oxford Rd	30
-	Corsham; Park La	30
-	Larkhill; The Packway	40
-	Swindon; Merlin Way	30
-	Swindon; Moredon Rd	30
-	Trowbridge; Wiltshire Dr	30
-	Trowbridge; Woodmarsh, North Bradley	30

SCOTLAND

Central Scotland

Road number	Location	Speed limit (mph)
M9	at M876 (northbound)	70
M9	Polmont (northbound)	70
M9	Stirling (northbound)	70
M80	Denny (northbound)	70
M876	Torwood, Larbert (northbound)	70
A9	Dunblane (southbound)	70
A82	Crianlarich	30
A706	Linlithgow Rd, Bo'ness	30
A907	Cambus	40
A908	Devonside, Tillicoultry	30
A908	Sauchie	30
A993	Dean Rd, Bo'ness	30

Dumfries and Galloway

Road number	Location	Speed limit (mph)
A74(M)	Multiple sites	70
A7	south of Langholm	60
A75	Multiple sites	n/a
A76	Auldgirth/Blackwood	60
A76	Closeburn to Thornhill	60
A76	Gateside (3km east of Kirkconnel)	60
A76	Glasgow Rd, Dumfries	30
A77	Balyett (south of Innermessan)	60
A77	Cairnryan (north for 2km)	30
A77	Whiteleys (1km south of Stranraer)	60
A701	south of Moffat	30
A701	north and south of St Ann's	60
A709	Burnside (1.5km west of Lochmaben)	60
A711	Tongland Rd, Kirkcudbright	30
A716	north of Stoneykirk	60
A718	Craichmore (1km south-east of B798 jct)	60
B721	Eastriggs	30

Fife

Road number	Location	Speed limit (mph)
A91	Deer Centre to Stratheden (Hospital) jct	60
A91	Guardbridge to St Andrews	60
A92	Cadham (Glenrothes) to New Inn (near A912/A914 jct)	50
A92	Cardenden overbridge to A910 jct	70
A92	Cowdenbeath to Lochgelly	70
A92	Freuchie to Annsmuir (south of A91 jct)	60
A92	A91 jct to 1.5km north of Fernie	60
A92	Rathillet (south) to Easter Kinnear (1km south-west of B946)	60
A823	St Margaret Dr, Dunfermline	40
A823	Queensferry Rd, Dunfermline	30
A907	Halbeath Rd, Dunfermline	30
A911	Glenrothes to Leslie	n/a
A911	Glenrothes to Milton of Balgonie	60
A914	Forgan (near A92) to St Michaels (A919 jct)	60
A914	Kettlebridge to Kingskettle	60
A914	Pitlessie to Cupar	60
A915	Checkbar jct (Coaltown of Wemyss) to B930 jct	60
A921	Esplanade, Kirkcaldy	30
A921	High St/The Path, Kirkcaldy	30
A921	Rosslyn St/St Clair St, Kirkcaldy	30
A955	Methilhaven Rd, Buckhaven	30
A955	Methilhaven Rd, Methil	30
A955	Dysart to Coaltown of Wemyss	40
A977	Feregait, Kincardine	30
A985	Culross (west) to Valleyfield	60
A985	Admiralty Rd, Rosyth	30
A985	Waulkmill (east of Crombie) to Brankholm (Rosyth)	60
B914	Redcraigs to Greenknowes (east of A823)	60
B920	Crosshill to Ballingry	30
B933	Glenlyon Rd, Leven	30
B942	east of Colinsburgh	60
B980	Castlandhill Rd, Rosyth	30
B981	Broad St, Cowdenbeath	30
B981	Dunnikier Way, Kirkcaldy	40
B9157	north of Aberdour	60
B9157	east of Balmule	60
B9157	east of Kirkcaldy	60
-	Dunfermline; Townhill Rd/Kingseat Rd	30
-	Dunfermline; Masterton Rd	30
-	Glenrothes; Formonthills Rd	30
-	Glenrothes; Woodside Rd	30
-	Glenrothes; Woodside Way	30
-	Kirkcaldy; Hendry Rd	30

Lothian and Borders

Road number	Location	Speed limit (mph)
A7	Crookston (near B6368)	60
A7	north of Galashiels (Buckholmside to Bowland)	NSL
A7	Commercial Rd/Wilton Hill, Hawick	30
A7	Stow to Bowland	30
A8	Ratho Station, Edinburgh	40
A68	Jedburgh	30
A68	Soutra Hill	NSL
A70	Balerno	30
A71	Breich	30
A71	Polbeth	30
A72	Castlecraig (near Blyth Bridge)	NSL
A72	Innerleithen Rd, Peebles	30
A72	Holylee (near Walkerburn)	NSL
A89	West Main St, Armadale	30
A90	Cramond Bridge (Burnshot flyover to Cammo Rd) (southbound)	40
A697	Greenlaw and southern approach	30
A697	Ploughlands to Hatchednize (either side of B6461)	NSL
A697	Orange La (at B6461)	NSL
A697	Coldstream	30
A698	Denholm to A6088 jct	NSL
A698	Crailing to Eckford	NSL
A699	Maxton village	40
A701	Blyth Bridge to Cowdenburn (1km north-east of Lamancha)	NSL
A701	Rachan Mill, Broughton to A72	30
A702	Comiston Rd, Edinburgh	30
A702	Dolphinton north to Medwyn Mains	NSL
A703	Eddleston and approaches	30
A703	Leadburn south to Shiplaw	NSL
A703	Edinburgh Rd, Peebles	30
A703	Peebles north to Milkieston	30
A705	Whitburn to East Whitburn	30
A706	Longridge Village	30
A706	Whitburn (at Cairnie Pl)	30
A720	City Bypass, east of Gogar roundabout, Edinburgh	50
A899	south of Deer Park roundabout (M8 jct 3) Livingston	50
A899	north of Lizzie Bryce roundabout, Livingston	50
A901	Lower Granton Rd, Edinburgh	30
A6091	Melrose Bypass	NSL
A6105	Gordon and approaches	30
B6374	Galashiels, Station Bridge to Lowood Bridge	30
B7015	Howden South Rd, Livingston	30
B7069	West Main St, Whitburn	30
-	Edinburgh; Muirhouse Parkway	30
-	Edinburgh; West Approach Rd (Morrison St to Dundee St)	40
-	Edinburgh; West Granton Rd	30

North East Scotland

Road number	Location	Speed limit (mph)
A90	Ellon Rd, Aberdeen	30
A90	Newtonhill to South Damhead, Kincorth, Aberdeen	70
A90	South Damhead to Whitestripes Ave Roundabout, Aberdeen	40
A90	south of Leys (near Ellon) to Blackhills (near Longhaven)	60
A90	Upper Criggie (3km south-west of A92 jct) to Mill of Barnes (2.5km south-west of A937 jct)	70
A92	Johnshaven to Inverbervie	60
A92	Kinneff, north to Mill of Uras	60
A93	Banchory, east from caravan site	40
A93	Banchory, west from church	30
A93	Kincardine O'Neil, south-east to Haugh of Sluie	60
A93	Aboyne	30
A93	Aboyne to Dinnet	60
A93	Dinnet to Cambus o'May	60
A95	Cornhill	30
A95	Keith to Davoch of Grange	60
A96	Great Northern Rd, Aberdeen	30
A96	Haudagain Roundabout to Chapel of Stoneywood, Aberdeen	30
A96	south of Port Elphinstone	70
A96	north of Inverurie	60
A96	Old Rayne to 2km east of Bainshole	60
A96	near Thomastown	60
A96	Huntly (A920 to B9002)	60
A96	approx 2.5km north-west of Cairnie	60
A96	Fochabers to Forgie	60
A96	Mosstodloch to Lhanbryde (east)	60
A98	Fochabers to Mill of Tynet	60
A98	Mill of Tynet to Barhill Rd jct, Buckie	60
A98	from Carnoch Farm Rd, Buckie to Cullen	60
A98	Banff	30
A941	Elgin to Lossiemouth	60
A941	Elgin to Rothes	60
A944	Gairloch (B9126 jct) to Westhill Roundabout	60/ 40/30
A947	Fyvie to Tulloch	60
A947	Whiterashes to Newmacher	60
A948	Ellon to Auchnagatt	60
A952	New Leeds to A90	60
A956	Ellon Rd, Aberdeen	30
A956	King St, Aberdeen	30
A956	North Esplanade West, Aberdeen	30
A956	Wellington Rd, Aberdeen	40
A978	St Machar Dr, Aberdeen	30
B9005	Craigs Rd, Ellon	30
B9040	Silver Sands Caravan Park, Lossiemouth to B9012 jct	60
B9077	Great Southern Rd, Aberdeen	30
B9089	Kinloss north-east to Roseisle Maltings crossroads	60
-	Aberdeen; Beach Blvd/Wales St/Links Rd	30
-	Aberdeen; Springhill Rd	30
-	Aberdeen; West Tullos Rd	40

Northern Scotland

Road number	Location	Speed limit (mph)
A9	Cuaich, north-east of Dalwhinnie	60
A9	near Dalwhinnie (either side of A889 jct)	60
A9	Daviot	70
A9	Caulmaillie Farm, near Golspie	60
A9	south of The Mound (Loch Fleet near Golspie)	60
A9	Altnasleanach, near Inverness	60
A9	North Kessock jct	70
A9	near Fearn jct, south of Tain	60
A82	3km north of Temple Pier, Drumnadrochit	60
A82	1.5km north of Kings House Hotel, Glencoe	60
A82	Invergarry Power Station	60
A82	1.5km south of Alltsigh Youth Hostel, north of Invermoriston	60
A82	near White Corries, Rannoch Moor	60
A87	1.5km west of Bun Loyn jct (A887)	60
A95	Drumuillie, near Boat of Garten	60
A95	approx 5km north of Cromdale	60
A95	Congash Farm, near Speybridge, Grantown-on-Spey	60
A96	Auldearn Bypass, western jct	60
A96	Auldearn Bypass, eastern jct	60
A96	west of Allanfearn jct (near Culloden)	60
A96	Gollanfield	60
A99	Hempriggs, south of Wick	60
A834	near Foddery Bridge, west of Dingwall	60
A834	Strathpeffer Rd, Dingwall	30
A835	Inverlael straight, south of Ullapool	60
A939	Dava Moor	60
B9006	Sunnyside, Culloden	60

Strathclyde

Road number	Location	Speed limit (mph)
M74	Jct 13 (Abington), northbound	70
A70	East Tarelgin (approx 5km west of Ochiltree)	60
A73	Carlisle Rd, Airdrie	30
A76	near Lime Rd, New Cumnock	30
A78	Main Rd, Fairlie	30
A82	Bridge of Orchy (Loch Tulla)	60
A82	Dumbarton Rd/Stirling Rd, Milton	40
A85	5.5km west of Tyndrum	60
A89	Forrest St, Airdrie	30
A706	south of Forth	60
A730	Blairbeth Rd, Rutherglen	30
A730	Glasgow Rd, Rutherglen	30
A730	Mill St, Rutherglen	30
A737	New St/Kilwinning Rd, Dalry	30

Road number	Location	Speed limit (mph)
A749	East Kilbride Rd, (Cathkin Rd (B759) to Cairnmuir Rd)	40
A761	Glasgow Rd, Paisley at Newtyle Rd	30
A807	Balmore Rd, Bardowie	30
A809/ A810	Drymen Rd/Duntocher Rd, Bearsden	30
A814	Glasgow Rd, Clydebank	30
A814	Cardross Rd, Dumbarton	30
A815	near Ardkinglas (near A83 jct)	60
B749	Craigend Rd, Troon	30
B768	Burnhill St, Rutherglen	30
B803	Coatbridge Rd, Glenmavis	30
B814	Duntocher Rd, Clydebank (Singer Rd to Overton Rd)	30
B7078	Blackwood	30
B8048	Waterside Rd, Kirkintilloch	30
-	Barrhead; Aurs Rd	30
-	Bishopbriggs; Woodhill Rd	30
-	Coatbridge; Townhead Rd	30
-	East Kilbride; Maxwellton Rd	30
-	Johnstone; Beith Rd	30
-	Neilston; Kingston Rd	30
-	Newton Mearns; Mearns Rd	30

Tayside

Road number	Location	Speed limit (mph)
M90	Jct 6	70
A9	north-east of Aberuthven	70
A9	Cairnie Braes (south-west of B934)	70
A9	Tibbermore jct	70
A9	near Inveralmond Industrial Est, Perth	70
A9	Killiecrankie	60
A90	near M90 jct 11	70
A90	Westown (4km west of Inchture)	70
A90	Inchture	70
A90	Kingsway West, Dundee (Myrekirk Rd to Gourdie Pl)	50
A90	Kingsway West, Dundee (west of A923 to Strathmartine Rd)	50
A90	Kingsway, Dundee (Caird Park)	50
A91	Dalqueich (2.5km west of M90 jct 7)	60
A92	East Dock St, Dundee	40
A92	Greendykes Rd, Dundee (Arbroath Rd to Craigie Ave)	30
A92	West Newton (2km north of Marywell)	60
A92	Inverkeilor	60
A92	Hawkhill (3km north of Inverkeilor)	60
A93	Scones Lethendry (3.5km south of Guildtown)	60
A93	Cargill	60
A93	Meikleour	60
A94	Perth Aerodrome	60
A94	Balbeggie	60
A94	Burrelton	60
A822	Drummond Castle	60
A923	River Isla bridge	60
A923	Kettins	60
A923	Leys	60
A923	Lundie	60
A933	Colliston Mill	60
A933	Legaston (1km south of Friockheim)	60
A933	Redford (4km south of Brechin)	60
A935	Montrose to House of Dun	60
A972	Kingsway East, Dundee (Forfar Rd to Pitairlie Rd)	40
A977	Balado House (2.5km west of M90, jct 6)	60
B961	Drumgeith Rd, Dundee	30
B996	Gairney Bank (north of B9097)	60
-	Dundee; Broughty Ferry Rd	30
-	Dundee; Charleston Dr	30
-	Dundee; Laird St	30
-	Dundee; Old Glamis Rd (A90 to Gilburn Rd)	30
-	Dundee; Perth Rd	30
-	Dundee; Strathmartine Rd (A90 to Balgowan Ave)	30

WALES

Mid and South Wales

Road number	Location	Speed limit (mph)
M4	Toll Plaza	50
M4	3km east of jct 24, Llanmartin overbridge	70
M4	approx 5km east of jct 32, Cherry Orchard Rd overbridge	70
M4	1km east of jct 32, Rhiwbina Hill overbridge	70
M4	1.1km east of jct 33, Llantrisant Rd overbridge	70
M4	2km east of jct 35 (overbridge)	70
M4	east of jct 36 (overbridge)	70
A40	Bancyfelin Bypass	70
A40	opposite Llangattock Lodge (southeast of Abergavenny)	70
A40	Llanhamlach	60
A40	Llansantffraed	60
A40	Rhosmaen (B4302 jct to national speed limit)	40
A40	Scethrog	60
A44	Forest Bends (5km south-east of Llandegley)	60
A44	Llanbadarn Fawr, Aberystwyth	30
A44	Sweet Lamb (west of Llangurig)	60
A48	Dinas Baglan Rd, Baglan	30
A48	Castleton (near motel)	50
A48	south of Cwmgwili	70
A48	Foelgastell	70
A48	Chepstow Rd, Langstone	40
A48	Llanddarog	70
A48	Clasemont Rd, Morriston, Swansea	30
A48	Nant-y-Caws	70
A48	Parkwall (near B4525 jct, Caldicot)	60
A48	north of Pont Abraham (M4 jct 49)	70
A48	Bolgoed Rd, Pontarddulais	30
A48	Margam Rd, Port Talbot (near Rhanallt St)	30
A438	Three Cocks	40
A449	Cat's Ash, Newport	70
A449	Llandenny	70
A458	Cefn Bridge	60
A458	Llanfair Caereinion (Neuadd Bridge)	60
A458	Trewern	40
A466	Chepstow (High Beech Roundabout to Old Hospital)	30
A466	Hereford Rd, Monmouth	30
A466	St Arvans	30
A467	Aberbeeg Rd, north-east of Aberbeeg	30
A467	Aberbeeg Rd, Abertillery	60
A467	Abertillery Rd, Blaina	40
A468	Caerphilly Rd, Rhiwderyn	30
A469	Lower Rhymney Valley Relief Rd, Llanbradach	70
A469	New Rd, Tir-y-Birth (north of Hengoed)	30
A470	Aberfan (overbridge)	70
A470	Aberduhonw (2km east of Builth Wells)	60
A470	near Alltmawr (south of Builth Wells)	60
A470	Argoed Mill (south of Rhayader)	60
A470	Beacons Reservoir (near A4059 jct)	60
A470	2.5km south of A4215 jct	60
A470	Ash Gr, Whitchurch, Cardiff	40
A470	north of Cilfynydd (overbridge)	70
A470	Erwood (south)	60
A470	Llandinam to Caersws jct	60
A470	Llanidloes to Llandinam	60
A470	Newbridge to Rhayader	60
A470	Rhydyfelin (overbridge, Dynea Rd)	70
A470	near Taffs Well	70
A470	Ysgiog (4km south of Builth Wells)	60
A472	Hafod-yr-ynys Rd, Hafodyrynys	30
A472	Main Rd, Maesycwmmer	30
A472	Monkswood	60
A472	Pontymoel Gyratory	50
A472	Ystrad Mynach to Nelson	30
A473	Bryntirion Hill, Bridgend	30
A473	New Rd, Bryncae	30
A473	Main Rd, Church Village	30
A473	Penybont Rd, Pencoed	30
A474	Graig Rd, Alltwen	40
A474	Glanffrwd Estate jct to 40mph speed limit, Garnant	30
A474	Briton Ferry Rd, Neath	50
A474	Penywern Rd, Neath	30
A474	Commercial St, Rhyd-y-fro	30
A475	Pentrebach, Lampeter	40
A475	Lampeter (central)	30
A475	Llanwnnen	30
A476	Carmel north to NSL, Temple Bar	40
A476	Ffairfach	30
A476	Thomas Arms, Llanelli to NSL, Swiss Valley	30
A476	Erw Non jct to Clos Rebecca jct, Llannon	30
A476	Llannon Rd/Bethania Rd, Upper Tumble	30
A478	Llandissilio	40
A478	Pentlepoir	30
A482	Lampeter Rd, Aberaeron	30
A482	Lampeter (central)	30
A483	Pen-y-banc Rd, Ammanford	30
A483	north of Crossgates	60
A483	Ffairfach	30
A483	Garthmyl	60
A483	Rhosmaen St, Llandeilo	30
A483	Midway Bends, Llandrindod Wells to Crossgates	60
A483	Fabian Way, Swansea (western end)	40
A484	Cenarth	30
A485	Cwmann (from A482 jct to NSL)	30
A484	Cwmffrwd (first bend on entering from the north)	40
A484	Idole (from B4309 jct to NSL)	40
A484	Sandy Rd, Llanelli (Wauneos Rd to Denham Ave)	30
A484	Llanelli (Trostre Roundabout to Berwick Roundabout)	60
A484	Newcastle Emlyn (from 80m west of New Rd jct east to NSL)	30
A485	Llanllwni	40
A486	Well St, Llandysul	30
A486	New Quay (central)	30
A487	Aberaeron (central)	30
A487	Aberystwyth (at A4120 jct)	30
A487	Penglais Hill/Waunfawr, Aberystwyth	30
A487	Bow Street	30
A487	Eglwyswrw	30
A487	Furnace	40
A487	Alma St, Llanarth	40
A487	Llanfarian	30
A487	Llanrhystud (southern approach)	40
A487	Newgale	30
A487	Newport	30
A487	Penparc	40
A487	Rhydyfelin	40
A487	Rhyd-y-pennau	30
A487	Tal-y-bont	30
A489	Caersws jct to Penstrowed	60
A489	Glanmule (at garage)	60
A489	Newtown to Penstrowed	60
A489	Newtown (west of Hafren College)	40
A4042	Mamhilad (near A472 jct)	60
A4043	Cwmavon Rd, Abersychan	40
A4043	St Lukes Rd, Pontnewynydd, Pontypool	30
A4046	College Rd, Ebbw Vale	30
A4046	Ebbw Vale (near Tesco)	30
A4046	Station Rd, Waunllwyd	30
A4047	Beaufort Hill/King St, Brynmawr	30
A4048	Blackwood Rd, Pontllanfraith	30
A4050	Jenner Rd, Barry	30
A4054	Cardiff Rd, Merthyr Vale	30
A4054	Cardiff Rd, Upper Boat	30
A4054	Oxford St, Nantgarw	30
A4054	Pentrebach Rd, Pontypridd	30
A4055	Gladstone Rd, Barry	30
A4058	The Broadway, Pontypridd	30
A4058	Trehafod	30
A4059	New Rd, Mountain Ash	30
A4061	Cemetery Rd/Blackmill Rd, Ogmore Vale	30
A4063	Sarn Bypass near jct with Bryncoch Rd	50
A4067	Abercraf	60
A4067	Crai	60
A4067	Mumbles Rd, Swansea (Sketty La to St Helens Sports Ground)	40
A4069	Station Rd, Brynamman (county bdy to Remploy factory)	30
A4069	Brynamman Rd, south of Brynamman	30
A4069	Broad St, Llandovery	30
A4075	Carew	30
A4076	Johnston	30
A4076	St Lawrence Hill, Milford Haven	30
A4076	Steynton Rd, Milford Haven	40
A4093	Gilfach Rd, Hendreforgan (near B4564 jct)	30
A4102	Goatmill Rd, Merthyr Tydfil	30
A4107	High St, Abergwynfi	30
A4109	Glynneath	30
A4119	Llantrisant Rd (at M4)	60
A4139	Orange Way, Pembroke	30
A4139	Bush St, Pembroke Dock	30
A4139	Marsh Rd, Tenby	30
A4216	Cockett Rd, Cockett, Swansea	30
A4222	Cowbridge Rd, Brynsadler	30
B4223	Gelli Rd, Gelli (Rhondda)	30
B4223	Maindy Rd, Ton Pentre (Rhondda)	30
B4236	Caerleon Rd, Llanfrechfa	30
B4237	Cardiff Rd, Newport (at hospital)	30
B4237	Chepstow Rd, Newport (near Aberthaw Rd)	30
B4237	Chepstow Rd, Newport (near Royal Oak Hill)	30
B4237	Maes-glas, Newport	30
B4237	Wharf Rd, Newport	30
B4239	Lighthouse Rd, Maes-glas, Newport	30
B4245	Leechpool (near Caldicot)	60
B4245	Magor (west)	30
B4245	west of Rogiet (at Green Farm bend)	40
B4246	New Rd, Garndiffaith, Abersychan	30
B4248	Garn Rd, Blaenavon	40
B4251	Kendon Rd, Oakdale	30
B4254	Church Rd, Gelligaer	30
B4254	Pengam Rd, Penpedairheol (near Gelligaer)	30
B4265	Llantwit Major Bypass	50
B4267	Leckwith Rd, Cardiff	30
B4275	Abercynon Rd, Abercynon	30
B4278	Dinas Rd, Dinas (near Tonypandy)	30
B4278	Penrhiw-fer Rd, Tonyrefail	30
B4282	Bridgend Rd/Castle St, Maesteg	30
B4283	Heol Fach, North Cornelly, Pyle	30
B4290	New Rd, Jersey Marine	30
B4290	Burrows Rd, Skewen, Neath	30
B4293	Devauden	30
B4293	Monmouth Rd, Trellech	30
B4295	Cwmbach Rd, Cockett, Swansea	30
B4295	New Rd, Crofty	30
B4296	Goetre Fawr Rd, Killay, Swansea	30
B4297	Bynea (Loughor Bridge Roundabout to Station Rd jct)	30
B4297	Capel Hendre	30
B4297	Llangennech (Cleviston Park to Park La)	30
B4297	Llwynhendy (Capel Soar to the Police Station)	30
B4303	Dafen Roundabout to Felinfoel Roundabout, Llanelli	30
B4304	Copperworks Roadbridge to Morfa Roundabout, Llanelli	40
B4304	Lower Trostre Rd Roundabout to Trostre Rd Roundabout, Llanelli	30
B4309	Cynheidre	30
B4314	Moorfield Rd, Narberth	30
B4320	Hundleton	30
B4325	Honeyborough Rd, Neyland	30
B4336	Llanfihangel-ar-Arth	30
B4436	Northway, Bishopston	40
B4337	Talsarn	40
B4350	north-east of Glasbury	60
B4471	Commercial Rd, Llanhilleth	30
B4478	Letchworth Rd, Pleasant View, Ebbw Vale	30
B4486	Steelworks Rd, Ebbw Vale	30
B4548	Aberystwyth Rd, Cardigan	30
B4556	Cae'r bryn, near Ammanford	30
B4591	High Cross, Newport (near jct 27)	30
B4591	Risca Rd, Pontymister, Risca (at Welsh Oak pub)	30
B4591	Risca Rd, Pontymister, Risca (opposite power station)	30
B4596	Caerleon Rd, Newport (south of M4)	30
B4596	Caerleon Rd, Newport (east of Beaufort Rd)	30
B4599	Ystradgynlais	30
B4603	Clydach Rd, Ynystawe	30
B4623	Mountain Rd, Caerphilly	30
-	Abergavenny; Hereford Rd	30
-	Abergwili (Ambulance Station to the Bypass roundabout)	30
-	Aberystwyth; Park Ave	30
-	Ammanford; New Rd/Pantyffynnon Rd	30
-	Barry; Barry Rd	30
-	Barry; Buttrills Rd	30
-	Barry; Winston Rd	30
-	Beaufort; Bryn Awelon	30
-	Beddau; Gwaunmiskin Rd	30
-	Bridgend; Brackla Way, Brackla	30
-	Caldicot; Chepstow Rd/Sandy La	30
-	Cardiff; Colchester Ave, Pen-y-lan	30
-	Cardiff; Maes-y-Coed Rd, Heath	30
-	Cardiff; Excalibur Dr, Thornhill	30
-	Cardiff; Lake Rd East, Roath Park	30
-	Cardiff; Lake Rd West, Roath Park	30
-	Cardiff; Wentloog Ave, Rumney	30
-	Cardiff; St Fagans Rd, Fairwater	30
-	Cardiff; Willowbrook Dr, St Mellons	30
-	Carmarthen; Lime Grove Ave/Fountain Head Terrace	30
-	Cefneithin (west of Gorslas)	30
-	Chepstow; Mathern Rd	30
-	Church Village; Station Rd	30
-	Cwmbran; Avondale Rd	30
-	Cwmbran; Thornhill Rd	30
-	Cwmbran; Ty Gwyn Way/ Greenmeadow Way	30
-	Ebbw Vale; Newchurch Rd	30
-	Gorseinon; Frampton Rd	30
-	Haverfordwest; Pembroke Rd, Merlin's Bridge	30
-	Llanbradach; Coed-y-Brain Rd	30
-	Llanelli; Heol Goffa (A476 to A484)	30
-	Llangybi (south of Usk)	30
-	Llantwit Major; Llanmaes Rd	30
-	Merthyr Tydfil; High St, Dowlais	30
-	Merthyr Tydfil; Swansea Rd, Gellideg	30
-	Merthyr Tydfil; Pant Rd	30
-	Merthyr Tydfil; High St, Pen-y-Darren	30
-	Merthyr Tydfil; Rocky Rd	30
-	Milford Haven; Priory Rd	30
-	Nant-y-caws (from Heol Login along Nant-y-caws Hill)(east of Carmarthen)	60
-	Neath; Crymlyn Rd, Skewen	30
-	Newport; Corporation Rd	30
-	Pontypool; Leigh Rd	30
-	Pontypool; Newport Rd	30
-	Pontypool; Sunnybank Rd, Griffithstown	30
-	Port Talbot; Village Rd, Sandfields	30
-	Rogerstone; Tregwillym Rd	30
-	Swansea; Llethri Rd, Felinfoel	30
-	Swansea; Pentregethin Rd, Cadle (near Farm Shop)	30
-	Swansea; Mynydd Garnllwyd Rd/Caemawr Rd/Parry Rd/ Vicarage Rd	30
-	Swansea; Mynydd Newydd Rd	30

North Wales

Road number	Location	Speed limit (mph)
A5	Bangor to Llandygai	30/40
A5	Froncysyllte to Betws-y-Coed (seasonal)	30/ 40/60
A5	London Rd, Holyhead	30
A5	Menai Bridge to Gwalchmai	30/ 40/60
A5/ A483	Chirk to Ruabon	60
A5/ A5025	Holyhead to Llanfachraeth	50
A458	Cwm-Cewydd east to county boundary (seasonal)	60
A470	Dolgellau (A496 to east of A494)	40/60
A470	Llansanffraid Glan Conwy to Betws-y-Coed	30/60
A470	Llandudno to A55, jct 19	30/ 40/60
A470	Mallwyd to A487 (seasonal)	30/ 40/60
A470	North of Rhiwbrifdir to Congl-y-wal, Blaenau Ffestiniog	30/ 40/60
A483/ A5	Ruabon to Chirk	60
A487	Caernarfon to Dolbenmaen	30/40/ 50/60
A487	Pantperthog to A470 (seasonal)	30/ 40/60
A487	Penmorfa to Gellilydan	30/ 40/60
A494	Bala to Glan-yr-afon	40/60
A494	Llyn Tegid (Bala Lake)	30
A494	Ruthin to Corwen (seasonal)	30/ 40/60
A494	Ruthin to Llanferres	40/60
A496	Harlech to Llanbedr	30/ 40/60
A499	Pwllheli to Penrhos	30/ 40/60
A525	Llanfair Dyffryn Clwyd to Llandegla (near B5430)	30/ 40/60
A525	Ruthin to Denbigh	40/60
A525	St Asaph to Trefnant	30/ 40/60
A525	Vale Rd/Rhuddlan Rd, Rhyl	30
A525	Wrexham to Minera	30/60
A525	Wrexham to Redbrook	30/ 40/60
A534	Holt Rd, Wrexham	30
A539	Mill St, Llangollen	30/60
A539	Trevor to Erbistock (A528 jct)	30/ 40/60
A541	Caergwrle to Wrexham	30/40/ 60/70
A541	Mold to Caergwrle	30/40/ 60/70
A541	Mold Rd, Wrexham	30
A541	Trefnant to Bodfari	30/ 40/60
A542	Horseshoe Pass (seasonal)	60
A543	Denbigh to Pentrefoelas (seasonal)	30/60
A545	Menai Bridge to Beaumaris	30/40
A547	Colwyn Bay to Old Colwyn	30/ 40/50
A547	Prestatyn to Rhuddlan	30/ 40/60
A548	Dundonald Ave, Abergele	30
A548	Gronant to Flint (Oakenholt)	30/ 40/50/ 60/70
A548	Rhyl to Prestatyn	30/40
A548	Abergele to Kinmel Bay	30/40
A549	Mynydd Isa to Buckley	30/60
A550	Hawarden	30
A4080	Brynsiencyn to Rhosneigr (seasonal)	30/ 40/60
A4086	Cwm-y-Glo to Llanrug	30/ 40/60
A4086	Llanberis (seasonal)	30/ 40/60
A4212	Bala	30/60
A4212	Trawsfynydd to Llyn Celyn	60
A4244	Cwm-y-Glo to B4547	60
A5025	Amlwch to Menai Bridge	30/40/ 50/60
A5025/ A5	Llanfachraeth to Holyhead	50
A5104	Coed-Talon to Leeswood (A541 to B5101)	30
A5104	Coed-Talon to A494 (seasonal)	30
A5119	Flint to Mold	30/ 50/60
A5152	Chester Rd, Wrexham	30
A5152	Rhostyllen	30/40
A5154	Victoria Rd, Holyhead	30
B4501	Denbigh to Cerrigydrudion (seasonal)	30/ 40/60
B4545	Kingsland to Valley (via Trearddur Bay)	30/40
B5105	Ruthin to Cerrigydrudion (seasonal)	30/ 40/60
B5108	Brynteg to Benllech	30/60
B5109	Llangefni towards Bodffordd	30
B5113	Kings Rd/Kings Dr, Colwyn Bay	30
B5115	Llandudno Promenade to Penrhyn Bay	30/40
B5115	Llandudno Rd, Llandrillo-yn-Rhos	30
B5118	Rhyl Promenade, Rhyl	30
B5120	Pendyffryn Rd, Prestatyn	30
B5125	Hawarden	30
B5129	Kelsterton to Saltney Ferry	30/60
B5420	Menai Bridge (Four Crosses to Menai Bridge Sq)	30
B5425	Wrexham to Llay	30/60
B5445	Rossett	30
B5605	Johnstown to Ruabon	30/ 40/60
-	Holyhead; Prince of Wales Rd	30
-	Penrhyn Bay to Rhos Point (coast road)	30
-	Kinmel Bay; St Asaph Ave	30/60

Key to listing

- Motorway
- Primary route
- Other A road
- B road
- Minor road

Tourist sites with satnav friendly postcodes

ENGLAND

- Acorn Bank Garden **CA10 1SP** Cumb **391** G4
- Aldborough Roman Site **YO51 9ES** N York **357** E1
- Alfriston Clergy House **BN26 5TL** E Susx **57** E4
- Alton Towers **ST10 4DB** Staffs **293** E6
- Anglesey Abbey **CB25 9EJ** Cambs **198** A2
- Anne Hathaway's Cottage **CV37 9HH** Warwks **190** B4
- Antony House **PL11 2QA** Cnwll **10** D2
- Appuldurcombe House **PO38 3EW** IoW **37** E4
- Apsley House **W1J 7NT** Gt Lon **119** F4
- Arlington Court **EX31 4LP** Devon **61** F3
- Ascott **LU7 0PS** Bucks **168** B5
- Ashton Court Estate **BS41 9JN** N Som **109** G5
- Athelhampton House & Gardens **DT2 7LG** Dorset **47** E6
- Attingham Park **SY4 4TP** Shrops **234** D3
- Audley End House & Gardens **CB11 4JF** Essex **171** H2
- Avebury Manor & Garden **SN8 1RF** Wilts **112** D6
- Baconsthorpe Castle **NR25 6LN** Norfk **261** F4
- Baddesley Clinton Hall **B93 0DQ** Warwks **214** B5
- Bamburgh Castle **NE69 7DF** Nthumb **455** F2
- Barnard Castle **DL12 8PW** Dur **382** B1
- Barrington Court **TA19 0NQ** Somset **66** B6
- Basildon Park **RG8 9NR** W Berk **115** G4
- Bateman's **TN19 7DS** E Susx **79** H5
- Battle of Britain Memorial Flight **LN4 4SY** Lincs **299** G3
- Beamish Open Air Museum **DH9 0RG** Dur **405** F4
- Beatrix Potter Gallery **LA22 0NS** Cumb **378** C5
- Beaulieu House **SO42 7ZN** Hants **50** C4
- Belton House **NG32 2LS** Lincs **278** C2
- Belvoir Castle **NG32 1PD** Leics **277** H3
- Bembridge Windmill **PO35 5SQ** IoW **37** G3
- Beningbrough Hall & Gardens **YO30 1DD** N York **357** G3
- Benthall Hall **TF12 5RX** Shrops **235** F4
- Berkeley Castle **GL13 9BQ** Gloucs **135** F5
- Berrington Hall **HR6 0DW** Herefs **186** C2
- Berry Pomeroy Castle **TQ9 6NJ** Devon **20** A5
- Beth Chatto Gardens **CO7 7DB** Essex **175** E5
- Biddulph Grange Garden **ST8 7SD** Staffs **292** A3
- Bishop's Waltham Palace **SO32 1DH** Hants **51** G1
- Blackpool Pleasure Beach **FY4 1EZ** Bpool **337** F3
- Blenheim Palace **OX20 1PX** Oxon **139** G1
- Blickling Hall **NR11 6NF** Norfk **255** G2
- Blue John Cavern **S33 8WP** Derbys **313** F3
- Bodiam Castle **TN32 5UA** E Susx **80** A4
- Bolsover Castle **S44 6PR** Derbys **315** F5
- Boscobel House **ST19 9AR** Staffs **236** B3
- Bovington Tank Museum **BH20 6JG** Dorset **33** E2
- Bowes Castle **DL12 9LD** Dur **382** A2
- Bradgate Country Park **LE6 0HE** Leics **240** B2
- Bradley Manor **TQ12 6BN** Devon **20** A3
- Bramber Castle **BN44 3WW** W Susx **55** E2
- Brinkburn Priory **NE65 8AP** Nthumb **443** E5
- Bristol Zoo **BS8 3HA** Bristl **109** G5
- British Library **NW1 2DB** Gt Lon **119** G3
- British Museum **WC1B 3DG** Gt Lon **119** G3
- Brockhampton Estate **WR6 5TB** Herefs **187** F4
- Brough Castle **CA17 4EJ** Cumb **380** D2
- Buckfast Abbey **TQ11 0EE** Devon **19** F4
- Buckingham Palace **SW1A 1AA** Gt Lon **119** F4
- Buckland Abbey **PL20 6EY** Devon **17** G5
- Buscot Park **SN7 8BU** Oxon **138** C5
- Byland Abbey **YO61 4BD** N York **371** G4
- Caldicot Castle & Country Park **NP26 4HU** Mons **109** E2
- Calke Abbey **DE73 7LE** Derbys **275** F
- Canons Ashby House **NN11 3SD** Nhants **192** C4
- Canterbury Cathedral **CT1 2EH** Kent **100** C4
- Carisbrooke Castle **PO30 1XY** IoW **35** D3
- Carlyle's House **SW3 5HL** Gt Lon **119** F4
- Castle Drogo **EX6 6PB** Devon **25** H4
- Castle Howard **YO60 7DA** N York **372** D5
- Castle Rising Castle **PE31 6AH** Norfk **252** D3
- Charlecote Park **CV35 9ER** Warwks **190** D3
- Chartwell **TN16 1PS** Kent **96** C4
- Chastleton House **GL56 0SU** Oxon **164** C4
- Chatsworth **DE45 1PP** Derbys **314** B5
- Chedworth Roman Villa **GL54 3LJ** Gloucs **137** G2
- Chessington World of Adventures **KT9 2NE** Gt Lon **94** D2
- Chester Cathedral **CH1 2HU** Ches **289** F1
- Chester Zoo **CH2 1LH** Ches **309** F5
- Chesters Roman Fort **NE46 4EP** Nthumb **429** E5
- Chiswick House **W4 2RP** Gt Lon **119** E4
- Chysauster Ancient Village **TR20 8XA** Cnwll **3** E3
- Clandon Park **GU4 7RQ** Surrey **94** A4
- Claremont Landscape Garden **KT10 9JG** Surrey **94** C2
- Claydon House **MK18 2EY** Bucks **167** F4
- Cleeve Abbey **TA23 0PS** Somset **63** G3
- Clevedon Court **BS21 6QU** N Som **108** D5
- Cliveden **SL6 0JA** Bucks **117** F2
- Clouds Hill **BH20 7NQ** Dorset **33** E1
- Clumber Park **S80 3AZ** Notts **316** B5
- Colchester Zoo **CO3 0SL** Essex **174** C5
- Coleridge Cottage **TA5 1NQ** Somset **64** C4
- Coleton Fishacre **TQ6 0EQ** Devon **13** G2
- Compton Castle **TQ3 1TA** Devon **20** B5
- Conisbrough Castle **DN12 3HH** Donc **330** B5
- Corbridge Roman Site **NE45 5NT** Nthumb **404** A2
- Corfe Castle **BH20 5EZ** Dorset **33** H3
- Cornish Mines & Engines **TR15 3NP** Cnwll **6** C5
- Cotehele **PL12 6TA** Cnwll **17** F5
- Coughton Court **B49 5JA** Warwks **189** G2
- Courts Garden **BA14 6RR** Wilts **87** F2
- Cragside **NE65 7PX** Nthumb **442** D4
- Crealy Adventure Park **EX5 1DR** Devon **27** G4
- Cricket St Thomas Wildlife Park **TA20 4DB** Somset **44** D6
- Croft Castle **HR6 9PW** Herefs **186** A1
- Croome Park **WR8 9JS** Worcs **188** C5
- Deddington Castle **OX15 0TE** Oxon **165** H3
- Didcot Railway Centre **OX11 7NJ** Oxon **115** E1
- Dover Castle **CT16 1HU** Kent **83** F2
- Drayton Manor Theme Park **B78 3TW** Staffs **238** B4
- Dudmaston **WV15 6QN** Shrops **211** H2
- Dunham Massey **WA14 4SJ** Traffd **311** E2
- Dunstanburgh Castle **NE66 3TT** Nthumb **455** H5
- Dunster Castle **TA24 6SL** Somset **63** F3
- Durham Cathedral **DH1 3EH** Dur **395** F1
- Dyrham Park **SN14 8ER** S Glos **110** C4
- East Riddlesden Hall **BD20 5EL** Brad **342** A1
- Eden Project **PL24 2SG** Cnwll **8** D3
- Eltham Palace **SE9 5QE** Gt Lon **120** B5
- Emmetts Garden **TN14 6AY** Kent **96** C4
- Fairlands Valley Park **SG2 0BL** Herts **170** C5
- Farleigh Hungerford Castle **BA2 7RS** Somset **87** E3
- Farnborough Hall **OX17 1DU** Warwks **191** G5
- Felbrigg Hall **NR11 8PR** Norfk **261** G4
- Fenton House **NW3 6RT** Gt Lon **119** F2
- Finch Foundry **EX20 2NW** Devon **25** F4
- Finchale Priory **DH1 5SH** Dur **405** G5
- Fishbourne Roman Palace **PO19 3QR** W Susx **53** E4
- Flamingo Family Fun Park **TN34 3AR** E Susx **58** D5
- Flamingo Land **YO17 6UX** N York **373** E4
- Forde Abbey **TA20 4LU** Dorset **29** G1
- Fountains Abbey & Studley Royal **HG4 3DY** N York **370** B6
- Gawthorpe Hall **BB12 8UA** Lancs **340** C3
- Gisborough Priory **TS14 6HG** R & Cl **385** G1
- Glendurgan **TR11 5JZ** Cnwll **5** E3
- Goodrich Castle **HR9 6HY** Herefs **160** D6
- Great Chalfield Manor **SN12 8NH** Wilts **87** F2
- Great Yarmouth Pleasure Beach **NR30 3EH** Norfk **251** G3
- Greenway **TQ5 0ES** Devon **13** F1
- Greyfriars **WR1 2LZ** Worcs **188** C4
- Hailes Abbey **GL54 5PB** Gloucs **163** F3
- Ham House **TW10 7RS** Gt Lon **118** D5
- Hampton Court Palace **KT8 9AU** Gt Lon **118** D6
- Hanbury Hall **WR9 7EA** Worcs **188** D2
- Hardwick Hall **S44 5QJ** Derbys **295** F2
- Hardy's Cottage **DT2 8QJ** Dorset **32** C1
- Hare Hill **SK10 4QB** Ches **312** A4
- Hatchlands Park **GU4 7RT** Surrey **94** B4
- Heale Gardens **SP4 6NT** Wilts **70** C2
- Helmsley Castle **YO62 5AB** N York **372** B3
- Hereford Cathedral **HR1 2NG** Herefs **160** C2
- Hergest Croft Gardens **HR5 3EG** Herefs **185** E3
- Hever Castle & Gardens **TN8 7NG** Kent **96** C5
- Hidcote Manor Garden **GL55 6LR** Gloucs **190** B6
- Hill Top **LA22 0LF** Cumb **378** C5
- Hinton Ampner **SO24 0LA** Hants **73** E4
- Holkham Hall **NR23 1AB** Norfk **260** A3
- Housesteads Roman Fort **NE47 6NN** Nthumb **428** B6
- Howletts Wild Animal Park **CT4 5EL** Kent **100** C4
- Hughenden Manor **HP14 4LA** Bucks **142** B5
- Hurst Castle **SO41 0TR** Hants **35** H2
- Ickworth House & Gardens **IP29 5QE** Suffk **199** G2
- Ightham Mote **TN15 0NT** Kent **97** E4
- Ironbridge Gorge Museums **TF8 7DQ** Wrekin **235** F4
- Kedleston Hall **DE22 5JH** Derbys **275** E1
- Kenilworth Castle **CV8 1NE** Warwks **214** D5
- Kenwood House **NW3 7JR** Gt Lon **119** F2
- Kew Gardens **TW9 3AB** Gt Lon **118** D4
- Killerton House & Garden **EX5 3LE** Devon **27** F2
- King John's Hunting Lodge **BS26 2AP** Somset **84** D4
- Kingston Lacy **BH21 4EA** Dorset **48** B4
- Kirby Hall **NN17 3EN** Nhants **242** C6
- Knightshayes Court **EX16 7RQ** Devon **42** C4
- Knole **TN15 0RP** Kent **96** D4
- Knowsley Safari Park **L34 4AN** Knows **324** B6
- Lacock Abbey **SN15 2LG** Wilts **111** G6
- Lamb House **TN31 7ES** E Susx **59** F2
- Lanhydrock **PL30 5AD** Cnwll **15** F6
- Launceston Castle **PL15 7DR** Cnwll **23** G6
- Leeds Castle **ME17 1PL** Kent **98** C4
- Lindisfarne Castle **TD15 2SH** Nthumb **455** E1
- Lindisfarne Priory **TD15 2RX** Nthumb **455** E1
- Little Moreton Hall **CW12 4SD** Ches **291** G3
- Liverpool Cathedral **L1 7AZ** Lpool **309** E2
- London Zoo **NW1 4RY** Gt Lon **119** F3
- Long Crendon Courthouse **HP18 9AN** Bucks **141** E3
- Longleat **BA12 7NW** Wilts **87** E6
- Lost Gardens of Heligan **PL26 6EN** Cnwll **8** B4
- Ludgershall Castle **SP11 9QR** Wilts **89** G4
- Lydford Castle **EX20 4BH** Devon **24** D6
- Lyme Park **SK12 2NX** Ches **312** C3
- Lytes Cary Manor **TA11 7HU** Somset **67** E4
- Lyveden New Bield **PE8 5AT** Nhants **218** D2
- Maiden Castle **DT2 9PP** Dorset **32** B2
- Mapledurham House **RG4 7TR** Oxon **115** H4
- Marble Hill House **TW1 2NL** Gt Lon **118** D5
- Marwell Zoological Park **SO21 1JH** Hants **72** D5
- Melford Hall **CO10 9AA** Suffk **199** H5
- Merseyside Maritime Museum **L3 4AQ** Lpool **308** D2
- Minster Lovell Hall **OX29 0RN** Oxon **139** E2
- Mompesson House **SP1 2EL** Wilts **70** C4
- Monk Bretton Priory **S71 5QD** Barns **329** F3
- Montacute House **TA15 6XP** Somset **45** F4
- Morwellham Quay **PL19 8JL** Devon **17** F5
- Moseley Old Hall **WV10 7HY** Staffs **236** D4
- Mottisfont Abbey & Garden **SO51 0LP** Hants **71** G4
- Mottistone Manor Garden **PO30 4ED** IoW **36** C4
- Mount Grace Priory **DL6 3JG** N York **384** C5
- National Gallery **WC2N 5DN** Gt Lon **119** G3
- National Maritime Museum **SE10 9NF** Gt Lon **120** A4
- National Motorcycle Museum **B92 0EJ** Solhll **214** C3
- National Portrait Gallery **WC2H 0HE** Gt Lon **119** F3
- National Railway Museum **YO26 4XJ** York **358** A4
- National Space Centre **LE4 5NS** C Leic **240** C3
- Natural History Museum **SW7 5BD** Gt Lon **119** F4
- Needles Old Battery **PO39 0JH** IoW **35** H4
- Nether Alderley Mill **SK10 4TW** Ches **311** G4
- Netley Abbey **SO31 5FB** Hants **51** E3
- New Metroland **NE11 9YJ** Gatesd **405** F2
- Newtown Old Town Hall **PO30 4PA** IoW **36** C2
- North Leigh Roman Villa **OX29 6QB** Oxon **139** F2
- Norwich Cathedral **NR1 4DH** Norfk **250** A3
- Nostell Priory **WF4 1QE** Wakefd **329** G1
- Nunnington Hall **YO62 5UY** N York **372** C4
- Nymans **RH17 6EB** W Susx **77** E4
- Old Royal Naval College **SE10 9LW** Gt Lon **120** A4
- Old Sarum **SP1 3SD** Wilts **70** C3
- Old Wardour Castle **SP3 6RR** Wilts **69** F4
- Oldway Mansion **TQ3 2TD** Torbay **20** B5
- Orford Castle **IP12 2ND** Suffk **203** E5
- Ormesby Hall **TS7 9AS** R & Cl **385** E1
- Osborne House **PO32 6JY** IoW **51** F6
- Osterley Park & House **TW7 4RB** Gt Lon **118** C4
- Overbeck's **TQ8 8LW** Devon **12** C5
- Oxburgh Hall **PE33 9PS** Norfk **247** E4
- Packwood House **B94 6AT** Warwks **214** B5
- Paignton Zoo **TQ4 7EU** Torbay **20** B6
- Paycocke's **CO6 1NS** Essex **173** G5
- Peckover House & Garden **PE13 1JR** Cambs **245** G3
- Pendennis Castle **TR11 4LP** Cnwll **5** F2
- Petworth House & Park **GU28 0AE** W Susx **75** F5
- Pevensey Castle **BN24 5LE** E Susx **57** G4
- Peveril Castle **S33 8WQ** Derbys **313** G3
- Polesden Lacey **RH5 6BD** Surrey **94** C4
- Portland Castle **DT5 1AZ** Dorset **32** B5
- Portsmouth Historic Dockyard **PO1 3LJ** C Port **52** A4
- Powderham Castle **EX6 8JQ** Devon **27** F6
- Prior Park Landscape Garden **BA2 5AH** BaNES **86** D2
- Prudhoe Castle **NE42 6NA** Nthumb **404** C2
- Quarry Bank Mill **SK9 4LA** Ches **311** G3
- Quebec House **TN16 1TD** Kent **96** B4
- Ramsey Abbey Gatehouse **PE26 1BX** Cambs **220** C2

- Reculver Towers CT6 6SU Kent 100 D2
- Red House DA6 8JF Gt Lon 120 C4
- Restormel Castle PL22 0HN Cnwll 9 E1
- Richborough Roman Fort CT13 9JW Kent 101 F3
- Richmond Castle DL10 4QW N York 383 E4
- Roche Abbey S66 8NW Rothm 315 G1
- Rochester Castle ME1 1SX Medway 122 A6
- Rockbourne Roman Villa SP6 3PG Hants 49 E1
- Roman Baths & Pump Room BA1 1LZ BaNES 86 D2
- Royal Observatory Greenwich SE10 9NF Gt Lon 120 A4
- Rufford Old Hall L40 1SG Lancs 324 B1
- Runnymede SL4 2JJ W & M 117 G5
- Rushton Triangular Lodge NN14 1RP Nhants 218 A3
- Rycote Chapel OX9 2PA Oxon 141 E4
- Salisbury Cathedral SP1 2EJ Wilts 70 C4
- Saltram PL7 1UH C Plym 11 F2
- Sandham Memorial Chapel RG20 9JT Hants 90 D2
- Sandringham House & Grounds PE35 6EN Norfk 252 D2
- Saxtead Green Post Mill IP13 9QQ Suffk 202 B2
- Scarborough Castle YO11 1HY N York 374 C2
- Science Museum SW7 2DD Gt Lon 119 F4
- Scotney Castle TN3 8JN Kent 79 F2
- Shaw's Corner AL6 9BX Herts 144 A1
- Sheffield Park Garden TN22 3QX E Susx 77 H5
- Sherborne Old Castle DT9 3SA Dorset 46 B1
- Sissinghurst Castle Garden TN17 2AB Kent 80 B2
- Sizergh Castle & Garden LA8 8AE Cumb 365 G2
- Smallhythe Place TN30 7NG Kent 80 C3
- Snowshill Manor WR12 7JU Glouca 163 G3
- Souter Lighthouse SR6 7NH S Tyne 406 C2
- Speke Hall L24 1XD Lpool 309 F3
- Spinnaker Tower PO1 3TT C Port 52 A5
- SS Great Britain BS1 6TY Bristl 109 G5
- St Michael's Mount TR17 0HT Cnwll 3 F3
- St Paul's Cathedral EC4M 8AD Gt Lon 119 G3
- Stokesay Castle SY7 9AH Shrops 210 A3
- Stonehenge SP4 7DE Wilts 70 C1
- Stourhead BA12 6QD Wilts 68 C3
- Stowe Landscape Gardens MK18 5EH Bucks 167 E2
- Sudbury Hall DE6 5HT Derbys 274 B3
- Sulgrave Manor OX17 2SD Nhants 192 C5
- Sunnycroft TF1 2DR Wrekin 235 F2
- Sutton Hoo IP12 3DJ Suffk 202 B5
- Sutton House E9 6JQ Gt Lon 119 H2
- Tate Britain SW1P 4RG Gt Lon 119 G4
- Tate Liverpool L3 4BB Lpool 308 D2
- Tate Modern SE1 9TG Gt Lon 119 G3
- Tattershall Castle LN4 4LR Lincs 299 G3
- Tatton Park WA16 6QN Ches 311 E3
- The Lowry M50 3AZ Salfd 326 B5
- The Vyne RG24 9HL Hants 91 G3
- Thornton Abbey DN39 6TU N Linc 348 B6
- Thorpe Park KT16 8PN Surrey 118 A6
- Tilbury Fort RM18 7NR Thurr 121 F4
- Tintagel Castle PL34 0HE Cnwll 22 B5
- Tintinhull Garden BA22 8PZ Somset 67 E6
- Totnes Castle TQ9 5NU Devon 19 H6
- Tower of London EC3N 4AB Gt Lon 119 G3
- Townend LA23 1LB Cumb 378 D4
- Treasurer's House YO1 7JL York 358 B4
- Trelissick Garden TR3 6QL Cnwll 7 F6
- Trengwainton Garden TR20 8RZ Cnwll 2 D3
- Trerice TR8 4PG Cnwll 7 F2
- Twycross Zoo CV9 3PX Leics 239 E3
- Upnor Castle ME2 4XG Medway 122 B5
- Uppark GU31 5QR W Susx 74 B6
- Upton House & Garden OX15 6HT Warwks 191 F5
- Victoria & Albert Museum SW7 2RL Gt Lon 119 F4
- Waddesdon Manor HP18 0JH Bucks 141 F1
- Wakehurst Place RH17 6TN W Susx 77 F3
- Wall Roman Site WS14 0AW Staffs 237 G3
- Wallington House NE61 4AR Nthumb 429 G3
- Walmer Castle & Gardens CT14 7LJ Kent 101 G5
- Warkworth Castle NE65 0UJ Nthumb 443 G3
- Warwick Castle CV34 4QU Warwks 190 D2
- Washington Old Hall NE38 7LE Sundld 405 H3
- Waterperry Gardens OX33 1JZ Oxon 140 D3
- Weeting Castle IP27 0RQ Norfk 223 F2
- Weir Gardens HR4 7QF Herefs 160 A1
- Wenlock Priory TF13 6HS Shrops 235 E4
- West Midland Safari Park DY12 1LF Worcs 212 B4
- West Wycombe Park HP14 3AJ Bucks 142 A6
- Westbury Court Garden GL14 1PD Gloucs 135 G2
- Westminster Abbey SW1P 3PA Gt Lon 119 G4
- Westonbirt Arboretum GL8 8QS Gloucs 111 F2
- Westwood Manor BA15 2AF Wilts 87 E3
- Whipsnade Wild Animal Park LU6 2LF Beds 169 E6
- Whitby Abbey YO22 4JT N York 387 F2
- Wightwick Manor WV6 8EE Wolves 236 C5
- Wimpole Hall & Home Farm SG8 0BW Cambs 196 D4
- Winchester City Mill SO23 0EJ Hants 72 C4
- Windermere Lake Cruises LA23 3HE Cumb 378 C5
- Windsor Castle SL4 1NJ W & M 117 G4
- Winkworth Arboretum GU8 4AD Surrey 75 F1
- Wisley Garden GU23 6QB Surrey 94 B3
- Woburn Safari Park MK17 9QN Beds 168 D3
- Wookey Hole Caves BA5 1BB Somset 85 F5
- Woolsthorpe Manor NG33 5NR Lincs 278 C5
- Wordsworth House CA13 9RX Cumb 388 D3
- Wrest Park Gardens MK45 4HS Beds 169 F2
- Wroxeter Roman City SY5 6PR Shrops 234 D3
- Xscape Castleford WF10 4TA Wakefd 344 A5
- Yarmouth Castle PO41 0PB IoW 36 B3
- York Minster YO1 7JF York 358 B4

SCOTLAND

- Aberdour Castle KY3 0SL Fife 487 G2
- Alloa Tower FK10 1PP Clacks 498 D6
- Angus Folk Museum DD8 1RT Angus 527 E5
- Arbroath Abbey DD11 1EG Angus 515 G1
- Arduaine Garden PA34 4XQ Ag & B 492 D2
- Bachelors' Club KA5 5RB S Ayrs 445 F4
- Balmoral Castle Grounds AB35 5TB Abers 537 L4
- Balvenie Castle AB55 4DH Moray 568 E7
- Bannockburn Heritage Centre FK7 0LJ Stirlg 485 F1
- Blackness Castle EH49 7NH Falk 487 E3
- Blair Castle PH18 5TL P & K 524 C2
- Bothwell Castle G71 8BL S Lans 467 G3
- Branklyn Garden PH2 7BB P & K 512 D5
- Brodick Castle KA27 8HY N Ayrs 461 E2
- Brodie Castle IV36 2TE Moray 567 H5
- Broughton House & Garden DG6 4JX D & G 412 C4
- Burleigh Castle KY13 9GG P & K 500 B4
- Burrell Collection G43 1AT C Glas 467 E2
- Caerlaverock Castle DG1 4RU D & G 398 C1
- Cardoness Castle DG7 2EH D & G 412 A3
- Carnassarie Castle PA31 8RQ Ag & B 492 D5
- Castle Campbell FK14 7PP Clacks 499 F5
- Castle Fraser AB51 7LD Abers 556 C2
- Castle Kennedy & Gardens DG9 8BX D & G 415 E4
- Castle Menzies PH15 2JD P & K 524 B6
- Corgarff Castle AB36 8YL Abers 554 A3
- Craigievar Castle AB33 8JF Abers 555 G3
- Craigmillar Castle EH16 4SY C Edin 488 B5
- Crarae Garden PA32 8YA Ag & B 493 G5
- Crathes Castle & Garden AB31 5QJ Abers 556 C5
- Crichton Castle EH37 5QH Mdloth 471 G2
- Crossraguel Abbey KA19 8HQ S Ayrs 432 C3
- Culloden Battlefield IV2 5EU Highld 556 C7
- Culross Palace KY12 8JH Fife 486 C2
- Culzean Castle & Country Park KA19 8LE S Ayrs 432 B2
- Dallas Dhu Distillery IV36 2RR Moray 567 J5
- David Livingstone Centre G72 9BT S Lans 467 G3
- Dirleton Castle EH39 5ER E Loth 489 G3
- Doune Castle FK16 6EA Stirlg 498 A4
- Drum Castle AB31 5EY Abers 556 D4
- Dryburgh Abbey TD6 0RQ Border 452 A3
- Duff House AB45 3SX Abers 570 B3
- Dumbarton Castle G82 1JJ W Duns 483 F5
- Dundrennan Abbey DG6 4QH D & G 412 D5
- Dunnottar Castle AB39 2TL Abers 541 G3
- Dunstaffnage Castle PA37 1PZ Ag & B 506 E3
- Edinburgh Castle EH1 2NG C Edin 488 B5
- Edinburgh Zoo EH12 6TS C Edin 487 H5
- Edzell Castle DD9 7UE Angus 540 A6
- Elgin Cathedral IV30 1EL Moray 568 C3
- Falkland Palace & Garden KY15 7BU Fife 501 E3
- Fort George IV2 7TE Highld 566 D5
- Fyvie Castle AB53 8JS Abers 559 H2
- Georgian House EH2 4DR C Edin 488 A5
- Gladstone's Land EH1 2NT C Edin 488 B5
- Glamis Castle DD8 1RJ Angus 527 E5
- Glasgow Botanic Gardens G12 0UE C Glas 467 E1
- Glasgow Cathedral G4 0QZ C Glas 467 F1
- Glasgow Museum of Transport G3 8DP C Glas 467 E1
- Glasgow Science Centre G51 1EA C Glas 467 E1
- Glenluce Abbey DG8 0AF D & G 415 G5
- Greenbank Garden G76 8RB E Rens 467 E3
- Haddo House AB41 7EQ Abers 560 C3
- Harmony Garden TD6 9LJ Border 451 G3
- Hermitage Castle TD9 0LU Border 439 F5
- Highland Wildlife Park PH21 1NL Highld 536 B2
- Hill House G84 9AJ Ag & B 482 C3
- Hill of Tarvit Mansionhouse & Garden KY15 5PB Fife 502 B2
- Holmwood House G44 3YG C Glas 467 E3
- House of Dun DD10 9LQ Angus 529 E3
- House of The Binns EH49 7NA W Loth 487 E4
- Hunterian Museum G12 8QQ C Glas 467 E1
- Huntingtower Castle PH1 3JL P & K 512 C4
- Huntly Castle AB54 4SH Abers 558 C1
- Hutchesons' Hall G1 1EJ C Glas 467 E1
- Inchmahome Priory FK8 3RA Stirlg 497 E4
- Inveresk Lodge Garden EH21 7TE E Loth 488 C5
- Inverewe Garden IV22 2LG Highld 573 G7
- Inverlochy Castle PH33 7NR Highld 533 H7
- Kellie Castle & Garden KY10 2RF Fife 503 E3
- Kildrummy Castle AB33 8RA Abers 555 E1
- Killiecrankie Visitor Centre PH16 5LG P & K 524 D3
- Leith Hall & Garden AB54 4NQ Abers 558 C4
- Linlithgow Palace EH49 7AL W Loth 486 D4
- Loch Leven Castle KY13 8AS P & K 500 B4
- Logan Botanic Garden DG9 9ND D & G 408 B3
- Malleny Garden EH14 7AF C Edin 470 C1
- Melrose Abbey TD6 9LG Border 451 G3
- National Museum of Scotland EH1 1JF C Edin 488 B5
- Newark Castle PA14 5NH Inver 482 D5
- Palace of Holyroodhouse EH8 8DX C Edin 488 B5
- Pitmedden Garden AB41 7PD Abers 560 C4
- Preston Mill EH40 3DS E Loth 490 A4
- Priorwood Garden TD6 9PX Border 451 G3
- Robert Smail's Printing Works EH44 6HA Border 450 C2
- Rothesay Castle PA20 0DA Ag & B 464 B2
- Royal Botanic Garden Edinburgh EH3 5LR C Edin 488 A4
- Royal Yacht Britannia EH6 6JJ C Edin 488 B4
- Scone Palace PH2 6BD P & K 512 D4
- Smailholm Tower TD5 7PG Border 452 B3
- Souter Johnnie's Cottage KA19 8HY S Ayrs 432 B3
- St Andrew's Cathedral KY16 9QU Fife 503 E1
- Stirling Castle FK8 1EJ Stirlg 498 B6
- Sweetheart Abbey DG2 8BU D & G 398 B1
- Tantallon Castle EH39 5PN E Loth 490 A2
- Tenement House G3 6QN C Glas 467 E1
- The Lighthouse G1 3NU C Glas 467 E1
- Threave Castle DG7 1RX D & G 413 E2
- Threave Garden DG7 1RX D & G 413 E2
- Tolquhon Castle AB41 7LP Abers 560 C4
- Traquair House EH44 6PW Border 450 C2
- Urquhart Castle IV63 6XJ Highld 549 J4
- Weaver's Cottage PA10 2JG Rens 466 B2
- Whithorn Priory DG8 8PY D & G 410 D4

WALES

- Aberconwy House LL32 8AY Conwy 305 G4
- Aberdulais Falls SA10 8EU Neath 130 B5
- Beaumaris Castle LL58 8AP IoA 304 D4
- Big Pit National Coal Museum NP4 9XP Torfn 132 D3
- Bodnant Garden LL28 5RE Conwy 305 H5
- Caerleon Roman Amphitheatre NP18 1AE Newpt 107 F1
- Caernarfon Castle LL55 2AY Gwynd 283 E3
- Cardiff Castle CF10 3RB Cardif 106 C4
- Castell Coch CF15 7JS Cardif 106 B3
- Chirk Castle LL14 5AF Wrexhm 269 E2
- Colby Woodland Garden SA67 8PP Pembks 126 D3
- Conwy Castle LL32 8AY Conwy 305 G4
- Criccieth Castle LL52 0DP Gwynd 264 C2
- Dan-yr-Ogof Showcaves SA9 1GJ Powys 130 C1
- Dinefwr Park SA19 6RT Carmth 155 F5
- Dolaucothi Gold Mines SA19 8RR Carmth 155 G2
- Erddig LL13 0YT Wrexhm 288 D5
- Ffestiniog Railway LL49 9NF Gwynd 264 D2
- Harlech Castle LL46 2YH Gwynd 264 D3
- Llanerchaeron SA48 8DG Cerdgn 180 C2
- Penrhyn Castle LL57 4HN Gwynd 304 C5
- Plas Newydd LL61 6DQ IoA 283 F2
- Plas Yn Rhiw LL53 8AB Gwynd 262 C5
- Portmeirion LL48 6ET Gwynd 264 D2
- Powis Castle & Garden SY21 8RF Powys 232 D3
- Raglan Castle NP15 2BT Mons 133 H3
- Sygun Copper Mine LL55 4NE Gwynd 284 C5
- Tintern Abbey NP16 6SE Mons 134 C4
- Tudor Merchant's House SA70 7BX Pembks 126 C4
- Tŷ Mawr Wybrnant LL25 0HJ Conwy 285 G4
- Valle Crucis Abbey LL20 8DD Denbgs 288 B6

Traffic signs and road markings

Traffic signs

Signs giving orders

Signs with red circles are mostly prohibitive. Plates below signs qualify their message.

Entry to 20mph zone

End of 20mph zone

Maximum speed

National speed limit applies

School crossing patrol

Stop and give way

Give way to traffic on major road

Manually operated temporary STOP and GO signs

No entry for vehicular traffic

No vehicles except bicycles being pushed

No cycling

No motor vehicles

No buses (over 8 passenger seats)

No overtaking

No towed caravans

No vehicles carrying explosives

No vehicle or combination of vehicles over length shown

No vehicles over height shown

No vehicles over width shown

Give priority to vehicles from opposite direction

No right turn

No left turn

No U-turns

No goods vehicles over maximum gross weight shown (in tonnes) except for loading and unloading

WEAK BRIDGE
No vehicles over maximum gross weight shown (in tonnes)

Permit holders only
Parking restricted to permit holders

RED ROUTE
No stopping during period indicated except for buses

URBAN CLEARWAY Monday to Friday
No stopping during times shown except for as long as necessary to set down or pick up passengers

No waiting

No stopping (Clearway)

Signs with blue circles but no red border mostly give positive instruction.

Ahead only

Turn left ahead (right if symbol reversed)

Turn left (right if symbol reversed)

Keep left (right if symbol reversed)

Vehicles may pass either side to reach same destination

Mini-roundabout (roundabout circulation – give way to vehicles from the immediate right)

Route to be used by pedal cycles only

Segregated pedal cycle and pedestrian route

Minimum speed

End of minimum speed

Only
Buses and cycles only

Only
Trams only

TRAMWAY LOOK BOTH WAYS
Pedestrian crossing point over tramway

One-way traffic (note: compare circular 'Ahead only' sign)

With-flow bus and cycle lane

Contraflow bus lane

With-flow pedal cycle lane

Warning signs

Mostly triangular

STOP 100 yds
Distance to 'STOP' line ahead

Dual carriageway ends

Road narrows on right (left if symbol reversed)

Road narrows on both sides

GIVE WAY 50 yds
Distance to 'Give Way' line ahead

Crossroads

Junction on bend ahead

T-junction with priority over vehicles from the right

Staggered junction

Traffic merging from left ahead

The priority through route is indicated by the broader line.

Double bend first to left (symbol may be reversed)

Bend to right (or left if symbol reversed)

Roundabout

Uneven road

REDUCE SPEED NOW
Plate below some signs

Two-way traffic crosses one-way road

Two-way traffic straight ahead

Opening or swing bridge ahead

Low-flying aircraft or sudden aircraft noise

Falling or fallen rocks

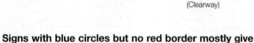
Traffic signals not in use

Traffic signals

Slippery road

Steep hill downwards

Steep hill upwards

Gradients may be shown as a ratio i.e. 20% = 1:5

Tunnel ahead

Trams crossing ahead

Level crossing with barrier or gate ahead

Level crossing without barrier or gate ahead

Level crossing without barrier

Downward pointing arrows mean 'Get in lane'
The left-hand lane leads to a different destination from the other lanes.

School crossing patrol ahead (some signs have amber lights which flash when crossings are in use)

Frail (or blind or disabled if shown) pedestrians likely to cross road ahead

Pedestrians in road ahead

Zebra crossing

Overhead electric cable; plate indicates maximum height of vehicles which can pass safely

The panel with the inclined arrow indicates the destinations which can be reached by leaving the motorway at the next junction

Signs on primary routes - green backgrounds

Available width of headroom indicated

On approaches to junctions

At the junction

Route confirmatory sign after junction

On approaches to junctions

On approach to a junction in Wales (bilingual)

Blue panels indicate that the motorway starts at the junction ahead.
Motorways shown in brackets can also be reached along the route indicated.
White panels indicate local or non-primary routes leading from the junction ahead.
Brown panels show the route to tourist attractions.
The name of the junction may be shown at the top of the sign.
The aircraft symbol indicates the route to an airport.
A symbol may be included to warn of a hazard or restriction along that route.

Sharp deviation of route to left (or right if chevrons reversed)

Light signals ahead at level crossing, airfield or bridge

Miniature warning lights at level crossings

Cattle

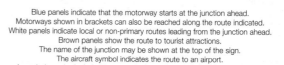

Primary route forming part of a ring road

Cattle

Wild animals

Wild horses or ponies

Accompanied horses or ponies

Cycle route ahead

Risk of ice

Traffic queues likely ahead

Distance over which road humps extend

Other danger; plate indicates nature of danger

Soft verges

Signs on non-primary and local routes - black borders

On approaches to junctions

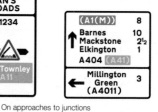

Market Walborough B 486

At the junction

Direction to toilets with access for the disabled

Green panels indicate that the primary route starts at the junction ahead.
Route numbers on a blue background show the direction to a motorway.
Route numbers on a green background show the direction to a primary route.

Direction signs

Mostly rectangular

Signs on motorways – blue backgrounds

At a junction leading directly into a motorway (junction number may be shown on a black background)

On approaches to junctions (junction number on black background)

Route confirmatory sign after junction

Note: Although this road atlas shows many of the signs commonly in use, a comprehensive explanation of our signing system is given in the Department of Transport's booklet *Know Your Traffic Signs*, which is on sale at booksellers. The booklet also illustrates and explains the vast majority of signs the road user in likely to encounter. The signs illustrated in this road atlas are not all drawn to the same scale. In Wales, bilingual versions of some signs are used including Welsh and English versions of place names. Some older designs of signs may still be seen on the roads.

Traffic signs and road markings

Other direction signs

Picnic site

Ancient monument in the care of English Heritage

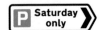

Direction to a car park

'Countdown' markers at exit from motorway (each bar represents 100 yards to the exit). Green-backed markers may be used on primary routes and white-backed markers with black bars on other routes. At approaches to concealed level crossings white-backed markers with red bars may be used. Although these will be erected at equal distances the bars do not represent 100 yard intervals.

Motorway service area sign showing the operator's name

Tourist attraction

Direction to camping and caravan site

Advisory route for lorries

Route for pedal cycles forming part of a network

Recommended route for pedal cycles to place shown

Route for pedestrians

Traffic has priority over oncoming vehicles

Hospital ahead with Accident and Emergency facilities

Tourist information point

No through road for vehicles

Symbols showing emergency diversion route for motorway and other main road traffic

Diversion route

Recommended route for pedal cycles

Home Zone Entry

Area in which cameras are used to enforce traffic regulations

Bus lane on road at junction ahead

Information signs

All rectangular

Entrance to controlled parking zone

Entrance to congestion charging zone

Greater London Low Emission Zone (LEZ)

Advance warning of restriction or prohibition ahead

Parking place for solo motorcycles

With-flow bus lane ahead which pedal cycles and taxis may also use

Lane designated for use by high occupancy vehicles (HOV) - see rule 142

Vehicles permitted to use an HOV lane ahead

End of motorway

Start of motorway and point from which motorway regulations apply

Appropriate traffic lanes at junction ahead

Traffic on the main carriageway coming from right has priority over joining traffic

Additional traffic joining from left ahead. Traffic on main carriageway has priority over joining traffic from right hand lane of slip road

Traffic in right hand lane of slip road joining the main carriageway has priority over left hand lane

---

Roadworks signs

Road works

Loose chippings

Temporary hazard at roadworks

Temporary lane closure (the number and position of arrows and red bars may be varied according to lanes open and closed)

Slow-moving or stationary works vehicle blocking a traffic lane. Pass in the direction shown by the arrow.

Mandatory speed limit ahead

Roadworks 1 mile ahead

End of roadworks and any temporary restrictions including speed limits

Signs used on the back of slow-moving or stationary vehicles warning of a lane closed ahead by a works vehicle. There are no cones on the road.

Lane restrictions at roadworks ahead

One lane crossover at contraflow roadworks

Road markings

Across the carriageway

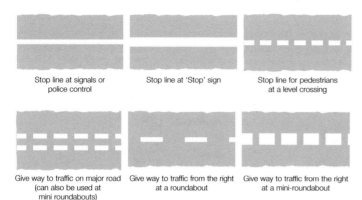

Stop line at signals or police control

Stop line at 'Stop' sign

Stop line for pedestrians at a level crossing

Give way to traffic on major road (can also be used at mini roundabouts)

Give way to traffic from the right at a roundabout

Give way to traffic from the right at a mini-roundabout

Along the carriageway

Edge line

Centre line
See Rule 127

Hazard warning line
See Rule 127

Double white lines
See Rules 128 and 129

See Rule 130

Lane line See Rule 131

Along the edge of the carriageway

Waiting restrictions

Waiting restrictions indicated by yellow lines apply to the carriageway, pavement and verge. You may stop to load or unload (unless there are also loading restrictions as described below) or while passengers board or alight. Double yellow lines mean no waiting at any time, unless there are signs that specifically indicate seasonal restrictions. The times at which the restrictions apply for other road markings are shown on nearby plates or on entry signs to controlled parking zones. If no days are shown on the signs, the restrictions are in force every day including Sundays and Bank Holidays. White bay markings and upright signs (see below) indicate where parking is allowed.

8 am - 6 pm →

Mon - Sat
8 am - 7 pm
20 mins
No return
within 40 mins

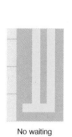
No waiting at any time

No waiting during times shown on sign

Waiting is limited to the duration specified during the days and times shown

Red Route stopping controls

Red lines are used on some roads instead of yellow lines. In London the double and single red lines used on Red Routes indicate that stopping to park, load/unload or to board and alight from a vehicle (except for a licensed taxi or if you hold a Blue Badge) is prohibited. The red lines apply to the carriageway, pavement and verge. The times that the red line prohibitions apply are shown on nearby signs, but the double red line ALWAYS means no stopping at any time. On Red Routes you may stop to park, load/unload in specially marked boxes and adjacent signs specify the times and purposes and duration allowed. A box MARKED IN RED indicates that it may only be available for the purpose specified for part of the day (e.g. between busy peak periods). A box MARKED IN WHITE means that it is available throughout the day.

RED AND SINGLE YELLOW LINES CAN ONLY GIVE A GUIDE TO THE RESTRICTIONS AND CONTROLS IN FORCE AND SIGNS, NEARBY OR AT A ZONE ENTRY, MUST BE CONSULTED.

RED ROUTE
No stopping
at any time

No stopping at any time

RED ROUTE
No stopping
Mon - Sat
7 am - 7 pm

No stopping during times shown on sign

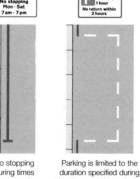

RED ROUTE
Mon - Sat
7 am - 7 pm
1 hour
No return within
2 hours

Parking is limited to the duration specified during the days and times shown

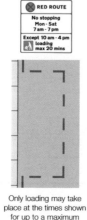

RED ROUTE
No stopping
Mon - Sat
7 am - 7 pm
Except 10 am - 4 pm
loading
max 20 mins

Only loading may take place at the times shown for up to a maximum duration of 20 mins

On the kerb or at the edge of the carriageway

Loading restrictions on roads other than Red Routes

Yellow marks on the kerb or at the edge of the carriageway indicate that loading or unloading is prohibited at the times shown on the nearby black and white plates. You may stop while passengers board or alight. If no days are indicated on the signs the restrictions are in force every day including Sundays and Bank Holidays.

ALWAYS CHECK THE TIMES SHOWN ON THE PLATES.

Lengths of road reserved for vehicles loading and unloading are indicated by a white 'bay' marking with the words 'Loading Only' and a sign with the white on blue 'trolley' symbol. This sign also shows whether loading and unloading is restricted to goods vehicles and the times at which the bay can be used. If no times or days are shown it may be used at any time. Vehicles may not park here if they are not loading or unloading.

No loading at any time

No loading or unloading at any time

No loading Mon - Sat 8.30 am - 6.30 pm

No loading or unloading at the times shown

Loading only
Loading bay

Other road markings

SCHOOL — KEEP — CLEAR

Keep entrance clear of stationary vehicles, even if picking up or setting down children

Warning of 'Give Way' just ahead

DOCTOR
Parking space reserved for vehicles named

BUS STOP
See Rule 243

BUS LANE
See Rule 141

Box junction - See Rule 174

KEEP CLEAR
Do not block that part of the carriageway indicated

CITY   A3   YORK ST
Indication of traffic lanes

Atlas symbols

Motoring information

M4	Motorway	A3	Primary route: dual, single carriageway		Toll road, steep gradient (arrows point downhill)
① ❸	Motorway numbered junction: full access, restricted access	① ❸	Primary route numbered junction: full access, restricted access		Roundabout
	Under construction	A25	Other A road: dual, single carriageway	▼ 4 ▼	Distance in miles between symbols
TOLL T4 Toll	Toll motorway with toll station	B382	B road: dual, single carriageway		Road under construction, in tunnel
BATH	Primary route destination		Minor road: more than 4 metres wide, less than 4 metres wide	or V	Vehicle ferry
Ⓢ Ⓢ	Service area: motorway, primary route		Narrow road with passing places (Scotland)		Fast vehicle ferry or catamaran
🍽	Transport café		Other road, drive or track: public, private or restricted access	✈ Ⓗ	Airport, airfield, heliport

Recreation and leisure Before visiting check opening times, to avoid disappointment.

	Sandy beach, heritage coast	C&CC site	Camping & Caravanning Club site (AA approved)		Bird collection
	National Park boundary	Sun Inn PH	AA recommended pub (selected for good food, real ale, character & comfort)	RSPB	Bird reserve (RSPB)
	Scenic area		Abbey, cathedral or priory		Castle
	Woodland		Abbey, cathedral or priory in ruins		Cave
	Heritage railway		Agricultural showground		Country park, picnic site
Tarka Trail	National Cycle Network (Sustrans)		Air show venue		Farm or animal centre
Pennine Way	Selection of national trails		Ancient monument		Garden
Hadrian's Wall	Ancient wall		Aquarium		Hill-fort
▲	AA approved campsite		Aqueduct or viaduct		Historic house
	AA approved caravan site		Arboretum		Industrial attraction
	AA approved caravan & campsite	✕	Battle site	⚓	Marina

Town and airport plans Refer to the recreation and leisure legend, above, for a complete list of symbols.

M8	Motorway		B road: dual, single carriageway		Road under construction
	Primary route: dual, single carriageway		Minor road: dual, single carriageway		Road in tunnel
	Other A road: dual, single carriageway	or	Other road, drive or track: (access may be restricted)		Track or footpath

Central London plan (see pages 612 - 619)

	Central London Congestion Charging Zone boundary		Charge-free routes through the Charging Zone		Theatre, Cinema

40	Speed camera site (fixed location) with speed limit in mph
30	Section of road with two or more fixed speed cameras, with speed limit in mph
30—30	Average speed (SPECS™) camera system with speed limit in mph
V	Fixed speed camera site with variable speed limit
	City, town, village or other built-up area
H	24-hour Accident & Emergency hospital
628 ▲ 459	Height in metres: peak, pass

P+	Park & Ride (at least 6 days per week)
	24-hour filling station
	Filling station, LPG station
———————	Railway line, in tunnel
—○——○—	Railway, DLR station
●	Underground station
⊖	London underground station

Fd ✳	Ford, level crossing
•—•—•—	Tramway
Borders **Cumbria**	National boundary
Devon **Cornwall**	County or unitary authority boundary
³10	National Grid reference
Miles ½ 1 / Km 1	1:100,000 scale bar
Miles ½ 1 / Km 1 2	1:150,000 scale bar

Monument	
Museum or gallery	
National Nature Reserve: England, Scotland, Wales	
Local nature reserve	
National Trust property	
National Trust for Scotland property	
English Heritage site	
Historic Scotland site	
Cadw (Welsh heritage) site	
Roman remains	
Steam railway	

Theme park	
Tourist Information Centre all year, seasonal	
Viewpoint	
Vineyard	
Visitor or heritage centre	
Windmill	
World Heritage Site (UNESCO)	
Zoo or wildlife collection	
Boxed symbols indicate in-town attractions	
Major shopping centre, other place of interest	
AA selected golf course	

Athletics	
County cricket	
Football	
Horse racing	
Ice hockey	
Rugby Union, League	
Ski slope: natural, artificial	
Motorsport, speedway	
Tennis	
Arena (indoor)	
Stadium	

Pedestrians only road	
One-way street, car park	
Park & Ride (at least 6 days per week)	
Building of interest	
24-hour Accident & Emergency hospital	
Junction numbers	
Church/chapel	
Public toilet	
Toilet with facilities for the less able	

AA inspected restaurant	
Public Library	

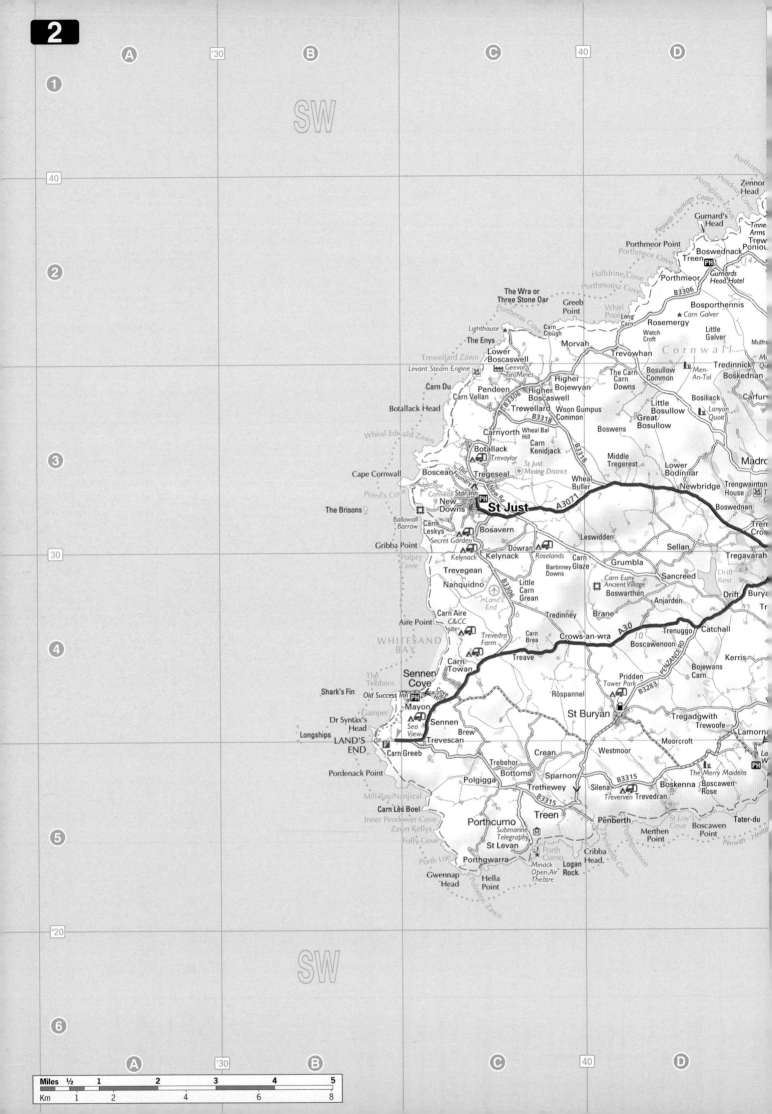

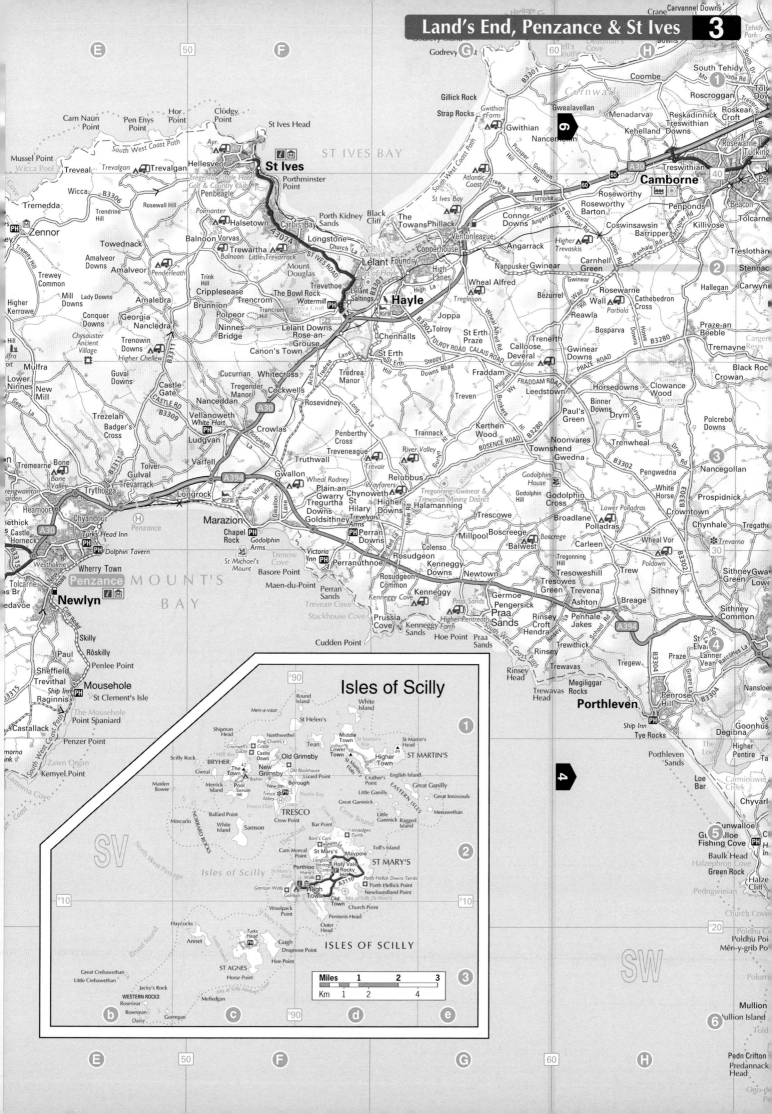

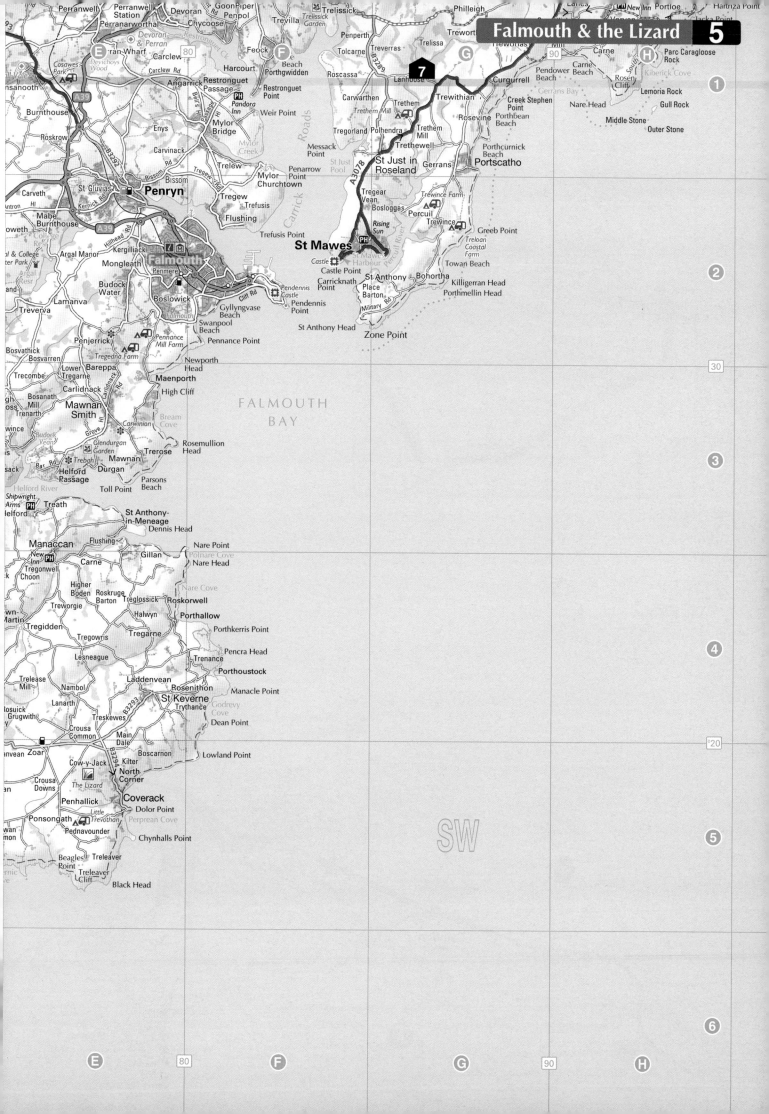

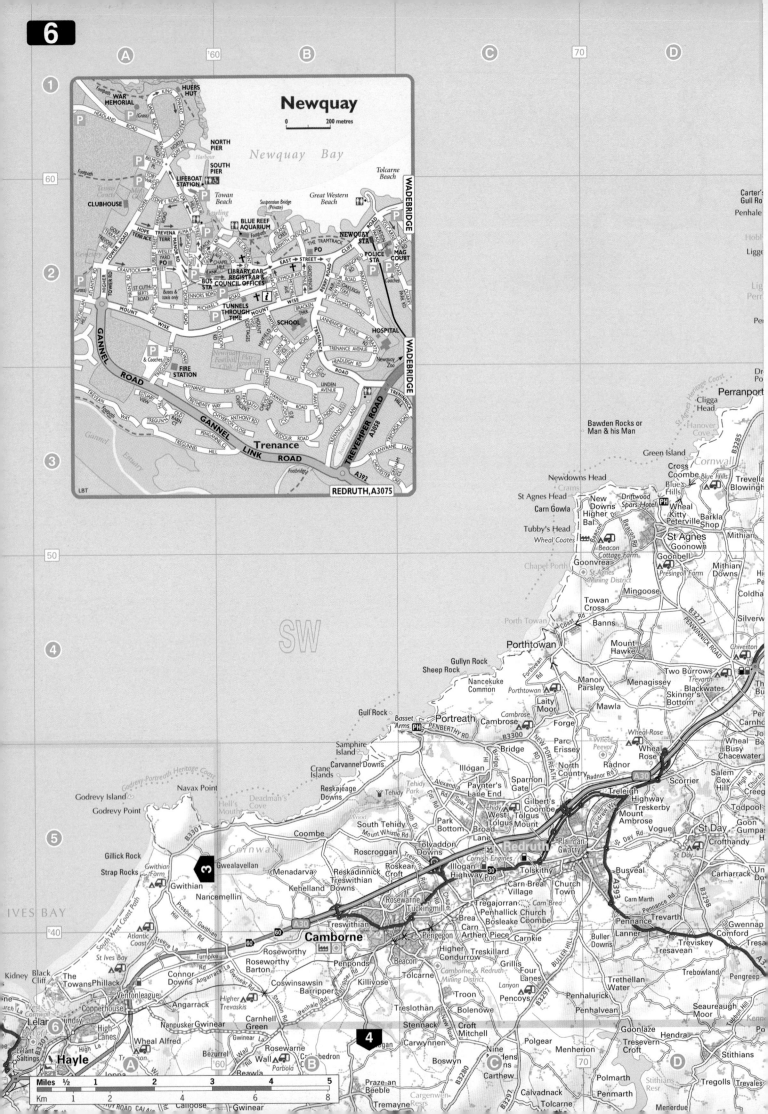

Newquay

0   200 metres

Newquay Bay

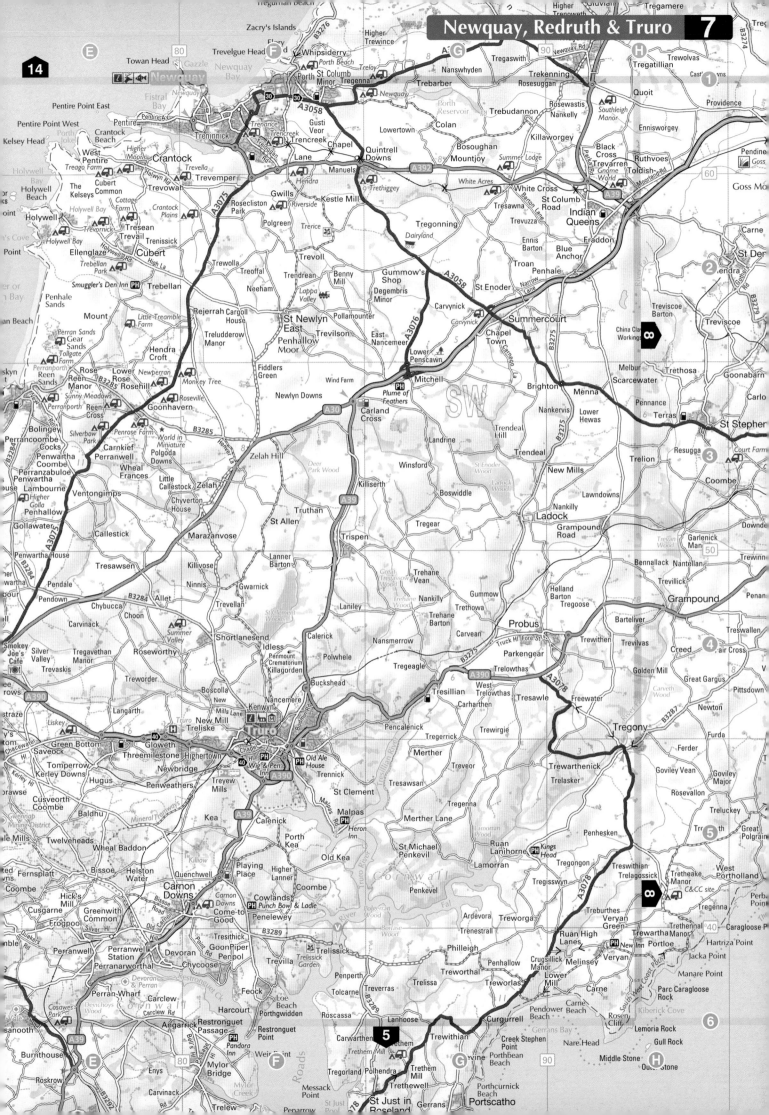

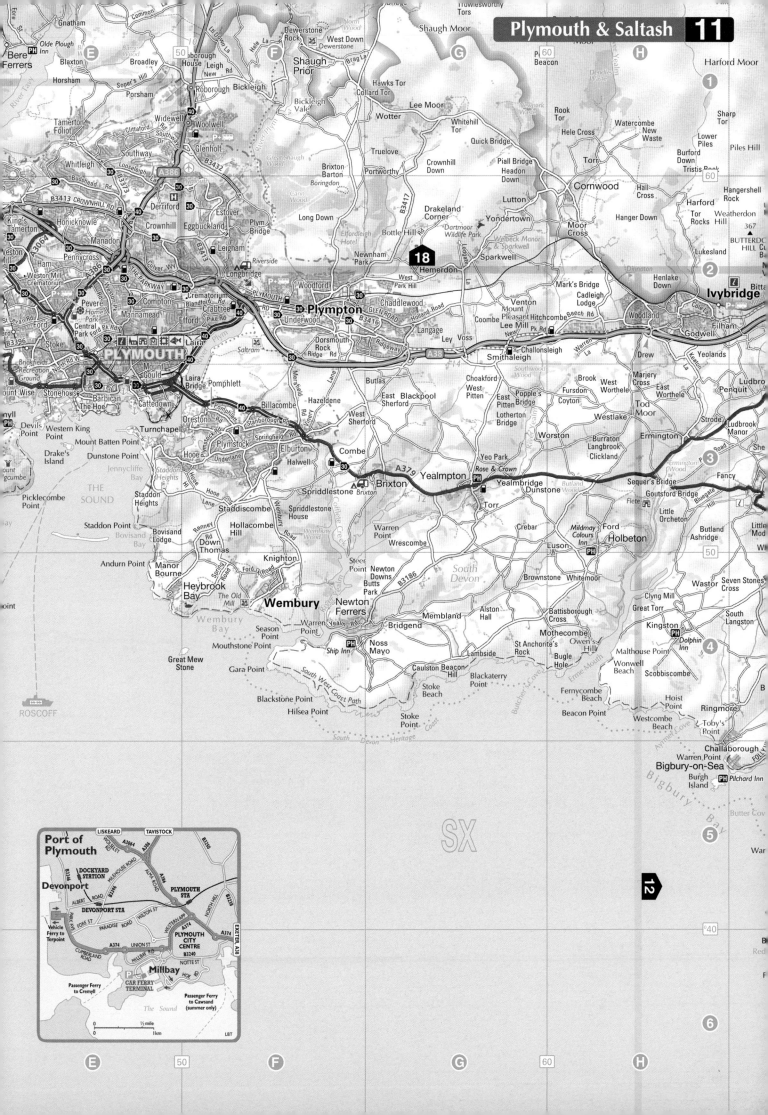

TOR BAY

Brixham

Brixham

Start Bay

SX

South Devon

Dartmouth

Kingswear

Stoke Fleming

Blackpool

Strete

Slapton

Torcross

Start Point

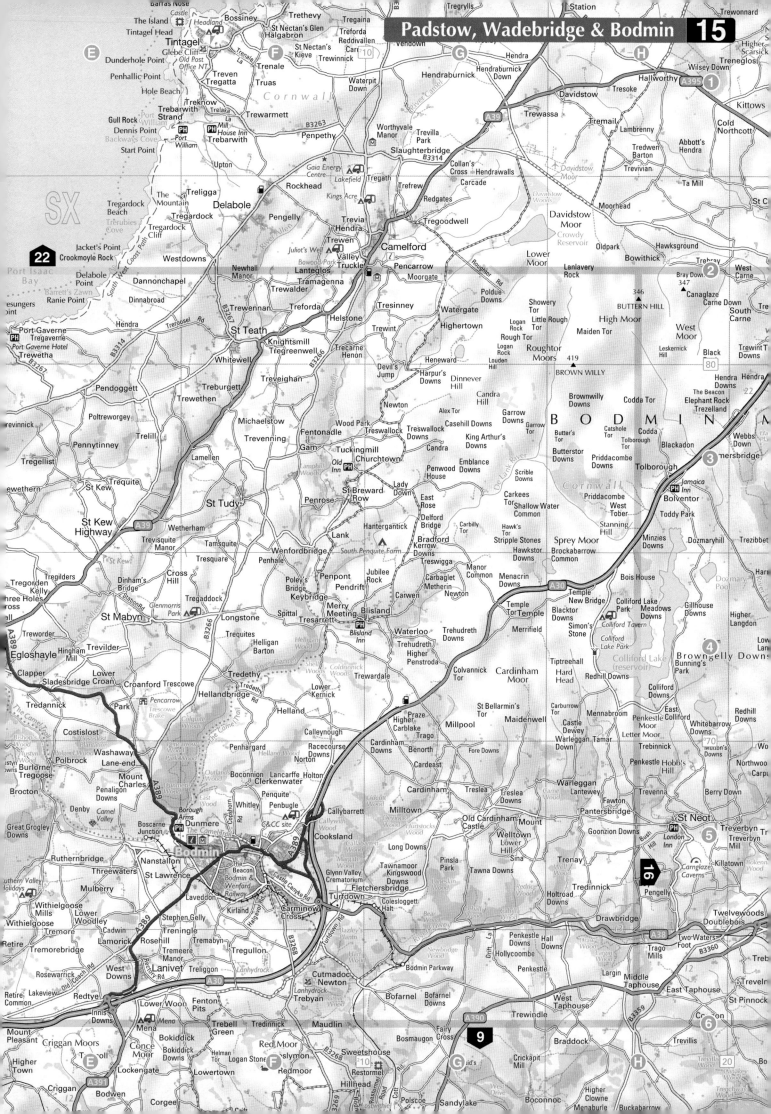

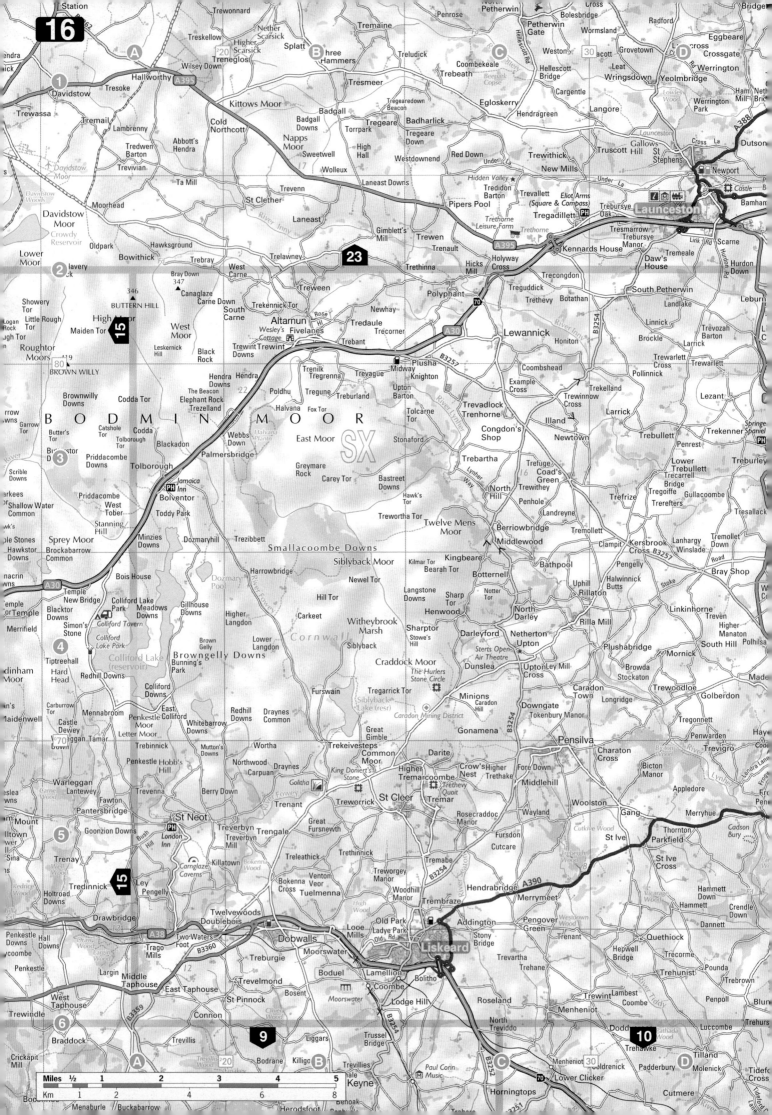

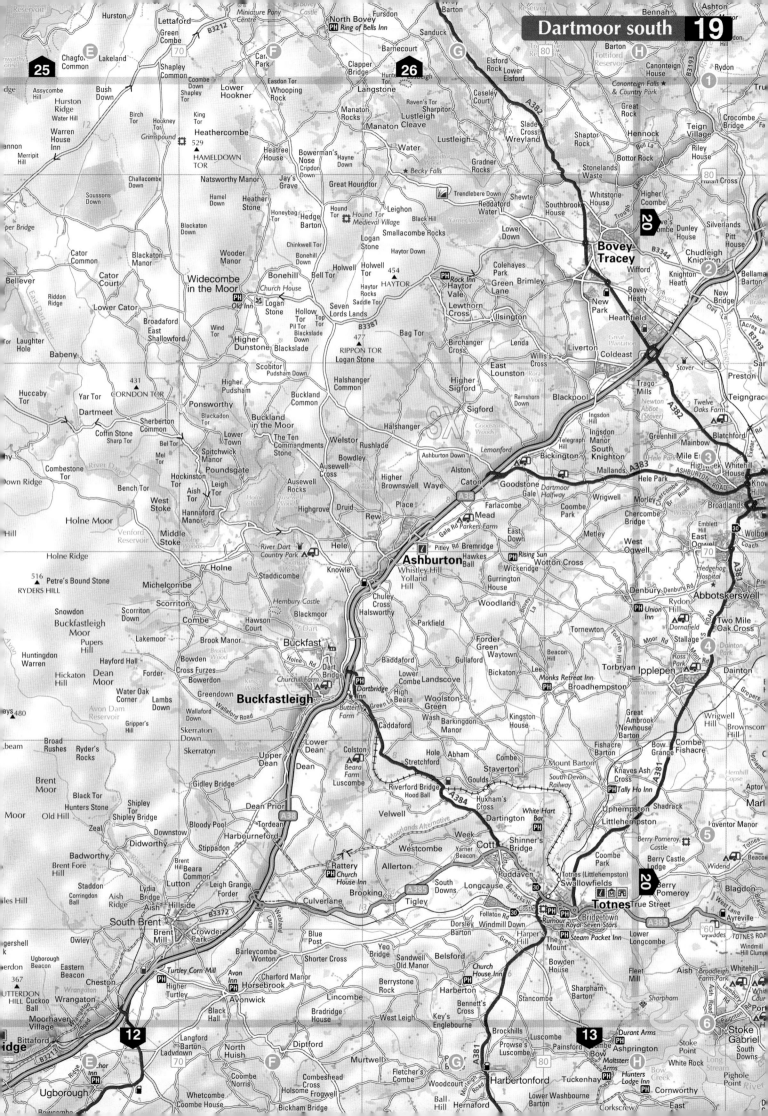

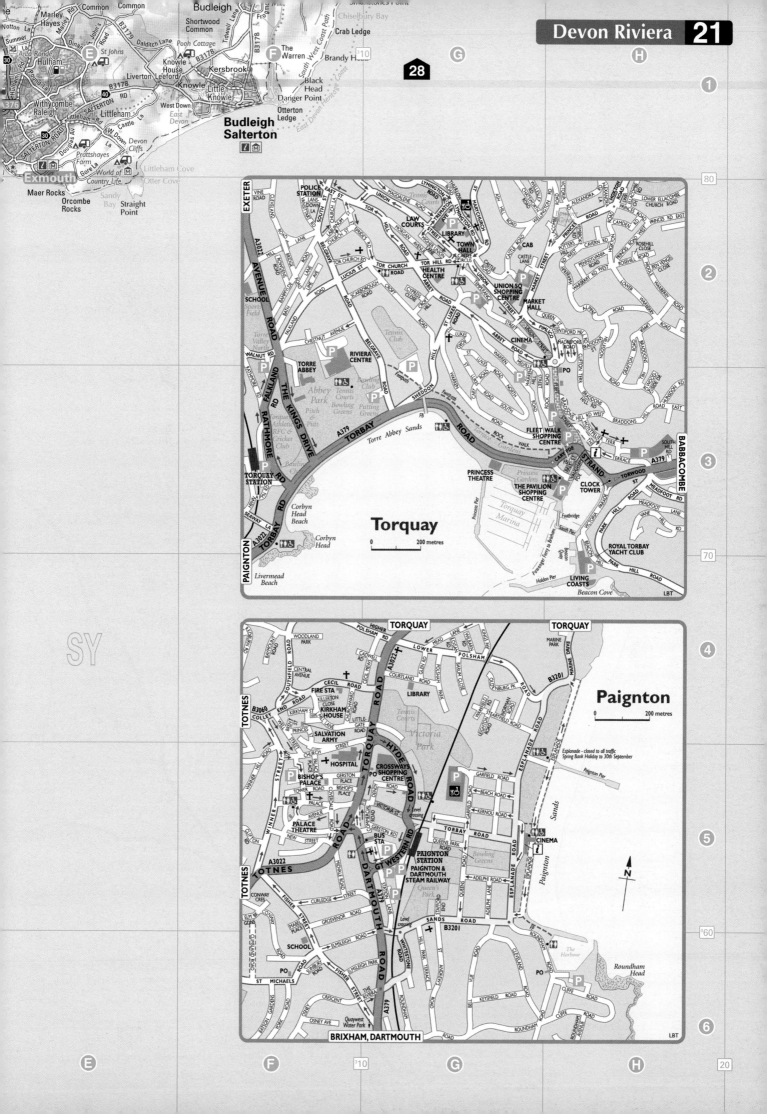

Torquay

0   200 metres

Paignton

0   200 metres

SY

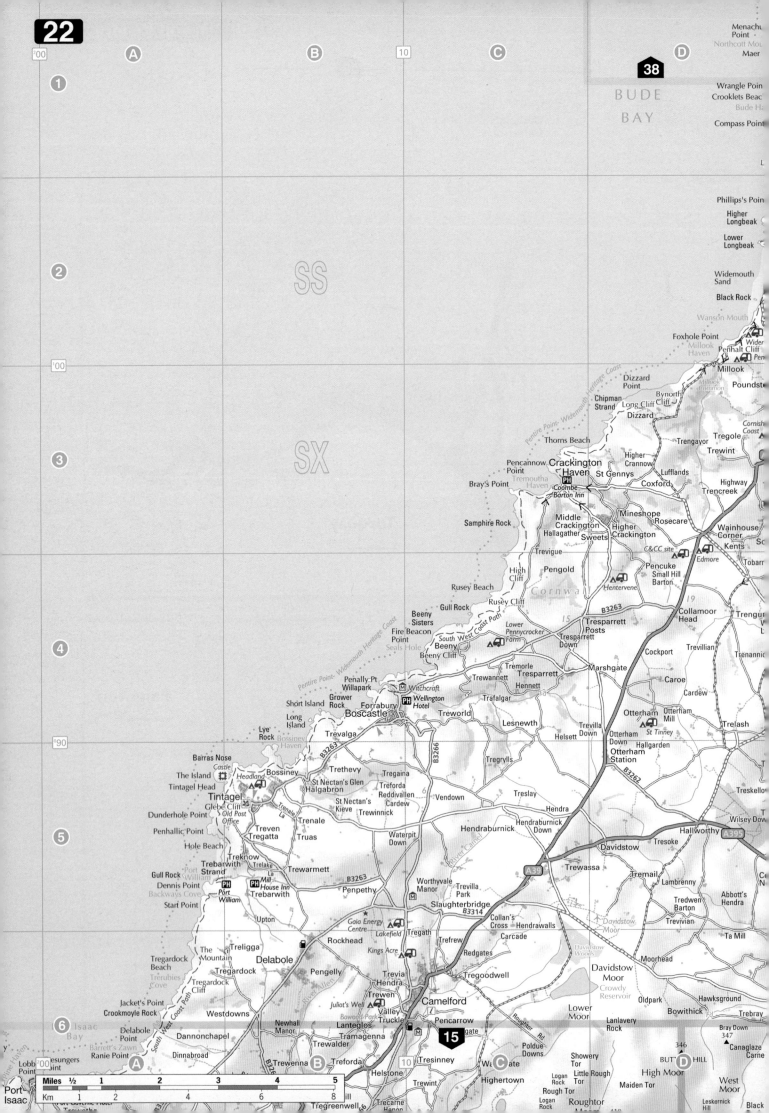

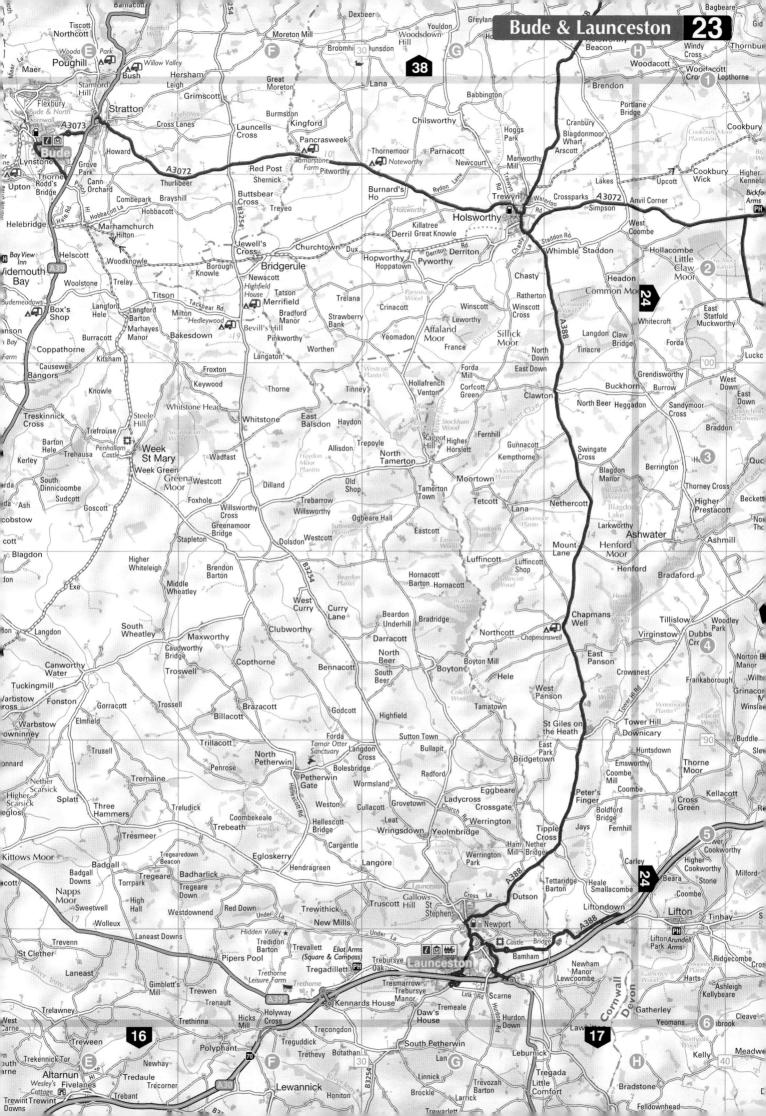

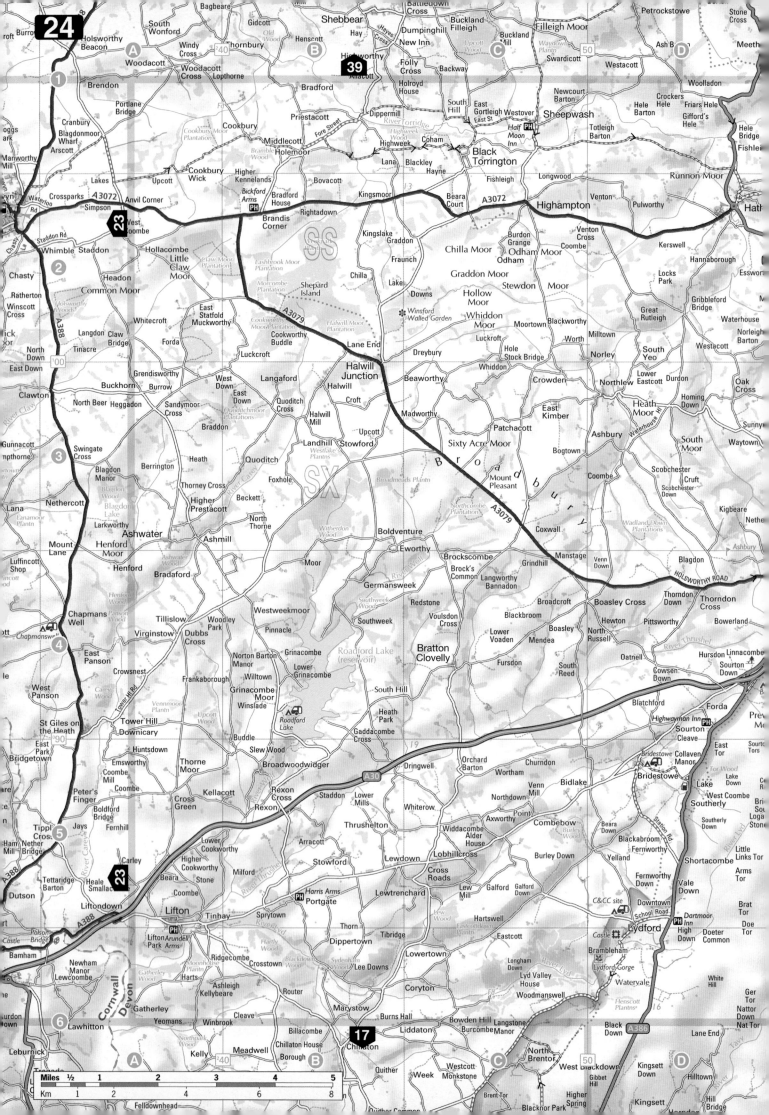

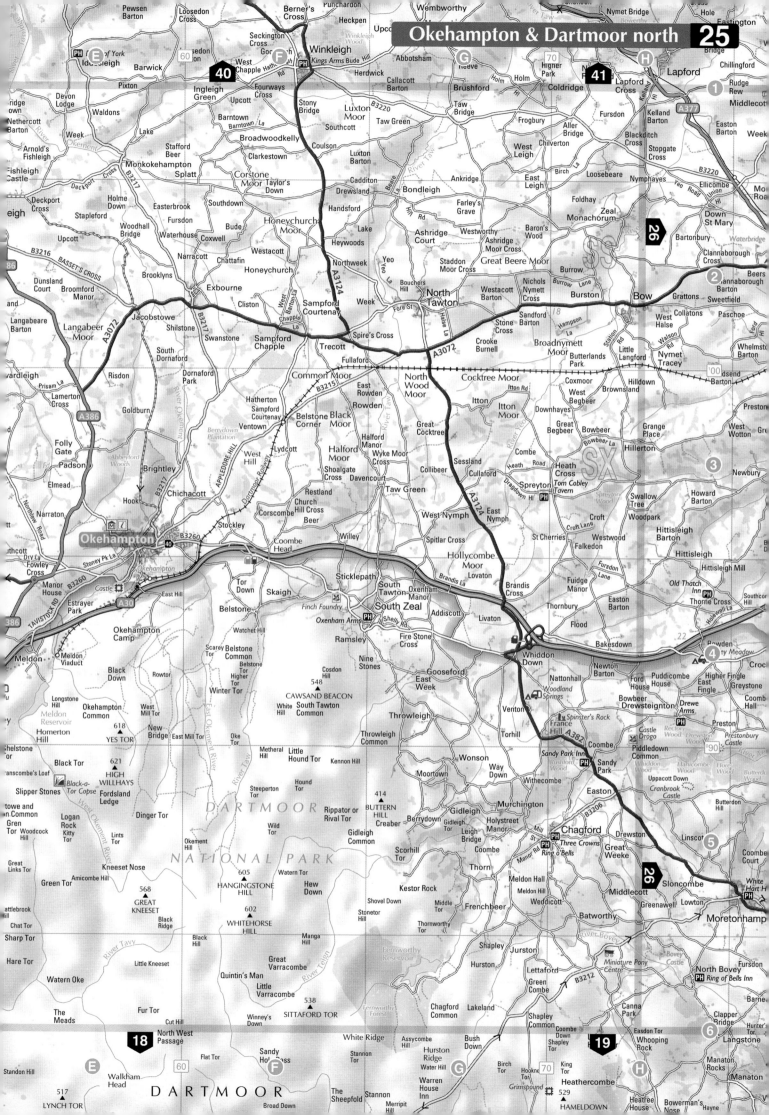

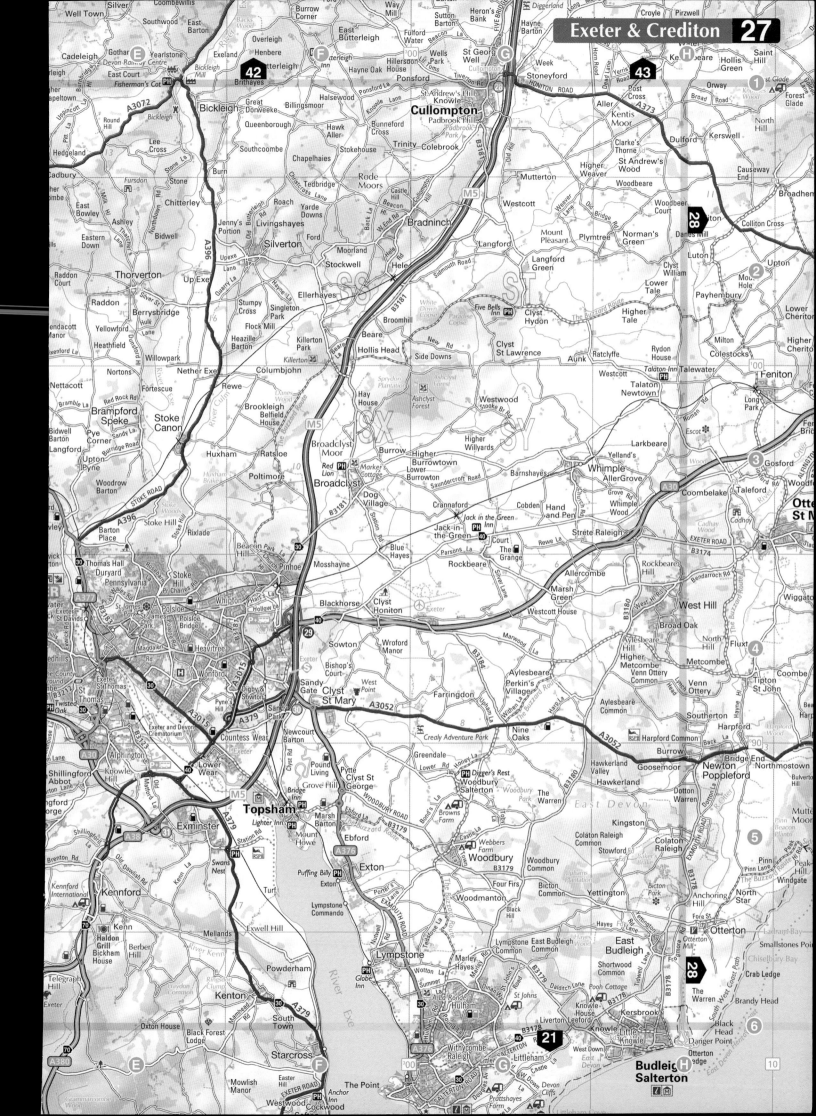

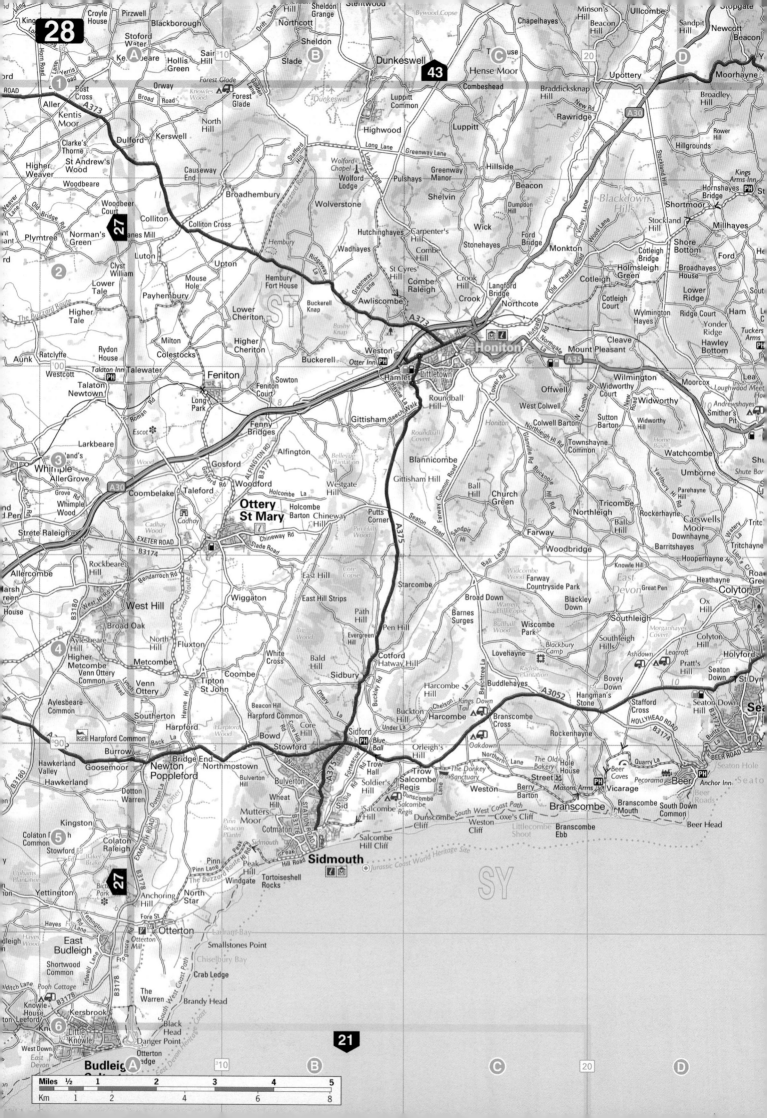

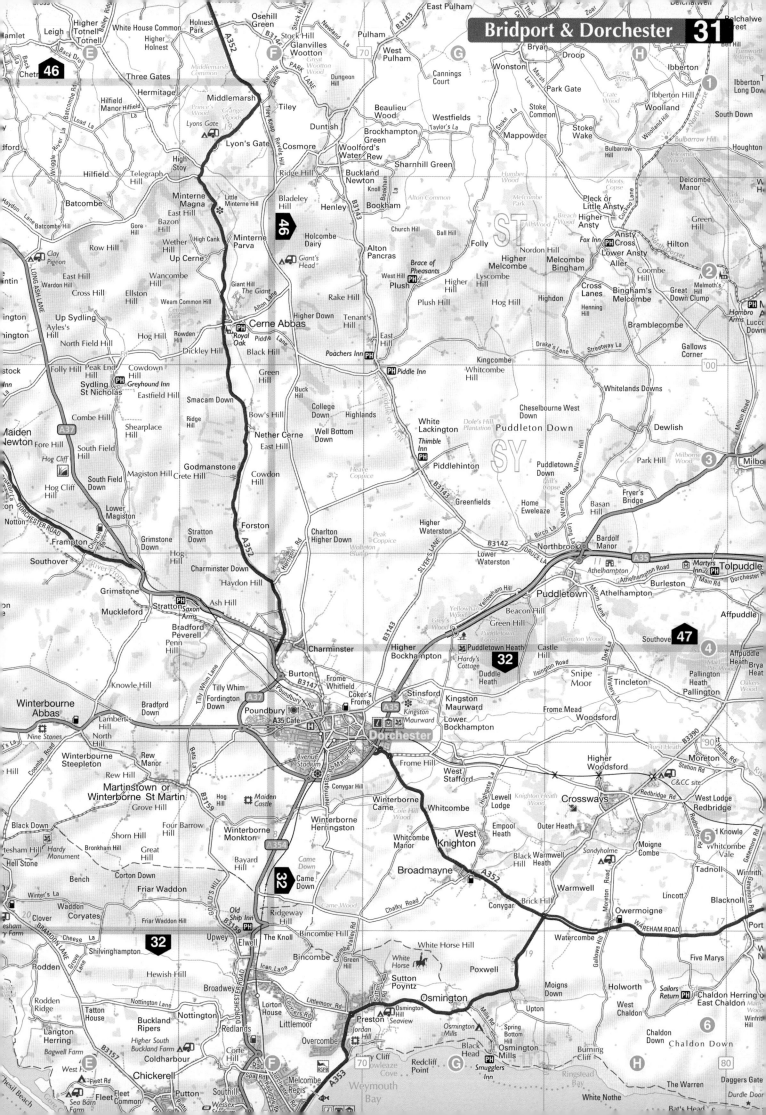

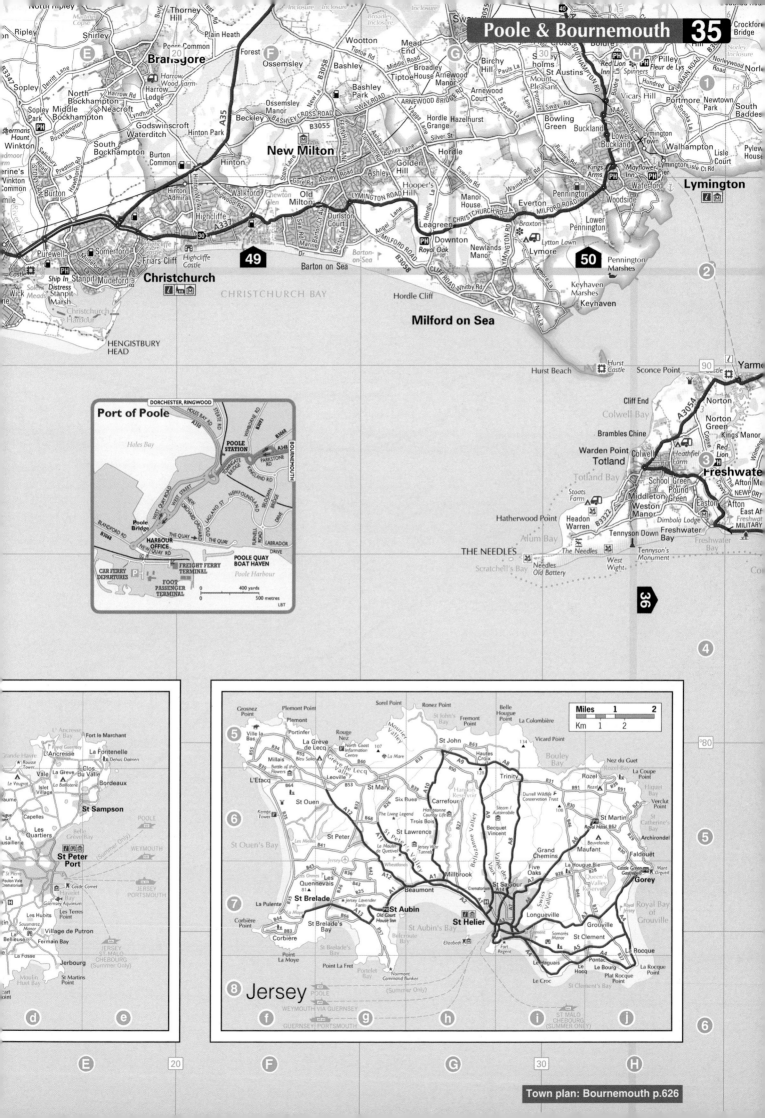

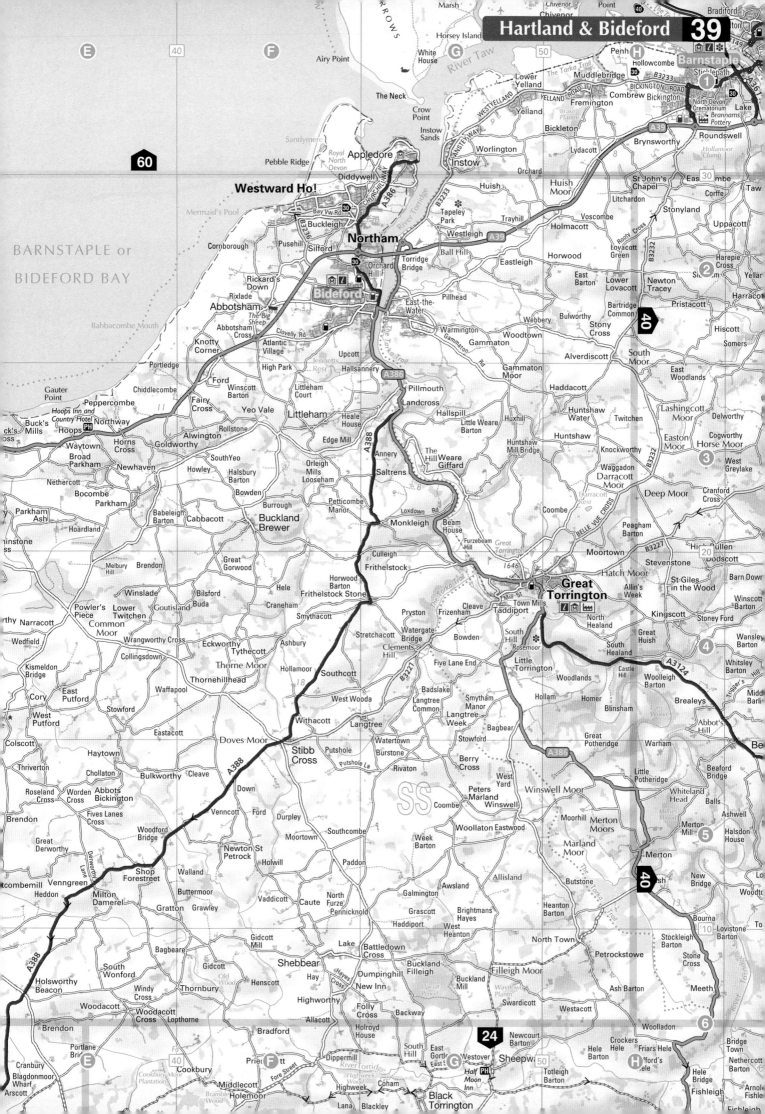

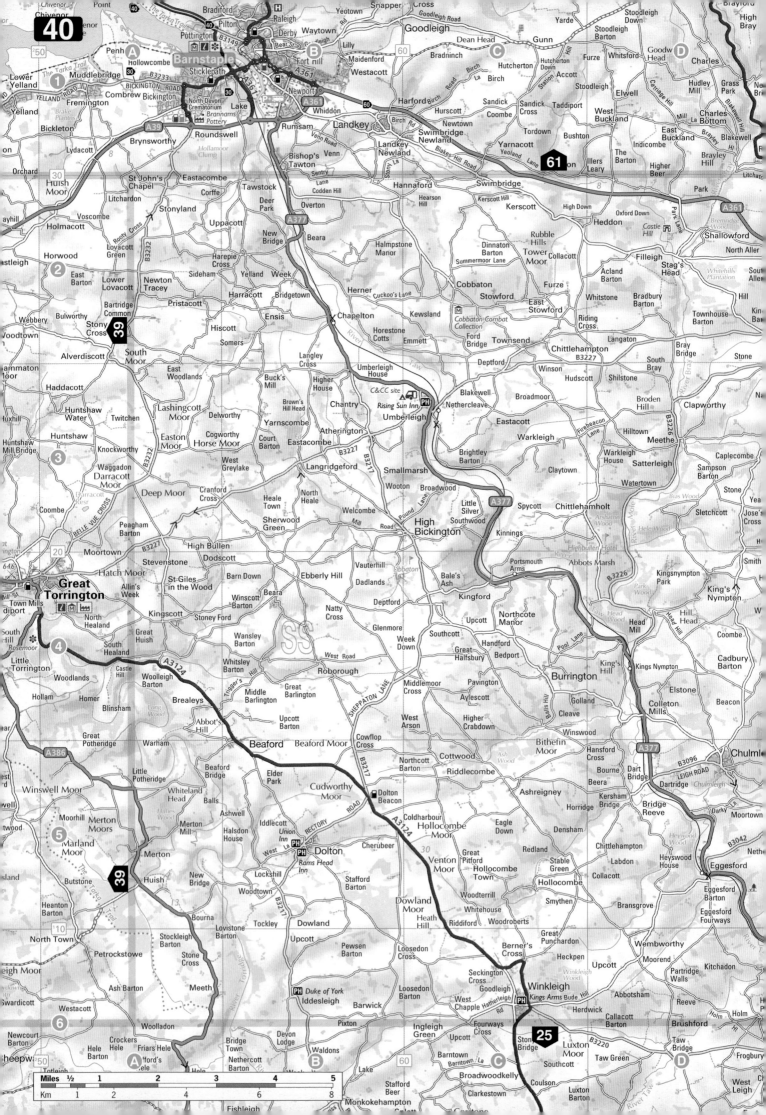

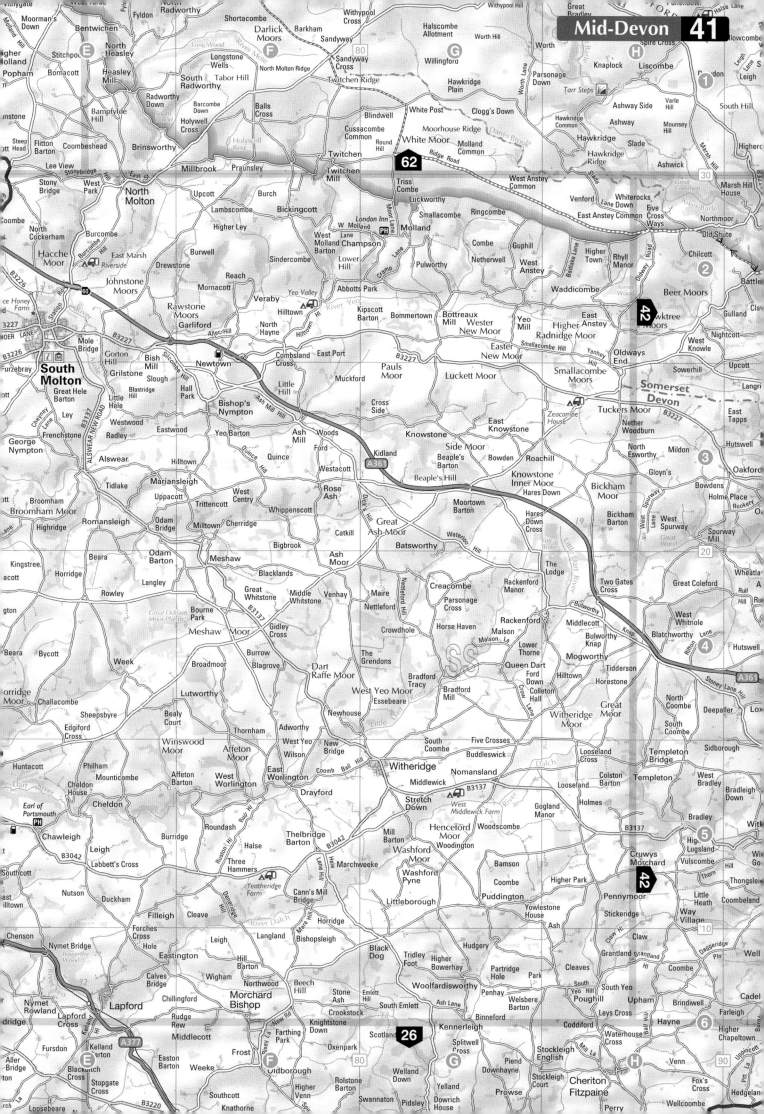

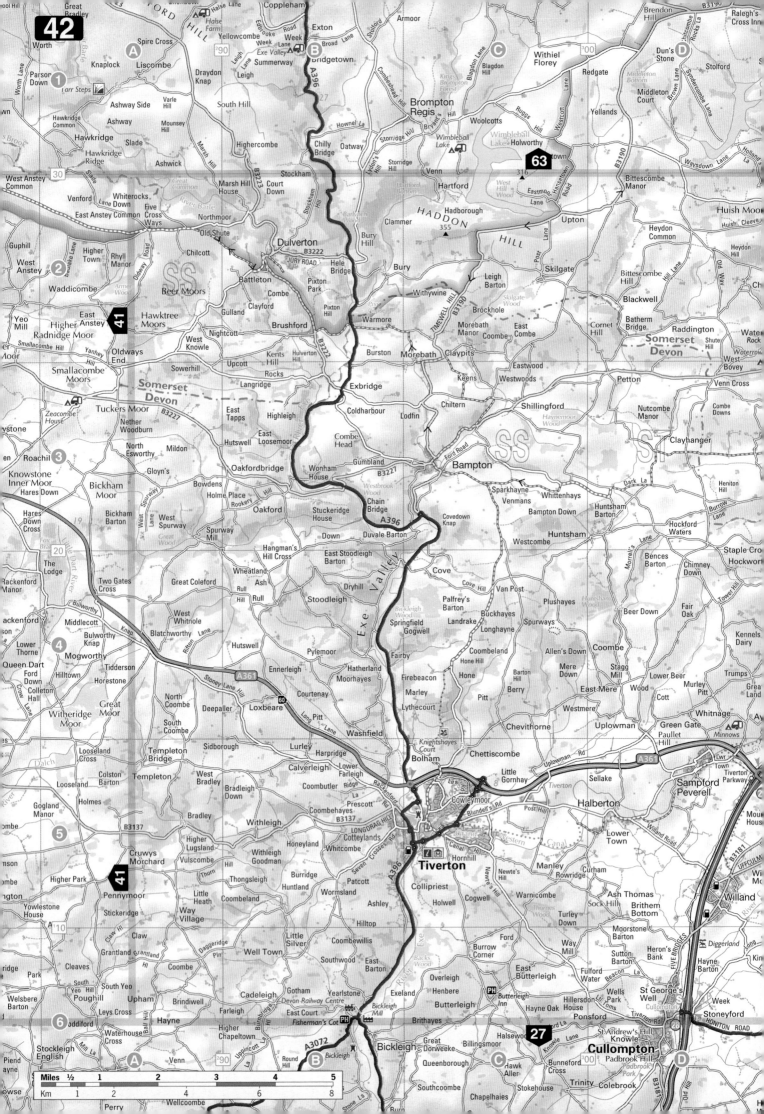

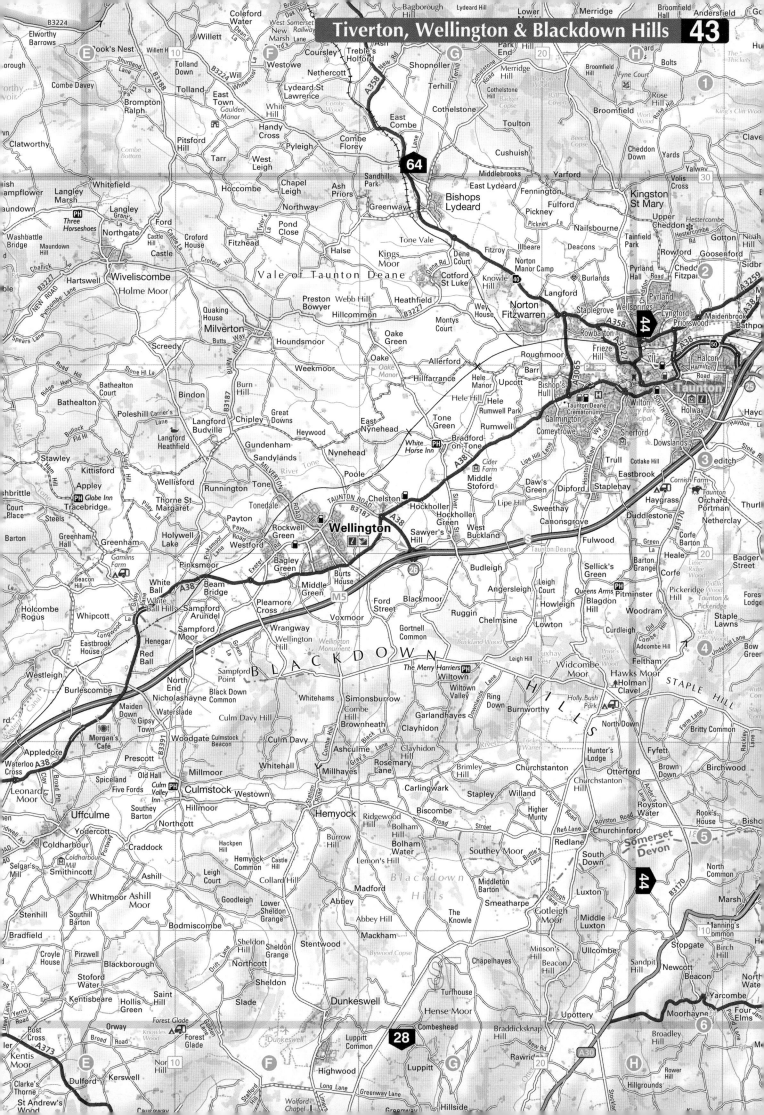

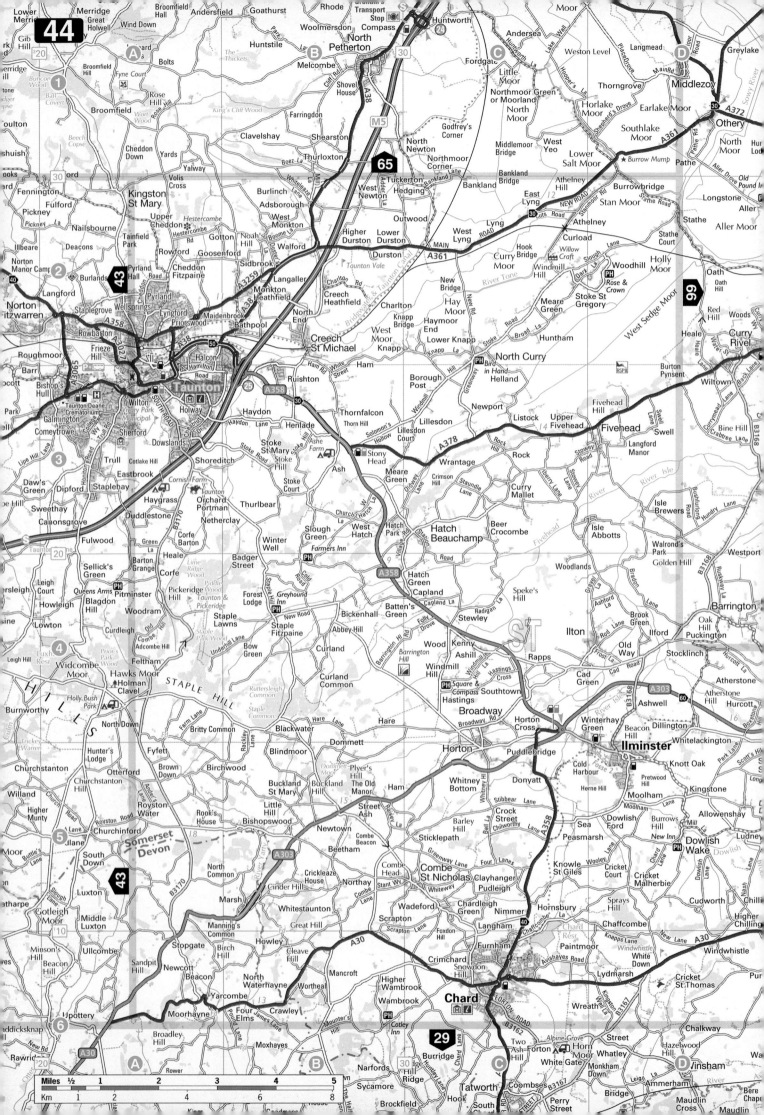

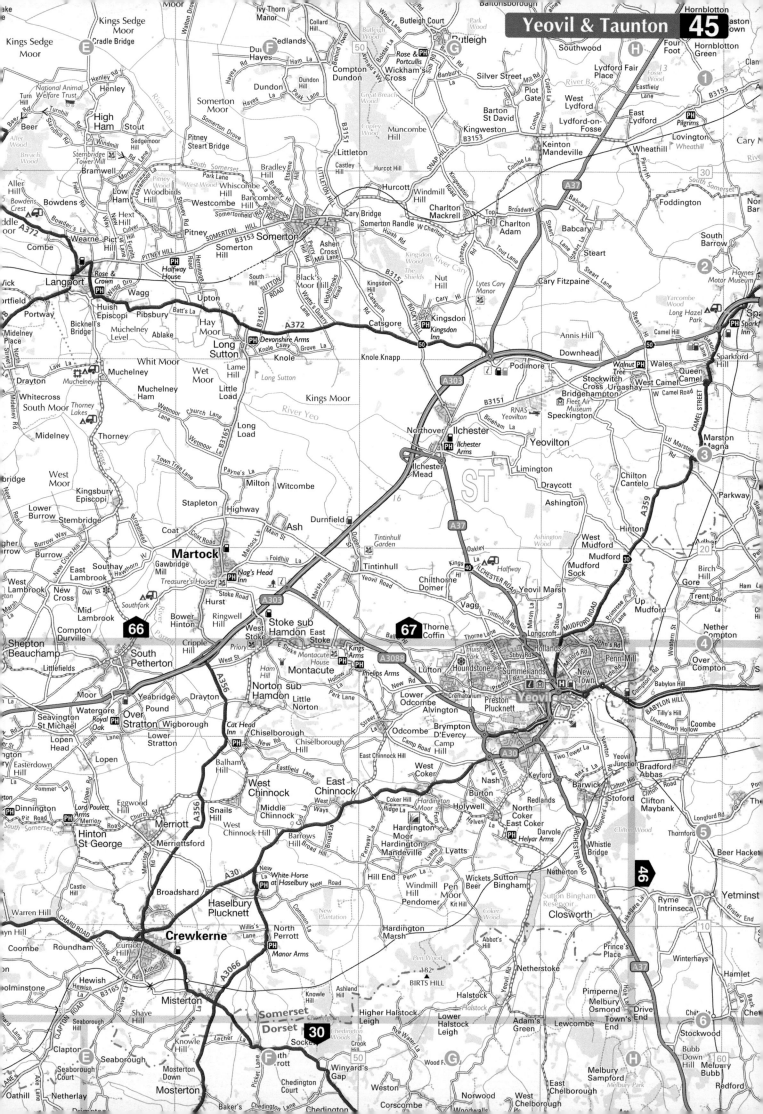

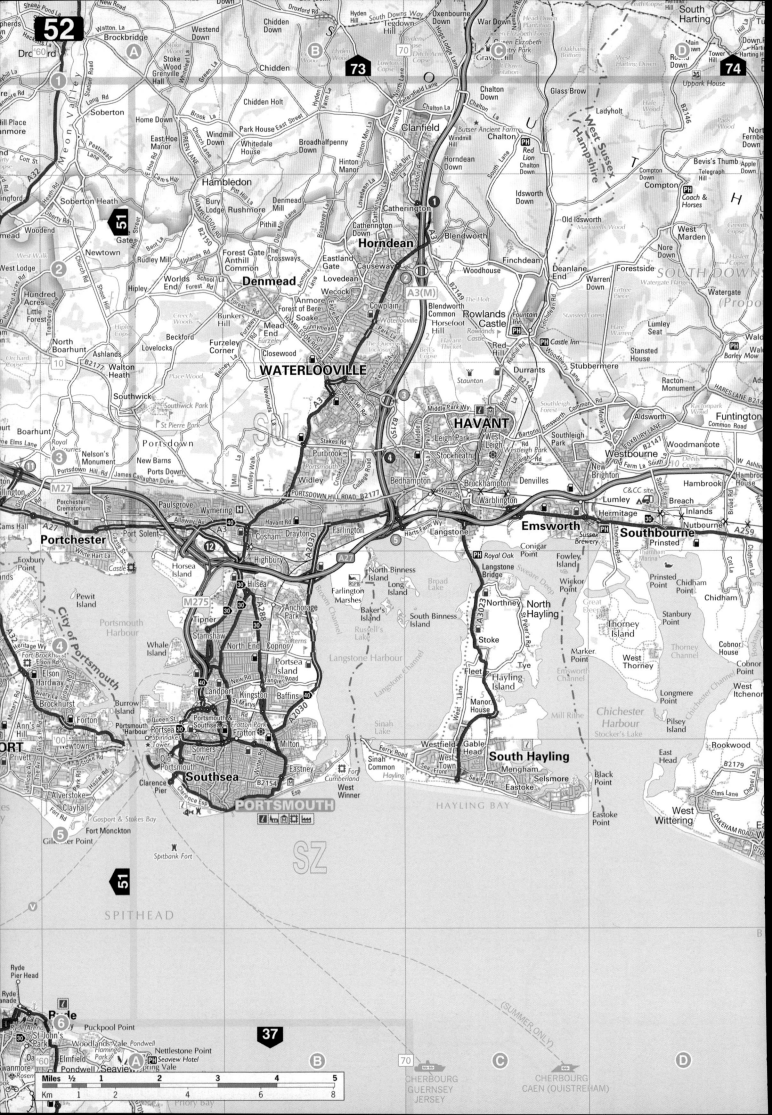

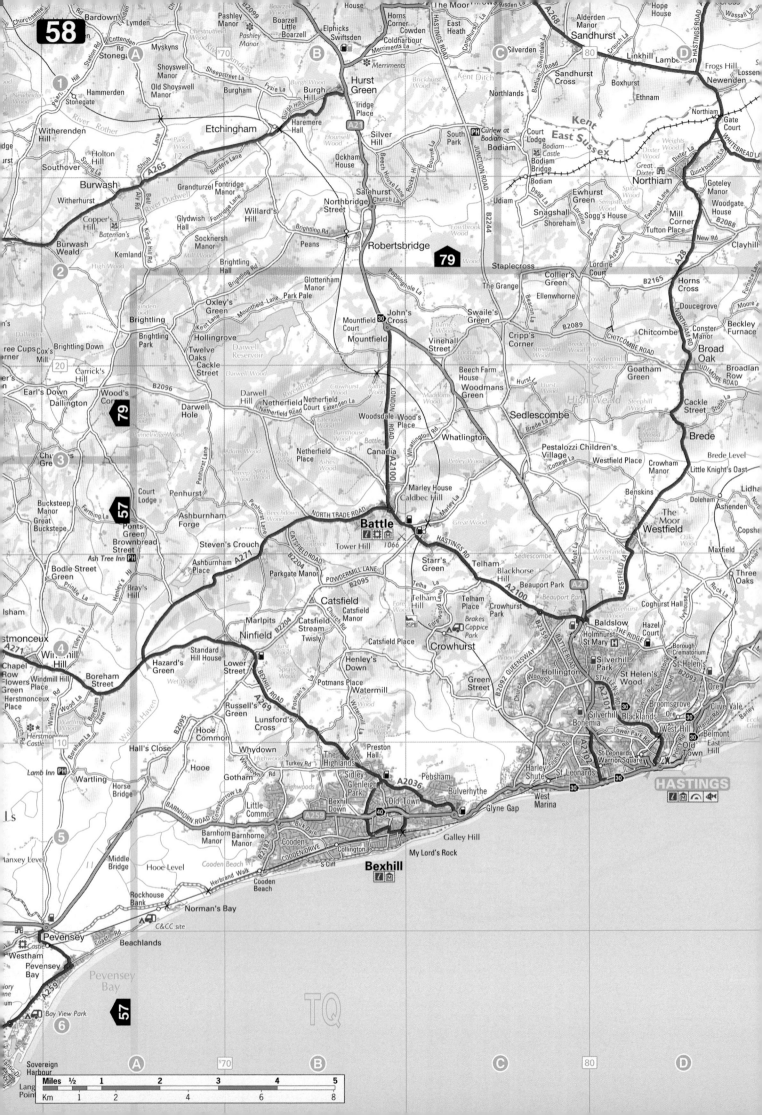

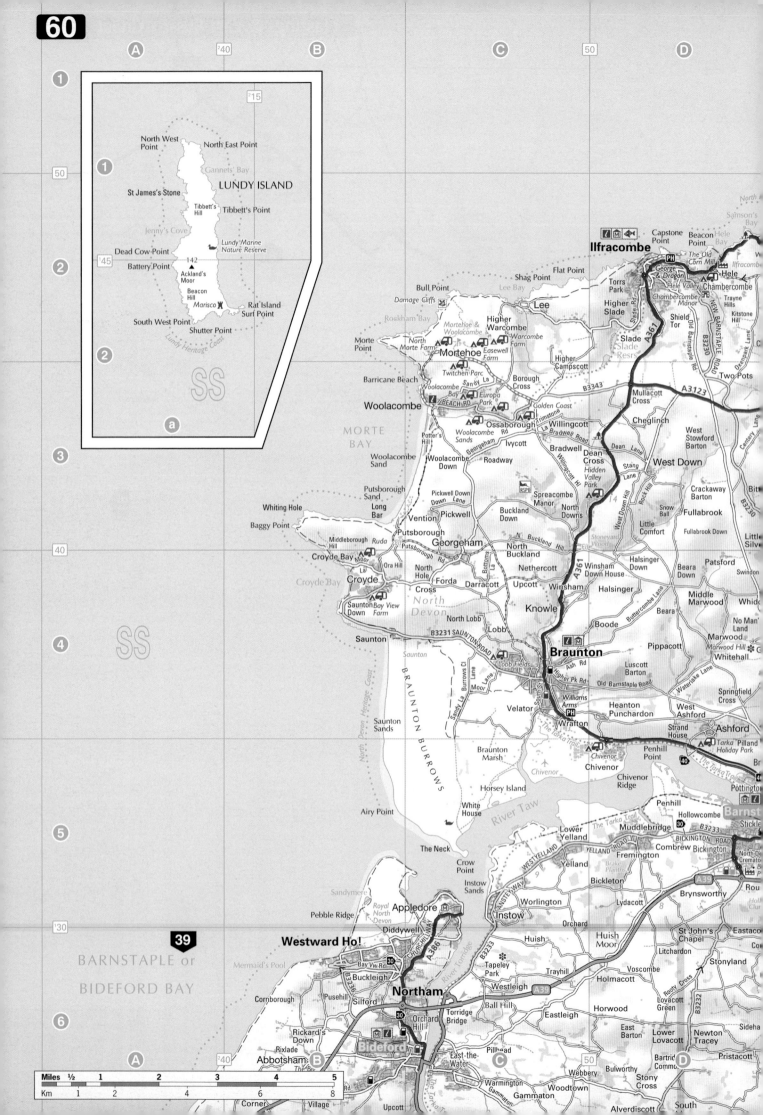

Ⓐ 40 Ⓑ Ⓒ 50 Ⓓ

1

50

2

3

40

4

5

30

6

Ⓐ 40 Ⓑ Ⓒ 50 Ⓓ

LUNDY ISLAND

North West Point
North East Point
Gannets' Bay
St James's Stone
Tibbett's Hill
Tibbett's Point
Jenny's Cove
Dead Cow Point
Lundy Marine Nature Reserve
Battery Point
142
Ackland's Moor
Beacon Hill
Marisco
Rat Island
Surf Point
South West Point
Shutter Point
Lundy Heritage Coast
SS

SS

BARNSTAPLE or BIDEFORD BAY

Ilfracombe
Capstone Point
Beacon Point
Hele Bay
The Old Corn Mill
Ilfracombe
George & Dragon
Hele
Chambercombe
Chambercombe Manor
Trayne Hills
Kitstone Hill
Torrs Park
Shag Point
Flat Point
Higher Slade
Shield Tor
Slade Resrs
Two Pots
Bull Point
Lee Bay
Lee
Damage Cliffs
Rockham Bay
Mortehoe & Woolacombe
Higher Warcombe
Warcombe Farm
Higher Campscott
B3343
Mullacott Cross
A3123
Cheglinch
West Stowford Barton
Morte Point
North Morte Farm
Mortehoe
Easewell Farm
Borough Cross
Twitchen Parc
Sandy La
Dean Lane
West Down
Barricane Beach
Woolacombe Bay
Golden Coast
Stang Lane
Crackaway Barton
Fullabrook
Woolacombe
BEACH RD
Ossaborough Rd
Willingcott
Bradwell Road
Dean Cross
Rock Hill
Snow Ball
Little Comfort
Fullabrook Down
MORTE BAY
Potter's Hill
Woolacombe Sands
Georgeham Rd
Ivycott
Bradwell
Hidden Valley Park
West Down Hill
Stang Lane
Woolacombe Down
Roadway
Spreacombe Manor
North Downs
Stoneyard Wood
Woolacombe Sand
Pickwell Down
Down Lane
Pickwell
Buckland Down
N. Buckland Hill
Putsborough Sand
Long Bar
Vention
RSPB
A361
Winsham Down House
Halsinger Down
Beara Down
Patsford
Whiting Hole
Middleborough Hill
Ruda
Putsborough
Georgeham
North Buckland
Winsham
Halsinger
Swindon
Baggy Point
Croyde Bay
Moor
Putsborough Rd
Nethercott
Middle Marwood
Croyde Bay
La
Ora Hill
North Hole
Bottoms La
Upcott
Winsham
Halsinger Lane
Beara
Croyde
Cross
Forda
Darracott
Knowle
Buttercombe Lane
Saunton Down
Bay View Farm
North Devon
Boode
Pippacott
Marwood
Saunton
North Lobb
Lobb
Boode
No Man's Land
Marwood Hill
Whitehall
B3231 SAUNTON ROAD
Lobb
Whid
Saunton
Lobb Fields
Braunton
Ash Rd
Luscott Barton
Springfield Cross
Little Silve
Saunton Sands
Higher Pk Rd
Old Barnstaple Road
Ashford
BRAUNTON BURROWS
Sandy La
Lane
Williams Arms
Heanton Punchardon
West Ashford
Moor
Velator
Wrafton
Strand House
Ashford
Saunton Sands
The Tarka Trail
Chivenor
Penhill Point
Tarka Pilland Holiday Park
Braunton Marsh
Chivenor
Pottington
Braunton Marsh
Chivenor Ridge
Penhill
Barnst
Horsey Island
The Tarka Trail
Hollowcombe
Airy Point
White House
Lower Yelland
Muddlebridge
Combrew
Bickington
River Taw
WESTLELAND
YELLAND ROAD
BICKINGTON ROAD
Stickle
The Neck
Fremington
Yelland
Brake Plantn
North Cremato
Crow Point
Instow Sands
Bickleton
A39
ANSTEY WAY
Worlington
Lydacott
Brynsworthy
Rou
Sandymere
Appledore
Instow
Orchard
St John's Chapel
Eastaco
Pebble Ridge
Royal North Devon
Diddywell
Huish
Huish Moor
Litchardon
Co
Westward Ho!
CHURCHILL WAY
A386
Tapeley Park
Westleigh
A39
Voscombe
Stonyland
Bay Vw Rd
Buckleigh
Trayhill
Holmacott
Roo
B3236
Northam
Silford
River Torridge
Ball Hill
Horwood
Lovacott Green
B3232
Cornborough
Pusehill
Torridge Bridge
Westleigh
Eastleigh
East Barton
Lower Lovacott
Newton Tracey
Sidehe
Rickard's Down
Orchard Hill
Pillhead
Bartrid Commo
Rixlade
Bideford
East-the-Water
Warmington
Webbery
Stony Cross
Abbotsham
The Bu
Gammaton
Woodtown
Gammaton
Pristacott
Corner
Village
Upcott
Alverdiscott
South

39

Miles ½ 1 2 3 4 5
Km 1 2 4 6 8

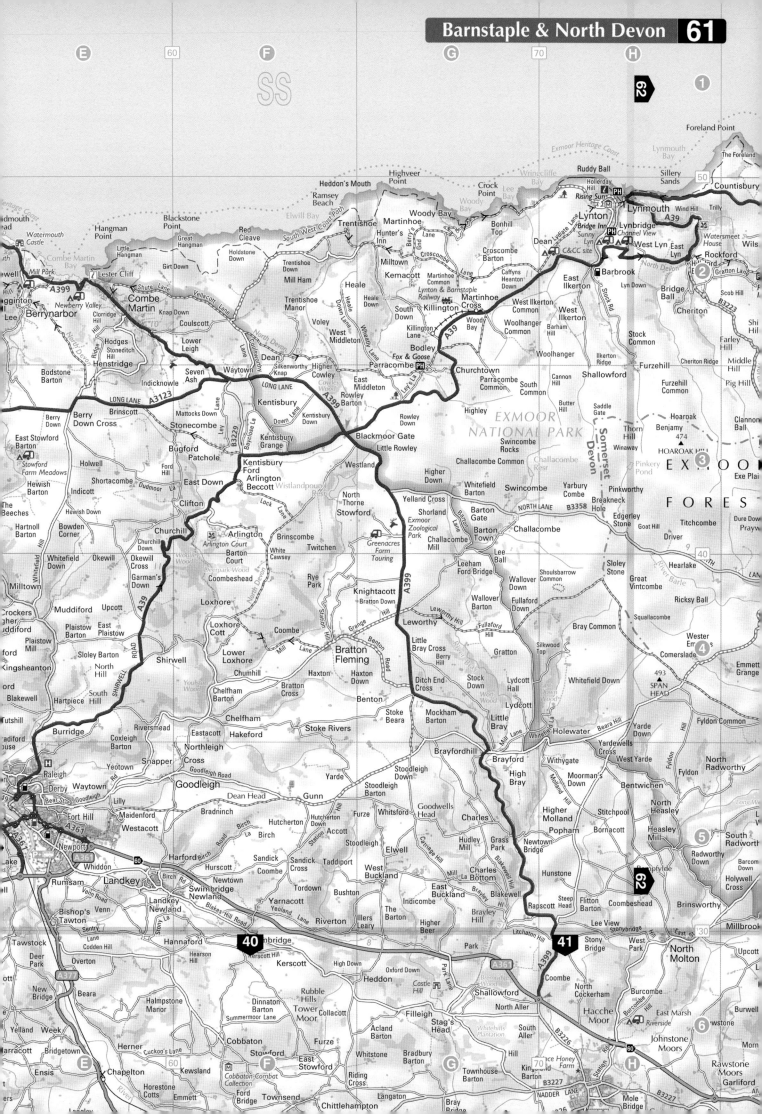

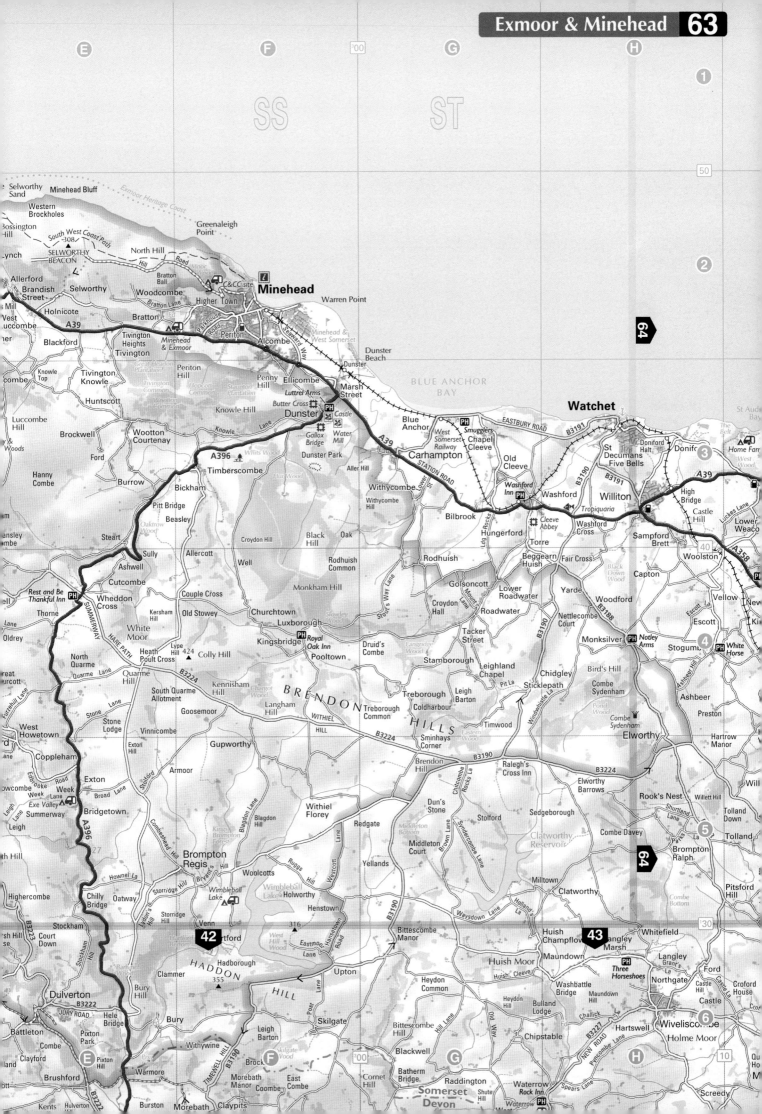

SS ST

E F S'00 G H

1

50

2

Minehead
Selworthy Sand
Minehead Bluff
Western Brockholes
Bossington Hill
Greenaleigh Point
South West Coast Path -308
SELWORTHY BEACON
Lynch
North Hill
Hill Road
Allerford
Brandish Street
Selworthy
Woodcombe
Bratton Ball
C&CC site
Higher Town
Warren Point

64

West Luccombe
Holnicote
A39
Bratton
Periton
Alcombe
Seaward Way
Dunster Beach
Blackford
Tivington Heights
Tivington
Minehead & Exmoor
Parkhouse Road
Periton Road
Minehead & West Somerset
BLUE ANCHOR BAY

Watchet

Knowle Top
Tivington Knowle
Periton Hill
Penny Hill
Ellicombe
Luttrel Arms
Marsh Street
St Audrie's Bay

The Belt
Home Farm

Luccombe Hill
Huntscott
Great Meadow Plantation
Butter Cross
Dunster
Castle
Blue Anchor
West Somerset Railway
Smugglers
Chapel Cleeve
EASTBURY ROAD
B3191
St Decumans
Five Bells
Doniford Halt
Doniford
West Wood

3

Brockwell
Wootton Courtenay
Knowle Hill
Knowle Lane
A39
STATION ROAD
Old Cleeve
Washford
Williton
A39

Hanny Combe
Ford
A396
Timberscombe
Whits Wood
Gallox Bridge
Water Mill
Dunster Park
Aller Hill
Withycombe
Lower St
Washford Inn
Cleeve Abbey
Washford Cross
Tropiquaria
High Bridge
Castle Hill
Luckes Lane
Lower Weaco

Burrow
Bickham
Beasley
Pitt Bridge
Hut Wood
Black Hill
Oak
Withycombe Hill
Bilbrook
Hungerford
Torre
Beggearn Huish
Fair Cross
Sampford Brett
Woolston
A358

Steart
Oaktrow Wood
Sully
Allercott
Well
Croydon Hill
Rodhuish Common
Rodhuish
Golsoncott
Lower Roadwater
Yarde
Woodford
Capton
Black Down Wood
Vellow
New

Ashwell
Rest and Be Thankful Inn
Cutcombe
Couple Cross
Monkham Hill
Shadley Copse
Croydon Hall
Roadwater
Nettlecombe Court
Monksilver
Notley Arms
Stogum
White Horse

4

Thorne
Wheddon Cross
Kersham Hill
Old Stowey
Churchtown
Luxborough
Stout's Way Lane
Tacker Street
Leighland Chapel
Chidgley
Sticklepath
Bird's Hill
Combe Sydenham
Ashbeer
Preston

Oldrey
White Moor
Lype Hill 424
Colly Hill
Kingsbridge
Royal Oak Inn
Pooltown
Druid's Combe
Langridge Wood
Stamborough
Leigh Barton
Timwood
Windwhistle La
Pond Wood
Combe Sydenham
Elworthy

North Quarme
Quarme Hill
Heath Poult Cross
B3224
Kennisham Hill
Chargot Wood
BRENDON
Treborough
Leigh Barton
Coldharbour
Timwood
Eastern Wood
Hartrow Manor

West Howetown
Stone Lodge
Vinnicombe
South Quarme Allotment
Goosemoor
Langham Hill
WITHIEL HILL
HILLS
Treborough Common
Sminhays Corner
B3224
Ralegh's Cross Inn
B3224
Elworthy Barrows
Rook's Nest
Willett Hill
Will

Coppleham
Exton Hill
Armoor
Stolford
Withiel Florey
Brendon Hill
B3190
Chicombe Rocks La
Syndercombe Lane
Sedgeborough
Elworthy
Shurtland Lane
Tolland Down

Exton
Broad Lane
Gupworthy
Redgate
Dun's Stone
Stolford
Clatworthy Reservoir
Combe Davey
Hartrow Manor

West Howetown
Edbrooke Week
Week Lane
Exe Valley
Summerway
Leigh
Bridgetown
Combeshead Lane
Blagdon Lane
Blagdon Hill
Withiel Florey
Middleton Bottom
Middleton Court
Brown Lane
Parks La
Brompton Ralph

64

5

Higher Combe
Hownel La
Storr/dge Hill
King's Brompton Forest
Bryant's Hill
Woolcotts
Ruggs Hill
Westcott
Yellands
Milltown
Clatworthy
Combe Bottom
Pitsford Hill

Chilly Bridge
Oatway
Storridge Hill
Brompton Regis
Wimbleball Lake
Holworthy
Henstown
B3190
Waysdown Lane
Holland La

Stockham
Lydon's Lane
Venn
316
West Hill Wood
Bittescombe Manor
Huish Champflower
Langley Marsh
Whitefield
'30

42
Court Down
Timewell Hill
HADDON
Hadborough
Eastmoor Lane
Upton
Maundown
43
Washbattle Bridge
Three Horseshoes
Northgate
Ford

Dulverton
B3222
JURY ROAD
Clammer
355
HILL
Skilgate
Heydon Common
Huish Moor
Heydon Hill
Bulland Lodge
Maundown Hill
Langley Grant's La
Castle
Croford House

6

Battleton
Hele Bridge
Pixton Park
Bury
Leigh Barton
Skilgate Wood
Bittescombe Hill
Chipstable
Challick
Pyncombe Lane
NEW ROAD
B3227
Hartswell
Wiveliscombe
Holme Moor
Qu

Clayford
Combe
Pixton Hill
Withywine
Brock
Morebath Manor
East Combe
Blackwell
Batherm Bridge
Raddington
Waterrow
Rock Inn
Spears Lane
Screedy
M

10

Brushford
Warmore
Withiwine
Morebath
Claypits
Cornet Hill
Somerset
Raddington
Shute Hill
Waterrow

Kents
Hulverton
Burston
Coombe
Devon

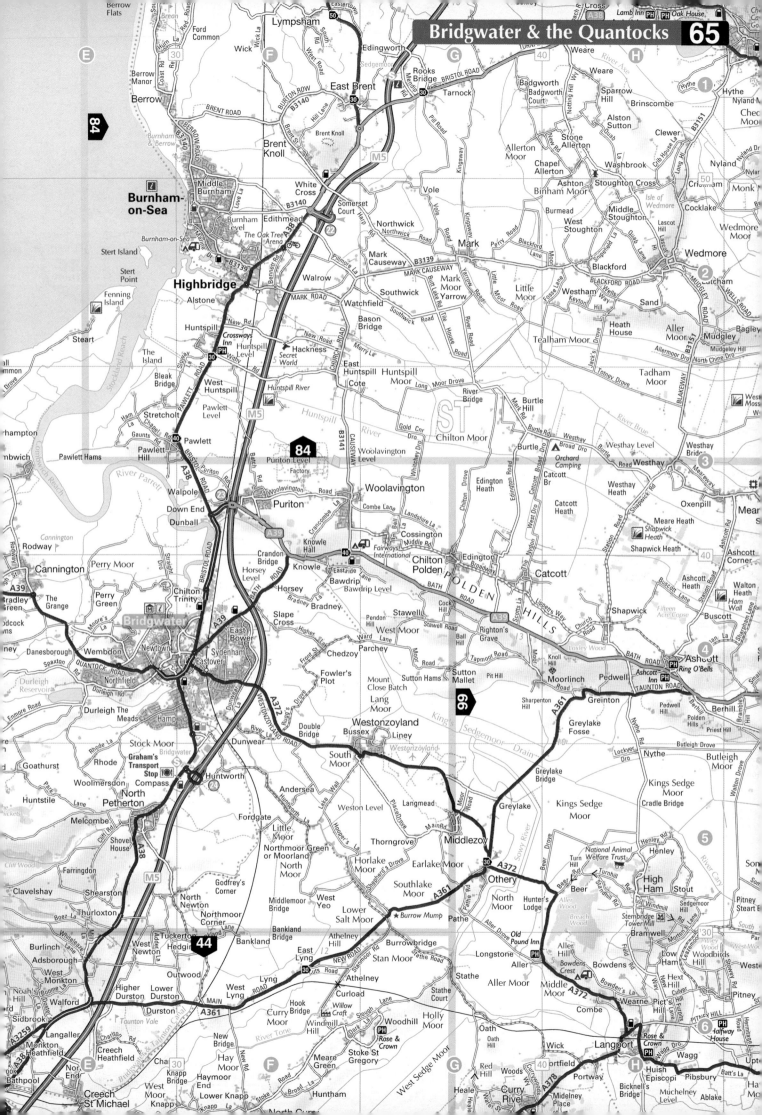

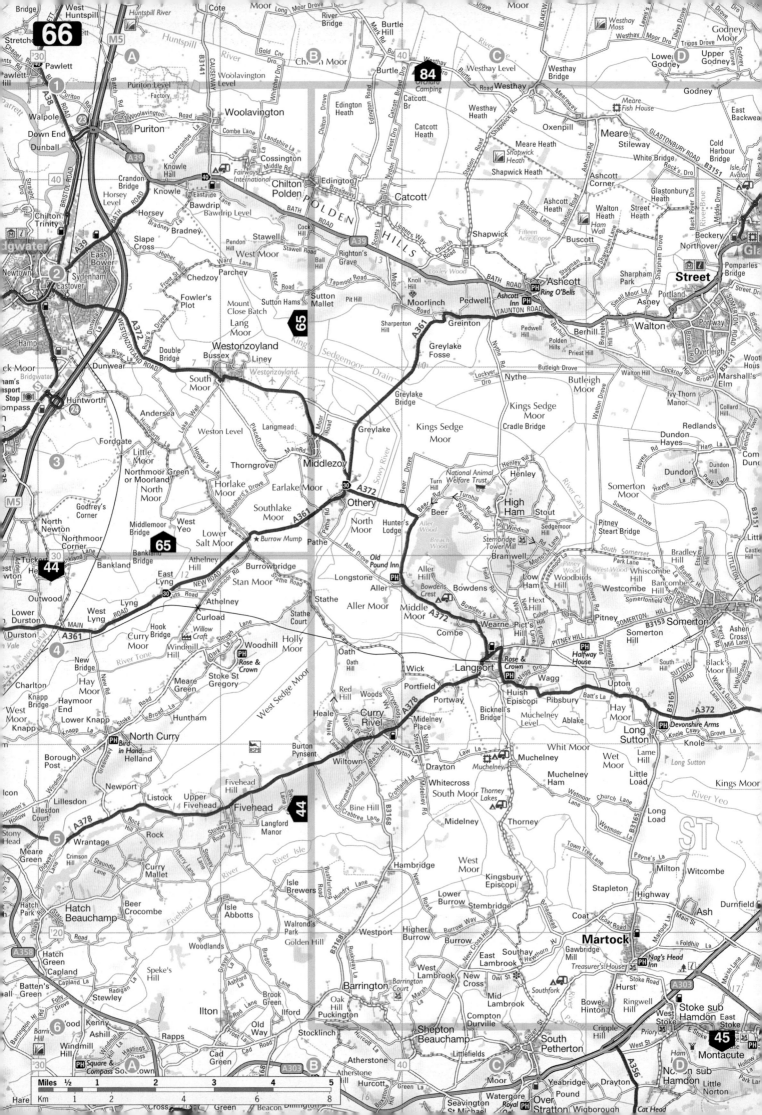

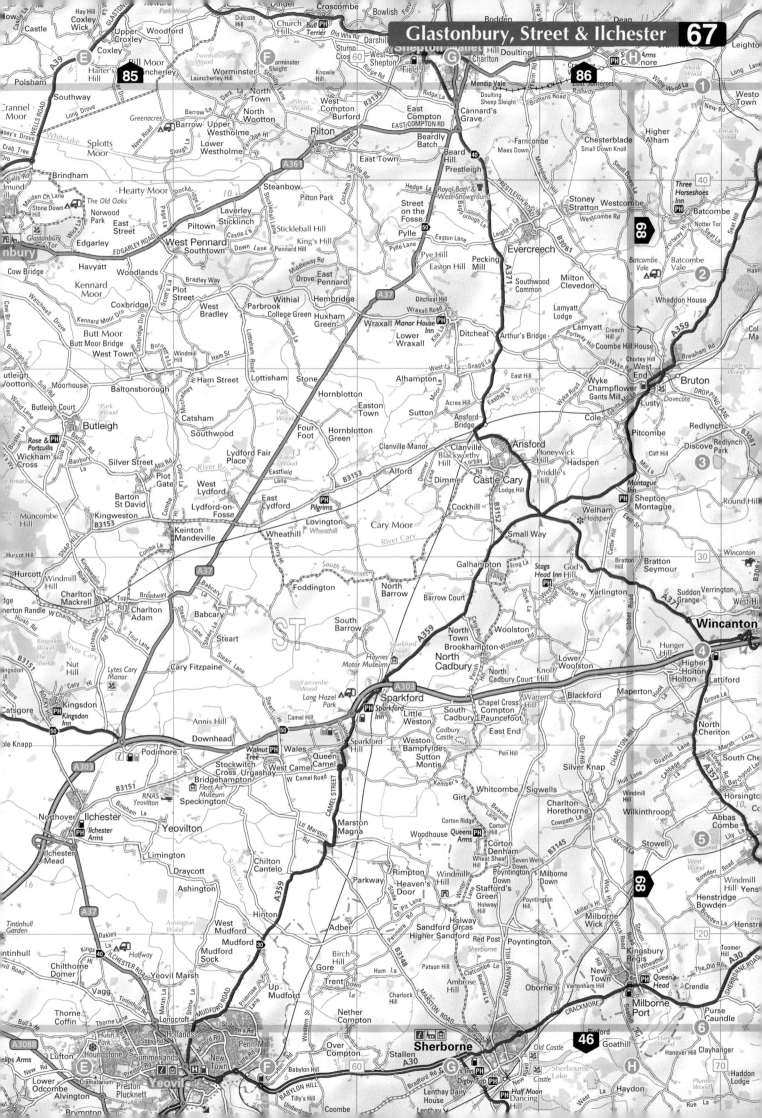

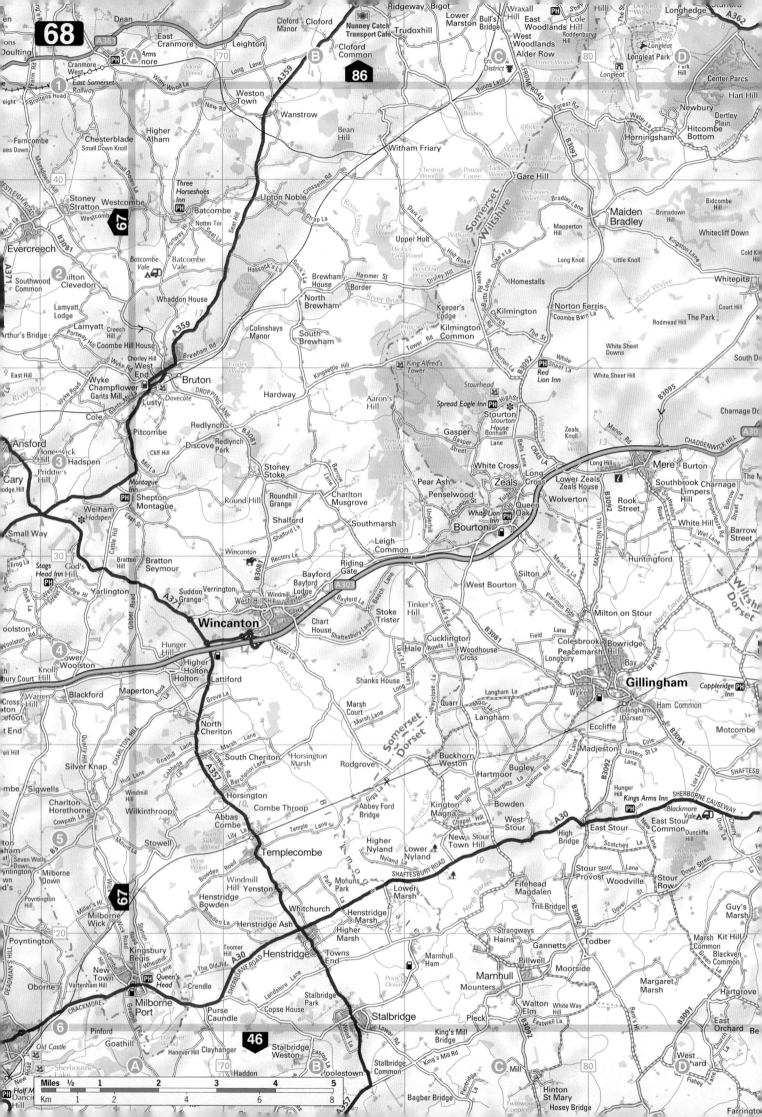

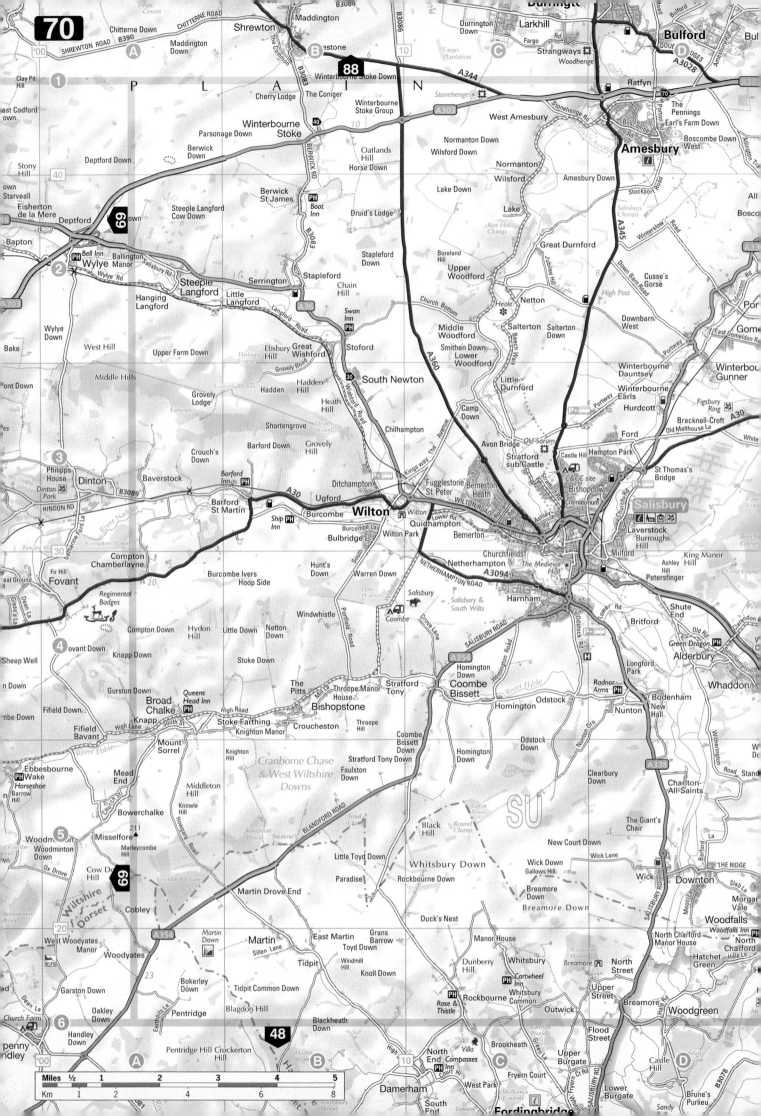

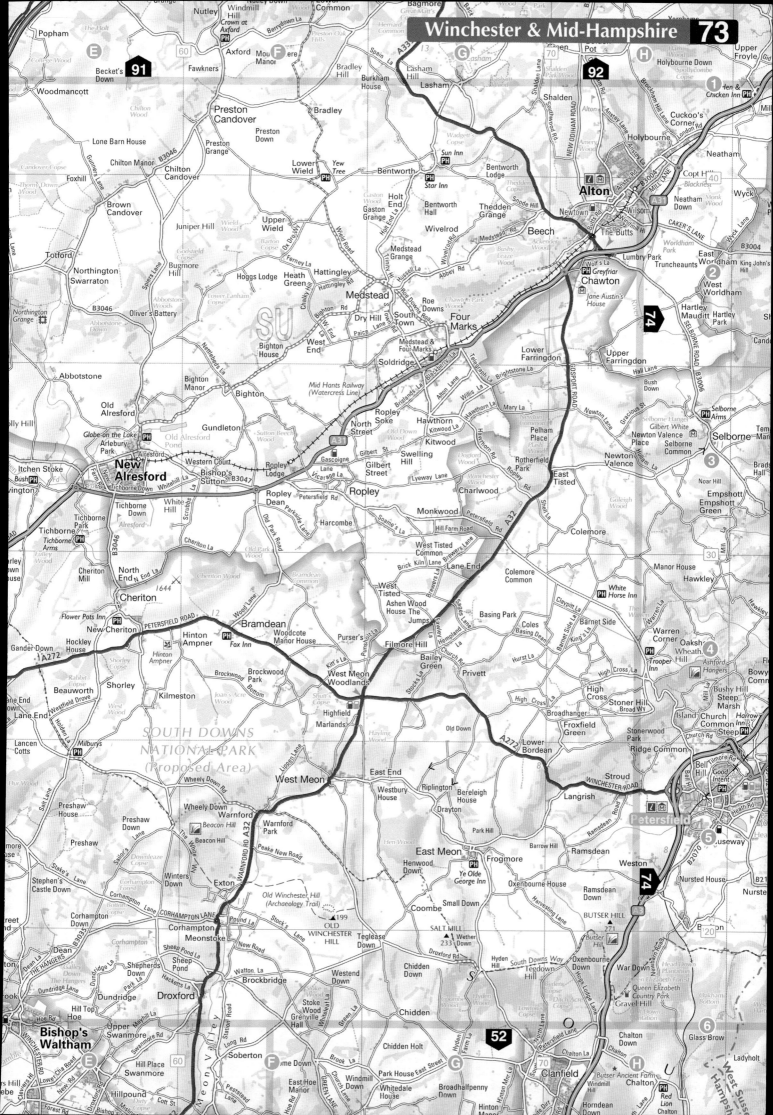

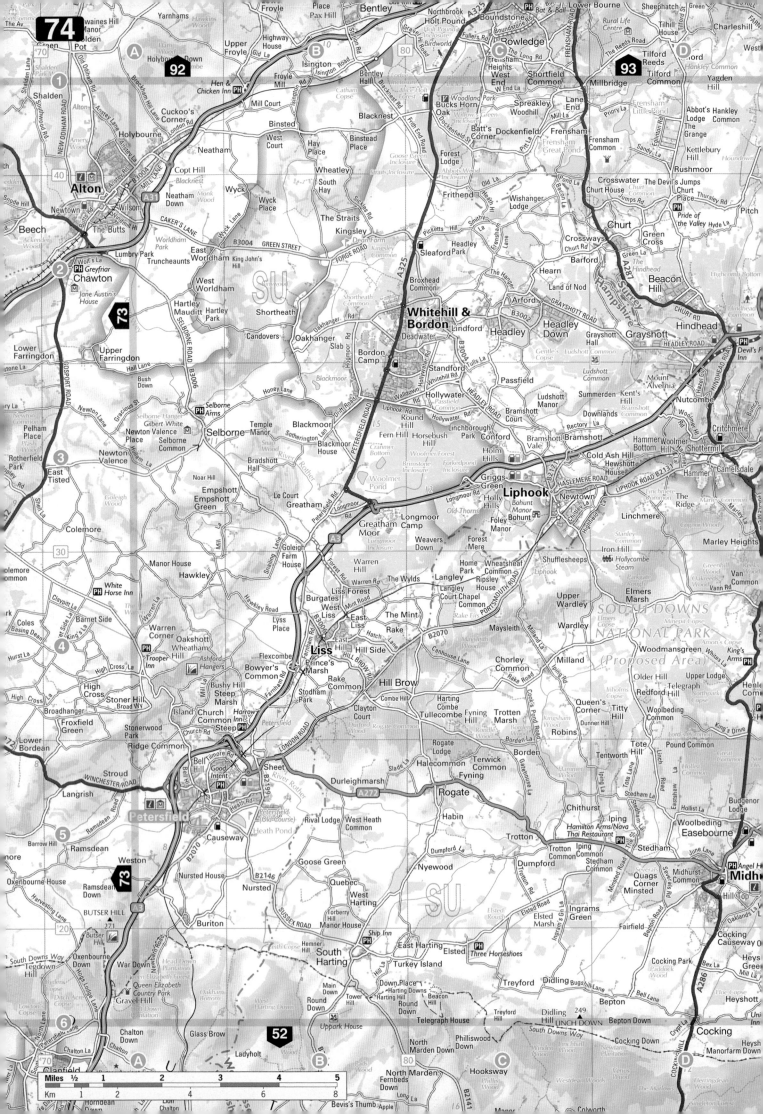

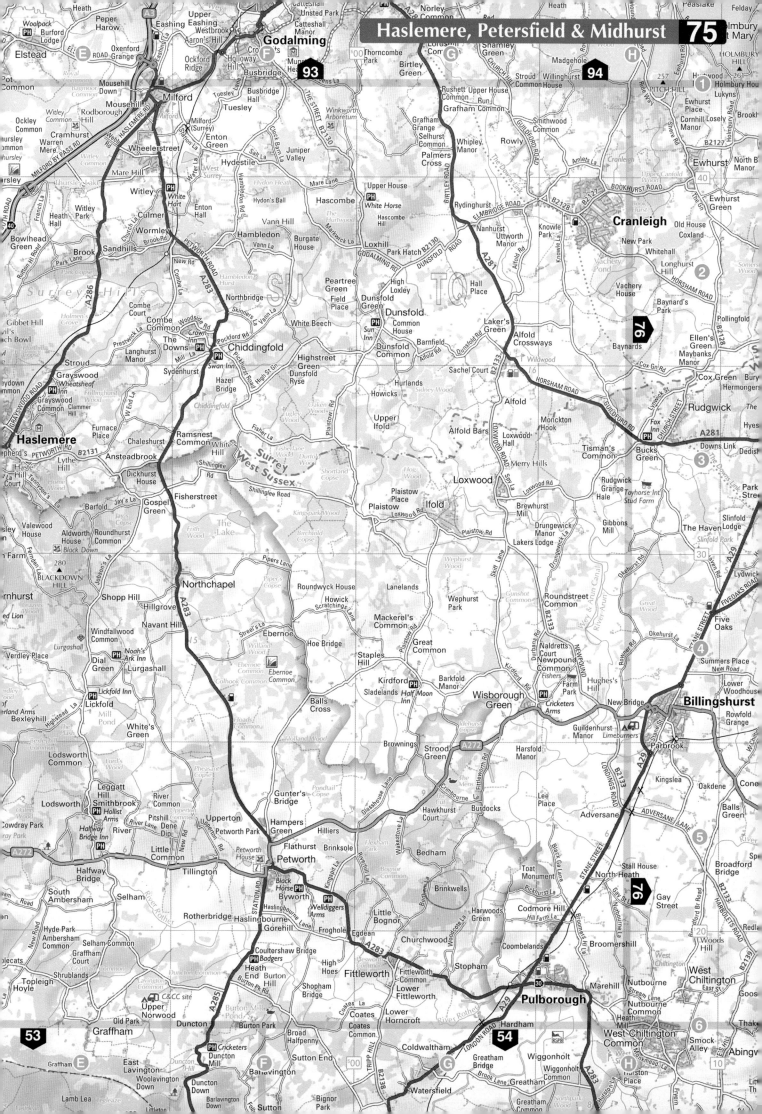

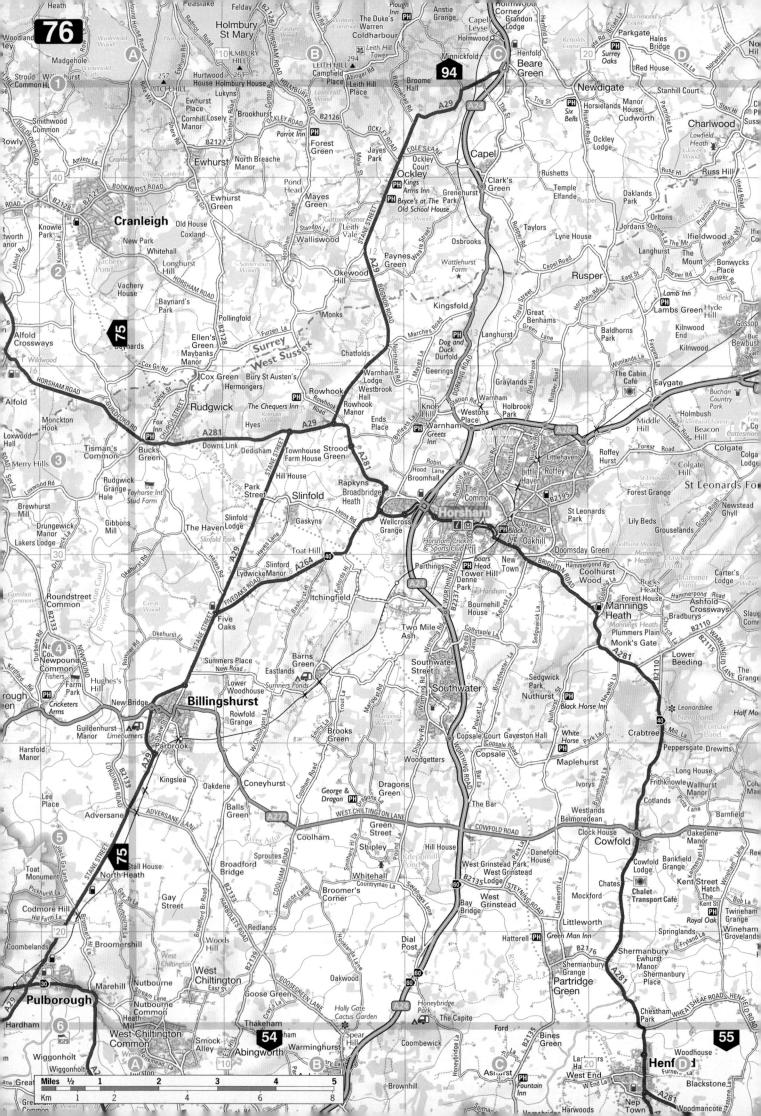

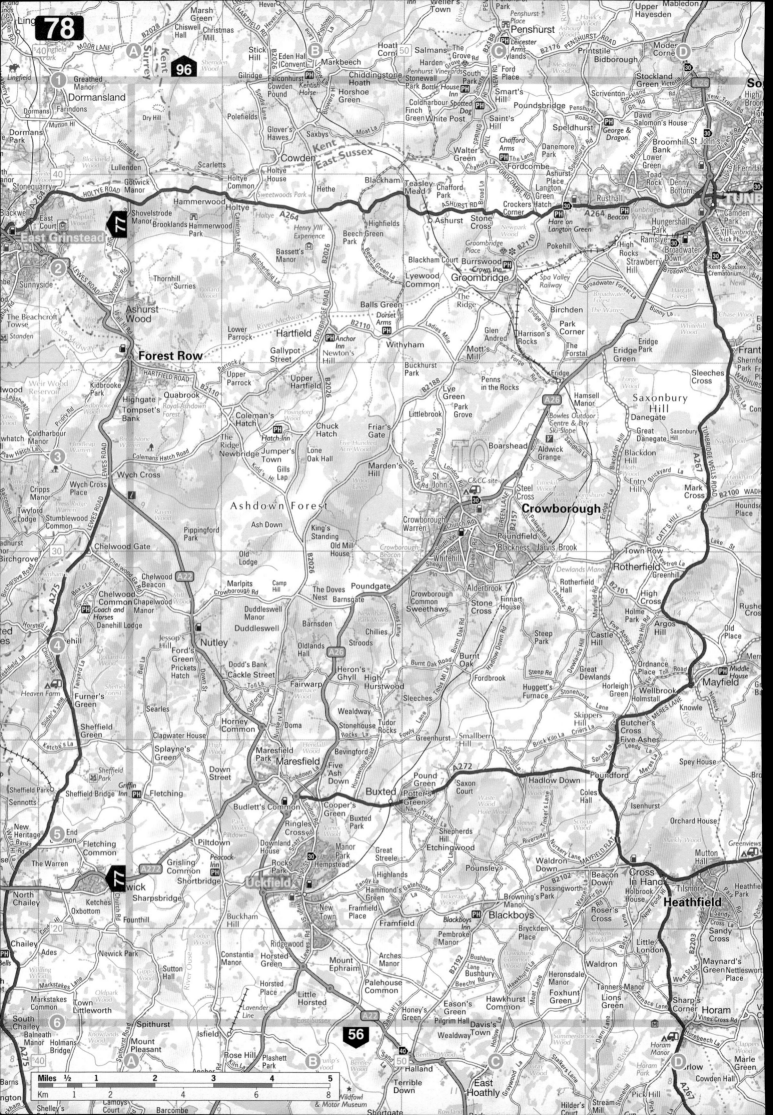

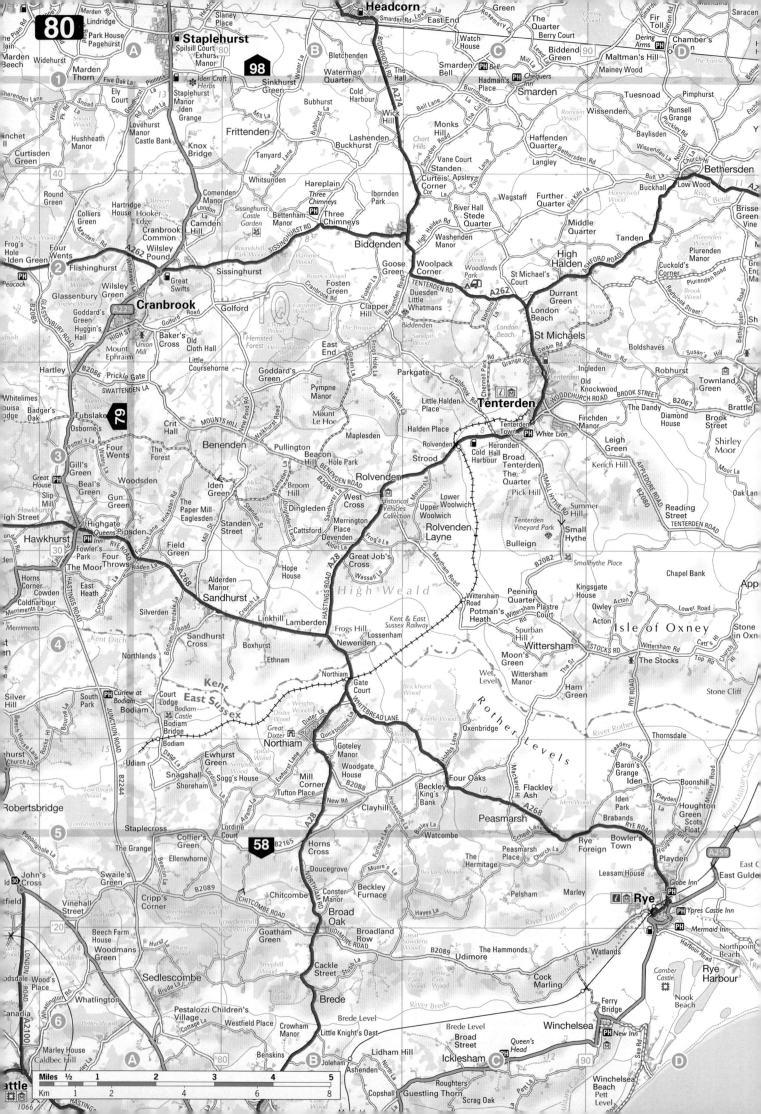

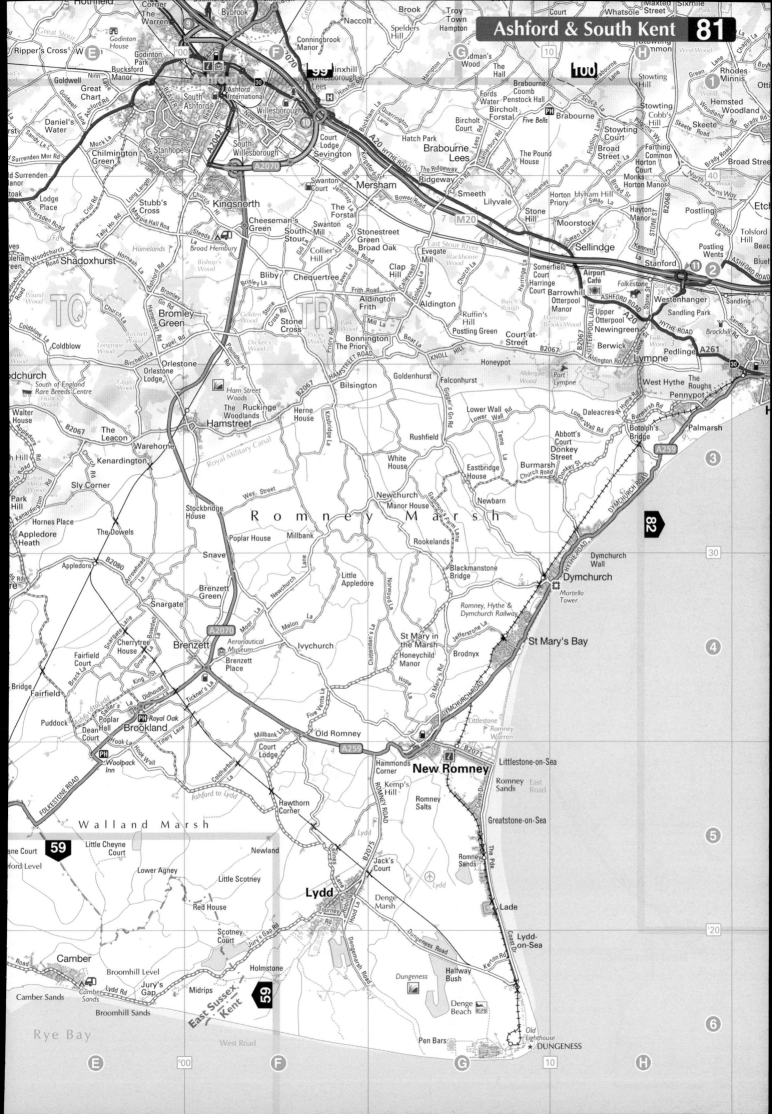

Rye Bay

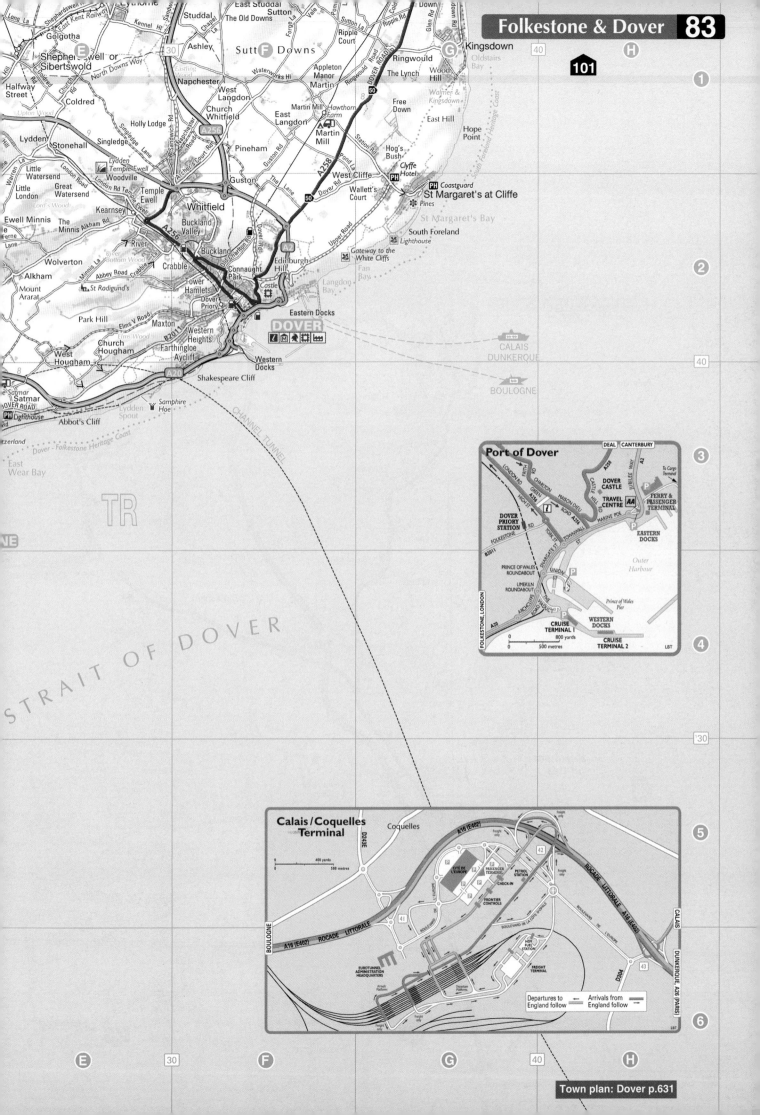

STRAIT OF DOVER

Port of Dover

Calais / Coquelles Terminal

Town plan: Dover p.631

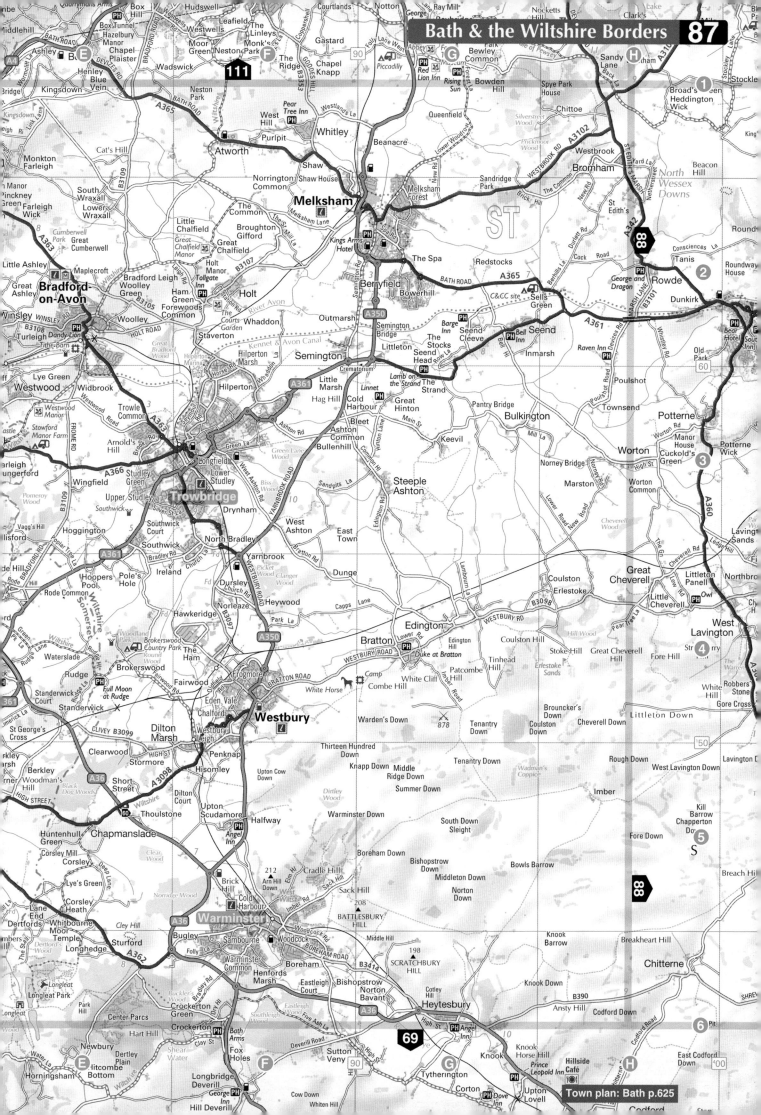

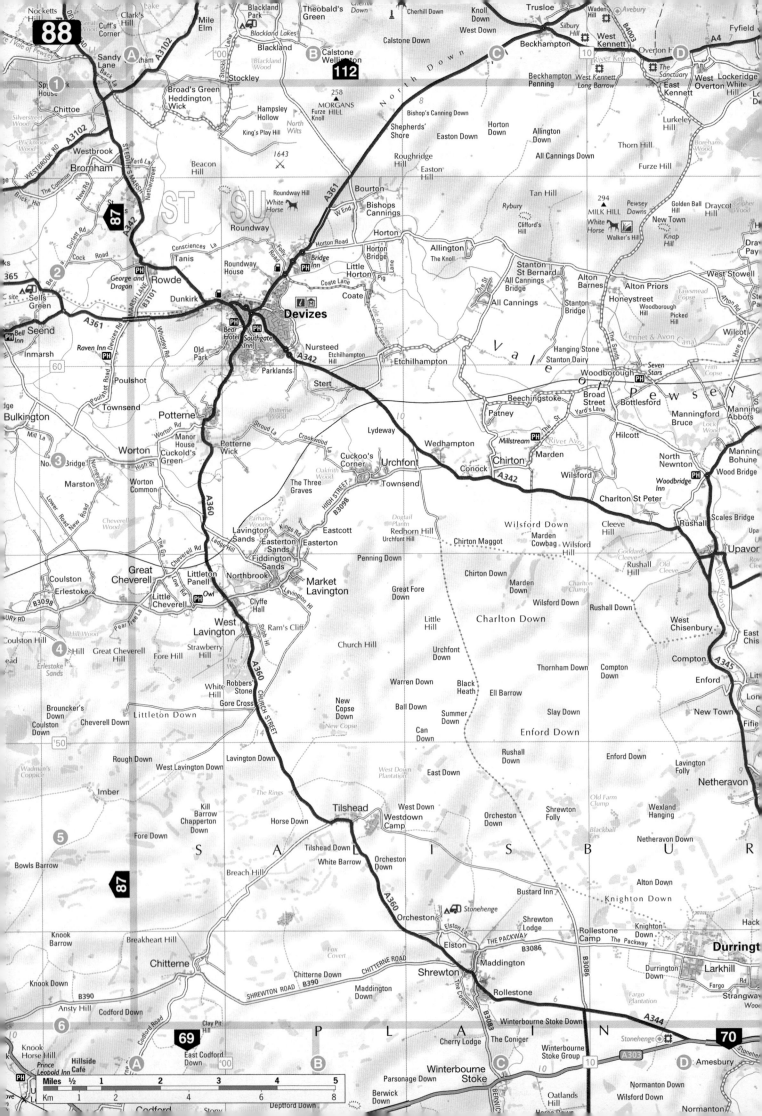

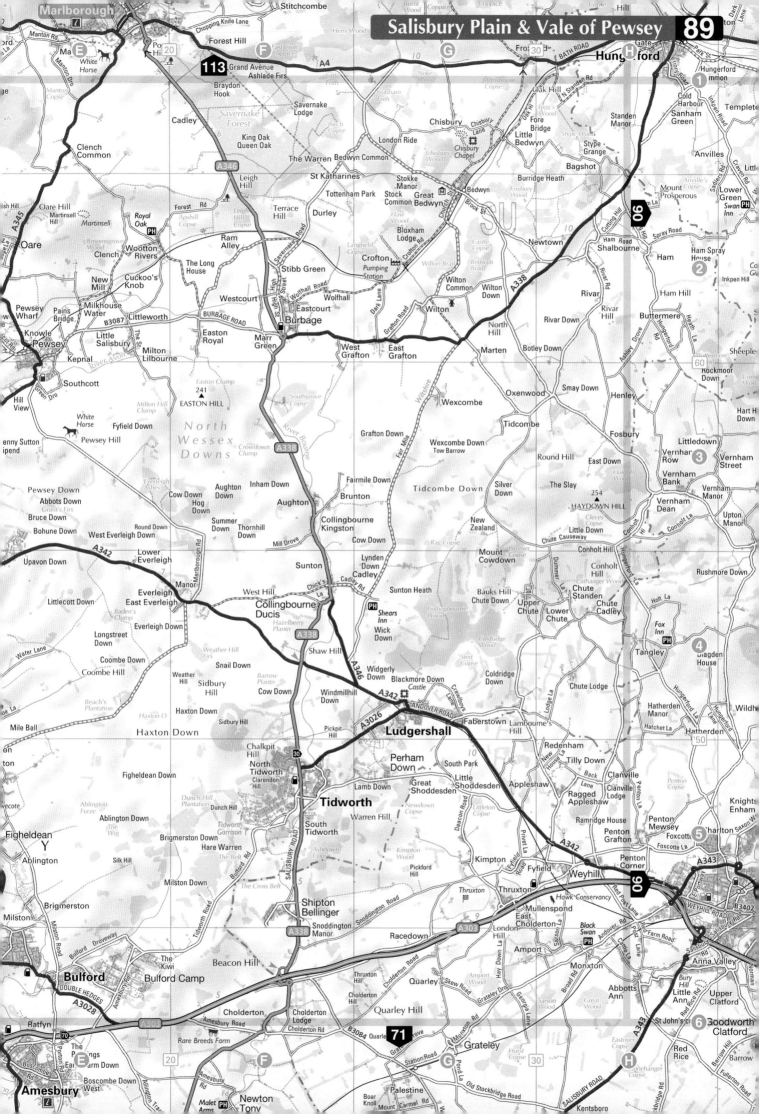

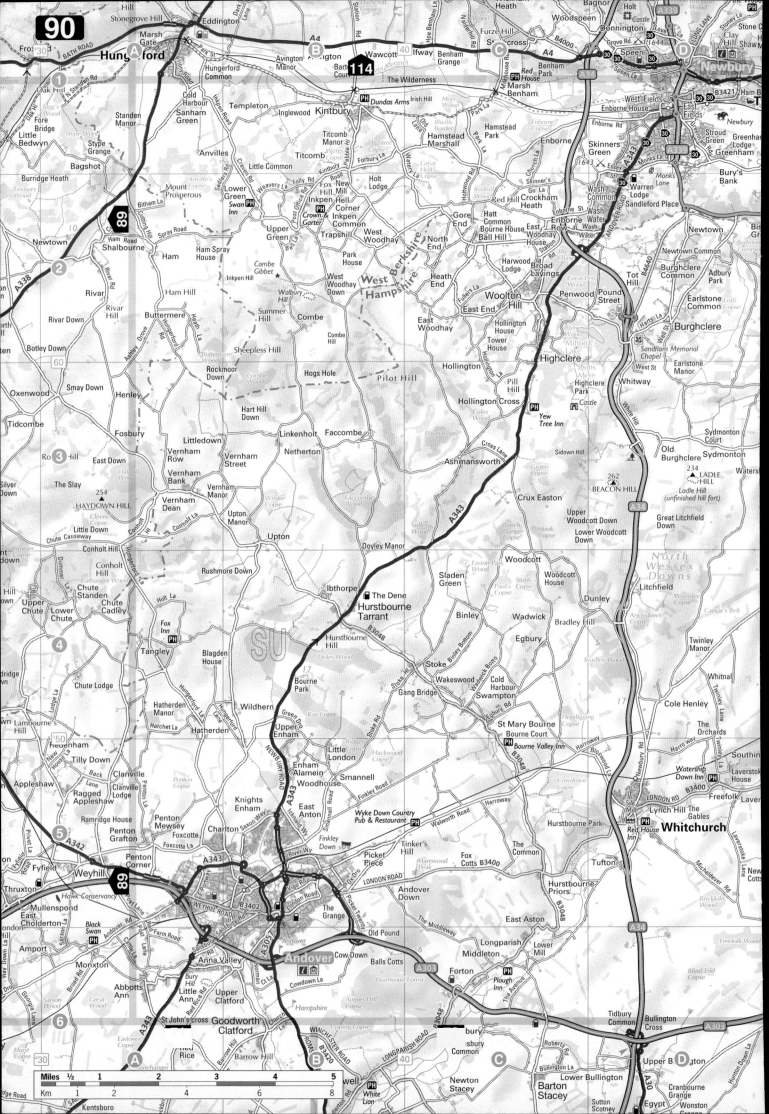

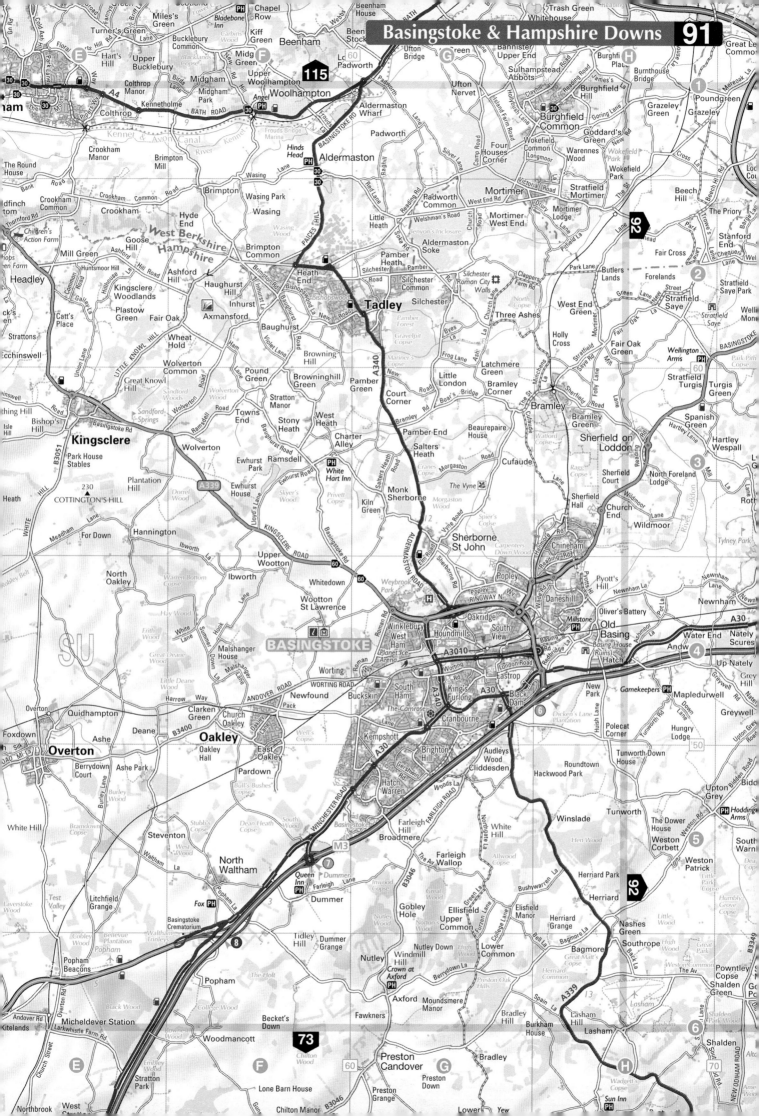

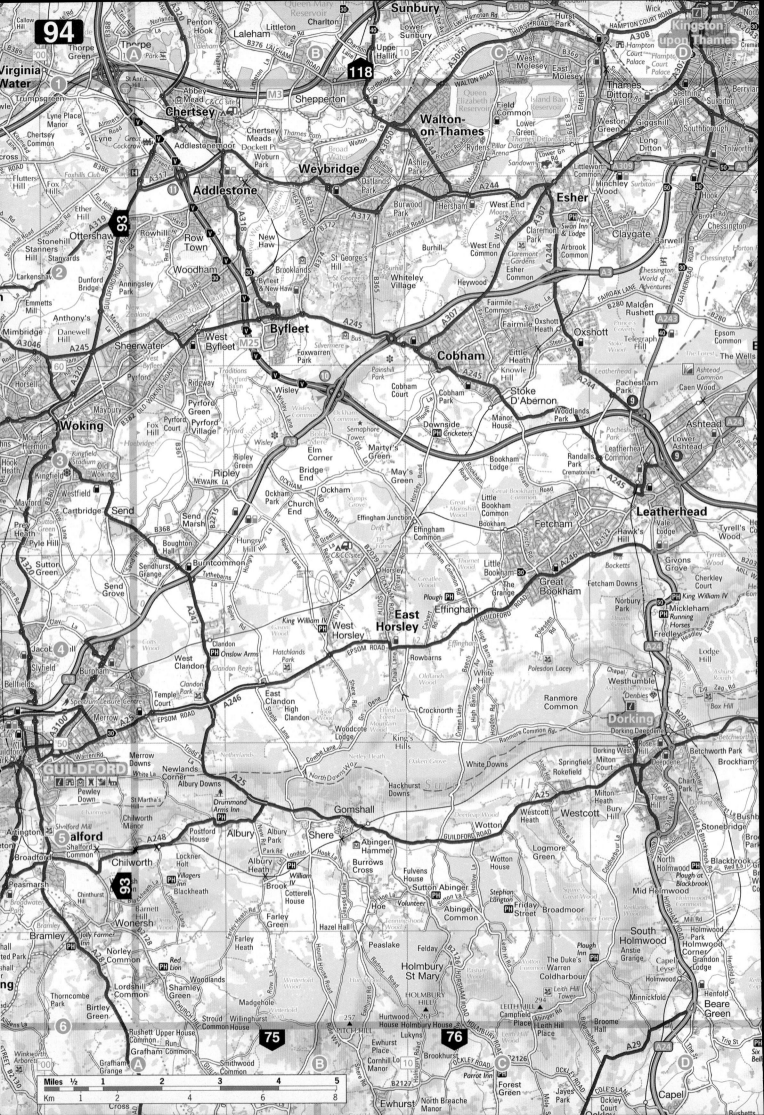

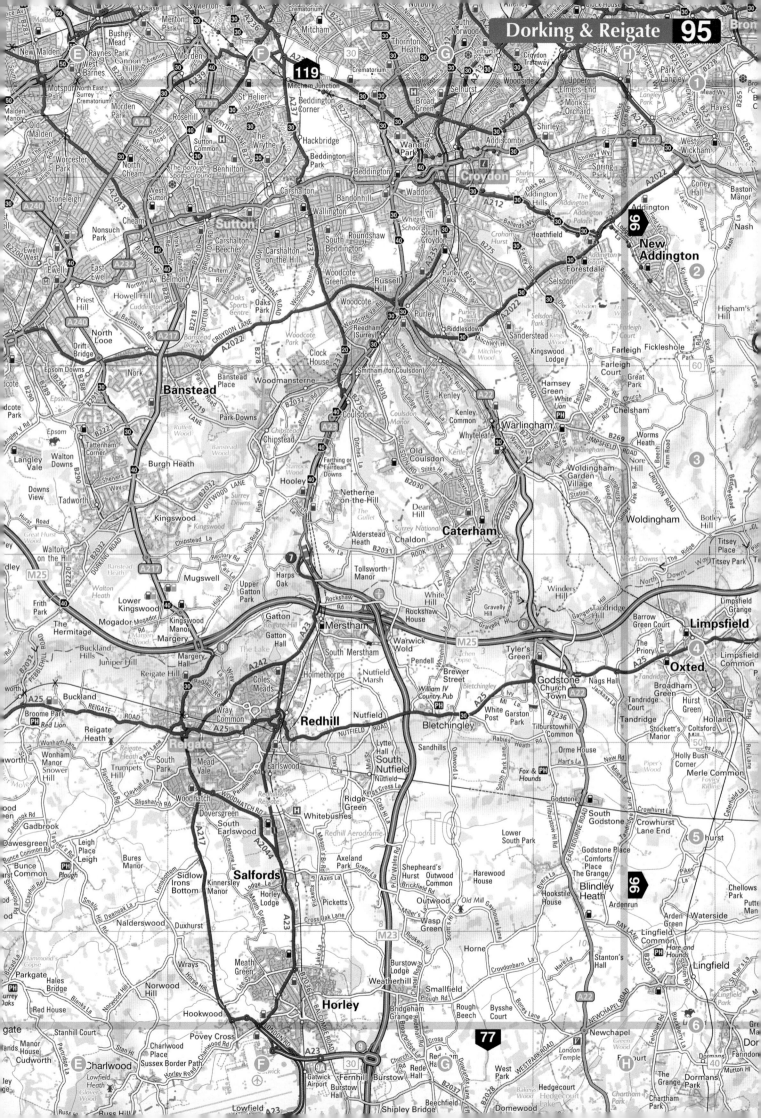

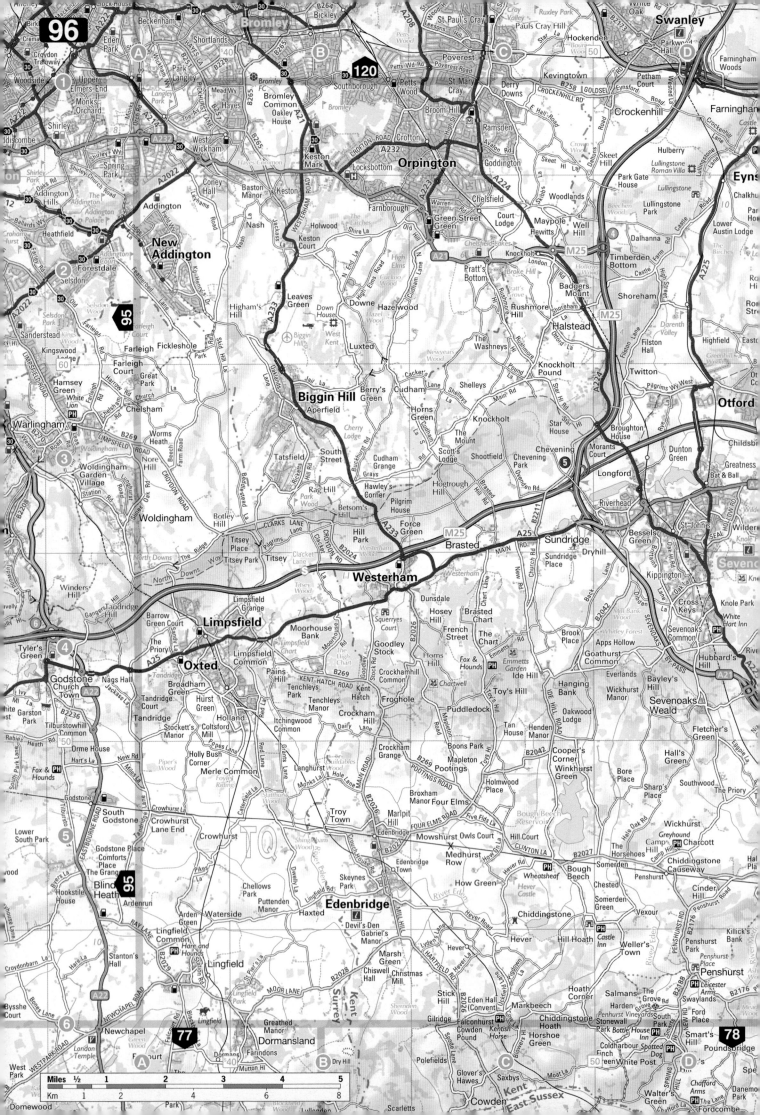

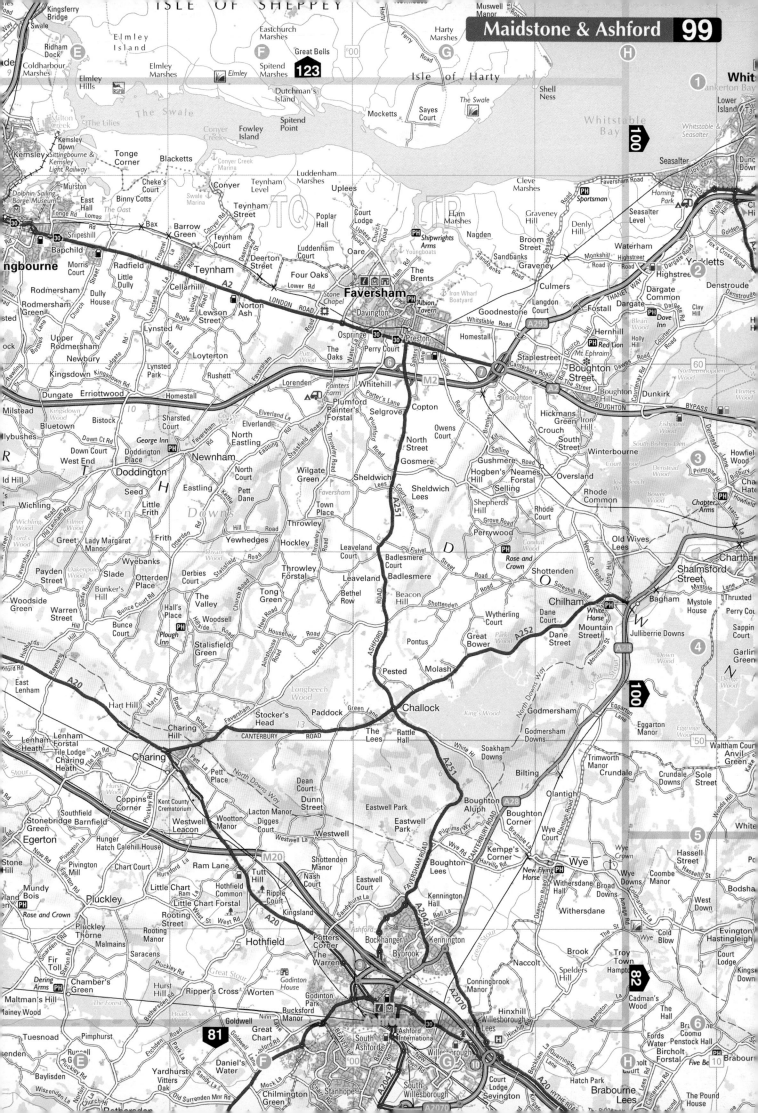

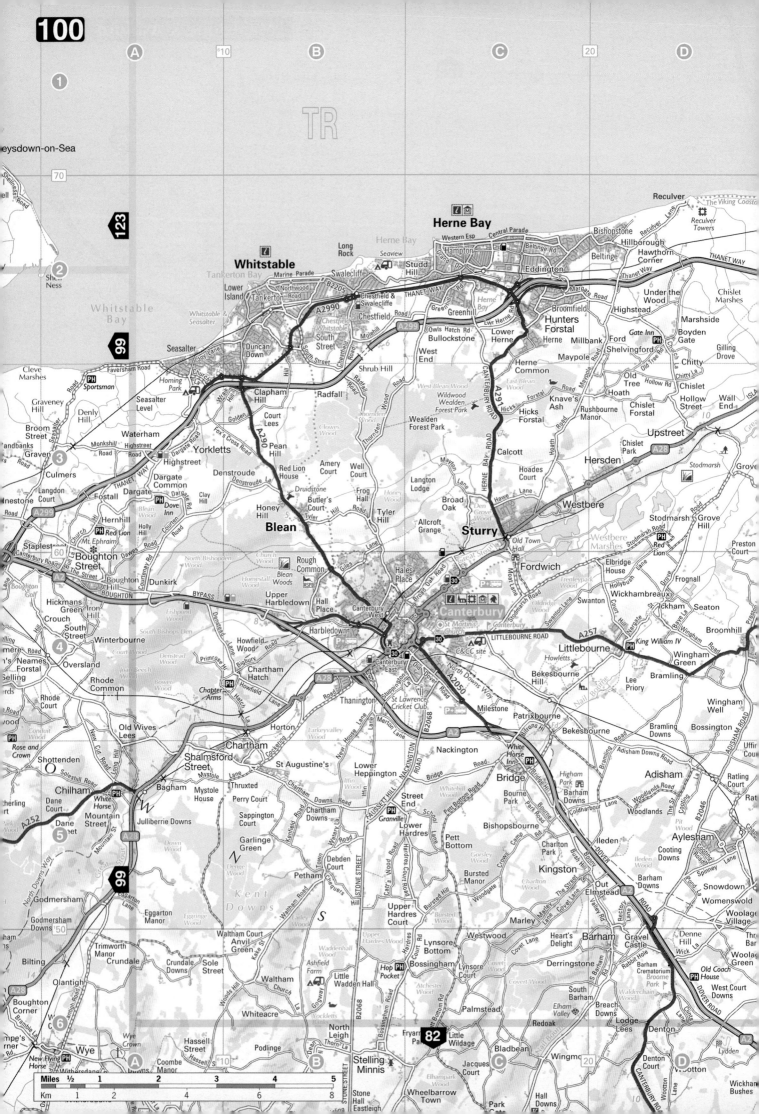

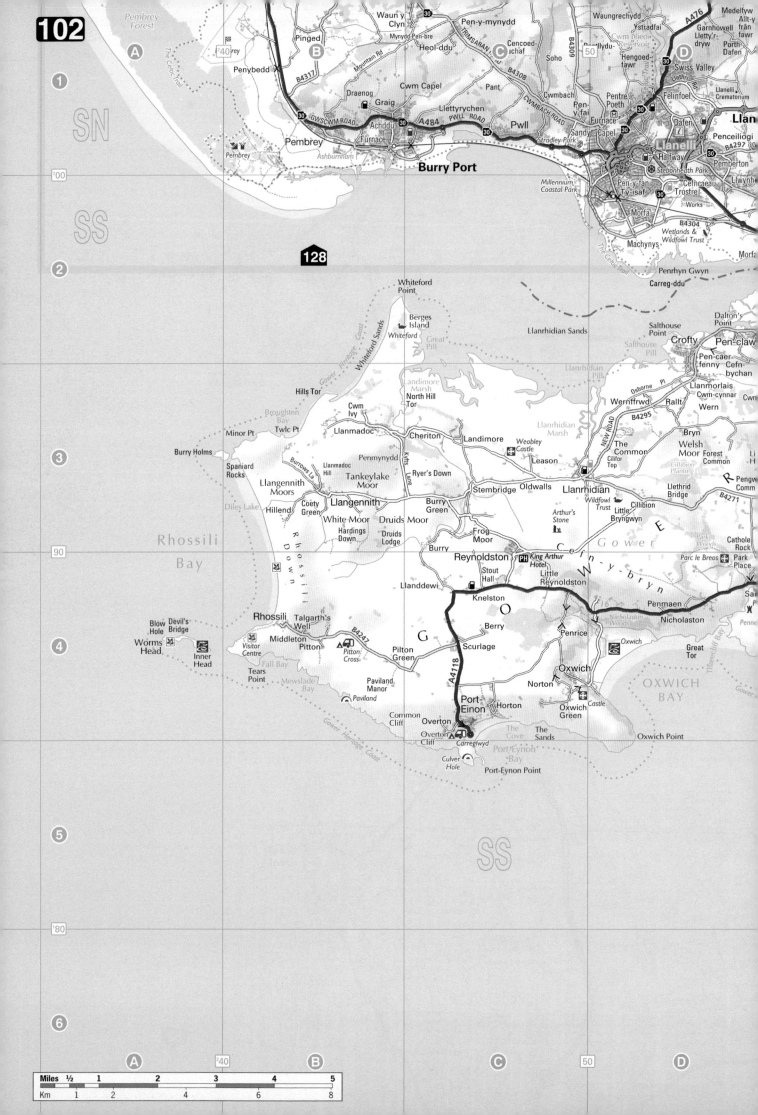

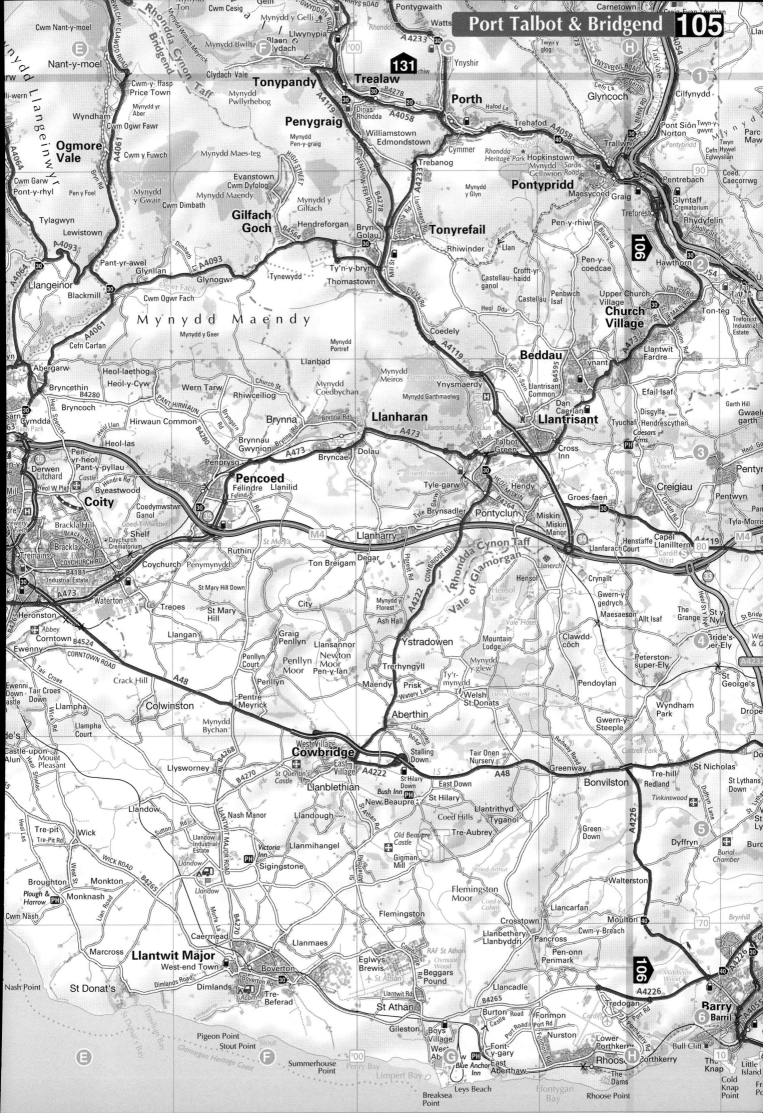

134
110
110
85

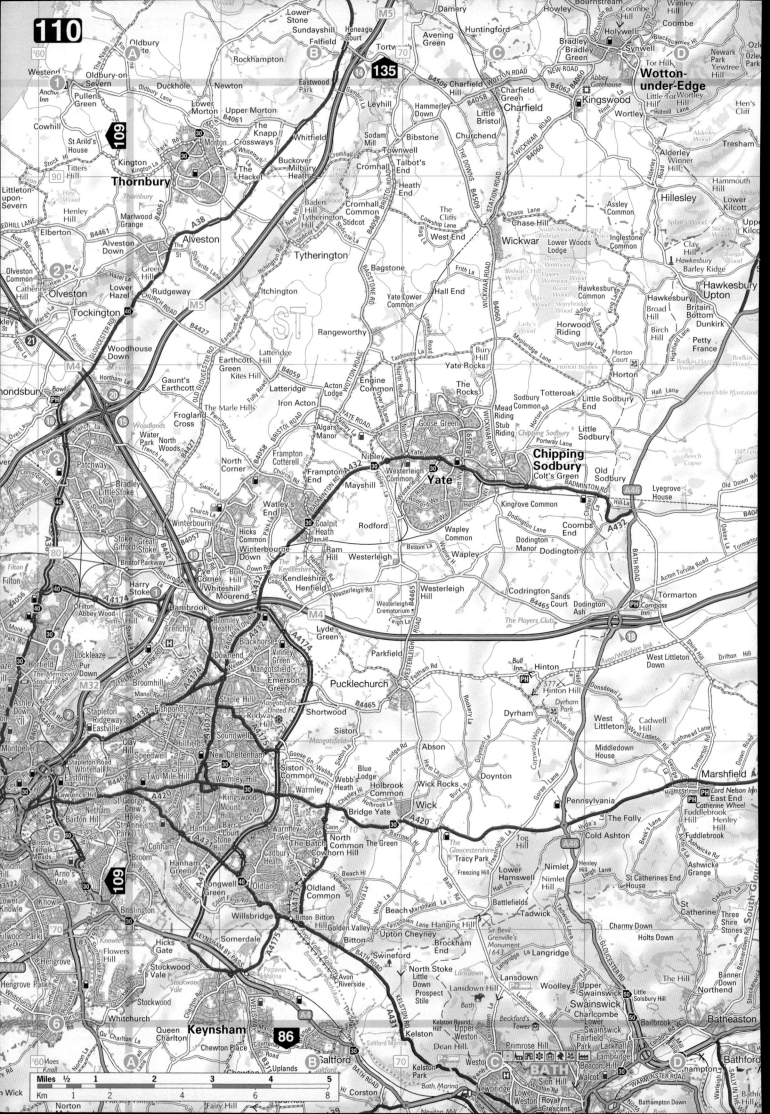

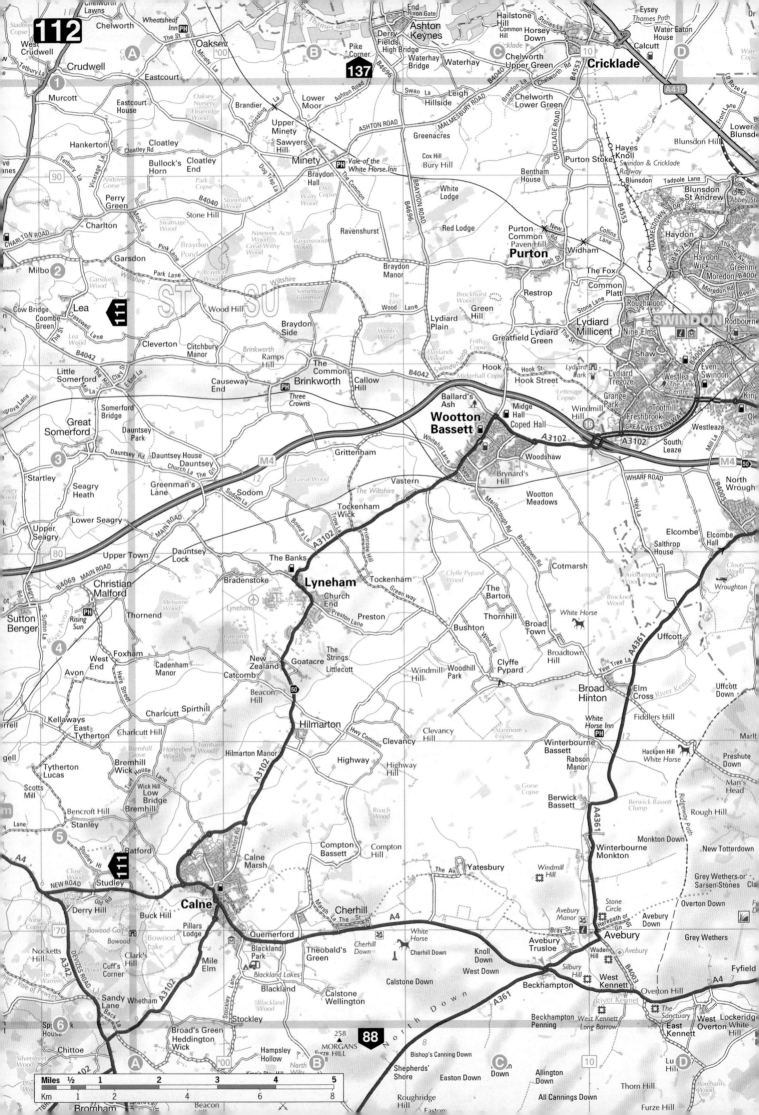

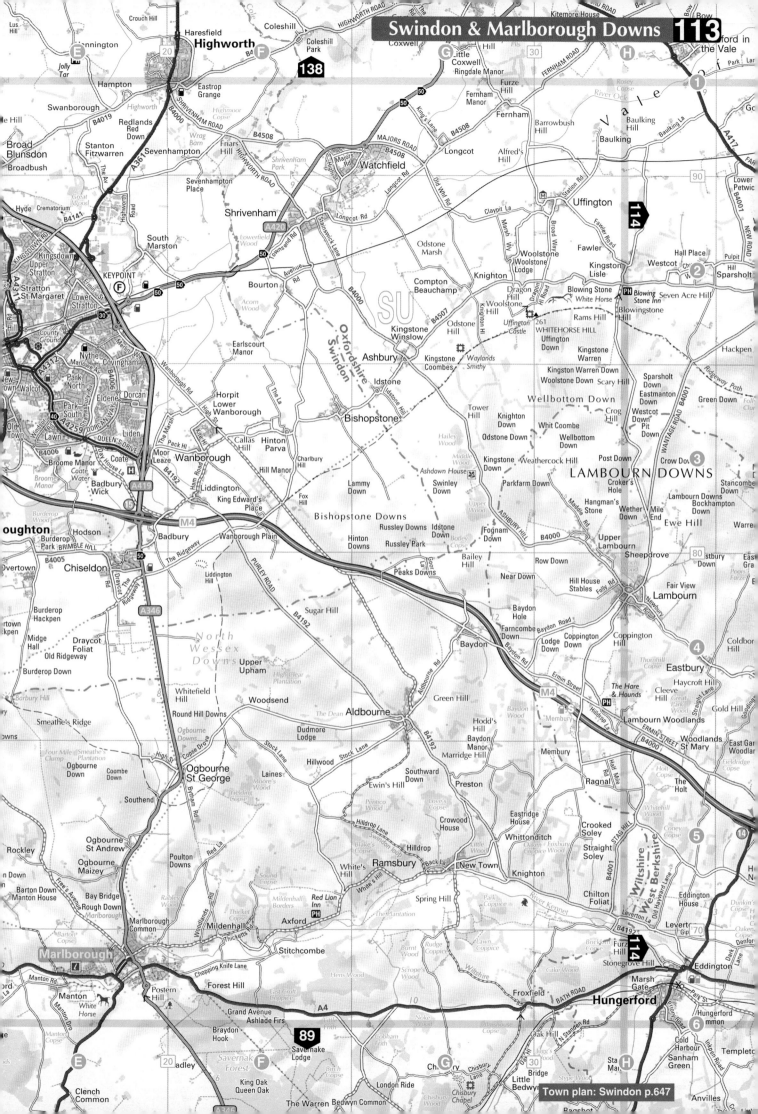

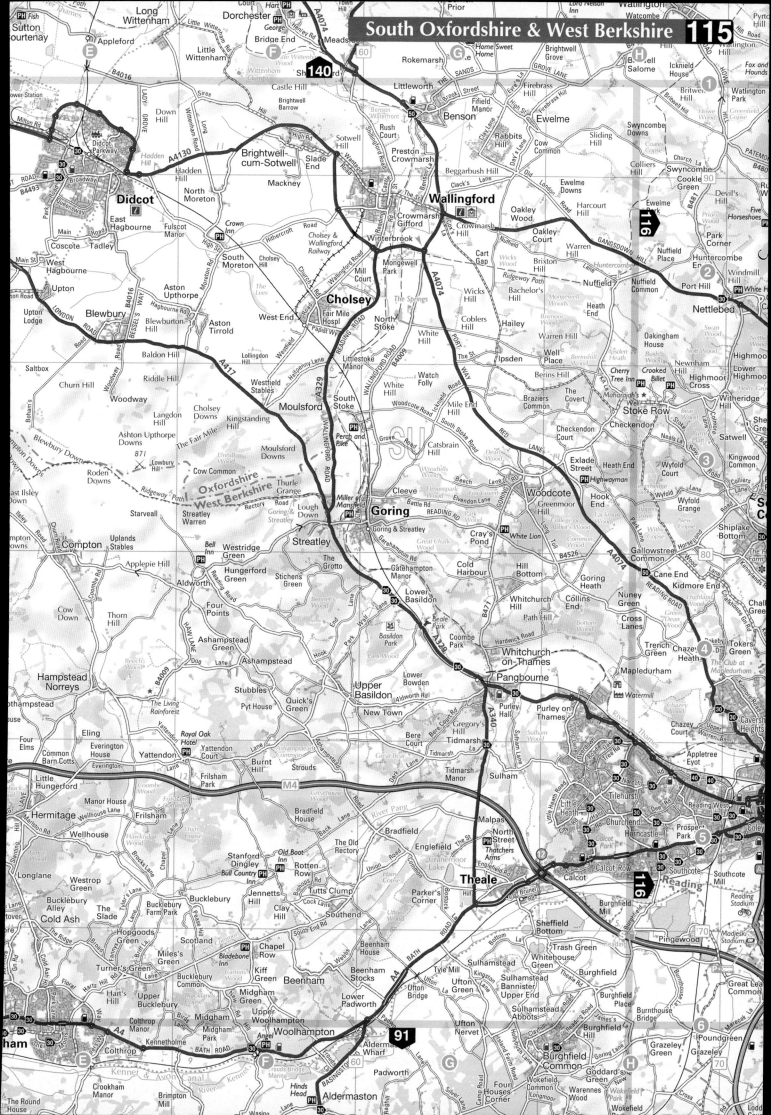

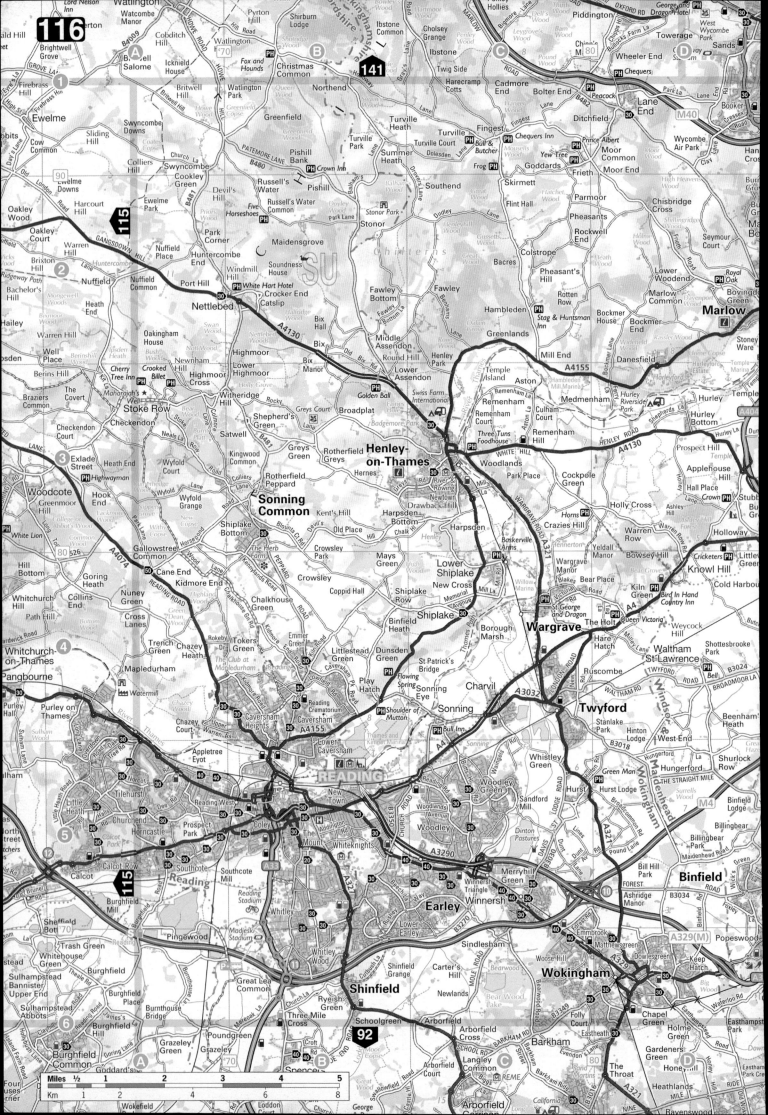

WALLASEA ISLAND

Crouch Corner

Crow Corner

The Quay

E West Hall

Paglesham Churchend

Clements Marsh

Churchend

F

G

Fisherman's Head

H

East Hall

East Wick

Plough & Sail

PH

Eastwick Head

148

Potton Point

Horseshoe Corner

FOULNESS ISLAND

Rugwood Head

East Hall

South Hall

Paglesham Eastend

Blackedge Point

POTTON ISLAND

New England Island

Shelford Head

Asplins Head

90

Barton Hall

Barling Marsh

Rushley Island

Havengore Island

Sharpness Head

bridge

Mucking Hall

Barling

Little Wakering

Little Wakering Hall

Havengore Head

TR

Stonebridge

Barrow Hall Road

Haven Point

Trotters

HIGH ST

New Rd

Samuel's Corner

Great Wakering

MAPLIN SANDS

1159

Bournes Green

B1017

Poynters

Lane

Black Grounds

2

North Shoebury

Pig's Bay

Thorpe Bay

Cambridge Town

Shoeburyness

SHOEBURY NESS

EA

SHOEBURYNESS

TQ

LONDON, CHELMSFORD

LIBRARY

VICTORIA AVE

SOUTHEND VICTORIA STATION

MUSEUM & PLANETARIUM

A13

LONDON

QUEENSWAY

Footbridge

Southend-on-Sea

Bowling Club

SHOEBURYNESS

H

3

QUEENSWAY

SUPERSTORE

VICTORIA PLAZA SHOPPING CENTRE

CINEMA

Buses Only (Southbound)

SOUTHCHURCH ROAD

SCHOOL

A13

0   200 metres

PO

SOUTHCHURCH ROAD

SWIMMING POOL

SCHOOL

80

UNIVERSITY OF ESSEX SOUTHEND

SOUTH EAST ESSEX COLLEGE

WHITEGATE

COUNTY COURT & INLAND REVENUE

QUEENSWAY

SOUTHEND CENTRAL STATION

MARKET

TRAVEL CENTRE

CAB

WOODGRANGE DRIVE

QUEENSWAY

SOUTHCHURCH AVENUE

THE ROYALS SHOPPING CENTRE

CHANCELLOR RD

Seaway Coach & Car Park

THE KURSAAL ENTERTAINMENT CENTRE

4

CLIFF LIFT

Never Never Land

FUNLAND

WESTERN

ESPLANADE

Adventure Island

MARINE PARADE

EASTERN ESPLANADE

B1016

SEALIFE ADVENTURE

SOUTHEND PIER

Adventure Island

LBT

Sheerness

Blue Town

Barton's Point

Scrapsgate

Mile Town

Marine Town

Sheerness

Royal Oak Point

Bugsby's Hole

West Minster

Halfway Houses

East End

Connetts

Warden Point

5

Holm Place

Minster

Brambledown

Norwood Manor

Berryfield

Thorn Hill

Warden

Barrows Hill

Furze Hill

South Lees

Rayham

The Bay

A245

Wallend

Eastchurch

High St

Bay View ROAD

B2231

Leysdown-on-Sea

Neats Court

Neatscourt Marshes

Southlees Marshes

Poors

Pump Hill

New Rides

LEYSDOWN

Bay View

Priory Hill

70

Kingsferry Bridge

Stray Marshes

HM PRISON

Newhouse

Muswell Manor

Priory Hill

Swale

Ridham Dock

ISLE OF SHEPPEY

Eastchurch Marshes

Harty Marshes

100

Coldharbour Marshes

Elmley Island

Great Bells

Harty Marshes

Shell Ness

6

Elmley Hills

RSPB

Elmley Marshes

Spitend Marshes

Isle of Harty

Whits

E

The Lilies

The Swale

99

Mocketts

The Swale

Sayes Court

G

Whitstable

H

Milton Creek

Dutchman's Island

Spitend Point

Whitstable Bay

Lower Island

Kemsley Down

Conyer Creek

Fowley Island

Seasalter

10

Sittingbourne

Tonge Corner

Blacketts

ST BRIDES BAY

150

A '70 B C 80 D

1

2

10

3

SM

4

SR

5

6

A '70 B C 80 D

Skomer Island / mainland labels:

Garland Stone

Pigstone Bay
SKOMER ISLAND
Pig Stone · Gorse Hill
Skomer Head
The Wick
Mew Stone
Shag Rock
Midland Isle

Broad Sound

Deadman's Bay
Marloes and Dale Heritage Coast
Rainy Rock

Little Bay Point
SKOKHOLM ISLAND
The Stack
Long Point
Mad Bay
Hog Bay
Long Nose
Quarry Point
The Head
Frank's Point

Marloes and Dale Heritage Coast

ROSSLARE HARBOUR

Stack Rocks
Howney Stone
Ticklas Point
Swan Inn & Borough Head
Mill Haven
Halfway Rock
Warey Haven
St Brides Haven
PEMBROKESHIRE COAST NATIONAL PARK
The Nab Head
Tower Point
St Brides
Windmill Park
South Hill
Hasguard Cross
Talb
Wooltack Point
Martin's Haven
Musselwick Sands
Orlandon
Winterton
Gay Lane
Marloes
B4327
Slatemill Bridge
Bicton
Marloes Court
St Ishmael's
Gateholm Stack
Marloes Sands
Gateholm Island
Red Cliff
Townsend
Musselwick
Lindsway Bay
Hooper's Point
Castle Wy
Dale
Watch House Point
Westdale Bay
Great Castle Head
Dale Roads
Long Point
Dale Point
Castlebeach Bay
Welshman's Bay
Watwick Point
Little Castle Point
Kete
Watwick Bay
Thorn Island
Frenchman's Bay
Mill Bay
West Blockhouse Point
West Ar
St Ann's Head
Rat Island
Castles Bay
Sheep Island
Parsonsquarry B
Pembrokeshire Coast Path

Rick

B

D

Scale:
Miles ½ 1 2 3 4 5
Km 1 2 4 6 8

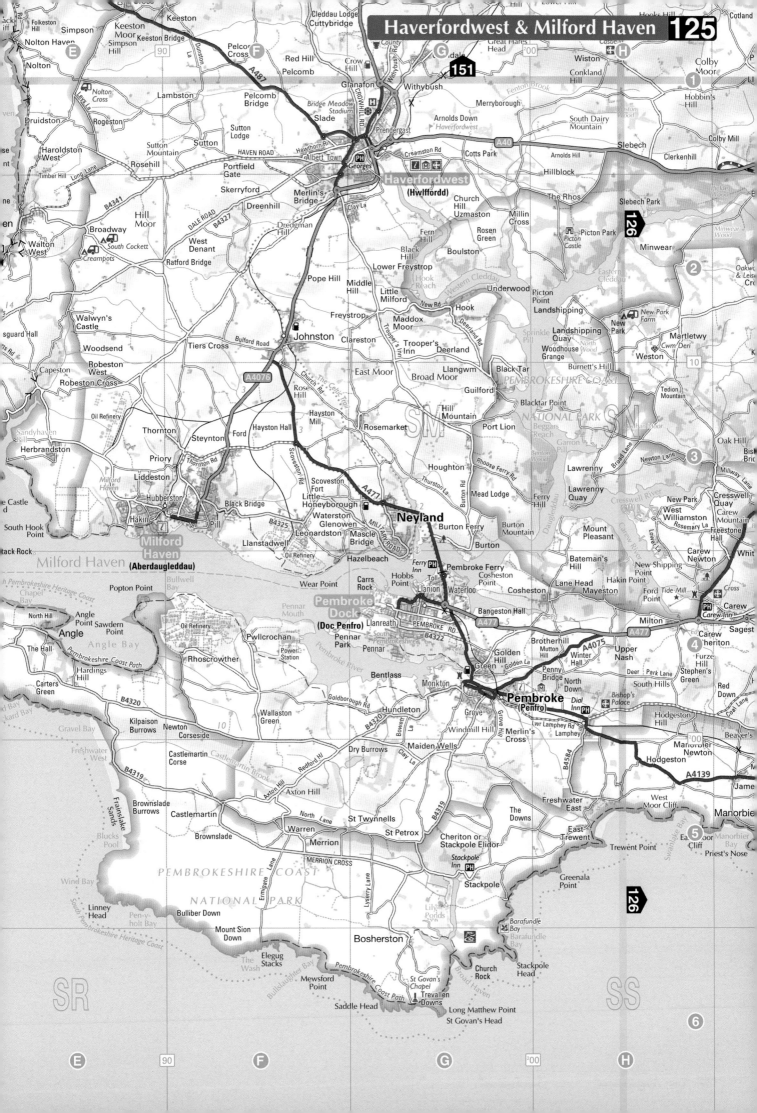

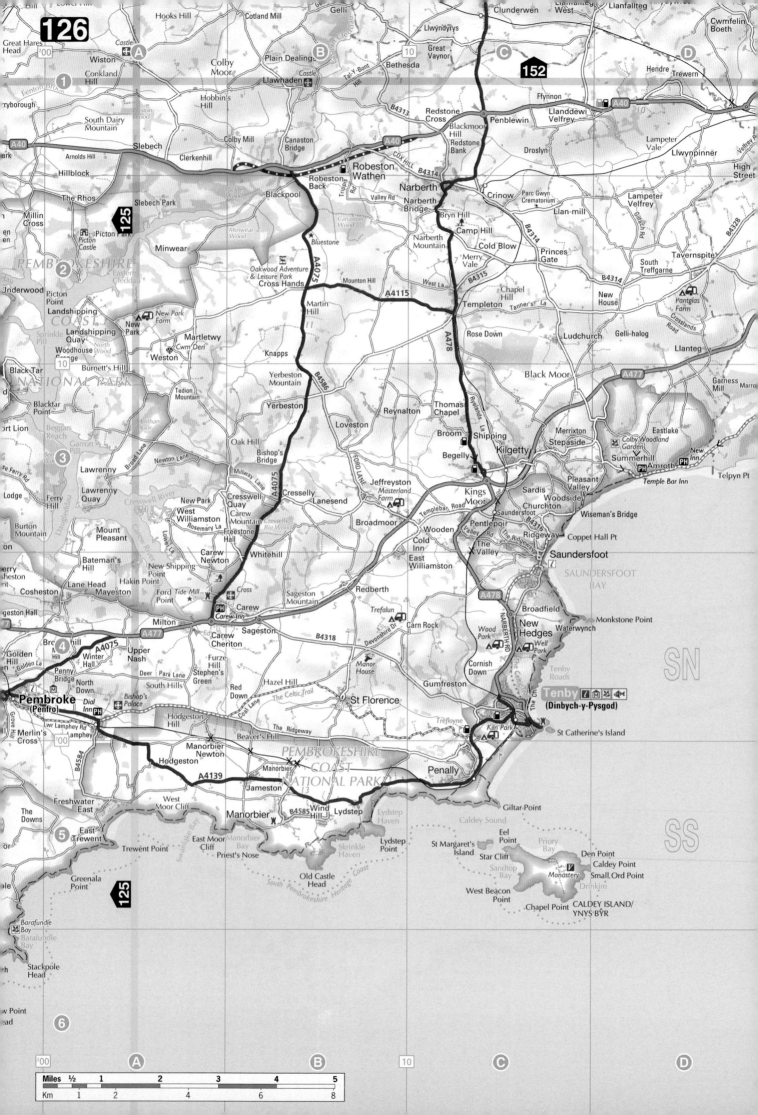

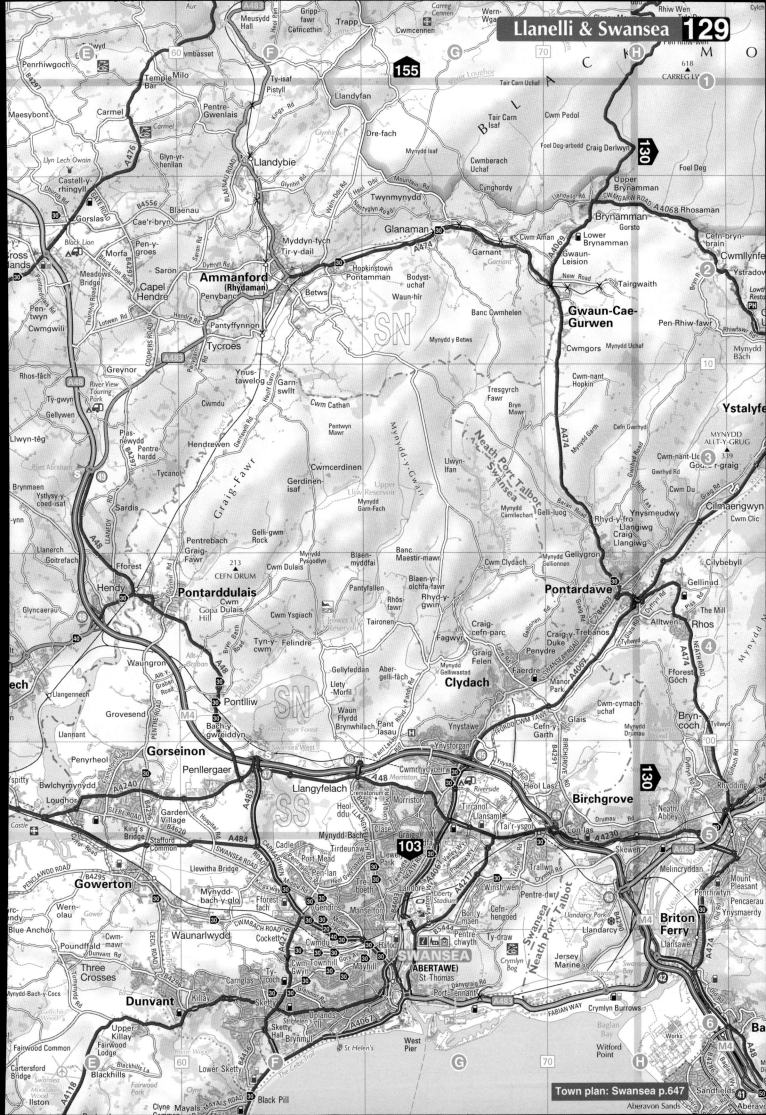

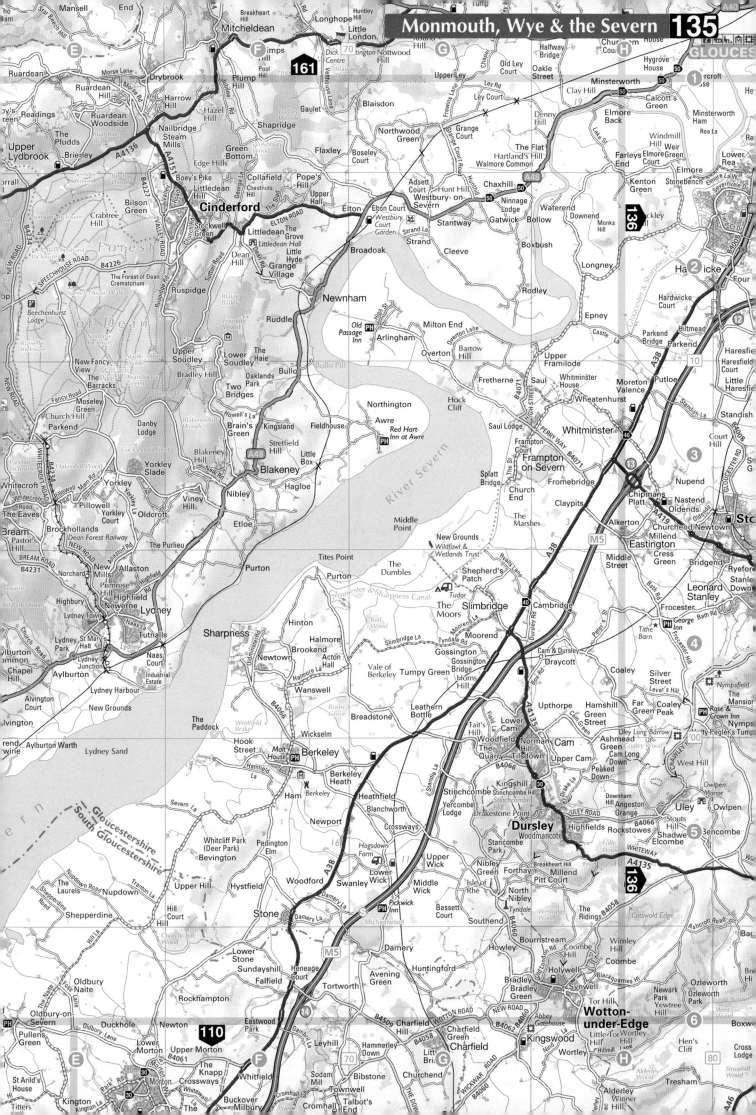

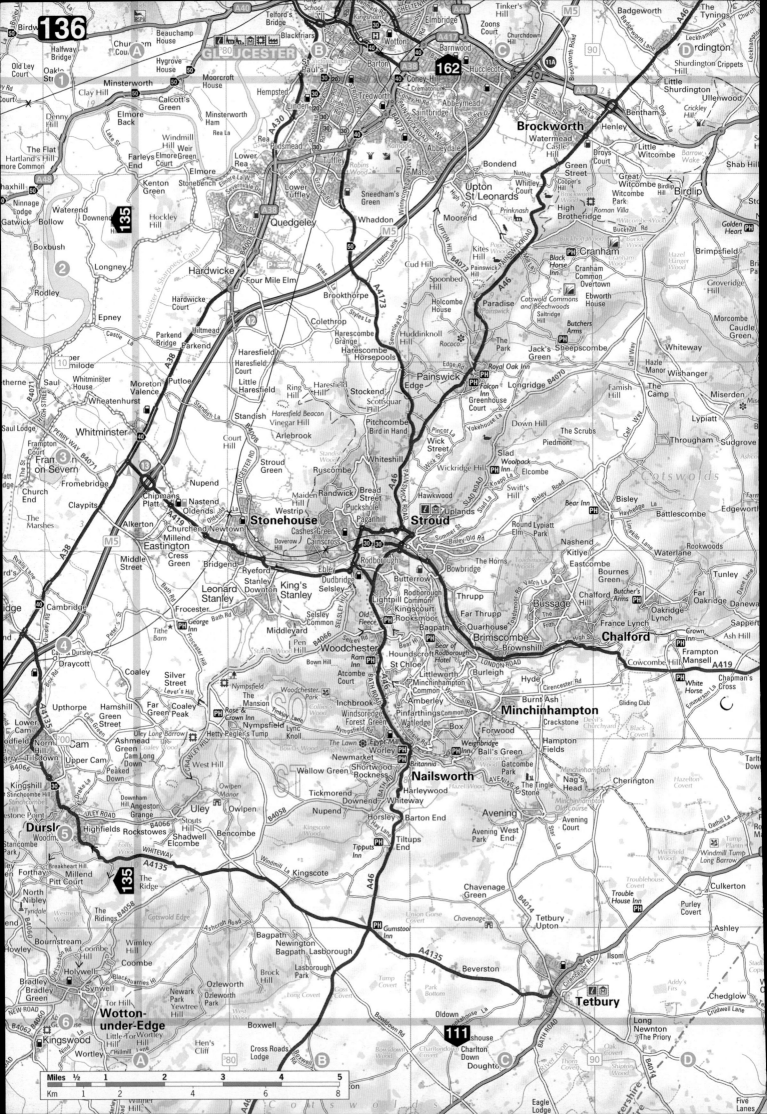

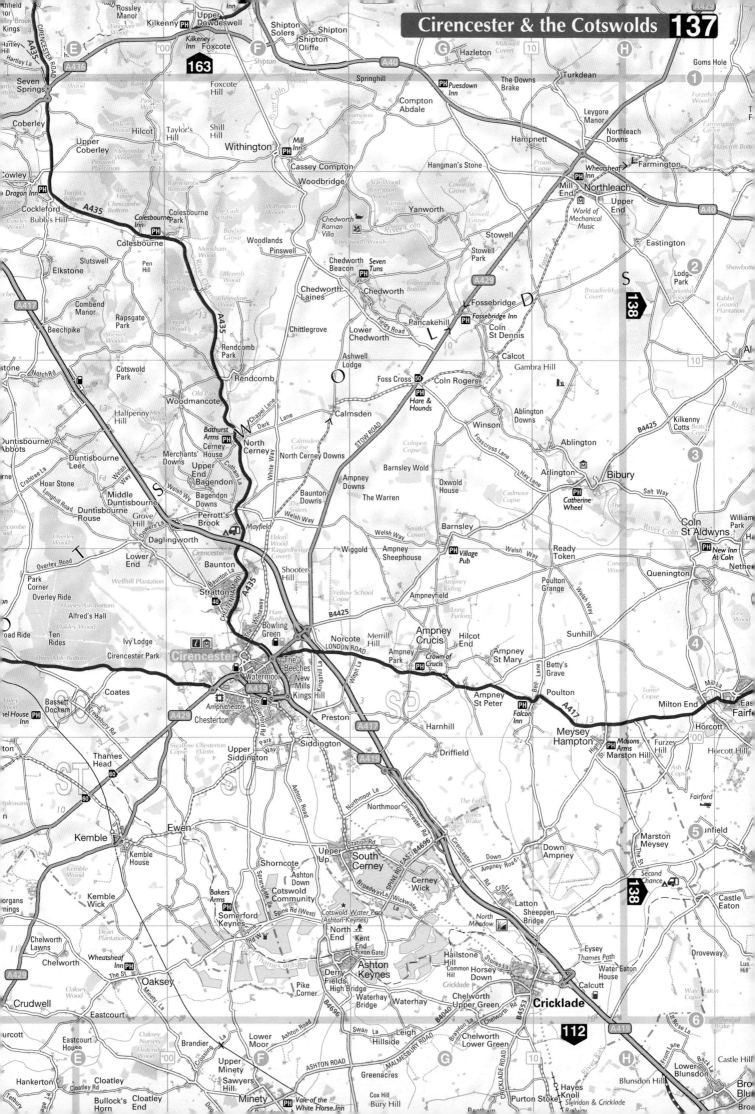

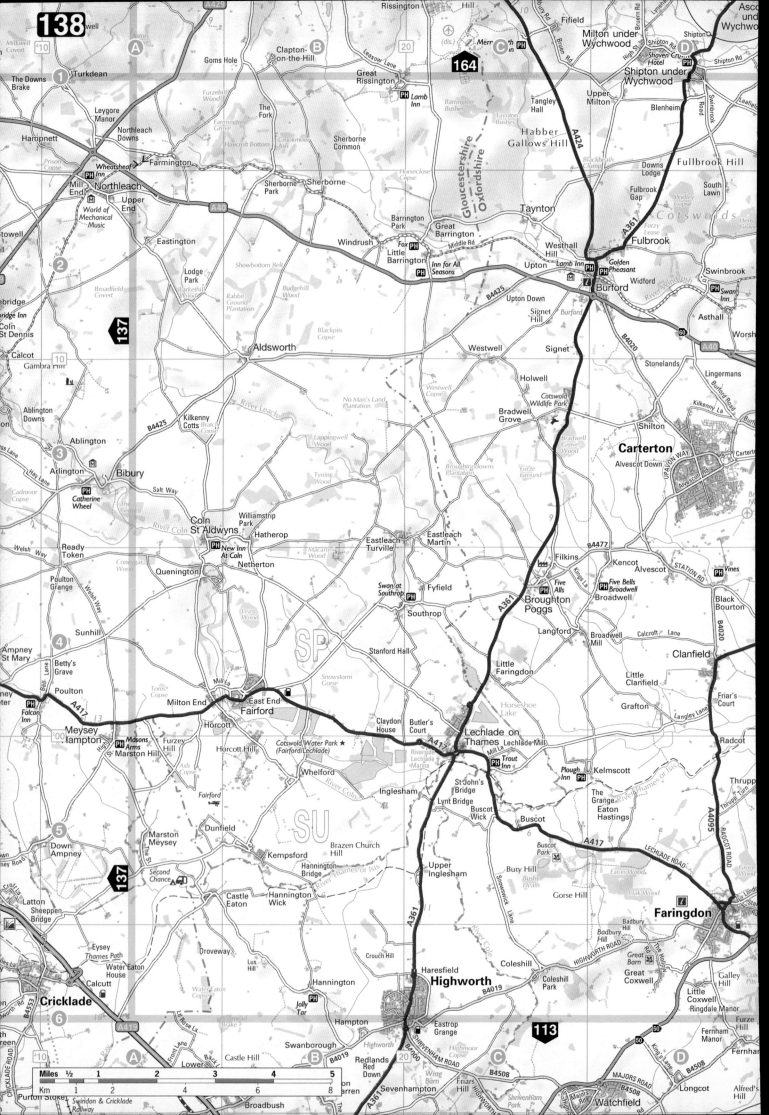

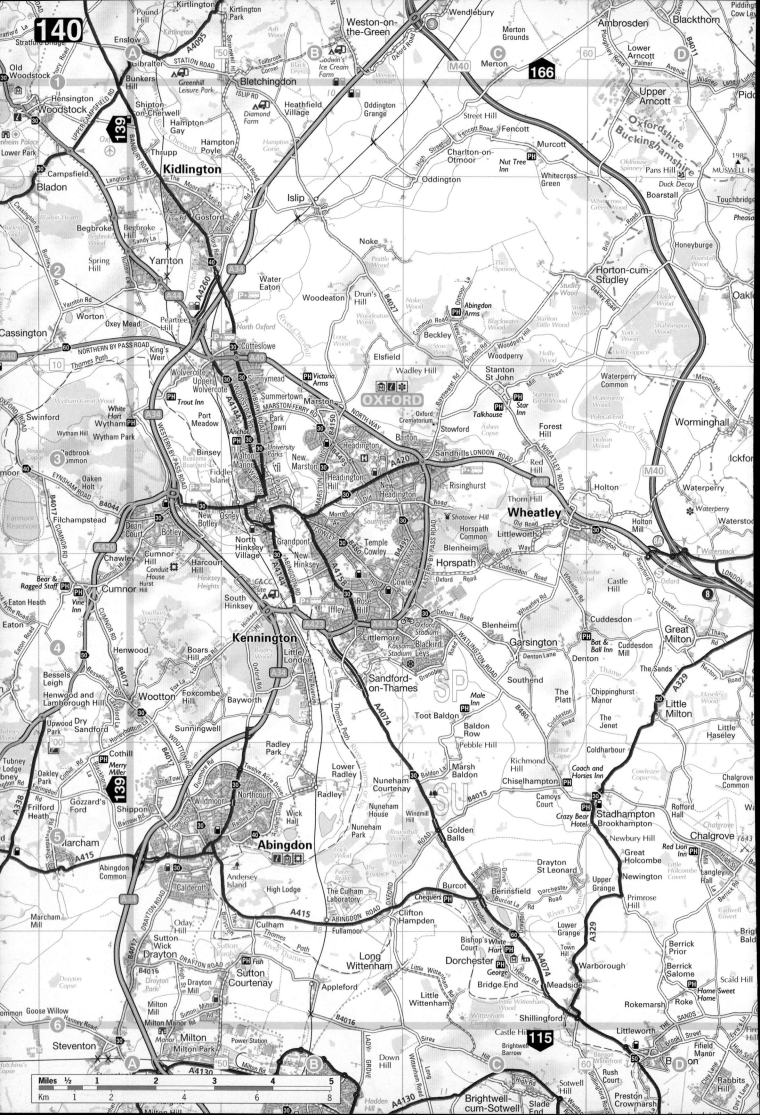

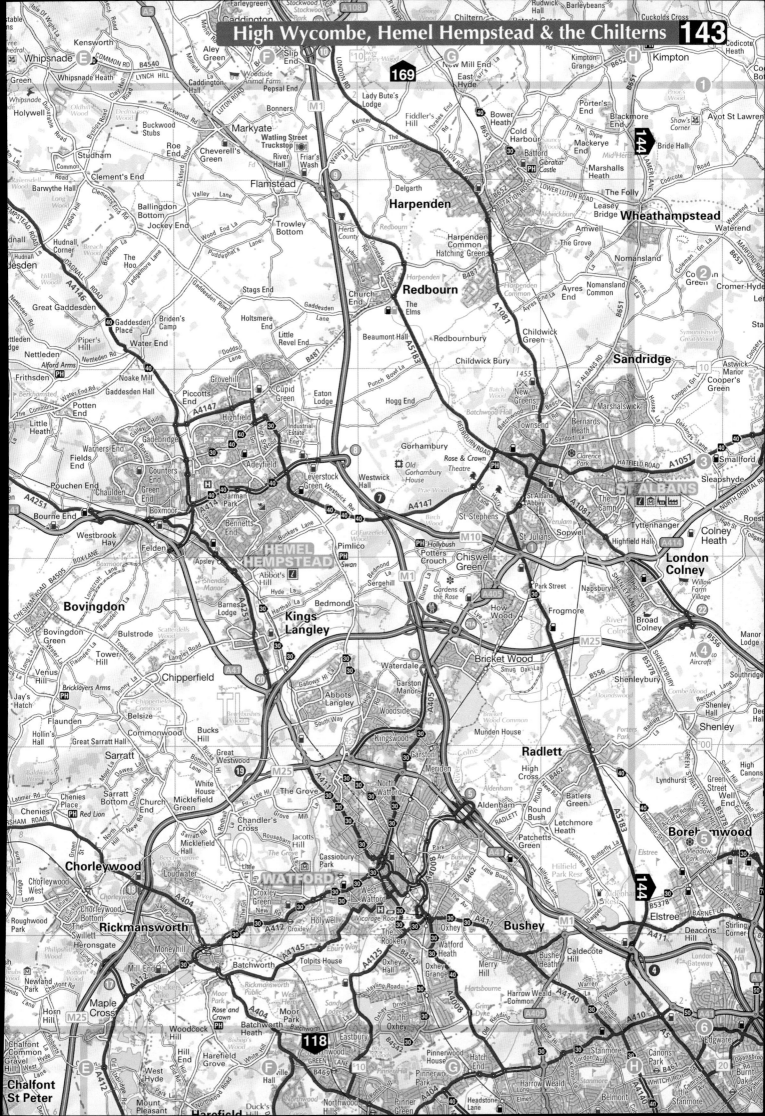

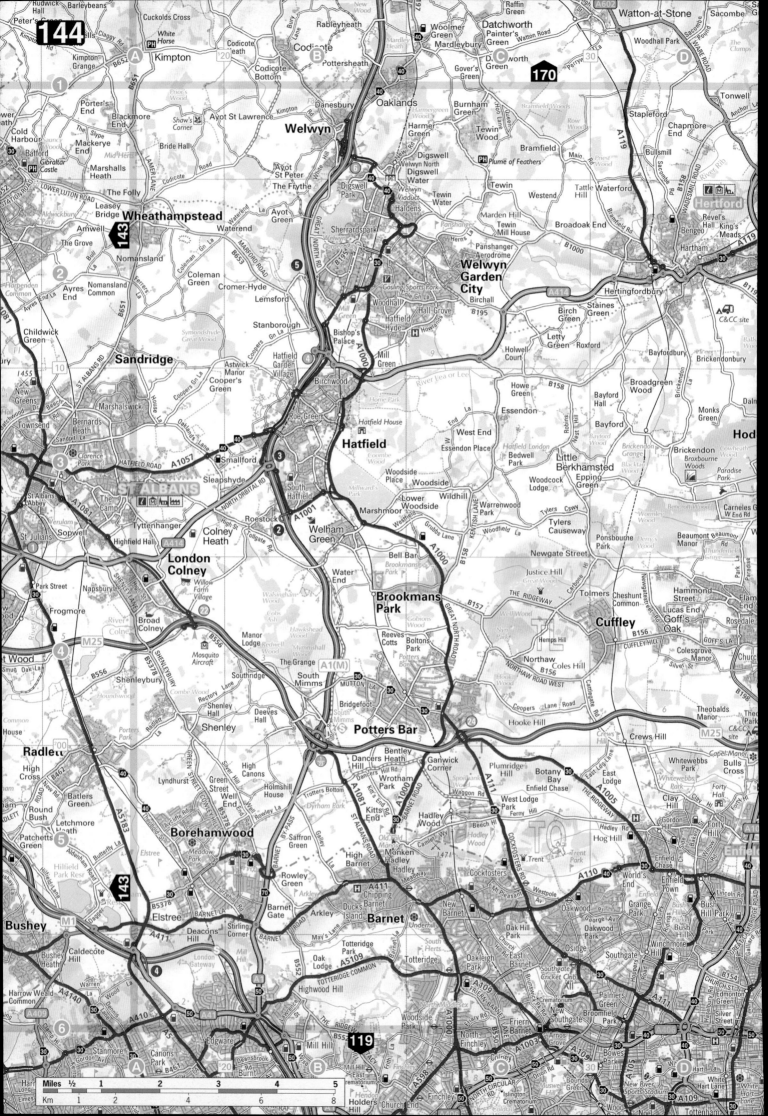

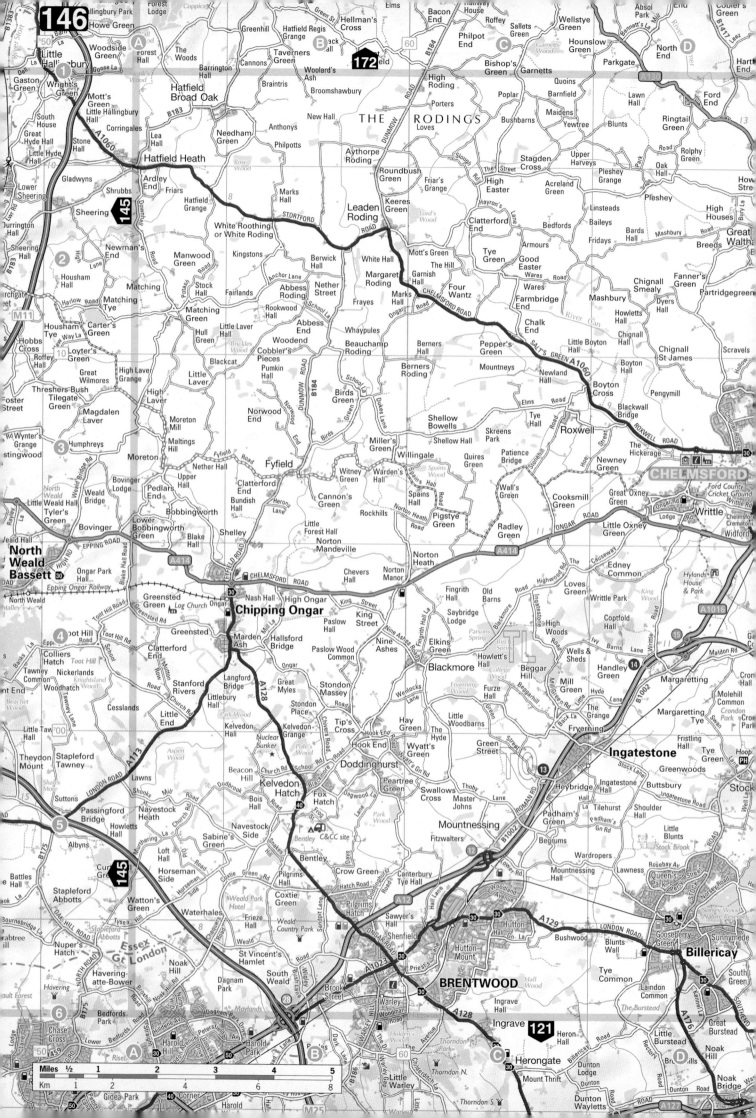

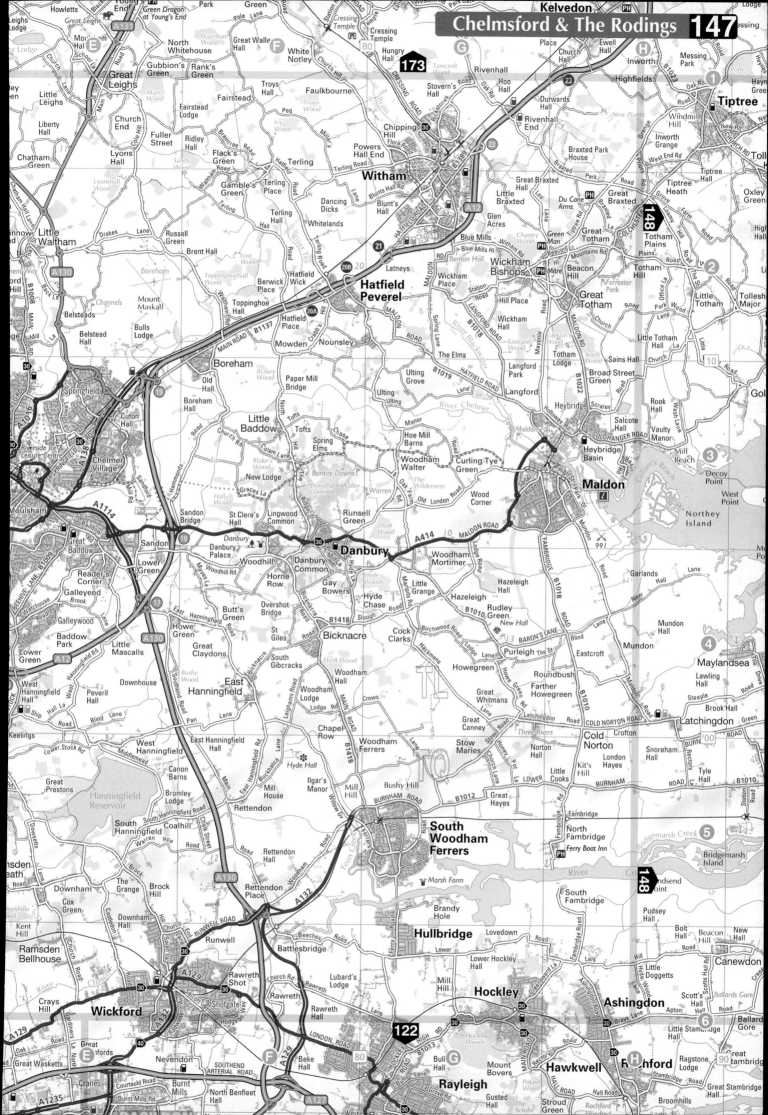

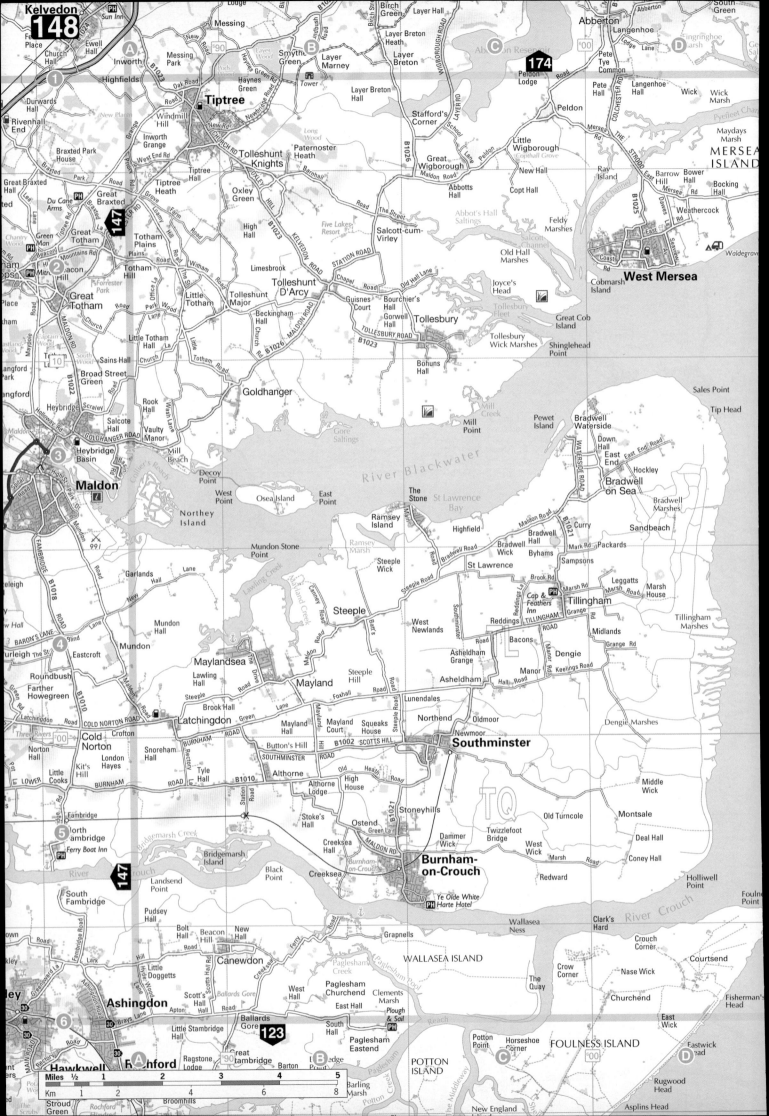

Aldboro Point
Rat Island
Ivy House
East Mersea
Cudmore Grove
Mersea Flats
Mersea Stone
Westmarsh Point
Colne Estuary
Colne Point
Lee-over-Sands
Sandy Point
St Osyth Stone Point
Point Clear
Cindery Island
St Osyth Marsh
Seawick
Mill Dam Lake

Alresford Creek
Brightlingsea
Morses
Hollybush Hill
Eastmarsh Point
Hurst Green
St Osyth
St Osyth Beach

175
176

CHURCH ROAD
BRIGHTLINGSEA ROAD
COLCHESTER ROAD
B1029
Regent Rd
Mill St
B1027
Clacton Rd
ST JOHN'S ROAD
Beach Rd
Daltes La
Golf Rd
Clay La
Frowick La
Dead La
Dial La
Wick La
Highbrich

Lodge
South Heath
St Osyth Heath
Riddles Wood
Milton Wood
Row Heath
Maldon Wood
Rectory
Hartley Woods
High Grove
Long Grove
Bovill's Hall
Earls Hall
Bocking's Elm
Coppins
Rush Green
Great Clacton
VALLEY
Burrsville Park
Highfield Grange
Little Clacton
Great Holland
Pond House
Holland-on-Sea
Holland Gap
Sandy Point
Chevaux de frise Point
Holland Haven

West Rd
Leas Rd
Rush Gn Road
Oxford Rd
THORPE ROAD
HOLLAND RD
FRINTON
B1442
B1027
B1032
Gorse La
CLACTON RD

A133
A133

Jaywick
Martello Beach

CLACTON-ON-SEA

B14
bury's old House

TM
TR

E F 10 G 20 H

1 2 10 3 4 200 5 6

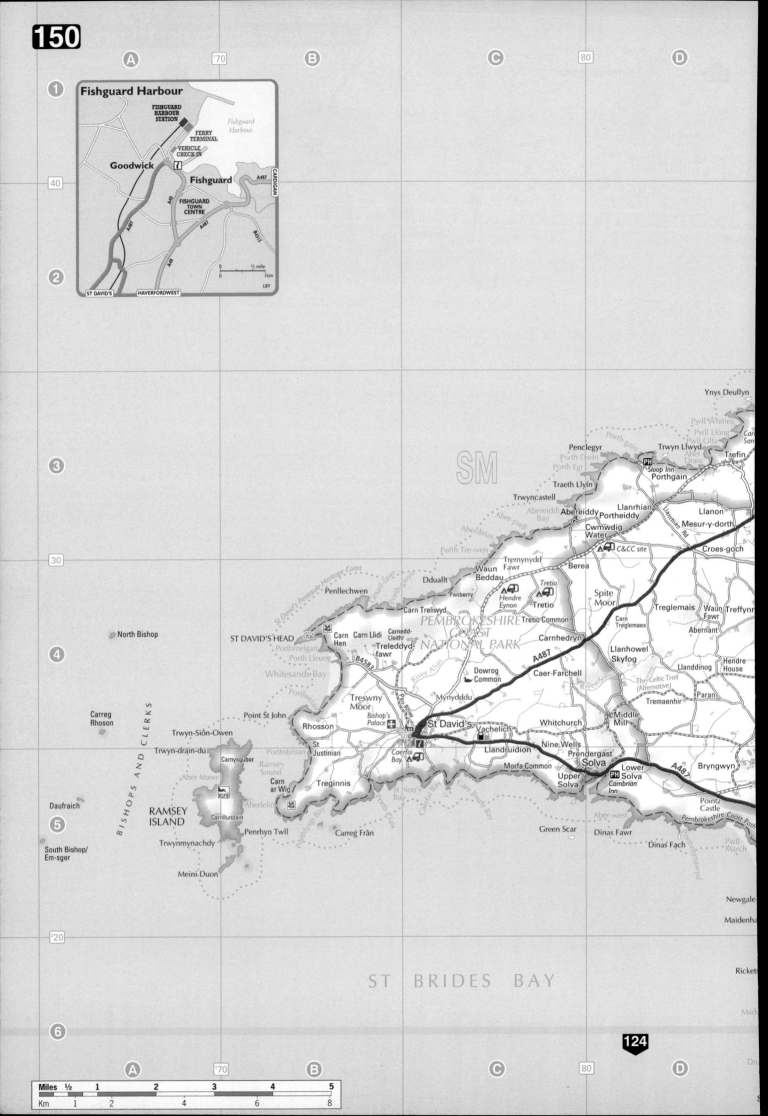

Fishguard Harbour

FISHGUARD HARBOUR STATION

FERRY TERMINAL

VEHICLE CHECK IN

Goodwick

Fishguard

Fishguard Harbour

FISHGUARD TOWN CENTRE

CARDIGAN

A487

A40

A40

B4313

ST DAVID'S

HAVERFORDWEST

½ mile
1km

LBT

Ynys Deullyn

Pwll Whiting
Pwll Llong
Pwll Olfa
Carn San

SM

Penclegyr
Porth Dwfn
Porth Egr
Porth-gain

Trwyn Llwyd

Trefin

Aber Draw

Sloop Inn
PH
Porthgain

Traeth Llyfn

Trwyncastell

Llanrhian
Abereiddi
Bay
Abereiddy
Portheiddy

Llanon

Cwmwdig
Water

Mesur-y-dorth

Aber-pwll

Aber-dinas

Porth Tre-wen

C&CC site

Croes-goch

30

Dduallt

Tremynydd
Fawr

Berea

Waun
Beddau

Penberry

Hendre
Eynon

Tretio

Tretio Common

Spite
Moor

Treglemais

Waun
Fawr

Treffynn

Abernant

Carn
Treglemaes

Penllechwen

Carn Treliwyd

PEMBROKESHIRE
COAST

Carnhedryn

North Bishop

St David's Peninsula Heritage Coast

Gesail fawr

Porthseswyn

ST DAVID'S HEAD

Carn
Hen

Carn Llidi

Carnedd-
Lleithr

NATIONAL PARK

Caer-Farchell

Llanhowel
Skyfog

Llanddinog

Hendre
House

Treleddyd
fawr

Porthmelgan

Porth Lleuog

B4583

Dowrog
Common

River Alun

A487

River Solva

Paran

The Celtic Trail
(Alternative)

Tremaenhir

Whitesands Bay

Porthsela

Treswny
Moor

Mynyddddu

Middle
Mill

Carreg
Rhoson

Trwyn-Siôn-Owen

Point St John

Rhosson

Bishop's
Palace

Pen Rhiw

St David's

Vachelich

Whitchurch

Trwyn-drain-du

Porthstinian

St
Justinian

Caerfai
Bay

Llandruidion

Nine Wells

Prendergast

Solva

Bryngwyn

Carnysgubor

Ramsey
Sound

Morfa Common

Lower
Solva

A487

Aber Mawr

Carn
ar Wig

Treginnis

Upper
Solva

PH
Cambrian
Inn

Daufraich

RSPB

Aberfelin

Porth Clais

Pointz
Castle

RAMSEY
ISLAND

Carnllundain

Penrhyn Twll

St Non's
Bay

Caer Bwdy Bay

Aber-west

Green Scar

Dinas Fawr

Pembrokeshire Coast Path

Pwll
March

BISHOPS AND CLERKS

Trwynmynachdy

Carreg Frân

Caerfai Bay

Dinas Fach

South Bishop/
Em-sger

Meini-Duon

Porthlysgi Bay

Porthmawr

Newgale

Maidenha

²20

ST BRIDES BAY

Ricketś

124

Madoḥ

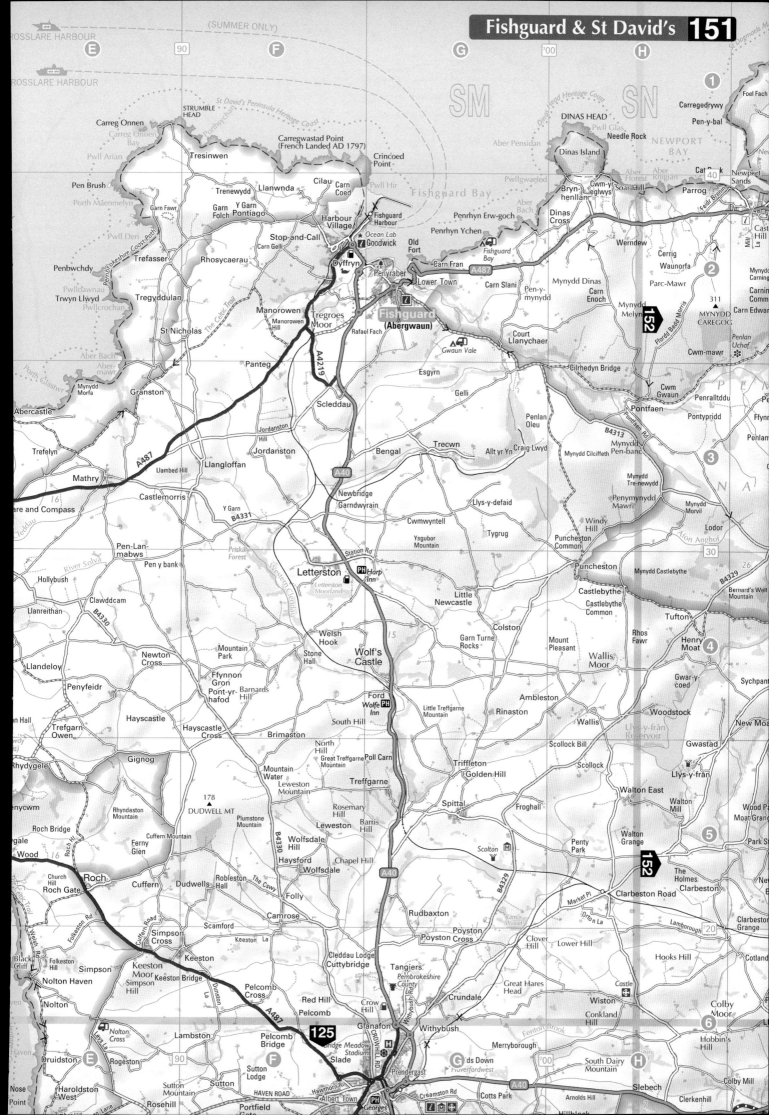

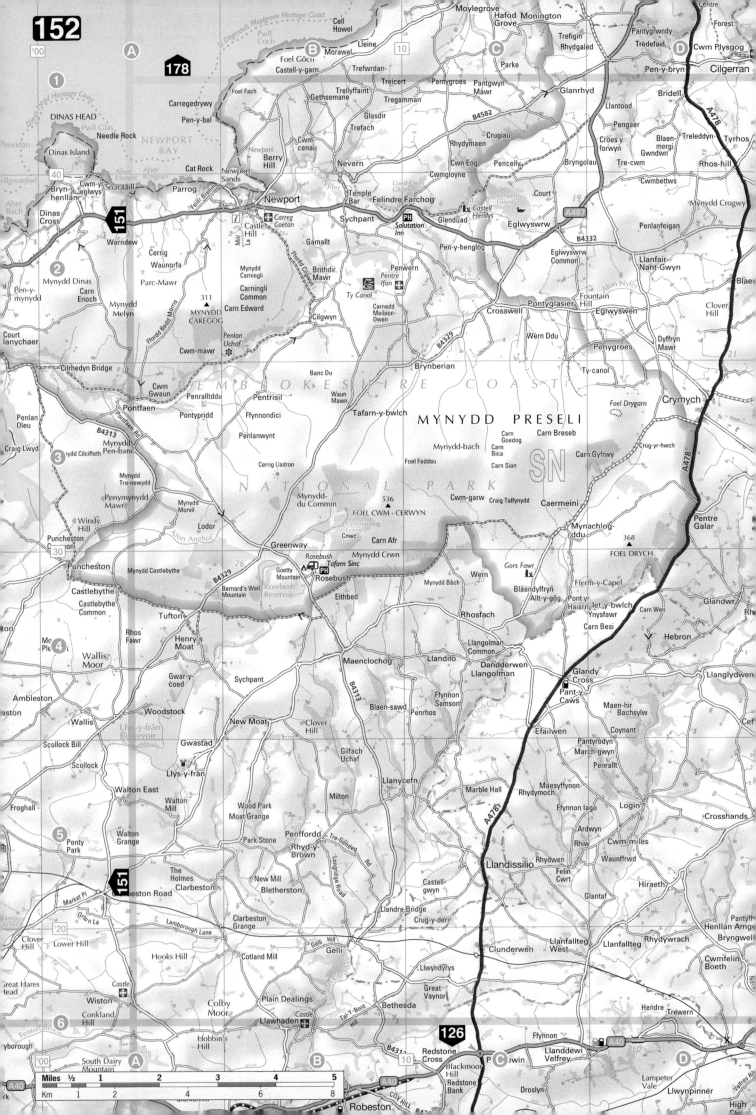

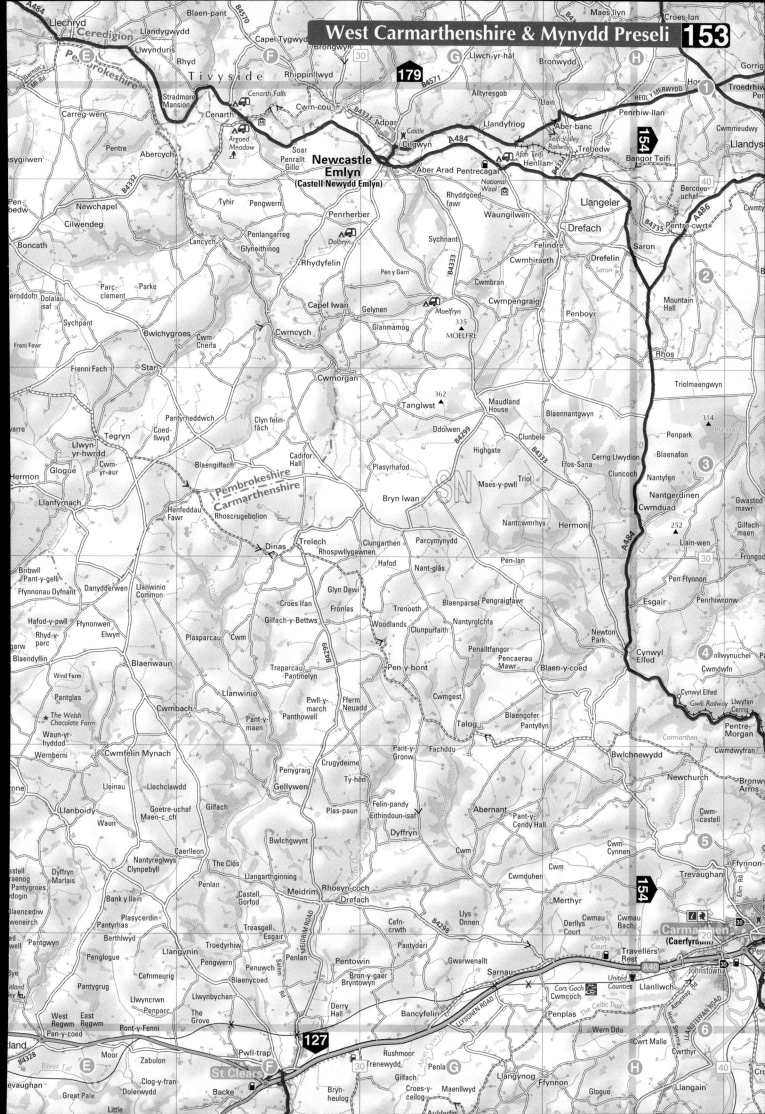

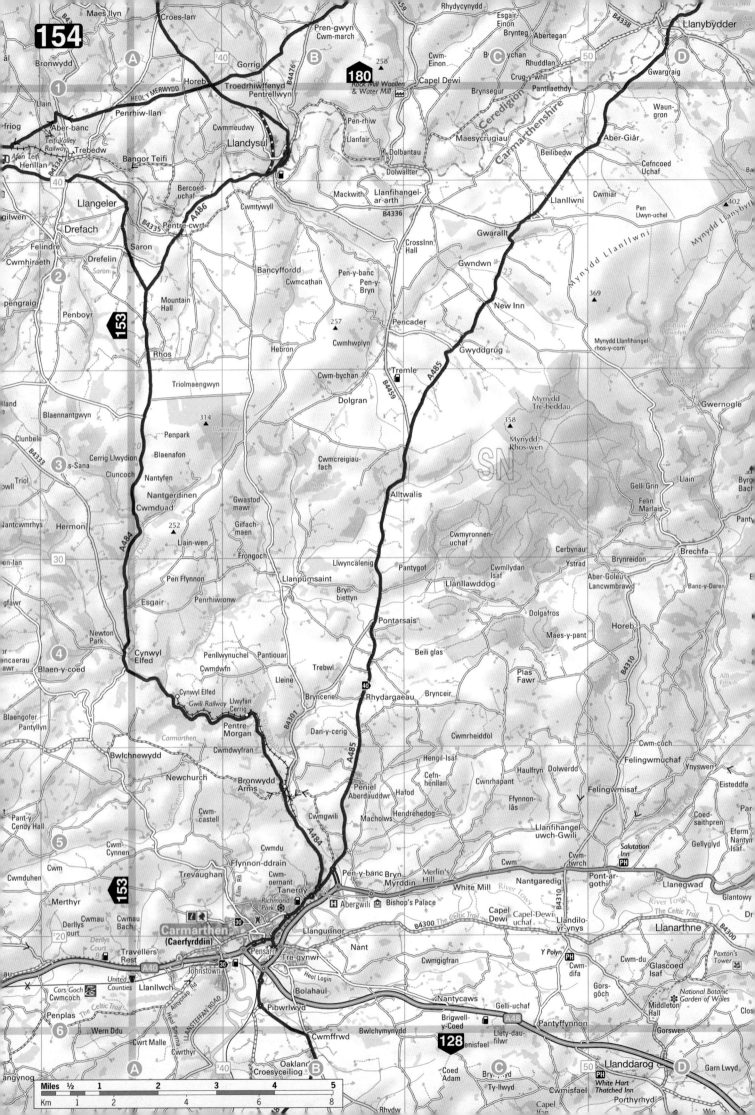

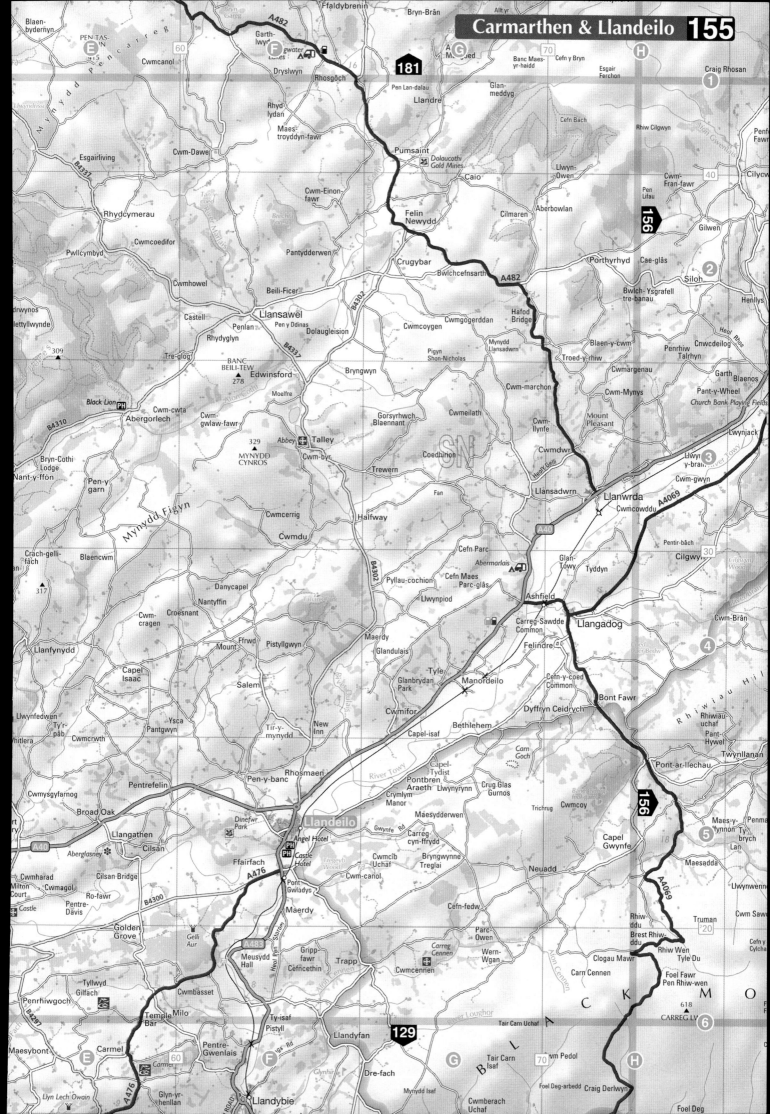

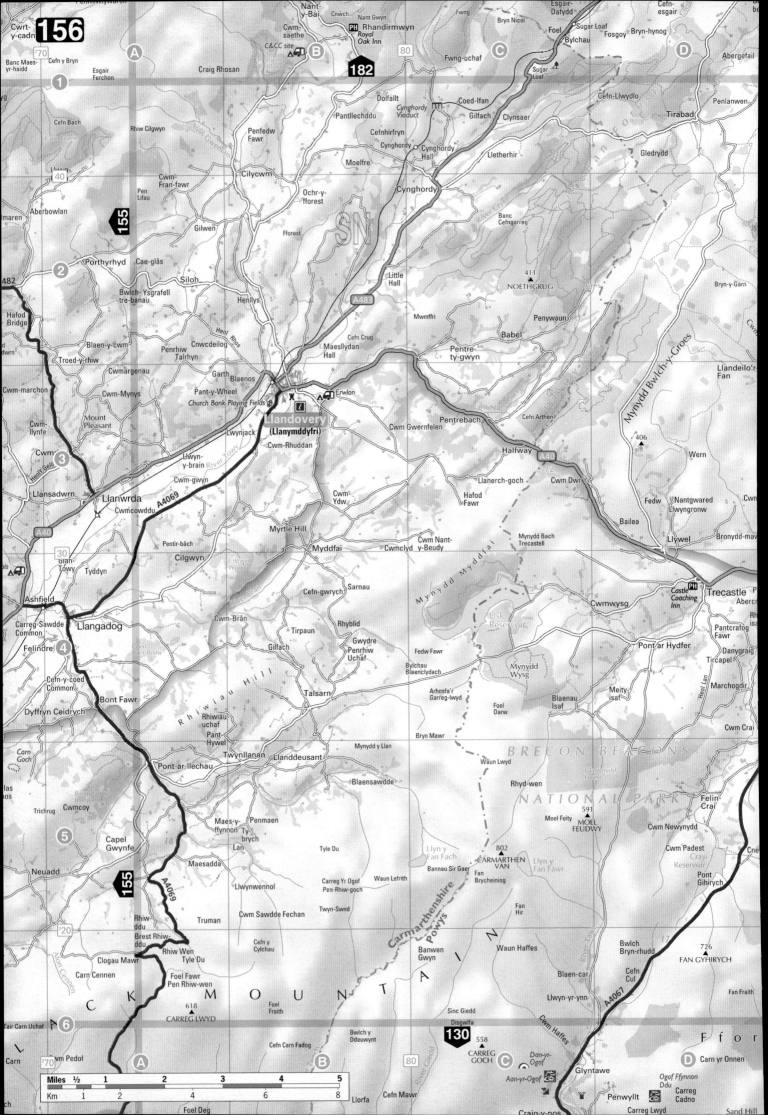

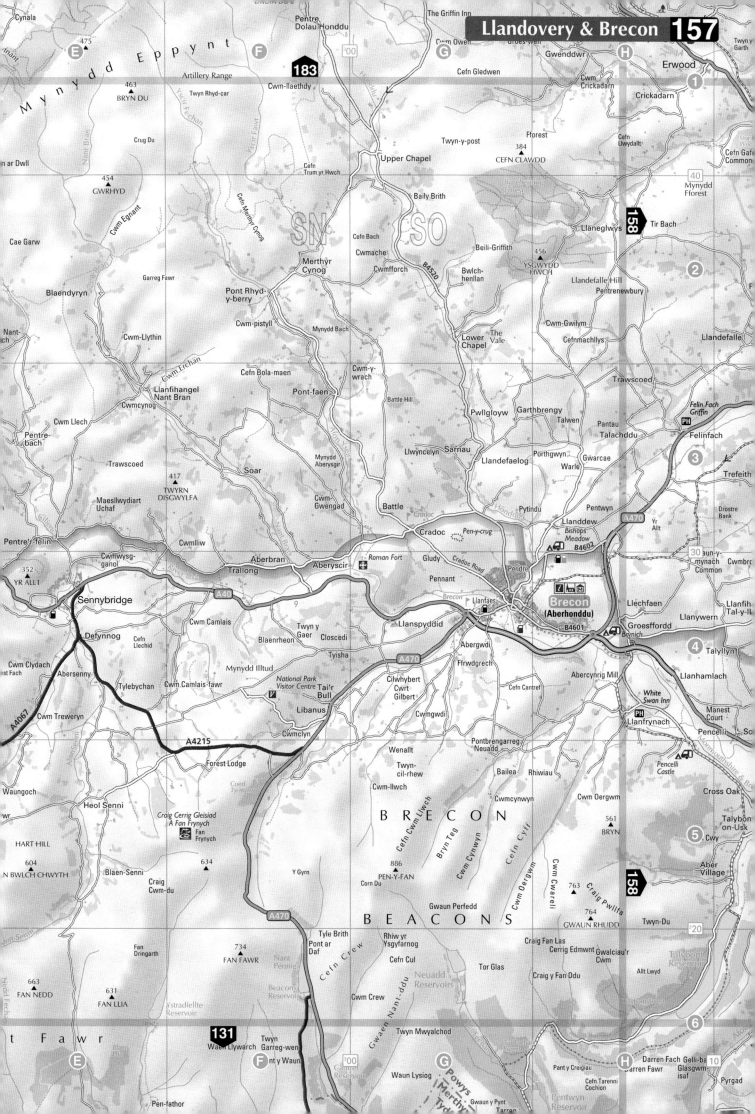

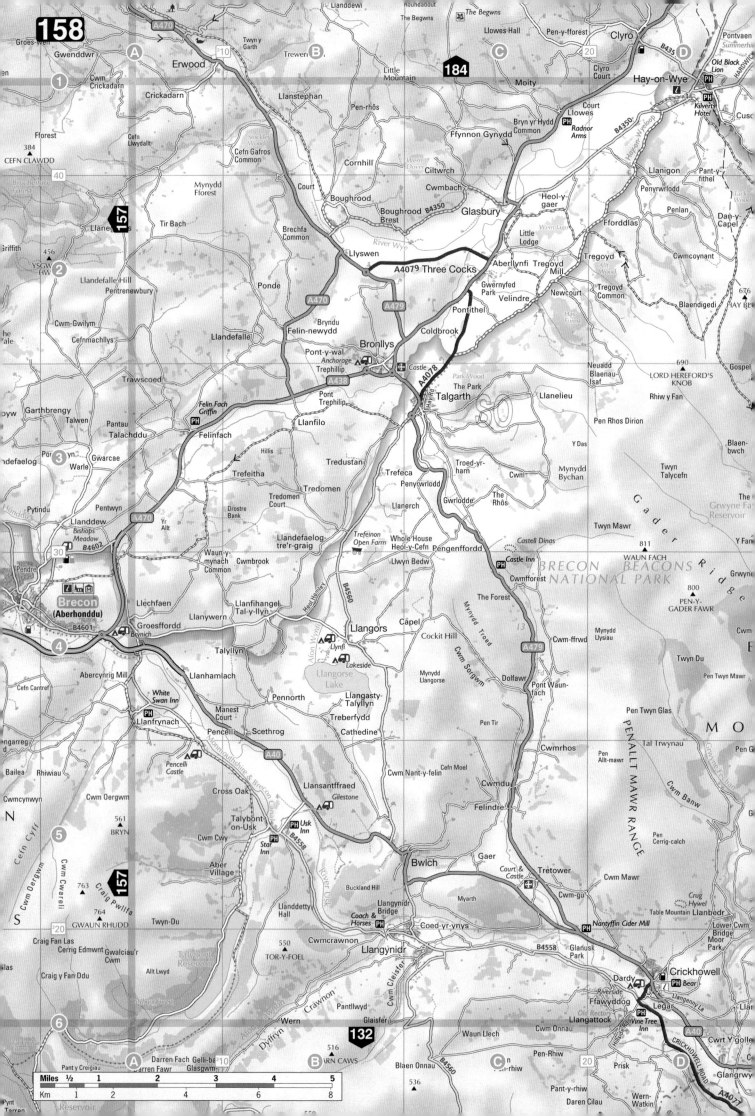

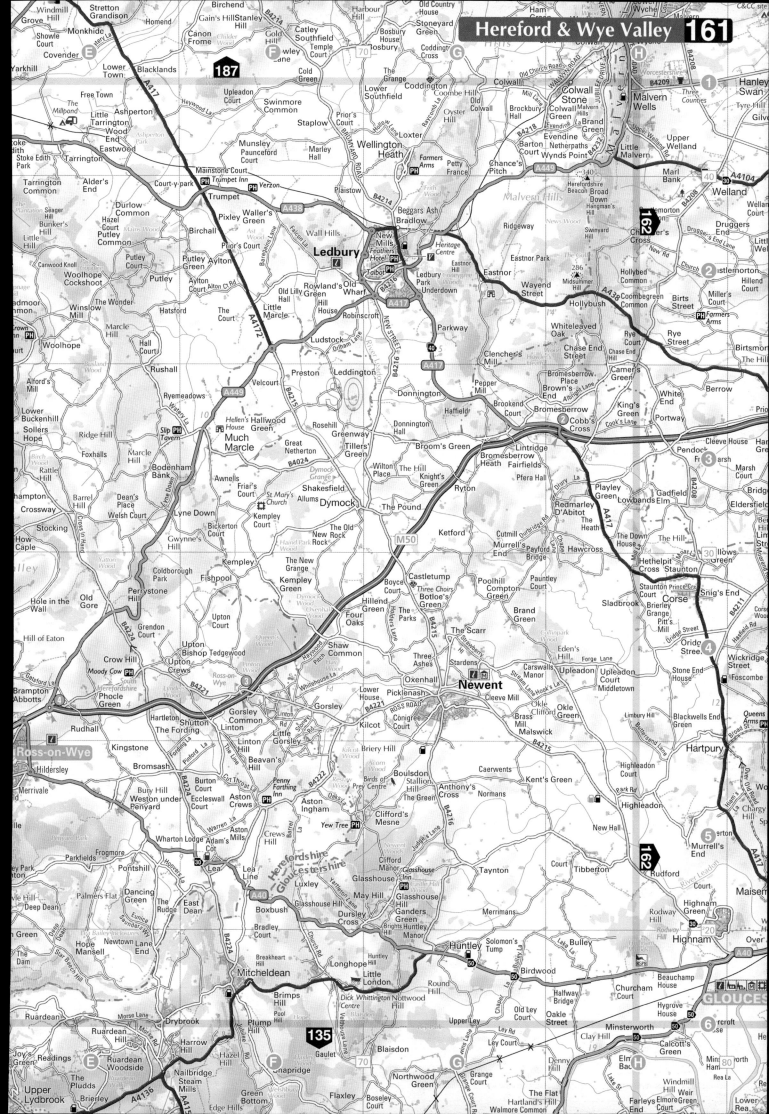

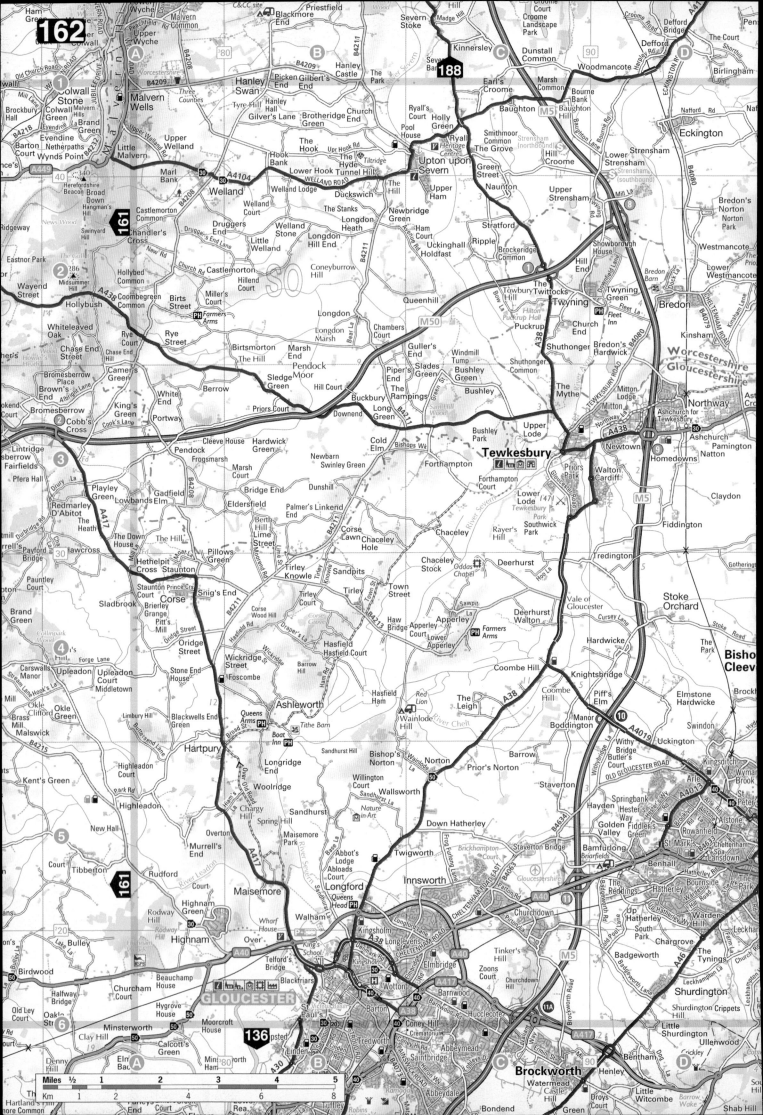

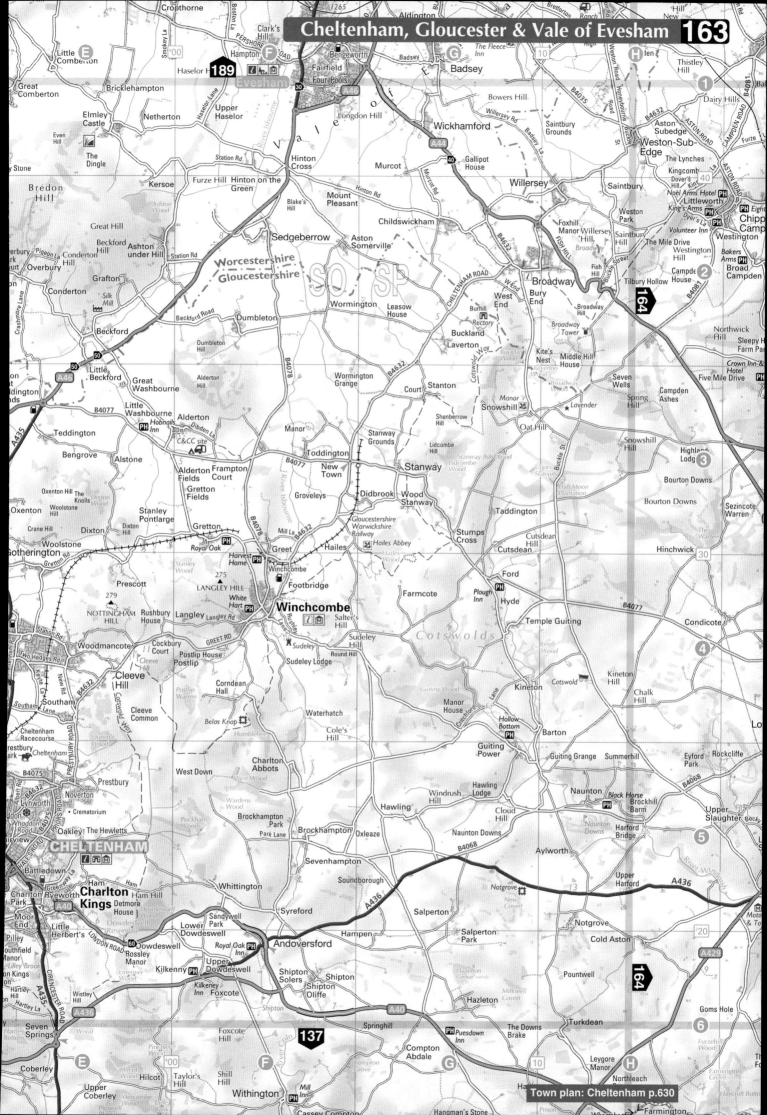

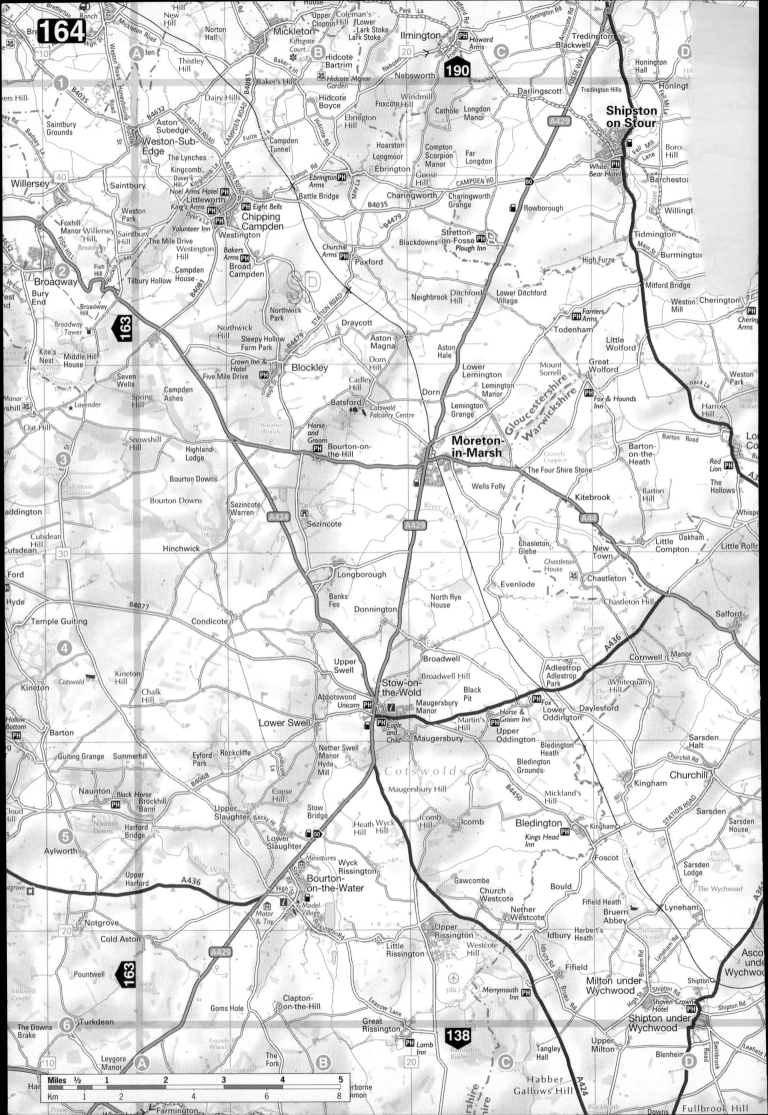

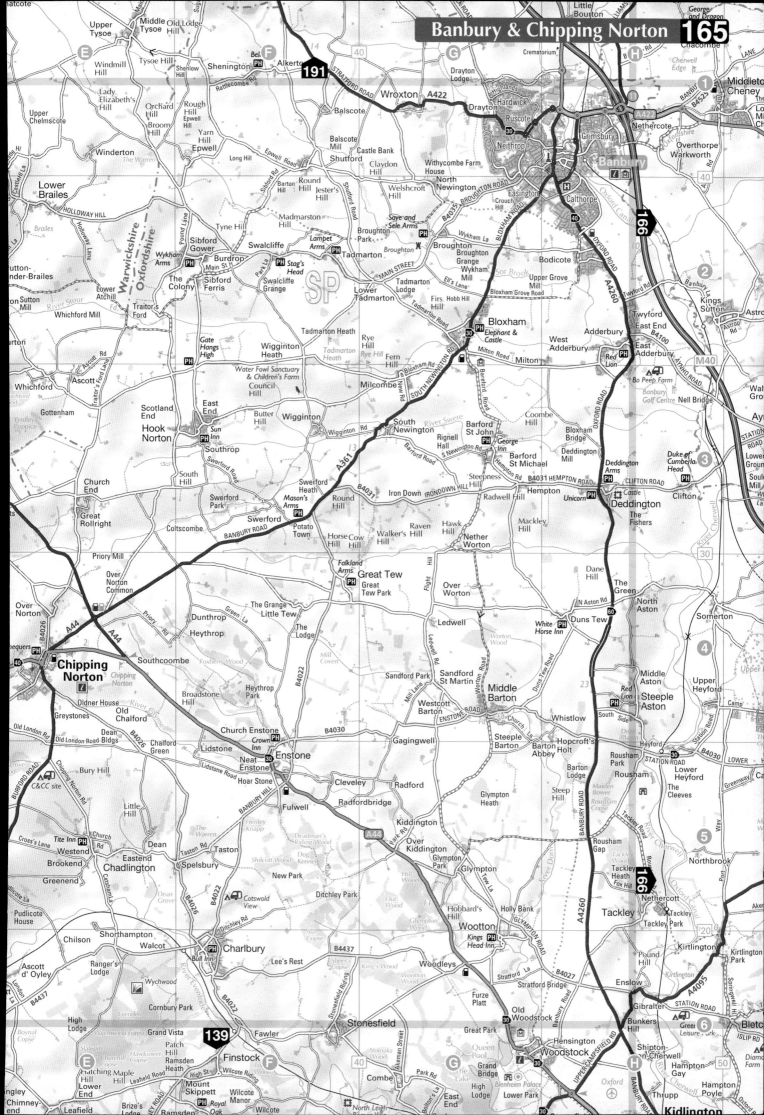

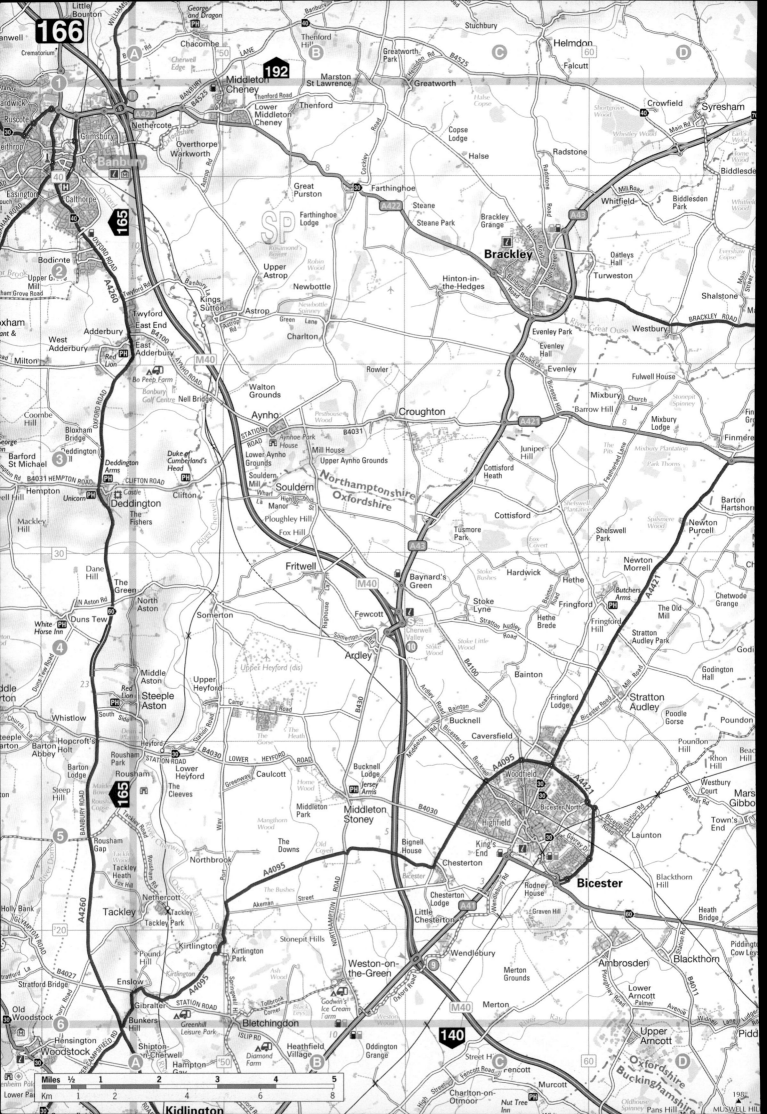

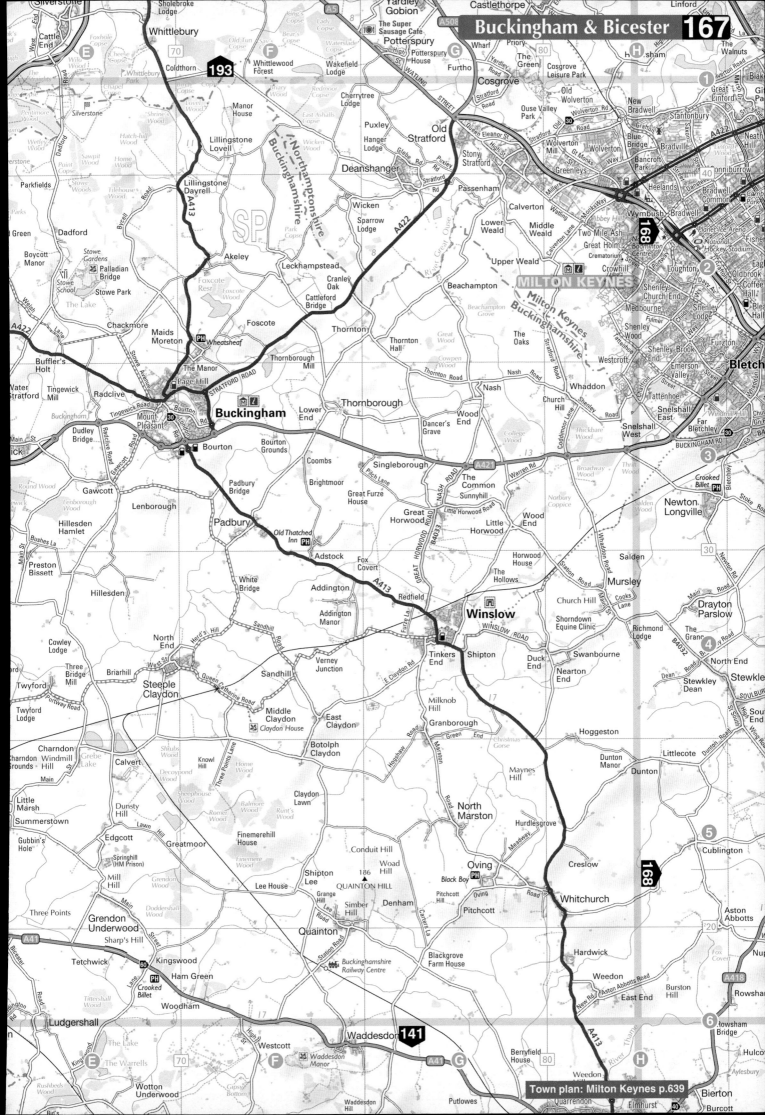

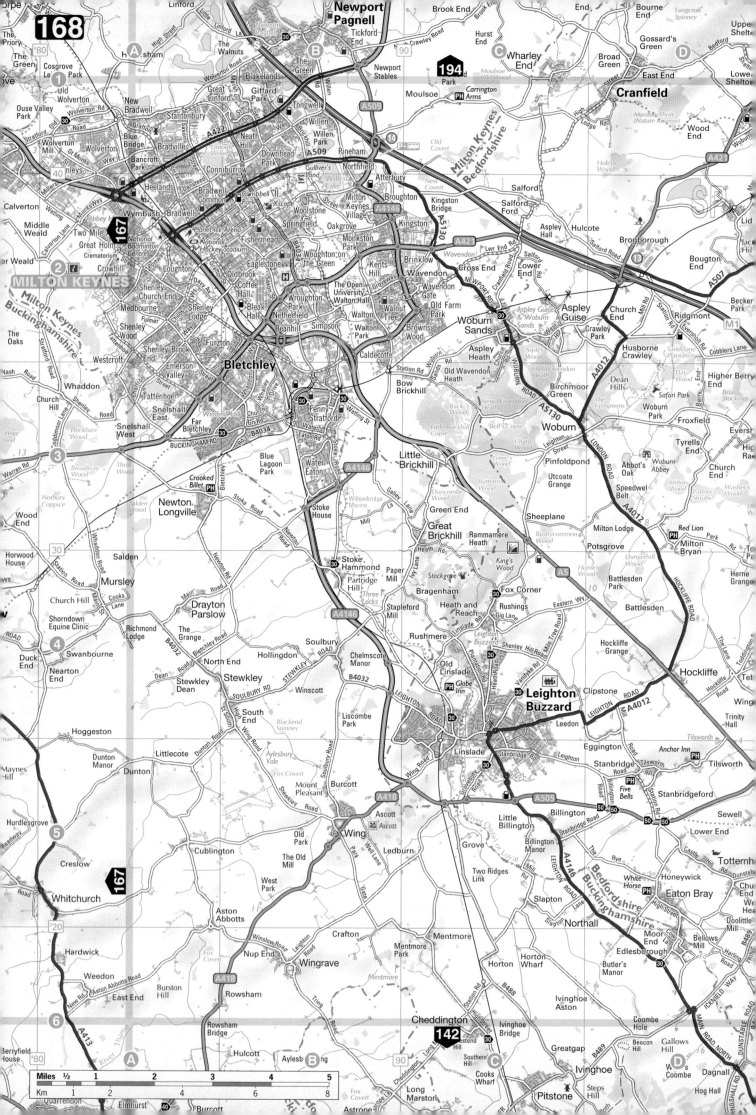

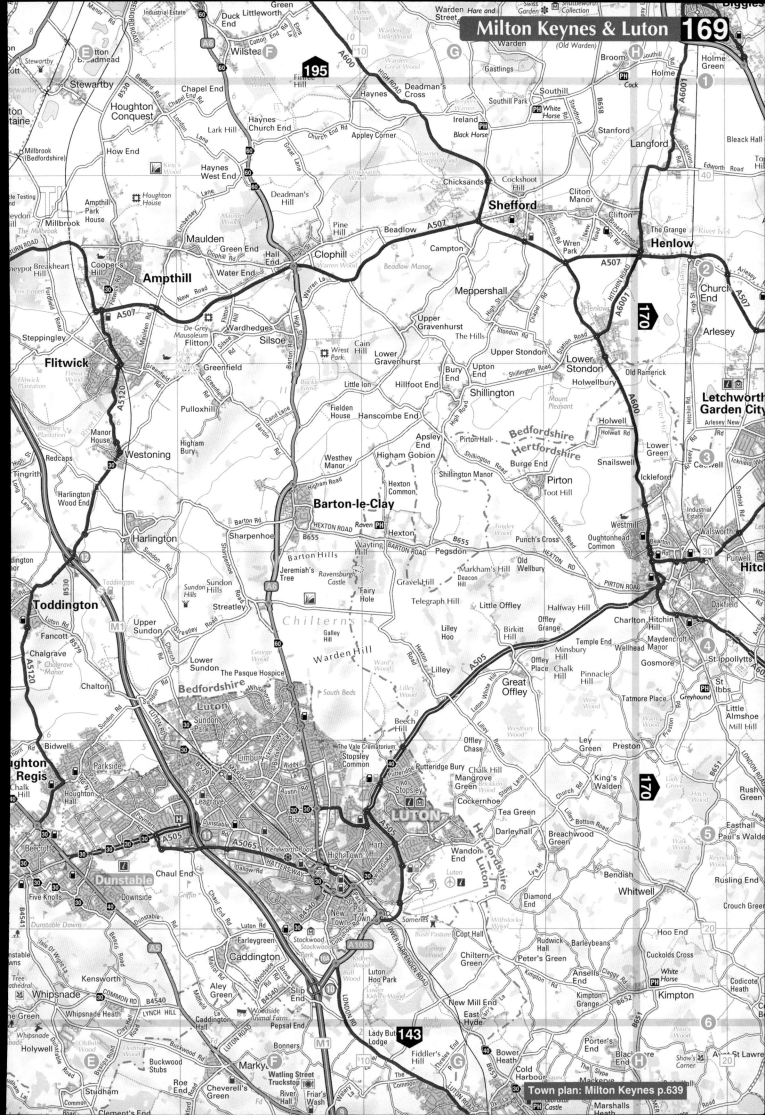

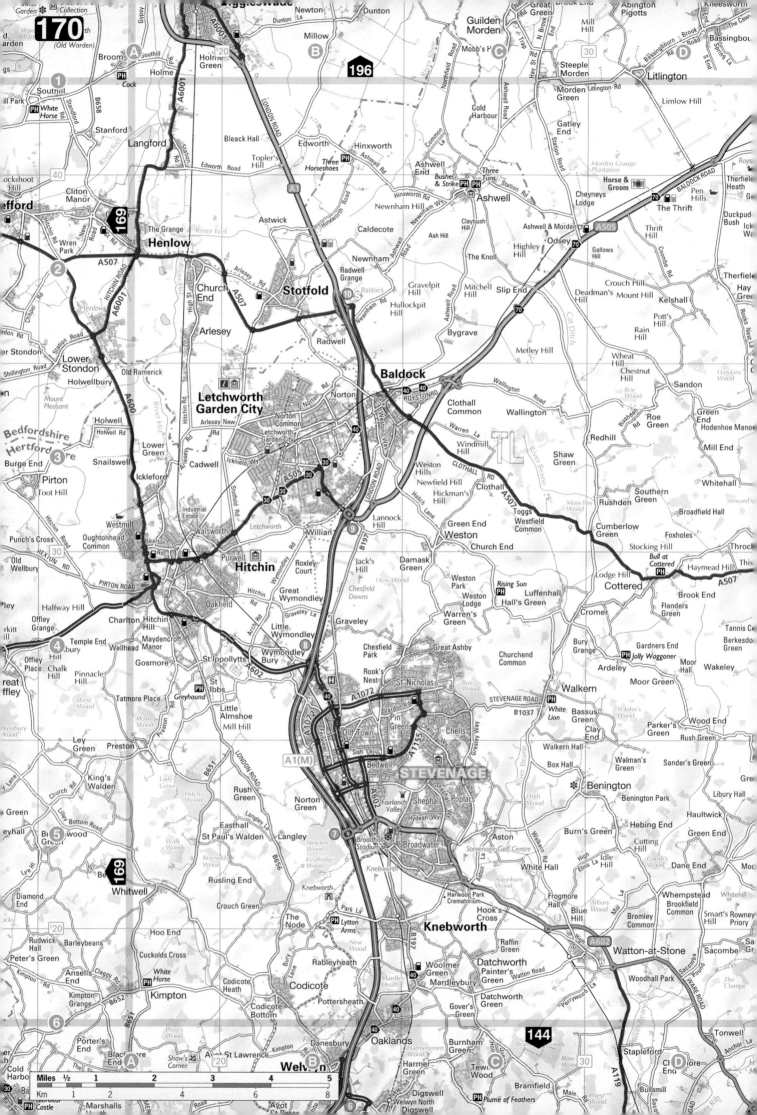

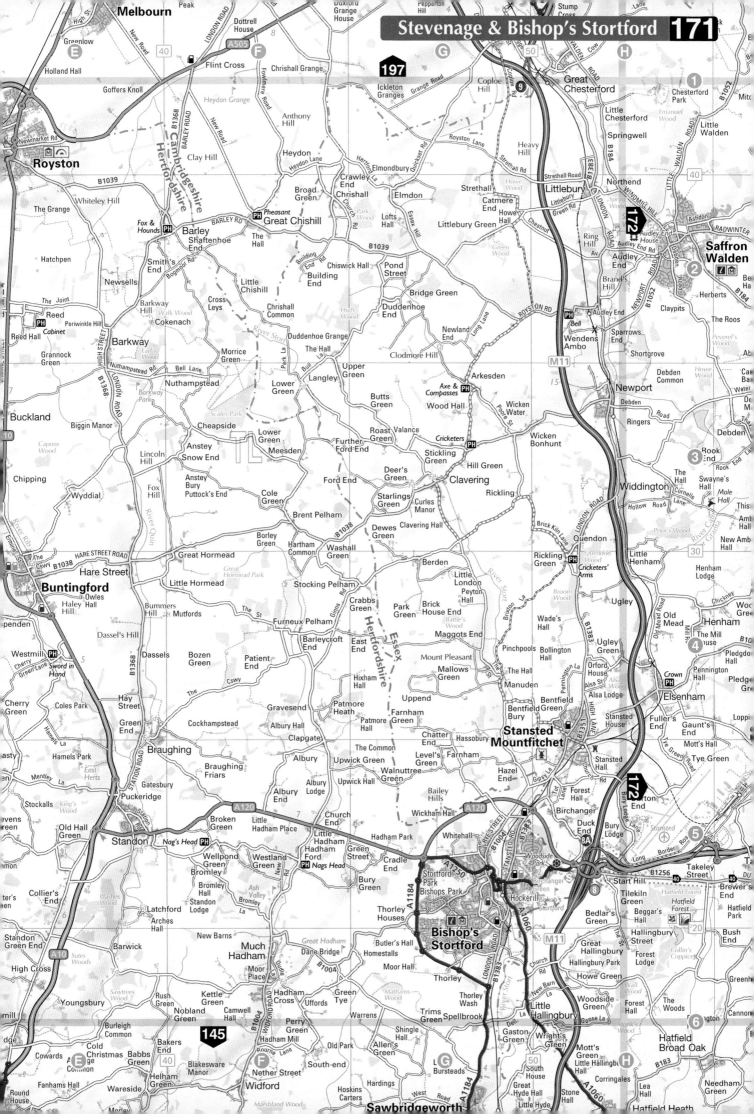

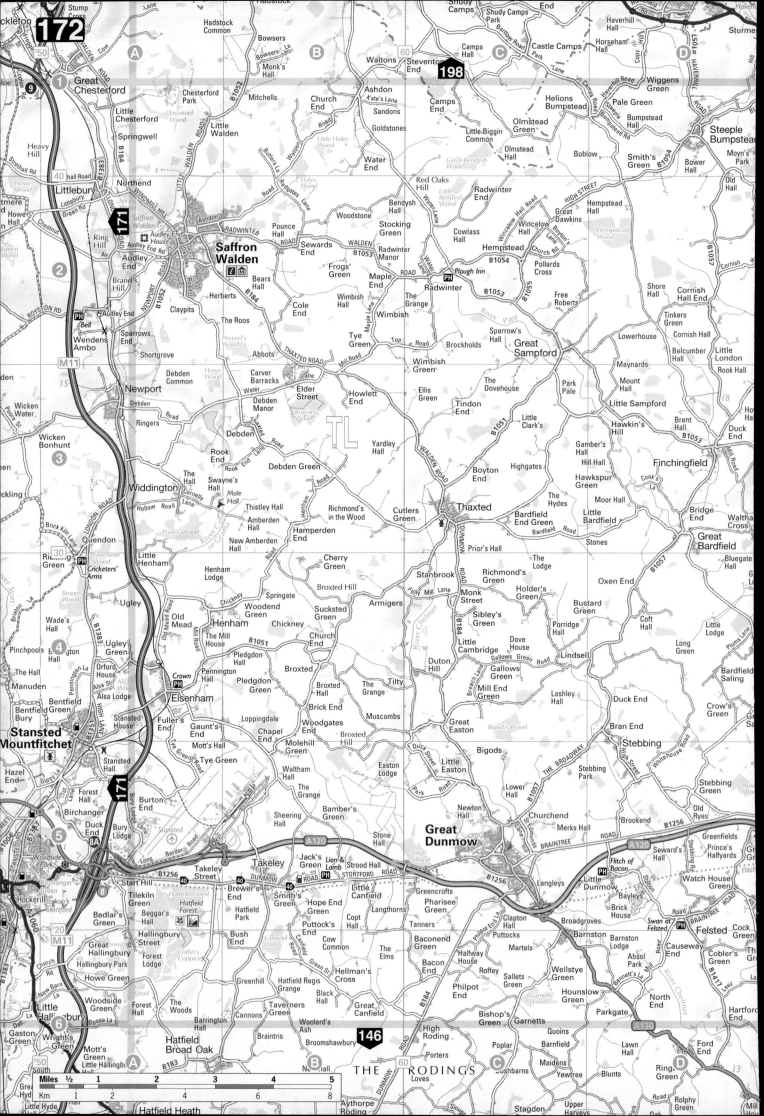

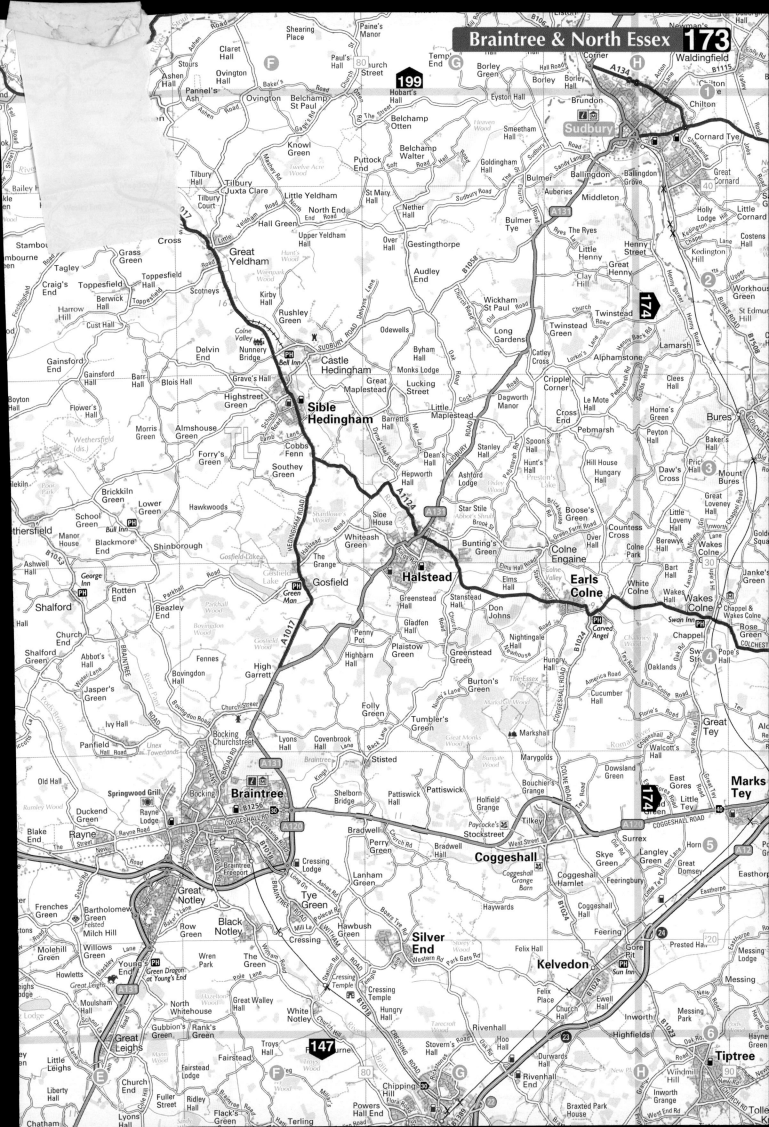

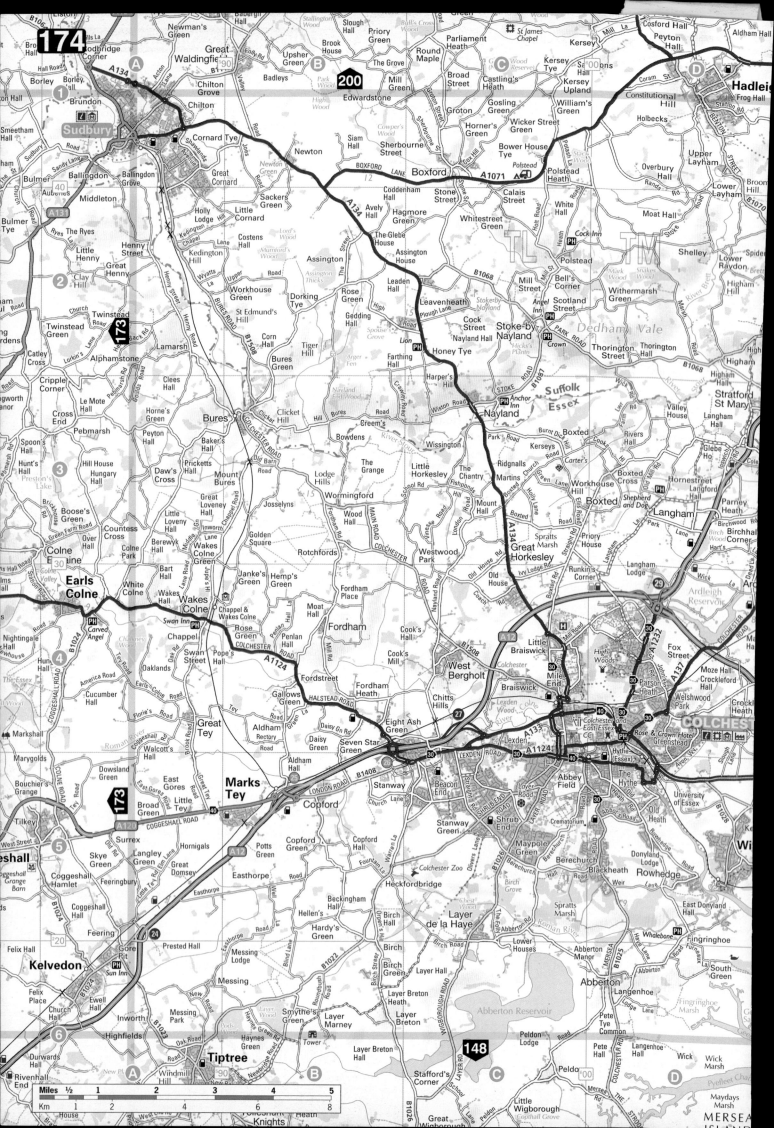

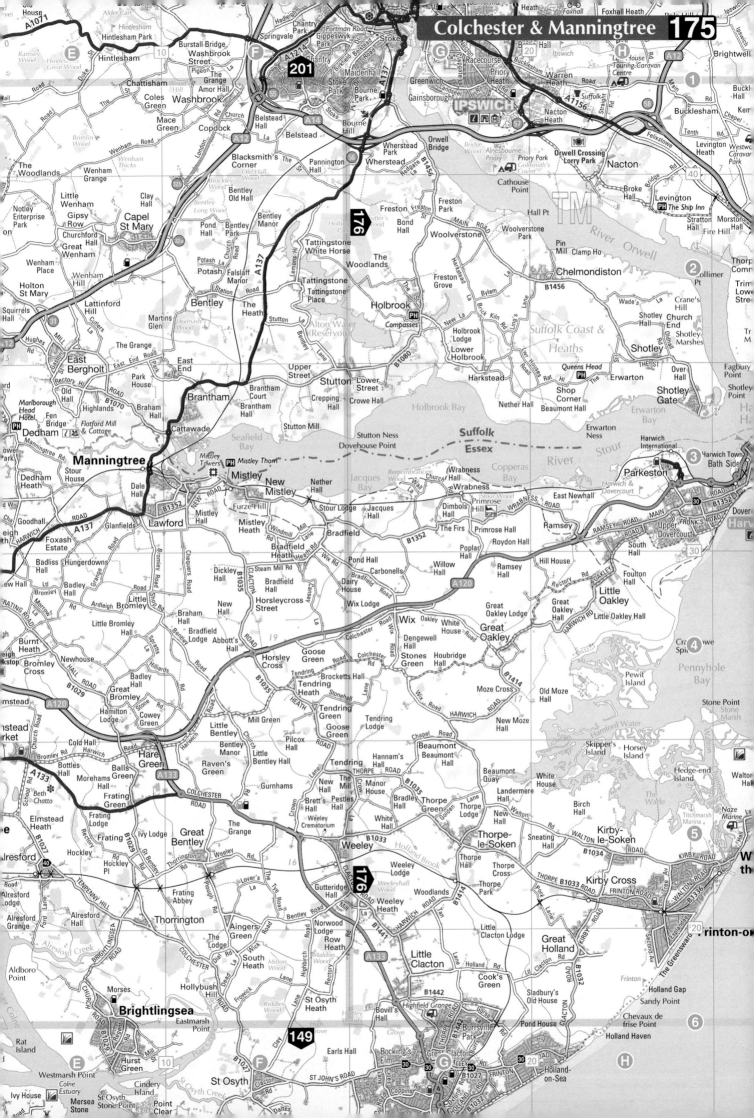

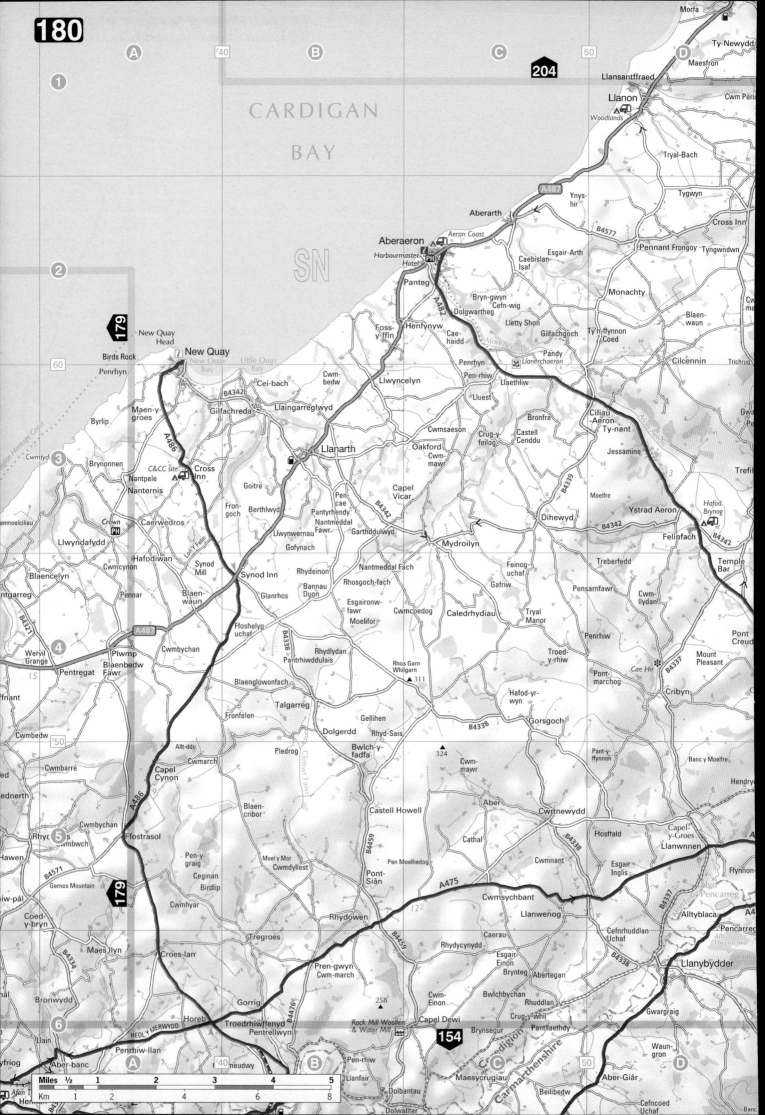

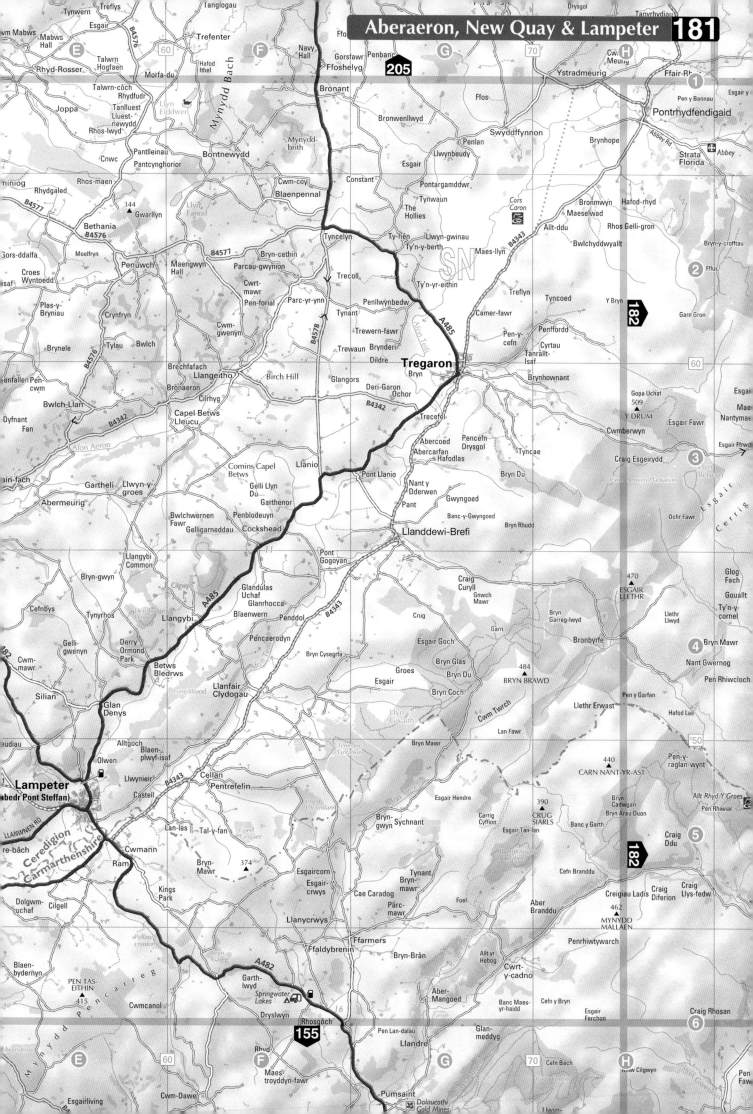

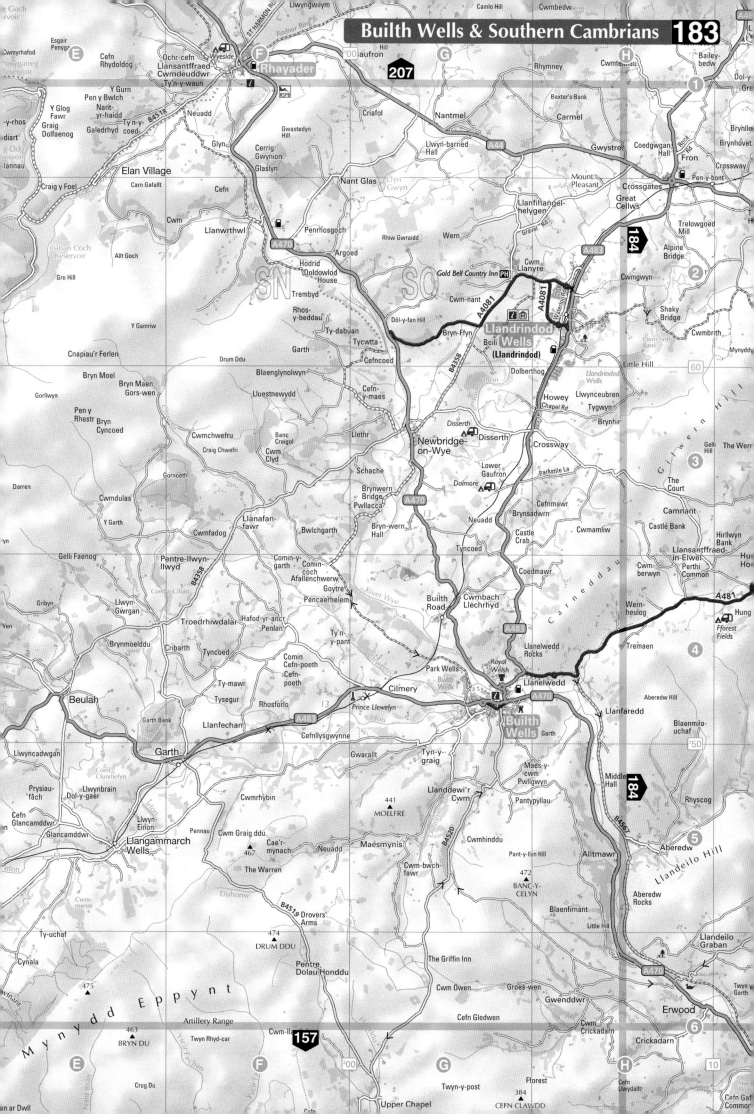

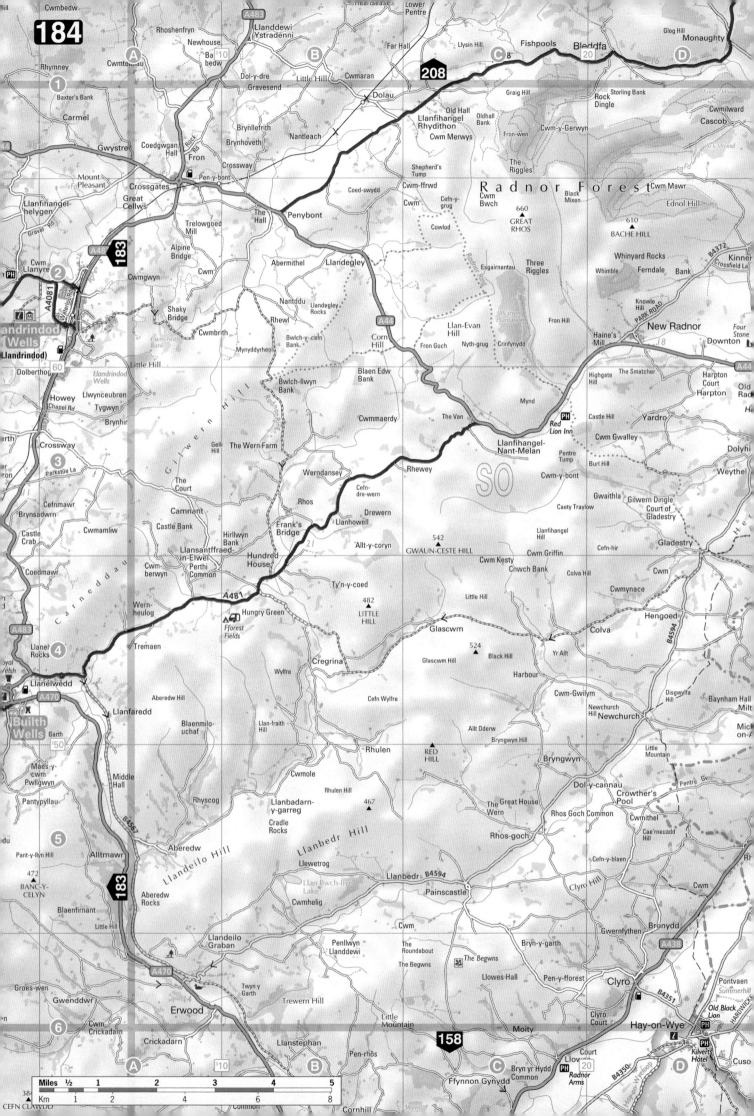

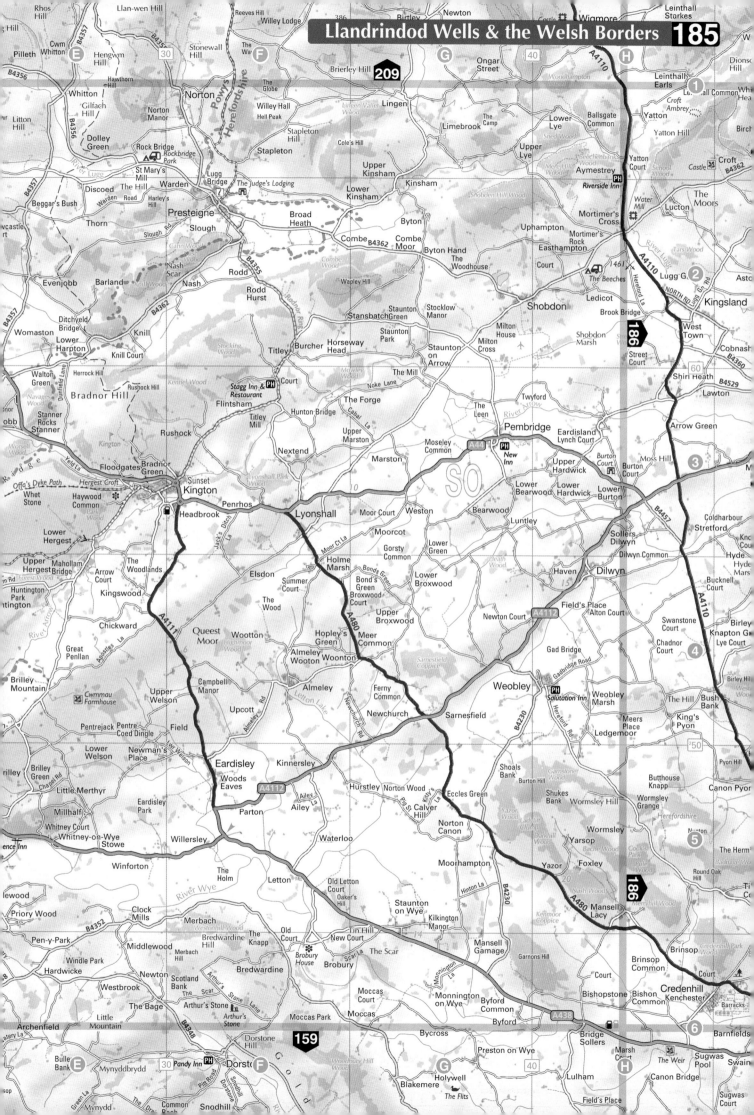

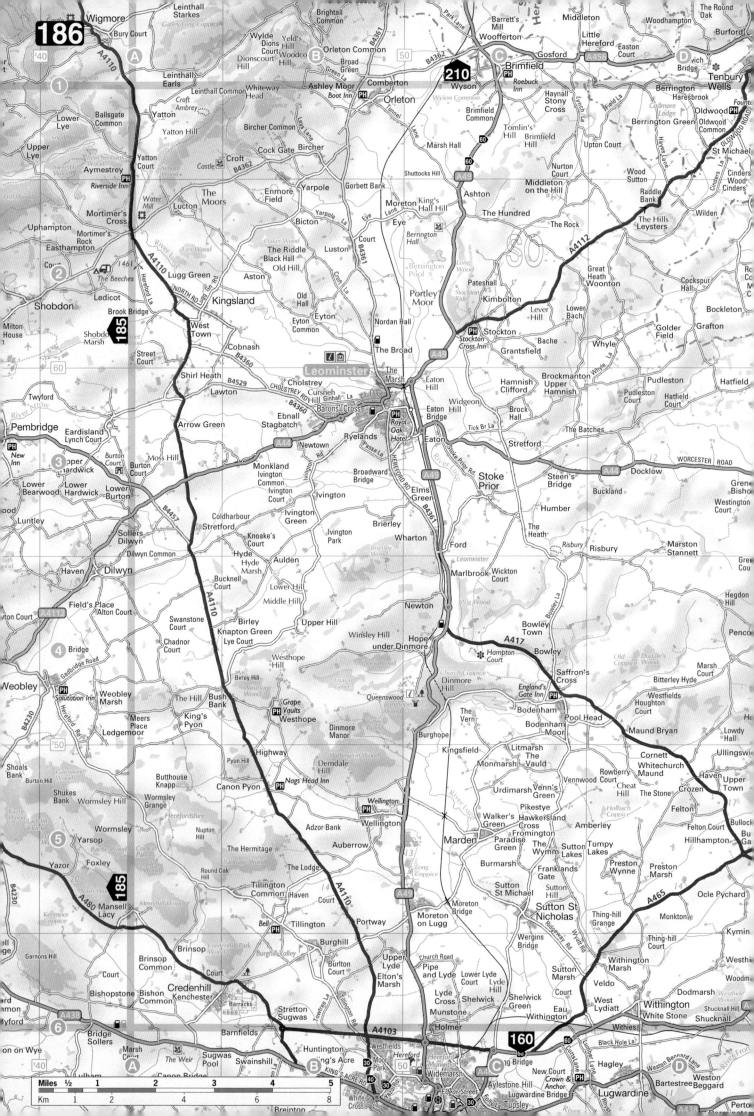

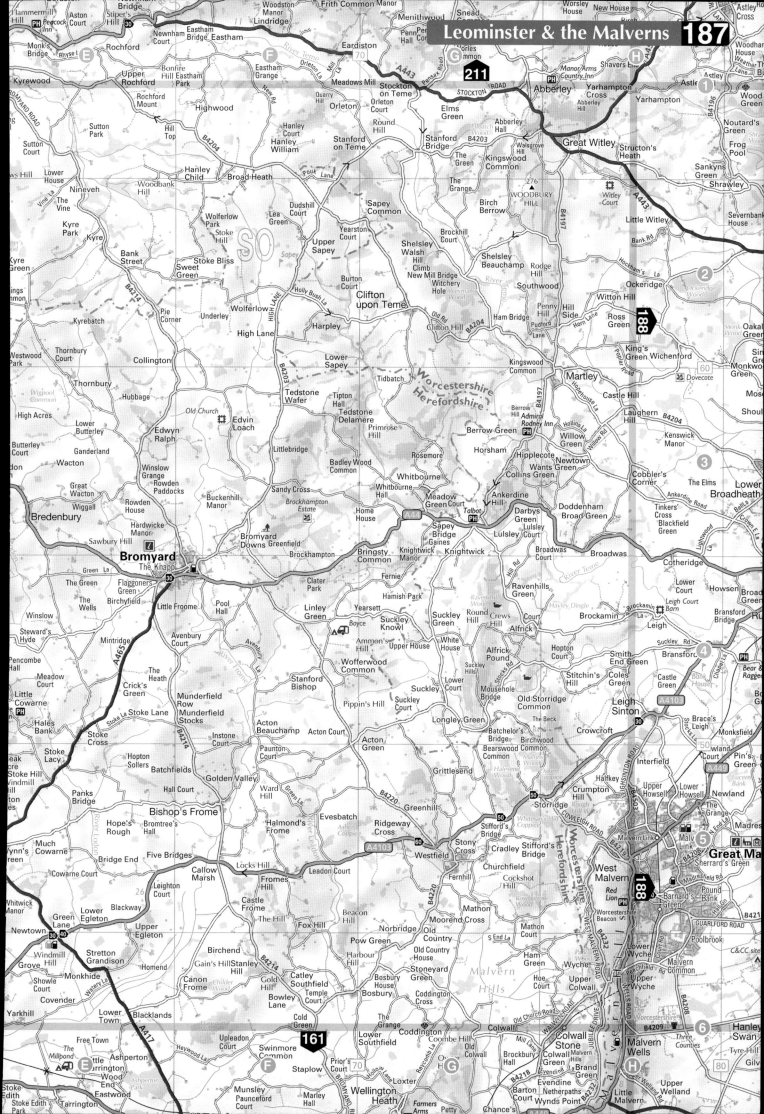

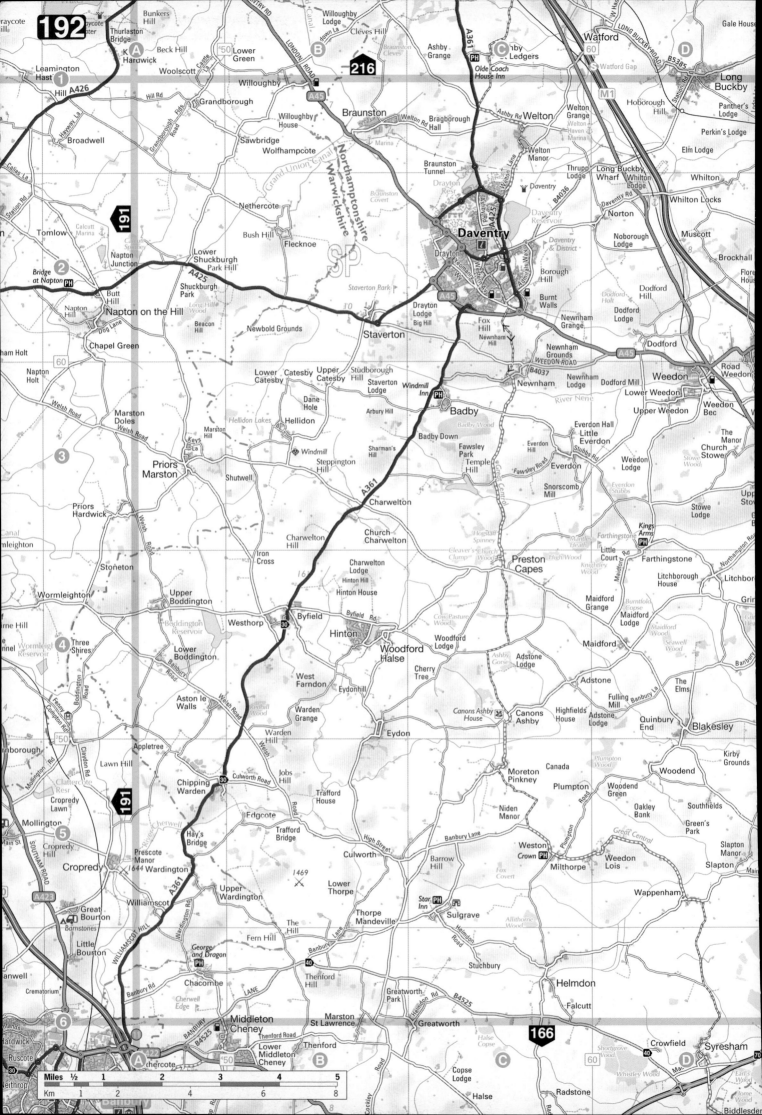

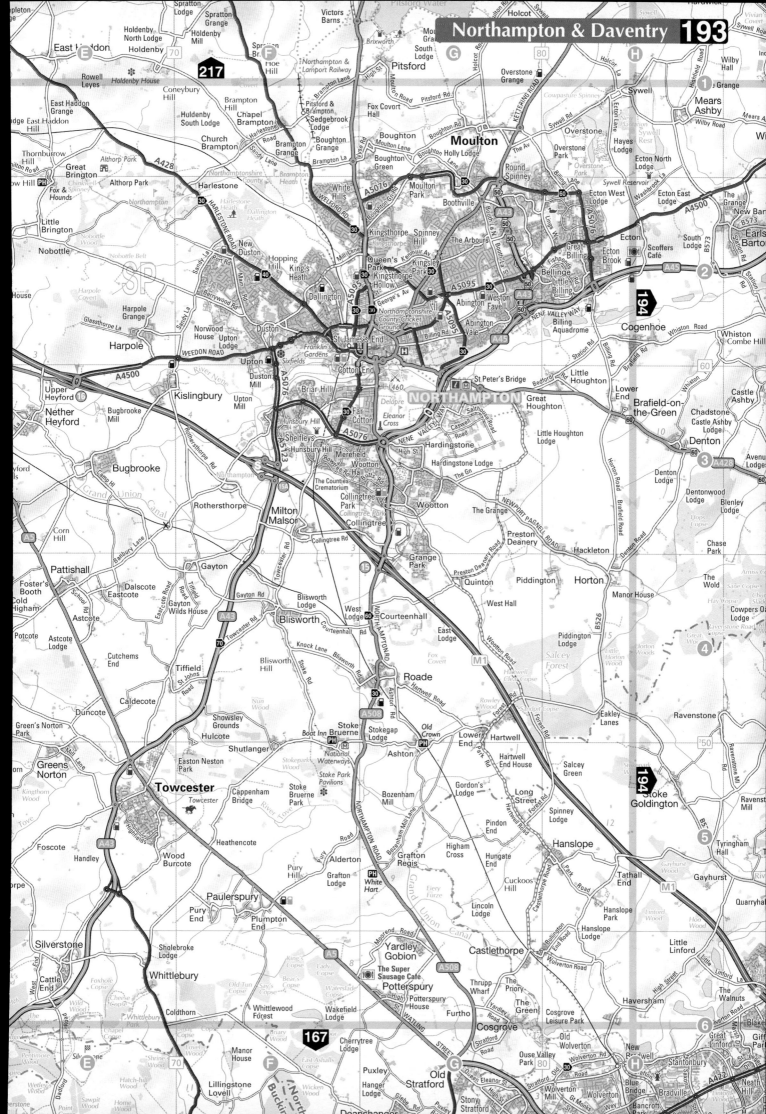

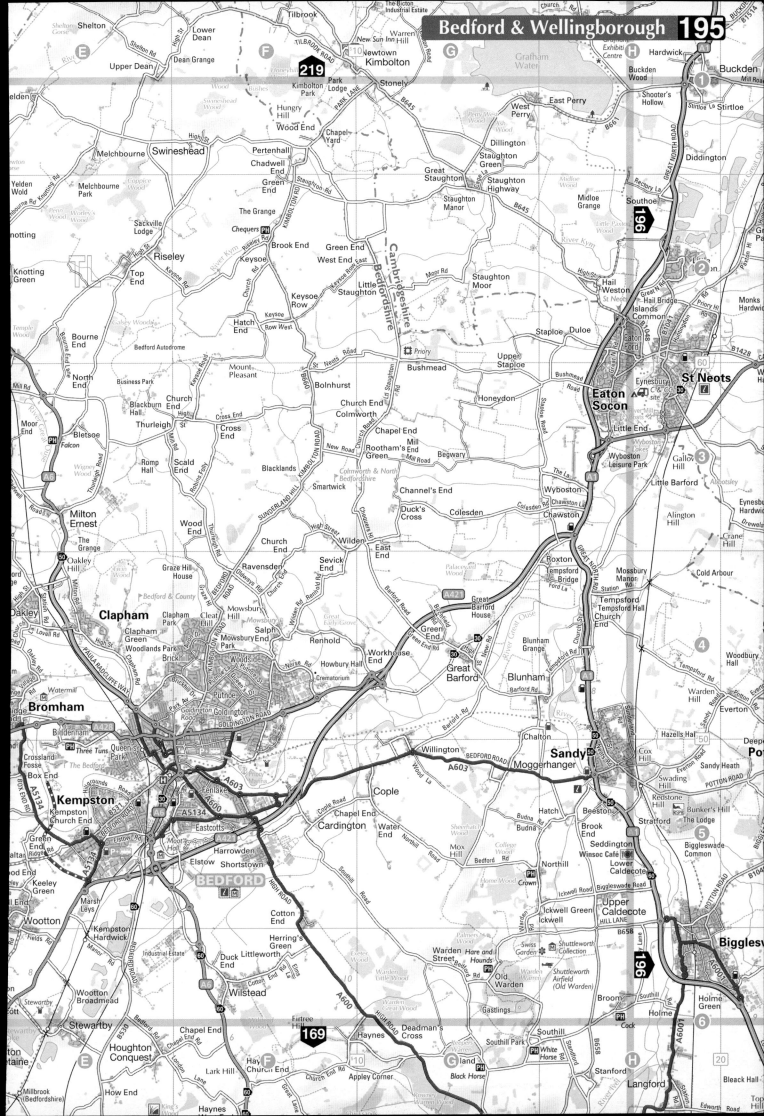

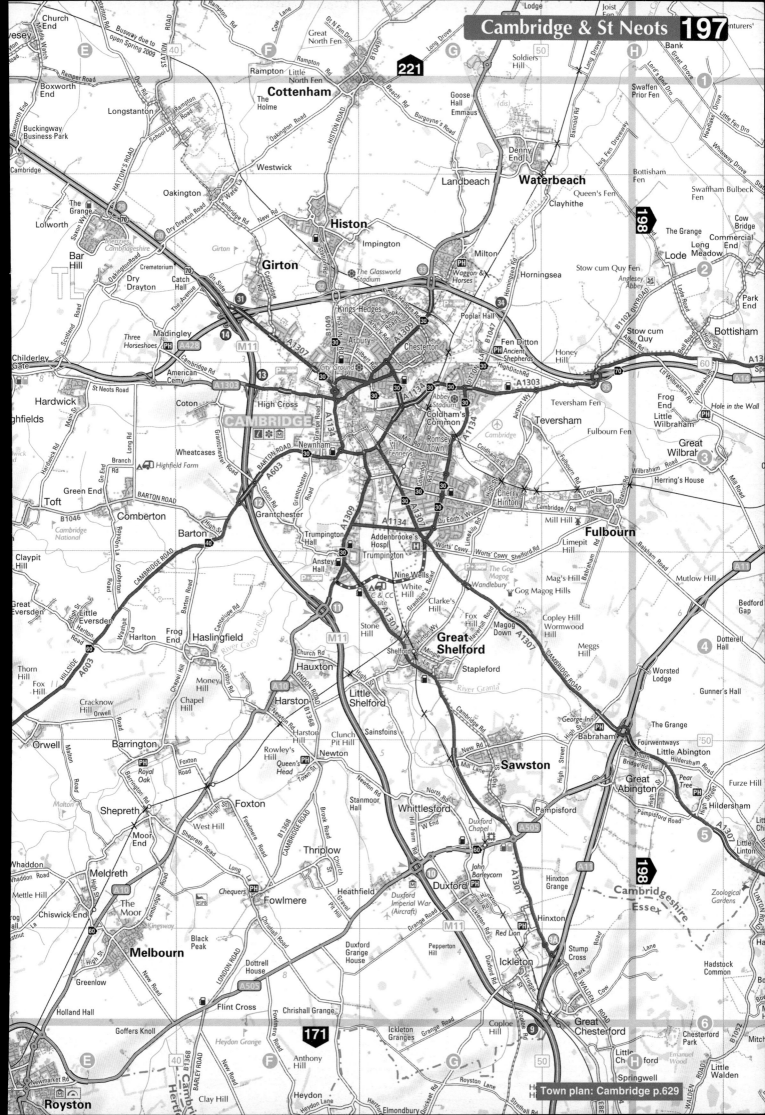

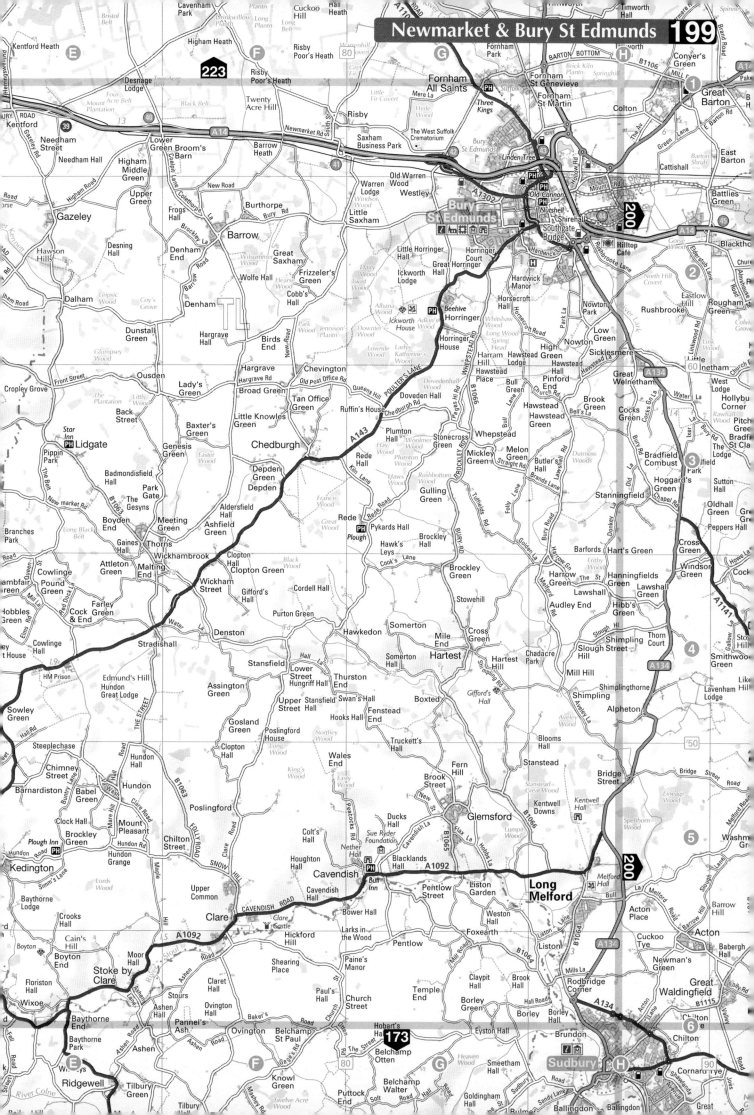

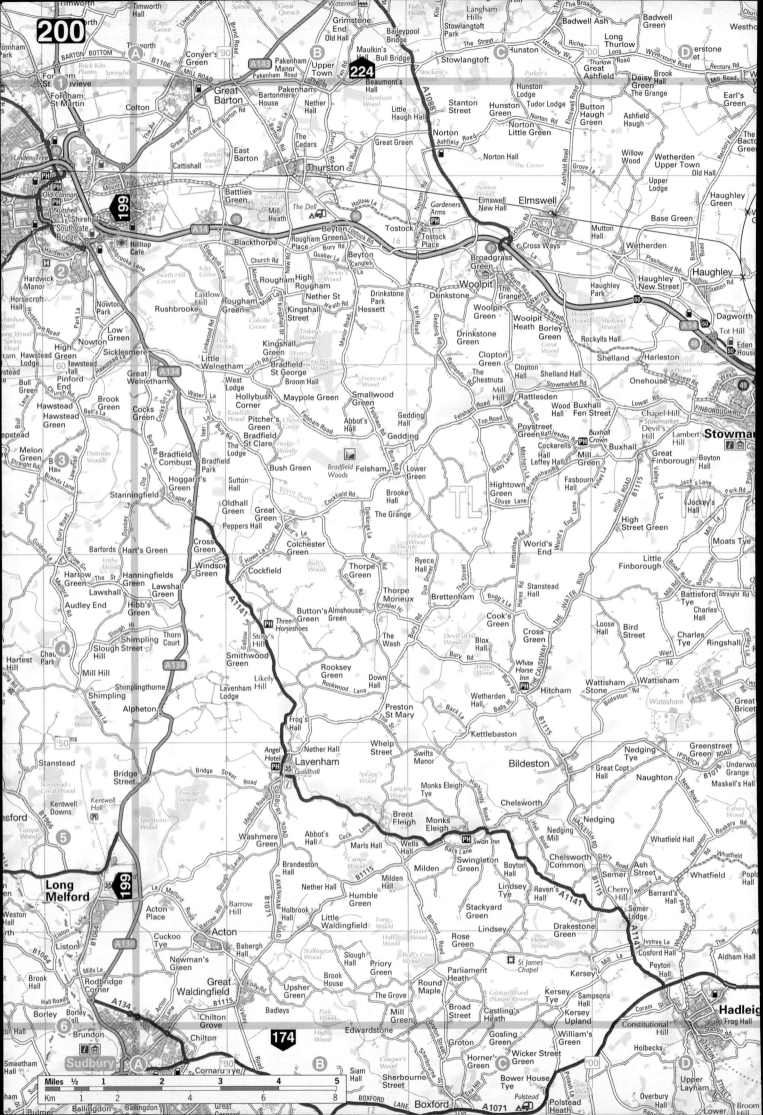

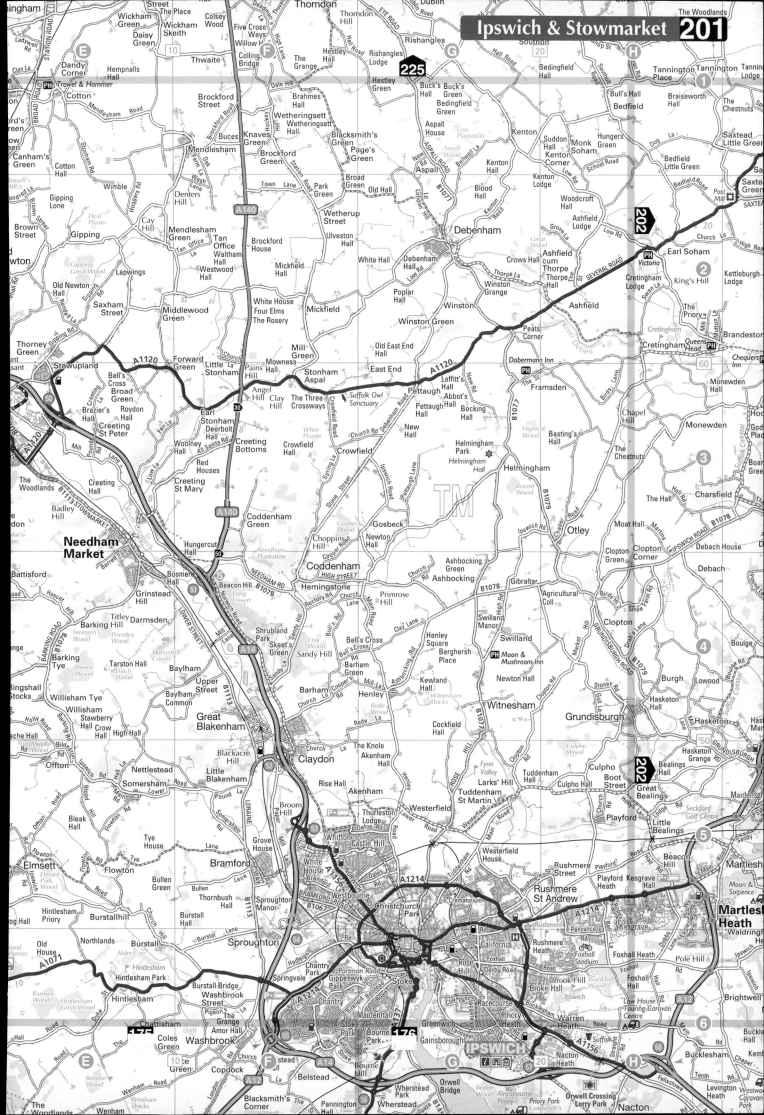

227

E **F** **G** **H**

1

Wesleton Rd
Westleton
The Grange **PH**
Westleton
YoxfordRd
Fenstreet Rd

Mount
Pleasant

Dunwich
Cliffs

OXFORD ROAD
Middle **E**
Moor
Middleton
Lindemoor Rd
Fordley Rd
Mill St
Title Rd
RECKFORD ROAD

Mill Rd

Dunwich
Heath

F Minsmere
Cliffs

Minsmere
Scottshall
Coverts
RSPB
Suffolk Coastal

The Warren

Vault Hill
Scott's
Hall
Coney Hill

LEISTON ROAD
Church Road

Minsmere Level

Eastbridge

The Sluice

Minsmere
Haven

2

60

Pretty Road
Onnen's
La
Theberton
B1122
Theberton
Woods
Moat Rd

The Grove

Ash
Wood

East Green
Harrow Lane

Goose
Hill

Clay Hills
Cakes
& Ale

Leiston
Abbey

Kenton
Hills

Knodishall Green
Buckle's
Wood
ABBEY ROAD

Lover's Lane
Valley Rd

Leiston
Common

SAXMUNDHAM ROAD

Grove
Wood

Power
Station

M

Leiston

Sizewell

Knodishall

Coldfair
Green

Ness House

721
Grove Rd
School Rd

Aldringham
B1353

Thorpe Ness

3

Knodishall
Common
Bull's
Hall
Parrot and
Punchbowl **PH**
Billeaford
Hall
ALDEBURGH ROAD

Thorpeness

Dolphin
Inn **PH**
Thorpeness

B1069
SNAPE ROAD

Great
Wood

The Meare

A 1094 ALDEBURGH ROAD
7

Hazlewood
Hall
LEISTON ROAD
B122
North
Warren **RSPB**

The Haven

Decoy
Wood

Hazelwood
Common

South Warren
Red
House
Aldeburgh

Black Heath Wood

Snape
Warren
Black Heath
Cliff
Plantation

Ham
Creek

Round
Hill

SAXMUNDHAM ROAD

Thorpe Rd

Mill
Inn

PH
Aldeburgh
i

Long Reach

Barber's
Point

Fort Green

Reach
Iken
Marshes

Yarn
Hill
Redlands
Covert

Aldeburgh
Marshes

ALDEBURGH
BAY

Iken
Sandy
La

High Street
Cowton

Slaughden

Fazeboons
Sudbourne
Great
Wood
Captain's
Wood
Lambert's La

Suffolk Coastal
Ferry Road

School Road
The Firs

Sudbourne Marshes

Sudbourne
Beach

4

Sudbourne
Birches
B1084

Snape Road
Hospital Rd

Town
Marshes
Raydon Hall

Lantern
Marshes

Radio
Station

River Alde

250

King's
Head **PH**

Orford
Kings
Marshes

Castle
PH
Jolly
Sailor Inn

ORFORD
NESS

Gedgrave
Marshes

5

Gedgrave
Marshes
Orfordness-
Havergate
Havergate Island
RSPB

Beach

Point

BAY

6

177

E **F** **50** **G** **H**

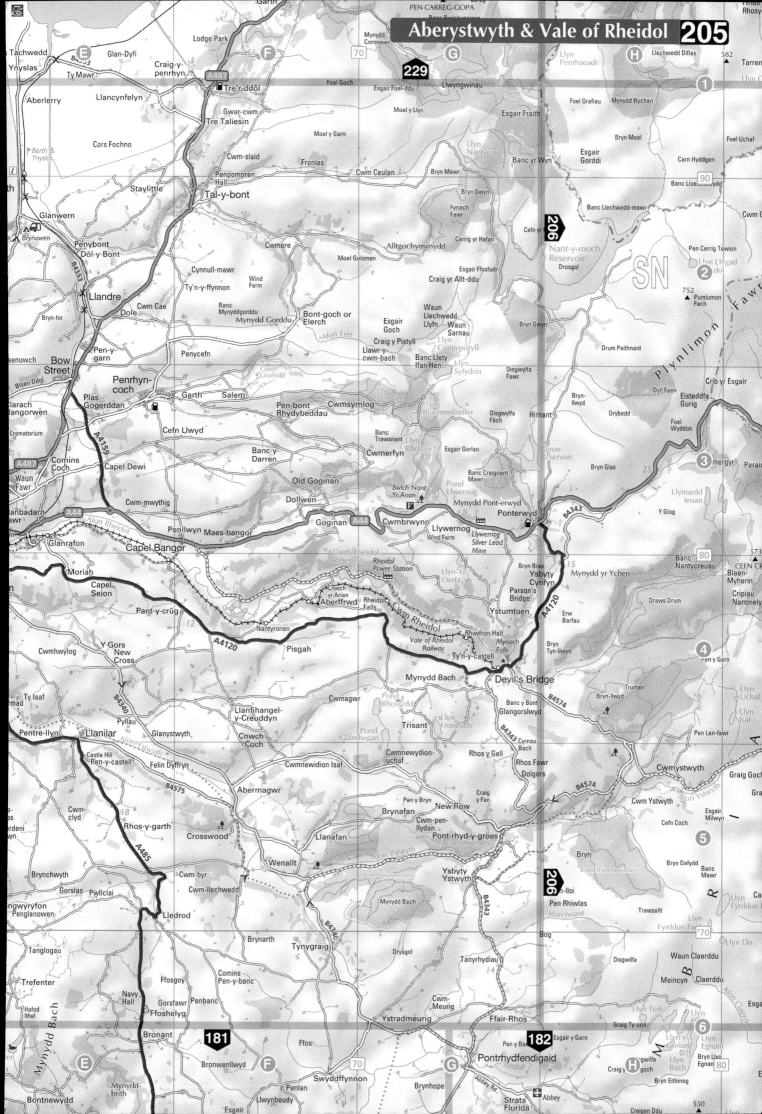

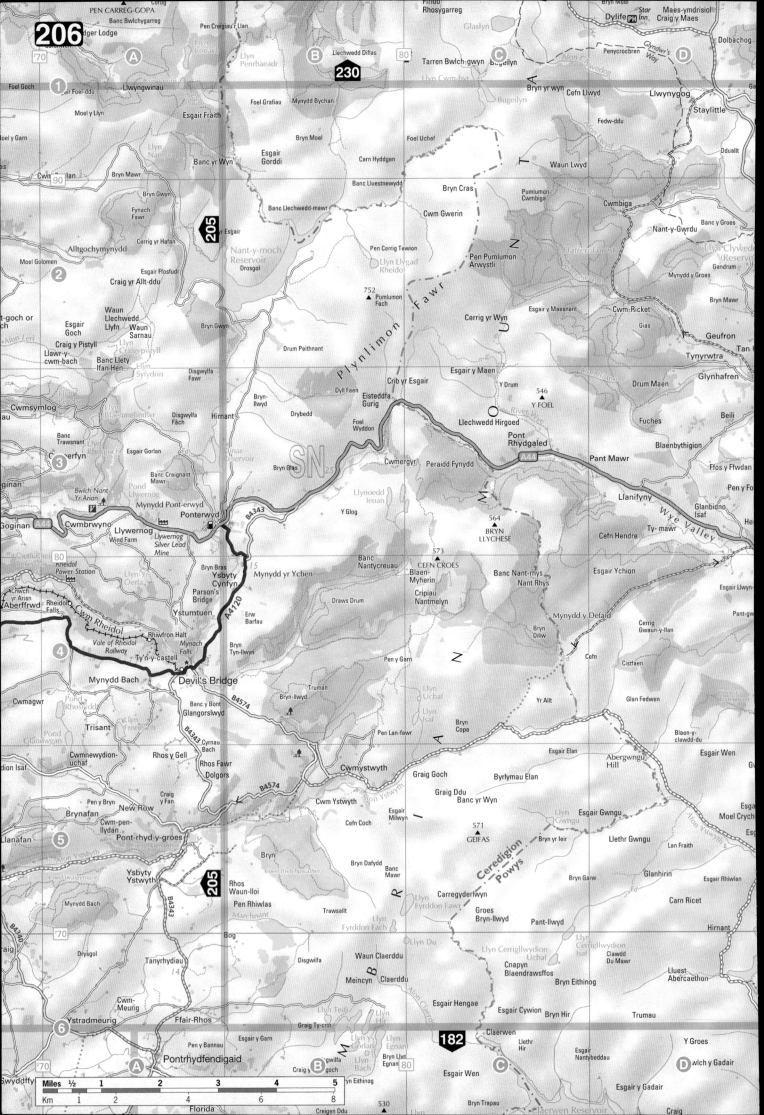

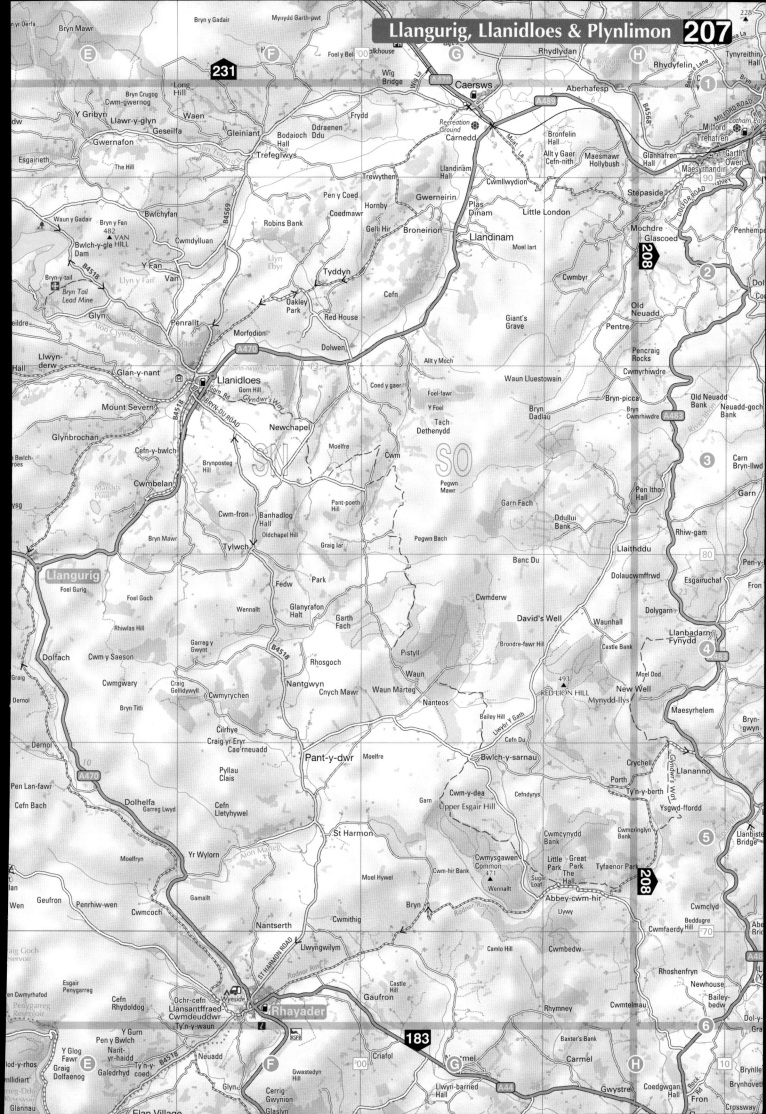

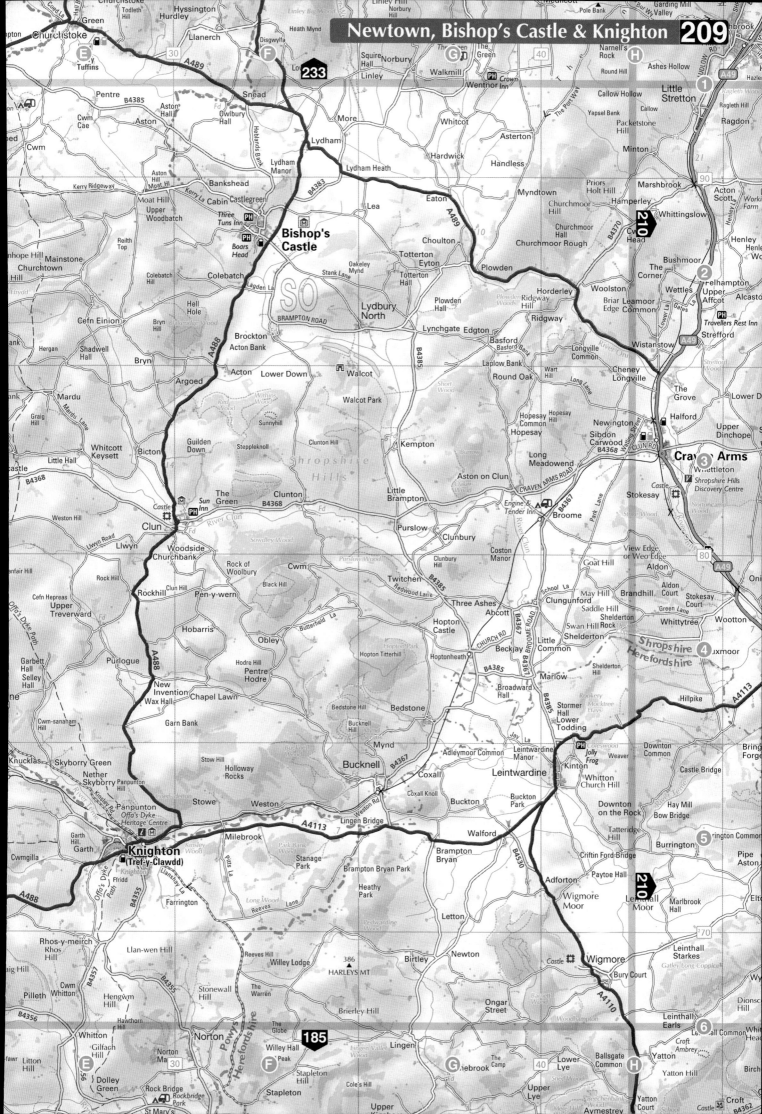

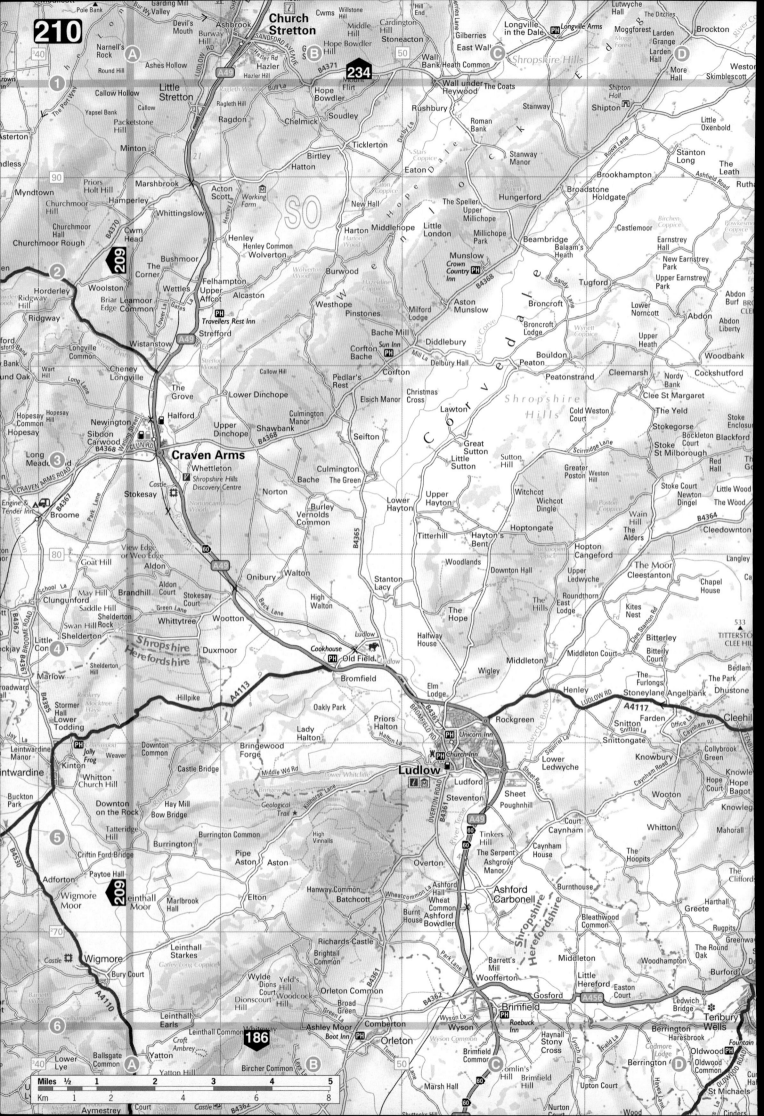

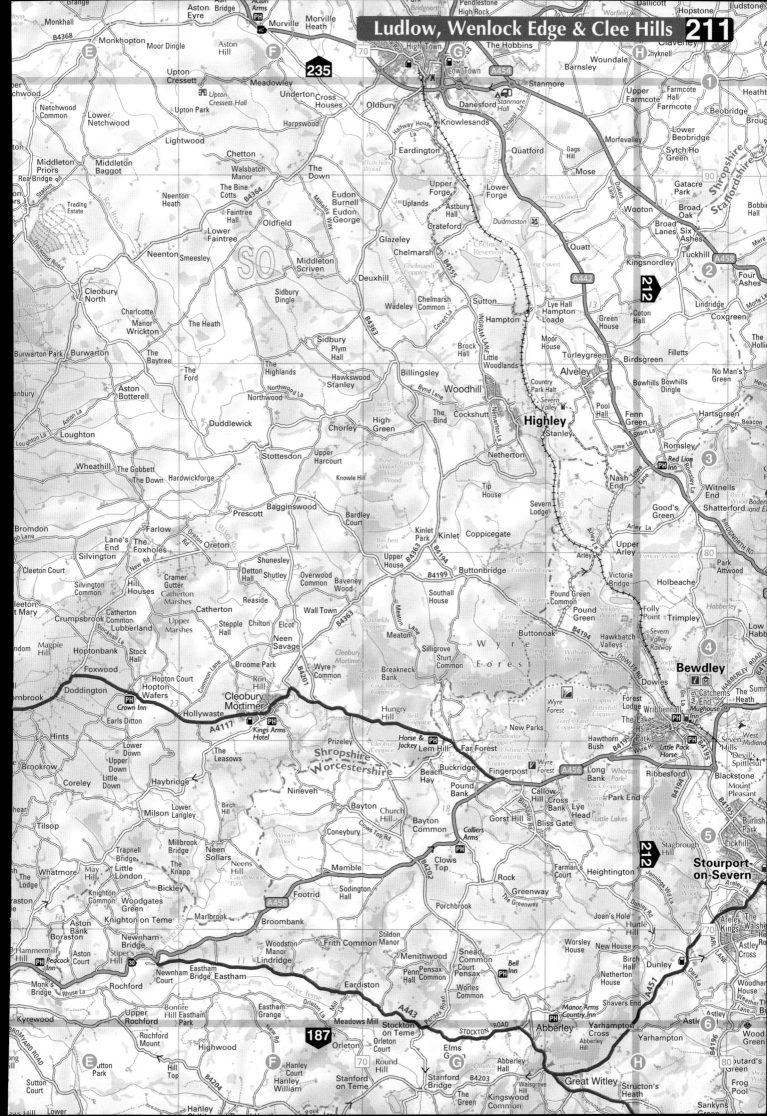

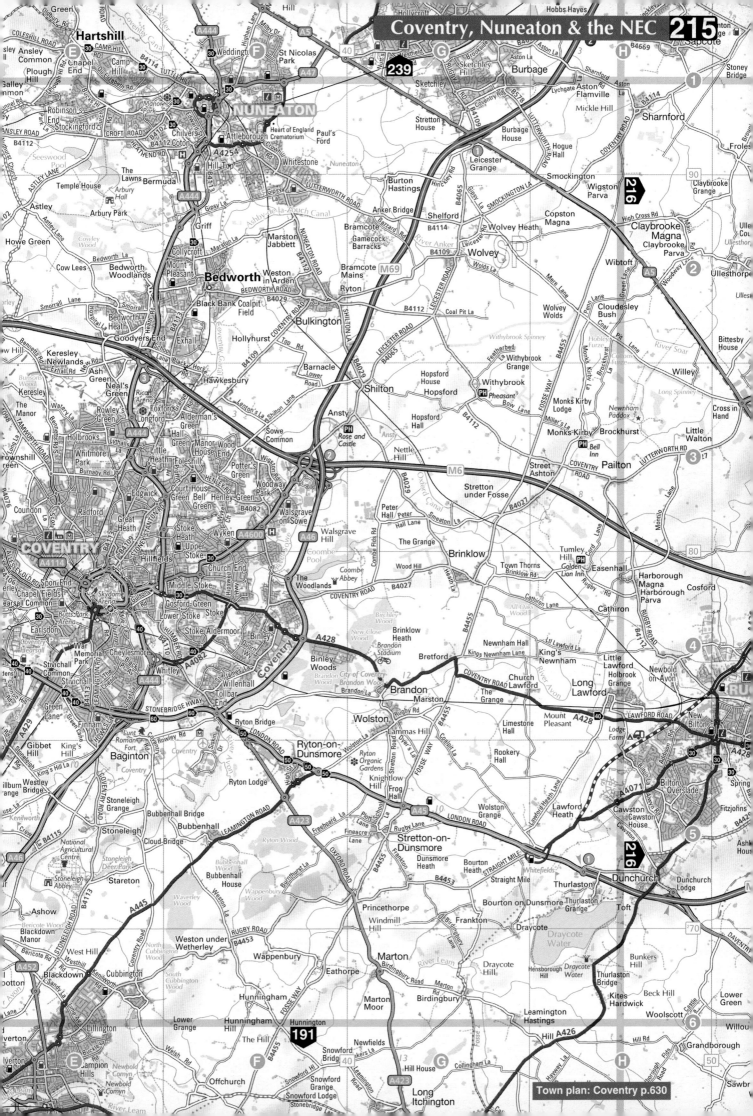

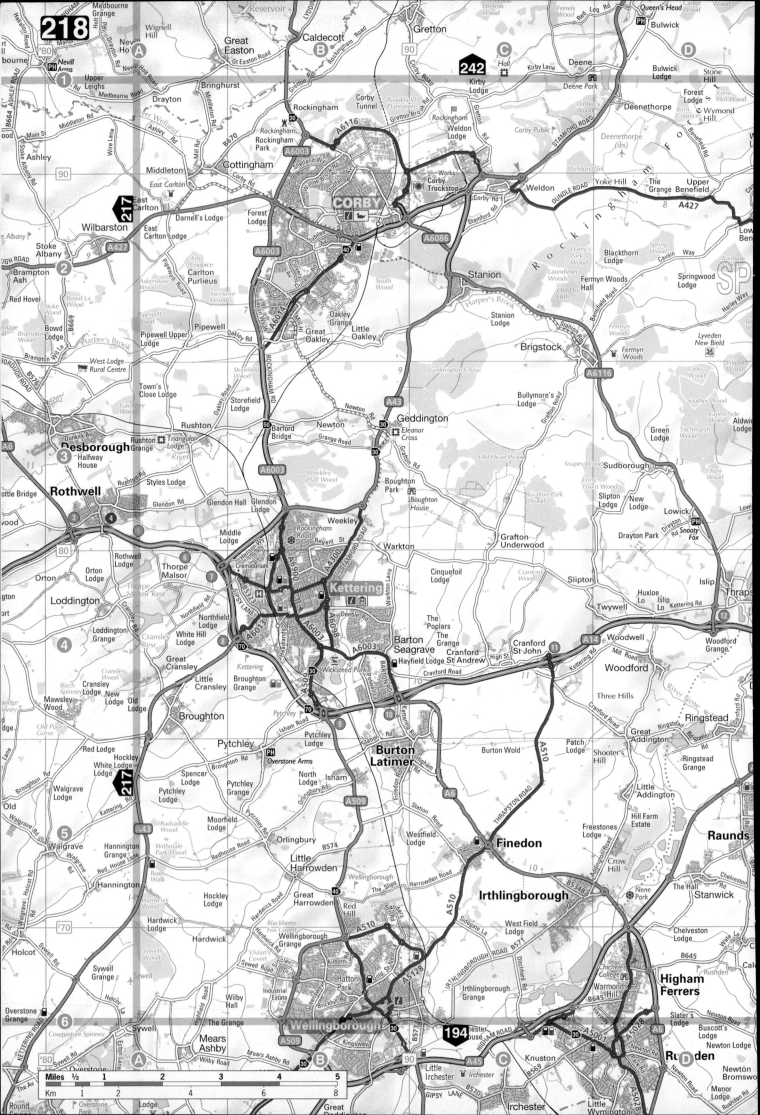

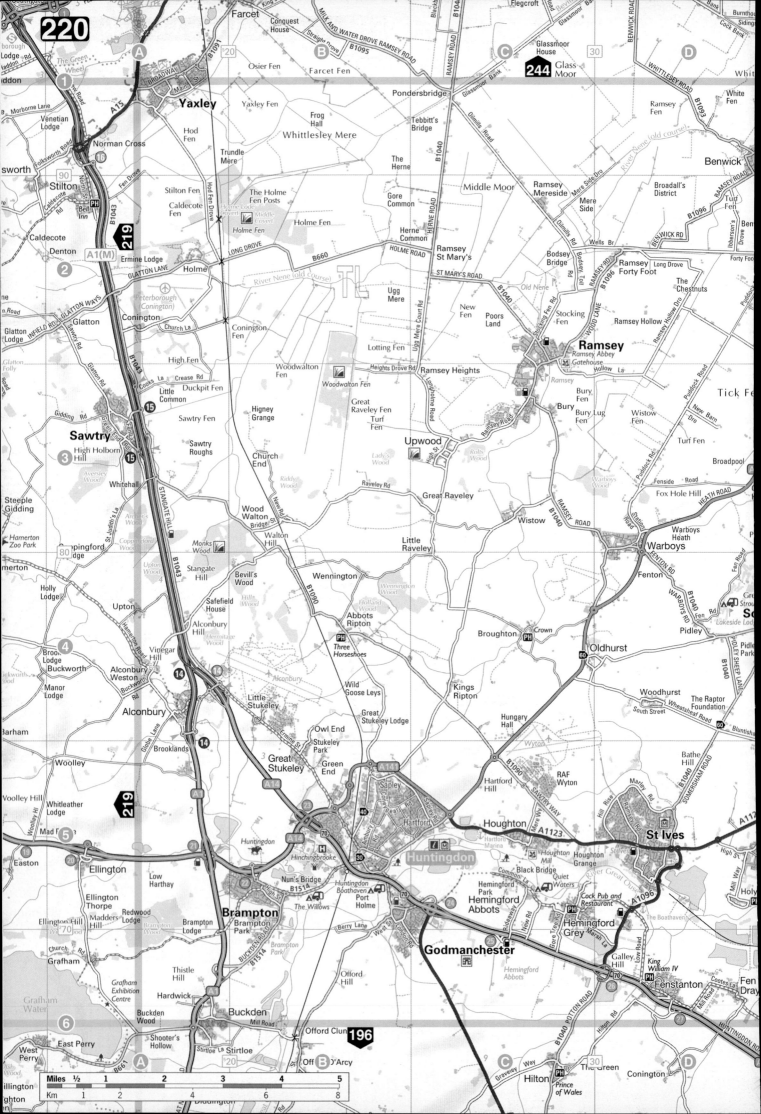

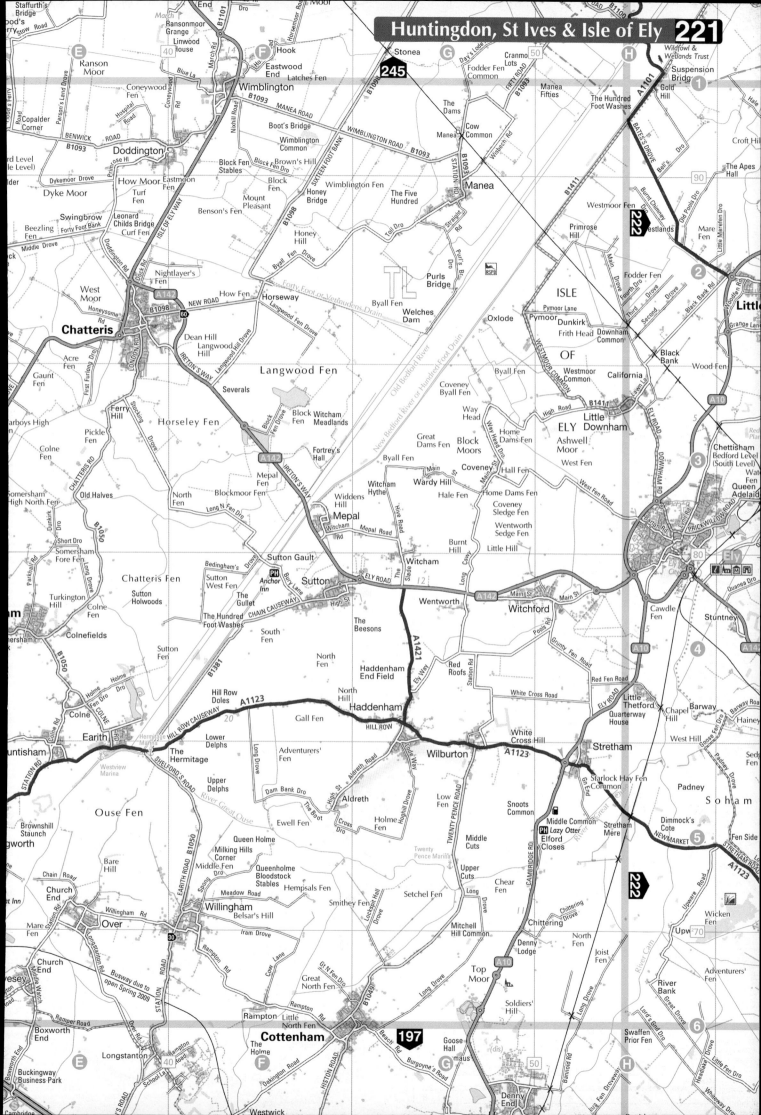

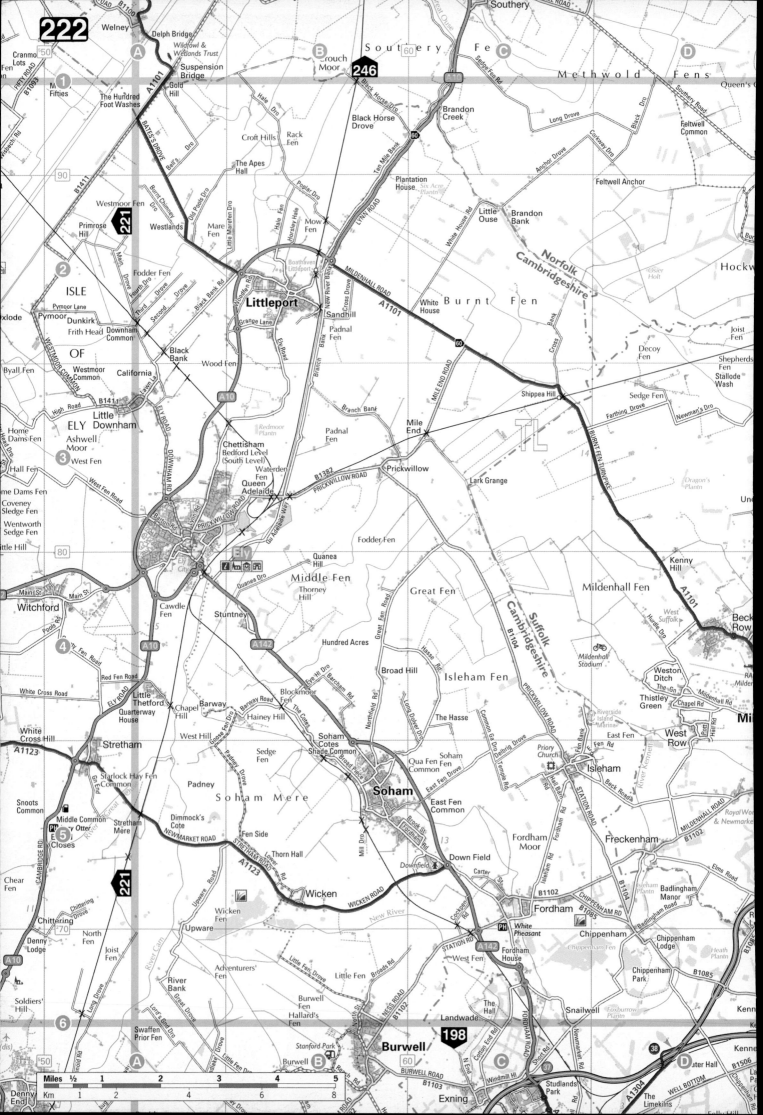

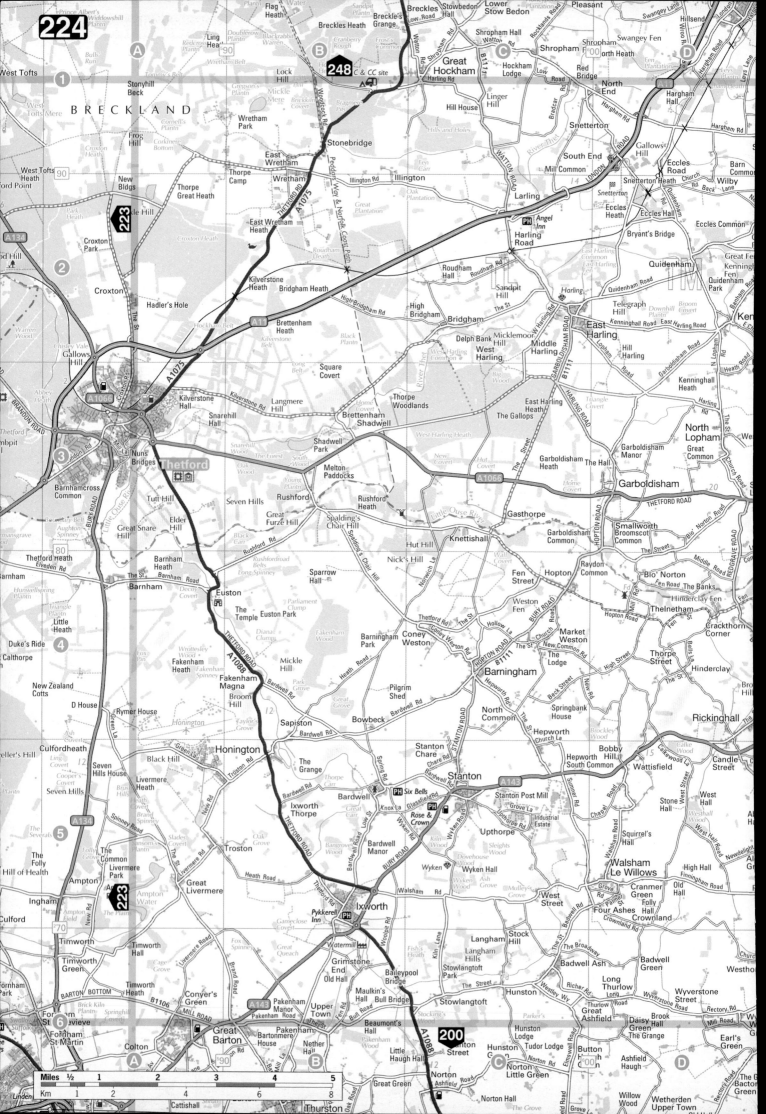

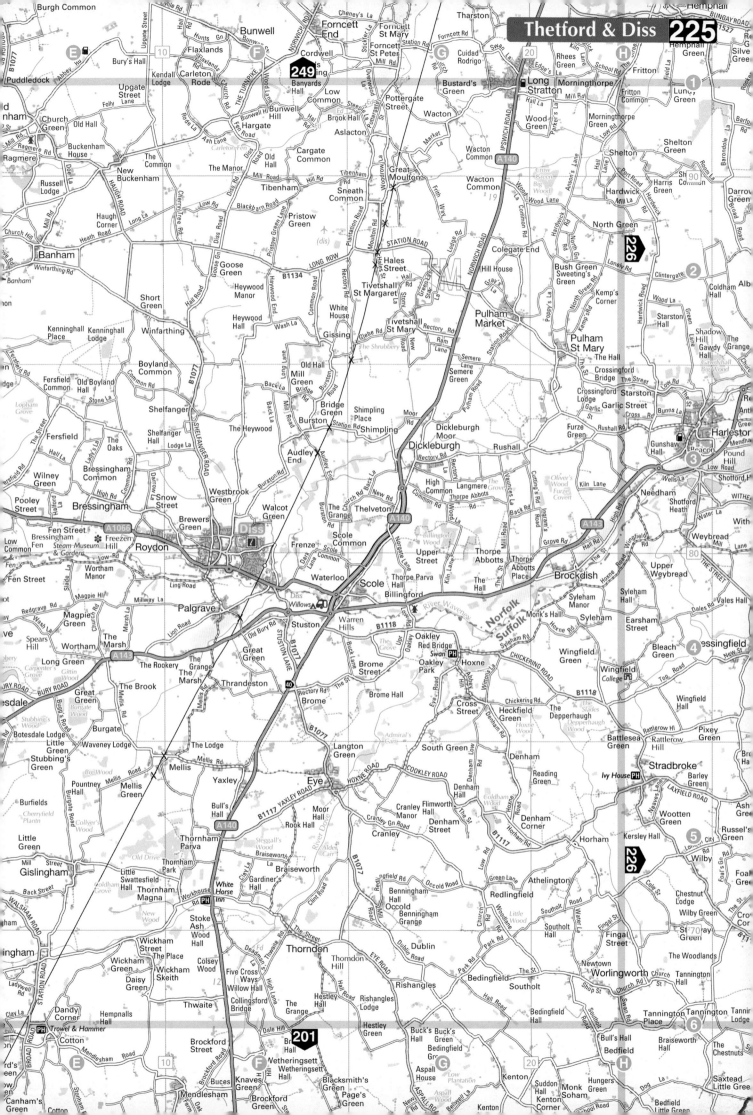

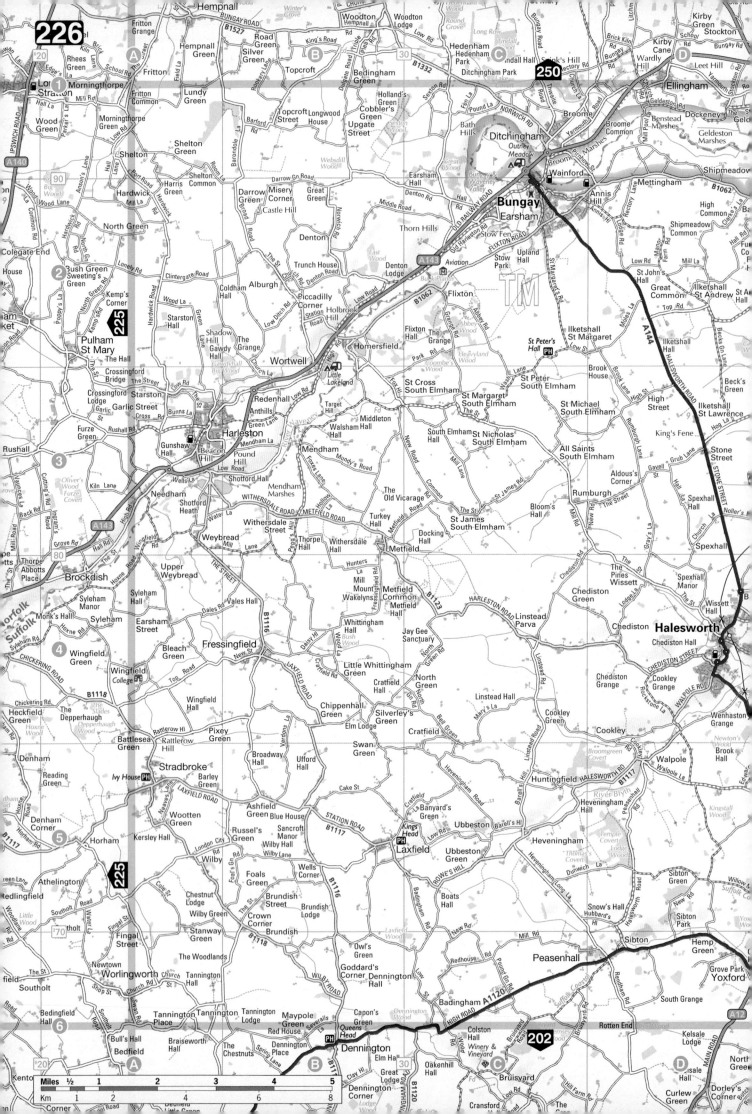

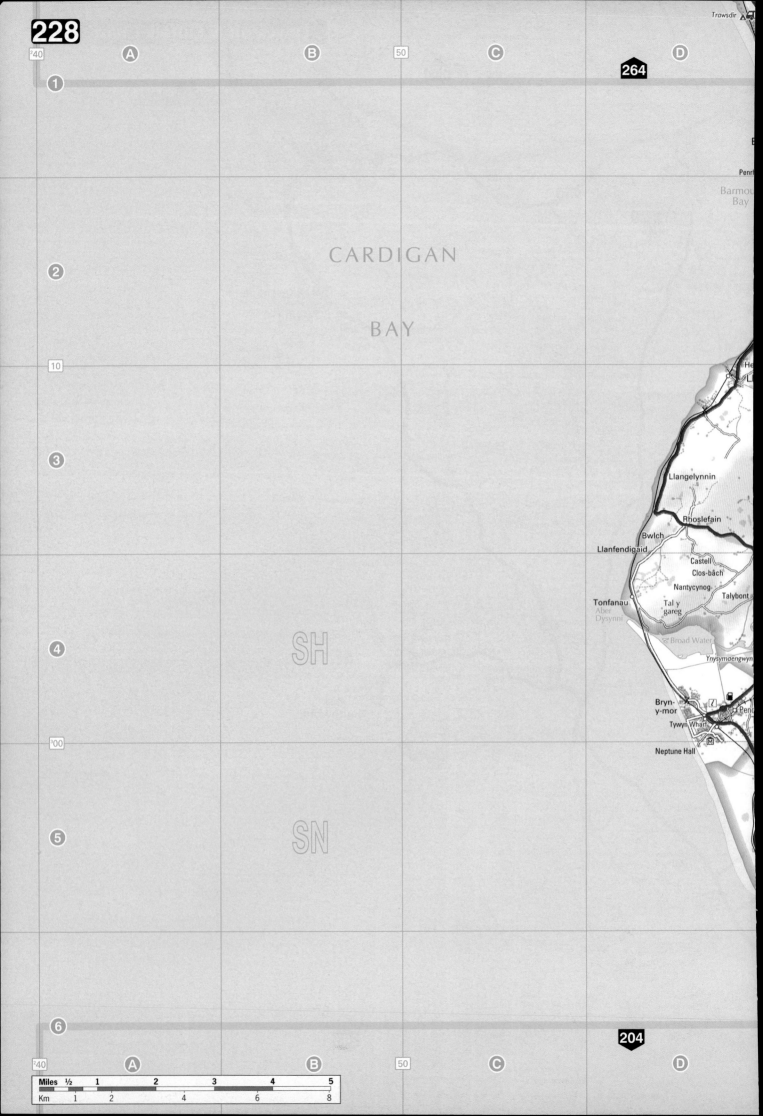

CARDIGAN

BAY

SH

SN

Trawsdir

264

204

Barmouth
Bay

Penrh

He
L

Llangelynnin

Rhoslefain

Bwlch

Llanfendigaid

Castell

Clos-bâch

Nantycynog

Tonfanau
Aber
Dysynni

Tal y
gareg

Talybont

Broad Water

Ynysymaengwyn

Bryn-
y-mor

Penc

Tywyn Wharf

Neptune Hall

Miles ½ 1 2 3 4 5
Km 1 2 4 6 8

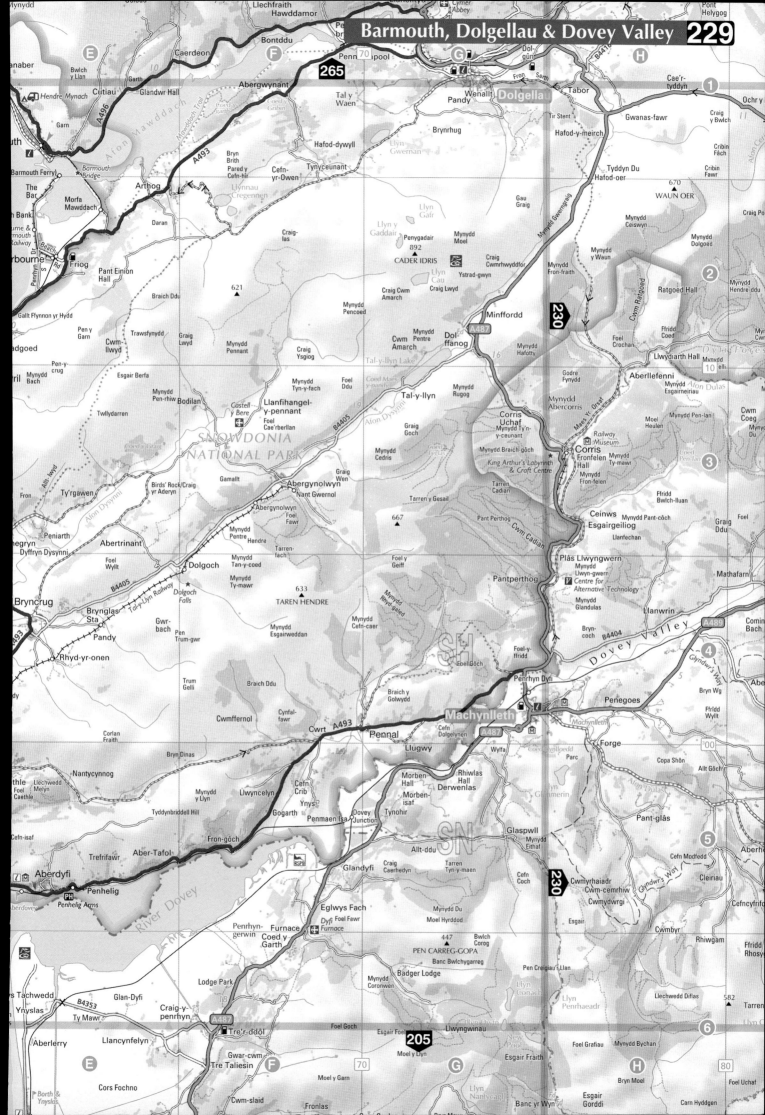

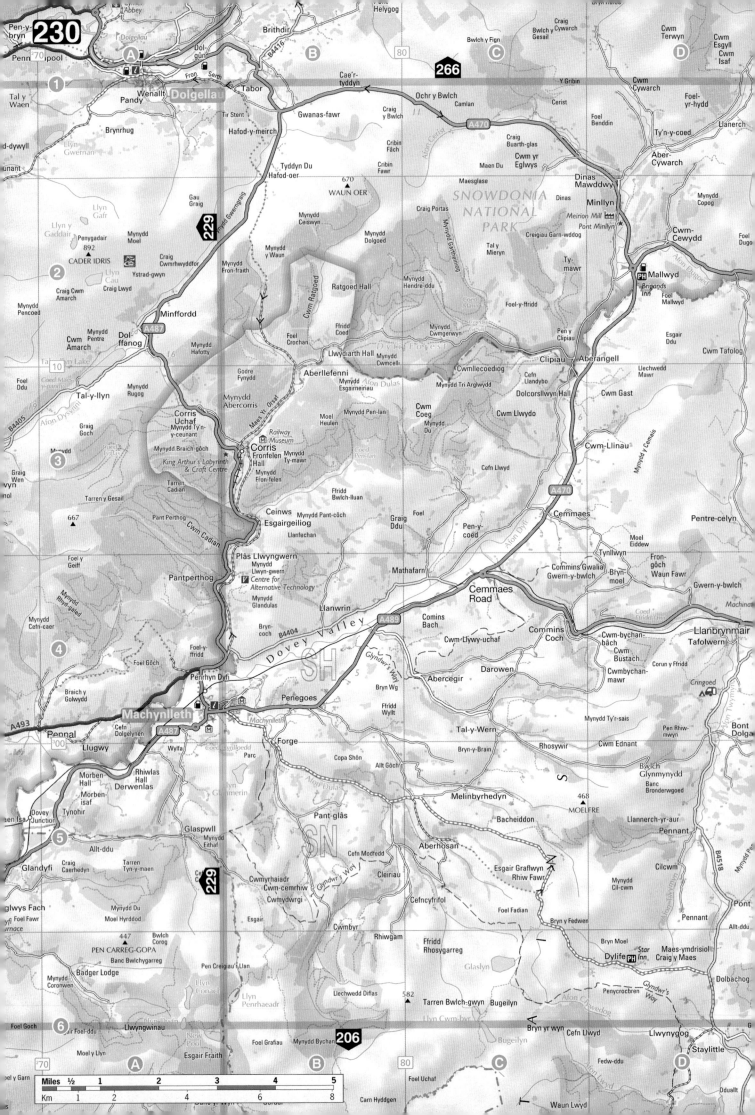

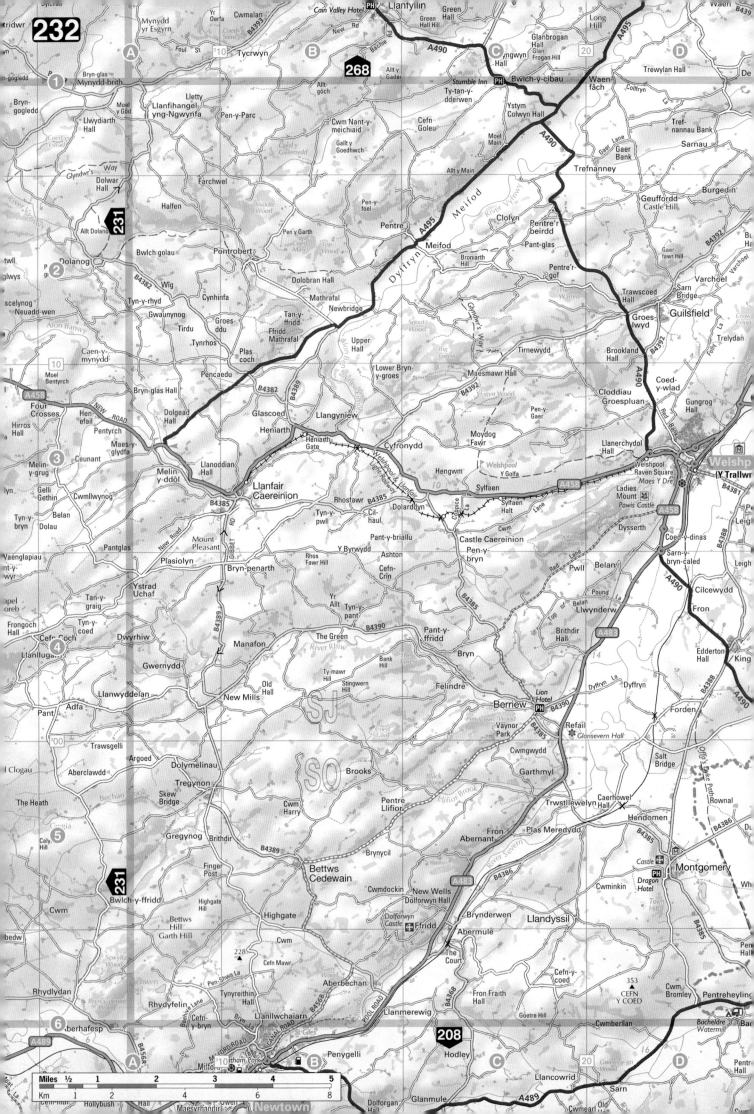

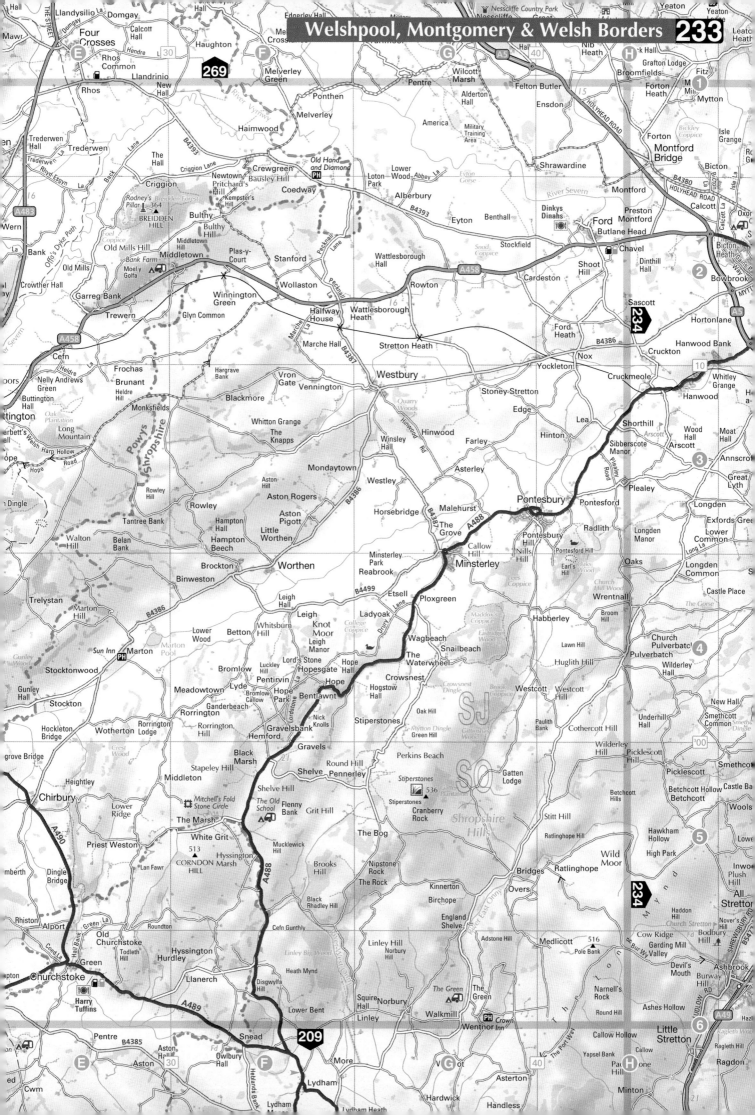

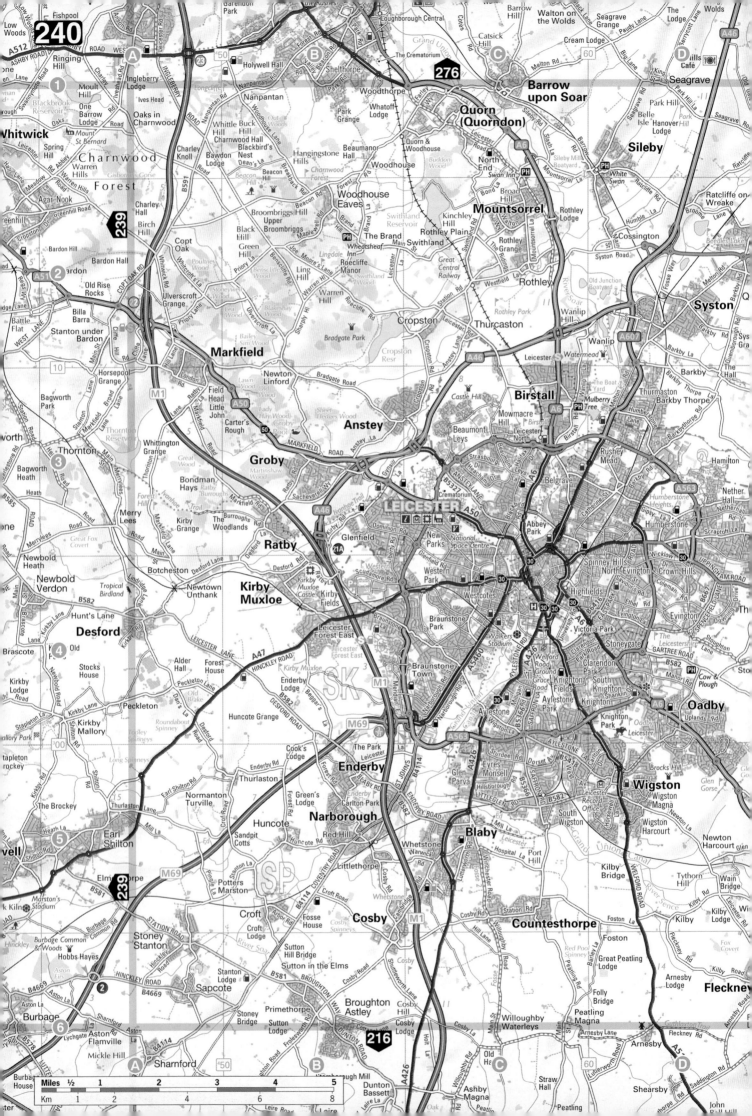

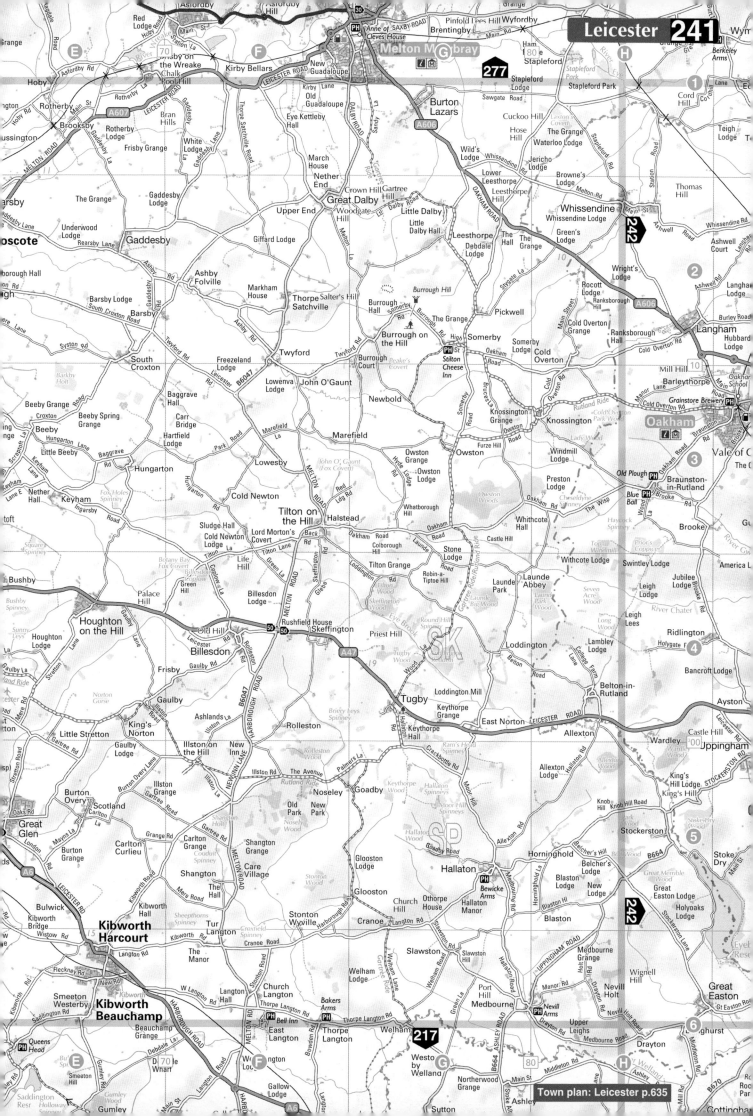

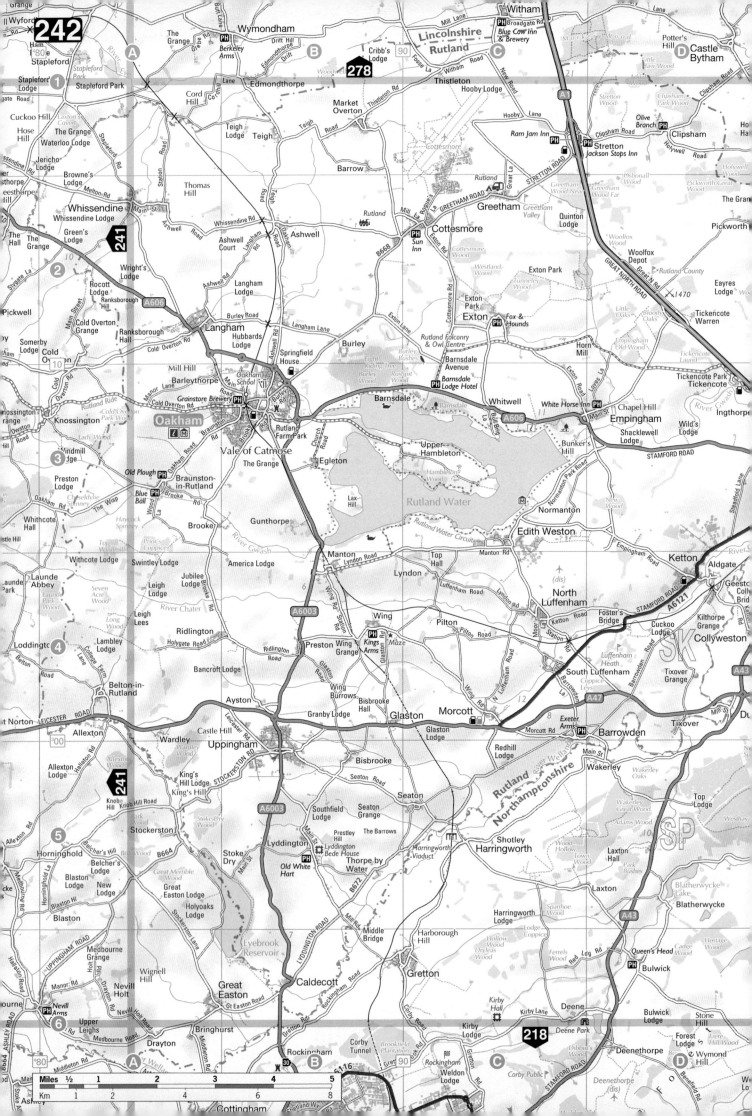

Rutland & Stamford 243

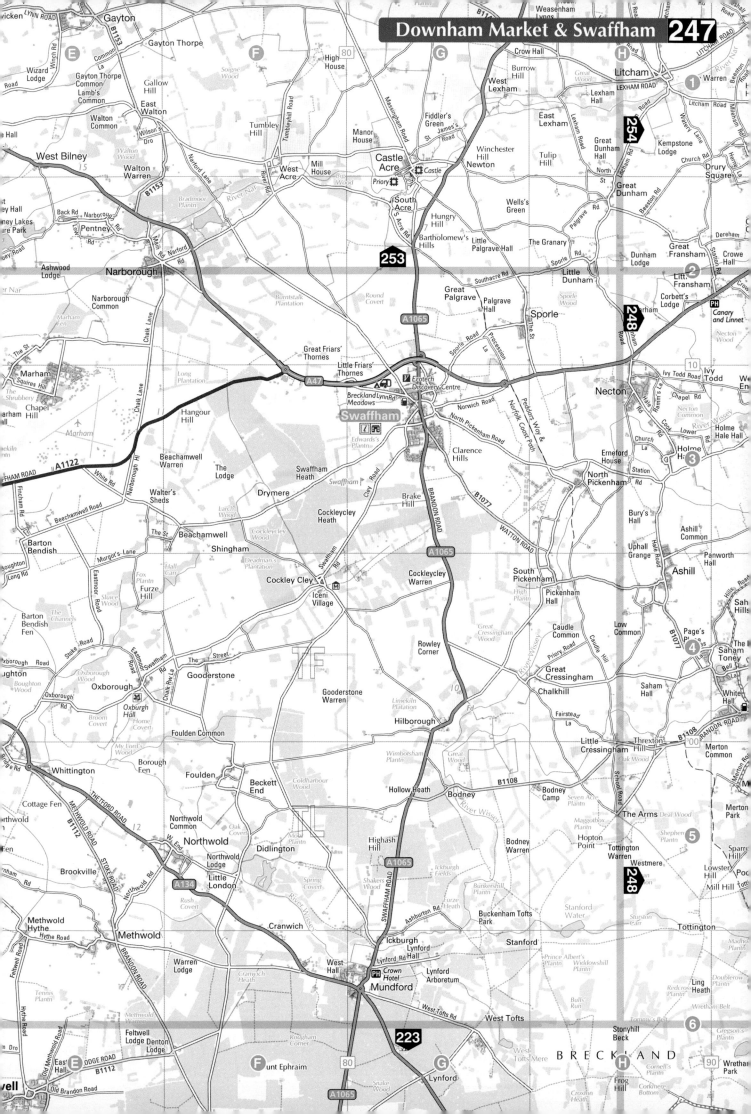

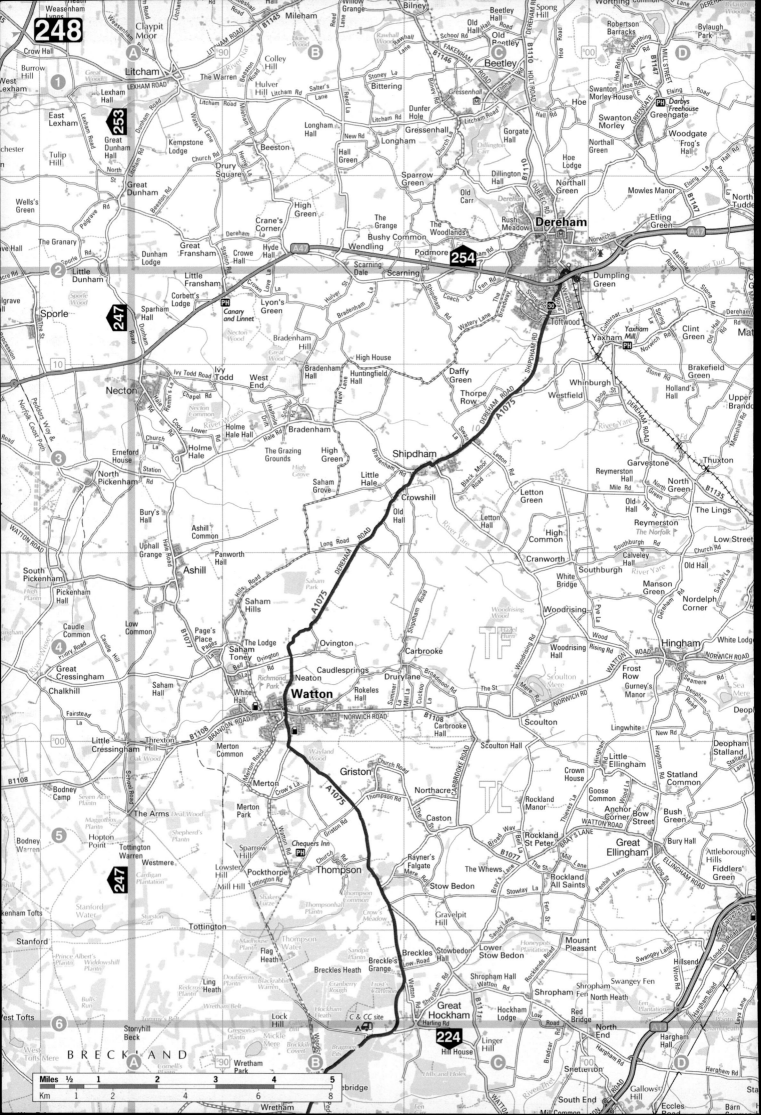

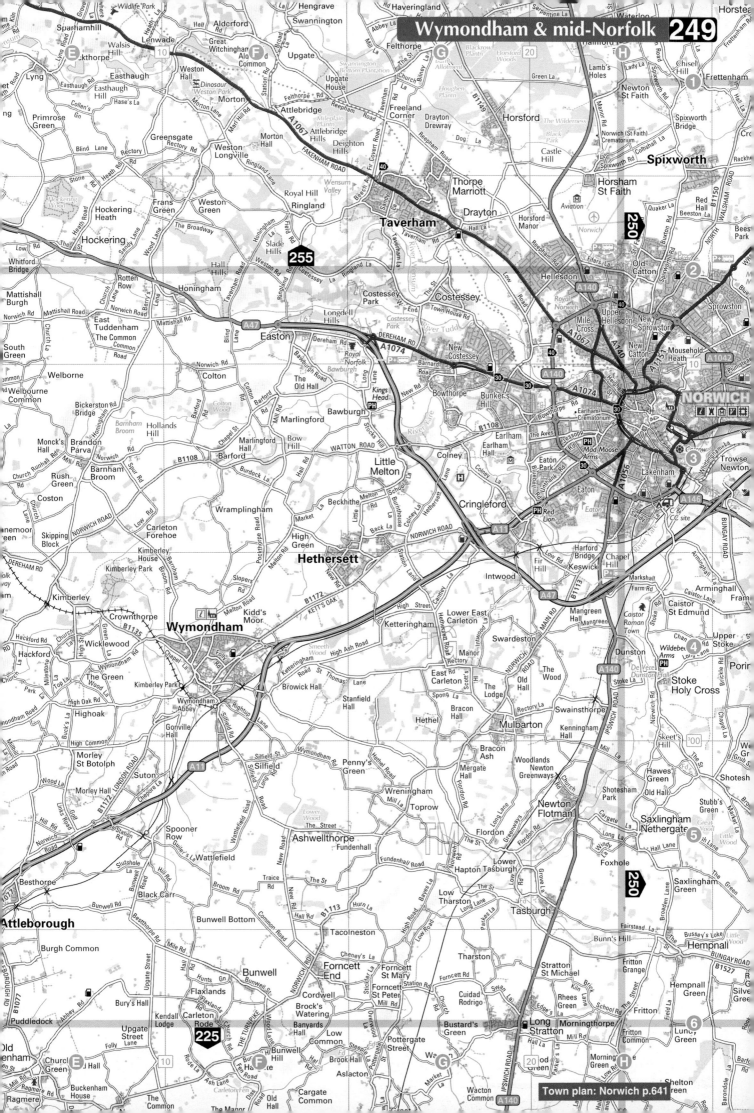

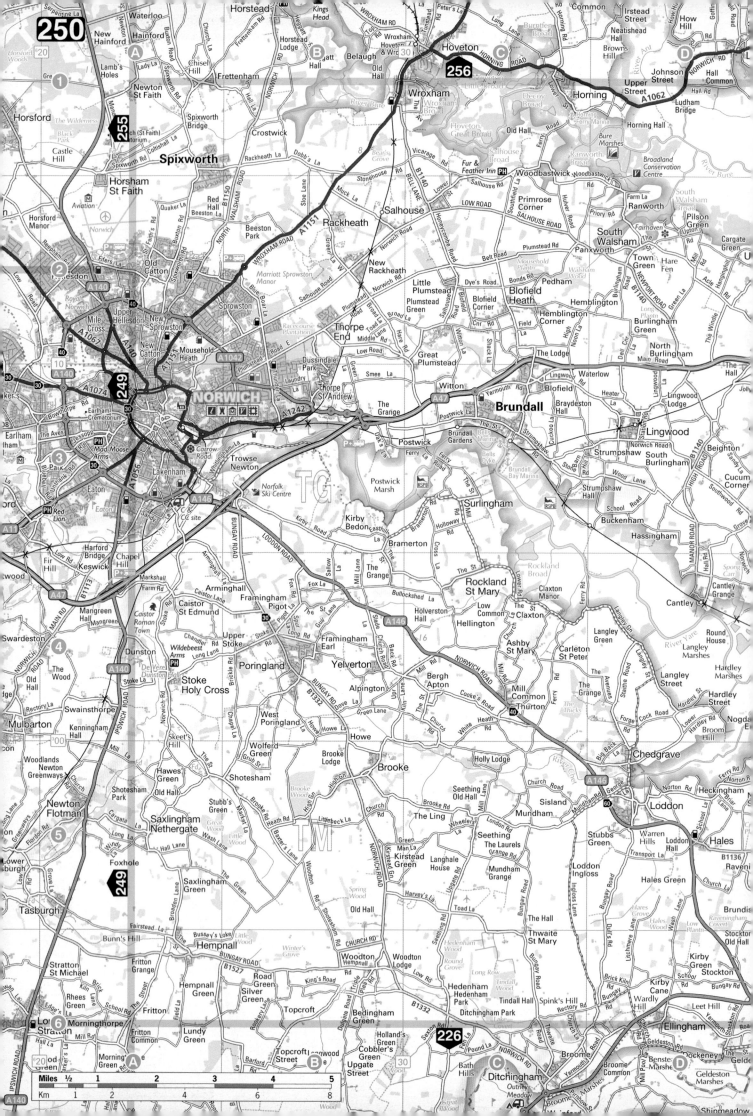

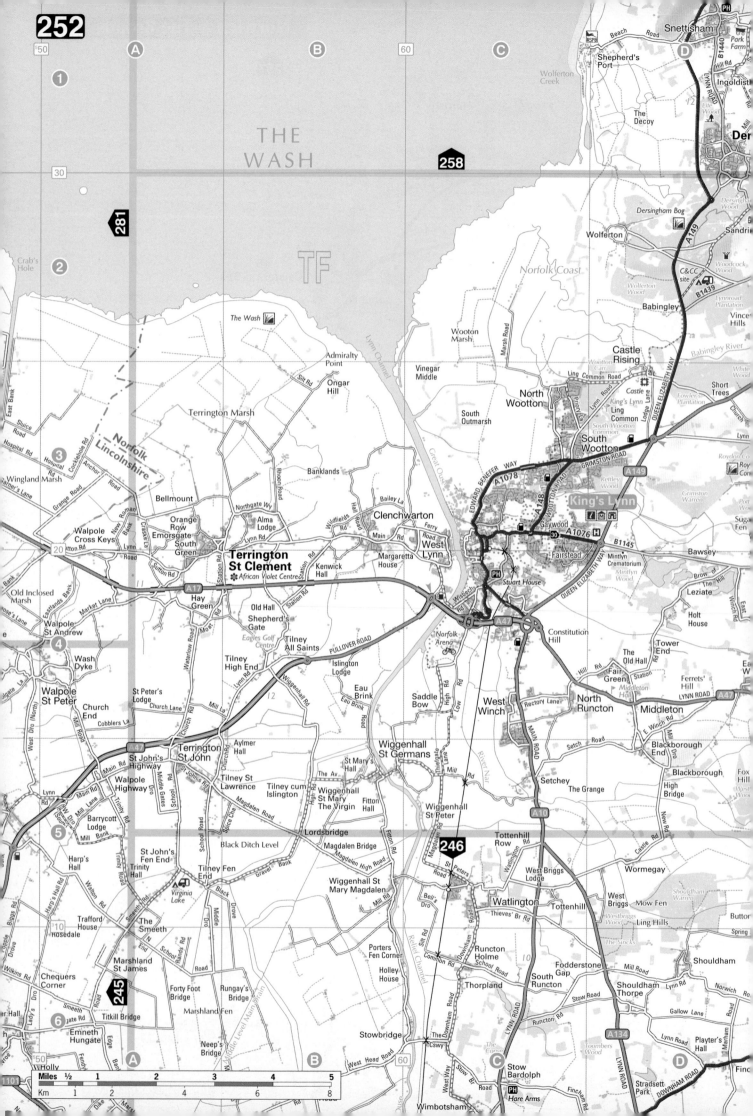

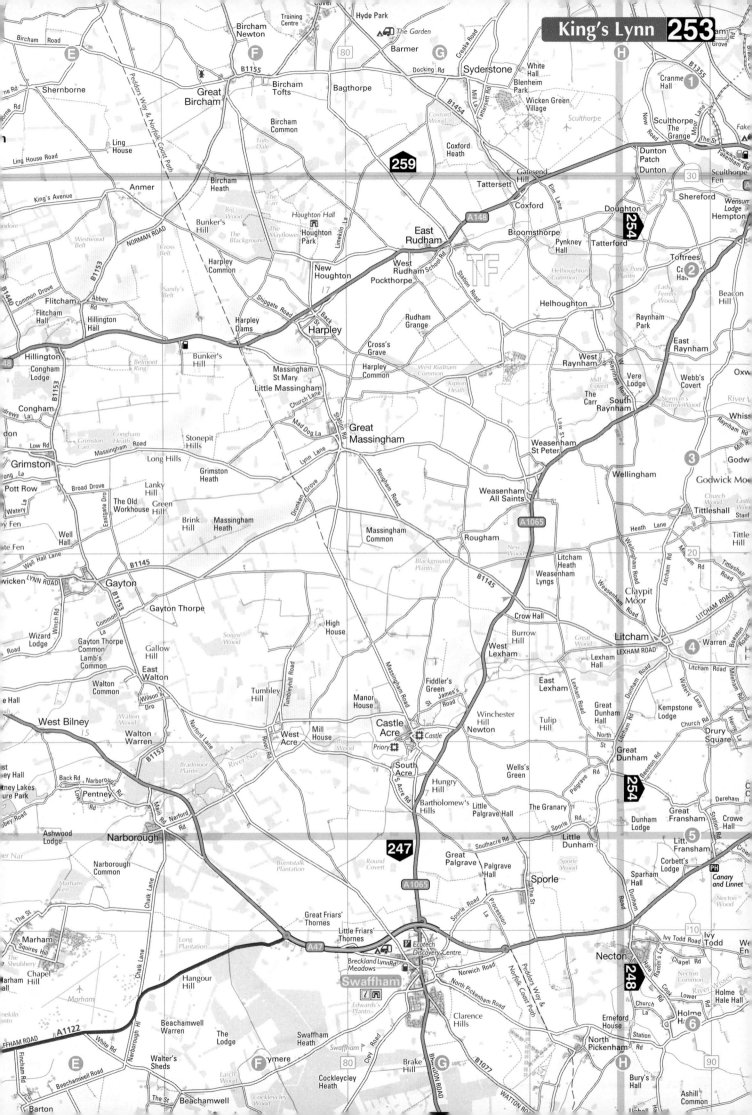

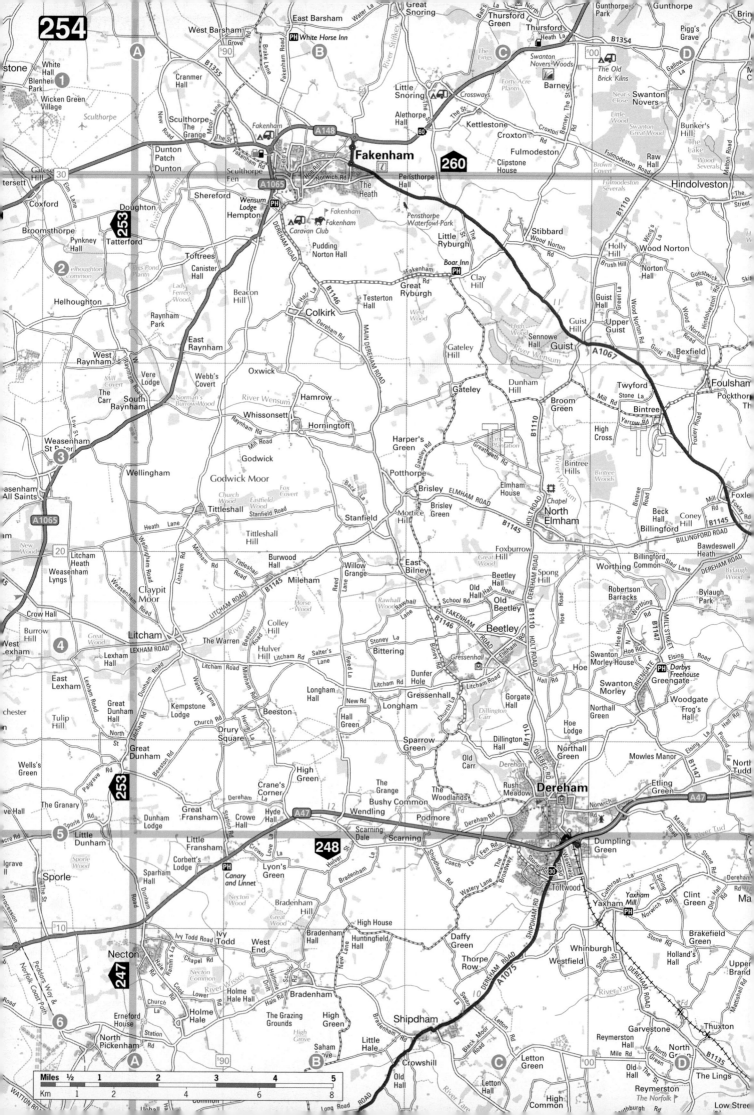

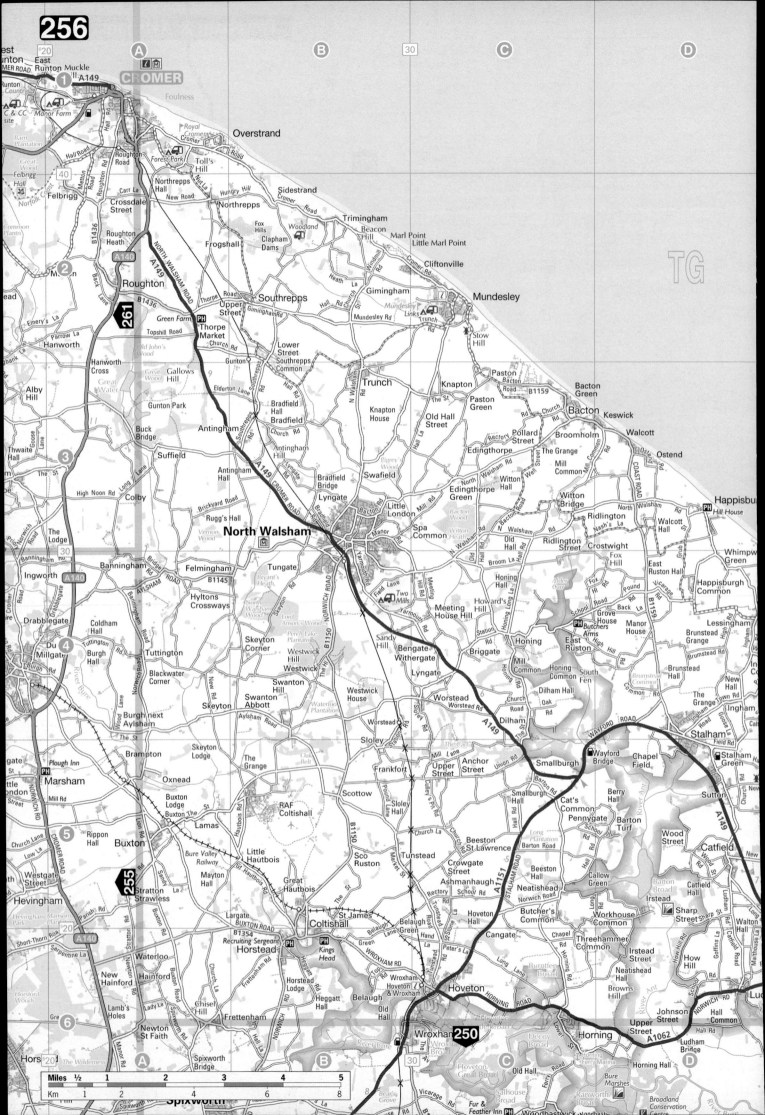

NORTH SEA

Eccles on Sea
North Gap
Hempstead
Marshes
Golden
Beach
Stalham Rd
Sea Palling
Waxham Road
The
Hall
Randall's
Mill
Great
Moss
Fen
Waxham
Marram
Hills
Hickling
Rd
Lambrigg
Mill
Norfolk Coast
Brograve
Level
Hickling
Eastfield Road
Hickling
Green
Stubb
Stubb Road
Hill
Common
Horsey
Mere
Horsey
Corner
Horsey
The
Hall
PH Nelson
Head
Horsey Mill
Bramble
Hill
Hickling
Heath
Stubb
Mill
Horsey
Windpump
Hundred Stream
Winterton
Ness
Hickling
Broad
THE
BROADS
Eelfleet
Wall
Somerton
Holmes
Winterton
Ness
Swim
Coots
Heigham
Sound
Horsey Road
Winterdon Dunes
Decoy Wood
Sound
Plantation
Heigham
Holmes
Church La
East
Somerton
Martham
Broad
Fishermans
Return
Potter
Heigham
High's
Mill
Ferrygate La
Damgate
Somerton
Road
West
Somerton
PH Winterton-
on-Sea
Fritton
Mustard
Hyrn
Cess
Collis Lane
Blood
Hills
Hemsby Rd
Repps
Level
Bastwick
Cess
Martham
Hemsby Road
Martham Rd
Bridge Rd
HIGH ROAD
Repps
Repps Road
Mill Rd
Beach
Rd
251
Repps Rd
Church
E
A149
Ashby
Hall
Heath Road
Heath
Rd
Martham
Rd
Back
Lane
Hemsby
Newport
Ormes
Broad
F
50
G
Dowe
Hill
Scratby
H
60
hurne
Church Rd
B1152
Thurne Road
Rollesby
MAIN ROAD
Ormesby
St Margaret
North Rd
Scratby
Hall
Scratby
California

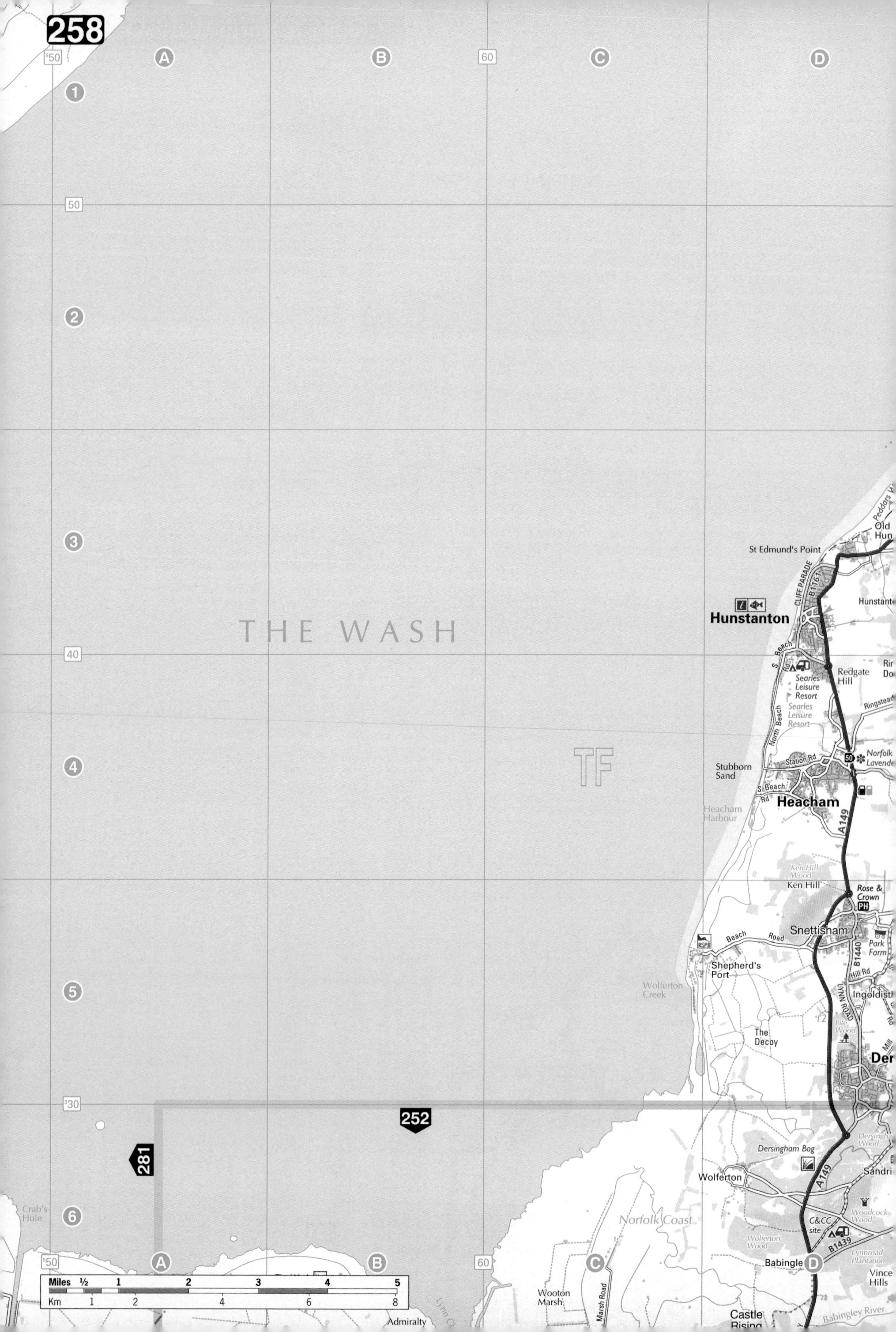

THE WASH

TF

St Edmund's Point

Old Hun

Peddars

CLIFF PARADE

B1161

Hunstant

Hunstanton

S. Beach

North Beach

Searles
Leisure
Resort

Searles
Leisure
Resort

Redgate
Hill

Rir
Do

Ringstead

Stubborn
Sand

S. Beach
Rd

Station Rd

50

Norfolk
Lavende

Heacham

Heacham
Harbour

A149

Ken Hill
Wood

Ken Hill

Rose &
Crown
PH

Snettisham

B1440

Park
Farm

RSPB

Beach
Road

Hill Rd

LYNN ROAD

Ingoldisth

Shepherd's
Port

Wolferton
Creek

The
Decoy

Life
Wood

Der

281

252

Crab's
Hole

Dersingham Bog

Dersingham
Wood

A149

Sandri

Wolferton

Norfolk Coast

C&CC
site

Woodcock
Wood

Wolferton
Wood

B1439

Lynnroad
Plantation

Babingle

Vince
Hills

Wooton
Marsh

Marsh Road

Castle
Rising

Babingley River

Lynn Cr

Admiralty

Miles ½	1		2		3		4		5
Km	1	2		4		6		8	

NORTH SEA

TG

Peddars Way & Norfolk Coast Path

Gramborough Hill
Salthouse
Great Hulver Hill
Bard Hill
The Hangs
Gallow Hill
Salthouse Heath
Swan Lodge
Cley Park
Pereer's Hills
Norfolk Coast
Holt
Common Hill
Ingmote Hill
King's Hills
Hunworth
The Green
Starlings' Hill
The Mount
Briston
John H Stracey
Edgefield Street
Nethergate
Old Hall
Chapel
Tyby
Guestwick
Guestwick Green
Jessa

The Quag
Kelling Hard
Muckleburgh Collection
Warborough Hill
Dun Cow
COAST ROAD
Kelling
Telegraph Hill
Holgate Hill
Kelling Heath Park
North Norfolk Railway
High Kelling
CROMER ROAD
Bodham Common
Lower Bodham
Wheatsheaf
Bodham
Bodham Hill
Baconsthorpe Castle
Red House
Baconsthorpe
Hempstead
Dam Hill
The Dale
Pond Hills
Edgefield
Plumstead Green
Plumstead Rd
Little Wood
Barningham Green
New Covert
Old Covert
Mannington Gardens
Moor Hall
Mossymere Wood
Itteringham
Walpole Arms
Elmerdale
Little London
Corpusty
Saxthorpe
River Bure
Thurning
Foundry Hill
Red Pits
Norton Corner
Crabgate
Earle Arms
Heydon
Wood Dalling Hall
Wood Dalling
Newhall Wood

Muckleburgh Hill
A149
SHERINGHAM RD
Weybourne
Station Rd
Sheringham Park
Howe's Hill
Bodham
The St
West Beckham
Osier La
Mill Road
Hell Hole
New Road
School Lane
Marliot Road
Plumstead Road
Northfield La
Plumstead
The St
Squallham
Little Barningham
Wolterton Park
Wolterton
Spa Lane
Oulton
Spink's La
Oak Grove
Oulton Street
Monson's Wood
The Beaselands Road
Heydon
Bluestone Plantn
Sankence Lodge

Dead Man's Hill
Robin Friend
Sheringham
Beeston Regis
Norfolk Shire Horse Centre
Upper Sheringham
Sheringwood
Pretty Corner
Stone Hill
Beacon Hill
East Beckham
Aylmerton
Church Rd
Gresham
Stonepit Hill
Plum Lane
Thurgarton Old Hall
Bessingham
Sustead
Up Wood
Watery La
Matlaske
Lower Street
Aldborough
Wickmere
Saracen's Head
Thwaite Hall
Calthorpe
Wall Rd
Erpingham
Blickling Hall
Blickling
Bunker's Hill
Itteringham Common
Abel Heath
Silvergate
Buckinghamshire Arms
Aylsham
Burgh Rd
River Bure
Burgh next Aylsham
Spa Lane

West Runton
CROMER ROAD
A1082
HOLWAY ROAD
Water La
East Runton
Muckle Hill
A149
Links Country Park
West Runton
C & CC site
Sandy La
Manor Farm
Barn Plantation
Great Wood
Felbrigg Hall
Felbrigg
Common Plantn
Metton
Norfolk Coast
Heligate La
Emery's La
Parrow La
Hanworth
Thurgarton
School Rd
Ringbank La
Alby Hill
Goose La
Hanworth Cross
Great Water
Great Wood
Gunton Park
Buck Bridge
Suffield
The Lodge
Colby
High Noon Rd
Priory Rd
Ingworth
A140
Banningham Rd
Drabblegate
Dunkirk
Coldham Hall
Millgate
Burgh Hall
Tuttington Rd

256
CROMER
Overstra
Royal Cromer Cromer
Forest Park
Toll's H'll
Northrepps Hall
New Road
Northrepps
Fox Hills
Crossdale Street
Carr La
Roughton Rd
Metton Rd
Roughton Heath
A140
A149
NORTH WALSHAM ROAD
Roughton
B1436
Thorpe Road
Upper Street
Gimingh
Green Farm
Thorpe Market
Church Rd
Gunton
Elderton Lane
Gallows Hill
Southrepps
Antingham
Buck Bridge
Antingham Hall
North W
Vernon Wood
Felmingham
B1145
Hyltons Crossways
North Walsham Rd
Skeyte
Tuttington
Blackwater Corner
Skeyton
Swant Abbott
New Rd

255
Itteringham Common
Thorgate
Banningham Rd
Blickling
Hercules Wood
Oulton Lodge
New Road
Church La
Oulton Street
Aylsham Rd
A140
256
AYLSHAM ROAD
Bridge Rd
Banningham

B1110
THORNAGE ROAD
B1149
NORWICH RD
Briston Rd
B1354
B1149
Reepham Road
Heydon Rd
Crow Hill
B1149
ROAD
Reepham Road

PH

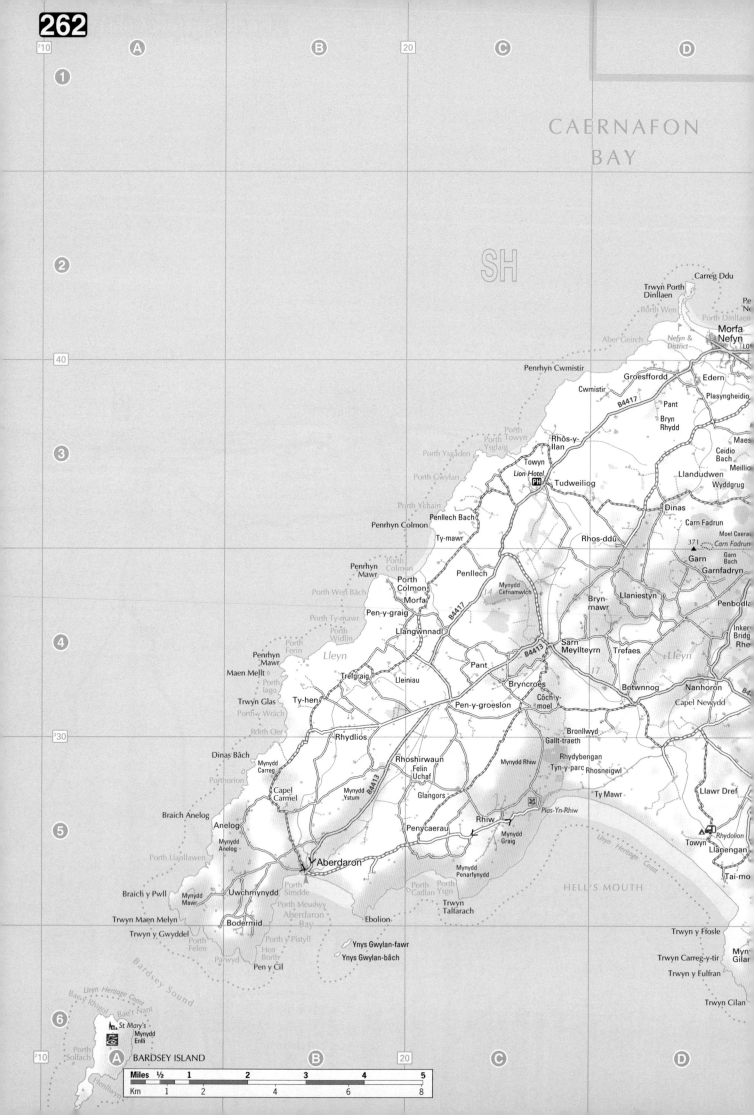

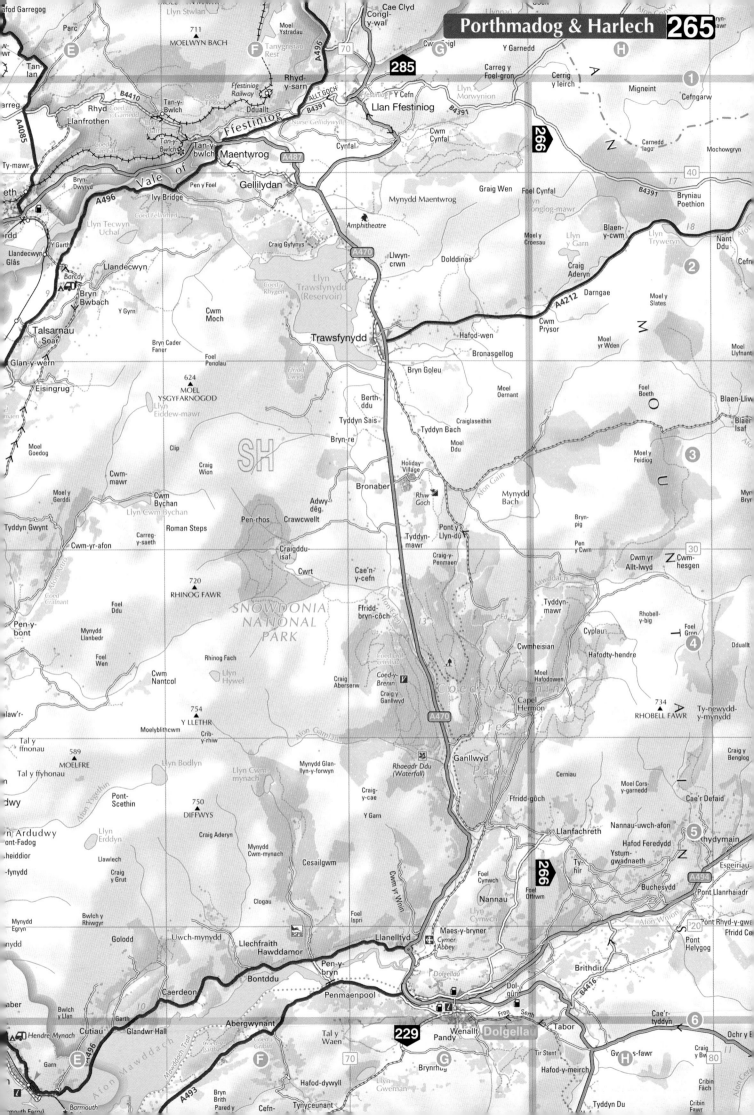

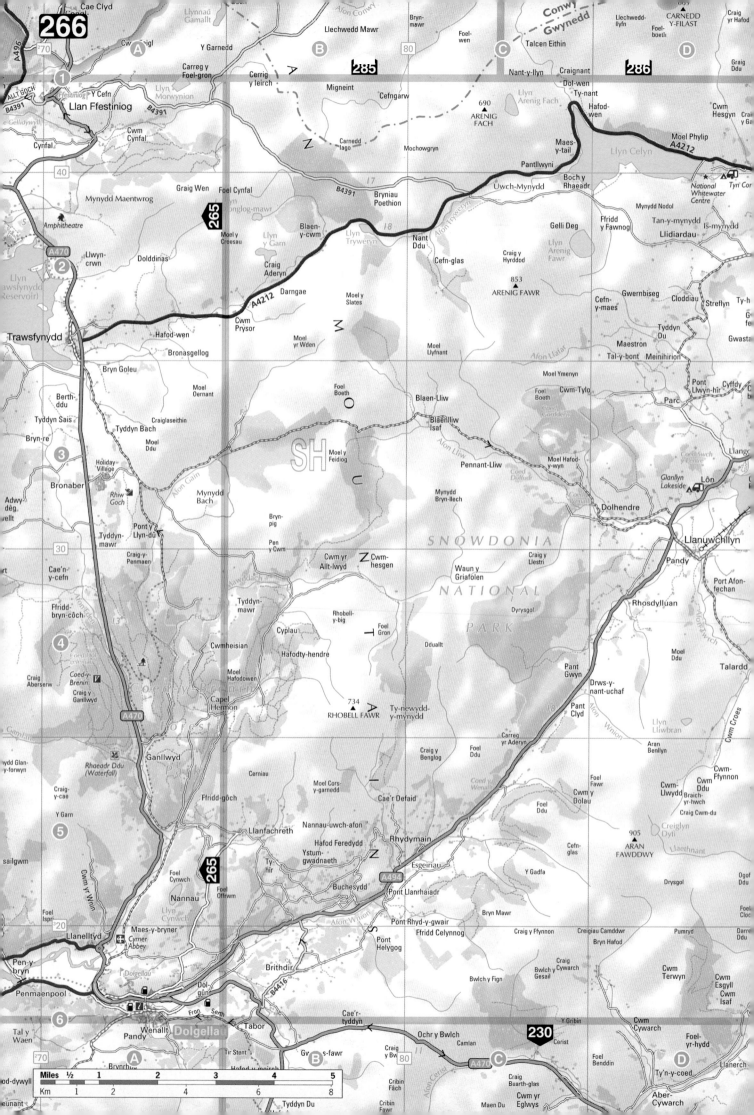

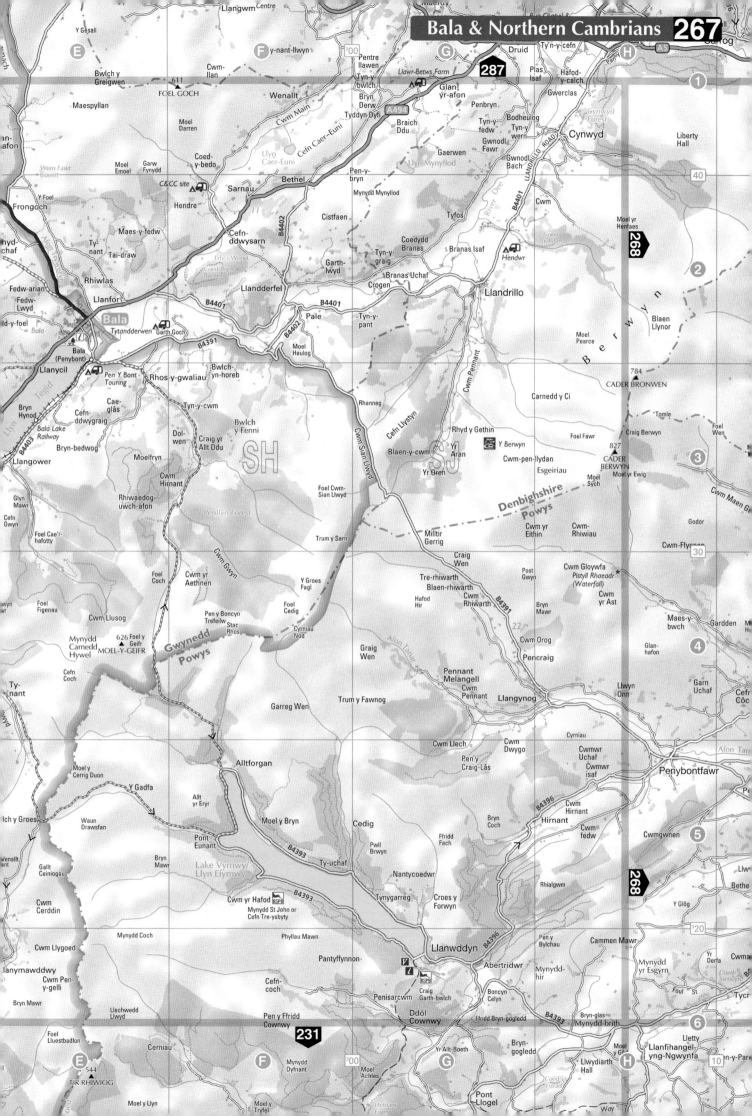

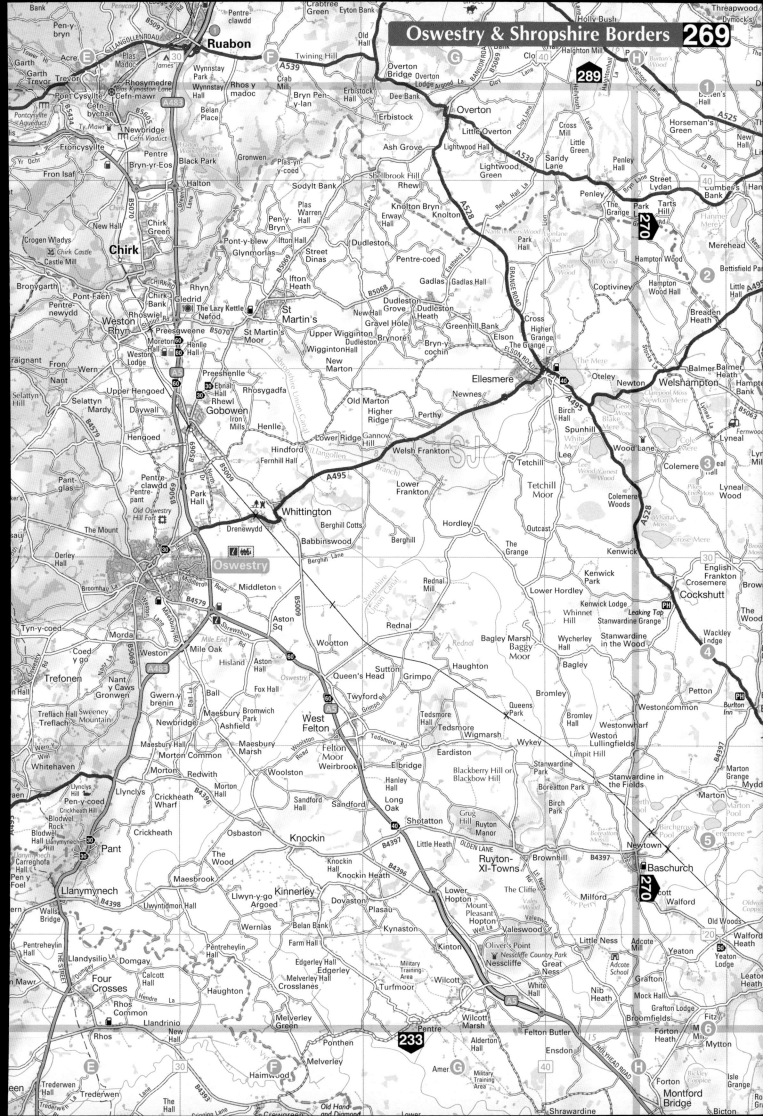

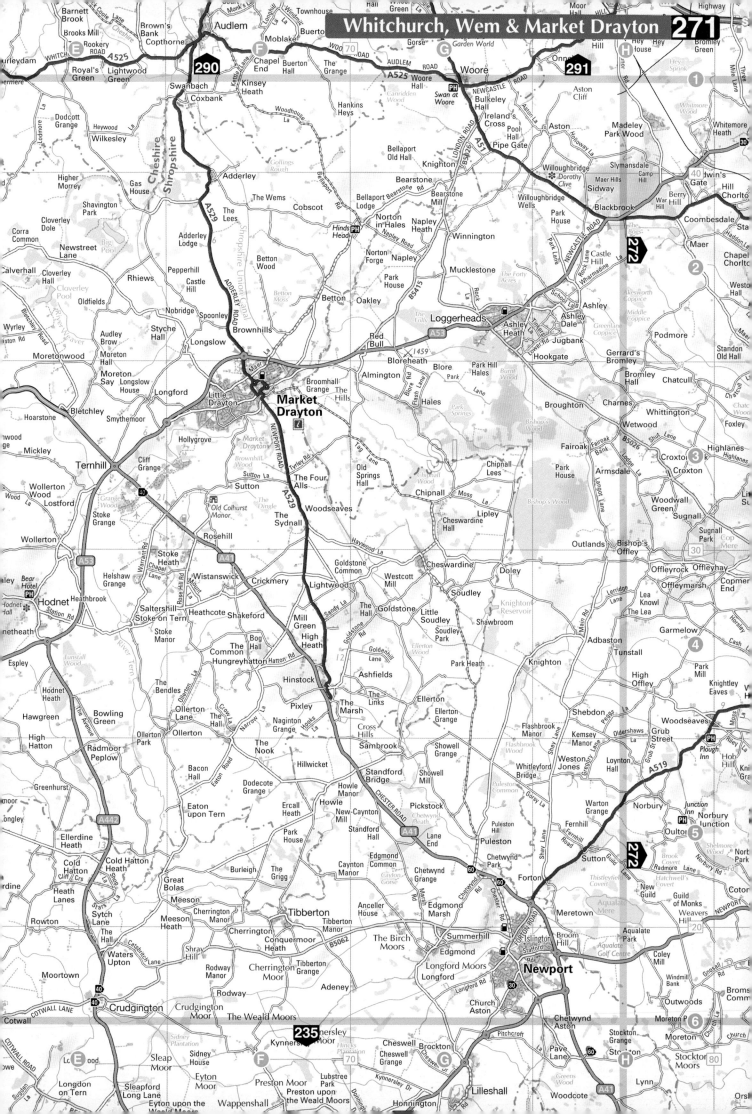

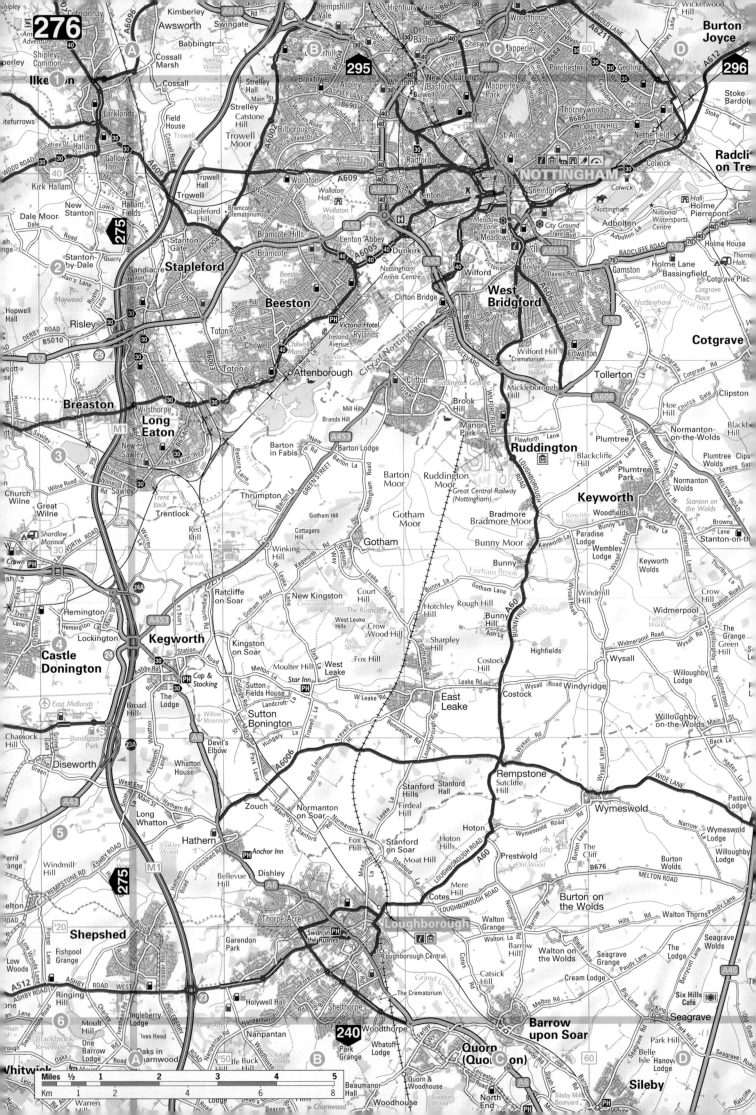

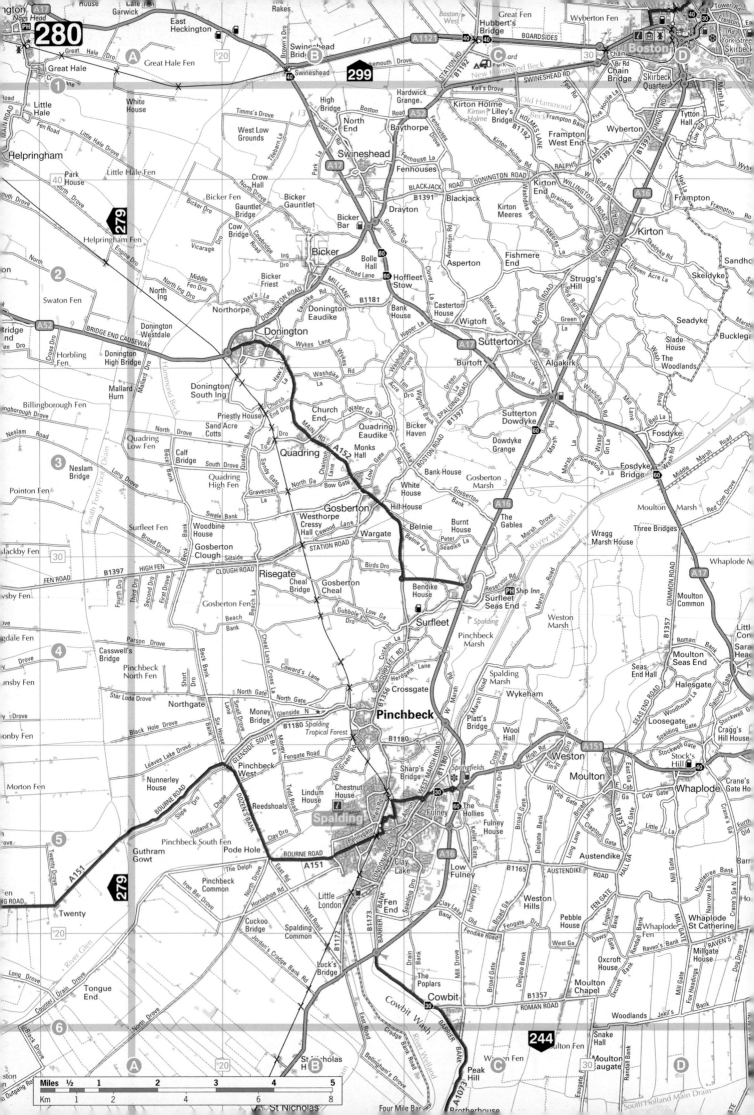

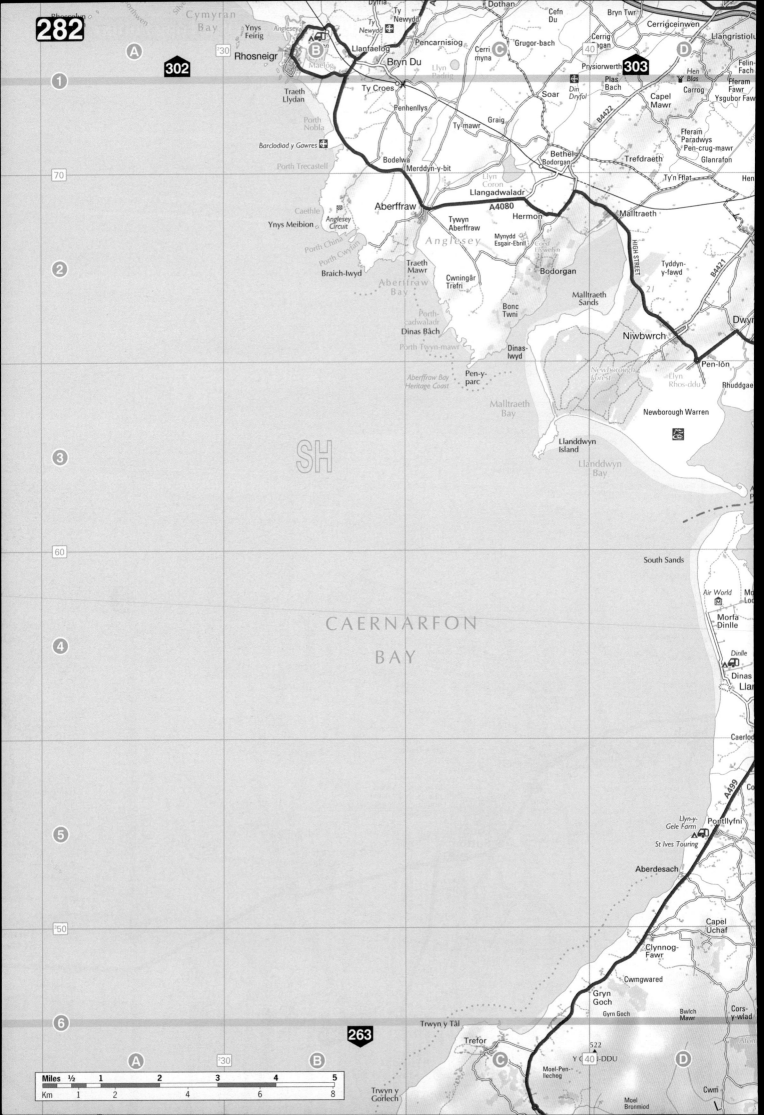

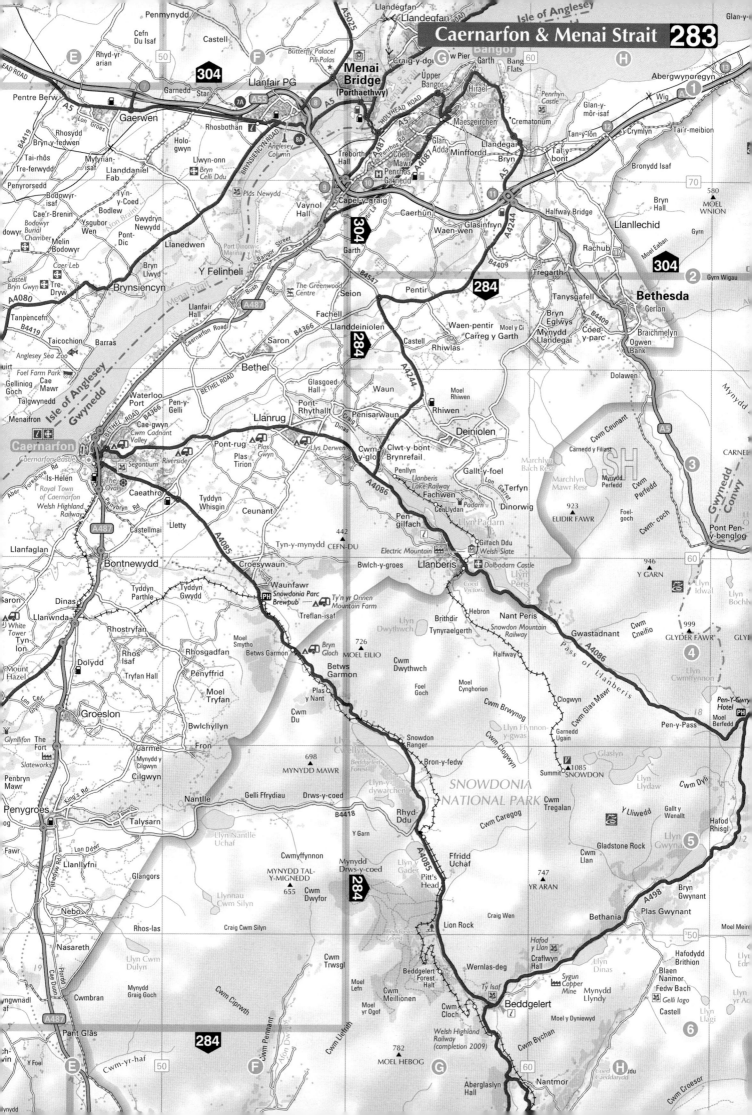

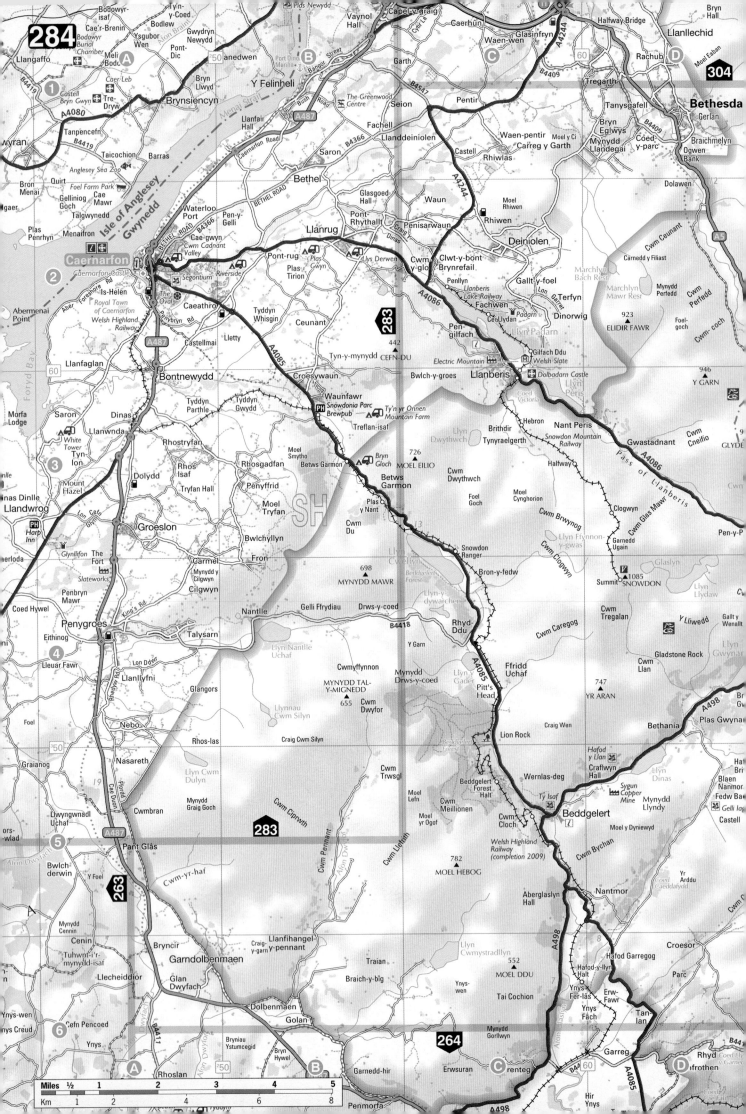

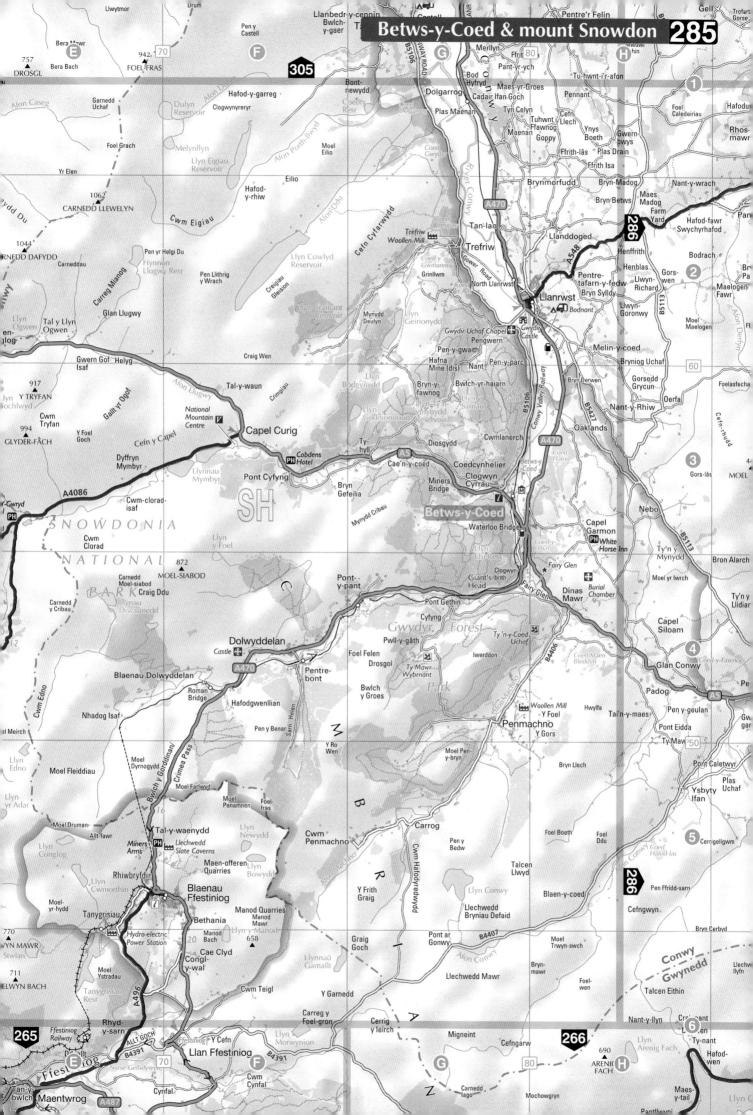

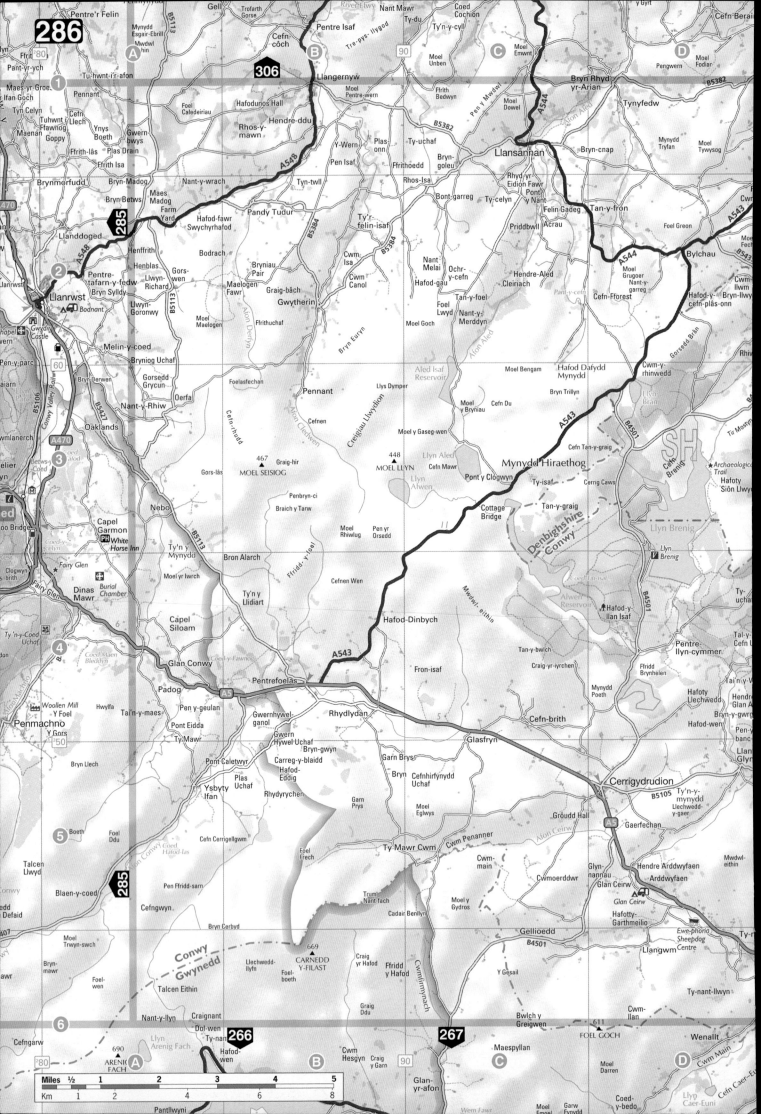

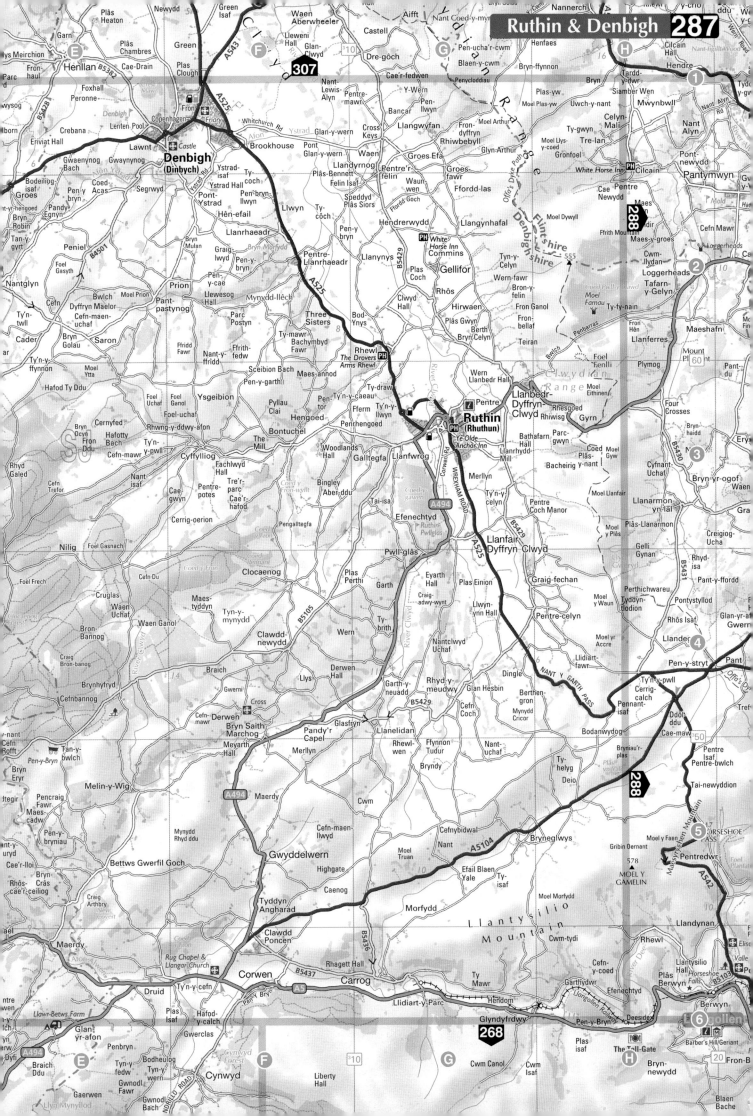

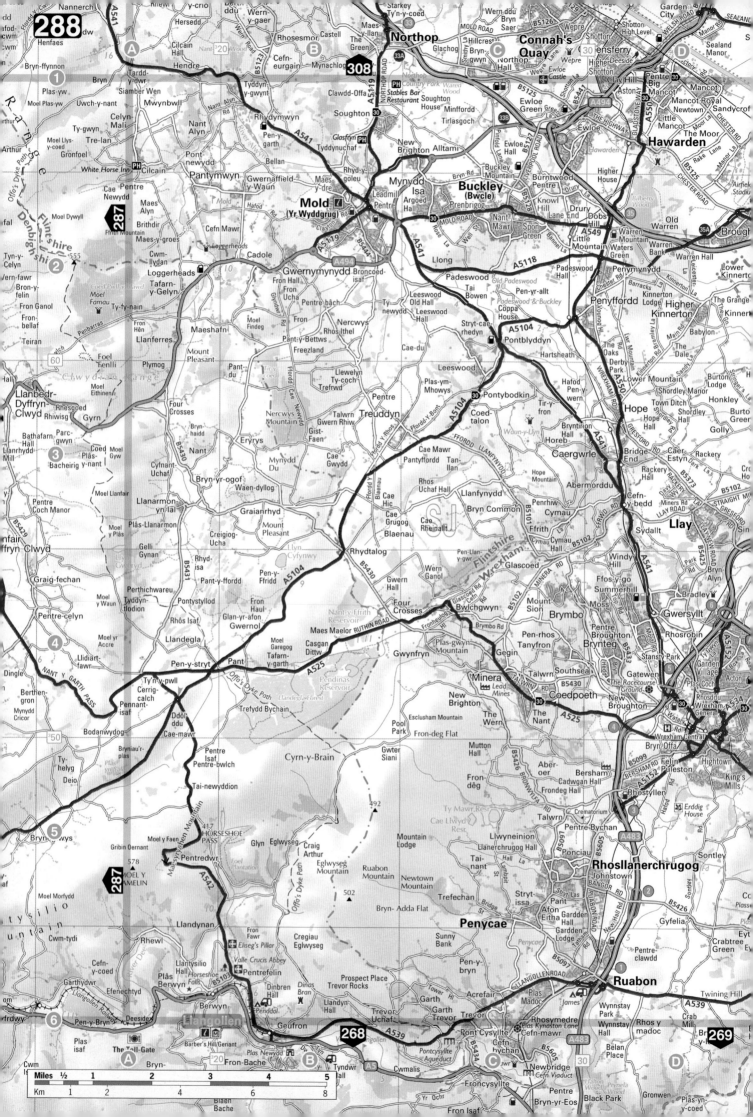

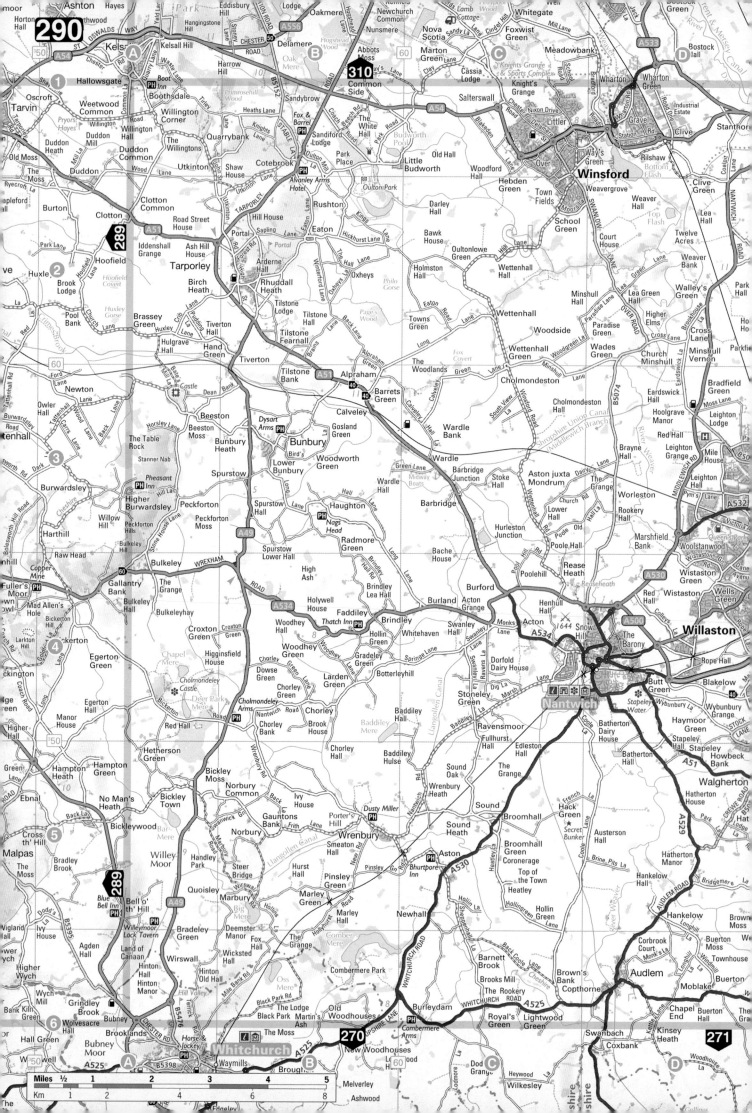

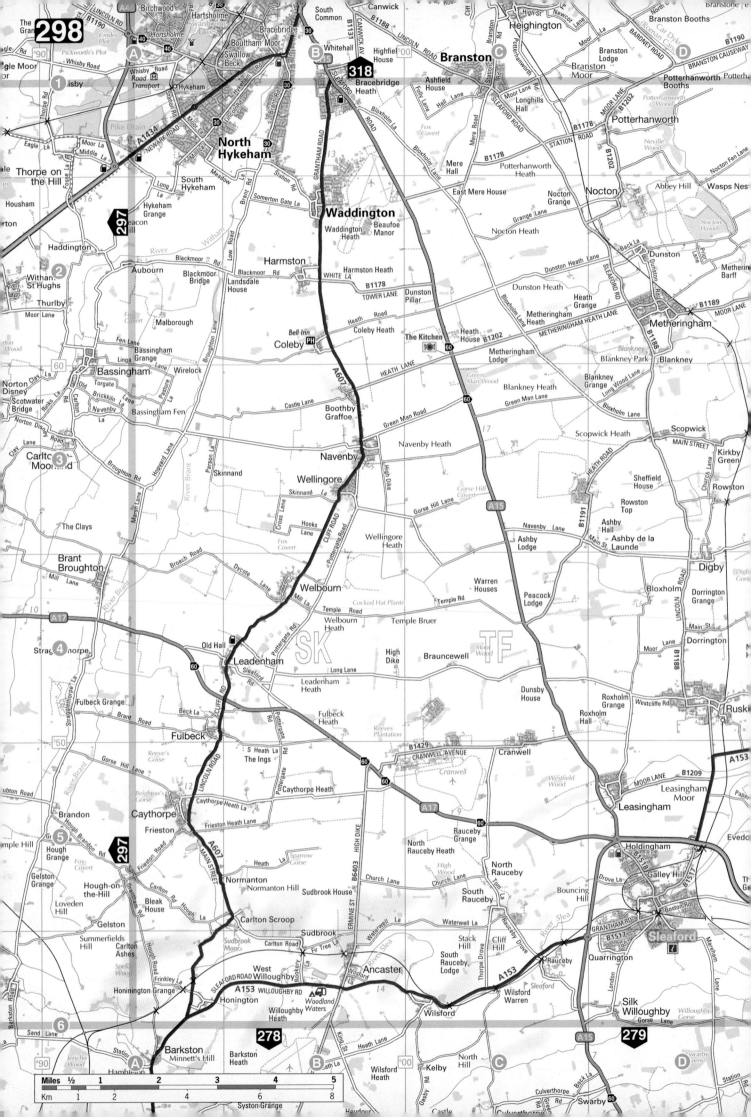

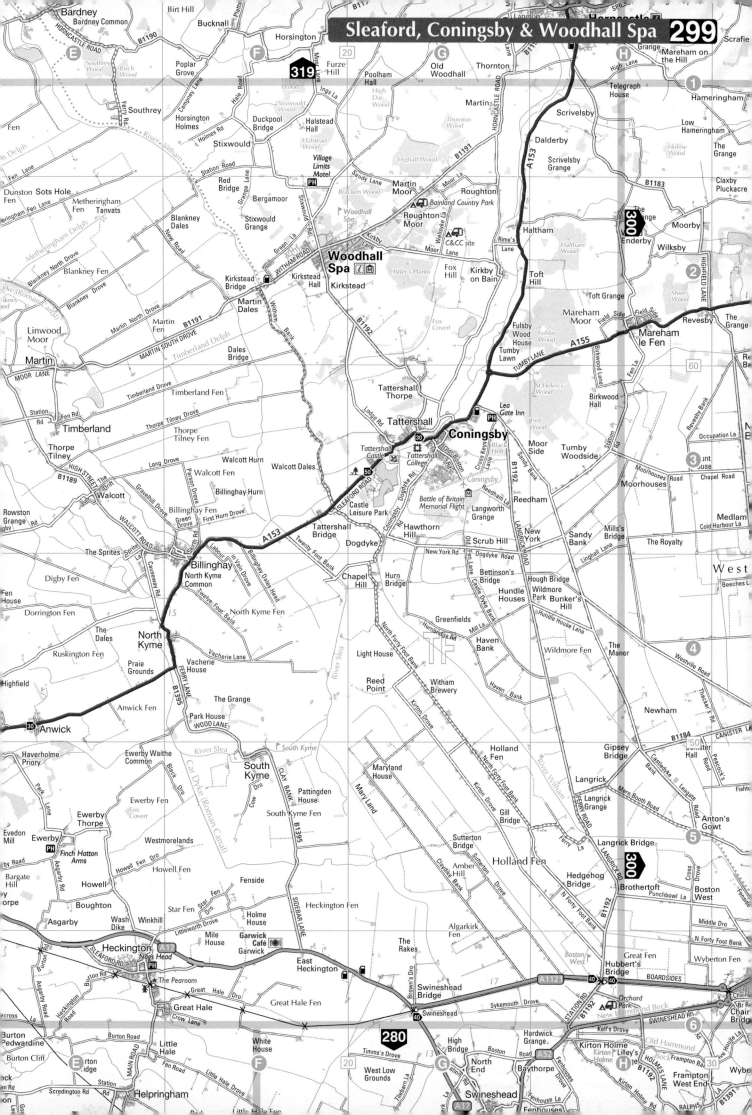

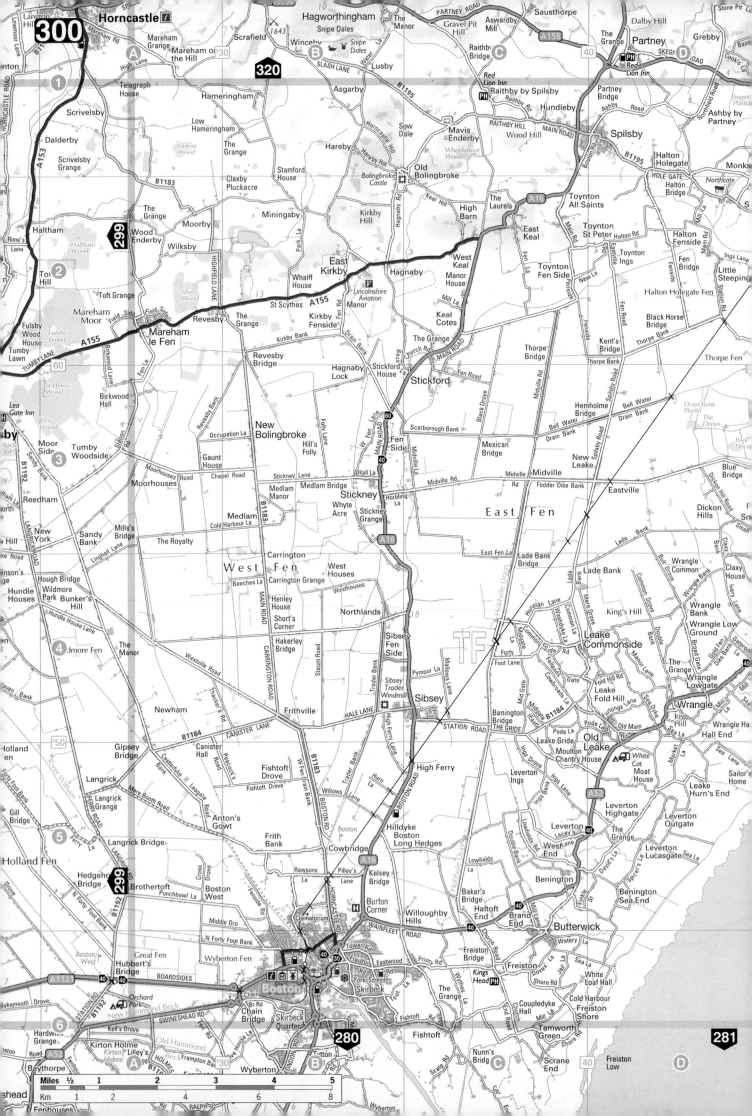

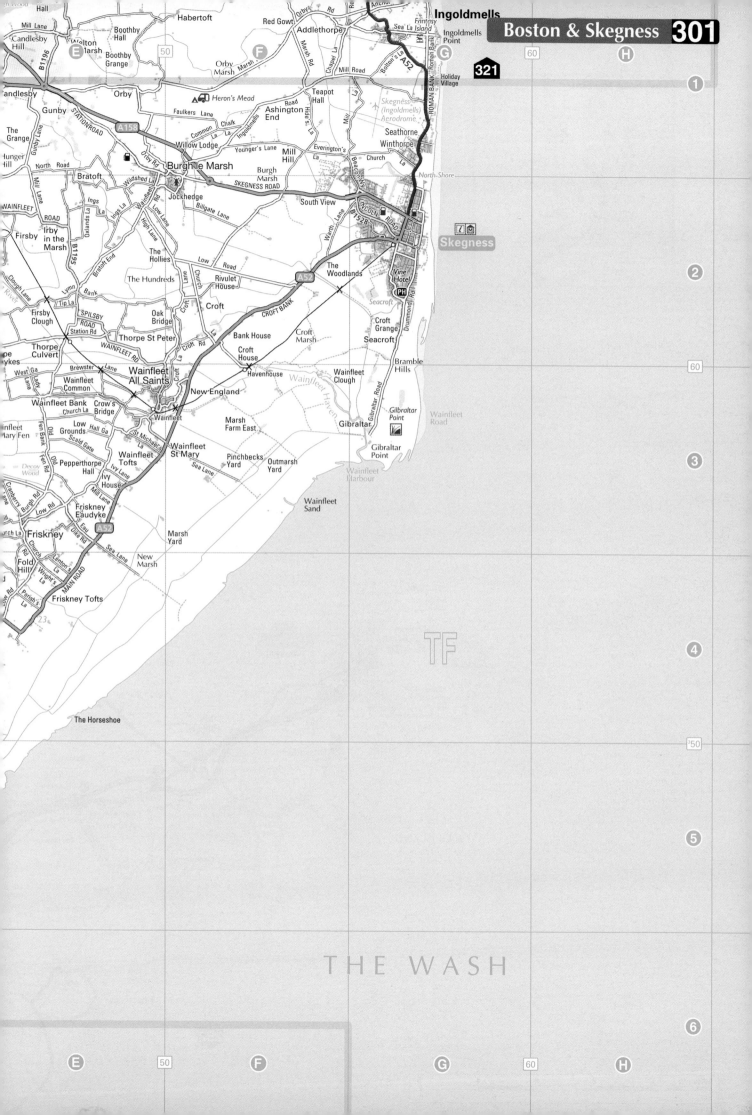

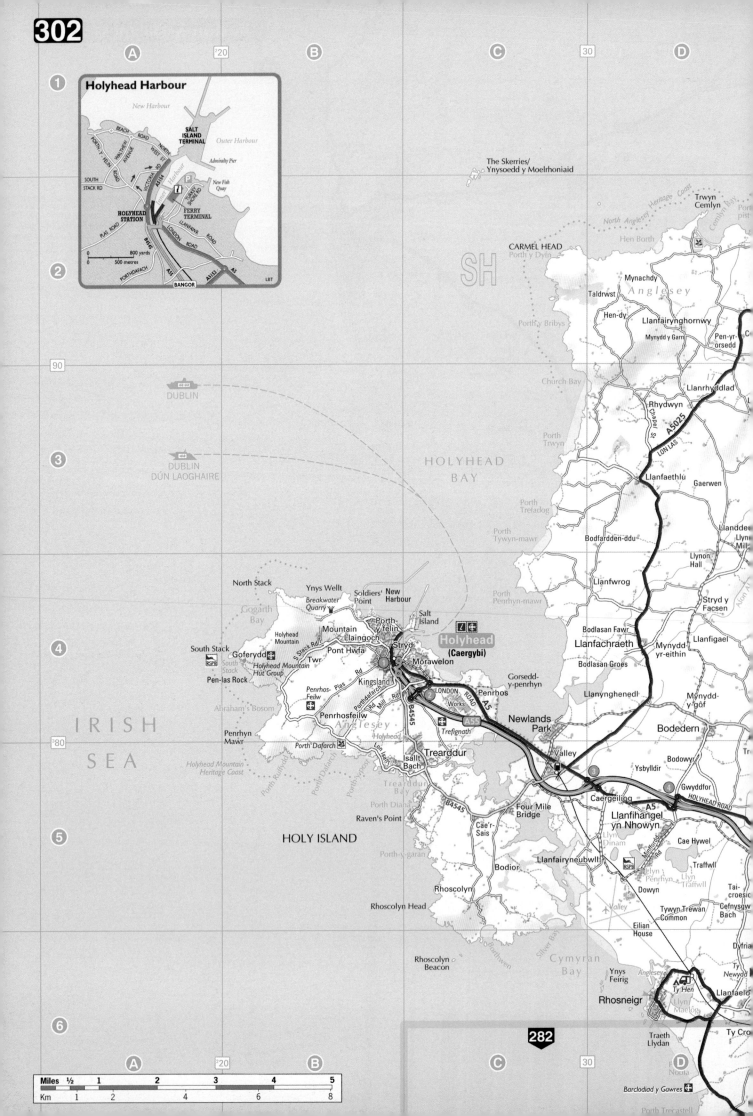

Holyhead Harbour

New Harbour

SALT ISLAND TERMINAL

Outer Harbour

Admiralty Pier

BEACH ROAD

PORTH-Y-FELIN ROAD

WALTHEW AVENUE

NORTH ST

WEST ST

VICTORIA RD

TUCKER

PORT RD

New Fish Quay

SOUTH STACK RD

P

Inner Harbour

FERRY TERMINAL

HOLYHEAD STATION

LLANFAWR

ROAD

LLANFAWR

PLAS ROAD

LONDON ROAD

B4545

A5154

PORTHDAFACH

A55

A5153

A5

BANGOR

LBT

800 yards

500 metres

A | ²20 | **B** | 30 | **C** | **D**

The Skerries/
Ynysoedd y Moelrhoniaid

CARMEL HEAD
Porth y Dyln

North Anglesey Heritage Coast

Cemlyn Bay

Trwyn
Cemlyn

Hen Borth

SH

Anglesey

Mynachdy

Taldrwst

Hen-dy

Llanfairynghornwy

Mynydd y Garn

Pen-yr-orsedd

DUBLIN

90

Porth y Bribys

Church Bay

Llanrhyddlad

Rhydwyn

A5025

LON LAS

CHAPEL ST

DUBLIN
DÚN LAOGHAIRE

3

HOLYHEAD
BAY

Porth
Trwyn

Llanfaethlu

Gaerwen

Porth
Trefadog

Llanddew

Llyn Mill

Porth
Tywyn-mawr

Bodfardden-ddu

Llynon
Hall

North Stack

Ynys Wellt

Soldiers'
Point

New
Harbour

Porth
Penrhyn-mawr

Llanfwrog

Stryd y
Facsen

Gogarth
Bay

Breakwater
Quarry

Holyhead
Mountain

Porth-
y-felin

Salt
Island

Holyhead
(Caergybi)

Bodlasan Fawr

Llanfachraeth

Mynydd-
yr-eithin

Llanfigael

South Stack

RSPB

Goferydd

Mountain

Llaingoch

Pont Hwfa

Stryd

Morawelon

Gorseddy-penrhyn

Bodlasan Groes

Twr

S Stack Rd

LONDON

ROAD

A5

Llanynghenedl

Mynydd-
y-gôf

Holyhead Mountain
Hut Group

Penrhos-
Feilw

Plas

Rd

Kingsland

Mill Rd

Penrhos
Works

Penrhos

4

Pen-las Rock

Porthdafarch

B4545

A55

Newlands
Park

Bodedern

Penrhosfeilw

Anglesey

Trefignath

Valley

Bodowyr

I R I S H

Abraham's Bosom

Holyhead

Ysbylldir

Penrhyn
Mawr

Lôn Isallt

Isallt
Bach

Trearddur

Caergeiliog

Gwyddfor

HOLYHEAD ROAD

S E A

Holyhead Mountain
Heritage Coast

Porth Dafarch

Trearddur
Bay

B4545

Four Mile
Bridge

A5

Llanfihangel
yn Nhowyn

Cae Hywel

Porth Diana

Cae'r-
Sais

Llyn
Dinam

Mintford Rd

Raven's Point

Porth-y-garan

Llanfairyneubwll

RSPB

Traffwll

5

HOLY ISLAND

Bodior

Llyn
Penrhyn

Llyn
Traffwll

Tai-
croesio

Dowyn

Cefnysgw
Bach

Rhoscolyn

Valley

Tywyn-Trewan
Common

Rhoscolyn Head

Eilian
House

Dyfria

Rhoscolyn
Beacon

Bodwen

Cymyran
Bay

Ynys
Feirig

Anglesey

Ty Hen

Ty
Newydd

Llanfaelo

Rhosneigr

Llyn
Maelog

6

282

Traeth
Llydan

Ty Cro

A | ²20 | **B** | **C** | 30 | **D**

Barclodiad y Gawres

Porth Trecastell

Miles ½ 1 2 3 4 5

Km 1 2 4 6 8

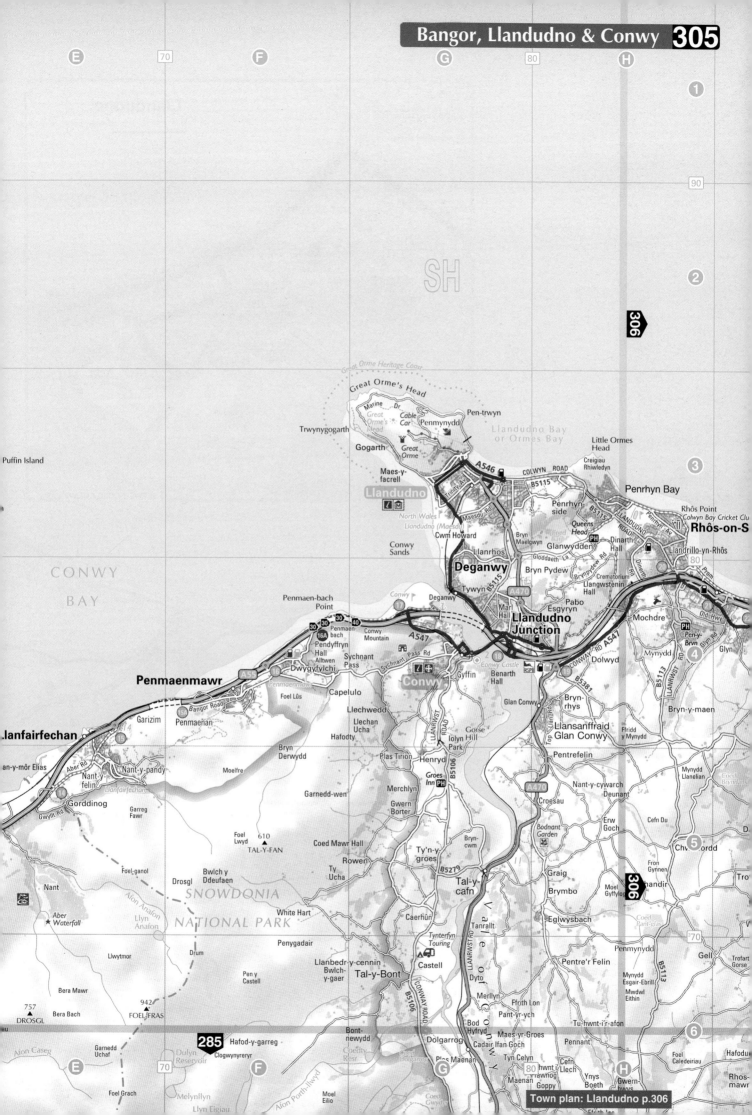

SH

306

Puffin Island

Great Orme Heritage Coast

Great Orme's Head

Marine Dr
Cable Car
Great Orme's Head

Pen-trwyn

Penmynydd

Trwynygogarth

Llandudno Bay or Ormes Bay

Gogarth

Great Orme

Little Ormes Head

Maes-y-facrell

Creigiau Rhiwledyn

A546

COLWYN ROAD

Llandudno

B5115

Penrhyn Bay

Penrhyn-side

North Wales

Llandudno (Maesdu)

Rhôs Point
Colwyn Bay Cricket Clu

Cwm Howard

Maesdu Rd

Queens Head

Penrhyn-side

B5115

LLANDUDNO

Rhôs-on-S

Conwy Sands

Cwm Howard

Llanrhos

Bryn Maelgwyn

Glanwydden

PH

Dinarth Hall

Llandrillo-yn-Rhôs

CONWY BAY

Deganwy

Gloddaeth La

Bryn Pydew

Brynydew Rd

Crematorium

Llangwstenin

Pabo

Esgyryn

Llandudno Junction

Mochdre

Old Hwy

Marl Hall

Tywyn B5115

A470

Penmaen-bach Point

Conwy

Deganwy

A547

Llandudno Junction

Dolwyd

Pen-y-Bryn

PH

Glyn

30 30 40

Penmaen-bach

Conwy Mountain

Conwy Castle

RSPB

CONWY RD A547

Mynydd

B5113

Glyn Rd

16A

Pendyffryn Hall

Alltwen

Sychnant Pass

Sychnant Pass Rd

Gyffin

Benarth Hall

A55 16

Dwygyfylchi

Conwy

Glan Conwy

Bryn-rhys

Bryn-y-maen

Penmaenmawr

Penmaenmawr

Foel Lûs

Capelulo

Llechwedd

LLANRWST ROAD

Llansanffraid Glan Conwy

Ffridd y Mynydd

Bangor Road

Garizim

Penmaenan

Llechan Ucha

Hafodty

Gorse Hill Park

Iolyn Hill

Pentrefin

Mynydd Llanelian

Coed Brynlâs

Llanfairfechan

an-y-môr Elias

Aber Rd

Nant-y-pandy

Bryn Derwydd

Moelfre

Plas Tirion

Henryd

B5106

Nant-y-cywarch

Deunant

Cefn Du

Nant-y-felin

Llanfairfechan

A470

Erw Goch

Gorddinog

Garreg Fawr

Garnedd-wen

Merchlyn

Croesau

Groes Inn

PH

Gwern Borter

Bryn-cwm

Bodnant Garden

Gwylt Rd

Foel-ganol

Foel Lwyd 610 TAL-Y-FAN

Coed Mawr Hall

Ty'n-y-groes

Graig

Fron Gynnen

Chw ordd

Nant

Drosgl

Ty Ucha

Rowen

Brymbo

Moel Gyffylog

306

Tro

handir

Aber ★ Waterfall

Llyn Anafon

SNOWDONIA

White Hart

B5279

Tal-y-cafn

Eglwysbach

Coed Pant-glas

Bera Mawr

NATIONAL PARK

Caerhûn

Tanrallt

Penmynydd

Llwytmor

Penygadair

Tynterfyn Touring

Pentre'r Felin

Gell

Bera Bach

Drum

Llanbedr-y-cennin Bwlch-y-gaer

Castell

Dyfo

Merllyn

Mynydd Esgair-Ebrill

B5113

Trofa Gorse

757 ▲ DROSGL

942 ▲ FOEL FRAS

Pen y Castell

Tal-y-Bont

CONWAY ROAD B5106

Ffrith Lon

Pant-yr-ych

Mwdwl Eithin

Hafodu

Garnedd Uchaf

285 Hafod-y-garreg

Bont-newydd

Tu-hwnt-i'r-afon

Dulyn Reservoir

Clogwynyreryr

Dôlgarrog

Cadair Ifan Goch

Tyn Celyn

Pennant

Foel Grach

Plas Maenan

Cefn Llech

Ynys Boeth

Gwern-hwus

Rhos-mawr

Afon Caseg

Melynllyn

Moel Eilio

Llyn Eigiau

80 hwnt i Trawnog Goppy

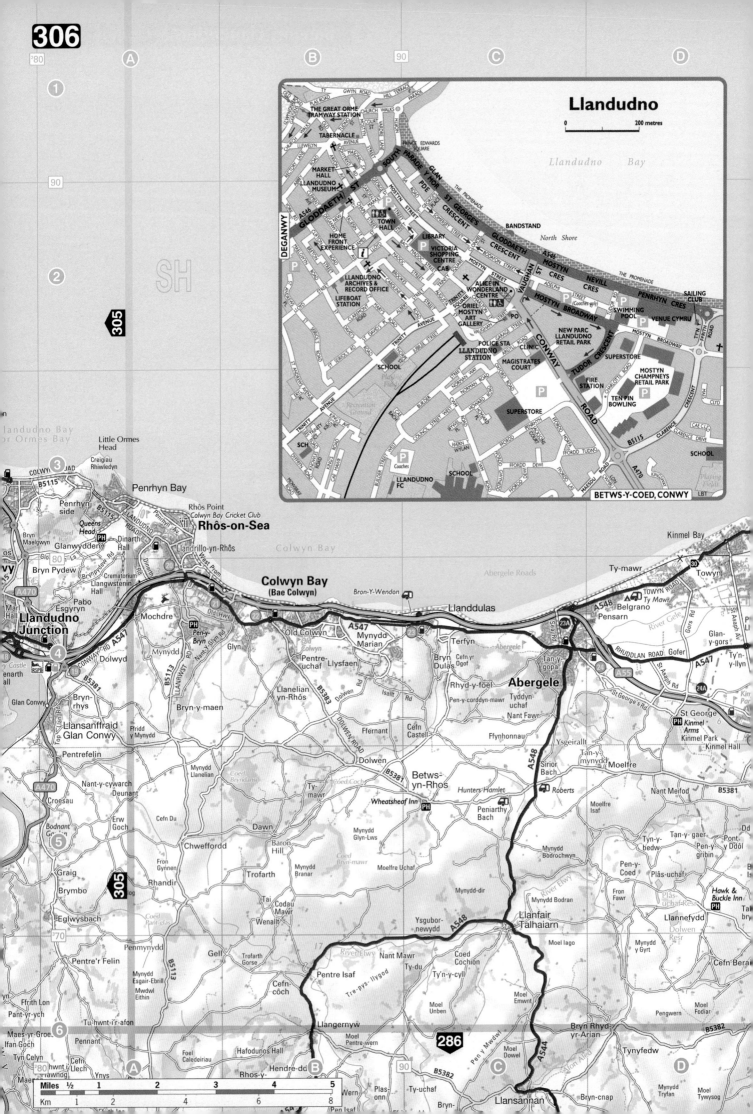

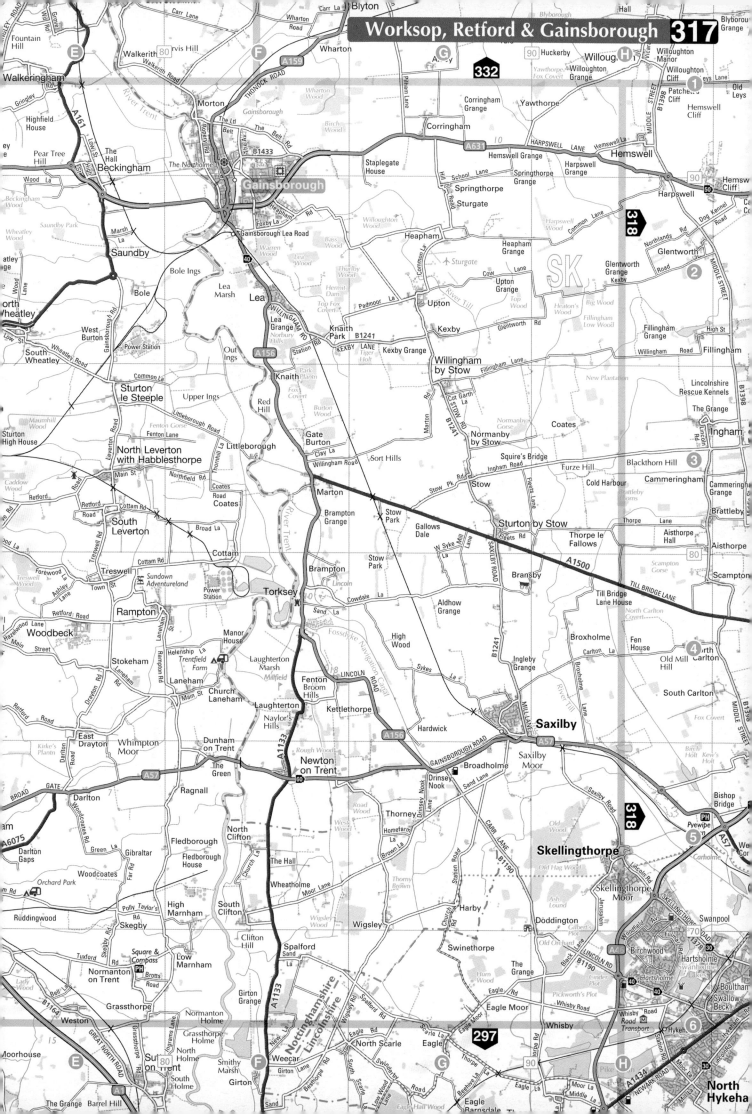

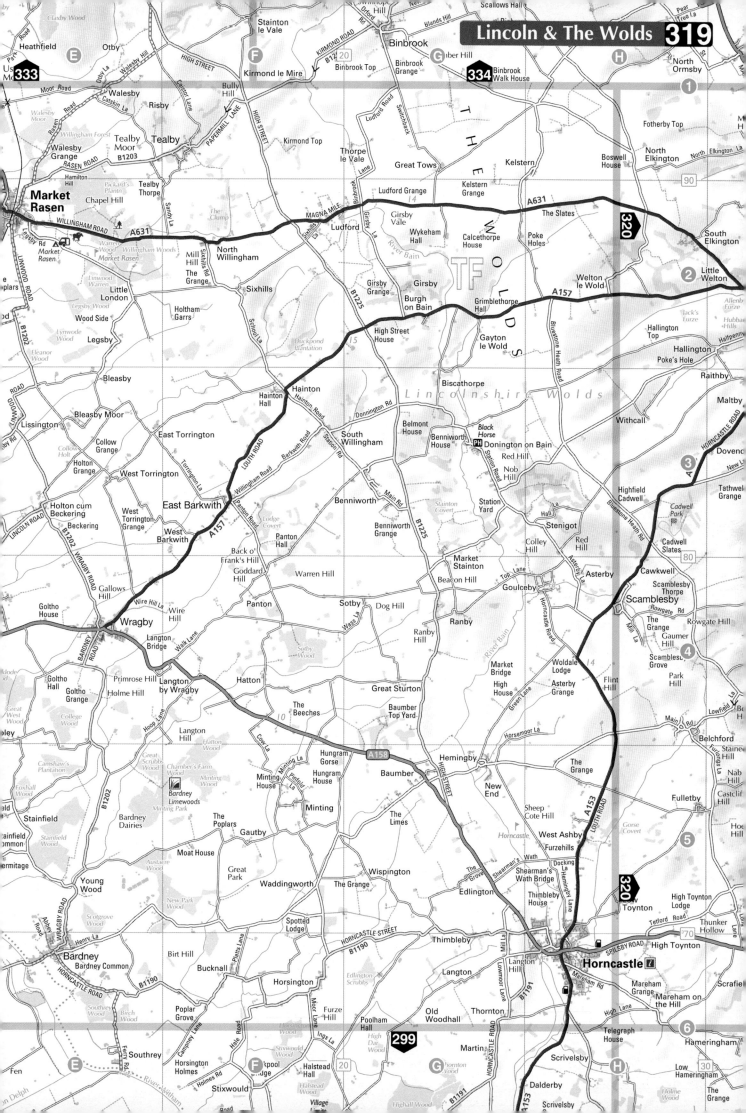

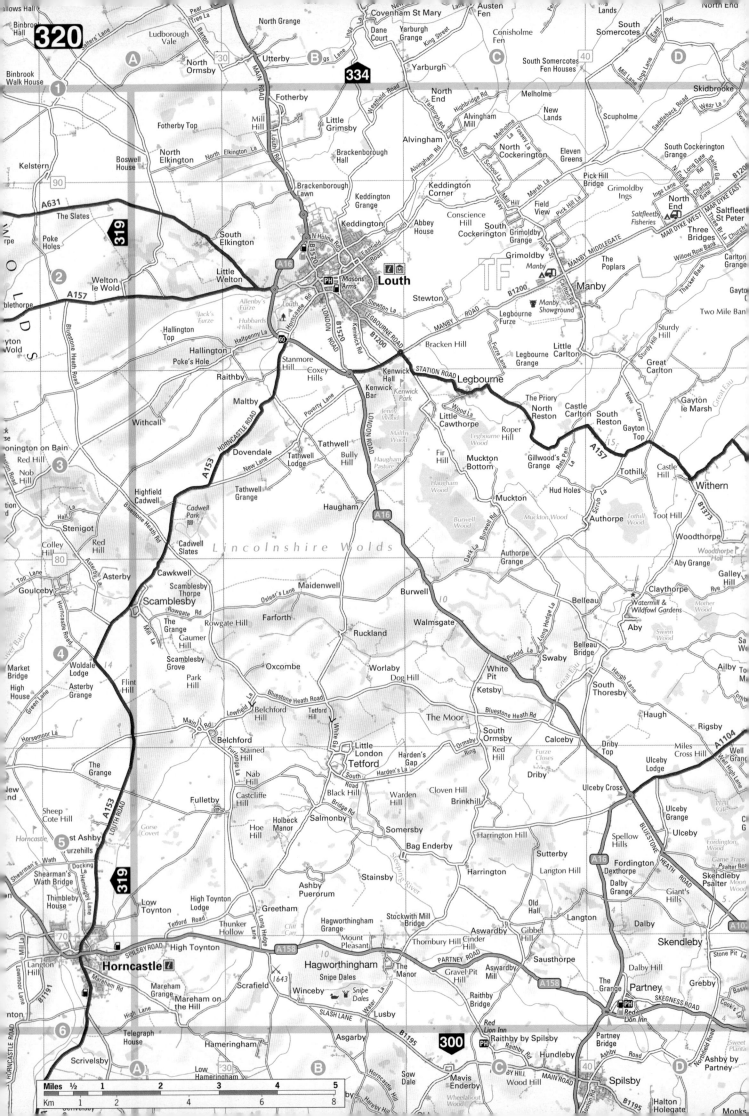

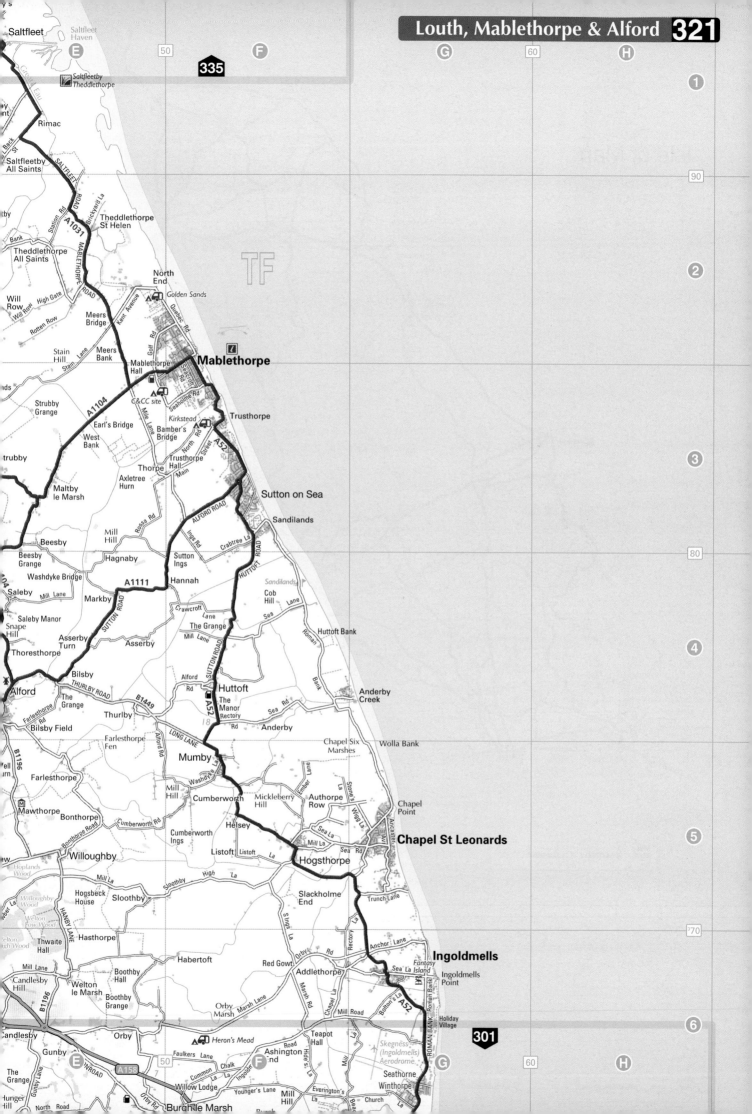

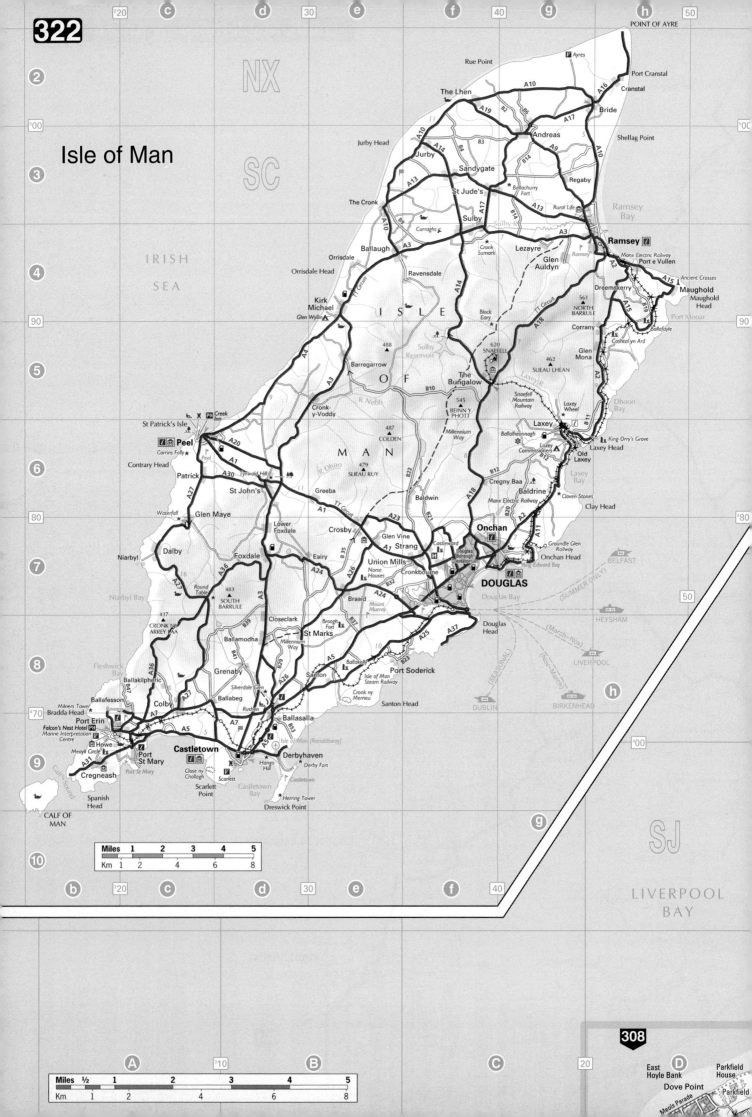

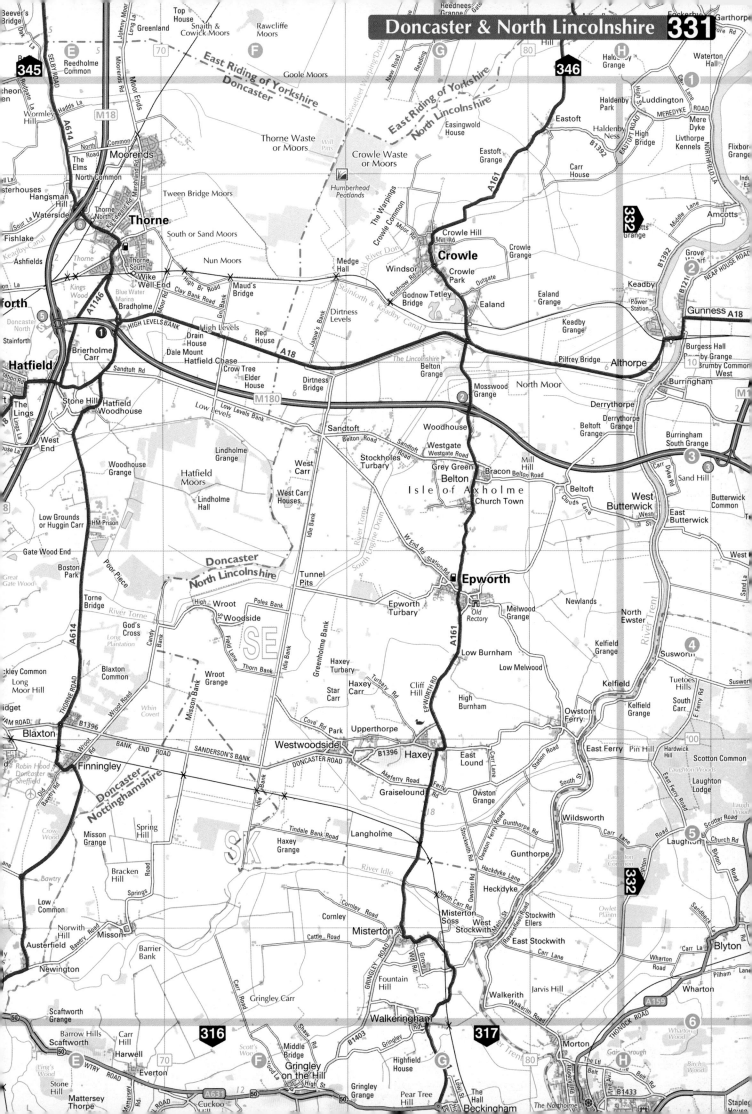

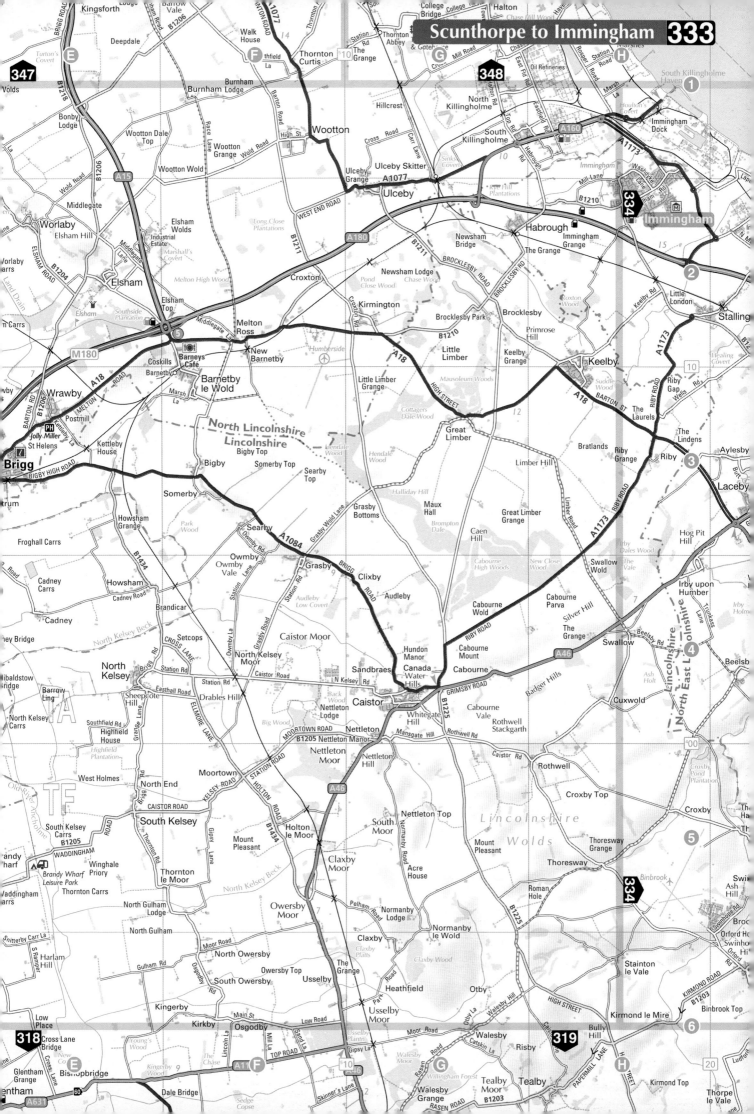

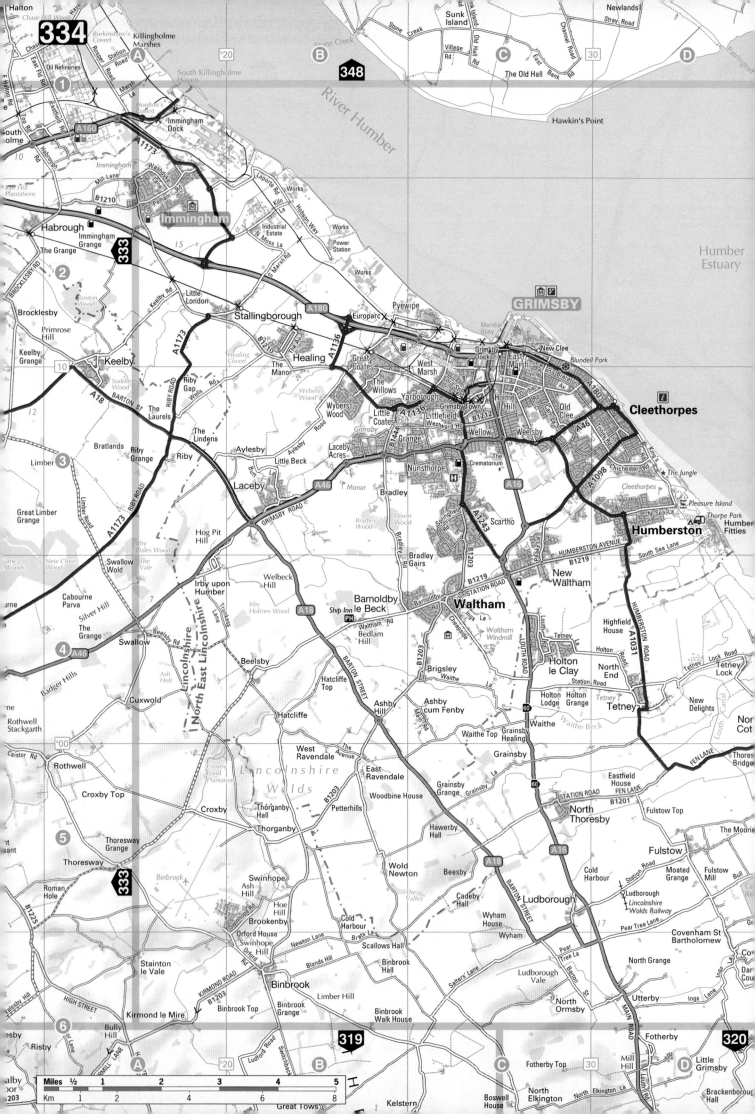

Skeffling
Easington
HULL ROAD
Winsetts

E   **F**   **349**   **G**   50   **H**

1

Long Bank
Bridge
Kilnsea
Grange
Spurn Heritage Coast
Kilnsea
Road
Kilnsea Warren
Spurn

2

SPURN HEAD

Mouth of the Humber

10

3

TA

4

Horse Shoe
Point

ney High Sands
Tetney
Haven
Northcoates
Point

Somercotes
Haven
Grainthorpe
Haven

The Fitties

North La

"00

Marshchapel
Donna
Nook
Porter's
Sluice
Donna
Nook

TF

Keyholme Lane
Eskham
Beacon Hill
Ivy House
Marsh
Grange
Marsh Lane
Low Gate
Coal La
Shore La
Marshchapel
Ings
Wragholme
Ark Road
Firebeacon Lane
Holmes Lane
Poplar Grove
Grainthorpe
Butt Gate
Marsh La
Bank End
Eau Bank
ROAD
North Somercotes
Sand
Haile
Flats

5

Biergate
29
Ludney
CONISHOLME
South Rd
A1031
WARREN ROAD
Fen Lane
Grainthorpe
Fen
Conisholme
Lowgate Road
Fen Lane
The
Poplars
Church La
Church End
Swancroft
Owe's Lane
Acre
Bridge La
Ing
Lands
Skidbrooke
North End
Toby's
Hill
Austen
Fen
Conisholme
Fen
South
Somercotes
East Rw
Church La
Louth Rd
Saltfleet
Saltfleet
Haven
Treasure
Lane
Mary
King Street
South Somercotes
Fen Houses
Mill Lane
Ings Lane
East La
Tilney Gate
Great Eau

6

North
End
urgh
Alvingham
Mill
E
Highbridge Rd
Melholme
New
Lands
40
Scupholme
Saddleback Road
Skidbrooke
F
West La
Queen's
Bridge
Saltfleetby
St Clement
Swallow Ga Rd
321
Saltfleetby
Theddlethorpe
G
Rimac
50
H
ham
Lock La
Tossey La
Manholme La
North Cockerington
Eleven
Greens
South Cockerington
Grange
Long Gate
Salter La
1200
Back St
Saltfleetby
All Saints

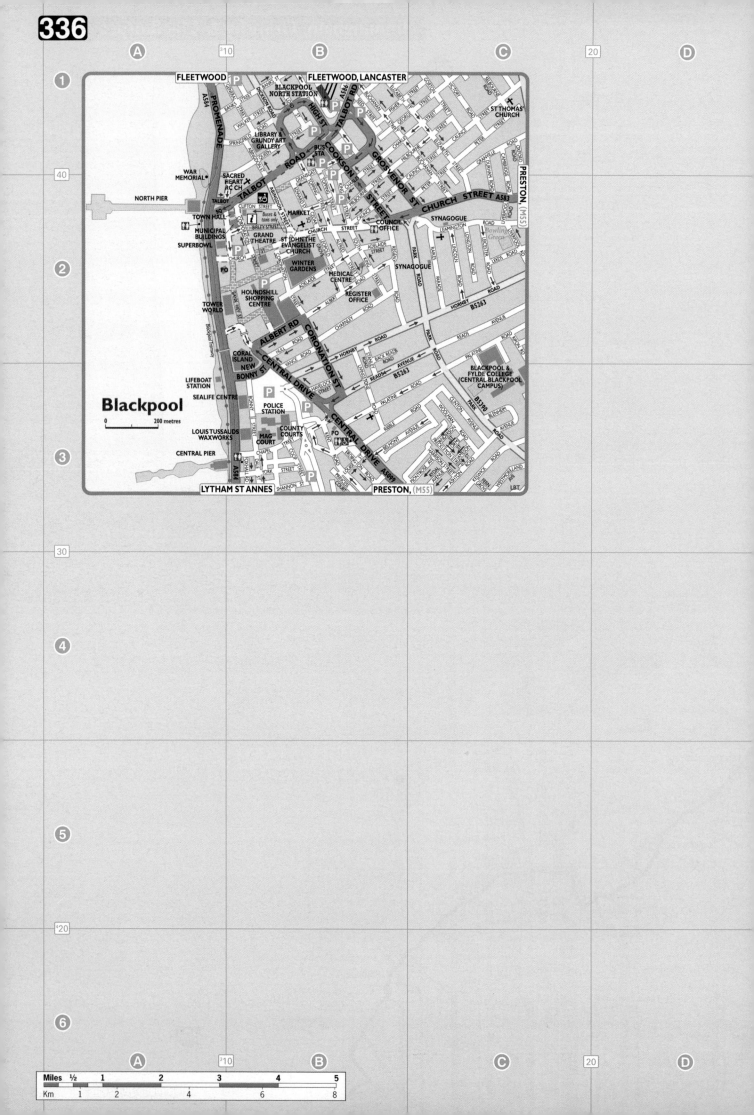

Blackpool

0 — 200 metres

FLEETWOOD
FLEETWOOD, LANCASTER
PRESTON (M55)
NORTH PIER
WAR MEMORIAL
SACRED HEART RC CH
BLACKPOOL NORTH STATION
LIBRARY & GRUNDY ART GALLERY
BUS STA
ST THOMAS CHURCH
TALBOT
TOWN HALL
MUNICIPAL BUILDINGS
SUPERBOWL
GRAND THEATRE
ST JOHN THE EVANGELIST CHURCH
MARKET
COUNCIL OFFICE
SYNAGOGUE
Bowling Green
WINTER GARDENS
MEDICAL CENTRE
REGISTER OFFICE
SYNAGOGUE
PO
HOUNDSHILL SHOPPING CENTRE
TOWER WORLD
ALBERT RD
CORONATION ST
B5263
CORAL ISLAND NEW
CENTRAL DRIVE
BONNY ST
HORNBY
BLACKPOOL & FYLDE COLLEGE (CENTRAL BLACKPOOL CAMPUS)
B5263
LIFEBOAT STATION
SEALIFE CENTRE
POLICE STATION
LOUIS TUSSAUDS WAXWORKS
MAG COURT
COUNTY COURTS
PO
CENTRAL PIER
A584
LYTHAM ST ANNES
PRESTON, (M55)
A5099
LBT

Miles ½ 1 2 3 4 5
Km 1 2 4 6 8

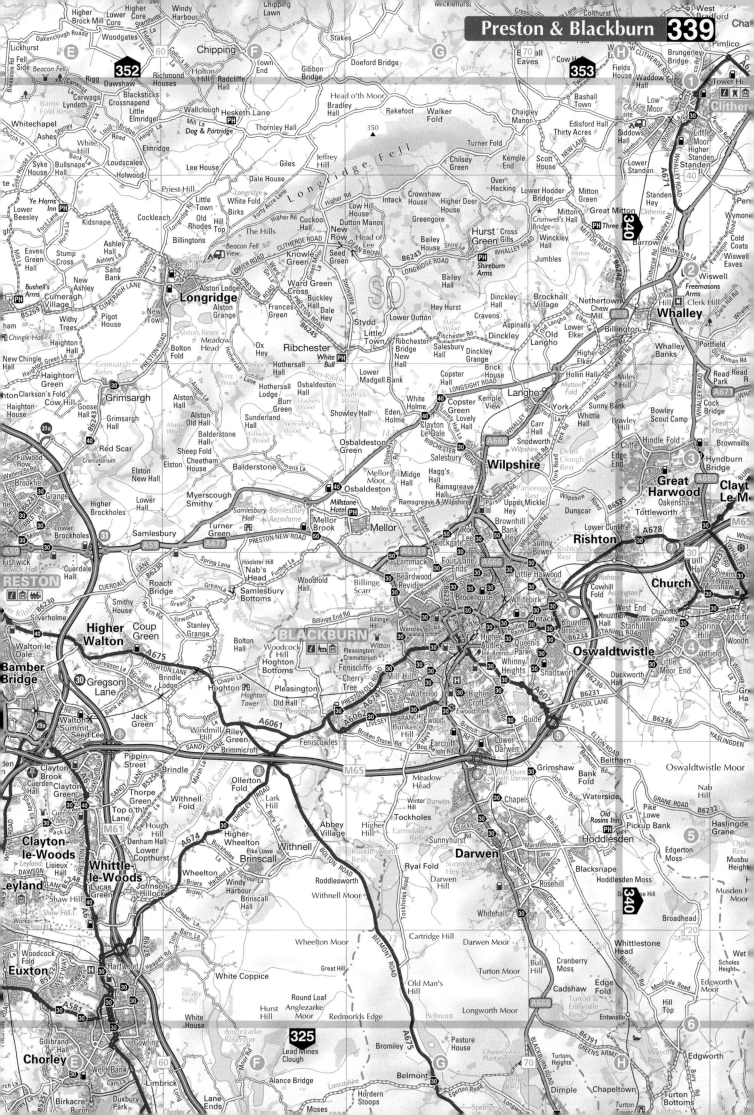

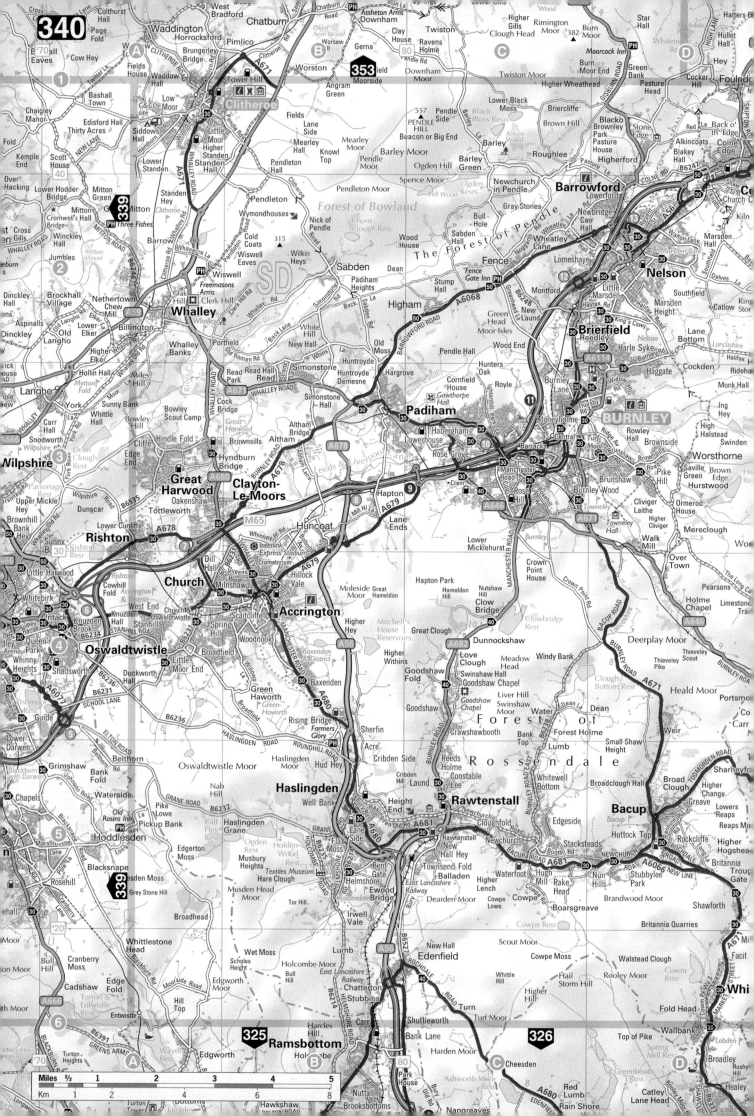

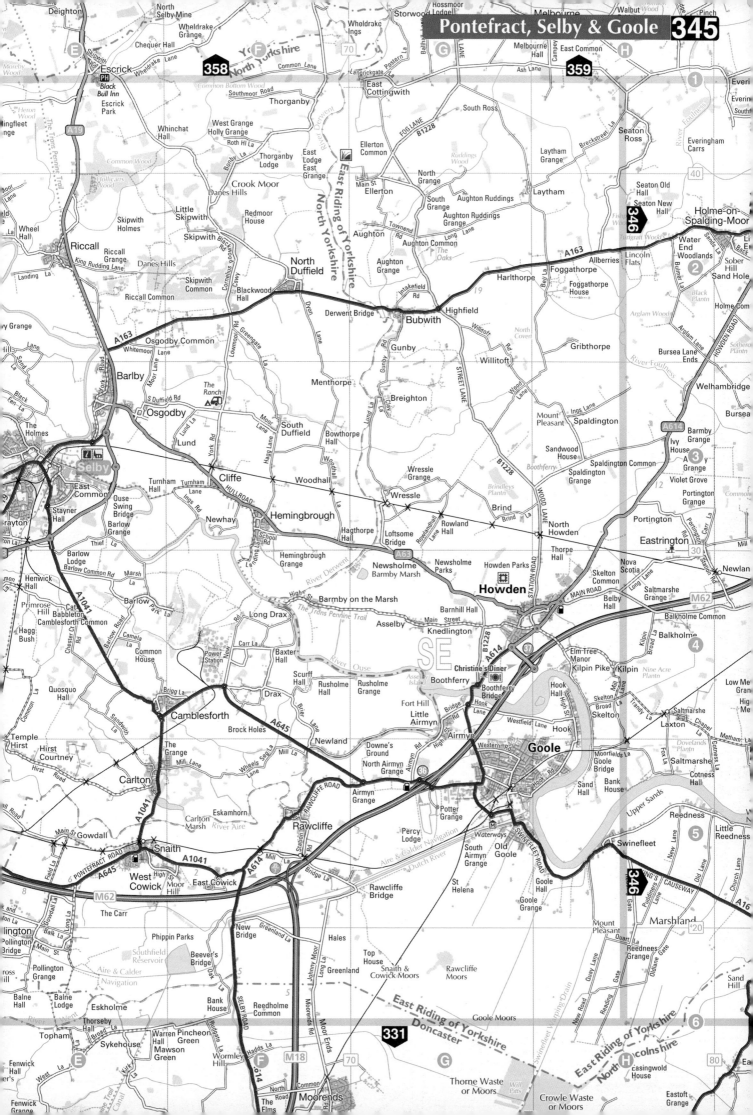

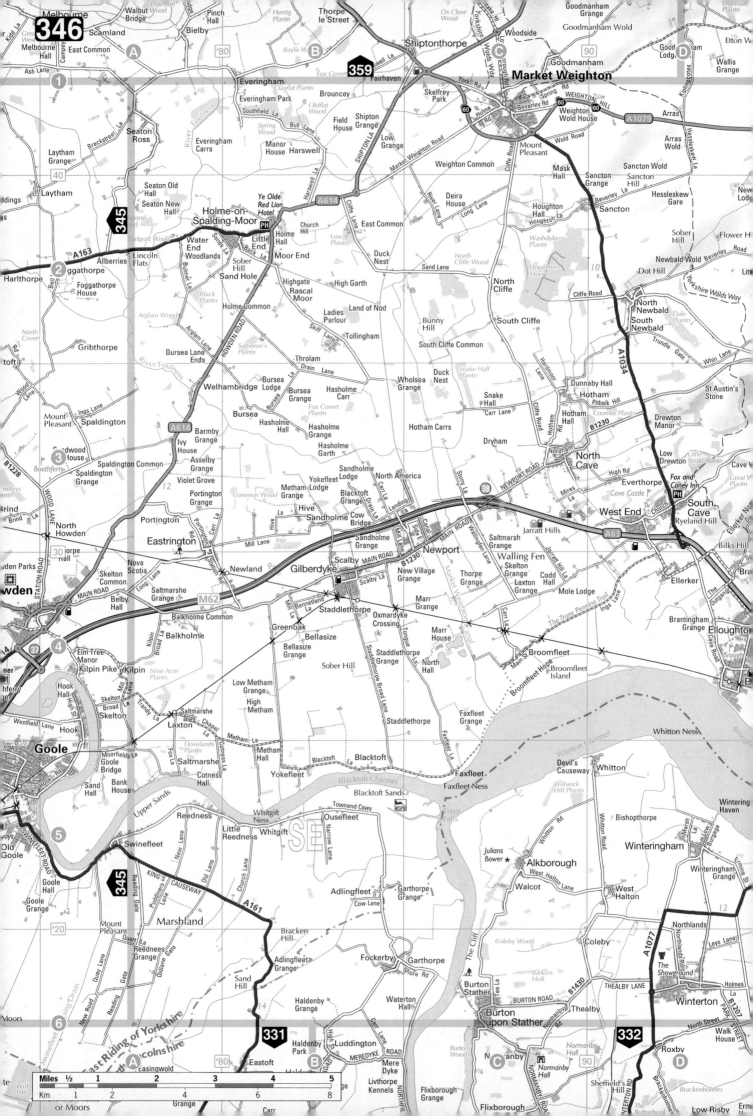

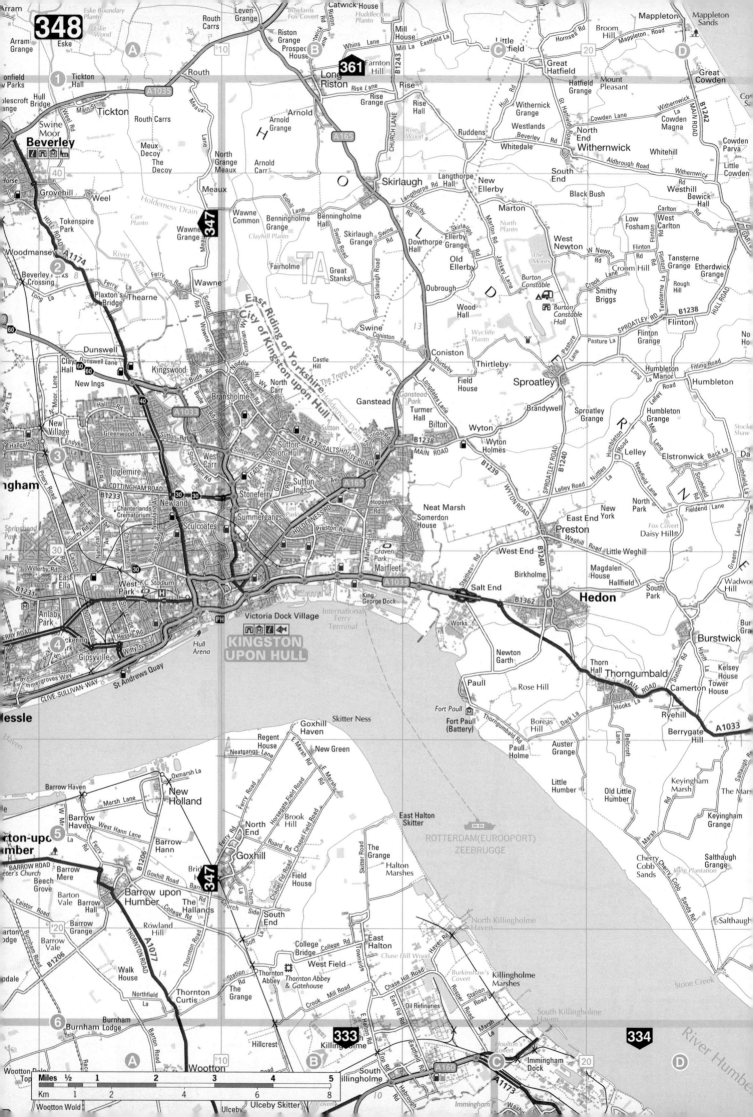

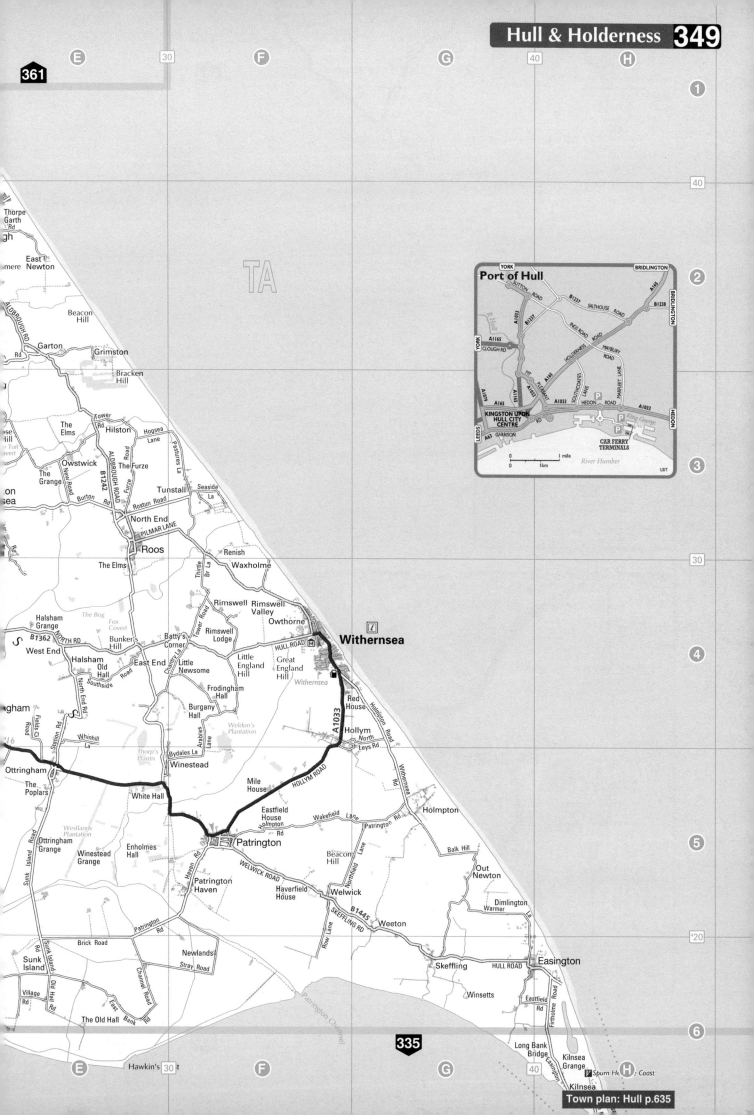

E · 30 · F · G · 40 · H

361

1

40

TA

East Newton

Thorpe Garth Rd

Beacon Hill

Garton Rd

Grimston

Bracken Hill

Tower Rd

Hilston

The Elms

Hogsea Lane

Pastures La

Owstwick

The Furze

Furze Road

ALDBROUGH ROAD

New Road

Burton Rd

Rostun Road

B1242

The Grange

Tunstall

Seaside La

North End

PILMAR LANE

Roos

The Elms

Renish

Waxholme

Thirtle Br La

Rimswell

Rimswell Valley

Owthorne

Withernsea

The Bog

Fox Covert

Halsham Grange

B1362

NORTH RD

Bunker's Hill

Batty's Corner

Chantry La

Tower Road

Rimswell Lodge

Hull Road

West End

Halsham Old Hall

East End

Southside Road

Little Newsome

Little England Hill

Great England Hill

Withernsea

Red House

Holmpton Road

North End Rd

Frodingham Hall

Burgany Hall

Weldon's Plantation

Arables Lane

A1033

Hollym

North Leys Rd

Whinhill La

Bydales La

Thorp's Plantn

Winestead

Mile House

HOLLYM ROAD

Withernsea Rd

Ottringham

Fields Cl

Station Rd

White Hall

Eastfield House

Holmpton Rd

Wakefield Lane

Patrington Rd

Holmpton

The Poplars

Westlands Plantation

Enholmes Hall

Patrington

Haven Rd

WELWICK ROAD

Beacon Hill

Northfield Lane

Balk Hill

Out Newton

Ottringham Grange

Winestead Grange

Patrington Haven

Haverfield House

Welwick

B1445

Weeton

Dimlington Warmer

Dimlington

Sunk Island Rd

Patrington Rd

Brick Road

SKEFFLING RD

Row Lane

Newlands

Stray Road

Channel Road

East Bank Rd

Old Hall Rd

Sunk Island

Skeffling

HULL ROAD

Easington

Winsetts

Eastfield Rd

Firtholme Road

Village Rd

The Old Hall

Patrington Channel

335

Long Bank Bridge

Kilnsea Grange

Spurn He... Coast

Kilnsea

E · Hawkin's · 30 · t · F · G · 40 · H

Port of Hull

YORK

BRIDLINGTON

SUTTON ROAD

B1237

SALTHOUSE ROAD

A165

BRIDLINGTON

B1238

A1033

B1237

INGS ROAD

A1165

CLOUGH RD

ROAD

MAYBURY ROAD

MT PLEASANT

A1165

HOLDERNESS

SOUTHCOATES LANE

MARFLEET LANE

A1079

A1165

A1033

HEDON

HEDON ROAD

A1033

HEDON

KINGSTON UPON HULL CITY CENTRE

LEEDS

A63

GARRISON

RD

King George Dock

CAR FERRY TERMINALS

River Humber

0 — 1 mile
0 — 1km

LBT

2

3

30

4

5

20

6

Town plan: Hull p.635

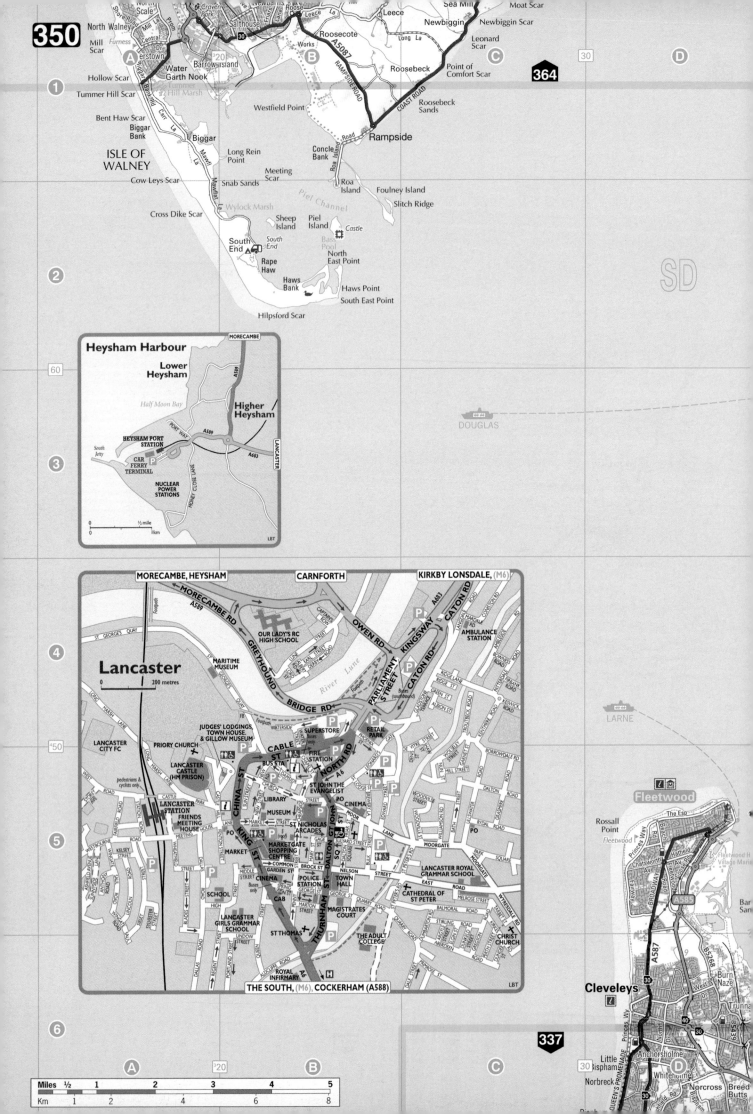

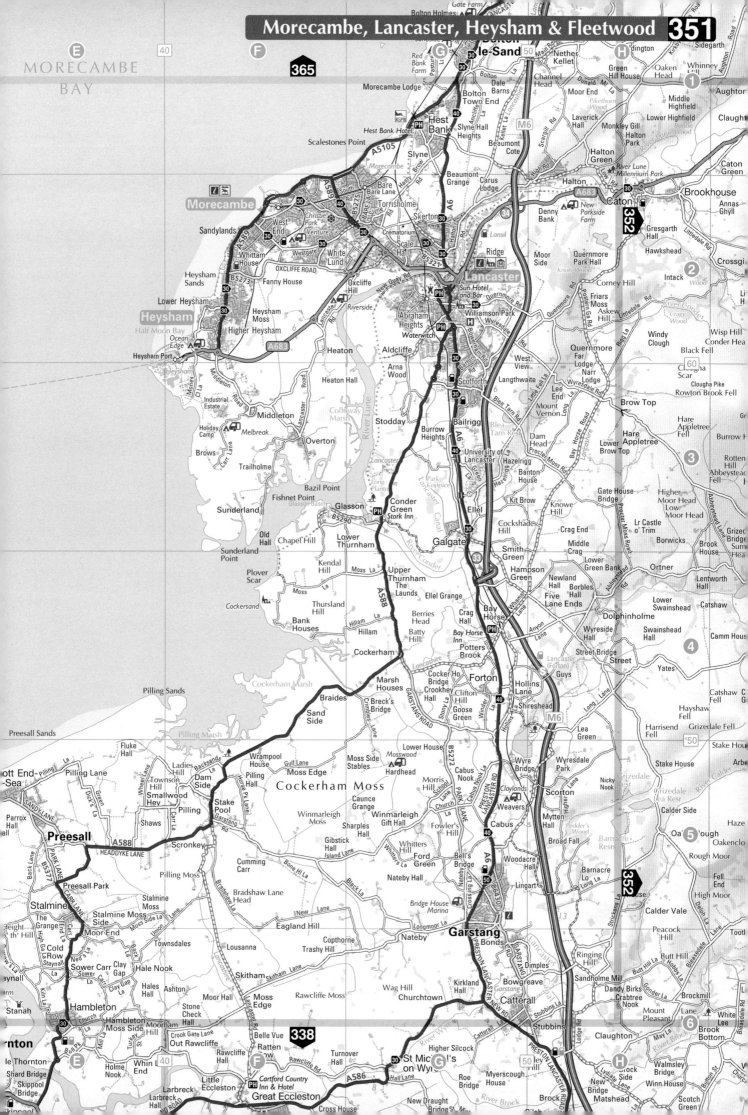

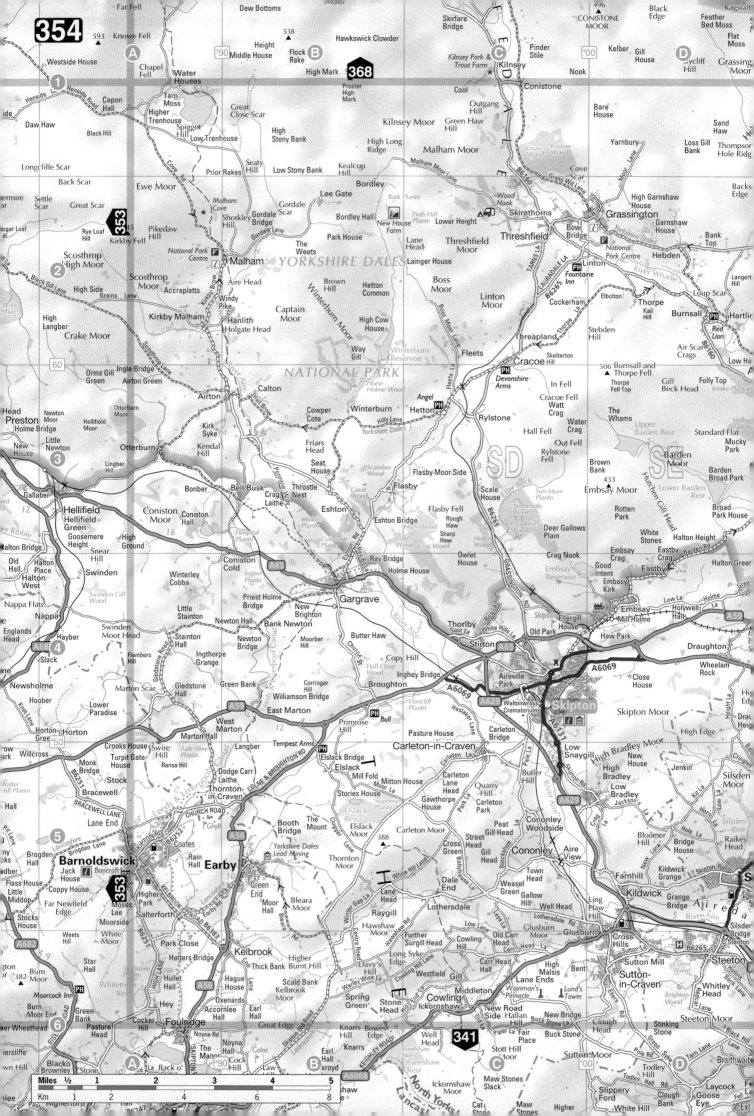

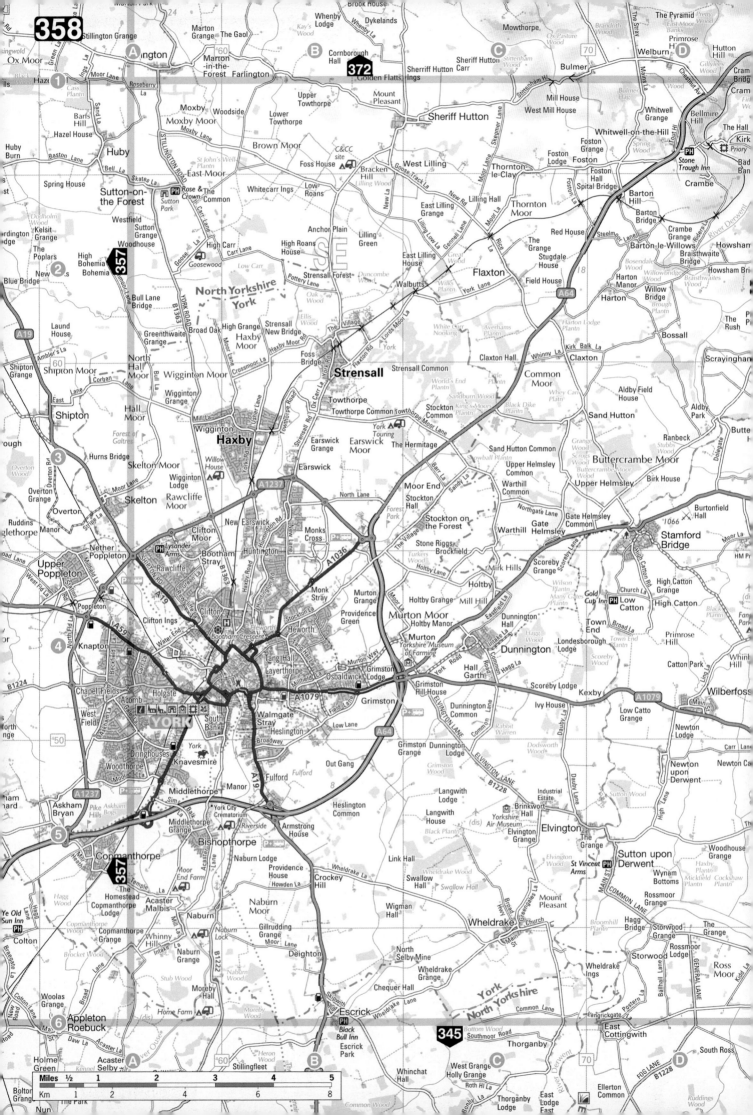

Town plan: York p.649

375

BRIDLINGTON BAY

TA

Bridlington

West Hill
Bessingby
Hilderthorpe
The Spa

Boynton

Carnaby

Haisthorpe

Thornholme

Burton Agnes

Thornholme Moor

Harpham
Moor

Gransmoor

Great Kelk

Park
House

Burtoncarr
House

Carnaby
Moor

North
Kingsfield

South
Kingsfield

Low
Stonehills

High
Stonehills

Industrial
Estate

Fraisthorpe
Sands

Fraisthorpe

Barmston

Barmston
Sands

Gransmoor
Lodge

Kelk Lane

Lissett

Lisset
Bridge

Beeford
Grange

Dringhoe

Upton

Beeford

Dunnington
Grange

Dunnington

Frodingham
Grange

Highthorns

Moor
Grange

Warleycross
Hill

Mount
Ephraim

Billings
Hill

Ulrome
Grange

East
End

Ulrome
West
End

Manor
House

Castle

Skipsea

Skipsea
Brough

Low
Bonwick

High
Bonwick

Dunnington

North End

Ulrome
Sands

Mill Farm

Skipsea
Sands

Skipsea
Grange

Skipsea

Low Skirlington

High
Skirlington

Low
Skirlington

Atwick
Sands

Atwick

Brandesburton

Dacre

Catwick
Grange

Leven

Old Hall

Little
Catwick

Catwick

Cobble
Hall

Field
House

The
Hall

Nunkeeling

Pasturefield
House

Harsell

Catfoss
Grange

Seaton
Hold

Bassymoor

Seaton
Grange

Brockholme

Seaton

Honeysuckle Farm

Arram
Hall

Little
Arram

Northfield
House

Hornsea
Mere

Hornsea

Hornsea
Burton

South Cliff

North Cliff

North
Cliff

Sigglesthorne

Goxhill

Sigglesthorne
Grange

Southorpe

Southorpe
Grange

Rolston

Rolston
Sands

Wassand
Hall

Wassand

Low
Wood

Southorpe

Riston
Grange

Prospect
House

Long
Riston

Arnold
Grange

Arnold

Rise
Grange

Rise
Hall

Mill
House

Farnton
Hill

Little
Hatfield

Great
Hatfield

Hatfield
Grange

Mount
Pleasant

Broom
Hill

Mappleton

Mappleton
Sands

Great
Cowden

Cowden
Sands

Cowden
Parva

Withernick
Grange

Westlands

Whitedale

Ruddens

North
End
Withernwick

Whitehill

Cow
Magna

Great
Cowden

348

Bondville Miniature Village

North Sands

Old Town

Bridlington
Harbour

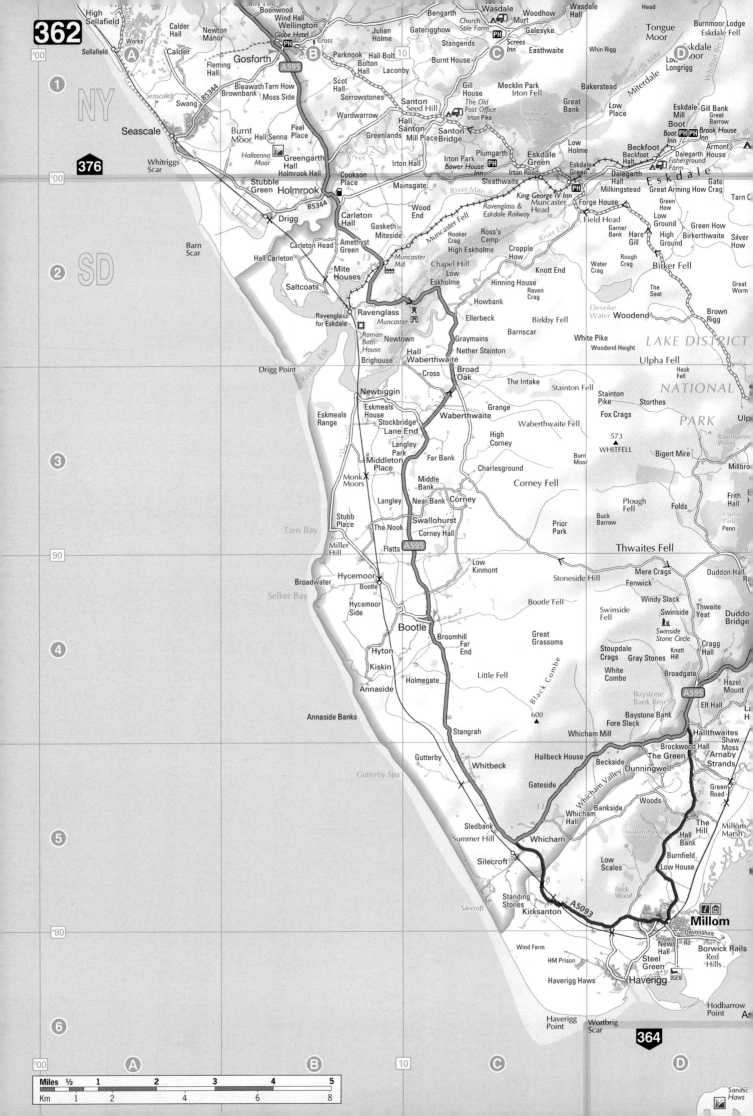

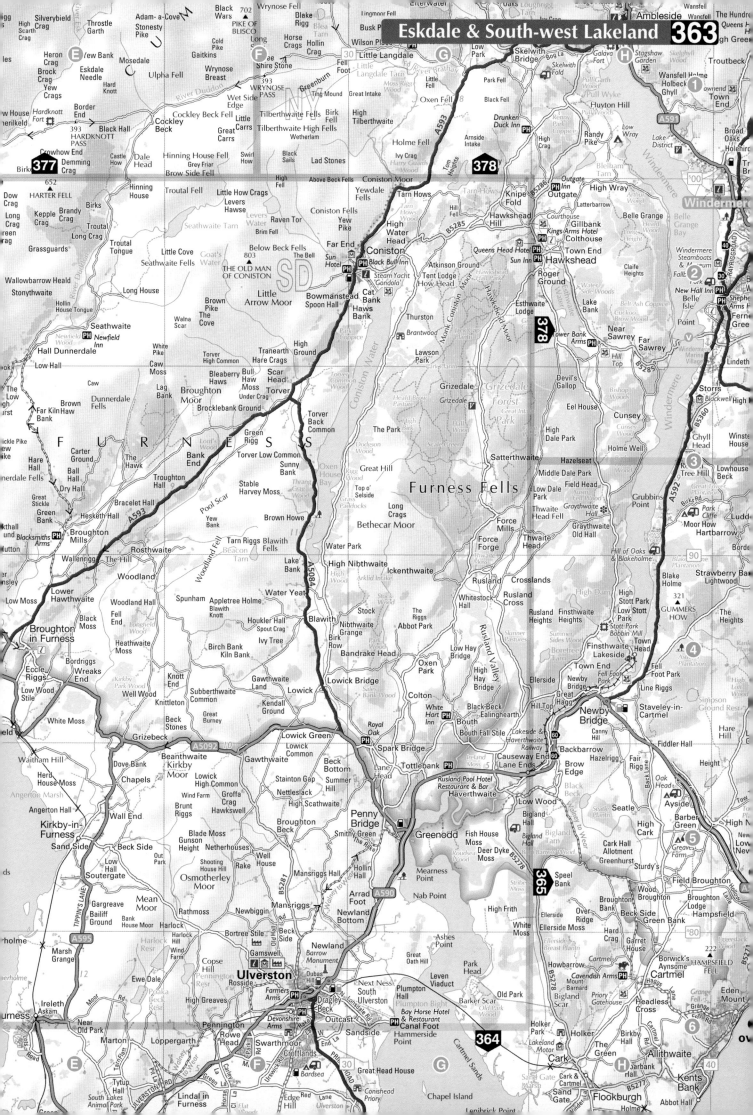

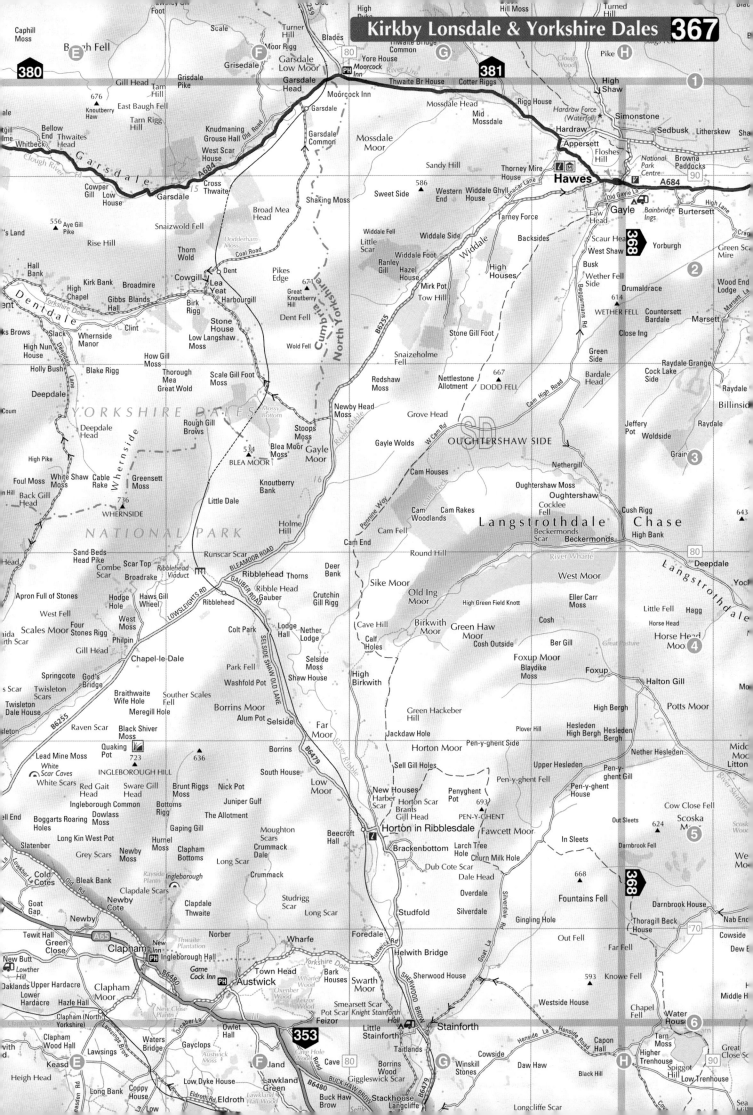

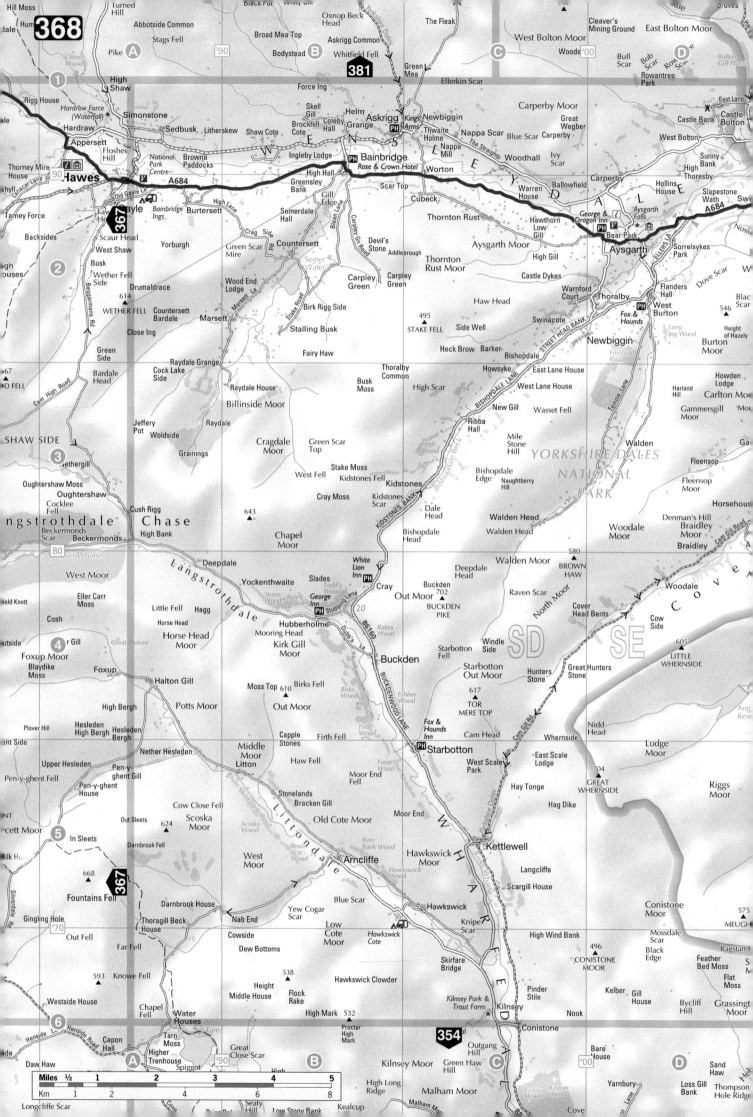

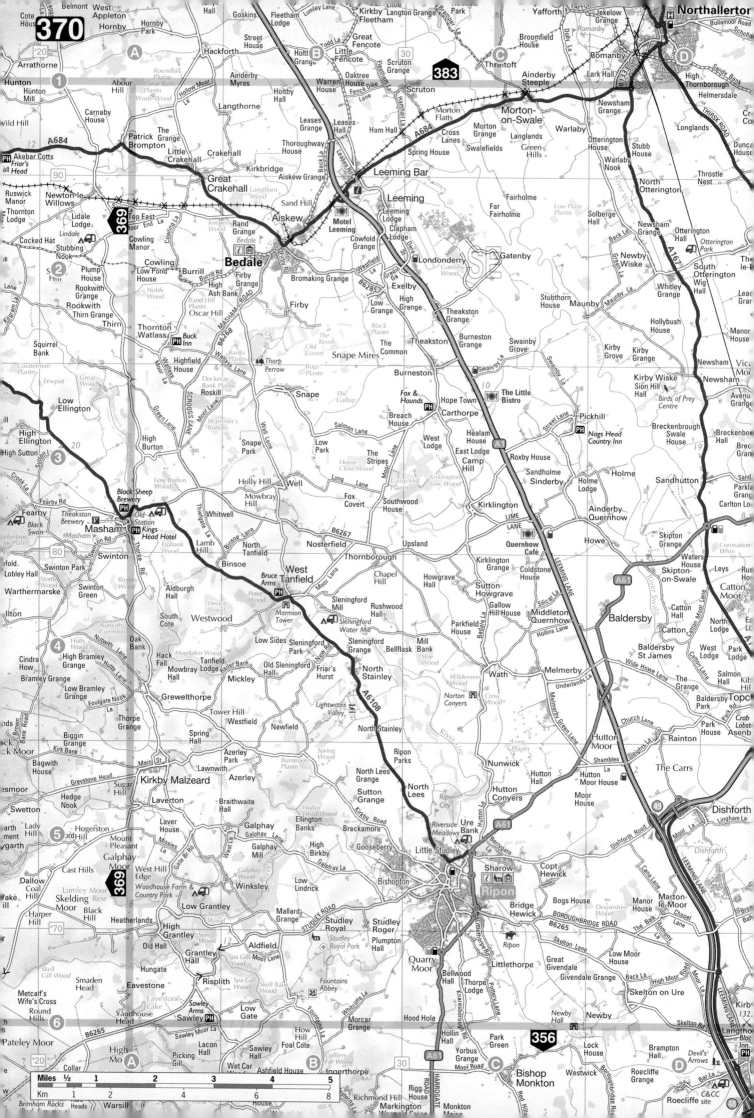

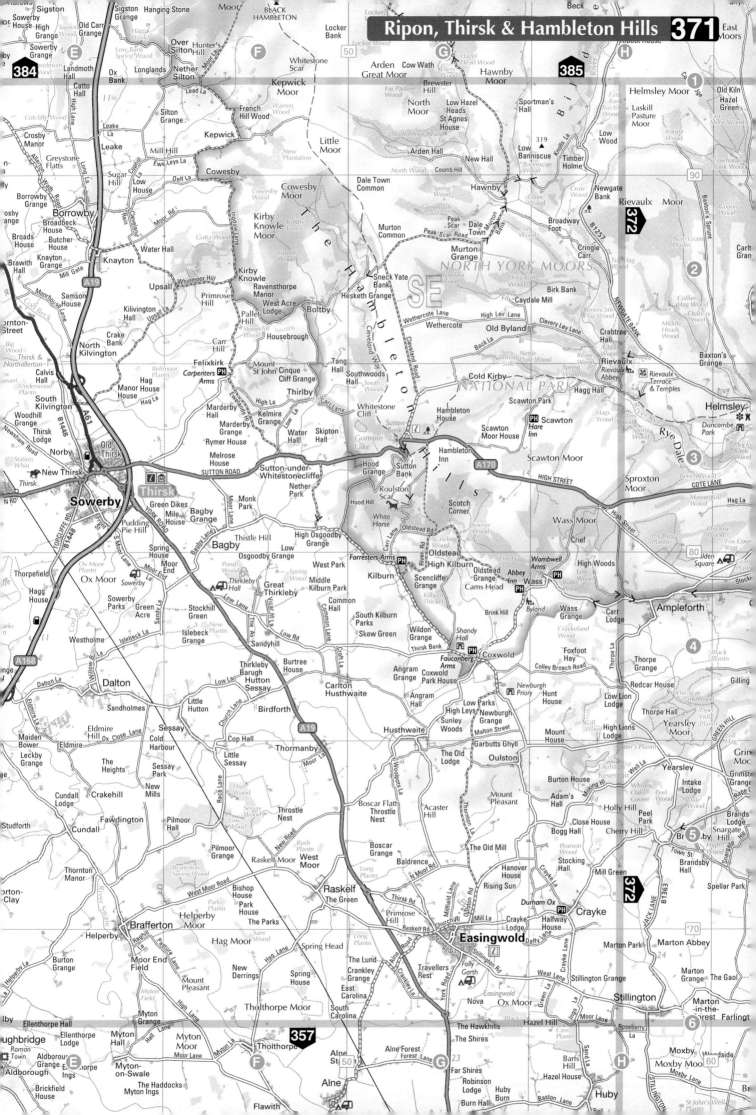

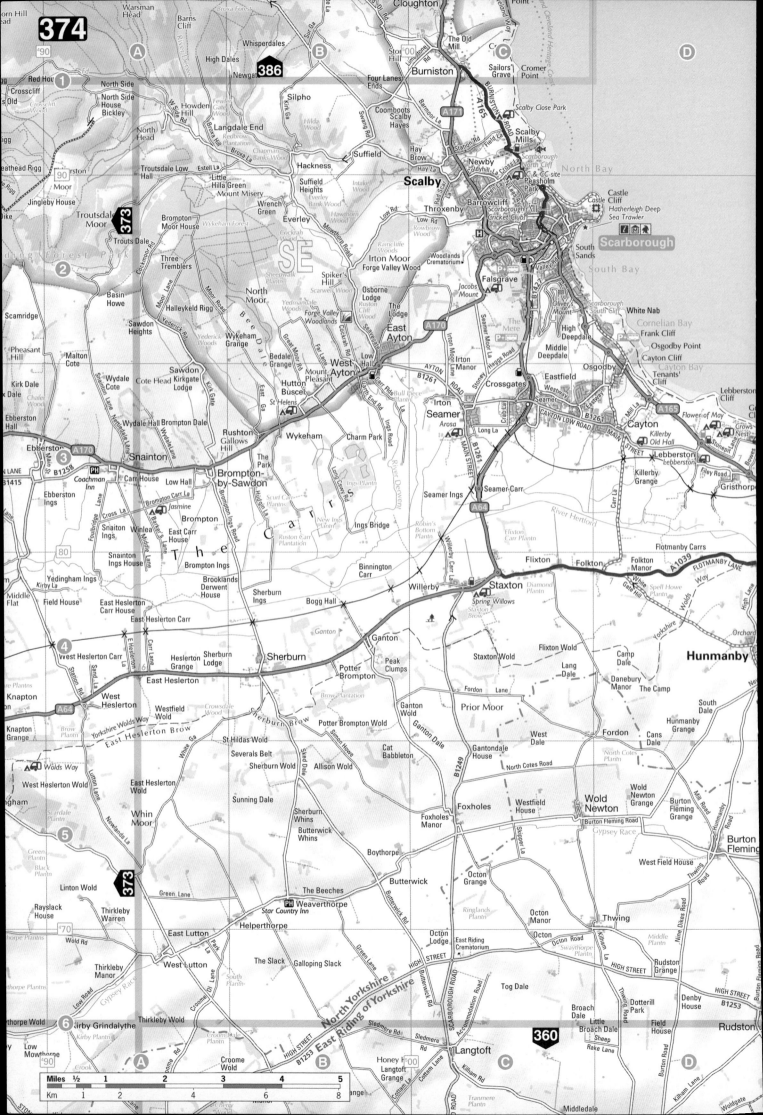

E   F   20   G   H

1

WHITBY

North Bay

ALEXANDRA BOWLS CENTRE

HOLLYWOOD PLAZA

90

CASTLE

ROMAN SIGNAL STATION

Cricket Ground

ANNE BRONTE'S GRAVE

2

ST PETER'S (RC)   ST MARY'S

SCHOOL

FIRE STA

YMCA TH   FRIARS WAY

METH CENTRAL HALL

COVERED MKT

LUNA PARK

HARBOUR OFFICE

FISH QUAY

TA

PO

TOWN HALL

FUTURIST CINEMA & THEATRE

RNLI

PO

MAG & LAW CTS

BRUNSWICK SHOPPING CENTRE

LIBRARY

LIGHTHOUSE & YACHT CLUB

CLINIC   POL STA

STEPHEN JOSEPH TH.

OLYMPIA LEISURE (SUPERBOWL)

South Bay

Scarborough

3

PO

SCARBOROUGH STATION SUPERSTORE

RADIO YORK

ROTUNDA MUS

ART GALLERY

WOOD END MUSEUM OF NATURAL HIST

THE SPA COMPLEX

0   200 metres

YORKSHIRE COAST COLLEGE

LBT

FILEY

PICKERING, MALTON   A64

Club Point North Cliff

Filey Brigg

Filey Sands

Filey

80

Centenary Way   *Muston Sands*

Muston Grange

Primrose Valley

Primrose Sands

Filey Bay

Hunmanby Sands

4

Hunmanby Moor

Moor House

Sands Rd

Reighton Gap   **Reighton Sands**

Sands Road

Reighton

Speeton Sands

Speeton Hills   Speeton Cliffs   Duley Dock   Buckton Cliffs

Beacon Hill

Speeton   Speeton Moor

Speeton Grange   Speeton Manor

Bempton Cliffs

Flamborough Head Heritage Coast

The Willows

Buckton Hall

Standard Hill   Bempton Grange

RSPB

A165   New Road   SPEETON GATE   B1229

5

Thornwick Bay

North Yorkshire

East Riding of Yorkshire

Buckton

Bolam La.

Bempton

FLAMBOROUGH ROAD

Dykes Plantn

Sixpenny Hill Plantn

North Cliff

The Grange

North Landing

Flamborough Head

Cradle Head

Selwicks Bay

Argham   Grindale

Grindale Road

East Leys

BEMPTON   The Grange

B1255

Lynhams

Seabirds Inn

B1259   Lighthouse

FLAMBOROUGH HEAD

Finley Hill

East Huntow

Norlands

North Mount

Flamborough Maltings   Fir Tree

The Crofts

PH

Flamborough

High Stacks

70

Little Argham

Fox Covert Plantn

West Huntow

The Grange

Cote Walls Plantn

B1255

South Sea

Highcliffe Manor

North Wood

The Poplars   Marton Lodge

Pinfold Lane

Sewerby Hall   Sewerby Church

Bridlington Links

Beacon Hill

East Crags Wood

Cottage Pasture Wood

North Wood

SCARBOROUGH ROAD

MARTON GATE

Bondville Miniature Village

Flamborough Head Heritage Coast

6

Boynton

B1255   Eastgate   **Sewerby**

North Sands

West Lawn Wood

Fish Pond Wood

Hallowkiln Wood

High Wood

Old Town

361

West Hill

Bridlington

Sands Wood

pe Hall   Plantn

W Bac

Carnaby

Church Lane

Bessingby   Hilderthorpe

The Spa

Bridlington Harbour

E   F   20   G   H   30

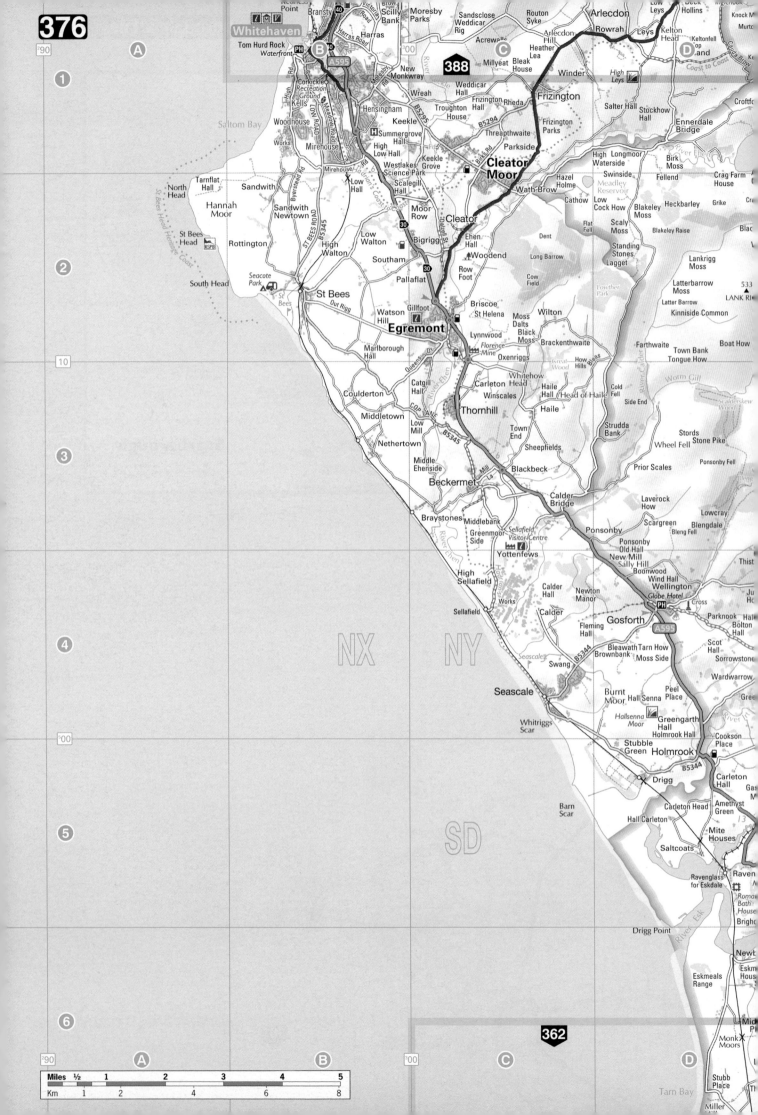

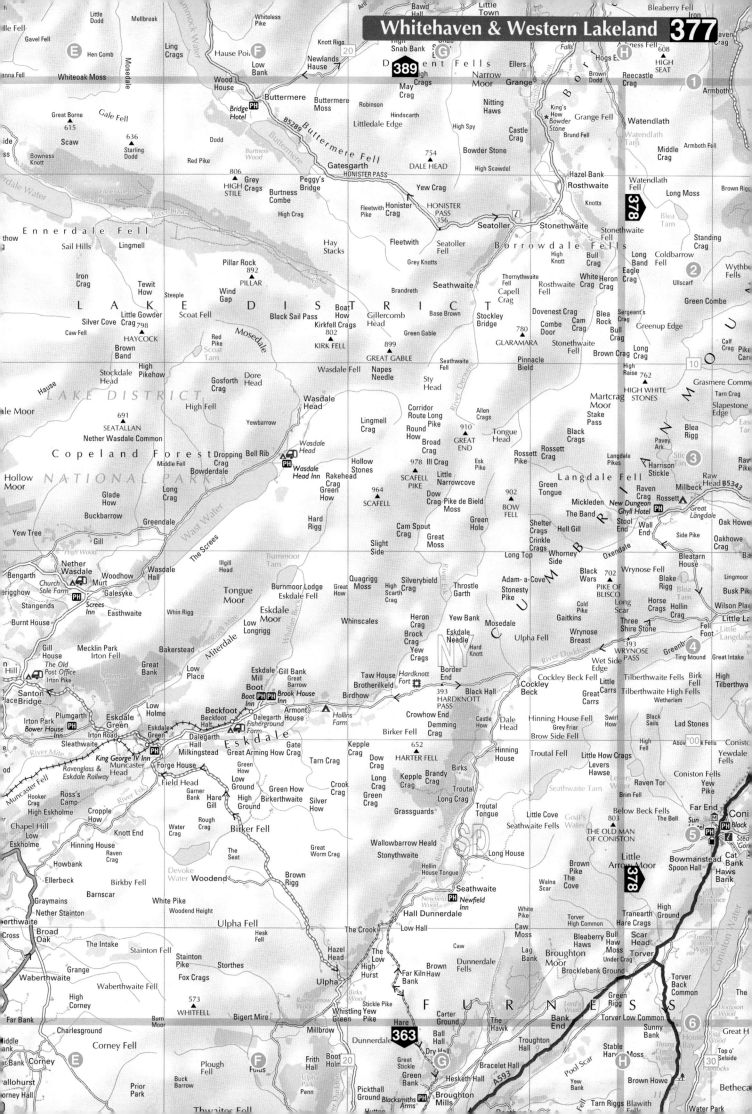

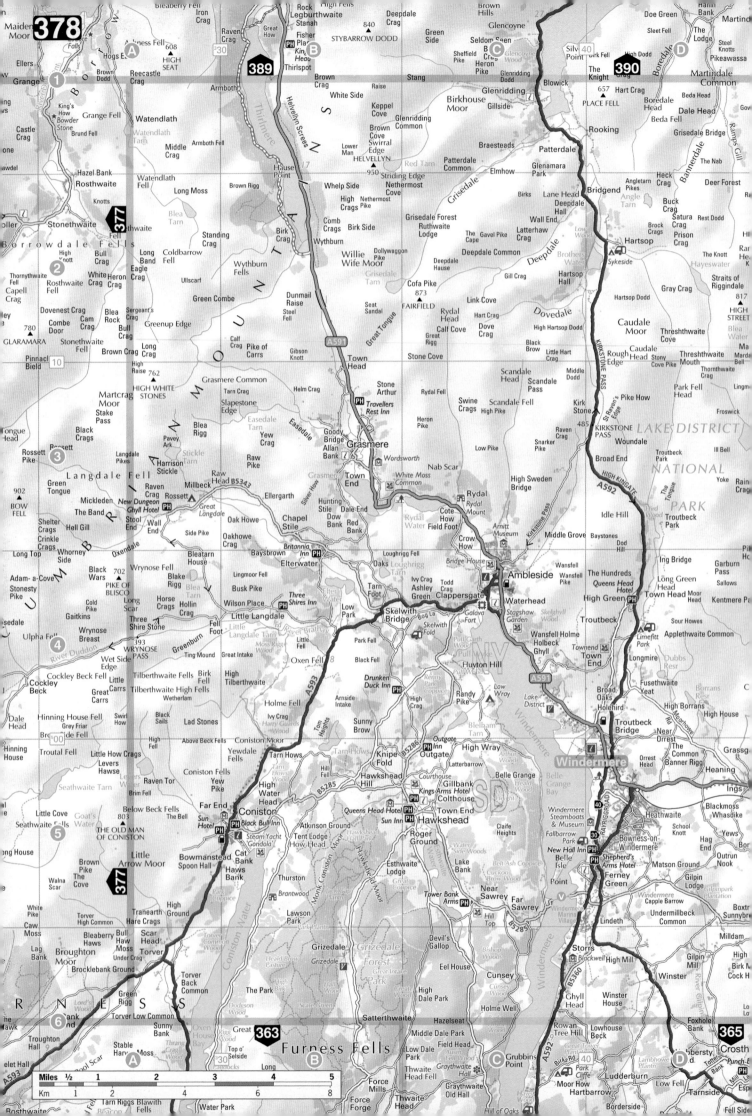

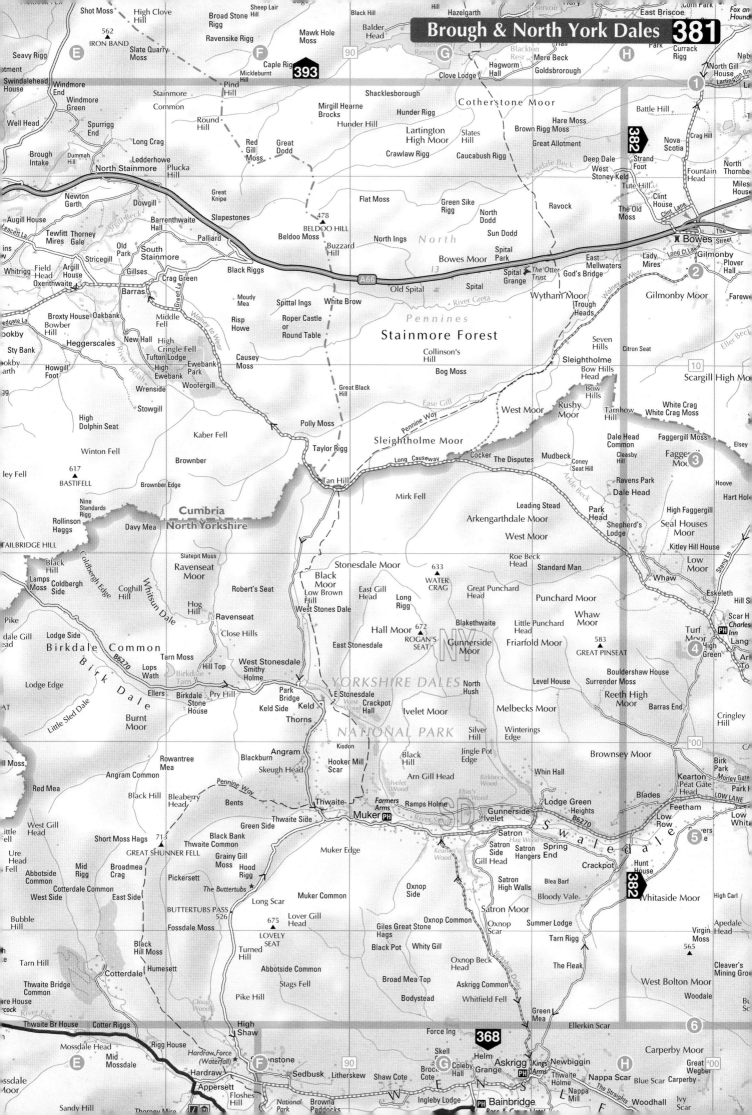

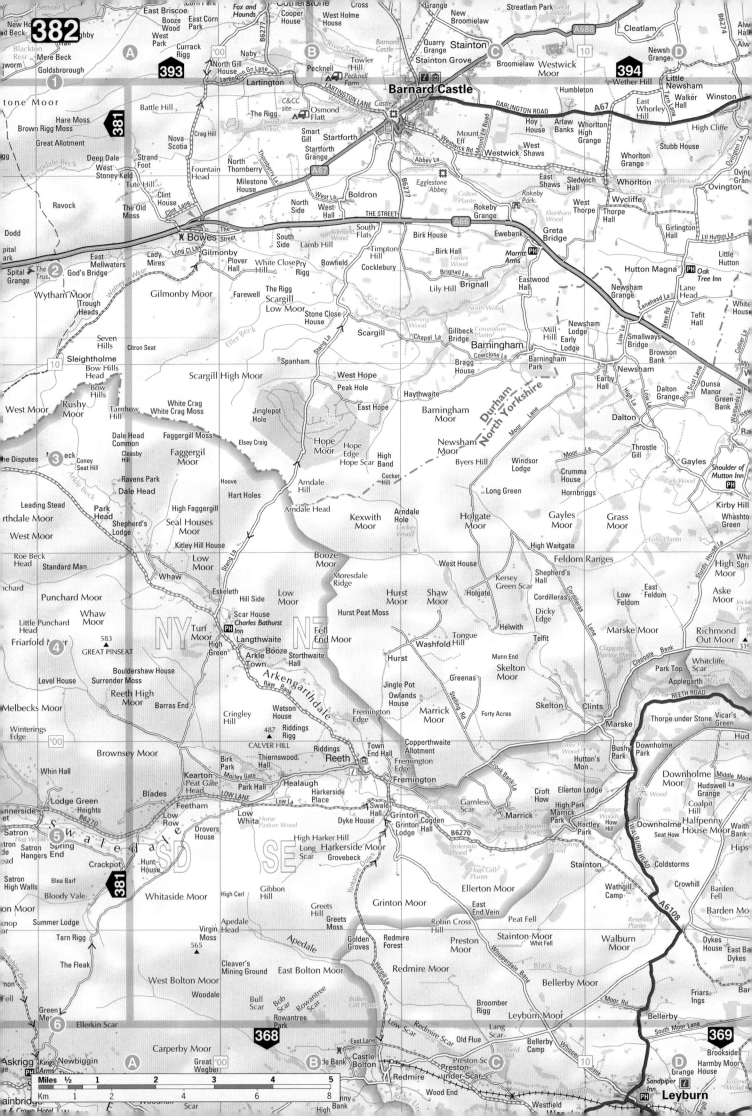

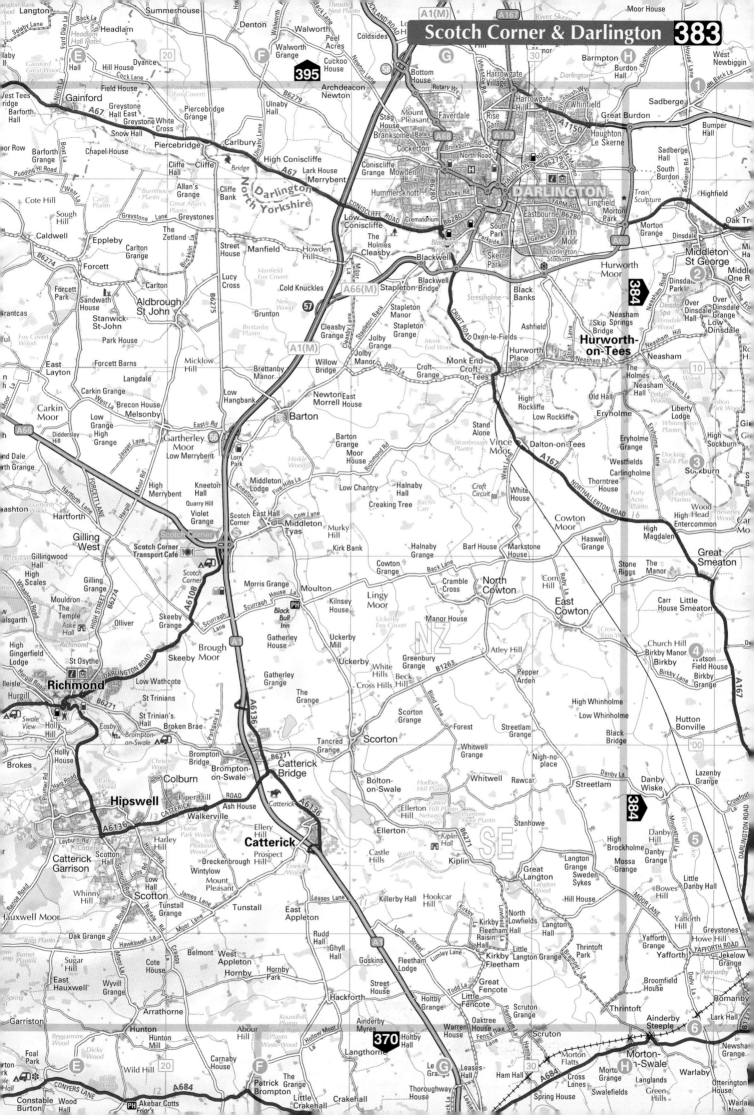

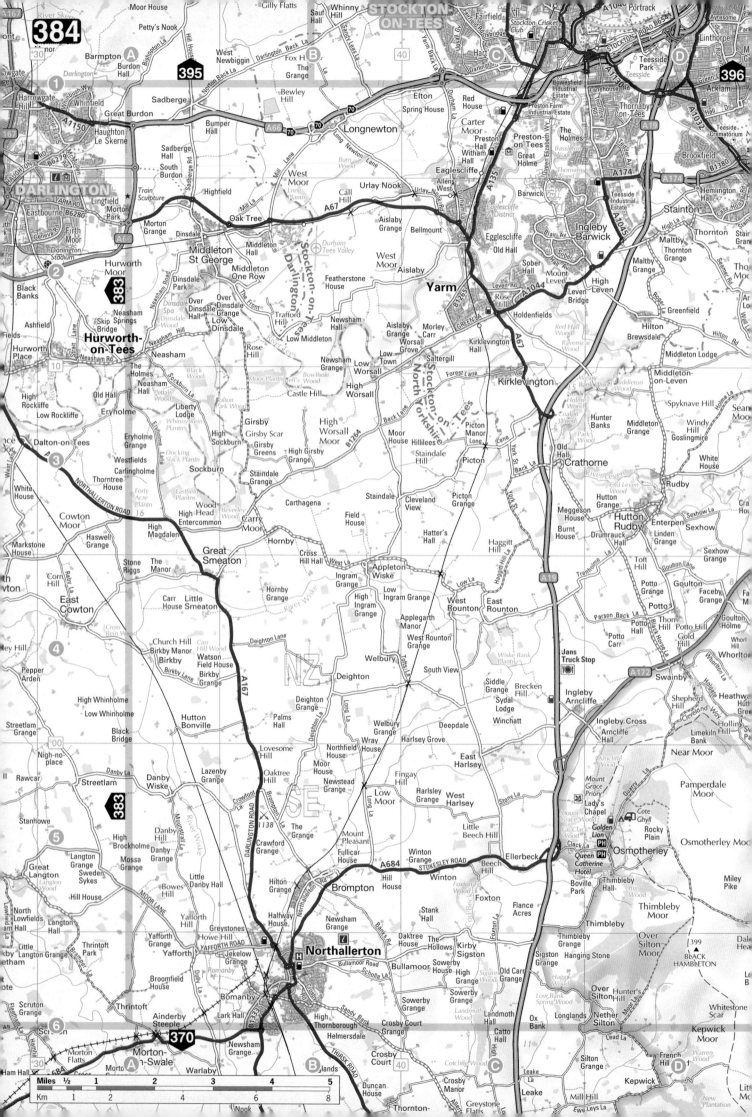

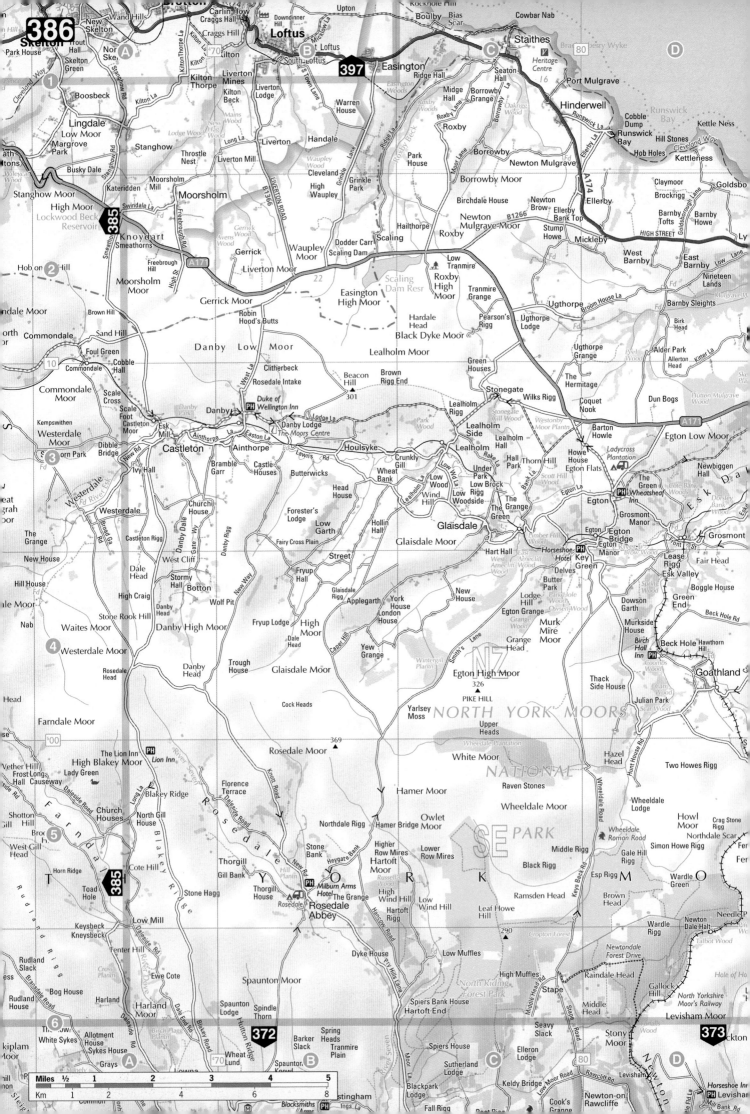

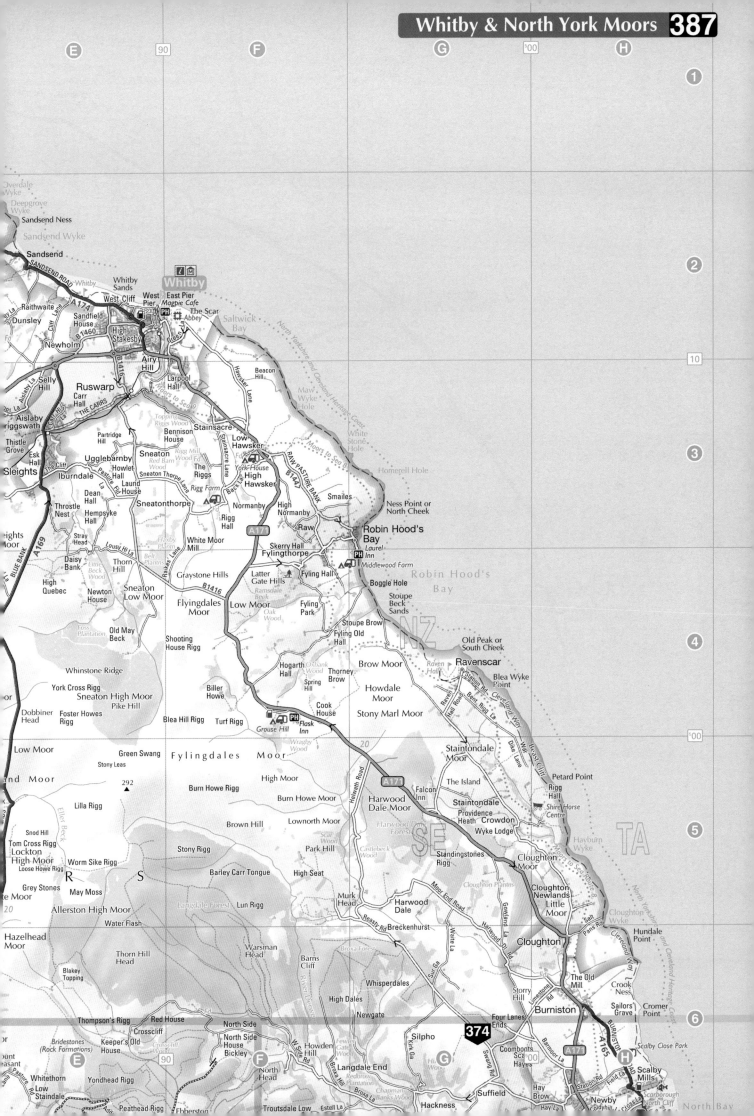

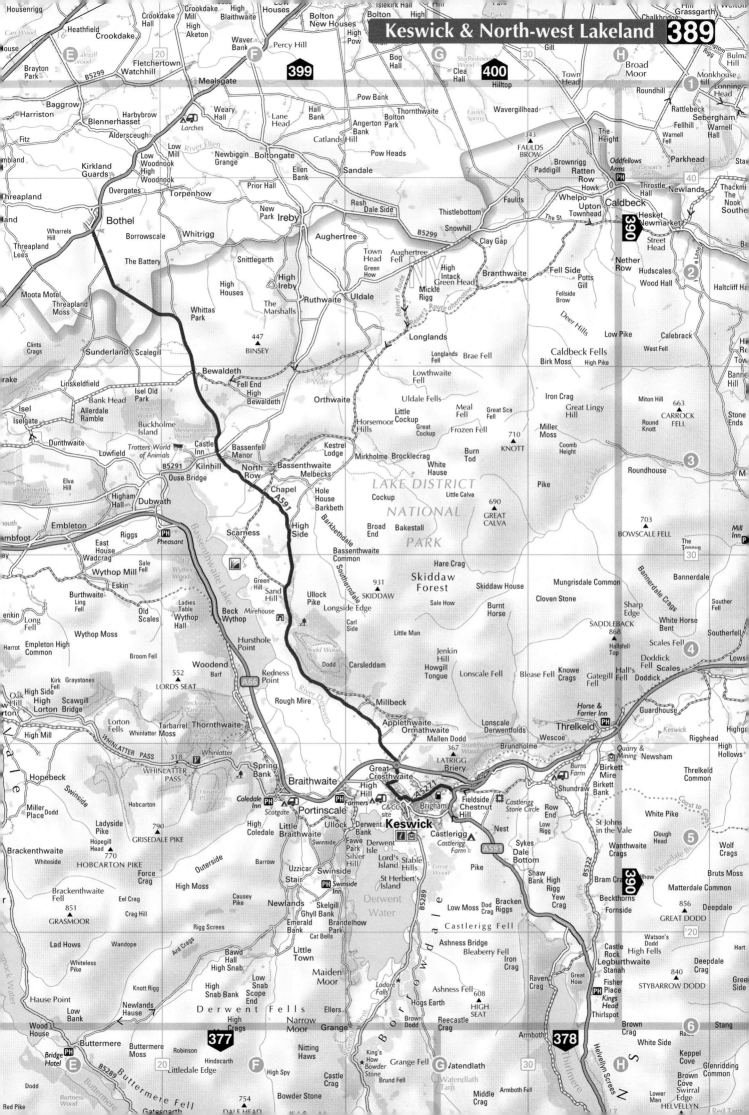

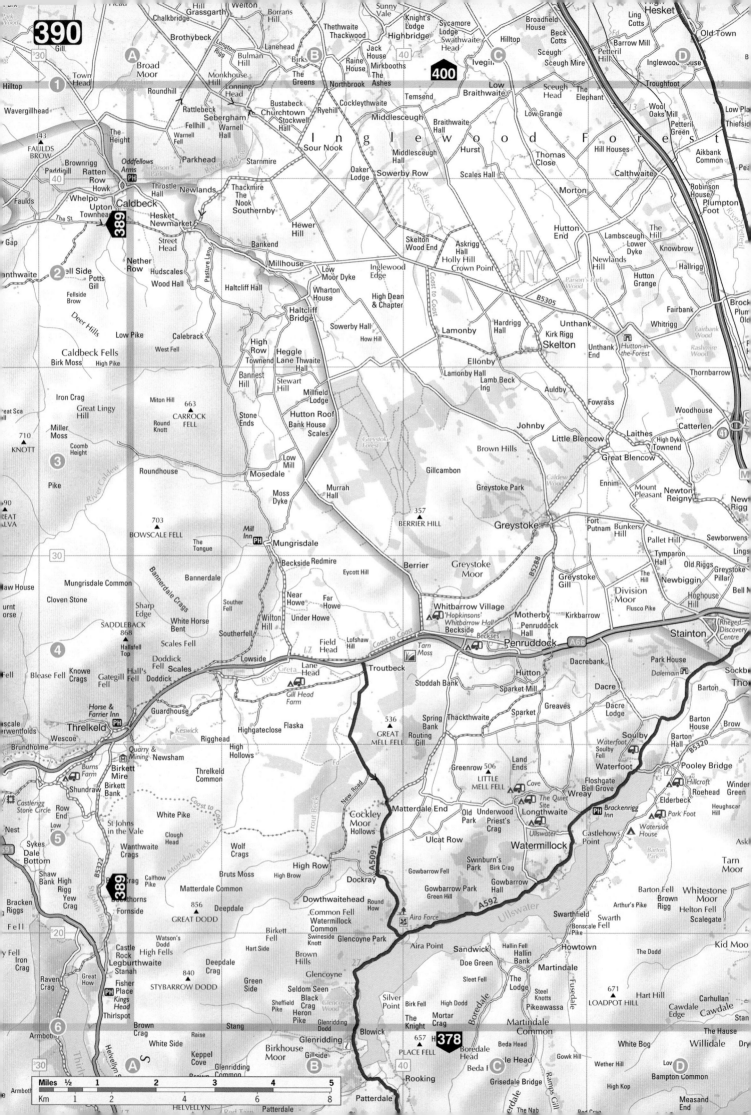

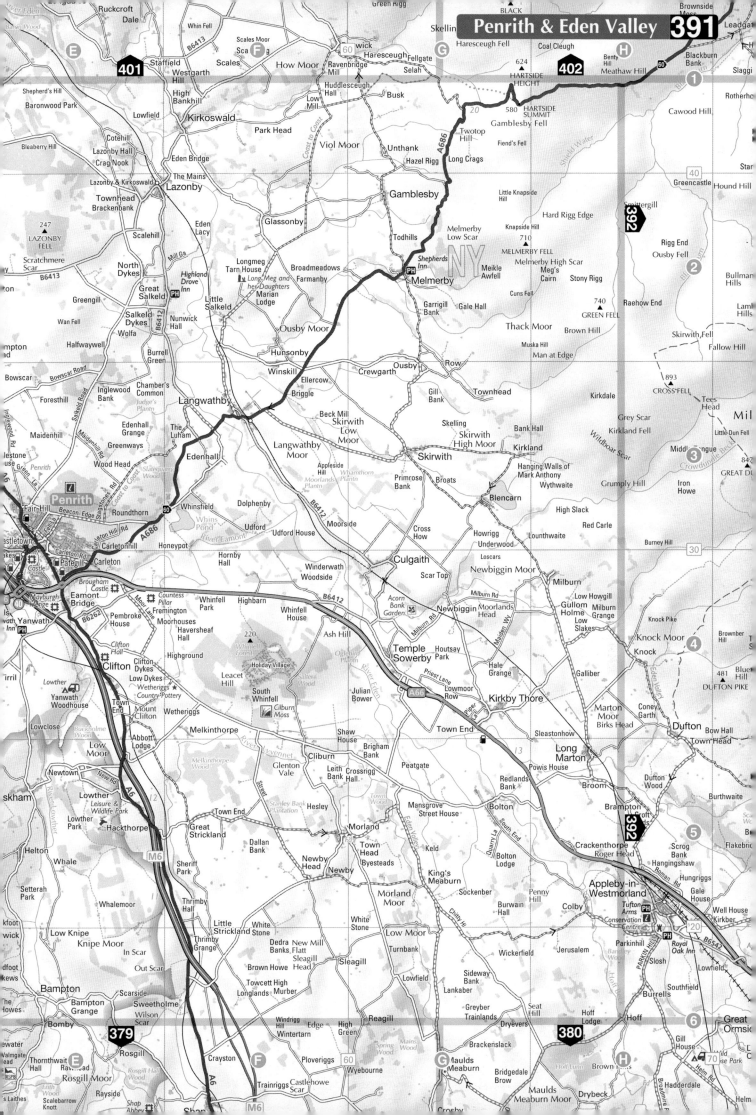

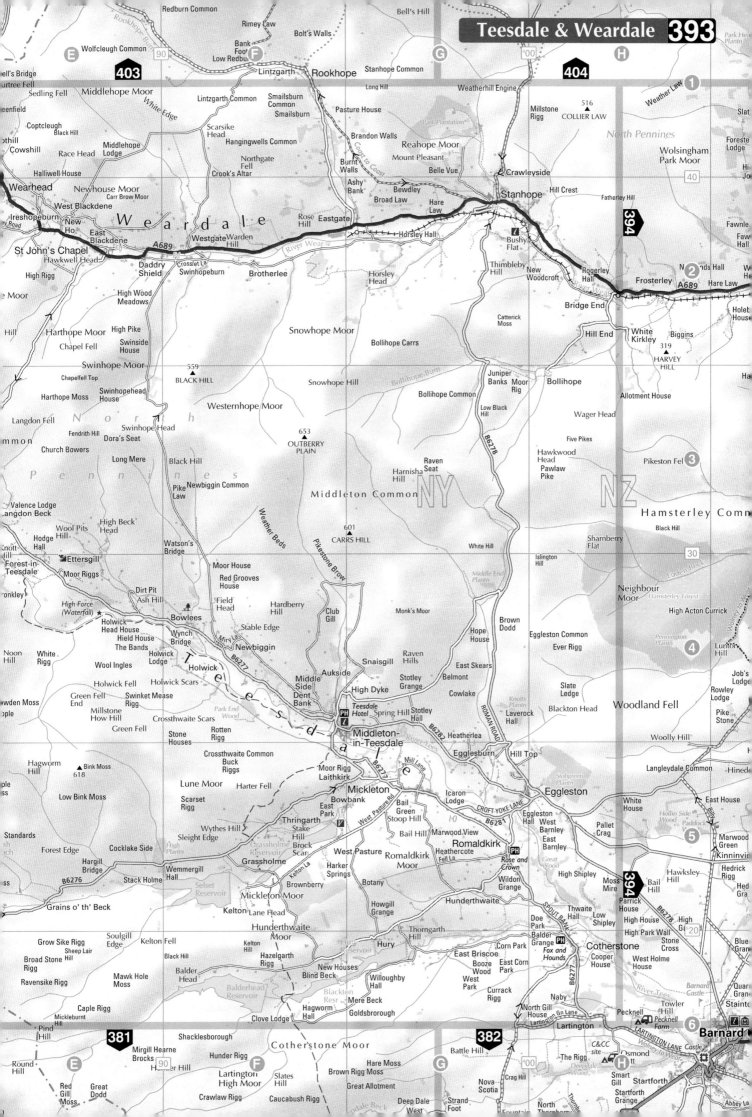

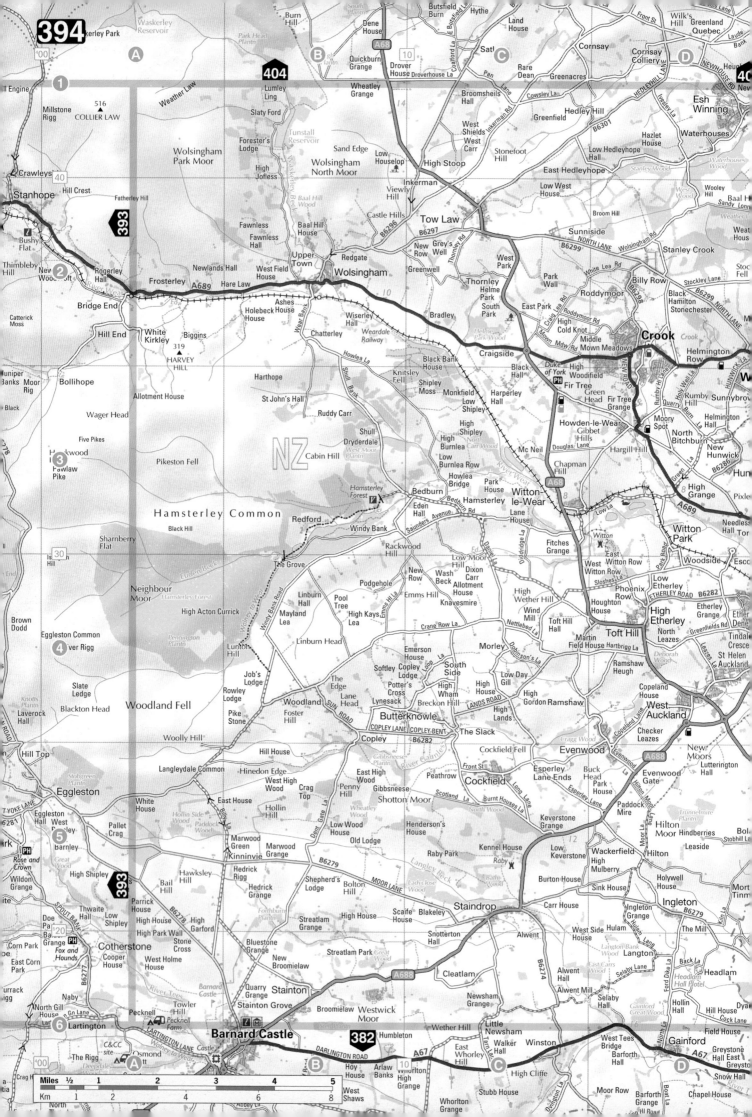

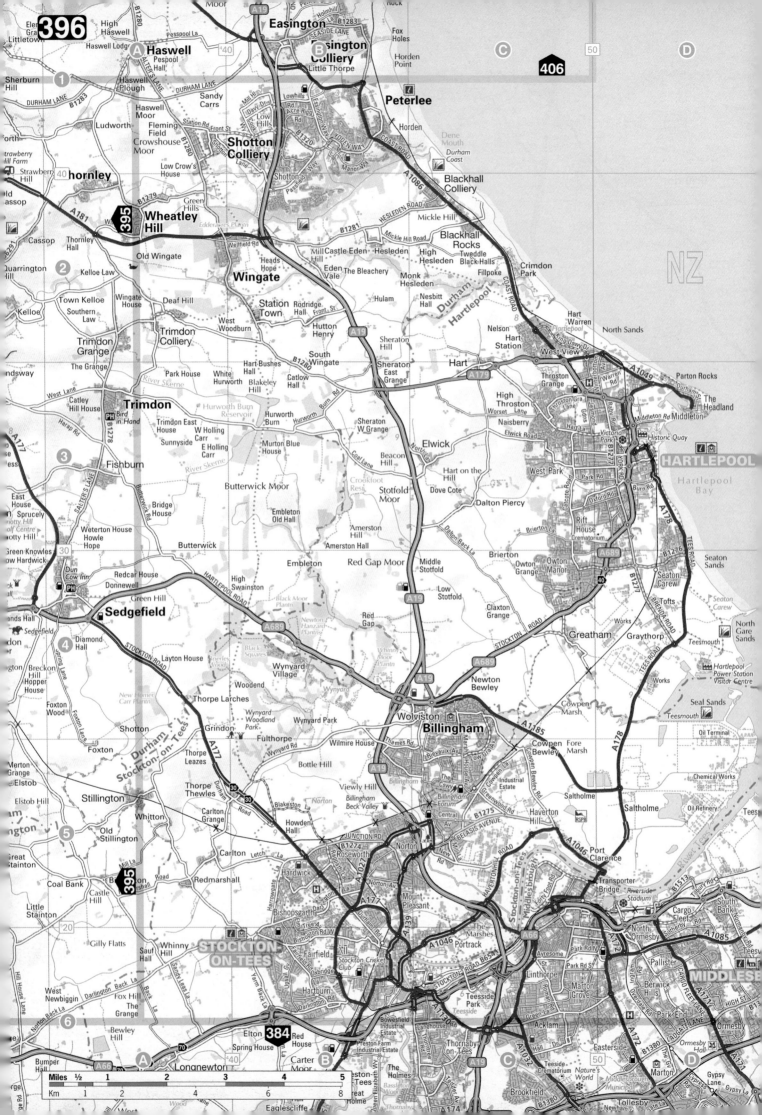

Middlesbrough

0   200 metres

NORTH ROAD

MIDDLESBROUGH STATION

HILL ST SHOPPING CENTRE

DUNDAS ARCADE SHOPPING CENTRE

SUPERSTORE

POSTAL SORTING OFFICE

RADIO CLEVELAND

GASHOLDERS

Cannon Park Industrial Estate

BUS STA

CAPTAIN COOK SQUARE

TOWN HALL

EMPIRE THEATRE

CINEMA

CIVIC REGISTER CENTRE

COMBINED COURTS

INLAND REVENUE OFFICE

THE MALL

PO

MIMA

LIBRARY

CLEVELAND BUSINESS CENTRE

VETERINARY HOSPITAL

SCHOOL

COMMUNITY CENTRE

POLICE STA & MAG COURT

UNIVERSITY OF TEESSIDE

CLINIC

INLAND REVENUE OFFICE

NEWLANDS MEDICAL CTR

SCH

COMMUNITY CENTRE

PO

UNIVERSITY OF TEESSIDE

UNIVERSITY OF TEESSIDE

SCHOOLS

HALLS OF RESIDENCE

CLAIRVILLE ROAD

SCHOOL

WAR MEMORIAL

DORMAN MUSEUM

Albert Park

CLAIRVILLE STADIUM

STOKESLEY

THE SOUTH, STOCKTON, SUNDERLAND

WHITBY REDCAR

MARTON ROAD

South Gare Breakwater

Tees Bay

Coatham Sands

Steel Works

Cleveland

Coatham

Warrenby

British Steel Redcar

Westfield

Broadway

Dormanstown

Redcar Central

Redcar

Redcar Sands

Redcar East

Marske Sands Stone Gap

Marske-by-the-Sea

Saltburn-by-the-Sea

Saltburn Sands

Hunt Cliff

NZ

Kirkleatham

Old Hall

Chemical Works

Yearby

Longbeck

New Marske

Marske Road

Saltburn

Marske Mill

Saltburn Sear

Saltburn Smugglers

Warsett Hill

Hunley Hall

Cattersty Sands

North Yorkshire and Cleveland Heritage Coast

Hummersea Scar

Lazenby

Wilton

Yearby Wood

Longbeck La

Errington Wood

New Marske

Hob Hill Lane

Saltburn-by-the-Sea

Marske Grange

Saltburn Grange

New Brotton

Wilton

Lazenby Bank

Eston Nab

Eston Moor

Wilton Moor Plantns

Court Green Wood

Dunsdale

Raisbeck Wood

Upleatham

Hollin Hill Wood

Village Wood

High St

New Skelton

Wand'l Hills

Brotton

Carlin How

Craggs Hall

Craggs Hall

Skinningrove

Downdinner Hill

Upton

Galinowe

Rockho

Boulb

Eston

Pinchinthorpe

Tocketts Mill

Skelton

Park House

Trout Hall

North Skelton

Skelton Green

Kilton

Loftus

East Loftus

South Loftus

Easington

Ridge H

Redcar Road

Skelton Ellers

Forge Fencote Wood

Cleveland Way

Boosbeck

Stanghow Rd

Kilton La

Kilton Thorpe

Kilton

Liverton Mines

Kilton Beck

Liverton Thorpe

Liverton Lodge

Handale

Waupley Wood

Park House

Roxby Woods

Lingdale

Low Moor

Margrove Park

Stanghow

Lodge Wood

Mains Wood

Liverton Mill

Town plan: Stockton-on-Tees p.645

Slapewath

Charltons

Rusky Dale

Guisborough

Hutton Gate

Rectory

Waterfall Wood

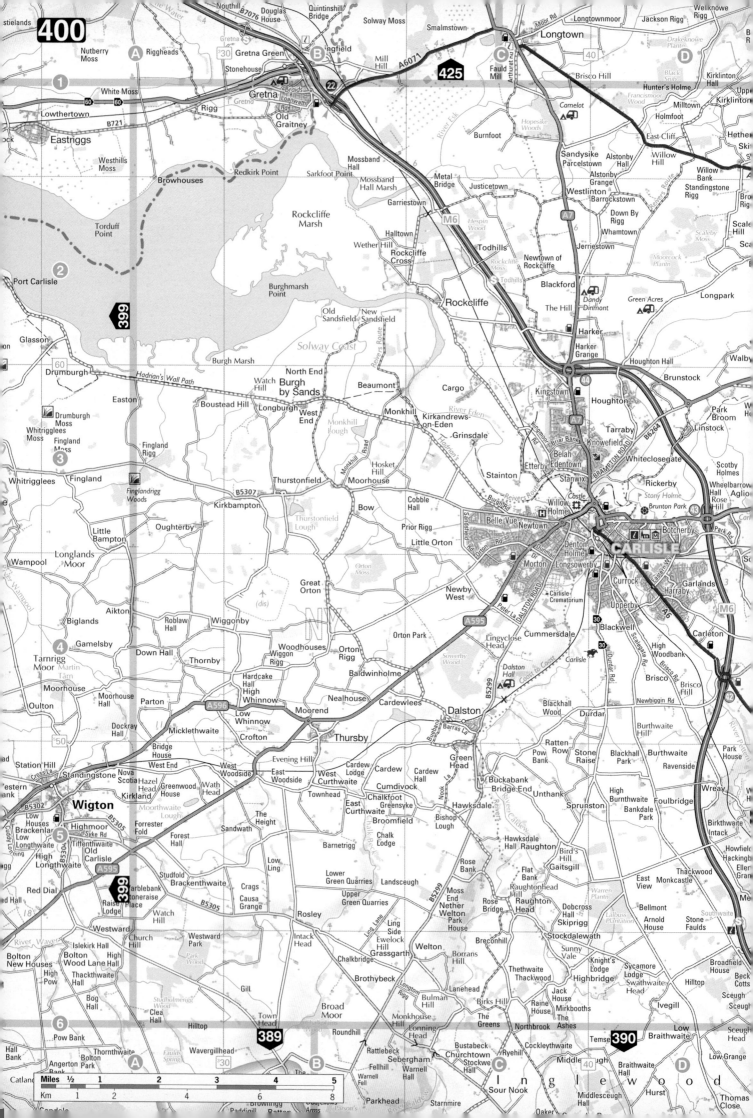

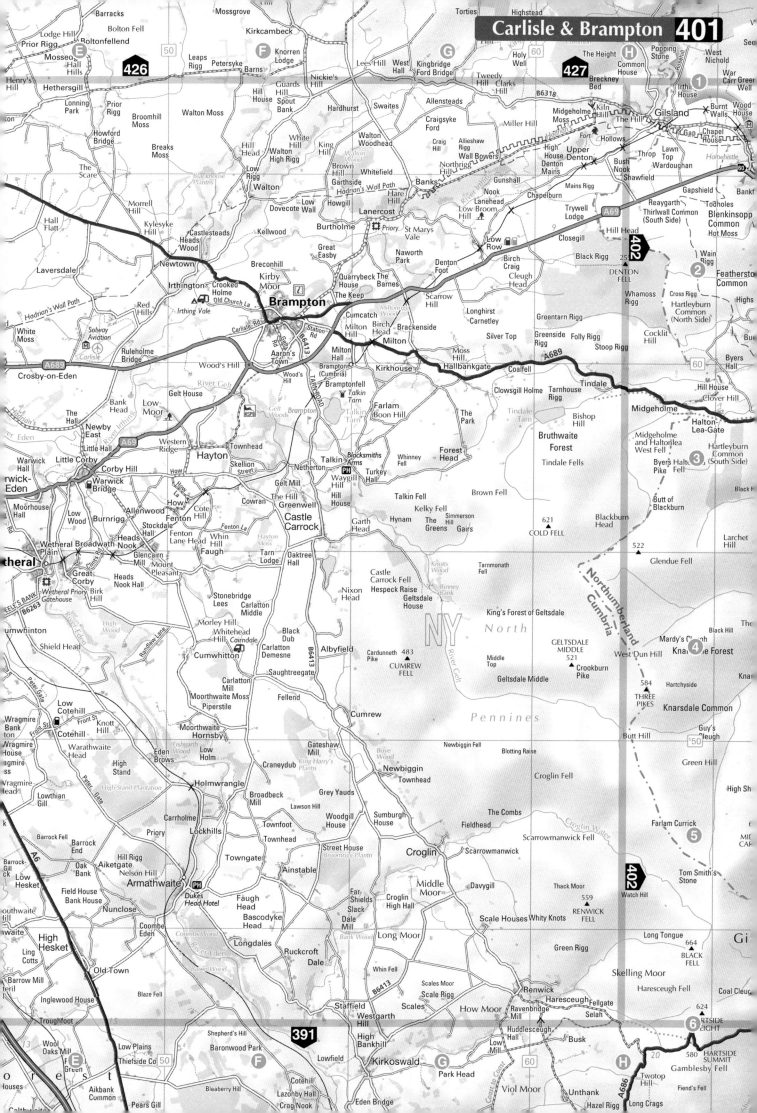

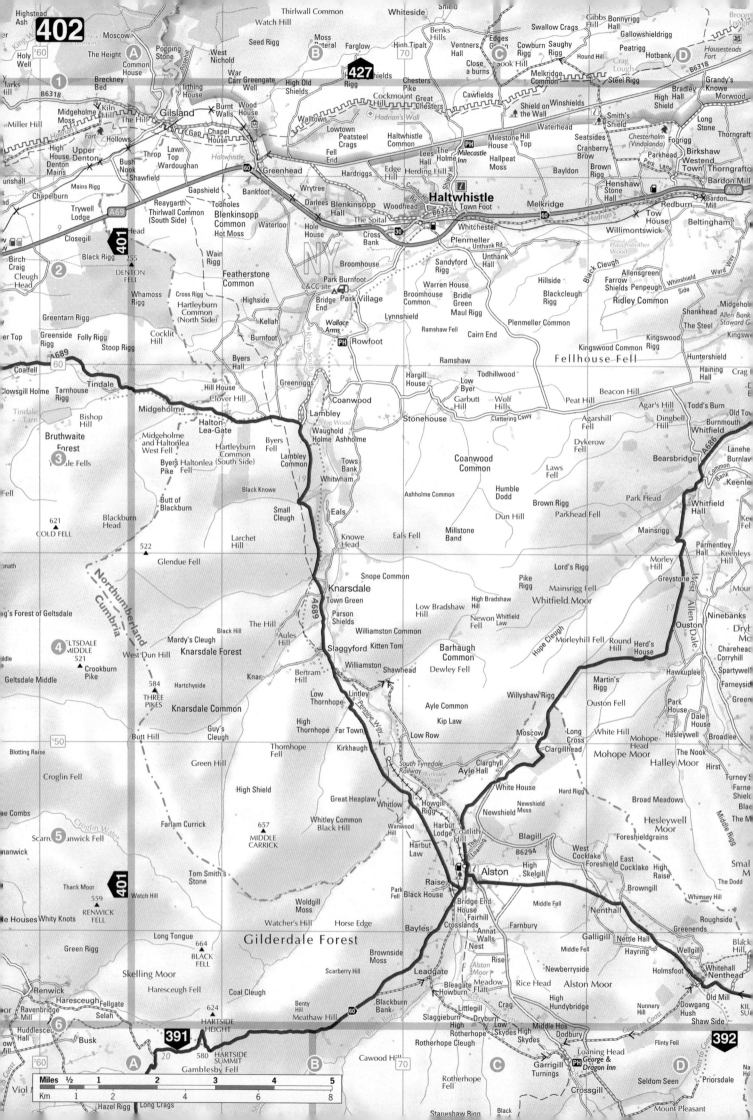

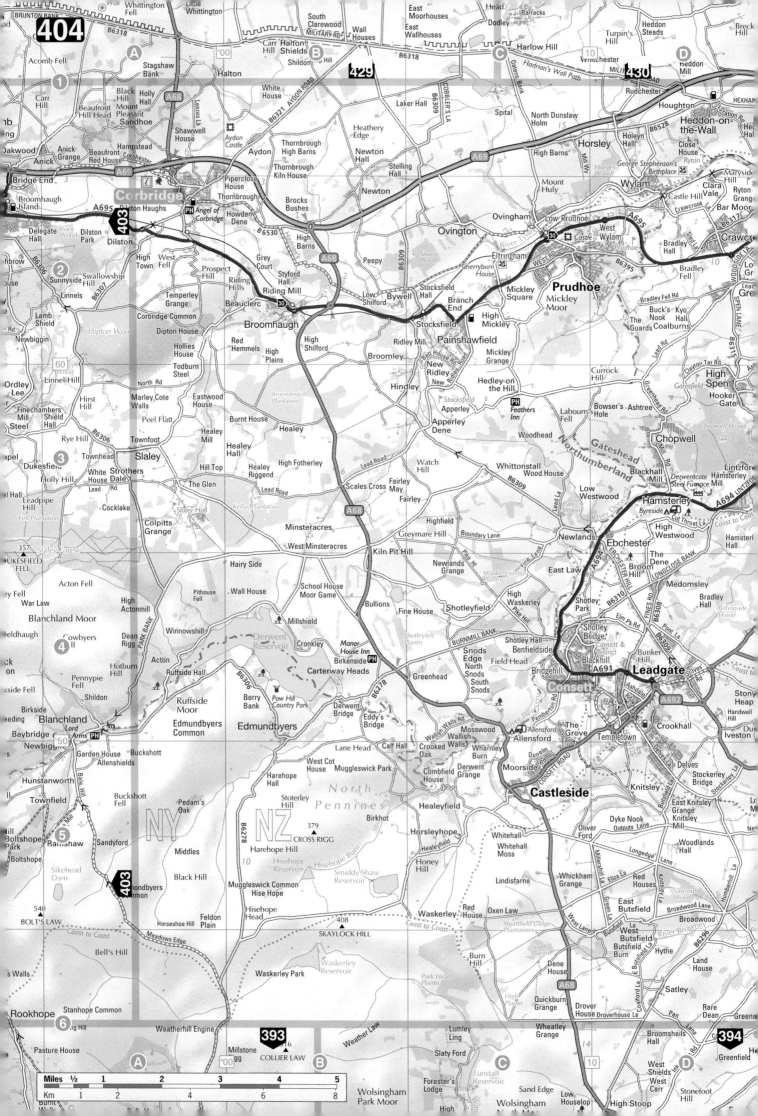

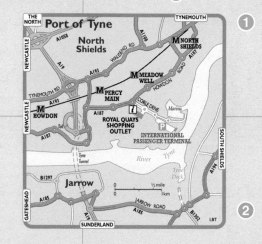

Port of Tyne

North Shields

TYNEMOUTH

THE NORTH

NEWCASTLE

A1058

A19

A193

WALLSEND RD

A187

M HOWDON

TYNEMOUTH RD

A193

M PERCY MAIN

M MEADOW WELL

HOWDON

A187

COBLE DENE

Toll

A187

ROYAL QUAYS SHOPPING OUTLET

i

Marina

M NORTH SHIELDS

A187

SOUTH SHIELDS

INTERNATIONAL PASSENGER TERMINAL

Tyne Dock

River   *Tyne*

GATESHEAD

B1297

Tyne Tunnel

JARROW ROAD

A185

Jarrow

A185

A19

SUNDERLAND

A185

B1302

LBT

0   ½ mile

0   1 km

2

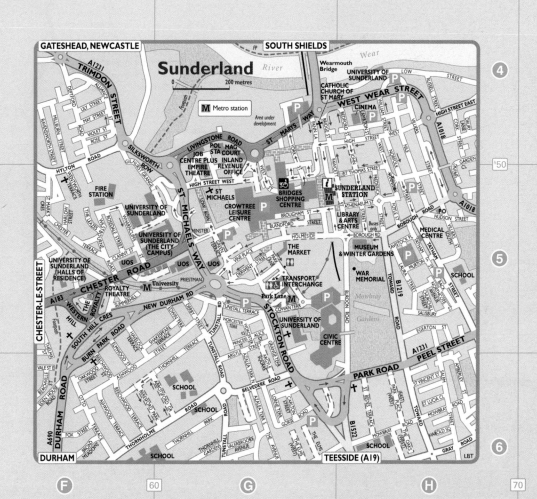

GATESHEAD, NEWCASTLE   FP   **SOUTH SHIELDS**   *Wear*

4

Sunderland   *River*

0   200 metres

Wearmouth Bridge

UNIVERSITY OF SUNDERLAND

LOW   STREET

A1231

TRIMDON STREET

DEPTFORD ROAD

LILY STREET

MAY STREET

VIOLET ST

ROSE ST

ALLIANCE

SILKSWORTH ROW

GIL HURST GRANGE

HYLTON ROAD

RAVENSWORTH STREET

MILLBURN ST

THE LEAZES

WESTBOURNE TERRACE

FIRE STATION

M Metro station

Area under development

LIVINGSTONE ROAD

JOB CENTRE PLUS

EMPIRE THEATRE

POL STA

MAG COURT

INLAND REVENUE OFFICE

HIGH STREET WEST

ST MARYS WAY

CATHOLIC CHURCH OF ST MARY

CINEMA

BRIDGE ST

WEST WEAR STREET

HIGH

ST

JOHN ST

FAWCETT ST

WEST SUNNISIDE

ST THOMAS STREET

VILLIERS ST

NILE ST

NORFOLK ST

HIGH STREET EAST

A1018

COKE DENE

GARDEN CL

50

P

P

P

P

P

P

ST MICHAELS

UNIVERSITY OF SUNDERLAND

CHESTER ROAD

ST MICHAELS WAY

ROSEDALE STREET

THE ELMS

CHESTER TERRACE

HARLOW ST

ST MARYS CRES

CLANNY ST

CROWTREE LEISURE CENTRE

BROUGHAM ST

BLANDFORD ST

BRIDGES SHOPPING CENTRE

i

M

SUNDERLAND STATION

ATHENAEUM ST

LIBRARY & ARTS CENTRE

FOYLE ST

Buses only

BOROUGH RD

PO

HUDSON ST

MEDICAL CENTRE

TATHAM

TAVISTOCK PL

SCHOOL

UNIVERSITY OF SUNDERLAND (THE CITY CAMPUS)

UOS

MINSTER

HOLMESIDE

BOROUGH RD

MUSEUM & WINTER GARDENS

WAR MEMORIAL

MURTON ST

LAURA ST

B1219

ST

UNIVERSITY OF SUNDERLAND (HALLS OF RESIDENCE)

UOS

UOS

PRIESTMAN

VINE PLACE

DERWENT

THE MARKET

Mowbray Gardens

SALISBURY

EGERTON ST

CHESTER-LE-STREET

A183

ROYALTY THEATRE

M University

THE ROYALTY

SUMMERHILL

NEW DURHAM RD

PRIESTMAN

TRANSPORT INTERCHANGE

Park Lane M

P

P

CIVIC CENTRE

BURDON ROAD

A1231

PEEL STREET

WESTERN HILL

SOUTH HILL CRES

COWAN TERR

TUNSTALL TERRACE

WORCESTER TERR

SHAKESPEARE TERRACE

DERBY ST

ALICE ST

TUNSTALL RD

TUNSTALL RD

STOCKTON ROAD

UNIVERSITY OF SUNDERLAND

TOWARD

PARK ROAD

ST VINCENT ST

ST LUCIA CL

DURHAM ROAD

A690

FOX ST

VALE ST E

BEECHILL

EDEN HOUSE RD

BURN PARK ROAD

OAKWOOD ST

ASHWOOD ST

ASHWOOD TERRACE

BROAD MEADOWS

BEDFORD RD

THORNHOLME

THORNHILL

THORNHILL GARDENS

VALEBROOKE AVENUE

SCHOOL

SCHOOL

PRINCESS ST

ARGYLE ST

AZALEA TERR

GRANGE TERR

BELVEDERE ROAD

THE CEDARS

THE OAKS

THE ELMS

BELVEDERE ROAD

PARK ROAD

CARLTON ST

ST BEDES TERRACE

B1522

MOWBRAY

PARK PLACE (WEST)

EAST

AMBERLEY ST

HAROLD SQ

SCHOOL

TOWARD RD

GRAY RD

MOWBRAY

DURHAM   **TEESSIDE (A19)**   LBT

SCHOOL

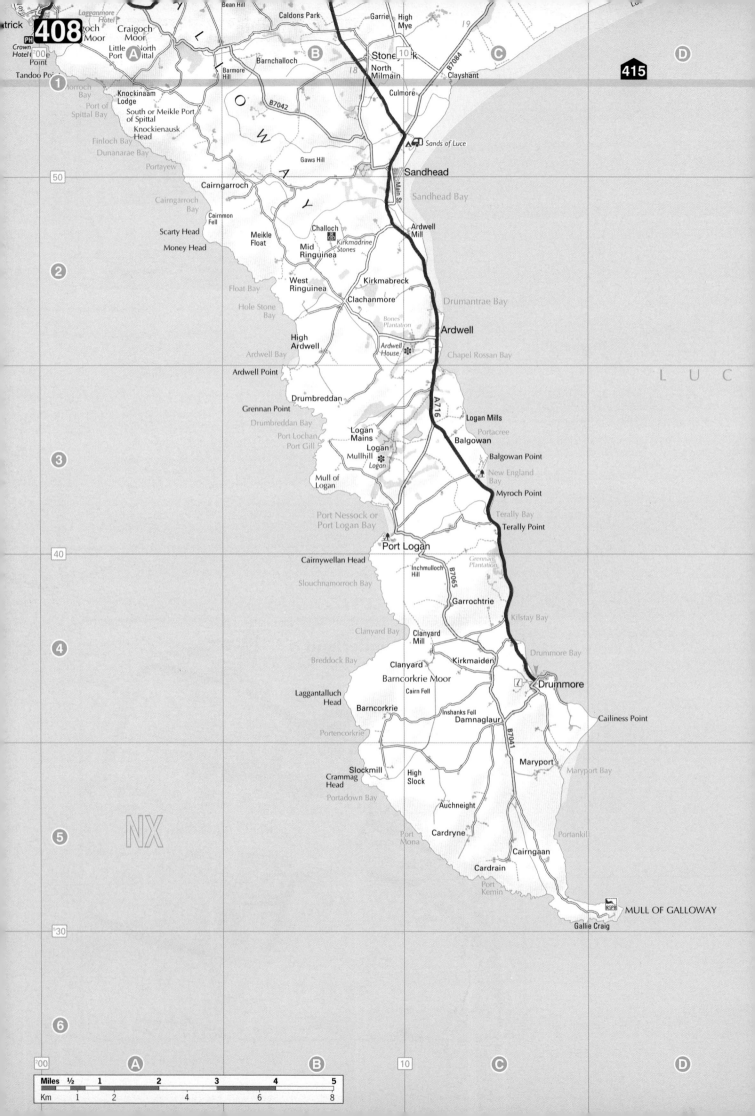

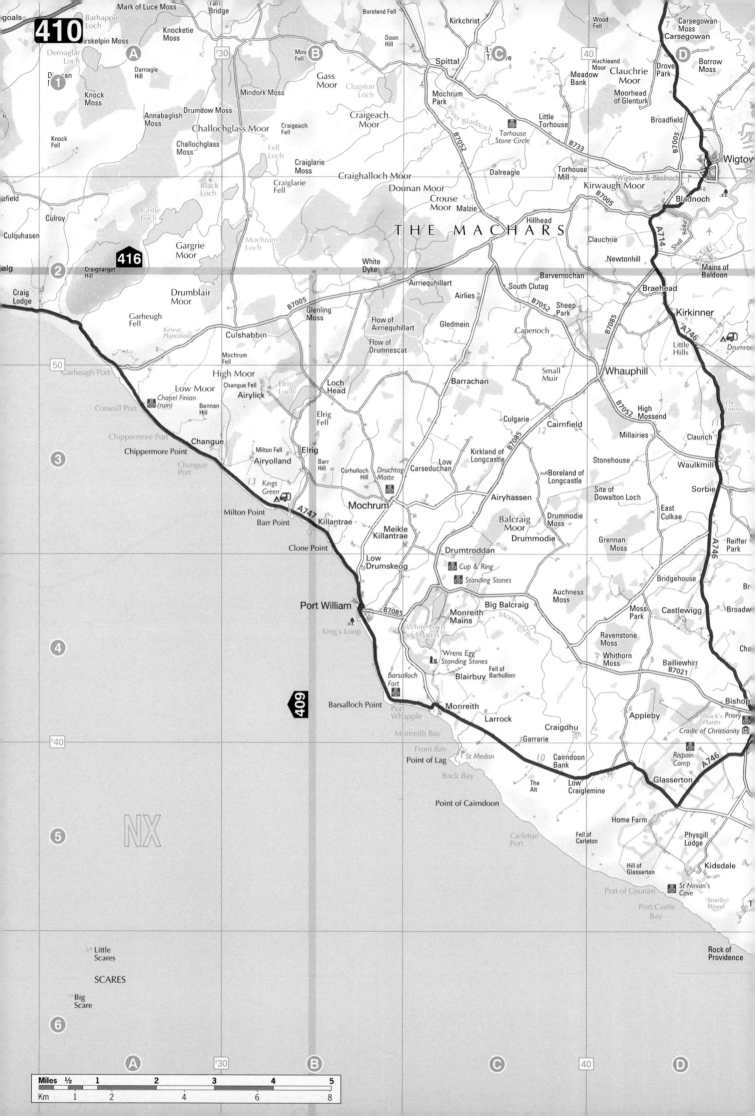

River Cree
Rock
Creetown
Creetown
Castle Cary
Knockeans Hill
Larg Hill
18
Carsluith
Carsluith
Castle
Birks Wood
Clash Wood

Glenquicken Moor
Shiel Hill
Corse of Slak
Strohnie Hill
Caml Hill
Cambret Moor
Blackmyre Moor
Glen
Doon Hill
Whiteside
455
CAIRNHARROW
Cairnholy Hill
Cairnholy Chambered Cairns
Barholm Hill
Ben John
Mill Knock
Lagganmullan
Skyreburn

Dalmaih Hill
Fore Hill
of Glengap
Fleet Valley
Ardwall
Killiegowan Wood
Anwoth
Anwoth
Cardoness Castle
Cally Lake
Skyreburn Bay
Cardoness Wood
Water of Fleet

Gatehouse
Disdow Wood
Gatehouse of Fleet
Fleet Bridge
Townhead
Bar Hill
Girthon
Barharrow

Meikle Culcaigrie Hill
Munwhall
Irelandton Moor
Knockendurrick
Carse
Moor Hill
Carsons Hill
Ingle Ston
Mark Hill
Auchenhay Hill
Boreland Bar
Kirko

E
F
G
H

1

2

50

60

A75

B796

B727

A755

8

417

412

Ravenshall Point
Auchenlarie
Mossyard
Mossyard Bay
Ringdoo Point
Garvellan Rocks
Dalavan Bay
Fleet Bay
Airds Bay
Sandgreen
Craigmore Point
Carrick Pt
Murray's Isles
Islands of Fleet
Barlocco Isle
Kendown Wood
Plunton Hill
Ardwall Isle
Bar Hill
Knockbrex
Cairn Hill
Castle Haven Bay
Kirkandrews Bay
Meggerland Pt
Kirkandrews
Muncraig Hill
Cairniehill
Blackcraig
Senwick Wood

Culscadden
Innerwell Port
Jultock Point
Port McGean
Penkiln
B7004
Cuttle Well Plantn
Millisle
Cairn Hill
Brown's Hole
Garlieston
Eggerness Point
Garlieston Bay
Pouton
W i g t o w n   B a y
Ringdoo Point
Borness
Borness Bar
Brighouse Bay
Balmangan Bar
Ma Bar
Manxman's Rock
Borness Point
Brighouse Bay
Mull of Ross   Ross
Ross Bay

3

B727

Gu Mi

Fox Craig
The Sound

4

Rigg or Cruggleton Bay
Sliddery Point
Gallow Hill
Baltier
Cruggleton Point
Palmallet Point
B7004
B7063
Port Allen
WhitePort
Auldbreck
Dunrod Point
Fauldbog Bay
Ross Ro

Sheddock
Portyerrock
Portyerrock Bay
Prestrie Plantn
Cairn Head
Prestrie
Stein Head
Boyach
Drummoral
Isle of Whithorn
PH
Steam Packet Inn
St Ninian's Chapel (ruin)
Cutreoch
Broom Point
Devil's Bridge
ROW EAD

40

NX

5

6

B7004

50
F
60
G
H
E

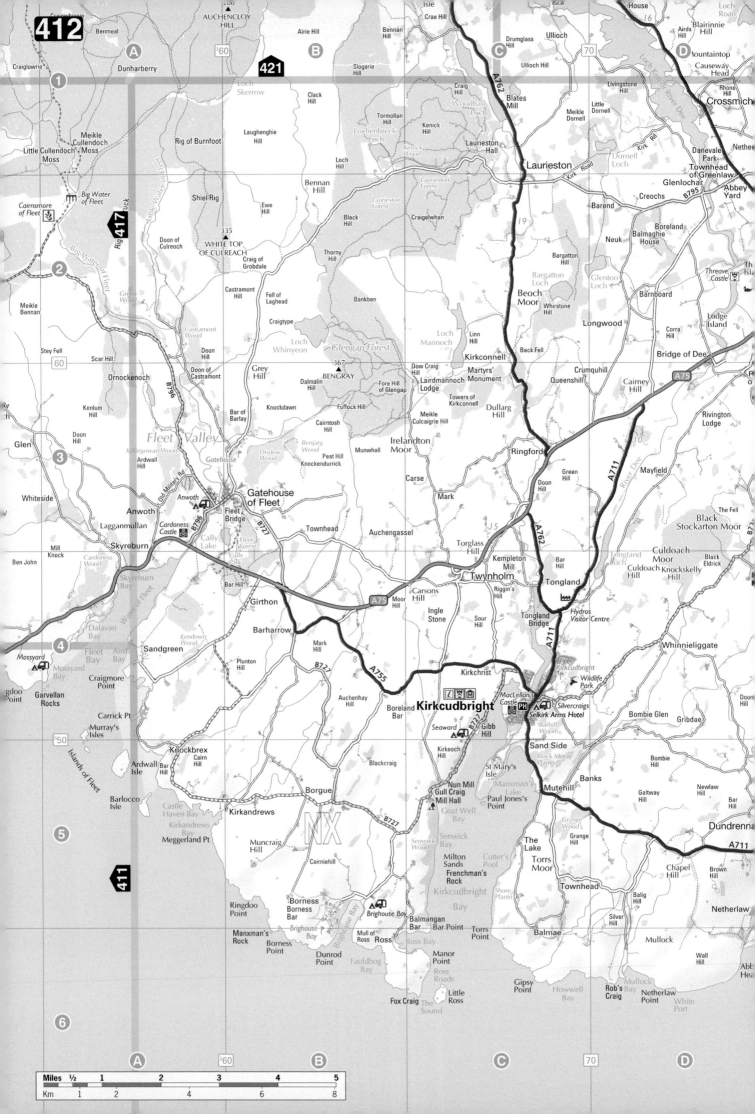

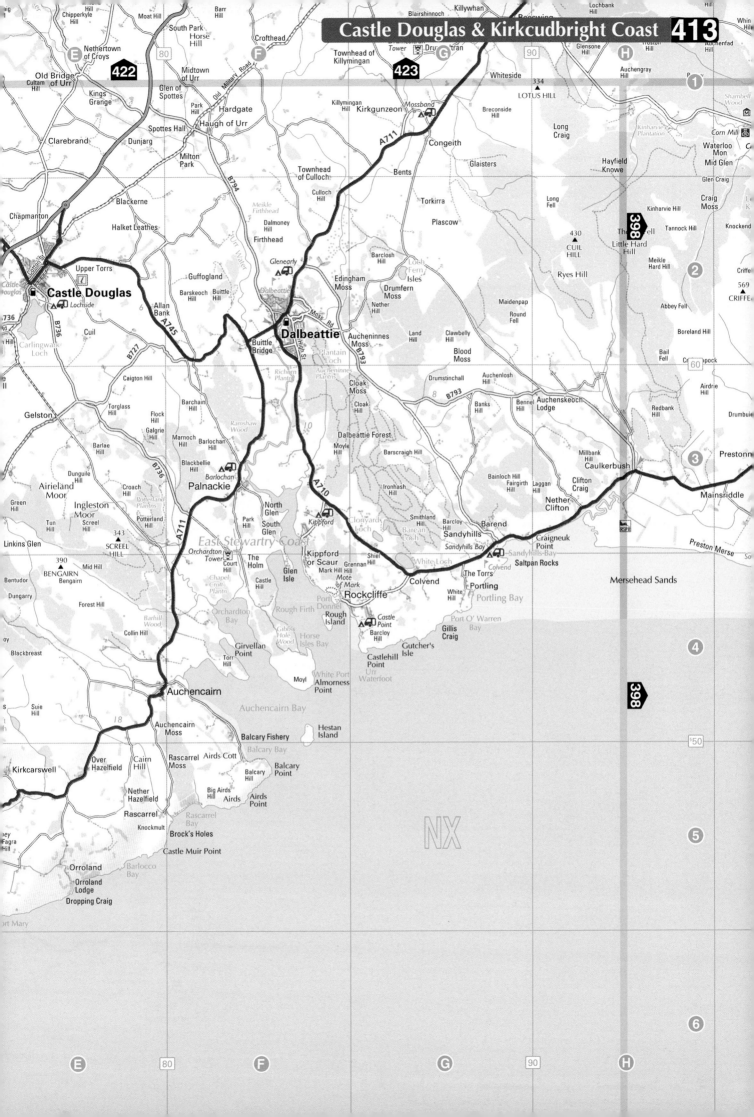

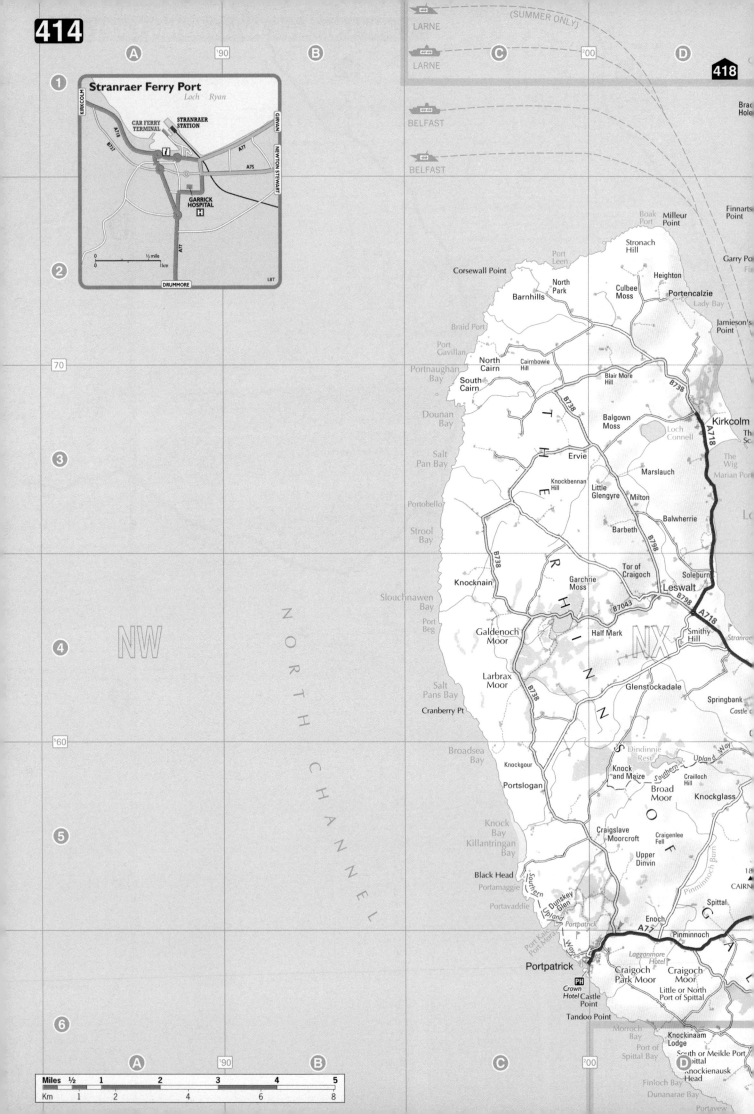

418

Stranraer Ferry Port

Loch Ryan

CAR FERRY TERMINAL

STRANRAER STATION

GARRICK HOSPITAL

KIRKCOLM

GIRVAN

NEWTON STEWART

A718

B731

A77

A75

A77

DRUMMORE

0   ½ mile

0   1 km

LBT

LARNE

(SUMMER ONLY)

LARNE

BELFAST

BELFAST

Brad
Hole

NW

NORTH CHANNEL

Corsewall Point

Port Leen

Boak Port

Milleur Point

Finnarts Point

Stronach Hill

Heighton

Garry Po

North Park

Culbee Moss

Portencalzie

Lady Bay

Barnhills

Jamieson's Point

Braid Port

Port Gavillan

North Cairn

Cairnbowie Hill

Blair More Hill

B738

Kirkcolm

Th
Sc

Portnaughan Bay

South Cairn

Balgown Moss

Loch Connell

A718

The Wig

Dounan Bay

B738

Ervie

Marslauch

Marian Por

Lo

Salt Pan Bay

Knockbennan Hill

Little Glengyre

Milton

Portobello

Barbeth

Balwherrie

B798

Strool Bay

B738

Tor of Craigoch

Soleburn

Knocknain

Garchrie Moss

Leswalt

B798

A718

Slouchnawen Bay

B7043

NX

Smithy Hill

Port Beg

Galdenoch Moor

Half Mark

Stranra

Salt Pans Bay

Larbrax Moor

B738

Glenstockadale

Springbank

Castle

Cranberry Pt

Broadsea Bay

Dindinnie Rest

Uplan Way

Knockgour

Knock and Maize

Southern

Crailloch Hill

Knock Bay

Portslogan

Broad Moor

Knockglass

Killantringan Bay

O

Craigslave Moorcroft

Craigenlee Fell

F

Black Head

Upper Dinvin

CAIRN

Portamaggie

Southern

Pinminnoch Burn

Spittal

Portavaddie

Dunskey Glen

Upland Way

18

Port Kale
Port Mora

Portpatrick

A77

Pinminnoch

Lagganmore Hotel

C

Enoch

Portpatrick

PH

Crown Hotel

Castle Point

Craigoch Park Moor

Craigoch Moor

Tandoo Point

Little or North Port of Spittal

Morroch Bay

Knockinaam Lodge

South or Meikle Port Spittal

Knockienausk Head

Finloch Bay

Dunanarae Bay

Portavew

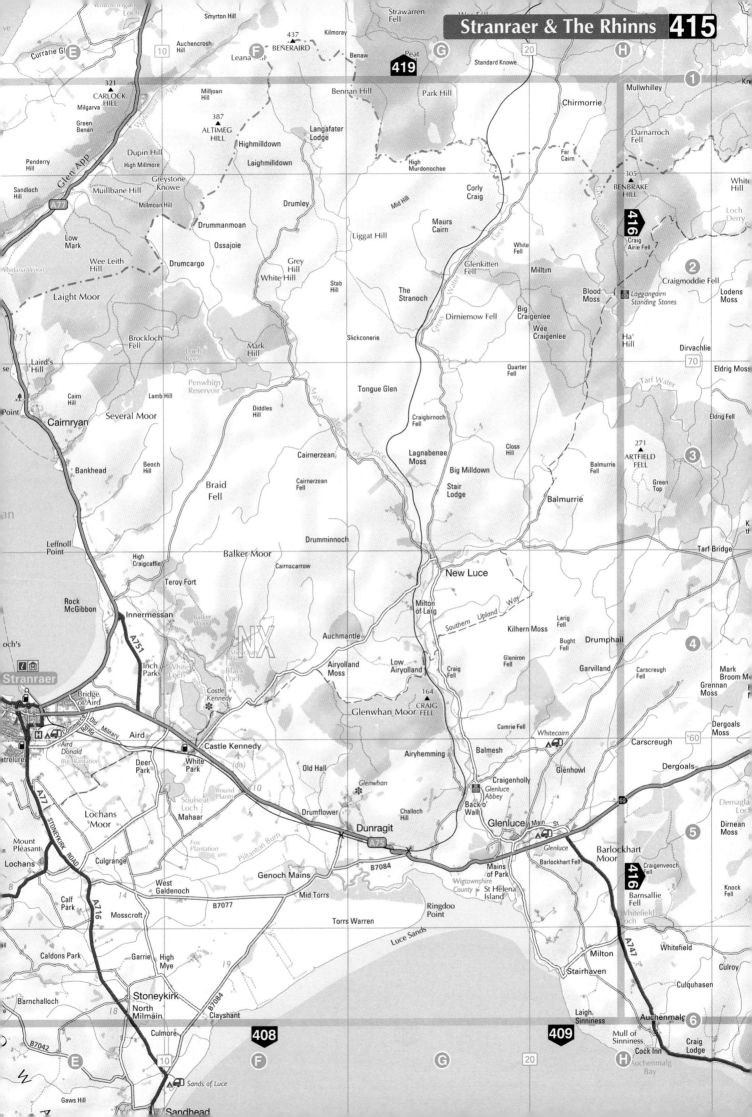

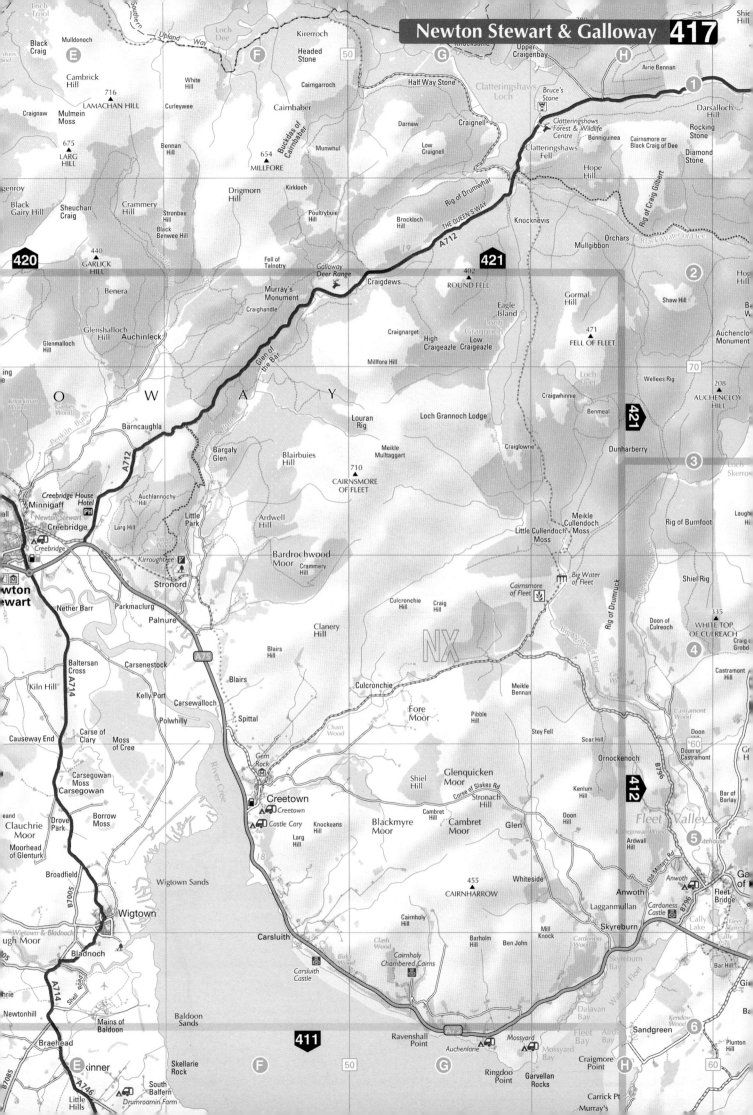

Ⓐ ²00 Ⓑ Ⓒ 10 Ⓓ

① NS

Swine
Holes

²00 ▲338
THE CAIRN ◊ Foreland Point
Stranny
Point [RSPB]
Ailsa Craig

② NX

③ A77

13

Carleton
Bay

90 Lendalfoot

Balsalloch
Hill

Games Knockormal
Loup Hill Moak
Hill

④ Balcreuchan Port Troax Lochton
Hill
Port Vad Claucha
Bennane Hill
Head Littleton Balhamie
Hill Hill
Knockdolian B734

Mossgavel Colmo

Cra
Hill

Cairn
Hill Kno
Heronsford

Ballantrae Cra
Bay Park End MAINS ROAD B7044 Craig
Wood
⑤ Ballantrae Glen

Garleffin Balkissoc
Leff
Dor
Crailoch
Little Balkissoc
Downan Point High Fell Hill
Kilphin Balrazzie Fells
Downan Hill Big Fell Millm
Smyrton
Meadow Park

80 Kilantringan Smyrton Hill
Loch

Dove Cove Auchencrosh 437
Hill BENERAIRD
Currarie Port Leana Hill
Currarie Glen

⑥

414 10 **415**

Brackness 321
Hole CARLOCK Milljoan
HILL Hill
Burn Milgarva
Foot Ⓒ C 10 387 Ⓓ
een ALTIMEG
Benan HILL Highmilldown Langa
Lodge

Miles ½ 1 2 3 4 5 Dupin Hill
Km 1 2 4 6 8 Turf High Millmore Penderry Laighmilldown
Hill Hill
App

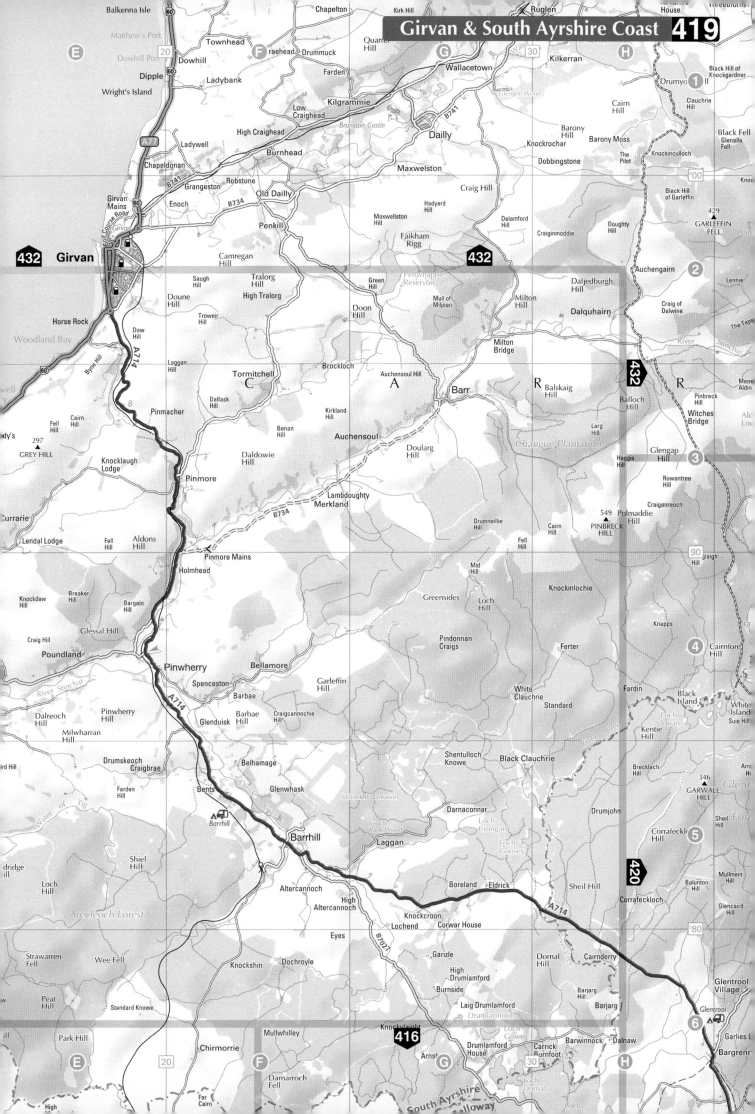

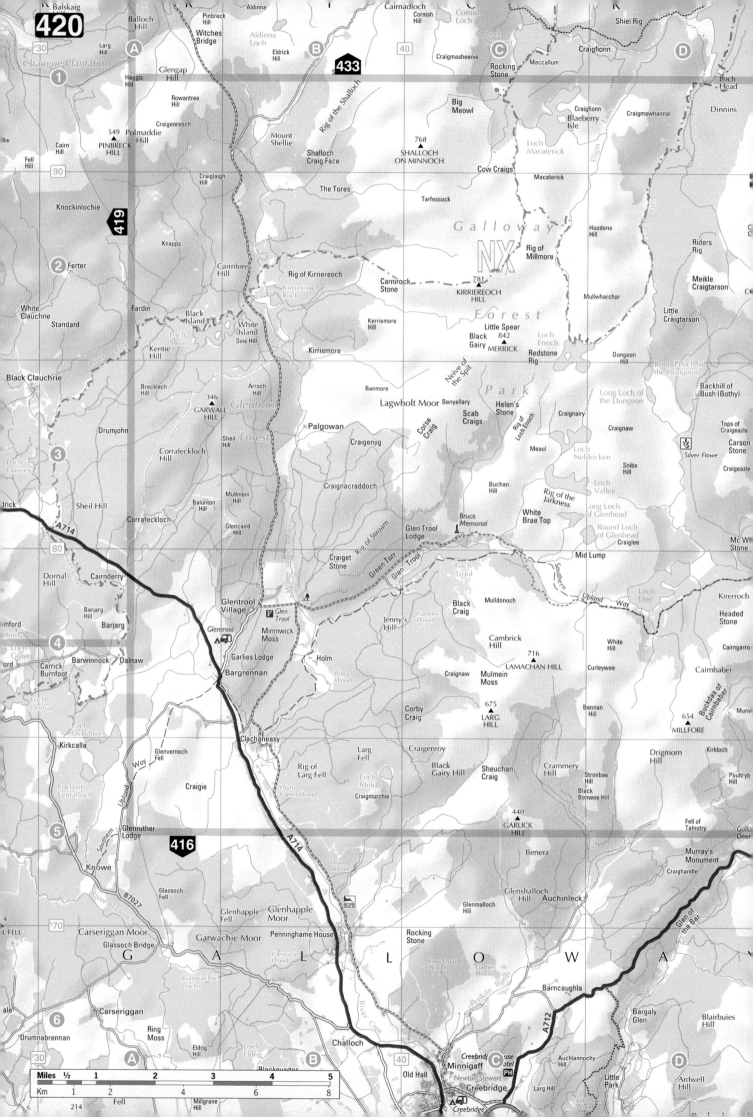

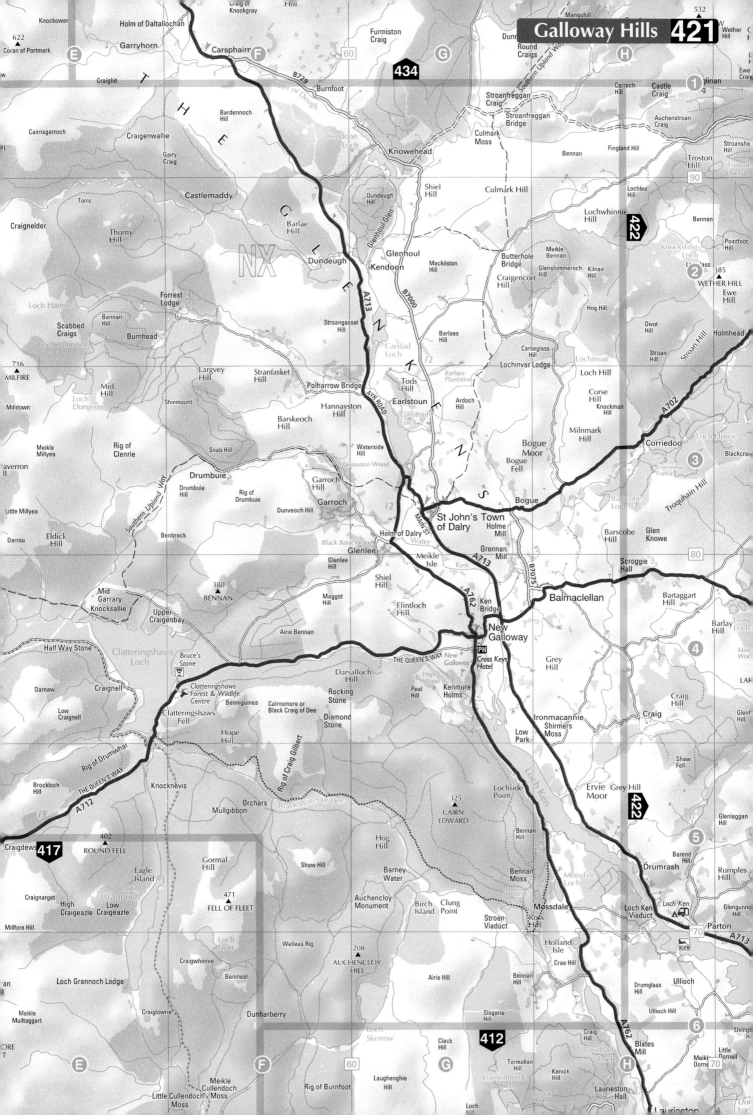

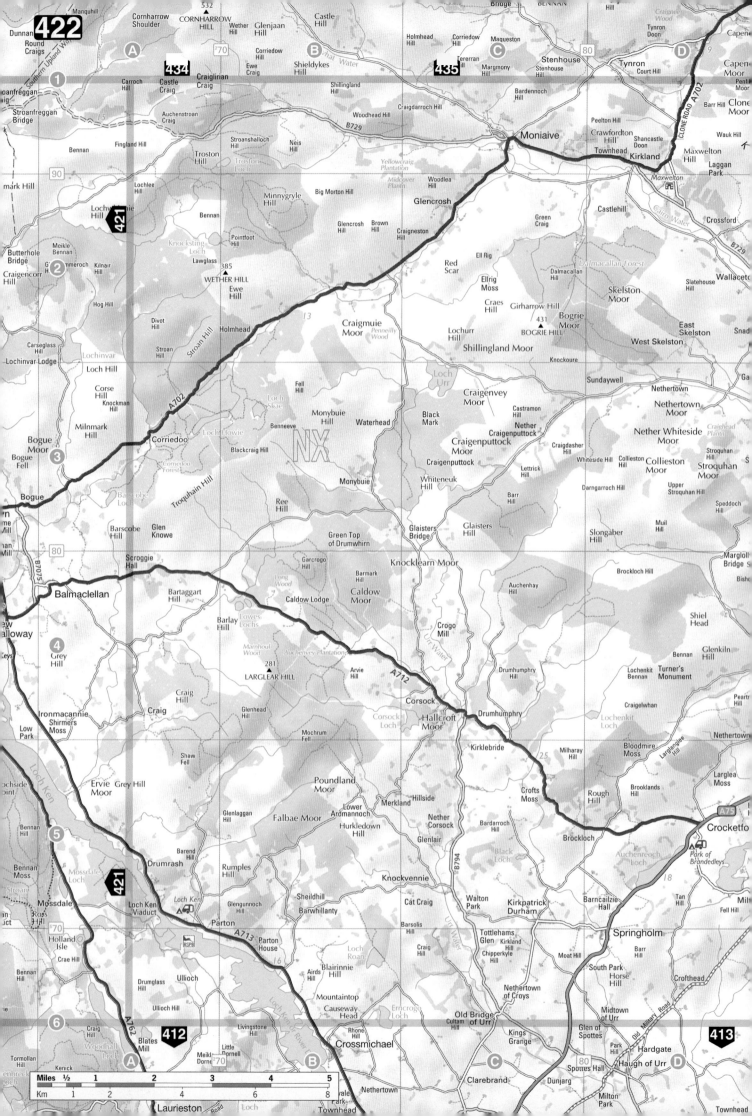

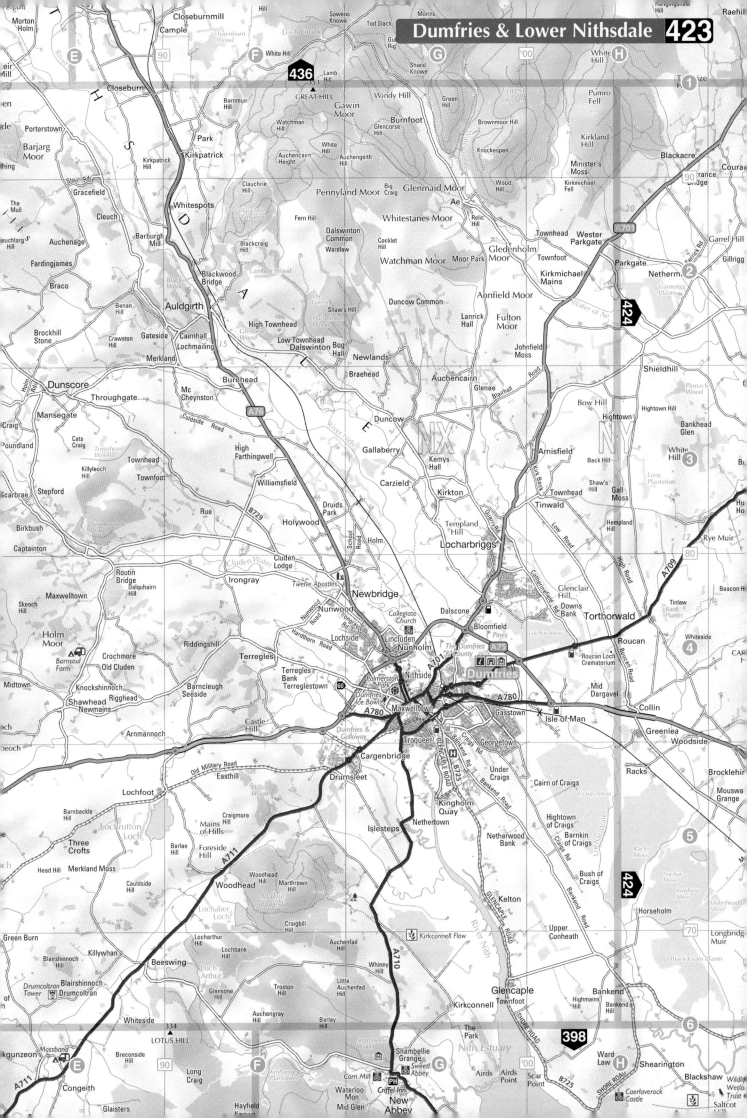

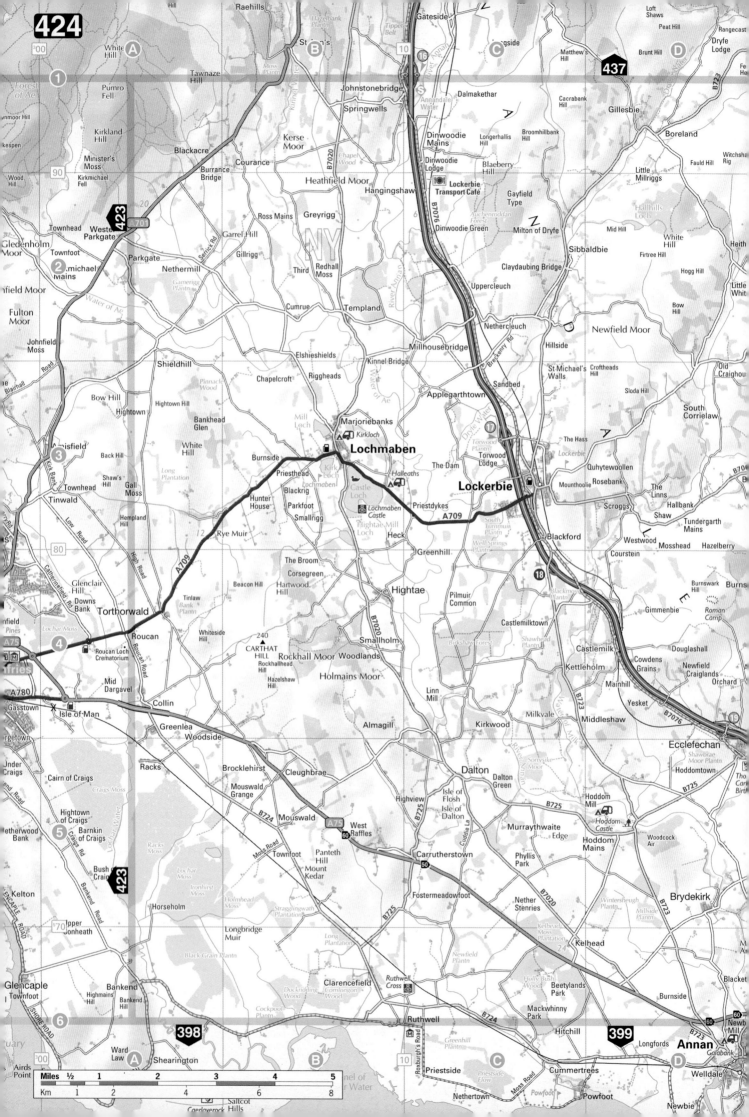

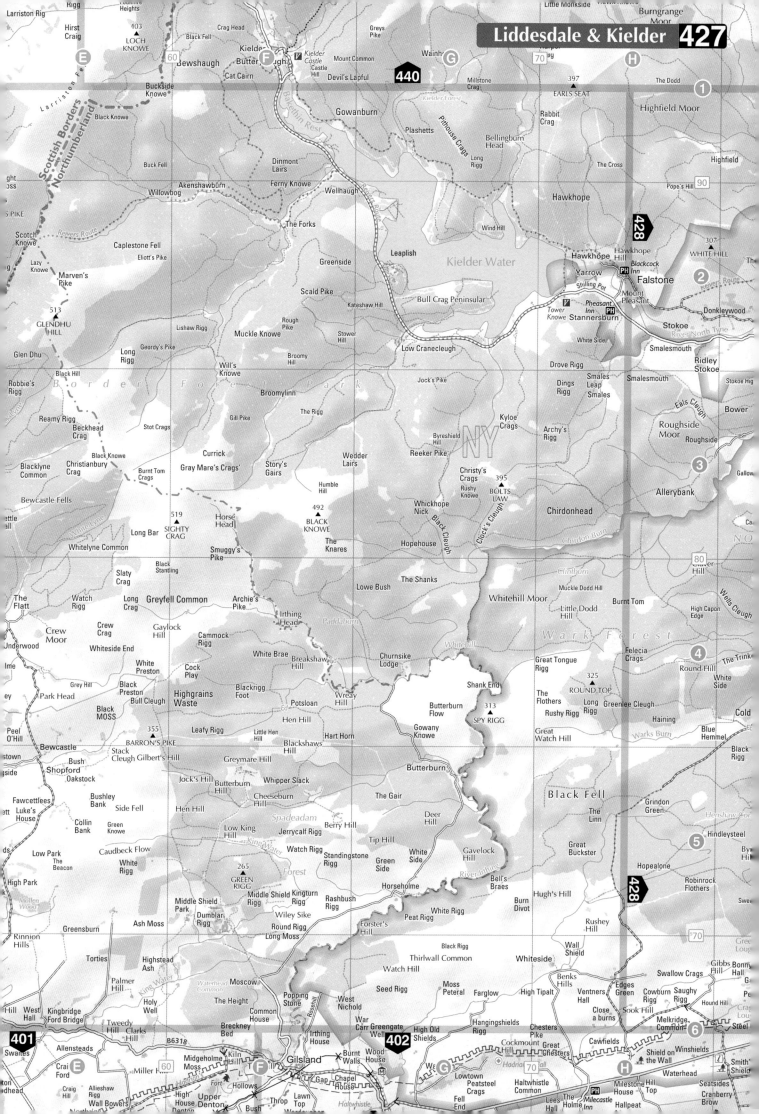

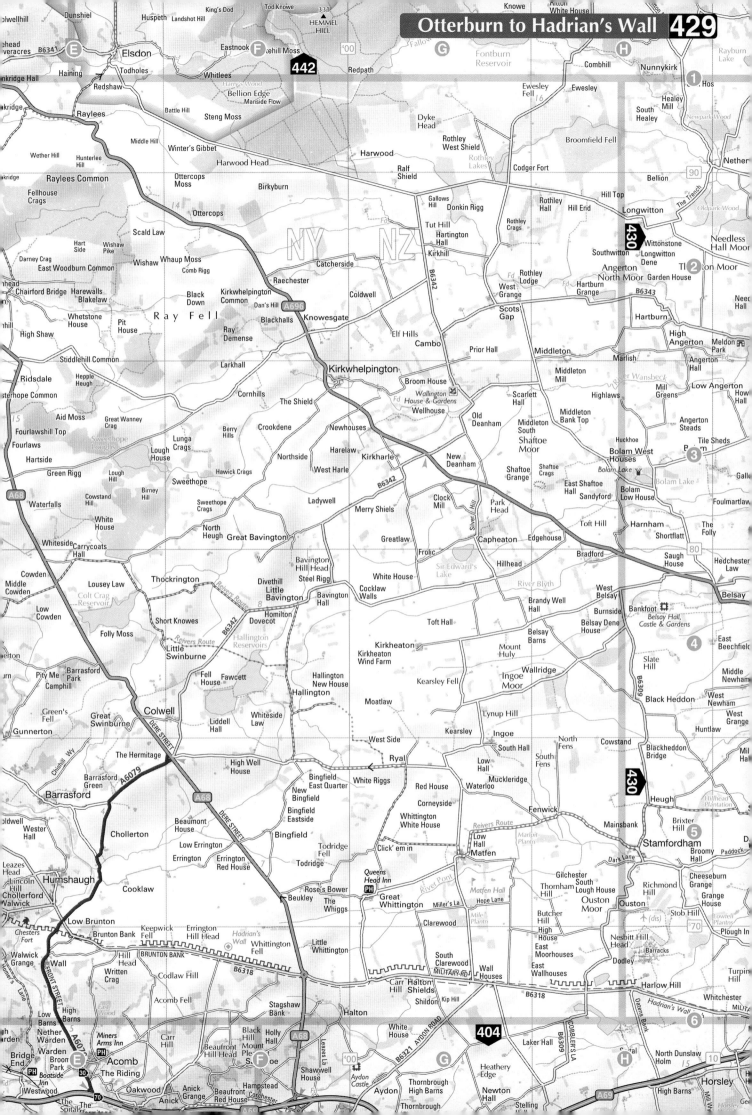

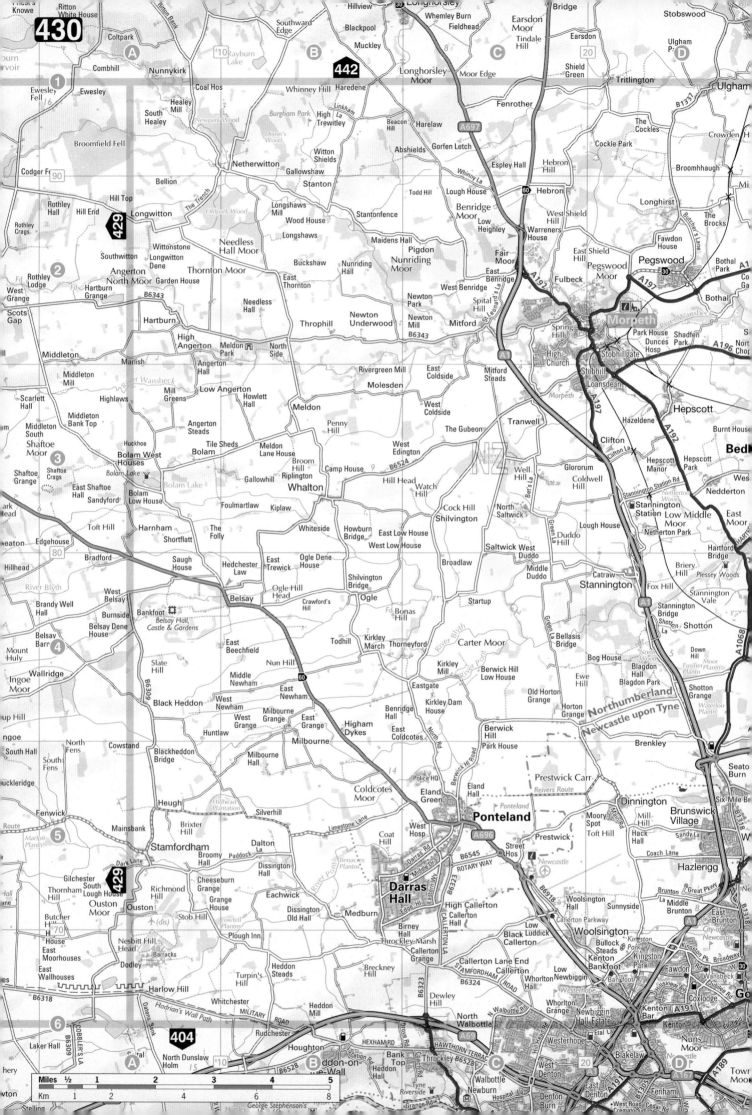

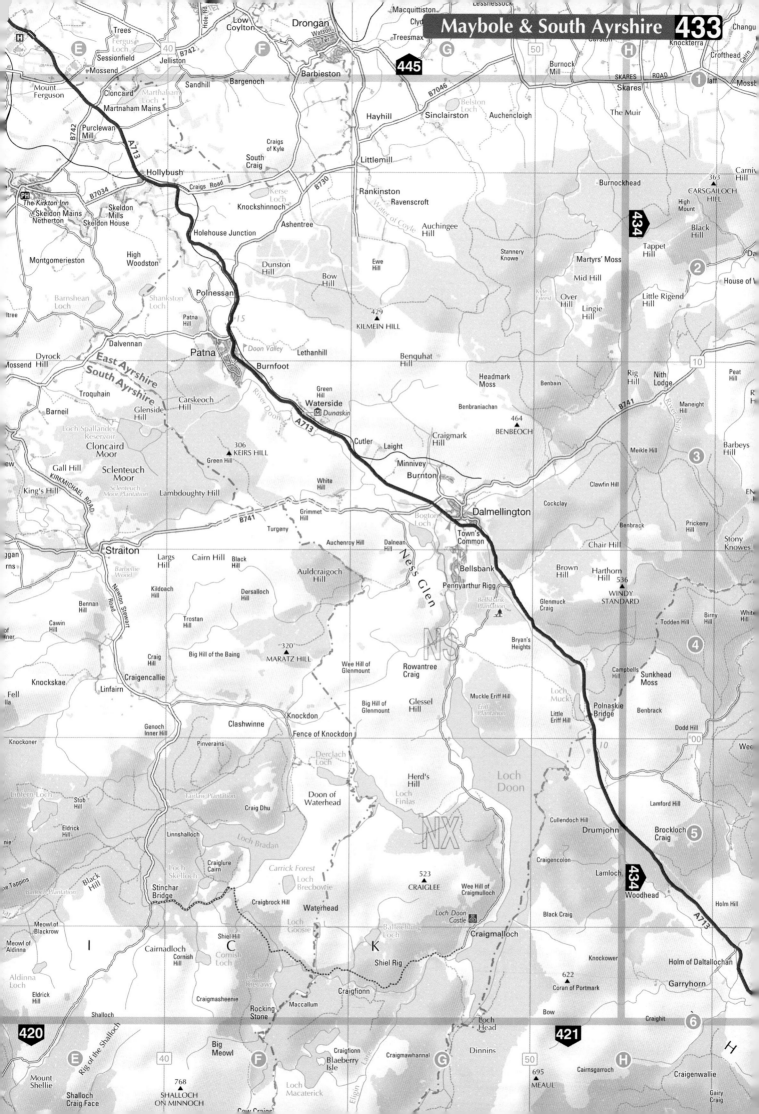

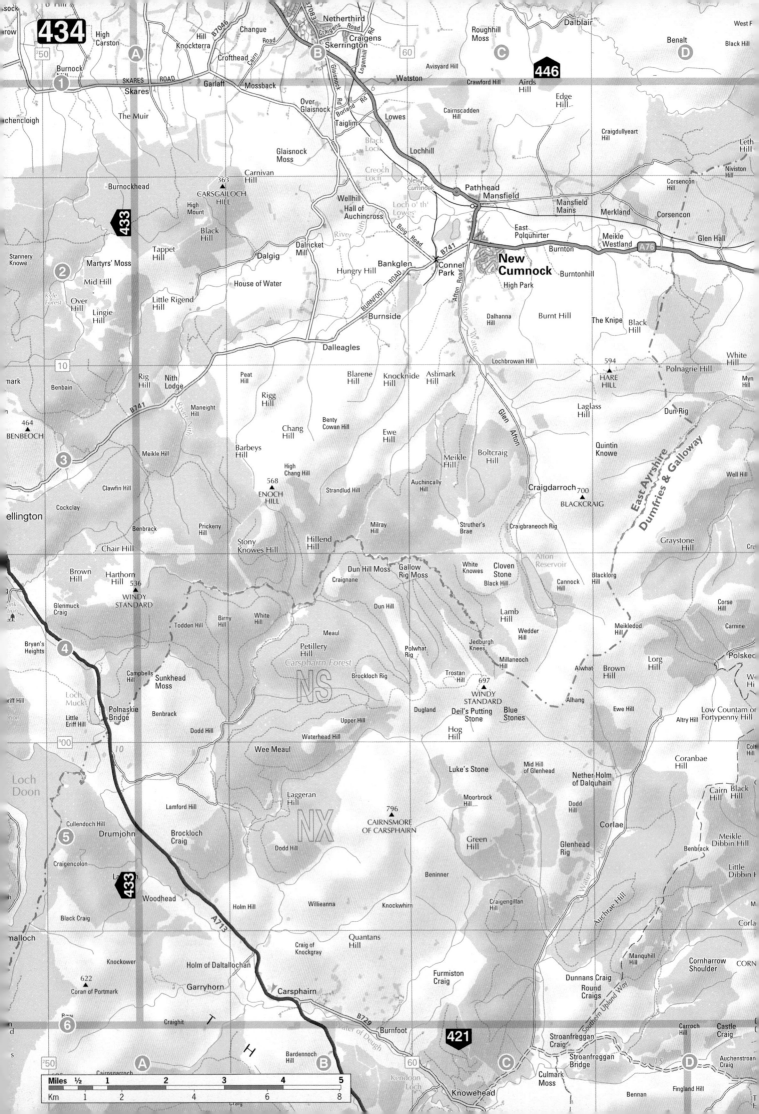

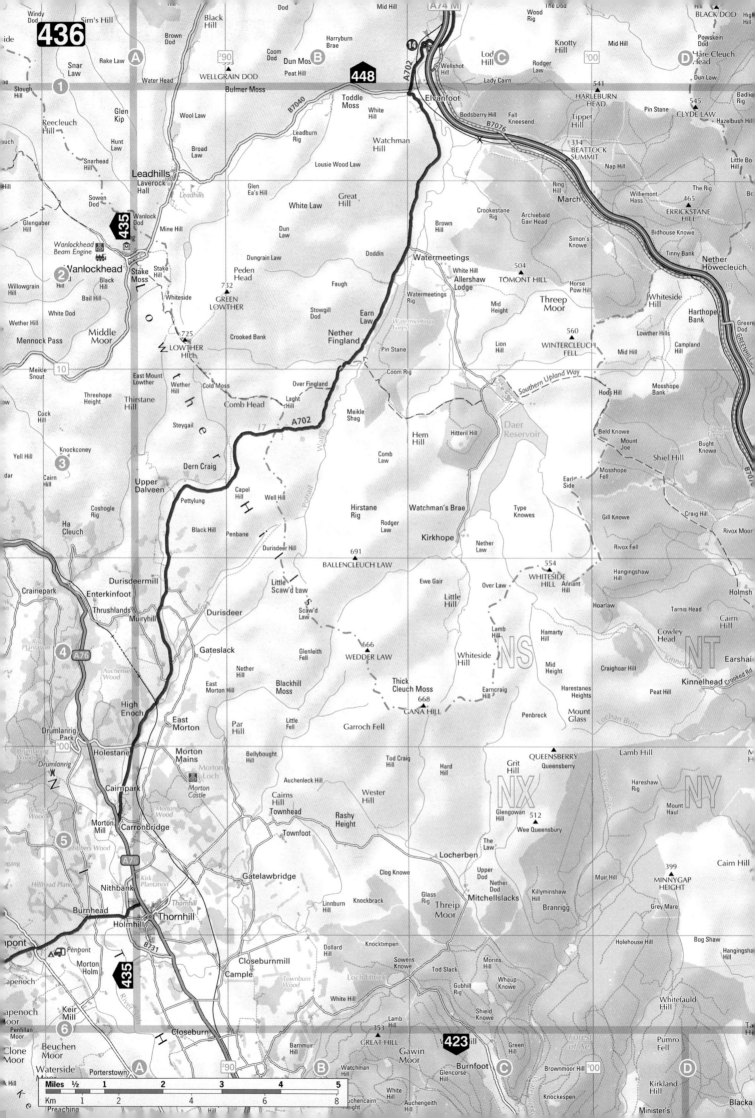

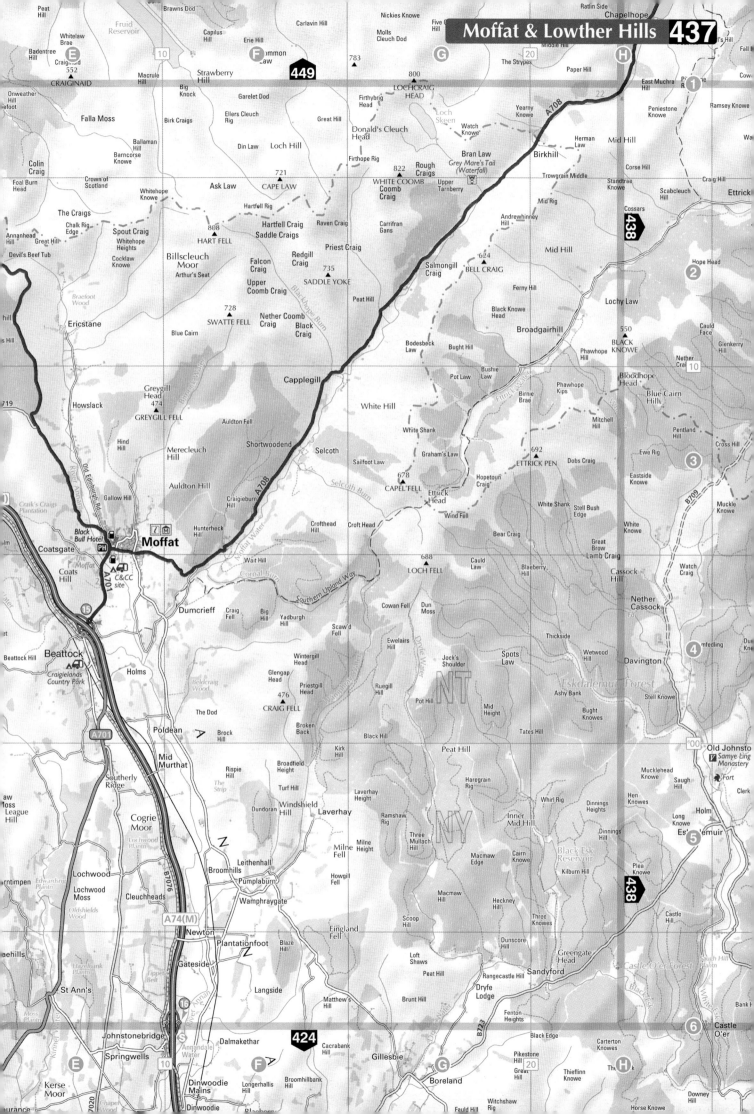

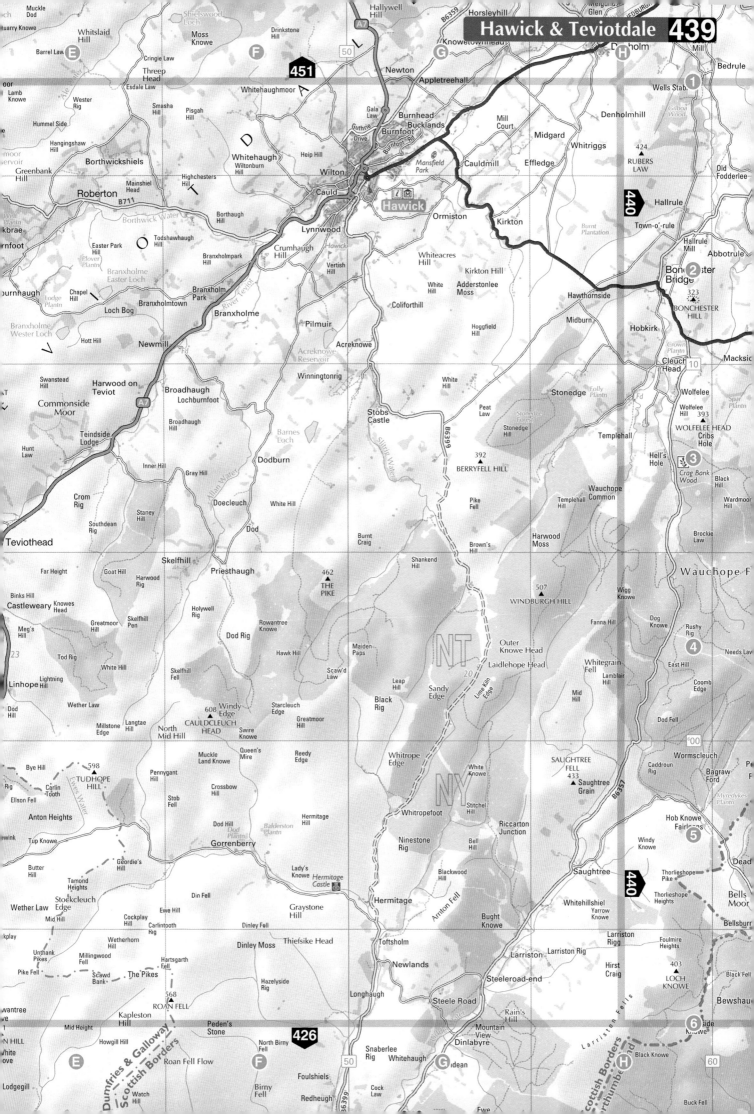

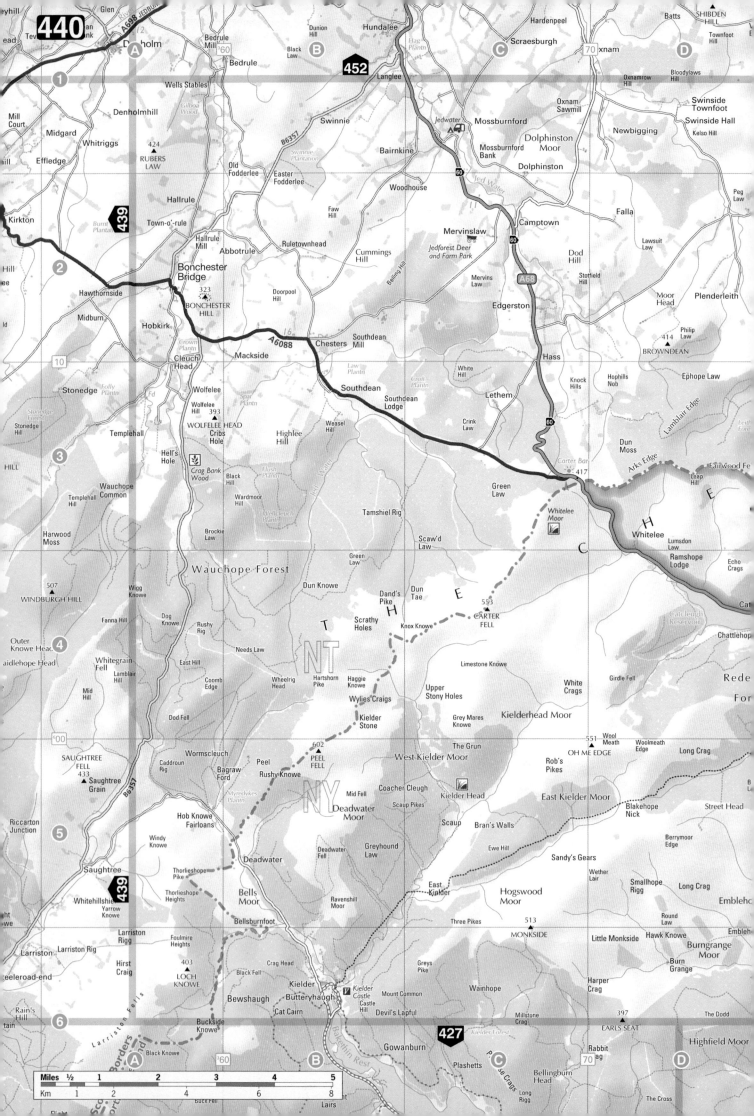

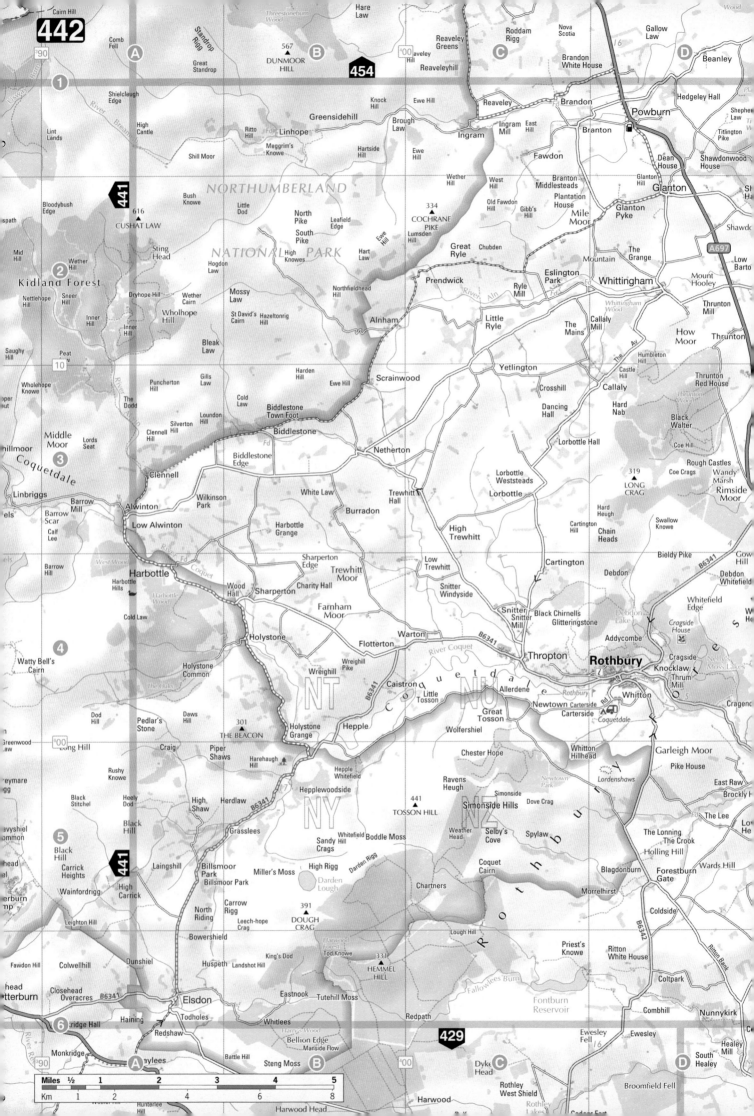

444

464

461

432

A   B   C   D

1

2

3

4

5

6

ARRAN (BRODICK)

Ardrossan
Ardrossan Harbour
Ardrossan Town
South Bay
Horse Isle
Broad Rock
North Bay
Clyde Marina
Argyle Rd
South Beach
Auchenharvie
Sandylands

Saltcoats

Stevenston or Ashgrove Loch
Whithurst
Middlepart
Ardeer
Burns
Stevenston
Dubbs
North Bay

Blair Rd
Crotihead
Montgre...
North Furgushill
Bensli...
Doura

C Castlehill
D **Kilwinning**
Eglinton
Dykehead
Irvine Ravenspark
Bogside Flats
Maritime
Fullarton
Irvine
Stanecastle
Shewalt...
Broon

Irvine

F I R T H   O F

C L Y D E

NS

NS

Irvine Bay

The Big Idea
The Magnum Leisure Centre
Beach Park
Western Gailes
Glasgow

Dundonald Camp
Kilmarnock (Barassie)
Barassie Sands
Barassie
Loans
Muirhead
DUNDONALD ROAD

North Bay
North Sands
Yacht Haven

Troon
South Bay
South Sands
Royal Troon
Little Craigs

(SUMMER ONLY)

Lady Isle

LARNE

Prestwick International Ai...
Prestwick
Prestwi...
Prestwick

Prestwick
St Nicholas

Woodfiel...
Newton on...
Wallacetown

Ayr

Seafield

Cunning Park
Longhill Point
Doonfoot
Belmo...
Kin...
Bower Hill
Craig Tara
Burns Cottage
Burns Monument
Alloway
Doonholm...
Millbrae
Bracken Bay
Heads of Ayr
DUNURE ROAD
Longhill Av.

A719
Fisherton
Station Rd
C
Brown Carrick Hill
Dunure
Blacktop Hill
Broad Craig
White...
Newark Hill
Brae of Auchendrane
Auchendran...
D

Miles ½   1   2   3   4   5

Km   1   2   4   6   8

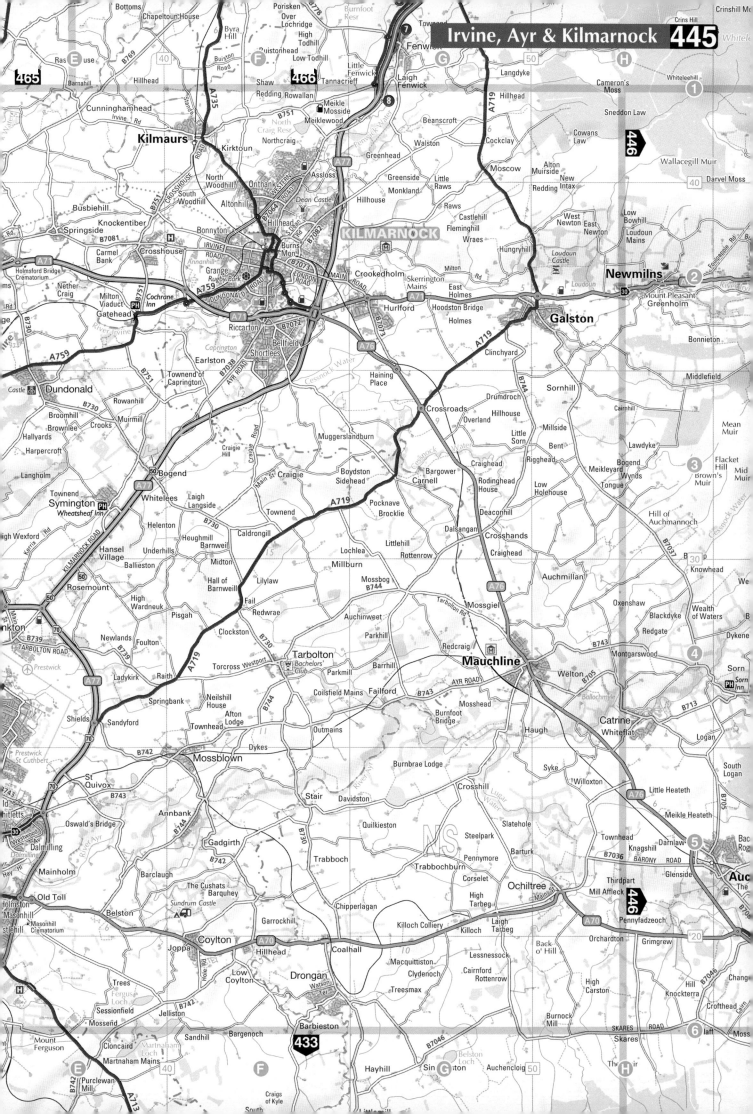

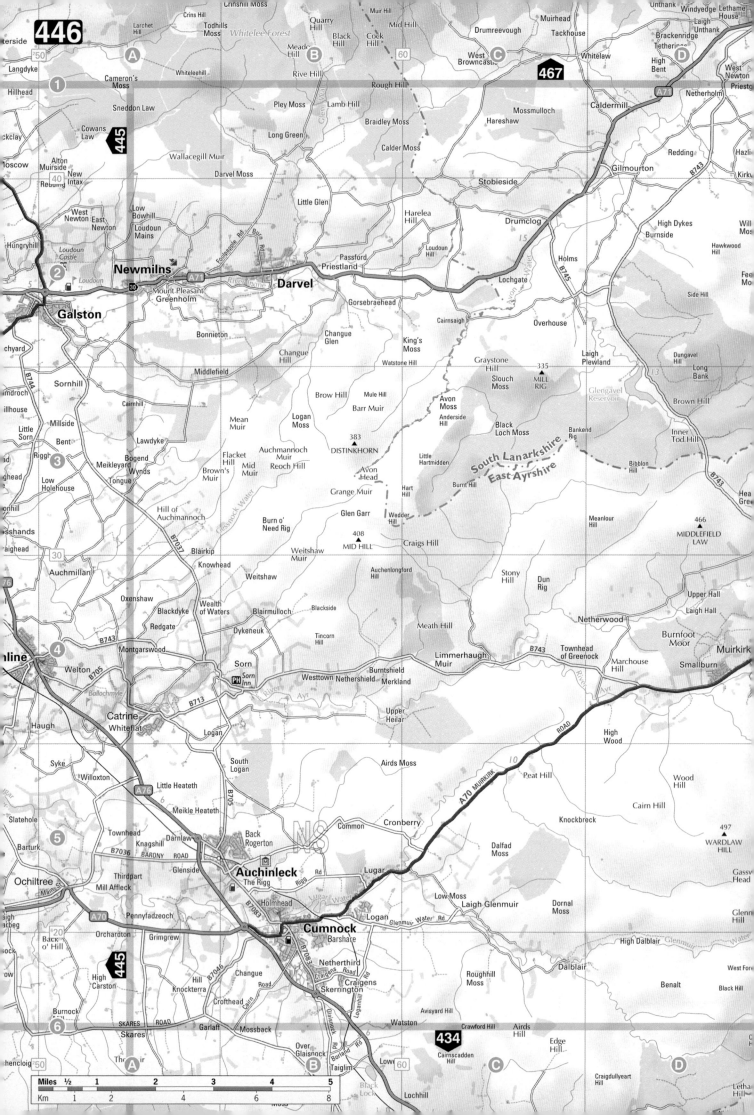

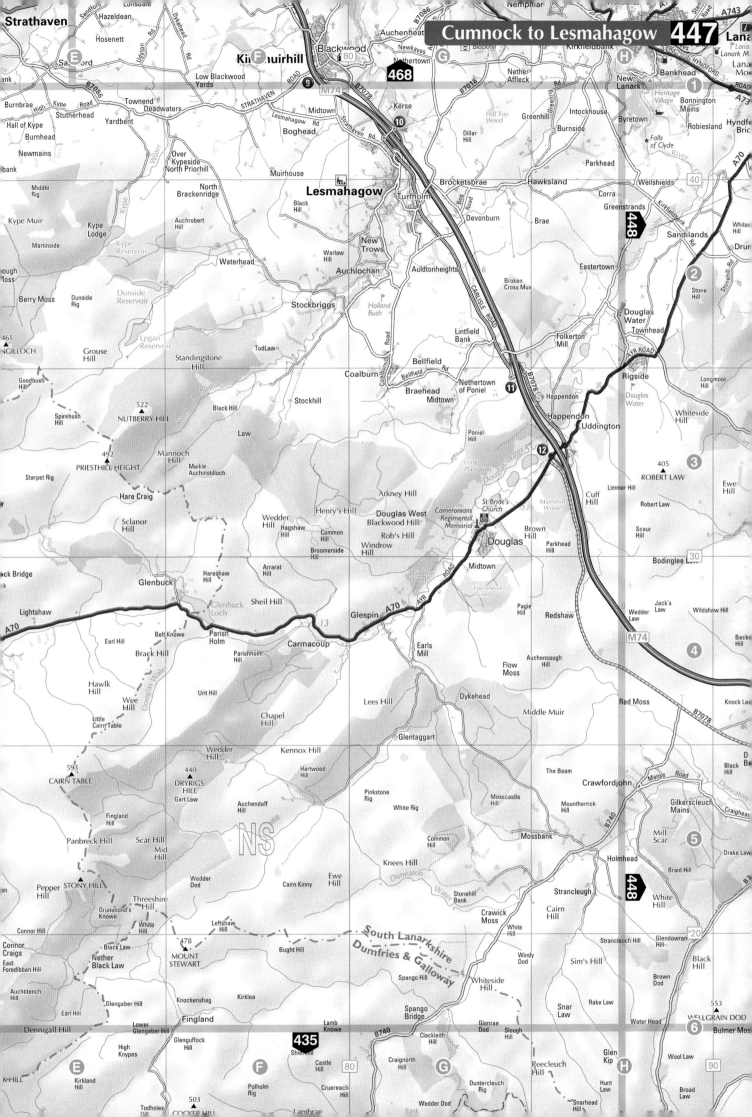

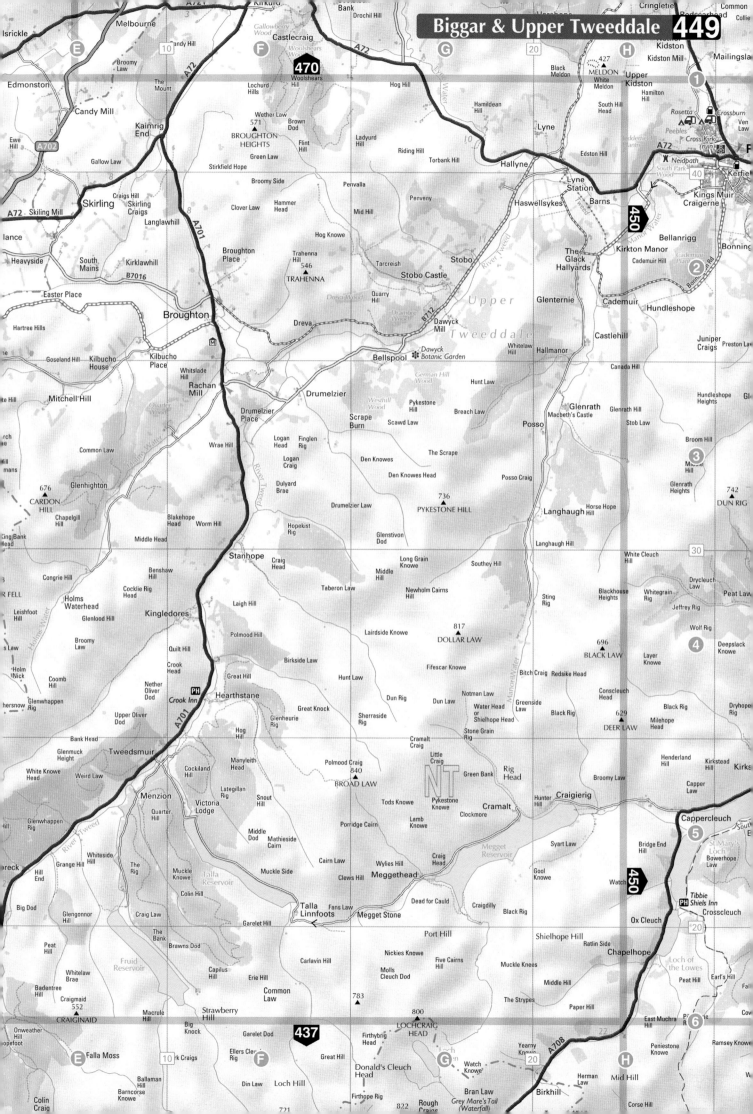

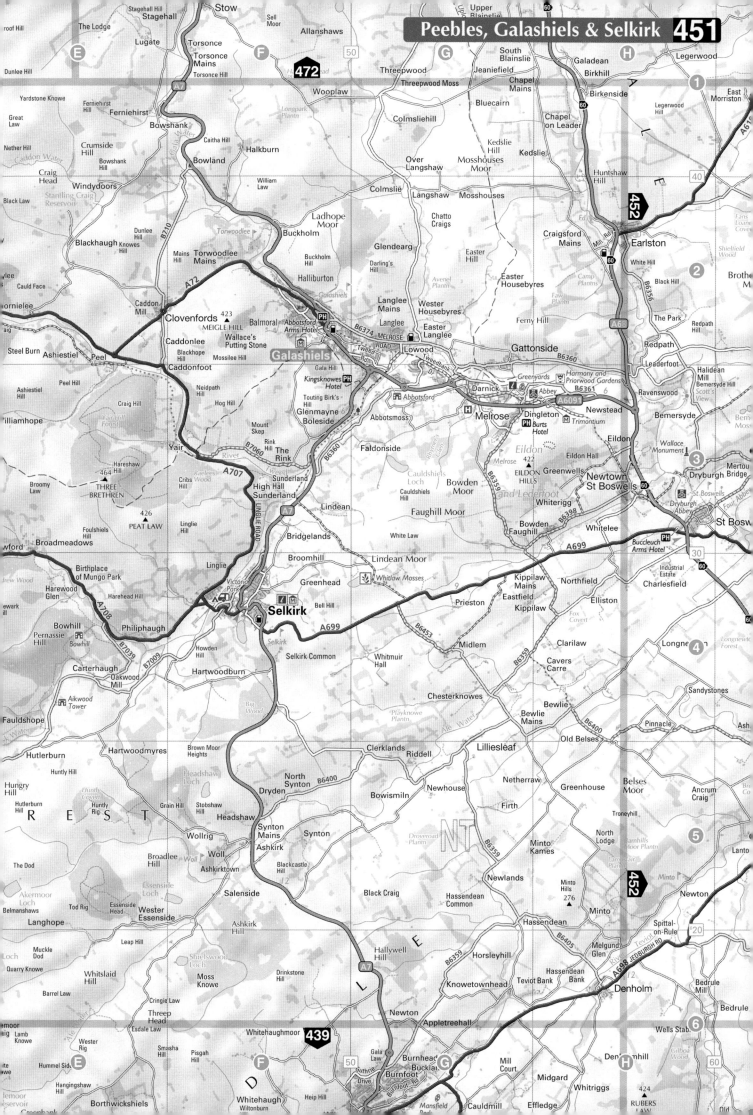

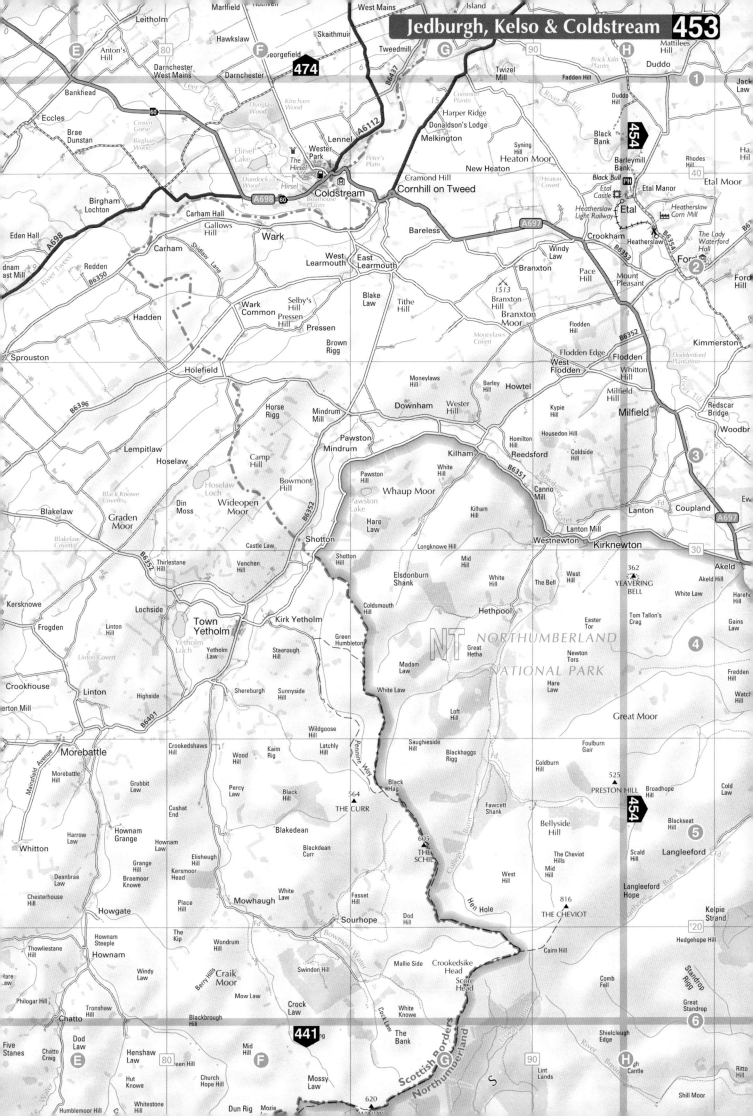

Port na Croise
Cnocan Gean
Port Corbert
Tangy Loch
Port nam Marbh
Tangy Lodge
Tangy
Cnoc a' Choire
Ske
Sk
Ranach Hill
Kilchenzie
Darlochan
Craigs
A83
Machrihanish Bay
Dhurrie
Campbeltown
Machrihanish
Aros Moss
East Backs
Machrihanish
Bleachfield
Machrihanish
Machrihanish Water
Ⓒ
Drumlemble
B843
6
Leac Bhuidhe
Ballygroggan
Skerry Fell Fad
Killypole Loch
Knockr
Killypole
Earadale Point
Tirfergus Hill
Beinn na Faire
B842
Creag nan Cuilean 385
THE SLATE
Killellan Park
Black Hill
446
CNOC MOY
Killellan Lo
Cnocan Biorach
Cnoc nan Gabhar
Connel Water
Rubha Dùin Bhàin
Achnaslishaig Hill
Dùn Bàn
Conie Glen
Port na h-Olainn
Cnoc Reamhar
Cnoc na Grèine
Glen Remuil
Cnoc Odhar
Rubh 'a' Mharaiche
Sliabh a' Bhiorain
Glen Breakevie
Remuil Hill
Amod Hill
Cnocan Lin
A'Chruach
Cnoc na Feudalach
Corr nan Long
North Carrine
Corr Bhàn
Strone Glen
'610
Lephenstrath Bridge
Cnoc Mòr
Glemanuilt Glen
Beinn Bhreac
Strone Water
428
Glenmanuilt Hill
BEINN NA LICE
Glenmanuilt
Carskiey
S
A
NR
South Point
Torr Mòr
Torr Dùbh
Carskey Bay
Keil Point
Dunaverty Bay
Bruner
Bay
Rubha na Lice
Beinn a' Theine
Rubha nan Scarlan
Port Mean
MULL OF KINTYRE
Sròn Uamha
Borgadalemore Point

Miles ½   1   2   3   4   5
Km   1   2   4   6   8

SGREADAN HILL

Easach Hill

Ugadale

Ugadale Point

Torbeg

ckwaterfoot

Nor

South Feorlir

Skeroblin Cruach

B842

Kildonald Bay

Island Ross

Kildonald Point

Drumadoo

Kilpatrick Point

Rubha Garbhard

Kilpat

1

Coul Hill

Glen Lussa

Black Bay

Carrick Point

Brown Head

Àird nan Ron

Peninve Bridge

Calliburn

Glenlussa Lodge

Rinn a' Chrubain

A'Chruach

Peninver

Ardnacross Bay

Torr a Ch

Port na Fea

Ballywilline Hill

460

2

Knockruan Loch

Aucha Lochy

Knock Scalbart

Knockruan Loch

20

Calton

Mill Knowe

HIGH ASKOMIL

B842

Macringan's Point

ltown

Askomill

Island Davaar

B842

Kilkerran

Trench Pt

Campbeltown Loch

Kilkerran Rd

Kildalloig Bay

Croshill Loch

Kildalloig

3

Tomaig Glen

352

BEINN GHUILEAN

Meall Mòr

Ballimenach Hill

Achinhoan Head

Achinhoan Hill

Arinarach Hill

Balnabraid Glen

n Kerran

Kerran Hill

Feochaig

Johnston's Point

4

Tod Hill

Glen Hervie

The Bastard

Kilchattan Hill

Eden Hill

Gartnagerach Point

10

Macharioch

Polliwilline Bay

Mill Park

Macharioch Bay

Cove Point

NR

5

Rubha MacShannuich

ound of Sanda

Sheep Island

Sanda Roads

Glunimore Island

Black Point

SANDA ISLAND

Prince Edward's Rock

6

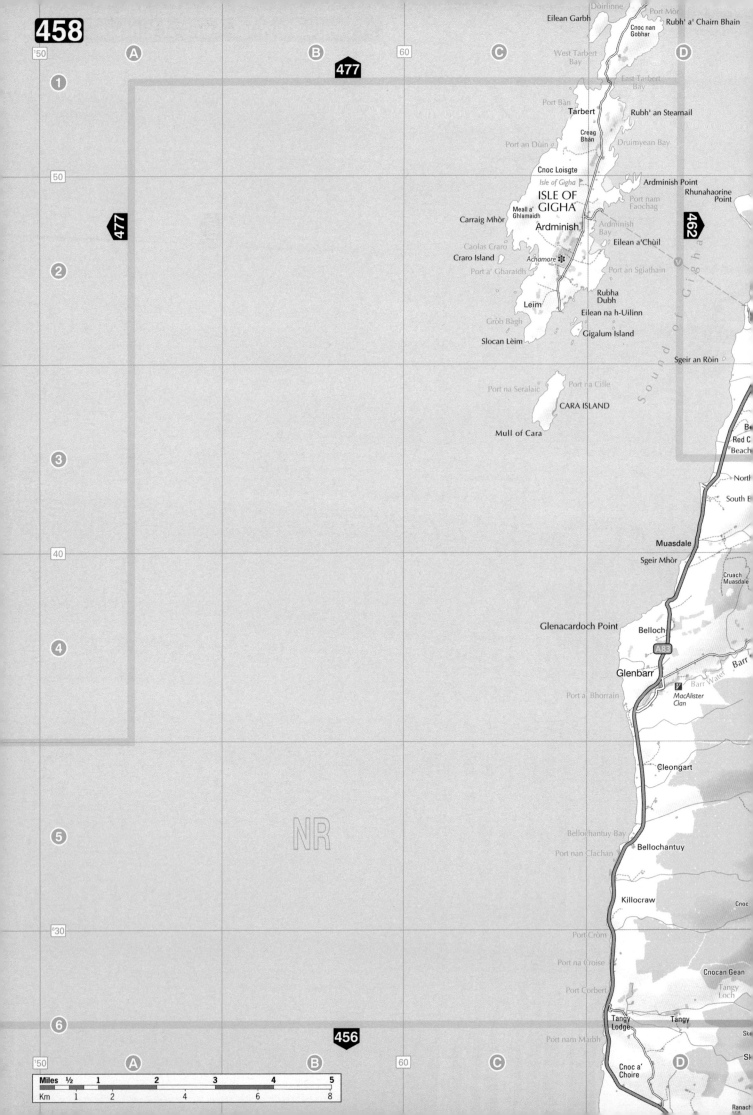

50

Ⓐ   Ⓑ   60   Ⓒ   Ⓓ

477

Dòirlinne

Eilean Garbh   Port Mòr

Cnoc nan Gobhar   Rubh' a' Chairn Bhain

West Tarbert Bay

East Tarbert Bay

Port Bàn

Tarbert   Rubh' an Stearnail

① 1

Creag Bhàn   Druimyean Bay

Port an Dùin

50

Cnoc Loisgte

Isle of Gigha   Ardminish Point

ISLE OF GIGHA   Rhunahaorine Point

477   Carraig Mhòr   Meall a' Ghlamaidh   Port nam Faochag

Ardminish   Ardminish Bay

② 2   Caolas Craro   Eilean a'Chùil

Craro Island   Achamore �֎   Port an Sgiathain

Port a' Gharaidh

462

Rubha Dubh

Leim   Eilean na h-Uilinn

Gròb Bàgh   Gigalum Island

Slocan Lèim   Sgeir an Ròin

Sound of Gigha

Port na Seralaic   Port na Cille

③ 3   **CARA ISLAND**   B...

Red C... Beach

Mull of Cara

Nort...

South ...

40

Muasdale

Sgeir Mhòr

Cruach Muasdale

④ 4   Glenacardoch Point   Belloch

A83

Glenbarr   Barr...

Port a' Bhorrain   Barr Water   MacAlister Clan

Cleongart

NR

Bellochantuy Bay

⑤ 5   Port nan Clachan   Bellochantuy

Killocraw   Cnoc...

30

Port Cròm

Port na Croise   Cnocan Gean

Tangy Loch

Port Corbert

⑥ 6   Tangy Lodge   Tangy

456

Port nam Marbh   Sk...

Cnoc a' Choire   Sh...

50

Ⓐ   Ⓑ   60   Ⓒ   Ⓓ

Miles   ½   1   2   3   4   5

Km   1   2   4   6   8

Argyll & Bute
North Ayrshire

E **F** **G** **H**

1

2

3

4

5

6

A83

Ballochroy
Ballochroy Glen

Bèiste
Loch Ciaran
Loch an Eilein Beag

Loch an Eilein Mòr
Fuar Larach
Loch Romain

Rubha na h-Airde Bàine
Eascairt Point

Creag Loisgte Talatoll
Cnoc Donn

Cruach na Seilcheig

Creag Eanaiche

Cru Bhreac

Creag Mhòr

Crossaig Glen

Port Alasdair Ruaidh

247
CRUACH MHIC GOUGAIN

Sròn Albannach

Cnoc a'Bhraidein

Loch a'Ghatha
Loch Garasdale

Cnoc Laoighscan

Crossaig

Port nan Gamhna
Port a' Mhiadair

Catacol
Catacol Bay

Cnoc nan Iteag

264
CNOC-AN T-SAMHLAIDH

Gleann Laoigh

Loch nam Breac

Cnoc na Buaile Salaich

Cnoc Dubh

Rubha Riabhach

Rubha Airigh Bheirg

Rhunahaorine

Cnoc Airigh Luachraich

Narachan Hill

Cnoc a'Mhinisteir

Beinn Bhreac
Loch a'Mhuilinn

Loch Tana

Cnoc Iaruinn

Cour

Cour Bay

Cour Island

Rubha Dearg-uillt

Rubha Glas

Thundergay

Meall Bhig

Braids

Loch Dirigadale

Loch Ulagadale

Loch an Fhraoich

Cnoc nan Craobh

Lorgie Hill

Cnoc Reamhar

Cnoc Rèilereidhe

Cnoc Dubh

Rubha Bàn

Meall Biorach

Meall Donn

Beinn Bhre

Cnoc Odhar Auchaluskin

Deucheran Hill

Cruach na Casaich

Cruach Ruadh

Cnoc Donn

Garrachcroit Bàgh
Grogport
Sgeir Bhuidhe
Port Raoin Mhòr

Pirnmill

Cruach Mhic-an t-Saoir

Cnoc Reamhar

Mullach Bu

354
CRUACH NAN GABHAR

Brackley

Eilean Grianain

Whitefarland Point

Whitefarland

BEINN BHARRAIN

Cnoc na Seilg

Meall Buidhe

Teanchoisin Glen

Kirnashie Hill

Ceann Reamhar

Coire nam Buabhall

Lag Kilmichael

Imachar Point

Imachar

Cnoc an t-Seilich

Diollaid Mhòr

Cnoc nan Gabhar

Ballekine

Cnoc Donn

Cnoc a' Choire Beag

Beinn Bhreac

Port na Cùile

Carradale

Rubha Airigh Dhughaill

High Dougarie

Cnoc Donn

Bridgend

B879
Carradale
Carradale House
Port Righ

Dougarie Point

Dougarie Lodge

Beinn Lochain

Meall Donn

Cnoc Breac

Waterfoot
Carradale Bay

Auchencar

Cnoc a' Choire Mhòir

Blary Hill

454
BEINN AN TUIRC

Dippen Bay
Torrisdale Bay

Carradale Point

Cnocan Cuallaich

Cnoc Eoghainn

Cnocmalavilach

Auchagallon
Stone Circle
Machrie

Cnoc a' Mhadaidh

Cnoc na Caillich

Greenhill

Rubha nan Sgarbh

Machrie Bay

329

Braid Hill

408
BÒRD MÒR

Saddell Glen

Tormore

Collusca

Meall Buidhe

Saddell

Cnocan a' Bhuachaill

Pluck Point

Saddell Bay

Torr Righ Mòr

oc nan Agh

Bord a Dubh

A'Chruach

396
SGREADAN HILL

Clachfin Glen

Torbeg

Easach Hill

Ugadale

Ugadale Point

Drumadoon Point
Shiskine

Blackwaterfoot

Skeroblin Cruach

Coul Hill

Glen Lussa

Kildonald Bay
Island Ross
Kildonald Point

ack Bay

Drumadoo

Kilpatrick Point
Rubha Garbhar

Kilpat

Peninve Bridge

Carrick Point

Glenlussa Lodge

Calliburn

462

460

457

NR

B842

80

50

40

30

90

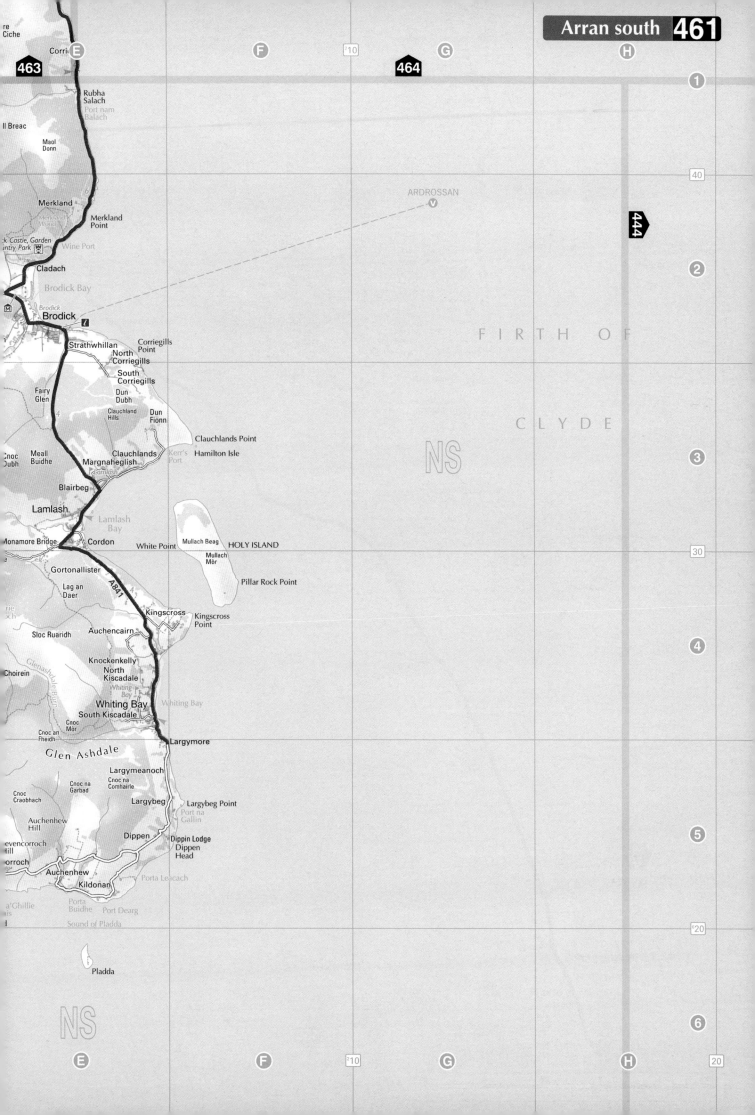

463

E

Corri
re
Ciche

Rubha
Salach
Port nam
Balach

Il Breac

Maol
Donn

Merkland

Merkland
Point

k Castle, Garden
untry Park

Wine Port

Cladach

Brodick Bay

Brodick

Strathwhillan

Corriegills
Point

North
Corriegills

South
Corriegills

Fairy
Glen

Dun
Dubh

Clauchland
Hills

Dun
Fionn

Cnoc
Dubh

Meall
Buidhe

Clauchlands

Margnaheglish

Clauchlands Point

Kerr's
Port

Hamilton Isle

Blairbeg

Lamlash

Lamlash
Bay

Monamore Bridge

Cordon

White Point

Mullach Beag

HOLY ISLAND

Mullach
Mòr

Gortonallister

Lag an
Daer

Pillar Rock Point

A841

Kingscross

Kingscross
Point

rie
och

Sloc Ruaridh

Auchencairn

Knockenkelly

North
Kiscadale

Choirein

Whiting
Bay

Whiting Bay

South Kiscadale

Whiting Bay

Cnoc an
Fheidh

Cnoc
Mòr

Largymore

Glen Ashdale

Largymeanoch

Cnoc na
Garbad

Cnoc na
Comhairle

Cnoc
Craobhach

Largybeg

Largybeg Point

Port na
Gallin

Auchenhew
Hill

Dippen

Dippin Lodge

evencorroch
ill

Dippen
Head

orroch

Auchenhew

Porta Leacach

Kildonan

a'Ghillie
is

Porta
Buidhe

Port Dearg

Sound of Pladda

NS

Pladda

FIRTH OF

CLYDE

NS

ARDROSSAN

444

464

E F 10 G H

1

40

2

3

30

4

5

20

6

E F 10 G H 20

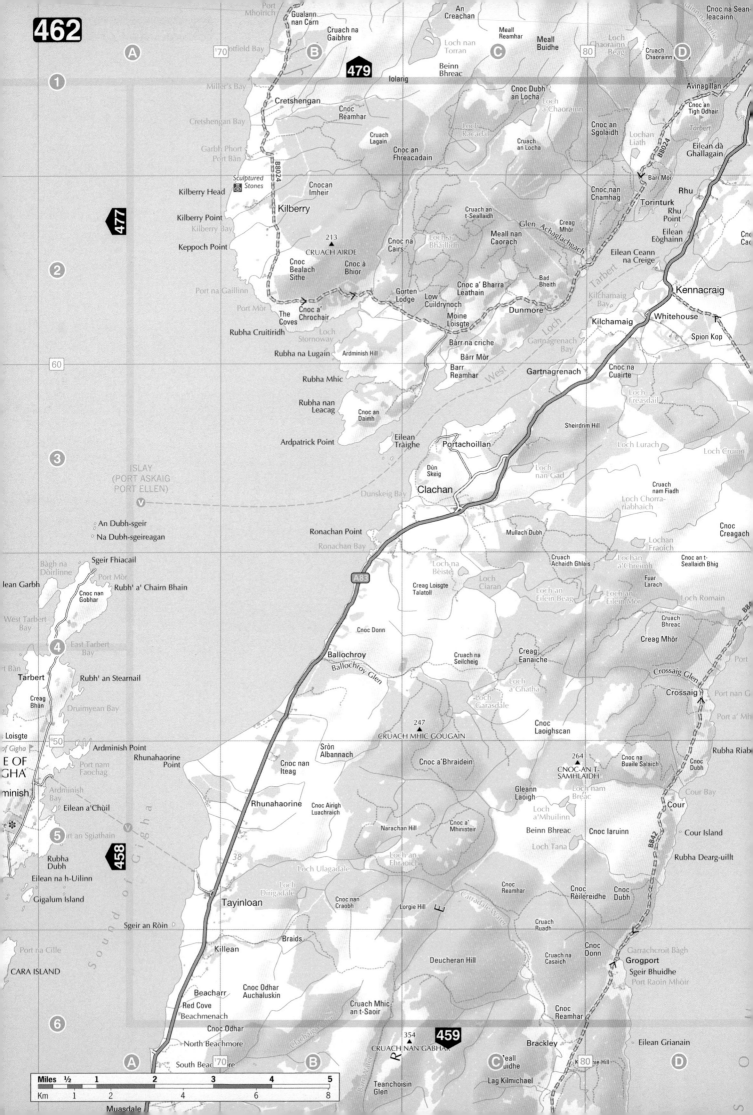

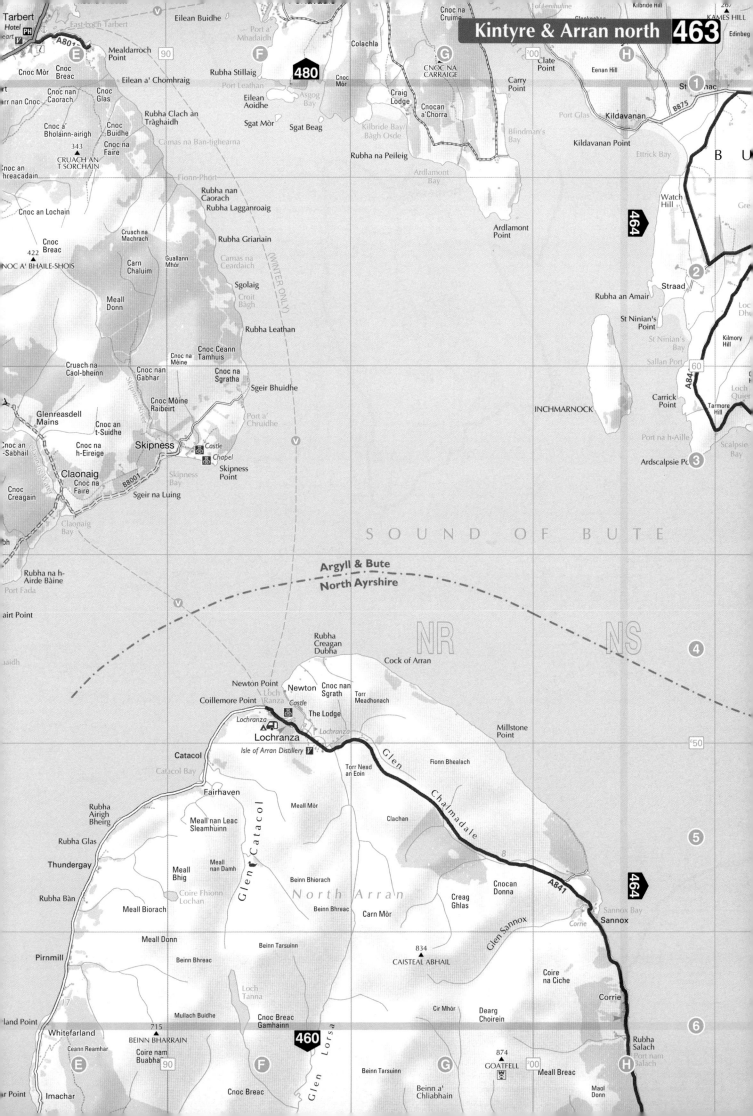

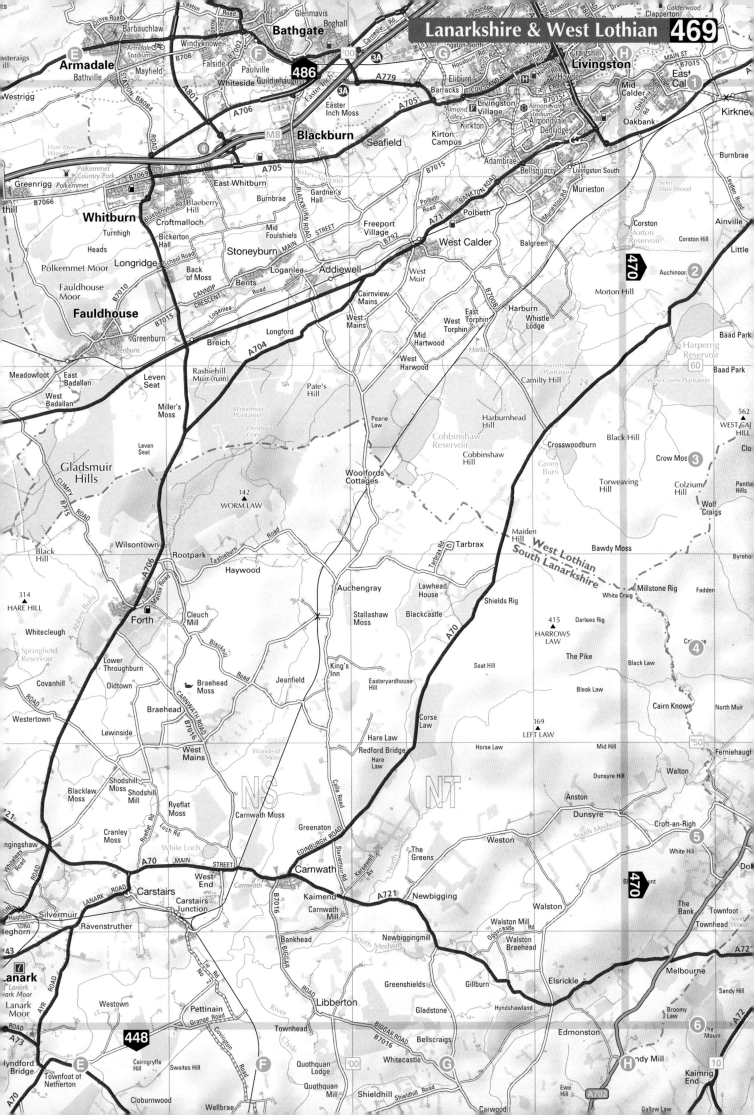

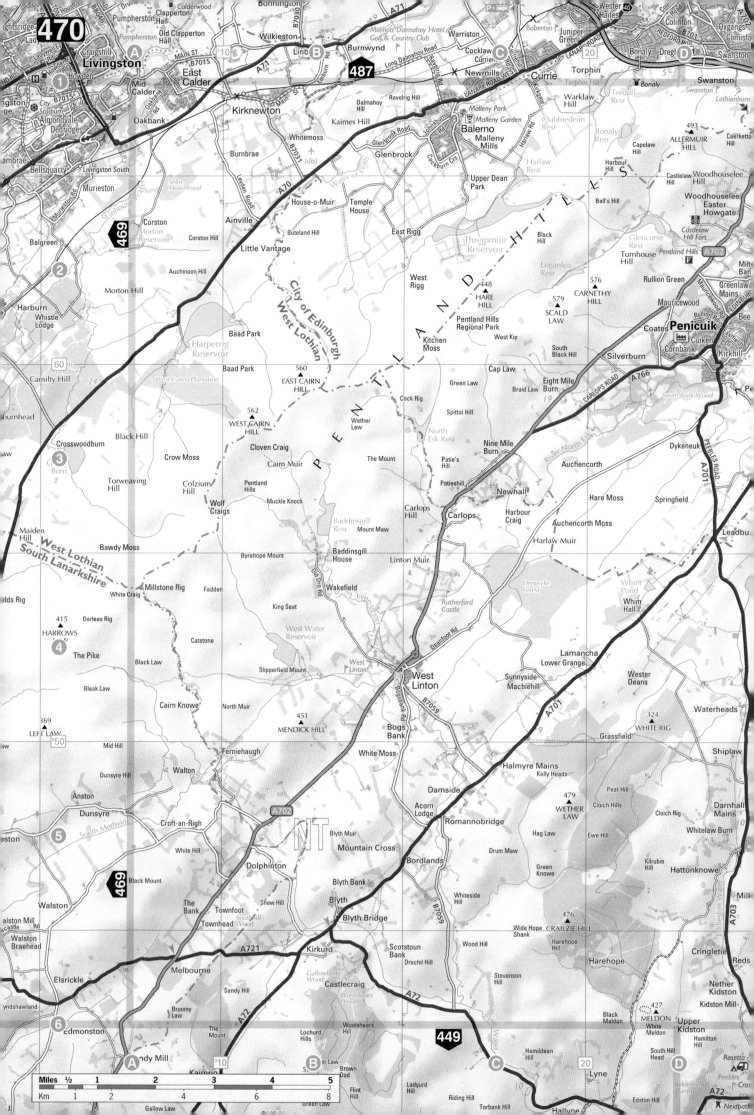

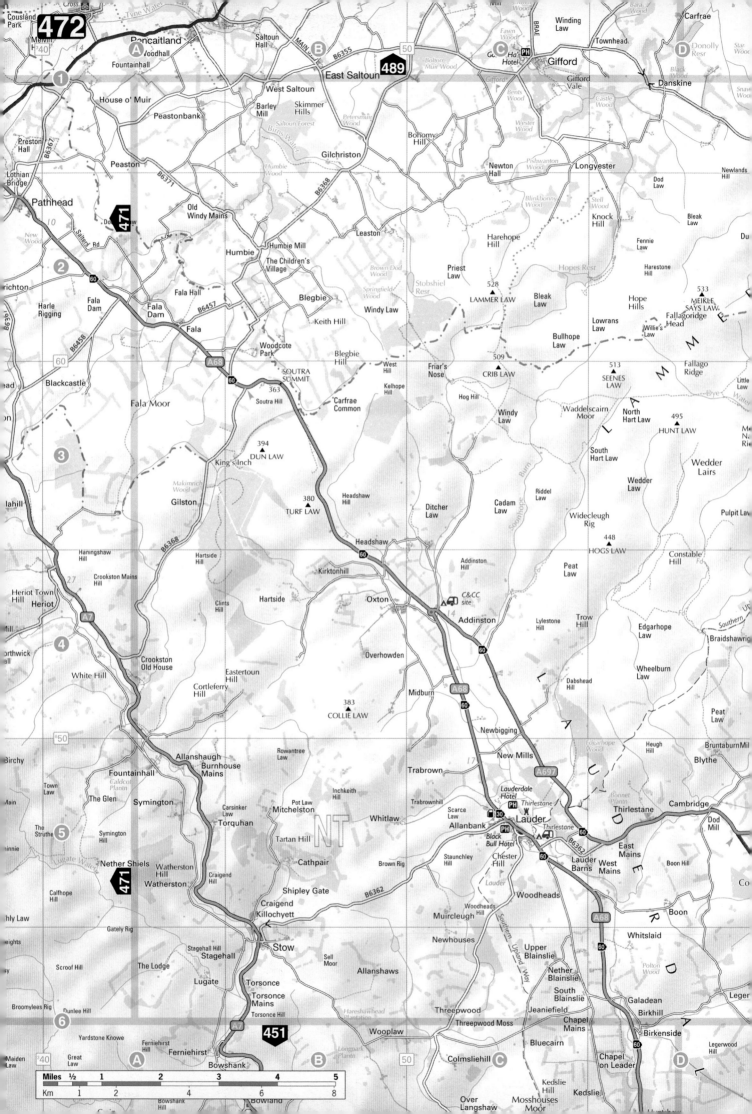

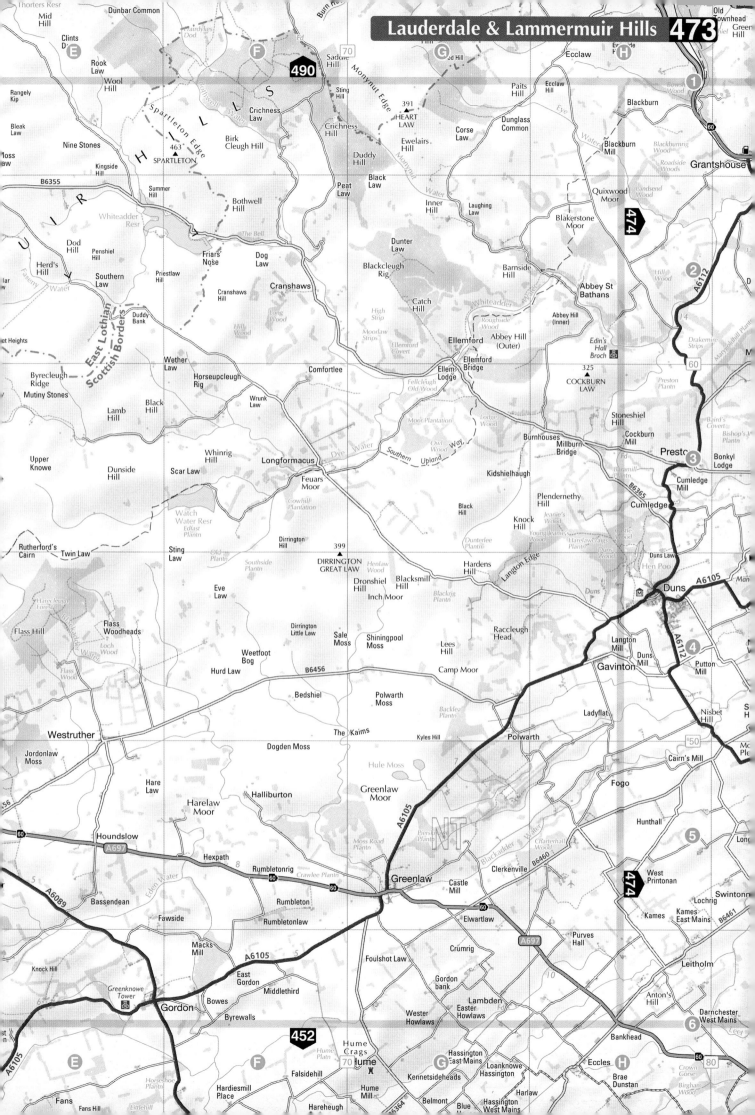

E '00 F 10 G H

1

NT NU 2

60

scout Point
Horse
Head
Fancove Head
es

outh Hill

Ross Ross Point 3

Hilton Bay
Lamberton
Moor Lamberton Beach

Lamberton 70

itches'
owe Marshall Meadows Marshall Meadows Bay

St John's Haven

North Northumberland
Heritage Coast

Brow of The Hill Highfields Brotherston's Hole
X 1333 Magdalene Fields Sharper's Head
dersbury DUNS ROAD A1167
Castle Ladies Skerrs
Royal Border Bridge Barracks **Berwick-upon-Tweed**
Fairney Flat 60 H Town Ramparts Meadow Haven 4
ew ills B6461 Shielfield Park Stadium Tweedmouth Sandstell Pt
ed Spittal
A698 Ord House Country Park East Ord Prior Park Bear's Head
Ord Mains METAL ROAD B635A Springhill La COW Rd Huds Head
Redshin Cove
Tweedmouthmoor 50
Scremerston

Ewe Hill Unthank Moor
Murton A1 5
Allerdean Mill Scremerston Hill
Shoreswood Hall
esdean West Allerdean Nabhill Cheswick
Allerdean Greens Cheswick Sands
Ancroft Allerdean Grange Cheswick Buildings Berwick-upon-Tweed (Goswick)
Northmoor East Ancroft Windmill Hill North Northumberland Heritage Coast
Goswick
Ancroft Mill Haggerston Castle Goswick Sands Coves
Berrington Law Bridge Mill Haggerston Snook Point Snipe Pt Haven Keel Head
B6525 Primrose Bank Emmanuel Head
Bowsden Moor Berrington New Haggerston Haggerston Burn Beal Point Lindisfarne Cswy **HOLY ISLAND**
Jacks Law Lickar Moor Beal Sands Holy Island Sands Chare Ends Lindisfarne Castle
454 Causeway flooded at High Tide **455** Lindisfarne Priory H Castle Point
Low Wood E Lickar Dean Lowick Mill West Mains Beal The Basin Hole Mouth
Bowsde '00 Lickar Lea F 60 Mount Hooley G Granary Point 10 Harbour Burrows Hole
Hazely Hill High Wood Coal Harbour Barmoor Hill Hunting Hall Fenhamhill Guile Point
Black West Fenwick

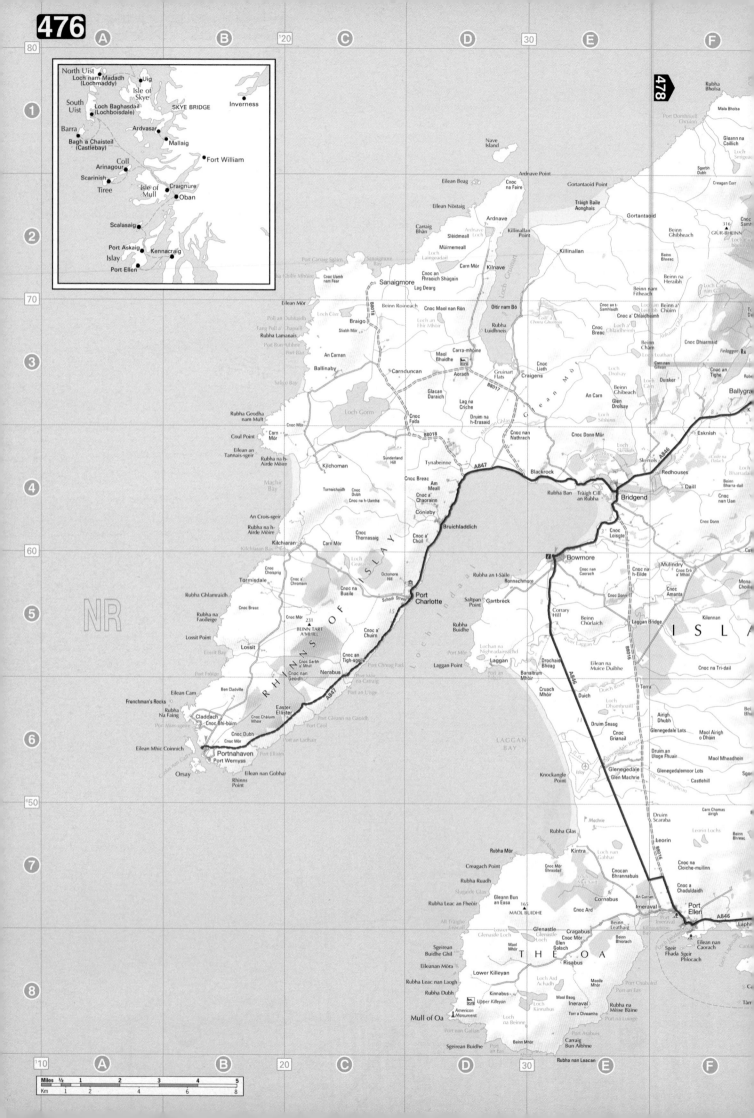

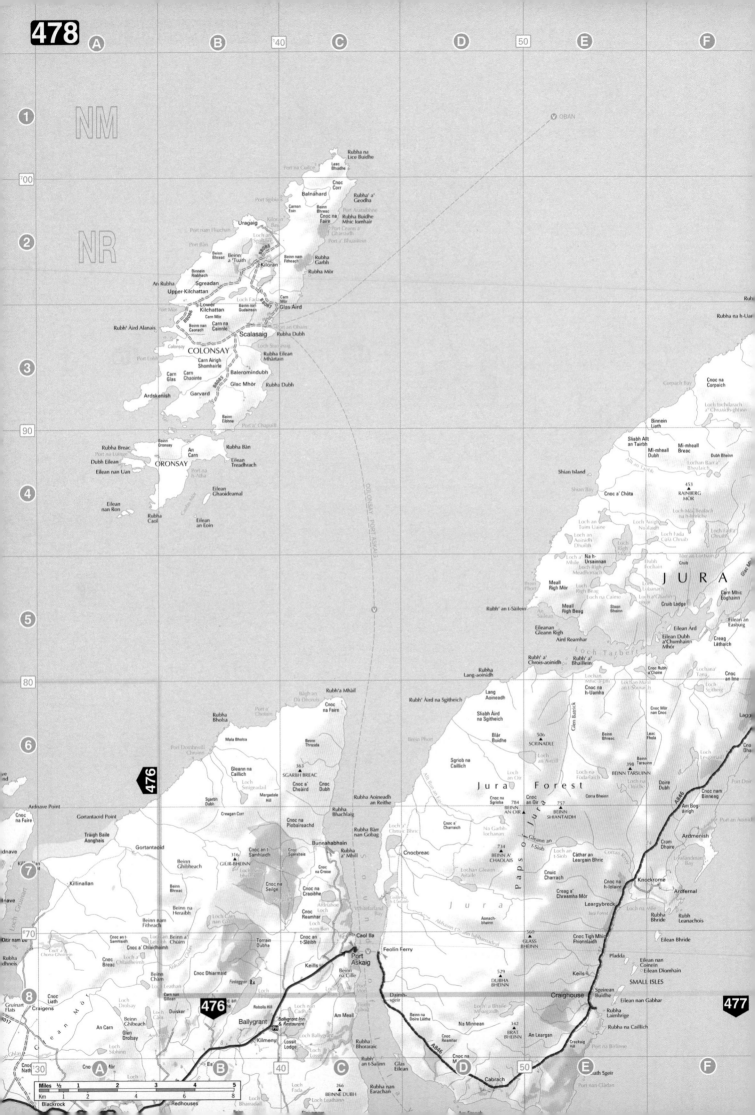

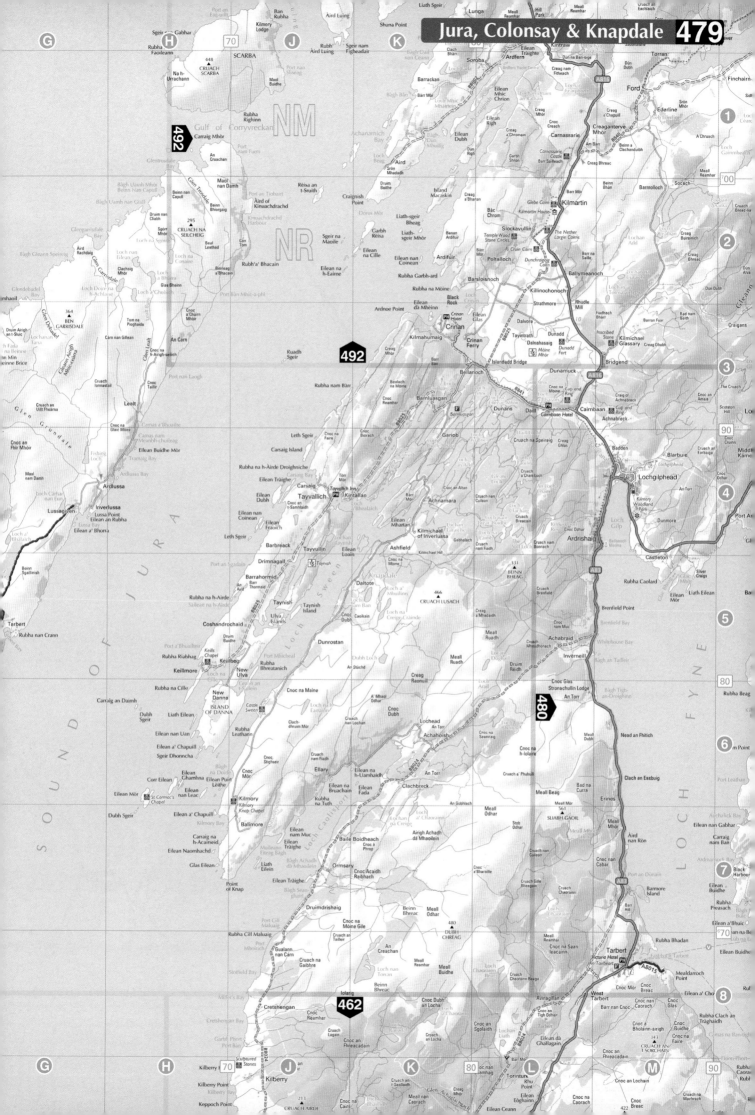

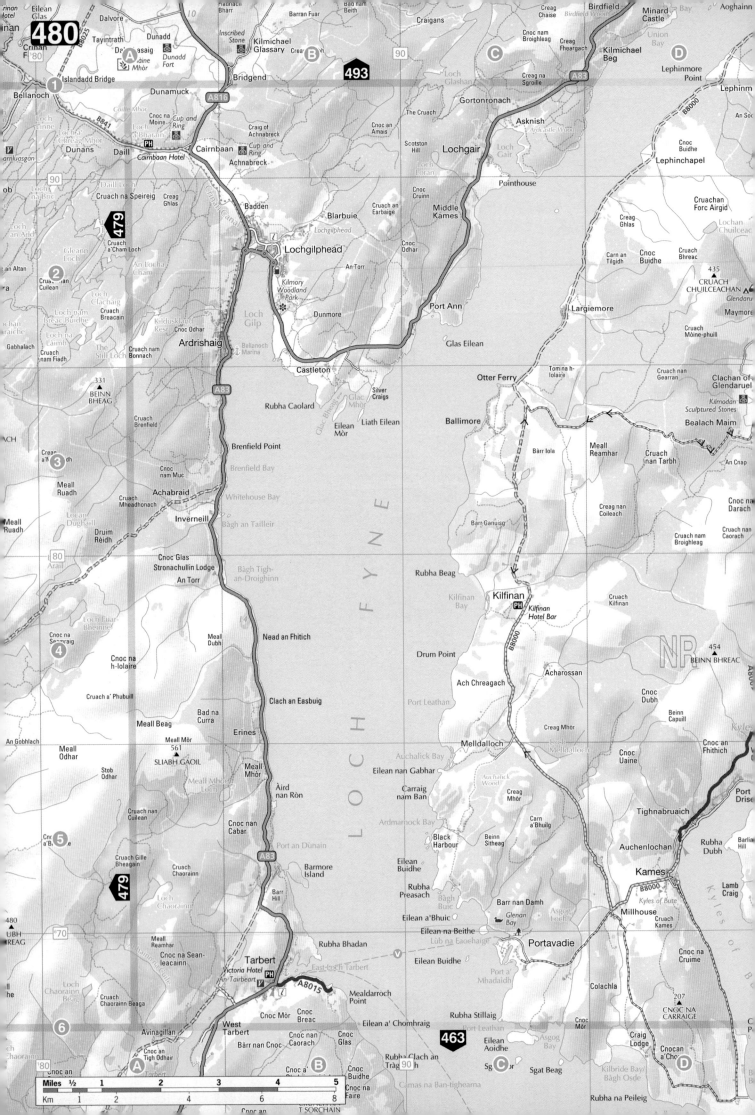

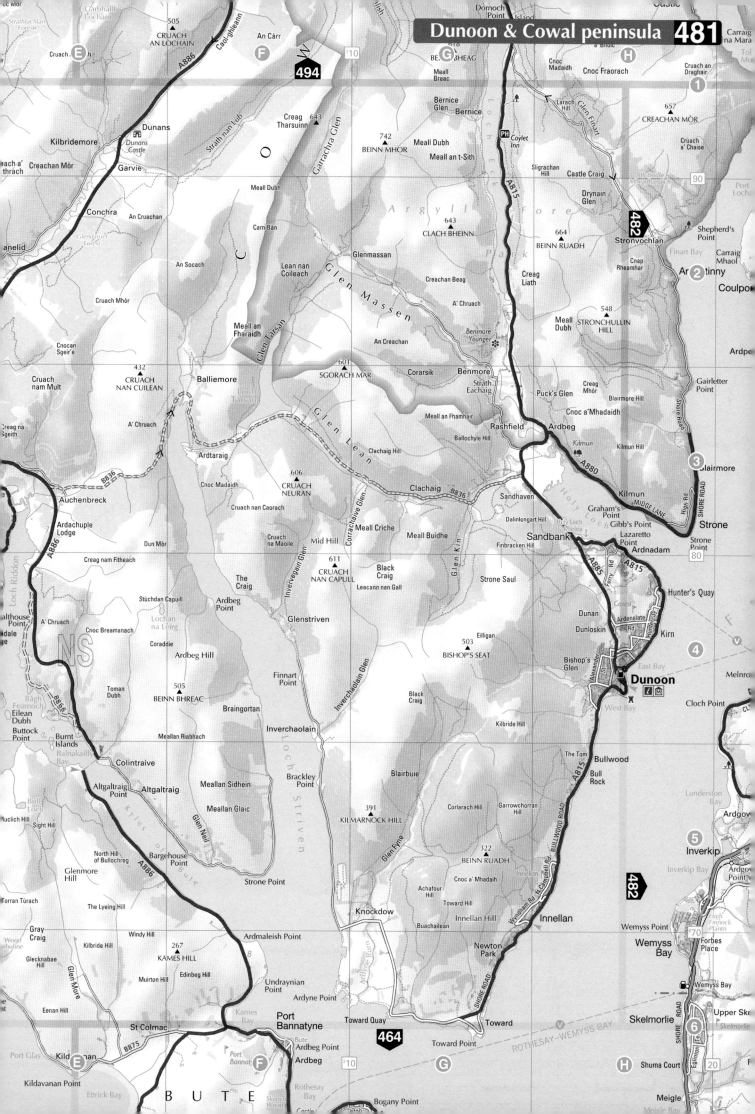

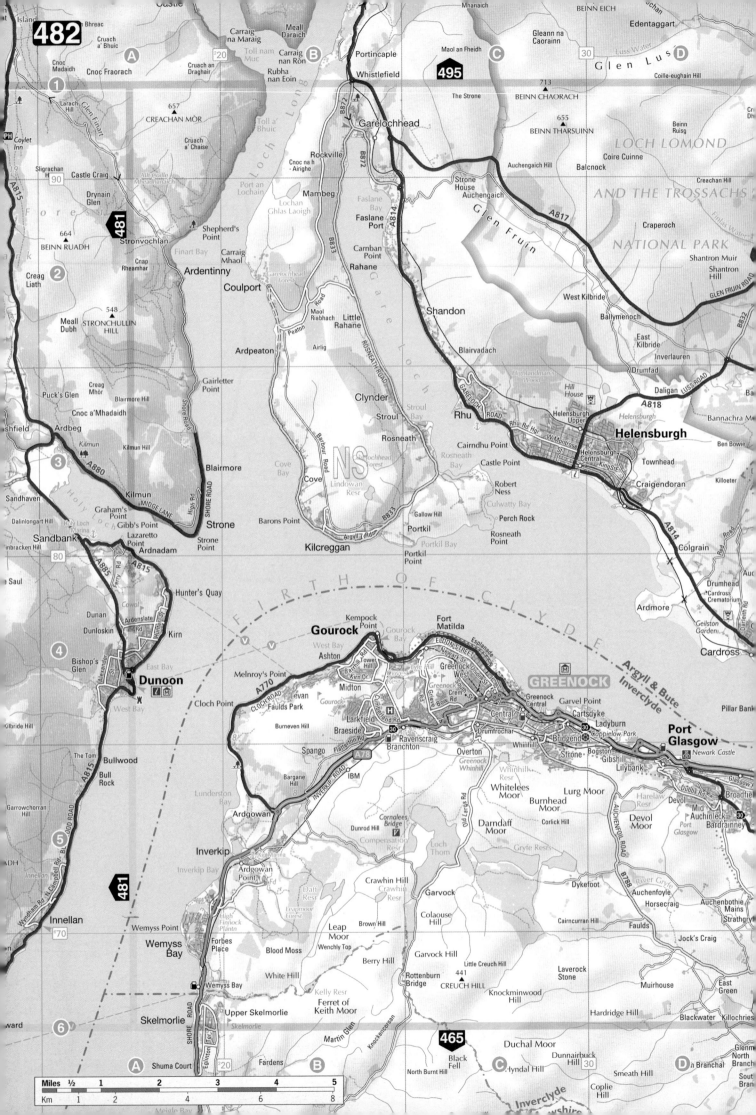

490

Bass Rock

Craigleith

Lamb

Brigs of Fidra

Longskelly Rocks
Longskelly Point
Broad Sands
Cowton Rocks
West Links
Scottish Seabird
Milsey Bay
North Berwick Bay
Leckmoram Ness
Gin Head
Tantallon Castle

Eldbotle Wood
Yellow Craig Plantn
Ware Rd
North Berwick
East Links
The Glen
A198

West Links
Duncan's Plantn
Castle & Gardens
North Berwick
NORTH BERWICK LAW
187
Meadowhead's Tantallon
Auldhame

The Honourable Company of Edinburgh Golfers
Broad Wood
Dirleton
Station Rd
B1347
Blackdykes
Scou

Gullane Bay
NT
Balgone Barns
Sheriff Hall
Gleghornie
New

Gullane Point
West Links
Kingston
East Craig
Whitekirk

Gullane Links
Saltcoats
B1345
Fenton Barns
Whitekirk Bridge

Gullane
West Fenton
East Fenton
Congalton Mains
Brownrigg
Old Stonelaws

Gullane Sands
Gala Law
Luffness Links
Park Hills
Binning Wood

Aberlady Bay
Luffness New
Avenue Road
Drem
B1377
Prora
West Fortune
East Fortune
B1347
Fortoun Bank
Oak Wood
Tyninghame
B1407

Aberlady Point
Craigelaw Point
Kilspindie
Aberlady
Motor
A6137
Chesters Hill Fort
Kilduff Hill
Camptoun
Athelstaneford
B1343
Museum of Flight
Pettro Burn
Markle
Drovers Inn
Preston Mill & Phantassie Doocot
Preston
K

Craigelaw
Craigelaw Point
Gosford Sands
Gosford Bay
A198
B1377
Ballencrieff
Spittal
Hopetown Monument
Garleton Hills
Abbey Mains
Amisfield Mains
PENCRAIG BRAE
A199
Pencraig Wood
Tyne
Brae Heads
Loan
East Linton

Seton Sands
LINKS ROAD
Longniddry
Longniddry
Bangly Hill
A6137
St Martin's Kirk (ruin)
Haddington
Sandy's Mill
Hailes Castle
River
Brae
Traprain
Hairy Craig
Traprain Law
Luggate Burn

Seton Sands
Seton Mains
Collegiate Church
B6363
Huntington
Lauderdale Aisle
St Mary's Church
West Bearford
Coldale
Standingstone

Meadowmill
Tranent
A199
Gladsmuir
Birk Hedges
Letham House
Lamblair Wood
Clerkington
Lennoxlove Mains
Lennoxlove
Mitchell Hall
Renton Hall
Mainshill
Lawhead Plantn
490
BLINDWELL BRAE
B6370

Macmerry
West Bank
Penston
Liberty Hall
Cuddie Wood
Whitelaw Hill
Garvald Grange
Garvald
Birks Plantn

New Winton
B6355
B6371
New Town
Samuelston
Begbie Wood
B6368
Colstoun Wood
Clacherdean Wood
Beech Hill
Morham Bank
Sled Hill
Nunraw Abbey
Blae

Market Cross
A6093
Samuelston South Mains
Bolton
Coulston Old Mill
Bara Wood
Winding Law
Carfrae
Donolly Rest
Star Wood
Robin Plantn

Pencaitland
Tyne Water
Woodhall
Fountainhall
Saltoun Hall
MAIN ST
Bolton Muir Wood
Fawn Wood
BRAE
Townhead
Black Wood

House o' Muir
Peastonbank
Peaston
East Saltoun
472
West Saltoun
Barley Mill
Skimmer Hills
B6355
Petersmuir Wood
Saltoun Forest
Birns Water
Gilchriston
Gilchrist
Bolton Muir Wood
Bohomy Hill
Goblin Ha' Hotel
PH
Gifford
Gifford Vale
Bents Wood
Wester Wood
Castle Wood
Danskine
Snawdon Wood
Mass Law

E 80 F G 90 H

1

90

2

NT

3

80

4

Point
ng Craig

ntonloch

5

Bilsdean
Creek

Reed
Point

Dunglass
Collegiate
Church

Cove Harbour

Cove

Pease Bay
Red Rock

Cockburnspath

Dovecot
Hall

Greenheugh
Point

Siccar Point

Fast Castle
Head

Wheat Stack

Meikle
Poo Craig

Telegraph
Hill

Fast
Castle

claw
l

Ewieside
Hill

60

Old Cambus
Townhead

Old
Townhead

Old Cambus

A1107

Dowlaw Road

70

Oatlee
Hill

St Abb's Head

Greenside
Hill

Meikle
Black Law

Old Cambus

196

BROWN RIG

Lumsdaine

Mire
Loch

Kirk
Hill

Horsecastle Bay

Ecclaw

Penmanshiel
Moor

Penmanshiel
Wood

Coldingham
Common

Laverlock
Law

Lumsdaine
Moor

Cross
Law

Coldingham
Loch

West Loch

Bell
Hill

Starney Bay

claw
l

Blowshiel
Wood

Hempark
Rd

Coldingham
Moor

Moorside
Plantn

Northfield

St Abbs

6

Eye

Blackburn

Gowel
Hill

474

W Loch Rd

B6438

St Abb's
Haven

Coldingham
Bay

E 80 F G 90 H

Water

Blackburn
Mill

Blackburning
Wood

Bell
Hill

Drone
Hill

SCHOOL

Temple
Hall

Scoutscroft

Yellow Craig

Grantshouse

Roadside
Wood

Brockholes

Three Burn
Grange

Abbey
Park

Coldingham

A1

Callercove
Point

Hairy

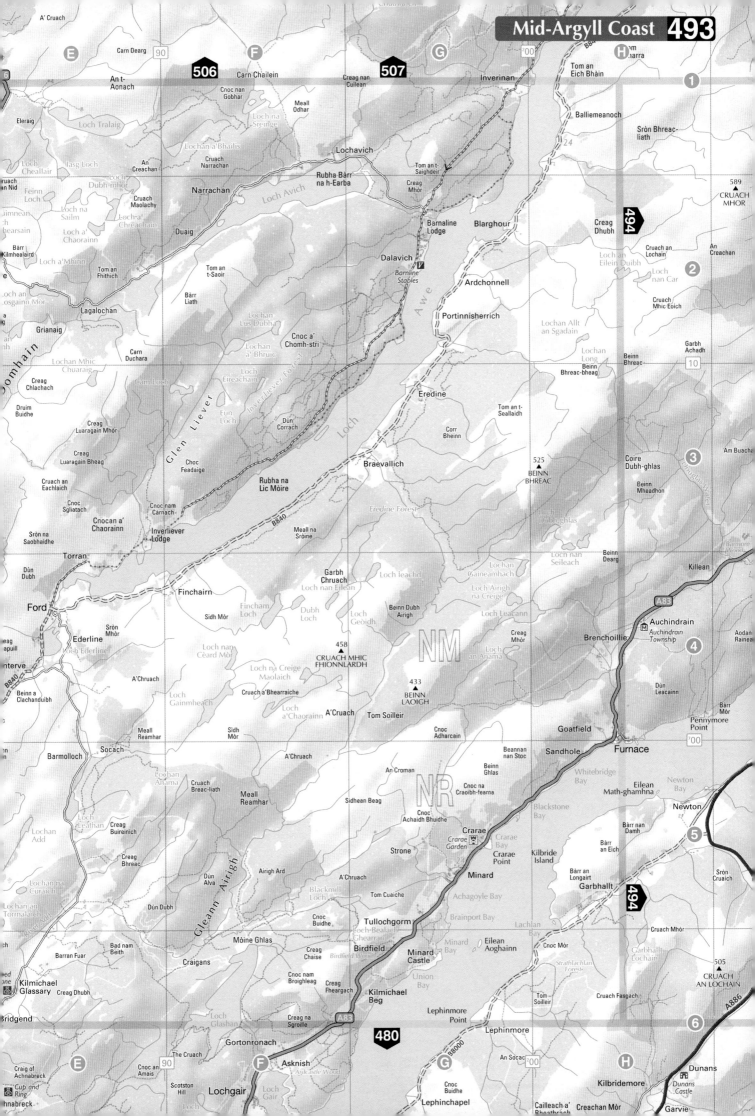

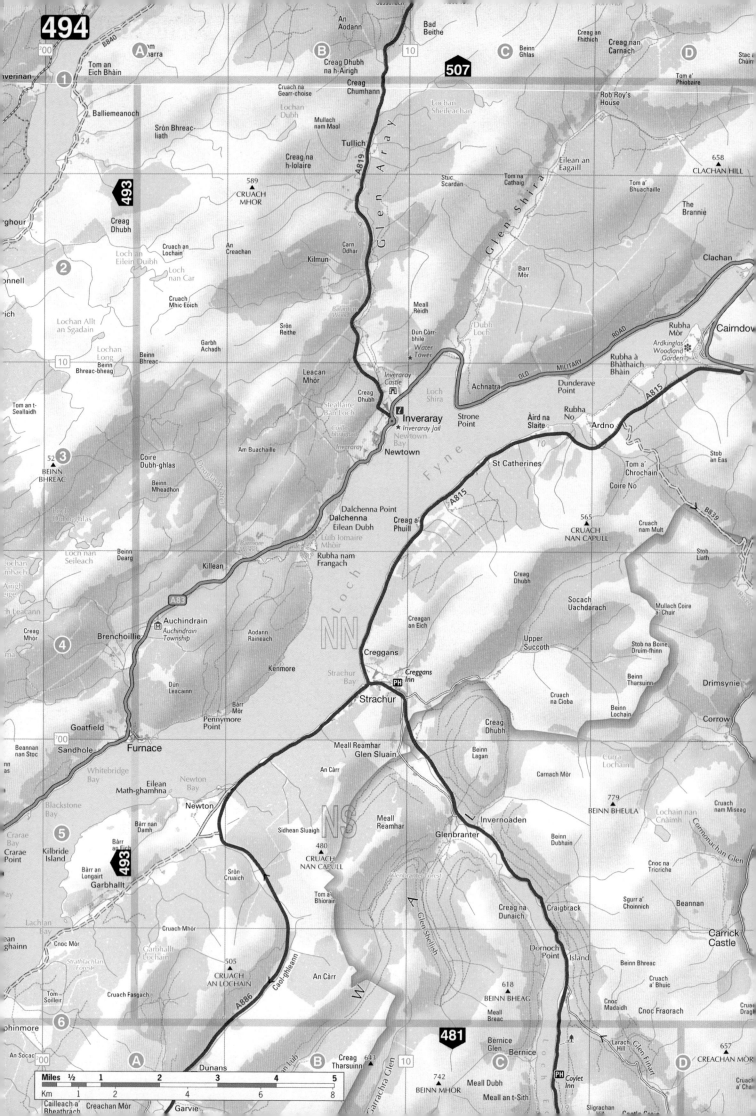

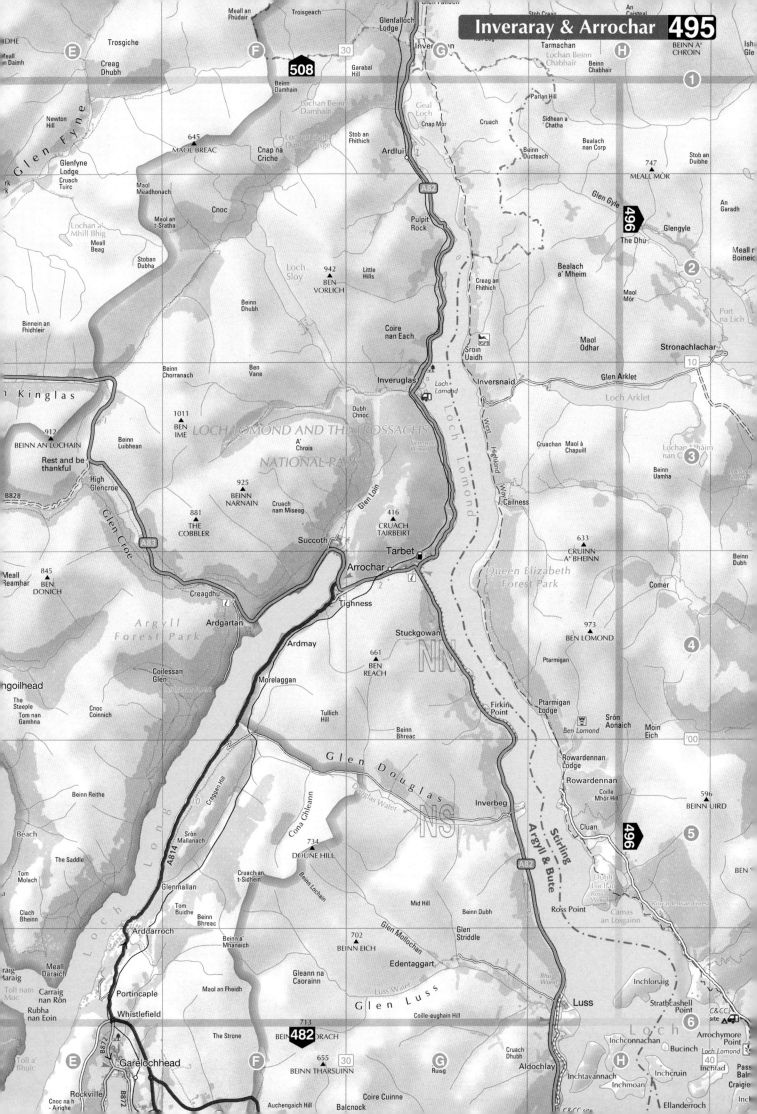

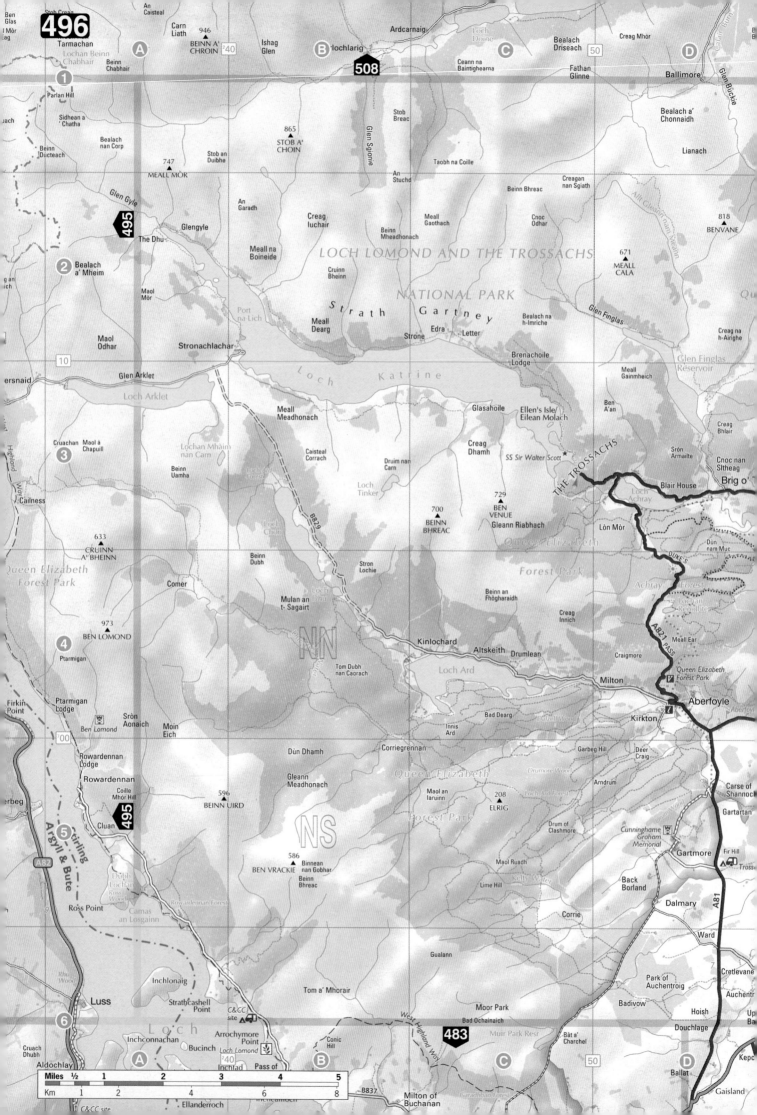

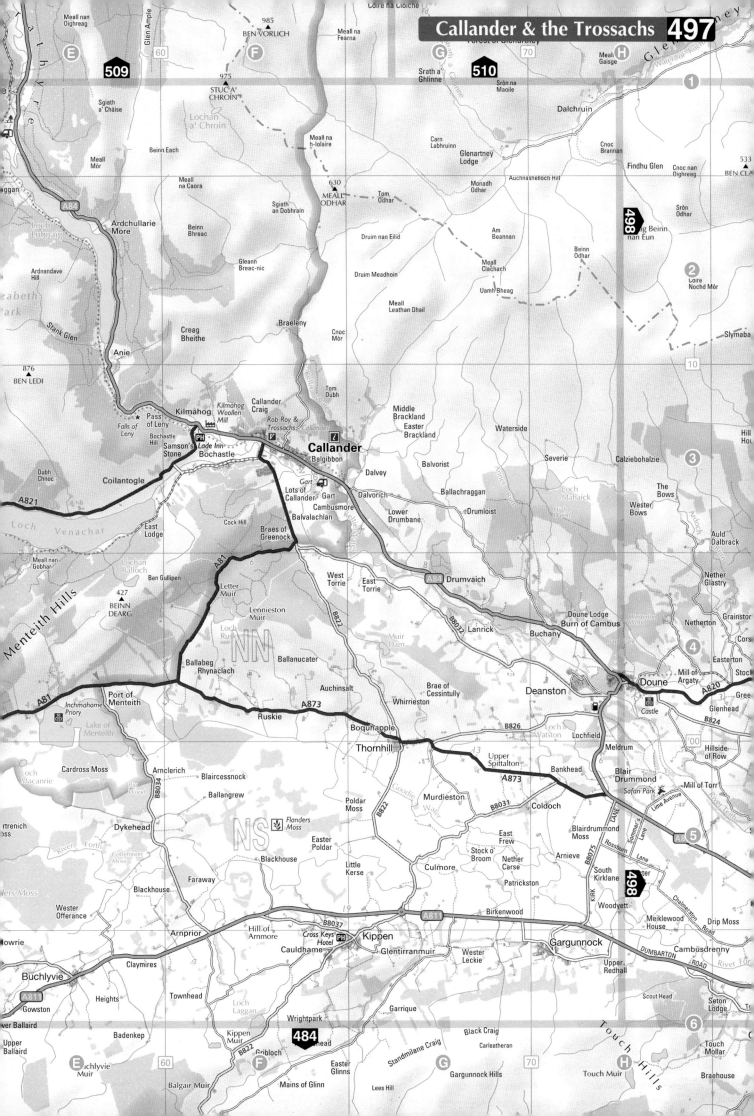

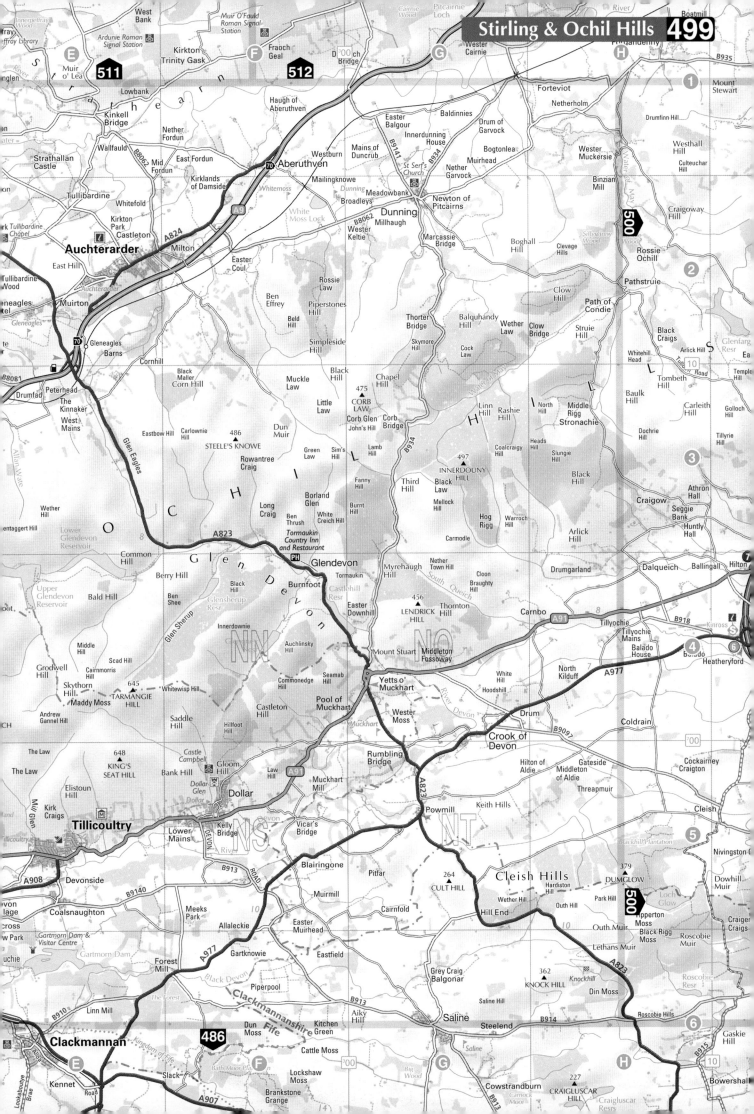

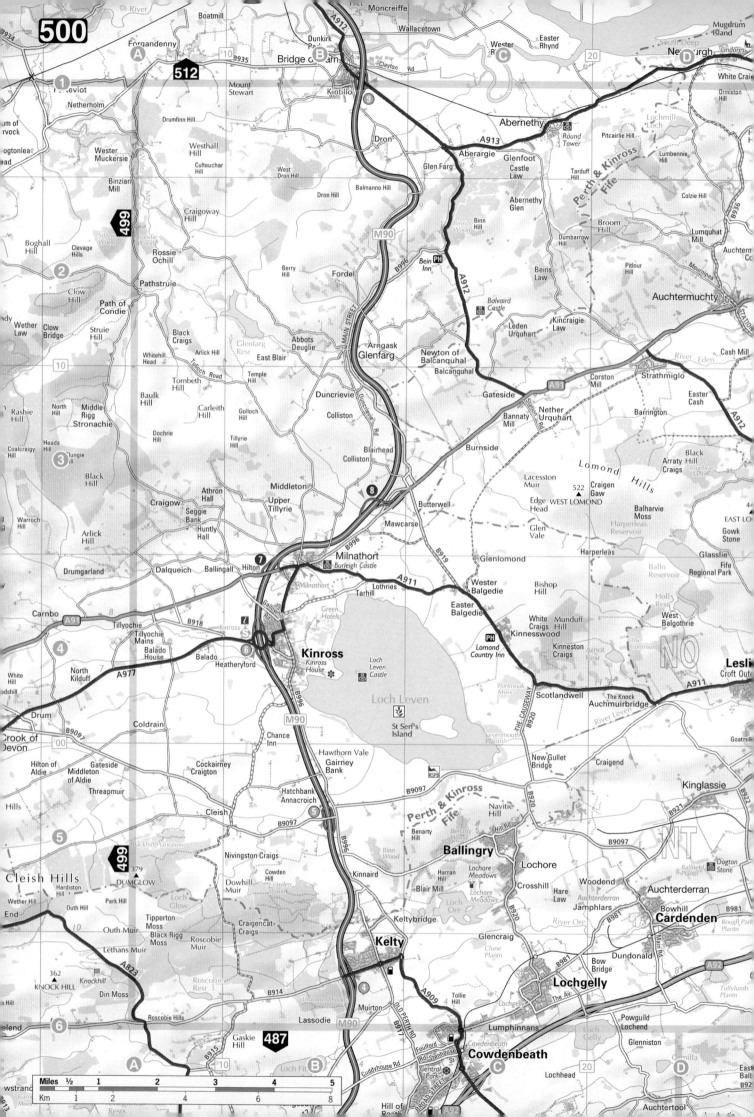

ST ANDREWS BAY

515

Castle
St Andrews
East Sands
Diamond Dr

The Grange
Brownhills
Kinkell Ness
The Rock and Spindle
Buddo Ness
Buddo Rock
St Andrews

Muir Park
Prior Muir
A917
Boarhills
Park Mill
Babbet Ness
Airbow Point

South Cambieletham
B9131
Bonnytown
Upper Kenley
Kilduncan
Kingsbarns
Cambo Sands
Cambo Ness
Kingsbarns

Brigton Gilmerton House
Stravithie
Law Drum
Barns Law
Kelly Water
Station Rd

Kinaldy
Dunino
Dunino Law
Kippo Planto
Cookston
Grassmiston
Blue Stone
Lochaber Rock
FIFE NESS
Balcomie

South Kinaldy
Cocklaw
Ragfield
B9171
B940
Crail

B940
Over Carnbee
Redwells Wood
Scotland's Secret Bunker
Toldrie
Troustrie
PH Crail
Golf Hotel
West Ness

Kellie Law
Carnbee
Spalefield
Balhouffie
Loanhead
Barnsmuir

Kittlenaked Wood
B9171
Pitkierie
Kilrenny Common

croach
Kellie Castle
Clephanton
Cauldcots
B9131
Kilrenny
Kilrenny Mill

Newton of Balcormo
Hamilton Wood
Crawhill
Dreel Tavern PH
Windmill
Cellardyke
Skinfast Haven
Anstruther Wester
Anstruther Easter

Sandyrigs Wood
B942
Abercrombie
A917
Anstruther
Billow Ness
Fisheries

albuthie
Pittenweem
Birnie Craig
St Monans
Partan Craig

NO

NT

North Ness
Tarbet Hole
Isle of May
South Ness

700

St Andrews

0 — 200 metres

THE BRITISH GOLF MUSEUM
P
SEA LIFE CENTRE
ST JAMES' RC CHURCH
ROYAL & ANCIENT GOLF CLUB
UNIVERSITY
CASTLE VISITOR CENTRE
CASTLE
Footpath
THE SCORES
THE LINKS

Links
FORTH ROAD BRIDGE, TAY ROAD BRIDGE
LINKS CRES
A917
NORTH STREET
UNIVERSITY
CINEMA
UNIV LIBRARY
ST SALVATORS HALL
UNIVERSITY
ST ANDREWS CATHEDRAL

PILMOUR LINKS
CITY ROAD
A915
PO
GREYFRIARS GDN
CRAWFORD ARTS CENTRE
POLICE STATION
MARKET STREET
ST ANDREWS PRESERVATION TRUST
GREGORY PLACE
REMAINS OF ST MARY'S CHURCH
ST LEONARDS CHAPEL
ST RULE'S TOWER

BUS STATION
COUNCIL OFFICES
BELL STREET
HOLY TRINITY CHURCH
PO
SOUTH STREET
SOUTH ST
Arches
The Pends

ST ANDREWS MUSEUM
ARGYLE STREET
BURGH CHAMBERS
BLACKFRIARS CHAPEL
ST MARY'S COLLEGE (UNIV)
BYRE THEATRE
ST LEONARDS SCHOOL
ST KATHERINES SCHOOL
East Sands
Footbridge

WEST PORT (Arch)
MADRAS COLLEGE
QUEENS GARDENS
ABBEY ST
ABBEY WALK
SCHOOL
The Shore
A917

BRIDGE STREET
A915
KINNESSBURN ROAD
BRAE
BONSE AVENUE
GLEBE ROAD
LANGLANDS ROAD
MEMORIAL HOSPITAL
WOODBURN PL

LBT
LEVEN, KIRKCALDY
CRAIL, ANSTRUTHER

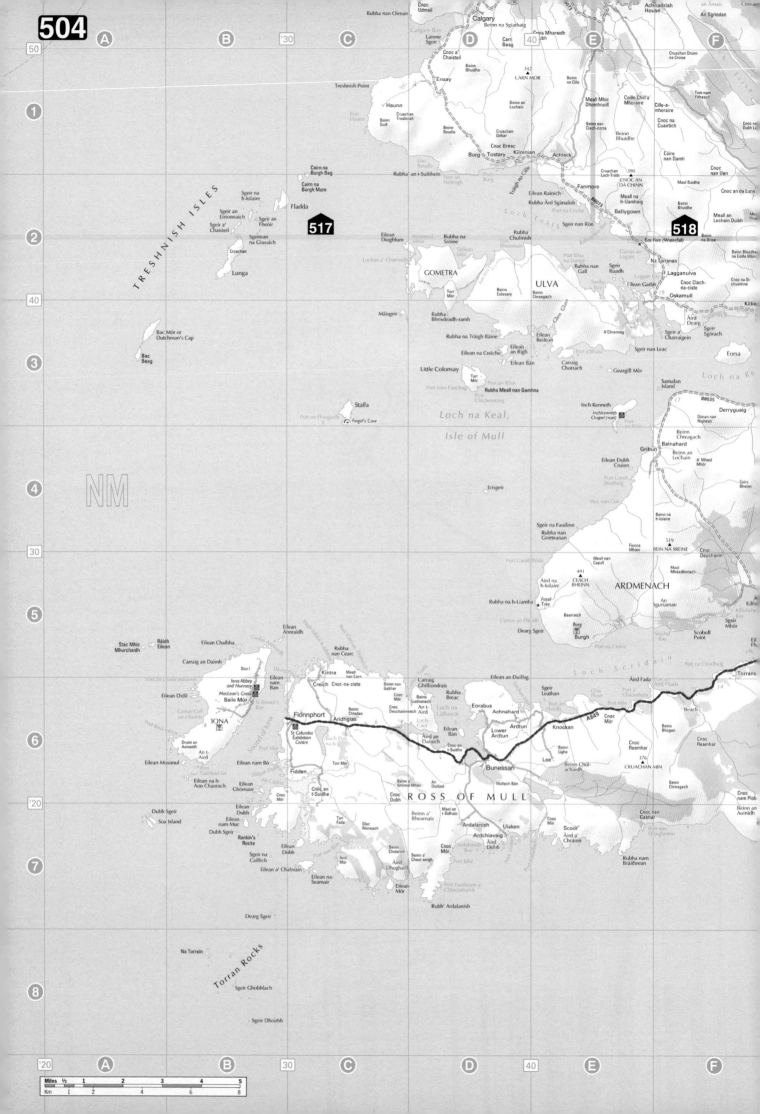

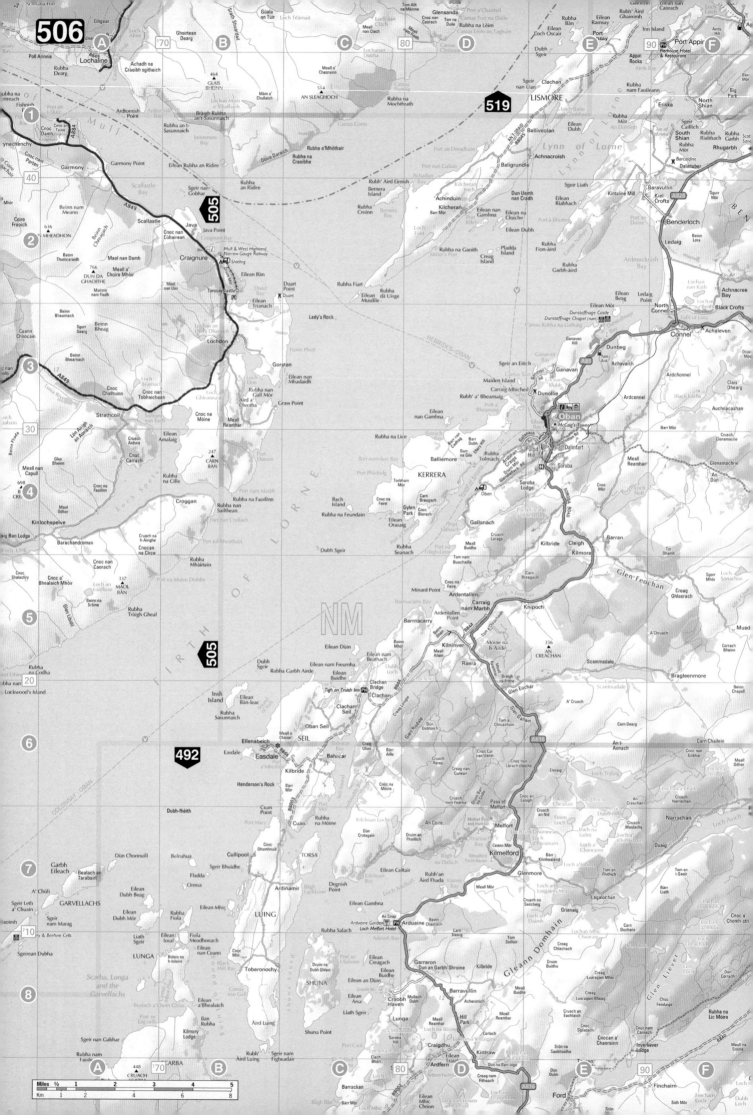

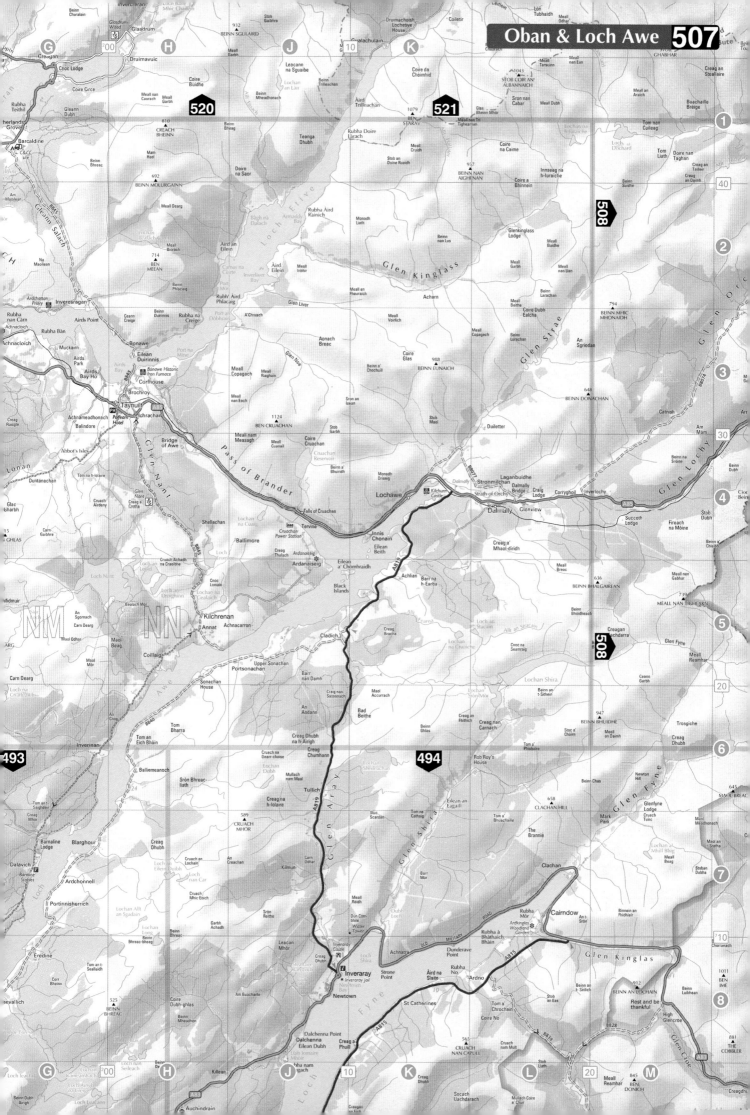

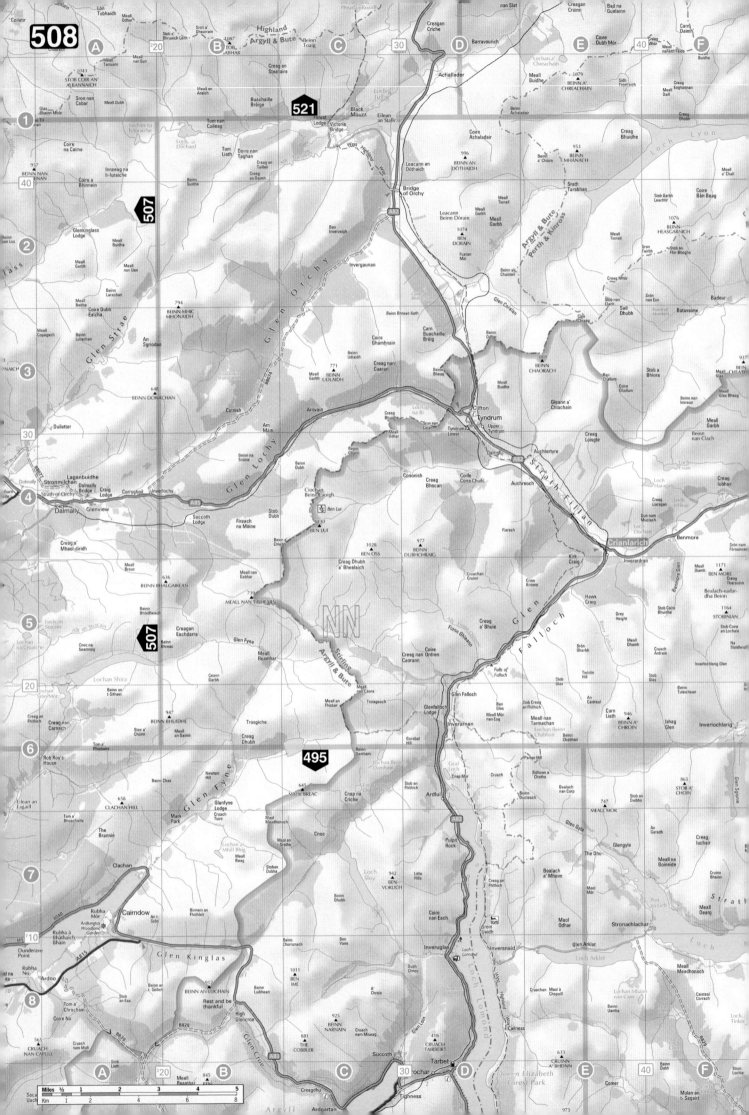

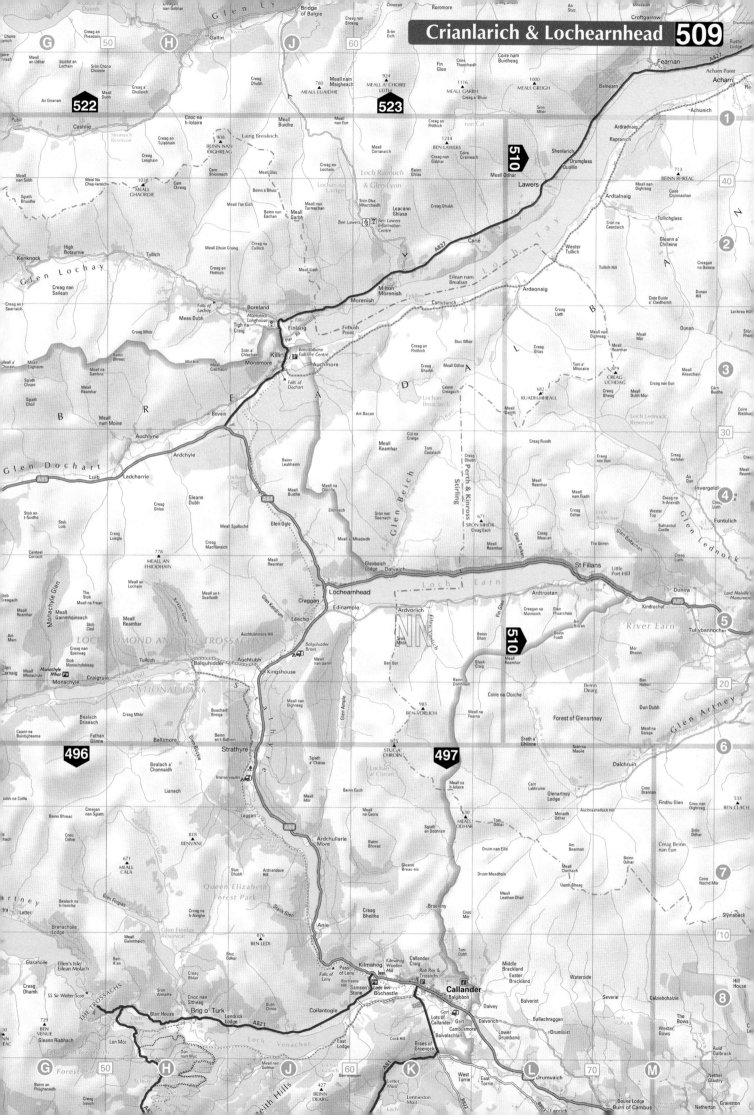

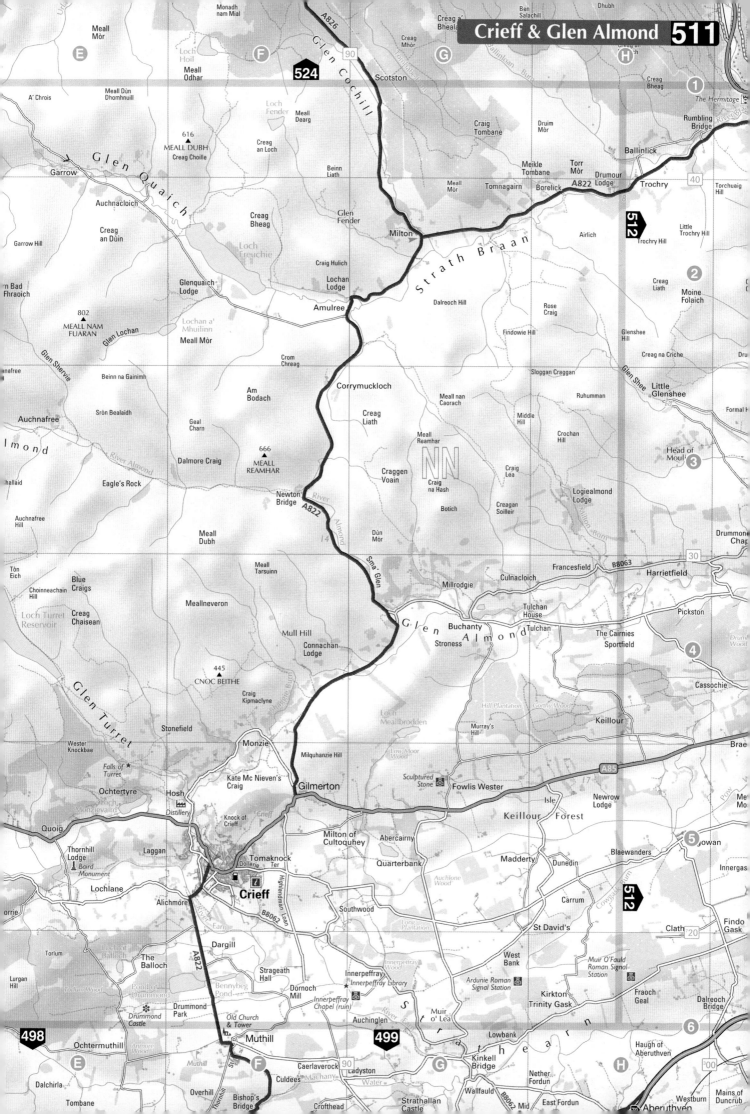

Meall Mòr

E

Monadh nam Mial

Loch Hoil

F

Meall Odhar

524

Scotston

90

Glen Cochill

A826

Creag a' Bheala

Creag Mhòr

G

Ben Salachill

Dhubh

H

Creag an Ech

Creag Bheag

1

The Hermitage

Rumbling Bridge

A' Chois

Meall Dùn Dhomhnuill

Loch Fender

Meall Dearg

Craig Tombane

Druim Mòr

Ballinlick

Garrow

Glen Quaich

616

MEALL DUBH

Creag Choille

Creag an Loch

Beinn Liath

Meikle Tombane

Torr Mòr

Drumour Lodge

A822

40

Trochry

Torchuaig Hill

Auchnacloich

Creag Bheag

Glen Fender

Meall Mòr

Borelick

512

Little Trochry Hill

Garrow Hill

Creag an Dùin

Milton

Tomnagairn

Trochry Hill

Airlich

Creag Liath

2

Moine Folaich

n Bad Fhraoich

Glenquaich Lodge

Loch Freuchie

Craig Hulich

Lochan Lodge

Strath Braan

Dalreoch Hill

Rose Craig

Glenshee Hill

Creag na Criche

Glen Shervie

802

MEALL NAM FUARAN

Beinn na Gainimh

Lochan a' Mhuilinn

Meall Mòr

Amulree

Crom Chreag

Corrymuckloch

Findowie Hill

Sloggan Craggan

Little Glenshee

Glen Shee

Auchnafree

Sròn Bealaidh

Geal Charn

Am Bodach

Creag Liath

Meall nan Caorach

Middle Hill

Ruhumman

Imond

Dalmore Craig

666

MEALL REAMHAR

Craggen Voain

NN

Meall Reamhar

Crochan Hill

Craig Lea

Head of Mouli

3

hallaid

Eagle's Rock

Craig na Hash

Botich

Creagan Soiller

Logiealmond Lodge

Auchnafree Hill

Meall Dubh

Newton Bridge

River

A822

Almond

Dùn Mòr

Drummon Chap

Tòn Eich

Choinneachain Hill

Blue Craigs

Meall Tarsuinn

Sma' Glen

Millrodgie

Culnacloich

Francesfield

B8063

30

Harrietfield

Loch Turret Reservoir

Creag Chaisean

Meallneveron

Tulchan House

Glen Almond

Tulchan

Pickston

Mull Hill

Buchanty

The Cairnies Sportfield

4

Glen Turret

445

CNOC BEITHE

Connachan Lodge

Stroness

Hill Plantation

Gorthy Wood

Keillour

Cassochie

Stonefield

Craig Kipmaclyne

Loch Meallbrodden

Murray's Hill

Wester Knockbae

Monzie

Shaggie Burn

Low Moor Wood

Keillour Forest

Newrow Lodge

Me Mo

Falls of Turret

Kate Mc Nieven's Craig

Milquhanzie Hill

Gilmerton

Sculptured Stone

Fowlis Wester

Isle

A85

Ochtertyre

Hosh

Distillery

Knock of Crieff

Crieff

Quoig

Thornhill Lodge

Baird Monument

Laggan

Milton of Cultoquhey

Abercairny

Madderty

Dunedin

Blaewanders

5

gowan

Innergas

Lochlane

Dollerie

Tomaknock

Ter

Quarterbank

Auchlone Wood

Crieff

West Bank

Innergas

Alichmore

B8062

Southwood

Carrum

512

Torlum

Dargill

Highlandman Loan

St David's

Clath

20

Findo Gask

Lurgan Hill

The Balloch

Strageath Hall

Bennybeg Pond

Dornoch Mill

Innerpeffray Wood

Innerpeffray Library

Muir O'Fauld Roman Signal Station

498

Drummond Park

Drummond Castle

Old Church & Tower

Innerpeffray Chapel (ruin)

Ardunie Roman Signal Station

Kirkton Trinity Gask

Fraoch Geal

Dalreoch Bridge

Ochtermuthill

E

Muthill

Anmore Wood

Muthill

F

Caerlaverock

499

Auchinglen

Muir o' Lea

Lowbank

Haugh of Aberuthven

H

6

Dalchirla

Tombane

Overhill

Bishop's Bridge

Culdees

Machany

Ladyston

90

Crofthead

Water

Strathallan Castle

Strathearn

Kinkell Bridge

Nether Fordun

Wallfauld

East Fordun

B8062 Mid

Westburn

Mains of Duncrub

Aberuthven

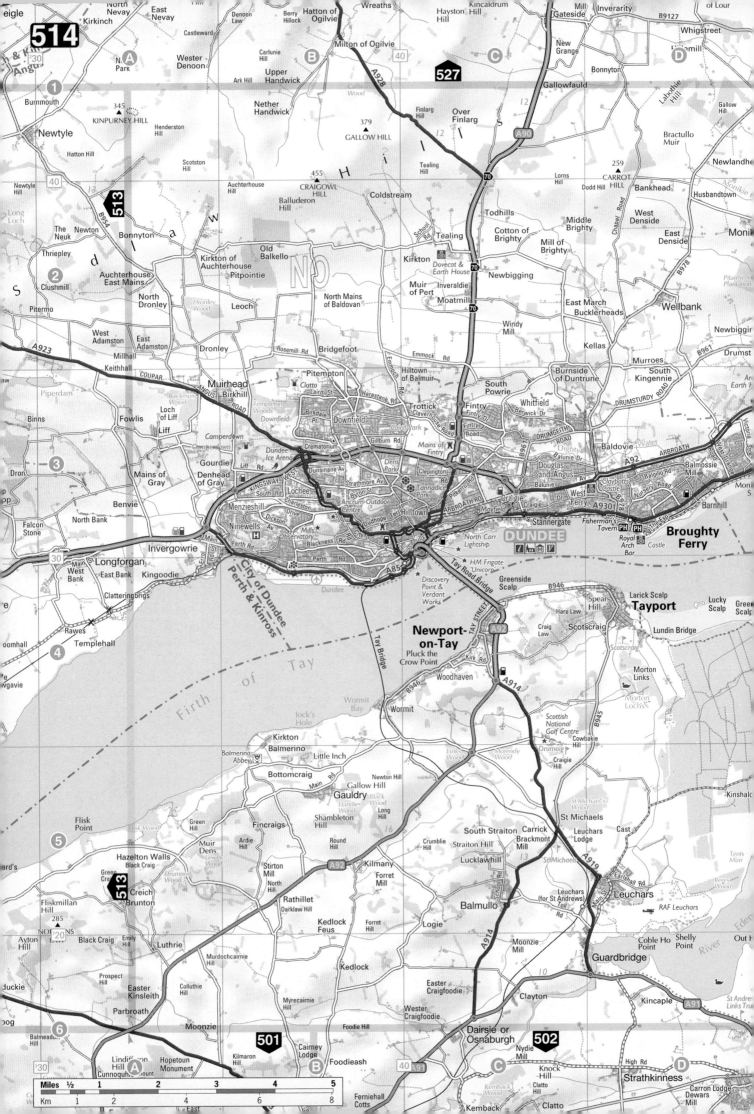

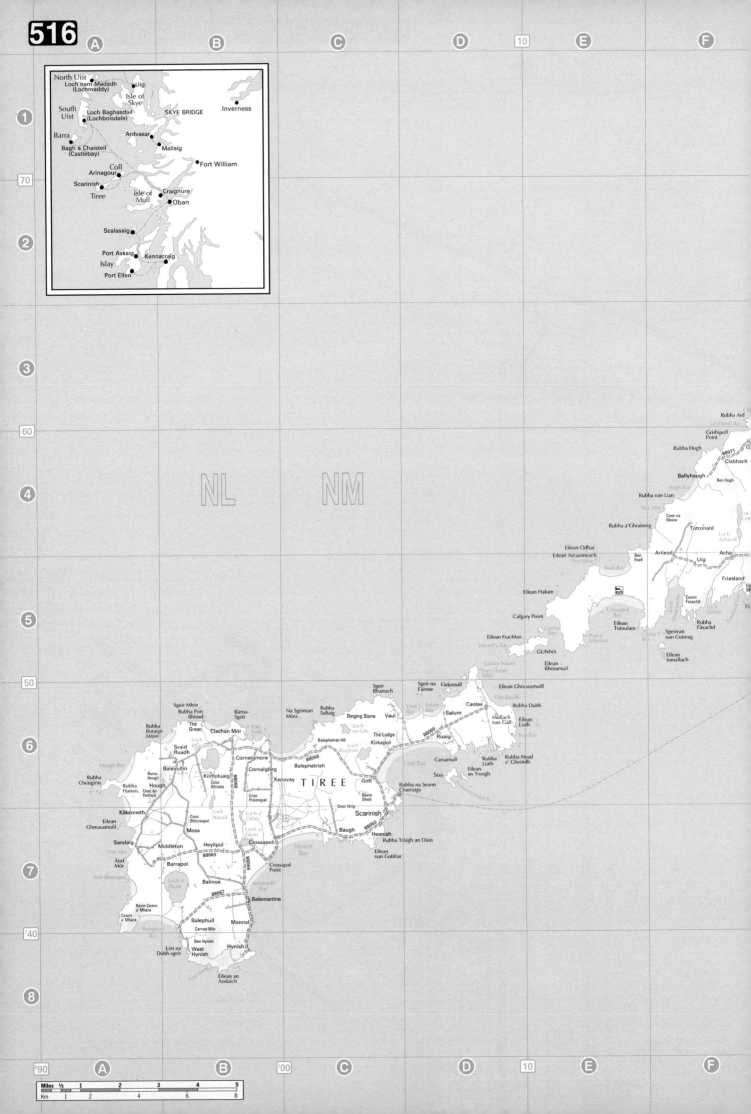

A B C D 10 E F

1

70

2

3

60

NL NM

4

5

50

6

7

40

8

A B 00 C D 10 E F

90

Inset map (top left):

North Uist
Loch nam Madadh
(Lochmaddy)
Uig
Isle of
Skye
SKYE BRIDGE
Inverness
South
Uist
Loch Baghasdail
(Lochboisdale)
Barra
Bagh a Chaisteil
(Castlebay)
Ardvasar
Mallaig
Fort William
Coll
Arinagour
Scarinish
Tiree
Isle of
Mull
Craignure
Oban
Scalasaig
Port Askaig
Kennacraig
Islay
Port Ellen

Main map labels:

Rubha Ard
Grishipoll Bay
Grishipoll
Point
Rubha Hogh
B8071
Clabhach
Ballyhaugh
Ben Hogh
Hogh Bay
Rubha nan Uan
Slic Mòr
Cnoc na
Moine
Rubha a'Ghraineig
Totronald
Loch
Anlaimh
Eilean Odhar
Eilean Ascaoineach
Port Mòr
Ben
Feall
Arileod
Uig
Acha
Feall Bay
Friesland
Eilean Halum
Ceann
Fasachd
Calgary Point
Crossapol
Bay
Ben
Fasachd
 Eilean
Ban
Caolas
Bàn
Port a'
Mhuirain
Eilean
Tomulam
Rubha
Fàsachd
Sgeirean
nan Cuiseag
Eilean Frachlan
Caolas a'
Soa
Eilean
Iomallach
Mcneil's Bay
GUNNA
Eilean
Bhoramuil
Gunna Sound
Port Chinn
Nèill
Fàdamull
Sgeir na
Fàinne
Eilean Ghreasamuill
Sgeir
Bharrach
Port Ruadh
Vaul
Caolas
Rubha Dubh
Eilean
Liath
Vaul Salum
Bay Bay
Salum
Sgeir Mhòr
Rubha Port
Bhiosd
Bàrna-
Sgeir
Na Sgeirean
Mòra
Rubha
Sithean
Ringing Stone
Vaul
Mùllach
nan Gall
Port Bàn
The
Green
Clachan Mòr
Port
Fada
Loch
na Gile
The Lodge
Salum
B8069
Ruaig
Rubha
Boraige
Mòire
Loch
Bhasapol
Balephetrish Hill
Kirkapol
Carsamull
Rubha
Liath
Rubha Nead
a' Gheòidh
Sraid
Ruadh
Balevullin
Cornaigmore
Cornaigbeg
Balephetrish
Gott Bay
Soa
Eilean
an Treogh
Sgeinneil Eulaich
Rubha
Chràiginis
Beinn
Hough
Hough
Cnoc an
Fhithich
Kilmoluaig
Cnoc
Bhiosta
Kenovay
TIREE
Gott
Rubha
Hanais
Loch
Riaghain
Beinn
Ghott
Rubha na Seann
Charraige
Cnoc
Fhòirnigial
Kilkenneth
Cnoc
Bhirceapol
Moss
Loch
Stànail
Loch a'
Chlàir
Cnoc Ibrig
Scarinish
Eilean
Ghreasamuill
Loch an
Eilein
B8065
Sandaig
Port Mòr
Middleton
Heylipol
Crossapol
Baugh
Heanish
Àird
Mòr
Barrapol
B8065
B8065
Rubha Tràigh an Dùin
Port Bharrapol
Balinoe
Crossapol
Point
Hynish
Bay
Eilean
nan Gobhar
B8067
Sorobaidh
Bay
Balemartine
Beinn Ceann
a' Mhara
Balephuil
Mannal
Ceann
a' Mhara
Carnan Mòr
Balephuil
Bay
Ben Hynish
Hynish
Lòn na
Dubh-sgeir
West
Hynish
Port Snoig
Eilean an
Aodaich

Scale (bottom left):

Miles ½ 1 2 3 4 5
Km 1 2 4 6 8

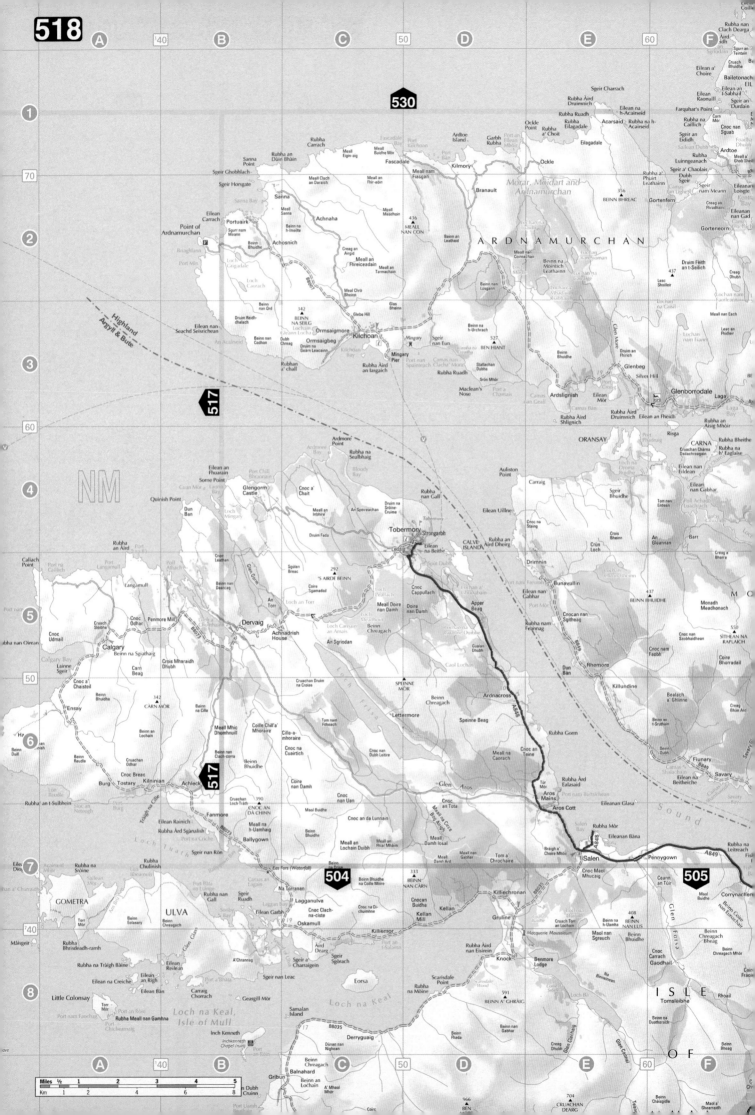

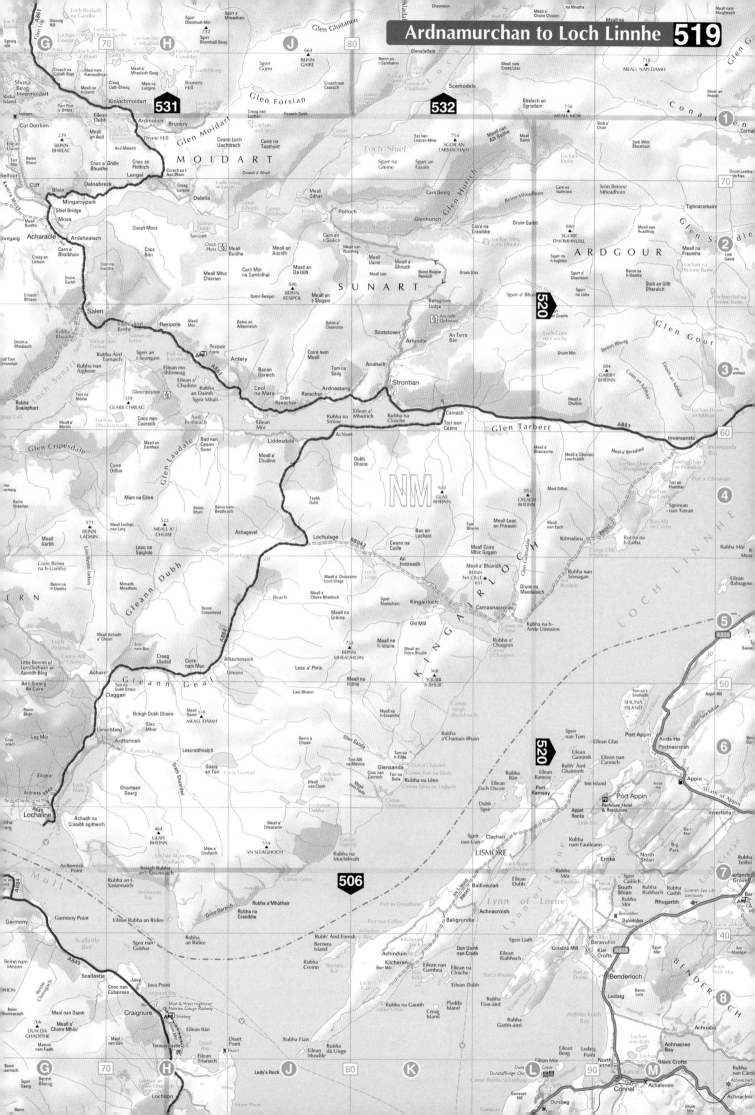

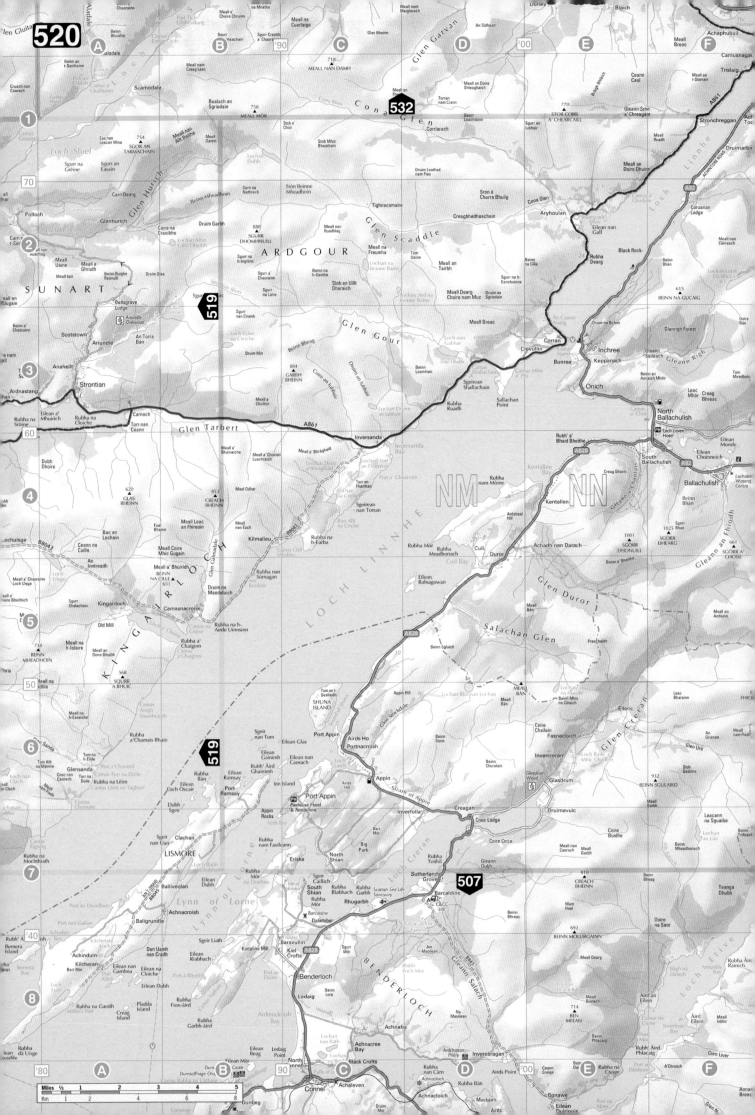

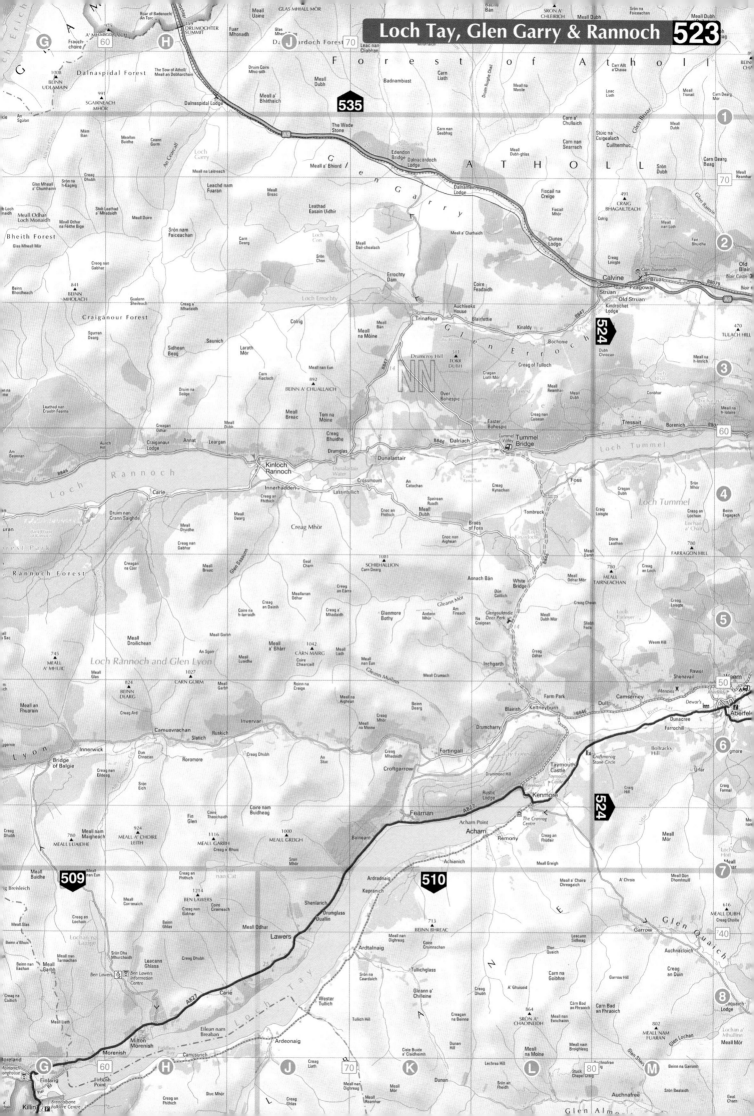

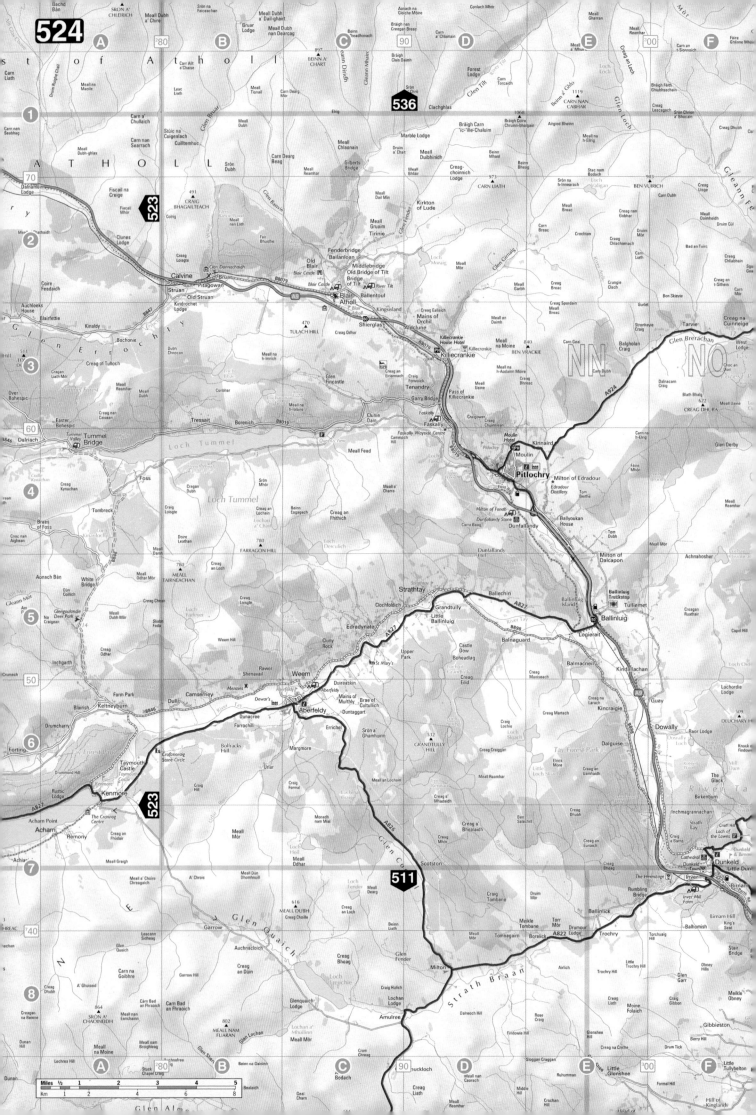

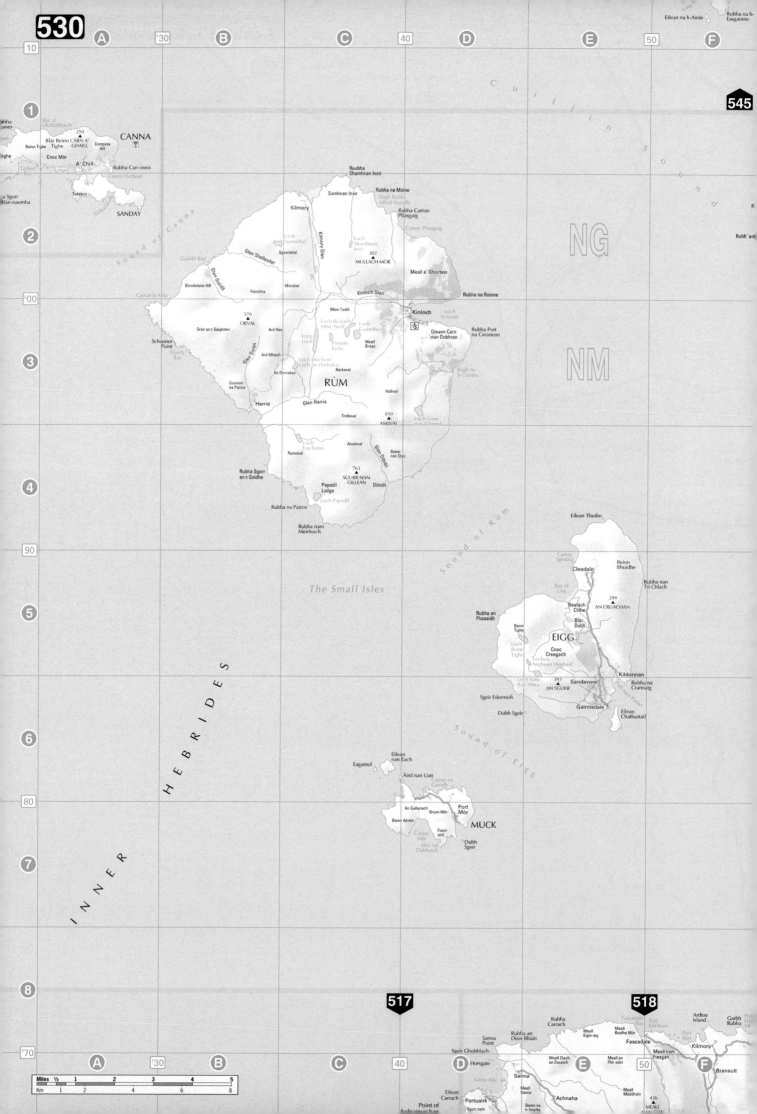

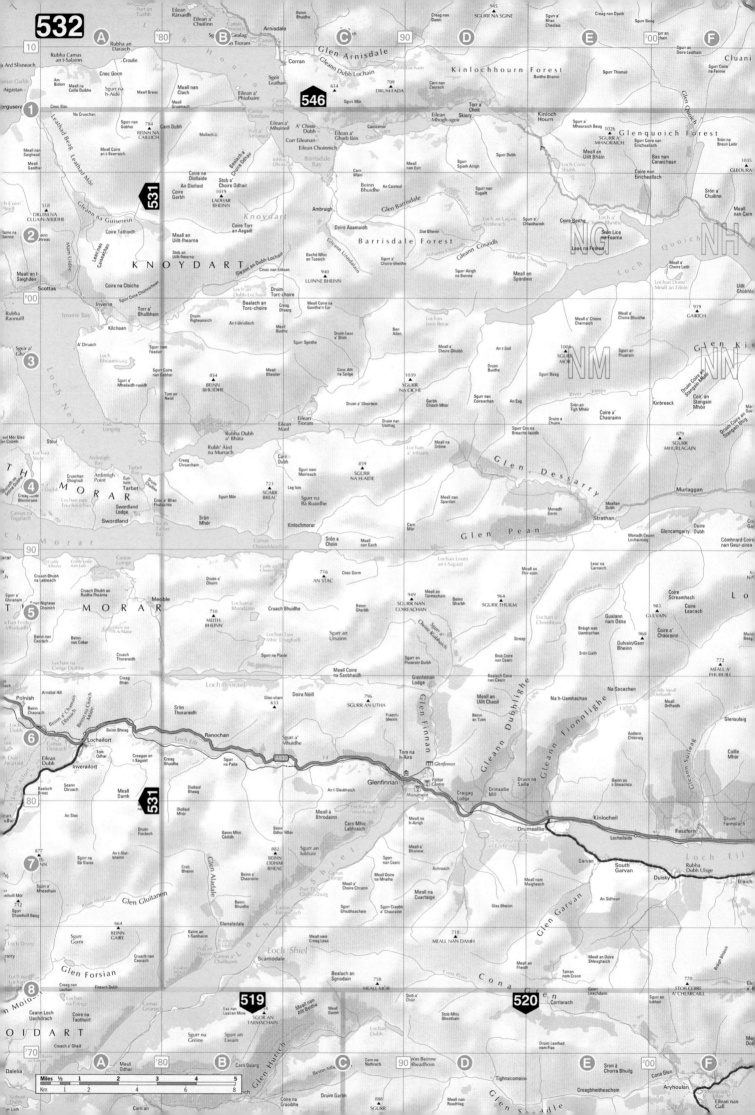

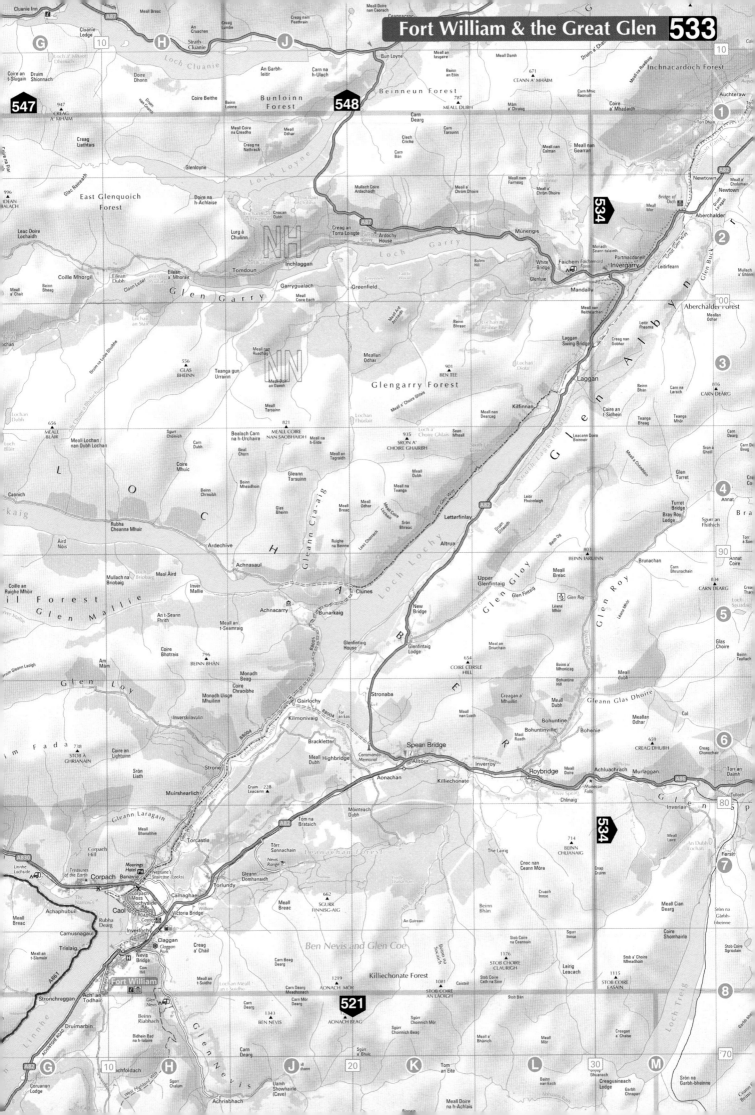

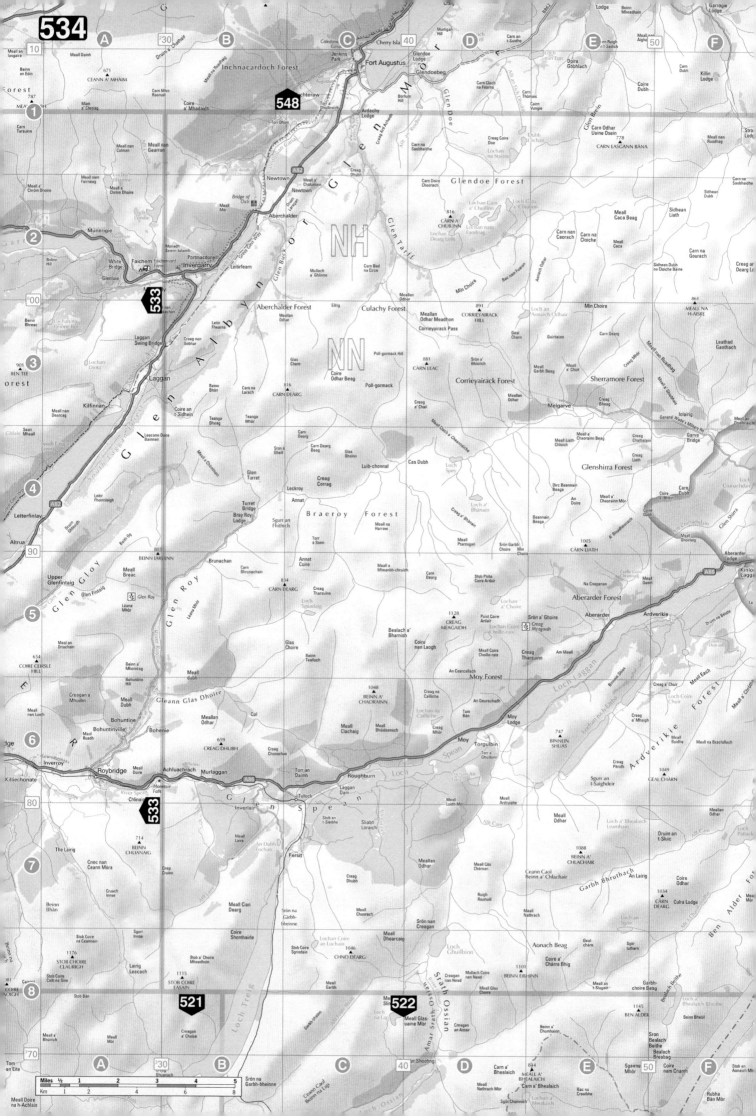

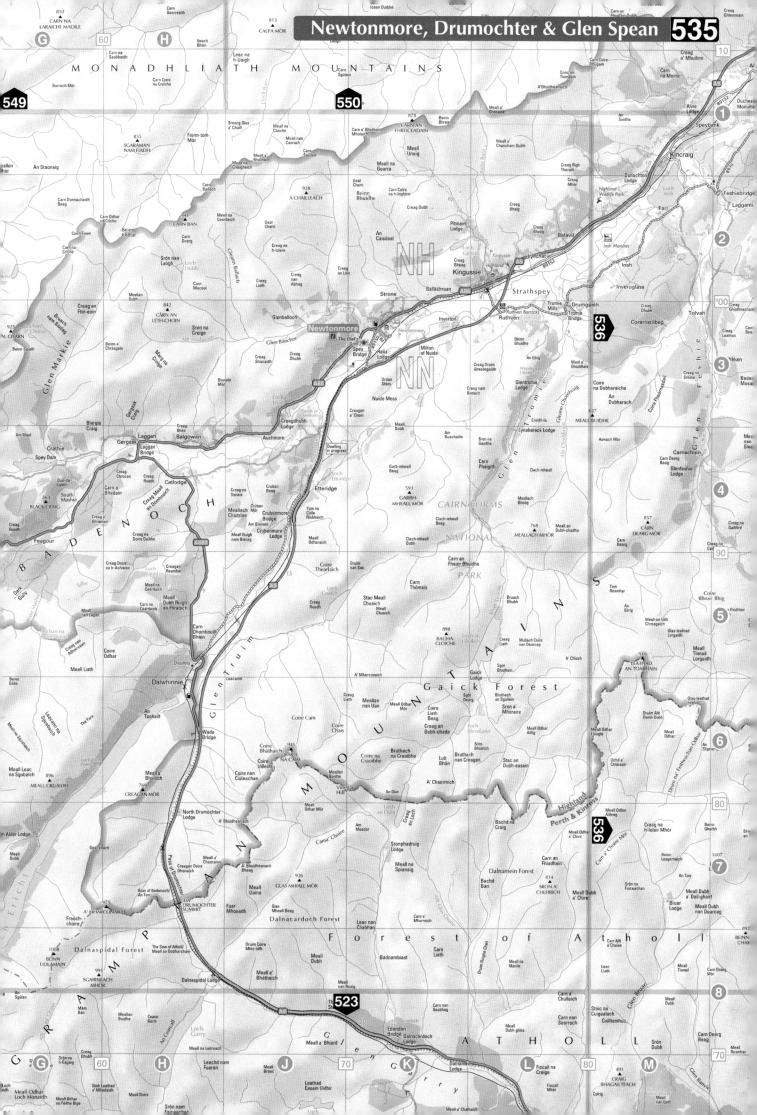

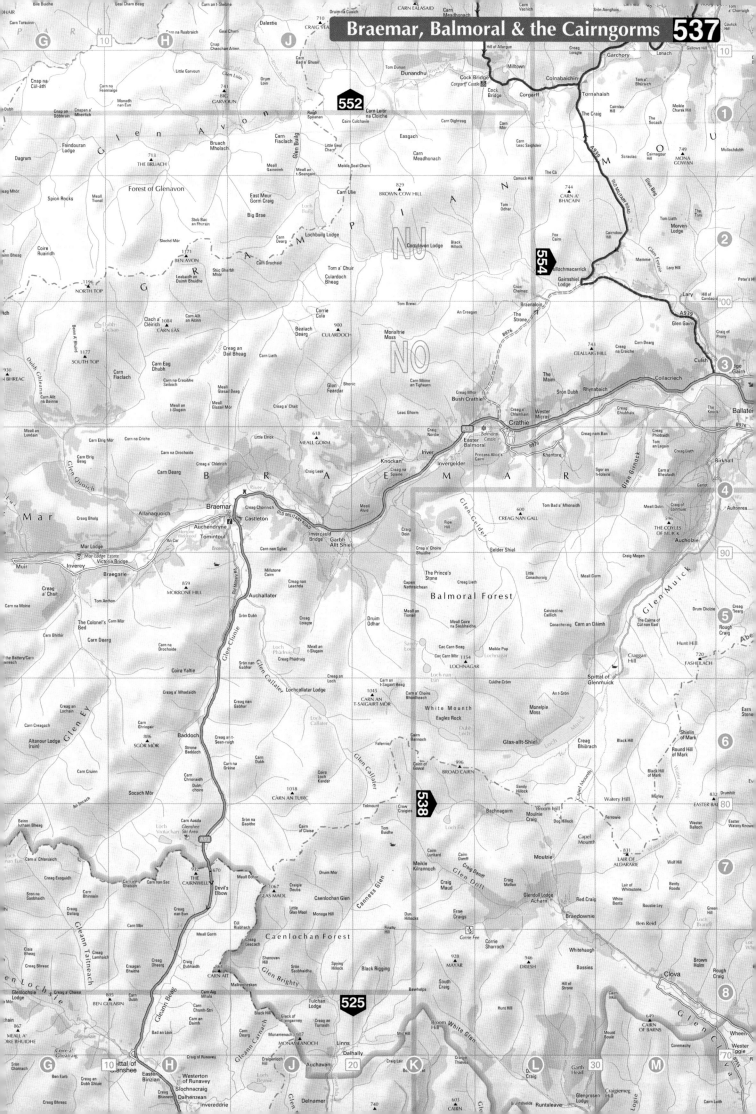

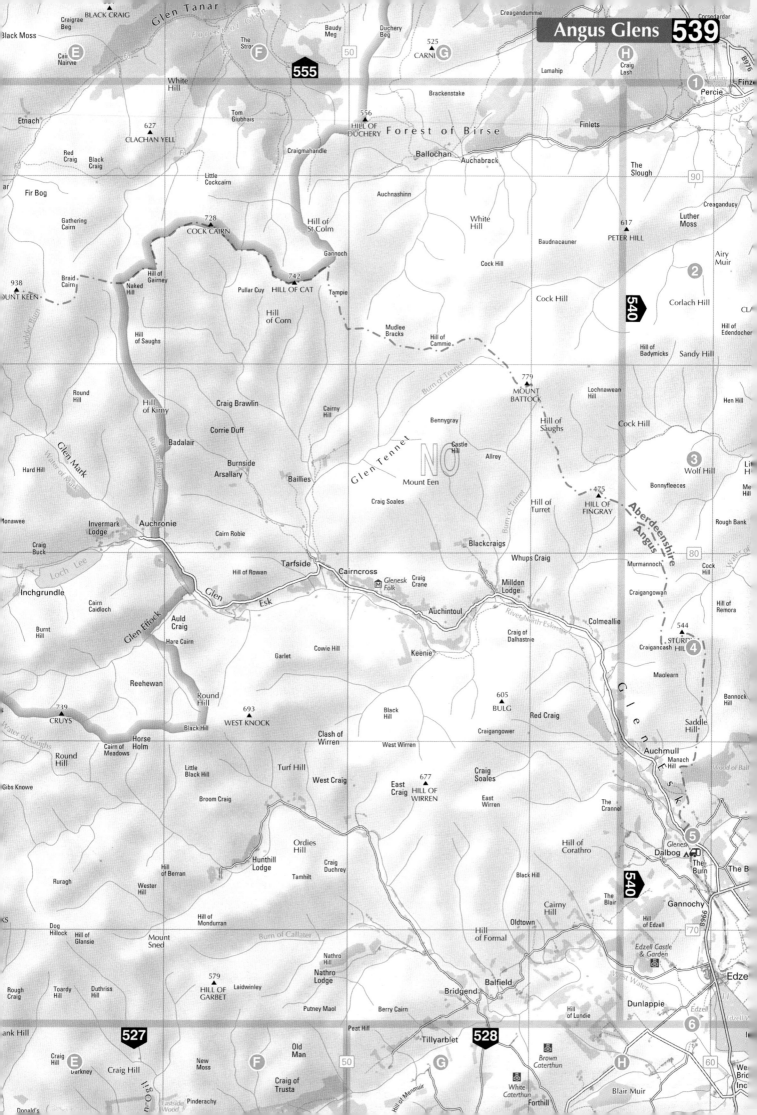

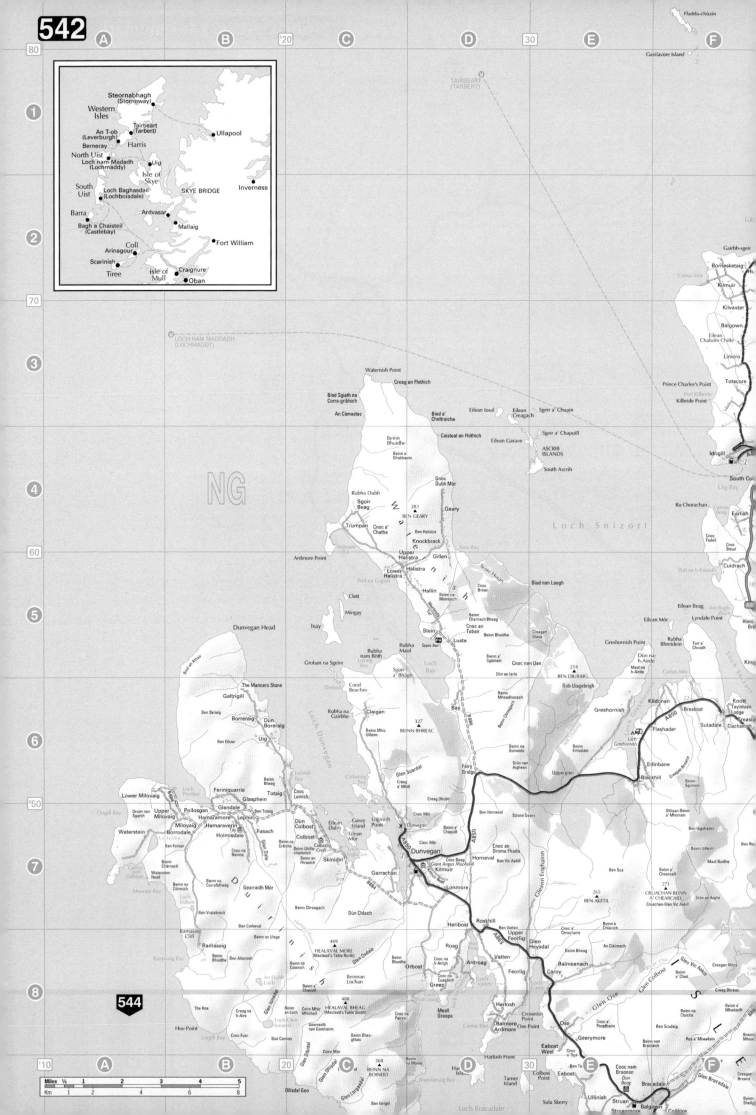

Fladda-chùain

Gaeilavore Island

A   B   '20   C   D   30   E   F

80

Western Isles

Steornabhagh
(Stornoway)

An T-ob
(Leverburgh)   Tairbeart
(Tarbert)   Ullapool

Berneray   Harris

North Uist
Loch nam Madadh
(Lochmaddy)   Uig

Isle of Skye

South Uist   Loch Baghasdail
(Lochboisdale)   SKYE BRIDGE   Inverness

Barra   Ardvasar

Bagh a Chaisteil
(Castlebay)   Mallaig

Coll   Fort William

Arinagour

Scarinish

Tiree   Isle of
Mull   Craignure

Oban

70

Gairbh-sgeir

Bornesketaig

Kilmuir

Kilvaxter

Balgown

Eilean
Chaluim Chille

Linicro

3   Waternish Point   Prince Charles's Point   Totscore

Creag an Fhithich   Port Kilbride
Kilbride Point

Biod Sgiath na
Corra-gribhich

An Càmastac   Biod a'
Choltraiche   Eilean Iosal   Eilean
Creagach   Sgeir a' Chuain

Beinn
Bhuidhe   Caisteal an Fhithich   Eilean Garave   Sgeir a' Chapuill   Idrigill

Beinn a'
Ghobhainn   ASCRIB
ISLANDS   South Cui

Gnoc
Dubh Mòr

NG   South Ascrib

4   Rubha Dubh   283   Geary   Ru Chorachan   Earlish
Sgoir
Beag   BEN GEARY   Cnoc
Fadail   Cnoc
Steud

Ben Halistra   Loch Snizort   Cuidrach

Trumpan   Cnoc a'
Chatha   Knockbreck   Aros Bay   Pull na h-Ealaidh

60   Upper
Halistra   Gillen   Eilean Beag   An Bagh
dhubh

Ardmore Point   Lower
Halistra   Scor Horan   Biod nan Laogh   Eilean Mòr   Lyndale Point   Hinni
Bre

Port na Cagain   Beinn na
Mointech   Cnoc
Breac   Greshornish Point   Rubha a'
Chruidh

5   Clett   Beinn
Charnach Bheag   Creagan
Glasa   Dùn na-
h-Airde   Torr a'
Chruidh

Mingay   Cnoc an
Tobair   Maol na
h-Airde   Camas Mòr   King

Dunvegan Head   Isay   Stein   Lusta   Beinn Bhuidhe   Dùn na-
Rubha   PH   Beinn a'   Kildonan   Knott
Biod an Athair   nam Bòth   Stein Inn   Sgùmain   Cnoc nan Uan   Gob Uisgebrigh   Tayinloan   Treaslo
Lodge   Clachamish

Rubha   Dùn an Iarla   214   Suladale
Groban na Sgeire   Maol   BEN DIUBAIG   A850

The Manners Stone   Sgurr   Lovaig   Beinn   Greshornish   Flashader
a' Bhàgh   Bay   Mheadhonach

Galtrigill   An   Loch
Doirish   Bay   Beinn na   Edinbane
Borreraig   Coral   Boineide   Sròn nan   Blackhill
Ben Skriaig   Beaches   327   Aighean   Upperglen
Dùn   Rubha na   BEINN BHREAC   Beinn   Beinn
Ben Ettow   Borreraig   Gairbhe   Claigan   Eirisalan   Sgùmain
Uig   Beinn Mhic   Bay
Uilleim   Fairy
Bridge

Leinish   Glen Suardal   Creag   Ben Horneval   Strone Gears   Sithean Beinn
50   Lower Milovaig   Bay   Creag   a' Mhill   a' Mhorrain
Druim nan   Upper   Feriniquarrie   Beinn   a' Mhill
Sgarbh   Milovaig   Bheag   Creag Dhubh   Ben Ugshader
Oisgill Bay   Totaig   A850
Pollosgan   Glasphein   Cnoc Mòr   Ben Re
Milovaig   Hamaramore   Garay   Uiginish   Dunvegan   Beinn a'
Borrodale   Glendale   Lephin   Dùn   Island   Point   Cnoc Mòr   Chapuill   Beinn Uilleim
Waterstein   Hamaraverin   Colbost   Eilean   Horneval   Maol Buidhe
Holmisdale   Fasach   Dubh   Cnoc an   Maol Buidhe
Ben Forsan   Colbost   Eilean   Droma Fhada
7   Ben Charnach   Colbost Ghille-   Skinidin   Mòr   Dunvegan   Ben Vic Askill   Beinn a'
choinnich   Giant Angus MacAskill   Chearcaill
Waterstein   Cnoc na   Garrachan   Kilmuir   Ben Sca   Sròn an Aighe
Head   Beinne   Beinn na   Fhraoich   265   CRUACHAN BEINN
Camas   Gearraidh Mòr   Lonmore   BEN AKETIL   A' CHEARCAILL
nan Sidhean   Cruachan-Glen Vic Askill
Mooinan Bay   Duirinish   Dùn Chlach   Heribost   Roskhill   Cnoc a'
Beinn Chreagach   Ben Vatten   Chrochaire   Beinn a
Ramasaig   Cnoc a   Chlèirich
Cliff   Beinn an Uisge   Dùn Chlach   Upper   Glen Heysdal   Beinn Bheag   An Cleireach   Creagan Mora
Ramasaig   Feorlig   Roag   Feorlig   River Ose   Glen Vic Askill
469   Vatten   Balmeanach   Glen Colbost   Cnoc
Ramasaig Bay   Beinn   HEALAVAL MORE   Beinn   Caroy   Beinn a' Chait   a' Chait
Bhuidhe   Ben Allarnish   (Macleod's Table North)   Bhuidhe   S
8   An Dubh   Glen Osdale   Orbost   Cnoc na   Ardroag   Creag Bhreac
Loch   h-Airigh   Caroy   Beinn na
Beinnan   Greep   Cnoc a'   Cloiche   Beinn a'
Lochan   Fhradhairc   Mhdaidh
488   Ben Connan   HEALAVAL BHEAG   Meall   Harlosh   Glen Ose   Ben Mheal
The Hoe   Coire Mhic   (Macleod's Table South)   Greepa   Crossnish   Ben Scodaig
Mhicheil   Point   Ose   Cnoc a'   Ros a' Mheallain
Hoe Point   Gearraidh   Cnoc Na   Ose Point   Fhradhairc
Cnoc Fuar   nan Gamhainn   Pairce   Camas Bàn
Coire Mòr   Eabost   Gearymore
Beinn Bhac-   West   Glen Bracadale
ghlais   Cnoc nam   Creaga
Brasonan   Creaga
368   Dùn   Mhea
A   '10   B   20   C   BEINN NA   D   30   E   Beag   F
BOINEID   Eabost
Colbost   Cnoc a'   Bracadale
Ollisdal Geo   Glen Dibidal   Point   Sga
Tarner   Harlosh Point   Glen Bracadale
Island   Ullinish   Coillore
Loch Bracadale   Sula Skerry   Struan   Balgown
Glen Lorgasdal   Struanmore

544

Miles ½   1   2   3   4   5
Km   1   2   4   6   8

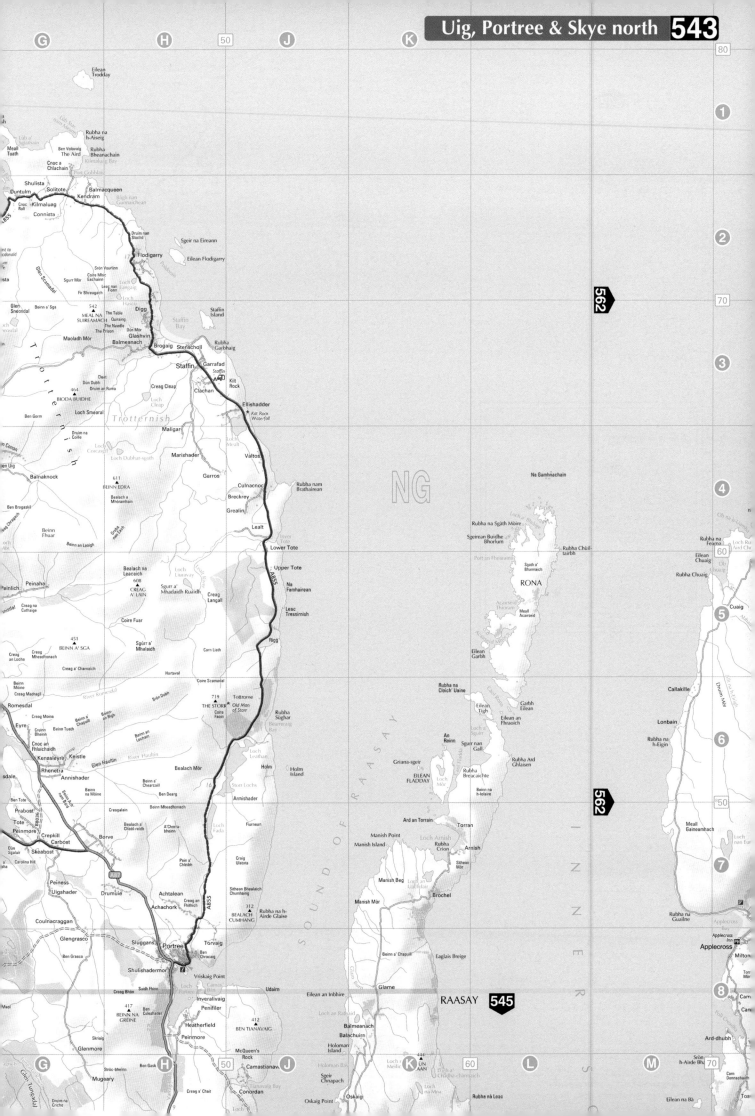

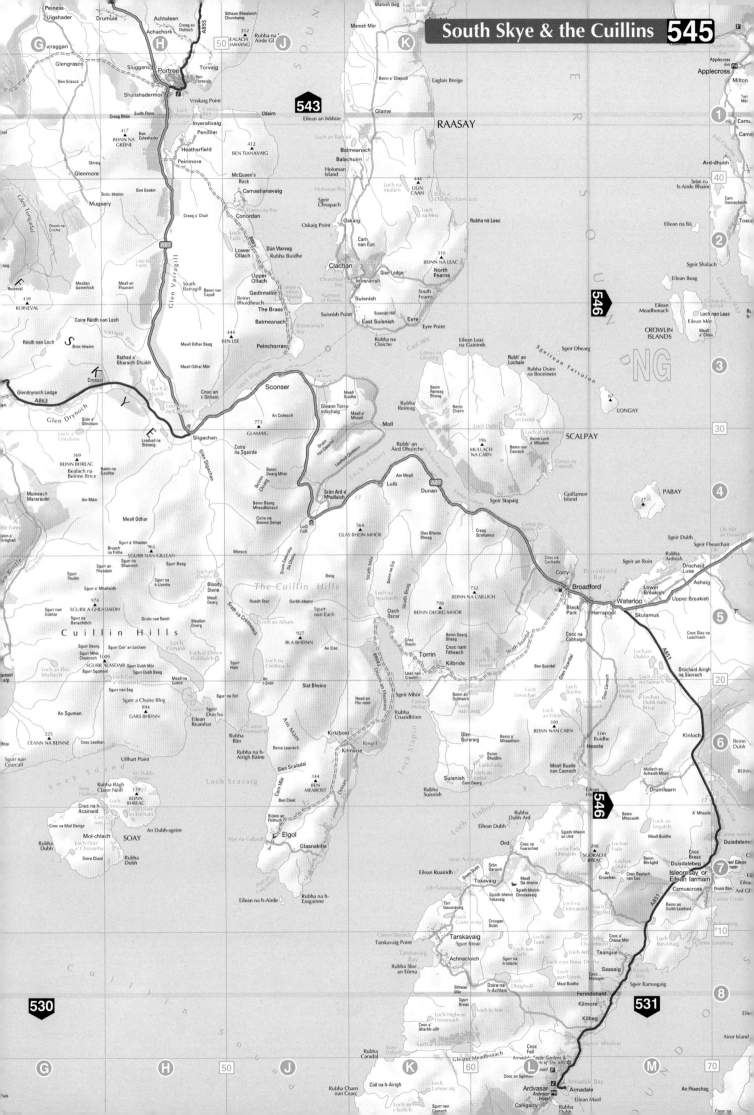

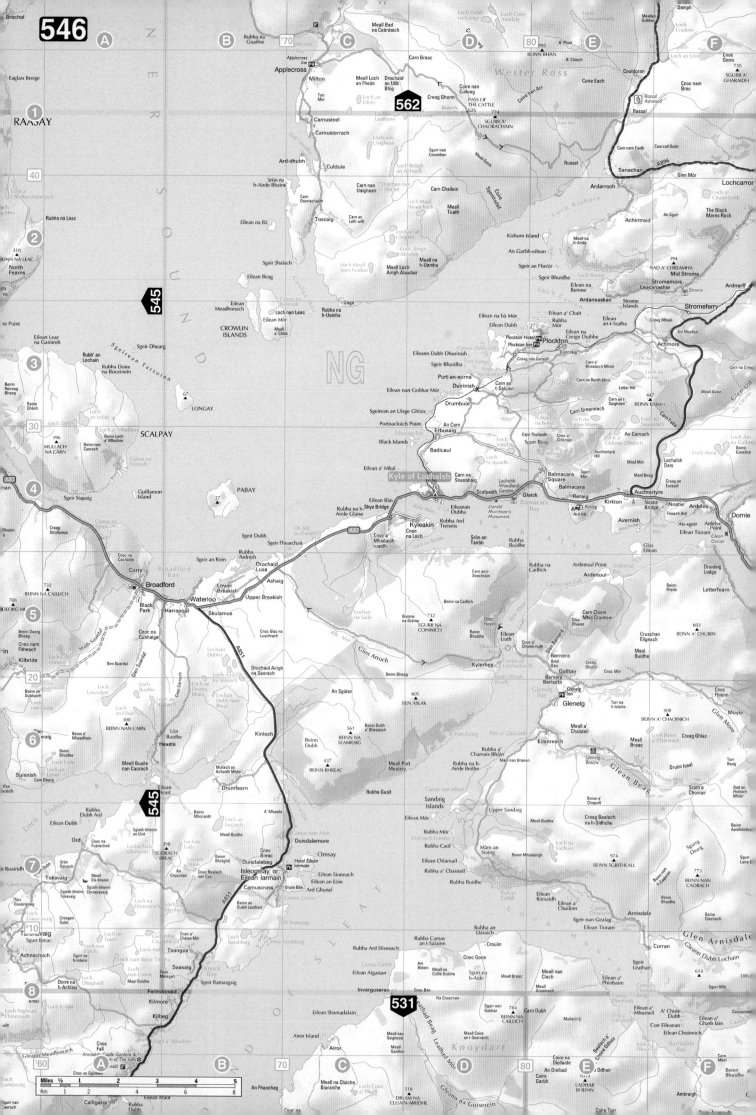

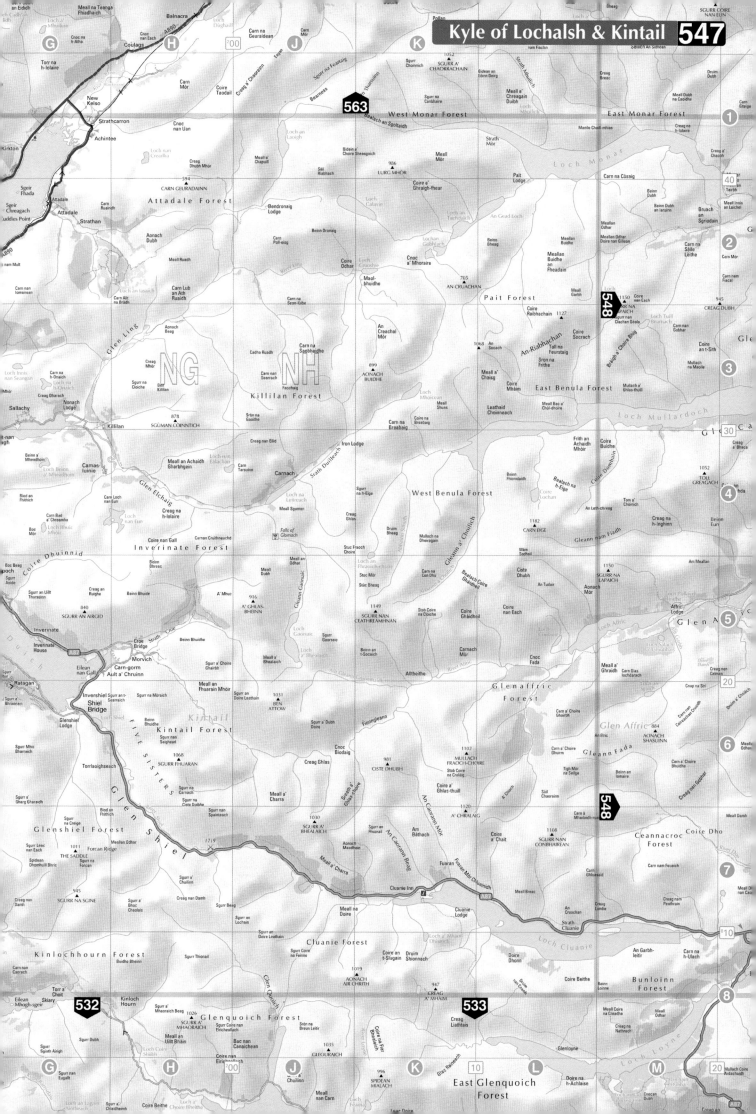

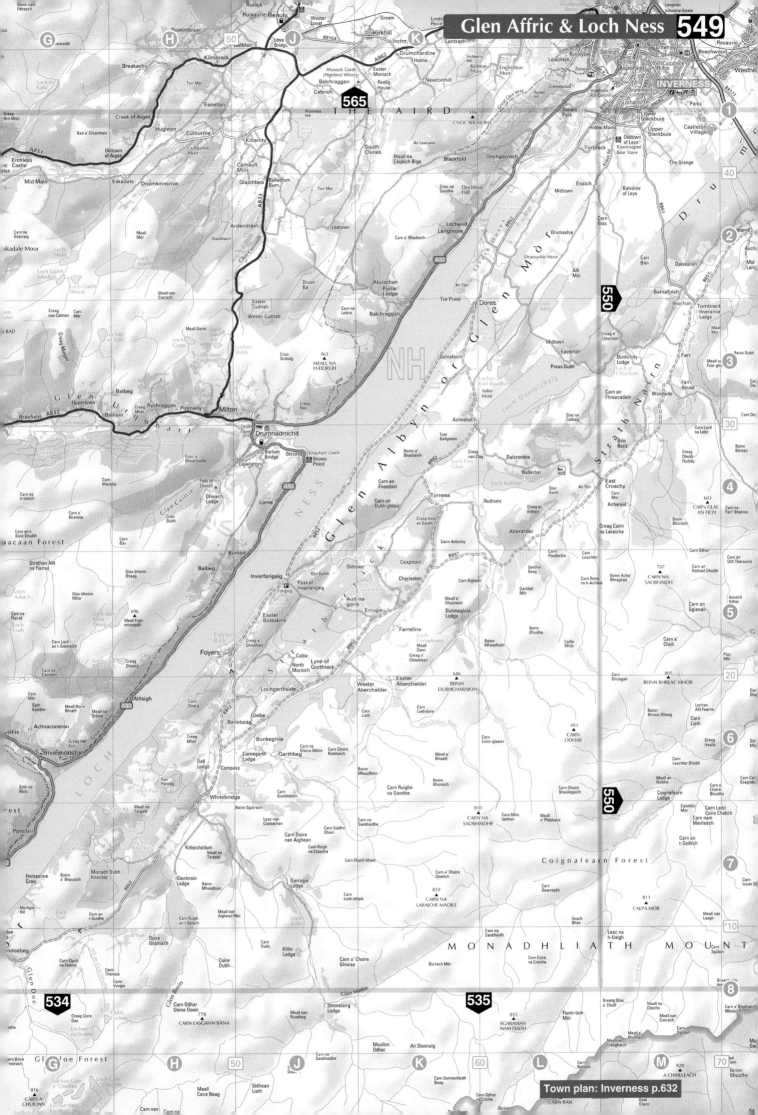

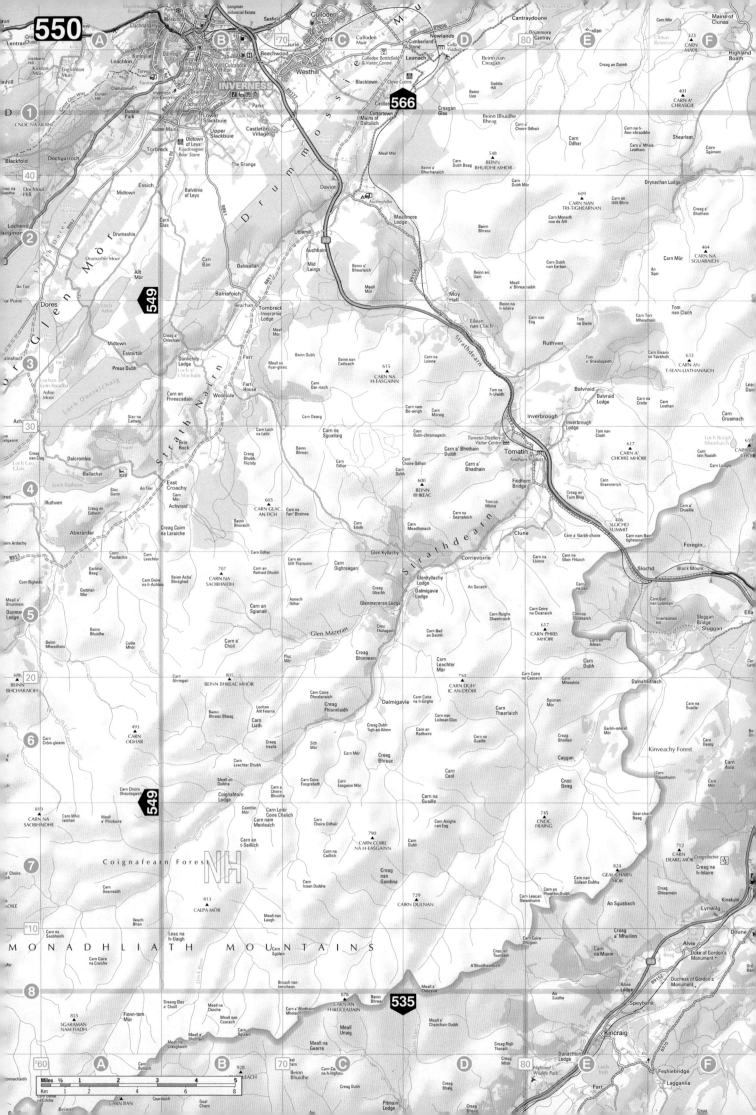

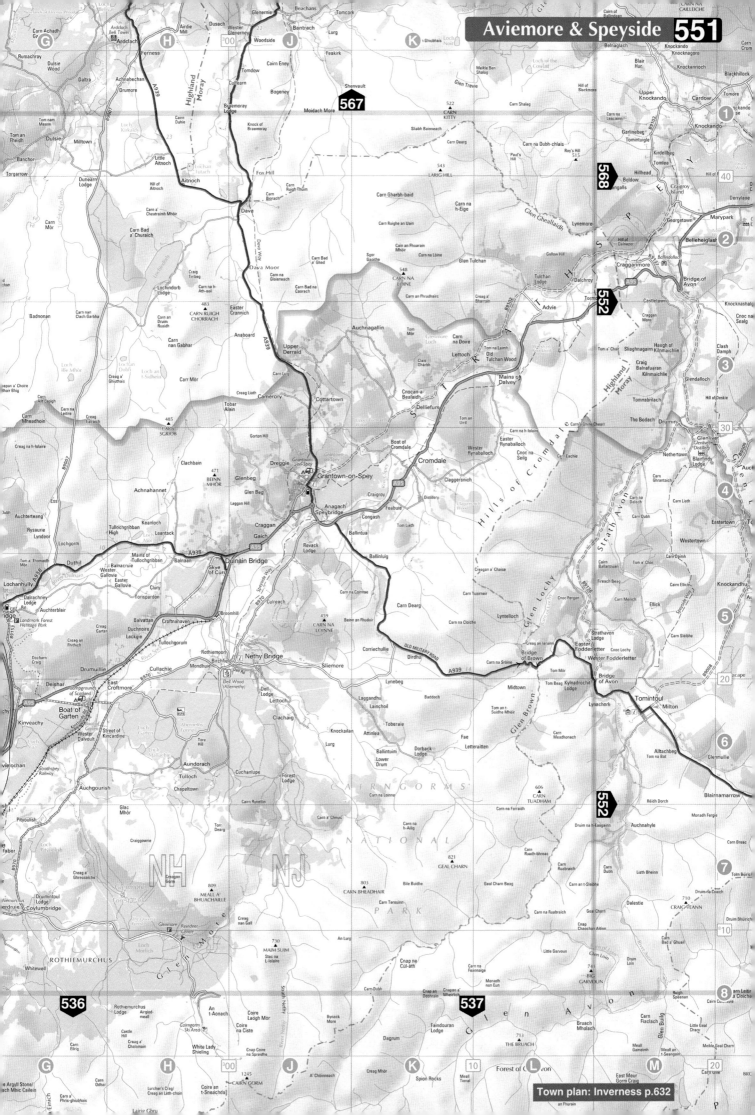

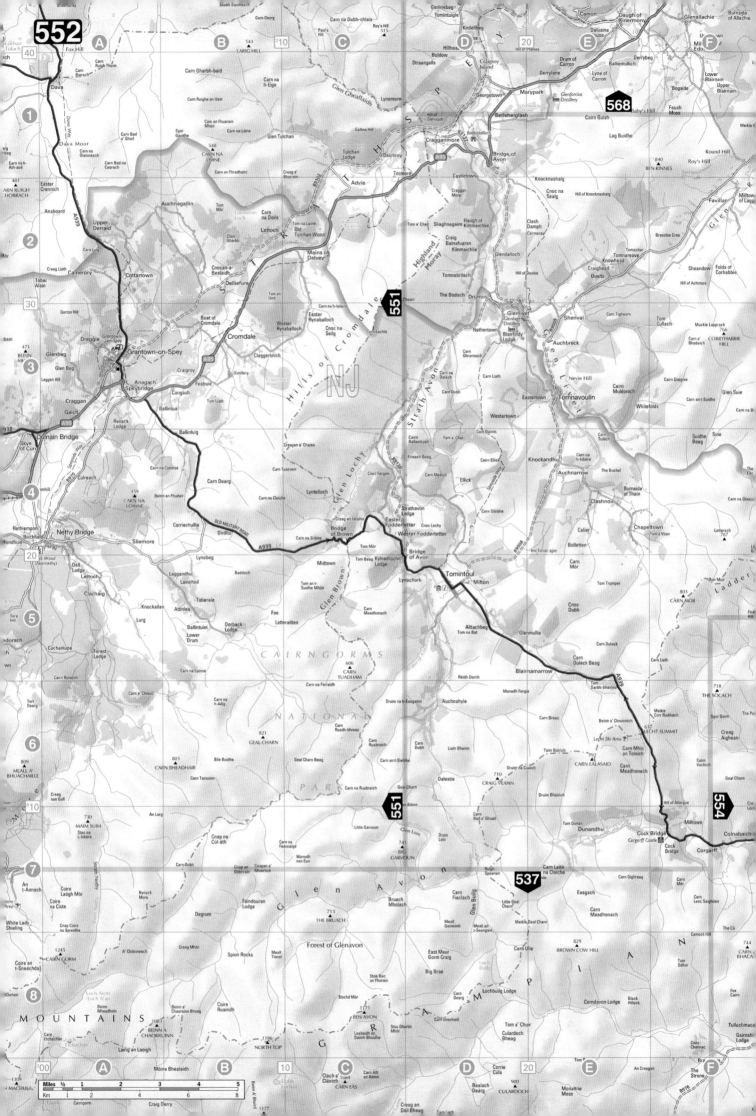

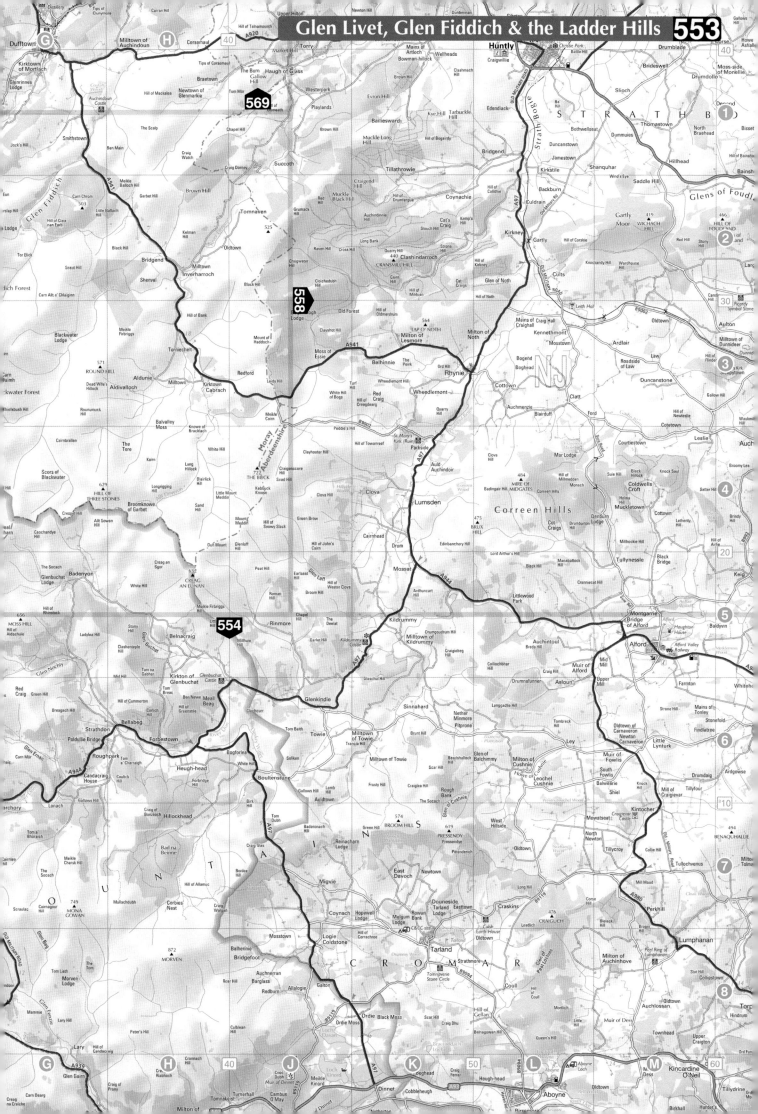

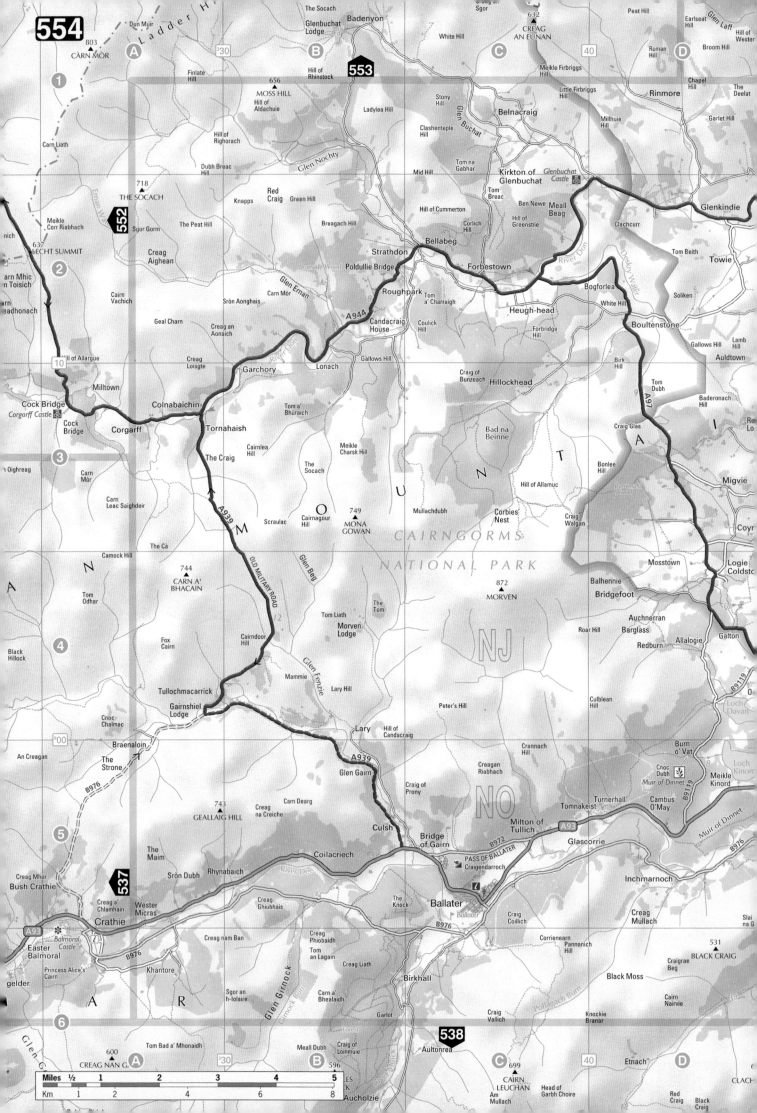

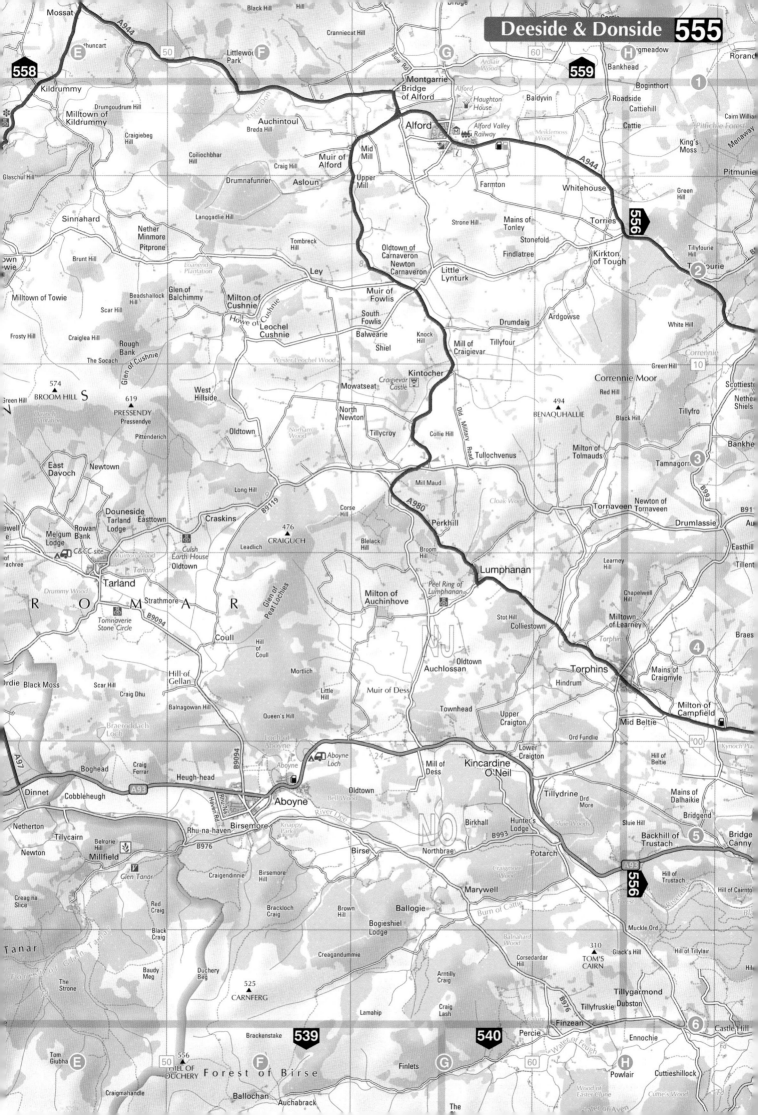

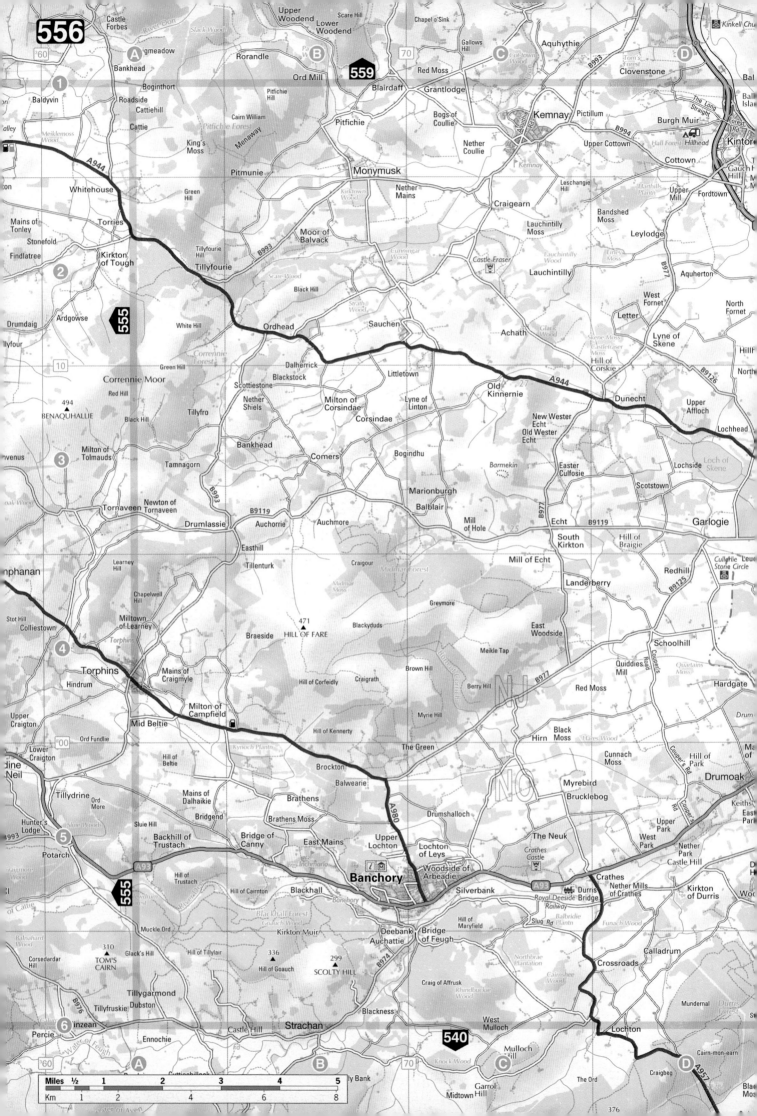

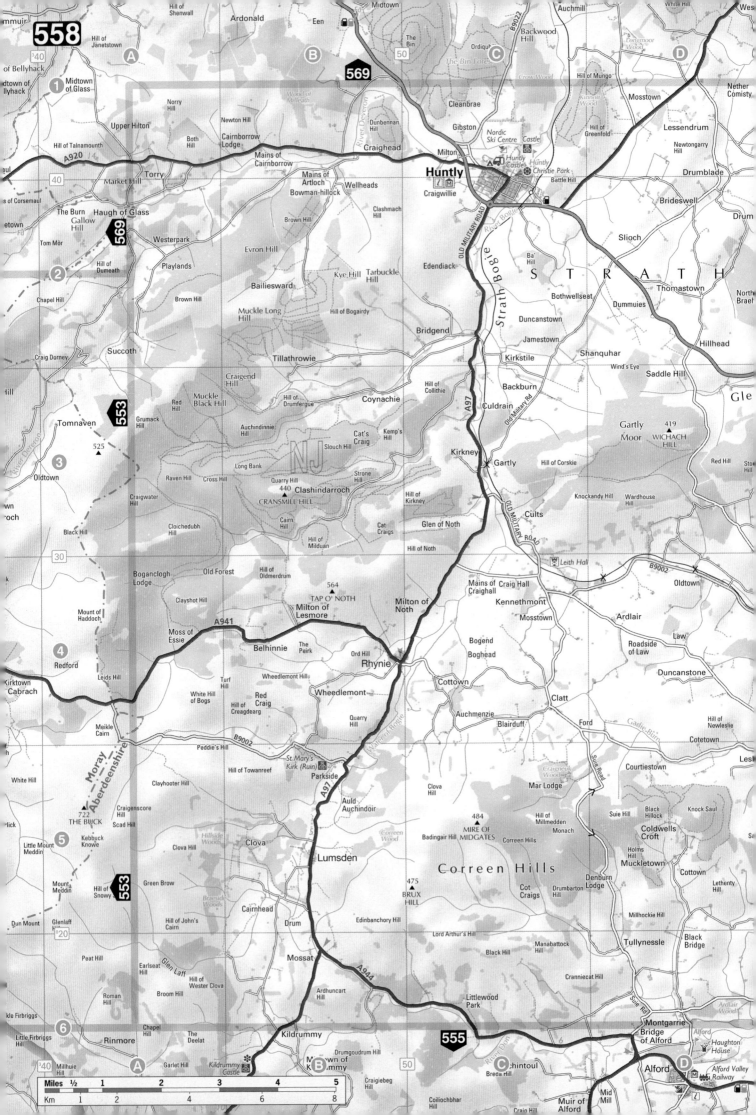

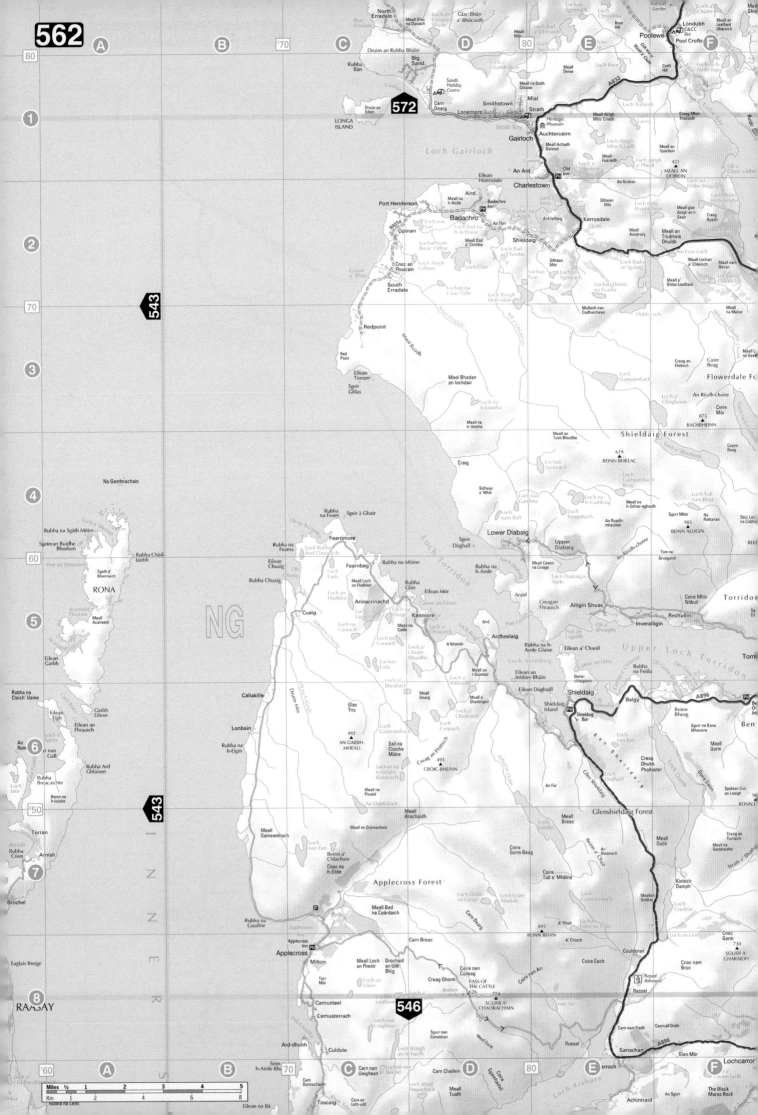

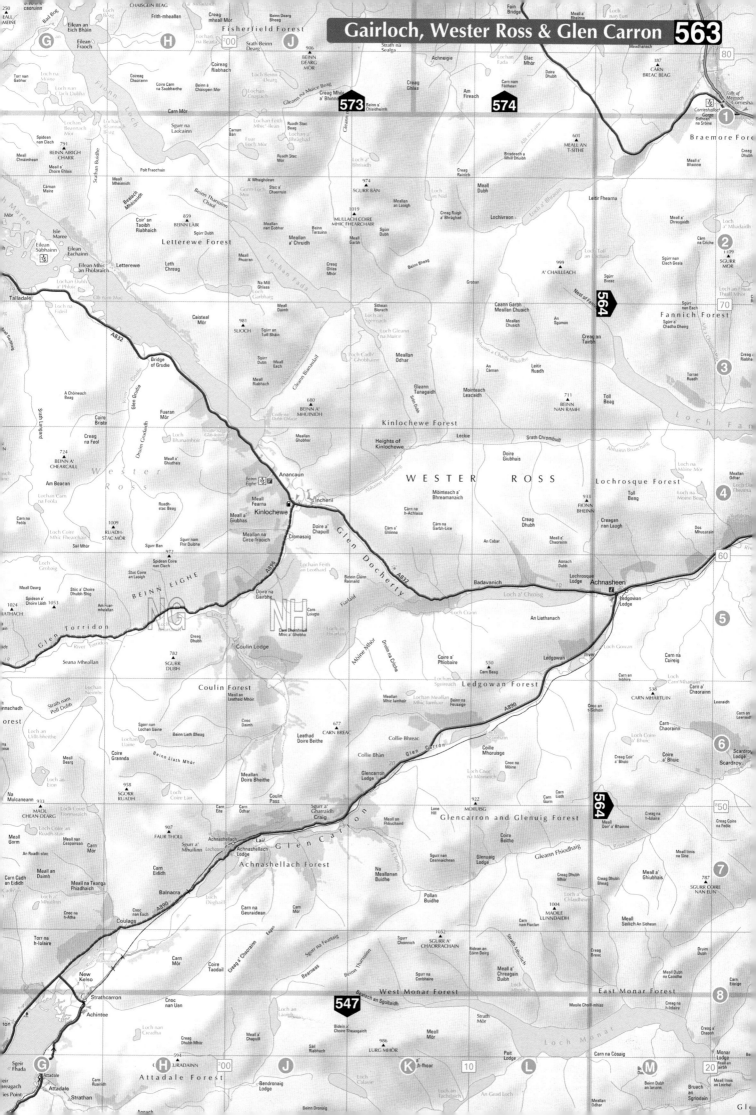

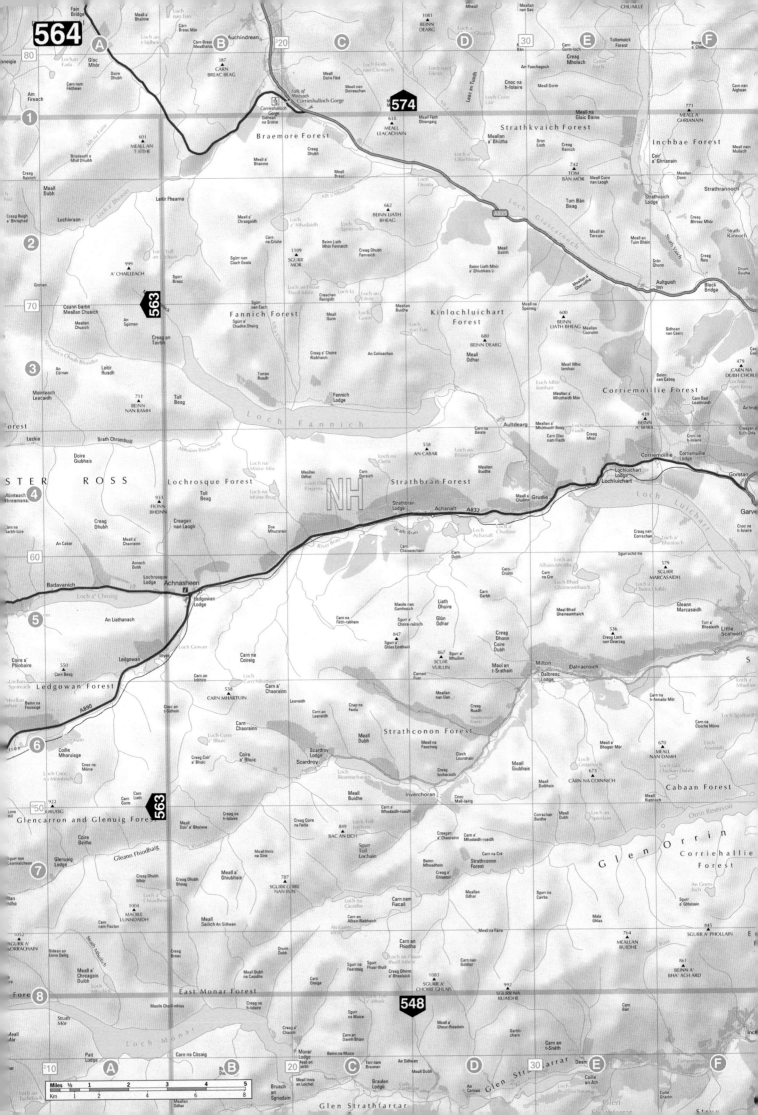

577

G   H   J

NH   NJ

568

Craag Mhaol

Culbin Sands   Findhorn

Findhorn Bay   Burghead Bay

Covesea
Clashach Cove   North Greer

Hopeman   Sweethillock
RAF Lossiemouth

Burghead Well   Cummingston   Duffus
Burghead   St Aethans   Backlands   St Peter's Kirk & Parish Cross   Crosshill

Clarkly Hill   Duffus Castle   Silverhills
Bennet Hill   Oldtown   Tappoch   Westerfolds   Salterhill

Charlestown   Roseisle   Bank of Roseisle   Midtown   Gilston
College of Roseisle   Kintrae

Lake of Moy   Standingstone   Quarrywood   Elgin
Coltfield   Longhillock   Wood Park   DUFFUS ROAD

Kincorth House   Hempriggs   Newton   Old Mills   Glen Moray Distillery
Wellhill   North Alves   WEST ROAD

Seafield   RAF Kinloss   Muirhead   Morayscairn   Alves   Pittendreich
Netherton   Grange Hill   Carden Hill   The Greens   Mosstowie

The Bar   Sea Park   Kinloss   East Grange   Monaughty   Wester Marchhead   Miltonduff
Milton of Grange

Cloddymoss   Kintessack   Grange Hall   Burgie Lodge   Brodieshill   Asliesk   Dykeside   Garrowslack   Muir of Miltonduff   Paddock
Springfield   Enterprise Park   Park of Dykeside

Muirtown   Wester Moy   **Forres**   Easter Newforres   Heldon Hill   Pluscarden   Torrieston   Nether Bogside   hill
Broom of Moy   Pilmuir   Sueno's Stone   Forres   Califer   Barnhill

Dyke   Chapeltonmoss   Wester Newforres   Tom Ruadh
Kingsteps   Brodie Castle   Newton of Dalvey   Sanquhar Mains   Rafford   Whitetree   Thistle Flat   Buinach Hill

Easterton   Macbeth's Hillock   Dallas Dhu Distillery   Oakwood   Miltown of Kellas   Leanoch   Middleton
Lochloy   Woodend   Blinkbonny   Little Tearie   Mundole   Kellas   Glenlatterach   Bardon

Hardmuir   Feddan   Berryley   Old Blairs   Woodside   Moor of Granary   Hill of Edinvale   Mossend   Mill Ou
Courage   Little Tearle   Cothall   Blackhills   Blackhills   Bauds

B9111   Garblies   Logiebuchany   Wardend House   Hill of the Wangie   Crofthead   Glen Latterach   Moss of Birnie   PIK
B9101   Auldearn   Whitemire   Fernielea   Dallas Lodge   Dallas   Mill Buie   Meikle Hill

Newton of Park   Easter Brightmony   Conicavel   Cluny   Branchill   Craigmill Lodge   CAIRN UISH   B9010
Brightmony   Milton   Muir of Logie   Craigroy   Romach Hill   365

Easter Arr   Newlands of Moynes   Dava Way   Burntack   371   MILL BUIE   Craigs of Sluggan   568
Braeside   Lethen House   Wester Clune   Logie Steading   Logie   Muckle Greens   Ballachraggan   Mannoch Hill

Fornighty   Wester Clune   Carnach   Wester Greens   Hill of Tomechole   Aultahurn   Soccach   Coldwells   B9010
Littlemill   Lethen Bar   Relugas   Hill of Gaschyle   Coldwells

Achnatone   Shaw Hill   Dunphail   Rochuln   Carnachie   Hill of Blackroads   CARN NA CAILLEICHE   400
Kronyhillock   Airdie Mill   Glenernie   Beachans   Tomcork   Cairn of Ballindean   Cairn of Clune

New Achamore   Ardclach Bell Tower   Dusach   Wester Glenerney   Lurg   Carn Ghiubhais   Loch Noir   Belnagloch   Belnagone   Lyne of Knockando   Blackhillock
Achavraat   Ardclach   Woodside   Bantrach   Feakirk   Belnaglach   Knocknagore   Tomore

Keppernach   Ferness   Cairn Eney   Cairn of Clune   Knockannioch
Rumachroy   Dulsie Wood   Tomdow   Meikle Ben Shalag   Blair Hur   Upper Knockando   Cardow

Daltra   Achnabechan   Culfearn   Shenvault   Glen Trevie   Hill of Slackmore   Tomore   Cardow
Drumore   Bogeney   522   Hill of Phones

Tom nam Meann   Cairn Duhie   Braemoray Lodge   Moidach More   CARN KITTY   Carn Shalag   Carn na Leacairn   Knockando
Dulsie   Highland / Moray   Roy's Hill   Garlinebeg

Milltown   Loch Kirkaldy   Knock of Braemoray   Sliabh Bainneach   543   LARIG HILL   Paul's Hill   515   Carn na Dubh-chlais   Tomintuigle   Kirdellbeg
Banchor   Lochan Tutach   Fox Hill   Carn Dearg   Carn Gharbh-bau   Carn na h-Eige   Tomlea   Hillhead

Torgarrow   Dunearn Lodge   Hill of Aitno   Aitnoch   Carn Biorach   Dava   Carn Ruighe an Uain   Boldow   Craigroy Island
Carn a' Cheatraimh Mhor   Straangalls   Derrylane   Marypark

Carn Mor   Carn Rad

551

G   H   J   K   L   M

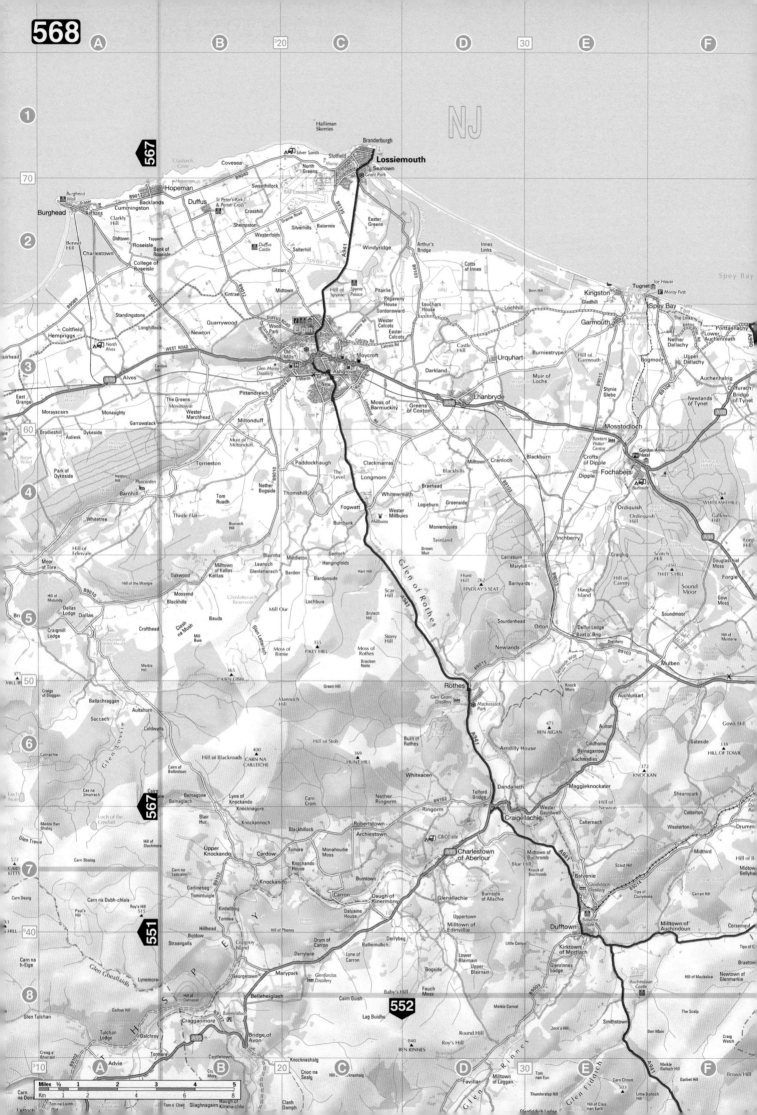

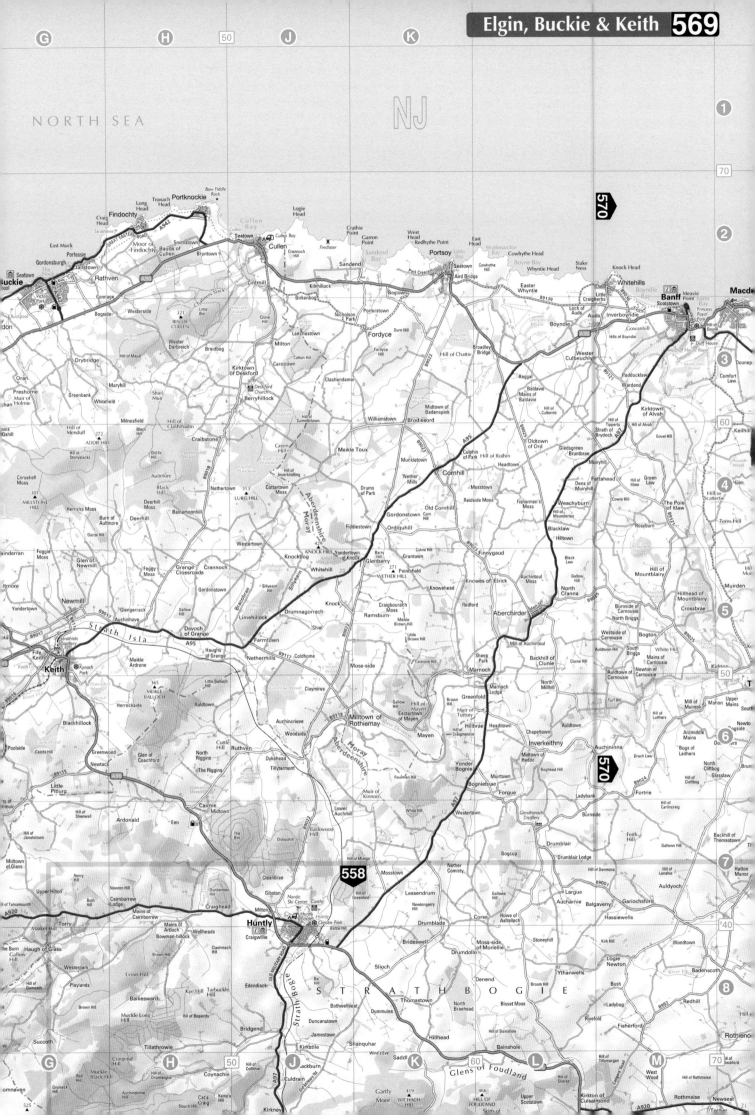

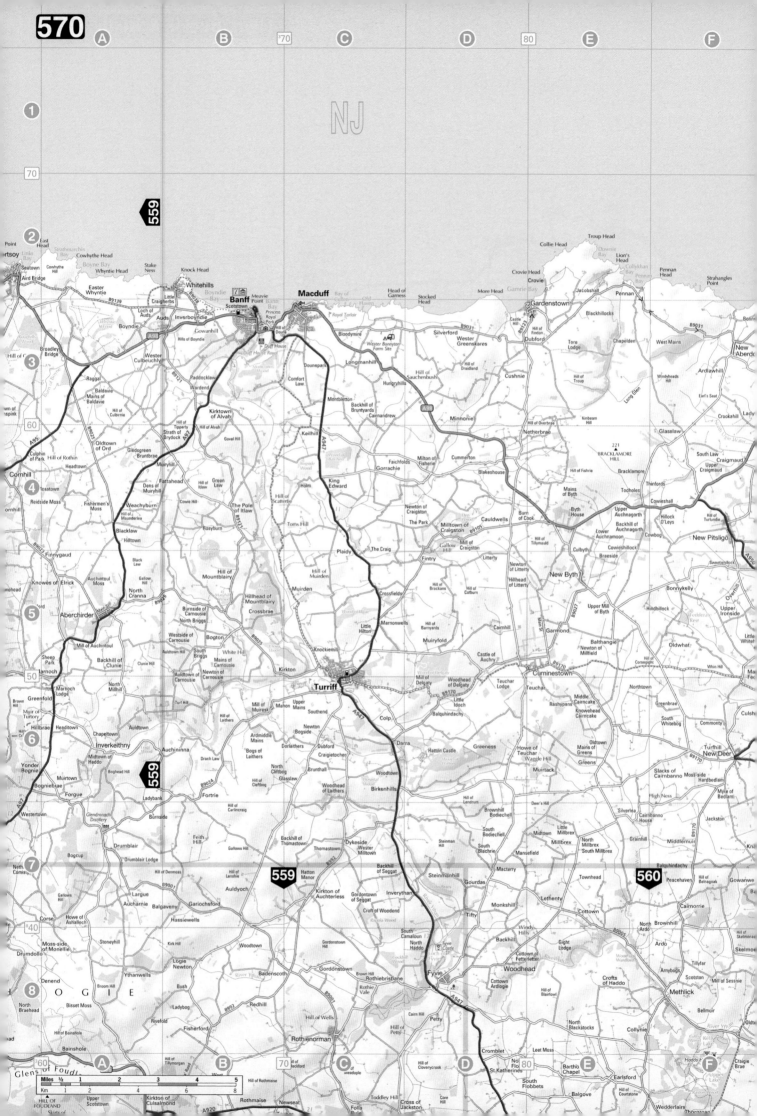

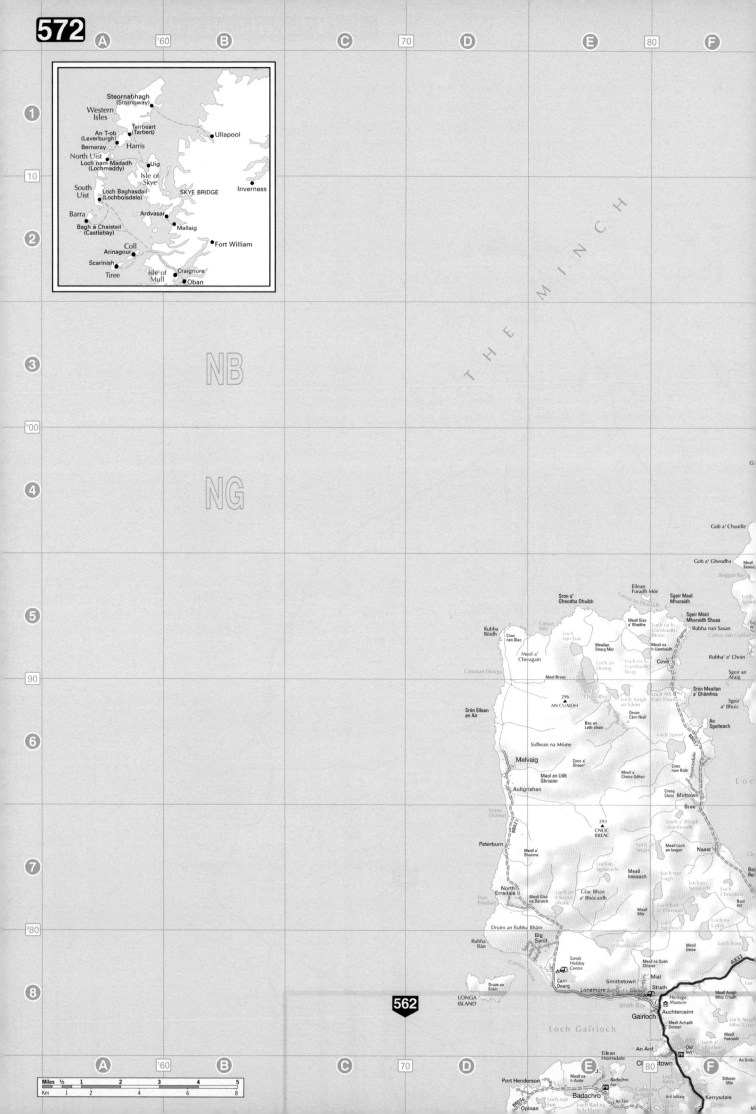

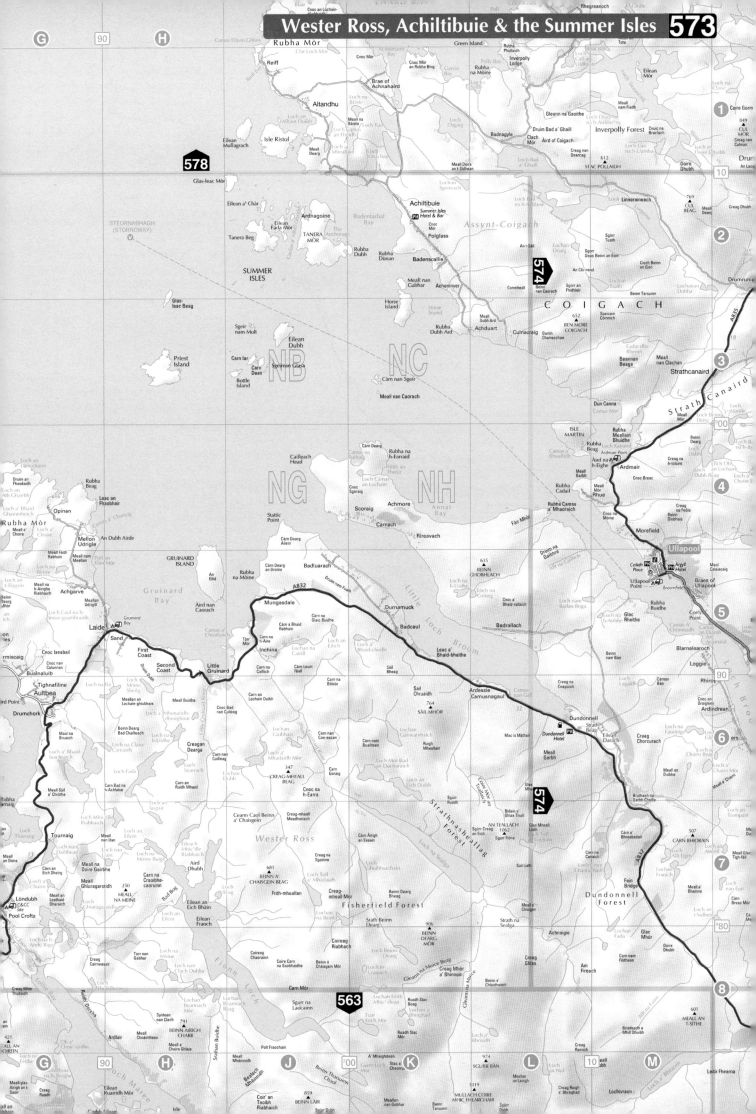

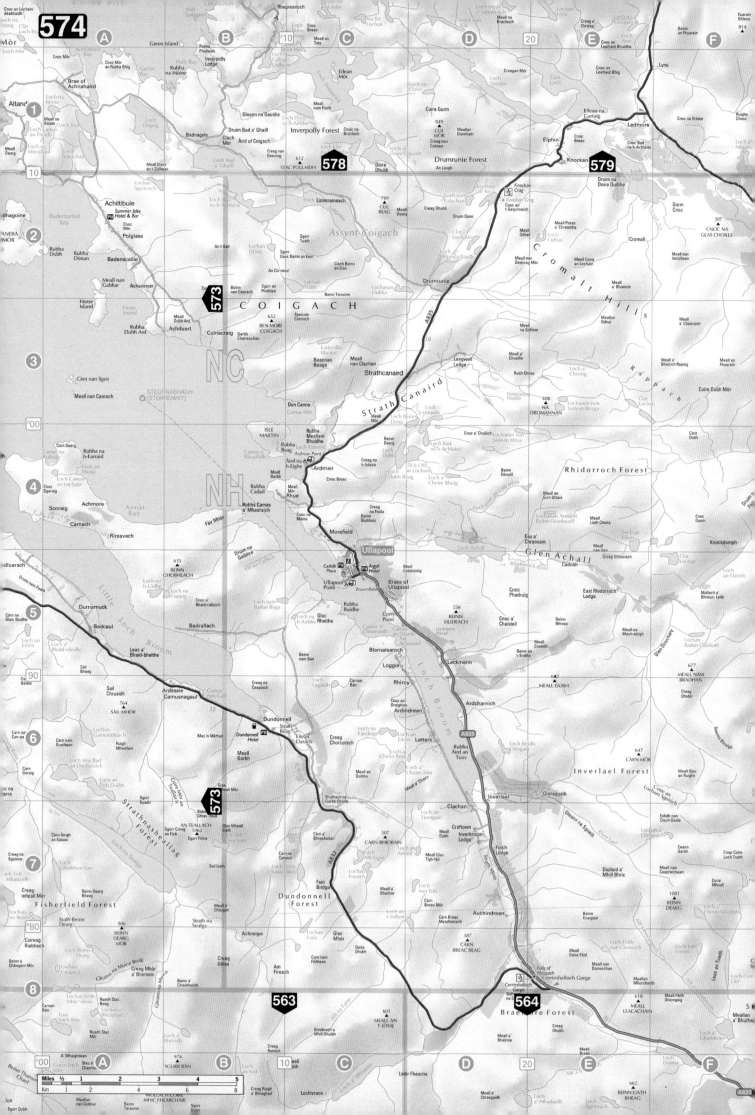

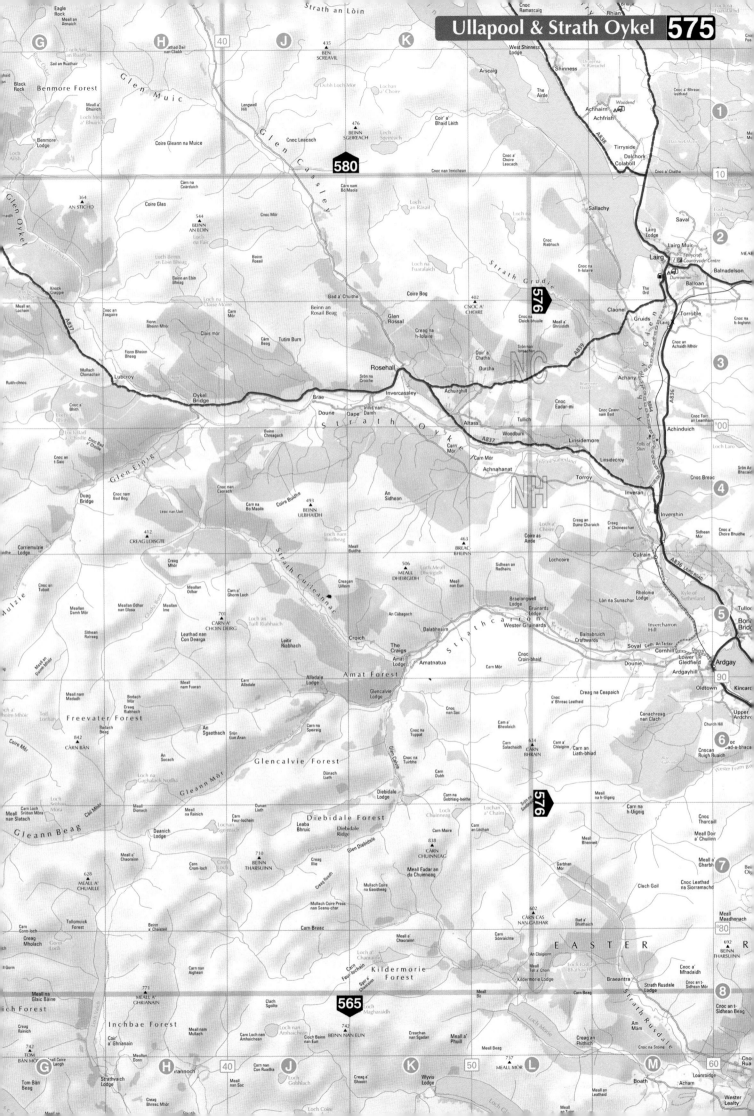

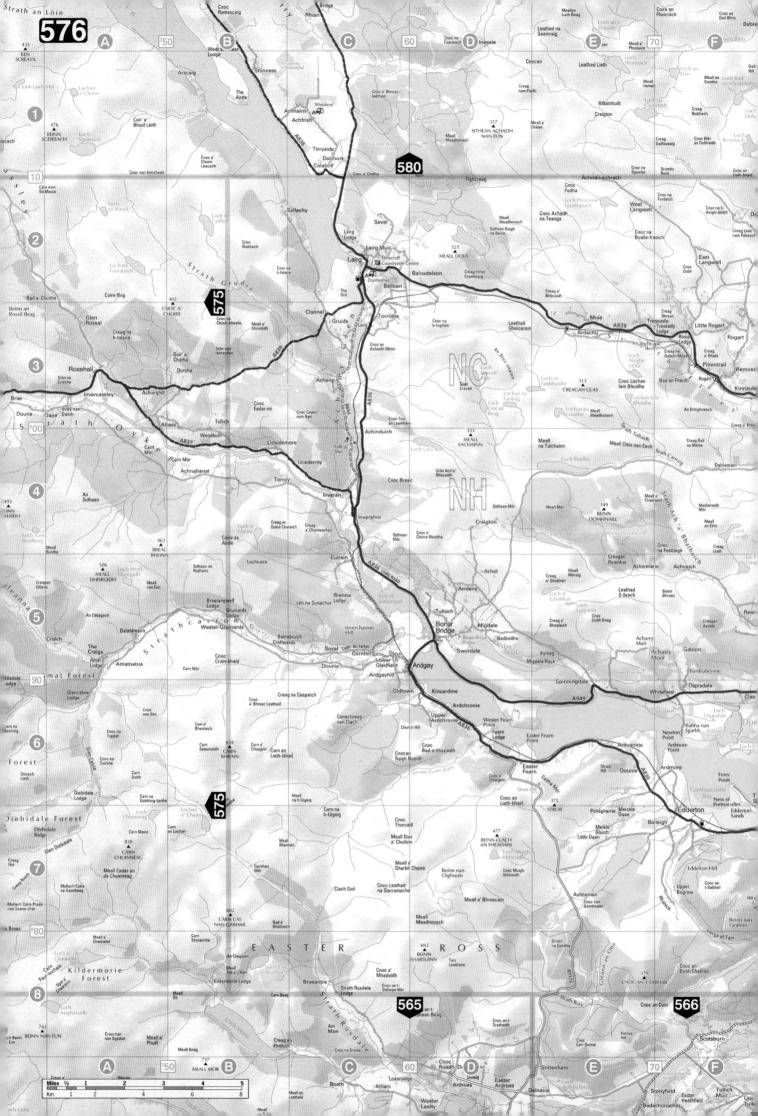

581

582

567

NC

ND

NH

NJ

Helmsdale
West Helmsdale
Navidale
Gartymore
Portgower
Culgower Hill
Lothmore
Sron Rubha na Gaoithe
Lothbeg
Lothbeg Point
Ballinreach
Creagan Mòr
Asc na Grèine
Achrimsdale
West Clyne
East Clyne
Dalchalm
Socach Hill
Killin Rock
Clynelish Moss
Clynelish
East Brora Muir
North Brora Muir
East Brora
Brora
Budgeon Park
Doll
Uppat
Strathsteven
Backies
Dunrobin Castle
Corn Liath
Golspie
Drummuie
Culmaily
Kirkton
Mound Rock
Silver Rock
Littleferry
Ferry Links
Skelbo
Skelbo Muir
Achavandra Muir
Fourpenny
Coul Links
Poles
Pronсy
Embo
Embo Muir
Heatherwood Park
Grannie's Heilan' Hame
Pitgrudy
Embo Street
Camore
Dornoch
Little Town
Historylinks
Dornoch Links
Lonemore
Royal Dornoch
Dornoch Point
Dornoch Sands
Cuthill Sands
Tarbat Ness
Port Buckie
Port Mòr
Wilkhaven Muir
Wilkhaven
Hilton
Port Uilleim
Bindal Muir
Bindal
Portmahomack
Balnabruach
Rockfield
Rockfield Mills
Inver Bay
Skinnerton
Inver
Gallow Hill
Lower Arboll
Tarrel
Creag Mhaol
Morrich More
Cnocan Mealbhain
Innis Mhòr
Whiteness Sands
Morangie
Glenmorangie Distillery
Moss Rd
Tain
Hilton
Hunting Hill
Miller's Place
Lochslin
Wester Arboll
Toulvaddie
Lower Pitkerrie
Balchery
Loandhu
Bogbain
Rhynie
Balaldie
Balmuchy
Lower Balaldie
Glen Aldie
Newfield
Logie Hill
Fearn
Clay of Allan
Fearn
Hilton of Cadboll Chapel (ruin)
Loans of Tullich
Hilton of Cadboll
Brenachie
Pitmaduthy
Shandwick
Kildary
Arabella
Cullisse
Shandwick
Balintore
Shandwick Mains
Ankerville
Chapelhill
Strath of Pitcalnie
Port an Righ

Strath Brora
Loch Fleet
Dornoch Firth
Loch Eye
BEN HORN
BEN LUNNDAIDH
BEN BHRAGGIE
CAGAR FEOSAIG
COL-BHEINN
Glen Sletdale
Glen Loth
Strath Brora
Meall na h-Amaite
Amat

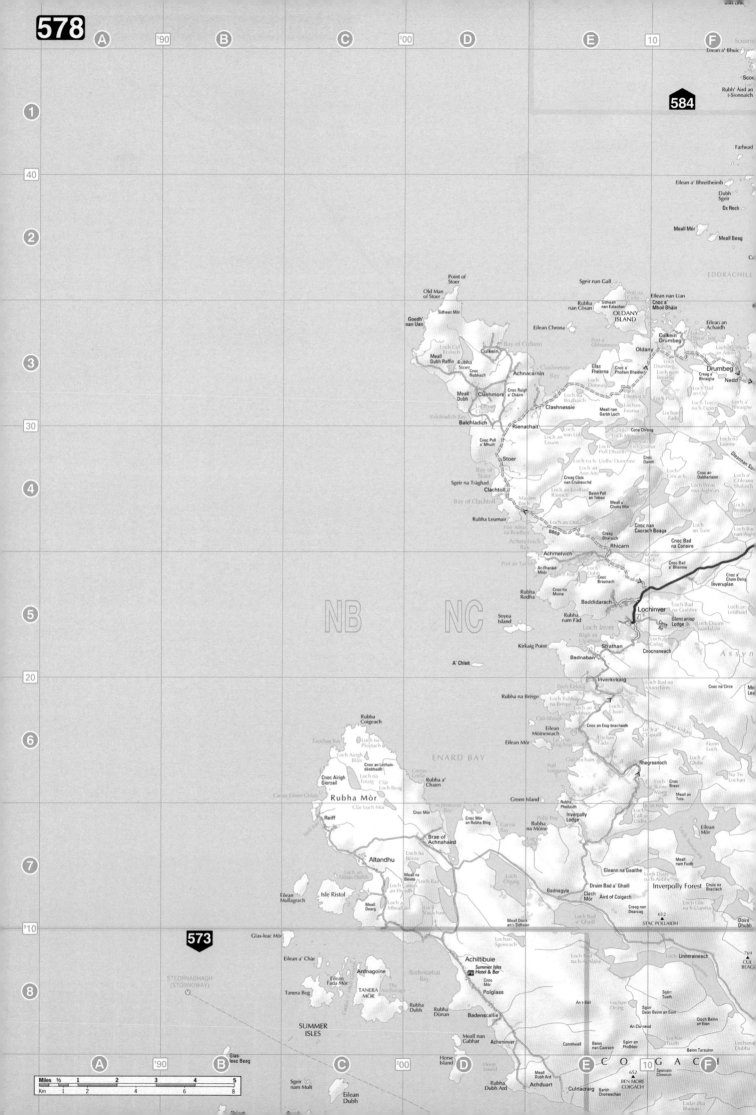

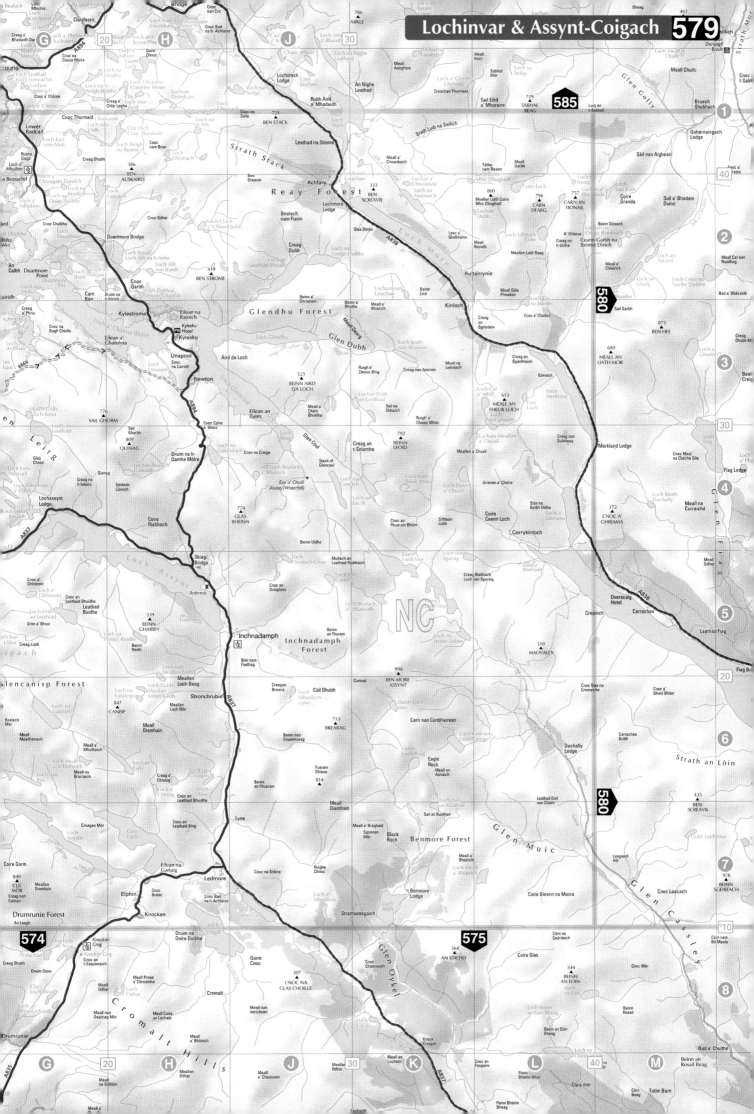

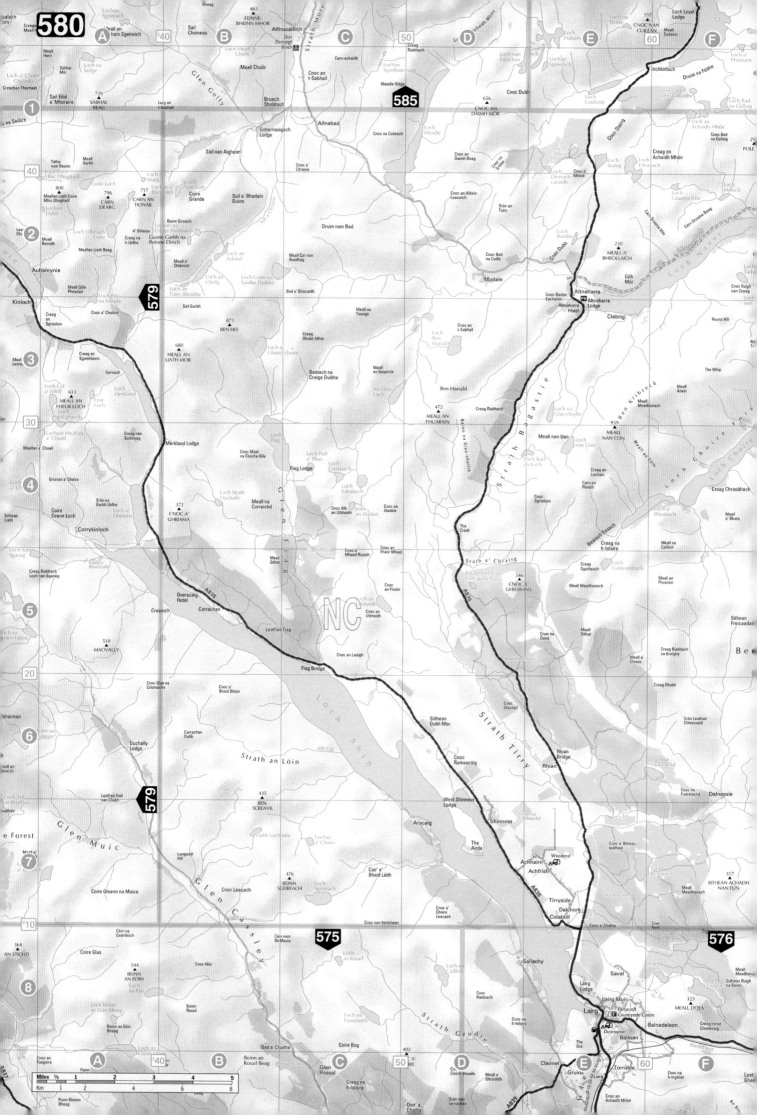

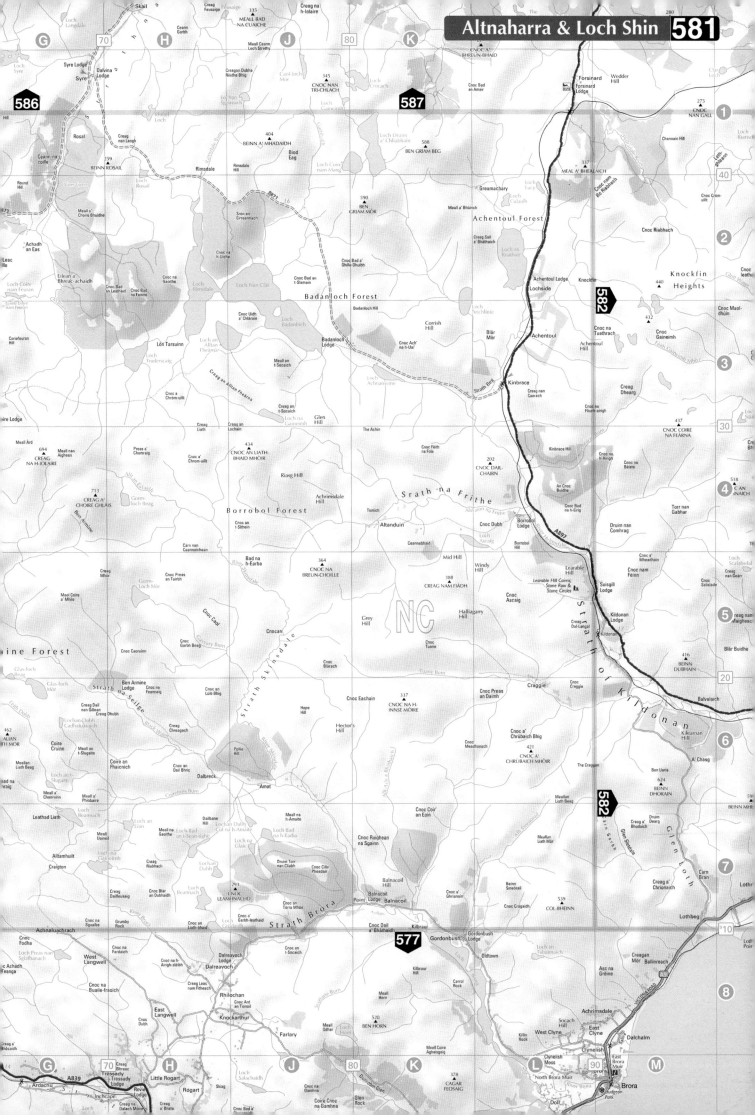

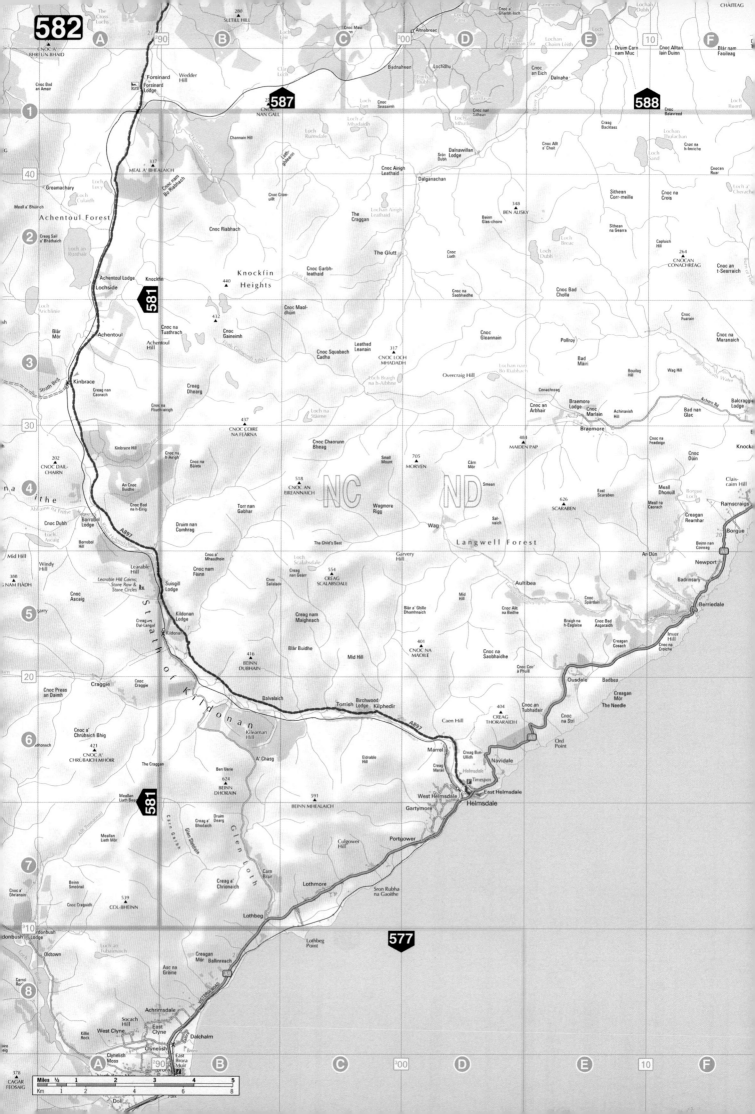

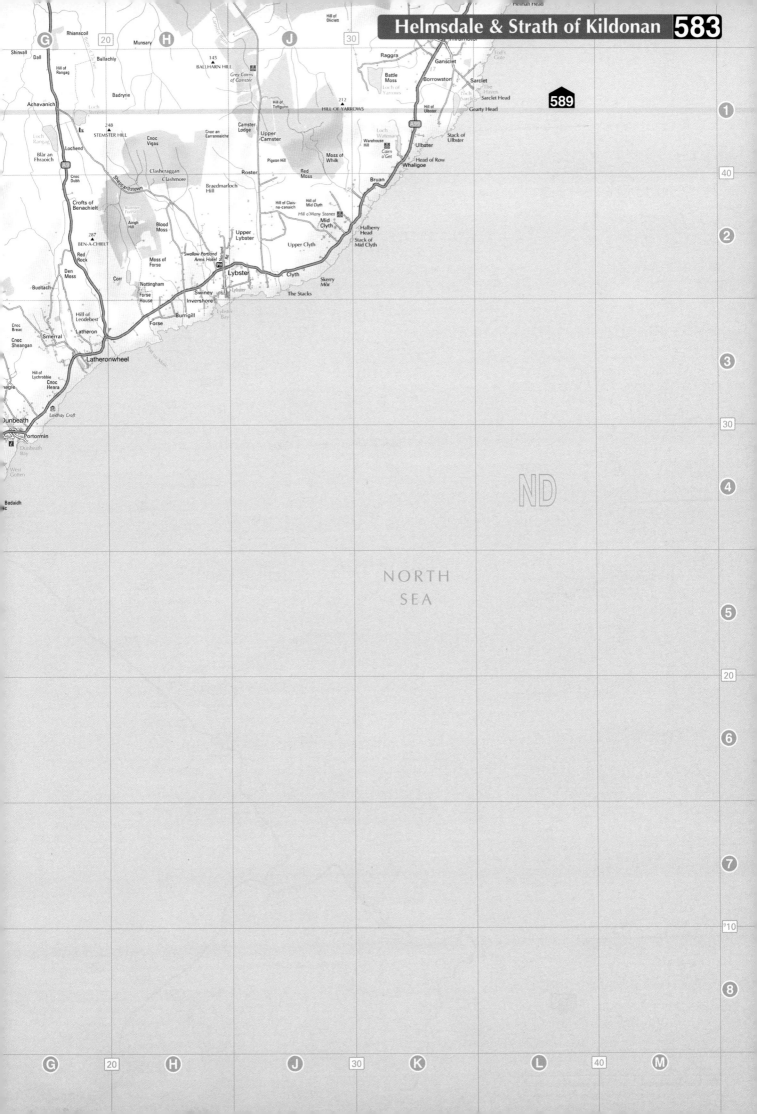

Helman Head

G · Rhianacoil · 20 · Munsary · H · J · 30 · Hill of Oliclett · Thrumster

Dall
Shinvall
Hill of Rangag
Ballachly
145
BALLHARN HILL
Grey Cairns of Camster
Raggra
Gansclet
7
Yod's Gate
Battle Moss
Borrowston
Sarclet
Loch of Yarrows
Badryrie
The Haven
Achavanich
248
STEMSTER HILL
Cnoc an Earrannaiche
Hill of Toftgunn
HILL OF YARROWS
Hill of Ulbster
Sarclet Head
Gearty Head
Loch Stemster
Camster Lodge
Warehouse Hill
Loch Watenan
589
Loch Rangag
Cnoc Vigas
Upper Camster
Cairn o'Get
Stack of Ulbster
Blàr an Fhraoich
Lochend
212
Ulbster
A9
Cnoc Dubh
Clashcraggan
Roster
Red Moss
Moss of Whilk
Head of Row
Whaligoe
Crofts of Benachielt
Clashmore
Braedmarloch Hill
Pigeon Hill
Bruan
Airigh Hill
287
BEN-A-CHIELT
Blood Moss
Hill of Clais-na-canaich
Hill of Mid Clyth
Mid Clyth
Halberry Head
Red Rock
Upper Lybster
Hill o'Many Stanes
Stack of Mid Clyth
Den Moss
Moss of Forse
Upper Clyth
Buoltach
Swallow Portland Arms Hotel
PH
Corr
Nottingham
Lybster
Clyth
Forse House
Swiney
Skerry Mòr
Hill of Leodebest
Invershore
Lybster
Burrigill
Forse
Lybster Bay
The Stacks
Cnoc Breac
Smerral
Latheron
Cnoc Sheangan
Latheronwheel
Hill of Lychrobbie
Cnoc Heara
Dunbeath
Portormin
Leidhay Croft
Dunbeath Bay
West Gotten
Badaidh
sc

ND

**NORTH
SEA**

G · 20 · H · J · 30 · K · L · 40 · M

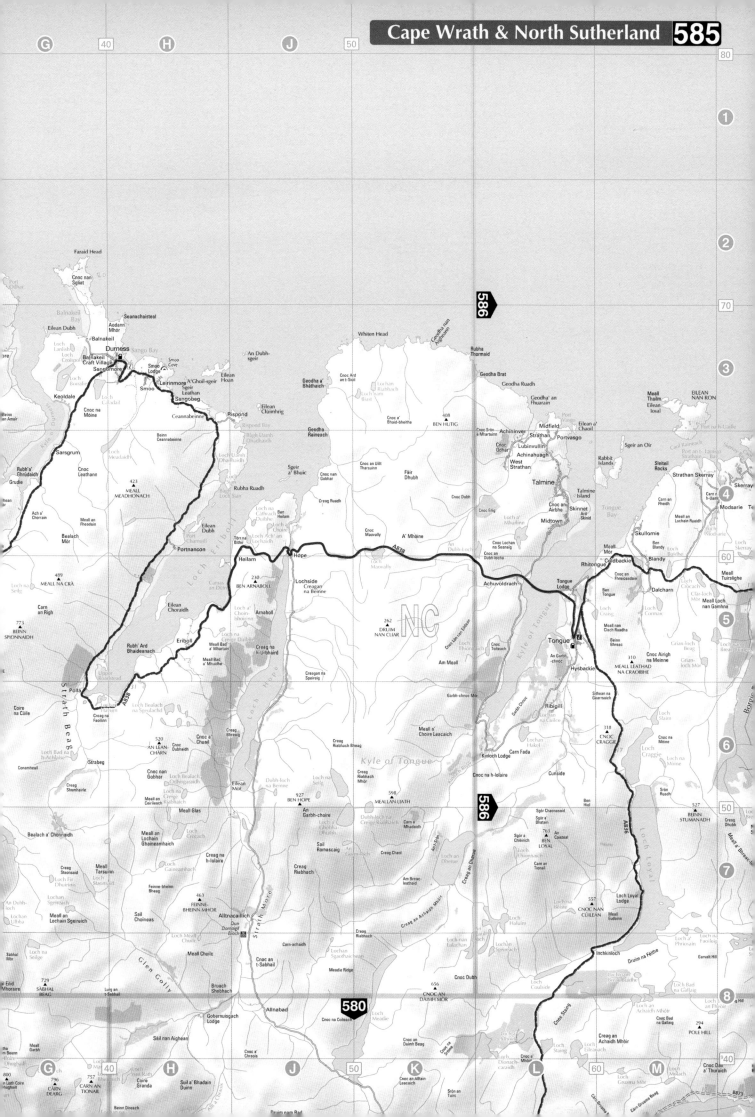

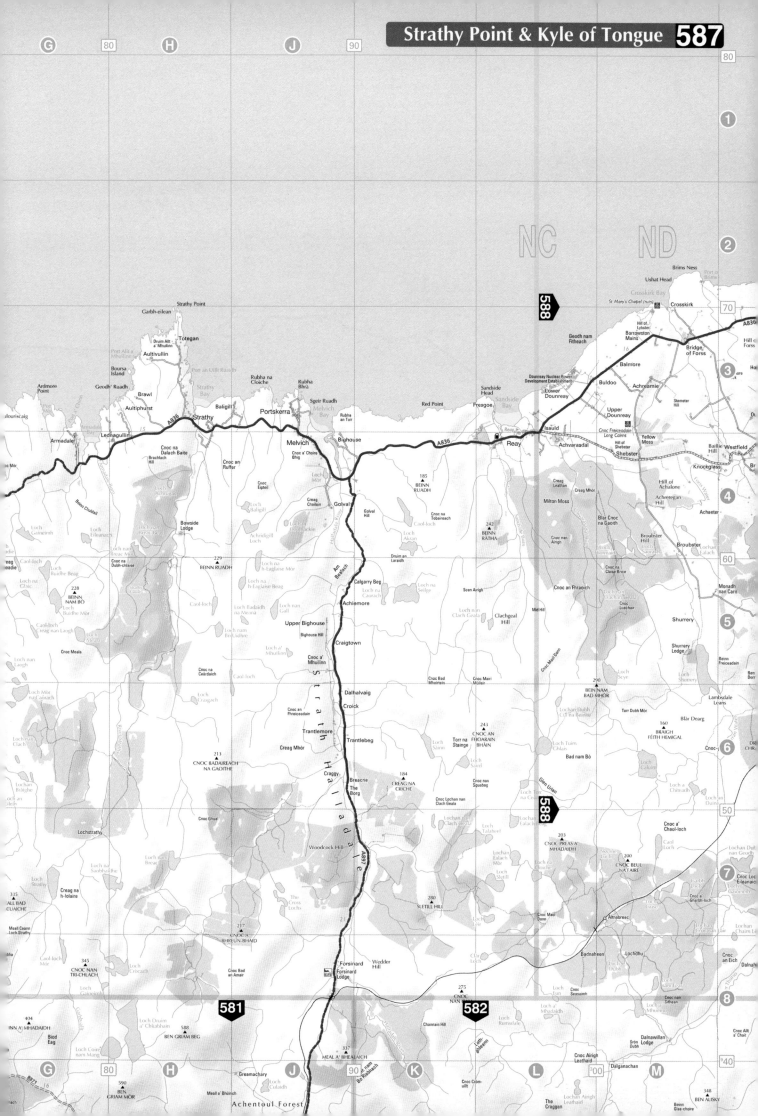

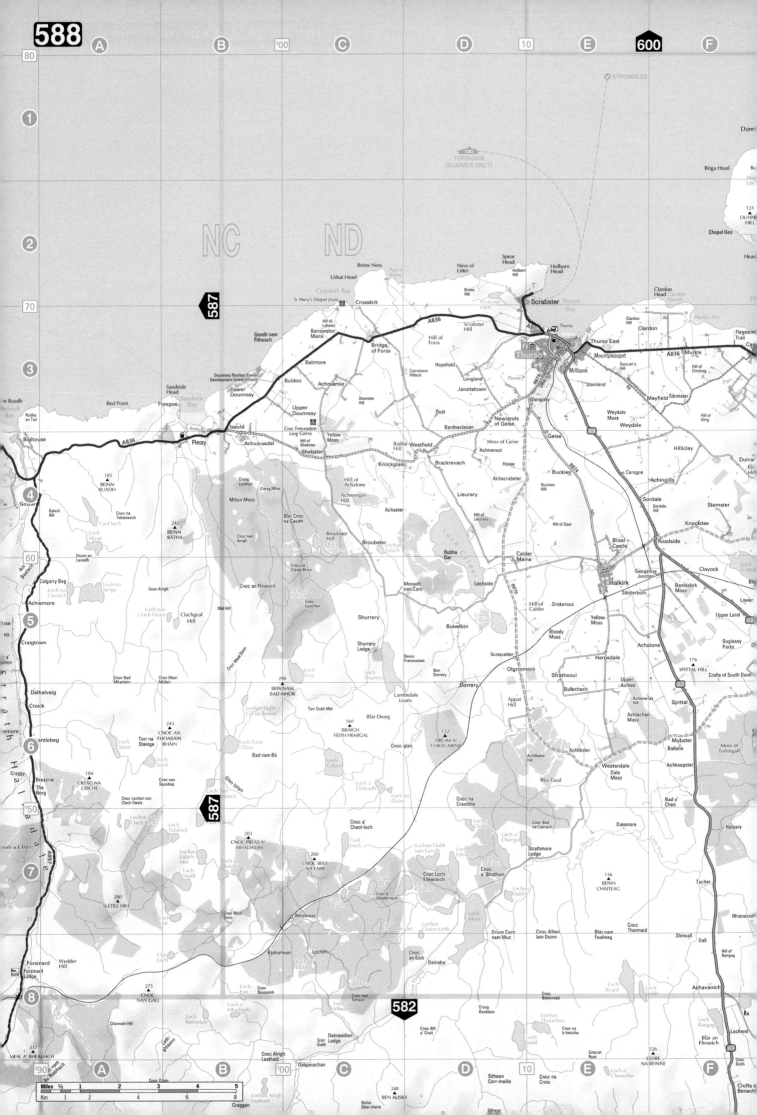

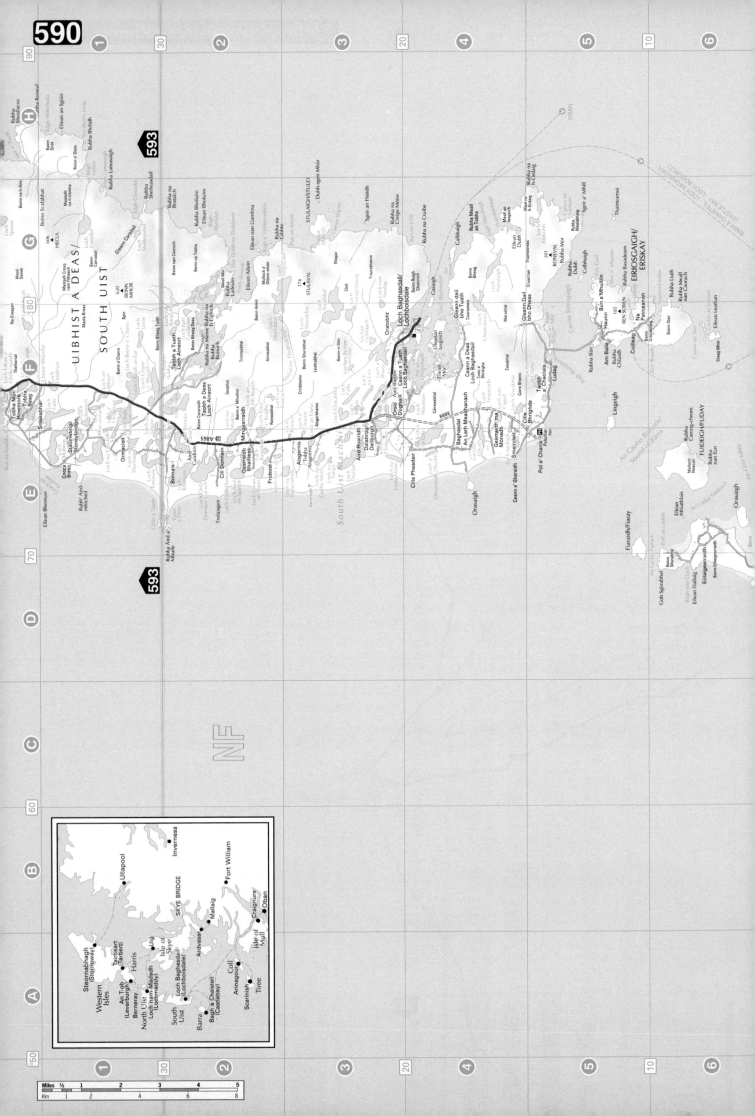

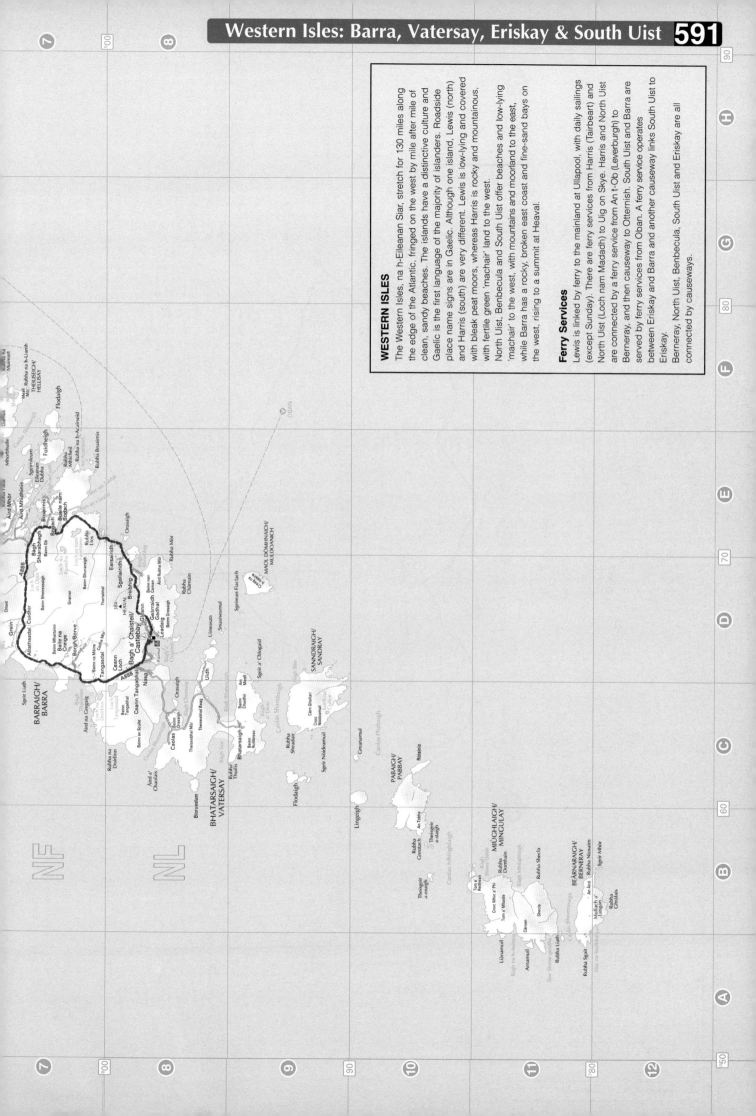

WESTERN ISLES

The Western Isles, na h-Eileanan Siar, stretch for 130 miles along the edge of the Atlantic, fringed on the west by mile after mile of clean, sandy beaches. The islands have a distinctive culture and Gaelic is the first language of the majority of islanders. Roadside place name signs are in Gaelic. Although one island, Lewis (north) and Harris (south) are very different. Lewis is low-lying and covered with bleak peat moors, whereas Harris is rocky and mountainous, with fertile green 'machair' land to the west. North Uist, Benbecula and South Uist offer beaches and low-lying 'machair' to the west, with mountains and moorland to the east, while Barra has a rocky, broken east coast and fine-sand bays on the west, rising to a summit at Heaval.

Ferry Services

Lewis is linked by ferry to the mainland at Ullapool, with daily sailings (except Sunday). There are ferry services from Harris (Tairbeart) and North Uist (Loch nam Madadh) to Uig on Skye. Harris and North Uist are connected by a ferry service from An t-Ob (Leverburgh) to Berneray, and then causeway to Otternish. South Uist and Barra are served by ferry services from Oban. A ferry service operates between Eriskay and Barra and another causeway links South Uist to Eriskay.

Berneray, North Uist, Benbecula, South Uist and Eriskay are all connected by causeways.

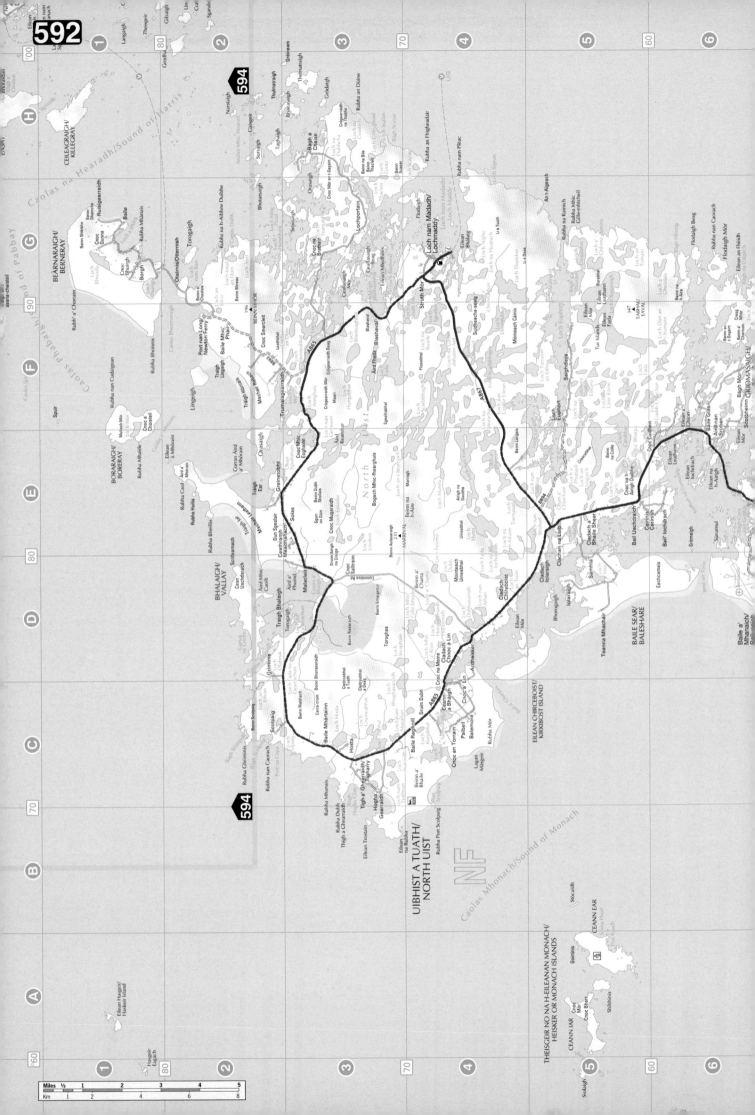

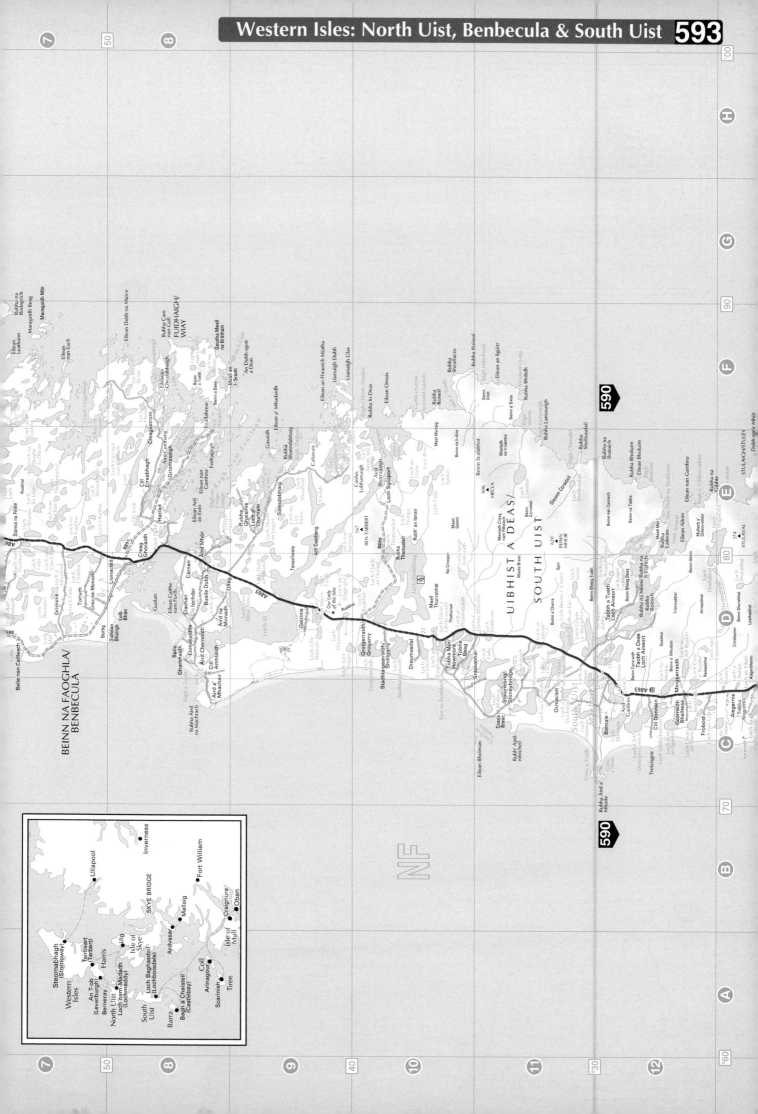

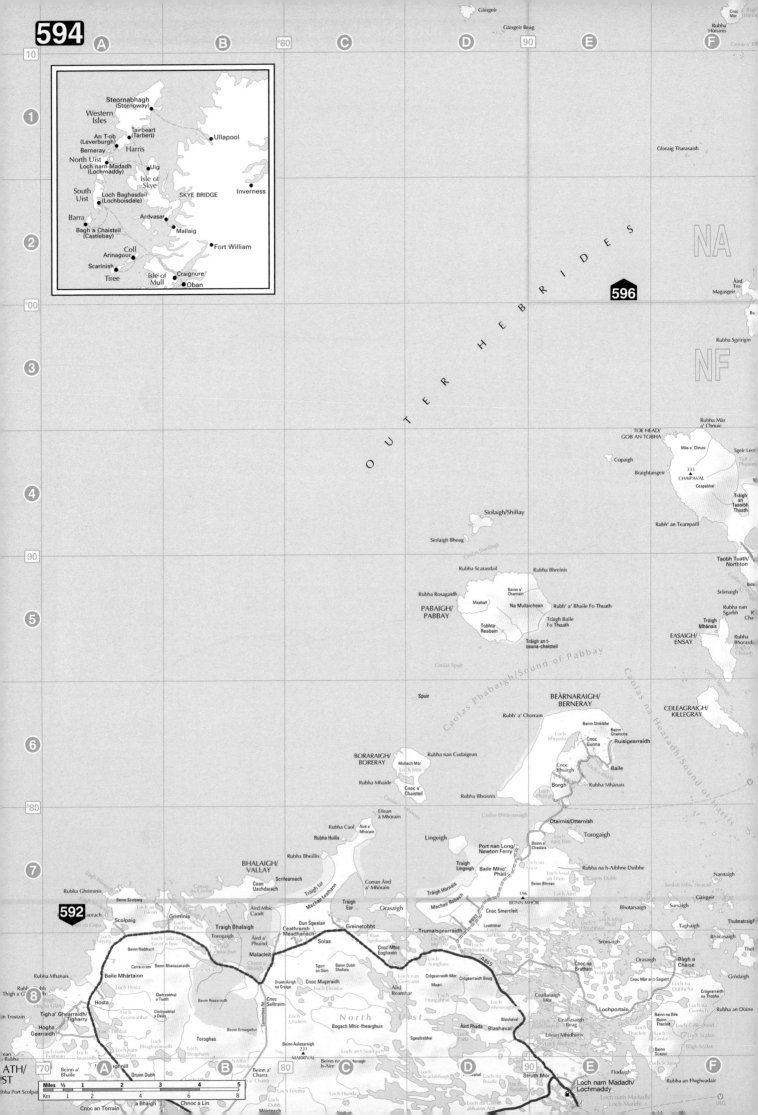

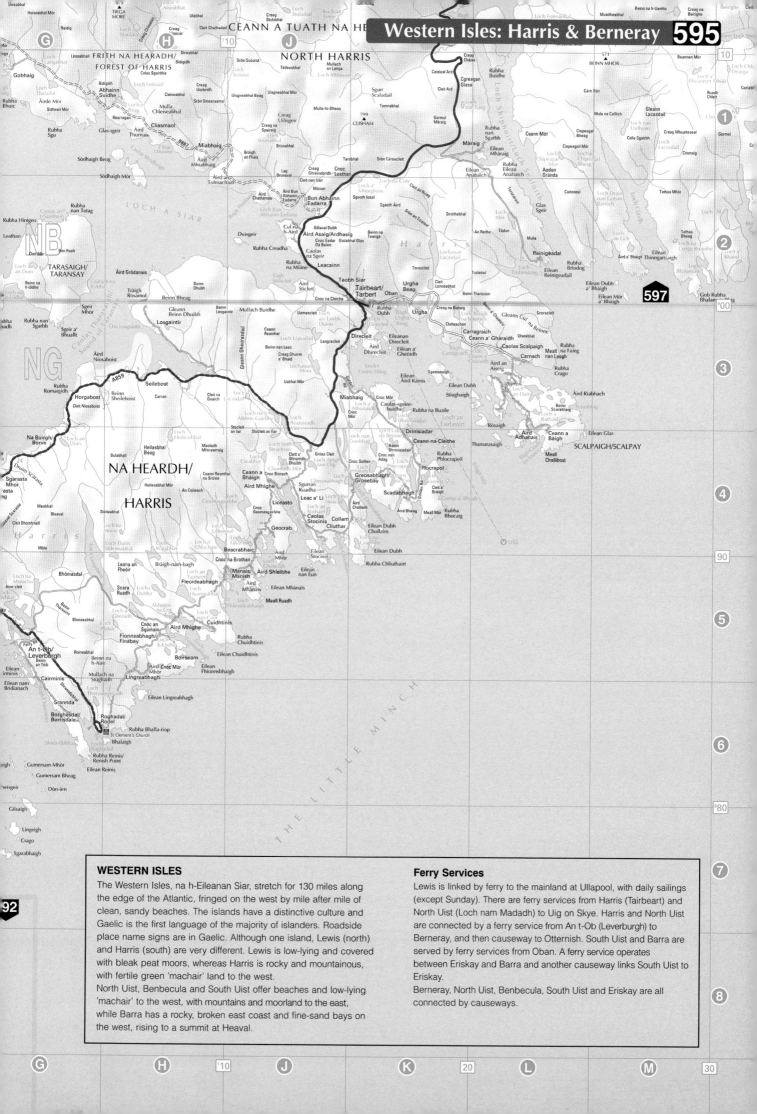

WESTERN ISLES

The Western Isles, na h-Eileanan Siar, stretch for 130 miles along the edge of the Atlantic, fringed on the west by mile after mile of clean, sandy beaches. The islands have a distinctive culture and Gaelic is the first language of the majority of islanders. Roadside place name signs are in Gaelic. Although one island, Lewis (north) and Harris (south) are very different. Lewis is low-lying and covered with bleak peat moors, whereas Harris is rocky and mountainous, with fertile green 'machair' land to the west.

North Uist, Benbecula and South Uist offer beaches and low-lying 'machair' to the west, with mountains and moorland to the east, while Barra has a rocky, broken east coast and fine-sand bays on the west, rising to a summit at Heaval.

Ferry Services

Lewis is linked by ferry to the mainland at Ullapool, with daily sailings (except Sunday). There are ferry services from Harris (Tairbeart) and North Uist (Loch nam Madadh) to Uig on Skye. Harris and North Uist are connected by a ferry service from An t-Ob (Leverburgh) to Berneray, and then causeway to Otternish. South Uist and Barra are served by ferry services from Oban. A ferry service operates between Eriskay and Barra and another causeway links South Uist to Eriskay.

Berneray, North Uist, Benbecula, South Uist and Eriskay are all connected by causeways.

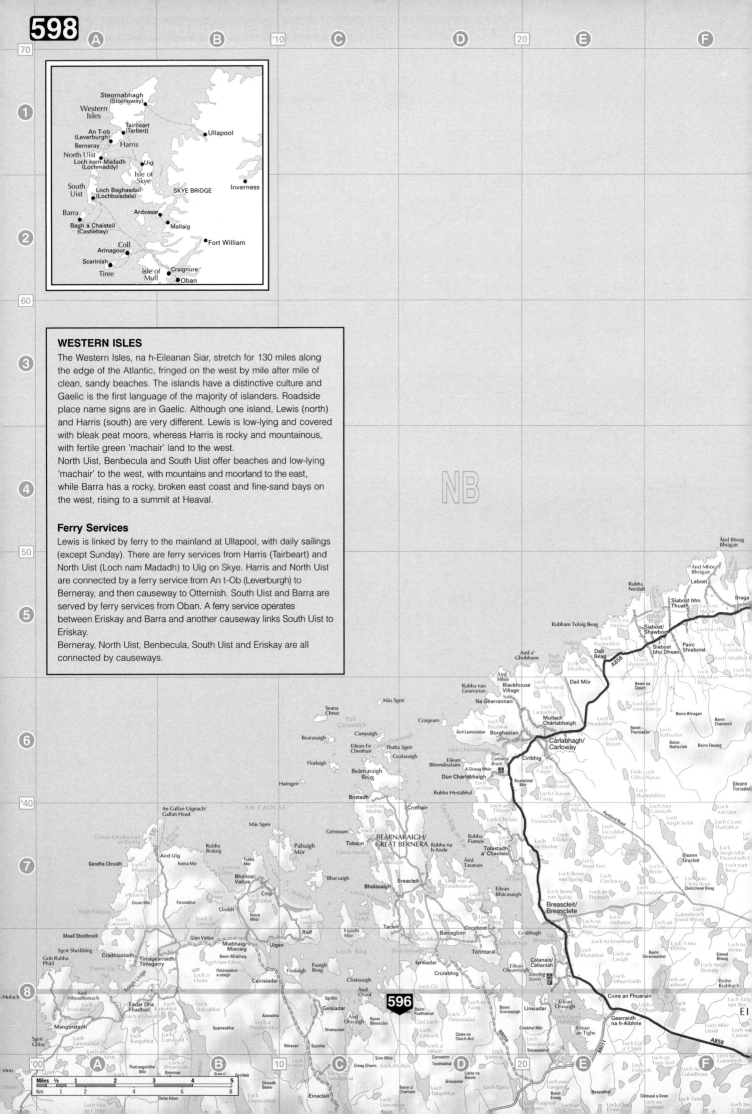

WESTERN ISLES

The Western Isles, na h-Eileanan Siar, stretch for 130 miles along the edge of the Atlantic, fringed on the west by mile after mile of clean, sandy beaches. The islands have a distinctive culture and Gaelic is the first language of the majority of islanders. Roadside place name signs are in Gaelic. Although one island, Lewis (north) and Harris (south) are very different. Lewis is low-lying and covered with bleak peat moors, whereas Harris is rocky and mountainous, with fertile green 'machair' land to the west.

North Uist, Benbecula and South Uist offer beaches and low-lying 'machair' to the west, with mountains and moorland to the east, while Barra has a rocky, broken east coast and fine-sand bays on the west, rising to a summit at Heaval.

Ferry Services

Lewis is linked by ferry to the mainland at Ullapool, with daily sailings (except Sunday). There are ferry services from Harris (Tairbeart) and North Uist (Loch nam Madadh) to Uig on Skye. Harris and North Uist are connected by a ferry service from An t-Ob (Leverburgh) to Berneray, and then causeway to Otternish. South Uist and Barra are served by ferry services from Oban. A ferry service operates between Eriskay and Barra and another causeway links South Uist to Eriskay.

Berneray, North Uist, Benbecula, South Uist and Eriskay are all connected by causeways.

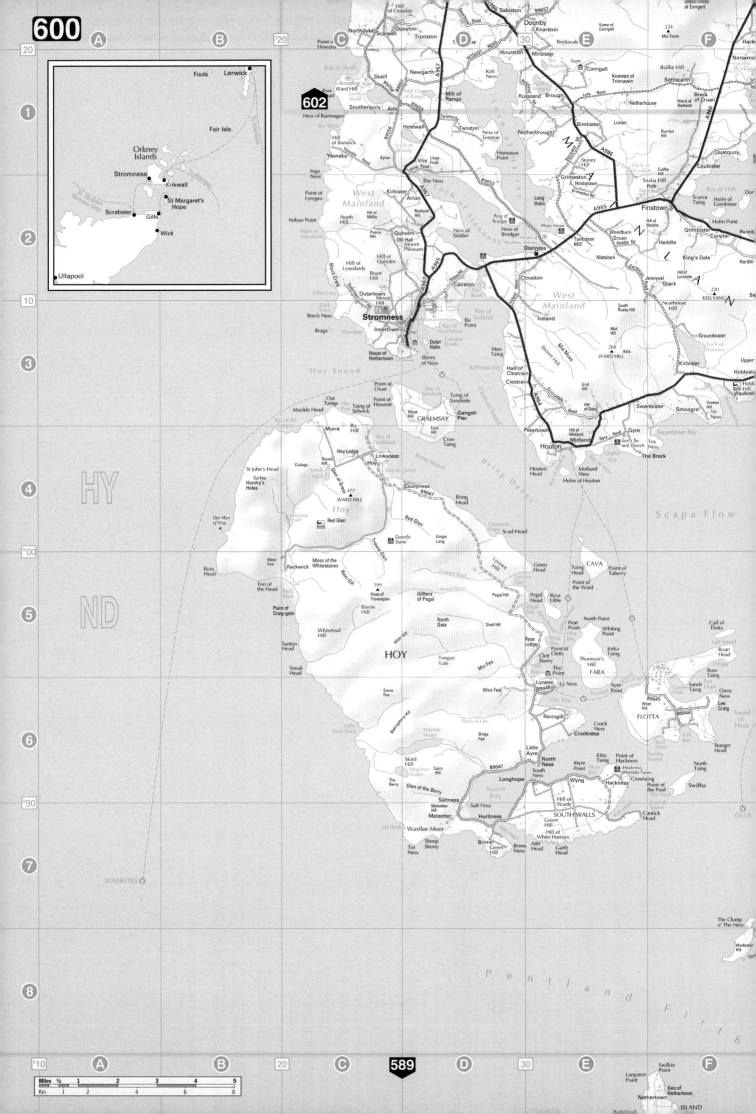

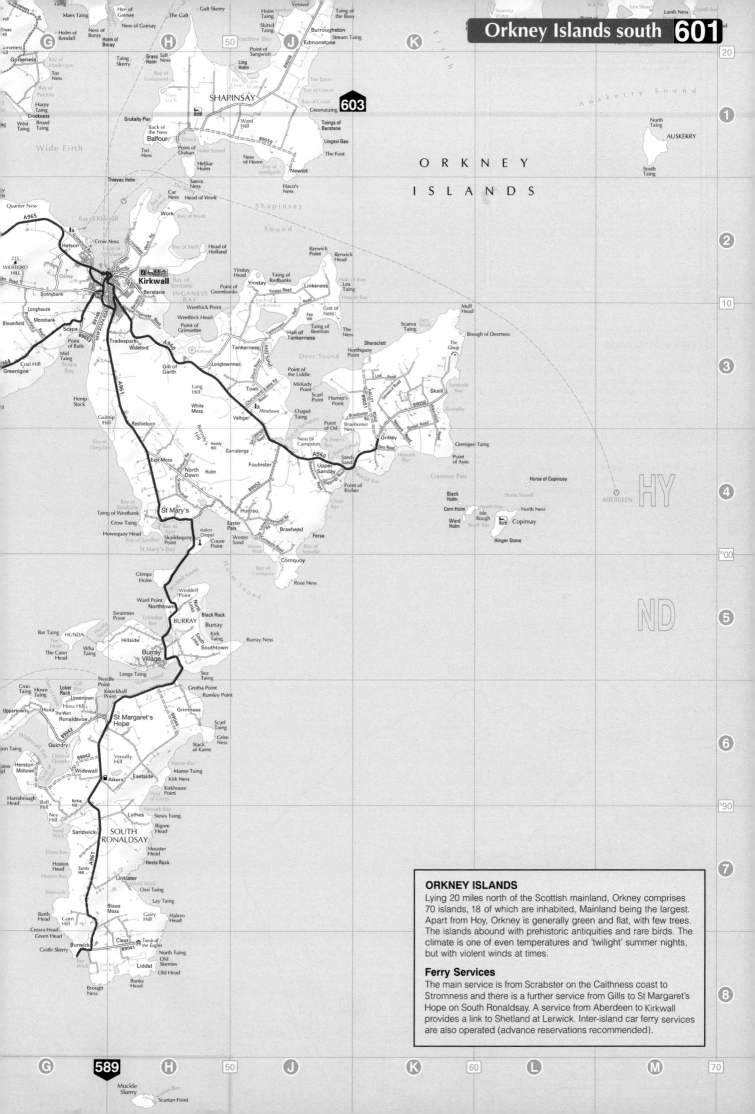

ORKNEY
ISLANDS

ORKNEY ISLANDS

Lying 20 miles north of the Scottish mainland, Orkney comprises 70 islands, 18 of which are inhabited, Mainland being the largest. Apart from Hoy, Orkney is generally green and flat, with few trees. The islands abound with prehistoric antiquities and rare birds. The climate is one of even temperatures and 'twilight' summer nights, but with violent winds at times.

Ferry Services

The main service is from Scrabster on the Caithness coast to Stromness and there is a further service from Gills to St Margaret's Hope on South Ronaldsay. A service from Aberdeen to Kirkwall provides a link to Shetland at Lerwick. Inter-island car ferry services are also operated (advance reservations recommended).

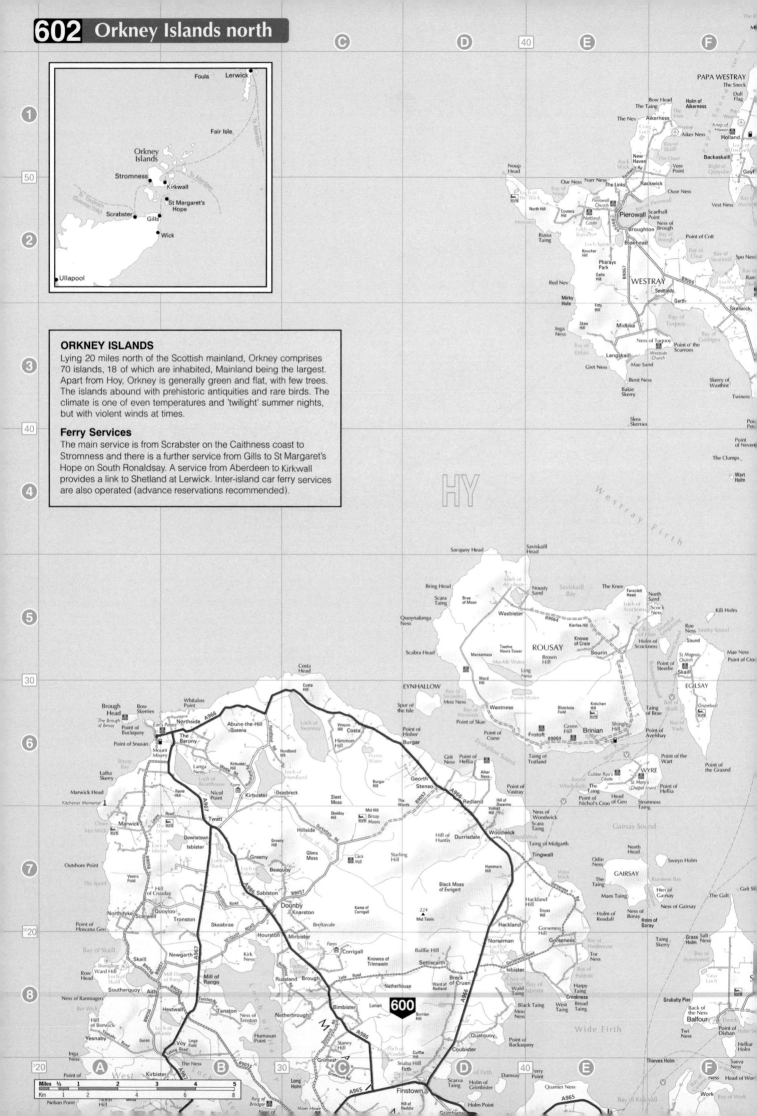

ORKNEY ISLANDS

Lying 20 miles north of the Scottish mainland, Orkney comprises 70 islands, 18 of which are inhabited, Mainland being the largest. Apart from Hoy, Orkney is generally green and flat, with few trees. The islands abound with prehistoric antiquities and rare birds. The climate is one of even temperatures and 'twilight' summer nights, but with violent winds at times.

Ferry Services

The main service is from Scrabster on the Caithness coast to Stromness and there is a further service from Gills to St Margaret's Hope on South Ronaldsay. A service from Aberdeen to Kirkwall provides a link to Shetland at Lerwick. Inter-island car ferry services are also operated (advance reservations recommended).

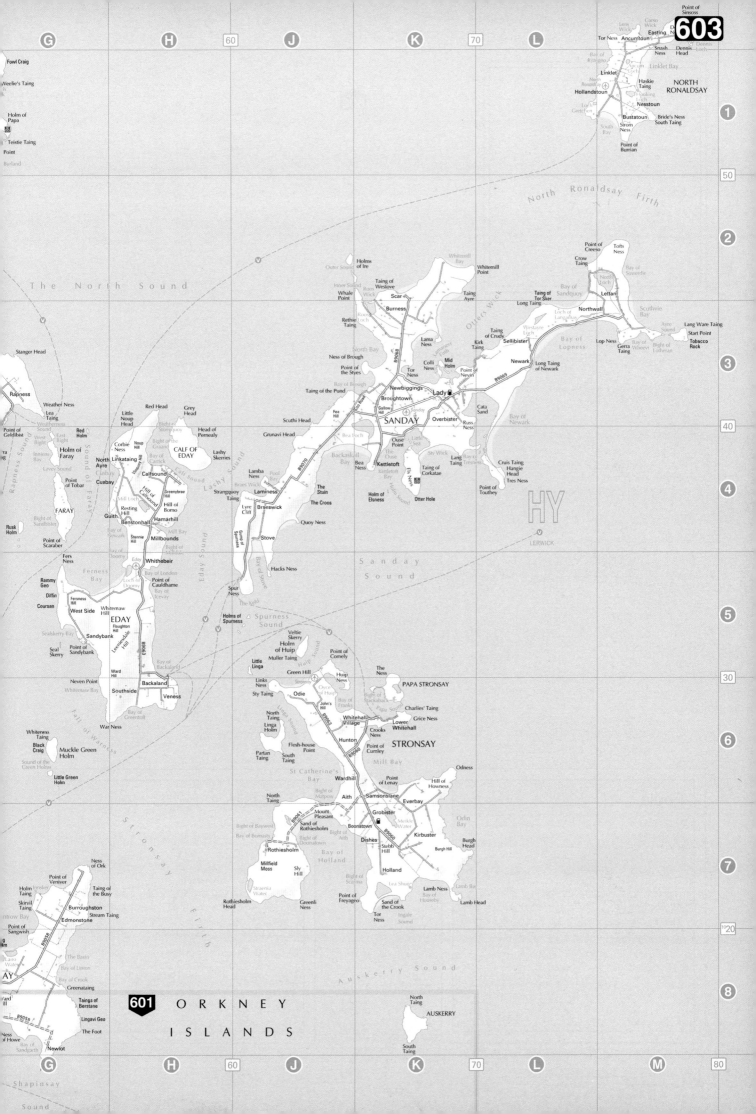

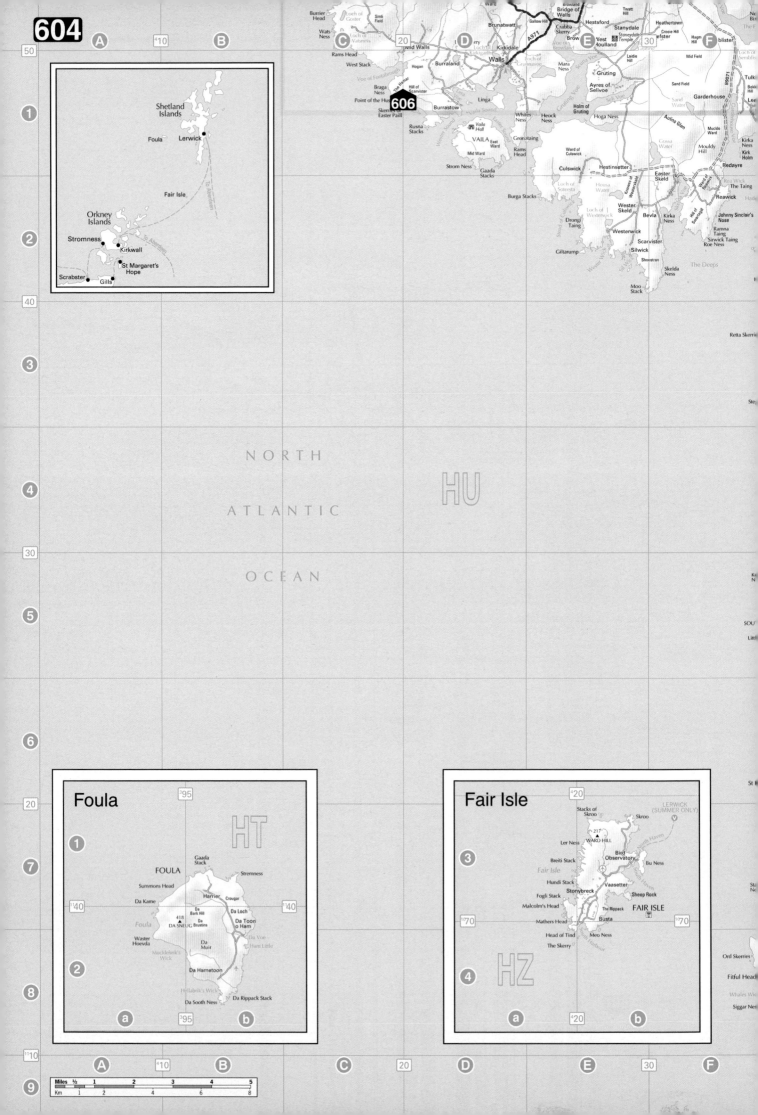

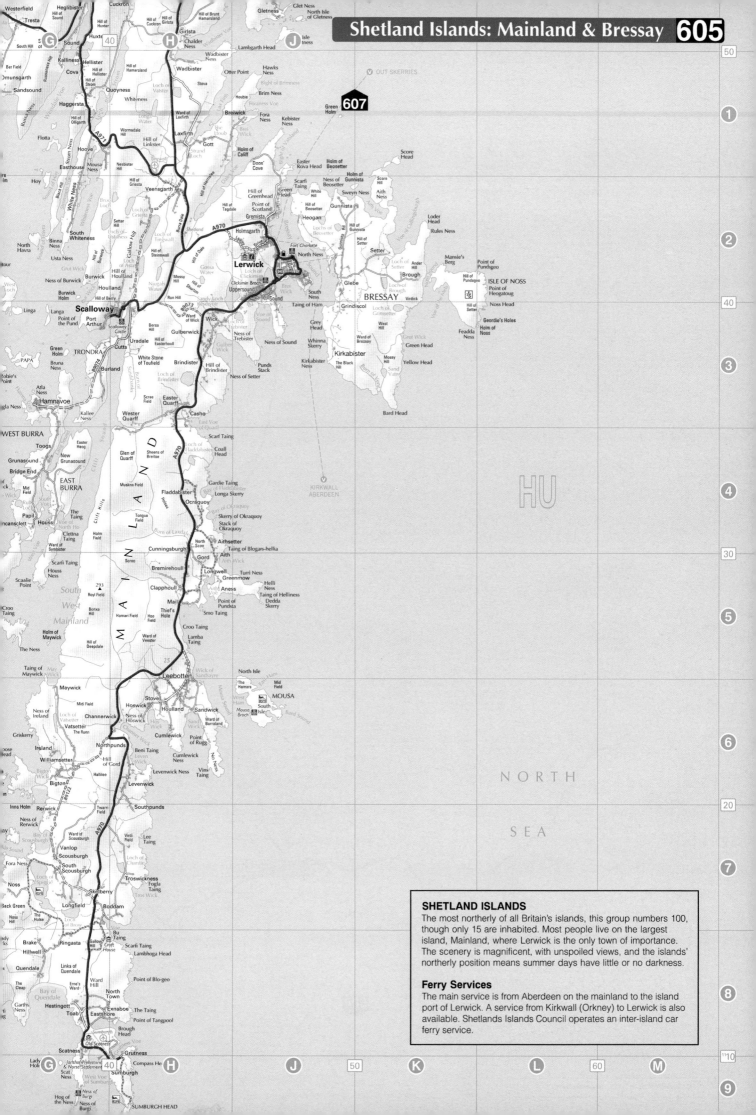

607

HU

N O R T H

S E A

SHETLAND ISLANDS

The most northerly of all Britain's islands, this group numbers 100, though only 15 are inhabited. Most people live on the largest island, Mainland, where Lerwick is the only town of importance. The scenery is magnificent, with unspoiled views, and the islands' northerly position means summer days have little or no darkness.

Ferry Services

The main service is from Aberdeen on the mainland to the island port of Lerwick. A service from Kirkwall (Orkney) to Lerwick is also available. Shetlands Islands Council operates an inter-island car ferry service.

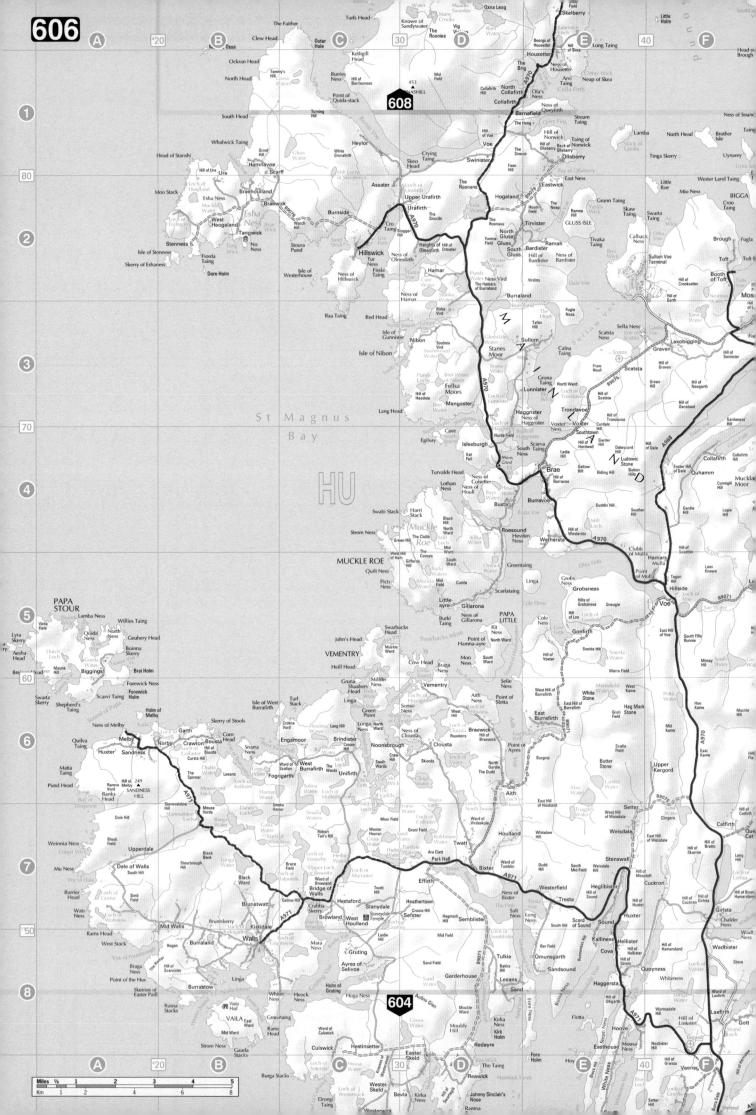

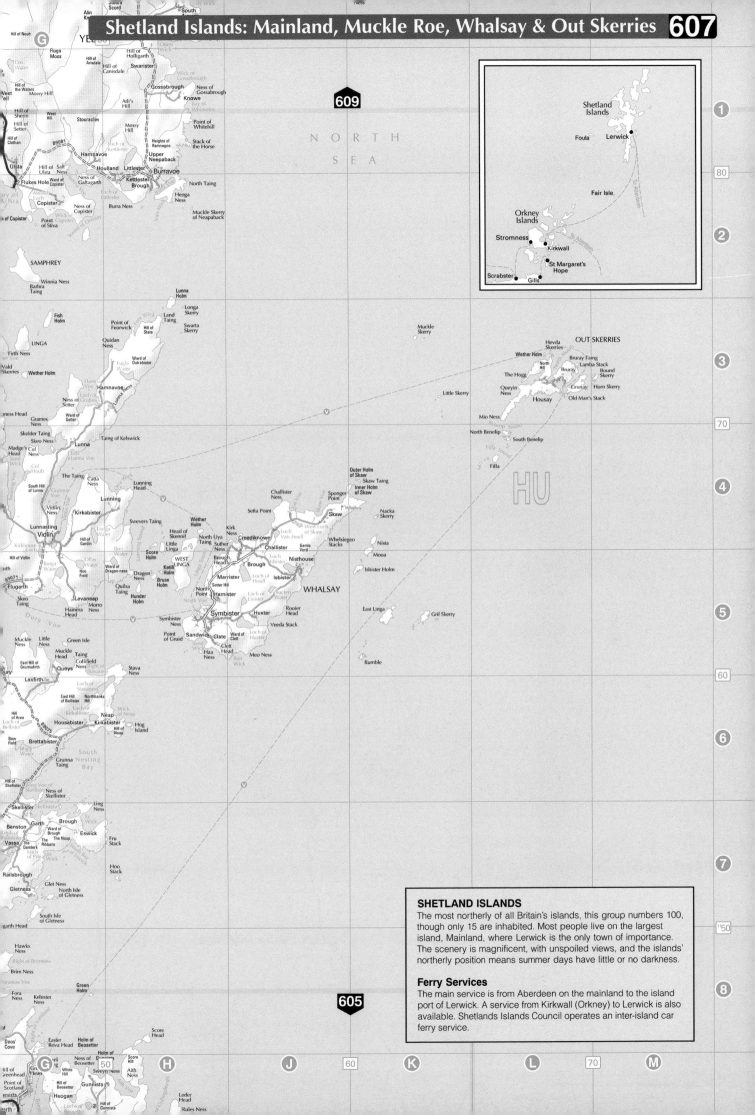

G YELL
Alin Knowe
Hill of Noub
Fluga Moss
Hill of Arisdale
Hill of Holligarth
South Aywick

Cro Water
Hill of the Waters
Mossy Hill
West Fell
Hill of Canisdale
Swarister
Otters Wick
Wick of Gossabrough

West Hill
Hill of Sherin
Gossabrough
Knowe
Ness of Gossabrough
Point of Whitehill

Hill of Setter
Stouraclev
Mossy Hill
Heights of Rannageo
Upper Neepaback
Stack of the Horse

Hill of Clothan
B9081
Loch of Kettlester
609

Harnavoe
Houlland
Littlester
Burravoe

Ulsta
Hill of Ulsta
Salt Ness
Ward of Copister
Kettlester Brough

Flukes Hole
Ness of Galtagarth
North Taing

Bay of Ulsta
Copister
Ness of Copister
Heoga Ness

Point of Stiva
Burra Ness
Muckle Skerry of Neapaback

of Copister

NORTH SEA

SAMPHREY

Winnia Ness
Barbra Taing

Muckle Skerry

Fish Holm
Lunna Holm
OUT SKERRIES

Point of Feorwick
Longa Skerry
Hevda Skerries
Bruray Taing

LINGA
Quidan Ness
Hill of State
Land Taing
Wether Holm
North Hill
Lamba Stack
Bound Skerry

Firth Ness
Ward of Outrabister
Swarta Skerry
The Hogg
Bruray
Grunay
Horn Skerry

Wald Skerries
Wether Holm
Fugla Water
Little Skerry
Queyin Ness
Housay
Old Man's Stack

Hamnavoe
Ness of Gruiwick
Lunna Ness
Mio Ness

Ness of Setter
Ward of Setter
North Benelip
South Benelip

Ness Head
Grames Ness
Taing of Kelswick
Filla

Skelder Taing
Skeo Ness
Lunning Head
HU

Madge's Head
Sand Wick
Cul Ness
Catta Ness
Outer Holm of Skaw
Skaw Taing

South Hill of Lunna
Grunna Voe
The Taing
Lunning
Inner Holm of Skaw

Vidlin Ness
Kirkabister
Challister Ness
Sponger Point
Skaw
Nacka Skerry

Lunnasting
Vidlin
Hill of Gardin
Swevers Taing
Sefta Point
West Loch of Skaw

Kirkhouse
Loch of Vidlin
Brei Water
Wether Holm
Head of Skennif
Kirk Ness
Creediknowe
Loch Vats-houll
Whelsiegeo Stacks

Hill of Vidlin
Burga Water
Offas Water
Little Linga
North Uya Taing
Suther Ness
Challister
Gamla Vord
Nista

Flugarth
Ward of Dragon-ness
Score Holm
Brough Head
Loch of Huxter
Mooa

B9071
Hoo Field
Dragon Ness
Ketill Holm
Marrister
Brough
Isbister
Nisthouse
Isbister Holm

Skeo Taing
Quilsa Taing
Bruse Holm
Setter Hill
Loch of Houll
WHALSAY

Levaneap
Hunder Holm
North Point
Hamister
Loch of Livister
East Linga
Grif Skerry

Hamera Head
Morro Ness
Symbister
Huxter
Sukkro Water
Rooier Head

Muckle Ness
Little Ness
Green Isle
Symbister Ness
Veeda Stack

Muckle Head
Taing
Point of Gruid
Sandwick
Clate
Ward of Clett
Rumble

East Hill of Grumafirth
Quoys
Collifield Ness
Haa Ness
Clett Head
Meo Ness

Laxfirth
Stava Ness
Brei Wick

Loch of Stavaness

East Hill of Bellister
Northbanks Hill
Wick of Neap

Hill of Area
Loch of Bellister
Neap
Ness of Neap
Hog Island

Housabister
Kirkabister
Hill of Neap

Bow Field
Brettabister
SOUTH NESTING BAY

Grunna Voe

Hill of Skellister
West Voe of Skellister
Ness of Skellister

Skellister
Ling Ness

Benston
Garth
Brough
Es Wick

Vassa
Ward of Brough
Eswick
Fru Stack

The Gamlers
The Noup
The Ribbans

Railsbrough
Glet Ness
North Isle of Gletness
Hoo Stack

Gletness

South Isle of Gletness

garth Head
Hawks Ness

Bight of Brimness

Brim Ness

Voraness Voe

Fora Ness
Kebister Ness
Green Holm
Score Head

Doos' Cove
Easter Rova Ness
Holm of Beosetter
605

Grti Head
Ness of Beosetter
Holm of Beosetter

Point of Scotland
ernista
White Ness
Sweyn Ness
Aith Ness

Gunnista
Heogan

G 50 **H** **J** 60 **K** **L** 70 **M**
Loder Head
Lochs of Gunnista
Rules Ness

Shetland Islands (inset map):
Shetland Islands
Foula
Lerwick
Fair Isle
Orkney Islands
Stromness
Kirkwall
St Margaret's Hope
Scrabster
Gills
To Aberdeen

SHETLAND ISLANDS

The most northerly of all Britain's islands, this group numbers 100, though only 15 are inhabited. Most people live on the largest island, Mainland, where Lerwick is the only town of importance. The scenery is magnificent, with unspoiled views, and the islands' northerly position means summer days have little or no darkness.

Ferry Services

The main service is from Aberdeen on the mainland to the island port of Lerwick. A service from Kirkwall (Orkney) to Lerwick is also available. Shetlands Islands Council operates an inter-island car ferry service.

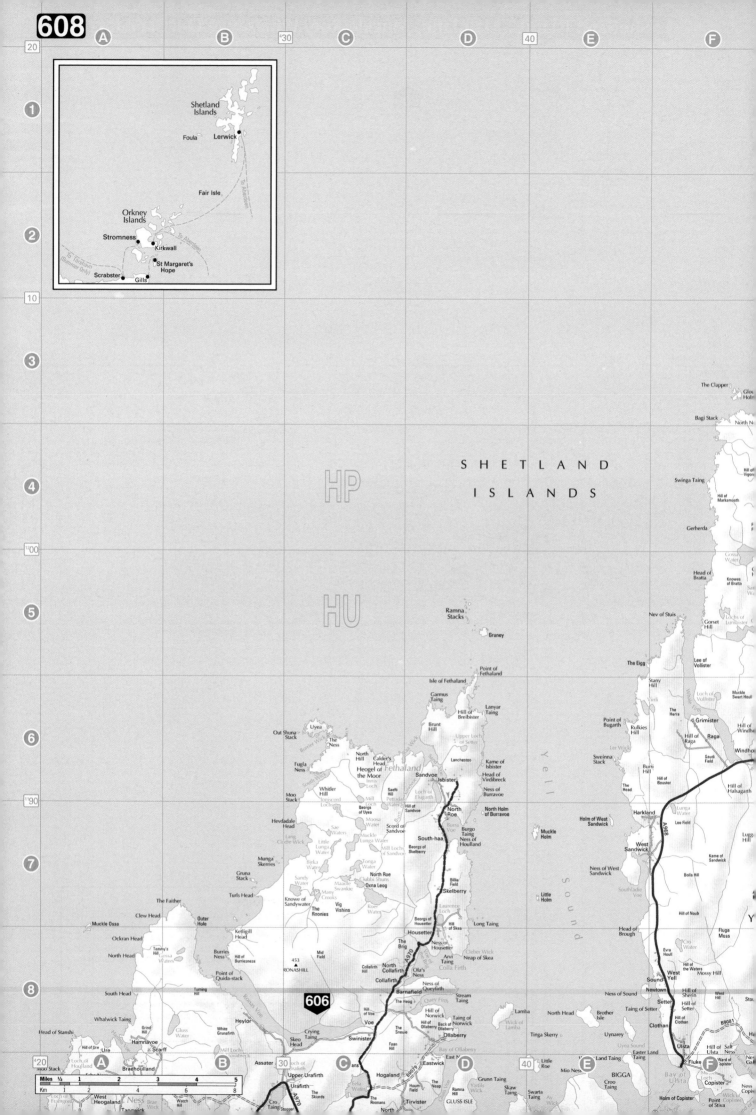

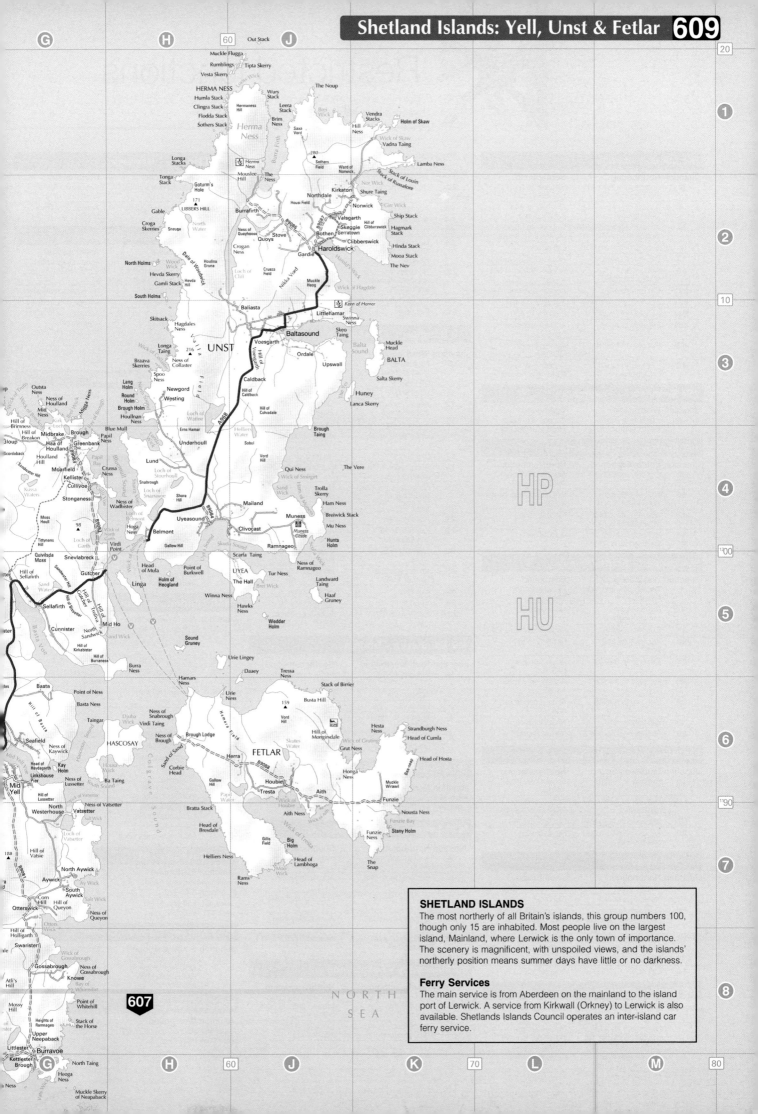

SHETLAND ISLANDS

The most northerly of all Britain's islands, this group numbers 100, though only 15 are inhabited. Most people live on the largest island, Mainland, where Lerwick is the only town of importance. The scenery is magnificent, with unspoiled views, and the islands' northerly position means summer days have little or no darkness.

Ferry Services

The main service is from Aberdeen on the mainland to the island port of Lerwick. A service from Kirkwall (Orkney) to Lerwick is also available. Shetlands Islands Council operates an inter-island car ferry service.

607

NORTH
SEA

Restricted junctions

Motorway and Primary Route junctions which have access or exit restrictions are shown thus ▨3▨ , ▨56▨ on the map pages.

M1 London - Leeds

Junction	Northbound	Southbound
2	Access only from A1 (*northbound*)	Exit only to A1 (*southbound*)
4	Access only from A41 (*northbound*)	Exit only to A41 (*southbound*)
6A	Access only from M25 (no link from A405)	Exit only to M25 (no link from A405)
7	Access only from M10	Exit only to M10
17	Exit only to M45	Access only from M45
19	Exit only to northbound M6	Access only from M6
21A	Exit only to A46	Access only from A46
23A	Access only from A42	Exit only to A42
24A	Access only from A50	Exit only to A50
35A	Exit only to A616	Access only from A616
43	Exit only to M621	Access only from M621
48	Exit only to A1(M) (*northbound*)	Access only from A1(M) (*southbound*)

M2 Rochester - Faversham

Junction	Westbound	Eastbound
1	Exit only to A289 (*eastbound*)	Access only from A289 (*westbound*)

M3 Sunbury - Southampton

Junction	Southwestbound	Northeastbound
8	Exit only to A303	Access only from A303
10	Access only from Winchester & A31	Exit only to Winchester & A31
13	Access only to M27 (westbound) & A33	No restriction
14	Exit only to M27 (eastbound) & A33	Access only

M4 London - South Wales

Junction	Westbound	Eastbound
1	Access only from A4 (*westbound*)	Exit only to A4 (*eastbound*)
4A	No exit to A4 (*westbound*)	No restriction
21	Exit only to M48	Access only from M48
23	Access only from M48	Exit only to M48
25	Exit only to B4596	Access only from B4596
25A	Exit only to A4042	Access only from A4042
29	Exit only to A48(M)	Access only from A48(M)
38	Exit only to A48	No restriction
39	Access only from A48	No access/exit

M5 Birmingham - Exeter

Junction	Southwestbound	Northeastbound
10	Exit only to A4019	Access only from A4019
11A	Exit only to A417 (*eastbound*)	Access only from A417 (*westbound*)
18A	Access only from M49	Exit only to M49
29	Access only from A30 (*westbound*)	No restriction

M6 Toll Motorway

Junction	Northbound	Southbound
T1	Access only	No access or exit
T2	No access or exit	Exit only
T3	Staggered junction; follow signs - access only from A38	Staggered junction; follow signs - no restriction
T5	Access only from A5127 (*southbound*)	Exit only to A5148 (*northbound*)
T7	Exit only	Access only
T8	Exit only	Access only

M6 Rugby - Carlisle

Junction	Northbound	Southbound
3A	Exit only	Access only
4	No access from M42 (*southbound*). No exit to M42 (*northbound*)	No access from M42 (*southbound*). No exit to M42
4A	Access only from M42 (*southbound*)	Exit only to M42
5	Exit only to A452	Access only from A452

(M1 continued)

Junction	Northbound	Southbound
10A	Exit only to M54	Access only from M54
11A	Access only	Exit only
20A (with M56)	No restriction	No access from M56 (*westbound*)
20	Access only from A50	No restriction
24	Access only from A58	Exit only to A58
25	Exit only	Access only
29	No direct access, use adjacent slip road to jct 29A	No direct exit, use adjacent slip road from jct 29A
29A	No direct exit, use adjacent slip road from jct 29	No direct access, use adjacent slip road to jct 29
30	Access only from M61	Exit only to M61
31A	Exit only	Access only

M8 Edinburgh - Bishopton

Junction	Westbound	Eastbound
8	No access from M73 (*southbound*) or from A8 (*eastbound*) & A89	No exit to M73 (*northbound*) or to A8 (*westbound*) & A89
9	Access only	Exit only
13	Access only from M80 (*southbound*)	Exit only to M80 (*northbound*)
14	Access only	Exit only
16	Exit only to A804	Access only from A879
17	Exit only to A82	No restriction
18	Access only from A82 (*eastbound*)	Exit only to A814
19	No access from A814 (*westbound*)	Exit only to A814 (*westbound*)
20	Exit only	Access only
21	Access only	Exit only to A8
22	Exit only to M77 (*southbound*)	Access only from M77 (*northbound*)
23	Exit only to B768	Access only from B768
25	No access or exit from or to A8	No access or exit from or to A8
25A	Exit only	Access only
28	Exit only	Access only
28A	Exit only to A737	Access only from A737

M9 Edinburgh - Dunblane

Junction	Northwestbound	Southeastbound
1A	Exit only to A90	Access only from A90
2	Access only	Exit only
3	Exit only	Access only
6	Access only from A904	Exit only to A905
8	Exit only to M876 (*southwestbound*)	Access only from M876 (*northeastbound*)

M10 St Albans - M1

Junction	Northwestbound	Southeastbound
with M1 (jct 7)	Exit only to M1 (*northbound*)	Access only from M1 (*southbound*)

M11 London - Cambridge

Junction	Northbound	Southbound
4	Access only from A406	Exit only to A406
5	Exit only to A1168	Access only from A1168
9	Access only to A11	Access only from A11
13	Exit only to A1303	Access only from A1303
14	Exit only to A14 (*eastbound*)	Access only from A14

M20 Swanley - Folkestone

Junction	Southeastbound	Northwestbound
2	Staggered junction; follow signs - exit only to A227	Staggered junction; follow signs - access only from A227
3	Access only from M26 (*eastbound*)	Exit only to M26 (*westbound*)
5	For access follow signs - exit only to A20	Access only from A20
6	For exit follow signs	No restriction
11A	Exit only	Access only

M23 Hooley - Crawley

Junction	Southbound	Northbound
7	Access only from A23 (*southbound*)	Exit only to A23 (*northbound*)
10A	Exit only to B2036	Access only from B2036

M25 London Orbital Motorway

Junction	Clockwise	Anticlockwise
1B	No direct access, use slip road to Jct 2. Exit only to A296	Access only from A296. No exit - use jct 2
5	No exit to M26	No access from M26
19	Exit only to A41	Access only from A41
21	Access only from M1 (*southbound*). Exit only to M1 (*northbound*)	Access only from M1 (*southbound*). Exit only to M1 (*northbound*)
31	No exit (use slip road via jct 30)	For access follow signs

M26 Sevenoaks - Wrotham

Junction	Eastbound	Westbound
with M25 (jct 5)	Access only from anticlockwise M25 (*eastbound*)	Exit only to clockwise M25 (*westbound*)
with M20 (jct 3)	Exit only to M20 (*southeastbound*)	Access only from M20 (*northwestbound*)

M27 Cadnam - Portsmouth

Junction	Eastbound	Westbound
4	Staggered junction; follow signs - access only from M3 (*southbound*). Exit only to M3 (*northbound*)	Staggered junction; follow signs - access only from M3 (*southbound*). Exit only to M3 (*northbound*)
10	Access only from A32	Exit only to A32
12	Staggered junction; follow signs - access only from M275 (*northbound*)	Staggered junction; follow signs - exit only to M275 (*southbound*)

M40 London - Birmingham

Junction	Northwestbound	Southeastbound
3	Exit only to A40	Access only from A40
7	Exit only to A329	Access only from A329
8	Exit only to A40	Access only from A40
13	Exit only to A452	Access only from A452
14	Access only from A452	Exit only to A452
16	Access only from A3400	Exit only to A3400

M42 Bromsgrove - Measham

Junction	Northeastbound	Southwestbound
1	Access only from A38	Exit only to A38
7	Exit only to M6 (*northwestbound*)	Access only from M6 (*northwestbound*)
7A	Exit only to M6 (*southeastbound*)	No access or exit
8	Access only from M6 (*southeastbound*)	Exit only to M6 (*northwestbound*)

M45 Coventry - M1

Junction	Eastbound	Westbound
unnumbered (Dunchurch)	Exit only to A45 & B4429	Access only from A45 & B4429
with M1 (jct 17)	Exit only to M1 (*southbound*)	Access only from M1 (*northbound*)

M53 Mersey Tunnel - Chester

Junction	Southeastbound	Northwestbound
11	Access only from M56 (*westbound*). Exit only to M56 (*eastbound*)	Access only from M56 (*westbound*). Exit only to M56 (*eastbound*)

M54 Telford

Junction	Westbound	Eastbound
with M6 (jct 10A)	Access only from M6 (*northbound*)	Exit only to M6 (*southbound*)

M56 North Cheshire

Junction	Westbound	Eastbound
1	Access only from M60 (*westbound*)	Exit only to M60 (*eastbound*) & A34 (*northbound*)
2	Exit only to A560	Access only from A560
3	Access only from A5103	Exit only to A5103 & A560
4	Exit only	Access only
9	Exit to M6 (*southbound*) via A50 interchange	Access from M6 (*northbound*) via A50 interchange
15	Exit only to M53	Access only from M53

M57 Liverpool Outer Ring Road

Junction	Northwestbound	Southeastbound
3	Access only from A526	Exit only to A526
5	Access only from A580 (*westbound*)	Exit only to A580

M58 Liverpool - Wigan

Junction	Eastbound	Westbound
1	Access only	Exit Only

M60 Manchester Orbital

Junction	Clockwise	Anticlockwise
2	Access only from A560	Exit only to A560
3	No access from M56	Access only from A34 (*northbound*)
4	Access only from A34 (*northbound*). Exit only to M56	Access only from M56 (*eastbound*). Exit only to A34 (*southbound*)
5	Access and exit only from and to A5103 (*northbound*)	Access and exit only from and to A5103 (*southbound*)
7	No direct access, use slip road to jct 8. Exit only to A56	Access only from A56. No exit - use jct 8
14	Access from A580 (*eastbound*)	Exit only to A580 (*westbound*)
16	Access only from A666	Exit only to A666
20	Exit only to A664	Access only from A664
22	No restriction	Exit only to A62
25	Exit only to A6017	No restriction
26	No restriction	No access or exit
27	Access only from A626	Exit only to A626

M61 Manchester - Preston

Junction	Northwestbound	Southeastbound
3	No access or exit	Exit only to A666
with M6 (jct 30)	Exit only to M6 (*northbound*)	Access only from M6 (*southbound*)

M62 Liverpool - Kingston upon Hull

Junction	Eastbound	Westbound
23	Exit only to A640	Access only from A640

M65 Preston - Colne

Junction	Northeastbound	Southwestbound
1	Access and exit to M6 only	Access and exit to M6 only
9	Exit only to A679	Access only from A679
11	Access only	Exit only

M66 Bury

Junction	Southbound	Northbound
with A56	Access only from A56 (*southbound*)	Exit only to A56 (*northbound*)
1	Access only from A56	Exit only to A56

M67 Hyde Bypass

Junction	Eastbound	Westbound
1	Exit only to A6017	Access only from A6017
2	Access only	Exit only to A57
3	No restriction	Exit only to A627

M69 Coventry - Leicester

Junction	Northbound	Southbound
2	Access only from B4669	Exit only to B4669

M73 East of Glasgow

Junction	Northbound	Southbound
2	No access from or exit to A89. No access from M8 (*eastbound*).	No access from or exit to A89. No exit to M8 (*westbound*)
3	Exit only to A80 (*northeastbound*)	Access only from A80 (*southwestbound*)

M74 and A74(M) Glasgow - Gretna

Junction	Southbound	Northbound
2	Access only from A763	Exit only to A763
3	Exit only	Access only
7	Exit only to A72	Access only from A72
9	Exit only to B7078	No access or exit
10	Access only from B7078	No restrictions
11	Exit only to B7078	Access only from B7078
12	Access only from A70	Exit only to A70
18	Access only from B723	Exit only to B723
21	Exit only to B6357	Access only from B6357
with B7076	Access only	Exit only
Gretna Green	Exit only	Access only
with A75	Access only from A75	Exit only to A75
with A6071	Exit only to A74 (*southbound*)	Access only from A74 (*northbound*)

M77 South of Glasgow

Junction	Southbound	Northbound
with M8 (jct 22)	No access from M8 (*eastbound*)	No exit to M8 (*westbound*)
4	Exit only	Access only
6	Exit only	Access only

M80 Stepps Bypass

Junction	Northeastbound	Southwestbound
1	Access only	No restriction
3	Exit only	Access only

M80 Bonnybridge - Stirling

Junction	Northbound	Southbound
5	Exit only to M876 (*northeastbound*)	Access only from M876 (*southwestbound*)

M90 Forth Road Bridge - Perth

Junction	Northbound	Southbound
2A	Exit only to A92 (*eastbound*)	Access only from A92 (*westbound*)
7	Access only from A91	Exit only to A91
8	Exit only to A91	Access only from A91
10	No access from A912. No exit to A912 (*southbound*)	No access from A912 (*northbound*). No exit to A912

M180 Doncaster - Grimsby

Junction	Eastbound	Westbound
1	Exit only A18	Access only from A18

M606 Bradford Spur

Junction	Northbound	Southbound
2	Exit only	No restriction

M621 Leeds - M1

Junction	Clockwise	Anticlockwise
2A	Access only	Exit only
4	Exit only	No restriction
5	Access only	Exit only
6	Exit only	Access only
with M1 (jct 43)	Exit only to M1 (*southbound*)	Access only from M1 (*northbound*)

M876 Bonnybridge - Kincardine Bridge

Junction	Northeastbound	Southwestbound
with M80 (jct 5)	Access only from M80 (*northbound*)	Exit only to M80 (*southbound*)
2	Exit only to A9	Access only from A9
with M9 (jct 8)	Exit only to M9 (*eastbound*)	Access only from M9 (*westbound*)

A1(M) South Mimms - Baldock

Junction	Northbound	Southbound
2	Exit only to A1001	Access only from A1001
3	No restriction	Exit only to A414
5	Access only	No access or exit

A1(M) East of Leeds

Junction	Northbound	Southbound
44	Access only from M1 (*northbound*)	Exit only to M1 (*southbound*)

A1(M) Scotch Corner - Newcastle upon Tyne

Junction	Northbound	Southbound
57	Exit only to A66(M) (*eastbound*)	Access only from A66(M) (*westbound*)
65	No access Exit only to A194(M) & A1 (*northbound*)	No exit Access only from A194(M) and A1 (*southbound*)

A3(M) Horndean - Havant

Junction	Southbound	Northbound
1	Exit only to A3	Access only from A3
4	Access only	Exit only

A48(M) Cardiff Spur

Junction	Westbound	Eastbound
29	Access only from M4 (*westbound*)	Exit only to M4 (*eastbound*)
29A	Exit only to A48 (*westbound*)	Access only from A48 (*eastbound*)

A66(M) Darlington Spur

Junction	Eastbound	Westbound
with A1(M) (jct 57)	Access only from A1(M) (*northbound*)	Exit only to A1(M) (*southbound*)

A194(M) Newcastle upon Tyne

Junction	Northbound	Southbound
with A1(M) (jct 65)	Access only from A1(M) (*northbound*)	Exit only to A1(M) (*southbound*)

A12 M25 - Ipswich

Junction	Northeastbound	Southwestbound
13	Access only from B1002	No restriction
14	Exit only	Access only
20A	Exit only to B1137	Access only from B1137
20B	Access only B1137	Exit only to B1137
21	No restriction	Access only from B1389
23	Exit only to B1024	Access only from B1024
24	Access only from B1024	Exit only from B1024
27	Exit only to A113	Access only from A113
unnumbered (with A120)	Exit only A120	Access only from A120
29	Access only from A120 and A1232	Exit only to A120 and A1232
unnumbered	Exit only	Access only

A14 M1 - Felixstowe

Junction	Eastbound	Westbound
With M1/M6 (jct19)	Access only from M6 and M1 (*southbound*)	Exit only to M6 and M1 (*northbound*)
4	Access only from B669	Exit only to B669
31	Access only from A428 & M11. Exit only to A1307	Exit only to A428 & M11. Access only from A1307
34	Exit only to B1047	Access only from B1047
unnumbered	No access from or exit to A1303	Access only from A1303
36	Access only from A11	Exit only to A11
38	Exit only to A11	Access only from A11
39	Access only from B1506	Exit only to B1506
49	Exit only to A1308	Access only from A1308
61	Exit only to A154	Access only from A154

A55 Holyhead - Chester

Junction	Eastbound	Westbound
8A	Access only from A5	Exit only to A5
23A	Exit only	Access only
24A	No access or exit	Exit only
33A	No access from or exit to B5126	Exit only to B5126
33B	Access only from A494	Exit only to A494
35A (west)	Exit only A5104	Access only from A5104
35B (east)	Access only from A5104	Exit only to A5104

Central London street index

In the index, street names are listed in alphabetical order and written in full, but may be abbreviated on the map. Each entry is followed by its Postcode District and each street name is preceded by the page number and the grid reference to the square in which the name is found.
Names are asterisked (*) in the index where there is insufficient space to show them on the map.

A

617 Q7 Abbey Orchard Street SW1P
619 Q7 Abbey Street SE1
619 P4 Abbots Lane SE1
617 K11 Abbots Manor SW1V
619 K11 Abbots Manor Estate SW1V
614 M10 Abchurch Lane EC4N
612 B5 Aberdeen Place W2
619 N9 Aberdour Street SE1
619 R10 Abingdon Close * SE1
614 A6 Abingdon Street SW1P
614 C3 Acton Street WC1X
612 A3 Ada Court W9
615 M8 Adams Court EC2N
617 J2 Adam's Row W1K
618 B2 Adam Street WC2N
618 D6 Addington Street SE1
614 H10 Addle Hill EC4V
615 K8 Addle Street * EC2V
618 A2 Adelaide Street * WC2N
612 Q7 Adeline Place WC1B
618 B2 Adelphi Terrace WC2N
612 B6 Adpar Street W2
614 D1 Affleck Street * N1
614 A2 Agar Street WC2N
614 G4 Agdon Street EC1V
613 N2 Air Street W1B
618 E4 Alaska Street SE1
613 M2 Albany Courtyard W1J
613 L2 Albany Street NW1
613 M2 Albemarle Street W1S
614 G5 Albemarle Way EC1V
611 H11 Alberta Estate SE17
611 H11 Alberta Estate SE17
618 B11 Albert Embankment SE1
616 G5 Albert Gate SW1X
612 E10 Albion Close W2
612 E10 Albion Gate W2
612 E10 Albion Mews W2
614 G6 Albion Place EC1M
612 E9 Albion Street W2
614 B1 Albion Walk N1
615 J7 Albion Way EC1A
619 P11 Aldbridge Street SE17
615 J8 Aldburgh Mews W1U
613 N1 Aldenham Street NW1
615 K8 Aldermanbury * EC2V
615 K7 Aldermanbury Square EC2V
615 L7 Alderney Mews SE1
617 K10 Alderney Street SW1V
615 J8 Aldersgate Street EC2V
616 H3 Aldford Street W1K
615 P9 Aldgate EC3M
615 R8 Aldgate Barrs * E1
615 Q9 Aldgate High Street EC3N
614 C9 Aldwych WC2B
616 D9 Alexander Place SW7
616 D9 Alexander Square SW3
616 B5 Alexandra Gate SW7
615 K1 Alford Place * N1
613 P6 Alfred Mews WC1E
613 P6 Alfred Place WC1E
619 N8 Alice Street SE1
615 R9 Alie Street E1
615 R1 Allerton Street N1
619 L2 Allhallows Lane EC4R
617 L8 Allington Street SW1W
617 M8 Allington Street SW1E
613 D1 Allitsen Road NW8
612 D1 Allitson Road NW8
612 G5 Allsop Place NW1
613 L7 All Souls' Place * W1B
619 R10 Alma Grove SE1
612 A2 Alma Square NW8
612 E4 Alpha Close NW1
619 N11 Alsace Road SE17
619 R8 Alscot Road SE1
619 Q9 Alscot Way SE1
619 N11 Alvey Street SE17
618 G11 Ambergate Street SE17
617 N8 Ambrosden Avenue SW1P
618 H11 Amelia Street SE17
614 H9 Amen Corner EC4M
614 H9 Amen Court EC4M
615 Q10 America Square EC3N
613 J4 America Street SE1
613 M1 Ampthill Estate NW1
613 N1 Ampthill Square NW1
614 C3 Ampton Street WC1X
614 E2 Amwell Street EC1R
615 K4 Anchor Yard * EC1V
615 F11 Anderson Street SW3
613 Q8 Andrew Borde Street * WC2H
615 R7 Angel Alley E1
615 M8 Angel Court EC2R
619 L2 Angel Passage EC4R
614 G1 Angel Square * EC1V
615 J8 Angel Street EC1A
613 P4 Anning Street E1
616 G6 Ann's Close SW1X
614 G9 Apothecary Street * EC4V
617 N3 Apple Tree Yard SW1Y
615 N6 Appold Street EC2A
617 K4 Apsley Way * W1J
618 F4 Aquinas Street SE1
613 P10 Archer Street W1D
612 E9 Archery Close W2
617 J2 Archibald Mews W1K
619 J8 Arch Street SE1
615 N1 Arden Estate N1
614 B2 Argyle Square WC1H
614 A2 Argyle Street WC1H
614 A3 Argyle Walk * WC1H
613 M9 Argyll Street W1D
619 P6 Archie Street SE1
617 M3 Arlington Street SW1A
614 F2 Arlington Way EC1R
614 B9 Arne Street WC2H
617 Q8 Arneway Street SW1P
614 D3 Arnold Circus E2
619 R6 Arnold Estate SE1
619 M2 Arthur Street EC4R
615 P7 Artillery Lane E2M
615 P7 Artillery Passage * E1
617 P8 Artillery Row SW1P
615 P8 Artizan Street E1
614 D10 Arundel Street WC2R
612 D5 Ashbridge Street NW8
614 H3 Ashby Street EC1V
615 N2 Ashford Street N1
612 H6 Ashland Place W1U
617 M8 Ashley Place SW1E
612 D6 Ashmill Street NW8
615 N2 Aske Street N1
619 K11 Asolando Drive * SE17
616 E11 Astell Street SW3
614 A9 Atherstone Mews SW7
617 Q10 Atterbury Street SW1P
614 E4 Attneave Street WC1X

617 J3 Audley Square * W1K
617 J3 Audley Street W1K
615 M8 Austin Friars EC2N
615 M8 Austin Friars Square * EC2N
615 Q3 Austin Street E2
618 G9 Austral Street SE11
618 D11 Aveline Street SE11
614 H9 Ave Marie Lane EC4M
617 K10 Avery Farm Row * SW1W
613 K10 Avery Row W1K
619 J7 Avonmouth Street SE1
612 H7 Aybrook Street W1U
614 G5 Aylesbury Street EC1R
617 P11 Aylesford Street SW1V
619 K5 Ayres Street SE1
616 B7 Ayrton Road SW7

B

617 P3 Babmaes Street SW1Y
615 M3 Bache's Street N1
614 F5 Back Hill EC1R
619 Q9 Bacon Grove SE1
615 R4 Bacon Street E2
619 L5 Baden Place SE1
615 Q8 Bainbridge Street WC1A
615 K4 Baird Street EC1Y
612 H8 Baker's Mews W1U
615 Q2 Bakers Rents E2
614 E5 Baker's Row EC1R
612 G5 Baker Street NW1
614 E5 Baker's Yard EC1R
615 R10 Balaclava Road SE1
612 F4 Balcombe Street NW1
613 J9 Balderton Street W1C
614 E6 Baldwin's Gardens WC1X
615 L3 Baldwin Street EC1V
614 B1 Balfe Street N1
617 J3 Balfour Mews W1K
617 J2 Balfour Place W1K
619 L9 Balfour Street SE1
615 J5 Baltic Street East EC1Y
615 J5 Baltic Street West EC1M
614 A10 Banbury Court * WC2E
619 K3 Bank End SE1
619 J2 Bankside SE1
615 K5 Banner Street EC1Y
614 B6 Barbon Close WC1N
618 F3 Barge House Street SE1
612 L2 Barlow Place W1J
615 M10 Barlow Street SE17
613 N1 Barnby Street NW1
619 P5 Barnham Street SE1
615 R2 Baroness Road E2
618 F6 Baron's Place SE1
614 F1 Baron Street N1
613 J9 Barrett Street W1U
612 D1 Barrow Hill Estate NW8
612 D1 Barrow Hill Road NW8
614 B7 Barter Street WC1A
615 J7 Bartholomew Close EC1A
615 M8 Bartholomew Lane EC2N
615 K4 Bartholomew Square EC1V
615 J7 Bartholomew Street SE1
614 F8 Bartlett Court * EC4A
617 R7 Barton Street SW1P
616 F6 Basil Street SW3
615 L8 Basinghall Avenue EC2V
615 L8 Basinghall Street EC2V
615 P2 Basing Place E2
614 H4 Bastwick Street EC1V
615 P9 Bateman's Buildings W1D
615 P4 Bateman's Row EC2A
615 P9 Bateman Street W1D
615 N3 Bath Place * EC2A
615 K3 Bath Street EC1V
619 J8 Bath Terrace SE1
612 C10 Bathurst Mews W2
612 C10 Bathurst Street W2
619 N4 Battle Bridge Lane SE1
613 P7 Bayley Street W1T
618 E7 Baylis Road SE1
616 A2 Bayswater Road W2
613 M10 Beak Street W1B
615 K3 Bear Gardens SE1
615 H3 Bear Lane SE1
613 Q10 Bear Street WC2H
616 E8 Beauchamp Place SW3
614 E7 Beauchamp Street EC1N
616 E7 Beaufort Gardens SW3
618 D10 Beaufoy Walk SE11
613 J6 Beaumont Mews * W1U
613 N4 Beaumont Place W1T
613 J6 Beaumont Street W1G
619 L7 Becket Street SE1
615 M10 Beckway Street SE17
619 L4 Bedale Street * SE1
613 Q7 Bedford Avenue WC1B
614 A10 Bedfordbury WC2N
618 A2 Bedford Court WC2N
614 A6 Bedford Place WC1B
614 D6 Bedford Row WC1R
613 Q7 Bedford Square WC1B
614 A10 Bedford Street WC2E
613 Q5 Bedford Way WC1H
612 C5 Bedlow Close NW8
615 J6 Beech Street (Below) EC2Y
617 L7 Belgrave Mews South SW1X
616 H7 Belgrave Mews West SW1X
617 J8 Belgrave Place SW1X
617 N10 Belgrave Road SW1V
616 H7 Belgrave Square SW1X
614 A2 Belgrave Street NW1
612 Q7 Bell Lane E1
612 D6 Bell Street W2
615 K2 Bell Wharf Lane EC4R
614 E9 Bell Yard WC2A
619 P6 Bell Yard Mews SE1
618 H6 Belvedere Buildings SE1
618 C5 Belvedere Road SE1
614 G6 Bendall Mews NW1
614 H10 Benjamin Street EC1M
617 M3 Bennet's Hill EC4V
613 J8 Bennet Street SW1A
613 J8 Bentinck Mews W1U
613 J8 Bentinck Street W1U
612 G8 Berkeley Mews W1H
617 L2 Berkeley Square W1J
617 L2 Berkeley Street W1J
619 N7 Bermondsey Street SE1
614 A5 Bernard Street WC1N
613 N7 Berners Mews W1T
613 N8 Berners Place W1T
613 N7 Berners Street W1T
618 H11 Bernhardt Crescent NW8
614 H3 Berry Place EC1V

614 H5 Berry Street EC1V
613 N9 Berwick Street W1F
617 Q11 Bessborough Gardens SW1V
617 P11 Bessborough Street SW1V
615 R4 Bethnal Green Road E2
614 A9 Betterton Street WC2H
615 M2 Bevenden Street N1
612 F7 Beverston Mews W1H
614 E1 Bevin Way WC1X
615 P8 Bevis Marks EC3A
612 G6 Bickenhall Street W1U
619 P6 Bickles Yard SE1
613 R3 Bidborough Street WC1H
615 P9 Billiter Square * EC3M
615 P9 Billiter Street EC3M
612 H6 Bingham Place W1U
613 J10 Binney Street W1K
615 M9 Birchin Lane EC3V
617 N6 Birdcage Walk SW1E
613 J9 Bird Street W1U
614 B2 Birkenhead Street NW1
615 G8 Bishop's Court EC4M
615 P7 Bishopsgate EC2M
615 N7 Bishopsgate Arcade * EC2M
618 F9 Bishops Terrace * SE11
618 F9 Bishop's Terrace SE11
619 J5 Bittern Street SE1
615 N4 Blackall Street EC2A
615 R2 Blackbird Yard E2
612 H2 Blackburne's Mews W1K
612 G2 Blackfriars Bridge EC4V
614 G9 Black Friars Lane EC4V
614 G10 Blackfriars Passage EC4V
615 G3 Blackfriars Road SE1
614 H10 Blackfriars Underpass EC4V
619 M8 Black Horse Court * SE1
615 F10 Blacklands Terrace SW3
615 R4 Blackmans Yard * E1
615 C10 Black Prince Road SE1
619 N5 Black Swan Yard SE1
615 L11 Blackwood Street SE17
612 E11 Blandford Square NW1
612 G8 Blandford Street W1H
614 F7 Bleeding Heart Yard * EC1N
615 K9 Blenheim Street W1S
615 K1 Bletchley Street N1
615 M7 Blomfield Street EC2M
613 L10 Bloomfield Place W1K
613 J11 Bloomfield Terrace SW1W
614 B7 Bloomsbury Place WC1A
614 B7 Bloomsbury Square WC1A
613 Q6 Bloomsbury Street WC1E
614 A7 Bloomsbury Way WC1A
615 P5 Blossom Street E1
615 M4 Blue Ball Yard SW1A
619 N7 Blue Lion Place SE1
612 D5 Boldero Place * NW8
613 D6 Bolney Gate SW7
613 L5 Bolsover Street W1W
614 F9 Bolt Court EC4A
617 L3 Bolton Street W1J
617 P11 Bonaparte Mews SW1V
615 M5 Bonhill Street EC2A
615 J10 Boot Street EC1V
614 H1 Boreas Walk N1
619 K6 Borough High Street SE1
619 K6 Borough Road SE1
619 J6 Borough Square SE1
617 J9 Boscobel Place SW1W
612 C6 Boscobel Street W2
619 Q5 Boss Street SE1
612 F5 Boston Place NW1
614 B6 Boswell Court WC1N
614 B6 Boswell Street WC1N
619 N2 Botolph Alley EC3R
619 N2 Botolph Lane EC3R
615 P4 Boundary Pass E1
615 Q3 Boundary Row E1
615 Q3 Boundary Street E2
618 P10 Bourchier Street W1D
613 L10 Bourdon Place W1K
613 L10 Bourdon Street W1K
613 M7 Bourlet Close W1W
614 E6 Bourne Estate * EC1N
616 H10 Bourne Street SW1W
612 C8 Bouverie Place W2
614 F9 Bouverie Street EC4Y
617 K9 Bow Churchyard * EC4M
618 F11 Bowden Street SE11
616 G6 Bowland Yard * SW1X
615 K9 Bow Lane EC4M
615 P5 Bowl Court * EC2A
619 L7 Bowling Green Lane EC1R
619 L5 Bowling Green Place * SE1
615 N2 Bowling Green Walk N1
614 B9 Bow Street WC2E
615 K6 Boyfield Street SE1
615 K6 Brackley Street EC2Y
614 F4 Brad Street SE1
615 R9 Braham Street E1
619 N4 Braidwood Street SE1
615 L6 Brandon Mews * EC2Y
619 K10 Brandon Street SE17
614 B1 Bravingtons Walk N1
611 F11 Bray Place SW3
615 K10 Bread Street EC4M
614 E8 Bream's Buildings WC2A
616 A11 Brechin Place SW7
614 A7 Bremner Road SW7
612 H8 Brendon Street W1H
617 L7 Bressenden Place SW1E
613 N10 Brewer Street W1B
614 H5 Brewery Square EC1V
619 Q4 Brewery Square SE1
614 G4 Brewhouse Yard EC1V
615 R5 Brick Court * EC4Y
615 R5 Brick Lane E1
614 K4 Brick Lane E1
614 G9 Bride Court EC4Y
614 G1 Bride Lane EC4Y
614 G1 Bridel Mews EC1V
612 D1 Bridewain Street SE1
614 G9 Bridewell Place EC4V
612 D1 Bridford Mews W1W
612 D1 Bridgeman Street NW8
611 L9 Bridge Place SW1V
618 A6 Bridge Street SW1A
613 J6 Bridgewater Square * EC2Y
613 J6 Bridgewater Street * EC2Y
613 N1 Bridgeway Street NW1
615 N10 Bridle Lane W1F
613 Q1 Brill Place NW1
614 G6 Brinton Walk SE1
615 J8 Briset Street EC1M
614 G5 Britannia Walk N1
615 L1 Britannia Walk N1
615 G5 Britton Street EC1M
613 K10 Broadbent Street * W1K
614 B9 Broad Court WC2E
612 D6 Broad Street * W2
612 H2 Bradley Terrace NW1
612 H7 Broadstone Place W1U
615 N7 Broad Street Avenue EC2M

615 M7 Broad Street Place EC2M
618 F3 Broadwall SE1
617 P6 Broadway SW1H
613 N10 Broadwick Street W1F
615 G5 Broad Yard EC1M
619 K7 Brockham Street SE1
615 R11 Brodie Street SE1
615 J10 Broken Wharf EC4V
617 F6 Brompton Arcade * SW3
616 E7 Brompton Place SW3
616 D9 Brompton Road SW3
616 D9 Brompton Square SW3
616 D7 Bronti Close SE17
618 F8 Brook Drive SE11
614 E7 Brooke Street EC1N
616 G2 Brook Gate W1K
612 A10 Brook Mews North W2
615 K10 Brook's Mews W1K
612 C10 Brook Street W2
613 J10 Brook Street W1K
613 J10 Brown Hart Gardens W1K
613 A5 Browning Close * W9
615 K11 Browning Street SE17
614 D4 Brownlow Mews WC1N
612 D7 Brownlow Street WC1V
612 F8 Brown Street W1H
612 F8 Brune Street E1
619 P6 Brunswick Court SE1
615 M3 Brunswick Mews W1H
613 J5 Brunswick Place NW1
615 M3 Brunswick Place N1
614 B4 Brunswick Square WC1N
615 P6 Brushfield Street E1
617 L2 Bruton Lane W1J
617 L2 Bruton Place W1J
617 L2 Bruton Street W1J
612 F7 Bryanston Mews East W1H
612 F7 Bryanston Mews West W1H
612 F7 Bryanston Place W1H
612 F8 Bryanston Square W1H
612 F9 Bryanston Street W1H
615 R2 Brydges Place WC2N
617 M7 Buckingham Gate SW1E
617 M7 Buckingham Mews * SW1E
617 K9 Buckingham Palace Road SW1W
617 M7 Buckingham Place SW1E
618 B2 Buckingham Street WC2N
615 M1 Buckland Street N1
615 L9 Bucklersbury * EC4N
615 R8 Buckle Street E1
613 R8 Buckhall Street WC1A
615 L10 Budge Row EC4N
617 R10 Bulinca Street * SW1P
619 L10 Bulleid Way SW1V
616 E9 Bull's Gardens SW3
613 J7 Bulstrode Place W1U
613 J8 Bulstrode Street W1U
615 L4 Bunhill Row EC1Y
616 H11 Bunhouse Place SW1W
619 L8 Burbage Close SE1
619 M8 Burge Street SE1
614 H9 Burgon Street EC4V
614 D4 Burleigh Street WC2E
617 M2 Burlington Arcade W1S
617 M2 Burlington Gardens W1S
612 R11 Burnell Walk * SE1
612 D6 Burne Street NW1
619 R10 Burnham Close SE1
616 E11 Burnsall Street SW3
613 G3 Burrell Street SE1
615 G5 Burrows Mews SE1
619 N4 Bursar Street * SE1
617 J10 Burton Mews SW1W
613 Q4 Burton Place WC1H
613 Q4 Burton Street WC1H
612 E8 Burwood Place W2
615 P8 Bury Court EC3A
614 A7 Bury Place WC1A
615 P9 Bury Street EC3A
617 M3 Bury Street SW1Y
615 D10 Bury Walk SW3
619 N8 Bushbaby Close SE1
615 L10 Bush Lane EC4R
619 R10 Bushwood Drive SE1
615 B9 Bute Street SW7
619 R5 Butlers & Colonial Wharf SE1
619 Q10 Buttermere Close SE1
615 M2 Buttesland Street N1
615 R5 Buxton Street E1
615 Q5 Byng Place WC1E
615 P2 Byward Street EC3R
616 F11 Bywater Street SW3
613 M7 Bywell Place * W1W

C

612 D7 Cabbell Street NW1
619 R8 Cadbury Way SE16
615 R1 Cadell Close E2
615 R11 Cadet Drive SE1
616 G10 Cadogan Gardens SW3
616 G9 Cadogan Gate SW1X
616 H8 Cadogan Lane SW1X
616 G7 Cadogan Place SW1X
616 F8 Cadogan Square SW1X
616 F10 Cadogan Street SW3
615 K5 Cahill Street * EC1Y
614 B1 Caledonia Street N1
613 Q11 Cale Street SW3
616 B7 Calendar Road SW7
614 D4 Calthorpe Street WC1X
615 P3 Calvert Avenue E1
615 N2 Calvin Street E1
613 Q9 Cambridge Circus W1D
615 K3 Cambridge Gate NW1
613 L3 Cambridge Gate Mews NW1
612 D8 Cambridge Square W2
617 L11 Cambridge Street SW1V
615 K3 Cambridge Terrace NW1
613 L3 Cambridge Terrace Mews * NW1
615 Q4 Camlet Street E2
615 N8 Camomile Street EC2N
615 R9 Camperdown Street E1
617 M3 Candover Street * W1W
615 J9 Cannon Street EC4V
619 Q8 Canon Murnane Road SE1
618 A6 Canon Row SW1A
614 H10 Canterbury Place SE17
613 N6 Canvey Street SE1
616 G6 Capeners Close SW1X
612 C4 Capland Street NW8
613 L6 Carburton Street W1W
614 E11 Cardigan Street SE11
619 M8 Cardinal Bourne Street * SE1
613 N2 Cardington Street NW1
615 J8 Carey Lane EC2V
617 P10 Carey Place SW1V
614 D9 Carey Street WC2A
615 P9 Carlisle Avenue EC3N

618 D7 Carlisle Lane SE1
617 M8 Carlisle Place SW1P
613 P9 Carlisle Street W1D
617 J2 Carlos Place W1K
617 P4 Carlton Gardens SW1Y
616 G7 Carlton House Terrace SW1Y
617 P2 Carlton Street SW1Y
616 G7 Carlton Tower Place SW1X
614 F10 Carmelite Street EC4Y
613 M9 Carnaby Street W1F
615 P2 Caroline Gardens E2
616 H10 Caroline Terrace SW1W
617 K2 Carpenter Street W1K
617 K4 Carrington Street W1J
617 P6 Carteret Street SW1H
614 C4 Carter Lane EC4V
615 J6 Carthusian Street EC1M
613 Q3 Carting Lane WC2R
613 Q3 Cartwright Gardens WC1H
615 R10 Cartwright Street E1
612 D3 Casey Close NW8
614 H10 Castle Baynard Street EC4V
618 G9 Castlebrook Close SE11
616 G7 Castle Court * EC3V
617 N6 Castle Lane SW1E
612 F8 Castlereagh Street W1H
618 H3 Castle Yard SE1
615 M10 Catesby Street SE17
619 L3 Cathedral Street SE1
614 F4 Catherine Griffiths Court EC1R
617 M7 Catherine Place SW1E
615 C10 Catherine Street * WC2B
617 M4 Catherine Wheel Alley E1
615 P7 Catherine Wheel Yard SW1A
612 E7 Cato Street W1H
617 Q10 Catton Street WC1B
612 C1 Causton Street SW1P
612 C2 Cavendish Avenue NW8
612 C2 Cavendish Close NW8
613 L6 Cavendish Mews North W1G
613 L7 Cavendish Mews South * W1W
613 L8 Cavendish Place W1G
613 L8 Cavendish Square W1G
615 L1 Cavendish Street N1
617 N7 Caxton Street SW1H
619 P5 Cayenne Court SE1
615 L3 Cayton Street EC1V
617 R2 Cecil Court WC2N
612 Q2 Cecil Court WC2N
618 D7 Centaur Street SE1
615 J2 Central Street EC1V
617 P8 Chadwell Street EC1R
617 P8 Chadwick Street SW1P
612 F5 Chagford Street NW1
613 Q2 Chalton Street NW1
615 R10 Chamber Street E1
615 R3 Chambord Street E2
614 G3 Chancel Street SE1
614 E9 Chancery Lane WC2A
615 Q4 Chance Street E2
618 A2 Chandos Place WC2N
613 L7 Chandos Street W1G
619 L5 Chapel Court SE1
613 K8 Chapel Place W1G
612 D7 Chapel Street NW1
617 J7 Chapel Street SW1X
618 F5 Chaplin Close SE1
617 P10 Chapter Street SW1P
617 R3 Charing Cross * WC2N
619 Q10 Charing Cross Road WC2H
617 P3 Charles II Street SW1Y
613 D7 Charles Lane NW8
613 N3 Charles Place * NW1
615 M3 Charles Square N1
615 M3 Charles Square Estate N1
617 K3 Charles Street W1J
615 K10 Charleston Street SE17
613 N6 Charlotte Mews W1T
617 N7 Charlotte Place SW1V
617 M10 Charlotte Place SW1V
613 N7 Charlotte Road EC2A
613 N6 Charlotte Street W1T
617 N10 Charlwood Place SW1V
617 N10 Charlwood Street SW1V
615 J5 Charterhouse Buildings EC1M
614 H6 Charterhouse Mews EC1M
614 F7 Charterhouse Street EC1N
615 M2 Chart Street N1
615 M2 Chatham Street SE17
619 R10 Chaucer Drive SE1
615 K9 Cheapside EC2V
616 D10 Chelsea Bridge Road SW1W
616 D11 Chelsea Manor Street SW3
614 A7 Cheltenham Terrace SW3
613 P5 Chenies Mews WC1E
613 P5 Chenies Street WC1E
615 K5 Chequer Street EC1Y
615 M1 Cherbury Street N1
615 K5 Cherry Tree Walk EC1Y
616 H8 Chesham Close SW1X
616 H7 Chesham Mews SW1X
616 H8 Chesham Place SW1X
616 H8 Chesham Street SW1X
613 J6 Chester Close SW1X
613 L2 Chester Close North NW1
613 L3 Chester Close South NW1
617 K3 Chesterfield Gardens * W1J
617 K3 Chesterfield Hill W1J
617 K3 Chesterfield Street W1J
613 K3 Chester Gate NW1
617 K7 Chester Mews SW1X
615 K2 Chester Place NW1
613 J3 Chester Road NW1
616 H10 Chester Row SW1W
617 J9 Chester Square SW1W
617 J9 Chester Square Mews * SW1W
617 J7 Chester Street SW1X
613 K2 Chester Terrace NW1
619 L7 Chester Way SE11
619 L7 Chettle Close SE1
616 H3 Cheval Place SW7
618 D5 Chicheley Street SE1
612 G6 Chicksand Street E1
612 G6 Chiltern Street W1U
615 R4 Chilton Street E2
612 A9 Chilworth Mews W2
612 A9 Chilworth Street W2
615 L6 Chiswell Street EC1Y
615 N6 Chitty Street W1T
615 N4 Christina Street EC2A
615 M5 Christopher Place * NW1
615 M5 Christopher Street EC2A
612 C4 Church Estate NW8
613 Q2 Church Street NW8
613 Q2 Churchway NW1
617 N10 Churton Place SW1V
617 N10 Churton Street SW1V
612 F6 Circus Mews * W1H
617 M3 Circus Place * EC2M
616 B2 Circus Road NW8
612 B2 Citadel Place SE11

Central London index: City Garden Row - Great Russell Street 621

614 H1 City Garden Row N1
614 G1 City Road EC1V
615 M6 City Road EC2A
619 N7 City Walk SE1
616 F8 Clabon Mews SW1X
614 F1 Claremont Close N1
614 E1 Claremont Square N1
613 L3 Clarence Gardens NW1
612 G4 Clarence Gate NW1
613 R1 Clarence Passage * NW1
612 G4 Clarence Terrace NW1
612 D10 Clarendon Close * W2
612 A5 Clarendon Gardens W9
612 D10 Clarendon Gate W2
612 D10 Clarendon Mews W2
612 D10 Clarendon Place W2
617 L11 Clarendon Street SW1V
612 A4 Clarendon Terrace W9
616 A10 Clareville Grove SW7
616 A10 Clareville Street SW7
617 K3 Clarges Mews W1J
617 L3 Clarges Street W1J
613 J6 Clarkes Mews W1G
613 M1 Clarkson Row NW1
612 G7 Clay Street W1U
618 F11 Cleaver Square SE11
618 E11 Cleaver Street SE11
614 D9 Clements Inn WC2A
615 M10 Clement's Lane EC4N
619 K5 Clennam Street * SE1
612 F8 Clenston Mews W1H
615 M4 Clere Place EC2A
615 M4 Clere Street EC2A
614 F4 Clerkenwell Close EC1R
614 G5 Clerkenwell Green EC1R
614 E5 Clerkenwell Road EC1R
613 M6 Cleveland Mews W1T
617 N3 Cleveland Place SW1Y
617 N4 Cleveland Row SW1A
613 L5 Cleveland Street NW1
612 A8 Cleveland Terrace W2
617 M2 Clifford Street W1S
612 C10 Clifton Place W2
612 A4 Clifton Road W9
615 N5 Clifton Street EC2A
619 L3 Clink Street SE1
613 M6 Clipstone Mews W1W
613 L6 Clipstone Street W1W
616 H9 Cliveden Place SW1W
615 K10 Cloak Lane EC4R
614 H7 Cloth Court EC1A
614 H7 Cloth Fair EC1A
615 P8 Clothier Street EC3A
615 J6 Cloth Street EC1A
615 Q3 Club Row E2
615 M1 Clunbury Street N1
619 N7 Cluny Estate SE1
619 N7 Cluny Place SE1
613 L10 Coach & Horses Yard W1S
615 Q8 Cobb Street E1
613 N3 Cobourg Street NW1
617 N9 Coburg Close SW1P
612 C1 Cochrane Mews NW8
612 C1 Cochrane Street NW8
614 G7 Cock Lane EC1A
617 Q3 Cockspur Court SW1A
617 Q3 Cockspur Street SW1Y
615 R8 Code Street E1
618 E3 Coin Street SE1
615 R8 Colchester Street E1
614 E5 Coldbath Square EC1R
612 G1 Colebrooke Row N1
615 L8 Coleman Street EC2V
619 K6 Cole Street SE1
614 D5 Coley Street WC1X
615 R7 College East * E1
615 K10 College Hill * EC4R
618 A7 College Mews SW1P
615 K10 College Street * EC4R
614 C1 Collier Street N1
619 J6 Collinson Street SE1
619 J6 Collinson Walk SE1
618 G8 Colnbrook Street SE1
618 G4 Colombo Street SE1
614 A5 Colonnade WC1N
613 L4 Colosseum Terrace NW1
615 Q2 Columbia Road E2
613 N7 Colville Place W1T
619 K10 Colworth Grove SE17
615 R8 Commercial Road E1
615 Q5 Commercial Street E1
613 L3 Compton Close NW1
614 H4 Compton Passage EC1V
614 G4 Compton Place WC1H
614 G4 Compton Street EC1V
619 N10 Comus Place SE17
618 D4 Concert Hall Approach SE1
614 A10 Conduit Court * WC2E
612 B9 Conduit Mews W2
612 B9 Conduit Passage W2
612 B9 Conduit Place W2
613 L10 Conduit Street W1S
619 N10 Congreve Street SE17
612 E9 Coniston Court * W2
612 D10 Connaught Close W2
612 E9 Connaught Square W2
612 E9 Connaught Street W2
618 F5 Cons Street * SE1
617 K5 Constitution Hill W1J
619 K10 Content Street SE17
613 M6 Conway Mews W1T
613 M5 Conway Street W1T
614 H1 Coombs Street N1
618 F6 Cooper Close SE1
613 Q1 Coopers Lane NW1
615 Q10 Cooper's Row EC3N
616 C11 Copenhagen Gardens SW3
618 H5 Copperfield Street SE1
619 Q4 Copper Row SE1
615 M8 Copthall Avenue EC2R
613 R7 Coptic Street WC1A
618 F6 Coral Street SE1
613 R5 Coram Street WC1H
615 Q6 Corbet Place E1
617 M2 Cork St Mews W1S
617 M2 Cork Street W1S
612 D6 Corlett Street NW1
615 M9 Cornhill EC3V
618 E3 Cornwall Road SE1
612 G5 Cornwall Terrace NW1
612 G5 Cornwall Terrace Mews NW1
615 N3 Coronet Street N1
614 F4 Corporation Row EC1R
615 M3 Corsham Street N1
613 K6 Cosmo Place WC1B
618 E7 Cosser Street SE1
612 E6 Cosway Street NW1
619 K10 Cotham Street SE17
616 D7 Cottage Place SW3
618 F7 Cottesloe Mews SE1
618 F11 Cottington Street SE11
618 G10 Cotton Gardens Estate SE11
615 P2 Cotton's Gardens E2
616 F11 Coulson Street SW3
619 N3 Counter Street SE1
619 K8 County Street SE1
618 D11 Courtenay Street SE11
615 L10 Cousin Lane EC4R
614 B10 Covent Garden WC2E
614 B10 Covent Garden Piazza WC2E
617 P2 Coventry Street W1D
614 G6 Cowcross Street EC1M
617 R8 Cowley Street SW1P
615 M4 Cowper Street EC1Y
619 Q6 Coxson Way SE1
615 Q1 Crabtree Close E2
617 R3 Craig's Court SW1A
619 M10 Crail Row SE17
613 J7 Cramer Street W1U
619 J11 Crampton Street SE17
613 Q10 Cranbourn Street WC2H
614 F9 Crane Court EC4A
613 N1 Cranleigh Street NW1
616 A11 Cranley Gardens SW7
616 A11 Cranley Mews SW7
616 B10 Cranley Place SW7
615 M3 Cranwood Street EC1V
612 A10 Craven Hill W2
612 A10 Craven Hill Mews W2
618 A3 Craven Passage WC2N
612 A10 Craven Road W2
618 A3 Craven Street WC2N
612 A10 Craven Terrace W2
614 E5 Crawford Passage EC1R
612 E7 Crawford Place W1H
612 F7 Crawford Street W1H
615 P8 Creechurch Lane EC3A
615 P9 Creechurch Place * EC3A
614 H9 Creed Lane EC4V
615 Q1 Cremer Street E2
615 Q10 Crescent EC3N
616 D9 Crescent Place SW3
615 J5 Crescent Row EC1Y
614 B2 Crestfield Street NW1
619 P8 Crimscott Street SE1
615 J6 Cripplegate Street * EC2Y
615 Q7 Crispin Street E1
614 B3 Cromer Street WC1H
612 B5 Crompton Street W2
616 C9 Cromwell Gardens SW7
616 C9 Cromwell Mews * SW7
616 C9 Cromwell Place SW7
616 B9 Cromwell Road SW7
615 M1 Crondall Street N1
612 A3 Cropthorne Court W9
619 L6 Crosby Row SE1
615 N9 Crosby Square EC3A
613 J7 Cross Keys Close W1U
619 N2 Cross Lane EC3R
619 M9 Crosslet Street SE17
615 Q10 Crosswall EC3N
614 B9 Crown Court WC2B
614 E10 Crown Office Row EC4Y
617 N4 Crown Passage SW1Y
615 N5 Crown Place EC2A
619 N5 Crucifix Lane SE1
614 E2 Cruickshank Street WC1X
615 P10 Crutched Friars EC3N
614 D3 Cubitt Street WC1X
616 G10 Culford Gardens SW3
615 N10 Cullum Street EC3M
616 H2 Culross Street W1K
612 D1 Culworth Street NW8
614 D2 Cumberland Gardens WC1X
612 F10 Cumberland Gate W2
613 K2 Cumberland Gate NW1
613 K2 Cumberland Market NW1
613 K2 Cumberland Place NW1
617 L11 Cumberland Street SW1V
613 K1 Cumberland Terrace NW1
613 K1 Cumberland Terrace Mews NW1
614 D1 Cumming Street N1
617 J10 Cundy Street SW1W
612 B4 Cunningham Place NW8
617 Q11 Cureton Street SW1P
619 Q5 Curlew Street SE1
614 E8 Cursitor Street EC4A
615 P3 Curtain Place EC2A
615 N3 Curtain Road EC2A
619 Q9 Curtis Street SE1
619 Q9 Curtis Way SE1
617 J4 Curzon Square W1J
617 J4 Curzon Street W1K
612 B5 Cuthbert Street W2
615 P8 Cutlers Gardens Arcade EC2M
615 P8 Cutler Street EC3A
615 R4 Cygnet Street E1
614 D1 Cynthia Street N1
614 H4 Cyrus Street EC1V

D

617 P7 Dacre Street SW1H
614 H4 Dallington Square EC1V
614 H5 Dallington Street EC1M
614 C7 Dane Street WC1R
613 P10 Dansey Place W1D
618 G9 Dante Road SE11
616 E11 Danube Street SW3
613 N9 D'Arblay Street W1F
617 P6 Dartmouth Street SW1H
619 M9 Darwin Street SE17
612 D6 Daventry Street NW1
618 G6 Davidge Street SE1
612 G6 David Mews W1U
613 K10 Davies Mews W1K
613 K10 Davies Street W1K
619 M11 Dawes Street SE17
615 R1 Dawson Street E2
619 J9 Deacon Way SE17
617 R8 Dean Bradley Street SW1P
613 P9 Deanery Mews * W1K
617 J3 Deanery Street W1K
613 Q7 Dean Farrar Street SW1H
617 R9 Dean Ryle Street SW1P
619 M10 Dean's Buildings SE17
614 H9 Dean's Court EC4M
613 L8 Dean's Mews * W1G
618 A8 Dean Stanley Street SW1P
613 P8 Dean Street W1D
617 Q7 Deans Yard SW1P
617 R8 Dean Trench Street SW1P
619 N7 Decima Street SE1
617 N10 Dell's Mews * SW1V
618 H11 Delverton Road SE17
617 M11 Denbigh Place SW1V
617 M10 Denbigh Street SW1V
617 N2 Denman Street W1D
613 Q9 Denmark Street WC2H
612 A2 Denning Close NW8
618 F11 Donny Crescent SE11
618 F11 Denny Street SE11
616 E9 Denyer Street SW3
618 A5 Derby Gate SW1A
617 J4 Derby Street W1J
615 P4 Dereham Place EC2A
613 K9 Dering Street W1C
619 L8 Deverell Street SE1
614 E10 Devereux Court WC2R
613 K6 Devonshire Close W1G
613 K6 Devonshire Mews South W1G
613 J5 Devonshire Mews West W1G
613 J5 Devonshire Place W1G
613 J5 Devonshire Place Mews W1G
615 P7 Devonshire Row EC2M
613 L5 Devonshire Row Mews W1W
615 P8 Devonshire Square EC2M
613 J6 Devonshire Street W1G
612 A10 Devonshire Terrace W2
613 J7 De Walden Street W1G
613 P8 Diadem Court W1F
613 L4 Diana Place NW1
614 G5 Dickens Mews EC1M
619 K7 Dickens Square SE1
615 K3 Dingley Place EC1V
615 J3 Dingley Road EC1V
619 K5 Disney Place SE1
619 K5 Disney Street SE1
615 Q1 Diss Street E2
615 J10 Distaff Lane EC4V
618 E10 Distin Street SE11
619 R6 Dockhead SE1
618 F6 Dodson Street SE1
618 H4 Dolben Street * SE1
614 C6 Dombey Street WC1N
615 J4 Domingo Street EC1V
615 M6 Dominion Street EC2M
614 D1 Donegal Street N1
616 E9 Donne Place SW3
618 E3 Doon Street SE1
613 P2 Doric Way NW1
614 E6 Dorrington Street EC1N
619 K5 Dorrit Street * SE1
614 G9 Dorset Buildings * EC4Y
612 F6 Dorset Close NW1
617 K7 Dorset Mews SW1X
614 F9 Dorset Rise EC4Y
612 F5 Dorset Square NW1
612 G7 Dorset Street W1U
614 C5 Doughty Mews WC1N
614 C4 Doughty Street WC1N
617 P10 Douglas Street SW1P
615 L9 Dove Court * EC2R
616 C11 Dovehouse Street SW3
617 L2 Dover Street W1S
617 L3 Dover Yard W1J
615 L10 Dowgate Hill EC4R
617 R5 Downing Street SW1A
617 K4 Down Street W1J
619 J5 Doyce Street * SE1
616 H9 D'Oyley Street SW1W
618 D10 Dragon Road SE11
614 C7 Drake Street WC1X
618 H9 Draper Estate SE1
616 E10 Draycott Avenue SW3
616 F10 Draycott Place SW3
616 F9 Draycott Terrace SW3
616 A11 Drayton Gardens SW10
619 Q5 Druid Street SE1
613 P2 Drummond Crescent NW1
617 Q11 Drummond Gate SW1V
613 M4 Drummond Street NW1
615 R8 Drum Street E1
614 A8 Drury Lane WC2B
614 B9 Dryden Street WC2E
615 P2 Drysdale Place N1
615 P3 Drysdale Street N1
615 R3 Ducal Street E2
613 L7 Duchess Mews W1G
613 L7 Duchess Street W1B
618 F3 Duchy Street SE1
613 P9 Duck Lane W1F
612 B7 Dudley Street * W2
616 C11 Dudmaston Mews SW3
615 L5 Dufferin Avenue EC1Y
615 K5 Dufferin Street EC1Y
613 N9 Dufour's Place W1F
618 G10 Dugard Way SE11
617 J6 Duke of Wellington Place SW1X
616 G11 Duke of York Square SW3
617 N3 Duke of York Street SW1Y
613 J8 Duke's Mews W1U
615 Q9 Duke's Place EC3A
613 Q3 Duke's Road NW1
613 J8 Duke Street W1U
619 M3 Duke Street Hill SE1
617 N3 Duke Street St James's W1J
613 J10 Duke's Yard W1K
617 R2 Duncannon Street WC2N
614 G1 Duncan Terrace N1
615 Q1 Dunloe Street E2
619 R8 Dunlop Place SE16
612 G10 Dunraven Street W1K
613 J6 Dunstable Mews W1G
615 N10 Dunster Court EC3R
619 M6 Dunsterville Way SE1
619 Q10 Dunton Road SE1
616 G6 Duplex Ride SW1X
618 B2 Durham House Street * WC2N
612 G6 Durweston Mews * W1U
612 F7 Durweston Street W1H
614 E7 Dyer's Buildings EC4A
613 Q7 Dyott Street WC1B
615 M5 Dysart Street EC2A

E

614 G6 Eagle Court EC1M
616 A11 Eagle Place SW7
614 C7 Eagle Street WC1V
613 Q9 Earlham Street WC2H
614 G2 Earlstoke Estate EC1V
614 G2 Earlstoke Street EC1V
615 N6 Earl Street EC2A
613 Q8 Earnshaw Street WC1A
613 J8 Easleys Mews W1U
612 A8 Eastbourne Mews W2
612 A8 Eastbourne Terrace W2
613 M8 Eastcastle Street W1W
615 M10 Eastcheap EC4N
614 F8 East Harding Street EC4A
614 E4 Easton Street WC1X
615 J6 East Passage EC1A
614 G7 East Poultry Avenue EC1M
615 M2 East Road N1
619 R2 East Smithfield E1W
619 K11 East Street SE17
615 R9 East Tenter Street E1
616 H9 Eaton Close SW1W
616 H9 Eaton Gate SW1W
617 L8 Eaton Lane SW1W
617 J8 Eaton Mews North SW1X
617 J9 Eaton Mews South SW1W
617 J9 Eaton Mews West SW1W
616 H8 Eaton Place SW1X
617 K7 Eaton Row SW1W
617 J8 Eaton Square SW1W
616 H9 Eaton Terrace SW1W
616 H9 Eaton Terrace Mews SW1W
615 L2 Ebenezer Street N1
615 Q4 Ebor Street E1
617 K11 Ebury Bridge SW1W
617 J9 Ebury Mews SW1W
617 K9 Ebury Mews East SW1W
617 K10 Ebury Square SW1W
617 J10 Ebury Street SW1W
617 J8 Eccleston Mews SW1X
617 K10 Eccleston Place SW1W
617 L10 Eccleston Square SW1V
617 L10 Eccleston Square Mews SW1V
617 J8 Eccleston Street SW1W
612 B5 Edgware Road W2
616 F5 Edinburgh Gate SW1X
613 P2 Edith Neville Cottages NW1
613 L2 Edward Mews * NW1
612 H9 Edwards Mews W1U
616 E9 Egerton Crescent SW3
616 D8 Egerton Gardens SW3
616 E8 Egerton Gardens Mews SW3
616 E8 Egerton Place * SW3
616 E8 Egerton Terrace SW3
619 K9 Elba Place * SE17
615 Q6 Elder Street E1
615 M7 Eldon Street EC2M
618 H9 Elephant & Castle SE1
619 J9 Elephant Road SE17
614 G1 Elia Mews N1
614 G1 Elia Street N1
619 N7 Elim Street SE1
617 K10 Elizabeth Bridge SW1W
612 A5 Elizabeth Close * W9
617 J9 Elizabeth Street SW1W
618 H9 Elliott's Row SE11
616 G9 Ellis Street SW1X
616 B11 Elm Place SW7
612 B10 Elms Mews W2
614 D5 Elm Street WC1X
612 B2 Elm Tree Close NW8
612 B2 Elm Tree Road NW8
619 M10 Elsted Street SE17
616 A8 Elvaston Mews SW7
616 A8 Elvaston Place SW7
617 P9 Elverton Street SW1P
614 F7 Ely Place EC1N
616 E11 Elystan Place SW3
616 D10 Elystan Street SW3
618 B3 Embankment Place WC2N
614 C6 Emerald Street WC1N
619 J3 Emerson Street SE1
617 N8 Emery Hill Street SW1P
618 F7 Emery Street SE1
619 L6 Empire Square SE1
614 H4 Enclave Court EC1V
613 R8 Endell Street WC2H
613 P4 Endsleigh Gardens WC1H
613 Q4 Endsleigh Place WC1H
613 Q4 Endsleigh Street WC1H
612 F6 Enford Street NW1
619 R7 Enid Street SE16
616 C7 Ennismore Gardens SW7
616 C7 Ennismore Gardens Mews SW7
616 D6 Ennismore Mews SW7
616 D7 Ennismore Street SW7
616 B11 Ensor Mews SW7
615 M5 Epworth Street EC2A
615 R3 Equity Square E2
617 Q10 Erasmus Street SW1P
615 K5 Errol Street EC1Y
614 E9 Essex Court * EC4Y
614 E9 Essex Street WC2R
617 P10 Esterbrooke Street SW1P
618 E10 Ethelred Estate SE11
619 K10 Ethel Street * SE17
615 J3 Europa Place EC1V
613 M4 Euston Centre NW1
613 M4 Euston Road NW1
613 R2 Euston Road WC1H
613 P3 Euston Square NW1
613 N4 Euston Street NW1
615 L1 Evelyn Walk N1
613 N1 Eversholt Street NW1
613 M3 Everton Buildings NW1
619 J4 Ewer Street SE1
617 Q2 Excel Court WC2H
615 N7 Exchange Arcade EC2M
618 B2 Exchange Court * WC2E
615 P6 Exchange Square * EC2A
614 B10 Exeter Street WC2E
616 C8 Exhibition Road SW7
614 E4 Exmouth Market EC1R
613 N3 Exmouth Mews * NW1
619 N10 Exon Street SE17
618 E4 Exton Street SE1
614 E5 Eyre Street Hill EC1R
615 R2 Ezra Street E2

F

615 L1 Fairbank Estate N1
615 P5 Fairchild Place * EC2A
615 P5 Fairchild Street EC2A
616 E7 Fairholt Street SW7
619 P5 Fair Street SE1
613 P8 Falconberg Court * W1D
618 H3 Falcon Close SE1
614 H1 Falcon Court N1
615 P1 Falkirk Street N1
619 K8 Falmouth Road SE1
615 J5 Fann Street EC1M
615 N2 Fanshaw Street N1
613 P8 Fareham Street * W1F
617 K2 Farm Street W1J
618 H4 Farnham Place SE1
614 F5 Farringdon Lane EC1R
614 E4 Farringdon Road EC1R
614 G8 Farringdon Street EC4A
615 Q7 Fashion Street E1
615 L4 Featherstone Street EC1Y
615 N9 Fenchurch Avenue EC3M
615 P9 Fenchurch Buildings EC3M
615 P10 Fenchurch Place * EC3M
615 N10 Fenchurch Street EC3M
619 P7 Fendall Street SE1
619 N5 Fenning Street SE1
614 E3 Fernsbury Street WC1X
614 F8 Fetter Lane EC4A
614 D7 Field Court WC1R
614 C2 Field Street WC1X
615 M9 Finch Lane EC3V
615 M7 Finsbury Avenue * EC2M
615 M7 Finsbury Circus EC2M
614 F3 Finsbury Estate EC1R
615 N5 Finsbury Market EC2A
615 M6 Finsbury Pavement EC2M
615 M5 Finsbury Square EC2A
615 L6 Finsbury Street EC1Y
616 E9 First Street SW3
614 C7 Fisher Street WC1R
612 B5 Fisherton Street NW8
619 M2 Fish Street Hill EC3R
618 D9 Fitzalan Street SE11
612 H8 Fitzhardinge Street W1H
617 L3 Fitzmaurice Place * W1J
613 M5 Fitzroy Mews W1T
613 M5 Fitzroy Square W1T
613 M6 Fitzroy Street W1T
613 Q3 Flaxman Terrace WC1H
614 G8 Fleet Place EC4A
614 C3 Fleet Square WC1X
614 E9 Fleet Street EC4Y
615 P5 Fleur de Lis Street E1
619 P11 Flinton Street SE17
619 M10 Flint Street SE17
613 Q9 Flitcroft Street WC2H
614 B10 Floral Street WC2E
615 R7 Flower & Dean Walk E1
613 M7 Foley Street W1W
615 P6 Folgate Street E1
615 L7 Fore Street EC2Y
612 E8 Forset Street W1H
619 R10 Fort Road SE1
615 P7 Fort Street * E1
615 K5 Fortune Street EC1Y
618 C5 Forum Magnum Square SE1
615 J8 Foster Lane EC2V
613 M9 Foubert's Place W1F
616 B10 Foulis Terrace SW7
613 M4 Foundry Mews NW1
615 Q6 Fournier Street E1
614 H6 Fox & Knot Street * EC1M
612 C5 Frampton Street NW8
617 N9 Francis Street SW1P
616 B8 Frankland Road SW7
616 G11 Franklin's Row SW3
618 E6 Frazier Street SE1
612 E10 Frederick Close W2
615 L9 Frederick's Place * EC2R
614 G2 Frederick's Row EC1V
614 C3 Frederick Street WC1X
616 H6 Frederic Mews * SW1X
619 N11 Freemantle Street SE17
615 P3 French Place EC2A
618 H3 Friars Close * SE1
615 J10 Friday Street EC4M
614 G2 Friend Street EC1V
613 P9 Frith Street W1D
615 K6 Frobisher Crescent * EC2Y
615 R7 Frostic Walk E1
615 P7 Frying Pan Alley E1
614 D7 Fullwood Place WC1R
613 M2 Fullwood's Mews N1
614 E8 Furnival Street EC4A
615 J10 Fye Foot Lane EC4V
617 P9 Fynes Street SW1P

G

618 E3 Gabriel's Wharf SE1
614 B6 Gage Street WC1N
619 Q4 Gainsford Street SE1
619 J5 Gaitskell Way SE1
614 B7 Galen Place WC1A
615 K3 Galway Street EC1V
618 H4 Gambia Street SE1
613 M10 Ganton Street W1B
613 J6 Garbutt Place * W1U
614 E10 Garden Court * EC4Y
612 A2 Garden Road NW8
618 G8 Garden Row SE1
617 P11 Garden Terrace SW1V
615 N4 Garden Walk EC2A
615 J10 Gardners Lane EC4V
614 H2 Gard Street EC1V
615 K10 Garlick Hill EC4V
614 F3 Garnault Mews EC1R
614 F3 Garnault Place EC1R
615 J4 Garrett Street EC1Y
614 A10 Garrick Street WC2E
613 R10 Garrick Yard WC2N
615 Q2 Gascoigne Place E2
612 D5 Gateforth Street NW8
619 M3 Gatehouse Square SE1
616 E6 Gate Mews SW7
614 C8 Gate Street WC2A
618 H7 Gaunt Street SE1
619 M9 Gavel Street * SE17
617 R8 Gayfere Street SW1P
618 H8 Gaywood Street SE1
619 Q7 Gedling Place SE1
613 J9 Gees Court W1U
615 J4 Gee Street EC1V
615 P1 Geffrye Estate N1
618 G9 George Mathers Road * SE11
613 M3 George Mews NW1
612 F8 George Street W1H
615 M9 George Yard EC3V
613 J10 George Yard W1K
615 R2 Georgina Gardens * E2
618 G8 Geraldine Street SE11
617 J9 Gerald Road SW1W
613 Q10 Gerrard Place * W1D
613 P10 Gerrard Street W1D
618 F6 Gerridge Street SE1
615 R3 Gibraltar Walk E2
618 D10 Gibson Road SE11
614 A7 Gilbert Place WC1A
618 F9 Gilbert Road SE11
613 J9 Gilbert Street W1K
617 L9 Gillingham Mews SW1V
617 M9 Gillingham Row SW1V
617 L10 Gillingham Street SW1V
612 A7 Gilpin Close W2
614 H8 Giltspur Street EC1A
618 G7 Gladstone Street SE1
618 H5 Glasshill Street SE1
617 N2 Glasshouse Street W1B
618 B11 Glasshouse Walk SE11
615 J5 Glasshouse Yard EC1M
616 B9 Glendower Place SW7
612 G5 Glentworth Street NW1
619 L6 Globe Street SE1
612 A9 Gloucester Mews W2
612 F4 Gloucester Place NW1
612 G7 Gloucester Place W1U
612 G7 Gloucester Place Mews W1H
616 A10 Gloucester Road SW7
612 C10 Gloucester Square W2
617 M11 Gloucester Street SW1V
612 B10 Gloucester Terrace W2
614 F3 Gloucester Way EC1R
616 E8 Glynde Mews SW3
616 E11 Godfrey Street SW3
614 H9 Godliman Street EC4V
618 C3 Golden Jubilee Bridge SE1
615 J4 Golden Lane EC1Y
615 J5 Golden Lane Estate EC1Y
613 N10 Golden Square W1F
615 K8 Goldsmith Street EC2V
613 N7 Goodge Place W1T
613 N7 Goodge Street W1T
615 Q10 Goodman's Yard EC3N
619 R8 Goodwin Close SE16
613 R10 Goodwins Court WC2N
615 L10 Gophir Lane * EC4R
613 P4 Gordon Square WC1H
613 P4 Gordon Street WC1H
616 A7 Gore Street SW7
615 P8 Goring Street EC3A
615 Q2 Gorsuch Place E2
615 Q2 Gorsuch Street E2
613 L6 Gosfield Street W1W
613 Q8 Goslett Yard W1D
614 H3 Goswell Place EC1V
614 H2 Goswell Road EC1V
614 F8 Gough Square EC4A
614 D4 Gough Street WC1X
615 Q8 Goulston Street E1
613 Q7 Gower Mews WC1E
613 N4 Gower Place WC1E
613 P5 Gower Street WC1E
615 M10 Gracechurch Street EC3V
612 A1 Graces Mews * NW8
619 N7 Graduate Place SE1
613 M5 Grafton Mews W1T
613 P3 Grafton Place NW1
617 L2 Grafton Street W1S
613 M6 Grafton Way W1T
614 H1 Graham Street N1
616 H10 Graham Terrace SW1W
615 R4 Granby Street E2
613 M1 Granby Terrace NW1
614 H6 Grand Avenue EC1M
615 J1 Grand Junction Wharf * N1
619 P8 Grange Road SE1
619 P7 Grange Walk SE1
619 P8 Grange Walk Mews SE1
619 Q8 Grange Yard SE1
617 K4 Grantham Place W1K
612 H9 Granville Place W1H
614 D3 Granville Street WC1X
614 A8 Grape Street WC2H
618 C11 Graphite Square SE11
615 Q8 Gravel Lane E1
614 B2 Gray's Inn Road WC1X
614 E6 Gray's Inn Square WC1R
613 J9 Gray's Yard * W1U
613 M8 Great Castle Street W1B
612 F6 Great Central Street NW1
613 P8 Great Chapel Street W1D
617 R7 Great College Street SW1P
612 F9 Great Cumberland Mews W1H
612 F8 Great Cumberland Place W1H
619 L7 Great Dover Street SE1
615 N3 Great Eastern Street EC2A
617 Q6 Great George Street SW1H
619 J4 Great Guildford Street SE1
614 C6 Great James Street WC1N
613 M9 Great Marlborough Street W1B
619 M4 Great Maze Pond SE1
614 F8 Great New Street * EC4A
614 B6 Great Ormond Street WC1N
614 D2 Great Percy Street WC1X
617 P8 Great Peter Street SW1P
613 L6 Great Portland Street W1W
613 N10 Great Pulteney Street W1F
614 B8 Great Queen Street WC2B
613 Q8 Great Russell Street WC1B

615 K10 Great St Thomas Apostle EC4V
617 R4 Great Scotland Yard SW1A
617 Q7 Great Smith Street SW1P
618 H4 Great Suffolk Street SE1
614 H5 Great Sutton Street EC1V
615 L8 Great Swan Alley EC2R
613 L6 Great Titchfield Street W1W
615 N10 Great Tower Street EC3R
615 K10 Great Trinity Lane EC4V
614 D7 Great Turnstile WC1V
615 M8 Great Winchester Street EC2N
617 P2 Great Windmill Street W1D
619 P5 Great Yard SE1
612 Q9 Greek Street W1D
618 G8 Green Arbour Court * EC1A
612 D1 Greenberry Street NW8
617 N9 Greencoat Place SW1P
617 N8 Greencoat Row SW1P
618 E6 Greenham Close SE1
614 G6 Greenhill's Rents * EC1M
615 P10 Green's Court W1F
612 G10 Green Street W1K
614 F3 Green Terrace EC1R
619 N8 Green Walk SE1
613 L5 Greenwell Street W1W
614 D4 Green Yard WC1X
618 F4 Greet Street SE1
612 D4 Grendon Street NW8
614 B5 Grenville Street WC1N
615 J8 Gresham Street EC2V
613 P7 Gresse Street W1T
614 F7 Greville Street EC1N
617 P8 Greycoat Place SW1P
617 P8 Greycoat Street SW1P
615 R5 Grey Eagle Street E1
619 P8 Grigg's Place SE1
615 R4 Grimsby Street E2
618 E6 Grindal Street SE1
615 L9 Grocers' Hall Court * EC2R
617 J7 Groom Place SW1X
616 H9 Grosvenor Cottages SW1X
617 J6 Grosvenor Crescent SW1X
616 H6 Grosvenor Crescent Mews SW1X
617 L8 Grosvenor Gardens SW1W
617 L7 Grosvenor Gardens East * SW1W
617 K8 Grosvenor Gardens Mews North * SW1W
616 G2 Grosvenor Gate W1K
613 K10 Grosvenor Hill W1K
612 J5 Grosvenor Place SW1X
613 J10 Grosvenor Square W1K
613 J10 Grosvenor Street W1K
619 J5 Grotto Court * SE1
612 H6 Grotto Passage W1U
612 B1 Grove End Road NW8
612 E3 Grove Gardens NW8
615 K9 Groveland Court EC4M
615 K8 Guildhall Buildings EC2V
615 K8 Guildhall Yard EC2V
617 M10 Guildhouse Street SW1V
614 C5 Guilford Place WC1N
614 C5 Guilford Street WC1N
619 N8 Guinness Square SE1
616 F10 Guinness Trust Estate SW3
617 Q7 Gun Street E1
615 R5 Gunthorpe Street E1
615 D11 Guthrie Street SW3
615 J8 Gutter Lane EC2V
619 M5 Guy Street SE1
614 D3 Gywnne Place WC1X

H
615 M2 Haberdasher Place N1
615 M2 Haberdasher Street N1
615 Q2 Hackney Road E2
615 R9 Half Moon Passage E1
617 L3 Half Moon Street W1J
616 H7 Halkin Arcade SW1X
616 H7 Halkin Mews * SW1X
616 H7 Halkin Place SW1X
617 J6 Halkin Street SW1X
613 L6 Hallam Mews W1W
613 L6 Hallam Street W1W
613 A3 Hall Gate NW8
612 B5 Hall Place W2
613 A3 Hall Road W9
614 H2 Hall Street EC1V
615 M10 Halpin Place SE17
616 F9 Halsey Street SW3
612 B3 Hamilton Close NW8
612 A2 Hamilton Gardens NW8
617 K5 Hamilton Mews W1J
617 J4 Hamilton Place W1K
619 M6 Hamlet Way SE1
615 Q10 Hammett Street EC3N
613 Q1 Hampden Close NW1
612 F9 Hampden Gurney Street W1H
613 M3 Hampstead Road NW1
618 H10 Hampton Street SE17
613 P10 Ham Yard * W1D
615 R6 Hanbury Street E1
614 D7 Hand Court WC1V
614 A4 Handel Street WC1N
619 M6 Hankey Place SE1
614 B9 Hanover Place WC2E
613 L9 Hanover Square W1S
612 E9 Hanover Steps * W2
613 L9 Hanover Street W1S
612 F3 Hanover Terrace NW1
612 E3 Hanover Terrace Mews NW1
616 F7 Hans Crescent SW1X
613 M6 Hanson Street W1W
616 F7 Hans Place SW1X
616 F7 Hans Road SW3
616 G8 Hans Street SW1X
619 P8 Hanway Place W1T
613 P8 Hanway Street W1T
612 C7 Harbet Road W2
614 E10 Harcourt Buildings * EC4Y
612 F7 Harcourt Street W1H
614 D3 Hardwick Mews * WC1X
614 F3 Hardwick Street EC1R
619 N5 Hardwidge Street SE1
614 E9 Hare Court * EC4Y
615 P1 Hare Walk N1
613 L9 Harewood Avenue NW1
613 L9 Harewood Place W1S
613 L9 Harewood Row NW1
613 K7 Harley Place W1G
613 K5 Harley Street W1G
619 R11 Harmony Place SE1
618 F8 Harmsworth Mews SE1
617 K7 Harper Road SE1
619 N2 Harp Lane EC3R
614 C6 Harpur Mews WC1N
614 C6 Harpur Street WC1N
616 G6 Harriet Street SW1X
616 G6 Harriet Walk SW1X
616 B9 Harrington Road SW7
613 M1 Harrington Street NW1
614 E3 Harrison Street WC1H
618 E9 Harrowby Street W1H
615 P8 Harrow Place E1
612 C7 Harrow Road Flyover W2
612 E6 Harrow Street * NW1
615 P10 Hart Street EC3R
615 E9 Hasker Street SW3
615 R1 Hassard Street E2
613 R3 Hastings Street WC1H
619 P6 Hatchers Mews SE1
618 F3 Hatfields SE1
617 N10 Hatherley Street SW1P

614 H5 Hat & Mitre Court EC1M
614 F6 Hatton Garden EC1N
614 F5 Hatton Place EC1N
612 C5 Hatton Row * NW8
612 C5 Hatton Street NW8
614 E6 Hatton Wall EC1N
613 K9 Haunch of Venison Yard * W1C
614 F1 Haverstock Place EC1V
614 H1 Haverstock Street N1
615 Q10 Haydon Street EC3N
615 Q9 Haydon Walk E1
612 E5 Hayes Place NW1
613 L2 Hay Hill W1J
618 G9 Hayles Street SE11
617 P2 Haymarket SW1Y
619 N6 Hay's Lane SE1
617 K2 Hay's Mews W1J
614 G5 Hayward's Place * EC1R
619 Q9 Hazel Way SE1
617 J2 Headfort Place SW1X
619 M10 Hearn's Buildings SE17
615 P5 Hearn Street EC2A
614 C4 Heathcote Street WC1N
617 M2 Heddon Street W1S
618 G9 Hedger Street SE11
615 K4 Helmet Row EC1V
614 M9 Hemp Walk SE17
612 B4 Henderson Drive NW8
619 P10 Hendre Road SE1
615 P9 Heneage Lane EC3A
615 R6 Heneage Street E1
619 R9 Henley Drive SE1
615 B4 Henrietta Mews WC1N
613 K8 Henrietta Place W1G
614 B10 Henrietta Street WC2E
619 L9 Henshaw Street SE17
618 G9 Heralds Place SE11
614 F5 Herbal Hill EC1R
616 G7 Herbert Crescent SW1X
619 R4 Herbrand Street WC1N
618 D8 Hercules Road SE1
614 A10 Hereford Square SW7
614 E1 Hermes Street N1
612 B7 Hermitage Street W2
614 G2 Hermit Street EC1V
617 Q10 Herrick Street SW1P
613 M5 Hertford Place W1T
617 K3 Hertford Street W1J
617 P5 Hewett Street EC2A
617 K9 Heygate Estate SE17
619 J10 Heygate Street SE17
617 P10 Hide Place SW1P
614 B8 High Holborn WC1V
615 J10 High Timber Street EC4V
614 E6 Highworth Street * NW1
619 M10 Hillery Close SE17
612 A1 Hill Road NW8
613 M9 Hills Place W1D
617 K3 Hill Street W1J
614 F9 Hind Court EC4A
613 J8 Hinde Mews * W1U
613 J8 Hinde Street W1U
617 K8 Hobart Place SW1W
615 Q3 Hocker Street * E2
615 M2 Hoffman Square * N1
612 B6 Hogan Mews W2
615 H11 Holbein Mews SW1W
615 H10 Holbein Place SW1W
614 E7 Holborn EC1N
614 F7 Holborn Circus EC1N
614 C7 Holborn Place WC1V
614 E7 Holborn Viaduct EC1A
614 E7 Holborn WC1R
614 C2 Holford Mews * WC1X
614 D2 Holford Street WC1X
614 E1 Holford Yard * WC1X
614 H3 Holland Street SE1
613 N9 Hollen Street W1F
613 L8 Holles Street W1G
613 L9 Holles Street W1C
618 E5 Holmes Terrace SE1
614 D5 Holsworthy Square WC1X
618 G9 Holyoak Road SE11
619 N4 Holyrood Street SE1
615 P4 Holywell Lane EC2A
615 N5 Holywell Row EC2A
615 N1 Homefield Street * N1
612 E7 Homer Row NW1
612 E7 Homer Street W1H
614 J4 Honduras Street EC1V
615 N7 Hope Square EC2M
615 R7 Hopetown Street * E1
617 R2 Hop Gardens WC2N
613 N9 Hopkins Street W1F
618 H3 Hoptons Gardens * SE1
618 H2 Hopton Street SE1
619 R1 Horatio Street E2
618 E9 Hornbeam Close SE11
617 P8 Horseferry Road SW1P
618 A4 Horse Guards Avenue SW1A
619 Q4 Horse Guards Road SW1A
619 Q4 Horselydown Lane SE1
614 G7 Hosier Lane EC1A
618 E11 Hotspur Street SE11
614 D9 Houghton Street * WC2A
615 P8 Houndsditch EC3A
618 H10 Howell Walk SE1
617 N8 Howick Place SW1E
613 N6 Howland Mews East W1T
613 N6 Howland Street W1T
614 A6 Howley Place W2
615 N3 Hoxton Market N1
615 N3 Hoxton Square N1
615 K10 Huggin Hill EC4V
617 M9 Hugh Mews SW1V
617 P9 Hugh Place SW1V
617 L10 Hugh Street SW1V
615 R6 Huguenot Place E1
615 J3 Hull Street EC1V
619 K6 Hulme Place SE1
619 Q11 Humphrey Street SE1
619 M8 Hunter Close SE1
614 B4 Hunter Street WC1N
615 N5 Hunter Street WC1E
619 N10 Huntsman Street SE17
612 F4 Huntsworth Mews NW1
614 F9 Hutton Street EC4Y
617 J5 Hyde Park Corner W1J
612 D9 Hyde Park Crescent W2
618 B9 Lambeth Bridge SW1P
612 C10 Hyde Park Gardens W2
612 C10 Hyde Park Gardens Mews W2
616 A6 Hyde Park Gate SW7
616 A6 Hyde Park Gate Mews * SW7
612 E10 Hyde Park Place W2
612 D9 Hyde Park Square W2
612 D10 Hyde Park Street W2

I
619 N2 Idol Lane EC3R
618 H11 Iliffe Street SE17
618 H11 Iliffe Yard SE17
616 B8 Imperial College Road SW7
615 Q9 India Street EC3N
613 N9 Ingestre Place W1F
614 E2 Inglebert Street EC1R
618 D9 Ingram Close SE11
612 H3 Inner Circle NW1
618 J5 Invicta Plaza SE1
615 L3 Ironmonger Lane EC2V
615 K3 Ironmonger Row EC1V
617 Q2 Irving Street WC2H
615 J3 Isaac Way SE1
615 G4 Isabella Street SE1
616 D10 Ives Street SW3
612 F5 Ivor Place NW1

619 Q11 Ivy Church Lane * SE17
616 D10 Ixworth Place SW3

J
619 R5 Jacob Street SE1
613 J8 Jacob's Well Mews W1U
613 J9 James Street W1U
614 A6 Jay Mews SW7
617 M3 Jermyn Street SW1Y
612 D4 Jerome Crescent NW8
615 Q6 Jerome Street E1
615 P1 Jerrold Street * N1
614 D6 Jerusalem Passage EC1V
615 Q9 Jewry Street EC3N
614 C8 Joan Street SE1
614 D6 Jockey's Fields WC1X
618 B3 Johanna Street * SE1
618 A6 John Adam Street WC2N
614 A6 John Aird Court W2
614 F10 John Carpenter Street EC4Y
617 Q11 John Islip Street SW1P
619 L9 John Maurice Close SE17
613 L8 John Prince's Street W1G
614 D5 John's Mews WC1N
614 C9 Johnson's Court EC4A
614 D5 John Street WC1N
615 J6 John Trundle Highwalk * EC2Y
619 M4 Joiner Street SE1
615 C11 Jonathan Street SE11
615 J7 Joseph Trotter Close EC1R
618 D4 Jubilee Gardens * SE1
618 E11 Jubilee Place SW3
614 A3 Judd Street WC1H
612 C8 Junction Mews W2
612 C8 Junction Place W2
618 D9 Juxon Street SE11

K
614 C9 Kean Street WC2B
619 Q10 Keats Close SE1
614 C9 Keeley Street WC2B
618 H7 Kell Street SE1
614 C9 Kemble Street WC2B
618 F10 Kempsford Road SE11
618 H7 Kendall Place W1U
612 E9 Kendal Steps * W2
612 E9 Kendal Street W2
615 B9 Kendrick Mews SW7
616 B10 Kendrick Place * SW7
615 M10 Kennedy Walk SE17
615 K10 Kennett Wharf Lane EC4V
618 F11 Kennings Way SE11
618 G11 Kennington Park Road SE11
618 E10 Kennington Road SE11
612 H6 Kenrick Place W1U
614 A6 Kensington Road SW7
614 A4 Kenton Street WC1H
612 F4 Kent Passage NW1
612 E3 Kent Terrace NW1
616 E6 Kent Yard SW7
613 Q6 Keppel Street WC1E
619 G8 Keyse Road SE1
615 B1 Keystone Crescent N1
618 H7 Keyworth Street SE1
615 M4 Kiffen Street EC2A
615 K11 King & Queen Street SE17
617 R3 King Charles I Island WC2R
617 Q5 King Charles Street SW1A
618 F7 King Edward Street EC1A
618 F7 King Edward Walk SE1
614 J8 Kinghorn Street EC1A
618 H6 King James Court SE1
618 H6 King James Street SE1
615 P4 King John Court EC2A
619 N11 Kinglake Estate * SE17
619 P11 Kinglake Street SE17
613 N10 Kingly Court * W1B
613 M9 Kingly Street W1B
615 K11 King & Queen Street * SE17
615 L8 King's Arms Yard EC2R
618 H5 King's Bench Street SE1
614 F10 King's Bench Walk * EC4Y
614 C10 Kingscote Street EC4V
614 B2 King's Court * SE1
614 C2 King's Cross Bridge * N1
614 C2 King's Cross Road WC1X
615 P1 Kingsland Road E2
613 D5 King's Mews WC1N
619 J6 King's Place SE1
613 J3 King Square EC1V
614 F10 Kings Reach * EC4Y
618 B4 Kings Reach SW1A
617 M8 King's Scholars' Passage SW1V
615 K9 King Street EC2V
614 A10 King Street SW1Y
617 N4 King Street SW1A
614 C9 Kingsway WC2B
614 F4 Kingsway Place * EC1R
615 M10 King William Street * EC4R
616 G6 Kinnerton Place North * SW1X
616 G6 Kinnerton Place South * SW1X
616 H6 Kinnerton Street SW1X
616 H6 Kinnerton Yard * SW1X
619 M6 Kipling Estate SE1
619 M6 Kipling Street SE1
619 N5 Kirby Grove SE1
614 E6 Kirby Street EC1N
615 R3 Kirton Gardens E2
614 H9 Knightrider Court * EC4V
614 H10 Knightrider Street EC4V
616 E6 Knightsbridge SW7
616 F6 Knightsbridge Green * SW1X
618 G10 Knights Walk SE11
612 F6 Knox Street NW1

L
615 M6 Lackington Street EC2A
619 Q5 Lafone Street SE1
613 J6 Lambeth Jones Mews * EC2Y
618 B9 Lambeth Bridge SW1P
618 C10 Lambeth High Street SE1
615 J10 Lambeth Hill EC4V
618 C7 Lambeth Palace Road SE1
618 E8 Lambeth Road SE1
618 D9 Lambeth Walk SE11
614 C6 Lamb's Conduit Passage WC1X
614 C5 Lamb's Conduit Street WC1N
615 L5 Lamb's Passage EC1Y
615 Q5 Lamb Street E1
619 N6 Lamb Walk SE1
618 E5 Lamlash Street SE11
612 A4 Lanark Place W9
615 K10 Lancashire Court W1K
612 A10 Lancaster Court W2
612 A10 Lancaster Mews W2
614 C2 Lancaster Place WC2E
614 C10 Lancaster Place SW7
618 D9 Lancaster Terrace W2
615 G6 Lancelot Place SW7
618 F6 Lancing Street NW1
617 P3 Landon Place SW1X
613 L7 Langford Place NW8
613 L7 Langham Place W1B
613 M7 Langham Street W1W
613 L7 Langham Street W1B
614 A10 Langley Court WC2E

614 A9 Langley Street WC2H
614 M8 Langthorn Court * EC2R
614 D3 Langton Close WC1X
619 M7 Lansdowne Place SE1
614 B5 Lansdowne Terrace WC1N
619 J5 Lant Street SE1
619 K10 Larcom Street SE17
615 M10 Larissa Street * SE17
615 K7 Lauderdale Place * EC2Y
614 C11 Laud Street SE11
618 E6 Launcelot Street SE1
615 L10 Laurence Pountney Hill EC4R
615 L10 Laurence Pountney Lane EC4R
618 H4 Lavington Street SE1
615 K9 Lawrence Lane EC2V
619 M7 Law Street SE1
613 L4 Laxton Place * NW1
614 E5 Laystall Street WC1X
614 A10 Lazenby Court * WC2E
615 N9 Leadenhall Place EC3V
615 N9 Leadenhall Street EC3V
618 D5 Leake Street SE1
615 R6 Leather Lane EC1N
619 N6 Leathermarket Court SE1
619 N6 Leathermarket Street SE1
616 B11 Lecky Street SW7
614 C2 Leeke Street WC1X
612 H10 Lees Place W1K
613 Q10 Leicester Place * WC2H
617 Q2 Leicester Square WC2H
613 Q10 Leicester Street WC2H
613 Q10 Leicester Street W1D
613 R4 Leigh Street WC1H
616 F8 Leman Street E1
616 F9 Lennox Gardens SW1X
615 F9 Lennox Gardens Mews SW1X
615 M4 Leonard Street EC2A
619 N9 Leroy Street SE1
616 E9 Leverett Street SW3
615 J3 Lever Street EC1V
613 N9 Lexington Street W1F
617 Q7 Leyden Street E1
618 H6 Library Street SE1
613 N1 Lidlington Place NW1
615 Q4 Ligonier Street E2
615 C10 Lilac Place SE11
612 D4 Lilestone Street NW8
615 N10 Lillington Gardens Estate SW1V
614 F6 Lily Place EC1M
614 G8 Limeburner Lane EC4M
615 N10 Lime Street EC3M
615 N9 Lime Street Passage * EC3V
614 C8 Lincoln's Inn Fields WC2A
614 F10 Lincoln Street SW3
617 Q11 Lindsay Square SW1V
614 H6 Lindsey Street EC1A
612 F4 Linhope Street NW1
615 R6 Links Yard E1
613 Q10 Lisle Street WC2H
612 C4 Lisson Grove NW8
612 D6 Lisson Street NW1
613 Q10 Litchfield Street WC2H
613 L4 Little Albany Street NW1
613 M9 Little Argyll Street * W1B
615 J7 Little Britain EC1A
617 K7 Little Chester Street SW1X
617 R7 Little Cloisters SW1P
617 R7 Little Deans Yard SW1P
617 K5 Little Dorrit Court SE1
613 L2 Little Edward Street * NW1
614 E10 Little Essex Street * WC2R
617 R6 Little George Street SW1P
613 M9 Little Marlborough Street * W1B
613 Q10 Little Newport Street WC2H
614 F8 Little New Street * EC4A
613 L8 Little Portland Street W1B
614 A7 Little Russell Street WC1A
617 M4 Little St James's Street SW1A
617 Q7 Little Smith Street SW1P
615 Q9 Little Somerset Street EC3N
613 M7 Little Titchfield Street W1W
615 K10 Little Trinity Lane EC4V
614 C7 Little Turnstile WC1V
615 N1 Liverpool Street EC2M
615 E3 Lizard Street EC1V
615 P9 Lloyd's Avenue EC3M
614 E2 Lloyd Baker Street WC1X
614 E2 Lloyd Square WC1X
614 E2 Lloyd's Row EC1R
614 E2 Lloyd Street WC1X
615 M6 Lockyer Street SE1
612 C3 Lodge Road NW8
615 Q7 Lolesworth Close E1
618 D9 Lollard Street SE11
618 H5 Loman Street SE1
614 F9 Lombard Lane EC4Y
615 M9 Lombard Street EC3V
619 M2 London Bridge EC4R
615 M4 London Bridge Street SE1
619 M3 London Bridge Walk * SE1
612 C9 London Mews W2
618 H7 London Road SE1
612 B8 London Street W2
615 P10 London Street * EC3M
615 K7 London Wall EC2V
615 M7 London Wall Buildings EC2M
614 A9 Long Acre WC2E
619 R10 Longfellow Way * SE1
619 R9 Longfield Estate SE1
614 L3 Longford Street NW1
614 H6 Long Lane EC1A
614 M6 Long Lane SE1
617 M10 Longmoore Street SW1V
619 Q1 Long Street E2
618 G9 Longville Road SE11
619 P7 Long Walk SE1
614 C5 Long Yard WC1N
617 R8 Lord North Street SW1P
612 D3 Lords View NW8
614 C2 Lorenzo Street WC1X
612 E3 Lorne Close NW8
615 L8 Lothbury EC2R
618 D11 Loughborough Street SE11
614 N10 Lovat Lane EC3R
615 K8 Love Lane EC2V
617 K7 Lower Belgrave Street SW1W
617 K7 Lower Grosvenor Place SW1W
613 N10 Lower James Street * W1F
613 N10 Lower John Street * W1F
618 E6 Lower Marsh SE1
619 N2 Lower Sloane Street SW1W
619 N2 Lower Thames Street EC3R
615 N9 Lowndes Close SE1
613 M9 Lowndes Court * W1F
618 H8 Lowndes Place * SW1X
616 G6 Lowndes Square SW1X
614 B3 Loxham Street * WC1H
614 D10 Lucan Place SW3
614 H9 Ludgate Broadway * EC4V
614 G9 Ludgate Circus EC4M
614 G9 Ludgate Hill EC4M
614 G9 Ludgate Square * EC4M
615 J4 Ludlow Street * EC1V
615 N4 Luke Street EC2A
614 C2 Lumley Street W1C
613 P11 Lupus Street SW1V
612 C8 Luton Street NW8
612 H6 Luxborough Street W1U
617 P3 Lyall Mews SW1X
616 H8 Lyall Mews West * SW1X
616 H8 Lyall Street SW1X
617 K8 Lygon Place * SW1W
619 P10 Lynton Estate SE1

619 R10 Lynton Road SE1
612 B5 Lyons Place NW8

M
613 Q3 Mabledon Place NW1
615 J2 Macclesfield Road EC1V
613 Q10 Macclesfield Street * W1D
613 J5 Mac Farren Place NW1
612 E1 Mackennal Street NW8
613 M2 Macklin Street * WC2B
613 M2 Mackworth Street NW1
615 L10 Maddox Street W1S
619 P11 Madron Street SE1
616 E3 Magazine Gate * W2
619 N4 Magdalen Street SE1
619 R5 Maguire Street SE1
612 A6 Maida Avenue W2
614 A4 Maida Vale W9
614 B10 Maiden Lane WC2E
614 K3 Maiden Lane SE1
619 K4 Maidstone Buildings Mews SE1
616 E10 Makins Street SW3
615 P5 Malet Street WC1E
612 E4 Mallory Street NW8
615 L4 Mallow Street EC1Y
614 G4 Malta Street EC1V
619 Q6 Maltby Street SE1
619 P5 Maltings Place SE1
614 D10 Maltravers Street WC2R
612 H7 Manchester Mews W1U
612 H8 Manchester Square W1H
612 H7 Manchester Street W1U
619 M6 Manciple Street SE1
619 P9 Mandela Way SE1
613 J8 Mandeville Place W1U
613 Q9 Manette Street W1D
614 G2 Manningford Close * EC1V
612 J11 Manor Place SE17
616 C11 Manresa Road SW3
615 R9 Mansell Street E1
613 K7 Mansfield Mews W1G
613 K7 Mansfield Street W1G
615 L9 Mansion House Place * EC4N
616 A10 Manson Mews SW7
616 B10 Manson Place SW7
614 N6 Maple Place W1T
613 M6 Maple Street W1T
619 R3 Marble Quay E1W
614 R4 Marchmont Street WC1H
619 P10 Marcia Road SE1
613 L8 Margaret Street W1G
614 E3 Margery Street EC1R
613 G2 Marigold Alley SE1
617 K4 Market Mews W1J
613 M8 Market Place W1W
619 N7 Market Yard Mews SE1
615 F11 Markham Place * SW3
616 F11 Markham Square SW3
615 E11 Markham Street SW3
615 P10 Mark Lane EC3R
615 N4 Mark Street EC2A
618 H10 Marlborough Close SE17
613 M10 Marlborough Court * W1B
616 B2 Marlborough Gate W2
617 N4 Marlborough Road SW1A
616 D10 Marlborough Street SW3
619 R8 Marshall's Place SE16
617 N1 Marshall Street * W1F
619 K5 Marshalsea Road SE1
617 Q9 Marsham Street SW1P
615 L4 Martha's Buildings EC1V
615 M10 Martin Lane EC4R
614 B9 Martlett Court WC2B
612 D7 Marylebone Flyover * W2
613 J7 Marylebone High Street W1G
613 J8 Marylebone Lane W1U
613 J7 Marylebone Mews W1G
613 N8 Marylebone Passage W1W
612 E6 Marylebone Road NW1
613 J7 Marylebone Street W1G
618 D10 Marylee Way SE11
613 L9 Mason's Arms Mews * W1S
615 L8 Mason's Avenue EC2V
614 H2 Mason's Place * EC1V
619 M10 Mason Street SE17
614 J4 Masons Yard SW1Y
617 N4 Masons Yard SW1Y
619 N10 Massinger Street SE17
613 R9 Mathews Yard * WC2H
618 H6 Mathieson Court SE1
617 P9 Maunsel Street SW1P
619 K4 Mayall Close SE1
617 L3 Mayfair Place W1J
617 R2 Mays Court WC2N
618 E7 McAuley Close SE1
619 J6 McCoid Way SE1
619 J8 Meadow Row SE1
618 E7 Mead Row SE1
617 P9 Meard Street W1F
614 C4 Mecklenburgh Place WC1N
614 C4 Mecklenburgh Square WC1N
614 C4 Mecklenburgh Street WC1N
617 P8 Medway Street SW1P
614 D9 Melbourne Place WC2B
612 F6 Melbury Terrace NW1
612 G5 Melcombe Place NW1
612 G5 Melcombe Street NW1
612 B3 Melina Place NW8
619 M5 Melior Place * SE1
619 M5 Melior Street SE1
613 N3 Melton Street NW1
613 J5 Memel Street EC1Y
618 D4 Mepham Street SE1
619 R9 Mercer Street SE1
614 C3 Meredith Street EC1R
614 E3 Merlin Street WC1X
619 L5 Mermaid Court SE1
617 L7 Merrick Square SE1
619 M11 Merrow Walk SE17
617 F8 Mertoun Terrace * W1H
615 Mews North SW1W
619 R3 Mews Street E1W
618 G4 Meymott Street SE1
613 J2 Micawber Street N1
615 P7 Middlesex Street E1
615 J6 Middle Street EC1A
614 E9 Middle Temple Lane EC4Y
613 M7 Middleton Place W1W
619 M3 Middle Yard SE1
613 N5 Midford Place * W1T
613 Q1 Midhope Street WC1H
613 Q1 Midland Road NW1
614 E10 Milford Lane WC2R
615 K8 Milk Street EC2V
617 R11 Millbank SW1P
617 Q10 Millbank Estate SW1P
619 J2 Millennium Bridge SE1
619 Q5 Millennium Square SE1
618 F4 Miller Walk SE1
614 C5 Millman Mews * WC1N
614 C5 Millman Place WC1N
614 C5 Millman Street WC1N
617 Q5 Milroy Walk SE1
619 Q6 Milstream Road SE1
613 L10 Mill Street W1S
617 R6 Milner Street SW3
618 F3 Milroy Walk SE1
615 L6 Milton Court EC2Y
615 L6 Milton Street EC2Y
615 N10 Mincing Lane EC3R
615 M6 Minera Mews SW1W
619 P10 Minnow Walk SE17
615 Q9 Minories EC3N

615 N10 Minster Court * EC3R
619 J5 Mint Street SE1
619 J4 Mitchell Street EC1V
618 F5 Mitre Road SE1
618 P9 Mitre Square EC3A
615 P9 Mitre Street EC3A
612 E7 Molyneux Street W1H
617 J9 Monck Street SW1P
616 D6 Moncorvo Close SW11
618 F9 Monkton Street SE11
615 K7 Monkwell Square EC2Y
613 Q9 Monmouth Street WC2H
619 L3 Montague Close SE1
613 Q6 Montague Place WC1E
615 R6 Montague Street EC1A
615 J7 Montague Street WC1B
612 G7 Montagu Mansions W1U
612 G7 Montagu Mews North W1H
612 G8 Montagu Mews South W1H
612 F8 Montagu Mews West W1H
612 F7 Montagu Place W1H
612 G7 Montagu Row W1U
612 G7 Montagu Square W1H
612 G8 Montagu Street W1H
615 Q3 Montclare Street E2
616 E7 Montpelier Mews SW7
616 E7 Montpelier Place SW7
616 E7 Montpelier Square SW7
616 E6 Montpelier Street SW7
616 E6 Montpelier Terrace SW7
616 E6 Montpelier Walk SW7
614 C10 Montreal Place WC2B
617 J6 Montrose Place SW1X
616 F9 Moore Street SW3
615 L7 Moorfields EC2M
615 L7 Moorfields Highwalk EC2Y
615 L8 Moorgate EC2R
615 L7 Moorgate EC2M
615 L8 Moorgate Place * EC2R
615 L7 Moor Lane EC2Y
613 Q9 Moor Street W1D
615 K3 Mora Street EC1V
619 K10 Morcambe Street SE17
614 H2 Moreland Street EC1V
619 N4 More London Place SE1
619 P4 More London Riverside SE1
617 N11 Moreton Place SW1V
617 N11 Moreton Street SW1V
617 N11 Moreton Terrace SW1V
617 N11 Moreton Terrace Mews South SW1V
619 N4 Morgans Lane SE1
618 F6 Morley Street SE1
619 N6 Morocco Street SE1
617 M8 Morpeth Terrace SW1P
618 F11 Morrells Yard SE11
613 L8 Mortimer Street W1W
618 E8 Morton Place SE1
613 P7 Morwell Street WC1B
616 E9 Mossop Street SW3
617 H7 Motcomb Street SW1X
614 H3 Mount Mills EC1V
614 D5 Mount Pleasant WC1X
617 K2 Mount Row W1K
616 H2 Mount Street W1K
612 H7 Moxon Street W1U
612 D5 Mulready Street NW8
615 N2 Mundy Street N1
613 L3 Munster Square NW1
619 K9 Munton Road SE17
618 E6 Murphy Street SE1
615 L1 Murray Grove N1
619 P2 Muscovy Street EC3R
614 A7 Museum Street WC1A
614 F2 Myddelton Passage EC1R
614 F2 Myddelton Square EC1R
614 F3 Myddelton Street EC1R
614 E2 Mylne Street EC1R
615 N1 Myrtle Street N1
615 N1 Myrtle Walk N1

N

614 E3 Naoroji Street WC1X
615 K1 Napier Grove N1
613 L2 Nash Street NW1
613 M7 Nassau Street W1W
615 R7 Nathaniel Close E1
614 F5 Navarre Street E2
615 Q2 Nazrul Street E2
614 A9 Neal Street WC2H
613 R9 Neal Yard WC2H
617 M9 Neathouse Place SW1V
619 R7 Neckinger SE16
619 R7 Neckinger Estate SE16
619 R6 Neckinger Street SE1
613 R9 Neils Yard * WC2H
614 H1 Nelson Place SE1
618 G5 Nelson Square SE1
614 H1 Nelson Terrace EC1V
613 M3 Netley Street NW1
616 B11 Neville Street SW7
616 B11 Neville Terrace * SW7
613 L10 New Bond Street W1J
614 G9 New Bridge Street EC4V
615 M7 New Broad Street EC2M
613 M9 Newburgh Street W1F
613 M10 New Burlington Mews W1S
613 M10 New Burlington Place W1S
613 M10 New Burlington Street W1S
618 D11 Newburn Street SE11
615 J7 Newbury Street EC1A
614 G8 Newcastle Close EC4A
612 C6 Newcastle Place W2
614 F5 Newcastle Row EC1R
613 J7 New Cavendish Street W1G
615 J9 New Change EC4M
614 H2 New Charles Street EC1V
619 L5 Newcomen Street SE1
613 Q9 New Compton Street * WC2H
614 E10 New Court * EC4Y
612 D1 Newcourt Street NW8
614 F8 New Fetter Lane EC4A
615 H8 Newgate Street EC1A
619 J3 New Globe Walk SE1
615 Q8 New Goulston Street E1
619 P6 Newham's Row SE1
619 K10 Newington Butts SE17
619 J7 Newington Causeway SE1
615 P4 New Inn Broadway * EC2A
615 P4 New Inn Square * EC2A
615 P4 New Inn Street EC2A
615 P4 New Inn Yard EC2A
619 K9 New Kent Road SE17
615 R2 Newling Estate E2
615 P10 New London Street * EC3R
614 D7 Newman's Row WC2A
613 N7 Newman Street W1T
618 E7 Newnham Terrace SE1
615 N4 New North Place EC2A
615 M1 New North Road N1
614 C6 New North Street WC1N
613 Q8 New Oxford Street WC1A
613 Q10 Newport Court WC2H
613 Q10 Newport Place * WC2H
615 C10 Newport Street SE11
612 G9 New Quebec Street W1H
615 R10 New Row WC2N
614 G8 New Square WC2A
612 P7 New Street EC2M
614 F8 New Street Square EC4A
615 M10 Newton Street WC2B
615 L7 New Union Street EC2Y
615 M10 Nicholas Lane EC4N
618 G4 Nicholson Street SE1
618 F9 Nightingale Mews SE11

615 L2 Nile Street N1
615 J8 Noble Street EC2V
613 N9 Noel Street W1F
612 D8 Norfolk Crescent W2
615 C8 Norfolk Place W2
618 C9 Norfolk Row SE1
612 C8 Norfolk Square W2
612 C9 Norfolk Square Mews W2
615 J3 Norman Street EC1V
617 P2 Norris Street SW1Y
614 F4 Northampton Road EC1R
614 F4 Northampton Row * EC1R
614 G3 Northampton Square EC1V
612 H10 North Audley Street W1K
612 D3 North Bank NW8
614 H5 Northburgh Street EC1V
612 E10 North Carriage Drive W2
613 N6 Northcourt W1T
613 P6 North Crescent EC1E
614 C1 Northdown Street N1
614 M3 North Gower Street NW1
614 C6 Northington Street WC1N
614 D5 North Mews WC1N
612 E9 North Rise * W2
612 G10 North Row W1K
615 R9 North Tenter Street E1
615 D9 North Terrace SW7
615 P9 Northumberland Alley * EC3M
618 A3 Northumberland Avenue WC2N
617 R3 Northumberland Street WC2N
612 B7 North Wharf Road W2
612 B4 Northwick Close NW8
612 B4 Northwick Terrace NW8
615 P5 Norton Folgate E1
614 E8 Norwich Street EC4A
614 A9 Nottingham Court WC2H
612 H5 Nottingham Place NW1
612 H6 Nottingham Street W1U
612 H5 Nottingham Terrace NW1
612 A1 Nugent Terrace NW8
619 L10 Nursery Row SE17
612 E8 Nutford Place W1H

O

618 F9 Oakden Street SE11
618 E7 Oakey Lane SE1
614 H1 Oakley Crescent * EC1V
615 R4 Oakley Yard * E2
612 C3 Oak Tree Road NW8
615 J8 Oat Lane EC2V
616 C7 Observatory Road SW7
619 J11 Occupation Road SE17
615 N7 Octagon Arcade * EC2M
614 A9 Odhams Walk * WC2H
613 M6 Ogle Street W1W
614 G9 Old Bailey EC4M
616 H5 Old Barrack Yard SW1X
617 M2 Old Bond Street W1S
615 M8 Old Broad Street EC2N
614 E8 Old Buildings WC2A
613 J6 Oldbury Place W1U
615 Q8 Old Castle Street E1
613 K9 Old Cavendish Street W1C
613 P10 Old Compton Street W1D
613 J10 Old Fish Street Hill * EC4V
614 G8 Old Fleet Lane EC4A
616 B6 Old Gloucester Street WC1N
615 L9 Old Jewry * EC2R
615 Q2 Old Market Square E2
612 E7 Old Marylebone Road NW1
614 F9 Old Mitre Court * EC4Y
615 Q4 Old Nichol Street E2
614 C6 Old North Street * WC1X
618 G9 Old Paradise Street SE11
617 J4 Old Park Lane W1K
617 P7 Old Pye Street SW1P
612 G9 Old Quebec Street W1H
614 Q6 Old Queen Street SW1H
614 G9 Old Sea Coal Lane EC4M
618 D8 Old Square WC2A
615 J4 Old Street EC1V
615 M4 Old Street EC1Y
615 M4 Oliver's Yard EC1Y
613 K4 O'Meara Street SE1
614 B1 Omega Place N1
616 C10 Onslow Crescent SW7
616 B11 Onslow Gardens SW7
616 B10 Onslow Mews East SW7
616 B10 Onslow Mews West SW7
616 B10 Onslow Square SW7
614 F5 Onslow Street EC1R
615 H8 Ontario Street SE1
618 G10 Opal Street SE11
617 Q2 Orange Street WC2H
616 C11 Oratory Lane * SW3
619 L10 Orb Street SE17
612 B5 Orchardson Street NW8
612 H9 Orchard Street W1H
614 C6 Orde Hall Street * WC1N
618 G9 Orient Street SE11
612 B6 Ormond Close WC1N
612 J10 Ormonde Place SW1W
613 N3 Ormond Yard SW1Y
613 D11 Orsett Street SE11
615 R7 Osborn Street E1
613 L5 Osnaburgh Street NW1
613 L4 Osnaburgh Terrace NW1
612 H6 Ossington Buildings * W1U
613 Q1 Ossulston Street NW1
618 H9 Oswin Street SE11
618 G11 Othello Close SE11
612 F4 Outer Circle NW1
615 P8 Outwich Street * EC3A
616 E8 Ovington Gardens SW3
616 E8 Ovington Mews SW3
616 E8 Ovington Square SW3
616 E8 Ovington Street SW3
615 G2 Owen's Row EC1V
614 F1 Owen Street EC1V
617 P2 Oxendon Street * W1D
615 L10 Oxford Court EC4N
612 D9 Oxford Square W2
612 H9 Oxford Street W1C
619 R11 Oxley Close SE1

P

615 R3 Padbury Court E2
612 B7 Paddington Green W2
612 H6 Paddington Street W1U
617 Q9 Page Street SW1P
615 N9 Page's Walk SE1
614 G2 Paget Street EC1V
617 M7 Pakenham Street WC1X
617 L7 Palace Place SW1E
617 E4 Palace Street SW1E
614 F4 Palgrave Gardens NW1
615 Q3 Palissy Street E2
617 P3 Pall Mall SW1Y
617 N4 Pall Mall East SW1Y
617 N7 Palmer Street SW1H
615 K9 Pancras Lane EC4N
617 K9 Panton Street SW1Y
614 F10 Paper Buildings * EC4Y
615 J2 President Street * EC1V
617 M9 Paragon Mews SE1
614 M7 Pardoner Street SE1
614 H4 Pardon Street EC1V
618 G3 Paris Garden SE1
616 F6 Park Close * SW7
613 K5 Park Crescent W1B

613 L5 Park Crescent Mews East W1W
613 K5 Park Crescent Mews West W1G
614 B8 Parker Mews * WC2B
619 R6 Parker's Row SE1
614 B8 Parker Street WC2B
616 H2 Park Lane W1K
612 G10 Park Lane W1C
612 M4 Park Place SW1A
612 A6 Park Place Villas W2
613 K4 Park Square East NW1
613 K5 Park Square Mews NW1
613 K4 Park Square West NW1
612 E10 Park Steps * W2
616 H2 Park Street W1K
612 E8 Park West W2
612 E8 Park West Place W2
617 P7 Parliament Court * E1
617 R6 Parliament Square SW1P
614 A5 Parliament Street SW1A
616 H10 Passmore Street SW1W
618 H9 Pastor Street SE11
615 J9 Paternoster Row EC4M
614 H9 Paternoster Square EC4M
614 N4 Paul Street EC2A
612 E3 Paveley Street NW8
616 G6 Pavilion Road SW1X
616 G6 Pavilion Street SW1X
614 F5 Peabody Estate * EC1R
614 F3 Peabody Estate * SE1
613 J3 Peabody Estate * SE1
613 K5 Peabody Estate * EC1Y
614 F5 Peabody Terrace * SE1
618 H10 Peacock Street SE17
618 H10 Peacock Yard SE17
618 F7 Pearman Street SE1
614 E5 Pear Place SE1
614 H4 Pear Tree Court EC1V
615 Q6 Pecks Yard * E1
615 R5 Pedley Street E1
615 L3 Peerless Street EC1V
616 D10 Pelham Crescent SW7
616 D9 Pelham Place SW7
616 C9 Pelham Street SW7
615 Q2 Pelter Street E2
617 F8 Pemberton Row EC4A
617 J6 Pembroke Close SW1X
612 D6 Penfold Place W2
612 C5 Penfold Street NW8
615 P10 Penry Street SE1
614 E1 Penton Grove N1
618 H10 Penton Place SE17
614 D2 Penton Rise WC1X
614 C1 Pentonville Road N1
613 J5 Pepper Street SE1
615 P10 Pepys Street EC3N
614 G4 Percival Street EC1V
613 P7 Percy Mews W1T
613 P7 Percy Street W1T
617 P7 Perkin's Rents SW1P
613 K3 Perkins Square SE1
615 J10 Peter's Hill EC4V
613 P10 Peter Street W1F
613 L4 Peto Place NW1
615 P7 Petticoat Lane E1
615 Q8 Petticoat Square E1
615 P8 Petticoat Tower * E1
617 N7 Petty France SW1E
617 P2 Petty Wales EC3R
618 E10 Petyward SW3
615 N10 Philpot Lane EC3M
617 K8 Phipp's Mews SW1W
615 N4 Phipp Street EC2A
614 D4 Phoenix Place WC1X
613 P2 Phoenix Road NW1
613 Q9 Phoenix Street WC2H
619 R6 Phoenix Wharf Road SE1
617 M3 Piccadilly W1J
617 M3 Piccadilly Arcade SW1Y
617 N2 Piccadilly Circus W1J
614 C7 Pickard Street EC1V
617 N4 Pickering Place * SW1A
613 J6 Pickwick Street SE1
613 J9 Picton Place W1U
614 G9 Pilgrim Street EC4V
619 K11 Pilton Place SE17
618 H11 Pimlico Road SW1W
615 N6 Pindar Street EC2A
617 M7 Pine Apple Court * SW1E
614 E4 Pine Street EC1R
615 N1 Pitfield Street N1
617 J4 Pitts Head Mews W1J
613 L5 Plantain Place SE1
615 N10 Plantation Lane EC3M
615 M4 Platina Street EC2A
613 J5 Playhouse Court SE1
614 G9 Playhouse Yard EC4V
615 K3 Pleydell Estate * EC1V
614 F9 Pleydell Street EC4Y
614 F8 Plough Place EC4A
615 P5 Plough Yard EC2A
614 E10 Plowden Buildings * EC4Y
617 F8 Plumtree Court EC4A
612 D5 Plympton Place * NW8
612 D5 Plympton Street NW8
618 G5 Pocock Street SE1
613 N8 Poland Street W1D
615 L9 Pollen Street W1S
612 B4 Pollitt Drive NW8
613 F9 Polperro Mews SE11
613 P1 Polygon Road NW1
615 R8 Pomell Way E1
618 D10 Pond Place SW3
617 Q11 Ponsonby Place SW1P
617 Q11 Ponsonby Terrace SW1P
617 F8 Pont Street SW1X
617 F8 Pont Street Mews SW1X
614 E5 Pooles Buildings WC1X
615 P6 Pope Street SE1
614 G9 Poppins Court EC4A
612 C8 Porchester Place W2
612 M5 Porlock Street SE1
612 G6 Porter Street W1U
612 K3 Porter Street SE1
612 A7 Porteus Road W2
613 N9 Portland Mews W1F
613 K5 Portland Place W1B
612 H8 Portman Close W1H
612 H2 Portman Gate NW1
612 H9 Portman Mews South W1H
612 G8 Portman Square W1H
612 H9 Portman Street W1H
612 G8 Portman Towers W1H
612 E6 Portpool Lane WC1X
612 E9 Portsea Mews W2
612 E9 Portsea Place W2
614 C8 Portsmouth Street WC2A
615 Q10 Portsoken Street EC3N
618 D9 Portugal Street SE11
619 M8 Potier Street SE1
615 P4 Potters Fields SE1
615 L9 Poultry EC2R
614 B5 Powis Mews W2
612 C8 Praed Mews W2
612 C8 Praed Street W2
618 D9 Pratt Walk SE11
612 R10 Prescot Street E1
615 J2 President Street * EC1V
615 N9 Preston Close SE1
615 K1 Prestwood Street * N1
618 H4 Price's Street SE1
614 D2 Prideaux Place WC1X
614 F9 Primrose Hill EC4Y
615 N6 Primrose Street EC2A

612 D2 Prince Albert Road NW8
616 B7 Prince Consort Road SW7
615 R6 Princelet Street E1
613 D5 Prince of Wales Gate SW7
613 M3 Prince of Wales Passage * NW1
613 M3 Prince Regent Mews NW1
617 N3 Princes Arcade W1J
616 C7 Princes Gardens SW7
616 C7 Princes Gate SW7
616 B6 Princes Gate Court SW7
616 C6 Princes Gate Mews SW7
616 C6 Princess Louise Close W2
612 H8 Princess Street SE1
615 L9 Princes Street EC2R
615 L9 Princes Street W1B
614 C7 Princeton Street WC1R
614 E8 Printers Inn Court EC4A
617 P3 Printing House Yard * SE1
619 M8 Prioress Street SE1
614 H9 Priory Court * EC4V
617 R6 Procter Street WC1R
613 J10 Providence Court SW1A
619 N5 Providence Square SE1
615 L2 Provost Estate N1
615 L3 Provost Street EC1V
615 M10 Pudding Lane EC3R
614 H10 Puddle Dock EC4V
615 Q6 Puma Court E1
614 E9 Pump Court * EC4Y
619 P7 Purbrook Street SE1

Q

617 N2 Quadrant Arcade W1B
615 Q5 Quaker Street E1
614 E8 Quality Court WC2A
613 G9 Quebec Mews W1H
613 L7 Queen Anne Mews W1G
617 P6 Queen Anne's Gate SW1H
613 K7 Queen Anne Street W1G
614 E10 Queen Elizabeth Buildings * EC4Y
619 P5 Queen Elizabeth Street SE1
619 K2 Queenhithe EC4V
614 H8 Queen Isabella Way EC1A
617 J4 Queen Mother Gate W1J
616 B9 Queensberry Mews West * SW7
616 B9 Queensberry Place SW7
616 B9 Queensberry Way * SW7
616 A6 Queens Gate SW7
616 A8 Queen's Gate Gardens SW7
616 A8 Queen's Gate Mews SW7
616 A8 Queen's Gate Place SW7
616 A8 Queen's Gate Place Mews SW7
616 A7 Queen's Gate Terrace * SW7
614 B5 Queen Square WC1N
617 K3 Queen Street W1J
615 K9 Queen Street EC4M
619 K2 Queen Street Place EC4R
615 N5 Queen's Yard W1T
614 G10 Queen Victoria Street EC4V
615 K9 Queen Victoria Street EC4N
614 H1 Quick Street N1
619 J5 Quilp Street SE1

R

619 P7 Radcliffe Road SE1
612 C9 Radnor Mews W2
612 D9 Radnor Place W2
615 K3 Radnor Street EC1V
619 L3 Railway Approach SE1
613 B1 Railway Street N1
612 D8 Rainsford Street W2
613 M9 Ramillies Place W1F
613 M9 Ramillies Street W1D
617 P11 Rampayne Street SW1V
614 C11 Randall Road SE11
614 C10 Randall Row SE11
612 A5 Randolph Mews W9
617 J11 Ranelagh Grove SW1W
615 Q9 Rangoon Street * EC3N
613 D6 Ranston Street NW1
616 F6 Raphael Street SW7
613 P7 Rathbone Place W1T
613 N8 Rathbone Street W1T
615 R1 Ravenscroft Street E2
615 N4 Raven Street EC2A
616 F9 Rawlings Street SW3
614 G2 Rawstorne Place * EC1V
614 G2 Rawstorne Street EC1V
614 D6 Raymond Buildings * WC1R
614 F4 Ray Street EC1R
614 F5 Ray Street Bridge * EC1R
615 K5 Redcross Way SE1
613 L1 Redhill Street NW1
614 F8 Red Lion Court EC4A
614 C8 Red Lion Square WC1R
614 C7 Red Lion Street WC1R
617 J3 Red Lion Yard * W1K
612 H10 Red Place W1K
615 P2 Redvers Street N1
615 B9 Reece Mews SW7
618 F10 Reedworth Street SE11
614 H2 Reeves Mews W1K
615 N4 Regan Way N1
617 P9 Regency Place SW1P
617 Q10 Regency Street SW1P
615 B11 Regency Terrace * SW7
612 A1 Regents Mews NW8
614 B3 Regent Square WC1H
613 M9 Regent Street W1B
617 P2 Regent Street SW1Y
615 N3 Regnart Buildings NW1
615 P4 Reliance Square EC2A
615 E7 Relton Mews SW7
616 H11 Rembrandt Close SW1W
614 H1 Remington Street N1
614 C8 Remnant Street WC2B
618 G9 Renfrew Road SE11
618 G3 Rennie Street SE1
619 M8 Rephidim Street SE1
615 P1 Retford Street * N1
617 J3 Rex Place W1K
615 R4 Rhoda Street E1
613 N9 Richardson's Mews W1T
613 P9 Richmond Buildings W1D
613 P9 Richmond Mews W1D
618 A5 Richmond Terrace SW1A
613 P6 Ridgmount Gardens WC1E
613 P6 Ridgmount Street WC1E
613 L8 Riding House Street W1B
618 Q7 Riley Road SE1
618 H5 Risborough Street SE1
614 E2 River Street EC1R
615 P3 Rivington Place EC1V
615 P3 Rivington Street EC2A
612 H8 Robert Adam Street W1U
612 A5 Robert Close W9
619 J10 Robert Dashwood Way SE17
615 H8 Roberts Mews * SW1X
614 F4 Robert's Place * EC1R
613 B2 Robert Street WC2N
615 Q3 Rochelle Street E2
617 N9 Rochester Row SW1P
617 P8 Rochester Street SW1P
619 L3 Rochester Walk * SE1
619 J8 Rockingham Street SE1
614 H1 Rocliffe Street N1

612 G7 Rodmarton Street W1U
615 K9 Rodney Place SE1
619 K10 Rodney Road SE17
616 D5 Roger Street WC1N
612 A11 Roland Gardens SW7
614 E8 Roland Way SW7
614 E8 Rolls Buildings EC4A
616 R11 Rolls Road SE1
613 Q10 Romilly Street W1D
617 Q8 Romney Street SW1P
615 N10 Rood Lane EC3M
615 L6 Ropemaker Street EC2Y
615 L6 Roper Lane SE1
616 A10 Rosary Gardens SW7
615 K5 Roscoe Street EC1Y
615 P7 Rose Alley EC2M
615 K3 Rose Alley SE1
617 N4 Rose & Crown Yard * SW1Y
614 E5 Rosebery Avenue EC1R
614 E5 Rosebery Court EC1R
615 Q7 Rose Court SE1
616 F10 Rosemoor Street SW3
614 A3 Rose Street WC2E
614 F4 Rosoman Place EC1R
614 F3 Rosoman Street EC1R
612 E5 Rossmore Close * NW1
612 E5 Rossmore Road NW1
618 G7 Rotary Street SE1
614 H4 Rotherham Walk * SE1
619 N7 Rothsay Street SE1
614 F4 Roupell Street SE1
619 Q11 Rowcross Street SE1
617 M2 Royal Arcade W1S
616 F11 Royal Avenue SW3
616 M9 Royal Court EC3V
615 R10 Royal Mint Place E1
615 R10 Royal Mint Street E1
619 N6 Royal Oak Yard SE1
617 P3 Royal Opera Arcade * SW1Y
618 D7 Royal Street SE1
613 N3 Rufus Street EC1V
614 C5 Rugby Street WC1N
613 P10 Rupert Court W1D
617 P2 Rupert Street W1D
618 H5 Rushworth Street SE1
615 N4 Russell Court W1A
613 Q6 Russell Square WC1B
618 B10 Russell Street WC2B
615 K9 Russia Row EC2V
617 P9 Rutherford Street SW1P
616 E7 Rutland Court SW7
616 E6 Rutland Gardens SW7
616 E6 Rutland Gardens Mews SW7
616 D6 Rutland Gate SW7
616 D6 Rutland Gate Mews * SW7
616 D7 Rutland Mews South * SW7
614 H6 Rutland Place * EC1M
616 E7 Rutland Street SW7
617 M3 Ryder Street SW1A
616 F7 Rysbrack Street SW3

S

617 M2 Sackville Street W1S
614 F6 Saffron Hill EC1N
614 F6 Saffron Street EC1N
614 C3 Sage Way WC1X
615 M4 St Agnes Well EC1Y
612 C6 St Alban's Mews W2
615 P2 St Alban's Street SW1Y
615 K7 St Alphage Gardens EC2Y
615 K7 St Alphage Highwalk EC2Y
614 H10 St Andrew's Hill EC4V
613 K4 St Andrew's Place NW1
614 F7 St Andrew Street EC1N
613 P9 St Annes Court W1F
617 Q7 St Ann's Street SW1P
617 J11 St Barnabas Street SW1W
617 R5 St Botolph Street EC3N
614 G8 St Bride Street EC4A
615 F3 St Catherines Mews SW3
614 B2 St Chad's Place WC1X
614 B2 St Chad's Street WC1H
613 J9 St Christopher's Place W1U
615 Q9 St Clare Street EC3
614 D9 St Clement's Lane WC2A
614 F6 St Cross Street EC1N
617 N3 St Dunstan's Hill * EC3R
617 N2 St Dunstan's Lane * EC3R
618 G6 St George's Circus SE1
617 L11 St George's Drive SW1V
612 E10 St Georges Fields W2
615 M10 St George's Lane * EC3R
618 G8 St George's Road SE1
618 G8 St George's Court * EC4M
617 N11 St George's Square SW1V
615 L10 St George Street W1S
615 K7 St Giles Churchyard * EC2Y
613 Q8 St Giles Circus W1D
613 Q8 St Giles Court WC2H
613 Q8 St Giles High Street WC2H
613 Q9 St Giles Passage WC2H
614 E3 St Helena Street * WC1X
615 N8 St Helen's Place EC3A
617 N3 St James's Court * SW1E
617 N3 St James's Chambers * SW1Y
617 N3 St James's Court SW1E
617 M3 St James's Gardens * SW1Y
617 P2 St James's Market * SW1Y
617 M4 St James's Place * SW1A
617 P3 St James's Square SW1A
617 M3 St James's Street SW1A
614 G4 St James Walk EC1R
615 Q5 St John's Estate N1
619 Q5 St John's Estate SE1
614 G3 St John's Lane EC1M
614 G5 St John's Place EC1M
614 G5 St John's Square EC1M
614 F1 St John Street EC1V
612 C1 St John's Wood High Street NW8
612 B4 St John's Wood Road NW8
619 R3 St Katharine's Way E1W
617 F11 St Leonards Terrace * SW3
615 L3 St Luke's Estate EC1V
615 K4 St Luke's Close SW3
615 D11 St Luke's Street SW3
618 A6 St Margaret Street SW1P
619 R9 St Mark Street E1
617 R2 St Martin-in-the-Fields * WC2N
613 R10 St Martins Court WC2N
613 R10 St Martin's Lane WC2N
615 J8 St Martin's le Grand EC1A
617 R2 St Martin's Place WC2N
617 Q2 St Martin's Street * WC2H
619 N2 St Mary at Hill EC3R
615 N9 St Mary Axe E3
617 R2 St Mary Graces Court * E1
618 F9 St Mary's Gardens SE11
612 A6 St Mary's Mansions W2
612 B6 St Mary's Square W2
612 B6 St Mary's Terrace W2
617 F9 St Mary's Walk SE1
617 P7 St Matthew Street SW1P
615 M9 St Michael's Alley EC3V
616 H10 St Michael's Mews SW1W
612 C8 St Michael's Street W2
615 L9 St Mildred's Court * EC2R
615 Q10 St Oswald's Place SE11
617 Q7 St Oswulf Street * SW1P
614 H9 St Pauls Church Yard EC4M
619 Q7 St Saviour's Estate SE1
615 A5 St Stephens Parade SW1A
615 L10 St Swithin's Lane EC4N
615 M4 St Thomas Street SE1
613 J7 St Vincent Street W1U

618 C10 Salamanca Place SE1
618 C10 Salamanca Street SE1
612 D7 Sale Place W2
619 L10 Salisbury Close SE17
614 F9 Salisbury Court EC4Y
612 F6 Salisbury Place W1H
612 G6 Salisbury Place W1U
614 F9 Salisbury Square * EC4Y
612 C5 Salisbury Street NW8
615 L10 Salters' Hall Court * EC4N
612 D5 Samford Street NW8
618 D11 Sancroft Street SE11
619 K5 Sanctuary Street SE1
618 E5 Sandell Street SE1
619 L11 Sandford Row SE17
614 D7 Sandland Street WC1R
613 R3 Sandwich Street WC1H
615 P7 Sandy's Row E1
614 G4 Sans Walk EC1R
618 D9 Saperton Walk SE11
615 P9 Saracen's Head Yard EC3M
615 P2 Sarah Street N1
614 C9 Sardinia Street WC2B
618 E9 Saunders Street SE11
612 P10 Savage Gardens EC3N
613 M10 Savile Row W1S
618 B2 Savoy Court * WC2R
618 C2 Savoy Hill WC2R
618 B2 Savoy Place WC2N
614 C10 Savoy Row WC2R
618 C2 Savoy Steps * WC2R
614 C10 Savoy Street WC2R
618 C2 Savoy Way WC2R
619 J5 Sawyer Street SE1
613 N6 Scala Street W1T
615 R9 Scarborough Street E1
615 R1 Scawfell Street E2
613 R1 Sclater Street E1
618 Q4 Scoresby Street SE1
614 F4 Scotswood Street * EC1R
615 L10 Scott's Yard EC4N
619 J6 Scovell Crescent * SE1
619 J6 Scovell Road SE1
615 N5 Scrutton Street EC2A
614 B3 Seaford Street WC1H
617 N7 Seaforth Place SW1E
618 M9 Searles Road SE1
618 F11 Seaton Close SE11
614 H3 Sebastian Street EC1V
614 E4 Secker Street SE1
618 N11 Sedan Way SE17
616 H9 Sedding Street SW1X
614 C3 Seddon Street WC1X
613 K9 Sedley Place W1C
615 P10 Seething Lane EC3N
614 G5 Sekforde Street EC1R
616 B11 Selwood Place SW7
616 B11 Selwood Terrace SW7
617 J10 Semley Place SW1W
614 F9 Serjeant's Inn * EC4Y
614 D8 Serle Street WC2A
615 J9 Sermon Lane EC4V
616 E4 Serpentine Road W2
619 Q9 Setchell Estate SE1
619 Q9 Setchell Road SE1
619 Q9 Setchell Way SE1
613 R9 Seven Dials WC2H
615 R6 Seven Stars Yard E1
616 G6 Seville Street SW1X
614 H4 Seward Street EC1V
612 H8 Seymour Mews W1H
612 F7 Seymour Place W1H
612 F9 Seymour Street W1H
615 R4 Shacklewell Street E2
619 Q4 Shad Thames SE1
613 P10 Shaftesbury Avenue W1D
615 J7 Shaftesbury Place * EC2Y
615 K1 Shaftesbury Street N1
619 F8 Shafto Mews SW1X
619 P4 Shand Street SE1
617 P2 Shavers Place * W1J
614 C9 Sheffield Street * WC2A
613 K9 Sheldon Square W2
612 A7 Shelton Street * WC2H
614 A9 Shelton Street W1K
617 K4 Shepherd Market * W1J
612 H10 Shepherds Place W1K
617 K4 Shepherd Street W1J
615 P1 Shenfield Street N1
615 K2 Shepherdess Place EC1V
615 K1 Shepherdess Walk N1
617 P9 Sheraton Street * W1F
615 L10 Sherborne Lane EC4N
612 H6 Sherlock Mews W1U
612 F7 Sherwood Court W1H
613 N10 Sherwood Street W1F
612 E7 Shillibeer Place W1H
619 M5 Ship & Mermaid Row * SE1
615 N10 Ship Tavern Passage EC3V
615 R2 Shipton Street E2
619 N4 Shipwright Yard * SE1
614 F8 Shoe Lane EC4A
615 P6 Shoreditch High Street E1
619 Q11 Shorncliffe Road SE1
615 Q10 Shorter Street EC3N
614 A9 Shorts Gardens * WC2H
618 F5 Short Street SE1
612 E7 Shouldham Street W1H
612 D6 Shroton Street NW1
614 B7 Sicilian Avenue * WC1A
612 G5 Siddons Lane NW1
618 D8 Sidford Place SE1
614 B3 Sidmouth Street WC1H
614 G1 Sidney Grove EC1V
615 L2 Silbury Street * N1
618 H6 Silex Street SE1
615 K6 Silk Street EC2Y
613 M1 Silverdale NW1
613 N9 Silver Place W1F
619 L6 Silvester Street SE1
615 M3 Singer Street EC1V
615 L9 Sise Lane * EC4N
616 H10 Skinner Place * SW1W
615 K10 Skinners Lane EC4V
614 G4 Skinner Street EC1R
619 R10 Slingsby Place WC2H
616 E10 Sloane Avenue SW3
616 H11 Sloane Court East SW3
616 H11 Sloane Court West SW3
616 H10 Sloane Gardens SW1W
616 G10 Sloane Square SW1X
616 G8 Sloane Street SW1X
616 G9 Sloane Terrace SW1X
612 B9 Smallbrook Mews W2
614 B8 Smart's Place WC1A
612 G7 Smithfield Street EC1A
613 P10 Smith's Court * W1D
617 R8 Smith Square SW1P
615 F11 Smith Street SW3
614 G7 Snow Hill EC1A
619 M5 Snowsfields SE1
613 P8 Soho Square W1D
613 P8 Soho Street W1D
613 D9 Somers Crescent W2
619 L6 Southall Place SE1
614 E7 Southampton Buildings * WC2A
614 B7 Southampton Place WC1A
614 A6 Southampton Row WC1B
614 B10 Southampton Street WC2E
617 J2 South Audley Street W1K
618 F2 South Bank SE1
616 D6 South Carriage Drive SW7
617 J9 South Eaton Place SW1W

616 C9 South Kensington Station Arcade SW7
613 K9 South Molton Lane W1K
613 K9 South Molton Street W1K
616 C11 South Parade SW3
615 M7 South Place EC2M
615 M7 South Place Mews EC2M
612 G10 South Rise * W2
614 E7 South Square WC1R
615 J3 South Street W1K
615 R10 South Tenter Street E1
616 D9 South Terrace SW7
619 K2 Southwark Bridge SE1
615 K3 Southwark Bridge Road SE1
619 R9 Southwark Park Road SE16
618 H3 Southwark Street SE1
618 B8 South Wharf Road W2
612 C8 Southwick Mews W2
612 D9 Southwick Place W2
612 D8 Southwick Street W2
612 E9 Southwick Yard * W2
614 E4 Spafield Street EC1R
614 F2 Spa Green Estate * EC1R
613 J8 Spanish Place * W1U
619 Q8 Spa Road SE16
614 A3 Speedy Place WC1H
618 E8 Spencer Place SW1P
614 G5 Spencer Street EC1V
617 N7 Spenser Street SW1E
615 P6 Spital Square * E1
615 P6 Spital Yard * E1
616 F11 Sprimont Place SW3
617 R3 Spring Gardens SW1A
613 G6 Spring Mews * W1U
612 B9 Spring Street W2
619 L7 Spurgeon Street SE1
618 E5 Spur Road SE1
617 M6 Spur Road SW1A
612 B3 Squire Gardens NW8
618 E11 Stables Way SE11
617 N5 Stable Yard Road SW1A
613 Q9 Stacey Street WC2H
616 F7 Stackhouse Street SW1X
617 M7 Stafford Place SW1E
617 M3 Stafford Street W1S
617 M7 Stag Place SW1E
619 M4 Stainer Street SE1
615 K8 Staining Lane EC2V
612 E6 Stalbridge Street NW1
618 E3 Stamford Street SE1
615 Q1 Stamper Place E2
615 P3 Standard Place EC2A
619 N10 Stanford Street SE17
617 P10 Stanford Street SW1V
614 A10 Stanhope Gardens SW7
612 F10 Stanhope Gate W1K
617 J4 Stanhope Gate W1K
616 A9 Stanhope Mews East SW7
616 A10 Stanhope Mews South SW7
616 A9 Stanhope Mews West SW7
613 L2 Stanhope Parade NW1
612 F10 Stanhope Place W2
617 K4 Stanhope Row * W1J
613 M2 Stanhope Street NW1
612 C10 Stanhope Terrace W2
613 R1 Stanley Passage * N1
619 Q6 Stanworth Street SE1
614 E7 Staple Inn WC1V
619 M6 Staple Street SE1
613 N3 Starcross Street NW1
619 R2 Star Place E1W
612 C8 Star Street W2
614 E8 Star Yard WC2A
612 H5 Station Approach * NW1
613 L5 Station Arcade * W1W
614 H9 Stationers Hall Court * EC4M
619 L10 Stead Street SE17
619 J10 Steedman Street SE17
613 P7 Stephen Mews W1T
613 N4 Stephenson Way NW1
613 P8 Stephen Street W1T
618 E6 Sterling Street SW7
619 L6 Sterry Street SE1
613 A7 Stevens Street SE1
616 C11 Stevens Grove * SW3
614 C11 Stewart's Grove SW3
613 J10 Stew Lane EC4V
617 N9 Stillington Street SW1P
614 D7 Stone Buildings WC2A
614 G8 Stonecutter Street EC4A
615 P8 Stone House Court EC2M
619 J6 Stones End Street SE1
615 P8 Stoney Lane EC3A
619 L3 Stoney Street SE1
613 P7 Store Street WC1E
617 Q6 Storeys Gate * SW1H
617 Q6 Storey's Gate SW1H
618 D10 Stoughton Close SE11
612 F9 Stourcliffe Street W1H
618 B2 Strand WC2N
614 C10 Strand WC2R
613 K9 Stratford Place W1C
613 D10 Strathearn Place W2
617 L3 Stratton Street W1J
613 R8 Streatham Street WC1A
615 Q2 Strout's Place E2
617 P7 Strutton Ground SW1H
615 Q7 Strype Street E1
615 G6 Studio Place SW1X
614 B8 Stukeley Street WC2B
619 J6 Sturge Street SE1
615 K1 Sturt Street N1
614 H1 Sudeley Street N1
619 J6 Sudrey Street SE1
615 L10 Suffolk Lane EC4R
617 Q3 Suffolk Street SW1Y
618 F9 Sullivan Road SE11
614 E5 Summers Street EC1R
616 C10 Sumner Place SW7
616 C10 Sumner Place Mews SW7
619 J3 Sumner Street SE1
615 M6 Sun Street EC2A
615 N7 Sun Street Passage EC2M
618 G5 Surrey Row * SE1
619 N11 Surrey Square SE17
614 D10 Surrey Street WC2R
619 P10 Surrey Terrace SE17
612 C10 Sussex Gardens W2
612 C10 Sussex Mews East * W2
612 C10 Sussex Mews West W2
612 C9 Sussex Place W2
612 F4 Sussex Place NW1
612 C10 Sussex Square W2
617 L11 Sutherland Row SW1V
617 L11 Sutherland Street SW1V
616 D11 Sutton Dwelling Estate SW3
614 H5 Sutton Lane EC1M
613 P8 Sutton Row W1D
612 K5 Tyburn Way W1H
612 C5 Swain Street NW8
613 L9 Swallow Place W1B
617 N2 Swallow Street W1B
619 Q3 Swan Lane EC4R
619 N3 Swan Mead SE1
619 R2 Swan Passage E1
619 K6 Swan Street SE1
619 R6 Sweeney Crescent SE1
614 C2 Swinton Place WC1X
614 C2 Swinton Street WC1X
615 J5 Sycamore Street EC1Y
616 C10 Sydney Close SW3
616 C10 Sydney Mews SW3
616 C10 Sydney Place SW7
616 D11 Sydney Street SW3
615 N3 Symister Mews * N1

616 G10 Symons Street SW3

T
619 L5 Tabard Garden Estate SE1
619 L6 Tabard Street SE1
615 M5 Tabernacle Street EC2A
617 N10 Tachbrook Street SW1V
615 M10 Talbot Court EC3V
612 B9 Talbot Square W2
615 L4 Talbot Yard SE1
614 F10 Tallis Street EC4Y
614 B3 Tankerton Houses * WC1H
614 B3 Tankerton Street WC1H
619 P6 Tanner Street SE1
618 E6 Tanswell Street * SE1
615 K1 Taplow Street N1
619 J8 Tarn Street SE1
612 F7 Tarrant Place W1H
619 M10 Tatum Street SE17
612 F5 Taunton Mews NW1
612 F4 Taunton Place NW1
614 B10 Tavistock Court * WC2E
613 Q4 Tavistock Place WC1H
614 Q4 Tavistock Square WC1H
614 B10 Tavistock Street WC2E
614 B3 Taviton Street WC1H
618 F11 Tavy Close SE11
615 L8 Telegraph Street EC2R
614 F10 Temple Avenue EC4Y
614 E10 Temple Gardens * EC4Y
614 F9 Temple Lane EC4Y
614 D10 Temple Place WC2R
618 E4 Tenison Way SE1
619 L5 Tennis Street SE1
613 L9 Tenterden Street W1S
615 Q7 Tenter Ground E1
619 L8 Terminus Place SW1W
619 P3 Thames Path EC3N
613 R11 Thames Path W1P
613 R3 Thanet Street WC1H
614 F8 Thavies Inn EC4A
613 J8 Thayer Street W1U
615 N7 The Arcade * EC2M
618 B3 The Arches * WC2N
614 H5 The Charterhouse * EC1M
618 F5 The Cut SE1
614 E8 Theed Street SE1
619 Q7 The Grange SE1
617 M5 The Mall SW1A
614 C6 Theobald's Road WC1R
615 L8 Theobald Street SE1
615 K7 The Postern * EC2Y
612 D8 The Quadrangle W2
619 P3 The Queens Walk SW1A
617 Q7 The Sanctuary SW1P
614 H1 Theseus Walk N1
612 D8 The Water Gardens W2
617 N8 Thirleby Road SW1P
618 G7 Thomas Doyle Street SE1
615 K2 Thoresby Street N1
617 P10 Thorndike Street * SW1V
614 A9 Thorney Street SW1P
613 Q5 Thornhaugh Street WC1H
612 F6 Thornton Place W1H
619 K4 Thrale Street SE1
615 R7 Thrawl Street E1
615 M9 Threadneedle Street EC2R
615 K10 Three Kings Yard W1K
615 Q5 Three Oak Lane SE1
615 M8 Throgmorton Avenue EC2N
615 M8 Throgmorton Street EC2N
619 J11 Thrush Street SE17
616 D9 Thurloe Close SW7
616 C9 Thurloe Place SW7
616 C9 Thurloe Place Mews * SW7
616 C9 Thurloe Square SW7
616 C9 Thurloe Street SW7
619 N11 Thurlow Walk SE17
617 J3 Tilney Street W1J
615 J4 Timber Street * EC1V
618 B11 Tinworth Street SE11
619 M10 Tisdall Place SE17
612 E9 Titchborne Row W2
619 J7 Tiverton Street SE1
615 L8 Tokenhouse Yard EC2R
613 N4 Tolmers Square NW1
615 R3 Tomlinson Close E2
614 C3 Tompion Street EC1V
614 A3 Tonbridge Street WC1H
614 E8 Took's Court EC4A
619 M3 Tooley Street SE1
617 E4 Topham Street * EC1R
614 G1 Torrens Street EC1V
613 N6 Torrington Place WC1E
613 Q5 Torrington Square WC1H
619 P6 Tothill Street SW1H
613 N5 Tottenham Court Road W1T
613 N6 Tottenham Mews * W1T
613 N7 Tottenham Street W1T
619 J6 Toulmin Street SE1
619 R3 Tower Bridge E1W
619 Q3 Tower Bridge Approach EC3N
619 N8 Tower Bridge Road SE1
619 R9 Tower Court * WC2H
619 R3 Tower Hill EC3N
619 P2 Tower Hill Terrace EC3R
615 K10 Tower Royal * EC4N
619 R9 Tower Street WC2H
619 L11 Townley Street SE17
619 M10 Townsend Street SE17
615 Q7 Toynbee Street E1
617 Q3 Trafalgar Square * SW1Y
619 L11 Trafalgar Street SE17
617 K3 Transept Street NW1
617 K3 Trebeck Street W1J
617 R8 Tresham Crescent NW8
618 H4 Treveris Street SE1
618 F6 Trevor Place SW7
618 F5 Trevor Square SW7
618 E6 Trevor Street SW7
615 J10 Trig Lane EC4V
615 K7 Trinity Church Square SE1
619 Q10 Trinity Place EC3N
619 P2 Trinity Square EC3N
619 J5 Trinity Street SE1
615 K6 Trio Place SE1
615 M4 Triton Square NW1
615 K9 Trump Street EC2V
619 J5 Trundle Street SE1
616 F11 Tryon Street SW3
614 F10 Tudor Street EC4Y
617 R8 Tufton Street SW1P
615 R8 Turks Row SW3
614 G8 Turnagain Lane * EC4A
614 H5 Turnmill Street EC1M
617 L11 Turpentine Lane SW1V
614 G4 Turquand Street SE17
615 Q4 Turville Street E2
612 G10 Tyburn Way W1H
619 N6 Tyers Gate SE1
618 C11 Tyers Street SE11
615 R8 Tyne Street E1
614 E3 Tysoe Street WC1X

U
617 N10 Udall Street SW1P
613 K5 Ufford Street SE1
613 K5 Ulster Place NW1
615 N9 Undershaft EC3A
615 K2 Underwood Row N1
615 K2 Underwood Street N1
615 N8 Union Court EC2N
618 H4 Union Street SE1

615 Q2 Union Walk E2
613 N5 University Street W1T
616 C7 Unwin Road SW7
612 A9 Upbrook Mews W2
619 P11 Upnor Way SE17
617 J7 Upper Belgrave Street SW1X
612 F9 Upper Berkeley Street W1H
612 H10 Upper Brook Street W1K
616 H2 Upper Grosvenor Street W1K
618 E3 Upper Ground SE1
613 J8 Upper Harley Street NW1
613 N10 Upper John Street W1F
618 D7 Upper Marsh SE1
612 F6 Upper Montagu Street W1H
617 R9 Upper St Martin's Lane WC2H
617 M9 Upper Tachbrook Street SW1V
619 J10 Upper Thames Street EC4V
613 J6 Upper Wimpole Street W1G
613 Q4 Upper Woburn Place WC1H

V
618 G5 Valentine Place SE1
617 N7 Vandon Street SW1H
615 N5 Vandy Street EC2A
613 M2 Varndell Street NW1
619 R8 Vauban Estate SE16
619 R8 Vauban Street SE16
613 Q2 Vaughan Estate * E2
617 M8 Vauxhall Bridge Road SW1X
619 Q11 Vauxhall Bridge Road SW1P
618 D11 Vauxhall Street SE11
618 C11 Vauxhall Walk SE11
613 C6 Venables Street W2
613 K9 Vere Street W1G
614 B7 Vernon Place WC1X
614 D7 Vernon Rise WC1X
614 E6 Vernon Square WC1X
614 E6 Verulam Street WC1X
615 L2 Vestry Street N1
617 L8 Victoria Arcade SW1E
614 F10 Victoria Embankment EC4Y
618 B5 Victoria Embankment SW1A
618 C11 Victoria Embankment Gardens * WC2N
612 C10 Victoria Gate W2
617 L7 Victoria Square SW1W
617 L8 Victoria Street SW1E
619 Q7 Victory Place SE17
617 M2 Vigo Street W1S
613 B3 Villiers Street WC2N
617 N9 Vincent Square SW1P
617 P9 Vincent Street SW1P
615 M3 Vince Street EC1V
614 E5 Vine Hill EC1R
617 N4 Vine Lane SE1
617 Q7 Vine Street SW1P
617 N5 Vinegar Yard SE1
614 F5 Vine Street EC3N
617 M2 Vine Street W1J
614 E4 Vineyard Mews * EC1R
614 E4 Vineyard Walk EC1R
618 D7 Virgil Street SE1
615 Q3 Virginia Road E2
615 J5 Viscount Street EC2Y

W
619 L10 Wadding Street SE17
614 A3 Wakefield Mews WC1H
614 B4 Wakefield Street WC1N
614 G2 Wakley Street EC1V
615 L10 Walbrook EC4N
619 K10 Walcorde Avenue SE17
618 F9 Walcot Square SE11
617 N9 Walcott Street * SW1P
613 P10 Walker's Court * W1F
615 K7 Wallside * EC2Y
618 E9 Walnut Tree Walk SE11
616 F11 Walpole Street SW3
616 F7 Walton Place SW3
616 E9 Walton Street SW3
619 J9 Walworth Road SE1
619 K10 Wansey Street SE17
613 J4 Wardens Grove SE1
613 N9 Wardour Mews W1F
613 N8 Wardour Street W1F
617 Q4 Wardrobe Place * EC4V
614 E5 Warner Street EC1R
614 E5 Warner Yard EC1R
613 M5 Warren Mews W1T
613 M5 Warren Street W1T
614 D7 Warwick Court WC1V
617 P3 Warwick House Street SW1Y
614 H8 Warwick Lane EC4M
617 M10 Warwick Place North * SW1V
617 M7 Warwick Row SW1E
617 M10 Warwick Square * EC4M
617 M10 Warwick Square Mews SW1V
613 N10 Warwick Street W1B
617 L11 Warwick Way SW1V
615 K5 Warwick Yard * EC1Y
614 G10 Watergate EC4Y
619 P2 Water Lane EC3R
618 C2 Waterloo Bridge WC2R
617 P3 Waterloo Place SW1Y
618 D3 Waterloo Road SE1
614 E10 Water Street WC2R
615 K9 Watling Court EC4M
615 J9 Watling Street EC4M
617 J3 Watson's Mews NW1
617 J3 Waverton Street W1K
619 P4 Weaver's Lane SE1
618 F6 Webber Row SE1
618 F5 Webber Street SE1
619 N8 Webb Street SE1
613 J10 Weighhouse Street W1K
613 Q2 Weirs Passage NW1
617 J7 Welbeck Street W1G
613 K8 Welbeck Way W1G
615 K9 Well Court EC4M
619 J5 Weller Street SE1
615 P3 Wellesley Place * NW1
615 K2 Wellesley Terrace N1
612 C2 Wellington Place NW8
612 C1 Wellington Road NW8
615 R2 Wellington Row E2
617 F11 Wellington Square SW3
614 B10 Wellington Street WC2E
614 N7 Wells Mews * W1T
614 C3 Wells Square WC1X
613 M7 Wells Street W1T
616 B7 Wells Way SW7
615 J1 Wenlock Road N1
615 K1 Wenlock Street N1
615 Q8 Wentworth Street E1
613 N1 Werrington Street NW1
618 H10 Wesley Close SE17
613 J7 Wesley Street W1G
612 B10 Westbourne Crescent W2
612 B10 Westbourne Crescent Mews W2
612 C10 Westbourne Gate W2
612 B10 Westbourne Street W2
612 A8 Westbourne Terrace W2
616 C4 West Carriage Drive W2
612 H9 West Central Street WC2H
616 H9 West Eaton Place SW1W
616 H9 West Eaton Place Mews SW1X
612 E8 West Garden Place W2
616 F9 West Halkin Street SW1X
614 F8 West Harding Street * EC4A
615 L2 Westland Place EC1V

617 L10 West Mews SW1V
618 B6 Westminster Bridge SW1A
618 D6 Westminster Bridge Road SE1
618 B6 Westminster Bridge Road SW1A
613 J7 Westmoreland Street W1G
617 L11 Westmoreland Terrace SW1V
613 D2 Weston Rise WC1X
619 M7 Weston Street SE1
614 G7 West Poultry Avenue EC1M
612 E10 West Rise * W2
615 J7 West Smithfield EC1A
618 G8 West Square SE11
615 Q9 West Street WC2H
615 R9 West Tenter Street E1
616 M10 West Warwick Place * SW1V
616 A10 Wetherby Place SW7
617 K2 Weymouth Mews W1G
613 J6 Weymouth Street W1G
615 J1 Wharf Road N1
614 D3 Wharton Cottages * WC1X
614 C3 Wharton Street WC1X
613 J7 Wheatley Street W1G
615 Q6 Wheeler Lane E1
615 Q5 Wheler Street E1
614 C9 Whetstone Park WC2A
614 E8 Whichcote Street * SE1
614 B3 Whidborne Street WC1H
615 R1 Whiskin Street EC1R
615 Q4 Whitby Street E1
613 P10 Whitcomb Street W1D
614 E5 White Bear Yard * EC1R
615 R8 Whitechapel High Street E1
615 J5 Whitecross Street EC1Y
614 F9 Whitefriars Street EC4Y
618 A4 Whitehall SW1A
618 A4 Whitehall Court SW1A
618 A4 Whitehall Gardens SW1A
618 A4 Whitehall Place SW1A
618 F11 White Hart Street SE11
615 L4 White Hart Yard SE1
612 D5 Whitehaven Street NW8
616 E10 Whiteheads Grove SW3
616 E11 Whitehead's Grove SW3
615 L4 White Horse Street W1J
615 P8 White Kennett Street EC3A
615 N9 White Lion Court EC3V
614 H10 White Lion Hill EC4V
615 N3 White Lion Street N1
615 J6 White Lyon Court EC1A
619 P5 White's Grounds SE1
619 P5 White's Grounds Estate SE1
615 Q7 White's Row * E1
617 M5 Whitfield Place W1T
613 N6 Whitfield Street W1T
613 C9 Whitgift Street SE11
616 H10 Whittaker Street SW1W
615 N9 Whittington Avenue EC3V
618 F4 Whittlesey Street SE1
615 C11 Wickham Street SE11
614 C2 Wicklow Street WC1X
615 P7 Widegate Street E1
613 K8 Wigmore Place * W1U
613 J8 Wigmore Street W1U
616 H9 Wilbraham Place SW1X
614 C8 Wild Court WC2B
619 N7 Wild's Rents SE1
614 B9 Wild Street WC2B
617 M7 Wilfred Street SW1E
615 R6 Wilkes Street E1
615 R1 Wilks Place N1
617 R2 William IV Street WC2N
616 G6 William Mews SW1X
613 M3 William Road NW1
617 N9 Willow Place SW1P
615 N4 Willow Street EC2A
619 P9 Willow Walk SE1
614 E3 Wilmington Square WC1X
614 E3 Wilmington Street WC1X
615 M6 Wilson Street EC2A
616 H6 Wilton Crescent SW1X
617 J7 Wilton Mews SW1X
616 H5 Wilton Place SW1X
618 L8 Wilton Road SW1V
616 H6 Wilton Row SW1X
617 K7 Wilton Street SW1X
616 H7 Wilton Terrace SW1X
613 K6 Wimpole Mews W1G
613 K7 Wimpole Street W1G
613 H10 Winchester Close * SE11
619 L3 Winchester Square SE1
617 L11 Winchester Street SW1V
619 L3 Winchester Walk SE1
618 F9 Wincott Street SE11
613 P7 Windmill Street W1T
617 P4 Windmill Walk * SE1
615 K2 Windsor Terrace N1
617 F8 Wine Office Court EC4A
613 P10 Winnett Street W1D
612 B8 Winsland Mews W2
612 B8 Winsland Street W2
612 M8 Winsley Street W1W
613 R4 Woburn Place WC1H
615 Q5 Woburn Square WC1H
613 Q3 Woburn Walk * WC1H
618 H9 Wollaston Close SE1
619 R6 Wolseley Street SE1
614 G4 Woodbridge Street EC1R
616 R6 Woodseer Street E1
615 C10 Wood's Mews W1K
619 P8 Wood's Place SE1
613 J7 Woodstock Mews W1G
613 K9 Woodstock Street W1C
615 K8 Wood Street EC2V
614 H6 Woolf Mews WC1H
618 F5 Wootton Street SE1
619 Q10 Wordsworth Road SE1
618 C11 Worgan Street SE11
615 N8 Wormwood Street EC2N
615 M5 Worship Street EC2A
614 D4 Wren Street WC1X
613 L4 Wybert Street NW1
614 G3 Wyclif Street EC1V
612 F7 Wyndham Mews W1H
612 F7 Wyndham Place W1H
612 F6 Wyndham Street NW1
618 D11 Wynyard Terrace SE11
614 G2 Wynyatt Street EC1V
612 F9 Wythburn Place W1H

Y
614 E3 Yardley Street WC1X
617 K4 Yarmouth Place W1J
616 E8 Yeoman's Row SW3
615 R10 Yeoman's Yard E1
612 H4 York Bridge NW1
612 D5 York Buildings WC2N
612 H5 York Gate NW1
612 D5 York Road SE1
614 C7 Yorkshire Grey Yard * WC1R
612 F7 York Street W1H
612 G6 York Street Chambers * W1U
612 H5 York Terrace East NW1
612 H5 York Terrace West NW1

Z
619 J3 Zoar Street SE1

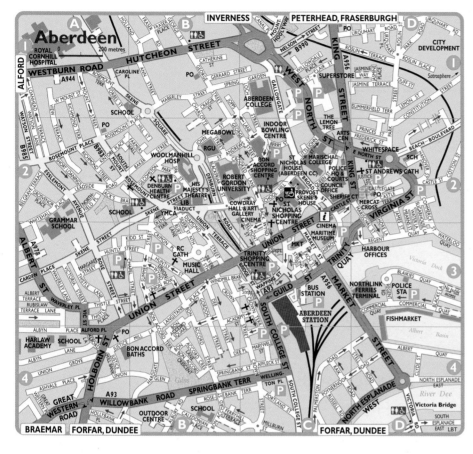

Aberdeen

Aberdeen is found on atlas page **557 G3**

C4	Affleck Street	A2	Kintore Place
A3	Albert Street	B3	Langstane Place
B4	Albury Road	C2	Little John Street
A4	Albyn Lane	C1	Loch Street
A4	Alford Place	B1	Maberley Street
C2	Back Wynd	D2	Marischal Street
D2	Beach Boulevard	C3	Market Street
C3	Belmont Street	C1	Mount Hooly Way
C2	Berry Street	A1	Mount Street
B2	Blackfriar Street	D4	North Esplanade West
D3	Blaikies Quay	D2	Park Street
B3	Bon Accord Street	C4	Portland Street
B3	Bon Accord Terrace	C2	Queen Street
C3	Bridge Street	D3	Regent Quay
C2	Broad Street	A2	Richmond Street
B4	Caledonian Place	A1	Richmond Terrace
D2	Castlegate	A3	Rose Street
B3	Chapel Street	A2	Rosemount Place
B1	Charlotte Street	B2	Rosemount Viaduct
D2	Commerce Street	C4	Russell Road
D3	Commercial Quay	B2	St Andrews Street
B3	Crimon Place	C1	St Clair Street
B2	Crooked Lane	C2	School Hill
B3	Crown Street	B3	Silver Street South
C3	Crown Terrace	B1	Skene Square
B3	Dee Street	A3	Skene Street
B2	Denburn Road	C3	South College Street
B3	Diamond Street	A2	South Mount Street
D2	East North Street	B2	Spa Street
A2	Esslemont Avenue	B1	Spring Garden
C3	Exchange Street	B4	Springbank Terrace
A1	Forbes Street	C3	Stirling Street
D2	Frederick Street	B3	Summer Street
C1	Gallowgate	C3	Trinity Quay
B1	George Street	A4	Union Glen
B2	Gilcomston Park	A4	Union Grove
C3	Guild Street	B3	Union Row
D2	Hanover Street	B3	Union Street
B4	Hardgate	B2	Union Terrace
A4	Holburn Street	D1	Urquhart Road
A3	Huntly Street	D4	Victoria Road
B1	Hutcheon Street	D2	Virginia Street
A2	Jack's Brae	C3	Wapping Street
D2	James Street	A3	Waverley Place
B2	John Street	C4	Wellington Place
B1	Jopps Lane	C1	West North Street
A4	Justice Mill Lane	A1	Westburn Road
C1	King Street	A4	Willowbank Road

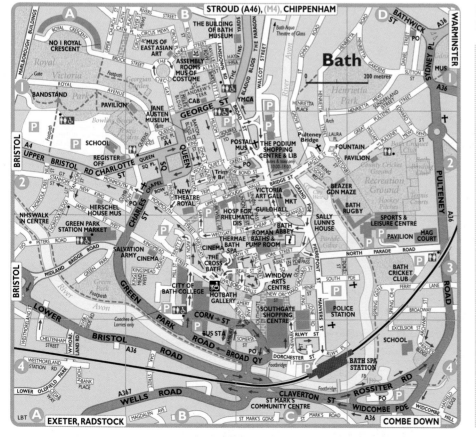

Bath

Bath is found on atlas page **86 C2**

C3	Abbey Square	A3	Lower Bristol Road
B1	Alfred Street	A4	Lower Oldfield Park
B4	Ambury	C3	Manvers Street
C2	Argyle Street	A3	Midland Bridge Road
B3	Avon Street	B3	Mill Street
B2	Barton Street	B2	Milsom Street
B3	Bath Street	A2	Monmouth Place
C3	Beau Street	B2	Monmouth Street
B1	Bennett Street	B2	New Bond Street
C1	Bladud Buildings	A2	New King Street
B2	Bridewell Lane	C3	New Orchard Street
C2	Bridge Street	D3	North Parade Road
B4	Broad Quay	B4	Oak Street
C2	Broad Street	C3	Old Orchard Street
D3	Broadway	C3	Pierrepont Street
A1	Brock Street	B2	Princes Street
B2	Chapel Row	D2	Pulteney Road
B3	Charles Street	B2	Queen Square
A2	Charlotte Street	B2	Queen Square Place
C3	Cheap Street	B2	Queen Street
B1	Circus Mews	B2	Quiet Street
C4	Claverton Street	C4	Railway Street
B3	Corn Street	D4	Rossiter Road
C4	Dorchester Street	A1	Royal Avenue
D2	Edward Street	A1	Royal Crescent
D3	Ferry Lane	B1	Russell Street
B1	Gay Street	C1	St John's Road
B1	George Street	B2	Saw Close
C2	Grand Parade	C3	South Parade
B2	Grange Grove	C4	Southgate Street
D2	Great Pulteney Street	C3	Stall Street
A2	Great Stanhope Street	D1	Sydney Place
A3	Green Park	B1	The Circus
B3	Green Park Road	C1	The Vineyards
B2	Green Street	B2	Trim Street
C2	Grove Street	C2	Union Passage
D1	Henrietta Gardens	C2	Union Street
D1	Henrietta Mews	B2	Upper Borough Walls
C1	Henrietta Road	A2	Upper Bristol Road
C1	Henrietta Street	A1	Upper Church Street
C3	Henry Street	C1	Walcot Street
A2	James Street West	B4	Wells Road
B2	John Street	B3	Westgate Buildings
B3	Kingsmead North	B3	Westgate Street
B3	Kingsmead Street	A4	Westmoreland Road
A2	Lansdown Road	D4	Widcombe Parade
A2	Little Stanhope Street	B2	Wood Street
B3	Lower Borough Walls	C3	York Street

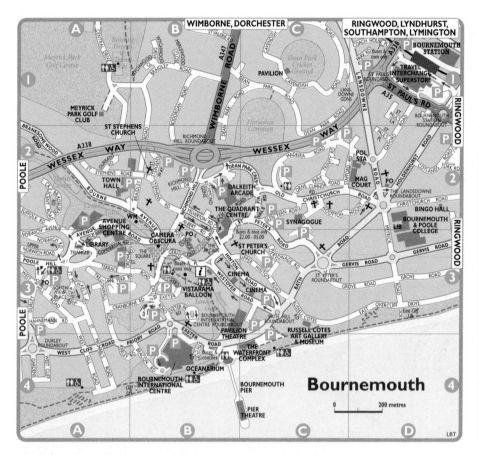

Bournemouth

Bournemouth is found on atlas page **34 C2**

B2	Albert Road	C3	Parsonage Road
A3	Avenue Lane	A3	Poole Hill
A3	Avenue Road	B3	Post Office Road
C3	Bath Road	B4	Priory Road
B4	Beacon Road	A3	Purbeck Road
B1	Bodorgan Road	B2	Richmond Gardens
A2	Bourne Avenue	B2	Richmond Hill
A2	Bradburne Road	B2	Richmond Hill Drive
B2	Braidley Road	C3	Russell Cotes Road
A2	Branksome Wood Road	A3	St Michael's Road
C1	Cavendish Road	D1	St Paul's Lane
A1	Central Drive	D2	St Paul's Place
D2	Christchurch Road	D1	St Paul's Road
D1	Coach House Place	C2	St Peter's Road
A3	Commercial Road	A2	St Stephens Road
C2	Cumnor Road	B2	St Stephens Way
D2	Cotlands Road	B1	St Valerie Road
A3	Cranborne Road	B4	South Cliff Road
A2	Crescent Road	A3	South View Place
B2	Dean Park Crescent	C2	Stafford Road
C1	Dean Park Road	A2	Suffolk Road
A3	Durley Road	A3	Terrace Road
A2	Durrant Road	B3	The Arcade
D3	East Overcliff Drive	B3	The Square
B3	Exeter Crescent	A3	The Triangle
B3	Exeter Park Road	A3	Tregonwell Road
B3	Exeter Road	C2	Trinity Road
C2	Fir Vale Road	C3	Upper Hinton Road
B3	Gervis Place	A3	Upper Norwich Road
D3	Gervis Road	A3	Upper Terrace Road
C2	Glen Fern Road	A2	Wessex Way
D3	Grove Road	A4	West Cliff Gardens
A3	Hahnemann Road	A4	West Cliff Road
B3	Hinton Road	A3	West Hill Road
D2	Holdenhurst Road	B3	Westover Road
A4	Kerley Road	B1	Wimborne Road
C1	Lansdowne Gardens	C2	Wootton Mount
D1	Lansdowne Road	B1	Wychwood Close
C2	Lorne Park Road	B1	Wychwood Drive
C2	Madeira Road	B2	Yelverton Road
B1	Merlewood Close	D2	York Road
D3	Meyrick Road		
A3	Norwich Avenue		
A3	Norwich Road		
B3	Old Christchurch Road		
A3	Orchard Street		
D2	Oxford Road		
D1	Park Road		

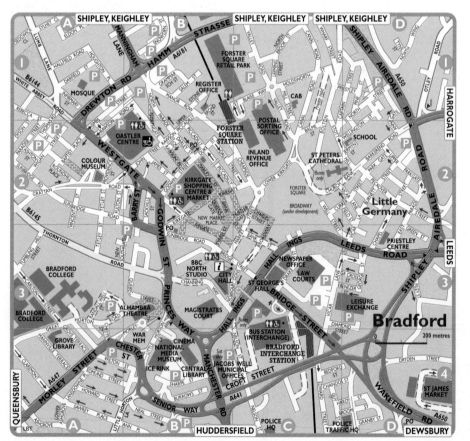

Bradford

Bradford is found on atlas page **342 C3**

B2	Bank Street	A1	Lumb Lane
D2	Barkerend Road	B4	Manchester Road
B2	Barry Street	B1	Manningham Lane
C2	Bolton Road	A4	Mannville Terrace
B3	Bridge Street	B1	Manor Row
C3	Broadway	C3	Market Street
D2	Burnett Street	A4	Morley Street
C2	Canal Road	B4	Neal Street
D1	Captain Street	C4	Nelson Street
A3	Carlton Street	B3	Norfolk Gardens
B3	Channing Way	C1	North Brook Street
D3	Chapel Street	B1	North Parade
C2	Charles Street	B1	Northgate
C2	Cheapside	D1	Otley Road
A4	Chester Street	D2	Peckover Street
C2	Church Bank	C2	Petergate
A4	Claremont	B2	Piccadilly
C4	Croft Street	B3	Princes Way
C2	Currer Street	A2	Providence Street
B2	Dale Street	B3	Quebec Street
A1	Darfield Street	B2	Rawson Place
B2	Darley Street	A2	Rawson Road
C3	Diamond Street	B2	Rawson Square
C3	Drake Street	C1	St Blaise Way
A1	Drewton Road	A2	St Thomas Road
D4	Dryden Street	B1	Salem Street
B2	Duke Street	B4	Senior Way
D3	East Parade	B4	Sharpe Street
D3	Ebenezer Street	D3	Shipley Airedale Road
A4	Edmund Street	A2	Simes Street
C4	Edward Street	C2	Stott Hill
C2	Forster Square	A2	Sunbridge Road
B2	Godwin Street	A3	Tetley Street
A2	Grattan Road	A3	Thornton Road
A3	Great Horton Road	A3	Tumbling Hill Street
C4	Guy Street	B3	Tyrrel Street
C3	Hall Ings	D2	Upper Parkgate
B1	Hamm Strasse	B2	Upper Piccadilly
C1	Holdsworth Street	C1	Valley Road
A1	Houghton Place	C3	Vicar Lane
A4	Howard Street	D4	Wakefield Road
B3	Ivegate	C2	Well Street
B2	James Street	D2	Wellington Street
B2	John Street	A2	Westgate
B2	Kirkgate	C1	Wharf Street
D3	Leeds Road	A1	White Abbey Road
B4	Little Horton Lane	A2	Wigan Street
C2	Lower Kirkgate	A4	Wilton Street

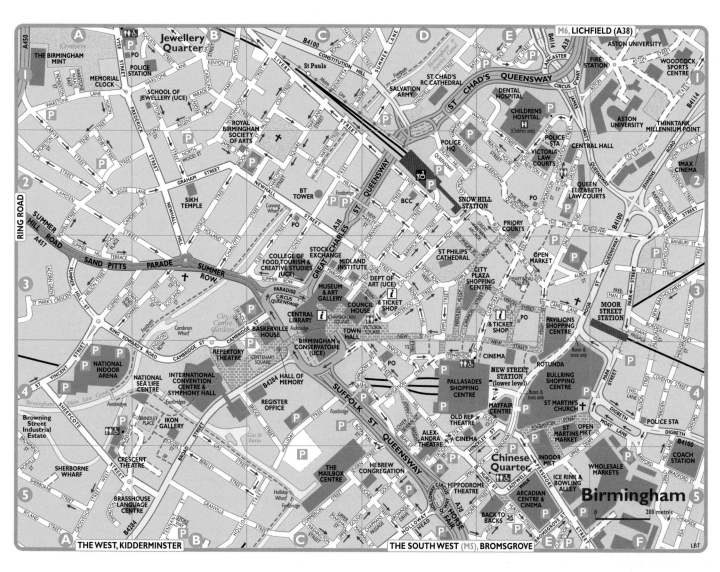

Birmingham

Birmingham is found on atlas page **213 G2**

A3 Acorn Grove	E3 Carrs Lane	B4 Gas Street	C3 Lionel Street	A1 Pemberton Street	B3 Summer Row
E3 Albert Street	A2 Carver Street	B2 George Street	C1 Livery Street	E5 Pershore Street	C4 Swallow Street
A2 Albion Street	C4 Centenary Square	D5 Gough Street	B3 Louisa Street	D4 Pinfold Street	D3 Temple Row
F4 Allison Street	C3 Chamberlain Square	B2 Graham Street	E1 Loveday Street	A2 Pope Street	D3 Temple Row West
A3 Arthur Place	D5 Chapmans Passage	B5 Granville Street	D4 Lower Severn Street	A2 Powell Street	D3 Temple Street
F1 Aston Street	B3 Charlotte Street	C3 Great Charles Street	C2 Ludgate Hill	E1 Price Street	A2 Tenby Street
B1 Augusta Street	F5 Cheapside	Queensway	C3 Margaret Street	E2 Printing House Street	A2 Tenby Street North
F3 Banbury Street	D2 Church Street	E2 Great Western Arcade	C5 Marshall Street	F5 Rea Street	B5 Tennant Street
F5 Barford Street	E5 Claybrook Street	F2 Grosvenor Street	E3 Martineau Square	B1 Regent Parade	E2 The Priory Queensway
F2 Bartholomew Row	A3 Clement Street	A5 Grosvenor Street West	C1 Mary Ann Street	B1 Regent Place	D5 Thorpe Street
F3 Bartholomew Street	F2 Coleshill Street	B1 Hall Street	B1 Mary Street	B2 Regent Street	A3 Townsend Way
D3 Barwick Street	E2 Colmore Circus	C1 Hampton Street	F4 Meriden Street	C4 Royal Mail Street	E3 Union Street
D1 Bath Street	Queensway	B3 Helena Street	F5 Mill Lane	A5 Ryland Street	E5 Upper Dean Street
D4 Beak Street	D3 Colmore Row	C1 Henrietta Street	F4 Moat Lane	D1 St Chad's Queensway	C5 Upper Gough Street
D3 Bennetts Hill	C5 Commercial Street	E3 High Street	E3 Moor Street Queensway	A3 St Mark's Crescent	C5 Upper Marshall Street
B5 Berkley Street	C1 Constitution Hill	D4 Hill Street	A2 Moreton Street	C2 St Paul's Square	E1 Vesey Street
D5 Blucher Street	D2 Cornwall Street	D5 Hinckley Street	A5 Morville Street	D3 St Philips Place	D3 Victoria Square
C1 Bond Street	E3 Corporation Street	B2 Holland Street	D4 Navigation Street	A4 St Vincent Street	B1 Vittoria Street
F3 Bordesley Street	F4 Coventry Street	B5 Holliday Street	D3 Needless Alley	A3 Sand Pitts	A1 Vyse Street
F5 Bradford Street	C1 Cox Street	D5 Holloway Circus	A3 Nelson Street	B3 Scotland Street	A1 Warstone Lane
C4 Bridge Street	E3 Dale End	Queensway	F3 New Bartholomew Street	C5 Severn Street	A1 Warstone Parade East
B3 Brindley Drive	E2 Dalton Street	D5 Holloway Head	F3 New Canal Street	D1 Shadwell Street	C5 Washington Street
B4 Brindley Place	F4 Digbeth	E5 Horse Fair	D2 New Market Street	F3 Shaws Passage	C2 Water Street
B5 Broad Street	E4 Dudley Street	E5 Hurst Street	D3 New Street	A4 Sheepcote Street	D3 Waterloo Street
E5 Bromsgrove Street	D3 Eden Place	E5 Inge Street	B2 Newhall Hill	A5 Sherborne Street	D1 Weaman Street
B2 Brook Street	E4 Edgbaston Street	B2 James Street	C2 Newhall Street	D5 Smallbrook Queensway	F4 Well Lane
A4 Browning Street	D3 Edmund Street	E1 James Watt Queensway	E2 Newton Street	D2 Snow Hill Queensway	E2 Whittall Street
D5 Brownsea Drive	A3 Edward Street	F2 Jennens Road	B2 Northwood Street	D5 Station Street	
C4 Brunel Street	D5 Ellis Street	D4 John Bright Street	F2 Nova Scotia Street	E2 Steelhouse Lane	
A4 Brunswick Street	A5 Essington Street	B1 Kenyon Street	E2 Old Square	D4 Stephenson Street	
E2 Bull Street	D4 Ethel Street	A3 King Edward's Road	B4 Oozel's Street	B5 Stoke Way	
B4 Cambridge Street	F3 Fazeley Street	B4 Kingston Row	F4 Oxford Street	C4 Suffolk Street Queensway	
A2 Camden Drive	C3 Fleet Street	E5 Ladywell Walk	B3 Parade	A2 Summer Hill Road	
A2 Camden Street	F2 Fox Street	E1 Lancaster Circus	C3 Paradise Circus	A3 Summer Hill Street	
D3 Cannon Street	B1 Frederick Street	Queensway	Queensway	A3 Summer Hill Terrace	
B1 Caroline Street	F3 Freeman Street	A2 Legge Lane	F4 Park Street	D1 Summer Lane	

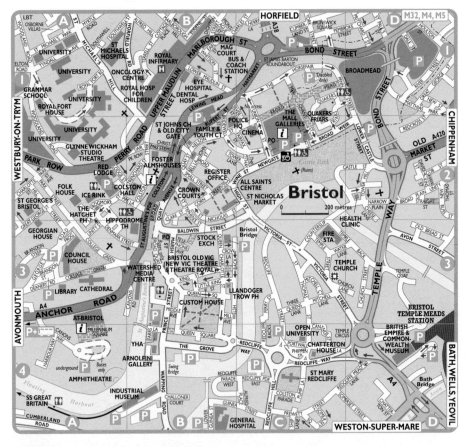

Bristol

Bristol is found on atlas page **109 G5**

A3	Anchor Road	A2	Park Row
B3	Baldwin Street	C1	Penn Street
C1	Barton Street	A2	Perry Road
C1	Bond Street	A2	Pipe Lane
A3	Brandon Street	C4	Portwall Lane
B2	Bridewell Street	B4	Prince Street
C1	Broad Mead	D1	Pritchard Street
B2	Broad Quay	C4	Pump Lane
B2	Broad Street	C1	Quakers Friars
C2	Broad Weir	B2	Quay Street
B3	Canons Road	B3	Queen Charlotte Street
A4	Canons Way	B4	Queen Square
D2	Castle Street	C3	Redcliff Street
C1	Charles Street	C4	Redcliffe Hill
B2	Christmas Steps	C4	Redcliffe Mead Lane
A3	College Green	C4	Redcliffe Parade East
B2	Colston Avenue	C4	Redcliffe Way
B2	Colston Street	D1	River Street
B2	Corn Street	A1	Royal Fort Road
C3	Countership	B2	Rupert Street
D1	Dale Street	B3	St Augustine's Parade
A3	Deanery Road	A3	St George's Road
A3	Denmark Street	D1	St Matthias Park
B1	Earl Street	A1	St Michael's Hill
C2	Fairfax Street	B2	St Nicholas Street
B4	Farrs Lane	D1	St Paul's Street
A2	Frogmore Street	B2	St Stephen's Street
A3	Great George Street	C3	St Thomas Street
B4	Guinea Street	C1	Silver Street
C1	Haymarket	B2	Small Street
C2	High Street	A1	Southwell Street
A2	Hill Street	C3	Temple Back
B1	Horfield Road	C3	Temple Street
B3	King Street	D3	Temple Way
B1	Lewins Mead	B1	Terrell Street
A2	Lodge Street	B4	The Grove
D2	Lower Castle Street	C1	The Horsefair
B1	Lower Maudlin Street	D2	Tower Hill
B2	Lower Park Row	B2	Trenchard Street
B1	Marlborough Street	A1	Tyndall Avenue
B3	Marsh Street	C1	Union Street
C1	Merchant Street	B1	Upper Maudlin Street
B1	Montague Street	C3	Victoria Street
D2	Narrow Plain	B4	Wapping Road
B2	Nelson Street	C3	Welsh Back
D1	Newfoundland Street	C2	Wine Street
C2	Newgate	A1	Woodland Road
D2	Old Market Street	C1	York Street

Cardiff

Cardiff is found on atlas page **106 C4**

D3	Adam Street	B4	Mill Lane
B3	Bakers Row	D2	Moira Place
C3	Barrack Lane	D2	Moira Terrace
B2	Boulevard de Nantes	B3	Morgan Arcade
C3	Bridge Street	B1	Museum Avenue
C4	Bute Street	B1	Museum Place
C3	Bute Terrace	D1	Newport Road
B4	Callaghan Square	C2	North Edward Street
B3	Caroline Street	A1	North Road
A3	Castle Street	D1	Oxford Lane
D4	Central Link	B1	Park Grove
B4	Central Square	B1	Park Lane
B2	Charles Street	B1	Park Place
B3	Church Street	B4	Penarth Road
C2	Churchill Way	A3	Quay Street
A1	City Hall Road	B2	Queen Street
D1	City Road	C1	Richmond Crescent
A1	College Road	C1	Richmond Road
B2	Crockherbtown Lane	B3	Royal Arcade
B4	Custom House Street	B1	St Andrew's Crescent
B2	Duke Street	C1	St Andrew's Lane
C2	Dumfries Place	B1	St Andrew's Place
C1	East Grove	B2	St John Street
D3	Ellen Street	B3	St Mary Street
D2	Fitzalan Place	C1	St Peter's Street
D2	Fitzalan Road	C1	Salisbury Road
A3	Fitzhamon Embankment	C3	Sandon Street
B3	Frederick Street	D4	Schooner Way
D1	Glossop Road	B1	Senghennydd Road
B3	Golate	C2	Station Terrace
B4	Great Western Lane	B2	Stuttgarter Strasse
B2	Greyfriars Place	C3	Taff Street
B2	Greyfriars Road	B2	The Friary
C3	Guildford Crescent	B3	The Hayes
C2	Guildford Street	C1	The Parade
B3	Hayes Bridge Road	B4	Tresillian Way
C4	Herbert Street	B3	Trinity Street
B3	High Street	D3	Tyndall Street
B3	Hill's Street	C1	West Grove
D2	Howard Gardens	A3	Westgate Street
D2	Howard Place	B3	Wharton Street
A1	King Edward VII Avenue	C2	Windsor Lane
B2	Kingsway	C2	Windsor Place
C2	Knox Road	D2	Windsor Road
C4	Lloyd George Avenue	A3	Womanby Street
C3	Longcross Street	B4	Wood Street
C3	Mary Ann Street	D1	Wordsworth Avenue
D2	Meteor Street	B3	Working Street

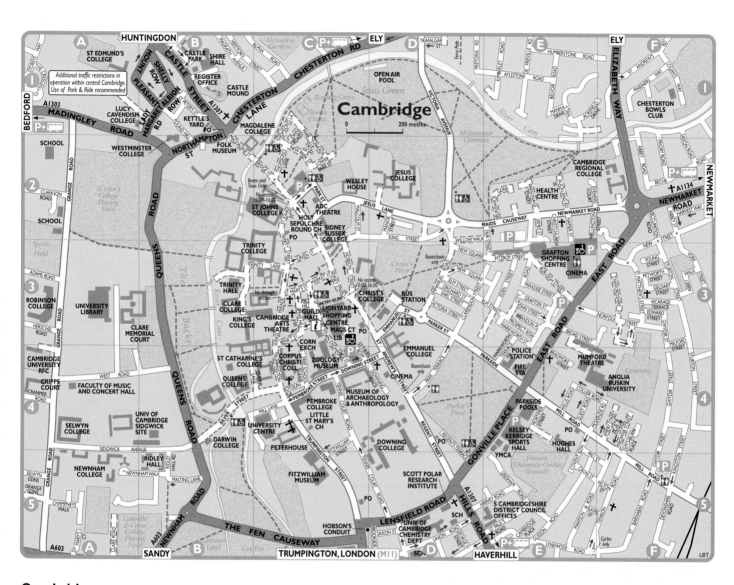

Cambridge

Cambridge is found on atlas page **197 F3**

F2	Abbey Road	F5	Devonshire Road	C3	Hobson Street	F3	New Street	F3	St Matthew's Street
F2	Abbey Street	F4	Ditchburn Place	E1	Humberstone Road	E2	Newmarket Road	E5	St Paul's Road
F3	Abbey Walk	D4	Downing Place	E2	James Street	B5	Newnham Road	B1	St Peter's Street
E1	Acrefield Drive	C4	Downing Street	C2	Jesus Lane	A5	Newnham Walk	C4	St Tibbs Row
A3	Adams Road	D3	Earl Street	E3	John Street	F3	Norfolk Street	F2	Saxon Road
B1	Albion Row	E4	East Road	E1	Kimberley Road	B2	Northampton Street	D5	Saxon Street
C1	Alpha Road	E3	Eden Street	D2	King Street	F2	Occupation Road	A5	Selwyn Gardens
E2	Auckland Road	F3	Edward Street	C3	Kings Parade	D3	Orchard Street	B1	Shelly Row
E1	Aylestone Road	F1	Elizabeth Way	F5	Kingston Street	E3	Paradise Street	A4	Sidgwick Avenue
F2	Beche Road	D3	Elm Street	B1	Lady Margaret Road	C1	Park Parade	C3	Sidney Street
E1	Belvoir Road	F4	Emery Road	D5	Lensfield Road	C2	Park Street	B4	Silver Street
C3	Bene't Street	F4	Emery Street	F1	Logan's Way	D4	Park Terrace	F3	Staffordshire Street
C4	Botolph Lane	D3	Emmanuel Road	C2	Lower Park Street	D3	Parker Street	A1	Storeys Way
E4	Bradmore Street	D3	Emmanuel Street	E5	Lynewode Road	E4	Parkside	F4	Sturton Street
E3	Brandon Place	E2	Evening Court	A1	Madingley Road	E2	Parsonage Street	F5	Tenison Road
C2	Bridge Street	E2	Fair Street	B2	Magdalene Street	C3	Peas Hill	C4	Tennis Court Road
E3	Broad Street	F5	Felton Street	B1	Magrath Avenue	C4	Pembroke Street	A1	The Crescent
D5	Brookside	E3	Fitzroy Street	E2	Maids Causeway	F4	Perowne Street	B5	The Fen Causeway
E2	Brunswick Gardens	C4	Fitzwilliam Street	C2	Malcolm Street	C3	Petty Cury	C1	Thomson's Lane
E3	Burleigh Street	C4	Free School Lane	B5	Malting Lane	F3	Petworth Street	D1	Trafalgar Street
E5	Cambridge Place	F3	Geldart Street	E1	Manhattan Drive	C2	Portugal Street	C3	Trinity Lane
B1	Castle Street	D5	George IV Street	D2	Manor Street	B1	Pound Hill	C2	Trinity Street
A5	Champneys Walk	E5	Glisson Road	F1	Mariners Way	D1	Pretoria Road	C4	Trumpington Street
B1	Chesterton Lane	D5	Gonville Place	C3	Market Hill	F2	Priory Road	D5	Union Road
C1	Chesterton Road	E3	Grafton Street	C3	Market Street	E3	Prospect Row	F3	Vicarage Terrace
E2	Christchurch Street	A5	Grange Gardens	E5	Mawson Road	C4	Queens Lane	D1	Victoria Avenue
E3	City Road	A5	Grange Road	E4	McKenzie Road	B4	Queens Road	D3	Victoria Street
A5	Clare Road	C3	Green Street	F3	Milford Street	D4	Regent Street	E3	Warkworth Street
D3	Clarendon Street	E5	Gresham Road	C4	Mill Lane	D4	Regents Terrace	E4	Warkworth Terrace
A2	Clarkson Road	E4	Guest Road	E4	Mill Road	B5	Ridley Hall Road	E2	Wellington Street
E4	Collier Road	F5	Gwydir Street	E5	Mill Street	D3	St Andrew's Street	A4	West Road
C3	Corn Exchange Street	D5	Harvey Road	E4	Mortimer Street	F1	St Andrew's Road	E5	Wilkins Street
E5	Covent Garden	E4	Harvest Way	B1	Mount Pleasant	F5	St Barnabas Road	E4	Willis Road
A4	Cranmer Road	A3	Herschel Road	E2	Napier Street	C2	St Johns Road	D2	Willow Walk
E5	Cross Street	B1	Hertford Street	C2	New Park Street	C2	St Johns Street	F3	York Street
E1	De Freiville Road	D5	Hills Road	D3	New Square	C3	St Mary's Street	F3	Young Street

University Colleges

C3	Christ's College
B3	Clare College
C4	Corpus Christi College
B4	Darwin College
D4	Downing College
D4	Emmanuel College
E4	Hughes Hall
D2	Jesus College
B3	King's College
A1	Lucy Cavendish College
B2	Magdalene College
A5	Newnham College
C4	Pembroke College
C4	Peterhouse
B4	Queen's College
B5	Ridley Hall
A3	Robinson College
C4	St Catharine's College
A1	St Edmund's College
C2	St John's College
A4	Selwyn College
C2	Sidney Sussex College
B3	Trinity College
B3	Trinity Hall
C2	Wesley House
B2	Westminster College

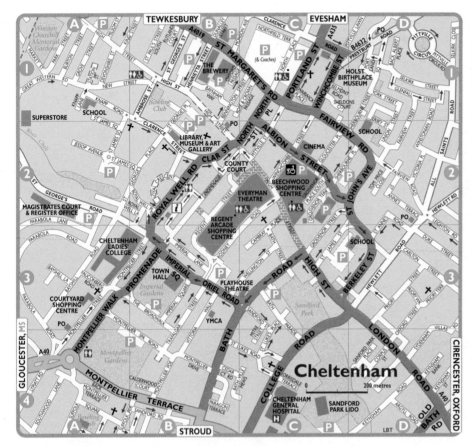

Cheltenham

Cheltenham is found on atlas page **163 E5**

C2	Albion Street	B3	Oriel Road
D2	All Saints Road	D3	Oxford Street
B1	Ambrose Street	A2	Parabola Lane
D1	Back Albert Place	A3	Parabola Road
C3	Bath Parade	A1	Park Street
B4	Bath Road	D1	Pittville Circus
C3	Bath Street	D1	Pittville Circus Road
B1	Baynham Way	D1	Pittville Lawn
A3	Bayshill Road	C2	Pittville Street
B1	Bennington Street	D1	Portland Square
D3	Berkeley Street	C1	Portland Street
A1	Burton Street	D1	Prestbury Road
C3	Cambray Place	D3	Priory Street
D3	Carlton Street	D3	Priory Terrace
C1	Clarence Road	D3	Priory Walk
B2	Clarence Street	B3	Promenade
C4	College Road	B3	Regent Street
A1	Devonshire Street	B3	Rodney Road
D3	Duke Street	B2	Royal Crescent
C2	Fairview Road	B2	Royal Well Place
D2	Fairview Street	B2	Royal Well Road
A3	Fauconberg Road	D3	St Anne's Road
D1	Glenfall Street	D2	St Anne's Terrace
C2	Gloucester Place	B2	St George's Place
A1	Great Western Road	A2	St George's Road
C2	Grosvenor Place South	B1	St George's Street
C3	Grosvenor Street	A2	St James Square
C2	Grosvenor Terrace	C3	St James Street
A1	Grove Street	D2	St John's Avenue
B1	Henrietta Street	C4	St Luke's Place
D3	Hewlett Road	C4	St Luke's Road
A1	High Street	B1	St Margaret's Road
B3	Imperial Lane	B1	St Paul's Street South
B3	Imperial Square	B4	Sandford Road
D4	Keynsham Road	C3	Sandford Street
A1	Knapp Road	D1	Selkirk Street
D4	London Road	C2	Sherbourne Place
B1	Monson Avenue	D1	Sherbourne Street
B4	Montpellier Drive	A4	Suffolk Square
B4	Montpellier Parade	D4	Sydenham Villas Road
A3	Montpellier Spa Road	B3	The Broadwalk
A3	Montpellier Street	B3	Trafalgar Street
A4	Montpellier Terrace	D2	Union Street
A4	Montpellier Walk	D2	Victoria Place
A1	New Street	B4	Vittoria Walk
C1	North Place	C3	Wellington Street
C2	North Street	C1	Winchcombe Street
C1	Northfield Terrace	D2	Winstonian Road

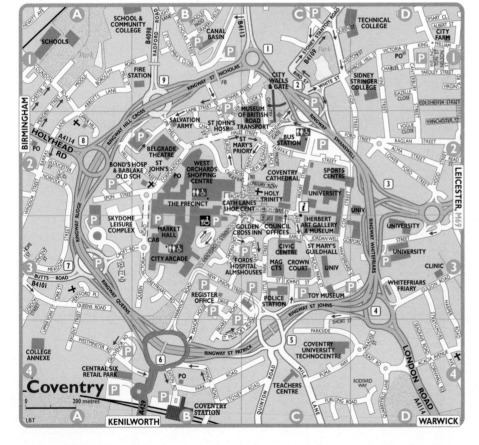

Coventry

Coventry is found on atlas page **215 E4**

A1	Abbotts Lane	A2	Meriden Street
D4	Acacia Avenue	A1	Middleborough Road
D2	Alma Street	C4	Mile Lane
A2	Barras Lane	C3	Much Park Street
C2	Bayley Lane	C2	New Buildings
C1	Bird Street	B3	New Union Street
B1	Bishop Street	A2	Norfolk Street
B2	Broadgate	B4	Park Road
B2	Burges	C4	Parkside
A3	Butts Road	D1	Primrose Hill Street
D1	Canterbury Street	C2	Priory Row
C2	Chantry Place	C2	Priory Street
B2	Chapel Street	C4	Puma Way
D1	Charles Street	D4	Quarryfield Lane
D1	Colchester Street	B3	Queen Victoria Road
C1	Cook Street	A3	Queens Road
B2	Corporation Street	C4	Quinton Road
A1	Coundon Road	B1	Radford Road
D1	Cox Street	D2	Raglan Street
A3	Croft Road	A4	Regent Street
B2	Cross Cheaping	A2	Ringway Hill Cross
C3	Earl Street	A3	Ringway Queens
B4	Eaton Road	A3	Ringway Rudge
C2	Fairfax Street	C3	Ringway St Johns
D2	Ford Street	B1	Ringway St Nicholas
B4	Friars Road	B4	Ringway St Patrick
C4	Furlong Road	C2	Ringway Swanswell
D3	Gosford Street	D3	Ringway Whitefriars
B3	Greyfriars Lane	C3	St John's Street
B3	Greyfriars Road	B1	St Nicholas Street
A4	Grosvenor Road	B4	St Patrick's Road
D3	Gulson Road	C3	Salt Lane
B2	Hales Street	B1	Silver Street
B2	Hay Lane	A2	Spon Street
B3	Hertford Street	B4	Stoney Road
C3	High Street	C1	Stoney Stanton Road
A2	Hill Street	D4	Strathmore Avenue
A2	Holyhead Road	C2	Swanswell Gate
D2	Hood Street	B1	Tower Street
C3	Jordan Well	C2	Trinity Street
D1	King William Street	B2	Upper Well Street
B1	Lamb Street	D1	Victoria Street
C3	Little Park Street	D1	Vine Street
D4	London Road	B3	Warwick Road
D2	Lower Ford Street	A4	Westminster Road
B3	Manor House Drive	C1	White Street
B4	Manor Road	C3	Whitefriars Street
A3	Meadow Street	D1	Yardley Street

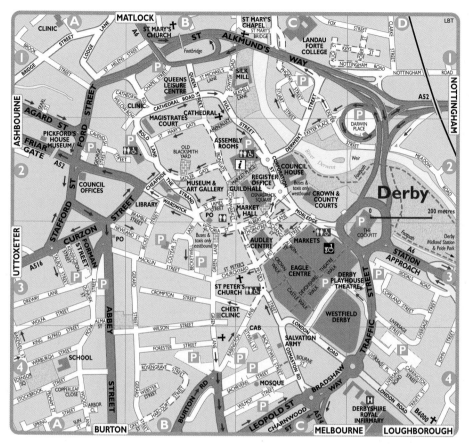

Derby

Derby is found on atlas page **275 F2**

A3	Abbey Street	C4	Leopold Street
A1	Agard Street	D4	Liversage Place
C2	Albert Street	D4	Liversage Road
C3	Albion Street	D3	Liversage Street
A3	Alma Street	A1	Lodge Lane
B2	Amen Alley	D4	London Road
B4	Babington Lane	B3	Macklin Street
C4	Back Sitwell Street	C2	Market Place
A4	Bakewell Street	D2	Meadow Road
B3	Becket Street	A4	Monk Street
B3	Becketwell Lane	C2	Morledge
B2	Bold Lane	A3	Newland Street
C4	Bradshaw Way	D1	Nottingham Road
B2	Bramble Street	B2	Old Blacksmith Yard
A1	Bridge Street	C4	Osmaston Road
A1	Brook Street	C2	Osnabrük Square
B4	Burton Road	C1	Phoenix Street
D4	Carrington Street	B1	Queen Street
C3	Castle Walk	B4	Sacheverel Street
B1	Cathedral Road	B2	Sadler Gate
A2	Cavendish Street	B1	St Alkmund's Way
B1	Chapel Street	A1	St Helens Street
C4	Charnwood Street	B2	St James Street
B2	Cheapside	C1	St Mary's Bridge
B3	Colyear Street	B2	St Mary's Gate
D3	Copeland Street	B1	St Michael's Lane
B2	Cornmarket	B3	St Peter's Churchyard
C2	Corporation Street	C3	St Peter's Street
C3	Crown Walk	D3	Siddals Road
A3	Curzon Street	C1	Silkmill Lane
D2	Darwin Place	C4	Sitwell Street
C2	Derwent Street	B1	Sowter Road
C3	Devonshire Walk	A3	Stafford Street
A3	Drewry Lane	D3	Station Approach
C3	East Street	A4	Stockbrook Street
C3	Exchange Street	C1	Stuart Street
C2	Exeter Place	A3	Talbot Street
C1	Exeter Street	D3	The Cockpitt
A2	Ford Street	B2	The Strand
B4	Forester Street	C3	Theatre Walk
A3	Forman Street	D4	Traffic Street
C1	Fox Street	D4	Trinity Street
A2	Friar Gate	B3	Victoria Street
B1	Full Street	B2	Wardwick
B3	Gerard Street	A4	Werburgh Street
B3	Green Lane	A1	Willow Row
B2	Irongate	C4	Wilmot Street
A4	King Alfred Street	B4	Wilson Street

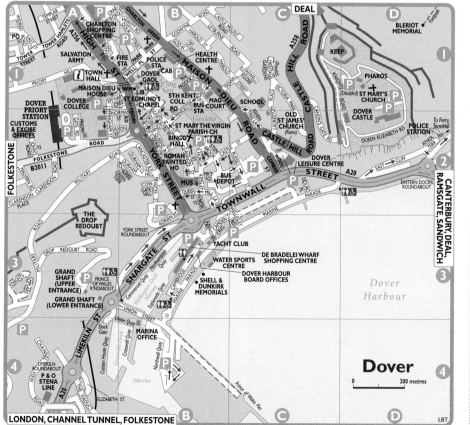

Dover

Dover is found on atlas page **83 F2**

B3	Adrian Street	B2	Market Square
C2	Ashen Tree Lane	A3	Military Road
D2	Athol Terrace	B2	Mill Lane
B2	Bench Street	B3	New Bridge
B2	Biggin Street	B2	New Street
B2	Bowling Green Terrace	A2	Norman Street
B3	Cambridge Road	B1	Park Place
B3	Camden Crescent	B1	Park Street
B2	Cannon Street	B1	Pencester Road
C2	Canon's Gate Road	B2	Princes Street
C2	Castle Hill Road	A2	Priory Gate Road
B1	Castle Mount Road	A1	Priory Hill
B2	Castle Street	B2	Priory Road
A4	Channel View Road	B2	Priory Street
B1	Charlton Green	D2	Queen Elizabeth Road
B2	Church Street	B2	Queen Street
A2	Clarendon Place	B2	Queens Gardens
A2	Clarendon Road	C2	Russell Street
B2	Cowgate Hill	A2	St John's Road
A1	Crafford Street	A2	Saxon Street
B1	Dour Street	B3	Snargate Street
C2	Douro Place	B2	Stem Brook
A3	Drop Redoubt Road	C1	Taswell Close
B2	Durham Close	C1	Taswell Street
B2	Durham Hill	A1	Templar Street
D2	East Cliff	B1	The Paddock
A1	East Street	A4	The Viaduct
A1	Effingham Crescent	A1	Tower Hamlets Road
A2	Effingham Street	A1	Tower Street
A4	Elizabeth Street	C2	Townwall Street
A2	Folkestone Road	B3	Union Street
B1	Godwyne Close	C1	Victoria Park
B1	Godwyne Road	C2	Wellesley Road
B1	Harold Street	A1	Widred Road
C1	Heritage Gardens	A1	Wood Street
B1	Hewitt Road	C2	Woolcomber Street
A1	High Street	B2	Worthington Street
B2	King Street	B2	York Street
C1	Knights Road		
A3	Knights Templars		
B1	Ladywell		
B2	Lancaster Road		
C2	Laureston Place		
B1	Leyburne Road		
A4	Limekiln Street		
B1	Maison Dieu Road		
A2	Malvern Road		
B3	Marine Parade		

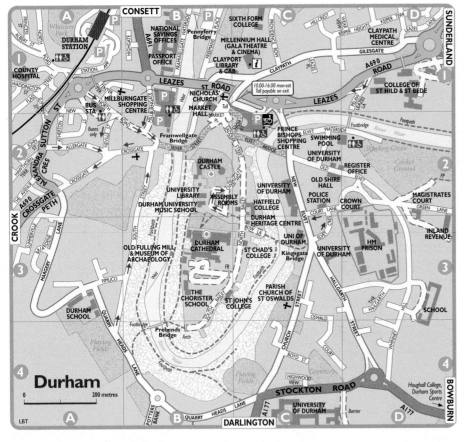

Durham

Durham is found on atlas page **395 F1**

A1	Albert Street	A3	Quarry Heads Lane
A2	Alexandra Crescent	B2	Saddler Street
A2	Allergate	B2	Silver Street
A2	Atherton Street	B3	South Bailey
C3	Bow Lane	B3	South Street
C4	Boyd Street	A1	Station Approach
A3	Briardene	C4	Stockton Road
C4	Church Street	A3	Summerville
C1	Claypath	A2	Sutton Street
C2	Court Lane	A1	Tenter Terrace
A2	Crossgate	A2	The Avenue
A2	Crossgate Peth	D3	The Hallgarth
C2	Elvet Bridge	A1	Waddington Street
C3	Elvet Crescent	D1	Wear View
C2	Elvet Waterside	D4	Whinney Hill
A1	Flass Street		
B1	Framwellgate Waterside		
B1	Freemans Place		
D1	Gilesgate		
D2	Green Lane		
C3	Hallgarth Street		
A2	Hawthorn Terrace		
B1	Highgate		
C2	High Street		
C4	Highwood View		
C1	Hillcrest		
A2	John Street		
D1	Keiper Heights		
D1	Keiper Terrace		
D1	Leazes Lane		
C1	Leazes Place		
B1	Leazes Road		
A3	Margery Lane		
B2	Market Place		
B1	Millburngate		
A2	Neville Street		
C2	New Elvet		
A1	New Street		
C3	North Bailey		
A1	North Road		
C2	Old Elvet		
C3	Oswald Court		
C2	Owengate		
D1	Pelaw Leazes Lane		
A3	Pimlico		
B4	Potters Bank		
A1	Princess Street		
C1	Providence Row		

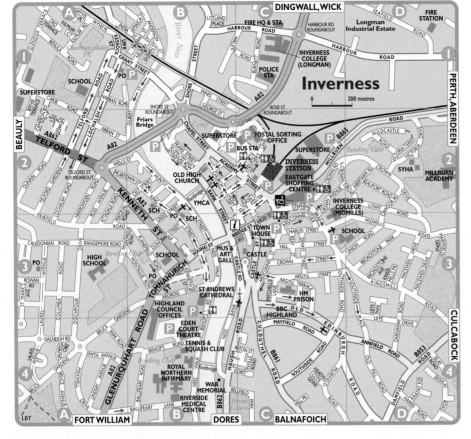

Inverness

Inverness is found on atlas page **566 B8**

D2	Abertarff Road	A4	Glenurquhart Road
B2	Academy Street	B1	Grant Street
B1	Anderson Street	B3	Greig Street
D4	Annfield Road	C1	Harbour Road
C3	Ardconnel Street	A2	Harrowden Road
C3	Ardconnel Terrace	B4	Haugh Road
B3	Ardross Street	C3	High Street
C3	Argyll Street	C3	Hill Street
C3	Argyll Terrace	B2	Huntley Street
A2	Attadale Road	A1	India Street
D2	Auldcastle Road	A2	Kenneth Street
B4	Ballifeary Lane	B2	King Street
B4	Ballifeary Road	D3	Kingsmills Road
B2	Bank Street	A3	Laurel Avenue
D2	Beaufort Road	D4	Leys Drive
A1	Benula Road	A2	Lochalsh Road
B4	Bishop's Road	D2	Lovat Road
C3	Bridge Street	A1	Lower Kessock Street
D3	Broadstone Park	D3	Macewen Drive
A4	Bruce Gardens	A4	Maxwell Drive
C1	Burnett Road	C4	Mayfield Road
A3	Caledonian Road	D3	Midmills Road
A2	Cameron Road	C2	Millburn Road
A1	Carse Road	B3	Montague Row
C3	Castle Road	C4	Muirfield Road
C3	Castle Street	A2	Muirtown Street
D2	Cawdor Road	B4	Ness Bank
B2	Celt Street	B4	Ness Walk
B2	Chapel Street	C3	Old Edinburgh Road
B2	Charles Street	D4	Old Mill Road
B2	Church Street	B3	Planefield Road
A3	Columba Road	A3	Rangemore Road
C2	Crown Avenue	D1	Seafield Road
C2	Crown Circus	B1	Shore Street
D2	Crown Drive	D3	Southside Place
C2	Crown Road	C4	Southside Road
C3	Crown Street	C2	Stephens Brae
C4	Culduthel Road	C2	Strother's Lane
A4	Dalneigh Road	A2	Telford Gardens
D4	Damfield Road	A2	Telford Road
D4	Darnaway Drive	A2	Telford Street
A3	Dochfour Drive	B3	Tomnahurich Street
B2	Douglas Row	D3	Union Road
A2	Dunain Road	C2	Union Street
A3	Fairfield Road	D2	Victoria Drive
B2	Friars Street	B1	Walker Road
B2	Gilbert Street	A2	Wells Street
A1	Glendoe Terrace	B3	Young Street

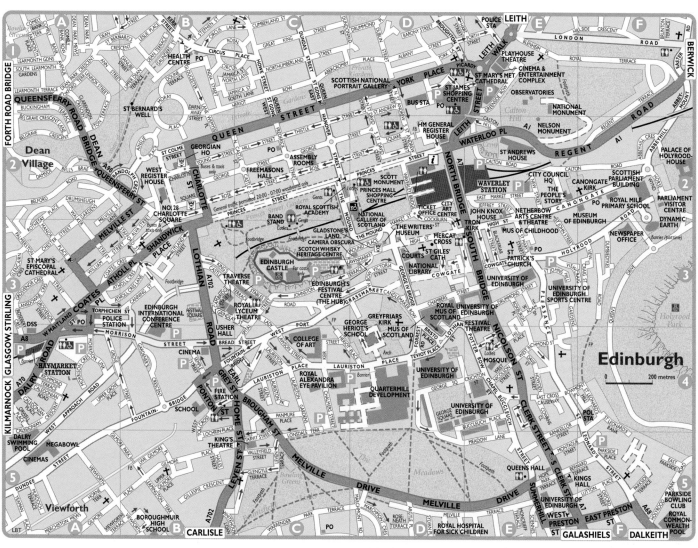

Edinburgh

Edinburgh is found on atlas page **488 B5**

F2 Abbeyhill	B3 Castle Terrace	E4 East Cross Causeway	B1 Jamaica Street North Lane	A4 Morrison Street	F5 St Leonard's Street
F2 Abbeyhill Crescent	C4 Chalmers Street	E2 East Market Street	C1 Jamaica Street South Lane	D3 Mound Place	E3 St Mary's Street
F1 Abbeymount	D3 Chambers Street	F5 East Preston Street	E2 Jeffrey Street	A5 Murdoch Terrace	B1 St Stephen Street
C1 Abercromby Place	E4 Chapel Street	A2 Eton Terrace	C3 Johnston Terrace	E2 New Street	B4 Semple Street
B2 Ainslie Place	B2 Charlotte Square	B3 Festival Square	C4 Keir Street	E4 Nicholson Street	B3 Shandwick Place
D1 Albany Street	A3 Chester Street Gardens	D4 Forrest Road	B1 Kerr Street	D2 North Bridge	E3 South Bridge
B3 Alva Street	B1 Circus Lane	E1 Forth Street	B3 King's Stables Road	C2 North Castle Street	E5 South Clerk Street
A1 Ann Street	B1 Circus Place	B4 Fountainbridge	C4 Lady Lawson Street	D1 North St Andrew Street	A1 South Learmonth Gardens
D5 Argyle Place	A1 Clarendon Crescent	C2 Frederick Street	A3 Lansdowne Crescent	D1 North St David Street	D2 South St Andrew Street
B3 Atholl Crescent	E4 Clerk Street	B4 Gardener's Crescent	C4 Lauriston Gardens	C1 Northumberland Street	D2 South St David Street
B3 Atholl Crescent Lane	A3 Coates Crescent	B4 George IV Bridge	C4 Lauriston Park	F5 Oxford Street	C4 Spital Street
A3 Atholl Place	A3 Coates Place	D4 George Square	C4 Lauriston Place	A3 Palmerston Street	B3 Stafford Street
D1 Barony Street	D2 Cockburn Street	B2 George Street	C4 Lauriston Street	F5 Parkside Terrace	E5 Summerhill
A2 Belford Road	A1 Comely Bank Avenue	B5 Gillespie Crescent	D3 Lawnmarket	E1 Picardy Place	C5 Tarvit Street
A2 Belgrave Crescent	D3 Cowgate	B5 Gilmore Park	B5 Leamington Terrace	E3 Pleasance	D4 Teviot Place
A2 Belgrave Crescent Lane	E4 Crichton Street	A5 Gilmore Place	A1 Learmonth Terrace	B4 Ponton Street	C2 The Mound
A2 Bells Brae	A4 Dalry Road	C4 Glen Street	E1 Leith Street	E4 Potter Row	C2 Thistle Street
E5 Bernard Terrace	A2 Damside	C5 Glengyle Terrace	E1 Leith Walk	C2 Princes Street	A3 Torphichen Street
E3 Blackfriar Street	B1 Danube Street	B1 Gloucester Lane	A1 Lennox Street	B2 Queen Street	B1 Upper Dean Terrace
E4 Bowmont Place	B1 Darnaway Street	D3 Grassmarket	B1 Leslie Place	C1 Queen Street	B5 Upper Gilmore Place
B4 Bread Street	E4 Davie Street	A3 Grindlay Street	C5 Leven Street		A4 Upper Grove Place
D4 Bristo Place	A2 Dean Bridge	A3 Grosvenor Crescent	C5 Leven Terrace	Gardens East / West	C5 Valleyfield Street
C4 Brougham Street	A1 Dean Park Crescent	A3 Grosvenor Street	B5 Lochrin Place	F3 Queen's Drive	D3 Victoria Street
D1 Broughton Street	A1 Dean Park Mews	A4 Grove Street	E1 London Road	A1 Queensferry Road	E3 Viewcraig Gardens
E4 Buccleuch Place	A1 Dean Park Street	C2 Hanover Street	C5 Lonsdale Terrace	A2 Queensferry Street	F3 Viewcraig Street
E4 Buccleuch Street	A1 Dean Street	C4 Heriot Place	B3 Lothian Road	B2 Randolph Crescent	A5 Viewforth
A1 Buckingham Terrace	B1 Dean Terrace	C1 Heriot Row	D4 Lothian Street	E4 Rankeillor Street	A3 Walker Street
A4 Caledonian Crescent	B1 Doune Terrace	D3 High Street	F5 Lutton Place	E2 Regent Road	C5 Warrender Park Terrace
A4 Caledonian Road	D1 Drummond Place	E4 Hill Place	A3 Manor Place	F2 Regent Terrace	E2 Waterloo Place
E2 Calton Hill	E3 Drummond Street	C2 Hill Street	D5 Marchmont Crescent	B2 Rose Street	D2 Waverley Bridge
E2 Calton Road	A2 Drumsheugh	F1 Hillside Crescent	D5 Marchmont Road	A3 Rothesay Place	A4 West Approach Road
B3 Cambridge Street	D1 Dublin Street	F5 Holyrood Park Road	D2 Market Street	E3 Roxburgh Place	D3 West Bow
D3 Candlemaker Row	F3 Dumbiedykes Road	E3 Holyrood Road	E5 Meadow Lane	B1 Royal Circus	A4 West Maitland Street
B3 Canning Street	C1 Dundas Street	C4 Home Street	C5 Melville Drive	F1 Royal Terrace	E4 West Nicholson Street
E2 Canongate	A5 Dundee Street	E5 Hope Park Terrace	A3 Melville Place	B3 Rutland Street	C4 West Port
C2 Castle Street	B4 Earl Grey Street	F2 Horse Wynd	A2 Melville Street	D2 St Andrew Square	E5 West Preston Street
		E4 Howden Street	A2 Melville Street Lane	A1 St Bernard's Crescent	E4 West Richmond Street
		C1 Howe Street	D5 Montague Street	B2 St Colme Street	B4 West Tollcross
		B1 India Street	E5 Montague Street	E3 St John Street	A3 William Street
			B1 Moray Place	E3 St Johns Hill	D1 York Place
			A4 Morrison Crescent	F4 St Leonard's Bank	B2 Young Street
			A4 Morrison Link		

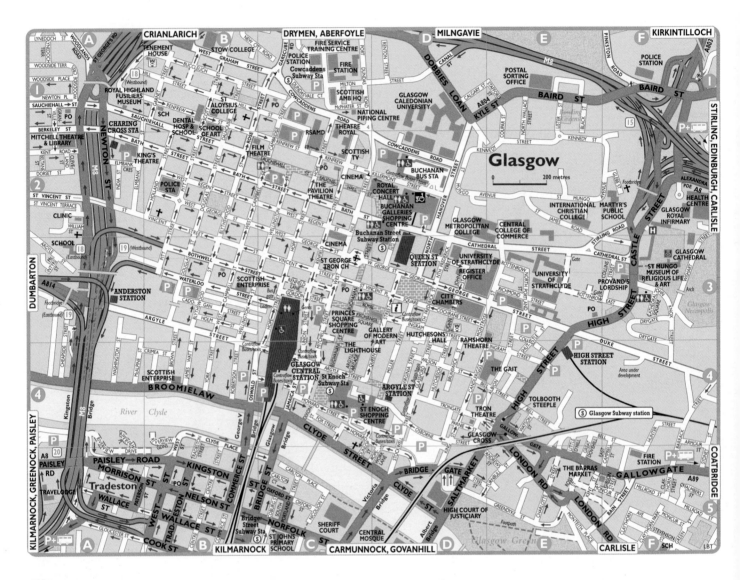

Glasgow

Glasgow is found on atlas page **467 E1**

E4	Albion Street	F5	Claythorn Avenue	A5	Gloucester Street	F5	Millroad Street	B2	Rose Street	B1	West Graham Street
F2	Alexandra Parade	F5	Claythorn Park	C3	Gordon Street	C1	Milton Street	E5	Ross Street	C3	West Nile Street
C4	Argyll Arcade	F5	Claythorn Street	A1	Granville Street	C3	Mitchell Street	E3	Rottenrow	B2	West Regent Street
B3	Argyle Street	A2	Cleveland Street	E5	Great Dovehill	E5	Moncur Street	E3	Rottenrow East	B4	West Street
F4	Armour Street	B4	Clyde Place	F5	Green Street	E5	Monteith Place	C3	Royal Exchange Square	A2	William Street
F5	Bain Street	D5	Clyde Street	E4	Greendyke Street	D3	Montrose Street	E5	St Andrews Street	D4	Wilson Street
E1	Baird Street	C5	Coburg Street	E4	High Street	A5	Morrison Street	A1	St Georges Road	F3	Wishart Street
F4	Barrack Street	D3	Cochrane Street	B1	Hill Street	B5	Nelson Street	E2	St James Road	A1	Woodlands Road
B2	Bath Street	E4	College Street	B2	Holland Street	B1	New City Road	E2	St Mungo Avenue	A1	Woodside Crescent
E4	Bell Street	F3	Collins Street	B3	Holm Street	A1	Newton Place	C3	St Vincent Place	A1	Woodside Place
A2	Beltane Street	B5	Commerce Street	C3	Hope Street	C5	Nicholson Street	A2	St Vincent Street	A1	Woodside Terrace
A1	Berkeley Street	B5	Cook Street	C4	Howard Street	C5	Norfolk Street	A2	St Vincent Terrace	B4	York Street
E1	Black Street	E1	Coupar Street	F4	Hunter Street	D3	North Frederick Street	D5	Saltmarket		
B3	Blythswood Street	C1	Cowcaddens Road	D4	Hutcheson Street	D3	North Hanover Street	A1	Sauchiehall Street		
B3	Bothwell Street	B4	Crimea Street	A2	India Street	E3	North Portland Street	B1	Scott Street		
D5	Bridgegate	B1	Dalhousie Street	D3	Ingram Street	E1	North Wallace Street	E4	Shuttle Street		
C5	Bridge Street	C4	Dixon Street	C4	Jamaica Street	D4	Osborne Street	D3	South Frederick Street		
B4	Broomielaw	D1	Dobbies Loan	B4	James Watt Street	B4	Oswald Street	C5	South Portland Street		
B4	Brown Street	A2	Dorset Street	F3	John Knox Street	C5	Oxford Street	E1	Stafford Street		
D4	Brunswick Street	B2	Douglas Street	D3	John Street	A5	Paisley Road	D5	Steel Street		
B1	Buccleuch Street	F3	Drygate	E2	Kennedy Street	D4	Parnie Street	F5	Stevenson Street		
C4	Buchanan Street	F4	Duke Street	A2	Kent Road	A5	Paterson Street	E3	Stirling Road		
B3	Cadogan Street	C1	Dundasvale Court	E5	Kent Street	F1	Pinkston Road	D5	Stockwell Street		
D1	Calgary Street	C5	Dunlop Street	D2	Killermont Street	B3	Pitt Street	F5	Sydney Street		
C2	Cambridge Street	F5	East Campbell Street	D5	King Street	C1	Port Dundas Road	B5	Tradeston Street		
D1	Canal Street	A2	Elmbank Crescent	B5	Kingston Street	C4	Queen Street	D4	Trongate		
D4	Candleriggs	A2	Elmbank Street	D1	Kyle Street	C3	Renfield Lane	E5	Turnbull Street		
C5	Carlton Court	C4	Fox Street	E1	Lister Street	C3	Renfield Street	C3	Union Street		
C5	Carlton Place	E4	Gallowgate	E4	Little Dovehill	B1	Renfrew Street	D4	Virginia Street		
F3	Castle Street	B1	Garnet Street	E5	London Road	D1	Renton Street	A5	Wallace Street		
F3	Cathedral Square	C1	Garscube Road	A1	Lynedoch Street	E3	Richmond Street	A4	Washington Street		
D3	Cathedral Street	D3	George Square	A1	Lynedoch Terrace	A5	Riverview Drive	B3	Waterloo Street		
B5	Centre Street	D3	George Street	A4	McAlpine Street	B4	Riverview Gardens	E4	Watson Street		
F5	Chambers Street	F5	Gibson Street	A3	McIntyre Street	A4	Riverview Place	B3	Wellington Street		
E5	Charlotte Street	D4	Glassford Street	C1	McPhater Street	B4	Robertson Street	B3	West Campbell Street		
A4	Cheapside Street	F2	Glebe Street	D4	Miller Street	D5	Ropework Lane	B2	West George Street		

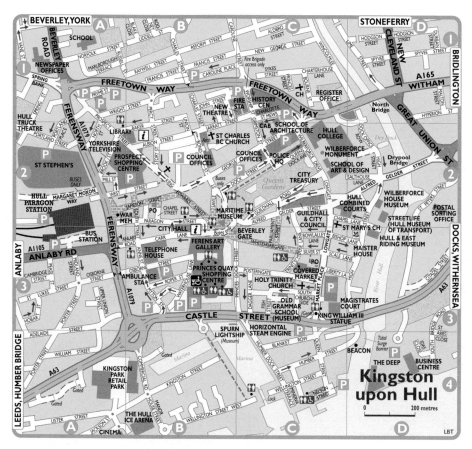

Kingston upon Hull

Kingston upon Hull is found on atlas page **347 G4**

A4	Adelaide Street		C3	Market Place
B2	Albion Street		A1	Marlborough Terrace
C2	Alfred Gelder Street		A3	Midland Street
A3	Anlaby Road		A2	Mill Street
B3	Anne Street		B3	Myton Street
B2	Baker Street		D1	New Cleveland Street
A1	Beverley Road		C1	New George Street
C3	Bishop Lane		A1	Norfolk Street
C4	Blanket Row		A3	Osborne Street
B2	Bond Street		B2	Paragon Street
C1	Bourne Street		C3	Parliament Street
C3	Bowlalley Lane		A3	Pease Street
A2	Brook Street		B1	Percy Street
B1	Caroline Place		A4	Porter Street
B1	Caroline Street		C3	Posterngate
B3	Carr Lane		C3	Princes Dock Street
B3	Castle Street		A1	Prospect Street
C2	Chapel Lane		C4	Queen Street
B1	Charles Street		C2	Queens Dock Avenue
C1	Charlotte Street Mews		B1	Raywell Street
C1	Charterhouse Lane		B1	Reform Street
D3	Citadel Street		B3	Roper Street
A2	Collier Street		A3	St Lukes Street
B4	Commercial Road		D2	St Peters Street
C3	Dagger Lane		B2	Savile Street
C2	Dock Street		C3	Scale Lane
A1	Ferensway		C3	Silver Street
C3	Fish Street		D4	South Bridge Road
A1	Freetown Way		C3	South Churchside
B2	George Street		B2	South Street
D2	Great Union Street		A1	Spring Bank
C2	Grimston Street		A1	Spring Street
C2	Guildhall Road		D1	Spyvee Street
D2	High Street		B2	Story Street
D1	Hodgson Street		C1	Sykes Street
C4	Humber Dock Street		C3	Trinity House Lane
C4	Humber Street		A3	Upper Union Street
D1	Hyperion Street		B3	Waterhouse Lane
B2	Jameson Street		C4	Wellington Street
B2	Jarratt Street		B4	Wellington Street West
B1	John Street		A2	West Street
B2	King Edward Street		C3	Whitefriargate
B4	Kingston Street		C2	Wilberforce Drive
C3	Liberty Lane		A4	William Street
D1	Lime Street		C1	Wincolmlee
A4	Lister Street		D1	Witham
C3	Lowgate		C1	Worship Street
B4	Manor House Street		A1	Wright Street

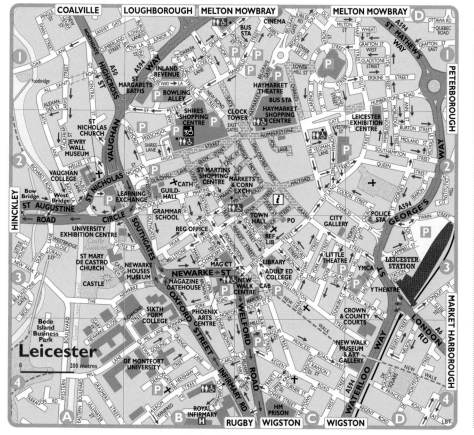

Leicester

Leicester is found on atlas page **240 C4**

C1	Abbey Street		C1	Mansfield Street
B2	Applegate		B2	Market Place
A2	Bath Lane		C3	Market Street
C1	Bedford Street South		C3	Marlborough Street
C3	Belvoir Street		A4	Mill Lane
C3	Bishop Street		C4	Mill Street
B4	Bonners Lane		B3	Millstone Lane
C3	Bowling Green Street		D4	Nelson Street
D3	Calais Hill		B3	Newarke Street
D3	Campbell Street		C4	Newtown Street
B4	Carlton Street		B3	Oxford Street
A3	Castle Street		B2	Peacock Lane
B1	Causeway Lane		C4	Pelham Street
C1	Charles Street		B3	Pocklingtons Walk
C3	Chatham Street		C4	Princess Road West
B1	Church Gate		C4	Regent Road
D2	Church Street		D4	Regent Street
C1	Clarence Street		C2	Rutland Street
C4	Crescent Street		A2	St Augustine Road
A1	Cumberland Street		D2	St George's Street
D4	De Montfort Street		D3	St George's Way
B4	Deacon Street		C1	St James Street
C3	Dover Street		D1	St Mathew's Way
B1	East Bond Street		A2	St Nicholas Circle
D3	East Street		B2	St Nicholas Place
C2	Every Street		B1	St Peter's Lane
B3	Friar Lane		C1	Sandiacre Street
C2	Gallowtree Gate		A1	Sanvey Gate
C2	Granby Street		B1	Short Street
B1	Great Central Street		B2	Silver Street
A1	Great Central Street		D3	South Albion Street
B2	Guildhall Lane		B3	Southgates
C2	Halford Street		A2	Talbot Lane
C1	Haymarket		B4	The Gateway
B2	High Street		A3	The Newarke
A1	Highcross Street		C4	Tower Street
C1	Hill Street		C4	Turner Street
C2	Horsefair Street		B3	Upper Brown Street
B2	Hotel Street		C4	Upper King Street
C2	Humberstone Gate		A2	Vaughan Way
D1	Humberstone Road		D4	Waterloo Way
B4	Infirmary Road		C3	Welford Road
C3	Jarrom Street		C3	Wellington Street
C3	King Street		C4	West Street
C1	Lee Street		D1	Wharf Street South
D4	London Road		D2	Wimbledon Street
B2	Loseby Lane		C2	Yeoman Street
C1	Lower Hill Street		B3	York Road

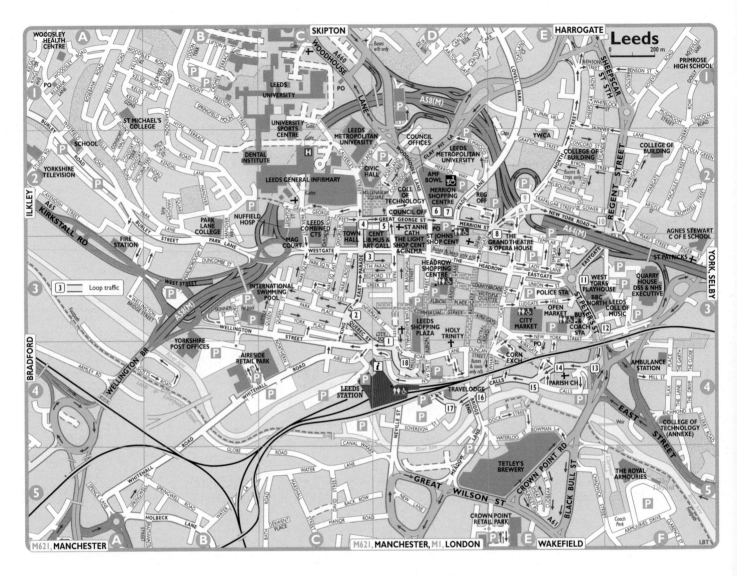

Leeds

Leeds is found on atlas page **343 E3**

C4 Aire Street	E2 Concord Street	C3 Infirmary Street	D4 Mill Hill	F3 St Mary's Street	B3 West Street
D3 Albion Place	A2 Consort Street	A1 Kelsall Grove	F4 Mill Street	C3 St Pauls Street	A1 Westfield Road
D4 Albion Street	A2 Consort Terrace	A1 Kelso Gardens	F2 Millwright Street	E3 St Peter's Street	C3 Westgate
F2 Argyle Street	A2 Consort Walk	A1 Kelso Place	B1 Mount Preston Street	E5 Sheaf Street	E4 Wharf Street
A4 Armley Road	D2 Cookridge Street	A1 Kelso Road	D4 Neville Street	E1 Sheepscar Grove	A5 Whitehall Road
F5 Armouries Drive	D3 County Arcade	A1 Kelso Street	D3 New Briggate	F1 Sheepscar Street South	E1 Whitelock Street
C5 Back Row	B1 Cromer Terrace	B2 Kendal Close	D5 New Lane	E1 Skinner Lane	C1 Woodhouse Lane
C5 Bath Road	F2 Cromwell Street	B2 Kendal Lane	D4 New Station Street	B3 Skinner Street	A1 Woodsley Road
C3 Bedford Street	B1 Cross Kelso Road	C3 King Street	C3 South Parade	C3 York Place
A2 Belle Vue Road	E5 Crown Point Road	A1 Kings Avenue	E2 New York Road	D4 Sovereign Street	
E1 Benson Street	E5 Cudbear Street	D3 Kirkgate	E3 New York Street	A5 Spence Lane	
E5 Black Bull Street	C5 David Street	A2 Kirkstall Road	E2 North Street	B1 Springfield Mount	
D4 Boar Lane	C5 Derwent Place	E3 Lady Lane	C4 Northern Street	B5 Springwell Road	
E4 Bowman Lane	E4 Dock Street	D3 Lands Lane	E1 Oatland Court	A5 Springwell Street	
B5 Braithwaite Street	F1 Dolly Lane	C2 Leighton Street	C3 Oxford Place	A2 Studio Road	
D4 Bridge End	D4 Duncan Street	E2 Leylands Road	C3 Oxford Row	E3 Templar Place	
E3 Bridge Street	B3 Duncombe Street	B1 Lifton Place	C3 Park Cross Street	E3 Templar Street	
D3 Briggate	C3 East Parade	F2 Lincoln Green	B2 Park Lane	F4 The Close	
F1 Bristol Street	F4 East Street	F1 Lincoln Road	C3 Park Place	F4 The Drive	
A1 Burley Road	E3 Eastgate	B3 Lisbon Street	D3 Park Row	F4 The Garth	
A2 Burley Street	F4 Ellerby Road	C3 Little Queen Street	C3 Park Square East	D3 The Headrow	
E2 Byron Street	D2 Elmwood Road	E1 Lovell Park	C3 Park Square North	F4 The Lane	
E4 Calls	F4 Flax Place	E1 Lovell Park Hill	C3 Park Square West	E2 Trafalgar Street	
C2 Calverley Street	B5 Globe Road	D3 Lower Basinghall Street	C2 Park Street	E3 Union Street	
C4 Canal Wharf	B4 Gotts Road	E3 Ludgate Hill	D2 Portland Crescent	D3 Upper Basinghall Street	
D1 Carlton Carr	E2 Gower Street	B1 Lyddon Terrace	C2 Portland Way	E3 Vicar Lane	
D1 Carlton Gate	E2 Grafton Street	F2 Mabgate	C3 Quebec Street	E3 Victoria Quarter	
D1 Carlton Rise	C2 Great George Street	F2 Macauley Street	C3 Queen Street	B2 Victoria Street	
A2 Cavendish Street	D5 Great Wilson Street	C5 Manor Road	F2 Regent Street	A2 Victoria Terrace	
E3 Central Road	D3 Greek Street	B3 Marlborough Street	F4 Richmond Street	D2 Wade Lane	
E5 Chadwick Street	B2 Hanover Avenue	D5 Marshall Street	F3 Rider Street	B5 Water Lane	
F2 Cherry Row	B2 Hanover Square	D5 Meadow Lane	A1 Rillbank Lane	E4 Waterloo Street	
F5 Clarence Street	B2 Hanover Way	E2 Melbourne Street	A1 Rosebank Road	D1 Well Close Rise	
B2 Clarendon Road	B5 Holbeck Lane	D2 Merrion Street	F1 Roseville Road	A4 Wellington Bridge	
D2 Clay Pit Lane	E5 Hunslet Road	D2 Merrion Way	F1 Roseville Way	A3 Wellington Bridge Street	
D3 Commercial Street	B1 Hyde Terrace	D2 Millennium Square	A1 St John's Road	B3 Wellington Street	

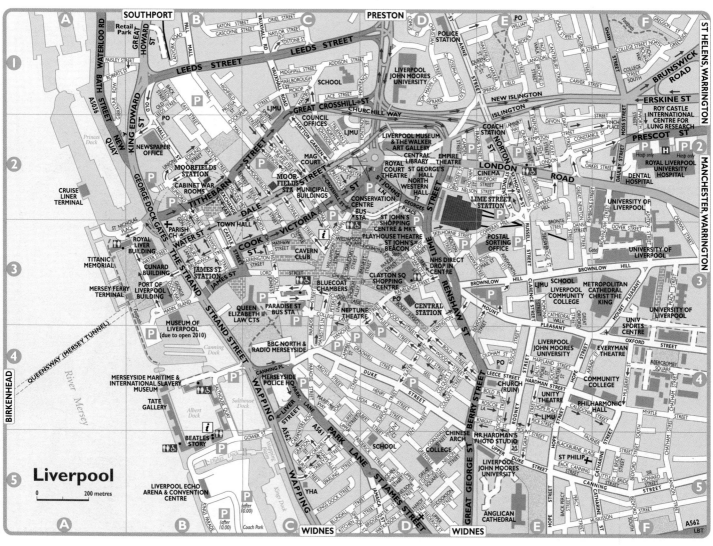

Liverpool

Liverpool is found on atlas page **308 D2**

F4	Abercromby Square	C3	Church Alley	D3	Fleet Street	B3	James Street	E2	Norton Street	E2	Seymour Street
C1	Addison Street	C3	Church Street	D2	Fontenoy Street	E1	John Street	F2	Oakes Street	F1	Shaw Street
E3	Ainsworth Street	C1	Churchill Way	E2	Fraser Street	C2	Johnson Street	B1	Old Hall Street	C5	Shaws Alley
C4	Argyle Street	E3	Clarence Street	B1	Gascoyne Street	E2	Kempston Street	B1	Old Leeds Street	C2	Sir Thomas Street
E4	Arrad Street	B2	Cockspur Street	B2	George Dock Gates	D4	Kent Street	E4	Oldham Street	D3	Skelhorne Street
F2	Ashton Street	C3	College Lane	B3	George Dock Way	B2	King Edward Street	F4	Oxford Street	D4	Slater Street
E2	Audley Street	F1	College Street North	D1	Gerard Street	C5	Kings Dock Street	A1	Paisley Street	C2	Smithfield Street
D3	Basnett Street	F1	College Street South	A1	Gibraltar Row	E4	Knight Street	B1	Pall Mall	E1	Soho Street
A1	Bath Street	D4	Colquitt Street	D4	Gilbert Street	C1	Lace Street	C4	Paradise Street	C3	South John Street
F5	Bedford Street South	E2	Constance Street	E2	Gildart Street	E1	Langsdale Street	C4	Park Lane	C5	Sparling Street
E3	Benson Street	C3	Cook Street	E2	Gill Street	E4	Leece Street	D3	Parker Street	E1	Springfield
D4	Berry Street	D5	Cookson Street	C1	Gladstone Street	B1	Leeds Street	F3	Peach Street	E2	Stafford Street
B2	Bixteth Street	E2	Copperas Hill	C5	Gower Street	D3	Lime Street	E2	Pembroke Street	C2	Stanley Street
E5	Blackburne Place	C5	Cornhill	D4	Gradwell Street	C4	Liver Street	C3	Peters Lane	B3	Strand Street
C5	Blundell Street	D5	Cornwallis Street	D3	Great Charlotte Street	B1	Liver Street	E5	Pilgrim Street	D4	Suffolk Street
D3	Bold Street	B3	Covent Garden	C1	Great Crosshill Street	D3	London Road	E3	Pomona Street	C4	Surrey Street
D3	Bolton Street	E2	Craven Street	D5	Great George Street	D2	Lord Nelson Street	F2	Prescot Street	C5	Tabley Street
E2	Bridport Street	C2	Crosshill Street	B1	Great Howard Street	C3	Lord Street	C2	Preston Street	B2	Tarleton Street
E3	Bronte Street	F3	Crown Street	E2	Great Newton Street	D4	Lydia Ann Street	B1	Prussia Street	B2	Tempest Hey
E3	Brownlow Hill	C2	Cunliffe Street	E3	Great Orford Street	C2	Manchester Street	D2	Pudsey Street	C2	Temple Court
F3	Brownlow Street	C2	Dale Street	E2	Greek Street	C4	Manesty's Lane	D3	Raneleigh Street	C2	Temple Street
F1	Brunswick Road	E3	Dansie Street	F1	Greenside	B3	Mann Island	D3	Renshaw Street	B3	The Strand
B3	Brunswick Street	F2	Daulby Street	F1	Gregson Street	C1	Marlborough Street	E4	Rice Street	B2	Tithebarn Street
E4	Caledonia Street	E2	Devon Street	D5	Grenville Street	A1	Marybone	C3	Richmond Street	D1	Tom Mann Close
D2	Camden Street	F3	Dover Street	B2	Hackins Hey	E4	Maryland Street	A1	Roberts Street	E3	Trowbridge Street
C4	Campbell Street	B3	Drury Lane	C4	Hanover Street	C3	Mathew Street	E4	Rodney Street	C2	Trueman Street
C4	Canning Place	D4	Duke Street	E4	Hardman Street	B1	Midghall Street	E3	Roscoe Street	B2	Union Street
F5	Canning Street	B1	East Street	E1	Harker Street	C2	Moorfields	E3	Royal Mail Street	E5	Upper Duke Street
E1	Canterbury Street	C2	Eberle Street	E3	Harrington Street	F2	Moss Street	B2	Rumford Street	C4	Upper Frederick Street
C5	Carpenters Row	B2	Edmund Street	E2	Hart Street	E3	Mount Pleasant	E3	Russell Street	D5	Upper Pitt Street
E1	Carver Street	D3	Elliot Street	C2	Hatton Garden	E5	Mount Street	D1	St Anne Street	C1	Vauxhall Road
B3	Castle Street	F2	Epworth Street	D3	Hawke Street	F4	Mulberry Street	D2	St Georges Place	C3	Vernon Street
F5	Catharine Street	F1	Erskine Street	E1	Henry Street	F4	Myrtle Street	D5	St James Street	C3	Victoria Street
C2	Chatham Street	B2	Exchange Street East	B1	Highfield Street	C1	Naylor Street	D2	St Johns Lane	E1	Wakefield Street
C2	Cheapside	E5	Falkner Street	E4	Hope Place	D5	Nelson Street	D1	St Josephs Crescent	C4	Wapping
D1	Christian Street	B3	Fenwick Street	E5	Hope Street	E1	New Islington	E2	St Vincent Street	B3	Water Street
				D2	Hotham Street	A2	New Quay	B4	Salisbury Quay	A1	Waterloo Road
				C5	Hurst Street	D3	Newington	F5	Sandon Street	C3	Whitechapel
				F5	Huskisson Street	C3	North John Street	C3	School Lane	C3	Williamson Street
				E1	Islington	C2	North Street	D4	Seel Street	D4	Wood Street
				D5	Jamaica Street					C4	York Street

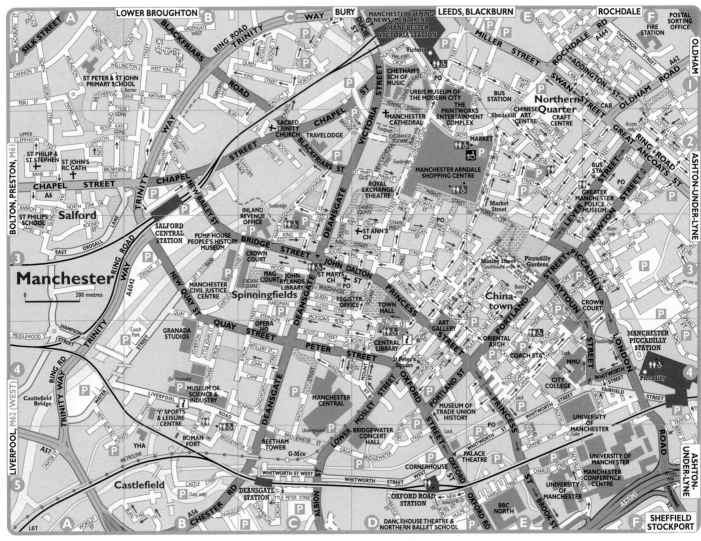

Manchester

Manchester is found on atlas page **326 B5**

E1	Addington Street
D3	Albert Square
C5	Albion Street
E1	Angel Street
A1	Arlington Street
C4	Artillery Street
B4	Atherton Street
C3	Atkinson Street
E3	Aytoun Street
E3	Back George Street
E3	Back Piccadilly
A2	Bank Street
A2	Barrow Street
F1	Bendix Street
F5	Berry Street
A1	Blackburn Street
B1	Blackfriars Road
C2	Blackfriars Street
B2	Bloom Street
E4	Bloom Street
F2	Blossom Street
F4	Boad Street
C1	Boond Street
C2	Booth Street
D3	Booth Street
C4	Bootle Street
C3	Brazennose Street
F3	Brewer Street
C3	Bridge Street
B5	Bridgewater Street
A1	Briggs Street
E5	Brook Street
A1	Brotherton Drive
D3	Brown Street
A2	Browning Street
B2	Bury Street

C4	Byrom Street
E1	Cable Street
D5	Cambridge Street
C4	Camp Street
E4	Canal Street
A1	Cannon Street
B1	Canon Green Drive
B5	Castle Street
C1	Caygill Street
A2	Chapel Street
D3	Chapel Walks
E5	Charles Street
E3	Charlotte Street
E3	Chatham Street
D5	Chepstow Street
B5	Chester Road
F3	China Lane
E4	Chorlton Street
E2	Church Street
A2	Cleminson Street
C2	Clowes Street
F4	Cobourg Street
C5	Commercial Street
E2	Copperas Street
F1	Cornell Street
D2	Corporation Street
F2	Cotton Street
F1	Cross Keys Street
D3	Cross Street
E2	Dale Street
E1	Dantzic Street
F2	Dean Street
C4	Deansgate
C2	Dearman's Place
D4	Dickenson Street
F5	Downing Street
F3	Ducie Street

B5	Duke Street
E1	Dyche Street
A3	East Ordsall Lane
E2	Edge Street
D2	Exchange Square
F4	Fairfield Street
E4	Faulkner Street
D1	Fennel Street
A2	Ford Street
D3	Fountain Street
B1	Garden Lane
B3	Gartside Street
F2	George Leigh Street
D4	George Street
F1	Goulden Street
E5	Granby Row
C1	Gravel Lane
F2	Great Ancoats Street
C5	Great Bridgewater Street
D1	Great Ducie Street
D5	Great Marlborough Street
C1	Greengate
B1	Greengate West
A4	Hampson Street
E1	Hanover Street
C3	Hardman Street
E2	Henry Street
E2	High Street
E3	Hilton Street
E3	Hope Street
F2	Houldsworth Street
D5	Hulme Street
D1	Hunts Bank
A2	Islington Way
C3	Jackson's Row
A3	James Street
C3	John Dalton Street
E2	John Street
C5	Jordan Street
F3	Jutland Street
A2	Kays Gardens

D3	Kennedy Street
C1	King Street
C3	King Street
C3	King Street West
F3	Laystall Street
B3	Left Bank
F3	Lena Street
E3	Lever Street
B4	Little John Street
C5	Little Peter Street
B4	Liverpool Road
C3	Lloyd Street
F4	London Road
D1	Long Millgate
C4	Longworth Street
B4	Lower Byrom Street
C5	Lower Mosley Street
E1	Ludgate Street
E4	Major Street
D3	Marble Street
D2	Market Street
D3	Marsden Street
F1	Marshall Street
A1	Mayan Avenue
E1	Mayes Street
A4	Middlewood Street
E1	Miller Street
E3	Minshull Street
C1	Mirabel Street
D4	Mosley Street
B1	Mount Street
D4	Mount Street
D4	Museum Street
B1	Nathan Drive
B2	New Bailey Street
C1	New Bridge Street
A4	New Elm Road
D2	New Market
B3	New Quay Street
D5	New Wakefield Street
F3	Newton Street

D3	Nicholas Street
D2	Norfolk Street
A1	North George Street
A1	North Hill Street
A2	North Star Drive
C1	Norton Street
E2	Oak Street
F1	Oldham Road
E2	Oldham Street
E5	Oxford Road
D4	Oxford Street
D3	Pall Mall
E3	Parker Street
C2	Parsonage
F3	Paton Street
A1	Peru Street
C4	Peter Street
E3	Piccadilly
C3	Police Street
F2	Port Street
E4	Portland Street
A5	Potato Wharf
D3	Princess Street
B4	Quay Street
C1	Queen Street
C3	Queen Street
E1	Richmond Street
E1	Rochdale Road
A3	Rodney Street
A2	Rosamond Drive
E4	Sackville Street
D2	St Ann's Square
C3	St Ann's Street
D4	St James Street
C4	St John Street
D2	St Mary's Gate
C3	St Mary's Parsonage
C2	St Mary's Street
B2	St Stephen Street
E5	Samuel Ogden Street
E1	Sharp Street

F1	Sherratt Street
E2	Shudehill
A1	Silk Street
B2	Sillavan Way
C3	South King Street
C4	Southmill Street
F4	Sparkle Street
B2	Spaw Street
E2	Spear Street
D3	Spring Gardens
B3	Stanley Street
F4	Store Street
E1	Swan Street
F3	Tariff Street
E2	Thomas Street
F1	Thompson Street
E2	Tib Street
D1	Todd Street
C4	Tonman Street
F4	Travis Street
A4	Trinity Way
E2	Turner Street
A1	Tysoe Gardens
A2	Upper Cleminson Street
C1	Viaduct Street
C2	Victoria Bridge Street
D2	Victoria Street
D1	Walkers Croft
A4	Water Street
C4	Watson Street
B1	Wellington Street
B1	West King Street
D3	West Mosley Street
E5	Whitworth Street
C5	Whitworth Street West
B2	William Street
C4	Windmill Street
D2	Withy Grove
C3	Wood Street
D3	York Street

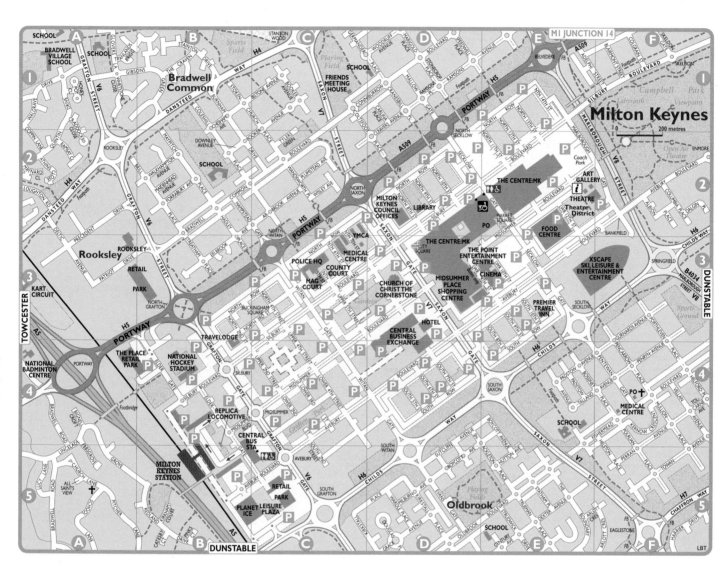

Milton Keynes

Milton Keynes is found on atlas page **168 A2**

E1	Adelphi Street	A2	Dansteed Way	E2	Lower 12th Street	C2	Plumstead Avenue	B1	The Craven
F2	Albion Place	A2	Deltic Avenue	A5	Lucy Lane	F4	Polruan Place	F4	Tolcarne Avenue
A5	All Saints View	E5	Dexter Avenue	B2	Maidenhead Avenue	F3	Porthleven Place	F5	Towan Avenue
C2	Arbrook Avenue	D5	Douglas Place	D1	Mallow Gate	A4	Portway	A1	Tranlands Brigg
E5	Arlott Crescent	D5	Downley Avenue	D1	Marigold Place	A3	Precedent Drive	E5	Trueman Place
A2	Athins Close	A5	Ebbsgrove	E2	Market Square	A2	Quintin Drive	C2	Tylers Green
C5	Avebury Boulevard	B3	Eelbrook Avenue	E2	Marlborough Gate	A2	Ramsay Close	C4	Upper 2nd Street
A4	Bignell Croft	B4	Elder Gate	E1	Marlborough Street	D1	Ramsons Avenue	C4	Upper 4th Street
F1	Blairmont Street	D5	Evans Gate	A2	Maynard Close	D1	Ramsons Place	C3	Upper 5th Street
B2	Booker Avenue	F4	Fishermead Boulevard	B2	Maypitch Place	B5	Redland Drive	F4	Vellan Avenue
E4	Bossiney Place	B2	Forrabury Avenue	B4	Midsummer Boulevard	D3	Saxon Gate	A1	Walgrave Drive
D5	Boycott Avenue	C1	Germander Place	D5	Milburn Avenue	C1	Saxon Street	B2	Walkhampton Avenue
B2	Bradwell Common	A1	Gibsons Green	F4	Mullion Place	E4	Saxon Street	C2	Wandsworth Place
	Boulevard	A1	Glovers Lane	B3	North 2nd Street	A5	School Lane	D5	Wardle Place
A5	Bradwell Road	D5	Grace Avenue	C3	North 3rd Street	D2	Secklow Gate	A1	Whetstone Close
B2	Brill Place	B4	Grafton Gate	C3	North 4th Street	D4	Shackleton Place	C2	Wisley Avenue
B3	Buckingham Square	A1	Grafton Street	C3	North 5th Street	B4	Silbury Boulevard	C3	Witan Gate
B1	Burnham Drive	F3	Gurnards Avenue	C3	North 6th Street	F1	Skeldon Gate	D1	Woodruff Avenue
D1	Caruna Place	B2	Hadley Place	C2	North 7th Street	C5	South 2nd Street		
B5	Catesby Court	B2	Hampstead Gate	D2	North 8th Street	D4	South 5th Street		
E5	Century Avenue	F5	Harrier Drive	D2	North 9th Street	D4	South 6th Street		
F5	Chaffron Way	F4	Helford Place	D2	North 10th Street	D4	South 7th Street		
B1	Chesham Avenue	F5	Helston Place	E2	North 11th Street	E3	South 8th Street		
D5	Childs Way	A1	Honey Pot Close	E1	North 12th Street	E3	South 9th Street		
A5	Church Lane	E5	Hutton Avenue	E1	North 13th Street	E3	South 10th Street		
D3	City Square	C1	Ibstone Avenue	E1	North 14th Street	D4	South Row		
D1	Cleavers Avenue	F4	Kernow Crescent	B3	North Row	D1	Speedwell Place		
B1	Coleshill Place	B5	Kirkham Court	D5	Oldbrook Boulevard	B1	Stainton Drive		
F1	Colgrain Street	C5	Kirkstall Place	E4	Padstow Avenue	E5	Statham Place		
C1	Coltsfoot Place	A5	Lincelade Grove	A3	Patriot Drive	B1	Stokenchurch Place		
C1	Columbia Place	A2	Loughton Road	F4	Pencarrow Place	D1	Stonecrop Place		
C1	Conniburrow Boulevard	C4	Lower 2nd Street	F4	Penryn Avenue	B3	Streatham Place		
A2	Coppin Lane	C4	Lower 3rd Street	F4	Pentewan Gate	E5	Strudwick Drive		
A1	Craddocks Close	C4	Lower 4th Street	F5	Perran Avenue	D5	Sutcliffe Avenue		
D1	Cransbill Place	D3	Lower 9th Street	B5	Pinks Court	E4	Talland Avenue		
F2	Dalgin Place	E3	Lower 10th Street	A5	Pitcher Lane	E5	The Boundary		

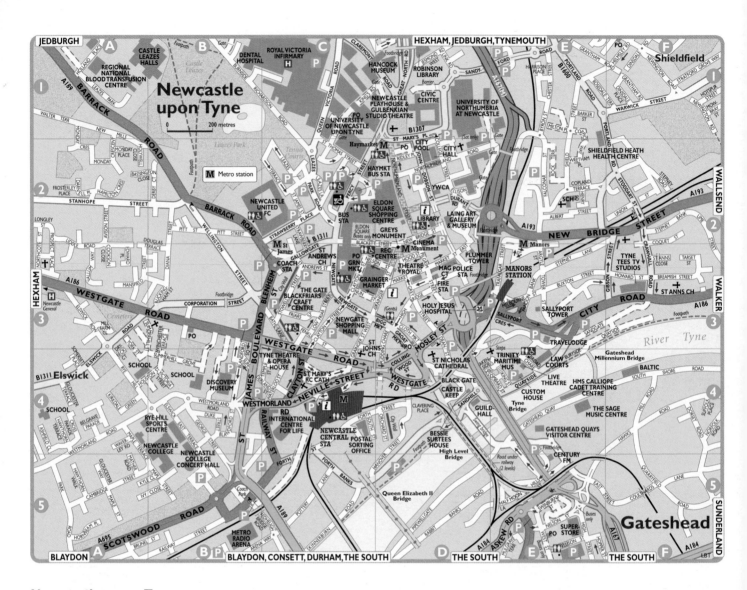

Newcastle upon Tyne

Newcastle upon Tyne is found on atlas page **405 F2**

D4 Akenside Hill	E1 Coppice Way	A5 Gloucester Way	C2 Leazes Park Road	D4 Orchard Street	A4 Somerset Place
E2 Albert Street	F2 Coquet Street	D3 Grainger Street	C2 Leazes Terrace	E3 Pandon Bank	F4 South Shore Road
B5 Arena Way	B3 Corporation Street	C3 Grainger Street West	A3 Liddle Road	A5 Park Road	C4 South Street
E3 Argyle Street	F5 Coulthards Lane	E1 Grantham Road	F2 Lime Street	C4 Peel Lane	A2 Stanhope Street
A4 Ashfield Close	F3 Crawhall Road	D1 Great North Road	D1 Link Road	C2 Percy Street	F2 Stepney Bank
E5 Askew Road	A4 Cross Parade	D3 Grey Street	E4 Lombard Street	D3 Pilgrim Street	E3 Stepney Lane
A2 Avison Street	A2 Darnell Place	D3 Groat Market	A2 Longley Street	D5 Pipewellgate	F2 Stepney Road
E1 Barker Street	D3 Dean Street	E5 Half Moon Lane	C3 Low Friar Street	B2 Pitt Street	F2 Stoddart Street
A1 Barrack Road	B2 Derby Court	A2 Hamilton Crescent	A3 Mansfield Street	E1 Portland Road	C3 Stowell Street
A2 Bassington Close	B3 Diana Street	D5 Hanover Street	B5 Maple Street	C5 Pottery Lane	F1 Stratford Grove Way
C3 Bath Lane	F1 Dinsdale Place	E1 Harrison Place	A4 Maple Terrace	A2 Pudding Chare	C2 Strawberry Lane
A4 Belgrave Parade	F1 Dinsdale Road	F4 Hawks Road	D3 Market Street	D4 Pudding Chare	C2 Strawberry Place
D3 Bigg Market	F4 Dorset Road	A4 Hawthorn Terrace	D3 Market Street East	F5 Quarryfield Road	F4 Suffolk Place
C2 Blackett Street	B3 Douglas Terrace	A5 Hawthorn Walk	A5 Mather Road	E4 Quayside	B4 Summerhill Grove
B4 Blandford Square	A4 Drybeck Court	F1 Helmsley Road	E3 Melbourne Street	C1 Queen Victoria Road	B3 Summerhill Street
B4 Blandford Street	B4 Duke Street	E2 Henry Square	A3 Mill Farm Close	D5 Rabbit Banks Road	B4 Sunderland Street
C3 Blenheim Street	D2 Durant Road	D3 High Bridge	F4 Mill Road	B5 Railway Street	E5 Swinburne Street
F3 Breamish Street	E5 East Street	E5 High Street	E1 Milton Street	C5 Redheugh Bridge Road	F3 Tarset Street
E4 Broad Chare	A3 Edward Place	E5 Hills Street	A2 Monday Crescent	B1 Richardson Road	C4 Temple Street
A5 Brunel Street	C2 Eldon Square	A1 Holland Place	A2 Monday Place	D2 Ridley Place	D4 The Close
B3 Buckingham Street	D2 Ellison Place	A2 Holywell Close	D3 Mosley Street	E2 Rock Terrace	E3 Tower Street
B1 Burnside	E5 Ellison Street	D3 Hood Street	F1 Mowbray Street	E1 Rosedale Terrace	E3 Trafalgar Street
E4 Buryside	B4 Elswick East Terrace	E5 Hopper Street	E5 Mulgrave Terrace	A4 Rye Hill	F2 Union Street
E3 Buxton Street	A4 Elswick Road	A5 Hornbeam Place	C3 Nelson Street	C3 St Andrews Street	A3 Vallum Way
E1 Byron Street	A3 Elswick Row	F1 Hotspur Street	E5 Nelson Street (Gateshead)	F3 St Anns Close	B4 Victoria Street
A5 Cambridge Street	E2 Falconar Street	A4 Houston Street	C4 Neville Street	B4 St James Boulevard	A1 Walter Terrace
E1 Chester Street	C3 Fenckle Street	F3 Howard Street	D2 New Bridge Street	C2 St James Street	F1 Warwick Street
E3 City Road	C5 Forth Banks	A5 Ivy Close	E2 New Bridge Street	D1 St Mary's Place	C4 Waterloo Street
C1 Claremont Road	C4 Forth Street	D1 Jesmond Road West	A1 New Mills	C2 St Thomas Street	A4 Waverley Road
D4 Clavering Place	C3 Friars Street	D2 John Dobson Street	C3 Newgate	E3 Sallyport Crescent	B2 Wellington Street
C4 Clayton Street	A2 Frosterley Place	C1 King's Road	F1 Newington Road	E3 Sandgate	E5 West Street
D3 Cloth Market	C3 Gallowgate	E4 King Street	F4 Norfolk Road	D4 Sandhill	A3 Westgate Road
D2 College Street	E4 Gateshead Quay	A4 Kirkdale Green	A3 Northcote Street	D1 Sandyford Road	A4 Westmorland Road
D4 Collingwood Street	B4 George Street	A5 Kyle Close	D2 Northumberland Road	A5 Scotswood Road	B3 Winchester Terrace
A3 Cookson Close	F3 Gibson Street	C2 Leazes Lane	D2 Northumberland Street	E2 Shield Street	E2 Wretham Place
E2 Copland Terrace	A4 Gloucester Terrace	A1 Leazes Park	C3 Nun Street	C5 Skinnerburn Road	A3 York Street

Norwich

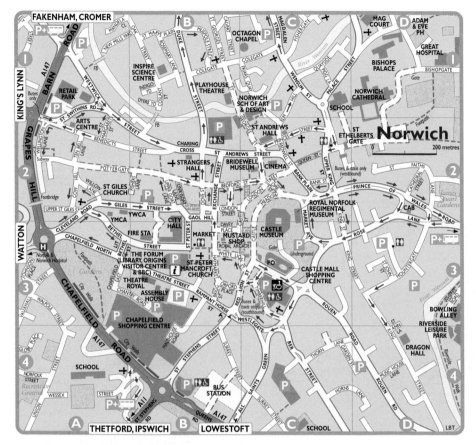
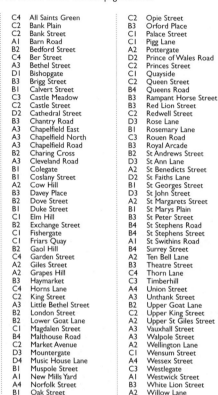

Norwich is found on atlas page **250 A3**

C4	All Saints Green	C2	Opie Street
C2	Bank Plain	B3	Orford Place
C2	Bank Street	C1	Palace Street
A1	Barn Road	C1	Pigg Lane
B2	Bedford Street	A2	Pottergate
C4	Ber Street	D2	Prince of Wales Road
A3	Bethel Street	C2	Princes Street
D1	Bishopgate	C1	Quayside
B3	Brigg Street	C2	Queen Street
B1	Calvert Street	B4	Queens Road
C3	Castle Meadow	B3	Rampant Horse Street
C2	Castle Street	B3	Red Lion Street
D2	Cathedral Street	C2	Redwell Street
B3	Chantry Road	D3	Rose Lane
A3	Chapelfield East	B1	Rosemary Lane
A3	Chapelfield North	C3	Rouen Road
A3	Chapelfield Road	B3	Royal Arcade
B2	Charing Cross	B2	St Andrews Street
A3	Cleveland Road	D3	St Ann Lane
B1	Colegate	A2	St Benedicts Street
B1	Coslany Street	D2	St Faiths Lane
A2	Cow Hill	B1	St Georges Street
B3	Davey Place	D3	St John Street
B2	Dove Street	A2	St Margarets Street
B1	Duke Street	B1	St Marys Plain
C1	Elm Hill	B3	St Peter Street
B2	Exchange Street	B4	St Stephens Road
C1	Fishergate	B4	St Stephens Street
C1	Friars Quay	A1	St Swithins Road
B2	Gaol Hill	B4	Surrey Street
C4	Garden Street	A2	Ten Bell Lane
A2	Giles Street	B3	Theatre Street
A2	Grapes Hill	C4	Thorn Lane
B3	Haymarket	C3	Timberhill
C4	Horns Lane	A4	Union Street
C2	King Street	A3	Unthank Street
A3	Little Bethel Street	B2	Upper Goat Lane
B2	London Street	C2	Upper King Street
B2	Lower Goat Lane	A2	Upper St Giles Street
C1	Magdalen Street	A3	Vauxhall Street
B4	Malthouse Road	A3	Walpole Street
C2	Market Avenue	A2	Wellington Lane
D3	Mountergate	C1	Wensum Street
D4	Music House Lane	A4	Wessex Street
B1	Muspole Street	C3	Westlegate
A1	New Mills Yard	A1	Westwick Street
A4	Norfolk Street	B3	White Lion Street
B1	Oak Street	A2	Willow Lane

Nottingham

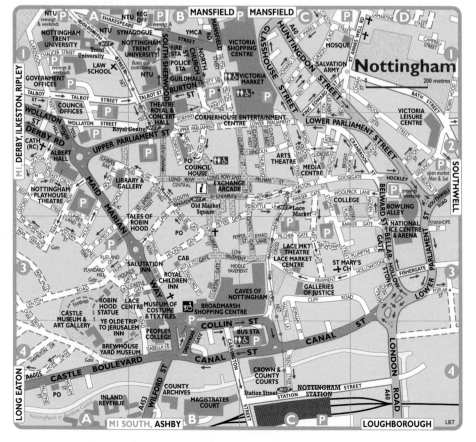

Nottingham is found on atlas page **276 C2**

B3	Albert Street	C1	Huntingdon Street
B2	Angel Row	C1	King Edward Street
C3	Barker Gate	B2	King Street
D1	Bath Street	D2	Lennox Street
B2	Beastmarket Hill	C2	Lincoln Street
C1	Beck Street	B3	Lister Gate
D3	Bellargate	D4	London Road
D2	Belward Street	B2	Long Row Central
C2	Bridlesmith Gate	B2	Long Row East
C2	Broad Street	B3	Low Pavement
A2	Bromley Place	C2	Lower Parliament Street
D1	Brook Street	A2	Maid Marion Way
B1	Burton Street	B1	Mansfield Road
B4	Canal Street	B2	Market Street
C2	Carlton Street	C3	Middle Hill
B4	Carrington Street	B1	Milton Street
A4	Castle Boulevard	A3	Mount Street
B3	Castle Gate	C2	Old Lenton Street
A3	Castle Road	A3	Park Row
A1	Chaucer Street	C2	Pelham Street
B2	Cheapside	D3	Pemberton Street
C3	Cliff Road	C3	Pilcher Gate
C2	Clinton Street East	D3	Plumptre Street
A1	Clarendon Street	B2	Queen Street
C2	Clumber Street	D1	St Annes Well Road
B4	Collin Street	A3	St James's Street
C1	Conuent Street	C1	St Marks Street
D2	Cranbrook Street	C2	St Mary's Gate
A2	Cumberland Place	B3	St Peters Gate
C1	Curzon Place	A1	Shakespeare Street
A2	Derby Road	B2	South Parade
A2	East Circus Street	B1	South Sherwood Street
C2	East Street	C4	Station Street
D3	Fishergate	C2	Stoney Street
C3	Fletcher Gate	A1	Talbot Street
B2	Forman Street	C2	Thurland Street
A3	Friar Lane	A2	Toll House Hill
D2	Gedling Street	C4	Trent Street
C2	George Street	B1	Trinity Square
C1	Glasshouse Street	A2	Upper Parliament Street
A1	Goldsmith Street	C2	Victoria Street
C2	Goosegate	C2	Warser Gate
B4	Greyfriar Gate	C3	Weekday Cross
C2	Heathcote Street	A2	Wellington Circus
C3	High Pavement	B2	Wheeler Gate
C2	High Street	B4	Wilford Street
D2	Hockley	A2	Wollaton Street
D3	Hollowstone	C2	Woolpack Lane

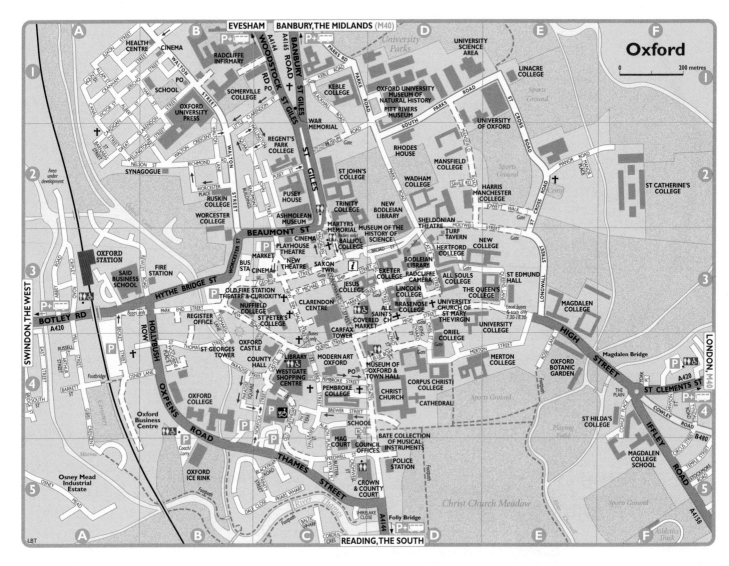

Oxford

Oxford is found on atlas page **140 B3**

A3	Abbey Road	C5	Faulkner Street	B4	Paradise Square	F4	Tyndale Road
A1	Albert Street	C5	Friars Wharf	B4	Paradise Street	A1	Victor Street
C4	Albion Place	C3	George Street	B3	Park End Street	B2	Walton Crescent
D4	Alfred Street	A4	Gibbs Crescent	C1	Parks Road	B2	Walton Lane
A1	Allam Street	A2	Great Clarendon Street	C4	Pembroke Street	B1	Walton Street
A4	Arthur Street	B1	Hart Street	C4	Pike Terrace	C2	Wellington Square
C5	Baltic Wharf	D3	High Street	C2	Pusey Street	A2	Wellington Street
C1	Banbury Road	B3	Hollybush Row	C4	Queen Street	B4	Woodbine Place
A4	Barrett Street	D2	Holywell Street	E3	Queens Lane	C1	Woodstock Road
B2	Beaumont Buildings	B3	Hythe Bridge Street	B3	Rewley Road	B2	Worcester Place
C3	Beaumont Street	F4	Iffley Road	B2	Richmond Road	B3	Worcester Street
A3	Becket Street	A1	Jericho Street	E4	Rose Lane	F4	York Place
C5	Blackfriars Road	E2	Jowett Walk	C4	Rose Place		
C1	Blackhall Road	A1	Juxon Street	A4	Russell Street		
D4	Blue Boar Street	C1	Keble Road	D4	St Aldates		
A3	Botley Road	D3	King Edward Street	A2	St Barnabas Street		
F4	Boulter Street	B2	Little Clarendon Street	F4	St Clements Street		
C4	Brewer Street	E3	Longwall Street	E1	St Cross Road		
A4	Bridge Street	C3	Magdalen Street	C4	St Ebbe's Street		
D3	Broad Street	E2	Manor Place	C1	St Giles		
C5	Butterwyke Place	E2	Manor Road	C2	St John Street		
A1	Canal Street	D2	Mansfield Road	C3	St Michael Street		
A2	Cardigan Street	C3	Market Street	B4	St Thomas Street		
C4	Castle Street	D4	Merton Street	D2	Savile Road		
D3	Catte Street	A4	Mill Street	C3	Ship Street		
F5	Circus Street	A1	Mount Street	C5	Shirelake Close		
C5	Cobden Crescent	C2	Museum Road	A2	St Barnabas Street		
C3	Cornmarket Street	A2	Nelson Street	D1	South Parks Road		
F4	Cowley Place	C3	New Inn Hall Street	A4	South Street		
F4	Cowley Road	B3	New Road	C5	Speedwell Street		
A1	Cranham Street	C4	Norfolk Street	F5	Stockmore Road		
A3	Cripley Road	C4	Old Greyfriars Street	F5	Temple Street		
C5	Cromwell Street	D3	Oriel Street	C5	Thames Street		
C5	Dale Close	A4	Osney Lane	F4	The Plain		
C5	Dawson Street	A5	Osney Mead	B3	Tidmarsh Lane		
A4	East Street	B4	Oxpens Road	C5	Trinity Street		
				D3	Turl Street		

University Colleges

D3	All Souls College
C3	Balliol College
D3	Brasenose College
D4	Christ Church College
D4	Corpus Christi College
D3	Exeter College
D3	Hertford College
C3	Jesus College
C1	Keble College
E1	Linacre College
D3	Lincoln College
E3	Magdalen College
D2	Manchester College
D2	Mansfield College
E4	Merton College
D3	New College
B3	Nuffield College
D4	Oriel College
C4	Pembroke College
E3	Queen's College
C2	Regent's Park College
B2	Ruskin College
F2	St Catherine's College
E3	St Edmund Hall
F4	St Hilda's College
C2	St John's College
C3	St Peter's College
B1	Somerville College
C2	Trinity College
D3	University College
D2	Wadham College
B2	Worcester College

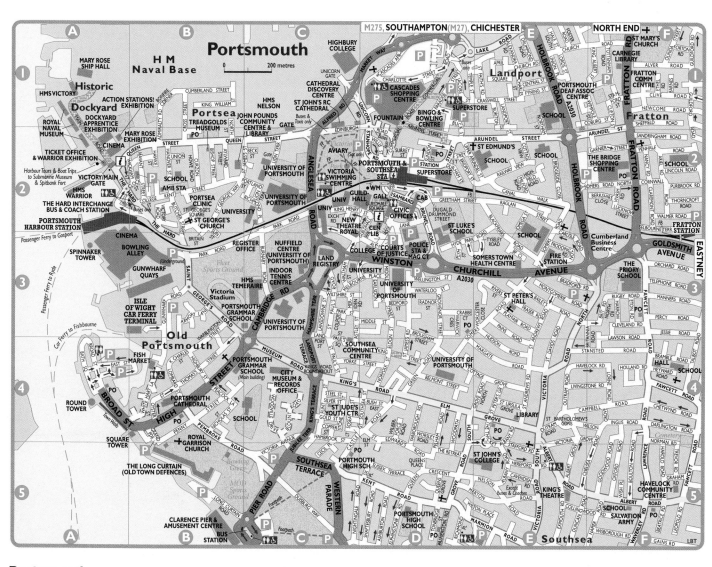

Portsmouth

Portsmouth is found on atlas page **52 A4**

B2	Admiralty Road	F4	Campbell Road	E5	Exmouth Road	C2	King Henry I Street	B4	Oyster Street	C5	Southsea Terrace
E5	Albany Road	E2	Canal Walk	F3	Fawcett Road	D4	King Street	E3	Painsthorpe Road	E5	Stafford Road
E5	Albert Grove	E3	Carlisle Road	C4	Flint Street	B1	King William Street	D5	Palmerston Road	D2	Stanhope Road
E5	Albert Road	D1	Cascades Approach	E3	Fraser Road	C4	King's Road	D1	Paradise Street	F4	Stansted Road
D3	Alec Rose Lane	C4	Castle Road	F1	Fratton Road	C4	King's Terrace	B3	Park Road	D2	Station Street
E1	Alexandra Road	E5	Cavendish Road	F2	Garnier Street	E1	Lake Road	C3	Park Street	C4	Stone Street
C1	Alfred Road	E1	Charles Street	E3	Gold Street	C3	Landport Street	B4	Peacock Lane	D2	Surrey Street
F1	Alver Road	D1	Charlotte Street	F3	Goldsmith Avenue	C4	Landport Terrace	D4	Pelham Road	D5	Sussex Terrace
C2	Angelsea Road	E5	Chelsea Road	F5	Goodwood Road	C3	Lansdowne Street	B4	Pembroke Road	F3	Telephone Road
E1	April Square	F4	Chetwynd Road	D4	Great Southsea Street	F5	Lawrence Road	F2	Penhale Road	D1	Temple Street
F2	Ariel Road	E1	Church Road	D4	Green Road	F3	Lawson Road	B4	Penny Street	A2	The Hard
B3	Armory Lane	F2	Claremont Road	D2	Greetham Street	C2	Lion Terrace	C5	Pier Road	D5	The Retreat
E2	Arundel Street	F3	Cleveland Road	D3	Grosvenor Street	C4	Little Southsea Street	E3	Playfair Road	E4	The Thicket
D5	Ashburton Road	F1	Clifton Street	E4	Grove Road North	E4	Livingstone Road	B2	Queen Street	D1	Unicorn Road
C3	Astley Street	F1	Clive Road	D5	Grove Road South	B4	Lombard Street	D5	Queens Crescent	E1	Union Place
B2	Aylward Street	E5	Collingwood Road	D2	Guildhall Square	B5	Long Curtain Road	D5	Queens Grove	D2	Upper Arundel Street
E3	Baileys Road	D2	Commercial Road	D2	Guildhall Walk	E1	Lords Street	D5	Queens Place	C5	Victoria Avenue
A4	Bath Square	F2	Cornwall Road	B3	Gunwharf Road	F4	Lorne Road	E2	Raglan Street	E4	Victoria Grove
D4	Belmont Street	D4	Cottage Grove	C4	Hambrook Street	F2	Lucknow Street	E2	Railway View	E4	Victoria Road North
B2	Bishop Street	E2	Cottage View	C3	Hampshire Terrace	D1	Market Way	F3	Rugby Road	E5	Victoria Road South
E2	Blackfriars Road	E1	Crasswell Street	B2	Hanover Street	E5	Marmion Road	E4	St Andrews Road	B2	Victory Road
C4	Blount Road	B1	Cross Street	F5	Harold Road	C3	Melbourne Place	E4	St Davids Road	F2	Vivash Road
A4	Broad Street	B1	Cumberland Street	B2	Havant Street	E5	Merton Road	D4	St Edward's Road	F2	Walmer Road
D3	Brougham Street	B2	Curzon Howe Road	E4	Havelock Road	D3	Middle Street	E1	St Faith's Road	C3	Waltham Street
D1	Buck Street	F4	Darlington Road	B2	Hawke Street	E2	Milford Road	B3	Saint George's Road	B3	Warblington Street
E1	Buriton Street	F3	Earlsdon Street	E5	Hereford Road	E3	Montgomerie Road	B2	St George's Way	D3	Warwick Crescent
C3	Burnaby Road	A4	East Street	E4	Heyward Road	C4	Museum Road	D4	St James's Road	D3	Waterloo Street
B2	Butcher Street	C2	Edinburgh Road	B4	High Street	F2	Nancy Road	C2	St James's Street	F5	Waverley Road
C3	Cambridge Road	D4	Eldon Street	E1	Highbury Street	F5	Napier Road	B4	St Nicholas Street	D3	Wellington Street
		D4	Elm Grove	E3	Holbrook Road	E5	Nelson Road	C3	St Paul's Road	C5	Western Parade
		D5	Elphinstone Road	E4	Hudson Road	F1	Newcome Road	C4	St Paul's Street	B4	White Hart Lane
				D3	Hyde Park Road	C5	Nightingale Road	E4	St Peter's Grove	B2	Wickham Street
				F4	Inglis Road	D4	Norfolk Street	B4	St Thomas's Street	D2	Willis Street
				D2	Isambard Brunel Road	F4	Norman Road	F2	Sandringham Road	F4	Wilson Grove
				D1	Jacobs Street	B2	North Street	F2	Selbourne Terrace	C3	Wiltshire Street
				F3	Jessie Road	F3	Orchard Road	D5	Shaftesbury Road	D3	Winston Churchill Avenue
				C4	Jubilee Terrace	E4	Outram Road	F1	Sheffield Road	F5	Wisborough Road
				D5	Kent Road	F5	Oxford Road	C4	Silver Street	D4	Woodpath
				B2	Kent Street			D2	Slindon Street	C4	Woodville Drive
				F1	King Albert Street			E3	Somers Road	D4	Yarborough Road
				B4	King Charles Street			F2	Somers Road North	C4	Yorke Street

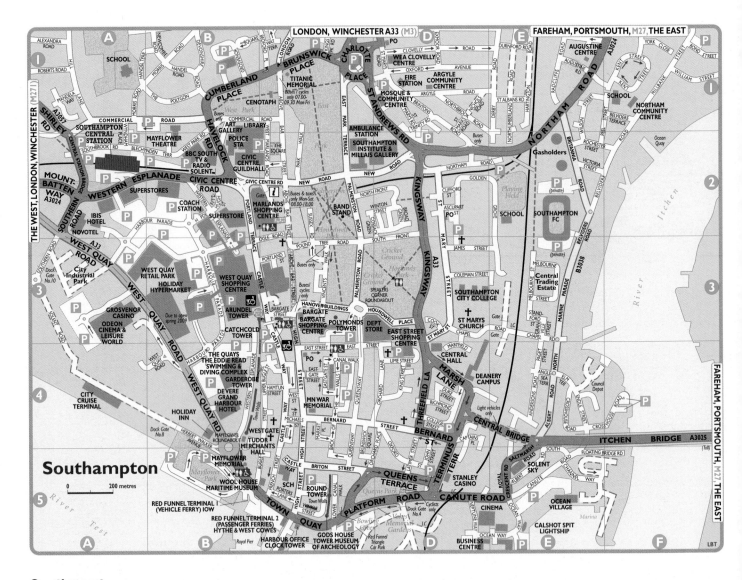

Southampton

Southampton is found on atlas page **50 D2**

C1	Above Bar Street	D3	Coleman Street	D5	John Street	C5	Platform Road	C2	West Marlands Road
E4	Albert Road North	D4	College Street	F1	Kent Street	C5	Porters Lane	B2	West Park Road
E5	Albert Road South	A1	Commercial Road	D4	King Street	C3	Portland Street	A3	West Quay Road
A1	Alexandra Road	D3	Cook Street	C1	Kings Park Road	B2	Portland Terrace	C4	West Street
E4	Andersons Road	D2	Cossack Green	D2	Kingsway	C3	Pound Tree Road	A2	Western Esplanade
E4	Anglesea Terrace	E4	Crosshouse Road	D5	Latimer Street	D5	Queens Terrace	F1	William Street
D1	Argyle Road	B1	Cumberland Place	D4	Lime Street	C4	Queensway	E1	Wilson Street
D2	Ascupart Street	E1	Derby Road	C1	London Road	E1	Radcliffe Road	C5	Winkle Street
C4	Back of the Walls	B1	Devonshire Road	C5	Lower Canal Walk	D4	Richmond Street	D2	Winton Street
C3	Bargate Street	D4	Duke Street	A1	Mandela Way	A1	Roberts Road	A2	Wyndham Place
C1	Bedford Place	E1	Durnford Road	E3	Marine Parade	E2	Rochester Street	F1	York Close
E2	Belvidere Road	C1	East Park Terrace	C4	Market Place	E5	Royal Crescent Road		
F1	Belvidere Terrace	C4	East Street	D4	Marsh Lane	E1	St Albans Road		
C4	Bernard Street	C4	Eastgate Street	D4	Maryfield	D1	St Andrews Road		
A2	Blechynden Terrace	E4	Elm Terrace	E3	Melbourne Street	D1	St Marks Road		
F1	Bond Street	E4	Endle Street	F1	Millbank Street	D2	St Mary Street		
D1	Brintons Road	D1	Exmoor Road	A1	Morris Road	D1	St Marys Road		
E2	Britannia Road	B2	Fitzhugh Street	A2	Mountbatten Way	C4	St Michaels Street		
C5	Briton Street	E5	Floating Bridge Road	D5	Neptune Way	E5	Saltmarsh Road		
D2	Broad Green	C5	French Street	C2	New Road	A1	Shirley Road		
C1	Brunswick Place	E2	Golden Grove	B1	Newcombe Road	A3	Solent Road		
C4	Brunswick Square	E3	Granville Road	D1	Nichols Road	D3	South Front		
B5	Bugle Street	B1	Grosvenor Square	C2	North Front	A2	Southbrook Road		
C4	Canal Walk	C4	Hamtun Street	D2	Northam Road	A2	Southern Road		
D5	Canute Road	B1	Handel Road	D1	Northbrook Road	E3	Standford Street		
D4	Captains Place	A1	Handel Terrace	E1	Northumberland Road	C2	Sussex Road		
C3	Castle Way	C3	Hanover Buildings	E5	Ocean Way	D5	Terminus Terrace		
D4	Central Bridge	A2	Harbour Parade	C2	Ogle Road	B1	The Polygon		
A2	Central Station Bridge	E1	Hartington Road	D4	Orchard Lane	C2	The Square		
E5	Channel Way	B2	Havelock Road	C5	Orchard Place	D4	Threefield Lane		
D3	Chapel Road	B4	Herbert Walker Avenue	D1	Oxford Avenue	C5	Town Quay		
C1	Charlotte Place	C3	High Street	D5	Oxford Street	D1	Trinity Road		
B2	Civic Centre Road	A1	Hill Lane	E4	Paget Street	C4	Upper Bugle Street		
D2	Clifford Street	D3	Houndwell Place	C2	Palmerston Road	E2	Victoria Street		
D1	Clovelly Road	F4	Itchen Bridge	C2	Park Walk	C3	Vincents Walk		
		D3	James Street	F1	Peel Street	C1	Waterloo Terrace		

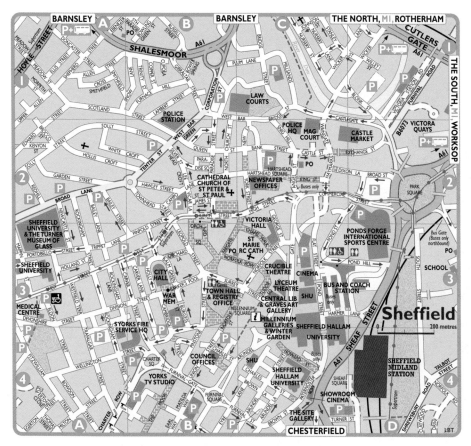

Sheffield

Sheffield is found on atlas page **314 D2**

A1	Allen Street	B1	Lambert Street
C2	Angel Street	B3	Leopold Street
C4	Arundel Gate	A1	Meadow Street
C4	Arundel Street	A4	Milton Street
A2	Bailey Lane	C2	New Street
B3	Balm Green	A2	Newcastle Street
C2	Bank Street	B3	Norfolk Row
B3	Barker's Pool	C3	Norfolk Street
D1	Blonk Street	B2	North Church Street
C1	Bridge Street	C1	Nursery Street
A2	Broad Lane	B3	Orchard Square
D2	Broad Street	B2	Paradise Square
C4	Brown Street	B2	Paradise Street
B3	Burgess Street	D2	Park Square
B3	Cambridge Street	C4	Paternoster Row
B2	Campo Lane	B3	Pinfold Street
B3	Carver Street	B4	Pinstone Street
C2	Castle Street	B1	Plum Lane
C1	Castlegate	C3	Pond Street
C3	Chapel Walk	A3	Portobello Street
B4	Charles Street	B2	Queen Street
B4	Charter Square	A2	Rockingham Street
B2	Church Street	B1	Russell Street
C2	Commercial Street	B2	St James Street
B1	Corporation Street	A1	Scotland Street
A3	Devonshire Street	B1	Shalesmoor
A3	Division Street	C4	Sheaf Street
A1	Doncaster Street	A1	Shepherd Street
A3	Eldon Street	C2	Snig Hill
D2	Exchange Street	B1	Snow Lane
B4	Eyre Lane	A2	Solly Street
B3	Fargate	D3	South Street
A4	Fitzwilliam Street	B1	Spring Street
C3	Flat Street	C1	Stanley Street
B1	Furnace Hill	B3	Surrey Street
D1	Furnival Road	B2	Townhead Street
B4	Furnival Street	A4	Trafalgar Street
A2	Garden Street	A3	Trippet Lane
C2	George Street	C3	Tudor Square
B1	Gibraltar Street	B4	Union Street
C3	Harmer Lane	C2	Waingate
B2	Hawley Street	A4	Wellington Street
C2	Haymarket	B1	West Bar
C2	High Street	B2	West Bar Green
A2	Hollis Croft	A3	West Street
B3	Holly Street	D1	Wicker
A1	Hoyle Street	C1	Wicker Lane
C2	King Street	C2	York Street

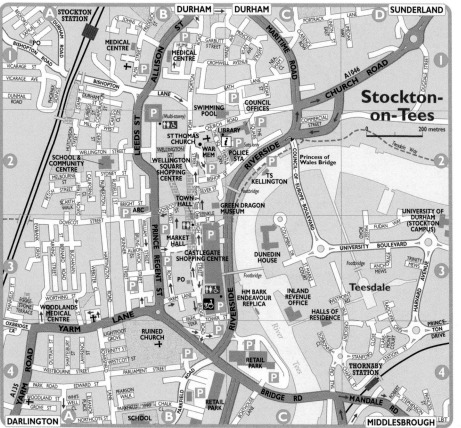

Stockton-on-Tees

Stockton-on-Tees is found on atlas page **396 B6**

B1	Allison Street	A2	Palmerston Street
B1	Alma Street	A4	Park Road
C1	Bath Lane	B3	Park Terrace
B2	Bishop Street	B4	Parkfield Road
A1	Bishopton Lane	B4	Parkfield Way
A1	Bishopton Road	B4	Parliament Street
C4	Boathouse Lane	A2	Petch Street
A4	Bowesfield Lane	A1	Phoenix Sidings
B3	Bridge Road	C1	Portrack Lane
B2	Bright Street	B3	Prince Regent Street
B3	Brunswick Street	C1	Princess Avenue
A3	Buchanan Street	D4	Princeton Drive
B4	Chalk Close	D3	Radcliffe Crescent
D4	Chapel Street	C3	Riverside
B2	Church Road	B2	Russell Street
D4	Claremont Court	C1	Ryan Avenue
C1	Clarence Row	A3	St Bernard Road
C3	Columbia Drive	B1	St Johns Close
C2	Commercial Street	C3	St Marks Court
A2	Corporation Street	A4	Shaftesbury Street
C2	Council of Europe Boulevard	B2	Silver Street
B1	Cromwell Avenue	B3	Skinner Street
A2	Derby Street	B2	Smith Street
A2	Dixon Street	A1	Stamp Street
A3	Dovecot Street	D4	Stanford Close
A1	Durham Road	D4	Station Street
A1	Durham Street	A2	Sydney Street
A4	Edward Street	A3	Tarring Street
A3	Ewbank Drive	B2	The Square
B3	Finkle Street	C2	Thistle Green
B1	Frederick Street	B3	Tower Street
D3	Fudan Way	C1	Union Street East
B1	Garbutt Street	D3	University Boulevard
A3	Hartington Road	A1	Vicarage Avenue
D3	Harvard Avenue	A1	Vicarage Street
B2	High Street	C1	Wade Avenue
B1	Hume Street	A3	Webster Close
A2	Hutchison Street	B2	Wellington Square
A4	Lawrence Street	A2	Wellington Street
B2	Leeds Street	B3	West Row
D4	Mandale Road	A4	Westbourne Street
C1	Maritime Road	C3	Westpoint Road
D3	Massey Road	B3	William Street
A2	Melbourne Street	A4	Woodland Street
A2	Mill Street West	A3	Worthing Street
B1	Norton Road	D3	Yale Crescent
A4	Outram Street	A4	Yarm Lane
A4	Oxbridge Lane	A4	Yarm Road

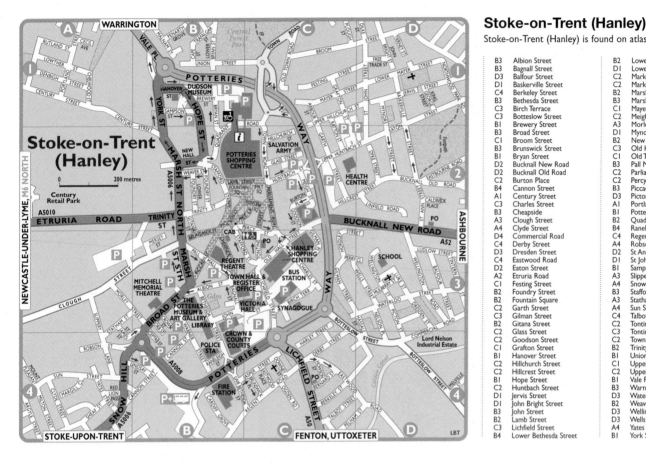

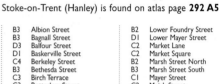

Stoke-on-Trent (Hanley)

Stoke-on-Trent (Hanley) is found on atlas page **292 A5**

B3	Albion Street	B2	Lower Foundry Street
B3	Bagnall Street	D1	Lower Mayer Street
D3	Balfour Street	C2	Market Lane
D1	Baskerville Street	C2	Market Square
C4	Berkeley Street	B2	Marsh Street North
B3	Bethesda Street	B3	Marsh Street South
C3	Birch Terrace	C1	Mayer Street
C3	Botteslow Street	C2	Meigh Street
B1	Brewery Street	A3	Morley Street
B3	Broad Street	D1	Mynors Street
C1	Broom Street	B2	New Hall Street
B3	Brunswick Street	C3	Old Hall Street
B1	Bryan Street	C1	Old Town Road
D2	Bucknall New Road	B3	Pall Mall
D2	Bucknall Old Road	C2	Parliament Row
C2	Burton Place	C2	Percy Street
B4	Cannon Street	B3	Piccadilly
A1	Century Street	D3	Picton Street
C3	Charles Street	A1	Portland Street
B3	Cheapside	B1	Potteries Way
A3	Clough Street	B2	Quadrant Road
A4	Clyde Street	B4	Raneleigh Street
D4	Commercial Road	C4	Regent Road
C4	Derby Street	A4	Robson Street
D3	Dresden Street	D2	St Ann Street
C4	Eastwood Road	D1	St John Street
D2	Eaton Street	B1	Sampson Street
A2	Etruria Road	A3	Slippery Lane
C1	Festing Street	A4	Snow Hill
B2	Foundry Street	B3	Stafford Street
B2	Fountain Square	A3	Statham Street
C2	Garth Street	A4	Sun Street
C3	Gilman Street	C4	Talbot Street
B2	Gitana Street	C2	Tontine Square
C2	Glass Street	C3	Tontine Street
C2	Goodson Street	C2	Town Road
C1	Grafton Street	B2	Trinity Street
B1	Hanover Street	B1	Union Street
C2	Hillchurch Street	C1	Upper Hillchurch Street
C2	Hillcrest Street	C2	Upper Huntbach Street
B1	Hope Street	B1	Vale Place
C2	Huntbach Street	B3	Warner Street
D1	Jervis Street	D3	Waterloo Street
D1	John Bright Street	B2	Weaver Street
B3	John Street	D3	Wellington Road
B2	Lamb Street	D3	Wells Street
C3	Lichfield Street	A4	Yates Street
B4	Lower Bethesda Street	B1	York Street

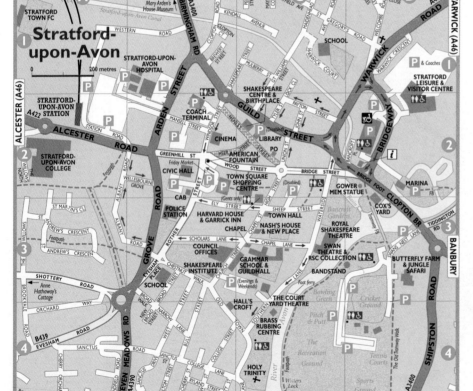

Stratford-upon-Avon

Stratford-upon-Avon is found on atlas page **190 C4**

A3	Albany Road	B4	New Broad Street
A2	Alcester Road	B4	New Street
B2	Arden Street	B3	Old Town
C1	Avenue Road	A4	Orchard Way
D2	Bancroft Place	C2	Payton Street
B1	Birmingham Road	C1	Percy Street
A4	Bordon Place	B3	Rother Street
B1	Brewery Street	D1	Rowley Crescent
D2	Bridge Foot	B4	Ryland Street
C2	Bridge Street	A3	St Andrew's Crescent
D2	Bridgeway	C1	St Gregory's Road
B3	Broad Street	A3	St Martin's Close
B3	Broad Walk	B4	Sanctus Drive
A3	Brookvale Road	A4	Sanctus Road
B4	Bull Street	B4	Sanctus Street
D1	Cedar Close	A4	Sandfield Road
C3	Chapel Lane	B3	Scholars Lane
C3	Chapel Street	A4	Seven Meadows Road
A4	Cherry Orchard	B1	Shakespeare Street
B4	Cherry Street	C3	Sheep Street
B3	Chestnut Walk	D4	Shipston Road
B3	Church Street	A3	Shottery Road
D3	Clopton Bridge	C4	Southern Lane
B1	Clopton Court	A2	Station Road
B1	Clopton Road	D3	Swans Nest Lane
B4	College Lane	A3	The Willows
B4	College Street	A2	The Willows North
B3	Ely Street	D3	Tiddington Road
B3	Evesham Place	B4	Trinity Street
A4	Evesham Road	C2	Tyler Street
C1	Great Williams Street	C2	Union Street
B2	Greenhill Street	C1	Warwick Court
B3	Grove Road	D1	Warwick Crescent
C2	Guild Street	D1	Warwick Road
B2	Henley Street	C3	Waterside
C2	High Street	D1	Welcombe Road
B4	Holtom Street	B2	Wellesbourne Grove
C2	John Street	B4	West Street
B1	Kendall Avenue	A1	Western Road
C1	Lock Close	B2	Windsor Street
C1	Maidenhead Road	B2	Wood Street
B2	Mansell Street		
C1	Mayfield Avenue		
C1	Mayfield Court		
B2	Meer Street		
C4	Mill Lane		
C1	Mulberry Street		
B4	Narrow Lane		

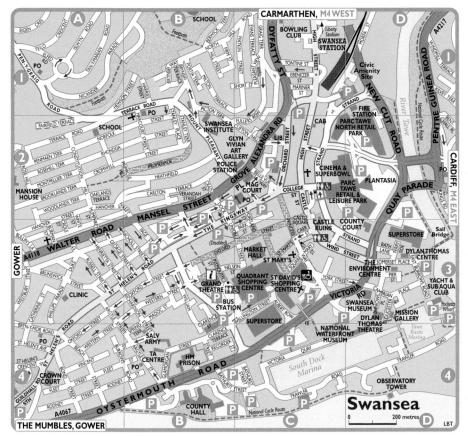

Swansea

Swansea is found on atlas page **103 G3**

C3	Albert Row	A1	Nicander Parade
C2	Alexandra Road	B3	Nicholl Street
A3	Argyle Street	A2	Norfolk Street
D3	Bath Lane	B1	North Hill
B4	Bathurst Street	C2	Orchard Street
A4	Beach Street	A4	Oxford Street
C2	Belle Vue Way	A4	Oystermouth Road
A4	Bond Street	B3	Page Street
A2	Brooklands Terrace	A1	Pen y Graig Road
A3	Brunswick Street	A2	Penmaen Terrace
B1	Brynsifi Terrace	D2	Pentre Guinea Road
A4	Burrows Road	A3	Phillips Parade
C3	Caer Street	B1	Picton Terrace
D3	Cambrian Place	D3	Pier Street
A2	Carlton Terrace	B3	Plymouth Street
C3	Castle Square	C2	Portland Street
C2	Castle Street	B1	Portia Terrace
A3	Catherine Street	B2	Primrose Hill
C2	Clifton Hill	C3	Princess Way
C2	College Street	B2	Promenade
A2	Constitution Hill	D2	Quay Parade
A2	Cromwell Street	A2	Rhondda Street
B2	Dock Union Street	B3	Richardson Street
A3	Duke Street	A4	Rodney Street
C1	Dyfatty Street	A2	Rosehill Terrace
D3	East Burrows Road	A3	Russell Street
A2	Fairfield Terrace	A3	St Helen's Road
A4	Fleet Street	C3	St Mary Street
C2	Fullers Row	C3	St Mary's Square
A3	George Street	D3	Somerset Place
B4	Glamorgan Street	B2	Stanley Place
D3	Gloucester Place	C2	Strand
C1	Graig Terrace	A1	Tan-y-Marian Road
C2	Grove Place	A2	Terrace Road
A3	Hanover Street	B3	The Kingsway
B2	Harcourt Street	C1	Tontine Street
B2	Heathfield	C4	Trawler Road
A3	Henrietta Street	C4	Victoria Quay
A1	Hewson Street	C3	Victoria Road
C1	High Street	A4	Vincent Street
A1	Islwyn Road	A3	Walter Road
B3	Madoc Street	C1	Watkin Street
B2	Mansel Street	C3	Wellington Street
B1	Milton Terrace	A4	Western Street
A2	Montpellier Terrace	B3	William Street
B2	Mount Pleasant	C3	Wind Street
B3	Nelson Street	A2	Woodlands Terrace
D1	New Cut Road	C3	York Street

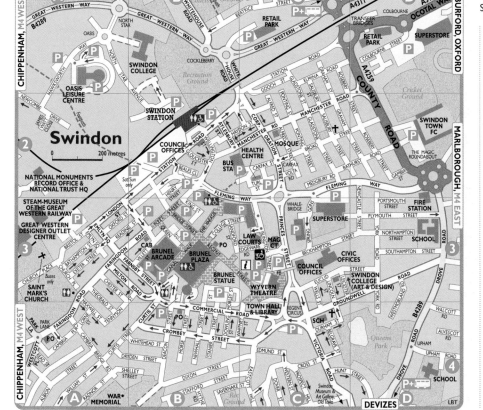

Swindon

Swindon is found on atlas page **113 E2**

C2	Alfred Street	B3	Havelock Street
B2	Aylesbury Street	A1	Hawksworth Way
A3	Bathampton Street	C2	Haydon Street
C2	Bathurst Road	B2	Henry Street
B2	Beales Close	C4	Hunt Street
C1	Beatrice Street	C3	Islington Street
C3	Beckhampton Street	A2	James Watt Close
C4	Belgrave Street	B3	King Street
B2	Bridge Street	C3	Leicester Street
A3	Bristol Street	C3	Lincoln Street
C2	Broad Street	A3	London Street
A4	Cambria Bridge Road	C2	Manchester Road
A4	Cambria Place	A4	Maxwell Street
B3	Canal Walk	A3	Milton Road
C2	Carfax Street	B3	Morley Street
A3	Chester Street	B4	Morse Street
A3	Church Place	D3	Newcastle Street
D1	Colbourne Street	A2	Newcombe Drive
B3	College Street	B4	Newhall Street
B4	Commercial Road	A1	North Star Avenue
C2	Corporation Street	D1	Ocotal Way
D1	County Road	A3	Oxford Street
B4	Crombey Street	A4	Park Lane
C4	Cross Street	D3	Plymouth Street
A4	Curtis Street	C2	Ponting Street
B4	Deacon Street	C3	Princes Street
B4	Dixon Street	B3	Queen Street
B4	Dowling Street	A3	Reading Street
D4	Drove Road	B3	Regent Street
B4	Dryden Street	C1	Rosebery Street
C4	Durham Street	C1	Salisbury Street
C4	Eastcott Hill	B3	Sandford Street
C3	Edgeware Road	D3	Southampton Street
B2	Edmund Street	B4	Stafford Street
C1	Elmina Road	B4	Stanier Street
A3	Emlyn Square	B2	Station Road
C3	Euclid Street	A4	Tennyson Street
A3	Exeter Street	B3	The Parade
A4	Faringdon Road	A3	Theobald Street
A3	Farnsby Street	C4	Victoria Road
B3	Fleet Street	B3	Villett Street
B2	Fleming Way	B2	Wellington Street
C1	Gladstone Street	C3	Wells Street
B2	Gloucester Street	A4	Westcott Place
C1	Gooch Street	B4	Whitehead Street
C1	Graham Street	B1	Whitehouse Road
A1	Great Western Way	C4	Whitney Street
C3	Groundwell Road	D3	York Road

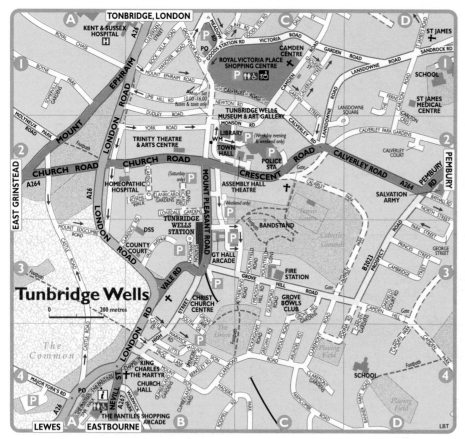

Tunbridge Wells

Tunbridge Wells is found on atlas page **78 D2**

C4	Arundel Road	B1	Lime Hill Road
D4	Banner Farm Road	B4	Little Mount Sion
D2	Bayhall Road	A2	London Road
B1	Belgrave Road	B2	Lonsdale Gardens
B4	Berkeley Road	B4	Madeira Park
A1	Boyne Park	A4	Major York's Road
C4	Buckingham Road	C3	Meadow Hill Road
C2	Calverley Park	B1	Meadow Road
D2	Calverley Park Gardens	A2	Molyneux Park Road
B1	Calverley Road	B2	Monson Road
C1	Calverley Street	A3	Mount Edgcumbe Road
D3	Cambridge Street	A2	Mount Ephraim
D3	Camden Gardens	B1	Mount Ephraim Road
D3	Camden Hill	B2	Mount Pleasant Road
D4	Camden Park	B4	Mount Sion
C1	Camden Road	C3	Mountfield Gardens
D2	Carlton Crescent	C3	Mountfield Road
D1	Carlton Road	A4	Nevill Street
A4	Castle Road	B1	Newton Road
B3	Castle Street	C4	Norfolk Road
B4	Chapel Place	D2	North Street
A2	Church Road	D3	Oakfield Court Road
B2	Clanricarde Gardens	D3	Park Street
B2	Clanricarde Road	D2	Pembury Road
C4	Claremont Gardens	C4	Poona Road
B4	Claremont Road	D3	Princes Street
B2	Clarence Road	D3	Prospect Road
C2	Crescent Road	B1	Rock Villa Road
B1	Culverden Street	B4	Rodmell Road
B4	Cumberland Gardens	B2	Rosehill Walk
B4	Cumberland Yard	A1	Royal Chase
B1	Dudley Road	D1	St James's Road
C4	Farmcombe Road	D1	Sandrock Road
B4	Frog Lane	A1	Somerville Gardens
C1	Garden Road	B3	South Grove
C1	Garden Street	B4	Spencer Mews
B1	Goods Station Road	B3	Station Approach
C4	Grecian Road	D1	Stone Street
B1	Grosvenor Road	B3	Sutherland Road
B3	Grove Avenue	D1	The Ferns
C3	Grove Hill Gardens	A4	The Pantiles Lower
C3	Grove Hill Road		Walk
C1	Grover Street	A4	The Pantiles
C3	Guildford Road	B3	Vale Avenue
B1	Hanover Road	B3	Vale Road
B4	High Street	C1	Victoria Road
C1	Lansdowne Road	B4	Warwick Road
C2	Lansdowne Square	B2	York Road

Wolverhampton

Wolverhampton is found on atlas page **236 D5**

A3	Alexandra Street	B3	Peel Street
A1	Bath Avenue	B4	Penn Road
A2	Bath Road	D2	Piper's Row
B3	Bell Street	B3	Pitt Street
C2	Berry Street	C2	Princess Street
C3	Bilston Street	C2	Queen Square
B2	Birch Street	C2	Queen Street
C2	Broad Street	C4	Raby Street
C2	Castle Street	A3	Raglan Street
A2	Chapel Ash	D2	Railway Drive
B2	Cheapside	B2	Red Lion Street
B4	Church Lane	A4	Retreat Street
B4	Church Street	A2	Ring Road St Andrews
B2	Clarence Road	D2	Ring Road St Davids
B2	Clarence Street	C4	Ring Road St Georges
D4	Cleveland Road	B4	Ring Road St Johns
B3	Cleveland Street	A3	Ring Road St Marks
D2	Corn Hill	C1	Ring Road St Patricks
B2	Corporation Street	B1	Ring Road St Peters
D1	Culwell Street	A4	Russell Street
A4	Dale Street	C3	St George's Parade
B2	Darlington Street	C4	St John's Square
C4	Dudley Road	A3	St Mark's Road
C2	Dudley Street	A3	St Mark's Street
B3	Fold Street	B1	St Peter's Square
C2	Fryer Street	B3	Salop Street
C3	Garrick Street	B4	School Street
A4	Graiseley Street	B3	Skinner Street
A4	Great Brickkiln Street	C3	Snow Hill
C1	Great Western Street	C1	Stafford Street
A4	Hallet Drive	A3	Stephenson Street
D2	Horseley Fields	B4	Stewart Street
C2	King Street	B3	Summer Row
C2	Lichfield Street	D4	Sutherland Place
C1	Littles Lane	C3	Tempest Street
C2	Long Street	B3	Temple Street
A3	Lord Street	B4	Thomas Street
C3	Market Street	C1	Thornley Street
A4	Merridale Street	C3	Tower Street
D3	Middle Cross	D4	Vicarage Road
B2	Mitrefold	B3	Victoria Street
B1	Molineux Street	B1	Waterloo Road
A1	New Hampton East	D1	Wednesfield Road
B2	North Street	B1	Whitmore Hill
C3	Old Hall Street	C1	Whitmore Street
A1	Park Avenue	B4	Worcester Street
A1	Park Road East	C2	Wulfruna Street
B2	Paternoster Row	A4	Zoar Street

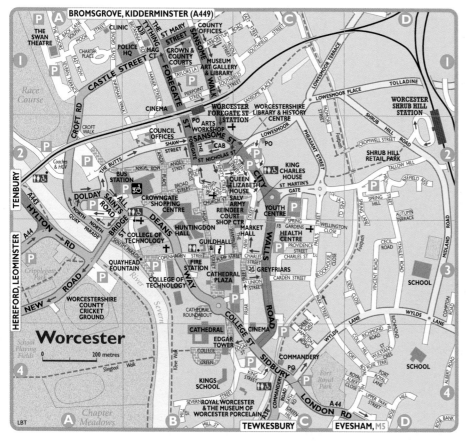

Worcester

Worcester is found on atlas page **188 B3**

A2	All Saints Road	A3	New Road
B2	Angel Place	C3	New Street
B2	Angel Row	A3	North Parade
B2	Angel Street	A2	North Quay
B1	Arboretum Road	C3	Park Street
C4	Bath Road	C2	Pheasant Street
A3	Bridge Street	B1	Pierpoint Street
B1	Britannia Road	C3	Providence Street
B2	Broad Street	B3	Pump Street
D2	Byefield Rise	C2	Queen Street
C3	Carden Street	D4	Richmond Hill
A1	Castle Street	D4	Richmond Road
D3	Cecil Road	D4	Rose Terrace
C3	Charles Street	C2	St James Close
A1	Charter Place	C2	St Martin's Gate
B2	Church Street	B1	St Mary Street
C2	City Walls Road	B2	St Nicholas Street
D4	Cole Hill	C3	St Paul's Street
B4	College Green	B2	St Swithuns Street
B3	College Street	D4	St Wulstan's Crescent
C4	Commandery Road	C1	Sansome Place
B3	Copenhagen Street	B2	Sansome Street
A2	Croft Road	B1	Sansome Walk
D2	Cromwell Street	B4	Severn Street
B3	Deans Way	A1	Severn Terrace
D3	Dent Close	B2	Shaw Street
A2	Dolday	D2	Shrub Hill Road
A1	Easy Row	C4	Sidbury
B1	Farrier Street	A3	South Parade
B1	Foregate Street	C1	Southfield Street
D4	Fort Royal Hill	C3	Spring Gardens
C3	Friar Street	D2	Spring Hill
C4	Green Hill	D2	Spring Lane
C4	Hamilton Road	D3	Stanley Road
B3	High Street	D2	Tallow Hill
D2	Hill Street	B1	Taylors Lane
A2	Hylton Road	A2	The Butts
A1	Infirmary Walk	B2	The Cross
C4	King Street	B2	The Foregate
B1	Little Southfield Street	C3	The Shambles
C4	London Road	B1	The Tything
A1	Love's Grove	D1	Tolladine
C2	Lowesmoor	B2	Trinity Street
C1	Lowesmoor Place	C3	Union Street
C1	Lowesmoor Terrace	D4	Upper Park Street
B1	Middle Street	D3	Vincent Road
D3	Midland Road	C3	Wellington Close
A1	Moor Street	C4	Wylds Lane

York

York is found on atlas page **358 A4**

C1	Aldwark	B3	Low Ousegate
B4	Baile Hill Terrace	C1	Low Petergate
A3	Barker Lane	D3	Margaret Street
C2	Bartle Garth	C2	Market Street
A3	Bishophill Junior	B1	Marygate
B3	Bishophill Senior	A3	Micklegate
B4	Bishopgate Street	D4	Mill Street
B2	Blake Street	C1	Minster Yard
A4	Blossom Street	C1	Monkgate
B1	Bootham	B2	Museum Street
B1	Bootham Row	D3	Navigation Road
C3	Castlegate	B4	Newton Terrace
C2	Church Street	B2	North Street
B4	Clementhorpe	A3	Nunnery Lane
C3	Clifford Street	A4	Nunthorpe Road
C1	College Street	C1	Ogleforth
C2	Colliergate	D4	Paragon Street
B2	Coney Street	C2	Parliament Street
C3	Coppergate	C2	Pavement
B4	Cromwell Road	D2	Peasholme Green
A4	Dale Street	D3	Peel Street
B2	Davygate	D3	Percy's Lane
C1	Deangate	C3	Piccadilly
B1	Duncombe Place	B4	Price's Lane
D4	Fawcett Street	A3	Priory Street
C2	Feasegate	A3	Queen Street
B3	Fetter Lane	B2	Rougier Street
D4	Fishergate	C2	St Andrewgate
D1	Foss Bank	C2	St Denys Road
D2	Foss Islands Road	B2	St Helens Square
C3	Fossgate	B1	St Leonards Place
A1	Frederic Street	B3	St Martins Lane
C2	Garden Place	C1	St Maurice's Road
B2	George Hudson Street	C2	St Saviourgate
D3	George Street	C2	Shambles
B1	Gillygate	B3	Skeldergate
C2	Goodramgate	C2	Spen Lane
C2	Grape Lane	A3	Station Road
C3	High Ousegate	B2	Stonegate
B1	High Petergate	A4	Swann Street
D4	Hope Street	C2	Swinegate
D4	Kent Street	A3	Tanner Row
C2	Kings Square	C2	The Stonebow
B3	Kings Staith	A3	Toft Green
D4	Leadmill Lane	C3	Tower Street
A2	Leeman Road	A3	Trinity Lane
B2	Lendal	B4	Victor Street
C1	Lord Mayor's Walk	C3	Walmgate

London Heathrow Airport – 16 miles west of London

Telephone: 0870 000 0123 or visit *www.heathrowairport.com*
Parking: short-stay, long-stay and business parking is available.
For charge details tel: 0870 000 1000
Public Transport: coach, bus, rail and London Underground.
There are several 4-star and 3-star hotels within easy reach of the airport.
Car hire facilities are available.

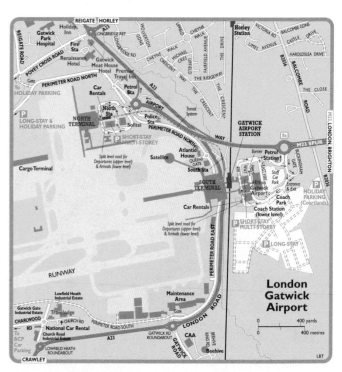

London Gatwick Airport – 35 miles south of London

Telephone: 0870 000 2468 or visit *www.gatwickairport.com*
Parking: short and long-stay parking is available at both the North and South terminals.
For charge details tel: 0870 000 1000
Public Transport: coach, bus and rail.
There are several 4-star and 3-star hotels within easy reach of the airport.
Car hire facilities are available.

London Stansted Airport – 36 miles north east of London

Telephone: 0870 000 0303 or visit *www.stanstedairport.com*
Parking: short, mid and long-stay open-air parking is available.
For charge details tel: 0870 000 1000
Public Transport: coach, bus and direct rail link to London on the Stansted Express.
There are several hotels within easy reach of the airport.
Car hire facilities are available.

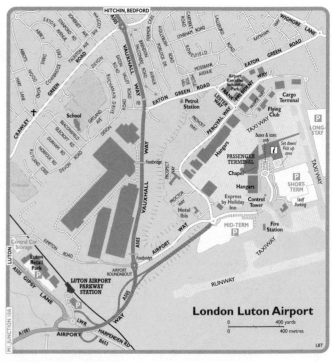

London Luton Airport – 33 miles north of London

Telephone: 01582 405100 or visit *www.london-luton.co.uk*
Parking: short-term, mid-term and long-stay parking is available.
For charge details tel: 0870 606 7050
Public Transport: coach, bus and rail.
There are several hotels within easy reach of the airport.
Car hire facilities are available.

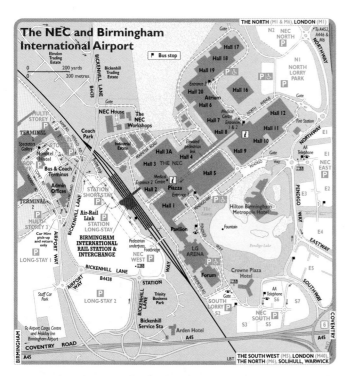

Birmingham International Airport – 8 miles east of Birmingham

Telephone: 0870 733 5511 or visit *www.bhx.co.uk*
Parking: short and long-stay parking is available. For charge details tel: 0870 733 5511
Public Transport: Air-Rail Link service operates every 2 minutes to and from Birmingham International Railway Station & Interchange.
There is one 3-star hotel adjacent to the airport and several 4 and 3-star hotels within easy reach of the airport. Car hire facilities are available.

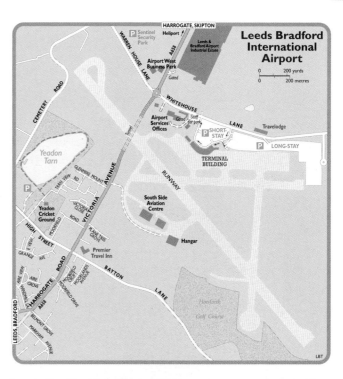

Leeds Bradford International Airport – 7 miles north east of Bradford and 9 miles north west of Leeds

Telephone: 0113 250 9696 or visit *www.lbia.co.uk*
Parking: short and long-stay parking is available. For charge details tel: 0113 250 9696
Public Transport: bus service operates every 30 minutes from Bradford, Leeds and Otley.
There are several 4-star and 3-star hotels within easy reach of the airport.
Car hire facilities are available.

Manchester Airport – 10 miles south of Manchester

Telephone: 0161 489 3000 or visit *www.manchesterairport.co.uk*
Parking: short and long-stay parking is available.
For charge details tel: 0161 489 3723
Public Transport: bus, coach and rail.
There are several 4-star and 3-star hotels within easy reach of the airport.
Car hire facilities are available.

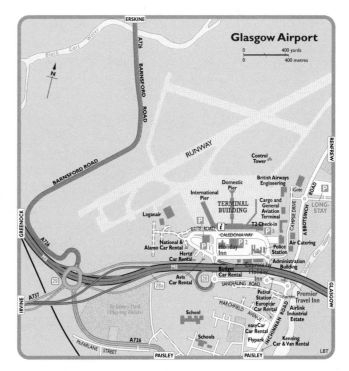

Glasgow Airport – 8 miles west of Glasgow

Telephone: 0870 040 0008 or visit *www.glasgowairport.com*
Parking: short and long-stay parking is available.
For charge details tel: 0870 000 1000
Public Transport: regular coach services operate direct to central Glasgow and Edinburgh.
There are several 3-star hotels within easy reach of the airport.
Car hire facilities are available.

Using the National Grid

With an Ordnance Survey National Grid reference you can pinpoint anywhere in the country using this atlas. The blue grid lines which divide the main-map pages into 5km squares for ease of indexing also match the National Grid. A National Grid reference gives two letters and some figures. This example shows how to find the summit of mount Snowdon using its 4-figure grid reference of **SH6154**.

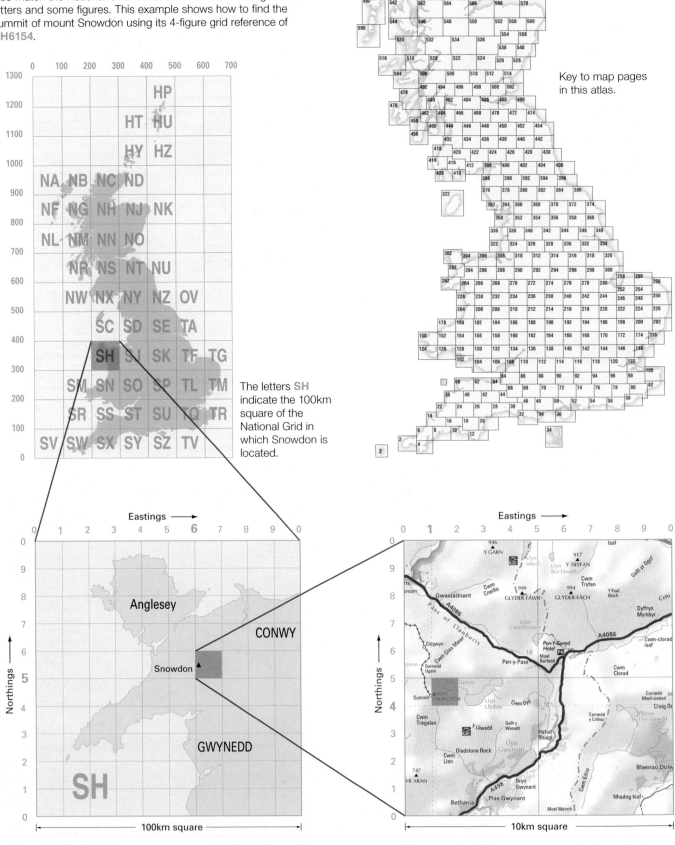

Key to map pages in this atlas.

The letters **SH** indicate the 100km square of the National Grid in which Snowdon is located.

Eastings →

Eastings →

Anglesey

CONWY

Snowdon

GWYNEDD

SH

100km square

10km square

In a 4-figure grid reference the first two figures (eastings) are read along the map from left to right, the second two (northings) up the map. The figures **6** and **5**, the first and third figures of the Snowdon reference, indicate the 10km square within the **SH** square, lying above (north) and right (east) of the intersection of the vertical (easting) line **6** and horizontal (northing) line **5**.

The summit is finally pinpointed by figures **1** and **4** which locate a 1km square within the 10km square.

At road atlas mapping scales these grid lines are normally estimated by eye.

Gazetteer of map entries

Both sections of this gazetteer list entries appearing in the main-map section of the atlas in alphabetical order. The reference before each name gives the atlas page number and grid reference of the square in which the place appears. The map shows counties, unitary authorities and administrative areas, together with a list of the abbreviated name forms used in the gazetteer. The recreation and leisure index lists places of tourist interest including airports and airfields, National Parks, main physical features, campsites, golf courses and cycle routes. Organisation affiliations are shown as follows: CADW Cadw, EH English Heritage, HS Historic Scotland, NT National Trust, NTS National Trust for Scotland, UNESCO. The city, town and village index lists settlements.

Scotland

Abers	Aberdeenshire
Ag & B	Argyll & Bute
Angus	Angus
Border	Scottish Borders
C Aber	City of Aberdeen
C Dund	City of Dundee
C Edin	City of Edinburgh
C Glas	City of Glasgow
Clacks	Clackmannanshire (1)
D & G	Dumfries & Galloway
E Ayrs	East Ayrshire
E Duns	East Dunbartonshire (2)
E Loth	East Lothian
E Rens	East Renfrewshire (3)
Falk	Falkirk
Fife	Fife
Highld	Highland
Inver	Inverclyde (4)
Mdloth	Midlothian (5)
Moray	Moray
N Ayrs	North Ayrshire
N Lans	North Lanarkshire (6)
Ork	Orkney Islands
P & K	Perth & Kinross
Rens	Renfrewshire (7)
S Ayrs	South Ayrshire
Shet	Shetland Islands
S Lans	South Lanarkshire
Stirlg	Stirling
W Duns	West Dunbartonshire (8)
W Isls	Western Isles
W Loth	West Lothian

Wales

Blae G	Blaenau Gwent (9)
Brdgnd	Bridgend (10)
Caerph	Caerphilly (11)
Cardif	Cardiff
Carmth	Carmarthenshire
Cerdgn	Ceredigion
Conwy	Conwy
Denbgs	Denbighshire
Flints	Flintshire
Gwynd	Gwynedd
IoA	Isle of Anglesey
Mons	Monmouthshire
Myr Td	Merthyr Tydfil (12)
Neath	Neath Port Talbot (13)
Newpt	Newport (14)
Pembks	Pembrokeshire
Powys	Powys
Rhondd	Rhondda Cynon Taff (15)
Swans	Swansea
Torfn	Torfaen (16)
V Glam	Vale of Glamorgan (17)
Wrexhm	Wrexham

Channel Islands & Isle of Man

Guern	Guernsey
Jersey	Jersey
IoM	Isle of Man

England

BaNES	Bath & N E Somerset (18)
Barns	Barnsley (19)
Beds	Bedfordshire
Birm	Birmingham
Bl w D	Blackburn with Darwen (20)
Bmouth	Bournemouth
Bolton	Bolton (21)
Bpool	Blackpool
Brad	Bradford (22)
Br & H	Brighton and Hove (23)
Br For	Bracknell Forest (24)
Bristl	City of Bristol
Bucks	Buckinghamshire
Bury	Bury (25)
C Derb	City of Derby
C KuH	City of Kingston upon Hull
C Leic	City of Leicester
C Nott	City of Nottingham
C Pete	City of Peterborough
C Plym	City of Plymouth
C Port	City of Portsmouth
C Sotn	City of Southampton
C Stke	City of Stoke
Calder	Calderdale (26)
Cambs	Cambridgeshire
Ches	Cheshire
Cnwll	Cornwall
Covtry	Coventry
Cumb	Cumbria
Darltn	Darlington (27)
Derbys	Derbyshire
Devon	Devon
Donc	Doncaster (28)
Dorset	Dorset
Dudley	Dudley (29)
Dur	Durham
E R Yk	East Riding of Yorkshire
E Susx	East Sussex

Essex	Essex
Gatesd	Gateshead (30)
Gloucs	Gloucestershire
Gt Lon	Greater London
Halton	Halton (31)
Hants	Hampshire
Hartpl	Hartlepool (32)
Herefs	Herefordshire
Herts	Hertfordshire
IoS	Isles of Scilly
IoW	Isle of Wight
Kent	Kent
Kirk	Kirklees (33)
Knows	Knowsley (34)
Lancs	Lancashire
Leeds	Leeds
Leics	Leicestershire
Lincs	Lincolnshire
Lpool	Liverpool
Luton	Luton
M Keyn	Milton Keynes
Manch	Manchester
Medway	Medway
Middsb	Middlesbrough
NE Lin	North East Lincolnshire
N Linc	North Lincolnshire
N Som	North Somerset (35)
N Tyne	North Tyneside (36)
N u Ty	Newcastle upon Tyne
N York	North Yorkshire
Nhants	Northamptonshire
Norfk	Norfolk
Notts	Nottinghamshire
Nthumb	Northumberland
Oldham	Oldham (37)
Oxon	Oxfordshire
Poole	Poole
R & Cl	Redcar and Cleveland
Readg	Reading
Rochdl	Rochdale (38)
Rothm	Rotherham (39)
Rutlnd	Rutland
S Glos	South Gloucestershire (40)
S on T	Stockton-on-Tees (41)
S Tyne	South Tyneside (42)
Salfd	Salford (43)
Sandw	Sandwell (44)
Sefton	Sefton (45)
Sheff	Sheffield
Shrops	Shropshire
Slough	Slough (46)
Solhll	Solihull (47)
Somset	Somerset
St Hel	St Helens (48)
Staffs	Staffordshire
Sthend	Southend-on-Sea
Stockp	Stockport (49)
Sundld	Sunderland
Surrey	Surrey
Swindn	Swindon
Tamesd	Tameside (50)
Thurr	Thurrock (51)
Torbay	Torbay
Traffd	Trafford (52)
W & M	Windsor & Maidenhead (53)
W Berk	West Berkshire
W Susx	West Sussex
Wakefd	Wakefield (54)
Warrtn	Warrington (55)
Warwks	Warwickshire
Wigan	Wigan (56)
Wilts	Wiltshire
Wirral	Wirral (57)
Wokham	Wokingham (58)
Wolves	Wolverhampton (59)
Worcs	Worcestershire
Wrekin	Telford and Wrekin (60)
Wsall	Walsall (61)
York	York

Recreation and leisure index

A

314 C3 Abbeydale Golf Club Sheff
324 A3 Abbey Farm Caravan Park Lancs
110 C1 Abbey Gatehouse EH Gloucs
167 H2 Abbey Hill Golf Club M Keyn
213 G6 Abbey Hotel & Country Club Worcs
197 G3 Abbey Stadium Cambs
112 D2 Abbey Stadium Swindn
30 D5 Abbotsbury Castle Dorset
30 D6 Abbotsbury Swannery Dorset
451 G3 Abbotsford House Border
196 A3 Abbotsley Golf Hotel & Country Club Cambs
131 G4 Aberdare Golf Club Rhondd
131 F4 Aberdare Park Rhondd
557 F2 Aberdeen airport C Aber
487 G2 Aberdour Castle HS Fife
487 G3 Aberdour Golf Club Fife
229 E5 Aberdovey Golf Club Gwynd
130 B5 Aberdulais Falls NT Neath
263 G3 Abererch Sands Holiday Centre Gwynd
524 C6 Aberfeldy Caravan Park P & K
524 C6 Aberfeldy Golf Club P & K
496 D4 Aberfoyle Golf Club Stirlg
133 E2 Abergavcenny Castle Mons
133 E1 Abergavenny & Border Counties showground Mons
306 C4 Abergele Golf Club Conwy
155 E5 Aberglasney Garden Carmth
182 C3 Abergwesyn Common NT Powys
229 F3 Abergynolwyn railway station Gwynd
489 F4 Aberlady Caravan Park E Loth
155 E4 Abermarlais Caravan Park Carmth
551 J5 Abernethy Golf Club Highld
500 C1 Abernethy Round Tower HS P & K
106 B2 Aber railway station Caerph
263 E5 Abersoch Golf Club Gwynd
305 E5 Aber Waterfall Gwynd
204 D4 Aberystwyth & District showground Cerdgn
204 D3 Aberystwyth Castle Cerdgn
204 D3 Aberystwyth Golf Club Cerdgn
448 B4 Abington service area S Lans
555 F5 Aboyne Golf Club Abers
555 F5 Aboyne Loch Caravan Park Abers
145 G5 Abridge Golf & Country Club Essex
340 A4 Accrington & District Golf Club Lancs
458 C2 Achamore Gardens Ag & B
480 B1 Achnabreck Cup and Ring HS Ag & B
507 G3 Achnacloich Garden Ag & B
563 J7 Achnashellach railway station Highld
250 D3 Acle railway station Norfk
391 G4 Acorn Bank Garden NT Cumb
105 F6 Acorn Camping & Caravan Site V Glam
234 C4 Acton Burnell Castle EH Shrops
34 A5 Acton Field Camping Site Dorset
210 B2 Acton Scott Working Farm museum Shrops
269 H6 Adcote School Shrops
213 G2 Adderley Park railway station Birm
95 H2 Addington Court golf course Gt Lon
95 H2 Addington Palace Golf Club Gt Lon
571 H6 Aden Country Park Abers
49 E5 Adventure Wonderland Dorset
180 C2 Aeron Coast Caravan Park Cerdgn
130 C6 Afan Argoed Country Park Neath
130 C5 Afan Forest Park Neath
153 G1 Afon Teifi Caravan & Camping Park Cerdgn
252 B4 African Violet Centre Norfk
36 B3 Afton Down NT & Compton Down NT IoW
212 B4 Aggborough Worcs
451 E4 Aikwood Tower Border
323 G5 Aintree racecourse Sefton
390 C5 Aira Force NT Cumb
468 B3 Airbles railway station N Lans
297 F3 Aircraft museum Notts
415 E4 Aird Donald Caravan Park D & G
468 B1 Airdrie Golf Club N Lans
288 D2 Airfields Stadium Flints
118 C4 Airlinks Golf Club Gt Lon
282 D4 Air World museum Gwynd
27 G6 A La Ronde NT Devon
120 C5 Albany Park railway station Gt Lon
308 D2 Albert Dock Lpool
220 B4 Alconbury airfield Cambs
357 E1 Aldborough Roman Town EH N York
203 E3 Aldeburgh Golf Club Suffk
143 G5 Aldenham Golf & Country Club Herts
71 E4 Aldenbury Caravan & Camping Park Wilts
311 G4 Alderley Edge Golf Club Ches
324 D6 Alder Root Golf Club Warrtn
357 F1 Alders Caravan Park N York
289 G3 Aldersey Green Golf Club Ches
357 F2 Aldwark Manor Golf Club N York
143 H2 Aldwickbury Park Golf Club Herts
213 G1 Alexander Stadium Birm
467 F1 Alexandra Golf Club C Glas
467 F1 Alexandra Parade railway station C Glas
291 E4 Alexandra Stadium Ches
555 G1 Alford Golf Club Abers
555 G1 Alford Valley Railway Abers
294 D3 Alfreton Golf Club Derbys
57 E4 Alfriston Clergy House NT E Susx
133 G3 Alice Springs Golf Club Mons
237 G6 Alison Nicholas Golf Academy Birm
557 H4 Allan Park C Aber
402 D2 Allen Banks and Staward Gorge NT Nthumb
403 E4 Allendale Golf Club Nthumb
404 C4 Allensford Caravan & Camping Park Dur
384 C2 Allens West railway station S on T
359 E5 Allerthorpe Park golf course E R Yk
357 E3 Allerton Park N York

309 F2 Allerton Park Golf Club Lpool
275 E1 Allestree Park golf course C Derb
499 E6 Alloa Golf Club Clacks
486 A1 Alloa Tower NTS Clacks
129 F4 Allt-y-Graban golf course Swans
487 E6 Almondell & Calderwood Country Park W Loth
469 G1 Almondvale Stadium W Loth
469 G1 Almond Valley heritage centre W Loth
176 C1 Alnesbourne Priory golf course Suffk
566 B2 Alness Golf Club Highld
443 H2 Alnmouth Golf Club Nthumb
443 G2 Alnmouth Village Golf Club Nthumb
443 F2 Alnwick Castle Nthumb
443 F2 Alnwick Golf Club Nthumb
29 F1 Alpine Grove Touring Park Somset
73 E3 Alresford Golf Club Hants
73 E3 Alresford railway station Hants
291 G4 Alsager Golf & Country Club Ches
12 C4 Alston Farm Camping & Caravanning Site Devon
402 C6 Alston Moor Golf Club Cumb
560 C3 Altar Tomb of William Forbes HS Abers
193 E1 Althorp Park Nhants
588 C7 Altnabreac railway station Highld
73 H1 Alton Golf Club Hants
293 E6 Alton Towers Staffs
311 F2 Altrincham Golf Club Traffd
311 F2 Altrincham Ice Dome Traffd
498 D5 Alva Golf Club Clacks
343 F1 Alwoodley Golf Club Leeds
54 B2 Amberley Museum W Susx
295 E6 American Adventure Derbys
273 E4 Amerton Railway Staffs
118 C5 Amida golf course Gt Lon
72 A5 Ampfield Par Three Golf Club Hants
158 B2 Anchorage Caravan Park Powys
514 B3 Ancrum Outdoor Centre C Dund
467 E1 Anderston railway station C Glas
310 C4 Anderton Boat Lift Ches
90 B6 Andover Golf Club Hants
28 D3 Andrewshayes Caravan Park Devon
323 G6 Anfield Lpool
405 G3 Angel of the North Gatesd
119 H1 Angel Road railway station Gt Lon
303 F4 Anglesey IoA
198 A2 Anglesey Abbey NT Cambs
282 B2 Anglesey Circuit IoA
302 D6 Anglesey Golf Club IoA
303 F5 Anglesey showground IoA
223 F5 Anglo-Saxon Village Reconstruction Suffk
527 E5 Angus Folk Museum NTS Angus
191 G5 Anita's Touring Caravan Park Oxon
437 F4 Annandale D & G
424 C1 Annandale Water service area D & G
445 F2 Annanhill Golf Club E Ayrs
190 B4 Anne Hathaway's Cottage Warwks
503 F4 Anstruther Golf Club Fife
215 G3 Ansty Golf Centre Warwks
480 B6 An Tairbeart visitor centre Ag & B
485 G4 Antonine Wall HS Falk
10 D2 Antony NT Cnwll
310 C3 Antrobus Golf Club Ches
412 A3 Anwoth Caravan & Campsite D & G
392 B6 Appleby Golf Club Cumb
81 E4 Appledore railway station Kent
37 E4 Appuldurcombe Gardens Caravan & Camping Park IoW
37 E4 Appuldurcombe House EH IoW
143 F4 Apsley railway station Herts
271 H6 Aqualate Golf Centre Staffs
398 B3 Arbigland Gardens D & G
293 G2 Arbor Low Stone Circle EH Derbys
515 G2 Arbroath golf course Angus
215 E2 Arbury Hall Warwks
559 F4 Archaeolink museum Abers
430 D4 Arcot Hall Golf Club Nthumb
507 J4 Ardanaiseig Gardens Ag & B
507 G2 Ardchattan Priory HS Ag & B
567 H7 Ardclach Bell Tower NT Highld
465 F6 Ardeer Golf Club N Ayrs
464 C2 Ardencraig Gardens Ag & B
515 E3 Ardestie Earth House HS Angus
492 D2 Ardfern Yacht Centre Ag & B
576 D5 Ardgay Golf Club Highld
520 C2 Ardgour Highld
494 D2 Ardkinglas Woodland Garden Ag & B
574 C4 Ardmair Point Camping & Caravan Park Highld
518 E2 Ardnamurchan Highld
444 B1 Ardrossan Harbour railway station N Ayrs
444 B1 Ardrossan South Beach railway station N Ayrs
444 B1 Ardrossan Town railway station N Ayrs
492 C2 Arduaine Garden NTS Ag & B
511 G6 Ardunie Roman Signal Station HS P & K
579 H5 Ardvreck Castle Highld
408 C2 Ardwell House Gardens D & G
121 E3 Arena Essex Raceway Thurr
5 E2 Argal & College Water Park Cnwll
153 F1 Argoed Meadow Caravan and Camping Site Carmth
467 F1 Argyle Street railway station C Glas
495 E4 Argyll Forest Park Ag & B
531 J5 Arisaig Highld
144 B5 Arkley Golf Club Gt Lon
310 D3 Arley Hall Ches
211 H4 Arley railway station Worcs
61 F3 Arlington Court NT Devon
57 F3 Arlington Stadium E Susx
531 H2 Armadale Castle Gardens & Museum of The Isles Highld
486 B6 Armdale Stadium W Loth
378 C3 Armitt Museum Cumb
93 E4 Army Golf Club Hants
374 C3 Arosa Caravan & Camping Park N York
460 D2 Arran N Ayrs
37 E3 Arreton Manor IoW
308 C2 Arrowe Park golf course Wirral
234 A3 Arscott Golf Club Shrops

185 F6 Arthur's Stone (Dorstone) Herefs
102 C3 Arthur's Stone (Reynoldston) Swans
54 B3 Arundel Park cricket ground W Susx
117 F6 Ascot racecourse W & M
168 B5 Ascott House NT Bucks
293 G5 Ashbourne Golf Club Derbys
128 B4 Ashburnham Golf Club E Susx
24 D4 Ashbury Golf Hotel Devon
326 C5 Ashburys railway station Manch
332 B3 Ashby Decoy Golf Club N Linc
239 F1 Ashby-de-la-Zouch Castle EH Leics
162 D3 Ashchurch for Tewkesbury railway station Gloucs
27 G3 Ashclyst Forest NT Devon
28 D4 Ashdown Caravan Park Devon
113 G3 Ashdown House NT Oxon
44 B3 Ashe Farm Camping & Caravan Site Somset
238 B5 Ash End House Warwks
379 E5 Ashes Lane campsite Cumb
100 B6 Ashfield Farm campsite Kent
484 B6 Ashfield railway station C Glas
484 B6 Ashfield Stadium C Glas
455 E4 Ashfield Golf Club Kent
81 E4 Ashford International railway station Kent
118 B5 Ashford Manor Golf Club Surrey
81 E4 Ashford to Lydd cycle route Kent
162 B4 Ashleworth Tithe Barn NT Gloucs
93 E4 Ash railway station Surrey
142 D2 Ashridge Estate NT Herts
142 D2 Ashridge Golf Club Herts
338 C3 Ashton & Lea Golf Club Lancs
109 G5 Ashton Court Country Park N Som
109 G5 Ashton Gate Bristl
324 D5 Ashton-in-Makerfield Golf Club St Hel
325 H6 Ashton on Mersey Golf Club Traffd
327 E4 Ashton-under-Lyne Golf Club Tamesd
50 B2 Ashurst New Forest railway station Hants
171 F5 Ash Valley Golf Club Herts
170 C2 Ashwell & Morden railway station Cambs
363 E6 Askam railway station Cumb
383 E4 Aske Hall N York
590 E3 Askernish Golf Club W Isls
168 C2 Aspley Guise & Woburn Sands Golf Club Beds
291 H2 Astbury Golf Club Ches
325 G5 Astley Green Colliery Museum Wigan
47 E6 Athelhampton House Dorset
239 E5 Atherstone Golf Club Warwks
524 C3 Atholl Country Collection museum P & K
3 G1 Atlantic Coast Caravan Park Cnwll
343 F6 Atlantic Solutions Stadium Wakefd
547 G2 Attadale railway station Highld
234 C2 Attingham Park NT Shrops
460 B3 Auchagallon Stone Circle HS N Ayrs
540 C4 Auchenblae golf course Abers
485 F2 Auchenbowie Caravan & Camping Site Stirlg
411 F2 Auchenlarie Holiday Park D & G
568 E8 Auchindoun Castle HS Moray
494 A4 Auchindrain Township museum Ag & B
510 D6 Auchingarrich Wildlife Centre P & K
557 F3 Auchmill golf course C Aber
550 C2 Auchnahillin Caravan and Camping Park Highld
499 E2 Auchterarder Golf Club P & K
500 D5 Auchterderran Fife
395 E3 Auckland Castle Dur
172 A2 Audley End House EH Essex
171 H2 Audley End railway station Essex
96 D2 Austin Lodge Golf Club Kent
112 D6 Avebury (UNESCO) Wilts
112 C5 Avebury Manor NT Wilts
112 D5 Avebury Stone Circle EH Wilts
32 B2 Avenue Stadium Dorset
72 D3 Avington Park Hants
54 A3 Avisford Park golf course W Susx
213 E6 Avoncroft museum Worcs
85 G2 Avon Cycleway BaNES
108 D6 Avon Cycleway N Som
109 G2 Avon Cycleway S Glos
49 E4 Avon Heath Country Park Dorset
110 B6 Avon Riverside railway station BaNES
110 B6 Avon Valley Railway S Glos
110 D4 Avon Wiltshire link cycle route S Glos
29 E5 Axe Cliff Golf Club Devon
404 B1 Aydon Castle EH Nthumb
142 B1 Aylesbury Golf Centre Bucks
141 H2 Aylesbury Park Golf Club Bucks
168 B5 Aylesbury Vale Golf Club Bucks
166 B3 Aynhoe Park House Nhants
3 F1 Ayr Holiday Park Cnwll
445 E5 Ayr racecourse S Ayrs
368 D2 Aysgarth Falls N York

B

20 C4 Babbacombe Model Village Torbay
487 G6 Baberton Golf Club C Edin
232 D6 Basildon Park NT W Berk
445 F4 Bachelors' Club NTS S Ayrs
309 F6 Bache railway station Ches
48 D4 Back of Beyond Touring Park Dorset
431 F5 Backworth Golf Club N Tyne
261 F4 Baconsthorpe Castle EH Norfk
340 D5 Bacup Golf Club Lancs
138 D6 Badbury Hill Oxon
48 B4 Badbury Rings Dorset
214 B5 Baddesley Clinton NT Warwks
116 B3 Badgemore Park Golf Club Oxon
328 C3 Badgworth Golf Club Kirk
236 C6 Baggeridge Country Park Staffs
32 A3 Bagwell Farm Touring Park Dorset

342 B1 Baildon Golf Club Brad
368 A2 Bainbridge Ings Caravan & Camping Site N York
299 G2 Bainland Country Park Lincs
314 A6 Bakewell Golf Club Derbys
313 H6 Bakewell showground Derbys
267 E2 Bala (Penybont) railway station Gwynd
267 E2 Bala Golf Club Gwynd
267 E3 Bala Lake Railway Gwynd
501 E4 Balbirnie Park Golf Club Fife
170 B2 Baldock service area Herts
322 g3 Ballabeg IoM
322 h4 Ballafayle IoM
322 e8 Ballakelly IoM
322 g6 Ballalheannagh IoM
148 B6 Ballards Gore Golf & Country Club Essex
554 C5 Ballater Golf Club Abers
552 D1 Ballindalloch Castle Moray
483 E3 Balloch Castle Country Park W Duns
445 H4 Ballochmyle Golf Club E Ayrs
2 C3 Ballowall Barrow EH Cnwll
561 E6 Balmedie Country Park Abers
514 B5 Balmerino Abbey NTS Fife
460 C3 Balmichael visitor centre N Ayrs
571 L6 Balmoor Stadium Abers
537 L4 Balmoral Castle Abers
484 B5 Balmore Golf Club E Duns
557 H3 Balnagask golf course C Aber
3 F2 Balnoon Camping Site Cnwll
509 J5 Balquhidder Braes Holiday Park Stirlg
500 C2 Balvaird Castle HS P & K
568 E7 Balvenie Castle HS Moray
455 F2 Bamburgh Castle Nthumb
455 F2 Bamburgh Castle Golf Club Nthumb
313 H3 Bamford railway station Derbys
166 A3 Banbury Golf Centre Oxon
556 B5 Banchory Golf Club Abers
353 H5 Bancroft Mill Lancs
289 E6 Bangor-on-Dee racecourse Wrexhm
225 E2 Banham Zoo Norfk
233 E2 Bank Farm Caravan Park Powys
323 F6 Bank Hall railway station Lpool
188 A4 Bank House Hotel & Country Club Worcs
293 G4 Bank Top Farm campsite Derbys
485 F1 Bannockburn Battlefield & Heritage Centre NTS Stirlg
95 F2 Banstead Downs Golf Club Surrey
3 d2 Bant's Carn EH IoS
125 G6 Barafundle Bay NT Pembks
113 E4 Barbury Castle Wilts
113 E4 Barbury Hill viewpoint Wilts
506 F1 Barcaldine Castle Ag & B
265 E2 Barcdy Touring Caravan & Camping Park Gwynd
282 B1 Barclodiad Y Gawres CADW IoA
355 E3 Barden Tower N York
402 D2 Bardon Mill railway station Nthumb
364 C4 Bardsea Leisure Park Cumb
262 A6 Bardsey Island Gwynd
351 G2 Bare Lane railway station Lancs
132 B4 Bargoed Golf Club Caerph
171 E3 Barkway Park Golf Club Herts
272 C2 Barlaston Golf Club Staffs
26 A4 Barley Meadow Caravan & Camping Park Devon
413 F3 Barlochan Caravan Park D & G
556 C3 Barmekin hill fort Abers
98 A3 Barming railway station Kent
229 E1 Barmouth Bridge Gwynd
382 B1 Barnard Castle EH Dur
394 A6 Barnard Castle Golf Club Dur
120 D4 Barnehurst golf course Gt Lon
333 F3 Barnetby railway station N Linc
249 E3 Barnham Broom Hotel & Golf Club Norfk
467 F1 Barnhill railway station C Glas
493 G2 Barnline Stables visitor centre Ag & B
479 K3 Barnluasgan visitor centre Ag & B
329 E2 Barnsley Golf Club Barns
423 E4 Barnsoul Farm Campsite D & G
191 H5 Barnstones Caravan & Camping Site Oxon
219 E2 Barnwell Country Park Nhants
304 C4 Baron Hill Golf Club IoA
591 C7 Barra W Isls
590 E6 Barra airport W Isls
591 C7 Barraigh W Isls
237 G5 Barr Beacon viewpoint Wsall
466 C3 Barrhead railway station E Rens
419 F5 Barrhill Holiday Park S Ayrs
66 B6 Barrington Court NT Somset
364 B5 Barrow Golf Club Cumb
347 G5 Barrow Haven railway station N Linc
315 E4 Barrow Hill Railway Centre Derbys
136 D1 Barrow Wake viewpoint Gloucs
106 B6 Barry Island Railway V Glam
515 E3 Barry Links railway station Angus
515 E3 Barry Mill NTS Angus
410 B4 Barsalloch Fort HS D & G
466 D2 Barshaw Golf Club Rens
49 H6 Barton-on-Sea Golf Club Hants
121 H2 Basildon Golf Club Essex
115 G4 Basildon Park NT W Berk
91 H4 Basing House (Ruins) Hants
91 F5 Basingstoke Golf Club Hants
308 A4 Basingwerk Abbey CADW Flints
96 D3 Bat & Ball railway station Kent
143 G3 Batchwood Hall Golf & Tennis Centre Herts
68 A2 Batcombe Vale Caravan and Camping Park Somset
79 F5 Bateman's NT E Susx
486 C6 Bathgate Golf Club W Loth
86 D2 Bath golf course BaNES
376 D5 Bath House (Ravenglass) roman site EH Cumb
86 C1 Bath Marina & Caravan Park BaNES
110 C6 Bath racecourse BaNES

86 D2 Bath Spa railway station BaNES
385 E2 Battersby Junction railway station N York
58 B3 Battle golf course E Susx
299 G3 Battle of Britain Memorial Flight museum Lincs
82 D3 Battle of Britain museum Kent
35 f6 Battle of the Flowers museum Jersey
249 G3 Bawburgh Golf Club Norfk
331 E5 Bawtry Golf Club Donc
340 B4 Baxenden & District Golf Club Lancs
568 A4 Baxters Visitor Centre Moray
13 F2 Bayard's Cove Fort EH Devon
79 F2 Bayham Old Abbey EH Kent
60 B4 Bay View Farm Caravan & Camping Park Devon
57 G4 Bay View Park campsite E Susx
502 B4 Bayview Stadium Fife
263 E5 Beach View Caravan Park Gwynd
57 F5 Beachy Head E Susx
57 F5 Beachy Head Countryside Centre E Susx
6 D3 Beacon Cottage Farm Touring Park Cnwll
324 C3 Beacon Country Park Lancs
352 B6 Beacon Fell Country Park Lancs
339 F2 Beacon Fell View Holiday Park Lancs
201 F4 Beacon Hill service area Suffk
48 B6 Beacon Hill Touring Park Dorset
240 B2 Beacon Hill viewpoint Leics
324 C3 Beacon Park Public Golf Centre Lancs
270 C6 Beaconsfield Farm Caravan Park Shrops
117 G1 Beaconsfield Golf Club Bucks
117 G2 Beaconsfield service area Bucks
169 G2 Beadlow Manor Hotel & Country Club Beds
546 D1 Bealach-na-Ba viewpoint Highld
115 G4 Beale Park W Berk
405 F4 Beamish Open Air Museum Dur
405 F4 Beamish Park Golf Club Dur
19 F5 Beara Farm Caravan & Camping Site Devon
484 A5 Bearsden Bath House HS E Duns
484 A5 Bearsden Golf Club C Glas
98 B3 Bearsted Golf Club Kent
98 C4 Bearsted vineyard Kent
116 C6 Bearwood Golf Club Wokham
531 K6 Beasdale railway station Highld
436 C1 Beattock Summit S Lans
314 C3 Beauchief golf course Sheff
237 F2 Beau Desert Golf Club Staffs
50 C4 Beaulieu House and Abbey Hants
50 B3 Beaulieu Road railway station Hants
565 J7 Beauly Priory HS Highld
304 D4 Beaumaris Castle (UNESCO) IoA
58 C4 Beauport Park Golf Club E Susx
35 J6 Beauvelande campsite Jersey
309 E3 Bebington cycle route Wirral
227 E1 Beccles Golf Club Suffk
120 A5 Beckenham Hill railway station Gt Lon
120 A5 Beckenham Place Park golf course Gt Lon
377 F4 Beckfoot Halt railway station Cumb
163 E2 Beckford Silk Mill Worcs
86 C1 Beckford's Tower museum BaNES
390 C4 Beckses Caravan Park Cumb
19 G1 Becky Falls Devon
370 B2 Bedale Golf Club N York
195 E4 Bedford & County Golf Club Beds
194 D5 Bedfordshire Golf Club Beds
79 G3 Bedgebury National Pinetum and Garden Kent
431 E3 Bedlingtonshire Golf Club Nthumb
89 G2 Bedwyn railway station Wilts
135 E2 Beechenhurst Lodge visitor centre Gloucs
486 D5 Beecraigs Caravan & Camping Site W Loth
486 D5 Beecraigs Country Park W Loth
240 D2 Beetles Lake Golf Centre Leics
238 C1 Beehive Farm Woodland Lakes campsite Derbys
28 D5 Beer Caves Devon
290 A3 Beeston Castle EH Ches
276 B2 Beeston Fields Golf Club Notts
276 B2 Beeston Marina Notts
593 C7 Beinn na Faoghla W Isls
465 H3 Beith Golf Club N Ayrs
117 F1 Bekonscot Model Village Bucks
163 F4 Belas Knap Long Barrow EH Gloucs
122 C2 Belfairs golf course Sthend
490 C4 Belhaven Bay Caravan & Camping Park E Loth
121 E3 Belhus Park golf course Thurr
121 E3 Belhus Woods Country Park Gt Lon
480 B2 Bellanoch Marina Ag & B
444 D6 Belleisle golf course S Ayrs
307 E3 Belle Vue Denbgs
326 C5 Belle Vue Manch
467 F2 Bellgrove railway station C Glas
428 C3 Bellingham Golf Club Nthumb
250 C3 Bells Dyke Marina Norfk
468 A3 Bellshill Golf Club N Lans
571 H2 Bellslea Park Abers
250 C3 Bells Marina Norfk
274 B4 Belmont golf course Staffs
160 B2 Belmont Lodge & Golf Herefs
430 A4 Belsay Hall Castle & Gardens EH Nthumb
278 C2 Belton House NT Lincs
278 C2 Belton Park Golf Club Lincs
277 H3 Belvoir Castle Leics
278 A3 Belvoir Ride cycle route Leics
37 G3 Bembridge Down viewpoint IoW
37 H3 Bembridge Lifeboat Station IoW
37 G3 Bembridge Windmill NT IoW
264 D5 Benar Beach Camping & Touring Park Gwynd
593 C7 Benbecula W Isls

592 D6 Benbecula airport W Isls
357 G3 Beningbrough Hall NT N York
509 K2 Ben Lawers Information Centre NTS P & K
495 H4 Ben Lomond NTS Stirlg
481 G2 Benmore Younger Botanic Garden Ag & B
32 A4 Bennetts Water Gardens Dorset
521 H1 Ben Nevis Highld
355 F5 Ben Rhydding Golf Club Brad
115 G1 Benson Waterfront Marina Oxon
235 H4 Benthall Hall NT Shrops
366 D5 Bentham Golf Club N York
366 D6 Bentham railway station N York
146 B3 Bentley Golf Club Essex
56 D1 Bentley Wildfowl & Motor Museum E Susx
147 G2 Benton Hall golf course Essex
202 C4 Bentwaters airfield (dis) Suffk
135 F5 Berkeley Castle Gloucs
142 D3 Berkhamsted Castle EH Herts
143 E3 Berkhamsted Golf Club Herts
214 C4 Berkswell railway station Solhll
214 D4 Berkswell windmill Solhll
251 E3 Berney Arms railway station Norfk
251 F4 Berney Arms Windmill EH Norfk
186 C2 Berrington Hall NT Herefs
20 A5 Berry Pomeroy Castle EH Devon
57 E3 Berwick railway station E Susx
475 G5 Berwick-upon-Tweed (Goswick) Golf Club Nthumb
475 H4 Berwick-upon-Tweed Barracks EH Nthumb
475 H4 Berwick-upon-Tweed Castle EH Nthumb
323 G2 Bescar Lane railway station Lancs
237 F5 Bescot Stadium Wsall
237 F5 Bescot Stadium railway station Wsall
295 H4 Bestwood Country Park Notts
94 D5 Betchworth Park Golf Club Surrey
95 E4 Betchworth railway station Surrey
175 E5 Beth Chatto Gardens Essex
283 F4 Betws Garmon railway station Gwynd
285 G3 Betws-y-Coed Golf Club Conwy
227 F2 Beulah Hall Caravan Park Suffk
33 H4 Beuvelande Camp Site Jersey
118 C6 Beverex Stadium Gt Lon
347 F2 Beverley & East Riding Golf Club E R Yk
20 B6 Beverley Parks Caravan & Camping Park Torbay
347 F2 Beverley racecourse E R Yk
79 F3 Bewl Water visitor centre E Susx
120 C5 Bexleyheath Golf Club Gt Lon
166 C5 Bicester Golf & Country Club Oxon
166 C5 Bicester North railway station Oxon
27 E1 Bickleigh Castle Devon
42 B6 Bickleigh Mill Devon
27 H5 Bicton Park Gardens Devon
80 C2 Biddenden vineyard Kent
292 A3 Biddulph Grange Garden NT Staffs
189 H4 Bidford Grange Golf Club Warwks
308 C1 Bidston Golf Club Wirral
12 B4 Bigbury Golf Club Devon
448 D2 Biggar Golf Club S Lans
96 B2 Biggin Hill airport Gt Lon
96 B2 Biggin Hill airshow venue Gt Lon
364 D3 Bigland Hall Caravan Park Cumb
54 A2 Bignor Roman Villa W Susx
132 D3 Big Pit Torfn
417 H4 Big Water of Fleet D & G
396 B5 Billingham Beck Valley Country Park S on T
396 C5 Billingham Forum (Ice Hockey) S on T
396 B5 Billingham Golf Club S on T
356 C3 Bilton Park campsite N York
334 A5 Binbrook airfield Lincs
33 F2 Bindon Abbey Dorset
342 A2 Bingley St Ives Golf Club Brad
260 C3 Binham Priory & Market Cross EH Norfk
171 H5 Birchanger Green service area Herts
237 F1 Birches Valley Forest Centre Staffs
174 C5 Birch Grove Golf Club Essex
314 D4 Birch Hall golf course Derbys
101 E2 Birchington-on-Sea railway station Kent
326 B3 Birch service area Rochdl
325 E6 Birchwood Golf Club Warrtn
120 D5 Birchwood Park Golf Centre Kent
33 G1 Birchwood Tourist Golf Dorset
117 E5 Bird Hills Golf Centre W & M
401 H1 Birdoswald Roman Fort Cumb
92 D6 Birdworld Hants
119 H6 Birkbeck railway station Gt Lon
308 D2 Birkenhead Central railway station Wirral
308 C1 Birkenhead North railway station Wirral
486 C4 Birkhill Claymine Falk
315 E3 Birley Wood Golf Club Sheff
214 B3 Birmingham airport Solhll
214 B3 Birmingham International railway station Solhll
240 C3 Birstall Golf Club C Leic
468 C5 Birthplace of General Roy S Lans
405 G4 Birtley Golf Club Gatesd
395 E3 Bishop Auckland Golf Club Dur
484 C5 Bishopbriggs Golf Club E Duns
91 E2 Bishops Green Farm campsite Hants
157 H3 Bishops Meadow Caravan Park Powys
125 H4 Bishop's Palace CADW Pembks
150 B4 Bishop's Palace CADW Pembks
171 H5 Bishop's Stortford Golf Club Herts
51 G1 Bishop's Waltham Palace EH Hants
91 F2 Bishopswood golf course Hants
110 B5 Bitton railway station S Gloucs
339 G4 Blackburn Golf Club Bl w D
339 G4 Blackburn Ice Arena Bl w D
339 G5 Blackburn with Darwen service area Bl w D
28 C4 Blackbury Camp EH Devon
92 D3 Blackbushe airport Hants
43 G4 Blackdown Hills Devon
75 E3 Black Down NT W Susx
488 B5 Blackford Hill viewpoint C Edin
36 D5 Blackgang Chine IoW
498 C2 Blackhall Camps Roman site P & K
405 G3 Blackham's Hill railway station Sundld
468 C6 Blackhill NTS S Lans
119 H2 Blackhorse Road railway station Gt Lon
599 G5 Blackhouse museum HS W Isls
566 B4 Black Isle Highld
565 J7 Black Isle showground Highld
565 L6 Black Isle Wildlife & Country Park Highld
112 B6 Blackland Lakes Holiday & Leisure Centre Wilts
326 C4 Blackley Golf Club Manch
129 E2 Black Lion Caravan & Camping Park Carmth
428 B1 Black Middens Bastle House EH Nthumb
74 B3 Blackmoor Golf Club Hants
68 D5 Blackmore Vale Caravan & Camping Park Dorset
156 A6 Black Mountain Carmth
159 E4 Black Mountains Powys
487 E3 Blackness Castle HS Falk
74 A2 Blacknest Golf Club Hants
117 H3 Black Park Country Park Bucks
337 F3 Blackpool airport Lancs
337 F2 Blackpool Cricket Club Bpool
337 F2 Blackpool Model Village Bpool
337 F2 Blackpool North railway station Bpool
337 F2 Blackpool North Shore Golf Club Bpool
337 F2 Blackpool Park Golf Club Bpool
337 F3 Blackpool Pleasure Beach railway station Bpool
337 F3 Blackpool South railway station Bpool
465 E5 Blackshaw Farm Park N Ayrs
369 G3 Black Swan Holiday Park N York
383 G2 Blackwell Grange Golf Club Darltn
378 C6 Blackwell museum Cumb
132 C5 Blackwood Golf Club Caerph
132 D3 Blaenavon Ironworks CADW Torfn
524 C3 Blair Atholl Golf Club P & K
467 F3 Bairbeth Golf Club C Glas
524 C2 Blair Castle P & K
524 C2 Blair Castle Caravan Park P & K
498 A5 Blair Drummond Safari Park Stirlg
526 A6 Blairgowrie Golf Club P & K
109 G4 Blaise Hamlet NT Bristl
260 D3 Blakeney Guildhall EH Norfk
260 D2 Blakeney Point NT Norfk
237 H4 Blake Street railway station Birm
403 H4 Blanchland Abbey Nthumb
298 D2 Blankney Golf Club Lincs
139 G1 Blenheim Palace (UNESCO) Oxon
95 G4 Bletchingley Golf Club Surrey
35 g5 Bleu Soleil campsite Jersey
255 G2 Blickling Hall NT Norfk
235 F4 Blists Hill Victorian Town Wrekin
322 F6 Block Eary IoM
237 E4 Bloxwich Golf Club Wsall
237 E4 Bloxwich North railway station Wsall
77 G3 Bluebell Railway W Susx
374 D3 Blue Dolphin Holiday Park N York
6 D3 Blue Hills Touring Park Cnwll
313 F3 Blue John Cavern Derbys
117 E5 Blue Mountain Golf Centre Br for
33 G3 Blue Pool Dorset
331 E2 Blue Water Marina Donc
121 E5 Bluewater Park Kent
334 C2 Blundell Park NE Lin
323 F5 Blundellsands & Crosby railway station Sefton
309 G1 Blundells Hill Golf Club St Hel
112 D2 Blunsdon railway station Wilts
431 E3 Blyth Golf Club Nthumb
316 B2 Blyth service area Notts
222 B2 Boathaven Littleport Cambs
567 G5 Boath Doocot Highld
551 G6 Boat of Garten Golf Club Highld
405 H4 Bobby Shafto Caravan Park Gatesd
94 D4 Bocketts Farm Park Surrey
307 E5 Bodelwyddan Castle Denbgs
212 B3 Bodenham Arboretum and Earth Centre Worcs
80 A4 Bodiam Castle NT E Susx
80 A4 Bodiam railway station E Susx
9 H3 Bodigga Cliff NT Cnwll
15 F5 Bodmin & Wenford Railway Cnwll
16 A3 Bodmin Moor Cnwll
15 G6 Bodmin Parkway railway station Cnwll
285 H2 Bodnant Caravan Park Conwy
305 H5 Bodnant Garden NT Conwy
282 C1 Bodorgan railway station IoA
283 E2 Bodowyr Burial Chamber CADW IoA
53 H4 Bognor Regis Golf Club W Susx
482 D5 Bogston railway station Inver
74 C3 Bohunt Manor Hants
430 A3 Bolam Lake Country Park Nthumb
12 B5 Bolberry House Farm Caravan & Camping Park Devon
237 G5 Boldmere golf course Birm
406 B2 Boldon Golf Club S Tyne
120 B3 Boleyn Ground Gt Lon
300 B2 Bolingbroke Castle EH Lincs
315 F5 Bolsover Castle EH Derbys
325 F3 Bolton Golf Club Bolton
325 F2 Bolton Old Links Golf Club Bolton
355 E4 Bolton Priory N York
325 E2 Bolton West service area Lancs
487 H6 Bonaly Country Park C Edin
576 D5 Bonar Bridge Highld
507 H3 Bonawe Historic Iron Furnace NT Ag & B
315 G4 Bondhay Golf & Fishing Club Derbys
375 F6 Bondville Miniature Village E R Yk
486 C4 Bo'ness & Kinneil Railway Falk
3 E3 Bone Valley Caravan & Camping Park Cnwll
467 E4 Bonnyton Golf Club E Rens
77 E5 Bookers vineyard W Susx
94 C3 Bookham railway station Surrey
358 A4 Bootham Crescent York
345 H3 Boothferry Golf Club E R Yk
323 F5 Bootle Golf Club Sefton
323 F5 Bootle New Strand railway station Sefton
323 F6 Bootle Oriel Road railway station Sefton
362 B4 Bootle railway station Cumb
166 A3 Bo Peep Farm Caravan Park Oxon
77 F4 Borde Hill Gardens W Susx
427 E3 Border Forest Park
452 D3 Border Union showground Border
147 E2 Boreham airfield Essex
18 B6 Borgindon Camp Devon
568 C3 Borough Briggs Moray
388 A4 Borough Park Cumb
205 E1 Borth & Ynyslas Golf Club Cerdgn
15 E5 Boscarne Junction railway station Cnwll
22 B4 Boscastle Witchcraft museum Cnwll
236 B3 Boscobel House EH Shrops
3 G3 Boscrege Caravan & Camping Park Cnwll
140 A3 Bossoms Boatyard Oxon
300 B5 Boston Golf Club Lincs
299 H6 Boston West Golf Centre Lincs
239 F4 Bosworth battlefield Leics
239 G5 Bosworth Battlefield Country Park Leics
239 F3 Bosworth Trail cycle route Leics
467 H3 Bothwell (southbound only) service area S Lans
467 G3 Bothwell Castle Golf Club S Lans
467 G2 Bothwell Castle HS S Lans
51 F2 Botley Park Hotel Golf & Country Club Hants
99 G3 Boughton Golf Club Kent
218 C3 Boughton House Nhants
326 D3 Boundary Park Oldham
49 E5 Bournemouth airport Dorset
196 D3 Bourn golf course Cambs
196 D3 Bourn Post Mill Cambs
164 B5 Bourton-on-the-Water Model Village Gloucs
26 A6 Bovey Castle golf course Devon
33 E2 Bovington Tank museum Dorset
364 B5 Bow Bridge EH Cumb
19 H5 Bowden House Devon
66 C4 Bowdens Crest Caravan & Camping Park Somset
377 H1 Bowder Stone Cumb
326 D4 Bower Fold Tamesd
405 G3 Bowes Railway & Museum Sundld
569 H2 Bow Fiddle Rock Moray
451 H2 Bowhill House Border
78 C3 Bowles Outdoor Centre & Dry Ski Slope E Susx
111 H6 Bowood Golf & Country Club Wilts
111 H6 Bowood House Wilts
15 F2 Bowood Park golf course Cnwll
309 F1 Bowring Park Golf Club Knows
53 G3 Boxgrove Priory EH W Susx
94 D4 Box Hill country park NT Surrey
143 E3 Boxmoor Golf Club Herts
187 F4 Boyce Caravan Park Herefs
122 B2 Boyce Hill Golf Club Essex
199 E6 Boyton vineyard Suffk
355 E4 Bracken Ghyll Golf Club Brad
308 D3 Brackenwood Golf Club Wirral
325 G4 Brackley Municipal Golf Club Salfd
342 C3 Bradford & Bingley Stadium Brad
342 C3 Bradford Golf Club Leeds
342 C3 Bradford Moor Golf Club Brad
240 B2 Bradgate Park Country Park Leics
342 C5 Bradley Park golf course Kirk
466 D2 Braehead C Glas
498 D6 Braehead Golf Club Clacks
537 J4 Braemar Castle Abers
537 J4 Braemar Golf Club Abers
488 B6 Braid Hills golf course C Edin
425 G6 Braids Caravan Park D & G
165 E2 Brailes Golf Club Warwks
173 F5 Braintree Freeport railway station Essex
173 F5 Braintree Golf Club Essex
58 C4 Brakes Coppice Park campsite E Susx
314 D2 Bramall Lane Sheff
312 A2 Bramall Park Golf Club Stockp
312 B3 Bramall Golf Club Stockp
343 H1 Bramham Park Leeds
93 H5 Bramley Golf Club Surrey
401 F3 Brampton (Cumbria) railway station Cumb
227 E3 Brampton (Suffolk) railway station Suffk
401 F3 Brampton Golf Club Cumb
193 F1 Brampton Heath Golf Centre Nhants
220 B6 Brampton Park Golf Club Cambs
71 F6 Bramshaw Commons NT Hants
49 H2 Bramshaw Golf Club Hants
395 E2 Brancepeth Castle Golf Club Dur
213 E2 Brandhall golf course Sandw
223 F2 Brandon Country Park Suffk
343 F1 Brandon golf course Leeds
215 G4 Brandon Stadium Warwks
559 H5 Brandsbutt Symbol Stone HS Abers
97 E2 Brands Hatch Kent
333 E5 Brandy Wharf Leisure Park Lincs
512 D5 Branklyn Garden NTS P & K
60 D5 Brannams Pottery Devon
259 F3 Branodunum Roman Fort NT Norfk
341 G2 Branshaw Golf Club Brad
274 C5 Branston Golf & Country Club Staffs
378 B5 Brantwood House Cumb
87 G4 Bratton Camp EH Wilts
192 B1 Braunston Marina Nhants
150 D5 Brawdy airfield (dis) Pembks
50 A6 Braxton Gardens Hants
509 J3 Breadalbane Folklore Centre Stirlg
302 B4 Breakwater Quarry Country Park IoA
56 C3 Breaky Bottom vineyard E Susx
70 D6 Breamore House Hants
84 A3 Brean Down Tropical Bird Garden Somset
84 A4 Brean Golf Club Somset
528 C3 Brechin Castle & Pictavia visitor centre Angus
528 D2 Brechin Golf & Squash Club Angus
247 G3 Breckland Meadows Touring Park Norfk
157 G5 Brecon Beacons Powys
157 H5 Brecon Beacons National Park
157 F4 Brecon Beacons National Park visitor centre Powys
157 G4 Brecon Gaer Fort Roman Site CADW Powys
157 G4 Brecon Golf Club Powys
131 H2 Brecon Mountain Railway Powys
275 G5 Breedon Priory Golf Centre Leics
325 H2 Breightmet Golf Club Bury
63 G4 Brendon Hills Somset
118 C3 Brent Valley Golf Club Gt Lon
81 F4 Brenzett Aeronautical Museum Kent
605 K2 Bressay Shet
225 E3 Bressingham Steam Museum & Gardens Norfk
174 D2 Brett Vale Golf Club Suffk
251 E4 Breydon Water campsite Norfk
162 D5 Briarfields campsite Gloucs
144 D3 Brickendon Grange Golf Club Herts
37 F2 Brickfields Horse Country IoW
11 E3 Brickfields Recreation Ground C Plym
162 C5 Brickhampton Court Golf Club Gloucs
373 G1 Bridestones (Rock Formation) N York
24 D5 Bridestowe Caravan Park Devon
134 B3 Bridge Caravan Park & Camping Site Mons
498 C6 Bridgehaugh Park Stirlg
351 G5 Bridge House Marina & Caravan Park Lancs
378 C4 Bridge House NT Cumb
125 G1 Bridge Meadow Stadium Pembks
291 E6 Bridgemere Garden World Ches
498 B5 Bridge of Allan Golf Club Stirlg
534 B2 Bridge of Oich HS Highld
235 G6 Bridgnorth Castle Shrops
235 G6 Bridgnorth Golf Club Shrops
65 E5 Bridgwater service area Somset
361 F1 Bridlington Golf Club E R Yk
361 F1 Bridlington Harbour Marina E R Yk
375 G6 Bridlington Links golf course E R Yk
30 B4 Bridport & West Dorset Golf Club Dorset
145 F2 Briggens House Hotel golf course Herts
412 B6 Brighouse Bay golf course D & G
412 B5 Brighouse Bay Holiday Park campsite D & G
55 G3 Brighton & Hove Golf Club Br & H
56 A3 Brighton racecourse Br & H
355 H2 Brimham Rocks N York
292 C3 Brindley Mill Staffs
443 E5 Brinkburn Priory EH Nthumb
112 B2 Brinkworth golf course Wilts
109 F5 Bristol & Clifton golf course N Som
85 F1 Bristol airport N Som
110 B6 Bristol and Bath Avon Cycleway S Glos
109 G3 Bristol golf course S Glos
109 H4 Bristol Parkway railway station S Glos
109 G5 Bristol Temple Meads railway station Bristl
292 A6 Britannia Stadium C Stke
22 C5 British Cycling museum Cnwll
104 B2 British Steel Port Talbot golf course Neath
397 E5 British Steel Redcar railway station R & Cl
11 F3 Brixton Caravan & Camping Park Devon
217 G6 Brixworth Country Park Nhants
138 D3 Brize Norton airport Oxon
77 E3 Broadfield Stadium W Susx
170 B5 Broadhall Stadium Herts
81 F2 Broad Hembury Holiday Park Kent
250 D1 Broadland Conservation Centre Norfk
71 H5 Broadlands Hants
20 B6 Broadleigh Farm Park campsite Devon
48 C5 Broadstone (Dorset) Golf Club Poole
93 G5 Broadwater Park Golf Club Surrey
163 H3 Broadway Golf Club Gloucs
84 D4 Broadway Hoad Holiday Caravan & Camping Park Somset
163 H2 Broadway Tower Country Park Worcs
485 E5 Broadwood Stadium N Lans
185 F6 Brobury House Gardens Herefs
187 F3 Brockhampton Estate NT Herefs
82 B3 Brockhill Country Park Kent
240 D5 Brocks Hill Country Park Leics
273 E6 Brocton Hall Golf Club Staffs
461 E2 Brodick Castle Garden & Country Park NTS N Ayrs
461 E2 Brodick Golf Club N Ayrs
567 H5 Brodie Castle NTS Moray
330 B3 Brodsworth Hall and Gardens EH Donc
330 B3 Brodsworth Welfare FC Donc
96 C2 Broke Hill Golf Club Kent
50 A4 Brokenhurst Manor Golf Club Hants
87 E4 Brokerswood Country Park campsite Wilts
308 D3 Bromborough Golf Club Wirral
308 D3 Bromborough Rake railway station Wirral
195 E4 Bromham Watermill museum Beds
120 B6 Bromley FC Gt Lon
96 B1 Bromley golf course Gt Lon
383 E4 Brompton-on-Swale Caravan & Camping Park N York
213 E5 Bromsgrove Golf Centre Worcs
158 B3 Bronllys Castle CADW Powys
306 C4 Bron-Y-Wendon Caravan Park Conwy
322 e8 Brough Fort IoM
326 D4 Brookdale Golf Club Oldham
85 E2 Brook Lodge Farm Camping & Caravan Park N Som
337 G6 Brooklyn Park and Country Club camping Lancs
144 B4 Brookmans Park Golf Club Herts
113 E3 Broome Manor Golf Complex Swindn
100 D6 Broome Park Golf Club Kent
574 C5 Broomfield Holiday Park Highld
551 H5 Broomhill railway station Highld
471 F1 Broomieknowe Golf Club Mdloth
577 K2 Brora Golf Club Highld
391 E4 Brougham Castle EH Cumb
380 D2 Brough Castle EH Cumb
346 D4 Brough Golf Club E R Yk
405 G2 Brough Park N u Ty
165 G2 Broughton Castle Oxon
514 D3 Broughty Castle HS C Dund
528 C1 Brown Caterthun HS Angus
237 F3 Brownhills West railway station Staffs
540 D4 Brownmuir Caravan Park Abers
428 C3 Brown Rigg Caravan & Camping Park Nthumb
34 B3 Brownsea Island NT Dorset
27 G5 Browns Farm Caravan Park Devon
485 G2 Brucefields Family Golfing Centre Stirlg
119 G1 Bruce Grove railway station Gt Lon
425 F5 Bruce's Cave Caravan & Camping Park D & G
421 F4 Bruce's Stone NTS D & G
202 C1 Bruisyard Winery & Vineyard Suffk
250 C3 Brundall Bay Marina Norfk
250 C3 Brundall Gardens railway station Norfk
432 C4 Brunston Castle golf course S Ayrs
309 E2 Brunswick railway station Lpool
216 C2 Bruntingthorpe airfield Leics
455 G4 Brunton airfield Nthumb
400 D3 Brunton Park Cumb
487 G4 Bruntsfield Links Golfing Society C Edin
68 A3 Bruton Dovecote NT Somset
3 C1 Bryher IoS
3 c2 Bryher campsite IoS
263 E5 Bryn Bach Caravan & Camping Site Gwynd
132 B3 Bryn Bach Country Park Blae G
283 F1 Bryn Celli Ddu CADW IoA
105 E2 Bryngarw Country Park Brdgnd
283 F4 Bryn Gloch Caravan & Camping Park Gwynd
106 B6 Brynhill Golf Club V Glam
267 E3 Bryn Hynod railway station Gwynd
157 H4 Brynich Caravan Park Powys
132 B5 Bryn Meadows Golf & Country Hotel Caerph
287 F2 Bryn Morfydd Hotel Golf Club Denbgs
205 E2 Brynowen Holiday Park Cerdgn
207 E2 Bryn Tail Lead Mine CADW Powys
483 G2 Buchanan Castle Golf Club Stirlg
76 D3 Buchan Country Park W Susx
19 F4 Buckfast Butterfly Farm Devon
167 E3 Buckingham Golf Club Bucks
118 A2 Buckinghamshire Golf Club Bucks
167 F6 Buckinghamshire Railway Centre Bucks
17 G5 Buckland Abbey NT Devon
163 G2 Buckland Rectory Gloucs
85 E5 Bucklegrove Caravan & Camping Park Somset
98 A2 Buckmore Park Kent
569 G3 Buckpool Golf Club Moray
23 E1 Bude & North Cornwall Golf Club Cnwll
23 E2 Budemeadows Touring Holiday Park Cnwll
5 E3 Budock Vean Hotel on the River golf course Cnwll
235 E4 Buildwas Abbey EH Shrops
183 G4 Builth Wells Golf Club Powys
47 E3 Bulbarrow Hill viewpoint Dorset
48 A6 Bulbury Woods Golf Club Dorset
303 F2 Bull Bay Golf Club IoA
134 C6 Bulwark Camp CADW Mons
295 C5 Bulwell Forest Golf Club C Nott
276 C1 Bulwell railway station C Nott
24 D4 Bundu Camping & Caravan Park Devon
226 C1 Bungay & Waveney Valley Golf Club Suffk
147 F3 Bunsay Downs Golf Club Essex
239 H6 Burbage Common & Woods Country Park Leics
85 F5 Burcott Mill Somset
256 A5 Bure Valley Railway Norfk
138 C2 Burford Golf Club Oxon
77 F5 Burgess Hill Golf Centre W Susx
430 B1 Burgham Park Golf & Leisure Club Nthumb
251 F4 Burgh Castle EH Norfk
251 F4 Burgh Castle Marina Norfk
567 L3 Burghead Well HS Moray
186 B6 Burghill Valley golf course Herefs
12 A4 Burgh Island Devon
243 E3 Burghley C Pete
243 E3 Burghley Park Golf Club C Pete
94 C2 Burhill Golf Club Surrey
500 B4 Burleigh Castle HS P & K
49 G4 Burley Golf Club Hants
343 E2 Burley Park railway station Leeds
359 F5 Bunby Hall Gardens E R Yk
84 B4 Burnham & Berrow Golf Club Somset
117 F3 Burnham Beeches Golf Club Bucks
148 B5 Burnham-on-Crouch Golf Club Essex
84 B5 Burnham-on-Sea Holiday Village Somset
340 C3 Burnley Barracks railway station Lancs
340 C3 Burnley Central railway station Lancs
340 C3 Burnley Golf Club Lancs
340 C3 Burnley Manchester Road railway station Lancs

444 D6 Burns Cottage museum S Ayrs
389 H5 Burns Farm Caravan Park Cumb
568 E4 Burnside Caravan Park Moray
467 F2 Burnside railway station S Lancs
424 D4 Burnswark Hill Roman Camp D & G
488 A2 Burntisland Golf House Club Fife
296 A4 Burntstump Country Park Notts
241 G2 Burrough Hill country park Leics
241 G2 Burrough Hill Fort Leics
62 D2 Burrowhayes Farm Caravan & Camping Site Somset
65 G5 Burrow Mump Somset
324 A2 Burscough Junction railway station Lancs
292 A4 Burslem Golf Club C Stke
348 C2 Burton Constable Hall E R Yk
348 C2 Burton Constable Holiday Park & Arboretum E R Yk
185 H3 Burton Court Herefs
191 F4 Burton Dassett Country Park Warwks
365 H4 Burton-in-Kendal (northbound only) service area Lancs
274 D5 Burton upon Trent Golf Club Derbys
310 B1 Burtonwood service area Warrtn
326 B3 Bury Golf Club Bury
90 A6 Bury Hill Hants
199 G1 Bury St Edmunds Golf Club Suffk
270 D4 Bury Walls Shrops
138 C5 Buscot Park NT Oxon
143 G6 Bushey Golf & Country Club Herts
143 G5 Bushey Hall Golf Club Herts
144 D5 Bush Hill Park Golf Club Gt Lon
195 G2 Bushmead Priory EH Beds
464 B1 Bute Ag & B
464 B1 Bute Golf Club Ag & B
237 H5 Butlers Lane railway station Birm
52 C1 Butser Ancient Farm Hants
63 F3 Butter Cross EH Somset
281 F5 Butterfly & Wildlife Park Lincs
304 B5 Butterfly Palace (Pili Palas) IoA
37 E2 Butterfly World IoW
295 E4 Butterley railway station Derbys
381 F5 Buttertubs Pass N York
215 E4 Butts Park Arena Covtry
313 E5 Buxton & High Peak Golf Club Derbys
256 A5 Buxton railway station Norfk
205 G3 Bwlch Nant Yr Arian visitor centre Cerdgn
94 B2 Byfleet & New Haw railway station Surrey
371 H4 Byland Abbey N York
404 D3 Byreside Caravan Site Dur
20 A5 Byslades International Touring & Camping Park Devon

C

118 C3 C & L Golf & Country Club Gt Lon
109 E5 Cadbury Camp N Som
67 G4 Cadbury Castle hill fort Somset
213 F3 Cadbury World visitor centre Birm
28 A3 Cadhay Devon
126 D5 Cadley Island Pembks
186 D1 Cadmore Lodge Hotel & Country Club Worcs
16 D5 Cadson Bury Cnwll
320 A3 Cadwell Park Lincs
303 G5 Cae Bob Parry IoA
180 D4 Cae Hir Garden Cerdgn
234 B5 Caer Caradoc hill fort Shrops
150 C5 Caerfai Bay Caravan & Tent Park Pembks
398 C1 Caeriaverock Castle HS D & G
283 E2 Caer Leb CADW IoA
107 F1 Caerleon golf course Newpt
283 E3 Caernarfon Castle (UNESCO) Gwynd
106 C2 Caerphilly Castle CADW Caerph
106 C2 Caerphilly Golf Club Caerph
514 C3 Caird Park golf course C Dund
401 F4 Cairndale Caravan Park Cumb
536 E2 Cairngorm Mountains Highld
536 E1 Cairngorm Ski Area Highld
551 K7 Cairngorms National Park Highld
417 G6 Cairn Holy Chambered Cairns HS D & G
583 K1 Cairn o'Get HS Highld
540 B3 Cairn O'Mount Abers
486 C5 Cairnpapple Hill HS W Loth
251 G2 Caister Castle Norfk
250 A4 Caistor Roman Town Norfk
512 C4 Caithness Glass P & K
203 E2 Cakes & Ale campsite Suffk
115 H5 Calcot Park Golf Club W Berk
191 H2 Calcutt Marina Warwks
251 F4 Caldecott Hall Golf & Leisure Norfk
467 G2 Calderbraes Golf Club N Lans
237 F5 Calderfields Golf Academy Wsall
467 G4 Calderglen Country Park S Lans
126 C5 Caldey Monastery visitor centre Pembks
466 B4 Caldwell Golf Club E Rens
308 B3 Caldy Golf Club Wirral
548 F7 Caledonian Canal visitor centre Highld
528 D3 Caledonian Railway Angus
566 B7 Caley Marina Highld
236 D3 Calf Heath Marina Staffs
92 C1 California Chalet & Touring Park Wokham
92 C1 California Country Park Wokham
275 F5 Calke Abbey NT Derbys
497 F3 Callander Golf Club Stirlg
486 A4 Callendar Park Falk
3 G2 Calloose Caravan & Camping Park Cnwll
51 E4 Calshot Castle EH Hants
51 E4 Calshot Velodrome Hants
17 F5 Calstock Viaduct Cnwll
342 D2 Calverley Golf Club Leeds
135 H4 Cam & Dursley railway station Gloucs
59 F3 Camber Castle EH E Susx
93 E3 Camberley Heath Golf Club Surrey
59 G3 Camber Sands campsite E Susx

6 C6 Camborne & Redruth Mining District (UNESCO) Cnwll
182 B2 Cambrian Mountains
197 G3 Cambridge airport Cambs
197 E3 Cambridge National golf course Cambs
197 E1 Cambridge service area Cambs
6 C4 Cambrose Touring Park Cnwll
498 C6 Cambuskenneth Abbey Stirlg
32 B2 Came Down Golf Club Dorset
324 C1 Camelot Lancs
400 C1 Camelot Caravan Park Cumb
15 E5 Camel Valley vineyard Cnwll
483 E3 Cameron House Marina W Duns
168 B2 Campbell Park M Keyn
456 D2 Campbeltown airport Ag & B
514 B3 Camperdown Country Park C Dund
514 B3 Camperdown golf course C Dund
551 G6 Campgrounds of Scotland Highld
9 G3 Camping Caradon Touring Park Cnwll
484 B3 Campsie Fells E Duns
484 C4 Campsie Golf Club E Duns
51 G3 Cants Hall Estate Golf Club Hants
531 H5 Camusdarach Campsite Highld
236 D5 Canal Path cycle route Wolves
104 D4 Candleston Castle Brdgnd
48 C5 Canford Magna Golf Club Poole
487 E2 Canmore Golf Club Fife
544 D8 Canna Highld
548 E3 Cannich Caravan and Camping Park Highld
65 E3 Cannington golf course Somset
273 E6 Cannock Chase Staffs
237 F2 Cannock Chase museum Staffs
237 E2 Cannock Park golf course Staffs
328 D3 Cannon Hall Farm Barns
192 C4 Canons Ashby House NT Nhants
145 F2 Canons Brook Golf Club Essex
20 A1 Canonteign Falls & Country Park Devon
100 B4 Canterbury East railway station Kent
100 C4 Canterbury Golf Club Kent
100 B4 Canterbury West railway station Kent
380 B5 Cantley Spout waterfall Cumb
234 C3 Cantlop Bridge EH Shrops
318 B6 Canwick Park Golf Club Lincs
2 C3 Cape Cornwall Golf & Country Club Cnwll
285 H4 Capel Garmon Burial Chamber CADW Conwy
144 D5 Capel Manor Gardens Gt Lon
311 G5 Capesthorne Hall Ches
311 G5 Capesthorne Hall campsite Ches
482 C4 Cappielow Park Inver
445 F2 Caprington Golf Club E Ayrs
16 C4 Caradon Mining District (UNESCO) Cnwll
254 B2 Caravan Club M.V.C. Site Norfk
105 H6 Cardiff airport V Glam
106 C4 Cardiff Athletic Stadium Cardif
106 C4 Cardiff Caravan Park Cardif
106 C4 Cardiff Castle Cardif
106 D3 Cardiff Gate service area Cardif
106 C3 Cardiff Golf Club Cardif
106 C4 Cardiff Queen Street railway station Cardif
106 A4 Cardiff West service area Cardif
178 D4 Cardigan Golf Club Cerdgn
178 D3 Cardigan Island Coastal Farm Park Cerdgn
412 A3 Cardoness Castle HS D & G
482 D4 Cardross Golf Club Ag & B
126 B4 Carew Castle Pembks
126 B4 Carew Cross CADW Pembks
109 E1 Carewent Roman Town CADW Mons
126 A4 Carew Tide Mill Pembks
318 B5 Carholme Golf Club Lincs
36 D3 Carisbrooke Castle EH IoW
365 E4 Cark & Cartmel railway station Cumb
401 E2 Carlisle airport Cumb
400 C3 Carlisle Castle EH Cumb
400 D3 Carlisle Golf Club Cumb
400 D4 Carlisle racecourse Cumb
468 C4 Carluke Golf Club S Lans
515 E2 Carlungie Earth House HS Angus
119 F4 Carlyle's House NT Gt Lon
8 D3 Carlyon Bay Caravan & Camping Park Cnwll
8 D3 Carlyon Bay Hotel Golf Club Cnwll
154 B5 Carmarthen Castle Carmth
154 A5 Carmarthen Golf Club Carmth
448 B2 Carmichael visitor centre S Lans
492 D4 Carnassarie Castle HS Ag & B
460 D4 Carn Ban HS N Ayrs
6 C5 Carn Brea hill fort Cnwll
2 D4 Carn Euny Ancient Village EH Cnwll
14 B4 Carnevas Holiday Park & Farm Cottages Cnwll
262 D3 Carn Fadrum hill fort Gwynd
16 A5 Carnglaze Caverns Cnwll
155 G5 Carn Goch hill fort Carmth
577 J3 Carn Liath HS Highld
7 F5 Carnon Downs Caravan & Camping Park Cnwll
515 F3 Carnoustie Golf Links Angus
469 F5 Carnwath Golf Club S Lans
459 G4 Carradale Bay Caravan Park Ag & B
459 G4 Carradale Golf Club Ag & B
459 G4 Carradale House Gardens Ag & B
428 D5 Carrawburgh: Temple of Mithras Roman site Nthumb
551 G5 Carrbridge Golf Club Highld
155 G6 Carreg Cennen Castle Carmth
152 B2 Carreg Coetan CADW Pembks
102 C4 Carreglwyd Camping & Caravan Park Swans
150 D3 Carreg Sampson Pembks
419 F3 Carrick S Ayrs
487 H5 Carrick Knowe golf course C Edin
250 A3 Carrow Road Norfk
294 B5 Carsington Fields Caravan Park Derbys
294 A4 Carsington visitor centre Derbys
417 F6 Carsluith Castle HS D & G

139 E5 Carswell Golf & Country Club Oxon
440 C3 Carter Bar viewpoint Border
174 C3 Carter's vineyard Essex
365 E4 Cartmel racecourse Cumb
379 F6 Carus Green & Driving Range Cumb
7 G2 Carvynick Country Club campsite Cnwll
5 E3 Carwinion Gardens Cnwll
322 h5 Cashtal yn Ard IoM
106 B3 Castell Coch CADW Cardif
158 C3 Castell Dinas Powys
152 C2 Castell Henllys Pembks
229 F3 Castell y Bere CADW Gwynd
253 G4 Castle Acre Castle EH Norfk
253 G5 Castle Acre Priory EH Norfk
118 D3 Castle Bar Park railway station Gt Lon
283 E2 Castle Bryn Gwyn CADW IoA
499 F5 Castle Campbell HS Clacks
417 F5 Castle Cary Holiday Park D & G
111 F4 Castle Coombe Wilts
35 d3 Castle Cornet Guern
413 E2 Castle Douglas Golf Club D & G
25 H4 Castle Drogo NT Devon
556 C2 Castle Fraser NTS Abers
589 K6 Castle Girnigoe & Sinclair Highld
326 C2 Castle Hawk Golf Club Rochdl
40 D2 Castle Hill Devon
240 C3 Castle Hill Country Park C Leic
372 D5 Castle Howard N York
92 D5 Castle Keep EH Surrey
415 F4 Castle Kennedy Gardens D & G
470 D2 Castlelaw Hill Fort HS Mdloth
589 H2 Castle of Mey Highld
589 K7 Castle of Old Wick HS Highld
415 E4 Castle of St John D & G
330 D4 Castle Park Donc
413 G4 Castle Point Caravan Park D & G
122 B3 Castle Point Golf Club Essex
389 G5 Castlerigg Farm Camping & Caravan Site Cumb
389 G5 Castlerigg Stone Circle EH Cumb
237 F2 Castle Ring Staffs
252 D3 Castle Rising Castle EH Norfk
465 H3 Castle Semple Collegiate Church HS Rens
479 J6 Castle Sween HS Ag & B
326 C2 Castleton (Greater Manchester) railway station Rochdl
386 A3 Castleton Moor railway station N York
322 d9 Castletown Golf Links IoM
322 f7 Castletown IoM
309 H3 Catalyst museum Halton
312 D5 Cat and Fiddle Ches
467 E3 Cathcart Castle Golf Club E Rens
467 F3 Cathkin Braes Golf Club S Lans
357 E3 Cattal railway station N York
383 E5 Catterick Golf Club N York
383 F5 Catterick racecourse N York
392 D4 Cauldron Snout (Waterfall) Dur
9 G2 Causeland railway station Cnwll
142 A6 Causeway Stadium Bucks
405 F3 Causey Arch Dur
403 G2 Causey Hill Caravan Park Nthumb
346 D3 Cave Castle Hotel & Country Club E R Yk
312 D5 Cavendish Golf Club E Duns
484 C5 Cawder Golf Club E Duns
566 E7 Cawdor Castle Highld
344 D2 Cawood Park campsite N York
596 E5 Ceann a Tuath na Hearadh W Isls
130 B4 Cefn Coed Colliery Museum Neath
269 E1 Cefn Viaduct Wrexhm
178 C4 Ceibwr Bay Pembks
284 C2 Cei Llydan railway station Gwynd
467 F2 Celtic Park C Glas
153 F1 Cenarth Falls Holiday Park Cerdgn
375 E4 Centenary Way Camping & Caravan Park N York
292 A5 Central Forest Park viewpoint C Stke
119 F5 Central London Golf Centre Gt Lon
487 G1 Central Park (Cowdenbeath FC) Fife
230 B4 Centre for Alternative Technology Powys
291 H5 Ceramica visitor centre C Stke
145 E2 Chadwell Springs Golf Club Herts
169 E4 Chalgrave Manor Golf Club Beds
140 D5 Chalgrove airfield Oxon
60 D2 Chambercombe Manor Devon
119 G4 Champion Hill Gt Lon
54 D2 Chanctonbury Ring W Susx
147 E2 Channels Golf Club Essex
61 H2 Channel View Caravan and Camping Park Devon
312 D3 Chapel-en-le-Frith Golf Club Derbys
409 F2 Chapel Finian (ruin) HS D & G
23 H4 Chapmanswell Caravan Park Devon
174 A4 Chappel & Wakes Colne railway station Essex
119 G3 Charing Cross railway station Gt Lon
190 D3 Charlecote Park NT Warwks
56 D3 Charleston Farmhouse museum E Susx
8 C3 Charlestown (UNESCO) Cnwll
502 D4 Charleton golf course Fife
324 D1 Charnock Richard Golf Club Lancs
324 C1 Charnock Richard service area Lancs
240 B1 Charnwood Forest Golf Club Leics
48 B5 Charris Camping & Caravan Park Dorset
77 G1 Chartham Park golf course Surrey
80 C1 Chart Hills Golf Club Kent
142 C4 Chartridge Park Golf Club Bucks
96 C4 Chartwell NT Kent
237 F3 Chasetown Church Street railway station Staffs
237 F3 Chasewater Heaths railway station Staffs
325 H6 Chassen Road railway station Traffd
164 C4 Chastleton House NT Oxon
468 A4 Chatelherault Country Park S Lans
314 B5 Chatsworth Derbys
136 C5 Chavenage Gloucs

311 H2 Cheadle Golf Club Stockp
85 E4 Cheddar Bridge Touring Park Somset
85 E4 Cheddar Caves & Gorge Somset
30 B1 Chedington Court Golf Club Dorset
137 G2 Chedworth Roman Villa NT Gloucs
146 D4 Chelmsford Golf Club Essex
96 C2 Chelsfield Lakes Golf Centre Gt Lon
163 E5 Cheltenham racecourse Gloucs
163 E4 Cheltenham Racecourse railway station Gloucs
162 D5 Cheltenham Spa railway station Gloucs
134 C6 Chepstow Castle CADW Mons
134 C5 Chepstow racecourse Mons
112 B6 Cherhill Down hill fort NT Wilts
404 C2 Cherryburn NT Nthumb
96 B3 Cherry Lodge Golf Club Gt Lon
192 A6 Cherwell Edge Golf Club Nhants
166 C4 Cherwell Valley service area Oxon
170 B4 Chesfield Downs Golf Club Herts
142 D4 Chesham & Ley Hill Golf Club Bucks
289 G5 Cheshire Cycleway Ches
288 D1 Cheshire Cycleway Flints
145 E4 Cheshunt Park golf course Herts
32 A3 Chesil Beach Dorset
36 B3 Chessell Pottery IoW
94 D2 Chessington Golf Centre Gt Lon
94 D2 Chessington World of Adventures Gt Lon
289 F1 Chester Castle EH Ches
314 D6 Chesterfield Golf Club Derbys
295 E2 Chesterfield service area Derbys
289 E2 Chester Golf Club Ches
402 D1 Chesterholm (Vindolanda) Roman site Nthumb
405 G4 Chester-le-Street Golf Club Dur
289 E1 Chester racecourse Ches
237 H6 Chester Road railway station Birm
309 G4 Chester service area Ches
429 E5 Chesters Fort Roman site Nthumb
489 G4 Chesters Hill Fort HS E Loth
289 E2 Chester Southerly Caravan Park Ches
291 G5 Chesterton Raceway Staffs
236 A5 Chesterton Valley Golf Club Shrops
191 E3 Chesterton windmill Warwks
100 B2 Chestfield & Swaliecliffe railway station Kent
100 B2 Chestfield (Whitstable) Golf Club Kent
313 E3 Chestnut Centre Derbys
46 A3 Chetnole railway station Dorset
37 F4 Cheverton Copse Holiday Park Cnwll
355 H6 Chevin Forest Park Leeds
294 C6 Chevin Golf Club Derbys
49 G6 Chewton Glen Hotel golf course Hants
218 D6 Chichele College Nhants
53 F3 Chichester airfield W Susx
53 E4 Chichester Golf Club W Susx
53 E4 Chichester Marina W Susx
75 F3 Chiddingfold golf course Surrey
96 C5 Chiddingstone Castle Kent
114 D5 Chieveley service area W Berk
145 F6 Chigwell Golf Club Essex
91 E2 Children's Action Farm Hants
198 B5 Chilford Hundred vineyard Cambs
454 D4 Chillingham Wild Cattle Park Nthumb
142 B2 Chiltern Forest Golf Club Bucks
141 G5 Chiltern Hills
276 B2 Chilwell Manor Golf Club Notts
72 B6 Chilworth Golf Club Hants
10 D1 China Fleet Country Club Cnwll
339 E2 Chingle Hall Lancs
141 G4 Chinnor & Princes Risborough Railway Oxon
111 G4 Chippenham Golf Club Wilts
165 E4 Chipping Norton Golf Club Oxon
110 C3 Chipping Sodbury golf course S Glos
95 F3 Chipstead Golf Club Surrey
269 E2 Chirk Castle NT Wrexhm
269 E2 Chirk Golf Club Wrexhm
89 G1 Chisbury Chapel EH Wilts
120 B5 Chislehurst Golf Club Gt Lon
119 E4 Chiswick House EH Gt Lon
60 C5 Chivenor airfield Devon
60 D5 Chivenor Caravan Park Devon
6 D4 Chiverton Caravan & Touring Park Cnwll
93 G3 Chobham Golf Club Surrey
71 E1 Cholderton Rare Breeds Farm Wilts
290 A4 Cholmondeley Castle Gardens Ches
115 F2 Cholsey & Wallingford Railway Oxon
325 E1 Chorley Golf Club Lancs
143 E5 Chorleywood Golf Club Herts
311 G1 Chorlton-cum-Hardy Golf Club Manch
471 G2 Christon Castle HS Mdloth
49 F6 Christchurch Castle EH Dorset
558 C5 Christie Park Abers
351 F2 Christie Park Lancs
40 D5 Chulmleigh Golf Club Devon
340 A4 Church & Oswaldtwistle railway station Lancs
48 C2 Church and Earthworks EH Dorset
156 B3 Church Bank Playing Fields Carmth
48 B1 Church Farm Caravan & Camping Park Dorset
212 C4 Churchill & Blakedown Golf Club Worcs
19 F4 Churchill Farm campsite Devon
118 B3 Church Road Gt Lon
377 E4 Church Stile Farm campsite Cumb
234 D3 Church Stretton Golf Club Shrops
292 C4 Churnet Valley Railway Staffs
292 D5 Churnet Valley Railway Staffs
13 F1 Churston Golf Club Torbay
13 F1 Churston railway station Torbay
268 D2 Chwarel Wynne Mine Wrexhm

4 D5 Chy-Carne Holiday Park Cnwll
3 E2 Chysauster Ancient Village EH Cnwll
178 D5 Cilgerran Castle CADW Cerdgn
181 F4 Cilgwyn Golf Club Cerdgn
137 F4 Cirencester Amphitheatre roman site EH Gloucs
137 F4 Cirencester Golf Club Gloucs
54 D5 Cissbury Ring W Susx
120 B3 City airport Gt Lon
276 C2 City Ground C Nott
197 G3 City Ground Cambs
215 F4 City of Coventry-Brandon Wood Golf Club Warwks
326 C5 City of Manchester Stadium Manch
430 D6 City of Newcastle Golf Club N u Ty
255 H5 City of Norwich Aviation museum Norfk
343 F6 City of Wakefield Golf Club Wakefd
96 B4 Clacket Lane service area Surrey
486 B1 Clackmannan Tower HS Clacks
149 G2 Clacton Golf Club Essex
533 H8 Claggan Park Highld
531 H2 Clan Donald visitor centre Highld
524 B2 Clan Donnachaidh museum P & K
94 A4 Clandon Park NT Surrey
94 A4 Clandon railway station Surrey
94 A4 Clandon Regis Golf Club Surrey
565 K4 Clanland & Seapoint visitor centre Highld
367 E6 Clapham (North Yorkshire) railway station N York
119 F4 Clapham Junction railway station Gt Lon
19 E2 Clapper Bridge Devon
119 G5 Clapton railway station Gt Lon
199 F5 Clare Castle Country Park Suffk
94 C2 Claremont Gardens NT Surrey
143 H3 Clarence Park Herts
421 F4 Clatteringshaws Forest & Wildlife Centre D & G
514 B3 Clatto Country Park C Dund
566 D8 Clava Cairns HS Highld
167 F4 Claydon House NT Bucks
351 G5 Claylands Caravan Park Lancs
31 E2 Clay Pigeon Caravan Park Dorset
514 D3 Claypotts Castle HS C Dund
289 E4 Clays Golf Centre Wrexhm
342 B3 Clayton Golf Club Brad
8 C2 Clay Trail Bugle to Eden cycle route Cnwll
134 D3 Clearwell Caves Gloucs
342 C4 Cleckheaton & District Golf Club Kirk
210 D4 Clee Hills viewpoint Shrops
334 D3 Cleethorpes Golf Club NE Lin
63 G3 Cleeve Abbey EH Somset
163 E4 Cleeve Hill Golf Club Gloucs
212 D3 Clent Hills viewpoint Worcs
211 F4 Cleobury Mortimer Golf Club Shrops
108 D5 Clevedon Court NT N Som
108 D5 Clevedon Golf Club N & CI
397 E4 Cleveland Golf Club R & CI
371 G1 Cleveland Hills N York
371 G2 Cleveland Way N York
87 E6 Cley Hill Wilts
605 J2 Clickimin Broch HS Shet
602 C7 Click Mill HS Ork
178 D3 Cliff Hotel Golf Course Cerdgn
391 E4 Clifton Hall EH Cumb
468 A2 Cliftonhill Stadium N Lans
326 A4 Clifton railway station Salfd
251 E2 Clippesby Hall campsite Norfk
340 A2 Clitheroe Golf Club Lancs
117 F2 Cliveden NT Bucks
484 A4 Clober Golf Club E Duns
119 H6 Clock House railway station Gt Lon
284 D3 Closeburn railway station Gwynd
322 C9 Close ny Chollagh hill fort IoM
62 B2 Cloud Farm campsite Somset
33 E1 Clouds Hill NT Dorset
322 g6 Cloven Stones IoM
313 E5 Clover Fields Touring Caravan Park Derbys
316 B5 Clumber Park NT Notts
209 E3 Clun Castle EH Shrops
287 G1 Clwydian Range Flints
483 H5 Clydebank & District golf course W Duns
483 G5 Clydebank Municipal golf course W Duns
444 B1 Clyde Marina N Ayrs
103 F3 Clyne Golf Club Swans
588 C3 Cnoc Freiceadain Long Cairns HS Highld
235 F4 Coalbrookdale Iron Museum Wrekin
235 F4 Coalport China Musuem Wrekin
452 C3 Coast & Castles South cycle route Border
388 C6 Coast to Coast cycle route Cumb
403 C5 Coast to Coast cycle route Dur
405 H2 Coast to Coast cycle route Gatesd
406 A3 Coast to Coast cycle route Sundld
20 C3 Coast View Holiday Park Devon
468 A1 Coatbridge Sunnyside railway station N Lans
113 E3 Coate Water Country Park Swindn
40 C2 Cobbaton Combat Collection Devon
94 B2 Cobham Bus Museum Surrey
98 A3 Cobtree Manor Park golf course Kent
466 B2 Cochrane Castle Golf Club Rens
389 E3 Cockermouth Golf Club Cumb
351 F4 Cockersand Abbey Lancs
486 C5 Cockleroy viewpoint W Loth
213 G4 Cocks Moors Woods Golf Club Birm
265 G4 Coed-Brenin Forest Park Gwynd
265 G4 Coed-y-Brenin visitor centre Gwynd
105 E3 Coed-Y-Mwstwr Golf Club Brdgnd
20 D2 Cofton Country Holiday Park Devon
173 G5 Coggeshall Grange Barn NT Essex
574 C3 Coigach Highld
105 E3 Coity Castle CADW Brdgnd

542 C7 Colbost Croft museum Highld
126 D3 Colby Woodland Garden NT Pembks
174 C4 Colchester and East Essex Cricket Club Essex
174 C4 Colchester Golf Club Essex
174 C5 Colchester Zoo Essex
216 D4 Cold Ashby Golf Club Nhants
43 E5 Coldharbour Mill museum Devon
64 C4 Coleridge Cottage NT Somset
15 G5 Colesloggett Halt railway station Cnwll
13 G2 Coleton Fishacre House NT Devon
516 F4 Coll Ag & B
162 D5 College Ground cricket ground Gloucs
316 A4 College Pines golf course Notts
56 B2 College vineyard E Susx
15 H4 Colliford Lake Park Cnwll
15 H4 Colliford Tavern Campsite Cnwll
58 B5 Collington railway station E Susx
193 G3 Collingtree Park golf course Nhants
195 F3 Colmworth & North Bedfordshire golf course Beds
341 E1 Colne Golf Club Lancs
173 H4 Colne Valley Golf Club Essex
173 F2 Colne Valley Railway Essex
478 B3 Colonsay Ag & B
478 B3 Colonsay Golf Club Ag & B
413 G4 Colvend Golf Club D & G
468 B3 Colville Park Golf Club N Lans
276 D2 Colwick Country Park N Nott
306 A3 Colwyn Bay Cricket Club Conwy
90 B2 Combe Gibbet W Berk
139 G1 Combe railway station Oxon
64 A4 Combe Sydenham Country Park Somset
385 H2 Commondale railway station N York
326 C5 Commonwealth Indoor Stadium Manch
510 D5 Comrie Golf Club P & K
314 D1 Concord Park Golf Club Sheff
528 D6 Condor ski slope Angus
140 A4 Conduit House EH Oxon
292 A2 Congleton Golf Club Ches
299 G3 Coningsby airfield Lincs
330 B5 Conisbrough Castle EH Donc
364 D4 Conishead Priory Cumb
239 E1 Conkers visitor centre Leics
292 D5 Consall railway station Staffs
404 D4 Consett & District Golf Club Dur
369 G1 Constable Burton Hall Caravan Park N York
308 D2 Conway Park railway station Wirral
305 G4 Conwy (Caernarvonshire) Golf Club Conwy
305 G4 Conwy Castle (UNESCO) Conwy
285 H3 Conwy Valley Railway Conwy
285 G3 Conwy Valley Railway museum Conwy
99 F1 Conyer Creek Marina Kent
58 B5 Cooden Beach Golf Club E Susx
58 B5 Cooden Beach railway station E Susx
343 E1 Cookridge Hall Golf Club Leeds
215 F4 Coombe Abbey Country Park Warwks
119 E5 Coombe Hill Golf Club Gt Lon
70 B4 Coombe Touring Park Wilts
119 E5 Coombe Wood Golf Club Gt Lon
313 F2 Coopers Camp & Caravan Park Derbys
214 B4 Copt Heath Golf Club Solhll
77 F2 Copthorne Golf Club W Susx
442 D4 Coquetdale Caravan Park Nthumb
404 A2 Corbridge Roman site Nthumb
218 C1 Corby Public golf course Nhants
33 H3 Corfe Castle NT Dorset
552 F7 Corgarff Castle HS Abers
73 E6 Corhampton Golf Club Hants
466 D2 Corkerhill railway station C Glas
376 B1 Corkickle railway station Cumb
215 E2 Corley service area Warwks
482 B5 Cornalees Bridge visitor centre Inver
22 D3 Cornish Coast Caravan & Camping Park Cnwll
6 C5 Cornish Engines NT Cnwll
44 A3 Cornish Farm Touring Park Somset
463 E4 Corrie Golf Club N Ayrs
548 F3 Corrimony Chambered Cairn HS Highld
322 c6 Corris Folly IoM
230 B3 Corris Railway museum Powys
522 C2 Corrour railway station Highld
111 F1 Corsham Court Wilts
210 C3 Corvedale Shrops
7 E6 Cosawes Park campsite Cnwll
240 C6 Cosby Golf Club Leics
236 A4 Cosford airfield Shrops
236 A3 Cosford railway station Shrops
106 C6 Cosmeston Lakes Country Park & Medieval Village V Glam
249 G2 Costessey Park golf course Norfk
384 D4 Cote Ghyll Caravan & Camping Park N York
17 F5 Cotehele NT Cnwll
276 D2 Cotgrave Place Golf Club Notts
217 E5 Coton Manor Garden Nhants
136 A5 Cotswold Edge golf course Gloucs
164 B3 Cotswold Falconry Centre Gloucs
163 H4 Cotswold Farm Park Gloucs
136 D1 Cotswold Hills Golf Club Gloucs
164 B5 Cotswold Motoring Museum & Toy Collection Gloucs
137 E3 Cotswolds
165 F5 Cotswold View Touring park Oxon
137 F5 Cotswold Water Park (Ashton Keynes section) Wilts
138 B5 Cotswold Water Park (Fairford-Lechlade Section) Gloucs
163 E4 Cotswold Way Gloucs
110 C5 Cotswold Way S Glos
138 C5 Cotswold Wildlife Park Oxon
313 F5 Cottage Farm Caravan Park Derbys

7 E2 Cottage Farm Touring Park Cnwll
217 F5 Cottesbrooke Hall Nhants
242 C1 Cottesmore airfield Rutlnd
76 D3 Cottesmore Golf & Country Club W Susx
347 F3 Cottingham Parks Golf & Country Club E R Yk
343 E3 Cottingley railway station Leeds
106 A5 Cottrell Park Golf Club V Glam
341 H1 Cougar Park Brad
189 G2 Coughton Court NT Warwks
95 G3 Coulsdon Manor Hotel golf course Gt Lon
448 D2 Coulter Motte HS S Lans
391 E4 Countess Pillar EH Cumb
211 G3 Country Park Halt railway station Shrops
84 B2 Country View Caravan Park N Som
113 E2 County Ground Swindn
8 B3 Court Farm Holidays Cnwll
390 C5 Cove Caravan & Camping Park Cumb
215 F5 Coventry airport Warwks
215 E5 Coventry Golf Club Warwks
215 E4 Coventry Hearsall Golf Club Covtry
368 D3 Coverdale N York
494 B6 Cowal Ag & B
482 A4 Cowal Golf Club Ag & B
487 G1 Cowdenbeath Golf Club Fife
74 D5 Cowdray Park Golf Club W Susx
51 E5 Cowes Golf Club IoW
466 D2 Cowglen Golf Club C Glas
250 B3 Cow Tower EH Norfk
295 G3 Coxmoor Golf Club Notts
157 G3 Cradoc Golf Club Powys
442 D4 Cragside House NT Nthumb
557 F2 Craibstone Golf Centre C Aber
488 B4 Craigentinny golf course C Edin
512 D5 Craigie Hill Golf Club P & K
437 E4 Craigielands Country Park campsite D & G
555 G3 Craigievar Castle NTS Abers
488 B5 Craigmillar Castle HS C Edin
488 B5 Craigmillar Park Golf Club C Edin
468 C3 Craignethan Castle HS S Lans
505 K2 Craignure Golf Club Ag & B
444 D6 Craig Tara Holiday Park S Ayrs
502 D2 Craigtoun Country Park Fife
502 D2 Craigtoun Meadows Holiday Park Fife
503 D3 Crail Golfing Society Fife
47 H1 Cranborne Chase Dorset
26 A5 Cranbrook Castle Devon
48 D3 Crane Valley Golf Club Dorset
168 D1 Cranfield airfield Beds
75 H1 Cranleigh Golf & Leisure Club Surrey
86 B6 Cranmore railway station Somset
86 B6 Cranmore West railway station Somset
7 F2 Crantock Plains Touring Park Cnwll
298 C5 Cranwell airfield Lincs
492 C3 Craobh Marina Ag & B
493 G5 Crarae Garden NTS Ag & B
159 E2 Craswall Abbey Herefs
556 C5 Crathes Castle NTS Abers
119 E4 Craven Cottage Gt Lon
348 B3 Craven Park C KuH
364 A6 Craven Park Cumb
120 C6 Cray Valley Golf Club Gt Lon
259 H4 Creake Abbey EH Norfk
27 G4 Crealy Adventure Park Devon
14 C5 Crealy Great Adventure Park Cnwll
125 E2 Creampots Touring Caravan & Camping Park Pembks
417 E3 Creebridge Caravan Park D & G
417 F5 Creetown Caravan Park D & G
106 A3 Creigiau Golf Club Cardif
173 F6 Cressing Temple Essex
309 E2 Cressington railway station Lpool
315 G5 Creswell Crags Derbys
202 A2 Cretingham Golf Club Suffk
291 E3 Crewe Golf Club Ches
144 D4 Crews Hill Golf Club Gt Lon
109 G3 Cribbs Causeway S Glos
264 C2 Criccieth Castle CADW Gwynd
264 C2 Criccieth Golf Club Gwynd
137 G6 Cricklade Hotel & Country Club golf course Wilts
136 D1 Crickley Hill Country Park Gloucs
511 F5 Crieff Golf Club P & K
230 D4 Cringoed Caravan Park Powys
186 A1 Croft Ambrey hill fort Herefs
186 A1 Croft Castle NT Herefs
383 G3 Croft Circuit N York
8 C2 Croft Farm Holiday Park Cnwll
605 G8 Croft House museum Shet
523 L6 Croftmoraig Stone Circle P & K
119 H5 Crofton Park railway station Gt Lon
89 G2 Crofton Pumping Station Wilts
431 F3 Croft Park Nthumb
347 E3 Croft Park campsite E R Yk
95 G2 Croham Hurst Golf Club Gt Lon
515 E1 Cromble Country Park Angus
294 B3 Cromford Mill Derbys
294 C3 Cromford railway station Derbys
326 D3 Crompton & Royton Golf Club Oldham
339 H2 Cromwell's Bridge Lancs
3 C1 Cromwell's Castle EH IoS
146 D4 Crondon Park Golf Club Essex
322 e8 Cronk ny Merrieu hill fort IoM
322 f4 Cronk Sumark hill fort IoM
394 D2 Crook Golf Club Dur
405 G6 Crook Hall Dur
330 B5 Crookhill Park Municipal golf course Donc
466 D2 Crookston castle HS C Glas
188 C6 Croome Park NT Worcs
327 H2 Crosland Heath Golf Club Kirk
450 A1 Crossburn Caravan Park Border
467 E2 Crosshill railway station C Glas
380 B3 Cross Keys Temperance Inn NT Cumb
450 B1 Cross Kirk (ruin) HS Border
432 C3 Crossraguel Abbey NTS S Ayrs
260 C5 Crossways Caravan & Camping Park Norfk
119 G2 Crouch Hill railway station Gt Lon
78 C4 Crowborough Beacon Golf Club E Susx

374 D3 Crows Nest Caravan Park N York
484 D6 Crow Wood Golf Club N Lans
273 G2 Croxden Abbey EH Staffs
323 H6 Croxteth Hall Country Park Lpool
432 C2 Croy Brae (Electric Brae) S Ayrs
507 J4 Cruachan Power Station Ag & B
360 D4 Cruckley Animal Farm E R Yk
561 G2 Cruden Bay Golf Club Abers
158 D5 Craig Hywel hill fort Powys
602 E6 Cubbie Roo's Castle HS Ork
328 C2 Cuckoos Nest railway station Kirk
95 E2 Cuddington Golf Club Gt Lon
149 E1 Cudmore Grove Country Park Essex
339 E5 Cuerden Valley Country Park Lancs
545 H5 Cuillin Hills Highld
484 C2 Culcreuch Country Park Stirlg
569 J2 Cullen Bay Holiday Park Moray
569 J2 Cullen Golf Club Moray
556 D4 Cullerlie Stone Circle HS Abers
566 C8 Culloden Battlefield NTS Highld
566 D7 Culloden Viaduct Highld
42 D6 Cullompton service area Devon
486 C2 Culross Abbey HS Fife
486 C2 Culross Palace NTS Fife
555 F3 Culsh Earth House HS Abers
102 C5 Culver Hole Swans
432 B2 Culzean Castle & Country Park NTS S Ayrs
87 E2 Cumberwell Park golf course Wilts
377 G4 Cumbrian Mountains Cumb
465 H5 Cunningham N Ayrs
496 D5 Cunninghame Graham Memorial NTS Stirlg
502 B2 Cupar Golf Club Fife
322 H4 Curraghs Wildlife Park IoM
487 G6 Currichill railway station C Edin
283 E3 Cwm Cadnant Valley campsite Gwynd
132 D5 Cwmcarn Forest Drive Caerph
132 D6 Cwmcarn Forest Drive Campsite Caerph
126 A2 Cwm Deri vineyard Pembks
185 E4 Cwmmau Farmhouse NT Herefs
131 E2 Cwm Porth Caves Powys
179 H2 Cwmtydu Smugglers Cove Cerdgn
265 G6 Cymer Abbey CADW Gwynd
156 C1 Cynghordy railway station Carmth
156 C1 Cynghordy Viaduct Carmth
154 A4 Cynwyl Elfed railway station Carmth

D

361 E5 Dacre Lakeside Park E R Yk
120 C3 Dagenham Dock railway station Gt Lon
20 A4 Dainton Park Golf Club Devon
7 G2 Dairyland Farm World Cnwll
326 D4 Daisy Nook Country Park Oldham
413 F2 Dalbeattie Golf Club D & G
373 G2 Dalby Forest Drive N York
373 G2 Dalby Forest visitor centre N York
377 H4 Dalegarth railway station Cumb
79 F3 Dale Hill Hotel & Golf Club E Susx
390 D4 Dalemain House Cumb
465 F5 Dalgarven Mill museum N Ayrs
487 F3 Dalgety Bay railway station Fife
488 C6 Dalkeith Park Country Park Mdloth
567 J5 Dallas Dhu Distillery HS Moray
507 K4 Dalmally golf course Ag & B
487 G4 Dalmeny House C Edin
445 E5 Dalmilling Golf Club S Ayrs
183 G3 Dalmore Camping & Caravanning Park Powys
525 G1 Dalmunzie Golf Club P & K
483 E4 Dalreoch railway station W Duns
400 C4 Dalton Hall Caravan Park Cumb
406 C5 Dalton Park Dur
535 H5 Dalwhinnie Distillery Highld
60 C2 Damage Cliffs NT Devon
214 B3 Damson Park Solhll
147 F3 Danbury Country Park Essex
400 D2 Dandy Dinmont Caravan & Camping Park Cumb
71 G2 Danebury Ring Hants
106 B4 Danescourt railway station Cardif
130 A1 Dan-yr-Ogof Caves Powys
213 H6 Danzey railway station Warwks
96 D2 Darenth Valley golf course Kent
274 B1 Darley Moor Derbys
395 G6 Darlington Golf Club Darltn
383 H2 Darlington Stadium Darltn
314 D2 Darnall railway station Sheff
120 D5 Dartford Golf Club Kent
13 F2 Dart Marina Devon
18 D2 Dartmoor Forest Devon
19 E2 Dartmoor National Park Devon
18 C6 Dartmoor Wildlife Park Devon
13 F2 Dartmouth Castle EH Devon
13 E2 Dartmouth Golf & Country Club Devon
237 F6 Dartmouth Golf Club Sandw
339 G5 Darwen Golf Club Bl w D
117 G4 Datchet Golf Club W & M
567 J6 Dava Way Moray
312 B3 Davenport Golf Club Ches
192 C2 Daventry & District Golf Club Nhants
192 C2 Daventry Country Park Nhants
467 G3 David Livingstone Centre NTS S Lans
22 D5 Davidson Moor airfield Cnwll
325 G5 Davyhulme Park Golf Club Traffd
449 G2 Dawyck Botanic Garden Border
445 F2 Dean Castle Country Park E Ayrs
325 F3 Dean Golf Club Bolton
74 B2 Dean Farm Golf Club Hants
135 E3 Dean Forest Railway Gloucs

122 B5 Deangate Ridge Golf Club Medway
326 C4 Dean Lane railway station Manch
71 F4 Dean railway station Wilts
324 C3 Dean Wood Golf Club Lancs
165 H3 Deddington Castle EH Oxon
242 C6 Deene Park Nhants
218 D1 Deenethorpe airfield Nhants
338 D3 Deepdale Lancs
292 C4 Deep Hayes Country Park Staffs
571 H6 Deer Abbey HS Abers
13 F3 Deer Park Caravan and Camping Devon
486 D6 Deer Park Golf & Country Club W Loth
557 F4 Deeside Golf Club C Aber
308 D6 Deeside Leisure Centre (Ice Hockey) Flints
268 C1 Deeside railway station Denbgs
308 C6 Deeside Stadium Flints
305 G4 Deganwy railway station Conwy
169 F2 De Grey Mausoleum EH Beds
35 e1 Dehus Dolmen Guern
342 C6 Deighton railway station Kirk
510 D5 Deil's Caldron (Waterfall) P & K
310 B5 Delamere Forest Golf Club Ches
310 A5 Delamere Forest Park Ches
193 G3 Delapre Golf Centre Nhants
94 D4 Denbies vineyard Surrey
287 F1 Denbigh Castle CADW Denbgs
287 F1 Denbigh Friary CADW Denbgs
287 E1 Denbigh Golf Club Denbgs
294 D5 Denby Potteries Derbys
118 A2 Denham Golf Club Bucks
53 G3 Denman's Garden W Susx
119 G4 Denmark Hill railway station Gt Lon
14 C4 Dennis Cove Camping Cnwll
514 C3 Dens Park C Dund
308 C6 Denton Golf Club Tamesd
367 F2 Dent railway station Cumb
322 d9 Derby Fort IoM
201 G6 Derby Road railway station Suffk
275 G3 Derby service area Derbys
275 F2 Derbyshire County Cricket Ground C Derb
254 C5 Dereham Golf Club Norfk
254 D5 Dereham windmill Norfk
326 D3 Derker railway station Oldham
153 H6 Derllys Court Golf Club Carmth
287 F4 Derwen Cross CADW Denbgs
404 D3 Derwentcote Steel Furnace Dur
388 A4 Derwent Park Cumb
275 F2 Derwent Valley Mills (UNESCO) C Derb
294 C3 Derwent Valley Mills (UNESCO) Derbys
294 C5 Derwent Valley Mills (UNESCO) Derbys
405 E2 Derwent Walk Country Park Gatesd
389 G5 Derwent Water Cumb
569 J3 Deskford Church HS Moray
365 G6 Detron Gate Farm campsite Lancs
263 E5 Deucoch Touring Park Gwynd
278 C2 De Vere Belton Woods Hotel golf course Lincs
289 G4 De Vere Carden Park Hotel Golf Resort & Spa Ches
250 A4 De Vere Dunston Hall Hotel golf course Norfk
337 F2 De Vere Herons Reach golf course Bpool
312 A4 De Vere Mottram Hall golf course Ches
404 A3 De Vere Slaley Hall Hotel Golf Resort & Spa Nthumb
356 D1 Devil's Arrows N York
55 G2 Devil's Dyke NT W Susx
4 D6 Devil's Frying Pan Cnwll
21 E1 Devon Cliffs Holiday Park Devon
42 B6 Devon Railway Centre Devon
57 G5 Devonshire Park E Susx
7 E6 Devoran & Perran (UNESCO) Cnwll
524 B6 Dewars P & K
18 B5 Dewerstone NT Devon
78 D4 Dewlands Manor golf course E Susx
342 D6 Dewsbury District Golf Club Kirk
109 E2 Dewstow Golf Club Mons
140 B1 Diamond Farm Caravan & Camping Park Oxon
115 E1 Didcot Parkway railway station Oxon
311 G1 Didsbury Golf Club Manch
27 F4 Digby & Sowton railway station Devon
42 D6 Diggerland Devon
405 F5 Diggerland Dur
122 B6 Diggerland Medway
292 C6 Dilhorne Park railway station Staffs
36 A3 Dimbola Lodge museum IoW
288 B6 Dinas Bran Castle Denbgs
106 C5 Dinas Powis Golf Club V Glam
105 G1 Dinas Rhondda railway station Rhondd
282 C1 Din Dryfol CADW IoA
155 F5 Dinefwr Park NT Carmth
106 C5 Dingle Road railway station V Glam
282 D4 Dinlle Caravan Park Gwynd
303 G3 Din Lligwy CADW IoA
11 H2 Dinosaur Park Devon
255 F4 Dinosaur Norfk
37 G3 Dinosaur Isle visitor centre IoW
384 A2 Dinsdale railway station Darltn
384 A2 Dinsdale Spa Golf Club Darltn
69 H3 Dinton Park NT Wilts
116 C5 Dinton Pastures Country Park Wokham
489 G3 Dirleton Castle & Gardens HS E Loth
514 C4 Discovery Point & Verdant Works C Dund
370 D5 Dishforth airfield N York
312 C2 Disley Golf Club Ches
183 G3 Disserth Caravan & Camping Park Powys
225 F4 Diss Golf Club Norfk
55 H2 Ditchling Beacon viewpoint E Susx
366 B5 Docker Park Farm Lancs
11 E2 Dockyard railway station C Plym
38 B3 Docton Mill Gardens Devon
500 D5 Dogton Stone HS Fife

155 G1 Dolaucothi Gold Mines roman site NT Carmth
284 C3 Dolbadarn Castle CADW Gwynd
10 C1 Dolbeare Caravan and Camping Park Cnwll
153 F2 Dolbryn Camping & Caravanning Carmth
58 D3 Doleham railway station E Susx
232 C5 Dolforwyn Castle CADW Powys
265 G6 Dolgellau Golf Club Gwynd
229 F4 Dolgoch Falls Gwynd
499 F5 Dollar Glen NTS Clacks
499 F5 Dollar Golf Club Clacks
99 E2 Dolphin Sailing Barge Museum Kent
285 F4 Dolwyddelan Castle CADW Conwy
131 H2 Dol-y-gaer railway station Powys
546 D4 Donald Murchison's Monument Highld
330 D5 Doncaster Golf Club Donc
331 E2 Doncaster North service area Donc
330 C4 Doncaster racecourse Donc
330 D4 Doncaster Town Moor Golf Club Donc
64 A3 Doniford Halt railway station Somset
239 G2 Donington Le Heath Leics
275 G4 Donington Park Leics
275 G4 Donington Park Farmhouse Hotel Leics
275 H4 Donington Park service area Leics
114 D6 Donnington Castle EH W Berk
114 D5 Donnington Valley golf course W Berk
314 D2 Don Valley Stadium Sheff
527 G3 Doocot NTS Angus
490 C4 Doonhill Homestead HS E Loth
433 F2 Doon Valley golf course E Ayrs
314 C3 Dore & Totley Golf Club Sheff
94 D4 Dorking Deepdene railway station Surrey
94 D5 Dorking Golf Club Surrey
94 D5 Dorking West railway station Surrey
77 G1 Dormans railway station Surrey
20 A4 Dornafield campsite Devon
117 F4 Dorney Court Bucks
577 G7 Dornoch Firth Caravan Park Highld
271 H2 Dorothy Clive Garden Staffs
48 D2 Dorset Heavy Horse Centre Dorset
8 D3 Doubletrees Farm campsite Cnwll
322 f7 Douglas Golf Club IoM
484 B5 Douglas Park Golf Club E Duns
448 A3 Douglas Water Golf Club S Lans
498 A4 Doune Castle HS Stirlg
528 D1 Dovecot Caravan Park Abers
83 F2 Dover Castle EH Kent
83 F2 Dover Priory railway station Kent
229 F5 Dovey Junction railway station Powys
134 D1 Doward Park Camp Site Herefs
272 D2 Down Banks NT Staffs
26 C3 Downes Crediton Golf Club Devon
514 B3 Downfield Golf Club C Dund
222 C5 Downfield windmill Cambs
96 B2 Down House EH Gt Lon
92 D1 Downshire Golf Complex Br For
86 B4 Downside Abbey Somset
55 F1 Downs Link cycle route W Susx
215 H6 Draycote Water Country Park Warwks
118 D3 Drayton Green railway station Gt Lon
238 B4 Drayton Manor Staffs
238 B4 Drayton Park Golf Club Staffs
140 A6 Drayton Park golf course Oxon
360 C3 Driffield Golf Club E R Yk
360 C3 Driffield showground E R Yk
94 B3 Drift Golf Club Surrey
188 D2 Droitwich Boat Centre Worcs
188 D2 Droitwich Golf & Country Club Worcs
410 B3 Druchtag Motte HS D & G
237 G4 Druids Heath Golf Club Wsall
369 G4 Druid's Temple N York
100 B3 Druidstone Park Kent
556 D4 Druim Castle NTS Abers
423 E6 Drumcoltran Tower NTS D & G
549 J4 Drum Farm Highld
482 C4 Drumfrochar railway station Inver
435 H5 Drumlanrig Castle D & G
488 D5 Drum Mohr Caravan Park E Loth
511 E6 Drummond Castle Gardens P & K
535 H7 Drumochter Summit Highld
514 C5 Drumoig Hotel & golf course Fife
566 C8 Drumossie Muir Highld
467 H1 Drumpellier Country Park N Lans
467 H1 Drumpellier Golf Club N Lans
410 D2 Drumpamin Farm Camping & Touring Site D & G
527 E4 Drumshademuir Caravan Park Angus
410 C4 Drumtrodden Cup & Ring HS D & G
410 C4 Drumtrodden Standing Stones HS D & G
524 F7 Drunkeld Cathedral HS P & K
443 H5 Druridge Bay Country Park Nthumb
57 E4 Drusillas Park E Susx
388 A5 Dryburgh Abbey HS Border
155 E5 Dryslwyn Castle CADW Carmth
506 B2 Duart Castle Ag & B
140 D1 Duck Decoy NT Bucks
194 D4 Duck End Post Mill Beds
213 G2 Duddeston railway station Birm
488 B5 Duddingston Golf Club C Edin
577 K3 Dudgeon Park Highld
212 D1 Dudley Castle Dudley
213 E2 Dudley Golf Club Sandw
211 G2 Dudmaston NT Shrops
49 E5 Dudmoor Farm Golf Course Dorset
49 E5 Dudsbury Golf Club Dorset
570 B3 Duff House HS Abers
570 B3 Duff House Royal golf course Abers
568 E8 Dufftown Golf Club Moray
566 D4 Duffus Castle HS Moray
502 D2 Duke's Course golf course Fife

467 F1 Duke Street railway station
C Glas
327 E5 Dukinfield Golf Club Tamesd
485 E4 Dullatur Golf Club N Lans
119 G5 Dulwich & Sydenham Hill
Golf Club Gt Lon
483 E5 Dumbarton Castle HS W Duns
483 E4 Dumbarton Central railway
station W Duns
483 F4 Dumbarton East railway
station W Duns
483 E4 Dumbarton Golf Club W Duns
423 G4 Dumfries & Galloway Golf
Club D & G
423 G4 Dumfries Ice Bowl D & G
91 F5 Dummer Golf Club Hants
101 G2 Dumpton Park railway
station Kent
492 D6 Dunadd Fort HS Ag & B
481 E1 Dunans Castle Ag & B
433 F3 Dunaskin museum E Ayrs
456 D5 Dunaverty Golf Club Ag & B
490 C4 Dunbar Golf Club E Loth
544 E2 Dun Beag HS Highld
498 B4 Dunblane New Golf Club
Stirlg
598 D6 Dun Carloway Broch HS
W Isls
492 D5 Dunchraigaig Cairn HS
Ag & B
372 B3 Duncombe Park N York
546 E3 Duncraig railway station
Highld
53 G1 Duncton Hill viewpoint
W Susx
86 D2 Dundas Aqueduct BaNES
487 F4 Dundas Parks Golf Club
C Edin
514 B4 Dundee airport C Dund
514 B3 Dundee Ice Arena C Dund
445 E3 Dundonald Castle HS S Ayrs
585 J8 Dun Dornaigil Broch HS
Highld
412 G5 Dundrennan Abbey HS D & G
524 D4 Dunfallandy Stone HS P & K
487 E2 Dunfermline Golf Club Fife
487 E2 Dunfermline Town railway
station Fife
81 G6 Dungeness Kent
81 G6 Dungeness Old Lighthouse
Kent
312 C4 Dunge Valley Gardens Ches
491 E5 Dunglass Collegiate Church
HS Border
311 F2 Dunham Forest Golf &
Country Club Traffd
311 E2 Dunham Massey NT Traffd
524 F7 Dunkeld & Birnam Golf Club
P & K
512 B1 Dunkeld Town NTS P & K
28 B1 Dunkeswell airfield Devon
363 E6 Dunnerholme Golf Club
Cumb
559 E4 Dunnideer Fort Abers
501 E6 Dunnikier Park Golf Club Fife
499 F2 Dunning Golf Club P & K
541 G3 Dunnottar Casle Abers
506 E3 Dunollie Castle Ag & B
576 C2 Dunroamin Caravan and
Camping Park Highld
577 J3 Dunrobin Castle Highld
577 H3 Dunrobin Castle railway
station Highld
325 G2 Dunscar Golf Club Bolton
473 H4 Duns Golf Club Border
169 E5 Dunstable Downs Golf Club
Beds
506 E3 Dunstaffnage Castle HS
Ag & B
455 G5 Dunstanburgh Castle Golf
Club Nthumb
455 H5 Dunstanburgh Castle NT
Nthumb
63 F3 Dunster Castle NT Somset
63 F3 Dunster railway station
Somset
63 F3 Dunster Water Mill NT
Somset
542 C7 Dunvegan Castle Highld
71 G5 Dunwood Manor Golf Club
Hants
17 E5 Dupath Well House EH Cnwll
33 E3 Durdle Door Dorset
395 F1 Durham Castle & Cathedral
(UNESCO) Dur
395 F2 Durham City Golf Club Dur
395 G2 Durham service area Dur
384 B2 Durham Tees Valley airport
S on T
34 B5 Durlston Country Park
Dorset
579 J2 Durness Golf Club Highld
35 i6 Durrell Wildlife Conservation
Trust Jersey
324 D1 Duxbury Jubilee Park Golf
Club Lancs
197 G5 Duxford airfield Cambs
197 G5 Duxford Chapel EH Cambs
197 G5 Duxford Imperial War
(Aircraft) museum Cambs
600 C4 Dwarfie Stane HS Ork
557 F1 Dyce Symbol Stones HS
C Aber
264 D5 Dyffryn Ardudwy Burial
Chamber CADW Gwynd
264 D5 Dyffryn Ardudwy railway
station Gwynd
106 A5 Dyffryn Gardens V Glam
229 F5 Dyfi Furnace CADW Cerdgn
55 G3 Dyke Golf Club Br & H
81 H4 Dymchurch Martello Tower
EH Kent
161 F3 Dymock Grange Golf Club
Gloucs
144 B5 Dyrham Park Country Club
golf course Herts
110 C4 Dyrham Park NT S Glos

E

487 G4 Eagle Rock HS C Edin
384 C2 Eaglescliffe & District Golf
Club S on T
252 B4 Eagles Golf Centre Norfk
118 D3 Ealing Golf Club Gt Lon
600 E4 Earl's Bu and Church HS Ork
119 F4 Earls Court Gt Lon
602 B6 Earl's Palace HS Ork
213 G5 Earlswood (West Midlands)
railway station Warwks
103 H3 Earlswood golf course Neath
315 E1 Earth Arena Rothm
330 B5 Earth Centre Donc
579 J4 Eas a' Chual Aluinn
(Waterfall) Highld
383 E4 Easby Abbey N York
60 C2 Easby Abbey N York
504 E2 Eas Fors (Waterfall) Ag & B
371 G6 Easingwold Golf Club N York
527 E5 Eassie Sculptured Stone HS
Angus
557 H1 East Aberdeenshire Golf
Centre Abers
92 D2 East Berkshire Golf Club
Wokham
342 C4 East Bierley Golf Club Kirk
57 F5 Eastbourne Downs Golf Club
E Susx

529 F1 East Bowstrips Caravan
Park Abers
120 D2 Eastbrookend Country Park
Gt Lon
218 A2 East Carlton Country Park
Nhants
33 G3 East Creech Camping &
Caravan Park Dorset
8 D3 East Crinnis Camping &
Caravan Park Cnwll
21 F1 East Devon Golf Club Devon
487 F2 East End Park Fife
559 G5 Easter Aquhorthies Stone
Circle HS Abers
468 B1 Easter Moffat Golf Club
N Lans
488 B5 Easter Road C Edin
576 C8 Easter Ross Highld
32 A4 East Fleet Farm Touring
Park Dorset
309 E3 Eastham Country Park Wirral
337 G4 Eastham Hall Caravan Site
Wirral
309 E3 Eastham Lodge Golf Club
Wirral
308 D4 Eastham Rake railway
station Wirral
171 E5 East Herts Golf Club Herts
72 D6 East Horton Golf Centre
Hants
467 F3 East Kilbride Golf Club S Lans
340 B6 East Lancashire Railway
Lancs
275 H4 East Midlands airport Leics
52 B5 Eastney Beam Engine House
museum C Port
161 G2 Eastnor Castle Herefs
243 G5 East of England
showground C Pete
202 B3 Easton Farm Park Suffk
466 D4 East Renfrewshire Golf Club
E Rens
442 A1 East Riddlesden Hall NT Brad
86 B6 East Somerset Railway
Somset
78 B6 East Sussex National Golf
Resort & Spa E Susx
466 D4 Eastwood Golf Club E Rens
289 G2 Eaton Golf Club Ches
249 H3 Eaton Golf Club Norfk
121 F5 Ebbsfleet International
railway station Kent
143 F6 Ebury Way cycle route Herts
294 B4 Ecclesbourne Valley Railway
Derbys
309 G1 Eccleston Park Golf Club
St Hel
247 G3 Ecotech Discovery Centre
Norfk
603 H5 Eday Ork
603 H5 Eday airport Ork
55 F2 Edburton Hill viewpoint
W Susx
96 B5 Edenbridge railway station
Kent
96 B5 Edenbridge Town railway
station Kent
373 E5 Eden Camp museum N York
401 E3 Eden golf course Cumb
8 C3 Eden Project Cnwll
391 G5 Eden Valley cycle route
Cumb
380 C4 Eden Valley Railway Cumb
160 C1 Edgar Street Herefs
213 G3 Edgbaston Cricket Ground
Birm
213 G3 Edgbaston Golf Club Birm
191 F5 Edgehill battlefield Warwks
191 G5 Edgehill Country Park
Warwks
312 A2 Edgeley Park Stockp
488 B5 Edinburgh Castle HS C Edin
487 G5 Edinburgh Park railway
station C Edin
473 H2 Edin's Hall Broch HS Border
443 E3 Edlingham Castle EH Nthumb
144 D6 Edmonton Green railway
station Gt Lon
22 D3 Edmore Tourist Park Cnwll
524 E4 Edradour Distillery P & K
474 B3 Edrom Church HS Border
187 F3 Edvin Loach Old Church EH
Herefs
276 D2 Edwalton Municipal golf
course Notts
540 B6 Edzell airfield (dis) Abers
540 A6 Edzell Castle & Garden HS
Angus
540 A6 Edzell Golf Club Angus
94 C4 Effingham Golf Club Surrey
94 C4 Effingham Junction railway
station Surrey
77 F2 Effingham Park Golf Club
W Susx
382 C1 Egglestone Abbey EH Dur
444 D1 Eglinton Castle N Ayrs
444 D1 Eglinton Country Park N Ayrs
386 D3 Egton railway station N York
530 E5 Eigg Highld
546 F4 Eilean Donan Highld
597 J1 Eilean Leodhais W Isls
264 C2 Eisteddfa campsite Gwynd
513 E5 Elcho Castle HS P & K
466 C2 Elderslie Golf Club Rens
218 B3 Eleanor Cross EH Nhants
284 C2 Electric Mountain Gwynd
406 B5 Elemore golf course Sundld
18 B6 Elfordleigh Hotel Golf &
Country Club Devon
188 B3 Elgar museum Worcs
568 C3 Elgin Golf Club Moray
100 C6 Elham Valley vineyard Kent
288 B6 Eliseg's Pillar CADW Denbgs
35 h7 Elizabeth Castle Jersey
342 A5 Elland Golf Club Calder
343 E3 Elland Road Leeds
142 A3 Ellesborough Golf Club Bucks
325 H4 Ellesmere Golf Club Salfd
309 E4 Ellesmere Port Golf Centre
Ches
53 E5 Ellscott Park campsite
W Susx
97 H1 Elmhaven Marina Medway
501 G2 Elmwood golf course Fife
329 F5 Elsecar Workshops Rothm
333 E2 Elsham Golf Club N Linc
144 A5 Elstree Golf & Country Club
Herts
120 B5 Eltham Place Gt Lon
120 B5 Eltham Warren Golf Club
Gt Lon
277 G1 Elton & Orston railway
station Notts
243 G6 Elton Furze Golf Club Cambs
243 F6 Elton Hall Cambs
222 A4 Ely City Golf Club Cambs
354 D4 Embsay & Bolton Abbey
Steam Railway N York
194 B4 Emberton Country Park
M Keyn
455 G5 Embleton & Newton Links
NT Nthumb
119 G2 Emirates Stadium Gt Lon
96 C4 Emmetts Garden NT Kent
240 B5 Enderby golf course Leics
144 D5 Enfield Chase railway
station Gt Lon
144 D5 Enfield Golf Club Gt Lon
209 H3 Engine & Tender Inn
campsite Shrops

64 D4 Enmore Park Golf Club
Somset
340 A6 Entwistle railway station
Bl w D
212 B2 Enville Golf Club Staffs
145 F5 Epping Forest Essex
145 H4 Epping Ongar Railway Essex
95 E3 Epsom Downs railway
station Surrey
95 E3 Epsom Golf Club Surrey
95 E3 Epsom racecourse Surrey
331 G4 Epworth Old Rectory N Linc
288 D5 Erddig NT Wrexhm
276 A2 Erewash Valley golf course
Derbys
78 C3 Eridge railway station E Susx
87 H4 Erlestoke Sands golf course
Wilts
483 F5 Erskine Golf Club Rens
156 B3 Erwlon Caravan & Camping
Park Carmth
28 A3 Escot Gardens Devon
425 G1 Eskdale D & G
377 E5 Eskdale Green railway
station Cumb
484 B5 Esporta Dougalston Golf
Club E Duns
453 H2 Etal Castle EH Nthumb
82 C2 Etchinghill golf course Kent
312 C1 Etherow Country Park
Stockp
450 D5 Ettrick Forest Border
132 C2 Eugene Cross Park Blae G
60 C3 Europa Caravan & Camping
Park Powys
339 E6 Euxton Balshaw Lane
railway station Lancs
189 E5 Evesham Golf Club Worcs
95 E2 Ewell West railway station
Surrey
327 E5 Ewen Fields Tamesd
105 E4 Ewenny Abbey CADW
Brdgnd
286 D5 Ewe-phoria Sheepdog
Centre Conwy
425 H2 Ewes Water Caravan &
Camping Park D & G
288 C1 Ewloe Castle CADW Flints
339 G4 Ewood Park Bl w D
50 D4 Exbury Gardens Hants
27 F5 Exeter Golf & Country Club
Devon
27 E6 Exeter racecourse Devon
27 E4 Exeter St Davids railway
station Devon
27 E4 Exeter St Thomas railway
station Devon
27 F4 Exeter service area Devon
63 E5 Exe Valley Caravan site
Somset
62 A3 Exmoor Forest Somset
62 B4 Exmoor National Park
61 G3 Exmoor Zoological Park
27 F5 Exton railway station Devon
313 H4 Eyam Hall Derbys
314 A4 Eyam Moor Derbys
313 H4 Eyam museum Derbys
475 E2 Eyemouth Golf Club Border
96 D1 Eynsford Castle EH Kent

F

533 L2 Faichemard Farm Camping
& Caravan Site Highld
229 E2 Fairbourne & Barmouth
Steam Railway Gwynd
326 D5 Fairfield Golf & Sailing Club
Tamesd
138 A5 Fairford airshow venue
Gloucs
250 D2 Fairhaven Garden Norfk
337 G4 Fairhaven Golf Club Lancs
604 b3 Fair Isle airport Shet
604 b3 Fair Isle NTS Shet
170 C5 Fairlands Valley Country
Park Herts
103 E3 Fairwood Park Golf Club
Swans
285 H4 Fairy Glen Conwy
260 B5 Fakenham Camp Site Norfk
254 B2 Fakenham Golf Club Norfk
254 B2 Fakenham racecourse Norfk
485 H3 Falkirk Golf Club Falk
486 A4 Falkirk High railway station
Falk
486 B3 Falkirk Stadium Falk
485 H3 Falkirk Tryst Golf Club Falk
485 H4 Falkirk Wheel Falk
501 E3 Falkland Golf Club Fife
501 E3 Falkland Palace NTS Fife
378 C5 Fallbarrow Park campsite
Cumb
448 A1 Falls of Clyde S Lans
507 J4 Falls of Cruachan railway
station Ag & B
549 H4 Falls of Divach Highld
509 J3 Falls of Dochart Stirlg
508 D5 Falls of Falloch Stirlg
547 J4 Falls of Glomach NTS Highld
497 E3 Falls of Leny Stirlg
509 H2 Falls of Lochay Stirlg
574 E8 Falls of Measach Highld
576 C4 Falls of Shin Highld
511 E5 Falls of Turret P & K
29 H2 Falmouth Golf Club Cnwll
147 H5 Fambridge railway station
Essex
358 D4 Fangfoss Park campsite
E R Yk
321 G6 Fantasy Island Lincs
549 J5 Farigaig visitor centre Highld
95 H2 Farleigh Court Golf Club
Surrey
87 E3 Farleigh Hungerford Castle
EH Somset
72 B4 Farley Mount Country Park
Hants
69 G3 Farmer Giles Farmstead Wilts
93 E4 Farnborough airshow
venue Hants
93 E3 Farnborough North railway
station Hants
455 H2 Farne Islands Nthumb
93 E5 Farnham Golf Club Surrey
117 G3 Farnham Park Golf Club
Bucks
92 D5 Farnham Park golf course
Surrey
121 E6 Farningham Road railway
station Kent
86 A4 Farrington Golf & Country
Club Somset
192 D3 Farthingstone Hotel golf
course Nhants
524 D3 Faskally Caravan Park P & K
524 D3 Faskally Wayside Centre
P & K
540 B4 Fasque Abers
491 E6 Fast Castle Border
34 c3 Fauxquets Valley Farm
campsite Guern
99 F3 Faversham Golf Club Kent
323 E3 Fazakerley railway station
Lpool
577 H8 Fearn railway station Highld
261 G4 Felbrigg Hall NT Norfk
179 E3 Felinwynt Rainforest &
Butterfly Centre Cerdgn

177 F2 Felixstowe Ferry Golf Club
Suffk
365 E2 Fell Foot Park NT Cumb
158 D5 Felsted vineyard Essex
223 E2 Feltwell Golf Club Norfk
244 B2 Fenland City Farm Lincs
197 G3 Fenner's Cambs
191 G4 Fenny Marina Warwks
119 F2 Fenton House NT Gt Lon
466 C3 Fereneze Golf Club E Rens
218 D2 Fermyn Woods Country
Park Nhants
48 D4 Ferndown Forest Golf Club
Dorset
48 D5 Ferndown Golf Club Dorset
270 B3 Fernwood Caravan Park
Shrops
347 E4 Ferriby railway station
Highld
344 B5 Ferrybridge service area
Wakefd
576 C2 Ferrycroft Countryside
Centre Highld
243 G5 Ferry Meadows Country
Park C Pete
243 H5 Ferry Meadows railway
station C Pete
609 J6 Fetlar Shet
265 E3 Ffestiniog Golf Club Gwynd
265 F1 Ffestiniog Railway Gwynd
184 B4 Fforest Fields Caravan &
Camping Park Powys
47 E2 Fiddleford Manor EH Dorset
310 B2 Fiddlers Ferry Yacht Haven
Warrtn
295 G2 Field Mill Notts
501 E2 Fife Animal Park Fife
501 E6 Fife Ice Arena Fife
70 D3 Figsbury Ring NT Wilts
375 E3 Filey Brigg Touring Caravan
& Country Park N York
375 E4 Filey Golf Club N York
109 H4 Filton Abbey Wood railway
station S Glos
109 G3 Filton airfield S Glos
109 G4 Filton golf course S Glos
110 A3 Filton Link cycle route S Glos
405 G5 Finchale Priory EH Dur
79 G2 Finchcocks Kent
25 F4 Finch Foundry NT Devon
119 E1 Finchley Golf Club Gt Lon
567 J4 Findhorn Bay Holiday Park
Hants
550 E4 Findhorn Viaduct Highld
569 J2 Findlater Castle Abers
504 C3 Fingal's Cave Ag & B
369 G1 Finghall railway station
N York
26 C4 Fingle Glen Golf Hotel Devon
90 B5 Finkley Down Farm Park
Hants
478 B8 Finlaggan Ag & B
483 E5 Finlaystone Country Estate
Inver
484 B6 Firhill C Glas
56 D3 Firle Place E Susx
468 B3 Fir Park N Lans
486 A3 Firs Park Falk
375 F5 Fir Tree Caravan Park E R Yk
53 E4 Fishbourne Roman Palace
EH W Susx
377 F4 Fisherground Farm
campsite Cumb
503 F4 Fisheries museum Fife
75 H4 Fishers Farm Park W Susx
151 G2 Fishguard Bay Caravan &
Camping Park Pembks
151 G2 Fishguard Harbour railway
station Pembks
339 E4 Fishwick Hall Golf Club Lancs
49 E6 Fitness First Stadium at
Dean Court Bmouth
148 B2 Five Lakes Resort golf
course Essex
213 G2 Five Ways railway station
Birm
117 E1 Flackwell Heath Golf Club
Bucks
244 B5 Flag Fen Bronze Age Centre
C Pete
4 C3 Flambards Cnwll
375 H5 Flamborough Head E R Yk
375 H5 Flamborough Head Golf
Club E R Yk
373 E4 Flamingo Land N York
175 E3 Flatford Mill & Cottage NT
Suffk
67 F5 Fleet Air Arm museum
Somset
92 C3 Fleet service area Hants
350 D5 Fleetwood Golf Club Lancs
350 D5 Fleetwood Harbour Village
Marina Lancs
72 B6 Fleming Park Golf Club Hants
223 E5 Flempton Golf Club Suffk
12 A2 Flete Estate Devon
308 B5 Flint Castle CADW Flints
308 B5 Flint Golf Club Flints
292 C4 Flint Mill Staffs
172 D5 Flitch Way cycle route Essex
325 H6 Flixton Golf Club Traffd
452 D3 Floors Castle Border
376 C2 Florence Mine Cumb
374 D3 Flower of May Holiday Park
N York
152 D3 Foel Drygarn hill fort
Pembks
81 H2 Folkestone racecourse Kent
82 D3 Folkestone West railway
station Kent
72 B3 Folly Farm Touring Caravan
Park Hants
371 G6 Folly Garth campsite N York
69 E6 Fontmell & Melbury Downs
NT Dorset
53 G3 Fontwell Park racecourse
W Susx
147 E3 Ford County Cricket Ground
Essex
29 G1 Forde Abbey Dorset
100 C4 Fordwich Old Town Hall Kent
281 F6 Foremans Bridge Caravan
Park Lincs
202 D5 Forest Camping Suffk
49 E4 Forest Edge Touring Park
Dorset
28 B1 Forest Glade Holiday Park
Devon
240 A3 Forest Hill Golf Club Leics
134 D2 Forest Hills Golf Club Gloucs
355 H3 Forest Moor N York
135 E2 Forest of Dean Gloucs
134 D2 Forest of Dean Golf Club &
Bells Hotel Gloucs
358 A3 Forest of Galtres Golf Club
York
256 A1 Forest Park Caravan Site
Norfk
358 B3 Forest Park Golf Club N Linc
332 C3 Forest Pines Golf Club
N Linc
213 F6 Forge Mill Worcs
323 E3 Formby Golf Club Sefton
323 E3 Formby Hall Golf & Country
Club Sefton
323 E3 Formby Ladies Golf Club
Sefton
567 K5 Forres golf course Moray

147 H2 Forrester Park Golf Club
Essex
122 B6 Fort Amherst Medway
548 F8 Fort Augustus Golf Club
Highld
51 G4 Fort Brockhurst EH Hants
605 J2 Fort Charlotte HS Shet
52 B5 Fort Cumberland EH C Port
566 D5 Fort George HS Highld
34 b3 Fort Grey Shipwreck
museum Guern
485 E4 Forth & Clyde Canal cycle
route N Lans
498 C5 Forthbank Stadium Stirlg
566 C5 Fortrose Cathedral HS Highld
348 C4 Fort Paull museum E R Yk
35 i7 Fort Regent Jersey
566 C5 Fortrose & Rosemarkie Golf
Club Highld
533 H7 Fort William Golf Club Highld
144 D5 Forty Hall Gt Lon
86 C3 Fosse 2 cycle route BaNES
240 C4 Fosse 2 cycle route N Leic
137 H2 Fosse 2 cycle route Gloucs
240 C6 Fosse 2 cycle route Leics
164 D2 Fosse 2 cycle route Warwks
86 B4 Fosseway Golf Course BaNES
504 E5 Fossil Tree Ag & B
604 E2 Foula Shet
604 E2 Foula Shet
604 b7 Foula airfield Shet
474 D3 Foulden Tithe Barn HS
Border
123 G1 Foulness Essex
118 D4 Fountain Leisure Centre
Gt Lon
370 B6 Fountains Abbey NT N York
452 B3 Four Abbeys cycle route
Border
237 H5 Four Oaks railway station
Birm
184 D2 Four Stone Powys
197 H5 Fourwentways service area
Cambs
511 G5 Fowlis Wester Sculptured
Stone HS P & K
292 C6 Foxfield Light Railway Staffs
201 H6 Foxhall Stadium Suffk
93 H2 Foxhills Club & Resort golf
course Surrey
372 B3 Foxholme Caravan &
Camping Park N York
111 G6 Fox Talbot museum NT Wilts
202 B2 Framlingham Castle EH Suffk
4 D4 Franchis' Holiday Park Cnwll
213 E3 Frankley service area Worcs
193 F2 Franklin's Gardens Nhants
79 E2 Frant railway station E Susx
571 H2 Fraserburgh Castle
Lighthouse and Museum HS
Abers
571 J2 Fraserburgh Golf Club Abers
52 B4 Fratton Park C Port
36 B3 Freshwater Bay Golf Club
IoW
30 B5 Freshwater Beach Holiday
Park Dorset
139 G5 Frilford Heath Golf Club
Oxon
176 D3 Frinton Golf Club Essex
251 F4 Fritton Lake Countryworld
Norfk
136 A4 Frocester Tithe Barn Gloucs
309 H4 Frodsham Golf Club Ches
117 G4 Frogmore House W & M
86 D6 Frome & District
showground Somset
86 D5 Frome Golf Club Somset
91 F1 Frouds Bridge Marina W Berk
358 B5 Fulford Golf Club York
213 G5 Fulford Heath Golf Club
Worcs
342 D3 Fulneck Golf Club Leeds
118 C5 Fulwell Golf Club Gt Lon
377 H6 Furness Cumb
364 B5 Furness Abbey EH Cumb
364 A6 Furness Golf Club Cumb
27 E2 Furzdon House Devon
52 B2 Furzeley golf course Hants
49 H2 Furzey Gardens Hants
64 D5 Fyne Court NT Somset
201 G5 Fynn Valley Golf Club Suffk
559 F4 Fyvie Castle NTS Abers

G

22 B5 Gaia Energy Centre Cnwll
317 F1 Gainsborough Golf Club Lincs
317 F2 Gainsborough Lea Road
railway station Lincs
332 D1 Gainsthorpe Medieval
Village EH N Linc
562 D1 Gairloch Caravan & Camping
Park Highld
562 E1 Gairloch Golf Club Highld
562 E1 Gairloch Heritage Museum
Highld
399 F1 Gaisbank Caravan &
Camping Group D & G
451 F2 Galashiels Golf Club Border
378 C4 Galava Fort Roman Site EH
Cumb
353 C3 Gallaber Park campsite
N York
416 D3 Galloway D & G
417 F2 Galloway Deer Range D & G
420 C2 Galloway Forest Park D & G
412 C4 Galloway Wildlife
Conservation Park D & G
63 F3 Gallox Bridge EH Somset
13 F1 Galmpton Touring Park
Devon
328 B1 Galpharm Stadium Kirk
43 E4 Gamlins Farm Caravan Park
Somset
348 C3 Ganstead Park Golf Club
E R Yk
374 B4 Ganton Golf Club N York
304 C3 Gaol & Courthouse museum
IoA
143 G4 Gardens of the Rose Herts
404 D3 Garesfield Golf Club Gatesd
343 H2 Garforth Golf Club Leeds
568 E3 Garmouth & Kingston Golf
Club Moray
129 G2 Garnant Park Golf Club
Carmth
263 E3 Garn Boduan hill fort Gwynd
303 G4 Garnedd Touring Park IoS
3 d2 Garrison campsite IoS
3 c2 Garrison Walls EH IoS
483 H6 Garscadden railway station
C Glas
367 F1 Garstale railway station
Cumb
351 G6 Garstang Country Hotel &
Golf Club Lancs
497 F3 Gart Caravan Park Stirlg
499 E6 Gartmorn Dam Country Park
& Visitor Centre Clacks
241 G4 Gartree Ride cycle route
Leics
505 K8 Garvellachs Ag & B
104 D1 Garw Fechan Woodland
Park Brdgnd
131 F2 Garwnant Forest Centre
Rhondd
412 B3 Gatehouse Golf Club D & G
97 F3 Gate House Wood Touring
Park Kent

405 G2 Gateshead International Stadium Gatesd
293 G5 Gateway Caravan Park Derbys
83 F2 Gateway to the White Cliffs visitor centre NT Kent
324 C3 Gathurst Golf Club Wigan
311 G2 Gatley Golf Club Stockp
76 B2 Gatton Manor Hotel Golf & Country Club Surrey
77 E1 Gatwick airport W Susx
77 E1 Gatwick Airport railway station W Susx
188 D2 Gaudet Luce Golf Club Worcs
64 B5 Gaulden Manor Somset
340 C3 Gawthorpe Hall NT Lancs
213 G4 Gay Hill Golf Club Worcs
234 C2 Gay Meadow Shrops
244 D2 Gedney Hill golf course Lincs
2 C3 Geevor Tin Mines Cnwll
482 D4 Geilston Garden NTS Ag & B
326 B2 Gelder Wood Country Park Rochdl
155 F6 Gelli Aur Country Park Carmth
284 D5 Gelli lago NT Gwynd
417 F5 Gem Rock museum D & G
210 B5 Geological Trail Herefs
588 F5 Georgemas Junction railway station Highld
404 D1 George Stephenson's Birthplace NT Nthumb
405 H3 George Washington Golf & Country Club Sundld
34 c4 German Occupation museum Guern
34 C3 German Underground Hospital Guern
117 H2 Gerrards Cross Golf Club Bucks
354 A5 Ghyll Golf Club Lancs
542 D7 Giant Angus MacAskill museum Highld
46 C4 Giant's Head Caravan & Camping Park Dorset
405 E3 Gibside NT Gatesd
472 C1 Gifford Golf Club E Loth
199 C4 Gifford's Hall vineyard Suffk
326 B3 Gigg Lane Bury
74 A3 Gilbert White museum Hants
158 B5 Gilestone Camping & Caravan Park Powys
284 C2 Gilfach Ddu railway station Gwynd
132 C5 Gilfach Fargoed railway station Caerph
390 B4 Gill Head Farm Caravan & Camping Park Cumb
68 D4 Gillingham (Dorset) railway station Dorset
98 B1 Gillingham Golf Club Medway
484 B6 Gilshochill railway station C Glas
119 G5 Gipsy Hill railway station Gt Lon
197 F2 Girton Golf Club Cambs
432 A5 Girvan Golf Club S Ayrs
527 E5 Glamis Castle Angus
106 C6 Glamorganshire Golf Club V Glam
286 D5 Glan Ceirw Caravan Park Conwy
305 H4 Glan Conwy railway station Conwy
332 B2 Glanford Park N Linc
266 D3 Glanllyn Flag railway station Gwynd
266 D3 Glanllyn Lakeside Caravan & Camping Park Gwynd
232 C4 Glansevern Hall Gardens Powys
466 C1 Glasgow airport Rens
444 D2 Glasgow Golf Club S Ayrs
467 E1 Glasgow Queen Street railway station C Glas
351 F3 Glasson Basin Marina Lancs
67 E2 Glastonbury Tor NT Somset
364 C5 Gleaston Watermill Cumb
492 D5 Glebe Cairn HS Ag & B
528 D2 Glebe Park Angus
483 E5 Gleddoch Golf & Country Club Rens
549 K3 Glen Albyn or Glen Mòr Highld
485 G3 Glenbervie Golf Club Falk
554 C2 Glenbuchat Castle HS Abers
521 G4 Glencoe Folk museum Highld
521 K5 Glencoe Ski Centre Highld
521 G4 Glen Coe visitor centre NTS Highld
471 E2 Glencorse Golf Club Mdloth
506 E4 Glencruitten Golf Club Ag & B
480 D2 Glendaruel Caravan Park Ag & B
569 L7 Glendronach Distillery Abers
5 E3 Glendurgan Garden NT Cnwll
499 E2 Gleneagles golf course P & K
499 E2 Gleneagles railway station P & K
413 F2 Glenearly Caravan Park D & G
546 E6 Glenelg Brochs HS Highld
540 A5 Glenesk Caravan Park Abers
539 G4 Glenesk Folk museum Angus
568 C8 Glenfarclas Distillery Moray
568 E7 Glenfiddich Distillery Moray
343 H1 Glenfield Caravan Park Leeds
532 D6 Glenfinnan Monument NTS Highld
532 D6 Glenfinnan Viaduct Highld
532 D6 Glenfinnan Visitor Centre NTS Highld
533 K2 Glen Garry viewpoint Highld
490 A2 Glen Golf Club E Loth
240 D5 Glen Gorse Golf Club Leics
523 L5 Glengoulandie Deer Park P & K
568 D6 Glen Grant Distillery Moray
466 C2 Gleniffer Braes Country Park Rens
552 D3 Glenlivet Distillery Moray
415 G5 Glenluce Abbey HS D & G
415 H5 Glenluce Holiday Park D & G
322 C7 Glen Maye waterfall IoM
577 G7 Glenmorangie Distillery Highld
568 B3 Glen Moray Distillery Moray
551 H7 Glenmore Forest Park Highld
551 H7 Glenmore visitor centre Highld
15 F4 Glenmorris Park campsite Cnwll
521 G1 Glen Nevis Caravan & Camping Park Highld
565 J6 Glen Ord Distillery Highld
501 E5 Glenrothes Golf Club Fife
501 E5 Glenrothes with Thornton railway station Fife
537 H7 Glenshee Ski Area Abers
555 E5 Glen Tanar visitor centre Abers
420 B4 Glentrool Holiday Park D & G
420 B4 Glen Trool visitor centre D & G
134 C2 Glen Trothy Caravan & Camping Park Mons
511 F5 Glenturret Distillery P & K
415 G5 Glenwhan Gardens D & G
322 e4 Glen Wyllin campsite IoM

455 F3 Glororum Caravan Park Nthumb
327 G6 Glossop & District Golf Club Derbys
162 C5 Gloucestershire airport Gloucs
109 G4 Gloucestershire County Ground Bristl
163 F3 Gloucestershire Warwickshire Railway Gloucs
128 C3 Glyn Abbey Golf Club Carmth
56 D3 Glynde Place E Susx
207 F3 Glyndwr's Way Powys
129 F1 Glynhir Golf Club Carmth
120 C2 Glyn Hopkin Stadium Gt Lon
283 E4 Glynllifon Country Park Gwynd
131 E3 Glynneath Golf Club Powys
268 D2 Glyn Valley Tramway Museum Wrexhm
39 E4 Gnome Reserve and Wildflower Garden Devon
7 H2 Gnome World Caravan & Camping Site Cnwll
93 F3 Goal Farm Golf Club Surrey
460 D1 Goatfell Mountain NTS N Ayrs
99 F6 Godinton House Kent
4 B2 Godolphin House NT Cnwll
95 G4 Godstone Farm & Play Barn Surrey
95 H5 Godstone railway station Surrey
166 B6 Godwin's Ice Cream Farm Caravan Park Oxon
488 B4 Goldenacre C Edin
257 E4 Golden Beach Holiday Centre campsite Norfk
29 H4 Golden Cap Caravan Park Dorset
29 H4 Golden Cap NT Dorset
60 C3 Golden Coast Holiday Village Devon
291 H4 Golden Hill golf course C Stke
321 E2 Golden Sands Holiday Park Lincs
20 D2 Golden Sands Holiday Park campsite Devon
372 B4 Golden Square Touring Caravan Park N York
195 F4 Goldington Road Beds
502 D4 Golf House Club Fife
515 F3 Golf Street railway station Angus
577 H4 Goispie Golf Club Highld
323 G6 Golson Park Lpool
160 D6 Goodrich Castle Herefs
340 C4 Goodshaw Chapel EH Lancs
53 F3 Goodwood W Susx
53 F3 Goodwood House W Susx
53 F2 Goodwood racecourse W Susx
4 D4 Goonhilly Satellite Earth Station Cnwll
358 A2 Goosewood Caravan Park N York
109 F4 Gordano service area N Som
144 D5 Gordon Hill railway station Gt Lon
115 F3 Goring & Streatley Golf Club W Berk
115 G3 Goring & Streatley railway station Oxon
251 G4 Gorleston Golf Club Norfk
152 C4 Gors Fawr Pembks
531 J5 Gorten Sands Caravan Site Highld
173 F4 Gosfield Lake Golf Club Essex
431 E6 Gosforth Golf Club N u Ty
144 B2 Gosling Sports Park visitor centre Herts
51 H5 Gosport & Stokes Bay Golf Club Hants
343 E3 Cotts Park Golf Club Leeds
482 B4 Gourock Golf Club Inver
102 D3 Gower Swans
103 E2 Gower Golf Club Swans
102 D4 Gower visitor centre Swans
240 C4 Grace Road cricket ground C Leic
219 H6 Grafham Exhibition Centre Cambs
535 H6 Grampian Mountains Highld
275 G4 Grand Prix Collection museum Leics
488 A5 Grange Cricket Club C Edin
365 E4 Grange Fell Golf Club Cumb
486 B4 Grangemouth Golf Club Falk
365 F4 Grange-over-Sands Golf Club Cumb
332 B4 Grange Park Golf Club N Linc
329 F6 Grange Park Golf Club Rothm
324 B6 Grange Park Golf Club St Hel
577 H5 Grannie's Heilan' Hame Holiday Park Highld
278 B2 Grantham North service area Lincs
551 J4 Grantown on Spey Caravan Park Highld
551 J4 Grantown-on-Spey Golf Club Highld
568 C1 Grant Park Moray
566 B7 Grant Street Park Highld
235 G2 Granville Country Park Wrekin
315 E6 Grassmoor Golf Centre Derbys
515 G2 Grayfield Park Angus
365 E1 Graythwaite Hall Gardens Cumb
138 D6 Great Barn NT Oxon
237 F5 Great Barr Golf Club Wsall
216 C2 Great Central Cycle Ride Fosse 2 Braid Leics
192 D5 Great Central cycle route Nhants
240 C2 Great Central Railway Leics
276 C3 Great Central Railway (Nottingham) Notts
87 F2 Great Chalfield Manor NT Wilts
94 A1 Great Cockcrow Steam Centre Surrey
464 C3 Great Cumbrae Island N Ayrs
80 B4 Great Dixter E Susx
549 G6 Great Glen Way Highld
171 F6 Great Hadham Golf & Country Club Herts
340 A3 Great Harwood Golf Club Lancs
9 F3 Great Kellow Farm campsite Cnwll
378 A3 Great Langdale NT campsite Cumb
173 E6 Great Leighs racecourse Essex
325 G3 Great Lever & Farnworth Golf Club Bolton
305 G3 Great Orme Country Park Conwy
305 G3 Great Orme's Head viewpoint Conwy
128 C5 Great Pill Carmth
52 B4 Great Salterns Public Golf Course C Port
39 G4 Great Torrington Golf Club Devon
136 C2 Great Witcombe Roman Villa EH Gloucs
251 G2 Great Yarmouth & Caister Golf Club Norfk

251 G2 Great Yarmouth racecourse Norfk
356 C4 Great Yorkshire showground N York
365 E3 Greaves Farm Caravan Park Cumb
67 E1 Greenacres Camping Somset
264 C2 Greenacres campsite Gwynd
400 D2 Green Acres Caravan Park Worcs
61 G3 Greenacres Farm Touring Caravan Park Devon
467 E3 Greenbank Garden NTS E Rens
469 E2 Greenburn Golf Club W Loth
308 A4 Greenfield Valley Country Park Flints
340 B4 Green Haworth Golf Club Lancs
402 B1 Greenhead Roman Army museum Nthumb
71 F6 Greenhill Farm Camping & Caravan Park Wilts
166 A6 Greenhill Leisure Park campsite Oxon
313 G6 Greenhills Holiday Park Derbys
500 B4 Green Hotels golf course P & K
473 E6 Greenknowe Tower HS Border
308 D2 Green Lane railway station Wirral
133 E5 Greenmeadow Community Farm Torfn
133 F5 Green Meadow Golf & Country Club Mons
482 C4 Greenock Central railway station Inver
482 C4 Greenock Golf Club Inver
482 C4 Greenock Whinhill Golf Club Inver
50 B1 Green Pastures Farm campsite Hants
362 D5 Green Road railway station Cumb
329 E4 Greensprings Touring Park Barns
146 A4 Greensted Log Church Essex
78 D5 Greenviews Caravan Park E Susx
292 A3 Greenway Country Park Staffs
292 B4 Greenway Hall Golf Club Staffs
13 F2 Greenway NT Devon
451 G3 Greenyards Border
242 C2 Greetham Valley Golf Club Rutlnd
254 C4 Gressenhall museum Norfk
400 B1 Gretna Golf Club D & G
425 G6 Gretna service area D & G
589 H8 Grey Cairns Of Camster HS Highld
437 G2 Grey Mare's Tail (waterfall) NTS D & G
116 B3 Greys Court NT Oxon
169 F5 Griffin Golf Club Beds
118 D4 Griffin Park Gt Lon
223 G1 Grimes Graves EH Norfk
334 C2 Grimsby Docks railway station NE Lin
334 B3 Grimsby Golf Club NE Lin
334 C3 Grimsby Town railway station NE Lin
143 G6 Grims Dyke Golf Club Gt Lon
19 F1 Grimspound Medieval Village EH Devon
314 B4 Grindleford railway station Derbys
378 B6 Grizedale Forest Park Cumb
378 B6 Grizedale visitor centre Cumb
566 C5 Groam House museum Highld
283 E5 Groeslon Slateworks Gwynd
78 C2 Groombridge Place Gardens Kent
159 H5 Grosmont Castle CADW Mons
294 B1 Grouse & Claret campsite Derbys
387 F4 Grouse Hill Caravan Park N York
49 E6 Grove Farm Meadow Holiday Caravan Park Dorset
573 H5 Gruinard Bay Caravan Park Highld
117 G6 Guards Polo Club W & M
34 c3 Guernsey airport Guern
95 G5 Guildford Cricket Club Surrey
385 F2 Guisborough Forest visitor centre R & Cl
489 F3 Gullane Golf Club E Loth
294 B3 Gulliver's Kingdom Derbys
168 B2 Gulliver's Land M Keyn
256 B2 Gunton railway station Norfk
14 D3 Gunvenna Caravan Park Cnwll
240 D6 Guthlaxton Trail cycle route Leics
151 G2 Gwaun Vale Touring Park Pembks
4 D3 Gweek Seal Sanctuary Cnwll
4 D5 Gwendreath Farm Holiday Park Cnwll
7 E5 Gwennap Mining District (UNESCO) Cnwll
133 G4 Gwent Rural Life museum Mons
154 A4 Gwili Railway Carmth
3 G1 Gwithian Farm campsite Cnwll
285 G2 Gwydir Castle Conwy
285 G2 Gwydir Uchaf Chapel CADW Conwy
285 G4 Gwydyr Forest Park Conwy
385 E1 Gypsy Lane railway station R & Cl

H

212 B4 Habberley Golf Club Worcs
290 C5 Hack Green Secret Bunker Ches
600 E6 Hackness Martello Tower HS Ork
141 F3 Haddenham & Thame Parkway railway station Bucks
115 E1 Hadden Hill Golf Club Oxon
489 G5 Haddington Golf Club E Loth
251 F5 Haddiscoe railway station Norfk
560 C2 Haddo House NTS Abers
294 A1 Haddon Hall Derbys
122 B2 Hadleigh Castle Country Park Essex
122 C2 Hadleigh Castle EH Essex
144 C5 Hadley Wood Golf Club Gt Lon
376 B1 Hadrian's Coast to Coast cycle route Cumb
402 D2 Hadrian's Cycleway Cumb
405 E2 Hadrian's Cycleway N u Ty
428 D6 Hadrian's Cycleway Nthumb
429 F6 Hadrian's Wall (UNESCO) Nthumb
401 E2 Hadrian's Wall Path Cumb

428 C5 Hadrian's Wall Path Nthumb
67 H3 Hadspen Garden Somset
180 D3 Hafod Brynog campsite Cerdgn
284 D5 Hafod y Llan NT Gwynd
475 F6 Haggerston Castle campsite Nthumb
467 E2 Haggs Castle Golf Club C Glas
212 D3 Hagley Golf & Country Club Worcs
212 D3 Hagley Hall Worcs
323 G1 Hagley Road railway station Birm
324 D3 Haigh Hall Golf Complex Wigan
163 G3 Hailes Abbey NT Gloucs
489 H4 Hailes Castle HS E Loth
145 G6 Hainault Forest Country Park Gt Lon
145 G6 Hainault Forest Golf Complex Gt Lon
361 E5 Hainsworth Park Golf Club E R Yk
122 C3 Halcon Marine Essex
70 D1 Hale Purlieu NT Hants
213 E3 Halesowen Golf Club Dudley
226 D4 Halesworth Golf Club Suffk
236 B6 Halfpenny Green Vineyards Staffs
67 E6 Halfway Caravan & Camping Park Somset
284 C3 Halfway railway station Gwynd
342 A5 Halifax Bradley Hall Golf Club Calder
341 H3 Halifax Golf Club Calder
314 D2 Hallam FM Arena Sheff
314 C2 Hallamshire Golf Club Sheff
424 B3 Halleaths Caravan Site D & G
395 F5 Hall Garth & Country Club Hotel Darltn
213 H3 Hall Green railway station Birm
4 D4 Halliggye Fogou EH Cnwll
310 C2 Halliwell Jones Stadium Warrtn
365 H4 Hall More Caravan Park Cumb
314 D4 Hallowes Golf Club Derbys
120 D5 Hall Place & Gardens Gt Lon
323 F4 Hall Road railway station Sefton
62 D5 Halse Farm Caravan & Camping Park Somset
45 G6 Halstock golf course Dorset
309 H2 Halton Stadium Halton
402 B1 Haltwhistle golf course Nthumb
116 C3 Hambleden Mill Marina Bucks
51 E3 Hamble Point Marina Hants
51 E3 Hamble railway station Hants
219 G3 Hamerton Zoo Park Cambs
45 F4 Ham Hill Country Park Somset
118 C5 Ham House NT Gt Lon
467 H3 Hamilton (northbound only) service area S Lans
467 H3 Hamilton Central railway station S Lans
468 A4 Hamilton Golf Club S Lans
325 F4 Hamilton Park Wigan
467 H3 Hamilton racecourse S Lans
308 D2 Hamilton Square railway station Wirral
467 H3 Hamilton West railway station S Lans
54 C4 Ham Manor Golf Club W Susx
78 A2 Hammerwood Park E Susx
467 E2 Hampden Park C Glas
90 B6 Hampshire Golf Club Hants
119 F2 Hampstead Golf Club Gt Lon
186 C4 Hampton Court Gardens Herefs
118 D6 Hampton Court Palace Gt Lon
118 D6 Hampton Court Palace Golf Club Gt Lon
35 h6 Hamptonne Country Life museum Jersey
71 E5 Hamptworth Golf & Country Club Wilts
213 G1 Hamstead railway station Birm
394 B3 Hamsterley Forest visitor centre Dur
139 G2 Hanborough railway station Oxon
188 D2 Hanbury Hall NT Worcs
145 E1 Hanbury Manor Golf & Country Club Herts
213 F1 Handsworth Golf Club Birm
343 E5 Hanging Heaton Golf Club Kirk
322 d9 Hango Hill IoM
93 E6 Hankley Common Golf Club Surrey
447 H3 Happendon service area S Lans
213 F3 Harborne Church Farm Golf Club Birm
213 F3 Harborne Golf Club Birm
469 G2 Harburn Golf Club W Loth
377 G4 Hardknott Fort roman site EH Cumb
377 G4 Hardknott Pass Cumb
367 H1 Hardraw Force waterfall N York
395 G4 Hardwick Hall Country Park Dur
295 F2 Hardwick Hall NT Derbys
31 E5 Hardy Monument NT Dorset
32 C1 Hardy's Cottage NT Dorset
312 A4 Hare Hill NT Ches
136 B3 Haresfield Beacon Gloucs
142 D5 Harewood Downs Golf Club Bucks
356 C6 Harewood House Leeds
18 B2 Harford Bridge Holiday Park Devon
264 D3 Harlech Castle (UNESCO) Gwynd
116 D3 Harleyford Estate Marina Bucks
116 D3 Harleyford Golf Club Bucks
224 C2 Harling vineyard Norfk
356 B4 Harlow Carr Gardens N York
145 G2 Harlow Mill railway station Essex
559 H5 Harlow Park Abers
145 F2 Harlow Town railway station Essex
14 B3 Harlyn Sands Holiday Park Cnwll
589 K7 Harmsworth Park Highld
134 B3 Harold's Stone Mons
143 G2 Harpenden Common Golf Club Herts
143 G2 Harpenden Golf Club Herts
242 C5 Harringworth Viaduct Nhants
595 H4 Harris W Isls
356 C3 Harrogate Golf Club N York
49 F5 Harrow Wood Farm campsite Hants
220 C5 Hartford Marina Cambs
469 E2 Harthill service area N Lans
38 B3 Hartland Abbey & Garden Devon

38 C4 Hartland Forest Golf Club Devon
212 B5 Hartlebury Castle Worcs
396 C2 Hartlepool Golf Club Hartpl
396 D4 Hartlepool Power Station Visitor Centre Hartpl
92 C3 Hartley Wintney Golf Club Hants
143 G6 Hartsbourne Golf & Country Club Herts
342 C5 Hartshead Moor service area Calder
239 E6 Hartshill Hayes Country Park Warwks
318 A6 Hartsholme Country Park Lincs
391 G1 Hartside Summit Cumb
146 C6 Hartswood Golf Club Essex
212 C5 Harvington Hall Worcs
176 D3 Harwich & Dovercourt Golf Club Essex
176 D3 Harwich International railway station Essex
177 E3 Harwich Town railway station Essex
325 H2 Harwood Golf Club (Bolton) Bolton
37 E3 Haseley Manor IoW
124 D2 Hasguard Cross Caravan Park Pembks
55 H1 Hassocks Golf Club W Susx
55 H1 Hassocks railway station W Susx
118 B1 Haste Hill golf course Gt Lon
214 B3 Hatchford Brook golf course Birm
94 B4 Hatchlands Park NT Surrey
330 D2 Hatfield & Stainforth railway station Donc
172 A5 Hatfield Forest country park NT Essex
172 A5 Hatfield House Herts
144 C3 Hatfield London Country Club golf course Herts
374 C2 Hatherleigh Deep Sea Trawler N York
190 C1 Hatton (Warwickshire) railway station Warwks
190 C1 Hatton Country World Warwks
234 C1 Haughmond Abbey EH Shrops
555 G1 Haughton House Country Park Abers
301 F3 Havenhouse railway station Lincs
125 G1 Haverfordwest Golf Club Pembks
198 D6 Haverhill Golf Club Essex
145 H6 Havering Country Park Gt Lon
288 D1 Hawarden airport Flints
288 D1 Hawarden Golf Club Flints
188 B2 Hawford Dovecote NT Worcs
439 F2 Hawick Golf Club Border
466 C2 Hawkhead railway station Rens
79 H3 Hawkhurst Golf Club Kent
378 C5 Hawkshead Courthouse NT Cumb
270 D4 Hawkstone Park Shrops
270 D4 Hawkstone Park Hotel & Golf Centre Shrops
368 B5 Hawkswick Cote Caravan Park N York
83 F1 Hawthorn Farm Caravan Park Kent
227 E5 Haw Wood Farm Caravan Park Suffk
324 D5 Haydock Park Golf Club Wigan
324 D5 Haydock Park racecourse St Hel
119 F5 Haydons Road railway station Gt Lon
118 B4 Hayes & Harlington railway station Gt Lon
52 C5 Hayling Golf Club Hants
52 C4 Hayling Island Hants
488 A5 Haymarket railway station C Edin
67 G4 Haynes Motor museum Somset
158 D1 Hay-on-Wye loop cycle route Powys
97 E5 Haysden Country Park Kent
484 C5 Hayston Golf Club E Duns
77 F4 Haywards Heath Golf Club W Susx
77 F5 Haywards Heath railway station W Susx
312 B2 Hazel Grove Golf Club Stockp
557 F3 Hazlehead golf course C Aber
142 B5 Hazlemere Golf Club Bucks
343 E1 Headingley Golf Club Leeds
343 E2 Headingley Stadium Leeds
394 D6 Headlam Hall Hotel golf course Dur
22 B5 Headland Caravan & Camping Park Cnwll
95 E4 Headley Common NT Surrey
342 A3 Headley Golf Club Brad
444 C6 Heads of Ayr Farm Park S Ayrs
118 C1 Headstone Lane railway station Gt Lon
365 G5 Heald Brow NT Lancs
70 C2 Heale Garden Wilts
600 E6 Heart of Neolithic Orkney (UNESCO) Ork
454 A2 Heatherslaw Corn Mill Nthumb
453 H2 Heatherslaw Light Railway Nthumb
454 A2 Heatherslaw railway station Nthumb
36 A3 Heathfield Farm Camping IoW
106 C3 Heath High Level railway station Cardif
227 G2 Heathland Beach Caravan Park Suffk
106 C3 Heath Low Level railway station Cardif
118 B4 Heath Park Golf Club Gt Lon
118 B5 Heathrow airport Gt Lon
118 B5 Heathrow Terminal 4 railway station Gt Lon
118 B4 Heathrow Terminal 5 railway station Gt Lon
118 B4 Heathrow Terminals 1 2 & 3 railway station Gt Lon
326 B4 Heaton Hall Manch
311 H1 Heaton Moor Golf Club Stockp
326 B4 Heaton Park Golf Centre Manch
77 H4 Heaven Farm campsite E Susx
341 G4 Hebden Bridge Golf Club Calder
284 C3 Hebron railway station Gwynd
299 E6 Heckington windmill Lincs
23 F2 Hedleywood Caravan & Camping Park Devon
294 B3 Heights of Abraham Derbys
482 C5 Helensburgh Central railway station Ag & B

482 D3 **Helensburgh Golf Club** Ag & B
482 C3 **Helensburgh Upper railway station** Ag & B
20 A3 **Hele Park Golf Club** Devon
60 D2 **Hele Valley Holiday Park** Devon
8 B4 **Heligan Woods campsite** Cnwll
161 F3 **Hellen's House** Herefs
142 A6 **Hell Fire Caves** Bucks
192 B3 **Hellidon Lakes Hotel & Country Club** Nhants
201 G3 **Helmingham Hall Gardens** Suffk
582 D6 **Helmsdale Golf Club** Highld
340 B5 **Helmshore Mills Textiles Museum** Lancs
309 G5 **Helsby Golf Club** Ches
19 F4 **Hembury Castle** Devon
28 B2 **Hembury Fort** Devon
220 C6 **Hemingford Abbots golf course** Cambs
80 B2 **Hemsted Forest Golf Club** Kent
282 D1 **Hen Blas Country Park** IoA
109 G4 **Henbury golf course** Bristl
119 E1 **Hendon Golf Club** Gt Lon
7 F1 **Hendra Holiday Park** Cnwll
150 C4 **Hendre Eynon Camping & Caravan Site** Pembks
229 E1 **Hendre Mynach Touring Caravan & Camping Park** Gwynd
267 G2 **Hendwr Country Park** campsite Denbgs
228 D4 **Hen-dy railway station** Gwynd
133 G1 **Hen-Gwrt (Moat) CADW** Mons
232 B3 **Heniarth Gate railway station** Powys
190 B1 **Henley Golf & Country Club** Warwks
116 C3 **Henley Golf Club** Oxon
169 H2 **Henlow airfield** Beds
116 C3 **Hennerton Golf Club** Wokham
130 D2 **Henrhyd Falls** Powys
78 B2 **Henry VIII Experience museum** E Susx
344 D5 **Hensall railway station** N York
22 D4 **Hentervene Holiday Park** campsite Cnwll
160 C1 **Hereford Municipal golf course** Herefs
160 C1 **Hereford racecourse** Herefs
186 A5 **Herefordshire Golf Club** Herefs
185 E3 **Hergest Croft Gardens** Herefs
191 F4 **Heritage Motor Centre museum** Warwks
467 E3 **Heritage Park** S Lans
342 D5 **Heritage Road** Kirk
439 F5 **Hermitage Castle HS** Border
221 E5 **Hermitage Marina** Cambs
100 C2 **Herne Bay Golf Club** Kent
301 F1 **Heron's Mead Fishing Lake & Touring Park** Lincs
322 d9 **Herring Tower** IoM
57 G2 **Herstmonceux Castle Gardens** E Susx
34 B5 **Herston Hall railway station** Dorset
143 F2 **Herts County showground** Herts
347 E3 **Hessle Golf Club** E R Yk
44 A2 **Hestercombe Gardens** Somset
118 C4 **Heston service area** Gt Lon
308 C3 **Heswall Golf Club** Wirral
96 C5 **Hever Castle** Kent
96 C5 **Hever Castle Golf Club** Kent
96 C6 **Hever railway station** Kent
405 H2 **Heworth Golf Club** Gatesd
358 B4 **Heworth Golf Club** York
403 G2 **Hexham Golf Club** Nthumb
403 G2 **Hexham racecourse** Nthumb
403 G2 **Hexham Racecourse Caravan Site** Nthumb
171 F1 **Heydon Grange Golf & Country Club** Cambs
166 A5 **Heyford railway station** Oxon
311 E4 **Heyrose Golf Club** Ches
351 E3 **Heysham Golf Club** Lancs
351 F2 **Heysham Port railway station** Lancs
117 F3 **H F Marina** Bucks
330 A3 **Hickleton Golf Club** Donc
190 B6 **Hidcote Manor Garden NT** Gloucs
23 F6 **Hidden Valley** Cnwll
60 D3 **Hidden Valley Park campsite** Devon
313 E6 **Hi Edge Raceway** Derbys
100 C5 **Higham Park** Kent
145 F5 **High Beech golf course** Essex
78 D1 **High Brooms railway station** Kent
40 D3 **Highbullen Hotel Golf & Country Club** Devon
90 C3 **Highclere Castle** Hants
49 G6 **Highcliffe Castle** Dorset
49 F6 **Highcliffe golf course** Dorset
96 B2 **High Elms golf course** Gt Lon
3 E2 **Higher Chellew Holiday Park** Cnwll
7 E3 **Higher Golla Touring & Caravan Park** Cnwll
18 B3 **Higher Longford Caravan & Camping Park** Devon
7 E1 **Higher Moor campsite** Cnwll
3 G4 **Higher Pentreath Farm campsite** Cnwll
12 C5 **Higher Rew Caravan & Camping Park** Devon
31 F6 **Higher South Buckland Farm campsite** Dorset
6 B6 **Higher Trevaskis Caravan Park** Cnwll
20 B6 **Higher Well Farm Holiday Park** Devon
197 E1 **Highfield Farm Touring Park** Cambs
176 C6 **Highfield Grange campsite** Essex
23 F2 **Highfield House Camping & Caravanning** Devon
393 E4 **High Force (Waterfall)** Dur
212 B2 **Highgate Common Country Park** Staffs
119 F2 **Highgate Golf Club** Gt Lon
535 L2 **Highland Folk museum** Highld
565 H5 **Highland Museum of Childhood** Highld
30 B4 **Highlands End Farm Holiday Park** Dorset
536 B2 **Highland Wildlife Park** Highld
311 E3 **High Legh Park Golf Club** Ches
223 G2 **High Lodge Forest Centre** Suffk
356 A3 **High Moor Park Farm campsite** N York
294 D3 **Highoredish viewpoint** Derbys
313 F1 **High Peak** Derbys

293 H3 **High Peak Trail cycle route** Derbys
70 D2 **High Post Golf Club** Wilts
441 F5 **High Rochester (Bremenium) Roman site** Nthumb
101 F4 **Highway Marina** Kent
174 D4 **High Woods Country Park** Essex
58 B5 **Highwoods Golf Club** E Susx
113 E1 **Highworth Golf Centre** Swindn
54 D3 **Hill Barn Golf Club** W Susx
49 E2 **Hill Cottage Farm Camping and Caravan Park** Dorset
390 D5 **Hillcroft Caravan & Camping Site** Cumb
71 F3 **Hill Farm Caravan Park** Hants
484 B5 **Hillfoot railway station** E Duns
556 D1 **Hillhead Caravan Park** Abers
482 D3 **Hill House NTS** Ag & B
72 A5 **Hillier arboretum** Hants
118 C3 **Hillingdon Cycle Circuit** Gt Lon
118 B3 **Hillingdon Golf Club** Gt Lon
466 D2 **Hillington East railway station** C Glas
466 D1 **Hillington West railway station** Rens
365 E1 **Hill of Oaks & Blakeholme campsite** Cumb
502 B2 **Hill of Tarvit NTS** Fife
583 J2 **Hill o'Many Stanes HS** Highld
314 C1 **Hillsborough** Sheff
314 C1 **Hillsborough Golf Club** Sheff
323 F2 **Hillside Golf Club** Sefton
378 C5 **Hill Top NT** Cumb
213 F1 **Hilltop Public golf course** Sandw
290 A6 **Hill Valley Golf & Country Club** Shrops
87 F3 **Hilperton Marina** Wilts
566 F1 **Hilton of Cadboll Chapel (ruin) HS** Highld
484 A4 **Hilton Park Golf Club** E Duns
237 E3 **Hilton Park service area** Staffs
162 C2 **Hilton Puckrup Hall golf course** Gloucs
212 C1 **Himley Hall Golf Centre** Staffs
212 C1 **Himley Hall Park** Staffs
220 B5 **Hinchingbrooke Country Park** Cambs
239 G6 **Hinckley Golf Club** Leics
325 E3 **Hindley Hall Golf Club** Wigan
140 B4 **Hinksey Heights golf course** Oxon
201 E6 **Hintlesham Golf Club** Suffk
49 G6 **Hinton Admiral railway station** Hants
73 E4 **Hinton Ampner Garden NT** Hants
453 F2 **Hirsel Golf Club** Border
80 B3 **Historic Vehicles Collection museum** Kent
577 G6 **Historylinks museum** Highld
514 C4 **HM Frigate 'Unicorn'** C Dund
273 H5 **Hoar Cross Hall Health Spa Golf Academy** Staffs
314 B6 **Hob Hurst's House EH** Derbys
405 E3 **Hobson Golf Club** Dur
72 C4 **Hockley Golf Club** Hants
424 D5 **Hoddom Castle Caravan Park** D & G
271 E4 **Hodnet Hall Gardens** Shrops
94 A3 **Hoebridge Golf Centre** Surrey
339 F4 **Hoghton Tower** Lancs
135 G5 **Hogsdon Farm Caravan & Camping Park** Gloucs
217 E6 **Holdenby House Gardens** Nhants
348 B1 **Holderness** E R Yk
386 D6 **Hole of Horcum viewpoint** N York
365 G4 **Holgate's Caravan Park** Cumb
364 A5 **Holker Street** Cumb
260 A3 **Holkham Hall** Norfk
447 G2 **Holland Bush Golf Club** S Lans
55 H3 **Hollingbury Park Golf Club** Br & H
326 D2 **Hollingworth Lake Caravan Park** Rochdl
326 D1 **Hollingworth Lake Country Park** Rochdl
377 F4 **Hollins Farm Campsite** Cumb
310 D1 **Holly Bank Caravan Park** Traffd
43 H4 **Holly Bush Park campsite** Somset
74 D4 **Hollycombe Steam** W Susx
76 B6 **Holly Gate Cactus Garden** W Susx
20 B1 **Holmans Wood Holiday Park** campsite Devon
399 F4 **Holm Cultram Abbey** Cumb
332 C3 **Holme Hall Golf Club** N Linc
327 G4 **Holme Moss** Kirk
327 H4 **Holme Moss viewpoint** Kirk
366 A4 **Holme Park Fell NT** Cumb
276 D2 **Holme Pierrepont House** Notts
94 D6 **Holmwood railway station** Surrey
23 G2 **Holsworthy Golf Club** Devon
261 E4 **Holt Lowes Country Park** Norfk
33 G1 **Holton Heath railway station** Dorset
78 B2 **Holtye Golf Club** E Susx
302 C4 **Holyhead Golf Club** IoA
302 B4 **Holyhead Mountain Hut Group CADW** IoA
302 B5 **Holy Island** IoA
475 H6 **Holy Island** Nthumb
481 H3 **Holy Loch Marina** Ag & B
7 E2 **Holywell Bay Golf Park** Cnwll
7 E2 **Holywell Bay Holiday Park** Cnwll
308 A5 **Holywell Golf Club** Flints
358 A6 **Home Farm Caravan & Camping** N York
30 C5 **Home Farm Caravan and Campsite** Dorset
304 B3 **Home Farm Caravan Park** IoA
64 B3 **Home Farm Holiday Centre camping** Somset
81 E2 **Homelands Bettergolf Centre** Kent
11 E2 **Home Park** C Plym
85 F5 **Homestead Park camping** Somset
100 A3 **Homing Park campsite** Kent
76 C6 **Honeybridge Park campsite** W Susx
48 C4 **Honeybrook Farm** Dorset
361 F5 **Honeysuckle Farm** E R Yk
224 A4 **Honington airfield** Suffk
377 G2 **Honister Pass** Cumb
28 C3 **Honiton Golf Club** Devon
235 F2 **Hoo Farm** Wrekin
29 F4 **Hook Farm Caravan & Camping Park** Devon
122 B5 **Hoo Marina** Medway
568 B2 **Hopeman Golf Club** Moray
313 G3 **Hope showground** Derbys
487 E4 **Hopetoun House** W Loth
97 G5 **Hop Farm Family Park** Kent

390 C4 **Hopkinsons Whitbarrow Hall Caravan Park** Cumb
209 G4 **Hoptonheath railway station** Shrops
213 F5 **Hopwood Park service area** Worcs
57 H1 **Horam Manor Touring Park** E Susx
57 F1 **Horam Park golf course** E Susx
356 C4 **Hornbeam Park railway station** N York
319 G5 **Horncastle Golf Club** Lincs
120 D3 **Hornchurch Country Park** Gt Lon
250 C1 **Horning Ferry Marina** Norfk
361 G5 **Hornsea Golf Club** E R Yk
118 D3 **Horsenden Hill Golf Club** Gt Lon
288 A6 **Horseshoe Falls** Denbgs
288 A5 **Horseshoe Pass** Denbgs
257 F5 **Horsey Windpump NT** Norfk
342 D1 **Horsforth Golf Club** Leeds
76 C3 **Horsham Cricket & Sports Club** W Susx
76 C4 **Horsham Golf & Fitness** W Susx
294 D6 **Horsley Lodge Golf Club** Derbys
94 B4 **Horsley railway station** Surrey
77 G4 **Horsted Keynes railway station** W Susx
94 D2 **Horton Country Park** Surrey
110 D2 **Horton Court NT** S Glos
94 D2 **Horton Park Golf & Country Club** Surrey
325 E3 **Horwich Parkway railway station** Bolton
253 F2 **Houghton Hall** Norfk
169 E2 **Houghton House EH** Beds
406 B5 **Houghton-le-Spring Golf Club** Sundld
71 G3 **Houghton Lodge Gardens** Hants
220 C5 **Houghton Mill NT** Cambs
324 C4 **Houghwood Golf** St Hel
326 C6 **Houldsworth Golf Club** Stockp
19 F2 **Hound Tor Medieval Village EH** Devon
118 C5 **Hounslow Heath golf course** Gt Lon
529 E3 **House of Dun NTS** Angus
428 B6 **Housesteads Fort museum NT** Nthumb
256 C6 **Hoveton & Wroxham railway station** Norfk
372 C5 **Howardian Hills** N York
355 E3 **Howgill Lodge campsite** N York
443 G1 **Howick Hall Gardens** Nthumb
100 C4 **Howletts Wild Animal Park** Kent
343 H4 **Howley Hall Golf Club** Leeds
466 A2 **Howwood (Renfrewshire) railway station** Rens
600 C5 **Hoy** Ork
308 B2 **Hoylake Golf Club** Wirral
342 B6 **Huddersfield Golf Club** Kirk
142 B5 **Hughenden Manor NT** Bucks
484 B6 **Hughenden Stadium** C Glas
566 D3 **Hugh Miller's Cottage NTS** Highld
45 A4 **Huish Park** Somset
347 G4 **Hull Arena** C KuH
347 F4 **Hull Golf Club** E R Yk
347 F4 **Humber Bridge Country Park** E R Yk
333 F2 **Humberside airport** N Linc
240 D3 **Humberstone Heights Golf Club** C Leic
452 D1 **Hume Castle** Border
326 A5 **Humphrey Park railway station** Traffd
397 G5 **Hunley Hall Golf Club** R & Cl
193 F3 **Hunsbury Hill Country Park** Nhants
258 D3 **Hunstanton Golf Club** Norfk
464 D4 **Hunterston Power Station** N Ayrs
115 H2 **Huntercombe Golf Club** Oxon
306 C5 **Hunters Hamlet Caravan Park** Conwy
48 B6 **Huntick Farm Caravan Park** Dorset
220 B5 **Huntingdon Boathaven & Caravan Park** Cambs
220 B5 **Huntingdon racecourse** Cambs
512 C4 **Huntingtower Castle HS** P & K
558 F2 **Huntly Castle Caravan Park** Abers
558 F1 **Huntly Castle HS** Abers
558 C1 **Huntly Golf Club** Abers
17 G3 **Hurdwick Golf Club** Devon
116 D3 **Hurley Riverside Park** campsite W & M
323 H2 **Hurlston Hall Country Caravan Park** Lancs
323 G2 **Hurlston Hall Golf Club** Lancs
35 H3 **Hurst Castle EH** Hants
93 F5 **Hurtmore Golf Club** Surrey
390 D2 **Hutton-in-the-Forest** Cumb
372 D2 **Hutton-le-Hole Caravan Park** N York
309 G1 **Huyton & Prescot Golf Club** Knows
147 F5 **Hyde Hall Gardens** Essex
412 C4 **Hydros Visitor Centre** D & G
298 A1 **Hykeham railway station** Lincs
146 D4 **Hylands House & Park** Essex
399 E4 **Hylton Caravan Park** Cumb
406 B3 **Hylton Castle EH** Sundld
484 B6 **Hyndland railway station** C Glas
174 D5 **Hythe (Essex) railway station** Essex
82 C4 **Hythe Imperial golf course** Kent

I

482 B5 **IBM railway station** Inver
467 E2 **Ibrox** C Glas
49 F2 **Ibsley Common** Hants
199 G2 **Ickworth House NT** Suffk
199 G2 **Ickworth vineyard** Suffk
80 A1 **Iden Croft Herbs** Kent
76 D2 **Ifield Golf & Country Club** W Susx
97 E4 **Ightham Mote NT** Kent
293 H4 **Ilam Park NT** Staffs
120 B2 **Ilford Golf Club** Gt Lon
23 G5 **Ilfracombe Golf Club** Devon
355 E5 **Ilkley Golf Club** N York
497 E1 **Immeroin Caravan and Camping Park** Stirlg
334 A1 **Immingham Golf Club** NE Lin
295 E3 **Impact Arena** Derbys
309 G4 **Ince & Elton railway station** Ches
324 D4 **Ince railway station** Wigan
487 G3 **Inchcolm Abbey HS** Fife
504 D3 **Inchkenneth Chapel (ruin) HS** Ag & B

497 E4 **Inchmahome Priory HS** Stirlg
556 B5 **Inchmarlo Golf Centre** Abers
129 G4 **Inco Golf Club** Swans
273 E5 **Ingestre Park Golf Club** Staffs
367 F5 **Ingleborough Caves** N York
388 C6 **Inglenook Caravan Park** Cumb
338 D3 **Ingol Golf Club** Lancs
190 C3 **Ingon Manor Golf & Country** Warwks
341 H2 **Ingrow (West) railway station** Brad
481 H5 **Innellan golf course** Ag & B
530 A7 **Inner Hebrides** Highld
450 C2 **Innerleithen Golf Club** Border
511 G6 **Innerpeffray Chapel (ruin) HS** P & K
511 F6 **Innerpeffray Library** P & K
3 d2 **Innisidgen Tomb EH** IoS
559 E4 **Insch Golf Club** Abers
340 B3 **Interlink Express Stadium** Lancs
571 J3 **Inverallochy Golf Club** Abers
494 B3 **Inveraray Castle** Ag & B
494 B3 **Inveraray golf course** Ag & B
494 B3 **Inveraray Jail** Ag & B
521 G4 **Invercoe Caravan & Camping Park** Highld
488 C5 **Inveresk Lodge Garden NTS** E Loth
573 G7 **Inverewe Garden NTS** Highld
566 B3 **Invergordon Golf Club** Highld
488 A5 **Inverleith Ground** C Edin
533 H7 **Inverlochy Castle HS** Highld
512 B1 **Inver Mill Farm Caravan Park** P & K
566 D6 **Inverness (Dalcross) airport** Highld
566 B8 **Inverness Golf Club** Highld
566 B8 **Inverness Ice Centre** Highld
559 H5 **Inverurie Golf Club** Abers
504 B6 **Iona** Ag & B
504 B6 **Iona Abbey and Nunnery HS** Ag & B
37 E5 **IOW Glass** IoW
201 H6 **Ipswich Golf Club** Suffk
194 C1 **Irchester Country Park** Nhants
276 B2 **Ireland Avenue** Notts
235 F4 **Ironbridge Gorge (UNESCO)** Shrops
235 F4 **Iron Bridge museum EH** Shrops
99 G2 **Iron Wharf Boatyard** Kent
401 F2 **Irthing Vale Holiday Park** Cumb
377 E5 **Irton Road railway station** Cumb
444 D1 **Irvine Golf Club** N Ayrs
444 D1 **Irvine Ravenspark Golf Club** N Ayrs
190 A3 **Island Meadow Caravan Park** Warwks
476 F5 **Islay** Ag & B
476 E6 **Islay airport** Ag & B
222 C5 **Isleham Priory Church EH** Cambs
463 F5 **Isle of Arran Distillery visitor centre** N Ayrs
66 D2 **Isle of Avalon Touring Caravan Park** Somset
221 H2 **Isle of Ely** Cambs
506 F1 **Isle Of Eriska golf course** Ag & B
458 C2 **Isle of Gigha** Ag & B
458 C2 **Isle of Gigha Golf Club** Ag & B
122 D4 **Isle of Grain** Medway
597 J1 **Isle of Lewis** W Isls
51 E1 **Isle Of Man (Ronaldsway) airport** IoM
322 e8 **Isle of Man Steam Railway** IoM
505 J3 **Isle of Mull** Ag & B
34 A4 **Isle of Purbeck** Dorset
34 B4 **Isle of Purbeck Golf Club** Dorset
123 F6 **Isle Of Sheppey** Kent
545 G2 **Isle of Skye** Highld
545 J3 **Isle of Skye Golf Club** Highld
101 F2 **Isle of Thanet** Kent
350 A1 **Isle of Walney** Cumb
84 D5 **Isle of Wedmore Golf Club** Somset
37 E3 **Isle of Wight** IoW
37 F3 **Isle of Wight Steam Railway** IoW
3 d2 **Isles of Scilly** IoS
3 d2 **Isles of Scilly (St Mary's) airport** IoS
239 G2 **Itchen Valley Country Park** Hants
117 H3 **Iver Golf Club** Bucks
272 C3 **Izaak Walton Golf Club** Staffs
272 C4 **Izaak Walton's Cottage museum** Staffs

J

291 G5 **Jack Barker's Keele Golf Centre** Staffs
365 G5 **Jack Scout NT** Lancs
374 C2 **Jacobs Mount Caravan Park** N York
214 D3 **Jaguar Daimler Heritage Centre museum** Covtry
288 C6 **James' Caravan Park** Wrexhm
73 H2 **Jane Austen's House museum** Hants
605 G9 **Jarlshof Prehistoric & Norse Settlement HS** Shet
374 A3 **Jasmine Caravan Park** N York
452 B6 **Jedburgh Golf Club** Border
440 C2 **Jedforest Deer and Farm Park** Border
440 C1 **Jedwater Caravan Park** Border
35 g6 **Jersey airport** Jersey
35 g7 **Jersey Lavender Farm** Jersey
35 h6 **Jersey War Tunnels** Jersey
369 G2 **Jervaulx Abbey** N York
55 H2 **Jill windmill** W Susx
324 D3 **JJB Stadium** Wigan
311 F5 **Jodrell Bank** Ches
309 F3 **John Lennon airport** Lpool
490 B4 **John Muir Country Park** E Loth
116 D6 **John Nike Leisuresport Complex** Br For
196 B5 **John O'Gaunt Golf Club** Beds
589 E6 **John O'Groats Caravan Site** Highld
32 B3 **Jordan Hill EH** Dorset
346 C5 **Julians Bower** N Linc
22 B6 **Juliot's Well Holiday Park** Cnwll
325 G2 **Jumbles Country Park** Bolton
478 F5 **Jura** Ag & B
478 D6 **Jura Forest** Ag & B
29 G4 **Jurassic Coast World Heritage Site (UNESCO)** Dorset

33 F4 **Jurassic Coast World Heritage Site (UNESCO)** Dorset

K

450 B2 **Kailzie Gardens** Border
12 B5 **Karragreen Caravan & Camping Park** Devon
140 C4 **Kassam Stadium** Oxon
275 E1 **Kedleston Hall NT** Derbys
275 E1 **Kedleston Park Golf Club** Derbys
291 G6 **Keele service area** Staffs
341 H1 **Keighley & Worth Valley Railway** Brad
355 E6 **Keighley Golf Club** Brad
479 H5 **Keills Chapel HS** Ag & B
568 F7 **Keith & Dufftown Railway** Moray
569 G5 **Keith Golf Club** Moray
465 E3 **Kelburn Country Centre** N Ayrs
379 G2 **Keld Chapel NT** Cumb
503 E3 **Kellie Castle NTS** Fife
261 F3 **Kelling Heath Park railway station** Norfk
217 F4 **Kelmarsh Hall** Nhants
452 E2 **Kelso Golf Club** Border
452 D2 **Kelso racecourse** Border
467 E1 **Kelvin Hall International Sports Arena** C Glas
2 C3 **Kelynack Caravan & Camping Park** Cnwll
556 C1 **Kemnay Golf Club** Abers
528 B4 **Kemp's Castle** Angus
118 C6 **Kempton Park racecourse** Surrey
35 f6 **Kempt Tower visitor centre** Jersey
99 E1 **Kemsley Down railway station** Kent
379 F6 **Kendal Golf Club** Cumb
214 D5 **Kenilworth Castle EH** Warwks
215 E5 **Kenilworth Golf Club** Warwks
169 F5 **Kenilworth Road** Luton
95 G3 **Kenley airfield** Gt Lon
523 L6 **Kenmore golf course** P & K
7 E6 **Kennall Vale** Cnwll
3 G4 **Kenneggy Cove Holiday Park** Cnwll
198 D1 **Kennett railway station** Cambs
27 E5 **Kennford International Caravan Park** Devon
119 F3 **Kensington Palace** Gt Lon
119 H5 **Kent County Cricket Ground** Gt Lon
98 C3 **Kent County showground** Kent
119 H6 **Kent House railway station** Gt Lon
101 F2 **Kent international airport** Kent
97 G6 **Kent National Golf and Country Club** Kent
199 H5 **Kentwell Hall** Suffk
320 B3 **Kenwick Park Golf Club** Lincs
119 F2 **Kenwood House EH** Gt Lon
506 D4 **Kerrera** Ag & B
227 G2 **Kessingland Beach Holiday Park** Suffk
390 A4 **Keswick Golf Club** Cumb
218 B4 **Kettering Golf Club** Nhants
118 D4 **Kew Gardens** Gt Lon
118 D4 **Kew Palace** Gt Lon
11 E2 **Keyham railway station** C Plym
241 E6 **Kibworth Golf Club** Leics
212 B4 **Kidderminster Golf Club** Worcs
128 B3 **Kidwelly Castle CADW** Carmth
440 B6 **Kielder Castle visitor centre** Nthumb
190 B6 **Kiftsgate Court Gardens** Gloucs
462 B2 **Kilberry Sculptured Stones HS** Ag & B
465 G4 **Kilbirnie Place Golf Club** N Ayrs
507 K4 **Kilchurn Castle HS** Ag & B
477 H6 **Kildalton Cross HS** Ag & B
582 B5 **Kildonan railway station** Highld
555 E1 **Kildrummy Castle HS** Abers
574 D3 **Kilberby Old Hall campsite** N York
27 F2 **Killerton NT** Devon
403 F6 **Killhope Lead Mining Centre** Dur
402 D6 **Killhope Summit** Cumb
524 D3 **Killiecrankie visitor centre NTS** P & K
9 G3 **Killigarth Manor Holiday Park** Cnwll
509 J3 **Killin Golf Club** Stirlg
366 B1 **Killington Lake (southbound only) service area** Cumb
61 G2 **Killington Lane railway station** Devon
7 F5 **Killiow golf course** Cnwll
483 E6 **Kilmacolm Golf Club** Rens
497 F3 **Kilmahog Woollen Mill** Stirlg
444 D3 **Kilmarnock (Barassie) Golf Club** N Ayrs
492 D5 **Kilmartin House museum** Ag & B
492 D2 **Kilmelford Yacht Haven** Ag & B
493 E6 **Kilmichael Glassary Inscribed Stone HS** Ag & B
480 D3 **Kilmodan Sculptured Stones HS** Ag & B
479 J6 **Kilmory Knap Chapel HS** Ag & B
480 B2 **Kilmory Woodland Park** Ag & B
481 H3 **Kilmun Arboretum** Ag & B
126 C4 **Kiln Park Holiday Centre** Pembks
368 C6 **Kilnsey Park & Trout Farm** N York
359 F4 **Kilnwick Percy Golf Club** E R Yk
460 C4 **Kilpatrick Dun HS** N Ayrs
483 G5 **Kilsyth Lennox Golf Club** W Duns
316 B3 **Kilton Forest Golf Club** Notts
543 J3 **Kilt Rock Waterfall** Highld
216 D3 **Kilworth Springs Golf Club** Leics
249 F4 **Kimberley Park railway station** Norfk
306 D4 **Kinmel Park golf course** Denbgs
519 K5 **Kingarroch** Highld
68 B2 **King Alfred's Tower NT** Wilts
230 B3 **King Arthur's Labyrinth & Craft Centre** Gwynd
3 C1 **King Charles's Castle EH** IoS
16 B5 **King Doniert's Stone EH** Cnwll
93 H3 **Kingfield Stadium** Surrey
356 C2 **Kingfisher Caravan Park** N York

164 D5 Kingham railway station Oxon
488 B2 Kinghorn Golf Club Fife
512 D5 King James VI Golf Club P & K
84 D4 King John's Hunting Lodge NT Somset
322 h6 King Orry's Grave IoM
22 C6 Kings Acre campsite Cnwll
503 G2 Kingsbarns Golf Links Fife
77 G2 Kingscote railway station W Susx
87 E1 Kingsdown golf course Wilts
28 C4 Kingsdown Tail Caravan & Camping Park Devon
409 G2 Kings Green Caravan Site D & G
97 G4 Kings Hill Golf Club Kent
162 B6 Kingsholm Gloucs
487 H6 Kingsknowe Golf Club C Edin
292 D5 Kingsley & Froghall railway station Staffs
557 H3 Kings Links golf course C Aber
252 D3 Kings Lynn Golf Club Norfk
297 E4 Kings Marina Notts
213 G5 Kings Norton Golf Club Worcs
40 D4 Kings Nympton railway station Devon
162 B6 King's School cricket ground Gloucs
193 G2 Kingsthorpe Golf Club Nhants
347 G4 Kingston Communications Stadium C KuH
48 B4 Kingston Lacy NT Dorset
32 C1 Kingston Maurward Gardens Dorset
430 D6 Kingston Park N u Ty
30 D5 Kingston Russell Stone Circle EH Dorset
197 E5 Kingsway Golf Centre Cambs
95 F3 Kingswood Golf & Country Club Surrey
331 E2 Kings Wood golf course Donc
185 H3 Kington Golf Club Herefs
535 L2 Kingussie Golf Club Highld
560 A6 Kinkell Church HS Abers
486 C3 Kinneil House HS Falk
486 C3 Kinneil railway station Falk
512 D5 Kinnoull Tower P & K
500 B4 Kinross House Gardens P & K
500 B4 Kinross service area P & K
547 H6 Kintail Highld
557 F1 Kintore golf course Abers
459 E4 Kintyre Ag & B
189 H3 Kinwarton Dovecote NT Warwks
383 F3 Kiplin Hall N York
482 B5 Kip Marina Inver
413 F3 Kippford Holiday Park D & G
242 C6 Kirby Hall EH Nhants
240 B4 Kirby Muxloe Golf Club Leics
370 D3 Kirby Wiske Birds of Prey Centre N York
366 C3 Kirkby Lonsdale Golf Club Cumb
372 C2 Kirkbymoorside Golf Club N York
240 B4 Kirkby Muxloe Castle EH Leics
488 B1 Kirkcaldy Golf Club Fife
412 C4 Kirkcudbright Golf Club D & G
338 B3 Kirkham & Wesham railway station Lancs
358 D1 Kirkham Priory EH N York
467 F3 Kirkhill Golf Club S Lans
467 F2 Kirkhill railway station S Lans
484 C5 Kirkintilloch Golf Club E Duns
328 C2 Kirklees Light Railway Kirk
424 B3 Kirkloch Caravan and Camping Park D & G
408 B2 Kirkmadrine Stones HS D & G
343 E2 Kirkstall Abbey Leeds
321 F3 Kirkstead Holiday Park Lincs
378 D3 Kirkstone Pass Cumb
601 H3 Kirkwall airport Ork
527 E4 Kirriemuir Camera Obscura NTS Angus
527 E3 Kirriemuir Golf Club Angus
417 F4 Kirroughtree visitor centre D & G
166 A6 Kirtlington Golf Club Oxon
280 C1 Kirton Holme golf course Lincs
591 D6 Kisimul Castle HS W Isls
37 E2 Kite Hill Farm Caravan Park IoW
17 E4 Kit Hill Country Park Cnwll
98 A2 Kit's Coty EH Kent
146 B5 Klevedon Hatch Nuclear Bunker Essex
88 D2 Knap Hill Wilts
602 F1 Knap of Howar HS Ork
356 D3 Knaresborough Golf Club N York
170 B5 Knebworth Golf Club Herts
170 B5 Knebworth House Herts
351 E6 Kneps Farm Holiday Park Lancs
209 E6 Knighton Golf Club Powys
48 C5 Knighton Heath Golf Club Poole
290 C1 Knights Grange & Sports Complex & golf course Ches
42 C4 Knightshayes Court NT Devon
353 G1 Knight Stainforth Hall Caravan & Campsite N York
484 A6 Knightswood Golf Club C Glas
574 D2 Knockan Crag viewpoint Highld
57 F3 Knockhatch E Susx
499 H6 Knockhill Fife
96 C2 Knockholt railway station Gt Lon
550 B1 Knocknagael Boar Stone HS Highld
96 D4 Knole NT Kent
96 D3 Knole Park Golf Club Kent
350 D5 Knott End Golf Club Lancs
395 G3 Knotty Hill Golf Centre Dur
109 H6 Knowle golf course Bristl
324 B5 Knowsley Road St Hel
324 B6 Knowsley Safari Park Knows
532 B2 Knoydart Highld
208 D5 Knucklas Viaduct Powys
311 F4 Knutsford Golf Club Ches
311 E4 Knutsford service area Ches
546 D5 Kylerhea Otter Haven Highld
480 D5 Kyles of Bute Golf Club Ag & B
569 G5 Kynoch Park Moray

L

35 d2 La Bailloterie Camping & Leisure Guern
111 G3 Lackham Countryside Centre Wilts
111 G6 Lacock Abbey NT Wilts
236 D5 Ladbroke Stadium Wolves
213 H5 Ladbroke Park Golf Club Warwks
292 C3 Ladderedge County Park Staffs

90 D3 Ladle Hill (unfinished hill fort) Hants
501 F2 Ladybank Golf Club Fife
55 F4 Lady Bee Marina W Susx
386 D3 Ladycross Plantation Caravan Park N York
20 D2 Lady's Mile Holiday Park camping Devon
416 A2 Laggangairn Standing Stones HS D & G
414 D6 Lagganmore Hotel Golf Course D & G
466 C2 Lagoon Leisure Centre Rens
34 C2 La Grand Mare Golf & Country Club Guern
583 G3 Laidhay Croft museum Highld
121 G2 Laindon railway station Essex
576 C3 Lairg railway station Highld
377 F2 Lake District Cumb
377 E3 Lake District National Park Cumb
378 C4 Lake District Visitor Centre Cumb
22 B5 Lakefield Caravan Park Cnwll
365 E5 Lakeland Leisure Park Cumb
365 E4 Lakeland Motor museum Cumb
388 D4 Lakeland Sheep & Wool Centre Cumb
365 H4 Lakeland Wildlife Oasis
291 E3 Lakemore Country Park Ches
225 E3 Lakenheath airfield Suffk
121 E4 Lakeside Thurr
364 D2 Lakeside & Haverthwaite Railway Cumb
158 B4 Lakeside Caravan Park Powys
246 C4 Lakeside Caravan Park & Fisheries Norfk
104 C3 Lakeside golf course Neath
93 E3 Lakeside Leisure Club Surrey
220 D4 Lakeside Lodge Golf Club Cambs
118 A6 Laleham Golf Club Surrey
35 g5 La Mare vineyard Jersey
310 C6 Lamb Cottage Caravan Park Ches
79 F2 Lamberhurst Golf Club Kent
114 A3 Lambourn Downs W Berk
461 E3 Lamlash Golf Club N Ayrs
473 E2 Lammermuir Hills E Loth
35 F7 La Moye Golf Club Jersey
125 H4 Lamphey railway station Pembks
217 G5 Lamport Hall Nhants
469 E6 Lanark Golf Club S Lans
469 E6 Lanark Moor Country Park S Lans
339 H2 Lancashire Cycleway Lancs
351 H4 Lancaster (Forton) service area Lancs
351 G3 Lancaster Golf Club Lancs
55 E3 Lancing College Chapel W Susx
37 F4 Landguard Camping Park IoW
177 E3 Landguard Fort Museum EH Suffk
551 G5 Landmark Forest Heritage Park Highld
2 B4 Land's End Cnwll
2 C4 Land's End airport Cnwll
401 G4 Lanercost Priory EH Cumb
121 G2 Langdon Hills Country Park Thurr
121 G2 Langdon Hills Golf Club Thurr
425 H3 Langholm Golf Club D & G
103 F4 Langland Bay Golf Club Swans
234 C5 Langley Chapel EH Shrops
96 A1 Langley Park Golf Club Gt Lon
18 B3 Langstone Manor Camping & Caravan Park Devon
15 F6 Lanhydrock Golf Club Cnwll
15 F6 Lanhydrock NT Cnwll
110 C6 Lansdown golf course BaNES
351 G2 Lansil Golf Club Lancs
6 C6 Lanyon Holiday Park Cnwll
2 D3 Lanyon Quoit Cnwll
7 F2 Lappa Valley Steam Railway Cnwll
214 B5 Lapworth railway station Warwks
389 F1 Larches Caravan Park Cumb
465 E3 Largs Golf Club N Ayrs
465 E3 Largs Yacht Haven N Ayrs
468 B4 Larkhall Golf Club S Lans
92 A6 Larkham airfield Hants
488 C6 Lasswade Butterfly Farm Mdloth
208 B1 Latham Park Powys
472 D5 Lauderdale Border
489 G3 Lauderdale Aisle St Mary's Church HS E Loth
472 C5 Lauder golf course Border
127 G2 Laugharne Castle CADW Carmth
23 G6 Launceston Castle EH Cnwll
23 G5 Launceston golf course Cnwll
487 H4 Lauriston Castle C Edin
78 B6 Lavender Line E Susx
117 E6 Lavender Park Golf Centre Br For
200 B5 Lavenham Guildhall NT Suffk
109 H5 Lawrence Hill railway station Bristl
322 g6 Laxey Commissioners campsite IoM
322 g5 Laxey Wheel IoM
174 B6 Layer Marney Tower Essex
174 C5 Layer Road Essex
391 E2 Lazonby & Kirkoswald railway station Cumb
28 D4 Leacroft Caravan Park Devon
436 A2 Leadhills Golf Club S Lans
20 D2 Leadstone Camping Devon
238 C6 Lea Marston Hotel & Leisure Complex & golf course Warwks
191 E2 Leamington & County Golf Club Warwks
581 L5 Learable Hill Cairns; Stone Rows & Stone Circles Highld
308 C1 Leasowe Golf Club Wirral
94 D3 Leatherhead Golf Club Surrey
374 D3 Lebberston Touring Park N York
552 E6 Lecht Ski Area Abers
552 E6 Lecht Summit Moray
71 H2 Leckford Golf Club Hants
161 G2 Ledbury Heritage Centre Herefs
342 D1 Leeds Bradford airport Leeds
98 C4 Leeds Castle Kent
98 C4 Leeds Castle golf course Kent
343 F1 Leeds Golf Centre Leeds
343 F2 Leeds Golf Club Leeds
292 C4 Leek Golf Club Staffs
295 G5 Leen Valley Golf Centre Notts
51 G4 Lee-on-the-Solent Golf Club Hants
309 F2 Lee Park Golf Club Lpool
314 D3 Lees Hall Golf Club Sheff
145 E6 Lee Valley Camping & Caravan Park Gt Lon

145 E5 Lee Valley campsite Essex
145 E3 Lee Valley Caravan Park Herts
120 A2 Lee Valley Cycle Circuit Gt Lon
145 E6 Lee Valley Leisure golf course Gt Lon
145 E2 Lee Valley Marina Stanstead Abbotts Herts
145 E4 Lee Valley Park Essex
145 F6 Lee Valley Stadium Gt Lon
117 F5 Legoland W & M
241 E4 Leicester airfield Leics
240 C5 Leicester cycle route Leics
240 B4 Leicester Forest East service area Leics
239 H2 Leicester (Markfield) service area Leics
240 C3 Leicester North railway station C Leic
240 D5 Leicester racecourse Leics
240 D6 Leicester Record Office museum Leics
240 C2 Leicester service area Leics
188 A4 Leigh Court Barn EH Worcs
111 F4 Leigh Delamere service area Wilts
325 E5 Leigh Golf Club Warrtn
168 C4 Leighton Buzzard Golf Club Beds
365 G5 Leighton Hall Lancs
203 E2 Leiston Abbey EH Suffk
338 B6 Leisure Lakes Lancs
558 C4 Leith Hall NTS Abers
94 C6 Leith Hill Tower NT Surrey
3 F2 Lelant Saltings railway station Cnwll
19 G3 Lemonford Caravan Park Devon
35 g6 Le Moulin de Quetivel Jersey
489 G5 Lennoxlove House E Loth
484 D5 Lenzie Golf Club E Duns
186 C4 Leominster Golf Club Herefs
76 D4 Leonardslee Lakes and Gardens W Susx
500 D4 Leslie Golf Club Fife
35 f6 Les Meilles Golf & Country Club Jersey
35 g7 Les Ormes Golf Club Jersey
170 B3 Letchworth Garden City railway station Herts
170 B3 Letchworth Golf Club Herts
528 D5 Letham Grange Resort golf course Angus
467 F1 Lethamhill Golf Club C Glas
237 G3 Letocetum Baths roman site NT Staffs
514 C5 Leuchars (for St Andrews) railway station Fife
2 C3 Levant Steam Engine NT Cnwll
35 d2 Le Vaugrat campsite Guern
502 B4 Leven Links golf course Fife
365 G2 Levens Hall Cumb
373 F1 Levisham railway station N York
56 C2 Lewes Castle EH E Susx
56 C2 Lewes Golf Club E Susx
174 C4 Lexden Wood Golf Club Essex
339 E5 Leyland Golf Club Lancs
40 C4 Libbaton Golf Club Devon
488 B5 Liberton Golf Club C Edin
49 F4 Liberty Raptor & Reptile Centre Hants
103 G2 Liberty Stadium Swans
237 H3 Lichfield City railway station Staffs
238 A3 Lichfield Trent Valley railway station Staffs
213 E4 Lickey Hills golf course Worcs
294 C3 Lickpenny Caravan Site Derbys
426 C3 Liddesdale Border
342 B4 Lightcliffe Golf Club Calder
370 B4 Lightwater Valley N York
235 G2 Lilleshall Abbey EH Wrekin
235 H2 Lilleshall Hall Golf Club Shrops
163 E6 Lilley Brook Golf Club Gloucs
76 A4 Limeburners Arms campsite W Susx
378 D4 Limefitt Park campsite Cumb
313 E5 Lime Tree Park campsite Derbys
118 C3 Lime Trees Park Golf Club Gt Lon
96 B4 Limpsfield Chart Golf Club Surrey
423 G4 Lincluden Collegiate Church HS D & G
139 F4 Lincoln Farm Park campsite Oxon
317 F4 Lincoln Golf Club Lincs
300 B2 Lincolnshire Aviation visitor centre Lincs
318 A6 Lincolnshire Road Transport museum Lincs
318 B4 Lincolnshire showground Lincs
334 D5 Lincolnshire Wolds Railway Lincs
369 H2 Lindale Holiday Park N York
443 F5 Linden Hall golf course Nthumb
455 E1 Lindisfarne Castle NT Nthumb
455 E1 Lindisfarne Priory EH Nthumb
513 F6 Lindores Abbey Fife
240 B2 Lingdale Golf Club Leics
96 A6 Lingfield Park Golf Club Surrey
96 A6 Lingfield racecourse Surrey
256 C2 Links Caravan Site Norfk
261 G3 Links Country Park Hotel & Golf Club Norfk
198 C2 Links Golf Club Cambs
529 F3 Links Park Angus
486 C4 Linlithgow Golf Club W Loth
310 B5 Linmere visitor centre Ches
533 G7 Linnhe Lochside Holidays campsite Highld
467 E3 Linn Park Gardens C Glas
467 E3 Linn Park Golf Club C Glas
198 B5 Linton Zoological Gardens Cambs
487 F6 Linwater Caravan Park C Edin
344 A5 Lionheart Stadium Wakefd
310 D4 Lion Salt Works Ches
74 C4 Liphook Golf Club W Susx
7 E4 Liskey Holiday Park Cnwll
519 L7 Lismore Ag & B
106 C3 Lisvane & Thornhill railway station Cardif
237 G5 Little Aston Golf Club Staffs
14 D4 Little Bodieve Holiday Park Cnwll
143 E6 Little Chalfont Golf Club Bucks
13 F2 Little Cotton Caravan Park Devon
135 F2 Littledean Hall Gloucs
54 B4 Littlehampton Golf Club W Susx
76 C3 Littlehaven railway station W Susx
484 C6 Littlehill golf course C Glas

226 B3 Little Lakeland Caravan Park Norfk
211 H5 Little Lakes Golf & Country Club Worcs
291 G3 Little Moreton Hall NT Ches
245 G3 Little Ranch Leisure campsite Herefs
83 E3 Little Satmar Holiday Park Kent
32 B4 Littlesea Holiday Park Dorset
82 D3 Little Switzerland Camping & Caravan Site Kent
7 E2 Little Treamble Farm Touring Park Cnwll
3 F2 Little Trevarrack Tourist Park Cnwll
5 E5 Little Trevothan Caravan & Camping Park Cnwll
308 D1 Liverpool Central railway station Lpool
309 E2 Liverpool Cricket Club Lpool
308 D1 Liverpool James Street railway station Lpool
309 E1 Liverpool Lime Street railway station Lpool
308 D1 Liverpool Moorfields railway station Lpool
323 G5 Liverpool Municipal Golf Club Knows
119 G3 Liverpool St railway station Gt Lon
486 D6 Livingston North railway station W Loth
469 H1 Livingston South railway station W Loth
406 B2 Lizard Lane Caravan & Camping Site S Tyne
204 D3 Llanbadarn railway station Cerdgn
284 C2 Llanberis Lake Railway Gwynd
208 C5 Llanbister Road railway station Powys
132 B5 Llancaiach Fawr Myr Td
106 B4 Llandaf railway station Cardif
103 H2 Llandarcy Park Neath
265 E2 Llandecwyn railway station Gwynd
156 B3 Llandovery Castle Carmth
105 F5 Llandow V Glam
105 F5 Llandow Touring Caravan Park V Glam
183 H2 Llandrindod Wells Golf Club Powys
305 G3 Llandudno (Maesdu) Golf Club Conwy
180 C3 Llanerchaeron NT Cerdgn
105 H4 Llanerch vineyard V Glam
305 E5 Llanfairfechan Golf Club Conwy
129 E4 Llangennech railway station Carmth
287 H6 Llangollen Railway Denbgs
208 D5 Llangynllo railway station Powys
106 C3 Llanishen Golf Club Cardif
307 F5 Llannerch Park golf course Denbgs
127 H2 Llansteffan Castle CADW Carmth
105 G3 Llantrisant & Pontyclun Golf Club Rhondd
108 C2 Llanwern Golf Club Newpt
269 E5 Llanymynech Golf Club Powys
126 B1 Llawhaden Castle CADW Pembks
267 G1 Llawr-Betws Farm Caravan Park Gwynd
285 F5 Llechwedd Slate Caverns Gwynd
263 E3 Lleyn Peninsula Gwynd
154 B4 Llwyfan Cerrig railway station Carmth
264 B2 Llwyn-Bugeilydd Caravan & Camping Site Gwynd
286 D4 Llyn Brenig visitor centre Conwy
158 B4 Llynfi Holiday Park campsite Powys
129 E1 Llyn Lech Owain Country Park Carmth
282 D5 Llyn-y-Gele Farm camp site Gwynd
283 F3 Llys Derwen Caravan & Camping Site Gwynd
205 G3 Llywernog Silver Lead Mine Cerdgn
559 G4 Loanhead Stone Circle HS Abers
60 C4 Lobb Fields Caravan & Camping Park Devon
326 C1 Lobden Golf Club Lancs
533 J5 Lochaber Highld
520 F4 Lochaber Watersports Centre Highld
546 D4 Lochalsh Woodland Garden NTS Highld
563 J7 Lochcarron Golf Club Highld
433 G5 Loch Doon Castle HS E Ayrs
533 G7 Loch Eil (Outward Bound) railway station Highld
532 F2 Locheilside railway station Highld
500 C4 Lochgelly Golf Club Fife
480 B2 Lochgilphead golf course Ag & B
542 E6 Loch Greshornish Caravan Site Highld
422 A5 Loch Ken Holiday Park D & G
500 B4 Loch Leven Castle HS P & K
483 E1 Loch Lomond
496 C1 Loch Lomond and the Trossachs National Park
483 E2 Loch Lomond Golf Club Ag & B
495 G3 Loch Lomond Holiday Park Ag & B
483 E3 Loch Lomond Marina W Duns
424 B3 Lochmaben Castle HS D & G
424 B3 Lochmaben golf course D & G
549 J4 Loch Ness Highld
550 B1 Loch Ness golf course Highld
524 F7 Loch of the Lowes visitor centre P & K
500 C5 Lochore Meadows Country Park Fife
500 C5 Lochore Meadows Country Park golf course Fife
463 F4 Lochranza Caravan & Camping Site N Ayrs
463 F4 Lochranza Castle HS N Ayrs
463 F4 Lochranza Golf N Ayrs
483 F3 Lochs & Glens North cycle route W Duns
465 G4 Lochs & Glens South cycle route N Ayrs
413 E2 Lochside Caravan & Camping Site D & G
465 G3 Lochwinnoch Golf Club Rens
424 C3 Lockerbie Golf Club D & G
216 A4 Lodge Farm campsite Warwks
389 G6 Lodore Falls Cumb
343 F4 Lofthouse Hill Golf Club Wakefd
119 E3 Loftus Road Gt Lon
408 B3 Logan Gardens D & G
288 A2 Loggerheads Country Park Denbgs

567 J6 Logie Steading visitor centre Moray
483 E3 Lomond Woods Holiday Park W Duns
120 A4 London Arena Gt Lon
80 C2 London Beach Hotel & Golf Club Kent
119 G3 London Bridge railway station Gt Lon
119 G3 London Fields railway station Gt Lon
144 A6 London Gateway service area Gt Lon
244 A5 London Road C Pete
55 H3 London Road (Brighton) railway station Br & H
119 E5 London Scottish Golf Club Gt Lon
77 G1 London Temple visitor centre Surrey
109 F5 Long Ashton golf course N Som
397 F5 Longbeck railway station R & C
240 F5 Longcliffe Golf Club Leics
141 E3 Long Crendon Courthouse NT Bucks
14 D3 Long Cross Victorian Gardens Cnwll
50 C2 Longdown Dairy Farm Hants
67 F4 Long Hazel Park campsite Somset
87 E6 Longleat House and Safari Park Wilts
328 B1 Longley Park Golf Club Kirk
566 B7 Longman Yacht Haven Highld
190 B5 Long Marston Warwks
391 F2 Long Meg and her Daughters Cumb
489 E4 Longniddry Golf Club E Loth
291 H5 Longport railway station C Stke
339 F2 Longridge Golf Club Lancs
314 B4 Longshaw Estate country park NT Derbys
571 K6 Longside heliport Abers
3 d2 Longstone heritage centre IoS
455 G2 Longstone Lighthouse Nthumb
66 D5 Long Sutton golf course Somset
159 F4 Longtown Castle Herefs
9 H2 Looe Golf Club Cnwll
93 E1 Look Out Discovery Centre Br For
33 G2 Lookout Holiday Park Dorset
442 D5 Lordenshaws hill fort Nthumb
119 F3 Lords Cricket Ground Gt Lon
389 E4 Lorton Vale Cumb
93 G5 Loseley Park Surrey
9 E1 Lostwithiel Hotel Golf & Country Club Cnwll
344 A2 Lotherton Hall Leeds
470 D1 Lothianburn Golf Club C Edin
445 H2 Loudoun Castle E Ayrs
445 H2 Loudoun Gowf Club golf course E Ayrs
276 B6 Loughborough Central railway station Leics
129 E5 Loughor Castle CADW Swans
145 F5 Loughton Golf Club Essex
29 E3 Loughwood Meeting House NT Devon
320 B2 Louth Golf Club Lincs
37 F4 Lower Hyde Holiday Park IoW
270 C3 Lower Lacon Caravan Park Shrops
22 C4 Lower Pennycrocker Farm Cnwll
4 B2 Lower Polladras Touring Park Cnwll
326 B2 Lowes Park Golf Club Bury
76 D1 Lowfield Heath windmill
176 D1 Low House Touring Caravan Centre Suffk
343 E5 Low Laithes Golf Club Wakefd
361 F4 Low Skirlington Leisure Park E R Yk
367 E6 Lower Hill Caravan Park N York
436 B3 Lowther Hills D & G
391 E4 Lowther Holiday Park Cumb
391 E5 Lowther Leisure & Wildlife Park Cumb
378 C4 Low Wray NT campsite Cumb
334 D5 Ludborough railway station Lincs
89 G4 Ludgershall Castle EH Wilts
210 C5 Ludlow Castle Shrops
210 B4 Ludlow Golf Club Shrops
210 B4 Ludlow racecourse Shrops
74 D2 Ludshott Common NT Hants
242 D4 Luffenham Heath Golf Club Rutlnd
489 F3 Luffness New Golf Club E Loth
545 J4 Luib Folk museum Highld
492 B2 Luing Ag & B
96 D2 Lullingstone Castle Kent
96 D1 Lullingstone Roman Villa EH Kent
33 F3 Lulworth Castle Dorset
33 E3 Lulworth Cove visitor centre Dorset
502 C4 Lundin Golf Club Fife
502 C4 Lundin Ladies Golf Club Fife
492 A3 Lunga Ag & B
215 E4 Lunt Roman Fort Warwks
75 E4 Lurgashall vineyard W Susx
19 G1 Lurkbell hill fort Devon
169 G5 Luton airport Luton
216 B3 Lutterworth Golf Club Leics
8 D2 Luxulyan Valley (UNESCO) Cnwll
583 J2 Lybster Golf Club Highld
81 G5 Lydd airport Kent
82 D1 Lydden Kent
81 G5 Lydd Golf Club Kent
242 B5 Lyddington Bede House EH Rutlnd
24 D6 Lydford Castle EH Devon
24 D6 Lydford Gorge NT Devon
112 D3 Lydiard Park Swindn
112 D3 Lydiard Park Country Park Swindn
135 E4 Lydney Golf Club Gloucs
135 E4 Lydney Junction railway station Gloucs
135 E4 Lydney Town railway station Gloucs
482 C4 Lyle Hill viewpoint Inver
312 C3 Lyme Park NT Ches
29 F4 Lyme Regis Golf Club Dorset
50 B5 Lymington Pier railway station Hants
50 B5 Lymington Town railway station Hants
310 D2 Lymm Golf Club Warrtn
310 D3 Lymm service area Warrtn
27 F5 Lympstone Commando railway station Devon
112 B4 Lyneham airport Wilts
61 G2 Lynton & Barnstaple Railway Devon

31 F1 Lyons Gate Caravan and Camping Park Dorset
67 E4 Lytes Cary Manor NT Somset
337 G4 Lytham Green Drive Golf Club Lancs
234 B3 Lyth Hill Country Park Shrops
50 A6 Lytton Lawn Touring Park Hants
218 D2 Lyveden New Bield NT Nhants

M

458 D4 MacAlister Clan visitor centre Ag & B
506 E3 McCaig's Tower Ag & B
312 B5 Macclesfield Golf Club Ches
512 C4 McDiarmid Park P & K
561 E3 McDonald Golf Club Abers
82 D2 Macfarlanes Butterfly Centre Kent
230 D4 Machinations museum Powys
460 B3 Machrie Bay golf course N Ayrs
476 E7 Machrie Hotel & Golf Links Ag & B
460 C3 Machrie Moor Stone Circles HS N Ayrs
456 D2 Machrihanish Golf Club Ag & B
230 B4 Machynlleth Golf Club Powys
568 D6 Mackessock Park Moray
504 B6 MacLean's Cross HS Ag & B
412 C4 Maclellan's Castle HS D & G
116 B6 Madjeski Stadium Readg
307 G4 Maen Achwyfaen Cross CADW Flints
264 D4 Maes Artro Centre Gwynd
600 E2 Maes Howe HS Ork
85 H1 Maes Knoll hill fort BaNES
104 C1 Maesteg Golf Club Brdgnd
232 D3 Maes Y Dre Powys
475 E4 Magdalene Fields Golf Club Nthumb
571 J2 Maggie's Hoosie Abers
315 E1 Magna Sheff
108 D2 Magor service area Mons
191 F4 Magpie Hill viewpoint Warwks
313 G6 Magpie Mine Derbys
116 A3 Maharajah's Well Oxon
31 F5 Maiden Castle EH Dorset
117 E3 Maidenhead Golf Club W & M
559 G5 Maiden Stone HS Abers
98 B3 Maidstone Barracks railway station Kent
98 B3 Maidstone East railway station Kent
98 C3 Maidstone service area Kent
98 B3 Maidstone West railway station Kent
293 E4 Mainifold Trail cycle route Staffs
600 F2 Mainland Ork
606 E3 Mainland Shet
514 C3 Mains of Fintry C Dund
528 C2 Maison Dieu Chapel (ruin) HS Angus
119 E6 Malden Golf Club Gt Lon
95 E1 Malden Manor railway station Gt Lon
147 G3 Maldon Golf Club Essex
354 A2 Malham Cove N York
291 F3 Malkins Bank golf course Ches
531 J3 Mallaig heritage centre Highld
470 C1 Malleny Garden NTS C Edin
470 C1 Malleny Park C Edin
239 G4 Mallory Park Leics
373 E5 Malton & Norton Golf Club N York
197 E5 Malton golf course Cambs
187 H6 Malvern Hills
188 A5 Malvern Link railway station Worcs
547 G6 Mam Ratagan Highld
313 F3 Mam Tor hill fort Derbys
320 C2 Manby Caravan Park Lincs
320 C2 Manby showground Lincs
311 G3 Manchester airport Manch
311 G2 Manchester Airport railway station Manch
326 A5 Manchester Golf Club Rochdl
326 C5 Manchester Indoor Tennis Centre Manch
326 C5 Manchester Velodrome Manch
326 B5 Manchester Victoria railway station Manch
474 B4 Manderston House Border
221 G1 Manea railway station Cambs
110 B4 Mangotsfield Golf Club S Glos
110 B4 Mangotsfield United FC S Glos
76 D4 Mannings Heath Golf Club W Susx
76 D4 Mannings Heath Hotel W Susx
261 F5 Mannington Gardens Norfk
126 B5 Manorbier Castle Pembks
126 B5 Manorbier railway station Pembks
261 H3 Manor Farm Caravan & Campsite Norfk
51 E2 Manor Farm Country Park Hants
29 G4 Manor Farm Holiday Centre Dorset
325 H4 Manor Golf Club Bolton
334 B3 Manor Golf Club NE Lin
273 G3 Manor Golf Club Staffs
126 B4 Manor House Wildlife Park Pembks
215 F1 Manor Park Warwks
308 B2 Manor Road railway station Wirral
405 G2 Manors railway station N u Ty
289 G3 Manor Wood Country Caravan Park Ches
439 G1 Mansfield Rofe Golf Club
101 F2 Manston Caravan & Camping Park Kent
27 E5 Manstree vineyard Devon
322 g6 Manx Electric Railway IoM
115 H4 Mapledurham House Oxon
30 C3 Mapperton Gardens Dorset
310 D4 Marbury Country Park Ches
245 F6 March Golf Club Cambs
104 C2 Margam Country Park Neath
104 C2 Margam Stones museum CADW Neath
247 E3 Marham airfield Norfk
322 b9 Marine Interpretation Centre IoM
60 a2 Marisco Castle Devon
27 F3 Marker's Cottage NT Devon
239 G4 Market Bosworth Country Park Leics
271 F3 Market Drayton Golf Club Shrops
217 F3 Market Harborough Golf Club Nhants
294 A2 Market House NT Derbys
319 E2 Market Rasen & District Golf Club Lincs

319 E2 Market Rasen racecourse Lincs
326 C2 Marland Park Golf Club Rochdl
113 E6 Marlborough Golf Club Wilts
79 F2 Marle Place Gardens Kent
537 G5 Mar Lodge Estate NTS Abers
370 B4 Marmion Tower N York
312 C2 Marple Golf Club Stockp
275 F1 Marriott Breadsall Priory Hotel & Country Club Derbys
487 F6 Marriott Dalmahoy Hotel Golf & Country Club C Edin
214 C3 Marriott Forest of Arden Golf & Country Club Warwks
53 F3 Marriott Goodwood Park Hotel & Country Club golf course W Susx
342 C1 Marriott Hollins Hall Hotel & Country Club Brad
51 G2 Marriott Meon Valley Hotel & Country Club golf course Hants
250 B2 Marriott Sprowston Manor Hotel & Country Club Norfk
98 C4 Marriott Tudor Park Hotel & Country Club golf course Kent
325 G4 Marriott Worsley Park Hotel & Country Club golf course Salfd
340 D2 Marsden Park golf course Lancs
327 F2 Marsden Golf Club Kirk
202 D2 Marsh Farm Caravan Site Suffk
147 G5 Marsh Farm Country Park Essex
272 D5 Marston Road Staffs
239 G5 Marston's Stadium Leics
149 F2 Martello Beach Holiday Park campsite Essex
83 F1 Martin Mill railway station Kent
89 E2 Martinsell hill fort Wilts
117 E6 Martins Heron railway station Br For
337 F3 Marton Mere Holiday Village Bpool
72 D5 Marwell Zoo Hants
60 D4 Marwood Hill Gardens Devon
190 B3 Mary Arden's House Warwks
120 A3 Maryland railway station Gt Lon
119 F3 Marylebone (London) railway station Gt Lon
388 B2 Maryport Fort Roman site Cumb
388 C2 Maryport Golf Club Cumb
369 H3 Masham Golf Club N York
294 B3 Masson Mills Derbys
126 B3 Masterland Farm Touring Caravan Park Pembks
120 A2 Matchroom Stadium Gt Lon
429 G5 Matfen Hall Country House Hotel & Golf Club Nthumb
294 C3 Matlock Golf Club Derbys
294 B2 Matlock Riverside railway station Derbys
316 D2 Mattersey Abbey EH Notts
249 E3 Mattishall golf course Norfk
326 C6 Mauldeth Road railway station Manch
356 C5 Maustin Caravan Park N York
606 D4 Mavis Grind Shet
229 E1 Mawddach Trail cycle route Gwynd
214 C2 Maxstoke Park Golf Club Warwks
467 E2 Maxwell Park railway station C Glas
422 D2 Maxwelton (Glencairn Castle) D & G
432 D3 Maybole Collegiate Church HS S Ayrs
432 C3 Maybole Municipal Golf Club S Ayrs
391 E4 Mayburgh Henge EH Cumb
514 C3 Mayfield C Dund
137 F3 Mayfield Touring Park Glosss
121 E1 Maylands Golf & Country Club Gt Lon
275 H2 Maywood golf course Derbys
488 B5 Meadowbank Stadium C Edin
314 D1 Meadowhall Sheff
488 B6 Meadowheads Mortonhall Caravan & Camping Park C Edin
489 H3 Meadowhead's Tantallon Caravan & Camping E Loth
276 C2 Meadow Lane Notts
144 A5 Meadow Park Herts
48 C3 Meadow View Caravan Park Dorset
66 D1 Meare Fish House EH Somset
322 b9 Meayll Circle IoM
73 G2 Medstead & Four Marks railway station Hants
98 A1 Medway Bridge Marina Medway
98 C2 Medway service area Medway
488 A5 Meggetland C Edin
513 E2 Meikleour Beech Hedge P & K
230 D2 Meirion Mill Gwynd
351 F3 Melbreak Caravan Park Lancs
430 B2 Meldon Park Nthumb
25 E4 Meldon Viaduct railway station Devon
199 H5 Melford Hall NT Suffk
492 D2 Melfort Pier and Harbour Ag & B
452 C2 Mellerstain House Border
209 E1 Mellington Hall Caravan Park Powys
312 C2 Mellor & Townscliffe Golf Club Stockp
451 G3 Melrose Abbey HS Border
451 G3 Melrose Golf Club Border
327 H3 Meltham Golf Club Kirk
277 G5 Melton Mowbray Golf Club Leics
113 H4 Membury service area W Berk
571 H3 Memsie Cairn HS Abers
15 E6 Mena Caravan & Camping Site Cnwll
2 D3 Men-An-Tol Cnwll
326 B5 MEN Arena Manch
85 H5 Mendip Golf Club N Som
84 D2 Mendip Spring Golf Club N Som
67 G1 Mendip Vale railway station Somset
10 A1 Menheniot railway station Cnwll
498 C5 Menstrie Castle NTS Clacks
168 B6 Mentmore Golf & Country Club Bucks
197 E2 Menzies Cambridgeshire Golf Club Cambs
524 B6 Menzies Castle P & K
190 C3 Menzies Welcombe Hotel golf course Warwks
323 G1 Meols Cop railway station Sefton
488 A5 Merchants of Edinburgh Golf Club C Edin

311 E3 Mere Golf & Country Club Ches
334 B3 Meridian Quay NE Lin
425 F5 Merkland Cross HS D & G
48 C5 Merley Court Touring Park Poole
14 B5 Merlin golf course Cnwll
79 G4 Merrimens Graden E Susx
93 G4 Merrist Wood Golf Club Surrey
18 C3 Merrivale Stone Circle EH Devon
212 D2 Merry Hill Dudley
148 D1 Mersea Island Essex
310 A2 Mersey Valley Golf & Country Club St Hel
309 H4 Mersey View viewpoint Ches
131 G3 Merthyr Tydfil Golf Club Myr Td
452 B8 Mertoun Gardens Border
405 F2 Metro Centre Gatesd
405 F2 Metro Radio Arena N u Ty
135 G5 Michaelwood service area Gloucs
57 F3 Michelham Priory EH E Susx
275 E3 Mickleover Golf Club C Derb
142 C4 Mid Chiltern Villages cycle route Bucks
189 G5 Middle Littleton Tithe Barn NT Worcs
385 E2 Middlesbrough Golf Club Middsb
385 E1 Middlesbrough Municipal Golf Centre Middsb
238 C5 Middleton Hall Warwks
252 D4 Middleton Hall Golf Club Norfk
343 E4 Middleton Park Municipal Golf Club Leeds
343 F4 Middleton Railway Leeds
71 G2 Middle Wallop airshow venue Hants
387 F4 Middlewood Farm Holiday Park N York
73 F3 Mid Hants Railway (Watercress Line) Hants
143 H1 Mid Herts golf course Herts
121 F5 Mid Kent Golf Club Kent
215 F4 Midland Air museum Warwks
295 E4 Midland Railway Centre Derbys
248 D4 Mid Norfolk Railway Norfk
56 A1 Mid Sussex Golf Club E Susx
290 C3 Midway Boats Ches
344 B5 Mid Yorkshire golf course Wakefd
269 F4 Mile End golf course Shrops
75 F1 Milford (Surrey) railway station Surrey
75 F1 Milford Golf Club Surrey
125 E3 Milford Haven Golf Club Pembks
38 D3 Milky Way Adventure Park Devon
444 D5 Millbrae S Ayrs
169 E1 Millbrook (Bedfordshire) railway station Beds
568 C4 Millbuies Country Park Moray
322 f6 Millenium Way IoM
77 F3 Millennium Seedbank W Susx
106 C4 Millennium Stadium Cardif
64 D3 Mill Farm Caravan & Camping Park Somset
361 F3 Mill Farm Country Park E R Yk
234 D5 Mill Farm Holiday Park Shrops
317 F4 Millfield Golf Complex Lincs
144 B2 Mill Green Golf Club Herts
144 B6 Mill Hill Golf Club Gt Lon
218 D4 Mill Marina Nhants
315 E1 Millmoor Rothm
61 E2 Mill Park Campsite Devon
464 D3 Millport Golf Club N Ayrs
117 F5 Mill Ride Golf Club Br For
326 C3 Mills Hill railway station Rochdl
514 B3 Mills Observatory C Dund
500 B4 Milnathort Golf Club P & K
322 B8 Milners Tower IoM
484 A4 Milngavie Golf Club E Duns
47 E4 Milton Abbey Dorset
114 D1 Milton Manor Oxon
524 D4 Milton of Fonab Caravan Site P & K
2 C5 Minack Open Air Theatre Cnwll
136 C5 Minchinhampton golf course Gloucs
136 C5 Minchinhampton Old Course golf course Gloucs
222 D4 Mindenhall Stadium Suffk
63 E2 Minehead & Exmoor Caravan & Camping Park Somset
63 F2 Minehead & West Somerset Golf Club Somset
601 J3 Minehowe Ork
288 C4 Minera Lead Mines Wrexhm
7 E5 Mineral Tramways cycle route Cnwll
518 D3 Mingary Castle Highld
25 H6 Miniature Pony Centre Devon
66 C5 Miniature World museum Gloucs
42 D4 Minnows Touring Park Devon
139 E2 Minster Lovell Hall EH Oxon
31 F2 Mintern Gardens Dorset
452 A5 Minto Golf Club Border
389 F4 Mirehouse Cumb
136 D3 Miserden Park Gardens Gloucs
175 F3 Misery Towers EH Essex
119 F6 Mitcham Golf Club Gt Lon
119 F6 Mitcham Junction railway station Gt Lon
233 F5 Mitchell's Fold Stone Circle EH Shrops
559 F5 Mither Tap hill fort Abers
202 B4 Moat Barn Touring Caravan Park Suffk
311 F3 Mobberley railway station Ches
287 H2 Moel Famau Country Park Denbgs
153 G2 Moelfryn Caravan & Camping Site Carmth
519 H1 Moidart Highld
509 J3 Moirlanich Longhouse NTS Stirlg
288 A2 Mold Golf Club Flints
172 A3 Mole Hall Wildlife Park Essex
236 D5 Molineux Wolves
550 B8 Monadhliath Mountains Highld
505 J9 Monastery & Beehive Cells HS Ag & B
14 C5 Monessie Falls Highld
565 K8 Moniack Castle (Highland Winery) Highld
515 E3 Monifieth Golf Links Angus
515 E2 Monikie Country Park Angus
329 F3 Monk Bretton Priory EH Barns
10 A3 Monkey Sanctuary Cnwll
7 F3 Monkey Tree Holiday Park Cnwll
33 E2 Monkey World Dorset
56 C3 Monk's House NT E Susx

90 D1 Monks Lane W Berk
134 C2 Monmouth Castle CADW Mons
134 C2 Monmouth Golf Club Mons
133 E2 Monmouthshire Golf Club Mons
134 C2 Monmouthshire showground Mons
45 F4 Montacute House NT Somset
232 D5 Montgomery Castle CADW Powys
35 j7 Mont Orgueil Jersey
529 F3 Montrose Golf Links Angus
202 B5 Moon & Sixpence campsite Suffk
343 F1 Moor Allerton Golf Club Leeds
358 A5 Moor End Farm campsite York
94 C2 Moore Place Golf Club Surrey
238 A5 Moor Hall Golf Club Birm
19 G5 Moorlands Alternative cycle route Devon
343 G1 Moor Lodge Park campsite Leeds
143 F6 Moor Park Golf Club Herts
343 F3 Moor Road railway station Leeds
325 H4 Moorside railway station Salfd
387 F5 Moors to Sea 8 cycle route N York
387 E3 Moors to Sea 9 cycle route N York
49 E3 Moors Valley Country Park Dorset
49 E3 Moors Valley golf course Dorset
16 B6 Moorswater Viaduct Cnwll
343 E1 Moortown Golf Club Leeds
12 C2 Moor View Touring Park Devon
195 E5 Moot Hall museum Beds
568 C1 Moray Golf Club Moray
351 G1 Morecambe Golf Club Lancs
308 C1 Moreton (Merseyside) railway station Wirral
270 D5 Moreton Corbet Castle EH Shrops
229 E2 Morfa Mawddach railway station Gwynd
131 H3 Morlais Castle Golf Club Myr Td
275 G1 Morley Hayes golf course Derbys
430 C3 Morpeth Golf Club Nthumb
129 G5 Morriston Golf Club Swans
260 D3 Morston Marshes NT Norfk
60 C2 Mortehoe & Woolacombe Golf Club Devon
186 A2 Mortimer's Cross Water Mill EH Herefs
436 A5 Morton Castle HS D & G
488 B6 Mortonhall Golf Club C Edin
17 F5 Morwellham Quay Devon
213 G3 Moseley Golf Club Birm
236 D4 Moseley Old Hall NT Staffs
213 G3 Moseley Rugby Union Birm
325 H3 Moses Gate Country Park Bolton
144 A4 Mosquito Aircraft museum Herts
413 G1 Mossband Caravan Park D & G
567 J5 Mosset Park Moray
460 C3 Moss Farm Road Stone Circle HS N Ayrs
311 F2 Moss Lane Traffd
323 H4 Mossock Hall Golf Club Lancs
312 B5 Moss Rose Ches
351 G5 Mosswood Caravan Park Lancs
411 F2 Mossyard Caravan & Camping Park D & G
98 B4 Mote Cricket Club Kent
413 F4 Mote of Mark D & G
71 G4 Mottisfont Abbey NT Hants
131 G4 Mountain Ash Golf Club Rhondd
106 B3 Mountain Lakes & Castell Heights golf course Cardif
11 E3 Mount Edgcumbe Country Park Cnwll
485 E6 Mount Ellen Golf Club N Lans
384 C5 Mount Grace Priory NT N York
322 e8 Mount Murray Hotel & Country Club IoM
395 F1 Mount Oswald Manor golf course Dur
169 H3 Mount Pleasant golf course Beds
239 H1 Mount St Bernard Leics
12 D3 Mounts Farm Touring Park Devon
464 C3 Mount Stuart Ag & B
448 B5 Mount View Caravan Park S Lans
605 J6 Mousa Broch HS Shet
291 H3 Mow Cop NT Staffs
195 F4 Mowsbury Golf Club Beds
99 H2 Mt Ephraim Gardens Kent
66 C5 Muchelney Abbey EH Somset
66 C5 Muchelney Caravan & Camping Site Somset
530 D7 Muck Highld
499 G4 Muckhart Golf Club Clacks
261 F3 Muckleburgh Collection museum Norfk
517 L2 Muck visitor centre Highld
484 A4 Mugdock Country Park Stirlg
486 C4 Muiravonside Country Park W Loth
486 C4 Muiravonside Country Park visitor centre Falk
512 A6 Muir O'Fauld Roman Signal Station HS P & K
565 J7 Muir of Ord Golf Club Highld
465 G2 Muirshiel Country Park Rens
3 E2 Muifra Quoit Cnwll
506 B2 Mull & West Highland Narrow Gauge Railway Ag & B
4 C4 Mullion Golf Club Cnwll
4 D5 Mullion Holiday Park Cnwll
377 E5 Muncaster Castle Cumb
376 D5 Muncaster Mill Cumb
256 C2 Mundesley Golf Club Norfk
609 J4 Muness Castle HS Shet
557 H2 Murcar Golf Club N Aber
264 D5 Murmur-yr-Afon Touring Park Conwy
488 C4 Murrayfield C Edin
487 H5 Murrayfield Golf Club C Edin
488 A5 Murrayfield Ice Rink C Edin
513 E4 Murrayshall Country House Hotel golf course P & K
127 E3 Museum of Speed Carmth
14 C5 Music Water Touring Park campsite Cnwll
488 C5 Musselburgh Golf Club E Loth
488 D5 Musselburgh Links golf course E Loth
488 D5 Musselburgh racecourse E Loth
119 F1 Muswell Hill Golf Club Gt Lon
498 D1 Muthill Golf Club P & K
498 D1 Muthill Old Church & Tower HS P & K
178 D2 Mwnt Beach NT Cerdgn
205 B4 Mynach Falls Cerdgn

152 C3 Mynydd Preseli Pembks
488 A5 Myreside C Edin
489 F4 Myreton Motor Museum E Loth
339 H3 Mytton Fold Hotel & Golf Complex Lancs

N

358 A6 Naburn Lock Caravan Park York
595 H4 Na Heardh W Isls
566 F5 Nairn Dunbar Golf Club Highld
229 F3 Nant Gwernol railway station Gwynd
205 H4 Nantyronen railway station Cerdgn
215 E5 National Agricultural Centre Warwks
66 C3 National Animal Welfare Trust Somset
168 A2 National Badminton Centre M Keyn
154 D6 National Botanic Garden of Wales Carmth
328 D1 National Coal Mining Museum Kirk
191 G5 National Herb Centre Warwks
168 A2 National Hockey Stadium M Keyn
276 C1 National Ice Centre C Nott
213 G2 National Indoor Arena Birm
106 C4 National Indoor Athletics Centre Cardif
314 D2 National Indoor Athletics Centre Sheff
238 B2 National Memorial arboretum Staffs
214 C3 National Motorcycle museum Solhll
50 C4 National Motor Museum Hants
285 F3 National Mountain Centre Conwy
489 H4 National Museum of Flight Scotland E Loth
467 F3 National Museum of Rural Life Scotland NTS S Lans
93 F3 National Shooting Centre Surrey
240 C3 National Space Centre C Leic
119 G5 National Sports Centre Gt Lon
326 C5 National Squash Centre Manch
294 B3 National Stone Centre Derbys
198 C2 National Stud visitor centre Suffk
294 C3 National Tramway museum Derbys
276 D2 National Watersports Centre Notts
193 F5 National Waterways museum Nhants
266 D2 National Whitewater Centre Gwynd
309 F2 National Wildfowl Centre Lpool
162 B5 Nature in Art museum Gloucs
384 D1 Nature's World Middsb
163 H5 Naunton Downs Golf Club Gloucs
311 F2 Navigation Road railway station Traffd
145 F3 Nazeing Golf Club Essex
177 E5 Naze Marine campsite Essex
130 B5 Neath Golf Club Neath
214 B3 NEC Solhll
35 G4 Needles Old Battery NT IoW
262 D2 Nefyn & District Golf Club Gwynd
450 A1 Neidpath Castle Border
340 D2 Nelson Golf Club Lancs
218 D5 Nene Park Nhants
243 G5 Nene Valley Railway C Pete
533 H7 Neptune's Staircase (Locks) Highld
308 D4 Ness Botanic Gardens Ches
269 G6 Nesscliffe Country Park Shrops
605 G9 Ness of Burgi HS Shet
311 G4 Nether Alderley Watermill NT Ches
88 D5 Netheravon Dovecote EH Wilts
199 G5 Nether Hall Suffk
51 E3 Netley Abbey EH Hants
78 D2 Nevill Golf Club Kent
533 J7 Nevis Range Ski Centre Highld
398 B1 New Abbey Corn Mill HS D & G
297 E3 Newark Castle railway station Notts
297 G4 Newark Golf Club Notts
482 D5 Newark HS Inver
471 F1 Newbattle Golf Club Mdloth
61 E2 Newberry Valley Park campsite Devon
431 F2 Newbiggin Golf Club Nthumb
191 E1 Newbold Comyn Country Park Warwks
191 E1 Newbold Comyn Golf Club Warwks
468 B1 New Broomfield N Lans
235 F2 New Buck's Head Wrekin
561 F4 Newburgh on Ythan Golf Club Abers
371 G4 Newburgh Priory N York
405 F1 Newburn Hall Motor Museum N u Ty
90 D1 Newbury & Crookham Golf Club W Berk
90 D1 Newbury racecourse W Berk
114 D5 Newbury showground W Berk
365 E2 Newby Bridge railway station Cumb
370 C6 Newby Hall N York
430 C5 Newcastle airport N u Ty
153 C1 Newcastle Emlyn castle Cerdgn
430 D5 Newcastle racecourse N u Ty
426 C2 Newcastleton Golf Club Border
291 G3 Newcastle-under-Lyme Golf Club Staffs
405 F1 Newcastle United Golf Club N u Ty
334 C2 New Clee railway station NE Lin
434 C2 New Cumnock Golf Club E Ayrs
467 H3 New Douglas Park S Lans
50 A3 New Forest Hants
50 B3 New Forest Golf Club Hants
49 G3 New Forest National Park Hants
50 C5 New Forest Otter, Owl & Wildlife Park Hants
421 G4 New Galloway Golf Club D & G
296 C4 New Hall Farm Touring Park Notts
147 G3 New Hall vineyard Essex
56 C4 Newhaven Fort E Susx

56 C4 Newhaven Harbour railway station E Susx
293 M3 Newhaven Holiday Camping & Caravan Park Derbys
326 F2 New Hey railway station Rochdl
366 C4 New House Caravan Park Lancs
468 D6 New Lanark World Heritage Village (UNESCO) S Lans
29 G4 Newlands Caravan & Camping Park Dorset
557 F1 Newmachar Golf Club Abers
198 C2 Newmarket racecourse Suffk
312 C2 New Mills Golf Club Derbys
312 C3 New Mills Newtown railway station Derbys
216 A3 Newnham Paddox Warwks
326 C3 New North Manchester Golf Club Rochdl
126 A2 New Park Farm campsite Pembks
351 H2 New Parkside Farm Caravan Park Lancs
7 E3 Newperran Holiday Park Cnwll
323 F1 New Pleasureland Sefton
152 B1 Newport (Pemb) Golf Club Pembks
37 E3 Newport Golf Club IoW
107 E2 Newport Golf Club Newpt
194 B6 Newport Pagnell service area M Keyn
107 F2 Newport Stadium Newpt
342 D3 New Pudsey railway station Leeds
14 B6 Newquay airport Cnwll
7 F1 Newquay Golf Club Cnwll
7 G1 Newquay Holiday Park Cnwll
119 G1 New River Sports Stadium Gt Lon
295 G4 Newstead Abbey Notts
467 G2 Newton (Lanarkshire) railway station S Lans
20 A3 Newton Abbot (Stover) Golf Club Devon
20 B3 Newton Abbot racecourse Devon
386 D6 Newtondale Forest Drive N York
386 D6 Newton Dale Halt railway station N York
327 E5 Newton for Hyde railway station Tamesd
174 B1 Newton Green Golf Club Suffk
86 C2 Newton Mill campsite BaNES
535 K3 Newtonmore Golf Club Highld
417 E3 Newton Stewart Golf Club D & G
94 A2 New Zealand Golf Club Surrey
369 F6 Nidderdale N York
487 E5 Niddry Castle Golf Club W Loth
294 A2 Nine Ladies EH Derbys
14 C5 Nine Maidens Cnwll
31 E4 Nine Stones EH Dorset
37 F4 Ninham Country Holidays campsite IoW
106 C4 Ninian Park Cardif
106 C4 Ninian Park railway station Cardif
435 H5 Nithsdale D & G
97 E4 Nizels golf course Kent
109 E5 Noah's Ark Zoo Farm N Som
37 G3 Nodes Point Holiday Park IoW
35 g8 Noirmont Command Bunker Jersey
602 E2 Noltland Castle HS Ork
125 E1 Nolton Cross Caravan Park Pembks
135 E4 Norchard railway station Gloucs
558 C1 Nordic Ski Centre Wrekin
226 C2 Norfolk & Suffolk Aviation museum Suffk
252 B4 Norfolk Arena Norfk
260 C4 Norfolk Coast Cycleway Norfk
258 D4 Norfolk Lavender Norfk
261 G3 Norfolk Shire Horse Centre Norfk
250 B3 Norfolk Ski Centre Norfk
255 E4 Norfolk Wildlife Park Norfk
474 D5 Norham Castle EH Nthumb
332 B1 Normanby Hall N Linc
332 B1 Normanby Hall Golf Club N Linc
332 B2 Normanby Road N Linc
361 E2 Norman Manor House E R Yk
343 F5 Normanton Golf Club Wakefd
322 e7 Norse Houses IoM
567 L4 North Alves Caravan Park Moray
84 A3 Northam Farm Caravan & Touring Park Somset
217 F6 Northampton & Lamport Railway Nhants
193 E2 Northampton Golf Club Nhants
193 F2 Northamptonshire County Cricket Ground Nhants
193 F2 Northamptonshire County Golf Club Nhants
489 G2 North Berwick Golf Club E Loth
514 C3 North Carr Lightship C Dund
342 B2 Northcliffe Golf Club Brad
300 D2 Northcote Heavy Horse Centre Lincs
61 E2 North Devon cycle route Devon
47 E4 North Dorset cycle route Dorset
99 G3 North Downs
95 H4 North Downs Golf Club Surrey
99 E4 North Downs Way Kent
94 B5 North Downs Way Surrey
119 G5 North Dulwich railway station Gt Lon
254 C3 North Elmham Chapel EH Norfk
311 G1 Northenden Golf Club Manch
101 G2 North Foreland Golf Club Kent
92 D3 North Hants Golf Club Hants
596 E6 North Harris W Isls
80 B4 North Inch golf course E Susx
512 D5 North Inch golf course P & K
73 E2 Northington Grange EH Hants
139 F1 North Leigh Roman Villa EH Oxon
285 G2 North Llanrwst railway station Conwy
144 C6 North Middlesex Golf Club Gt Lon
60 C2 North Morte Farm Caravan & Camping Park Devon
261 E3 North Norfolk Railway Norfk
118 C3 Northolt aerodrome Gt Lon
118 C2 Northolt Park railway station Gt Lon
308 C6 Northop Country Park Golf Club Flints
140 B2 North Oxford Golf Club Oxon

373 G2 North Riding Forest Park N York
383 G2 North Road railway station Darltn
603 M1 North Ronaldsay Ork
603 M1 North Ronaldsay airport Ork
301 G2 North Shore Hotel & Golf Club Lincs
592 B4 North Uist W Isls
430 D5 Northumberland Golf Club N u Ty
441 H4 Northumberland National Park Nthumb
119 G1 Northumberland Park railway station Gt Lon
305 G3 North Wales Golf Club Conwy
238 D5 North Warwickshire Cycleway Warwks
214 C3 North Warwickshire Golf Club Solhll
145 G4 North Weald airshow venue Essex
145 H3 North Weald Golf Club Essex
145 G4 North Weald railway station Essex
513 F5 North West Trail cycle route P & K
88 B1 North Wilts Golf Club Wilts
118 B1 Northwood Golf Club Gt Lon
213 H4 North Worcestershire golf course Birm
385 F5 North York Moors N York
386 B4 North York Moors National Park
386 D6 North Yorkshire Moor's Railway N York
237 F3 Norton Canes service area Staffs
370 C2 Norton Conyers N York
396 B5 Norton golf course S on T
237 F3 Norton Lakeside railway station Staffs
296 C4 Norwood Park golf course Notts
255 H5 Norwich airport Norfk
343 H6 Nostell Priory NT Wakefd
23 G1 Noseworthy Caravan and Campsite Devon
163 G5 Notgrove Long Barrow EH Gloucs
32 B4 Nothe Fort Dorset
276 D2 Nottingham airfield Notts
295 G4 Nottingham City Golf Club C Nott
276 D2 Nottingham racecourse C Nott
297 F3 Nottinghamshire showground Notts
276 B2 Nottingham Tennis Centre C Nott
295 G3 Notts Golf Club Notts
215 F1 Nuneaton Golf Club Warwks
86 C5 Nunney Castle EH Somset
372 C4 Nunnington Hall NT N York
490 A5 Nunraw Abbey E Loth
37 F3 Nunwell House IoW
95 G5 Nutfield railway station Surrey
53 G5 Nyewood Lane W Susx
77 E4 Nymans NT W Susx
136 A4 Nympsfield Monument EH Gloucs

O

240 D4 Oadby Golf Club Leics
425 H5 Oakbank Lakes campsite Cumb
356 B3 Oakdale Golf Club N York
132 C5 Oakdale golf course Caerph
28 C4 Oakdown Touring & Holiday Caravan Park Devon
43 G3 Oake Manor Golf Club Somset
235 F2 Oakengates railway station Wrekin
242 B3 Oakham School cricket ground Rutlnd
365 E3 Oak Head Caravan Park Cumb
142 D6 Oakland Park Golf Club Bucks
395 F5 Oakleaf Golf Complex Dur
296 B4 Oakmere Park golf course Notts
92 D5 Oak Park Golf Club Hants
214 D1 Oakridge golf course Warwks
95 F2 Oaks Sports Centre golf course Gt Lon
329 F3 Oakwell Barns
342 D4 Oakwell Hall Country Park Kirk
126 B2 Oakwood Adventure & Leisure Park Pembks
97 G2 Oastpark golf course Kent
506 D4 Oban Caravan & Camping Park Ag & B
351 F2 Ocean Edge Leisure Park campsite Lancs
151 F2 Ocean Lab Pembks
204 D3 Ocean View Caravan Park Cerdgn
499 G3 Ochil Hills P & K
485 H3 Ochilview Park Falk
162 C4 Oddas Chapel EH Gloucs
117 F2 Odds Farm Park Rare Breeds Centre Bucks
92 B5 Odiham airfield Hants
92 B4 Odiham Castle Hants
342 C4 Odsall Stadium Brad
209 E5 Offa's Dyke Heritage Centre museum Shrops
288 B4 Offa's Dyke Path Denbgs
185 E3 Offa's Dyke Path Herefs
134 B2 Offa's Dyke Path Mons
233 E2 Offa's Dyke Path Powys
113 F5 Ogbourne Downs Golf Club Wilts
104 D4 Ogmore Castle CADW V Glam
25 E4 Okehampton Castle EH Devon
25 E4 Okehampton Golf Club Devon
37 F4 Old Barn Touring Park IoW
105 G5 Old Beaupre Castle CADW V Glam
3 C1 Old Blockhouse EH IoS
97 E3 Oldbury hill fort Kent
293 E6 Old Churnet Railway Trail cycle route Staffs
271 F3 Old Colhurst Manor Shrops
306 B4 Old Colwyn Golf Club Conwy
466 A2 Old Course Ranfurly Golf Club Rens
118 D4 Old Deer Park Gt Lon
86 A4 Old Down Touring Park Somset
144 B5 Old Fold Manor Golf Club Gt Lon
143 G3 Old Gorhambury House EH Herts
366 A5 Old Hall Caravan Park Lancs
397 E5 Old Hall museum R & Cl
327 E4 Oldham Golf Club Oldham
326 D4 Oldham Mumps railway station Oldham
240 D2 Old Junction Boatyard Leics
8 C2 Old Kerrow Farm Holiday Park Cnwll
600 B4 Old Man of Hoy Ork

543 J6 Old Man of Storr Highld
560 B4 Oldmeldrum Golf Club Abers
454 D2 Old Mill Caravan Site Nthumb
220 C2 Old Nene Golf & Country Club Cambs
269 E3 Old Oswestry Hill Fort EH Shrops
288 C2 Old Padeswood Golf Club Flints
104 C1 Old Parish Ground Brdgnd
365 G5 Old Rectory EH Lancs
158 D6 Old Rectory Golf Club Powys
323 G5 Old Roan railway station Sefton
70 C3 Old Sarum EH Wilts
605 G8 Old Scatness museum Shet
37 E4 Old Smithy & Gardens museum IoW
97 F4 Old Soar Manor NT Kent
370 A3 Old Station Caravan Park N York
74 C3 Old Thorns Hotel Golf & Country Estate Cumb
36 C2 Old Town Hall NT IoW
498 B6 Old Town Jail Stirlg
326 B5 Old Trafford Traffd
326 B5 Old Trafford Cricket Ground Traffd
69 F4 Old Wardour Castle EH Wilts
73 F5 Old Winchester Hill (Archaeology Trail) Hants
374 C2 Oliver's Mount N York
214 A3 Olton Golf Club Solhll
119 E4 Olympia Gt Lon
212 B6 Ombersley Golf Club Worcs
121 G2 One Tree Hill Country Park Essex
146 B4 Ongar railway station Essex
291 F6 Onneley Golf Club Staffs
49 E6 Open Golf Centres Dorset
84 D6 Orchard Camping Somset
375 E4 Orchard Farm Holiday Village N York
86 D4 Orchardleigh golf course Somset
299 H6 Orchard Park campsite Lincs
317 E5 Orchard Park Touring Caravan & Camping Park Notts
36 C3 Orchards Holiday Caravan Park IoW
413 F4 Orchardton Tower NTS D & G
475 E4 Ord House Country Park Nthumb
58 D4 Ore railway station E Susx
203 E5 Orford Castle EH Suffk
305 G5 Oriel Ynys Mon museum IoA
601 G2 Orkney Golf Club Ork
601 K1 Orkney Islands Ork
385 E1 Ormesby Hall NT R & Cl
489 E6 Ormiston Market Cross HS E Loth
295 E5 Ormonde Fields Golf & Country Club Derbys
324 A3 Ormskirk Golf Club Lancs
323 G5 Orrell Park railway station Lpool
323 F5 Orrell Park railway station Sefton
121 G3 Orsett Golf Club Thurr
243 H5 Orton Meadows Golf Centre C Pete
243 H5 Orton Mere railway station C Pete
51 F5 Osborne Golf Club IoW
51 F6 Osborne House EH IoW
32 C3 Osmington Mills Holidays campsite Dorset
118 C4 Osterley Park NT Gt Lon
269 F4 Oswestry Golf Club Shrops
355 G6 Otley Golf Club Leeds
441 G6 Otterburn Mill Nthumb
370 D2 Otterington Park campsite N York
28 A5 Otterton Mill visitor centre Devon
251 G6 Oulton Broad North railway station Suffk
227 G1 Oulton Broad South railway station Suffk
290 B2 Oulton Park Ches
343 G4 Oulton Park golf course Leeds
219 E2 Oundle Golf Club Nhants
593 D9 Our Lady of the Isles W Isls
77 F4 Ouse Valley Viaduct W Susx
594 D3 Outer Hebrides W Isls
327 G1 Outlane Golf Club Kirk
226 C1 Outney Meadow Caravan Park Suffk
95 G5 Outwood windmill Surrey
12 C5 Overbecks Museum & Garden NT Devon
193 H1 Overstone Park golf course Nhants
91 E4 Overton railway station Hants
314 C2 Owlerton Stadium Sheff
79 F2 Owl House Gardens Kent
136 A5 Owlpen Manor Gloucs
330 B2 Owston Park golf course Donc
247 E4 Oxburgh Hall NT Norfk
139 H1 Oxford airport Oxon
140 D4 Oxford service area Oxon
140 C4 Oxford Stadium Oxon
236 D4 Oxley Park Golf Club Wolves
234 B2 Oxon Hall Touring Park Shrops
102 C4 Oxwich Castle CADW Swans

P

94 D3 Pachesham Park Golf Centre Surrey
198 D2 Packhorse Bridge EH Suffk
214 B5 Packwood House NT Warwks
284 C2 Padarn Country Park Gwynd
27 G1 Padbrook Park Golf Club Devon
288 C2 Padeswood & Buckley Golf Club Flints
14 C4 Padstow Holiday Park Cnwll
14 C4 Padstow Park Cnwll
13 F2 Paignton and Dartmouth Steam Railway Devon
20 B5 Paignton Queen's Park railway station Torbay
94 B2 Painshill Park Surrey
136 C2 Painswick Golf Club Gloucs
99 F3 Painters Farm Caravan & Camping Site Kent
329 E1 Painthorpe House Golf & Country Club Wakefd
466 C2 Paisley Canal railway station Rens
466 C2 Paisley Gilmour Street railway station Rens
466 C2 Paisley Golf Club Rens
466 C2 Paisley St James railway station Rens
224 B6 Pakenham Watermill Suffk
485 F5 Palacerigg Country Park N Lans
130 B2 Palleg Golf Club Powys
423 G4 Palmerston D & G
106 D1 Pandy Park Caerph
515 E3 Panmure Golf Club Angus

356 C4 Pannal Golf Club N York
144 C2 Panshanger Golf & Squash Complex Herts
126 D2 Pantglas Farm Caravan Park Pembks
602 F1 Papa Westray airport Ork
296 A4 Papplewick Pumping Station Notts
144 D3 Paradise Park Herts
56 C4 Paradise Park Gardens E Susx
4 B1 Parbola Holiday Park Cnwll
132 B4 Parc Cwm Darran Country Park Caerph
355 E2 Parcevall Hall Gardens N York
107 E3 Parc golf course Newpt
102 D4 Parc Le Breos CADW Swans
54 C2 Parham W Susx
204 D3 Park Avenue Cerdgn
106 C3 Park Cefn Onn Country Park Cardif
365 E1 Park Cliffe Camping & Caravan Estate Cumb
19 G3 Parkers Farm Holiday Park Devon
390 D5 Park Foot Caravan & Camping Park Cumb
343 F4 Park Halt railway station Leeds
240 D1 Park Hill Golf Club Leics
431 E5 Parklands golf course N u Ty
326 A4 Park Lane Bury
422 D5 Park of Brandedleys campsite D & G
34 B2 Parkstone Golf Club Poole
143 G4 Park Street railway station Herts
120 C4 Park View Road Gt Lon
96 B3 Park Wood Golf Club Surrey
49 E5 Parley golf course Dorset
8 D3 Par railway station Cnwll
82 C1 Parsonage Farm Rural heritage centre Kent
109 G5 Parson Street railway station Bristl
79 G4 Pashley Manor Gardens
562 D8 Pass of the Cattle Highld
275 E3 Pastures Golf Club Derbys
236 A5 Patshull Park Hotel Golf & Country Club Staffs
466 D3 Patterton railway station E Rens
9 H1 Paul Corin Music museum Cnwll
50 B1 Paultons Golf Centre Hants
50 B1 Paultons Park Hants
194 D3 Pavenham Park golf course Beds
102 B4 Paviland Cave Swans
77 G4 Paxhill Park Golf Club W Susx
474 D4 Paxton House Border
173 G5 Paycockes NT Essex
56 C4 Peacehaven Golf Club E Susx
313 F3 Peak Cavern Derbys
313 G1 Peak District National Park
294 B2 Peak Railway Derbys
33 G1 Pear Tree Touring Park Dorset
77 E3 Pease Pottage service area W Susx
32 B4 Pebble Bank Caravan Park Dorset
119 G4 Peckham Rye railway station Gt Lon
394 A4 Pecknell Farm Caravan Park Dur
28 D5 Pecorama Railway Devon
62 D2 Pedal Around Porlock cycle route Somset
247 G3 Pedars Way & Norfolk Coast Path Norfk
450 A1 Peebles Golf Club Border
322 C6 Peel Golf Club IoM
555 G4 Peel Ring Of Lumphanan HS Abers
177 E3 Peewit Caravan Park Suffk
324 D4 Pemberton railway station Wigan
128 B4 Pembrey Carmth
128 B4 Pembrey Country Park Carmth
128 B4 Pembrey ski slope Carmth
124 D3 Pembrokeshire Coast National Park Pembks
151 E2 Pembrokeshire Coast Path Pembks
151 G6 Pembrokeshire County showground Pembks
15 E4 Pencarrow House Cnwll
158 A5 Pencelli Castle Caravan & Camping Park Powys
288 B6 Penddol Caravan Park Denbgs
5 F2 Pendennis Castle EH Cnwll
3 E2 Penderleath Caravan & Camping Park Cnwll
9 E3 Penhale Caravan & Camping Park Cnwll
23 E3 Penhallam Castle EH Cnwll
22 D2 Penhalt Farm Holiday Park Cnwll
8 C4 Penhaven Touring Park Cnwll
108 D1 Penhow Castle Newpt
96 D6 Penhurst Vineyards Kent
307 F4 Penisar Mynydd Caravan Park Denbgs
341 G2 Penistone Hill Country Park Brad
5 E2 Penjerrick Garden Cnwll
152 B2 Penlan Uchaf Gardens Pembks
284 C2 Penllyn railway station Gwynd
285 G4 Penmachno Woollen Mill Conwy
305 F4 Penmaenmawr Golf Club Conwy
9 E3 Penmarlam Caravan & Camping Park Cnwll
5 E2 Penmere railway station Cnwll
304 D3 Penmon Priory CADW IoA
5 E2 Pennance Mill Farm Touring Park Cnwll
102 D4 Pennard Castle Swans
102 D4 Pennard Golf Club Swans
263 G3 Penrarth Fawr CADW Gwynd
236 C6 Penn Golf Club Staffs
341 F2 Pennines
453 G5 Pennine Way Border
341 E3 Pennine Way Calder
392 B2 Pennine Way Cumb
313 E1 Pennine Way Derbys
367 G3 Pennine Way N York
441 F6 Pennine Way Nthumb
325 E5 Pennington Flash Country Park Wigan
93 E2 Pennyhill Park Hotel & Country Club golf course Surrey
12 B2 Pennymoor Camping & Caravan Park Devon
441 E2 Pennymuir Roman Camps Border
435 H6 Penpont Caravan & Camping Park D & G
302 B4 Penrhos-Feilw CADW IoA

204 C6 Penrhos Golf & Country Club Cerdgn
304 D5 Penrhyn NT Gwynd
229 E1 Penrhyn Point (Barmouth Ferry) railway station Gwynd
391 E4 Penrith Caste EH Cumb
391 E4 Penrith Golf Club Cumb
391 E4 Penrith North Lakes railway station Cumb
7 E3 Penrose Farm Touring Park Cnwll
8 B4 Pensagillas Farm campsite
406 A4 Penshaw monument NT Sundld
96 D6 Penshurst Place Kent
96 D5 Penshurst railway station Kent
254 B2 Pensthorpe Waterfowl Park Norfk
8 C4 Pentewan Sands Holiday Park Cnwll
470 C2 Pentland Hills C Edin
470 D2 Pentland Hills visitor centre Mdloth
131 H4 Pentre-Bach railway station Myr T
152 B2 Pentre Ifan CADW Pembks
266 D3 Pentrepiod railway station Gwynd
338 D4 Penwortham Golf Club Lancs
184 A2 Pen-y-bont railway station Powys
267 E3 Pen Y Bont Touring & Camping Park Gwynd
287 E5 Pen-y-Bryn Farm Park Denbgs
288 C6 Penycae Golf Club Wrexhm
157 G3 Pen-y-crug hill fort Powys
132 C4 Pen-y-fan-pond Country Park Caerph
264 D2 Pen-y-Mount railway station Gwynd
3 E3 Penzance heliport Cnwll
311 E5 Peover Golf Club Ches
71 E5 Pepperbox Hill NT Wilts
20 D2 Peppermint Park campsite Devon
188 C3 Perdiswell Park golf course Worcs
118 D3 Perivale Park golf course Gt Lon
7 E3 Perranporth Camping & Touring Park Cnwll
7 E3 Perranporth Golf Club Cnwll
7 E2 Perran Sands Holiday Park Cnwll
213 G1 Perry Barr railway station Birm
134 D3 Perrygrove Railway Gloucs
189 E5 Pershore railway station Worcs
512 D4 Perth racecourse P & K
512 C3 Perthshire visitor centre P & K
236 C5 Perton Park Golf Club Staffs
220 A2 Peterborough (Conington) airport Cambs
243 G5 Peterborough Milton Golf Club C Pete
243 G5 Peterborough service area Cambs
557 E5 Peterculter golf course C Aber
571 L6 Peterhead Golf Club Abers
56 C4 Peter Leonard Marina E Susx
74 B4 Petersfield Golf Club (New Course) Hants
74 B5 Petersfield Golf Club (Old Course) Hants
107 E3 Peterstone Lakes Golf Club Newpt
251 E4 Pettitts Crafts & Animal Adventure Park Norfk
75 F5 Petworth House NT W Susx
57 G4 Pevensey & Westham railway station E Susx
313 G3 Peveril Castle EH Derbys
315 E1 Phoenix Golf Club Rothm
559 E3 Picardy Symbol Stone HS Abers
111 G6 Piccadilly Caravan Park Wilts
373 E3 Pickering Castle EH N York
125 H2 Picton Castle Pembks
350 B2 Piel Castle EH Cumb
383 F1 Piercebridge Roman Bridge N York
602 E2 Pierowall Church HS Ork
357 H5 Pike Hills Golf Club York
179 G4 Pilbach Holiday Park Cerdgn
94 C1 Pillar Data rugby union ground Surrey
29 H2 Pilsdon Pen hill fort Dorset
78 A5 Piltdown Golf Club E Susx
313 G3 Pindale Farm Outdoor Centre Derbys
98 C4 Pine Lodge Touring Park Kent
93 F3 Pine Ridge Golf Club Surrey
423 G4 Pines Golf Centre D & G
118 C1 Pinner Hill Golf Club Gt Lon
274 D4 Pirelli Stadium Staffs
267 H4 Pistyll Rhaeadr (Waterfall) Powys
189 F1 Pitcheroak Golf Club Worcs
577 G5 Pitgrudy Caravan Park Highld
524 D3 Pitlochry golf course P & K
560 C4 Pitmedden Garden NTS Abers
487 F2 Pitreavie Golf Club Fife
122 A2 Pitsea railway station Essex
193 F1 Pitsford & Brampton railway station Nhants
142 C1 Pitstone windmill Bucks
557 G3 Pittodrie C Aber
102 B4 Pitton Cross Caravan & Camping Park Swans
20 C4 Plainmoor Torbay
468 B1 Plains Country Park N Lans
243 H4 Planet Ice Arena C Pete
91 G4 Planet Ice Arena Hants
168 A2 Planet Ice Arena M Keyn
283 F3 Plas Gwyn Caravan Park Gwynd
269 E1 Plas Kynaston Lane Wrexhm
268 D1 Plas Newydd Denbgs
283 F2 Plas Newydd NT IoA
288 D5 Plassey Golf Club Wrexhm
283 F4 Plas y Nant railway station Gwynd
262 C5 Plas-Yn-Rhiw NT Gwynd
339 F4 Pleasington Golf Club Bl w D
334 D3 Pleasure Island NE Lin
91 G4 Pleasurewood Hills Suffk
430 D4 Plessey Woods Country Park Nthumb
56 B1 Plumpton racecourse E Susx
567 L5 Pluscarden Abbey Moray
18 B5 Plymouth airport C Plym
14 B4 Point Curlew Chalet & Touring Park Cnwll
10 A2 Polborder House Caravan & Camping Park Cnwll
4 C2 Poldark Mine Cnwll
4 B3 Poldown Caravan Park Cnwll
94 C4 Polesdon Lacy NT Surrey
9 E3 Polglaze Farm campsite Cnwll
469 E1 Polkemmet Country Park W Loth

469 E1 **Polkemmet Country Park golf course** W Loth
466 D2 **Pollok Country Park** C Glas
467 E2 **Pollok Golf Club** C Glas
466 D2 **Pollok House NTS** C Glas
3 F2 **Polmanter Tourist Park** Cnwll
486 B4 **Polmont Golf Club** Falk
9 G3 **Polperro Model Village** Cnwll
9 E3 **Polruan Holidays-Camping & Caravanning** Cnwll
27 E4 **Polsloe Bridge railway station** Devon
23 H6 **Polson Bridge** Cnwll
174 C1 **Polstead Touring Park** Suffk
37 G2 **Pondwell Camp Site** IoW
129 E3 **Pont Abraham service area** Carmth
129 H4 **Pontardawe Golf Club** Neath
269 E1 **Pontcysyllte Aqueduct** Wrexhm
344 A5 **Pontefract & District Golf Club** Wakefd
344 A5 **Pontefract Baghill railway station** Wakefd
344 A5 **Pontefract racecourse** Wakefd
344 B5 **Pontefract Tanshelf railway station** Wakefd
430 C5 **Ponteland Golf Club** Nthumb
155 F5 **Pont Gwladys railway station** Carmth
133 G3 **Pont Kemys Caravan & Camping Park** Mons
230 D2 **Pont Minllyn** Gwynd
133 E5 **Pontnewydd Golf Club** Torfn
133 F4 **Pontypool & New Inn railway station** Torfn
133 E4 **Pontypool Golf Club** Torfn
106 A1 **Pontypridd Golf Club** Rhondd
27 H6 **Pooh Cottage Holiday Park** Devon
312 D5 **Poole's Cavern** Derbys
34 B2 **Poole Stadium** Poole
91 E6 **Popham airfield** Hants
178 D4 **Poppit Sands** Pembks
357 H4 **Poppleton railway station** York
9 F2 **Porfell Animal Land** Cnwll
62 D2 **Porlock Caravan Park** Somset
290 B2 **Portal Golf & Country Club** Ches
110 B6 **Portavon Marina** S Glos
464 B1 **Port Bannatyne Golf Club** Ag & B
51 H4 **Portchester Castle roman site EH** Hants
283 F2 **Port Dinorwic Marina** Gwynd
143 H4 **Porters Park Golf Club** Herts
31 E5 **Portesham Dairy Farm campsite** Dorset
482 D6 **Port Glasgow Golf Club** Inver
51 E3 **Port Hamble Marina** Hants
14 A6 **Porth Beach Tourist Park** Cnwll
302 B5 **Porth Dafarch NT** IoA
3 d2 **Porth Hellick Downs Tombs EH** IoS
264 C2 **Porthmadog Golf Club** Gwynd
264 D2 **Porthmadog Harbour railway station** Gwynd
8 C3 **Porthpean Golf Club** Cnwll
6 C4 **Porthtowan Tourist Park** Cnwll
32 B5 **Portland** Dorset
32 B6 **Portland Bill Lighthouse** Dorset
32 B5 **Portland Castle EH** Dorset
32 B5 **Portland Museum & Shipwreck Centre** Dorset
557 G5 **Portlethen Golf Club** Abers
81 H3 **Port Lympne Wild Animal Park** Kent
201 G6 **Portman Road** Suffk
97 H1 **Port Medway Marina** Medway
264 D2 **Portmeirion** Gwynd
488 C5 **Portobello golf course** C Edin
3 F2 **Port of Hayle (UNESCO)** Cnwll
414 C6 **Portpatrick Golf Club** D & G
14 D3 **Portreath Bee Centre** Cnwll
322 C9 **Port St Mary Golf Club** IoM
52 A4 **Portsmouth & Southsea railway station** C Port
40 C4 **Portsmouth Arms railway station** Devon
52 B3 **Portsmouth golf course** Hants
52 A4 **Portsmouth Harbour railway station** C Port
484 B6 **Possilpark & Parkhouse railway station** C Glas
159 G2 **Poston Mill Caravan & Camping Park** Herefs
144 B4 **Potters Bar Golf Club** Herts
337 G1 **Poulton Le Fylde Golf Club** Lancs
310 C1 **Poulton Park golf course** Warrtn
97 F5 **Poult Wood Golf Centre** Kent
8 D2 **Powderham Castle Tourist Park** Cnwll
399 E1 **Powfoot Golf Club** D & G
404 B4 **Pow Hill Country Park** Dur
232 D3 **Powis Castle NT** Powys
312 B3 **Poynton showground** Ches
3 G4 **Praa Sands Golf Club** Cnwll
21 E1 **Prattshayes Farm National Trust campsite** Devon
502 B3 **Praytis Country Park** Fife
243 F5 **Prebendal Manor House** Nhants
4 C5 **Predannack airfield** Cnwll
270 C3 **Prees railway station** Shrops
308 D2 **Prenton Golf Club** Wirral
308 D2 **Prenton Park** Wirral
302 D4 **Presaddfed CADW** IoA
6 D4 **Presingoll Farm Caravan & Camping Park** Cnwll
307 F3 **Prestatyn Golf Club** Denbgs
312 A4 **Prestbury Golf Club** Ches
307 G3 **Presthaven Sands campsite** Flints
26 A4 **Prestonbury Castle** Devon
488 B5 **Prestonfield Golf Club** C Edin
338 D3 **Preston Golf Club** Lancs
488 D5 **Preston Grange Industrial Heritage Museum** E Loth
338 D4 **Preston Marina** Lancs
488 D5 **Preston Market Cross HS** E Loth
490 A4 **Preston Mill and Phantassie Doocot NTS** E Loth
55 G3 **Preston Park railway station** Br & H
455 F4 **Preston Pele Tower** Nthumb
326 B4 **Prestwich Golf Club** Bury
445 E4 **Prestwick airport** S Ayrs
444 D4 **Prestwick Golf Club** S Ayrs
444 D4 **Prestwick International Airport railway station** S Ayrs
445 E5 **Prestwick St Cuthbert Golf Club** S Ayrs
444 D5 **Prestwick St Nicholas Golf Club** S Ayrs
444 D4 **Prestwick Town railway station** S Ayrs
20 A4 **Prickley Ball Farm Hedgehog Hospital** Devon

14 C3 **Prideaux Place** Cnwll
275 F2 **Pride Park** C Derb
122 B6 **Priestfield Stadium** Medway
466 D2 **Priesthill & Darnley railway station** C Glas
375 E4 **Primrose Valley Holiday Park** N York
531 K6 **Prince Charlie's Cairn** Highld
101 G5 **Prince's Golf Club** Kent
300 D4 **Princes golf course** IoA
570 B3 **Princess Royal Park** Abers
136 C2 **Prinknash Abbey** Gloucs
86 D2 **Prior Park NT** BaNES
451 H3 **Priorwood Garden NTS** Border
159 E4 **Priory Abbey CADW** Mons
365 E4 **Priory Gatehouse NT** Cumb
123 G5 **Priory Hill campsite** Kent
57 G4 **Priory Lane** E Susx
195 F5 **Priory Marina** Beds
176 C1 **Priory Park campsite** Suffk
151 F3 **Priskilly Forest Golf Club** Pembks
467 G1 **Provan Hall NTS** C Glas
404 C2 **Prudhoe Castle EH** Nthumb
404 D2 **Prudhoe Golf Club** Nthumb
289 H1 **Pryors Hayes Golf Club** Ches
343 F6 **Pugneys Country Park** Wakefd
142 A4 **Pulpit Hill** Bucks
487 E6 **Pumpherston Golf Club** W Loth
239 E6 **Purley Chase Golf Club** Warwks
95 G2 **Purley Downs Golf Club** Gt Lon
95 G2 **Purley Oaks railway station** Gt Lon
84 B3 **Purn International Holiday Park** N Som
93 F5 **Puttenham Golf Club** Surrey
263 F4 **Pwllheli Golf Club** Gwynd
55 G2 **Pyecombe Golf Club** W Susx
104 C3 **Pyle & Kenfig Golf Club** Brdgnd
238 A6 **Pype Hayes Golf Club** Birm
94 B3 **Pyrford Basin Marina** Surrey
94 A3 **Pyrford Golf Club** Surrey
133 E1 **Pyscodlyn Farm Caravan & Camping Site** Mons
218 B4 **Pytchley Golf Lodge** Nhants

Q

64 C4 **Quantock Hills** Somset
64 B4 **Quantock Orchard Caravan Park** Somset
311 G3 **Quarry Bank Mill NT** Ches
273 F1 **Quarry Walk Park campsite** Staffs
37 F4 **Queen Bower Dairy Caravan Park** IoW
73 H6 **Queen Elizabeth Country Park** Hants
496 C3 **Queen Elizabeth Forest Park** Stirlg
496 D4 **Queen Elizabeth Forest Park visitor centre** Stirlg
342 B4 **Queensbury Golf Club** Brad
566 D5 **Queen's Own Highlanders Regimental museum** Highld
119 E3 **Queens Park (London) railway station** Gt Lon
49 E6 **Queen's Park golf course** Bmouth
290 D3 **Queen's Park golf course** Ches
483 H3 **Queen's View (Stirling) viewpoint** Stirlg
524 C4 **Queen's View visitor centre** P & K
186 C4 **Queenswood Country Park** Herefs
101 F2 **Quex Caravan Park** Kent
220 C5 **Quiet Waters Caravan Park** Cambs
41 E2 **Quince Honey Farm** Devon
240 B1 **Quorn & Woodhouse railway station** Leics

R

545 K1 **Raasay** Highld
394 C5 **Raby Castle** Dur
319 E2 **Racecourse Caravan Park** Lincs
117 F4 **Racecourse Yacht Basin** W & M
276 D2 **Radcliffe (Nottinghamshire) railway station** Notts
277 E2 **Radcliffe-on-Trent Golf Club** Notts
184 C3 **Radnor Forest** Powys
185 F2 **Radnor Ring cycle route** Herefs
207 F6 **Radnor Ring cycle route** Powys
106 B3 **Radyr Golf Club** Cardif
438 B5 **Raeburnfoot Roman Fort** D & G
567 K4 **RAF Kinloss airfield** Moray
514 C3 **RAF Leuchars** Fife
568 C2 **RAF Lossiemouth airfield** Moray
222 D4 **RAF Mildenhall** Suffk
119 E1 **RAF Museum (Hendon)** Gt Lon
105 G6 **RAF St Athan Golf Club** V Glam
133 H3 **Raglan Castle CADW** Mons
133 H3 **Raglan Parc Golf Club** Mons
189 G3 **Ragley Hall** Warwks
98 C1 **Rainham (Kent) railway station** Medway
466 D2 **Rainhill Golf Club** Rens
136 C1 **Ramada Hotel & Resort Gloucester golf course** Gloucs
296 A5 **Ramsdale Park Golf Centre** Notts
220 C2 **Ramsey Abbey Gatehouse NT** Cambs
220 C3 **Ramsey Golf & Bowls Club** Cambs
322 g4 **Ramsey Golf Club** IoM
150 A5 **Ramsey Island** Pembks
339 G3 **Ramsgreave & Wilpshire railway station** Lancs
405 H6 **Ramside Hall Golf Club** Dur
189 H6 **Ranch Caravan Park** Worcs
466 A1 **Ranfurly Castle Golf Club** Rens
521 L5 **Rannoch Moor** Highld
522 D4 **Rannoch railway station** P & K
487 G5 **Rathro Park Golf Club** C Edin
298 C6 **Rauceby railway station** Lincs
487 H5 **Ravelston Golf Club** C Edin
377 E5 **Ravenglass & Eskdale Railway** Cumb
376 D5 **Ravenglass for Eskdale railway station** Cumb
387 G4 **Raven Hall Hotel golf course** N York
120 A5 **Ravensbourne railway station** Gt Lon

169 F4 **Ravensburgh Castle** Herts
405 G3 **Ravensworth Golf Club** Gatesd
340 C5 **Rawtenstall railway station** Lancs
116 B4 **Reading Golf Club** Readg
115 H6 **Reading service area** W Berk
116 B5 **Reading West railway station** Readg
290 C4 **Reaseheath Golf Club** Ches
587 L3 **Reay Golf Club** Highld
100 D2 **Reculver Towers EH** Kent
86 D2 **Recreation Ground** BaNES
93 E4 **Recreation Ground** Hants
207 G1 **Recreation Ground** Powys
121 F4 **Recreation Ground** Thurr
376 B1 **Recreation Ground (Whitehaven RLFC)** Cumb
498 D6 **Recreation Park (Alloa Athletic FC)** Clacks
119 G2 **Rectory Road railway station** Gt Lon
365 G6 **Red Bank Farm campsite** Lancs
143 G2 **Redbourn Golf Club** Herts
50 C2 **Redbridge railway station** C Soton
397 F5 **Redcar Central railway station** R & Cl
397 F5 **Redcar East railway station** R & Cl
397 F5 **Redcar racecourse** R & Cl
326 D6 **Reddish Vale Golf Club** Stockp
189 F1 **Redditch Golf Club** Worcs
441 F5 **Redesdale** Nthumb
95 F5 **Redhill & Reigate Golf Club** Surrey
95 F5 **Redhill aerodrome** Surrey
276 A4 **Red Hill Marina** Notts
125 E2 **Redlands Caravan & Camping Park** Pembks
97 E1 **Redlibbets Golf Club** Kent
162 C4 **Red Lion Caravan Park** Gloucs
269 G4 **Rednal airfield** Shrops
49 F3 **Red Shoot Camping Park** Hants
325 E3 **Reebok Stadium** Bolton
95 G2 **Reedham (Surrey) railway station** Gt Lon
526 C4 **Reekie Linn Falls** Angus
325 F3 **Regent Park golf course** Bolton
69 H4 **Regimental Badges chalk figures (Fovant)** Wilts
147 E2 **Regiment Way Golf Centre** Essex
95 E5 **Reigate Heath Golf Club** Surrey
95 F4 **Reigate Hill Golf Club** Surrey
375 E4 **Reighton Sands Holiday Park** N York
551 H8 **Reindeer Centre** Highld
400 C3 **Reivers Route cycle route** Cumb
431 G5 **Reivers Route cycle route** Nthumb
92 C1 **REME museum** Wokham
483 G6 **Renfrew Golf Club** Rens
315 E4 **Renishaw Park Golf Club** Derbys
546 E4 **Reraig Caravan Site** Highld
519 H3 **Resipole Farm campsite** Highld
527 G4 **Restenneth Priory HS** Angus
9 E1 **Restormel Castle EH** Cnwll
4 D2 **Retanna Holiday Park** Cnwll
316 C4 **Retford (Gamston) airport** Notts
316 C4 **Retford Golf Club** Notts
314 D4 **Revolution House** Derbys
265 G5 **Rhaeadr Ddu (Waterfall) NT** Gwynd
390 D4 **Rheged Discovery Centre** Cumb
205 G4 **Rheidol Falls railway station** Cerdgn
205 G4 **Rheidol Power Station** Cerdgn
49 H4 **Rhinefield Ornamental Drive** Hants
476 C5 **Rhinns of Islay** Ag & B
205 G4 **Rhiwfron Halt railway station** Cerdgn
265 G3 **Rhiw Goch Ski Centre** Gwynd
181 G6 **Rhondda Golf Club** Rhondd
105 G1 **Rhondda Heritage Park** Rhondd
131 F5 **Rhondda Valley** Rhondd
304 B4 **Rhos Caravan Park** IoA
306 A3 **Rhos-on-Sea Golf Club** Conwy
102 B4 **Rhossili Visitor Centre NT** Swans
39 G4 **RHS Garden Rosemoor** Devon
307 E4 **Rhuddlan Castle CADW** Denbgs
307 E4 **Rhuddlan Golf Club** Denbgs
262 D5 **Rhydolion campsite** Gwynd
307 E3 **Rhyl Golf Club** Denbgs
367 H4 **Ribblehead railway station** N York
367 H4 **Ribblehead Viaduct** N York
353 G3 **Ribblesdale** N York
323 G5 **Rice Lane railway station** Lpool
101 F3 **Richborough Roman Fort EH** Kent
118 A4 **Richings Park Golf Club** Bucks
383 E4 **Richmond Golf Club** N York
154 B5 **Richmond Park** Carmth
248 B4 **Richmond Golf Club** Norfk
119 E3 **Richmond Park golf course** Gt Lon
143 F6 **Rickmansworth Public golf course** Herts
215 E3 **Ricoh Arena** Covtry
492 D5 **Ri Cruin Cairn HS** Ag & B
355 E6 **Riddlesden Golf Club** Brad
95 G2 **Riddlesdown railway station** Gt Lon
33 G2 **Ridge Farm Camping & Caravan Park** Dorset
160 C2 **Ridge Hill Caravan and campsite** Herefs
142 D3 **Ridgeway Path** Bucks
114 A3 **Ridgeway Path** Oxon
115 G2 **Ridgeway Path** W Berk
372 A3 **Rievaulx Abbey** N York
372 A3 **Rievaulx Terrace & Temples NT** N York
387 F3 **Rigg Farm Caravan Park** N York
353 G3 **Rimington Caravan Park** Lancs
600 D2 **Ring of Brodgar HS** Ork
311 F2 **Ringway Golf Club** Trafd
356 B2 **Ripley Caravan Park** N York
370 C5 **Ripon City Golf Club** N York
370 C6 **Ripon racecourse** N York
186 C3 **Risbury hill fort** Herefs
120 D1 **Risebridge Golf Centre** Gt Lon
340 A4 **Rishton Golf Club** Lancs
428 D2 **Risinghan (Habitancum) Roman site** Nthumb

431 F6 **Rising Sun Country Park** N Tyne
410 D3 **Rispain Camp HS** D & G
309 E4 **Rivacre Park** Ches
293 G3 **Rivendale Touring Caravan & Leisure Park** Derbys
116 C3 **River & Rowing museum** Oxon
19 F3 **River Dart Country Park** Devon
19 F4 **River Dart Country Park campsite** Devon
351 H1 **River Lune Millennium Park** Lancs
195 H3 **River Mill Boats** Cambs
283 F3 **Riverside Camping** Gwynd
41 E2 **Riverside Caravan & Camping Park** Devon
158 D6 **Riverside Caravan & Camping Park** Powys
358 B5 **Riverside Caravan & Camping Park** York
18 B6 **Riverside Caravan Park** C Plym
351 F2 **Riverside Caravan Park** Lancs
366 D6 **Riverside Caravan Park** N York
129 G3 **Riverside Caravan Park** Swans
188 B5 **Riverside Caravan Park** Worcs
122 C6 **Riverside Country Park** Medway
405 G4 **Riverside cricket ground** Dur
7 F2 **Riverside Holiday Park** Cnwll
338 B6 **Riverside Holiday Park** Lancs
51 E3 **Riverside Holidays campsite** Hants
147 E3 **Riverside Ice & Leisure Centre** Essex
222 D4 **Riverside Island Marina** Cambs
138 C5 **Riverside Lechlade Marina** Gloucs
370 C5 **Riverside Meadows Country Caravan Park** N York
396 D5 **Riverside Stadium** Middsb
524 C2 **River Tilt Caravan Park** P & K
3 G3 **River Valley Country Park** Cnwll
8 C3 **River Valley Holiday Park** Cnwll
515 E3 **Riverview Caravan Park** Angus
129 E3 **River View Touring Park** Carmth
67 E5 **RNAS Yeovilton airshow venue** Somset
24 B4 **Roadford Lake campsite** Devon
306 C5 **Roberts Caravan Park** Conwy
450 C2 **Robert Smail's Printing Works NTS** Border
37 E3 **Robin Hill Countryside Adventure Park** IoW
372 D5 **Robin Hood Caravan & Camping Park** N York
331 E6 **Robin Hood Doncaster Sheffield airport** Donc
214 A3 **Robin Hood Golf Club** Solhll
136 B2 **Robins Wood Hill viewpoint** Gloucs
497 F3 **Rob Roy And Trossachs visitor centre** Stirlg
326 C2 **Rochdale Golf Club** Rochdl
315 G2 **Roche Abbey EH** Rothm
8 B1 **Roche railway station** Cnwll
121 H6 **Rochester & Cobham Park Golf Club** Kent
122 D1 **Rochford Hundred Golf Club** Essex
49 E1 **Rockbourne Roman Villa** Hants
185 E1 **Rockbridge Park campsite** Powys
49 F3 **Rockford Common NT** Hants
218 C1 **Rockingham** Nhants
218 B1 **Rockingham Castle** Nhants
218 B3 **Rockingham Motor Speedway** Nhants
34 A2 **Rockley Park campsite** Poole
154 B1 **Rock Mill Woollen & Water Mill** Cerdgn
136 C2 **Rococo Gardens** Gloucs
107 F2 **Rodney Parade** Newpt
162 A5 **Rodway Hill golf course** Gloucs
37 F2 **Roebeck Camping and Caravan Park** IoW
576 F3 **Rogart railway station** Highld
565 G5 **Rogie Falls** Highld
382 C2 **Rokeby Park** Dur
93 G4 **Roker Park golf course** Surrey
164 D3 **Rollright Stones EH** Oxon
80 C3 **Rolvenden railway station** Kent
285 F4 **Roman Bridge railway station** Conwy
384 A6 **Romanby Golf & Country Club** N York
120 D1 **Romford Golf Club** Gt Lon
120 D2 **Romford Ice Rink** Gt Lon
312 B1 **Romiley Golf Club** Stockp
81 G4 **Romney; Hythe & Dymchurch Railway** Kent
81 G3 **Romney Marsh** Kent
81 G5 **Romney Sands railway station** Kent
81 G4 **Romney Warren Golf Club** Kent
71 G5 **Romsey Abbey** Hants
71 H6 **Romsey Golf Club** Hants
543 L5 **Rona** Highld
227 G1 **Rookery Park Golf Club** Suffk
37 E4 **Rookley Country Park campsite** IoW
364 B6 **Roose railway station** Cumb
122 D2 **Roots Hall** Sthend
454 D4 **Ros Castle NT** Nthumb
405 F4 **Roseberry Grange golf course** Dur
84 B5 **Rosebush Caravan Park** Pembks
386 B5 **Rosedale Caravan & Camping Park** N York
251 F4 **Rose Farm Touring & Camping Park** Norfk
312 C2 **Rose Hill Marple railway station** Stockp
2 C3 **Roselands Caravan Park** Cnwll
37 F2 **Rosemary vineyard** IoW
14 D3 **Roserrow Golf & Country Club** Cnwll
450 A1 **Rosetta Caravan & Camping Park** Border
7 E3 **Roseville Holiday Park** Cnwll
340 B5 **Rossendale Golf Club** Lancs
323 F5 **Rosset Park** Lpool
504 D6 **Ross of Mull** Ag & B
161 F4 **Ross-on-Wye Golf Club** Herefs
20 A4 **Ross Park campsite** Devon
442 D5 **Rothbury Forest** Nthumb
442 D4 **Rothbury Golf Club** Nthumb
329 G6 **Rotherham Central railway station** Rothm
329 H5 **Rotherham Golf Club** Rothm
193 F3 **Rothersthorpe service area** Nhants

315 F3 **Rother Valley Country Park** Rothm
315 F3 **Rother Valley Golf Centre** Rothm
464 B2 **Rothesay Castle HS** Ag & B
464 B2 **Rothesay Golf Club** Ag & B
568 D6 **Rothes Golf Club** Moray
551 G7 **Rothiemurchus visitor centre** Highld
240 C2 **Rothley Park Golf Club** Leics
261 H3 **Roughton Road railway station** Norfk
466 D3 **Rouken Glen Park** E Rens
343 F2 **Roundhay Golf Club** Leeds
322 C7 **Round Table** IoM
36 D4 **Round the Island cycle route** IoW
602 E5 **Rousay** Ork
166 A5 **Rousham Park** Oxon
35 d1 **Rousse Tower** Guern
464 D2 **Routenburn Golf Club** N Ayrs
322 c9 **Rowany Golf Club** IoM
52 C2 **Rowlands Castle Golf Club** Hants
47 F6 **Rowlands Wait Touring Park** Dorset
198 C2 **Rowley Mile service area** Suffk
72 A6 **Rownhams service area** Hants
557 H2 **Royal Aberdeen Golf Club** C Aber
236 A3 **Royal Air Force museum** Shrops
51 H3 **Royal Armouries museum** Leeds
117 F6 **Royal Ascot Golf Club** W & M
78 A3 **Royal Ashdown Forest Golf Club** E Susx
67 G2 **Royal Bath and West Showground** Somset
120 B5 **Royal Blackheath Golf Club** Gt Lon
118 D4 **Royal Botanic Gardens (UNESCO)** Gt Lon
487 G4 **Royal Burgess Golfing Society of Edinburgh** C Edin
101 G5 **Royal Cinque Ports Golf Club** Kent
14 D4 **Royal Cornwall showground** Cnwll
256 A1 **Royal Cromer Golf Club** Norfk
556 C5 **Royal Deeside Railway** Abers
577 H5 **Royal Dornoch Golf Club** Highld
57 F5 **Royal Eastbourne Golf Club** E Susx
145 E5 **Royal Epping Forest Golf Club** Gt Lon
487 F5 **Royal Highland showground (Ingliston)** C Edin
35 j7 **Royal Jersey Golf Club** Jersey
308 B2 **Royal Liverpool Golf Club** Wirral
93 F3 **Royal Logistics Corps Transport museum** Surrey
337 F4 **Royal Lytham & St Annes Golf Club** Lancs
118 D4 **Royal Mid-Surrey Golf Club** Gt Lon
488 D5 **Royal Musselburgh Golf Club** E Loth
249 G2 **Royal Norfolk showground** Norfk
60 B5 **Royal North Devon Golf Club** Devon
249 H2 **Royal Norwich Golf Club** Norfk
488 B5 **Royal Observatory visitor centre** C Edin
104 C4 **Royal Porthcawl Golf Club** Brdgnd
406 A1 **Royal Quays Marina** N Tyne
264 D3 **Royal St Davids Golf Club** Gwynd
101 G4 **Royal St George's Golf Club** Kent
47 H3 **Royal Signals museum** Dorset
570 C3 **Royal Tarlair Golf Club** Abers
283 E3 **Royal Town Of Caernarfon Golf Club** Gwynd
444 D4 **Royal Troon Golf Club** S Ayrs
338 D6 **Royal Umpire Caravan Park** Lancs
51 E3 **Royal Victoria Country Park** Hants
183 G4 **Royal Welsh showground** Powys
259 F2 **Royal West Norfolk Golf Club** Norfk
119 E5 **Royal Wimbledon Golf Club** Gt Lon
72 C4 **Royal Winchester Golf Club** Hants
223 E5 **Royal Worlington & Newmarket Golf Club** Suffk
488 B4 **Royal Yacht Britannia** C Edin
145 F2 **Roydon Mill Leisure Park campsite** Essex
170 D1 **Royston Golf Club** Herts
35 j6 **Rozel Camping Park** Jersey
60 B4 **Ruda Holiday Park** Devon
356 C4 **Rudding Holiday Park** N York
356 C4 **Rudding Park Hotel golf course** N York
276 C3 **Ruddington Grange Golf Club** Notts
296 B2 **Rufford Abbey EH** Notts
296 B2 **Rufford Country Park** Notts
324 B1 **Rufford Old Hall NT** Lancs
296 C2 **Rufford Park Golf & Country Club** Notts
216 B4 **Rugby Golf Club** Warwks
445 F2 **Rugby Park** E Ayrs
287 F6 **Rug Chapel and Llangar Church CADW** Denbgs
273 F6 **Rugeley Trent Valley railway station** Staffs
118 B2 **Ruislip Golf Club** Gt Lon
530 C3 **Rùm** Highld
310 B3 **Runcorn East railway station** Halton
309 H3 **Runcorn Golf Club** Halton
202 D6 **Run Cottage Touring Park** Suffk
117 H5 **Runnymede NT** Surrey
109 E1 **Runston Chapel CADW** Mons
322 g3 **Rural Life museum** IoM
218 D6 **Rushden Golf Club** Nhants
326 B6 **Rushen Abbey** IoM
201 H6 **Rushmere Golf Club** Suffk
69 G6 **Rushmore golf course** Wilts
76 D2 **Rusper golf course** Surrey
470 C4 **Rutherford Castle Golf Club** Border
15 E5 **Ruthern Valley Holidays** Cnwll
287 G3 **Ruthin-Pwllglas Golf Club** Denbgs
535 L3 **Ruthven Barracks HS** Highld
424 C6 **Ruthwell Cross HS** D & G
242 C2 **Rutland Caravan & Camping Park** Rutlnd
242 C2 **Rutland County Golf Club** Rutlnd
242 C2 **Rutland Falconry & Owl Centre** Rutlnd
243 E2 **Rutland Open Air Theatre** Rutlnd

242 B2 Rutland Railway Museum Rutlnd
241 E4 Rutland Ride cycle route Leics
242 C3 Rutland Water Circuit cycle route Rutlnd
120 C6 Ruxley Park Golf Centre Gt Lon
341 H5 Ryburn Golf Club Calder
88 C2 Rybury hill fort Wilts
141 E4 Rycote Chapel EH Oxon
378 D4 Rydal Mount Cumb
51 G6 Ryde Arena IoW
51 G6 Ryde Esplanade railway station IoW
51 G6 Ryde Golf Club IoW
51 G6 Ryde Pier Head railway station IoW
326 C5 Ryder Brow railway station Manch
59 F3 Rye Golf Club E Susx
165 G3 Rye Hill Golf Club Oxon
145 E3 Rye House Stadium Herts
246 C4 Ryston Park golf course Norfk
404 D1 Ryton Golf Club Nthumb
215 G5 Ryton Organic Gardens Warwks

S

243 F4 Sacrewell Farm & Country Centre C Pete
459 F5 Saddell Abbey Ag & B
327 E3 Saddleworth Golf Club Oldham
327 E2 Saddleworth Moor Rochdl
172 A2 Saffron Walden Golf Club Essex
491 H6 St Abb's Head NTS Border
3 C3 St Agnes IoS
6 D4 St Agnes Mining District (UNESCO) Cnwll
143 G3 St Albans Abbey railway station Herts
213 G2 St Andrews Birm
503 E2 St Andrews Bay Golf Resort & Spa Fife
503 E1 St Andrews Botanic Gardens Fife
503 E1 St Andrews Castle HS Fife
514 D6 St Andrews Links Trust golf course Fife
106 B5 St Andrews Major golf course V Glam
109 F4 St Andrews Road railway station Bristl
337 F3 St Annes Old Links golf course Lancs
337 F4 St Annes-on-the-Sea railway station Lancs
105 G6 St Athan airfield V Glam
101 F3 St Augustine's Cross EH Kent
101 F3 St Augustine's Golf Club Kent
8 B3 St Austell Golf Club Cnwll
376 B2 St Bees Golf Club Cumb
464 B4 St Blane's Church HS Ag & B
452 A3 St Boswells Golf Club Border
14 D5 St Breock Downs Monolith EH Cnwll
134 D4 St Briavels Castle EH Gloucs
447 G3 St Bride's Church HS S Lans
487 G3 St Bridget's Kirk HS Fife
9 E3 St Catherine's Castle EH Cnwll
30 D6 St Catherines Chapel EH Dorset
36 D5 St Catherine's Down NT IoW
36 D5 St Catherine's Lighthouse IoW
36 D5 St Catherine's Oratory IoW
36 D5 St Catherine's Point NT IoW
405 G3 St Clement Golf & Sports Centre Sundld
35 I7 St Clement golf course Jersey
595 H6 St Clement's Church HS W Isls
121 G3 St Clere's Hall Golf Club Thurr
504 C6 St Columba Exhibition Centre HS Ag & B
479 H6 St Cormac's Chapel HS Ag & B
454 D2 St Cuthbert's Cave NT Nthumb
263 G2 St Cybi's Well CADW Gwynd
6 D5 St Day Holiday Park Cnwll
304 C5 St Deiniol Golf Club Gwynd
178 D4 St Dogmaels Abbey CADW Pembks
14 C3 St Enodoc Golf Club Cnwll
510 C5 St Fillans Golf Club P & K
94 B2 St George's Hill Golf Club Surrey
188 B3 St Georges Lane Worcs
208 B1 St Giles Golf Club Powys
342 D1 St Helena's Caravan Park Leeds
103 F3 St Helen's Swans
374 B3 St Helens Caravan Park N York
103 F3 St Helen's cricket ground Swans
324 C6 St Helens Junction railway station St Hel
77 G2 Saint Hill Manor W Susx
207 F2 St Idloes Golf Club Powys
3 G2 St Ives Bay Holiday Park Cnwll
220 D5 St Ives Golf Club Cambs
282 D5 St Ives Touring Caravan Park Gwynd
200 C6 St James Chapel EH Suffk
27 E4 St James Park Devon
405 F2 St James' Park N Ty
27 E4 St James' Park railway station Devon
119 H2 St James Street railway station Gt Lon
27 G6 St Johns Caravan & Camping Park Devon
2 C3 St Just Mining District (UNESCO) Cnwll
15 E4 St Kew golf course Cnwll
100 C4 St Lawrence Cricket Club
48 D4 St Leonards Farm Caravan & Camping Park Dorset
58 D5 St Leonards Warrior Square railway station E Susx
602 F5 St Magnus Church HS Ork
3 d1 St Martin's IoS
100 C4 St Martin's Church (UNESCO) Kent
489 G5 St Martin's Kirk (ruin) HS E Loth
3 d2 St Mary's IoS
262 A6 St Mary's Abbey Gwynd
464 B2 St Mary's Chapel (ruin) HS Ag & B
588 C2 St Mary's Chapel (ruin) HS Highld
602 E6 St Mary's Chapel (ruin) HS Ork
524 C5 St Mary's Church P & K
161 F3 St Mary's Church EH Gloucs
135 E4 St Mary's Hotel railway station Gloucs
105 F3 St Mary's Golf Club
558 B5 St Mary's Kirk (ruin) HS Abers

431 G4 St Mary's Lighthouse N Tyne
50 D2 St Mary's Stadium C Sotn
5 F2 St Mawes Castle EH Cnwll
410 C5 St Medan Golf Club D & G
17 E5 St Mellion Hotel Golf & Country Club Cnwll
106 D3 St Mellons Golf Club Newpt
307 F3 St Melyd Golf Club Denbgs
309 H2 St Michael Jubilee golf course Halton
514 C5 St Michaels Golf Club Fife
3 F4 St Michael's Mount NT Cnwll
309 E2 St Michaels railway station Lpool
466 C2 Saint Mirren Park Rens
196 A2 St Neots Golf Club Cambs
101 E2 St Nicholas Camping Site Kent
410 D5 St Ninian's Cave HS D & G
411 E5 St Ninian's Chapel (ruin) HS D & G
251 E5 St Olaves' Priory EH Norfk
527 F4 St Orland's Stone HS Angus
347 F5 St Peter's Church EH N Linc
568 B2 St Peter's Kirk & Parish Cross HS Moray
109 F1 St Pierre golf course Guern
35 d3 St Pierre Park Golf Club Guern
52 A3 St Pierre Park Golf Club Hants
105 F5 St Quentin's Castle CADW V Glam
83 E2 St Radigund's Abbey Kent
499 G2 St Serf's Church HS P & K
237 G1 St Thomas's Priory Golf Club Staffs
141 F3 St Tiggywinkles Wildlife Hospital Bucks
22 D4 St Tinney Farm Holidays Cnwll
488 B5 St Triduana's Chapel HS C Edin
308 A4 St Winefride's Well CADW Flints
28 B5 Salcombe Regis Caravan & Camping Park Devon
311 G1 Sale Golf Club Traffd
326 B5 Salford Central railway station Salfd
326 B5 Salford Crescent railway station Salfd
486 D1 Saline Golf Club Fife
70 C4 Salisbury & South Wilts Golf Club Wilts
88 C4 Salisbury Plain Wilts
70 C4 Salisbury racecourse Wilts
101 G2 Salmestone Grange Kent
342 B2 Salmon (UNESCO) Brad
397 G5 Saltburn by the Sea Golf Club R & Cl
397 G5 Saltburn railway station R & Cl
397 G5 Saltburn Smugglers visitor centre R & Cl
314 D5 Saltergate Derbys
320 D2 Saltfleetby Fisheries campsite Lincs
86 B1 Salford golf course BaNES
86 B1 Saltford Marina BaNES
346 A4 Saltmarshe railway station E R Yk
11 F2 Saltram House NT C Plym
338 C3 Salwick railway station Lancs
35 I7 Samarès Manor Jersey
339 F3 Samlesbury aerodrome Lancs
339 F3 Samlesbury Hall Lancs
25 F3 Sampford Courtenay railway station Devon
83 E3 Samphire Hoe Country Park Kent
438 B5 Samye Ling Monastery visitor centre D & G
343 F6 Sandal & Agbrigg railway station Wakefd
603 K3 Sanday Ork
603 K3 Sanday airport Ork
291 F2 Sandbach service area Ches
33 G1 Sandford Holiday Park Dorset
91 E3 Sandford Springs golf course Hants
90 D2 Sandham Memorial Chapel NT Hants
406 B1 Sandhaven Caravan & Camping Park S Tyne
329 G3 Sandhill Golf Club Barns
323 F6 Sandhills railway station Lpool
321 F4 Sandilands Golf Club Lincs
310 C5 Sandiway Golf Club Ches
82 B3 Sandling railway station Kent
92 C1 Sand Martins Golf Club Wokham
343 F1 Sand Moor Golf Club Leeds
94 C1 Sandown racecourse Surrey
9 G2 Sandplace railway station Cnwll
572 E8 Sands Holiday Centre Highld
365 G6 Sandside Caravan & Camping Park Lancs
408 C1 Sands of Luce Holiday Park D & G
213 E1 Sandwell & Dudley railway station Sandw
213 F1 Sandwell Park Golf Club Birm
213 F1 Sandwell Valley Country Park Sandw
101 F4 Sandwich Leisure Park campsite Kent
49 F2 Sandy Balls Holiday Centre Hants
413 G3 Sandyhills Bay Leisure Park D & G
32 D2 Sandyholme Caravan Park Dorset
444 C1 Sandylands campsite N Ayrs
143 F6 Sandy Lodge Golf Club Herts
38 B5 Sandymouth Bay Holiday Park Cnwll
310 B2 Sankey for Penketh railway station Warrtn
189 F5 Sankey Marina Worcs
310 B1 Sankey Valley Country Park Warrtn
435 F3 Sanquhar Golf Club D & G
435 F2 Sanquhar Tolbooth Museum D & G
194 D3 Santa Pod Raceway Beds
187 F2 Sapey Golf Club Herefs
105 H2 Sardis Road Rhondd
213 G3 Sarehole Mill museum Birm
105 E3 Sarn Park service area Brdgnd
153 H2 Saron golf course Carmth
198 D3 Sascombe vineyard Cambs
34 C2 Saumarez Park Folk museum Guern
126 C3 Saundersfoot railway station Pembks
289 E1 Saunders Honda Stadium Flints
141 H5 Saunton railway station Bucks
60 C4 Saunton Golf Club Devon
35 H3 Sausmarez Manor Guern
117 G5 Savill Garden Surrey
353 F5 Sawley Abbey EH Lancs
50 D2 Saxon Wharf Marina C Sotn

202 B2 Saxtead Green Post Mill EH Suffk
377 G3 Scafell Pike Cumb
374 C1 Scalby Close Park campsite N York
605 H3 Scalloway Castle HS Shet
545 L4 Scalpay Highld
492 B4 Scarba Ag & B
374 D2 Scarborough Castle EH N York
374 C2 Scarborough Cricket Club
374 C1 Scarborough North Cliff Golf Club N York
374 C2 Scarborough South Cliff Golf Club N York
343 G1 Scarcroft Golf Club Leeds
344 B2 Scarthingwell Golf Club N York
151 G5 Scolton Country Park Pembks
512 D4 Scone Palace P & K
502 B4 Scoonie golf course Fife
383 F4 Scotch Corner Caravan Park N York
383 F3 Scotch Corner service area N York
389 F5 Scotgate Holiday Park Cumb
503 F3 Scotland's Secret Bunker Fife
467 H3 Scotland's Theme Park N Lans
79 F2 Scotney Castle NT Kent
588 D5 Scotscalder railway station Highld
514 D4 Scotscraig Golf Club Fife
501 G2 Scotstarvit Tower HS Fife
484 A6 Scotstounhill railway station C Glas
484 A6 Scotstoun Stadium C Glas
501 F2 Scottish Deer Centre Fife
444 D2 Scottish Maritime Museum (Irvine) N Ayrs
471 F2 Scottish Mining Museum Mdloth
514 C4 Scottish National Golf Centre Fife
498 C5 Scottish National Tennis Centre Stirlg
489 H2 Scottish Seabird Centre E Loth
145 E2 Scott's Grotto Herts
452 A3 Scott's View viewpoint Border
474 D1 Scoutscroft Holiday Centre Border
241 E3 Scraptoft Golf Club Leics
251 F1 Scratby Hall Caravan Park Norfk
526 C6 Sculptured Stone Museum HS P & K
528 B3 Sculptured Stones HS Angus
259 H5 Sculthorpe airfield Norfk
32 A3 Sea Barn Farm campsite Dorset
188 B5 Seaborne Leisure Worcs
376 B2 Seacote Park campsite Cumb
301 G2 Seacroft Golf Club Lincs
56 D4 Seaford Golf Club E Susx
56 D5 Seaford Head golf course E Susx
28 D4 Seaton Flamingo Park IoW
37 G2 Sea View Holiday Park Cnwll
2 C4 Sea View Holiday Park Dorset
32 C3 Seaview Holiday Village Kent
100 B2 Sea View International Caravan & Camping Park
8 B5 Seaward Caravan Park D & G
304 B2 Seawatch Centre IoA
202 B5 Seckford Golf Centre Suffk
138 A5 Second Chance Touring Park Wilts
2 C3 Secret Garden Caravan & Camping Park Cnwll
84 B5 Secret World Animal Rescue Somset
366 D1 Sedbergh Golf Club Cumb
395 G4 Sedgefield racecourse Dur
84 C4 Sedgemoor service area Somset
212 D1 Sedgley Golf Centre Staffs
58 C3 Sedlescombe Golf Club E Susx
237 H2 Seedy Mill Golf Club Staffs
283 E3 Segontium roman site NT Gwynd
344 D4 Selby Golf Club N York
119 G6 Selhurst Park Gt Lon
451 G4 Selkirk Golf Club Border
376 C4 Sellafield railway station Cumb
376 C3 Sellafield Visitor Centre Cumb
95 G2 Selsdon Park Hotel golf course Gt Lon
53 F6 Selsey Golf Club W Susx
94 B3 Semaphore Tower Surrey
82 C3 Sene Valley Golf Club Kent
316 B2 Serlby Park golf course Notts
489 E4 Seton Collegiate Church HS E Loth
489 E4 Seton Sands Holiday Village E Loth
353 G2 Settle Golf Club N York
86 D6 Seven Acres Caravan & Camping Site Somset
57 E5 Seven Sisters Country Park E Susx
119 G2 Seven Sisters railway station Gt Lon
235 F3 Severn Gorge Park Wrekin
109 E2 Severn Tunnel Junction railway station Mons
211 H3 Severn Valley Country Park Shrops
212 A4 Severn Valley Railway Worcs
109 G2 Severn View service area S Glos
375 G6 Serwerby Hall E R Yk
131 E3 Sgwd yr Eira (Waterfall) Rhondd
93 H5 Shalford Mill NT Surrey
49 E4 Shamba Holiday Park Dorset
371 G4 Shandy Hall N York
37 F4 Shanklin & Sandown Golf Club IoW
37 F4 Shanklin Chine IoW
379 F1 Shap Abbey EH Cumb
603 G8 Shapinsay Ork
379 G2 Shap Summit Cumb
295 F2 Shardaroba Caravan Park Notts

275 G3 Shardlow Marina Caravan Park Derbys
214 A4 Sharmans Cross Roads Solhll
20 A6 Sharpham vineyard Devon
326 D3 Shaw & Crompton railway station Oldham
270 C6 Shawbury airfield Shrops
270 B4 Sleap airfield Shrops
323 G2 Shaw Hall Caravan Park Lancs
339 E5 Shaw Hill Hotel Golf & Country Club Lancs
144 A1 Shaw's Corner NT Herts
202 B2 Shawsgate vineyard Suffk
356 C3 Shaws Trailer Park N York
123 E5 Sheerness railway station Kent
77 H5 Sheffield Park EH E Susx
77 H5 Sheffield Park railway station E Susx
214 B3 Sheldon Country Park Birm
197 G4 Shelford railway station Cambs
143 F4 Shendish Manor Golf Club Herts
67 G6 Sherborne Golf Club Dorset
46 B1 Sherbourne Castle NT Dorset
324 C6 Sherdley Park golf course St Hel
261 F3 Sheringham Golf Club Norfk
261 F3 Sheringham Park NT Norfk
296 B3 Sherwood Forest Notts
316 B6 Sherwood Forest Country Park Notts
296 A2 Sherwood Forest Golf Club Notts
296 B2 Sherwood Pines visitor centre Notts
605 H2 Shetland Islands Shet
608 E4 Shetland Islands Shet
342 B4 Shibden Hall Calder
475 E4 Shielfield Park Stadium Nthumb
506 B2 Shieling Holidays campsite Ag & B
235 H3 Shifnal Golf Club Shrops
54 B4 Ship & Anchor Marina campsite W Susx
54 B4 Ship and Anchor Marina W Susx
121 E4 Ship Lane Thurr
295 E6 Shipley Country Park Derbys
342 B2 Shipley Golf Club Brad
222 C3 Shippea Hill railway station Cambs
163 F6 Shipton golf course Gloucs
210 D1 Shipton Hall Shrops
164 D6 Shipton railway station Oxon
109 F4 Shirehampton Park golf course Bristl
294 D3 Shirland Golf Club Derbys
214 A4 Shirley Golf Club Solhll
95 G1 Shirley Park Golf Club Gt Lon
213 H4 Shirley railway station Solhll
460 B4 Shiskine Golf Club N Ayrs
120 B4 Shooters Hill Golf Club Gt Lon
55 E3 Shoreham airport W Susx
121 G5 Shorne Wood Country Park Kent
140 C3 Shotover Hill Country Park Oxon
308 D6 Shotton High Level railway station Flints
308 D6 Shotton railway station Flints
468 D2 Shotts Golf Club N Lans
234 B3 Shrewsbury Golf Club Shrops
312 B4 Shrigley Hall Hotel Golf & Country Club Ches
113 F1 Shrivenham Park Golf Club Oxon
210 A3 Shropshire Hills Discovery Centre Shrops
29 E4 Shrubbery Touring Park Devon
273 E5 Shugborough Lodge NT Staffs
492 C3 Shuna Ag & B
29 E3 Shute Barton NT Devon
195 H6 Shuttleworth Airfield (Old Warden) Beds
195 H6 Shuttleworth Collection museum Beds
300 B4 Sibsey Trader EH Lincs
313 H3 Sickleholme Golf Club Derbys
120 C5 Sidcup Golf Club Gt Lon
28 B5 Sidlaw Hills Angus
28 B5 Sidmouth Golf Club Devon
112 C6 Silbury Hill EH Wilts
91 G2 Silchester Roman City Walls EH Hants
240 C1 Sileby Mill Boatyard Leics
362 C5 Silecroft Golf Club Cumb
329 E3 Silkstone Golf Club Barns
399 E4 Silloth on Solway Golf Club Cumb
355 E5 Silsden Golf Club Brad
7 E3 Silverbow Park campsite Cnwll
412 C4 Silvercraigs Caravan & Camping Site D & G
322 d8 Silverdale Glen IoM
365 G4 Silverdale Golf Club Lancs
487 H4 Silverknowes golf course C Edin
50 D1 Silverlake Stadium Hants
94 B2 Silvermere Golf Club Surrey
4 D5 Silver Sands Holiday Park Cnwll
568 C1 Silver Sands Leisure Park Moray
167 E1 Silverstone Bucks
167 E1 Silverstone golf course Bucks
144 D6 Silver Street railway station Gt Lon
318 B5 Sincil Bank Lincs
275 F3 Sinfin golf course C Derb
483 G5 Singer railway station W Duns
55 G1 Singing Hills golf course W Susx
80 B2 Sissinghurst Castle Garden NT Kent
99 E1 Sittingbourne & Kemsley Light Railway Kent
98 D2 Sittingbourne & Milton Regis Golf Club Kent
99 E1 Sittingbourne Viaduct railway station Kent
315 F1 Sitwell Park Golf Club Rothm
193 F2 Sixfields Nhants
277 E5 Six Hills Golf Club Leics
188 C3 Sixways Stadium Worcs
365 G2 Sizergh Castle NT Cumb
602 A8 Skara Brae (UNESCO) Ork
301 G1 Skegness (Ingoldmells) aerodrome Lincs
482 B6 Skelmorlie Golf Club N Ayrs
378 C4 Skelwith Fold Caravan Park Cumb
160 B5 Skenfrith Castle CADW Herefs
463 F3 Skipness Castle HS Ag & B
463 F3 Skipness Chapel HS Ag & B
361 F3 Skipsea Castle EH E R Yk
361 F4 Skipsea Golf Club E R Yk
354 C4 Skipton Golf Club N York
124 B3 Skokholm Island Pembks
124 B3 Skomer Island Pembks
4 C4 Skyburriowe Farm campsite Cnwll

215 E4 Skydome Arena Covtry
542 F2 Skye Museum of Island Life Highld
561 H2 Slains Castle Abers
471 E2 Slatebarns Caravan Club Site Mdloth
298 C6 Sleaford Golf Club Lincs
360 A2 Sledmere House E R Yk
370 B4 Sleningford Water Mill Caravan & Camping Park N York
76 B3 Slinfold Park Golf & Country Club W Susx
550 E4 Slochd Summit Highld
117 G4 Slough Ice Arena Slough
452 B3 Smailholm Tower HS Border
37 F2 Smallbrook Junction railway station IoW
37 F2 Smallbrook Stadium IoW
80 C4 Smallhythe Place NT Kent
213 F2 Smethwick Rolfe Street railway station Sandw
95 G3 Smitham (for Coulsdon) railway station Gt Lon
325 F2 Smithills Hall Bolton
585 H3 Smoo Cave Highld
322 g5 Snaefell Mountain Railway IoM
327 G6 Snake Pass Derbys
114 D5 Snelsmore Common Country Park W Berk
224 D2 Snetterton Norfk
258 D5 Snettisham Park Farm Norfk
239 G2 Snibston Discovery Park museum Leics
320 B6 Snipe Dales Country Park Lincs
284 D4 Snowdon Gwynd
266 C4 Snowdonia National Park
284 C3 Snowdon Mountain Railway Gwynd
284 C3 Snowdon Ranger railway station Gwynd
284 D4 Snowdon visitor centre Gwynd
163 H3 Snowshill Lavender Farm Gloucs
163 G3 Snowshill Manor NT Gloucs
545 H7 Soay Highld
35 E2 Solent Meads Golf Centre Bmouth
313 E5 Solomon's Temple Derbys
401 E2 Solway Aviation museum Cumb
398 B3 Solway Links Golf Course D & G
169 F4 Someries Castle Beds
251 F5 Somerleyton Hall & Gardens Suffk
44 A2 Somerset County Ground Somset
444 D5 Somerset Park S Ayrs
116 C5 Sonning Golf Club Wokham
432 B3 Souter Johnnie's Cottage NTS S Ayrs
406 C2 Souter Lighthouse NT S Tyne
51 E1 Southampton airport Hants
50 D1 Southampton Airport Parkway railway station Hants
50 D1 Southampton Municipal golf course C Sotn
169 F4 South Beds Golf Club Beds
119 H4 South Bermondsey railway station Gt Lon
342 C4 South Bradford Golf Club Brad
144 D5 Southbury railway station Gt Lon
125 E2 South Cockett Caravan & Camping Park Pembks
19 H5 South Devon Railway Devon
56 B3 South Downs
73 G5 South Downs National Park (Proposed Area)
72 D4 South Downs Way Hants
122 D2 Southend airport Essex
350 B2 South End Caravan Park Cumb
122 D2 Southend East railway station Sthend
122 D2 Southend-on-Sea Cricket Club Sthend
122 D2 Southend Victoria railway station Sthend
104 D4 Southerndown Golf Club V Glam
398 B4 Southerness Golf Club D & G
398 B4 Southerness Holiday Village D & G
472 C5 Southern Upland Way Border
421 E3 Southern Upland Way D & G
436 C3 Southern Upland Way S Lans
121 G5 Southern Valley golf course Kent
347 E5 South Ferriby Marina N Linc
140 B3 Southfield Golf Club Oxon
83 G2 South Foreland Lighthouse NT Kent
66 C6 Southfork Caravan Park Somset
144 C6 Southgate Cricket Club Gt Lon
161 E4 South Herefordshire Golf Club Herefs
144 C6 South Herts Golf Club Gt Lon
118 D2 South Kenton railway station Gt Lon
299 F5 South Kyme Golf Club Lincs
364 B4 South Lakes Animal Park Cumb
37 F4 Southland Camping Park IoW
343 E4 South Leeds Golf Club Leeds
343 F4 South Leeds Stadium Leeds
7 H1 Southleigh Manor Tourist Park Cnwll
48 B6 South Lytchett Manor Caravan Park Dorset
144 B4 South Mimms service area Herts
405 F4 South Moor Golf Club Dur
81 E3 South of England Rare Breeds Centre Kent
77 F3 South of England showground W Susx
125 G4 South Pembrokeshire Golf Club Pembks
15 G3 South Penquite Farm campsite Cnwll
323 F2 Southport & Ainsdale Golf Club Sefton
337 F6 Southport Municipal Golf Club Sefton
337 F6 Southport Old Links Golf Club Sefton
601 H7 South Ronaldsay Ork
406 B2 South Shields Golf Club S Tyne
45 E5 South Somerset cycle route Somset
302 A4 South Stack viewpoint IoA
236 C4 South Staffordshire Golf Club Wolves
402 B5 South Tynedale Railway Nthumb
593 E1 South Uist W Isls
400 D5 Southwaite service area Cumb
296 D4 Southwell racecourse Notts

3 G2 **South West Coast Path** Cnwll
87 E3 **Southwick Country Park** Wilts
52 A3 **Southwick Park golf course** Hants
72 C4 **South Winchester Golf Club** Hants
14 C3 **South Winds Caravan & Camping Park** Cnwll
227 F4 **Southwold Golf Club** Suffk
93 E4 **Southwood golf course** Hants
472 B3 **Soutra Summit** Mdloth
371 E4 **Sowerby Caravan Park** N Yrk
280 C2 **Spalding Golf Club** Lincs
280 B4 **Spalding Tropical Forest** Lincs
78 C2 **Spa Valley Railway** E Susx
93 H4 **Spectrum Leisure Centre** Surrey
313 F3 **Speedwell Cavern** Derbys
309 F3 **Speke Hall NT** Lpool
188 C4 **Spetchley Park and Gardens** Worcs
568 B1 **Spey Bay golf course** Moray
52 A5 **Spinnaker Tower** C Port
50 B5 **Spinners** Hants
25 H4 **Spinster's Rock** Devon
52 A5 **Spitbank Fort** C Port
101 F2 **Spitfire & Hurricane Memorial Museum** Kent
356 D4 **Spofforth Castle EH** N York
326 C2 **Spotland** Rochdl
26 B4 **Springfield Holiday Park campsite** Devon
280 C2 **Springfields Festival Gardens** Lincs
48 B5 **Springfield Touring Park** Dorset
347 F3 **Springhead Park Golf Club (Municipal)** E R Yk
213 H3 **Spring Road railway station** Birm
296 B5 **Springwater Golf Club** Notts
181 F6 **Springwater Lakes campsite** Carmth
374 C4 **Spring Willows Touring Caravan Park** N York
452 D3 **Springwood Caravan Park** Border
335 F1 **Spurn Heritage Coast visitor centre** E R Yk
568 C2 **Spynie Palace HS** Moray
96 B4 **Squerryes Court** Kent
496 C3 **SS Sir Walter Scott** Stirlg
589 L2 **Stacks of Duncansby** Highld
11 E3 **Staddon Heights Golf Club** C Plym
406 B3 **Stadium of Light** Sundld
543 H3 **Staffin Camping & Caravanning** Highld
272 C3 **Stafford (northbound) service area** Staffs
272 C3 **Stafford (southbound) service area** Staffs
272 D5 **Stafford Castle Golf Club** Staffs
273 E4 **Staffordshire County showground** Staffs
238 A3 **Staffordshire Regiment museum** Staffs
378 C4 **Stagshaw Garden NT** Cumb
295 F1 **Stainsby Mill NT** Derbys
387 H5 **Staintondale Shire Horse Centre** N York
386 C1 **Staithes heritage centre** N York
119 F4 **Stamford Bridge** Gt Lon
327 E4 **Stamford Golf Club** Tamesd
327 F2 **Standedge Experience visitor centre** Kirk
77 G2 **Standen NT** W Susx
326 A3 **Stand Golf Club** Bury
598 E8 **Standing Stones HS** W Isls
324 D2 **Standish Court Golf Club** Wigan
314 C6 **Stanedge Golf Club** Derbys
606 C7 **Staneydale Temple HS** Shet
216 C4 **Stanford Hall** Leics
198 B1 **Stanford Park campsite** Cambs
343 G5 **Stanley Ferry Marina** Wakefd
309 F4 **Stanlow & Thornton railway station** Ches
118 D1 **Stanmore Golf Club** Gt Lon
211 G1 **Stanmore Hall Touring Park** Shrops
172 A5 **Stansted airport** Essex
85 G2 **Stanton Drew Stone Circle EH** BaNES
276 D3 **Stanton on the Wolds Golf Club** Notts
399 E4 **Stanwix Park Holiday Centre** Cumb
290 D4 **Stapeley Water Gardens** Ches
145 H6 **Stapleford Abbotts Golf Club** Essex
277 H6 **Stapleford Park golf course** Leics
109 H5 **Stapleton Road railway station** Bristl
488 B1 **Stark's Park** Fife
527 G4 **Station Park** Angus
566 F5 **Station Park** Highld
52 C3 **Staunton Country Park** Hants
275 F5 **Staunton Harold NT** Leics
192 B2 **Staverton Park golf course** Nhants
35 i6 **Steam & Automobile museum** Jersey
378 B5 **Steam Yacht Gondola NT** Cumb
128 D4 **Stebonheath Park** Carmth
354 D6 **Steeton & Silsden railway station** Brad
344 B3 **Steeton Hall Gatehouse EH** N York
599 H4 **Steinacleit Cairn & Stone Circle HS** W Isls
66 C3 **Stembridge Tower Mill NT** Somset
16 C4 **Sterts Open-Air Theatre** Cnwll
170 C5 **Stevenage Golf Centre** Herts
195 E6 **Stewartby Country Park** Beds
55 E2 **Steyning Golf Club** W Susx
135 H5 **Stinchcombe Hill golf course** Gloucs
498 B6 **Stirling Castle HS** Stirlg
498 B6 **Stirling Golf Club** Stirlg
485 F2 **Stirling service area** Stirlg
35 H3 **Stoats Farm Camping** IoW
146 D5 **Stock Brook Golf & Country Club** Essex
118 B3 **Stockley Park Golf Club** Gt Lon
312 B2 **Stockport Golf Club** Stockp
328 D5 **Stocksbridge & District Golf Club** Sheff
404 C3 **Stocksfield Golf Club** Nthumb
142 D2 **Stocks Hotel & Golf Club** Herts
328 B2 **Stocksmoor railway station** Kirk
396 B6 **Stockton Cricket Club** S on T
169 F6 **Stockwood museum** Luton

169 F6 **Stockwood Park Golf Club** Luton
110 A6 **Stockwood Vale golf course** BaNES
217 G2 **Stoke Albany golf course** Nhants
174 C2 **Stoke by Nayland Golf Club** Suffk
117 G3 **Stoke Park Club golf course** Bucks
193 F5 **Stoke Park Pavilions** Nhants
278 C4 **Stoke Rochford Golf Club** Lincs
278 C4 **Stoke Rochford Hall** Lincs
210 A3 **Stokesay Castle EH** Shrops
45 F4 **Stoke sub Hamdon Priory NT** Somset
214 C3 **Stonebridge Golf Club** Warwks
121 F5 **Stonebridge Road** Kent
99 F2 **Stone Chapel EH** Kent
79 F4 **Stonegate railway station** E Susx
272 C4 **Stone Golf Club** Staffs
50 D1 **Stoneham Golf Club** Hants
541 G2 **Stonehaven Golf Club** Abers
70 C1 **Stonehenge (UNESCO)** Wilts
88 C5 **Stonehenge Touring Park** Wilts
215 E5 **Stoneleigh Abbey** Warwks
215 E5 **Stoneleigh Deer Park Golf Club** Warwks
51 E3 **Stone Pier Yard Marina** Hants
86 C3 **Stoney Littleton Long Barrow EH** BaNES
116 B2 **Stonor Park** Oxon
400 D3 **Stony Holme Municipal Golf Club** Cumb
82 B3 **Stop 24 service area** Kent
599 K8 **Stornoway airport** W Isls
599 J8 **Stornoway Golf Club** W Isls
365 E2 **Stott Park Bobbin Mill EH** Cumb
212 D3 **Stourbridge Golf Club** Dudley
212 D3 **Stourbridge Junction railway station** Dudley
212 D3 **Stourbridge Town railway station** Dudley
68 C3 **Stourhead NT** Wilts
212 B6 **Stourport Marina** Worcs
68 C3 **Stourton House Gardens** Wilts
20 A2 **Stover Country Park** Devon
167 E2 **Stowe Gardens NT** Bucks
167 E2 **Stowe School cricket ground** Bucks
61 E3 **Stowford Farm Meadows campsite** Devon
87 E3 **Stowford Manor Farm campsite** Wilts
200 D3 **Stowmarket Golf Club** Suffk
256 C2 **Stow Mill windmill** Norfk
528 D1 **Stracathro service area** Angus
251 E3 **Stracey Arms Windpump** Norfk
128 C4 **Stradley Park rugby ground** Carmth
414 D4 **Stranraer Golf Club** D & G
182 A1 **Strata Florida Abbey CADW** Cerdgn
92 A2 **Stratfield Saye** Hants
190 C3 **Stratford Oaks golf course** Warwks
190 C3 **Stratford-upon-Avon Butterfly Farm** Warwks
190 C4 **Stratford-upon-Avon Cricket Club** Warwks
190 C3 **Stratford-upon-Avon Golf Club** Warwks
190 B4 **Stratford-upon-Avon racecourse** Warwks
467 H5 **Strathaven Golf Club** S Lans
558 D2 **Strathbogie** Abers
468 A3 **Strathclyde Country Park** N Lans
467 H3 **Strathclyde Country Park Camping & Caravan** N Lans
483 F5 **Strathclyde Homes Stadium** W Duns
468 A3 **Strathclyde Park Golf Club** S Lans
483 G5 **Strathendrick Golf Club** Stirlg
569 G5 **Strathisla Distillery** Moray
569 H2 **Strathiene Golf Club** Moray
527 G3 **Strathmore** Angus
526 D5 **Strathmore Golf Centre** P & K
565 H5 **Strathpeffer Spa Golf Club** Highld
551 L2 **Strathspey** Highld
551 L6 **Strathspey Railway** Highld
524 D5 **Strathtay Golf Club** P & K
395 G1 **Strawberry Hill Farm Camping & Caravan Park** Dur
118 D5 **Strawberry Hill Golf Club** Gt Lon
162 C1 **Strensham (northbound) service area** Worcs
162 C1 **Strensham (southbound) service area** Worcs
383 G2 **Stressholme Golf Club** Darltn
546 F2 **Strome Castle NTS** Highld
600 D3 **Stromness Golf Club** Ork
603 K6 **Stronsay** Ork
603 J5 **Stronsay airport** Ork
220 D4 **Stroud Hill Park campsite** Cambs
576 D6 **Struie Hill viewpoint** Highld
370 B6 **Studley Royal Park (UNESCO)** N York
140 C2 **Studley Wood Golf Club** Oxon
355 E2 **Stump Cross Caverns** N York
317 G2 **Sturgate airfield** Lincs
48 A4 **Sturminster Marshall golf course** Dorset
311 G3 **Styal country park NT** Ches
311 G3 **Styal Golf Club** Ches
2 C5 **Submarine Telegraph museum** Cnwll
298 B6 **Sudbrook Moor Golf Club** Lincs
118 D3 **Sudbury Golf Club** Gt Lon
274 B3 **Sudbury Hall NT** Derbys
163 F4 **Sudeley Castle** Gloucs
567 K5 **Sueno's Stone HS** Moray
199 G5 **Sue Ryder Foundation museum** Suffk
227 F6 **Suffolk Coastal cycle route** Suffk
201 F3 **Suffolk Owl Sanctuary** Suffk
176 D1 **Suffolk showground** Suffk
227 G2 **Suffolk Wildlife Park** Suffk
182 C6 **Sugar Loaf railway station** Powys
133 E1 **Sugar Loaf Viewpoint** Mons
605 G8 **Sumburgh airport** Shet
184 D6 **Summerhill golf course** Herefs
468 A1 **Summerlee Heritage Trust** N Lans
7 G1 **Summer Lodge Holiday Park** Cnwll
7 E4 **Summer Valley campsite** Cnwll
284 D4 **Summit railway station** Gwynd
76 B4 **Sumners Ponds Fishery & Campsite** W Susx
519 K2 **Sunart** Highld
118 B6 **Sunbury Golf Centre** Surrey

169 F4 **Sundon Hills Country Park** Beds
317 E4 **Sundown Adventureland** Notts
120 B5 **Sundridge Park Golf Club** Gt Lon
445 F5 **Sundrum Castle Holiday Park** S Ayrs
14 B5 **Sun Haven Valley Holiday Park** Cnwll
93 G1 **Sunningdale Golf Club** W & M
93 G1 **Sunningdale Ladies Golf Club** W & M
61 H2 **Sunny Lyn Holiday Park** Devon
7 E3 **Sunny Meadows Tourist Park** Cnwll
487 G5 **Suntrap Garden** C Edin
8 C4 **Sun Valley Holiday Park** Cnwll
94 D2 **Surbiton Golf Club** Surrey
314 A4 **Surprise View viewpoint** Derbys
95 F3 **Surrey Downs Golf Club** Surrey
95 G3 **Surrey National Golf Club** Surrey
55 G3 **Sussex County Cricket Ground** Br & H
371 G3 **Sutton Bank viewpoint** N York
281 G5 **Sutton Bridge Golf Club** Lincs
237 G5 **Sutton Coldfield Golf Club** Birm
95 F1 **Sutton Common railway station** Gt Lon
93 H3 **Sutton Green Golf Club** Surrey
310 A4 **Sutton Hall golf course** Ches
202 B5 **Sutton Hoo visitor centre NT** Suffk
358 A2 **Sutton Park** N York
348 B3 **Sutton Park Golf Club** C KuH
295 G3 **Sutton Parkway railway station** Notts
315 E6 **Sutton Scarsdale Hall EH** Derbys
72 C2 **Sutton Scotney service area** Hants
98 C5 **Sutton Valence EH** Kent
247 G3 **Swaffham Golf Club** Norfk
106 C4 **SWALEC stadium cricket ground** Cardif
381 H5 **Swaledale** N York
99 F2 **Swale Marina** Kent
123 E6 **Swale railway station** Kent
383 E4 **Swale View Caravan Park** N York
358 C5 **Swallow Hall golf course** York
199 G1 **Swallow Suffolk Hotel Golf & Country Club** Suffk
34 B5 **Swanage Coastal Park campsite** Dorset
34 A5 **Swanage Railway** Dorset
103 E3 **swansea airport** Swans
103 H3 **Swansea Bay Golf Club** Neath
129 F5 **Swansea West service area** Swans
470 D1 **Swanston Golf Club** C Edin
295 E4 **Swanwick Junction railway station** Derbys
443 F4 **Swarland Hall golf course** Nthumb
398 B1 **Sweetheart Abbey HS** D & G
78 B2 **Sweetwoods Park golf course** E Susx
112 D1 **Swindon & Cricklade Railway** Wilts
212 B1 **Swindon Golf Club** Staffs
113 G6 **Swindon Loop cycle route** Wilts
299 G6 **Swineshead railway station** Lincs
93 F1 **Swinley Forest Golf Club** Br For
362 D4 **Swinside Stone Circle** Cumb
326 A4 **Swinton (Greater Manchester) railway station** Salfd
326 A4 **Swinton Park Golf Club** Salfd
116 C5 **Swiss Farm International Camping** Oxon
195 H6 **Swiss Garden** Beds
284 D5 **Sygun Copper Mine** Gwynd
378 D2 **Sykeside Camping Park** Cumb
232 C3 **Sylfaen Halt railway station** Powys
134 D1 **Symonds Yat Caravan & Camping Park** Herefs
118 D4 **Syon House** Gt Lon
118 D4 **Syon Lane railway station** Gt Lon
217 H6 **Sywell airfield** Nhants
194 A1 **Sywell Reservoir Country Park** Nhants

T

311 E4 **Tabley House** Ches
166 A5 **Tackley railway station** Oxon
165 F2 **Tadmarton Heath Golf Club** Oxon
577 G7 **Tain Golf Club** Highld
104 B2 **Talbot Athletic Ground** Neath
401 F3 **Talkin Tarn Country Park** Cumb
155 F3 **Talley Abbey CADW** Carmth
85 E1 **Tall Pines Golf Club** N Som
229 E4 **Tal-y-Llyn Railway** Gwynd
38 C5 **Tamar Lake campsite** Cnwll
23 F5 **Tamar Otter Sanctuary** Cnwll
23 F1 **Tamarstone Farm campsite** Devon
17 F5 **Tamar Valley Mining District (UNESCO)** Cnwll
237 F6 **Tame Bridge Parkway railway station** Sandw
238 C5 **Tame View Caravan Site** Warwks
238 C4 **Tamworth Municipal golf course** Warwks
238 C4 **Tamworth service area** Warwks
327 F4 **Tandle Hill Country Park** Oldham
96 A4 **Tandridge Golf Club** Surrey
405 F3 **Tanfield Railway** Dur
399 E4 **Tanglewood Caravan Park** Cumb
606 B2 **Tangwick museum** Shet
329 E5 **Tankersley Park Golf Club** Barns
514 C3 **Tannadice Park** C Dund
490 A3 **Tantallon Castle HS** E Loth
265 F1 **Tan-y-Bwlch Gardens** Gwynd
265 F1 **Tan-y-Bwlch railway station** Gwynd
285 E6 **Tanygrisiau Hydro-electric Power Station** Gwynd
37 G3 **Tapeley Park** Devon
314 D5 **Tapton Park Golf Club** Derbys
462 D1 **Tarbert Golf Club** Ag & B
60 D5 **Tarka Holiday Park** Devon
555 E4 **Tarland Golf Club** Abers
95 E3 **Tattenham Corner railway station** Surrey
299 G3 **Tattershall Castle NT** Lincs

299 G3 **Tattershall College EH** Lincs
311 E3 **Tatton Park NT** Ches
44 A4 **Taunton & Pickeridge Golf Club** Somset
43 G3 **Taunton Deane service area** Somset
44 A3 **Taunton racecourse** Somset
44 B2 **Taunton Vale Golf Club** Somset
17 G4 **Tavistock Golf Club** Devon
523 L3 **Tay Forest Park** P & K
523 L6 **Taymouth Castle golf course** P & K
514 C2 **Tealing Dovecot & Earth House HS** Angus
379 H3 **Tebay Caravan Site** Cumb
379 H3 **Tebay service area** Cumb
393 F4 **Teesdale** Dur
396 C6 **Teesside Golf Club** S on T
312 B5 **Tegg's Nose Country Park** Ches
6 B5 **Tehidy Country Park** Cnwll
6 C5 **Tehidy Holiday Park** Cnwll
153 H1 **Teifi Valley Railway** Cerdgn
20 C2 **Teignmouth Golf Club** Devon
26 C6 **Teign Valley Golf Club** Devon
235 G4 **Telford Golf & Country Club** Wrekin
235 F3 **Telford Ice Rink** Wrekin
235 G3 **Telford service area** Shrops
116 D3 **Temple Golf Club** W & M
116 D3 **Temple Marina** Bucks
343 G3 **Temple Newsam** Leeds
343 F3 **Temple-Newsam Golf Club** Leeds
492 D5 **Temple Wood Stone Circle HS** Ag & B
126 C4 **Tenby Castle** Pembks
126 C5 **Tenby Golf Club** Pembks
9 G3 **Tencreek Holiday Park** Cnwll
4 C5 **Teneriffe Farm Caravan Park** Cnwll
80 C3 **Tenterden Golf Club** Kent
80 C3 **Tenterden Town railway station** Kent
80 C3 **Tenterden Vineyard Park** Kent
91 E5 **Test Valley Golf Club** Hants
71 G4 **Test Way cycle route** Hants
343 E5 **Tetley's Stadium** Kirk
334 D4 **Tetney Golf Club** Lincs
439 F2 **Teviotdale** Border
452 D4 **Teviot Water Gardens** Border
162 C3 **Tewkesbury Park Hotel Golf & Country Club** Gloucs
116 B5 **Thames and Kennet Marina** Oxon
120 B4 **Thames Barrier visitor centre** Gt Lon
94 C1 **Thames Ditton & Esher Golf Club** Surrey
94 B1 **Thames Path** Gt Lon
139 H3 **Thames Path** Oxon
137 H6 **Thames Path** Wilts
120 C3 **Thamesview Golf Centre** Gt Lon
95 H2 **The Addington Golf Club** Gt Lon
549 K1 **The Aird** Highld
369 H3 **Theakston Brewery visitor centre** N York
119 E5 **The All England Lawn Tennis & Croquet Club** Gt Lon
526 C5 **The Alyth Golf Club** P & K
47 H3 **The Ashley Wood Golf Club** Dorset
239 F4 **The Battlefield Line** Leics
195 E5 **The Bedford Golf Club** Beds
185 H2 **The Beeches Touring Caravan Site** Herefs
184 C6 **The Begwns NT** Powys
455 E3 **The Belford Golf Club** Nthumb
559 F5 **The Bennachie Centre** Abers
93 F1 **The Berkshire Golf Club** Br For
444 D2 **The Big Idea visitor centre** N Ayrs
39 F2 **The Big Sheep** Devon
213 E5 **The Blackwell Golf Club** Worcs
220 D5 **The Boathaven** Cambs
240 D3 **The Boat Yard** Leics
95 F2 **The Borough Sports Ground** Gt Lon
105 E3 **The Brewery Field** Brdgnd
251 F3 **The Broads** Norfk
602 A6 **The Brough Of Birsay HS** Ork
142 A3 **The Bucks Goat Centre** Bucks
146 D6 **The Burstead Golf Club** Essex
326 D5 **The Butchers Arms** Tamesd
381 F5 **The Buttertubs** N York
27 F3 **The Buzzard cycle route** Devon
537 H7 **The Cairnwell** P & K
14 D4 **The Camel Trail cycle route** Cnwll
91 G4 **The Camrose** Hants
374 B3 **The Carrs** N York
49 E4 **The Castleman Trailway cycle route** Dorset
108 C1 **The Celtic Manor Resort golf course** Newpt
153 H6 **The Celtic Trail cycle route** Carmth
131 F5 **The Celtic Trail cycle route** Rhondd
53 F2 **The Centurion Way cycle route** W Susx
31 F2 **The Cerne Giant** Dorset
237 E2 **The Chase Golf Club** Staffs
440 B4 **The Cheviot Hills**
309 F2 **The Childwall Golf Club** Lpool
19 F2 **The Church House NT** Devon
116 A4 **The Club at Mapledurham golf course** Oxon
34 C2 **The Club at Meyrick Park golf course** Bmouth
87 F2 **The Courts Garden NT** Wilts
523 L7 **The Cramog Centre museum** P & K
274 C4 **The Craythorne golf course** Staffs
19 H3 **The Dartmoor Halfway Inn Caravan Park** Devon
200 B3 **The Dell Touring & Caravan Park** Cnwll
119 H4 **The Den** Gt Lon
238 B5 **The De Vere Belfry golf course** Warwks
120 A3 **The Dome** Gt Lon
28 C5 **The Donkey Sanctuary** Devon
33 F1 **The Dorset Golf & Country Club** Dorset
75 G1 **The Downs Link cycle route** Surrey
56 C3 **The Dripping Pan** E Susx
423 G4 **The Dumfries & County Golf Club** D & G
37 G3 **The Duver NT** IoW
330 C4 **The Earth Stadium** Donc
145 G4 **The Epping golf course** Essex
173 G4 **The Essex Golf & Country Club** Essex
65 G3 **The Fairways International C & C Park** Somset
212 C4 **The Falconry Centre (Hagley)** Worcs

189 G6 **The Fleece Inn NT** Worcs
259 G5 **The Garden Caravan Site** Norfk
17 G5 **The Garden House** Devon
197 F2 **The Glassworld Stadium** Cambs
421 G2 **The Glenkens** D & G
110 C5 **The Gloucestershire golf course** S Glos
601 K3 **The Gloup** Ork
130 B5 **The Gnoll** Neath
197 G4 **The Gog Magog Golf Club** Cambs
233 G6 **The Green Caravan Park** Shrops
243 G4 **The Green Wheel cycle route** C Pete
283 F2 **The Greenwood Centre** Gwynd
143 F5 **The Grove golf course** Herts
371 G2 **The Hambleton Hills** N York
89 H5 **The Hawk Conservancy Trust** Hants
213 F1 **The Hawthorns** Sandw
512 B1 **The Hermitage NTS** P & K
337 G6 **The Hesketh Golf Club** Sefton
74 D2 **The Hindhead Golf Club** Surrey
453 F1 **The Hirsel Country Park** Border
122 B6 **The Historic Dockyard Chatham** Medway
489 F3 **The Honourable Company of Edinburgh Golfers** E Loth
487 E4 **The House of the Binns NTS** W Loth
16 C4 **The Hurlers Stone Circle EH** Cnwll
47 G4 **The Inside Park campsite** Dorset
160 D6 **The Jubilee Park** Herefs
185 F2 **The Jugle's Lodging** Powys
334 D3 **The Jungle** NE Lin
344 A4 **The Jungle** Wakefd
110 B4 **The Kendleshire golf course** S Glos
134 C2 **The Kymin NT** Mons
454 A2 **The Lady Waterford Hall museum** Nthumb
213 H5 **The Lakes (Warwickshire) railway station** Warwks
238 C4 **The Lamb Ground** Staffs
117 F3 **The Lambourne Club golf course** Bucks
14 D4 **The Laurels Holiday Park** Cnwll
136 B5 **The Lawn** Gloucs
240 D4 **The Leicestershire Golf Club** C Leic
331 G2 **The Lincolnshire golf course** N Linc
112 D3 **The Link Centre** Swindn
35 g6 **The Living Legend** Jersey
115 E4 **The Living Rainforest** W Berk
97 E2 **The London Golf Club** Kent
57 E4 **The Long Man of Wilmington** E Susx
8 B4 **The Lost Gardens of Heligan** Cnwll
416 D6 **The Machars** D & G
444 D2 **The Magnum Leisure Centre** N Ayrs
202 D3 **The Maltings** Suffk
111 E4 **The Manor House Hotel & Golf Club** Wilts
70 C4 **The Medieval Hall** Wilts
109 G4 **The Memorial Stadium** Bristl
2 D5 **The Merry Maidens** Cnwll
119 E1 **The Metro Golf Centre** Gt Lon
169 E2 **The Millbrook Golf Club** Beds
161 E1 **The Millpond campsite** Herefs
21 E1 **The Model Railway (Exmouth)** Devon
437 E4 **The Moffat Golf Club** D & G
566 F5 **The Nairn Golf Club** Highld
161 G5 **The National Birds of Prey Centre** Gloucs
35 H3 **The Needles Park** IoW
492 D5 **The Nether Largie Cairns HS** Ag & B
248 D3 **The Norfolk Golf & Country Club** Norfk
317 F1 **The Northolme** Lincs
476 E8 **The Oa** Ag & B
345 G2 **The Oaks Golf Club** E R Yk
84 B5 **The Oak Tree Arena** Somset
99 E2 **The Oast Golf Centre** Kent
145 E4 **Theobalds Grove railway station** Herts
28 C5 **The Old Bakery NT** Devon
260 D5 **The Old Brick Kilns campsite** Norfk
60 D2 **The Old Corn Mill and Pottery** Devon
16 E4 **The Old Mill NT** Devon
67 E2 **The Old Oaks Touring Park** Somset
377 E4 **The Old Post Office Campsite** Cumb
233 F5 **The Old School Caravan Park** Shrops
56 C4 **The Old Shipyard Marina** E Susx
381 G2 **The Otter Trust** Dur
119 G4 **The Oval** Gt Lon
283 E3 **The Oval** Gwynd
141 E4 **The Oxfordshire Golf Club** Oxon
584 E3 **The Parph** Highld
484 A6 **The Pavillion** C Glas
106 C2 **The Pavillion** Caerph
326 A5 **The Pavillion** Salfd
299 E6 **The Pearoom** Lincs
188 D5 **The Pershore to Worcester cycle route** Worcs
486 A2 **The Pineapple NTS** Falk
83 G2 **The Pines Garden** Kent
288 D5 **The Plassey Leisure Park campsite** Wrexhm
110 C4 **The Players Club golf course** S Glos
18 C3 **The Plume Of Feathers Inn campsite** Devon
375 F6 **The Poplars Touring Park** E R Yk
77 G3 **The Priest House Museum EH** W Susx
162 D2 **The Priory Gardens** Kemerton
119 E4 **The Queen's Club** Gt Lon
390 C5 **The Quiet Site campsite** Cumb
288 D4 **The Racecourse Ground** Wrexhm
345 F3 **The Ranch Caravan Park** N York
120 C5 **The Red House NT** Gt Lon
177 E3 **The Redoubt** Essex
414 C3 **The Rhinns of Galloway** D & G
118 D5 **The Richmond Golf Club** Gt Lon
259 F4 **The Rickels Caravan & Camping Park** Norfk
98 C4 **The Ridge Golf Club** Kent
134 B2 **The Rolls of Monmouth Golf Club** Mons
51 E2 **The Rose Bowl** Hants
452 C4 **The Roxburghe golf course** Border

323 F2 The Royal Birkdale Golf Club Sefton
276 B4 The Rushcliffe Golf Club Notts
112 D6 The Sanctuary EH Wilts
342 A5 The Shay Calder
235 G2 The Shropshire Golf Centre Wrekin
53 H2 The South Downs Way cycle route W Susx
115 G2 The Springs Hotel & Golf Club Oxon
293 E5 The Star Caravan & Camping Park Staffs
131 H5 The Taff Trail cycle route Myr Td
60 C4 The Tarka Trail cycle route Devon
223 G2 Thetford Forest Park
223 G3 Thetford Golf Club Norfk
328 D4 The Trans Pennine Trail cycle route Barns
327 F5 The Trans Pennine Trail cycle route Derbys
330 D2 The Trans Pennine Trail cycle route Donc
346 C4 The Trans Pennine Trail cycle route E R Yk
309 G3 The Trans Pennine Trail cycle route Halton
323 F3 The Trans Pennine Trail cycle route Lancs
323 G6 The Trans Pennine Trail cycle route Lpool
345 E1 The Trans Pennine Trail cycle route N York
323 F2 The Trans Pennine Trail cycle route Sefton
328 D5 The Trans Pennine Trail cycle route Sheff
57 G2 The Truggery E Susx
53 F2 The Trundle W Susx
312 B4 The Tytherington Club golf course Ches
80 A2 The Union Mill windmill Kent
120 B4 The Valley Gt Lon
100 D2 The Viking Coastal Trail cycle route Kent
343 F1 The Village golf course Leeds
91 G3 The Vyne NT Hants
214 D6 The Warwickshire golf course Warwks
272 C2 The Wedgwood Story visitor centre C Stke
160 A1 The Weir NT Herefs
153 E4 The Welsh Chocolate Farm Carmth
485 F4 The Westerwood Hotel golf course N Lans
432 B3 The Westin Turnberry Resort golf course S Ayrs
464 D5 The West Kilbride Golf Club N Ayrs
119 E4 The Wetland Centre Gt Lon
220 B5 The Willows Caravan Park Cambs
112 B3 The Wiltshire Golf & Country Club Wilts
319 G2 The Wolds (Lincolnshire) Lincs
360 B5 The Wolds (Yorkshire) E R Yk
188 A6 The Worcestershire Golf Club Worcs
235 E3 The Wrekin Wrekin
164 D5 The Wychwood Golf Club Oxon
145 F4 Theydon Bois Golf Club Essex
371 F4 Thirkleby Hall Caravan Park N York
472 C5 Thirlestane Castle Border
472 C5 Thirlestane Castle Caravan & Camping Site Border
371 E2 Thirsk & Northallerton golf course N York
371 E3 Thirsk racecourse N York
424 D5 Thomas Carlyle's Birthplace (museum) NTS D & G
110 A2 Thornbury golf course S Glos
121 F1 Thorndon North Country Park Essex
121 F1 Thorndon Park Golf Club Essex
121 F1 Thorndon South Country Park Essex
331 E2 Thorne Golf Club Donc
331 E2 Thorne North railway station Donc
331 E2 Thorne South railway station Donc
50 D6 Thorness Bay Holiday Park IoW
244 C3 Thorney Golf Centre C Pete
52 D4 Thorney Island W Susx
66 C5 Thorney Lakes Caravan Park Somset
118 A4 Thorney Park Golf Club Bucks
46 A2 Thornford railway station Dorset
52 D4 Thornham Marina W Susx
313 E4 Thornheyes Farm Campsite Derbys
436 A5 Thornhill Golf Club D & G
330 C2 Thornhurst Park Golf Club Donc
348 B6 Thornton Abbey & Gatehouse EH N Linc
348 B6 Thornton Abbey railway station N Linc
501 F5 Thornton Golf Club Fife
276 D2 Thornton's Holt Camping Park Notts
375 E6 Thorpe Hall Caravan & Camping Site E R Yk
123 E2 Thorpe Hall Golf Club Sthend
203 F2 Thorpeness Hotel & Golf Club Suffk
118 A6 Thorpe Park Surrey
334 D3 Thorpe Park Holiday Centre NE Lin
243 H5 Thorpe Wood golf course C Pete
370 B2 Thorp Perrow arboretum N York
412 D2 Threave Castle NTS D & G
413 E2 Threave Garden NTS D & G
161 G4 Three Choirs vineyard Gloucs
188 A6 Three Counties showground Worcs
236 D3 Three Hammers Short Course golf course Staffs
416 B3 Three Lochs Holiday Park D & G
168 B4 Three Locks Golf Club Bucks
147 G4 Three Rivers Golf & Country Club Essex
324 D4 Three Sisters Race Circuit Wigan
389 H5 Threlkeld Quarry & Mining museum Cumb
251 F2 Thrigby Hall Wildlife Gardens Norfk
342 D3 Throstle Nest Stadium Leeds
89 G5 Thruxton Hants
330 A5 Thrybergh Country Park Rothm
12 B4 Thurlestone Golf Club Devon
121 E4 Thurrock service area Thurr
260 C5 Thursford museum Norfk
588 E3 Thurso Caravan & Camping Site Highld

588 D3 Thurso Golf Club Highld
490 D5 Thurston Manor Holiday Home Park E Loth
202 B5 Tidemill Yacht Harbour Suffk
89 F5 Tidworth Garrison Golf Club Wilts
121 G4 Tilbury Fort EH Thurr
77 E2 Tilgate Forest Golf Centre W Susx
77 E2 Tilgate Park Country Park W Susx
499 E5 Tillicoultry Golf Club Clacks
168 D5 Tilsworth Golf Centre Beds
162 B1 Tiltridge vineyard Worcs
582 D6 Timespan visitor centre Highld
605 H1 Tingwall airport Shet
106 A5 Tinkinswood CADW V Glam
315 E2 Tinsley Park Municipal Golf Club Sheff
22 A5 Tintagel Castle EH Cnwll
22 B5 Tintagel Old Post Office NT Cnwll
134 C5 Tintern Abbey CADW Mons
67 E6 Tintinhull Garden NT Somset
519 G1 Tioram Castle Highld
516 C6 Tiree Ag & B
516 C6 Tiree airport Ag & B
51 F3 Titchfield Abbey EH Hants
176 D5 Titchmarsh Marina Essex
87 E2 Tithe Barn (Bradford-on-Avon) EH Wilts
42 C5 Tiverton Castle Devon
42 C5 Tiverton Golf Club Devon
42 D5 Tiverton Parkway railway station Devon
518 D4 Tobermory Golf Club Ag & B
169 E4 Toddington service area Beds
400 C2 Todhills service area Cumb
341 E4 Todmorden Golf Club Calder
243 F1 Toft Hotel Golf Club Lincs
357 G2 Tollerton Holiday Park N York
7 E2 Tollgate Farm Caravan & Camping Park Cnwll
560 C4 Tolquhon Castle HS Abers
550 D4 Tomatin Distillery Visitor Centre Highld
601 H8 Tomb of the Eagles Ork
555 E4 Tomnaverie Stone Circle HS Abers
145 H4 Toot Hill Golf Club Essex
371 E4 Topcliffe airfield N York
121 E3 Top Meadow golf course Gt Lon
416 D5 Torhouse Stone Circle HS D & G
506 B2 Torosay railway station Ag & B
486 C5 Torphichen Perceptory HS W Loth
487 H6 Torphin Hill Golf Club C Edin
555 H4 Torphins Golf Club Abers
20 C4 Torquay Golf Club Torbay
460 C5 Torr A Chaisteal Fort HS N Ayrs
467 G4 Torrance House golf course S Lans
563 G5 Torridon Countryside Centre NTS Highld
460 D5 Torrylin Cairn HS N Ayrs
565 L8 Torvean Caravan Park Highld
565 L8 Torvean Golf Club Highld
451 F2 Torwoodlee Golf Club Border
90 D2 Tot Hill service area Hants
19 H5 Totnes (Littlehempston) railway station Devon
19 G5 Totnes Castle EH Devon
193 F5 Towcester racecourse Nhants
427 H2 Tower Knowe visitor centre Nthumb
2 D4 Tower Park Caravans & Camping Cnwll
340 D3 Towneley Golf Club Lancs
340 D3 Towneley Hall museum Lancs
378 D4 Townend NT Cumb
232 D5 Town Hill viewpoint Powys
76 A3 Toyhorse International Stud Farm W Susx
94 A3 Traditions golf course Surrey
325 H5 Trafford Centre Traffd
531 J5 Tralgel golf course Highld
383 A4 Train Sculpture Darltn
490 A5 Traprain Law E Loth
450 C2 Traquair House Border
264 D6 Trawsdir Touring & Camping Park Gwynd
265 G2 Trawsfynydd Amphitheatre Roman site Gwynd
7 E1 Treago Farm Caravan Site Cnwll
313 F3 Treak Cliff Cavern Derbys
66 D6 Treasurer's House NT Somset
533 G7 Treasures of the Earth Highld
5 E3 Trebah Gardens Cnwll
7 E2 Trebellan Park campsite Cnwll
132 B3 Tredegar & Rhymney Golf Club Caerph
107 E2 Tredegar House Newpt
107 E2 Tredegar Park Golf Club Newpt
169 E6 Tree Cathedral arboretum NT Beds
126 B4 Trefalun campsite Pembks
158 B3 Trefeinon Open Farm Powys
302 C4 Trefignath CADW IoA
126 C4 Trefloyne Golf Club Pembks
285 G2 Trefriw Woollen Mill Conwy
14 B4 Tregavone Touring Park Cnwll
5 E2 Tregedna Farm Touring Caravan & Tent Park Cnwll
3 F2 Tregenna Castle Hotel Golf & Country Club Cnwll
3 G2 Treglisson Camping & Caravan Park Cnwll
2 A4 Tregony golf course Cnwll
9 H2 Tregoad Park campsite Cnwll
3 G3 Tregonning Gwinear & Trewavas Mining District (UNESCO) Cnwll
9 G3 Trelay Farmpark campsite Cnwll
8 C5 Trelispen Caravan & Camping Park Cnwll
7 F6 Trelissick Garden NT Cnwll
14 B6 Treloan Coastal Farm Holidays Cnwll
7 F1 Treloy Touring Park Cnwll
8 B4 Trenance Holiday Park Cnwll
8 B4 Trencreek Farm Country Holiday Park Cnwll
7 F1 Trencreek Holiday Park Cnwll
2 D3 Trengwainton Garden NT Cnwll
276 C2 Trent Bridge Notts
144 C5 Trent Country Park Gt Lon
317 F4 Trentfield Farm campsite Notts
272 C1 Trentham Club HS C Stke
272 C1 Trentham Park Golf Club Staffs
276 A3 Trent Lock Golf Centre Derbys
144 C5 Trent Park Golf Club Gt Lon
263 F2 Tre'r Ceiri hill fort Gwynd
7 F2 Trerice NT Cnwll
3 c2 Tresco IoS

3 c2 Tresco Abbey Gardens IoS
3 c2 Tresco heliport IoS
517 H7 Treshnish Isles Ag & B
5 G1 Trethem Mill Touring Park Cnwll
16 C5 Trethevy Quoit EH Cnwll
7 G2 Trethiggey Touring Park Cnwll
23 F6 Trethorne Golf Club Cnwll
23 F6 Trethorne Leisure Farm Cnwll
150 C4 Tretio Caravan & Camping Park Pembks
158 C5 Tretower Court & Castle CADW Powys
3 G3 Trevair Touring Park Cnwll
3 E1 Trevalgan Touring Park Cnwll
4 B2 Trevarno Manor Gardens Cnwll
14 B5 Trevarrian Holiday Park Cnwll
6 D4 Trevarth Holiday Park Cnwll
2 C3 Trevaylor Caravan & Camping Park Cnwll
8 C5 Treveague Farm Caravan & Camping Site Cnwll
14 B4 Trevean Caravan & Camping Park Cnwll
2 C4 Trevedra Farm Caravan & Camping Site Cnwll
7 F2 Trevella Tourist Park Cnwll
8 B5 Treveor Farm Caravan & Camping Site Cnwll
7 E2 Treverven Touring Caravan & Camping Park Cnwll
7 E2 Trevornick Holiday Park Cnwll
14 B4 Trevose Golf Club Cnwll
14 C4 Trewince Farm Holiday Park Cnwll
5 G2 Trewince Farm Touring Park Cnwll
218 A3 Triangular Lodge EH Nhants
92 D2 Trilakes Animal Park Br For
451 H3 Trimontium museum Border
114 B4 Trindledown Farm Animal Retirement Centre W Berk
14 C3 Tristram Caravan & Camping Park Cnwll
444 D3 Troon Municipal Golf Club S Ayrs
444 D3 Troon Yacht Haven S Ayrs
239 H4 Tropical Birdland Leics
343 F2 Tropical World Roundhay Park Leeds
97 F2 Trosley Country Park Kent
496 C3 Trossachs Stirlg
496 D5 Trossachs Holiday Park Stirlg
389 F3 Trotters World of Animals Cumb
276 A1 Trowell service area Notts
7 F4 Truro Golf Club Cnwll
322 e6 TT Circuit IoM
135 G4 Tudor Caravan & Camping Gloucs
568 F2 Tugnet Ice House museum Moray
486 B2 Tulliallan Golf Club Fife
499 E2 Tullibardine Chapel HS P & K
534 C6 Tulloch railway station Highld
566 B7 Tullock Caledonian Stadium Highld
523 L4 Tummel Valley Holiday Park P & K
78 D2 Tunbridge Wells Cricket Club Kent
78 D2 Tunbridge Wells Golf Club Kent
326 D2 Tunshill Golf Club Rochdl
340 D3 Turf Moor Lancs
145 E5 Turkey Street railway station Gt Lon
487 G5 Turnhouse Golf Club C Edin
570 C6 Turriff Golf Club Abers
325 G2 Turton Golf Club Bl w D
325 G1 Turton Tower Bl w D
535 K3 Turus Tim museum Highld
274 C4 Tutbury & Hatton railway station Derbys
449 H2 Tweed Cycleway Border
448 C2 Tweed Cycleway S Lans
423 F4 Twelve Apostles D & G
20 A3 Twelve Oaks Farm Caravan Park Devon
221 G5 Twenty Pence Marina Cambs
86 C2 Twerton Park BaNES
118 D5 Twickenham Gt Lon
118 D5 Twickenham Stoop Gt Lon
60 C3 Twitchen Parc campsite Devon
101 F2 Two Chimneys Caravan Park Kent
256 B4 Two Mills Touring Park Norfk
239 E3 Twycross Zoo Leics
97 G5 Twyford Bridge Marina Kent
245 F1 Tydd St Giles Golf & Leisure Centre Cambs
264 B1 Tyddyn Cethin Caravan Park Gwynd
303 G3 Tyddyn Isaf Caravan Park IoA
264 B1 Tyddyn Morthwyl Camping & Caravan Site Gwynd
106 C3 Ty Glas railway station Cardif
265 E3 Tygwyn railway station Gwynd
302 D6 Ty Hen campsite IoA
284 C5 Ty Isaf NT Gwynd
92 B3 Tylney Park Golf Club Hants
269 E1 Ty Mawr Country Park Wrexhm
306 D4 Ty Mawr Holiday Park Conwy
285 G4 Ty Mawr Wybrnant NT Conwy
266 D2 Tyn Cornel Camping & Caravan Park Gwynd
508 D3 Tyndrum Lower railway station Stirlg
488 A5 Tynecastle C Edin
403 G2 Tyne Green Country Park Nthumb
33 F3 Tyneham Village museum Dorset
431 G6 Tynemouth Priory & Castle EH N Tyne
431 G6 Tynemouth Golf Club N Tyne
405 H4 Tyne Riverside Country Park N u Ty
431 F5 Tyneside cycle route N Tyne
404 D2 Tyneside Golf Club Gatesd
302 D6 Ty Newydd CADW IoA
304 B3 Ty Newydd Leisure Park IoA
303 G3 Ty'n Rhos Caravan Park IoA
305 G6 Tynterfyn Touring Caravan Park Conwy
109 F5 Tyntesfield NT N Som
322 d6 Tynwald Hill IoM
285 H4 Ty 'n-y-Coed Uchaf NT Conwy
283 F4 Ty'n yr Onnen Mountain Farm Caravan & Camping Gwynd
94 D3 Tyrrells Wood Golf Club Surrey
267 E2 Tytandderwen Caravan Park Gwynd
268 D1 Ty-Ucha Caravan Park Denbgs

228 D4 Tywyn Wharf railway station Gwynd

U

113 G2 Uffington Castle EH Oxon
202 B4 Ufford Park Hotel Golf & Leisure Suffk
20 B2 Ugbrooke Park Devon
593 D11 Uibhist a Deas W Isls
592 B4 Uibhist a Tuath W Isls
136 A4 Uley Long Barrow Monument EH Gloucs
216 B2 Ullesthorpe campsite Leics
216 B2 Ullesthorpe Golf Club Leics
390 C5 Ullswater Cumb
390 C5 Ullswater Caravan Camping & Marine Park Cumb
364 D4 Ulverston railway station Cumb
34 B4 Ulwell Cottage Caravan Park Dorset
144 C5 Underhill Gt Lon
173 E4 Unex Towerlands Golf Club Essex
153 H6 United Counties showground Carmth
51 E3 Universal Marina Hants
140 B3 University Parks cricket ground Oxon
213 F3 University railway station Birm
609 H3 Unst Shet
89 E3 Upavon Golf Club Wilts
98 C1 Upchurch River Valley Golf Centre Kent
487 E5 Uphall Golf Club W Loth
324 C4 Upholland railway station Lancs
121 G2 Upminster Golf Club Gt Lon
122 B5 Upnor Castle EH Medway
74 B6 Uppark NT W Susx
373 F3 Upper Carr Touring Park N York
166 B4 Upper Heyford airfield (dis) Oxon
23 E1 Upper Lynstone Caravan Park Cnwll
18 C4 Upper Plym Valley EH Devon
508 D3 Upper Tyndrum railway station Stirlg
309 F6 Upton-by-Chester Golf Club Ches
211 F1 Upton Cressett Hall Shrops
191 F5 Upton House NT Warwks
162 C1 Upton upon Severn heritage centre Worcs
549 J4 Urquhart Castle HS Highld
273 H3 Uttoxeter Golf Club Staffs
273 H3 Uttoxeter racecourse Staffs
504 E2 Uvla Ag & B
118 B2 Uxbridge Cricket Ground Gt Lon
118 B2 Uxbridge golf course Gt Lon

V

189 F4 Vale Golf Club Worcs
105 G4 Vale Hotel Golf & Spa Resort V Glam
277 H2 Vale of Belvoir Leics
307 F6 Vale of Clwyd Denbgs
483 F3 Vale of Leven Golf Club W Duns
268 D1 Vale of Llangollen Golf Club Denbgs
88 D3 Vale of Pewsey Wilts
88 B2 Vale of Pewsey cycle route Wilts
373 G3 Vale of Pickering Caravan Park N York
205 G4 Vale of Rheidol Railway Cerdgn
139 F6 Vale of White Horse Oxon
291 H4 Vale Park C Stke
288 B6 Valle Crucis Abbey CADW Denbgs
302 D5 Valley airfield IoA
117 G6 Valley Gardens Surrey
213 F6 Valley Stadium Worcs
251 G3 Vauxhall Holiday Park Norfk
37 E5 Ventnor Botanic Garden IoW
37 E5 Ventnor Down NT IoW
37 E5 Ventnor Golf Club IoW
351 F2 Venture Caravan Park Lancs
143 H3 Verulam Golf Club Herts
143 G3 Verulamium Roman Theatre Herts
143 G5 Vicarage Road Herts
309 G6 Vicars Cross Golf Club Ches
119 F4 Victoria (London) railway station Gt Lon
162 B6 Victoria Basin Marina Gloucs
396 D3 Victoria Park Hartpl
565 K5 Victoria Park Moray
324 A2 Victoria Park Lancs
569 G3 Victoria Park Moray
308 D1 Victoria Park Wirral
451 F4 Victoria Park Caravan & Camping Park Border
310 D5 Victoria Stadium Ches
465 E3 Vikingar visitor centre N Ayrs
101 G3 Viking Ship 'Hugin' Kent
213 G1 Villa Park Birm
297 E2 Vina Cooke Dolls museum Notts
246 A2 Virginia Lake Caravan Park Norfk
106 C2 Virginia Park Caerph
44 A3 Vivary Park Municipal golf course Somset
471 G2 Vogrie Country Park Mdloth
471 G2 Vogrie golf course Mdloth

W

141 F1 Waddesdon Manor NT Bucks
301 E3 Wainfleet railway station Lincs
329 E1 Wakefield Golf Club Wakefd
343 F5 Wakefield Kirkgate railway station Wakefd
343 F5 Wakefield Westgate railway station Wakefd
77 F3 Wakehurst Place NT W Susx
90 B2 Walbury Hill W Berk
148 D2 Waldegraves Holiday Park Essex
405 F5 Waldridge Fell Country Park Dur
202 B6 Waldringfield Golf Club Suffk
106 C4 Wales National Ice Rink Cardif
240 C4 Walkers Stadium C Leic
323 E6 Wallasey Golf Club Wirral
323 E6 Wallasey Grove Road railway station Wirral
308 C1 Wallasey Village railway station Wirral
405 H1 Wallsend EH N Tyne
83 G1 Walmer & Kingsdown Golf Club Kent
101 G5 Walmer Castle EH Kent
326 B2 Walmersley Golf Club Lancs

238 A6 Walmley Golf Club Birm
364 A5 Walney airfield Cumb
405 F6 Walney to Wear cycle route Dur
406 B2 Walney to Wear cycle route Sundld
237 F5 Walsall Golf Club Wsall
260 B4 Walsingham railway station Norfk
334 C4 Waltham Windmill Golf Club NE Lin
334 C4 Waltham Windmill museum NE Lin
323 G6 Walton (Merseyside) railway station Lpool
310 B3 Walton Hall and Gardens Warrtn
310 B3 Walton Hall golf course Warrtn
95 E4 Walton Heath Golf Club Surrey
93 F4 Wanborough railway station Surrey
197 G4 Wandlebury Country Park Cambs
119 F6 Wandle Trail cycle route Gt Lon
435 H2 Wanlockhead Beam Engine HS D & G
435 H2 Wanlockhead Lead Mining museum D & G
431 E2 Wansbeck Riverside Country Park Nthumb
243 F5 Wansford railway station Cambs
120 B2 Wanstead Golf Club Gt Lon
120 B2 Wanstead Park railway station Gt Lon
60 C2 Warcombe Farm Caravan & Camping Park Devon
33 F1 Wareham Forest Tourist Park Dorset
33 G2 Wareham Golf Club Dorset
455 E3 Waren Caravan Park Nthumb
260 B3 Warham St Mary railway station Norfk
443 G3 Warkworth Castle & Hermitage EH Nthumb
121 E1 Warley Park Golf Club Essex
213 F2 Warley Woods Golf Club Sandw
53 E6 Warner Farm Touring Park W Susx
76 C3 Warnham railway station W Susx
84 B3 Warren Farm Holiday Centre Somset
20 D2 Warren Golf Club Devon
147 G3 Warren Golf Club Essex
323 E6 Warren Golf Club Wirral
223 G3 Warren Lodge EH Norfk
310 B2 Warrington Bank Quay railway station Warrtn
310 C3 Warrington Golf Club Warrtn
338 B4 Warton airfield Lancs
190 D2 Warwick Castle Warwks
190 D2 Warwick Golf Club Warwks
190 D1 Warwick Parkway railway station Warwks
190 D1 Warwick racecourse Warwks
191 E3 Warwick service area Warwks
191 F2 Warwickshire Exhibition Centre Warwks
377 F3 Wasdale Head NT campsite Cumb
405 G4 Washington service area Gatesd
26 B2 Waterbridge golf course Devon
390 D5 Waterfoot Caravan Park Cumb
165 F3 Water Fowl Sanctuary & Children's Farm Oxon
14 A5 Watergate Bay Tourist Park Cnwll
55 G3 Waterhall Golf Club Br & H
119 G4 Waterloo railway station Gt Lon
52 B2 Waterlooville Golf Club Hants
240 D2 Watermead Country Park Leics
320 D4 Watermill & Wildfowl Gardens Lincs
61 E2 Watermouth Castle Devon
61 E2 Watermouth Cove Holiday Park Devon
487 H5 Water of Leith visitor centre C Edin
140 D3 Waterperry Gardens Oxon
42 D2 Waterrow Touring Park Somset
366 A3 Waters Edge Caravan Park Cumb
390 D5 Waterside House campsite Cumb
62 A2 Watersmeet House NT Devon
140 D3 Waterstock golf course Oxon
345 G5 Waterways museum E R Yk
216 D6 Watford Gap service area Nhants
329 G5 Wath Golf Club Rothm
295 G5 Watnall Road Notts
200 D4 Wattisham airfield Suffk
76 C2 Wattlehurst Farm Surrey
122 A2 Wat Tyler Country Park Essex
106 B4 Waun-gron Park railway station Cardif
288 C3 Waun-y-Llyn viewpoint Flints
168 C2 Wavendon Golf Centre M Keyn
251 E2 Waveney River Centre Norfk
93 E5 Waverley Abbey EH Surrey
309 E1 Wavertree Technology Park railway station Lpool
3 G2 Wayfarers Caravan & Camping Park Cnwll
113 G2 Waylands Smithy EH Oxon
373 E2 Wayside Caravan Park N York
53 F2 Weald & Downland Open Air Museum EH W Susx
146 B6 Weald Country Park Essex
98 C5 Weald of Kent golf course Kent
146 B5 Weald Park Hotel Golf & Country Club Essex
393 F2 Weardale Dur
394 B2 Weardale Railway Dur
406 A3 Wearside Golf Club Sundld
466 A2 Weavers Cottage NTS Rens
27 G5 Webbers Farm Caravan & Camping Park Devon
188 D1 Webbs of Wychbold Worcs
272 C2 Wedgwood railway station Staffs
223 F2 Weeting Castle EH Norfk
356 B5 Weeton railway station N York
18 C6 Welbeck Manor & Sparkwell golf club Devon
240 C4 Welford Road Ground C Leic
218 B5 Wellingborough Golf Club Nhants
92 B2 Wellington Country Park Hants
92 B2 Wellington Country Park campsite Hants
92 D2 Wellingtonia Avenue arboretum Wokham
43 F4 Wellington Monument viewpoint Somset

71 G5 **Wellow golf course** Hants
126 C4 **Well Park Caravan & Camping site** Pembks
260 B4 **Wells & Walsingham Light Railway** Norfk
85 G5 **Wells (Somerset) Golf Club** Somset
57 F2 **Wellshurst Golf & Country Club** E Susx
260 B3 **Wells railway station** Norfk
285 E3 **Welsh Highland Railway** Gwynd
284 C5 **Welsh Highland Railway** Gwynd
106 B4 **Welsh Life & Gardens museum** Cardif
107 F2 **Welsh National Cycling Centre** Newpt
106 D4 **Welsh National Tennis Centre** Cardif
232 B3 **Welshpool & Llanfair Light Railway** Powys
232 C3 **Welshpool Golf Club** Powys
232 D3 **Welshpool Raven Square railway station** Powys
284 C2 **Welsh Slate museum** Gwynd
192 C1 **Welton Haven Marina** Nhants
144 B2 **Welwyn Garden City Golf Club** Herts
144 B1 **Welwyn North railway station** Herts
144 B2 **Welwyn Viaduct** Herts
118 D2 **Wembley Arena & Conference Centre** Gt Lon
118 D2 **Wembley Stadium** Gt Lon
482 A6 **Wemyss Bay railway station** Inver
4 C2 **Wendron Mining District (UNESCO)** Cnwll
235 E4 **Wenlock Priory EH** Shrops
368 C1 **Wensleydale** N York
369 F2 **Wensleydale Railway** N York
255 G5 **Wensum Valley Hotel Golf & Country Club** Norfk
117 G6 **Wentworth Club golf course** Surrey
106 B5 **Wenvoe Castle Golf Club** V Glam
102 C3 **Weobley Castle CADW** Swans
308 C6 **Wepre Country Park** Flints
236 C4 **Wergs Golf Club** Wolves
133 F1 **Wernddu Golf Centre** Mons
326 D4 **Werneth Low Golf Club** Oldham
327 E6 **Werneth Low Golf Club** Tamesd
327 E6 **Werneth Low viewpoint** Tamesd
16 B2 **Wesley's Cottage** Cnwll
32 B3 **Wessex Stadium** Dorset
309 E2 **West Allerton railway station** Lpool
30 B4 **West Bay Holiday Park camping** Dorset
114 C4 **West Berkshire golf course** W Berk
342 C4 **West Bowling Golf Club** Brad
342 B3 **West Bradford Golf Club** Brad
135 G2 **Westbury Court NT** Gloucs
94 A2 **West Byfleet Golf Club** Surrey
76 A6 **West Chiltington Golf Club** W Susx
3 F2 **West Cornwall Golf Club** Cnwll
53 F2 **West Dean Gardens** W Susx
323 H6 **West Derby Golf Club** Lpool
84 C3 **West End Farm campsite** N Som
341 H4 **West End Golf Club** Calder
570 C3 **Wester Bonnyton Farm Site** Abers
96 C4 **Westerham Golf Club** Kent
430 C6 **Westerhope Golf Club** N u Ty
62 C4 **Westermill Farm campsite** Somset
444 D2 **Western Gailes Golf Club** N Ayrs
240 B4 **Western golf course** C Leic
563 L4 **Wester Ross** Highld
484 A5 **Westerton railway station** E Duns
145 E2 **West Essex Golf Club** Essex
32 A3 **West Fleet Holiday Farm** Dorset
101 F2 **Westgate & Birchington Golf Club** Kent
101 F2 **Westgate-on-Sea railway station** Kent
92 B3 **West Green House NT** Hants
57 G4 **Westham Castle EH** E Susx
143 F6 **West Herts Golf Club** Herts
521 G2 **West Highland Way** Highld
496 B6 **West Highland Way** Stirlg
557 E3 **Westhill Golf Club** Abers
93 G3 **West Hill Golf Club** Surrey
3 E4 **Westholme** Cnwll
325 E3 **Westhoughton Golf Club** Bolton
55 G3 **West Hove Golf Club** Br & H
112 D6 **West Kennett Long Barrow EH** Wilts
96 B2 **West Kent Golf Club** Gt Lon
323 F4 **West Lancashire Golf Club** Sefton
338 B5 **West Lancashire Light Railway** Lancs
52 C3 **Westleigh Park** Devon
121 G2 **Westley Heights Country Park** Thurr
470 B4 **West Linton Golf Club** Border
217 H3 **West Lodge Rural Centre** Nhants
486 D4 **West Lothian Golf Club** Falk
97 G3 **West Malling Golf Club** Kent
118 C3 **West Middlesex Golf Club** Gt Lon
41 G5 **West Middlewick Farm Caravan & Camping Site** Devon
214 C4 **West Midlands Golf Club** Solhll
212 B4 **West Midlands Safari Park** Worcs
132 C2 **West Monmouthshire Golf Club** Blae G
366 A3 **Westmorland showground** Cumb
111 E2 **Westonbirt arboretum** Gloucs
111 F2 **Westonbirt golf course** Gloucs
84 C2 **Weston Gateway Caravan Site** N Som
84 B2 **Weston Milton railway station** N Som
236 B2 **Weston Park** Staffs
255 F4 **Weston Park Golf Club** Norfk
84 B3 **Weston-Super-Mare Golf Club** N Som
142 B2 **Weston Turville Golf Club** Bucks
65 G5 **Westonzoyland airfield** Somset
27 F4 **West Point showground** Devon
602 F2 **Westray** Ork
602 F1 **Westray airport** Ork
261 G3 **West Runton railway station** Norfk
602 F3 **Westside Church HS** Ork

63 G3 **West Somerset Railway** Somset
222 D4 **West Suffolk Golf Centre** Suffk
75 F1 **West Surrey Golf Club** Surrey
54 C1 **West Sussex Golf Club** W Susx
95 F2 **West Sutton railway station** Gt Lon
221 E5 **Westview Marina** Cambs
35 H3 **West Wight NT** IoW
87 F5 **West Wilts Golf Club** Wilts
292 C3 **Westwood (Leek) golf course** Staffs
177 E1 **Westwood Caravan Park** Suffk
87 E3 **Westwood Manor NT** Wilts
142 A6 **West Wycombe Park NT** Bucks
401 E4 **Wetheral Priory Gatehouse EH** Cumb
356 D5 **Wetherby Golf Club** Leeds
357 E5 **Wetherby racecourse** Leeds
356 C3 **Wetherby Road** N York
391 F4 **Wetheriggs Country Pottery** Cumb
173 E3 **Wethersfield airfield (dis)** Essex
128 D5 **Wetlands & Wildfowl Trust** Carmth
117 G3 **Wexham Park Golf Club** Bucks
91 G4 **Weybrook Park Golf Club** Hants
32 B4 **Weymouth Golf Club** Dorset
163 E5 **Whaddon Road** Gloucs
340 A2 **Whalley Golf Club** Lancs
607 J5 **Whalsay** Shet
607 J4 **Whalsay Golf Club** Shet
355 F5 **Wharfedale** Brad
162 B6 **Wharf House visitor centre** Gloucs
359 G2 **Wharram Percy Deserted Medieval Village EH** N York
211 H5 **Wharton Park Golf Club** Worcs
294 C4 **Whatstandwell railway station** Derbys
6 D3 **Wheal Coates** Cnwll
8 C2 **Wheal Martyn Heritage Centre** Cnwll
6 D5 **Wheal Peevor (UNESCO)** Cnwll
3 F3 **Wheal Rodney Holiday Park** Cnwll
6 D5 **Wheal Rose Caravan & Camping Park** Cnwll
67 F3 **Wheathill Golf Club** Somset
35 d1 **Wheatlands Golf Club** Guern
35 g6 **Wheatlands Golf Club** Jersey
330 D3 **Wheatley Golf Club** Donc
343 H3 **Wheatley Park Golf Club** Leeds
386 D5 **Wheeldale Roman Road** N York
240 C5 **Whetstone Golf Club** Leics
405 E3 **Whickham Golf Club** Gatesd
482 C4 **Whinhill railway station** Inver
389 F1 **Whinlatter Pass** Cumb
389 F5 **Whinlatter visitor centre** Cumb
142 D1 **Whipsnade Park golf course** Bucks
143 E1 **Whipsnade Zoo** Beds
292 D5 **Whiston Hall Golf Club** Staffs
309 G1 **Whiston railway station** Knows
406 C2 **Whitburn Golf Club** S Tyne
387 F2 **Whitby Abbey EH** N York
387 E2 **Whitby Golf Club** N York
106 C3 **Whitchurch (Cardiff) Golf Club** Cardif
106 B3 **Whitchurch (Cardiff) railway station** Cardif
90 D5 **Whitchurch Silk Mill** Hants
7 G2 **White Acres Holiday Park** Cnwll
202 D2 **Whitearch Touring Caravan Park** Suffk
324 D2 **White Bear Marina** Lancs
415 H5 **Whitecairn Holiday Park** D & G
133 G1 **White Castle CADW** Mons
300 D5 **White Cat Caravan & Camping Park** Lincs
528 B1 **White Caterthun HS** Angus
37 G3 **Whitecliff Bay Holiday Park** IoW
326 B3 **Whitefield Golf Club** Bury
215 H5 **Whitefields Golf Club** Warwks
132 A5 **Whitehall Golf Club** Myr Td
119 G1 **White Hart Lane** Gt Lon
119 G1 **White Hart Lane railway station** Gt Lon
20 B6 **Whitehill Country Park** Torbay
170 D5 **Whitehill golf course** Herts
88 D2 **White Horse Alton Barnes chalk figure** Wilts
112 C4 **White Horse Broad Town chalk figure** Wilts
112 B6 **White Horse Cherhill chalk figure** Wilts
88 B2 **White Horse Devizes chalk figure** Wilts
112 D5 **White Horse Hackpen chalk figure** Wilts
113 E6 **White Horse Marlborough chalk figure** Wilts
371 G3 **White Horse Oldstead chalk figure** N York
89 E3 **White Horse Pewsey chalk figure** Wilts
32 C3 **White Horse Sutton Poyntz chalk figure** Dorset
113 H2 **White Horse Uffington chalk figure** Oxon
87 F4 **White Horse Westbury chalk figure** Wilts
490 A3 **Whitekirk Golf & Country Club** E Loth
236 B3 **White Ladies Priory EH** Shrops
141 H4 **Whiteleaf Golf Club** Bucks
33 E2 **Whitemead Caravan Park** Dorset
378 B3 **White Moss Common NT** Cumb
499 F2 **Whitemoss golf course** P & K
296 B3 **White Post Modern Farm Centre** Notts
343 H4 **White Rose** Leeds
54 B4 **White Rose Touring Park** W Susx
367 E3 **White Scar Caves** N York
283 E4 **White Tower Caravan Park** Gwynd
144 D5 **Whitewebbs Park golf course** Gt Lon
95 G2 **Whitgift School cricket ground** Gt Lon
410 D4 **Whithorn Cradle of Christianity museum** D & G
410 D4 **Whithorn Priory HS** D & G
461 E4 **Whitley Bay Golf Club** N Ayrs
153 E6 **Whitland Abbey** Carmth
431 F5 **Whitley Bay Golf Club** N Tyne
250 B3 **Whitlingham Country Park** Norfk
10 D3 **Whitsand Bay Holiday Park** Cnwll

10 C3 **Whitsand Bay Hotel Golf & Country Club** Cnwll
100 B2 **Whitstable & Seasalter Golf Club** Kent
326 D1 **Whittaker Golf Club** Rochdl
238 A3 **Whittington Heath Golf Club** Staffs
193 E6 **Whittlebury Park Golf & Country Club** Nhants
188 A3 **Wichenford Dovecote NT** Worcs
51 G2 **Wickham Park Golf Club** Hants
51 F2 **Wickham vineyard** Hants
53 F4 **Wicks Farm Holiday Park** W Susx
218 B4 **Wicksteed Park** Nhants
20 B5 **Widdicombe Farm Tourist Park** Devon
22 D2 **Widemouth Bay Caravan Park** Cnwll
20 B5 **Widend Touring Park** Devon
309 H2 **Widnes Golf Club** Halton
214 B4 **Widney Manor Golf Club** Solhll
214 B4 **Widney Manor railway station** Solhll
236 C5 **Wigan Golf Club** Bolton
260 B4 **Wighton railway station** Norfk
236 C5 **Wightwick Manor NT** Wolves
209 H6 **Wigmore Castle EH** Herefs
417 E6 **Wigtown & Bladnoch Golf Club** D & G
415 G5 **Wigtownshire County Golf Club** D & G
251 F4 **Wild Duck Holiday Park** Norfk
97 E3 **Wildernesse Golf Club** Kent
135 G3 **Wildfowl & Wetlands Trust** Gloucs
324 A2 **Wildfowl & Wetlands Trust** Lancs
246 A6 **Wildfowl & Wetlands Trust** Norfk
406 A3 **Wildfowl & Wetlands Trust** Sundld
54 B3 **Wildfowl & Wetlands Trust** W Susx
398 D1 **Wildlife & Wetlands Trust Centre** D & G
98 B3 **Wildlife Trust Tyland Barn visitor centre** Kent
380 B1 **Wild Rose Park campsite** Cumb
75 G2 **Wildwood Country Club golf course** Surrey
100 C3 **Wildwood Wealden Forest Park** Kent
48 C4 **Wilksworth Farm Caravan Park** Dorset
294 B3 **Willersley Castle** Derbys
239 E1 **Willesley Park Golf Club** Leics
467 E3 **Williamwood Golf Club** E Rens
325 H6 **William Wroe Municipal golf course** Traffd
57 F4 **Willingdon Golf Club** E Susx
323 F2 **Willowbank Holiday Home & Touring Park** Surrey
168 B3 **Willowbridge Marina** Bucks
144 A4 **Willow Farm Village** Bucks
358 A3 **Willow House Caravan Park** York
116 C4 **Willow Marina** Wokham
276 A4 **Willow Moorings Marina** Notts
225 F4 **Willows Camping & Caravan Park** Norfk
342 C5 **Willow Valley Golf Club** Calder
38 B6 **Willow Valley Holiday Park** Cnwll
311 G4 **Wilmslow Golf Club** Ches
339 G3 **Wilpshire Golf Club** Lancs
397 E6 **Wilton Golf Club** R & Cl
70 B3 **Wilton House** Wilts
87 F1 **Wiltshire Cycleway** Wilts
63 F5 **Wimbleball Lake campsite** Somset
119 E6 **Wimbledon Chase railway station** Gt Lon
119 E5 **Wimbledon Common Golf Club** Gt Lon
119 E5 **Wimbledon Park Golf Club** Gt Lon
119 F5 **Wimbledon Stadium** Gt Lon
196 D4 **Wimpole Hall & Home Farm NT** Cambs
68 B4 **Wincanton racecourse** Somset
163 F4 **Winchcombe railway station** Gloucs
72 C4 **Winchester Castle EH** Hants
72 D2 **Winchester service area** Hants
378 D5 **Windermere Golf Club** Cumb
378 C5 **Windermere Marina Village** Cumb
378 D5 **Windermere Steamboats & Museum** Cumb
93 F2 **Windlemere Golf Club** Surrey
93 F2 **Windlesham golf course** Surrey
324 A1 **Windmill Animal Farm** Lancs
112 C5 **Windmill Hill EH** Wilts
168 A3 **Windmill Hill Golf Centre** M Keyn
213 E4 **Windmill Hill viewpoint** Worcs
136 D5 **Windmill Tump Long Barrow NT** Gloucs
214 D3 **Windmill Village Hotel Golf & Leisure Club** Covtry
192 B3 **Windmill vineyard** Nhants
117 G4 **Windsor Castle** W & M
117 F4 **Windsor racecourse** W & M
44 D6 **Windwhistle Golf Club** Somset
483 H5 **Windyhill Golf Club** E Duns
226 A4 **Wingfield College** Suffk
294 D4 **Wingfield Manor** Derbys
242 B4 **Wing Maze** Rutlnd
75 F1 **Winkworth Arboretum NT** Surrey
116 C5 **Winnersh Triangle Railway Station** Wokham
24 B2 **Winsford Walled Garden** Devon
566 B2 **Winter Alternative cycle route** Highld
490 C4 **Winterfield Golf Club** E Loth
117 E2 **Winter Hill Golf Club** W & M
346 D6 **Winterton Showground** N Linc
308 C2 **Wirral**
308 B3 **Wirral Country Park** Wirral
308 C2 **Wirral Ladies Golf Club** Wirral
468 B3 **Wishaw Golf Club** N Lans
238 B6 **Wishaw golf course** Birm
94 B3 **Wisley** Surrey
151 H6 **Wiston Castle CADW** Pembks
498 C5 **Witches Craig Caravan & Camping Park** Stirlg
55 G3 **Withdean Stadium** Br & H
349 H4 **Withernsea Golf Club** E R Yk
311 G1 **Withington Golf Club** Manch

75 E1 **Witley Common visitor centre NT** Surrey
187 H2 **Witley Court EH** Worcs
139 E3 **Witney Lakes golf course** Oxon
140 C6 **Wittenham Clumps viewpoint** Oxon
243 E4 **Wittering airfield** Nhants
80 C4 **Wivelsfield Road railway station** Kent
394 D3 **Witton Castle** Dur
339 G4 **Witton Country Park** Bl w D
213 G1 **Witton railway station** Birm
77 F6 **Wivelsfield railway station** W Susx
168 D3 **Woburn Abbey** Beds
168 D3 **Woburn Safari Park** Beds
92 A1 **Wokefield Park Golf Club** W Berk
93 G3 **Woking Golf Club** Surrey
95 H3 **Woldingham Golf Club** Surrey
373 C5 **Wolds Way Caravan and Camping** N York
276 B2 **Wollaton Hall** C Nott
276 B2 **Wollaton Park Golf Club** C Nott
451 F5 **Woll golf course** Border
291 C5 **Wolstanton Golf Club** Staffs
261 G5 **Wolterton Park** Norfk
212 B1 **Wolverhampton Business airport** Staffs
236 D4 **Wolverhapmton racecourse** Wolves
38 B6 **Wooda Farm Park campsite** Cnwll
315 F3 **Woodall service area** Rothm
202 C5 **Woodbridge airfield (dis)** Suffk
202 B5 **Woodbridge Golf Club** Suffk
580 E7 **Woodbury Park Hotel Golf & Country Club** Devon
136 B4 **Woodchester Park NT** Gloucs
80 D2 **Woodchurch Windmill** Kent
366 C4 **Woodclose Caravan Park** Cumb
95 F2 **Woodcote Park Golf Club** Gt Lon
580 E7 **Woodend Caravan & Camping Site** Highld
29 G4 **Wood Farm Caravan & Camping Park** Dorset
145 E6 **Woodford Golf Club** Gt Lon
213 F3 **Woodgate Valley Country Park** Birm
120 B2 **Woodgarston Park railway station** Gt Lon
342 D2 **Woodhall Hills Golf Club** Leeds
299 F2 **Woodhall Spa Golf Club** Lincs
395 F4 **Woodham Golf & Country Club** Dur
328 B4 **Woodhead Pass** Barns
88 D6 **Woodhenge EH** Wilts
370 A5 **Woodhouse Farm & Country Park campsite** N York
133 F4 **Woodlake Park Golf & Country Club** Mons
33 G3 **Woodland Caravan & Camping Park** Dorset
502 C4 **Woodland Gardens Caravan & Camping Site** Fife
256 B2 **Woodland Leisure Park** Norfk
74 C1 **Woodland Park visitor centre** Hants
33 F2 **Woodlands Camping Park** Dorset
180 D1 **Woodlands Caravan Park** Cerdgn
110 A3 **Woodlands golf course** S Glos
13 E2 **Woodlands Leisure Park** Devon
13 E2 **Woodlands Leisure Park campsite** Devon
97 E2 **Woodlands Manor Golf Club** Kent
311 E5 **Woodlands Park campsite** Ches
80 C2 **Woodlands Park campsite** Kent
25 G4 **Woodland Springs Adult Touring Park** Devon
134 D3 **Woodlands View Camping & Caravan Park** Gloucs
298 B6 **Woodland Waters campsite** Lincs
354 C2 **Wood Nook Caravan Park** N York
17 F4 **Woodovis Park campsite** Devon
126 C4 **Wood Park Caravans campsite** Pembks
169 F6 **Woodside Animal Farm** Herts
171 H5 **Woodside Park** Herts
328 B2 **Woodsome Hall Golf Club** Kirk
109 F6 **Woodspring Golf & Country Club** N Som
84 B3 **Woodspring Park** N Som
320 D3 **Woodthorpe Hall Golf Club** Lincs
61 G2 **Woody Bay railway station** Devon
85 F5 **Wookey Hole** Somset
60 C3 **Woolacombe Bay Holiday Village** Devon
60 C3 **Woolacombe Sands Holiday Park** Devon
454 B4 **Wooler Golf Club** Nthumb
329 E2 **Woolley Edge service area** Wakefd
329 E2 **Woolley Park golf course** Wakefd
48 D4 **Woolsbridge Manor Farm Caravan Park** Dorset
278 C5 **Woolsthorpe Manor NT** Lincs
145 F5 **Woolston Manor Golf Club** Essex
309 F2 **Woolton Golf Club** Lpool
188 B3 **Worcester Foregate Street railway station** Worcs
188 B4 **Worcester Golf & Country Club** Worcs
188 B3 **Worcester racecourse** Worcs
188 B4 **Worcestershire County Cricket Ground** Worcs
188 C3 **Worcester Shrub Hill railway station** Worcs
378 B3 **Wordsworth museum** Cumb
235 H6 **Worfield golf course** Shrops
388 B4 **Workington Golf Club** Cumb
316 B4 **Worksop Golf Club** Notts
74 A2 **Worldham Park golf course** Hants
7 E3 **World in Miniature** Cnwll
21 E1 **World Of Country Life museum** Devon
137 H2 **World of Mechanical Music museum** Gloucs
84 B2 **Worlebury Golf Club** N Som
84 C2 **Worle railway station** N Som
93 G3 **Worplesdon Golf Club** Surrey
325 H5 **Worsley Golf Club** Salfd
256 B4 **Worstead railway station** Norfk
54 D3 **Worthing Golf Club** W Susx
329 E4 **Wortley Golf Club** Barns
113 F1 **Wrag Barn Golf Club** Swindn
19 E6 **Wrangaton (S Devon) Golf Club** Devon

235 E3 **Wrekin Golf Club** Wrekin
410 C4 **Wrens Egg Standing Stones** D & G
372 C5 **Wrens of Ryedale Touring Park** N York
169 F2 **Wrest Park EH** Beds
288 D4 **Wrexham Central railway station** Wrexhm
288 D4 **Wrexham General railway station** Wrexhm
289 E4 **Wrexham Golf Club** Wrexhm
97 F5 **Wrotham Heath Golf Club** Kent
112 D4 **Wroughton airshow venue** Swindn
234 D3 **Wroxeter Roman City EH** Shrops
256 C6 **Wroxham railway station** Norfk
378 A4 **Wrynose Pass** Cumb
195 H3 **Wyboston Lakes golf course** Beds
341 E2 **Wycoller country park** Lancs
117 F1 **Wycombe Heights Golf Centre** Bucks
99 H5 **Wye Crown chalk figure** Kent
207 F6 **Wyeside Caravan & Camping Park** Powys
134 C4 **Wye Valley Forest of Dean cycle route** Mons
118 D4 **Wyke Green Golf Club** Gt Lon
224 C5 **Wyken vineyard** Suffk
237 H6 **Wylde Green railway station** Birm
249 F4 **Wymondham Abbey railway station** Norfk
396 B4 **Wynyard Golf Club** S on T
396 B4 **Wynyard Woodland Park** S on T
212 B5 **Wyre Forest Golf Club** Worcs
211 G5 **Wyre Forest visitor centre** Worcs
213 G4 **Wythall railway station** Worcs
311 G2 **Wythenshawe Hall** Manch
220 C4 **Wyton airfield** Cambs

X

168 B2 **Xscape sports complex** M Keyn
466 D1 **Xscape sports complex** Rens
344 A5 **Xscape sports complex** Wakefd

Y

36 C4 **Yafford Watermill Farm Park** IoW
97 G4 **Yalding railway station** Kent
36 B3 **Yarmouth Castle EH** IoW
311 E6 **Yatehouse Farm Caravan Park** Ches
92 D3 **Yateley Common Country Park** Hants
110 C3 **Yate railway station** S Glos
41 F5 **Yeatheridge Farm Caravan Park** Devon
608 F7 **Yell** Shet
18 B4 **Yelverton Golf Club** Devon
41 F2 **Yeo Valley Holiday Park** Devon
45 H4 **Yeovil Golf Club** Dorset
45 H5 **Yeovil Junction railway station** Dorset
228 D4 **Ynysmaengwyn Caravan Park** Gwynd
358 B2 **York Golf Club** York
387 F3 **York House Caravan Park** N York
358 A5 **York racecourse** York
117 E3 **York Road** W & M
358 C5 **Yorkshire Air museum** York
367 E2 **Yorkshire Dales Cycleway** Cumb
368 C5 **Yorkshire Dales Cycleway** N York
354 B5 **Yorkshire Dales Lead Mining museum** Lancs
368 A4 **Yorkshire Dales National Park** N York
354 D2 **Yorkshire Dales National Park Centre (Grassington)** N York
368 A2 **Yorkshire Dales National Park Centre (Hawes)** N York
354 A2 **Yorkshire Dales National Park Centre (Malham)** N York
366 D1 **Yorkshire Dales National Park Centre (Sedbergh)** Cumb
356 B2 **Yorkshire Hussar Inn Holiday Caravan Park** N York
358 C4 **Yorkshire Museum of Farming** York
328 D2 **Yorkshire Sculpture Park** Wakefd
346 D2 **Yorkshire Wolds Way** E R Yk
373 H4 **Yorkshire Wolds Way** N York
300 B6 **York Street** Lincs
358 B3 **York Touring Caravan Site** York
99 G2 **Youngboats Marina** Kent
131 F6 **Ystrad Rhondda railway station** Rhondd
264 D2 **Y Traeth Stadium** Gwynd

Z

41 H3 **Zeacombe House Caravan Park** Devon

City, town and village index

A

93 G6 Aaron's Hill Surrey
68 A5 Abbas Combe Somset
187 G1 Abberley Worcs
174 C6 Abberton Essex
189 E4 Abberton Worcs
443 E2 Abberwick Nthumb
146 B2 Abbess End Essex
146 B2 Abbess Roding Essex
43 F5 Abbey Devon
207 H5 Abbey-cwm-hir Powys
136 C1 Abbeydale Gloucs
314 C3 Abbeydale Sheff
314 C3 Abbeydale Park Sheff
159 G3 Abbey Dore Herefs
174 C5 Abbey Field Essex
29 E3 Abbey Gate Devon
98 B3 Abbey Gate Kent
270 C3 Abbey Green Shrops
292 C3 Abbey Green Staffs
326 C5 Abbey Hey Manch
488 B5 Abbeyhill C Edin
44 B4 Abbey Hill Somset
292 B5 Abbey Hulton C Stke
136 C1 Abbeymead Gloucs
94 A1 Abbey Mead Surrey
473 H2 Abbey St Bathans Border
352 B4 Abbeystead Lancs
399 F4 Abbey Town Cumb
339 F5 Abbey Village Lancs
120 C4 Abbey Wood Gt Lon
412 D2 Abbey Yard D & G
440 A2 Abbotrule Border
39 E5 Abbots Bickington Devon
273 G5 Abbots Bromley Staffs
30 D5 Abbotsbury Dorset
77 E5 Abbotsford W Susx
39 F2 Abbotsham Devon
20 A4 Abbotskerswell Devon
143 F4 Abbots Langley Herts
12 D3 Abbotsleigh Devon
109 F5 Abbots Leigh N Som
196 B3 Abbotsley Cambs
309 E6 Abbot's Meads Ches
189 F4 Abbots Morton Worcs
220 B4 Abbots Ripton Cambs
189 G4 Abbot's Salford Warwks
73 E3 Abbotstone Hants
71 H5 Abbotswood Hants
72 C3 Abbots Worthy Hants
89 H6 Abbotts Ann Hants
209 G4 Abcott Shrops
210 D2 Abdon Shrops
329 G5 Abdy Rothm
180 C5 Aber Cerdgn
180 B2 Aberaeron Cerdgn
131 G4 Aberaman Rhondd
230 C2 Aberangell Gwynd
153 G1 Aber Arad Carmth
534 E5 Aberarder Highld
549 L4 Aberarder Highld
500 C1 Aberargie P & K
180 C2 Aberarth Cerdgn
104 B1 Aberavon Neath
153 H1 Aber-banc Cerdgn
132 C4 Aberbargoed Caerph
232 B6 Aberbechan Powys
132 C4 Aberbeeg Blae G
157 F4 Aberbran Powys
131 G4 Abercanaid Myr Td
132 C6 Abercarn Caerph
151 E3 Abercastle Pembks
230 C4 Abercegir Powys
534 B2 Aberchalder Highld
569 L5 Aberchirder Abers
487 E4 Abercorn W Loth
130 C2 Abercraf Powys
130 C5 Abercregan Neath
503 E4 Abercrombie Fife
131 G5 Abercwmboi Rhondd
153 E1 Abercych Pembks
131 H5 Abercynon Rhondd
230 D1 Aber-Cywarch Gwynd
512 C6 Aberdalgie P & K
131 F4 Aberdare Rhondd
262 B5 Aberdaron Gwynd
557 G3 Aberdeen C Aber
282 D5 Aberdesach Gwynd
487 G3 Aberdour Fife
130 B5 Aberdulais Neath
229 E5 Aberdyfi Gwynd
184 A5 Aberedw Powys
150 C3 Abereiddy Pembks
263 G3 Abererch Gwynd
131 H4 Aberfan Myr Td
524 C6 Aberfeldy P & K
282 B2 Aberffraw IoA
205 F4 Aberffrwd Cerdgn
133 F3 Aberffrwd Mons
343 H2 Aberford Leeds
496 D4 Aberfoyle Stirlg
105 E3 Abergarw Brdgnd
130 B4 Abergarwed Neath
133 F2 Abergavenny Mons
306 C4 Abergele Conwy
154 D1 Aber-Giâr Carmth
155 E3 Abergorlech Carmth
182 C4 Abergwesyn Powys
154 B5 Abergwili Carmth
229 F1 Abergwynant Gwynd
130 D5 Abergwynfi Neath
304 D5 Abergwyngregyn Gwynd
229 F3 Abergynolwyn Gwynd
207 H1 Aberhafesp Powys
230 C5 Aberhosan Powys
104 D3 Aberkenfig Brdgnd
489 F4 Aberlady E Loth
528 B3 Aberlemno Angus
205 E1 Aberlerry Cerdgn
230 B3 Aberllefenni Gwynd
158 C2 Aberllynfi Powys
205 F5 Abermagwr Cerdgn
181 E3 Abermeurig Cerdgn
288 C3 Abermorddu Flints
232 C6 Abermule Powys
268 B5 Abernaint Powys
153 G5 Abernant Carmth
232 C5 Abernant Powys
131 G4 Abernant Rhondd
500 C1 Abernethy P & K
513 F3 Abernyte P & K
288 C5 Aber-oer Wrexhm
179 F3 Aberporth Cerdgn
262 D5 Abersoch Gwynd
133 E4 Abersychan Torfn
229 E5 Aber-Tafol Gwynd
105 G4 Aberthin V Glam
132 D3 Abertillery Blae G
106 B2 Abertridwr Caerph
267 G6 Abertridwr Powys
229 E3 Abertrinant Gwynd
132 B3 Abertysswg Caerph
499 F1 Aberuthven P & K
158 A5 Aber Village Powys
157 F4 Aberyscir Powys
204 D3 Aberystwyth Cerdgn
596 C6 Abhainn Suidhe W Isls
140 B5 Abingdon Oxon
94 C5 Abinger Common Surrey
94 B5 Abinger Hammer Surrey
193 G2 Abington Nhants
448 B5 Abington S Lans
196 D6 Abington Pigotts Cambs
193 G2 Abington Vale Nhants
54 D1 Abingworth W Susx
277 F5 Ab Kettleby Leics
189 F4 Ab Lench Worcs
137 H3 Ablington Gloucs
89 E5 Ablington Wilts
313 G4 Abney Derbys
555 F5 Aboyne Abers
351 G2 Abraham Heights Lancs
325 E4 Abram Wigan
549 K2 Abriachan Highld
145 G5 Abridge Essex
485 F4 Abronhill N Lans
51 F3 Abshot Hants
110 C5 Abson S Glos
192 D5 Abthorpe Nhants
602 B6 Abune-the-Hill Ork
320 D4 Aby Lincs
518 E1 Acarsaid Highld
358 A5 Acaster Malbis York
344 D1 Acaster Selby N York
340 B4 Accrington Lancs
516 F5 Acha Ag & B
480 A3 Achabraid Ag & B
543 H7 Achachork Highld
520 E4 Achadh nan Darach Highld
479 K6 Achahoish Ag & B
506 F3 Achaleven Ag & B
521 L7 Achallader Ag & B
588 E5 Achalone Highld
597 J2 Acha Mòr W Isls
564 D4 Achanalt Highld
565 L2 Achandunie Highld
481 E2 Achanelid Ag & B
520 F1 Ach' an Todhair Highld
576 C3 Achany Highld
533 G7 Achaphubuil Highld
519 G2 Acharacle Highld
586 F6 Achargary Highld
538 B4 Acharn Angus
519 G5 Acharn Highld
523 K7 Acharn P & K
556 C2 Achath Abers
577 G5 Achavandra Muir Highld
588 F8 Achavanich Highld
128 B4 Achddu Carmth
573 L3 Achduart Highld
581 L3 Achentoul Highld
579 J2 Achfary Highld
580 E7 Achfrish Highld
573 G5 Achgarve Highld
584 F3 Achiemore Highld
587 J5 Achiemore Highld
544 D8 A' Chill Highld
573 K2 Achiltibuie Highld
586 F4 Achina Highld
586 C4 Achinahuagh Highld
576 C4 Achinduich Highld
506 D2 Achinduin Ag & B
588 F4 Achingills Highld
586 C4 Achininver Highld
547 G1 Achintee Highld
546 E2 Achintraid Highld
517 L6 Achleck Ag & B
534 B6 Achluachrach Highld
584 D6 Achlyness Highld
578 E5 Achmelvich Highld
546 F3 Achmore Highld
573 K4 Achmore Highld
597 J2 Achmore W Isls
506 F2 Achnaba Ag & B
578 D3 Achnacarnin Highld
533 J5 Achnacarry Highld
507 G3 Achnacloich Ag & B
545 K8 Achnacloich Highld
549 G6 Achnaconeran Highld
506 F2 Achnacree Bay Ag & B
506 E1 Achnacroish Ag & B
518 B5 Achnadrish House Ag & B
566 B2 Achnagarron Highld
518 C2 Achnaha Highld
575 L4 Achnahanat Highld
551 H4 Achnahannet Highld
504 D6 Achnahard Ag & B
580 D7 Achnairn Highld
576 E2 Achnaluachrach Highld
479 K4 Achnamara Ag & B
533 J5 Achnasaul Highld
563 L5 Achnasheen Highld
518 B2 Achosnich Highld
588 C3 Achreamie Highld
521 G2 Achriabhach Highld
584 E6 Achriesgill Highld
577 J2 Achrimsdale Highld
543 H7 Achtalean Highld
193 H5 Achterneed Highld
586 E4 Achtoty Highld
219 E3 Achurch Nhants
586 C5 Achuvoldrach Highld
576 F5 Achvaich Highld
588 B4 Achvarasdal Highld
365 H3 Ackenthwaite Cumb
589 K6 Ackergill Highld
384 D1 Acklam Middsb
359 E2 Acklam N York
235 H5 Ackleton Shrops
443 G4 Acklington Nthumb
343 H5 Ackton Wakefd
329 G1 Ackworth Moor Top Wakefd
250 D2 Acle Norfk
213 H3 Acock's Green Birm
101 F2 Acol Kent
403 G1 Acomb Nthumb
357 H4 Acomb York
160 C3 Aconbury Herefs
340 B5 Acre Lancs
326 D3 Acre Oldham
288 C6 Acrefair Wrexhm
291 G4 Acres Nook Staffs
290 C4 Acton Ches
34 A5 Acton Dorset
119 E3 Acton Gt Lon
209 F3 Acton Shrops
272 B1 Acton Staffs
200 A6 Acton Suffk
188 B1 Acton Worcs
288 D4 Acton Wrexhm
187 F4 Acton Beauchamp Herefs
310 B4 Acton Bridge Ches
234 C4 Acton Burnell Shrops
187 G4 Acton Green Herefs
234 C4 Acton Pigott Shrops
200 A5 Acton Place Suffk
270 C5 Acton Reynald Shrops
235 E5 Acton Round Shrops
210 A2 Acton Scott Shrops
272 D6 Acton Trussell Staffs
111 E3 Acton Turville S Glos
599 L2 Adabroc W Isls
469 G1 Adambrae W Loth
30 C1 Adam's Green Dorset
380 B5 Adamthwaite Cumb
271 H4 Adbaston Staffs
67 F5 Adber Dorset
276 D2 Adbolton Notts
165 H2 Adderbury Oxon
271 F2 Adderley Shrops
292 B5 Adderley Green C Stke
455 E3 Adderstone Nthumb
469 F2 Addiewell W Loth
355 E4 Addingham Brad
355 E5 Addingham Moorside Brad
167 F4 Addington Bucks
16 C5 Addington Cnwll
96 A2 Addington Gt Lon
97 G3 Addington Kent
472 C4 Addinston Border
95 G1 Addiscombe Gt Lon
94 A2 Addlestone Surrey
94 A1 Addlestonemoor Surrey
321 F6 Addlethorpe Lincs
343 E2 Adel Leeds
271 F6 Adeney Wrekin
143 F3 Adeyfield Herts
231 H4 Adfa Powys
209 H5 Adforton Herefs
37 F3 Adgestone IoW
100 D5 Adisham Kent
164 C4 Adlestrop Gloucs
346 B5 Adlingfleet E R Yk
312 B3 Adlington Ches
325 E2 Adlington Lancs
324 D2 Adlington Park Lancs
273 F5 Admaston Staffs
235 E2 Admaston Wrekin
190 B5 Admington Warwks
153 G1 Adpar Cerdgn
44 B2 Adsborough Somset
64 C4 Adscombe Somset
167 F4 Adstock Bucks
192 C4 Adstone Nhants
312 A2 Adswood Stockp
75 H5 Adversane W Susx
551 L3 Advie Highld
342 D4 Adwalton Leeds
141 E5 Adwell Oxon
330 B3 Adwick le Street Donc
329 H4 Adwick upon Dearne Donc
571 G5 Adziel Abers
423 G2 Ae D & G
325 H2 Affetside Bury
560 C5 Affleck Abers
47 E6 Affpuddle Dorset
288 C5 Afon Eitha Wrexhm
307 G5 Afon-Wen Flints
263 G3 Afon Wen Gwynd
36 B3 Afton IoW
239 G2 Agar Nook Leics
212 B4 Aggborough Worcs
369 E2 Agglethorpe N York
400 D3 Aglionby Cumb
307 G6 Aifft Denbgs
309 E2 Aigburth Lpool
599 K8 Aiginis W Isls
360 C5 Aike E R Yk
602 E1 Aikerness Ork
601 H6 Aikers Ork
401 E5 Aiketgate Cumb
399 H4 Aikton Cumb
320 D4 Ailby Lincs
185 F5 Ailey Herefs
190 C4 Ailstone Warwks
243 G5 Ailsworth C Pete
145 E4 Aimes Green Essex
370 D3 Ainderby Quernhow N York
370 C1 Ainderby Steeple N York
175 F5 Aingers Green Essex
323 F2 Ainsdale Sefton
323 E2 Ainsdale-on-Sea Sefton
401 F5 Ainstable Cumb
325 H3 Ainsworth Bury
386 B3 Ainthorpe N York
323 G5 Aintree Sefton
470 B2 Ainville W Loth
492 C4 Aird Ag & B
415 E4 Aird D & G
562 D2 Aird Highld
593 D7 Aird W Isls
599 M7 Aird W Isls
595 L4 Àird Adhanais W Isls
593 C8 Aird a' Mhachair W Isls
596 F5 Aird a' Mhulaidh W Isls
596 E7 Aird Asaig W Isls
593 D8 Aird Choinnich W Isls
599 K2 Aird Dhail W Isls
576 D5 Airdens Highld
591 E7 Aird Mhidhinis W Isls
595 H5 Aird Mhighe W Isls
595 J4 Aird Mhighe W Isls
591 E7 Aird Mhòr W Isls
593 D8 Aird Mhòr W Isls
593 D8 Aird na Monadh W Isls
592 E6 Aird nan Srùban W Isls
505 G5 Aird of Kinloch Ag & B
531 G2 Aird of Sleat Highld
468 B1 Airdrie N Lans
468 B1 Airdriehill N Lans
590 E3 Àird Ruairidh W Isls
507 G3 Airds Bay Ho Ag & B
595 J5 Àird Shleibhe W Isls
520 C6 Airds Ho Ag & B
599 K7 Aird Thunga W Isls
586 E4 Airdtorrisdale Highld
598 B7 Aird Uig W Isls
344 B4 Airedale Wakefd
354 C5 Aire View N York
597 G4 Airidh a Bhruaich W Isls
526 D4 Airlie Angus
345 G4 Airmyn E R Yk
512 C2 Airntully P & K
531 K1 Airor Highld
486 A2 Airth Falk
498 C5 Airthrey Castle Stirlg
354 A3 Airton N York
410 C3 Airyhassen D & G
387 E3 Airy Hill N York
409 G2 Airylick D & G
409 G2 Airyolland D & G
279 E2 Aisby Lincs
332 B6 Aisby Lincs
590 E3 Aisgernis W Isls
19 E5 Aish Devon
20 A6 Aish Devon
64 C4 Aisholt Somset
370 B2 Aiskew N York
373 E2 Aislaby N York
387 E3 Aislaby N York
384 B2 Aislaby S on T
318 A3 Aisthorpe Lincs
602 A8 Aith Ork
603 J6 Aith Ork
605 H5 Aith Shet
606 D6 Aith Shet
609 J6 Aith Shet
268 D5 Aithnen Powys
605 H4 Aithsetter Shet
551 H2 Aitnoch Highld
454 A4 Akeld Nthumb
167 F2 Akeley Bucks
201 F5 Akenham Suffk
405 G3 Albany Sundld
17 F4 Albaston Cnwll
233 G2 Alberbury Shrops
125 F1 Albert Town Pembks
275 E6 Albert Village Leics
55 G1 Albourne W Susx
55 G1 Albourne Green W Susx
236 B4 Albrighton Shrops
270 B6 Albrighton Shrops
178 D4 Albro Castle Pembks
226 B2 Alburgh Norfk
171 F5 Albury Herts
94 B5 Albury Surrey
171 F5 Albury End Herts
94 B5 Albury Heath Surrey
401 F4 Albyfield Cumb
261 G5 Alby Hill Norfk
565 K5 Alcaig Highld
210 B2 Alcaston Shrops
68 D5 Alcester Dorset
189 G3 Alcester Warwks
213 G3 Alcester Lane's End Birm
56 D3 Alciston E Susx
63 F2 Alcombe Somset
110 D6 Alcombe Wilts
219 H4 Alconbury Cambs
219 H4 Alconbury Weston Cambs
357 E1 Aldborough N York
261 G5 Aldborough Norfk
120 C2 Aldborough Hatch Gt Lon
113 F4 Aldbourne Wilts
348 D2 Aldbrough E R Yk
383 E2 Aldbrough St John N York
142 D2 Aldbury Herts
351 G2 Aldcliffe Lancs
524 D3 Aldclune P & K
203 F3 Aldeburgh Suffk
251 F6 Aldeby Norfk
143 G5 Aldenham Herts
78 C4 Alderbrook E Susx
70 D4 Alderbury Wilts
295 E5 Aldercar Derbys
255 F4 Alderford Norfk
325 H4 Alder Forest Salfd
49 E2 Alderholt Dorset
110 D1 Alderley Gloucs
311 G4 Alderley Edge Ches
215 F3 Alderman's Green Covtry
91 F1 Aldermaston W Berk
91 G2 Aldermaston Soke Hants
91 G1 Aldermaston Wharf W Berk
190 C5 Alderminster Warwks
50 C1 Aldermoor C Sotn
274 C4 Alder Moor Staffs
48 C6 Alderney Poole
86 D6 Alder Row Somset
120 B2 Aldersbrook Gt Lon
161 E2 Alder's End Herefs
289 G3 Aldersey Green Ches
237 H3 Aldershawe Staffs
92 D4 Aldershot Hants
163 F3 Alderton Gloucs
193 E5 Alderton Nhants
270 B5 Alderton Shrops
177 F1 Alderton Suffk
111 E3 Alderton Wilts
163 F3 Alderton Fields Gloucs
294 C4 Alderwasley Derbys
370 B6 Aldfield N York
289 F3 Aldford Ches
242 D4 Aldgate Rutlnd
174 B4 Aldham Essex
200 D6 Aldham Suffk
561 G1 Aldie Abers
53 G3 Aldingbourne W Susx
364 C5 Aldingham Cumb
81 G2 Aldington Kent
189 G6 Aldington Worcs
81 F2 Aldington Frith Kent
553 H3 Aldivalloch Moray
482 D1 Aldochlay Ag & B
210 A4 Aldon Shrops
399 E5 Aldoth Cumb
221 F5 Aldreth Cambs
237 G4 Aldridge Wsall
203 E2 Aldringham Suffk
55 G3 Aldrington Br & H
138 B2 Aldsworth Gloucs
553 H3 Aldunie Moray
294 A3 Aldwark Derbys
357 F2 Aldwark N York
329 G5 Aldwarke Rothm
53 G5 Aldwick W Susx
219 E3 Aldwincle Nhants
115 F4 Aldworth W Berk
208 D3 Ale Oak Shrops
483 E3 Alexandria W Duns
64 C4 Aley Somset
169 F6 Aley Green Beds
38 C5 Alfardisworthy Devon
28 B3 Alfington Devon
75 G3 Alfold Surrey
75 G3 Alfold Bars W Susx
75 G2 Alfold Crossways Surrey
555 G1 Alford Abers
321 E4 Alford Lincs
67 G3 Alford Somset
212 D5 Alfred's Well Worcs
295 E3 Alfreton Derbys
187 G4 Alfrick Worcs
187 G4 Alfrick Pound Worcs
57 E4 Alfriston E Susx
280 C2 Algakirk Lincs
67 G3 Alhampton Somset
531 K7 Alisary Highld
346 C5 Alkborough N Linc
135 H3 Alkerton Gloucs
191 F6 Alkerton Oxon
83 E2 Alkham Kent
270 C2 Alkington Shrops
274 B2 Alkmonton Derbys
326 C4 Alkrington Garden Village Rochdl
13 E2 Allaleigh Devon
537 H4 Allanaquoich Abers
472 C5 Allanbank Border
468 C3 Allanbank N Lans
565 L6 Allangrange Mains Highld
472 A5 Allanshaugh Border
472 B6 Allanshaws Border
474 C4 Allanton Border
468 C3 Allanton N Lans
468 A4 Allanton S Lans
541 F5 Allardice Abers
135 E4 Allaston Gloucs
591 D7 Allathasdal W Isls
72 C5 Allbrook Hants
88 C2 All Cannings Wilts
403 E3 Allendale Town Nthumb
238 B5 Allen End Warwks
403 F5 Allenheads Nthumb
404 C4 Allensford Dur
145 G1 Allen's Green Herts
160 B2 Allensmore Herefs
275 F3 Allenton C Derb
401 E3 Allenwood Cumb
20 B4 Aller Devon
27 H1 Aller Devon
47 E4 Aller Dorset
66 B4 Aller Somset
388 C2 Allerby Cumb
27 G4 Allercombe Devon
43 G2 Allerford Somset
63 E2 Allerford Somset
27 H3 Aller Grove Devon
20 B4 Aller Park Devon
373 G3 Allerston N York
359 E5 Allerthorpe E R Yk
342 B3 Allerton Brad
19 G5 Allerton Devon
309 F2 Allerton Lpool
343 H4 Allerton Bywater Leeds
357 E3 Allerton Mauleverer N York
214 D3 Allesley Covtry
275 E2 Allestree C Derb
7 E4 Allet Cnwll
241 H4 Allexton Leics
292 C1 Allgreave Ches
122 C4 Allhallows Medway
122 C4 Allhallows-on-Sea Medway
562 E5 Alligin Shuas Highld
272 C6 Allimore Green Staffs
30 B4 Allington Dorset
98 A3 Allington Kent
278 B1 Allington Lincs
70 D2 Allington Wilts
88 C2 Allington Wilts
111 F4 Allington Wilts
111 F5 Allington Bar Wilts
365 E4 Allithwaite Cumb
580 C1 Allnabad Highld
498 D6 Alloa Clacks
398 D6 Allonby Cumb
311 E5 Allostock Ches
444 D6 Alloway S Ayrs
44 D5 Allowenshay Somset
29 E2 All Saints Devon
226 C3 All Saints South Elmham Suffk
235 G5 Allscot Shrops
235 E2 Allscott Wrekin
234 B5 All Stretton Shrops
129 E4 Allt Carmth
288 C1 Alltami Flints
521 H5 Alltchaorunn Highld
267 F5 Alltforgan Powys
183 H5 Alltmawr Powys
585 H7 Alltnacaillich Highld
547 G4 Allt-nan-Sùgh Highld
533 K6 Alltour Highld
549 H6 Alltsigh Highld
154 B3 Alltwalis Carmth
130 A4 Alltwen Neath
180 D5 Alltyblaca Cerdgn
107 E2 Allt-yr-yn Newpt
224 D5 Allwood Green Suffk
295 F4 Alma Notts
424 B4 Almagill D & G
185 F4 Almeley Herefs
185 F4 Almeley Wooton Herefs
47 H5 Almer Dorset
330 C3 Almholme Donc
271 G3 Almington Staffs
38 D3 Alminstone Cross Devon
512 C4 Almondbank P & K
328 B1 Almondbury Kirk
109 G3 Almondsbury S Glos
469 G1 Almondvale W Loth
173 E3 Almshouse Green Essex
357 F1 Alne N York
189 H3 Alne End Warwks
189 H2 Alne Hills Warwks
565 L2 Alness Highld
566 B3 Alnessferry Highld
357 F1 Alne Station N York
442 B2 Alnham Nthumb
443 G2 Alnmouth Nthumb
443 F2 Alnwick Nthumb
118 D3 Alperton Gt Lon
173 H2 Alphamstone Essex
199 H4 Alpheton Suffk
27 E5 Alphington Devon
250 B4 Alpington Norfk
293 H2 Alport Derbys
233 E5 Alport Powys
290 B3 Alpraham Ches
175 E5 Alresford Essex
238 B2 Alrewas Staffs
291 F3 Alsager Ches
291 F5 Alsagers Bank Staffs
141 G4 Alscot Bucks
293 G3 Alsop en le Dale Derbys
402 C5 Alston Cumb
29 E2 Alston Devon
162 D5 Alstone Gloucs
163 E3 Alstone Gloucs
84 B5 Alstone Somset
293 F3 Alstonefield Staffs
84 D4 Alston Sutton Somset
41 E3 Alswear Devon
326 D4 Alt Oldham
578 C7 Altandhu Highld
581 K4 Altanduin Highld
16 B2 Altarnun Cnwll
575 K3 Altass Highld
160 D4 Altbough Herefs
557 H4 Altens C Aber
589 H3 Alterwall Highld
481 E5 Altgaltraig Ag & B
340 B3 Altham Lancs
326 D4 Alt Hill Tamesd
148 B5 Althorne Essex
331 H3 Althorpe N Linc
117 E4 Altmore W & M
521 J4 Altnafeadh Highld
580 E2 Altnaharra Highld
343 G5 Altofts Wakefd
294 D2 Alton Derbys
73 H2 Alton Hants
273 G1 Alton Staffs
88 D5 Alton Wilts
88 C2 Alton Barnes Wilts
445 F2 Altonhill E Ayrs
46 D4 Alton Pancras Dorset
88 D2 Alton Priors Wilts
311 F2 Altrincham Traffd
533 K4 Altrua Highld
496 C4 Altskeith Stirlg
213 H2 Alum Rock Birm
498 D5 Alva Clacks
309 G5 Alvanley Ches
275 F3 Alvaston C Derb
213 F5 Alvechurch Worcs
238 C4 Alvecote Warwks
69 G5 Alvediston Wilts
211 H3 Alveley Shrops
39 H2 Alverdiscott Devon
51 H5 Alverstoke Hants
37 F3 Alverstone IoW
343 F5 Alverthorpe Wakefd
277 G1 Alverton Notts
567 L4 Alves Moray
138 D4 Alvescot Oxon
110 A2 Alveston S Glos
190 C3 Alveston Warwks
109 H2 Alveston Down S Glos
190 C4 Alveston Hill Warwks
550 F8 Alvie Highld
320 B1 Alvingham Lincs
135 E4 Alvington Gloucs

45 G4 Alvington Somst
243 G5 Alwalton C Pete
107 F2 Alway Newpt
46 C3 Alweston Dorset
39 F3 Alwington Devon
441 H3 Alwinton Nthumb
343 E2 Alwoodley Leeds
343 F1 Alwoodley Gates Leeds
343 E1 Alwoodley Park Leeds
526 B5 Alyth P & K
3 E2 Amalebra Cnwll
3 E2 Amalveor Cnwll
575 K5 Amatnatua Highld
590 F5 Am Baile W Isls
275 G3 Ambaston Derbys
294 D4 Ambergate Derbys
136 B4 Amberley Gloucs
186 C5 Amberley Herefs
54 B2 Amberley W Susx
443 H4 Amble Nthumb
212 C2 Amblecote Dudley
378 C4 Ambleside Cumb
151 G4 Ambleston Pembks
166 D6 Ambrosden Oxon
332 A2 Amcotts N Linc
116 D6 Amen Corner Br For
142 C5 Amersham Bucks
142 D5 Amersham Common Bucks
142 C5 Amersham Old Town Bucks
142 D5 Amersham on the Hill Bucks
273 E4 Amerton Staffs
86 A3 Amesbury BaNES
70 D1 Amesbury Wilts
48 D4 Ameysford Dorset
238 C4 Amington Staffs
423 H3 Amisfield D & G
303 F2 Amlwch IoA
303 G2 Amlwch Port IoA
129 F2 Ammanford Carmth
29 G1 Ammerham Somst
373 E5 Amotherby N York
72 B5 Ampfield Hants
372 A4 Ampleforth N York
137 G4 Ampney Crucis Gloucs
137 G4 Ampney St Mary Gloucs
137 G4 Ampney St Peter Gloucs
89 G6 Amport Hants
169 E2 Ampthill Beds
223 H5 Ampton Suffk
126 D3 Amroth Pembks
511 F2 Amulree P & K
143 H2 Amwell Herts
551 J4 Anagach Highld
519 K3 Anaheilt Highld
563 J4 Anancaun Highld
562 D1 An Ard Highld
298 B6 Ancaster Lincs
208 C3 Anchor Shrops
52 B4 Anchorage Park C Port
248 D5 Anchor Corner Norfk
337 F1 Anchorsholme Bpool
256 C5 Anchor Street Norfk
599 K8 An Cnoc W Isls
599 L2 An Cnoc Ard W Isls
326 B5 Ancoats Manch
475 F5 Ancroft Nthumb
475 K5 Ancroft Northmoor Nthumb
452 B5 Ancrum Border
54 A4 Ancton W Susx
603 M1 Ancumtoun Ork
321 F4 Anderby Lincs
321 G4 Anderby Creek Lincs
65 F5 Andersea Somst
64 D5 Andersfield Somst
47 G5 Anderson Dorset
310 C4 Anderton Ches
10 D3 Anderton Cnwll
325 F2 Anderton Lancs
324 C2 Andertons Mill Lancs
90 B6 Andover Hants
90 B5 Andover Down Hants
163 F6 Andoversford Gloucs
322 g3 Andreas IoM
92 A4 Andwell Hants
262 A5 Anelog Gwynd
119 G6 Anerley Gt Lon
605 H5 Aness Shet
323 G6 Anfield Lpool
3 G2 Angarrack Cnwll
5 E1 Angarrick Cnwll
210 D4 Angelbank Shrops
43 G4 Angersleigh Somst
399 G3 Angerton Cumb
125 E4 Angle Pembks
599 J8 An Gleann Ur W Isls
54 C4 Angmering W Susx
357 G5 Angram N York
381 F5 Angram N York
403 G1 Anick Nthumb
497 E2 Anie Stirlg
187 G3 Ankerdine Hill Worcs
566 E2 Ankerville Highld
347 F4 Anlaby E R Yk
347 F4 Anlaby Park C KuH
590 E4 An Leth Meadhanach W Isls
253 E2 Anmer Norfk
52 B2 Anmore Hants
399 F1 Annan D & G
362 B4 Annaside Cumb
507 H5 Annat Ag & B
562 F6 Annat Highld
90 A6 Anna Valley Hants
445 E5 Annbank S Ayrs
295 G4 Annesley Notts
295 F4 Annesley Woodhouse Notts
405 E4 Annfield Plain Dur
484 A6 Anniesland C Glas
543 G6 Annishader Highld
226 D2 Annis Hill Suffk
431 E5 Annitsford N Tyne
560 D1 Annochie Abers
234 B3 Annscroft Shrops
51 G4 Ann's Hill Hants
275 E6 Annwell Place Derbys
337 F4 Ansdell Lancs
169 H6 Ansford Somst
67 G3 Ansford Somst
215 E1 Ansley Warwks
239 E6 Ansley Common Warwks
274 C5 Anslow Staffs
274 B4 Anslow Gate Staffs
75 E3 Ansteadbrook Surrey
171 F3 Anstey Hants
240 B3 Anstey Leics
503 F4 Anstruther Easter Fife
503 F4 Anstruther Wester Fife
77 E5 Ansty W Susx
215 F3 Ansty Warwks
69 G4 Ansty Wilts
69 G4 Ansty Coombe Wilts
47 E4 Ansty Cross Dorset
52 B2 Anthill Common Hants
93 H2 Anthony's Surrey
161 G5 Anthony's Cross Gloucs
399 F3 Anthorn Cumb
256 A3 Antingham Norfk
595 G5 An t-Ob W Isls
300 A3 Anton's Gowt Lincs
486 A3 Antonshill Falk
10 D3 Antony Cnwll
10 D2 Antony Passage Cnwll

310 C4 Antrobus Ches
100 B6 Anvil Green Kent
90 A1 Anvilles W Berk
299 E4 Anwick Lincs
417 H5 Anwoth D & G
533 K6 Aonachan Highld
291 G5 Apedale Staffs
96 B3 Aperfield Gt Lon
213 E5 Apes Dale Worcs
243 E5 Apethorpe Nhants
272 C6 Apeton Staffs
319 E4 Apley Lincs
235 G5 Apley Forge Shrops
314 D4 Apperknowle Derbys
162 C4 Apperley Gloucs
404 C3 Apperley Dene Nthumb
367 H1 Appersett N York
520 C6 Appin Ag & B
410 D4 Appleby D & G
332 D2 Appleby N Linc
391 H5 Appleby-in-Westmorland Cumb
239 E3 Appleby Magna Leics
239 E3 Appleby Parva Leics
562 B8 Applecross Highld
43 E5 Appledore Devon
60 B5 Appledore Devon
80 D4 Appledore Kent
81 E3 Appledore Heath Kent
140 B6 Appleford Oxon
424 C3 Applegarthtown D & G
116 D3 Applehouse Hill W & M
50 D3 Appleshaw Hants
89 G5 Applethwaite Cumb
389 G4 Appleton Halton
309 H2 Appleton Oxon
139 G4 Appleton-le-Moors N York
372 D2 Appleton-le-Street N York
372 D5 Appleton Park Warrtn
310 C3 Appleton Roebuck N York
344 D1 Appleton Thorn Warrtn
310 C3 Appleton Wiske N York
384 B4 Appletreehall Border
439 G1 Appletreewick N York
354 D2 Appley IoW
37 G2 Appley Somset
43 E3 Appley Bridge Lancs
324 C3 Apse Heath IoW
37 F4 Apsey Green Suffk
202 B2 Apsley End Beds
169 G3 Apuldram W Susx
53 E4 Aqueduct Wrekin
235 F3 Aquhythie Abers
559 G6 Arabella Highld
566 D1 Arbirlot Angus
515 G1 Arborfield Wokham
92 C1 Arborfield Cross Wokham
92 C1 Arborfield Garrison Wokham
92 C2 Arbourthorne Sheff
314 D2 Arbroath Angus
515 G1 Arbury Cambs
197 F2 Arbuthnott Abers
541 E4 Archdeacon Newton Darltn
383 F1 Archenfield Herefs
159 E1 Archiestown Moray
568 C7 Archirondel Jersey
35 j6 Arclid Ches
291 F2 Arclid Green Ches
291 F2 Ardachu Highld
576 E3 Ardalanish Ag & B
504 D7 Ardallie Abers
561 F2 Ardanaiseig Ag & B
507 J5 Ardaneaskan Highld
546 E2 Ardarroch Highld
546 E2 Ardbeg Ag & B
464 B1 Ardbeg Ag & B
477 G7 Ardbeg Ag & B
481 H3 Ardcharnich Highld
574 D6 Ardchiavaig Ag & B
504 D7 Ardchonnell Ag & B
493 G2 Ardchronie Highld
576 D6 Ardchullarie More Stirlg
497 E2 Ardchyle Stirlg
509 H4 Ardclach Highld
567 H7 Ard-Dhubh Highld
495 E6 Ardarroch Ag & B
546 B1 Ardbeg Ag & B
232 D1 Ardleen Powys
533 H4 Ardechive Highld
170 D4 Ardeley Herts
546 F4 Ardelve Highld
483 E3 Arden Ag & B
466 D3 Arden C Glas
549 H2 Ardendrain Highld
312 B1 Arden Park Stockp
189 H4 Ardens Grafton Warwks
506 D5 Ardentallen Ag & B
482 A2 Ardentinny Ag & B
510 B2 Ardeonaig Stirlg
566 D6 Ardersier Highld
519 J3 Ardery Highld
573 K6 Ardessie Highld
492 D4 Ardfern Ag & B
478 F7 Ardfernal Ag & B
495 F4 Ardgartan Ag & B
576 D5 Ardgay Highld
576 C5 Ardgayhill Highld
482 B5 Ardgowan Inver
596 E7 Ardhasig W Isls
592 D4 Ardheisker W Isls
562 D5 Ardheslaig Highld
492 C5 Ardifuir Ag & B
492 B2 Ardinamir Ag & B
574 C6 Ardindrean Highld
77 F4 Ardingly W Susx
114 C2 Ardington Oxon
114 C2 Ardington Wick Oxon
546 E5 Ardintoul Highld
558 D4 Ardlair Abers
570 F3 Ardlawhill Abers
174 D4 Ardleigh Essex
120 D2 Ardleigh Green Gt Lon
175 E3 Ardleigh Heath Essex
513 G1 Ardler P & K
166 B4 Ardley Oxon
146 A2 Ardley End Essex
495 G1 Ardlui Ag & B
479 G4 Ardlussa Ag & B
574 C4 Ardmair Highld
495 F4 Ardmay Ag & B
478 F7 Ardmenish Ag & B
458 C2 Ardminish Ag & B
519 H1 Ardmolich Highld
477 H6 Ardmore Ag & B
482 D4 Ardmore Ag & B
544 D1 Ardmore Highld
576 F6 Ardmore Highld
518 D6 Ardnacross Ag & B
482 A3 Ardnadam Ag & B
573 J2 Ardnagoine Highld
565 J7 Ardnagrask Highld
546 F2 Ardnarff Highld
519 J3 Ardnastang Highld
476 D2 Ardnave Ag & B
494 C3 Ardno Ag & B
560 C2 Ardo Abers
483 E4 Ardoch Ag & B
512 C2 Ardoch P & K
569 H7 Ardonald Abers
559 F4 Ardoyne Abers
482 B2 Ardpeaton Ag & B
480 A2 Ardrishaig Ag & B

542 D8 Ardroag Highld
565 L2 Ardross Highld
444 B1 Ardrossan N Ayrs
519 G2 Ardshealach Highld
478 A3 Ardskenish Ag & B
329 F3 Ardsley Barns
518 E3 Ardslignish Highld
477 H6 Ardtalla Ag & B
510 C2 Ardtalnaig P & K
518 F1 Ardtoe Highld
519 H6 Ardtornish Highld
544 E3 Ardtreck Highld
510 B5 Ardtrostan P & K
504 D6 Ardtun Ag & B
492 D2 Arduaine Ag & B
565 K4 Ardullie Highld
576 E6 Ardvannie Highld
534 E5 Ardvasar Highld
534 E5 Ardverikie Highld
509 K5 Ardvorlich P & K
596 F5 Ardvourlie W Isls
408 C2 Ardwell D & G
326 C5 Ardwick Manch
531 H8 Arean Highld
212 A5 Areley Kings Worcs
74 C2 Arford Hants
132 C4 Argoed Caerph
209 E1 Argoed Powys
209 F3 Argoed Shrops
269 F5 Argoed Shrops
78 D4 Argos Hill E Susx
597 G4 Aribruach W Isls
504 C6 Aridhglas Ag & B
516 F5 Arileod Ag & B
562 C5 Arinacrinachd Highld
517 G4 Arinagour Ag & B
600 D2 Arion Ork
531 J5 Arisaig Highld
519 K3 Ariundle Highld
519 G2 Arivegaig Highld
356 D2 Arkendale N York
171 G3 Arkesden Essex
366 B5 Arkholme Lancs
388 D2 Arkleby Cumb
425 H1 Arkleton D & G
382 B4 Arkle Town N York
144 B5 Arkley Gt Lon
330 C3 Arksey Donc
315 E5 Arkwright Town Derbys
162 D5 Arle Gloucs
136 B3 Arlebrook Gloucs
388 B6 Arlecdon Cumb
191 F5 Arlescote Warwks
170 A2 Arlesey Beds
235 F2 Arleston Wrekin
310 D3 Arley Ches
310 D3 Arley Green Ches
135 G2 Arlingham Gloucs
61 F3 Arlington Devon
57 E3 Arlington E Susx
137 H3 Arlington Gloucs
61 F3 Arlington Beccott Devon
531 H2 Armadale Highld
587 G4 Armadale Highld
486 B6 Armadale W Loth
401 E5 Armathwaite Cumb
172 B4 Armigers Essex
250 A4 Aminghall Norfk
237 G1 Armitage Staffs
328 A2 Armitage Bridge Kirk
343 E3 Armley Leeds
190 C6 Armscote Warwks
271 H3 Armsdale Staffs
292 B5 Armshead Staffs
219 F2 Armston Nhants
330 D4 Armthorpe Donc
516 F3 Arnabost Ag & B
362 D5 Arnaby Cumb
368 B5 Arncliffe N York
503 E3 Arncroach Fife
568 D6 Arndilly House Moray
33 H2 Arne Dorset
216 D1 Arnesby Leics
500 B2 Arngask P & K
459 E4 Arnicle Ag & B
546 E7 Arnisdale Highld
543 K7 Arnish Highld
471 F2 Arniston Mdloth
599 G5 Arnol W Isls
348 B1 Arnold E R Yk
296 A5 Arnold Notts
109 H5 Arno's Vale Bristl
497 F6 Arnprior Stirlg
365 F4 Arnside Cumb
518 E6 Aros Cott Ag & B
518 E6 Aros Mains Ag & B
270 B2 Arowry Wrexhm
565 K6 Arpafeelie Highld
82 C3 Arpinge Kent
364 D3 Arrad Foot Cumb
360 C6 Arram E R Yk
383 E4 Arrathorne N York
37 E3 Arreton IoW
196 D4 Arrington Cambs
495 G4 Arrochar Ag & B
189 G3 Arrow Warwks
308 C2 Arrowe Hill Wirral
213 F5 Arrowfield Top Worcs
186 A3 Arrow Green Herefs
328 A3 Arrunden Kirk
580 D7 Arscaig Highld
234 A3 Arscott Shrops
565 L7 Artafallie Highld
311 E2 Arthill Ches
356 B6 Arthington Leeds
217 G3 Arthingworth Nhants
229 E2 Arthog Gwynd
561 E2 Arthrath Abers
343 G2 Arthursdale Leeds
526 C6 Arthurstone P & K
93 G5 Artington Surrey
561 F3 Artrochie Abers
54 B3 Arundel W Susx
520 E2 Aryhoulan Highld
388 C5 Asby Cumb
464 C2 Ascog Ag & B
117 F6 Ascot W & M
165 E3 Ascott Warwks
165 G5 Ascott D' Oyley Oxon
164 D6 Ascott Earl Oxon
164 D6 Ascott-under-Wychwood Oxon
526 D3 Ascreavie Angus
370 D4 Asenby N York
277 F6 Asfordby Leics
277 F6 Asfordby Hill Leics
299 E5 Asgarby Lincs
300 B1 Asgarby Lincs
13 E5 Ash Devon
30 B3 Ash Dorset
47 G2 Ash Dorset
97 E2 Ash Kent
101 E4 Ash Kent
44 B1 Ash Somset
66 D5 Ash Somset
93 E4 Ash Surrey
546 B5 Ashaig Highld
115 F3 Ashampstead W Berk
115 F3 Ashampstead Green W Berk
98 C4 Ashbank Kent
292 B5 Ash Bank Staffs
64 A4 Ashbeer Somset
201 G4 Ashbocking Suffk

293 G5 Ashbourne Derbys
43 G5 Ashbrittle Somst
444 B1 Ashbrook Shrops
406 B3 Ashbrooke Sundld
58 A3 Ashburnham Forge E Susx
19 G4 Ashburton Devon
24 D3 Ashbury Devon
113 G2 Ashbury Oxon
332 B3 Ashby N Linc
300 D1 Ashby by Partney Lincs
334 C4 Ashby cum Fenby NE Lin
298 D3 Ashby de la Launde Lincs
239 E1 Ashby-de-la-Zouch Leics
241 F2 Ashby Folville Leics
334 B4 Ashby Hill NE Lin
216 C1 Ashby Magna Leics
216 B2 Ashby Parva Leics
320 B5 Ashby Puerorum Lincs
216 C6 Ashby St Ledgers Nhants
250 C4 Ashby St Mary Norfk
162 D3 Ashchurch Gloucs
20 C2 Ashcombe Devon
84 B2 Ashcombe Park N Som
66 D1 Ashcott Somset
66 D1 Ashcott Corner Somset
43 F5 Ashculme Devon
172 B1 Ashdon Essex
91 E4 Ashe Hants
148 C4 Asheldham Essex
173 E1 Ashen Essex
141 F2 Ashendon Bucks
142 C4 Asheridge Bucks
37 F3 Ashey IoW
380 C4 Ash Fell Cumb
479 K4 Ashfield Ag & B
155 G4 Ashfield Carmth
71 H6 Ashfield Hants
160 D5 Ashfield Herefs
269 F4 Ashfield Shrops
498 B4 Ashfield Stirlg
201 H2 Ashfield Suffk
201 H2 Ashfield cum Thorpe Suffk
199 F3 Ashfield Green Suffk
226 B5 Ashfield Green Suffk
271 G4 Ashfields Shrops
76 D4 Ashfold Crossways W Susx
355 F1 Ashfold Side N York
12 B3 Ashford Devon
60 D3 Ashford Devon
49 E2 Ashford Hants
81 F1 Ashford Kent
118 B5 Ashford Surrey
210 C5 Ashford Bowdler Shrops
210 C5 Ashford Carbonell Shrops
118 B5 Ashford Common Surrey
118 B5 Ashford Hill Hants
313 G6 Ashford in the Water Derbys
314 D5 Ashgate Derbys
468 B5 Ashgill S Lans
93 F5 Ash Green Surrey
215 E3 Ash Green Warwks
86 B3 Ashgrove BaNES
568 C3 Ashgrove Moray
269 G1 Ash Grove Wrexhm
280 C3 Ash Hill Devon
451 E2 Ashiestiel Border
43 E5 Ashill Devon
248 A4 Ashill Norfk
44 C4 Ashill Somset
147 H6 Ashingdon Essex
430 D2 Ashington Nthumb
48 C5 Ashington Poole
67 F5 Ashington Somset
54 D1 Ashington W Susx
301 F1 Ashington End Lincs
451 F5 Ashkirk Border
51 E4 Ashlett Hants
162 B4 Ashleworth Gloucs
198 D2 Ashley Cambs
311 F3 Ashley Ches
49 E4 Ashley Dorset
136 D6 Ashley Dorset
49 H5 Ashley Hants
72 A3 Ashley Hants
101 F6 Ashley Kent
217 G1 Ashley Nhants
271 H2 Ashley Staffs
111 E6 Ashley Wilts
271 H2 Ashley Dale Staffs
109 G4 Ashley Down Bristl
142 D3 Ashley Green Bucks
89 E4 Ashley Heath Dorset
271 G2 Ashley Heath Staffs
311 F2 Ashley Heath Traffd
188 E1 Ashley Moor Herefs
94 C1 Ashley Park Surrey
227 G2 Ash Magna Shrops
256 C5 Ashmanhaugh Norfk
90 C3 Ashmansworth Hants
38 D2 Ashmansworthy Devon
135 H5 Ashmead Green Gloucs
24 A3 Ashmill Devon
41 F3 Ash Mill Devon
41 F4 Ash Moor Devon
69 F6 Ashmore Dorset
114 D6 Ashmore Green W Berk
237 E4 Ashmore Lake Wsall
237 E4 Ashmore Park Wolves
313 G2 Ashopton Derbys
191 E3 Ashorne Warwks
294 C2 Ashover Derbys
294 D2 Ashover Hay Derbys
214 E5 Ashow Warwks
270 D2 Ash Parva Shrops
161 E1 Asperton Herefs
13 E1 Ashprington Devon
43 F2 Ash Priors Somset
40 C5 Ashreigney Devon
25 G2 Ashridge Court Devon
200 D5 Ash Street Suffk
94 D3 Ashtead Surrey
42 D5 Ash Thomas Devon
243 G3 Ashton C Pete
309 H6 Ashton Ches
4 B3 Ashton Cnwll
72 C6 Ashton Hants
186 C2 Ashton Herefs
482 B4 Ashton Inver
193 G5 Ashton Nhants
219 F2 Ashton Nhants
84 D5 Ashton Somset
87 F3 Ashton Common Wilts
109 G5 Ashton Gate Bristl
56 D2 Ashton Green E Susx
310 B4 Ashton Heath Ches
324 D5 Ashton-in-Makerfield Wigan
137 G6 Ashton Keynes Wilts
163 E2 Ashton under Hill Worcs
326 A6 Ashton-under-Lyne Tamesd
326 A6 Ashton upon Mersey Traffd
109 G5 Ashton Vale Bristl
50 B2 Ashurst Hants
78 C2 Ashurst Kent
324 B3 Ashurst Lancs
55 H1 Ashurst W Susx
77 H2 Ashurst Wood W Susx
20 B3 Ashwater Devon

170 C2 Ashwell Herts
242 B3 Ashwell Rutlnd
44 D4 Ashwell Somset
170 C1 Ashwell End Herts
249 F5 Ashwellthorpe Norfk
86 A5 Ashwick Somset
253 E4 Ashwicken Norfk
212 C2 Ashwood Staffs
362 D6 Askam in Furness Cumb
330 C2 Askern Donc
30 C4 Askerswell Dorset
297 F5 Askerton Hill Notts
141 H3 Askett Bucks
391 E5 Askham Cumb
316 D5 Askham Notts
357 H5 Askham Bryan York
357 G5 Askham Richard York
480 C1 Asknish Ag & B
457 E2 Askomill Ag & B
368 B1 Askrigg N York
355 G5 Askwith N York
279 F3 Aslackby Lincs
225 F1 Aslacton Norfk
277 F1 Aslockton Notts
555 F2 Asloun Abers
66 D2 Asney Somset
201 G1 Aspall Suffk
388 D1 Aspatria Cumb
171 E4 Aspenden Herts
280 C2 Asperton Lincs
276 B1 Aspley C Nott
272 B3 Aspley Staffs
168 C2 Aspley Guise Beds
168 C2 Aspley Heath Beds
213 G5 Aspley Heath Warwks
325 E3 Aspull Wigan
325 E5 Aspull Common Wigan
606 C2 Assater Shet
345 G4 Asselby E R Yk
321 E4 Asserby Lincs
321 E4 Asserby Turn Lincs
174 B2 Assington Suffk
199 F4 Assington Green Suffk
291 G2 Astbury Ches
193 E4 Astcote Nhants
319 H4 Asterby Lincs
233 G3 Asterley Shrops
209 G1 Asterton Shrops
138 D2 Asthall Oxon
139 E2 Asthall Leigh Oxon
311 G5 Astle Ches
270 C6 Astley Shrops
215 E3 Astley Warwks
325 G4 Astley Worcs
212 A6 Astley Worcs
235 G5 Astley Abbotts Shrops
325 G2 Astley Bridge Bolton
212 B6 Astley Cross Worcs
325 G5 Astley Green Wigan
310 A3 Astmoor Halton
310 A3 Aston Birm
215 G2 Aston Ches
290 C5 Aston Ches
310 B4 Aston Ches
274 B3 Aston Derbys
313 G3 Aston Derbys
288 D1 Aston Flints
269 F4 Aston Herefs
210 B5 Aston Herefs
170 C5 Aston Herts
139 E4 Aston Oxon
209 E1 Aston Powys
315 F3 Aston Rothm
236 B6 Aston Shrops
270 C4 Aston Shrops
271 H1 Aston Staffs
272 C5 Aston Staffs
116 C3 Aston Wokham
235 E3 Aston Wrekin
168 A5 Aston Abbotts Bucks
211 E5 Aston Bank Worcs
211 E5 Aston Botterell Shrops
272 D3 Aston-by-Stone Staffs
190 A3 Aston Cantlow Warwks
142 B2 Aston Clinton Bucks
161 F5 Aston Crews Herefs
162 D3 Aston Cross Gloucs
235 E6 Aston Eyre Shrops
213 E6 Aston Fields Worcs
215 H1 Aston Flamville Leics
161 F5 Aston Ingham Herefs
290 C3 Aston Juxta Mondrum Ches
192 A4 Aston le Walls Nhants
164 B2 Aston Magna Gloucs
210 C2 Aston Munslow Shrops
162 D3 Aston on Carrant Gloucs
209 G3 Aston on Clun Shrops
275 G4 Aston-on-Trent Derbys
233 F3 Aston Pigott Shrops
233 F3 Aston Rogers Shrops
141 F5 Aston Rowant Oxon
141 G3 Aston Sandford Bucks
163 F2 Aston Somerville Worcs
269 F4 Aston Sq Shrops
164 A1 Aston Subedge Gloucs
115 F2 Aston Tirrold Oxon
115 F2 Aston Upthorpe Oxon
166 B2 Astrop Nhants
142 B1 Astrope Herts
170 B2 Astwick Beds
295 E2 Astwith Derbys
194 D5 Astwood M Keyn
188 C3 Astwood Worcs
188 C3 Astwood Worcs
189 F2 Astwood Bank Worcs
215 E5 Aswarby Lincs
320 C5 Aswarby Lincs
234 C3 Atcham Shrops
189 F4 Atch Lench Worcs
47 E6 Athelhampton Dorset
225 G5 Athelington Suffk
40 C5 Athelney Somset
25 D2 Athelstaneford E Loth
200 D5 Atherfield Green IoW
40 B3 Atherington Devon
54 B4 Atherington W Susx
329 F3 Athersley North Barns
329 F3 Athersley South Barns
44 D4 Atherstone Somset
239 E3 Atherstone Warwks
190 B4 Atherstone on Stour Warwks
325 F4 Atherton Wigan
294 A5 Atlow Derbys
30 A3 Atrim Dorset
547 G2 Attadale Highld
276 B3 Attenborough Notts
168 B2 Atterby M Keyn
332 D6 Atterby Lincs
314 D2 Attercliffe Sheff
235 E5 Atterley Shrops
235 E3 Atterton Leics
234 D3 Attingham Shrops
249 G6 Attleborough Norfk
215 F1 Attleborough Warwks
255 F4 Attlebridge Norfk
199 E4 Attleton Green Suffk
361 F1 Atwick E R Yk
87 F1 Atworth Wilts
80 B2 Auberrow Herefs
186 B5 Aubourn Lincs
297 H2 Auchagallon N Ayrs
460 B3 Auchallater N Ayrs
537 J5 Auchallater Abers
559 E1 Aucharnie Abers

City, town and village index: Auchattie - Barkby Thorpe 671

556 B6 Auchattie Abers
525 J2 Auchavan Angus
552 E3 Auchbreck Moray
466 C3 Auchenback E Rens
435 G5 Auchenbainzie D & G
540 D4 Auchenblae Abers
435 F5 Auchenbrack D & G
481 E3 Auchenbreck Ag & B
413 F4 Auchencairn D & G
423 G3 Auchencairn D & G
461 E4 Auchencairn N Ayrs
460 B2 Auchencar N Ayrs
483 F3 Auchencarroch W Duns
474 C2 Auchencrow Border
471 E2 Auchendinny Mdloth
537 H4 Auchendryne Abers
469 F4 Auchengray S Lans
435 G3 Auchengruith D & G
568 F3 Auchenhalrig Moray
444 C1 Auchenharvie N Ayrs
468 C6 Auchenheath S Lans
435 F5 Auchenhessnane D & G
461 E5 Auchenhew N Ayrs
480 D5 Auchenlochan Ag & B
416 A6 Auchenmalg D & G
419 F3 Auchensoul S Ayrs
467 G4 Auchentibber S Lans
465 H5 Auchentiber N Ayrs
551 G6 Auchgourish Highld
484 C6 Auchinairn C Glas
569 G5 Auchinderran Moray
494 A4 Auchindrain Ag & B
574 D7 Auchindrean Highld
569 L6 Auchininna Abers
417 E2 Auchinleck D & G
446 B5 Auchinleck E Ayrs
526 B3 Auchinleish Angus
484 D5 Auchinloch N Lans
467 G3 Auchinraith S Lans
484 D4 Auchinreoch E Duns
485 E4 Auchinstarry N Lans
555 F1 Auchintoul Abers
536 C3 Auchlean Highld
557 F5 Auchlee Abers
561 F2 Auchleuchries Abers
559 E5 Auchleven Abers
447 F2 Auchlochan S Lans
555 G4 Auchlossan Abers
557 F5 Auchlunies Abers
509 H4 Auchlyne Stirlg
561 E3 Auchmacoy Abers
445 H4 Auchmillan E Ayrs
529 E6 Auchmithie Angus
509 J3 Auchmore Stirlg
500 D4 Auchmuirbridge Fife
540 A5 Auchmull Angus
501 E4 Auchmuty Fife
527 G2 Auchnacree Angus
511 E3 Auchnafree P & K
551 K3 Auchnagallin Highld
560 D1 Auchnagatt Abers
552 E4 Auchnarrow Moray
538 C1 Aucholzie Abers
539 E3 Auchronie Angus
499 E2 Auchterarder P & K
548 F8 Auchteraw Highld
562 E1 Auchtercairn Highld
500 D5 Auchterderran Fife
513 H2 Auchterhouse Angus
500 D2 Auchtermuchty Fife
487 H1 Auchtertool Fife
546 E4 Auchtertyre Highld
509 J5 Auchtubh Stirlg
589 K4 Auckengill Highld
330 D4 Auckley Donc
326 D5 Audenshaw Tamesd
290 D6 Audlem Ches
291 F4 Audley Staffs
171 H2 Audley End Essex
173 G2 Audley End Essex
225 F3 Audley End Norfk
199 H4 Audley End Suffk
569 L3 Auds Abers
389 F2 Aughertree Cumb
345 G2 Aughton E R Yk
323 G4 Aughton Lancs
352 B1 Aughton Lancs
315 F2 Aughton Rothm
89 F3 Aughton Wilts
323 H3 Aughton Park Lancs
393 F4 Aukside Dur
411 E4 Auldbreck D & G
567 G6 Auldearn Highld
186 B4 Aulden Herefs
423 F2 Auldgirth D & G
490 A3 Auldhame E Loth
467 F4 Auldhouse S Lans
559 F1 Auldyoch Abers
547 G5 Ault a' Chruinn Highld
579 K2 Aultanrynie Highld
573 G6 Aultbea Highld
564 D3 Aultdearg Highld
572 D6 Aultgrishan Highld
295 F1 Ault Hucknall Derbys
582 D5 Aultibea Highld
587 H3 Aultiphurst Highld
587 H3 Aultivullin Highld
569 G5 Aultmore Moray
549 J5 Ault-na-Goire Highld
559 E4 Aulton Abers
565 J7 Aultvaich Highld
243 E2 Aunby Lincs
551 H6 Aundorach Highld
27 G2 Aunk Devon
279 E2 Aunsby Lincs
560 B4 Auquhorthies Abers
109 G2 Aust S Glos
280 C5 Austendike Lincs
335 E6 Austen Fen Lincs
117 G2 Austenwood Bucks
331 E6 Austerfield Donc
327 E3 Austerlands Oldham
238 D3 Austrey Warwks
367 F6 Austwick N York
320 D3 Authorpe Lincs
321 F5 Authorpe Row Lincs
112 D6 Avebury Wilts
112 C6 Avebury Trusloe Wilts
121 E4 Aveley Thurr
136 C5 Avening Gloucs
135 G6 Avening Green S Glos
297 E4 Averham Notts
546 E4 Avernish Highld
120 B5 Avery Hill Gt Lon
12 B3 Aveton Gifford Devon
551 G6 Avielochan Highld
550 F7 Aviemore Highld
72 D3 Avington Hants
114 B6 Avington W Berk
566 C6 Avoch Highld
49 E5 Avon Hants
111 H4 Avon Wilts
486 A5 Avonbridge Falk
49 E4 Avon Castle Dorset
86 D3 Avoncliff Wilts
191 G5 Avon Dassett Warwks
109 F4 Avonmouth Bristl
19 F6 Avonwick Devon
71 G5 Awbridge Hants
109 G2 Awkley S Glos
28 B2 Awliscombe Devon
135 G3 Awre Gloucs
295 F6 Awsworth Notts
84 D4 Axbridge Somset
91 G6 Axford Hants
113 F5 Axford Wilts
91 F2 Axmansford Hants
29 E3 Axminster Devon
29 E4 Axmouth Devon
307 F4 Axton Flints
18 B4 Axtown Devon
405 E2 Axwell Park Gatesd
83 F2 Aycliff Kent
395 F5 Aycliffe Village Dur
404 B1 Aydon Nthumb
405 G6 Aykley Heads Dur
135 E4 Aylburton Gloucs
135 E4 Aylburton Common Gloucs
402 C5 Ayle Nthumb
27 G4 Aylesbeare Devon
141 G2 Aylesbury Bucks
334 B3 Aylesby NE Lin
97 H3 Aylesford Kent
100 D5 Aylesham Kent
240 C4 Aylestone C Leic
160 C1 Aylestone Hill Herefs
240 C4 Aylestone Park C Leic
261 G4 Aylmerton Norfk
255 G2 Aylsham Norfk
161 F2 Aylton Herefs
163 G5 Aylworth Gloucs
185 H1 Aymestrey Herefs
166 B3 Aynho Nhants
144 B2 Ayot Green Herts
144 A1 Ayot St Lawrence Herts
144 B1 Ayot St Peter Herts
444 D5 Ayr S Ayrs
143 H2 Ayres End Herts
606 C8 Ayres of Selivoe Shet
406 B3 Ayres Quay Sundld
368 D2 Aysgarth N York
42 D4 Ayshford Devon
365 E3 Ayside Cumb
242 B4 Ayston Rutlnd
146 B1 Aythorpe Roding Essex
474 D2 Ayton Border
405 G3 Ayton Sundld
474 D2 Ayton Castle Border
609 G7 Aywick Shet
370 B5 Azerley N York

B

20 C4 Babbacombe Torbay
295 F6 Babbington Notts
269 F3 Babbinswood Shrops
145 E1 Babbs Green Herts
67 F4 Babcary Somset
156 C2 Babel Carmth
199 E5 Babel Green Suffk
307 G5 Babell Flints
19 E2 Babeny Devon
252 D2 Babingley Norfk
197 H4 Babraham Cambs
316 C3 Babworth Notts
599 K6 Bac W Isls
303 F4 Bachau IoA
210 B3 Bache Shrops
208 D1 Bacheldre Powys
58 D4 Bachelor's Bump E Susx
210 B2 Bache Mill Shrops
129 F4 Bach-y-Gwreiddyn Swans
603 H6 Backaland Ork
602 F1 Backaskaill Ork
365 E3 Backbarrow Cumb
327 E6 Backbower Tamesd
541 F1 Backburn Abers
558 C3 Backburn Abers
127 F1 Backe Carmth
571 J5 Backfolds Abers
309 E5 Backford Ches
309 E5 Backford Cross Ches
560 A2 Backhill Abers
561 F2 Backhill Abers
571 G6 Backhill of Clackriach Abers
569 L5 Backhill of Clunie Abers
561 E1 Backhill of Fortrie Abers
556 A5 Backhill of Trustach Abers
577 H3 Backies Highld
567 L3 Backlands Moray
588 F6 Backlass Highld
502 C3 Backmuir of New Gilston Fife
531 H5 Back of Keppoch Highld
293 E4 Back O'th' Brook Staffs
446 B5 Back Rogerton E Ayrs
199 E3 Back Street Suffk
109 E6 Backwell N Som
109 E5 Backwell Common N Som
109 E6 Backwell Green N Som
431 E5 Backworth N Tyne
172 C6 Bacon End Essex
172 C6 Baconend Green Essex
214 B2 Bacon's End Solhll
261 F4 Baconsthorpe Norfk
159 G3 Bacton Herefs
256 C3 Bacton Norfk
201 E1 Bacton Suffk
256 C3 Bacton Green Norfk
200 D1 Bacton Green Suffk
340 D5 Bacup Lancs
566 B2 Badachonacher Highld
562 D2 Badachro Highld
563 L5 Badavanich Highld
113 E3 Badbury Swindn
113 E3 Badbury Wick Swindn
192 C3 Badby Nhants
584 D5 Badcall Highld
573 K5 Badcaul Highld
292 B4 Baddeley Edge C Stke
292 B4 Baddeley Green C Stke
214 B5 Baddesley Clinton Warwks
238 D5 Baddesley Ensor Warwks
578 E5 Baddidarach Highld
537 H6 Baddoch Abers
147 E4 Baddow Park Essex
573 K2 Badenscallie Highld
559 F2 Badenscoth Abers
557 F5 Badentoy Park Abers
553 G5 Badenyon Abers
23 E5 Badgall Cnwll
245 F5 Badgeney Cambs
235 H5 Badger Shrops
3 E3 Badger's Cross Cnwll
189 F5 Badger's Hill Worcs
96 C2 Badgers Mount Kent
44 B4 Badger Street Somset
162 D6 Badgeworth Gloucs
84 C4 Badgworth Somset
23 F5 Badharlick Cnwll
546 D4 Badicaul Highld
226 C6 Badingham Suffk
99 G4 Badlesmere Kent
589 G7 Badlipster Highld
573 J5 Badluarach Highld
111 E3 Badminton S Glos
578 E5 Badnaban Highld
583 G3 Badnagie Highld
577 G5 Badninish Highld
573 L5 Badrallach Highld
189 G6 Badsey Worcs
483 F2 Badshalloch W Duns
93 E5 Badshot Lea Surrey
329 H1 Badsworth Wakefd
224 C6 Badwell Ash Suffk
224 D6 Badwell Green Suffk
19 E5 Badworthy Devon
52 B4 Baffins C Port
47 E2 Bagber Dorset
371 F3 Bagby N York
371 F3 Bagby Grange N York
320 C5 Bag Enderby Lincs
137 F3 Bagendon Gloucs
211 F3 Bagginswood Shrops
389 E1 Baggrow Cumb
592 H3 Bàgh a Chàise W Isls
591 D8 Bàgh a' Chaisteil W Isls
100 A5 Bagham Kent
590 E4 Baghasdal W Isls
592 F6 Bàgh Mòr W Isls
591 D7 Bàgh Shiarabhagh W Isls
308 B4 Bagillt Flints
215 E5 Baginton Warwks
104 B1 Baglan Neath
342 D2 Bagley Leeds
269 H4 Bagley Shrops
85 E5 Bagley Somset
43 F4 Bagley Green Somset
269 G4 Bagley Marsh Shrops
91 H6 Bagmore Hants
292 B4 Bagnall Staffs
114 C6 Bagnor W Berk
136 B6 Bagpath Gloucs
136 C4 Bagpath Gloucs
313 E3 Bagshaw Derbys
93 F2 Bagshot Surrey
89 H1 Bagshot Wilts
93 F2 Bagshot Heath Surrey
326 C2 Bagslate Moor Rochdl
110 B2 Bagstone S Glos
259 F5 Bagthorpe Norfk
295 F4 Bagthorpe Notts
311 G2 Baguley Manch
239 G3 Bagworth Leics
160 A4 Bagwyllydiart Herefs
524 C2 Bailanloan P & K
599 J3 Bail Àrd Bhuirgh W Isls
86 D1 Bailbrook BaNES
342 B2 Baildon Brad
342 B2 Baildon Green Brad
594 E6 Baile W Isls
597 H3 Baile Ailein W Isls
592 D6 Baile a' Mhanaich W Isls
599 H4 Baile an Truiseil W Isls
549 H6 Bailebeag Highld
479 J7 Baile Boidheach Ag & B
593 D8 Baile Gharbhaidh W Isls
592 E6 Baile Glas W Isls
592 C3 Baile Mhàrtainn W Isls
594 D7 Baile Mhic' Phàil W Isls
504 B6 Baile Mòr Ag & B
591 D7 Baile na Creige W Isls
593 C7 Baile nan Cailleach W Isls
592 C4 Baile Raghnill W Isls
531 H8 Bailetonach Highld
73 G4 Bailey Green Hants
558 B2 Bailiesward Abers
592 E6 Bail' Iochdrach W Isls
467 G2 Bailleston C Glas
351 G3 Bailrigg Lancs
592 E5 Bail Uachdraich W Isls
599 L5 Bail' Ur Tholastaidh W Isls
368 B1 Bainbridge N York
486 A3 Bainsford Falk
559 E2 Bainshole Abers
243 F3 Bainton C Pete
360 B4 Bainton E R Yk
166 C4 Bainton Oxon
501 F4 Baintown Fife
440 B1 Bairnkine Border
80 A2 Baker's Cross Kent
145 E1 Bakers End Herts
134 D2 Baker's Hill Gloucs
121 F3 Baker Street Thurr
118 A2 Baker's Wood Bucks
23 E2 Bakesdown Cnwll
315 G4 Bakestone Moor Derbys
313 H6 Bakewell Derbys
267 E2 Bala Gwynd
545 J1 Balachuirn Highld
597 H3 Balallan W Isls
273 G3 Balance Hill Staffs
535 L2 Balavil Highld
549 H3 Balbeg Highld
549 H5 Balbeg Highld
513 E4 Balbeggie P & K
560 A6 Balbithan Abers
556 C3 Balblair Abers
565 J7 Balblair Highld
566 C3 Balblair Highld
503 E4 Balbuthie Fife
330 C4 Balby Donc
515 F2 Balcathie Angus
577 H7 Balcherry Highld
578 D3 Balchladich Highld
549 K3 Balchraggan Highld
565 J8 Balchraggan Highld
584 C4 Balchrick Highld
77 E3 Balcombe W Susx
77 F3 Balcombe Lane W Susx
503 G3 Balcomie Fife
501 F4 Balcurvie Fife
370 D4 Baldersby N York
370 D4 Baldersby St James N York
339 F3 Balderstone Lancs
326 D2 Balderstone Rochdl
289 E2 Balderton Ches
297 F4 Balderton Notts
7 E5 Baldhu Cnwll
326 A2 Baldingstone Bury
502 C2 Baldinnie Fife
170 B3 Baldock Herts
140 C4 Baldon Row Oxon
514 D3 Baldovie C Dund
322 g6 Baldrine IoM
58 D4 Baldslow E Susx
322 f6 Baldwin IoM
400 B4 Baldwinholme Cumb
272 A2 Baldwin's Gate Staffs
77 G2 Baldwins Hill W Susx
260 D4 Bale Norfk
516 B7 Balemartine Ag & B
592 C4 Balemore W Isls
516 C6 Balephetrish Ag & B
516 B7 Balephuil Ag & B
470 C1 Balerno C Edin
478 B3 Baleromindubh Ag & B
516 B6 Balevullin Ag & B
539 G6 Balfield Angus
601 H1 Balfour Ork
484 B2 Balfron Stirlg
483 H2 Balfron Station Stirlg
559 E1 Balgaveny Abers
528 B4 Balgavies House Angus
501 E4 Balgeddie Fife
499 G6 Balgonar Fife
560 B3 Balgove Abers
408 C3 Balgowan D & G
535 H4 Balgowan Highld
512 A5 Balgowan P & K
542 F3 Balgown Highld
544 E2 Balgown Highld
484 C4 Balgrochan E Duns
565 L7 Balgunearie Highld
565 L7 Balgunloune Highld
562 E6 Balgy Highld
559 H5 Balhalgardy Abers
119 F5 Balham Gt Lon
526 C5 Balhary P & K
609 J3 Baliasta Shet
587 H3 Baligill Highld
506 D1 Baligrundle Ag & B
479 J7 Balimore Ag & B
516 B7 Balinoe Ag & B
526 C3 Balintore Angus
566 F1 Balintore Highld
566 C2 Balintraid Highld
592 D6 Balivanich W Isls
526 D6 Balkeerie Angus
316 D3 Balk Field Notts
346 A4 Balkholme E R Yk
529 F4 Balkiellie Angus
418 D5 Balkissock S Ayrs
14 D4 Ball Cnwll
269 F4 Ball Shrops
322 d8 Ballabeg IoM
520 F4 Ballachulish Highld
340 C5 Balladen Lancs
322 b8 Ballafesson IoM
322 c8 Ballakilpheric IoM
322 d8 Ballamodha IoM
418 C5 Ballantrae S Ayrs
112 C3 Ballard's Ash Wilts
123 E1 Ballards Gore Essex
214 D1 Ballard's Green Warwks
322 d9 Ballasalla IoM
554 C5 Ballater Abers
322 e4 Ballaugh IoM
524 D5 Ballechin P & K
576 E7 Balleigh Highld
489 F4 Ballencrieff E Loth
486 C5 Ballencrieff Toll W Loth
524 C2 Ballentoul P & K
292 A4 Ball Green C Stke
292 C3 Ball Haye Green Staffs
38 C3 Ballhill Devon
90 C2 Ball Hill Hants
293 H4 Ballidon Derbys
460 B2 Balliekine N Ayrs
481 F3 Balliemore Ag & B
506 D4 Balliemore Ag & B
566 B8 Ballifeary Highld
480 C3 Ballimore Ag & B
507 J4 Ballimore Ag & B
509 H6 Ballimore Stirlg
476 C3 Ballinaby Ag & B
513 G4 Ballindean P & K
173 H1 Ballingdon Suffk
143 E2 Ballingdon Bottom Herts
142 C4 Ballinger Bottom Bucks
142 C4 Ballinger Bottom (South) Bucks
142 C4 Ballinger Common Bucks
160 D3 Ballingham Herefs
160 D3 Ballingham Hill Herefs
500 C5 Ballingry Fife
512 A1 Ballinlick P & K
524 E5 Ballinluig P & K
525 H4 Ballintuim P & K
506 D1 Balliveolan Ag & B
576 C2 Balloan Highld
526 D3 Balloch Angus
566 C7 Balloch Highld
485 E5 Balloch N Lans
483 E3 Balloch W Duns
539 G1 Ballochan Abers
484 B2 Ballochearn Stirlg
464 B2 Ballochgoy Ag & B
462 B4 Ballochroy Ag & B
309 G2 Ball O' Ditton Halton
555 G5 Ballogie Abers
75 F4 Balls Cross W Susx
78 B2 Balls Green E Susx
175 E5 Balls Green Essex
136 C5 Ball's Green Gloucs
76 B5 Balls Green W Susx
237 E6 Balls Hill Sandw
518 B7 Ballygown Ag & B
476 F3 Ballygrant Ag & B
516 F4 Ballyhaugh Ag & B
492 D5 Ballymeanoch Ag & B
546 E4 Balmacara Highld
546 E4 Balmacara Square Highld
421 H4 Balmaclellan D & G
524 E5 Balmacneil P & K
543 G2 Balmacqueen Highld
412 C6 Balmae D & G
483 F1 Balmaha Stirlg
501 F3 Balmalcolm Fife
485 E4 Balmalloch N Lans
527 G5 Balmashanner Angus
542 E8 Balmeanach Highld
543 H3 Balmeanach Highld
545 J1 Balmeanach Highld
545 J3 Balmeanach Highld
561 E6 Balmedie Abers
270 A3 Balmer Shrops
270 A3 Balmer Heath Shrops
514 B5 Balmerino Fife
50 B4 Balmerlawn Hants
460 C3 Balmichael N Ayrs
451 F2 Balmoral Border
484 C5 Balmore E Duns
544 D1 Balmore Highld
588 C3 Balmore Highld
514 C5 Balmullo Fife
566 C5 Balmungie Highld
415 H3 Balmurrie D & G
526 D1 Balnaboth Angus
577 J7 Balnabruach Highld
582 F4 Balnabruich Highld
581 K7 Balnacoil Highld
563 H7 Balnacra Highld
576 D2 Balnadelson Highld
550 B2 Balnafoich Highld
557 H4 Balnagask C Aber
524 D5 Balnaguard P & K
566 B2 Balnaguisich Highld
478 C2 Balnahard Ag & B
504 F4 Balnahard Ag & B
549 G3 Balnain Highld
585 G3 Balnakeil Highld
585 G3 Balnakeil Craft Village Highld
525 G3 Balnakilly P & K
543 G4 Balnaknock Highld
570 F4 Balnamoon Abers
528 B2 Balnamoon Angus
566 D3 Balnapaling Highld
344 D6 Balne N York
3 E2 Balnoon Cnwll
484 C6 Balornock C Glas
509 H5 Balquhidder Stirlg
214 C4 Balsall Solhll
214 C4 Balsall Common Solhll
213 G3 Balsall Heath Birm
214 C4 Balsall Street Solhll
165 F1 Balscote Oxon
198 B4 Balsham Cambs
121 G3 Balstonia Thurr
609 J3 Baltasound Shet
291 F5 Balterley Staffs
291 F4 Balterley Green Staffs
291 E4 Balterley Heath Staffs
570 E5 Balthangie Abers
502 B2 Baltilly Fife
67 E3 Baltonsborough Somset
565 J6 Balvaird Highld
525 G3 Balvarran P & K
568 E7 Balvenie Moray
492 C1 Balvicar Ag & B
550 E3 Balvraid Highld
565 J6 Balvraid Highld
3 G3 Balwest Cnwll
339 E4 Bamber Bridge Lancs
172 B5 Bamber's Green Essex
455 F2 Bamburgh Nthumb
526 B4 Bamff P & K
313 H3 Bamford Derbys
326 C2 Bamford Rochdl
162 C5 Bamfurlong Gloucs
324 D4 Bamfurlong Wigan
391 E6 Bampton Cumb
42 C3 Bampton Devon
139 E4 Bampton Oxon
391 E6 Bampton Grange Cumb
533 H7 Banavie Highld
165 H1 Banbury Oxon
128 C2 Bancffosfelen Carmth
556 B5 Banchory Abers
557 G4 Banchory-Devenick Abers
128 B2 Bancycapel Carmth
205 F3 Banc-y-Darren Cerdgn
153 G6 Bancyfelin Carmth
154 B2 Bancyffordd Carmth
95 F2 Bandonhill Gt Lon
364 C2 Bandrake Head Cumb
570 B3 Banff Abers
304 C5 Bangor Gwynd
289 E5 Bangor on Dee Wrexhm
23 E3 Bangors Cnwll
153 H1 Bangor Teifi Cerdgn
225 E2 Banham Norfk
50 A3 Bank Hants
233 E2 Bank Powys
362 D4 Bank End Cumb
377 H6 Bank End Cumb
388 B2 Bank End Cumb
423 H6 Bankend D & G
339 H5 Bank Fold Bl w D
512 C2 Bankfoot P & K
434 B2 Bankglen E Ayrs
556 B3 Bankhead Abers
514 D2 Bankhead Angus
557 F3 Bankhead C Aber
485 G3 Bankhead Falk
468 D6 Bankhead S Lans
469 F6 Bankhead S Lans
339 G3 Bank Hey Bl w D
351 F4 Bank Houses Lancs
44 C2 Bankland Somset
326 B1 Bank Lane Bury
354 B4 Bank Newton N York
485 F4 Banknock Falk
401 G2 Banks Cumb
412 C5 Banks D & G
337 G5 Banks Lancs
189 E1 Bank's Green Worcs
209 F2 Bankshead Shrops
424 D3 Bankshill D & G
486 A3 Bankside Falk
187 E2 Bank Street Worcs
325 G2 Bank Top Bolton
342 C2 Bank Top Brad
291 H4 Bank Top C Stke
342 B5 Bank Top Calder
324 C3 Bank Top Lancs
404 D1 Bank Top N u Ty
237 G5 Banners Gate Birm
390 B3 Bannest Hill Cumb
255 H2 Banningham Norfk
172 D5 Bannister Green Essex
485 G1 Bannockburn Stirlg
6 D4 Banns Cnwll
95 E3 Banstead Surrey
485 H4 Bantaskin Falk
12 B4 Bantham Devon
485 F4 Banton N Lans
567 J7 Bantrach Moray
84 C3 Banwell N Som
99 E2 Bapchild Kent
212 D2 Baptist End Dudley
69 G2 Bapton Wilts
599 H5 Barabhas W Isls
599 G5 Barabhas Iarach W Isls
531 H8 Baramore Highld
444 D3 Barassie S Ayrs
506 E2 Baravullin Ag & B
566 C2 Barbaraville Highld
486 B6 Barbauchlaw W Loth
313 F2 Barber Booth Derbys
365 E3 Barber Green Cumb
338 C6 Barber's Moor Lancs
599 H4 Barbhas Uarach W Isls
11 E3 Barbican C Plym
445 F6 Barbieston S Ayrs
366 C3 Barbon Cumb
188 B3 Barbourne Worcs
479 J4 Barbreack Ag & B
290 C3 Barbridge Ches
61 H2 Barbrook Devon
216 B5 Barby Nhants
216 C5 Barby Nortoft Nhants
507 G1 Barcaldine Ag & B
9 G3 Barcelona Cnwll
164 D2 Barcheston Warwks
400 D2 Barclose Cumb
56 C2 Barcombe E Susx
56 C1 Barcombe Cross E Susx
341 G2 Barcroft Brad
382 D6 Barden N York
97 E5 Barden Park Kent
172 C3 Bardfield End Green Essex
172 D4 Bardfield Saling Essex
606 E2 Bardister Shet
319 E6 Bardney Lincs
239 H2 Bardon Leics
402 D2 Bardon Mill Nthumb
484 B5 Bardowie E Duns
79 F4 Bardown E Susx
482 D5 Bardrainney Inver
364 D5 Bardsea Cumb
356 D6 Bardsey Leeds
326 D4 Bardsley Oldham
224 B5 Bardwell Suffk
351 G2 Bare Lancs
64 D5 Bare Ash Somset
453 G2 Bareless Nthumb
413 G3 Barend D & G
72 C4 Bar End Hants
388 B4 Barepot Cumb
5 E3 Bareppa Cnwll
74 C2 Barford Hants
249 F3 Barford Norfk
190 D2 Barford Warwks
165 G3 Barford St John Oxon
70 A3 Barford St Martin Wilts
165 G3 Barford St Michael Oxon
101 E5 Barfrestone Kent
483 G5 Bargarran Rens
294 D5 Bargate Derbys
467 G2 Bargeddie N Lans
132 B5 Bargoed Caerph
420 B4 Bargrennan D & G
219 G4 Barham Cambs
100 C6 Barham Kent
201 F4 Barham Suffk
412 B4 Barharrow D & G
197 E2 Bar Hill Cambs
291 F6 Bar Hill Staffs
243 F2 Barholm Lincs
240 D3 Barkby Leics
240 D3 Barkby Thorpe Leics

270 C4 Barkers Green Shrops
69 F4 Barkers Hill Wilts
277 G3 Barkestone-le-Vale Leics
92 C1 Barkham Wokham
120 B3 Barking Gt Lon
201 E4 Barking Suffk
120 B2 Barkingside Gt Lon
201 E4 Barking Tye Suffk
341 H6 Barkisland Calder
6 D3 Barkla Shop Cnwll
278 C1 Barkston Lincs
344 B2 Barkston Ash N York
171 E2 Barkway Herts
86 B5 Barlake Somset
467 G2 Barlanark C Glas
185 E2 Barland Powys
103 E4 Barland Common Swans
272 C2 Barlaston Staffs
53 H1 Barlavington W Susx
315 H4 Barlborough Derbys
345 E3 Barlby N York
239 G3 Barlestone Leics
171 F5 Barley Herts
340 C1 Barley Lancs
171 F4 Barleycroft End Herts
142 D2 Barley End Bucks
340 C1 Barley Green Lancs
405 G4 Barley Mow Gatesd
242 A3 Barleythorpe Rutlnd
123 E2 Barling Essex
318 D5 Barlings Lincs
314 C5 Barlow Derbys
405 E2 Barlow Gatesd
345 E4 Barlow N York
326 B6 Barmber Moor Manch
359 E5 Barmby Moor E R Yk
345 F4 Barmby on the Marsh E R Yk
259 G5 Barmer Norfk
97 H3 Barming Heath Kent
404 D2 Bar Moor Gatesd
228 D1 Barmouth Gwynd
395 G6 Barmpton Darltn
361 F3 Barmston E R Yk
405 H3 Barmston Sundld
484 C6 Barmulloch C Glas
227 F4 Barnaby Green Suffk
243 F4 Barnack C Pete
215 F3 Barnacle Warwks
606 D1 Barnafield Shet
382 B1 Barnard Castle Dur
139 G2 Barnard Gate Oxon
199 E5 Barnardiston Suffk
188 A5 Barnard's Green Worcs
107 F2 Barnardtown Newpt
343 G2 Barnbow Carr Leeds
330 A4 Barnburgh Donc
227 F2 Barnby Suffk
330 D3 Barnby Dun Donc
297 F4 Barnby in the Willows Notts
316 C3 Barnby Moor Notts
467 H4 Barncluith S Lans
408 B4 Barncorkrie D & G
10 D2 Barne Barton C Plym
120 C4 Barnehurst Gt Lon
119 E4 Barnes Gt Lon
120 D4 Barnes Cray Gt Lon
329 E5 Barnes Hall Sheff
97 F5 Barnes Street Kent
144 B5 Barnet Gt Lon
333 F3 Barnetby le Wold N Linc
144 B5 Barnet Gate Gt Lon
290 C6 Barnett Brook Ches
212 C4 Barnettbrook Worcs
260 C5 Barney Norfk
99 E5 Barnfield Kent
160 A1 Barnfields Herefs
292 C3 Barnfields Staffs
223 H4 Barnham Suffk
53 H4 Barnham W Susx
249 E3 Barnham Broom Norfk
529 E3 Barnhead Angus
514 D3 Barnhill C Dund
289 G4 Barnhill Ches
567 L5 Barnhill Moray
512 D5 Barnhill P & K
414 C2 Barnhills D & G
382 C2 Barningham Dur
224 C4 Barningham Suffk
261 F5 Barningham Green Norfk
479 K3 Barnluasgan Ag & B
190 B2 Barnmoor Green Warwks
334 B4 Barnoldby le Beck NE Lin
353 H5 Barnoldswick Lancs
366 D5 Barnoldswick N York
449 H2 Barns Border
242 B3 Barnsdale Rutlnd
76 B4 Barns Green W Susx
328 B3 Barnside Kirk
329 E3 Barnsley Barns
137 G3 Barnsley Gloucs
235 H6 Barnsley Shrops
101 K4 Barnsole Kent
60 D5 Barnstaple Devon
172 C6 Barnston Essex
308 C3 Barnston Wirral
277 F2 Barnstone Notts
213 F5 Barnt Green Worcs
487 G4 Barnton C Edin
310 C4 Barnton Ches
219 E3 Barnwell Nhants
162 C6 Barnwood Gloucs
502 D4 Barnyards Fife
186 B3 Barons' Cross Herefs
419 G3 Barr S Ayrs
43 G3 Barr Somset
410 C3 Barrachan D & G
467 G2 Barrachnie C Glas
560 C1 Barrack Abers
107 F2 Barrack Hill Newpt
598 D8 Barraglom W Isls
479 J5 Barrahormid Ag & B
506 E4 Barran Ag & B
516 B7 Barrapol Ag & B
381 E2 Barras Cumb
429 E5 Barrasford Nthumb
492 D3 Barravullin Ag & B
237 G4 Barr Common Wsall
322 e5 Barregarrow IoM
290 B3 Barrets Green Ches
466 D3 Barrhead E Rens
419 F5 Barrhill S Ayrs
197 E5 Barrington Cambs
66 B6 Barrington Somset
6 B6 Barripper Cnwll
465 H4 Barrmill N Ayrs
506 D5 Barrnacarry Ag & B
589 G2 Barrock Highld
162 C5 Barrow Gloucs
340 A2 Barrow Lancs
329 F5 Barrow Rothm
242 B1 Barrow Rutlnd
235 F4 Barrow Shrops
67 F1 Barrow Somset
199 F2 Barrow Suffk
246 B4 Barroway Drove Norfk
325 F2 Barrow Bridge Bolton
441 G2 Barrowburn Nthumb
278 B2 Barrowby Lincs
374 C2 Barrowcliff N York
109 F6 Barrow Common N Som
242 D4 Barrowden Rutlnd

340 C2 Barrowford Lancs
99 F2 Barrow Green Kent
109 F6 Barrow Gurney N Som
347 G5 Barrow Hann N Linc
347 G5 Barrow Haven N Linc
315 E4 Barrow Hill Derbys
48 A5 Barrow Hill Dorset
81 G2 Barrowhill Kent
364 C5 Barrow-in-Furness Cumb
364 A6 Barrow Island Cumb
309 G6 Barrowmore Estate Ches
324 A4 Barrow Nook Lancs
290 D3 Barrows Green Ches
365 H2 Barrows Green Cumb
310 A2 Barrow's Green Halton
295 F4 Barrows Green Notts
68 D3 Barrow Street Wilts
347 G5 Barrow upon Humber N Linc
240 C1 Barrow upon Soar Leics
275 E4 Barrow upon Trent Derbys
86 A2 Barrow Vale BaNES
515 E3 Barry Angus
106 A6 Barry V Glam
106 B6 Barry Dock V Glam
106 B6 Barry Island V Glam
241 E2 Barsby Leics
226 D2 Barsham Suffk
446 B6 Barshare E Ayrs
492 C5 Barsloisnoch Ag & B
121 H2 Barstable Essex
214 C4 Barston Solhll
160 D1 Bartestree Herefs
560 B3 Barthol Chapel Abers
173 E5 Bartholomew Green Essex
291 F4 Barthomley Ches
50 B2 Bartley Hants
213 F3 Bartley Green Birm
198 B5 Bartlow Cambs
197 F3 Barton Cambs
289 F4 Barton Ches
162 B6 Barton Gloucs
163 H4 Barton Gloucs
37 E3 Barton IoW
323 F3 Barton Lancs
338 D2 Barton Lancs
84 C3 Barton N Som
383 F1 Barton N York
140 B3 Barton Oxon
20 C4 Barton Torbay
189 H4 Barton Warwks
165 G5 Barton Abbey Oxon
247 E3 Barton Bendish Norfk
161 G1 Barton Court Herefs
136 B5 Barton End Gloucs
61 G3 Barton Gate Devon
274 B6 Barton Gate Staffs
274 B6 Barton Green Staffs
166 D3 Barton Hartshorn Bucks
109 H5 Barton Hill Bristl
358 D2 Barton Hill N York
276 B3 Barton in Fabis Notts
239 F3 Barton in the Beans Leics
169 F3 Barton-le-Clay Beds
372 D5 Barton-le-Street N York
358 D2 Barton-le-Willows N York
223 E5 Barton Mills Suffk
325 G5 Barton Moss Salfd
49 G6 Barton on Sea Hants
164 D3 Barton-on-the-Heath Warwks
67 E3 Barton St David Somset
218 B4 Barton Seagrave Nhants
160 C2 Bartonsham Herefs
72 B1 Barton Stacey Hants
61 G3 Barton Town Devon
256 D5 Barton Turf Norfk
274 C6 Barton Turn Staffs
274 B6 Barton-under-Needwood Staffs
347 F5 Barton-upon-Humber N Linc
325 H5 Barton upon Irwell Salfd
347 F5 Barton Waterside N Linc
329 E3 Barugh Barns
329 E3 Barugh Green Barns
599 H5 Barvas W Isls
222 A4 Barway Cambs
94 D2 Barwell Gt Lon
239 G5 Barwell Leics
40 B6 Barwick Devon
171 E6 Barwick Herts
45 H5 Barwick Somset
343 H2 Barwick in Elmet Leeds
270 A5 Bascodyke Head Cumb
191 G2 Bascote Warwks
191 F2 Bascote Heath Warwks
200 D2 Base Green Suffk
209 G2 Basford Shrops
291 H5 Basford Green Staffs
292 C4 Basford Green Staffs
352 D6 Bashall Eaves Lancs
49 G5 Bashley Hants
49 G5 Bashley Park Hants
122 A2 Basildon Essex
91 F4 Basingstoke Hants
314 A5 Baslow Derbys
84 B5 Bason Bridge Somset
107 E2 Bassaleg Newpt
389 F3 Bassenthwaite Cumb
50 D1 Bassett C Sotn
314 B3 Bassett Sheff
50 D1 Bassett Green C Sotn
196 D6 Bassingbourn Cambs
276 D2 Bassingfield Notts
297 H3 Bassingham Lincs
278 D4 Bassingthorpe Lincs
170 C4 Bassus Green Herts
609 C6 Basta Shet
97 F3 Basted Kent
243 G2 Baston Lincs
188 B4 Bastonford Worcs
257 E6 Bastwick Norfk
272 D5 Baswich Staffs
84 B3 Batch Somset
210 B5 Batchcott Shrops
187 E5 Batchfields Herefs
189 F1 Batchley Worcs
143 F6 Batchworth Herts
143 F6 Batchworth Heath Herts
31 E2 Batcombe Dorset
68 A2 Batcombe Somset
310 D4 Bate Heath Ches
213 G4 Bateman's Green Worcs
125 H4 Bateman's Hill Pembs
314 D3 Batemoor Sheff
143 G1 Batford Herts
86 C1 Bath BaNES
86 D1 Bathampton BaNES
43 E3 Bathealton Somset
110 D6 Batheaston BaNES
86 D1 Bathford BaNES
486 C6 Bathgate W Loth
297 E3 Bathley Notts
16 C4 Bathpool Cnwll
44 B2 Bathpool Somset
176 D3 Bath Side Essex
291 H2 Bath Vale Ches
486 B6 Bathville W Loth
85 G4 Bathway Somset
86 D2 Bathwick BaNES
143 H5 Batlers Green Herts

342 D5 Batley Kirk
342 D5 Batley Carr Kirk
164 B3 Batsford Gloucs
12 C5 Batson Devon
41 G3 Batsworthy Devon
44 B4 Batten's Green Somset
188 B1 Battenton Green Worcs
385 F3 Battersby N York
119 F4 Battersea Gt Lon
201 E4 Battisford Suffk
200 D4 Battisford Tye Suffk
58 B3 Battle E Susx
157 G3 Battle Powys
163 E5 Battledown Gloucs
39 G6 Battledown Cross Devon
467 E2 Battlefield C Glas
234 C1 Battlefield Shrops
431 E6 Battle Hill N Tyne
147 F6 Battlesbridge Essex
136 D3 Battlescombe Gloucs
168 A3 Battlesden Beds
225 H4 Battlesea Green Suffk
42 B2 Battleton Somset
200 B2 Battlies Green Suffk
239 G3 Battram Leics
50 A5 Battramsley Hants
50 B5 Battramsley Cross Hants
74 C1 Batt's Corner Hants
342 C5 Battyeford Kirk
25 H5 Battyford Kirk
569 H2 Bauds of Cullen Moray
516 C7 Baugh Ag & B
162 C1 Baughton Worcs
91 F2 Baughurst Hants
113 H1 Baulking Oxon
319 C3 Baumber Lincs
137 F4 Baunton Gloucs
70 A3 Baverstock Wilts
249 F3 Bawburgh Norfk
254 A3 Bawdeswell Norfk
65 F4 Bawdrip Somset
177 F1 Bawdsey Suffk
252 D4 Bawsey Norfk
330 D5 Bawtry Donc
340 B4 Baxenden Lancs
215 F3 Baxterley Warwks
199 F3 Baxter's Green Suffk
68 A3 Bay Dorset
542 D6 Bay Highld
72 B6 Baybridge Hants
403 G4 Baybridge Nthumb
364 C5 Baycliff Cumb
113 G4 Baydon Wilts
144 D3 Bayford Herts
68 B4 Bayford Somset
353 E5 Bay Gate Lancs
351 G4 Bay Horse Lancs
402 C5 Bayles Cumb
96 D4 Bayley's Hill Kent
201 E4 Baylham Suffk
213 G5 Baylis Green Worcs
75 H2 Baynards Surrey
166 C4 Baynard's Green Oxon
188 C3 Baynhall Worcs
160 D4 Baysham Herefs
234 B3 Bayston Hill Shrops
119 F3 Bayswater Gt Lon
199 E6 Baythorne End Essex
280 B1 Baythorpe Lincs
211 F5 Bayton Worcs
211 G5 Bayton Common Worcs
123 G5 Bay View Kent
140 B4 Bayworth Oxon
110 B5 Beach S Glos
167 G2 Beachampton Bucks
247 F3 Beachamwell Norfk
462 A6 Beacharr Ag & B
211 H5 Beach Hay Worcs
57 H4 Beachlands E Susx
109 G1 Beachley Gloucs
6 B6 Beacon Cnwll
28 C2 Beacon Devon
44 A6 Beacon Devon
78 D5 Beacon Down E Susx
174 C5 Beacon End Essex
86 C1 Beacon Hill BaNES
142 C6 Beacon Hill Bucks
364 B5 Beacon Hill Cumb
48 B6 Beacon Hill Dorset
147 H2 Beacon Hill Essex
80 B3 Beacon Hill Kent
297 F4 Beacon Hill Notts
430 D4 Beacon Hill Nthumb
202 A5 Beacon Hill Suffk
74 D2 Beacon Hill Surrey
405 G2 Beacon Lough Gatesd
141 G5 Beacon's Bottom Bucks
117 F1 Beaconsfield Bucks
272 D5 Beaconside Staffs
595 H4 Beacrabhaic W Isls
372 B3 Beadlam N York
169 G2 Beadlow Beds
455 G4 Beadnell Nthumb
40 B5 Beaford Devon
344 C4 Beal N York
454 D1 Beal Nthumb
480 D3 Bealach Maim Ag & B
17 E5 Bealbury Cnwll
79 H3 Beal's Green Kent
17 E3 Bealsmill Cnwll
210 C2 Beambridge Shrops
43 F4 Beam Bridge Somset
274 C4 Beam Hill Staffs
273 F2 Beamhurst Staffs
273 G2 Beamhurst Lane Staffs
30 B2 Beaminster Dorset
405 F4 Beamish Dur
142 C5 Beamond End Bucks
355 E4 Beamsley N York
121 E5 Bean Kent
87 G1 Beanacre Wilts
486 B4 Beancross Falk
168 B2 Beanhill M Keyn
454 D6 Beanley Nthumb
363 E5 Beanthwaite Cumb
602 B7 Beaquoy Ork
48 C5 Bear Cross Bmouth
67 G1 Beard Hill Somset
67 G1 Beardly Batch Somset
339 G4 Beardwood Bl w D
27 F2 Beare Devon
94 D6 Beare Green Surrey
190 B2 Bearley Warwks
190 B2 Bearley Cross Warwks
405 F6 Bearpark Dur
402 D3 Bearsbridge Nthumb
483 H5 Bearsden E Duns
98 B3 Bearsted Kent
271 G2 Bearstone Shrops
213 F2 Bearwood Birm
185 G3 Bearwood Herefs
48 C5 Bearwood Poole
291 E4 Beasley Staffs
437 E4 Beattock D & G
146 B2 Beauchamp Roding Essex
314 C3 Beauchief Sheff
404 B2 Beauclerc Nthumb
190 B1 Beaudesert Warwks
132 C2 Beaufort Blae G
50 C4 Beaulieu Hants
46 D3 Beaulieu Wood Dorset
565 J7 Beauly Highld
304 C4 Beaumaris IoA

400 B3 Beaumont Cumb
176 C5 Beaumont Essex
35 g7 Beaumont Jersey
117 G5 Beaumont W & M
395 F6 Beaumont Hill Darltn
240 C3 Beaumont Leys C Leic
214 C5 Beausale Warwks
295 F5 Beauvale Notts
295 G5 Beauvale Notts
73 E4 Beauworth Hants
161 F5 Beavan's Hill Herefs
24 C3 Beaworthy Devon
173 E4 Beazley End Essex
309 E3 Bebington Wirral
431 E3 Bebside Nthumb
227 E2 Beccles Suffk
338 B5 Becconsall Lancs
364 C3 Beck Bottom Cumb
343 F5 Beck Bottom Wakefd
235 H4 Beckbury Shrops
120 A6 Beckenham Gt Lon
376 C3 Beckermet Cumb
367 H3 Beckermonds N York
66 D2 Beckery Somset
247 F5 Beckett End Norfk
377 F4 Beckfoot Cumb
379 H5 Beck Foot Cumb
398 D5 Beckfoot Cumb
163 E2 Beckford Worcs
112 C6 Beckhampton Wilts
365 F3 Beck Head Cumb
386 D4 Beck Hole N York
379 G5 Beck Houses Cumb
297 G4 Beckingham Lincs
317 E1 Beckingham Notts
86 D4 Beckington Somset
209 G4 Beckjay Shrops
80 C5 Beckley E Susx
49 G5 Beckley Hants
140 C2 Beckley Oxon
58 D2 Beckley Furnace E Susx
222 D4 Beck Row Suffk
365 E3 Beck Side Cumb
365 E3 Beck Side Cumb
366 C2 Beckside Cumb
120 B3 Beckton Gt Lon
356 B4 Beckwith N York
356 B4 Beckwithshaw N York
120 C2 Becontree Gt Lon
35 h6 Becquet Vincent Jersey
370 B2 Bedale N York
394 C3 Bedburn Dur
47 F1 Bedchester Dorset
105 G3 Beddau Rhondd
284 C5 Beddgelert Gwynd
56 C3 Beddingham E Susx
95 G1 Beddington Gt Lon
95 F1 Beddington Corner Gt Lon
201 H1 Bedfield Suffk
195 F3 Bedford Beds
325 F5 Bedford Wigan
119 E4 Bedford Park Gt Lon
74 A5 Bedgebury Cross Kent
79 G3 Bedgrove Bucks
142 A2 Bedgrove Bucks
52 B3 Bedham W Susx
225 G6 Bedingfield Suffk
250 B6 Bedingham Green Norfk
356 B2 Bedlam N York
86 D5 Bedlam Somset
55 G1 Bedlam Street W Susx
171 H5 Bedlar's Green Essex
430 D3 Bedlington Nthumb
431 E3 Bedlington Station Nthumb
132 A4 Bedlinog Myr Td
109 G5 Bedminster Bristl
109 G6 Bedminster Down Bristl
143 F4 Bedmond Herts
273 E6 Bednall Staffs
237 E1 Bednall Head Staffs
452 B6 Bedrule Border
209 G4 Bedstone Shrops
106 C2 Bedwas Caerph
170 B5 Bedwell Herts
289 E5 Bedwell Wrexhm
132 E5 Bedwellty Caerph
132 B3 Bedwellty Pits Blae G
268 D2 Bedwlwyn Wrexhm
215 F2 Bedworth Warwks
215 E2 Bedworth Heath Warwks
215 E2 Bedworth Woodlands Warwks
241 E3 Beeby Leics
73 G2 Beech Hants
272 B2 Beech Staffs
272 C2 Beechcliff Staffs
355 E6 Beechcliffe Brad
86 C2 Beechen Cliff BaNES
92 A2 Beech Hill W Berk
324 D3 Beech Hill Wigan
88 C3 Beechingstoke Wilts
213 F2 Beech Lanes Birm
310 A4 Beechwood Halton
566 B8 Beechwood Highld
343 F2 Beechwood Leeds
107 F2 Beechwood Newpt
214 D4 Beechwood Solhll
169 E5 Beecroft Beds
114 D4 Beedon W Berk
114 D4 Beedon Hill W Berk
361 E4 Beeford E R Yk
314 B6 Beeley Derbys
334 B4 Beelsby NE Lin
115 F6 Benham W Berk
116 D4 Benham's Heath W & M
115 F6 Benham Stocks W Berk
22 C4 Beeny Cnwll
28 D3 Beer Devon
66 C3 Beer Somset
44 C3 Beer Crocombe Somset
46 A2 Beer Hackett Dorset
13 E4 Beesands Devon
321 E3 Beesby Lincs
470 D2 Beeslack Mdloth
13 E4 Beeson Devon
195 H5 Beeston Beds
290 A3 Beeston Ches
343 E3 Beeston Leeds
254 B4 Beeston Norfk
276 B2 Beeston Notts
343 E3 Beeston Hill Leeds
343 E4 Beeston Park Side Leeds
343 E5 Beeston Regis Norfk
343 E3 Beeston Royds Leeds
256 C5 Beeston St Lawrence Norfk
423 E6 Beeswing D & G
365 G4 Beetham Cumb
44 B5 Beetham Somset
254 C4 Beetley Norfk
272 B6 Beffcote Staffs
106 D3 Began Cardif
139 H2 Begbroke Oxon
245 G3 Begdale Cambs
156 C3 Begelly Pembs
146 C4 Beggar Hill Essex
343 E5 Beggarington Hill Kirk
161 G2 Beggars Ash Herefs
55 E3 Beggars Bush W Susx
105 G6 Beggars Pound V Glam
63 G4 Beggearn Huish Somset
208 C4 Beguildy Powys
250 D3 Beighton Norfk
315 E3 Beighton Sheff
460 C5 Beith N Ayrs

133 F2 Beili-Glas Mons
597 L2 Beinn Casgro W Isls
465 G4 Beith N Ayrs
100 C4 Bekesbourne Kent
100 C4 Bekesbourne Hill Kent
400 C3 Belah Cumb
232 D4 Belan Powys
256 B6 Belaugh Norfk
71 H5 Belbins Hants
212 D4 Belbroughton Worcs
47 E3 Belchalwell Dorset
47 E3 Belchalwell Street Dorset
173 G1 Belchamp Otten Essex
173 F1 Belchamp St Paul Essex
173 G1 Belchamp Walter Essex
239 G3 Belcher's Bar Leics
320 A4 Belchford Lincs
571 J4 Belfatton Abers
326 C2 Belfield Rochdl
455 E3 Belford Nthumb
306 D4 Belgrano Conwy
240 C3 Belgrave C Leic
289 E2 Belgrave Ches
238 C4 Belgrave Staffs
498 E3 Belhaven E Loth
557 G1 Belhelvie Abers
558 B4 Belhinnie Abers
554 C2 Bellabeg Abers
466 D2 Bellahouston C Glas
419 F4 Bellamore S Ayrs
479 K3 Bellanoch Ag & B
450 A2 Bellanrigg Border
346 B4 Bellasize E R Yk
526 B3 Bellaty Angus
144 B4 Bell Bar Herts
501 G2 Bellbrae Fife
354 B3 Bell Busk N York
145 H4 Bell Common Essex
320 C4 Belleau Lincs
296 C3 Belle Eau Park Notts
329 F3 Belle Green Barns
552 D1 Belleheiglash Moray
343 F4 Belle Isle Leeds
212 D4 Bell End Worcs
382 D6 Bellerby N York
213 H3 Belle Vale Dudley
309 F2 Belle Vale Lpool
19 E2 Bellever Devon
388 D3 Belle Vue Cumb
400 C3 Belle Vue Cumb
330 C4 Belle Vue Manch
326 C5 Belle Vue Manch
234 B2 Belle Vue Shrops
343 F6 Belle Vue Wakefd
213 E5 Bellevue Worcs
445 F2 Bellfield E Ayrs
447 G2 Bellfield S Lans
93 G4 Bellfields Surrey
215 F3 Bell Green Covtry
119 H5 Bell Green Gt Lon
213 E4 Bell Heath Worcs
74 A5 Bell Hill Hants
528 C2 Belliehill Angus
142 C3 Bellingdon Bucks
193 G2 Bellinge Nhants
119 H5 Bellingham Gt Lon
428 C3 Bellingham Nthumb
252 A3 Bellmount Norfk
458 D4 Belloch Ag & B
458 D5 Bellochantuy Ag & B
289 H5 Bell O' Th' Hill Ches
433 G4 Bellsbank E Ayrs
405 E2 Bell's Close N u Ty
174 C2 Bell's Corner Suffk
468 A3 Bellshill N Lans
455 E3 Bellshill Nthumb
468 C3 Bellside N Lans
483 F4 Bellsmyre W Duns
449 G2 Bellspool Border
469 G1 Bellsquarry W Loth
79 E2 Bells Yew Green E Susx
85 H2 Belluton BaNES
487 F2 Bellyeoman Fife
566 B5 Belmaduthy Highld
243 E3 Belmesthorpe Rutlnd
325 F1 Belmont Bl w D
405 H6 Belmont Dur
58 D4 Belmont E Susx
95 E2 Belmont Gt Lon
118 D1 Belmont Gt Lon
114 B2 Belmont Oxon
444 D5 Belmont S Ayrs
609 H4 Belmont Shet
554 C1 Belnacraig Abers
280 C3 Belnie Lincs
8 B1 Belowda Cnwll
294 D5 Belper Derbys
294 C5 Belper Lane End Derbys
315 G4 Belph Derbys
430 B4 Belsay Nthumb
19 G6 Belsford Devon
143 E4 Belsize Herts
175 F1 Belstead Suffk
445 E5 Belston S Ayrs
25 F4 Belstone Devon
25 F3 Belstone Corner Devon
339 H5 Belthorn Lancs
100 D2 Beltinge Kent
411 H8 Beltingham Nthumb
331 H3 Beltoft N Linc
275 G5 Belton Leics
278 C2 Belton Lincs
331 G3 Belton N Linc
251 F4 Belton Norfk
241 H4 Belton-in-Rutland Rutlnd
97 G5 Beltring Kent
120 C4 Belvedere Gt Lon
486 C6 Belvedere W Loth
277 H3 Belvoir Leics
37 H3 Bembridge IoW
452 A2 Bemersyde Border
70 C3 Bemerton Wilts
70 C3 Bemerton Heath Wilts
375 F5 Bempton E R Yk
227 G3 Benacre Suffk
435 E5 Benbuie D & G
311 G2 Benchill Manch
164 A5 Bencombe Gloucs
506 F2 Benderloch Ag & B
170 B3 Bendish Herts
80 A3 Benenden Kent
405 D4 Benfield E R Yk
404 C4 Benfieldside Dur
151 G3 Bengal Pembs
256 B4 Bengate Norfk
144 D2 Bengeo Herts
189 F6 Bengeworth Worcs
162 D5 Benhall Gloucs
202 D2 Benhall Green Suffk
202 D2 Benhall Street Suffk
95 F1 Benhilton Gt Lon
541 F6 Benholm Abers
357 G3 Beningbrough N York
170 D5 Benington Herts
300 C5 Benington Lincs
300 D5 Benington Sea End Lincs
304 B3 Benllech IoA
481 G3 Benmore Ag & B
508 F4 Benmore Stirlg
23 F4 Bennacott Cnwll
26 C6 Bennah Devon
460 C5 Bennecarrigan N Ayrs

City, town and village index: Bennett End - Blackwell 673

141 G5 **Bennett End** Bucks
143 F3 **Bennetts End** Herts
319 F3 **Benniworth** Lincs
97 H5 **Benover** Kent
355 F5 **Ben Rhydding** Brad
405 F2 **Bensham** Gatesd
465 G6 **Benslie** N Ayrs
115 G1 **Benson** Oxon
607 G7 **Benston** Shet
603 H4 **Benstonhall** Ork
86 A5 **Benter** Somset
171 G4 **Bentfield Bury** Essex
171 H4 **Bentfield Green** Essex
340 B5 **Bent Gate** Lancs
326 D2 **Bentgate** Rochdl
235 F4 **Benthall** Shrops
136 D1 **Bentham** Gloucs
557 E4 **Benthoul** C Aber
292 B5 **Bentilee** C Stke
125 G4 **Bentlass** Pembks
233 F4 **Bentlawnt** Shrops
330 C3 **Bentley** Donc
347 F2 **Bentley** E R Yk
146 B5 **Bentley** Essex
92 C6 **Bentley** Hants
175 F2 **Bentley** Suffk
238 D5 **Bentley** Warwks
237 E5 **Bentley** Wsall
238 D5 **Bentley Common** Warwks
144 B5 **Bentley Heath** Herts
214 B4 **Bentley Heath** Solhll
330 C4 **Bentley Rise** Donc
61 F4 **Benton** Devon
214 D4 **Benton Green** Solhll
425 G1 **Bentpath** D & G
469 F2 **Bents** W Loth
61 H5 **Bentwichen** Devon
73 G1 **Bentworth** Hants
513 H3 **Benvie** Angus
30 C2 **Benville** Dorset
405 F2 **Benwell** N u Ty
220 D1 **Benwick** Cambs
212 A1 **Beobridge** Shrops
213 G6 **Beoley** Worcs
531 J4 **Beoraidbeg** Highld
74 D6 **Bepton** W Susx
171 G4 **Berden** Essex
150 C4 **Berea** Pembks
17 G5 **Bere Alston** Devon
174 C5 **Berechurch** Essex
17 G6 **Bere Ferrers** Devon
561 E2 **Berefold** Abers
4 C4 **Berepper** Cnwll
47 F5 **Bere Regis** Dorset
250 C4 **Bergh Apton** Norfk
117 F2 **Berghers Hill** Bucks
66 C2 **Berhill** Somset
140 C5 **Berinsfield** Oxon
135 F5 **Berkeley** Gloucs
135 F5 **Berkeley Heath** Gloucs
142 D3 **Berkhamsted** Herts
87 E5 **Berkley** Somset
86 D5 **Berkley Down** Somset
87 E5 **Berkley Marsh** Somset
214 C4 **Berkswell** Solhll
119 G4 **Bermondsey** Gt Lon
215 E2 **Bermuda** Warwks
143 H3 **Bernards Heath** Herts
546 E5 **Bernera** Highld
40 C6 **Berner's Cross** Devon
79 G3 **Berner's Hill** E Susx
146 B3 **Berners Roding** Essex
481 G1 **Bernice** Ag & B
542 F7 **Bernisdale** Highld
140 D6 **Berrick Prior** Oxon
140 D6 **Berrick Salome** Oxon
582 F5 **Berriedale** Highld
390 C4 **Berrier** Cumb
232 C4 **Berriew** Powys
475 F6 **Berrington** Nthumb
234 C3 **Berrington** Shrops
186 D1 **Berrington** Worcs
186 D1 **Berrington Green** Worcs
16 C3 **Berriowbridge** Cnwll
84 A4 **Berrow** Somset
162 A3 **Berrow** Worcs
187 G3 **Berrow Green** Worcs
102 C4 **Berry** Swans
328 A2 **Berry Brow** Kirk
39 G5 **Berry Cross** Devon
61 E3 **Berry Down Cross** Devon
87 G2 **Berryfield** Wilts
348 D4 **Berrygate Hill** E R Yk
292 A5 **Berry Hill** C Stke
134 D2 **Berry Hill** Gloucs
295 H3 **Berry Hill** Notts
152 B1 **Berry Hill** Pembks
188 C2 **Berry Hill** Worcs
569 J3 **Berryhillock** Moray
94 D1 **Berrylands** Gt Lon
328 D4 **Berry Moor** Barns
61 E2 **Berrynarbor** Devon
20 A5 **Berry Pomeroy** Devon
27 E2 **Berrysbridge** Devon
96 B3 **Berry's Green** Gt Lon
288 C5 **Bersham** Wrexhm
601 H2 **Berstane** Ork
53 G4 **Bersted** W Susx
308 B6 **Berth-Ddu** Flints
307 G4 **Berthengam** Flints
57 E3 **Berwick** E Susx
81 H2 **Berwick** Kent
109 F3 **Berwick** S Glos
112 C5 **Berwick Bassett** Wilts
430 C4 **Berwick Hill** Nthumb
396 D6 **Berwick Hills** Middsb
70 B2 **Berwick St James** Wilts
69 F5 **Berwick St John** Wilts
69 F3 **Berwick St Leonard** Wilts
475 F4 **Berwick-upon-Tweed** Nthumb
234 C2 **Berwick Wharf** Shrops
288 A6 **Berwyn** Denbgs
277 H4 **Bescaby** Leics
323 G2 **Bescar** Lancs
237 F5 **Bescot** Wsall
270 D5 **Besford** Shrops
188 D6 **Besford** Worcs
330 D4 **Bessacarr** Donc
96 D3 **Bessels Green** Kent
139 H4 **Bessels Leigh** Oxon
326 B3 **Besses O' Th' Barn** Bury
361 F1 **Bessingby** E R Yk
261 G4 **Bessingham** Norfk
79 E3 **Best Beech Hill** E Susx
249 E5 **Besthorpe** Norfk
297 F2 **Besthorpe** Notts
295 H5 **Bestwood** C Nott
295 H5 **Bestwood Village** Notts
360 C5 **Beswick** E R Yk
326 C5 **Beswick** Manch
234 A5 **Betchcott** Shrops
291 F2 **Betchton Heath** Ches
94 D5 **Betchworth** Surrey
181 E2 **Bethania** Cerdgn
284 D4 **Bethania** Gwynd
285 F5 **Bethania** Gwynd
10 B2 **Bethany** Cnwll
8 C3 **Bethel** Cnwll
267 F2 **Bethel** Gwynd
283 F3 **Bethel** Gwynd
282 C1 **Bethel** IoA
80 D1 **Bethersden** Kent
284 D1 **Bethesda** Gwynd
152 B6 **Bethesda** Pembks
155 G4 **Bethlehem** Carmth
119 G3 **Bethnal Green** Gt Lon
291 F5 **Betley** Staffs
291 E5 **Betley Common** Staffs
121 E5 **Betsham** Kent
101 F5 **Betteshanger** Kent
29 G2 **Bettiscombe** Dorset
270 B2 **Bettisfield** Wrexhm
233 F4 **Betton** Shrops
271 F2 **Betton** Shrops
234 C3 **Betton Strange** Shrops
104 D2 **Bettws** Brdgnd
159 E6 **Bettws** Mons
107 E1 **Bettws** Newpt
232 B5 **Bettws Cedewain** Powys
287 E5 **Bettws Gwerfil Goch** Denbgs
133 G3 **Bettws Newydd** Mons
208 D3 **Bettws-y-Crwyn** Shrops
586 F4 **Bettyhill** Highld
129 F2 **Betws** Carmth
181 E4 **Betws Bledrws** Cerdgn
283 F4 **Betws Garmon** Gwynd
179 F4 **Betws Ifan** Cerdgn
285 G3 **Betws-y-Coed** Conwy
306 C5 **Betws-yn-Rhos** Conwy
179 F4 **Beulah** Cerdgn
183 E4 **Beulah** Powys
56 A3 **Bevendean** Br & H
316 C5 **Bevercotes** Notts
188 B3 **Bevere** Worcs
347 F1 **Beverley** E R Yk
136 C6 **Beverston** Gloucs
135 F5 **Bevington** Gloucs
604 E2 **Bevla** Shet
389 F3 **Bewaldeth** Cumb
76 D2 **Bewbush** W Susx
427 E5 **Bewcastle** Cumb
212 A4 **Bewdley** Worcs
355 F2 **Bewerley** N York
111 G6 **Bewley Common** Wilts
451 H4 **Bewlie** Border
451 G4 **Bewlie Mains** Border
310 B2 **Bewsey** Warrtn
254 D2 **Bexfield** Norfk
58 B5 **Bexhill** E Susx
120 C5 **Bexley** Gt Lon
120 C4 **Bexleyheath** Gt Lon
75 E4 **Bexleyhill** W Susx
98 D3 **Bexon** Kent
246 C4 **Bexwell** Norfk
200 B2 **Beyton** Suffk
200 B2 **Beyton Green** Suffk
598 C7 **Bhalasaigh** W Isls
598 B7 **Bhaltos** W Isls
591 C9 **Bhatarsaigh** W Isls
110 C1 **Bibstone** S Glos
137 H3 **Bibury** Gloucs
166 C5 **Bicester** Oxon
44 B4 **Bickenhall** Somset
214 B3 **Bickenhill** Solhll
280 B2 **Bicker** Lincs
280 B2 **Bicker Bar** Lincs
280 B2 **Bicker Gauntlet** Lincs
325 E4 **Bickershaw** Wigan
324 A4 **Bickerstaffe** Lancs
289 H4 **Bickerton** Ches
13 E5 **Bickerton** Devon
357 E4 **Bickerton** N York
236 C2 **Bickford** Staffs
63 E3 **Bickham** Somset
41 F2 **Bickingcott** Devon
19 G3 **Bickington** Devon
60 D5 **Bickington** Devon
18 B5 **Bickleigh** Devon
27 E1 **Bickleigh** Devon
60 D5 **Bickleton** Devon
120 B6 **Bickley** Gt Lon
211 E5 **Bickley** Worcs
290 A5 **Bickley Moss** Ches
290 A5 **Bickley Town** Ches
289 H5 **Bickleywood** Ches
189 H5 **Bickmarsh** Worcs
147 F4 **Bicknacre** Essex
64 B4 **Bicknoller** Somset
98 D3 **Bicknor** Kent
49 E2 **Bickton** Hants
186 B2 **Bicton** Herefs
124 D3 **Bicton** Pembks
209 E3 **Bicton** Shrops
234 A1 **Bicton** Shrops
234 A2 **Bicton Heath** Shrops
97 E6 **Bidborough** Kent
92 B5 **Bidden** Hants
80 B2 **Biddenden** Kent
98 D6 **Biddenden Green** Kent
195 E4 **Biddenham** Beds
111 E5 **Biddestone** Wilts
405 H3 **Biddick** Sundld
406 B2 **Biddick Hall** S Tyne
84 C4 **Biddisham** Somset
166 D1 **Biddlesden** Bucks
442 B3 **Biddlestone** Nthumb
291 H3 **Biddulph** Staffs
292 B3 **Biddulph Moor** Staffs
39 F2 **Bideford** Devon
189 H4 **Bidford-on-Avon** Warwks
24 C5 **Bidlake** Devon
308 C1 **Bidston** Wirral
308 C2 **Bidston Hill** Wirral
169 E5 **Bidwell** Beds
359 E6 **Bielby** E R Yk
557 F4 **Bieldside** C Aber
342 C3 **Bierley** Brad
37 E5 **Bierley** IoW
142 A1 **Bierton** Bucks
410 C4 **Big Balcraig** D & G
12 B3 **Bigbury** Devon
12 A4 **Bigbury-on-Sea** Devon
333 F3 **Bigby** Lincs
117 E3 **Bigfrith** W & M
350 A1 **Biggar** Cumb
448 D2 **Biggar** S Lans
468 B2 **Biggar Road** N Lans
293 G3 **Biggin** Derbys
294 B5 **Biggin** Derbys
344 C3 **Biggin** N York
121 F4 **Biggin** Thurr
606 A5 **Biggings** Shet
96 B3 **Biggin Hill** Gt Lon
196 A6 **Biggleswade** Beds
587 J4 **Bighouse** Highld
73 F3 **Bighton** Hants
399 H4 **Biglands** Cumb
288 D1 **Big Mancot** Flints
291 G4 **Bignall End** Staffs
54 A2 **Bignor** W Susx
172 C5 **Bigods** Essex
376 C2 **Bigrigg** Cumb
572 E8 **Big Sand** Highld
605 G6 **Bigton** Shet
8 C1 **Bilberry** Cnwll
276 B1 **Bilborough** C Nott
63 G3 **Bilbrook** Somset
236 C4 **Bilbrook** Staffs
357 G5 **Bilbrough** N York
589 H6 **Bilbster** Highld
589 H6 **Bilbster Mains** Highld
316 B3 **Bilby** Notts
394 D5 **Bildershaw** Dur
200 C5 **Bildeston** Suffk
11 F3 **Billacombe** C Plym
23 F4 **Billacott** Cnwll
146 D6 **Billericay** Essex
241 F4 **Billesdon** Leics
213 G3 **Billesley** Birm
190 A3 **Billesley** Warwks
213 G3 **Billesley Common** Birm
279 G3 **Billingborough** Lincs
324 C4 **Billinge** St Hel
225 G4 **Billingford** Norfk
254 D3 **Billingford** Norfk
396 C4 **Billingham** S on T
299 F4 **Billinghay** Lincs
329 G4 **Billingley** Barns
76 A4 **Billingshurst** W Susx
211 G3 **Billingsley** Shrops
168 C5 **Billington** Beds
339 H2 **Billington** Lancs
272 C5 **Billington** Staffs
251 E2 **Billockby** Norfk
405 G2 **Bill Quay** Gatesd
442 A5 **Billsmoor Park** Nthumb
431 F6 **Billy Mill** N Tyne
394 D2 **Billy Row** Dur
270 B4 **Bilmarsh** Shrops
338 C1 **Bilsborrow** Lancs
321 E4 **Bilsby** Lincs
321 E4 **Bilsby Field** Lincs
26 C4 **Bilsdon** Devon
53 H4 **Bilsham** W Susx
81 F3 **Bilsington** Kent
135 E2 **Bilson Green** Gloucs
296 B2 **Bilsthorpe** Notts
296 B3 **Bilsthorpe Moor** Notts
471 E2 **Bilston** Mdloth
236 D5 **Bilston** Wolves
239 F3 **Bilstone** Leics
99 G5 **Bilting** Kent
348 C3 **Bilton** E R Yk
356 C3 **Bilton** N York
443 G2 **Bilton** Nthumb
216 A5 **Bilton** Warwks
357 F5 **Bilton Haggs** N York
357 F4 **Bilton in Ainsty** N York
600 E1 **Bimbister** Ork
334 B6 **Binbrook** Lincs
395 E3 **Binchester Blocks** Dur
32 B3 **Bincombe** Dorset
64 C4 **Bincombe** Somset
577 K7 **Bindal** Highld
43 F3 **Bindon** Somset
85 H5 **Binegar** Somset
55 E1 **Bines Green** W Susx
116 D5 **Binfield** Br For
116 B4 **Binfield Heath** Oxon
429 F5 **Bingfield** Nthumb
488 B5 **Bingham** C Edin
277 F1 **Bingham** Notts
47 E4 **Bingham's Melcombe** Dorset
342 B2 **Bingley** Brad
270 C6 **Bings Heath** Shrops
260 C4 **Binham** Norfk
215 F4 **Binley** Covtry
90 C4 **Binley** Hants
215 F4 **Binley Woods** Warwks
33 F2 **Binnegar** Dorset
485 H5 **Binniehill** Falk
93 G5 **Binscombe** Surrey
140 A3 **Binsey** Oxon
370 A4 **Binsoe** N York
37 F2 **Binstead** IoW
74 B1 **Binsted** Hants
54 A3 **Binsted** W Susx
190 A4 **Binton** Warwks
254 D3 **Bintree** Norfk
233 F4 **Binweston** Shrops
174 B6 **Birch** Essex
326 C3 **Birch** Rochdl
213 G5 **Birch Acre** Worcs
161 F2 **Birchall** Herefs
292 C4 **Birchall** Staffs
259 F5 **Bircham Newton** Norfk
259 F5 **Bircham Tofts** Norfk
212 B5 **Birchan Coppice** Worcs
171 H5 **Birchanger** Essex
187 G2 **Birch Berrow** Worcs
460 C4 **Birchburn** N Ayrs
273 H3 **Birch Cross** Staffs
78 C2 **Birchden** E Susx
577 G5 **Birchen** Highld
187 F6 **Birchend** Herefs
273 G2 **Birchendale** Staffs
186 B1 **Bircher** Herefs
213 H1 **Birches Green** Birm
292 A5 **Birches Head** C Stke
79 F3 **Birchett's Green** E Susx
213 G1 **Birchfield** Birm
174 B6 **Birch Green** Essex
144 C2 **Birch Green** Herts
324 B3 **Birch Green** Lancs
188 C5 **Birch Green** Worcs
106 C3 **Birchgrove** Cardif
129 H5 **Birchgrove** Swans
77 G4 **Birchgrove** W Susx
174 D3 **Birchhall Corner** Essex
290 A2 **Birch Heath** Ches
93 E1 **Birch Hill** Br For
29 F2 **Birchill** Devon
237 F5 **Birchills** Wsall
101 E2 **Birchington** Kent
238 D6 **Birchley Heath** Warwks
238 C4 **Birchmoor** Warwks
168 C3 **Birchmoor Green** Beds
81 G1 **Bircholt Forstal** Kent
294 A2 **Birchover** Derbys
312 D2 **Birch Vale** Derbys
144 B3 **Birchwood** Herts
318 A6 **Birchwood** Lincs
44 A5 **Birchwood** Somset
310 C1 **Birchwood** Warrtn
50 A5 **Birchy Hill** Hants
316 B1 **Bircotes** Notts
172 D1 **Birdbrook** Essex
69 F5 **Birdbush** Wilts
493 G6 **Birdfield** Ag & B
371 F4 **Birdforth** N York
53 E4 **Birdham** W Susx
314 D6 **Birdholme** Derbys
215 G6 **Birdingbury** Warwks
136 D2 **Birdlip** Gloucs
604 b3 **Bird Observatory** Shet
359 F1 **Birdsall** N York
328 C3 **Birds Edge** Kirk
199 F2 **Birds End** Suffk
146 B3 **Birds Green** Essex
211 H2 **Birdsgreen** Shrops
29 G2 **Birdsmoorgate** Dorset
484 C4 **Birdston** E Duns
200 D4 **Bird Street** Suffk
329 E4 **Birdwell** Barns
161 G6 **Birdwood** Gloucs
453 E2 **Birgham** Border
324 D1 **Birkacre** Lancs
388 C2 **Birkby** Cumb
342 B6 **Birkby** Kirk
384 A4 **Birkby** N York
323 F1 **Birkdale** Sefton
308 C2 **Birkenhead** Wirral
570 C6 **Birkenhills** Abers
342 D4 **Birkenshaw** Kirk
467 G2 **Birkenshaw** N Lans
468 B5 **Birkenshaw** S Lans
451 H1 **Birkenside** Border
389 H5 **Birkett Mire** Cumb
554 B6 **Birkhall** Abers
514 B3 **Birkhill** Angus
472 D6 **Birkhill** Border
437 H1 **Birkhill** D & G
278 D5 **Birkholme** Lincs
342 C5 **Birkhouse** Calder
344 C4 **Birkin** N York
366 C1 **Birks** Cumb
343 E4 **Birks** Leeds
402 D1 **Birkshaw** Nthumb
186 B4 **Birley** Herefs
314 C1 **Birley Carr** Sheff
329 E6 **Birley Edge** Sheff
314 D3 **Birleyhay** Derbys
97 G2 **Birling** Kent
443 H3 **Birling** Nthumb
57 F5 **Birling Gap** E Susx
188 D6 **Birlingham** Worcs
213 F2 **Birmingham** Birm
512 B1 **Birnam** P & K
561 E3 **Birness** Abers
467 F4 **Birniehill** S Lans
555 G5 **Birse** Abers
555 F5 **Birsemore** Abers
342 D4 **Birstall** Kirk
240 C3 **Birstall** Leics
356 A3 **Birstwith** N York
279 G3 **Birthorpe** Lincs
326 B2 **Birtle** Rochdl
405 G3 **Birtley** Gatesd
209 G6 **Birtley** Herefs
428 D4 **Birtley** Nthumb
210 B1 **Birtley** Shrops
93 H6 **Birtley Green** Surrey
162 B2 **Birtsmorton** Worcs
162 A2 **Birts Street** Worcs
242 B5 **Bisbrooke** Rutlnd
319 G3 **Biscathorpe** Lincs
43 G5 **Biscombe** Somset
169 F5 **Biscot** Luton
8 D3 **Biscovey** Cnwll
117 E2 **Bisham** W & M
189 E4 **Bishampton** Worcs
41 E2 **Bish Mill** Devon
186 A6 **Bishon Common** Herefs
395 E4 **Bishop Auckland** Dur
318 C1 **Bishopbridge** Lincs
484 B5 **Bishopbriggs** E Duns
347 E1 **Bishop Burton** E R Yk
70 C3 **Bishopdown** Wilts
565 J6 **Bishop Kinkell** Highld
395 G3 **Bishop Middleham** Dur
568 C3 **Bishopmill** Moray
356 C1 **Bishop Monkton** N York
332 D6 **Bishop Norton** Lincs
100 C5 **Bishopsbourne** Kent
88 B2 **Bishops Cannings** Wilts
209 F2 **Bishop's Castle** Shrops
46 D2 **Bishop's Caundle** Dorset
162 D4 **Bishop's Cleeve** Gloucs
46 C2 **Bishop's Down** Dorset
187 E5 **Bishop's Frome** Herefs
396 B5 **Bishopsgarth** S on T
117 G5 **Bishopsgate** Surrey
172 C6 **Bishop's Green** Essex
90 D2 **Bishop's Green** Hants
43 G3 **Bishop's Hull** Somset
191 F3 **Bishop's Itchington** Warwks
43 G2 **Bishops Lydeard** Somset
162 B5 **Bishop's Norton** Gloucs
41 F3 **Bishop's Nympton** Devon
271 H3 **Bishop's Offley** Staffs
171 G5 **Bishops Park** Herts
4 D3 **Bishop's Quay** Cnwll
171 G6 **Bishop's Stortford** Herts
73 F3 **Bishop's Sutton** Hants
191 E2 **Bishop's Tachbrook** Warwks
61 E5 **Bishop's Tawton** Devon
20 C3 **Bishopsteignton** Devon
72 C6 **Bishopstoke** Hants
109 G4 **Bishopston** Bristl
103 E4 **Bishopston** Swans
141 H2 **Bishopstone** Bucks
56 D4 **Bishopstone** E Susx
185 H6 **Bishopstone** Herefs
100 D2 **Bishopstone** Kent
113 F3 **Bishopstone** Swindn
70 B4 **Bishopstone** Wilts
87 F6 **Bishopstrow** Wilts
85 G3 **Bishop Sutton** BaNES
51 G1 **Bishop's Waltham** Hants
44 B5 **Bishopswood** Somset
236 B3 **Bishop's Wood** Staffs
109 G6 **Bishopsworth** Bristl
356 B2 **Bishop Thornton** N York
358 A5 **Bishopthorpe** York
410 D4 **Bishopton** D & G
395 H5 **Bishopton** Darltn
370 B5 **Bishopton** N York
483 F5 **Bishopton** Rens
190 B3 **Bishopton** Warwks
406 B3 **Bishopwearmouth** Sundld
359 E4 **Bishop Wilton** E R Yk
107 F2 **Bishpool** Newpt
108 C2 **Bishton** Newpt
273 F5 **Bishton** Staffs
136 D3 **Bisley** Gloucs
93 G3 **Bisley** Surrey
93 F3 **Bisley Camp** Surrey
337 E1 **Bispham** Bpool
324 B2 **Bispham Green** Lancs
7 E5 **Bissoe** Cnwll
5 E2 **Bissom** Cnwll
49 E4 **Bisterne** Hants
49 G4 **Bisterne Close** Hants
97 E4 **Bitchet Green** Kent
278 D4 **Bitchfield** Lincs
60 D3 **Bittadon** Devon
12 B1 **Bittaford** Devon
254 B4 **Bittering** Norfk
210 D4 **Bitterley** Shrops
50 D2 **Bitterne** C Sotn
50 D2 **Bitterne Park** C Sotn
238 B4 **Bitterscote** Staffs
216 B2 **Bitteswell** Leics
69 E4 **Bittles Green** Dorset
110 B6 **Bitton** S Glos
116 B2 **Bix** Oxon
606 D7 **Bixter** Shet
240 C5 **Blaby** Leics
424 A1 **Blackacre** D & G
474 B4 **Blackadder** Border
13 E2 **Blackawton** Devon
222 A2 **Black Bank** Cambs
215 F2 **Black Bank** Warwks
383 G2 **Black Banks** Darltn
281 F4 **Black Barn** Lincs
376 C3 **Blackbeck** Cumb
43 E6 **Blackborough** Devon
252 D5 **Blackborough** Norfk
252 D5 **Blackborough End** Norfk
138 D4 **Black Bourton** Oxon
78 C5 **Blackboys** E Susx
294 C5 **Blackbrook** Derbys
313 E3 **Blackbrook** Derbys
324 C5 **Blackbrook** St Hel
271 H2 **Blackbrook** Staffs
94 D5 **Blackbrook** Surrey
557 E2 **Blackburn** Abers
339 F4 **Blackburn** Bl w D
568 E4 **Blackburn** Moray
329 F6 **Blackburn** Rothm
469 F1 **Blackburn** W Loth
430 C6 **Black Callerton** N u Ty
249 E5 **Black Carr** Norfk
471 H3 **Blackcastle** Mdloth
419 G5 **Black Clauchrie** S Ayrs
506 F3 **Black Crofts** Ag & B
7 H1 **Black Cross** Cnwll
91 G4 **Black Dam** Hants
311 F5 **Blackden Heath** Ches
139 G3 **Blackditch** Oxon
557 H2 **Blackdog** Abers
41 G6 **Black Dog** Devon
29 G2 **Blackdown** Dorset
72 D5 **Blackdown** Hants
215 E6 **Blackdown** Warwks
399 E4 **Blackdyke** Cumb
490 A3 **Blackdykes** E Loth
329 F4 **Blacker Hill** Barns
99 E1 **Blacketts** Kent
405 G3 **Blackfell** Sundld
120 C5 **Blackfen** Gt Lon
50 D4 **Blackfield** Hants
549 K1 **Blackfold** Highld
400 C2 **Blackford** Cumb
424 C3 **Blackford** D & G
498 D3 **Blackford** P & K
210 D3 **Blackford** Shrops
63 E2 **Blackford** Somset
67 H4 **Blackford** Somset
84 D5 **Blackford** Somset
326 A3 **Blackford Bridge** Bury
275 E6 **Blackfordby** Leics
36 D5 **Blackgang** IoW
556 B5 **Blackhall** Abers
487 H5 **Blackhall** C Edin
466 C2 **Blackhall** Rens
396 C2 **Blackhall Colliery** Dur
404 D3 **Blackhall Mill** Gatesd
396 C2 **Blackhall Rocks** Dur
78 B2 **Blackham** E Susx
451 E2 **Blackhaugh** Border
174 D5 **Blackheath** Essex
120 A4 **Blackheath** Gt Lon
213 E2 **Blackheath** Sandw
227 E5 **Blackheath** Suffk
120 A4 **Blackheath Park** Gt Lon
430 A4 **Black Heddon** Nthumb
571 K4 **Blackhill** Abers
341 G1 **Black Hill** Brad
404 C4 **Blackhill** Dur
71 F6 **Blackhill** Hants
542 E6 **Blackhill** Highld
569 G6 **Blackhillock** Moray
103 E3 **Blackhills** Swans
27 F4 **Blackhorse** Devon
110 B4 **Blackhorse** S Glos
222 B1 **Black Horse Drove** Cambs
571 L6 **Blackhouse** Abers
598 D6 **Blackhouse Village** W Isls
140 C4 **Blackird Leys** Oxon
280 C2 **Blackjack** Lincs
237 E6 **Black Lake** Sandw
112 B6 **Blackland** Wilts
58 D4 **Blacklands** E Susx
187 E6 **Blacklands** Herefs
326 A3 **Black Lane** Bury
569 L4 **Blacklaw** Abers
338 C3 **Blackleach** Lancs
326 C4 **Blackley** Manch
525 H3 **Blacklunans** P & K
233 F5 **Black Marsh** Shrops
160 C2 **Blackmarstone** Herefs
105 E2 **Blackmill** Brdgnd
189 G6 **Blackminster** Worcs
85 G2 **Blackmoor** BaNES
74 B3 **Blackmoor** Hants
324 B2 **Black Moor** Lancs
343 E2 **Black Moor** Leeds
85 E2 **Blackmoor** N Som
43 G4 **Blackmoor** Somset
325 F4 **Blackmoor** Wigan
327 G2 **Blackmoorfoot** Kirk
61 F3 **Blackmoor Gate** Devon
146 C4 **Blackmore** Essex
233 F3 **Blackmore** Shrops
173 E3 **Blackmore End** Essex
143 H1 **Blackmore End** Herts
188 B6 **Blackmore End** Worcs
521 K7 **Black Mount** Ag & B
487 E2 **Black Muir** Fife
78 C3 **Blackness** E Susx
487 E4 **Blackness** Falk
74 B1 **Blacknest** Hants
117 G6 **Blacknest** W & M
30 A3 **Blackney** Dorset
32 D2 **Blacknoll** Dorset
173 F5 **Black Notley** Essex
340 D1 **Blacko** Lancs
270 C2 **Blackoe** Shrops
545 L5 **Black Park** Highld
269 F1 **Black Park** Wrexhm
103 F3 **Black Pill** Swans
338 C2 **Black Pole** Lancs
188 C3 **Blackpole** Worcs
337 E2 **Blackpool** Bpool
11 G3 **Blackpool** Devon
13 F3 **Blackpool** Devon
19 H3 **Blackpool** Devon
126 B2 **Blackpool** Pembks
29 F3 **Blackpool Corner** Devon
426 D4 **Blackpool Gate** Cumb
468 D1 **Blackridge** W Loth
476 E4 **Blackrock** Ag & B
85 H1 **Blackrock** BaNES
56 A4 **Black Rock** Br & H
4 B2 **Black Rock** Cnwll
132 D2 **Blackrock** Mons
325 E2 **Blackrod** Bolton
398 C1 **Blackshaw** D & G
341 E4 **Blackshaw Head** Calder
292 C3 **Blackshaw Moor** Staffs
175 F1 **Blacksmith's Corner** Suffk
201 F1 **Blacksmith's Green** Suffk
339 H5 **Blacksnape** Bl w D
55 F1 **Blackstone** W Susx
212 A5 **Blackstone** Worcs
227 G2 **Black Street** Suffk
125 G3 **Black Tar** Pembks
166 D6 **Blackthorn** Oxon
200 B2 **Blackthorpe** Suffk
346 B5 **Blacktoft** E R Yk
557 F4 **Blacktop** C Aber
24 C1 **Black Torrington** Devon
106 D3 **Blacktown** Newpt
106 D1 **Black Vein** Caerph
294 B5 **Blackwall** Derbys
120 A3 **Blackwall** Gt Lon
6 D4 **Blackwater** Cnwll
49 E5 **Blackwater** Dorset
92 D2 **Blackwater** Hants
37 E3 **Blackwater** IoW
255 E3 **Blackwater** Norfk
44 B4 **Blackwater** Somset
460 B4 **Blackwaterfoot** N Ayrs
106 C4 **Blackweir** Cardif
400 D4 **Blackwell** Cumb
383 G2 **Blackwell** Darltn
295 E3 **Blackwell** Derbys
313 F5 **Blackwell** Derbys
42 D2 **Blackwell** Somset
77 G2 **Blackwell** W Susx
190 C6 **Blackwell** Warwks

213 E5 Blackwell Worcs
132 C5 Blackwood Caerph
468 B6 Blackwood S Lans
310 C1 Blackwood Warrtn
292 B3 Blackwood Hill Staffs
309 E6 Blacon Ches
82 C1 Bladbean Kent
382 A5 Blades N York
417 E6 Bladnoch D & G
139 G2 Bladon Oxon
179 E4 Blaenannerch Cerdgn
129 E2 Blaenau Carmth
288 B3 Blaenau Flints
285 E4 Blaenau Dolwyddelan Conwy
285 F5 Blaenau Ffestiniog Gwynd
132 D4 Blaenau-Gwent Blae G
133 E3 Blaenavon Torfn
179 H3 Blaenbedw Fawr Cerdgn
130 D6 Blaencaerau Neath
179 G3 Blaencelyn Cerdgn
131 F6 Blaen Clydach Rhondd
131 E5 Blaencwm Rhondd
157 E2 Blaendyryn Powys
152 D2 Blaenffos Pembks
104 D1 Blaengarw Brdgnd
130 D3 Blaengwrach Neath
130 D5 Blaengwynfi Neath
179 F5 Blaen-Pant Cerdgn
181 F2 Blaenpennal Cerdgn
204 D4 Blaenplwyf Cerdgn
179 F4 Blaenporth Cerdgn
131 E5 Blaenrhondda Rhondd
153 E4 Blaenwaun Carmth
180 A4 Blaen-Waun Cerdgn
153 G4 Blaen-y-Coed Carmth
132 B2 Blaen-y-cwm Blae G
23 E4 Blagdon Cnwll
85 F3 Blagdon N Som
20 A5 Blagdon Torbay
43 H4 Blagdon Hill Somset
402 C5 Blagill Cumb
324 A3 Blaguegate Lancs
532 F7 Blaich Highld
519 G2 Blain Highld
132 D3 Blaina Blae G
501 F6 Blair Fife
524 C3 Blair Atholl P & K
461 E3 Blairbeg N Ayrs
486 C2 Blairburn Fife
410 C4 Blairbuy D & G
556 B1 Blairdaff Abers
497 H5 Blair Drummond Stirlg
525 J6 Blairgowrie P & K
486 D2 Blairhall Fife
467 H1 Blairingone P & K
499 F5 Blairland N Ayrs
465 F5 Blairlinn N Lans
485 F5 Blairlogie Stirlg
498 C5 Blairlogie Stirlg
482 A3 Blairmore Ag & B
584 C4 Blairmore Highld
552 D5 Blairnamarrow Moray
565 H5 Blairninich Highld
484 B4 Blairskaith E Duns
135 G1 Blaisdon Gloucs
109 F4 Blaise Hamlet Bristl
212 B4 Blakebrook Worcs
212 C4 Blakedown Worcs
173 E5 Blake End Essex
194 B6 Blakelands M Keyn
453 E3 Blakelaw Border
405 F1 Blakelaw N u Ty
212 C1 Blakeley Staffs
292 C5 Blakeley Lane Staffs
290 D4 Blakelow Ches
159 G1 Blakemere Herefs
237 F4 Blakenall Heath Wsall
135 F3 Blakeney Gloucs
260 D3 Blakeney Norfk
291 E5 Blakenhall Ches
236 D5 Blakenhall Wolves
212 B3 Blakeshall Worcs
192 D4 Blakesley Nhants
403 G4 Blanchland Nthumb
47 H3 Blandford Camp Dorset
47 G3 Blandford Forum Dorset
47 G4 Blandford St Mary Dorset
355 H4 Bland Hill N York
586 D5 Blandy Highld
484 A4 Blanefield Stirlg
474 B3 Blanerne Border
291 G5 Blank Bank Staffs
298 D2 Blankney Lincs
28 C3 Blannicombe Devon
467 G3 Blantyre S Lans
521 G2 Blàr a' Chaorainn Highld
480 B2 Blarbuie Ag & B
553 G2 Blarghour Ag & B
520 F2 Blarmachfoldach Highld
574 C5 Blarnalearoch Highld
146 D2 Blasford Hill Essex
592 F3 Blashaval W Isls
49 E3 Blashford Hants
241 H5 Blaston Leics
86 D5 Blatchbridge Somset
242 D5 Blatherwycke Nhants
364 C2 Blawith Cumb
202 D3 Blaxhall Suffk
331 E4 Blaxton Donc
405 E2 Blaydon Gatesd
405 E2 Blaydon Burn Gatesd
405 E2 Blaydon Haughs Gatesd
388 A6 Bleachgreen Cumb
226 A4 Bleach Green Suffk
85 E5 Bleadney Somset
84 B3 Bleadon N Som
187 E5 Bleak Acre Herefs
168 B2 Bleak Hall M Keyn
327 F2 Bleak Hey Nook Oldham
49 E2 Bleak Hill Hants
100 B3 Blean Kent
319 E3 Bleasby Lincs
296 D5 Bleasby Notts
319 E3 Bleasby Moor Lincs
352 B5 Bleasdale Lancs
380 C2 Bleatarn Cumb
502 C2 Blebocraigs Fife
208 C6 Bleddfa Powys
164 C5 Bledington Gloucs
141 G4 Bledlow Bucks
141 G5 Bledlow Ridge Bucks
87 F3 Bleet Wilts
472 B2 Blegbie E Loth
38 B2 Blegbury Devon
391 G3 Blencarn Cumb
399 F5 Blencogo Cumb
52 C2 Blendworth Hants
140 C3 Blenheim Oxon
140 C4 Blenheim Oxon
402 B2 Blenkinsopp Hall Nthumb
389 E1 Blennerhasset Cumb
140 B1 Bletchingdon Oxon
95 G4 Bletchingley Surrey
168 B3 Bletchley M Keyn
271 E3 Bletchley Shrops
152 B5 Bletherston Pembks
195 E3 Bletsoe Beds
115 E2 Blewbury Oxon
81 F2 Bliby Kent
255 G2 Blickling Norfk
296 A3 Blidworth Notts
296 A3 Blidworth Bottoms Notts

295 H4 Blidworth Dale Notts
441 F2 Blindburn Nthumb
389 E3 Blindcrake Cumb
95 H5 Blindley Heath Surrey
44 B5 Blindmoor Somset
513 G6 Blinkbonny Fife
15 F4 Blisland Cnwll
49 F2 Blissford Hants
211 G5 Bliss Gate Worcs
235 F4 Blists Hill Wrekin
193 H4 Blisworth Nhants
273 G5 Blithbury Staffs
399 E4 Blitterlees Cumb
164 B3 Blockley Gloucs
250 C3 Blofield Norfk
250 C2 Blofield Heath Norfk
224 D4 Blo' Norton Norfk
251 G5 Bloodman's Corner Suffk
86 B3 Bloomfield BaNES
86 C2 Bloomfield BaNES
236 D6 Bloomfield Sandw
119 F3 Bloomsbury Gt Lon
271 E3 Blore Staffs
293 F5 Blore Staffs
271 G3 Bloreheath Staffs
214 A4 Blossomfield Solhll
273 G3 Blount's Green Staffs
323 F1 Blowick Sefton
6 D3 Blowinghouse Cnwll
165 G2 Bloxham Oxon
298 D4 Bloxholm Lincs
237 E4 Bloxwich Wsall
47 G6 Bloxworth Dorset
355 G3 Blubberhouses N York
7 H2 Blue Anchor Cnwll
63 G3 Blue Anchor Somset
103 E3 Blue Anchor Swans
234 D2 Bluebell Shrops
98 A2 Blue Bell Hill Kent
451 G1 Bluecairn Border
170 C5 Blue Hill Herts
99 E3 Bluetown Kent
123 E4 Blue Town Kent
111 E6 Blue Vein Wilts
121 E5 Bluewater Kent
323 E5 Blundellsands Sefton
251 G5 Blundeston Suffk
212 B2 Blundies Staffs
195 G4 Blunham Beds
112 D2 Blunsdon St Andrew Swindn
212 C5 Bluntington Worcs
221 E5 Bluntisham Cambs
16 D6 Blunts Cnwll
214 A6 Blunt's Green Warwks
29 H3 Bluntshay Dorset
272 C1 Blurton C Stke
332 C6 Blyborough Lincs
227 E4 Blyford Suffk
236 B2 Blymhill Staffs
470 B5 Blyth Border
316 B2 Blyth Notts
431 F3 Blyth Nthumb
470 B5 Blyth Bridge Border
227 F4 Blythburgh Suffk
472 D5 Blythe Border
272 D1 Blythe Bridge Staffs
273 E1 Blythe Marsh Staffs
214 C1 Blyth End Warwks
483 G6 Blythswood Rens
332 B6 Blyton Lincs
503 F2 Boarhills Fife
51 G3 Boarhunt Hants
340 C5 Boarsgreave Lancs
78 C3 Boarshead E Susx
324 D3 Boar's Head Wigan
140 A4 Boars Hill Oxon
140 D2 Boarstall Bucks
24 D4 Boasley Cross Devon
565 K2 Boath Highld
551 G6 Boat of Garten Highld
98 D1 Bobbing Kent
212 B1 Bobbington Staffs
146 A3 Bobbingworth Essex
224 D5 Bobby Hill Suffk
9 F2 Bocaddon Cnwll
497 F3 Bochastle Stirlg
99 G6 Bockhanger Kent
173 F5 Bocking Essex
173 F4 Bocking Churchstreet Essex
149 G1 Bocking's Elm Essex
186 D2 Bockleton Worcs
116 D2 Bockmer End Bucks
39 E3 Bocombe Devon
9 E1 Boconnoc Cnwll
561 H1 Boddam Abers
605 G7 Boddam Shet
86 A6 Bodden Somset
529 F4 Boddin Angus
162 C4 Boddington Gloucs
302 D4 Bodedern IoA
14 C4 Bodellick Cnwll
8 D3 Bodelva Cnwll
307 E4 Bodelwyddan Denbgs
186 C4 Bodenham Herefs
70 D4 Bodenham Wilts
161 E3 Bodenham Bank Herefs
186 C4 Bodenham Moor Herefs
262 B6 Bodermid Gwynd
303 E2 Bodewryd IoA
307 F5 Bodfari Denbgs
303 F5 Bodffordd IoA
263 E3 Bodfuan Gwynd
261 F3 Bodham Norfk
79 H4 Bodiam E Susx
165 G2 Bodicote Oxon
14 D4 Bodieve Cnwll
8 C2 Bodiggo Cnwll
4 C2 Bodilly Cnwll
9 E3 Bodinnick Cnwll
302 C5 Bodior IoA
57 H2 Bodle Street Green E Susx
61 G2 Bodley Devon
15 E5 Bodmin Cnwll
43 E5 Bodmiscombe Devon
247 G5 Bodney Norfk
282 C2 Bodorgan IoA
82 B1 Bodsham Kent
16 B6 Boduel Cnwll
8 C1 Bodwen Cnwll
238 B5 Bodymoor Heath Warwks
15 G6 Bofarnel Cnwll
591 E7 Bogach W Isls
565 L6 Bogallan Highld
561 F2 Bogbrae Abers
295 F5 Bogend Notts
445 E3 Bogend S Ayrs
470 D2 Boghall Mdloth
486 C6 Boghall W Loth
447 F1 Boghead S Lans
568 E3 Bogmoor Moray
569 K6 Bogniebrae Abers
53 C5 Bognor Regis W Susx
559 G6 Bograxie Abers
470 B4 Bogs Bank Border
468 C4 Bogside N Lans
570 B5 Bogton Abers
421 G3 Bogue D & G
58 C4 Bohemia E Susx
71 E6 Bohemia Wilts
533 L6 Bohenie Highld
17 F5 Bohetherick Cnwll
5 G2 Bohortha Cnwll
533 L6 Bohuntine Highld

533 L6 Bohuntinville Highld
595 H5 Boirseam W Isls
8 C1 Bokiddick Cnwll
154 B6 Bolahaul Carmth
394 D5 Bolam Dur
430 A3 Bolam Nthumb
429 H3 Bolam West Houses Nthumb
12 B5 Bolberry Devon
310 A2 Bold Heath St Hel
237 H6 Boldmere Birm
406 B2 Boldon S Tyne
406 A2 Boldon Colliery S Tyne
50 B5 Boldre Hants
382 B2 Boldron Dur
24 B3 Boldventure Devon
317 E2 Bole Notts
238 C4 Bolehall Staffs
294 B3 Bolehill Derbys
314 C5 Bole Hill Derbys
315 E5 Bolehill Derbys
314 C3 Bolehill Sheff
6 C6 Bolenowe Cnwll
7 E3 Bolham Devon
4 C2 Bolitho Cnwll
393 H3 Bollihope Dur
312 B4 Bollington Ches
312 B4 Bollington Cross Ches
135 G2 Bollow Gloucs
77 E5 Bolney W Susx
195 F3 Bolnhurst Beds
77 F5 Bolnore W Susx
528 D4 Bolshan Angus
315 F5 Bolsover Derbys
328 D5 Bolsterstone Sheff
160 D3 Bolstone Herefs
371 F2 Boltby N York
116 C1 Bolter End Bucks
325 G3 Bolton Bolton
342 C2 Bolton Brad
391 G5 Bolton Cumb
489 G5 Bolton E Loth
359 E4 Bolton E R Yk
443 E2 Bolton Nthumb
355 E4 Bolton Abbey N York
355 E4 Bolton Bridge N York
353 F5 Bolton-by-Bowland Lancs
426 C6 Boltonfellend Cumb
389 F1 Boltongate Cumb
324 C1 Bolton Green Lancs
338 B3 Bolton Houses Lancs
365 G6 Bolton-le-Sands Lancs
399 G6 Bolton Low Houses Cumb
399 G6 Bolton New Houses Cumb
383 G5 Bolton-on-Swale N York
344 C1 Bolton Percy N York
351 G1 Bolton Town End Lancs
329 H4 Bolton upon Dearne Barns
399 H6 Bolton Wood Lane Cumb
342 C2 Bolton Woods Brad
403 G5 Boltshope Park Dur
16 A3 Bolventor Cnwll
431 E3 Bomarsund Nthumb
379 F1 Bomby Cumb
270 B6 Bomere Heath Shrops
487 H6 Bonaly C Edin
576 D5 Bonar Bridge Highld
507 H3 Bonawe Ag & B
333 E1 Bonby N Linc
153 E2 Boncath Pembks
440 A2 Bonchester Bridge Border
37 F5 Bonchurch IoW
136 C1 Bondend Gloucs
274 A6 Bond End Staffs
25 G2 Bondleigh Devon
240 A3 Bondman Hays Leics
351 G6 Bonds Lancs
19 F2 Bonehill Devon
238 B4 Bonehill Staffs
486 C5 Bo'ness Falk
237 F2 Boney Hay Staffs
483 F4 Bonhill W Duns
236 B4 Boningale Shrops
452 B5 Bonjedward Border
468 C3 Bonkle N Lans
379 E5 Bonning Gate Cumb
450 B2 Bonnington C Edin
487 F6 Bonnington Kent
81 F2 Bonnington Kent
501 G4 Bonnybank Fife
485 G3 Bonnybridge Falk
570 F5 Bonnykelly Abers
471 F2 Bonnyrigg Mdloth
559 F3 Bonnyton Abers
513 H2 Bonnyton Angus
529 E3 Bonnyton Angus
445 F2 Bonnyton E Ayrs
515 F2 Bonnyton Smiddy Angus
294 B3 Bonsall Derbys
64 D3 Bonson Somset
159 G6 Bont Mons
265 F6 Bontddu Gwynd
230 D4 Bont Dolgadfan Powys
155 H4 Bont Fawr Carmth
205 F2 Bont-Goch or Elerch Cerdgn
321 E5 Bonthorpe Lincs
181 F1 Bontnewydd Cerdgn
307 E5 Bont-Newydd Conwy
283 E4 Bontnewydd Gwynd
287 F3 Bontuchel Denbgs
105 H5 Bonvilston V Glam
103 G2 Bon-y-Maen Swans
60 D4 Boode Devon
116 D1 Booker Bucks
46 D4 Bookham Dorset
270 D4 Booley Shrops
270 D4 Booleybank Shrops
472 D5 Boon Border
291 G4 Boon Hill Staffs
51 F2 Boorley Green Hants
385 H1 Boosbeck R & Cl
173 H3 Boose's Green Essex
377 F4 Boot Cumb
341 G4 Booth Calder
273 F4 Booth Green
358 A4 Bootham Stray York
311 E2 Booth Bridge N York
354 B5 Booth Bridge N York
298 B3 Boothby Graffoe Lincs
278 D3 Boothby Pagnell Lincs
291 H6 Boothen C Stke
345 G4 Boothferry E R Yk
294 D5 Boothgate Derbys
312 B3 Booth Green Ches
606 F2 Booth of Toft Shet
342 D5 Boothroyd Kirk
290 A1 Boothsdale Ches
325 G3 Boothstown Salfd
342 A4 Boothtown Calder
193 G2 Boothville Nhants
327 F1 Booth Wood Calder
362 B4 Bootle Cumb
323 F5 Bootle Sefton
255 F3 Booton Norfk
311 F5 Booth Green Ches
201 H5 Boot Street Suffk
382 B4 Booze N York

484 A2 Boquhan Stirlg
497 G4 Boquhapple Stirlg
4 C2 Boquio Cnwll
211 E6 Boraston Shrops
211 E5 Boraston Dale Shrops
35 e2 Bordeaux Guern
98 D2 Borden Kent
74 C5 Borden W Susx
399 F4 Border Cumb
213 G2 Bordesley Birm
213 G2 Bordesley Green Birm
470 C5 Bordlands Border
354 B2 Bordley N York
74 B2 Bordon Camp Hants
147 F3 Boreham Essex
87 F6 Boreham Wilts
57 H2 Boreham Street E Susx
144 A5 Borehamwood Herts
424 D1 Boreland D & G
501 F6 Boreland Fife
509 J3 Boreland Stirlg
188 B1 Boreley Worcs
485 F5 Borestone Stirlg
3 c2 Borough IoS
357 E1 Boroughbridge N York
97 E3 Borough Green Kent
116 C4 Borough Marsh Wokham
238 C3 Borough Park Staffs
44 C3 Borough Post Somset
288 D4 Borras Wrexhm
289 E4 Borras Head Wrexhm
542 B6 Borreraig Highld
595 G6 Borrisdale W Isls
542 B7 Borrodale Highld
275 G3 Borrowash Derbys
371 E2 Borrowby N York
386 C1 Borrowby N York
557 E6 Borrowfield Abers
589 J8 Borrowston Highld
486 C3 Borrowstoun Mains Falk
98 A1 Borstal Medway
205 E2 Borth Cerdgn
471 G3 Borthwick Mdloth
438 D2 Borthwickbrae Border
439 E1 Borthwickshiels Border
264 D2 Borth-y-Gest Gwynd
543 G8 Borve Highld
591 D7 Borve W Isls
595 G4 Borve W Isls
366 A5 Borwick Lancs
362 D6 Borwick Rails Cumb
2 C3 Bosavern Cnwll
187 G6 Bosbury Herefs
4 C2 Boscadjack Cnwll
22 B4 Boscastle Cnwll
2 C3 Boscean Cnwll
34 D2 Boscombe Bmouth
70 D2 Boscombe Wilts
236 D2 Boscomoor Staffs
8 C3 Boscoppa Cnwll
3 G3 Boscreege Cnwll
53 E4 Bosham W Susx
53 E4 Bosham Hoe W Susx
125 G6 Bosherston Pembks
2 D3 Boskednan Cnwll
2 D5 Boskenna Cnwll
6 C5 Bosleake Cnwll
292 B1 Bosley Ches
5 D1 Boslowick Cnwll
7 G1 Boslymon Cnwll
2 D2 Bosoughan Cnwll
358 D2 Bossall N York
22 B5 Bossiney Cnwll
100 C6 Bossingham Kent
71 G3 Bossington Hants
100 D4 Bossington Kent
62 D2 Bossington Somset
2 D5 Bostadh W Isls
310 D6 Bostock Green Ches
300 B6 Boston Lincs
300 B6 Boston Lincs
299 E5 Boston Long Hedges Lincs
357 E5 Boston Spa Leeds
300 A5 Boston West Lincs
2 D2 Boswednack Cnwll
4 C2 Boswin Cnwll
8 B5 Boswinger Cnwll
4 C1 Boswyn Cnwll
2 C3 Botallack Cnwll
144 C3 Botany Bay Gt Lon
134 C4 Botany Bay Mons
400 D3 Botcherby Cumb
240 A4 Botcheston Leics
225 E4 Botesdale Suffk
430 D2 Bothal Nthumb
115 G3 Bothampstead W Berk
316 C5 Bothamsall Notts
389 E2 Bothel Cumb
609 J2 Bothen Shet
30 B4 Bothenhampton Dorset
467 G3 Bothwell S Lans
142 D4 Botley Bucks
51 F2 Botley Hants
140 A3 Botley Oxon
161 G4 Botloe's Green Gloucs
167 F5 Botolph Claydon Bucks
55 E3 Botolphs W Susx
565 H4 Bottacks Highld
16 C4 Botternell Cnwll
277 H2 Bottesford Leics
332 B3 Bottesford N Linc
198 A2 Bottisham Cambs
88 D3 Bottlesford Wilts
343 G5 Bottom Boat Wakefd
514 B5 Bottomcraig Fife
292 D4 Bottom House Staffs
341 H6 Bottomley Calder
338 C4 Bottom of Hutton Lancs
325 F2 Bottom O' Th' Moor Bolton
98 D3 Bottom Pond Kent
2 C5 Bottoms Cnwll
386 A4 Botton N York
352 D2 Botton Head Lancs
41 G2 Botteaux Mill Devon
238 C6 Botts Green Warwks
10 D1 Botusfleming Cnwll
262 D4 Botwnnog Gwynd
96 C5 Bough Beech Kent
158 B2 Boughrood Powys
158 B2 Boughrood Brest Powys
134 D5 Boughspring Gloucs
289 F1 Boughton Ches
299 E5 Boughton Lincs
193 G1 Boughton Nhants
247 E4 Boughton Norfk
316 C6 Boughton Notts
99 G5 Boughton Aluph Kent
99 G5 Boughton Corner Kent
98 B4 Boughton Green Kent

289 F1 Boughton Heath Ches
99 G5 Boughton Lees Kent
98 D5 Boughton Malherbe Kent
98 B4 Boughton Monchelsea Kent
99 H3 Boughton Street Kent
168 D2 Bougton End Beds
386 C1 Boulby R & Cl
164 C5 Bould Oxon
341 G5 Boulder Clough Calder
36 B3 Bouldnor IoW
210 C2 Bouldon Shrops
443 H2 Boulmer Nthumb
161 G5 Boulsdon Gloucs
154 D2 Boulston Pembks
554 D2 Boultenstone Abers
318 B6 Boultham Lincs
318 B6 Boultham Moor Lincs
275 F3 Boulton C Derb
275 F3 Boulton Moor C Derb
275 E6 Boundary Derbys
292 C6 Boundary Staffs
92 D6 Boundstone Surrey
196 D3 Bourn Cambs
213 F3 Bournbrook Birm
279 F5 Bourne Lincs
85 E3 Bourne N Som
194 D6 Bourne End Beds
195 E2 Bourne End Beds
117 E2 Bourne End Bucks
143 E3 Bourne End Herts
34 C2 Bournemouth Bmouth
136 D4 Bournes Green Gloucs
123 E2 Bournes Green Sthend
212 D5 Bournes Green Worcs
237 G5 Bourne Vale Wsall
48 D6 Bourne Valley Poole
212 D5 Bournheath Worcs
405 H4 Bournmoor Dur
162 D5 Bournside Gloucs
135 G6 Bournstream Gloucs
213 F3 Bournville Birm
167 F3 Bourton Bucks
68 C3 Bourton Dorset
84 C2 Bourton N Som
113 F2 Bourton Oxon
234 D5 Bourton Shrops
88 B2 Bourton Wilts
215 G5 Bourton on Dunsmore Warwks
164 B3 Bourton-on-the-Hill Gloucs
164 B5 Bourton-on-the-Water Gloucs
444 D2 Bourtreehill N Ayrs
517 H3 Bousd Ag & B
606 B6 Bousta Shet
400 A3 Boustead Hill Cumb
364 D2 Bouth Cumb
369 F5 Bouthwaite N York
189 F3 Bouts Worcs
117 F4 Boveney Bucks
48 D2 Boveridge Dorset
105 F6 Boverton V Glam
19 H2 Bovey Tracey Devon
143 E4 Bovingdon Herts
143 E4 Bovingdon Green Bucks
143 E4 Bovingdon Green Herts
145 H3 Bovinger Essex
33 G2 Bovington Camp Dorset
400 B3 Bow Cumb
13 E1 Bow Devon
25 H2 Bow Devon
119 H3 Bow Gt Lon
139 E6 Bow Oxon
393 F5 Bowbank Dur
224 B4 Bowbeck Suffk
168 B3 Bow Brickhill M Keyn
136 C4 Bowbridge Gloucs
234 A2 Bow Broom Rothm
329 G5 Bow Broom Rothm
395 F2 Bowburn Dur
36 D3 Bowcombe IoW
119 H3 Bow Common Gt Lon
28 B4 Bowd Devon
451 E2 Bowden Border
13 E3 Bowden Devon
68 C5 Bowden Dorset
87 G1 Bowden Hill Wilts
66 C4 Bowdens Somset
380 B4 Bowderdale Cumb
311 F2 Bowdon Traffd
589 G4 Bower Highld
428 B3 Bower Nthumb
109 G5 Bower Ashton Bristl
69 H5 Bowerchalke Wilts
143 G1 Bower Heath Herts
87 G2 Bowerhill Wilts
66 C6 Bower Hinton Somset
450 B5 Bowerhope Border
174 C1 Bower House Tye Suffk
589 G4 Bowermadden Highld
272 B2 Bowers Staffs
122 A2 Bowers Gifford Essex
487 E1 Bowershall Fife
589 G4 Bowertower Highld
382 A2 Bowes Dur
119 G1 Bowes Park Gt Lon
351 G6 Bowgreave Lancs
311 E2 Bowgreen Traffd
451 E4 Bowhill Border
500 D5 Bowhill Fife
468 D3 Bowhousebog or Liquo N Lans
309 F2 Bowing Park Knows
451 G5 Bowismiln Border
22 D6 Bowithick Cnwll
323 G4 Bowker's Green Lancs
451 F1 Bowland Border
365 F2 Bowland Bridge Cumb
111 G4 Bowldown Wilts
326 B3 Bowlee Rochdl
393 F4 Bowlees Dur
59 F2 Bowler's Town E Susx
186 C4 Bowley Herefs
187 F6 Bowley Lane Herefs
186 C4 Bowley Town Herefs
75 E2 Bowlhead Green Surrey
342 C3 Bowling Brad
483 G5 Bowling W Duns
92 C5 Bowling Alley Hants
289 E5 Bowling Bank Wrexhm
8 C2 Bowling Green Cnwll
17 E2 Bowling Green Cnwll
212 D2 Bowling Green Cnwll
137 F4 Bowling Green Dudley
50 B5 Bowling Green Hants
271 E4 Bowling Green Shrops
188 B4 Bowling Green Worcs
85 H6 Bowlish Somset
120 D5 Bowmans Kent
378 A5 Bowmanstead Cumb
476 E5 Bowmore Ag & B
399 G2 Bowness-on-Solway Cumb
378 D5 Bowness-on-Windermere Cumb
501 E2 Bow of Fife Fife
68 D4 Bowridge Hill Dorset
528 B5 Bowriefauld Angus
454 B1 Bowsden Nthumb
116 D4 Bowsey Hill Wokham
451 E1 Bowshank Border
379 F5 Bowston Cumb
205 E3 Bow Street Cerdgn
248 D5 Bow Street Norfk

City, town and village index: Bowthorpe - Broadhaven 675

249 G3 Bowthorpe Norfk
74 B4 Bowyer's Common Hants
136 C4 Box Gloucs
111 E6 Box Wilts
135 G2 Boxbush Gloucs
195 E5 Box End Beds
174 C1 Boxford Suffk
114 C5 Boxford W Berk
53 G3 Boxgrove W Susx
94 D4 Box Hill Surrey
111 E6 Box Hill Wilts
98 B3 Boxley Kent
143 E3 Boxmoor Herts
23 E2 Box's Shop Cnwll
174 C3 Boxted Essex
174 D3 Boxted Essex
199 G4 Boxted Suffk
174 D3 Boxted Cross Essex
214 A5 Box Trees Solhll
111 E1 Boxwell Gloucs
196 D2 Boxworth Cambs
197 E1 Boxworth End Cambs
411 E5 Boyach D & G
72 C5 Boyatt Wood Hants
199 E3 Boyden End Suffk
100 D2 Boyden Gate Kent
225 E3 Boyland Common Norfk
274 B2 Boylestone Derbys
274 B2 Boylestonfield Derbys
569 L3 Boyndie Abers
571 G3 Boyndlie Abers
117 E3 Boyn Hill W & M
375 E6 Boynton E R Yk
528 D5 Boysack Angus
46 C2 Boys Hill Dorset
105 G6 Boys Village V Glam
314 D5 Boythorpe Derbys
23 G4 Boyton Cnwll
202 D5 Boyton Suffk
69 F2 Boyton Wilts
146 D3 Boyton Cross Essex
172 C3 Boyton End Essex
199 E6 Boyton End Suffk
194 C3 Bozeat Nhants
171 F4 Bozen Green Herts
322 e7 Braaid IoM
588 E4 Braal Castle Highld
202 B2 Brabling Green Suffk
81 H1 Brabourne Kent
81 G1 Brabourne Lees Kent
589 J3 Brabster Highld
589 G4 Brabsterdorran Highld
544 E2 Bracadale Highld
531 K4 Bracara Highld
243 F2 Braceborough Lincs
318 B6 Bracebridge Lincs
298 B1 Bracebridge Heath Lincs
279 E2 Braceby Lincs
353 H5 Bracewell Lancs
341 G2 Bracken Bank Brad
392 B6 Brackenber Cumb
367 G5 Brackenbottom N York
294 D3 Brackenfield Derbys
342 B6 Brackenhall Kirk
399 G5 Brackenlands Cumb
389 E5 Brackenthwaite Cumb
400 A5 Brackenthwaite Cumb
356 B4 Brackenthwaite N York
105 E4 Brackla (Bragle) Brdgnd
53 E5 Bracklesham W Susx
533 J6 Brackletter Highld
459 F3 Brackley Ag & B
166 C2 Brackley Nhants
117 E6 Bracknell Br For
588 D4 Brackrevach Highld
498 C3 Braco P & K
569 J5 Bracobrae Moray
331 G3 Bracon N Linc
249 G5 Bracon Ash Norfk
531 K4 Bracorina Highld
24 A4 Bradaford Devon
293 H4 Bradbourne Derbys
395 G4 Bradbury Dur
192 D5 Bradden Nhants
9 F1 Braddock Cnwll
292 A3 Braddocks Hay Staffs
292 A4 Bradeley C Stke
290 A6 Bradeley Green Ches
142 A5 Bradenham Bucks
248 B3 Bradenham Norfk
112 B4 Bradenstoke Wilts
213 E1 Brades Village Sandw
43 E6 Bradfield Devon
175 F3 Bradfield Essex
256 B3 Bradfield Norfk
115 G5 Bradfield W Berk
200 A3 Bradfield Combust Suffk
290 D3 Bradfield Green Ches
175 F3 Bradfield Heath Essex
200 B3 Bradfield St Clare Suffk
200 B3 Bradfield St George Suffk
342 C3 Bradford Brad
15 G3 Bradford Cnwll
293 H2 Bradford Derbys
24 B1 Bradford Devon
326 C5 Bradford Manch
455 E3 Bradford Nthumb
46 A2 Bradford Abbas Dorset
87 E2 Bradford Leigh Wilts
87 E2 Bradford-on-Avon Wilts
43 G3 Bradford-on-Tone Somset
31 E4 Bradford Peverell Dorset
329 G6 Bradgate Rothm
60 D5 Bradiford Devon
37 G3 Brading IoW
293 H5 Bradley Derbys
135 G6 Bradley Gloucs
73 F1 Bradley Hants
342 C5 Bradley Kirk
334 B3 Bradley NE Lin
272 C6 Bradley Staffs
237 E5 Bradley Wolves
288 D4 Bradley Wrexhm
85 E4 Bradley Cross Somset
325 H3 Bradley Fold Bury
135 G6 Bradley Green Gloucs
65 E4 Bradley Green Somset
238 D4 Bradley Green Warwks
189 E2 Bradley Green Worcs
273 F1 Bradley in the Moors Staffs
312 B4 Bradley Mount Ches
109 H3 Bradley Stoke S Glos
161 G2 Bradlow Herefs
276 C3 Bradmore Notts
236 C5 Bradmore Wolves
235 H5 Bradney Shrops
65 F4 Bradney Somset
27 F2 Bradninch Devon
214 C4 Bradnock's Marsh Solhll
292 D3 Bradnop Staffs
185 E3 Bradnor Green Herefs
30 B4 Bradpole Dorset
325 G2 Bradshaw Bolton
342 A4 Bradshaw Calder
327 G2 Bradshaw Kirk
292 B3 Bradshaw Staffs
17 E2 Bradstone Devon
168 A1 Bradville M Keyn
291 E2 Bradwall Green Ches
314 C4 Bradway Sheff
313 G3 Bradwell Derbys
60 C3 Bradwell Devon
173 F5 Bradwell Essex
168 A2 Bradwell M Keyn
168 A2 Bradwell Common M Keyn
138 C3 Bradwell Grove Oxon
313 G3 Bradwell Hills Derbys
148 D3 Bradwell on Sea Essex
148 C3 Bradwell Waterside Essex
38 D5 Bradworthy Devon
566 B4 Brae Highld
572 F7 Brae Highld
575 J3 Brae Highld
606 E4 Brae Shet
576 C8 Braeantra Highld
538 B4 Braedownie Angus
485 F3 Braeface Falk
549 G3 Braefield Highld
565 L5 Braefindon Highld
537 G5 Braegarie Abers
512 B5 Braegrum P & K
410 D2 Braehead D & G
601 J4 Braehead Ork
602 E2 Braehead Ork
444 D5 Braehead S Ayrs
447 G3 Braehead S Lans
467 E3 Braehead S Lans
469 E4 Braehead S Lans
485 G1 Braehead Stirlg
529 E4 Braehead of Lunan Angus
606 B2 Braehoulland Shet
537 H4 Braemar Abers
582 E4 Braemore Highld
578 D7 Brae of Achnahaird Highld
528 D1 Brae of Pert Angus
487 G4 Braepark C Edin
560 D2 Braeside Abers
557 G4 Braeside C Aber
482 B4 Braeside Inver
526 C3 Braes of Coul Angus
574 C5 Braes of Ullapool Highld
603 J4 Braeswick Ork
493 G3 Braevallich Ag & B
606 B2 Braewick Shet
606 D6 Braewick Shet
395 F5 Brafferton Darltn
371 E5 Brafferton N York
194 A3 Brafield-on-the-Green Nhants
598 F5 Bragar W Isls
168 C4 Bragenham Bucks
506 F5 Bragleenmore Ag & B
284 D1 Braichmelyn Gwynd
206 D1 Braichyfedw Powys
351 F4 Braides Lancs
467 F2 Braidfauld C Glas
368 D3 Braidley N York
468 C5 Braidwood S Lans
599 K8 Bràigh na H-Aoidhe W Isls
476 C3 Braigo Ag & B
274 D1 Brailsford Derbys
274 C1 Brailsford Green Derbys
135 F3 Brain's Green Gloucs
173 F5 Braintree Essex
225 F5 Braiseworth Suffk
72 A4 Braishfield Hants
174 C4 Braiswick Essex
341 G1 Braithwaite Brad
389 F5 Braithwaite Cumb
330 D2 Braithwaite Donc
330 B6 Braithwell Donc
605 G8 Brake Shet
248 D3 Brakefield Green Norfk
329 G1 Brakenhill Wakefd
55 E2 Bramber W Susx
47 E4 Bramblecombe Dorset
72 C5 Brambridge Hants
276 B2 Bramcote Notts
215 F2 Bramcote Warwks
276 B2 Bramcote Hills Notts
215 F2 Bramcote Mains Warwks
73 F4 Bramdean Hants
250 B3 Bramerton Norfk
144 C1 Bramfield Herts
227 E5 Bramfield Suffk
236 D6 Bramford Dudley
201 F5 Bramford Suffk
312 A2 Bramhall Stockp
312 B2 Bramhall Moor Stockp
312 A2 Bramhall Park Stockp
357 E6 Bramham Leeds
356 B6 Bramhope Leeds
315 E4 Bramley Derbys
91 G3 Bramley Hants
342 D3 Bramley Leeds
330 A6 Bramley Rothm
93 G6 Bramley Surrey
91 G3 Bramley Corner Hants
91 H3 Bramley Green Hants
355 F3 Bramley Head N York
295 F1 Bramley Vale Derbys
100 D4 Bramling Kent
27 E3 Brampford Speke Devon
220 A5 Brampton Cambs
391 H5 Brampton Cumb
401 F2 Brampton Cumb
314 D5 Brampton Derbys
317 F4 Brampton Lincs
255 H3 Brampton Norfk
329 G4 Brampton Rothm
227 E3 Brampton Suffk
161 E4 Brampton Abbotts Herefs
217 G2 Brampton Ash Nhants
209 G5 Brampton Bryan Herefs
315 F2 Brampton en le Morthen Rothm
220 B5 Brampton Park Cambs
227 E3 Brampton Street Suffk
273 G3 Bramshall Staffs
49 H1 Bramshaw Hants
92 B2 Bramshill Hants
74 C3 Bramshott Hants
66 C4 Bramwell Somset
518 D2 Branault Highld
97 G5 Branbridges Kent
259 F3 Brancaster Norfk
259 F3 Brancaster Staithe Norfk
395 E2 Brancepeth Dur
404 C2 Branch End Nthumb
567 K6 Branchill Moray
482 B5 Branchton Inver
300 C5 Brand End Lincs
568 C1 Branderburgh Moray
361 E5 Brandesburton E R Yk
202 B2 Brandeston Suffk
161 G4 Brand Green Gloucs
161 H1 Brand Green Herefs
209 H4 Brandhill Shrops
24 B2 Brandis Corner Devon
63 E2 Brandish Street Somset
255 F3 Brandiston Norfk
388 D4 Brandlingill Cumb
395 E2 Brandon Dur
297 H5 Brandon Lincs
442 C1 Brandon Nthumb
223 F2 Brandon Suffk
215 G4 Brandon Warwks
222 C2 Brandon Bank Norfk
222 C1 Brandon Creek Norfk
249 E3 Brandon Parva Norfk
372 A5 Brandsby N York
117 H4 Brands Hill Slough
270 B4 Brandwood Shrops
213 G4 Brandwood End Birm
343 F5 Brandy Carr Wakefd
147 G5 Brandy Hole Essex
333 E5 Brandy Wharf Lincs
2 D4 Brane Cnwll
172 D4 Bran End Essex
383 G1 Branksome Darltn
34 C2 Branksome Poole
34 C2 Branksome Park Poole
72 B1 Bransbury Hants
317 G4 Bransby Lincs
28 C5 Branscombe Devon
188 A4 Bransford Worcs
49 F5 Bransgore Hants
498 D6 Branshill Clacks
347 G3 Bransholme C KuH
213 G5 Branson's Cross Worcs
277 H4 Branston Leics
318 C6 Branston Lincs
274 C5 Branston Staffs
318 D6 Branston Booths Lincs
37 E4 Branstone IoW
388 A6 Bransty Cumb
297 H4 Brant Broughton Lincs
175 F3 Brantham Suffk
388 C5 Branthwaite Cumb
389 G2 Branthwaite Cumb
388 C5 Branthwaite Edge Cumb
346 D4 Brantingham E R Yk
330 D4 Branton Donc
442 C1 Branton Nthumb
357 E2 Branton Green N York
439 F2 Branxholme Border
453 G2 Branxton Nthumb
239 G4 Brascote Leics
290 A2 Brassey Green Ches
294 A4 Brassington Derbys
96 C3 Brasted Kent
96 C4 Brasted Chart Kent
556 B5 Brathens Abers
301 E2 Bratoft Lincs
80 D3 Brattle Kent
318 A3 Brattleby Lincs
63 E2 Bratton Somset
87 G4 Bratton Wilts
235 E2 Bratton Wrekin
24 C4 Bratton Clovelly Devon
61 F4 Bratton Fleming Devon
68 A4 Bratton Seymour Somset
171 E5 Braughing Herts
171 F5 Braughing Friars Herts
298 C4 Brauncewell Lincs
192 B1 Braunston Nhants
240 C4 Braunstone Town Leics
242 A3 Braunston-in-Rutland Rutlnd
60 C4 Braunton Devon
372 D4 Brawby N York
385 E3 Brawith N York
587 H3 Brawl Highld
588 D5 Brawlbin Highld
117 F4 Bray W & M
217 G3 Braybrooke Nhants
112 B2 Braydon Side Wilts
61 G5 Brayford Devon
61 G5 Brayfordhill Devon
16 D4 Bray Shop Cnwll
376 C3 Braystones Cumb
188 B5 Brayswick Worcs
356 A5 Braythorn N York
345 E3 Brayton N York
33 E2 Braytown Dorset
117 E4 Bray Wick W & M
117 E4 Braywoodside W & M
23 F4 Brazacott Cnwll
272 C5 Brazenhill Staffs
6 C5 Brea Cnwll
86 A2 Breach BaNES
98 C1 Breach Kent
52 D3 Breach W Susx
169 H5 Breachwood Green Herts
598 C7 Breacleit W Isls
270 A2 Breaden Heath Shrops
275 F2 Breadsall Derbys
275 F2 Breadsall Hilltop C Derb
135 G4 Breadstone Gloucs
136 B3 Bread Street Gloucs
4 B3 Breage Cnwll
565 H8 Breakachy Highld
18 C6 Brealeys Devon
135 E3 Bream Gloucs
70 D6 Breamore Hants
134 D3 Bream's Meend Gloucs
84 A3 Brean Somset
596 B2 Breanais W Isls
356 C2 Brearton N York
598 E7 Breascleit W Isls
598 E7 Breasclete W Isls
275 H3 Breaston Derbys
154 D3 Brechfa Carmth
528 D2 Brechin Angus
248 B6 Breckles Norfk
602 D8 Breck of Cruan Ork
543 J4 Breckrey Highld
315 F1 Brecks Rothm
157 H4 Brecon Powys
312 B1 Bredbury Stockp
312 B1 Bredbury Green Stockp
58 D3 Brede E Susx
187 E3 Bredenbury Herefs
202 B4 Bredfield Suffk
98 D2 Bredgar Kent
98 B2 Bredhurst Kent
162 D2 Bredon Worcs
162 D2 Bredon's Hardwick Worcs
162 D2 Bredon's Norton Worcs
185 F6 Bredwardine Herefs
275 G5 Breedon on the Hill Leics
146 D2 Breeds Essex
337 F1 Breedy Butts Lancs
599 K7 Breibhig W Isls
591 D8 Brèibhig W Isls
469 F2 Breich W Loth
325 G3 Breightmet Bolton
345 G3 Breighton E R Yk
160 B1 Breinton Common Herefs
605 H1 Breiwick Shet
160 D5 Breiston Green Herefs
111 H5 Bremhill Wilts
111 H5 Bremhill Wick Wilts
605 H5 Bremirehoull Shet
566 D1 Brenachie Highld
79 F1 Brenchley Kent
493 H4 Brenchoillie Ag & B
23 H1 Brendon Devon
39 E5 Brendon Devon
62 B2 Brendon Devon
596 B2 Brenish W Isls
430 D5 Brenkley N u Ty
9 G3 Brent Cnwll
200 B5 Brent Eleigh Suffk
118 D4 Brentford Gt Lon
277 G6 Brentingby Leics
84 B4 Brent Knoll Somset
19 E6 Brent Mill Devon
171 F3 Brent Pelham Herts
109 G4 Brentry Bristl
146 C6 Brentwood Essex
81 E4 Brenzett Kent
81 F4 Brenzett Green Kent
237 G1 Brereton Staffs
237 G1 Brereton Cross Staffs
291 F2 Brereton Green Ches
291 F2 Brereton Heath Ches
237 F1 Breretonhill Staffs
225 E3 Bressingham Norfk
225 E3 Bressingham Common Norfk
274 D5 Bretby Derbys
215 G4 Bretford Warwks
189 G6 Bretforton Worcs
379 G3 Bretherdale Head Cumb
338 C5 Bretherton Lancs
607 G6 Brettabister Shet
224 B3 Brettenham Norfk
200 C4 Brettenham Suffk
243 H4 Bretton C Pete
313 H4 Bretton Derbys
289 E2 Bretton Flints
172 B5 Brewer's End Essex
225 F3 Brewers Green Norfk
95 G4 Brewer Street Surrey
526 A2 Brewlands Bridge Angus
236 C3 Brewood Staffs
47 F6 Briantspuddle Dorset
193 F3 Briar Hill Nhants
172 B4 Brick End Essex
144 D3 Brickendon Herts
143 G4 Bricket Wood Herts
188 C3 Brickfields Worcs
195 E4 Brickhill Beds
93 G2 Brick Hill Surrey
171 G4 Brick House End Essex
291 F2 Brickhouses Ches
314 C3 Brick Houses Sheff
296 A3 Brick-Kiln End Notts
173 E3 Brickkiln Green Essex
163 E1 Bricklehampton Worcs
322 h2 Bride IoM
388 D3 Bridekirk Cumb
152 D1 Bridell Pembks
24 D5 Bridestowe Devon
558 D2 Brideswell Abers
26 C5 Bridford Devon
26 C5 Bridfordmills Devon
4 D3 Bridge Cnwll
6 C5 Bridge Cnwll
100 C5 Bridge Kent
29 G1 Bridge Somset
62 A2 Bridge Ball Devon
195 E4 Bridge End Beds
400 C5 Bridge End Cumb
12 B3 Bridge End Devon
28 A5 Bridge End Devon
393 H2 Bridge End Dur
172 D3 Bridge End Essex
288 D3 Bridge End Flints
187 E5 Bridge End Herefs
279 G2 Bridge End Lincs
403 G1 Bridge End Nthumb
403 G2 Bridge End Nthumb
140 C6 Bridge End Oxon
605 G4 Bridge End Shet
94 B3 Bridge End Surrey
190 D2 Bridge End Warwks
162 B3 Bridge End Worcs
557 F2 Bridgefield C Aber
554 D4 Bridgefoot Abers
514 B2 Bridgefoot Angus
388 C4 Bridgefoot Cumb
171 G2 Bridge Green Essex
225 F3 Bridge Green Norfk
67 F5 Bridgehampton Somset
370 C5 Bridge Hewick N York
404 C4 Bridgehill Dur
312 D3 Bridgeholm Green Derbys
355 F1 Bridgehouse Gate N York
451 F3 Bridgelands Border
51 G4 Bridgemary Hants
291 E5 Bridgemere Ches
312 C3 Bridgemont Derbys
558 C2 Bridgend Abers
459 F4 Bridgend Ag & B
476 E4 Bridgend Ag & B
493 E6 Bridgend Ag & B
527 E5 Bridgend Angus
539 G6 Bridgend Angus
104 D3 Bridgend Brdgnd
178 D4 Bridgend Cerdgn
9 E2 Bridgend Cnwll
378 D2 Bridgend Cumb
11 G4 Bridgend Devon
502 B2 Bridgend Fife
136 A4 Bridgend Gloucs
482 C4 Bridgend Inver
553 H2 Bridgend Moray
484 D5 Bridgend N Lans
486 D4 Bridgend W Loth
526 C4 Bridgend of Lintrathen Angus
486 D3 Bridgeness Falk
555 G1 Bridge of Alford Abers
498 C5 Bridge of Allan Stirlg
552 D1 Bridge of Avon Moray
552 D4 Bridge of Avon Moray
507 H4 Bridge of Awe Ag & B
523 G6 Bridge of Balgie P & K
551 L5 Bridge of Brown Highld
525 H5 Bridge of Cally P & K
556 B5 Bridge of Canny Abers
526 C4 Bridge of Craigisla Angus
412 D2 Bridge of Dee D & G
557 G2 Bridge of Don C Aber
529 E3 Bridge of Dun Angus
540 C2 Bridge of Dye Abers
512 D6 Bridge of Earn P & K
522 F4 Bridge of Ericht P & K
556 C6 Bridge of Feugh Abers
588 C3 Bridge of Forss Highld
554 C5 Bridge of Gairn Abers
522 F4 Bridge of Gaur P & K
541 G1 Bridge of Muchalls Abers
508 D2 Bridge of Orchy Ag & B
524 C2 Bridge of Tilt P & K
568 F3 Bridge of Tynet Moray
606 C7 Bridge of Walls Shet
466 A1 Bridge of Weir Rens
40 D5 Bridge Reeve Devon
23 F2 Bridgerule Devon
8 C2 Bridges Cnwll
233 G5 Bridges Shrops
159 H1 Bridge Sollers Herefs
199 H5 Bridge Street Suffk
467 F2 Bridgeton C Glas
23 G5 Bridgetown Cnwll
19 H5 Bridgetown Devon
63 E5 Bridgetown Somset
190 C4 Bridge Town Warwks
309 G5 Bridge Trafford Ches
110 B5 Bridge Yate S Glos
224 C2 Bridgham Norfk
235 G6 Bridgnorth Shrops
237 E3 Bridgtown Staffs
65 E4 Bridgwater Somset
361 F1 Bridlington E R Yk
30 A4 Bridport Dorset
160 D5 Bridstow Herefs
340 C2 Brierfield Lancs
331 E2 Brierholme Carr Donc
329 G2 Brierley Barns
135 E1 Brierley Gloucs
186 B3 Brierley Herefs
212 D2 Brierley Hill Dudley
396 C4 Brierton Hartpl
389 G5 Briery Cumb
132 C3 Briery Hill Blae G
328 C1 Briestfield Kirk
366 C1 Brigflatts Cumb
333 E3 Brigg N Linc
256 C4 Briggate Norfk
387 E3 Briggswath N York
388 C3 Brigham Cumb
389 G5 Brigham Cumb
360 D4 Brigham E R Yk
342 B5 Brighouse Calder
36 C4 Brighstone IoW
294 B3 Brightgate Derbys
139 F4 Brighthampton Oxon
328 D6 Brightholmlee Sheff
25 E3 Brightley Devon
79 F5 Brightling E Susx
175 E6 Brightlingsea Essex
55 G4 Brighton Br & H
7 G3 Brighton Cnwll
91 G5 Brighton Hill Hants
323 E5 Brighton le Sands Sefton
486 B4 Brightons Falk
314 D2 Brightside Sheff
114 C4 Brightwalton W Berk
114 C4 Brightwalton Green W Berk
114 C4 Brightwalton Holt W Berk
202 B6 Brightwell Suffk
140 D6 Brightwell Baldwin Oxon
115 F1 Brightwell-cum-Sotwell Oxon
89 E5 Brigmerston Wilts
382 C2 Brignall Dur
496 D3 Brig O' Turk Stirlg
334 C4 Brigsley NE Lin
365 G2 Brigsteer Cumb
218 C2 Brigstock Nhants
141 E2 Brill Bucks
4 D3 Brill Cnwll
185 E5 Brilley Herefs
185 E4 Brilley Mountain Powys
151 F4 Brimaston Pembks
210 C6 Brimfield Herefs
315 E5 Brimington Derbys
315 E5 Brimington Common Derbys
19 G2 Brimley Devon
29 F2 Brimley Devon
136 D2 Brimpsfield Gloucs
161 F6 Brimps Hill Gloucs
91 F2 Brimpton W Berk
91 F2 Brimpton Common W Berk
600 D7 Brims Ork
136 C4 Brimscombe Gloucs
145 E5 Brimsdown Gt Lon
308 C3 Brimstage Wirral
314 C2 Brincliffe Sheff
345 G3 Brind E R Yk
67 E1 Brindham Somset
605 H3 Brindister Shet
606 C6 Brindister Shet
339 E5 Brindle Lancs
326 B4 Brindle Heath Salfd
290 B4 Brindley Ches
292 A4 Brindley Ford C Stke
314 C4 Brindwoodgate Derbys
236 B2 Brineton Staffs
210 B5 Bringewood Forge Herefs
218 A1 Bringhurst Leics
187 F3 Bringsty Common Herefs
219 F4 Brington Cambs
602 E6 Brinian Ork
260 D5 Brininngham Norfk
320 C5 Brinkhill Lincs
198 C4 Brinkley Cambs
296 D4 Brinkley Notts
160 D3 Brinkley Hill Herefs
168 C2 Brinklow M Keyn
215 G4 Brinklow Warwks
112 B3 Brinkworth Wilts
312 B1 Brinnington Stockp
339 F5 Brinscall Lancs
84 D4 Brinscombe Somset
84 D2 Brinsea N Som
236 D4 Brinsford Staffs
295 F5 Brinsley Notts
186 A6 Brinsop Herefs
186 A6 Brinsop Common Herefs
315 E1 Brinsworth Rothm
62 A5 Brinsworthy Devon
260 D4 Brinton Norfk
400 D4 Brisco Cumb
376 C2 Briscoe Cumb
356 B4 Briscoerigg N York
254 C3 Brisley Norfk
109 H5 Brislington Bristl
80 D2 Brissenden Green Kent
213 E2 Bristnall Fields Sandw
109 G4 Bristol Bristl
261 E5 Briston Norfk
110 D2 Britain Bottom S Glos
340 D5 Britannia Lancs
70 D4 Britford Wilts
132 B4 Brithdir Caerph
179 G4 Brithdir Cerdgn
266 B6 Brithdir Gwynd
42 D5 Brithem Bottom Devon
132 D4 Brithish Torfn
130 A5 Briton Ferry Neath
86 B3 Britten's BaNES
117 F3 Britwell Slough
141 E6 Britwell Salome Oxon
13 G1 Brixham Torbay
11 G3 Brixton Devon
119 G4 Brixton Gt Lon
69 E2 Brixton Deverill Wilts
217 F5 Brixworth Nhants
139 E3 Brize Norton Oxon
212 C6 Broad Alley Worcs
113 E1 Broad Blunsdon Swindn
327 E6 Broadbottom Tamesd
53 E3 Broadbridge W Susx
76 B3 Broadbridge Heath W Susx
113 E1 Broadbush Swindn
164 B2 Broad Campden Gloucs
70 A4 Broad Chalke Wilts
340 D5 Broad Clough Lancs
27 F3 Broadclyst Devon
144 A4 Broad Colney Herts
212 C6 Broad Common Worcs
482 D5 Broadfield Inver
338 D5 Broadfield Lancs
340 A4 Broadfield Lancs
126 C4 Broadfield Pembks
326 B2 Broadfield Rochdl
77 E3 Broadfield W Susx
545 L5 Broadford Highld
79 G2 Broad Ford Kent
93 G5 Broadford Surrey
76 A5 Broadford Bridge W Susx
437 G2 Broadgairhill Border
72 B5 Broadgate Hants
200 C2 Broadgrass Green Suffk
194 D6 Broad Green Beds
198 D3 Broad Green Cambs
171 F2 Broad Green Essex
174 A5 Broad Green Essex
95 G1 Broad Green Gt Lon
309 F1 Broad Green Lpool
199 F3 Broad Green Suffk
201 E3 Broad Green Suffk
187 H3 Broad Green Worcs
213 E5 Broad Green Worcs
144 D3 Broadgreen Wood Herts
326 C2 Broadhalgh Rochdl
96 A4 Broadham Green Surrey
439 F3 Broadhaugh Border
589 K6 Broadhaven Highld

676 City, town and village index: Broad Haven - Bulphan

124 D2 Broad Haven Pembks
185 F2 Broad Heath Powys
272 C4 Broad Heath Staffs
311 F2 Broadheath Traffd
187 F2 Broad Heath Worcs
28 B2 Broadhembury Devon
19 H4 Broadhempston Devon
222 B4 Broad Hill Cambs
112 C4 Broad Hinton Wilts
294 C5 Broadholm Derbys
317 G5 Broadholme Lincs
359 F4 Broad Ings E R Yk
58 D3 Broadland Row E Susx
20 A3 Broadlands Devon
4 B2 Broadlane Cnwll
6 C5 Broad Lane Cnwll
212 A2 Broad Lanes Shrops
127 H3 Broadlay Carmth
90 C2 Broad Layings Hants
326 C1 Broadley Lancs
568 F3 Broadley Moray
145 F3 Broadley Common Essex
190 A5 Broad Marston Worcs
32 C2 Broadmayne Dorset
451 E3 Broadmeadows Border
91 G5 Broadmere Hants
126 B3 Broadmoor Pembks
94 C5 Broadmoor Surrey
161 E2 Broadmoor Common Herefs
188 B4 Broadmore Green Worcs
155 E5 Broad Oak Carmth
377 E6 Broad Oak Cumb
27 H4 Broad Oak Devon
30 A3 Broadoak Dorset
47 E2 Broad Oak Dorset
58 D2 Broad Oak E Susx
79 E5 Broad Oak E Susx
135 G2 Broadoak Gloucs
51 E2 Broadoak Hants
92 C4 Broad Oak Hants
160 B5 Broad Oak Herefs
81 F2 Broad Oak Kent
100 C3 Broad Oak Kent
212 A2 Broad Oak Shrops
234 B1 Broadoak Shrops
324 C5 Broad Oak St Hel
289 E3 Broadoak Wrexhm
144 C2 Broadoak End Herts
325 H4 Broadoak Park Salfd
39 E3 Broad Parkham Devon
116 B3 Broadplat Oxon
134 C5 Broadrock Gloucs
13 F1 Broadsands Torbay
571 H2 Broadsea Abers
146 D2 Broad's Green Essex
88 A1 Broad's Green Wilts
45 E5 Broadshard Somset
101 H2 Broadstairs Kent
98 D5 Broadstone Kent
134 C4 Broadstone Mons
48 B5 Broadstone Poole
210 C2 Broadstone Shrops
59 E3 Broad Street E Susx
81 H1 Broad Street Kent
82 C2 Broad Street Kent
98 C3 Broad Street Kent
122 B5 Broad Street Medway
200 C6 Broad Street Suffk
88 C3 Broad Street Wilts
108 C3 Broadstreet Common Newpt
147 H3 Broad Street Green Essex
80 C3 Broad Tenterden Kent
112 C4 Broad Town Wilts
187 H4 Broadwas Worcs
170 C5 Broadwater Herts
54 D4 Broadwater W Susx
78 D2 Broadwater Down Kent
212 B4 Broadwaters Worcs
401 E3 Broadwath Cumb
127 G2 Broadway Carmth
128 A3 Broadway Carmth
125 E2 Broadway Pembks
44 C4 Broadway Somset
226 D4 Broadway Suffk
163 G2 Broadway Worcs
160 C3 Broadway Lands Herefs
134 D2 Broadwell Gloucs
163 G4 Broadwell Gloucs
138 D4 Broadwell Oxon
191 H1 Broadwell Warwks
31 F6 Broadwey Dorset
30 A2 Broadwindsor Dorset
25 F1 Broadwoodkelly Devon
24 B5 Broadwoodwidger Devon
185 F6 Brobury Herefs
599 M7 Brocair W Isls
543 K7 Brochel Highld
507 H3 Brochroy Ag & B
338 D1 Brock Lancs
187 H4 Brockamin Worcs
73 F6 Brockbridge Hants
225 H4 Brockdish Norfk
212 C5 Brockencote Worcs
50 B4 Brockenhurst Hants
447 G2 Brocketsbrae S Lans
29 E1 Brockfield Devon
201 F1 Brockford Green Suffk
201 F1 Brockford Street Suffk
192 D2 Brockhall Nhants
339 H2 Brockhall Village Lancs
94 D5 Brockham Surrey
110 C6 Brockham End BaNES
94 D5 Brockham Park Surrey
162 D4 Brockhampton Gloucs
163 F5 Brockhampton Gloucs
52 C3 Brockhampton Hants
160 D3 Brockhampton Herefs
46 C3 Brockhampton Green Dorset
450 D5 Brockhill Border
147 E5 Brock Hill Essex
328 A2 Brockholes Kirk
135 E3 Brockhollands Gloucs
294 C2 Brockhurst Derbys
51 G4 Brockhurst Hants
215 H3 Brockhurst Warwks
424 A5 Brocklehirst D & G
333 G2 Brocklesby Lincs
119 H5 Brockley Gt Lon
85 E1 Brockley N Som
223 G5 Brockley Corner Suffk
199 E5 Brockley Green Suffk
199 G4 Brockley Green Suffk
390 D2 Brockleymoor Cumb
186 C3 Brockmanton Herefs
212 D2 Brockmoor Dudley
24 C4 Brockscombe Devon
91 E2 Brock's Green Hants
249 F6 Brock's Watering Norfk
209 F2 Brockton Shrops
233 F4 Brockton Shrops
234 D6 Brockton Shrops
235 G4 Brockton Shrops
272 B3 Brockton Staffs
235 G1 Brockton Wrekin
134 C4 Brockweir Gloucs
63 E3 Brockwell Somset
136 C1 Brockworth Gloucs
15 E5 Brocton Cnwll
273 E6 Brocton Staffs
461 E2 Brodick N Ayrs
569 K3 Brodiesord Abers
330 A3 Brodsworth Donc
543 H3 Brogaig Highld
168 D2 Brogborough Beds
201 G6 Broke Hall Suffk
111 G2 Brokenborough Wilts
310 D5 Broken Cross Ches
312 A5 Broken Cross Ches
171 F5 Broken Green Herts
87 E4 Brokerswood Wilts
383 E5 Brokes N York
104 B2 Brombil Neath
309 E3 Bromborough Wirral
308 D3 Bromborough Pool Wirral
211 E3 Bromdon Shrops
225 F4 Brome Suffk
161 G3 Bromesberrow Gloucs
161 G3 Bromesberrow Heath Gloucs
225 G4 Brome Street Suffk
202 B4 Bromeswell Suffk
399 F5 Bromfield Cumb
210 B4 Bromfield Shrops
213 H1 Bromford Birm
195 E4 Bromham Beds
87 H1 Bromham Wilts
329 E5 Bromley Barns
212 D2 Bromley Dudley
119 H3 Bromley Gt Lon
120 B6 Bromley Gt Lon
171 F5 Bromley Herts
235 G5 Bromley Shrops
269 G4 Bromley Shrops
96 B1 Bromley Common Gt Lon
325 G2 Bromley Cross Bolton
175 E4 Bromley Cross Essex
81 E2 Bromley Green Kent
272 A3 Bromley Hall Staffs
110 A4 Bromley Heath S Glos
120 A6 Bromley Park Gt Lon
273 H5 Bromley Wood Staffs
233 F4 Bromlow Shrops
119 F4 Brompton Gt Lon
122 B6 Brompton Medway
374 A3 Brompton N York
384 B5 Brompton N York
234 C3 Brompton Shrops
374 A3 Brompton-by-Sawdon N York
383 F5 Brompton-on-Swale N York
64 A5 Brompton Ralph Somset
63 F5 Brompton Regis Somset
161 E5 Bromsash Herefs
213 E5 Bromsgrove Worcs
272 B6 Bromstead Common Staffs
101 G2 Bromstone Kent
187 E4 Bromyard Herefs
187 F3 Bromyard Downs Herefs
265 G3 Bronaber Gwynd
181 F1 Bronant Cerdgn
210 C2 Broncroft Shrops
119 E3 Brondesbury Gt Lon
119 E3 Brondesbury Park Gt Lon
207 G2 Broneirion Powys
179 G4 Brongest Cerdgn
179 F5 Brongwyn Cerdgn
270 B2 Bronington Wrexhm
158 B2 Bronllys Powys
179 G5 Bronwydd Cerdgn
154 B5 Bronwydd Arms Carmth
184 D5 Bronydd Powys
269 E2 Bronygarth Shrops
127 F3 Brook Carmth
17 G4 Brook Devon
26 C4 Brook Devon
50 A2 Brook Hants
71 G4 Brook Hants
36 B4 Brook IoW
99 H6 Brook Kent
75 E2 Brook Surrey
94 B5 Brook Surrey
312 C2 Brook Bottom Derbys
338 D1 Brook Bottom Lancs
327 E4 Brook Bottom Tamesd
250 B5 Brooke Norfk
242 A3 Brooke Rutlnd
334 B5 Brookenby Lincs
195 F2 Brook End Beds
195 H5 Brook End Beds
219 F5 Brook End Cambs
134 D5 Brookend Gloucs
135 F4 Brookend Gloucs
170 D4 Brook End Herts
194 C6 Brook End M Keyn
165 E5 Brookend Oxon
111 E3 Brook End Wilts
188 C5 Brook End Worcs
327 F5 Brookfield Derbys
339 E3 Brookfield Lancs
384 D1 Brookfield Middsb
466 B2 Brookfield Rens
342 B5 Brookfoot Calder
36 B4 Brookgreen IoW
199 H3 Brook Green Suffk
140 D5 Brookhampton Oxon
210 D2 Brookhampton Shrops
67 G4 Brookhampton Somset
49 H2 Brook Hill Hants
276 C3 Brook Hill Notts
339 G4 Brookhouse Bl w D
341 H4 Brookhouse Calder
312 B4 Brookhouse Ches
287 F1 Brookhouse Denbgs
352 A2 Brookhouse Lancs
315 G2 Brookhouse Rothm
291 G2 Brookhouse Green Ches
312 D2 Brookhouses Derbys
292 C6 Brookhouses Staffs
308 D3 Brookhurst Wirral
19 F5 Brooking Devon
81 E4 Brookland Kent
343 F2 Brooklands Leeds
270 C1 Brooklands Shrops
94 B2 Brooklands Surrey
311 F1 Brooklands Traffd
27 F3 Brookleigh Devon
144 B4 Brookmans Park Herts
54 B4 Brookpits W Susx
93 G2 Brook Place Surrey
211 E5 Brookrow Shrops
9 F1 Brooks Cnwll
232 B5 Brooks Powys
326 A1 Brooksbottoms Bury
241 E1 Brooksby Leics
101 E2 Brooks End Kent
76 B4 Brooks Green W Susx
117 F5 Brookside Br For
314 C5 Brookside Derbys
235 F3 Brookside Wrekin
146 B6 Brook Street Essex
80 D3 Brook Street Kent
97 E5 Brook Street Kent
199 G5 Brook Street Suffk
77 F4 Brook Street W Susx
136 B2 Brookthorpe Gloucs
310 A3 Brookvale Halton
247 E5 Brookville Norfk
69 F5 Brook Waters Wilts
93 F3 Brookwood Surrey
195 H6 Broom Beds
391 H5 Broom Cumb
29 F2 Broom Dorset
466 D3 Broom E Rens
501 G4 Broom Fife
126 C3 Broom Pembks
315 E1 Broom Rothm
189 G4 Broom Warwks
211 F5 Broombank Worcs
226 C1 Broome Norfk
209 H3 Broome Shrops
234 C5 Broome Shrops
212 D4 Broome Worcs
311 E2 Broomedge Warrtn
443 E2 Broome Park Nthumb
76 B5 Broomer's Corner W Susx
75 H6 Broomershill W Susx
560 D3 Broomfield Abers
400 B5 Broomfield Cumb
146 D2 Broomfield Essex
98 C4 Broomfield Kent
100 C2 Broomfield Kent
64 D5 Broomfield Somset
111 F4 Broomfield Wilts
269 H6 Broomfields Shrops
346 C4 Broomfleet E R Yk
254 C3 Broom Green Norfk
290 C5 Broomhall Ches
93 G1 Broomhall W & M
290 C5 Broomhall Green Ches
57 E2 Broomham E Susx
404 B2 Broomhaugh Nthumb
451 F4 Broomhill Border
110 A4 Broomhill Bristl
110 A5 Broom Hill Bristl
309 G6 Broomhill Ches
48 C4 Broom Hill Dorset
404 D4 Broom Hill Dur
96 C1 Broom Hill Gt Lon
566 C2 Broomhill Highld
100 D4 Broomhill Kent
246 C4 Broomhill Norfk
295 G5 Broomhill Notts
443 G4 Broomhill Nthumb
202 B5 Broom Hill Suffk
212 D4 Broom Hill Worcs
78 D1 Broomhill Bank Kent
256 C3 Broomholm Norfk
467 G2 Broomhouse C Glas
444 D2 Broomlands N Ayrs
404 B2 Broomley Nthumb
395 E1 Broompark Dur
485 F1 Broomridge Stirlg
199 F1 Broom's Barn Suffk
161 G3 Broom's Green Gloucs
58 D4 Broomsgrove E Susx
253 G2 Broomsthorpe Norfk
99 G2 Broom Street Kent
160 B2 Broomy Hill Herefs
293 E5 Broomyshaw Staffs
577 K3 Brora Highld
235 F4 Broseley Shrops
125 G4 Brotherhill Pembks
244 C1 Brotherhouse Bar Lincs
162 B1 Brotheridge Green Worcs
393 F2 Brotherlee Dur
299 H5 Brothertoft Lincs
344 B4 Brotherton N York
400 B6 Brothybeck Cumb
397 G6 Brotton R & Cl
588 C4 Broubster Highld
380 D2 Brough Cumb
313 G3 Brough Derbys
346 D4 Brough E R Yk
589 G2 Brough Highld
297 F3 Brough Notts
602 C8 Brough Ork
605 K2 Brough Shet
606 F2 Brough Shet
607 G7 Brough Shet
607 H2 Brough Shet
607 J5 Brough Shet
609 G4 Brough Shet
270 D1 Broughall Shrops
380 D2 Brough Sowerby Cumb
449 E2 Broughton Border
142 A2 Broughton Bucks
488 B5 Broughton C Edin
220 C4 Broughton Cambs
288 D2 Broughton Flints
71 G3 Broughton Hants
338 D2 Broughton Lancs
168 B2 Broughton M Keyn
332 D3 Broughton N Linc
354 B4 Broughton N York
373 E5 Broughton N York
218 A4 Broughton Nhants
602 E2 Broughton Ork
165 G2 Broughton Oxon
212 B1 Broughton Shrops
271 H3 Broughton Staffs
105 E5 Broughton V Glam
240 B6 Broughton Astley Leics
364 C3 Broughton Beck Cumb
332 D2 Broughton Common N Linc
388 C3 Broughton Cross Cumb
87 F2 Broughton Gifford Wilts
189 E2 Broughton Green Worcs
188 D4 Broughton Hackett Worcs
363 E4 Broughton in Furness Cumb
277 F5 Broughton Lodges Leics
363 E3 Broughton Mills Cumb
388 C3 Broughton Moor Cumb
326 B4 Broughton Park Salfd
138 C4 Broughton Poggs Oxon
603 K3 Broughtown Ork
514 D3 Broughty Ferry C Dund
365 E3 Brow Edge Cumb
400 A2 Browhouses D & G
606 C7 Browland Shet
355 H4 Brown Bank N York
380 C3 Brownber Cumb
57 H1 Brownbread Street E Susx
73 E2 Brown Candover Hants
291 F2 Brownedge Ches
323 G2 Brown Edge Lancs
324 B6 Brown Edge St Hel
292 A4 Brown Edge Staffs
289 G2 Brown Heath Ches
43 F4 Brownheath Devon
51 F1 Brown Heath Hants
270 B4 Brownheath Shrops
188 C2 Brownheath Common Worcs
560 C1 Brownhill Abers
339 G3 Brownhill Bl w D
269 G5 Brownhill Shrops
503 E1 Brownhills Fife
271 F2 Brownhills Shrops
237 G3 Brownhills Wsall
455 F5 Brownieside Nthumb
91 F3 Browninghill Green Hants
289 G4 Brown Knowl Ches
291 H3 Brown Lees Staffs
291 G2 Brownlow Ches
324 C4 Brownlow Wigan
325 F2 Brownlow Fold Bolton
291 G2 Brownlow Heath Ches
343 G3 Brown Moor Leeds
290 C6 Brown's Bank Ches
161 G3 Brown's End Gloucs
213 F1 Brown's Green Birm
136 C4 Brownshill Gloucs
215 E3 Brownshill Green Covtry
340 D3 Brownside Lancs
216 B4 Brownsover Warwks
12 B2 Brownston Devon
201 E2 Brown Street Suffk
168 C2 Browns Wood M Keyn
468 B2 Browsburn N Lans
388 C5 Browtop Cumb
352 A3 Brow Top Lancs
145 E3 Broxbourne Herts
490 C4 Broxburn E Loth
487 E5 Broxburn W Loth
443 G1 Broxfield Nthumb
317 H4 Broxholme Lincs
172 B4 Broxted Essex
289 G4 Broxton Ches
276 B1 Broxtowe C Nott
56 D2 Broyle Side E Susx
599 G5 Brù W Isls
599 H8 Bruach Màiri W Isls
591 E7 Bruairnis W Isls
583 K2 Bruan Highld
524 B2 Bruar P & K
487 E2 Brucefield Fife
483 E4 Brucehill W Duns
310 C2 Bruche Warrtn
556 C5 Brucklebog Abers
289 F2 Bruera Ches
164 D5 Bruern Abbey Oxon
476 D4 Bruichladdich Ag & B
202 C1 Bruisyard Suffk
332 B3 Brumby N Linc
233 E3 Brunant Powys
606 B7 Brunatwatt Shet
293 F2 Brund Staffs
250 C3 Brundall Norfk
250 D5 Brundish Norfk
226 B6 Brundish Suffk
226 B5 Brundish Street Suffk
173 H1 Brundon Suffk
519 H1 Brunery Highld
3 F2 Brunnion Cnwll
340 D3 Brunshaw Lancs
488 C5 Brunstane C Edin
400 D3 Brunstock Cumb
430 D5 Brunswick Village N u Ty
342 D4 Bruntcliffe Leeds
216 C1 Bruntingthorpe Leics
513 H5 Brunton Fife
455 G5 Brunton Nthumb
89 F3 Brunton Wilts
311 H2 Bruntwood Hall Stockp
327 E5 Brushes Tamesd
313 G5 Brushfield Derbys
25 G1 Brushford Devon
42 B2 Brushford Somset
68 A3 Bruton Somset
471 F2 Bryans Mdloth
212 C6 Bryan's Green Worcs
47 G3 Bryanston Dorset
142 B4 Bryant's Bottom Bucks
424 D5 Brydekirk D & G
305 H5 Brymbo Conwy
288 C4 Brymbo Wrexhm
45 G4 Brympton D'Evercy Somset
132 C5 Bryn Caerph
128 D4 Bryn Carmth
310 C5 Bryn Ches
304 C5 Bryn Gwynd
104 C1 Bryn Neath
232 C4 Bryn Powys
131 E3 Bryn Rhondd
209 E2 Bryn Shrops
102 D3 Bryn Swans
324 D4 Bryn Wigan
205 G5 Brynafan Cerdgn
129 H2 Brynamman Carmth
106 C1 Brynawel Caerph
152 C3 Brynberian Pembks
130 B6 Brynbryddan Neath
265 E2 Bryn Bwbach Gwynd
105 F3 Bryncae Rhondd
308 A4 Bryn Celyn Flints
304 D4 Bryn Celyn IoA
105 E3 Bryncethin Brdgnd
284 A6 Bryncir Gwynd
105 E3 Bryncoch Brdgnd
130 A4 Bryn-Coch Neath
288 C3 Bryn Common Flints
262 C4 Bryncroes Gwynd
229 E4 Bryncrug Gwynd
232 C5 Brynderwen Powys
128 D3 Bryndu Carmth
302 D6 Bryn Du IoA
306 C4 Bryn Dulas Conwy
287 G5 Bryneglwys Denbgs
284 D1 Bryn Eglwys Gwynd
307 H5 Brynford Flints
324 D4 Bryn Gates Wigan
107 F1 Brynglas Newpt
229 E4 Brynglas Sta Gwynd
105 G2 Bryn Golau Rhondd
152 D6 Bryngwelltyn Carmth
303 E5 Bryngwran IoA
179 F4 Bryngwyn Cerdgn
133 G3 Bryngwyn Mons
150 D5 Bryngwyn Pembks
184 C5 Bryngwyn Powys
151 H2 Bryn-Henllan Pembks
130 C6 Brynheulog Brdgnd
179 G3 Brynhoffnant Cerdgn
307 F3 Bryniau Denbgs
338 B4 Bryning Lancs
132 D4 Brynithel Blae G
153 G3 Bryn Iwan Carmth
208 B2 Brynllywarch Powys
132 C2 Brynmawr Blae G
262 C4 Bryn-mawr Gwynd
268 D6 Bryn Mawr Powys
104 D2 Brynmenyn Brdgnd
103 F3 Brynmill Swans
285 G2 Brynmorfudd Conwy
154 B5 Bryn Myrddin Carmth
105 F3 Brynna Rhondd
105 F3 Brynnau Gwynion Rhondd
268 C1 Bryn-newydd Denbgs
288 D5 Bryn Offa Wrexhm
269 G2 Brynore Shrops
232 B4 Bryn-penarth Powys
269 F1 Bryn Pen-y-Lan Wrexhm
305 G4 Bryn Pydew Conwy
284 C2 Brynrefail Gwynd
303 G3 Brynrefail IoA
286 C1 Bryn Rhyd-yr-Arian Conwy
305 H4 Bryn-rhys Conwy
105 G3 Brynsadler Rhondd
287 F4 Bryn Saith Marchog Denbgs
283 E2 Brynsiencyn IoA
60 D5 Brynsworthy Devon
268 D5 Bryn Tanat Powys
303 G4 Brynteg IoA
288 C4 Brynteg Wrexhm
104 D3 Bryntirion Brdgnd
269 G2 Bryn-y-Cochin Shrops
133 F1 Brynygwenin Mons
306 A4 Bryn-y-maen Conwy
228 D4 Bryn-y-mor Gwynd
269 E1 Bryn-yr-Eos Wrexhm
288 A3 Bryn-yr-ogof Denbgs
593 D8 Buaile Dubh W Isls
591 E7 Buaile nam Bodach W Isls
544 F5 Bualintur Highld
573 G5 Bualnaluib Highld
215 F5 Bubbenhall Warwks
314 A5 Bubnell Derbys
345 G2 Bubwith E R Yk
438 C2 Buccleuch Border
483 G2 Buchanan Smithy Stirlg
571 L6 Buchanhaven Abers
511 G4 Buchanty P & K
497 G4 Buchany Stirlg
484 B5 Buchley E Duns
497 E6 Buchlyvie Stirlg
400 C5 Buckabank Cumb
162 B3 Buckbury Worcs
220 A6 Buckden Cambs
368 B4 Buckden N York
250 D3 Buckenham Norfk
28 B2 Buckerell Devon
72 B5 Bucket Corner Hants
19 F4 Buckfast Devon
19 F4 Buckfastleigh Devon
30 B2 Buckham Dorset
501 G5 Buckhaven Fife
112 A5 Buck Hill Wilts
451 F2 Buckholm Border
134 B1 Buckholt Mons
23 H3 Buckhorn Devon
68 C5 Buckhorn Weston Dorset
80 B1 Buckhurst Kent
145 F5 Buckhurst Hill Essex
145 F6 Buckhurst Hill Essex
569 G2 Buckie Moray
588 E4 Buckies Highld
167 F3 Buckingham Bucks
142 B2 Buckland Bucks
12 B4 Buckland Devon
20 B3 Buckland Devon
163 G2 Buckland Gloucs
50 B5 Buckland Hants
171 E3 Buckland Herts
83 F2 Buckland Kent
139 E5 Buckland Oxon
95 E4 Buckland Surrey
39 F3 Buckland Brewer Devon
142 C3 Buckland Common Bucks
86 D4 Buckland Dinham Somset
86 C4 Buckland Down Somset
214 A2 Buckland End Birm
39 G6 Buckland Filleigh Devon
19 F3 Buckland in the Moor Devon
139 E5 Buckland Marsh Oxon
17 G5 Buckland Monachorum Devon
46 C3 Buckland Newton Dorset
31 E6 Buckland Ripers Dorset
439 G1 Bucklands Border
44 B5 Buckland St Mary Somset
83 F2 Buckland Valley Kent
142 B2 Bucklandwharf Bucks
115 F5 Bucklebury W Berk
115 E5 Bucklebury Alley W Berk
280 D2 Bucklegate Lincs
39 F3 Buckleigh Devon
514 C2 Bucklerheads Angus
50 C5 Bucklers Hard Hants
176 D1 Bucklesham Suffk
288 C2 Buckley Flints
326 D2 Buckley Rochdl
190 B1 Buckley Green Warwks
323 F5 Buckley Hill Sefton
311 E3 Bucklow Hill Ches
278 B5 Buckminster Leics
142 A4 Buckmoorend Bucks
292 B5 Bucknall C Stke
319 F6 Bucknall Lincs
166 C4 Bucknell Oxon
209 F5 Bucknell Shrops
309 H5 Buckoak Ches
110 B1 Buckover S Glos
212 C2 Buckpool Dudley
569 G2 Buckpool Moray
211 G5 Buckridge Worcs
557 F3 Bucksburn C Aber
38 D3 Buck's Cross Devon
76 A3 Bucks Green W Susx
143 F4 Bucks Hill Herts
74 C1 Bucks Horn Oak Hants
91 F4 Buckskin Hants
39 E3 Buck's Mills Devon
375 F5 Buckton E R Yk
209 G5 Buckton Herefs
454 D2 Buckton Nthumb
327 E4 Buckton Vale Tamesd
219 H4 Buckworth Cambs
190 C1 Budbrooke Warwks
316 B6 Budby Notts
291 E5 Buddileigh Staffs
23 E1 Bude Cnwll
10 B2 Budge's Shop Cnwll
455 F3 Budle Nthumb
43 G4 Budleigh Somset
21 F1 Budleigh Salterton Devon
78 B5 Budlett's Common E Susx
5 E2 Budock Water Cnwll
310 D4 Budworth Heath Ches
326 D2 Buersil Head Rochdl
290 D6 Buerton Ches
167 E3 Buffler's Holt Bucks
239 F3 Bufton Leics
193 E3 Bugbrooke Nhants
61 E3 Bugford Devon
487 G5 Bughtlin C Edin
291 H2 Buglawton Ches
8 C2 Bugle Cnwll
212 B6 Bugle Gate Worcs
68 C5 Bugley Dorset
87 F6 Bugley Wilts
359 E3 Bugthorpe E R Yk
171 F2 Building End Essex
235 E4 Buildwas Shrops
183 G4 Builth Road Powys
183 G4 Builth Wells Powys
142 C2 Bulbourne Herts
70 B3 Bulbridge Wilts
279 F4 Bulby Lincs
296 C6 Bulcote Notts
588 C3 Buldoo Highld
89 E6 Bulford Wilts
89 E6 Bulford Camp Wilts
290 A4 Bulkeley Ches
271 G1 Bulkeley Hall Shrops
215 F2 Bulkington Warwks
87 G3 Bulkington Wilts
39 E5 Bulkworthy Devon
384 B6 Bullamoor N York
294 C4 Bullbridge Derbys
117 E6 Bullbrook Br For
80 C3 Bulleign Kent
87 F3 Bullenhill Wilts
161 H6 Bulley Gloucs
388 C2 Bullgill Cumb
50 B5 Bull Hill Hants
294 B6 Bullhurst Hill Derbys
160 C2 Bullinghope Herefs
318 D4 Bullington Lincs
135 F3 Bullo Gloucs
112 A1 Bullock's Horn Wilts
100 C2 Bullockstone Kent
144 D5 Bulls Cross Gt Lon
251 E6 Bull's Green Norfk
86 C5 Bulls Green Somset
160 D5 Bull's Hill Herefs
481 H5 Bullwood Ag & B
134 B5 Bullyhole Bottom Mons
173 G1 Bulmer Essex
372 C6 Bulmer N York
173 G2 Bulmer Tye Essex
121 F2 Bulphan Thurr

City, town and village index: Bulstrode - Cameron 677

143 E4 **Bulstrode** Herts
233 F2 **Bulthy** Shrops
58 C5 **Bulverhythe** E Susx
28 B5 **Bulverton** Devon
109 F1 **Bulwark** Mons
295 G5 **Bulwell** C Nott
295 G5 **Bulwell Forest** C Nott
241 E5 **Bulwick** Leics
242 D6 **Bulwick** Nhants
145 E3 **Bumble's Green** Essex
596 E7 **Bun Abhainn Eadarra** W Isls
531 J5 **Bunacaimb** Highld
590 F5 **Bun a'mhuillin** W Isls
533 J5 **Bunarkaig** Highld
518 E5 **Bunavullin** Highld
290 B3 **Bunbury** Ches
290 A3 **Bunbury Heath** Ches
95 E5 **Bunce Common** Surrey
565 L7 **Bunchrew** Highld
546 F4 **Bundalloch** Highld
504 D6 **Bunessan** Ag & B
226 C2 **Bungay** Suffk
549 J6 **Bunkegivie** Highld
245 F3 **Bunker's Hill** Cambs
299 H4 **Bunker's Hill** Lincs
249 G3 **Bunker's Hill** Norfk
165 H6 **Bunkers Hill** Oxon
312 B2 **Bunkers Hill** Stockp
251 G4 **Bunker's Hill** Suffk
549 H5 **Bunloit** Highld
478 C7 **Bunnahabhain** Ag & B
276 C4 **Bunny** Notts
276 C4 **Bunny Hill** Notts
520 E3 **Bunree** Highld
72 B5 **Bunstead** Hants
548 F3 **Buntait** Highld
171 E4 **Buntingford** Herts
173 G3 **Bunting's Green** Essex
249 F6 **Bunwell** Norfk
249 F5 **Bunwell Bottom** Norfk
225 F1 **Bunwell Hill** Norfk
312 D5 **Burbage** Derbys
239 G6 **Burbage** Leics
89 F2 **Burbage** Wilts
185 F2 **Burcher** Herefs
116 D3 **Burchett's Green** W & M
70 B3 **Burcombe** Wilts
140 C5 **Burcot** Oxon
213 E5 **Burcot** Worcs
235 G6 **Burcote** Shrops
142 A1 **Burcott** Bucks
168 B5 **Burcott** Bucks
85 F5 **Burcott** Somset
359 G2 **Burdale** N York
471 E1 **Burdiehouse** C Edin
406 B4 **Burdon** Sundld
106 B5 **Burdonshill** V Glam
165 F2 **Burdrop** Oxon
174 A3 **Bures** Essex
174 B2 **Bures Green** Suffk
290 C4 **Burford** Ches
38 C3 **Burford** Devon
138 D2 **Burford** Oxon
210 D6 **Burford** Shrops
67 F1 **Burford** Somset
517 K6 **Burg** Ag & B
602 D6 **Burgar** Ork
225 E4 **Burgate** Suffk
74 B4 **Burgates** Hants
232 D2 **Burgedin** Powys
169 G3 **Burge End** Herts
77 F6 **Burgess Hill** W Susx
504 E5 **Burgh** Ag & B
202 A4 **Burgh** Suffk
400 B3 **Burgh by Sands** Cumb
251 F4 **Burgh Castle** Norfk
90 D2 **Burghclere** Hants
90 D2 **Burghclere Common** Hants
249 E6 **Burgh Common** Norfk
567 L3 **Burghead** Moray
115 H6 **Burghfield** W Berk
91 H1 **Burghfield Common** W Berk
91 H1 **Burghfield Hill** W Berk
95 E3 **Burgh Heath** Surrey
57 E2 **Burgh Hill** E Susx
79 G4 **Burgh Hill** E Susx
186 B6 **Burghill** Herefs
301 F1 **Burgh le Marsh** Lincs
556 D1 **Burgh Muir** Abers
255 H2 **Burgh next Aylsham** Norfk
319 G2 **Burgh on Bain** Lincs
251 F6 **Burgh St Peter** Norfk
260 D5 **Burgh Stubbs** Norfk
330 B2 **Burghwallis** Donc
14 C4 **Burgois** Cnwll
98 A2 **Burham** Kent
97 H2 **Burham Court** Kent
74 A5 **Buriton** Hants
290 C4 **Burland** Ches
605 G3 **Burland** Shet
14 D4 **Burlawn** Cnwll
136 C4 **Burleigh** Gloucs
43 E4 **Burlescombe** Devon
47 E6 **Burleston** Dorset
13 E3 **Burlestone** Devon
49 G4 **Burley** Hants
343 E3 **Burley** Leeds
242 B2 **Burley** Rutlnd
210 B3 **Burley** Shrops
49 F4 **Burley Beacon** Hants
290 C6 **Burleydam** Ches
186 D5 **Burley Gate** Herefs
355 F5 **Burley in Wharfedale** Brad
49 G4 **Burley Lawn** Hants
49 G4 **Burley Street** Hants
355 G6 **Burley Woodhead** Brad
44 B2 **Burlinch** Somset
250 D2 **Burlingham Green** Norfk
184 D3 **Burlingjobb** Powys
212 B5 **Burlish Park** Worcs
15 E5 **Burlorne Tregoose** Cnwll
57 F1 **Burlow** E Susx
270 B4 **Burlton** Shrops
186 C5 **Burmarsh** Herefs
81 G3 **Burmarsh** Kent
164 D2 **Burmington** Warwks
344 D4 **Burn** N York
23 G2 **Burnard's Ho** Devon
274 D3 **Burnaston** Derbys
467 G3 **Burnbank** S Lans
356 B4 **Burn Bridge** N York
359 F5 **Burnby** E R Yk
329 E5 **Burncross** Sheff
54 A3 **Burndell** W Susx
325 G3 **Burnden** Bolton
326 D2 **Burnedge** Rochdl
379 F5 **Burneside** Cumb
603 K3 **Burness** Ork
370 B3 **Burneston** N York
88 B1 **Burnett** BaNES
439 E2 **Burnfoot** Border
439 G1 **Burnfoot** Border
423 G1 **Burnfoot** D & G
425 F5 **Burnfoot** D & G
425 G2 **Burnfoot** D & G
433 F3 **Burnfoot** E Ayrs
468 A1 **Burnfoot** N Lans
499 F4 **Burnfoot** P & K
314 D2 **Burngreave** Sheff
117 F3 **Burnham** Bucks
333 F4 **Burnham** N Linc
117 F3 **Burnham** Slough
259 G3 **Burnham Deepdale** Norfk
144 C1 **Burnham Green** Herts
259 G3 **Burnham Market** Norfk
259 G3 **Burnham Norton** Norfk
148 C5 **Burnham-on-Crouch** Essex
84 A5 **Burnham-on-Sea** Somset
259 H3 **Burnham Overy Staithe** Norfk
259 G3 **Burnham Overy Town** Norfk
259 H3 **Burnham Thorpe** Norfk
557 F6 **Burnhead** Abers
439 G1 **Burnhead** Border
423 F3 **Burnhead** D & G
435 H5 **Burnhead** D & G
432 B4 **Burnhead** S Ayrs
559 G6 **Burnhervie** Abers
236 A4 **Burnhill Green** Staffs
405 E5 **Burnhope** Dur
466 A4 **Burnhouse** N Ayrs
472 A5 **Burnhouse Mains** Border
14 D4 **Burniere** Cnwll
568 E3 **Burniestrype** Moray
387 H6 **Burniston** N York
327 H3 **Burnlee** Kirk
340 D3 **Burnley** Lancs
340 C3 **Burnley Lane** Lancs
340 C3 **Burnley Wood** Lancs
474 D2 **Burnmouth** Border
350 D6 **Burn Naze** Lancs
497 H4 **Burn of Cambus** Stirlg
405 E3 **Burnopfield** Dur
401 E3 **Burnrigg** Cumb
354 D2 **Burnsall** N York
170 C5 **Burn's Green** Herts
527 F3 **Burnside** Angus
527 G4 **Burnside** Angus
434 B2 **Burnside** E Ayrs
500 C3 **Burnside** Fife
512 B4 **Burnside** P & K
606 C2 **Burnside** Shet
406 A4 **Burnside** Sundld
487 E5 **Burnside** W Loth
514 C3 **Burnside of Duntrune** Angus
38 D3 **Burnstone** Devon
424 D4 **Burnswark** D & G
136 C4 **Burnt Ash** Gloucs
94 A4 **Burntcommon** Surrey
274 C3 **Burntheath** Derbys
175 E4 **Burnt Heath** Essex
115 F5 **Burnt Hill** W Berk
5 E1 **Burnthouse** Cnwll
488 A3 **Burntisland** Fife
122 A1 **Burnt Mills** Essex
78 C4 **Burnt Oak** E Susx
119 E1 **Burnt Oak** Gt Lon
433 G3 **Burnton** E Ayrs
213 E1 **Burnt Tree** Sandw
237 G3 **Burntwood** Staffs
237 G3 **Burntwood Green** Staffs
288 C2 **Burntwood Pentre** Flints
356 B2 **Burnt Yates** N York
43 G4 **Burnworthy** Somset
487 F6 **Burnwynd** W Loth
93 H4 **Burpham** Surrey
54 B3 **Burpham** W Susx
431 E5 **Burradon** N Tyne
442 B3 **Burradon** Nthumb
609 J2 **Burrafirth** Shet
606 B8 **Burraland** Shet
606 D2 **Burraland** Shet
4 C1 **Burras** Cnwll
606 B8 **Burrastow** Shet
10 D2 **Burraton** Cnwll
10 D2 **Burraton Coombe** Cnwll
606 E4 **Burravoe** Shet
607 H1 **Burravoe** Shet
601 H5 **Burray Village** Ork
392 A6 **Burrells** Cumb
513 F2 **Burrelton** P & K
29 F1 **Burridge** Devon
61 E4 **Burridge** Devon
51 F2 **Burridge** Hants
583 H3 **Burrigill** Highld
370 A2 **Burrill** N York
332 A3 **Burringham** N Linc
40 C4 **Burrington** Devon
210 A5 **Burrington** Herefs
85 E3 **Burrington** N Som
198 C3 **Burrough End** Cambs
198 C3 **Burrough Green** Cambs
241 G2 **Burrough on the Hill** Leics
116 D2 **Burroughs Grove** Bucks
603 G7 **Burroughston** Ork
27 F3 **Burrow** Devon
27 H5 **Burrow** Devon
63 E3 **Burrow** Somset
66 C6 **Burrow** Somset
44 D2 **Burrowbridge** Somset
93 G2 **Burrowhill** Surrey
94 B5 **Burrows Cross** Surrey
277 F1 **Burrowsmoor Holt** Notts
149 G1 **Burrsville Park** Essex
78 C2 **Burrswood** Kent
102 C3 **Burry** Swans
102 C3 **Burry Green** Swans
128 C4 **Burry Port** Carmth
38 D3 **Burscott** Devon
324 A2 **Burscough** Lancs
323 H2 **Burscough Bridge** Lancs
38 C4 **Bursdon** Devon
346 B3 **Bursea** E R Yk
360 D5 **Burshill** E R Yk
51 E3 **Bursledon** Hants
291 H5 **Burslem** C Stke
201 E6 **Burstall** Suffk
201 E5 **Burstallhill** Suffk
29 H2 **Burstock** Dorset
25 H2 **Burston** Devon
225 F3 **Burston** Norfk
272 D3 **Burston** Staffs
77 F1 **Burstow** Surrey
348 D4 **Burstwick** E R Yk
368 A2 **Burtersett** N York
401 F2 **Burtholme** Cumb
199 F2 **Burthorpe** Suffk
400 D5 **Burthwaite** Cumb
84 C6 **Burtle** Somset
84 C6 **Burtle Hill** Somset
280 C2 **Burtoft** Lincs
289 H2 **Burton** Ches
308 D5 **Burton** Ches
32 B1 **Burton** Dorset
49 F6 **Burton** Dorset
318 B5 **Burton** Lincs
455 F3 **Burton** Nthumb
125 G3 **Burton** Pembks
45 G5 **Burton** Somset
64 C3 **Burton** Somset
105 G6 **Burton** V Glam
68 D3 **Burton** Wilts
111 E4 **Burton** Wilts
289 E3 **Burton** Wrexhm
361 E2 **Burton Agnes** E R Yk
30 B5 **Burton Bradstock** Dorset
300 B5 **Burton Corner** Lincs
191 F4 **Burton Dassett** Warwks
198 C4 **Burton End** Cambs
172 A5 **Burton End** Essex
125 G3 **Burton Ferry** Pembks
374 D5 **Burton Fleming** E R Yk
214 D4 **Burton Green** Warwks
288 D3 **Burton Green** Wrexhm
215 G2 **Burton Hastings** Warwks
366 A4 **Burton-in-Kendal** Cumb
366 C5 **Burton in Lonsdale** N York
296 B6 **Burton Joyce** Notts
218 B5 **Burton Latimer** Nhants
241 G1 **Burton Lazars** Leics
278 D4 **Burton-le-Coggles** Lincs
356 C2 **Burton Leonard** N York
272 D5 **Burton Manor** Staffs
276 C5 **Burton on the Wolds** Leics
241 E5 **Burton Overy** Leics
279 G1 **Burton Pedwardine** Lincs
349 E3 **Burton Pidsea** E R Yk
344 B4 **Burton Salmon** N York
173 G4 **Burton's Green** Essex
346 C6 **Burton Stather** N Linc
332 B1 **Burton upon Stather** N Linc
274 D5 **Burton upon Trent** Staffs
234 D5 **Burton Westwood** Shrops
310 B1 **Burtonwood** Warrtn
289 H3 **Burwardsley** Ches
211 E2 **Burwarton** Shrops
79 F5 **Burwash** E Susx
79 E5 **Burwash Common** E Susx
79 F5 **Burwash Weald** E Susx
198 B1 **Burwell** Cambs
320 B4 **Burwell** Lincs
303 F2 **Burwen** IoA
601 G8 **Burwick** Ork
605 G2 **Burwick** Shet
210 B2 **Burwood** Shrops
94 B2 **Burwood Park** Surrey
326 A2 **Bury** Bury
220 C3 **Bury** Cambs
42 B2 **Bury** Somset
54 B2 **Bury** W Susx
2 D4 **Buryas Br** Cnwll
272 C2 **Burybank** Staffs
169 G3 **Bury End** Beds
194 D4 **Bury End** Beds
163 G2 **Bury End** Worcs
144 D4 **Bury Green** Herts
171 G5 **Bury Green** Herts
54 B2 **Bury Hollow** W Susx
199 G2 **Bury St Edmunds** Suffk
90 D2 **Bury's Bank** W Berk
359 E2 **Burythorpe** N York
445 E2 **Busbiehill** E Ayrs
93 G6 **Busbridge** Surrey
467 E3 **Busby** E Rens
512 B4 **Busby** P & K
138 C5 **Buscot** Oxon
66 C2 **Buscott** Somset
529 G1 **Bush** Abers
38 B6 **Bush** Cnwll
186 A4 **Bush Bank** Herefs
94 D5 **Bushbury** Surrey
236 D4 **Bushbury** Wolves
241 E4 **Bushby** Leics
537 K3 **Bush Crathie** Abers
172 B6 **Bush End** Essex
256 D4 **Bush Estate** Norfk
34 A4 **Bushey** Dorset
143 G5 **Bushey** Herts
139 E3 **Bushey Ground** Oxon
143 G6 **Bushey Heath** Herts
119 E6 **Bushey Mead** Gt Lon
426 C3 **Bushfield** Cumb
225 H2 **Bush Green** Norfk
248 D5 **Bush Green** Norfk
200 B3 **Bush Green** Suffk
144 D5 **Bush Hill Park** Gt Lon
162 C3 **Bushley** Worcs
162 C3 **Bushley Green** Worcs
195 G3 **Bushmead** Beds
210 A2 **Bushmoor** Shrops
112 C4 **Bushton** Wilts
254 B5 **Bushy Common** Norfk
391 G1 **Busk** Cumb
326 D3 **Busk** Oldham
318 D2 **Buslingthorpe** Lincs
136 C4 **Bussage** Gloucs
65 F4 **Bussex** Somset
604 b3 **Busta** Shet
606 D4 **Busta** Shet
172 C4 **Bustard Green** Essex
225 G1 **Bustard's Green** Norfk
603 M1 **Bustatoun** Ork
6 D5 **Busveal** Cnwll
256 C5 **Butcher's Common** Norfk
78 D4 **Butcher's Cross** E Susx
85 F2 **Butcombe** N Som
132 A3 **Bute Town** Caerph
106 C4 **Butetown** Cardif
233 H2 **Butlane Head** Shrops
67 E3 **Butleigh** Somset
67 E3 **Butleigh Wootton** Somset
270 D5 **Butlersbank** Shrops
142 A3 **Butler's Cross** Bucks
142 D6 **Butlers Cross** Bucks
295 G5 **Butler's Hill** Notts
190 D5 **Butlers Marston** Warwks
202 D4 **Butley** Suffk
202 D5 **Butley High Corner** Suffk
202 D5 **Butley Low Corner** Suffk
312 B4 **Butley Town** Ches
51 E3 **Butlocks Heath** Hants
272 C5 **Butter Bank** Staffs
427 G5 **Butterburn** Cumb
358 D3 **Buttercrambe** N York
4 D2 **Butteriss Gate** Cnwll
394 B4 **Butterknowle** Dur
42 C6 **Butterleigh** Devon
294 C2 **Butterley** Derbys
295 E4 **Butterley** Derbys
377 F1 **Buttermere** Cumb
90 A2 **Buttermere** Wilts
136 B4 **Butterrow** Gloucs
291 G4 **Butters Green** Staffs
342 B4 **Buttershaw** Brad
525 G6 **Butterstone** P & K
272 B1 **Butterton** Staffs
293 E3 **Butterton** Staffs
390 D6 **Butterwick** Cumb
396 A3 **Butterwick** Dur
300 C5 **Butterwick** Lincs
372 D4 **Butterwick** N York
374 B5 **Butterwick** N York
440 B6 **Butteryhaugh** Nthumb
290 D4 **Butt Green** Ches
233 E3 **Buttington** Powys
291 G4 **Butt Lane** Staffs
211 G4 **Buttonbridge** Shrops
200 C1 **Button Haugh Green** Suffk
211 G4 **Buttonoak** Shrops
200 B4 **Button's Green** Suffk
26 B5 **Butts** Devon
50 D3 **Buttsash** Hants
23 F2 **Buttsbear Cross** Cnwll
146 D5 **Buttsbury** Essex
147 F4 **Butt's Green** Essex
171 G3 **Butts Green** Essex
71 F4 **Butt's Green** Hants
101 F5 **Buttsole** Kent
366 B6 **Butt Yeats** Lancs
200 D3 **Buxhall** Suffk
200 C3 **Buxhall Fen Street** Suffk
474 B4 **Buxley** Border
78 B5 **Buxted** E Susx
313 E5 **Buxton** Derbys
255 H3 **Buxton** Norfk
312 D3 **Buxworth** Derbys
308 A5 **Bwlch** Flints
228 D3 **Bwlch** Gwynd
158 C5 **Bwlch** Powys
263 H1 **Bwlch-Derwin** Gwynd
288 C4 **Bwlchgwyn** Wrexhm
181 E3 **Bwlch-Llan** Cerdgn
153 H5 **Bwlchnewydd** Carmth
262 D5 **Bwlchtocyn** Gwynd
232 C1 **Bwlch-y-Cibau** Powys
106 B3 **Bwlch-y-cwm** Cardif
268 C5 **Bwlchyddar** Powys
180 B5 **Bwlch-y-Fadfa** Cerdgn
231 H5 **Bwlch-y-Ffridd** Powys
231 G5 **Bwlch y Garreg** Powys
153 E2 **Bwlchygroes** Pembks
283 F4 **Bwlchyllyn** Gwynd
129 E5 **Bwlchymynydd** Carmth
208 D4 **Bwlch-y-Plain** Powys
207 G5 **Bwlch-y-Sarnau** Powys
99 G6 **Bybrook** Kent
159 G1 **Bycross** Herefs
105 E3 **Byeastwood** Brdgnd
142 B2 **Bye Green** Bucks
403 F5 **Byerhope** Nthumb
405 E3 **Byermoor** Gatesd
395 E3 **Byers Green** Dur
192 B4 **Byfield** Nhants
94 B2 **Byfleet** Surrey
185 G6 **Byford** Herefs
185 G6 **Byford Common** Herefs
170 C2 **Bygrave** Herts
405 G2 **Byker** N u Ty
286 D2 **Bylchau** Conwy
311 E6 **Byley** Ches
128 D5 **Bynea** Carmth
344 B4 **Byram** N York
441 E4 **Byrness** Nthumb
219 F4 **Bythorn** Cambs
185 G2 **Byton** Herefs
185 G2 **Byton Hand** Herefs
404 B2 **Bywell** Nthumb
75 F5 **Byworth** W Susx

C

39 F3 **Cabbacott** Devon
117 E5 **Cabbage Hill** Br For
597 K3 **Cabharstadh** W Isls
209 F2 **Cabin** Shrops
333 G4 **Cabourne** Lincs
477 H4 **Cabrach** Ag & B
553 H3 **Cabrach** Moray
565 J8 **Cabrich** Highld
351 G5 **Cabus** Lancs
281 E4 **Cackle Hill** Lincs
58 A3 **Cackle Street** E Susx
58 D3 **Cackle Street** E Susx
78 B4 **Cackle Street** E Susx
27 E2 **Cadbury** Devon
40 D4 **Cadbury Barton** Devon
110 B5 **Cadbury Heath** S Glos
484 C5 **Cadder** E Duns
169 F6 **Caddington** Beds
451 F3 **Caddonfoot** Border
451 E2 **Caddonlee** Border
330 B4 **Cadeby** Donc
239 G4 **Cadeby** Leics
42 B6 **Cadeleigh** Devon
449 H2 **Cademuir** Border
287 E2 **Cader** Denbgs
79 E5 **Cade Street** E Susx
527 G3 **Cadger Path** Angus
44 C4 **Cad Green** Somset
4 D6 **Cadgwith** Cnwll
501 E4 **Cadham** Fife
311 E1 **Cadishead** Salfd
103 F2 **Cadle** Swans
338 D3 **Cadley** Lancs
89 F1 **Cadley** Wilts
89 F4 **Cadley** Wilts
116 C1 **Cadmore End** Bucks
50 B2 **Cadnam** Hants
333 E4 **Cadney** N Linc
270 B3 **Cadney Bank** Wrexhm
288 B2 **Cadole** Flints
106 B6 **Cadoxton** V Glam
130 B5 **Cadoxton-Juxta-Neath** Neath
339 H6 **Cadshaw** Bl w D
170 A3 **Cadwell** Herts
467 H4 **Cadzow** S Lans
283 E3 **Caeathro** Gwynd
285 F6 **Cae Clyd** Gwynd
130 C2 **Caehopkin** Powys
178 D4 **Caemorgan** Cerdgn
318 C2 **Caenby** Lincs
130 D6 **Caerau** Brdgnd
106 B4 **Caerau** Cardif
107 E2 **Caerau Park** Newpt
130 C2 **Cae'r-bont** Powys
129 E2 **Cae'r-Bryn** Carmth
265 E6 **Caerdeon** Gwynd
288 D3 **Caer-Estyn** Flints
150 C4 **Caer-Farchell** Pembks
302 D5 **Caergeiliog** IoA
288 C3 **Caergwrle** Flints
104 B1 **Caerhendy** Neath
304 C6 **Caerhûn** Gwynd
130 B2 **Cae'r-Lan** Powys
107 F1 **Caerleon** Newpt
134 B3 **Caer Llan** Mons
105 F6 **Caermead** V Glam
152 C3 **Caermeini** Pembks
283 E3 **Caernarfon** Gwynd
106 C2 **Caerphilly** Caerph
207 G1 **Caersws** Powys
180 A3 **Caerwedros** Cerdgn
109 E1 **Caerwent** Mons
109 E2 **Caerwent Brook** Mons
307 G5 **Caerwys** Flints
229 E5 **Caethle** Gwynd
97 E5 **Cage Green** Kent
159 G6 **Caggle Street** Mons
304 D3 **Caim** IoA
136 B3 **Cainscross** Gloucs
155 G2 **Caio** Carmth
592 E5 **Cairinis** W Isls
598 B8 **Cairisiadar** W Isls
595 G6 **Cairminis** W Isls
480 A1 **Cairnbaan** Ag & B
560 C4 **Cairnbrogie** Abers
571 J2 **Cairnbulg** Abers
539 F4 **Cairncross** Angus
474 C2 **Cairncross** Border
494 D2 **Cairndow** Ag & B
571 J3 **Cairness** Abers
486 D2 **Cairneyhill** Fife
410 C3 **Cairnfield** D & G
408 C5 **Cairngaan** D & G
408 A2 **Cairngarroch** D & G
559 F3 **Cairnhill** Abers
468 B2 **Cairnhill** N Lans
559 H7 **Cairnie** Abers
560 D2 **Cairnleith Crofts** Abers
560 C1 **Cairnorrie** Abers
560 B6 **Cairnpark** Abers
435 H5 **Cairnpark** D & G
415 E3 **Cairnryan** D & G
600 D2 **Cairston** Ork
251 G2 **Caister-on-Sea** Norfk
333 G4 **Caistor** Lincs
250 A4 **Caistor St Edmund** Norfk
442 B4 **Caistron** Nthumb
212 C5 **Cakebole** Worcs
174 C2 **Calais Street** Suffk
598 E8 **Calanais** W Isls
597 L4 **Calbost** W Isls
36 C3 **Calbourne** IoW
320 C4 **Calceby** Lincs
307 H5 **Calcoed** Flints
137 G2 **Calcot** Gloucs
115 H5 **Calcot** W Berk
115 H5 **Calcot Row** W Berk
100 C3 **Calcott** Kent
234 A2 **Calcott** Shrops
136 A1 **Calcott's Green** Gloucs
356 C3 **Calcutt** N York
137 H6 **Calcutt** Wilts
609 J3 **Caldback** Shet
389 H2 **Caldbeck** Cumb
369 E2 **Caldbergh** N York
196 D3 **Caldecote** Cambs
219 G2 **Caldecote** Cambs
170 B2 **Caldecote** Herts
193 E4 **Caldecote** Nhants
239 E6 **Caldecote** Warwks
143 H6 **Caldecote Hill** Herts
218 D6 **Caldecott** Nhants
140 A5 **Caldecott** Oxon
242 B6 **Caldecott** Rutlnd
168 B2 **Caldecotte** M Keyn
376 C4 **Calder** Cumb
468 B2 **Calderbank** N Lans
376 C3 **Calder Bridge** Cumb
341 E6 **Calderbrook** Rochdl
485 G6 **Caldercruix** N Lans
329 E1 **Calder Grove** Wakefd
588 D4 **Calder Mains** Highld
446 D1 **Caldermill** S Lans
326 D1 **Caldermoor** Rochdl
309 E2 **Calderstones** Lpool
352 A5 **Calder Vale** Lancs
467 F3 **Calderwood** S Lans
527 G5 **Caldhame** Angus
109 E2 **Caldicot** Mons
237 F5 **Caldmore** Wsall
238 C1 **Caldwell** Derbys
383 E2 **Caldwell** N York
308 B2 **Caldy** Wirral
180 C4 **Caledrhydiau** Cerdgn
312 A2 **Cale Green** Stockp
7 F5 **Calenick** Cnwll
236 D3 **Calf Heath** Staffs
199 E5 **Calford Green** Suffk
603 H4 **Calfsound** Ork
517 K5 **Calgary** Ag & B
567 K5 **Califer** Moray
213 F3 **California** Birm
221 H3 **California** Cambs
486 B4 **California** Falk
251 G1 **California** Norfk
201 G6 **California** Suffk
12 B2 **California Cross** Devon
275 F5 **Calke** Derbys
556 D6 **Calladrum** Abers
562 B6 **Callakille** Highld
442 D3 **Callaly** Nthumb
497 F3 **Callander** Stirlg
310 B1 **Callands** Warrtn
598 E8 **Callanish** W Isls
235 E5 **Callaughton** Shrops
430 C6 **Callerton** N u Ty
430 C6 **Callerton Lane End** N u Ty
7 E3 **Callestick** Cnwll
531 H2 **Calligarry** Highld
17 E5 **Callington** Cnwll
274 B5 **Callingwood** Staffs
3 G2 **Calloose** Cnwll
294 B4 **Callow** Derbys
160 B3 **Callow** Herefs
188 B5 **Callow End** Worcs
134 C1 **Callow Hill** Herefs
85 F6 **Callow Hill** Somset
112 B3 **Callow Hill** Wilts
211 G5 **Callow Hill** Worcs
187 F5 **Callow Marsh** Herefs
50 B2 **Calmore** Hants
137 F3 **Calmsden** Gloucs
112 A5 **Calne** Wilts
112 B5 **Calne Marsh** Wilts
315 E5 **Calow** Derbys
315 E6 **Calow Green** Derbys
312 B5 **Calrofold** Ches
51 E4 **Calshot** Hants
17 F5 **Calstock** Cnwll
112 B6 **Calstone Wellington** Wilts
261 G5 **Calthorpe** Norfk
165 H2 **Calthorpe** Oxon
390 D1 **Calthwaite** Cumb
457 E2 **Calton** Ag & B
467 E2 **Calton** C Glas
354 B3 **Calton** N York
293 F4 **Calton** Staffs
314 A6 **Calton Lees** Derbys
4 C1 **Calvadnack** Cnwll
290 B3 **Calveley** Ches
314 A5 **Calver** Derbys
271 E2 **Calverhall** Shrops
185 G5 **Calver Hill** Herefs
42 B5 **Calverleigh** Devon
342 D2 **Calverley** Leeds
314 A4 **Calver Sough** Derbys
167 E5 **Calvert** Bucks
167 G2 **Calverton** M Keyn
296 B5 **Calverton** Notts
524 B2 **Calvine** P & K
399 E4 **Calvo** Cumb
135 H5 **Cam** Gloucs
533 H7 **Camaghael** Highld
547 G4 **Camas-Luinie** Highld
519 L5 **Camasnacroise** Highld
545 J2 **Camastianavaig** Highld
549 J1 **Camault Muir** Highld
609 G6 **Camb** Shet
59 G3 **Camber** E Susx
93 E2 **Camberley** Surrey
119 G4 **Camberwell** Gt Lon
345 F4 **Camblesforth** N York
429 G2 **Cambo** Nthumb
431 E3 **Cambois** Nthumb
6 B6 **Camborne** Cnwll
196 D3 **Cambourne** Cambs
472 D5 **Cambridge** Border
197 F3 **Cambridge** Cambs
135 H4 **Cambridge** Gloucs
355 H5 **Cambridge** Leeds
109 F6 **Cambridge Batch** N Som
123 E3 **Cambridge Town** Sthend
6 C4 **Cambrose** Cnwll
498 D6 **Cambus** Clacks
485 F1 **Cambusbarron** Stirlg
498 A6 **Cambusdrenny** Stirlg
498 C6 **Cambuskenneth** Stirlg
467 F3 **Cambuslang** S Lans
468 C3 **Cambusnethan** N Lans
448 D2 **Cambuswallace** S Lans
80 A2 **Camden Hill** Kent
78 D2 **Camden Park** Kent
119 F3 **Camden Town** Gt Lon
85 H3 **Cameley** BaNES
22 C6 **Camelford** Cnwll
49 E2 **Camel Green** Dorset
485 H3 **Camelon** Falk
74 D3 **Camelsdale** W Susx
97 G1 **Camer** Kent
501 F5 **Cameron** Fife

678 City, town and village index: Cameron Bridge - Chalfont Common

501 F5 Cameron Bridge Fife
551 J3 Camerory Highld
161 H3 Camer's Green Worcs
86 B3 Camerton BaNES
388 B3 Camerton Cumb
348 D4 Camerton E R Yk
30 B3 Camesworth Dorset
522 F4 Camghouran P & K
557 F6 Cammachmore Abers
318 A3 Cammeringham Lincs
184 A3 Camnant Powys
484 A2 Camoquhill Stirlg
577 G5 Camore Highld
297 G4 Camp Lincs
464 D4 Campbelton N Ayrs
456 D2 Campbeltown Ag & B
141 E4 Camp Corner Oxon
431 E5 Camperdown N Tyne
313 G4 Camphill Derbys
309 F2 Camp Hill Lpool
370 C3 Camp Hill N York
126 C2 Camp Hill Pembks
239 E6 Camp Hill Warwks
191 E1 Campion Hills Warwks
436 A6 Cample D & G
513 F2 Campmuir P & K
330 B2 Campsall Donc
202 C3 Campsea Ashe Suffk
172 C1 Camps End Cambs
139 H2 Campsfield Oxon
251 G6 Camps Heath Suffk
169 G2 Campton Beds
489 G4 Camptoun E Loth
440 C2 Camptown Border
151 F5 Camrose Pembks
524 B6 Camserney P & K
546 B7 Camuscross Highld
533 G8 Camusnagaul Highld
573 L6 Camusnagaul Highld
546 C1 Camusteel Highld
546 C1 Camusterrach Highld
523 H6 Camusvrachan P & K
71 F6 Canada Hants
333 G4 Canada Lincs
58 B3 Canadia E Susx
364 D4 Canal Foot Cumb
301 E1 Candlesby Lincs
224 D5 Candle Street Suffk
449 E1 Candy Mill S Lans
116 A4 Cane End Oxon
57 F3 Caneheath E Susx
148 A6 Canewdon Essex
34 C3 Canford Cliffs Poole
48 C6 Canford Heath Poole
48 C5 Canford Magna Poole
256 C6 Cangate Norfk
201 E1 Canham's Green Suffk
312 D5 Canholes Derbys
589 K2 Canisbay Highld
315 E1 Canklow Rothm
214 D4 Canley Covtry
69 E5 Cann Dorset
14 C5 Cannalidgey Cnwll
67 G1 Cannard's Grave Somset
69 E5 Cann Common Dorset
548 E3 Cannich Highld
65 E4 Cannington Somset
120 A3 Canning Town Gt Lon
236 D2 Cannock Staffs
237 F2 Cannock Wood Staffs
146 B3 Cannon's Green Essex
134 D2 Cannop Gloucs
426 A4 Canonbie D & G
160 A1 Canon Bridge Herefs
187 F6 Canon Frome Herefs
186 A5 Canon Pyon Herefs
192 C4 Canons Ashby Nhants
43 G3 Canonsgrove Somset
118 D1 Canons Park Gt Lon
3 F2 Canon's Town Cnwll
100 C4 Canterbury Kent
330 D4 Cantley Donc
250 D4 Cantley Norfk
234 C3 Cantlop Shrops
106 C4 Canton Cardif
566 D7 Cantraydoune Highld
566 D7 Cantraywood Highld
366 C5 Cantsfield Lancs
122 B3 Canvey Island Essex
318 B6 Canwick Lincs
23 E4 Canworthy Water Cnwll
533 H7 Caol Highld
516 D6 Caolas Ag & B
591 C8 Caolas W Isls
595 L3 Caolas Scalpaigh W Isls
595 J4 Caolas Stocinis W Isls
478 C8 Caol Ila Ag & B
128 D4 Capel Carmth
97 F6 Capel Kent
158 B4 Capel Powys
76 C1 Capel Surrey
205 E3 Capel Bangor Cerdgn
181 F3 Capel Betws Lleucu Cerdgn
303 F4 Capel Coch IoA
79 G1 Capel Cross Kent
285 F3 Capel Curig Conwy
180 A5 Capel Cynon Cerdgn
154 C5 Capel Dewi Carmth
180 C6 Capel Dewi Cerdgn
205 E3 Capel Dewi Cerdgn
285 H3 Capel Garmon Conwy
202 D5 Capel Green Suffk
179 G4 Capel Gwnda Cerdgn
302 D5 Capel Gwyn IoA
155 H5 Capel Gwynfe Carmth
129 E2 Capel Hendre Carmth
155 E4 Capel Isaac Carmth
153 F2 Capel Iwan Carmth
82 D3 Capel-le-Ferne Kent
35 d2 Capelles Guern
106 A3 Capel Llanilltern Cardif
282 D1 Capel Mawr IoA
303 G3 Capel Parc IoA
202 D5 Capel St Andrew Suffk
175 E2 Capel St Mary Suffk
128 D2 Capel Seion Carmth
205 E4 Capel Seion Cerdgn
286 A4 Capel Siloam Conwy
179 F5 Capel Tygwydd Cerdgn
282 D5 Capel Uchaf Gwynd
305 F4 Capelulo Conwy
180 B3 Capel Vicar Cerdgn
159 E3 Capel-y-Ffin Powys
283 F2 Capel-y-Graig Gwynd
309 E5 Capenhurst Ches
366 A5 Capernwray Lancs
429 G3 Capheaton Nthumb
44 C4 Capland Somset
450 A5 Cappercleuch Border
437 F3 Capplegill D & G
98 B2 Capstone Medway
326 C2 Captain Fold Rochdl
13 E2 Capton Devon
64 A4 Capton Somset
512 C2 Caputh P & K
16 C4 Caradon Town Cnwll
3 F2 Carbis Bay Cnwll
544 F3 Carbost Highld
485 F5 Carbrain N Lans
314 D2 Carbrook Sheff
248 C4 Carbrooke Norfk
316 B5 Carburton Notts
528 D3 Carcary Angus
8 C3 Carclaze Cnwll
7 E6 Carclew Cnwll
296 D6 Car Colston Notts
330 B2 Carcroft Donc
500 D5 Cardenden Fife
233 G2 Cardeston Shrops
400 B5 Cardew Cumb
400 B4 Cardewlees Cumb
106 D4 Cardiff Cardif
178 D4 Cardigan Cerdgn
198 C5 Cardinal's Green Cambs
195 F5 Cardington Beds
234 C5 Cardington Shrops
15 G5 Cardinham Cnwll
466 D2 Cardonald C Glas
568 B7 Cardow Moray
408 C5 Cardrain D & G
450 B2 Cardrona Border
482 D4 Cardross Ag & B
408 C5 Cardryne D & G
399 F3 Cardurnock Cumb
243 E1 Careby Lincs
528 B2 Careston Angus
241 F5 Care Village Leics
126 B4 Carew Pembks
126 A4 Carew Cheriton Pembks
126 A4 Carew Newton Pembks
160 D3 Carey Herefs
5 G3 Carey Park Cnwll
468 B3 Carfin N Lans
490 A6 Carfrae E Loth
2 D3 Carfury Cnwll
225 F1 Cargate Common Norfk
423 G5 Cargenbridge D & G
512 D2 Cargill P & K
400 C3 Cargo Cumb
396 D5 Cargo Fleet Middsb
10 D1 Cargreen Cnwll
453 E2 Carham Nthumb
63 G3 Carhampton Somset
6 D5 Carharrack Cnwll
509 K2 Carie P & K
523 H4 Carie P & K
592 E5 Carinish W Isls
36 D3 Carisbrooke IoW
365 E4 Cark Cumb
10 D1 Carkeel Cnwll
598 E6 Càrlabhagh W Isls
7 F3 Carland Cross Cnwll
383 F1 Carlbury Darltn
243 F2 Carlby Lincs
328 B4 Carlecotes Barns
4 B2 Carleen Cnwll
438 D4 Carlenrig Border
369 G5 Carlesmoor N York
376 C3 Carleton Cumb
391 E4 Carleton Cumb
400 D4 Carleton Cumb
337 F2 Carleton Lancs
344 B5 Carleton Wakefd
249 E3 Carleton Forehoe Norfk
376 D5 Carleton Hall Cumb
354 B5 Carleton-in-Craven N York
249 F6 Carleton Rode Norfk
250 C4 Carleton St Peter Norfk
406 B3 Carley Hill Sundld
5 E3 Carlidnack Cnwll
86 B3 Carlingcott BaNES
43 G5 Carlingwark Devon
397 G6 Carlin How R & Cl
400 D3 Carlisle Cumb
8 B3 Carloggas Cnwll
14 B3 Carloggas Cnwll
470 C3 Carlops Border
598 E6 Carloway W Isls
329 F3 Carlton Barns
194 D3 Carlton Beds
198 C4 Carlton Cambs
343 F4 Carlton Leeds
239 F4 Carlton Leics
345 E5 Carlton N York
369 E3 Carlton N York
372 B2 Carlton N York
276 D1 Carlton Notts
396 A5 Carlton S on T
202 D2 Carlton Suffk
227 G1 Carlton Colville Suffk
241 E5 Carlton Curlieu Leics
198 C4 Carlton Green Cambs
371 F4 Carlton Husthwaite N York
384 D4 Carlton in Cleveland N York
316 A3 Carlton in Lindrick Notts
297 H3 Carlton-le-Moorland Lincs
370 D3 Carlton Miniott N York
297 E2 Carlton-on-Trent Notts
218 A2 Carlton Purlieus Nhants
298 B5 Carlton Scroop Lincs
8 C2 Carluddon Cnwll
468 D4 Carluke S Lans
8 D3 Carlyon Bay Cnwll
447 F4 Carmacoup S Lans
154 A5 Carmarthen Carmth
129 E1 Carmel Carmth
307 H4 Carmel Flints
283 E5 Carmel Gwynd
303 E4 Carmel IoA
183 H1 Carmel Powys
448 B2 Carmichael S Lans
15 F5 Carminow Cross Cnwll
541 F3 Carmont Abers
467 F3 Carmunnock C Glas
467 G2 Carmyle C Glas
528 B6 Carmyllie Angus
361 E1 Carnaby E R Yk
547 J4 Carnach Highld
573 K4 Carnach Highld
567 J7 Carnach Moray
595 L3 Carnach W Isls
536 B4 Carnachuin Highld
586 F6 Carnachy Highld
593 D8 Càrnan W Isls
6 C5 Carn Arthen Cnwll
492 D4 Carnassarie Ag & B
503 E3 Carnbee Fife
499 G4 Carnbo P & K
6 C5 Carn Brea Village Cnwll
468 A2 Carnbroe N Lans
476 C3 Carnduncan Ag & B
5 E4 Carne Cnwll
7 H6 Carne Cnwll
8 B2 Carne Cnwll
4 D2 Carnebone Cnwll
207 G1 Carnedd Powys
515 E1 Carnegie Angus
445 G3 Carnell S Ayrs
131 H6 Carnetown Rhondd
365 G5 Carnforth Lancs
103 F3 Carnglas Swans
547 H5 Carn-Gorm Highld
150 C4 Carnhedryn Pembks
6 B6 Carnhell Green Cnwll
6 D4 Carnhot Cnwll
557 E3 Carnie Abers
4 D2 Carnkie Cnwll
6 C6 Carnkie Cnwll
7 E3 Carnkief Cnwll
231 F5 Carno Powys
486 D2 Carnock Fife
7 E5 Carnon Downs Cnwll
515 F3 Carnoustie Angus
8 C2 Carnsmerry Cnwll
2 C4 Carn Towan Cnwll
467 F2 Carntyne C Glas
466 D3 Carnwadric C Glas
469 F5 Carnwath S Lans
2 C3 Carnyorth Cnwll
22 D4 Caroe Cnwll
214 D4 Carol Green Solhll
542 E8 Caroy Highld
8 B3 Carpalla Cnwll
213 G5 Carpenter's Hill Worcs
368 D2 Carperby N York
368 B2 Carpley Green N York
326 A1 Carr Bury
315 G1 Carr Rothm
459 G4 Carradale Ag & B
595 K3 Carragraich W Isls
506 D5 Carraig nam Marbh Ag & B
365 G4 Carr Bank Cumb
550 F5 Carrbridge Highld
327 E4 Carrbrook Tamesd
323 G2 Carr Cross Lancs
35 h6 Carrefour Jersey
303 E3 Carreglefn IoA
153 E1 Carreg-Wen Pembks
284 C1 Carreg y Garth Gwynd
343 F5 Carr Gate Wakefd
311 E2 Carr Green Traffd
405 G2 Carr Hill Gatesd
323 F4 Carr Houses Sefton
514 C5 Carrick Fife
494 D6 Carrick Castle Ag & B
486 D3 Carriden Falk
276 C1 Carrington C Nott
300 B4 Carrington Lincs
471 F2 Carrington Mdloth
325 G6 Carrington Traffd
285 G5 Carrog Conwy
287 F6 Carrog Denbgs
486 A3 Carron Falk
568 C7 Carron Moray
435 H5 Carronbridge D & G
485 E3 Carron Bridge Falk
486 A3 Carronshore Falk
238 A4 Carroway Head Staffs
108 D1 Carrow Hill Mons
403 E5 Carrshield Nthumb
424 C5 Carrutherstown D & G
315 F6 Carr Vale Derbys
405 H6 Carrville Dur
479 J4 Carsaig Ag & B
505 G6 Carsaig Ag & B
416 A5 Carscreugh D & G
417 E5 Carsegowan D & G
528 B4 Carsegownie Angus
527 G4 Carse Gray Angus
416 C3 Carseriggan D & G
398 B3 Carsethorn D & G
95 F2 Carshalton Gt Lon
95 F2 Carshalton Beeches Gt Lon
95 F2 Carshalton on the Hill Gt Lon
294 A4 Carsington Derbys
456 D5 Carskiey Ag & B
417 F6 Carsluith D & G
434 B6 Carsphairn D & G
469 E5 Carstairs S Lans
469 F5 Carstairs Junction S Lans
139 E5 Carswell Marsh Oxon
93 H3 Cartbridge Surrey
451 E4 Carterhaugh Border
314 C3 Carter Knowle Sheff
71 F5 Carter's Clay Hants
145 H2 Carter's Green Essex
116 C6 Carter's Hill Wokham
134 D2 Carterspiece Gloucs
138 D3 Carterton Oxon
404 B4 Carterway Heads Nthumb
17 E3 Carthamartha Cnwll
4 C1 Carthew Cnwll
8 C2 Carthew Cnwll
370 C3 Carthorpe N York
442 C4 Cartington Nthumb
468 D5 Cartland S Lans
314 C4 Cartledge Derbys
365 E4 Cartmel Cumb
365 F2 Cartmel Fell Cumb
482 C4 Cartsdyke Inver
328 A3 Cartworth Kirk
128 C3 Carway Carmth
426 A5 Carwinley Cumb
4 C1 Carwynnen Cnwll
67 E4 Cary Fitzpaine Somset
423 G3 Carzield D & G
184 D1 Cascob Powys
136 B3 Cashes Green Gloucs
509 G1 Cashlie P & K
48 B2 Cashmoor Dorset
605 H3 Casho Shet
501 E4 Caskieberran Fife
137 F1 Cassey Compton Gloucs
139 G2 Cassington Oxon
395 G2 Cassop Dur
3 E4 Castallack Cnwll
34 c3 Castel Guern
305 G6 Castell Conwy
307 G6 Castell Denbgs
304 B5 Castell IoA
180 B5 Castell Howell Cerdgn
133 E6 Castell-y-Bwch Torfn
129 E2 Castell-y-Rhingyll Carmth
366 C4 Casterton Cumb
29 F2 Castle Devon
43 E2 Castle Somset
85 F6 Castle Somset
253 G4 Castle Acre Norfk
194 B3 Castle Ashby Nhants
591 D8 Castlebay W Isls
368 D1 Castle Bolton N York
214 A2 Castle Bromwich Solhll
278 D6 Castle Bytham Lincs
151 H4 Castlebythe Pembks
232 C3 Castle Caereinion Powys
198 C6 Castle Camps Cambs
320 C3 Castle Carlton Lincs
401 F3 Castle Carrock Cumb
485 F4 Castlecary Falk
67 G3 Castle Cary Somset
111 E4 Castle Combe Wilts
470 B6 Castlecraig Border
566 E3 Castlecraig Highld
236 C5 Castlecroft Wolves
275 H4 Castle Donington Leics
413 E2 Castle Douglas D & G
314 C3 Castle Dyke Sheff
138 B5 Castle Eaton Swindn
396 B2 Castle Eden Dur
243 G5 Castle End C Pete
310 A3 Castlefields Halton
234 C2 Castle Fields Shrops
344 A4 Castleford Wakefd
187 F5 Castle Frome Herefs
3 E3 Castle Gate Cnwll
328 D4 Castle Green Barns
120 C3 Castle Green Gt Lon
209 F2 Castlegreen Shrops
93 G2 Castle Green Surrey
274 D6 Castle Gresley Derbys
466 C2 Castlehead Rens
173 F2 Castle Hedingham Essex
449 H2 Castlehill Border
78 D4 Castle Hill E Susx
588 F3 Castlehill Highld
97 G6 Castle Hill Kent
513 G3 Castlehill P & K
445 E5 Castlehill S Ayrs
326 D6 Castle Hill Stockp
201 F5 Castle Hill Suffk
483 E4 Castlehill W Duns
187 H3 Castle Hill Worcs
415 F5 Castle Kennedy D & G
421 F2 Castlemaddy D & G
125 F5 Castlemartin Pembks
467 F3 Castlemilk C Glas
424 C4 Castlemilk D & G
151 E3 Castlemorris Pembks
162 A2 Castlemorton Worcs
425 F1 Castle O'er D & G
309 H4 Castle Park Ches
389 G5 Castlerigg Cumb
252 D3 Castle Rising Norfk
404 C5 Castleside Dur
341 E4 Castle Street Calder
193 G6 Castlethorpe M Keyn
332 D3 Castlethorpe N Linc
537 J4 Castleton Abers
480 B3 Castleton Ag & B
526 D5 Castleton Angus
313 G3 Castleton Derbys
386 A3 Castleton N York
107 E3 Castleton Newpt
499 E2 Castleton P & K
326 C2 Castleton Rochdl
550 B1 Castleton Village Highld
289 F4 Castletown Ches
391 E3 Castletown Cumb
32 B5 Castletown Dorset
588 F3 Castletown Highld
322 c9 Castletown IoM
272 C5 Castletown Staffs
406 B3 Castletown Sundld
55 E3 Castle Town W Susx
161 G4 Castletump Gloucs
105 E5 Castle-upon-Alun V Glam
214 A1 Castle Vale Birm
439 E4 Castleweary Border
410 D4 Castlewigg D & G
356 B5 Castley N York
200 C6 Castling's Heath Suffk
248 C5 Caston Norfk
243 G5 Castor C Pete
103 E4 Caswell Swans
463 F5 Catacol N Ayrs
378 B5 Cat Bank Cumb
109 G3 Catbrain S Glos
134 C4 Catbrook Mons
308 B5 Catch Flints
2 D4 Catchall Cnwll
214 D4 Catchems Corner Solhll
212 A4 Catchems End Worcs
405 E4 Catchgate Dur
589 H5 Catchory Highld
440 D4 Catcleugh Nthumb
315 E2 Catcliffe Rothm
112 B4 Catcomb Wilts
66 B2 Catcott Somset
95 G3 Caterham Surrey
192 B3 Catesby Nhants
256 D5 Catfield Norfk
606 F7 Catfirth Shet
120 A5 Catford Gt Lon
338 C2 Catforth Lancs
106 C4 Cathays Cardif
106 C4 Cathays Park Cardif
467 E2 Cathcart C Glas
158 B4 Cathedine Powys
214 B3 Catherine-de-Barnes Solhll
342 A4 Catherine Slack Brad
52 B2 Catherington Hants
29 G4 Catherston Leweston Dorset
211 F4 Catherton Shrops
328 C3 Cat Hill Barns
215 H4 Cathiron Warwks
366 C1 Catholes Cumb
472 B5 Cathpair Border
51 F3 Catisfield Hants
326 C1 Catley Lane Head Rochdl
187 F6 Catley Southfield Herefs
535 H4 Catlodge Highld
426 C4 Catlowdy Cumb
171 G2 Catmere End Essex
114 C3 Catmore W Berk
19 G3 Caton Devon
351 H2 Caton Lancs
352 B1 Caton Green Lancs
19 E2 Cator Court Devon
445 H4 Catrine E Ayrs
108 C1 Cat's Ash Newpt
256 C5 Cat's Common Norfk
292 B4 Cats Edge Staffs
58 B4 Catsfield E Susx
58 B4 Catsfield Stream E Susx
67 E4 Catsgore Somset
67 F3 Catsham Somset
328 C4 Catshaw Barns
213 E5 Catshill Worcs
237 G4 Catshill Wsall
272 B3 Cat's Hill Cross Staffs
450 C4 Catslackburn Border
116 B2 Catslip Oxon
235 G5 Catstree Shrops
357 E4 Cattal N York
175 F3 Cattawade Suffk
11 E3 Cattedown C Plym
351 G6 Catterall Lancs
383 F5 Catterick N York
383 F5 Catterick Bridge N York
383 E5 Catterick Garrison N York
390 D3 Catterlen Cumb
541 G4 Catterline Abers
357 G5 Catterton N York
93 G6 Catteshall Surrey
216 B4 Catthorpe Leics
30 D3 Cattistock Dorset
193 E6 Cattle End Nhants
370 D4 Catton N York
403 E3 Catton Nthumb
361 E5 Catwick E R Yk
219 F5 Catworth Cambs
136 D2 Caudle Green Gloucs
248 B4 Caudlesprings Norfk
194 D6 Caulcott Beds
166 B5 Caulcott Oxon
439 F2 Cauld Border
486 D4 Cauldcoats Holdings Falk
528 D5 Cauldcots Angus
497 F6 Cauldhame Stirlg
439 G1 Cauldmill Border
293 E5 Cauldon Staffs
293 E5 Cauldon Lowe Staffs
570 D4 Cauldwells Abers
413 H3 Caulkerbush D & G
426 B3 Caulside D & G
46 C2 Caundle Marsh Dorset
212 B3 Caunsall Worcs
296 D2 Caunton Notts
52 B2 Causeway Hants
74 A5 Causeway Hants
364 D3 Causeway End Cumb
365 G2 Causeway End Cumb
172 D6 Causeway End Essex
448 D2 Causewayend S Lans
112 A3 Causeway End Wilts
341 H3 Causeway Foot Calder
328 B2 Causeway Foot Kirk
213 E2 Causeway Green Sandw
498 B5 Causewayhead Stirlg
234 C5 Causewaywood Shrops
405 F3 Causey Dur
560 D6 Causeyend Abers
443 F6 Causey Park Bridge Nthumb
39 F5 Caute Devon
380 B5 Cautley Cumb
199 F5 Cavendish Suffk
275 G4 Cavendish Bridge Leics
223 F6 Cavenham Suffk
451 H4 Cavers Carre Border
166 C4 Caversfield Oxon
116 B4 Caversham Readg
116 B4 Caversham Heights Readg
292 C6 Caverswall Staffs
566 E6 Cawdor Highld
360 B4 Cawkeld E R Yk
320 A4 Cawkwell Lincs
344 D2 Cawood N York
10 D3 Cawsand Cnwll
255 F3 Cawston Norfk
215 H5 Cawston Warwks
328 D3 Cawthorne Barns
373 E2 Cawthorne N York
279 F5 Cawthorpe Lincs
372 B4 Cawton N York
196 D3 Caxton Cambs
210 C5 Caynham Shrops
297 H5 Caythorpe Lincs
296 C5 Caythorpe Notts
374 D3 Cayton N York
592 C4 Ceann a Bhàigh W Isls
595 J4 Ceann a Bhàigh W Isls
595 L4 Ceann a Bhàigh W Isls
597 L1 Ceann a' Chòinich W Isls
590 F4 Ceann a Deas Loch Baghasdail W Isls
595 K3 Ceann a' Gharaidh W Isls
599 J6 Ceann a-Muigh Chuil W Isls
599 K7 Ceann a-Staigh Chuil W Isls
590 F3 Ceann a Tuath Loch Baghasdail W Isls
591 D8 Ceann Loch W Isls
595 K4 Ceann-na-Cleithe W Isls
597 L1 Ceann nam Buailtean W Isls
597 H4 Ceann Shiphoirt W Isls
591 C8 Ceann Tangabhal W Isls
597 G4 Ceann Tarabhaigh W Isls
597 J4 Cearsiadair W Isls
592 D2 Ceathramh Meadhanach W Isls
267 G5 Cedig Powys
107 E2 Cefn Newpt
233 E2 Cefn Powys
306 D6 Cefn Berain Conwy
286 C4 Cefn-Brith Conwy
130 A2 Cefn-Bryn-Brain Carmth
102 D3 Cefn-Bychan Swans
269 E1 Cefn-Bychan Wrexhm
128 D5 Cefncaeau Carmth
268 D3 Cefn Canol Powys
306 B6 Cefn-Coch Conwy
231 H4 Cefn Coch Powys
268 B4 Cefn Coch Powys
131 G3 Cefn-Coed-y-Cymmer Myr Td
132 D5 Cefn-Crib Torfn
104 D3 Cefn Cribwr Brdgnd
104 D3 Cefn Cross Brdgnd
267 F2 Cefn-Ddwysarn Gwynd
209 E2 Cefn Einion Shrops
128 D2 Cefneithin Carmth
308 B6 Cefn-Eurgain Flints
132 B5 Cefn Fforest Caerph
104 D3 Cefn Glas Brdgnd
132 B3 Cefn Golau Blae G
182 D5 Cefn-Gorwydd Powys
132 B5 Cefn Hengoed Caerph
103 G2 Cefn-Hengoed Swans
205 E3 Cefn Llwyd Cerdgn
269 E1 Cefn-mawr Wrexhm
131 G4 Cefnpennar Rhondd
131 E3 Cefn Rhigos Rhondd
288 D3 Cefn-y-Bedd Flints
129 G4 Cefn-y-Garth Swans
152 D4 Cefn-y-Pant Carmth
180 B3 Cei-Bach Cerdgn
303 F3 Ceidio IoA
303 G5 Ceint IoA
230 B3 Ceinws Powys
181 F5 Cellan Cerdgn
503 F4 Cellardyke Fife
292 C5 Cellarhead Staffs
99 F2 Cellarhill Kent
287 H1 Celyn-Mali Flints
303 E2 Cemaes IoA
230 C3 Cemmaes Powys
230 C4 Cemmaes Road Powys
153 F1 Cenarth Carmth
263 H2 Cenin Gwynd
482 C4 Central Inver
519 J3 Ceol na Mara Highld
597 K3 Ceòs W Isls
502 C2 Ceres Fife
31 F2 Cerne Abbas Dorset
137 G5 Cerney Wick Gloucs
303 F6 Cerrigceinwen IoA
130 B6 Cerrig Llwydion Neath
303 G2 Cerrig-Mân IoA
286 D5 Cerrigydrudion Conwy
257 E6 Cess Norfk
452 D5 Cessford Border
283 F3 Ceunant Gwynd
162 C3 Chaceley Gloucs
162 B3 Chaceley Hole Gloucs
162 C4 Chaceley Stock Gloucs
6 D5 Chacewater Cnwll
167 E2 Chackmore Bucks
192 A6 Chacombe Nhants
189 F5 Chadbury Worcs
326 C3 Chadderton Oldham
326 C3 Chadderton Fold Oldham
275 F2 Chaddesden C Derb
212 C5 Chaddesley Corbett Worcs
17 F3 Chaddlehanger Devon
11 G2 Chaddlewood C Plym
114 B4 Chaddleworth W Berk
312 B2 Chadkirk Stockp
165 E5 Chadlington Oxon
191 F4 Chadshunt Warwks
237 E2 Chadsmoor Staffs
194 A3 Chadstone Nhants
213 F2 Chad Valley Birm
277 G5 Chadwell Leics
195 F1 Chadwell End Beds
120 C2 Chadwell Heath Gt Lon
121 F4 Chadwell St Mary Thurr
212 B6 Chadwick Worcs
214 C5 Chadwick End Solhll
324 C5 Chadwick Green St Hel
44 D5 Chaffcombe Somset
121 E4 Chafford Hundred Thurr
25 H5 Chagford Devon
77 G6 Chailey E Susx
245 F4 Chainbridge Cambs
300 B6 Chain Bridge Lincs
98 A5 Chainhurst Kent
48 C3 Chalbury Dorset
48 C3 Chalbury Common Dorset
95 G3 Chaldon Surrey
32 D3 Chaldon Herring or East Chaldon Dorset
36 D5 Chale IoW
36 D5 Chale Green IoW
117 H1 Chalfont Common Bucks

117 G1 Chalfont Grove Bucks
142 D6 Chalfont St Giles Bucks
117 H1 Chalfont St Peter Bucks
136 D4 Chalford Gloucs
141 F4 Chalford Oxon
87 F4 Chalford Wilts
136 C4 Chalford Hill Gloucs
169 E4 Chalgrave Beds
140 D5 Chalgrove Oxon
121 G5 Chalk Kent
146 C2 Chalk End Essex
400 B5 Chalkfoot Cumb
247 H3 Chalkhill Norfk
116 B4 Chalkhouse Green Oxon
142 A3 Chalkshire Bucks
82 D2 Chalksole Kent
29 G1 Chalkway Somset
98 D2 Chalkwell Kent
122 C2 Chalkwell Sthend
12 A4 Challaborough Devon
61 G3 Challacombe Devon
607 J4 Challister Shet
416 D3 Challoch D & G
99 G4 Challock Kent
30 D2 Chalmington Dorset
169 E4 Chalton Beds
195 G5 Chalton Beds
52 C1 Chalton Hants
122 A2 Chalvedon Essex
117 G4 Chalvey Slough
57 E3 Chalvington E Susx
60 D2 Chambercombe Devon
99 E6 Chamber's Green Kent
486 D4 Champany Falk
29 G3 Champernhayes Marsh Dorset
41 F2 Champson Devon
501 G2 Chance Inn Fife
204 D4 Chancery Cerdgn
161 G1 Chance's Pitch Herefs
143 F5 Chandler's Cross Herts
161 H2 Chandler's Cross Worcs
72 B5 Chandler's Ford Hants
92 B3 Chandlers Green Hants
409 F2 Changue D & G
435 F4 Chanlockfoot D & G
195 G3 Channel's End Beds
82 C3 Channel Tunnel Terminal Kent
605 G6 Channerwick Shet
40 B3 Chantry Devon
86 C5 Chantry Somset
201 F6 Chantry Suffk
7 F1 Chapel Cnwll
389 F3 Chapel Cumb
500 D6 Chapel Fife
343 F2 Chapel Allerton Leeds
84 C4 Chapel Allerton Somset
14 D3 Chapel Amble Cnwll
193 F1 Chapel Brampton Nhants
272 B2 Chapel Chorlton Staffs
63 G3 Chapel Cleeve Somset
79 E5 Chapel Cross E Susx
169 F1 Chapel End Beds
195 F5 Chapel End Beds
195 G3 Chapel End Beds
219 G3 Chapel End Cambs
290 D6 Chapel End Ches
172 B4 Chapel End Essex
219 G2 Chapel End Nhants
239 E6 Chapel End Warwks
313 E3 Chapel-en-le-Frith Derbys
326 A3 Chapel Field Bury
256 D5 Chapel Field Norfk
215 E4 Chapel Fields Covtry
357 H4 Chapel Fields York
281 F5 Chapelgate Lincs
170 D3 Chapel Green Herts
191 H2 Chapel Green Warwks
214 D2 Chapel Green Warwks
116 D6 Chapel Green Wokham
344 D4 Chapel Haddlesey N York
468 B2 Chapelhall N Lans
220 D3 Chapel Head Cambs
561 G2 Chapel Hill Abers
135 E4 Chapel Hill Gloucs
566 E2 Chapelhill Highld
299 F4 Chapel Hill Lincs
134 C5 Chapel Hill Mons
512 B3 Chapelhill P & K
513 E5 Chapelhill P & K
449 H6 Chapelhope Border
324 B3 Chapel House Lancs
111 F6 Chapel Knapp Wilts
425 G5 Chapelknowe D & G
209 F4 Chapel Lawn Shrops
367 E4 Chapel-le-Dale N York
43 F2 Chapel Leigh Somset
451 G1 Chapel Mains Border
313 E3 Chapel Milton Derbys
132 D5 Chapel of Ease Caerph
559 G5 Chapel of Garioch Abers
557 F2 Chapel of Stoneywood C Aber
451 H1 Chapel on Leader Border
111 E6 Chapel Plaister Wilts
57 G2 Chapel Row E Susx
147 F4 Chapel Row Essex
115 F6 Chapel Row W Berk
339 G5 Chapels Bl w D
363 E5 Chapels Cumb
321 G5 Chapel St Leonards Lincs
378 B3 Chapel Stile Cumb
329 E1 Chapelthorpe Wakefd
557 F6 Chapelton Abers
528 D5 Chapelton Angus
40 B2 Chapelton Devon
467 G5 Chapelton S Lans
325 G1 Chapeltown Bl w D
7 G2 Chapel Town Cnwll
343 F2 Chapeltown Leeds
552 E4 Chapeltown Moray
329 E5 Chapeltown Sheff
213 E4 Chapman's Hill Worcs
87 E5 Chapmanslade Wilts
79 E6 Chapman's Town E Susx
23 H4 Chapmans Well Devon
144 D1 Chapmore End Herts
174 A4 Chappel Essex
16 D5 Charaton Cross Cnwll
96 D5 Charcott Kent
44 C6 Chard Somset
29 F2 Chard Junction Somset
44 C5 Chardleigh Green Somset
29 F2 Chardstock Devon
110 C1 Charfield S Glos
110 C1 Charfield Green S Glos
110 C1 Charfield Hill S Glos
213 E6 Chargrove Worcs
162 D6 Chargrove Gloucs
99 E5 Charing Kent
99 E5 Charing Heath Kent
99 E4 Charing Hill Kent
164 B2 Charingworth Gloucs
165 F6 Charlbury Oxon
110 C6 Charlcombe BaNES
112 A4 Charlcutt Wilts
190 D3 Charlecote Warwks
237 F6 Charlemont Sandw
61 G5 Charles Devon
61 G5 Charles Bottom Devon
452 A4 Charlesfield Border
93 E6 Charleshill Surrey

527 E5 Charleston Angus
466 C2 Charleston Rens
571 J3 Charlestown Abers
342 C2 Charlestown Brad
557 G4 Charlestown C Aber
341 F4 Charlestown Calder
8 C3 Charlestown Cnwll
312 D1 Charlestown Derbys
32 A4 Charlestown Dorset
487 E3 Charlestown Fife
562 D2 Charlestown Highld
565 L7 Charlestown Highld
326 C2 Charlestown Manch
567 L3 Charlestown Moray
326 B5 Charlestown Salfd
568 D7 Charlestown of Aberlour Moray
200 A4 Charles Tye Suffk
327 F6 Charlesworth Derbys
120 B6 Charlton Gt Lon
90 A5 Charlton Hants
169 H4 Charlton Herts
166 B2 Charlton Nhants
428 C3 Charlton Nthumb
114 C2 Charlton Oxon
44 B2 Charlton Somset
86 A6 Charlton Somset
86 B4 Charlton Somset
118 B6 Charlton Surrey
53 F2 Charlton W Susx
69 F5 Charlton Wilts
111 H2 Charlton Wilts
189 F5 Charlton Worcs
212 B5 Charlton Worcs
234 D2 Charlton Wrekin
163 F5 Charlton Abbots Gloucs
67 E4 Charlton Adam Somset
70 D5 Charlton-All-Saints Wilts
329 E5 Charltonbrook Sheff
67 H5 Charlton Horethorne Somset
163 E5 Charlton Kings Gloucs
67 E4 Charlton Mackrell Somset
47 H4 Charlton Marshall Dorset
68 B3 Charlton Musgrove Somset
140 C1 Charlton-on-Otmoor Oxon
47 G4 Charlton on the Hill Dorset
163 E5 Charlton Park Gloucs
385 G1 Charltons R & Cl
88 D3 Charlton St Peter Wilts
77 G3 Charlwood E Susx
73 G3 Charlwood Surrey
76 D1 Charlwood Surrey
64 D4 Charlynch Somset
48 D6 Charminster Bmouth
32 B1 Charminster Dorset
29 G4 Charmouth Dorset
68 D3 Charnage Wilts
167 E5 Charndon Bucks
271 H3 Charnes Staffs
139 F6 Charney Bassett Oxon
324 C1 Charnock Green Lancs
314 D3 Charnock Hall Sheff
324 C1 Charnock Richard Lancs
202 A3 Charsfield Suffk
98 B4 Chart Corner Kent
91 F3 Charter Alley Hants
85 E3 Charterhouse Somset
485 F2 Chartershall Stirlg
139 E2 Charterville Allotments Oxon
100 B5 Chartham Kent
100 B4 Chartham Hatch Kent
98 B5 Chart Hill Kent
142 C4 Chartridge Bucks
98 B4 Chart Sutton Kent
116 C4 Charvil Wokham
192 B3 Charwelton Nhants
120 D1 Chase Cross Gt Lon
161 H2 Chase End Street Worcs
110 C2 Chase Hill Gloucs
237 F3 Chase Terrace Staffs
237 G3 Chasetown Staffs
164 C4 Chastleton Oxon
23 G2 Chasty Devon
353 F6 Chatburn Lancs
272 A3 Chatcull Staffs
234 B3 Chatford Shrops
106 D2 Chatham Caerph
98 A1 Chatham Medway
147 E1 Chatham Green Essex
342 B3 Chat Hill Brad
455 F4 Chathill Nthumb
188 C2 Chatley Worcs
122 B5 Chattenden Medway
171 G4 Chatter End Essex
221 E2 Chatteris Cambs
291 G4 Chatterley Staffs
118 B5 Chattern Hill Surrey
340 B6 Chatterton Lancs
175 E1 Chattisham Suffk
214 B1 Chattle Hill Warwks
453 E6 Chatto Border
454 D4 Chatton Nthumb
143 E3 Chaulden Herts
169 E5 Chaul End Beds
233 H2 Chavel Shrops
136 C5 Chavenage Green Gloucs
117 E6 Chavey Down Br For
41 E5 Chawleigh Devon
139 H4 Chawley Oxon
188 C2 Chawson Worcs
195 H3 Chawston Beds
73 H2 Chawton Hants
135 G2 Chaxhill Gloucs
116 A4 Chazey Heath Oxon
292 D6 Cheadle Staffs
311 H2 Cheadle Stockp
311 H2 Cheadle Heath Stockp
311 H2 Cheadle Hulme Stockp
292 D6 Cheadle Park Staffs
95 E2 Cheam Gt Lon
171 F3 Cheapside Herts
117 F6 Cheapside W & M
141 F2 Chearsley Bucks
272 C4 Chebsey Staffs
115 H3 Checkendon Oxon
291 E5 Checkley Ches
160 D2 Checkley Herefs
273 F2 Checkley Staffs
291 E5 Checkley Green Ches
199 F3 Chedburgh Suffk
85 E4 Cheddar Somset
142 C1 Cheddington Bucks
292 C4 Cheddleton Staffs
292 C4 Cheddleton Heath Staffs
44 A2 Cheddon Fitzpaine Somset
136 D6 Chedglow Wilts
250 D5 Chedgrave Norfk
30 B1 Chedington Dorset
226 D4 Chediston Suffk
226 C4 Chediston Green Suffk
137 G2 Chedworth Gloucs
137 F2 Chedworth Laines Gloucs
65 F4 Chedzoy Somset
87 F2 Cheeseman's Green Kent
326 B4 Cheetham Hill Manch
60 D3 Cheglinch Devon
98 C4 Chegworth Kent
41 E5 Cheldon Devon
311 G4 Chelford Ches
275 F3 Chellaston C Derb

292 A4 Chell Heath C Stke
194 D3 Chellington Beds
170 C4 Chells Herts
211 G2 Chelmarsh Shrops
147 E3 Chelmer Village Essex
210 B1 Chelmick Shrops
176 D2 Chelmondiston Suffk
313 F5 Chelmorton Derbys
146 D3 Chelmsford Essex
43 G4 Chelmsine Somset
214 B2 Chelmsley Wood Solhll
119 F4 Chelsea Gt Lon
96 C2 Chelsfield Gt Lon
95 H3 Chelsham Surrey
43 G3 Chelston Somset
20 B5 Chelston Torbay
200 C5 Chelsworth Suffk
200 C5 Chelsworth Common Suffk
163 E5 Cheltenham Gloucs
218 D6 Chelveston Nhants
109 E6 Chelvey N Som
85 E1 Chelvey Batch N Som
86 A2 Chelwood BaNES
77 H4 Chelwood Common E Susx
77 H3 Chelwood Gate E Susx
137 E6 Chelworth Wilts
112 C1 Chelworth Lower Green Wilts
137 G6 Chelworth Upper Green Wilts
86 B6 Chelynch Somset
209 H3 Cheney Longville Shrops
3 G2 Chenhalls Cnwll
143 E5 Chenies Bucks
134 C6 Chepstow Mons
325 F3 Chequerbent Bolton
344 B5 Chequerfield Wakefd
245 H3 Chequers Corner Norfk
81 F2 Chequertree Kent
112 B5 Cherhill Wilts
136 D5 Cherington Gloucs
164 D2 Cherington Warwks
38 C2 Cheristow Devon
62 A2 Cheriton Devon
73 E4 Cheriton Hants
82 C3 Cheriton Kent
102 C3 Cheriton Swans
26 B4 Cheriton Bishop Devon
26 D1 Cheriton Fitzpaine Devon
125 G5 Cheriton or Stackpole Elidor Pembks
271 F6 Cherrington Wrekin
512 C5 Cherrybank P & K
347 E1 Cherry Burton E R Yk
172 B4 Cherry Green Essex
171 E4 Cherry Green Herts
197 G3 Cherry Hinton Cambs
234 B2 Cherry Orchard Shrops
188 C4 Cherry Orchard Worcs
339 F4 Cherry Tree Bl w D
312 C1 Cherry Tree Stockp
275 F2 Cherrytree Hill C Derb
318 C5 Cherry Willingham Lincs
94 A1 Chertsey Surrey
94 B1 Chertsey Meads Surrey
142 D4 Chesham Bucks
326 B2 Chesham Bury
142 D5 Chesham Bois Bucks
145 E4 Cheshunt Herts
98 D2 Chesley Kent
237 E3 Cheslyn Hay Staffs
214 B5 Chessetts Wood Warwks
94 D2 Chessington Gt Lon
142 D4 Chessmount Bucks
237 G2 Chestall Staffs
289 E1 Chester Ches
67 H1 Chesterblade Somset
314 C5 Chesterfield Derbys
237 G3 Chesterfield Staffs
471 G1 Chesterhill Mdloth
428 D2 Chesterhope Nthumb
451 G4 Chesterknowes Border
405 G4 Chester-le-Street Dur
405 G5 Chester Moor Dur
440 B2 Chesters Border
452 B5 Chesters Border
197 G2 Chesterton Cambs
243 G5 Chesterton Cambs
137 F4 Chesterton Gloucs
166 C5 Chesterton Oxon
236 A5 Chesterton Shrops
291 G5 Chesterton Staffs
191 F3 Chesterton Warwks
191 E3 Chesterton Green Warwks
403 E1 Chesterwood Nthumb
100 B2 Chestfield Kent
389 G5 Chestnut Hill Cumb
98 D2 Chestnut Street Kent
19 E6 Cheston Devon
271 G4 Cheswardine Shrops
235 G1 Cheswell Wrekin
475 F5 Cheswick Nthumb
475 F5 Cheswick Buildings Nthumb
214 A4 Cheswick Green Solhll
46 B3 Chetnole Dorset
42 C5 Chettiscombe Devon
222 A3 Chettisham Cambs
48 A2 Chettle Dorset
211 F1 Chetton Shrops
166 D4 Chetwode Bucks
271 H6 Chetwynd Aston Wrekin
198 D2 Cheveley Cambs
96 C3 Chevening Kent
143 F1 Cheverell's Green Herts
355 G6 Chevin End Brad
199 F3 Chevington Suffk
42 C4 Chevithorne Devon
85 G2 Chew Magna BaNES
325 F3 Chew Moor Bolton
85 G2 Chew Stoke BaNES
86 B1 Chewton Keynsham BaNES
85 G4 Chewton Mendip Somset
215 E4 Cheylesmore Covtry
25 E3 Chichacott Devon
194 C5 Chicheley M Keyn
53 F4 Chichester W Susx
32 A3 Chickerell Dorset
69 F3 Chicklade Wilts
169 G2 Chicksands Beds
185 E4 Chickward Herefs
73 G6 Chidden Hants
75 F2 Chiddingfold Surrey
57 E2 Chiddingly E Susx
96 C5 Chiddingstone Kent
96 D5 Chiddingstone Causeway Kent
96 C6 Chiddingstone Hoath Kent
29 H4 Chideock Dorset
63 G4 Chidham W Susx
52 D4 Chidswell Kirk
343 E5 Chidswell Kirk
114 D5 Chieveley W Berk
146 D2 Chignall St James Essex
146 D2 Chignall Smealy Essex
145 H3 Chigwell Essex
145 G6 Chigwell Row Essex
72 A2 Chilbolton Hants
72 B1 Chilbolton Down Hants
134 C2 Chilbridge Dorset
72 D4 Chilcomb Hants
30 C4 Chilcombe Dorset

64 B4 Chilcombe Somset
86 A4 Chilcompton Somset
238 D2 Chilcote Leics
121 F2 Childerditch Essex
197 E2 Childerley Gate Cambs
309 E4 Childer Thornton Ches
47 F2 Child Okeford Dorset
114 B2 Childrey Oxon
96 D3 Childsbridge Kent
119 E2 Child's Hill Gt Lon
163 G2 Childswickham Worcs
309 F2 Childwall Lpool
143 G2 Childwick Bury Herts
143 G2 Childwick Green Herts
30 D5 Chilfrome Dorset
53 E2 Chilgrove W Susx
99 H4 Chilham Kent
22 D5 Chillaton Devon
101 E5 Chillenden Kent
36 D4 Chillerton IoW
202 D4 Chillesford Suffk
454 D4 Chillingham Nthumb
12 D4 Chillington Devon
44 D5 Chillington Somset
79 F1 Chilmark Kent
69 G3 Chilmark Wilts
81 E1 Chilmington Green Kent
57 G2 Chilsham E Susx
165 E6 Chilson Oxon
29 F2 Chilson Common Somset
17 F4 Chilsworthy Cnwll
23 G1 Chilsworthy Devon
169 G6 Chiltern Green Beds
67 E6 Chilthorne Domer Somset
67 E6 Chiltington E Susx
141 E2 Chilton Bucks
395 F4 Chilton Dur
101 G3 Chilton Kent
114 D2 Chilton Oxon
174 A1 Chilton Suffk
73 E1 Chilton Candover Hants
67 F5 Chilton Cantelo Somset
113 H5 Chilton Foliat Wilts
200 A6 Chilton Grove Suffk
395 F3 Chilton Lane Dur
405 H5 Chilton Moor Sundld
65 G4 Chilton Polden Somset
199 F5 Chilton Street Suffk
65 E4 Chilton Trinity Somset
215 F1 Chilvers Coton Warwks
276 B2 Chilwell Notts
72 B6 Chilworth Hants
93 H5 Chilworth Surrey
72 A6 Chilworth Old Village Hants
139 E4 Chimney Oxon
139 E1 Chimney-End Oxon
199 E5 Chimney Street Suffk
91 H3 Chineham Hants
145 E6 Chingford Gt Lon
145 E6 Chingford Green Gt Lon
312 D3 Chinley Derbys
313 E3 Chinley Head Derbys
141 F4 Chinnor Oxon
43 F3 Chipley Somset
136 A3 Chipmans Platt Gloucs
271 G3 Chipnall Shrops
226 B4 Chippenhall Green Suffk
222 C6 Chippenham Cambs
111 G5 Chippenham Wilts
143 E4 Chipperfield Herts
171 E3 Chipping Herts
352 C6 Chipping Lancs
144 B5 Chipping Barnet Gt Lon
164 B2 Chipping Campden Gloucs
147 G1 Chipping Hill Essex
165 E4 Chipping Norton Oxon
146 B4 Chipping Ongar Essex
110 C3 Chipping Sodbury S Glos
192 A5 Chipping Warden Nhants
42 D2 Chipstable Somset
95 F3 Chipstead Surrey
233 E5 Chirbury Shrops
269 E2 Chirk Wrexhm
269 E2 Chirk Bank Shrops
269 E2 Chirk Green Wrexhm
415 H1 Chirmorrie S Ayrs
474 C3 Chirnside Border
474 B3 Chirnsidebridge Border
431 F6 Chirton N Tyne
88 C5 Chirton Wilts
116 D2 Chisbridge Cross Bucks
89 G1 Chisbury Wilts
45 F4 Chiselborough Somset
113 H4 Chiseldon Swindn
140 C5 Chiselhampton Oxon
341 G4 Chiserley Calder
120 B5 Chislehurst Gt Lon
120 B5 Chislehurst West Gt Lon
100 D3 Chislet Kent
100 D3 Chislet Forstal Kent
32 B5 Chiswell Dorset
143 G4 Chiswell Green Herts
119 E4 Chiswick Gt Lon
197 E5 Chiswick End Cambs
312 C1 Chisworth Derbys
58 D2 Chitcombe E Susx
74 C5 Chithurst W Susx
221 G5 Chittering Cambs
27 E2 Chitterley Devon
88 A6 Chitterne Wilts
40 C3 Chittlehamholt Devon
40 C2 Chittlehampton Devon
87 H1 Chittoe Wilts
174 C4 Chitts Hills Essex
100 D3 Chitty Kent
12 D5 Chivelstone Devon
60 C5 Chivenor Devon
142 B3 Chivery Bucks
93 G2 Chobham Surrey
89 F6 Cholderton Wilts
142 C3 Cholesbury Bucks
429 E5 Chollerford Nthumb
429 E5 Chollerton Nthumb
290 C3 Cholmondeston Ches
115 F2 Cholsey Oxon
186 B3 Cholstrey Herefs
85 H3 Cholwell BaNES
385 F5 Chop Gate N York
431 E3 Choppington Nthumb
404 D3 Chopwell Gatesd
290 B4 Chorley Ches
324 D1 Chorley Lancs
211 F3 Chorley Shrops
237 G2 Chorley Staffs
74 C4 Chorley Common W Susx
143 E5 Chorleywood Herts
143 E5 Chorleywood Bottom Herts
143 E5 Chorleywood West Herts
291 E4 Choriton Ches
326 B6 Choriton-cum-Hardy Manch
289 G3 Choriton Lane Ches
209 G2 Choulton Shrops
405 G3 Chowdene Gatesd
289 G3 Chowley Ches
77 F5 Chownes Mead W Susx
171 F2 Chrishall Essex
245 G5 Christchurch Cambs
35 E2 Christchurch Dorset
134 C2 Christchurch Gloucs
107 F2 Christchurch Newpt
201 G5 Christchurch Park Suffk
263 G3 Christ... Wilts
111 H4 Christian Malford Wilts

289 F1 Christleton Ches
141 F6 Christmas Common Oxon
84 C3 Christon N Som
455 F5 Christon Bank Nthumb
26 C6 Christow Devon
484 D5 Chryston N Lans
18 B4 Chub Tor Devon
78 B3 Chuck Hatch E Susx
20 B2 Chudleigh Devon
20 A2 Chudleigh Knighton Devon
40 D5 Chulmleigh Devon
312 D1 Chunal Derbys
340 A4 Church Lancs
161 H6 Churcham Gloucs
271 G6 Church Aston Wrekin
209 E4 Churchbank Shrops
193 F1 Church Brampton Nhants
9 G2 Churchbridge Cnwll
237 E3 Churchbridge Staffs
380 D2 Church Brough Cumb
274 C3 Church Broughton Derbys
192 B3 Church Charwelton Nhants
340 D2 Church Clough Lancs
74 A4 Church Common Hants
6 C5 Church Coombe Cnwll
4 D6 Church Cove Cnwll
92 D4 Church Crookham Hants
162 D6 Churchdown Gloucs
272 B6 Church Eaton Staffs
168 D2 Church End Beds
168 D3 Church End Beds
168 D5 Church End Beds
170 A2 Church End Beds
195 E3 Church End Beds
195 F3 Church End Beds
195 F4 Church End Beds
195 H4 Church End Beds
141 F3 Church End Bucks
142 C2 Church End Bucks
219 F5 Church End Cambs
220 B3 Church End Cambs
221 E5 Church End Cambs
221 E6 Church End Cambs
245 E3 Church End Cambs
215 F4 Church End Covtry
360 D4 Church End E R Yk
147 E1 Church End Essex
148 D6 Church End Essex
172 B1 Church End Essex
172 B4 Church End Essex
172 C5 Church End Essex
173 E4 Church End Essex
135 G3 Church End Gloucs
136 A3 Church End Gloucs
162 C2 Church End Gloucs
119 E1 Church End Gt Lon
119 E3 Church End Gt Lon
91 H3 Church End Hants
143 E5 Church End Herts
143 F2 Church End Herts
170 C3 Church End Herts
171 F5 Church End Herts
280 B3 Church End Lincs
335 F5 Church End Lincs
245 H1 Church End Norfk
139 F3 Church End Oxon
165 E3 Church End Oxon
115 H5 Church End Readg
110 C1 Church End S Glos
176 D2 Church End Suffk
94 B3 Church End Surrey
214 D1 Church End Warwks
112 B4 Church End Wilts
162 B1 Church End Worcs
165 F4 Church Enstone Oxon
79 E6 Churches Green E Susx
344 C2 Church Fenton N York
187 G5 Churchfield Herefs
237 F6 Churchfield Sandw
70 C4 Churchfields Wilts
144 D4 Churchgate Herts
145 G2 Churchgate Street Essex
28 C3 Church Green Devon
225 E1 Church Green Norfk
274 D6 Church Gresley Derbys
139 G2 Church Hanborough Oxon
125 G2 Church Hill Pembks
237 E6 Church Hill Ches
237 F2 Church Hill Staffs
213 G6 Church Hill Worcs
83 E2 Church Hougham Kent
385 H5 Church Houses N York
29 E2 Churchill Devon
61 E3 Churchill Devon
84 D3 Churchill N Som
164 D5 Churchill Oxon
188 D4 Churchill Worcs
212 C4 Churchill Worcs
84 D2 Churchill Green N Som
43 H5 Churchinford Somset
33 G3 Church Knowle Dorset
317 F4 Church Laneham Notts
241 F6 Church Langton Leics
215 G4 Church Lawford Warwks
291 G3 Church Lawton Ches
273 F2 Church Leigh Staffs
189 F4 Church Lench Worcs
293 G6 Church Mayfield Staffs
290 D2 Church Minshull Ches
209 G2 Churchmoor Rough Shrops
53 F5 Church Norton W Susx
91 F4 Church Oakley Hants
216 B3 Churchover Warwks
234 C5 Church Preen Shrops
234 A4 Church Pulverbatch Shrops
43 G5 Church Stanton Somset
233 E6 Churchstoke Powys
12 C3 Churchstow Devon
192 D3 Church Stowe Nhants
199 F6 Church Street Essex
121 H5 Church Street Kent
234 B6 Church Stretton Shrops
126 C3 Churchtown Pembks
6 C5 Church Town Cnwll
15 F3 Churchtown Cnwll
390 B1 Churchtown Cumb
294 B2 Churchtown Derbys
23 F2 Churchtown Devon
61 G3 Churchtown Devon
351 G6 Churchtown Lancs
239 F1 Church Town Leics
331 G3 Churchtown N Linc
337 G6 Churchtown Sefton
209 E2 Churchtown Shrops
63 F4 Churchtown Somset
95 H4 Churchtown Surrey
105 H2 Church Village Rhondd
315 H6 Church Warsop Notts
164 C5 Church Westcote Gloucs
83 F1 Church Whitfield Kent
275 G3 Church Wilne Derbys
75 G6 Churchwood W Susx
292 C4 Churnet Grange Staffs
20 B5 Churscombe Torbay
13 G1 Churston Ferrers Torbay
74 D2 Churt Surrey
289 F3 Churton Ches
343 E4 Churwell Leeds
89 H4 Chute Cadley Wilts
89 H4 Chute Standen Wilts
306 A5 Chwefforddd Conwy
263 G3 Chwilog Gwynd
3 E3 Chyandour Cnwll

4 C4 Chyanvounder Cnwll
7 E6 Chycoose Cnwll
4 B2 Chynhale Cnwll
3 F3 Chynoweth Cnwll
4 C4 Chyvarloe Cnwll
134 C4 Cicelyford Mons
262 D6 Cilan Uchaf Gwynd
151 F2 Cilau Pembks
288 A2 Cilcain Flints
180 D2 Cilcennin Cerdgn
232 D4 Cilcewydd Powys
130 B4 Cilfrew Neath
106 A1 Cilfynydd Rhondd
178 D5 Cilgerran Pembks
156 A4 Cilgwyn Carmth
153 G1 Cilgwyn Cerdgn
283 E5 Cilgwyn Gwynd
180 D3 Ciliau-Aeron Cerdgn
593 D6 Cill Amhlaidh W Isls
590 E2 Cill Donnain W Isls
590 F5 Cille Bhrighde W Isls
593 E8 Cill Eireabhagh W Isls
590 E4 Cill Eireabhagh W Isls
130 A3 Cilmaengwyn Neath
183 G4 Cilmery Powys
155 E5 Cilsan Carmth
158 C1 Ciltwrch Powys
153 E2 Cilwendeg Pembks
130 A4 Cilybebyll Neath
156 B2 Cilycwm Carmth
263 E5 Cim Gwynd
130 B5 Cimla Neath
135 F2 Cinderford Gloucs
325 H3 Cinder Hill Bolton
295 C6 Cinderhill C Nott
294 D5 Cinderhill Derbys
96 D5 Cinder Hill Kent
77 C4 Cinder Hill W Susx
236 D6 Cinder Hill Wolves
310 C1 Cinnamon Brow Warrtn
117 F3 Cippenham Slough
178 C4 Cippyn Pembks
598 D8 Circebost W Isls
137 F4 Cirencester Gloucs
598 E6 Ciribhig W Isls
208 D2 City Powys
105 F4 City V Glam
303 G3 City Dulas IoA
516 F4 Clabhach Ag & B
481 G3 Clachaig Ag & B
551 J6 Clachaig Highld
462 C3 Clachan Ag & B
494 D2 Clachan Ag & B
506 C6 Clachan Ag & B
519 L7 Clachan Ag & B
543 H3 Clachan Highld
545 J2 Clachan Highld
574 D7 Clachan Highld
586 F4 Clachan Highld
593 D8 Clachan W Isls
516 B6 Clachan Mòr Ag & B
408 B2 Clachanmore D & G
592 D5 Clachan na Luib W Isls
484 C4 Clachan of Campsie E Duns
480 D3 Clachan of Glendaruel Ag & B
506 C6 Clachan-Seil Ag & B
479 K6 Clachbreck Ag & B
565 L7 Clachnaharry Highld
578 D4 Clachtoll Highld
486 B1 Clackmannan Clacks
568 C4 Clackmarras Moray
149 G2 Clacton-on-Sea Essex
461 E2 Cladach N Ayrs
592 E5 Cladach a' Bhaile Shear W Isls
592 D4 Cladach Chirebost W Isls
592 D4 Cladach Chnoc a Lin W Isls
592 D5 Cladach Iolaraigh W Isls
476 B6 Claddach Ag & B
507 J5 Cladich Ag & B
189 F3 Cladswell Worcs
519 G6 Claggan Highld
533 H8 Claggan Highld
542 C6 Claigan Highld
188 B3 Claines Worcs
17 F6 Clamoak Devon
86 B3 Clandown BaNES
52 B1 Clanfield Hants
138 D4 Clanfield Oxon
141 H3 Clanking Bucks
89 H5 Clanville Hants
67 G3 Clanville Somset
111 G4 Clanville Wilts
408 B4 Clanyard D & G
463 E3 Claonaig Ag & B
576 C3 Claonel Highld
48 C4 Clapgate Dorset
171 F5 Clapgate Herts
195 E4 Clapham Beds
26 D5 Clapham Devon
119 F4 Clapham Gt Lon
367 E6 Clapham N York
54 C3 Clapham W Susx
195 E4 Clapham Green Beds
356 A3 Clapham Green N York
100 B3 Clapham Hill Kent
119 F5 Clapham Park Gt Lon
81 G2 Clap Hill Kent
15 E4 Clapper Cnwll
80 B2 Clapper Hill Kent
474 D3 Clappers Border
378 C4 Clappersgate Cumb
605 H5 Clapphoull Shet
29 H1 Clapton Somset
86 A4 Clapton Somset
114 B5 Clapton W Berk
109 E5 Clapton in Gordano N Som
164 B6 Clapton-on-the-Hill Gloucs
119 H2 Clapton Park Gt Lon
40 D3 Clapworthy Devon
205 E3 Clarach Cerdgn
404 D2 Clara Vale Gatesd
152 A5 Clarbeston Pembks
151 H5 Clarbeston Road Pembks
316 D3 Clarborough Notts
588 E3 Clardon Highld
141 E5 Clare Oxon
199 F5 Clare Suffk
413 E1 Clarebrand D & G
236 C4 Claregate Wolves
94 C2 Claremont Park Surrey
424 B6 Clarencefield D & G
84 B2 Clarence Park N Som
240 C4 Clarendon Park C Leic
125 F2 Clareston Pembks
451 H4 Clarilaw Border
91 F4 Clarken Green Hants
312 B4 Clark Green Ches
326 D4 Clarksfield Oldham
76 C2 Clark's Green Surrey
281 E5 Clark's Hill Lincs
189 F6 Clark's Hill Lincs
467 E3 Clarkston E Rens
468 B1 Clarkston N Lans
129 G5 Clase Swans
565 J7 Clashandorran Highld
558 B3 Clashindarroch Abers
576 F6 Clashmore Highld
578 D3 Clashmore Highld
578 E3 Clashnessie Highld
552 E4 Clashnoir Moray
607 H5 Clate Shet

112 D6 Clatford Wilts
71 G2 Clatford Oakcuts Hants
512 A5 Clathy P & K
558 F4 Clatt Abers
231 F6 Clatter Powys
36 D3 Clatterford IoW
146 A4 Clatterford End Essex
146 B3 Clatterford End Essex
146 C2 Clatterford End Essex
540 C4 Clatterin' Brig Abers
502 C1 Clatto Fife
63 H5 Clatworthy Somset
461 E3 Clauchlands N Ayrs
338 D1 Claughton Lancs
352 B1 Claughton Lancs
308 D2 Claughton Wirral
65 E5 Clavelshay Somset
190 B2 Claverdon Warwks
84 D1 Claverham N Som
145 F4 Claverhambury Essex
171 G3 Clavering Essex
236 A6 Claverley Shrops
86 D2 Claverton BaNES
86 D2 Claverton Down BaNES
105 H4 Clawdd-Côch V Glam
287 F4 Clawdd-Newydd Denbgs
287 F6 Clawdd Poncen Denbgs
366 A4 Clawthorpe Cumb
23 G3 Clawton Devon
333 G6 Claxby Lincs
320 D5 Claxby St Andrew Lincs
358 C2 Claxton N York
250 C4 Claxton Norfk
227 F3 Clay Common Suffk
216 C4 Clay Coton Nhants
294 D2 Clay Cross Derbys
162 D3 Claydon Gloucs
201 F5 Claydon Suffk
170 C4 Clay End Herts
426 A4 Claygate D & G
97 F4 Claygate Kent
97 H6 Claygate Kent
94 D2 Claygate Surrey
120 B1 Claygate Cross Kent
51 H5 Clayhall Hants
42 D3 Clayhanger Devon
44 C5 Clayhanger Somset
237 F4 Clayhanger Wsall
43 G4 Clayhidon Devon
109 H5 Clay Hill Bristl
80 B5 Clay Hill E Susx
144 D5 Clay Hill Gt Lon
50 B3 Clay Hill Hants
115 F5 Clay Hill W Berk
197 H2 Clayhithe Cambs
515 E2 Clayholes Angus
280 B5 Clay Lake Lincs
484 A2 Clayland Stirlg
274 D4 Clay Mills Staffs
588 F5 Clayock Highld
566 E1 Clay of Allan Highld
197 E4 Claypit Hill Cambs
42 C2 Claypits Devon
135 H3 Claypits Gloucs
100 D4 Claypits Kent
223 E3 Claypits Suffk
297 F5 Claypole Lincs
86 C2 Clays End BaNES
320 D4 Claythorpe Lincs
342 B3 Clayton Brad
329 H3 Clayton Donc
514 C6 Clayton Fife
326 C5 Clayton Manch
291 G6 Clayton Staffs
55 H2 Clayton W Susx
339 E5 Clayton Brook Lancs
339 E5 Clayton Green Lancs
342 B3 Clayton Heights Brad
339 G3 Clayton le Dale Lancs
340 B3 Clayton-le-Moors Lancs
339 E5 Clayton-le-Woods Lancs
328 D2 Clayton West Kirk
316 D2 Clayworth Notts
530 E5 Cleadale Highld
406 B2 Cleadon S Tyne
406 B2 Cleadon Park S Tyne
18 B4 Clearbrook Devon
134 D3 Clearwell Gloucs
106 D2 Clearwell Newpt
87 E5 Clearwood Wilts
383 G2 Cleasby N York
601 H8 Cleat Ork
394 C6 Cleatlam Dur
376 C3 Cleator Cumb
376 C1 Cleator Moor Cumb
28 D2 Cleave Devon
580 E3 Clebrig Highld
342 C5 Cleckheaton Kirk
134 C4 Cleddon Mons
210 D3 Cleedownton Shrops
210 D4 Cleehill Shrops
468 B3 Cleekhimin N Lans
210 D3 Cleemarsh Shrops
210 D3 Clee St Margaret Shrops
210 D4 Cleestanton Shrops
334 D3 Cleethorpes NE Lin
211 E4 Cleeton St Mary Shrops
135 G2 Cleeve Gloucs
85 E1 Cleeve N Som
115 G3 Cleeve Oxon
163 E4 Cleeve Hill Gloucs
189 G5 Cleeve Prior Worcs
469 E6 Clehonger Herefs
160 B2 Cleigh Ag & B
506 E4 Cleish P & K
500 A5 Cleland N Lans
468 B3 Cleland N Lans
143 E1 Clement's End Beds
134 D3 Clements End Gloucs
120 D5 Clement Street Kent
89 E2 Clench Wilts
89 E1 Clench Common Wilts
161 G2 Clencher's Mill Herefs
252 B3 Clenchwarton Norfk
442 A3 Clennell Nthumb
212 D4 Clent Worcs
211 F4 Cleobury Mortimer Shrops
211 E2 Cleobury North Shrops
458 D5 Cleongart Ag & B
566 E6 Clephanton Highld
15 F5 Clerkenwater Cnwll
342 D5 Clerk Green Kirk
571 L6 Clerkhill Abers
451 G5 Clerklands Border
487 G5 Clermiston C Edin
600 D3 Clestrain Ork
440 A2 Cleuch Head Border
424 B5 Cleughbrae D & G
112 B5 Clevancy Wilts
465 H1 Clevans Rens
108 C5 Clevedon N Som
165 F5 Cleveley Oxon
350 C6 Cleveleys Lancs
112 A2 Cleverton Wilts
84 D4 Clewer Somset
117 F4 Clewer Green W & M
117 F4 Clewer New Town W & M
117 F4 Clewer Village W & M
260 D3 Cley next the Sea Norfk
591 D7 Cliad W Isls

596 D6 Cliasmaol W Isls
609 J2 Clibberswick Shet
391 F5 Cliburn Cumb
91 G5 Cliddesden Hants
312 D2 Cliff Highld
519 G2 Cliff Highld
238 C5 Cliff Warwks
515 H1 Cliffburn Angus
340 A3 Cliffe Lancs
122 A4 Cliffe Medway
59 E4 Cliffe N York
122 A5 Cliffe N York
38 D3 Cliff End E Susx
184 D5 Cliffe Herefs
357 E6 Cliffe Leeds
190 B4 Clifford Chambers Warwks
161 G5 Clifford's Mesne Gloucs
101 F3 Cliff's End Kent
122 D2 Clifftown Sthend
169 H2 Clifton Beds
109 G5 Clifton Bristl
276 C3 Clifton C Nott
342 C5 Clifton Calder
309 H4 Clifton Ches
391 E4 Clifton Cumb
293 G6 Clifton Derbys
61 F3 Clifton Devon
330 B5 Clifton Donc
338 C3 Clifton Lancs
355 G5 Clifton N York
430 D3 Clifton Nthumb
166 A3 Clifton Oxon
329 G6 Clifton Rothm
325 H4 Clifton Salfd
508 D5 Clifton Stirlg
188 B5 Clifton Worcs
358 A4 Clifton York
238 D2 Clifton Campville Staffs
326 A4 Clifton Green Salfd
140 B5 Clifton Hampden Oxon
326 A4 Clifton Junction Salfd
46 A2 Clifton Maybank Dorset
358 A3 Clifton Moor York
194 C4 Clifton Reynes M Keyn
216 B4 Clifton upon Dunsmore Warwks
187 F2 Clifton upon Teme Worcs
101 G1 Cliftonville Kent
468 A2 Cliftonville N Lans
256 C2 Cliftonville Norfk
54 A4 Climping W Susx
324 C5 Clinkham Wood St Hel
66 C5 Clint Somset
356 B3 Clint N York
557 E2 Clinterty C Aber
248 D2 Clint Green Norfk
452 B3 Clintmains Border
382 C4 Clints N York
598 B7 Cliobh W Isls
230 C2 Clipiau Gwynd
251 E2 Clippesby Norfk
248 D2 Clippings Green Norfk
242 D1 Clipsham Rutlnd
217 E3 Clipston Nhants
276 D3 Clipston Notts
168 C4 Clipstone Beds
296 A2 Clipstone Notts
340 B1 Clitheroe Lancs
169 H2 Cliton Manor Beds
595 J4 Cliuthar W Isls
290 D1 Clive Ches
270 C5 Clive Shrops
290 D2 Clive Green Ches
58 D4 Clive Vale E Susx
609 J4 Clivocast Shet
333 G4 Clixby Lincs
112 A1 Cloatley Wilts
112 A1 Cloatley End Wilts
287 F4 Clocaenog Denbgs
569 G3 Clochan Moray
309 H1 Clock Face St Hel
95 F2 Clock House Gt Lon
185 E5 Clock Mills Herefs
232 D3 Cloddiau Powys
567 H4 Cloddymoss Moray
159 F4 Clodock Herefs
86 C6 Cloford Somset
86 C6 Cloford Common Somset
285 G3 Clogwyn Cyrrau Conwy
128 B2 Cloigyn Carmth
571 J7 Clola Abers
232 C2 Clonrae Powys
169 F2 Clophill Beds
201 H4 Clopton Suffk
202 A3 Clopton Suffk
199 F4 Clopton Green Suffk
200 C2 Clopton Green Suffk
35 d2 Clos Du Valle Guern
423 E1 Closeburn D & G
436 B6 Closeburnmill D & G
322 d8 Closeclark IoM
395 E4 Close House Dur
45 H5 Closworth Somset
170 C3 Clothall Herts
170 C3 Clothall Common Herts
607 G1 Clothan Shet
289 H2 Clotton Ches
290 A2 Clotton Common Ches
215 H2 Cloudesley Bush Warwks
160 D2 Clouds Herefs
292 B2 Cloud Side Staffs
327 G2 Clough Kirk
326 D3 Clough Oldham
326 D1 Clough Rochdl
405 E3 Clough Dene Dur
340 C5 Cloughfold Lancs
341 E5 Clough Foot Calder
291 G4 Clough Hall Staffs
341 H5 Clough Head Calder
327 G1 Clough Head Kirk
387 G6 Cloughton N York
387 G5 Cloughton Newlands N York
606 D6 Clousta Shet
600 D2 Clouston Ork
558 B5 Clova Abers
538 C5 Clova Angus
38 D3 Clovelly Devon
451 E2 Clovenfords Border
559 H6 Clovenstone Abers
520 D3 Clovullin Highld
4 B2 Clowance Wood Cnwll
340 C4 Clow Bridge Lancs
315 F4 Clowne Derbys
211 G5 Clows Top Worcs
289 E6 Cloy Wrexhm
323 G6 Clubmoor Lpool
23 F4 Clubworthy Cnwll
235 E2 Cluddley Wrekin
209 E3 Clun Shrops
209 G3 Clunbury Shrops
152 C6 Clunderwen Carmth
550 D4 Clune Highld
533 K5 Clunes Highld
209 H4 Clungunford Shrops
525 H7 Clunie P & K
209 F3 Clunton Shrops
500 D5 Cluny Fife
86 A3 Clutton BaNES
289 G4 Clutton Ches
86 A3 Clutton Hill BaNES
284 C2 Clwt-y-Bont Gwynd

131 G3 Clwydfagwyr Myr Td
132 D2 Clydach Mons
129 G4 Clydach Swans
132 C2 Clydach Terrace Blae G
131 F6 Clydach Vale Rhondd
483 G5 Clydebank W Duns
112 C4 Clyffe Pypard Wilts
482 B3 Clynder Ag & B
130 C4 Clyne Neath
577 J2 Clynelish Highld
282 D6 Clynnog-Fawr Gwynd
184 D6 Clyro Powys
27 H3 Clyst Honiton Devon
27 G2 Clyst Hydon Devon
27 F5 Clyst St George Devon
27 G2 Clyst St Lawrence Devon
27 F4 Clyst St Mary Devon
583 J2 Clyth Highld
598 B7 Cnip W Isls
592 C4 Cnoc a' Lin W Isls
592 C4 Cnoc an Torrain W Isls
599 K6 Cnoc an t-Solais W Isls
478 D7 Cnocbreac Ag & B
599 H8 Cnoc Màiri W Isls
599 J8 Cnoc nan Gobhar W Isls
565 J2 Cnwch Coch Cerdgn
16 C3 Coad's Green Cnwll
314 D3 Coal Aston Derbys
395 G5 Coal Bank Darltn
132 C3 Coalbrookvale Blae G
447 F3 Coalburn S Lans
404 D7 Coalburns Gatesd
403 E5 Coalcleugh Nthumb
135 H4 Coaley Gloucs
136 A4 Coaley Peak Gloucs
557 E5 Coalford Abers
445 F6 Coalhall E Ayrs
147 E5 Coalhill Essex
235 F3 Coalmoor Wrekin
215 F2 Coalpit Field Warwks
110 B3 Coalpit Heath S Glos
291 G4 Coalpit Hill Staffs
237 F4 Coal Pool Wsall
499 E5 Coalsnaughton Clacks
501 E5 Coaltown of Balgonie Fife
501 F3 Coaltown of Burnturk Fife
501 F5 Coaltown of Wemyss Fife
239 G2 Coalville Leics
134 D2 Coalway Gloucs
402 B3 Coanwood Nthumb
12 C2 Coarsewell Devon
66 C5 Coat Somset
467 H2 Coatbridge N Lans
468 B2 Coatdyke N Lans
113 E3 Coate Swindn
88 B2 Coate Wilts
244 D5 Coates Cambs
137 E4 Coates Gloucs
354 A5 Coates Lancs
317 H3 Coates Lincs
470 D2 Coates Mdloth
317 F3 Coates Notts
75 F4 Coates W Susx
397 E4 Coatham R & Cl
395 F6 Coatham Mundeville Darltn
437 E3 Coatsgate D & G
29 F4 Cobb Dorset
40 C2 Cobbaton Devon
187 H3 Cobbler's Corner Worcs
226 B1 Cobbler's Green Norfk
146 B2 Cobbler's Pieces Essex
134 B4 Cobbler's Plain Mons
310 C2 Cobbs Warrtn
161 H3 Cobb's Cross Gloucs
173 F3 Cobbs Fenn Essex
355 G4 Cobby Syke N York
137 E1 Coberley Gloucs
160 B2 Cobhall Common Herefs
121 G6 Cobham Kent
94 C2 Cobham Surrey
251 G3 Cobholm Island Norfk
172 D6 Cobler's Green Essex
69 H5 Cobley Dorset
213 F5 Cobley Hill Worcs
186 B2 Cobnash Herefs
34 C2 Cobo Guern
291 H5 Cobridge C Stke
271 F2 Cobscot Shrops
199 E4 Cock & End Suffk
315 E5 Cock Alley Derbys
385 G5 Cockayne N York
196 C5 Cockayne Hatley Beds
288 D5 Cock Bank Wrexhm
189 F4 Cock Bevington Warwks
552 E7 Cock Bridge Abers
491 K6 Cockburnspath Border
147 G4 Cock Clarks Essex
340 C1 Cockden Lancs
488 D4 Cockenzie and Port Seton E Loth
338 C5 Cocker Bar Lancs
351 E4 Cockerham Lancs
388 D3 Cockermouth Cumb
169 G5 Cockernhoe Herts
342 D4 Cockersdale Leeds
383 G1 Cockerton Darltn
103 F3 Cockett Swans
394 C5 Cockfield Dur
200 B4 Cockfield Suffk
144 C5 Cockfosters Gt Lon
186 B1 Cock Gate Herefs
172 D6 Cock Green Essex
357 G3 Cock Hill N York
67 G3 Cockhill Somset
53 F1 Cocking W Susx
74 D6 Cocking Causeway W Susx
20 B5 Cockington Torbay
84 D5 Cocklake Somset
137 E2 Cockleford Gloucs
377 G4 Cockley Beck Cumb
247 F4 Cockley Cley Norfk
342 C6 Cockley Hill Kirk
59 E3 Cock Marling E Susx
33 G3 Cocknowle Dorset
116 C3 Cockpole Green Wokham
7 E3 Cocks Cnwll
199 H3 Cocks Green Suffk
181 F3 Cockshead Cerdgn
160 D2 Cockshoot Herefs
210 D3 Cockshutford Shrops
211 G3 Cockshutt Shrops
270 A4 Cockshutt Shrops
98 B4 Cock Street Kent
174 C2 Cock Street Suffk
260 C3 Cockthorpe Norfk
3 F3 Cockwells Cnwll
20 D1 Cockwood Devon
64 D3 Cockwood Somset
312 D4 Cockyard Ches
159 H3 Cockyard Herefs
201 F3 Coddenham Suffk
201 F3 Coddenham Green Suffk
289 F3 Coddington Ches
161 G1 Coddington Herefs
297 F4 Coddington Notts
69 G2 Codford St Mary Wilts
69 G1 Codford St Peter Wilts
170 B6 Codicote Herts
170 B6 Codicote Bottom Herts
142 D2 Codmore Bucks
75 G5 Codmore Hill W Susx

295 E5 Codnor Derbys
295 E5 Codnor Breach Derbys
295 E4 Codnor Gate Derbys
295 E4 Codnor Park Derbys
110 C4 Codrington S Glos
236 C3 Codsall Staffs
236 B4 Codsall Wood Staffs
62 D4 Codsend Somset
132 D3 Coedcae Blae G
133 E3 Coedcae Torfn
133 H5 Coed Cwnwr Mons
285 G3 Coedcynhelier Conwy
105 G2 Coedely Rhondd
133 E6 Coed Eva Torfn
104 C3 Coed Hirwaun Neath
107 E3 Coedkernew Newpt
304 C5 Coed Mawr Gwynd
133 F2 Coed Morgan Mons
288 C3 Coedpoeth Wrexhm
288 C3 Coed-Talon Flints
233 F2 Coedway Powys
108 C1 Coed-y-caerau Newpt
134 A3 Coed-y-fedw Mons
229 F6 Coed y Garth Cerdgn
269 E4 Coed y go Gwynd
133 F5 Coed-y-paen Mons
284 D1 Coed-y-parc Gwynd
158 C5 Coed-yr-ynys Powys
284 D5 Coed Ystumgwern Gwynd
232 D3 Coed-y-Wlad Powys
130 C2 Coelbren Powys
168 B2 Coffee Hall M Keyn
213 F4 Coffinswell Devon
20 D1 Cofton Devon
213 F4 Cofton Common Birm
213 F4 Cofton Hackett Worcs
106 C6 Cog V Glam
106 C5 Cogan V Glam
193 H2 Cogenhoe Nhants
139 F3 Cogges Oxon
173 G5 Coggeshall Essex
173 H5 Coggeshall Hamlet Essex
79 E4 Coggins Mill E Susx
599 L1 Coig Peighinnean W Isls
599 H3 Coig Peighinnean Bhuirgh W Isls
554 B5 Coilacriech Abers
497 E3 Coilantogle Stirlg
507 H5 Coillaig Ag & B
590 F5 Coilleag W Isls
533 G2 Coille Mhorgil Highld
544 F2 Coillore Highld
597 G1 Coire an Fhuarain W Isls
315 E3 Coisley Hill Sheff
105 E3 Coity Brdgnd
171 E2 Cokenach Herts
274 D4 Cokhay Green Derbys
599 K7 Col W Isls
580 E7 Colaboll Highld
7 G1 Colan Cnwll
27 H5 Colaton Raleigh Devon
542 C7 Colbost Highld
383 K5 Colburn N York
385 E5 Colby Cumb
391 H5 Colby Cumb
322 c8 Colby IoM
261 H5 Colby Norfk
174 D4 Colchester Essex
200 B3 Colchester Green Suffk
106 B6 Colcot V Glam
115 E5 Cold Ash W Berk
217 E4 Cold Ashby Nhants
74 C3 Cold Ash Hill Hants
110 D5 Cold Ashton S Glos
163 H6 Cold Aston Gloucs
586 D5 Coldbackie Highld
120 C5 Coldblow Gt Lon
126 C5 Cold Blow Pembks
194 C4 Cold Brayfield M Keyn
158 C2 Coldbrook Powys
145 E1 Cold Christmas Herts
367 E5 Cold Cotes N York
56 A3 Coldean Br & H
19 H2 Coldeast Devon
293 F3 Coldeaton Derbys
162 B3 Cold Elm Worcs
341 F4 Colden Calder
72 C5 Colden Common Hants
203 E2 Coldfair Green Suffk
245 F4 Coldham Cambs
236 C3 Coldham Staffs
197 G3 Coldham's Common Cambs
318 C3 Cold Hanworth Lincs
6 D4 Coldharbour Cnwll
43 E5 Coldharbour Devon
32 A3 Coldharbour Dorset
33 F2 Cold Harbour Dorset
134 D4 Coldharbour Gloucs
120 D4 Coldharbour Gt Lon
143 G1 Cold Harbour Herts
97 E4 Coldharbour Kent
98 D1 Cold Harbour Kent
278 D3 Cold Harbour Lincs
115 G4 Cold Harbour Oxon
94 C6 Coldharbour Surrey
116 D4 Cold Harbour W & M
87 F3 Cold Harbour Wilts
87 F5 Cold Harbour Wilts
271 E5 Cold Hatton Wrekin
271 E5 Cold Hatton Heath Wrekin
406 C5 Cold Hesledon Dur
329 F2 Cold Hiendley Wakefd
193 E4 Cold Higham Nhants
474 D1 Coldingham Border
126 C3 Cold Inn Pembks
371 G3 Cold Kirby N York
272 C3 Coldmeece Staffs
291 F2 Cold Moss Heath Ches
241 F3 Cold Newton Leics
22 D5 Cold Northcott Cnwll
147 H5 Cold Norton Essex
497 H5 Coldoch Stirlg
241 H2 Cold Overton Leics
108 C3 Coldra Newpt
500 A4 Coldrain P & K
83 E1 Coldred Kent
25 G1 Coldridge Devon
351 E6 Cold Row Lancs
514 B2 Coldstream Angus
453 F2 Coldstream Border
8 B2 Coldvreath Cnwll
54 B1 Coldwaltham W Susx
237 G2 Cold Well Staffs
561 H1 Coldwells Abers
558 D5 Coldwells Croft Abers
67 H3 Cole Somset
209 F2 Colebatch Shrops
27 G1 Colebrook Devon
26 B3 Colebrooke Devon
298 B2 Coleby Lincs
332 D6 Coleby N Linc
346 C6 Cole End Essex
172 B2 Cole End Warwks
214 C5 Cole End Warwks
26 B2 Coleford Devon
134 D2 Coleford Gloucs
64 B5 Coleford Somset
86 B5 Coleford Water Somset
225 G2 Colegate End Norfk
171 F3 Cole Green Herts
214 A2 Colehall Birm
90 D4 Cole Henley Hants
48 C4 Colehill Dorset
144 A2 Coleman Green Herts

City, town and village index: Coleman's Hatch - Coxbridge 681

78 B3 Coleman's Hatch E Susx
270 A3 Colemere Shrops
73 H3 Colemore Hants
235 G5 Colemore Green Shrops
275 F6 Coleorton Leics
239 G1 Coleorton Moor Leics
118 D5 Cole Park Gt Lon
111 E5 Colerne Wilts
137 E2 Colesbourne Gloucs
68 C4 Colesbrook Dorset
12 D3 Cole's Cross Devon
29 G2 Cole's Cross Dorset
195 G3 Colesden Beds
175 E1 Coles Green Suffk
202 B2 Cole's Green Suffk
187 H4 Coles Green Worcs
142 C5 Coleshill Bucks
138 C6 Coleshill Oxon
214 C2 Coleshill Warwks
95 F4 Coles Meads Surrey
28 A2 Colestocks Devon
136 B2 Colethrop Gloucs
85 G3 Coley BaNES
342 B4 Coley Calder
116 B5 Coley Readg
76 D3 Colgate W Susx
482 D3 Colgrain Ag & B
118 B3 Colham Green Gt Lon
119 E2 Colindale Gt Lon
502 D4 Colinsburgh Fife
487 H6 Colinton C Edin
481 E5 Colintraive Ag & B
254 B2 Colkirk Norfk
513 F3 Collace P & K
135 F2 Collafield Gloucs
606 F4 Collafirth Shet
608 C8 Collafirth Shet
595 J4 Collam W Isls
22 D4 Collamoor Head Cnwll
12 C5 Collaton Devon
20 B5 Collaton St Mary Torbay
467 F3 College Milton S Lans
567 L3 College of Roseisle Moray
93 E2 College Town Br For
444 D3 Collennan S Ayrs
501 E2 Collessie Fife
40 D4 Colleton Mills Devon
245 G3 Collett's Br Cambs
188 B4 Collett's Green Worcs
120 C1 Collier Row Gt Lon
171 E5 Collier's End Herts
58 C2 Collier's Green E Susx
145 H4 Colliers Hatch Essex
97 H5 Collier Street Kent
119 F5 Collier's Wood Gt Lon
406 A5 Colliery Row Sundld
561 F4 Collieston Abers
424 A4 Collin D & G
89 F4 Collingbourne Ducis Wilts
89 F3 Collingbourne Kingston Wilts
356 D5 Collingham Leeds
297 F2 Collingham Notts
187 E2 Collington Herefs
193 F3 Collingtree Nhants
193 F3 Collingtree Park Nhants
431 E4 Collingwood Nthumb
115 H4 Collins End Oxon
324 D6 Collins Green Warrtn
187 G3 Collins Green Worcs
42 C5 Collipriest Devon
528 D5 Colliston Angus
28 A2 Colliton Devon
215 F2 Collycroft Warwks
501 E4 Collydean Fife
326 B5 Collyhurst Manch
560 B2 Collynie Abers
242 D4 Collyweston Nhants
418 D4 Colmonell S Ayrs
451 G2 Colmslie Border
451 G1 Colmsliehill Border
195 F3 Colmworth Beds
554 A3 Colnabaichin Abers
117 H4 Colnbrook Slough
221 E4 Colne Cambs
340 D2 Colne Lancs
340 D1 Colne Edge Lancs
173 H3 Colne Engaine Essex
221 E4 Colnefields Cambs
249 G3 Colney Norfk
119 F1 Colney Hatch Gt Lon
144 A3 Colney Heath Herts
137 G3 Coln Rogers Gloucs
138 A3 Coln St Aldwyns Gloucs
137 G2 Coln St Dennis Gloucs
570 C6 Colp Abers
404 A3 Colpitts Grange Nthumb
559 E3 Colpy Abers
39 E5 Colscott Devon
356 D3 Colshaw Staffs
369 F3 Colsterdale N York
278 C5 Colsterworth Lincs
484 B6 Colston E Duns
151 G4 Colston Pembks
277 F3 Colston Bassett Notts
116 C2 Coltrope Bucks
567 L4 Coltfield Moray
92 B4 Colt Hill Hants
378 C5 Colthouse Cumb
91 E1 Colthrop W Berk
256 B5 Coltishall Norfk
468 C3 Coltness N Lans
364 D2 Colton Cumb
343 G3 Colton Leeds
357 G6 Colton N York
249 F3 Colton Norfk
273 F5 Colton Staffs
199 H1 Colton Suffk
236 D5 Colton Hills Staffs
364 C5 Colt Park Cumb
110 C3 Colt's Green S Glos
97 F6 Colt's Hill Kent
599 K7 Col Uarach W Isls
405 H3 Columbia Sundld
27 F3 Columbjohn Devon
184 D4 Colva Powys
413 G4 Colvend D & G
609 G5 Colvister Shet
161 G1 Colwall Herefs
161 H1 Colwall Green Herefs
161 H1 Colwall Stone Herefs
35 H3 Colwell IoW
429 E4 Colwell Nthumb
273 F5 Colwich Staffs
276 D1 Colwick Notts
105 E4 Colwinston V Glam
53 G4 Colworth W Susx
194 D2 Colworth Ho Beds
306 B4 Colwyn Bay Conwy
29 E4 Colyford Devon
28 D4 Colyton Devon
441 E6 Comb Nthumb
11 F3 Combe Devon
12 C5 Combe Devon
19 F4 Combe Devon
79 E4 Combe E Susx
185 F2 Combe Herefs
139 G1 Combe Oxon
66 C4 Combe Somset
90 B2 Combe W Berk
48 B5 Combe Almer Dorset
24 C5 Combebow Devon
75 E2 Combe Common Surrey
86 D2 Combe Down BaNES
20 A5 Combe Fishacre Devon
64 B5 Combe Florey Somset
86 C3 Combe Hay BaNES
20 C3 Combeinteignhead Devon
61 E2 Combe Martin Devon
185 G2 Combe Moor Herefs
20 C4 Combe Pafford Torbay
28 C2 Combe Raleigh Devon
310 C4 Comberbach Ches
238 B3 Comberford Staffs
197 E3 Comberton Cambs
186 B1 Comberton Herefs
212 B4 Comberton Worcs
44 C5 Combe St Nicholas Somset
68 B5 Combe Throop Somset
29 E4 Combpyne Devon
60 D5 Combrew Devon
273 G2 Combridge Staffs
191 E4 Combrook Warwks
312 D4 Combs Derbys
342 D6 Combs Kirk
200 D3 Combs Suffk
201 E3 Combs Ford Suffk
64 D3 Combwich Somset
556 B3 Comers Abers
7 F5 Come-To-Good Cnwll
43 G3 Comeytrowe Somset
6 D6 Comford Cnwll
4 D3 Comfort Cnwll
188 B1 Comhampton Worcs
205 E3 Comins Coch Cerdgn
488 A6 Comiston C Edin
234 B5 Comley Shrops
198 A2 Commercial End Cambs
287 G2 Commins Denbgs
230 C4 Commins Coch Powys
133 F6 Common Cefn-Llwyn Mons
385 G2 Commondale N York
337 F3 Common Edge Bpool
388 B5 Common End Cumb
295 E2 Common End Derbys
160 D3 Common Hill Herefs
16 B5 Common Moor Cnwll
112 D2 Common Platt Wilts
290 B1 Common Side Ches
310 A5 Commonside Ches
274 C1 Commonside Derbys
295 E5 Common Side Derbys
314 C4 Common Side Derbys
295 F3 Commonside Notts
143 E4 Commonwood Herts
270 B4 Commonwood Shrops
289 E4 Commonwood Wrexhm
108 D2 Common-y-Coed Mons
97 F3 Comp Kent
65 E5 Compass Somset
312 C1 Compstall Stockp
11 E2 Compton C Plym
293 G5 Compton Derbys
20 B5 Compton Devon
71 G4 Compton Hants
72 C4 Compton Hants
356 D6 Compton Leeds
212 B3 Compton Staffs
93 E5 Compton Surrey
93 G5 Compton Surrey
115 E3 Compton W Berk
52 D2 Compton W Susx
88 D4 Compton Wilts
236 C5 Compton Wolves
69 E6 Compton Abbas Dorset
137 G1 Compton Abdale Gloucs
112 B5 Compton Bassett Wilts
113 G2 Compton Beauchamp Oxon
84 C3 Compton Bishop Somset
69 H4 Compton Chamberlayne Wilts
86 A2 Compton Common BaNES
86 A2 Compton Dando BaNES
66 D3 Compton Dundon Somset
66 C6 Compton Durville Somset
72 C4 Compton End Hants
161 G4 Compton Green Gloucs
109 G3 Compton Greenfield S Glos
85 F3 Compton Martin BaNES
67 G4 Compton Pauncefoot Somset
30 D4 Compton Valence Dorset
486 D2 Comrie Fife
510 D5 Comrie P & K
330 A5 Conanby Donc
481 E2 Conchra Ag & B
405 H3 Concord Sundld
314 D1 Concord Park Sheff
525 G7 Concraigie P & K
351 G3 Conder Green Lancs
163 E2 Conderton Worcs
164 A4 Condicote Gloucs
485 E5 Condorrat N Lans
234 B3 Condover Shrops
30 B4 Coneygar Dorset
96 A2 Coney Hall Gt Lon
136 B1 Coney Hill Gloucs
76 B5 Coneyhurst W Susx
372 C5 Coneysthorpe N York
356 D3 Coneythorpe N York
224 B4 Coney Weston Suffk
74 C3 Conford Hants
16 C3 Congdon's Shop Cnwll
413 G1 Congeith D & G
97 G5 Congelow Kent
239 F3 Congerstone Leics
253 E3 Congham Norfk
291 H2 Congleton Ches
292 A2 Congleton Edge Ches
285 F6 Congl-y-wal Gwynd
84 D2 Congresbury N Som
236 D2 Congreve Staffs
110 A5 Conham S Glos
567 H6 Conicavel Moray
299 G3 Coningsby Lincs
196 D1 Conington Cambs
219 H2 Conington Cambs
330 B5 Conisbrough Donc
476 D4 Conisby Ag & B
335 E5 Conisholme Lincs
378 B5 Coniston Cumb
348 C2 Coniston E R Yk
354 B4 Coniston Cold N York
354 C1 Conistone N York
86 D2 Conkwell Wilts
308 C6 Connah's Quay Flints
506 F3 Connel Ag & B
434 C2 Connel Park E Ayrs
168 A1 Conniburrow M Keyn
543 G2 Connista Highld
16 A6 Connon Cnwll
3 G2 Connor Downs Cnwll
88 C3 Conock Wilts
565 J6 Conon Bridge Highld
354 C5 Cononley N York
354 C5 Cononley Woodside N York
528 C5 Cononsyth Angus
545 J2 Conordan Highld
271 F6 Conquermoor Heath Wrekin
292 C5 Consall Staffs
404 C4 Consett Dur
369 G1 Constable Burton N York
340 C5 Constable Lee Lancs
4 D3 Constantine Cnwll
14 B4 Constantine Bay Cnwll
565 G5 Contin Highld
557 E4 Contlaw C Aber
305 G4 Conwy Conwy
99 F2 Conyer Kent
224 A6 Conyer's Green Suffk
58 B5 Cooden E Susx
24 B1 Cookbury Devon
24 A1 Cookbury Wick Devon
117 E3 Cookham W & M
117 E3 Cookham Dean W & M
117 E3 Cookham Rise W & M
189 F3 Cookhill Worcs
429 E5 Cooklaw Nthumb
226 D4 Cookley Suffk
212 B3 Cookley Worcs
116 A2 Cookley Green Oxon
557 F6 Cookney Abers
342 D1 Cookridge Leeds
56 C2 Cooksbridge E Susx
212 D6 Cooksey Corner Worcs
212 C6 Cooksey Green Worcs
176 C6 Cook's Green Essex
200 C4 Cook's Green Suffk
292 B6 Cookshill Staffs
15 F5 Cooksland Cnwll
146 C3 Cooksmill Green Essex
310 B5 Cooksongreen Ches
76 B5 Coolham W Susx
76 C4 Coolhurst Wood W Susx
122 B4 Cooling Medway
82 D3 Coolinge Kent
122 A5 Cooling Street Medway
142 A3 Coombe Bucks
6 B5 Coombe Cnwll
7 E5 Coombe Cnwll
7 F5 Coombe Cnwll
8 A3 Coombe Cnwll
16 B6 Coombe Cnwll
38 B5 Coombe Cnwll
20 C3 Coombe Devon
28 B4 Coombe Devon
42 D4 Coombe Devon
29 G3 Coombe Dorset
135 H6 Coombe Gloucs
118 D5 Coombe Gt Lon
73 G5 Coombe Hants
101 E4 Coombe Kent
45 E6 Coombe Somset
69 E5 Coombe Wilts
88 D4 Coombe Wilts
70 C4 Coombe Bissett Wilts
109 F4 Coombe Dingle Bristl
162 C4 Coombe Hill Gloucs
33 E3 Coombe Keynes Dorset
27 H3 Coombelake Devon
93 E4 Coombes W Susx
272 A2 Coombesdale Staffs
213 E2 Coombeswood Dudley
97 G2 Coomb Hill Kent
110 C3 Coombs End S Glos
29 F1 Coombses Somset
145 G4 Coopersale Common Essex
96 C5 Cooper's Corner Kent
78 B5 Cooper's Green E Susx
144 A3 Cooper's Green Herts
169 E2 Cooper's Hill Beds
117 G5 Cooper's Hill Surrey
101 F4 Cooper Street Kent
325 E3 Cooper Turning Bolton
54 C2 Cootham W Susx
188 C2 Copcut Worcs
175 F1 Copdock Suffk
112 C3 Coped Hall Wilts
287 E1 Copenhagen Denbgs
174 B5 Copford Essex
174 B5 Copford Green Essex
356 C2 Copgrove N York
607 G2 Copister Shet
571 L6 Coplandhill Abers
195 G5 Cople Beds
342 A5 Copley Calder
394 B4 Copley Dur
327 E5 Copley Tamesd
342 D4 Copley Hill Kirk
313 G4 Coplow Dale Derbys
357 H5 Copmanthorpe York
272 B4 Copmere End Staffs
52 B4 Copnor C Port
338 B2 Copp Lancs
23 E2 Coppathorne Cnwll
291 E3 Coppenhall Ches
272 D6 Coppenhall Staffs
291 E3 Coppenhall Moss Ches
3 G2 Copperhouse Cnwll
326 D4 Coppice Oldham
211 G3 Coppicegate Shrops
219 H3 Coppingford Cambs
99 E5 Coppins Corner Kent
63 E5 Coppleham Somset
26 B2 Copplestone Devon
324 D2 Coppull Lancs
324 D2 Coppull Moor Lancs
76 C5 Copsale W Susx
119 E5 Copse Hill Gt Lon
339 G3 Copster Green Lancs
215 H2 Copston Magna Warwks
101 E4 Cop Street Kent
214 B6 Copt Green Warwks
145 F4 Copthall Green Essex
214 B4 Copt Heath Solhll
370 C5 Copt Hewick N York
393 E1 Copthill Dur
290 C6 Copthorne Ches
23 F4 Copthorne Cnwll
234 B2 Copthorne Shrops
77 F2 Copthorne W Susx
269 H2 Coptiviney Shrops
240 A2 Copt Oak Leics
99 G3 Copton Kent
260 B4 Copy's Green Norfk
50 B2 Copythorne Hants
536 B3 Corarnstilbeg Highld
121 E2 Corbets Tey Gt Lon
35 f7 Corbière Jersey
403 H2 Corbridge Nthumb
315 E6 Corbriggs Derbys
218 B2 Corby Nhants
279 E4 Corby Glen Lincs
401 E3 Corby Hill Cumb
461 E3 Cordon N Ayrs
249 F6 Cordwell Norfk
211 E5 Coreley Shrops
117 F2 Cores End Bucks
44 A4 Corfe Somset
33 H3 Corfe Castle Dorset
48 B5 Corfe Mullen Dorset
507 H3 Corfhouse Ag & B
210 B3 Corfton Shrops
210 B2 Corfton Bache Shrops
552 F7 Corgarff Abers
8 C1 Corgee Cnwll
73 E6 Corhampton Hants
434 D5 Corlae D & G
104 B1 Corlannau Neath
214 D2 Corley Warwks
214 D2 Corley Ash Warwks
214 D3 Corley Moor Warwks
476 E7 Cornabus Ag & B
516 B6 Cornaigbeg Ag & B
516 B6 Cornaigmore Ag & B
174 A1 Cornard Tye Suffk
470 D2 Cornbank Mdloth
211 E4 Cornbrook Shrops
338 B2 Corner Row Lancs
186 D5 Cornett Herefs
362 C3 Corney Cumb
395 G3 Cornforth Dur
569 K4 Cornhill Abers
557 G3 Cornhill C Aber
292 A4 Cornhill C Stke
576 C5 Cornhill Highld
158 B1 Cornhill Powys
453 G2 Cornhill on Tweed Nthumb
340 D4 Cornholme Calder
172 D2 Cornish Hall End Essex
601 J5 Cornquoy Ork
392 D1 Cornriggs Dur
404 D6 Cornsay Dur
405 E6 Cornsay Colliery Dur
498 B5 Cornton Stirlg
565 K5 Corntown Highld
105 E4 Corntown V Glam
164 D4 Cornwell Oxon
18 D6 Cornwood Devon
13 E1 Cornworthy Devon
533 G7 Corpach Highld
255 F2 Corpusty Norfk
520 E3 Corran Highld
546 F8 Corran Highld
322 g5 Corrany IoM
463 H6 Corrie N Ayrs
425 E2 Corrie Common D & G
460 C5 Corriecravie N Ayrs
422 A3 Corriedoo D & G
564 E4 Corriemoillie Highld
550 D5 Corrievorrie Highld
602 C8 Corrigall Ork
548 F3 Corrimony Highld
317 G1 Corringham Lincs
121 H3 Corringham Thurr
230 B3 Corris Gwynd
229 G3 Corris Uchaf Gwynd
494 D4 Corrow Ag & B
545 L5 Corry Highld
525 H2 Corrydon P & K
579 L4 Corrykinloch Highld
511 F3 Corrymuckloch P & K
505 J2 Corrynachenchy Ag & B
565 H7 Corry of Ardnagrask Highld
589 G2 Corsback Highld
25 F3 Corscombe Devon
30 C1 Corscombe Dorset
558 D1 Corse Abers
162 A4 Corse Gloucs
162 B3 Corse Lawn Worcs
111 F6 Corsham Wilts
512 D5 Corsiehill P & K
556 B3 Corsindae Abers
87 E5 Corsley Wilts
87 E5 Corsley Heath Wilts
422 C4 Corsock D & G
86 B1 Corston BaNES
111 G3 Corston Wilts
487 H5 Corstorphine C Edin
527 E3 Cortachy Angus
251 G5 Corton Suffk
69 F1 Corton Wilts
67 G5 Corton Denham Somset
329 G5 Cortworth Rothm
287 F6 Corwen Denbgs
39 E4 Cory Devon
31 E5 Coryates Dorset
106 B3 Coryton Cardif
24 C6 Coryton Devon
29 E3 Coryton Devon
122 A3 Coryton Thurr
240 B5 Cosby Leics
115 E2 Coscote Oxon
236 D6 Coseley Dudley
216 A4 Cosford Warwks
167 G1 Cosgrove Nhants
52 B3 Cosham C Port
479 H5 Coshandrochaid Ag & B
125 G4 Cosheston Pembks
106 C6 Cosmeston V Glam
46 C3 Cosmore Dorset
276 A1 Cossall Notts
295 F6 Cossall Marsh Notts
240 D2 Cossington Leics
65 G3 Cossington Somset
602 C6 Costa Ork
249 G2 Costessey Norfk
249 G2 Costessey Park Norfk
316 A2 Costhorpe Notts
15 E4 Costislost Cnwll
276 C4 Costock Notts
278 B5 Coston Leics
249 E3 Coston Norfk
6 B6 Coswinsawsin Cnwll
139 F4 Cote Oxon
84 B6 Cote Somset
54 D3 Cote W Susx
290 B1 Cotebrook Ches
380 B4 Cotegill Cumb
401 E4 Cotehill Cumb
365 G2 Cotes Cumb
276 C5 Cotes Leics
272 B3 Cotes Staffs
216 B3 Cotesbach Leics
272 B3 Cotes Heath Staffs
295 E4 Cotes Park Derbys
28 B4 Cotford Devon
43 G2 Cotford St Luke Somset
276 D2 Cotgrave Notts
557 F1 Cothall Abers
109 G5 Cotham Bristl
297 E5 Cotham Notts
64 C5 Cothelstone Somset
188 A4 Cotheridge Worcs
393 H6 Cotherstone Dur
139 H5 Cothill Oxon
134 B4 Cotland Mons
28 C2 Coteigh Devon
295 F6 Cotmanhay Derbys
112 C4 Cotmarsh Wilts
28 B5 Cotmaton Devon
197 F3 Coton Cambs
217 E5 Coton Nhants
270 C3 Coton Shrops
238 B4 Coton Staffs
272 B5 Coton Staffs
273 E3 Coton Staffs
272 C5 Coton Clanford Staffs
273 E3 Coton Hayes Staffs
234 B2 Coton Hill Shrops
273 E3 Coton Hill Staffs
274 B4 Coton in the Clay Staffs
238 C1 Coton in the Elms Derbys
274 D6 Coton Park Derbys
270 C2 Cotonwood Shrops
272 B5 Cotonwood Staffs
137 F5 Cotswold Community Wilts
39 C5 Cott Devon
338 D3 Cottam Lancs
317 F4 Cottam Notts
551 J3 Cottartown Highld
197 F1 Cottenham Cambs
119 E6 Cottenham Park Gt Lon
381 E6 Cotterdale N York
170 D4 Cottered Herts
315 H3 Cotterhill Woods Rothm
213 F3 Cotteridge Birm
219 E1 Cotterstock Nhants
217 E5 Cottesbrooke Nhants
242 C2 Cottesmore Rutlnd
42 B5 Cotteylands Devon
347 F3 Cottingham E R Yk
218 A1 Cottingham Nhants
342 B2 Cottingley Brad
166 C3 Cottisford Oxon
293 E5 Cotton Staffs
201 E1 Cotton Suffk
195 F5 Cotton End Beds
193 F3 Cotton End Nhants
514 C2 Cotton of Brighty Angus
528 C5 Cotton of Gardyne Angus
341 G5 Cotton Stones Calder
341 E2 Cotton Tree Lancs
71 H2 Cottonworth Hants
556 D1 Cottown Abers
558 C4 Cottown Abers
560 B1 Cottown Abers
513 F5 Cottown P & K
17 F5 Cotts Devon
40 C5 Cottwood Devon
235 E1 Cotwall Wrekin
272 D3 Cotwalton Staffs
600 F1 Coubister Ork
72 D3 Couch Green Hants
9 E2 Couch's Mill Cnwll
160 D5 Coughton Herefs
189 G2 Coughton Warwks
189 G3 Coughton Fields Warwks
563 H7 Coulags Highld
385 E2 Coulby Newham Middsb
376 B3 Coulderton Cumb
563 J5 Coulin Lodge Highld
555 F4 Coull Abers
543 G7 Coulnacraggan Highld
565 H6 Coul of Fairburn Highld
482 B2 Coulport Ag & B
95 F3 Coulsdon Gt Lon
87 H4 Coulston Wilts
448 D3 Coulter S Lans
64 D3 Coultings Somset
372 B5 Coulton N York
234 D4 Cound Shrops
234 D4 Coundlane Shrops
234 D4 Coundmoor Shrops
215 E3 Coundon Covtry
395 E4 Coundon Dur
395 E4 Coundongate Dur
395 E4 Coundon Grange Dur
143 E3 Counters End Herts
368 B2 Countersett N York
173 H3 Countess Cross Essex
27 E4 Countess Wear Devon
240 C5 Countesthorpe Leics
62 A2 Countisbury Devon
513 F1 Coupar Angus P & K
339 E4 Coup Green Lancs
392 B6 Coupland Cumb
454 A3 Coupland Nthumb
462 D5 Cour Ag & B
424 B1 Courance D & G
64 B5 Coursley Somset
81 G2 Court-at-Street Kent
26 C5 Court Barton Devon
104 D3 Court Colman Brdgnd
91 G3 Court Corner Hants
531 J3 Courteachan Highld
193 G4 Courteenhall Nhants
155 E5 Court Henry Carmth
309 F1 Court Hey Knows
215 F3 Court House Green Covtry
30 B4 Court Orchard Dorset
148 D6 Courtsend Essex
64 D5 Courtway Somset
488 D6 Cousland Mdloth
79 F3 Cousley Wood E Susx
606 E8 Cova Shet
482 B3 Cove Ag & B
491 E5 Cove Border
42 C4 Cove Devon
92 D3 Cove Hants
572 F5 Cove Highld
557 G4 Cove Bay C Aber
227 F4 Cove Bottom Suffk
227 G3 Covehithe Suffk
236 D3 Coven Staffs
187 E6 Covender Herefs
221 G3 Coveney Cambs
334 D6 Covenham St Bartholomew Lincs
334 D6 Covenham St Mary Lincs
236 D3 Coven Heath Staffs
236 C3 Coven Lawn Staffs
215 E4 Coventry Covtry
5 E5 Coverack Cnwll
4 C2 Coverack Bridges Cnwll
369 F2 Coverham N York
568 B1 Covesea Moray
113 E3 Covingham Swindn
219 F5 Covington Cambs
448 C2 Covington S Lans
366 C4 Cowan Bridge Lancs
352 D5 Cow Ark Lancs
57 G2 Cowbeech E Susx
57 G2 Cowbeech Hill E Susx
280 C6 Cowbit Lincs
300 B5 Cowbridge Lincs
105 F5 Cowbridge V Glam
342 B6 Cowcliffe Kirk
78 B1 Cowden Kent
510 D5 Cowden P & K
487 G1 Cowdenbeath Fife
379 E5 Cowen Head Cumb
294 C5 Cowers Lane Derbys
51 E5 Cowes IoW
371 F1 Cowesby N York
71 F5 Cowesfield Green Wilts
76 D5 Cowfold W Susx
367 F2 Cowgill Cumb
201 E1 Cow Green Suffk
48 B5 Cowgrove Dorset
294 D5 Cowhill Derbys
339 E3 Cow Hill Lancs
109 G1 Cowhill S Glos
110 B5 Cowhorn Hill S Glos
541 G2 Cowie Abers
485 G2 Cowie Stirlg
467 F1 Cowlairs C Glas
7 F5 Cowlands Cnwll
139 E4 Cowleaze Corner Oxon
314 C4 Cowley Derbys
26 D3 Cowley Devon
137 E2 Cowley Gloucs
118 B3 Cowley Gt Lon
140 B4 Cowley Oxon
42 C5 Cowleymoor Devon
118 B3 Cowley Peachy Gt Lon
324 D1 Cowling Lancs
354 C6 Cowling N York
370 A2 Cowling N York
199 E4 Cowlinge Suffk
313 E5 Cowlow Derbys
328 B1 Cowmes Kirk
340 C5 Cowpe Lancs
431 E3 Cowpen Nthumb
396 C5 Cowpen Bewley S on T
52 B2 Cowplain Hants
142 D2 Cow Roast Herts
393 E1 Cowshill Dur
85 E2 Cowslip Green N Som
486 D1 Cowstrandburn Fife
357 E4 Cowthorpe N York
209 G5 Coxall Herefs
271 F1 Coxbank Ches
294 D6 Coxbench Derbys
67 E2 Coxbridge Somset

226 D3 Cox Common Suffk
485 F1 Coxet Hill Stirlg
50 C2 Coxford C Sotn
22 D3 Coxford Cnwll
253 G2 Coxford Norfk
325 G2 Cox Green Bolton
212 A2 Coxgreen Staffs
76 A3 Cox Green Surrey
117 E4 Cox Green W & M
98 A4 Coxheath Kent
6 D5 Cox Hill Cnwll
395 G2 Coxhoe Dur
85 F6 Coxley Somset
328 D1 Coxley Wakefd
85 F6 Coxley Wick Somset
430 D6 Coxlodge N u Ty
295 G3 Cox Moor Notts
17 E4 Coxpark Cnwll
146 B5 Coxtie Green Essex
371 G4 Coxwold N York
105 E4 Coychurch Brdgnd
445 F6 Coylton S Ayrs
551 G7 Coylumbridge Highld
554 D3 Coynach Abers
558 B3 Coynachie Abers
104 D2 Coytrahen Brdgnd
77 F2 Crabbet Park W Susx
83 E2 Crabble Kent
189 F2 Crabbs Cross Worcs
171 F4 Crabbs Green Herts
255 E2 Crabgate Norfk
48 D3 Crab Orchard Dorset
11 F2 Crabtree C Plym
76 D4 Crabtree W Susx
288 D6 Crabtree Green Wrexhm
391 H5 Crackenthorpe Cumb
22 C3 Crackington Haven Cnwll
291 G4 Crackley Staffs
214 D5 Crackley Warwks
235 H2 Crackleybank Shrops
50 C2 Cracknore Hard Hants
381 H5 Crackpot N York
224 D4 Crackthorn Corner Suffk
354 C2 Cracoe N York
291 F5 Cracow Moss Staffs
43 E5 Craddock Devon
598 A8 Cradhlastadh W Isls
341 H2 Cradle Edge Brad
171 G5 Cradle End Herts
212 D3 Cradley Dudley
187 G5 Cradley Herefs
212 D2 Cradley Heath Sandw
157 G3 Cradoc Powys
10 C3 Crafthole Cnwll
168 B6 Crafton Bucks
476 E8 Cragabus Ag & B
365 G5 Crag Bank Lancs
365 G5 Crag Foot Lancs
551 J4 Craggan Highld
509 J5 Craggan Stirlg
552 D1 Cragganmore Moray
581 L6 Craggie Highld
341 G5 Cragg Vale Calder
405 F4 Craghead Dur
4 C2 Crahan Cnwll
156 D5 Crai Powys
569 H4 Craibstone Moray
527 G5 Craichie Angus
422 A4 Craig D & G
563 J7 Craig Highld
132 A5 Craig Berthlwyd Myr Td
129 G4 Craig-Cefn-Parc Swans
513 G4 Craigdallie P & K
560 B3 Craigdam Abers
434 C3 Craigdarroch E Ayrs
565 G5 Craigdarroch Highld
492 D3 Craigdhu Ag & B
410 C4 Craigdhu D & G
450 B5 Craig Douglas Border
556 C2 Craigearn Abers
568 D7 Craigellachie Moray
515 F2 Craigend Angus
472 B5 Craigend Border
467 G1 Craigend C Glas
512 D5 Craigend P & K
485 F2 Craigend Stirlg
482 D3 Craigendoran Ag & B
466 B1 Craigends Rens
422 C3 Craigenputtock D & G
476 D3 Craigens Ag & B
446 B6 Craigens E Ayrs
488 B4 Craigentinny C Edin
450 A2 Craigerne Border
557 E6 Craiggie Cat Abers
525 J6 Craighall P & K
483 G3 Craighat Stirlg
558 B1 Craighead Abers
477 J3 Craighouse Ag & B
560 D6 Craigie Abers
514 C3 Craigie C Dund
512 D5 Craigie P & K
525 H7 Craigie P & K
444 D5 Craigie S Ayrs
445 F3 Craigie S Ayrs
557 F3 Craigiebuckler C Aber
487 G4 Craigiehall C Edin
489 E4 Craigielaw E Loth
449 H5 Craigierig Border
487 H5 Craigleith C Edin
129 H3 Craig Llangiwg Neath
268 D4 Craig-Llwyn Shrops
487 H5 Craiglockhart C Edin
433 G6 Craigmalloch E Ayrs
570 F4 Craigmaud Abers
515 F2 Craigmill Angus
498 C5 Craigmill Stirlg
488 B5 Craigmillar C Edin
464 C1 Craigmore Ag & B
269 E2 Craignant Shrops
468 B1 Craigneuk N Lans
468 B3 Craigneuk N Lans
505 L3 Craignure Ag & B
529 E2 Craigo Angus
500 A3 Craigow P & K
565 L7 Craigrory Highld
501 G2 Craigrothie Fife
509 G5 Craigruie Stirlg
173 E2 Craig's End Essex
451 H2 Craigsford Mains Border
487 E6 Craigshill W Loth
394 C2 Craigside Dur
515 E2 Craigton Angus
526 D4 Craigton Angus
557 E4 Craigton C Aber
466 D2 Craigton C Glas
566 B7 Craigton Highld
576 D4 Craigton Highld
587 J5 Craigtown Highld
304 C5 Craig-y-Don IOA
129 H4 Craig-y-Duke Neath
130 C1 Craig-y-Nos Powys
229 E6 Craig-y-Penrhyn Cerdgn
106 C2 Craig-y-Rhacca Caerph
438 C3 Craik Border
503 G3 Crail Fife
452 C5 Crailing Border
452 D5 Crailinghall Border
370 A1 Crakehall N York
371 E5 Crakehill N York
273 G2 Crakemarsh Staffs
449 G5 Cramalt Border
358 D2 Crambe N York
358 D1 Crambeck N York

75 E1 Cramhurst Surrey
431 E4 Cramlington Nthumb
487 G4 Cramond C Edin
487 G4 Cramond Bridge C Edin
72 A5 Crampmoor Hants
311 E6 Cranage Ches
272 B2 Cranberry Staffs
48 D2 Cranborne Dorset
117 F5 Cranbourne Br For
91 G4 Cranbourne Hants
120 B2 Cranbrook Ct Lon
80 A2 Cranbrook Kent
80 A2 Cranbrook Common Kent
329 E4 Crane Moor Barns
121 H1 Cranes Essex
254 B5 Crane's Corner Norfk
168 D1 Cranfield Beds
38 D3 Cranford Devon
118 C4 Cranford Gt Lon
218 C4 Cranford St Andrew Nhants
218 C4 Cranford St John Nhants
136 C2 Cranham Gloucs
121 E2 Cranham Gt Lon
467 F1 Cranhill C Glas
190 A4 Cranhill Warwks
324 C5 Crank St Hel
325 E4 Crankwood Wigan
75 H2 Cranleigh Surrey
225 G5 Cranley Suffk
119 F2 Cranley Gardens Gt Lon
568 D4 Cranloch Moray
224 D5 Cranmer Green Suffk
36 B2 Cranmore IoW
86 B6 Cranmore Somset
569 H5 Crannoch Moray
241 G5 Cranoe Leics
202 C2 Cransford Suffk
473 F2 Cranshaws Border
322 h2 Cranstal IoM
360 C4 Cranswick E R Yk
7 E1 Crantock Cnwll
298 C5 Cranwell Lincs
247 F5 Cranwich Norfk
248 C4 Cranworth Norfk
492 C3 Craobh Haven Ag & B
18 B4 Crapstone Devon
493 G5 Crarae Ag & B
586 F4 Crask Highld
555 F3 Craskins Abers
549 H1 Crask of Aigas Highld
455 H6 Craster Nthumb
159 E3 Craswall Herefs
211 G2 Crateford Shrops
236 D3 Crateford Staffs
226 C4 Cratfield Suffk
556 D5 Crathes Abers
537 L3 Crathie Abers
535 G4 Crathie Highld
384 C3 Crathorne N York
210 A3 Craven Arms Shrops
404 D2 Crawcrook Gatesd
324 B4 Crawford Lancs
448 C5 Crawford S Lans
468 D5 Crawforddyke S Lans
447 H5 Crawfordjohn S Lans
435 F2 Crawick D & G
44 B6 Crawley Devon
72 B3 Crawley Hants
139 E2 Crawley Oxon
77 E2 Crawley W Susx
77 F2 Crawley Down W Susx
171 F2 Crawley End Essex
93 E3 Crawley Hill Surrey
393 J1 Crawleyside Dur
328 C2 Crawshaw Kirk
340 C4 Crawshawbooth Lancs
541 G4 Crawton Abers
606 B6 Crawton Shet
368 B4 Cray N York
525 H3 Cray P & K
120 D5 Crayford Gt Lon
371 H5 Crayke N York
260 D5 Craymere Beck Norfk
147 E6 Crays Hill Essex
115 G3 Cray's Pond Oxon
116 C3 Crazies Hill Wokham
41 G4 Creacombe Devon
520 D7 Creagan Ag & B
492 D4 Creaganterve Mhòr Ag & B
593 B8 Creagastrom W Isls
593 D8 Creag Ghoraidh W Isls
524 F3 Creag na Cuinneige P & K
270 C3 Creamore Bank Shrops
2 C5 Crean Cnwll
217 F5 Creaton Nhants
425 E5 Creca D & G
186 A6 Credenhill Herefs
26 C2 Crediton Devon
26 C3 Crediton Devon
417 E3 Creebridge D & G
33 G3 Creech Dorset
33 G3 Creech Bottom Dorset
44 B2 Creech Heathfield Somset
44 B2 Creech St Michael Somset
8 A4 Creed Cnwll
607 J4 Creediknowe Shet
6 D5 Creegbrawse Cnwll
48 B6 Creekmoor Poole
120 C3 Creekmouth Gt Lon
148 B5 Creeksea Essex
201 F3 Creeting Hills Suffk
201 E3 Creeting St Mary Suffk
201 E3 Creeting St Peter Suffk
279 E5 Creeton Lincs
417 F5 Creetown D & G
494 B4 Creggans Ag & B
322 b9 Cregneash IoM
322 f6 Cregny Baa IoM
184 B4 Cregrina Powys
504 C6 Creich Ag & B
513 H5 Creich Fife
134 B5 Creigau Mons
273 G2 Creighton Staffs
106 A3 Creigiau Cardif
4 C2 Crelly Cnwll
10 D3 Cremyll Cnwll
48 D2 Crendell Dorset
543 G7 Crepkill Highld
167 H5 Creslow Bucks
234 D4 Cressage Shrops
313 G5 Cressbrook Derbys
126 B3 Cresselly Pembks
116 D1 Cressex Bucks
136 A4 Cress Green Gloucs
173 F6 Cressing Essex
443 H6 Cresswell Nthumb
273 E2 Cresswell Staffs
126 B3 Cresswell Quay Pembks
315 G5 Creswell Derbys
272 D5 Creswell Staffs
237 G2 Creswell Green Staffs
202 A2 Cretingham Suffk
462 B1 Cretshengan Ag & B
291 E4 Crewe Ches
289 F4 Crewe-by-Farndon Ches
391 G4 Crewgarth Cumb
233 F1 Crewgreen Powys
45 E6 Crewkerne Somset
144 D4 Crews Hill Gt Lon
109 H5 Crew's Hole Bristl
275 F3 Crewton C Derb
508 E4 Crianlarich Stirlg
340 B5 Cribden Side Lancs

180 D4 Cribyn Cerdgn
264 B2 Criccieth Gwynd
294 D4 Crich Derbys
294 C4 Crich Carr Derbys
571 G7 Crichie Abers
471 G2 Crichton Mdloth
109 E1 Crick Mons
216 C5 Crick Nhants
158 A1 Crickadarn Powys
92 D3 Cricket Hill Hants
44 D5 Cricket Malherbie Somset
44 D6 Cricket St Thomas Somset
84 D5 Crickham Somset
269 E5 Crickheath Shrops
269 E5 Crickheath Wharf Shrops
158 D6 Crickhowell Powys
137 G6 Cricklade Wilts
119 E2 Cricklewood Gt Lon
271 F4 Crickmery Shrops
187 E4 Crick's Green Herefs
49 F2 Criddlestyle Hants
344 C5 Cridling Stubbs N York
36 D4 Cridmore IoW
511 F5 Crieff P & K
8 C1 Criggan Cnwll
233 E2 Criggion Powys
329 E1 Crigglestone Wakefd
326 C2 Crimble Rochdl
44 C6 Crimchard Somset
396 C2 Crimdon Park Dur
571 J4 Crimond Abers
571 J4 Crimonmogate Abers
38 B4 Crimp Cnwll
246 C4 Crimplesham Norfk
190 C5 Crimscote Warwks
492 C6 Crinan Ag & B
492 C6 Crinan Ferry Ag & B
107 F2 Crindau Newpt
468 C3 Crindledyke N Lans
249 G3 Cringleford Norfk
354 D5 Cringles Brad
470 D6 Cringletie Border
126 C2 Crinow Pembks
173 G3 Cripple Corner Essex
3 F2 Cripplesease Cnwll
48 D2 Cripplestyle Dorset
58 C2 Cripp's Corner E Susx
312 D3 Crist Derbys
71 F4 Critchell's Green Hants
86 D5 Critchill Somset
74 D3 Critchmere Surrey
80 A3 Crit Hall Kent
160 A3 Crizeley Herefs
15 E4 Croanford Cnwll
376 D1 Croasdale Cumb
96 D1 Crockenhill Kent
116 B2 Crocker End Oxon
51 G3 Crockerhill Hants
53 G3 Crockerhill W Susx
26 B4 Crockernwell Devon
61 E4 Crockers Devon
134 C1 Crocker's Ash Herefs
68 D1 Crockerton Wilts
87 E6 Crockerton Green Wilts
422 D5 Crocketford D & G
358 B5 Crockey Hill York
90 C2 Crockham Heath W Berk
96 B4 Crockham Hill Kent
97 F6 Crockhurst Street Kent
174 D4 Crockleford Heath Essex
600 E6 Crockness Ork
44 C5 Crock Street Somset
268 D4 Croesau Bach Shrops
130 D5 Croes-Goch Pembks
150 D3 Croes-Hywel Mons
133 F2 Croes-Lan Cerdgn
180 A6 Croes-Lan Cerdgn
133 F3 Croes Lanfair Mons
284 D6 Croesor Gwynd
132 C5 Croespenmaen Caerph
307 C5 Croes-Wian Flints
128 B1 Croesyceiliog Carmth
133 E5 Croesyceiliog Torfn
107 F1 Croes-y-mwyalch Torfn
133 F4 Croes y Pant Mons
283 F4 Croesywaun Gwynd
186 B1 Croft Herefs
240 B5 Croft Leics
301 F2 Croft Lincs
325 E6 Croft Warrtn
485 G2 Croftamie Stirlg
467 E2 Croftfoot C Glas
523 K6 Croftgarrow P & K
6 D5 Crofthandy Cnwll
364 C4 Croftlands Cumb
469 E2 Croftmalloch W Loth
4 C1 Croft Mitchell Cnwll
565 L7 Croftnacriech Highld
400 B4 Crofton Cumb
96 B1 Crofton Gt Lon
343 G6 Crofton Wakefd
89 G2 Crofton Wilts
383 G3 Croft-on-Tees N York
500 D4 Croft Outerly Fife
325 H5 Crofts Bank Traffd
583 G2 Crofts of Benachielt Highld
568 E4 Crofts of Dipple Moray
560 B2 Crofts of Haddo Abers
577 G8 Crofts of Kingscauseway Highld
102 D2 Crofty Swans
505 L5 Croggan Ag & B
401 G5 Croglin Cumb
575 K5 Croich Highld
587 J6 Croick Highld
590 F3 Crois Dùghaill W Isls
566 D3 Cromarty Highld
487 E2 Crombie Fife
560 A2 Cromblet Abers
551 K4 Cromdale Highld
170 C4 Cromer Herts
261 H3 Cromer Norfk
144 A2 Cromer-Hyde Herts
294 B3 Cromford Derbys
110 B1 Cromhall S Glos
110 B2 Cromhall Common S Glos
597 L3 Cromor W Isls
327 E3 Crompton Fold Oldham
297 E2 Cromwell Notts
342 B5 Cromwell Bottom Calder
446 B5 Cronberry E Ayrs
92 C5 Crondall Hants
322 h10 Cronkbourne IoM
322 e5 Cronk-y-Voddy IoM
309 G2 Cronton Knows
379 E5 Crook Cumb
28 C2 Crook Devon
394 D2 Crook Dur
399 F6 Crookdake Cumb
324 D3 Crooke Wigan
445 G2 Crookedholm E Ayrs
113 H5 Crooked Soley Wilts
48 C3 Crooked Withies Dorset
314 C2 Crookes Sheff
314 C2 Crookesmoor Sheff
466 D3 Crookfur E Rens
405 E3 Crookgate Bank Dur
166 B3 Crookhall Dur
453 H2 Crookham Nthumb
91 E2 Crookham W Berk
92 C4 Crookham Village Hants
405 E2 Crookhill Gatesd
453 E4 Crookhouse Border

366 A3 Crooklands Cumb
499 G5 Crook of Devon P & K
466 C2 Crookston C Glas
191 H5 Cropredy Oxon
240 B2 Cropston Leics
189 E6 Cropthorne Worcs
373 E2 Cropton N York
277 E2 Cropwell Bishop Notts
277 E2 Cropwell Butler Notts
599 L2 Cros W Isls
597 K3 Crosbost W Isls
376 D1 Crosby Cumb
380 E3 Crosby IoM
332 B2 Crosby N Linc
323 E5 Crosby Sefton
370 D1 Crosby Court N York
380 E3 Crosby Garrett Cumb
401 E3 Crosby-on-Eden Cumb
379 H1 Crosby Ravensworth Cumb
388 C2 Crosby Villa Cumb
85 G6 Croscombe Somset
270 A4 Crosemere Shrops
327 A4 Crosland Edge Kirk
327 H2 Crosland Hill Kirk
327 H1 Crosland Moor Kirk
364 B5 Croslands Park Cumb
60 C4 Cross Devon
61 F5 Cross Devon
269 E5 Cross Shrops
84 D4 Cross Somset
462 D4 Crossaig Ag & B
516 B7 Crossapol Ag & B
159 H6 Cross Ash Mons
98 B5 Cross-at-Hand Kent
211 H5 Cross Bank Worcs
570 B5 Crossbrae Abers
485 H5 Crossburn Falk
54 B3 Crossbush W Susx
388 C2 Crosscanonby Cumb
6 D3 Cross Coombe Cnwll
365 H2 Crosscrake Cumb
261 H4 Crossdale Street Norfk
195 H3 Cross End Beds
173 H3 Cross End Beds
168 C2 Cross End M Keyn
337 G5 Crossens Sefton
342 B1 Crossflatts Brad
487 E2 Crossford Fife
468 C5 Crossford S Lans
23 G5 Crossgate Cnwll
280 B4 Crossgate Lincs
272 D2 Crossgate Staffs
54 B2 Cross Gate W Susx
342 A2 Cross Gates Brad
388 C2 Crossgates Cumb
487 F2 Crossgates Fife
343 G3 Cross Gates Leeds
374 C3 Crossgates N York
183 H2 Crossgates Powys
392 B1 Crossgill Cumb
392 B1 Crossgill Lancs
24 A5 Cross Green Devon
234 B1 Crossgreen Shrops
199 G4 Cross Green Suffk
200 A3 Cross Green Suffk
200 C4 Cross Green Suffk
235 E2 Cross Green Wrekin
139 G2 Crosshands Carmth
152 D5 Crosshands Carmth
445 G3 Crosshands E Ayrs
126 B2 Cross Hands Pembks
291 G5 Cross Heath Staffs
15 E4 Cross Hill Cnwll
295 E5 Cross Hill Derbys
445 G5 Crosshill E Ayrs
500 C5 Crosshill Fife
134 D5 Cross Hills Gloucs
432 D3 Crosshill S Ayrs
354 D6 Cross Hills N York
385 F5 Cross Holme N York
445 E2 Crosshouse E Ayrs
211 F1 Cross Houses Shrops
234 C3 Cross Houses Shrops
426 C4 Crossings Cumb
78 D5 Cross in Hand E Susx
127 F2 Cross Inn Carmth
180 A3 Cross Inn Cerdgn
180 D2 Cross Inn Cerdgn
105 H3 Cross Inn Rhondd
106 D1 Cross Keys Caerph
96 D4 Cross Keys Kent
111 F5 Cross Keys Wilts
588 C2 Crosskirk Highld
364 D2 Crosslands Cumb
290 D2 Cross Lane Ches
235 G5 Cross Lane Head Shrops
4 C4 Cross Lanes Cnwll
47 E4 Cross Lanes Dorset
357 G2 Cross Lanes N York
115 H4 Cross Lanes Oxon
269 F6 Crosslanes Shrops
289 E5 Cross Lanes Wrexhm
450 C6 Crosslee Rens
466 B1 Crosslee Rens
160 A4 Crosslyde Herefs
412 D1 Crossmichael D & G
466 D3 Crossmill E Rens
338 B2 Crossmoor Lancs
467 E2 Crossmyloof C Glas
158 A5 Cross Oak Powys
559 G3 Cross of Jackston Abers
294 B3 Cross O'th Hands Derbys
289 G5 Cross O' Th' Hill Ches
77 E5 Crosspost W Susx
556 D6 Crossroads Abers
24 C5 Cross Roads Devon
445 G3 Crossroads E Ayrs
501 G5 Crossroads Fife
225 G4 Cross Street Suffk
311 F4 Crosston Angus
38 A5 Crosstown Cnwll
105 G5 Crosstown V Glam
74 D2 Crosswater Surrey
161 E3 Crossway Herefs
160 A6 Crossway Mons
183 H3 Crossway Powys
134 C6 Crossway Green Mons
212 B6 Crossway Green Worcs
32 D2 Crossways Dorset
121 E4 Crossways Kent
159 F6 Crossways Mons
110 B1 Crossways S Glos
74 C2 Crossways Surrey
152 C2 Crosswell Pembks
205 F3 Crosswood Cerdgn
365 F1 Crosthwaite Cumb
338 C2 Croston Lancs
250 B1 Crostwick Norfk
256 C3 Crostwight Norfk
598 D7 Crothair W Isls
97 F3 Crouch Kent
99 H3 Crouch Kent
119 F2 Crouch End Gt Lon
53 E4 Crouchers W Susx
70 B4 Croucheston Wilts
46 D2 Crouch Hill Dorset
166 B3 Croughton Nhants
570 E2 Crovie Abers
49 F4 Crow Hants
4 B2 Crowan Cnwll
78 D5 Crowborough E Susx
292 B3 Crowborough Staffs

78 C3 Crowborough Warren E Susx
64 B4 Crowcombe Somset
187 H4 Crowcroft Worcs
293 E4 Crowdecote Derbys
327 G5 Crowden Derbys
24 C3 Crowden Devon
19 F6 Crowder Park Devon
72 C5 Crowdhill Hants
97 E3 Crowdieham Kent
387 G5 Crowdon N York
328 B4 Crow Edge Barns
141 F5 Crowell Oxon
141 G5 Crowell Hill Oxon
166 D1 Crowfield Nhants
201 F3 Crowfield Suffk
256 C5 Crowgate Street Norfk
235 H5 Crowgreaves Shrops
146 B3 Crow Green Essex
161 E4 Crow Hill Herefs
167 H2 Crowhill M Keyn
326 D5 Crowhill Tamesd
314 C4 Crowhole Derbys
58 C4 Crowhurst E Susx
96 A5 Crowhurst Surrey
96 A5 Crowhurst Lane End Surrey
244 B2 Crowland Lincs
3 F3 Crowlas Cnwll
331 F5 Crowle N Linc
188 D3 Crowle Worcs
188 D3 Crowle Green Worcs
331 G2 Crowle Hill N Linc
331 G2 Crowle Park N Linc
115 G2 Crowmarsh Gifford Oxon
566 B8 Crown Highld
226 B5 Crown Corner Suffk
188 B4 Crown East Worcs
141 G5 Crownfield Bucks
11 E2 Crownhill C Plym
240 D4 Crown Hills C Leic
224 D5 Crownland Suffk
93 G6 Crownpits Surrey
249 G6 Crownthorpe Norfk
4 B2 Crowntown Cnwll
93 E1 Crown Wood Br For
2 C4 Crows-an-Wra Cnwll
172 D4 Crow's Green Essex
248 B3 Crowshill Norfk
116 B4 Crowsley Oxon
16 C5 Crow's Nest Cnwll
233 G4 Crowsnest Shrops
184 D5 Crowther's Pool Powys
92 D2 Crowthorne Br For
310 B5 Crowton Ches
309 H2 Crow Wood Halton
238 B2 Croxall Staffs
334 A5 Croxby Lincs
333 H5 Croxby Top Lincs
395 F2 Croxdale Dur
273 G2 Croxden Staffs
143 F5 Croxley Green Herts
323 H6 Croxteth Lpool
196 B3 Croxton Cambs
333 F2 Croxton N Linc
223 H2 Croxton Norfk
260 C5 Croxton Norfk
272 A3 Croxton Staffs
272 B3 Croxtonbank Staffs
290 A4 Croxton Green Ches
278 A4 Croxton Kerrial Leics
566 D7 Croy Highld
485 E1 Croy N Lans
60 B4 Croyde Devon
60 B4 Croyde Bay Devon
196 D5 Croydon Cambs
95 G2 Croydon Gt Lon
186 D5 Crozen Herefs
233 H3 Cruckmeole Shrops
234 A2 Cruckton Shrops
561 G2 Cruden Bay Abers
271 E6 Crudgington Wrekin
137 E6 Crudwell Wilts
208 C5 Crug Powys
130 B4 Crugau Neath
14 C3 Crugmeer Cnwll
155 G2 Crugybar Carmth
189 F2 Cruise Hill Worcs
598 D8 Crùlabhig W Isls
132 D5 Crumlin Caerph
9 G3 Crumplehorn Cnwll
326 B4 Crumpsall Manch
211 E4 Crumpsbrook Shrops
187 H5 Crumpton Hill Herefs
99 H5 Crundale Kent
151 G6 Crundale Pembks
41 H5 Cruwys Morchard Devon
90 C3 Crux Easton Hants
30 D3 Cruxton Dorset
128 C2 Crwbin Carmth
142 B5 Cryers Hill Bucks
152 D3 Crymych Pembks
130 B4 Crynant Neath
562 C5 Cuaig Highld
492 C5 Cuan Ag & B
215 E6 Cubbington Warwks
368 C2 Cubeck N York
7 E2 Cubert Cnwll
120 A4 Cubitt Town Gt Lon
328 C4 Cubley Barns
274 B2 Cubley Common Derbys
168 A5 Cublington Bucks
77 E5 Cuckfield W Susx
68 C4 Cucklington Somset
315 H5 Cuckney Notts
227 F3 Cuckold's Green Suffk
88 A3 Cuckold's Green Wilts
251 G5 Cuckoo Green Suffk
74 A1 Cuckoo's Corner Hants
88 B3 Cuckoo's Corner Suffk
89 E2 Cuckoo's Knob Wilts
200 A6 Cuckoo Tye Suffk
606 E7 Cuckron Shet
250 D3 Cucumber Corner Norfk
140 D4 Cuddesdon Oxon
141 F2 Cuddington Bucks
310 B5 Cuddington Ches
289 G5 Cuddington Heath Ches
338 C2 Cuddy Hill Lancs
96 B3 Cudham Gt Lon
18 B2 Cudliptown Devon
329 F3 Cudworth Barns
44 D5 Cudworth Somset
76 D1 Cudworth Surrey
329 F3 Cudworth Common Barns
339 E5 Cuerden Lancs
310 A2 Cuerdley Cross Warrtn
91 G3 Cufaude Hants
151 E5 Cuffern Pembks
144 B3 Cuffley Herts
568 F3 Cuffurach Moray
543 D7 Cuidhir W Isls
595 H5 Cuidhtinis W Isls
542 F5 Cuidrach Highld
470 D2 Cuiken Mdloth
520 H4 Cuil Highld
565 L4 Culbo Highld
565 L6 Culbokie Highld
549 H1 Culburnie Highld
566 F6 Culcabock Highld
566 F6 Culcharry Highld
325 F6 Culcheth Warrtn
519 G1 Cùl Doirlinn Highld
558 C3 Culdrain Abers

City, town and village index: Culduie - Dhail Bho Dheas 683

546 C1 **Culduie** Highld
223 G5 **Culford** Suffk
223 G5 **Culfordheath** Suffk
391 G4 **Culgaith** Cumb
140 B5 **Culham** Oxon
578 D3 **Culkein** Highld
578 F3 **Culkein Drumbeg** Highld
136 D5 **Culkerton** Gloucs
551 H5 **Cullachie** Highld
569 J2 **Cullen** Moray
431 G5 **Cullercoats** N Tyne
565 L4 **Cullicudden** Highld
341 H2 **Cullingworth** Brad
492 B2 **Cullipool** Ag & B
566 E1 **Cullisse** Highld
609 G4 **Cullivoe** Shet
510 D6 **Culloch** P & K
566 C7 **Culloden** Highld
27 F1 **Cullompton** Devon
577 H4 **Culmaily** Highld
43 F5 **Culm Davy** Devon
75 E2 **Culmer** Surrey
99 H2 **Culmers** Kent
210 B3 **Culmington** Shrops
497 G5 **Culmore** Stirlg
43 F5 **Culmstock** Devon
543 J4 **Culnacnoc** Highld
573 L3 **Culnacraig** Highld
201 H5 **Culpho** Suffk
576 C5 **Culrain** Highld
599 J8 **Culrigrein** W Isls
486 C2 **Culross** Fife
432 D2 **Culroy** S Ayrs
411 E3 **Culscadden** D & G
554 B5 **Culsh** Abers
570 F6 **Culsh** Abers
409 G1 **Culshabbin** D & G
604 E1 **Culswick** Shet
560 D5 **Culterculien** Abers
558 C3 **Cults** Abers
557 F4 **Cults** C Aber
510 D6 **Cultybraggan** P & K
19 F5 **Culverlane** Devon
97 F2 **Culverstone Green** Kent
279 E1 **Culverthorpe** Lincs
192 B5 **Culworth** Nhants
170 D3 **Cumberlow Green** Herts
485 F5 **Cumbernauld** N Lans
485 E4 **Cumbernauld Village** N Lans
270 A2 **Cumber's Bank** Wrexhm
321 F5 **Cumberworth** Lincs
400 B5 **Cumdivock** Cumb
339 E2 **Cumeragh Village** Lancs
570 E5 **Cuminestown** Abers
474 A3 **Cumledge** Border
605 H6 **Cumlewick** Shet
400 C4 **Cummersdale** Cumb
399 E1 **Cummertrees** D & G
557 G3 **Cummings Park** C Aber
567 L3 **Cummingston** Moray
446 B6 **Cumnock** E Ayrs
139 H4 **Cumnor** Oxon
140 A4 **Cumnor Hill** Oxon
401 G4 **Cumrew** Cumb
401 E4 **Cumwhinton** Cumb
401 F4 **Cumwhitton** Cumb
371 E5 **Cundall** N York
329 E5 **Cundy Hos** Barns
445 E1 **Cunninghamhead** N Ayrs
605 H4 **Cunningsburgh** Shet
609 G5 **Cunnister** Shet
502 B2 **Cupar** Fife
501 G2 **Cupar Muir** Fife
71 H5 **Cupernham** Hants
143 F3 **Cupid Green** Herts
159 G4 **Cupid's Hill** Mons
314 B5 **Curbar** Derbys
238 A2 **Curborough** Staffs
51 F2 **Curbridge** Hants
139 E3 **Curbridge** Oxon
51 F2 **Curdridge** Hants
238 B6 **Curdworth** Warwks
7 G6 **Curgurrell** Cnwll
44 B4 **Curland** Somset
44 B4 **Curland Common** Somset
202 D1 **Curlew Green** Suffk
147 G3 **Curling Tye Green** Essex
44 C2 **Curload** Somset
419 E3 **Currarie** S Ayrs
8 B2 **Currian Vale** Cnwll
114 D5 **Curridge** W Berk
487 G6 **Currie** C Edin
400 D4 **Currock** Cumb
23 F4 **Curry Lane** Cnwll
44 C3 **Curry Mallet** Somset
66 B4 **Curry Rivel** Somset
600 F2 **Cursiter** Ork
80 C2 **Curteis' Corner** Kent
79 G1 **Curtisden Green** Kent
12 C2 **Curtisknowle** Devon
145 H5 **Curtismill Green** Essex
4 C4 **Cury** Cnwll
603 G4 **Cusbay** Ork
7 E5 **Cusgarne** Cnwll
570 D3 **Cushnie** Abers
64 C5 **Cushuish** Somset
158 D1 **Cusop** Herefs
50 A3 **Custards** Hants
7 E5 **Cusveorth Coombe** Cnwll
330 B4 **Cusworth** Donc
411 E6 **Cutcloy** D & G
63 E4 **Cutcombe** Somset
326 C2 **Cutgate** Rochdl
488 D5 **Cuthill** E Loth
229 E1 **Cutiau** Gwynd
172 B3 **Cutlers Green** Essex
85 G4 **Cutler's Green** Somset
15 F6 **Cutmadoc** Cnwll
10 B1 **Cutmere** Cnwll
212 C6 **Cutnall Green** Worcs
411 E5 **Cutreoch** D & G
163 G3 **Cutsdean** Gloucs
343 H5 **Cutsyke** Wakefd
140 B2 **Cutteslowe** Oxon
314 C5 **Cutthorpe** Derbys
605 H3 **Cutts** Shet
151 F6 **Cuttybridge** Pembks
571 J5 **Cuttyhill** Abers
141 E5 **Cuxham** Oxon
97 H1 **Cuxton** Medway
333 H4 **Cuxwold** Lincs
132 C3 **Cwm** Blae G
307 F4 **Cwm** Denbgs
130 C6 **Cwm** Neath
209 E1 **Cwm** Powys
231 H5 **Cwm** Powys
209 F4 **Cwm** Shrops
104 B1 **Cwmafan** Neath
131 G5 **Cwmaman** Rhondd
181 E5 **Cwmann** Carmth
133 E3 **Cwmavon** Torfn
153 E4 **Cwmbach** Carmth
158 C2 **Cwmbach** Powys
181 G4 **Cwmbach** Rhondd
183 G4 **Cwmbach Llechrhyd** Powys
207 E3 **Cwmbelan** Powys
133 E5 **Cwmbran** Torfn
205 G3 **Cwmbrwyno** Cerdgn
128 B4 **Cwm Capel** Carmth
132 D6 **Cwmcarn** Caerph
134 B3 **Cwmcarvan** Mons
132 D3 **Cwm-celyn** Blae G
129 F3 **Cwmcerdinen** Swans
230 D2 **Cwm-Cewydd** Gwynd
179 G4 **Cwmcoednerth** Cerdgn
153 F1 **Cwm-cou** Cerdgn
158 B6 **Cwmcrawnon** Powys
153 F2 **Cwmcych** Carmth
131 F4 **Cwmdare** Rhondd
132 C5 **Cwm Dows** Caerph
155 F3 **Cwmdu** Carmth
158 C5 **Cwmdu** Powys
103 F3 **Cwmdu** Swans
154 A3 **Cwmduad** Carmth
129 F4 **Cwm Dulais** Swans
155 G3 **Cwmdwr** Carmth
205 G3 **Cwmerfyn** Cerdgn
104 D2 **Cwmfelin** Brdgnd
132 A4 **Cwmfelin** Myr Td
152 D6 **Cwmfelin Boeth** Carmth
106 C1 **Cwmfelinfach** Caerph
153 E5 **Cwmfelin Mynach** Carmth
128 B1 **Cwmffrwd** Carmth
133 E4 **Cwm Ffrwd-oer** Torfn
133 E4 **Cwm-Fields** Torfn
132 C5 **Cwm Gelli** Caerph
130 B2 **Cwmgiedd** Powys
129 H2 **Cwmgors** Neath
129 E2 **Cwmgwili** Carmth
130 D4 **Cwmgwrach** Neath
103 F3 **Cwm Gwyn** Swans
209 H2 **Cwm Head** Shrops
153 G2 **Cwmhiraeth** Carmth
131 E3 **Cwm-hwnt** Rhondd
155 G4 **Cwmifor** Carmth
182 C5 **Cwm Irfon** Powys
128 C1 **Cwmisfael** Carmth
230 C3 **Cwm-Llinau** Powys
130 A2 **Cwmllynfell** Neath
128 D2 **Cwm-mawr** Carmth
152 D5 **Cwm-Miles** Carmth
132 D2 **Cwm Nant-gam** Mons
132 C5 **Cwmnantyrodyn** Caerph
153 F3 **Cwmorgan** Carmth
131 E5 **Cwmparc** Rhondd
153 G2 **Cwmpengraig** Carmth
285 F5 **Cwm Penmachno** Conwy
131 G4 **Cwmpennar** Rhondd
178 D5 **Cwm Plysgog** Pembks
158 C5 **Cwmrhos** Powys
129 G5 **Cwmrhydyceirw** Swans
180 C5 **Cwmsychbant** Cerdgn
132 C4 **Cwmsyfiog** Caerph
205 F3 **Cwmsymlog** Cerdgn
132 D3 **Cwmtillery** Blae G
130 B2 **Cwm-twrch Isaf** Powys
130 B2 **Cwm-twrch Uchaf** Powys
150 C3 **Cwmwdig Water** Pembks
156 C4 **Cwmwysg** Powys
284 C2 **Cwm-y-glo** Gwynd
133 E5 **Cwmynyscoy** Torfn
159 E5 **Cwmyoy** Mons
206 B5 **Cwmystwyth** Cerdgn
229 F4 **Cwrt** Gwynd
180 C5 **Cwrtnewydd** Cerdgn
181 G6 **Cwrt-y-Cadno** Carmth
132 D1 **Cwrt y Gollen** Powys
287 F3 **Cyffylliog** Denbgs
232 B3 **Cyfronydd** Powys
288 C3 **Cymau** Flints
105 E3 **Cymdda** Brdgnd
130 D5 **Cymer** Neath
105 G1 **Cymmer** Rhondd
106 C3 **Cyncoed** Cardif
156 B2 **Cynghordy** Carmth
128 C3 **Cynheidre** Carmth
130 C6 **Cynonville** Neath
106 B4 **Cyntwell** Cardif
267 H1 **Cynwyd** Denbgs
154 A4 **Cynwyl Elfed** Carmth

D

20 B4 **Daccombe** Devon
390 D4 **Dacre** Cumb
355 G2 **Dacre** N York
355 G2 **Dacre Banks** N York
393 E2 **Daddry Shield** Dur
167 E2 **Dadford** Bucks
239 G5 **Dadlington** Leics
128 D4 **Dafen** Carmth
248 C3 **Daffy Green** Norfk
273 G3 **Dagdale** Staffs
120 C3 **Dagenham** Gt Lon
49 E2 **Daggons** Dorset
137 E3 **Daglingworth** Gloucs
142 D1 **Dagnall** Bucks
189 F2 **Dagtail End** Worcs
200 D2 **Dagworth** Suffk
604 b2 **Da Hametoon** Shet
598 E5 **Dail Beag** W Isls
599 K2 **Dail Bho Thuath** W Isls
476 F4 **Daill** Ag & B
479 L3 **Daill** Ag & B
432 C4 **Dailly** S Ayrs
598 E6 **Dail Mòr** W Isls
20 A4 **Dainton** Devon
502 C1 **Dairsie or Osnaburgh** Fife
224 D6 **Daisy Green** Suffk
225 E6 **Daisy Green** Suffk
325 E4 **Daisy Hill** Bolton
342 B3 **Daisy Hill** Brad
326 D4 **Daisy Nook** Oldham
590 E3 **Dalabrog** W Isls
493 G2 **Dalavich** Ag & B
413 F2 **Dalbeattie** D & G
446 C6 **Dalblair** E Ayrs
540 A5 **Dalbog** Angus
274 D3 **Dalbury** Derbys
322 c7 **Dalby** IoM
320 D5 **Dalby** Lincs
372 B5 **Dalby** N York
577 K2 **Dalchalm** Highld
586 D5 **Dalcharn** Highld
494 B3 **Dalchenna** Ag & B
580 E7 **Dalchork** Highld
548 D7 **Dalchreichart** Highld
497 H1 **Dalchruin** P & K
299 H1 **Dalderby** Lincs
401 F6 **Dale** Cumb
327 E3 **Dale** Oldham
124 D3 **Dale** Pembks
275 G2 **Dale Abbey** Derbys
294 D2 **Dalebank** Derbys
389 G5 **Dale Bottom** Cumb
312 B4 **Dale Brow** Ches
293 H2 **Dale End** Derbys
354 C5 **Dale End** N York
378 D1 **Dale Head** Cumb
381 H3 **Dale Head** N York
79 G3 **Dale Hill** E Susx
519 H2 **Dalelia** Highld
275 G2 **Dale Moor** Derbys
606 A7 **Dale of Walls** Shet
325 H4 **Dales Brow** Salfd
291 G3 **Dales Green** Staffs
295 G2 **Dalestorth** Notts
551 G7 **Dalfaber** Highld
484 B2 **Dalfoil** Stirlg
465 F5 **Dalgarven** N Ayrs
487 G3 **Dalgety Bay** Fife
434 B2 **Dalgig** E Ayrs
510 D5 **Dalginross** P & K
524 E6 **Dalguise** P & K
525 J1 **Dalhally** Angus
587 J6 **Dalhalvaig** Highld
199 E2 **Dalham** Suffk
525 H2 **Dalhenzean** P & K
590 E3 **Daliburgh** W Isls
506 E4 **Dalintart** Ag & B
471 F1 **Dalkeith** Mdloth
310 B1 **Dallam** Warrtn
567 L6 **Dallas** Moray
434 B2 **Dalleagles** E Ayrs
235 H6 **Dallicott** Shrops
51 F6 **Dallimores** IoW
202 B3 **Dallinghoo** Suffk
79 F6 **Dallington** E Susx
193 F2 **Dallington** Nhants
369 G5 **Dallow** N York
507 L4 **Dalmally** Ag & B
467 F2 **Dalmarnock** C Glas
496 D5 **Dalmary** Stirlg
433 G3 **Dalmellington** E Ayrs
487 F4 **Dalmeny** C Edin
550 C6 **Dalmigavie** Highld
445 E5 **Dalmilling** S Ayrs
515 E3 **Dalmore** Angus
566 B3 **Dalmore** Highld
483 G5 **Dalmuir** W Duns
519 G2 **Dalnabreck** Highld
564 E5 **Dalnacroich** Highld
565 L2 **Dalnavie** Highld
566 B8 **Dalneigh** Highld
521 H5 **Dalness** Highld
580 F6 **Dalnessie** Highld
604 b2 **Da Loch** Shet
500 A4 **Dalqueich** P & K
419 H2 **Dalquhairn** S Ayrs
576 F2 **Dalreavoch** Highld
523 K4 **Dalriach** P & K
488 A5 **Dalry** C Edin
465 F5 **Dalry** N Ayrs
432 D2 **Dalrymple** E Ayrs
193 E4 **Dalscote** Nhants
468 B4 **Dalserf** S Lans
609 G5 **Dalsetter** Shet
485 E5 **Dalshannon** N Lans
400 C4 **Dalston** Cumb
119 G3 **Dalston** Gt Lon
423 F2 **Dalswinton** D & G
366 A4 **Dalton** Cumb
424 C5 **Dalton** D & G
328 B1 **Dalton** Kirk
324 B3 **Dalton** Lancs
371 E4 **Dalton** N York
382 D3 **Dalton** N York
403 G3 **Dalton** Nthumb
430 B5 **Dalton** Nthumb
329 H6 **Dalton** Rothm
467 G3 **Dalton** S Lans
364 B5 **Dalton-in-Furness** Cumb
406 C5 **Dalton-le-Dale** Dur
329 H6 **Dalton Magna** Rothm
383 G3 **Dalton-on-Tees** N York
329 H6 **Dalton Parva** Rothm
396 C3 **Dalton Piercy** Hartpl
479 K5 **Daltote** Ag & B
526 A1 **Dalvanie** Angus
509 K5 **Dalveich** Stirlg
535 H6 **Dalwhinnie** Highld
28 D2 **Dalwood** Devon
170 B4 **Damask Green** Herts
341 G2 **Damems** Brad
48 D1 **Damerham** Hants
135 G6 **Damery** Gloucs
251 E3 **Damgate** Norfk
257 F6 **Damgate** Norfk
225 E2 **Dam Green** Norfk
559 G4 **Damhead** Abers
342 A4 **Dam Head** Calder
471 E1 **Damhead Holdings** Mdloth
236 C4 **Dam Mill** Staffs
408 C4 **Damnaglaur** D & G
470 C5 **Damside** Border
351 F5 **Dam Side** Lancs
98 D2 **Danaway** Kent
147 F4 **Danbury** Essex
147 F4 **Danbury Common** Essex
386 A3 **Danby** N York
384 A5 **Danby Wiske** N York
105 H3 **Dan Caerlan** Rhondd
144 B5 **Dancers Hill** Herts
161 E5 **Dancing Green** Herefs
568 D6 **Dandalieth** Moray
152 C4 **Dandderwen** Pembks
488 C6 **Danderhall** Mdloth
225 E6 **Dandy Corner** Suffk
312 C3 **Danebank** Ches
326 C5 **Dane Bank** Tamesd
292 C2 **Danebridge** Ches
170 D5 **Dane End** Herts
78 D3 **Danegate** E Susx
77 H4 **Danehill** E Susx
292 A2 **Dane in Shaw** Ches
249 E3 **Danemoor Green** Norfk
144 B1 **Danesbury** Herts
116 D2 **Danesfield** Bucks
211 G1 **Danesford** Shrops
91 H4 **Daneshill** Hants
295 E2 **Danesmoor** Derbys
312 B5 **Danes Moss** Ches
99 H4 **Dane Street** Kent
136 D4 **Daneway** Gloucs
324 C2 **Dangerous Corner** Lancs
325 E4 **Dangerous Corner** Wigan
81 E1 **Daniel's Water** Kent
15 E2 **Dannonchapel** Cnwll
472 D1 **Danskine** E Loth
348 D3 **Danthorpe** E R Yk
158 D2 **Dan-y-Capel** Powys
106 D1 **Danygraig** Caerph
213 H6 **Danzey Green** Warwks
273 F4 **Dapple Heath** Staffs
213 E2 **Darby End** Dudley
92 D2 **Darby Green** Hants
187 G3 **Darbys Green** Worcs
213 E2 **Darby's Hill** Sandw
325 G3 **Darcy Lever** Bolton
158 D6 **Dardy** Powys
121 E5 **Darenth** Kent
310 B3 **Daresbury** Halton
310 B3 **Daresbury Delph** Halton
329 G4 **Darfield** Barns
315 H4 **Darfoulds** Notts
99 H2 **Dargate** Kent
100 A3 **Dargate Common** Kent
511 F6 **Dargill** P & K
16 C5 **Darite** Cnwll
568 D3 **Darkland** Moray
289 E3 **Darland** Wrexhm
237 E5 **Darlaston** Wsall
237 E5 **Darlaston Green** Wsall
355 H3 **Darley** N York
235 F5 **Darley** Shrops
275 F2 **Darley Abbey** C Derb
294 B2 **Darley Bridge** Derbys
294 B2 **Darley Dale** Derbys
16 C4 **Darleyford** Cnwll
214 B5 **Darley Green** Solhll
169 G5 **Darleyhall** Herts
355 G3 **Darley Head** N York
294 B2 **Darley Hillside** Derbys
164 C1 **Darlingscott** Warwks
383 G2 **Darlington** Darltn
270 D3 **Darliston** Shrops
456 D2 **Darlochan** Ag & B
317 E5 **Darlton** Notts
201 E4 **Darmsden** Suffk
314 D2 **Darnall** Sheff
238 A3 **Darnford** Staffs
470 D5 **Darnhall Mains** Border
326 B2 **Darn Hill** Rochdl
451 G3 **Darnick** Border
230 C4 **Darowen** Powys
570 C6 **Darra** Abers
23 G4 **Darracott** Cnwll
38 B4 **Darracott** Devon
60 C4 **Darracott** Devon
430 B5 **Darras Hall** Nthumb
344 B5 **Darrington** Wakefd
226 B2 **Darrow Green** Norfk
227 E6 **Darsham** Suffk
85 H6 **Darshill** Somset
120 D5 **Dartford** Kent
121 E4 **Dartford Crossing** Kent
19 G5 **Dartington** Devon
19 E3 **Dartmeet** Devon
13 F2 **Dartmouth** Devon
119 F2 **Dartmouth Park** Gt Lon
329 E2 **Darton** Barns
446 B2 **Darvel** E Ayrs
141 H5 **Darvillshill** Bucks
58 A3 **Darwell Hole** E Susx
339 G5 **Darwen** Bl w D
171 E4 **Dassels** Herts
117 G4 **Datchet** W & M
117 G4 **Datchet Common** W & M
170 C6 **Datchworth** Herts
170 C6 **Datchworth Green** Herts
604 b2 **Da Toon o Ham** Shet
325 G3 **Daubhill** Bolton
568 C7 **Daugh of Kinermony** Moray
112 A3 **Dauntsey** Wilts
112 A4 **Dauntsey Lock** Wilts
551 J2 **Dava** Highld
310 C5 **Davenham** Ches
291 G1 **Davenport** Ches
312 A2 **Davenport** Stockp
311 G4 **Davenport Green** Ches
311 F2 **Davenport Green** Traffd
192 C2 **Daventry** Nhants
487 H4 **Davidson's Mains** C Edin
22 D5 **Davidstow** Cnwll
97 F2 **David Street** Kent
207 G4 **David's Well** Powys
438 A4 **Davington** D & G
99 G2 **Davington** Kent
559 H4 **Daviot** Abers
550 C2 **Daviot** Highld
57 E1 **Davis's Town** E Susx
569 H5 **Davoch of Grange** Moray
325 H5 **Davyhulme** Traffd
356 B4 **Daw Cross** N York
406 C5 **Dawdon** Dur
237 F4 **Daw End** Wsall
95 E5 **Dawesgreen** Surrey
344 D2 **Dawker Hill** N York
235 F3 **Dawley** Wrekin
20 D2 **Dawlish** Devon
20 D2 **Dawlish Warren** Devon
306 B5 **Dawn** Conwy
174 A3 **Daw's Cross** Essex
43 G3 **Daw's Green** Somset
122 C2 **Daws Heath** Essex
188 B4 **Dawshill** Worcs
23 G6 **Daw's House** Cnwll
281 F3 **Dawsmere** Lincs
296 A5 **Daybrook** Notts
291 F3 **Day Green** Ches
273 E3 **Dayhills** Staffs
213 E4 **Dayhouse Bank** Worcs
164 C4 **Daylesford** Gloucs
269 E3 **Daywall** Shrops
307 G5 **Ddol** Flints
267 G6 **Ddôl Cownwy** Powys
144 A5 **Deacons Hill** Herts
169 G1 **Deadman's Cross** Beds
273 F2 **Deadman's Green** Staffs
74 B2 **Deadwater** Hants
440 B5 **Deadwater** Nthumb
396 A2 **Deaf Hill** Dur
101 G5 **Deal** Kent
488 A5 **Dean** C Edin
388 C4 **Dean** Cumb
19 F5 **Dean** Devon
61 F2 **Dean** Devon
61 G2 **Dean** Devon
48 B1 **Dean** Dorset
72 B3 **Dean** Hants
73 E6 **Dean** Hants
340 D4 **Dean** Lancs
165 E5 **Dean** Oxon
86 B6 **Dean** Somset
395 F3 **Dean Bank** Dur
439 E2 **Deanburnhaugh** Border
139 H3 **Dean Court** Oxon
60 C3 **Dean Cross** Devon
325 F3 **Deane** Bolton
91 E4 **Deane** Hants
48 B1 **Deanend** Dorset
328 D4 **Dean Head** Barns
69 G6 **Deanland** Dorset
52 C2 **Deanlane End** W Susx
466 D1 **Dean Park** Rens
19 F5 **Dean Prior** Devon
311 H3 **Dean Row** Ches
486 D6 **Deans** W Loth
98 D2 **Deans Bottom** Kent
388 C4 **Deanscales** Cumb
310 D2 **Deansgreen** Ches
214 A6 **Dean's Green** Warwks
167 F1 **Deanshanger** Nhants
98 D2 **Deans Hill** Kent
497 G4 **Deanston** Stirlg
98 A4 **Dean Street** Kent
388 C2 **Dearham** Cumb
326 D1 **Dearnley** Rochdl
326 D1 **Debach** Suffk
326 C5 **Debdale** Manch
172 B3 **Debden** Essex
145 F5 **Debden Green** Essex
172 B3 **Debden Green** Essex
201 G2 **Debenham** Suffk
188 B5 **Deblin's Green** Worcs
486 D5 **Dechmont** W Loth
165 H3 **Deddington** Oxon
175 E3 **Dedham** Essex
175 E3 **Dedham Heath** Essex
469 H1 **Dedridge** W Loth
117 F4 **Dedworth** W & M
556 B6 **Deebank** Abers
242 C6 **Deene** Nhants
218 D1 **Deenethorpe** Nhants
328 D5 **Deepcar** Sheff
327 F5 **Deepclough** Derbys
93 F3 **Deepcut** Surrey
196 B5 **Deepdale** Beds
367 E3 **Deepdale** Cumb
368 A4 **Deepdale** N York
94 D5 **Deepdene** Surrey
206 D6 **Deepfields** Dudley
243 G3 **Deeping Gate** C Pete
243 H3 **Deeping St James** Lincs
244 B1 **Deeping St Nicholas** Lincs
365 H3 **Deepthwaite** Cumb
109 E2 **Deepweir** Mons
569 H4 **Deerhill** Moray
162 C4 **Deerhurst** Gloucs
162 C4 **Deerhurst Walton** Gloucs
125 G2 **Deerland** Pembks
171 G3 **Deer's Green** Essex
355 E4 **Deerstones** N York
99 F2 **Deerton Street** Kent
188 D6 **Defford** Worcs
157 E4 **Defynnog** Powys
305 G4 **Deganwy** Conwy
105 G4 **Degar** Rhondd
4 B3 **Degibna** Cnwll
384 B4 **Deighton** N York
358 B6 **Deighton** York
284 C2 **Deiniolen** Gwynd
551 G6 **Deishar** Highld
22 B6 **Delabole** Cnwll
310 B6 **Delamere** Ches
561 E5 **Delfrigs** Abers
551 G7 **Dell** Highld
551 K3 **Delliefure** Highld
53 E4 **Dell Quay** W Susx
139 F2 **Delly End** Oxon
525 J2 **Delnamer** Angus
327 E3 **Delph** Oldham
404 D5 **Delves** Dur
512 D1 **Delvine** P & K
173 F2 **Delvin End** Essex
279 E2 **Dembleby** Lincs
14 D6 **Demelza** Cnwll
330 A5 **Denaby Main** Donc
501 G5 **Denbeath** Fife
287 E1 **Denbigh** Denbgs
19 H4 **Denbury** Devon
294 D5 **Denby** Derbys
294 D5 **Denby Bottles** Derbys
295 E5 **Denby Common** Derbys
328 C3 **Denby Dale** Kirk
114 B1 **Denchworth** Oxon
364 B5 **Dendron** Cumb
558 D2 **Denend** Abers
97 E4 **Dene Park** Kent
406 C5 **Deneside** Dur
218 D4 **Denford** Nhants
292 C4 **Denford** Staffs
148 C4 **Dengie** Essex
118 A2 **Denham** Bucks
167 G5 **Denham** Bucks
199 F2 **Denham** Suffk
225 G5 **Denham** Suffk
225 G5 **Denham Corner** Suffk
199 F2 **Denham End** Suffk
118 A2 **Denham Green** Bucks
225 G5 **Denham Street** Suffk
561 E3 **Denhead** Abers
571 H5 **Denhead** Abers
502 D2 **Denhead** Fife
515 F1 **Denhead of Arbirlot** Angus
514 A3 **Denhead of Gray** C Dund
451 H6 **Denholm** Border
341 H3 **Denholme** Brad
341 H3 **Denholme Gate** Brad
439 H1 **Denholmhill** Border
52 B2 **Denmead** Hants
557 G2 **Denmore** C Aber
202 B1 **Dennington** Suffk
202 B1 **Dennington Corner** Suffk
226 B6 **Dennington Hall** Suffk
467 F1 **Dennistoun** C Glas
485 G3 **Denny** Falk
78 D2 **Denny Bottom** Kent
197 G1 **Denny End** Cambs
485 G3 **Dennyloanhead** Falk
483 E4 **Dennystown** W Duns
501 E1 **Den of Lindores** Fife
327 E2 **Denshaw** Oldham
557 E5 **Denside** Abers
82 D2 **Densole** Kent
199 F4 **Denston** Suffk
273 G1 **Denstone** Staffs
100 A3 **Denstroude** Kent
367 E2 **Dent** Cumb
393 F4 **Dent Bank** Dur
219 H2 **Denton** Cambs
395 E6 **Denton** Darltn
56 D4 **Denton** E Susx
82 D1 **Denton** Kent
121 G5 **Denton** Kent
278 B3 **Denton** Lincs
355 F5 **Denton** N York
194 A3 **Denton** Nhants
226 B2 **Denton** Norfk
140 C4 **Denton** Oxon
326 D6 **Denton** Tamesd
405 E1 **Denton Burn** N u Ty
400 C3 **Denton Holme** Cumb
324 B5 **Denton's Green** St Hel
246 C4 **Denver** Norfk
52 C3 **Denvilles** Hants
443 G2 **Denwick** Nthumb
248 D4 **Deopham** Norfk
248 D5 **Deopham Green** Norfk
248 D5 **Deopham Stalland** Norfk
199 F3 **Depden** Suffk
199 F3 **Depden Green** Suffk
191 F3 **Deppers Bridge** Warwks
119 H4 **Deptford** Gt Lon
406 B3 **Deptford** Sundld
69 H2 **Deptford** Wilts
275 E2 **Derby** C Derb
61 E5 **Derby** Devon
322 d9 **Derbyhaven** IoM
324 C6 **Derbyshire Hill** St Hel
254 C5 **Dereham** Norfk
416 A5 **Dergoals** D & G
132 B4 **Deri** Caerph
11 E2 **Derriford** C Plym
23 G2 **Derril** Devon
100 C6 **Derringstone** Kent
210 D1 **Derrington** Shrops
272 C5 **Derrington** Staffs
23 G2 **Derriton** Devon
96 C1 **Derry Downs** Gt Lon
137 F6 **Derry Fields** Wilts
504 F3 **Derryguaig** Ag & B
111 H5 **Derry Hill** Wilts
331 H3 **Derrythorpe** N Linc
258 D5 **Dersingham** Norfk
87 E5 **Dertfords** Wilts
518 B5 **Dervaig** Ag & B
105 E3 **Derwen** Brdgnd
287 F4 **Derwen** Denbgs
229 G5 **Derwenlas** Powys
217 H3 **Desborough** Nhants
239 H4 **Desford** Leics
454 D2 **Detchant** Nthumb
98 B3 **Detling** Kent
527 G2 **Deuchar** Angus
268 D6 **Deuddwr** Powys
211 F2 **Deuxhill** Shrops
134 B5 **Devauden** Mons
3 G2 **Deveral** Cnwll
205 G4 **Devil's Bridge** Cerdgn
214 D1 **Devitts Green** Warwks
88 B2 **Devizes** Wilts
482 D5 **Devol** Inver
10 D2 **Devonport** C Plym
499 E5 **Devonside** Clacks
499 E5 **Devon Village** Clacks
7 E6 **Devoran** Cnwll
471 G2 **Dewartown** Mdloth
171 G3 **Dewes Green** Essex
48 D3 **Dewlands Common** Dorset
47 E5 **Dewlish** Dorset
342 D5 **Dewsbury** Kirk
599 K2 **Dhail Bho Dheas** W Isls

684 City, town and village index: Dhustone - Dunn Street

210 D4 Dhustone Shrops
75 E4 Dial Green W Susx
76 B6 Dial Post W Susx
30 B2 Dibberford Dorset
50 D3 Dibden Hants
50 C3 Dibden Purlieu Hants
213 H4 Dickens Heath Solhll
225 G3 Dickleburgh Norfk
225 G3 Dickleburgh Moor Norfk
300 D3 Dickon Hills Lincs
163 G3 Didbrook Gloucs
115 E2 Didcot Oxon
196 A1 Diddington Cambs
210 C2 Diddlebury Shrops
39 F2 Diddywell Devon
160 B3 Didley Herefs
74 C6 Didling W Susx
247 F5 Didlington Norfk
111 E2 Didmarton Gloucs
311 G1 Didsbury Manch
19 E5 Didworthy Devon
213 G2 Digbeth Birm
298 D4 Digby Lincs
543 H3 Digg Highld
327 F3 Diggle Oldham
188 B4 Diglis Worcs
324 B4 Digmoor Lancs
144 C1 Digswell Herts
144 B2 Digswell Park Herts
144 C1 Digswell Water Herts
180 C3 Dihewyd Cerdgn
256 C4 Dilham Norfk
292 C6 Dilhorne Staffs
340 A4 Dill Hall Lancs
195 G1 Dillington Cambs
44 D4 Dillington Somset
403 H2 Dilston Nthumb
87 E4 Dilton Marsh Wilts
185 H4 Dilwyn Herefs
105 F6 Dimlands V Glam
67 G3 Dimmer Somset
325 G1 Dimple Bolton
294 B2 Dimple Derbys
291 G5 Dimsdale Staffs
17 F4 Dimson Cnwll
153 F3 Dinas Carmth
14 C4 Dinas Cnwll
262 D3 Dinas Gwynd
264 B2 Dinas Gwynd
283 E4 Dinas Gwynd
151 H2 Dinas Cross Pembks
282 D4 Dinas Dinlle Gwynd
230 C2 Dinas Mawddwy Gwynd
285 H4 Dinas Mawr Conwy
106 B5 Dinas Powys V Glam
339 G2 Dinckley Lancs
85 G6 Dinder Somset
160 C2 Dinedor Herefs
160 C2 Dinedor Cross Herefs
188 B3 Dines Green Worcs
134 A2 Dingestow Mons
84 D3 Dinghurst N Som
309 E2 Dingle Lpool
80 B3 Dingleden Kent
451 G3 Dingleton Border
217 G2 Dingley Nhants
565 J5 Dingwall Highld
426 D1 Dinlabyre Border
286 D6 Dinmael Conwy
555 E5 Dinnet Abers
430 D5 Dinnington N u Ty
315 G2 Dinnington Rothm
45 E5 Dinnington Somset
284 C2 Dinorwig Gwynd
141 G2 Dinton Bucks
69 H3 Dinton Wilts
424 C1 Dinwoodie Mains D & G
38 D4 Dinworthy Devon
43 H3 Dipford Somset
92 B3 Dipley Hants
461 E5 Dippen N Ayrs
92 D5 Dippenhall Surrey
24 B6 Dippertown Devon
38 D4 Dipple Devon
568 E4 Dipple Moray
432 A4 Dipple S Ayrs
12 C1 Diptford Devon
404 D4 Dipton Dur
403 G2 Diptonmill Nthumb
595 K3 Direcleit W Isls
489 G3 Dirleton E Loth
525 G3 Dirnanean P & K
403 F5 Dirt Pot Nthumb
185 E2 Discoed Powys
68 A3 Discove Somset
275 H5 Diseworth Leics
603 K7 Dishes Ork
370 D5 Dishforth N York
276 B5 Dishley Leics
312 C3 Disley Ches
225 F3 Diss Norfk
183 G3 Disserth Powys
388 B5 Distington Cumb
70 B3 Ditchampton Wilts
67 G2 Ditcheat Somset
116 C1 Ditchfield Bucks
226 C1 Ditchingham Norfk
56 A1 Ditchling E Susx
234 C2 Ditherington Shrops
111 E6 Ditteridge Wilts
13 F2 Dittisham Devon
309 G2 Ditton Halton
97 H3 Ditton Kent
198 D3 Ditton Green Cambs
211 E2 Ditton Priors Shrops
57 G4 Dittons E Susx
163 E3 Dixton Gloucs
134 C2 Dixton Mons
22 D3 Dizzard Cnwll
327 E3 Dobcross Oldham
288 D2 Dobs Hill Flints
270 B3 Dobson's Bridge Shrops
16 B6 Dobwalls Cnwll
26 B5 Doccombe Devon
549 L1 Dochgarroch Highld
226 D1 Dockeney Norfk
127 D1 Dockenfield Surrey
366 B5 Docker Lancs
259 F4 Docking Norfk
186 D3 Docklow Herefs
390 B5 Dockray Cumb
341 G2 Dockroyd Brad
38 B3 Docton Devon
12 C4 Dodbrooke Devon
439 F3 Dodburn Border
187 H3 Doddenham Worcs
146 B5 Doddinghurst Essex
221 E1 Doddington Cambs
99 E3 Doddington Kent
317 H5 Doddington Lincs
454 B3 Doddington Nthumb
211 E4 Doddington Shrops
26 C5 Doddiscombsleigh Devon
258 D5 Doddshill Norfk
10 B1 Doddycross Cnwll
192 D2 Dodford Nhants
212 D5 Dodford Worcs
110 C4 Dodington S Glos
64 C3 Dodington Somset
289 E2 Dodleston Ches
186 D6 Dodmarsh Herefs
40 A4 Dodscott Devon
273 F3 Dods Leigh Staffs
329 E3 Dodworth Barns
329 E4 Dodworth Bottom Barns
237 H5 Doe Bank Birm
310 A2 Doe Green Warrtn
294 D3 Doehole Derbys
295 F1 Doe Lea Derbys
325 F2 Doffcocker Bolton
323 G5 Dog & Gun Lpool
299 F3 Dogdyke Lincs
327 E3 Dog Hill Oldham
237 E2 Dogingtree Estate Staffs
92 C4 Dogmersfield Hants
244 A4 Dogsthorpe C Pete
27 F3 Dog Village Devon
231 H2 Dolanog Powys
184 B1 Dolau Powys
105 G3 Dolau Rhondd
284 B6 Dolbenmaen Gwynd
205 E2 Dole Cerdgn
86 D2 Dolemeads BaNES
271 G4 Doley Staffs
207 E4 Dolfach Powys
231 E4 Dol-fâch Powys
229 G2 Dol-ffanog Gwynd
208 B2 Dolfor Powys
285 G1 Dolgarrog Conwy
229 G1 Dolgellau Gwynd
180 B4 Dolgerdd Cerdgn
229 F4 Dolgoch Gwynd
154 B3 Dolgran Carmth
207 E5 Dolhelfa Powys
266 D3 Dolhendre Gwynd
577 J3 Doll Highld
499 F5 Dollar Clacks
185 E1 Dolley Green Powys
119 E2 Dollis Hill Gt Lon
205 F3 Dollwen Cerdgn
308 A5 Dolphin Flints
488 D5 Dolphingstone E Loth
351 H4 Dolphinholme Lancs
440 C1 Dolphinston Border
470 B5 Dolphinton S Lans
40 B5 Dolton Devon
306 B5 Dolwen Conwy
231 F3 Dolwen Powys
305 H4 Dolwyd Conwy
285 F4 Dolwyddelan Conwy
205 E2 Dôl-y-Bont Cerdgn
184 C5 Dol-y-Cannau Powys
283 E4 Dolydd Gwynd
184 D3 Dolyhir Powys
232 A5 Dolymelinau Powys
268 D2 Dolywern Wrexhm
77 F1 Domewood Surrey
269 E6 Domgay Powys
44 B5 Dommett Somset
330 D4 Doncaster Donc
330 C4 Doncaster Carr Donc
310 B4 Dones Green Ches
69 F5 Donhead St Andrew Wilts
69 E5 Donhead St Mary Wilts
487 G2 Donibristle Fife
64 A3 Doniford Somset
280 B2 Donington Lincs
236 B4 Donington Shrops
280 B2 Donington Eaudike Lincs
239 G2 Donington le Heath Leics
319 G3 Donington on Bain Lincs
280 A3 Donington South Ing Lincs
239 E2 Donisthorpe Leics
173 G4 Don Johns Essex
81 H3 Donkey Street Kent
93 F2 Donkey Town Surrey
335 F5 Donna Nook Lincs
164 B4 Donnington Gloucs
161 G3 Donnington Herefs
234 D3 Donnington Shrops
114 D6 Donnington W Berk
53 F4 Donnington W Susx
235 G2 Donnington Wrekin
235 G2 Donnington Wood Wrekin
405 G3 Donwell Sundld
44 C5 Donyatt Somset
76 C3 Doomsday Green W Susx
444 D6 Doonfoot S Ayrs
432 D1 Doonholm S Ayrs
92 D5 Dora's Green Hants
113 E3 Dorcan Swindn
32 C1 Dorchester Dorset
140 C6 Dorchester Oxon
212 D5 Dordale Worcs
238 D4 Dordon Warwks
314 C3 Dore Sheff
549 L3 Dores Highld
94 D4 Dorking Surrey
174 B2 Dorking Tye Suffk
202 D1 Dorley's Corner Suffk
77 H1 Dormansland Surrey
77 G1 Dormans Park Surrey
397 E5 Dormanstown R & Cl
118 C3 Dormer's Wells Gt Lon
160 D1 Dormington Herefs
189 E3 Dormston Worcs
164 C3 Dorn Gloucs
117 F4 Dorney Bucks
117 F4 Dorney Reach Bucks
546 F4 Dornie Highld
577 H6 Dornoch Highld
399 G1 Dornock D & G
588 D6 Dorrery Highld
214 B4 Dorridge Solhll
298 D4 Dorrington Lincs
234 B4 Dorrington Shrops
190 A5 Dorsington Warwks
159 F1 Dorstone Herefs
141 E2 Dorton Bucks
235 F3 Doseley Wrekin
238 C4 Dosthill Staffs
303 E6 Dothan IoA
30 B3 Dottery Dorset
16 A5 Doublebois Cnwll
86 C3 Double Hill BaNES
111 F1 Doughton Gloucs
253 H2 Doughton Norfk
322 f7 Douglas IoM
447 G3 Douglas S Lans
514 C3 Douglas and Angus C Dund
527 F5 Douglastown Angus
448 A2 Douglas Water S Lans
447 G3 Douglas West S Lans
86 A6 Doulting Somset
602 B7 Dounby Ork
550 F8 Doune Highld
575 J3 Doune Highld
498 A4 Doune Stirlg
555 E3 Douneside Abers
576 C5 Dounie Highld
576 E6 Dounie Highld
465 G6 Doura N Ayrs
18 B4 Dousland Devon
269 F5 Dovaston Shrops
309 F1 Dovecot Lpool
466 D3 Dovecothall E Rens
295 F4 Dove Green Notts
313 E4 Dove Holes Derbys
388 C3 Dovenby Cumb
320 B3 Dovendale Lincs
308 B1 Dove Point Wirral
83 F2 Dover Kent
325 E4 Dover Wigan
177 E3 Dovercourt Essex
188 B1 Doverdale Worcs
62 D2 Doverhay Somset
273 H3 Doveridge Derbys
95 F5 Doversgreen Surrey
524 F6 Dowally P & K
467 E1 Dowanhill C Glas
338 B3 Dowbridge Lancs
163 E6 Dowdeswell Gloucs
251 G1 Dowe Hill Norfk
432 B4 Dowhill S Ayrs
132 A3 Dowlais Myr Td
131 H3 Dowlais Top Myr Td
40 B5 Dowland Devon
212 A4 Dowles Worcs
116 D6 Dowlesgreen Wokham
44 D5 Dowlish Ford Somset
44 D5 Dowlish Wake Somset
324 D4 Downall Green St Hel
137 H5 Down Ampney Gloucs
10 B3 Downderry Cnwll
96 B2 Downe Gt Lon
136 B5 Downend Gloucs
37 E3 Downend IoW
110 A4 Downend S Glos
65 E3 Down End Somset
114 D4 Downend W Berk
514 B3 Downfield C Dund
222 C5 Down Field Cambs
16 C4 Downgate Cnwll
17 E4 Downgate Cnwll
400 A4 Down Hall Cumb
147 E5 Downham Essex
120 A5 Downham Gt Lon
353 F6 Downham Lancs
453 G3 Downham Nthumb
246 C4 Downham Market Norfk
162 C5 Down Hatherley Gloucs
67 F4 Downhead Somset
86 B5 Downhead Somset
168 B1 Downhead Park M Keyn
14 B5 Downhill Cnwll
406 B3 Downhill Sundld
323 G3 Downholland Cross Lancs
382 D5 Downholme N York
23 H4 Downicary Devon
557 G5 Downies Abers
307 H4 Downing Flints
23 E4 Downinney Cnwll
142 A5 Downley Bucks
77 F2 Down Park W Susx
106 B5 Downs V Glam
26 A2 Down St Mary Devon
169 E5 Downside Beds
57 F4 Downside E Susx
85 E1 Downside N Som
86 A4 Downside Somset
86 A6 Downside Somset
94 C3 Downside Surrey
78 A5 Down Street E Susx
11 F3 Down Thomas Devon
49 H6 Downton Hants
184 D2 Downton Powys
234 C2 Downton Shrops
70 D5 Downton Wilts
209 H5 Downton on the Rock Herefs
279 G4 Dowsby Lincs
244 C2 Dowsdale Lincs
44 A3 Dowslands Somset
390 B5 Dowthwaitehead Cumb
272 D5 Doxey Staffs
406 B4 Doxford Park Sundld
110 C5 Doynton S Glos
255 G2 Drabblegate Norfk
106 D2 Draethen Caerph
468 B5 Draffan S Lans
364 C4 Dragley Beck Cumb
332 B2 Dragonby N Linc
76 B5 Dragons Green W Susx
29 F4 Dragon's Hill Dorset
315 E3 Drakehouse Sheff
18 C6 Drakeland Corner Devon
212 B3 Drakelow Worcs
561 E2 Drakemyre Abers
465 F4 Drakemyre N Ayrs
188 D5 Drakes Broughton Worcs
213 G4 Drakes Cross Worcs
200 C5 Drakestone Green Suffk
17 F4 Drakewalls Cnwll
354 D4 Draughton N York
217 G4 Draughton Nhants
15 H5 Drawbridge Cnwll
345 F4 Drax N York
140 D3 Draycot Oxon
111 G4 Draycot Cerne Wilts
215 G6 Draycote Warwks
88 D2 Draycot Fitz Payne Wilts
113 E4 Draycot Foliat Swindn
275 G3 Draycott Derbys
135 H4 Draycott Gloucs
164 B2 Draycott Gloucs
236 B6 Draycott Shrops
67 E5 Draycott Somset
85 E4 Draycott Somset
188 C5 Draycott Worcs
274 B4 Draycott in the Clay Staffs
273 E1 Draycott in the Moors Staffs
41 F5 Drayford Devon
52 B3 Drayton C Port
218 A1 Drayton Leics
280 B2 Drayton Lincs
192 C2 Drayton Nhants
255 G5 Drayton Norfk
140 A6 Drayton Oxon
165 G1 Drayton Oxon
45 F4 Drayton Somset
66 C5 Drayton Somset
190 B3 Drayton Warwks
212 D4 Drayton Worcs
238 B4 Drayton Bassett Staffs
142 C2 Drayton Beauchamp Bucks
168 A4 Drayton Parslow Bucks
140 C5 Drayton St Leonard Oxon
355 E3 Drebley N York
322 h4 Dreemskerry IoM
125 F2 Dreenhill Pembks
128 D2 Drefach Carmth
155 F5 Drefach Carmth
153 H2 Drefach Carmth
129 G1 Dre-Fach Carmth
153 H2 Drefelin Carmth
551 J4 Dreggie Highld
487 H6 Dreghorn C Edin
444 D2 Dreghorn N Ayrs
307 G6 Dre-gôch Denbgs
82 D2 Drellingore Kent
489 G4 Drem E Loth
272 D1 Dresden C Stke
593 D10 Dreumasdal W Isls
25 H4 Drewsteignton Devon
320 C5 Driby Lincs
360 C3 Driffield E R Yk
137 G5 Driffield Gloucs
2 D4 Drift Cnwll
376 D5 Drigg Cumb
342 D4 Drighlington Leeds
479 J5 Drimnagall Ag & B
518 E5 Drimnin Highld
29 H2 Drimpton Dorset
494 D4 Drimsynie Ag & B
361 E3 Dringhoe E R Yk
357 H5 Dringhouses York
595 K4 Drinisiadar W Isls
200 C2 Drinkstone Suffk
200 C2 Drinkstone Green Suffk
46 A3 Drive End Dorset
546 B5 Drochaid Lusa Highld
273 F4 Drointon Staffs
188 C2 Droitwich Worcs
584 C5 Droman Highld
500 B1 Dron P & K
314 D4 Dronfield Derbys
314 C4 Dronfield Woodhouse Derbys
445 F6 Drongan E Ayrs
514 A2 Dronley Angus
47 E3 Droop Dorset
106 B4 Drope V Glam
329 F6 Dropping Well Rothm
73 E6 Droxford Hants
326 C5 Droylsden Tamesd
342 C4 Drub Kirk
162 A2 Druggers End Worcs
287 E6 Druid Denbgs
125 E1 Druidston Pembks
520 F1 Druimarbin Highld
520 E7 Druimavuic Ag & B
479 J7 Druimdrishaig Ag & B
531 J6 Druimindarroch Highld
549 H2 Druimkinnerras Highld
488 B6 Drum C Edin
499 G4 Drum P & K
448 B2 Drumalbin S Lans
578 F3 Drumbeg Highld
558 D1 Drumblade Abers
569 L7 Drumblair Abers
408 B3 Drumbreddan D & G
421 F3 Drumbuie D & G
546 D3 Drumbuie Highld
399 H3 Drumburgh Cumb
483 H5 Drumchapel C Glas
565 K8 Drumchardine Highld
573 G6 Drumchork Highld
446 C2 Drumclog S Lans
558 D2 Drumdollo Abers
502 C4 Drumeldrie Fife
449 F3 Drumelzier Border
546 B6 Drumfearn Highld
468 B1 Drumgelloch N Lans
527 F4 Drumgley Angus
535 L3 Drumguish Highld
552 D2 Drumin Moray
433 H5 Drumjohn D & G
556 A3 Drumlassie Abers
456 D2 Drumlemble Ag & B
557 G1 Drumligair Abers
541 E3 Drumlithie Abers
323 G2 Drummersdale Lancs
410 C3 Drummodie D & G
565 K3 Drummond Highld
566 B8 Drummond Highld
411 E5 Drummoral D & G
408 C4 Drummore D & G
577 H4 Drummuie Highld
568 F7 Drummuir Moray
528 C6 Drummygar Angus
549 J4 Drumnadrochit Highld
569 J5 Drumnagorrach Moray
556 D5 Drumoak Abers
467 H1 Drumpellier N Lans
415 H4 Drumphail D & G
422 A5 Drumrash D & G
574 D2 Drumrunie Highld
483 H5 Drumry W Duns
561 E5 Drums Abers
532 D7 Drumsallie Highld
432 C2 Drumshang S Ayrs
423 F5 Drumsleet D & G
565 L7 Drumsmittal Highld
514 D2 Drumsturdy Angus
410 C3 Drumtroddan D & G
543 G7 Drumuie Highld
551 G5 Drumuillie Highld
497 G4 Drumvaich Stirlg
560 D2 Drumwhindle Abers
529 E5 Drunkendub Angus
288 C2 Drury Flints
248 B4 Drurylane Norfk
289 G6 Drury Lane Wrexhm
254 A4 Drury Square Norfk
380 B1 Drybeck Cumb
569 G3 Drybridge Moray
444 D2 Drybridge N Ayrs
135 E1 Drybrook Gloucs
452 A3 Dryburgh Border
451 F5 Dryden Border
297 G5 Dry Doddington Lincs
197 E2 Dry Drayton Cambs
73 F2 Dry Hill Hants
96 C4 Dryhill Kent
450 B5 Dryhope Border
487 H4 Drylaw C Edin
4 B2 Drym Cnwll
483 G2 Drymen Stirlg
247 F3 Drymere Norfk
571 G6 Drymuir Abers
87 F3 Drynham Wilts
565 K6 Drynie Park Highld
544 F3 Drynoch Highld
139 H4 Dry Sandford Oxon
154 D5 Dryslwyn Carmth
121 H2 Dry Street Essex
234 D3 Dryton Shrops
24 A4 Dubbs Cross Devon
570 D3 Dubford Abers
557 G2 Dubford C Aber
565 L2 Dublin Highld
225 G6 Dublin Suffk
528 C4 Dubton Angus
389 E3 Dubwath Cumb
202 D5 Duck Corner Suffk
194 D4 Duck End Beds
195 F6 Duck End Beds
167 G4 Duck End Bucks
196 B2 Duck End Cambs
171 H5 Duck End Essex
172 D3 Duck End Essex
172 D4 Duck End Essex
173 E5 Duckend Green Essex
110 A1 Duckhole S Glos
289 G4 Duckington Ches
139 F3 Ducklington Oxon
315 E5 Duckmanton Derbys
195 G3 Duck's Cross Beds
144 B5 Ducks Island Gt Lon
162 B2 Duckswich Worcs
136 B4 Dudbridge Gloucs
119 E2 Dudden Hill Gt Lon
171 G2 Duddenhoe End Essex
488 B5 Duddingston C Edin
242 D4 Duddington Nhants
43 H3 Duddlestone Somset
78 B4 Duddleswell E Susx
211 F3 Duddlewick Shrops
474 D6 Duddo Nthumb
289 H1 Duddon Ches
362 D4 Duddon Bridge Cumb
289 H1 Duddon Common Ches
269 F2 Dudleston Shrops
269 G2 Dudleston Grove Shrops
269 G2 Dudleston Heath Shrops
212 D2 Dudley Dudley
431 E5 Dudley N Tyne
342 C3 Dudley Hill Brad
213 E1 Dudley Port Sandw
237 E4 Dudley's Fields Wsall
212 D2 Dudley Wood Dudley
310 C3 Dudlows Green Warrtn
48 D5 Dudsbury Dorset
142 D3 Dudswell Herts
151 E5 Dudwells Pembks
38 D4 Duerdon Devon
294 C6 Duffield Derbys
294 D6 Duffieldbank Derbys
130 C5 Duffryn Neath
107 E2 Duffryn Newpt
208 D3 Duffryn Shrops
557 G5 Duff's Hill Abers
568 E7 Dufftown Moray
568 B2 Duffus Moray
392 A4 Dufton Cumb
359 G1 Duggleby N York
546 D3 Duirinish Highld
546 B7 Duisdalebeg Highld
546 C7 Duisdalemore Highld
532 F7 Duisky Highld
214 C2 Duke End Warwks
403 G3 Dukesfield Nthumb
132 B2 Dukestown Blae G
326 D5 Dukinfield Tamesd
303 G3 Dulas IoA
85 G6 Dulcote Somset
27 H1 Dulford Devon
524 B6 Dull P & K
485 E4 Dullatur N Lans
198 C3 Dullingham Cambs
198 C3 Dullingham Ley Cambs
551 H5 Dulnain Bridge Highld
487 F2 Duloch Fife
195 H2 Duloe Beds
9 G2 Duloe Cnwll
551 G1 Dulsie Highld
42 B2 Dulverton Somset
119 G5 Dulwich Gt Lon
119 G5 Dulwich Village Gt Lon
483 F4 Dumbarton W Duns
163 F2 Dumbleton Gloucs
467 E2 Dumbreck C Glas
437 F4 Dumcrieff D & G
423 G4 Dumfries D & G
483 H3 Dumgoyne Stirlg
91 F5 Dummer Hants
74 C5 Dumpford W Susx
39 F6 Dumpinghill Devon
248 D2 Dumpling Green Norfk
325 H5 Dumplington Traffd
101 G2 Dumpton Kent
529 E3 Dun Angus
523 K4 Dunalastair P & K
480 A1 Dunamuck Ag & B
545 K4 Dunan Highld
552 E7 Dunandhu Abers
479 L3 Dunans Ag & B
481 E1 Dunans Ag & B
65 E3 Dunball Somset
490 C4 Dunbar E Loth
583 G3 Dunbeath Highld
506 E3 Dunbeg Ag & B
498 B4 Dunblane Stirlg
513 G6 Dunbog Fife
542 B6 Dùn Boreraig Highld
71 G4 Dunbridge Hants
605 G4 Duncansclett Shet
565 K5 Duncanston Highld
558 D4 Duncanstone Abers
598 D6 Dùn Chàrlabhaigh W Isls
26 D5 Dunchideock Devon
215 H5 Dunchurch Warwks
542 C7 Dùn Colbost Highld
338 C2 Duncombe Lancs
193 E4 Duncote Nhants
423 G3 Duncow D & G
500 B3 Duncrievie P & K
53 H1 Duncton W Susx
514 C3 Dundee C Dund
421 F2 Dundeugh D & G
66 D3 Dundon Somset
500 D6 Dundonald Fife
445 E3 Dundonald S Ayrs
444 D3 Dundonald Camp N Ayrs
66 D3 Dundon Hayes Somset
574 B6 Dundonnell Highld
399 G5 Dundraw Cumb
548 E7 Dundreggan Highld
412 D5 Dundrennan D & G
73 E6 Dundridge Hants
85 F1 Dundry N Som
498 C2 Dunduff P & K
467 H2 Dundyvan N Lans
556 D3 Dunecht Abers
524 D4 Dunfallandy P & K
487 F2 Dunfermline Fife
138 A5 Dunfield Gloucs
328 A4 Dunford Bridge Barns
592 D6 Dùn Gainmhich W Isls
99 E3 Dungate Kent
87 F4 Dunge Wilts
314 B2 Dungworth Sheff
309 G5 Dunham-on-the-Hill Ches
317 F5 Dunham on Trent Notts
188 D2 Dunhampstead Worcs
188 B1 Dunhampton Worcs
311 E2 Dunham Town Traffd
311 E2 Dunham Woodhouses Traffd
318 C4 Dunholme Lincs
503 E2 Dunino Fife
485 G3 Dunipace Falk
510 C5 Dunira P & K
524 F7 Dunkeld P & K
527 E5 Dunkenny Angus
86 C3 Dunkerton BaNES
43 F6 Dunkeswell Devon
356 B5 Dunkeswick N York
276 B2 Dunkirk C Nott
221 H2 Dunkirk Cambs
309 E5 Dunkirk Ches
100 A4 Dunkirk Kent
255 G2 Dunkirk Norfk
110 D2 Dunkirk S Glos
291 G4 Dunkirk Staffs
88 A2 Dunkirk Wilts
97 F4 Dunk's Green Kent
540 A6 Dunlappie Angus
90 C4 Dunley Hants
212 A6 Dunley Worcs
466 B5 Dunlop E Ayrs
15 F5 Dunmere Cnwll
462 C2 Dunmore Ag & B
486 A2 Dunmore Falk
565 J7 Dunmore Highld
362 D6 Dunnerholme Cumb
589 G2 Dunnet Highld
528 B5 Dunnichen Angus
501 E6 Dunnikier Fife
499 G2 Dunning P & K
361 F4 Dunnington E R Yk
189 G4 Dunnington Warwks
358 C4 Dunnington York
362 D5 Dunningwell Cumb
340 C4 Dunnockshaw Lancs
37 F5 Dunnose IoW
234 B1 Dunnsheath Shrops
98 B2 Dunn Street Kent

99 F5 Dunn Street Kent
506 E2 Dunollie Ag & B
482 A4 Dunoon Ag & B
415 G5 Dunragit D & G
479 J5 Dunrostan Ag & B
474 A4 Duns Border
314 A5 Dunsa Derbys
36 B4 Dunsbury IoW
279 G4 Dunsby Lincs
325 G2 Dunscar Bolton
423 E3 Dunscore D & G
330 D3 Dunscroft Donc
397 F6 Dunsdale R & Cl
116 B4 Dunsden Green Oxon
38 D6 Dunsdon Devon
75 G2 Dunsfold Surrey
75 G2 Dunsfold Common Surrey
75 G2 Dunsfold Green Surrey
26 C5 Dunsford Devon
501 E2 Dunshalt Fife
295 F2 Dunsill Notts
513 E3 Dunsinnan P & K
16 C4 Dunslea Cnwll
387 E2 Dunsley N York
212 C3 Dunsley Staffs
142 A3 Dunsmore Bucks
216 B4 Dunsmore Warwks
352 D4 Dunsop Bridge Lancs
169 E5 Dunstable Beds
273 G4 Dunstall Staffs
274 B5 Dunstall Staffs
188 C6 Dunstall Common Worcs
199 E2 Dunstall Green Suffk
236 D4 Dunstall Hill Wolves
455 G6 Dunstan Nthumb
63 F3 Dunster Somset
165 H4 Duns Tew Oxon
314 D5 Dunston Derbys
405 F2 Dunston Gatesd
298 D2 Dunston Lincs
249 H4 Dunston Norfk
272 D6 Dunston Staffs
11 G3 Dunstone Devon
12 D4 Dunstone Devon
272 D6 Dunston Heath Staffs
405 F2 Dunston Hill Gatesd
330 D3 Dunsville Donc
347 G2 Dunswell E R Yk
469 H5 Dunsyre S Lans
17 E3 Dunterton Devon
165 F4 Dunthrop Oxon
137 E3 Duntisbourne Abbots Gloucs
137 E3 Duntisbourne Leer Gloucs
137 E3 Duntisbourne Rouse Gloucs
46 C3 Duntish Dorset
483 G5 Duntocher W Duns
196 B6 Dunton Beds
167 H5 Dunton Bucks
260 A5 Dunton Norfk
216 B1 Dunton Bassett Leics
96 D3 Dunton Green Kent
260 A5 Dunton Patch Norfk
121 F1 Dunton Wayletts Essex
543 G2 Duntulm Highld
432 C1 Dunure S Ayrs
103 E3 Dunvant Swans
542 D7 Dunvegan Highld
14 D4 Dunveth Cnwll
65 F5 Dunwear Somset
227 F5 Dunwich Suffk
292 B3 Dunwood Staffs
8 C3 Duporth Cnwll
400 C4 Durdar Cumb
513 F5 Durdie P & K
5 E3 Durgan Cnwll
79 E3 Durgates E Susx
395 H1 Durham Dur
436 A4 Durisdeer D & G
435 H4 Durisdeermill D & G
329 E1 Durkar Wakefd
65 E4 Durleigh Somset
74 B5 Durleighmarsh W Susx
51 F1 Durley Hants
89 F2 Durley Wilts
72 D6 Durley Street Hants
101 E4 Durlock Kent
161 E2 Durlow Common Herefs
326 D1 Durn Rochdl
573 K5 Durnamuck Highld
585 G3 Durness Highld
66 D5 Durnfield Somset
559 G4 Durno Abers
50 A5 Durns Town Hants
520 D4 Duror Highld
588 F4 Durran Highld
80 C2 Durrant Green Kent
52 C3 Durrants Hants
54 D4 Durrington W Susx
88 D6 Durrington Wilts
54 D4 Durrington-on-Sea W Susx
602 D7 Durrisdale Ork
556 D5 Durris Ho Abers
135 G5 Dursley Gloucs
87 F4 Dursley Wilts
161 F5 Dursley Cross Gloucs
44 B2 Durston Somset
47 G3 Durweston Dorset
607 G5 Dury Shet
27 E4 Duryard Devon
193 F2 Duston Nhants
122 B3 Dutch Village Essex
551 G5 Duthil Highld
208 D4 Dutlas Powys
172 C4 Duton Hill Essex
23 G5 Dutson Cnwll
310 B4 Dutton Ches
197 G5 Duxford Cambs
139 F5 Duxford Oxon
210 A4 Duxmoor Shrops
305 F4 Dwygyfylchi Conwy
282 D2 Dwyran IoA
231 H4 Dwyrhiw Powys
557 F2 Dyce C Aber
64 C3 Dyche Somset
403 G3 Dye House Nthumb
109 F3 Dyer's Common S Glos
196 D5 Dyer's Green Cambs
130 C6 Dyffryn Brdgnd
153 G5 Dyffryn Carmth
179 F3 Dyffryn Cerdgn
151 F2 Dyffryn Pembks
106 A5 Dyffryn V Glam
264 D5 Dyffryn Ardudwy Gwynd
179 F3 Dyffryn-bern Cerdgn
155 G4 Dyffryn Ceidrych Carmth
130 C3 Dyffryn Cellwen Neath
279 G5 Dyke Lincs
567 H5 Dyke Moray
527 E2 Dykehead Angus
468 D3 Dykehead N Lans
497 E5 Dykehead Stirlg
526 B3 Dykend Angus
570 C7 Dykeside Abers
230 D6 Dylife Powys
81 H4 Dymchurch Kent
161 F3 Dymock Gloucs

110 C4 Dyrham S Glos
501 F6 Dysart Fife
307 E4 Dyserth Denbgs

E

544 E2 Eabost Highld
544 E1 Eabost West Highld
101 E4 Each End Kent
213 E4 Eachway Worcs
430 B5 Eachwick Nthumb
596 C1 Eadar Dha Fhadhail W Isls
351 F6 Eagland Hill Lancs
297 G1 Eagle Lincs
297 G1 Eagle Barnsdale Lincs
317 G6 Eagle Moor Lincs
384 C1 Eaglescliffe S on T
388 C4 Eaglesfield Cumb
425 E5 Eaglesfield D & G
467 E4 Eaglesham E Rens
168 B2 Eaglestone M Keyn
219 F1 Eaglethorpe Nhants
294 A2 Eagle Tor Derbys
325 G2 Eagley Bolton
322 e7 Eairy IoM
296 C2 Eakring Notts
331 G2 Ealand N Linc
118 D4 Ealing Gt Lon
402 B3 Eals Nthumb
391 E4 Eamont Bridge Cumb
354 A5 Earby Lancs
339 G5 Earcroft Bl w D
211 G1 Eardington Shrops
185 H3 Eardisland Herefs
185 F5 Eardisley Herefs
269 G5 Eardiston Shrops
211 F6 Eardiston Worcs
221 E4 Earith Cambs
454 B4 Earle Nthumb
278 B2 Earlesfield Lincs
324 D5 Earlestown St Hel
116 C5 Earley Wokham
249 G3 Earlham Norfk
542 F4 Earlish Highld
194 B2 Earls Barton Nhants
173 H4 Earls Colne Essex
189 E3 Earl's Common Worcs
162 C1 Earl's Croome Worcs
215 E4 Earlsdon Covtry
79 E6 Earl's Down E Susx
502 D5 Earlsferry Fife
119 F5 Earlsfield Gt Lon
560 B3 Earlsford Abers
200 D1 Earl's Green Suffk
239 H5 Earl Shilton Leics
202 A2 Earl Soham Suffk
293 E1 Earl Sterndale Derbys
452 A2 Earlston Border
445 F2 Earlston E Ayrs
90 D2 Earlstone Common Hants
201 F3 Earl Stonham Suffk
421 G3 Earlstoun D & G
134 A5 Earlswood Mons
95 F5 Earlswood Surrey
213 H5 Earlswood Warwks
53 E5 Earnley W Susx
467 G4 Earnock S Lans
338 D5 Earnshaw Bridge Lancs
591 D8 Earsairidh W Isls
431 F5 Earsdon D & G
436 D4 Earshaig D & G
226 C2 Earsham Norfk
226 A4 Earsham Street Suffk
358 B3 Earswick York
53 G3 Eartham W Susx
110 A2 Earthcott Green S Glos
385 F3 Easby N York
492 B1 Easdale Ag & B
74 D5 Easebourne W Susx
215 H4 Easenhall Warwks
93 H6 Eashing Surrey
141 E2 Easington Bucks
406 C6 Easington Dur
349 H6 Easington E R Yk
352 D4 Easington Lancs
455 E2 Easington Nthumb
141 E5 Easington Oxon
165 G2 Easington Oxon
397 H6 Easington R & Cl
406 C6 Easington Colliery Dur
406 B5 Easington Lane Sundld
371 G6 Easingwold N York
78 C6 Eason's Green E Susx
526 D5 Eassie Angus
105 G6 East Aberthaw V Glam
40 A2 Eastacombe Devon
40 B3 Eastacombe Devon
40 C3 Eastacott Devon
119 E3 East Acton Gt Lon
166 A2 East Adderbury Oxon
12 D3 East Allington Devon
41 H2 East Anstey Devon
90 B5 East Anton Hants
383 F5 East Appleton N York
343 E4 East Ardsley Leeds
53 E3 East Ashling W Susx
90 C5 East Aston Hants
557 E3 East Auchronie Abers
374 B2 East Ayton N York
515 F2 East Balmirmer Angus
23 F3 East Balsdon Cnwll
132 D3 East Bank Blae G
319 E3 East Barkwith Lincs
97 H4 East Barming Kent
386 D2 East Barnby N York
144 C6 East Barnet Gt Lon
260 B5 East Barsham Norfk
200 B1 East Barton Suffk
53 F6 East Beach W Susx
261 G3 East Beckham Norfk
118 B5 East Bedfont Gt Lon
460 D5 East Bennan N Ayrs
175 E3 East Bergholt Suffk
342 C4 East Bierley Kirk
254 B4 East Bilney Norfk
393 E2 East Blackdene Dur
56 D5 East Blatchington E Susx
47 G6 East Bloxworth Dorset
50 C4 East Boldon S Tyne
383 G2 East Boldre Hants
57 G5 Eastbourne Darltn
65 F4 Eastbourne E Susx
84 B4 East Bower Somset
203 F1 East Brent Somset
296 C6 Eastbridge Suffk
393 G6 East Bridgford Notts
43 H3 East Briscoe Dur
106 C5 East Brora Highld
61 G5 East Buckland Devon
27 H6 East Budleigh Devon
360 B3 Eastburn E R Yk
117 F3 East Burnham Bucks
606 E6 East Burrafirth Shet
33 E2 East Burton Dorset
118 B1 Eastbury Herts
114 A4 Eastbury W Berk
89 G2 East Butsfield Dur
92 C6 East Butterleigh Devon
198 D4 East Butterwick N Linc

354 D4 Eastby N York
540 C4 East Cairnbeg Abers
470 A1 East Calder W Loth
249 G4 East Carleton Norfk
355 H6 East Carlton Leeds
217 H2 East Carlton Nhants
114 B2 East Challow Oxon
12 D4 East Charleton Devon
30 D1 East Chelborough Dorset
56 B2 East Chiltington E Susx
45 F5 East Chinnock Somset
88 D4 East Chisenbury Wilts
89 G5 East Cholderton Hants
123 F5 Eastchurch Kent
94 B4 East Clandon Surrey
167 F4 East Claydon Bucks
108 D5 East Clevedon N Som
577 J2 East Clyne Highld
45 G5 East Coker Somset
136 C4 Eastcombe Gloucs
64 C5 East Combe Somset
345 E3 East Common N York
69 E6 East Compton Dorset
67 G1 East Compton Somset
13 E1 East Cornworthy Devon
118 C2 Eastcote Gt Lon
193 E4 Eastcote Nhants
214 B4 Eastcote Solhll
118 C2 Eastcote Village Gt Lon
38 C4 Eastcott Cnwll
88 B3 Eastcott Wilts
345 G1 East Cottingwith E R Yk
195 F5 Eastcotts Beds
89 F2 Eastcourt Wilts
137 E6 Eastcourt Wilts
51 F5 East Cowes IoW
345 F5 East Cowick E R Yk
383 H4 East Cowton N York
431 E4 East Cramlington Nthumb
86 B6 East Cranmore Somset
33 G3 East Creech Dorset
550 B4 East Croachy Highld
551 G6 East Croftmore Highld
400 B5 East Curthwaite Cumb
555 E3 East Davoch Abers
57 F5 East Dean E Susx
161 F5 East Dean Gloucs
71 F4 East Dean Hants
53 G2 East Dean W Susx
329 G6 East Dene Rothm
514 D2 East Denside Angus
405 E1 East Denton N u Ty
311 G1 East Didsbury Manch
20 D2 Eastdon Devon
13 E3 Eastdown Devon
61 F3 East Down Devon
317 E4 East Drayton Notts
119 G5 East Dulwich Gt Lon
85 G1 East Dundry N Som
347 G4 East Ella C KuH
194 D6 East End Beds
195 G3 East End Beds
167 H6 East End Bucks
48 B5 East End Dorset
348 C3 East End E R Yk
349 E4 East End E R Yk
361 F3 East End E R Yk
145 F2 Eastend Essex
148 D3 East End Essex
138 B4 East End Gloucs
50 C5 East End Hants
73 G5 East End Hants
90 C2 East End Hants
171 G4 East End Herts
80 B2 East End Kent
98 D6 East End Kent
123 F5 East End Kent
194 C6 East End M Keyn
109 E5 East End N Som
139 F2 East End Oxon
139 G1 East End Oxon
165 E5 Eastend Oxon
165 F3 East End Oxon
166 A2 East End Oxon
110 D5 East End S Glos
67 G4 East End Somset
85 G4 East End Somset
86 B5 East End Somset
175 F2 East End Suffk
201 G3 East End Suffk
549 K6 Easter Aberchalder Highld
565 L2 Easter Ardross Highld
500 C4 Easter Balgedie P & K
537 K4 Easter Balmoral Abers
525 H2 Easter Binzian P & K
549 J5 Easter Boleskine Highld
109 G3 Easter Compton S Glos
525 H7 Easter Essendy P & K
576 D6 Easter Fearn Highld
551 L5 Easter Fodderletter Moray
566 E7 Easter Galcantray Highld
53 G3 Eastergate W Susx
467 G1 Easterhouse C Glas
451 E2 Easter Housebyres Border
470 D2 Easter Howgate Mdloth
501 E2 Easter Kilwhiss Fife
565 K5 Easter Kinkell Highld
513 H6 Easter Kinsleith Fife
515 F2 Easter Knox Angus
451 G2 Easter Langlee Border
526 D2 Easter Lednathie Angus
527 G5 Easter Meathie Angus
214 D4 Easter Green Covtry
557 E4 Easter Ord Abers
605 H3 Easter Quarff Shet
384 D1 Easterside Middsb
604 F1 Easter Skeld Shet
452 D3 Easter Softlaw Border
88 B3 Easterton Wilts
88 B3 Easterton Sands Wilts
84 B4 Eastertown Somset
569 L2 Easter Whyntie Abers
89 E4 East Everleigh Wilts
95 E2 East Ewell Surrey
98 A4 East Farleigh Kent
217 F3 East Farndon Nhants
222 C5 East Fen Common Cambs
331 H5 East Ferry Lincs
451 G4 Eastfield Border
109 G4 Eastfield Bristl
244 A4 Eastfield C Pete
468 D2 Eastfield N Lans
374 C3 Eastfield N York
431 E4 Eastfield Nthumb
467 F2 Eastfield S Lans
443 G3 Eastfield Hall Nthumb
90 D1 East Fields W Berk
501 E5 East Finglassie Fife
318 C2 East Firsby Lincs
32 A4 East Fleet Dorset
343 H3 East Garforth Leeds
114 B4 East Garston W Berk
393 E2 Eastgate Dur
244 A5 Eastgate N Linc
255 F3 Eastgate Norfk
405 G2 East Gateshead Gatesd
114 C2 East Ginge Oxon
174 A5 East Gores Essex
240 D2 East Goscote Leics
89 G2 East Grafton Wilts
92 C6 East Green Hants
198 D4 East Green Suffk
203 E1 East Green Suffk

71 E4 East Grimstead Wilts
77 G2 East Grinstead W Susx
59 F2 East Guldeford E Susx
217 E6 East Haddon Nhants
115 E2 East Hagbourne Oxon
170 A5 Easthall Herts
348 B6 East Halton Lincs
120 B3 East Ham Gt Lon
309 E3 Eastham Wirral
211 F6 Eastham Worcs
309 E3 Eastham Ferry Wirral
53 G3 East Hampnett W Susx
117 E6 Easthampstead Br For
185 H2 Easthampton Herefs
114 C1 East Hanney Oxon
147 F4 East Hanningfield Essex
344 B6 East Hardwick Wakefd
224 C2 East Harling Norfk
384 C5 East Harlsey N York
85 G3 East Harptree BaNES
431 E4 East Hartford Nthumb
74 B6 East Harting W Susx
198 C4 East Hatch Wilts
196 C4 East Hatley Cambs
255 E4 Easthaugh Norfk
383 E6 East Hauxwell N York
515 F2 East Haven Angus
92 C1 East Heath W Berk
299 F6 East Heckington Lincs
394 C1 East Hedleyhope Dur
582 D6 East Helmsdale Highld
114 D2 East Hendred Oxon
329 H6 East Herringthorpe Rothm
406 B4 East Herrington Sundld
374 A4 East Heslerton N York
84 C2 East Hewish N Som
97 E2 East Hill Kent
528 B5 East Hills Angus
57 E1 East Hoathly E Susx
33 F2 East Holme Dorset
33 H1 East Holton Dorset
431 F5 East Holywell N Tyne
234 D5 Easthope Shrops
234 D5 Easthopewood Shrops
121 F2 East Horndon Essex
174 B5 Easthorpe Essex
277 H2 Easthorpe Leics
296 D4 Easthorpe Notts
85 G5 East Horrington Somset
94 B4 East Horsley Surrey
454 C3 East Horton Nthumb
605 G1 Easthouse Shet
471 F1 Easthouses Mdloth
48 D5 East Howe Bmouth
84 B5 East Huntspill Somset
169 G6 East Hyde Beds
61 H2 East Ilkerton Devon
114 D3 East Ilsley W Berk
603 M1 Easting Ork
41 E6 Eastington Devon
136 A3 Eastington Gloucs
138 A2 Eastington Gloucs
300 C2 East Keal Lincs
88 D1 East Kennett Wilts
356 D6 East Keswick Leeds
467 G4 East Kilbride S Lans
24 C3 East Kimber Devon
54 C4 East Kingston W Susx
300 B2 East Kirkby Lincs
373 G4 East Knapton N York
33 E2 East Knighton Dorset
41 G3 East Knowstone Devon
69 E3 East Knoyle Wilts
405 E4 East Kyo Dur
66 C6 East Lambrook Somset
576 F8 East Lamington Highld
52 B2 Eastland Gate Hants
83 F1 East Langdon Kent
217 F1 East Langton Leics
576 F2 East Langwell Highld
53 F3 East Lavant W Susx
53 G1 East Lavington W Susx
404 C4 East Law Dur
383 E2 East Layton N York
138 C3 Eastleach Martin Gloucs
138 B3 Eastleach Turville Gloucs
276 C4 East Leake Notts
453 G2 East Learmouth Nthumb
12 B2 East Leigh Devon
25 G1 East Leigh Devon
39 G2 East Leigh Devon
72 C6 Eastleigh Devon
253 H4 East Lexham Norfk
454 C5 East Lilburn Nthumb
99 F3 Eastling Kent
490 A4 East Linton E Loth
74 B4 East Liss Hants
114 C2 East Lockinge Oxon
397 H6 East Loftus R & Cl
9 H3 East Looe Cnwll
331 G5 East Lound N Linc
19 G3 East Lounston Devon
33 F3 East Lulworth Dorset
374 A6 East Lutton N York
43 G2 East Lydeard Somset
67 F3 East Lydford Somset
44 C2 East Lyng Somset
556 B5 East Mains Abers
513 H2 East Mains Angus
472 D5 East Mains Border
467 F4 East Mains S Lans
528 B4 East Mains of Burnside Angus
97 H3 East Malling Kent
97 G3 East Malling Heath Kent
514 C2 East March Angus
53 E2 East Marden W Susx
316 D5 East Markham Notts
334 C2 East Marsh NE Lin
70 B6 East Martin Hants
354 B4 East Marton N York
69 E5 East Melbury Dorset
73 G5 East Meon Hants
42 C4 East Mere Devon
149 E2 East Mersea Essex
95 F4 East Molesey Surrey
343 F5 East Moor Wakefd
106 D4 East Moors Cardif
47 H5 East Morden Dorset
355 E6 East Morton Brad
436 A4 East Morton D & G
56 A3 East Moulsecoomb Br & H
372 C4 East Ness N York
526 D6 East Nevay Angus
349 E2 East Newton E R Yk
372 B4 East Newton N York
52 B5 Eastney C Port
161 G2 Eastnor Herefs
241 G4 East Norton Leics
43 G3 East Nynehead Somset
91 F5 East Oakley Hants
331 H1 Eastoft N Linc
20 A3 East Ogwell Devon
52 C5 Eastoke Hants
109 H5 Easton Bristl
219 G5 Easton Cambs
399 H3 Easton Cumb
426 B5 Easton Cumb
12 B3 Easton Devon
25 H5 Easton Devon
32 B5 Easton Dorset
72 D3 Easton Hants

36 A3 Easton IoW
278 C4 Easton Lincs
249 F2 Easton Lincs
85 F5 Easton Somset
202 B3 Easton Suffk
114 C5 Easton W Berk
111 F5 Easton Wilts
111 F2 Easton Wilts
109 F4 Easton-in-Gordano N Som
194 B3 Easton Maudit Nhants
243 E4 Easton on the Hill Nhants
89 F2 Easton Royal Wilts
67 G3 Easton Town Somset
111 F2 Easton Town Wilts
68 D6 East Orchard Dorset
475 E4 East Ord Nthumb
65 F4 Eastover Somset
23 H4 East Panson Devon
48 D5 East Parley Dorset
97 G5 East Peckham Kent
67 F2 East Pennard Somset
195 H1 East Perry Cambs
8 B5 East Portholland Cnwll
12 C5 East Portlemouth Devon
12 D5 East Prawle Devon
398 B3 East Preston D & G
54 C4 East Preston W Susx
46 D3 East Pulham Dorset
39 E4 East Putford Devon
64 B3 East Quantoxhead Somset
406 A5 East Rainton Sundld
254 A2 East Ravendale NE Lin
244 C5 East Raynham Norfk
399 H1 Eastrea Cambs
356 D6 East Rigton Leeds
346 A3 Eastrington E R Yk
111 E5 Eastrip Wilts
84 C2 East Rolstone N Som
91 G4 Eastrop Hants
384 C4 East Rounton N York
253 G2 East Rudham Norfk
261 G3 East Runton Norfk
256 C4 East Ruston Norfk
101 F5 Eastry Kent
472 B1 East Saltoun E Loth
119 E4 East Sheen Gt Lon
605 G8 Eastshore Shet
601 H6 Eastside Ork
422 D2 East Skelston D & G
431 E3 East Sleekburn Nthumb
257 F5 East Somerton Norfk
405 F4 East Stanley Dur
331 G6 East Stockwith Lincs
33 F2 East Stoke Dorset
296 D5 East Stoke Notts
66 D6 East Stoke Somset
68 D5 East Stour Dorset
68 D5 East Stour Common Dorset
101 E3 East Stourmouth Kent
40 C2 East Stowford Devon
72 D2 East Stratton Hants
101 F4 East Street Kent
67 E2 East Street Somset
101 F6 East Studdal Kent
545 K3 East Suisnish Highld
16 A6 East Taphouse Cnwll
39 G2 East-the-Water Devon
452 B2 East Third Border
443 F5 East Thirston Nthumb
121 G4 East Tilbury Thurr
73 H3 East Tisted Hants
319 E3 East Torrington Lincs
64 B5 East Town Somset
67 G1 East Town Somset
87 F3 East Town Wilts
125 H5 East Trewent Pembks
249 E2 East Tuddenham Norfk
71 F4 East Tytherley Hants
111 H4 East Tytherton Wilts
26 C2 East Village Devon
105 F5 East Village V Glam
109 H4 Eastville Bristl
300 D3 Eastville Lincs
234 C6 East Wall Shrops
253 E4 East Walton Norfk
85 F4 East Water Somset
25 G4 East Week Devon
277 G4 Eastwell Leics
71 G5 East Wellow Hants
99 G5 Eastwell Park Kent
501 F5 East Wemyss Fife
469 F2 East Whitburn W Loth
513 E2 East Whitefield P & K
145 F2 Eastwick Herts
606 E2 Eastwick Shet
120 C4 East Wickham Gt Lon
126 C4 East Williamston Pembks
252 D4 East Winch Norfk
71 E3 East Winterslow Wilts
52 D5 East Wittering W Susx
369 F2 East Witton N York
341 F4 Eastwood Calder
161 E1 Eastwood Herefs
295 F5 Eastwood Notts
329 G6 Eastwood Rothm
122 C2 Eastwood Sthend
428 D2 East Woodburn Nthumb
245 F6 Eastwood End Cambs
295 F5 Eastwood Hall Notts
90 C2 East Woodhay Hants
86 D6 East Woodlands Somset
74 A2 East Worldham Hants
41 F5 East Worlington Devon
55 E4 East Worthing W Susx
224 B1 East Wretham Norfk
38 C4 East Youlstone Devon
215 F6 Eathorpe Warwks
290 B2 Eaton Ches
291 H1 Eaton Ches
186 C3 Eaton Herefs
277 G4 Eaton Leics
249 H3 Eaton Norfk
316 D4 Eaton Notts
139 G4 Eaton Oxon
209 G2 Eaton Shrops
210 C1 Eaton Shrops
160 A2 Eaton Bishop Herefs
168 D5 Eaton Bray Beds
234 D3 Eaton Constantine Shrops
195 H2 Eaton Ford Cambs
289 F2 Eaton Hall Ches
138 D5 Eaton Hastings Oxon
234 C3 Eaton Mascott Shrops
195 H3 Eaton Socon Cambs
271 F5 Eaton upon Tern Shrops
252 B4 Eau Brink Norfk
186 C6 Eau Withington Herefs
214 D3 Eaves Green Solhll
369 H6 Eavestone N York
40 B4 Ebberly Hill Devon
373 G3 Ebberston N York
69 G5 Ebbesbourne Wake Wilts
49 E3 Ebblake Dorset
132 B5 Ebbw Vale Blae G
404 D3 Ebchester Dur
84 C2 Ebdon N Som
75 F4 Ebernoe W Susx
27 F5 Ebford Devon
136 B4 Ebley Gloucs
289 G5 Ebnal Ches
186 B3 Ebnall Herefs
234 C1 Ebreywood Shrops

164 B1	**Ebrington** Gloucs
91 E2	**Ecchinswell** Hants
491 E6	**Ecclaw** Border
424 D5	**Ecclefechan** D & G
363 E4	**Eccle Riggs** Cumb
453 E1	**Eccles** Border
98 A2	**Eccles** Kent
325 H5	**Eccles** Salfd
314 C3	**Ecclesall** Sheff
329 E6	**Ecclesfield** Sheff
529 F1	**Ecclesgreig** Abers
272 B4	**Eccleshall** Staffs
342 C2	**Eccleshill** Brad
487 E5	**Ecclesmachan** W Loth
257 E4	**Eccles on Sea** Norfk
224 D1	**Eccles Road** Norfk
289 F2	**Eccleston** Ches
324 C1	**Eccleston** Lancs
324 B5	**Eccleston** St Hel
324 B6	**Eccleston Park** St Hel
68 D4	**Eccliffe** Dorset
356 B6	**Eccup** Leeds
556 C3	**Echt** Abers
452 D4	**Eckford** Border
452 D4	**Eckfordmoss** Border
315 E4	**Eckington** Derbys
162 D1	**Eckington** Worcs
57 E2	**Ecklands** Barns
328 C4	**Eckworthy** Devon
39 F4	**Eckworthy** Devon
193 H2	**Ecton** Nhants
293 E3	**Ecton** Staffs
193 H2	**Ecton Brook** Nhants
313 F2	**Edale** Derbys
313 G2	**Edale End** Derbys
64 D3	**Edbrook** Somset
55 F2	**Edburton** W Susx
399 E5	**Edderside** Cumb
576 F7	**Edderton** Highld
100 C2	**Eddington** Kent
114 A6	**Eddington** W Berk
470 D5	**Eddleston** Border
467 H4	**Eddlewood** S Lans
96 B5	**Edenbridge** Kent
340 C6	**Edenfield** Lancs
391 F3	**Edenhall** Cumb
279 F5	**Edenham** Lincs
365 H4	**Eden Mount** Cumb
119 H6	**Eden Park** Gt Lon
314 A6	**Edensor** Derbys
495 G6	**Edentaggart** Ag & B
330 D3	**Edenthorpe** Donc
400 C3	**Edentown** Cumb
396 B2	**Eden Vale** Dur
87 F4	**Eden Vale** Wilts
493 E4	**Edern** Ag & B
262 D3	**Edern** Gwynd
86 B5	**Edford** Somset
67 E2	**Edgarley** Somset
213 G3	**Edgbaston** Birm
192 B5	**Edgcote** Nhants
167 E5	**Edgcott** Bucks
62 C4	**Edgcott** Somset
4 D2	**Edgcumbe** Cnwll
136 B3	**Edge** Gloucs
233 G3	**Edge** Shrops
270 D5	**Edgebolton** Shrops
134 D2	**Edge End** Gloucs
339 H3	**Edge End** Lancs
261 E5	**Edgefield** Norfk
261 E5	**Edgefield Street** Norfk
339 H6	**Edge Fold** Bl w D
325 F3	**Edge Fold** Bolton
289 G4	**Edge Green** Ches
224 D3	**Edge Green** Norfk
324 D5	**Edge Green** Wigan
309 E2	**Edge Hill** Lpool
191 F5	**Edgehill** Warwks
238 C5	**Edge Hill** Warwks
312 A2	**Edgeley** Stockp
328 D6	**Edge Mount** Sheff
269 F6	**Edgerley** Shrops
440 C2	**Edgerston** Border
342 B6	**Edgerton** Kirk
340 C5	**Edgeside** Lancs
136 D3	**Edgeworth** Gloucs
20 B4	**Edginswell** Torbay
189 F2	**Edgiock** Worcs
271 G6	**Edgmond** Wrekin
271 G5	**Edgmond Marsh** Wrekin
209 G2	**Edgton** Shrops
118 D1	**Edgware** Gt Lon
215 E3	**Edgwick** Covtry
325 G1	**Edgworth** Bl w D
237 G3	**Edial** Staffs
509 J5	**Edinample** Stirlg
542 E6	**Edinbane** Highld
488 B4	**Edinburgh** C Edin
238 C2	**Edingale** Staffs
296 C3	**Edingley** Notts
256 C3	**Edingthorpe** Norfk
256 C3	**Edingthorpe Green** Norfk
66 B2	**Edington** Somset
87 G4	**Edington** Wilts
84 C4	**Edingworth** Somset
38 B3	**Edistone** Devon
84 B5	**Edithmead** Somset
242 C3	**Edith Weston** Rutlnd
293 G6	**Edlaston** Derbys
168 D6	**Edlesborough** Bucks
443 E3	**Edlingham** Nthumb
319 G5	**Edlington** Lincs
48 C2	**Edmondsham** Dorset
405 F5	**Edmondsley** Dur
105 G1	**Edmondstown** Rhondd
242 B1	**Edmondthorpe** Leics
449 E1	**Edmonston** S Lans
603 G7	**Edmonstone** Ork
14 D4	**Edmonton** Cnwll
144 D6	**Edmonton** Gt Lon
404 B4	**Edmundbyers** Dur
452 D2	**Ednam** Border
274 C1	**Ednaston** Derbys
146 D4	**Edney Common** Essex
524 C5	**Edradynate** P & K
474 B3	**Edrom** Border
270 C3	**Edstaston** Shrops
190 B2	**Edstone** Warwks
187 F3	**Edvin Loach** Herefs
276 C2	**Edwalton** Notts
174 B1	**Edwardstone** Suffk
132 A5	**Edwardsville** Myr Td
155 F3	**Edwinsford** Carmth
296 B1	**Edwinstowe** Notts
170 B1	**Edworth** Beds
187 E3	**Edwyn Ralph** Herefs
540 B6	**Edzell** Angus
130 B5	**Efail-Fach** Neath
106 A3	**Efail Isaf** Rhondd
263 F3	**Efailnewydd** Gwynd
268 C4	**Efail-Rhyd** Powys
152 C4	**Efailwen** Carmth
287 G3	**Efenechtyd** Denbgs
94 C4	**Effingham** Surrey
606 D7	**Effirth** Shet
439 G1	**Effledge** Border
238 B1	**Efflinch** Staffs
11 E2	**Efford** C Plym
26 D2	**Efford** Devon
90 C4	**Egbury** Hants
188 D4	**Egdon** Worcs
325 G2	**Egerton** Bolton
99 E5	**Egerton** Kent

98 D5	**Egerton Forstal** Kent
289 H4	**Egerton Green** Ches
86 D5	**Egford** Somset
23 G5	**Eggbeare** Cnwll
344 C5	**Eggborough** N York
18 B6	**Eggbuckland** C Plym
40 D5	**Eggesford** Devon
168 C5	**Eggington** Beds
274 D4	**Egginton** Derbys
274 D4	**Egginton Common** Derbys
393 G5	**Egglesburn** Dur
384 C2	**Egglescliffe** S on T
393 H5	**Eggleston** Dur
117 G5	**Egham** Surrey
117 H5	**Egham Hythe** Surrey
117 G6	**Egham Wick** Surrey
242 B3	**Egleton** Rutlnd
454 D6	**Eglingham** Nthumb
15 E4	**Egloshayle** Cnwll
23 F5	**Egloskerry** Cnwll
305 H5	**Eglwysbach** Conwy
105 G6	**Eglwys-Brewis** V Glam
270 B1	**Eglwys Cross** Wrexhm
229 F5	**Eglwys Fach** Cerdgn
152 D2	**Eglwyswen** Pembks
152 C2	**Eglwyswrw** Pembks
316 D6	**Egmanton** Notts
260 A4	**Egmere** Norfk
376 B2	**Egremont** Cumb
308 D1	**Egremont** Wirral
386 D3	**Egton** N York
386 D3	**Egton Bridge** N York
342 A3	**Egypt** Brad
117 G2	**Egypt** Bucks
72 C1	**Egypt** Hants
114 C4	**Egypt** W Berk
174 B4	**Eight Ash Green** Essex
405 G3	**Eighton Banks** Gatesd
160 C2	**Eign Hill** Herefs
546 E6	**Eilanreach** Highld
451 H3	**Eildon** Border
507 H3	**Eilean Duirinnis** Ag & B
596 E2	**Einacleit** W Isls
597 J5	**Eisgein** W Isls
265 E3	**Eisingrug** Gwynd
430 C5	**Eland Green** Nthumb
183 E1	**Elan Village** Powys
109 H2	**Elberton** S Glos
84 C3	**Elborough** N Som
269 G5	**Elbridge** Shrops
53 G4	**Elbridge** W Susx
11 F3	**Elburton** C Plym
189 F2	**Elcock's Brook** Worcs
136 A5	**Elcombe** Gloucs
112 D3	**Elcombe** Swindn
114 B6	**Elcot** W Berk
113 E3	**Eldene** Swindn
244 D5	**Eldernell** Cambs
162 B3	**Eldersfield** Worcs
466 B2	**Elderslie** Rens
172 B3	**Elder Street** Essex
395 E4	**Eldon** Dur
395 E4	**Eldon Lane** Dur
353 F1	**Eldroth** N York
342 B1	**Eldwick** Brad
406 B5	**Elemore Vale** Sundld
455 F3	**Elford** Nthumb
238 B2	**Elford** Staffs
221 H5	**Elford Closes** Cambs
568 C3	**Elgin** Moray
545 J7	**Elgol** Highld
82 C2	**Elham** Kent
486 D6	**Eliburn** W Loth
502 D5	**Elie** Fife
303 E4	**Elim** IoA
50 C2	**Eling** Hants
115 E4	**Eling** W Berk
441 G5	**Elishaw** Nthumb
316 C4	**Elkesley** Notts
216 D4	**Elkington** Nhants
146 C4	**Elkins Green** Essex
137 E2	**Elkstone** Gloucs
20 C5	**Ellacombe** Torbay
550 F5	**Ellan** Highld
342 B5	**Elland** Calder
342 B5	**Elland Lower Edge** Calder
479 J6	**Ellary** Ag & B
293 F6	**Ellastone** Staffs
351 G3	**Ellel** Lancs
473 G2	**Ellemford** Border
506 B6	**Ellenabeich** Ag & B
388 B2	**Ellenborough** Cumb
7 E2	**Ellenglaze** Cnwll
272 B4	**Ellenhall** Staffs
76 A2	**Ellen's Green** Surrey
384 C5	**Ellerbeck** N York
373 F3	**Ellerburn** N York
386 D2	**Ellerby** N York
271 E5	**Ellerdine** Wrekin
271 E5	**Ellerdine Heath** Wrekin
27 F2	**Ellerhayes** Devon
520 E6	**Elleric** Ag & B
346 D4	**Ellerker** E R Yk
345 G2	**Ellerton** E R Yk
383 G5	**Ellerton** N York
271 G4	**Ellerton** Shrops
142 A3	**Ellesborough** Bucks
269 G3	**Ellesmere** Shrops
326 A5	**Ellesmere Park** Salfd
309 F4	**Ellesmere Port** Ches
63 F3	**Ellicombe** Somset
49 E3	**Ellingham** Hants
226 D1	**Ellingham** Norfk
455 F4	**Ellingham** Nthumb
369 G3	**Ellingstring** N York
219 H5	**Ellington** Cambs
431 E1	**Ellington** Nthumb
219 H5	**Ellington Thorpe** Cambs
515 G2	**Elliot** Angus
86 D5	**Elliots Green** Somset
132 C4	**Elliot's Town** Caerph
91 G5	**Ellisfield** Hants
543 J3	**Ellishadder** Highld
476 B6	**Ellister** Ag & B
451 H4	**Elliston** Border
239 G2	**Ellistown** Leics
561 E3	**Ellon** Abers
390 C2	**Ellonby** Cumb
227 E2	**Ellough** Suffk
227 E2	**Ellough Moor** Suffk
346 D4	**Elloughton** E R Yk
134 D3	**Ellwood** Gloucs
245 G3	**Elm** Cambs
162 C6	**Elmbridge** Gloucs
212 D6	**Elmbridge** Worcs
94 B3	**Elm Corner** Surrey
112 D4	**Elm Cross** Wilts
171 G2	**Elmdon** Essex
214 B3	**Elmdon** Solhll
214 B3	**Elmdon Heath** Solhll
54 A4	**Elmer** W Susx
119 H6	**Elmers End** Gt Lon
324 B3	**Elmers Green** Lancs
74 D4	**Elmers Marsh** W Susx
239 H5	**Elmesthorpe** Leics
37 G2	**Elmfield** IoW
68 D4	**Elm Hill** Dorset
141 H1	**Elmhurst** Bucks
237 H2	**Elmhurst** Staffs
163 E1	**Elmley Castle** Worcs
212 C6	**Elmley Lovett** Worcs
136 A2	**Elmore** Gloucs
135 H1	**Elmore Back** Gloucs

120 D2	**Elm Park** Gt Lon
38 B3	**Elmscott** Devon
201 E5	**Elmsett** Suffk
186 C3	**Elms Green** Herefs
187 G1	**Elms Green** Worcs
365 G4	**Elmslack** Lancs
175 E3	**Elmstead** Essex
120 B5	**Elmstead** Gt Lon
175 E5	**Elmstead Heath** Essex
175 E4	**Elmstead Market** Essex
82 B1	**Elmsted** Kent
101 E3	**Elmstone** Kent
162 D4	**Elmstone Hardwicke** Gloucs
360 B3	**Elmswell** E R Yk
200 C2	**Elmswell** Suffk
315 G5	**Elmton** Derbys
579 H7	**Elphin** Highld
488 D5	**Elphinstone** E Loth
557 E3	**Elrick** Abers
409 G2	**Elrig** D & G
403 F2	**Elrington** Nthumb
185 F4	**Elsdon** Herefs
442 A6	**Elsdon** Nthumb
329 F4	**Elsecar** Barns
172 A4	**Elsenham** Essex
140 B2	**Elsfield** Oxon
333 E2	**Elsham** N Linc
255 E4	**Elsing** Norfk
354 B5	**Elslack** N York
51 H4	**Elson** Hants
269 G2	**Elson** Shrops
469 H6	**Elsrickle** S Lans
93 F6	**Elstead** Surrey
74 C6	**Elsted** W Susx
395 G5	**Elstob** Dur
26 B2	**Elston** Devon
297 E5	**Elston** Notts
88 C6	**Elston** Wilts
40 D4	**Elstone** Devon
195 F5	**Elstow** Beds
144 A5	**Elstree** Herts
348 D3	**Elstronwick** E R Yk
338 B2	**Elswick** Lancs
405 F2	**Elswick** N u Ty
338 B2	**Elswick Leys** Lancs
196 D2	**Elsworth** Cambs
378 B4	**Elterwater** Cumb
120 B5	**Eltham** Gt Lon
196 C3	**Eltisley** Cambs
326 A2	**Elton** Bury
243 F6	**Elton** Cambs
309 F4	**Elton** Ches
293 H2	**Elton** Derbys
135 F2	**Elton** Gloucs
210 B5	**Elton** Herefs
277 G2	**Elton** Notts
384 C1	**Elton** S on T
309 F4	**Elton Green** Ches
186 B6	**Elton's Marsh** Herefs
404 C2	**Eltringham** Nthumb
436 C1	**Elvanfoot** S Lans
275 G3	**Elvaston** Derbys
223 G4	**Elveden** Suffk
92 C3	**Elvetham Heath** Hants
395 F1	**Elvet Hill** Dur
489 F5	**Elvingston** E Loth
101 E5	**Elvington** Kent
358 C5	**Elvington** N York
61 G5	**Elwell** Devon
31 F6	**Elwell** Dorset
396 C3	**Elwick** Hartpl
455 E2	**Elwick** Nthumb
291 E2	**Elworth** Ches
63 H5	**Elworthy** Somset
222 B4	**Ely** Cambs
106 B4	**Ely** Cardif
194 B5	**Emberton** M Keyn
389 E3	**Embleton** Cumb
396 B4	**Embleton** Cumb
455 G5	**Embleton** Nthumb
577 H5	**Embo** Highld
85 H4	**Emborough** Somset
577 G5	**Embo Street** Highld
354 D4	**Embsay** N York
120 D2	**Emerson Park** Gt Lon
110 B4	**Emerson's Green** S Glos
168 A3	**Emerson Valley** M Keyn
49 H3	**Emery Down** Hants
328 C2	**Emley** Kirk
116 C6	**Emmbrook** Wokam
116 B4	**Emmer Green** Readg
315 E4	**Emmett Carr** Derbys
141 H4	**Emmington** Oxon
245 G3	**Emneth** Norfk
245 H3	**Emneth Hungate** Norfk
252 A3	**Emorsgate** Norfk
242 D3	**Empingham** Rutlnd
74 A3	**Empshott** Hants
74 A3	**Empshott Green** Hants
190 D1	**Emscote** Warwks
234 C2	**Emstrey** Shrops
52 C3	**Emsworth** Hants
90 C1	**Enborne** W Berk
90 C2	**Enborne Row** W Berk
234 C5	**Enchmarsh** Shrops
240 B5	**Enderby** Leics
366 A3	**Endmoor** Cumb
292 B4	**Endon** Staffs
292 B4	**Endon Bank** Staffs
106 B2	**Energlyn** Caerph
144 D5	**Enfield** Gt Lon
213 F6	**Enfield** Worcs
145 E5	**Enfield Highway** Gt Lon
145 E5	**Enfield Lock** Gt Lon
144 D5	**Enfield Town** Gt Lon
145 E5	**Enfield Wash** Gt Lon
88 D4	**Enford** Wilts
606 C6	**Engamoor** Shet
303 E5	**Engedi** IoA
110 B3	**Engine Common** S Glos
115 G5	**Englefield** W Berk
117 G5	**Englefield Green** Surrey
291 E4	**Englesea-Brook** Ches
134 D1	**English Bicknor** Gloucs
86 C2	**Englishcombe** BaNES
270 A4	**English Frankton** Shrops
14 B5	**Engollan** Cnwll
90 B5	**Enham Alamein** Hants
64 D5	**Enmore** Somset
186 B2	**Enmore Field** Herefs
69 E5	**Enmore Green** Dorset
376 D1	**Ennerdale Bridge** Cumb
8 B2	**Enniscaven** Cnwll
525 G3	**Enochdhu** P & K
517 K6	**Ensay** Ag & B
48 D5	**Ensbury** Bmouth
48 D6	**Ensbury Park** Bmouth
233 H1	**Ensdon** Shrops
40 B2	**Ensis** Devon
165 H6	**Ensiow** Oxon
165 F5	**Enstone** Oxon
435 H4	**Enterkinfoot** D & G
384 D3	**Enterpen** N York
75 F1	**Enton Green** Surrey
212 B2	**Enville** Staffs
590 D6	**Eòlaigearraidh** W Isls
504 D6	**Eorabus** Ag & B
599 L2	**Eòropaidh** W Isls
135 H2	**Epney** Gloucs
296 C5	**Epperstone** Notts
145 G4	**Epping** Essex
145 F3	**Epping Green** Essex
144 C3	**Epping Green** Herts

145 F4	**Epping Upland** Essex
333 E2	**Eppleby** N York
347 H2	**Eppleworth** E R Yk
94 D2	**Epsom** Surrey
165 F1	**Epwell** Oxon
331 G4	**Epworth** N Linc
331 G4	**Epworth Turbary** N Linc
269 G1	**Erbistock** Wrexhm
549 G1	**Erbusaig** Highld
549 H1	**Erchless Castle** Highld
213 H1	**Erdington** Birm
493 G3	**Eredine** Ag & B
585 H5	**Eriboll** Highld
437 E2	**Ericstane** D & G
78 D2	**Eridge Green** E Susx
480 B4	**Erines** Ag & B
520 C7	**Eriska** Ag & B
223 E4	**Eriswell** Suffk
120 D4	**Erith** Gt Lon
87 H4	**Erlestoke** Wilts
318 B5	**Ermine** Lincs
12 A2	**Ermington** Devon
10 D2	**Ernesettle** C Plym
261 G5	**Erpingham** Norfk
99 E3	**Erriottwood** Kent
549 K5	**Errogie** Highld
513 G5	**Errol** P & K
483 G5	**Erskine** Rens
483 F5	**Erskine Bridge** Rens
414 C3	**Ervie** D & G
176 D3	**Erwarton** Suffk
184 A6	**Erwood** Powys
383 H3	**Eryholme** N York
288 B3	**Eryrys** Denbgs
394 D4	**Escomb** Dur
64 A4	**Escott** Somset
358 B6	**Escrick** N York
154 A4	**Esgair** Carmth
230 B3	**Esgairgeiliog** Powys
305 H4	**Esgyryn** Conwy
405 E6	**Esh** Dur
94 C2	**Esher** Surrey
450 B2	**Eshiels** Border
342 C1	**Esholt** Brad
443 G5	**Eshott** Nthumb
354 B3	**Eshton** N York
394 D1	**Esh Winning** Dur
549 H2	**Eskadale** Highld
471 F4	**Eskbank** Mdloth
377 E4	**Eskdale Green** Cumb
438 A5	**Eskdalemuir** D & G
335 E5	**Eskham** Lincs
345 E6	**Eskholme** Donc
476 F4	**Esknish** Ag & B
386 D4	**Esk Valley** N York
442 C2	**Eslington Park** Nthumb
394 C5	**Esperley Lane Ends** Dur
338 B2	**Esprick** Lancs
243 E2	**Essendine** Rutlnd
144 C3	**Essendon** Herts
549 L2	**Essich** Highld
236 D4	**Essington** Staffs
560 D3	**Esslemont** Abers
397 E6	**Eston** R & Cl
18 B6	**Estover** C Plym
607 G7	**Eswick** Shet
453 H2	**Etal** Nthumb
88 B2	**Etchilhampton** Wilts
79 F4	**Etchingham** E Susx
82 C3	**Etchinghill** Kent
273 F6	**Etchinghill** Staffs
78 C5	**Etchingwood** E Susx
394 D4	**Etherley Dene** Dur
529 E5	**Ethie Mains** Angus
254 D5	**Etling Green** Norfk
135 F3	**Etloe** Gloucs
117 G4	**Eton** W & M
117 G4	**Eton Wick** W & M
291 H5	**Etruria** C Stke
233 G4	**Etsell** Shrops
400 C3	**Etterby** Cumb
535 J4	**Etteridge** Highld
393 E4	**Ettersgill** Dur
291 E4	**Ettiley Heath** Ches
236 D5	**Ettingshall** Wolves
236 D6	**Ettingshall Park** Wolves
190 D5	**Ettington** Warwks
243 G3	**Etton** C Pete
360 B6	**Etton** E R Yk
438 B2	**Ettrick** Border
450 D5	**Ettrickbridge** Border
438 B2	**Ettrickhill** Border
274 D3	**Etwall** Derbys
274 D3	**Etwall Common** Derbys
211 F2	**Eudon Burnell** Shrops
211 F2	**Eudon George** Shrops
224 A4	**Euston** Suffk
339 E6	**Euxton** Lancs
105 F2	**Evanstown** Brdgnd
565 K3	**Evanton** Highld
298 D5	**Evedon** Lincs
212 D1	**Eve Hill** Dudley
577 G5	**Evelix** Highld
161 G1	**Evendine** Herefs
185 E2	**Evenjobb** Powys
166 C3	**Evenley** Nhants
164 C4	**Evenlode** Gloucs
160 D2	**Even Pits** Herefs
112 D3	**Even Swindon** Swindn
394 C5	**Evenwood** Dur
394 D5	**Evenwood Gate** Dur
603 K6	**Everbay** Ork
67 G2	**Evercreech** Somset
192 C3	**Everdon** Nhants
346 B1	**Everingham** E R Yk
89 E4	**Everleigh** Wilts
374 B2	**Everley** N York
168 D3	**Eversholt** Beds
30 D2	**Evershot** Dorset
122 A2	**Eversley** Essex
92 C2	**Eversley** Hants
92 C2	**Eversley Centre** Hants
92 C2	**Eversley Cross** Hants
346 C2	**Everthorpe** E R Yk
196 A4	**Everton** Beds
50 A6	**Everton** Hants
309 E1	**Everton** Lpool
316 C1	**Everton** Notts
425 H4	**Evertown** D & G
187 F5	**Evesbatch** Herefs
164 D1	**Evesham** Worcs
240 D4	**Evington** C Leic
82 B2	**Evington** Kent
388 B2	**Ewanrigg** Cumb
329 E3	**Ewden Village** Sheff
95 E2	**Ewell** Surrey
99 G3	**Ewell Minnis** Kent
115 G1	**Ewelme** Oxon
137 F5	**Ewen** Gloucs
105 E4	**Ewenny** V Glam
299 E5	**Ewerby** Lincs
299 E5	**Ewerby Thorpe** Lincs
425 H1	**Ewes** D & G
76 A1	**Ewhurst** Surrey
80 A5	**Ewhurst Green** E Susx
76 A2	**Ewhurst Green** Surrey
288 C1	**Ewloe** Flints
288 C1	**Ewloe Green** Flints
339 G4	**Ewood** Bl w D
340 B5	**Ewood Bridge** Lancs
24 B4	**Eworthy** Devon
92 D5	**Ewshot** Hants
159 G4	**Ewyas Harold** Herefs

25 F2	**Exbourne** Devon
42 B3	**Exbridge** Devon
50 D4	**Exbury** Hants
57 E5	**Exceat** E Susx
370 B2	**Exelby** N York
26 D4	**Exeter** Devon
62 C4	**Exford** Somset
234 A3	**Exfords Green** Shrops
189 H4	**Exhall** Warwks
215 F2	**Exhall** Warwks
115 H3	**Exlade Street** Oxon
342 A5	**Exley** Calder
341 G1	**Exley Head** Brad
27 E3	**Exminster** Devon
21 E2	**Exmouth** Devon
605 G8	**Exnaboe** Shet
198 C1	**Exning** Suffk
82 C2	**Exted** Kent
27 F5	**Exton** Devon
73 F5	**Exton** Hants
242 C2	**Exton** Rutlnd
63 E3	**Exton** Somset
26 D4	**Exwick** Devon
313 H4	**Eyam** Derbys
192 B6	**Eydon** Nhants
244 B4	**Eye** C Pete
186 B2	**Eye** Herefs
225 F5	**Eye** Suffk
244 B4	**Eye Green** C Pete
474 D2	**Eyemouth** Border
196 B5	**Eyeworth** Beds
98 C4	**Eyhorne Street** Kent
202 C4	**Eyke** Suffk
196 A3	**Eynesbury** Cambs
544 F4	**Eynort** Highld
96 D2	**Eynsford** Kent
139 G3	**Eynsham** Oxon
30 A4	**Eype** Dorset
30 A4	**Eype's Mouth** Dorset
543 G6	**Eyre** Highld
545 K3	**Eyre** Highld
240 C5	**Eyres Monsell** C Leic
101 E6	**Eythorne** Kent
186 B2	**Eyton** Herefs
209 G2	**Eyton** Shrops
233 G2	**Eyton** Shrops
288 D6	**Eyton** Wrexhm
234 D3	**Eyton on Severn** Shrops
235 E1	**Eyton upon the Weald Moors** Wrekin

F

89 G4	**Faberstown** Wilts
90 B3	**Faccombe** Hants
384 D4	**Faceby** N York
283 F2	**Fachell** Gwynd
284 C2	**Fachwen** Gwynd
340 D6	**Facit** Lancs
295 F3	**Fackley** Notts
290 B4	**Faddiley** Ches
372 C2	**Fadmoor** N York
129 G4	**Faerdre** Swans
342 C3	**Fagley** Brad
129 G4	**Fagwyr** Swans
533 L2	**Faichem** Highld
483 H5	**Faifley** W Duns
109 F5	**Failand** N Som
445 G4	**Failford** S Ayrs
326 C4	**Failsworth** Oldham
229 E2	**Fairbourne** Gwynd
98 A4	**Fairbourne Heath** Kent
344 B4	**Fairburn** N York
144 D4	**Fair Cross** Gt Lon
326 B2	**Fairfield** Bury
498 D6	**Fairfield** Clacks
313 E5	**Fairfield** Derbys
81 E4	**Fairfield** Kent
309 E1	**Fairfield** Lpool
396 B6	**Fairfield** S on T
326 C5	**Fairfield** Tamesd
189 F6	**Fairfield** Worcs
212 B4	**Fairfield** Worcs
212 D4	**Fairfield** Worcs
86 C1	**Fairfield Park** BaNES
161 G3	**Fairfields** Gloucs
138 B4	**Fairford** Gloucs
252 D4	**Fair Green** Norfk
337 F4	**Fairhaven** Lancs
463 F5	**Fairhaven** N Ayrs
391 E3	**Fair Hill** Cumb
467 H4	**Fairhill** S Lans
93 G4	**Fairlands** Surrey
37 E2	**Fairlie** IoW
465 E3	**Fairlie** N Ayrs
59 E4	**Fairlight** E Susx
59 E4	**Fairlight Cove** E Susx
120 C1	**Fairlop** Gt Lon
49 E6	**Fairmile** Dorset
94 C2	**Fairmile** Surrey
488 A6	**Fairmilehead** C Edin
430 C2	**Fair Moor** Nthumb
132 C5	**Fairoak** Caerph
72 C6	**Fair Oak** Hants
91 E2	**Fair Oak** Hants
352 C5	**Fair Oak** Lancs
271 H3	**Fairoak** Staffs
91 H2	**Fair Oak Green** Hants
97 F2	**Fairseat** Kent
147 F1	**Fairstead** Essex
252 C4	**Fairstead** Norfk
163 E5	**Fairview** Gloucs
78 B4	**Fairwarp** E Susx
106 B4	**Fairwater** Cardif
133 E6	**Fairwater** Torfn
87 F4	**Fairwood** Wilts
39 F3	**Fairy Cross** Devon
260 B5	**Fakenham** Norfk
224 A4	**Fakenham Magna** Suffk
472 A2	**Fala** Mdloth
472 A2	**Fala Dam** Mdloth
471 G3	**Falahill** Border
160 D3	**Falcon** Herefs
238 C5	**Falcon Lodge** Birm
120 B4	**Falconwood** Gt Lon
192 C6	**Falcutt** Nhants
318 D3	**Faldingworth** Lincs
451 G3	**Faldonside** Border
35 J6	**Faldouët** Jersey
135 F6	**Falfield** S Glos
177 E2	**Falkenham** Suffk
177 E2	**Falkenham Sink** Suffk
485 H4	**Falkirk** Falk
501 E3	**Falkland** Fife
440 D2	**Falla** Border
294 C2	**Fallgate** Derbys
485 G1	**Fallin** Stirlg
294 B1	**Fallinge** Derbys
237 E5	**Fallings Heath** Wsall
326 B6	**Fallowfield** Manch
467 H2	**Fallside** N Lans
56 B3	**Falmer** E Susx
5 E2	**Falmouth** Cnwll
438 D3	**Falnash** Border
374 C2	**Falsgrave** N York
486 C6	**Falside** W Loth
428 A2	**Falstone** Nthumb
584 C7	**Fanagmore** Highld
169 E4	**Fancott** Beds
565 H8	**Fanellan** Highld
385 F6	**Fangdale Beck** N York

359 E4 Fangfoss E R Yk
485 F3 Fankerton Falk
517 L7 Fanmore Ag & B
146 D2 Fanner's Green Essex
452 B1 Fans Border
311 H5 Fanshowe Ches
98 A5 Fant Kent
365 F4 Far Arnside Cumb
330 D2 Far Bank Donc
338 B5 Far Banks Lancs
244 B6 Farcet Cambs
239 F4 Far Coton Leics
193 F3 Far Cotton Nhants
210 A4 Farden Shrops
51 G3 Fareham Hants
378 A5 Far End Cumb
237 G2 Farewell Staffs
211 G5 Far Forest Worcs
320 B4 Farforth Lincs
136 A4 Far Green Gloucs
294 D3 Farhill Derbys
274 A5 Far Hoarcross Staffs
138 D5 Faringdon Oxon
338 D5 Farington Lancs
338 D5 Farington Moss Lancs
401 G3 Farlam Cumb
313 E2 Farlands Booth Derbys
577 G2 Farlary Highld
294 D5 Far Laund Derbys
109 E6 Farleigh N Som
95 H2 Farleigh Surrey
95 H3 Farleigh Court Surrey
97 H4 Farleigh Green Kent
87 E3 Farleigh Hungerford Somset
91 G5 Farleigh Wallop Hants
87 E2 Farleigh Wick Wilts
321 E5 Farlesthorpe Lincs
366 A3 Farleton Cumb
352 B1 Farleton Lancs
294 B2 Farley Derbys
108 D5 Farley N Som
233 C5 Farley Shrops
235 E4 Farley Shrops
236 A5 Far Ley Staffs
293 E6 Farley Staffs
71 E4 Farley Wilts
199 E4 Farley Green Suffk
94 B5 Farley Green Surrey
92 C2 Farley Hill Wokham
135 H1 Farleys End Gloucs
52 B3 Farlington C Port
372 B6 Farlington N York
211 E3 Farlow Shrops
86 B2 Farmborough BaNES
146 C2 Farmbridge End Essex
163 G4 Farmcote Gloucs
212 A4 Farmcote Shrops
138 A1 Farmington Gloucs
139 G3 Farmoor Oxon
324 C4 Far Moor Wigan
4 C2 Farms Common Cnwll
239 F1 Farm Town Leics
569 J5 Farmtown Moray
294 C5 Farnah Green Derbys
96 B2 Farnborough Gt Lon
92 D4 Farnborough Hants
114 C3 Farnborough W Berk
191 G5 Farnborough Warwks
93 E3 Farnborough Green Hants
93 E3 Farnborough Park Hants
93 E3 Farnborough Street Hants
93 G5 Farncombe Surrey
194 C2 Farndish Beds
289 F4 Farndon Ches
297 E4 Farndon Notts
528 D3 Farnell Angus
48 B1 Farnham Dorset
171 G5 Farnham Essex
356 C2 Farnham N York
202 D3 Farnham Suffk
92 D5 Farnham Surrey
117 G2 Farnham Common Bucks
171 G4 Farnham Green Essex
117 G3 Farnham Park Bucks
117 G3 Farnham Royal Bucks
354 D5 Farnhill N York
96 D1 Farningham Kent
343 E3 Farnley Leeds
355 H5 Farnley N York
328 B2 Farnley Bank Kirk
328 B2 Farnley Tyas Kirk
296 C3 Farnsfield Notts
325 G3 Farnworth Bolton
309 G2 Farnworth Halton
136 D4 Far Oakridge Gloucs
536 B2 Farr Highld
550 B3 Farr Highld
586 F4 Farr Highld
549 K5 Farraline Highld
27 G4 Farringdon Devon
406 B4 Farringdon Sundld
47 F1 Farrington Dorset
85 H3 Farrington Gurney BaNES
343 E3 Far Royds Leeds
378 C5 Far Sawrey Cumb
342 D2 Farsley Leeds
342 D3 Farsley Beck Bottom Leeds
147 G4 Farther Howegreen Essex
98 C2 Farthing Corner Medway
98 C5 Farthing Green Kent
166 B2 Farthinghoe Nhants
83 E2 Farthingloe Kent
192 D4 Farthingstone Nhants
136 C4 Far Thrupp Gloucs
28 C3 Farway Devon
29 F2 Farway Marsh Devon
542 B7 Fasach Highld
562 F5 Fasag Highld
518 C1 Fascadale Highld
524 D3 Faskally P & K
482 B2 Faslane Port Ag & B
520 E6 Fasnacloich Ag & B
540 B4 Fasque Abers
532 F7 Fassfern Highld
405 H4 Fatfield Sundld
569 L4 Fattahead Abers
487 E5 Faucheldean W Loth
401 F4 Faugh Cumb
401 F5 Faugh Head Cumb
451 G3 Faughill Border
274 B4 Fauld Staffs
469 E2 Fauldhouse W Loth
451 E4 Fauldshope Border
147 F1 Faulkbourne Essex
86 C4 Faulkland Somset
270 D3 Fauls Shrops
383 G1 Faverdale Darltn
99 F2 Faversham Kent
552 F2 Favillar Moray
371 E5 Fawdington N York
430 D6 Fawdon N u Ty
442 C1 Fawdon Nthumb
293 E2 Fawfieldhead Staffs
97 E1 Fawkham Green Kent
113 H2 Fawler Oxon
139 F1 Fawler Oxon
116 C2 Fawley Bucks
51 E4 Fawley Hants
114 B3 Fawley W Berk
116 B2 Fawley Bottom Bucks
160 D4 Fawley Chapel Herefs
346 C5 Faxfleet E R Yk

76 D3 Faygate W Susx
323 G5 Fazakerley Lpool
238 C4 Fazeley Staffs
535 G4 Feagour Highld
369 G3 Fearby N York
566 F1 Fearn Highld
523 K7 Fearnan P & K
562 C5 Fearnbeg Highld
310 C1 Fearnhead Warrtn
562 C4 Fearnmore Highld
343 F2 Fearnville Leeds
236 D4 Featherstone Staffs
343 H5 Featherstone Wakefd
189 F2 Feckenham Worcs
304 C3 Fedw Fawr IoA
173 H5 Feering Essex
382 A5 Feetham N York
292 A4 Fegg Hayes C Stke
353 F1 Feizor N York
77 G2 Felbridge Surrey
261 H4 Felbrigg Norfk
77 G1 Felcourt Surrey
143 E3 Felden Herts
101 F4 Felderland Kent
310 D4 Feldy Ches
210 A2 Felhampton Shrops
156 D5 Felin-Crai Powys
128 C2 Felindre Carmth
153 G2 Felindre Carmth
154 D5 Felindre Carmth
155 G4 Felindre Carmth
158 C5 Felindre Powys
208 C3 Felindre Powys
232 C4 Felindre Powys
105 F3 Felindre Rhondd
129 F4 Felindre Swans
152 B2 Felindre Farchog Pembks
180 D3 Felinfach Cerdgn
158 A3 Felinfach Powys
128 D4 Felinfoel Carmth
154 D5 Felingwmisaf Carmth
154 D5 Felingwmuchaf Carmth
155 G2 Felin Newydd Carmth
268 D4 Felin Newydd Powys
158 B2 Felin-Newydd Powys
288 D5 Felin Puleston Wrexhm
179 G4 Felin-Wnda Cerdgn
371 F3 Felixkirk N York
177 F3 Felixstowe Suffk
177 F2 Felixstowe Ferry Suffk
474 D6 Felkington Nthumb
329 F2 Felkirk Wakefd
388 C6 Felldyke Cumb
380 C5 Fell End Cumb
405 H2 Fellgate S Tyne
380 B2 Fell Head Cumb
405 G2 Felling Gatesd
405 G2 Felling Shore Gatesd
341 G1 Fell Lane Brad
389 H2 Fell Side Cumb
405 E3 Fellside Gatesd
194 D3 Felmersham Beds
256 A4 Felmingham Norfk
122 A2 Felmore Essex
53 H4 Felpham W Susx
200 B3 Felsham Suffk
172 D6 Felsted Essex
118 B5 Feltham Gt Lon
43 H4 Feltham Somset
118 B5 Felthamhill Surrey
255 G4 Felthorpe Norfk
186 D5 Felton Herefs
85 F1 Felton N Som
443 F4 Felton Nthumb
233 G1 Felton Butler Shrops
222 D1 Feltwell Norfk
328 B1 Fenay Bridge Kirk
340 C2 Fence Lancs
405 H4 Fence Houses Sundld
140 C1 Fencott Oxon
524 C2 Fenderbridge P & K
197 G2 Fen Ditton Cambs
220 D6 Fen Drayton Cambs
280 B5 Fen End Lincs
214 C5 Fen End Solhll
244 B5 Fengate C Pete
255 G3 Fengate Norfk
405 F1 Fenham N u Ty
280 B1 Fenhouses Lincs
339 F4 Feniscliffe Bl w D
339 F4 Feniscowles Bl w D
28 A3 Feniton Devon
195 F5 Fenlake Beds
211 H3 Fenn Green Shrops
43 G2 Fennington Somset
270 C2 Fenn's Bank Wrexhm
122 B4 Fenn Street Medway
293 G5 Fenny Bentley Derbys
28 B3 Fenny Bridges Devon
191 G4 Fenny Compton Warwks
239 F5 Fenny Drayton Leics
168 B3 Fenny Stratford M Keyn
430 C1 Fenrother Nthumb
300 B3 Fen Side Lincs
220 D6 Fenstanton Cambs
199 G4 Fenstead End Suffk
225 E3 Fen Street Norfk
224 C4 Fen Street Suffk
225 E4 Fen Street Suffk
292 A6 Fenton C Stke
220 B4 Fenton Cambs
401 E3 Fenton Cumb
297 G4 Fenton Lincs
317 F4 Fenton Lincs
454 B3 Fenton Nthumb
15 F3 Fentonadle Cnwll
489 G3 Fenton Barns E Loth
292 A5 Fenton Low C Stke
15 F6 Fenton Pits Cnwll
211 G5 Fengest Bucks
116 C1 Fengest Bucks
330 C1 Fenwick Donc
466 C6 Fenwick E Ayrs
429 G5 Fenwick Nthumb
454 D1 Fenwick Nthumb
457 F4 Feochaig Ag & B
7 F6 Feock Cnwll
478 C8 Feolin Ferry Ag & B
542 D8 Feorlig Highld
466 C2 Ferguslie Park Rens
531 H1 Ferindonald Highld
542 B6 Feriniquarrie Highld
35 d3 Fermain Bay Guern
527 G2 Fern Angus
117 E2 Fern Bucks
327 E5 Fern Bank Tamesd
78 D1 Ferndale Kent
131 F5 Ferndale Rhondd
48 D5 Ferndown Dorset
69 F5 Ferne Wilts
567 H8 Ferness Highld
378 D5 Ferney Green Cumb
113 G1 Fernham Oxon
326 B2 Fernhill Bury
131 G5 Fernhill Rhondd
199 G5 Fernhill W Susx
77 E1 Fernhill W Susx
325 F3 Fernhill Gate Bolton
188 C3 Fernhill Heath Worcs
75 E4 Fernhurst W Susx
501 F1 Fernie Fife
468 A4 Ferniegair S Lans
451 E2 Ferniehirst Border
544 F3 Fernilea Highld
312 D1 Fernilee Derbys

7 E5 Fernsplatt Cnwll
356 D2 Ferrensby N York
347 E5 Ferriby Sluice N Linc
54 C4 Ferring W Susx
344 B5 Ferrybridge Wakefd
529 F3 Ferryden Angus
557 G3 Ferryhill C Aber
221 E3 Ferry Hill Cambs
395 F3 Ferryhill Dur
395 F3 Ferryhill Station Dur
127 H2 Ferryside Carmth
225 E3 Fersfield Norfk
534 C7 Fersit Highld
536 C2 Feshiebridge Highld
94 C3 Fetcham Surrey
571 H5 Fetterangus Abers
540 B5 Fettercairn Abers
565 K6 Fettes Highld
166 B4 Fewcott Oxon
355 G4 Fewston N York
355 G4 Fewston Bents N York
155 F5 Ffairfach Carmth
205 G6 Ffair-Rhos Cerdgn
181 F6 Ffaldybrenin Carmth
181 G6 Ffarmers Carmth
158 D6 Ffawyddog Powys
287 G2 Ffordd-Las Denbgs
158 D2 Fforddlas Powys
104 D3 Ffordd-y-Gyfraith Brdgnd
129 E4 Fforest Carmth
103 F2 Fforest-fach Swans
130 A4 Fforest Gôch Neath
205 E6 Ffoshelyg Cerdgn
179 H4 Ffostrasol Cerdgn
131 H3 Ffos-y-frân Myr Td
288 D4 Ffos-y-go Wrexhm
232 C5 Ffridd Powys
284 C4 Ffridd Uchaf Gwynd
288 C3 Ffrith Flints
127 G1 Ffynnon Carmth
154 B5 Ffynnon-ddrain Carmth
151 F4 Ffynnon Gron Pembks
307 G3 Ffynnongroyw Flints
158 C1 Ffynnon Gynydd Powys
96 A2 Fickleshole Surrey
504 C6 Fidden Ag & B
541 F3 Fiddes Abers
162 D3 Fiddington Gloucs
42 D2 Fiddington Somset
88 B4 Fiddington Sands Wilts
47 F2 Fiddleford Dorset
337 G5 Fiddler's Ferry Sefton
310 B2 Fiddler's Ferry Warrtn
571 K3 Fiddler's Green Abers
162 D5 Fiddler's Green Gloucs
160 D2 Fiddler's Green Herefs
248 D5 Fiddler's Green Norfk
145 G4 Fiddlers Hamlet Essex
599 M7 Fidigeadh W Isls
185 F4 Field Herefs
85 H6 Field Somset
273 F3 Field Staffs
139 E2 Field Assarts Oxon
365 E3 Field Broughton Cumb
94 C1 Field Common Surrey
260 D4 Field Dalling Norfk
80 A3 Field Green Kent
240 A3 Field Head Leics
143 E3 Fields End Herts
185 H4 Field's Place Herefs
68 C5 Fifehead Magdalen Dorset
47 E2 Fifehead Neville Dorset
47 E2 Fifehead St Quintin Dorset
569 G5 Fife Keith Moray
164 C6 Fifield Oxon
117 F4 Fifield W & M
88 D4 Fifield Wilts
69 H4 Fifield Bavant Wilts
89 E5 Figheldean Wilts
111 G2 Filands Wilts
251 F2 Filby Norfk
251 F2 Filby Heath Norfk
139 H3 Filchampstead Oxon
57 F4 Filching E Susx
375 E3 Filey N York
30 A3 Filford Dorset
194 B5 Filgrave M Keyn
12 A1 Filham Devon
138 C4 Filkins Oxon
40 D2 Filleigh Devon
41 E5 Filleigh Devon
318 A2 Fillingham Lincs
214 D2 Fillongley Warwks
73 G4 Filmore Hill Hants
109 G4 Filton S Glos
109 G6 Filwood Park Bristl
359 G2 Fimber E R Yk
527 G3 Finavon Angus
493 F4 Finchairn Ag & B
309 F1 Fincham Lpool
246 D3 Fincham Norfk
92 C3 Finchampstead Wokham
52 C2 Finchdean Hants
172 D3 Finchingfield Essex
119 F1 Finchley Gt Lon
514 B5 Fincraigs Fife
275 E3 Findern Derbys
567 J4 Findhorn Moray
569 H2 Findochty Moray
512 B5 Findo Gask P & K
557 G5 Findon Abers
54 D3 Findon W Susx
565 L4 Findon Mains Highld
54 D3 Findon Valley W Susx
218 C5 Finedon Nhants
159 F2 Fine Street Herefs
225 H6 Fingal Street Suffk
559 H4 Fingask Abers
211 G5 Fingest Bucks
281 E5 Finghall N York
121 E5 Fingland Cumb
51 G4 Fingland D & G
101 F5 Finglesham Kent
174 D5 Fingringhoe Essex
215 E4 Finham Covtry
329 E5 Finkle Street Barns
509 J3 Finlarig Stirlg
166 D3 Finmere Oxon
522 F4 Finnart P & K
311 H3 Finney Green Ches
225 E6 Finney Green Staffs
225 H6 Finningham Suffk
330 C5 Finningley Donc
571 G6 Finnygaud Abers
595 H5 Finsbay W Isls
119 G3 Finsbury Gt Lon
119 G3 Finsbury Park Gt Lon
213 E6 Finstall Worcs
365 E2 Finsthwaite Cumb
139 F1 Finstock Oxon
600 E2 Finstown Ork
570 D5 Fintry Abers
514 C3 Fintry C Dund
484 C1 Fintry Stirlg
214 B6 Finwood Warwks
540 B5 Finzean Abers
504 C6 Fionnphort Ag & B
595 H5 Fionnsabhagh W Isls
379 H6 Firbank Cumb
315 H2 Firbeck Rothm
358 D1 Firby N York
370 B2 Firby N York

326 D2 Firgrove Rochdl
565 L3 Firhill Highld
56 D3 Firle E Susx
301 E2 Firsby Lincs
71 E3 Firsdown Wilts
325 E4 Firs Lane Highld
573 H5 First Coast Highld
326 B6 Firswood Traffd
451 G5 Firth Border
606 F3 Firth Shet
383 H2 Firth Moor Darltn
528 C6 Firth Muir of Boysack Angus
314 D1 Firth Park Sheff
99 E6 Fir Toll Kent
394 C3 Fir Tree Dur
314 D1 Fir Vale Sheff
325 G2 Firwood Fold Bolton
51 G6 Fishbourne IoW
53 E4 Fishbourne W Susx
395 H3 Fishburn Dur
499 E5 Fishcross Clacks
559 F2 Fisherford Abers
168 B2 Fishermead M Keyn
488 C5 Fisherrow E Loth
55 G3 Fishersgate W Susx
72 C5 Fisher's Pond Hants
75 F3 Fisherstreet W Susx
566 C6 Fisherton Highld
432 C1 Fisherton S Ayrs
69 G2 Fisherton de la Mere Wilts
566 F5 Fishertown Highld
238 B3 Fisherwick Staffs
117 E3 Fishery W & M
151 G2 Fishguard Pembks
331 E2 Fishlake Donc
24 D1 Fishleigh Devon
25 E1 Fishleigh Castle Devon
251 E2 Fishley Norfk
237 E4 Fishley Wsall
280 C2 Fishmere End Lincs
29 G3 Fishpond Bottom Dorset
110 A4 Fishponds Bristl
326 B3 Fishpool Bury
161 F4 Fishpool Gloucs
356 A5 Fishpool N York
208 C6 Fishpools Powys
281 E1 Fishtoft Lincs
300 B5 Fishtoft Drove Lincs
474 D4 Fishwick Border
339 E4 Fishwick Lancs
544 E3 Fiskavaig Highld
318 C5 Fiskerton Lincs
296 D4 Fiskerton Notts
348 D3 Fitling E R Yk
88 D5 Fittleton Wilts
75 F6 Fittleworth W Susx
245 F2 Fitton End Cambs
326 D4 Fitton Hill Oldham
270 A6 Fitz Shrops
43 F2 Fitzhead Somset
329 G1 Fitzwilliam Wakefd
518 F6 Fiunary Highld
134 D2 Five Acres Gloucs
78 B5 Five Ash Down E Susx
78 D5 Five Ashes E Susx
63 H3 Five Bells Somset
187 E5 Five Bridges Herefs
310 A4 Fivecrosses Ches
44 D3 Fivehead Somset
36 C3 Five Houses IoW
351 H4 Five Lane Ends Lancs
16 B2 Fivelanes Cnwll
109 E1 Five Lanes Mons
97 F5 Five Oak Green Kent
35 i7 Five Oaks Jersey
75 H5 Five Oaks W Susx
128 C3 Five Roads Carmth
214 C6 Five Ways Warwks
98 C4 Five Wents Kent
342 B5 Fixby Kirk
80 C5 Flackley Ash E Susx
147 F1 Flack's Green Essex
117 E2 Flackwell Heath Bucks
189 E5 Fladbury Worcs
189 E5 Fladbury Cross Worcs
605 H4 Fladdabister Shet
313 F6 Flagg Derbys
187 E4 Flaggoners Green Herefs
375 G5 Flamborough E R Yk
143 F2 Flamstead Herts
144 D4 Flamstead End Herts
53 H4 Flansham W Susx
343 F5 Flanshaw Wakefd
341 H2 Flappit Spring Brad
354 B3 Flasby N York
292 D1 Flash Staffs
542 F6 Flashader Highld
75 F5 Flathurst W Susx
143 E4 Flaunden Herts
297 E6 Flawborough Notts
357 F1 Flawith N York
109 F6 Flax Bourton N Som
356 D3 Flaxby N York
275 F1 Flaxholme Derbys
249 F6 Flaxlands Norfk
135 F1 Flaxley Gloucs
340 B5 Flax Moss Lancs
64 B4 Flaxpool Somset
358 C2 Flaxton N York
240 D6 Fleckney Leics
192 B2 Flecknoe Warwks
317 F5 Fledborough Notts
32 A3 Fleet Dorset
52 C4 Fleet Hants
92 D4 Fleet Hants
281 E5 Fleet Lincs
121 E5 Fleet Downs Kent
51 F3 Fleetend Hants
281 E5 Fleet Hargate Lincs
51 G4 Fleetlands Hants
354 C2 Fleets N York
350 D5 Fleetwood Lancs
251 E2 Fleggburgh Norfk
599 L7 Fleisirin W Isls
396 A1 Fleming Field Dur
101 F4 Flemings Kent
105 G5 Flemingston V Glam
467 G3 Flemington S Lans
467 H6 Flemington S Lans
223 G6 Flempton Suffk
599 E3 Fleoideabhagh W Isls
15 F5 Fletchersbridge Cnwll
96 D4 Fletcher's Green Kent
399 F6 Fletchertown Cumb
78 A5 Fletching E Susx
77 H5 Fletching Common E Susx
132 C5 Fleur-de-Lis Caerph
23 E1 Flexbury Cnwll
72 B5 Flexford Hants
93 F5 Flexford Surrey
388 B3 Flimby Cumb
79 G3 Flimwell E Susx
308 C5 Flint Flints
197 F6 Flint Cross Cambs
296 D5 Flintham Notts
405 E4 Flint Hill Dur
308 B5 Flint Mountain Flints
348 D2 Flinton E R Yk
214 D3 Flint's Green Solhll
185 F3 Flintsham Herefs
79 H2 Flishinghurst Kent

253 E2 Flitcham Norfk
380 D2 Flitholme Cumb
169 F2 Flitton Beds
169 E3 Flitwick Beds
332 B1 Flixborough N Linc
332 B2 Flixborough Stather N Linc
374 C4 Flixton N York
226 C2 Flixton Suffk
325 G6 Flixton Traffd
328 C2 Flockton Kirk
328 D1 Flockton Green Kirk
328 C2 Flockton Moor Kirk
592 E6 Flodaigh W Isls
453 H2 Flodden Nthumb
543 H2 Flodigarry Highld
185 E3 Floodgates Herefs
245 E6 Flood's Ferry Cambs
49 E1 Flood Street Hants
365 E4 Flookburgh Cumb
249 G5 Flordon Norfk
192 D3 Flore Nhants
272 D1 Florence C Stke
442 B4 Flotterton Nthumb
142 A5 Flowers Bottom Bucks
57 G2 Flowers Green E Susx
326 D5 Flowery Field Tamesd
201 E5 Flowton Suffk
484 B5 Fluchter E Duns
607 G5 Flugarth Shet
607 G5 Flukes Hole Shet
327 H3 Flush House Kirk
571 J6 Flushing Abers
5 F2 Flushing Cnwll
28 A4 Fluxton Devon
189 E4 Flyford Flavell Worcs
226 B5 Foals Green Suffk
121 H3 Fobbing Thurr
568 E4 Fochabers Moray
132 B3 Fochriw Caerph
346 B6 Fockerby N Linc
246 C3 Fodderstone Gap Norfk
565 J5 Fodderty Highld
67 F4 Foddington Somset
231 F2 Foel Powys
128 D2 Foel-Gastell Carmth
527 F5 Foffarty Angus
345 H2 Foggathorpe E R Yk
312 B2 Foggbrook Stockp
473 H5 Fogo Border
606 B6 Fogrigarth Shet
568 C4 Fogwatt Moray
584 C7 Foindle Highld
526 A2 Folda Angus
340 D6 Fold Head Lancs
301 E4 Fold Hill Lincs
328 D6 Foldrings Sheff
273 F2 Fole Staffs
215 F3 Foleshill Covtry
46 C2 Folke Dorset
82 D3 Folkestone Kent
279 F3 Folkingham Lincs
57 E4 Folkington E Susx
219 G1 Folksworth Cambs
374 C4 Folkton N York
559 G3 Folla Rule Abers
356 C4 Follifoot N York
405 H2 Follingsby Gatesd
211 F5 Folley Shrops
46 D4 Folly Dorset
151 F5 Folly Pembks
39 F6 Folly Cross Devon
25 E3 Folly Gate Devon
173 F4 Folly Green Essex
105 G6 Fonmon V Glam
23 E4 Fonston Cnwll
69 F3 Fonthill Bishop Wilts
69 F3 Fonthill Gifford Wilts
47 G1 Fontmell Magna Dorset
47 F2 Fontmell Parva Dorset
53 H3 Fontwell W Susx
105 G6 Font-y-Gary V Glam
502 B1 Foodieash Fife
313 G4 Foolow Derbys
163 F4 Footbridge Gloucs
237 G4 Footherley Staffs
211 F5 Footrid Worcs
120 C5 Foots Cray Gt Lon
554 C2 Forbestown Abers
364 D1 Force Forge Cumb
96 B3 Force Green Kent
364 D1 Force Mills Cumb
383 E2 Forcett N York
493 E4 Ford Ag & B
141 G3 Ford Bucks
11 E2 Ford C Plym
315 E3 Ford Derbys
11 H3 Ford Devon
12 D4 Ford Devon
28 D2 Ford Devon
39 F3 Ford Devon
163 G4 Ford Gloucs
186 C3 Ford Herefs
100 D2 Ford Kent
454 A2 Ford Nthumb
151 G4 Ford Pembks
323 F5 Ford Sefton
233 H2 Ford Shrops
43 E2 Ford Somset
85 G4 Ford Somset
293 E4 Ford Staffs
54 B4 Ford W Susx
70 D3 Ford Wilts
111 E5 Ford Wilts
24 D4 Forda Devon
60 C4 Forda Devon
214 B2 Fordbridge Solhll
78 C1 Fordcombe Kent
500 B2 Fordel P & K
487 G2 Fordell Fife
232 D4 Forden Powys
146 D1 Ford End Essex
171 F3 Ford End Essex
10 D2 Forder Cnwll
19 G4 Forder Green Devon
65 F5 Fordgate Somset
292 A4 Ford Green C Stke
351 G5 Ford Green Lancs
222 C5 Fordham Cambs
174 B4 Fordham Essex
246 C5 Fordham Norfk
174 B4 Fordham Heath Essex
233 H2 Ford Heath Shrops
454 B2 Ford Hill Nthumb
236 D4 Fordhouses Wolves
510 D5 Fordie P & K
49 E1 Fordingbridge Hants
320 D5 Fordington Lincs
431 E5 Fordley N Tyne
374 D4 Fordon E R Yk
540 D4 Fordoun Abers
78 A4 Ford's Green E Susx
201 E1 Ford's Green Suffk
174 B4 Fordstreet Essex
43 G4 Ford Street Somset
26 C3 Fordton Devon
29 F2 Fordwater Devon
138 D2 Fordwells Oxon
100 C4 Fordwich Kent
569 K3 Fordyce Abers
272 C5 Forebridge Staffs
367 G6 Foredale N York
550 F4 Foregin Highld

688 City, town and village index: Forehill - Gateford

444 D5 **Forehill** S Ayrs
37 G3 **Foreland Fields** IoW
275 E4 **Foremark** Derbys
34 C4 **Forest** Guern
353 F4 **Forest Becks** Lancs
442 D5 **Forestburn Gate** Nthumb
159 E5 **Forest Coal Pit** Mons
95 H2 **Forestdale** Gt Lon
120 B2 **Forest Gate** Gt Lon
52 A2 **Forest Gate** Hants
136 B4 **Forest Green** Gloucs
76 B1 **Forest Green** Surrey
431 E6 **Forest Hall** N Tyne
401 G3 **Forest Head** Cumb
119 H5 **Forest Hill** Gt Lon
140 C3 **Forest Hill** Oxon
113 F6 **Forest Hill** Wilts
340 C4 **Forest Holme** Lancs
393 E4 **Forest-in-Teesdale** Dur
356 C3 **Forest Lane Head** N York
499 E6 **Forest Mill** Clacks
356 C3 **Forest Moor** N York
39 E5 **Forestreet** Devon
78 A2 **Forest Row** E Susx
36 D3 **Forest Side** IoW
52 D2 **Forestside** W Susx
295 H2 **Forest Town** Notts
87 E2 **Forewoods Common** Wilts
527 G4 **Forfar** Angus
512 C6 **Forgandenny** P & K
6 C4 **Forge** Cnwll
230 B5 **Forge** Powys
133 E5 **Forge Hammer** Torfn
132 D3 **Forge Side** Torfn
468 A3 **Forgewood** N Lans
568 F5 **Forgie** Moray
569 L6 **Forgue** Abers
213 F4 **Forhill** Worcs
323 E3 **Formby** Sefton
249 F6 **Forncett End** Norfk
249 G6 **Forncett St Mary** Norfk
249 G6 **Forncett St Peter** Norfk
525 G6 **Forneth** P & K
199 G1 **Fornham All Saints** Suffk
223 H6 **Fornham St Genevieve** Suffk
199 H1 **Fornham St Martin** Suffk
22 B4 **Forrabury** Cnwll
567 J5 **Forres** Moray
468 D1 **Forrestfield** N Lans
173 F3 **Forry's Green** Essex
273 E1 **Forsbrook** Staffs
583 H3 **Forse** Highld
213 G5 **Forshaw Heath** Warwks
587 J8 **Forsinard** Highld
98 A3 **Forstal** Kent
31 F3 **Forston** Dorset
548 F8 **Fort Augustus** Highld
526 A2 **Forter** Angus
499 H1 **Forteviot** P & K
566 D5 **Fort George** Highld
469 E4 **Forth** S Lans
162 C3 **Forthampton** Gloucs
135 G5 **Forthay** Gloucs
61 E5 **Fort Hill** Devon
34 b2 **Fort Hommet** Guern
487 F4 **Forth Road Bridge** C Edin
523 K6 **Fortingall** P & K
119 F2 **Fortis Green** Gt Lon
35 e1 **Fort le Marchant** Guern
482 C4 **Fort Matilda** Inver
51 H4 **Forton** Hants
90 C6 **Forton** Hants
351 G4 **Forton** Lancs
234 A1 **Forton** Shrops
29 F1 **Forton** Somset
271 G5 **Forton** Staffs
234 A1 **Forton Heath** Shrops
561 E1 **Fortrie** Abers
570 B6 **Fortrie** Abers
566 C5 **Fortrose** Highld
32 B5 **Fortuneswell** Dorset
533 H8 **Fort William** Highld
117 F1 **Forty Green** Bucks
141 G4 **Forty Green** Bucks
144 D5 **Forty Hill** Gt Lon
201 E2 **Forward Green** Suffk
136 C4 **Forwood** Gloucs
89 H3 **Fosbury** Wilts
164 D5 **Foscot** Oxon
167 F2 **Foscote** Bucks
193 E5 **Foscote** Nhants
111 F4 **Foscote** Wilts
280 D3 **Fosdyke** Lincs
280 D3 **Fosdyke Bridge** Lincs
523 L4 **Foss** P & K
137 G2 **Fossebridge** Gloucs
180 B2 **Foss-y-Ffin** Cerdgn
99 H2 **Fostall** Kent
80 B2 **Fosten Green** Kent
331 E2 **Fosterhouses** Donc
193 E4 **Foster's Booth** Nhants
189 E1 **Foster's Green** Worcs
145 G3 **Foster Street** Essex
274 B3 **Foston** Derbys
240 D6 **Foston** Leics
297 G6 **Foston** Lincs
358 C1 **Foston** N York
361 E3 **Foston on the Wolds** E R Yk
320 B1 **Fotherby** Lincs
388 B3 **Fothergill** Cumb
243 F6 **Fotheringhay** Nhants
601 J4 **Foubister** Ork
245 G1 **Foul Anchor** Cambs
400 D5 **Foulbridge** Cumb
474 D3 **Foulden** Border
247 F5 **Foulden** Norfk
166 C4 **Foul End** Warwks
238 C6 **Foulford** Hants
49 F3 **Foul Mile** E Susx
57 F1 **Foulrice** E Susx
57 F4 **Foulride Green** E Susx
354 A6 **Foulridge** Lancs
254 D3 **Foulsham** Norfk
3 G2 **Foundry** Cnwll
255 E2 **Foundry Hill** Norfk
104 D3 **Fountain** Brdgnd
471 H5 **Fountainhall** Border
142 B5 **Four Ashes** Bucks
214 A4 **Four Ashes** Solhll
212 B4 **Four Ashes** Staffs
236 D3 **Four Ashes** Staffs
224 D5 **Four Ashes** Suffk
34 c3 **Four Cabots** Guern
231 G3 **Four Crosses** Powys
269 E6 **Four Crosses** Powys
237 E3 **Four Crosses** Staffs
288 B4 **Four Crosses** Wrexhm
44 B6 **Four Elms** Devon
96 C5 **Four Elms** Kent
67 F3 **Four Foot** Somset
64 D4 **Four Forks** Somset
325 E3 **Four Gates** Bolton
245 F1 **Four Gotes** Cambs
91 G1 **Four Houses Corner** W Berk
328 D4 **Four Lane End** Barns
339 G4 **Four Lane Ends** Bl w D
342 B3 **Four Lane Ends** Brad
325 H2 **Four Lane Ends** Bury
6 C6 **Four Lanes** Cnwll
291 G3 **Fourlanes End** Ches
73 G2 **Four Marks** Hants
302 C5 **Four Mile Bridge** IoA
136 B2 **Four Mile Elm** Gloucs
80 C5 **Four Oaks** E Susx
161 F4 **Four Oaks** Gloucs
99 F2 **Four Oaks** Kent
214 C3 **Four Oaks** Solhll
237 H5 **Four Oaks Park** Birm
577 H5 **Fourpenny** Highld
115 F4 **Four Points** W Berk
163 F1 **Four Pools** Worcs
128 C3 **Four Roads** Carmth
428 D6 **Fourstones** Nthumb
79 H4 **Four Throws** Kent
146 C2 **Four Wantz** Essex
79 H2 **Four Wents** Kent
79 H3 **Four Wents** Kent
69 H4 **Fovant** Wilts
561 E5 **Foveran** Abers
9 E3 **Fowey** Cnwll
65 F4 **Fowler's Plot** Somset
325 F5 **Fowley Common** Warrtn
513 H3 **Fowlis** Angus
511 G5 **Fowlis Wester** P & K
197 F5 **Fowlmere** Cambs
160 D3 **Fownhope** Herefs
175 E3 **Foxash Estate** Essex
466 C2 **Foxbar** Rens
120 B5 **Foxbury** Gt Lon
140 A4 **Foxcombe Hill** Oxon
168 C4 **Fox Corner** Beds
93 G4 **Fox Corner** Surrey
163 F6 **Foxcote** Gloucs
86 C3 **Foxcote** Somset
322 d7 **Foxdale** IoM
91 E4 **Foxdown** Hants
199 G6 **Foxearth** Essex
97 G1 **Foxendown** Kent
363 E4 **Foxfield** Cumb
215 E3 **Foxford** Covtry
111 H4 **Foxham** Wilts
146 B5 **Fox Hatch** Essex
86 D2 **Fox Hill** BaNES
187 F5 **Fox Hill** Herefs
50 B2 **Foxhills** Hants
8 B3 **Foxhole** Cnwll
23 F3 **Foxhole** Cnwll
249 H5 **Foxhole** Norfk
103 E4 **Fox Hole** Swans
374 C5 **Foxholes** N York
69 E1 **Fox Holes** Wilts
78 C6 **Foxhunt Green** E Susx
93 E3 **Fox Lane** Hants
185 H5 **Foxley** Herefs
254 D3 **Foxley** Norfk
291 F4 **Foxley** Staffs
111 F2 **Foxley** Wilts
189 F1 **Foxlydiate** Worcs
342 D6 **Fox Royd** Kirk
174 D4 **Fox Street** Essex
292 D5 **Foxt** Staffs
197 F5 **Foxton** Cambs
395 H5 **Foxton** Dur
217 F2 **Foxton** Leics
384 C5 **Foxton** N York
367 H4 **Foxup** N York
310 C6 **Foxwist Green** Ches
211 E4 **Foxwood** Shrops
160 D4 **Foy** Herefs
549 H5 **Foyers** Highld
3 G3 **Fraddam** Cnwll
7 H2 **Fraddon** Cnwll
238 A2 **Fradley** Staffs
238 A2 **Fradley Junction** Staffs
238 A2 **Fradley South** Staffs
273 E3 **Fradswell** Staffs
361 F2 **Fraisthorpe** E R Yk
78 B5 **Framfield** E Susx
250 B4 **Framingham Earl** Norfk
250 B4 **Framingham Pigot** Norfk
202 B2 **Framlingham** Suffk
31 E3 **Frampton** Dorset
280 D2 **Frampton** Lincs
110 B3 **Frampton Cotterell** S Glos
163 F3 **Frampton Court** Gloucs
110 B3 **Frampton End** S Glos
136 D4 **Frampton Mansell** Gloucs
135 H3 **Frampton on Severn** Gloucs
280 C1 **Frampton West End** Lincs
201 G3 **Framsden** Suffk
405 G6 **Framwellgate Moor** Dur
136 D4 **France Lynch** Gloucs
212 B4 **Franche** Worcs
310 C4 **Frandley** Ches
308 B2 **Frankby** Wirral
256 B5 **Frankfort** Norfk
186 C5 **Franklands Gate** Herefs
213 E3 **Frankley** Worcs
213 E3 **Frankley Green** Worcs
213 E4 **Frankley Hill** Worcs
184 B3 **Frank's Bridge** Powys
215 G5 **Frankton** Warwks
234 B2 **Frankwell** Shrops
255 E5 **Frans Green** Norfk
78 D2 **Frant** E Susx
571 J2 **Fraserburgh** Abers
175 E5 **Frating** Essex
175 E5 **Frating Green** Essex
52 B4 **Fratton** C Port
238 C5 **Freasley** Warwks
10 C3 **Freathy** Cnwll
314 D3 **Frecheville** Sheff
222 D5 **Freckenham** Suffk
338 B4 **Freckleton** Lancs
94 D4 **Fredley** Surrey
314 C5 **Freebirch** Derbys
277 H6 **Freeby** Leics
90 D5 **Freefolk** Hants
273 F1 **Freehay** Staffs
139 G2 **Freeland** Oxon
483 G6 **Freeland** Rens
255 G4 **Freeland Corner** Norfk
50 C2 **Freemantle** C Sotn
469 G2 **Freeport Village** W Loth
606 F7 **Freester** Shet
251 E3 **Freethorpe** Norfk
326 B2 **Free Town** Bury
145 E5 **Freezy Water** Gt Lon
300 C6 **Freiston** Lincs
300 C6 **Freiston Shore** Lincs
60 D5 **Fremington** Devon
382 B5 **Fremington** N York
110 A4 **Frenchay** S Glos
25 G5 **Frenchbeer** Devon
173 E5 **Frenches Green** Essex
71 F4 **Frenchmoor** Hants
96 C4 **French Street** Kent
338 D4 **Frenchwood** Lancs
74 C1 **Frensham** Surrey
225 F3 **Frenze** Norfk
587 K3 **Fresgoe** Highld
112 D3 **Freshbrook** Swindn
323 E3 **Freshfield** Sefton
86 D2 **Freshford** BaNES
36 A3 **Freshwater** IoW
36 A3 **Freshwater Bay** IoW
125 H5 **Freshwater East** Pembks
226 A4 **Fressingfield** Suffk
176 C2 **Freston** Suffk
589 K3 **Freswick** Highld
135 G3 **Fretherne** Gloucs
256 A6 **Frettenham** Norfk
501 E3 **Freuchie** Fife
526 B2 **Freuchies** Angus
125 F2 **Freystrop** Pembks
64 C4 **Friarn** Somset
237 F6 **Friar Park** Sandw
49 F6 **Friars Cliff** Dorset
78 B3 **Friar's Gate** E Susx
59 E4 **Friar's Hill** E Susx
512 D5 **Friarton** P & K
31 E5 **Friar Waddon** Dorset
245 G3 **Friday Bridge** Cambs
145 E6 **Friday Hill** Gt Lon
202 C4 **Friday Street** Suffk
202 D2 **Friday Street** Suffk
94 C5 **Friday Street** Surrey
359 G3 **Fridaythorpe** E R Yk
144 C6 **Friern Barnet** Gt Lon
516 F5 **Friesland** Ag & B
318 D3 **Friesthorpe** Lincs
298 A5 **Frieston** Lincs
116 C2 **Frieth** Bucks
43 H2 **Frieze Hill** Somset
295 F4 **Friezeland** Notts
139 G5 **Frilford** Oxon
139 G5 **Frilford Heath** Oxon
115 E5 **Frilsham** W Berk
93 E3 **Frimley** Surrey
93 E3 **Frimley Green** Surrey
93 E3 **Frimley Ridge** Surrey
122 A6 **Frindsbury** Medway
259 E5 **Fring** Norfk
166 C4 **Fringford** Oxon
98 C3 **Friningham** Kent
173 E2 **Frinkle Green** Essex
98 D3 **Frinsted** Kent
176 D6 **Frinton-on-Sea** Essex
528 C5 **Friockheim** Angus
229 E2 **Friog** Gwynd
241 E4 **Frisby** Leics
277 E6 **Frisby on the Wreake** Leics
301 E3 **Friskney** Lincs
301 E3 **Friskney Eaudyke** Lincs
301 E4 **Friskney Tofts** Lincs
57 E5 **Friston** E Susx
203 E2 **Friston** Suffk
294 D4 **Fritchley** Derbys
99 E3 **Frith** Kent
49 G2 **Fritham** Hants
300 B5 **Frith Bank** Lincs
211 F6 **Frith Common** Worcs
39 G4 **Frithelstock** Devon
39 F4 **Frithelstock Stone** Devon
74 C2 **Frithend** Hants
142 C4 **Frith-Hill** Bucks
93 G6 **Frith Hill** Surrey
143 E3 **Frithsden** Herts
300 B4 **Frithville** Lincs
80 B1 **Frittenden** Kent
13 E4 **Frittiscombe** Devon
250 A6 **Fritton** Norfk
251 F4 **Fritton** Norfk
257 E6 **Fritton** Norfk
166 B4 **Fritwell** Oxon
342 B2 **Frizinghall** Brad
376 C1 **Frizington** Cumb
199 F2 **Frizzeler's Green** Suffk
590 E2 **Frobost** W Isls
136 A4 **Frocester** Gloucs
233 E3 **Frochas** Powys
234 C4 **Frodesley** Shrops
332 B2 **Frodingham** N Linc
310 A4 **Frodsham** Ches
197 E4 **Frog End** Cambs
198 A3 **Frog End** Cambs
314 A4 **Froggatt** Derbys
292 D5 **Froghall** Staffs
49 F2 **Frogham** Hants
100 D5 **Frogham** Kent
96 B4 **Froghole** Kent
82 C3 **Frogholt** Kent
110 A3 **Frogland Cross** S Glos
102 C3 **Frog Moor** Swans
12 D4 **Frogmore** Devon
73 G5 **Frogmore** Hants
92 D2 **Frogmore** Hants
143 H4 **Frogmore** Herts
87 F4 **Frogmore** Wilts
444 D4 **Frognal** S Ayrs
243 H2 **Frognall** Lincs
7 E5 **Frogpool** Cnwll
188 B1 **Frog Pool** Worcs
172 B2 **Frogs' Green** Essex
256 A2 **Frogshall** Norfk
16 D5 **Frogwell** Cnwll
216 B1 **Frolesworth** Leics
86 D5 **Frome** Somset
135 H3 **Fromebridge** Gloucs
86 D5 **Fromefield** Somset
30 D2 **Frome St Quintin** Dorset
187 F5 **Fromes Hill** Herefs
186 C5 **Fromington** Herefs
287 F1 **Fron** Denbgs
263 F3 **Fron** Gwynd
283 F5 **Fron** Gwynd
184 A1 **Fron** Powys
231 E4 **Fron** Powys
232 C5 **Fron** Powys
232 D4 **Fron** Powys
269 E2 **Fron** Shrops
268 D1 **Fron-Bache** Denbgs
269 E1 **Froncysyllte** Wrexhm
288 C5 **Fron-dêg** Wrexhm
267 E2 **Frongoch** Gwynd
269 E1 **Fron Isaf** Wrexhm
26 B1 **Frost** Devon
227 F3 **Frostenden** Suffk
227 F3 **Frostenden Corner** Suffk
394 A2 **Frosterley** Dur
84 D2 **Frost Hill** N Som
50 D3 **Frostlane** Hants
248 D4 **Frost Row** Norfk
602 E6 **Frotoft** Ork
168 D3 **Froxfield** Beds
113 G6 **Froxfield** Wilts
73 H4 **Froxfield Green** Hants
72 B5 **Fryern Hill** Hants
146 C4 **Fryerning** Essex
121 H2 **Fryerns** Essex
372 C4 **Fryton** N York
70 C3 **Fugglestone St Peter** Wilts
298 A4 **Fulbeck** Lincs
430 C2 **Fulbeck** Nthumb
197 H3 **Fulbourn** Cambs
138 D2 **Fulbrook** Oxon
72 C4 **Fulflood** Hants
43 H2 **Fulford** Somset
273 E2 **Fulford** Staffs
358 B5 **Fulford** York
119 E4 **Fulham** Gt Lon
55 F2 **Fulking** W Susx
60 D3 **Fullabrook** Devon
467 F2 **Fullarton** C Glas
444 D2 **Fullarton** N Ayrs
172 A4 **Fuller's End** Essex
289 G4 **Fuller's Moor** Ches
147 E1 **Fuller Street** Essex
71 H2 **Fullerton** Hants
320 A5 **Fulletby** Lincs
328 C4 **Fullshaw** Barns
358 D3 **Full Sutton** E R Yk
120 B1 **Fullwell Cross** Gt Lon
466 B4 **Fullwood** E Ayrs
326 D3 **Fullwood** Oldham
260 C5 **Fulmodeston** Norfk
342 D3 **Fulneck** Leeds
318 D4 **Fulnetby** Lincs
280 C5 **Fulney** Lincs
190 D5 **Fulready** Warwks
311 G3 **Fulshaw Park** Ches
328 B3 **Fulstone** Kirk
334 D5 **Fulstow** Lincs
396 B5 **Fulthorpe** S on T
165 F5 **Fulwell** Oxon
406 B3 **Fulwell** Sundld
338 D3 **Fulwood** Lancs
314 C2 **Fulwood** Sheff
43 H3 **Fulwood** Somset
314 B2 **Fulwood Hall** Sheff
314 B3 **Fulwood Head** Sheff
249 F5 **Fundenhall** Norfk
52 D3 **Funtington** W Susx
51 G3 **Funtley** Hants
510 C4 **Funtulich** P & K
609 K6 **Funzie** Shet
30 B3 **Furleigh Cross** Dorset
29 E2 **Furley** Devon
493 H5 **Furnace** Ag & B
128 B4 **Furnace** Carmth
128 D4 **Furnace** Carmth
229 F5 **Furnace** Cerdgn
214 C1 **Furnace End** Warwks
77 E2 **Furnace Green** W Susx
77 F2 **Furnace Wood** W Susx
77 H4 **Furner's Green** E Susx
312 D3 **Furness Vale** Derbys
171 F4 **Furneux Pelham** Herts
44 C6 **Furnham** Somset
171 F3 **Further Ford End** Essex
80 C2 **Further Quarter** Kent
193 G6 **Furtho** Nhants
40 C2 **Furze** Devon
33 G3 **Furzebrook** Dorset
119 F5 **Furzedown** Gt Lon
71 H4 **Furzedown** Hants
62 A3 **Furzehill** Devon
48 C4 **Furzehill** Dorset
49 F2 **Furze Hill** Hants
52 A2 **Furzeley Corner** Hants
117 E3 **Furze Platt** W & M
50 C4 **Furzey Lodge** Hants
50 A1 **Furzley** Hants
168 A2 **Furzton** M Keyn
44 A5 **Fyfett** Somset
146 B3 **Fyfield** Essex
138 C4 **Fyfield** Gloucs
89 G5 **Fyfield** Hants
139 G5 **Fyfield** Oxon
112 D6 **Fyfield** Wilts
387 F4 **Fylingthorpe** N York
74 C5 **Fyning** W Susx
559 H2 **Fyvie** Abers

G

106 C4 **Gabalfa** Cardif
599 J3 **Gabhsann Bho Dheas** W Isls
599 J3 **Gabhsann Bho Thuath** W Isls
52 C5 **Gable Head** Hants
576 F5 **Gablon** Highld
466 C4 **Gabroc Hill** E Ayrs
95 E5 **Gadbrook** Surrey
241 E2 **Gaddesby** Leics
143 E3 **Gadebridge** Herts
303 G3 **Gadfa** IoA
162 A3 **Gadfield Elm** Worcs
445 F5 **Gadgirth** S Ayrs
269 G2 **Gadlas** Shrops
131 F4 **Gadlys** Rhondd
121 H5 **Gadshill** Kent
107 E2 **Gaer** Newpt
158 C5 **Gaer** Powys
134 A5 **Gaer-Fawr** Mons
134 A5 **Gaerllwyd** Mons
283 E1 **Gaerwen** IoA
165 G5 **Gagingwell** Oxon
551 J4 **Gaich** Highld
236 D2 **Gailey** Staffs
236 D2 **Gailey Wharf** Staffs
139 E5 **Gainfield** Oxon
383 E1 **Gainford** Dur
97 G5 **Gain Hill** Kent
317 F2 **Gainsborough** Lincs
176 C1 **Gainsborough** Suffk
173 E2 **Gainsford End** Essex
562 D1 **Gairloch** Highld
533 J6 **Gairlochy** Highld
500 B5 **Gairney Bank** P & K
380 A3 **Gaisgill** Cumb
400 C5 **Gaitsgill** Cumb
472 D6 **Galadean** Border
451 F2 **Galashiels** Border
308 B5 **Galdlys** Flints
326 D1 **Gale** Rochdl
351 G3 **Galgate** Lancs
67 G4 **Galhampton** Somset
423 G3 **Gallaberry** D & G
506 D4 **Gallanach** Ag & B
517 G3 **Gallanach** Ag & B
289 H4 **Gallantry Bank** Ches
501 E6 **Gallatown** Fife
215 E1 **Galley Common** Warwks
147 E4 **Galleyend** Essex
298 D5 **Galley Hill** Lincs
320 D4 **Galley Hill** Lincs
147 E4 **Galleywood** Essex
402 C6 **Galligill** Cumb
522 F6 **Gallin** P & K
514 C1 **Gallowfauld** Angus
467 E3 **Gallowhill** C Glas
466 C1 **Gallowhill** Rens
571 K5 **Gallowhills** Abers
120 D1 **Gallows Corner** Gt Lon
172 C4 **Gallows Green** Essex
174 B4 **Gallows Green** Essex
273 G1 **Gallows Green** Staffs
132 D3 **Gallowsgreen** Torfn
188 D2 **Gallows Green** Worcs
115 H3 **Gallowstree Common** Oxon
546 E5 **Galltair** Highld
287 G3 **Galltegfa** Denbgs
284 C2 **Gallt-y-Foel** Gwynd
78 B2 **Gallypot Street** E Susx
43 H3 **Galmington** Somset
530 E6 **Galmisdale** Highld
12 B4 **Galmpton** Devon
13 F1 **Galmpton** Torbay
131 G3 **Galon Uchaf** Myr Td
370 B5 **Galphay** N York
445 H2 **Galston** E Ayrs
542 B6 **Galtrigill** Highld
15 F3 **Gam** Cnwll
343 E3 **Gamble Hill** Leeds
391 G2 **Gamblesby** Cumb
147 F2 **Gamble's Green** Essex
399 H4 **Gamelsby** Cumb
327 E6 **Gamesley** Derbys
196 B4 **Gamlingay** Cambs
196 B4 **Gamlingay Cinques** Cambs
196 B4 **Gamlingay Great Heath** Cambs
39 G2 **Gammaton** Devon
39 G3 **Gammaton Moor** Devon
368 D3 **Gammersgill** N York
276 D2 **Gamston** Notts
316 D4 **Gamston** Notts
134 C1 **Ganarew** Herefs
506 E3 **Ganavan** Ag & B
161 G5 **Ganders Green** Gloucs
16 D5 **Gang** Cnwll
600 D3 **Gangsti Pier** Ork
265 G5 **Ganllwyd** Gwynd
68 C6 **Gannetts** Dorset
540 A5 **Gannochy** Angus
512 D5 **Gannochy** P & K
589 J8 **Gansclet** Highld
348 B3 **Ganstead** E R Yk
372 C5 **Ganthorpe** N York
374 B4 **Ganton** N York
120 B2 **Gants Hill** Gt Lon
144 C5 **Ganwick Corner** Herts
505 J3 **Gaodhail** Ag & B
20 B2 **Gappah** Devon
565 G3 **Garbat** Highld
493 H5 **Garbhallt** Ag & B
537 J4 **Garbh Allt Shiel** Abers
224 D3 **Garboldisham** Norfk
554 B3 **Garchory** Abers
132 C3 **Garden City** Blae G
308 D6 **Garden City** Flints
92 D1 **Gardeners Green** Wokham
570 E3 **Gardenstown** Abers
328 D5 **Garden Village** Sheff
129 E5 **Garden Village** Swans
288 D4 **Garden Village** Wrexhm
606 D8 **Garderhouse** Shet
347 E1 **Gardham** E R Yk
609 G6 **Gardie** Shet
609 J2 **Gardie** Shet
68 C1 **Gare Hill** Somset
482 B1 **Garelochhead** Ag & B
139 G5 **Garford** Oxon
343 H3 **Garforth** Leeds
354 B4 **Gargrave** N York
497 H6 **Gargunnock** Stirlg
479 K4 **Gariob** Ag & B
589 F1 **Gariochsford** Abers
305 E4 **Garizim** Conwy
8 C3 **Garker** Cnwll
43 G4 **Garlandhayes** Devon
400 D4 **Garlands** Cumb
418 C5 **Garleffin** S Ayrs
225 H3 **Garlic Street** Norfk
411 E3 **Garlieston** D & G
41 F2 **Garliford** Devon
101 F2 **Garlinge** Kent
100 B5 **Garlinge Green** Kent
556 D3 **Garlogie** Abers
272 A4 **Garmelow** Staffs
570 E5 **Garmond** Abers
395 G3 **Garmondsway** Dur
505 K2 **Garmony** Ag & B
568 E3 **Garmouth** Moray
235 E3 **Garmston** Shrops
262 D4 **Garn** Gwynd
208 B3 **Garn** Powys
129 G2 **Garnant** Carmth
132 D4 **Garndiffaith** Torfn
284 A6 **Garndolbenmaen** Gwynd
379 F5 **Garnett Bridge** Cumb
172 C6 **Garnetts** Essex
262 D4 **Garnfadryn** Gwynd
484 D6 **Garnkirk** N Lans
132 C2 **Garnlydan** Blae G
281 F5 **Garnsgate** Lincs
129 F3 **Garn-swllt** Swans
132 D3 **Garn-yr-erw** Torfn
599 K8 **Garrabost** W Isls
542 C7 **Garrachan** Highld
543 H3 **Garrafad** Highld
492 D3 **Garraron** Ag & B
4 D4 **Garras** Cnwll
307 G4 **Garreg** Flints
265 E1 **Garreg** Gwynd
233 E2 **Garreg Bank** Powys
214 A2 **Garrets Green** Birm
498 C2 **Garrick** P & K
392 B1 **Garrigill** Cumb
383 E6 **Garriston** N York
421 F3 **Garroch** D & G
408 C4 **Garrochtrie** D & G
543 H4 **Garros** Highld
511 E1 **Garrow** P & K
467 G2 **Garrowhill** C Glas
533 J2 **Garrygualach** Highld
434 A6 **Garryhorn** D & G
367 E2 **Garsdale** Cumb
367 F1 **Garsdale Head** Cumb
111 H2 **Garsdon** Wilts
273 E3 **Garshall Green** Staffs
140 C4 **Garsington** Oxon
351 G6 **Garstang** Lancs
143 G5 **Garston** Herts
309 F3 **Garston** Lpool
476 D5 **Gartbreck** Ag & B
484 D6 **Gartcosh** N Lans
104 D1 **Garth** Brdgnd
205 F3 **Garth** Cerdgn
307 G3 **Garth** Flints
304 C5 **Garth** Gwynd
133 F6 **Garth** Mons
107 E2 **Garth** Newpt
183 E5 **Garth** Powys
209 E5 **Garth** Powys
606 B6 **Garth** Shet
607 G7 **Garth** Shet
288 C6 **Garth** Wrexhm
467 G1 **Garthamlock** C Glas
549 J6 **Garthbeg** Highld
157 G3 **Garthbrengy** Powys
557 G4 **Garthdee** C Aber
181 E3 **Gartheli** Cerdgn
232 C5 **Garthmyl** Powys
278 A5 **Garthorpe** Leics
346 C6 **Garthorpe** N Linc
208 A1 **Garth Owen** Powys
379 F5 **Garth Row** Cumb
288 C6 **Garth Trevor** Wrexhm
468 B2 **Gartlea** N Lans
467 G1 **Gartloch** C Glas
558 C3 **Gartly** Abers
496 D5 **Gartmore** Stirlg
462 C3 **Gartnagrenach** Ag & B
468 B2 **Gartness** N Lans
483 G2 **Gartness** Stirlg
483 F2 **Gartocharn** W Duns
349 E2 **Garton** E R Yk
360 B3 **Garton-on-the-Wolds** E R Yk
467 H1 **Gartsherrie** N Lans
582 D7 **Gartymore** Highld
490 A5 **Garvald** E Loth
478 B3 **Garvard** Ag & B
564 F4 **Garve** Highld
248 D3 **Garvestone** Norfk
481 E1 **Garvie** Ag & B
540 D5 **Garvock** Abers
482 C5 **Garvock** Inver
487 F2 **Garvock Hill** Fife
160 B5 **Garway** Herefs
160 A4 **Garway Hill** Herefs
597 K4 **Garyvard** W Isls
68 C3 **Gasper** Wilts
111 F6 **Gastard** Wilts
224 C3 **Gasthorpe** Norfk
145 G1 **Gaston Green** Essex
212 A2 **Gatacre Park** Shrops
36 D4 **Gatcombe** IoW
309 F2 **Gateacre** Lpool
366 A2 **Gatebeck** Cumb
317 F3 **Gate Burton** Lincs
315 H3 **Gateford** Notts

315 H3 Gateford Common Notts
344 D4 Gateforth N York
445 E2 Gatehead E Ayrs
358 C3 Gate Helmsley N York
428 B2 Gatehouse Nthumb
412 B3 Gatehouse of Fleet D & G
436 B5 Gatelawbridge D & G
254 C3 Gateley Norfk
370 C2 Gatenby N York
377 F1 Gatesgarth Cumb
405 F2 Gateshead Gatesd
289 G2 Gatesheath Ches
527 F6 Gateside Angus
437 F6 Gateside D & G
466 C3 Gateside E Rens
500 C3 Gateside Fife
465 H4 Gateside N Ayrs
436 A4 Gateslack D & G
288 D4 Gatewen Wrexhm
24 A6 Gatherley Devon
324 C3 Gathurst Wigan
133 F6 Gatley Manch
311 G2 Gatlas Newpt
170 C1 Gatley End Cambs
95 F4 Gatton Surrey
451 G2 Gattonside Border
135 G2 Gatwick Gloucs
207 G6 Gaufron Powys
241 E4 Gaulby Leics
514 B5 Gauldry Fife
512 C3 Gauls P & K
290 B5 Gauntons Bank Ches
48 C3 Gaunt's Common Dorset
110 A3 Gaunt's Earthcott S Glos
172 A4 Gaunt's End Essex
319 F5 Gautby Lincs
473 H4 Gavinton Border
329 E3 Gawber Barns
167 E3 Gawcott Bucks
312 A5 Gawsworth Ches
328 B1 Gawthorpe Kirk
343 E5 Gawthorpe Wakefd
366 D2 Gawthrop Cumb
363 F5 Gawthwaite Cumb
147 F4 Gay Bowers Essex
191 F4 Gaydon Warwks
602 F1 Gayfield Ork
194 A5 Gayhurst M Keyn
367 H2 Gayle N York
382 D3 Gayles N York
76 A5 Gay Street W Susx
193 H4 Gayton Nhants
253 E4 Gayton Norfk
273 G4 Gayton Staffs
308 C3 Gayton Wirral
320 C3 Gayton Engine Lincs
320 D3 Gayton le Marsh Lincs
319 G2 Gayton le Wold Lincs
253 E4 Gayton Thorpe Norfk
252 C3 Gaywood Norfk
199 E2 Gazeley Suffk
590 E2 Gearraidh Bhailteas W Isls
597 K4 Gearraidh Bhaird W Isls
591 D8 Gearraidh Gadhal W Isls
590 E4 Gearraidh ma Mònadh W Isls
597 G1 Gearraidh na h-Aibhne W Isls
542 D4 Geary Highld
544 E1 Gearymore Highld
200 B3 Gedding Suffk
218 B3 Geddington Nhants
202 D5 Gedgrave Hall Suffk
545 J2 Gedintailor Highld
296 B6 Gedling Notts
281 F5 Gedney Lincs
281 E5 Gedney Broadgate Lincs
281 G5 Gedney Drove End Lincs
281 F4 Gedney Dyke Lincs
244 D2 Gedney Hill Lincs
326 D6 Gee Cross Tamesd
242 D4 Geeston Rutlnd
288 C4 Gegin Wrexhm
482 D4 Geilston Ag & B
307 F6 Geinas Denbgs
593 D9 Geirinis W Isls
588 E4 Geise Highld
596 E1 Geisiadar W Isls
226 D1 Geldeston Norfk
306 A6 Gell Conwy
152 B6 Gelli Pembks
131 F4 Gelli Rhondd
131 G3 Gellideg Myr Tyd
287 G2 Gellifor Denbgs
132 B5 Gelligaer Caerph
130 B6 Gelli-Gaer Neath
132 C6 Gelligroes Caerph
132 C5 Gelli-hâf Caerph
265 F2 Gellilydan Gwynd
130 A4 Gellinud Neath
286 C6 Gellioedd Conwy
512 C2 Gellyburn P & K
129 H4 Gellygron Neath
153 F5 Gellywen Carmth
275 G6 Gelsmoor Leics
413 E3 Gelston D & G
297 H5 Gelston Lincs
361 E3 Gembling E R Yk
310 B1 Gemini Warrtn
103 F2 Gendros Swans
199 E3 Genesis Green Suffk
415 F5 Genoch Mains D & G
237 G2 Gentleshaw Staffs
595 J4 Geocrab W Isls
425 F1 Georgefield D & G
117 H3 George Green Bucks
60 C3 Georgeham Devon
41 E3 George Nympton Devon
132 B3 Georgetown Blae G
423 G5 Georgetown D & G
3 E2 Georgia Cnwll
602 D6 Georth Ork
129 F3 Gerdinen-isaf Swans
535 H4 Gergask Highld
284 D1 Gerlan Gwynd
24 B4 Germansweek Devon
467 F1 Germiston C Glas
3 G4 Germoe Cnwll
145 G4 Gernon Bushes Essex
5 G1 Gerrans Cnwll
271 H2 Gerrard's Bromley Staffs
117 G2 Gerrards Cross Bucks
386 B2 Gerrick R & Cl
207 E1 Geseilfa Powys
173 G2 Gestingthorpe Essex
232 D2 Geuffordd Powys
268 D1 Geufron Denbgs
206 D2 Geufron Powys
215 E5 Gibbet Hill Covtry
216 B3 Gibbet Hill Leics
310 C4 Gibb Hill Ches
512 B2 Gibbieston P & K
213 F2 Gib Heath Birm
195 E5 Gibraltar Beds
141 F2 Gibraltar Bucks
82 D3 Gibraltar Kent
301 F3 Gibraltar Lincs
166 A6 Gibraltar Oxon
482 D5 Gibshill Inver
296 D5 Gibsmere Notts
111 F5 Giddeahall Wilts
33 E2 Giddy Green Dorset
120 D1 Gidea Park Gt Lon

120 D2 Gidea Park Gt Lon
25 G5 Gidleigh Devon
168 B1 Giffard Park M Keyn
467 E3 Giffnock E Rens
489 G6 Gifford E Loth
501 E2 Giffordtown Fife
326 B3 Gigg Bury
212 C1 Giggetty Staffs
353 F2 Giggleswick N York
94 D1 Giggshill Surrey
151 E5 Gignog Pembks
346 B4 Gilberdyke E R Yk
6 C5 Gilbert's Coombe Cnwll
188 B6 Gilbert's End Worcs
213 H5 Gilbert's Green Warwks
214 A3 Gilbertstone Birm
73 F3 Gilbert Street Hants
472 B1 Gilchriston E Loth
388 D2 Gilcrux Cumb
342 D4 Gildersome Leeds
342 D4 Gildersome Street Leeds
315 G2 Gildingwells Rothm
405 G6 Gilesgate Dur
405 G6 Gilesgate Moor Dur
105 G6 Gileston V Glam
132 B5 Gilfach Caerph
159 F3 Gilfach Herefs
105 F2 Gilfach Goch Rhondd
180 A3 Gilfachreda Cerdgn
388 B5 Gilgarran Cumb
354 C6 Gill N York
372 C2 Gillamoor N York
5 E4 Gillan Cnwll
606 D5 Gillarona Shet
378 C5 Gillbank Cumb
311 H3 Gillbent Stockp
542 D5 Gillen Highld
424 D1 Gillesbie D & G
372 B4 Gilling East N York
68 D4 Gillingham Dorset
98 B1 Gillingham Medway
227 E1 Gillingham Norfk
383 E3 Gilling West N York
323 G5 Gillmoss Lpool
601 H3 Gill of Garth Ork
291 H3 Gillow Heath Staffs
589 J2 Gills Highld
79 H3 Gill's Green Kent
238 C3 Gillway Staffs
450 C5 Gilmanscleuch Border
488 B6 Gilmerton C Edin
511 F5 Gilmerton P & K
382 A2 Gilmonby Dur
216 C2 Gilmorton Leics
446 D1 Gilmourton S Lans
325 C3 Gilnow Bolton
329 E4 Gilroyd Barns
402 A1 Gilsland Nthumb
214 B2 Gilson Warwks
342 B2 Gilstead Brad
472 A3 Gilston Border
145 F2 Gilston Herts
295 F5 Giltbrook Notts
162 B1 Gilver's Lane Worcs
145 E5 Gilwell Park Essex
132 D2 Gilwern Mons
256 B2 Gimingham Norfk
312 C4 Ginclough Ches
57 G2 Ginger's Green E Susx
596 E2 Giosla W Isls
201 E2 Gipping Suffk
299 H5 Gipsey Bridge Lincs
175 E2 Gipsy Row Suffk
347 G4 Gipsyville C KuH
343 F3 Gipton Leeds
444 D1 Girdle Toll N Ayrs
342 B3 Girlington Brad
606 F7 Girlsta Shet
319 G2 Girsby Lincs
384 B3 Girsby N York
67 G5 Girt Somset
412 B4 Girthon D & G
197 F2 Girton Cambs
297 F1 Girton Notts
419 E2 Girvan S Ayrs
353 G5 Gisburn Lancs
227 G2 Gisleham Suffk
225 E5 Gislingham Suffk
225 F2 Gissing Norfk
28 B3 Gittisham Devon
94 D4 Givons Grove Surrey
565 K6 Glackmore Highld
478 B3 Glac Mhòr Ag & B
184 D3 Gladestry Powys
489 F5 Gladsmuir E Loth
549 J2 Glaichbeg Highld
546 D4 Glaick Highld
129 H4 Glais Swans
386 C3 Glaisdale N York
543 K8 Glame Highld
527 E5 Glamis Angus
304 C5 Glan Adda Gwynd
125 F1 Glanafon Pembks
129 G2 Glanaman Carmth
286 A4 Glan Conwy Conwy
181 E4 Glan Denys Cerdgn
260 D3 Glandford Norfk
132 D4 Glandwr Caerph
152 D4 Glandwr Pembks
284 A6 Glan Dwyfach Gwynd
152 A4 Glandy Cross Carmth
229 F5 Glandyfi Cerdgn
132 D1 Glangrwyney Powys
231 E5 Glanhanog Powys
208 C1 Glanmule Powys
205 E3 Glanrafon Cerdgn
152 C1 Glanrhyd Pembks
130 B3 Glan-Rhyd Powys
443 E3 Glantlees Nthumb
442 D2 Glanton Nthumb
442 D2 Glanton Pyke Nthumb
46 C3 Glanvilles Wootton Dorset
205 E2 Glanwern Cerdgn
305 H3 Glanwydden Conwy
307 H4 Glan-y-don Flints
106 B3 Glan-y-llyn Rhondd
127 G2 Glan-y-môr Carmth
132 B5 Glan-y-nant Caerph
207 E3 Glan-y-nant Powys
307 G3 Glan-yr-afon Flints
267 E1 Glan-yr-afon Gwynd
267 G1 Glan-yr-afon Gwynd
304 D3 Glan-yr-afon IoA
268 D5 Glan-yr-afon Shrops
265 E3 Glan-y-wern Gwynd
219 E1 Glapthorn Nhants
295 F1 Glapwell Derbys
478 C3 Glas Àird Ag & B
538 B3 Glas-Allt-Shiel Abers
158 C2 Glasbury Powys
306 D5 Glascoed Denbgs
133 F4 Glascoed Mons
208 A2 Glascoed Powys
232 B3 Glascoed Powys
288 C4 Glascoed Powys
154 D6 Glascoed Isaf Carmth
554 C5 Glascorrie Abers
238 C4 Glascote Staffs
184 C4 Glascwm Powys
307 G3 Glasdir Flints
520 E6 Glasdrum Ag & B
286 C5 Glasfryn Conwy

179 G4 Glasgoed Cerdgn
467 E2 Glasgow C Glas
543 H3 Glashvin Highld
304 C6 Glasinfryn Gwynd
107 E2 Glasllwch Newpt
531 J3 Glasnacardoch Highld
545 J7 Glasnakille Highld
229 G5 Glaspwll Powys
548 F3 Glassburn Highld
79 H2 Glassenbury Kent
410 D5 Glasserton D & G
468 A5 Glassford S Lans
344 A5 Glass Houghton Wakefd
161 F5 Glasshouse Gloucs
161 G5 Glasshouse Hill Gloucs
355 G2 Glasshouses N York
570 F4 Glasslaw Abers
500 D3 Glasslie Fife
388 B2 Glasson Cumb
399 G2 Glasson Lancs
351 F3 Glasson Lancs
391 F2 Glassonby Cumb
528 C4 Glasterlaw Angus
66 D2 Glastonbury Somset
219 H2 Glatton Cambs
310 D1 Glazebrook Warrtn
325 F5 Glazebury Warrtn
211 G2 Glazeley Shrops
314 D3 Gleadless Sheff
314 D3 Gleadless Valley Sheff
311 G6 Gleadsmoss Ches
591 D8 Gleann W Isls
590 F4 Gleann dail bho Dheas W Isls
590 F4 Gleann dail bho Tuath W Isls
599 L6 Gleann Tholastaidh W Isls
364 C5 Gleaston Cumb
51 F1 Glebe Hants
549 J6 Glebe Highld
605 J2 Glebe Shet
405 H3 Glebe Sundld
343 F2 Gledhow Leeds
269 E2 Gledrid Shrops
490 A3 Gleghornie E Loth
207 F1 Gleiniant Powys
199 G5 Glemsford Suffk
417 G5 Glen D & G
568 D7 Glenallachie Moray
531 J4 Glenancross Highld
476 E8 Glenastle Ag & B
322 g4 Glenbarr Ag & B
458 D4 Glenbarry Abers
569 K5 Glenbeg Abers
518 E3 Glenbeg Highld
551 J4 Glenbeg Highld
542 F7 Glen Bernisdale Highld
541 E3 Glenbervie Abers
485 E6 Glenboig N Lans
518 F3 Glenborrodale Highld
494 C5 Glenbranter Ag & B
448 D5 Glenbreck Border
470 B1 Glenbrock C Edin
447 E4 Glenbuck E Ayrs
466 C2 Glenburn Rens
430 B4 Glencaple D & G
513 E5 Glencarse P & K
487 G5 Glenceitlein Highld
520 F4 Glencoe Highld
205 F3 Glencraig Fife
422 C2 Glencrosh D & G
542 B7 Glendale Highld
451 G2 Glendearg Border
499 F4 Glendevon P & K
549 G8 Glendoebeg Highld
513 G6 Glendoick P & K
513 G6 Glenduckie Fife
499 E2 Gleneagles Hotel P & K
476 E6 Glenegedale Ag & B
546 E6 Glenelg Highld
500 B2 Glenfarg P & K
240 B3 Glenfield Leics
532 C6 Glenfinnan Highld
500 C1 Glenfoot P & K
465 H4 Glengarnock N Ayrs
518 B4 Glengorm Castle Ag & B
543 G8 Glengrasco Highld
542 D8 Glen Heysdal Highld
18 B5 Glenholt C Plym
421 G2 Glenhoul D & G
519 K2 Glenhurich Highld
438 B2 Glenkerry Border
554 D2 Glenkindie Abers
421 F3 Glenlee D & G
58 B5 Glenleigh Park E Susx
498 B2 Glenlichorn P & K
552 D3 Glenlivet Moray
412 D2 Glenlochar D & G
500 C4 Glenlomond P & K
415 G5 Glenluce D & G
526 B2 Glenmarkie Lodge Angus
485 E6 Glenmavis N Lans
486 C6 Glenmavis W Loth
322 c6 Glen Maye IoM
451 F3 Glenmayne Border
322 g5 Glen Mona IoM
492 D2 Glenmore Ag & B
545 G1 Glenmore Highld
527 E2 Glenmoy Angus
567 G2 Glen of Newmill Moray
527 F2 Glenogil Angus
125 F3 Glenowen Pembks
240 C5 Glen Parva Leics
526 D1 Glenprosen Village Angus
527 F2 Glenquiech Angus
449 H3 Glenrath Border
463 E3 Glenreasdell Mains Ag & B
378 C1 Glenridding Cumb
575 K3 Glen Rossal Highld
501 E4 Glenrothes Fife
519 K6 Glensanda Highld
500 C4 Glensaugh Abers
486 B3 Glensburgh Falk
494 B5 Glen Sluain Ag & B
414 D4 Glenstockadale D & G
481 F4 Glenstriven Ag & B
449 H2 Glenternie Border
318 C1 Glentham Lincs
559 E5 Glenton Abers
450 B2 Glentress Border
420 B4 Glentrool Village D & G
318 A2 Glentworth Lincs
531 J7 Glenuig Highld
507 L4 Glenview Ag & B
486 A4 Glen Village Falk
322 e7 Glen Vine IoM
447 G4 Glespin S Lans
607 G7 Gletness Shet
160 C5 Glewstone Herefs
597 G5 Glib Cheòis W Isls
243 H3 Glinton C Pete
326 D4 Glodwick Oldham
153 E3 Glogue Pembks
241 G5 Glooston Leics
455 F3 Gliororum Nthumb
327 H6 Glossop Derbys
443 H4 Gloster Hill Nthumb
162 A6 Gloucester Gloucs
609 G4 Gloup Shet
7 E5 Gloweth Cnwll
354 C6 Glusburn N York

606 D2 Gluss Shet
293 E1 Glutton Bridge Derbys
14 C6 Gluvian Cnwll
165 G5 Glympton Oxon
134 B5 Glyn Mons
207 E2 Glyn Powys
179 G4 Glynarthen Cerdgn
207 E3 Glynbrochan Powys
130 C4 Glyn Castle Neath
268 D2 Glyn Ceiriog Wrexhm
105 H1 Glyncoch Rhondd
132 C2 Glyncoed Blae G
130 D5 Glyncorrwg Neath
56 C3 Glynde E Susx
56 D2 Glyndebourne E Susx
268 B1 Glyndyfrdwy Denbgs
58 C5 Glyne Gap E Susx
132 C3 Glyn Etwy Blae G
206 D3 Glynhafren Powys
105 E2 Glynllan Brdgnd
269 F2 Glynmorlas Shrops
130 D3 Glynneath Neath
105 F2 Glynogwr Brdgnd
106 A2 Glyntaff Rhondd
130 C1 Glyntawe Powys
272 B5 Gnosall Staffs
272 B5 Gnosall Heath Staffs
275 G2 Goadby Leics
277 G4 Goadby Marwood Leics
112 B4 Goatacre Wilts
493 H4 Goatfield Ag & B
58 D3 Goatham Green E Susx
46 C1 Goathill Dorset
386 D2 Goathland N York
65 E5 Goathurst Somset
96 C4 Goathurst Common Kent
596 C6 Gobhaig W Isls
91 G5 Gobley Hole Hants
269 F3 Gobowen Shrops
93 G6 Godalming Surrey
116 C1 Goddards Bucks
226 B6 Goddard's Corner Suffk
80 B3 Goddard's Green Kent
91 H1 Goddard's Green W Berk
77 E5 Goddards' Green W Susx
97 E3 Godden Green Kent
96 C1 Goddington Gt Lon
166 D4 Godington Oxon
327 E5 Godley Tamesd
292 C6 Godleybrook Staffs
327 E6 Godley Hill Tamesd
77 G6 Godleys Green E Susx
220 C6 Godmanchester Cambs
31 F3 Godmanstone Dorset
99 G4 Godmersham Kent
66 D1 Godney Somset
3 G3 Godolphin Cross Cnwll
130 A3 Godre'r-Graig Neath
49 F2 Godshill Hants
37 E4 Godshill IoW
95 H4 Godstone Surrey
49 F5 Godswinscroft Hants
12 A1 Godwell Devon
254 B3 Godwick Norfk
133 F3 Goetre Mons
302 B4 Goferydd IoA
144 D4 Goff's Oak Herts
487 G5 Gogar C Edin
205 F3 Goginan Cerdgn
284 B6 Golan Gwynd
180 C4 Golant Cnwll
16 D4 Golberdon Cnwll
325 E5 Golborne Wigan
327 G1 Golcar Kirk
307 H4 Golch Flints
108 C3 Goldcliff Newpt
140 C5 Golden Balls Oxon
57 E2 Golden Cross E Susx
57 E2 Golden Cross E Susx
97 F5 Golden Green Kent
155 E6 Golden Grove Carmth
109 G4 Golden Hill Bristl
291 G4 Golden Hill C Stke
49 H5 Golden Hill Hants
125 G4 Golden Hill Pembks
151 G5 Golden Hill Pembks
38 B3 Golden Park Devon
92 B6 Golden Pot Hants
295 E4 Golden Valley Derbys
162 D5 Golden Valley Gloucs
187 F5 Golden Valley Herefs
186 D2 Golder Field Herefs
119 E2 Golders Green Gt Lon
91 E2 Goldfinch Bottom W Berk
173 F4 Goldhanger Essex
47 F2 Gold Hill Dorset
234 C4 Golding Shrops
195 F4 Goldington Beds
356 D3 Goldsborough N York
386 D2 Goldsborough N York
85 G2 Gold's Cross BaNES
237 E6 Golds Green Sandw
3 F3 Goldsithney Cnwll
271 G4 Goldstone Shrops
236 D5 Goldthorn Park Wolves
329 H4 Goldthorpe Barns
39 E3 Goldworthy Devon
80 A2 Golford Kent
308 C5 Golftyn Flints
101 E6 Golgotha Kent
568 F3 Gollachy Moray
566 E6 Gollanfield Highld
7 E3 Gollawater Cnwll
369 F3 Gollingith Foot N York
288 D3 Golly Wrexhm
63 G4 Golsoncott Somset
577 H3 Golspie Highld
587 J4 Golval Highld
132 D4 Golynos Torfn
70 D2 Gomeldon Wilts
342 C4 Gomersal Kirk
94 B5 Gomshall Surrey
296 C5 Gonalston Notts
296 D6 Gonamena Cnwll
16 C4 Gonerby Hill Foot Lincs
278 C2 Gonfirth Shet
606 E5 Good Easter Essex
146 C2 Goodleigh Devon
55 E5 Gooderstone Norfk
61 F5 Goodleigh Devon
96 B4 Goodley Stock Kent
80 B3 Goodmanham E R Yk
120 C2 Goodmayes Gt Lon
99 G2 Goodnestone Kent
101 E5 Goodnestone Kent
160 D6 Goodrich Herefs
20 B6 Goodrington Torbay
212 A3 Good's Green Worcs
340 C4 Goodshaw Lancs
340 C4 Goodshaw Chapel Lancs
340 C4 Goodshaw Fold Lancs
19 G3 Goodstone Devon
151 G2 Goodwick Pembks
71 H1 Goodworth Clatford Hants
215 E2 Goodyers End Warwks
398 D5 Goodyhills Cumb
345 G5 Goole E R Yk
189 H4 Goom's Hill Worcs
8 A3 Goonabarn Cnwll
6 D5 Goonbell Cnwll
7 E3 Goonhavern Cnwll

4 C3 Goonhusband Cnwll
4 D1 Goonlaze Cnwll
6 D3 Goonown Cnwll
7 F6 Goon Piper Cnwll
6 C4 Goonvrea Cnwll
146 D6 Gooseberry Green Essex
341 G1 Goose Eye Brad
25 G4 Gooseford Devon
366 A3 Goose Green Cumb
175 F4 Goose Green Essex
50 B3 Goose Green Hants
145 E3 Goose Green Herts
80 B2 Goose Green Kent
97 F4 Goose Green Kent
338 C5 Goose Green Lancs
225 F2 Goose Green Norfk
110 C3 Goose Green S Glos
74 B5 Goose Green W Susx
76 B6 Goose Green W Susx
324 D4 Goose Green Wigan
38 B4 Gooseham Cnwll
38 B4 Gooseham Mill Cnwll
91 E2 Goose Hill Hants
343 G5 Goosehill Worcs
188 D2 Goosehill Green Worcs
27 H5 Goosemoor Devon
272 B6 Goosemoor Staffs
237 G2 Goosemoor Green Staffs
44 A2 Goosenford Somset
160 B2 Goose Pool Herefs
60 D2 Goosewell Devon
114 B1 Goosey Oxon
338 D2 Goosnargh Lancs
311 F5 Goostrey Ches
467 E2 Gorbals C Glas
213 G6 Gorcott Hill Warwks
605 H5 Gord Shet
305 E5 Gorddinog Gwynd
473 E6 Gordon Border
577 H2 Gordonbush Highld
569 G2 Gordonsburgh Moray
559 G2 Gordonstown Abers
569 K4 Gordonstown Abers
67 F6 Gore Dorset
101 E4 Gore Kent
471 F2 Gorebridge Mdloth
90 C2 Gore End Hants
245 F2 Gorefield Cambs
75 F5 Gorehill W Susx
173 H6 Gore Pit Essex
101 E2 Gore Street Kent
35 J7 Gorey Jersey
477 F5 Gorgie C Edin
143 G3 Gorhambury Herts
115 G3 Goring Oxon
54 D4 Goring-by-Sea W Susx
115 H4 Goring Heath Oxon
251 G4 Gorleston-on-Sea Norfk
212 D1 Gornalwood Dudley
570 C4 Gorrachie Abers
8 C5 Gorran Haven Cnwll
8 B5 Gorran High Lanes Cnwll
439 F5 Gorrenberry Border
180 B6 Gorrig Cerdgn
310 D1 Gorse Covert Warrtn
307 G4 Gorsedd Flints
113 E2 Gorse Hill Swindn
326 B5 Gorse Hill Traffd
129 E5 Gorseinon Swans
602 E8 Gorseness Ork
296 A1 Gorsethorpe Notts
294 B4 Gorseybank Derbys
180 C4 Gorsgoch Cerdgn
129 E2 Gorslas Carmth
161 F4 Gorsley Gloucs
161 F4 Gorsley Common Herefs
310 C5 Gorstage Ches
564 F4 Gorstan Highld
289 E2 Gorstella Ches
506 B3 Gorsten Ag & B
237 G3 Gorstey Ley Staffs
211 G5 Gorst Hill Worcs
291 E4 Gorstyhill Ches
273 H4 Gorsty Hill Staffs
476 E2 Gortantaoid Ag & B
518 F2 Gorteneorn Highld
518 E2 Gortenfern Highld
326 C5 Gorton Manch
461 E4 Gortonallister N Ayrs
480 C1 Gortonronach Ag & B
201 G3 Gosbeck Suffk
280 B3 Gosberton Lincs
280 B4 Gosberton Cheal Lincs
280 A3 Gosberton Clough Lincs
237 F4 Goscote Wsall
275 E5 Goseley Dale Derbys
173 F4 Gosfield Essex
28 A3 Gosford Devon
210 C6 Gosford Herefs
140 C2 Gosford Oxon
215 F4 Gosford Green Covtry
376 D4 Gosforth Cumb
430 D6 Gosforth N u Ty
314 C4 Gosforth Valley Derbys
199 F4 Gosland Green Suffk
174 C1 Gosling Green Suffk
99 G3 Gosmere Kent
170 A4 Gosmore Herts
212 B1 Gospel Ash Staffs
236 D6 Gospel End Village Staffs
75 E3 Gospel Green W Susx
119 F2 Gospel Oak Gt Lon
51 G5 Gosport Hants
72 A5 Gosport Hants
609 G8 Gossabrough Shet
194 D6 Gossard's Green Beds
135 G4 Gossington Gloucs
76 D2 Gossops Green W Susx
475 G6 Goswick Nthumb
48 D2 Gotham Dorset
58 A5 Gotham E Susx
276 B3 Gotham Notts
64 D4 Gotheiney Green Somset
163 E4 Gotherington Gloucs
8 B2 Gothers Cnwll
516 C6 Gott Ag & B
605 H1 Gott Shet
44 A2 Gotton Somset
79 G2 Goudhurst Kent
319 G4 Goulceby Lincs
384 D4 Goulton N York
559 H1 Gourdas Abers
514 A3 Gourdie C Dund
541 F5 Gourdon Abers
482 F5 Gourock Inver
466 D1 Govan C Glas
97 F4 Gover Hill Kent
296 C3 Goverton Notts
12 D3 Goveton Devon
133 E2 Govilon Mons
571 J3 Gowanbank Angus
527 G4 Gowanhill Abers
560 C1 Gowanwell Abers
345 G3 Gowdall E R Yk
103 E2 Gowerton Swans
312 D3 Gowhole Derbys
487 E2 Gowkhall Fife
468 B4 Gowkthrapple N Lans
359 E4 Gowthorpe E R Yk
361 F6 Goxhill E R Yk
348 B5 Goxhill N Linc
348 B4 Goxhill Haven N Linc

690 City, town and village index: Goytre - Grubb Street

104 B2 Goytre Neath
139 H5 Gozzard's Ford Oxon
597 K4 Grabhair W Isls
279 F4 Graby Lincs
8 C2 Gracca Cnwll
488 B6 Gracemount C Edin
4 D6 Grade Cnwll
53 G1 Graffham W Susx
219 H6 Grafham Cambs
75 G1 Grafham Surrey
160 B2 Grafton Herefs
357 E2 Grafton N York
138 D4 Grafton Oxon
269 H6 Grafton Shrops
163 E2 Grafton Worcs
186 D2 Grafton Worcs
189 E3 Grafton Flyford Worcs
193 G5 Grafton Regis Nhants
218 C3 Grafton Underwood Nhants
98 D5 Grafty Green Kent
486 A3 Grahamston Falk
288 B3 Graianrhyd Denbgs
128 B4 Graig Carmth
305 H5 Graig Conwy
307 F5 Graig Denbgs
105 H2 Graig Rhondd
268 D2 Graig Wrexhm
129 F4 Graig-Fawr Swans
287 G4 Graig-Fechan Denbgs
129 G4 Graig Felen Swans
105 F4 Graig Penllyn V Glam
103 G2 Graig Trewyddfa Swans
122 D4 Grain Medway
327 E3 Grains Bar Oldham
334 C5 Grainsby Lincs
393 E5 Grains O' Th' Beck Dur
335 E5 Grainthorpe Lincs
335 E5 Grainthorpe Fen Lincs
331 G5 Graiselound N Linc
592 E6 Gramasdail W Isls
8 A4 Grampound Cnwll
7 H3 Grampound Road Cnwll
167 G4 Granborough Bucks
277 G2 Granby Notts
192 A1 Grandborough Warwks
35 i6 Grand Chemins Jersey
34 c2 Grandes Rocques Guern
140 B3 Grandpont Oxon
524 D5 Grandtully P & K
377 G1 Grange Cumb
48 C4 Grange Dorset
445 F2 Grange E Ayrs
309 H3 Grange Halton
36 C4 Grange IoW
339 E3 Grange Lancs
122 B6 Grange Medway
368 B1 Grange N York
334 B3 Grange NE Lin
513 G4 Grange P & K
310 C1 Grange Warrtn
308 B2 Grange Wirral
569 H5 Grange Crossroads Moray
49 E4 Grange Estate Dorset
395 E4 Grange Hill Dur
120 B1 Grange Hill Essex
294 A3 Grangemill Derbys
328 C1 Grange Moor Kirk
486 C3 Grangemouth Falk
500 D1 Grange of Lindores Fife
365 F4 Grange-over-Sands Cumb
486 D3 Grangepans Falk
144 D5 Grange Park Gt Lon
193 G4 Grange Park Nhants
324 B6 Grange Park St Hel
112 D3 Grange Park Swindn
106 C5 Grangetown Cardif
396 D5 Grangetown R & Cl
397 E5 Grangetown R & Cl
406 B4 Grangetown Sundld
405 F4 Grange Villa Dur
135 F2 Grange Village Gloucs
551 G7 Granish Highld
361 E3 Gransmoor E R Yk
172 D5 Gransmore Green Essex
151 E3 Granston Pembks
197 F3 Grantchester Cambs
278 C2 Grantham Lincs
370 A6 Grantley Hall N York
556 C1 Grantlodge Abers
487 H4 Granton C Edin
551 J4 Grantown-on-Spey Highld
186 C2 Grantsfield Herefs
474 A1 Grantshouse Border
310 C2 Grappenhall Warrtn
310 C2 Grappenhall Heys Warrtn
333 F4 Grasby Lincs
378 B3 Grasmere Cumb
327 E4 Grasscroft Oldham
309 E2 Grassendale Lpool
378 D5 Grassgarth Cumb
400 B6 Grassgarth Cumb
173 E2 Grass Green Essex
393 F5 Grassholme Dur
354 D2 Grassington N York
294 D1 Grassmoor Derbys
317 E6 Grassthorpe Notts
406 A4 Grasswell Sundld
71 F1 Grateley Hants
39 E5 Gratton Devon
273 F3 Gratwich Staffs
290 D1 Gravel Ches
100 D6 Gravel Castle Kent
196 C2 Graveley Cambs
170 B4 Graveley Herts
117 H1 Gravel Hill Bucks
234 B2 Gravelhill Shrops
326 D3 Gravel Hole Oldham
269 G2 Gravel Hole Shrops
213 G1 Gravelly Hill Birm
233 F5 Gravels Shrops
233 F4 Gravelsbank Shrops
606 F3 Graven Shet
99 G2 Graveney Kent
171 F4 Gravesend Herts
121 F5 Gravesend Kent
314 D3 Graves Park Sheff
597 K4 Gravir W Isls
314 A2 Grayingham Lincs
332 C5 Grayrigg Cumb
379 G5 Grays Thurr
121 F4 Grayshott Hants
74 D2 Grayson Green Cumb
388 A5 Grayswood Surrey
75 E3 Graythorp Hartpl
396 D4 Grazeley Wokham
92 A1 Grazeley Green W Berk
92 A1 Grealin Highld
543 J4 Greasbrough Rothm
329 G5 Greasby Wirral
308 B2 Greasley Notts
295 F5 Great Abington Cambs
198 A5 Great Addington Nhants
218 D4 Great Alne Warwks
189 H3 Great Altcar Lancs
323 F3 Great Amwell Herts
380 B2 Great Asby Cumb
170 C4 Great Ashby Herts
224 C6 Great Ashfield Suffk
87 E2 Great Ashley Wilts
385 E2 Great Ayton N York
147 E3 Great Baddow Essex
172 D3 Great Bardfield Essex
195 G4 Great Barford Beds
237 F6 Great Barr Sandw
138 C2 Great Barrington Gloucs
309 G6 Great Barrow Ches
200 A1 Great Barton Suffk
372 D4 Great Barugh N York
429 F3 Great Bavington Nthumb
202 A5 Great Bealings Suffk
89 G2 Great Bedwyn Wilts
175 F5 Great Bentley Essex
121 G2 Great Berry Essex
193 H2 Great Billing Nhants
259 F5 Great Bircham Norfk
201 F4 Great Blakenham Suffk
390 D3 Great Blencow Cumb
271 E5 Great Bolas Wrekin
94 C4 Great Bookham Surrey
2 D3 Great Bosullow Cnwll
191 H5 Great Bourton Oxon
217 F2 Great Bowden Leics
99 G4 Great Bower Kent
198 D4 Great Bradley Suffk
147 H2 Great Braxted Essex
200 D4 Great Bricett Suffk
168 C3 Great Brickhill Bucks
237 E6 Great Bridge Sandw
272 C4 Great Bridgeford Staffs
193 E1 Great Brington Nhants
175 E4 Great Bromley Essex
388 C3 Great Broughton Cumb
385 F3 Great Broughton N York
97 G2 Great Buckland Kent
310 D4 Great Budworth Ches
383 H1 Great Burdon Darltn
121 G1 Great Burstead Essex
385 E3 Great Busby N York
172 B6 Great Canfield Essex
320 D2 Great Carlton Lincs
243 E3 Great Casterton Rutlnd
183 H2 Great Cellws Powys
87 F2 Great Chalfield Wilts
81 E1 Great Chart Kent
236 A2 Great Chatwell Staffs
291 H4 Great Chell C Stke
171 H1 Great Chesterford Essex
79 G1 Great Cheveney Kent
88 A4 Great Cheverell Wilts
395 F3 Great Chilton Dur
171 F2 Great Chishill Cambs
149 G1 Great Clacton Essex
147 F4 Great Claydons Essex
388 B4 Great Clifton Cumb
334 B2 Great Coates NE Lin
163 E1 Great Comberton Worcs
226 D2 Great Common Suffk
75 G4 Great Common W Susx
401 E4 Great Corby Cumb
174 A1 Great Cornard Suffk
361 G6 Great Cowden E R Yk
138 D6 Great Coxwell Oxon
370 A2 Great Crakehall N York
218 A4 Great Cransley Nhants
247 H4 Great Cressingham Norfk
323 F5 Great Crosby Sefton
389 G5 Great Crosthwaite Cumb
274 B2 Great Cubley Derbys
241 F2 Great Dalby Leics
194 B1 Great Doddington Nhants
134 C1 Great Doward Herefs
253 H5 Great Dunham Norfk
172 C5 Great Dunmow Essex
70 C2 Great Durnford Wilts
172 C4 Great Easton Essex
242 A6 Great Easton Leics
338 B1 Great Eccleston Lancs
372 D3 Great Edstone N York
248 D5 Great Ellingham Norfk
86 C5 Great Elm Somset
406 B5 Great Eppleton Sundld
197 E4 Great Eversden Cambs
383 G6 Great Fencote N York
112 C2 Greatfield Wilts
200 D3 Great Finborough Suffk
243 F2 Greatford Lincs
254 A5 Great Fransham Norfk
143 E2 Great Gaddesden Herts
142 C1 Greatgap Bucks
273 G1 Great Gate Staffs
219 G3 Great Gidding Cambs
359 F4 Great Givendale E R Yk
202 C2 Great Glemham Suffk
241 E5 Great Glen Leics
278 C2 Great Gonerby Lincs
196 C3 Great Gransden Cambs
196 C6 Great Green Cambs
200 B3 Great Green Suffk
225 E4 Great Green Suffk
225 F4 Great Green Suffk
373 E4 Great Habton N York
299 F6 Great Hale Lincs
171 H6 Great Hallingbury Essex
74 B3 Greatham Hants
396 C4 Greatham Hartpl
54 B1 Greatham W Susx
142 A4 Great Hampden Bucks
218 B5 Great Harrowden Nhants
340 A3 Great Harwood Lancs
140 D4 Great Haseley Oxon
361 F6 Great Hatfield E R Yk
256 B5 Great Hautbois Norfk
273 F5 Great Haywood Staffs
215 E3 Great Heath Covtry
344 D5 Great Heck N York
173 H2 Great Henny Essex
87 G3 Great Hinton Wilts
142 D4 Great Hivings Bucks
248 C6 Great Hockham Norfk
140 D5 Great Holcombe Oxon
176 D6 Great Holland Essex
117 E6 Great Hollands Br For
167 H2 Great Holm M Keyn
174 C3 Great Horkesley Essex
171 F4 Great Hormead Herts
342 B3 Great Horton Brad
167 G3 Great Horwood Bucks
329 G3 Great Houghton Barns
193 G3 Great Houghton Nhants
326 D1 Great Howarth Rochdl
313 G4 Great Hucklow Derbys
80 B4 Great Job's Cross Kent
361 E3 Great Kelk E R Yk
360 C2 Great Kendale E R Yk
142 A3 Great Kimble Bucks
142 B5 Great Kingshill Bucks
383 G5 Great Langton N York
116 B6 Great Lea Common Wokham
147 E1 Great Leighs Essex
325 G3 Great Lever Bolton
333 G3 Great Limber Lincs
168 A1 Great Linford M Keyn
224 A5 Great Livermere Suffk
313 H5 Great Longstone Derbys
405 G5 Great Lumley Dur
234 B3 Great Lyth Shrops
121 G3 Great Malgraves Thurr
188 A5 Great Malvern Worcs
173 G3 Great Maplestead Essex
337 F2 Great Marton Bpool
337 F3 Great Marton Moss Lancs
253 G3 Great Massingham Norfk
140 D4 Great Milton Oxon
142 B4 Great Missenden Bucks
339 H2 Great Mitton Lancs
101 F5 Great Mongeham Kent
167 E5 Greatmoor Bucks
236 B5 Great Moor Staffs
312 B2 Great Moor Stockp
225 G1 Great Moulton Norfk
170 D5 Great Munden Herts
380 D2 Great Musgrave Cumb
96 D3 Greatness Kent
269 G6 Great Ness Shrops
173 E5 Great Notley Essex
133 G3 Great Oak Mons
176 C4 Great Oakley Essex
218 B2 Great Oakley Nhants
169 G4 Great Offley Herts
380 C1 Great Ormside Cumb
400 B4 Great Orton Cumb
357 E2 Great Ouseburn N York
217 F3 Great Oxendon Nhants
146 D3 Great Oxney Green Essex
247 G2 Great Palgrave Norfk
145 F3 Great Parndon Essex
98 A5 Great Pattenden Kent
196 B2 Great Paxton Cambs
337 G3 Great Plumpton Lancs
250 C2 Great Plumstead Norfk
278 C3 Great Ponton Lincs
343 H4 Great Preston Leeds
166 B2 Great Purston Nhants
220 C3 Great Raveley Cambs
164 B6 Great Rissington Gloucs
165 E3 Great Rollright Oxon
254 B2 Great Ryburgh Norfk
442 C2 Great Ryle Nthumb
234 B4 Great Ryton Shrops
172 D4 Great Saling Essex
391 E2 Great Salkeld Cumb
172 C2 Great Sampford Essex
310 B2 Great Sankey Warrtn
237 E3 Great Saredon Staffs
199 F2 Great Saxham Suffk
114 B4 Great Shefford W Berk
197 G4 Great Shelford Cambs
89 G5 Great Shoddesden Hants
384 A4 Great Smeaton N York
260 B5 Great Snoring Norfk
111 H3 Great Somerford Wilts
395 G5 Great Stainton Darltn
123 E1 Great Stambridge Essex
195 G1 Great Staughton Cambs
300 D2 Great Steeping Lincs
110 A3 Great Stoke S Glos
101 F4 Great Stonar Kent
81 G5 Greatstone-on-Sea Kent
241 E4 Great Stretton Leics
391 F5 Great Strickland Cumb
220 B5 Great Stukeley Cambs
319 G4 Great Sturton Lincs
309 E4 Great Sutton Ches
210 C3 Great Sutton Shrops
429 E4 Great Swinburne Nthumb
165 F4 Great Tew Oxon
174 A4 Great Tey Essex
371 F4 Great Thirkleby N York
198 D4 Great Thurlow Suffk
39 H4 Great Torrington Devon
442 C4 Great Tosson Nthumb
147 H2 Great Totham Essex
319 G1 Great Tows Lincs
9 H2 Great Tree Cnwll
364 C5 Great Urswick Cumb
123 E2 Great Wakering Essex
200 B6 Great Waldingfield Suffk
260 B4 Great Walsingham Norfk
146 D2 Great Waltham Essex
121 E1 Great Warley Essex
163 E3 Great Washbourne Gloucs
25 H5 Great Weeke Devon
199 H3 Great Welnetham Suffk
175 E2 Great Wenham Suffk
429 G5 Great Whittington Nthumb
148 C1 Great Wigborough Essex
198 A3 Great Wilbraham Cambs
275 G3 Great Wilne Derbys
70 B2 Great Wishford Wilts
255 F3 Great Witchingham Norfk
136 D2 Great Witcombe Gloucs
187 H1 Great Witley Worcs
164 C3 Great Wolford Warwks
166 C1 Greatworth Nhants
198 D5 Great Wratting Suffk
170 B4 Great Wymondley Herts
237 E3 Great Wyrley Staffs
270 D6 Great Wytheford Shrops
251 G3 Great Yarmouth Norfk
173 F2 Great Yeldham Essex
340 D5 Greave Lancs
312 B1 Greave Stockp
320 D6 Grebby Lincs
322 e6 Greeba IoM
307 F6 Green Denbgs
125 G4 Green Pembks
233 E6 Green Powys
326 D3 Greenacres Oldham
310 C5 Greenbank Ches
365 E3 Green Bank Cumb
485 H4 Greenbank Falk
609 G4 Greenbank Shet
7 E5 Green Bottom Cnwll
135 F1 Green Bottom Gloucs
469 E2 Greenburn W Loth
367 E6 Green Close N York
160 C2 Green Crize Herefs
405 E4 Greencroft Dur
74 D2 Green Cross Surrey
312 A4 Greendale Ches
29 E2 Green Down Devon
85 G4 Greendown Somset
454 D4 Greendykes Nthumb
169 F2 Green End Beds
195 E5 Green End Beds
195 F2 Green End Beds
195 G4 Green End Beds
141 H5 Green End Bucks
168 C3 Green End Bucks
197 E3 Green End Cambs
220 B5 Green End Cambs
143 E3 Green End Herts
170 C3 Green End Herts
170 D3 Green End Herts
170 D5 Green End Herts
171 E4 Green End Herts
354 B5 Green End Lancs
468 A2 Greenend N Lans
386 D4 Green End N York
165 E5 Greenend Oxon
214 D2 Green End Warwks
570 D6 Greeness Abers
485 E5 Greenfaulds N Lans
169 F3 Greenfield Beds
467 F2 Greenfield C Glas
308 A4 Greenfield Flints
308 B4 Greenfield Flints
533 K2 Greenfield Highld
327 E4 Greenfield Oldham
116 B1 Greenfield Oxon
569 K6 Greenfold Moray
485 E6 Greenfoot N Lans
118 C3 Greenford Gt Lon
485 F5 Greengairs N Lans
376 D4 Greengarth Hall Cumb
42 D4 Green Gate Devon
254 D4 Greengate Norfk
326 D1 Greengate Rochdl
342 C2 Greengates Brad
388 C2 Greengill Cumb
142 A4 Green Hailey Bucks
337 G2 Greenhalgh Lancs
467 G3 Greenhall S Lans
29 H2 Greenham Dorset
43 E3 Greenham Somset
90 D1 Greenham W Berk
357 F3 Green Hammerton N York
428 B2 Greenhaugh Nthumb
340 B4 Green Haworth Lancs
451 F4 Greenhead Border
400 C5 Green Head Cumb
468 C4 Greenhead N Lans
402 B1 Greenhead Nthumb
292 C5 Greenhead Staffs
237 E2 Green Heath Staffs
325 F4 Greenheys Salfd
424 C4 Greenhill D & G
406 B5 Greenhill Dur
485 G4 Greenhill Falk
118 D2 Greenhill Gt Lon
187 G5 Greenhill Herefs
98 B4 Green Hill Kent
100 C2 Greenhill Kent
344 A2 Green Hill Leeds
239 G2 Greenhill Leics
278 B2 Green Hill Lincs
448 B3 Greenhill S Lans
314 C3 Greenhill Sheff
112 C2 Green Hill Wilts
189 F5 Greenhill Worcs
212 B4 Greenhill Worcs
269 G2 Greenhill Bank Shrops
295 E5 Greenhillocks Derbys
467 F4 Greenhills S Lans
121 E4 Greenhithe Kent
446 A2 Greenholm E Ayrs
379 G3 Greenholme Cumb
451 H5 Greenhouse Border
355 F2 Greenhow N York
601 G3 Greenigoe Ork
589 G3 Greenland Highld
314 D2 Greenland Sheff
589 G3 Greenland Mains Highld
116 C2 Greenlands Bucks
189 F1 Greenlands Worcs
215 E4 Green Lane Covtry
19 G2 Green Lane Devon
187 E5 Green Lane Herefs
189 G2 Green Lane Worcs
473 G5 Greenlaw Border
470 D2 Greenlaw Mains Mdloth
424 A4 Greenlea D & G
167 H1 Greenleys M Keyn
498 C3 Greenloaning P & K
289 G2 Greenlooms Ches
112 A3 Greenman's Lane Wilts
112 D2 Greenmeadow Swindn
133 E5 Greenmeadow Torfn
328 D5 Green Moor Barns
325 H2 Greenmount Bury
605 H5 Greenmow Shet
346 B4 Greenoak E R Yk
482 C4 Greenock Inver
482 C4 Greenock West Inver
364 D3 Greenodd Cumb
85 G4 Green Ore Somset
86 C4 Green Parlour Somset
379 E4 Green Quarter Cumb
469 E2 Greenrigg W Loth
399 E4 Greenrow Cumb
570 E6 Greens Abers
426 C2 Greens Border
212 B2 Greensforge Staffs
255 E4 Greensgate Norfk
469 G6 Greenshields S Lans
380 C4 Greenside Cumb
314 D4 Greenside Derbys
404 D2 Greenside Gatesd
328 B1 Greenside Kirk
328 B2 Green Side Kirk
343 E3 Green Side Leeds
326 C5 Greenside Tamesd
442 B1 Greensidehill Nthumb
193 E5 Greens Norton Nhants
568 D3 Greens of Coxton Moray
528 C4 Greens of Gardyne Angus
8 B2 Greensplat Cnwll
174 D4 Greenstead Essex
173 G4 Greenstead Green Essex
146 A4 Greensted Essex
146 A4 Greensted Green Essex
58 C4 Green Street E Susx
146 C5 Green Street Essex
135 H4 Green Street Gloucs
136 C1 Green Street Gloucs
144 A5 Green Street Herts
171 F5 Green Street Herts
76 B5 Green Street W Susx
162 C1 Green Street Worcs
188 C5 Green Street Worcs
96 C2 Green Street Green Gt Lon
121 E5 Green Street Green Kent
200 D5 Greenstreet Green Suffk
171 F6 Green Tye Herts
161 F3 Greenway Gloucs
152 B3 Greenway Pembks
43 G2 Greenway Somset
105 H5 Greenway V Glam
211 G5 Greenway Worcs
401 F3 Greenwell Cumb
451 H3 Greenwells Border
120 A4 Greenwich Gt Lon
176 C1 Greenwich Suffk
69 F3 Greenwich Wilts
7 E5 Greenwith Common Cnwll
146 D5 Greenwoods Essex
602 B7 Greeny Ork
542 D8 Greep Highld
163 F3 Greet Gloucs
99 E3 Greet Kent
210 D5 Greete Shrops
320 B5 Greetham Lincs
242 C2 Greetham Rutlnd
342 A5 Greetland Calder
341 H5 Greetland Wall Nook Calder
332 C4 Greetwell N Linc
339 E4 Gregson Lane Lancs
232 A5 Gregynog Powys
591 D7 Grein W Isls
592 E2 Greinetobht W Isls
66 C2 Greinton Somset
605 J2 Gremista Shet
322 c8 Grenaby IoM
194 B2 Grendon Nhants
238 D5 Grendon Warwks
186 D3 Grendon Bishop Herefs
238 D5 Grendon Common Warwks
186 D3 Grendon Green Herefs
167 E6 Grendon Underwood Bucks
17 G4 Grenofen Devon
329 E6 Grenoside Sheff
595 K4 Greosabhagh W Isls
289 E4 Gresford Wrexhm
261 G4 Gresham Norfk
542 E6 Greshornish Highld
254 C4 Gressenhall Norfk
366 B6 Gressingham Lancs
382 C2 Greta Bridge Dur
400 B1 Gretna D & G
425 G6 Gretna Green D & G
163 F3 Gretton Gloucs
242 C6 Gretton Nhants
234 C5 Gretton Shrops
163 F3 Gretton Fields Gloucs
370 A4 Grewelthorpe N York
86 A3 Greyfield BaNES
369 G5 Greygarth N York
331 G3 Grey Green N Linc
66 B3 Greylake Somset
66 C2 Greylake Fosse Somset
129 E3 Greynor Carmth
424 B2 Greyrigg D & G
116 B3 Greys Green Oxon
388 C4 Greysouthen Cumb
428 B2 Greystead Nthumb
390 C3 Greystoke Cumb
390 C4 Greystoke Gill Cumb
528 B6 Greystone Angus
365 H4 Greystone Cumb
366 D6 Greystonegill N York
314 C3 Greystones Sheff
189 G5 Greystones Warwks
160 D4 Greytree Herefs
92 B4 Greywell Hants
599 K6 Griais W Isls
599 J7 Grianan W Isls
29 G2 Gribb Dorset
345 H2 Gribthorpe E R Yk
504 E4 Gribun Ag & B
215 F2 Griff Warwks
213 F3 Griffins Hill Birm
133 E5 Griffithstown Torfn
275 G6 Griffydam Leics
98 D6 Grigg Kent
74 C3 Griggs Green Hants
6 C6 Grillis Cnwll
41 E3 Grilstone Devon
600 F2 Grimbister Ork
325 E2 Grimeford Village Lancs
213 G4 Grimes Hill Worcs
314 D2 Grimesthorpe Sheff
600 E2 Grimeston Ork
329 G3 Grimethorpe Barns
593 D7 Griminis W Isls
592 D2 Griminis W Isls
608 F6 Grimister Shet
188 B2 Grimley Worcs
601 H6 Grimness Ork
320 C2 Grimoldby Lincs
269 G4 Grimpo Shrops
339 E3 Grimsargh Lancs
165 H1 Grimsbury Oxon
334 C2 Grimsby NE Lin
192 D4 Grimscote Nhants
23 F1 Grimscott Cnwll
597 K2 Grimshader W Isls
339 H5 Grimshaw Bl w D
324 B2 Grimshaw Green Lancs
279 F5 Grimsthorpe Lincs
349 E2 Grimston E R Yk
277 E5 Grimston Leics
253 E3 Grimston Norfk
358 B4 Grimston York
31 E4 Grimstone Dorset
224 B6 Grimstone End Suffk
24 B4 Grinacombe Moor Devon
375 E5 Grindale E R Yk
605 J3 Grindiscol Shet
235 H4 Grindle Shrops
314 A4 Grindleford Derbys
353 E5 Grindleton Lancs
273 F4 Grindley Staffs
289 H6 Grindley Brook Shrops
313 G4 Grindlow Derbys
474 D6 Grindon Nthumb
396 A4 Grindon S on T
293 E4 Grindon Staffs
406 B4 Grindon Sundld
313 F2 Grindsbrook Booth Derbys
316 D1 Gringley on the Hill Notts
400 C3 Grinsdale Cumb
270 C5 Grinshill Shrops
201 E4 Grinstead Hill Suffk
382 B5 Grinton N York
595 E8 Griomasaigh W Isls
597 K2 Griomsidar W Isls
380 D6 Grisedale Cumb
516 F4 Grishipoll Ag & B
78 A5 Grisling Common E Susx
374 D3 Gristhorpe N York
248 B5 Griston Norfk
601 K4 Gritley Ork
112 B3 Grittenham Wilts
187 G5 Grittlesend Herefs
111 E3 Grittleton Wilts
363 E4 Grizebeck Cumb
378 B6 Grizedale Cumb
603 K7 Grobister Ork
606 E5 Grobsness Shet
240 B3 Groby Leics
287 E2 Groes Conwy
104 B2 Groes Neath
287 G1 Groes Efa Denbgs
105 H3 Groes-faen Rhondd
287 G1 Groes-fawr Denbgs
262 D3 Groesffordd Gwynd
158 A4 Groesffordd Powys
283 E4 Groeslon Gwynd
159 F5 Groes-Lwyd Mons
232 D2 Groes-Lwyd Powys
232 D3 Groespluan Powys
106 B2 Groes-Wen Caerph
593 D10 Grogarry W Isls
462 D6 Grogport Ag & B
593 D10 Groigearraidh W Isls
202 D3 Gromford Suffk
307 F3 Gronant Flints
269 E4 Gronwen Shrops
78 C2 Groombridge E Susx
595 K4 Grosebay W Isls
159 G5 Grosmont Mons
386 D3 Grosmont N York
191 F3 Gross Green Warwks
174 C1 Groton Suffk
327 E4 Grotton Oldham
35 j7 Grouville Jersey
168 C5 Grove Bucks
32 B5 Grove Dorset
187 E6 Grove Herefs
100 D3 Grove Kent
316 D4 Grove Notts
114 C1 Grove Oxon
125 G4 Grove Pembks
238 B6 Grove End Birm
98 D2 Grove End Kent
164 D2 Grove End Warwks
98 B3 Grove Green Kent
347 G2 Grovehill E R Yk
57 F2 Grove Hill E Susx
143 F3 Grovehill Herts
100 D3 Grove Hill Kent
120 B5 Grove Park Gt Lon
101 E4 Groves Kent
129 E4 Grovesend Swans
344 B5 Grove Town Wakefd
237 F6 Grove Vale Sandw
121 E6 Grubb Street Kent

272 A4 Grub Street Staffs
564 E4 Grudie Highld
576 C3 Gruids Highld
544 F4 Grula Highld
505 G2 Cruline Ag & B
2 D4 Grumbla Cnwll
605 G4 Grunasound Shet
201 H4 Grundisburgh Suffk
353 F4 Grunsagill Lancs
606 C8 Gruting Shet
605 H8 Grutness Shet
282 D6 Gryn Goch Gwynd
521 G6 Gualachulain Highld
514 D6 Guardbridge Fife
341 G1 Guard House Brad
188 B5 Guarlford Worcs
524 F6 Guay P & K
173 E6 Gubbion's Green Essex
142 C2 Gubblecote Herts
59 E4 Guestling Green E Susx
59 E3 Guestling Thorn E Susx
255 E2 Guestwick Norfk
255 E2 Guestwick Green Norfk
339 G4 Guide Bl w D
326 D5 Guide Bridge Tamesd
431 E3 Guide Post Nthumb
196 C6 Guilden Morden Cambs
309 G6 Guilden Sutton Ches
93 H5 Guildford Surrey
93 G5 Guildford Park Surrey
469 F1 Guildiehaugh W Loth
512 D3 Guildtown P & K
515 E2 Guildy Angus
125 G3 Guilford Pembks
217 E5 Guilsborough Nhants
232 D2 Guilsfield Powys
315 E2 Guithwaite Rothm
101 E4 Guilton Kent
60 D4 Guineaford Devon
385 G1 Guisborough R & Cl
342 C1 Guiseley Leeds
254 C2 Guist Norfk
603 G4 Guith Ork
163 G5 Guiting Power Gloucs
605 H3 Gulberwick Shet
489 F3 Gullane E Loth
162 C2 Guller's End Worcs
199 G3 Gulling Green Suffk
391 H4 Gullom Holme Cumb
3 E3 Gulval Cnwll
17 F4 Gulworthy Devon
126 C4 Gumfreston Pembks
217 E1 Gumley Leics
7 G2 Gummow's Shop Cnwll
345 G2 Gunby E R Yk
278 C5 Gunby Lincs
301 E1 Gunby Lincs
43 F3 Gundenham Somset
73 F3 Gundleton Hants
79 H3 Gun Green Kent
57 F2 Gun Hill E Susx
61 F5 Gunn Devon
381 G5 Gunnerside N York
429 E4 Gunnerton Nthumb
332 A2 Gunness N Linc
17 F4 Gunnislake Cnwll
605 J2 Gunnista Shet
236 C4 Gunstone Staffs
213 E1 Guns Village Sandw
75 F5 Gunter's Bridge W Susx
244 A4 Gunthorpe C Pete
331 G5 Gunthorpe N Linc
260 D5 Gunthorpe Norfk
296 C6 Gunthorpe Notts
242 B3 Gunthorpe Rutlnd
251 G5 Gunton Suffk
14 D3 Gunvenna Cnwll
36 D3 Gunville IoW
4 B4 Gunwalloe Cnwll
4 B4 Gunwalloe Fishing Cove Cnwll
63 F5 Gupworthy Somset
51 E5 Gurnard IoW
312 B5 Gurnett Ches
85 H5 Gurney Slade Somset
131 G3 Gurnos Myr Td
130 B3 Gurnos Powys
99 G3 Gushmere Kent
48 C2 Gussage All Saints Dorset
48 B2 Gussage St Andrew Dorset
48 B2 Gussage St Michael Dorset
83 F2 Guston Kent
609 G5 Gutcher Shet
280 A5 Guthram Gowt Lincs
528 C4 Guthrie Angus
245 F4 Guyhirn Cambs
245 E4 Guyhirn Gull Cambs
190 D1 Guy's Cliffe Warwks
281 G4 Guy's Head Lincs
68 D5 Guy's Marsh Dorset
443 G4 Guyzance Nthumb
106 B3 Gwaelod-y-Garth Cardif
307 F3 Gwaenysgor Flints
303 E5 Gwalchmai IoA
303 E5 Gwalchmai Uchaf IoA
3 F3 Gwallon Cnwll
154 C2 Gwaralt Carmth
152 A5 Gwastad Pembks
228 D2 Gwastadgoed Gwynd
284 D3 Gwastadnant Gwynd
129 H2 Gwaun-Cae-Gurwen Neath
129 H2 Gwaun-Leision Neath
4 C3 Gwavas Cnwll
4 D6 Gwavas Cnwll
178 D4 Gwbert Cerdgn
4 B2 Gwedna Cnwll
4 C3 Gweek Cnwll
133 G4 Gwehelog Mons
304 B4 Gweithdy IoA
183 H6 Gwenddwr Powys
6 D5 Gwennap Cnwll
4 D5 Gwenter Cnwll
288 B2 Gwernaffield-y-Waun Flints
207 E1 Gwernafon Powys
207 G2 Gwerneirin Powys
208 C3 Gwerneirin Powys
133 H4 Gwernesney Mons
154 D3 Gwernogle Carmth
288 B4 Gwernol Denbgs
269 E4 Gwern y Brenin Shrops
232 A4 Gwernydd Powys
288 B2 Gwernymynydd Flints
105 H4 Gwern-y-Steeple V Glam
288 D4 Gwersyllt Wrexhm
307 F3 Gwespyr Flints
7 F2 Gwills Cnwll
3 G2 Gwinear Cnwll
4 B1 Gwinear Downs Cnwll
3 G1 Gwithian Cnwll
154 C2 Gwndwn Carmth
303 E3 Gwredog IoA
132 C5 Gwrhay Caerph
287 F5 Gwyddelwern Denbgs
154 C2 Gwyddgrug Carmth
288 B4 Gwynfryn Wrexhm
183 H1 Gwystre Powys
286 B2 Gwytherin Conwy
288 D5 Gyfelia Wrexhm

305 G4 Gyffin Conwy
600 E4 Gyre Ork
287 H3 Gyrn Denbgs

H

609 G4 Haa of Houlland Shet
233 G4 Habberley Shrops
212 B4 Habberley Worcs
340 C3 Habergham Lancs
321 F6 Habertoft Lincs
74 C5 Habin W Susx
333 G2 Habrough NE Lin
20 B3 Haccombe Devon
279 E2 Haceby Lincs
202 B3 Hacheston Suffk
95 F1 Hackbridge Gt Lon
315 E3 Hackenthorpe Sheff
249 E4 Hackford Norfk
383 F6 Hackforth N York
290 C5 Hack Green Ches
602 D7 Hackland Ork
193 H3 Hackleton Nhants
101 F5 Hacklinge Kent
212 C4 Hackman's Gate Worcs
374 B1 Hackness N York
600 E6 Hackness Ork
84 B5 Hackness Somset
119 G3 Hackney Gt Lon
318 B3 Hackthorn Lincs
88 D5 Hackthorn Wilts
391 E5 Hackthorpe Cumb
593 E8 Haclait W Isls
279 G4 Haconby Lincs
120 D3 Hacton Gt Lon
39 H3 Haddacott Devon
453 E2 Hadden Border
141 F3 Haddenham Bucks
221 F4 Haddenham Cambs
221 G4 Haddenham End Field Cambs
489 G5 Haddington E Loth
297 H2 Haddington Lincs
251 E5 Haddiscoe Norfk
219 G1 Haddon Cambs
328 A3 Hade Edge Kirk
238 B3 Hademore Staffs
213 E2 Haden Cross Sandw
327 F5 Hadfield Derbys
171 F6 Hadham Cross Herts
171 F5 Hadham Ford Herts
122 C2 Hadleigh Essex
200 D6 Hadleigh Suffk
144 B5 Hadley Gt Lon
188 C2 Hadley Worcs
235 F2 Hadley Wrekin
235 F2 Hadley Castle Wrekin
273 H5 Hadley End Staffs
144 C5 Hadley Wood Gt Lon
78 C5 Hadlow Down E Susx
97 F5 Hadlow Stair Kent
270 C5 Hadnall Shrops
67 H3 Hadspen Somset
198 B6 Hadstock Essex
443 H5 Hadston Nthumb
314 D5 Hady Derbys
188 D2 Hadzor Worcs
80 C1 Haffenden Quarter Kent
103 G3 Hafod Swans
286 B4 Hafod-Dinbych Conwy
178 C5 Hafod Grove Pembks
180 A4 Hafodiwan Cerdgn
307 E5 Hafod-y-Green Denbgs
132 D5 Hafodyrnys Caerph
325 F4 Hag Fold Wigan
340 D3 Haggate Lancs
326 D3 Haggate Oldham
426 C5 Haggbeck Cumb
606 E8 Haggersta Shet
119 G3 Haggerston Gt Lon
475 F6 Haggerston Nthumb
61 E2 Hagginton Hill Devon
606 D3 Haggrister Shet
485 F4 Haggs Falk
467 F1 Haghill C Glas
160 D1 Hagley Herefs
212 B3 Hagley Worcs
135 F3 Hagloe Gloucs
174 B2 Hagmore Green Suffk
300 B2 Hagnaby Lincs
321 E4 Hagnaby Lincs
300 B3 Hagnaby Lock Lincs
312 C2 Hague Bar Derbys
320 B6 Hagworthingham Lincs
328 D2 Haigh Barns
325 E3 Haigh Wigan
343 E5 Haigh Moor Leeds
339 E3 Haighton Green Lancs
339 E3 Haighton Top Lancs
376 C3 Haile Cumb
163 F3 Hailes Gloucs
145 E2 Hailey Herts
115 G2 Hailey Oxon
139 F2 Hailey Oxon
57 F3 Hailsham E Susx
137 G6 Hailstone Hill Wilts
195 H2 Hail Weston Cambs
233 F1 Haimwood Powys
120 C1 Hainault Gt Lon
101 G2 Haine Kent
255 H4 Hainford Norfk
68 C6 Hains Dorset
319 F3 Hainton Lincs
341 H2 Hainworth Shaw Brad
467 F4 Hairmyres S Lans
361 E2 Haisthorpe E R Yk
61 F4 Hakeford Devon
125 E3 Hakin Pembks
4 D2 Halabezack Cnwll
296 C4 Halam Notts
5 G3 Halamanning Cnwll
487 F2 Halbeath Fife
42 C5 Halberton Devon
44 A2 Halcon Somset
601 H3 Halcro Highld
144 B2 Haldens Herts
365 G4 Hale Cumb
309 G3 Hale Halton
70 D6 Hale Hants
101 E2 Hale Kent
98 B1 Hale Medway
68 C4 Hale Somset
92 D5 Hale Surrey
311 F2 Hale Traffd
309 G3 Hale Bank Halton
311 F2 Hale Barns Traffd
74 C5 Halecommon W Susx
84 D3 Hale Coombe N Som
120 A1 Hale End Gt Lon
57 F2 Hale Green E Susx
6 D5 Hale Mills Cnwll
351 E6 Hale Nook Lancs
250 D5 Hales Norfk
271 G3 Hales Staffs
187 E4 Hales Bank Herefs
235 G4 Halesfield Wrekin
280 D4 Halesgate Lincs
274 B1 Hales Green Derbys
250 D5 Hales Green Norfk
44 A3 Halesowen Dudley
211 H4 Hales Park Worcs

100 B4 Hales Place Kent
225 G2 Hales Street Norfk
97 G5 Hale Street Kent
160 D3 Hales Wood Herefs
226 D4 Halesworth Suffk
309 F2 Halewood Knows
26 D3 Half Moon Village Devon
210 A3 Halford Shrops
190 D5 Halford Warwks
366 A2 Halfpenny Cumb
127 F2 Halfpenny Furze Carmth
212 B1 Halfpenny Green Staffs
128 D4 Halfway Carmth
155 F3 Halfway Carmth
156 C3 Halfway Carmth
315 E3 Halfway Sheff
114 B6 Halfway W Berk
87 F5 Halfway Wilts
75 E5 Halfway Bridge W Susx
233 F2 Halfway House Shrops
325 H3 Halfway Houses Bury
123 E5 Halfway Houses Kent
83 E1 Halfway Street Kent
22 B5 Halgabron Cnwll
342 B5 Halifax Calder
542 C5 Halistra Highld
451 F1 Halkburn Border
466 B4 Halket E Ayrs
588 E5 Halkirk Highld
308 B5 Halkyn Flints
308 A5 Halkyn Mountain Flints
275 H2 Hall Fields Derbys
57 E1 Halland E Susx
241 G5 Hallaton Leics
86 A3 Hallatrow BaNES
401 G3 Hallbankgate Cumb
328 A2 Hall Bower Kirk
314 B2 Hall Broom Sheff
338 B3 Hall Cross Lancs
377 G5 Hall Dunnerdale Cumb
109 F3 Hallen S Glos
169 F2 Hall End Beds
195 E5 Hall End Beds
300 D4 Hall End Lincs
110 C2 Hall End S Glos
190 A1 Hallend Warwks
238 D4 Hall End Warwks
8 C2 Hallew Cnwll
294 D3 Hallfield Gate Derbys
213 E5 Hall Flat Worcs
405 H6 Hallgarth Dur
358 C4 Hall Garth York
486 A4 Hallglen Falk
213 H3 Hall Green Birm
291 G3 Hall Green Ches
215 F3 Hall Green Covtry
173 F2 Hall Green Essex
324 C3 Hall Green Lancs
338 C4 Hall Green Lancs
237 F6 Hall Green Sandw
329 E2 Hall Green Wakefd
270 B1 Hall Green Wrexhm
144 C2 Hall Grove Herts
451 F2 Halliburton Border
473 F5 Halliburton Border
542 D5 Hallin Highld
97 H2 Halling Medway
172 A6 Hallingbury Street Essex
320 A2 Hallington Lincs
429 F4 Hallington Nthumb
325 G2 Hall I' Th' Wood Bolton
325 G2 Halliwell Bolton
571 L6 Hallmoss Abers
600 D3 Hall of Clestrain Ork
601 J3 Hall of Tankerness Ork
235 G3 Hallon Shrops
235 H5 Hallonsford Shrops
296 C4 Halloughton Notts
188 B3 Hallow Worcs
188 B3 Hallow Heath Worcs
289 H1 Hallowsgate Ches
440 A2 Hallrule Border
490 C5 Halls E Loth
13 E5 Hallsands Devon
376 D4 Hall Santon Cumb
57 H3 Hall's Close E Susx
146 B4 Hallsford Bridge Essex
145 F3 Halls Green Essex
170 C4 Hall's Green Herts
96 D5 Hall's Green Kent
39 G3 Hallspill Devon
362 D4 Hallthwaites Cumb
377 E5 Hall Waberthwaite Cumb
161 F3 Hallwood Green Gloucs
22 D5 Hallworthy Cnwll
449 H2 Hallyards Border
449 G1 Hallyne Border
291 F5 Halmer End Staffs
187 F5 Halmond's Frome Herefs
135 F4 Halmore Gloucs
470 C5 Halmyre Mains Border
53 G3 Halnaker W Susx
323 G2 Halsall Lancs
193 F3 Halse Nhants
166 C1 Halse Nhants
43 F2 Halse Somset
3 F2 Halsetown Cnwll
26 D4 Halsfordwood Devon
349 E4 Halsham E R Yk
60 D4 Halsinger Devon
173 G4 Halstead Essex
96 C2 Halstead Kent
241 F3 Halstead Leics
45 G6 Halstock Dorset
64 B4 Halsway Somset
390 B2 Haltcliff Bridge Cumb
71 H5 Halterworth Hants
299 G2 Haltham Lincs
141 G3 Halton Bucks
309 G3 Halton Halton
351 H1 Halton Lancs
343 F3 Halton Leeds
429 F6 Halton Nthumb
269 F2 Halton Wrexhm
17 F5 Halton Barton Cnwll
309 H3 Halton Brook Halton
354 D4 Halton East N York
300 D2 Halton Fenside Lincs
368 A4 Halton Gill N York
351 H1 Halton Green Lancs
300 D1 Halton Holegate Lincs
402 A3 Halton-Lea-Gate Nthumb
343 F3 Halton Moor Leeds
429 G6 Halton Shields Nthumb
310 A2 Halton View Halton
353 G4 Halton West N York
402 C2 Haltwhistle Nthumb
251 E3 Halvergate Norfk
4 D2 Halvosso Cnwll
12 D2 Halwell Devon
24 B3 Halwill Devon
24 B3 Halwill Junction Devon
4 C2 Halwyn Cnwll
11 E2 Ham C Plym
28 D2 Ham Devon
135 F5 Ham Gloucs
163 E5 Ham Gloucs
118 D5 Ham Gt Lon
589 G2 Ham Highld
101 F5 Ham Kent
44 A3 Ham Somset
44 B5 Ham Somset

86 B5 Ham Somset
90 A2 Ham Wilts
606 D2 Hamar Shet
542 B7 Hamaramore Highld
542 B7 Hamaraverin Highld
603 H4 Hamarhill Ork
606 F5 Hamars Shet
116 C2 Hambleden Bucks
52 A2 Hambledon Hants
75 F2 Hambledon Surrey
51 E3 Hamble-le-Rice Hants
351 E6 Hambleton Lancs
344 C3 Hambleton N York
355 E4 Hambleton N York
337 G1 Hambleton Moss Side Lancs
66 B5 Hambridge Somset
110 A4 Hambrook S Glos
52 D3 Hambrook W Susx
68 D4 Ham Common Dorset
300 A1 Hameringham Lincs
219 G4 Hamerton Cambs
167 E6 Ham Green Bucks
72 B3 Ham Green Hants
187 G6 Ham Green Herefs
80 C4 Ham Green Kent
122 C6 Ham Green Kent
109 F4 Ham Green N Som
87 E2 Ham Green Wilts
189 F2 Ham Green Worcs
97 G2 Ham Hill Kent
467 G3 Hamilton S Lans
607 H5 Hamister Shet
28 B3 Hamlet Devon
46 B3 Hamlet Dorset
74 B3 Hammer W Susx
74 D3 Hammer Bottom Hants
54 C3 Hammerpot W Susx
294 D4 Hammersmith Derbys
119 E4 Hammersmith Gt Lon
237 G3 Hammerwich Staffs
78 A2 Hammerwood E Susx
101 E4 Hammill Kent
144 D4 Hammond Street Herts
47 F2 Hammoon Dorset
605 G3 Hamnavoe Shet
606 B1 Hamnavoe Shet
607 G1 Hamnavoe Shet
607 G1 Hamnavoe Shet
607 G3 Hamnavoe Shet
186 C3 Hamnish Clifford Herefs
65 E4 Hamp Somset
57 G4 Hampden Park E Susx
163 F6 Hampen Gloucs
172 B3 Hamperden End Essex
209 H2 Hamperley Shrops
75 F5 Hampers Green W Susx
443 F3 Hampeth Nthumb
137 G1 Hampnett Gloucs
330 A2 Hampole Donc
48 C5 Hampreston Dorset
365 E3 Hampsfield Cumb
351 G4 Hampson Green Lancs
119 F2 Hampstead Gt Lon
119 E2 Hampstead Garden Suburb Gt Lon
115 E4 Hampstead Norreys W Berk
356 B3 Hampsthwaite N York
29 E3 Hampton Devon
118 C5 Hampton Gt Lon
100 C2 Hampton Kent
211 G2 Hampton Shrops
113 E1 Hampton Swindn
189 F6 Hampton Worcs
270 B3 Hampton Bank Shrops
233 F3 Hampton Beech Shrops
160 D2 Hampton Bishop Herefs
136 C5 Hampton Fields Gloucs
140 A1 Hampton Gay Oxon
289 H5 Hampton Green Ches
243 H6 Hampton Hargate C Pete
289 H5 Hampton Heath Ches
118 C5 Hampton Hill Gt Lon
214 C3 Hampton in Arden Solhll
211 G2 Hampton Loade Shrops
188 C1 Hampton Lovett Worcs
190 C3 Hampton Lucy Warwks
190 D1 Hampton Magna Warwks
190 D2 Hampton on the Hill Warwks

50 D1 Hampton Park C Sotn
160 C2 Hampton Park Herefs
140 A1 Hampton Poyle Oxon
97 F4 Hamptons Kent
118 D6 Hampton Wick Gt Lon
71 E6 Hamptworth Wilts
254 B3 Hamrow Norfk
56 C2 Hamsey E Susx
95 H3 Hamsey Green Surrey
135 H4 Hamshill Gloucs
273 H6 Hamstall Ridware Staffs
36 C2 Hamstead IoW
237 F6 Hamstead Birm
90 C1 Hamstead Marshall W Berk
394 C3 Hamsterley Dur
404 D3 Hamsterley Dur
81 F3 Hamstreet Kent
67 F3 Ham Street Somset
34 A2 Hamworthy Poole
274 B4 Hanbury Staffs
189 E2 Hanbury Worcs
274 B4 Hanbury Woodend Staffs
279 E3 Hanby Lincs
198 C5 Hanchett Village Suffk
272 B1 Hanchurch Staffs
386 B1 Handale R & Cl
27 G3 Hand and Pen Devon
289 F1 Handbridge Ches
77 E4 Handcross W Susx
311 G3 Handforth Ches
290 A1 Hand Green Ches
209 G1 Handless Shrops
289 G3 Handley Ches
294 D2 Handley Derbys
146 D4 Handley Green Essex
237 G1 Handsacre Staffs
213 F1 Handsworth Birm
315 E2 Handsworth Sheff
213 F1 Handsworth Wood Birm
116 D1 Handy Cross Bucks
64 B5 Handy Cross Somset
272 C1 Hanford C Stke
47 F2 Hanford Dorset
49 F3 Hangersley Hants
96 C4 Hanging Bank Kent
239 E1 Hanging Heaton Kirk
217 F5 Hanging Houghton Nhants
70 A2 Hanging Langford Wilts
450 D3 Hangingshaw Border
424 B2 Hangingshaw D & G
55 G3 Hangleton Br & H
54 C4 Hangleton W Susx
331 E2 Hangsman Hill Donc
110 A5 Hanham S Glos
110 A5 Hanham Green S Glos
290 D5 Hankelow Ches
111 H1 Hankerton Wilts
57 G3 Hankham E Susx
292 A5 Hanley C Stke
188 B6 Hanley Castle Worcs
187 F1 Hanley Child Worcs
162 B1 Hanley Swan Worcs
187 F1 Hanley William Worcs
354 B2 Hanlith N York
270 B2 Hanmer Wrexhm

40 B2 Hannaford Devon
9 G3 Hannafore Cnwll
321 F4 Hannah Lincs
199 H4 Hanningfields Green Suffk
91 E3 Hannington Hants
217 H5 Hannington Nhants
138 B6 Hannington Swindn
138 B5 Hannington Wick Swindn
169 F3 Hanscombe End Beds
13 E3 Hansel Devon
445 E4 Hansel Village S Ayrs
293 E6 Hansley Cross Staffs
193 H5 Hanslope M Keyn
279 F5 Hanthorpe Lincs
118 D4 Hanwell Gt Lon
191 G6 Hanwell Oxon
234 A3 Hanwood Shrops
234 A2 Hanwood Bank Shrops
93 E1 Hanworth Br For
118 C5 Hanworth Gt Lon
261 G4 Hanworth Norfk
447 H3 Happendon S Lans
256 D3 Happisburgh Norfk
256 D4 Happisburgh Common Norfk
309 G5 Hapsford Ches
86 D5 Hapsford Somset
340 B3 Hapton Lancs
249 G5 Hapton Norfk
19 G6 Harberton Devon
12 D1 Harbertonford Devon
100 B4 Harbledown Kent
213 F3 Harborne Birm
216 A4 Harborough Magna Warwks
216 A4 Harborough Parva Warwks
441 H4 Harbottle Nthumb
56 C5 Harbour Heights E Susx
98 B3 Harbourland Kent
19 F5 Harbourneford Devon
189 E1 Harbours Hill Worcs
151 F2 Harbour Village Pembks
49 E3 Harbridge Hants
49 E2 Harbridge Green Hants
469 G2 Harburn W Loth
191 F2 Harbury Warwks
277 F3 Harby Leics
317 G5 Harby Notts
20 B1 Harcombe Devon
28 C4 Harcombe Devon
29 F3 Harcombe Bottom Devon
7 F6 Harcourt Cnwll
140 A4 Harcourt Hill Oxon
328 A4 Harden Barns
342 A2 Harden Brad
237 F4 Harden Wsall
379 G2 Hardendale Cumb
311 G4 Harden Park Ches
556 D4 Hardgate Abers
413 F1 Hardgate D & G
356 B2 Hardgate N York
483 H5 Hardgate W Duns
313 F4 Hardgatewall Derbys
54 B1 Hardham W Susx
337 G2 Hardhorn Lancs
248 D4 Hardingham Norfk
293 E2 Hardings Booth Staffs
193 G3 Hardingstone Nhants
291 G4 Hardings Wood Staffs
86 C4 Hardington Somset
45 G5 Hardington Mandeville Somset
45 G6 Hardington Marsh Somset
45 G5 Hardington Moor Somset
38 B3 Hardisworthy Devon
50 D4 Hardley Hants
250 D4 Hardley Street Norfk
194 C5 Hardmead M Keyn
367 H1 Hardraw N York
295 E2 Hardstoft Derbys
295 E2 Hardstoft Common Derbys
51 G4 Hardway Hants
68 B3 Hardway Somset
167 H6 Hardwick Bucks
197 E3 Hardwick Cambs
220 A6 Hardwick Cambs
218 A6 Hardwick Nhants
225 H2 Hardwick Norfk
139 F3 Hardwick Oxon
165 G1 Hardwick Oxon
166 C4 Hardwick Oxon
315 F2 Hardwick Rothm
396 B5 Hardwick S on T
209 G1 Hardwick Shrops
237 G5 Hardwick Wsall
136 A2 Hardwicke Gloucs
162 C4 Hardwicke Gloucs
185 E6 Hardwicke Herefs
162 B3 Hardwick Green Worcs
316 B4 Hardwick Village Notts
174 B5 Hardy's Green Essex
44 B4 Hare Somset
352 A3 Hare Appletree Lancs
300 B1 Hareby Lincs
342 A2 Harecroft Brad
352 C4 Hareden Lancs
314 C5 Hare Edge Derbys
51 E2 Harefield C Sotn
118 B1 Harefield Gt Lon
118 B1 Harefield Grove Gt Lon
292 C3 Haregate Staffs
175 E5 Hare Green Essex
116 D4 Hare Hatch Wokham
274 B2 Harehill Derbys
343 F3 Harehills Leeds
470 D6 Harehope Border
454 D5 Harehope Nthumb
405 E4 Harelaw Dur
468 B4 Hareleeshill S Lans
80 B2 Hareplain Kent
401 H6 Haresceugh Cumb
136 B2 Harescombe Gloucs
136 B2 Haresfield Gloucs
138 C6 Haresfield Swindn
324 C5 Haresfinch St Hel
468 C3 Hareshaw N Lans
484 D5 Harestanes E Duns
72 C3 Harestock Hants
145 F3 Hare Street Essex
171 E4 Hare Street Herts
356 C5 Harewood Leeds
160 C4 Harewood End Herefs
18 D6 Harford Devon
61 E3 Harford Devon
225 F1 Hargate Norfk
327 F6 Hargate Hill Derbys
289 G2 Hargrave Ches
219 E5 Hargrave Nhants
199 F3 Hargrave Suffk
400 C2 Harker Cumb
388 C3 Harker Marsh Cumb
608 E7 Harkland Shet
145 F3 Harknett's Gate Essex
176 C3 Harkstead Suffk
238 C2 Harlaston Staffs
278 B3 Harlaxton Lincs
264 D3 Harlech Gwynd
277 E2 Harlequin Notts
234 C1 Harlescott Shrops
119 E3 Harlesden Gt Lon
315 F4 Harlesthorpe Derbys
12 D4 Harleston Devon
226 A3 Harleston Norfk
200 D3 Harleston Suffk

692 City, town and village index: Harlestone - Hemsworth

193 F2 Harlestone Nhants
340 D2 Harle Syke Lancs
329 F5 Harley Rothm
234 D4 Harley Shrops
58 C5 Harley Shute E Susx
136 B5 Harleywood Gloucs
224 C2 Harling Road Norfk
169 E3 Harlington Beds
330 A4 Harlington Donc
118 B4 Harlington Gt Lon
544 D1 Harlosh Highld
145 F3 Harlow Essex
145 G2 Harlowbury Essex
356 B4 Harlow Carr N York
405 G3 Harlow Green Gatesd
356 B4 Harlow Hill N York
430 A6 Harlow Hill Nthumb
345 G2 Harlthorpe E R Yk
197 E4 Harlton Cambs
14 B3 Harlyn Cnwll
98 D2 Harman's Corner Kent
33 H3 Harman's Cross Dorset
117 E6 Harmans Water Br For
369 F2 Harmby N York
144 C1 Harmer Green Herts
270 B5 Harmer Hill Shrops
118 B4 Harmondsworth Gt Lon
298 B2 Harmston Lincs
234 D4 Harnage Shrops
430 A3 Harnham Nthumb
70 C4 Harnham Wilts
137 G4 Harnhill Gloucs
120 D1 Harold Hill Gt Lon
121 E1 Harold Park Gt Lon
125 E1 Haroldston West Pembks
609 J2 Haroldswick Shet
120 D1 Harold Wood Gt Lon
372 B3 Harome N York
143 G2 Harpenden Herts
143 G2 Harpenden Common Herts
325 G3 Harper Green Bolton
405 E4 Harperley Dur
292 B3 Harper's Gate Staffs
254 B3 Harper's Green Norfk
28 A4 Harpford Devon
360 D2 Harpham E R Yk
253 F2 Harpley Norfk
187 F2 Harpley Worcs
193 E2 Harpole Nhants
559 F5 Harpsdale Highld
116 C3 Harpsden Oxon
116 B3 Harpsden Bottom Oxon
318 A2 Harpswell Lincs
184 D3 Harpton Powys
326 C4 Harpurhey Manch
313 E5 Harpur Hill Derbys
400 D4 Harraby Cumb
30 B2 Harracott Devon
546 B5 Harrapool Highld
388 A6 Harras Cumb
405 G4 Harraton Sundld
604 b1 Harrier Shet
512 A4 Harrietfield P & K
98 D4 Harrietsham Kent
119 G2 Harringay Gt Lon
388 A4 Harrington Cumb
320 C5 Harrington Lincs
217 G4 Harrington Nhants
242 C5 Harringworth Nhants
530 B3 Harris Highld
291 H3 Harriseahead Staffs
389 E1 Harriston Cumb
356 B3 Harrogate N York
194 C3 Harrold Beds
327 F3 Harrop Dale Oldham
118 C2 Harrow Gt Lon
17 E4 Harrowbarrow Cnwll
18 B4 Harrowbeer Devon
278 C3 Harrowby Lincs
195 F5 Harrowden Beds
383 G1 Harrowgate Hill Darltn
395 F6 Harrowgate Village Darltn
199 H4 Harrow Green Suffk
135 F1 Harrow Hill Gloucs
118 D2 Harrow on the Hill Gt Lon
118 C1 Harrow Weald Gt Lon
110 A4 Harry Stoke S Glos
197 F4 Harston Cambs
278 A3 Harston Leics
346 B1 Harswell E R Yk
396 C3 Hart Hartpl
365 E1 Hartbarrow Cumb
430 A2 Hartburn Nthumb
396 B6 Hartburn S on T
109 G6 Hartcliffe Bristl
325 E4 Hart Common Bolton
199 G4 Hartest Suffk
199 G4 Hartest Hill Suffk
78 B2 Hartfield E Susx
220 B5 Hartford Cambs
310 C5 Hartford Ches
42 C2 Hartford Somset
310 C5 Hartfordbeach Ches
92 C3 Hartfordbridge Hants
172 E3 Hartford End Essex
383 E3 Hartforth N York
68 D6 Hartgrove Dorset
144 D2 Hartham Herts
289 H3 Harthill Ches
169 G5 Hart Hill Luton
469 E2 Harthill N Lans
315 F3 Harthill Rothm
293 F2 Hartington Derbys
38 B3 Hartland Devon
38 B3 Hartland Quay Devon
212 D4 Hartle Worcs
235 G5 Hartlebury Shrops
212 B5 Hartlebury Worcs
212 B5 Hartlebury Common Worcs
396 D3 Hartlepool Hartpl
380 D3 Hartley Cumb
79 G3 Hartley Kent
121 F6 Hartley Kent
431 F4 Hartley Nthumb
121 E6 Hartley Green Kent
273 E4 Hartley Green Staffs
74 A2 Hartley Mauditt Hants
92 A3 Hartley Wespall Hants
92 C3 Hartley Wintney Hants
354 D2 Hartlington N York
98 C2 Hartlip Kent
68 C5 Hartmoor Dorset
577 G8 Hartmount Highld
386 C6 Hartoft End N York
358 D2 Harton N York
406 B2 Harton S Tyne
210 B2 Harton Shrops
162 A5 Hartpury Gloucs
212 A3 Hartsgreen Shrops
199 H3 Hart's Green Suffk
342 C5 Hartshead Kirk
327 E4 Hartshead Green Tamesd
342 C4 Hartshead Moor Top Kirk
327 E4 Hartshead Pike Tamesd
291 H5 Hartshill C Stke
212 D2 Hart's Hill Dudley
239 E6 Hartshill Warwks
239 E6 Hartshill Green Warwks
318 A6 Hartsholme Lincs
275 E5 Hartshorne Derbys
287 E5 Hartsop Cumb
396 C2 Hart Station Hartpl
43 E2 Hartswell Somset
193 G4 Hartwell Nhants
272 D2 Hartwell Staffs
355 H2 Hartwith N York
339 E6 Hartwood Lancs
468 C3 Hartwood N Lans
451 F4 Hartwoodburn Border
451 E5 Hartwoodmyres Border
97 F2 Harvel Kent
214 D3 Harvest Hill Covtry
237 E6 Harvills Hawthorn Sandw
189 G5 Harvington Worcs
212 C5 Harvington Worcs
316 C1 Harwell Notts
114 D2 Harwell Oxon
177 E3 Harwich Essex
325 G2 Harwood Bolton
392 D3 Harwood Dur
429 G1 Harwood Nthumb
387 G5 Harwood Dale N York
325 G2 Harwood Lee Bolton
439 E3 Harwood on Teviot Border
316 B1 Harworth Notts
213 E3 Hasbury Dudley
75 F2 Hascombe Surrey
217 F4 Haselbech Nhants
45 F5 Haselbury Plucknett Somset
214 C6 Haseley Warwks
214 C6 Haseley Green Warwks
214 C5 Haseley Knob Warwks
189 H3 Haselor Warwks
162 B4 Hasfield Gloucs
124 D3 Hasguard Pembks
323 F3 Haskayne Lancs
202 A4 Hasketon Suffk
314 D6 Hasland Derbys
314 D6 Hasland Green Derbys
75 E3 Haslemere Surrey
75 F5 Haslingbourne W Susx
340 B5 Haslingden Lancs
340 B5 Haslingden Grane Lancs
197 F4 Haslingfield Cambs
291 E3 Haslington Ches
213 H4 Hasluck's Green Solhll
440 C2 Hass Border
291 F3 Hassall Ches
291 F3 Hassall Green Ches
82 A1 Hassell Street Kent
451 G5 Hassendean Border
559 F1 Hassiewells Abers
250 D3 Hassingham Norfk
55 G1 Hassocks W Susx
313 H5 Hassop Derbys
321 E6 Hasthorpe Lincs
589 G4 Hastigrow Highld
406 B4 Hasting Hill Sundld
82 A2 Hastingleigh Kent
58 D5 Hastings E Susx
44 C4 Hastings Somset
145 G3 Hastingwood Essex
142 C3 Hastoe Herts
270 C5 Haston Shrops
406 B6 Haswell Dur
396 A1 Haswell Moor Dur
395 H1 Haswell Plough Dur
449 G2 Haswellsykes Border
195 G5 Hatch Beds
12 C3 Hatch Devon
91 H4 Hatch Hants
44 C3 Hatch Beauchamp Somset
51 E2 Hatch Bottom Hants
195 F2 Hatch End Beds
118 C1 Hatch End Gt Lon
50 C4 Hatchet Gate Hants
70 D6 Hatchet Green Hants
74 D4 Hatch Farm Hill W Susx
44 C4 Hatch Green Somset
143 G2 Hatching Green Herts
310 B5 Hatchmere Ches
91 G5 Hatch Warren Hants
334 B4 Hatcliffe NE Lin
237 F6 Hateley Heath Sandw
331 E3 Hatfield Donc
186 D3 Hatfield Herefs
144 B3 Hatfield Herts
188 C4 Hatfield Worcs
146 A1 Hatfield Broad Oak Essex
331 F3 Hatfield Chase Donc
144 B2 Hatfield Garden Village Herts
146 A1 Hatfield Heath Essex
144 B2 Hatfield Hyde Herts
147 F2 Hatfield Peverel Essex
331 E3 Hatfield Woodhouse Donc
139 E6 Hatford Oxon
90 A4 Hatherden Hants
24 D2 Hatherleigh Devon
162 D5 Hatherley Gloucs
276 A5 Hathern Leics
138 B3 Hatherop Gloucs
314 A3 Hathersage Derbys
314 A3 Hathersage Booths Derbys
326 D4 Hathershaw Oldham
290 D5 Hatherton Ches
236 D2 Hatherton Staffs
196 C4 Hatley St George Cambs
601 G2 Hatson Ork
10 C1 Hatt Cnwll
327 E6 Hattersley Tamesd
71 G4 Hatt Hill Hants
73 F2 Hattingley Hants
561 G2 Hatton Abers
274 C3 Hatton Derbys
319 F4 Hatton Lincs
210 B1 Hatton Shrops
310 B3 Hatton Warrtn
190 C1 Hatton Warwks
560 B5 Hattoncrook Abers
235 H4 Hatton Grange Shrops
289 G2 Hatton Heath Ches
93 F2 Hatton Hill Surrey
470 D5 Hattonknowe Border
557 E1 Hatton of Fintray Abers
527 E6 Hatton of Ogilvie Angus
218 B6 Hatton Park Nhants
445 G4 Haugh E Ayrs
320 D4 Haugh Lincs
326 D2 Haugh Rochdl
320 B3 Haugham Lincs
450 C2 Haugh-Head Border
454 C4 Haugh Head Nthumb
200 D2 Haughley Suffk
200 D2 Haughley Green Suffk
200 D2 Haughley New Street Suffk
569 G8 Haugh of Glass Moray
413 F1 Haugh of Urr D & G
290 B3 Haughton Ches
316 C5 Haughton Notts
269 F6 Haughton Powys
234 D1 Haughton Shrops
235 F5 Haughton Shrops
235 G3 Haughton Shrops
269 G4 Haughton Shrops
272 C5 Haughton Staffs
326 D6 Haughton Green Tamesd
383 H1 Haughton le Skerne Darltn
91 F2 Haughurst Hill Hants
170 D5 Haultwick Herts
517 J6 Haunn Ag & B
590 F5 Haunn W Isls
238 C2 Haunton Staffs
35 h5 Hautes Croix Jersey
197 F4 Hauxton Cambs
291 H2 Havannah Ches
52 C3 Havant Hants
185 H4 Haven Herefs
186 D5 Haven Herefs
299 G4 Haven Bank Lincs
37 F3 Havenstreet IoW
329 F2 Havercroft Wakefd
125 G2 Haverfordwest Pembks
198 D5 Haverhill Suffk
362 D6 Haverigg Cumb
145 H6 Havering-atte-Bower Gt Lon
255 G4 Haveringland Norfk
193 H6 Haversham M Keyn
364 D3 Haverthwaite Cumb
396 C5 Haverton Hill S on T
97 H5 Haviker Street Kent
67 E2 Havyatt Somset
85 E2 Havyatt Green N Som
288 D1 Hawarden Flints
188 D5 Hawbridge Worcs
173 F5 Hawbush Green Essex
364 B5 Hawcoat Cumb
161 H3 Hawcross Gloucs
265 F6 Hawddamor Gwynd
179 G4 Hawen Cerdgn
367 H2 Hawes N York
250 A5 Hawes' Green Norfk
337 F3 Hawes Side Bpool
188 B2 Hawford Worcs
271 E4 Hawgreen Shrops
439 G2 Hawick Border
29 F2 Hawkchurch Devon
199 F4 Hawkedon Suffk
78 D2 Hawkenbury Kent
98 B6 Hawkenbury Kent
87 F4 Hawkeridge Wilts
27 H5 Hawkerland Devon
186 C5 Hawkersland Cross Herefs
110 D2 Hawkesbury S Glos
215 F3 Hawkesbury Warwks
110 D2 Hawkesbury Upton S Glos
214 D3 Hawkes End Covtry
213 F4 Hawkesley Birm
312 C2 Hawk Green Stockp
388 B4 Hawk Hill Cumb
443 G2 Hawkhill Nthumb
427 H2 Hawkhope Nthumb
79 G3 Hawkhurst Kent
78 C6 Hawkhurst Common E Susx
82 D3 Hawkinge Kent
172 D3 Hawkin's Hill Essex
74 A4 Hawkley Hants
324 D4 Hawkley Wigan
62 D5 Hawkridge Somset
400 C5 Hawksdale Cumb
237 E2 Hawks Green Staffs
325 H1 Hawkshaw Bury
378 C5 Hawkshead Cumb
378 B5 Hawkshead Hill Cumb
117 F2 Hawks Hill Bucks
94 D3 Hawk's Hill Surrey
447 G2 Hawksland S Lans
172 C3 Hawkspur Green Essex
341 E4 Hawks Stones Calder
368 C5 Hawkswick N York
342 C1 Hawksworth Leeds
343 E2 Hawksworth Leeds
297 E6 Hawksworth Notts
122 D1 Hawkwell Essex
92 D3 Hawley Hants
120 D5 Hawley Kent
28 D2 Hawley Bottom Devon
93 E3 Hawley Lane Hants
163 G5 Hawling Gloucs
371 G2 Hawnby N York
213 E3 Hawne Dudley
341 G2 Haworth Brad
378 B5 Haws Bank Cumb
199 G3 Hawstead Suffk
199 H3 Hawstead Green Suffk
406 C5 Hawthorn Dur
73 G3 Hawthorn Hants
106 A2 Hawthorn Rhondd
100 D2 Hawthorn Corner Kent
117 E5 Hawthorn Hill Br For
299 G3 Hawthorn Hill Lincs
279 E4 Hawthorpe Lincs
297 E4 Hawton Notts
358 A3 Haxby York
331 G5 Haxey N Linc
331 G4 Haxey Carr N Linc
96 B5 Haxted Surrey
89 E5 Haxton Wilts
14 D4 Hay Cnwll
211 E5 Haybridge Shrops
85 F5 Haybridge Somset
235 F2 Haybridge Wrekin
162 C5 Hayden Gloucs
324 D5 Haydock St Hel
86 B4 Haydon BaNES
46 C1 Haydon Dorset
44 B3 Haydon Somset
85 G5 Haydon Somset
112 D2 Haydon Swindn
403 E2 Haydon Bridge Nthumb
112 D2 Haydon Wick Swindn
16 D4 Haye Cnwll
96 A1 Hayes Gt Lon
118 B3 Hayes Gt Lon
293 E2 Hayes Staffs
118 B3 Hayes End Gt Lon
112 D1 Hayes Knoll Wilts
312 D2 Hayfield Derbys
330 D5 Hay Field Donc
501 E6 Hayfield Fife
330 D5 Hayfield Green Donc
235 E2 Haygate Wrekin
44 A3 Haygrass Somset
146 B4 Hay Green Essex
170 D2 Hay Green Herts
252 A4 Hay Green Norfk
433 G1 Hayhill E Ayrs
515 E1 Hayhillock Angus
37 F2 Haylands IoW
3 G2 Hayle Cnwll
212 D3 Hayley Green Worcs
213 H3 Hay Mills Birm
44 C2 Haymoor End Somset
290 D4 Haymoor Green Ches
26 D1 Hayne Devon
169 G1 Haynes Beds
169 F1 Haynes Church End Beds
169 F1 Haynes West End Beds
158 D1 Hay-on-Wye Powys
151 E4 Hayscastle Pembks
151 F4 Hayscastle Cross Pembks
151 F5 Haysford Pembks
515 G1 Hayshead Angus
484 C5 Hayston E Duns
450 B2 Haystoun Border
171 E4 Hay Street Herts
48 C3 Haythorne Dorset
557 G3 Hayton C Aber
388 D1 Hayton Cumb
401 F3 Hayton Cumb
359 F5 Hayton E R Yk
316 D3 Hayton Notts
210 C3 Hayton's Bent Shrops
19 G2 Haytor Vale Devon
39 E5 Haytown Devon
77 F5 Haywards Heath W Susx
330 C2 Haywood Donc
469 F4 Haywood S Lans
296 B3 Haywood Oaks Notts
58 A4 Hazard's Green E Susx
468 C6 Hazelbank S Lans
125 F4 Hazelbeach Pembks
46 D3 Hazelbury Bryan Dorset
147 G4 Hazeleigh Essex
171 G5 Hazel End Essex
92 B3 Hazeley Hants
92 B3 Hazeley Bottom Hants
92 C3 Hazeley Heath Hants
92 B3 Hazeley Lea Hants
312 B2 Hazel Grove Stockp
325 H1 Hazelhurst Bury
49 H5 Hazelhurst Hants
325 H4 Hazelhurst Salfd
327 E4 Hazelhurst Tamesd
454 D3 Hazelrigg Nthumb
365 G4 Hazelslack Cumb
237 F2 Hazelslade Staffs
79 F2 Hazel Street Kent
98 D3 Hazel Street Kent
198 C5 Hazel Stub Suffk
513 H5 Hazelton Walls Fife
294 C5 Hazelwood Derbys
12 C2 Hazelwood Devon
96 B2 Hazelwood Gt Lon
328 B4 Hazlehead Barns
142 B5 Hazlemere Bucks
234 B6 Hazler Shrops
430 D5 Hazlerigg N u Ty
292 C5 Hazles Staffs
292 D5 Hazlescross Staffs
163 G6 Hazleton Gloucs
355 E4 Hazlewood N York
443 F4 Hazon Nthumb
258 D4 Heacham Norfk
72 C3 Headbourne Worthy Hants
185 F3 Headbrook Herefs
98 C6 Headcorn Kent
343 E2 Headingley Leeds
140 B3 Headington Oxon
140 B3 Headington Hill Oxon
394 D6 Headlam Dur
365 E4 Headless Cross Cumb
189 F1 Headless Cross Worcs
74 C2 Headley Hants
91 E2 Headley Hants
95 E4 Headley Surrey
74 C2 Headley Down Hants
213 G4 Headley Heath Worcs
109 G6 Headley Park Bristl
485 G3 Head of Muir Falk
23 H2 Headon Devon
316 D4 Headon Notts
467 H5 Heads S Lans
451 F5 Headshaw Border
401 E3 Heads Nook Cumb
118 C2 Headstone Gt Lon
487 E2 Headwell Fife
294 D5 Heage Derbys
357 F5 Healaugh N York
382 B5 Healaugh N York
311 H2 Heald Green Stockp
326 C3 Healds Green Oldham
61 F2 Heale Devon
44 A4 Heale Somset
66 B4 Heale Somset
86 B6 Heale Somset
369 G3 Healey N York
404 B3 Healey Nthumb
326 C1 Healey Rochdl
343 E6 Healey Wakefd
443 E4 Healey Cote Nthumb
404 C5 Healeyfield Dur
404 B3 Healey Hall Nthumb
334 B2 Healing NE Lin
3 E3 Heamoor Cnwll
378 D5 Heaning Cumb
516 C7 Heanish Ag & B
295 E5 Heanor Derbys
295 E5 Heanor Gate Derbys
60 D4 Heanton Punchardon Devon
326 B2 Heap Bridge Rochdl
317 G2 Heapham Lincs
74 C2 Hearn Hants
98 C5 Hearnden Green Kent
449 F4 Hearthstane Border
294 C3 Hearthstone Derbys
98 D2 Hearts Delight Kent
62 A5 Heasley Mill Devon
545 L6 Heaste Highld
106 A4 Heath Cardif
295 E1 Heath Derbys
309 H3 Heath Halton
168 C4 Heath and Reach Beds
324 D2 Heath Charnock Lancs
54 D2 Heath Common W Susx
293 F2 Heathcote Derbys
271 F4 Heathcote Shrops
191 E2 Heathcote Warwks
25 H3 Heath Cross Devon
26 C4 Heath Cross Devon
142 B5 Heath End Bucks
142 D3 Heath End Bucks
90 C2 Heath End Hants
91 F2 Heath End Hants
275 F5 Heath End Leics
110 B2 Heath End S Glos
92 D5 Heath End Surrey
75 F6 Heath End W Susx
190 C2 Heath End Warwks
237 F4 Heath End Wsall
239 F2 Heather Leics
19 F1 Heathercombe Devon
545 H1 Heatherfield Highld
92 B4 Heather Row Hants
93 F3 Heatherside Surrey
197 F5 Heathfield Cambs
19 H2 Heathfield Devon
78 D5 Heathfield E Susx
135 G5 Heathfield Gloucs
51 G3 Heathfield Hants
333 G6 Heathfield Lincs
465 G2 Heathfield Rens
444 D5 Heathfield S Ayrs
43 G2 Heathfield Somset
140 B1 Heathfield Village Oxon
73 F2 Heath Green Hants
213 G5 Heath Green Worcs
237 F2 Heath Hayes Staffs
235 H2 Heath Hill Shrops
84 D5 Heath House Somset
92 D1 Heathlands Wokham
271 E5 Heath Lanes Wrekin
120 D2 Heath Park Gt Lon
557 F3 Heathryfold C Aber
120 D5 Heath Side Kent
28 D2 Heathstock Devon
212 B1 Heathton Shrops
274 C3 Heathtop Derbys
236 D5 Heath Town Wolves
378 D5 Heathwaite Cumb
384 D4 Heathwaite N York
273 G4 Heatley Staffs
311 E2 Heatley Warrtn
325 F3 Heaton Bolton
342 B2 Heaton Brad
351 F2 Heaton Lancs
405 G1 Heaton N u Ty
292 C2 Heaton Staffs
326 C6 Heaton Chapel Stockp
311 H1 Heaton Mersey Stockp
311 H1 Heaton Moor Stockp
312 A1 Heaton Norris Stockp
342 B2 Heaton Royds Brad
323 H2 Heaton's Bridge Lancs
67 G5 Heaven's Door Somset
97 E3 Heaverham Kent
312 B2 Heaviley Stockp
27 E4 Heavitree Devon
405 H2 Hebburn S Tyne
405 H1 Hebburn Colliery S Tyne
405 G2 Hebburn New Town S Tyne
354 D2 Hebden N York
341 F4 Hebden Bridge Calder
290 C2 Hebden Green Ches
170 D5 Hebing End Herts
152 D4 Hebron Carmth
303 G4 Hebron IoA
430 C2 Hebron Nthumb
424 B3 Heck D & G
331 G5 Heckdyke Notts
92 B2 Heckfield Hants
225 G4 Heckfield Green Suffk
174 B5 Heckfordbridge Essex
250 D5 Heckingham Norfk
299 E6 Heckington Lincs
342 D5 Heckmondwike Kirk
88 A1 Heddington Wick Wilts
600 F2 Heddle Ork
40 D2 Heddon Devon
404 D1 Heddon-on-the-Wall Nthumb
250 C6 Hedenham Norfk
47 F3 Hedge End Dorset
51 E2 Hedge End Hants
299 H5 Hedgehog Bridge Lincs
117 G2 Hedgerley Bucks
117 G2 Hedgerley Green Bucks
117 G2 Hedgerley Hill Bucks
44 B2 Hedging Somset
354 C1 Hedley Hill Dur
404 C3 Hedley on the Hill Nthumb
237 F2 Hednesford Staffs
348 C4 Hedon E R Yk
117 F2 Hedsor Bucks
406 A2 Hedworth S Tyne
168 A2 Heelands M Keyn
314 D3 Heeley Sheff
186 D4 Hegdon Hill Herefs
381 E2 Heggerscales Cumb
390 B2 Heggle Lane Cumb
606 E7 Heglibister Shet
395 F5 Heighington Darltn
318 C6 Heighington Lincs
291 F5 Heighley Staffs
340 B5 Height End Lancs
211 H5 Heightington Worcs
327 E3 Heights Oldham
565 J4 Heights of Brae Highld
563 K4 Heights of Kinlochewe Highld
585 J5 Heilam Highld
452 D3 Heiton Border
380 D1 Helbeck Cumb
19 F3 Hele Devon
23 G4 Hele Devon
27 F2 Hele Devon
60 D2 Hele Devon
43 G3 Hele Somset
20 C4 Hele Torbay
23 E2 Helebridge Cnwll
482 D3 Helensburgh Ag & B
4 D3 Helford Cnwll
5 E3 Helford Passage Cnwll
145 E1 Helham Green Herts
253 H2 Helhoughton Norfk
172 C1 Helions Bumpstead Essex
315 G1 Hellaby Rothm
15 F4 Helland Cnwll
44 C3 Helland Somset
15 F4 Hellandbridge Cnwll
90 B2 Hell Corner W Berk
249 H2 Hellesdon Norfk
3 F1 Hellesveor Cnwll
192 B3 Hellidon Nhants
353 H3 Hellifield N York
353 H3 Hellifield Green N York
57 F2 Hellingly E Susx
250 C4 Hellington Norfk
606 E8 Hellister Shet
172 B6 Hellman's Cross Essex
368 B1 Helm N York
450 D5 Helmburn Border
192 C6 Helmdon Nhants
327 G2 Helme Kirk
201 G3 Helmingham Suffk
394 D2 Helmington Row Dur
582 D7 Helmsdale Highld
340 B5 Helmshore Lancs
366 D2 Helmside Cumb
372 A3 Helmsley N York
371 E6 Helperby N York
374 B5 Helperthorpe N York
279 G1 Helpringham Lincs
243 G3 Helpston C Pete
309 G4 Helsby Ches
23 E2 Helscott Cnwll
321 F5 Helsey Lincs
4 C3 Helston Cnwll
15 F2 Helstone Cnwll
7 E5 Helston Water Cnwll
391 E5 Helton Cumb
357 G6 Helwith Bridge N York
250 C2 Hemblington Norfk
250 C2 Hemblington Corner Norfk
67 F2 Hembridge Somset
143 F4 Hemel Hempstead Herts
11 G2 Hemerdon Devon
233 F4 Hemford Shrops
272 C1 Hem Heath C Stke
345 F3 Hemingbrough N York
319 G5 Hemingby Lincs
329 F4 Hemingfield Barns
220 C5 Hemingford Abbots Cambs
220 C6 Hemingford Grey Cambs
201 F4 Hemingstone Suffk
275 H4 Hemington Leics
219 F2 Hemington Nhants
86 C4 Hemington Somset
177 E1 Hemley Suffk
384 D2 Hemlington Middsb
226 D6 Hemp Green Suffk
360 D4 Hempholme E R Yk
250 A6 Hempnall Norfk
250 A6 Hempnall Green Norfk
567 L4 Hempriggs Moray
174 B4 Hemp's Green Essex
295 G6 Hempshill Vale C Nott
172 C2 Hempstead Essex
98 B2 Hempstead Medway
257 E4 Hempstead Norfk
261 E4 Hempstead Norfk
136 B1 Hempsted Gloucs
254 B2 Hempton Norfk
165 G3 Hempton Oxon
143 G4 Hempton Wainhill Oxon
251 F1 Hemsby Norfk
82 B2 Hemsted Kent
317 H1 Hemswell Lincs
318 B2 Hemswell Cliff Lincs
48 B3 Hemsworth Dorset
314 D3 Hemsworth Sheff
329 G2 Hemsworth Wakefd

43 F5 **Hemyock** Devon
38 B4 **Henaford** Devon
304 C5 **Hen Bentref Llandegfan** IoA
188 D1 **Henbrook** Worcs
109 G4 **Henbury** Bristl
312 A5 **Henbury** Ches
48 B5 **Henbury** Dorset
452 D2 **Hendersyde Park** Border
232 D5 **Hendomen** Powys
119 E2 **Hendon** Gt Lon
406 C3 **Hendon** Sundld
3 G4 **Hendra** Cnwll
4 C2 **Hendra** Cnwll
4 D1 **Hendra** Cnwll
4 D5 **Hendra** Cnwll
8 A2 **Hendra** Cnwll
8 B3 **Hendra** Cnwll
14 D6 **Hendra** Cnwll
22 B6 **Hendra** Cnwll
16 C5 **Hendrabridge** Cnwll
22 C5 **Hendraburnick** Cnwll
7 E2 **Hendra Croft** Cnwll
308 A6 **Hendre** Flints
228 D3 **Hendre** Gwynd
231 F5 **Hendre** Powys
286 B1 **Hendre-Ddu** Conwy
106 B2 **Hendredenny Park** Caerph
105 F2 **Hendreforgan** Rhondd
287 G2 **Hendrerwydd** Denbgs
129 F3 **Hendrewen** Swans
129 E4 **Hendy** Carmth
105 G3 **Hendy** Rhondd
287 F2 **Hên-Efail** Denbgs
303 F5 **Heneglwys** IoA
110 B4 **Henfield** S Glos
55 F1 **Henfield** W Susx
23 H4 **Henford** Devon
87 F6 **Henfords Marsh** Wilts
180 C2 **Henfynyw** Cerdgn
132 B5 **Hengoed** Caerph
287 F3 **Hengoed** Denbgs
184 D4 **Hengoed** Powys
269 E3 **Hengoed** Shrops
255 F4 **Hengrave** Norfk
223 G6 **Hengrave** Suffk
109 G6 **Hengrove** Bristl
109 G6 **Hengrove Park** Bristl
172 A4 **Henham** Essex
232 B3 **Heniarth** Powys
44 B3 **Henlade** Somset
109 G4 **Henleaze** Bristl
46 C4 **Henley** Dorset
136 D1 **Henley** Gloucs
210 B2 **Henley** Shrops
210 C4 **Henley** Shrops
66 C3 **Henley** Somset
201 F4 **Henley** Suffk
74 D4 **Henley** W Susx
89 H3 **Henley** Wilts
111 E6 **Henley** Wilts
74 D4 **Henley Common** W Susx
215 F3 **Henley Green** Covtry
190 A1 **Henley-in-Arden** Warwks
116 B3 **Henley-on-Thames** Oxon
93 F4 **Henley Park** Surrey
58 B4 **Henley's Down** E Susx
97 G1 **Henley Street** Kent
153 G1 **Henllan** Cerdgn
307 E6 **Henllan** Denbgs
152 D6 **Henllan Amgoed** Carmth
269 F3 **Henlle** Shrops
133 E6 **Henllys** Torfn
133 E6 **Henllys Vale** Torfn
170 A2 **Henlow** Beds
19 H1 **Hennock** Devon
173 H2 **Henny Street** Essex
305 G5 **Henryd** Conwy
152 A4 **Henry's Moat** Pembks
329 B5 **Hensall** N York
342 D1 **Henshaw** Leeds
402 D2 **Henshaw** Nthumb
376 B1 **Hensingham** Cumb
139 H1 **Hensington** Oxon
227 F2 **Henstead** Suffk
72 C5 **Hensting** Hants
61 E3 **Henstridge** Devon
68 B6 **Henstridge** Somset
68 B5 **Henstridge Ash** Somset
68 A5 **Henstridge Bowden** Somset
68 B5 **Henstridge Marsh** Somset
141 G4 **Henton** Oxon
85 E5 **Henton** Somset
16 C4 **Henwood** Cnwll
139 H4 **Henwood** Oxon
139 H4 **Henwood and Lamborough Hill** Oxon
79 E1 **Henwood Green** Kent
605 J2 **Heogan** Shet
128 C4 **Heol-Ddu** Carmth
129 F5 **Heol-Ddu** Swans
131 G3 **Heolgerrig** Myr Td
105 E3 **Heol-Laethog** Brdgnd
105 E3 **Heol-Las** Brdgnd
129 G5 **Heol Las** Swans
157 E5 **Heol Senni** Powys
105 E3 **Heol-y-Cyw** Brdgnd
158 C2 **Heol-y-Gaer** Powys
104 D5 **Heol-y-Mynydd** V Glam
454 D5 **Hepburn** Nthumb
442 B4 **Hepple** Nthumb
430 D3 **Hepscott** Nthumb
294 D2 **Hepthorne Lane** Derbys
341 F4 **Heptonstall** Calder
328 B3 **Hepworth** Kirk
224 C4 **Hepworth** Suffk
125 E3 **Herbrandston** Pembks
160 C2 **Hereford** Herefs
542 D7 **Heribost** Highld
543 G2 **Heribusta** Highld
471 G4 **Heriot** Border
487 G6 **Hermiston** C Edin
439 G5 **Hermitage** Border
31 E1 **Hermitage** Dorset
115 E5 **Hermitage** W Berk
52 D3 **Hermitage** W Susx
325 E6 **Hermitage Green** Warrtn
329 E4 **Hermit Hill** Barns
153 H3 **Hermon** Carmth
282 C2 **Hermon** IoA
153 E3 **Hermon** Pembks
12 D1 **Hernaford** Devon
100 C2 **Herne** Kent
100 C2 **Herne Bay** Kent
100 C3 **Herne Common** Kent
119 G5 **Herne Hill** Gt Lon
97 G4 **Herne Pound** Kent
40 B2 **Herner** Devon
99 H2 **Hernhill** Kent
4 D2 **Herniss** Cnwll
9 G1 **Herodsfoot** Cnwll
101 E5 **Heronden** Kent
121 F1 **Herongate** Essex
418 D5 **Heronsford** S Ayrs
143 E6 **Heronsgate** Herts
78 B4 **Heron's Ghyll** E Susx
85 F3 **Herons Green** BaNES
105 E4 **Heronston** Brdgnd
609 H6 **Herra** Shet
91 H5 **Herriard** Hants
251 F5 **Herringfleet** Suffk
195 F6 **Herring's Green** Beds
223 E6 **Herringswell** Suffk
315 E1 **Herringthorpe** Rothm
100 C3 **Hersden** Kent
38 B6 **Hersham** Cnwll
94 C2 **Hersham** Surrey
57 G2 **Herstmonceux** E Susx
34 B5 **Herston** Dorset
601 G6 **Herston** Ork
144 D2 **Hertford** Herts
145 E2 **Hertford Heath** Herts
144 D2 **Hertingfordbury** Herts
338 B5 **Hesketh Bank** Lancs
339 F1 **Hesketh Lane** Lancs
338 B5 **Hesketh Moss** Lancs
390 A2 **Hesket Newmarket** Cumb
324 C1 **Heskin Green** Lancs
396 B2 **Hesleden** Dur
428 C3 **Hesleyside** Nthumb
358 B4 **Heslington** York
357 G4 **Hessay** York
10 B2 **Hessenford** Cnwll
200 B2 **Hessett** Suffk
347 F4 **Hessle** E R Yk
344 A6 **Hessle** Wakefd
606 C7 **Hestaford** Shet
351 G1 **Hest Bank** Lancs
162 D5 **Hester's Way** Gloucs
605 G8 **Hestingott** Shet
604 E1 **Hestinsetter** Shet
118 C4 **Heston** Gt Lon
600 D1 **Hestwall** Ork
308 C3 **Heswall** Wirral
166 C4 **Hethe** Oxon
249 G4 **Hethel** Norfk
162 A4 **Hethelpit Cross** Gloucs
249 F4 **Hethersett** Norfk
401 E1 **Hethersgill** Cumb
400 D1 **Hetherside** Cumb
290 A5 **Hetherson Green** Ches
453 G4 **Hethpool** Nthumb
395 F2 **Hett** Dur
354 C3 **Hetton** N York
406 B5 **Hetton Downs** Sundld
406 B5 **Hetton-le-Hill** Sundld
406 B5 **Hetton-le-Hole** Sundld
430 A5 **Heugh** Nthumb
554 C2 **Heugh-Head** Abers
226 C5 **Heveningham** Suffk
96 C6 **Hever** Kent
365 G3 **Heversham** Cumb
255 G3 **Hevingham** Norfk
8 B4 **Hewas Water** Cnwll
134 D4 **Hewelsfield** Gloucs
134 C4 **Hewelsfield Common** Gloucs
390 B2 **Hewer Hill** Cumb
356 A3 **Hew Green** N York
84 D2 **Hewish** N Som
45 E6 **Hewish** Somset
29 G2 **Hewood** Dorset
405 G2 **Heworth** Gatesd
358 B4 **Heworth** York
403 G2 **Hexham** Nthumb
120 D5 **Hextable** Kent
330 C4 **Hexthorpe** Donc
169 G3 **Hexton** Herts
18 D3 **Hexworthy** Devon
354 A6 **Hey** Lancs
146 C5 **Heybridge** Essex
147 H3 **Heybridge** Essex
147 H3 **Heybridge Basin** Essex
11 F4 **Heybrook Bay** Devon
171 F1 **Heydon** Cambs
255 F2 **Heydon** Norfk
279 E2 **Heydour** Lincs
327 F2 **Hey Green** Kirk
327 E4 **Heyheads** Tamesd
337 F4 **Hey Houses** Lancs
516 B7 **Heylipol** Ag & B
606 C1 **Heylor** Shet
208 D5 **Heyop** Powys
327 E5 **Heyrod** Tamesd
351 E2 **Heysham** Lancs
355 G2 **Heyshaw** N York
74 D6 **Heyshott** W Susx
74 D6 **Heyshott Green** W Susx
326 D3 **Heyside** Oldham
87 G6 **Heytesbury** Wilts
165 F4 **Heythrop** Oxon
326 B2 **Heywood** Rochdl
87 F4 **Heywood** Wilts
332 D4 **Hibaldstow** N Linc
199 H4 **Hibb's Green** Suffk
199 F6 **Hickford Hill** Essex
330 A4 **Hickleton** Donc
257 E5 **Hickling** Norfk
277 E4 **Hickling** Notts
257 E5 **Hickling Green** Norfk
257 E5 **Hickling Heath** Norfk
277 E4 **Hickling Pastures** Notts
99 H3 **Hickmans Green** Kent
100 C3 **Hicks Forstal** Kent
110 A6 **Hicks Gate** BaNES
7 E5 **Hick's Mill** Cnwll
77 E6 **Hickstead** W Susx
190 B6 **Hidcote Bartrim** Gloucs
164 B1 **Hidcote Boyce** Gloucs
235 G5 **Hifnal** Shrops
326 D3 **Higginshaw** Oldham
344 A6 **High Ackworth** Wakefd
294 D3 **Higham** Derbys
121 H5 **Higham** Kent
340 B2 **Higham** Lancs
174 D2 **Higham** Suffk
199 E1 **Higham** Suffk
329 E3 **Higham Common** Barns
430 B4 **Higham Dykes** Nthumb
218 D6 **Higham Ferrers** Nhants
169 G3 **Higham Gobion** Beds
119 H1 **Higham Hill** Gt Lon
239 F5 **Higham on the Hill** Leics
24 C2 **Highampton** Devon
120 A1 **Highams Park** Gt Lon
97 F5 **Higham Wood** Kent
430 A2 **High Angerton** Nthumb
408 B2 **High Ardwell** D & G
391 F1 **High Bankhill** Cumb
485 E4 **High Banton** N Lans
300 C2 **High Barn** Lincs
144 B5 **High Barnet** Gt Lon
406 B3 **High Barns** Sundld
145 F5 **High Beach** Essex
366 D6 **High Bentham** N York
40 C3 **High Bickington** Devon
366 B4 **High Biggins** Cumb
367 G4 **High Birkwith** N York
355 H3 **High Birstwith** N York
467 G3 **High Blantyre** S Lans
485 G4 **High Bonnybridge** Falk
328 D6 **High Bradfield** Sheff
354 D5 **High Bradley** N York
61 G5 **High Bray** Devon
400 C6 **Highbridge** Cumb
72 C5 **Highbridge** Hants
533 J6 **Highbridge** Highld
84 A5 **Highbridge** Somset
237 F4 **Highbridge** Wsall
77 G3 **Highbrook** W Susx
78 D1 **High Brooms** Kent
136 C2 **High Brotheridge** Gloucs
40 A3 **High Bullen** Devon
328 B2 **Highburton** Kirk
52 B4 **Highbury** C Port
119 G2 **Highbury** Gt Lon
86 B5 **Highbury** Somset
295 G6 **Highbury Vale** C Nott
443 G3 **High Buston** Nthumb
430 C5 **High Callerton** Nthumb
365 E3 **High Cark** Cumb
366 C4 **High Casterton** Cumb
358 D4 **High Catton** E R Yk
430 C2 **High Church** Nthumb
90 C3 **Highclere** Hants
313 H4 **Highcliffe** Derbys
49 G6 **Highcliffe** Dorset
139 F3 **High Cogges** Oxon
248 C3 **High Common** Norfk
383 F1 **High Coniscliffe** Darltn
326 D2 **High Crompton** Oldham
197 F3 **High Cross** Cambs
4 D3 **High Cross** Cnwll
78 D4 **High Cross** E Susx
73 H4 **High Cross** Hants
143 G5 **High Cross** Herts
171 E6 **High Cross** Herts
107 E2 **High Cross** Newpt
76 D6 **High Cross** W Susx
190 B1 **High Cross** Warwks
467 F2 **High Crosshill** S Lans
378 C6 **High Cunsey** Cumb
460 B2 **High Dougarie** N Ayrs
405 H5 **High Dubmire** Sundld
393 G4 **High Dyke** Dur
146 C2 **High Easter** Essex
344 D5 **High Eggborough** N York
369 G3 **High Ellington** N York
435 H4 **High Enoch** D & G
68 A1 **Higher Alham** Somset
47 E4 **Higher Ansty** Dorset
26 D5 **Higher Ashton** Devon
339 G4 **Higher Audley** Bl w D
6 D3 **Higher Bal** Cnwll
337 G3 **Higher Ballam** Lancs
338 D3 **Higher Bartle** Lancs
308 D2 **Higher Bebington** Wirral
168 D3 **Higher Berry End** Beds
326 B4 **Higher Blackley** Manch
326 C3 **Higher Boarshaw** Rochdl
32 C1 **Higher Bockhampton** Dorset
2 C3 **Higher Bojewyan** Cnwll
2 C3 **Higher Boscaswell** Cnwll
13 G1 **Higher Brixham** Torbay
326 B4 **Higher Broughton** Salfd
66 C5 **Higher Burrow** Somset
27 G3 **Higher Burrowtown** Devon
289 H3 **Higher Burwardsley** Ches
270 D6 **High Ercall** Wrekin
30 D2 **Higher Chalmington** Dorset
28 B2 **Higher Cheriton** Devon
44 D5 **Higher Chillington** Somset
312 C1 **Higher Chisworth** Derbys
9 G2 **Highercliff** Cnwll
38 D3 **Higher Clovelly** Devon
6 C6 **Higher Condurrow** Cnwll
22 D3 **Higher Crackington** Cnwll
14 D5 **Higher Cransworth** Cnwll
339 G4 **Higher Croft** Bl w D
117 H2 **Higher Denham** Bucks
327 F5 **Higher Dinting** Derbys
312 C3 **Higher Disley** Ches
3 G3 **Higher Downs** Cnwll
19 F2 **Higher Dunstone** Devon
44 B2 **Higher Durston** Somset
324 C4 **Higher End** Wigan
30 A4 **Higher Eype** Dorset
325 F4 **Higher Folds** Wigan
340 D1 **Higherford** Lancs
20 C4 **Higher Gabwell** Devon
325 G4 **Higher Green** Wigan
45 G6 **Higher Halstock Leigh** Dorset
351 F2 **Higher Heysham** Lancs
340 D5 **Higher Hogshead** Lancs
68 A4 **Higher Holton** Somset
312 B4 **Higher Hurdsfield** Ches
30 C3 **Higher Kingcombe** Dorset
288 D2 **Higher Kinnerton** Flints
68 B5 **Higher Marsh** Somset
46 D4 **Higher Melcombe** Dorset
8 C2 **Higher Menadew** Cnwll
27 H4 **Higher Metcombe** Devon
61 H5 **Higher Molland** Devon
61 E4 **Higher Muddiford** Devon
68 B5 **Higher Nyland** Dorset
338 D4 **Higher Penwortham** Lancs
69 E2 **Higher Pertwood** Wilts
8 C3 **Higher Porthpean** Cnwll
312 B3 **Higher Poynton** Ches
24 A3 **Higher Prestacott** Devon
168 D3 **Higher Rads End** Beds
269 G3 **Higher Ridge** Shrops
20 B4 **Higher Rocombe Barton** Devon
48 C4 **Higher Row** Dorset
309 H3 **Higher Runcorn** Halton
67 G6 **Higher Sandford** Dorset
308 D6 **Higher Shotton** Flints
310 D5 **Higher Shurlach** Ches
19 G3 **Higher Sigford** Devon
60 D2 **Higher Slade** Devon
64 B3 **Higher Street** Somset
27 H2 **Higher Tale** Devon
14 B5 **Higher Tolcarne** Cnwll
46 B3 **Higher Totnell** Dorset
7 F5 **Highertown** Cnwll
8 C1 **Higher Town** Cnwll
15 G2 **Highertown** Cnwll
3 d1 **Higher Town** IoS
63 F2 **Higher Town** Somset
16 B5 **Higher Tremarcoombe** Cnwll
64 B4 **Higher Vexford** Somset
17 G4 **Higher Walreddon** Devon
339 E4 **Higher Walton** Lancs
310 B2 **Higher Walton** Warrtn
44 B6 **Higher Wambrook** Somset
60 C2 **Higher Warcombe** Devon
27 G1 **Higher Weaver** Devon
47 F4 **Higher Whatcombe** Dorset
339 F5 **Higher Wheelton** Lancs
310 C3 **Higher Whitley** Ches
310 D4 **Higher Wincham** Ches
32 D2 **Higher Woodsford** Dorset
32 D2 **Higher Wraxall** Dorset
289 G6 **Higher Wych** Ches
394 D4 **High Etherley** Dur
300 C5 **High Ferry** Lincs
325 G3 **Highfield** Bolton
50 D2 **Highfield** C Sotn
345 G2 **Highfield** E R Yk
404 D3 **Highfield** Gatesd
135 E4 **Highfield** Gloucs
143 F3 **Highfield** Herts
353 E4 **High Field** Lancs
465 G4 **Highfield** N Ayrs
166 C5 **Highfield** Oxon
314 C2 **Highfield** Sheff
324 C4 **Highfield** Wigan
240 C4 **Highfields** C Leic
197 E3 **Highfields** Cambs
295 E1 **Highfields** Derbys
330 B3 **Highfields** Donc
147 H1 **Highfields** Essex
135 H5 **Highfields** Gloucs
475 E4 **Highfields** Nthumb
272 D5 **Highfields** Staffs
405 F4 **High Forge** Dur
405 E3 **High Friarside** Dur
484 C5 **High Gallowhill** E Duns
173 F4 **High Garrett** Essex
213 G2 **Highgate** Birm
77 H3 **Highgate** E Susx
119 F2 **Highgate** Gt Lon
79 H3 **Highgate** Kent
232 B5 **Highgate** Powys
394 D3 **High Grange** Dur
370 A5 **High Grantley** N York
378 C4 **High Green** Cumb
328 B2 **High Green** Kirk
248 B3 **High Green** Norfk
249 F3 **High Green** Norfk
254 B5 **High Green** Norfk
329 E5 **High Green** Sheff
211 G3 **High Green** Shrops
199 H2 **High Green** Suffk
188 C5 **High Green** Worcs
80 C2 **High Halden** Kent
122 B4 **High Halstow** Medway
66 C3 **High Ham** Somset
405 F4 **High Handenhold** Dur
388 B4 **High Harrington** Cumb
356 C3 **High Harrogate** N York
406 B6 **High Haswell** Dur
271 E5 **High Hatton** Shrops
443 H4 **High Hauxley** Nthumb
387 F3 **High Hawsker** N York
271 F4 **High Heath** Shrops
237 F4 **High Heath** Wsall
401 E6 **High Hesket** Cumb
396 C2 **High Hesleden** Dur
389 G5 **High Hill** Cumb
146 D2 **High Houses** Essex
367 G2 **High Houses** N York
328 D3 **High Hoyland** Barns
347 E2 **High Hunsley** E R Yk
78 B4 **High Hurstwood** E Susx
373 E6 **High Hutton** N York
389 F2 **High Ireby** Cumb
261 F3 **High Kelling** Norfk
371 G4 **High Kilburn** N York
566 F8 **Highland Boath** Highld
30 A4 **Highlands** Dorset
312 A6 **Highlane** Ches
315 E3 **Highlane** Derbys
187 F2 **High Lane** Herefs
312 B2 **High Lane** Stockp
3 G2 **High Lanes** Cnwll
14 B4 **Highlanes** Cnwll
272 A3 **Highlanes** Staffs
146 A3 **High Laver** Essex
399 E5 **Highlaws** Cumb
161 H5 **Highleadon** Gloucs
311 E3 **High Legh** Ches
53 E5 **Highleigh** W Susx
384 D2 **High Leven** S on T
211 G3 **Highley** Shrops
86 A3 **High Littleton** BaNES
399 G5 **High Longthwaite** Cumb
389 E4 **High Lorton** Cumb
410 D5 **High Mains** D & G
373 F4 **High Marishes** N York
317 F5 **High Marnham** Notts
330 B4 **High Melton** Donc
404 C2 **High Mickley** Nthumb
399 H5 **Highmoor** Cumb
315 F3 **High Moor** Derbys
324 C2 **High Moor** Lancs
116 B2 **Highmoor** Oxon
116 A3 **Highmoor Cross** Oxon
109 E2 **Highmoor Hill** Mons
406 A5 **High Moorsley** Sundld
162 A6 **Highnam** Gloucs
162 A5 **Highnam Green** Gloucs
134 D2 **High Nash** Gloucs
365 F3 **High Newton** Cumb
455 G4 **High Newton-by-the-Sea** Nthumb
364 C2 **High Nibthwaite** Cumb
249 E4 **Highoak** Norfk
366 C1 **High Oaks** Cumb
272 A4 **High Offley** Staffs
146 B4 **High Ongar** Essex
236 B1 **High Onn** Staffs
236 B1 **High Onn Wharf** Staffs
366 A1 **High Park** Cumb
323 G1 **High Park** Sefton
109 G6 **Highridge** Bristl
85 G1 **Highridge** N Som
332 C2 **High Risby** N Linc
341 H4 **Highroad Well Moor** Calder
146 C1 **High Roding** Essex
200 B2 **High Rougham** Suffk
390 B2 **High Row** Cumb
390 B5 **High Row** Cumb
352 C2 **High Salter** Lancs
54 D3 **High Salvington** W Susx
399 F5 **High Scales** Cumb
376 C4 **High Sellafield** Cumb
367 H1 **High Shaw** N York
406 B1 **High Shields** S Tyne
395 F1 **High Shincliffe** Dur
389 F3 **High Side** Cumb
406 B3 **High Southwick** Sundld
404 D3 **High Spen** Gatesd
387 E2 **High Stakesby** N York
100 D2 **Highstead** Kent
98 D2 **Highsted** Kent
394 C1 **High Stoop** Dur
8 B3 **High Street** Cnwll
79 G3 **High Street** Kent
100 A3 **Highstreet** Kent
126 D1 **High Street** Pembks
203 E3 **High Street** Suffk
226 D3 **High Street** Suffk
227 E5 **High Street** Suffk
173 F3 **Highstreet Green** Essex
200 D3 **High Street Green** Suffk
75 F2 **Highstreet Green** Surrey
451 F3 **High Sunderland** Border
424 B4 **Hightae** D & G
213 G4 **Highter's Heath** Birm
396 C3 **High Throston** Hartpl
51 E2 **Hightown** C Sotn
291 H2 **Hightown** Ches
49 F3 **Hightown** Hants
169 F5 **High Town** Luton
323 E3 **Hightown** Sefton
235 G6 **High Town** Shrops
237 E2 **High Town** Staffs
288 D5 **Hightown** Wrexhm
200 C3 **Hightown Green** Suffk
320 A6 **High Toynton** Lincs
442 C3 **High Trewhitt** Nthumb
405 F4 **High Urpeth** Dur
486 D2 **High Valleyfield** Fife
376 B2 **High Walton** Cumb
403 G1 **High Warden** Nthumb
378 B5 **High Water Head** Cumb
6 D5 **Highway** Cnwll
186 B5 **Highway** Herefs
66 D5 **Highway** Somset
117 E3 **Highway** W & M
112 B5 **Highway** Wilts
20 A3 **Highweek** Devon
404 D3 **High Westwood** Dur
400 B4 **High Whinnow** Cumb
28 B1 **Highwood** Devon
33 F2 **Highwood** Dorset
49 F3 **Highwood** Hants
187 F1 **Highwood** Worcs
144 B6 **Highwood Hill** Gt Lon
134 D5 **High Woolaston** Gloucs
384 B3 **High Worsall** N York
138 C6 **Highworth** Swindn
39 F6 **Highworthy** Devon
378 C5 **High Wray** Cumb
145 G2 **High Wych** Herts
142 B6 **High Wycombe** Bucks
247 G4 **Hilborough** Norfk
137 E1 **Hilcot** Gloucs
295 F3 **Hilcote** Derbys
137 G4 **Hilcot End** Gloucs
88 D3 **Hilcott** Wilts
97 E5 **Hildenborough** Kent
97 E5 **Hilden Park** Kent
198 A5 **Hildersham** Cambs
161 E5 **Hildersley** Herefs
272 D3 **Hilderstone** Staffs
361 F1 **Hilderthorpe** E R Yk
31 E2 **Hilfield** Dorset
246 C5 **Hilgay** Norfk
237 H5 **Hill** Birm
135 E5 **Hill** S Glos
191 H1 **Hill** Warwks
344 C4 **Hillam** N York
125 H2 **Hillblock** Pembks
100 D2 **Hillborough** Kent
115 G4 **Hill Bottom** Oxon
48 C6 **Hillbourne** Poole
560 A5 **Hillbrae** Abers
569 K6 **Hillbrae** Abers
74 B4 **Hill Brow** W Susx
48 B4 **Hillbutts** Dorset
272 B2 **Hill Chorlton** Staffs
310 C2 **Hillcliffe** Warrtn
294 B5 **Hillcliffane** Derbys
257 E5 **Hill Common** Norfk
43 F2 **Hillcommon** Somset
87 E5 **Hill Corner** Somset
162 C1 **Hill Croome** Worcs
275 E3 **Hillcross** C Derb
324 B2 **Hill Dale** Lancs
69 E1 **Hill Deverill** Wilts
300 B5 **Hilldyke** Lincs
527 G5 **Hillend** Angus
393 H2 **Hill End** Dur
487 F3 **Hillend** Fife
499 G5 **Hill End** Fife
162 C2 **Hill End** Gloucs
118 B1 **Hill End** Gt Lon
468 C1 **Hillend** N Lans
84 C3 **Hill End** N Som
355 E4 **Hill End** N York
236 B6 **Hillend** Shrops
45 G5 **Hill End** Somset
102 B3 **Hillend** Swans
188 D2 **Hill End** Worcs
161 F4 **Hillend Green** Gloucs
134 D2 **Hillersland** Gloucs
25 H3 **Hillerton** Devon
167 E4 **Hillesden** Bucks
167 E3 **Hillesden Hamlet** Bucks
110 D2 **Hillesley** Gloucs
43 G3 **Hillfarrance** Somset
13 E2 **Hillfield** Devon
214 A4 **Hillfield** Solhll
110 A5 **Hillfields** Bristl
215 E4 **Hillfields** Covtry
342 D3 **Hillfoot** Leeds
169 G3 **Hillfoot End** Beds
189 E5 **Hill Furze** Worcs
160 B4 **Hill Gate** Herefs
171 G3 **Hill Green** Essex
98 C2 **Hill Green** Kent
114 D4 **Hillgreen** W Berk
75 E4 **Hillgrove** W Susx
186 D5 **Hillhampton** Herefs
556 D2 **Hillhead** Abers
558 D5 **Hillhead** Abers
560 A5 **Hillhead** Abers
8 D1 **Hillhead** Cnwll
13 G2 **Hillhead** Devon
445 F2 **Hillhead** E Ayrs
51 F4 **Hill Head** Hants
445 F6 **Hillhead** S Ayrs
571 G4 **Hillhead of Auchentumb** Abers
571 K7 **Hillhead of Cocklaw** Abers
570 B5 **Hillhead of Mountblairy** Abers
96 C6 **Hill Hoath** Kent
237 G4 **Hill Hook** Birm
211 E4 **Hill Houses** Shrops
238 A2 **Hilliard's Cross** Staffs
588 F4 **Hilliclay** Highld
118 B3 **Hillingdon** Gt Lon
118 B3 **Hillingdon Heath** Gt Lon
466 D2 **Hillington** C Glas
253 E2 **Hillington** Norfk
51 E6 **Hillis Corner** IoW
43 F5 **Hillmoor** Devon
216 B5 **Hillmorton** Warwks
125 G3 **Hill Mountain** Pembks
554 C3 **Hillockhead** Abers
340 B4 **Hillock Vale** Lancs
487 F1 **Hill of Beath** Fife
498 B5 **Hill of Drip** Stirlg
577 H8 **Hill of Fearn** Highld
570 B5 **Hill of Mountblairy** Abers
51 F3 **Hill Park** Hants
96 B3 **Hill Park** Kent
212 C4 **Hillpool** Worcs
51 G1 **Hillpound** Hants
273 G6 **Hill Ridware** Staffs
314 C1 **Hillsborough** Sheff
557 G5 **Hillside** Abers
529 E2 **Hillside** Angus
328 C4 **Hill Side** Barns
19 E5 **Hillside** Devon
28 C1 **Hillside** Devon
74 B4 **Hill Side** Hants
92 C4 **Hillside** Hants
328 B1 **Hill Side** Kirk
601 H5 **Hillside** Ork
602 C7 **Hillside** Ork
323 F2 **Hillside** Sefton
606 F5 **Hillside** Shet
210 D2 **Hillside** Shrops
112 C1 **Hillside** Wilts
187 H2 **Hill Side** Worcs
274 A3 **Hill Somersal** Derbys
315 F6 **Hills Town** Derbys
50 B1 **Hillstreet** Hants
82 B1 **Hill Street** Kent
606 C2 **Hillswick** Shet
328 D3 **Hill Top** Barns
132 C3 **Hilltop** Blae G
342 A3 **Hill Top** Brad
142 D4 **Hilltop** Bucks
294 C2 **Hilltop** Derbys
314 D4 **Hill Top** Derbys
330 A5 **Hill Top** Donc
393 G5 **Hill Top** Dur
405 E4 **Hill Top** Dur
405 F6 **Hill Top** Dur
50 D4 **Hill Top** Hants
327 G2 **Hill Top** Kirk
343 E3 **Hill Top** Leeds
355 G2 **Hill Top** N York
356 B2 **Hill Top** N York
295 F5 **Hill Top** Notts
329 F6 **Hill Top** Rothm
325 G4 **Hill Top** Salfd

237 E6 Hill Top Sandw
314 B2 Hill Top Sheff
236 C3 Hill Top Staffs
74 D5 Hill Top W Susx
214 D1 Hill Top Warwks
215 F1 Hill Top Warwks
514 B3 Hilltown C Dund
48 B5 Hill View Dorset
406 B4 Hillview Sundld
37 G3 Hillway IoW
605 G8 Hillwell Shet
237 H4 Hill Wood Birm
215 E6 Hill Wootton Warwks
50 C1 Hillyfields Hants
512 C5 Hillyland P & K
112 B4 Hilmarton Wilts
87 F3 Hilperton Wilts
87 F2 Hilperton Marsh Wilts
52 B4 Hilsea C Port
349 E3 Hilston E R Yk
72 B5 Hiltingbury Hants
560 D3 Hilton Abers
474 C4 Hilton Border
557 G3 Hilton C Aber
196 C1 Hilton Cambs
392 B5 Hilton Cumb
274 C3 Hilton Derbys
47 E4 Hilton Dorset
394 D5 Hilton Dur
566 B8 Hilton Highld
577 G7 Hilton Highld
577 K6 Hilton Highld
384 D2 Hilton S on T
236 A5 Hilton Shrops
237 G4 Hilton Staffs
325 E3 Hilton House Bolton
566 F1 Hilton of Cadboll Highld
326 B4 Hilton Park Bury
212 C1 Himbleton Worcs
236 C4 Himley Staffs
365 H3 Hincaster Cumb
94 D2 Hinchley Wood Surrey
328 A3 Hinchliffe Mill Kirk
164 A3 Hinchwick Gloucs
239 G6 Hinckley Leics
30 B3 Hincknowle Dorset
224 D4 Hinderclay Suffk
308 D4 Hinderton Ches
386 C1 Hinderwell N York
269 F3 Hindford Shrops
74 D2 Hindhead Surrey
340 A3 Hindle Fold Lancs
404 B3 Hindley Nthumb
325 E4 Hindley Wigan
325 E4 Hindley Green Wigan
188 C3 Hindlip Worcs
254 D2 Hindolveston Norfk
69 F3 Hindon Wilts
364 A6 Hindpool Cumb
260 C4 Hindringham Norfk
325 F4 Hindsford Wigan
248 D4 Hingham Norfk
271 F4 Hinstock Shrops
201 E6 Hintlesham Suffk
135 F4 Hinton Gloucs
49 G5 Hinton Hants
159 F2 Hinton Herefs
192 B4 Hinton Nhants
110 C4 Hinton S Glos
233 H3 Hinton Shrops
67 F5 Hinton Somset
73 F4 Hinton Ampner Hants
85 G3 Hinton Blewett BaNES
86 D3 Hinton Charterhouse BaNES
163 F1 Hinton Cross Worcs
166 C2 Hinton-in-the-Hedges Nhants
48 C3 Hinton Martell Dorset
163 F2 Hinton on the Green Worcs
48 B4 Hinton Parva Dorset
113 F3 Hinton Parva Swindn
45 E5 Hinton St George Somset
47 E1 Hinton St Mary Dorset
139 F5 Hinton Waldrist Oxon
211 E4 Hints Shrops
238 B4 Hints Staffs
194 C2 Hinwick Beds
233 G3 Hinwood Shrops
99 G6 Hinxhill Kent
197 G5 Hinxton Cambs
170 B1 Hinxworth Herts
342 B4 Hipperholme Calder
187 G3 Hipplecote Worcs
443 G2 Hipsburn Nthumb
383 E5 Hipswell N York
304 C5 Hirael Gwynd
152 D5 Hiraeth Carmth
556 C4 Hirn Abers
267 H5 Hirnant Powys
468 D2 Hirst N Lans
431 E2 Hirst Nthumb
345 E5 Hirst Courtney N York
287 G2 Hirwaen Denbgs
131 E3 Hirwaun Rhondd
105 E3 Hirwaun Common Brdgnd
40 A2 Hiscott Devon
438 D4 Hislop Border
87 F5 Hisomley Wilts
197 F2 Histon Cambs
200 C4 Hitcham Suffk
399 E1 Hitchill D & G
170 B4 Hitchin Herts
170 A4 Hitchin Hill Herts
68 D1 Hitcombe Bottom Wilts
120 A5 Hither Green Gt Lon
26 A3 Hittisleigh Devon
26 A3 Hittisleigh Barton Devon
346 B3 Hive E R Yk
273 F4 Hixon Staffs
101 E4 Hoaden Kent
159 G5 Hoaldalbert Mons
274 A5 Hoar Cross Staffs
160 C4 Hoarwithy Herefs
100 D3 Hoath Kent
96 C6 Hoath Corner Kent
209 F4 Hobarris Shrops
600 F3 Hobbister Ork
237 F3 Hobble End Staffs
199 E4 Hobbles Green Suffk
145 G2 Hobbs Cross Essex
145 G5 Hobbs Cross Essex
86 B3 Hobbs Wall BaNES
289 G4 Hob Hill Ches
440 A2 Hobkirk Border
327 F6 Hobroyd Derbys
405 E3 Hobson Dur
241 E1 Hoby Leics
43 F2 Hoccombe Somset
120 C6 Hockenden Gt Lon
171 G5 Hockerill Herts
255 E5 Hockering Norfk
255 E5 Hockering Heath Norfk
296 D3 Hockerton Notts
43 G3 Hockholler Somset
43 G3 Hockholler Green Somset
312 B3 Hockley Ches
214 D4 Hockley Covtry
147 G6 Hockley Essex
148 D3 Hockley Essex
99 F3 Hockley Kent
238 C4 Hockley Staffs
214 B5 Hockley Heath Solhll

168 D4 Hockliffe Beds
223 E2 Hockwold cum Wilton Norfk
42 D4 Hockworthy Devon
72 B5 Hocombe Hants
144 D3 Hoddesdon Herts
339 H5 Hoddlesden Bl w D
424 C5 Hoddom Mains D & G
189 G5 Hoden Worcs
292 B4 Hodgefield Staffs
213 H2 Hodgehill Birm
311 G6 Hodgehill Ches
126 A5 Hodgeston Pembks
528 D5 Hodgeton Angus
208 C1 Hodley Powys
271 E4 Hodnet Shrops
271 E4 Hodnetheath Shrops
316 B2 Hodsock Notts
97 F2 Hodsoll Street Kent
113 E3 Hodson Swindn
315 G4 Hodthorpe Derbys
73 H6 Hoe Hants
254 C4 Hoe Norfk
94 B5 Hoe Surrey
114 C6 Hoe Benham W Berk
51 H2 Hoe Gate Hants
392 A6 Hoff Cumb
280 B2 Hoffleet Stow Lincs
606 D2 Hogaland Shet
99 G3 Hogben's Hill Kent
467 F1 Hogganfield C Glas
200 A3 Hoggard's Green Suffk
167 H4 Hoggeston Bucks
87 E3 Hoggington Wilts
214 C1 Hoggrill's End Warwks
592 B3 Hogha Gearraidh W Isls
92 D5 Hog Hatch Surrey
390 D4 Hoghouse Hill Cumb
339 F4 Hoghton Lancs
327 H3 Hoghton Bottoms Lancs
293 H4 Hognaston Derbys
321 F5 Hogsthorpe Lincs
48 A3 Hogstock Dorset
281 E4 Holbeach Lincs
281 E4 Holbeach Bank Lincs
280 D4 Holbeach Clough Lincs
244 D2 Holbeach Drove Lincs
212 A4 Holbeache Worcs
281 E4 Holbeach Hurn Lincs
280 D6 Holbeach St Johns Lincs
281 E3 Holbeach St Marks Lincs
281 F3 Holbeach St Matthew Lincs
343 E3 Holbeck Leeds
315 G5 Holbeck Notts
315 G5 Holbeck Woodhouse Notts
189 F3 Holberrow Green Worcs
11 H3 Holbeton Devon
97 G2 Holborough Kent
294 D6 Holbrook Derbys
315 E3 Holbrook Sheff
176 C2 Holbrook Suffk
110 B5 Holbrook Common S Glos
294 D5 Holbrook Moor Derbys
215 E3 Holbrooks Covtry
365 H4 Holbury Hants
327 H3 Holcombe Bury
20 D3 Holcombe Devon
86 B5 Holcombe Somset
325 H2 Holcombe Brook Bury
43 E4 Holcombe Rogus Devon
217 G6 Holcot Nhants
145 E5 Holdbrook Gt Lon
353 F5 Holden Lancs
217 E6 Holdenby Nhants
326 D3 Holden Fold Oldham
48 D5 Holdenhurst Bmouth
172 C4 Holder's Green Essex
119 E1 Holders Hill Gt Lon
162 C2 Holdfast Worcs
210 D2 Holdgate Shrops
298 D5 Holdingham Lincs
29 F2 Holditch Dorset
342 A4 Holdsworth Calder
314 B1 Holdworth Sheff
341 G2 Hole Brad
38 D4 Hole Devon
341 E4 Hole Bottom Calder
453 F3 Holefield Border
468 B1 Holehills N Lans
312 D1 Holehouse Derbys
161 E4 Hole in the Wall Herefs
527 G6 Holemill Angus
24 B1 Holemoor Devon
17 F5 Hole's Hole Devon
435 H5 Holestane D & G
294 C2 Holestone Derbys
54 D2 Hole Street W Susx
61 H4 Holewater Devon
64 C3 Holford Somset
358 A4 Holgate York
365 E4 Holker Cumb
260 A3 Holkham Norfk
24 A2 Hollacombe Devon
26 C2 Hollacombe Devon
11 F3 Hollacombe Hill Devon
602 F1 Holland Ork
603 K7 Holland Ork
96 A4 Holland Surrey
299 G5 Holland Fen Lincs
324 C3 Holland Lees Lancs
149 H1 Holland-on-Sea Essex
45 G4 Hollands Ork
603 L1 Hollandstoun Ork
425 F6 Hollee D & G
202 C6 Hollesley Suffk
20 B5 Hollicombe Torbay
272 B5 Hollies Common Staffs
140 D3 Hollin Oxon
310 C1 Hollinfare Warrtn
98 C3 Hollingbourne Kent
55 H3 Hollingbury Br & H
55 H3 Hollingdean Br & H
168 B4 Hollingdon Bucks
58 A2 Hollingrove E Susx
329 E2 Hollington Derbys
274 C2 Hollington Derbys
58 C4 Hollington E Susx
90 C3 Hollington Staffs
273 G2 Hollington Staffs
274 C2 Hollington Grove Derbys
315 E5 Hollingwood Derbys
327 E5 Hollingworth Tamesd
341 E2 Hollin Hall Lancs
343 F2 Hollin Park Leeds
325 G3 Hollins Bolton
326 B3 Hollins Bury
366 D1 Hollins Cumb
314 C5 Hollins Derbys
291 G4 Hollins Staffs
292 B3 Hollins Staffs
292 C5 Hollins Staffs
293 E1 Hollinsclough Staffs
314 D3 Hollins End Sheff
291 E2 Hollinsgreen Ches
310 D1 Hollins Green Warrtn
351 G4 Hollins Lane Lancs
235 G3 Hollinswood Wrekin
326 D4 Hollinwood Oldham
270 C2 Hollinwood Shrops
43 E6 Hollis Green Devon
27 F2 Hollis Head Devon

40 C5 Hollocombe Devon
40 C5 Hollocombe Town Devon
294 C3 Holloway Derbys
116 D3 Holloway W & M
69 E3 Holloway Wilts
93 G6 Holloway Hill Surrey
85 G2 Hollow Brook BaNES
217 E5 Hollowell Nhants
314 A2 Hollow Meadows Sheff
309 G6 Hollowmoor Heath Ches
47 F6 Hollow Oak Dorset
425 H4 Hollows D & G
100 D3 Hollow Street Kent
237 G4 Holly Bank Wsall
214 D3 Hollyberry End Solhll
85 F5 Holly Brook Somset
292 A6 Hollybush C Stke
132 C4 Hollybush Caerph
433 E2 Hollybush E Ayrs
133 E6 Hollybush Torfn
161 H2 Hollybush Worcs
289 F6 Holly Bush Wrexhm
117 G2 Hollybush Corner Bucks
200 B3 Hollybush Corner Suffk
99 E3 Hollybushes Kent
117 G3 Hollybush Hill Bucks
175 F6 Hollybush Hill Essex
239 G6 Hollycroft Leics
116 D3 Holly Cross W & M
245 H3 Holly End Norfk
141 G4 Holly Green Bucks
162 C1 Holly Green Worcs
383 E4 Holly Hill N York
234 B5 Hollyhurst Shrops
215 F2 Hollyhurst Warwks
349 F4 Hollywaste Shrops
211 F4 Hollywater Hants
213 G4 Hollywood Worcs
39 H2 Holmacott Devon
43 H4 Holman Clavel Somset
327 H3 Holmbridge Kirk
94 C6 Holmbury St Mary Surrey
8 C3 Holmbush Cnwll
29 G2 Holmbush Dorset
272 D4 Holmcroft Staffs
196 A6 Holme Beds
342 C3 Holme Brad
220 A2 Holme Cambs
365 H4 Holme Cumb
327 H3 Holme Kirk
332 C3 Holme N Linc
370 D3 Holme N York
297 F3 Holme Notts
33 F2 Holmebridge Dorset
340 D4 Holme Chapel Lancs
196 A6 Holme Green Beds
344 C1 Holme Green N York
92 D1 Holme Green Wokham
248 A3 Holme Hale Norfk
334 C3 Holme Hill NE Lin
160 D2 Holme Lacy Herefs
276 D2 Holme Lane Notts
185 F4 Holme Marsh Herefs
365 H4 Holme Mills Cumb
259 E3 Holme next the Sea Norfk
346 B2 Holme-on-Spalding-Moor E R Yk
360 B5 Holme on the Wolds E R Yk
276 D2 Holme Pierrepont Notts
160 C1 Holmer Herefs
142 C5 Holmer Green Bucks
338 B6 Holmes Lancs
398 D5 Holme St Cuthbert Cumb
291 F1 Holmes Chapel Ches
314 D4 Holmesdale Derbys
314 C4 Holmesfield Derbys
339 E3 Holme Slack Lancs
57 E2 Holmes's Hill E Susx
324 A1 Holmeswood Lancs
95 F4 Holmethorpe Surrey
342 C3 Holme Wood Brad
295 E1 Holmewood Derbys
341 H4 Holmfield Calder
328 A3 Holmfirth Kirk
446 B5 Holmhead E Ayrs
435 H5 Holmhead D & G
542 B7 Holmisdale Highld
314 D4 Holmley Common Derbys
349 G5 Holmpton E R Yk
376 D5 Holmrook Cumb
605 J2 Holmsgarth Shet
405 F5 Holmside Dur
28 D2 Holmsleigh Green Devon
445 E5 Holmston S Ayrs
94 D6 Holmwood Corner Surrey
401 F5 Holmwrangle Cumb
19 F4 Holne Devon
46 C3 Holnest Dorset
63 E2 Holnicote Somset
23 G2 Holsworthy Devon
39 E6 Holsworthy Beacon Devon
48 C4 Holt Dorset
92 B4 Holt Hants
261 E4 Holt Norfk
309 G1 Holt St Hel
87 F2 Holt Wilts
188 B3 Holt Worcs
289 F4 Holt Wrexhm
358 C4 Holtby York
73 G2 Holt End Hants
213 G6 Holt End Worcs
188 B2 Holt Fleet Worcs
323 G4 Holt Green Lancs
327 G2 Holt Head Kirk
48 D4 Holt Heath Dorset
188 B2 Holt Heath Worcs
274 A4 Holt Hill Staffs
140 D3 Holton Oxon
68 A4 Holton Somset
227 E4 Holton Suffk
319 E3 Holton cum Beckering Lincs
334 C4 Holton le Clay Lincs
333 F5 Holton le Moor Lincs
175 E2 Holton St Mary Suffk
343 E1 Holt Park Leeds
92 D6 Holt Pound Hants
326 D4 Holts Oldham
117 F1 Holtspur Bucks
81 E4 Holt Wood Dorset
78 B2 Holtye E Susx
29 G3 Holway Dorset
308 A4 Holway Flints
44 A3 Holway Somset
46 C2 Holwell Dorset
169 H3 Holwell Herts
138 C3 Holwell Leics
86 C5 Holwell Oxon
169 H3 Holwellbury Beds
393 F4 Holwick Dur
32 D3 Holworth Dorset
73 H1 Holy City Devon
29 E2 Holy Cross N Tyne
431 F6 Holy Cross Worcs
212 D4 Holyfield Essex
145 E4 Holyfield Essex
28 D4 Holyford Devon
302 C4 Holyhead IoA
450 D2 Holylee Border
314 C6 Holymoorside Derbys
117 F4 Holyport W & M

442 B4 Holystone Nthumb
468 B2 Holytown N Lans
3 d2 Holy Vale IoS
143 E1 Holywell Beds
220 D5 Holywell Cambs
7 E2 Holywell Cnwll
30 D2 Holywell Dorset
308 A4 Holywell Flints
135 H6 Holywell Gloucs
159 G1 Holywell Herefs
143 F5 Holywell Herts
431 F5 Holywell Nthumb
45 G5 Holywell Somset
190 B1 Holywell Warwks
341 H6 Holywell Green Calder
43 E3 Holywell Lake Somset
223 E4 Holywell Row Suffk
423 F3 Holywood D & G
162 D3 Homedowns Gloucs
235 E4 Homer Shrops
323 F4 Homer Green Sefton
226 B2 Homersfield Suffk
119 H2 Homerton Gt Lon
160 D5 Hom Green Herefs
70 C4 Homington Wilts
189 G6 Honeybourne Worcs
25 F2 Honeychurch Devon
195 G3 Honeydon Beds
84 D2 Honey Hall N Som
100 B3 Honey Hill Kent
92 D1 Honeyhill Wokham
88 D2 Honeystreet Wilts
174 C2 Honey Tye Suffk
168 D5 Honeywick Beds
11 E2 Honicknowle C Plym
214 C5 Honiley Warwks
256 C4 Honing Norfk
249 F2 Honingham Norfk
298 A6 Honington Lincs
224 A5 Honington Suffk
164 D1 Honington Warwks
28 C2 Honiton Devon
288 D3 Honkley Wrexhm
328 A2 Honley Kirk
328 A2 Honley Moor Kirk
119 G5 Honor Oak Gt Lon
119 H5 Honor Oak Park Gt Lon
326 D1 Honresfeld Rochdl
101 E3 Hoo Kent
202 B3 Hoo Suffk
212 B5 Hoobrook Worcs
329 E4 Hood Green Barns
329 F5 Hood Hill Rothm
310 B2 Hood Manor Warrtn
11 F3 Hooe C Plym
58 A5 Hooe E Susx
170 A6 Hoo End Herts
289 H2 Hoofield Ches
311 E3 Hoo Green Ches
341 G4 Hoo Hole Calder
245 F6 Hook Cambs
29 F1 Hook Devon
345 H4 Hook E R Yk
94 D2 Hook Gt Lon
51 F3 Hook Hants
92 B4 Hook Hants
125 G2 Hook Pembks
112 C3 Hook Wilts
234 B3 Hook-a-Gate Shrops
162 B1 Hook Bank Worcs
30 C3 Hooke Dorset
146 B5 Hook End Essex
115 H3 Hook End Oxon
214 C3 Hook End Solhll
404 D3 Hooker Gate Gatesd
271 H2 Hookgate Staffs
79 F2 Hook Green Kent
97 F1 Hook Green Kent
120 D5 Hook Green Kent
121 F5 Hook Green Kent
93 G3 Hook Heath Surrey
165 E3 Hook Norton Oxon
51 E4 Hook Park Hants
170 C5 Hook's Cross Herts
135 F5 Hook Street Gloucs
112 C3 Hook Street Wilts
53 E1 Hooksway W Susx
26 D3 Hookway Devon
95 F6 Hookwood Surrey
289 F1 Hoole Ches
309 F6 Hoole Bank Ches
95 F3 Hooley Surrey
326 B2 Hooley Bridge Rochdl
326 C2 Hooley Brow Rochdl
326 D5 Hooley Hill Tamesd
18 B4 Hoo Meavy Devon
134 C3 Hoop Mons
87 E4 Hoopers Pool Wilts
39 E3 Hoops Devon
122 B5 Hoo St Werburgh Medway
309 E4 Hooton Ches
315 G1 Hooton Levitt Rothm
330 A3 Hooton Pagnell Donc
330 A5 Hooton Roberts Rothm
605 G1 Hoove Shet
165 H5 Hopcroft's Holt Oxon
313 G3 Hope Derbys
288 D3 Hope Flints
585 J5 Hope Highld
233 E3 Hope Powys
233 F4 Hope Shrops
293 F3 Hope Staffs
210 D5 Hope Bagot Shrops
389 E5 Hopebeck Cumb
210 B1 Hope Bowdler Shrops
293 F4 Hopedale Staffs
172 B5 Hope End Green Essex
312 B3 Hope Green Ches
568 B2 Hopeman Moray
161 E6 Hope Mansell Herefs
233 F4 Hope Park Shrops
209 G3 Hopesay Shrops
233 F4 Hopesgate Shrops
122 B2 Hope's Green Essex
187 E5 Hope's Rough Herefs
186 C4 Hope under Dinmore Herefs
115 E6 Hopgoods Green W Berk
105 G1 Hopkinstown Rhondd
233 F4 Hopley's Green Herefs
357 E3 Hopperton N York
244 A2 Hop Pole Lincs
215 G3 Hopsford Warwks
236 A6 Hopstone Shrops
294 B4 Hopton Derbys
269 G5 Hopton Derbys
272 D4 Hopton Staffs
224 C4 Hopton Staffs
211 E4 Hoptonbank Shrops
210 C3 Hopton Cangeford Shrops
209 G4 Hopton Castle Shrops
210 C3 Hoptongate Shrops
273 H4 Hopton Heath Staffs
251 G4 Hopton on Sea Norfk
211 E4 Hopton Wafers Shrops
238 B3 Hopwas Staffs
326 C2 Hopwood Rochdl
213 F5 Hopwood Worcs
23 G2 Hopworthy Devon
78 D6 Horam E Susx
279 G2 Horbling Lincs

343 E6 Horbury Wakefd
138 A4 Horcott Gloucs
209 G2 Horderley Shrops
49 H5 Hordle Hants
269 G3 Hordley Shrops
128 C3 Horeb Carmth
154 D4 Horeb Carmth
180 A6 Horeb Cerdgn
288 C3 Horeb Flints
109 G4 Horfield Bristl
595 G3 Horgabost W Isls
225 H5 Horham Suffk
347 E6 Horkstow N Linc
347 E6 Horkstow Wolds N Linc
191 G6 Horley Oxon
95 F6 Horley Surrey
29 G2 Horn Ash Dorset
67 F3 Hornblotton Somset
67 F3 Hornblotton Green Somset
366 B6 Hornby Lancs
383 F6 Hornby N York
384 B3 Hornby N York
319 H6 Horncastle Lincs
115 H5 Horncastle Readg
120 D2 Hornchurch Gt Lon
474 D5 Horncliffe Nthumb
474 C5 Horndean Border
52 B2 Horndean Hants
18 B1 Horndon Devon
121 G3 Horndon on the Hill Thurr
95 G6 Horne Surrey
62 D2 Horner Somset
147 F4 Horne Row Essex
174 C1 Horner's Green Suffk
174 D3 Hornestreet Essex
542 D7 Horneval Highld
78 B4 Horney Common E Susx
143 E6 Horn Hill Bucks
64 D3 Horn Hill Somset
8 B3 Hornick Cnwll
527 F2 Horniehaugh Angus
250 C1 Horning Norfk
241 G5 Horninghold Leics
274 C4 Horninglow Staffs
197 G2 Horningsea Cambs
68 D1 Horningsham Wilts
254 B3 Horningtoft Norfk
9 H1 Horningtops Cnwll
44 C5 Hornsbury Somset
401 F4 Hornsby Cumb
39 E3 Horns Cross Devon
58 D2 Horns Cross E Susx
361 G5 Hornsea E R Yk
361 G5 Hornsea Burton E R Yk
119 G2 Hornsey Gt Lon
119 G2 Hornsey Vale Gt Lon
96 C3 Horns Green Gt Lon
82 C3 Horn Street Kent
97 G2 Horn Street Kent
191 F6 Hornton Oxon
113 F3 Horpit Swindn
18 B3 Horrabridge Devon
199 G2 Horringer Suffk
325 F2 Horrocks Fold Bolton
353 E6 Horrocksford Lancs
98 D4 Horsalls Kent
17 F4 Horsebridge Devon
71 G3 Horsebridge Hants
233 G3 Horsebridge Shrops
292 C4 Horse Bridge Staffs
19 F6 Horsebrook Devon
236 C2 Horsebrook Staffs
84 D1 Horsecastle N Som
111 E4 Horsedown Wilts
4 B2 Horsedowns Cnwll
235 F3 Horsehay Wrekin
198 B5 Horseheath Cambs
368 D3 Horsehouse N York
237 E6 Horseley Heath Sandw
93 G3 Horsell Surrey
93 G3 Horsell Birch Surrey
270 A1 Horseman's Green Wrexhm
146 A5 Horseman Side Essex
54 A4 Horsemere Green W Susx
141 G4 Horsenden Bucks
136 B2 Horsepools Gloucs
221 F2 Horseway Cambs
185 F2 Horseway Head Herefs
257 F5 Horsey Norfk
65 F4 Horsey Somset
257 F5 Horsey Corner Norfk
137 G6 Horsey Down Wilts
255 G4 Horsford Norfk
342 D2 Horsforth Leeds
76 C3 Horsham W Susx
187 G3 Horsham Worcs
255 H5 Horsham St Faith Norfk
78 B1 Horshoe Green Kent
319 F6 Horsington Lincs
68 B5 Horsington Somset
294 D6 Horsley Derbys
136 B5 Horsley Gloucs
404 C1 Horsley Nthumb
441 F5 Horsley Nthumb
175 F4 Horsley Cross Essex
175 F4 Horsleycross Street Essex
451 G6 Horsleyhill Border
406 B1 Horsley Hill S Tyne
404 C5 Horsleyhope Dur
141 G5 Horsleys Green Bucks
294 D5 Horsley Woodhouse Derbys
79 F1 Horsmonden Kent
140 C4 Horspath Oxon
256 B6 Horstead Norfk
78 B6 Horsted Green E Susx
77 G4 Horsted Keynes W Susx
168 C6 Horton Bucks
48 C3 Horton Dorset
100 B4 Horton Kent
353 H4 Horton Lancs
193 H4 Horton Nhants
110 D3 Horton S Glos
270 B3 Horton Shrops
44 C5 Horton Somset
236 D3 Horton Staffs
102 C4 Horton Swans
117 H4 Horton W & M
88 B2 Horton Wilts
235 F2 Horton Wrekin
48 D3 Horton Common Dorset
44 C4 Horton Cross Somset
140 D2 Horton-cum-Studley Oxon
289 G4 Horton Green Ches
48 D3 Horton Heath Dorset
51 E1 Horton Heath Hants
367 G5 Horton in Ribblesdale N York
121 E6 Horton Kirby Kent
234 A2 Hortonlane Shrops
168 C6 Hortonwharf Bucks
235 F2 Hortonwood Wrekin
325 E2 Horwich Bolton
312 D3 Horwich End Derbys
39 H2 Horwood Devon
110 C2 Horwood Riding S Glos
324 B2 Hoscar Lancs
277 F4 Hose Leics
453 E3 Hoselaw Border
96 C4 Hosey Hill Kent
511 E6 Hosh P & K
515 G1 Hospitalfield Angus
592 C3 Hosta W Isls

605 H6 Hoswick Shet
346 C3 Hotham E R Yk
99 F6 Hothfield Kent
142 B4 Hotley Bottom Bucks
276 C5 Hoton Leics
109 G5 Hotwells Bristl
609 J6 Houbie Shet
516 A6 Hough Ag & B
291 E4 Hough Ches
311 H4 Hough Ches
297 G6 Hougham Lincs
309 G2 Hough Green Halton
297 H5 Hough-on-the-Hill Lincs
220 C5 Houghton Cambs
400 D3 Houghton Cumb
71 G3 Houghton Hants
404 D1 Houghton Nthumb
125 G3 Houghton Pembks
54 B2 Houghton W Susx
395 E5 Houghton Bank Darltn
169 E1 Houghton Conquest Beds
80 D5 Houghton Green E Susx
310 C1 Houghton Green Warrtn
395 E5 Houghton-le-Side Darltn
406 A5 Houghton-le-Spring Sundld
241 E4 Houghton on the Hill Leics
168 D5 Houghton Regis Beds
260 B4 Houghton St Giles Norfk
324 C4 Houghwood St Hel
605 G2 Houlland Shet
605 H5 Houlland Shet
606 D7 Houlland Shet
607 G3 Houlland Shet
386 B3 Houlsyke N York
51 E3 Hound Hants
92 B3 Hound Green Hants
48 B4 Hound Hill Dorset
91 G4 Houndmills Hants
136 B4 Houndscroft Gloucs
473 E5 Houndslow Border
43 F2 Houndsmoor Somset
45 G4 Houndstone Somset
474 B2 Houndwood Border
50 C2 Hounsdown Hants
85 F2 Hounsley Batch N Som
118 C4 Hounslow Gt Lon
172 C6 Hounslow Green Essex
118 C4 Hounslow West Gt Lon
602 B8 Hourston Ork
607 G6 Housabister Shet
471 H1 House O' Muir E Loth
328 C1 Houses Hill Kirk
608 D8 Housetter Shet
145 H2 Housham Tye Essex
605 G4 Houss Shet
466 B1 Houston Rens
582 F2 Houstry Highld
600 E4 Houton Ork
55 G4 Hove Br & H
342 B5 Hove Edge Calder
296 C5 Hoveringham Notts
256 C6 Hoveton Norfk
372 C4 Hovingham N York
401 E3 How Cumb
290 D5 Howbeck Bank Ches
329 E5 Howbrook Barns
161 E3 How Caple Herefs
345 G4 Howden E R Yk
487 E6 Howden W Loth
342 D4 Howden Clough Kirk
394 C3 Howden-le-Wear Dur
406 C3 Howdon N Tyne
406 A1 Howdon Pans N Tyne
589 J4 Howe Highld
322 b9 Howe IoM
370 C3 Howe N York
250 B4 Howe Norfk
325 F4 Howe Bridge Wigan
147 E4 Howe Green Essex
147 G4 Howegreen Essex
171 H6 Howe Green Essex
215 E2 Howe Green Warwks
299 E5 Howell Lincs
169 E1 How End Beds
570 D6 Howe of Teuchar Abers
146 D2 Howe Street Essex
172 D3 Howe Street Essex
183 H3 Howey Powys
450 C2 Howford Border
453 E5 Howgate Border
388 A5 Howgate Cumb
470 D3 Howgate Mdloth
380 A5 Howgill Cumb
353 G5 Howgill Lancs
355 E3 Howgill N York
96 C5 How Green Kent
256 D6 How Hill Norfk
134 C5 Howick Mons
455 H6 Howick Nthumb
338 C4 Howick Cross Lancs
271 F5 Howle Wrekin
43 G4 Howleigh Somset
172 B3 Howlett End Essex
135 G6 Howley Gloucs
44 B6 Howley Somset
310 C2 Howley Warrtn
593 D10 Howmore W Isls
453 E6 Hownam Border
438 C3 Howpasley Border
188 A4 Howsen Worcs
353 E4 Howsham N Linc
358 D2 Howsham N York
453 G3 Howtel Nthumb
98 D1 Howt Green Kent
159 H4 Howton Herefs
390 C6 Howtown Cumb
143 G4 How Wood Herts
466 A3 Howwood Rens
601 G6 Hoxa Ork
225 G4 Hoxne Suffk
600 C4 Hoy Ork
308 B2 Hoylake Wirral
329 F4 Hoyland Common Barns
329 F5 Hoyland Nether Barns
328 D3 Hoylandswaine Barns
75 E6 Hoyle W Susx
329 F3 Hoyle Mill Barns
96 D4 Hubbard's Hill Kent
368 B4 Hubberholme N York
125 E3 Hubberston Pembks
365 F1 Hubbersty Head Cumb
299 H6 Hubbert's Bridge Lincs
356 B5 Huby N York
357 H1 Huby N York
162 C6 Hucclecote Gloucs
98 C3 Hucking Kent
295 G5 Hucknall Notts
327 H1 Huddersfield Kirk
188 D3 Huddington Worcs
38 D4 Huddisford Devon
238 B2 Huddlesford Staffs
340 B6 Hud Hey Lancs
143 E2 Hudnall Herts
134 C4 Hudnalls Gloucs
382 D4 Hudswell N York
111 F6 Hudswell Wilts
359 G3 Huggate E R Yk
38 C3 Hugglepit Devon
239 G2 Hugglescote Leics
142 B5 Hughenden Valley Bucks
234 D5 Hughley Shrops
340 C5 Hugh Mill Lancs
549 H1 Hughton Highld
3 d2 Hugh Town IoS
7 E5 Hugus Cnwll
39 G2 Huish Devon
40 A5 Huish Devon
88 D2 Huish Wilts
43 E2 Huish Champflower Somset
66 C4 Huish Episcopi Somset
596 B5 Huisinis W Isls
168 C2 Hulcote Beds
193 F4 Hulcote Nhants
142 B1 Hulcott Bucks
27 G6 Hulham Devon
294 A5 Hulland Moss Derbys
294 A5 Hulland Village Derbys
294 B5 Hulland Ward Derbys
111 F3 Hullavington Wilts
147 G6 Hullbridge Essex
313 E3 Hull End Derbys
292 B5 Hulme Staffs
310 C1 Hulme Warrtn
293 E3 Hulme End Staffs
291 G1 Hulme Walfield Ches
311 E3 Hulseheath Ches
36 B4 Hulverstone IoW
227 F2 Hulver Street Suffk
20 B2 Humber Devon
186 C3 Humber Herefs
334 D3 Humberston NE Lin
240 D3 Humberstone C Leic
334 D3 Humberston Fitties NE Lin
472 B2 Humbie E Loth
406 B4 Humbledon Sundld
200 B5 Humble Green Suffk
348 D3 Humbleton E R Yk
454 B4 Humbleton Nthumb
279 E3 Humby Lincs
452 D1 Hume Border
383 G2 Hummersknott Darltn
429 E5 Humshaugh Nthumb
589 K2 Huna Highld
340 B3 Huncoat Lancs
240 B5 Huncote Leics
452 B6 Hundalee Border
314 D4 Hundall Derbys
393 G5 Hunderthwaite Dur
160 B2 Hunderton Herefs
300 C1 Hundleby Lincs
299 G4 Hundle Houses Lincs
450 A2 Hundleshope Border
125 G4 Hundleton Pembks
199 E5 Hundon Suffk
51 G2 Hundred Acres Hants
338 B5 Hundred End Lancs
184 B4 Hundred House Powys
241 E3 Hungarton Leics
343 G4 Hungate Leeds
210 C2 Hungerford Shrops
63 G3 Hungerford Somset
116 D5 Hungerford W & M
113 H6 Hungerford W Berk
115 F4 Hungerford Green W Berk
114 B5 Hungerford Newtown W Berk
325 F3 Hunger Hill Bolton
324 C2 Hunger Hill Lancs
78 D2 Hungershall Park Kent
160 A2 Hungerstone Herefs
278 B3 Hungerton Lincs
542 F2 Hungladder Highld
271 F4 Hungreyhatton Shrops
374 D4 Hunmanby N York
375 E4 Hunmanby Moor N York
215 F6 Hunningham Warwks
191 F1 Hunningham Hill Warwks
213 E3 Hunnington Worcs
36 D3 Hunny Hill IoW
145 F2 Hunsdon Herts
145 F2 Hunsdonbury Herts
357 E4 Hunsingore N York
343 F3 Hunslet Leeds
391 F2 Hunsonby Cumb
589 G2 Hunspow Highld
258 D3 Hunstanton Norfk
403 G5 Hunstanworth Dur
290 D5 Hunsterson Ches
224 C6 Hunston Suffk
53 F4 Hunston W Susx
200 C1 Hunston Green Suffk
86 A2 Hunstrete BaNES
342 C4 Hunsworth Kirk
189 F2 Hunt End Worcs
87 E5 Huntenhull Green Wilts
116 A2 Huntercombe End Oxon
100 C2 Hunters Forstal Kent
482 A4 Hunter's Quay Ag & B
44 C2 Huntham Somset
220 B5 Huntingdon Cambs
226 C5 Huntingfield Suffk
68 D4 Huntingford Dorset
135 G6 Huntingford Gloucs
289 F2 Huntington Ches
489 F5 Huntington E Loth
160 B1 Huntington Herefs
185 E4 Huntington Herefs
237 E2 Huntington Staffs
235 E3 Huntington Wrekin
358 B4 Huntington York
512 C5 Huntingtower P & K
512 C4 Huntingtower Haugh P & K
161 G6 Huntley Gloucs
273 E1 Huntley Staffs
558 C1 Huntly Abers
72 C2 Hunton Hants
97 H5 Hunton Kent
369 G1 Hunton N York
603 J6 Hunton Ork
224 D2 Hunt's Corner Norfk
63 E3 Huntscott Somset
309 F3 Hunt's Cross Lpool
142 B4 Hunt's Green Bucks
114 C6 Hunt's Green W Berk
238 B5 Hunts Green Warwks
42 C3 Huntsham Devon
39 H3 Huntshaw Devon
39 H3 Huntshaw Water Devon
142 A5 Hunt's Hill Bucks
239 H4 Hunt's Lane Leics
84 B5 Huntspill Somset
65 E5 Huntstile Somset
65 F5 Huntworth Somset
394 D3 Hunwick Dur
261 E4 Hunworth Norfk
44 D4 Hurcott Somset
67 E4 Hurcott Somset
212 C4 Hurcott Worcs
70 D3 Hurdcott Wilts
233 E6 Hurdley Powys
312 B5 Hurdsfield Ches
383 E4 Hurgill N York
466 D2 Hurlet C Glas
116 D3 Hurley W & M
238 C5 Hurley Warwks
116 D3 Hurley Bottom W & M
238 C5 Hurley Common Warwks
445 G2 Hurlford E Ayrs
600 D7 Hurliness Ork
323 G2 Hurlston Lancs
323 G2 Hurlston Green Lancs
49 E5 Hurn Dorset
347 F1 Hurn E R Yk
29 H2 Hursey Dorset
72 B4 Hursley Hants
390 C1 Hurst Cumb
32 D1 Hurst Dorset
382 B4 Hurst N York
56 C3 Hurst Somset
326 D4 Hurst Tamesd
116 C5 Hurst Wokham
90 C5 Hurstbourne Priors Hants
90 B4 Hurstbourne Tarrant Hants
326 D1 Hurstead Rochdl
213 E2 Hurst Green Dudley
79 G4 Hurst Green E Susx
149 E1 Hurst Green Essex
339 G2 Hurst Green Lancs
96 A4 Hurst Green Surrey
236 D6 Hurst Hill Dudley
185 F5 Hurstley Herefs
118 C6 Hurst Park Surrey
55 G1 Hurstpierpoint W Susx
55 G1 Hurst Wickham W Susx
340 D3 Hurstwood Lancs
601 J4 Hurtiso Ork
93 G5 Hurtmore Surrey
383 H2 Hurworth-on-Tees Darltn
383 G2 Hurworth Place Darltn
393 G6 Hury Dur
216 D3 Husbands Bosworth Leics
168 D2 Husborne Crawley Beds
371 G4 Husthwaite N York
12 D2 Hutcherleigh Devon
467 E2 Hutchesontown C Glas
344 D5 Hut Green N York
295 F3 Huthwaite Notts
451 E5 Hutlerburn Border
340 D5 Huttock Top Lancs
321 F4 Huttoft Lincs
474 D4 Hutton Border
390 C4 Hutton Cumb
360 C4 Hutton E R Yk
146 C6 Hutton Essex
84 B3 Hutton N Som
384 A4 Hutton Bonville N York
374 B3 Hutton Buscel N York
370 C5 Hutton Conyers N York
360 C4 Hutton Cranswick E R Yk
390 C2 Hutton End Cumb
385 F1 Hutton Gate R & Cl
369 G2 Hutton Hang N York
396 B2 Hutton Henry Dur
372 D2 Hutton-le-Hole N York
382 D2 Hutton Magna Dur
146 C6 Hutton Mount Essex
366 B4 Hutton Roof Cumb
390 B3 Hutton Roof Cumb
384 D3 Hutton Rudby N York
373 E6 Huttons Ambo N York
371 F4 Hutton Sessay N York
385 G2 Hutton Village R & Cl
357 G4 Hutton Wandesley N York
27 E3 Huxham Devon
67 F2 Huxham Green Somset
289 G2 Huxley Ches
606 A6 Huxter Shet
606 E7 Huxter Shet
607 J5 Huxter Shet
309 G1 Huyton Knows
309 F1 Huyton Park Knows
309 G1 Huyton Quarry Knows
309 F1 Huyton-with-Roby Knows
362 B4 Hycemoor Cumb
30 B4 Hyde Dorset
136 C4 Hyde Gloucs
163 G4 Hyde Gloucs
49 F2 Hyde Hants
72 C3 Hyde Hants
186 B4 Hyde Herefs
327 E6 Hyde Tamesd
147 F4 Hyde Chase Essex
91 F2 Hyde End W Berk
142 C4 Hyde Heath Bucks
272 D5 Hyde Lea Staffs
330 C4 Hyde Park Donc
75 F1 Hydestile Surrey
406 B3 Hylton Castle Sundld
406 B3 Hylton Red House Sundld
256 A4 Hyltons Crossways Norfk
340 A3 Hyndburn Bridge Lancs
448 B1 Hyndford Bridge S Lans
450 D5 Hyndhope Border
516 B8 Hynish Ag & B
586 C5 Hysbackie Highld
233 F6 Hyssington Powys
135 F5 Hystfield Gloucs
50 D3 Hythe Hants
82 C4 Hythe Kent
84 D4 Hythe Somset
117 H5 Hythe End W & M
571 J5 Hythie Abers
362 B4 Hyton Cumb

I

569 G2 Ianstown Moray
598 D8 Iarsiadar W Isls
47 E3 Ibberton Dorset
294 A3 Ible Derbys
467 E2 Ibrox C Glas
49 F3 Ibsley Hants
239 G2 Ibstock Leics
141 G6 Ibstone Bucks
90 B4 Ibthorpe Hants
387 E3 Iburndale N York
91 F4 Ibworth Hants
84 C1 Icelton N Som
507 H3 Ichrachan Ag & B
247 G6 Ickburgh Norfk
118 B2 Ickenham Gt Lon
364 D2 Ickenthwaite Cumb
140 D3 Ickford Bucks
100 D4 Ickham Kent
170 A3 Ickleford Herts
59 E3 Icklesham E Susx
197 G6 Ickleton Cambs
223 F5 Icklingham Suffk
354 C6 Ickornshaw N York
195 G5 Ickwell Beds
195 H5 Ickwell Green Beds
164 C5 Icomb Gloucs
12 B3 Icy Park Devon
164 C6 Idbury Oxon
40 B6 Iddesleigh Devon
26 D4 Ide Devon
20 B2 Ideford Devon
96 C4 Ide Hill Kent
80 D5 Iden E Susx
79 G2 Iden Green Kent
80 A3 Iden Green Kent
342 C2 Idle Brad
342 C2 Idle Moor Brad
7 F4 Idless Cnwll
190 D6 Idlicote Warwks
70 D2 Idmiston Wilts
128 B1 Idole Carmth
294 B5 Idridgehay Derbys
294 B5 Idridgehay Green Derbys
542 F4 Idrigill Highld
113 G3 Idstone Oxon
528 B5 Idvies Angus
152 D4 Iet-y-Bwlch Carmth
140 B4 Iffley Oxon
76 D2 Ifield W Susx
77 E2 Ifield Green W Susx
76 D2 Ifieldwood W Susx
75 G3 Ifold W Susx
49 E6 Iford Bmouth
56 C3 Iford E Susx
269 F2 Ifton Heath Shrops
270 D2 Ightfield Shrops
270 D2 Ightfield Heath Shrops
97 E3 Ightham Kent
97 E3 Igtham Common Kent
203 E3 Iken Suffk
293 F4 Ilam Staffs
67 E5 Ilchester Somset
67 E5 Ilchester Mead Somset
454 C5 Ilderton Nthumb
100 D5 Ileden Kent
120 B2 Ilford Gt Lon
44 D4 Ilford Somset
60 D2 Ilfracombe Devon
275 G1 Ilkeston Derbys
226 D2 Ilketshall St Andrew Suffk
226 D3 Ilketshall St Lawrence Suffk
226 C2 Ilketshall St Margaret Suffk
355 F5 Ilkley Brad
16 C3 Illand Cnwll
213 E3 Illey Dudley
291 F2 Illidge Green Ches
224 B2 Illington Norfk
341 H4 Illingworth Calder
6 C5 Illogan Cnwll
6 C5 Illogan Highway Cnwll
214 A5 Illshaw Heath Solhll
241 F5 Illston on the Hill Leics
141 G3 Ilmer Bucks
190 B6 Ilmington Warwks
44 D5 Ilminster Somset
19 G2 Ilsington Devon
103 E3 Ilston Swans
369 G4 Ilton N York
44 C4 Ilton Somset
460 B1 Imachar N Ayrs
87 H5 Imber Wilts
476 E7 Imeraval Ag & B
334 A2 Immingham NE Lin
334 A1 Immingham Dock NE Lin
197 G2 Impington Cambs
309 G4 Ince Ches
323 F4 Ince Blundell Sefton
324 D4 Ince-in-Makerfield Wigan
528 D1 Inchbare Angus
568 E4 Inchberry Moray
529 E3 Inchbraoch Angus
136 B4 Inchbrook Gloucs
563 J4 Incheril Highld
539 E4 Inchgrundle Angus
573 J5 Inchina Highld
483 G6 Inchinnan Rens
533 J2 Inchlaggan Highld
554 D5 Inchmarnoch Abers
548 F1 Inchmore Highld
565 K7 Inchmore Highld
579 J5 Inchnadamph Highld
520 E3 Inchree Highld
14 D6 Inchs Cnwll
513 G4 Inchture P & K
513 E5 Inchyra P & K
7 H2 Indian Queens Cnwll
476 E8 Ineraval Ag & B
146 D5 Ingatestone Essex
328 C3 Ingbirchworth Barns
356 B1 Ingerthorpe N York
273 E5 Ingestre Staffs
318 A3 Ingham Lincs
256 D4 Ingham Norfk
223 G5 Ingham Suffk
256 D4 Ingham Corner Norfk
245 G2 Ingleborough Norfk
275 E4 Ingleby Derbys
384 C4 Ingleby Arncliffe N York
384 C2 Ingleby Barwick S on T
384 D4 Ingleby Cross N York
385 F3 Ingleby Greenhow N York
25 F1 Ingleigh Green Devon
347 G3 Inglemire C KuH
86 B2 Inglesbatch BaNES
138 B5 Inglesham Swindn
394 D5 Ingleton Dur
366 D5 Ingleton N York
338 D2 Inglewhite Lancs
527 F5 Ingliston Angus
487 F5 Ingliston C Edin
357 E4 Ingmanthorpe N York
429 G4 Ingoe Nthumb
338 D3 Ingol Lancs
258 D5 Ingoldisthorpe Norfk
321 G6 Ingoldmells Lincs
279 E3 Ingoldsby Lincs
190 C3 Ingon Warwks
442 C1 Ingram Nthumb
74 C5 Ingrams Green W Susx
121 F1 Ingrave Essex
341 G2 Ingrow Brad
378 D5 Ings Cumb
109 G2 Ingst S Glos
242 D3 Ingthorpe Rutlnd
255 G2 Ingworth Norfk
91 F2 Inhurst Hants
189 F3 Inkberrow Worcs
394 B2 Inkerman Dur
315 E5 Inkersall Derbys
315 E5 Inkersall Green Derbys
213 G5 Inkford Worcs
560 D2 Inkhorn Abers
90 B2 Inkpen W Berk
90 B2 Inkpen Common W Berk
589 H2 Inkstack Highld
52 D3 Inlands W Susx
87 G2 Inmarsh Wilts
481 H5 Innellan Ag & B
523 J4 Innerhadden P & K
12 B5 Inner Hope Devon
450 C2 Innerleithen Border
502 B5 Innerleven Fife
415 E4 Innermessan D & G
600 C3 Innertown Ork
490 D5 Innerwick E Loth
523 G6 Innerwick P & K
507 K4 Innis Chonain Ag & B
86 D5 Innox Hill Somset
162 B5 Innsworth Gloucs
559 E4 Insch Abers
536 B2 Insh Highld
584 D5 Inshegra Highld
584 F3 Inshore Highld
338 C2 Inskip Lancs
338 C2 Inskip Moss Side Lancs
330 C2 Instoneville Donc
60 C5 Instow Devon
10 D3 Insworke Cnwll
339 H4 Intack Bl w D
330 C4 Intake Donc
314 D3 Intake Sheff
188 A5 Interfield Worcs
249 G4 Intwood Norfk
537 K4 Inver Abers
577 J7 Inver Highld
512 B1 Inver P & K
531 L6 Inverailort Highld
545 H1 Inveralivaig Highld
562 E5 Inveralligin Highld
571 J2 Inverallochy Abers
559 G5 Inveramsay Abers
576 C4 Inveran Highld
494 B3 Inveraray Ag & B
545 K2 Inverarish Highld
527 G6 Inverarity Angus
508 D6 Inverarnan Stirlg
495 G5 Inverbeg Ag & B
541 F5 Inverbervie Abers
570 B3 Inverboyndie Abers
550 E3 Inverbrough Highld
575 K3 Invercassley Highld
481 F4 Inverchaolain Ag & B
521 G6 Invercharnan Highld
564 C6 Inverchoran Highld
520 E6 Invercreran Ag & B
551 G7 Inverdruie Highld
560 D3 Inverebrie Abers
525 H2 Invereddrie P & K
488 C5 Inveresk E Loth
507 G2 Inveresragan Ag & B
537 G5 Inverey Abers
549 J5 Inverfarigaig Highld
520 C7 Inverfolla Ag & B
534 B2 Invergarry Highld
537 K4 Invergelder Abers
510 C4 Invergeldie P & K
566 C3 Invergordon Highld
514 A3 Invergowrie P & K
546 C8 Inverguseran Highld
553 H2 Inverharroch Moray
531 L3 Inverie Highld
507 G6 Inverinan Ag & B
547 G5 Inverinate Highld
529 E5 Inverkeilor Angus
487 F3 Inverkeithing Fife
569 L6 Inverkeithny Abers
482 A5 Inverkip Inver
578 E6 Inverkirkaig Highld
574 D6 Inverlael Highld
534 B7 Inverlair Highld
488 A4 Inverleith C Edin
508 F6 Inverlochlarig Stirlg
533 H8 Inverlochy Highld
479 G4 Inverlussa Ag & B
531 J8 Invermoidart Highld
549 G6 Invermoriston Highld
586 E4 Invernaver Highld
480 A3 Inverneill Ag & B
566 B8 Inverness Highld
571 L7 Invernettie Abers
494 C5 Invernoaden Ag & B
527 E3 Inverquharity Angus
571 J6 Inverquhomery Abers
533 L6 Inverroy Highld
520 C4 Inversanda Highld
547 G6 Invershiel Highld
576 C4 Invershin Highld
583 H3 Invershore Highld
495 G3 Inversnaid Stirlg
571 K6 Inverugie Abers
495 G3 Inveruglas Ag & B
536 B2 Inveruglass Highld
559 G5 Inverurie Abers
523 J6 Invervar P & K
559 G1 Inverythan Abers
24 D3 Inwardleigh Devon
234 B5 Inwood Shrops
173 H6 Inworth Essex
593 D8 Iochdar W Isls
592 D5 Iolaraigh W Isls
74 D5 Iping W Susx
20 A4 Ipplepen Devon
115 G2 Ipsden Oxon
189 G1 Ipsley Worcs
292 D5 Ipstones Staffs
176 C1 Ipswich Suffk
308 C3 Irby Wirral
301 E2 Irby in the Marsh Lincs
334 A4 Irby upon Humber NE Lin
194 C1 Irchester Nhants
389 F2 Ireby Cumb
366 D4 Ireby Lancs
169 G1 Ireland Beds
600 E3 Ireland Ork
605 G6 Ireland Shet
87 E4 Ireland Wilts
271 G1 Ireland's Cross Shrops
343 E2 Ireland Wood Leeds
363 E6 Ireleth Cumb
393 E2 Ireshopeburn Dur
294 B5 Ireton Wood Derbys
325 G6 Irlam Salfd
279 E4 Irnham Lincs
110 B3 Iron Acton S Glos
245 G5 Iron Bridge Cambs
235 F4 Ironbridge Wrekin
189 F4 Iron Cross Warwks
423 F4 Irongray D & G
421 H4 Ironmacannie D & G
95 F5 Irons Bottom Surrey
295 E4 Ironville Derbys
256 D5 Irstead Norfk
256 D6 Irstead Street Norfk
401 F2 Irthington Cumb
218 C5 Irthlingborough Nhants
374 C3 Irton N York
444 D2 Irvine N Ayrs
340 B5 Irwell Vale Lancs
431 E3 Isabella Pit Nthumb
302 B5 Isallt Bach IoA
588 B3 Isauld Highld
602 B7 Isbister Ork
602 D8 Isbister Ork
607 J5 Isbister Shet
608 D6 Isbister Shet
389 E3 Isel Cumb
56 C1 Isfield E Susx
218 B5 Isham Nhants
92 C6 Isington Hants
332 D3 Island Carr N Linc
196 A2 Islands Common Cambs
44 D3 Isle Abbotts Somset
44 D3 Isle Brewers Somset
222 C5 Isleham Cambs
423 H4 Isle of Man D & G
411 E5 Isle of Whithorn D & G
546 B7 Isleornsay or Eilean Iarmain Highld
606 D4 Islesburgh Shet
423 G5 Islesteps D & G
35 d2 Islet Village Guern
118 C4 Isleworth Gt Lon
275 G5 Isley Walton Leics
596 B2 Islibhig W Isls
119 G2 Islington Gt Lon
271 G6 Islington Wrekin
218 D4 Islip Nhants
140 B2 Islip Oxon
596 B2 Islivig W Isls
235 E2 Isombridge Wrekin
121 F6 Istead Rise Kent
289 F4 Isycoed Wrexhm
50 D2 Itchen C Sotn
72 D3 Itchen Abbas Hants
73 E3 Itchen Stoke Hants
76 B4 Itchingfield W Susx
110 B2 Itchington S Glos
261 F5 Itteringham Norfk
255 G2 Itteringham Common Norfk
25 G3 Itton Devon
134 B5 Itton Mons
134 B5 Itton Common Mons
400 D6 Ivegill Cumb
381 G5 Ivelet N York
118 A3 Iver Bucks
118 A3 Iver Heath Bucks
212 C3 Iverley Staffs

404 D4 Iveston Dur
236 B2 Ivetsey Bank Staffs
142 C1 Ivinghoe Bucks
168 C6 Ivinghoe Aston Bucks
186 B3 Ivington Herefs
186 B3 Ivington Green Herefs
12 A1 Ivybridge Devon
145 G4 Ivy Chimneys Essex
81 F4 Ivychurch Kent
69 E5 Ivy Cross Dorset
97 E4 Ivy Hatch Kent
248 A3 Ivy Todd Norfk
123 E6 Iwade Kent
47 F2 Iwerne Courtney or Shroton Dorset
47 G2 Iwerne Minster Dorset
84 D2 Iwood N Som
224 B5 Ixworth Suffk
224 B5 Ixworth Thorpe Suffk

J

339 E4 Jack Green Lancs
355 G4 Jack Hill N York
27 G3 Jack-in-the-Green Devon
295 E4 Jacksdale Notts
172 B5 Jack's Green Essex
136 C2 Jack's Green Gloucs
328 B3 Jackson Bridge Kirk
559 G3 Jackstown Abers
467 E4 Jackton S Lans
22 D3 Jacobstow Cnwll
25 E2 Jacobstowe Devon
93 G4 Jacobs Well Surrey
342 A6 Jagger Green Calder
126 B5 Jameston Pembks
438 B5 Jamestown D & G
565 H5 Jamestown Highld
483 E3 Jamestown W Duns
500 C5 Jamphlars Fife
588 D3 Janetstown Highld
589 J6 Janetstown Highld
174 B4 Janke's Green Essex
406 A1 Jarrow S Tyne
78 C3 Jarvis Brook E Susx
173 E4 Jasper's Green Essex
505 L3 Java Ag & B
485 G5 Jawcraig Falk
343 E5 Jaw Hill Leeds
149 F2 Jaywick Essex
117 E5 Jealott's Hill Br For
472 C6 Jeaniefield Border
452 B5 Jedburgh Border
126 B3 Jeffreyston Pembks
566 C3 Jemimaville Highld
115 F5 Jennetts Hill W Berk
356 B3 Jennyfield N York
35 d4 Jerbourg Guern
326 B2 Jericho Bury
103 H3 Jersey Marine Neath
468 C5 Jerviswood S Lans
405 G1 Jesmond N u Ty
57 F4 Jevington E Susx
23 F2 Jewell's Cross Devon
134 B2 Jingle Street Mons
143 E2 Jockey End Herts
311 F5 Jodrell Bank Ches
390 C3 Johnby Cumb
241 F3 John O'Gaunt Leics
589 K2 John o' Groats Highld
58 B2 John's Cross E Susx
529 G1 Johnshaven Abers
325 F2 Johnson Fold Bolton
339 E5 Johnson's Hillock Lancs
256 D6 Johnson Street Norfk
125 F2 Johnston Pembks
466 B2 Johnstone Rens
424 B1 Johnstonebridge D & G
154 A6 Johnstown Carmth
288 D5 Johnstown Wrexhm
6 D4 Jolly's Bottom Cnwll
488 C5 Joppa C Edin
181 E1 Joppa Cerdgn
3 G2 Joppa Cnwll
445 F6 Joppa S Ayrs
255 E3 Jordan Green Norfk
117 G1 Jordans Bucks
151 F3 Jordanston Pembks
314 D3 Jordanthorpe Sheff
329 G6 Jordon Rothm
484 A6 Jordonhill C Glas
120 D5 Joyden's Wood Kent
134 D2 Joyford Gloucs
135 E1 Joy's Green Gloucs
326 D2 Jubilee Oldham
271 H2 Jugbank Staffs
329 F4 Jump Barns
49 E6 Jumpers Common Dorset
78 B3 Jumper's Town E Susx
403 G3 Juniper Nthumb
487 G6 Juniper Green C Edin
322 f3 Jurby IoM
25 G6 Jurston Devon
59 G3 Jury's Gap E Susx

K

380 D2 Kaber Cumb
469 F5 Kaimend S Lans
488 B6 Kaimes C Edin
557 G4 Kaimhill C Aber
449 E1 Kaimrig End Border
606 E8 Kalliness Shet
480 D5 Kames Ag & B
446 D4 Kames E Ayrs
213 E1 Kates Hill Dudley
7 F5 Kea Cnwll
332 A2 Keadby N Linc
300 C2 Keal Cotes Lincs
356 C5 Kearby Town End N York
356 C5 Kearby with Netherby N York
83 E2 Kearnsey Kent
325 H4 Kearsley Bolton
366 B4 Kearstwick Cumb
382 A5 Kearton N York
584 E2 Kearvaig Highld
353 E1 Keasden N York
341 G5 Kebroyd Calder
310 B3 Keckwick Halton
320 B2 Keddington Lincs
320 C2 Keddington Corner Lincs
199 E5 Kedington Suffk
275 L1 Kedleston Derbys
514 B6 Kedlock Fife
514 B5 Kedlock Feus Fife
451 G1 Kedslie Border
376 B1 Keekle Cumb
174 D5 Keelars Tye Essex
333 H2 Keelby Lincs
291 G6 Keele Staffs
195 E5 Keeley Green Beds
342 A3 Keelham Brad
402 D3 Keenley Nthumb
64 D4 Keenthorne Somset
146 B2 Keeres Green Essex
151 F6 Keeston Pembks
87 G3 Keevil Wilts
276 A4 Kegworth Leics

6 B5 Kehelland Cnwll
559 E6 Keig Abers
341 H1 Keighley Brad
498 D6 Keilarsbrae Clacks
570 C4 Keilhill Abers
479 H5 Keillbeg Ag & B
479 H5 Keillmore Ag & B
513 G1 Keillor P & K
511 H4 Keillour P & K
478 C8 Keils Ag & B
478 E8 Keils Ag & B
67 F3 Keinton Mandeville Somset
435 H6 Keir Mill D & G
279 E4 Keisby Lincs
589 J4 Keiss Highld
543 G6 Keith Moray
569 G5 Keith Inch Abers
571 L6 Keithick P & K
528 C2 Keithock Angus
354 B6 Kelbrook Lancs
465 E3 Kelburn N Ayrs
279 E1 Kelby Lincs
355 G6 Kelcliffe Leeds
379 F2 Keld Cumb
389 F2 Keld N York
372 D2 Keldholme N York
355 F2 Keld Houses N York
331 H4 Kelfield N Linc
344 D2 Kelfield N York
297 E3 Kelham Notts
424 C6 Kelhead D & G
24 A5 Kellacott Devon
338 B4 Kellamergh Lancs
505 G2 Kellan Ag & B
505 G2 Kellan Mill Ag & B
514 C2 Kellas Angus
568 B5 Kellas Moray
12 D5 Kellaton Devon
111 H4 Kellaways Wilts
380 B3 Kelleth Cumb
360 C3 Kelleythorpe E R Yk
261 E3 Kelling Norfk
344 C5 Kellingley N York
344 D5 Kellington N York
609 G4 Kellister Shet
395 G2 Kelloe Dur
435 E2 Kelloholm D & G
376 B1 Kells Cumb
15 E4 Kelly Cnwll
17 E2 Kelly Devon
17 E4 Kelly Bray Cnwll
217 F4 Kelmarsh Nhants
138 D5 Kelmscott Oxon
202 D1 Kelsale Suffk
309 H6 Kelsall Ches
170 D2 Kelshall Herts
399 F4 Kelsick Cumb
452 D3 Kelso Border
294 C2 Kelstedge Derbys
319 G1 Kelstern Lincs
308 C5 Kelsterton Flints
86 C1 Kelston BaNES
523 L6 Keltneyburn P & K
423 G5 Kelton D & G
393 F5 Kelton Dur
500 B6 Kelty Fife
500 B5 Keltybridge P & K
173 G6 Kelvedon Essex
146 B5 Kelvedon Hatch Essex
467 F4 Kelvin S Lans
484 B6 Kelvindale C Glas
484 B6 Kelvinside C Glas
2 C4 Kelynack Cnwll
61 G2 Kemacott Devon
502 C1 Kemback Fife
235 G4 Kemberton Shrops
137 E5 Kemble Gloucs
137 E5 Kemble Wick Gloucs
162 D2 Kemerton Worcs
133 F4 Kemeys Commander Mons
311 G6 Kemincham Ches
556 C1 Kemnay Abers
99 G5 Kempe's Corner Kent
161 F4 Kempley Gloucs
161 F4 Kempley Green Gloucs
188 C5 Kempsey Worcs
138 B5 Kempsford Gloucs
214 A5 Kemps Green Warwks
91 G4 Kempshott Hants
195 E5 Kempston Beds
195 E5 Kempston Church End Beds
195 E6 Kempston Hardwick Beds
194 D5 Kempston West End Beds
209 G3 Kempton Shrops
55 H4 Kemp Town Br & H
97 E3 Kemsing Kent
99 E1 Kemsley Kent
98 C2 Kemsley Street Kent
81 E3 Kenardington Kent
186 A6 Kenchester Herefs
138 D4 Kencot Oxon
379 F6 Kendal Cumb
213 E5 Kendal End Worcs
159 H4 Kenderchurch Herefs
110 B4 Kendleshire S Glos
132 C5 Kendon Caerph
421 G2 Kendoon D & G
543 G2 Kendram Highld
329 F4 Kendray Barns
104 B3 Kenfig Brdgnd
104 C3 Kenfig Hill Brdgnd
214 D5 Kenilworth Warwks
509 G2 Kenknock Stirlg
95 G3 Kenley Gt Lon
234 D4 Kenley Shrops
562 D5 Kenmore Highld
523 L6 Kenmore P & K
27 E5 Kenn Devon
108 D6 Kenn N Som
108 D6 Kenn Moor Gate N Som
462 D2 Kennacraig Ag & B
23 F6 Kennards House Cnwll
3 G4 Kenneggy Cnwll
3 G4 Kenneggy Downs Cnwll
26 C1 Kennerleigh Devon
486 B1 Kennet Clacks
198 D1 Kennet End Cambs
558 C4 Kennethmont Abers
222 D6 Kennett Cambs
27 E5 Kennford Devon
224 D2 Kenninghall Norfk
119 G4 Kennington Gt Lon
99 G6 Kennington Kent
140 B4 Kennington Oxon
466 D2 Kennoway Fife
44 C4 Kenny Somset
222 D4 Kenny Hill Suffk
359 E1 Kennythorpe N York
516 B6 Kenovay Ag & B
543 G6 Kensaleyre Highld
119 E3 Kensal Green Gt Lon
119 F4 Kensington Gt Lon
309 E1 Kensington Lpool
169 E6 Kensworth Beds
520 E4 Kentallen Highld
159 H4 Kentchurch Herefs
199 E1 Kentford Suffk
43 E6 Kentisbeare Devon
61 F3 Kentisbury Devon
61 F3 Kentisbury Ford Devon
378 D4 Kentmere Cumb
27 E6 Kenton Devon

118 D2 Kenton Gt Lon
405 F1 Kenton N u Ty
201 G1 Kenton Suffk
430 D6 Kenton Bankfoot N u Ty
430 D6 Kenton Bar N u Ty
201 H1 Kenton Corner Suffk
136 A2 Kenton Green Gloucs
518 F2 Kentra Highld
379 F6 Kentrigg Cumb
22 D3 Kents Cnwll
365 E4 Kents Bank Cumb
161 G5 Kent's Green Gloucs
168 B2 Kents Hill M Keyn
71 G5 Kent's Oak Hants
97 G4 Kent Street Kent
76 D5 Kent Street W Susx
269 H3 Kenwick Shrops
269 H4 Kenwick Park Shrops
7 F4 Kenwyn Cnwll
325 E5 Kenyon Warrtn
585 G3 Keoldale Highld
497 E6 Kepdowrie Stirlg
89 E3 Kepnal Wilts
520 E3 Keppanach Highld
547 G5 Keppoch Highld
371 F1 Kepwick N York
255 E3 Kerdiston Norfk
215 E3 Keresley Covtry
215 E2 Keresley Newlands Warwks
450 B2 Kerfield Border
7 E5 Kerley Downs Cnwll
12 D4 Kernborough Devon
160 D6 Kerne Bridge Herefs
312 B4 Kerridge Ches
312 B5 Kerridge-End Ches
2 D4 Kerris Cnwll
548 E3 Kerrow Highld
208 B2 Kerry Powys
464 B2 Kerrycroy Ag & B
292 B5 Kerry Hill Staffs
562 E2 Kerrysdale Highld
159 G3 Kerry's Gate Herefs
326 B4 Kersal Salfd
296 D2 Kersall Notts
27 H6 Kersbrook Devon
16 D3 Kersbrook Cross Cnwll
40 C2 Kerscott Devon
200 C6 Kersey Suffk
200 C6 Kersey Tye Suffk
200 C6 Kersey Upland Suffk
597 J4 Kershader W Isls
426 C3 Kershopefoot Cumb
163 E2 Kersoe Worcs
28 A1 Kerswell Devon
188 C5 Kerswell Green Worcs
3 G3 Kerthen Wood Cnwll
201 H6 Kesgrave Suffk
227 G2 Kessingland Suffk
227 G2 Kessingland Beach Suffk
8 B4 Kestle Cnwll
7 F2 Kestle Mill Cnwll
96 B2 Keston Gt Lon
96 B1 Keston Mark Gt Lon
389 G5 Keswick Cumb
249 H4 Keswick Norfk
256 D3 Keswick Norfk
124 D4 Kete Pembks
161 G3 Ketford Gloucs
235 F2 Ketley Wrekin
235 F2 Ketley Bank Wrekin
320 C4 Ketsby Lincs
218 B4 Kettering Nhants
249 G4 Ketteringham Norfk
513 F2 Kettins P & K
200 C4 Kettlebaston Suffk
501 F3 Kettlebridge Fife
238 C4 Kettlebrook Staffs
202 B2 Kettleburgh Suffk
97 H4 Kettle Corner Kent
171 F6 Kettle Green Herts
501 F3 Kettlehill Fife
424 C4 Kettleholm D & G
386 D1 Kettleness N York
312 C4 Kettleshulme Ches
355 H3 Kettlesing N York
356 A3 Kettlesing Bottom N York
607 H2 Kettlester Shet
260 C2 Kettlestone Norfk
317 F4 Kettlethorpe Lincs
329 E1 Kettlethorpe Wakefd
603 K4 Kettletoft Ork
368 C3 Kettlewell N York
242 D4 Ketton Rutlnd
120 C6 Kevingtown Gt Lon
118 D4 Kew Gt Lon
85 F6 Keward Somset
84 B2 Kewstoke N Som
328 D3 Kexbrough Barns
317 G2 Kexby Lincs
358 C4 Kexby York
15 F4 Keybridge Cnwll
98 D2 Keycol Kent
86 D5 Keyford Somset
292 A2 Key Green Ches
386 C4 Key Green N York
241 E3 Keyham Leics
35 H2 Keyhaven Hants
571 K4 Keyhead Abers
348 D4 Keyingham E R Yk
55 H1 Keymer W Susx
86 A1 Keynsham BaNES
145 E3 Keysers Estate Essex
79 F2 Key's Green Kent
195 F2 Keysoe Beds
195 F2 Keysoe Row Beds
219 E4 Keyston Cambs
98 D2 Key Street Kent
276 C3 Keyworth Notts
405 F3 Kibblesworth Gatesd
241 E6 Kibworth Beauchamp Leics
241 E6 Kibworth Harcourt Leics
120 B4 Kidbrooke Gt Lon
388 C5 Kidburngill Cumb
343 H2 Kiddal Lane End Leeds
236 B3 Kiddemore Green Staffs
212 B4 Kidderminster Worcs
165 G5 Kiddington Oxon
571 G7 Kiddshill Abers
249 F4 Kidd's Moor Norfk
140 A1 Kidmore End Oxon
116 A4 Kidmore End Oxon
289 G5 Kidnal Ches
410 D5 Kidsdale D & G
291 G4 Kidsgrove Staffs
368 B3 Kidstones N York
128 B3 Kidwelly Carmth
506 F2 Kiel Crofts Ag & B
440 B6 Kielder Nthumb
115 F6 Kiff Green W Berk
466 B2 Kilbarchan Rens
531 H1 Kilbeg Highld
462 B2 Kilberry Ag & B
465 G4 Kilbirnie N Ayrs
483 G5 Kilbowie W Duns
492 C1 Kilbride Ag & B
506 E4 Kilbride Ag & B
545 K5 Kilbride Highld
481 E1 Kilbridemore Ag & B
294 C5 Kilburn Derbys
119 E3 Kilburn Gt Lon
371 G3 Kilburn N York
240 D5 Kilby Leics
240 D5 Kilby Bridge Leics

462 D2 Kilchamaig Ag & B
464 C3 Kilchattan Ag & B
456 D2 Kilchattan Bay Ag & B
506 D2 Kilcheran Ag & B
476 B4 Kilchiaran Ag & B
518 C3 Kilchoan Highld
507 H5 Kilchoan Highld
476 C4 Kilchoman Ag & B
507 H5 Kilchrenan Ag & B
502 D4 Kilconquhar Fife
161 F4 Kilcot Gloucs
565 K6 Kilcoy Highld
482 B3 Kilcreggan Ag & B
385 F3 Kildale N York
457 F3 Kildalloig Ag & B
566 D1 Kildary Highld
463 H1 Kildavanan Ag & B
542 E6 Kildonan Highld
461 E5 Kildonan N Ayrs
530 E5 Kildonnan Highld
485 F5 Kildrum N Lans
555 E1 Kildrummy Abers
354 D5 Kildwick N York
480 C4 Kilfinan Ag & B
533 L3 Kilfinnan Highld
126 C3 Kilgetty Pembks
432 B4 Kilgrammie S Ayrs
134 B5 Kilgwrrwg Common Mons
8 D2 Kilhallon Cnwll
360 C2 Kilham E R Yk
440 B6 Kilham Nthumb
516 A7 Kilkenneth Ag & B
163 E6 Kilkenny Gloucs
457 E3 Kilkerran Ag & B
432 D4 Kilkerran S Ayrs
38 C5 Kilkhampton Cnwll
315 E3 Killamarsh Derbys
410 B3 Killantrae D & G
7 G1 Killaworgy Cnwll
103 F3 Killay Swans
462 A6 Killean Ag & B
484 A2 Killearn Stirlg
456 D3 Killellan Park Ag & B
566 B5 Killen Highld
394 D6 Killerby Darltn
522 F4 Killichonan P & K
533 K6 Killiechonate Highld
505 G2 Killiechronan Ag & B
524 D3 Killiecrankie P & K
504 F3 Killiemor Ag & B
547 G3 Killilan Highld
589 J5 Killimster Highld
509 J3 Killin Stirlg
476 E2 Killinallan Ag & B
356 B3 Killinghall N York
366 C2 Killington Cumb
61 G2 Killington Devon
431 E5 Killingworth N Tyne
431 E5 Killingworth Moor N Tyne
431 E5 Killingworth Village N Tyne
492 D5 Killinochonoch Ag & B
6 B6 Killivose Cnwll
472 B5 Killochyett Border
458 D5 Killocraw Ag & B
518 E6 Killundine Highld
483 E6 Kilmacolm Inver
497 F3 Kilmahog Stirlg
492 C5 Kilmahumaig Ag & B
520 B4 Kilmalieu Highld
543 G2 Kilmaluag Ag & B
514 B5 Kilmany Fife
545 J6 Kilmarie Highld
445 F2 Kilmarnock E Ayrs
492 D5 Kilmartin Ag & B
445 E1 Kilmaurs E Ayrs
492 D2 Kilmelford Ag & B
476 F3 Kilmeny Ag & B
86 B4 Kilmersdon Somset
73 E4 Kilmeston Hants
493 E6 Kilmichael Beg Ag & B
493 E6 Kilmichael Glassary Ag & B
479 K4 Kilmichael of Inverlussa Ag & B
29 E3 Kilmington Devon
68 C2 Kilmington Wilts
68 C2 Kilmington Common Wilts
516 B6 Kilmoluaig Ag & B
533 J6 Kilmonivaig Highld
565 H8 Kilmorack Highld
506 E4 Kilmore Ag & B
531 H1 Kilmore Highld
479 J6 Kilmory Ag & B
518 D1 Kilmory Highld
530 C2 Kilmory Highld
460 D5 Kilmory N Ayrs
542 D7 Kilmuir Highld
542 F2 Kilmuir Highld
566 B7 Kilmuir Highld
566 D2 Kilmuir Highld
481 H3 Kilmun Ag & B
476 D2 Kilnave Ag & B
468 C5 Kilncadzow S Lans
79 G2 Kilndown Kent
161 E6 Kiln Green Herefs
116 D4 Kiln Green Wokham
389 F3 Kilnhill Cumb
329 G5 Kilnhurst Rothm
517 K6 Kilninian Ag & B
517 K6 Kilninver Ag & B
404 B4 Kiln Pit Hill Nthumb
335 F1 Kilnsea E R Yk
368 C4 Kilnsey N York
359 F4 Kilnwick E R Yk
359 E4 Kilnwick Percy E R Yk
478 B2 Kiloran Ag & B
460 C4 Kilpatrick N Ayrs
160 A3 Kilpeck Herefs
582 C6 Kilphedir Highld
345 H4 Kilpin E R Yk
345 H4 Kilpin Pike E R Yk
503 F4 Kilrenny Fife
216 C5 Kilsby Nhants
513 F4 Kilspindie P & K
485 E4 Kilsyth N Lans
549 J1 Kiltarlity Highld
316 A4 Kilton Notts
397 H6 Kilton R & Cl
64 C3 Kilton Somset
397 G6 Kilton Thorpe R & Cl
542 F3 Kilvaxter Highld
64 C3 Kilve Somset
297 H6 Kilvington Notts
465 G6 Kilwinning N Ayrs
249 E4 Kimberley Norfk
295 F6 Kimberley Notts
329 G6 Kimberworth Rothm
329 G6 Kimberworth Park Rothm
405 F5 Kimblesworth Dur
141 G3 Kimble Wick Bucks
219 G6 Kimbolton Cambs
186 C2 Kimbolton Herefs
71 G4 Kimbridge Hants
216 C2 Kimcote Leics
33 G4 Kimmeridge Dorset
454 A2 Kimmerston Nthumb
89 G5 Kimpton Hants
170 A6 Kimpton Herts
38 D5 Kimworthy Devon
565 L4 Kinbeachie Highld
581 L3 Kinbrace Highld
498 B4 Kinbuck Stirlg
514 D6 Kincaple Fife
486 B2 Kincardine Fife

576 D6 Kincardine Highld
486 B2 Kincardine Br Fife
555 G5 Kincardine O'neil Abers
513 E2 Kinclaven P & K
557 F5 Kincluny Abers
557 G4 Kincorth C Aber
536 B1 Kincraig Highld
524 E6 Kincraigie P & K
524 E5 Kindallachan P & K
328 D4 Kine Moor Barns
163 G4 Kineton Gloucs
191 E4 Kineton Warwks
214 A3 Kineton Green Solhll
513 E5 Kinfauns P & K
519 K5 Kingairloch Highld
464 B3 Kingarth Ag & B
37 E5 Kingates IoW
16 C4 Kingbeare Cnwll
134 A3 Kingcoed Mons
85 F2 Kingdown N Som
570 C4 King Edward Abers
333 E6 Kingerby Lincs
93 G3 Kingfield Surrey
23 F1 Kingford Devon
40 C4 Kingford Devon
164 D5 Kingham Oxon
69 E4 Kinghay Wilts
425 G5 Kingholm Quay D & G
488 B2 Kinghorn Fife
500 D5 Kinglassie Fife
449 E4 Kingledores Border
160 B1 King's Acre Herefs
10 D3 Kingsand Cnwll
142 B3 Kingsash Bucks
503 F2 Kingsbarns Fife
12 C4 Kingsbridge Devon
63 F4 Kingsbridge Somset
238 A1 King's Bromley Staffs
542 F5 Kingsburgh Highld
118 D2 Kingsbury Gt Lon
238 C5 Kingsbury Warwks
66 C5 Kingsbury Episcopi Somset
67 H6 Kingsbury Regis Somset
160 D4 King's Caple Herefs
486 D4 Kingscavil W Loth
91 E3 Kingsclere Hants
91 E2 Kingsclere Woodlands Hants
243 G3 King's Cliffe Nhants
136 B5 Kingscote Gloucs
40 A4 Kingscott Devon
189 G3 King's Coughton Warwks
136 B4 Kingscourt Gloucs
461 E4 Kingscross N Ayrs
600 F2 King's Dale Ork
162 D5 Kingsditch Gloucs
29 E4 Kingsdon Devon
67 E4 Kingsdon Somset
99 E3 Kingsdown Kent
101 G6 Kingsdown Kent
113 E2 Kingsdown Swindn
87 E1 Kingsdown Wilts
244 B5 King's Dyke Cambs
487 F1 Kingseat Fife
487 F1 Kingseathill Fife
166 C5 King's End Oxon
188 B4 King's End Worcs
18 B1 Kingsett Devon
141 F3 Kingsey Bucks
186 C5 Kingsfield Herefs
338 D4 Kingsfold Lancs
76 C2 Kingsfold W Susx
466 B5 Kingsford E Ayrs
212 B3 Kingsford Worcs
347 F6 Kingsforth N Linc
91 G4 King's Furlong Hants
101 G1 Kingsgate Kent
161 H3 King's Green Gloucs
187 H2 King's Green Worcs
200 B2 Kingshall Green Suffk
200 B2 Kingshall Street Suffk
61 E4 Kingsheanton Devon
213 G3 King's Heath Birm
193 F2 King's Heath Nhants
197 F2 Kings Hedges Cambs
135 G5 Kingshill Gloucs
137 F4 Kings Hill Gloucs
97 G3 King's Hill Kent
112 D3 Kingshill Swindn
237 E5 King's Hill Wsall
162 B6 Kingsholm Gloucs
509 J5 Kingshouse Stirlg
214 B2 Kingshurst Solhll
399 E4 Kingside Hill Cumb
20 B4 Kingskerswell Devon
501 E3 Kingskettle Fife
487 G5 Kingsknowe C Edin
30 A3 Kingsland Dorset
186 A2 Kingsland Herefs
302 B4 Kingsland IoA
234 B2 Kingsland Shrops
143 F4 Kings Langley Herts
310 B5 Kingsley Ches
74 B2 Kingsley Hants
292 D5 Kingsley Staffs
74 D3 Kingsley Green W Susx
292 D5 Kingsley Holt Staffs
292 C5 Kingsley Moor Staffs
193 G2 Kingsley Park Nhants
236 A5 Kingslow Shrops
252 C3 King's Lynn Norfk
391 G5 King's Meaburn Cumb
54 C3 Kings Mead Hants
54 C3 King's Mills Guern
275 C4 King's Mills Lincs
288 D5 King's Mills Wrexhm
145 F3 Kingsmoor Essex
324 C4 Kings Moss St Hel
527 G5 Kingsmuir Angus
450 A2 Kings Muir Border
215 H4 King's Newnham Warwks
275 H4 King's Newton Derbys
211 H2 Kingsnordley Shrops
81 F2 Kingsnorth Kent
122 C5 Kingsnorth Medway
213 G4 King's Norton Birm
241 E4 King's Norton Leics
40 D4 King's Nympton Devon
49 E6 King's Park Bmouth
467 F3 Kings Park C Glas
186 A4 Kings Pyon Herefs
220 C4 Kings Ripton Cambs
71 H3 King's Somborne Hants
46 D2 King's Stag Dorset
136 B4 King's Stanley Gloucs
166 A2 King's Sutton Nhants
11 E2 King's Tamerton C Plym
237 G6 Kingstanding Birm
20 B3 Kingsteignton Devon
567 G5 Kingsteps Highld
313 E5 King Sterndale Derbys
160 B3 King's Thorn Herefs
193 G2 Kingsthorpe Nhants
193 G2 Kingsthorpe Hollow Nhants
52 B4 Kingston C Port
196 D3 Kingston Cambs
12 A3 Kingston Devon
13 F2 Kingston Devon
27 H5 Kingston Devon
33 H4 Kingston Dorset
47 E3 Kingston Dorset
489 G3 Kingston E Loth

49 E4 **Kingston** Hants
36 D4 **Kingston** IoW
100 C5 **Kingston** Kent
168 B2 **Kingston** M Keyn
568 E2 **Kingston** Moray
202 B5 **Kingston** Suffk
326 D5 **Kingston** Tamesd
139 G5 **Kingston Bagpuize** Oxon
141 F5 **Kingston Blount** Oxon
55 F3 **Kingston by Sea** W Susx
68 D2 **Kingston Deverill** Wilts
160 A2 **Kingstone** Herefs
161 E5 **Kingstone** Herefs
44 D5 **Kingstone** Somset
273 G4 **Kingstone** Staffs
113 G2 **Kingston Winslow** Oxon
54 C4 **Kingston Gorse** W Susx
113 H2 **Kingston Lisle** Oxon
32 C1 **Kingston Maurward** Dorset
56 B3 **Kingston Near Lewes** E Susx
276 B4 **Kingston on Soar** Notts
430 D6 **Kingston Park** N u Ty
30 D4 **Kingston Russell** Dorset
43 H2 **Kingston St Mary** Somset
84 C1 **Kingston Seymour** N Som
141 F4 **Kingston Stert** Oxon
348 B4 **Kingston upon Hull** C KuH
118 D6 **Kingston upon Thames** Gt Lon
119 E5 **Kingston Vale** Gt Lon
400 C3 **Kingstown** Cumb
146 B4 **King Street** Essex
169 H5 **King's Walden** Herts
86 C2 **Kingsway** BaNES
309 H2 **Kingsway** Halton
13 F2 **Kingswear** Devon
557 F3 **Kingswells** C Aber
212 C2 **Kingswinford** Dudley
167 E6 **Kingswood** Bucks
347 G3 **Kingswood** C KuH
121 H2 **Kingswood** Essex
110 C1 **Kingswood** Gloucs
185 E4 **Kingswood** Herefs
143 G4 **Kingswood** Herts
98 C4 **Kingswood** Kent
232 D4 **Kingswood** Powys
110 B5 **Kingswood** S Glos
64 B4 **Kingswood** Somset
95 E3 **Kingswood** Surrey
310 B1 **Kingswood** Warrtn
214 B5 **Kingswood** Warwks
214 B5 **Kingswood Brook** Warwks
236 B4 **Kingswood Common** Staffs
187 G1 **Kingswood Common** Worcs
72 C3 **Kings Worthy** Hants
185 F3 **Kington** Herefs
109 H1 **Kington** S Glos
189 E3 **Kington** Worcs
111 G4 **Kington Langley** Wilts
68 C5 **Kington Magna** Dorset
111 F4 **Kington St Michael** Wilts
535 K2 **Kingussie** Highld
67 E3 **Kingweston** Somset
560 D3 **Kinharrachie** Abers
540 D4 **Kinkell** Abers
499 E1 **Kinkell Bridge** P & K
561 F1 **Kinknockie** Abers
426 D4 **Kinkry Hill** Cumb
211 G3 **Kinlet** Shrops
501 E2 **Kinloch** Fife
530 D3 **Kinloch** Highld
546 B6 **Kinloch** Highld
579 K3 **Kinloch** Highld
525 H7 **Kinloch** P & K
526 C6 **Kinloch** P & K
496 C4 **Kinlochard** Stirlg
588 D5 **Kinlochbervie** Highld
532 E7 **Kinlocheil** Highld
563 J4 **Kinlochewe** Highld
532 E1 **Kinloch Hourn** Highld
534 F5 **Kinloch Laggan** Highld
521 H3 **Kinlochleven** Highld
531 K8 **Kinlochmoidart** Highld
521 H3 **Kinlochmore** Highld
523 J4 **Kinloch Rannoch** P & K
505 J5 **Kinlochspelve** Ag & B
531 J5 **Kinloid** Highld
567 K4 **Kinloss** Moray
306 D3 **Kinmel Bay** Conwy
560 B6 **Kinmuck** Abers
560 C6 **Kinmundy** Abers
565 L8 **Kinmylies** Highld
571 H7 **Kinnadie** Abers
513 F4 **Kinnaird** P & K
524 E4 **Kinnaird** P & K
576 F3 **Kinnauld** Highld
541 G5 **Kinneff** Abers
486 C3 **Kinneil** Falk
436 D4 **Kinnelhead** D & G
528 D4 **Kinnell** Angus
269 F5 **Kinnerley** Shrops
185 F5 **Kinnersley** Herefs
188 C6 **Kinnersley** Worcs
184 D2 **Kinnerton** Powys
288 D2 **Kinnerton Green** Flints
500 C4 **Kinnesswood** P & K
394 B5 **Kinninvie** Dur
527 E4 **Kinnordy** Angus
277 E3 **Kinoulton** Notts
500 B4 **Kinross** P & K
513 E3 **Kinrossie** P & K
271 F1 **Kinsey Heath** Ches
185 G2 **Kinsham** Herefs
162 D2 **Kinsham** Worcs
329 G2 **Kinsley** Wakefd
48 D5 **Kinson** Bmouth
479 J4 **Kintallan** Ag & B
90 B1 **Kintbury** W Berk
567 H4 **Kintessack** Moray
500 B1 **Kintillo** P & K
555 G3 **Kintocher** Abers
209 H5 **Kinton** Herefs
269 G6 **Kinton** Shrops
556 D1 **Kintore** Abers
477 G6 **Kintour** Ag & B
476 E7 **Kintra** Ag & B
504 C5 **Kintra** Ag & B
492 D3 **Kintraw** Ag & B
551 G6 **Kinveachy** Highld
212 B3 **Kinver** Staffs
214 D2 **Kinwalsey** Warwks
405 F4 **Kip Hill** Dur
383 G5 **Kippax** N York
343 H3 **Kippax** Leeds
497 G6 **Kippen** Stirlg
413 F4 **Kippford or Scaur** D & G
451 G4 **Kippilaw** Border
451 G4 **Kippilaw Mains** Border
79 E2 **Kipping's Cross** Kent
96 D4 **Kippington** Kent
600 C2 **Kirbister** Ork
600 F3 **Kirbister** Ork
602 B6 **Kirbister** Ork
603 K7 **Kirbuster** Ork
250 B3 **Kirby Bedon** Norfk
277 F6 **Kirby Bellars** Leics
250 D6 **Kirby Cane** Norfk
214 D4 **Kirby Corner** Covtry
176 D5 **Kirby Cross** Essex
240 B4 **Kirby Fields** Leics
250 D6 **Kirby Green** Norfk
359 H1 **Kirby Grindalythe** N York
370 D6 **Kirby Hill** N York

382 D3 **Kirby Hill** N York
371 F2 **Kirby Knowle** N York
176 D5 **Kirby-le-Soken** Essex
373 E4 **Kirby Misperton** N York
240 B4 **Kirby Muxloe** Leics
384 C6 **Kirby Sigston** N York
359 E3 **Kirby Underdale** E R Yk
370 D3 **Kirby Wiske** N York
75 G4 **Kirdford** W Susx
589 H5 **Kirk** Highld
605 J3 **Kirkabister** Shet
607 G4 **Kirkabister** Shet
607 G6 **Kirkabister** Shet
412 B5 **Kirkandrews** D & G
400 C3 **Kirkandrews-on-Eden** Cumb
516 C6 **Kirkapol** Ag & B
609 J2 **Kirkaton** Shet
400 A3 **Kirkbampton** Cumb
398 B3 **Kirkbean** D & G
388 B2 **Kirkborough** Cumb
330 D2 **Kirk Bramwith** Donc
399 G3 **Kirkbride** Cumb
370 B1 **Kirkbridge** N York
528 B6 **Kirkbuddo** Angus
450 B2 **Kirkburn** Border
360 B3 **Kirkburn** E R Yk
328 B2 **Kirkburton** Kirk
323 H5 **Kirkby** Knows
333 F6 **Kirkby** Lincs
385 E3 **Kirkby** N York
300 B2 **Kirkby Fenside** Lincs
383 G6 **Kirkby Fleetham** N York
298 D3 **Kirkby Green** Lincs
295 F3 **Kirkby in Ashfield** Notts
363 E5 **Kirkby-in-Furness** Cumb
299 E5 **Kirkby la Thorpe** Lincs
366 C4 **Kirkby Lonsdale** Cumb
354 A2 **Kirkby Malham** N York
239 H4 **Kirkby Mallory** Leics
370 A5 **Kirkby Malzeard** N York
372 D2 **Kirkby Mills** N York
372 C2 **Kirkbymoorside** N York
299 G2 **Kirkby on Bain** Lincs
380 D3 **Kirkby Overblow** N York
391 G4 **Kirkby Stephen** Cumb
425 G4 **Kirkby Thore** Cumb
279 F4 **Kirkby Underwood** Lincs
425 E5 **Kirkby Wharfe** N York
295 F4 **Kirkby Woodhouse** Notts
198 D3 **Kirkcaldy** Fife
426 D6 **Kirkcambeck** Cumb
413 E5 **Kirkcarswell** D & G
414 D3 **Kirkcolm** D & G
435 E2 **Kirkconnel** D & G
412 C2 **Kirkconnell** D & G
423 G6 **Kirkconnell** D & G
416 C4 **Kirkcowan** D & G
412 C4 **Kirkcudbright** D & G
323 F6 **Kirkdale** Lpool
356 D4 **Kirk Deighton** N York
347 F4 **Kirk Ella** E R Yk
468 D6 **Kirkfieldbank** S Lans
501 E4 **Kirkforthar Feus** Fife
413 G1 **Kirkgunzeon** D & G
275 G2 **Kirk Hallam** Derbys
338 B3 **Kirkham** Lancs
358 D1 **Kirkham** N York
343 E5 **Kirkhamgate** Wakefd
357 F3 **Kirk Hammerton** N York
326 B4 **Kirkhams** Bury
429 G3 **Kirkharle** Nthumb
342 C6 **Kirkheaton** Kirk
429 G4 **Kirkheaton** Nthumb
529 E2 **Kirkhill** Angus
467 E3 **Kirkhill** E Rens
565 K7 **Kirkhill** Highld
470 D2 **Kirkhill** Highld
487 E5 **Kirkhill** W Loth
326 C2 **Kirkholt** Rochdl
436 C5 **Kirkhope** Border
450 C3 **Kirkhope** S Lans
213 E3 **Kirkhouse** Border
401 G3 **Kirkhouse** Cumb
545 J6 **Kirkibost** Highld
606 B7 **Kirkidale** Shet
526 D6 **Kirkinch** Angus
410 D2 **Kirkinner** D & G
484 D5 **Kirkintilloch** E Duns
294 B4 **Kirk Ireton** Derbys
388 C6 **Kirkland** Cumb
391 G3 **Kirkland** Cumb
399 H5 **Kirkland** Cumb
422 D1 **Kirkland** D & G
435 E2 **Kirkland** D & G
501 G4 **Kirkland** Fife
501 G4 **Kirkland** Fife
389 E1 **Kirkland Dam** Fife
274 D2 **Kirkland Guards** Cumb
397 E5 **Kirk Langley** Derbys
326 A2 **Kirkleatham** R & Cl
384 C3 **Kirklees** Bury
227 G1 **Kirklevington** S on T
370 C3 **Kirkley** Suffk
296 C3 **Kirklington** N York
400 D1 **Kirklington** Notts
487 F5 **Kirkliston** C Edin
408 B2 **Kirkmabreck** D & G
408 C4 **Kirkmaiden** D & G
395 F3 **Kirk Merrington** Dur
322 e4 **Kirk Michael** IoM
525 G3 **Kirkmichael** P & K
432 D3 **Kirkmichael** S Ayrs
423 H2 **Kirkmichael Mains** D & G
468 B6 **Kirkmuirhill** S Lans
453 H3 **Kirknewton** Nthumb
470 B1 **Kirknewton** W Loth
558 C3 **Kirkney** Abers
468 C2 **Kirk of Shotts** N Lans
391 F1 **Kirkoswald** Cumb
432 B3 **Kirkoswald** S Ayrs
423 F1 **Kirkpatrick** D & G
422 C5 **Kirkpatrick Durham** D & G
425 F6 **Kirkpatrick-Fleming** D & G
330 D3 **Kirk Sandall** Donc
362 C5 **Kirksanton** Cumb
467 H2 **Kirkshaw** N Lans
330 B1 **Kirk Smeaton** N York
343 E2 **Kirkstall** Leeds
450 B5 **Kirkstead** Border
299 F2 **Kirkstead** Lincs
558 C2 **Kirkstile** Abers
589 J2 **Kirkstyle** Highld
559 E4 **Kirkton** Abers
570 B5 **Kirkton** Abers
571 L5 **Kirkton** Abers
514 C2 **Kirkton** Angus
515 G1 **Kirkton** Angus
527 F5 **Kirkton** Angus
439 G2 **Kirkton** Border
423 G3 **Kirkton** D & G
488 A2 **Kirkton** Fife
514 B4 **Kirkton** Fife
546 E4 **Kirkton** Highld
547 G1 **Kirkton** Highld
577 G4 **Kirkton** Highld
511 H6 **Kirkton** P & K
496 D4 **Kirkton** Stirlg
469 G1 **Kirkton** W Loth
483 K5 **Kirktonhill** W Duns
449 H2 **Kirkton Manor** Border
526 D4 **Kirkton of Airlie** Angus

514 A2 **Kirkton of Auchterhouse** Angus
559 G1 **Kirkton of Auchterless** Abers
566 E7 **Kirkton of Barevan** Highld
560 B5 **Kirkton of Bourtie** Abers
513 E3 **Kirkton of Collace** P & K
529 E3 **Kirkton of Craig** Angus
559 E3 **Kirkton of Culsalmond** Abers
501 F3 **Kirkton of Cults** Fife
556 D5 **Kirkton of Durris** Abers
554 C2 **Kirkton of Glenbuchat** Abers
526 B2 **Kirkton of Glenisla** Angus
526 D4 **Kirkton of Kingoldrum** Angus
512 D1 **Kirkton of Lethendy** P & K
561 E4 **Kirkton of Logie Buchan** Abers
524 D2 **Kirkton of Lude** P & K
557 F5 **Kirkton of Maryculter** Abers
528 B2 **Kirkton of Menmuir** Angus
515 E2 **Kirkton of Monikie** Angus
559 F4 **Kirkton of Oyne** Abers
559 F3 **Kirkton of Rayne** Abers
557 E3 **Kirkton of Skene** Abers
555 H2 **Kirkton of Tough** Abers
445 F1 **Kirktoun** E Ayrs
571 K5 **Kirktown** Abers
570 B3 **Kirktown of Alvah** Abers
569 J3 **Kirktown of Deskford** Moray
541 F2 **Kirktown of Fetteresso** Abers
568 E8 **Kirktown of Mortlach** Moray
470 B6 **Kirkurd** Border
601 H2 **Kirkwall** Ork
429 F3 **Kirkwhelpington** Nthumb
424 C4 **Kirkwood** D & G
467 H2 **Kirkwood** N Lans
453 F4 **Kirk Yetholm** Border
333 G2 **Kirmington** N Linc
333 H6 **Kirmond le Mire** Lincs
482 A4 **Kirn** Ag & B
527 E4 **Kirriemuir** Angus
250 B5 **Kirstead Green** Norfk
425 E5 **Kirtlebridge** D & G
425 F3 **Kirtleton** D & G
198 D3 **Kirtling** Cambs
198 D3 **Kirtling Green** Cambs
166 A6 **Kirtlington** Oxon
586 F4 **Kirtomy** Highld
280 D2 **Kirton** Lincs
316 C6 **Kirton** Notts
177 E2 **Kirton** Suffk
469 G1 **Kirton Campus** W Loth
280 C2 **Kirton End** Lincs
280 C1 **Kirton Holme** Lincs
332 C5 **Kirton in Lindsey** N Linc
502 C4 **Kirton of Largo or Upper Largo** Fife
362 B4 **Kiskin** Cumb
193 E3 **Kislingbury** Nhants
29 F2 **Kitbridge** Devon
328 C3 **Kitchenroyd** Kirk
164 C3 **Kitebrook** Warwks
190 B1 **Kite Green** Warwks
37 F2 **Kite Hill** IoW
215 H6 **Kites Hardwick** Warwks
68 D6 **Kit Hill** Dorset
136 C4 **Kitlye** Gloucs
98 A2 **Kit's Coty** Kent
324 D3 **Kitt Green** Wigan
43 E3 **Kittisford** Somset
103 E4 **Kittle** Swans
144 B5 **Kitts End** Herts
214 A2 **Kitt's Green** Birm
312 A3 **Kitt's Moss** Stockp
29 G2 **Kittwhistle** Dorset
557 G3 **Kittybrewster** C Aber
213 E3 **Kitwell** Birm
73 G3 **Kitwood** Hants
160 B3 **Kivernoll** Herefs
315 F3 **Kiveton Park** Rothm
317 F3 **Knaith** Lincs
317 F2 **Knaith Park** Lincs
72 B5 **Knap** Hants
513 G3 **Knap** P & K
44 B2 **Knapp** Somset
70 A4 **Knapp** Wilts
69 E4 **Knapp Hill** Dorset
296 D3 **Knapthorpe** Notts
216 D2 **Knaptoft** Leics
256 C3 **Knapton** Norfk
357 H4 **Knapton** York
186 A4 **Knapton Green** Herefs
196 D2 **Knapwell** Cambs
356 D3 **Knaresborough** N York
402 B4 **Knarsdale** Nthumb
602 C7 **Knarston** Ork
97 E2 **Knatts Valley** Kent
570 F7 **Knaven** Abers
100 C3 **Knave's Ash** Kent
201 F1 **Knaves Green** Suffk
358 A5 **Knavesmire** York
371 E2 **Knayton** N York
170 C6 **Knebworth** Herts
345 H4 **Knedlington** E R Yk
296 D2 **Kneesall** Notts
196 D6 **Kneesworth** Cambs
296 D5 **Kneeton** Notts
102 C4 **Knelston** Swans
272 D2 **Knenhall** Staffs
224 C3 **Knettishall** Suffk
61 F4 **Knightacott** Devon
191 F4 **Knightcote** Warwks
84 C3 **Knightcott** N Som
272 B4 **Knightley** Staffs
272 B5 **Knightley Dale** Staffs
240 C4 **Knighton** C Leic
11 F4 **Knighton** Devon
46 B2 **Knighton** Dorset
113 G2 **Knighton** Oxon
48 D5 **Knighton** Poole
209 E5 **Knighton** Powys
64 C3 **Knighton** Somset
271 G1 **Knighton** Staffs
271 G4 **Knighton** Staffs
113 G5 **Knighton** Wilts
189 F3 **Knighton** Worcs
240 C4 **Knighton Fields** C Leic
211 E5 **Knighton on Teme** Worcs
8 C2 **Knightor** Cnwll
162 C4 **Knightsbridge** Gloucs
119 F4 **Knightsbridge** Gt Lon
245 F6 **Knight's End** Cambs
90 B5 **Knights Enham** Hants
15 F2 **Knightsmill** Cnwll
486 D6 **Knightsridge** W Loth
483 H6 **Knightswood** C Glas
187 H3 **Knightwick** Worcs
185 E2 **Knill** Herefs
300 C4 **Knipe Bank** Lincs
355 F1 **Knipe Fold** Cumb
312 D5 **Knipton** Leics
7 G3 **Knitsley** Dur
72 B5 **Kniveton** Derbys
603 K3 **Knock** Ag & B
505 G3 **Knock** Cumb
432 B4 **Knock** Highld
569 J5 **Knock** Moray

582 F4 **Knockally** Highld
537 K4 **Knockan** Abers
504 E6 **Knockan** Ag & B
579 H7 **Knockan** Highld
552 E4 **Knockandhu** Highld
568 B7 **Knockando** Moray
576 F2 **Knockarthur** Highld
565 J8 **Knockbain** Highld
565 L5 **Knockbain** Highld
569 J5 **Knockbog** Moray
552 D4 **Knockbreck** Highld
412 A5 **Knockbrex** D & G
588 F4 **Knockdee** Highld
418 D4 **Knockdolian** S Ayrs
481 G5 **Knockdow** Ag & B
111 E2 **Knockdown** Wilts
559 E4 **Knockenbaird** Abers
461 E4 **Knockenkelly** N Ayrs
445 E2 **Knockentiber** E Ayrs
294 A4 **Knockerdown** Derbys
565 J5 **Knockfarrel** Highld
414 D5 **Knockglass** Highld
588 C4 **Knockglass** Highld
121 E5 **Knockhall** Kent
96 C3 **Knockholt** Kent
96 C3 **Knockholt Pound** Kent
269 F5 **Knockin** Shrops
269 F5 **Knockin Heath** Shrops
442 D4 **Knocklaw** Nthumb
97 E2 **Knockmill** Kent
456 D3 **Knocknaha** Ag & B
414 C4 **Knocknain** D & G
478 E7 **Knockrome** Ag & B
456 D4 **Knockstapple** Ag & B
422 B5 **Knockvennie** D & G
203 E2 **Knodishall** Suffk
203 E2 **Knodishall Common** Suffk
66 D5 **Knole** Somset
108 D2 **Knollbury** Mons
64 D4 **Knoll Green** Somset
311 G4 **Knolls Green** Ches
355 G1 **Knoll Top** N York
269 G2 **Knolton** Wrexhm
269 G2 **Knolton Bryn** Wrexhm
69 F1 **Knook** Wilts
241 H3 **Knossington** Leics
312 D6 **Knotbury** Staffs
542 F6 **Knott** Highld
351 E5 **Knott End-on-Sea** Lancs
195 E2 **Knotting** Beds
195 E2 **Knotting Green** Beds
344 B5 **Knottingley** Wakefd
326 D4 **Knott Lanes** Oldham
44 D5 **Knott Oak** Somset
353 F4 **Knotts** Lancs
309 F1 **Knotty Ash** Lpool
39 F2 **Knotty Corner** Devon
117 F1 **Knotty Green** Bucks
210 D5 **Knowbury** Shrops
416 C2 **Knowe** D & G
609 G8 **Knowe** Shet
400 C3 **Knowefield** Cumb
421 G1 **Knowehead** D & G
490 B4 **Knowes** E Loth
429 F2 **Knowesgate** Nthumb
432 C2 **Knoweside** S Ayrs
569 K5 **Knowes of Elrick** Abers
468 A3 **Knowetop** N Lans
451 G6 **Knowetownhead** Border
291 F5 **Knowl Bank** Staffs
109 H5 **Knowle** Bristl
21 E1 **Knowle** Devon
26 B2 **Knowle** Devon
27 G1 **Knowle** Devon
60 C4 **Knowle** Devon
210 D5 **Knowle** Shrops
214 B4 **Knowle** Solhll
65 F4 **Knowle** Somset
89 E2 **Knowle** Wilts
189 F3 **Knowle Fields** Worcs
210 D5 **Knowlegate** Shrops
339 F2 **Knowle Green** Lancs
118 A5 **Knowle Green** Surrey
214 B5 **Knowle Grove** Solhll
93 G1 **Knowle Hill** Surrey
341 H1 **Knowle Park** Brad
44 C5 **Knowle St Giles** Somset
211 G1 **Knowlesands** Shrops
20 B3 **Knowles Hill** Devon
51 G3 **Knowle Village** Hants
173 F1 **Knowl Green** Essex
116 D4 **Knowl Hill** W & M
48 C3 **Knowlton** Dorset
101 E5 **Knowlton** Kent
272 B2 **Knowl Wall** Staffs
341 E5 **Knowl Wood** Calder
323 H5 **Knowsley** Knows
41 G3 **Knowstone** Devon
80 A1 **Knox Bridge** Kent
209 E5 **Knucklas** Powys
194 C1 **Knuston** Nhants
311 F4 **Knutsford** Ches
291 G5 **Knutton** Staffs
339 H4 **Knuzden Brook** Lancs
292 A3 **Knypersley** Staffs
341 H6 **Krumlin** Calder
4 D5 **Kuggar** Cnwll
546 D4 **Kyleakin** Highld
546 C4 **Kyle of Lochalsh** Highld
467 G2 **Kylepark** S Lans
546 D5 **Kylerhea** Highld
579 H3 **Kylesku** Highld
579 H3 **Kylestrome** Highld
186 D6 **Kymin** Herefs
134 C2 **Kymin** Mons
160 C4 **Kynaston** Herefs
269 G5 **Kynaston** Shrops
235 F1 **Kynnersley** Wrekin
187 E2 **Kyre** Worcs
187 E2 **Kyre Green** Worcs
187 E2 **Kyre Park** Worcs
211 E6 **Kyrewood** Worcs

482 D4 **Ladyburn** Inver
23 G5 **Ladycross** Cnwll
214 D5 **Ladyes Hill** Warwks
448 B4 **Ladygill** S Lans
323 F4 **Lady Green** Sefton
362 D4 **Lady Hall** Cumb
210 B4 **Lady Halton** Shrops
326 D2 **Lady House** Rochdl
474 C5 **Ladykirk** Border
233 G4 **Ladyoak** Shrops
405 F3 **Lady Park** Gatesd
160 D3 **Ladyridge** Herefs
570 F3 **Ladysford** Abers
199 F3 **Lady's Green** Suffk
270 B3 **Ladywell** Gt Lon
209 F3 **Ladywell** Shrops
486 D6 **Ladywell** W Loth
213 F2 **Ladywood** Birm
343 F2 **Lady Wood** Leeds
188 C2 **Ladywood** Worcs
324 C5 **Laffak** St Hel
35 e1 **La Fontenelle** Guern
35 d4 **La Fosse** Guern
518 F3 **Laga** Highld
507 L4 **Laganbuidhe** Ag & B
476 F7 **Lagavulin** Ag & B
478 F6 **Lagg** Ag & B
460 C5 **Lagg** N Ayrs
476 D5 **Laggan** Ag & B
533 L3 **Laggan** Highld
535 H4 **Laggan** Highld
419 G5 **Laggan** S Ayrs
536 C2 **Lagganlia** Highld
504 F2 **Lagganulva** Ag & B
53 F4 **Lagness** W Susx
35 d2 **La Greve** Guern
35 f5 **La Grève de Lecq** Jersey
35 i7 **La Hougue Bie** Jersey
34 b3 **La Houguette** Guern
573 G5 **Laide** Highld
467 G5 **Laigh Carnduff** S Lans
466 C6 **Laigh Fenwick** E Ayrs
444 D6 **Laigh Glengall** S Ayrs
446 C5 **Laigh Glenmuir** E Ayrs
467 H4 **Laighstonehall** S Lans
121 G2 **Laindon** Essex
563 J7 **Lair** Highld
11 F2 **Laira** C Plym
576 C2 **Lairg** Highld
549 K2 **Lairgmore** Highld
576 C2 **Lairg Muir** Highld
390 D3 **Laithes** Cumb
393 F5 **Laithkirk** Dur
6 C4 **Laity Moor** Cnwll
24 D5 **Lake** Devon
39 F6 **Lake** Devon
61 E5 **Lake** Devon
37 F4 **Lake** IoW
34 A2 **Lake** Poole
70 C2 **Lake** Wilts
117 F4 **Lake End** Bucks
250 A3 **Lakenham** Norfk
223 E3 **Lakenheath** Suffk
75 G2 **Laker's Green** Surrey
245 H5 **Lakes End** Norfk
365 E2 **Lakeside** Cumb
121 E4 **Lakeside** Thurr
189 G1 **Lakeside** Worcs
118 B6 **Laleham** Surrey
104 D3 **Laleston** Brdgnd
470 C4 **Lamancha** Border
5 E2 **Lamanva** Cnwll
174 A2 **Lamarsh** Essex
256 A5 **Lamas** Norfk
174 D3 **Lamb Corner** Essex
473 G6 **Lambden** Border
80 B4 **Lamberden** Kent
324 C4 **Lamberhead Green** Wigan
79 F2 **Lamberhurst** Kent
79 F2 **Lamberhurst Quarter** Kent
475 E3 **Lamberton** Border
213 E1 **Lambert's End** Sandw
119 G4 **Lambeth** Gt Lon
199 E4 **Lambfair Green** Suffk
389 E3 **Lambfoot** Cumb
484 B6 **Lambhill** C Glas
296 B5 **Lambley** Notts
402 B3 **Lambley** Nthumb
114 A4 **Lambourn** W Berk
7 E3 **Lambourne** Cnwll
145 G5 **Lambourne** Essex
145 G6 **Lambourne End** Essex
113 H4 **Lambourn Woodlands** W Berk
86 D1 **Lambridge** BaNES
30 B3 **Lambrook** Dorset
98 B5 **Lamb's Cross** Kent
48 B5 **Lambs Green** Dorset
76 D2 **Lambs Green** W Susx
125 E1 **Lambston** Pembks
405 G3 **Lambton** Sundld
16 B6 **Lamellion** Cnwll
17 G3 **Lamerton** Devon
405 F3 **Lamesley** Gatesd
603 J4 **Laminess** Ork
566 C1 **Lamington** Highld
448 C3 **Lamington** S Lans
461 K3 **Lamlash** N Ayrs
8 C5 **Lamledra** Cnwll
339 G4 **Lammack** Bl w D
390 C2 **Lamonby** Cumb
15 E6 **Lamorick** Cnwll
2 D4 **Lamorna** Cnwll
7 G5 **Lamorran** Cnwll
181 E5 **Lampeter** Cerdgn
126 D2 **Lampeter Velfrey** Pembks
388 C5 **Lamplugh** Cumb
217 F5 **Lamport** Nhants
118 C4 **Lamyatt** Somset
67 H2 **Lamyatt** Somset
23 G1 **Lana** Devon
23 G3 **Lana** Devon
469 E6 **Lanark** S Lans
351 G2 **Lancaster** Lancs
405 E5 **Lanchester** Dur
55 E4 **Lancing** W Susx
35 d1 **L'Ancresse** Guern
197 G2 **Landbeach** Cambs
39 G3 **Landcross** Devon
556 C4 **Landerberry** Abers
71 F6 **Landford** Wilts
71 F6 **Landfordwood** Wilts
324 D4 **Land Gate** Wigan
37 F4 **Landguard Manor** IoW
24 B3 **Landhill** Devon
308 C2 **Landican** Wirral
102 C3 **Landimore** Swans
61 E5 **Landkey** Devon
61 E5 **Landkey Newland** Devon
103 G2 **Landore** Swans
52 A4 **Landport** C Port
56 C2 **Landport** E Susx
10 C1 **Landrake** Cnwll
19 G4 **Landscove** Devon
125 H2 **Landshipping** Pembks
125 H2 **Landshipping Quay** Pembks
327 E5 **Landslow Green** Tamesd
10 D1 **Landulph** Cnwll
222 C6 **Landwade** Suffk
237 E3 **Landywood** Staffs
7 F1 **Lane** Cnwll
23 E6 **Laneast** Cnwll
341 H2 **Lane Bottom** Brad

340 D2 Lane Bottom Lancs
341 G2 Lane End Brad
116 D1 Lane End Bucks
15 E5 Lane-End Cnwll
376 D6 Lane End Cumb
295 E2 Lane End Derbys
24 B2 Lane End Devon
33 F1 Lane End Dorset
288 C2 Lane End Flints
73 E4 Lane End Hants
73 G4 Lane End Hants
161 E6 Lane End Herefs
37 H3 Lane End IoW
121 E5 Lane End Kent
353 H5 Lane End Lancs
329 F5 Lane End Sheff
74 C1 Lane End Surrey
87 E5 Lane End Wilts
291 E3 Lane Ends Ches
312 C3 Lane Ends Ches
364 D3 Lane Ends Cumb
274 C3 Lane Ends Derbys
325 E1 Lane Ends Lancs
340 B3 Lane Ends Lancs
353 E4 Lane Ends Lancs
342 D2 Lane Ends Leeds
354 C6 Lane Ends N York
230 C4 Lane Ends Stockp
236 C4 Lane Green Staffs
317 F4 Laneham Notts
313 G4 Lane Head Derbys
392 D1 Lane Head Dur
328 B3 Lane Head Kirk
428 B2 Lanehead Nthumb
125 H4 Lane Head Pembks
325 E5 Lane Head Wigan
237 E4 Lane Head Wsall
338 B2 Lane Heads Lancs
32 B4 Lanehouse Dorset
401 G2 Lanercost Cumb
8 D2 Lanescot Cnwll
142 C3 Lanes End Bucks
126 B3 Lanesend Pembks
211 E3 Lane's End Shrops
236 D5 Lanesfield Wolves
341 E1 Laneshaw Bridge Lancs
340 B5 Lane Side Lancs
237 E3 Laney Green Staffs
24 B3 Langafer Devon
11 G2 Langage Highld
519 H1 Langal Highld
44 B2 Langaller Somset
277 F3 Langar Notts
483 E5 Langbank Rens
355 E4 Langbar N York
385 E2 Langbaurgh N York
353 G2 Langcliffe N York
374 A1 Langdale End N York
393 E3 Langdon Beck Dur
121 G2 Langdon Hills Essex
50 D3 Langdown Hants
501 F4 Langdyke Fife
174 D6 Langenhoe Essex
169 H1 Langford Beds
27 E3 Langford Devon
27 G2 Langford Devon
147 G3 Langford Essex
297 H3 Langford Notts
138 C4 Langford Oxon
43 H2 Langford Somset
43 F3 Langford Budville Somset
27 G2 Langford Green Devon
85 E3 Langford Green N Som
68 C4 Langham Dorset
174 D3 Langham Essex
260 D3 Langham Norfk
242 A2 Langham Rutlnd
44 C5 Langham Somset
224 C6 Langham Suffk
449 H3 Langhaugh Border
339 G3 Langho Lancs
425 H3 Langholm D & G
331 G5 Langholme N Linc
451 E5 Langhope Border
103 E4 Langland Swans
451 G2 Langlee Border
454 A5 Langleeford Nthumb
451 G2 Langlee Mains Border
486 A3 Langlees Falk
312 B5 Langley Bucks
295 E5 Langley Derbys
171 F3 Langley Essex
163 F4 Langley Gloucs
50 D4 Langley Hants
170 B5 Langley Herts
98 C4 Langley Kent
403 E2 Langley Nthumb
139 E1 Langley Oxon
326 C3 Langley Rochdl
213 E2 Langley Sandw
117 H4 Langley Slough
43 E2 Langley Somset
74 C4 Langley W Susx
190 B2 Langley Warwks
111 G4 Langley Burrell Wilts
274 D2 Langley Common Derbys
92 C1 Langley Common Wokham
117 H3 Langley Corner Bucks
274 D2 Langley Green Derbys
174 A5 Langley Green Essex
213 E2 Langley Green Sandw
77 E2 Langley Green W Susx
190 B2 Langley Green Warwks
98 C4 Langley Heath Kent
43 E2 Langley Marsh Somset
295 E5 Langley Mill Derbys
395 F1 Langley Moor Dur
405 F6 Langley Park Dur
250 D4 Langley Street Norfk
95 E3 Langley Vale Surrey
467 H2 Langloan N Lans
57 G4 Langney E Susx
316 A2 Langold Notts
23 F5 Langore Cnwll
66 C4 Langport Somset
299 H5 Langrick Lincs
299 H5 Langrick Bridge Lincs
110 C6 Langridge BaNES
40 B3 Langridgeford Devon
380 D2 Langrigg Cumb
399 F5 Langrigg Cumb
73 H5 Langrish Hants
328 C4 Langsett Barns
451 G2 Langshaw Border
467 E2 Langside C Glas
602 E3 Langskaill Ork
19 F1 Langstone Devon
52 C3 Langstone Hants
108 C1 Langstone Newpt
370 A1 Langthorne N York
356 D1 Langthorpe N York
382 B4 Langthwaite N York
360 C1 Langtoft E R Yk
243 G2 Langtoft Lincs
394 D6 Langton Dur
319 G6 Langton Lincs
320 C5 Langton Lincs
359 E1 Langton N York
319 E4 Langton by Wragby Lincs

47 G3 Langton Long Blandford Dorset
34 B5 Langton Matravers Dorset
39 F4 Langtree Devon
39 G4 Langtree Week Devon
391 F3 Langwathby Cumb
315 G6 Langwith Derbys
315 G6 Langwith Junction Derbys
318 C4 Langworth Lincs
173 F5 Lanham Green Essex
15 E6 Lanivet Cnwll
8 B3 Lanjeth Cnwll
14 D6 Lanjew Cnwll
15 F3 Lank Cnwll
8 D2 Lanlivery Cnwll
6 D6 Lanner Cnwll
9 F2 Lanreath Cnwll
497 G4 Lanrick Stirlg
9 F3 Lansallos Cnwll
106 C2 Lansbury Park Caerph
110 C6 Lansdown BaNES
162 D5 Lansdown Gloucs
15 F2 Lanteglos Cnwll
9 E3 Lanteglos Highway Cnwll
452 B5 Lanton Border
454 A3 Lanton Nthumb
14 D5 Lantuel Cnwll
9 E2 Lantyan Cnwll
213 E3 Lapal Dudley
35 d2 La Passee Guern
41 E6 Lapford Devon
41 E6 Lapford Cross Devon
476 F7 Laphroaig Ag & B
236 C2 Lapley Staffs
35 f7 La Pulente Jersey
214 B5 Lapworth Warwks
519 G6 Larachbeg Highld
485 G3 Larbert Falk
337 G1 Larbreck Lancs
338 C3 Larches Lancs
290 B4 Larden Green Ches
559 E3 Largie Abers
480 C2 Largiemore Ag & B
502 D3 Largoward Fife
464 D2 Largs N Ayrs
559 E1 Largue Abers
461 E5 Largybeg N Ayrs
461 E5 Largymeanoch N Ayrs
461 F5 Largymore N Ayrs
27 H3 Larkbeare Devon
482 B4 Larkfield Inver
97 H3 Larkfield Kent
342 D2 Larkfield Leeds
86 D1 Larkhall BaNES
468 B4 Larkhall S Lans
325 F4 Lark Hill Wigan
88 D6 Larkhill Wilts
275 H1 Larklands Derbys
201 G5 Larks' Hill Suffk
224 C2 Larling Norfk
35 j7 La Rocque Jersey
35 d2 La Rousaillerie Guern
160 D2 Larport Herefs
16 D3 Larrick Cnwll
439 G6 Larriston Border
410 C4 Larrock D & G
382 B1 Lartington Dur
554 B4 Lary Abers
136 B6 Lasborough Gloucs
73 G1 Lasham Hants
80 B1 Lashenden Kent
292 B3 Lask Edge Staffs
500 B6 Lassodie Fife
471 F1 Lasswade Mdloth
372 D1 Lastingham N York
84 D5 Latcham Somset
10 C2 Latchbrook Cnwll
171 E5 Latchford Herts
141 E4 Latchford Oxon
310 C2 Latchford Warrtn
148 A4 Latchingdon Essex
17 F4 Latchley Cnwll
91 G2 Latchmere Green Hants
325 F5 Lately Common Warrtn
194 B5 Lathbury M Keyn
583 G3 Latheron Highld
583 G3 Latheronwheel Highld
324 B2 Lathom Lancs
502 D3 Lathones Fife
142 D5 Latimer Bucks
110 B3 Latteridge S Glos
68 A4 Lattiford Somset
175 E2 Lattinford Hill Suffk
137 G5 Latton Wilts
145 G3 Latton Bush Essex
556 C2 Lauchintilly Abers
472 C5 Lauder Border
472 C5 Lauder Barns Border
127 F2 Laugharne Carmth
187 H3 Laughern Hill Worcs
317 H2 Laughterton Lincs
57 E2 Laughton E Susx
217 E2 Laughton Leics
279 F3 Laughton Lincs
332 A5 Laughton Lincs
56 D2 Laughton Common E Susx
315 G2 Laughton Common Rothm
315 G2 Laughton en le Morthen Rothm
23 F1 Launcells Cross Cnwll
23 G6 Launceston Cnwll
85 F6 Launcherley Somset
340 C5 Laund Lancs
241 G4 Launde Abbey Leics
166 D5 Launton Oxon
540 D5 Laurencekirk Abers
412 C1 Laurieston D & G
486 B3 Laurieston Falk
194 C4 Lavendon M Keyn
200 B5 Lavenham Suffk
437 F5 Laverhay D & G
450 B2 Laverlaw Border
67 F2 Laverley Somset
106 C6 Lavernock V Glam
401 E2 Laversdale Cumb
70 D3 Laverstock Wilts
90 D5 Laverstoke Hants
163 G2 Laverton Gloucs
370 A5 Laverton N York
86 D4 Laverton Somset
34 c3 La Villette Guern
88 B3 Lavington Sands Wilts
289 E3 Lavister Wrexhm
8 C2 Lavrean Cnwll
468 C4 Law S Lans
510 B2 Lawers P & K
510 D5 Lawers P & K
175 E3 Lawford Essex
64 B4 Lawford Somset
215 H5 Lawford Heath Warwks
468 C4 Law Hill S Lans
17 E2 Lawhitton Cnwll
353 F1 Lawkland N York
353 F1 Lawkland Green N York
234 C5 Lawley Shrops
235 F3 Lawley Wrekin
113 E3 Lawn Swindn
272 B4 Lawnhead Staffs
343 F5 Lawns Wakefd
287 E1 Lawnt Denbgs
107 F2 Lawrence Hill Newpt
109 F4 Lawrence Weston Bristl
125 H3 Lawrenny Pembks

125 H3 Lawrenny Quay Pembks
199 H4 Lawshall Suffk
200 A4 Lawshall Green Suffk
186 A3 Lawton Herefs
210 C3 Lawton Shrops
291 G3 Lawton-Gate Ches
291 F3 Lawton Heath End Ches
597 J3 Laxay W Isls
599 J8 Laxdale W Isls
322 g6 Laxey IoM
226 B5 Laxfield Suffk
605 H1 Laxfirth Shet
607 G6 Laxfirth Shet
584 D7 Laxford Bridge Highld
606 F5 Laxo Shet
606 F3 Laxobigging Shet
346 A4 Laxton E R Yk
242 D5 Laxton Nhants
296 D1 Laxton Notts
341 G1 Laycock Brad
174 B6 Layer Breton Essex
174 C5 Layer de la Haye Essex
174 B6 Layer Marney Essex
358 B4 Laythorpe York
29 G2 Laymore Dorset
117 G1 Layters Green Bucks
345 H2 Laytham E R Yk
337 F2 Layton Bpool
397 E6 Lazenby R & Cl
391 F2 Lazonby Cumb
294 C3 Lea Derbys
28 D3 Lea Devon
161 F5 Lea Herefs
338 C3 Lea Lancs
317 F2 Lea Lincs
209 G2 Lea Shrops
233 H3 Lea Shrops
111 H2 Lea Wilts
119 H2 Lea Bridge Gt Lon
295 E4 Leabrooks Derbys
309 E5 Lea by Backford Ches
596 F2 Leacainn W Isls
595 J4 Leac a' Li W Isls
546 E2 Leacanashie Highld
565 L8 Leachkin Highld
591 D8 Leadaig W Isls
470 D3 Leadburn Mdloth
272 D2 Leadendale Staffs
298 B4 Leadenham Lincs
146 B2 Leaden Roding Essex
402 C6 Leadgate Cumb
404 D4 Leadgate Dur
435 H1 Leadhills S Lans
98 D4 Leadingcross Green Kent
313 H3 Leadmill Derbys
288 B2 Leadmill Flints
213 F5 Lea End Worcs
139 E1 Leafield Oxon
111 F6 Leafield Wilts
291 E5 Lea Forge Ches
169 F5 Leagrave Luton
49 H6 Leagreen Hants
309 H1 Lea Green St Hel
214 A2 Lea Hall Birm
273 F4 Lea Heath Staffs
371 E1 Leake N York
300 C4 Leake Commonside Lincs
300 D4 Leake Fold Hill Lincs
300 D5 Leake Hurn's End Lincs
386 C3 Lealholm N York
386 C3 Lealholm Side N York
161 F5 Lea Line Herefs
479 H3 Lealt Ag & B
543 J4 Lealt Highld
314 A4 Leam Derbys
238 C6 Lea Marston Warwks
215 G6 Leamington Hastings Warwks
191 E2 Leamington Spa Warwks
237 G3 Leamonsley Staffs
209 H2 Leamoor Common Shrops
237 E4 Leamore Wsall
405 H5 Leamside Dur
566 D8 Leanach Highld
212 B5 Leapgate Worcs
478 E7 Leargybreck Ag & B
386 D4 Lease Rigg N York
143 H2 Leasey Bridge Herts
365 G3 Leasgill Cumb
298 D5 Leasingham Lincs
395 F4 Leasingthorne Dur
102 C3 Leason Swans
308 C1 Leasowe Wirral
94 D3 Leatherhead Surrey
94 D3 Leatherhead Common Surrey
135 G4 Leathern Bottle Gloucs
356 A5 Leathley N York
270 B6 Leaton Shrops
235 E2 Leaton Wrekin
270 B6 Leaton Heath Shrops
338 C3 Lea Town Lancs
99 F4 Leaveland Kent
174 C2 Leavenheath Suffk
359 E2 Leavening N York
96 B2 Leaves Green Gt Lon
367 F2 Lea Yeat Cumb
374 D3 Lebberston N York
34 C3 Le Bigard N York
34 c3 Le Bourg Guern
35 j8 Le Bourg Jersey
16 D2 Leburnick Cnwll
138 C5 Lechlade on Thames Gloucs
366 C4 Leck Lancs
72 A2 Leckford Hants
586 F5 Leckfurin Highld
167 F2 Leckhampstead Bucks
114 C4 Leckhampstead W Berk
114 C4 Leckhampstead Thicket W Berk
162 D6 Leckhampton Gloucs
574 D5 Leckmelm Highld
106 B5 Leckwith V Glam
360 C6 Leconfield E R Yk
506 F2 Ledaig Ag & B
518 C4 Ledaig Ag & B
168 B5 Ledburn Bucks
161 F2 Ledbury Herefs
509 H4 Ledcharrie Stirlg
161 F3 Leddington Gloucs
185 H4 Ledgemoor Herefs
185 H2 Ledicot Herefs
579 H7 Ledmore Highld
577 G5 Lednabirichen Highld
587 G4 Lednagullin Highld
309 E5 Ledsham Ches
344 B4 Ledsham Leeds
344 A4 Ledston Leeds
12 C3 Ledstone Devon
344 A3 Ledston Luck Leeds
165 G4 Ledwell Oxon
504 E6 Lee Ag & B
60 C2 Lee Devon
61 E2 Lee Devon
120 A5 Lee Gt Lon
71 H6 Lee Hants
352 B3 Lee Lancs
403 G3 Lee Nthumb
269 H3 Lee Shrops
606 D8 Leeans Shet
213 G2 Lee Bank Birm
605 H5 Leebotten Shet
234 B5 Leebotwood Shrops

270 C4 Lee Brockhurst Shrops
364 B6 Leece Cumb
121 G2 Lee Chapel Essex
109 E2 Leechpool Mons
142 C4 Lee Clump Bucks
142 C4 Lee Common Bucks
98 C4 Leeds Kent
343 F3 Leeds Leeds
3 G5 Leedstown Cnwll
62 B2 Leeford Devon
142 B3 Lee Gate Bucks
354 B2 Lee Gate N York
235 F2 Leegomery Wrekin
51 F3 Lee Ground Hants
395 E3 Lee Head Derbys
365 G3 Leeholme Dur
292 C3 Leek Staffs
292 C4 Leekbrook Staffs
214 D6 Leek Wootton Warwks
11 G2 Lee Mill Devon
341 G3 Leeming Brad
370 B2 Leeming N York
370 B1 Leeming Bar N York
353 E5 Leemings Lancs
18 C5 Lee Moor Devon
343 F4 Lee Moor Wakefd
51 F4 Lee-on-the-Solent Hants
149 F2 Lee-over-Sands Essex
274 D2 Lees Derbys
327 E4 Lees Oldham
241 G2 Leesthorpe Leics
288 C3 Leeswood Flints
513 F5 Leetown P & K
310 D5 Leftwich Ches
158 D6 Legar Powys
320 C3 Legbourne Lincs
389 H6 Legburthwaite Cumb
472 D6 Legerwood Border
75 E5 Leggatt Hill W Susx
34 c3 Le Gron Guern
319 E2 Legsby Lincs
35 i8 Le Haguais Jersey
35 i8 Le Hocq Jersey
240 B3 Leicester C Leic
240 B4 Leicester Forest East Leics
215 G1 Leicester Grange Warwks
41 E5 Leigh Devon
46 B3 Leigh Dorset
47 E3 Leigh Dorset
48 C5 Leigh Dorset
97 E5 Leigh Kent
233 F4 Leigh Shrops
95 E5 Leigh Surrey
325 F4 Leigh Wigan
112 C1 Leigh Wilts
188 A4 Leigh Worcs
122 C3 Leigh Beck Essex
68 B3 Leigh Common Somset
111 F4 Leigh Delamere Wilts
80 D3 Leigh Green Kent
63 G4 Leighland Chapel Somset
122 C2 Leigh-on-Sea Sthend
52 C3 Leigh Park Hants
187 H4 Leigh Sinton Worcs
237 G4 Leighswood Wsall
111 E1 Leigh Woods N Som
369 G4 Leighton N York
232 D3 Leighton Powys
235 E3 Leighton Shrops
86 C6 Leighton Somset
219 G4 Leighton Bromswold Cambs
168 C4 Leighton Buzzard Beds
528 D2 Leightonhill Angus
86 B5 Leigh upon Mendip Somset
109 F5 Leigh Woods N Som
458 C2 Leim Ag & B
210 A6 Leinthall Earls Herefs
210 A6 Leinthall Starkes Herefs
209 G5 Leintwardine Herefs
216 B1 Leire Leics
585 H3 Leirinmore Highld
203 F2 Leiston Suffk
526 C5 Leitfie P & K
488 B4 Leith C Edin
474 A6 Leitholm Border
3 F2 Lelant Cnwll
3 F2 Lelant Downs Cnwll
348 D3 Lelley E R Yk
211 G5 Lem Hill Worcs
405 E1 Lemington N u Ty
453 E3 Lempitlaw Border
597 K5 Lemreway W Isls
144 B2 Lemsford Herts
366 D2 Lenacre Cumb
167 E3 Lenborough Bucks
189 F5 Lenchwick Worcs
418 D4 Lendalfoot S Ayrs
98 D4 Lenham Kent
99 E4 Lenham Forstal Kent
99 E5 Lenham Heath Kent
549 J4 Lenie Highld
453 F1 Lennel Border
484 C4 Lennoxtown E Duns
117 F3 Lent Bucks
287 E1 Lenten Pool Denbgs
276 C2 Lenton C Nott
279 E3 Lenton Lincs
276 B2 Lenton Abbey C Nott
565 K7 Lentran Highld
117 F3 Lent Rise Bucks
255 E4 Lenwade Norfk
484 D5 Lenzie E Duns
485 F5 Lenziemill N Lans
514 B2 Leoch Angus
555 F2 Leochel Cushnie Abers
186 B3 Leominster Herefs
136 A4 Leonard Stanley Gloucs
125 F3 Leonardston Pembks
476 F7 Leorin Ag & B
35 g6 Leoville Jersey
50 D5 Lepe Hants
542 B7 Lephin Highld
480 D1 Lephinchapel Ag & B
480 D1 Lephinmore Ag & B
359 E2 Leppington N York
328 B1 Lepton Kirk
34 b3 L'Erée Guern
9 E2 Lerryn Cnwll
605 J2 Lerwick Shet
34 b3 Les Arquêts Guern
443 G2 Lesbury Nthumb
35 d3 Les Hubits Guern
558 D5 Leslie Abers
500 D4 Leslie Fife
34 c3 Les Lohiers Guern
447 F2 Lesmahagow S Lans
34 b4 Les Murchez Guern
22 C4 Lesnewth Cnwll
34 c3 Les Nicolles Guern
35 d2 Les Quartiers Guern
35 g7 Les Quennevais Jersey
34 b3 Les Sages Guern
558 D1 Lessendrum Abers
256 D6 Lessingham Norfk
120 C4 Lessness Heath Gt Lon
399 G4 Lessonhall Cumb
34 c4 Les Villets Guern
414 D4 Leswalt D & G
35 f6 L'Etacq Jersey
143 H5 Letchmore Heath Herts
170 A3 Letchworth Garden City Herts

114 B2 Letcombe Bassett Oxon
114 B2 Letcombe Regis Oxon
528 B5 Letham Angus
486 A5 Letham Falk
501 F2 Letham Fife
512 C5 Letham P & K
528 D5 Letham Grange Angus
440 C3 Lethem Border
560 B1 Lethenty Abers
202 B3 Letheringham Suffk
251 E2 Letheringsett Norfk
25 G6 Lettaford Devon
603 M2 Letter Abers
556 D2 Letter Abers
563 H2 Letterewe Highld
546 F5 Letterfearn Highld
533 K4 Letterfinlay Highld
531 K5 Lettermorar Highld
518 C6 Lettermore Ag & B
574 D6 Letters Highld
151 H4 Letterston Pembks
551 J6 Lettoch Highld
551 K3 Lettoch Highld
185 H2 Letton Herefs
209 G5 Letton Herefs
248 C3 Letton Green Norfk
104 D2 Letty Brongu Brdgnd
144 C2 Letty Green Herts
315 H2 Letwell Rothm
361 E5 Leuchars Fife
597 K5 Leumrabhagh W Isls
597 K2 Leurbost W Isls
8 C4 Levalsa Meor Cnwll
482 B4 Levan Inver
607 G5 Levaneap Shet
236 C1 Levedale Staffs
107 E2 Level of Mendalgief Newpt
171 G5 Level's Green Essex
361 E5 Leven E R Yk
502 B4 Leven Fife
460 D5 Levencorroch N Ayrs
488 D5 Levenhall E Loth
502 B4 Leven Links Fife
365 G2 Levens Cumb
469 E3 Leven Seat W Loth
171 E5 Levens Green Herts
326 C6 Levenshulme Manch
342 B3 Leventhorpe Brad
605 H6 Levenwick Shet
595 G5 Leverburgh W Isls
325 G3 Lever Edge Bolton
245 E2 Leverington Cambs
245 F3 Leverington Common Cambs
143 F3 Leverstock Green Herts
300 C5 Leverton Lincs
114 A5 Leverton W Berk
300 D5 Leverton Highgate Lincs
300 D5 Leverton Lucasgate Lincs
300 D5 Leverton Outgate Lincs
34 C2 Le Villocq Guern
176 D2 Levington Suffk
373 F1 Levisham N York
549 G6 Levishie Highld
139 E3 Lew Oxon
16 C2 Lewannick Cnwll
30 D1 Lewcombe Dorset
24 B5 Lewdown Devon
56 B2 Lewes E Susx
151 F5 Leweston Pembks
120 A5 Lewisham Gt Lon
549 J4 Lewiston Highld
105 E2 Lewistown Brdgnd
141 F5 Lewknor Oxon
61 G4 Leworthy Devon
99 F2 Lewson Street Kent
338 C2 Lewth Lancs
19 G2 Lewthorn Cross Devon
24 B5 Lewtrenchard Devon
174 C4 Lexden Essex
555 F2 Ley Abers
16 A5 Ley Cnwll
62 C4 Ley Somset
97 G3 Leybourne Kent
369 F1 Leyburn N York
291 F5 Leycett Staffs
238 B3 Leyfields Staffs
169 H5 Ley Green Herts
312 C2 Ley Hey Park Stockp
257 H5 Ley Hill Hants
142 D4 Ley Hill Bucks
110 B1 Leyhill S Glos
339 E5 Leyland Lancs
556 D2 Leylodge Abers
327 H1 Leymoor Kirk
571 J5 Leys Abers
388 C6 Leys Cumb
513 F2 Leys P & K
292 D5 Leys Staffs
123 G5 Leysdown-on-Sea Kent
160 D6 Leys Hill Herefs
528 D5 Leysmill Angus
527 E5 Leys of Cossans Angus
186 D2 Leysters Herefs
120 A2 Leyton Midland Road Gt Lon
16 D3 Lezant Cnwll
322 g4 Lezayre IoM
4 C2 Lezerea Cnwll
252 D4 Leziate Norfk
568 D3 Lhanbryde Moray
157 F4 Libanus Powys
469 F6 Libberton S Lans
188 D3 Libbery Worcs
488 B6 Liberton C Edin
595 J4 Liceasto W Isls
238 A2 Lichfield Staffs
213 E4 Lickey Worcs
213 E5 Lickey End Worcs
75 E4 Lickfold W Susx
212 A5 Lickhill Worcs
17 F2 Liddaton Devon
601 H8 Liddel Ork
519 J4 Liddesdale Highld
125 E3 Liddeston Pembks
113 F3 Liddington Swindn
314 C4 Lidgate Derbys
199 E3 Lidgate Suffk
331 H4 Lidget Donc
296 F3 Lidgett Notts
343 F3 Lidget Park Leeds
58 D3 Lidham Hill E Susx
168 D2 Lidlington Beds
53 G4 Lidsey W Susx
98 B2 Lidsing Kent
165 F5 Lidstone Oxon
588 D4 Lieurary Highld
514 A3 Liff Angus
213 G4 Lifford Birm
24 A5 Lifton Devon
23 H5 Liftondown Devon
342 D4 Lightcliffe Calder
270 C3 Lighteach Shrops
338 D3 Lightfoot Green Lancs
191 E3 Lighthorne Warwks
191 E3 Lighthorne Heath Warwks
191 E3 Lighthorne Rough Warwks
235 F2 Lightmoor Wrekin
292 B4 Light Oaks C Stke
136 B4 Lightpill Gloucs
93 F2 Lightwater Surrey
314 D3 Lightwood Derbys
211 E1 Lightwood Shrops

City, town and village index: Lightwood - Llandefaelog 699

271 F4 Lightwood Shrops
292 D6 Lightwood Staffs
290 C6 Lightwood Green Ches
269 G1 Lightwood Green Wrexhm
216 C4 Lilbourne Nhants
325 F4 Lilford Wigan
44 C3 Lillesdon Somset
235 G1 Lilleshall Wrekin
169 G4 Lilley Herts
114 C4 Lilley W Berk
451 G5 Lilliesleaf Border
167 F2 Lillingstone Dayrell Bucks
167 F1 Lillingstone Lovell Bucks
46 B2 Lillington Dorset
191 E1 Lillington Warwks
34 B3 Lilliput Poole
64 C3 Lilstock Somset
482 D5 Lilybank Inver
235 G2 Lilyhurst Shrops
81 G2 Lilyvale Kent
324 D1 Limbrick Lancs
169 F5 Limbury Luton
185 G1 Limebrook Herefs
326 B2 Limefield Bury
569 J5 Limehillock Moray
326 D4 Limehurst Tamesd
467 H4 Limekilnburn S Lans
315 F5 Limekiln Field Derbys
487 E3 Limekilns Fife
485 G5 Limerigg Falk
36 C4 Limerstone IoW
326 D4 Lime Side Oldham
402 D4 Limestone Brae Nthumb
162 B3 Lime Street Worcs
214 D4 Lime Tree Park Covtry
67 E5 Limington Somset
446 C4 Limmerhaugh Muir E Ayrs
250 D4 Limpenhoe Norfk
251 E4 Limpenhoe Hill Norfk
68 D3 Limpers Hill Wilts
86 D2 Limpley Stoke Wilts
96 A4 Limpsfield Surrey
96 B4 Limpsfield Common Surrey
441 G3 Linbriggs Nthumb
487 F6 Linburn W Loth
295 G4 Linby Notts
74 D3 Linchmere W Susx
423 G4 Lincluden D & G
318 B5 Lincoln Lincs
212 B6 Lincomb Worcs
12 C4 Lincombe Devon
19 F6 Lincombe Devon
365 F3 Lindale Cumb
364 C4 Lindal in Furness Cumb
451 F3 Lindean Border
136 B1 Linden Gloucs
77 F4 Lindfield W Susx
74 C2 Lindford Hants
342 B6 Lindley Kirk
356 A5 Lindley N York
501 E1 Lindores Fife
311 G4 Lindow End Ches
211 F6 Lindridge Worcs
172 C4 Lindsell Essex
200 C6 Lindsey Suffk
200 C5 Lindsey Tye Suffk
342 A5 Lindwell Calder
188 B1 Lineholt Worcs
188 B1 Lineholt Common Worcs
65 G4 Liney Somset
327 E3 Linfitts Oldham
49 F3 Linford Hants
121 G4 Linford Thurr
342 A2 Lingbob Brad
385 H1 Lingdale R & Cl
185 G1 Lingen Herefs
383 H2 Lingfield Darltn
96 A6 Lingfield Surrey
96 A6 Lingfield Common Surrey
310 B2 Lingley Green Warrtn
310 B1 Lingley Mere Warrtn
595 H6 Lingreabhagh W Isls
250 D3 Lingwood Norfk
439 E4 Linhope Border
442 B1 Linhope Nthumb
542 F3 Linicro Highld
85 E3 Link N Som
603 H4 Linkataing Ork
162 B3 Linkend Worcs
90 B3 Linkenholt Hants
80 B4 Linkhill Kent
16 D4 Linkinhorne Cnwll
601 H7 Linklater Ork
603 M1 Linklet Ork
600 C4 Linksness Ork
601 J2 Linksness Ork
488 B1 Linktown Fife
233 G6 Linley Shrops
235 F5 Linley Shrops
235 F5 Linley Brook Shrops
187 F4 Linley Green Herefs
235 F5 Linleygreen Shrops
486 D4 Linlithgow W Loth
486 C4 Linlithgow Bridge W Loth
565 K6 Linnie Highld
525 J1 Linns Angus
325 G4 Linnyshaw Salfd
441 G3 Linshiels Nthumb
597 G1 Linsiadar W Isls
576 B4 Linsidemore Highld
168 C5 Linslade Beds
226 C4 Linstead Parva Suffk
400 D3 Linstock Cumb
396 C6 Linthorpe Middsb
213 E5 Linthurst Worcs
327 H2 Linthwaite Kirk
474 B3 Lintlaw Border
569 J2 Lintmill Moray
453 E4 Linton Border
198 B5 Linton Cambs
238 D1 Linton Derbys
161 F4 Linton Herefs
98 B4 Linton Kent
356 D5 Linton Leeds
354 C2 Linton N York
431 E1 Linton Nthumb
238 D1 Linton Heath Derbys
161 F5 Linton Hill Herefs
357 F2 Linton-on-Ouse N York
161 G3 Lintridge Gloucs
405 E3 Lintz Dur
404 D3 Lintzford Gatesd
403 G6 Lintzgarth Dur
49 F3 Linwood Hants
318 D2 Linwood Lincs
466 B2 Linwood Rens
593 D8 Lionacleit W Isls
593 D8 Lionacuidhe W Isls
599 L2 Lional W Isls
78 D6 Lions Green E Susx
74 C3 Liphook Hants
271 G3 Lipley Shrops
145 E5 Lippitts Hill Essex
86 B4 Lipyeate Somset
308 C1 Liscard Wirral
62 D5 Liscombe Somset
16 C6 Liskeard Cnwll
74 B4 Liss Hants
361 E3 Lissett E R Yk
74 B4 Liss Forest Hants
319 E3 Lissington Lincs
315 F1 Listerdale Rothm
44 C3 Listock Somset
321 F5 Listoft Lincs
199 H6 Liston Essex
199 G5 Liston Garden Essex
106 C3 Lisvane Cardif
107 F2 Liswerry Newpt
253 H4 Litcham Norfk
105 E3 Litchard Brdgnd
192 D4 Litchborough Nhants
90 D4 Litchfield Hants
275 F3 Litchurch C Derb
323 F5 Litherland Sefton
196 D6 Litlington Cambs
57 E4 Litlington E Susx
186 C5 Litmarsh Herefs
198 A5 Little Abington Cambs
218 D5 Little Addington Nhants
345 G4 Little Airmyn N York
170 A4 Little Almshoe Herts
190 A2 Little Alne Warwks
323 F3 Little Altcar Sefton
90 A6 Little Ann Hants
270 B1 Little Arowry Wrexhm
380 B3 Little Asby Cumb
87 E2 Little Ashley Wilts
237 G4 Little Aston Staffs
36 D4 Little Atherfield IoW
600 E6 Little Ayre Ork
606 D5 Little-Ayre Shet
385 F2 Little Ayton N York
147 F3 Little Baddow Essex
111 E3 Little Badminton S Glos
524 D5 Little Ballinluig P & K
399 H3 Little Bampton Cumb
172 C3 Little Bardfield Essex
196 A3 Little Barford Beds
261 F5 Little Barningham Norfk
138 B2 Little Barrington Gloucs
309 G5 Little Barrow Ches
373 E4 Little Barugh N York
429 F4 Little Bavington Nthumb
79 E2 Little Bayham E Susx
202 A5 Little Bealings Suffk
163 E3 Little Beckford Worcs
89 G1 Little Bedwyn Wilts
175 F4 Little Bentley Essex
144 C3 Little Berkhamsted Herts
193 H2 Little Billing Nhants
168 C5 Little Billington Beds
160 C3 Little Birch Herefs
337 F1 Little Bispham Bpool
201 F5 Little Blakenham Suffk
390 C3 Little Blencow Cumb
237 F4 Little Bloxwich Wsall
75 G5 Little Bognor W Susx
294 B4 Little Bolehill Derbys
311 E2 Little Bollington Ches
326 A5 Little Bolton Salfd
94 C4 Little Bookham Surrey
41 G5 Littleborough Devon
317 F3 Littleborough Notts
326 D1 Littleborough Rochdl
2 D3 Little Bosullow Cnwll
100 C4 Littlebourne Kent
191 H6 Little Bourton Oxon
217 F2 Little Bowden Leics
142 C5 Little Boys Heath Bucks
198 D4 Little Bradley Suffk
174 C4 Little Braiswick Essex
389 F5 Little Braithwaite Cumb
209 G3 Little Brampton Shrops
147 G2 Little Braxted Essex
61 G4 Little Bray Devon
528 C2 Little Brechin Angus
30 D5 Littlebredy Dorset
168 B3 Little Brickhill M Keyn
272 C4 Little Bridgeford Staffs
193 E2 Little Brington Nhants
110 C1 Little Bristol S Glos
189 H4 Little Britain Warwks
175 E4 Little Bromley Essex
213 H2 Little Bromwich Birm
388 C3 Little Broughton Cumb
290 C1 Little Budworth Ches
121 G1 Little Burstead Essex
171 H2 Littlebury Essex
171 G2 Littlebury Green Essex
279 E6 Little Bytham Lincs
172 C4 Little Cambridge Essex
172 B5 Little Canfield Essex
48 C5 Little Canford Dorset
337 F2 Little Carleton Bpool
320 C2 Little Carlton Lincs
297 E3 Little Carlton Notts
243 E3 Little Casterton Rutlnd
361 E6 Little Catwick E R Yk
219 F5 Little Catworth Cambs
320 C3 Little Cawthorpe Lincs
87 F2 Little Chalfield Wilts
142 D5 Little Chalfont Bucks
99 E5 Little Chart Kent
99 F5 Little Chart Forstal Kent
291 H4 Little Chell C Stke
275 E2 Little Chester C Derb
171 H1 Little Chesterford Essex
166 C5 Little Chesterton Oxon
88 A4 Little Cheverell Wilts
171 F2 Little Chishill Cambs
176 C6 Little Clacton Essex
138 D4 Little Clanfield Oxon
326 D2 Little Clegg Rochdl
388 C4 Little Clifton Cumb
334 B3 Little Coates NE Lin
189 E6 Little Comberton Worcs
16 D2 Little Comfort Cnwll
58 B5 Little Common E Susx
280 D4 Little Common Lincs
209 G4 Little Common Shrops
75 E5 Little Common W Susx
164 D3 Little Compton Warwks
401 E3 Little Corby Cumb
174 B2 Little Cornard Suffk
168 A5 Littlecote Bucks
88 D4 Littlecott Wilts
187 E4 Little Cowarne Herefs
138 D6 Little Coxwell Oxon
370 A1 Little Crakehall N York
218 A4 Little Cransley Nhants
194 C5 Little Crawley M Keyn
217 F5 Little Creaton Nhants
247 H5 Little Cressingham Norfk
323 F4 Little Crosby Sefton
274 B2 Little Cubley Derbys
241 G2 Little Dalby Leics
235 F3 Little Dawley Wrekin
135 F2 Littledean Gloucs
135 F2 Littledean Hill Gloucs
571 K7 Little Dens Abers
160 C3 Little Dewchurch Herefs
198 D3 Little Ditton Cambs
134 C1 Little Doward Herefs
49 E6 Littledown Bmouth
90 A3 Littledown Hants
221 H3 Little Downham Cambs
271 F3 Little Drayton Shrops
360 C3 Little Driffield E R Yk
134 D3 Little Drybrook Gloucs
247 H2 Little Dunham Norfk
512 B1 Little Dunkeld P & K
172 C5 Little Dunmow Essex
70 C3 Little Durnford Wilts
188 B3 Little Eastbury Worcs
172 C5 Little Easton Essex
275 F1 Little Eaton Derbys
338 B1 Little Eccleston Lancs
248 D5 Little Ellingham Norfk
195 H3 Little End Cambs
346 B2 Little End E R Yk
146 A4 Little End Essex
192 C3 Little Everdon Nhants
197 E4 Little Eversden Cambs
138 C4 Little Faringdon Oxon
383 G6 Little Fencote N York
344 C2 Little Fenton N York
577 H4 Littleferry Highld
334 C3 Littlefield NE Lin
93 F4 Littlefield Common Surrey
116 D4 Littlefield Green W & M
200 D4 Little Finborough Suffk
248 A2 Little Fransham Norfk
99 E3 Little Frith Kent
142 D2 Little Gaddesden Herts
236 A5 Littlegain Shrops
219 G3 Little Gidding Cambs
202 C3 Little Glemham Suffk
512 A3 Little Glenshee P & K
161 F4 Little Gorsley Herefs
196 C4 Little Gransden Cambs
196 C5 Little Green Cambs
296 D6 Little Green Notts
86 C5 Little Green Somset
225 E5 Little Green Suffk
270 B1 Little Green Wrexhm
320 B1 Little Grimsby Lincs
316 D3 Little Gringley Notts
573 H5 Little Gruinard Highld
372 D4 Little Habton N York
171 F5 Little Hadham Herts
279 G1 Little Hale Lincs
248 B3 Little Hale Norfk
275 H1 Little Hallam Derbys
171 G6 Little Hallingbury Essex
21 E1 Littleham Devon
39 F3 Littleham Devon
609 J3 Littlehamar Shet
142 B4 Little Hampden Bucks
54 B4 Littlehampton W Susx
136 B3 Little Haresfield Gloucs
218 B5 Little Harrowden Nhants
339 G4 Little Harwood Bl w D
140 D4 Little Haseley Oxon
361 F6 Little Hatfield E R Yk
256 B5 Little Hautbois Norfk
124 D2 Little Haven Pembks
76 C3 Little Haven W Susx
237 H4 Little Hay Staffs
312 D2 Little Hayfield Derbys
273 F5 Little Haywood Staffs
289 F1 Little Heath Ches
215 E3 Little Heath Covtry
120 C2 Little Heath Gt Lon
143 E3 Little Heath Herts
272 C6 Little Heath Staffs
94 C2 Little Heath Surrey
115 H5 Little Heath W Berk
344 D5 Little Heck N York
19 H5 Littlehempston Devon
172 A4 Little Henham Essex
173 H2 Little Henny Essex
163 E6 Little Herbert's Gloucs
210 C6 Little Hereford Herefs
160 B4 Little Hill Herefs
44 B5 Little Hill Somset
50 D4 Little Holbury Hants
125 F3 Little Honeyborough Pembks
338 C5 Little Hoole Moss Houses Lancs
174 C3 Little Horkesley Essex
171 F4 Little Hormead Herts
78 B6 Little Horsted E Susx
342 B3 Little Horton Brad
88 B2 Little Horton Wilts
167 G3 Little Horwood Bucks
329 G3 Little Houghton Barns
193 H3 Little Houghton Nhants
443 G1 Littlehoughton Nthumb
313 G4 Little Hucklow Derbys
325 G4 Little Hulton Salfd
115 E5 Little Hungerford W Berk
141 E3 Little Ickford Bucks
120 B2 Little Ilford Gt Lon
273 E5 Little Ingestre Staffs
189 F3 Little Inkberrow Worcs
194 C1 Little Irchester Nhants
86 D5 Little Keyford Somset
141 H3 Little Kimble Bucks
191 E4 Little Kineton Warwks
142 B5 Little Kingshill Bucks
21 F1 Little Knowle Devon
199 F3 Little Knowles Green Suffk
378 B4 Little Langdale Cumb
70 B2 Little Langford Wilts
146 A3 Little Laver Essex
215 H4 Little Lawford Warwks
337 F2 Little Layton Bpool
310 C4 Little Leigh Ches
147 E1 Little Leighs Essex
328 C2 Little Lepton Kirk
360 D5 Little Leven E R Yk
325 G3 Little Lever Bolton
333 G2 Little Limber Lincs
194 A6 Little Linford M Keyn
66 D5 Little Load Somset
342 C2 Little London Brad
140 D2 Little London Bucks
142 B3 Little London Bucks
245 F5 Little London Cambs
78 D6 Little London E Susx
171 G4 Little London Essex
172 D2 Little London Essex
161 F6 Little London Gloucs
90 B5 Little London Hants
91 G3 Little London Hants
280 B5 Little London Lincs
281 F5 Little London Lincs
319 E2 Little London Lincs
320 B5 Little London Lincs
247 F5 Little London Norfk
255 G3 Little London Norfk
256 B3 Little London Norfk
261 F5 Little London Norfk
140 B4 Little London Oxon
207 G2 Little London Powys
210 C2 Little London Shrops
67 F3 Little London Somset
201 E3 Little London Suffk
211 E5 Little London Worcs
313 G5 Little Longstone Derbys
555 G2 Little Lynturk Abers
234 B3 Little Lyth Shrops
291 F5 Little Madeley Staffs
161 H1 Little Malvern Worcs
288 D1 Little Mancot Flints
173 G3 Little Maplestead Essex
161 F2 Little Marcle Herefs
117 E2 Little Marlow Bucks
340 D2 Little Marsden Lancs
167 E5 Little Marsh Bucks
260 D4 Little Marsh Norfk
87 F3 Little Marsh Wilts
337 G3 Little Marton Bpool
147 E4 Little Mascalls Essex
253 F3 Little Massingham Norfk
249 G3 Little Melton Norfk
185 E5 Little Merthyr Herefs
125 G2 Little Milford Pembks
433 G1 Littlemill E Ayrs
567 G6 Littlemill Highld
97 G5 Little Mill Kent
133 F4 Little Mill Mons
140 D4 Little Milton Oxon
139 E2 Little Minster Oxon
142 C5 Little Missenden Bucks
101 F5 Little Mongeham Kent
294 D2 Littlemoor Derbys
32 B3 Littlemoor Dorset
340 A1 Little Moor Lancs
312 B2 Little Moor Stockp
340 A4 Little Moor End Lancs
140 B4 Littlemore Oxon
191 E3 Little Morrell Warwks
326 D5 Littlemoss Tamesd
288 C2 Little Mountain Flints
380 D2 Little Musgrave Cumb
269 H6 Little Ness Shrops
308 C4 Little Neston Ches
151 G4 Little Newcastle Pembks
394 C6 Little Newsham Dur
56 C2 Little Norlington E Susx
45 F4 Little Norton Somset
176 D4 Little Oakley Essex
218 B2 Little Oakley Nhants
194 D3 Little Odell Beds
169 G4 Little Offley Herts
236 B1 Little Onn Staffs
380 C1 Little Ormside Cumb
400 C3 Little Orton Cumb
239 E3 Little Orton Leics
222 C2 Little Ouse Cambs
357 E2 Little Ouseburn N York
275 E3 Littleover C Derb
269 G1 Little Overton Wrexhm
146 D3 Little Oxney Green Essex
214 C3 Little Packington Warwks
196 A2 Little Paxton Cambs
14 C4 Little Petherick Cnwll
569 G6 Little Pitlurg Moray
337 G3 Little Plumpton Lancs
250 C2 Little Plumstead Norfk
278 C3 Little Ponton Lincs
222 B2 Littleport Cambs
51 F4 Little Posbrook Hants
337 G2 Little Poulton Lancs
98 A3 Little Preston Kent
343 G3 Little Preston Leeds
290 C1 Littler Ches
482 B2 Little Rahane Ag & B
220 B3 Little Raveley Cambs
346 B5 Little Reedness E R Yk
102 C4 Little Reynoldston Swans
356 D4 Little Ribston N York
164 B6 Little Rissington Gloucs
576 F3 Little Rogart Highld
164 D3 Little Rollright Oxon
254 C2 Little Ryburgh Norfk
442 C2 Little Ryle Nthumb
234 B4 Little Ryton Shrops
89 E2 Little Salisbury Wilts
391 F2 Little Salkeld Cumb
172 D3 Little Sampford Essex
92 D2 Little Sandhurst Br For
236 D3 Little Saredon Staffs
199 G2 Little Saxham Suffk
564 F5 Little Scatwell Highld
325 E2 Little Scotland Bolton
197 F4 Little Shelford Cambs
89 G5 Little Shoddesden Hants
190 C1 Little Shrewley Warwks
136 D1 Little Shurdington Gloucs
42 B6 Little Silver Devon
60 D3 Little Silver Devon
337 G2 Little Singleton Lancs
345 F2 Little Skipwith N York
330 B1 Little Smeaton N York
384 A4 Little Smeaton N York
260 B5 Little Snoring Norfk
110 C3 Little Sodbury S Glos
110 C3 Little Sodbury End S Glos
72 A3 Little Somborne Hants
111 H3 Little Somerford Wilts
271 G4 Little Soudley Shrops
353 G1 Little Stainforth N York
395 G5 Little Stainton Darltn
118 D1 Little Stanmore Gt Lon
309 F5 Little Stanney Ches
195 G2 Little Staughton Beds
116 B4 Littlestead Green Oxon
300 D2 Little Steeping Lincs
607 H1 Littlester Shet
109 H3 Little Stoke S Glos
272 D3 Little Stoke Staffs
81 G5 Littlestone-on-Sea Kent
201 F3 Little Stonham Suffk
241 E4 Little Stretton Leics
210 A1 Little Stretton Shrops
391 F5 Little Strickland Cumb
370 C5 Little Studley N York
220 B4 Little Stukeley Cambs
272 B3 Little Sugnall Staffs
309 E4 Little Sutton Ches
281 G5 Little Sutton Lincs
210 C3 Little Sutton Shrops
429 F4 Little Swinburne Nthumb
161 E1 Little Tarrington Herefs
165 F4 Little Tew Oxon
174 A5 Little Tey Essex
221 H4 Little Thetford Cambs
261 E4 Little Thornage Norfk
337 G1 Little Thornton Lancs
406 C6 Little Thorpe Dur
342 C5 Little Thorpe Kirk
240 B5 Littlethorpe Leics
370 C6 Littlethorpe N York
198 D4 Little Thurlow Suffk
198 D4 Little Thurlow Green Suffk
121 F4 Little Thurrock Thurr
85 F2 Littleton BaNES
289 F1 Littleton Ches
47 G4 Littleton Dorset
72 C3 Littleton Hants
513 G3 Littleton P & K
66 D3 Littleton Somset
93 G5 Littleton Surrey
118 B6 Littleton Surrey
87 G2 Littleton Wilts
118 B5 Littleton Common Surrey
111 E3 Littleton Drew Wilts
88 A4 Littleton Panell Wilts
109 G2 Littleton-upon-Severn S Glos
576 F4 Little Torboll Highld
39 G4 Little Torrington Devon
148 A2 Little Totham Essex
389 F6 Little Town Cumb
28 C3 Littletown Devon
406 A6 Littletown Dur
577 H6 Little Town Highld
37 E2 Littletown IoW
342 C5 Littletown Kirk
339 G2 Little Town Lancs
325 E6 Little Town Warrtn
142 C2 Little Tring Herts
239 E3 Little Twycross Leics
364 C5 Little Urswick Cumb
470 B2 Little Vantage W Loth
123 E2 Little Wakering Essex
172 A1 Little Walden Essex
200 B5 Little Waldingfield Suffk
260 B4 Little Walsingham Norfk
147 E2 Little Waltham Essex
216 A3 Little Walton Warwks
121 E1 Little Warley Essex
238 D4 Little Warton Warwks
163 E3 Little Washbourne Gloucs
347 E3 Little Weighton E R Yk
162 B2 Little Welland Worcs
200 A2 Little Welnetham Suffk
320 A2 Little Welton Lincs
175 E2 Little Wenham Suffk
235 E3 Little Wenlock Wrekin
67 G4 Little Weston Somset
36 D2 Little Whitehouse IoW
226 B4 Little Whittingham Green Suffk
116 D4 Littlewick Green W & M
148 C1 Little Wigborough Essex
198 A3 Little Wilbraham Cambs
30 A2 Littlewindsor Dorset
279 G3 Little Wisbeach Lincs
136 D1 Little Witcombe Gloucs
187 H2 Little Witley Worcs
140 C6 Little Wittenham Oxon
164 D2 Little Wolford Warwks
237 E3 Littlewood Staffs
142 C4 Little Wood Corner Bucks
189 G2 Littlewood Green Warwks
33 H3 Little Woolgarston Dorset
195 F6 Littleworth Beds
330 D5 Littleworth Donc
136 C4 Littleworth Gloucs
164 A2 Littleworth Gloucs
115 G1 Littleworth Oxon
139 E5 Littleworth Oxon
140 C3 Littleworth Oxon
237 F2 Littleworth Staffs
272 D5 Littleworth Staffs
76 C5 Littleworth W Susx
190 C2 Littleworth Warwks
89 E2 Littleworth Wilts
188 C5 Littleworth Worcs
189 E2 Littleworth Worcs
117 F2 Littleworth Common Bucks
233 F3 Little Worthen Shrops
238 B5 Littleworth End Warwks
198 D5 Little Wratting Suffk
194 C1 Little Wymington Beds
170 B4 Little Wymondley Herts
237 F3 Little Wyrley Staffs
270 D6 Little Wytheford Shrops
173 F2 Little Yeldham Essex
146 D1 Littley Green Essex
313 G5 Litton Derbys
368 B5 Litton N York
85 G4 Litton Somset
30 D4 Litton Cheney Dorset
313 G5 Litton Mill Derbys
597 K2 Liurbost W Isls
20 C5 Livermead Torbay
308 D2 Liverpool Lpool
342 C5 Liversedge Kirk
19 H2 Liverton Devon
386 B1 Liverton R & Cl
397 H6 Liverton Mines R & Cl
98 D4 Liverton Street Kent
97 H4 Livesey Street Kent
27 F2 Livingshayes Devon
487 E6 Livingston W Loth
469 G1 Livingston Village W Loth
307 H5 Lixwm Flints
4 D6 Lizard Cnwll
180 B3 Llaingarreglwyd Cerdgn
302 B4 Llaingoch IoA
207 H3 Llaithddu Powys
105 E4 Llampha V Glam
265 E6 Llanaber Gwynd
263 F2 Llanaelhaearn Gwynd
205 F5 Llanafan Cerdgn
183 F3 Llanafan-Fawr Powys
303 G4 Llanallgo IoA
304 B2 Llanallgo IoA
208 A5 Llananno Powys
263 G3 Llanarmon Gwynd
268 B3 Llanarmon Dyffryn Ceiriog Wrexhm
268 B4 Llanarmon Mynydd-mawr Powys
288 A3 Llanarmon-yn-Lal Denbgs
180 B3 Llanarth Cerdgn
133 G2 Llanarth Mons
154 D5 Llanarthne Carmth
307 F3 Llanasa Flints
303 E3 Llanbabo IoA
105 F3 Llanbad Rhondd
205 E3 Llanbadarn Fawr Cerdgn
208 A4 Llanbadarn Fynydd Powys
184 B5 Llanbadarn-y-garreg Powys
133 G4 Llanbadoc Mons
303 E2 Llanbadrig IoA
108 C1 Llanbeder Newpt
264 D4 Llanbedr Gwynd
158 D5 Llanbedr Powys
184 B5 Llanbedr Powys
287 G3 Llanbedr-Dyffryn-Clwyd Denbgs
303 G4 Llanbedrgoch IoA
263 E4 Llanbedrog Gwynd
305 F6 Llanbedr-y-cennin Conwy
284 C3 Llanberis Gwynd
105 G6 Llanbethery V Glam
208 B5 Llanbister Powys
105 F5 Llanblethian V Glam
153 E5 Llanboidy Carmth
106 B1 Llanbradach Caerph
230 D4 Llanbrynmair Powys
105 G6 Llancadle V Glam
132 B5 Llancaiach Caerph
105 H5 Llancarfan V Glam
133 G4 Llancayo Mons
160 B5 Llancloudy Herefs
208 C1 Llancowrid Powys
205 E1 Llancynfelyn Cerdgn
132 C4 Llan-dafal Blae G
106 C4 Llandaff Cardif
106 B4 Llandaff North Cardif
264 D4 Llandanwg Gwynd
103 H3 Llandarcy Neath
127 F2 Llandawke Carmth
283 E1 Llanddaniel Fab IoA
128 D1 Llanddarog Carmth
204 D5 Llanddeiniol Cerdgn
283 F2 Llanddeiniolen Gwynd
267 F2 Llandderfel Gwynd
156 B5 Llanddeusant Carmth
302 D3 Llanddeusant IoA
157 H3 Llanddew Powys
102 B4 Llanddewi Swans
181 G3 Llanddewi-Brefi Cerdgn
133 F5 Llanddewi Fach Mons
183 G5 Llanddewi'r Cwm Powys
133 F2 Llanddewi Rhydderch Mons
133 F1 Llanddewi Skirrid Mons
126 C1 Llanddewi Velfrey Pembks
208 B6 Llanddewi Ystradenni Powys
285 H2 Llanddoged Conwy
304 C4 Llanddona IoA
127 F2 Llanddowror Carmth
306 C4 Llanddulas Conwy
264 D5 Llanddwywe Gwynd
304 B4 Llanddyfnan IoA
265 E2 Llandecwyn Gwynd
157 G3 Llandefaelog Powys

700 City, town and village index: Llandefaelog-tre'r-graig - Loudwater

158 B3 Llandefaelog-tre'r-graig Powys
158 A2 Llandefalle Powys
304 C5 Llandegai Gwynd
304 C5 Llandegfan IoA
288 A4 Llandegla Denbgs
184 B2 Llandegley Powys
133 F5 Llandegveth Mons
155 F5 Llandeilo Carmth
184 A6 Llandeilo Graban Powys
156 D3 Llandeilo'r-Fan Powys
151 E4 Llandeloy Pembks
133 H4 Llandenny Mons
133 H4 Llandenny Walks Mons
108 D1 Llandevaud Newpt
108 C2 Llandevenny Mons
152 C4 Llandilo Pembks
154 C5 Llandilo-yr-ynys Carmth
160 C4 Llandinabo Herefs
207 G2 Llandinam Powys
152 C5 Llandissilio Pembks
134 C4 Llandogo Mons
105 F5 Llandough V Glam
106 C5 Llandough V Glam
156 B3 Llandovery Carmth
105 E5 Llandow V Glam
155 G1 Llandre Carmth
205 E2 Llandre Cerdgn
267 G2 Llandrillo Denbgs
306 A3 Llandrillo-yn-Rhôs Conwy
183 G2 Llandrindod Wells Powys
269 E6 Llandrinio Powys
150 C5 Llandruidion Pembks
305 G3 Llandudno Conwy
305 G4 Llandudno Junction Conwy
262 D3 Llandudwen Gwynd
282 D4 Llandwrog Gwynd
129 F1 Llandybie Carmth
128 B2 Llandyfaelog Carmth
129 F1 Llandyfan Carmth
153 G1 Llandyfriog Cerdgn
303 F3 Llandyfrydog IoA
179 E5 Llandygwydd Cerdgn
288 A6 Llandynan Denbgs
287 F1 Llandyrnog Denbgs
269 E6 Llandysilio Powys
232 C5 Llandyssil Powys
154 B1 Llandysul Cerdgn
106 C4 Llanedeyrn Cardif
106 D3 Llanedeyrn Cardif
283 F2 Llanedwen IoA
157 H2 Llaneglwys Powys
229 E3 Llanegryn Gwynd
154 D5 Llanegwad Carmth
303 G2 Llaneilian IoA
306 B4 Llanelian yn-Rhôs Conwy
287 G4 Llanelidan Denbgs
158 C3 Llanelieu Powys
133 E2 Llanellen Mons
128 D4 Llanelli Carmth
265 G6 Llanelltyd Gwynd
132 D1 Llanelly Mons
132 D2 Llanelly Hill Mons
183 G4 Llanelwedd Powys
264 D5 Llanenddwyn Gwynd
262 B4 Llanengan Gwynd
233 F6 Llanerch Powys
268 C5 Llanerchemrys Powys
303 F4 Llanerchymedd IoA
231 G3 Llanerfyl Powys
303 F2 Llaneuddog IoA
132 B6 Llanfabon Caerph
132 D6 Llanfach Caerph
302 C4 Llanfachraeth IoA
266 B5 Llanfachreth Gwynd
302 D6 Llanfaelog IoA
304 D4 Llanfaes IoA
157 G4 Llanfaes Powys
302 D3 Llanfaethlu IoA
283 E3 Llanfaglan Gwynd
264 D4 Llanfair Gwynd
232 B3 Llanfair Caereinion Powys
181 F4 Llanfair Clydogau Cerdgn
287 G4 Llanfair Dyffryn Clwyd Denbgs
305 E4 Llanfairfechan Conwy
133 F3 Llanfair Kilgeddin Mons
152 D2 Llanfair-Nant-Gwyn Pembks
305 B4 Llanfair Pwllgwyngyll IoA
306 C5 Llanfair Talhaiarn Conwy
208 D4 Llanfair Waterdine Shrops
302 C5 Llanfairyneubwll IoA
302 D2 Llanfairynghornwy IoA
152 D6 Llanfallteg Carmth
152 C5 Llanfallteg West Carmth
183 H4 Llanfaredd Powys
204 D2 Llanfarian Cerdgn
268 C5 Llanfechain Powys
183 F4 Llanfechan Powys
303 E2 Llanfechell IoA
228 D3 Llanfendigaid Gwynd
288 A2 Llanferres Denbgs
265 G1 Llan Ffestiniog Gwynd
303 F5 Llanfflewyn IoA
302 D4 Llanfigael IoA
154 B2 Llanfihangel-ar-arth Carmth
286 D5 Llanfihangel Glyn Myfyr Conwy
183 G2 Llanfihangel-Helygen Powys
157 E3 Llanfihangel Nant Bran Powys
184 C3 Llanfihangel-Nant-Melan Powys
184 C1 Llanfihangel Rhydithon Powys
108 D2 Llanfihangel Rogiet Mons
158 B4 Llanfihangel Tal-y-Llyn Powys
134 A4 Llanfihangel Tor y Mynydd Mons
154 C5 Llanfihangel uwch-Gwili Carmth
205 F4 Llanfihangel-y-Creuddyn Cerdgn
232 A1 Llanfihangel-yng-Ngwynfa Powys
302 D5 Llanfihangel yn Nhowyn IoA
229 F3 Llanfihangel-y-Pennant Gwynd
284 B6 Llanfihangel-y-Pennant Gwynd
158 B3 Llanfilo Powys
133 E2 Llanfoist Mons
267 E2 Llanfor Gwynd
133 F6 Llanfrechfa Torfn
265 E1 Llanfrothen Gwynd
158 A4 Llanfrynach Powys
287 G3 Llanfwrog Denbgs
302 D4 Llanfwrog IoA
268 B6 Llanfyllin Powys
155 E4 Llanfynydd Carmth
288 C3 Llanfynydd Flints
153 E3 Llanfyrnach Pembks
231 F2 Llangadfan Powys
128 B3 Llangadog Carmth
155 H4 Llangadog Carmth
282 C2 Llangadwaladr IoA
268 C3 Llangadwaladr Powys
282 D2 Llangaffo IoA
128 A1 Llangain Carmth
183 E5 Llangammarch Wells Powys
105 E4 Llangan V Glam
160 C5 Llangarron Herefs
158 B4 Llangasty-Talyllyn Powys
155 E5 Llangathen Carmth
158 C6 Llangattock Powys
159 F5 Llangattock Lingoed Mons
134 A1 Llangattock-Vibon-Avel Mons
268 C5 Llangedwyn Powys
303 G5 Llangefni IoA
105 E2 Llangeinor Brdgnd
181 F3 Llangeitho Cerdgn
153 H2 Llangeler Carmth
228 D3 Llangelynin Gwynd
128 D4 Llangennech Carmth
102 B3 Llangennith Swans
158 D6 Llangenny Powys
306 B6 Llangernyw Conwy
133 G4 Llangeview Mons
262 D5 Llangian Gwynd
129 H3 Llangiwg Neath
151 F3 Llangloffan Pembks
152 D4 Llanglydwen Carmth
304 D4 Llangoed IoA
178 D4 Llangoedmor Cerdgn
268 C1 Llangollen Denbgs
152 C4 Llangolman Pembks
158 B4 Llangors Powys
205 E3 Llangorwen Cerdgn
134 B3 Llangovan Mons
267 E3 Llangower Gwynd
178 C4 Llangranog Cerdgn
303 F6 Llangristiolus IoA
160 C6 Llangrove Herefs
159 G4 Llangua Mons
208 C5 Llangunllo Powys
154 B5 Llangunnor Carmth
207 E4 Llangurig Powys
286 D6 Llangwm Conwy
133 H4 Llangwm Mons
125 G3 Llangwm Pembks
262 B4 Llangwnnadl Gwynd
287 G1 Llangwyfan Denbgs
303 F5 Llangwyllog IoA
205 E5 Llangwyryfon Cerdgn
181 E4 Llangybi Cerdgn
263 G2 Llangybi Gwynd
133 G5 Llangybi Mons
129 F5 Llangyfelach Swans
128 C2 Llangyndeyrn Carmth
287 G2 Llangynhafal Denbgs
158 B6 Llangynidr Powys
232 B3 Llangyniew Powys
153 E6 Llangynin Carmth
127 G1 Llangynog Carmth
267 G4 Llangynog Powys
104 D2 Llangynwyd Brdgnd
158 A4 Llanhamlach Powys
105 G3 Llanharan Rhondd
105 G3 Llanharry Rhondd
107 F1 Llanhennock Mons
132 D4 Llanhilleth Blae G
150 D4 Llanhowel Pembks
207 F3 Llanidloes Powys
262 D4 Llaniestyn Gwynd
206 D3 Llanifyny Powys
158 D1 Llanigon Powys
205 E4 Llanilar Cerdgn
105 F3 Llanilid Rhondd
181 F3 Llanio Cerdgn
125 G4 Llanion Pembks
106 C3 Llanishen Cardif
134 B4 Llanishen Mons
154 C4 Llanllawddog Carmth
304 D6 Llanllechid Gwynd
133 G5 Llanllowell Mons
231 G4 Llanllugan Powys
154 A6 Llanllwch Carmth
232 B6 Llanllwchaiarn Powys
154 C2 Llanllwni Carmth
208 C3 Llanllwyd Shrops
283 E5 Llanllyfni Gwynd
102 B3 Llanmadoc Swans
106 B4 Llanmaes Cardif
105 F6 Llanmaes V Glam
108 C2 Llanmartin Newpt
232 B6 Llanmerewig Powys
105 F5 Llanmihangel V Glam
126 C2 Llan-Mill Pembks
127 F3 Llanmiloe Carmth
102 D3 Llanmorlais Swans
306 D5 Llannefydd Conwy
308 A4 Llannerch-y-Môr Flints
128 D3 Llannon Carmth
263 F3 Llannor Gwynd
180 D1 Llanon Cerdgn
150 D3 Llanon Pembks
133 F3 Llanover Mons
154 B4 Llanpumsaint Carmth
125 G4 Llanreath Pembks
287 F2 Llanrhaeadr Denbgs
268 B4 Llanrhaeadr-ym-Mochnant Powys
150 D3 Llanrhian Pembks
102 C3 Llanrhidian Swans
305 G3 Llanrhos Conwy
302 D3 Llanrhyddlad IoA
204 C6 Llanrhystud Cerdgn
160 B6 Llanrothal Herefs
283 F3 Llanrug Gwynd
106 D3 Llanrumney Cardif
285 H2 Llanrwst Conwy
127 F2 Llansadurnen Carmth
155 G3 Llansadwrn Carmth
304 C4 Llansadwrn IoA
128 A3 Llansaint Carmth
129 G5 Llansamlet Swans
305 H4 Llansanffraid Glan Conwy Conwy
286 C1 Llansannan Conwy
105 F4 Llansannor V Glam
204 C6 Llansantffraed Cerdgn
158 B5 Llansantffraed Powys
207 E6 Llansantffraed-Cwmdeuddwr Powys
184 A3 Llansantffraed-in-Elwel Powys
268 D5 Llansantffraid-ym-Mechain Powys
155 F2 Llansawel Carmth
130 A6 Llansawel Neath
268 D4 Llansilin Powys
134 A4 Llansoy Mons
157 G4 Llanspyddid Powys
125 F3 Llanstadwell Pembks
127 G2 Llansteffan Carmth
158 B1 Llanstephan Powys
133 E6 Llantarnam Torfn
159 F5 Llanteems Mons
126 D2 Llanteg Pembks
159 E4 Llanthony Mons
133 G1 Llantilio Crossenny Mons
133 F1 Llantilio Pertholey Mons
303 E4 Llantrisant IoA
133 G5 Llantrisant Mons
105 H3 Llantrisant Rhondd
105 G5 Llantrithyd V Glam
130 B5 Llantwit Neath
106 A2 Llantwit Fardre Rhondd
105 E6 Llantwit Major V Glam
266 D3 Llanuwchllyn Gwynd
108 D1 Llanvaches Newpt
134 A6 Llanvair Discoed Mons
133 G2 Llanvapley Mons
133 G1 Llanvetherine Mons
159 E3 Llanveynoe Herefs
159 F5 Llanvihangel Crucorney Mons
133 F3 Llanvihangel Gobion Mons
134 A2 Llanvihangel-Ystern-Llewern Mons
160 B4 Llanwarne Herefs
267 G6 Llanwddyn Powys
133 E2 Llanwenarth Mons
180 C5 Llanwenog Cerdgn
108 C2 Llanwern Newpt
153 F4 Llanwinio Carmth
283 E4 Llanwnda Gwynd
151 F2 Llanwnda Pembks
180 D5 Llanwnnen Cerdgn
231 G6 Llanwnog Powys
155 H3 Llanwrda Carmth
230 B4 Llanwrin Powys
183 F2 Llanwrthwl Powys
182 D5 Llanwrtyd Powys
182 D5 Llanwrtyd Wells Powys
231 H4 Llanwyddelan Powys
268 D5 Llanyblodwel Shrops
127 G2 Llanybri Carmth
180 D6 Llanybydder Carmth
152 B5 Llanycefn Pembks
151 G2 Llanychaer Pembks
267 E3 Llanycil Gwynd
181 F5 Llanycrwys Carmth
267 E6 Llanymawddwy Gwynd
269 E5 Llanymynech Shrops
302 C4 Llanynghenedl IoA
287 G2 Llanynys Denbgs
289 E4 Llan-y-Pwll Wrexhm
133 E5 Llanyrafon Torfn
183 G2 Llanyre Powys
263 H3 Llanystumdwy Gwynd
158 A4 Llanywern Powys
126 B1 Llawhaden Pembks
268 D3 Llawnt Shrops
262 D5 Llawr Dref Gwynd
207 E1 Llawr-y-Glyn Powys
288 D3 Llay Wrexhm
303 E4 Llechcynfarwy IoA
263 H2 Llecheiddior Gwynd
158 A4 Llechfaen Powys
265 F6 Llechfraith Gwynd
132 B3 Llechrhyd Caerph
179 E5 Llechryd Cerdgn
268 D3 Llechrydau Wrexhm
305 F4 Llechwedd Conwy
205 E5 Lledrod Cerdgn
128 C4 Llettyrychen Carmth
103 G2 Llewelyn Park Swans
154 D2 Llidiad-Nenog Carmth
266 D2 Llidiardau Gwynd
287 G6 Llidiart-y-Parc Denbgs
263 E2 Llithfaen Gwynd
307 G4 Lloc Flints
288 C2 Llong Flints
158 C1 Llowes Powys
208 D4 Lloyney Powys
229 G5 Llugwy Gwynd
180 D3 Llundain-Fach Cerdgn
179 G5 Llwch-yr-hâl Cerdgn
104 C1 Llwydarth Brdgnd
131 F4 Llwydcoed Rhondd
287 F2 Llwyn Denbgs
209 E3 Llwyn Shrops
180 B3 Llwyncelyn Cerdgn
179 H2 Llwyndafydd Cerdgn
232 C4 Llwynderw Powys
207 E2 Llwyn-derw Powys
133 E1 Llwyn-du Mons
179 E5 Llwynduris Cerdgn
263 F2 Llwyndyrys Gwynd
288 C5 Llwyneinion Wrexhm
228 D3 Llwyngwril Gwynd
128 D5 Llwynhendy Carmth
268 D2 Llwynmawr Wrexhm
131 G2 Llwyn-on Village Myr Td
126 D1 Llwynpinner Pembks
129 E3 Llwyn-têg Carmth
126 D1 Llwyn-y-brain Carmth
269 F5 Llwyn-y-go Shrops
206 D1 Llwynygog Powys
181 E3 Llwyn-y-groes Cerdgn
131 F6 Llwynypia Rhondd
153 E3 Llwyn-yr-hwrdd Pembks
269 E5 Llynclys Shrops
303 F5 Llynfaes IoA
304 C5 Llyn Gors IoA
306 B4 Llysfaen Conwy
158 B2 Llyswen Powys
105 E5 Llysworney V Glam
152 A5 Llys-y-frân Pembks
156 D3 Llywel Powys
205 G3 Llywernog Cerdgn
314 B2 Load Brook Sheff
486 C4 Loan Falk
577 H8 Loandhu Highld
474 D4 Loanend Nthumb
471 E1 Loanhead Mdloth
444 D3 Loans S Ayrs
430 D3 Loansdean Nthumb
566 F1 Loans of Tullich Highld
60 C4 Lobb Devon
24 C5 Lobhillcross Devon
405 F2 Lobley Hill Gatesd
278 C5 Lobthorpe Lincs
593 E9 Loch a' Charnain W Isls
597 J2 Loch a' Ghainmhich W Isls
531 L6 Lochailort Highld
519 G7 Lochaline Highld
551 G5 Lochanhully Highld
415 E5 Lochans D & G
423 G3 Locharbriggs D & G
566 B8 Lochardil Highld
493 F1 Lochavich Ag & B
507 K4 Lochawe Ag & B
590 F4 Loch Baghasdail W Isls
590 F4 Lochboisdale W Isls
505 J6 Lochbuie Ag & B
546 F2 Lochcarron Highld
505 L4 Lochdon Ag & B
479 K6 Lochead Ag & B
509 J5 Lochearnhead Stirlg
514 B3 Lochee C Dund
488 B5 Lochend C Edin
549 K2 Lochend Highld
589 H3 Lochend Highld
436 C5 Locherben D & G
592 F5 Loch Euphort W Isls
423 E5 Lochfoot D & G
480 C1 Lochgair Ag & B
549 J6 Lochgarthside Highld
500 C6 Lochgelly Fife
480 B2 Lochgilphead Ag & B
495 E4 Lochgoilhead Ag & B
410 B3 Loch Head D & G
568 D3 Lochhill Moray
490 B3 Lochhouses E Loth
578 E5 Lochinver Highld
515 G1 Lochlands Angus
511 E5 Lochlane P & K
564 E4 Lochluichart Highld
424 B3 Lochmaben D & G
592 G4 Lochmaddy W Isls
592 G4 Loch nam Madadh W Isls
500 C5 Lochore Fife
592 G3 Lochportain W Isls
463 F4 Lochranza N Ayrs
593 E10 Loch Sgioport W Isls
529 F2 Lochside Abers
423 F4 Lochside D & G
566 E6 Lochside Highld
581 L2 Lochside Highld
585 J5 Lochside Highld
444 D5 Lochside S Ayrs
577 H7 Lochslin Highld
541 E1 Lochton Abers
556 C5 Lochton of Leys Abers
512 C4 Lochty P & K
519 J4 Lochuisge Highld
465 H3 Lochwinnoch Rens
467 G1 Lochwood C Glas
437 E5 Lochwood D & G
533 H7 Lochyside Highld
8 C1 Lockengate Cnwll
424 C3 Lockerbie D & G
112 D6 Lockeridge Wilts
88 D1 Lockeridge Dene Wilts
71 F4 Lockerley Hants
401 F5 Lockhills Cumb
84 C3 Locking N Som
310 C1 Locking Stumps Warrtn
360 B5 Lockington E R Yk
275 H4 Lockington Leics
109 H4 Lockleaze Bristl
96 B1 Locksbottom Gt Lon
86 C2 Locksbrook BaNES
36 C2 Locksgreen IoW
51 E3 Locks Heath Hants
373 F2 Lockton N York
328 A1 Lockwood Kirk
241 G4 Loddington Leics
217 H4 Loddington Nhants
12 C3 Loddiswell Devon
250 D5 Loddon Norfk
250 C5 Loddon Ingloss Norfk
198 A2 Lode Cambs
214 B3 Lode Heath Solhll
30 B4 Loders Dorset
270 D4 Lodgebank Shrops
381 H5 Lodge Green N York
214 D3 Lodge Green Solhll
213 F3 Lodge Hill Birm
16 B6 Lodge Hill Cnwll
343 E5 Lodge Hill Wakefd
100 D6 Lodge Lees Kent
314 B2 Lodge Moor Sheff
189 F1 Lodge Park Worcs
75 E5 Lodsworth W Susx
75 E5 Lodsworth Common W Susx
109 F4 Lodway N Som
343 F4 Lofthouse Leeds
369 F5 Lofthouse N York
343 F5 Lofthouse Gate Wakefd
397 H6 Loftus R & Cl
408 B3 Logan D & G
446 B5 Logan E Ayrs
469 F2 Loganlea W Loth
408 B3 Logan Mains D & G
288 A2 Loggerheads Denbgs
271 G2 Loggerheads Staffs
574 C5 Loggie Highld
529 E2 Logie Angus
514 C5 Logie Fife
567 J6 Logie Moray
554 D4 Logie Coldstone Abers
566 D1 Logie Hill Highld
559 F2 Logie Newton Abers
529 E2 Logie Pert Angus
524 E5 Logierait P & K
152 D5 Login Carmth
94 C5 Logmore Green Surrey
197 E2 Lolworth Cambs
340 C2 Lomeshaye Lancs
266 D3 Lôn Gwynd
562 B6 Lonbain Highld
359 G5 Londesborough E R Yk
119 F3 London Gt Lon
8 C3 London Apprentice Cnwll
80 C2 London Beach Kent
144 A4 London Colney Herts
370 C2 Londonderry N York
213 F2 Londonderry Sandw
212 D1 London Fields Dudley
50 A2 London Minstead Hants
278 C2 Londonthorpe Lincs
573 G7 Londubh Highld
572 E8 Lonemore Highld
577 G6 Lonemore Highld
109 F5 Long Ashton N Som
211 H5 Long Bank Worcs
465 G4 Longbar N Ayrs
310 C1 Longbarn Warrtn
297 F6 Long Bennington Lincs
431 E6 Longbenton N Tyne
164 B4 Longborough Gloucs
30 D4 Long Bredy Dorset
213 F4 Longbridge Birm
11 F2 Longbridge C Plym
190 D2 Longbridge Warwks
69 E1 Longbridge Deverill Wilts
291 G4 Longbridge Hayes Staffs
192 D1 Long Buckby Nhants
192 D1 Long Buckby Wharf Nhants
400 B3 Longburgh Cumb
46 B2 Longburton Dorset
19 G5 Longcause Devon
277 F4 Long Clawson Leics
294 A3 Longcliffe Derbys
51 F1 Long Common Hants
272 C5 Long Compton Staffs
164 D3 Long Compton Warwks
113 G1 Longcot Oxon
141 E3 Long Crendon Bucks
48 B2 Long Crichel Dorset
399 G3 Longcroft Cumb
485 F4 Longcroft Falk
17 F3 Longcross Devon
93 G1 Longcross Surrey
68 C3 Long Cross Wilts
380 A4 Longdale Cumb
401 F6 Longdales Cumb
111 F4 Long Dean Wilts
234 A3 Longden Shrops
234 A4 Longden Common Shrops
94 D1 Long Ditton Surrey
237 G2 Longdon Staffs
162 B2 Longdon Worcs
237 G2 Longdon Green Staffs
162 B2 Longdon Heath Worcs
162 B2 Longdon Hill End Worcs
235 E1 Longdon on Tern Wrekin
26 D4 Longdown Devon
4 D2 Longdowns Cnwll
345 F4 Long Drax N York
315 E5 Long Duckmanton Derbys
276 A3 Long Eaton Derbys
121 F6 Longfield Kent
605 G7 Longfield Shet
87 F3 Longfield Wilts
121 F6 Longfield Hill Kent
34 B2 Longfleet Poole
215 E3 Longford Covtry
274 C2 Longford Derbys
162 B5 Longford Gloucs
118 A4 Longford Gt Lon
96 D3 Longford Kent
271 E3 Longford Shrops
310 C1 Longford Warrtn
271 G6 Longford Wrekin
274 C2 Longfordlane Derbys
513 H4 Longforgan P & K
473 F3 Longformacus Border
443 E4 Longframlington Nthumb
173 G2 Long Gardens Essex
353 F3 Long Gill N York
309 G5 Long Green Ches
225 E4 Long Green Suffk
162 B3 Long Green Worcs
48 D5 Longham Dorset
254 B4 Longham Norfk
139 G2 Long Hanborough Oxon
561 G2 Longhaven Abers
87 E6 Longhedge Wilts
430 D2 Longhirst Nthumb
161 F6 Longhope Gloucs
600 D6 Longhope Ork
443 F6 Longhorsley Nthumb
443 G1 Longhoughton Nthumb
86 B2 Longhouse BaNES
191 G1 Long Itchington Warwks
389 G2 Longlands Cumb
120 B5 Longlands Gt Lon
274 C2 Longlane Derbys
115 E5 Longlane W Berk
235 E1 Long Lane Wrekin
215 H4 Long Lawford Warwks
342 A1 Long Lee Brad
162 B6 Longlevens Gloucs
341 G5 Longley Calder
328 A3 Longley Kirk
314 C1 Longley Estate Sheff
187 G4 Longley Green Worcs
66 D5 Long Load Somset
570 C3 Longmanhill Abers
142 C1 Long Marston Herts
357 G4 Long Marston N York
190 B5 Long Marston Warwks
391 H5 Long Marton Cumb
198 A2 Long Meadow Cambs
209 G3 Long Meadowend Shrops
199 H5 Long Melford Suffk
74 B3 Longmoor Camp Hants
568 C4 Longmorn Moray
312 A5 Longmoss Ches
111 G1 Long Newnton Gloucs
452 A4 Longnewton Border
384 B1 Longnewton S on T
135 H2 Longney Gloucs
489 E4 Longniddry E Loth
234 B4 Longnor Shrops
236 C2 Longnor Staffs
293 E2 Longnor Staffs
234 B4 Longnor Park Shrops
269 G5 Long Oak Shrops
90 C6 Longparish Hants
400 D2 Longpark Cumb
72 B3 Long Park Hants
353 G3 Long Preston N York
136 C3 Longridge Gloucs
339 F2 Longridge Lancs
236 D1 Longridge Staffs
469 E2 Longridge W Loth
162 B5 Longridge End Gloucs
485 G5 Longrigg N Lans
485 G5 Longriggend N Lans
348 B1 Long Riston E R Yk
3 E3 Longrock Cnwll
330 D3 Long Sandall Donc
355 H3 Longscales N York
292 B4 Longsdon Staffs
293 E5 Longshaw Staffs
324 C4 Longshaw Wigan
571 J6 Longside Abers
326 C5 Longsight Manch
271 F2 Longslow Shrops
400 C4 Longsowerby Cumb
197 E1 Longstanton Cambs
71 G2 Longstock Hants
487 H5 Longstone C Edin
3 F2 Longstone Cnwll
15 F4 Longstone Cnwll
66 B4 Longstone Somset
196 C3 Longstowe Cambs
225 G1 Long Stratton Norfk
193 G5 Long Street M Keyn
88 D4 Longstreet Wilts
92 B5 Long Sutton Hants
281 F5 Long Sutton Lincs
66 D4 Long Sutton Somset
243 H5 Longthorpe C Pete
224 D6 Long Thurlow Suffk
390 C5 Longthwaite Cumb
292 A6 Longton C Stke
338 C4 Longton Lancs
426 A6 Longtown Cumb
159 F4 Longtown Herefs
35 I7 Longueville Jersey
324 A6 Longview Knows
234 C6 Longville in the Dale Shrops
294 C4 Longway Bank Derbys
605 H5 Longwell Shet
110 A5 Longwell Green S Glos
276 A5 Long Whatton Leics
141 G3 Longwick Bucks
140 B6 Long Wittenham Oxon
430 A2 Longwitton Nthumb
412 C2 Longwood D & G
139 F5 Longworth Oxon
472 C1 Longyester E Loth
129 H5 Lon-Las Swans
571 J4 Lonmay Abers
542 D7 Lonmore Highld
9 H3 Looe Cnwll
16 B6 Looe Mills Cnwll
98 B4 Loose Kent
25 H1 Loosebeare Devon
280 D4 Loosegate Lincs
98 B4 Loose Hill Kent
141 H4 Loosley Row Bucks
71 E2 Lopcombe Corner Wilts
45 E5 Lopen Somset
45 E5 Lopen Head Somset
364 B4 Loppergarth Cumb
270 B4 Loppington Shrops
17 G6 Lopwell Devon
442 C3 Lorbottle Nthumb
246 B2 Lordsbridge Norfk
50 C1 Lord's Hill C Sotn
93 H6 Lordshill Common Surrey
50 D1 Lordswood C Sotn
98 B2 Lords Wood Medway
525 J6 Lornty P & K
295 E5 Loscoe Derbys
343 H5 Loscoe Wakefd
30 C3 Loscombe Dorset
595 H3 Losgaintir W Isls
568 C1 Lossiemouth Moray
476 B5 Lossit Ag & B
271 E3 Lostford Shrops
325 F3 Lostock Bolton
310 D4 Lostock Gralam Ches
310 D5 Lostock Green Ches
338 D5 Lostock Hall Lancs
325 F3 Lostock Junction Bolton
9 E2 Lostwithiel Cnwll
582 B7 Lothbeg Highld
354 C5 Lothersdale N York
471 F2 Lothianbridge Mdloth
582 C7 Lothmore Highld
67 F3 Lottisham Somset
117 F1 Loudwater Bucks

City, town and village index: Loudwater - Lyons Hall 701

143 E5 **Loudwater** Herts
276 B6 **Loughborough** Leics
129 E5 **Loughor** Swans
168 A2 **Loughton** M Keyn
211 E3 **Loughton** Shrops
279 F6 **Lound** Lincs
316 C2 **Lound** Notts
251 G5 **Lound** Suffk
314 D5 **Loundsley Green** Derbys
275 F6 **Lount** Leics
320 B2 **Louth** Lincs
18 B4 **Lovaton** Devon
340 C4 **Love Clough** Lancs
52 B2 **Lovedean** Hants
118 A3 **Love Green** Bucks
71 E5 **Lover** Wilts
330 C5 **Loversall** Donc
146 C4 **Loves Green** Essex
126 B3 **Loveston** Pembks
67 F3 **Lovington** Somset
329 H1 **Low Ackworth** Wakefd
441 H3 **Low Alwinton** Nthumb
430 A3 **Low Angerton** Nthumb
161 H3 **Lowbands** Gloucs
318 D5 **Low Barlings** Lincs
366 D6 **Low Bentham** N York
366 C4 **Low Biggins** Cumb
467 G3 **Low Blantyre** S Lans
379 H4 **Low Borrowbridge** Cumb
314 B1 **Low Bradfield** Sheff
354 D5 **Low Bradley** N York
390 C1 **Low Braithwaite** Cumb
112 A5 **Low Bridge** Wilts
429 E5 **Low Brunton** Nthumb
331 G4 **Low Burnham** N Linc
388 A5 **Lowca** Cumb
358 D4 **Low Catton** E R Yk
225 F1 **Low Common** Norfk
326 D3 **Low Compton** Oldham
383 F2 **Low Coniscliffe** Darltn
401 E4 **Low Cotehill** Cumb
445 F6 **Low Coylton** S Ayrs
289 G4 **Lowcross Hill** Ches
373 G2 **Low Dalby** N York
296 C5 **Lowdham** Notts
384 A2 **Low Dinsdale** Darltn
380 C5 **Low Dovengill** Cumb
410 B4 **Low Drumskeog** D & G
270 B3 **Lowe** Shrops
314 C3 **Lowedges** Sheff
292 C3 **Lowe Hill** Staffs
405 G3 **Low Eighton** Gatesd
369 H3 **Low Ellington** N York
64 D4 **Lower Aisholt** Somset
235 G5 **Lower Allscot** Shrops
343 G5 **Lower Altofts** Wakefd
14 D4 **Lower Amble** Cnwll
47 E4 **Lower Ansty** Dorset
577 J7 **Lower Arboll** Highld
504 D6 **Lower Ardtun** Ag & B
166 D6 **Lower Arncott** Oxon
94 D3 **Lower Ashtead** Surrey
26 C6 **Lower Ashton** Devon
116 B3 **Lower Assendon** Oxon
568 F3 **Lower Auchenreath** Moray
579 G1 **Lower Badcall** Highld
337 G3 **Lower Ballam** Lancs
338 C3 **Lower Bartle** Lancs
115 G4 **Lower Basildon** W Berk
278 D4 **Lower Bassingthorpe** Lincs
185 G3 **Lower Bearwood** Herefs
308 D3 **Lower Bebington** Wirral
76 D4 **Lower Beeding** W Susx
218 D2 **Lower Benefield** Nhants
189 E1 **Lower Bentley** Worcs
212 A1 **Lower Beobridge** Shrops
134 D2 **Lower Berry Hill** Gloucs
190 B4 **Lower Binton** Warwks
295 E4 **Lower Birchwood** Derbys
97 E4 **Lower Bitchet** Kent
47 G3 **Lower Blandford St Mary** Dorset
112 D1 **Lower Blunsdon** Swindn
145 H3 **Lower Bobbingworth Green** Essex
32 C1 **Lower Bockhampton** Dorset
192 A4 **Lower Boddington** Nhants
261 F4 **Lower Bodham** Norfk
2 D3 **Lower Bodinnar** Cnwll
142 D4 **Lower Bois** Bucks
73 G5 **Lower Bordean** Hants
2 C2 **Lower Boscaswell** Cnwll
92 D6 **Lower Bourne** Surrey
237 E5 **Lower Bradley** Wolves
165 E5 **Lower Brailes** Warwks
546 B5 **Lower Breakish** Highld
312 B1 **Lower Bredbury** Stockp
160 B2 **Lower Breinton** Herefs
188 B3 **Lower Broadheath** Worcs
71 G4 **Lower Brook** Hants
326 B5 **Lower Broughton** Salfd
185 G4 **Lower Broxwood** Herefs
129 H2 **Lower Brynamman** Neath
14 D6 **Lower Brynn** Cnwll
161 E3 **Lower Buckenhill** Herefs
50 B5 **Lower Buckland** Hants
160 C2 **Lower Bullingham** Herefs
72 B1 **Lower Bullington** Hants
290 B3 **Lower Bunbury** Ches
49 F1 **Lower Burgate** Hants
66 C5 **Lower Burrow** Somset
185 H3 **Lower Burton** Herefs
120 G1 **Lower Bush** Medway
141 H4 **Lower Cadsden** Bucks
195 E5 **Lower Caldecote** Beds
135 G4 **Lower Cam** Gloucs
84 C3 **Lower Canada** N Som
289 G4 **Lower Carden** Ches
192 B3 **Lower Catesby** Nhants
19 E2 **Lower Cator** Devon
116 B5 **Lower Caversham** Readg
157 G2 **Lower Chapel** Powys
137 F2 **Lower Chedworth** Gloucs
28 B2 **Lower Cheriton** Devon
69 G3 **Lower Chicksgrove** Wilts
89 H4 **Lower Chute** Wilts
119 H2 **Lower Clapton** Gt Lon
212 D3 **Lower Clent** Worcs
10 A1 **Lower Clicker** Cnwll
190 B3 **Lower Clopton** Warwks
91 G6 **Lower Common** Hants
92 C2 **Lower Common** Hants
132 D1 **Lower Common** Mons
234 A3 **Lower Common** Shrops
339 E5 **Lower Copthurst** Lancs
79 F3 **Lower Cousley Wood** E Susx
98 C2 **Lower Cox Street** Kent
26 C2 **Lower Creedy** Devon
15 E4 **Lower Croan** Cnwll
312 D3 **Lower Crossings** Derbys
328 C3 **Lower Cumberworth** Kirk
48 D2 **Lower Daggons** Hants
339 G5 **Lower Darwen** Bl w D
219 F6 **Lower Dean** Beds
19 F5 **Lower Dean** Devon
328 C3 **Lower Denby** Kirk
14 B5 **Lower Denzell** Cnwll
562 D4 **Lower Diabaig** Highld
57 E2 **Lower Dicker** E Susx
210 B3 **Lower Dinchope** Shrops
588 B3 **Lower Dounreay** Highld
163 F5 **Lower Dowdeswell** Gloucs
209 F3 **Lower Down** Shrops
357 E2 **Lower Dunsforth** N York
44 B2 **Lower Durston** Somset
116 B5 **Lower Earley** Wokham
249 G4 **Lower East Carleton** Norfk
214 D4 **Lower Eastern Green** Covtry
187 E5 **Lower Egleton** Herefs
293 E3 **Lower Elkstone** Staffs
293 F6 **Lower Ellastone** Staffs
168 D5 **Lower End** Beds
141 E3 **Lower End** Bucks
167 F3 **Lower End** Bucks
137 E4 **Lower End** Gloucs
168 C2 **Lower End** M Keyn
193 G4 **Lower End** Nhants
193 H3 **Lower End** Nhants
194 B2 **Lower End** Nhants
139 E1 **Lower End** Oxon
89 E4 **Lower Everleigh** Wilts
30 A4 **Lower Eype** Dorset
101 E6 **Lower Eythorne** Kent
109 F5 **Lower Failand** N Som
211 F2 **Lower Faintree** Shrops
177 E2 **Lower Falkenham** Suffk
73 G2 **Lower Farringdon** Hants
118 B5 **Lower Feltham** Gt Lon
75 G6 **Lower Fittleworth** W Susx
340 C2 **Lowerford** Lancs
211 G2 **Lower Forge** Shrops
322 d7 **Lower Foxdale** IoM
269 G3 **Lower Frankton** Shrops
125 G2 **Lower Freystrop** Pembks
92 C6 **Lower Froyle** Hants
20 C4 **Lower Gabwell** Devon
576 C5 **Lower Gledfield** Highld
85 E6 **Lower Godney** Somset
101 E3 **Lower Goldstone** Kent
212 D1 **Lower Gornal** Dudley
342 B3 **Lower Grange** Brad
169 G2 **Lower Gravenhurst** Beds
147 E4 **Lower Green** Essex
171 F3 **Lower Green** Essex
173 E3 **Lower Green** Essex
170 A3 **Lower Green** Herts
171 F3 **Lower Green** Herts
78 D1 **Lower Green** Kent
79 E1 **Lower Green** Kent
260 C4 **Lower Green** Norfk
236 D3 **Lower Green** Staffs
199 E1 **Lower Green** Suffk
94 C1 **Lower Green** Surrey
90 B2 **Lower Green** W Berk
216 B6 **Lower Green** Warwks
325 G5 **Lower Green** Wigan
160 C4 **Lower Grove Common** Herefs
202 C3 **Lower Hacheston** Suffk
542 C5 **Lower Halistra** Highld
45 G6 **Lower Halstock Leigh** Dorset
98 D1 **Lower Halstow** Kent
110 C5 **Lower Hamswell** S Glos
34 A3 **Lower Hamworthy** Poole
100 B5 **Lower Hardres** Kent
185 H3 **Lower Hardwick** Herefs
185 E2 **Lower Harpton** Herefs
98 C2 **Lower Hartlip** Kent
294 D4 **Lower Hartshay** Derbys
141 G2 **Lower Hartwell** Bucks
272 B2 **Lower Hatton** Staffs
363 E4 **Lower Hawthwaite** Cumb
97 E5 **Lower Haysden** Kent
210 B3 **Lower Hayton** Shrops
109 H2 **Lower Hazel** S Glos
291 H2 **Lower Heath** Ches
100 B5 **Lower Heppington** Kent
185 E3 **Lower Hergest** Herefs
100 C2 **Lower Herne** Kent
166 A5 **Lower Heyford** Oxon
351 E2 **Lower Heysham** Lancs
121 H5 **Lower Higham** Kent
116 B3 **Lower Highmoor** Oxon
176 C2 **Lower Holbrook** Suffk
29 F2 **Lower Holditch** Dorset
48 D2 **Lower Holwell** Dorset
162 B1 **Lower Hook** Worcs
19 F1 **Lower Hookner** Devon
342 C6 **Lower Hopton** Kirk
269 G5 **Lower Hopton** Shrops
269 G4 **Lower Hordley** Shrops
75 G6 **Lower Horncroft** W Susx
57 F2 **Lower Horsebridge** E Susx
312 B4 **Lowerhouse** Ches
309 G3 **Lower House** Halton
340 B3 **Lowerhouse** Lancs
328 B1 **Lower Houses** Kirk
188 A5 **Lower Howsell** Worcs
213 E3 **Lower Illey** Dudley
100 B2 **Lower Island** Kent
326 B4 **Lower Kersal** Salfd
294 D5 **Lower Kilburn** Derbys
478 B3 **Lower Kilchattan** Ag & B
110 D2 **Lower Kilcott** Gloucs
476 D8 **Lower Killeyan** Ag & B
30 D3 **Lower Kingcombe** Dorset
95 E4 **Lower Kingswood** Surrey
288 D2 **Lower Kinnerton** Ches
185 F2 **Lower Kinsham** Herefs
44 C2 **Lower Knapp** Somset
109 G5 **Lower Knowle** Bristl
84 D2 **Lower Langford** N Som
502 C4 **Lower Largo** Fife
174 D1 **Lower Layham** Suffk
210 C5 **Lower Ledwyche** Shrops
273 F2 **Lower Leigh** Staffs
164 C3 **Lower Lemington** Gloucs
162 C3 **Lower Lode** Gloucs
39 H2 **Lower Lovacott** Devon
61 F4 **Lower Loxhore** Devon
134 D1 **Lower Lydbrook** Gloucs
185 H1 **Lower Lye** Herefs
106 D2 **Lower Machen** Newpt
159 F3 **Lower Maes-coed** Herefs
499 F5 **Lower Mains** Clacks
48 D3 **Lower Mannington** Dorset
68 B5 **Lower Marsh** Somset
86 D6 **Lower Marston** Somset
134 C4 **Lower Meend** Gloucs
8 C2 **Lower Menadue** Cnwll
64 C5 **Lower Merridge** Somset
166 B1 **Lower Middleton Cheney** Nhants
275 E5 **Lower Midway** Derbys
7 G6 **Lower Mill** Cnwll
542 A6 **Lower Milovaig** Highld
85 F5 **Lower Milton** Somset
112 B1 **Lower Moor** Wilts
189 E5 **Lower Moor** Worcs
110 A1 **Lower Morton** S Glos
288 D3 **Lower Mountain** Flints
145 E3 **Lower Nazeing** Essex
211 E1 **Lower Netchwood** Shrops
133 F5 **Lower New Inn** Torfn
3 E3 **Lower Ninnes** Cnwll
273 F3 **Lower Nobut** Staffs
142 B5 **Lower North Dean** Bucks
190 C2 **Lower Norton** Warwks
68 B5 **Lower Nyland** Dorset
106 D2 **Lower Ochrwyth** Caerph
45 G4 **Lower Odcombe** Somset
164 C4 **Lower Oddington** Gloucs
545 J2 **Lower Ollach** Highld
115 F6 **Lower Padworth** W Berk
106 C5 **Lower Penarth** V Glam
236 C5 **Lower Penn** Staffs
50 B6 **Lower Pennington** Hants
338 D4 **Lower Penwortham** Lancs
311 E5 **Lower Peover** Ches
312 A5 **Lower Pexhill** Ches
295 E2 **Lower Pilsley** Derbys
577 J7 **Lower Pitkerrie** Highld
326 D2 **Lower Place** Rochdl
141 F2 **Lower Pollicot** Bucks
105 H6 **Lower Porthkerry** V Glam
8 C3 **Lower Porthpean** Cnwll
190 B5 **Lower Quinton** Warwks
184 D4 **Lower Rabber** Powys
133 E4 **Lower Race** Torfn
140 B5 **Lower Radley** Oxon
98 C1 **Lower Rainham** Medway
71 G5 **Lower Ratley** Hants
174 D2 **Lower Raydon** Suffk
136 B1 **Lower Rea** Gloucs
28 D2 **Lower Ridge** Devon
269 F3 **Lower Ridge** Shrops
63 G4 **Lower Roadwater** Somset
7 E3 **Lower Rose** Cnwll
48 C4 **Lower Row** Dorset
352 C2 **Lower Salter** Lancs
187 F2 **Lower Sapey** Worcs
111 H3 **Lower Seagry** Wilts
145 G2 **Lower Sheering** Essex
194 D6 **Lower Shelton** Beds
116 C4 **Lower Shiplake** Oxon
192 A2 **Lower Shuckburgh** Warwks
103 F3 **Lower Sketty** Swans
550 B1 **Lower Slackbuie** Highld
72 A4 **Lower Slackstead** Hants
164 B5 **Lower Slaughter** Gloucs
150 D5 **Lower Solva** Pembks
343 E5 **Lower Soothill** Kirk
135 F2 **Lower Soudley** Gloucs
161 G1 **Lower Southfield** Herefs
111 G3 **Lower Stanton St Quintin** Wilts
215 E4 **Lower Stoke** Covtry
122 C4 **Lower Stoke** Medway
169 H3 **Lower Stondon** Beds
135 F6 **Lower Stone** Gloucs
237 G4 **Lower Stonnall** Staffs
248 C6 **Lower Stow Bedon** Norfk
45 E5 **Lower Stratton** Somset
113 E2 **Lower Stratton** Swindn
58 A4 **Lower Street** E Susx
256 B2 **Lower Street** Norfk
261 G5 **Lower Street** Norfk
176 C3 **Lower Street** Suffk
199 F4 **Lower Street** Suffk
162 D1 **Lower Strensham** Worcs
310 C3 **Lower Stretton** Warrtn
30 B3 **Lower Strode** Dorset
87 F3 **Lower Studley** Wilts
118 B6 **Lower Sunbury** Surrey
169 F4 **Lower Sundon** Beds
86 C1 **Lower Swainswick** BaNES
51 E3 **Lower Swanwick** Hants
164 B4 **Lower Swell** Gloucs
119 H5 **Lower Sydenham** Gt Lon
165 F2 **Lower Tadmarton** Oxon
27 H2 **Lower Tale** Devon
249 G5 **Lower Tasburgh** Norfk
273 F2 **Lower Tean** Staffs
192 B5 **Lower Thorpe** Nhants
289 F6 **Lower Threapwood** Ches
251 E5 **Lower Thurlton** Norfk
351 F3 **Lower Thurnham** Lancs
274 C2 **Lower Thurvaston** Derbys
209 H4 **Lower Todding** Herefs
543 J4 **Lower Tote** Highld
4 C3 **Lowertown** Cnwll
8 D1 **Lowertown** Cnwll
24 C6 **Lowertown** Devon
42 D5 **Lower Town** Devon
187 E6 **Lower Town** Herefs
3 d1 **Lower Town** IoS
151 G2 **Lower Town** Pembks
188 C3 **Lower Town** Worcs
16 D3 **Lower Trebullett** Cnwll
136 B2 **Lower Tuffley** Gloucs
49 E3 **Lower Turmer** Hants
39 E4 **Lower Twitchen** Devon
122 C6 **Lower Twydall** Medway
191 E5 **Lower Tysoe** Warwks
72 D6 **Lower Upham** Hants
122 B5 **Lower Upnor** Medway
64 B4 **Lower Vexford** Somset
141 G4 **Lower Wainhill** Oxon
310 C2 **Lower Walton** Warrtn
113 F3 **Lower Wanborough** Swindn
64 B3 **Lower Weacombe** Somset
167 G2 **Lower Weald** M Keyn
27 E5 **Lower Wear** Devon
84 D4 **Lower Weare** Somset
192 D3 **Lower Weedon** Nhants
185 E5 **Lower Welson** Herefs
67 F1 **Lower Westholme** Somset
366 D5 **Lower Westhouse** N York
162 D2 **Lower Westmancote** Worcs
86 C1 **Lower Weston** BaNES
47 F4 **Lower Whatcombe** Dorset
86 C5 **Lower Whatley** Somset
603 K6 **Lower Whitehall** Ork
310 C4 **Lower Whitley** Ches
135 G5 **Lower Wick** Gloucs
188 B4 **Lower Wick** Worcs
73 F1 **Lower Wield** Hants
57 F4 **Lower Willingdon** E Susx
311 G5 **Lower Withington** Ches
188 D4 **Lower Wolverton** Worcs
559 F6 **Lower Woodend** Abers
116 D2 **Lower Woodend** Bucks
70 C2 **Lower Woodford** Wilts
15 E5 **Lower Woodley** Cnwll
144 B3 **Lower Woodside** Herts
67 H4 **Lower Woolston** Somset
15 E6 **Lower Woon** Cnwll
30 D2 **Lower Wraxall** Dorset
67 G2 **Lower Wraxall** Somset
87 E2 **Lower Wraxall** Wilts
289 G6 **Lower Wych** Ches
187 H6 **Lower Wyche** Worcs
342 C4 **Lower Wyke** Brad
60 C5 **Lower Yelland** Devon
68 C3 **Lower Zeals** Wilts
395 F1 **Lowes Barn** Dur
241 F3 **Lowesby** Leics
227 G1 **Lowestoft** Suffk
388 D5 **Loweswater** Cumb
394 D4 **Low Etherley** Dur
405 G3 **Low Fell** Gatesd
314 D2 **Lowfield** Sheff
77 E1 **Lowfield Heath** W Susx
342 D2 **Low Fold** Leeds
51 E2 **Lowford** Hants
280 C5 **Low Fulney** Lincs
386 B3 **Low Garth** N York
370 B6 **Low Gate** N York
403 F2 **Low Gate** Nthumb
379 H5 **Lowgill** Cumb
352 D2 **Lowgill** Lancs
370 A5 **Low Grantley** N York
355 H3 **Low Green** N York
199 H2 **Low Green** Suffk
404 D2 **Low Greenside** Gatesd
212 B4 **Low Habberley** Worcs
66 C4 **Low Ham** Somset
443 H4 **Low Hauxley** Nthumb
387 F3 **Low Hawsker** N York
401 E5 **Low Hesket** Cumb
442 D5 **Low Hesleyhurst** Nthumb
236 D4 **Low Hill** Wolves
359 E1 **Low Hutton** N York
364 C2 **Lowick** Cumb
218 D3 **Lowick** Nhants
454 C2 **Lowick** Nthumb
364 C2 **Lowick Bridge** Cumb
364 C2 **Lowick Green** Cumb
391 E6 **Low Knipe** Cumb
355 G2 **Low Laithe** N York
329 F4 **Low Laithes** Barns
133 E5 **Lowlands** Torfn
312 D2 **Low Leighton** Derbys
389 E4 **Low Lorton** Cumb
410 D5 **Low Mains** D & G
373 F4 **Low Marishes** N York
317 F6 **Low Marnham** Notts
386 A5 **Low Mill** N York
342 C4 **Low Moor** Brad
340 A1 **Low Moor** Lancs
406 A5 **Low Moorsley** Sundld
388 A5 **Low Moresby** Cumb
372 C1 **Lowna** N York
365 F3 **Low Newton** Cumb
455 G5 **Low Newton-by-the-Sea** Nthumb
527 G5 **Lownie Moor** Angus
451 G2 **Lowood** Border
404 C2 **Low Prudhoe** Nthumb
332 C1 **Low Risby** N Linc
399 F6 **Low Row** Cumb
401 G2 **Low Row** Cumb
382 A5 **Low Row** N York
354 C5 **Low Snaygill** N York
214 B6 **Lowsonford** Warwks
248 D3 **Low Street** Norfk
121 G4 **Low Street** Thurr
249 G5 **Low Tharston** Norfk
391 E5 **Lowther** Cumb
399 G1 **Lowthertown** D & G
37 F5 **Lowtherville** IoW
405 E2 **Low Thornley** Gatesd
360 D2 **Lowthorpe** E R Yk
43 G4 **Lowton** Somset
325 E5 **Lowton** Wigan
325 E5 **Lowton Common** Wigan
325 E5 **Lowton Heath** Wigan
325 E5 **Lowton St Mary's** Wigan
486 D2 **Low Torry** Fife
235 G6 **Low Town** Shrops
320 A5 **Low Toynton** Lincs
329 G4 **Low Valley** Barns
486 C2 **Low Valleyfield** Fife
376 B2 **Low Walton** Cumb
467 H4 **Low Waters** S Lans
404 C3 **Low Westwood** Dur
400 B4 **Low Whinnow** Cumb
382 B5 **Low Whita** N York
364 D3 **Low Wood** Cumb
384 B2 **Low Worsall** N York
42 B4 **Loxbeare** Devon
120 B2 **Loxford** Gt Lon
75 G2 **Loxhill** Surrey
61 F4 **Loxhore** Devon
61 F4 **Loxhore Cott** Devon
314 C2 **Loxley** Sheff
190 D4 **Loxley** Warwks
273 G3 **Loxley Green** Staffs
161 G1 **Loxter** Herefs
84 C3 **Loxton** N Som
75 G3 **Loxwood** W Susx
145 H2 **Loyter's Green** Essex
99 F2 **Loyterton** Kent
213 G2 **Lozells** Birm
211 E4 **Lubberland** Shrops
575 H3 **Lubcroy** Highld
217 E2 **Lubenham** Leics
586 C4 **Lubinvullin** Highld
144 D4 **Lucas End** Herts
339 E5 **Lucas Green** Lancs
93 F3 **Lucas Green** Surrey
62 D3 **Luccombe** Somset
37 F4 **Luccombe Village** IoW
455 F3 **Lucker** Nthumb
17 E4 **Luckett** Cnwll
173 G3 **Lucking Street** Essex
111 E3 **Luckington** Wilts
514 C5 **Lucklawhill** Fife
62 D4 **Luckwell Bridge** Somset
186 A2 **Lucton** Herefs
590 F5 **Ludag** W Isls
334 C5 **Ludborough** Lincs
12 B2 **Ludbrook** Devon
126 C2 **Ludchurch** Pembks
341 G4 **Luddenden** Calder
341 G5 **Luddenden Foot** Calder
365 F1 **Ludderburn** Cumb
97 G1 **Luddesdown** Kent
332 A1 **Luddington** N Linc
190 B4 **Luddington** Warwks
219 G3 **Luddington in the Brook** Nhants
319 F2 **Ludford** Lincs
210 C5 **Ludford** Shrops
141 E1 **Ludgershall** Bucks
89 G4 **Ludgershall** Wilts
3 F3 **Ludgvan** Cnwll
256 D6 **Ludham** Norfk
210 B5 **Ludlow** Shrops
335 E5 **Ludney** Lincs
44 D5 **Ludney** Somset
161 F2 **Ludstock** Herefs
236 B6 **Ludstone** Shrops
69 F5 **Ludwell** Wilts
395 H1 **Ludworth** Dur
170 C4 **Luffenhall** Herts
23 G4 **Luffincott** Devon
45 G4 **Lufton** Somset
446 B5 **Lugar** E Ayrs
472 A6 **Lugate** Border
490 A5 **Luggate Burn** E Loth
186 A2 **Lugg Green** Herefs
485 F5 **Luggiebank** N Lans
309 H3 **Lugsdale** Halton
466 B4 **Lugton** E Ayrs
160 D1 **Lugwardine** Herefs
545 K4 **Luib** Highld
509 G4 **Luib** Stirlg
159 H1 **Lulham** Herefs
238 D2 **Lullington** Derbys
86 D4 **Lullington** Somset
85 F1 **Lulsgate Bottom** N Som
187 G3 **Lulsley** Worcs
33 E3 **Lulworth Camp** Dorset
328 B2 **Lumb** Kirk
340 B6 **Lumb** Lancs
17 G4 **Lumburn** Devon
341 E5 **Lumbutts** Calder
344 B3 **Lumby** N York
52 D3 **Lumley** W Susx
405 G4 **Lumley Thicks** Dur
484 C5 **Lumloch** E Duns
555 G4 **Lumphanan** Abers
487 G1 **Lumphinnans** Fife
491 G6 **Lumsdaine** Border
558 B5 **Lumsden** Abers
529 E4 **Lunan** Angus
527 G4 **Lunanhead** Angus
512 C4 **Luncarty** P & K
360 B5 **Lund** E R Yk
345 F3 **Lund** N York
609 H4 **Lund** Shet
513 G2 **Lundie** Angus
502 C4 **Lundin Links** Fife
329 F3 **Lundwood** Barns
226 A1 **Lundy Green** Norfk
492 C3 **Lunga** Ag & B
607 G4 **Lunna** Shet
607 G4 **Lunnasting** Shet
607 G4 **Lunning** Shet
606 E3 **Lunnister** Shet
102 D4 **Lunnon** Swans
97 G3 **Lunsford** Kent
58 B4 **Lunsford's Cross** E Susx
323 F4 **Lunt** Sefton
185 G3 **Luntley** Herefs
309 H2 **Lunts Heath** Halton
238 A1 **Lupin** Staffs
28 C1 **Luppitt** Devon
12 C2 **Lupridge** Devon
343 F6 **Lupset** Wakefd
366 B3 **Lupton** Cumb
75 E4 **Lurgashall** W Susx
42 B5 **Lurley** Devon
320 B6 **Lusby** Lincs
234 C5 **Lushcott** Shrops
11 G3 **Luson** Devon
495 H6 **Luss** Ag & B
479 G4 **Lussagiven** Ag & B
542 D5 **Lusta** Highld
19 G1 **Lustleigh** Devon
19 G1 **Lustleigh Cleave** Devon
186 B2 **Luston** Herefs
68 A3 **Lusty** Somset
540 C6 **Luthermuir** Abers
514 A6 **Luthrie** Fife
212 D3 **Lutley** Dudley
20 C2 **Luton** Devon
28 A2 **Luton** Devon
169 G5 **Luton** Luton
98 B1 **Luton** Medway
38 B4 **Lutsford** Devon
216 B2 **Lutterworth** Leics
18 C6 **Lutton** Devon
19 E5 **Lutton** Devon
281 F4 **Lutton** Lincs
219 G2 **Lutton** Nhants
281 F5 **Lutton Gowts** Lincs
41 F4 **Lutworthy** Devon
63 F4 **Luxborough** Somset
161 F5 **Luxley** Gloucs
96 B2 **Luxted** Gt Lon
43 H5 **Luxton** Devon
8 D2 **Luxulyan** Cnwll
327 E4 **Luzley** Tamesd
326 D3 **Luzley Brook** Oldham
45 G5 **Lyatts** Somset
583 H2 **Lybster** Highld
134 D1 **Lydbrook** Gloucs
209 G2 **Lydbury North** Shrops
61 G4 **Lydcott** Devon
81 F5 **Lydd** Kent
83 E1 **Lydden** Kent
101 F2 **Lydden** Kent
242 B5 **Lyddington** Rutlnd
81 G6 **Lydd-on-Sea** Kent
233 F4 **Lyde** Shrops
64 B5 **Lydeard St Lawrence** Somset
186 C6 **Lyde Cross** Herefs
92 B3 **Lyde Green** Hants
110 B4 **Lyde Green** S Glos
24 D6 **Lydford** Devon
67 F3 **Lydford Fair Place** Somset
67 F3 **Lydford-on-Fosse** Somset
341 E4 **Lydgate** Calder
327 E4 **Lydgate** Oldham
209 F1 **Lydham** Shrops
112 C2 **Lydiard Green** Wilts
112 C2 **Lydiard Millicent** Wilts
112 C2 **Lydiard Plain** Wilts
112 D3 **Lydiard Tregoze** Swindn
323 G4 **Lydiate** Sefton
213 E4 **Lydiate Ash** Worcs
46 D2 **Lydlinch** Dorset
44 D6 **Lydmarsh** Somset
135 E4 **Lydney** Gloucs
126 B5 **Lydstep** Pembks
212 D3 **Lye** Dudley
85 E2 **Lye Cross** N Som
142 D4 **Lye Green** Bucks
78 C3 **Lye Green** E Susx
190 B1 **Lye Green** Warwks
87 E3 **Lye Green** Wilts
211 H5 **Lye Head** Worcs
85 F2 **Lye Hole** N Som
78 C2 **Lyewood Common** E Susx
139 F6 **Lyford** Oxon
82 B2 **Lymbridge Green** Kent
312 B5 **Lyme Green** Ches
29 F4 **Lyme Regis** Dorset
438 D4 **Lymiecleuch** Border
82 C2 **Lyminge** Kent
50 B6 **Lymington** Hants
54 B4 **Lyminster** W Susx
310 D2 **Lymm** Warrtn
50 A6 **Lymore** Hants
81 H2 **Lympne** Kent
84 B4 **Lympsham** Somset
27 F6 **Lympstone** Devon
61 H2 **Lynbridge** Devon
90 D5 **Lynch** Hants
63 E2 **Lynch** Somset
535 L2 **Lynchat** Highld
209 G2 **Lynchgate** Shrops
90 D5 **Lynch Hill** Hants
117 F3 **Lynch Hill** Slough
50 B3 **Lyndhurst** Hants
242 B4 **Lyndon** Rutlnd
214 A2 **Lyndon Green** Birm
449 H1 **Lyne** Border
93 H1 **Lyne** Surrey
270 A3 **Lyneal** Shrops
270 B3 **Lyneal Mill** Shrops
270 A3 **Lyneal Wood** Shrops
161 E3 **Lyne Down** Herefs
164 D5 **Lyneham** Oxon
112 B4 **Lyneham** Wilts
431 F1 **Lynemouth** Nthumb
549 J5 **Lyne of Gorthleck** Highld
556 D2 **Lyne of Skene** Abers
600 E6 **Lyness** Ork
449 H2 **Lyne Station** Border
223 G1 **Lynford** Norfk
255 E4 **Lyng** Norfk
44 C2 **Lyng** Somset
256 B3 **Lyngate** Norfk
256 C4 **Lyngate** Norfk
44 A2 **Lyngford** Somset
61 H2 **Lynmouth** Devon
237 G4 **Lynn** Staffs
236 A1 **Lynn** Wrekin
465 F5 **Lynn Glen** N Ayrs
439 F2 **Lynnwood** Border
100 C6 **Lynsore Bottom** Kent
99 E2 **Lynsted** Kent
23 E1 **Lynstone** Cnwll
61 H2 **Lynton** Devon
550 F7 **Lynwilg** Highld
163 E5 **Lynworth** Gloucs
406 B5 **Lyons** Sundld
31 F1 **Lyon's Gate** Dorset
248 B2 **Lyon's Green** Norfk
147 E1 **Lyons Hall** Essex

185 F3 Lyonshall Herefs
136 D3 Lypiatt Gloucs
188 C3 Lyppard Grange Worcs
48 A5 Lytchett Matravers Dorset
48 A6 Lytchett Minster Dorset
589 H4 Lyth Highld
337 G4 Lytham Lancs
337 F3 Lytham Moss Lancs
337 F4 Lytham St Anne's Lancs
234 B3 Lythbank Shrops
386 D2 Lythe N York
601 H7 Lythes Ork

M

5 E2 Mabe Burnthouse Cnwll
97 E6 Mabledon Kent
321 F3 Mablethorpe Lincs
312 A5 Macclesfield Ches
312 C5 Macclesfield Forest Ches
570 C2 Macduff Abers
500 D4 Macedonia Fife
175 E1 Mace Green Suffk
468 B4 Machan S Lans
457 E5 Macharioch Ag & B
106 D2 Machen Caerph
263 E5 Machrie N Ayrs
456 C2 Machrihanish Ag & B
263 E5 Machroes Gwynd
229 G4 Machynlleth Powys
128 D5 Machynys Carmth
75 G4 Mackerel's Common W Susx
143 H1 Mackerye End Herts
43 G6 Mackham Devon
115 F2 Mackney Oxon
440 B2 Mackside Border
275 E2 Mackworth C Derb
489 E5 Macmerry E Loth
511 G5 Madderty P & K
88 C6 Maddington Wilts
486 B4 Maddiston Falk
125 G2 Maddox Moor Pembks
54 A2 Madehurst W Susx
291 F6 Madeley Staffs
235 F4 Madeley Wrekin
291 F5 Madeley Heath Staffs
213 E4 Madeley Heath Worcs
271 H1 Madeley Park Wood Staffs
16 D4 Maders Cnwll
43 F5 Madford Devon
197 E2 Madingley Cambs
68 C5 Madjeston Dorset
159 H2 Madley Herefs
188 B5 Madresfield Worcs
2 D3 Madron Cnwll
303 G4 Maenaddwyn IoA
132 B4 Maenclochog Pembks
105 G4 Maendy V Glam
5 E3 Maenporth Cnwll
265 F1 Maentwrog Gwynd
180 A3 Maen-y-Groes Cerdgn
38 B6 Maer Cnwll
272 A2 Maer Staffs
155 F5 Maerdy Carmth
287 E6 Maerdy Conwy
131 F5 Maerdy Rhondd
205 F3 Maes-bangor Cerdgn
269 E5 Maesbrook Shrops
269 F4 Maesbury Shrops
269 F5 Maesbury Marsh Shrops
304 C5 Maesgeirchen Gwynd
107 E2 Maes-glas Newpt
152 D5 Maesgwynne Carmth
288 A2 Maeshafn Denbgs
179 H5 Maes llyn Cerdgn
185 G3 Maesmynis Powys
307 H4 Maes Pennant Flints
104 C1 Maesteg Brdgnd
129 E1 Maesybont Carmth
105 H2 Maesycoed Rhondd
154 C1 Maesycrugiau Carmth
132 C6 Maesycwmmer Caerph
288 B2 Maes-y-Dre Flints
132 D2 Maesygwartha Mons
231 F5 Maesypandy Powys
208 A1 Maesyrhandir Powys
145 H3 Magdalen Laver Essex
568 E6 Maggieknockater Moray
171 G4 Maggots End Essex
57 G2 Magham Down E Susx
323 G4 Maghull Sefton
108 D2 Magor Mons
225 E4 Magpie Green Suffk
119 F3 Maida Vale Gt Lon
77 E2 Maidenbower W Susx
68 D2 Maiden Bradley Wilts
20 C4 Maidencombe Torbay
201 F6 Maidenhall Suffk
29 E3 Maidenhayne Devon
85 G1 Maiden Head N Som
117 E3 Maidenhead W & M
117 E3 Maidenhead Court W & M
405 E5 Maiden Law Dur
31 E3 Maiden Newton Dorset
486 C3 Maidenpark Falk
432 B3 Maidens S Ayrs
202 B5 Maidensgrave Suffk
117 E5 Maiden's Green Br For
116 B2 Maidensgrove Oxon
443 G5 Maiden's Hall Nthumb
15 G4 Maidenwell Cnwll
320 B4 Maidenwell Lincs
125 G5 Maiden Wells Pembks
192 C4 Maidford Nhants
167 E2 Maids Moreton Bucks
98 B3 Maidstone Kent
217 F4 Maidwell Nhants
605 H5 Mail Shet
609 J4 Mailand Shet
470 D6 Mailingsland Border
107 F2 Maindee Newpt
106 C4 Maindy Cardif
445 E5 Mainholm S Ayrs
388 C5 Mains Cumb
395 G3 Mainsforth Dur
515 E3 Mains of Ardestie Angus
528 B4 Mains of Balgavies Angus
528 B2 Mains of Balhall Angus
527 E4 Mains of Ballindarg Angus
566 F7 Mains of Clunas Highld
551 L3 Mains of Dalvey Highld
540 D3 Mains of Dellavaird Abers
556 D5 Mains of Drum Abers
570 F5 Mains of Fedderate Abers
557 F2 Mains of Grandhome C Aber
514 A3 Mains of Gray C Dund
571 J6 Mains of Kinmundy Abers
561 F3 Mains of Leask Abers
528 B3 Mains of Melgund Angus
524 D3 Mains of Orchil P & K
540 C5 Mains of Thornton Abers
529 F3 Mains of Usan Angus
398 A3 Mainsriddle D & G
209 E2 Mainstone Shrops
162 B5 Maisemore Gloucs
213 G4 Major's Green Worcs
294 D6 Makeney Derbys
452 C3 Makerstoun Border
592 D2 Malacleit W Isls
12 B5 Malborough Devon
313 E3 Malcoff Derbys
94 D2 Malden Rushett Gt Lon
147 H3 Maldon Essex
233 G3 Malehurst Shrops
354 B2 Malham N York
543 H4 Maligar Highld
314 C2 Malinbridge Sheff
235 F3 Malinslee Wrekin
291 F3 Malkin's Bank Ches
531 J3 Mallaig Highld
531 J3 Mallaig Bheag Highld
531 J3 Mallaigmore Highld
470 C1 Malleny Mills C Edin
171 G4 Mallows Green Essex
282 D2 Malltraeth IoA
230 D2 Mallwyd Gwynd
111 G2 Malmesbury Wilts
62 B2 Malmsmead Devon
289 G5 Malpas Ches
7 F5 Malpas Cnwll
107 E1 Malpas Newpt
115 G5 Malpas W Berk
161 G4 Malswick Gloucs
320 B3 Maltby Lincs
330 B6 Maltby Rothm
384 D2 Maltby S on T
321 E3 Maltby le Marsh Lincs
199 E4 Malting End Suffk
99 E6 Maltman's Hill Kent
373 E5 Malton N York
188 A6 Malvern Common Worcs
188 A5 Malvern Link Worcs
161 H1 Malvern Wells Worcs
482 B2 Mambeg Ag & B
211 F5 Mamble Worcs
133 F4 Mamhilad Mons
5 E3 Manaccan Cnwll
11 E2 Manadon C Plym
232 B4 Manafon Powys
595 J5 Manais W Isls
19 G1 Manaton Devon
320 C2 Manby Lincs
239 E5 Mancetter Warwks
326 B5 Manchester Manch
288 D1 Mancot Flints
288 D1 Mancot Royal Flints
533 L2 Mandally Highld
221 G2 Manea Cambs
237 H5 Maney Birm
383 F2 Manfield N York
606 D3 Mangaster Shet
30 B3 Mangerton Dorset
110 B4 Mangotsfield S Glos
169 G5 Mangrove Green Herts
596 C1 Mangurstadh W Isls
4 C2 Manhay Cnwll
178 D4 Manian-Fawr Pembks
595 J5 Manish W Isls
341 F5 Mankinholes Calder
309 H5 Manley Ches
42 C5 Manley Devon
309 H5 Manley Common Ches
132 C4 Manmoel Caerph
516 B7 Mannal Ag & B
11 E2 Mannamead C Plym
486 D4 Mannerston Falk
88 D3 Manningford Abbots Wilts
88 D3 Manningford Bohune Wilts
88 D3 Manningford Bruce Wilts
342 B3 Manningham Brad
76 D4 Mannings Heath W Susx
48 C3 Mannington Dorset
175 E3 Manningtree Essex
557 G4 Mannofield C Aber
126 B5 Manorbier Pembks
126 A5 Manorbier Newton Pembks
11 E4 Manor Bourne Devon
155 G4 Manordeilo Carmth
314 D2 Manor Estate Sheff
452 C3 Manorhill Border
281 F6 Manor Hill Corner Lincs
215 F3 Manor House Covtry
151 F2 Manorowen Pembks
355 G5 Manor Park Brad
141 H2 Manor Park Bucks
291 E1 Manor Park Ches
78 B5 Manor Park E Susx
120 B2 Manor Park Gt Lon
310 A3 Manor Park Halton
276 C3 Manor Park Notts
314 D2 Manor Park Sheff
117 G3 Manor Park Slough
6 C4 Manor Parsley Cnwll
77 E2 Manor Royal W Susx
173 E2 Man's Cross Essex
423 E3 Mansegate D & G
103 E4 Manselfield Swans
185 G6 Mansell Gamage Herefs
185 H5 Mansell Lacy Herefs
103 F2 Manselton Swans
366 B3 Mansergh Cumb
467 E2 Mansewood C Glas
434 C2 Mansfield E Ayrs
295 G2 Mansfield Notts
295 H2 Mansfield Woodhouse Notts
248 D4 Manson Green Norfk
364 C3 Mansriggs Cumb
47 F1 Manston Dorset
101 F2 Manston Kent
343 G3 Manston Leeds
48 B3 Manswood Dorset
243 F1 Manthorpe Lincs
278 C2 Manthorpe Lincs
142 C5 Mantles Green Bucks
332 C4 Manton N Linc
316 A4 Manton Notts
242 B4 Manton Rutlnd
113 E6 Manton Wilts
332 C3 Manton Warren N Linc
171 G4 Manuden Essex
146 A2 Manwood Green Essex
341 H2 Manywells Height Brad
67 H4 Maperton Somset
296 C2 Maplebeck Notts
143 E6 Maple Cross Herts
115 H4 Mapledurham Oxon
92 A4 Mapledurwell Hants
172 B2 Maple End Essex
76 C5 Maplehurst W Susx
293 G5 Mapleton Derbys
296 A6 Mapperley C Nott
295 E6 Mapperley Derbys
276 C1 Mapperley Park C Nott
30 C3 Mapperton Dorset
47 G5 Mapperton Dorset
189 G1 Mappleborough Green Warwks
361 G6 Mappleton E R Yk
329 E3 Mapplewell Barns
46 D3 Mappowder Dorset
596 F6 Màraig W Isls
7 F3 Marazanvose Cnwll
3 F3 Marazion Cnwll
597 L4 Marbhig W Isls
290 B5 Marbury Ches
245 F5 March Cambs
436 C2 March S Lans
139 H5 Marcham Oxon
270 D4 Marchamley Shrops
270 D3 Marchamley Wood Shrops
274 A3 Marchington Staffs
273 H4 Marchington Woodlands Staffs
289 E5 Marchwiel Wrexhm
50 C2 Marchwood Hants
105 E6 Marcross V Glam
528 B3 Marcus Angus
186 C5 Marden Herefs
98 A6 Marden Kent
431 F5 Marden N Tyne
88 C3 Marden Wilts
146 B4 Marden Ash Essex
98 A6 Marden Beech Kent
78 B3 Marden's Hill E Susx
98 B6 Marden Thorn Kent
170 C6 Mardleybury Herts
209 E3 Mardu Shrops
133 F1 Mardy Mons
269 E3 Mardy Shrops
241 F3 Marefield Leics
300 A2 Mareham le Fen Lincs
320 A6 Mareham on the Hill Lincs
294 D5 Marehay Derbys
75 H6 Marehill W Susx
78 B5 Maresfield E Susx
78 B5 Maresfield Park E Susx
348 B4 Marfleet C KuH
289 E3 Marford Wrexhm
104 B2 Margam Neath
68 D6 Margaret Marsh Dorset
146 B2 Margaret Roding Essex
146 D4 Margaretting Essex
146 D4 Margaretting Tye Essex
101 F1 Margate Kent
95 E4 Margery Surrey
461 E3 Margnaheglish N Ayrs
385 H1 Margrove Park R & Cl
247 E3 Marham Norfk
23 E2 Marhamchurch Cnwll
243 G4 Marholm C Pete
307 F4 Marian Flints
307 F4 Marian Cwm Denbgs
304 C3 Mariandyrys IoA
304 B3 Marian-glas IoA
41 E3 Mariansleigh Devon
123 E5 Marine Town Kent
556 C3 Marionburgh Abers
543 H4 Marishader Highld
424 B3 Marjoriebanks D & G
84 C5 Mark Somset
96 C6 Markbeech Kent
321 E4 Markby Lincs
84 C5 Mark Causeway Somset
78 D3 Mark Cross E Susx
275 E2 Markeaton C Derb
239 G4 Market Bosworth Leics
243 G2 Market Deeping Lincs
271 F3 Market Drayton Shrops
217 F2 Market Harborough Leics
88 B4 Market Lavington Wilts
242 B1 Market Overton Rutlnd
319 E2 Market Rasen Lincs
319 G4 Market Stainton Lincs
315 H6 Market Warsop Notts
359 G6 Market Weighton E R Yk
224 C4 Market Weston Suffk
240 A2 Markfield Leics
145 G2 Mark Hall North Essex
145 G2 Mark Hall South Essex
132 C4 Markham Caerph
316 D5 Markham Moor Notts
501 F4 Markinch Fife
356 B1 Markington N York
325 F3 Markland Hill Bolton
489 H4 Markle E Loth
86 B2 Marksbury BaNES
36 D2 Mark's Corner IoW
120 C1 Marks Gate Gt Lon
174 B5 Marks Tey Essex
10 C2 Markwell Cnwll
143 F1 Markyate Herts
326 C2 Marland Rochdl
160 A4 Marlas Herefs
162 A1 Marl Bank Worcs
113 E6 Marlborough Wilts
186 C4 Marlbrook Herefs
213 E5 Marlbrook Worcs
189 G4 Marlcliff Warwks
20 B5 Marldon Devon
57 F1 Marle Green E Susx
162 D5 Marle Hill Gloucs
202 C3 Marlesford Suffk
100 C5 Marley Kent
101 F5 Marley Kent
290 B5 Marley Green Ches
74 D3 Marley Heights W Susx
405 F3 Marley Hill Gatesd
406 B3 Marley Pots Sundld
249 F3 Marlingford Norfk
124 C3 Marloes Pembks
116 D2 Marlow Bucks
209 G4 Marlow Herefs
116 D2 Marlow Bottom Bucks
116 D2 Marlow Common Bucks
96 B5 Marlpit Hill Kent
83 B4 Marlpits E Susx
295 E6 Marlpool Derbys
68 C6 Marnhull Dorset
569 K5 Marnoch Abers
485 E6 Marnock N Lans
312 B2 Marple Stockp
312 C2 Marple Bridge Stockp
312 C2 Marpleridge Stockp
330 B3 Marr Donc
582 D6 Marrel Highld
89 F2 Marr Green Wilts
382 C5 Marrick N York
607 H5 Marrister Shet
127 E3 Marros Carmth
327 G2 Marsden Kirk
406 B2 Marsden S Tyne
340 D2 Marsden Height Lancs
368 A2 Marsett N York
341 G2 Marsh Brad
141 H3 Marsh Bucks
44 A5 Marsh Devon
327 H1 Marsh Kirk
475 E3 Marshall Meadows Nthumb
309 H1 Marshall's Cross St Hel
66 D3 Marshall's Elm Somset
143 H1 Marshalls Heath Herts
29 G2 Marshalsea Dorset
143 H3 Marshalswick Herts
255 G3 Marsham Norfk
352 B4 Marshaw Lancs
140 C5 Marsh Baldon Oxon
90 C1 Marsh Benham W Berk
101 F4 Marshborough Kent
210 A2 Marshbrook Shrops
335 E5 Marshchapel Lincs
109 G3 Marsh Common S Glos
162 B2 Marsh End Worcs
107 E3 Marshfield Newpt
110 D5 Marshfield S Glos
290 D3 Marshfield Bank Ches
22 C4 Marshgate Cnwll
114 A6 Marsh Gate W Berk
166 D5 Marsh Gibbon Bucks
309 H4 Marsh Green Ches
27 G4 Marsh Green Devon
96 B6 Marsh Green Kent
291 H3 Marsh Green Staffs
324 C3 Marsh Green Wigan
235 E2 Marsh Green Wrekin
351 G4 Marsh Houses Lancs
245 H3 Marshland St James Norfk
315 E4 Marsh Lane Derbys
134 D3 Marsh Lane Gloucs
64 C4 Marsh Mills Somset
144 B3 Marshmoor Herts
100 D2 Marshside Kent
259 F3 Marsh Side Norfk
337 G6 Marshside Sefton
63 F3 Marsh Street Somset
29 G3 Marshwood Dorset
382 D4 Marske N York
397 F5 Marske-by-the-Sea R & Cl
310 D4 Marston Ches
185 G3 Marston Herefs
297 G6 Marston Lincs
140 B3 Marston Oxon
236 B2 Marston Staffs
272 D4 Marston Staffs
215 G4 Marston Warwks
238 B6 Marston Warwks
87 H3 Marston Wilts
86 D6 Marston Bigot Somset
191 H3 Marston Doles Warwks
86 D5 Marston Gate Somset
214 B2 Marston Green Solhll
137 H5 Marston Hill Wilts
215 F2 Marston Jabbett Warwks
67 F5 Marston Magna Somset
138 A5 Marston Meysey Wilts
274 A2 Marston Montgomery Derbys
168 D1 Marston Moretaine Beds
274 C4 Marston on Dove Derbys
192 B6 Marston St Lawrence Nhants
186 D3 Marston Stannett Herefs
217 E2 Marston Trussell Nhants
160 D6 Marstow Herefs
142 C2 Marsworth Bucks
89 G2 Marten Wilts
311 G4 Marthall Ches
257 E6 Martham Norfk
366 C1 Marthwaite Cumb
70 B6 Martin Hants
83 F1 Martin Kent
299 E2 Martin Lincs
299 G1 Martin Lincs
390 C6 Martindale Cumb
299 F2 Martin Dales Lincs
70 B5 Martin Drove End Hants
61 G2 Martinhoe Devon
61 G2 Martinhoe Cross Devon
188 C3 Martin Hussingtree Worcs
83 F1 Martin Mill Kent
299 G2 Martin Moor Lincs
310 C2 Martinscroft Warrtn
291 G2 Martin's Moss Ches
31 E5 Martinstown or Winterborne St Martin Dorset
202 B5 Martlesham Suffk
202 A5 Martlesham Heath Suffk
126 A2 Martletwy Pembks
187 H3 Martley Worcs
66 C6 Martock Somset
311 H6 Marton Ches
364 B4 Marton Cumb
348 C2 Marton E R Yk
317 F3 Marton Lincs
385 E1 Marton Middsb
357 E2 Marton N York
372 D3 Marton N York
233 E4 Marton Shrops
270 A5 Marton Shrops
215 G6 Marton Warwks
372 A6 Marton Abbey N York
310 C6 Marton Green Ches
396 C6 Marton Grove Middsb
372 A6 Marton-in-the-Forest N York
370 D5 Marton-le-Moor N York
215 G6 Marton Moor Warwks
337 F3 Marton Moss Side Bpool
94 B3 Martyr's Green Surrey
72 D3 Martyr Worthy Hants
602 A7 Marwick Ork
60 D4 Marwood Devon
565 H6 Marybank Highld
566 C1 Marybank Highld
565 J5 Maryburgh Highld
10 D2 Maryfield Cnwll
474 B2 Marygold Border
484 B6 Maryhill C Glas
529 E1 Marykirk Abers
134 C3 Maryland Mons
324 D3 Marylebone Wigan
568 B8 Marypark Moray
388 B2 Maryport Cumb
408 C5 Maryport D & G
24 B6 Marystow Devon
18 B2 Mary Tavy Devon
527 E4 Maryton Angus
529 E3 Maryton Angus
555 G5 Marywell Abers
557 G5 Marywell Abers
528 D6 Marywell Angus
329 G6 Masbrough Rothm
125 G3 Mascle Bridge Pembks
369 H3 Masham N York
146 C2 Mashbury Essex
366 D4 Masongill N York
445 E5 Masonhill S Ayrs
315 F4 Mastin Moor Derbys
557 F3 Mastrick C Aber
189 G1 Matchborough Worcs
145 H2 Matching Essex
146 A2 Matching Green Essex
145 H2 Matching Tye Essex
429 G5 Matfen Nthumb
79 F1 Matfield Kent
109 F1 Mathern Mons
187 G5 Mathon Herefs
151 E3 Mathry Pembks
261 G5 Matlaske Norfk
327 E5 Matley Tamesd
294 B3 Matlock Derbys
294 C2 Matlock Bank Derbys
294 B3 Matlock Bath Derbys
294 B3 Matlock Bridge Derbys
294 C3 Matlock Cliff Derbys
294 B3 Matlock Dale Derbys
30 C4 Matravers Dorset
338 D1 Matshead Lancs
136 C2 Matson Gloucs
390 B5 Matterdale End Cumb
316 C2 Mattersey Notts
316 C1 Mattersey Thorpe Notts
116 D6 Matthewsgreen Wokham
92 B3 Mattingley Hants
248 D2 Mattishall Norfk
249 E2 Mattishall Burgh Norfk
445 G4 Mauchline E Ayrs
571 G6 Maud Abers
8 D1 Maudlin Cnwll
29 G1 Maudlin Dorset
53 F3 Maudlin W Susx
29 G1 Maudlin Cross Dorset
35 i6 Maufant Jersey
164 C5 Maugersbury Gloucs
322 h4 Maughold IoM
169 F2 Maulden Beds
380 A1 Maulds Meaburn Cumb
370 C2 Maunby N York
186 D4 Maund Bryan Herefs
43 E2 Maundown Somset
470 D2 Mauricewood Mdloth
251 F2 Mautby Norfk
237 G1 Mavesyn Ridware Staffs
300 C1 Mavis Enderby Lincs
398 D5 Mawbray Cumb
324 B2 Mawdesley Lancs
104 B3 Mawdlam Brdgnd
4 D4 Mawgan Cnwll
14 A5 Mawgan Porth Cnwll
291 E3 Maw Green Ches
6 D4 Mawla Cnwll
5 E3 Mawnan Cnwll
5 E3 Mawnan Smith Cnwll
330 D1 Mawson Green Donc
321 E5 Mawthorpe Lincs
243 G3 Maxey C Pete
214 C2 Maxstoke Warwks
82 B2 Maxted Street Kent
452 B3 Maxton Border
83 E2 Maxton Kent
423 G4 Maxwelltown D & G
432 C4 Maxwelston S Ayrs
23 F4 Maxworthy Cnwll
93 G3 Mayals Swans
291 H5 May Bank Staffs
432 D3 Maybole S Ayrs
93 H3 Maybury Surrey
50 C2 Maybush C Sotn
569 K6 Mayen Moray
213 F1 Mayer's Green Sandw
76 B2 Mayes Green Surrey
125 H4 Mayeston Pembks
119 F3 Mayfair Gt Lon
78 D4 Mayfield E Susx
588 E3 Mayfield Highld
471 G2 Mayfield Mdloth
431 E4 Mayfield Nthumb
293 F5 Mayfield Staffs
486 B6 Mayfield W Loth
93 G3 Mayford Surrey
161 F5 May Hill Gloucs
134 C2 May Hill Mons
103 F3 Mayhill Swans
148 B4 Mayland Essex
148 A4 Maylandsea Essex
78 D6 Maynard's Green E Susx
2 C4 Mayon Cnwll
96 C2 Maypole Gt Lon
3 d2 Maypole IoS
100 C2 Maypole Kent
120 D5 Maypole Kent
134 B1 Maypole Mons
174 C5 Maypole Green Essex
251 E5 Maypole Green Norfk
200 B3 Maypole Green Suffk
226 B6 Maypole Green Suffk
84 C2 May's Green N Som
116 B4 Mays Green Oxon
94 B3 May's Green Surrey
110 B3 Mayshill S Glos
328 B3 Maythorn Barns
296 C3 Maythorne Notts
605 G6 Maywick Shet
19 G3 Mead Devon
38 B4 Mead Devon
49 H5 Mead End Hants
52 B2 Mead End Hants
69 H5 Mead End Wilts
86 B3 Meadgate BaNES
141 H3 Meadle Bucks
488 B5 Meadowbank C Edin
310 C6 Meadowbank Ches
173 E1 Meadowend Essex
395 E2 Meadowfield Dur
465 E5 Meadowfoot N Ayrs
187 G3 Meadow Green Herefs
314 C3 Meadow Head Sheff
211 F1 Meadowley Shrops
489 E5 Meadowmill E Loth
276 C2 Meadows C Nott
233 F4 Meadowtown Shrops
57 G5 Meads E Susx
140 C6 Meadside Oxon
95 F5 Mead Vale Surrey
17 F2 Meadwell Devon
272 C2 Meaford Staffs
355 G3 Meagill N York
599 K8 Mealabost W Isls
599 J3 Mealabost Bhuirgh W Isls
596 B3 Mealasta W Isls
379 F5 Meal Bank Cumb
328 B3 Meal Hill Kirk
399 E5 Mealrigg Cumb
389 F1 Mealsgate Cumb
343 E2 Meanwood Leeds
353 G2 Mearbeck N York
66 D1 Meare Somset
44 B3 Meare Green Somset
44 C2 Meare Green Somset
86 B3 Mearns BaNES
466 D3 Mearns E Rens
194 A1 Mears Ashby Nhants
329 F3 Measborough Dike Barns
239 E2 Measham Leics
95 F6 Meath Green Surrey
365 F3 Meathop Cumb
347 G2 Meaux E R Yk
4 C5 Meaver Cnwll
18 B4 Meavy Devon
241 G6 Medbourne Leics
167 H2 Medbourne M Keyn
430 B5 Medburn Nthumb
38 C4 Meddon Devon
315 H6 Meden Vale Notts
96 C5 Medhurst Row Kent
300 B3 Medlam Lincs
338 B2 Medlar Lancs
233 H6 Medlicott Shrops
4 D2 Medlyn Cnwll
116 C3 Medmenham Bucks
404 D4 Medomsley Dur
73 F2 Medstead Hants
292 C2 Meerbrook Staffs
185 G4 Meer Common Herefs
214 C5 Meer End Solhll
30 B2 Meerhay Dorset
314 C3 Meersbrook Sheff
171 F3 Meesden Herts
271 F5 Meeson Wrekin
271 E5 Meeson Heath Wrekin
40 A6 Meeth Devon
40 D3 Meethe Devon
571 L6 Meethill Abers
199 E3 Meeting Green Suffk
256 C4 Meeting House Hill Norfk
449 G5 Meggethead Border
153 F5 Meidrim Carmth
232 C2 Meifod Powys
464 D1 Meigle N Ayrs
526 C6 Meigle P & K
467 H4 Meikle Earnock S Lans
464 B3 Meikle Kilchattan Butts Ag & B
410 B3 Meikle Killantrae D & G
513 E2 Meikleour P & K
540 B5 Meikle Strath Abers
561 E4 Meikle Tarty Abers
569 J4 Meikle Toux Abers
559 G3 Meikle Wartle Abers
513 E3 Meikle Whitefield P & K
128 C2 Meinciau Carmth
272 D1 Meir C Stke

City, town and village index: Meir Heath - Minster 703

272 D1 Meir Heath Staffs
197 E6 Melbourn Cambs
275 F4 Melbourne Derbys
359 E6 Melbourne E R Yk
470 A6 Melbourne S Lans
69 E5 Melbury Abbas Dorset
30 D1 Melbury Bubb Dorset
45 H6 Melbury Osmond Dorset
30 D1 Melbury Sampford Dorset
606 A6 Melby Shet
195 E1 Melchbourne Beds
65 E5 Melcombe Somset
47 E4 Melcombe Bingham Dorset
32 B3 Melcombe Regis Dorset
25 E4 Meldon Devon
430 B3 Meldon Nthumb
197 E5 Meldreth Cambs
492 D2 Melfort Ag & B
534 E3 Melgarve Highld
307 F3 Meliden Denbgs
230 C5 Melinbyrhedyn Powys
132 B5 Melin Caiach Myr Td
130 C4 Melincourt Neath
130 A5 Melincryddan Neath
7 H6 Melinsey Cnwll
285 H2 Melin-y-coed Conwy
232 A3 Melin-y-ddôl Powys
287 E5 Melin-y-Wig Denbgs
453 G1 Melkington Nthumb
391 F4 Melkinthorpe Cumb
402 C2 Melkridge Nthumb
87 F2 Melksham Wilts
87 G2 Melksham Forest Wilts
4 C3 Mellangoose Cnwll
480 C5 Melldalloch Ag & B
114 D4 Mell Green W Berk
400 D5 Mellguards Cumb
366 B5 Melling Lancs
323 G4 Melling Sefton
14 C4 Mellingey Cnwll
323 H4 Melling Mount Sefton
225 F5 Mellis Suffk
225 E5 Mellis Green Suffk
573 G5 Mellon Charles Highld
573 G4 Mellon Udrigle Highld
339 G3 Mellor Lancs
312 C2 Mellor Stockp
339 F3 Mellor Brook Lancs
86 C5 Mells Somset
226 D4 Mells Suffk
86 C5 Mells Green Somset
391 G2 Melmerby Cumb
369 E2 Melmerby N York
370 C4 Melmerby N York
199 G3 Melon Green Suffk
30 B3 Melplash Dorset
451 G3 Melrose Border
600 D7 Melsetter Ork
383 E3 Melsonby N York
327 G2 Meltham Kirk
327 H2 Meltham Mills Kirk
347 E4 Melton E R Yk
202 B4 Melton Suffk
359 E4 Meltonby E R Yk
260 D5 Melton Constable Norfk
277 G6 Melton Mowbray Leics
333 F2 Melton Ross N Linc
572 D6 Melvaig Highld
233 F1 Melverley Shrops
269 F6 Melverley Green Shrops
587 J4 Melvich Highld
11 G4 Membland Devon
29 E2 Membury Devon
571 H3 Memsie Abers
527 F3 Memus Angus
8 C1 Mena Cnwll
8 D3 Menabilly Cnwll
6 B5 Menadarva Cnwll
6 D4 Menagissey Cnwll
304 B5 Menai Bridge IoA
226 B3 Mendham Suffk
201 F1 Mendlesham Suffk
201 E2 Mendlesham Green Suffk
373 E6 Menethorpe N York
52 C5 Mengham Hants
16 C6 Menheniot Cnwll
4 C1 Menherion Cnwll
211 G6 Menithwood Worcs
7 H3 Menna Cnwll
435 G3 Mennock D & G
355 G6 Menston Brad
498 C5 Menstrie Clacks
345 F3 Menthorpe N York
168 C6 Mentmore Bucks
514 B3 Menzieshill C Dund
449 E5 Menzion Border
531 L5 Meoble Highld
234 B2 Meole Brace Shrops
308 B2 Meols Wirral
51 F4 Meon Hants
73 F6 Meonstoke Hants
97 F1 Meopham Kent
97 F1 Meopham Green Kent
121 F6 Meopham Station Kent
221 F3 Mepal Cambs
169 G2 Meppershall Beds
185 F5 Merbach Herefs
294 B6 Mercaton Derbys
342 C4 Merchant Fields Kirk
488 A5 Merchiston C Edin
311 E3 Mere Ches
68 D3 Mere Wilts
338 B6 Mere Brow Lancs
340 D3 Mereclough Lancs
237 H5 Mere Green Birm
188 D2 Mere Green Worcs
270 A2 Merehead Wrexhm
310 D5 Mere Heath Ches
98 C2 Meresborough Medway
337 F3 Mereside Bpool
271 H5 Meretown Staffs
97 G4 Mereworth Kent
541 E2 Mergie Abers
143 G5 Meriden Herts
214 C3 Meriden Solhll
544 F3 Merkadale Highld
566 B7 Merkinch Highld
461 E2 Merkland N Ayrs
419 F3 Merkland S Ayrs
96 A5 Merle Common Surrey
48 C5 Merley Poole
125 F2 Merlin's Bridge Pembks
125 G4 Merlin's Cross Pembks
236 C5 Merridale Wolves
64 D5 Merridge Somset
37 F4 Merrie Gardens IoW
13 E3 Merrifield Devon
23 F2 Merrifield Devon
270 B5 Merrington Shrops
125 F5 Merrion Pembks
30 C3 Merriott Dorset
45 E5 Merriott Somset
45 E5 Merriottsford Somset
49 E5 Merritown Dorset
18 B2 Merrivale Devon
161 E5 Merrivale Herefs
93 H4 Merrow Surrey
383 F2 Merrybent Darltn
48 C4 Merry Field Hill Dorset
143 G6 Merry Hill Herts
236 C5 Merry Hill Wolves
116 C5 Merryhill Green Wokham
467 E3 Merrylee E Rens
239 H3 Merry Lees Leics
16 C5 Merrymeet Cnwll
15 F4 Merry Meeting Cnwll
50 D2 Merry Oak C Sotn
81 F2 Mersham Kent
95 F4 Merstham Surrey
53 F4 Merston W Susx
37 E4 Merstone IoW
7 G5 Merther Cnwll
7 G5 Merther Lane Cnwll
153 H5 Merthyr Carmth
157 F2 Merthyr Cynog Powys
106 B5 Merthyr Dyfan V Glam
104 D4 Merthyr Mawr Brdgnd
131 G4 Merthyr Tydfil Myr Td
132 A5 Merthyr Vale Myr Td
40 A5 Merton Devon
119 F6 Merton Gt Lon
248 B5 Merton Norfk
166 C6 Merton Oxon
119 E6 Merton Park Gt Lon
440 C2 Mervinslaw Border
41 F4 Meshaw Devon
174 A6 Messing Essex
332 B4 Messingham N Linc
237 E5 Mesty Croft Sandw
150 D3 Mesur-y-Dorth Pembks
395 F2 Metal Bridge Dur
28 A4 Metcombe Devon
226 B3 Metfield Suffk
226 B4 Metfield Common Suffk
17 F5 Metherell Cnwll
298 D2 Metheringham Lincs
202 B5 Methersgate Suffk
502 B5 Methil Fife
501 G4 Methilhill Fife
343 E2 Methley Leeds
343 G4 Methley Junction Leeds
343 G4 Methley Lanes Wakefd
560 C2 Methlick Abers
512 B4 Methven P & K
247 E6 Methwold Norfk
247 E5 Methwold Hythe Norfk
226 D2 Mettingham Suffk
261 H4 Metton Norfk
8 C5 Mevagissey Cnwll
353 E1 Mewith Head N York
329 H4 Mexborough Donc
589 H2 Mey Highld
34 C2 Meyrick Park Bmouth
137 H5 Meysey Hampton Gloucs
595 J3 Miabhaig W Isls
596 D6 Miabhaig W Isls
598 B8 Miabhaig W Isls
572 F8 Mial Highld
598 B8 Miavaig W Isls
160 C4 Michaelchurch Herefs
159 F3 Michaelchurch Escley Herefs
184 D4 Michaelchurch-on-Arrow Powys
106 B5 Michaelston-le-Pit V Glam
106 B4 Michaelston-super-Ely Cardif
106 D3 Michaelston-y-Fedw Newpt
15 F3 Michaelstow Cnwll
19 E4 Michelcombe Devon
72 D2 Micheldever Hants
91 E6 Micheldever Station Hants
71 G4 Michelmersh Hants
201 F2 Mickfield Suffk
330 B6 Micklebring Donc
386 C2 Mickleby N York
117 E1 Micklefield Bucks
344 A3 Micklefield Leeds
143 E5 Micklefield Green Herts
94 D4 Mickleham Surrey
327 E4 Micklehurst Tamesd
275 E2 Mickleover C Derb
342 B1 Micklethwaite Brad
400 A4 Micklethwaite Cumb
393 G5 Mickleton Dur
190 B6 Mickleton Gloucs
343 G4 Mickletown Leeds
309 F6 Mickle Trafford Ches
314 C4 Mickley Derbys
370 B4 Mickley N York
271 E3 Mickley Shrops
199 G3 Mickley Green Suffk
404 C2 Mickley Square Nthumb
50 D2 Midanbury C Sotn
571 G3 Mid Ardlaw Abers
482 D5 Mid Auchinleck Inver
602 E3 Midbea Ork
555 H4 Mid Beltie Abers
609 G4 Midbrake Shet
469 H1 Mid Calder W Loth
583 J2 Mid Clyth Highld
116 B2 Middle Assendon Oxon
166 A4 Middle Aston Oxon
513 F4 Middlebank P & K
165 G4 Middle Barton Oxon
214 C3 Middle Bickenhill Solhll
425 E4 Middlebie D & G
49 F5 Middle Bockhampton Dorset
92 D5 Middle Bourne Surrey
109 E4 Middle Bridge N Som
524 C2 Middlebridge P & K
514 C2 Middle Brighty Angus
84 B5 Middle Burnham Somset
373 E5 Middlecave N York
45 F5 Middle Chinnock Somset
167 F4 Middle Claydon Bucks
292 C4 Middle Cliff Staffs
329 G4 Middlecliffe Barns
24 B1 Middlecott Devon
25 H5 Middlecott Devon
26 A1 Middlecott Devon
22 C3 Middle Crackington Cnwll
315 E5 Middlecroft Derbys
528 C3 Middle Drums Angus
137 E3 Middle Duntisbourne Gloucs
557 G3 Middlefield C Aber
486 A3 Middlefield Falk
338 D4 Middleforth Green Lancs
571 L6 Middle Grange Abers
117 H3 Middle Green Bucks
43 F4 Middle Green Somset
199 E1 Middle Green Suffk
369 F2 Middleham N York
315 E4 Middle Handley Derbys
224 C2 Middle Harling Norfk
406 B4 Middle Herrington Sundld
16 C5 Middlehill Cnwll
125 F2 Middle Hill Pembks
111 E6 Middlehill Wilts
210 B2 Middlehope Shrops
480 C2 Middle Kames Ag & B
189 G5 Middle Littleton Worcs
43 H5 Middle Luxton Devon
159 F3 Middle Maes-coed Herefs
31 F1 Middlemarsh Dorset
60 D4 Middle Marwood Devon
293 F6 Middle Mayfield Staffs
130 D4 Middle Mill Pembks
560 D5 Middlemuir Abers
570 F4 Middlemuir Abers
570 F7 Middlemuir Abers
291 H5 Middleport C Stke
80 C2 Middle Quarter Kent
406 A5 Middle Rainton Sundld
318 D2 Middle Rasen Lincs
486 B4 Middlerig Falk
20 C4 Middle Rocombe Devon
352 C2 Middle Salter Lancs
396 D6 Middlesbrough Middsb
390 B1 Middlesceugh Cumb
366 B2 Middleshaw Cumb
424 C4 Middleshaw D & G
393 F4 Middle Side Dur
369 E5 Middlesmoor N York
43 G3 Middle Stoford Somset
215 F4 Middle Stoke Covtry
19 E3 Middle Stoke Devon
122 C4 Middle Stoke Medway
395 F3 Middlestone Dur
395 E3 Middlestone Moor Dur
84 D5 Middle Stoughton Somset
328 D1 Middlestown Wakefd
486 B5 Middle Strath W Loth
135 H4 Middle Street Gloucs
15 H6 Middle Taphouse Cnwll
358 A5 Middlethorpe York
560 B6 Middleton Abers
516 A7 Middleton Ag & B
528 C5 Middleton Angus
366 C2 Middleton Cumb
293 G2 Middleton Derbys
294 B3 Middleton Derbys
173 H2 Middleton Essex
90 C6 Middleton Hants
396 D3 Middleton Hartpl
210 C6 Middleton Herefs
35 H3 Middleton IoW
351 F3 Middleton Lancs
343 E4 Middleton Leeds
471 G3 Middleton Mdloth
354 C6 Middleton N York
355 F5 Middleton N York
373 E2 Middleton N York
218 A1 Middleton Nhants
252 D4 Middleton Norfk
429 H2 Middleton Nthumb
454 D2 Middleton Nthumb
500 B3 Middleton P & K
525 H6 Middleton P & K
326 B3 Middleton Rochdl
210 C4 Middleton Shrops
233 E5 Middleton Shrops
269 F4 Middleton Shrops
227 E6 Middleton Suffk
102 B4 Middleton Swans
238 B5 Middleton Warwks
211 E1 Middleton Baggot Shrops
166 B1 Middleton Cheney Nhants
273 E2 Middleton Green Staffs
454 B4 Middleton Hall Nthumb
393 G5 Middleton-in-Teesdale Dur
326 C4 Middleton Junction Oldham
227 E6 Middleton Moor Suffk
525 H4 Middleton of Dalrulzian P & K
384 B2 Middleton One Row Darltn
384 D3 Middleton-on-Leven N York
53 H5 Middleton-on-Sea W Susx
186 C2 Middleton on the Hill Herefs
360 B5 Middleton-on-the-Wolds E R Yk
557 G2 Middleton Park C Aber
362 B3 Middleton Place Cumb
211 E1 Middleton Priors Shrops
370 C4 Middleton Quernhow N York
384 A2 Middleton St George Darltn
211 F2 Middleton Scriven Shrops
166 B5 Middleton Stoney Oxon
383 F3 Middleton Tyas N York
376 B3 Middletown Cumb
3 d1 Middle Town IoS
108 D5 Middletown N Som
233 E2 Middletown Powys
189 G2 Middletown Warwks
191 E6 Middle Tysoe Warwks
71 F2 Middle Wallop Hants
167 G2 Middle Weald M Keyn
291 E1 Middlewich Ches
135 G5 Middle Wick Gloucs
111 F5 Middlewick Wilts
71 E3 Middle Winterslow Wilts
312 B3 Middlewood Ches
16 C3 Middlewood Cnwll
184 D5 Middlewood Herefs
185 E6 Middlewood Herefs
314 C1 Middlewood Sheff
70 C2 Middle Woodford Wilts
201 E2 Middlewood Green Suffk
136 B4 Middleyard Gloucs
65 G5 Middlezoy Somset
395 F4 Middridge Dur
66 C5 Midelney Somset
586 C3 Midfield Highld
86 D2 Midford BaNES
439 H1 Midgard Border
338 D5 Midge Hall Lancs
341 F4 Midgehole Calder
402 A3 Midgeholme Cumb
115 E6 Midgham W Berk
115 F6 Midgham Green W Berk
341 G4 Midgley Calder
328 D2 Midgley Wakefd
609 G5 Mid Ho Shet
94 D5 Mid Holmwood Surrey
328 C5 Midhopestones Sheff
74 D5 Midhurst W Susx
66 C6 Mid Lambrook Somset
600 E4 Midland Ork
53 E3 Mid Lavant W Susx
451 G4 Midlem Border
448 C5 Midlock S Lans
549 G2 Mid Main Highld
437 E5 Mid Murthat D & G
408 B2 Mid Ringuinea D & G
86 A4 Midsomer Norton BaNES
546 F2 Mid Strome Highld
482 B4 Midton Inver
572 F6 Midtown Highld
586 C4 Midtown Highld
566 F7 Mid Urchany Highld
300 C3 Midville Lincs
606 B7 Mid Walls Shet
312 B3 Midway Ches
86 A5 Midway Somset
609 G6 Mid Yell Shet
576 D5 Migdale Highld
554 D3 Migvie Abers
20 B3 Milber Devon
68 A6 Milborne Port Somset
47 F5 Milborne St Andrew Dorset
67 H5 Milborne Wick Somset
430 B5 Milbourne Nthumb
111 G2 Milbourne Wilts
391 H4 Milburn Cumb
110 B1 Milbury Heath S Glos
371 E6 Milby N York
173 E5 Milch Hill Essex
9 G2 Milcombe Cnwll
165 G3 Milcombe Oxon
200 C5 Milden Suffk
222 D4 Mildenhall Suffk
113 F5 Mildenhall Wilts
209 F5 Milebrook Powys
98 B5 Milebush Kent
249 H2 Mile Cross Norfk
112 A6 Mile Elm Wilts
222 B3 Mile End Cambs
20 A3 Mile End Devon
174 C4 Mile End Essex
134 D2 Mile End Gloucs
119 H3 Mile End Gt Lon
199 G4 Mile End Suffk
254 B4 Mileham Norfk
55 F3 Mile Oak Br & H
97 G6 Mile Oak Kent
269 F4 Mile Oak Shrops
238 B4 Mile Oak Staffs
30 A4 Miles Cross Dorset
291 G5 Miles Green Staffs
93 F3 Miles Green Surrey
343 E2 Miles Hill Leeds
487 E2 Milesmark Fife
326 C4 Miles Platting Manch
115 E6 Miles's Green W Berk
123 E5 Mile Town Kent
453 H3 Milfield Nthumb
294 D5 Milford Derbys
38 B3 Milford Devon
208 A1 Milford Powys
269 H5 Milford Shrops
273 E5 Milford Staffs
75 E1 Milford Surrey
70 D4 Milford Wilts
125 E3 Milford Haven Pembks
35 G2 Milford on Sea Hants
89 E2 Milkhouse Water Wilts
470 D5 Milkieston Border
134 D3 Milkwall Gloucs
69 F5 Milkwell Wilts
35 f5 Millais Jersey
74 C4 Milland W Susx
466 C2 Millarston Rens
557 E5 Millbank Abers
341 G5 Mill Bank Calder
588 E3 Millbank Highld
100 C2 Millbank Kent
389 G4 Millbeck Cumb
603 H4 Millbounds Ork
571 J6 Millbreck Abers
570 E7 Millbrex Abers
74 D1 Millbridge Surrey
169 E2 Millbrook Beds
50 C2 Millbrook C Sotn
10 D3 Millbrook Cnwll
29 F3 Millbrook Devon
62 B5 Millbrook Devon
35 h7 Millbrook Jersey
327 E5 Millbrook Tamesd
312 C2 Mill Brow Stockp
445 F4 Millburn S Ayrs
250 C4 Mill Common Norfk
80 B5 Mill Corner E Susx
566 B2 Millcraig Highld
293 F4 Milldale Derbys
366 D6 Mill Dam N York
406 B1 Mill Dam S Tyne
557 H1 Millden Abers
528 B4 Milldens Angus
116 C2 Mill End Bucks
198 D3 Mill End Cambs
135 H5 Millend Gloucs
136 A3 Millend Gloucs
137 H2 Mill End Gloucs
143 E6 Mill End Herts
170 D3 Mill End Herts
172 C4 Mill End Green Essex
9 H3 Millendreath Cnwll
488 C6 Millerhill Mdloth
313 F5 Miller's Dale Derbys
294 B4 Millers Green Derbys
146 B3 Miller's Green Essex
484 D5 Millersneuk E Duns
484 C6 Millerston C Glas
555 E5 Millfield Abers
244 A4 Millfield C Pete
406 B3 Millfield Sundld
340 D6 Millgate Lancs
255 G2 Millgate Norfk
388 C5 Millgillhead Cumb
198 C5 Mill Green Cambs
146 C4 Mill Green Essex
91 E2 Mill Green Hants
144 B2 Mill Green Herts
225 F3 Mill Green Norfk
271 F4 Mill Green Shrops
237 G4 Mill Green Staffs
200 B6 Mill Green Suffk
200 C3 Mill Green Suffk
201 F2 Mill Green Suffk
185 E5 Millhalf Herefs
97 H3 Millhall Kent
28 D2 Millhayes Devon
43 F5 Millhayes Devon
365 G5 Millhead Lancs
468 A4 Millheugh S Lans
339 G4 Mill Hill Bl w D
325 G3 Mill Hill Bolton
17 G4 Millhill Devon
57 G4 Mill Hill E Susx
147 G6 Mill Hill Essex
134 D3 Mill Hill Gloucs
119 E1 Mill Hill Gt Lon
101 G5 Mill Hill Kent
301 F1 Mill Hill Lincs
199 H4 Mill Hill Suffk
202 B5 Mill Hills Suffk
355 G2 Mill Hirst N York
366 B1 Millholme Cumb
480 D5 Millhouse Ag & B
390 B2 Millhouse Cumb
424 C2 Millhousebridge D & G
328 C4 Millhouse Green Barns
314 C3 Millhouses Sheff
466 B2 Millikenpark Rens
125 G2 Millin Cross Pembks
359 F4 Millington E R Yk
294 B5 Millington Green Derbys
411 E3 Millisle D & G
457 E2 Mill Knowe Ag & B
92 C4 Mill Lane Hants
272 B3 Millmeece Staffs
43 F5 Millmoor Devon
565 J5 Millnain Highld
366 A3 Millness Cumb
514 C2 Mill of Brighty Angus
556 C4 Mill of Echt Abers
483 F3 Mill of Haldane W Duns
540 C4 Mill of Kincardine Abers
560 B4 Mill of Kingodie Abers
528 B3 Mill of Marcus Angus
557 F5 Mill of Monquich Abers
559 G4 Mill of Pitcaple Abers
602 B8 Mill of Rango Ork
362 D5 Millom Cumb
22 D3 Millook Cnwll
196 B6 Millow Beds
457 E5 Mill Park Ag & B
3 G3 Millpool Cnwll
15 G4 Millpool Cnwll
464 D3 Millport N Ayrs
501 F2 Mills Fife
343 E3 Mill Shaw Leeds
365 F3 Mill Side Cumb
561 F3 Mills of Leask Abers
97 G3 Mill Street Kent
255 E4 Mill Street Norfk
174 C2 Mill Street Suffk
314 C4 Millthorpe Derbys
279 G3 Millthorpe Lincs
366 D1 Millthrop Cumb
557 E4 Milltimber C Aber
552 F7 Milltown Abers
8 D2 Milltown Cnwll
15 G5 Milltown Cnwll
425 G4 Milltown D & G
294 C2 Milltown Derbys
61 E4 Milltown Devon
512 C5 Milltown of Aberdalgie P & K
568 F7 Milltown of Auchindoun Moray
570 D4 Milltown of Craigston Abers
568 D7 Milltown of Edinvillie Moray
555 E1 Milltown of Kildrummy Abers
569 J6 Milltown of Rothiemay Moray
554 D2 Milltown of Towie Abers
119 H4 Millwall Gt Lon
29 F3 Millway Rise Devon
566 B3 Milnafua Highld
500 B4 Milnathort P & K
289 G2 Milners Heath Ches
483 H5 Milngavie E Duns
485 G4 Milnquarter Falk
326 D2 Milnrow Rochdl
340 A4 Milnshaw Lancs
365 G3 Milnthorpe Cumb
329 E1 Milnthorpe Wakefd
468 A3 Milnwood N Lans
155 E6 Milo Carmth
542 B7 Milovaig Highld
211 E5 Milson Shrops
99 E3 Milstead Kent
89 E5 Milston Wilts
192 C5 Milthorpe Nhants
527 E5 Milton Angus
329 F4 Milton Barns
484 B6 Milton C Glas
52 B5 Milton C Port
292 B4 Milton C Stke
197 G2 Milton Cambs
366 A3 Milton Cumb
401 G2 Milton Cumb
415 H6 Milton D & G
422 D5 Milton D & G
275 E4 Milton Derbys
549 H3 Milton Highld
550 F7 Milton Highld
562 C8 Milton Highld
564 E5 Milton Highld
565 K7 Milton Highld
566 D2 Milton Highld
567 H6 Milton Highld
589 J6 Milton Highld
121 G5 Milton Kent
552 D5 Milton Moray
569 J3 Milton Moray
84 B2 Milton N Som
108 C2 Milton Newpt
316 D5 Milton Notts
114 D1 Milton Oxon
165 G2 Milton Oxon
499 F2 Milton P & K
511 G2 Milton P & K
126 A4 Milton Pembks
184 D4 Milton Powys
66 D5 Milton Somset
496 D4 Milton Stirlg
483 F5 Milton W Duns
69 E3 Milton Wilts
47 F4 Milton Abbas Dorset
17 F3 Milton Abbot Devon
471 E2 Milton Bridge Mdloth
168 D3 Milton Bryan Beds
67 H2 Milton Clevedon Somset
561 E2 Milton Coldwells Abers
17 G5 Milton Combe Devon
141 E4 Milton Common Oxon
39 E5 Milton Damerel Devon
568 B3 Miltonduff Moray
135 G2 Milton End Gloucs
138 A4 Milton End Gloucs
195 E3 Milton Ernest Beds
289 F3 Milton Green Ches
17 F3 Milton Green Devon
114 D1 Milton Heights Oxon
20 C2 Milton Hill Devon
114 D1 Milton Hill Oxon
167 G2 Milton Keynes M Keyn
168 B2 Milton Keynes Village M Keyn
89 E2 Milton Lilbourne Wilts
193 F3 Milton Malsor Nhants
509 K2 Milton Morenish P & K
555 G4 Milton of Auchinhove Abers
501 F4 Milton of Balgonie Fife
483 F1 Milton of Buchanan Stirlg
556 A4 Milton of Campfield Abers
484 C4 Milton of Campsie E Duns
556 B3 Milton of Corsindae Abers
511 F5 Milton of Cultoquhey P & K
555 F2 Milton of Cushnie Abers
524 E5 Milton of Dalcapon P & K
540 D3 Milton of Dellavaird Abers
524 E4 Milton of Edradour P & K
527 G3 Milton of Finavon Angus
566 D6 Milton of Gollanfield Highld
558 B4 Milton of Lesmore Abers
557 F4 Milton of Murtle C Aber
558 B4 Milton of Noth Abers
527 E6 Milton of Ogilvie Angus
554 C5 Milton of Tullich Abers
68 D4 Milton on Stour Dorset
114 D1 Milton Park Oxon
98 D1 Milton Regis Kent
57 E4 Milton Street E Susx
164 C6 Milton under Wychwood Oxon
43 F2 Milverton Somset
191 E1 Milverton Warwks
273 E3 Milwich Staffs
308 A5 Milwr Flints
93 G2 Mimbridge Surrey
493 G5 Minard Ag & B
493 G6 Minard Castle Ag & B
48 B2 Minchington Dorset
136 C4 Minchinhampton Gloucs
453 F3 Mindrum Nthumb
63 F2 Minehead Somset
288 C4 Minera Wrexhm
22 D3 Mineshope Cnwll
112 B1 Minety Wilts
229 G2 Minffordd Gwynd
265 E2 Minffordd Gwynd
304 C5 Minffordd Gwynd
519 G2 Mingarrypark Highld
590 E2 Mingearraidh W Isls
6 D4 Mingoose Cnwll
300 B2 Miningsby Lincs
16 C4 Minions Cnwll
432 D2 Minishant S Ayrs
92 D3 Minley Manor Hants
230 C2 Minllyn Gwynd
560 D5 Minnes Abers
417 E3 Minnigaff D & G
570 D3 Minnonie Abers
147 E2 Minnow End Essex
290 D2 Minshull Vernon Ches
356 D2 Minskip N York
49 H2 Minstead Hants
74 D5 Minsted W Susx
101 E3 Minster Kent

704 City, town and village index: Minster - Muswell Hill

123 E5 **Minster** Kent
404 B3 **Minsteracres** Nthumb
233 G4 **Minsterley** Shrops
139 E2 **Minster Lovell** Oxon
135 H1 **Minsterworth** Gloucs
31 E2 **Minterne Magna** Dorset
31 F2 **Minterne Parva** Dorset
319 F5 **Minting** Lincs
571 J6 **Mintlaw** Abers
571 H6 **Mintlaw Station** Abers
451 H5 **Minto** Border
451 G5 **Minto Kames** Border
209 H1 **Minton** Shrops
379 F6 **Mintsfeet** Cumb
126 A2 **Minwear** Pembks
214 B1 **Minworth** Birm
602 C8 **Mirbister** Ork
376 B1 **Mirehouse** Cumb
589 J4 **Mireland** Highld
342 C6 **Mirfield** Kirk
136 D3 **Miserden** Gloucs
226 B2 **Misery Corner** Norfk
105 G3 **Miskin** Rhondd
131 G5 **Miskin** Rhondd
69 H5 **Misselfore** Wilts
331 E6 **Misson** Notts
216 C3 **Misterton** Leics
331 G6 **Misterton** Notts
45 E6 **Misterton** Somset
331 E6 **Misterton Soss** Notts
175 F3 **Mistley** Essex
175 F3 **Mistley Heath** Essex
119 F6 **Mitcham** Gt Lon
161 F6 **Mitcheldean** Gloucs
7 G3 **Mitchell** Cnwll
449 E3 **Mitchell Hill** Border
436 C5 **Mitchellslacks** D & G
472 B5 **Mitchelston** Border
182 B2 **Mitchel Troy** Mons
376 D5 **Mite Houses** Cumb
430 C2 **Mitford** Nthumb
6 D3 **Mithian** Cnwll
6 D4 **Mithian Downs** Cnwll
162 D3 **Mitton** Gloucs
236 C1 **Mitton** Staffs
166 D3 **Mixbury** Oxon
341 H4 **Mixenden** Calder
292 D3 **Mixon** Staffs
9 E3 **Mixtow** Cnwll
609 G4 **Moarfield** Shet
426 B5 **Moat** Cumb
514 C2 **Moatmill** Angus
200 D3 **Moats Tye** Suffk
311 F4 **Mobberley** Ches
273 F1 **Mobberley** Staffs
290 D6 **Moblake** Ches
142 B4 **Mobwell** Bucks
185 F6 **Moccas** Herefs
306 A4 **Mochdre** Conwy
207 H2 **Mochdre** Powys
410 B3 **Mochrum** D & G
49 F3 **Mockbeggar** Hants
82 B2 **Mockbeggar** Kent
122 A5 **Mockbeggar** Medway
388 C5 **Mockerkin** Cumb
12 B2 **Modbury** Devon
292 B2 **Moddershall** Staffs
315 G5 **Model Village** Derbys
191 G2 **Model Village** Warwks
97 E6 **Modest Corner** Kent
586 E4 **Modsarie** Highld
306 D5 **Moelfre** Conwy
304 B2 **Moelfre** IoA
268 C4 **Moelfre** Powys
283 F4 **Moel Tryfan** Gwynd
308 A6 **Moel-y-Crio** Flints
437 E3 **Moffat** D & G
468 B2 **Moffat Mills** N Lans
95 E4 **Mogador** Surrey
195 G5 **Moggerhanger** Beds
41 H4 **Mogworthy** Devon
239 E1 **Moira** Leics
158 C1 **Moity** Powys
99 G4 **Molash** Kent
545 G7 **Mol-Chlach** Highld
288 B2 **Mold** Flints
172 B5 **Molehill Green** Essex
173 E6 **Molehill Green** Essex
347 F1 **Molescroft** E R Yk
431 E4 **Molesden** Nthumb
219 F4 **Molesworth** Cambs
8 C2 **Molinnis** Cnwll
545 K3 **Moll** Highld
41 G2 **Molland** Devon
309 E6 **Mollington** Ches
191 G5 **Mollington** Oxon
485 E5 **Mollinsburn** N Lans
303 F6 **Mona** IoA
180 D2 **Monachty** Cerdgn
509 G6 **Monachyle** Stirlg
208 D6 **Monaughty** Powys
540 D4 **Monboddo** Abers
512 D6 **Moncreiffe** P & K
512 D5 **Moncrieffe** P & K
233 F3 **Mondaytown** Shrops
541 E4 **Mondynes** Abers
509 J3 **Monemore** Stirlg
202 A3 **Monewden** Suffk
466 B4 **Moneyacres** E Ayrs
512 C4 **Moneydie** P & K
143 E6 **Moneyhill** Herts
275 F6 **Money Hill** Leics
117 E4 **Moneyrow Green** W & M
292 D5 **Moneystone** Staffs
5 E2 **Mongleath** Cnwll
422 C1 **Moniaive** D & G
515 E3 **Monifieth** Angus
514 D2 **Monikie** Angus
501 E2 **Monimail** Fife
178 C5 **Monington** Pembks
329 F3 **Monk Bretton** Barns
383 G2 **Monk End** N York
144 B5 **Monken Hadley** Gt Lon
344 C4 **Monk Fryston** N York
396 B2 **Monk Hesleden** Dur
187 E6 **Monkhide** Herefs
400 B3 **Monkhill** Cumb
344 B5 **Monkhill** Wakefd
235 E6 **Monkhopton** Shrops
186 B3 **Monkland** Herefs
39 G3 **Monkleigh** Devon
234 C2 **Monkmoor** Shrops
105 E5 **Monknash** V Glam
25 E1 **Monkokehampton** Devon
17 E4 **Monkscross** Cnwll
431 F5 **Monkseaton** N Tyne
200 C5 **Monks Eleigh** Suffk
76 D4 **Monk's Gate** W Susx
311 G5 **Monk's Heath** Ches
91 G3 **Monk Sherborne** Hants
560 A1 **Monkshill** Abers
80 C1 **Monks Hill** Kent
63 H4 **Monksilver** Somset
215 H3 **Monks Kirby** Warwks
201 H1 **Monk Soham** Suffk
95 H1 **Monks Orchard** Gt Lon
111 F6 **Monk's Park** Wilts
214 B5 **Monkspath** Solhll
141 G4 **Monks Risborough** Bucks
300 D1 **Monksthorpe** Lincs
168 B2 **Monkston Park** M Keyn
501 E3 **Monkstown** Fife
172 C4 **Monk Street** Essex
343 F2 **Monkswood** Leeds
471 F2 **Monkswood** Mdloth
133 F4 **Monkswood** Mons
28 C2 **Monkton** Devon
101 E2 **Monkton** Kent
125 G4 **Monkton** Pembks
445 E4 **Monkton** S Ayrs
405 H2 **Monkton** S Tyne
105 E5 **Monkton** V Glam
86 D2 **Monkton Combe** BaNES
69 E2 **Monkton Deverill** Wilts
87 E1 **Monkton Farleigh** Wilts
488 C5 **Monktonhall** E Loth
44 B2 **Monkton Heathfield** Somset
48 C2 **Monkton Up Wimborne** Dorset
29 F3 **Monkton Wyld** Dorset
406 B3 **Monkwearmouth** Sundld
30 A3 **Monkwood** Dorset
73 G3 **Monkwood** Hants
188 B3 **Monkwood Green** Worcs
186 C5 **Monmarsh** Herefs
236 D5 **Monmore Green** Wolves
134 B2 **Monmouth** Mons
159 G4 **Monmouth Cap** Mons
185 G6 **Monnington on Wye** Herefs
410 C4 **Monreith** D & G
410 C4 **Monreith Mains** D & G
45 F4 **Montacute** Somset
325 F2 **Montcliffe** Bolton
464 C2 **Montford** Ag & B
233 H2 **Montford** Shrops
234 A1 **Montford Bridge** Shrops
555 G1 **Montgarrie** Abers
232 D5 **Montgomery** Powys
93 E4 **Montgomery Lines** Hants
465 G6 **Montgreenan** N Ayrs
325 H5 **Monton** Salfd
109 G5 **Montpelier** Bristl
501 G3 **Montrave** Fife
529 F3 **Montrose** Angus
34 b3 **Mont Saint** Guern
148 D5 **Montsale** Essex
214 D1 **Monwode Lea** Warwks
89 H6 **Monxton** Hants
293 F1 **Monyash** Derbys
556 B1 **Monymusk** Abers
511 F5 **Monzie** P & K
484 D5 **Moodiesburn** N Lans
44 D5 **Moolham** Somset
80 C4 **Moon's Green** Kent
213 G6 **Moon's Moat** Worcs
501 F1 **Moonzie** Fife
45 E4 **Moor** Somset
69 G3 **Mooray** Wilts
30 A3 **Moorbath** Dorset
300 A2 **Moorby** Lincs
388 A4 **Moorclose** Cumb
326 C3 **Moorclose** Rochdl
116 D1 **Moor Common** Bucks
185 G3 **Moorcot** Herefs
48 B3 **Moor Crichel** Dorset
18 D6 **Moor Cross** Devon
48 D6 **Moordown** Bmouth
310 B3 **Moore** Halton
342 A2 **Moor Edge** Brad
328 D4 **Moor End** Barns
116 D1 **Moor End** Bucks
168 D6 **Moor End** Bucks
341 G4 **Moor End** Calder
197 E5 **Moor End** Cambs
400 B4 **Moorend** Cumb
425 E5 **Moorend** D & G
293 H5 **Moorend** Derbys
405 G6 **Moor End** Dur
346 B2 **Moor End** E R Yk
135 G4 **Moorend** Gloucs
136 C2 **Moorend** Gloucs
163 E5 **Moor End** Gloucs
351 E6 **Moor End** Lancs
357 E5 **Moor End** Leeds
344 D2 **Moor End** N York
356 D2 **Moor End** N York
110 A4 **Moorend** S Glos
312 C2 **Moorend** Stockp
188 D3 **Moor End** Worcs
358 C3 **Moor End** York
187 G5 **Moorend Cross** Herefs
371 E6 **Moor End Field** N York
331 E1 **Moorends** Donc
327 F6 **Moorfield** Derbys
255 G2 **Moorgate** Norfk
315 E1 **Moorgate** Rothm
213 G3 **Moor Green** Birm
51 E1 **Moorgreen** Hants
170 D4 **Moor Green** Herts
295 F5 **Moorgreen** Notts
273 E1 **Moor Green** Staffs
111 F6 **Moor Green** Wilts
295 G2 **Moorhaigh** Notts
237 H5 **Moor Hall** Birm
314 C5 **Moorhall** Derbys
185 G5 **Moorhampton** Herefs
19 E6 **Moorhaven Village** Devon
44 A6 **Moorhayne** Devon
342 B2 **Moorhead** Brad
328 C2 **Moor Head** Kirk
342 D4 **Moor Head** Leeds
326 D4 **Moorhey** Oldham
315 E3 **Moorhole** Sheff
399 H4 **Moorhouse** Cumb
400 B3 **Moorhouse** Cumb
330 A2 **Moorhouse** Donc
297 E1 **Moorhouse** Notts
96 B4 **Moorhouse Bank** Surrey
299 H3 **Moorhouses** Lincs
85 G2 **Moorledge** BaNES
66 C2 **Moorlinch** Somset
357 G3 **Moor Monkton** N York
357 G3 **Moor Monkton Moor** N York
556 B2 **Moor of Balvack** Abers
567 K5 **Moor of Granary** Moray
388 C2 **Moor Park** Cumb
186 B1 **Moor Park** Herefs
143 F6 **Moor Park** Herts
93 E5 **Moor Park** Surrey
376 C2 **Moor Row** Cumb
399 G5 **Moor Row** Cumb
386 A2 **Moorsholm** R & Cl
342 C4 **Moor Side** Brad
308 C4 **Moorside** Ches
68 C6 **Moorside** Dorset
404 C5 **Moorside** Dur
338 B3 **Moor Side** Lancs
338 C2 **Moor Side** Lancs
342 D2 **Moorside** Leeds
342 D4 **Moorside** Leeds
299 G3 **Moor Side** Lincs
327 E3 **Moorside** Oldham
325 H4 **Moorside** Salfd
81 H2 **Moorstock** Kent
98 C1 **Moor Street** Medway
16 B6 **Moorswater** Cnwll
329 H2 **Moorthorpe** Wakefd
342 C5 **Moor Top** Kirk
18 B3 **Moortown** Devon
23 G3 **Moortown** Devon
39 H4 **Moortown** Devon
49 F4 **Moortown** Hants
36 C4 **Moortown** IoW
343 F2 **Moortown** Leeds
333 F5 **Moortown** Lincs
271 E6 **Moortown** Wrekin
577 G7 **Morangie** Highld
531 J4 **Morar** Highld
275 G2 **Moravian Settlement** Derbys
302 C4 **Môrawelon** IoA
219 G1 **Morborne** Cambs
41 F6 **Morchard Bishop** Devon
26 B2 **Morchard Road** Devon
29 G4 **Morcombelake** Dorset
242 C4 **Morcott** RutInd
269 E4 **Morda** Shrops
47 H5 **Morden** Dorset
119 F6 **Morden** Gt Lon
170 C1 **Morden Green** Cambs
95 E1 **Morden Park** Gt Lon
160 D2 **Mordiford** Herefs
474 D3 **Mordington Holdings** Border
395 G4 **Mordon** Dur
209 F1 **More** Shrops
42 B2 **Morebath** Devon
453 E5 **Morebattle** Border
351 F2 **Morecambe** Lancs
112 D2 **Moredon** Swindn
488 B6 **Moredun** C Edin
574 C4 **Morefield** Highld
82 D3 **Morehall** Kent
12 D2 **Moreleigh** Devon
509 J2 **Morenish** P & K
388 B6 **Moresby Parks** Cumb
72 D4 **Morestead** Hants
32 D2 **Moreton** Dorset
145 H3 **Moreton** Essex
186 B2 **Moreton** Herefs
139 G4 **Moreton** Oxon
141 E4 **Moreton** Oxon
236 A1 **Moreton** Staffs
274 A4 **Moreton** Staffs
308 C1 **Moreton** Wirral
270 C5 **Moreton Corbet** Shrops
26 A5 **Moretonhampstead** Devon
164 C3 **Moreton-in-Marsh** Gloucs
186 D5 **Moreton Jeffries** Herefs
191 E3 **Moreton Morrell** Warwks
186 C5 **Moreton on Lugg** Herefs
191 E4 **Moreton Paddox** Warwks
192 C5 **Moreton Pinkney** Nhants
271 E3 **Moreton Say** Shrops
135 H3 **Moreton Valence** Gloucs
271 E2 **Moretonwood** Shrops
128 D5 **Morfa** Carmth
129 E2 **Morfa** Carmth
179 G3 **Morfa** Cerdgn
262 B4 **Morfa** Gwynd
128 D5 **Morfa Bacas** Carmth
127 H2 **Morfa Bach** Carmth
264 C2 **Morfa Bychan** Gwynd
282 D4 **Morfa Dinlle** Gwynd
130 D3 **Morfa Glas** Neath
262 D2 **Morfa Nefyn** Gwynd
287 G5 **Morfydd** Denbgs
106 B3 **Morganstown** Cardif
70 D5 **Morgan's Vale** Wilts
205 E4 **Moriah** Cerdgn
134 D3 **Mork** Gloucs
391 F5 **Morland** Cumb
311 G3 **Morley** Ches
275 F1 **Morley** Derbys
394 C4 **Morley** Dur
343 E4 **Morley** Leeds
311 G3 **Morley Green** Ches
275 F1 **Morleymoor** Derbys
294 D5 **Morley Park** Derbys
249 E5 **Morley St Botolph** Norfk
275 F1 **Morley Smithy** Derbys
16 D4 **Mornick** Cnwll
488 A5 **Morningside** C Edin
468 C3 **Morningside** N Lans
225 H1 **Morningthorpe** Norfk
430 D2 **Morpeth** Nthumb
529 F2 **Morphie** Abers
274 A6 **Morrey** Staffs
292 D4 **Morridge Side** Staffs
273 E2 **Morrilow Heath** Staffs
129 G5 **Morriston** Swans
106 C5 **Morristown** V Glam
260 D3 **Morston** Norfk
60 C2 **Mortehoe** Devon
315 F2 **Morthen** Rothm
91 G2 **Mortimer** W Berk
185 H2 **Mortimer's Cross** Herefs
91 G2 **Mortimer West End** Hants
119 E4 **Mortlake** Gt Lon
329 E5 **Mortomley** Sheff
390 C2 **Morton** Cumb
400 C4 **Morton** Cumb
294 D2 **Morton** Derbys
37 G3 **Morton** IoW
279 G5 **Morton** Lincs
297 G2 **Morton** Lincs
317 F1 **Morton** Lincs
255 F4 **Morton** Norfk
296 D4 **Morton** Notts
110 A1 **Morton** S Glos
269 E5 **Morton** Shrops
189 H2 **Morton Bagot** Warwks
269 E5 **Morton Common** Shrops
436 A5 **Morton Mains** D & G
270 D5 **Morton Mill** Shrops
370 C1 **Morton-on-Swale** N York
189 F4 **Morton Spirt** Worcs
394 D5 **Morton Tinmouth** Dur
189 F3 **Morton Underhill** Worcs
2 C2 **Morvah** Cnwll
9 H2 **Morval** Cnwll
547 H5 **Morvich** Highld
577 G3 **Morvich** Highld
235 F6 **Morville** Shrops
235 F6 **Morville Heath** Shrops
17 F5 **Morwellham Quay** Cnwll
38 B4 **Morwenstow** Cnwll
315 E3 **Mosborough** Sheff
445 G1 **Moscow** E Ayrs
211 H1 **Mose** Shrops
390 B3 **Mosedale** Cumb
213 G5 **Moseley** Birm
236 D5 **Moseley** Wolves
188 B3 **Moseley** Worcs
325 G3 **Moses Gate** Bolton
325 G4 **Mosley Common** Wigan
516 B7 **Moss** Ag & B
330 C2 **Moss** Donc
519 G2 **Moss** Highld
288 D4 **Moss** Wrexhm
558 B6 **Mossat** Abers
310 A2 **Moss Bank** Halton
606 F2 **Mossbank** Shet
324 C5 **Moss Bank** St Hel
388 A4 **Mossbay** Cumb
445 F5 **Mossblown** S Ayrs
311 E2 **Mossbrow** Traffd
440 C1 **Mossburnford** Border
421 G5 **Mossdale** D & G
426 C6 **Mossedge** Cumb
351 F5 **Moss Edge** Lancs
351 F6 **Moss Edge** Lancs
117 E5 **Moss End** Br For
310 D4 **Moss End** Ches
468 B2 **Mossend** N Lans
388 D5 **Mosser** Cumb
388 D4 **Mosser Mains** Cumb
272 D2 **Mossgate** Staffs
445 G4 **Mossgiel** E Ayrs
451 G2 **Mosshouses** Border
312 A5 **Moss Houses** Ches
527 F4 **Mosside** Angus
312 B5 **Moss Lane** Ches
291 H2 **Mossley** Ches
327 E4 **Mossley** Tamesd
309 E2 **Mossley Hill** Lpool
311 G2 **Moss Nook** Manch
324 C6 **Moss Nook** St Hel
568 C3 **Moss of Barmuckity** Moray
466 D2 **Mosspark** C Glas
272 D5 **Moss Pit** Staffs
399 F4 **Moss Side** Cumb
566 F6 **Moss-Side** Highld
324 A5 **Moss Side** Knows
337 G3 **Moss Side** Lancs
338 D5 **Moss Side** Lancs
326 B5 **Moss Side** Manch
569 J5 **Moss-Side** Moray
323 G4 **Moss Side** Sefton
559 E2 **Moss-Side of Monellie** Abers
568 E3 **Mosstodloch** Moray
528 B6 **Mosston** Angus
324 C2 **Mossy Lea** Lancs
30 A1 **Mosterton** Dorset
309 E5 **Moston** Ches
326 C4 **Moston** Manch
270 D4 **Moston** Shrops
291 E2 **Moston Green** Ches
307 G3 **Mostyn** Flints
68 D4 **Motcombe** Dorset
11 G4 **Mothecombe** Devon
390 C4 **Motherby** Cumb
468 B3 **Motherwell** N Lans
95 E1 **Motspur Park** Gt Lon
120 B5 **Mottingham** Gt Lon
71 G4 **Mottisfont** Hants
36 B4 **Mottistone** IoW
327 E5 **Mottram in Longdendale** Tamesd
327 E5 **Mottram Rise** Tamesd
311 H4 **Mottram St Andrew** Ches
145 H1 **Mott's Green** Essex
78 C2 **Mott's Mill** E Susx
34 c3 **Mouilpied** Guern
309 H5 **Mouldsworth** Ches
524 D4 **Moulin** P & K
56 A3 **Moulsecoomb** Br & H
115 F3 **Moulsford** Oxon
147 E3 **Moulsham** Essex
168 C1 **Moulsoe** M Keyn
310 C6 **Moulton** Ches
280 C5 **Moulton** Lincs
383 F4 **Moulton** N York
193 G1 **Moulton** Nhants
198 D2 **Moulton** Suffk
105 H5 **Moulton** V Glam
280 C6 **Moulton Chapel** Lincs
244 D1 **Moulton Eaugate** Lincs
193 G2 **Moulton Park** Nhants
250 D3 **Moulton St Mary** Norfk
280 D4 **Moulton Seas End** Lincs
538 B4 **Moulzie** Angus
7 E2 **Mount** Cnwll
15 G5 **Mount** Cnwll
302 B4 **Mountain** IoA
132 B3 **Mountain Air** Blae G
131 H5 **Mountain Ash** Rhondd
111 E4 **Mountain Bower** Wilts
470 B5 **Mountain Cross** Border
99 H4 **Mountain Street** Kent
6 D5 **Mount Ambrose** Cnwll
109 E2 **Mount Ballan** Mons
450 B4 **Mountbenger** Border
450 B4 **Mountbengerburn** Border
483 G5 **Mountblow** W Duns
122 C1 **Mount Bovers** Essex
174 A3 **Mount Bures** Essex
8 C3 **Mount Charles** Cnwll
15 E5 **Mount Charles** Cnwll
89 G4 **Mount Cowdown** Wilts
145 G4 **Mount End** Essex
78 B6 **Mount Ephraim** E Susx
68 C6 **Mounters** Dorset
58 B2 **Mountfield** E Susx
565 K4 **Mountgerald** Highld
11 E3 **Mount Gould** C Plym
6 D4 **Mount Hawke** Cnwll
4 D5 **Mount Hermon** Cnwll
93 G3 **Mount Hermon** Surrey
566 B4 **Mount High** Highld
110 B5 **Mount Hill** S Glos
7 G1 **Mountjoy** Cnwll
23 H3 **Mount Lane** Devon
146 C5 **Mountnessing** Essex
134 C6 **Mounton** Mons
167 E3 **Mount Pleasant** Bucks
292 A6 **Mount Pleasant** C Stke
291 G3 **Mount Pleasant** Ches
8 C1 **Mount Pleasant** Cnwll
238 D1 **Mount Pleasant** Derbys
275 E4 **Mount Pleasant** Derbys
294 C5 **Mount Pleasant** Derbys
28 C2 **Mount Pleasant** Devon
392 D1 **Mount Pleasant** Dur
395 F3 **Mount Pleasant** Dur
348 D2 **Mount Pleasant** E R Yk
56 C1 **Mount Pleasant** E Susx
56 D4 **Mount Pleasant** E Susx
308 B5 **Mount Pleasant** Flints
405 G2 **Mount Pleasant** Gatesd
118 A1 **Mount Pleasant** Gt Lon
588 E3 **Mountpleasant** Highld
101 E2 **Mount Pleasant** Kent
385 E2 **Mount Pleasant** Middsb
132 A5 **Mount Pleasant** Myr Td
130 B5 **Mount Pleasant** Neath
248 C6 **Mount Pleasant** Norfk
125 H3 **Mount Pleasant** Pembks
396 B5 **Mount Pleasant** S on T
234 B2 **Mount Pleasant** Shrops
199 E5 **Mount Pleasant** Suffk
215 F2 **Mount Pleasant** Warwks
163 F2 **Mount Pleasant** Worcs
189 E2 **Mount Pleasant** Worcs
207 E3 **Mount Severn** Powys
288 C4 **Mount Sion** Wrexhm
139 F1 **Mount Skippett** Oxon
571 G4 **Mountsolie** Abers
240 C2 **Mountsorrel** Leics
70 A5 **Mount Sorrel** Wilts
341 H4 **Mount Tabor** Calder
467 G2 **Mount Vernon** C Glas
10 D3 **Mount Wise** C Plym
75 E1 **Mousehill** Surrey
3 E4 **Mousehole** Cnwll
455 E3 **Mousen** Nthumb
214 C6 **Mousley End** Warwks
424 B5 **Mouswald** D & G
38 C2 **Mouth Mill** Devon
338 B3 **Mowbreck** Lancs
291 H3 **Mow Cop** Staffs
383 G1 **Mowden** Darltn
147 F2 **Mowden** Essex
453 F5 **Mowhaugh** Border
240 C3 **Mowmacre Hill** C Leic
96 C5 **Mowshurst** Kent
216 D2 **Mowsley** Leics
358 A1 **Moxby** N York
237 E5 **Moxley** Wsall
534 D6 **Moy** Highld
568 C3 **Moycroft** Moray
550 D2 **Moy Hall** Highld
546 F6 **Moyle** Highld
178 C5 **Moylegrove** Pembks
467 E2 **Mt Florida** C Glas
458 D3 **Muasdale** Ag & B
541 H1 **Muchalls** Abers
160 C3 **Much Birch** Herefs
187 E5 **Much Cowarne** Herefs
160 B3 **Much Dewchurch** Herefs
66 C5 **Muchelney** Somset
66 C5 **Muchelney Ham** Somset
171 F6 **Much Hadham** Herts
338 C5 **Much Hoole** Lancs
338 C5 **Much Hoole Moss Houses** Lancs
338 C5 **Much Hoole Town** Lancs
9 G2 **Muchlarnick** Cnwll
161 F3 **Much Marcle** Herefs
548 D3 **Muchrachd** Highld
235 E5 **Much Wenlock** Shrops
121 G3 **Mucking** Thurr
31 E4 **Muckleford** Dorset
271 G2 **Mucklestone** Staffs
259 G4 **Muckleton** Norfk
270 D5 **Muckleton** Shrops
558 D5 **Muckletown** Abers
235 E5 **Muckley** Shrops
237 G3 **Muckley Corner** Staffs
235 E5 **Muckley Cross** Shrops
320 C3 **Muckton** Lincs
320 C3 **Muckton Bottom** Lincs
580 D2 **Mudale** Highld
327 E6 **Mudd** Tamesd
61 E4 **Muddiford** Devon
60 D5 **Muddlebridge** Devon
57 E2 **Muddles Green** E Susx
35 E2 **Mudeford** Dorset
67 F6 **Mudford** Somset
67 F6 **Mudford Sock** Somset
84 D5 **Mudgley** Somset
484 B4 **Mugdock** Stirlg
545 G2 **Mugeary** Highld
294 B6 **Mugginton** Derbys
294 B6 **Muggintonlane End** Derbys
95 F4 **Mugswell** Surrey
576 E3 **Muie** Highld
537 G5 **Muir** Abers
472 C5 **Muircleugh** Border
570 C5 **Muirden** Abers
515 E2 **Muirdrum** Angus
501 F5 **Muiredge** Fife
467 E3 **Muirend** C Glas
514 A3 **Muirhead** Angus
501 E3 **Muirhead** Fife
484 D6 **Muirhead** N Lans
444 D3 **Muirhead** S Ayrs
487 H4 **Muirhouse** C Edin
468 B4 **Muirhouse** N Lans
527 E3 **Muirhouses** Angus
486 D3 **Muirhouses** Falk
513 G5 **Muirhouses** P & K
446 D4 **Muirkirk** E Ayrs
555 F1 **Muir of Alford** Abers
565 H6 **Muir of Fairburn** Highld
555 G2 **Muir of Fowlis** Abers
568 E3 **Muir of Lochs** Moray
565 J6 **Muir of Ord** Highld
514 C2 **Muir of Pert** Angus
565 J6 **Muir of Tarradale** Highld
533 H6 **Muirshearlich** Highld
557 E5 **Muirskie** Abers
561 E2 **Muirtack** Abers
570 E6 **Muirtack** Abers
566 C4 **Muirton** Highld
499 E2 **Muirton** P & K
512 D4 **Muirton** P & K
565 H6 **Muirton Mains** Highld
525 J7 **Muirton of Ardblair** P & K
529 E2 **Muirton of Ballochy** Angus
570 D5 **Muiryfold** Abers
381 G5 **Muker** N York
249 G4 **Mulbarton** Norfk
568 F5 **Mulben** Moray
15 E5 **Mulberry** Cnwll
3 E3 **Mulfra** Cnwll
476 F5 **Mulindry** Ag & B
598 E6 **Mullach Chàrlabhaigh** W Isls
60 D3 **Mullacott Cross** Devon
89 G5 **Mullenspond** Hants
4 C5 **Mullion** Cnwll
4 C5 **Mullion Cove** Cnwll
103 F4 **Mumbles Hill** Swans
321 F5 **Mumby** Lincs
326 D3 **Mumps** Oldham
187 F4 **Munderfield Row** Herefs
187 F4 **Munderfield Stocks** Herefs
256 C2 **Mundesley** Norfk
247 G6 **Mundford** Norfk
250 C5 **Mundham** Norfk
147 H4 **Mundon** Essex
557 G2 **Mundurno** C Aber
99 E5 **Mundy Bois** Kent
533 L2 **Munerigie** Highld
609 J4 **Muness** Shet
573 J5 **Mungasdale** Highld
390 B3 **Mungrisdale** Cumb
566 B6 **Munlochy** Highld
161 F1 **Munsley** Herefs
210 C2 **Munslow** Shrops
186 C6 **Munstone** Herefs
106 C5 **Murch** V Glam
25 G5 **Murchington** Devon
163 G1 **Murcot** Worcs
140 C1 **Murcott** Oxon
111 H1 **Murcott** Wilts
497 G5 **Murdieston** Stirlg
310 B3 **Murdishaw** Halton
469 H2 **Murieston** W Loth
588 F3 **Murkle** Highld
532 F4 **Murlaggan** Highld
534 B6 **Murlaggan** Highld
600 C4 **Murra** Ork
487 H5 **Murrayfield** C Edin
424 C5 **Murraythwaite** D & G
92 B3 **Murrell Green** Hants
161 G3 **Murrell's End** Gloucs
162 A5 **Murrell's End** Gloucs
514 D2 **Murroes** Angus
245 E3 **Murrow** Cambs
167 H4 **Mursley** Bucks
99 E2 **Murston** Kent
527 G3 **Murthill** Angus
512 C2 **Murthly** P & K
392 B5 **Murton** Cumb
406 B5 **Murton** Dur
431 F5 **Murton** N Tyne
475 E5 **Murton** Nthumb
103 E4 **Murton** Swans
358 C4 **Murton** York
371 G2 **Murton Grange** N York
12 C1 **Murtwell** Devon
29 E4 **Musbury** Devon
48 D5 **Muscliff** Bmouth
372 C3 **Muscoates** N York
192 D2 **Muscott** Nhants
506 F5 **Musdale** Ag & B
212 D2 **Mushroom Green** Dudley
488 C5 **Musselburgh** E Loth
124 D3 **Musselwick** Pembks
257 E6 **Mustard Hyrn** Norfk
278 A2 **Muston** Leics
374 D4 **Muston** N York
212 C5 **Mustow Green** Worcs
119 F1 **Muswell Hill** Gt Lon

412 C5 Mutehill D & G
227 F2 Mutford Suffk
498 D1 Muthill P & K
27 G2 Mutterton Devon
78 D5 Mutton Hall E Susx
235 G2 Muxton Wrekin
307 H4 Mwdwl-eithin Flints
288 A1 Mwynbwll Flints
588 F6 Mybster Highld
156 B3 Myddfai Carmth
270 B5 Myddle Shrops
270 B5 Myddlewood Shrops
129 F2 Myddyn-Fych Carmth
180 C3 Mydroilyn Cerdgn
338 C2 Myerscough Lancs
339 F3 Myerscough Smithy Lancs
5 F1 Mylor Bridge Cnwll
6 F2 Mylor Churchtown Cnwll
106 C4 Mynachdy Cardif
131 G5 Mynachdy Rhondd
152 C3 Mynachlog-Ddu Pembks
209 G5 Mynd Shrops
209 G2 Myndtown Shrops
205 G4 Mynydd bach Cerdgn
134 B6 Mynydd-bach Mons
103 F2 Mynydd-bach Swans
103 F2 Mynydd-bach-y-glo Swans
303 G3 Mynydd Bodafon IoA
262 D6 Mynydd Gilan Gwynd
288 C2 Mynydd Isa Flints
132 C6 Mynyddislwyn Caerph
307 G5 Mynydd-llan Flints
284 D1 Mynydd Llandegai Gwynd
306 B4 Mynydd Marian Conwy
303 E3 Mynydd Mechell IoA
303 F4 Mynydd-Mwyn IoA
303 F4 Mynydd Mwyn Mawr IoA
302 D4 Mynydd-y-gof IoA
302 D4 Mynydd-yr-eithin IoA
263 E4 Mynytho Gwynd
556 C5 Myrebird Abers
589 H5 Myrelandhorn Highld
156 B3 Myrtle Hill Carmth
93 E3 Mytchett Surrey
93 E3 Mytchett Place Surrey
341 F4 Mytholm Calder
341 G4 Mytholmroyd Calder
337 G3 Mythop Lancs
190 D2 Myton Warwks
357 E1 Myton Hall N York
357 E1 Myton-on-Swale N York
234 A1 Mytton Shrops

N

572 F7 Naast Highld
342 C6 Nab Hill Kirk
339 F4 Nab's Head Lancs
595 G4 Na Buirgh W Isls
358 A5 Naburn York
342 B2 Nab Wood Brad
99 G6 Naccolt Kent
100 C5 Nackington Kent
176 D1 Nacton Suffk
26 D4 Nadderwater Devon
360 D3 Nafferton E R Yk
598 D6 Na Gearrannan W Isls
136 C5 Nag's Head Gloucs
307 H4 Naid-y-march Flints
135 E1 Nailbridge Gloucs
43 H2 Nailsbourne Somset
109 E6 Nailsea N Som
239 G3 Nailstone Leics
136 C5 Nailsworth Gloucs
86 C2 Nailwell BaNES
566 F5 Nairn Highld
95 E5 Nalderswood Surrey
3 F3 Nancedden Cnwll
4 B2 Nancegollan Cnwll
3 G1 Nancemellin Cnwll
4 D3 Nancenoy Cnwll
3 E2 Nancledra Cnwll
326 B1 Nangreaves Bury
262 D4 Nanhoron Gwynd
265 G5 Nannau Gwynd
307 H6 Nannerch Flints
240 B1 Nanpantan Leics
8 B2 Nanpean Cnwll
2 C4 Nanquidno Cnwll
15 E5 Nanstallon Cnwll
154 B6 Nant Carmth
288 A3 Nant Denbgs
269 E3 Nant Shrops
288 A1 Nant Alyn Flints
131 G2 Nant-ddu Powys
179 H2 Nanternis Cerdgn
154 C5 Nantgaredig Carmth
106 B2 Nantgarw Rhondd
154 A3 Nantgerdinen Carmth
183 F2 Nant Glas Powys
287 E2 Nantglyn Denbgs
207 F4 Nantgwyn Powys
4 C4 Nantithet Cnwll
283 F5 Nantlle Gwynd
288 C2 Nant Mawr Flints
268 D5 Nantmawr Shrops
183 G1 Nantmel Powys
284 D5 Nantmor Gwynd
284 C3 Nant Peris Gwynd
207 F5 Nantserth Powys
290 C4 Nantwich Ches
182 B6 Nant-y-Bai Carmth
132 B2 Nant-y-Bwch Blae G
130 C3 Nant-y-cafn Neath
154 C6 Nantycaws Carmth
269 E4 Nant y Caws Carmth
106 D2 Nant-y-ceisiad Caerph
133 F3 Nant-y-derry Mons
305 E5 Nant-y-felin Conwy
155 E3 Nant-y-Ffin Carmth
130 D6 Nantyffyllon Brdgnd
132 C2 Nantyglo Blae G
268 D4 Nant-y-gollen Shrops
131 E6 Nant-y-moel Brdgnd
305 E5 Nant-y-pandy Conwy
285 H3 Nant-y-Rhiw Conwy
590 F5 Na Pairceanan W Isls
83 F1 Napchester Kent
142 A5 Naphill Bucks
188 C5 Napleton Worcs
271 G2 Napley Staffs
271 G2 Napley Heath Staffs
353 G4 Nappa N York
368 C1 Nappa Scar N York
191 H2 Napton on the Hill Warwks
126 B2 Narberth Pembks
126 B2 Narberth Bridge Pembks
240 B5 Narborough Leics
247 E2 Narborough Norfk
29 E1 Narfords Devon
10 B2 Narkurs Cnwll
493 F2 Narrachan Ag & B
39 E4 Narracott Devon
251 E2 Narrowgate Corner Norfk
283 E6 Nasareth Gwynd
217 E4 Naseby Nhants
591 C8 Nasg W Isls
167 G3 Nash Bucks
96 B2 Nash Gt Lon
185 F2 Nash Herefs
101 E4 Nash Kent

107 F3 Nash Newpt
211 E5 Nash Shrops
45 G5 Nash Somset
136 C3 Nashend Gloucs
211 H3 Nash End Worcs
91 H5 Nashes Green Hants
142 A3 Nash Lee Bucks
57 F2 Nash Street E Susx
121 F6 Nash Street Kent
243 E5 Nassington Nhants
136 A3 Nastend Gloucs
171 E5 Nasty Herts
38 C3 Natcott Devon
380 D3 Nateby Cumb
351 G6 Nateby Lancs
92 B4 Nately Scures Hants
365 H2 Natland Cumb
162 D3 Natton Gloucs
200 D5 Naughton Suffk
163 H5 Naunton Gloucs
162 C2 Naunton Worcs
189 E4 Naunton Beauchamp Worcs
75 A4 Navant Hill W Susx
298 B3 Navenby Lincs
146 A5 Navestock Heath Essex
146 B5 Navestock Side Essex
582 D6 Navidale Highld
372 C3 Nawton N York
174 C3 Nayland Suffk
145 F3 Nazeing Essex
145 F3 Nazeing Gate Essex
145 F4 Nazeing Long Green Essex
145 E3 Nazeing Mead Essex
49 F5 Neacroft Hants
400 B4 Nealhouse Cumb
215 E3 Neal's Green Warwks
99 G3 Neames Forstal Kent
315 E3 Neap Shet
355 F1 Near Hardcastle N York
378 F3 Near Sawrey Cumb
167 H4 Nearton End Bucks
119 E2 Neasden Gt Lon
384 A2 Neasham Darltn
165 F5 Neat Enstone Oxon
130 B5 Neath Neath
130 A5 Neath Abbey Neath
74 A1 Neatham Hants
168 B1 Neath Hill M Keyn
256 C5 Neatishead Norfk
348 C3 Neat Marsh E R Yk
248 B4 Neaton Norfk
180 D1 Nebo Cerdgn
286 A3 Nebo Conwy
283 E5 Nebo Gwynd
303 G2 Nebo IoA
190 B6 Nebsworth Warwks
213 G2 Nechells Birm
247 H3 Necton Norfk
578 F3 Nedd Highld
430 D3 Nedderton Nthumb
85 G4 Nedge Hill Somset
200 C5 Nedging Suffk
200 D5 Nedging Tye Suffk
226 A3 Needham Norfk
146 A1 Needham Green Essex
201 E3 Needham Market Suffk
199 E1 Needham Street Suffk
220 D5 Needingworth Cambs
274 B5 Needwood Staffs
211 F4 Neen Savage Shrops
211 F5 Neen Sollars Shrops
211 E2 Neenton Shrops
269 F2 Nefod Shrops
263 E2 Nefyn Gwynd
86 A5 Neighbourne Somset
188 D3 Neight Hill Worcs
466 C3 Neilston E Rens
165 G1 Neithrop Oxon
132 B5 Nelson Caerph
340 D2 Nelson Lancs
431 E4 Nelson Village Nthumb
468 C6 Nemphlar S Lans
85 F2 Nempnett Thrubwell BaNES
244 C3 Nene Terrace Lincs
402 D5 Nenthall Cumb
402 D6 Nenthead Cumb
452 C2 Nenthorn Border
26 B3 Neopardy Devon
54 D3 Nepcote W Susx
388 C4 Nepgill Cumb
55 F1 Nep Town W Susx
476 C5 Nerabus Ag & B
288 B2 Nercwys Flints
467 F3 Nerston S Lans
454 B3 Nesbit Nthumb
308 D4 Ness Ches
269 G6 Nesscliffe Shrops
308 D4 Nessholt Ches
603 M1 Nesstoun Ork
308 C4 Neston Ches
111 F6 Neston Wilts
213 G2 Netchells Green Birm
109 H5 Nether Bristl
468 C5 Netheravon Wilts
88 D5 Nether Alderley Ches
311 G4 Netheravon Wilts
600 D1 Netherbrough Ork
277 E4 Nether Broughton Leics
468 C5 Netherburn S Lans
366 C4 Nether Burrow Lancs
274 D2 Nether Burrows Derbys
30 B3 Netherbury Dorset
426 A5 Netherby Cumb
356 C5 Netherby N York
438 A4 Nether Cassock D & G
31 F3 Nether Cerne Dorset
314 C5 Nether Chanderhill Derbys
44 A3 Netherclay Somset
413 H3 Nether Clifton D & G
67 F6 Nether Compton Dorset
165 H1 Nethercote Oxon
192 B2 Nethercote Warwks
23 H3 Nethercott Devon
60 C4 Nethercott Devon
166 A5 Nethercott Oxon
64 B5 Nethercott Somset
560 B5 Nether Crimond Abers
568 F3 Nether Dallachy Moray
529 E4 Nether Dysart Angus
314 C3 Nether Edge Sheff
314 B5 Nether End Derbys
134 D5 Netherend Gloucs
328 C3 Nether End Kirk
241 F2 Nether End Leics
27 E3 Nether Exe Devon
58 B3 Netherfield E Susx
168 B2 Netherfield M Keyn
276 D1 Netherfield Notts
436 B2 Nether Fingland S Lans
255 E2 Nethergate Norfk
240 D3 Nether Hall C Leic
70 C4 Netherhampton Wilts
315 E4 Nether Handley Derbys
514 B1 Nether Handwick Angus
440 D1 Nether Haugh Rothm
329 G5 Nether Headon Notts
316 D4 Nether Heage Derbys
216 C2 Nether Heyford Nhants
450 C2 Nether Horsburgh Border
436 D2 Nether Howcleuch S Lans

365 H6 Nether Kellet Lancs
470 D6 Nether Kidston Border
571 J7 Nether Kinmundy Abers
466 C3 Nether Kirkton E Rens
273 H3 Netherland Green Staffs
315 G5 Nether Langwith Notts
412 D5 Netherlaw D & G
29 H1 Netherley Dorset
561 F3 Nether Leask Abers
467 E3 Netherlee E Rens
557 F6 Netherley Abers
327 F2 Netherley Kirk
309 F2 Netherley Lpool
314 C6 Nether Loads Derbys
424 A2 Nethermill D & G
569 J5 Nethermills Moray
294 D1 Nether Moor Derbys
570 F7 Nethermuir Abers
95 F3 Netherne on-the-Hill Surrey
314 B4 Nether Padley Derbys
466 D3 Netherplace E Rens
357 H3 Nether Poppleton York
451 G5 Netherraw Border
568 C6 Nether Ringorm Moray
389 H2 Nether Row Cumb
200 B2 Nether St Suffk
238 D2 Netherseal Derbys
471 H5 Nether Shiels Border
384 D6 Nether Silton N York
209 E5 Nether Skyborry Shrops
45 G6 Netherstoke Dorset
237 H2 Nether Stowe Staffs
64 C4 Nether Stowey Somset
146 B2 Nether Street Essex
145 F1 Nether Street Herts
446 B6 Netherthird E Ayrs
328 A3 Netherthong Kirk
315 E5 Netherthorpe Derbys
528 B3 Netherton Angus
309 H4 Netherton Ches
16 C4 Netherton Cnwll
388 B2 Netherton Cumb
20 B3 Netherton Devon
212 D2 Netherton Dudley
138 B4 Netherton Gloucs
90 B3 Netherton Hants
160 C4 Netherton Herefs
327 H2 Netherton Kirk
468 B4 Netherton N Lans
442 B3 Netherton Nthumb
139 G5 Netherton Oxon
525 H5 Netherton P & K
323 G4 Netherton Sefton
211 G3 Netherton Shrops
484 B4 Netherton Stirlg
328 D1 Netherton Wakefd
163 E1 Netherton Worcs
376 B3 Nethertown Cumb
589 J1 Nethertown Highld
339 H2 Nethertown Lancs
273 H6 Nethertown Staffs
500 C3 Nether Urquhart Fife
71 G2 Nether Wallop Hants
403 G1 Nether Warden Nthumb
377 E4 Nether Wasdale Cumb
400 C5 Nether Welton Cumb
164 C5 Nether Westcote Gloucs
238 C6 Nether Whitacre Warwks
141 F2 Nether Winchendon or Lower Winchendon Bucks
430 B1 Netherwitton Nthumb
446 C4 Netherwood E Ayrs
165 G3 Nether Worton Oxon
551 J5 Nethy Bridge Highld
50 D3 Netley Hants
51 E2 Netley Hill Hants
50 B2 Netley Marsh Hants
27 E3 Nettacott Devon
145 F2 Netteswell Essex
116 A2 Nettlebed Oxon
86 B5 Nettlebridge Somset
30 C3 Nettlecombe Dorset
37 E5 Nettlecombe IoW
143 E2 Nettleden Herts
318 C4 Nettleham Lincs
97 G4 Nettlestead Kent
201 E5 Nettlestead Suffk
97 G4 Nettlestead Green Kent
37 G2 Nettlestone IoW
405 F5 Nettlesworth Dur
136 D2 Nettleton Gloucs
333 F4 Nettleton Lincs
111 E4 Nettleton Wilts
111 E4 Nettleton Green Wilts
111 E4 Nettleton Shrub Wilts
333 G5 Nettleton Top Lincs
111 E4 Netton Wilts
155 G5 Neuadd Carmth
122 A1 Neuadd Carmth
152 B1 Nevendon Essex
395 F1 Nevern Pembks
241 H6 Neville Holt Leics
398 B1 Nevilles Cross Dur
570 F3 New Abbey D & G
96 A2 New Aberdour Abers
355 H5 New Addington Gt Lon
311 G2 Newall Leeds
472 C6 Newall Green Manch
73 E3 New Alresford Hants
526 B5 New Alyth P & K
244 B4 Newark C Pete
603 L3 Newark Ork
297 F4 Newark-on-Trent Notts
214 D2 New Arley Warwks
360 C6 New Arram E R Yk
468 B3 Newarthill N Lans
97 F1 New Ash Green Kent
297 F4 New Balderton Notts
318 D4 Newball Lincs
82 C3 Newbarn Kent
121 F6 New Barn Kent
144 C5 New Barnet Gt Lon
333 F2 New Barnetby N Linc
364 B5 Newbarns Cumb
194 B2 New Barton Nhants
276 C1 New Basford C Nott
471 F1 Newbattle Mdloth
105 G5 New Beaupre V Glam
119 H5 New Beckenham Gt Lon
454 C4 New Bewick Nthumb
399 H1 Newbie D & G
364 C6 Newbiggin Cumb
366 B4 Newbiggin Cumb
376 D6 Newbiggin Cumb
390 D4 Newbiggin Cumb
391 G4 Newbiggin Cumb
401 G5 Newbiggin Cumb
393 H4 Newbiggin Dur
404 D3 Newbiggin Dur
368 C3 Newbiggin N York
368 C2 Newbiggin N York
403 G5 Newbiggin Nthumb
431 F2 Newbiggin-by-the-Sea Nthumb
513 G1 Newbigging Angus
514 C2 Newbigging Angus
514 D2 Newbigging Angus
440 D1 Newbigging Border
487 F4 Newbigging C Edin
469 G5 Newbigging S Lans
603 K3 Newbigging Ork
430 D2 Newbigging Hall Estate N u Ty
380 C3 Newbiggin-on-Lune Cumb

216 A4 New Bilton Warwks
314 D5 Newbold Derbys
241 D3 Newbold Leics
275 G6 Newbold Leics
326 D2 Newbold Rochdl
239 G4 Newbold Heath Leics
216 A4 Newbold on Avon Warwks
190 C5 Newbold-on-Stour Warwks
190 D3 Newbold-Pacey Warwks
236 D4 Newbolds Wolves
239 G4 Newbold Verdon Leics
300 B3 Newbolt Wolves
315 F5 New Bolingbroke Lincs
244 B3 Newborough C Pete
273 H4 Newborough Staffs
324 D5 New Boston St Hel
140 A3 New Botley Oxon
166 B2 Newbottle Nhants
406 A4 Newbottle Sundld
318 B5 New Boultham Lincs
202 B6 Newbourne Suffk
167 H1 New Bradwell M Keyn
395 E1 New Brancepeth Dur
86 C1 Newbridge BaNES
487 F5 Newbridge C Edin
132 D5 Newbridge Caerph
2 D3 Newbridge Cnwll
7 E5 Newbridge Cnwll
16 D5 Newbridge Cnwll
423 G4 Newbridge D & G
78 A3 Newbridge E Susx
50 A1 Newbridge Hants
36 C3 Newbridge IoW
340 C2 Newbridge Lancs
373 F2 Newbridge N York
139 F4 Newbridge Oxon
269 E4 Newbridge Shrops
236 C5 Newbridge Wolves
269 E1 Newbridge Wrexhm
162 B2 Newbridge Green Worcs
133 G6 Newbridge on Usk Mons
183 G3 Newbridge-on-Wye Powys
342 B2 New Brighton Brad
288 B1 New Brighton Flints
52 D3 New Brighton Hants
323 E6 New Brighton Wirral
288 C4 New Brighton Wrexhm
314 D5 New Brimington Derbys
295 F4 New Brinsley Notts
397 G5 New Brotton R & Cl
428 D6 Newbrough Nthumb
288 D4 New Broughton Wrexhm
225 E2 New Buckenham Norfk
86 B3 New Buildings BaNES
26 B2 Newbuildings Devon
34 A4 New Buildings Dorset
561 E5 Newburgh Abers
513 F6 Newburgh Fife
324 B2 Newburgh Lancs
405 E1 Newburn N u Ty
325 G3 New Bury Bolton
99 E2 Newbury Kent
86 B4 Newbury Somset
114 D6 Newbury W Berk
68 D1 Newbury Wilts
391 F5 Newby Cumb
353 G5 Newby Lancs
356 B5 Newby N York
367 E5 Newby N York
370 D6 Newby N York
374 C1 Newby N York
385 E2 Newby N York
365 E2 Newby Bridge Cumb
367 G5 Newby Cote N York
401 E3 Newby East Cumb
391 F5 Newby Head Cumb
570 E5 New Byth Abers
400 C4 Newby West Cumb
370 D2 Newby Wiske N York
104 D3 Newcastle Brdgnd
134 A1 Newcastle Mons
208 D3 Newcastle Shrops
153 F1 Newcastle Emlyn Carmth
426 C2 Newcastleton or Copshaw Holm Border
291 G5 Newcastle-under-Lyme Staffs
405 E2 Newcastle upon Tyne N u Ty
250 A2 New Catton Norfk
153 E2 Newchapel Pembks
207 F3 Newchapel Powys
291 H4 Newchapel Staffs
77 G1 Newchapel Surrey
110 A5 New Cheltenham S Glos
73 E4 New Cheriton Hants
132 C2 Newchurch Blae G
154 A5 Newchurch Carmth
185 G4 Newchurch Herefs
37 E3 Newchurch IoW
81 G3 Newchurch Kent
340 C5 Newchurch Lancs
134 A5 Newchurch Mons
184 D4 Newchurch Powys
274 A5 Newchurch Staffs
340 C2 Newchurch in Pendle Lancs
249 G2 New Costessey Norfk
44 A6 Newcott Devon
395 E3 New Coundon Dur
399 E5 New Cowper Cumb
488 C5 Newcraighall C Edin
329 F1 New Crofton Wakefd
205 E4 New Cross Cerdgn
119 H4 New Cross Gt Lon
116 C4 New Cross Oxon
66 C6 New Cross Somset
434 C2 New Cumnock E Ayrs
479 H6 New Danna Ag & B
570 F6 New Deer Abers
431 E4 New Delaval Nthumb
327 E3 New Delph Oldham
118 A3 New Denham Bucks
76 C1 Newdigate Surrey
2 C3 New Downs Cnwll
6 D3 New Downs Cnwll
193 F2 New Duston Nhants
358 B3 New Earswick York
295 F5 New Eastwood Notts
330 B5 New Edlington Donc
568 C3 New Elgin Moray
348 C2 New Ellerby E R Yk
117 E5 Newell Green Br For
120 B5 New Eltham Gt Lon
319 G5 New End Lincs
189 G3 New End Worcs
80 B4 Newenden Kent
244 A4 New England C Pete
198 D6 New England Essex
301 F3 New England Lincs
161 G4 Newent Gloucs
135 E4 Newerne Gloucs
342 D3 New Farnley Leeds
308 D2 New Ferry Wirral
291 H4 Newfield C Stke
395 E3 Newfield Dur
405 F4 Newfield Dur
566 D1 Newfield Highld
244 A5 New Fletton C Pete
91 F4 Newfound Hants
150 D5 Newgale Pembks
421 G4 New Galloway D & G
324 C3 Newgate Lancs
261 E3 Newgate Norfk

251 E2 Newgate Corner Norfk
144 C3 Newgate Street Herts
502 C3 New Gilston Fife
609 H3 Newgord Shet
143 G3 New Greens Herts
3 C2 New Grimsby IoS
142 D2 New Ground Herts
49 F2 Newgrounds Hants
488 C5 Newhailes E Loth
255 H4 New Hainford Norfk
290 B5 Newhall Ches
274 D5 Newhall Derbys
470 C3 Newhall Mdloth
310 B2 New Hall Warrtn
214 D2 Newhall Green Warwks
340 C5 New Hall Hey Lancs
300 A4 Newham Lincs
455 F4 Newham Nthumb
431 F4 New Hartley Nthumb
488 B4 Newhaven C Edin
293 G3 Newhaven Derbys
39 E3 Newhaven Devon
56 D4 Newhaven E Susx
94 B2 New Haw Surrey
345 F3 Newhay N York
140 B3 New Headington Oxon
453 G1 New Heaton Nthumb
126 C4 New Hedges Pembks
406 A4 New Herrington Sundld
326 D2 Newhey Rochdl
329 G5 Newhill Rothm
557 F3 Newhills C Aber
140 B4 New Hinksey Oxon
393 E2 New Ho Dur
259 H4 New Holkham Norfk
342 A2 New Holland Brad
347 G5 New Holland N Linc
387 E2 Newholm N York
312 D3 New Horwich Derbys
295 G1 New Houghton Derbys
253 F2 New Houghton Norfk
451 G5 Newhouse Border
121 F5 New House Kent
468 B2 Newhouse N Lans
472 C6 Newhouses Border
367 G5 New Houses N York
324 C4 New Houses Wigan
394 D3 New Hunwick Dur
366 B1 New Hutton Cumb
97 H3 New Hythe Kent
77 H5 Newick E Susx
81 H2 Newingreen Kent
488 B5 Newington C Edin
119 G4 Newington Gt Lon
82 C3 Newington Kent
98 C1 Newington Kent
101 G2 Newington Kent
331 E6 Newington Notts
140 D5 Newington Oxon
209 H3 Newington Shrops
136 B6 Newington Bagpath Gloucs
154 C2 New Inn Carmth
39 F6 New Inn Devon
134 B4 New Inn Mons
133 F4 New Inn Torfn
209 E4 New Invention Shrops
563 G8 New Kelso Highld
276 B4 New Kingston Notts
405 E4 New Kyo Dur
474 C5 New Ladykirk Border
468 D6 New Lanark S Lans
347 G3 Newland C KuH
364 C4 Newland Cumb
346 B4 Newland E R Yk
134 C3 Newland Gloucs
345 F5 Newland N York
139 F2 Newland Oxon
188 A5 Newland Worcs
364 C3 Newland Bottom Cumb
188 C2 Newland Common Worcs
99 E5 Newland Green Kent
514 D1 Newlandhead Angus
471 G2 Newlandrig Mdloth
439 G6 Newlands Border
451 G5 Newlands Border
467 E2 Newlands C Glas
389 F5 Newlands Cumb
390 A2 Newlands Cumb
423 G2 Newlands D & G
295 E5 Newlands Derbys
566 D7 Newlands Moray
568 D5 Newlands Moray
295 H2 Newlands Notts
404 C3 Newlands Nthumb
273 G5 Newlands Staffs
94 A5 Newlands Corner Surrey
467 F4 Newlandsmuir S Lans
588 D3 Newlands of Geise Highld
568 F5 Newlands of Tynet Moray
302 C4 Newlands Park IoA
324 A2 New Lane Lancs
324 E5 New Lane End Warrtn
425 G2 New Langholm D & G
300 C3 New Leake Lincs
571 H5 New Leeds Abers
487 F5 Newliston C Edin
500 D6 Newliston Fife
329 E3 New Lodge Barns
338 C4 New Longton Lancs
601 J1 Newlot Ork
415 G4 New Luce D & G
3 E4 Newlyn Cnwll
560 C6 Newmachar Abers
490 B3 New Mains E Loth
468 C3 Newmains N Lans
119 E6 New Malden Gt Lon
145 H2 Newman's End Essex
200 A6 Newman's Green Suffk
185 E5 Newman's Place Herefs
136 B5 Newmarket Gloucs
198 C2 Newmarket Suffk
599 J7 Newmarket W Isls
597 F5 New Marske R & Cl
140 B3 New Marston Oxon
269 F2 New Marton Shrops
344 A3 New Micklefield Leeds
439 E2 Newmill Border
3 E3 New Mill Cnwll
7 F4 New Mill Cnwll
376 D4 New Mill Dur
142 C2 New Mill Herts
328 B3 New Mill Kirk
89 E2 New Mill Wilts
169 G6 New Mill End Beds
527 F2 Newmill of Inshewan Angus
441 E5 New Mills Border
472 C5 New Mills C Edin
311 F3 New Mills Ches
7 H3 New Mills Cnwll
23 F5 New Mills Cnwll
312 C2 New Mills Derbys
436 D2 New Mills Gloucs
135 E4 New Mills Gloucs
161 G2 New Mills Herefs
566 B4 New Mills Highld
232 B4 New Mills Powys
512 D3 New Mills Powys
565 J6 Newmiln P & K
449 G5 Newmilns E Ayrs
49 G5 New Milton Hants
175 F3 New Mistley Essex
152 B4 New Moat Pembks
565 J6 Newmore Highld
326 C4 New Moston Manch

706 City, town and village index: Newnes - North Reston

269 G3 Newnes Shrops
146 D3 Newney Green Essex
197 F3 Newnham Cambs
135 F2 Newnham Gloucs
92 A4 Newnham Hants
170 B2 Newnham Herts
99 F3 Newnham Kent
192 C3 Newnham Nhants
190 B2 Newnham Warwks
211 E6 Newnham Bridge Worcs
316 C6 New Ollerton Notts
237 G6 New Oscott Birm
309 H5 New Pale Ches
19 H2 New Park Devon
356 B3 New Park N York
240 C3 New Parks C Leic
109 F2 New Passage S Glos
570 F4 New Pitsligo Abers
14 C3 New Polzeath Cnwll
291 H3 Newpool Staffs
23 G5 Newport Cnwll
61 E5 Newport Devon
47 G6 Newport Dorset
346 C4 Newport E R Yk
171 H3 Newport Essex
135 F5 Newport Gloucs
582 F5 Newport Highld
37 E3 Newport IoW
107 F3 Newport Newpt
251 G1 Newport Norfk
152 B2 Newport Pembks
44 C3 Newport Somset
271 G6 Newport Wrekin
514 C4 Newport-on-Tay Fife
194 B6 Newport Pagnell M Keyn
75 G4 Newpound Common W Susx
180 A2 New Quay Cerdgn
7 E1 Newquay Cnwll
250 B2 New Rackheath Norfk
184 D2 New Radnor Powys
404 C3 New Ridley Nthumb
354 C6 New Road Side N York
81 G5 New Romney Kent
330 D5 New Rossington Donc
205 G5 New Row Cerdgn
339 F2 New Row Lancs
275 H3 New Sawley Derbys
291 G1 Newsbank Ches
559 F3 Newseat Abers
571 K6 Newseat Abers
171 E2 Newsells Herts
311 E2 Newsham Lancs
370 D3 Newsham N York
382 D3 Newsham N York
431 E3 Newsham Nthumb
341 G2 Newsholme Brad
345 H4 Newsholme E R Yk
353 G4 Newsholme Lancs
406 B4 New Silksworth Sundld
397 G6 New Skelton R & Cl
313 E3 New Smithy Derbys
328 A2 Newsome Kirk
144 C6 New Southgate Gt Lon
325 E3 New Springs Wigan
250 A2 New Sprowston Norfk
275 H2 New Stanton Derbys
451 H3 Newstead Border
272 C1 Newstead C Stke
295 G4 Newstead Notts
353 G4 Newstead Nthumb
329 F2 Newstead Wakefd
468 B2 New Stevenston N Lans
97 F2 New Street Kent
293 E4 New Street Staffs
271 E2 Newstreet Lane Shrops
34 B4 New Swanage Dorset
239 G1 New Swannington Leics
20 B3 Newtake Devon
371 E3 New Thirsk N York
344 B3 Newthorpe N York
295 F5 Newthorpe Notts
295 F5 Newthorpe Common Notts
122 B2 New Thundersley Essex
318 C2 Newtoft Lincs
494 A5 Newton Ag & B
196 B6 Newton Beds
451 G6 Newton Border
452 A5 Newton Border
104 C4 Newton Brdgnd
197 F5 Newton Cambs
245 F2 Newton Cambs
106 D4 Newton Cardif
289 H3 Newton Ches
309 F6 Newton Ches
309 H4 Newton Ches
15 F6 Newton Cnwll
364 B5 Newton Cumb
425 F5 Newton D & G
437 F6 Newton D & G
295 E3 Newton Derbys
330 C4 Newton Donc
47 E2 Newton Dorset
159 G3 Newton Herefs
185 E6 Newton Herefs
186 C4 Newton Herefs
209 G6 Newton Herefs
566 C7 Newton Highld
566 D3 Newton Highld
579 H3 Newton Highld
589 K7 Newton Highld
337 F2 Newton Lancs
352 D4 Newton Lancs
366 B5 Newton Lancs
279 E2 Newton Lincs
568 B3 Newton Moray
463 F4 Newton N Ayrs
218 B3 Newton Nhants
253 G4 Newton Norfk
277 E1 Newton Notts
404 B2 Newton Nthumb
110 A1 Newton S Glos
448 B3 Newton S Lans
467 G2 Newton S Lans
237 F6 Newton Sandw
235 G5 Newton Shrops
269 H3 Newton Shrops
64 B4 Newton Somset
273 F4 Newton Staffs
174 B1 Newton Suffk
103 E4 Newton Swans
327 E5 Newton Tamesd
487 E4 Newton W Loth
216 B4 Newton Warwks
71 E5 Newton Wilts
308 B2 Newton Wirral
20 B3 Newton Abbot Devon
399 G4 Newton Arlosh Cumb
395 F5 Newton Aycliffe Dur
396 C4 Newton Bewley Hartpl
194 C4 Newton Blossomville M Keyn
194 D1 Newton Bromswold Nhants
239 F3 Newton Burgoland Leics
318 C2 Newton by Toft Lincs
151 E4 Newton Cross Pembks
11 F4 Newton Ferrers Devon
594 D7 Newton Ferry W Isls
249 H5 Newton Flotman Norfk
405 G5 Newton Grange Dur
471 F2 Newtongrange Mdloth
109 F1 Newton Green Mons
405 G5 Newton Hall Dur
404 B1 Newton Hall Nthumb
240 D5 Newton Harcourt Leics
326 C4 Newton Heath Manch
557 G6 Newtonhill Abers
565 K8 Newtonhill Highld
343 F5 Newton Hill Wakefd
273 G4 Newton Hurst Staffs
290 D1 Newtonia Ches
395 G5 Newton Ketton Darltn
357 F5 Newton Kyme N York
369 H2 Newton-le-Willows N York
324 D5 Newton-le-Willows St Hel
240 B3 Newton Linford Leics
168 A3 Newton Longville Bucks
466 D3 Newton Mearns E Rens
528 D2 Newtonmill Angus
535 J3 Newtonmore Highld
383 F3 Newton Morrell N York
166 D4 Newton Morrell Oxon
386 C1 Newton Mulgrave N York
518 F1 Newton of Ardtoe Highld
500 C2 Newton of Balcanquhal P & K
503 E4 Newton of Balcormo Fife
528 D5 Newton of Boysack Angus
501 E3 Newton of Falkland Fife
499 G2 Newton of Pitcairns P & K
444 D5 Newton on Ayr S Ayrs
357 G3 Newton-on-Ouse N York
373 F1 Newton-on-Rawcliffe N York
270 B5 Newton on the Hill Shrops
443 F3 Newton on the Moor Nthumb
317 F5 Newton on Trent Lincs
481 G6 Newton Park Ag & B
324 D6 Newton Park St Hel
48 A5 Newton Peveril Dorset
28 A5 Newton Poppleford Devon
166 D3 Newton Purcell Oxon
238 D3 Newton Regis Warwks
390 D3 Newton Reigny Cumb
390 D3 Newton Rigg Cumb
26 D3 Newton St Cyres Devon
250 A1 Newton St Faith Norfk
86 B2 Newton St Loe BaNES
39 F5 Newton St Petrock Devon
274 D4 Newton Solney Derbys
72 B1 Newton Stacey Hants
417 E4 Newton Stewart D & G
71 E1 Newton Tony Wilts
40 A2 Newton Tracey Devon
385 F2 Newton under Roseberry R & Cl
430 B2 Newton Underwood Nthumb
358 D5 Newton upon Derwent E R Yk
73 H3 Newton Valence Hants
338 C3 Newton-with-Scales Lancs
326 D5 Newton Wood Tamesd
314 C4 New Totley Sheff
494 B3 Newtown Ag & B
85 G2 New Town BaNES
86 D3 New Town BaNES
213 G2 Newtown Birm
132 C3 Newtown Blae G
142 D4 Newtown Bucks
488 B5 New Town C Edin
50 D2 New Town C Sotn
106 D1 Newtown Caerph
219 G6 Newtown Cambs
310 A4 Newtown Ches
3 G4 Newtown Cnwll
16 C3 Newtown Cnwll
398 D5 Newtown Cumb
400 C3 Newtown Cumb
401 E2 Newtown Cumb
312 C2 Newtown Derbys
27 H3 Newtown Devon
41 F3 Newtown Devon
30 B2 Newtown Dorset
48 B1 New Town Dorset
48 B3 New Town Dorset
68 C5 New Town Dorset
489 E5 New Town E Loth
78 B5 New Town E Susx
486 C3 Newtown Falk
135 F4 Newtown Gloucs
136 A3 Newtown Gloucs
162 D3 Newtown Gloucs
163 F3 New Town Gloucs
49 H2 Newtown Hants
51 E3 Newtown Hants
51 F1 Newtown Hants
51 H2 Newtown Hants
51 H5 Newtown Hants
71 F5 Newtown Hants
73 H2 Newtown Hants
74 C3 Newtown Hants
90 D2 Newtown Hants
160 C3 Newtown Herefs
187 E6 Newtown Herefs
534 B2 Newtown Highld
36 C2 Newtown IoW
97 G3 New Town Kent
120 D5 New Town Kent
338 D6 Newtown Lancs
339 E2 New Town Lancs
169 F5 New Town Luton
97 H2 New Town Medway
251 G3 Newtown Norfk
442 C4 Newtown Nthumb
454 C4 Newtown Nthumb
116 C3 Newtown Oxon
164 C3 New Town Oxon
48 C6 Newtown Poole
208 B1 Newtown Powys
116 B5 Newtown Readg
131 H5 Newtown Rhondd
406 A2 New Town S Tyne
325 H4 Newtown Salfd
213 E1 New Town Sandw
235 E4 Newtown Shrops
269 H5 Newtown Shrops
270 B3 Newtown Shrops
44 B5 Newtown Somset
45 H4 New Town Somset
65 E4 Newtown Somset
67 H6 New Town Somset
85 E5 New Town Somset
324 B5 Newtown St Hel
237 E4 Newtown Staffs
292 B2 Newtown Staffs
293 E2 Newtown Staffs
406 B5 New Town Sundld
113 E3 New Town Swindn
115 G4 New Town W Berk
76 C4 New Town W Susx
344 B5 New Town Wakefd
324 D3 Newtown Wigan
69 F4 Newtown Wilts
88 D4 New Town Wilts
89 G2 Newtown Wilts
113 G5 New Town Wilts
187 H3 Newtown Worcs
188 C2 Newtown Worcs
237 G3 New Town Wsall
4 D4 Newtown-in-St Martin Cnwll
451 H3 Newtown St Boswells Border
240 A4 Newton Unthank Leics
132 B4 New Tredegar Caerph
447 G2 New Trows S Lans
513 H1 Newtyle Angus
479 J5 New Ulva Ag & B
330 C3 New Village Donc
347 G3 New Village E R Yk
334 C4 New Waltham NE Lin
207 H4 New Well Powys
232 C5 New Wells Powys
314 D4 New Whittington Derbys
489 E5 New Winton E Loth
270 D1 New Woodhouses Shrops
235 F3 New Works Wrekin
139 F2 New Yatt Oxon
118 B2 Newyears Green Gt Lon
299 G3 New York Lincs
431 F5 New York N Tyne
355 G2 New York N York
112 B4 New Zealand Wilts
185 F3 Nextend Herefs
125 G3 Neyland Pembks
322 b7 Niarbyl IoM
269 H6 Nib Heath Shrops
135 F3 Nibley Gloucs
110 B3 Nibley S Glos
135 G5 Nibley Green Gloucs
606 D3 Nibon Shet
43 E4 Nicholashayne Devon
102 D4 Nicholaston Swans
356 C2 Nidd N York
488 B5 Niddrie C Edin
557 G4 Nigg C Aber
566 E2 Nigg Highld
566 D3 Nigg Ferry Highld
287 E3 Nilig Denbgs
326 D4 Nimble Nook Oldham
110 C5 Nimlet S Glos
44 C5 Nimmer Somset
146 B4 Nine Ashes Essex
402 D4 Ninebanks Nthumb
119 F4 Nine Elms Gt Lon
112 D2 Nine Elms Swindn
4 C1 Nine Maidens Downs Cnwll
27 G4 Nine Oaks Devon
187 E2 Nineveh Worcs
211 F5 Nineveh Worcs
514 B3 Ninewells C Dund
134 D2 Ninewells Gloucs
150 C5 Nine Wells Pembks
58 B4 Ninfield E Susx
36 B3 Ningwood IoW
36 B3 Ningwood Common IoW
3 F2 Ninnes Bridge Cnwll
452 C4 Nisbet Border
607 J5 Nisthouse Shet
435 H5 Nithbank D & G
423 G4 Nithside D & G
37 E5 Niton IoW
466 D2 Nitshill C Glas
282 D2 Niwbwrch IoA
97 E3 Noah's Arks Kent
189 E2 Noah's Green Worcs
121 G1 Noak Bridge Essex
121 G1 Noak Hill Essex
146 A6 Noak Hill Gt Lon
325 G3 Nob End Bolton
171 F6 Nobland Green Herts
234 B2 Nobold Shrops
193 E2 Nobottle Nhants
72 C5 Nob's Crook Hants
298 C2 Nocton Lincs
308 C2 Noctorum Wirral
114 C4 Nodmore W Berk
119 G1 Noel Park Gt Lon
250 D4 Nogdam End Norfk
338 C3 Nog Tow Lancs
140 B2 Noke Oxon
122 A5 Noke Street Medway
151 E6 Nolton Pembks
151 E6 Nolton Haven Pembks
289 H5 No Man's Heath Ches
238 D3 No Man's Heath Warwks
10 A2 No Man's Land Cnwll
41 G5 Nomansland Devon
72 D4 No Man's Land Hants
143 H2 Nomansland Herts
49 G1 Nomansland Wilts
270 B4 Noneley Shrops
566 B2 Nonikiln Highld
101 E5 Nonington Kent
366 A3 Nook Cumb
426 C4 Nook Cumb
606 C6 Noonsbrough Shet
311 G4 Noonsun Ches
3 G3 Noonvares Cnwll
527 G2 Noranside Angus
118 D6 Norbiton Gt Lon
337 E1 Norbreck Bpool
187 G5 Norbridge Herefs
290 B5 Norbury Ches
273 H1 Norbury Derbys
119 G6 Norbury Gt Lon
233 G6 Norbury Shrops
272 A5 Norbury Staffs
290 B5 Norbury Common Ches
272 A5 Norbury Junction Staffs
312 B2 Norbury Moor Stockp
371 E3 Norby N York
606 A6 Norby Shet
212 B6 Norchard Worcs
137 F4 Norcote Gloucs
310 C3 Norcott Brook Ches
337 F1 Norcross Lancs
246 B4 Nordelph Norfk
248 D4 Nordelph Corner Norfk
33 G3 Norden Dorset
326 C2 Norden Rochdl
235 F5 Nordley Shrops
474 D5 Norham Nthumb
474 D5 Norham West Mains Nthumb
95 E3 Nork Surrey
341 H5 Norland Town Calder
87 F4 Norleaze Wilts
310 B5 Norley Ches
24 D2 Norley Devon
93 H6 Norley Common Surrey
50 C5 Norleywood Hants
56 C2 Norlington E Susx
332 B1 Normanby N Linc
372 D3 Normanby N York
396 D6 Normanby R & Cl
318 C2 Normanby-by-Spital Lincs
317 G3 Normanby by Stow Lincs
333 G5 Normanby le Wold Lincs
219 H1 Norman Cross Cambs
93 F4 Normandy Surrey
135 G5 Norman Hill Gloucs
58 A5 Norman's Bay E Susx
27 H2 Norman's Green Devon
251 G6 Normanston Suffk
275 E3 Normanton C Derb
277 G1 Normanton Leics
298 B5 Normanton Lincs
296 D4 Normanton Notts
242 C3 Normanton Rutlnd
343 G5 Normanton Wakefd
70 C1 Normanton Wilts
239 F2 Normanton le Heath Leics
276 B5 Normanton on Soar Notts
276 D3 Normanton-on-the-Wolds Notts
317 E6 Normanton on Trent Notts
314 D3 Normanton Spring Sheff
240 A5 Normanton Turville Leics
337 F2 Normoss Lancs
93 F6 Norney Surrey
342 A2 Norr Brad
87 F2 Norrington Common Wilts
17 F5 Norris Green Cnwll
323 G6 Norris Green Lpool
239 E1 Norris Hill Leics
602 D8 Norseman Ork
248 C5 Northacre Norfk
119 E3 North Acton Gt Lon
168 C5 Northall Bucks
384 B6 Northallerton N York
254 C5 Northall Green Norfk
50 D2 Northam C Sotn
39 F2 Northam Devon
193 G3 Northampton Nhants
315 G3 North Anston Rothm
117 F5 North Ascot Br For
166 A4 North Aston Oxon
144 C4 Northaw Herts
29 G2 Northay Devon
44 B5 Northay Somset
603 G4 North Ayre Ork
609 G7 North Aywick Shet
72 A6 North Baddesley Hants
520 F3 North Ballachulish Highld
67 G4 North Barrow Somset
260 B4 North Barsham Norfk
279 F1 Northbeck Lincs
23 G4 North Beer Cnwll
122 B2 North Benfleet Essex
53 G4 North Bersted W Susx
489 G3 North Berwick E Loth
394 D3 North Bitchburn Dur
431 F3 North Blyth Nthumb
51 H2 North Boarhunt Hants
49 F5 North Bockhampton Dorset
243 G3 Northborough C Pete
48 D5 Northbourne Bmouth
101 F5 Northbourne Kent
26 A6 North Bovey Devon
30 A3 North Bowood Dorset
87 F3 North Bradley Wilts
17 G2 North Brentor Devon
68 B2 North Brewham Somset
78 D5 Northbridge Street E Susx
46 D5 Northbrook Dorset
72 D2 Northbrook Hants
72 D6 Northbrook Hants
166 A5 Northbrook Oxon
88 B4 Northbrook Wilts
196 C6 North Brook End Cambs
485 H3 North Broomage Falk
60 C3 North Buckland Devon
250 D2 North Burlingham Norfk
67 G4 North Cadbury Somset
414 C2 North Cairn D & G
93 E4 North Camp Hants
318 A4 North Carlton Lincs
316 A3 North Carlton Notts
456 D4 North Carrine Ag & B
346 C3 North Cave E R Yk
137 F3 North Cerney Gloucs
77 G5 North Chailey E Susx
75 F4 Northchapel W Susx
70 D6 North Charford Hants
455 F5 North Charlton Nthumb
95 E1 North Cheam Gt Lon
68 A4 North Cheriton Somset
29 H4 North Chideock Dorset
142 D3 Northchurch Herts
346 C2 North Cliffe E R Yk
317 F5 North Clifton Notts
395 F3 North Close Dur
320 C1 North Cockerington Lincs
45 G5 North Coker Somset
608 C8 North Collafirth Shet
110 B5 North Common S Glos
224 C4 North Common Suffk
506 F3 North Connel Ag & B
104 C3 North Cornelly Brdgnd
5 E5 North Corner Cnwll
110 B3 North Corner S Glos
461 E2 North Corriegills N Ayrs
28 C2 Northcote Devon
40 C4 Northcote Manor Devon
334 D4 North Cotes Lincs
38 B6 Northcott Cnwll
23 G4 Northcott Devon
43 E5 Northcott Devon
43 F6 Northcott Devon
6 C5 North Country Cnwll
140 B5 Northcourt Oxon
227 F2 North Cove Suffk
383 G4 North Cowton N York
529 E2 North Craigo Angus
569 L5 North Cranna Abers
194 C6 North Crawley M Keyn
120 C5 North Cray Gt Lon
259 H4 North Creake Norfk
44 C2 North Curry Somset
609 J2 Northdale Shet
359 H4 North Dalton E R Yk
16 C4 North Darley Cnwll
601 H4 North Dawn Ork
356 D4 North Deighton N York
251 G2 North Denes Norfk
101 G1 Northdown Kent
514 A2 North Dronley Angus
345 F2 North Duffield N York
602 A7 Northdyke Ork
391 E2 North Dykes Cumb
99 F3 North Eastling Kent
294 D2 Northedge Derbys
82 C2 North Elham Kent
320 A1 North Elkington Lincs
254 C3 North Elmham Norfk
330 A2 North Elmsall Wakefd
488 D5 North Elphinestone E Loth
85 H2 North End BaNES
110 D6 Northend BaNES
194 D5 North End Beds
195 E3 North End Beds
116 B1 Northend Bucks
167 E4 North End Bucks
168 A4 North End Bucks
52 B4 North End C Port
400 B3 North End Cumb
43 E4 North End Devon
68 D4 North End Dorset
405 G6 North End Dur
348 C1 North End E R Yk
349 E3 North End E R Yk
361 F4 North End E R Yk
148 C4 North End Essex
171 H2 Northend Essex
172 D6 North End Essex
173 F2 North End Essex
119 F2 North End Gt Lon
120 D4 North End Gt Lon
49 E1 North End Hants
73 E4 North End Hants
90 C2 North End Hants
240 C1 North End Leics
280 B1 North End Lincs
320 C1 North End Lincs
320 D2 North End Lincs
321 E2 North End Lincs
333 E5 North End Lincs
334 D4 North End Lincs
348 B5 North End N Linc
84 D1 North End N Som
224 D1 North End Norfk
443 E4 North End Nthumb
44 B2 North End Somset
54 A4 North End W Susx
54 D2 North End W Susx
77 G2 North End W Susx
191 F4 Northend Warwks
137 F6 North End Wilts
311 G1 Northenden Manch
311 G1 Northern Moor Manch
572 D7 North Erradale Highld
240 D4 North Evington C Leic
332 A4 North Ewster N Linc
147 H5 North Fambridge Essex
545 K2 North Fearns Highld
344 A5 North Featherstone Wakefd
118 C5 North Feltham Gt Lon
460 C4 North Feorline N Ayrs
347 E4 North Ferriby E R Yk
213 F4 Northfield Birm
451 H4 Northfield Border
474 D1 Northfield Border
557 F3 Northfield C Aber
488 B5 Northfield C Edin
347 F4 Northfield E R Yk
168 B1 Northfield M Keyn
65 E4 Northfield Somset
72 C4 Northfields Hants
119 F1 North Finchley Gt Lon
121 F5 Northfleet Kent
121 F5 Northfleet Green Kent
560 A3 North Flobbets Abers
101 H2 North Foreland Kent
361 E4 North Frodingham E R Yk
465 G6 North Furgushill N Ayrs
280 A4 Northgate Lincs
43 E2 Northgate Somset
77 E2 Northgate W Susx
606 D2 North Gluss Shet
49 F2 North Gorley Hants
225 H2 North Green Norfk
248 D3 North Green Norfk
202 C2 North Green Suffk
202 D1 North Green Suffk
226 C4 North Green Suffk
318 C5 North Greetwell Lincs
373 F6 North Grimston N York
97 G1 North Halling Medway
118 C2 North Harrow Gt Lon
52 C4 North Hayling Hants
62 A5 North Heasley Devon
114 D5 North Heath W Berk
75 H5 North Heath W Susx
16 C3 North Hill Cnwll
118 B3 North Hillingdon Gt Lon
140 B3 North Hinksey Village Oxon
94 D5 North Holmwood Surrey
71 G3 North Houghton Hants
345 H3 North Howden E R Yk
12 C1 North Huish Devon
118 C4 North Hyde Gt Lon
298 A1 North Hykeham Lincs
406 A3 North Hylton Sundld
80 B5 Northiam E Susx
195 H5 Northill Beds
512 D5 North Inch P & K
135 G3 Northington Gloucs
73 E2 Northington Hants
333 E4 North Kelsey Lincs
333 F4 North Kelsey Moor Lincs
566 B7 North Kessock Highld
333 G1 North Killingholme N Linc
371 E2 North Kilvington N York
216 D3 North Kilworth Leics
49 F4 North Kingston Hants
461 E4 North Kiscadale N Ayrs
299 E4 North Kyme Lincs
55 E3 North Lancing W Susx
375 G5 North Landing E R Yk
300 B4 Northlands Lincs
406 C4 Northlea Dur
137 H2 Northleach Gloucs
142 A3 North Lee Bucks
370 C5 North Lees N York
28 C3 Northleigh Devon
61 F5 Northleigh Devon
82 B1 North Leigh Kent
139 F2 North Leigh Oxon
317 E3 North Leverton with Habblesthorpe Notts
24 D3 Northlew Devon
189 G5 North Littleton Worcs
95 E2 North Looe Surrey
224 D3 North Lopham Norfk
242 C4 North Luffenham Rutlnd
52 D1 North Marden W Susx
167 G5 North Marston Bucks
471 G3 North Middleton Mdloth
454 B5 North Middleton Nthumb
415 E6 North Milmain D & G
41 E2 North Molton Devon
38 C4 Northmoor Devon
139 G4 Northmoor Oxon
65 F5 Northmoor Corner Somset
65 F5 Northmoor Green or Moorland Somset
115 F2 North Moreton Oxon
28 A5 Northmostown Devon
468 A3 North Motherwell N Lans
56 A3 North Moulsecoomb Br & H
527 E3 Northmuir Angus
53 F4 North Mundham W Susx
297 E3 North Muskham Notts
600 E6 North Ness Ork
526 D6 North Nevay Angus
346 D2 North Newbald E R Yk
165 G2 North Newington Oxon
88 D3 North Newnton Wilts
65 F5 North Newton Somset
52 C4 Northney Hants
135 G5 North Nibley Gloucs
91 E4 North Oakley Hants
121 E3 North Ockendon Gt Lon
118 C3 Northolt Gt Lon
308 B6 Northop Flints
308 C6 Northop Hall Flints
396 D6 North Ormesby Middsb
334 C6 North Ormsby Lincs
342 D5 Northorpe Kirk
243 F1 Northorpe Lincs
280 A2 Northorpe Lincs
332 B5 Northorpe Lincs
370 D2 North Otterington N York
66 D2 Northover Somset
67 E5 Northover Somset
333 F6 North Owersby Lincs
342 B4 Northowram Calder
45 F6 North Perrott Somset
65 E5 North Petherton Somset
23 F5 North Petherwin Cnwll
247 H3 North Pickenham Norfk
189 E4 North Piddle Worcs
30 C3 North Poorton Dorset
33 G2 Northport Dorset
49 F3 North Poulner Hants
605 G6 Northpunds Shet
487 F3 North Queensferry Fife
62 A5 North Radworthy Devon
298 C5 North Rauceby Lincs
559 F3 North Rayne Abers
326 C6 North Reddish Stockp
256 A2 Northrepps Norfk
320 C3 North Reston Lincs

356 B5 North Rigton N York
49 F5 North Ripley Hants
292 A1 North Rode Ches
608 D7 North Roe Shet
389 F5 North Row Cumb
252 C4 North Runcton Norfk
364 A6 North Scale Ches
297 G1 North Scarle Lincs
431 E2 North Seaton Nthumb
431 E2 North Seaton Colliery Nthumb
520 C7 North Shian Ag & B
431 F6 North Shields N Tyne
123 E2 North Shoebury Sthend
337 F2 North Shore Bpool
244 C5 North Side C Pete
388 B4 North Side Cumb
602 B6 Northside Ork
397 G6 North Skelton R & Cl
335 F5 North Somercotes Lincs
370 B4 North Stainley N York
381 E1 North Stainmore Cumb
28 A5 North Star Thurr
121 E3 North Stifford Thurr
110 C6 North Stoke BaNES
115 G2 North Stoke Oxon
54 B2 North Stoke W Susx
50 D1 North Stoneham Hants
70 D6 North Street Hants
73 F3 North Street Hants
99 G3 North Street Kent
122 C5 North Street Medway
115 G5 North Street W Berk
455 G3 North Sunderland Nthumb
451 F5 North Synton Border
23 G3 North Tamerton Cnwll
25 G2 North Tawton Devon
334 C5 North Thoresby Lincs
89 F5 North Tidworth Wilts
443 G4 North Togston Nthumb
594 F5 Northton W Isls
39 G6 North Town Devon
93 E4 North Town Hants
601 H5 Northtown Ork
605 G8 North Town Shet
67 F1 North Town Somset
67 G4 North Town Somset
117 E3 North Town W & M
254 D5 North Tuddenham Norfk
120 C4 Northumberland Heath Gt Lon
133 E5 Northville Torfn
430 C6 North Walbottle N u Ty
603 L3 Northwall Ork
364 A6 North Walney Cumb
256 A3 North Walsham Norfk
91 F5 North Waltham Hants
92 B4 North Warnborough Hants
529 E1 North Water Bridge Angus
44 B6 North Waterhayne Devon
143 G5 North Watford Herts
589 G5 North Watten Highld
39 E3 Northway Devon
162 D3 Northway Gloucs
43 F2 Northway Somset
103 E4 Northway Swans
145 G4 North Weald Bassett Essex
50 A4 North Weirs Hants
118 D2 North Wembley Gt Lon
609 G1 North Westerhouse Shet
109 E5 North Weston N Som
141 E3 North Weston Oxon
317 E2 North Wheatley Notts
20 B4 North Whilborough Devon
173 E6 North Whitehouse Essex
310 C5 Northwich Ches
85 G1 North Wick BaNES
109 G2 Northwick S Glos
84 C5 Northwick Somset
188 B3 Northwick Worcs
85 G3 North Widcombe BaNES
319 F2 North Willingham Lincs
295 E2 North Wingfield Derbys
278 C5 North Witham Lincs
247 F5 Northwold Norfk
292 A5 Northwood C Stke
294 B2 Northwood Derbys
118 B1 Northwood Gt Lon
51 E6 Northwood IoW
101 G2 Northwood Kent
323 H5 Northwood Knows
270 B3 Northwood Shrops
291 H6 Northwood Staffs
135 G1 Northwood Green Gloucs
118 B1 Northwood Hills Gt Lon
46 C2 North Wootton Dorset
252 C3 North Wootton Norfk
67 F1 North Wootton Somset
111 E4 North Wraxall Wilts
112 D3 North Wroughton Swindn
13 F2 Norton Devon
38 C2 Norton Devon
330 B2 Norton Donc
212 C3 Norton Dudley
56 D4 Norton E Susx
162 C5 Norton Gloucs
310 A3 Norton Halton
170 B3 Norton Herts
36 A3 Norton IoW
160 A5 Norton Mons
84 B2 Norton N Som
192 D2 Norton Nhants
315 H5 Norton Notts
185 F1 Norton Powys
396 B5 Norton S on T
314 D3 Norton Sheff
210 B3 Norton Shrops
234 D3 Norton Shrops
235 G4 Norton Shrops
200 C1 Norton Suffk
102 C4 Norton Swans
103 F4 Norton Swans
53 F5 Norton W Susx
53 G3 Norton W Susx
111 F3 Norton Wilts
188 C4 Norton Worcs
189 F5 Norton Worcs
99 F2 Norton Ash Kent
87 G6 Norton Bavant Wilts
272 C3 Norton Bridge Staffs
237 F3 Norton Canes Staffs
185 G5 Norton Canon Herefs
255 E2 Norton Corner Norfk
297 G3 Norton Disney Lincs
237 F3 Norton East Staffs
68 C2 Norton Ferris Wilts
43 G2 Norton Fitzwarren Somset
292 A4 Norton Green C Stke
170 B5 Norton Green Herts
36 A3 Norton Green IoW
214 B5 Norton Green Solhll
85 G2 Norton Hawkfield BaNES
146 C4 Norton Heath Essex
86 B4 Norton Hill BaNES
271 G2 Norton in Hales Shrops
292 A4 Norton-in-the-Moors C Stke
239 E3 Norton-Juxta-Twycross Leics
371 E5 Norton-le-Clay N York
190 C2 Norton Lindsey Warwks
200 C1 Norton Little Green Suffk
85 H1 Norton Malreward BaNES
146 B4 Norton Mandeville Essex

373 F5 Norton-on-Derwent N York
86 D3 Norton St Philip Somset
250 D5 Norton Subcourse Norfk
45 F4 Norton sub Hamdon Somset
108 D5 Norton's Wood N Som
314 D3 Norton Woodseats Sheff
297 E2 Norwell Notts
296 D2 Norwell Woodhouse Notts
250 A3 Norwich Norfk
609 K2 Norwick Shet
315 F3 Norwood Derbys
30 C1 Norwood Dorset
146 B3 Norwood End Essex
118 C4 Norwood Green Gt Lon
95 E6 Norwood Hill Surrey
119 G5 Norwood New Town Gt Lon
245 F5 Norwoodside Cambs
241 F5 Noseley Leics
589 K6 Noss Highld
605 G7 Noss Shet
11 G4 Noss Mayo Devon
370 B3 Nosterfield N York
198 C6 Nosterfield End Cambs
546 F4 Nostie Highld
163 H5 Notgrove Gloucs
104 C4 Nottage Brdgnd
10 C1 Notter Cnwll
276 C2 Nottingham C Nott
119 E3 Notting Hill Gt Lon
31 E6 Nottington Dorset
329 E2 Notton Wakefd
111 G6 Notton Wilts
147 F2 Nounsley Essex
188 A1 Noutard's Green Worcs
310 C6 Nova Scotia Ches
109 G6 Novers Park Bristl
163 E5 Noverton Gloucs
199 H2 Nowton Suffk
233 H2 Nox Shrops
179 E4 Noyadd Trefawr Cerdgn
179 E4 Noyadd Wilym Cerdgn
115 H2 Nuffield Oxon
344 C1 Nun Appleton N York
359 F5 Nunburnholme E R Yk
295 G4 Nuncargate Notts
401 E5 Nunclose Cumb
215 F1 Nuneaton Warwks
140 B5 Nuneham Courtenay Oxon
115 H4 Nuney Green Oxon
119 H4 Nunhead Gt Lon
340 D5 Nun Hills Lancs
423 G4 Nunholm D & G
357 G3 Nun Monkton N York
86 C5 Nunney Somset
86 C5 Nunney Catch Somset
372 C4 Nunnington N York
442 D6 Nunnykirk Nthumb
334 B3 Nunsthorpe NE Lin
385 E2 Nunthorpe Middsb
70 D4 Nunton Wilts
370 C5 Nunwick N York
428 D5 Nunwick Nthumb
423 F4 Nunwood D & G
135 E5 Nupdown S Glos
168 B6 Nup End Bucks
136 A3 Nupend Gloucs
136 B5 Nupend Gloucs
145 H6 Nuper's Hatch Essex
134 D4 Nuppend Gloucs
117 E5 Nuptown Br For
50 C1 Nursling Hants
74 B5 Nursted Hants
88 B2 Nursteed Wilts
105 H6 Nurston V Glam
236 B5 Nurton Staffs
236 B5 Nurton Hill Staffs
52 D3 Nutbourne W Susx
76 A6 Nutbourne W Susx
76 A6 Nutbourne Common W Susx
72 A5 Nutburn Hants
74 D3 Nutcombe Surrey
95 G4 Nutfield Surrey
324 B6 Nut Grove St Hel
295 G6 Nuthall Notts
171 E3 Nuthampstead Herts
76 C4 Nuthurst W Susx
214 A5 Nuthurst Warwks
78 A4 Nutley E Susx
91 G6 Nutley Hants
326 A1 Nuttall Bury
330 D4 Nutwell Donc
589 K4 Nybster Highld
84 D2 Nye N Som
53 F5 Nyetimber W Susx
74 C5 Nyewood W Susx
84 D4 Nyland Somset
41 E6 Nymet Rowland Devon
26 A2 Nymet Tracey Devon
136 B4 Nympsfield Gloucs
43 F3 Nynehead Somset
66 C3 Nythe Somset
113 E2 Nythe Swindn
53 G3 Nyton W Susx

O

240 D4 Oadby Leics
98 D2 Oad Street Kent
188 B2 Oakall Green Worcs
292 D6 Oakamoor Staffs
326 B3 Oak Bank Bury
470 A1 Oakbank W Loth
24 D3 Oak Cross Devon
132 C5 Oakdale Caerph
356 B3 Oakdale N York
48 C6 Oakdale Poole
43 G2 Oake Somset
43 G2 Oake Green Somset
236 C4 Oaken Staffs
352 A5 Oakenclough Lancs
235 G2 Oakengates Wrekin
308 B5 Oakenholt Flints
395 E2 Oakenshaw Dur
342 C4 Oakenshaw Kirk
340 A3 Oakenshaw Lancs
294 D4 Oakerthorpe Derbys
327 H1 Oakes Kirk
170 A4 Oakfield Herts
37 F2 Oakfield IoW
133 E6 Oakfield Torfn
180 C3 Oakford Cerdgn
42 B3 Oakford Devon
42 B3 Oakfordbridge Devon
312 B6 Oakgrove Ches
168 D2 Oakgrove M Keyn
242 A3 Oakham Rutlnd
213 E2 Oakham Sandw
291 F4 Oakhanger Ches
74 B2 Oakhanger Hants
291 H6 Oak Hill C Stke
86 A5 Oakhill Somset
202 D5 Oak Hill Suffk
76 C3 Oakhill W Susx
97 A4 Oakhurst Kent
197 E2 Oakington Cambs
128 B1 Oaklands Carmth
285 H3 Oaklands Conwy
144 B1 Oaklands Herts
144 C6 Oakleigh Park Gt Lon
161 H6 Oakle Street Gloucs

195 E4 Oakley Beds
140 D2 Oakley Bucks
486 D2 Oakley Fife
165 E5 Oakley Gloucs
141 F4 Oakley Hants
48 C5 Oakley Poole
271 G2 Oakley Staffs
225 G4 Oakley Suffk
115 G2 Oakley Court Oxon
117 F4 Oakley Green W & M
225 G4 Oakley Park Suffk
115 G2 Oakley Wood Oxon
310 B6 Oakmere Ches
91 G4 Oakridge Hants
136 D4 Oakridge Lynch Gloucs
233 H4 Oaks Shrops
137 E6 Oaksey Wilts
274 B3 Oaks Green Derbys
426 D4 Oakshaw Ford Cumb
74 A4 Oakshott Hants
240 A1 Oaks in Charnwood Leics
239 E2 Oakthorpe Leics
384 B2 Oak Tree Darltn
342 D4 Oakwell Kirk
275 F2 Oakwood C Derb
144 C5 Oakwood Gt Lon
343 F2 Oakwood Leeds
403 G1 Oakwood Nthumb
310 D1 Oakwood Warrtn
341 G2 Oakworth Brad
575 J3 Oape Highld
99 F2 Oare Kent
62 B2 Oare Somset
115 E5 Oare W Berk
89 E2 Oare Wilts
62 C2 Oareford Somset
279 E2 Oasby Lincs
66 B4 Oath Somset
29 H1 Oathill Dorset
527 G3 Oathlaw Angus
467 E2 Oatlands C Glas
356 C4 Oatlands N York
94 B2 Oatlands Park Surrey
506 E3 Oban Ag & B
596 F7 Oban W Isls
506 C6 Oban Seil Ag & B
209 F4 Obley Shrops
67 G6 Oborne Dorset
566 B3 Obsdale Park Highld
290 D2 Occlestone Green Ches
225 G5 Occold Suffk
50 D2 Ocean Village C Sotn
445 G5 Ochiltree E Ayrs
307 F4 Ochr-y-foel Denbgs
498 C1 Ochtermuthill P & K
511 E5 Ochtertyre P & K
275 G2 Ockbrook Derbys
237 E6 Ocker Hill Sandw
187 H2 Ockeridge Worcs
93 G6 Ockford Ridge Surrey
94 B3 Ockham Surrey
518 E1 Ockle Highld
76 B1 Ockley Surrey
186 D5 Ocle Pychard Herefs
605 H4 Ocraquoy Shet
41 E4 Odam Barton Devon
45 G4 Odcombe Somset
86 C2 Odd Down BaNES
379 G2 Oddendale Cumb
188 D3 Oddingley Worcs
140 C2 Oddington Oxon
194 D3 Odell Beds
24 C2 Odham Devon
603 J6 Odie Ork
92 B4 Odiham Hants
170 C2 Odsey Cambs
70 C4 Odstock Wilts
239 F3 Odstone Leics
191 F1 Offchurch Warwks
189 F5 Offenham Worcs
189 G5 Offenham Cross Worcs
312 B2 Offerton Stockp
406 A3 Offerton Sundld
312 B2 Offerton Green Stockp
56 B2 Offham E Susx
97 G3 Offham Kent
54 B3 Offham W Susx
272 A4 Offleyhay Staffs
272 A4 Offleymarsh Staffs
272 A4 Offleyrock Staffs
196 B1 Offord Cluny Cambs
196 B1 Offord D'arcy Cambs
201 E5 Offton Suffk
28 C3 Offwell Devon
113 E5 Ogbourne Maizey Wilts
113 E5 Ogbourne St Andrew Wilts
113 F5 Ogbourne St George Wilts
341 H3 Ogden Calder
49 F2 Ogdens Hants
527 F2 Ogil Angus
430 B4 Ogle Nthumb
309 F3 Oglet Lpool
104 D4 Ogmore V Glam
104 C5 Ogmore-by-Sea V Glam
105 E1 Ogmore Vale Brdgnd
47 F2 Okeford Fitzpaine Dorset
25 E3 Okehampton Devon
25 E4 Okehampton Camp Devon
294 B2 Oker Derbys
76 B2 Okewood Hill Surrey
161 H4 Okle Green Gloucs
112 D3 Okus Swindn
99 H5 Olantigh Kent
20 B2 Olchard Devon
217 G5 Old Nhants
557 G3 Old Aberdeen C Aber
73 E3 Old Alresford Hants
578 E3 Oldany Highld
214 D1 Old Arley Warwks
514 B2 Old Balkello Angus
484 C6 Old Balornock C Glas
295 H6 Old Basford C Nott
91 H4 Old Basing Hants
254 C4 Old Beetley Norfk
451 H5 Old Belses Border
189 H1 Oldberrow Warwks
454 D5 Old Bewick Nthumb
120 C5 Old Bexley Gt Lon
524 C2 Old Blair P & K
300 C1 Old Bolingbroke Lincs
26 B1 Oldborough Devon
324 D5 Old Boston St Hel
356 A6 Old Bramhope Leeds
314 C5 Old Brampton Derbys
524 C2 Old Bridge of Tilt P & K
422 C6 Old Bridge of Urr D & G
168 B2 Oldbrook M Keyn
225 E1 Old Buckenham Norfk
406 B4 Old Burdon Sundld
90 D3 Old Burghclere Hants
97 E3 Oldbury Kent
213 E2 Oldbury Sandw
211 G1 Oldbury Shrops
239 E6 Oldbury Warwks
135 E6 Oldbury Naite S Glos
135 E6 Oldbury-on-Severn S Glos
111 E6 Oldbury on the Hill Gloucs
371 G2 Old Byland N York
102 C3 Oldcastle Swans
195 H5 Old Cambus Border
491 F6 Old Cardinham Castle Cnwll
15 G5 Old Carlisle Cumb
399 H5 Old Cassop Dur
395 G2 Old Cassop Dur

159 F5 Oldcastle Mons
289 G5 Oldcastle Heath Ches
426 D1 Old Castleton Border
250 A2 Old Catton Norfk
165 E4 Old Chalford Oxon
233 E6 Old Churchstoke Powys
334 C3 Old Clee NE Lin
63 G3 Old Cleeve Somset
296 A2 Old Clipstone Notts
306 B4 Old Colwyn Conwy
234 B3 Old Coppice Shrops
569 K4 Old Cornhill Abers
316 A2 Oldcotes Notts
95 G3 Old Coulsdon Gt Lon
187 G6 Old Country Herefs
135 E3 Oldcroft Gloucs
79 F1 Old Cryals Kent
432 B5 Old Dailly S Ayrs
277 E5 Old Dalby Leics
313 F3 Old Dam Derbys
571 H6 Old Deer Abers
329 H5 Old Denaby Donc
85 F3 Old Ditch Somset
342 B3 Old Dolphin Brad
85 H4 Old Down Somset
330 B5 Old Edlington Donc
395 E4 Old Eldon Dur
348 C2 Old Ellerby E R Yk
136 A3 Oldends Gloucs
236 D4 Old Fallings Wolves
237 E2 Oldfallow Staffs
168 C2 Old Farm Park M Keyn
177 F2 Old Felixstowe Suffk
341 G2 Oldfield Brad
388 C4 Oldfield Cumb
328 A2 Oldfield Kirk
210 B4 Old Field Shrops
211 F2 Oldfield Shrops
188 B2 Oldfield Worcs
311 F2 Oldfield Brow Traffd
86 C2 Oldfield Park BaNES
244 A5 Old Fletton C Pete
405 G2 Old Fold Gatesd
119 H3 Old Ford Gt Lon
86 D1 Oldford Somset
160 D6 Old Forge Herefs
292 D6 Oldfurnace Staffs
133 E4 Old Furnace Torfn
281 F5 Old Gate Lincs
327 F6 Old Glossop Derbys
205 F3 Old Goginan Cerdgn
345 G5 Old Goole E R Yk
161 E4 Old Gore Herefs
400 B1 Old Graitney D & G
3 C1 Old Grimsby IoS
207 E3 Old Hall Powys
466 D2 Oldhall Rens
171 E5 Old Hall Green Herts
200 A3 Oldhall Green Suffk
256 C3 Old Hall Street Norfk
326 D4 Oldham Oldham
326 D3 Oldham Edge Oldham
490 D5 Oldhamstocks E Loth
145 G2 Old Harlow Essex
174 D5 Old Heath Essex
79 E5 Old Heathfield E Susx
213 E2 Old Hill Sandw
188 B5 Old Hills Worcs
258 D3 Old Hunstanton Norfk
220 C4 Oldhurst Cambs
366 B2 Old Hutton Cumb
235 G5 Oldington Shrops
438 A5 Old Johnstone D & G
7 F5 Old Kea Cnwll
483 F5 Old Kilpatrick W Duns
556 C3 Old Kinnernie Abers
110 B5 Oldland S Glos
110 B5 Oldland Common S Glos
339 H2 Old Langho Lancs
322 g6 Old Laxey IoM
300 C5 Old Leake Lincs
168 C4 Old Linslade Beds
95 E1 Old Malden Gt Lon
373 E5 Old Malton N York
269 F3 Old Marton Shrops
172 A4 Old Mead Essex
560 A4 Oldmeldrum Abers
17 E4 Old Mill Cnwll
49 G6 Old Milton Hants
191 E1 Old Milverton Warwks
84 B3 Oldmixon N Som
467 H2 Old Monkland N Lans
529 E3 Old Montrose Angus
452 C2 Old Nenthorn Border
51 E2 Old Netley Hants
207 H2 Old Neuadd Powys
201 E2 Old Newton Suffk
16 B5 Old Park Cnwll
235 F3 Old Park Wrekin
275 F6 Old Parks Leics
109 G2 Old Passage S Glos
236 C5 Old Perton Staffs
486 D4 Old Philpstoun W Loth
486 B4 Old Polmont Falk
52 A5 Old Portsmouth C Port
395 G2 Old Quarrington Dur
184 D3 Old Radnor Powys
559 F4 Old Rayne Abers
26 C3 Oldridge Devon
81 F4 Old Romney Kent
512 D4 Old Scone P & K
50 C2 Old Shirley C Sotn
584 C5 Oldshore Beg Highld
55 F3 Old Shoreham W Susx
584 D5 Oldshoremore Highld
343 H5 Old Snydale Wakefd
110 D3 Old Sodbury S Glos
278 C3 Old Somerby Lincs
371 G4 Oldstead N York
395 H5 Old Stillington S on T
187 G4 Old Storridge Common Worcs
167 G1 Old Stratford Nhants
524 B3 Old Struan P & K
309 E1 Old Swan Lpool
443 F4 Old Swarland Nthumb
212 C3 Old Swinford Dudley
327 E3 Old Tame Oldham
379 H3 Old Tebay Cumb
371 E3 Old Thirst N York
450 D4 Old Tinnis Border
445 E3 Old Toll S Ayrs
488 A5 Old Town C Edin
341 H4 Old Town Calder
366 B3 Old Town Cumb
401 E6 Old Town Cumb
375 F6 Old Town E R Yk
57 F5 Old Town E Susx
58 B5 Old Town E Susx
58 D5 Old Town E Susx
170 B4 Old Town Herts
576 C6 Oldtown Highld
3 d2 Old Town IoS
113 E3 Old Town Swindn
294 D1 Old Tupton Derbys
102 C3 Oldwalls Swans
195 G5 Old Warden Beds
288 D2 Old Warren Flints
44 D4 Old Way Somset
103 H4 Oldway Swans

20 B5 Oldway Torbay
41 H2 Oldways End Devon
559 F4 Old Westhall Abers
219 G4 Old Weston Cambs
161 F2 Old Wharf Herefs
570 F5 Oldwhat Abers
314 D5 Old Whittington Derbys
214 C5 Oldwich Lane Solhll
196 D4 Old Wimpole Cambs
117 G5 Old Windsor W & M
396 A2 Old Wingate Dur
99 H3 Old Wives Lees Kent
93 H3 Old Woking Surrey
167 H1 Old Wolverton M Keyn
186 D1 Oldwood Worcs
319 G6 Old Woodhall Lincs
290 B6 Old Woodhouses Shrops
165 G6 Old Woodstock Oxon
588 D5 Olgrinmore Highld
273 H6 Olive Green Staffs
72 C4 Oliver's Battery Hants
606 E1 Ollaberry Shet
593 D9 Ollag W Isls
313 F2 Ollerbrook Booth Derbys
311 F4 Ollerton Ches
296 C1 Ollerton Notts
271 G4 Ollerton Shrops
339 F5 Ollerton Fold Lancs
271 F4 Ollerton Lane Shrops
172 C1 Olmstead Green Cambs
194 B4 Olney M Keyn
214 A3 Olton Solhll
109 H2 Olveston S Glos
188 B2 Ombersley Worcs
296 C1 Ompton Notts
606 E8 Omunsgarth Shet
322 f7 Onchan IoM
292 D3 Onecote Staffs
200 D3 Onehouse Suffk
134 A2 Onen Mons
328 D6 Onesacre Sheff
252 B3 Ongar Hill Norfk
209 G6 Ongar Street Herefs
210 B4 Onibury Shrops
520 E3 Onich Highld
130 C2 Onllwyn Neath
291 F6 Onneley Staffs
93 G5 Onslow Village Surrey
445 F2 Onthank E Ayrs
326 C5 Openshaw Manch
294 D5 Openwoodgate Derbys
562 C2 Opinan Highld
573 C4 Opinan Highld
569 G3 Oran Moray
252 A3 Orange Row Norfk
597 K5 Orasaigh W Isls
590 F3 Oratobht W Isls
468 A3 Orbiston N Lans
542 C8 Orbost Highld
301 E1 Orby Lincs
39 G2 Orchard Hill Devon
142 D4 Orchard Leigh Bucks
44 A3 Orchard Portman Somset
88 B5 Orcheston Wilts
160 B4 Orcop Herefs
160 B4 Orcop Hill Herefs
545 L7 Ord Highld
566 C2 Ord Highld
609 J3 Ordale Shet
556 B2 Ordhead Abers
555 E4 Ordie Abers
569 K4 Ordiquhill Abers
568 E4 Ordiquish Moray
403 G3 Ordley Nthumb
559 F6 Ord Mill Abers
316 C3 Ordsall Notts
326 B5 Ordsall Salfd
58 D4 Ore E Susx
11 F3 Oreston C Plym
211 F3 Oreton Shrops
203 E5 Orford Suffk
310 C1 Orford Warrtn
33 C2 Organford Dorset
315 E2 Orgreave Sheff
238 A1 Orgreave Staffs
162 A4 Oridge Street Gloucs
124 D3 Orlandon Pembks
81 E3 Orleston Kent
186 B1 Orleton Herefs
187 F1 Orleton Worcs
210 B6 Orleton Common Herefs
218 B5 Orlingbury Nhants
593 C11 Ormacleit W Isls
389 G4 Ormathwaite Cumb
385 E1 Ormesby R & Cl
251 F1 Ormesby St Margaret Norfk
251 F2 Ormesby St Michael Norfk
480 D3 Ormidale Ag & B
573 G5 Ormiscaig Highld
439 G2 Ormiston Border
489 E6 Ormiston E Loth
518 C3 Ormsaigbeg Highld
518 C3 Ormsaigmore Highld
479 J7 Ormsary Ag & B
364 A5 Ormsgill Cumb
323 G3 Ormskirk Lancs
405 E5 Ornsby Hill Dur
96 B1 Orpington Gt Lon
323 F5 Orrell Sefton
324 C3 Orrell Wigan
324 C4 Orrell Post Wigan
322 e4 Orrisdale IoM
487 H2 Orrock Fife
413 E5 Orroland D & G
121 F3 Orsett Thurr
121 F4 Orsett Heath Thurr
236 B1 Orslow Staffs
277 G1 Orston Notts
389 F3 Orthwaite Cumb
352 A4 Ortner Lancs
379 H3 Orton Cumb
568 E5 Orton Moray
217 G4 Orton Nhants
236 C5 Orton Staffs
243 G5 Orton Brimbles C Pete
243 H5 Orton Goldhay C Pete
243 H5 Orton Longueville C Pete
243 H5 Orton Malbourne C Pete
239 E4 Orton-on-the-Hill Leics
400 B4 Orton Rigg Cumb
243 G6 Orton Southgate C Pete
243 H5 Orton Waterville C Pete
243 G5 Orton Wistow C Pete
197 E5 Orwell Cambs
339 F3 Osbaldeston Lancs
339 F3 Osbaldeston Green Lancs
358 B4 Osbaldwick York
239 G4 Osbaston Leics
269 F5 Osbaston Shrops
270 D6 Osbaston Wrekin
239 G3 Osbaston Hollow Leics
279 F2 Osbournby Lincs
289 G1 Oscroft Ches
544 E1 Ose Highld
46 C3 Osehill Green Dorset
275 G6 Osgathorpe Leics
318 D1 Osgodby Lincs
345 E3 Osgodby Lincs
345 E3 Osgodby N York
374 C3 Osgodby N York
345 E2 Osgodby Common N York
144 C6 Osidge Gt Lon
545 L3 Oskaig Highld
504 F2 Oskamull Ag & B

274 C2 **Osleston** Derbys
275 F3 **Osmaston** C Derb
293 G6 **Osmaston** Derbys
32 C3 **Osmington** Dorset
32 C3 **Osmington Mills** Dorset
384 D5 **Osmotherley** N York
140 A3 **Osney** Oxon
576 F6 **Ospisdale** Highld
99 F2 **Ospringe** Kent
60 C3 **Ossaborough** Devon
49 G5 **Ossemsley** Hants
343 E6 **Osset Spa** Wakefd
343 E5 **Ossett** Wakefd
296 D2 **Ossington** Notts
148 B5 **Ostend** Essex
256 D3 **Ostend** Norfk
118 C4 **Osterley** Gt Lon
372 B4 **Oswaldkirk** N York
339 H4 **Oswaldtwistle** Lancs
269 F4 **Oswestry** Shrops
594 E7 **Otairnis** W Isls
333 G6 **Otby** Lincs
269 H3 **Oteley** Shrops
96 D3 **Otford** Kent
98 B4 **Otham** Kent
98 C4 **Otham Hole** Kent
236 D2 **Otherton** Staffs
66 B3 **Othery** Somset
355 H5 **Otley** Leeds
201 H3 **Otley** Suffk
72 C5 **Otterbourne** Hants
353 H3 **Otterburn** N York
441 G6 **Otterburn** Nthumb
441 G5 **Otterburn Camp** Nthumb
99 E4 **Otterden Place** Kent
480 C3 **Otter Ferry** Ag & B
43 H5 **Otterford** Somset
22 D4 **Otterham** Cnwll
64 D3 **Otterhampton** Somset
98 C1 **Otterham Quay** Kent
22 D5 **Otterham Station** Cnwll
594 E7 **Otternish** W Isls
93 H2 **Ottershaw** Surrey
309 E2 **Otterspool** Lpool
609 G7 **Otterswick** Shet
28 A6 **Otterton** Devon
50 D4 **Otterwood** Hants
28 B3 **Ottery St Mary** Devon
82 C2 **Ottinge** Kent
349 E5 **Ottringham** E R Yk
400 A3 **Oughterby** Cumb
367 H3 **Oughtershaw** N York
388 D1 **Oughterside** Cumb
328 D6 **Oughtibridge** Sheff
310 D2 **Oughtrington** Warrtn
371 G5 **Oulston** N York
399 G4 **Oulton** Cumb
343 G4 **Oulton** Leeds
255 F2 **Oulton** Norfk
272 A5 **Oulton** Staffs
272 D2 **Oulton** Staffs
251 G6 **Oulton** Suffk
251 G6 **Oulton Broad** Suffk
272 D3 **Oultoncross** Staffs
272 D2 **Oulton Grange** Staffs
255 G2 **Oulton Street** Norfk
219 E2 **Oundle** Nhants
236 C6 **Ounsdale** Staffs
391 G3 **Ousby** Cumb
582 E6 **Ousdale** Highld
199 E3 **Ousden** Suffk
346 B5 **Ousefleet** E R Yk
355 F6 **Ousel Hole** Brad
405 G4 **Ouston** Dur
402 D4 **Ouston** Nthumb
429 H5 **Ouston** Nthumb
364 C4 **Outcast** Cumb
100 D5 **Out Elmstead** Kent
12 B4 **Outer Hope** Devon
600 C2 **Outertown** Ork
378 C5 **Outgate** Cumb
380 D4 **Outhgill** Cumb
189 H1 **Outhill** Warwks
271 H3 **Outlands** Staffs
342 A6 **Outlane** Kirk
309 F4 **Outlet Village** Ches
87 F2 **Outmarsh** Wilts
349 G5 **Out Newton** E R Yk
338 B1 **Out Rawcliffe** Lancs
245 H4 **Outwell** Norfk
70 C6 **Outwick** Hants
325 H3 **Outwood** Bury
44 B2 **Outwood** Somset
95 G5 **Outwood** Surrey
343 F5 **Outwood** Wakefd
275 F6 **Outwoods** Leics
272 A6 **Outwoods** Staffs
274 C5 **Outwoods** Staffs
214 C3 **Outwoods** Warwks
343 F4 **Ouzlewell Green** Leeds
342 A4 **Ovenden** Calder
221 E5 **Over** Cambs
290 C1 **Over** Ches
162 B6 **Over** Gloucs
109 G3 **Over** S Glos
603 K3 **Overbister** Ork
366 C4 **Over Burrow** Lancs
274 D2 **Over Burrows** Derbys
163 E2 **Overbury** Worcs
32 B3 **Overcombe** Dorset
46 A1 **Over Compton** Dorset
243 F6 **Over End** Cambs
314 B5 **Over End** Derbys
213 E3 **Overend** Sandw
514 C1 **Over Finlarg** Angus
238 B6 **Over Green** Birm
293 G1 **Over Haddon** Derbys
570 F5 **Overhill** Abers
325 F4 **Over Hulton** Bolton
365 H6 **Over Kellet** Lancs
165 G5 **Over Kiddington** Oxon
311 F4 **Over Knutsford** Ches
451 G1 **Over Langshaw** Border
66 D2 **Overleigh** Somset
238 B1 **Overley** Staffs
134 C2 **Over Monnow** Mons
292 C5 **Overmoor** Staffs
165 E4 **Over Norton** Oxon
311 F5 **Over Peover** Ches
309 E4 **Overpool** Ches
233 G5 **Overs** Shrops
238 D1 **Overseal** Derbys
384 D6 **Over Silton** N York
216 A5 **Overslade** Warwks
99 H3 **Oversland** Kent
189 G3 **Oversley Green** Warwks
193 H1 **Overstone** Nhants
64 C4 **Over Stowey** Somset
256 B1 **Overstrand** Norfk
45 E4 **Over Stratton** Somset
311 E3 **Over Tabley** Ches
342 D6 **Overthorpe** Kirk
166 A1 **Overthorpe** Nhants
557 F2 **Overton** C Aber
309 H4 **Overton** Ches
398 B2 **Overton** D & G
135 G2 **Overton** Gloucs
91 E5 **Overton** Hants
482 C5 **Overton** Inver
351 F3 **Overton** Lancs
357 H3 **Overton** N York
210 C5 **Overton** Shrops
273 F2 **Overton** Staffs
102 C4 **Overton** Swans
328 D1 **Overton** Wakefd
269 G1 **Overton** Wrexhm
289 E6 **Overton Bridge** Wrexhm
340 D2 **Over Town** Lancs
366 C4 **Overtown** N Lans
468 C4 **Overtown** N Lans
113 E4 **Overtown** Swindn
329 F1 **Overtown** Wakefd
71 F2 **Over Wallop** Hants
214 C1 **Over Whitacre** Warwks
165 G4 **Over Worton** Oxon
167 G5 **Oving** Bucks
53 G3 **Oving** W Susx
56 A4 **Ovingdean** Br & H
404 C2 **Ovingham** Nthumb
382 D2 **Ovington** Dur
173 F1 **Ovington** Essex
73 E3 **Ovington** Hants
248 B4 **Ovington** Norfk
404 C2 **Ovington** Nthumb
274 C4 **Owen's Bank** Staffs
50 B1 **Ower** Hants
32 D2 **Owermoigne** Dorset
315 E6 **Owlcotes** Derbys
220 B4 **Owl End** Cambs
314 B4 **Owler Bar** Derbys
314 C2 **Owlerton** Sheff
342 C2 **Owlet** Brad
136 A5 **Owlpen** Gloucs
93 E2 **Owlsmoor** Br For
141 G3 **Owlswick** Bucks
315 E3 **Owlthorpe** Sheff
333 F4 **Owmby** Lincs
318 C2 **Owmby-by-Spital** Lincs
114 C5 **Ownham** W Berk
72 D5 **Owslebury** Hants
330 B2 **Owston** Donc
241 H3 **Owston** Leics
331 H4 **Owston Ferry** N Linc
349 E3 **Owstwick** E R Yk
349 F4 **Owthorne** E R Yk
277 E3 **Owthorpe** Notts
396 C4 **Owton Manor** Hartpl
247 E4 **Oxborough** Norfk
30 B3 **Oxbridge** Dorset
315 E3 **Oxclose** Sheff
405 G3 **Oxclose** Sundld
320 B4 **Oxcombe** Lincs
315 F5 **Oxcroft** Derbys
315 F5 **Oxcroft Estate** Derbys
172 D4 **Oxen End** Essex
161 G4 **Oxenhall** Gloucs
366 A2 **Oxenholme** Cumb
341 G3 **Oxenhope** Brad
364 D2 **Oxen Park** Cumb
66 C1 **Oxenpill** Somset
163 E3 **Oxenton** Gloucs
89 G3 **Oxenwood** Wilts
291 H4 **Oxford** C Stke
140 B3 **Oxford** Oxon
484 D5 **Oxgang** E Duns
488 A6 **Oxgangs** C Edin
143 G5 **Oxhey** Herts
405 E4 **Oxhill** Dur
191 E5 **Oxhill** Warwks
236 D4 **Oxley** Wolves
148 B2 **Oxley Green** Essex
58 A2 **Oxley's Green** E Susx
221 G2 **Oxlode** Cambs
452 D6 **Oxnam** Border
256 A5 **Oxnead** Norfk
94 C2 **Oxshott** Surrey
328 D4 **Oxspring** Barns
96 A4 **Oxted** Surrey
472 B4 **Oxton** Border
357 G6 **Oxton** N York
296 B4 **Oxton** Notts
308 C2 **Oxton** Wirral
314 C5 **Oxton Rakes** Derbys
102 C4 **Oxwich** Swans
102 C4 **Oxwich Green** Swans
254 B3 **Oxwick** Norfk
575 H3 **Oykel Bridge** Highld
559 F4 **Oyne** Abers
103 H4 **Oystermouth** Swans
136 A6 **Ozleworth** Gloucs

P

599 L8 **Pabail Iarach** W Isls
599 L8 **Pabail Uarach** W Isls
305 H4 **Pabo** Conwy
94 D3 **Pachesham Park** Surrey
46 D2 **Packers Hill** Dorset
239 F2 **Packington** Leics
291 H4 **Packmoor** C Stke
190 D1 **Packmores** Warwks
214 B5 **Packwood** Solhll
214 B5 **Packwood Gullet** Solhll
527 F4 **Padanaram** Angus
167 F3 **Padbury** Bucks
310 C2 **Paddington** Warrtn
82 C2 **Paddlesworth** Kent
97 G2 **Paddlesworth** Kent
99 F4 **Paddock** Kent
327 H1 **Paddock** Kirk
568 C4 **Paddockhaugh** Moray
311 G4 **Paddockhill** Ches
97 G6 **Paddock Wood** Kent
270 B3 **Padolgreen** Shrops
288 C2 **Padeswood** Flints
327 F5 **Padfield** Derbys
310 C1 **Padgate** Warrtn
146 C5 **Padham's Green** Essex
340 C3 **Padiham** Lancs
222 A5 **Padney** Cambs
286 A4 **Padog** Conwy
355 G3 **Padside** N York
355 G3 **Padside Green** N York
25 E3 **Padson** Devon
14 C4 **Padstow** Cnwll
91 G1 **Padworth** W Berk
91 G2 **Padworth Common** W Berk
136 B3 **Paganhill** Gloucs
395 E2 **Page Bank** Dur
309 F1 **Page Moss** Knows
201 F1 **Page's Green** Suffk
53 F5 **Pagham** W Susx
148 B6 **Paglesham Churchend** Essex
123 E1 **Paglesham Eastend** Essex
592 H5 **Paibeil** W Isls
20 B5 **Paignton** Torbay
215 H3 **Pailton** Warwks
273 F3 **Painleyhill** Staffs
184 C5 **Painscastle** Powys
404 C2 **Painshawfield** Nthumb
96 B4 **Pains Hill** Surrey
359 F3 **Painsthorpe** E R Yk
136 C3 **Painswick** Gloucs
99 F3 **Painter's Forstal** Kent
170 C6 **Painter's Green** Herts
270 C1 **Painters Green** Wrexhm
329 E1 **Painthorpe** Wakefd
176 D3 **Paintmoor** Somset
598 F5 **Pairc Shiaboist** W Isls
466 F2 **Paisley** Rens
227 G1 **Pakefield** Suffk
200 B1 **Pakenham** Suffk
267 F2 **Pale** Gwynd
172 D1 **Pale Green** Essex
78 B6 **Palehouse Common** E Susx
71 F1 **Palestine** Hants
117 E4 **Paley Street** W & M
237 F5 **Palfrey** Wsall
420 B3 **Palgowan** D & G
225 F4 **Palgrave** Suffk
376 B2 **Pallaflat** Cumb
32 D1 **Pallington** Dorset
406 B3 **Pallion** Sundld
396 D6 **Pallister** Middsb
82 B4 **Palmarsh** Kent
274 A3 **Palmer Moor** Derbys
16 A3 **Palmersbridge** Cnwll
75 G1 **Palmers Cross** Surrey
236 C4 **Palmers Cross** Wolves
134 D3 **Palmer's Flat** Gloucs
144 D6 **Palmers Green** Gt Lon
79 F1 **Palmer's Green** Kent
106 B6 **Palmerstown** V Glam
431 E5 **Palmersville** N Tyne
100 C6 **Palmstead** Kent
413 F3 **Palnackie** D & G
417 E4 **Palnure** D & G
315 F6 **Palterton** Derbys
91 G3 **Pamber End** Hants
91 F3 **Pamber Green** Hants
91 G2 **Pamber Heath** Hants
162 D3 **Pamington** Gloucs
48 B4 **Pamphill** Dorset
197 G5 **Pampisford** Cambs
37 E3 **Pan** IoW
85 E5 **Panborough** Somset
515 F2 **Panbride** Angus
137 G2 **Pancakehill** Gloucs
23 F1 **Pancrasweek** Devon
105 G6 **Pancross** V Glam
229 E4 **Pandy** Gwynd
229 G1 **Pandy** Gwynd
266 D4 **Pandy** Gwynd
159 F5 **Pandy** Mons
231 E4 **Pandy** Powys
268 C2 **Pandy** Wrexhm
289 F6 **Pandy** Wrexhm
287 F4 **Pandy'r Capel** Denbgs
286 B2 **Pandy Tudur** Conwy
173 E4 **Panfield** Essex
115 G2 **Pangbourne** W Berk
187 E5 **Panks Bridge** Herefs
356 C4 **Pannal** N York
356 B4 **Pannal Ash** N York
199 F6 **Pannel's Ash** Essex
209 E5 **Panpunton** Shrops
288 B4 **Pant** Denbgs
307 G5 **Pant** Flints
262 C4 **Pant** Gwynd
131 H3 **Pant** Myr Td
231 G4 **Pant** Powys
269 E5 **Pant** Shrops
289 E3 **Pant** Wrexhm
307 G4 **Pantasaph** Flints
104 B1 **Pantdu** Neath
180 C2 **Panteg** Cerdgn
151 F3 **Panteg** Pembks
133 F5 **Panteg** Torfn
15 H5 **Pantersbridge** Cnwll
263 H1 **Pant Glâs** Gwynd
230 B5 **Pant-glas** Powys
269 E3 **Pant-glas** Shrops
179 E4 **Pantgwyn** Cerdgn
129 G4 **Pant-lasau** Swans
106 B3 **Pantmawr** Cardif
206 D3 **Pant Mawr** Powys
319 F4 **Panton** Lincs
287 E2 **Pant-pastynog** Denbgs
229 G4 **Pantperthog** Gwynd
132 D5 **Pantside** Caerph
152 C4 **Pant-y-Caws** Carmth
205 E4 **Pant-y-Crüg** Cerdgn
207 F5 **Pant-y-dwr** Powys
232 C4 **Pant-y-ffridd** Powys
129 F2 **Pantyffynnon** Carmth
154 C6 **Pantyffynnon** Carmth
133 E5 **Pantygasseg** Torfn
288 A2 **Pantymwyn** Flints
105 E3 **Pant-y-pyllau** Brdgnd
105 E2 **Pant-yr-awel** Brdgnd
307 G4 **Pant y Wacco** Flints
250 C2 **Panxworth** Norfk
388 D3 **Papcastle** Cumb
270 D4 **Papermill Bank** Shrops
589 K6 **Papigoe** Highld
605 G4 **Papil** Shet
219 G2 **Papley** Nhants
490 A5 **Papple** E Loth
295 G4 **Papplewick** Notts
196 C2 **Papworth Everard** Cambs
196 C2 **Papworth St Agnes** Cambs
8 D3 **Par** Cnwll
136 C2 **Paradise** Gloucs
186 C5 **Paradise Green** Herefs
8 B4 **Paramoor** Cnwll
101 E3 **Paramour Street** Kent
324 B2 **Parbold** Lancs
513 H6 **Parbroath** Fife
67 F2 **Parbrook** Somset
76 A5 **Parbrook** W Susx
266 D3 **Parc** Gwynd
6 C5 **Parc Erissey** Cnwll
103 E2 **Parc-hendy** Swans
154 D5 **Parc-Henri** Carmth
65 F4 **Parchey** Somset
303 G4 **Parciau** IoA
179 E3 **Parcllyn** Cerdgn
106 B1 **Parc Mawr** Caerph
108 D1 **Parc Seymour** Newpt
91 F5 **Pardown** Hants
388 C5 **Pardshaw** Cumb
388 D4 **Pardshaw Hall** Cumb
202 C2 **Parham** Suffk
15 E4 **Park** Cnwll
423 F1 **Park** D & G
26 C3 **Park** Devon
93 G4 **Park Barn** Surrey
543 G6 **Park Bernisdale** Highld
6 C5 **Park Bottom** Cnwll
96 C5 **Park Bridge** Tamesd
400 D3 **Park Broom** Cumb
354 A6 **Park Close** Lancs
86 D3 **Park Corner** BaNES
57 E2 **Park Corner** E Susx
78 C2 **Park Corner** E Susx
116 A2 **Park Corner** Oxon
194 D4 **Park End** Beds
198 B2 **Park End** Cambs
135 E3 **Parkend** Gloucs
136 A2 **Parkend** Gloucs
396 D6 **Park End** Middsb
428 D4 **Park End** Nthumb
418 C5 **Park End** S Ayrs
64 C5 **Park End** Somset
291 H4 **Park End** Staffs
211 H5 **Park End** Staffs
7 G4 **Parkengear** Cnwll
115 G5 **Parker's Corner** W Berk
170 D4 **Parker's Green** Herts
97 F5 **Parker's Green** Kent
176 D3 **Parkeston** Essex
16 D5 **Parkfield** Cnwll
110 B4 **Parkfield** S Glos
236 D5 **Parkfield** Wolves
485 E6 **Parkfoot** Falk
308 C4 **Parkgate** Ches
311 F5 **Parkgate** Ches
399 G5 **Parkgate** Cumb
423 H2 **Parkgate** D & G
46 D3 **Park Gate** Dorset
172 D6 **Parkgate** Essex
51 F3 **Park Gate** Hants
80 B3 **Parkgate** Kent
82 C1 **Park Gate** Kent
328 C2 **Park Gate** Kirk
329 G5 **Parkgate** Rothm
199 E3 **Park Gate** Suffk
95 E6 **Parkgate** Surrey
212 D5 **Park Gate** Worcs
171 G4 **Park Green** Essex
269 F3 **Park Hall** Shrops
483 G5 **Parkhall** W Duns
39 E3 **Parkham** Devon
39 E3 **Parkham Ash** Devon
557 F5 **Parkhead** Abers
467 F2 **Parkhead** C Glas
390 A1 **Parkhead** Cumb
391 F1 **Park Head** Cumb
294 D4 **Park Head** Derbys
328 B3 **Park Head** Kirk
381 H3 **Park Head** N York
314 C3 **Parkhead** Sheff
513 F6 **Parkhill** Fife
134 D5 **Parkhill** Gloucs
482 D5 **Parkhill** Inver
81 E3 **Park Hill** Kent
314 D2 **Park Hill** Sheff
324 B4 **Park Hill** St Hel
134 C4 **Parkhouse** Mons
295 E2 **Parkhouse Green** Derbys
36 D2 **Parkhurst** IoW
343 F2 **Parklands** Leeds
236 C3 **Park Lane** Staffs
269 H2 **Park Lane** Wrexhm
120 A6 **Park Langley** Gt Lon
483 G5 **Park Mains** Rens
102 D4 **Parkmill** Swans
487 E2 **Parkneuk** Fife
113 E3 **Park North** Swindn
118 D3 **Park Royal** Gt Lon
169 F5 **Parkside** Beds
376 C1 **Parkside** Cumb
406 C5 **Parkside** Dur
468 B3 **Parkside** N Lans
272 D4 **Parkside** Staffs
289 E4 **Parkside** Wrexhm
113 E4 **Park South** Swindn
34 B2 **Parkstone** Poole
76 B3 **Park Street** W Susx
169 F5 **Park Town** Luton
140 B3 **Park Town** Oxon
402 B2 **Park Village** Nthumb
236 D4 **Park Village** Wolves
161 G2 **Parkway** Herefs
67 F5 **Parkway** Somset
98 B4 **Park Wood** Kent
98 C2 **Park Wood** Medway
314 C2 **Parkwood Springs** Sheff
48 D5 **Parley Cross** Dorset
48 D5 **Parley Green** Dorset
200 C6 **Parliament Heath** Suffk
343 H2 **Parlington** Leeds
116 C2 **Parmoor** Bucks
23 G1 **Parnacott** Devon
174 D3 **Parney Heath** Essex
324 C6 **Parr** St Hel
61 G3 **Parracombe** Devon
325 G4 **Parr Brow** Wigan
152 A2 **Parrog** Pembks
142 A4 **Parslow's Hillock** Bucks
146 D2 **Parsonage Green** Essex
388 D2 **Parsonby** Cumb
314 C1 **Parson Cross** Sheff
245 E3 **Parson Drove** Cambs
119 E4 **Parsons Green** Gt Lon
174 D4 **Parson's Heath** Essex
466 D1 **Partick** C Glas
311 E1 **Partington** Traffd
320 D6 **Partney** Lincs
388 A5 **Parton** Cumb
400 A4 **Parton** Cumb
422 A5 **Parton** D & G
185 F5 **Parton** Herefs
146 D2 **Partridgegreen** Essex
76 C6 **Partridge Green** W Susx
159 E5 **Partrishow** Powys
293 G4 **Parwich** Derbys
236 B5 **Pasford** Staffs
167 G2 **Passenham** Nhants
74 C3 **Passfield** Hants
145 H5 **Passingford Bridge** Essex
145 F3 **Passmores** Essex
244 A4 **Paston** C Pete
256 C3 **Paston** Norfk
256 C3 **Paston Green** Norfk
273 E5 **Pasturefields** Staffs
24 C3 **Patchacott** Devon
55 H3 **Patcham** Br & H
143 G5 **Patchetts Green** Herts
54 C3 **Patching** W Susx
61 F3 **Patchole** Devon
109 H3 **Patchway** S Glos
356 A2 **Pateley Bridge** N York
148 B1 **Paternoster Heath** Essex
65 G5 **Pathe** Somset
468 B4 **Pather** N Lans
26 C4 **Pathfinder Village** Devon
434 C2 **Pathhead** E Ayrs
501 E6 **Pathhead** Fife
405 E2 **Path Head** Gatesd
471 G2 **Pathhead** Mdloth
190 B3 **Pathlow** Warwks
499 H3 **Path of Condie** P & K
500 A2 **Pathstruie** P & K
171 F4 **Patient End** Herts
171 F4 **Patmore Heath** Herts
433 F2 **Patna** E Ayrs
71 H4 **Patney** Wilts
322 c6 **Patrick** IoM
369 H1 **Patrick Brompton** N York
325 H5 **Patricroft** Salfd
349 F5 **Patrington** E R Yk
349 F5 **Patrington Haven** E R Yk
100 C4 **Patrixbourne** Kent
60 D4 **Patsford** Devon
378 C1 **Patterdale** Cumb
236 B5 **Pattingham** Staffs
193 E4 **Pattishall** Nhants
234 D5 **Pattiswick** Essex
379 F5 **Patton** Shrops
3 E4 **Patton Bridge** Cumb
193 F5 **Paul** Cnwll
348 C4 **Paulerspury** Nhants
64 C5 **Paull** E R Yk
4 B2 **Paul's Green** Cnwll
52 A3 **Paulsgrove** C Port
86 B3 **Paulton** BaNES
486 C6 **Paulville** W Loth
442 D5 **Pauperhaugh** Nthumb
235 H1 **Pave Lane** Wrekin
194 D3 **Pavenham** Beds
84 B6 **Pawlett** Somset
84 D5 **Pawlett Hill** Somset
453 F3 **Pawston** Nthumb
164 B2 **Paxford** Gloucs
474 D2 **Paxton** Border
99 E4 **Payden Street** Kent
28 A2 **Payhembury** Devon
76 B2 **Paynes Green** Surrey
17 E6 **Paynter's Cross** Cnwll
6 C5 **Paynter's Lane End** Cnwll
353 G6 **Paythorne** Lancs
43 F3 **Payton** Somset
56 C4 **Peacehaven** E Susx
56 C4 **Peacehaven Heights** E Susx
68 C4 **Peacemarsh** Dorset
313 E4 **Peak Dale** Derbys
313 F4 **Peak Forest** Derbys
244 C1 **Peak Hill** Lincs
243 H3 **Peakirk** C Pete
100 B3 **Pean Hill** Kent
68 C3 **Pear Ash** Somset
527 E3 **Pearsie** Angus
97 G6 **Pearson's Green** Kent
275 F3 **Pear Tree** C Derb
146 B5 **Peartree Green** Essex
160 D3 **Peartree Green** Herefs
75 F2 **Peartree Green** Surrey
342 A1 **Peas Acre** Brad
86 C3 **Peasedown St John** BaNES
295 E5 **Peasehill** Derbys
254 A4 **Peaseland Green** Norfk
114 D4 **Peasemore** W Berk
226 C6 **Pease Pottage** W Susx
77 E3 **Peas Hill** Cambs
245 F5 **Peaslake** Surrey
94 B6 **Peasley Cross** St Hel
324 C6 **Peasmarsh** E Susx
80 C5 **Peasmarsh** Somset
44 C5 **Peasmarsh** Surrey
93 G5 **Peaston** E Loth
471 H1 **Peastonbank** E Loth
472 A1 **Peathill** Abers
571 G2 **Peat Inn** Fife
502 D3 **Peatling Magna** Leics
240 C6 **Peatling Parva** Leics
216 C2 **Peaton** Shrops
210 C2 **Peatonstrand** Shrops
210 C3 **Pebmarsh** Essex
173 H3 **Pebsham** E Susx
58 C5 **Pebworth** Worcs
190 A5 **Pecket Well** Calder
341 F4 **Peckforton** Ches
290 A3 **Peckham** Gt Lon
119 G4 **Peckham Bush** Kent
97 G5 **Peckingill** Wilts
111 G5 **Pecking Mill** Somset
67 G2 **Peckleton** Leics
239 H4 **Pedair-Ffordd** Powys
268 B5 **Pedham** Norfk
250 C2 **Pedlars End** Essex
146 A3 **Pedlar's Rest** Shrops
210 B3 **Pedlinge** Kent
82 B3 **Pedmore** Dudley
212 D3 **Pednor Bottom** Bucks
142 C4 **Pednormead End** Bucks
66 C2 **Pedwell** Somset
450 B1 **Peebles** Border
451 E2 **Peel** IoM
322 c6 **Peel** Lancs
337 G3 **Peel Common** Hants
51 G4 **Peel Green** Salfd
325 G5 **Peel Hall** Manch
311 G2 **Peel Hill** Lancs
337 G3 **Peel Park** S Lans
467 F4 **Peene** Kent
82 C3 **Peening Quarter** Kent
80 C4 **Peggs Green** Leics
275 G6 **Pegsdon** Beds
169 G4 **Pegswood** Nthumb
430 D2 **Pegwell** Kent
101 G3 **Peinaha** Highld
543 G5 **Peinchorran** Highld
545 J3 **Peiness** Highld
543 G7 **Peinlich** Highld
543 G7 **Peinmore** Highld
545 H1 **Peinmore** Highld
405 G2 **Pelaw** Gatesd
151 F5 **Pelcomb** Pembks
125 F1 **Pelcomb Bridge** Pembks
151 F5 **Pelcomb Cross** Pembks
148 C1 **Peldon** Essex
51 G4 **Pelhamfield** IoW
79 E3 **Pell Green** E Susx
341 G4 **Pellon** Calder
237 F4 **Pelsall** Wsall
237 F4 **Pelsall Wood** Wsall
405 G4 **Pelton** Dur
405 G4 **Pelton Fell** Dur
399 E5 **Pelutho** Cumb
15 E2 **Pelynt** Cnwll
128 D4 **Pemberton** Carmth
98 D5 **Pembles Cross** Kent
128 B4 **Pembrey** Carmth
185 G3 **Pembridge** Herefs
125 F4 **Pembroke** Pembks
125 G4 **Pembroke Dock** Pembks
125 F4 **Pembroke Ferry** Pembks
79 E1 **Pembury** Kent
17 E3 **Pempwell** Cnwll
160 D3 **Pen-allt** Herefs
134 C2 **Penallt** Mons
126 C5 **Penally** Pembks
8 C5 **Penare** Cnwll
208 B2 **Penarron** Powys
106 C5 **Penarth** V Glam
106 C5 **Penarth Moors** Cardif
3 F2 **Penbeagle** Cnwll
307 H6 **Penbedw** Flints
153 E2 **Pen-bedw** Pembks
2 D5 **Penberth** Cnwll
159 F5 **Penbidwal** Mons
126 C1 **Penblewin** Pembks
262 D4 **Penbodlas** Cnwll
205 F3 **Pen-bont Rhydybeddau** Cerdgn
153 H2 **Penboyr** Carmth
179 F3 **Penbryn** Cerdgn
154 B2 **Pencader** Carmth
263 G2 **Pencaenewydd** Gwynd
130 B5 **Pencaerau** Neath
102 D2 **Pen-caer-fenny** Swans
489 E6 **Pencaitland** E Loth
303 E6 **Pencarnisiog** IoA
180 D6 **Pencarreg** Carmth
22 C6 **Pencarrow** Cnwll
128 D4 **Penceiliogi** Carmth
158 A4 **Pencelli** Powys
102 A3 **Pen-clawdd** Swans
105 F3 **Pencoed** Brdgnd
186 D6 **Pencombe** Herefs
131 E3 **Pen-common** Powys
160 C4 **Pencoyd** Herefs
6 C6 **Pencoys** Cnwll
160 D5 **Pencraig** Herefs
266 D2 **Pencraig** IoA
267 G4 **Pencraig** Powys
133 F3 **Pencroesoped** Mons
22 D4 **Pencuke** Cnwll
343 G2 **Pendas Fields** Leeds
2 C3 **Pendeen** Cnwll
194 D4 **Penderyn** Rhondd
127 E3 **Pendine** Carmth
326 A4 **Pendlebury** Salfd
340 B2 **Pendleton** Lancs
326 A5 **Pendleton** Salfd
162 A3 **Pendock** Worcs
15 E3 **Pendoggett** Cnwll

City, town and village index: Pendomer - Plasnewydd 709

45 G5 **Pendomer** Somset
105 H4 **Pendoylan** V Glam
105 E3 **Pendre** Brdgnd
228 D4 **Pendre** Gwynd
157 G4 **Pendre** Powys
15 F4 **Pendrift** Cnwll
230 B4 **Penegoes** Powys
7 F5 **Penelewey** Cnwll
98 B3 **Penenden Heath** Kent
152 B5 **Penffordd** Pembks
132 C5 **Pengam** Caerph
119 G5 **Penge** Gt Lon
6 C6 **Pengegon** Cnwll
22 B6 **Pengelly** Cnwll
158 C3 **Pengenffordd** Powys
3 G4 **Pengersick** Cnwll
284 C2 **Pen-gilfach** Gwynd
22 C4 **Pengold** Cnwll
303 G2 **Pengorffwysfa** IoA
16 C5 **Pengover Green** Cnwll
160 C5 **Penguithal** Herefs
307 E4 **Pengwern** Denbgs
4 C5 **Penhale** Cnwll
7 G2 **Penhale** Cnwll
4 B3 **Penhale Jakes** Cnwll
5 E5 **Penhallick** Cnwll
6 C5 **Penhallick** Cnwll
7 E3 **Penhallow** Cnwll
6 C6 **Penhalurick** Cnwll
6 C6 **Penhalvean** Cnwll
229 E5 **Penhelig** Gwynd
60 D5 **Penhill** Devon
112 D2 **Penhill** Swindn
108 D1 **Penhow** Newpt
58 A3 **Penhurst** E Susx
470 D2 **Penicuik** Mdloth
154 B5 **Peniel** Carmth
287 E2 **Peniel** Denbgs
545 H1 **Penifiler** Highld
457 E1 **Peninver** Ag & B
284 C2 **Penisarwaun** Gwynd
328 C4 **Penistone** Barns
5 E2 **Penjerrick** Cnwll
310 A2 **Penketh** Warrtn
291 H6 **Penkhull** C Stke
432 B5 **Penkill** S Ayrs
411 E3 **Penkiln** D & G
87 F5 **Penknap** Wilts
236 D2 **Penkridge** Staffs
103 F2 **Pen-lan** Swans
151 E3 **Pen-Lan-mabws** Pembks
269 H2 **Penley** Wrexhm
262 C4 **Penllech** Gwynd
129 F5 **Penllergaer** Swans
132 C5 **Penllwyn** Caerph
205 E3 **Penllwyn** Cerdgn
303 E4 **Pen-llyn** IoA
105 F4 **Penllyn** V Glam
282 D3 **Pen-lôn** IoA
285 G4 **Penmachno** Conwy
132 C5 **Penmaen** Caerph
102 D4 **Penmaen** Swans
305 F4 **Penmaenan** Conwy
305 E4 **Penmaenmawr** Conwy
265 F6 **Penmaenpool** Gwynd
105 H6 **Penmark** V Glam
4 D1 **Penmarth** Cnwll
14 C3 **Penmayne** Cnwll
304 D3 **Penmon** IoA
179 G3 **Penmorfa** Cerdgn
264 C1 **Penmorfa** Gwynd
303 G6 **Penmynydd** IoA
142 C6 **Penn** Bucks
29 F3 **Penn** Dorset
236 C5 **Penn** Wolves
229 G4 **Pennal** Gwynd
570 E2 **Pennan** Abers
6 D5 **Pennance** Cnwll
180 D2 **Pennant** Cerdgn
286 B3 **Pennant** Conwy
230 D5 **Pennant** Powys
267 G4 **Pennant Melangell** Powys
125 G4 **Pennar** Pembks
103 E4 **Pennard** Swans
125 F4 **Pennar Park** Pembks
142 C6 **Penn Bottom** Bucks
233 F5 **Pennerley** Shrops
364 C4 **Pennington** Cumb
50 B6 **Pennington** Hants
325 F5 **Pennington** Wigan
325 E3 **Pennington Green** Wigan
45 H4 **Penn Mill** Somset
158 B4 **Pennorth** Powys
142 C5 **Penn Street** Bucks
27 E4 **Pennsylvania** Devon
110 C5 **Pennsylvania** S Glos
364 D3 **Penny Bridge** Cumb
505 G5 **Pennycross** Ag & B
11 E2 **Pennycross** C Plym
256 C5 **Pennygate** Norfk
505 G5 **Pennyghael** Ag & B
518 F7 **Pennygown** Ag & B
315 G4 **Penny Green** Derbys
341 H6 **Penny Hill** Calder
281 E4 **Penny Hill** Lincs
324 B3 **Pennylands** Lancs
41 H5 **Pennymoor** Devon
82 B4 **Pennypot** Kent
249 F5 **Penny's Green** Norfk
15 E3 **Pennytinney** Cnwll
406 B3 **Pennywell** Sundld
105 H6 **Pen-onn** V Glam
179 E4 **Penparc** Cerdgn
150 D3 **Penparc** Pembks
204 D4 **Penparcau** Cerdgn
132 B5 **Penpedairheol** Caerph
133 F4 **Penpedairheol** Mons
133 F2 **Penpergym** Mons
133 F4 **Penperlleni** Mons
22 B5 **Penpethy** Cnwll
8 D2 **Penpillick** Cnwll
153 H6 **Penplas** Carmth
7 F6 **Penpol** Cnwll
9 E3 **Penpoll** Cnwll
6 B6 **Penponds** Cnwll
15 F4 **Penpont** Cnwll
435 G6 **Penpont** D & G
105 F3 **Penprysg** Brdgnd
12 A2 **Penquit** Devon
263 F3 **Penrallt** Gwynd
207 E2 **Penrallt** Powys
153 F2 **Penrherber** Carmth
106 D1 **Penrhiw** Caerph
131 G5 **Penrhiwceiber** Rhondd
130 A2 **Pen-Rhiw-fawr** Neath
132 D4 **Penrhiwgarreg** Blae G
155 E6 **Penrhiwgoch** Carmth
153 H1 **Penrhiw-llan** Cerdgn
179 G4 **Penrhiw-pâl** Cerdgn
130 A5 **Penrhiwtyn** Neath
263 E4 **Penrhos** Gwynd
185 F3 **Penrhos** Herefs
302 C4 **Penrhos** IoA
133 H2 **Penrhos** Mons
130 B2 **Penrhos** Powys
288 C4 **Pen-rhos** Wrexhm
302 B4 **Penrhosfeilw** IoA
304 C5 **Penrhos Garnedd** Gwynd
303 F2 **Penrhyd Lastra** IoA
306 A3 **Penrhyn Bay** Conwy
178 C4 **Penrhyn Castle** Pembks
205 E3 **Penrhyn-Coch** Cerdgn
264 D2 **Penrhyndeudraeth** Gwynd
305 H3 **Penrhyn-side** Conwy
131 F5 **Penrhys** Rhondd
102 C4 **Penrice** Swans
391 E3 **Penrith** Cumb
14 B4 **Penrose** Cnwll
15 F3 **Penrose** Cnwll
4 B3 **Penrose Hill** Cnwll
390 C4 **Penruddock** Cumb
5 E2 **Penryn** Cnwll
154 B6 **Pensarn** Carmth
306 D4 **Pensarn** Conwy
263 G2 **Pen-sarn** Gwynd
264 D4 **Pen-sarn** Gwynd
211 G6 **Pensax** Worcs
308 C3 **Pensby** Wirral
68 C3 **Penselwood** Somset
85 H2 **Pensford** BaNES
188 D6 **Pensham** Worcs
406 A4 **Penshaw** Sundld
96 D6 **Penshurst** Kent
16 C5 **Pensilva** Cnwll
212 D2 **Pensnett** Dudley
489 E5 **Penston** E Loth
26 B2 **Penstone** Devon
6 D4 **Penstraze** Cnwll
129 E2 **Pen-tyn** Carmth
8 C4 **Pentewan** Cnwll
208 D3 **Pentiken** Shrops
284 C1 **Pentir** Gwynd
7 E1 **Pentire** Cnwll
233 F4 **Pentirvin** Shrops
126 C3 **Pentlepoir** Pembks
199 G6 **Pentlow** Essex
199 G5 **Pentlow Street** Essex
253 E5 **Pentney** Norfk
89 H5 **Penton Corner** Hants
89 H5 **Penton Grafton** Hants
118 A6 **Penton Hook** Surrey
90 A5 **Penton Mewsey** Hants
119 G3 **Pentonville** Gt Lon
153 F6 **Pentowin** Carmth
304 B4 **Pentraeth** IoA
132 C4 **Pentrapeod** Caerph
128 D2 **Pentre** Carmth
287 G3 **Pentre** Denbgs
287 H2 **Pentre** Flints
288 B2 **Pentre** Flints
288 B3 **Pentre** Flints
308 D6 **Pentre** Flints
207 H2 **Pentre** Powys
209 E1 **Pentre** Powys
232 B2 **Pentre** Powys
232 D3 **Pentre** Powys
131 F5 **Pentre** Rhondd
233 G1 **Pentre** Shrops
268 D4 **Pentre** Shrops
269 E1 **Pentre** Wrexhm
156 C3 **Pentrebach** Carmth
181 E5 **Pentre-bâch** Cerdgn
131 H4 **Pentrebach** Myr Td
157 E3 **Pentre-bach** Powys
106 A2 **Pentrebach** Rhondd
129 F3 **Pentrebach** Swans
106 B4 **Pentrebane** Cardif
283 E1 **Pentre Berw** IoA
285 F4 **Pentre-bont** Conwy
288 D4 **Pentre Broughton** Wrexhm
288 C5 **Pentre Bychan** Wrexhm
153 G1 **Pentrecagal** Carmth
268 D4 **Pentre-cefn** Shrops
287 H4 **Pentre-celyn** Denbgs
230 D3 **Pentre-celyn** Powys
103 G3 **Pentre-chwyth** Swans
268 D2 **Pentre Cilgwyn** Wrexhm
269 E3 **Pentre-clawdd** Shrops
130 C3 **Pentreclwydau** Neath
269 G2 **Pentre-coed** Shrops
154 A2 **Pentre-cwrt** Carmth
183 F6 **Pentre Dolau Honddu** Powys
288 A5 **Pentredwr** Denbgs
103 G2 **Pentre-dwr** Swans
155 E5 **Pentrefelin** Carmth
181 F5 **Pentrefelin** Cerdgn
305 H5 **Pentrefelin** Conwy
288 B6 **Pentrefelin** Denbgs
264 C2 **Pentrefelin** Gwynd
303 F2 **Pentrefelin** IoA
308 C5 **Pentre-Ffwrndan** Flints
286 B4 **Pentrefoelas** Conwy
132 C5 **Pentref-y-groes** Caerph
152 D3 **Pentre Galar** Pembks
179 H3 **Pentregat** Cerdgn
129 F1 **Pentre-Gwenlais** Carmth
264 D4 **Pentre Gwynfryn** Gwynd
308 A5 **Pentre Halkyn** Flints
232 D6 **Pentreheyling** Shrops
209 F4 **Pentre Hodre** Shrops
306 B6 **Pentre Isaf** Conwy
287 F2 **Pentre-Llanrhaeadr** Denbgs
232 B5 **Pentre Llifior** Powys
154 B1 **Pentrellwyn** Cerdgn
304 C3 **Pentrellwyn** IoA
183 E4 **Pentre-Llwyn-llwyd** Powys
205 E4 **Pentre-llyn** Cerdgn
286 D4 **Pentre-llyn-cymmer** Conwy
289 E5 **Pentre Maelor** Wrexhm
105 F4 **Pentre Meyrick** V Glam
154 B4 **Pentre-Morgan** Carmth
269 E2 **Pentre-newydd** Shrops
128 D4 **Pentre-Poeth** Carmth
107 E2 **Pentre-poeth** Newpt
133 E4 **Pentre-poid** Torfn
232 C2 **Pentre'r beirdd** Powys
305 H6 **Pentre'r Felin** Conwy
287 G1 **Pentre'r-felin** Denbgs
157 E3 **Pentre'r-felin** Powys
285 H2 **Pentre-tafarn-y-fedw** Conwy
156 C2 **Pentre-ty-gwyn** Carmth
306 B4 **Pentre-uchaf** Conwy
263 F3 **Pentreuchaf** Gwynd
294 D4 **Pentrich** Derbys
70 A6 **Pentridge** Dorset
152 B3 **Pentrisil** Pembks
132 B4 **Pentwyn** Caerph
132 D4 **Pen-twyn** Caerph
106 A3 **Pentwyn** Cardif
106 D3 **Pentwyn** Cardif
133 E4 **Pen-twyn** Torfn
132 A5 **Pentwyn Berthlwyd** Myr Td
132 C5 **Pentwyn-mawr** Caerph
106 B3 **Pentyrch** Cardif
308 A5 **Pen-Uchar Plwyf** Flints
181 E2 **Penuwch** Cerdgn
7 E3 **Penwartha** Cnwll
7 E3 **Penwartha Coombe** Cnwll
7 E5 **Penweathers** Cnwll
8 C2 **Penwithick** Cnwll
90 C2 **Penwood** Hants
338 D4 **Penwortham Lane** Lancs
130 D1 **Penwyllt** Powys
307 H4 **Pen-y-Ball Top** Flints
129 F2 **Penybanc** Carmth
154 B5 **Pen-y-banc** Carmth
155 F5 **Pen-y-banc** Carmth
132 A4 **Pen-y-bank** Caerph
128 B4 **Penybedd** Carmth
132 D3 **Pen-y-bont** Blae G
153 G4 **Pen-y-bont** Carmth
205 E2 **Penybont** Cerdgn
265 E4 **Pen-y-bont** Gwynd
184 B2 **Penybont** Powys
268 A5 **Penybontfawr** Powys
268 D5 **Pen-y-bont Llanerch Emrys** Powys
132 B5 **Penybryn** Caerph
264 B2 **Pen-y-bryn** Gwynd
265 F6 **Pen-y-Bryn** Gwynd
178 D5 **Pen-y-bryn** Pembks
232 C5 **Pen-y-bryn** Powys
269 F2 **Pen-y-Bryn** Shrops
288 C6 **Pen-y-bryn** Wrexhm
105 E3 **Pen-y-cae** Brdgnd
104 B2 **Pen-y-cae** Neath
130 C2 **Pen-y-cae** Powys
288 C5 **Penycae** Wrexhm
133 G5 **Pen-y-Cae-mawr** Mons
262 C5 **Penycaerau** Gwynd
307 G4 **Pen-y-cefn** Flints
133 G3 **Pen-y-clawdd** Mons
269 E5 **Pen-y-coed** Shrops
105 H2 **Pen-y-coedcae** Rhondd
151 E5 **Penycwm** Pembks
131 H3 **Pen-y-Darren** Myr Td
129 G4 **Penydre** Swans
104 D3 **Pen-y-fai** Brdgnd
128 C4 **Pen-y-fai** Carmth
128 D4 **Pen-y-fan** Carmth
134 C3 **Pen-y-fan** Mons
151 E4 **Penyfeidr** Pembks
307 G6 **Pen-y-felin** Flints
307 E4 **Pen-y-ffordd** Denbgs
288 D2 **Penyffordd** Flints
307 G3 **Pen-y-ffordd** Flints
283 F4 **Penyffrid** Gwynd
269 E5 **Pen y foel** Powys
155 E3 **Pen-y-garn** Carmth
205 E2 **Pen-y-garn** Cerdgn
133 E4 **Penygarn** Torfn
304 B4 **Pen-y-garnedd** IoA
268 B5 **Penygarnedd** Powys
208 B1 **Penygelli** Powys
262 B4 **Pen-y-graig** Gwynd
105 F1 **Penygraig** Rhondd
303 F3 **Penygraigwen** IoA
129 E2 **Pen-y-groes** Carmth
283 E5 **Penygroes** Gwynd
152 D2 **Penygroes** Pembks
262 C4 **Pen-y-groeslon** Gwynd
106 C4 **Pen-y-lan** Cardif
107 E3 **Pen-y-lan** Newpt
105 F4 **Pen-y-lan** V Glam
308 A4 **Pen-y-maes** Flints
128 C4 **Pen-y-mynydd** Carmth
288 D2 **Penymynydd** Flints
185 E6 **Pen-y-Park** Herefs
151 G2 **Penyraber** Pembks
131 E5 **Pen-yr-englyn** Rhondd
105 E3 **Pen-yr-heol** Brdgnd
106 B2 **Penyrheol** Caerph
134 A2 **Pen-yr-heol** Mons
129 E5 **Penyrheol** Swans
133 E5 **Penyrheol** Torfn
105 H2 **Pen-y-rhiw** Rhondd
303 F2 **Penysarn** IoA
288 A4 **Pen-y-stryt** Denbgs
131 F4 **Penywaun** Rhondd
209 F4 **Pen-y-wern** Shrops
3 E4 **Penzance** Cnwll
188 D4 **Peopleton** Worcs
311 F5 **Peover Heath** Ches
93 F6 **Peper Harow** Surrey
271 E5 **Peplow** Shrops
39 E3 **Peppercombe** Devon
342 B4 **Pepper Hill** Calder
443 G1 **Peppermoor** Nthumb
146 C2 **Pepper's Green** Essex
444 D1 **Perceton** N Ayrs
540 A1 **Percie** Abers
5 G2 **Percuil** Cnwll
571 H2 **Percyhorner** Abers
406 A1 **Percy Main** N Tyne
34 b3 **Perelle** Guern
307 G4 **Per-ffordd-llan** Flints
89 G5 **Perham Down** Wilts
63 F2 **Periton** Somset
118 D3 **Perivale** Gt Lon
555 G3 **Perkhill** Abers
27 G4 **Perkin's Village** Devon
405 F4 **Perkinsville** Dur
316 B5 **Perlethorpe** Notts
7 E6 **Perranarworthal** Cnwll
7 E3 **Perrancoombe** Cnwll
3 F3 **Perran Downs** Cnwll
6 D3 **Perranporth** Cnwll
3 F4 **Perranuthnoe** Cnwll
7 E3 **Perranwell** Cnwll
7 E6 **Perranwell** Cnwll
7 E6 **Perranwell Station** Cnwll
7 E6 **Perran Wharf** Cnwll
7 E3 **Perranzabuloe** Cnwll
137 F3 **Perrott's Brook** Gloucs
237 G6 **Perry** Birm
26 D1 **Perry** Devon
101 E4 **Perry** Kent
213 G1 **Perry Barr** Birm
237 G6 **Perry Beeches** Birm
237 G6 **Perry Common** Birm
238 C4 **Perry Crofts** Staffs
212 D5 **Perryfields** Worcs
313 F3 **Perryfoot** Derbys
173 G5 **Perry Green** Essex
145 F1 **Perry Green** Herts
65 E4 **Perry Green** Somset
111 H2 **Perry Green** Wilts
86 C2 **Perrymead** BaNES
161 E4 **Perrystone Hill** Herefs
121 F5 **Perry Street** Kent
29 F1 **Perry Street** Somset
99 F3 **Perrywood** Kent
272 B4 **Pershall** Staffs
188 D5 **Pershore** Worcs
528 D1 **Pert** Angus
195 F1 **Pertenhall** Beds
512 C5 **Perth** P & K
131 G5 **Perthcelyn** Rhondd
269 G3 **Perthy** Shrops
160 D1 **Perton** Herefs
236 C5 **Perton** Staffs
58 C3 **Pestalozzi Children's Village** E Susx
99 G4 **Pested** Kent
244 B4 **Peterborough** C Pete
572 D7 **Peterburn** Highld
159 G2 **Peterchurch** Herefs
557 E4 **Peterculter** C Aber
571 L6 **Peterhead** Abers
396 B1 **Peterlee** Dur
468 B2 **Petersburn** N Lans
73 H5 **Petersfield** Hants
23 H5 **Peter's Finger** Devon
169 G6 **Peter's Green** Herts
39 G5 **Peters Marland** Devon
107 E3 **Peterstone Wentlooge** Newpt
106 A4 **Peterston-super-Ely** V Glam
160 D5 **Peterstow** Herefs
18 B2 **Peter Tavy** Devon
600 D4 **Petertown** Ork
6 D3 **Peterville** Cnwll
100 B5 **Petham** Kent
23 F5 **Petherwin Gate** Cnwll
39 H6 **Petrockstowe** Devon
194 B5 **Petsoe End** M Keyn
59 E4 **Pett** E Susx
201 G3 **Pettaugh** Suffk
82 B2 **Pett Bottom** Kent
100 C5 **Pett Bottom** Kent
79 F1 **Petteridge** Kent
469 F6 **Pettinain** S Lans
97 F2 **Pettings** Kent
202 B4 **Pettistree** Suffk
59 E4 **Pett Level** E Susx
42 D3 **Petton** Devon
270 A4 **Petton** Shrops
96 B1 **Petts Wood** Gt Lon
559 H2 **Petty** Abers
110 D2 **Petty France** S Glos
560 D5 **Pettymuick** Abers
255 E3 **Pettywell** Norfk
75 F5 **Petworth** W Susx
57 H4 **Pevensey** E Susx
57 G4 **Pevensey Bay** E Susx
11 E2 **Peverell** C Plym
89 E2 **Pewsey** Wilts
89 E2 **Pewsey Wharf** Wilts
310 C3 **Pewterspear** Warrtn
490 A4 **Phantassie** E Loth
172 C5 **Pharisee Green** Essex
116 C2 **Pheasants** Bucks
116 C2 **Pheasant's Hill** Bucks
237 G5 **Pheasey** Wsall
188 D3 **Phepson** Worcs
406 A4 **Philadelphia** Sundld
38 C3 **Philham** Devon
451 E4 **Philiphaugh** Border
3 G2 **Phillack** Cnwll
7 G6 **Philleigh** Cnwll
132 B4 **Phillip's Town** Caerph
172 C6 **Philpot End** Essex
486 D4 **Philpstoun** W Loth
161 E4 **Phocle Green** Herefs
92 B3 **Phoenix Green** Hants
394 D4 **Phoenix Row** Dur
66 C4 **Pibsbury** Somset
154 B6 **Pibwrlwyd** Carmth
388 B5 **Pica** Cumb
329 G5 **Piccadilly** Rothm
238 C5 **Piccadilly** Warwks
226 B2 **Piccadilly Corner** Norfk
143 F3 **Piccotts End** Herts
330 B3 **Pickburn** Donc
188 B6 **Picken End** Worcs
373 E3 **Pickering** N York
405 E3 **Pickering Nook** Dur
528 C4 **Pickerton** Angus
49 F3 **Picket Hill** Hants
90 B5 **Picket Piece** Hants
49 F3 **Picket Post** Hants
214 D3 **Pickford** Covtry
214 D3 **Pickford Green** Covtry
370 C3 **Pickhill** N York
161 G4 **Picklenash** Gloucs
234 A5 **Picklescott** Shrops
341 G2 **Pickles Hill** Brad
325 F4 **Pickley Green** Wigan
310 D4 **Pickmere** Ches
43 G2 **Pickney** Somset
271 G5 **Pickstock** Wrekin
340 A5 **Pickup Bank** Bl w D
60 C3 **Pickwell** Devon
241 G2 **Pickwell** Leics
111 F5 **Pickwick** Wilts
341 H5 **Pickwood Scar** Calder
279 E3 **Pickworth** Lincs
242 D2 **Pickworth** Rutlnd
309 F5 **Picton** Ches
307 G3 **Picton** Flints
384 C3 **Picton** N York
66 C4 **Pict's Hill** Somset
56 C4 **Piddinghoe** E Susx
141 G6 **Piddington** Bucks
193 G4 **Piddington** Nhants
140 D1 **Piddington** Oxon
46 D5 **Piddlehinton** Dorset
220 D4 **Pidley** Cambs
46 D3 **Pidney** Dorset
6 C6 **Piece** Cnwll
383 E1 **Piercebridge** Darltn
145 G5 **Piercing Hill** Essex
602 E2 **Pierowall** Ork
162 D4 **Piff's Elm** Gloucs
430 C2 **Pigdon** Nthumb
64 D4 **Pightley** Somset
48 C4 **Pig Oak** Dorset
146 C3 **Pigstye Green** Essex
341 G6 **Pike End** Calder
293 G3 **Pikehall** Derbys
340 D3 **Pike Hill** Lancs
327 F1 **Pike Law** Calder
50 A3 **Pikeshill** Hants
186 C5 **Pikestye** Herefs
48 C4 **Pilford** Dorset
146 B5 **Pilgrims Hatch** Essex
332 B6 **Pilham** Lincs
294 A1 **Pilhough** Derbys
109 F4 **Pill** N Som
125 F3 **Pill** Pembks
17 E6 **Pillaton** Cnwll
236 D2 **Pillaton** Staffs
191 E5 **Pillerton Hersey** Warwks
190 D5 **Pillerton Priors** Warwks
209 E6 **Pilleth** Powys
329 E4 **Pilley** Barns
163 E6 **Pilley** Gloucs
50 B5 **Pilley** Hants
50 B5 **Pilley Bailey** Hants
107 F2 **Pillgwenlly** Newpt
351 F5 **Pilling** Lancs
351 E5 **Pilling Lane** Lancs
39 G3 **Pillmouth** Devon
135 E3 **Pillowell** Gloucs
162 A4 **Pillows Green** Gloucs
68 C6 **Pillwell** Dorset
439 F2 **Pilmuir** Border
567 J5 **Pilmuir** Moray
109 G2 **Pilning** S Glos
488 B4 **Pilrig** C Edin
293 F2 **Pilsbury** Derbys
29 H3 **Pilsdon** Dorset
243 F3 **Pilsgate** C Pete
295 E2 **Pilsley** Derbys
314 A5 **Pilsley** Derbys
295 E2 **Pilsley Green** Derbys
250 D2 **Pilson Green** Norfk
78 A5 **Piltdown** E Susx
488 A4 **Pilton** C Edin
60 D5 **Pilton** Devon
219 E3 **Pilton** Nhants
242 C4 **Pilton** Rutlnd
67 F1 **Pilton** Somset
102 B4 **Pilton Green** Swans
67 F2 **Piltown** Somset
326 B2 **Pimhole** Bury
119 F4 **Pimlico** Gt Lon
143 F3 **Pimlico** Herts
353 F6 **Pimlico** Lancs
45 H6 **Pimperne** Dorset
47 G3 **Pimperne** Dorset
280 B4 **Pinchbeck** Lincs
280 B5 **Pinchbeck West** Lincs
331 E1 **Pincheon Green** Donc
385 F1 **Pinchinthorpe** R & Cl
87 E2 **Pinckney Green** Wilts
338 D6 **Pincock** Lancs
81 F3 **Pineham** Kent
168 B1 **Pineham** M Keyn
112 D2 **Pinehurst** Swindn
136 B4 **Pinfarthings** Gloucs
323 G2 **Pinfold** Lancs
328 D4 **Pinfold Hill** Barns
168 C3 **Pinfoldpond** Beds
199 H3 **Pinford End** Suffk
128 B4 **Pinged** Carmth
116 A6 **Pingewood** W Berk
170 B4 **Pin Green** Herts
27 F4 **Pinhoe** Devon
214 D3 **Pinkett's Booth** Covtry
213 G6 **Pink Green** Worcs
488 D5 **Pinkie Braes** E Loth
111 F2 **Pinkney** Wilts
116 D3 **Pinkneys Green** W & M
43 F4 **Pinksmoor** Somset
190 C1 **Pinley Green** Warwks
419 F3 **Pinmore** S Ayrs
145 F3 **Pinnacles** Essex
118 C2 **Pinner** Gt Lon
118 C1 **Pinner Green** Gt Lon
118 C1 **Pinnerwood Park** Gt Lon
188 B5 **Pin's Green** Worcs
290 B5 **Pinsley Green** Ches
210 B2 **Pinstones** Shrops
188 D5 **Pinvin** Worcs
239 E4 **Pinwall** Leics
419 E4 **Pinwherry** S Ayrs
295 E4 **Pinxton** Derbys
186 C6 **Pipe and Lyde** Herefs
210 B5 **Pipe Aston** Herefs
271 G1 **Pipe Gate** Shrops
237 G3 **Pipehill** Staffs
86 D3 **Pipehouse** BaNES
566 F6 **Piperhill** Highld
273 G6 **Pipe Ridware** Staffs
309 F6 **Piper's Ash** Ches
162 B3 **Piper's End** Worcs
189 E2 **Piper's Hill** Worcs
23 F6 **Pipers Pool** Cnwll
218 A2 **Pipewell** Nhants
60 D4 **Pippacott** Devon
339 E5 **Pippin Street** Lancs
121 G2 **Pipps Hill** Essex
79 H3 **Pipsden** Kent
93 F3 **Pirbright** Surrey
93 F3 **Pirbright Camp** Surrey
463 E6 **Pirnmill** N Ayrs
169 H3 **Pirton** Herts
188 C5 **Pirton** Worcs
205 F4 **Pisgah** Cerdgn
498 B4 **Pisgah** Stirlg
116 B2 **Pishill** Oxon
116 B1 **Pishill Bank** Oxon
314 D1 **Pismire Hill** Sheff
263 E2 **Pistyll** Gwynd
133 G3 **Pit** Mons
524 B2 **Pitagowan** P & K
571 H2 **Pitblae** Abers
512 C4 **Pitcairngreen** P & K
566 E2 **Pitcalnie** Highld
559 G4 **Pitcaple** Abers
136 B3 **Pitchcombe** Gloucs
167 G5 **Pitchcott** Bucks
200 B3 **Pitcher's Green** Suffk
234 C4 **Pitchford** Shrops
141 G4 **Pitch Green** Bucks
74 D2 **Pitch Place** Surrey
93 G4 **Pitch Place** Surrey
68 A3 **Pitcombe** Somset
487 F2 **Pitcorthie** Fife
86 B5 **Pitcot** Somset
104 D5 **Pitcot** V Glam
490 B4 **Pitcox** E Loth
513 F2 **Pitcur** P & K
514 B3 **Pitempton** C Dund
556 B1 **Pitfichie** Abers
541 F4 **Pitforthie** Abers
577 G5 **Pitgrudy** Highld
528 B4 **Pitkennedy** Angus
501 F3 **Pitlessie** Fife
524 D4 **Pitlochry** P & K
566 D1 **Pitmaduthy** Highld
560 C4 **Pitmedden** Abers
43 H4 **Pitminster** Somset
528 C5 **Pitmuies** Angus
556 B1 **Pitmunie** Abers
66 D4 **Pitney** Somset
514 B2 **Pitpointie** Angus
527 G5 **Pitreuchie** Angus
502 C2 **Pitscottie** Fife
122 A2 **Pitsea** Essex
326 D4 **Pitses** Oldham
217 G6 **Pitsford** Nhants
64 B5 **Pitsford Hill** Somset
314 D2 **Pitsmoor** Sheff
142 C1 **Pitstone** Bucks
142 C2 **Pitstone Hill** Bucks
72 C4 **Pitt** Hants
135 H5 **Pitt Court** Gloucs
568 B3 **Pittendreich** Moray
576 F3 **Pittentrail** Highld
503 F4 **Pittenweem** Fife
501 E5 **Pitteuchar** Fife
406 A6 **Pittington** Dur
102 B4 **Pitton** Swans
71 E3 **Pitton** Wilts
291 H4 **Pitts Hill** C Stke
571 H2 **Pittulie** Abers
162 D5 **Pittville** Gloucs
14 C3 **Pityme** Cnwll
405 G5 **Pity Me** Dur
226 A4 **Pixey Green** Suffk
188 B5 **Pixham** Worcs
161 F2 **Pixley** Herefs
271 F4 **Pixley** Shrops
97 G4 **Pizien Well** Kent
373 G5 **Place Newton** N York
570 C5 **Plaidy** Abers
9 H3 **Plaidy** Cnwll
3 F3 **Plain-an-Gwarry** Cnwll
6 C5 **Plain-an-Gwarry** Cnwll
152 B6 **Plain Dealings** Pembks
468 B1 **Plains** N Lans
64 C4 **Plainsfield** Somset
295 F4 **Plain Spot** Notts
14 D3 **Plain Street** Cnwll
234 C5 **Plaish** Shrops
120 A3 **Plaistow** Gt Lon
120 A5 **Plaistow** Gt Lon
75 G3 **Plaistow** W Susx
173 G4 **Plaistow Green** Essex
71 F6 **Plaitford** Hants
71 F5 **Plaitford Green** Hants
325 E4 **Plank Lane** Wigan
379 E5 **Plantation Bridge** Cumb
437 F6 **Plantationfoot** D & G
272 B5 **Plardiwick** Staffs
269 G5 **Plasau** Shrops
288 A6 **Plâs Berwyn** Denbgs
288 D4 **Plas Coch** Wrexhm
207 G2 **Plas Dinam** Powys
154 C4 **Plas Fawr** Carmth
205 E3 **Plas Gogerddan** Cerdgn
284 D4 **Plas Gwynant** Gwynd
120 B3 **Plashet** Gt Lon
127 F3 **Plashett** Carmth
232 A4 **Plasiolyn** Powys
230 B4 **Plâs Llwyngwern** Powys
231 E5 **Plâs Llysyn** Powys
288 C6 **Plas Madoc** Wrexhm
232 C5 **Plas Meredydd** Powys
268 C2 **Plas Nantyr** Wrexhm
231 F5 **Plasnewydd** Powys

303 G5 Plas Penmynydd IoA
85 F2 Plaster's Green BaNES
91 E2 Plastow Green Hants
97 F3 Platt Kent
325 E4 Platt Bridge Wigan
270 C2 Platt Lane Shrops
329 F4 Platts Common Barns
98 D4 Platt's Heath Kent
405 G5 Plawsworth Dur
97 F4 Plaxtol Kent
59 F2 Playden E Susx
201 H5 Playford Suffk
116 B4 Play Hatch Oxon
7 F5 Playing Place Cnwll
161 H3 Playley Green Gloucs
234 A3 Plealey Shrops
43 F4 Pleamore Cross Somset
485 G2 Plean Stirlg
126 C3 Pleasant Valley Pembks
339 F4 Pleasington Bl w D
295 G2 Pleasley Derbys
295 G2 Pleasleyhill Notts
46 D2 Pleck Dorset
68 C6 Pleck Dorset
237 E5 Pleck Wsall
339 G3 Pleckgate Bl w D
47 E4 Pleck or Little Ansty Dorset
172 B4 Pledgdon Green Essex
329 E1 Pledwick Wakefd
34 C2 Pleinheaume Guern
35 f5 Plemont Jersey
309 G5 Plemstall Ches
440 D2 Plenderleith Border
402 C2 Plenmeller Nthumb
146 D2 Pleshey Essex
546 E3 Plockton Highld
595 K4 Plocrapol W Isls
67 E3 Plot Gate Somset
67 E2 Plot Street Somset
239 E6 Plough Hill Warwks
209 G2 Plowden Shrops
233 G4 Ploxgreen Shrops
99 E5 Pluckley Kent
99 E6 Pluckley Thorne Kent
101 E3 Plucks Gutter Kent
389 E2 Plumbland Cumb
315 E3 Plumbley Sheff
99 F3 Plumford Kent
311 K4 Plumley Ches
135 F1 Plump Hill Gloucs
390 D2 Plumpton Cumb
56 B2 Plumpton E Susx
337 G3 Plumpton Lancs
192 C5 Plumpton Nhants
193 F5 Plumpton End Nhants
390 D2 Plumpton Foot Cumb
56 B1 Plumpton Green E Susx
391 E2 Plumpton Head Cumb
120 B4 Plumstead Gt Lon
261 F5 Plumstead Norfk
120 B4 Plumstead Common Gt Lon
261 F5 Plumstead Green Norfk
276 D3 Plumtree Notts
98 C5 Plumtree Green Kent
276 D3 Plumtree Park Notts
277 G3 Plungar Leics
46 D4 Plush Dorset
16 C3 Plusha Cnwll
16 D4 Plushabridge Cnwll
134 D5 Plusterwine Gloucs
179 H3 Plwmp Cerdgn
11 E2 Plymouth C Plym
11 F2 Plympton C Plym
11 F3 Plymstock C Plym
27 G2 Plymtree Devon
327 F3 Pobgreen Oldham
132 C3 Pochin Houses Blae G
325 E5 Pocket Nook Wigan
372 B2 Pockley N York
359 F5 Pocklington E R Yk
248 B5 Pockthorpe Norfk
253 G2 Pockthorpe Norfk
254 D3 Pockthorpe Norfk
255 E4 Pockthorpe Norfk
280 B5 Pode Hole Lincs
67 E5 Podimore Somset
194 C2 Podington Beds
212 C5 Podmoor Worcs
254 C5 Podmore Norfk
272 A2 Podmore Staffs
136 B1 Podsmead Gloucs
139 F2 Poffley End Oxon
329 E3 Pogmoor Barns
149 E1 Point Clear Essex
279 Q3 Pointon Lincs
34 D2 Pokesdown Bmouth
590 E5 Pol a' Charra W Isls
416 B2 Polbae D & G
10 B2 Polbathic Cnwll
469 G2 Polbeth W Loth
17 E6 Polborder Cnwll
15 E5 Polbrock Cnwll
437 E4 Poldean D & G
219 F2 Polebrook Nhants
188 B5 Pole Elm Worcs
57 F4 Polegate E Susx
327 G1 Pole Moor Kirk
577 G5 Poles Highld
43 E3 Poleshill Somset
87 E4 Pole's Hole Wilts
238 D4 Polesworth Warwks
4 C1 Polgear Cnwll
2 C5 Polgigga Cnwll
573 K2 Polglass Highld
8 B3 Polgooth Cnwll
54 B4 Poling W Susx
54 B3 Poling Corner W Susx
8 D3 Polkerris Cnwll
585 G6 Polla Highld
4 B2 Polladras Cnwll
256 C3 Pollard Street Norfk
98 D4 Polhill Kent
308 C3 Poll Hill Wirral
345 E6 Pollington E R Yk
519 J2 Polloch Highld
466 D2 Pollok C Glas
467 E2 Pollokshaws C Glas
467 E2 Pollokshields C Clas
542 B7 Polmassick Cnwll
467 E2 Polmadie C Glas
549 H3 Polmaily Highld
4 D1 Polmarth Cnwll
8 B4 Polmassick Cnwll
8 D3 Polmear Cnwll
486 B4 Polmont Falk
14 D4 Polmorla Cnwll
433 F2 Polnessan E Ayrs
531 K6 Polnish Highld
219 E4 Polopit Nhants
4 D3 Polpenwith Cnwll
3 F2 Polpeor Cnwll
9 G5 Polperro Cnwll
9 E3 Polruan Cnwll
85 F6 Polsham Somset
434 D4 Polskeoch D & G
27 E4 Polsloe Devon
174 C2 Polstead Suffk
174 C1 Polstead Heath Suffk
492 D5 Poltalloch Ag & B
4 D5 Poltesco Cnwll
27 F3 Poltimore Devon
471 E1 Polton Mdloth
473 G4 Polwarth Border

4 D3 Polwheveral Cnwll
16 C2 Polyphant Cnwll
14 C3 Polzeath Cnwll
470 D3 Pomathorn Mdloth
313 F6 Pomeroy Derbys
11 F3 Pomphlett C Plym
288 C5 Ponciau Wrexhm
43 F2 Pond Close Somset
158 B2 Ponde Powys
220 B1 Pondersbridge Cambs
145 E5 Ponders End Gt Lon
142 D4 Pond Park Bucks
171 G2 Pond Street Essex
37 G2 Pondwell IoW
2 D2 Poniou Cnwll
4 D3 Ponjeravah Cnwll
4 D1 Ponsanooth Cnwll
42 C6 Ponsford Devon
376 C3 Ponsonby Cumb
5 E5 Ponsongath Cnwll
19 F3 Ponsworthy Devon
9 E3 Pont Cnwll
35 j8 Pontac Jersey
129 F2 Pontamman Carmth
128 B2 Pontantwn Carmth
129 G4 Pontardawe Neath
129 E4 Pontarddulais Swans
154 D5 Pont-ar-gothi Carmth
156 D4 Pont ar hydfer Powys
156 A5 Pont-ar-llechau Carmth
154 B4 Pontarsais Carmth
288 C2 Pontblyddyn Flints
155 C5 Pontbren Araeth Carmth
106 C4 Pontcanna Cardif
180 D4 Pont Creuddyn Cerdgn
230 D6 Pont Crugnant Powys
285 F3 Pont Cyfyng Conwy
269 E1 Pont Cysyllte Denbgs
231 C6 Pontdolgoch Powys
344 B5 Pontefract Wakefd
430 C5 Ponteland Nthumb
205 G3 Ponterwyd Cerdgn
233 G3 Pontesbury Shrops
233 G3 Pontesbury Hill Shrops
233 H3 Pontesford Shrops
268 D2 Pontfadog Wrexhm
151 H3 Pontfaen Pembks
157 F3 Pont-Faen Powys
269 E2 Pont-Faen Shrops
179 G3 Pontgarreg Cerdgn
233 F1 Ponthen Shrops
128 C3 Pont Henri Carmth
133 F6 Ponthir Torfn
179 F4 Ponthirwaun Cerdgn
302 B4 Pont Hwfa IoA
151 F2 Pontiago Pembks
158 C2 Pontithel Powys
132 C5 Pontlanfraith Caerph
129 F4 Pontlliw Swans
231 G1 Pont Llogel Powys
282 D5 Pontllyfni Gwynd
132 B3 Pontlottyn Caerph
131 E3 Pontneddfechan Powys
128 B3 Pont-Newydd Carmth
288 A1 Pont-Newydd Flints
133 E5 Pontnewydd Torfn
133 E4 Pontnewynydd Torfn
284 D2 Pont Pen-y-Benglog Gwynd
182 A1 Pontrhydfendigaid Cerdgn
206 C3 Pont Rhydgaled Powys
157 F2 Pont Rhyd-y-berry Powys
104 D2 Pont Rhyd-y-cyff Brdgnd
130 B6 Pontrhydyfen Neath
205 G5 Pont-rhyd-y-groes Cerdgn
133 E5 Pontrhydyrun Torfn
283 F3 Pont-Rhythallt Gwynd
159 H4 Pontrilas Herefs
232 A2 Pontrobert Powys
283 F3 Pont-Rug Gwynd
57 H1 Ponts Green E Susx
161 E5 Pontshill Herefs
180 B5 Pont-Siân Cerdgn
106 A1 Pont Siôn Norton Rhondd
131 G2 Pontsticill Myr Td
130 D3 Pont-Walby Neath
128 C3 Pontyates Carmth
128 D2 Pontyberem Carmth
269 F2 Pont-y-blew Wrexhm
288 C3 Pontybodkin Flints
105 G3 Pontyclun Rhondd
104 D1 Pontycymer Brdgnd
152 C2 Pontyglasier Pembks
131 G6 Pontygwaith Rhondd
106 D1 Pontymister Caerph
133 E4 Pontymoel Torfn
285 H4 Pont-y-pant Conwy
133 E4 Pontypool Torfn
105 G2 Pontypridd Rhondd
151 F4 Pont-yr-hafod Pembks
105 E2 Pont-y-rhyl Brdgnd
287 F2 Pont-Ystrad Denbgs
158 B2 Pont-y-wal Powys
132 D6 Pontywaun Caerph
50 C2 Pooksgreen Hants
6 C5 Pool Cnwll
3 c2 Pool IoS
356 A6 Pool Leeds
188 A6 Poolbrook Worcs
573 G7 Pool Crofts Highld
344 B4 Poole N York
34 B3 Poole Poole
43 F3 Poole Somset
292 C3 Poolend Staffs
46 D1 Poolestown Dorset
572 F7 Poolewe Highld
390 D5 Pooley Bridge Cumb
225 E3 Pooley Street Norfk
292 A3 Poolfold Staffs
186 C4 Pool Head Herefs
270 B3 Poolhead Shrops
323 G1 Pool Hey Lancs
161 G4 Poolhill Gloucs
160 D5 Poolhill Herefs
499 F4 Pool of Muckhart Clacks
233 E2 Pool Quay Powys
315 E5 Poolsbrook Derbys
324 D4 Poolstock Wigan
63 F4 Pooltown Somset
96 C5 Pootings Kent
308 D3 Pope Hill Pembks
281 G5 Popeluton...
125 G2 Pope Hill Pembks
135 F2 Pope's Hill Gloucs
116 D6 Popeswood Br For
61 H5 Popham Devon
91 F6 Popham Hants
119 H3 Poplar Gt Lon
335 F5 Poplar Grove Lincs
170 C5 Poplars Herts
91 G4 Popley Hants
296 A6 Porchester Notts
36 C2 Porchfield IoW
250 B4 Poringland Norfk
4 C2 Porkellis Cnwll
62 D2 Porlock Somset
62 D2 Porlockford Somset
62 D2 Porlock Weir Somset

464 B1 Port Bannatyne Ag & B
488 B1 Port Brae Fife
20 B6 Port Bridge Devon
109 F5 Portbury N Som
399 G2 Port Carlisle Cumb
476 D5 Port Charlotte Ag & B
51 G3 Portchester Hants
549 G7 Portclair Highld
396 C5 Port Clarence S on T
480 D5 Port Driseach Ag & B
467 E1 Port Dundas C Glas
14 D3 Porteath Cnwll
487 F4 Port Edgar C Edin
476 F7 Port Ellen Ag & B
560 A6 Port Elphinstone Abers
414 D2 Portencalzie D & G
464 C5 Portencross N Ayrs
466 C1 Porterfield Rens
322 b9 Port Erin IoM
561 G2 Port Erroll Abers
143 H1 Porter's End Herts
30 D5 Portesham Dorset
569 J7 Portessie Moray
322 h4 Port E Vullen IoM
102 C4 Port-Eynon Swans
66 C4 Portfield Somset
53 F4 Portfield W Susx
125 F1 Portfield Gate Pembks
24 B5 Portgate Devon
15 E2 Port Gaverne Cnwll
482 D4 Port Glasgow Inver
568 F3 Portgordon Moray
582 C7 Portgower Highld
14 A6 Porth Cnwll
105 G1 Porth Rhondd
5 E4 Porthallow Cnwll
9 G3 Porthallow Cnwll
104 B4 Porthcawl Brdgnd
262 B4 Porth Colmon Gwynd
14 B4 Porthcothan Cnwll
2 C5 Porthcurno Cnwll
150 D3 Portheiddy Pembks
562 C2 Port Henderson Highld
150 D3 Porthgain Pembks
2 C5 Porthgwarra Cnwll
116 A2 Port Hill Oxon
234 B2 Porthill Shrops
14 C3 Porthilly Cnwll
7 F5 Port Kea Cnwll
106 A6 Porthkerry V Glam
4 B3 Porthleven Cnwll
303 F2 Porthllechog IoA
3 c2 Porthloo IoS
264 C2 Porthmadog Gwynd
2 D2 Porthmeor Cnwll
4 D3 Port Navas Cnwll
5 F4 Porthoustock Cnwll
6 C4 Porthtowan Cnwll
302 B4 Porth-y-Felin IoA
128 D1 Porthyrhyd Carmth
155 H2 Porthyrhyd Carmth
268 D5 Porth-y-waen Shrops
324 B6 Portico St Hel
495 E6 Portincaple Ag & B
35 f5 Portinfer Jersey
17 F3 Portington Devon
346 A3 Portington E R Yk
493 H2 Portinnisherrich Ag & B
389 F5 Portinscale Cumb
14 D2 Port Isaac Cnwll
108 D4 Portishead N Som
482 C3 Portkil Ag & B
569 G5 Portknockie Moray
569 H2 Portknockie Moray
66 D2 Portland Dorset
557 G5 Portlethen Abers
557 G5 Portlethen Village Abers
413 G4 Portling D & G
125 G3 Port Lion Pembks
8 A6 Portloe Cnwll
408 B3 Port Logan D & G
9 G3 Portlooe Cnwll
577 J7 Portmahomack Highld
103 F2 Port Mead Swans
8 C5 Portmellon Cnwll
599 M7 Port Mholair W Isls
530 D7 Port Mòr Highld
50 B5 Portmore Hants
386 C1 Port Mulgrave N York
520 C6 Portnacroish Ag & B
599 L7 Portnaguran W Isls
476 B6 Portnahaven Ag & B
544 F2 Portnalong Highld
531 H5 Portnaluchaig Highld
585 H4 Portnancon Highld
599 L7 Port nan Giuran W Isls
594 D7 Port nan Long W Isls
599 L2 Port Nis W Isls
488 C5 Portobello C Edin
405 G3 Portobello Gatesd
236 D5 Portobello Wolves
497 E4 Port of Menteith Stirlg
599 L2 Port of Ness W Isls
70 D2 Porton Wilts
583 G4 Portormin Highld
414 C6 Portpatrick D & G
14 D2 Port Quin Cnwll
396 C6 Portrack S on T
520 B6 Port Ramsay Ag & B
14 C5 Portreath Cnwll
543 H8 Portree Highld
464 D3 Portrye N Ayrs
322 c9 Port St Mary IoM
5 G1 Portscatho Cnwll
52 A4 Portsea C Port
599 L2 Port Sgiogarstaigh W Isls
587 J3 Portskerra Highld
109 E2 Portskewett Mons
55 G3 Portslade Br & H
55 F4 Portslade-by-Sea Br & H
55 F3 Portslade Village Br & H
414 C5 Portslogan D & G
52 B5 Portsmouth C Port
340 D4 Portsmouth Calder
322 e8 Port Soderick IoM
51 H3 Port Solent C Port
507 J5 Portsonachan Ag & B
569 K2 Portsoy Abers
308 D3 Port Sunlight Wirral
281 G5 Port Sutton Bridge Lincs
50 D2 Portswood C Sotn
104 A2 Port Talbot Neath
568 F3 Porttannachy Moray
103 G3 Port Tennant Swans
518 B2 Portuairk Highld
586 C4 Portvasgo Highld
33 E2 Portway Dorset
160 B2 Portway Herefs
186 B5 Portway Herefs
213 E2 Portway Sandw
66 C4 Portway Somset
66 D2 Portway Somset
162 A3 Portway Worcs
213 G5 Portway Worcs
476 B6 Port Wemyss Ag & B
409 G3 Port William D & G
312 B1 Portwood Stockp
10 C3 Portwrinkle Cnwll
411 E5 Portyerrock D & G
235 E4 Posenhall Shrops
199 F5 Poslingford Suffk
484 B6 Possil Park C Glas
449 G3 Posso Border

18 D2 Postbridge Devon
141 F5 Postcombe Oxon
48 A6 Post Green Dorset
82 B3 Postling Kent
163 F4 Postlip Gloucs
250 B3 Postwick Norfk
555 G5 Potarch Abers
175 F2 Potash Suffk
92 B4 Potbridge Hants
93 F6 Pot Common Surrey
80 C4 Potman's Heath Kent
168 D3 Potsgrove Beds
143 E3 Potten End Herts
101 E2 Potten Street Kent
374 B4 Potter Brompton N York
225 G1 Pottergate Street Norfk
298 D1 Potterhanworth Lincs
318 D6 Potterhanworth Booths Lincs
257 E6 Potter Heigham Norfk
277 F5 Potter Hill Leics
329 E5 Potter Hill Sheff
88 A3 Potterne Wilts
88 A3 Potterne Wick Wilts
144 B4 Potters Bar Herts
351 G4 Potters Brook Lancs
99 F6 Potters Corner Kent
143 G3 Potters Crouch Herts
98 D5 Potter's Forstal Kent
215 F3 Potter's Green Covtry
78 C5 Potter's Green E Susx
170 B6 Pottersheath Herts
85 F1 Potters Hill N Som
240 A5 Potters Marston Leics
274 A2 Potter Somersal Derbys
193 G6 Potterspury Nhants
145 G3 Potter Street Essex
557 G1 Potterton Abers
343 H2 Potterton Leeds
343 F3 Pottery Field Leeds
254 B3 Potthorpe Norfk
60 D5 Pottington Devon
384 D4 Potto N York
196 B5 Potton Beds
253 E3 Pott Row Norfk
312 B4 Pott Shrigley Ches
143 E3 Pouchen End Herts
38 B6 Poughill Cnwll
41 H6 Poughill Devon
49 F3 Poulner Hants
87 H3 Poulshot Wilts
289 E3 Poulton Ches
137 H4 Poulton Gloucs
308 C1 Poulton Wirral
308 D3 Poulton Wirral
337 F2 Poulton-le-Fylde Lancs
45 E4 Pound Somset
188 B4 Pound Bank Worcs
211 G5 Pound Bank Worcs
31 F4 Poundbury Dorset
103 E3 Poundffald Swans
78 C3 Poundfield E Susx
78 D5 Poundford E Susx
78 B4 Poundgate E Susx
91 F3 Pound Green E Susx
36 A3 Pound Green IoW
199 E4 Pound Green Suffk
92 A1 Poundgreen Wokham
211 H4 Pound Green Worcs
77 E2 Pound Hill W Susx
419 E4 Poundland S Ayrs
166 D4 Poundon Bucks
78 C1 Poundsbridge Kent
19 F3 Poundsgate Devon
15 H5 Poundstock Cnwll
90 D2 Pound Street Hants
78 C5 Pounsley E Susx
411 E3 Pouton D & G
120 C6 Poverest Gt Lon
77 E1 Povey Cross Surrey
442 D1 Powburn Nthumb
77 F6 Powderham Devon
97 E5 Powder Mills Kent
147 F1 Powers Hall End Essex
30 C2 Powerstock Dorset
399 E1 Powfoot D & G
187 F6 Pow Green Herefs
399 G3 Powhill Cumb
188 B4 Powick Worcs
39 E4 Powler's Piece Devon
499 G5 Powmill P & K
32 C3 Poxwell Dorset
143 E2 Poyle Slough
55 G2 Poynings W Susx
67 G6 Poyntington Dorset
312 B3 Poynton Ches
270 D6 Poynton Wrekin
270 D6 Poynton Green Wrekin
151 G6 Poyston Pembks
151 G6 Poyston Cross Pembks
200 C3 Poystreet Green Suffk
3 G4 Praa Sands Cnwll
543 G7 Prabost Highld
98 A3 Pratling Street Kent
96 C2 Pratt's Bottom Gt Lon
4 B1 Praze-an-Beeble Cnwll
270 C5 Prees Shrops
351 E5 Preesall Lancs
351 E5 Preesall Park Lancs
270 D3 Prees Green Shrops
269 E2 Preesgweene Shrops
270 D2 Prees Heath Shrops
269 F3 Preeshenlle Shrops
270 D2 Prees Higher Heath Shrops
270 D3 Prees Lower Heath Shrops
270 C3 Prees Wood Shrops
288 C2 Prenbrigog Flints
125 G1 Prendergast Pembks
150 C5 Prendergast Pembks
474 D3 Prenderguest Border
442 C2 Prendwick Nthumb
180 B6 Pren-gwyn Cerdgn
264 D7 Prenteg Gwynd
308 D2 Prenton Wirral
309 G1 Prescot Knows
43 E5 Prescott Devon
163 E4 Prescott Gloucs
211 F3 Prescott Shrops
270 A5 Prescott Shrops
145 E2 Presdales Herts
569 G3 Preshome Moray
526 A1 Presnerb Angus
294 D1 Press Derbys
453 F2 Pressen Nthumb
307 F3 Prestatyn Denbgs
312 A4 Prestbury Ches
163 E5 Prestbury Gloucs
185 F2 Presteigne Powys
234 D5 Presthope Shrops
67 G1 Prestleigh Somset
325 H3 Prestolee Bolton
474 A3 Preston Border
55 H1 Preston Br & H
20 B3 Preston Devon
32 B3 Preston Dorset
488 D5 Preston E Loth
490 A4 Preston E Loth
348 C3 Preston E R Yk
137 F4 Preston Gloucs
161 F3 Preston Gloucs

118 D2 Preston Gt Lon
169 H5 Preston Herts
99 G2 Preston Kent
101 E3 Preston Kent
339 E4 Preston Lancs
431 F6 Preston N Tyne
455 F4 Preston Nthumb
242 B4 Preston Rutlnd
20 B5 Preston Torbay
112 B4 Preston Wilts
113 G5 Preston Wilts
190 B1 Preston Bagot Warwks
167 E4 Preston Bissett Bucks
43 F2 Preston Bowyer Somset
270 C5 Preston Brockhurst Shrops
310 B3 Preston Brook Halton
73 F1 Preston Candover Hants
192 C4 Preston Capes Nhants
115 G1 Preston Crowmarsh Oxon
193 G3 Preston Deanery Nhants
488 B5 Prestonfield C Edin
190 B1 Preston Fields Warwks
431 F5 Preston Grange N Tyne
190 B1 Preston Green Warwks
270 B6 Preston Gubbals Shrops
395 G5 Preston-le-Skerne Dur
186 D5 Preston Marsh Herefs
398 B3 Prestonmill D & G
233 F4 Preston Montford Shrops
190 B5 Preston on Stour Warwks
384 C1 Preston-on-Tees S on T
310 B3 Preston on the Hill Halton
159 G1 Preston on Wye Herefs
488 D5 Prestonpans E Loth
45 G4 Preston Plucknett Somset
200 B4 Preston St Mary Suffk
369 E1 Preston-under-Scar N York
235 F1 Preston upon the Weald Moors Wrekin
186 D5 Preston Wynne Herefs
326 B4 Prestwich Bury
430 C5 Prestwick Nthumb
444 D4 Prestwick S Ayrs
276 C5 Prestwold Leics
142 B4 Prestwood Bucks
212 C2 Prestwood Staffs
273 H1 Prestwood Staffs
93 H3 Prey Heath Surrey
105 E1 Price Town Brdgnd
222 B3 Prickwillow Cambs
85 F4 Priddy Somset
24 B1 Priestacott Devon
313 F5 Priestcliffe Derbys
313 F5 Priestcliffe Ditch Derbys
85 H2 Priest Down BaNES
236 D5 Priestfield Wolves
188 B6 Priestfield Worcs
439 F4 Priesthaugh Border
466 D2 Priesthill C Glas
366 A5 Priest Hutton Lancs
446 B2 Priestland E Ayrs
342 B4 Priestley Green Calder
451 G4 Prieston Border
399 E1 Priestside D & G
233 E5 Priest Weston Shrops
117 E6 Priestwood Br For
97 F2 Priestwood Kent
97 F2 Priestwood Green Kent
240 B6 Primethorpe Leics
406 A2 Primrose S Tyne
250 C2 Primrose Corner Norfk
255 E4 Primrose Green Norfk
86 C1 Primrose Hill BaNES
212 D2 Primrose Hill Dudley
119 F3 Primrose Hill Gt Lon
323 G2 Primrose Hill Lancs
375 E4 Primrose Valley N York
188 C2 Primsland Worcs
291 E6 Prince Hill Ches
513 F1 Princeland P & K
342 B6 Prince Royd Kirk
237 E6 Princes End Sandw
126 C2 Princes Gate Pembks
74 B4 Prince's Marsh Hants
309 E2 Princes Park Lpool
141 H4 Princes Risborough Bucks
215 G5 Princethorpe Warwks
132 B3 Princetown Caerph
18 C3 Princetown Devon
52 D3 Prinsted W Susx
96 D6 Printstile Kent
287 F2 Prion Denbgs
503 E2 Prior Muir Fife
475 E4 Prior Park Nthumb
426 C6 Prior Rigg Cumb
160 D2 Prior's Frome Herefs
221 H6 Priors Halton Shrops
191 H3 Priors Hardwick Warwks
235 G2 Priorslee Wrekin
192 A3 Priors Marston Warwks
162 C3 Prior's Norton Gloucs
162 C3 Priors Park Gloucs
44 A2 Priorswood Somset
125 F3 Priory Pembks
200 B6 Priory Green Suffk
201 G4 Priory Heath Suffk
185 E5 Priory Wood Herefs
105 G4 Prisk V Glam
40 A2 Pristacott Devon
86 B2 Priston BaNES
225 F2 Pristow Green Norfk
122 D2 Prittlewell Sthend
51 G5 Privett Hants
73 G4 Privett Hants
60 D4 Prixford Devon
7 G4 Probus Cnwll
577 G5 Proncy Highld
388 C2 Prospect Cumb
237 F2 Prospect Village Staffs
4 B2 Prospidnick Cnwll
467 F1 Provanmill C Glas
41 F2 Prowse Devon
404 C2 Prudhoe Nthumb
3 G4 Prussia Cove Cnwll
86 A2 Publow BaNES
171 E5 Puckeridge Herts
66 B6 Puckington Somset
110 B4 Pucklechurch S Glos
72 A5 Pucknall Hants
162 C2 Puckrup Gloucs
136 B3 Puckshole Gloucs
19 G5 Puddaven Devon
311 E6 Puddinglake Ches
338 C3 Pudding Pie Nook Lancs
308 D3 Puddington Ches
41 G5 Puddington Devon
8 D2 Puddle Cnwll
44 C5 Puddlebridge Somset
96 C4 Puddledock Kent
120 D5 Puddledock Kent
225 E1 Puddledock Norfk
46 B6 Puddletown Dorset
44 C5 Pudleigh Somset
186 D3 Pudleston Herefs
341 E4 Pudsey Calder
342 D3 Pudsey Leeds
75 G6 Pulborough W Susx
342 A4 Pule Hill Calder
271 G5 Puleston Wrekin
289 E3 Pulford Ches
46 C3 Pulham Dorset
225 G2 Pulham Market Norfk
225 H2 Pulham St Mary Norfk

City, town and village index: Pullens Green - Rhostryfan 711

109 H1 Pullens Green S Glos
234 B3 Pulley Shrops
80 B3 Pullington Kent
169 F3 Pulloxhill Beds
506 D4 Pulpit Hill Ag & B
234 A4 Pulverbatch Shrops
487 E6 Pumpherston W Loth
155 G1 Pumsaint Carmth
151 H4 Puncheston Pembks
30 C5 Puncknowle Dorset
79 E5 Punnett's Town E Susx
52 B3 Purbrook Hants
49 F6 Purewell Dorset
121 E4 Purfleet Thurr
65 F3 Puriton Somset
147 G4 Purleigh Essex
95 G2 Purley Gt Lon
115 G4 Purley on Thames W Berk
549 K2 Purlie Lodge Highld
209 E4 Purlogue Shrops
87 F1 Purlpit Wilts
221 G2 Purls Bridge Cambs
84 B3 Purn N Som
68 A6 Purse Caundle Dorset
209 G3 Purslow Shrops
344 A6 Purston Jaglin Wakefd
44 D6 Purtington Somset
135 F4 Purton Gloucs
114 D4 Purton W Berk
112 C2 Purton Wilts
112 C2 Purton Common Wilts
112 C1 Purton Stoke Wilts
170 B4 Purwell Herts
193 F5 Pury End Nhants
139 F5 Pusey Oxon
161 E2 Putley Herefs
161 E2 Putley Common Herefs
161 F2 Putley Green Herefs
136 A3 Putloe Gloucs
119 E5 Putney Gt Lon
195 F4 Putnoe Beds
60 B3 Putsborough Devon
160 C2 Putson Herefs
142 B2 Puttenham Herts
93 F5 Puttenham Surrey
173 F1 Puttock End Essex
172 B5 Puttock's End Essex
32 A3 Putton Dorset
47 E2 Puxey Dorset
167 G1 Puxley Nhants
84 D2 Puxton N Som
128 C4 Pwll Carmth
232 C4 Pwll Powys
308 A5 Pwll-clai Flints
125 F4 Pwllcrochan Pembks
287 G4 Pwll-glâs Denbgs
157 G3 Pwllgloyw Powys
263 F4 Pwllheli Gwynd
106 D4 Pwll-mawr Cardif
308 A5 Pwll-melyn Flints
109 F1 Pwllmeyric Mons
127 F1 Pwll-trap Carmth
130 B6 Pwll-y-glaw Neath
106 C2 Pwllypant Caerph
295 E4 Pye Bridge Derbys
55 G2 Pyecombe W Susx
27 E3 Pye Corner Devon
98 D5 Pye Corner Kent
107 E2 Pye Corner Newpt
107 F2 Pye Corner Newpt
110 A4 Pye Corner S Glos
237 E2 Pye Green Staffs
295 E4 Pye Hill Notts
334 B2 Pyewipe NE Lin
104 C3 Pyle Brdgnd
36 D5 Pyle IoW
103 E4 Pyle Swans
72 C6 Pylehill Hants
93 G3 Pyle Hill Surrey
64 B5 Pyleigh Somset
67 G2 Pylle Somset
221 G2 Pymoor Cambs
30 B4 Pymore Dorset
213 H1 Pype Hayes Birm
93 H3 Pyrford Surrey
94 A3 Pyrford Green Surrey
94 A3 Pyrford Village Surrey
44 A2 Pyrland Somset
141 E5 Pyrton Oxon
218 A5 Pytchley Nhants
23 G2 Pyworthy Devon

Q

208 D3 Quabbs Shrops
78 A3 Quabrook E Susx
280 B3 Quadring Lincs
280 B3 Quadring Eaudike Lincs
74 D5 Quags Corner W Susx
167 F6 Quainton Bucks
152 A5 Quaker's Yard Myr Td
405 E4 Quaking Houses Dur
338 A6 Quality Corner Cumb
136 C4 Quarhouse Gloucs
89 G6 Quarley Hants
327 H1 Quarmby Kirk
275 E1 Quarndon Derbys
275 E1 Quarndon Common Derbys
466 B2 Quarrelton Rens
141 H1 Quarrendon Bucks
37 F2 Quarr Hill IoW
465 H1 Quarriers Village Inver
298 C6 Quarrington Lincs
395 G2 Quarrington Hill Dur
290 A1 Quarrybank Ches
212 D2 Quarry Bank Dudley
576 F7 Quarryhill Highld
238 C4 Quarry Hill Staffs
512 D4 Quarrymill P & K
568 B3 Quarrywood Moray
467 H4 Quarter S Lans
511 G5 Quarterbank P & K
211 G1 Quatford Shrops
600 F1 Quatquoy Ork
211 H2 Quatt Shrops
405 E6 Quebec Dur
74 B5 Quebec W Susx
136 B2 Quedgeley Gloucs
222 B3 Queen Adelaide Cambs
122 D5 Queenborough Kent
67 F5 Queen Camel Somset
86 A1 Queen Charlton BaNES
42 D4 Queen Dart Devon
162 B2 Queenhill Worcs
68 C3 Queen Oak Wilts
37 F4 Queen's Bower IoW
342 A3 Queensbury Brad
118 D2 Queensbury Gt Lon
74 C4 Queen's Corner W Susx
308 C6 Queensferry Flints
269 F4 Queen's Head Shrops
467 G1 Queenslie C Glas
195 E5 Queen's Park Beds
339 G4 Queen's Park Bl w D
289 F1 Queen's Park Ches
146 D5 Queen's Park Essex
193 G2 Queen's Park Nhants
337 F2 Queenstown Bpool
97 G5 Queen Street Kent
501 E4 Queensway Fife
484 D4 Queenzieburn N Lans
112 B6 Quemerford Wilts
605 G8 Quendale Shet
171 H3 Quendon Essex
240 D2 Queniborough Leics
138 A4 Quenington Gloucs
351 H2 Quernmore Lancs
237 G6 Queslett Birm
16 D6 Quethiock Cnwll
606 F4 Quham Shet
600 C2 Quholm Ork
327 E4 Quick Edge Tamesd
115 F4 Quick's Green W Berk
224 D2 Quidenham Norfk
91 E4 Quidhampton Hants
70 C3 Quidhampton Wilts
560 C2 Quilquox Abers
270 C3 Quina Brook Shrops
192 D4 Quinbury End Nhants
601 G6 Quindry Ork
213 E3 Quinton Dudley
193 G4 Quinton Nhants
7 G1 Quintrell Downs Cnwll
273 H1 Quixhill Staffs
24 B3 Quoditch Devon
511 E5 Quoig P & K
290 A5 Quoisley Ches
7 H1 Quoit Cnwll
240 C1 Quorn (Quorndon) Leics
448 C2 Quothquan S Lans
602 A7 Quoyloo Ork
600 D4 Quoyness Ork
606 E8 Quoyness Shet
607 G5 Quoys Shet
609 J2 Quoys Shet
606 F7 Quoys of Catfirth Shet

R

98 B5 Rabbit's Cross Kent
115 G1 Rabbits Hill Oxon
170 B6 Rableyheath Herts
399 F4 Raby Cumb
308 D4 Raby Wirral
201 G6 Racecourse Suffk
89 G6 Racedown Hants
449 F3 Rachan Mill Border
304 D6 Rachub Gwynd
139 G4 Rack End Oxon
41 G4 Rackenford Devon
54 C2 Rackham W Susx
250 B2 Rackheath Norfk
84 C4 Rackley Somset
424 A5 Racks D & G
600 C5 Rackwick Ork
602 E2 Rackwick Ork
274 D2 Radbourne Derbys
325 H3 Radcliffe Bury
443 H6 Radcliffe Nthumb
276 D1 Radcliffe on Trent Notts
167 E3 Radclive Bucks
138 D5 Radcot Oxon
566 C5 Raddery Highld
42 D2 Raddington Somset
27 E2 Raddon Devon
502 D3 Radernie Fife
100 B3 Radfall Kent
99 E2 Radfield Kent
86 B3 Radford BaNES
276 C1 Radford C Nott
215 E3 Radford Covtry
165 G5 Radford Oxon
189 F3 Radford Worcs
165 F5 Radfordbridge Oxon
191 E2 Radford Semele Warwks
32 B3 Radipole Dorset
64 D4 Radlet Somset
143 G5 Radlett Herts
140 B5 Radley Oxon
146 C3 Radley Green Essex
140 B5 Radley Park Oxon
233 H3 Radlith Shrops
295 G2 Radmanthwaite Notts
271 E5 Radmoor Shrops
290 B3 Radmore Green Ches
273 G4 Radmore Wood Staffs
141 G5 Radnage Bucks
6 D5 Radnor Cnwll
291 G1 Radnor Bridge Ches
483 G5 Radnor Park W Duns
86 B3 Radstock BaNES
166 C1 Radstone Nhants
191 F5 Radway Warwks
291 F3 Radway Green Ches
194 D3 Radwell Beds
170 B2 Radwell Herts
172 C2 Radwinter Essex
172 C2 Radwinter End Essex
106 B3 Radyr Cardif
437 E6 Raehills D & G
506 D5 Raera Ag & B
93 E3 Rafborough Hants
256 B5 Raf Coltishall Norfk
567 K5 Rafford Moray
608 F6 Raga Shet
277 E5 Ragdale Leics
210 A1 Ragdon Shrops
342 A3 Raggalds Brad
89 H5 Ragged Appleshaw Hants
589 J8 Raggra Highld
3 E4 Raginnis Cnwll
133 H3 Raglan Mons
225 E1 Ragmere Norfk
113 H5 Ragnal W Berk
317 F5 Ragnall Notts
482 B2 Rahane Ag & B
314 B2 Rails Sheff
607 G7 Railsbrough Shet
188 B3 Rainbow Hill Worcs
324 B4 Rainford St Hel
324 B4 Rainford Junction St Hel
120 D3 Rainham Gt Lon
98 C1 Rainham Medway
309 G1 Rainhill St Hel
309 G1 Rainhill Stoops St Hel
312 C4 Rainow Ches
312 B4 Rainowlow Ches
326 B1 Rain Shore Rochdl
326 B4 Rainsough Bury
370 D4 Rainton N York
406 A5 Rainton Bridge Sundld
405 H5 Rainton Gate Dur
296 A3 Rainworth Notts
380 A3 Raisbeck Cumb
402 C5 Raise Cumb
513 F4 Rait P & K
320 A3 Raithby Lincs
300 C1 Raithby by Spilsby Lincs
74 B4 Rake Hants
74 B4 Rake Common Hants
273 G6 Rake End Staffs
340 C5 Rake Head Lancs
273 G1 Rakes Dale Staffs
273 F1 Rakeway Staffs
326 D2 Rakewood Rochdl
61 E5 Raleigh Devon
102 D3 Rallt Swans
181 E5 Ram Carmth
606 E2 Ramah Shet
89 F2 Ram Alley Wilts
542 B8 Ramasaig Highld
4 D2 Rame Cnwll
10 D4 Rame Cnwll
110 B3 Ram Hill S Glos
99 F5 Ram Lane Kent
609 J4 Ramnageo Shet
30 D2 Rampisham Dorset
350 B1 Rampside Cumb
221 F6 Rampton Cambs
317 E4 Rampton Notts
325 H1 Ramsbottom Bury
569 K5 Ramsburn Moray
113 G5 Ramsbury Wilts
582 F4 Ramscraigs Highld
73 H5 Ramsdean Hants
91 F3 Ramsdell Hants
96 C1 Ramsden Gt Lon
139 E1 Ramsden Oxon
188 D5 Ramsden Worcs
147 E6 Ramsden Bellhouse Essex
147 E5 Ramsden Heath Essex
341 E5 Ramsden Wood Calder
220 C2 Ramsey Cambs
176 D3 Ramsey Essex
322 h4 Ramsey IoM
438 B2 Ramseycleuch Border
220 D2 Ramsey Forty Foot Cambs
220 C3 Ramsey Heights Cambs
148 B3 Ramsey Island Essex
220 C2 Ramsey Mereside Cambs
220 C2 Ramsey St Mary's Cambs
101 G3 Ramsgate Kent
369 F5 Ramsgill N York
394 C4 Ramshaw Dur
403 H5 Ramshaw Dur
177 F1 Ramsholt Suffk
293 E5 Ramshorn Staffs
25 F4 Ramsley Devon
78 D2 Ramslye Kent
75 F3 Ramsnest Common Surrey
597 K2 Ranais W Isls
319 G4 Ranby Lincs
316 C3 Ranby Notts
318 D4 Rand Lincs
136 B3 Randwick Gloucs
466 A2 Ranfurly Rens
274 B5 Rangemore Staffs
110 B2 Rangeworthy S Glos
433 G2 Rankinston E Ayrs
173 F6 Rank's Green Essex
314 C2 Ranmoor Sheff
94 C4 Ranmore Common Surrey
522 D4 Rannoch Station P & K
532 B6 Ranochan Highld
316 B2 Ranskill Notts
272 C5 Ranton Staffs
272 B5 Ranton Green Staffs
252 D2 Ranworth Norfk
599 J8 Raon na Crèadha W Isls
76 B3 Rapkyns W Susx
498 B6 Raploch Stirlg
603 G3 Rapness Ork
44 C4 Rapps Somset
346 B2 Rascal Moor E R Yk
413 E5 Rascarrel D & G
481 G3 Rashfield Ag & B
483 G5 Rashielee Rens
188 D1 Rashwood Worcs
371 F5 Raskelf N York
132 C2 Rassau Blae G
342 B5 Rastrick Calder
547 G6 Ratagan Highld
240 B3 Ratby Leics
239 E5 Ratcliffe Culey Leics
276 A4 Ratcliffe on Soar Notts
240 D2 Ratcliffe on the Wreake Leics
111 H5 Ratford Wilts
70 D1 Ratfyn Wilts
571 J3 Rathen Abers
514 B5 Rathillet Fife
353 G3 Rathmell N York
487 F5 Ratho C Edin
487 F5 Ratho Station C Edin
569 G2 Rathven Moray
72 B5 Ratlake Hants
191 F5 Ratley Warwks
100 D5 Ratling Kent
233 H5 Ratlinghope Shrops
27 F3 Ratsloe Devon
589 H2 Rattar Highld
389 H1 Ratten Row Cumb
400 C5 Ratten Row Cumb
338 B1 Ratten Row Lancs
19 F5 Rattery Devon
200 C3 Rattlesden Suffk
57 F4 Ratton Village E Susx
526 A5 Rattray P & K
400 C5 Raughton Cumb
400 C5 Raughton Head Cumb
218 D5 Raunds Nhants
487 H5 Ravelston C Edin
330 A5 Ravenfield Rothm
376 D5 Ravenglass Cumb
324 B6 Ravenhead St Hel
187 G4 Ravenhills Green Worcs
250 D5 Raveningham Norfk
387 G4 Ravenscar N York
342 C2 Ravenscliffe Brad
291 G4 Ravenscliffe C Stke
482 B4 Ravenscraig Inver
322 f4 Ravensdale IoM
195 F4 Ravensden Beds
381 F4 Ravenseat N York
175 F5 Raven's Green Essex
291 E5 Ravenshall Staffs
295 H4 Ravenshead Notts
290 C4 Ravensmoor Ches
243 H4 Ravensthorpe C Pete
342 D5 Ravensthorpe Kirk
217 E5 Ravensthorpe Nhants
239 F2 Ravenstone Leics
194 A4 Ravenstone M Keyn
380 C4 Ravenstonedale Cumb
365 E4 Ravenstown Cumb
469 E5 Ravenstruther S Lans
92 D1 Ravenswood Village Settlement Wokham
382 D3 Ravensworth N York
387 F3 Raw N York
345 F5 Rawcliffe E R Yk
358 A4 Rawcliffe York
345 G5 Rawcliffe Bridge E R Yk
342 D2 Rawdon Leeds
342 D2 Rawdon Carrs Leeds
342 C5 Rawfolds Kirk
328 D3 Raw Green Barns
403 G3 Rawgreen Nthumb
329 G5 Rawmarsh Rothm
237 F2 Rawnsley Staffs
147 F6 Rawreth Essex
147 F6 Rawreth Shot Essex
28 C1 Rawridge Devon
294 D5 Rawson Green Derbys
340 C5 Rawtenstall Lancs
342 C6 Rawthorpe Kirk
468 B1 Rawyards N Lans
175 E2 Raydon Suffk
354 B5 Raygill N York
429 E1 Raylees Nthumb
122 C1 Rayleigh Essex
29 F3 Raymond's Hill Devon
173 E5 Rayne Essex
118 C2 Rayners Lane Gt Lon
119 E6 Raynes Park Gt Lon
233 G4 Reabrook Shrops
198 B1 Reach Cambs
340 B3 Read Lancs
147 E4 Reader's Corner Essex
116 B5 Reading Readg
135 E1 Readings Gloucs
80 D3 Reading Street Kent
101 G2 Reading Street Kent
9 E3 Readymoney Cnwll
137 H4 Ready Token Gloucs
391 G6 Reagill Cumb
576 F5 Rearquhar Highld
241 E2 Rearsby Leics
318 D4 Reasby Lincs
290 C4 Rease Heath Ches
589 H3 Reaster Highld
604 F2 Reawick Shet
4 B1 Reawla Cnwll
587 L4 Reay Highld
562 F5 Rechullin Highld
100 D2 Reculver Kent
604 F1 Redayre Shet
43 E4 Red Ball Devon
126 B4 Redberth Pembks
143 G2 Redbourn Herts
143 G2 Redbournbury Herts
332 D4 Redbourne N Linc
50 C2 Redbridge C Sotn
32 D2 Redbridge Dorset
120 B2 Redbridge Gt Lon
365 G4 Red Bridge Lancs
134 C2 Redbrook Gloucs
270 C1 Redbrook Wrexhm
291 G3 Red Bull Ches
271 G2 Red Bull Staffs
565 K3 Redburn Highld
567 G7 Redburn Highld
402 D2 Redburn Nthumb
397 F5 Redcar R & Cl
529 E4 Redcastle Angus
565 K7 Redcastle Highld
108 D4 Redcliff Bay N Som
212 C5 Redcross Worcs
399 G5 Red Dial Cumb
238 A5 Reddicap Heath Birm
486 B4 Redding Falk
486 B4 Reddingmuirhead Falk
326 C6 Reddish Stockp
310 D2 Reddish Warrtn
213 G6 Redditch Worcs
199 F3 Rede Suffk
226 B3 Redenhall Norfk
89 H5 Redenham Hants
441 F5 Redesdale Camp Nthumb
428 D3 Redesmouth Nthumb
528 C6 Redford Angus
30 D1 Redford Dorset
394 B3 Redford Dur
74 D4 Redford W Susx
438 D1 Redfordgreen Border
512 C4 Redgorton P & K
224 D4 Redgrave Suffk
527 F2 Redheugh Angus
556 D4 Redhill Abers
559 F2 Redhill Abers
48 D5 Red Hill Bmouth
52 C2 Red Hill Hants
160 C2 Red Hill Herefs
170 D3 Redhill Herts
97 G4 Red Hill Kent
240 B5 Red Hill Leics
85 F2 Redhill N Som
295 H5 Redhill Notts
151 F6 Red Hill Pembks
234 B3 Redhill Shrops
235 G2 Redhill Shrops
272 B4 Redhill Staffs
95 F4 Redhill Surrey
344 A4 Red Hill Wakefd
190 A3 Red Hill Warwks
188 C4 Red Hill Worcs
235 G2 Redhill Wrekin
390 D4 Redhills Cumb
26 D4 Redhills Devon
77 G5 Red House Common E Susx
476 F4 Redhouses Ag & B
226 D3 Redisham Suffk
109 G4 Redland Bristl
602 D6 Redland Ork
142 A4 Redland End Bucks
31 F6 Redlands Dorset
66 D3 Redlands Somset
113 E1 Redlands Swindn
43 H5 Redlane Somset
225 G5 Redlingfield Suffk
222 D5 Red Lodge Suffk
326 B1 Red Lumb Rochdl
68 A3 Redlynch Somset
71 E5 Redlynch Wilts
388 D3 Redmain Cumb
161 H3 Redmarley D'Abitot Gloucs
396 A5 Redmarshall S on T
277 G2 Redmile Leics
368 D1 Redmire N York
38 C4 Redmonsford Devon
8 D1 Redmoor Cnwll
560 B3 Redmoss Abers
213 E4 Rednal Birm
269 G4 Rednal Shrops
452 A2 Redpath Border
255 E2 Red Pits Norfk
562 C3 Redpoint Highld
23 F1 Red Post Cnwll
160 C4 Red Rail Herefs
71 G1 Red Rice Hants
324 D3 Red Rock Wigan
127 E2 Red Roses Carmth
443 G5 Red Row Nthumb
6 C5 Redruth Cnwll
339 E3 Red Scar Lancs
470 D6 Redscarhead Border
87 G2 Redstocks Wilts
126 C1 Redstone Cross Pembks
291 G4 Red Street Staffs
15 E6 Redtye Cnwll
326 A3 Redvales Bury
304 B3 Red Wharf Bay IoA
108 D3 Redwick Newpt
109 E3 Redwick S Glos
269 F5 Redwith Shrops
395 E5 Redworth Darltn
171 E2 Reed Herts
170 D2 Reed End Herts
299 G3 Reedham Lincs
251 E4 Reedham Norfk
340 C2 Reedley Lancs
346 A5 Reedness E R Yk
299 G4 Reed Point Lincs
453 G3 Reedsford Nthumb
340 C5 Reeds Holme Lancs
26 C5 Reedy Devon
7 E3 Reen Manor Cnwll
318 C5 Reepham Lincs
255 F3 Reepham Norfk
382 B5 Reeth N York
214 D4 Reeves Green Solhll
232 C4 Refail Powys
322 g3 Regaby IoM
119 F3 Regent's Park Gt Lon
85 F2 Regil N Som
566 F6 Regoul Highld
578 C7 Reiff Highld
95 F5 Reigate Surrey
95 E4 Reigate Heath Surrey
375 E4 Reighton N York
597 G7 Reinigeadal W Isls
589 J6 Reiss Highld
7 F2 Rejerrah Cnwll
4 C2 Releath Cnwll
3 G3 Relubbus Cnwll
567 H7 Relugas Moray
116 C3 Remenham Wokham
116 C3 Remenham Hill Wokham
523 L7 Remony P & K
276 C5 Rempstone Notts
576 F3 Remusaig Highld
137 F3 Rendcomb Gloucs
202 D2 Rendham Suffk
202 C4 Rendlesham Suffk
466 C1 Renfrew Rens
195 F4 Renhold Beds
315 E4 Renishaw Derbys
455 F6 Rennington Nthumb
236 B3 Renshaw Wood Shrops
483 E4 Renton W Duns
401 G6 Renwick Cumb
251 E1 Repps Norfk
275 E4 Repton Derbys
546 E4 Reraig Highld
605 G7 Rerwick Shet
566 B7 Resaurie Highld
8 B5 Rescassa Cnwll
528 B4 Rescobie Angus
8 C2 Rescorla Cnwll
519 H3 Resipole Highld
6 B5 Reskadinnick Cnwll
566 B3 Resolis Highld
130 C4 Resolven Neath
488 B5 Restalrig C Edin
495 E3 Rest and be Thankful Ag & B
474 C2 Reston Border
379 E5 Reston Cumb
5 F1 Restronguet Passage Cnwll
112 C2 Restrop Wilts
8 C2 Resugga Green Cnwll
528 B4 Reswallie Angus
14 C5 Retallack Cnwll
316 D3 Retford Notts
15 E6 Retire Cnwll
147 F5 Rettendon Essex
147 F5 Rettendon Place Essex
300 A2 Revesby Lincs
300 B2 Revesby Bridge Lincs
339 G4 Revidge Bl w D
12 C5 Rew Devon
19 G3 Rew Devon
46 D3 Rew Dorset
27 E3 Rewe Devon
51 E6 Rew Street IoW
24 B5 Rexon Devon
24 B5 Rexon Cross Devon
111 G6 Reybridge Wilts
227 F4 Reydon Suffk
227 F4 Reydon Smear Suffk
248 D3 Reymerston Norfk
126 B3 Reynalton Pembks
102 C4 Reynoldston Swans
17 E3 Rezare Cnwll
265 F1 Rhyd-y-Sarn Gwynd
133 G4 Rhadyr Mons
306 A5 Rhandir Conwy
182 B6 Rhandirmwyn Carmth
207 F6 Rhayader Powys
262 D4 Rhedyn Gwynd
565 J7 Rheindown Highld
518 E5 Rhemore Highld
543 G6 Rhenetra Highld
308 A5 Rhes-y-Cae Flints
287 G2 Rhewl Denbgs
288 A6 Rhewl Denbgs
269 G2 Rhewl Wrexhm
307 G3 Rhewl-fawr Flints
307 G3 Rhewl-Mostyn Flints
580 E6 Rhian Highld
578 E4 Rhicarn Highld
584 E6 Rhiconich Highld
566 B2 Rhicullen Highld
271 E2 Rhiews Shrops
586 F7 Rhifail Highld
131 E3 Rhigos Rhondd
576 F2 Rhilochan Highld
179 F5 Rhippinllwyd Cerdgn
179 G3 Rhippinllwyd Cerdgn
574 C6 Rhiroy Highld
586 C5 Rhitongue Highld
566 C2 Rhives Highld
584 D6 Rhivichie Highld
262 C5 Rhiw Gwynd
287 G1 Rhiwbebyll Denbgs
106 C3 Rhiwbina Cardif
285 E5 Rhiwbryfdir Gwynd
105 F3 Rhiwceiliog Brdgnd
107 E2 Rhiwderin Newpt
284 C2 Rhiwen Gwynd
105 G2 Rhiwinder Rhondd
267 E2 Rhiwlas Gwynd
284 C1 Rhiwlas Gwynd
268 C3 Rhiwlas Powys
65 E5 Rhode Somset
99 H3 Rhode Common Kent
326 B3 Rhodes Rochdl
315 H3 Rhodesia Notts
82 B2 Rhodes Minnis Kent
204 D5 Rhodmad Cerdgn
131 F5 Rhondda Rhondd
412 D3 Rhonehouse or Kelton Hill D & G
105 H6 Rhoose V Glam
154 A2 Rhos Carmth
287 G2 Rhôs Denbgs
130 A4 Rhos Neath
233 E1 Rhos Powys
130 A2 Rhosaman Carmth
304 B4 Rhoscefnhir IoA
302 C5 Rhoscolyn IoA
269 E6 Rhôs Common Powys
125 F4 Rhoscrowther Pembks
262 C3 Rhos-ddû Gwynd
288 D4 Rhosddu Wrexhm
266 D4 Rhosdylluan Gwynd
308 B6 Rhosesmor Flints
152 C4 Rhosfach Pembks
263 F3 Rhos-fawr Gwynd
283 F4 Rhosgadfan Gwynd
303 F3 Rhosgoch IoA
184 C5 Rhos-goch Powys
263 H2 Rhosgyll Gwynd
180 D2 Rhos Haminiog Cerdgn
152 D1 Rhos-hill Pembks
262 B5 Rhoshirwaun Gwynd
283 E4 Rhos Isaf Gwynd
264 B1 Rhoslan Gwynd
228 D3 Rhoslefain Gwynd
288 D5 Rhosllanerchrugog Wrexhm
303 G3 Rhôs Lligwy IoA
155 F5 Rhosmaen Carmth
303 G5 Rhosmeirch IoA
302 D6 Rhosneigr IoA
288 D4 Rhosnesni Wrexhm
306 A3 Rhôs-on-Sea Conwy
288 D4 Rhosrobin Wrexhm
102 B4 Rhossili Swans
150 B4 Rhosson Pembks
303 F6 Rhostrehwfa IoA
283 E4 Rhostryfan Gwynd

288 D5 **Rhostyllen** Wrexhm
269 E2 **Rhoswiel** Shrops
303 F3 **Rhosybol** IoA
268 B5 **Rhos-y-brithdir** Powys
151 F2 **Rhoscaerau** Pembks
179 E4 **Rhosgadair Newydd** Cerdgn
269 F3 **Rhosgadfa** Shrops
205 E5 **Rhos-y-garth** Cerdgn
153 E1 **Rhosgilwen** Pembks
267 E3 **Rhos-y-gwaliau** Gwynd
262 C3 **Rhôs-y-llan** Gwynd
269 F1 **Rhos y madoc** Wrexhm
286 B1 **Rhos-maen** Conwy
288 C6 **Rhosymedre** Wrexhm
209 E6 **Rhos-y-meirch** Powys
153 F5 **Rhosyn-coch** Carmth
462 D2 **Rhu** Ag & B
482 C3 **Rhu** Ag & B
307 F4 **Rhualt** Denbgs
290 B2 **Rhuddall Heath** Ches
307 E4 **Rhuddlan** Denbgs
574 C4 **Rhue** Highld
506 F1 **Rhugarbh** Ag & B
184 B5 **Rhulen** Powys
462 B5 **Rhunahaorine** Ag & B
584 D6 **Rhuvoult** Highld
179 F5 **Rhyd** Cerdgn
265 E1 **Rhyd** Gwynd
231 F4 **Rhyd** Powys
154 B4 **Rhydargaeau** Carmth
155 E2 **Rhydcymerau** Carmth
188 B5 **Rhydd** Worcs
284 C4 **Rhyd-Ddu** Gwynd
188 B6 **Rhydd Green** Worcs
130 A5 **Rhydding** Neath
286 D2 **Rhydgaled** Conwy
179 G4 **Rhydlewis** Cerdgn
262 B5 **Rhydlios** Gwynd
286 B4 **Rhydlydan** Conwy
231 G6 **Rhydlydan** Powys
152 D4 **Rhydowen** Carmth
180 B5 **Rhydowen** Cerdgn
204 D6 **Rhyd-Rosser** Cerdgn
184 D5 **Rhydspence** Herefs
288 B4 **Rhydtalog** Flints
267 E2 **Rhyd-Uchaf** Gwynd
302 D3 **Rhydwyn** IoA
152 B5 **Rhyd-y-Brown** Pembks
263 E4 **Rhyd-y-clafdy** Gwynd
268 D3 **Rhydycroesau** Shrops
208 C3 **Rhyd-y-cwm** Shrops
153 F2 **Rhydyfelin** Carmth
204 D4 **Rhydyfelin** Cerdgn
232 A6 **Rhydyfelin** Powys
106 A2 **Rhydyfelin** Rhondd
306 C4 **Rhyd-y-foel** Conwy
129 H3 **Rhyd-y-fro** Neath
151 E5 **Rhydygele** Pembks
129 G4 **Rhyd-y-gwin** Swans
263 G3 **Rhyd-y-gwystl** Gwynd
266 B5 **Rhydymain** Gwynd
133 F3 **Rhyd-y-meirch** Mons
287 G4 **Rhyd-y-meudwy** Denbgs
288 B1 **Rhydymwyn** Flints
229 E4 **Rhyd-yr-onen** Gwynd
152 D6 **Rhydywrach** Carmth
307 E3 **Rhyl** Denbgs
132 B3 **Rhymney** Caerph
269 F2 **Rhyn** Shrops
513 E5 **Rhynd** P & K
558 B4 **Rhynie** Abers
577 H8 **Rhynie** Highld
212 A5 **Ribbesford** Worcs
367 F4 **Ribblehead** N York
338 D3 **Ribbleton** Lancs
338 B3 **Ribby** Lancs
339 F2 **Ribchester** Lancs
294 C3 **Riber** Derbys
586 C6 **Ribigill** Highld
334 A3 **Riby** Lincs
345 E2 **Riccall** N York
445 F2 **Riccarton** E Ayrs
210 B6 **Richards Castle** Herefs
101 F3 **Richborough Port** Kent
118 A4 **Richings Park** Bucks
118 D5 **Richmond** Gt Lon
383 E4 **Richmond** N York
315 E2 **Richmond** Sheff
34 b2 **Richmond Fort** Guern
172 C4 **Richmond's Green** Essex
64 B5 **Rich's Holford** Somset
39 F2 **Rickard's Down** Devon
541 F2 **Rickarton** Abers
400 D3 **Rickerby** Cumb
272 D5 **Rickerscote** Staffs
85 E3 **Rickford** N Som
224 D4 **Rickinghall** Suffk
405 G4 **Rickleton** Sundld
171 G3 **Rickling** Essex
171 H4 **Rickling Green** Essex
143 E5 **Rickmansworth** Herts
57 G3 **Rickney** E Susx
451 G5 **Riddell** Border
295 E4 **Riddings** Derbys
40 C5 **Riddlecombe** Devon
355 E6 **Riddlesden** Brad
467 F1 **Riddrie** C Glas
213 F3 **Ridgacre** Birm
85 G3 **Ridge** BaNES
29 E1 **Ridge** Devon
33 G2 **Ridge** Dorset
71 G6 **Ridge** Hants
351 G2 **Ridge** Lancs
69 G3 **Ridge** Wilts
73 H5 **Ridge Common** Hants
95 F5 **Ridge Green** Surrey
327 E5 **Ridge Hill** Tamesd
238 D5 **Ridge Lane** Warwks
142 D6 **Ridgemarsh** Bucks
82 D2 **Ridge Row** Kent
109 H4 **Ridgeway** Bristl
294 D4 **Ridgeway** Derbys
315 E3 **Ridgeway** Derbys
81 G2 **Ridgeway** Kent
107 E2 **Ridgeway** Newpt
126 C3 **Ridgeway** Pembks
86 C6 **Ridgeway** Somset
292 A4 **Ridgeway** Staffs
187 G5 **Ridgeway Cross** Herefs
315 E3 **Ridgeway Moor** Derbys
173 E1 **Ridgewell** Essex
33 G2 **Ridge Wharf** Dorset
78 B6 **Ridgewood** E Susx
168 D2 **Ridgmont** Beds
209 G2 **Ridgway** Shrops
94 A3 **Ridgway** Surrey
68 B4 **Riding Gate** Somset
404 B2 **Riding Mill** Nthumb
97 F2 **Ridley** Kent
402 D1 **Ridley** Nthumb
428 A2 **Ridley Stokoe** Nthumb
289 E4 **Ridleywood** Wrexhm
256 C3 **Ridlington** Norfk
242 A4 **Ridlington** Rutlnd
256 C3 **Ridlington Street** Norfk
429 E3 **Ridsdale** Nthumb
525 G6 **Riechip** P & K
578 D4 **Rienachait** Highld
371 H3 **Rievaulx** N York
133 E3 **Rifle Green** Torfn
396 C3 **Rift House** Hartpl
400 A1 **Rigg** D & G

485 F5 **Riggend** N Lans
320 D4 **Rigsby** Lincs
448 A3 **Rigside** S Lans
339 F4 **Riley Green** Lancs
237 H2 **Rileyhill** Staffs
16 C4 **Rilla Mill** Cnwll
16 C4 **Rillaton** Cnwll
373 F5 **Rillington** N York
321 E1 **Rimac** Lincs
501 E4 **Rimbleton** Fife
353 G5 **Rimington** Lancs
67 G5 **Rimpton** Somset
349 F4 **Rimswell** E R Yk
349 F4 **Rimswell Valley** E R Yk
151 G4 **Rinaston** Pembks
235 G5 **Rindleford** Shrops
605 G8 **Ringasta** Shet
412 C3 **Ringford** D & G
275 H6 **Ringing Hill** Leics
314 B3 **Ringinglow** Sheff
108 C2 **Ringland** Newpt
255 F5 **Ringland** Norfk
78 B5 **Ringles Cross** E Susx
98 A3 **Ringlestone** Kent
98 D3 **Ringlestone** Kent
325 H4 **Ringley** Bolton
56 C2 **Ringmer** E Susx
12 A3 **Ringmore** Devon
20 C3 **Ringmore** Devon
324 B2 **Ring O' Bells** Lancs
568 D7 **Ringorm** Moray
245 F4 **Ring's End** Cambs
226 D2 **Ringsfield** Suffk
226 D2 **Ringsfield Corner** Suffk
142 D2 **Ringshall** Herts
200 D4 **Ringshall** Suffk
201 E4 **Ringshall Stocks** Suffk
218 D4 **Ringstead** Nhants
259 E3 **Ringstead** Norfk
146 D1 **Ringtail Green** Essex
49 E3 **Ringwood** Hants
101 G6 **Ringwould** Kent
554 D1 **Rinmore** Abers
600 E6 **Rinnigill** Ork
3 G4 **Rinsey** Cnwll
3 G4 **Rinsey Croft** Cnwll
598 C8 **Riof** W Isls
57 E2 **Ripe** E Susx
295 E4 **Ripley** Derbys
49 F5 **Ripley** Hants
356 B2 **Ripley** N York
94 A3 **Ripley** Surrey
347 E3 **Riplingham** E R Yk
370 C5 **Ripon** N York
99 F6 **Ripper's Cross** Kent
279 F4 **Rippingale** Lincs
101 G6 **Ripple** Kent
162 C2 **Ripple** Worcs
341 G6 **Rippondon** Calder
573 K4 **Rireavach** Highld
476 E8 **Risabus** Ag & B
186 D3 **Risbury** Herefs
347 F3 **Risby** E R Yk
319 E1 **Risby** Lincs
199 G1 **Risby** Suffk
106 D1 **Risca** Caerph
348 B1 **Rise** E R Yk
383 G1 **Rise Carr** Darltn
79 G2 **Riseden** Kent
294 B3 **Rise End** Derbys
280 B4 **Risegate** Lincs
318 B5 **Riseholme** Lincs
388 B3 **Risehow** Cumb
195 E2 **Riseley** Beds
92 B2 **Riseley** Wokham
295 H5 **Rise Park** C Nott
120 D1 **Rise Park** Gt Lon
225 G6 **Rishangles** Suffk
339 H3 **Rishton** Lancs
341 G6 **Rishworth** Calder
340 B4 **Rising Bridge** Lancs
272 D5 **Risingbrook** Staffs
140 C3 **Risinghurst** Oxon
17 E4 **Rising Sun** Cnwll
275 H2 **Risley** Derbys
325 F6 **Risley** Warrtn
370 A6 **Risplith** N York
585 H3 **Rispond** Highld
89 H2 **Rivar** Wilts
173 G6 **Rivenhall** Essex
147 G1 **Rivenhall End** Essex
83 E2 **River** Kent
75 E5 **River** W Susx
222 A6 **River Bank** Cambs
96 D3 **Riverhead** Kent
47 E2 **Rivers' Corner** Dorset
10 D2 **Riverside** C Plym
106 C4 **Riverside** Cardif
498 B6 **Riverside** Highld
213 F6 **Riverside** Worcs
338 D4 **Riversway Docklands** Lancs
61 F5 **Riverton** Devon
121 G5 **Riverview Park** Kent
325 E2 **Rivington** Lancs
47 E2 **Rixon** Dorset
310 D1 **Rixton** Warrtn
339 E4 **Roach Bridge** Lancs
327 E4 **Roaches** Tamesd
41 G3 **Roachill** Devon
193 G4 **Roade** Nhants
28 D4 **Road Green** Devon
250 B6 **Road Green** Norfk
426 D5 **Roadhead** Cumb
468 D5 **Roadmeetings** S Lans
588 F4 **Roadside** Highld
541 G4 **Roadside of Catterline** Abers
541 F4 **Roadside of Kinneff** Abers
63 G4 **Roadwater** Somset
192 D3 **Road Weedon** Nhants
542 D8 **Roag** Highld
571 L6 **Roanheads** Abers
171 G3 **Roast Green** Essex
106 C4 **Roath** Cardif
106 C4 **Roath Park** Cardif
439 E2 **Roberton** Border
448 B4 **Roberton** S Lans
79 G5 **Robertsbridge** E Susx
568 C7 **Robertstown** Moray
131 G4 **Robertstown** Rhondd
126 B2 **Robeston Back** Pembks
125 E3 **Robeston Cross** Pembks
126 B2 **Robeston Wathen** Pembks
125 E3 **Robeston West** Pembks
80 D3 **Robhurst** Kent
292 B3 **Robin Hill** Staffs
314 B5 **Robin Hood** Derbys
324 C2 **Robin Hood** Lancs
324 C2 **Robin Hood** Lancs
356 C5 **Robin Hood** Leeds
172 D2 **Robinhood End** Essex
387 G3 **Robin Hood's Bay** N York
74 C4 **Robins** W Susx
215 E1 **Robinson's End** Warwks
18 B5 **Roborough** Devon
40 B4 **Roborough** Devon
484 C6 **Robroyston** C Glas
309 F1 **Roby** Knows
324 C3 **Roby Mill** Lancs
273 H2 **Rocester** Staffs
151 E5 **Roch** Pembks
326 B2 **Rochdale** Rochdl
8 B1 **Roche** Cnwll
292 C2 **Roche Grange** Staffs

121 H6 **Rochester** Medway
441 F5 **Rochester** Nthumb
122 D1 **Rochford** Essex
211 E6 **Rochford** Worcs
151 E5 **Roch Gate** Pembks
132 C5 **Rock** Caerph
14 C3 **Rock** Cnwll
29 E2 **Rock** Devon
130 B6 **Rock** Neath
455 G5 **Rock** Nthumb
44 C3 **Rock** Somset
54 D2 **Rock** W Susx
211 G5 **Rock** Worcs
27 G4 **Rockbeare** Devon
70 C6 **Rockbourne** Hants
400 C2 **Rockcliffe** D & G
413 F4 **Rockcliffe** D & G
340 D5 **Rockcliffe** Cumb
400 C2 **Rockcliffe** Lancs
400 D5 **Rockcliffe Cross** Cumb
292 A3 **Rock End** Staffs
308 D2 **Rock Ferry** Wirral
577 K7 **Rockfield** Highld
134 B2 **Rockfield** Mons
62 A2 **Rockford** Devon
49 F3 **Rockford** Hants
210 C4 **Rockgreen** Shrops
135 F6 **Rockhampton** S Glos
22 B6 **Rockhead** Cnwll
209 E4 **Rockhill** Shrops
218 B1 **Rockingham** Nhants
248 C5 **Rockland All Saints** Norfk
250 C4 **Rockland St Mary** Norfk
248 C5 **Rockland St Peter** Norfk
316 D5 **Rockley** Notts
113 E5 **Rockley** Wilts
86 C4 **Rockley Ford** Somset
136 B5 **Rockness** Gloucs
79 E3 **Rockrobin** E Susx
309 H3 **Rocksavage** Halton
78 B5 **Rocks Park** E Susx
135 H5 **Rockstowes** Gloucs
482 B1 **Rockville** Ag & B
116 C2 **Rockwell End** Bucks
43 F3 **Rockwell Green** Somset
3 d2 **Rocky Hill** IoS
236 D2 **Rodbaston** Staffs
136 B4 **Rodborough** Gloucs
112 D2 **Rodbourne** Swindn
111 G3 **Rodbourne** Wilts
111 G3 **Rodbourne Bottom** Wilts
199 H6 **Rodbridge Corner** Suffk
185 F2 **Rodd** Herefs
454 C5 **Roddam** Nthumb
31 E6 **Rodden** Dorset
185 F2 **Rodd Hurst** Herefs
394 C2 **Roddymoor** Dur
86 D4 **Rode** Somset
291 G3 **Rode Heath** Ches
292 A1 **Rodeheath** Ches
87 E4 **Rode Hill** Somset
595 G6 **Rodel** W Isls
234 D1 **Roden** Wrekin
110 B3 **Rodford** S Gloucs
68 B5 **Rodgrove** Somset
63 G4 **Rodhuish** Somset
234 D2 **Rodington** Wrekin
234 D2 **Rodington Heath** Wrekin
135 G2 **Rodley** Gloucs
342 D2 **Rodley** Leeds
136 D5 **Rodmarton** Gloucs
56 C3 **Rodmell** E Susx
341 E4 **Rodmer Clough** Calder
99 E2 **Rodmersham** Kent
99 E2 **Rodmersham Green** Kent
85 E5 **Rodney Stoke** Somset
274 C1 **Rodsley** Derbys
65 E3 **Rodway** Somset
271 F6 **Rodway** Wrekin
32 B4 **Rodwell** Dorset
327 E3 **Roebuck Low** Oldham
356 D1 **Roecliffe** N York
327 E5 **Roe Cross** Tamesd
56 A4 **Roedean** Br & H
143 E1 **Roe End** Herts
144 B3 **Roe Green** Herts
170 D3 **Roe Green** Herts
119 E5 **Roe Green** Salfd
339 G3 **Roe Lee** Bl w D
606 D4 **Roesound** Shet
144 B3 **Roestock** Herts
76 C3 **Roffey** W Susx
576 F3 **Rogart** Highld
74 C5 **Rogate** W Susx
378 C5 **Roger Ground** Cumb
107 E2 **Rogerstone** Newpt
467 F3 **Rogerton** S Lans
595 G6 **Roghadal** W Isls
109 E2 **Rogiet** Mons
140 D6 **Roke** Oxon
140 D6 **Roker** Sundld
251 E1 **Rollesby** Norfk
241 F4 **Rolleston** Leics
296 D4 **Rolleston** Notts
314 D3 **Rolleston** Staffs
88 C6 **Rollstone** Wilts
88 C6 **Rollstone Camp** Wilts
274 C4 **Rolleston on Dove** Staffs
47 E2 **Rolls Mill** Dorset
361 G5 **Rolston** E R Yk
84 C2 **Rolstone** N Som
80 B3 **Rolvenden** Kent
80 C3 **Rolvenden Layne** Kent
393 G5 **Romaldkirk** Dur
384 B6 **Romanby** N York
251 G6 **Roman Hill** Suffk
470 C5 **Romannobridge** Border
41 E3 **Romansleigh** Devon
543 G6 **Romesdal** Highld
48 D3 **Romford** Dorset
120 D2 **Romford** Gt Lon
79 E1 **Romford** Kent
312 C1 **Romiley** Stockp
96 D2 **Romney Street** Kent
71 G5 **Romsey** Hants
197 G3 **Romsey Town** Cambs
212 A3 **Romsley** Shrops
213 E4 **Romsley** Worcs
214 E4 **Romsley** Worcs
601 G6 **Ronaldsvoe** Ork
235 G3 **Rondlay** Wrekin
188 C4 **Ronkswood** Worcs
213 F2 **Rood End** Sandw
381 E2 **Rookby** Cumb
172 A3 **Rook End** Essex
403 G6 **Rookhope** Dur
378 D1 **Rooking** Cumb
37 E4 **Rookley** IoW
37 E4 **Rookley Green** IoW
84 C4 **Rooks Bridge** Somset
200 B4 **Rooksey Green** Suffk
97 E4 **Rooks Hill** Kent
136 B4 **Rooksmoor** Gloucs
64 A5 **Rook's Nest** Somset
68 D3 **Rook Street** Wilts
369 H2 **Rookwith** N York
52 D5 **Rookwood** W Susx
349 E3 **Roos** E R Yk
364 B6 **Roose** Cumb
364 B6 **Roosebeck** Cumb
364 B6 **Roosecote** Cumb
198 D6 **Roost End** Essex
565 K6 **Rootfield** Highld

195 G3 **Rootham's Green** Beds
99 E5 **Rooting Street** Kent
469 F4 **Rootpark** S Lans
73 F3 **Ropley** Hants
73 F3 **Ropley Dean** Hants
73 G3 **Ropley Soke** Hants
278 D3 **Ropsley** Lincs
571 K5 **Rora** Abers
559 F6 **Rorandle** Abers
233 F4 **Rorrington** Shrops
6 B5 **Roscroggan** Cnwll
7 E3 **Rose** Cnwll
98 B3 **Roseacre** Kent
338 B2 **Roseacre** Lancs
3 F2 **Rose-an-Grouse** Cnwll
41 F3 **Rose Ash** Devon
484 D5 **Rosebank** E Duns
468 C5 **Rosebank** S Lans
471 F3 **Rosebery** Mdloth
152 B4 **Rosebush** Pembks
22 D3 **Rosecare** Cnwll
144 D4 **Rosedale** Herts
386 B5 **Rosedale Abbey** N York
454 C5 **Roseden** Nthumb
14 C5 **Rosedinnick** Cnwll
38 C3 **Rosedown** Devon
566 F6 **Rosefield** Highld
174 B4 **Rose Green** Essex
174 B4 **Rose Green** Suffk
200 C6 **Rose Green** Suffk
53 G5 **Rose Green** W Susx
340 C3 **Rose Grove** Lancs
575 K3 **Rosehall** Highld
468 A2 **Rosehall** N Lans
571 G2 **Rosehearty** Abers
339 H5 **Rosehill** Bl w D
325 G3 **Rose Hill** Bolton
117 F3 **Rose Hill** Derbys
557 G3 **Rosehill** C Aber
275 E3 **Rose Hill** C Derb
7 E3 **Rosehill** Cnwll
15 E6 **Rosehill** Cnwll
56 D1 **Rose Hill** E Susx
95 F1 **Rosehill** Gt Lon
340 C3 **Rose Hill** Lancs
405 H1 **Rosehill** N Tyne
140 B4 **Rose Hill** Oxon
220 C6 **Rosehill** Rutlnd
271 F3 **Rosehill** Shrops
201 G6 **Rose Hill** Suffk
94 D5 **Rose Hill** Surrey
311 F2 **Rosehill** Traffd
567 L3 **Roseisle** Moray
16 C6 **Roseland** Cnwll
57 G4 **Roselands** E Susx
125 G3 **Rosemarket** Pembks
566 C5 **Rosemarkie** Highld
43 G5 **Rosemary Lane** Devon
8 C2 **Rosemelling** Cnwll
2 D2 **Rosemergy** Cnwll
557 G3 **Rosemount** C Aber
526 A6 **Rosemount** P & K
445 E4 **Rosemount** S Ayrs
14 D5 **Rosenannon** Cnwll
5 E4 **Rosenithon** Cnwll
78 D5 **Roser's Cross** E Susx
8 C2 **Rosevean** Cnwll
4 C4 **Rosevear** Cnwll
236 D6 **Roseville** Dudley
5 G1 **Rosevine** Cnwll
4 B1 **Rosewarne** Cnwll
6 B5 **Rosewarne** Cnwll
471 E2 **Rosewell** Mdloth
396 B5 **Roseworth** S on T
6 B6 **Roseworthy** Cnwll
7 E4 **Roseworthy** Cnwll
6 B6 **Roseworthy Barton** Cnwll
379 F1 **Rosgill** Cumb
121 F5 **Rosherville** Kent
531 K7 **Roshven** Highld
6 B5 **Roskear Croft** Cnwll
542 D7 **Roskhill** Highld
5 E4 **Roskorwell** Cnwll
400 B5 **Rosley** Cumb
471 E2 **Roslin** Mdloth
238 C1 **Rosliston** Derbys
482 B3 **Rosneath** Ag & B
475 E2 **Ross** Border
412 B6 **Ross** D & G
455 E2 **Ross** Nthumb
510 D5 **Ross** P & K
289 E3 **Rossett** Wrexhm
356 C4 **Rossett Green** N York
187 H2 **Ross Green** Worcs
529 E3 **Rossie Island** Angus
500 A2 **Rossie Ochill** P & K
330 D5 **Rossington** Donc
566 B3 **Rosskeen** Highld
483 F5 **Rossland** Rens
48 D6 **Rossmore** Poole
161 E5 **Ross-on-Wye** Herefs
583 J2 **Roster** Highld
311 E3 **Rostherne** Ches
330 C3 **Rostholme** Donc
363 E3 **Rosthwaite** Cumb
377 H2 **Rosthwaite** Cumb
274 A1 **Rostley** Derbys
3 G4 **Rosudgeon** Cnwll
487 F3 **Rosyth** Fife
174 B3 **Rotchfords** Essex
86 A3 **Rotcombe** BaNES
442 D4 **Rothbury** Nthumb
75 F5 **Rotherbridge** W Susx
241 E1 **Rotherby** Leics
78 D4 **Rotherfield** E Susx
116 B3 **Rotherfield Greys** Oxon
116 B3 **Rotherfield Peppard** Oxon
315 E1 **Rotherham** Rothm
119 H3 **Rotherhithe** Gt Lon
193 F3 **Rotherthorpe** Nhants
160 C2 **Rotherwas** Herefs
92 B3 **Rotherwick** Hants
568 D6 **Rothes** Moray
464 D6 **Rothesay** Ag & B
559 G2 **Rothiebrisbane** Abers
559 G2 **Rothienorman** Abers
603 J7 **Rothiesholm** Ork
240 C2 **Rothley** Leics
240 C2 **Rothley Plain** Leics
559 F3 **Rothmaise** Abers
559 E4 **Rothney** Abers
343 F4 **Rothwell** Leeds
333 H5 **Rothwell** Lincs
217 H3 **Rothwell** Nhants
360 D4 **Rotsea** E R Yk
538 D6 **Rottal** Angus
173 E4 **Rotten End** Essex
92 C5 **Rotten Green** Hants
214 B4 **Rotten Row** Solhll
115 F5 **Rotten Row** W Berk
56 B4 **Rottingdean** Br & H
376 B2 **Rottington** Cumb
213 F2 **Rotton Park** Birm
424 A4 **Roucan** D & G
37 E4 **Roud** IoW
253 G3 **Rougham** Norfk
200 B2 **Rougham** Suffk
200 A2 **Rougham Green** Suffk
326 D2 **Rough Bank** Rochdl
534 C6 **Roughburn** Highld
272 D2 **Rough Close** Staffs
100 B4 **Rough Common** Kent
292 B6 **Roughcote** Staffs

586 F7 **Rough Haugh** Highld
274 C5 **Rough Hay** Staffs
340 C1 **Roughlee** Lancs
237 H5 **Roughley** Birm
43 G2 **Roughmoor** Somset
112 D2 **Roughmoor** Swindn
554 B2 **Roughpark** Abers
485 G5 **Roughrigg** N Lans
426 D4 **Roughsike** Cumb
299 G2 **Roughton** Lincs
261 H4 **Roughton** Norfk
235 H6 **Roughton** Shrops
299 G2 **Roughton Moor** Lincs
97 F4 **Roughway** Kent
147 G4 **Roundbush** Essex
143 G5 **Round Bush** Herts
146 B2 **Roundbush Green** Essex
45 E6 **Roundham** Somset
343 F2 **Roundhay** Leeds
200 C6 **Round Maple** Suffk
212 D2 **Round Oak** Dudley
209 G3 **Round Oak** Shrops
213 E2 **Round's Green** Sandw
95 F2 **Roundshaw** Gt Lon
193 G1 **Round Spinney** Nhants
121 G6 **Round Street** Kent
75 H4 **Roundstreet Common** W Susx
60 D5 **Roundswell** Devon
311 G2 **Roundthorn** Manch
379 G4 **Roundthwaite** Cumb
88 B2 **Roundway** Wilts
527 E4 **Roundyhill** Angus
29 E4 **Rousdon** Devon
165 H5 **Rousham** Oxon
189 F4 **Rous Lench** Worcs
464 D2 **Routenburn** N Ayrs
360 D6 **Routh** E R Yk
141 G5 **Rout's Green** Bucks
15 F3 **Row** Cnwll
365 F2 **Row** Cumb
391 G5 **Row** Cumb
426 B4 **Rowanburn** D & G
162 D5 **Rowanfield** Gloucs
495 H5 **Rowardennan** Stirlg
312 D2 **Rowarth** Derbys
51 F2 **Row Ash** Hants
43 H2 **Rowbarton** Somset
85 E3 **Rowberrow** Somset
388 C2 **Row Brow** Cumb
88 A2 **Rowde** Wilts
25 F3 **Rowden** Devon
356 B3 **Rowden** N York
364 C4 **Rowe Head** Cumb
305 F5 **Rowen** Conwy
402 B2 **Rowfoot** Nthumb
44 A2 **Rowford** Somset
173 E5 **Row Green** Essex
175 F6 **Row Heath** Essex
174 D5 **Rowhedge** Essex
94 A2 **Rowhill** Surrey
76 B3 **Rowhook** W Susx
214 C6 **Rowington** Warwks
214 C6 **Rowington Green** Warwks
313 H5 **Rowland** Derbys
78 D5 **Rowlands Castle** Hants
405 E3 **Rowland's Gill** Gatesd
161 F2 **Rowland's Green** Herefs
92 D6 **Rowledge** Surrey
159 G4 **Rowlestone** Herefs
233 F3 **Rowley** Shrops
144 B5 **Rowley Green** Gt Lon
419 J5 **Rowley Hill** Kirk
272 D5 **Rowley Park** Staffs
213 E2 **Rowley Regis** Sandw
215 E3 **Rowley's Green** Covtry
101 E5 **Rowling** Kent
75 G1 **Rowly** Surrey
292 C5 **Rownall** Staffs
51 E4 **Rowner** Hants
213 F5 **Rowney Green** Worcs
50 C1 **Rownhams** Hants
311 G4 **Row-of-Trees** Ches
388 C6 **Rowrah** Cumb
168 B6 **Rowsham** Bucks
294 A1 **Rowsley** Derbys
114 D2 **Rowstock** Oxon
298 D3 **Rowston** Lincs
295 F2 **Rowthorne** Derbys
289 F2 **Rowton** Ches
233 G2 **Rowton** Shrops
271 E5 **Rowton** Wrekin
289 F2 **Rowton Moor** Ches
94 A2 **Row Town** Surrey
452 C3 **Roxburgh** Border
452 C3 **Roxburgh Mains** Border
332 C1 **Roxby** N Linc
386 C1 **Roxby** N York
118 C2 **Roxeth** Gt Lon
195 H4 **Roxton** Beds
146 C3 **Roxwell** Essex
97 H3 **Royal British Legion Village** Kent
395 E5 **Royal Oak** Darltn
323 H4 **Royal Oak** Lancs
375 E4 **Royal Oak** N York
290 C6 **Royal's Green** Ches
533 L6 **Roybridge** Highld
328 C2 **Roydhouse** Kirk
329 G2 **Royd Moor** Wakefd
145 F2 **Roydon** Essex
225 E3 **Roydon** Norfk
253 E3 **Roydon** Norfk
145 F3 **Roydon Hamlet** Essex
343 F4 **Royds Green** Leeds
329 E2 **Royston** Barns
467 F1 **Royston** C Glas
171 E1 **Royston** Herts
44 A5 **Royston Water** Somset
326 D3 **Royton** Oldham
35 I6 **Rozel** Jersey
288 D6 **Ruabon** Wrexhm
516 D6 **Ruaig** Ag & B
7 H6 **Ruan High Lanes** Cnwll
7 G5 **Ruan Lanihorne** Cnwll
4 D5 **Ruan Major** Cnwll
4 D5 **Ruan Minor** Cnwll
161 E6 **Ruardean** Gloucs
161 E6 **Ruardean Hill** Gloucs
161 E1 **Ruardean Woodside** Gloucs
213 E4 **Rubery** Worcs
593 E9 **Rubha Ghaisinis** W Isls
487 F1 **Ruchazie** C Glas
484 B6 **Ruchill** C Glas
401 F6 **Ruckcroft** Cumb
160 A2 **Ruckhall** Herefs
81 F3 **Ruckinge** Kent
320 B4 **Ruckland** Lincs
234 C4 **Ruckley** Shrops
151 G5 **Rudbaxton** Pembks
384 D1 **Rudby** N York
276 C3 **Ruddington** Notts
135 F2 **Ruddle** Gloucs
162 A5 **Rudford** Gloucs
236 B5 **Rudge** Shrops
87 E4 **Rudge** Somset
236 A5 **Rudge Heath** Shrops
110 A2 **Rudgeway** S Glos
76 A3 **Rudgwick** W Susx
161 E4 **Rudhall** Herefs
310 D3 **Rudheath** Ches
311 E5 **Rudheath Woods** Ches
147 G4 **Rudley Green** Essex

111 E6 **Rudloe** Wilts
106 C2 **Rudry** Caerph
360 D1 **Rudston** E R Yk
292 B3 **Rudyard** Staffs
270 B4 **Ruewood** Shrops
324 A1 **Rufford** Lancs
357 G4 **Rufforth** York
295 G5 **Ruffs** Notts
216 B4 **Rugby** Warwks
273 F6 **Rugeley** Staffs
43 G4 **Ruggin** Somset
432 C4 **Ruglen** S Ayrs
443 F2 **Rugley** Nthumb
565 J7 **Ruilick** Highld
565 J7 **Ruisaurie** Highld
44 B3 **Ruishton** Somset
594 E6 **Ruisigearraidh** W Isls
118 B2 **Ruislip** Gt Lon
118 B2 **Ruislip Common** Gt Lon
118 B2 **Ruislip Gardens** Gt Lon
118 C2 **Ruislip Manor** Gt Lon
212 D1 **Ruiton** Dudley
310 B5 **Ruloe** Ches
499 G5 **Rumbling Bridge** P & K
212 D4 **Rumbow Cottages** Worcs
226 C3 **Rumburgh** Suffk
213 H5 **Rumbush** Solhll
237 E3 **Rumer Hill** Staffs
14 B4 **Rumford** Cnwll
486 B4 **Rumford** Falk
106 D4 **Rumney** Cardif
61 E5 **Rumsam** Devon
43 G3 **Rumwell** Somset
309 H3 **Runcorn** Halton
53 F4 **Runcton** W Susx
246 C3 **Runcton Holme** Norfk
93 E5 **Runfold** Surrey
248 D3 **Runhall** Norfk
251 F2 **Runham** Norfk
251 G3 **Runham Vauxhall** Norfk
327 F3 **Running Hill Head** Oldham
43 F3 **Runnington** Somset
395 G1 **Running Waters** Dur
147 F3 **Runsell Green** Essex
338 D6 **Runshaw Moor** Lancs
386 D1 **Runswick Bay** N York
538 B6 **Runtaleave** Angus
147 F6 **Runwell** Essex
136 B3 **Ruscombe** Gloucs
116 C4 **Ruscombe** Wokham
165 G1 **Ruscote** Oxon
161 E3 **Rushall** Herefs
225 G3 **Rushall** Norfk
88 D3 **Rushall** Wilts
237 F4 **Rushall** Wsall
200 A2 **Rushbrooke** Suffk
210 C1 **Rushbury** Shrops
48 B5 **Rushcombe Bottom** Dorset
170 D3 **Rushden** Herts
194 D1 **Rushden** Nhants
123 E5 **Rushenden** Kent
78 D4 **Rusher's Cross** E Susx
240 D3 **Rushey Mead** C Leic
17 F3 **Rushford** Devon
224 B3 **Rushford** Norfk
149 G2 **Rush Green** Essex
120 D2 **Rush Green** Gt Lon
170 B5 **Rush Green** Herts
249 E3 **Rush Green** Norfk
310 D2 **Rushgreen** Warrtn
86 C2 **Rush Hill** BaNES
50 B2 **Rushington** Hants
79 E6 **Rushlake Green** E Susx
173 F2 **Rushley Green** Essex
168 C4 **Rushmere** Beds
227 F2 **Rushmere** Suffk
201 G5 **Rushmere St Andrew** Suffk
201 H5 **Rushmere Street** Suffk
74 D1 **Rushmoor** Surrey
235 E2 **Rushmoor** Wrekin
52 B2 **Rushmore** Hants
96 C2 **Rushmore Hill** Gt Lon
185 E3 **Rushock** Herefs
212 C5 **Rushock** Worcs
326 C6 **Rusholme** Manch
290 B2 **Rushton** Ches
33 F2 **Rushton** Dorset
374 A3 **Rushton** N York
218 A3 **Rushton** Nhants
235 E3 **Rushton** Shrops
292 B2 **Rushton Spencer** Staffs
188 B4 **Rushwick** Worcs
395 F4 **Rushyford** Dur
56 D2 **Rushy Green** E Susx
497 F4 **Ruskie** Stirlg
298 D4 **Ruskington** Lincs
364 D2 **Rusland** Cumb
364 D2 **Rusland Cross** Cumb
170 A5 **Rusling End** Herts
76 C2 **Rusper** W Susx
135 F2 **Ruspidge** Gloucs
95 G2 **Russell Hill** Gt Lon
58 B4 **Russell's Green** E Susx
212 D1 **Russell's Hall** Dudley
116 B2 **Russell's Water** Oxon
226 B5 **Russel's Green** Suffk
76 D1 **Russ Hill** Surrey
602 B8 **Russland** Ork
78 D2 **Rusthall** Kent
54 B4 **Rustington** W Susx
360 D2 **Ruston** E R Yk
387 E3 **Ruswarp** N York
210 D2 **Ruthall** Shrops
452 B3 **Rutherford** Border
467 E2 **Rutherglen** C Glas
15 E5 **Ruthernbridge** Cnwll
287 G3 **Ruthin** Denbgs
105 F4 **Ruthin** V Glam
557 G4 **Ruthrieston** C Aber
569 J6 **Ruthven** Abers
526 C5 **Ruthven** Angus
535 L3 **Ruthven** Highld
550 E3 **Ruthven** Highld
7 H1 **Ruthvoes** Cnwll
389 F2 **Ruthwaite** Cumb
399 E1 **Ruthwell** D & G
120 C5 **Ruxley** Gt Lon
160 D4 **Ruxton** Herefs
160 C6 **Ruxton Green** Herefs
269 G5 **Ruyton-XI-Towns** Shrops
429 G5 **Ryal** Nthumb
339 G5 **Ryal Fold** Bl w D
29 H4 **Ryall** Dorset
162 C1 **Ryall** Worcs
97 G3 **Ryarsh** Kent
549 H3 **Rychraggan** Highld
378 C3 **Rydal** Cumb
51 H6 **Ryde** IoW
94 C1 **Rydens** Surrey
93 G4 **Rydeshill** Surrey
20 B3 **Rydon** Devon
59 F2 **Rye** E Susx
92 C4 **Ryebank** Shrops
270 C9 **Rye Common** Hants
341 H2 **Ryecroft** Brad
329 G5 **Ryecroft** Rothm
292 B2 **Ryecroft Gate** Staffs
136 B4 **Ryeford** Gloucs
59 E2 **Rye Foreign** E Susx
59 F3 **Rye Harbour** E Susx
559 F4 **Ryehill** Abers
348 D4 **Ryehill** E R Yk
116 B6 **Ryeish Green** Wokham

186 B3 **Ryelands** Herefs
145 H2 **Rye Park** Herts
162 A2 **Rye Street** Worcs
163 E5 **Ryeworth** Gloucs
243 E2 **Ryhall** Rutlnd
329 F2 **Ryhill** Wakefd
406 C4 **Ryhope** Sundld
315 F6 **Rylah** Derbys
276 B2 **Rylands** Notts
354 C3 **Rylstone** N York
46 A3 **Ryme Intrinseca** Dorset
344 D2 **Ryther** N York
405 E2 **Ryton** Gatesd
161 G3 **Ryton** Gloucs
373 E4 **Ryton** N York
235 H4 **Ryton** Shrops
215 F2 **Ryton** Warwks
215 F5 **Ryton-on-Dunsmore** Warwks
404 D2 **Ryton Woodside** Gatesd

S

546 B8 **Saasaig** Highld
340 B2 **Sabden** Lancs
146 A5 **Sabine's Green** Essex
602 B7 **Sabiston** Ork
174 B2 **Sackers Green** Suffk
170 D6 **Sacombe** Herts
170 D6 **Sacombe Green** Herts
405 F5 **Sacriston** Dur
384 A1 **Sadberge** Darltn
459 F5 **Saddell** Ag & B
216 D1 **Saddington** Leics
252 C4 **Saddle Bow** Norfk
558 D3 **Saddle Hill** Abers
55 G2 **Saddlescombe** W Susx
29 G2 **Saddle Street** Dorset
379 E3 **Sadgill** Cumb
186 C4 **Saffron's Cross** Herefs
172 A2 **Saffron Walden** Essex
126 B4 **Sageston** Pembks
248 B4 **Saham Hills** Norfk
248 B4 **Saham Toney** Norfk
592 F5 **Saighdinis** W Isls
289 F2 **Saighton** Ches
474 D1 **St Abbs** Border
567 L3 **St Aethans** Moray
6 D3 **St Agnes** Cnwll
143 H3 **St Albans** Herts
7 F3 **St Allen** Cnwll
34 C3 **St Andrew** Guern
503 E1 **St Andrews** Fife
106 B5 **St Andrews' Major** V Glam
30 B4 **St Andrew's Well** Dorset
27 H1 **St Andrew's Wood** Devon
337 F4 **St Annes** Lancs
109 H5 **St Anne's Park** Bristl
276 C1 **St Ann's** C Nott
9 G1 **St Ann's** D & G
437 E6 **St Ann's** D & G
17 F4 **St Ann's Chapel** Cnwll
12 B3 **St Ann's Chapel** Devon
5 F2 **St Anthony** Cnwll
5 E3 **St Anthony-in-Meneage** Cnwll
405 G2 **St Anthony's** N u Ty
134 C5 **St Arvans** Mons
307 E5 **St Asaph** Denbgs
105 G6 **St Athan** V Glam
35 g7 **St Aubin** Jersey
100 B5 **St Augustine's** Kent
8 C3 **St Austell** Cnwll
50 B5 **St Austins** Hants
376 B2 **St Bees** Cumb
8 D2 **St Blazey** Cnwll
8 D3 **St Blazey Gate** Cnwll
452 B3 **St Boswells** Border
35 f7 **St Brelade** Jersey
35 f7 **St Brelade's Bay** Jersey
14 D4 **St Breock** Cnwll
15 F3 **St Breward** Cnwll
134 D4 **St Briavels** Gloucs
134 C4 **St Briavels Common** Gloucs
124 C2 **St Brides** Pembks
104 D5 **St Bride's Major** V Glam
106 A4 **St Bride's-super-Ely** V Glam
107 E3 **St Brides Wentlooge** Newpt
136 C1 **Saintbridge** Gloucs
10 D2 **St Budeaux** C Plym
163 H2 **Saintbury** Gloucs
2 C4 **St Buryan** Cnwll
110 D5 **St Catherine** BaNES
494 C3 **St Catherines** Ag & B
49 E5 **St Catherine's Hill** Dorset
136 B4 **St Chloe** Gloucs
127 F1 **St Clears** Carmth
16 B5 **St Cleer** Cnwll
7 F5 **St Clement** Cnwll
35 i7 **St Clement** Jersey
23 E6 **St Clether** Cnwll
464 A3 **St Colmac** Ag & B
14 C6 **St Columb Major** Cnwll
14 A6 **St Columb Minor** Cnwll
7 G2 **St Columb Road** Cnwll
571 K3 **St Combs** Abers
72 C4 **St Cross** Hants
226 C3 **St Cross South Elmham** Suffk
529 G2 **St Cyrus** Abers
511 H5 **St David's** P & K
150 C4 **St David's** Pembks
6 D5 **St Day** Cnwll
63 H3 **St Decumans** Somset
8 B2 **St Dennis** Cnwll
50 D2 **St Denys** C Sotn
133 E6 **St Dials** Torfn
178 C4 **St Dogmaels** Pembks
17 F5 **St Dominick** Cnwll
105 E6 **St Donat's** V Glam
28 D4 **St Dympna's** Devon
14 D3 **St Endellion** Cnwll
7 G2 **St Enoder** Cnwll
10 C2 **St Erney** Cnwll
3 G2 **St Erth** Cnwll
3 G2 **St Erth Praze** Cnwll
14 B4 **St Ervan** Cnwll
14 B5 **St Eval** Cnwll
8 B4 **St Ewe** Cnwll
106 B3 **St Fagans** Cardif
571 K5 **St Fergus** Abers
510 B5 **St Fillans** P & K
126 B4 **St Florence** Pembks
22 D3 **St Gennys** Cnwll
109 H5 **St George** Bristl
306 D4 **St George** Conwy
326 B5 **St George's** Manch
84 C2 **St Georges** N Som
106 B4 **St George's** V Glam
235 G2 **St George's** Wrekin
94 B2 **St George's Hill** Surrey
42 D6 **St George's Well** Devon
10 C2 **St Germans** Cnwll
119 G3 **St Giles** Gt Lon
318 B5 **St Giles** Lincs
405 G2 **St Giles in the Wood** Devon
40 A1 **St Giles on the Heath** Devon
72 C4 **St Giles's Hill** Hants
5 E2 **St Gluvias** Cnwll
213 E6 **St Godwalds** Worcs
207 F5 **St Harmon** Powys
238 D4 **St Helena** Warwks

394 D4 **St Helen Auckland** Dur
329 F3 **St Helen's** Barns
388 B3 **St Helens** Cumb
58 B4 **St Helen's** E Susx
37 G3 **St Helens** IoW
324 C5 **St Helens** St Hel
58 D4 **St Helen's Wood** E Susx
95 F1 **St Helier** Gt Lon
35 h7 **St Helier** Jersey
3 F3 **St Hilary** Cnwll
105 G5 **St Hilary** V Glam
43 E6 **Saint Hill** Devon
77 G2 **Saint Hill** W Susx
170 A4 **St Ibbs** Herts
132 D4 **St Illtyd** Blae G
170 A4 **St Ippollytts** Herts
127 H3 **St Ishmael's** Carmth
124 D3 **St Ishmael's** Pembks
14 C4 **St Issey** Cnwll
16 D5 **St Ive** Cnwll
16 D5 **St Ive Cross** Cnwll
220 D5 **St Ives** Cambs
3 F1 **St Ives** Cnwll
49 E4 **St Ives** Dorset
69 E5 **St James** Dorset
119 F3 **St James** Gt Lon
256 B5 **St James** Norfk
193 F2 **St James's End** Nhants
226 C3 **St James South Elmham**
14 C5 **St Jidgey** Cnwll
10 D3 **St John** Cnwll
35 h5 **St John** Jersey
78 C3 **St John's** E Susx
119 H4 **St Johns** Gt Lon
322 d6 **St John's** IoM
78 D1 **St John's** Kent
96 D3 **St John's** Kent
344 A2 **St John's** Leeds
93 G3 **St Johns** Surrey
214 D5 **St Johns** Warwks
188 B4 **St Johns** Worcs
39 H2 **St John's Chapel** Devon
393 E2 **St John's Chapel** Dur
246 A2 **St John's Fen End** Norfk
245 H2 **St John's Highway** Norfk
37 F2 **St John's Park** IoW
421 G3 **St John's Town of Dalry** D & G
119 F3 **St John's Wood** Gt Lon
322 f3 **St Jude's** IoM
143 G3 **St Julians** Herts
107 F2 **St Julians** Newpt
2 C3 **St Just** Cnwll
5 G1 **St Just in Roseland** Cnwll
89 F2 **St Katharines** Wilts
560 A3 **St Katherines** Abers
5 E4 **St Keverne** Cnwll
15 E3 **St Kew** Cnwll
15 E3 **St Kew Highway** Cnwll
9 G1 **St Keyne** Cnwll
15 E5 **St Lawrence** Cnwll
148 C4 **St Lawrence** Essex
37 E5 **St Lawrence** IoW
35 g6 **St Lawrence** Jersey
101 G2 **St Lawrence** Kent
142 C3 **St Leonards** Bucks
49 E4 **St Leonards** Dorset
58 C5 **St Leonards** E Susx
467 F4 **Saint Leonards** S Lans
97 G3 **St Leonard's Street** Kent
2 C5 **St Levan** Cnwll
275 E2 **St Luke's** C Derb
106 B5 **St Lythans** V Glam
15 E4 **St Mabyn** Cnwll
513 E5 **St Madoes** P & K
159 G3 **St Margarets** Herefs
83 G2 **St Margaret's at Cliffe** Kent
601 H6 **St Margaret's Hope** Ork
226 C3 **St Margaret South Elmham** Suffk
162 D5 **St Mark's** Gloucs
322 d8 **St Marks** IoM
4 D4 **St Martin** Cnwll
9 H2 **St Martin** Cnwll
35 d3 **St Martin** Guern
35 j6 **St Martin** Jersey
512 D3 **St Martins** P & K
269 F2 **St Martin's** Shrops
269 F2 **St Martin's Moor** Shrops
35 g6 **St Mary** Jersey
90 C4 **St Mary Bourne** Hants
20 C4 **St Marychurch** Torbay
96 C1 **St Mary Cray** Gt Lon
105 F4 **St Mary Hill** V Glam
122 C4 **St Mary Hoo** Medway
81 G4 **St Mary in the Marsh** Kent
3 d2 **St Mary's** IoS
601 H4 **St Mary's** Ork
81 G4 **St Mary's Bay** Kent
134 B1 **St Maughans** Mons
134 B1 **St Maughans Green** Mons
5 F2 **St Mawes** Cnwll
14 B5 **St Mawgan** Cnwll
17 E5 **St Mellion** Cnwll
106 D3 **St Mellons** Cardif
14 B4 **St Merryn** Cnwll
8 B3 **St Mewan** Cnwll
8 B5 **St Michael Caerhays** Cnwll
7 G5 **St Michael Penkevil** Cnwll
514 C5 **St Michaels** Fife
80 C2 **St Michaels** Kent
20 B6 **St Michaels** Torbay
186 D1 **St Michaels** Worcs
309 E2 **St Michael's Hamlet** Lpool
338 C1 **St Michael's on Wyre** Lancs
226 C3 **St Michael South Elmham** Suffk
14 D3 **St Minver** Cnwll
503 E4 **St Monans** Fife
16 A5 **St Neot** Cnwll
196 A3 **St Neots** Cambs
7 F2 **St Newlyn East** Cnwll
170 B4 **St Nicholas** Herts
151 E2 **St Nicholas** Pembks
106 A5 **St Nicholas** V Glam
101 E2 **St Nicholas at Wade** Kent
244 B1 **St Nicholas House** Lincs
226 C3 **St Nicholas South Elmham** Suffk
239 F6 **St Nicolas Park** Warwks
485 G1 **St Ninians** Stirlg
251 F5 **St Olaves** Norfk
149 F1 **St Osyth** Essex
175 F6 **St Osyth Heath** Essex
35 f6 **St Ouen** Jersey
160 C5 **St Owen's Cross** Herefs
162 B6 **St Paul's** Gloucs
120 C6 **St Paul's Cray** Gt Lon
170 A5 **St Paul's Walden** Herts
35 g6 **St Peter** Jersey
35 d2 **St Peter Port** Guern
162 D5 **St Peter's** Gloucs
34 b3 **St Peter's** Guern
101 G2 **St Peter's** Kent
405 G2 **St Peter's** N u Ty
226 C3 **St Peter South Elmham** Suffk
188 C4 **St Peter the Great** Worcs
125 J3 **St Petrox** Pembks
16 B6 **St Pinnock** Cnwll
445 E5 **St Quivox** S Ayrs
4 D6 **St Ruan** Cnwll

35 d2 **St Sampson** Guern
67 G5 **St Saviour** Guern
35 h7 **St Saviour** Jersey
8 A3 **Saint's Kent**
10 D2 **St Stephen** Cnwll
23 G5 **St Stephens** Cnwll
143 G3 **St Stephens** Herts
15 F2 **St Teath** Cnwll
27 E4 **St Thomas** Devon
103 G3 **St Thomas** Swans
15 F3 **St Tudy** Cnwll
125 F5 **St Twynnells** Pembks
9 E2 **St Veep** Cnwll
528 D6 **St Vigeans** Angus
146 B6 **St Vincent's Hamlet** Essex
14 D6 **St Wenn** Cnwll
160 B5 **St Weonards** Herefs
9 E2 **St Winnow** Cnwll
106 A4 **St y-Nyll** V Glam
307 G4 **Saith Ffynnon** Flints
12 C5 **Salcombe** Devon
28 B5 **Salcombe Regis** Devon
148 B2 **Salcott-cum-Virley** Essex
167 H4 **Salden** Bucks
311 G1 **Sale** Traffd
321 E4 **Saleby** Lincs
188 D3 **Sale Green** Worcs
79 G5 **Salehurst** E Susx
155 F4 **Salem** Carmth
205 F3 **Salem** Cerdgn
6 D5 **Salem** Cnwll
518 E7 **Salen** Ag & B
519 G3 **Salen** Highld
327 H1 **Salendine Nook** Kirk
451 F5 **Salenside** Border
339 G3 **Salesbury** Lancs
188 D3 **Saleway** Worcs
168 C2 **Salford** Beds
164 D4 **Salford** Oxon
326 A5 **Salford** Salfd
168 C2 **Salford Ford** Beds
189 G4 **Salford Priors** Warwks
95 F5 **Salfords** Surrey
250 B2 **Salhouse** Norfk
499 G6 **Saline** Fife
70 D3 **Salisbury** Wilts
391 E2 **Salkeld Dykes** Cumb
547 G3 **Sallachy** Highld
576 B2 **Sallachy** Highld
255 F3 **Salle** Norfk
96 D6 **Salmans** Kent
320 B5 **Salmonby** Lincs
515 F2 **Salmond's Muir** Angus
26 C3 **Salmonhutch** Devon
163 G5 **Salperton** Gloucs
163 G6 **Salperton Park** Gloucs
195 F4 **Salph End** Beds
468 C2 **Salsburgh** N Lans
273 E4 **Salt** Staffs
398 D5 **Salta** Cumb
348 C4 **Saltaire** Brad
10 C2 **Saltash** Cnwll
566 C3 **Saltburn** Highld
397 G5 **Saltburn-by-the-Sea** R & Cl
278 B4 **Saltby** Leics
399 F4 **Salt Coates** Cumb
376 D2 **Saltcoats** Cumb
489 F3 **Saltcoats** E Loth
444 B1 **Saltcoats** N Ayrs
337 G4 **Saltcotes** Lancs
56 B4 **Saltdean** Br & H
348 C4 **Salt End** E R Yk
388 A4 **Salterbeck** Cumb
354 A5 **Salterforth** Lancs
91 G3 **Salters Heath** Hants
271 E4 **Saltershill** Shrops
246 B4 **Salters Lode** Norfk
213 H5 **Salter Street** Solhll
290 C1 **Salterswall** Ches
70 C2 **Salterton** Wilts
335 G6 **Saltfleet** Lincs
321 E1 **Saltfleetby All Saints** Lincs
320 D1 **Saltfleetby St Clement** Lincs
320 D2 **Saltfleetby St Peter** Lincs
86 B1 **Saltford** BaNES
117 G3 **Salt Hill** Slough
364 B6 **Salthouse** Cumb
261 E3 **Salthouse** Norfk
213 G2 **Saltley** Birm
107 F3 **Saltmarsh** Newpt
346 A5 **Saltmarshe** E R Yk
600 D6 **Saltness** Ork
289 E2 **Saltney** Flints
372 D4 **Salton** N York
39 G3 **Saltrens** Devon
405 F2 **Saltwell** Gatesd
430 C3 **Saltwick** Nthumb
82 C3 **Saltwood** Kent
516 D6 **Salum** Ag & B
54 D3 **Salvington** W Susx
188 C2 **Salwarpe** Worcs
30 A3 **Salwayash** Dorset
189 F2 **Sambourne** Warwks
87 F6 **Sambourne** Wilts
271 G5 **Sambrook** Wrekin
592 D5 **Samhla** W Isls
339 E3 **Samlesbury** Lancs
339 F4 **Samlesbury Bottoms** Lancs
43 F4 **Sampford Arundel** Somset
25 F2 **Sampford Brett** Somset
25 F2 **Sampford Chapple** Devon
43 F4 **Sampford Courtenay** Devon
42 D5 **Sampford Moor** Somset
18 B3 **Sampford Peverell** Devon
603 K6 **Sampford Spiney** Devon
123 F2 **Samsonslane** Ork
489 F5 **Samuel's Corner** Essex
546 E1 **Samuelston** E Loth
476 C2 **Sanachan** Highld
2 D4 **Sanaigmore** Ag & B
346 D2 **Sancreed** Cnwll
573 H5 **Sancton** E R Yk
606 D8 **Sand** Highld
84 D5 **Sand** Shet
516 A7 **Sand** Somset
531 K2 **Sandaig** Ag & B
389 F1 **Sandaig** Highld
343 F6 **Sandale** Cumb
530 E6 **Sandal Magna** Wakefd
291 E2 **Sandavore** Highld
291 F2 **Sandbach** Ches
481 Q3 **Sandbach Heath** Ches
34 A3 **Sandbank** Ag & B
148 D3 **Sandbanks** Poole
273 H6 **Sandbeach** Essex
333 G4 **Sandborough** Staffs
569 J2 **Sandbraes** Lincs
95 G2 **Sandend** Abers
104 A1 **Sanderstead** Gt Lon
237 H3 **Sandfields** Neath
380 C1 **Sandfields** Staffs
26 C2 **Sandford** Cumb
33 G2 **Sandford** Devon
49 F4 **Sandford** Dorset
37 E4 **Sandford** Hants
84 D3 **Sandford** IoW
467 H6 **Sandford** N Som
269 F5 **Sandford** S Lans
270 D3 **Sandford** Shrops
188 C5 **Sandford** Shrops
84 D3 **Sandford Batch** N Som
561 H1 **Sandfordhill** Abers

140 B4 **Sandford-on-Thames** Oxon
67 G5 **Sandford Orcas** Dorset
165 G4 **Sandford St Martin** Oxon
365 E4 **Sand Gate** Cumb
82 D4 **Sandgate** Kent
412 A4 **Sandgreen** D & G
571 H2 **Sandhaven** Abers
408 C1 **Sandhead** D & G
329 E3 **Sandhill** Barns
167 F4 **Sandhill** Bucks
222 B2 **Sandhill** Cambs
30 D2 **Sandhills** Dorset
46 C2 **Sandhills** Dorset
343 G2 **Sandhills** Leeds
323 F6 **Sandhills** Lpool
140 C3 **Sandhills** Oxon
75 E2 **Sandhills** Surrey
403 H1 **Sandhoe** Nthumb
493 H5 **Sandhole** Ag & B
346 A2 **Sand Hole** E R Yk
346 B3 **Sandholme** E R Yk
280 D2 **Sandholme** Lincs
93 E2 **Sandhurst** Br For
162 B5 **Sandhurst** Gloucs
80 A4 **Sandhurst** Kent
80 A4 **Sandhurst Cross** Kent
358 D3 **Sand Hutton** N York
370 D3 **Sandhutton** N York
275 H2 **Sandiacre** Derbys
321 F3 **Sandilands** Lincs
448 A2 **Sandilands** S Lans
310 C5 **Sandiway** Ches
49 E2 **Sandleheath** Hants
98 B3 **Sandling** Kent
291 F1 **Sandlow Green** Ches
606 A6 **Sandness** Shet
147 E4 **Sandon** Essex
170 D3 **Sandon** Herts
272 D4 **Sandon** Staffs
272 D4 **Sandonbank** Staffs
37 G4 **Sandown** IoW
79 E1 **Sandown Park** Kent
30 A2 **Sandpit** Dorset
162 B4 **Sandpits** Gloucs
143 H2 **Sandridge** Herts
252 D2 **Sandringham** Norfk
142 A6 **Sands** Bucks
119 F4 **Sands End** Gt Lon
387 E2 **Sandsend** N York
363 E5 **Sand Side** Cumb
364 C4 **Sandside** Cumb
365 G3 **Sandside** Cumb
412 C5 **Sand Side** D & G
351 F4 **Sand Side** Lancs
606 E8 **Sandsound** Shet
331 F3 **Sandtoft** N Linc
608 D6 **Sandvoe** Shet
98 D4 **Sandway** Kent
213 F2 **Sandwell** Sandw
101 F4 **Sandwich** Kent
101 G4 **Sandwich Bay Estate** Kent
390 C6 **Sandwick** Cumb
601 G7 **Sandwick** Ork
605 H6 **Sandwick** Shet
607 H5 **Sandwick** Shet
597 L1 **Sandwick** W Isls
376 B2 **Sandwith** Cumb
376 B2 **Sandwith Newtown** Cumb
195 H5 **Sandy** Beds
128 C4 **Sandy** Carmth
299 H3 **Sandy Bank** Lincs
603 G5 **Sandybank** Ork
396 A1 **Sandy Carrs** Dur
288 D1 **Sandycroft** Flints
78 D6 **Sandy Cross** E Susx
93 E5 **Sandy Cross** Surrey
50 B5 **Sandy Down** Hants
291 H4 **Sandyford** C Stke
437 G6 **Sandyford** D & G
20 B3 **Sandygate** Devon
27 F4 **Sandy Gate** Devon
322 f3 **Sandygate** IoM
314 C2 **Sandygate** Sheff
124 D3 **Sandy Haven** Pembks
413 G3 **Sandyhills** D & G
9 E1 **Sandylake** Cnwll
351 F2 **Sandylands** Lancs
43 F3 **Sandylands** Somset
342 B2 **Sandy Lane** Brad
102 D4 **Sandylane** Swans
111 H6 **Sandy Lane** Wilts
269 H1 **Sandy Lane** Wrexhm
400 C1 **Sandysike** Cumb
36 D4 **Sandy Way** IoW
237 H3 **Sandyway** Staffs
585 H3 **Sangobeg** Highld
585 G3 **Sangomore** Highld
90 A1 **Sanham Green** W Berk
310 B2 **Sankey Bridges** Warrtn
188 A1 **Sankyns Green** Worcs
518 B2 **Sanna** Highld
593 E8 **Sanndabhaig** W Isls
597 L1 **Sanndabhaig** W Isls
463 H5 **Sannox** N Ayrs
435 F3 **Sanquhar** D & G
270 C5 **Sansaw Heath** Shrops
376 D4 **Santon** Cumb
322 d8 **Santon** IoM
332 C2 **Santon** N Linc
377 E4 **Santon Bridge** Cumb
223 G2 **Santon Downham** Suffk
240 A6 **Sapcote** Leics
187 G3 **Sapey Bridge** Herefs
187 G2 **Sapey Common** Herefs
224 B4 **Sapiston** Suffk
220 B5 **Sapley** Cambs
274 B3 **Sapperton** Derbys
136 D4 **Sapperton** Gloucs
279 E3 **Sapperton** Lincs
280 D2 **Saracen's Head** Lincs
589 J8 **Sarclet** Highld
129 E3 **Sardis** Carmth
126 C3 **Sardis** Pembks
51 F3 **Sarisbury** Hants
S am Brdgnd
105 E3 **Sarn** Powys
208 D1 **Sarn** Powys
153 G6 **Sarnau** Carmth
179 G3 **Sarnau** Cerdgn
267 F2 **Sarnau** Gwynd
231 D1 **Sarnau** Powys
232 D1 **Sarnau** Powys
263 E5 **Sarn Bach** Gwynd
185 G4 **Sarnesfield** Herefs
262 C4 **Sarn Meyllteyrn** Gwynd
129 E2 **Saron** Carmth
153 H2 **Saron** Carmth
287 E2 **Saron** Denbgs
283 E4 **Saron** Gwynd
283 F2 **Saron** Gwynd
143 E5 **Sarratt** Herts
143 E5 **Sarratt Bottom** Herts
101 F2 **Sarre** Kent
164 D5 **Sarsden** Oxon
164 D5 **Sarsden Halt** Oxon
585 G4 **Sarsgrum** Highld
234 A2 **Sascott** Shrops
404 D6 **Satley** Dur
83 E3 **Satmar** Kent
545 G3 **Satran** Highld
381 G5 **Satron** N York
40 D3 **Satterleigh** Devon
378 B2 **Satterthwaite** Cumb

116 A3 Satwell Oxon
556 B2 Sauchen Abers
513 E3 Saucher P & K
499 E6 Sauchie Clacks
540 C6 Sauchieburn Abers
432 D2 Saughall Ches
309 E5 Saughall Ches
308 B2 Saughall Massie Wirral
487 G5 Saughton C Edin
439 H5 Saughtree Border
135 G3 Saul Gloucs
317 E2 Saundby Notts
126 C4 Saundersfoot Pembks
141 G4 Saunderton Bucks
141 G5 Saunderton Lee Bucks
60 B4 Saunton Devon
320 C6 Sausthorpe Lincs
576 C2 Saval Highld
518 F6 Savary Highld
7 E5 Saveock Cnwll
273 E2 Saverley Green Staffs
342 A5 Savile Park Calder
342 D5 Savile Town Kirk
192 B1 Sawbridge Warwks
145 G1 Sawbridgeworth Herts
374 A3 Sawdon N York
275 H3 Sawley Derbys
353 F5 Sawley Lancs
370 A6 Sawley N York
341 G3 Sawood Brad
197 G5 Sawston Cambs
219 H3 Sawtry Cambs
43 G3 Sawyer's Hill Somset
112 B1 Sawyers Hill Wilts
277 H6 Saxby Leics
318 C2 Saxby Lincs
53 H4 Saxby W Susx
332 D1 Saxby All Saints N Linc
277 F5 Saxelbye Leics
201 E2 Saxham Street Suffk
317 H4 Saxilby Lincs
260 D4 Saxlingham Norfk
250 A5 Saxlingham Green Norfk
250 A5 Saxlingham Nethergate Norfk
202 D2 Saxmundham Suffk
277 E2 Saxondale Notts
198 D3 Saxon Street Cambs
202 B1 Saxtead Suffk
202 B1 Saxtead Green Suffk
202 B1 Saxtead Little Green Suffk
261 F5 Saxthorpe Norfk
344 B2 Saxton N York
77 E6 Sayers Common W Susx
372 B5 Scackleton N York
595 K4 Scadabhagh W Isls
316 C1 Scaftworth Notts
373 F5 Scagglethorpe N York
340 B4 Scaitcliffe Lancs
478 B3 Scalasaig Ag & B
346 B4 Scalby E R Yk
374 B2 Scalby N York
374 C1 Scalby Mills N York
195 F3 Scald End Beds
217 G5 Scaldwell Nhants
400 D2 Scaleby Cumb
400 D2 Scaleby Hill Cumb
351 G2 Scale Hall Lancs
401 G5 Scale Houses Cumb
364 C5 Scales Cumb
390 A4 Scales Cumb
401 G6 Scales Cumb
277 G5 Scalford Leics
386 B2 Scaling N York
505 K3 Scalista Ag & B
605 G3 Scalloway Shet
320 A4 Scamblesby Lincs
359 E6 Scamland E R Yk
532 B8 Scamodale Highld
373 G4 Scampston N York
318 B4 Scampton Lincs
601 G3 Scapa Ork
327 G1 Scapegoat Hill Kirk
603 K2 Scar Ork
374 D2 Scarborough N York
7 H3 Scarcewater Cnwll
315 F6 Scarcliffe Derbys
343 F1 Scarcroft Leeds
564 C6 Scardroy Highld
606 B1 Scarff Shet
589 H2 Scarfskerry Highld
382 B2 Scargill Dur
378 A6 Scar Head Cumb
516 C7 Scarinish Ag & B
323 G2 Scarisbrick Lancs
389 F3 Scarness Cumb
248 B2 Scarning Norfk
277 F1 Scarrington Notts
324 A3 Scarth Hill Lancs
344 B2 Scarthingwell N York
334 C3 Scartho NE Lin
604 E2 Scarvister Shet
602 A7 Scarwell Ork
605 G8 Scatness Shet
606 B3 Scatsta Shet
332 D3 Scawby N Linc
330 B4 Scawsby Donc
330 C3 Scawthorpe Donc
371 H3 Scawton N York
77 G5 Scayne's Hill W Susx
158 B4 Scethrog Powys
291 G3 Scholar Green Ches
342 B3 Scholemoor Brad
341 G2 Scholes Brad
328 B3 Scholes Kirk
342 C4 Scholes Kirk
343 G2 Scholes Leeds
329 F5 Scholes Rothm
395 E5 School Aycliffe Dur
290 C2 School Green Ches
173 E3 School Green Essex
36 A3 School Green IoW
92 B1 Schoolgreen Wokham
556 D4 Schoolhill Abers
557 G5 Schoolhill Abers
29 G2 School House Dorset
388 A6 Scilly Bank Cumb
328 D2 Scissett Kirk
151 F3 Scleddau Pembks
316 B3 Scofton Notts
225 G4 Scole Norfk
225 F3 Scole Common Norfk
592 C2 Scolpaig W Isls
512 D4 Scone P & K
545 J3 Sconser Highld
502 B4 Scoonie Fife
512 D5 Scoonieburn P & K
504 E7 Scoor Ag & B
298 D3 Scopwick Lincs
573 K4 Scoraig Highld
360 C5 Scorborough E R Yk
6 D5 Scorrier Cnwll
19 E4 Scorriton Devon
351 H5 Scorton Lancs
383 G4 Scorton N York
256 B5 Sco Ruston Norfk
592 E6 Scotbheinn W Isls
400 D4 Scotby Cumb
383 E3 Scotch Corner N York
294 C5 Scotches Derbys
351 G3 Scotforth Lancs
327 H2 Scotgate Kirk
291 G3 Scot Hay Staffs

318 C4 Scothern Lincs
241 E5 Scotland Leics
275 F5 Scotland Leics
279 E4 Scotland Leics
115 F6 Scotland W Berk
165 E3 Scotland End Oxon
431 E3 Scotland Gate Nthumb
236 D4 Scotlands Wolves
174 C2 Scotland Street Suffk
500 C4 Scotlandwell P & K
325 E3 Scot Lane End Wigan
566 C1 Scotsburn Highld
514 C4 Scotscraig Fife
429 G2 Scots' Gap Nthumb
540 D5 Scotston Abers
524 D7 Scotston P & K
483 H6 Scotstoun C Glas
519 K3 Scotstown Highld
405 F2 Scotswood N u Ty
93 F1 Scotswood W & M
531 K2 Scottas Highld
332 B4 Scotter Lincs
332 B4 Scotterthorpe Lincs
332 B5 Scotton Lincs
356 C3 Scotton N York
383 E5 Scotton N York
256 B5 Scottow Norfk
279 F2 Scott Willoughby Lincs
490 B3 Scoughall E Loth
464 C3 Scoulag Ag & B
248 C4 Scoulton Norfk
273 G4 Scounslow Green Staffs
584 D4 Scourie Highld
584 B8 Scourie More Highld
605 G7 Scousburgh Shet
628 C3 Scout Dike Barns
379 G3 Scout Green Cumb
327 E3 Scouthead Oldham
134 D2 Scowles Gloucs
588 E2 Scrabster Highld
452 C6 Scraesburgh Border
320 B6 Scrafield Lincs
98 C2 Scragged Oak Kent
442 B3 Scrainwood Nthumb
281 E1 Scrane End Lincs
123 E5 Scrapsgate Kent
241 E3 Scraptoft Leics
44 B5 Scrapton Somset
251 G1 Scratby Norfk
358 D2 Scrayingham N York
8 C3 Scredda Cnwll
279 F1 Scredington Lincs
43 E2 Screedy Somset
320 D6 Scremby Lincs
475 F5 Scremerston Nthumb
296 D6 Screveton Notts
299 H1 Scrivelsby Lincs
356 C3 Scriven N York
351 F5 Scronkey Lancs
316 B1 Scrooby Notts
274 B3 Scropton Derbys
299 G3 Scrub Hill Lincs
370 C1 Scruton N York
268 C5 Scrwgan Powys
426 B5 Scuggate Cumb
347 G3 Sculcoates C KuH
260 A5 Sculthorpe Norfk
332 C2 Scunthorpe N Linc
102 C4 Scurlage Swans
44 C5 Sea Somset
30 A1 Seaborough Dorset
291 G6 Seabridge Staffs
82 C4 Seabrook Kent
406 B3 Seaburn Sundld
308 D1 Seacombe Wirral
79 G3 Seacox Heath E Susx
343 F2 Seacroft Leeds
301 G2 Seacroft Lincs
280 D2 Seadyke Lincs
485 F5 Seafar N Lans
557 G4 Seafield C Aber
470 D2 Seafield Mdloth
444 D5 Seafield S Ayrs
609 G6 Seafield Shet
469 G1 Seafield W Loth
56 D5 Seaford E Susx
276 D6 Seagrave Leics
111 H3 Seagry Heath Wilts
406 C5 Seaham Dur
455 G3 Seahouses Nthumb
97 E3 Seal Kent
308 D6 Sealand Flints
93 E5 Seale Surrey
374 C3 Seamer N York
384 D2 Seamer N York
364 C6 Sea Mill Cumb
464 D5 Seamill N Ayrs
109 F4 Sea Mills Bristl
14 C4 Sea Mills Cnwll
257 E4 Sea Palling Norfk
333 F3 Searby Lincs
100 A2 Seasalter Kent
376 C4 Seascale Cumb
513 G5 Seaside P & K
301 G1 Seathorne Lincs
377 G2 Seathwaite Cumb
377 G5 Seathwaite Cumb
365 E3 Seatle Cumb
377 G2 Seatoller Cumb
515 H1 Seaton Angus
557 G3 Seaton C Aber
10 B3 Seaton Cnwll
388 B3 Seaton Cumb
28 D4 Seaton Devon
406 B4 Seaton Dur
361 F5 Seaton E R Yk
100 D4 Seaton Kent
242 B5 Seaton Rutlnd
430 D5 Seaton Burn N Tyne
396 D4 Seaton Carew Hartpl
431 F4 Seaton Delaval Nthumb
28 D3 Seaton Junction Devon
345 H1 Seaton Ross E R Yk
431 F4 Seaton Sluice Nthumb
29 H4 Seatown Dorset
568 C1 Seatown Moray
569 G2 Seatown Moray
6 D6 Seaureaugh Moor Cnwll
385 F4 Seave Green N York
37 G2 Seaview IoW
399 F4 Seaville Cumb
44 D5 Seavington St Mary Somset
45 E4 Seavington St Michael Somset
149 F2 Seawick Essex
133 E5 Sebastopol Torfn
390 A1 Sebergham Cumb
238 D3 Seckington Warwks
573 H5 Second Coast Highld
29 F3 Sector Devon
366 C1 Sedbergh Cumb
134 C6 Sedbury Gloucs
368 A1 Sedbusk N York
195 H5 Seddington Beds
163 F2 Sedgeberrow Worcs
278 B2 Sedgebrook Lincs
395 H4 Sedgefield Dur
259 E4 Sedgeford Norfk
69 E4 Sedgehill Wilts
214 C4 Sedgemere Solhll
236 D6 Sedgley Dudley
326 B4 Sedgley Park Bury
365 H2 Sedgwick Cumb

58 C3 Sedlescombe E Susx
141 G2 Sedrup Bucks
99 E3 Seed Kent
339 E4 Seed Lee Lancs
326 A5 Seedley Salfd
87 G2 Seend Wilts
87 G2 Seend Cleeve Wilts
87 G2 Seend Head Wilts
117 G1 Seer Green Bucks
250 C5 Seething Norfk
94 D1 Seething Wells Gt Lon
606 D7 Sefster Shet
88 D3 Sefton Sefton
214 A2 Sefton Park Lpool
275 G3 Shardlow Derbys
51 F3 Segensworth Hants
431 E5 Seghill Nthumb
210 B3 Seifton Shrops
272 C5 Seighford Staffs
595 H3 Seilebost W Isls
283 F2 Seion Gwynd
236 B6 Seisdon Staffs
599 L8 Seisiadar W Isls
269 E3 Selattyn Shrops
74 A3 Selborne Hants
345 E3 Selby N York
99 G3 Selgrove Kent
75 E5 Selham W Susx
95 G1 Selhurst Gt Lon
451 F4 Selkirk Border
160 D4 Sellack Herefs
160 D4 Sellack Boat Herefs
609 G5 Sellafirth Shet
2 D3 Sellan Cnwll
603 L3 Sellibister Ork
43 H4 Sellick's Green Somset
81 H2 Sellindge Kent
99 G3 Selling Kent
87 G2 Sells Green Wilts
387 E3 Selly Hill N York
213 F3 Selly Oak Birm
213 F3 Selly Park Birm
57 E3 Selmeston E Susx
95 H2 Selsdon Gt Lon
53 F6 Selsey W Susx
379 F5 Selside Cumb
367 F4 Selside N York
136 B4 Selsley Gloucs
52 C5 Selsmore Hants
101 F4 Selson Kent
82 D7 Selsted Kent
295 F4 Selston Notts
295 F4 Selston Common Notts
295 E4 Selston Green Notts
63 E2 Selworthy Somset
606 D7 Semblister Shet
200 D5 Semer Suffk
69 E4 Sem Hill Wilts
87 F2 Semington Wilts
69 E4 Semley Wilts
279 G1 Sempringham Lincs
93 H3 Send Surrey
93 H4 Send Grove Surrey
94 A3 Send Marsh Surrey
106 B1 Senghenydd Caerph
2 C4 Sennen Cnwll
2 C4 Sennen Cove Cnwll
157 E4 Sennybridge Powys
316 B2 Serlby Notts
70 B2 Serrington Wilts
371 E4 Sessay N York
252 C5 Setchey Norfk
50 B4 Setley Hants
489 E5 Seton E Loth
489 E4 Seton Mains E Loth
605 K2 Setter Shet
606 E7 Setter Shet
607 G1 Setter Shet
602 D8 Settiscarth Ork
353 G2 Settle N York
373 F5 Settrington N York
64 C5 Seven Ash Somset
163 F5 Sevenhampton Gloucs
113 E1 Sevenhampton Swindn
120 C2 Seven Kings Gt Lon
96 D4 Sevenoaks Kent
96 D4 Sevenoaks Common Kent
96 D4 Sevenoaks Weald Kent
130 C3 Seven Sisters Neath
137 E1 Seven Springs Gloucs
174 D4 Seven Star Green Essex
109 F3 Severn Beach S Glos
188 B6 Severn Stoke Worcs
195 F4 Sevick End Beds
81 F1 Sevington Kent
172 B2 Sewards End Essex
145 E5 Sewardstone Essex
145 E5 Sewardstonebury Essex
168 D5 Sewell Beds
375 F6 Sewerby E R Yk
4 D2 Seworgan Cnwll
278 B5 Sewstern Leics
384 D3 Sexhow N York
164 B3 Sezincote Gloucs
591 D8 Sgallairidh W Isls
595 G4 Sgarasta Bheag W Isls
595 G4 Sgarasta Mhor W Isls
584 C6 Sgeir Iosal Highld
599 L2 Sgiogarstaigh W Isls
542 C4 Sgor Beag Highld
478 B2 Sgreadan Ag & B
141 E3 Shabbington Bucks
136 D1 Shab Hill Gloucs
236 B3 Shackerley Shrops
239 F3 Shackerstone Leics
275 G3 Shacklecross Derbys
93 F5 Shackleford Surrey
341 F4 Shackleton Calder
119 G2 Shacklewell Gt Lon
341 E5 Shade Calder
395 G1 Shadforth Dur
227 E3 Shadingfield Suffk
81 E2 Shadoxhurst Kent
339 H4 Shadsworth Bl w D
136 A5 Shadwell Gloucs
119 H3 Shadwell Leeds
343 F2 Shadwell Leeds
224 B3 Shadwell Norfk
292 C4 Shaffalong Staffs
171 F2 Shaftenhoe End Herts
69 E5 Shaftesbury Dorset
329 F2 Shafton Barns
329 F2 Shafton Two Gates Barns
33 E3 Shaggs Dorset
271 H4 Shakeford Shrops
325 F4 Shakerley Wigan
161 F3 Shakesfield Gloucs
89 H2 Shalbourne Wilts
36 B3 Shalcombe IoW
73 G1 Shalden Hants
92 A6 Shalden Green Hants
20 C3 Shaldon Devon
36 C3 Shalfleet IoW
173 E4 Shalford Essex
68 B3 Shalford Somset
93 H5 Shalford Surrey
173 E4 Shalford Green Essex
40 D2 Shallowford Devon
61 H3 Shallowford Devon
272 C4 Shallowford Staffs
100 A5 Shalmsford Street Kent
166 D2 Shalstone Bucks
94 A6 Shamley Green Surrey
482 C2 Shandon Ag & B

566 F2 Shandwick Highld
241 F5 Shangton Leics
431 E4 Shankhouse Nthumb
37 F4 Shanklin IoW
557 F4 Shannaburn Abers
460 D5 Shannochie N Ayrs
558 C2 Shanquhar Abers
379 G1 Shap Cumb
135 F1 Shapridge Gloucs
48 A4 Shapwick Dorset
66 C2 Shapwick Somset
88 D3 Sharcott Wilts
214 A2 Shard End Birm
275 G3 Shardlow Derbys
236 D3 Shareshill Staffs
343 G6 Sharlston Wakefd
343 G6 Sharlston Common Wakefd
214 A4 Sharmans Cross Solhll
122 B5 Sharnal Street Medway
194 D3 Sharnbrook Beds
340 D5 Sharneyford Lancs
216 A1 Sharnford Leics
46 D3 Sharnhill Green Dorset
338 D3 Sharoe Green Lancs
370 C5 Sharow N York
169 F3 Sharpenhoe Beds
442 B4 Sharperton Nthumb
325 G2 Sharples Bolton
273 E2 Sharpley Heath Staffs
135 F4 Sharpness Gloucs
78 A5 Sharpsbridge E Susx
78 D6 Sharp's Corner E Susx
86 D3 Sharpstone BaNES
256 D5 Sharp Street Norfk
77 G3 Sharpthorne W Susx
16 C4 Sharptor Cnwll
188 D1 Sharpway Gate Worcs
260 D4 Sharrington Norfk
314 C2 Sharrow Sheff
311 G2 Sharston Manch
212 A3 Shatterford Worcs
101 K4 Shatterling Kent
313 G3 Shatton Derbys
18 B5 Shaugh Prior Devon
291 E4 Shavington Ches
341 G2 Shaw Brad
326 D3 Shaw Oldham
112 D2 Shaw Swindn
114 D6 Shaw W Berk
87 F1 Shaw Wilts
210 B3 Shawbank Shrops
235 E2 Shawbirch Wrekin
598 E5 Shawbost W Isls
270 C5 Shawbury Shrops
326 C2 Shawclough Rochdl
161 F4 Shaw Common Gloucs
442 D2 Shawdon Hall Nthumb
216 B3 Shawell Leics
326 C2 Shawfield Rochdl
293 E2 Shawfield Staffs
356 B4 Shawford Head N York
72 C5 Shawford Hants
86 D4 Shawford Somset
340 D5 Shawforth Lancs
170 C3 Shaw Green Herts
338 D6 Shaw Green Lancs
356 B4 Shaw Green N York
423 E4 Shawhead D & G
468 A2 Shawhead N Lans
311 F4 Shaw Heath Ches
312 A2 Shaw Heath Stockp
467 E2 Shawlands C Glas
356 A2 Shaw Mills N York
468 A4 Shawsburn S Lans
326 D3 Shaw Side Oldham
467 G5 Shawton S Lans
467 G5 Shawtonhill S Lans
398 C1 Shearington D & G
216 D1 Shearsby Leics
65 E3 Shearston Somset
39 F6 Shebbear Devon
271 H4 Shebdon Staffs
588 C4 Shebster Highld
467 E3 Sheddens E Rens
411 E5 Sheddock D & G
557 F3 Sheddocksley C Aber
51 F2 Shedfield Hants
293 F2 Sheen Staffs
314 D5 Sheepbridge Derbys
114 A4 Sheepdrove W Berk
405 E3 Sheep Hill Dur
168 C3 Sheeplane Beds
117 E2 Sheepridge Bucks
342 E2 Sheepridge Kirk
604 B3 Sheep Rock Shet
136 C2 Sheepscombe Gloucs
18 C4 Sheepstor Devon
24 C1 Sheepwash Devon
430 D2 Sheepwash Nthumb
109 H4 Sheepway N Som
239 E4 Sheepy Magna Leics
239 E4 Sheepy Parva Leics
145 H2 Sheering Essex
123 E4 Sheerness Kent
93 H2 Sheerwater Surrey
74 B5 Sheet Hants
210 C5 Sheet Shrops
93 F3 Sheets Heath Surrey
3 E4 Sheffield Cnwll
314 C2 Sheffield Sheff
115 G5 Sheffield Bottom W Berk
77 H4 Sheffield Green E Susx
314 D2 Sheffield Park Sheff
169 G2 Shefford Beds
114 B5 Shefford Woodlands W Berk
584 C4 Sheigra Highld
468 B3 Sheildmuir N Lans
235 E4 Sheinton Shrops
209 H4 Shelderton Shrops
214 B3 Sheldon Birm
313 G6 Sheldon Derbys
43 F6 Sheldon Devon
99 G3 Sheldwich Kent
99 G3 Sheldwich Lees Kent
105 E3 Shelf Brdgnd
342 B4 Shelf Calder
225 E3 Shelfanger Norfk
189 H2 Shelfield Warwks
237 F4 Shelfield Wsall
189 H2 Shelfield Green Warwks
193 F5 Shelfleys Nhants
277 E1 Shelford Notts
215 G2 Shelford Warwks
189 E3 Shell Worcs
200 D3 Shelland Suffk
239 E1 Shellbrook Leics
146 A3 Shelley Essex
328 C2 Shelley Kirk
174 D2 Shelley Suffk
328 C2 Shelley Woodhouse Kirk
310 A3 Shell Green Halton
139 E6 Shellingford Oxon
146 C3 Shellow Bowells Essex
94 D5 Shellwood Cross Surrey
187 G2 Shelsley Beauchamp Worcs
187 G2 Shelsley Walsh Worcs
276 B6 Shelthorpe Leics
219 E6 Shelton Beds
292 A5 Shelton C Stke
225 H1 Shelton Norfk
297 E6 Shelton Notts
234 B2 Shelton Shrops
226 A1 Shelton Green Norfk

275 F3 Shelton Lock C Derb
272 B2 Shelton under Harley Staffs
233 F5 Shelve Shrops
28 C2 Shelvin Devon
100 D2 Shelvingford Kent
186 C6 Shelwick Herefs
186 C6 Shelwick Green Herefs
146 B6 Shenfield Essex
191 F6 Shenington Oxon
144 A4 Shenley Herts
168 A2 Shenley Brook End M Keyn
143 H4 Shenleybury Herts
168 A2 Shenley Church End M Keyn
213 F3 Shenley Fields Birm
168 A2 Shenley Lodge M Keyn
167 H2 Shenley Wood M Keyn
159 G2 Shenmore Herefs
416 C4 Shennanton D & G
237 H4 Shenstone Staffs
212 C5 Shenstone Worcs
237 H4 Shenstone Woodend Staffs
239 F4 Shenton Leics
548 F4 Shenval Highld
552 E3 Shenval Moray
244 D2 Shepeau Stow Lincs
170 C5 Shephall Herts
119 E5 Shepherd's Bush Gt Lon
252 B4 Shepherd's Gate Norfk
116 B3 Shepherd's Green Oxon
75 E3 Shepherd's Hill Surrey
135 G4 Shepherd's Patch Gloucs
258 D5 Shepherd's Port Norfk
101 E6 Shepherdswell or Sibertswold Kent
328 B2 Shepley Kirk
135 E5 Shepperdine S Glos
94 B1 Shepperton Surrey
197 E5 Shepreth Cambs
275 H6 Shepshed Leics
45 E4 Shepton Beauchamp Somset
85 H6 Shepton Mallet Somset
68 A3 Shepton Montague Somset
98 B4 Shepway Kent
396 B3 Sheraton Dur
18 D3 Sherberton Devon
46 B1 Sherborne Dorset
138 B2 Sherborne Gloucs
85 G3 Sherborne Somset
91 G3 Sherborne St John Hants
190 D2 Sherbourne Warwks
174 B1 Sherbourne Street Suffk
395 G1 Sherburn Dur
374 B4 Sherburn N York
405 H6 Sherburn Grange Dur
395 G1 Sherburn Hill Dur
344 B3 Sherburn in Elmet N York
94 B5 Shere Surrey
254 A2 Shereford Norfk
71 F5 Sherfield English Hants
92 A3 Sherfield on Loddon Hants
340 A4 Sherfin Lancs
12 D4 Sherford Devon
47 H6 Sherford Dorset
43 H3 Sherford Somset
235 H2 Sheriffhales Shrops
405 G2 Sheriff Hill Gatesd
358 C1 Sheriff Hutton N York
189 F5 Sheriff's Lench Worcs
261 E3 Sheringham Norfk
194 B5 Sherington M Keyn
261 G3 Sheringwood Norfk
76 D6 Shermanbury W Susx
188 D2 Shernal Green Worcs
259 E5 Shernborne Norfk
188 A5 Sherrard's Green Worcs
144 B2 Sherrardspark Herts
69 G2 Sherrington Wilts
111 F2 Sherston Wilts
295 H6 Sherwood C Nott
40 B3 Sherwood Green Devon
79 E1 Sherwood Park Kent
467 F2 Shettleston C Glas
324 C3 Shevington Wigan
324 C2 Shevington Moor Wigan
324 C3 Shevington Vale Wigan
10 C2 Sheviock Cnwll
444 D2 Shewalton N Ayrs
342 A4 Shibden Head Brad
37 E3 Shide IoW
547 G6 Shiel Bridge Highld
562 D2 Shieldaig Highld
562 E6 Shieldaig Highld
466 D1 Shieldhall C Glas
424 A3 Shieldhill D & G
486 A4 Shieldhill Falk
448 D1 Shieldhill S Lans
405 F4 Shield Row Dur
519 G1 Shielfoot Highld
527 F3 Shielhill Angus
524 C3 Shierglas P & K
235 H3 Shifnal Shrops
443 F3 Shilbottle Nthumb
443 F3 Shilbottle Grange Nthumb
395 E4 Shildon Dur
466 B3 Shillford E Rens
593 D10 Shilligarry W Isls
42 C3 Shillingford Devon
140 C6 Shillingford Oxon
27 E5 Shillingford Abbot Devon
26 D5 Shillingford St George Devon
47 F2 Shillingstone Dorset
169 G3 Shillington Beds
441 G3 Shillmoor Nthumb
138 D3 Shilton Oxon
215 G3 Shilton Warwks
430 C3 Shilvington Nthumb
225 G3 Shimpling Norfk
199 H4 Shimpling Suffk
199 H4 Shimpling Street Suffk
173 E3 Shincliffe Dur
395 F1 Shincliffe Dur
405 H4 Shiney Row Sundld
116 B6 Shinfield Wokham
196 D5 Shingay Cambs
247 F3 Shingham Norfk
202 D6 Shingle Street Suffk
19 G5 Shinner's Bridge Devon
580 D7 Shinness Lodge Highld
97 E4 Shipbourne Kent
248 B3 Shipdham Norfk
84 C3 Shipham Somset
20 B4 Shiphay Torbay
116 C4 Shiplake Oxon
116 A3 Shiplake Bottom Oxon
116 B4 Shiplake Row Oxon
84 C3 Shiplate N Som
470 D5 Shiplaw Border
342 C2 Shipley Brad
295 E5 Shipley Derbys
236 B5 Shipley Shrops
76 B5 Shipley W Susx
77 F1 Shipley Bridge Surrey
295 E4 Shipley Common Derbys
472 B5 Shipley Gate Border
77 F1 Shipmeadow Suffk
139 H5 Shippon Oxon
164 D1 Shipston-on-Stour Warwks
163 F6 Shipton Gloucs
357 H3 Shipton N York

210 D1 **Shipton** Shrops
89 F5 **Shipton Bellinger** Hants
30 B4 **Shipton Gorge** Dorset
53 E5 **Shipton Green** W Susx
167 F5 **Shipton Lee** Bucks
111 F2 **Shipton Moyne** Gloucs
163 F6 **Shipton Oliffe** Gloucs
140 A1 **Shipton-on-Cherwell** Oxon
163 F6 **Shipton Solers** Gloucs
359 G6 **Shipthorpe** E R Yk
138 D1 **Shipton under Wychwood** Oxon
141 E5 **Shirburn** Oxon
323 G2 **Shirdley Hill** Lancs
295 G1 **Shirebrook** Derbys
314 C1 **Shirecliffe** Sheff
329 F6 **Shiregreen** Sheff
109 F4 **Shirehampton** Bristl
431 F5 **Shiremoor** N Tyne
134 B6 **Shirenewton** Mons
237 F4 **Shire Oak** Wsall
313 E3 **Shireoaks** Derbys
315 G3 **Shireoaks** Notts
486 D2 **Shires Mill** Fife
80 D2 **Shirkoak** Kent
294 D3 **Shirland** Derbys
235 F5 **Shirlett** Shrops
50 D2 **Shirley** C Sotn
274 C1 **Shirley** Derbys
95 H1 **Shirley** Gt Lon
49 F5 **Shirley** Hants
213 H4 **Shirley** Solhll
213 H4 **Shirley Heath** Solhll
50 A5 **Shirley Holms** Hants
50 C2 **Shirley Warren** C Sotn
186 A3 **Shirl Heath** Herefs
51 G2 **Shirrell Heath** Hants
51 E4 **Shirwell** Devon
460 C4 **Shiskine** N Ayrs
47 F6 **Shitterton** Dorset
185 G2 **Shobdon** Herefs
49 F3 **Shobley** Hants
274 C5 **Shobnall** Staffs
26 D2 **Shobrooke** Devon
277 E5 **Shoby** Leics
289 F5 **Shocklach** Ches
289 F5 **Shocklach Green** Ches
123 E3 **Shoeburyness** Sthend
101 G5 **Sholden** Kent
51 E2 **Sholing** C Sotn
51 E2 **Sholing Common** C Sotn
326 D2 **Sholver** Oldham
71 G5 **Shootash** Hants
142 D3 **Shootersway** Herts
233 H2 **Shoot Hill** Shrops
14 B4 **Shop** Cnwll
38 B5 **Shop** Cnwll
39 E5 **Shop** Devon
176 D3 **Shop Corner** Suffk
427 E1 **Shopford** Cumb
64 C5 **Shopnoller** Somset
75 E4 **Shopp Hill** W Susx
53 F4 **Shopwyke** W Susx
341 E4 **Shore** Calder
326 D1 **Shore** Rochdl
28 D2 **Shore Bottom** Devon
119 G3 **Shoreditch** Gt Lon
44 A3 **Shoreditch** Somset
380 D4 **Shoregill** Cumb
96 D2 **Shoreham** Kent
55 F4 **Shoreham Beach** W Susx
55 F4 **Shoreham-by-Sea** W Susx
475 E5 **Shoresdean** Nthumb
139 F2 **Shores Green** Oxon
474 D5 **Shoreswood** Nthumb
565 H1 **Shoreton** Highld
73 E4 **Shorley** Hants
82 C3 **Shorncliffe Camp** Kent
137 F5 **Shorncote** Gloucs
121 G5 **Shorne** Kent
121 G5 **Shorne Ridgeway** Kent
121 G5 **Shorne West** Kent
24 D5 **Shortacombe** Devon
10 A2 **Shortacross** Cnwll
78 A5 **Shortbridge** E Susx
213 E3 **Short Cross** Dudley
92 D6 **Shortfield Common** Surrey
56 D1 **Shortgate** E Susx
225 E2 **Short Green** Norfk
165 E6 **Shorthampton** Oxon
237 G6 **Short Heath** Birm
239 E2 **Short Heath** Derbys
74 B2 **Shortheath** Hants
92 D6 **Shortheath** Surrey
237 E4 **Short Heath** Wsall
233 H3 **Shorthill** Shrops
120 A6 **Shortlands** Gt Lon
7 F4 **Shortlanesend** Cnwll
445 F2 **Shortlees** E Ayrs
28 D2 **Shortmoor** Devon
30 B2 **Shortmoor** Dorset
20 B5 **Shorton** Torbay
466 C1 **Shortroods** Rens
134 C2 **Shortstanding** Gloucs
195 F5 **Shortstown** Beds
87 E5 **Short Street** Wilts
136 B5 **Shortwood** Gloucs
110 B4 **Shortwood** S Glos
36 D4 **Shorwell** IoW
86 B3 **Shoscombe** BaNES
86 B3 **Shoscombe Vale** BaNES
269 G5 **Shotatton** Shrops
250 B5 **Shotesham** Norfk
147 F6 **Shotgate** Essex
242 C5 **Shotley** Nhants
176 D2 **Shotley** Suffk
404 C4 **Shotley Bridge** Dur
404 C4 **Shotleyfield** Nthumb
176 D3 **Shotley Gate** Suffk
99 G4 **Shottenden** Kent
74 D3 **Shottermill** Surrey
190 B4 **Shottery** Warwks
191 G5 **Shotteswell** Warwks
202 C6 **Shotisham** Suffk
294 C5 **Shottle** Derbys
294 C5 **Shottlegate** Derbys
395 H4 **Shotton** Dur
396 B2 **Shotton** Dur
308 C6 **Shotton** Flints
430 D4 **Shotton** Nthumb
453 F3 **Shotton** Nthumb
396 B1 **Shotton Colliery** Dur
468 D2 **Shotts** N Lans
308 D5 **Shotwick** Ches
246 D3 **Shouldham** Norfk
246 D3 **Shouldham Thorpe** Norfk
188 B3 **Shoulton** Worcs
79 E3 **Shover's Green** E Susx
291 F5 **Shraleybrook** Staffs
233 H1 **Shrawardine** Shrops
188 A2 **Shrawley** Worcs
117 H3 **Shreding Green** Bucks
214 C6 **Shrewley** Warwks
234 C2 **Shrewsbury** Shrops
88 C6 **Shrewton** Wilts
53 G4 **Shripney** W Susx
113 F2 **Shrivenham** Oxon
248 C6 **Shropham** Norfk
174 C5 **Shrub End** Essex
93 G1 **Shrubs Hill** Surrey
186 D6 **Shucknall** Herefs
199 E2 **Shudy Camps** Cambs
543 H8 **Shulishadermor** Highld

543 G2 **Shulista** Highld
162 D6 **Shurdington** Gloucs
116 D5 **Shurlock Row** W & M
189 F2 **Shurnock** Worcs
588 C5 **Shurrery** Highld
64 D3 **Shurton** Somset
214 C3 **Shustoke** Warwks
26 D2 **Shute** Devon
28 D3 **Shute** Devon
70 D4 **Shute End** Wilts
165 F1 **Shutford** Oxon
272 C5 **Shut Heath** Staffs
162 C2 **Shuthonger** Gloucs
193 F5 **Shutlanger** Nhants
9 H3 **Shutta** Cnwll
236 C3 **Shutt Green** Staffs
238 D3 **Shuttington** Warwks
82 C2 **Shuttlesfield** Kent
315 F5 **Shuttlewood** Derbys
340 C6 **Shuttleworth** Bury
161 E4 **Shutton** Herefs
104 D2 **Shwt** Brdgnd
598 E5 **Siabost** W Isls
598 F5 **Siabost bho Dheas** W Isls
598 F5 **Siabost bho Thuath** W Isls
599 H4 **Siadar** W Isls
599 H4 **Siadar Iarach** W Isls
599 H4 **Siadar Uarach** W Isls
424 C2 **Sibbaldbie** D & G
217 E3 **Sibbertoft** Nhants
209 H3 **Sibdon Carwood** Shrops
165 F2 **Sibford Ferris** Oxon
165 F2 **Sibford Gower** Oxon
173 F3 **Sible Hedingham** Essex
172 C4 **Sibley's Green** Essex
300 C4 **Sibsey** Lincs
300 B4 **Sibsey Fen Side** Lincs
243 F5 **Sibson** Cambs
239 F4 **Sibson** Leics
297 E5 **Sibthorpe** Notts
316 D5 **Sibthorpe** Notts
226 D6 **Sibton** Suffk
199 H2 **Sicklesmere** Suffk
356 D5 **Sicklinghall** N York
28 B5 **Sid** Devon
44 B2 **Sidbrook** Somset
28 B4 **Sidbury** Devon
211 F2 **Sidbury** Shrops
84 D3 **Sidcot** N Som
120 C5 **Sidcup** Gt Lon
342 B5 **Siddal** Calder
388 B3 **Siddick** Cumb
311 G5 **Siddington** Ches
137 F5 **Siddington** Gloucs
311 G5 **Siddington Heath** Ches
213 E5 **Sidemoor** Worcs
325 Q2 **Side of the Moor** Bolton
256 B2 **Sidestrand** Norfk
292 A6 **Sideway** C Stke
28 B4 **Sidford** Devon
53 F5 **Sidlesham** W Susx
53 F4 **Sidlesham Common** W Susx
58 B5 **Sidley** E Susx
95 F5 **Sidlow** Surrey
28 B5 **Sidmouth** Devon
271 H2 **Sidway** Staffs
19 G3 **Sigford** Devon
361 F5 **Sigglesthorne** E R Yk
487 G5 **Sighthill** C Edin
467 E1 **Sighthill** C Glas
105 F5 **Sigingstone** V Glam
138 C2 **Signet** Oxon
67 G5 **Sigwells** Somset
91 G2 **Silchester** Hants
597 H4 **Sildinis** W Isls
240 D1 **Sileby** Leics
362 C5 **Silecroft** Cumb
249 F5 **Silfield** Norfk
39 F2 **Silford** Devon
181 E4 **Silian** Cerdgn
72 B5 **Silkstead** Hants
328 D3 **Silkstone** Barns
328 D4 **Silkstone Common** Barns
298 D6 **Silk Willoughby** Lincs
502 B4 **Sillerhole** Fife
399 E4 **Silloth** Cumb
569 J5 **Sillyearn** Moray
156 A2 **Siloh** Carmth
374 B1 **Silpho** N York
354 D5 **Silsden** Brad
169 F2 **Silsoe** Beds
68 C4 **Silton** Dorset
556 C2 **Silverbank** Abers
470 C2 **Silverburn** Mdloth
365 G4 **Silverdale** Lancs
291 G5 **Silverdale** Staffs
365 G5 **Silverdale Green** Lancs
212 D2 **Silver End** Dudley
173 G6 **Silver End** Essex
570 D3 **Silverford** Abers
255 G2 **Silvergate** Norfk
250 B6 **Silver Green** Norfk
58 C4 **Silverhill** E Susx
79 G4 **Silver Hill** E Susx
58 C4 **Silverhill Park** E Susx
67 H5 **Silver Knap** Somset
487 G4 **Silverknowes** C Edin
226 B4 **Silverley's Green** Suffk
469 E5 **Silvermuir** S Lans
193 E6 **Silverstone** Nhants
136 A4 **Silver Street** Gloucs
98 D3 **Silver Street** Kent
67 E3 **Silver Street** Somset
213 G4 **Silver Street** Worcs
27 F2 **Silverton** Devon
483 F4 **Silverton** W Duns
467 H4 **Silvertonhill** S Lans
120 B4 **Silvertown** Gt Lon
6 D4 **Silverwell** Cnwll
211 E4 **Silvington** Shrops
604 E2 **Silwick** Shet
328 D4 **Sim Hill** Barns
326 B3 **Simister** Bury
327 F6 **Simmondley** Derbys
309 H2 **Simm's Cross** Halton
324 C4 **Simm's Lane End** St Hel
428 D5 **Simonburn** Nthumb
62 B4 **Simonsbath** Somset
43 F4 **Simonsburrow** Devon
406 A2 **Simonside** S Tyne
340 B3 **Simonstone** Lancs
367 H1 **Simonstone** N York
474 D1 **Simprim** Border
313 E3 **Simpson** Derbys
365 G4 **Slack Head** Cumb
151 E6 **Simpson** M Keyn
151 E6 **Simpson** Pembks
474 B4 **Simpson Cross** Pembks
433 G1 **Sinclair's Hill** Border
501 E5 **Sinclairston** E Ayrs
370 C3 **Sinclairtown** Fife
370 C3 **Sinderby** N York
403 E4 **Sinderhope** Nthumb
311 E1 **Sinderland Green** Traffd
116 C6 **Sindlesham** Wokham
275 E3 **Sinfin** C Derb
275 E3 **Sinfin Moor** C Derb
86 C3 **Singleborough** Bucks
337 G2 **Singleton** Lancs
53 F2 **Singleton** W Susx
121 F5 **Singlewell** Kent
288 D3 **Singret** Wrexhm
80 B1 **Sinkhurst Green** Kent
555 E2 **Sinnahard** Abers

372 D2 **Sinnington** N York
188 B2 **Sinton** Worcs
188 B2 **Sinton Green** Worcs
86 C1 **Sion Hill** BaNES
118 B4 **Sipson** Gt Lon
132 B2 **Sirhowy** Blae G
250 C5 **Sisland** Norfk
80 A2 **Sissinghurst** Kent
110 B4 **Siston** S Glos
110 B4 **Siston Common** S Glos
4 B3 **Sithney** Cnwll
4 B3 **Sithney Common** Cnwll
4 B3 **Sithney Green** Cnwll
98 D2 **Sittingbourne** Kent
560 B5 **Sittyton** Abers
212 A2 **Six Ashes** Shrops
132 D4 **Six Bells** Blae G
276 D5 **Six Hills** Leics
319 F2 **Sixhills** Lincs
82 B2 **Sixmile** Kent
198 B3 **Six Mile Bottom** Cambs
48 B1 **Sixpenny Handley** Dorset
35 g6 **Six Rues** Jersey
203 F2 **Sizewell** Suffk
25 F4 **Skaigh** Devon
586 F7 **Skail** Highld
601 K3 **Skaill** Ork
602 A8 **Skaill** Ork
602 F5 **Skaill** Ork
433 H1 **Skares** E Ayrs
490 D4 **Skateraw** E Loth
607 J4 **Skaw** Shet
543 G7 **Skeabost** Highld
602 B7 **Skeabrae** Ork
385 F4 **Skeeby** N York
82 B2 **Skeete** Kent
241 F4 **Skeffington** Leics
349 G6 **Skeffling** E R Yk
295 F2 **Skegby** Notts
317 E5 **Skegby** Notts
609 J2 **Skeggie** Shet
301 G2 **Skegness** Lincs
605 G7 **Skelberry** Shet
317 E5 **Skelberry** Shet
608 D7 **Skelberry** Shet
577 G4 **Skelbo** Highld
577 G5 **Skelbo Muir** Highld
330 D2 **Skelbrooke** Donc
280 D2 **Skeldyke** Lincs
438 C4 **Skelfhill** Border
317 H5 **Skellingthorpe** Lincs
607 G7 **Skellister** Shet
312 B3 **Skellorn Green** Ches
330 B2 **Skellow** Donc
328 C2 **Skelmanthorpe** Kirk
324 B3 **Skelmersdale** Lancs
560 C2 **Skelmonae** Abers
482 A6 **Skelmorlie** N Ayrs
571 H7 **Skelmuir** Abers
586 F5 **Skelpick** Highld
390 C2 **Skelton** Cumb
345 H4 **Skelton** E R Yk
382 C4 **Skelton** N York
397 F6 **Skelton** R & Cl
357 H3 **Skelton** York
370 D6 **Skelton on Ure** N York
602 F3 **Skelwick** Ork
378 B4 **Skelwith Bridge** Cumb
320 D6 **Skendleby** Lincs
320 D5 **Skendleby Psalter** Lincs
160 A5 **Skenfrith** Mons
360 C3 **Skerne** E R Yk
383 G2 **Skerne Park** Darltn
456 D1 **Skeroblingarry** Ag & B
586 E4 **Skerray** Highld
584 D6 **Skerricha** Highld
446 B6 **Skerrington** E Ayrs
125 F2 **Skerryford** Pembks
351 G2 **Skerton** Lancs
215 G1 **Sketchley** Leics
103 F3 **Sketty** Swans
103 H2 **Skewen** Neath
14 D5 **Skewes** Cnwll
372 B5 **Skewsby** N York
256 A4 **Skeyton** Norfk
256 B4 **Skeyton Corner** Norfk
515 E1 **Skichen Muir** Angus
320 D1 **Skidbrooke** Lincs
335 F6 **Skidbrooke North End** Lincs
347 F3 **Skidby** E R Yk
42 C2 **Skilgate** Somset
30 B4 **Skilling** Dorset
278 B4 **Skillington** Lincs
399 E3 **Skinburness** Cumb
486 B3 **Skinflats** Falk
542 C7 **Skinidin** Highld
6 D4 **Skinner's Bottom** Cnwll
90 C1 **Skinners Green** W Berk
577 J7 **Skinnerton** Highld
586 C4 **Skinnet** Highld
397 H6 **Skinningrove** R & Cl
463 E3 **Skipness** Ag & B
337 G1 **Skippool** Lancs
400 C5 **Skiprigg** Cumb
361 F3 **Skipsea** E R Yk
361 F3 **Skipsea Brough** E R Yk
354 C4 **Skipton** N York
370 D4 **Skipton-on-Swale** N York
345 F2 **Skipwith** N York
300 B6 **Skirbeck** Lincs
300 B6 **Skirbeck Quarter** Lincs
354 C2 **Skirethorns** N York
348 B2 **Skirlaugh** E R Yk
449 E2 **Skirling** Border
116 C2 **Skirmett** Bucks
358 D3 **Skirpenbeck** E R Yk
391 G3 **Skirwith** Cumb
589 K3 **Skirza** Highld
400 D1 **Skitby** Cumb
11 G2 **Skitham** Lancs
141 G4 **Skittle Green** Bucks
546 B5 **Skulamus** Highld
586 D4 **Skullomie** Highld
209 E5 **Skyborry Green** Shrops
173 H5 **Skye Green** Essex
551 H5 **Skye of Curr** Highld
150 D4 **Skyfog** Pembks
417 H5 **Skyreburn** D & G
355 E2 **Skyreholme** N York
341 F4 **Slack** Calder
294 C2 **Slack** Derbys
327 G1 **Slack Kirk**
327 E8 **Slackcote** Oldham
313 E3 **Slackhall** Derbys
568 F3 **Slackhead** Moray
321 F5 **Slackholme End** Lincs
570 F6 **Slacks of Cairnbanno** Abers
136 C3 **Slad** Gloucs
161 H4 **Sladbrook** Gloucs
43 F6 **Slade** Devon
60 D2 **Slade** Devon
99 E4 **Slade** Kent
125 F1 **Slade** Pembks
115 F1 **Slade End** Oxon
120 D4 **Slade Green** Gt Lon
236 D3 **Slade Heath** Staffs
315 G2 **Slade Hooton** Rothm
90 C4 **Sladen Green** Hants
162 C5 **Slades Green** Worcs
402 B4 **Slaggyford** Nthumb
353 E4 **Slaidburn** Lancs
327 G2 **Slaithwaite** Kirk

294 B3 **Slaley** Derbys
404 A3 **Slaley** Nthumb
485 H5 **Slamannan** Falk
65 F4 **Slape Cross** Somset
385 G1 **Slapewath** R & Cl
168 C5 **Slapton** Bucks
13 E4 **Slapton** Devon
192 D5 **Slapton** Nhants
487 H5 **Slateford** C Edin
314 C6 **Slatepit Dale** Derbys
326 C3 **Slattocks** Rochdl
77 E4 **Slaugham** W Susx
22 C5 **Slaughterbridge** Cnwll
111 E5 **Slaughterford** Wilts
291 E3 **Slaughter Hill** Ches
241 G6 **Slawston** Leics
74 C2 **Sleaford** Hants
298 D6 **Sleaford** Lincs
391 F6 **Sleagill** Cumb
270 B4 **Sleap** Shrops
235 E1 **Sleapford** Wrekin
144 A3 **Sleapshyde** Herts
125 H1 **Sledge Green** Worcs
360 A2 **Sledmere** E R Yk
78 D3 **Sleeches Cross** E Susx
72 C4 **Sleepers Hill** Hants
426 C4 **Sleetbeck** Cumb
295 E4 **Sleet Moor** Derbys
48 B5 **Sleight** Dorset
381 H2 **Sleightholme** Dur
387 E3 **Sleights** N York
47 H6 **Slepe** Dorset
593 D7 **Sliabh na h-Airde** W Isls
589 H3 **Slickly** Highld
460 C5 **Sliddery** N Ayrs
213 E5 **Slideslow** Worcs
551 J5 **Sligachan** Highld
545 H4 **Slimbridge** Gloucs
135 G4 **Slindon** Staffs
272 B3 **Slindon** W Susx
53 H3 **Slinfold** W Susx
76 B3 **Sling** Gloucs
134 D3 **Slingsby** N York
372 C4 **Slioch** Abers
558 D2 **Slip End** Beds
169 F6 **Slip End** Herts
170 C2 **Slippery Ford** Brad
341 G1 **Slipton** Nhants
218 C4 **Slitting Mill** Staffs
237 F1 **Slochd** Highld
550 E5 **Slochnacraig** P & K
525 H2 **Slockavullin** Ag & B
492 D5 **Slockmill** D & G
408 B5 **Sloley** Norfk
256 B5 **Sloncombe** Devon
26 A5 **Sloothby** Lincs
321 E5 **Slough** Powys
185 F2 **Slough** Slough
117 G4 **Slough Green** Somset
44 B3 **Slough Green** W Susx
77 E4 **Slough Hill** Suffk
199 H4 **Sluggan** Highld
550 F5 **Sluggans** Highld
81 E3 **Sly Corner** Kent
93 G4 **Slyfield** Surrey
351 G1 **Slyne** Lancs
452 C2 **Smailholm** Border
326 D2 **Smallbridge** Rochdl
26 D3 **Smallbrook** Devon
134 D4 **Smallbrook** Gloucs
256 C5 **Smallburgh** Norfk
561 F1 **Smallburn** Abers
446 D4 **Smallburn** E Ayrs
313 E4 **Smalldale** Derbys
313 G3 **Smalldale** Derbys
55 F2 **Small Dole** W Susx
300 D3 **Small End** Lincs
295 E6 **Smalley** Derbys
275 G1 **Smalley Common** Derbys
295 E6 **Smalley Green** Derbys
95 G6 **Smallfield** Surrey
144 A3 **Smallford** Herts
213 G2 **Small Heath** Birm
424 B4 **Smallholm** D & G
80 C3 **Small Hythe** Kent
40 B3 **Smallmarsh** Devon
273 E3 **Smallrice** Staffs
29 E2 **Smallridge** Devon
326 D4 **Smallshaw** Tamesd
292 A4 **Smallthorne** C Stke
67 G3 **Small Way** Somset
291 G2 **Smallwood** Ches
189 F1 **Smallwood** Worcs
200 B3 **Smallwood Green** Suffk
351 E5 **Smallworth** Norfk
90 B5 **Smannell** Hants
380 C3 **Smardale** Cumb
80 C1 **Smarden** Kent
98 D6 **Smarden Bell** Kent
78 C1 **Smart's Hill** Kent
43 G5 **Smeatharpe** Devon
501 E6 **Smeaton** Fife
81 G2 **Smeeth** Kent
241 E6 **Smeeton Westerby** Leics
590 E4 **Smeircleit** W Isls
355 G2 **Smelthouses** N York
583 G3 **Smerral** Highld
212 B1 **Smestow** Staffs
234 A5 **Smethcott** Shrops
213 F2 **Smethwick** Sandw
291 G2 **Smethwick Green** Ches
528 B6 **Smiddy Hill** Angus
531 H7 **Smirisary** Highld
275 E6 **Smisby** Derbys
188 C3 **Smite Hill** Worcs
75 E5 **Smithbrook** W Susx
187 H4 **Smith End Green** Worcs
400 D1 **Smithfield** Cumb
351 G4 **Smith Green** Lancs
329 F3 **Smithies** Barns
43 E5 **Smithincott** Devon
329 F4 **Smithley** Barns
171 E2 **Smith's End** Herts
291 F4 **Smith's Green** Ches
311 G5 **Smiths Green** Ches
172 D1 **Smith's Green** Essex
572 E8 **Smithstown** Highld
566 C7 **Smithton** Highld
326 D1 **Smithy Bridge** Rochdl
308 A4 **Smithy Gate** Flints
311 E5 **Smithy Green** Ches
311 H2 **Smithy Green** Stockp
294 D5 **Smithy Houses** Derbys
323 G2 **Smithy Lane Ends** Lancs
54 C1 **Smock Alley** W Susx
215 H2 **Smockington** Leics
141 H3 **Smoky Row** Bucks
585 H3 **Smoo** Highld
600 F3 **Smoogro** Ork
174 B6 **Smythe's Green** Essex
80 A5 **Snagshall** E Susx
233 G4 **Snailbeach** Shrops
45 F5 **Snails Hill** Somset
169 H3 **Snailswell** Herts
222 C6 **Snailwell** Cambs
373 H3 **Snainton** N York
393 G4 **Snaisgill** Dur

345 E5 **Snaith** E R Yk
370 B3 **Snape** N York
202 D3 **Snape** Suffk
323 G2 **Snape Green** Lancs
329 G4 **Snape Hill** Barns
314 B4 **Snape Hill** Derbys
61 E5 **Snapper** Devon
120 A2 **Snaresbrook** Gt Lon
239 E3 **Snarestone** Leics
318 C3 **Snarford** Lincs
81 E4 **Snargate** Kent
133 E4 **Snatchwood** Torfn
81 F4 **Snave** Kent
188 C4 **Sneachill** Worcs
209 F1 **Snead** Powys
211 G6 **Snead Common** Worcs
212 C6 **Sneads Green** Worcs
225 F2 **Sneath Common** Norfk
387 E3 **Sneaton** N York
387 E3 **Sneatonthorpe** N York
276 C2 **Sneinton** C Nott
318 D3 **Snelland** Lincs
168 A3 **Snelshall East** M Keyn
167 H3 **Snelshall West** M Keyn
293 G6 **Snelston** Derbys
224 C1 **Snetterton** Norfk
258 D5 **Snettisham** Norfk
609 G5 **Snevlabreck** Shet
292 A5 **Sneyd Green** C Stke
109 G4 **Sneyd Park** Bristl
239 G2 **Snibston** Leics
162 A4 **Snig's End** Gloucs
99 E2 **Snipeshill** Kent
593 D11 **Sniseabhal** W Isls
442 C4 **Snitter** Nthumb
332 D6 **Snitterby** Lincs
190 C5 **Snitterfield** Warwks
294 B2 **Snitterton** Derbys
210 D4 **Snitton** Shrops
210 D5 **Snittongate** Shrops
159 F1 **Snodhill** Herefs
97 G2 **Snodland** Kent
404 C4 **Snods Edge** Nthumb
328 D4 **Snowden Hill** Barns
100 D5 **Snowdown** Kent
171 F3 **Snow End** Herts
290 C4 **Snow Hill** Ches
343 F5 **Snow Hill** Wakefd
342 A6 **Snow Lea** Kirk
163 G3 **Snowshill** Gloucs
225 E3 **Snow Street** Norfk
343 H5 **Snydale** Wakefd
52 B2 **Soake** Hants
12 C5 **Soar** Devon
265 E2 **Soar** Gwynd
282 C1 **Soar** IoA
157 F3 **Soar** Powys
51 H1 **Soberton** Hants
51 H2 **Soberton Heath** Hants
390 D4 **Sockbridge** Cumb
384 A3 **Sockburn** Darltn
30 B1 **Sockety** Dorset
307 F5 **Sodom** Denbgs
112 B3 **Sodom** Wilts
269 F2 **Sodylt Bank** Shrops
222 B5 **Soham** Cambs
222 B4 **Soham Cotes** Cambs
119 F3 **Soho** Gt Lon
213 F2 **Soho** Sandw
86 B5 **Soho** Somset
592 E3 **Solas** W Isls
38 D5 **Soldon Cross** Devon
73 G3 **Soldridge** Hants
100 A6 **Sole Street** Kent
121 F6 **Sole Street** Kent
214 B4 **Solihull** Solhll
213 G4 **Solihull Lodge** Solhll
543 G2 **Solitote** Highld
185 H3 **Sollers Dilwyn** Herefs
161 E3 **Sollers Hope** Herefs
338 B6 **Sollom** Lancs
150 C5 **Solva** Pembks
425 F4 **Solwaybank** D & G
241 G2 **Somerby** Leics
333 F3 **Somerby** Lincs
295 E4 **Somercotes** Derbys
110 B6 **Somerdale** BaNES
291 G1 **Somerford** Ches
49 F6 **Somerford** Dorset
236 C3 **Somerford** Staffs
137 F5 **Somerford Keynes** Gloucs
53 E5 **Somerley** W Susx
251 F5 **Somerleyton** Suffk
274 A3 **Somersal Herbert** Derbys
320 B5 **Somersby** Lincs
220 D4 **Somersham** Cambs
201 E5 **Somersham** Suffk
52 A5 **Somers Town** C Port
107 F2 **Somerton** Newpt
166 A4 **Somerton** Oxon
66 D4 **Somerton** Somset
199 G4 **Somerton** Suffk
66 D4 **Somerton** Somset
234 D2 **Somerwood** Shrops
55 E4 **Sompting** W Susx
55 E3 **Sompting Abbotts** W Susx
116 C4 **Sonning** Wokham
116 B3 **Sonning Common** Oxon
116 C4 **Sonning Eye** Oxon
288 D5 **Sontley** Wrexhm
295 G5 **Sookholme** Notts
49 F5 **Sopley** Hants
143 H3 **Sopwell** Herts
111 E2 **Sopworth** Wilts
410 D3 **Sorbie** D & G
588 E4 **Sordale** Highld
517 H3 **Sorisdale** Ag & B
12 C3 **Sorley** Devon
446 B4 **Sorn** E Ayrs
445 H3 **Sornhill** E Ayrs
492 C4 **Soroba** Ag & B
506 A4 **Soroba** Ag & B
589 H4 **Sortat** Highld
319 F4 **Sotby** Lincs
315 E3 **Sothall** Sheff
299 E2 **Sots Hole** Lincs
227 E3 **Sotterley** Suffk
210 B1 **Soudley** Shrops
271 G4 **Soudley** Shrops
328 B4 **Soughley** Barns
288 B1 **Soughton** Flints
168 B4 **Soulbury** Bucks
380 C2 **Soulby** Cumb
390 D4 **Soulby** Cumb
166 B3 **Souldern** Oxon
194 D2 **Souldrop** Beds
290 C5 **Sound** Ches
605 J2 **Sound** Shet
606 E7 **Sound** Shet
608 E8 **Sound** Shet
290 C5 **Sound Heath** Ches
110 A4 **Soundwell** S Glos
453 F5 **Sourhope** Border
602 E5 **Sourin** Ork
444 D1 **Sourlie** N Ayrs
390 B1 **Sour Nook** Cumb
24 D4 **Sourton** Devon
363 E5 **Soutergate** Cumb
253 G5 **South Acre** Norfk
118 D4 **South Acton** Gt Lon
82 D2 **South Alkham** Kent
118 C3 **Southall** Gt Lon
12 D5 **South Allington** Devon

486 A1 South Alloa Falk
376 B2 Southam Cumb
163 E4 Southam Gloucs
191 G2 Southam Warwks
75 E5 South Ambersham W Susx
50 C2 Southampton C Sotn
315 G3 South Anston Rothm
117 F6 South Ascot W & M
81 F1 South Ashford Kent
66 C6 Southay Somset
609 G7 South Aywick Shet
50 C5 South Baddesley Hants
520 E4 South Ballachulish Highld
396 D5 South Bank R & Cl
358 A4 South Bank York
67 F4 South Barrow Somset
263 F4 South Beach Gwynd
431 E4 South Beach Nthumb
95 F2 South Beddington Gt Lon
122 B2 South Benfleet Essex
406 C2 South Bents Sundld
53 G4 South Bersted W Susx
472 C6 South Blainslie Border
89 F5 South Bockhampton Dorset
94 D1 Southborough Gt Lon
96 B1 Southborough Gt Lon
78 D1 Southborough Kent
34 D2 Southbourne Bmouth
52 D3 Southbourne W Susx
30 A3 South Bowood Dorset
557 E6 South Brachmont Abers
330 D2 South Bramwith Donc
19 E5 South Brent Devon
68 B2 South Brewham Somset
120 A3 South Bromley Gt Lon
68 D3 Southbrook Wilts
485 H3 South Broomage Falk
443 G4 South Broomhill Nthumb
248 C4 Southburgh Norfk
250 D3 South Burlingham Norfk
360 B4 Southburn E R Yk
67 G4 South Cadbury Somset
414 C3 South Cairn D & G
318 A4 South Carlton Lincs
316 A3 South Carlton Notts
16 A2 South Carne Cnwll
346 D3 South Cave E R Yk
137 G5 South Cerney Gloucs
77 G6 South Chailey E Susx
29 F1 South Chard Somset
455 F5 South Charlton Nthumb
68 B5 South Cheriton Somset
395 E4 South Church Dur
123 E2 Southchurch Sthend
346 C2 South Cliffe E R Yk
317 F5 South Clifton Notts
549 K1 South Clunes Highld
320 C2 South Cockerington Lincs
557 F6 South Cookney Abers
165 H4 Southcoombe Oxon
104 C3 South Cornelly Brdgnd
461 E3 South Corriegills N Ayrs
424 D3 South Corrielaw D & G
116 A5 Southcote Readg
22 D3 Southcott Cnwll
39 F4 Southcott Devon
89 E3 Southcott Wilts
141 H2 Southcourt Bucks
227 G3 South Cove Suffk
259 H4 South Creake Norfk
189 F1 Southcrest Worcs
327 H2 South Crosland Kirk
241 E2 South Croxton Leics
95 G2 South Croydon Gt Lon
542 F4 South Cuil Highld
360 B5 South Dalton E R Yk
121 E6 South Darenth Kent
440 B3 Southdean Border
323 H5 Southdene Knows
251 G4 South Denes BaNES
86 C2 Southdown BaNES
10 D3 Southdown Cnwll
72 C5 South Down Hants
43 H5 South Down Somset
345 F3 South Duffield N York
95 F5 South Earlswood Surrey
56 C3 Southease E Susx
320 A2 South Elkington Lincs
329 H2 South Elmsall Wakefd
488 D5 South Elphinstone E Loth
456 D5 Southend Ag & B
116 C2 Southend Bucks
168 B4 South End Bucks
350 B2 South End Cumb
348 C1 South End E R Yk
135 G5 Southend Gloucs
120 A5 Southend Gt Lon
49 E1 South End Hants
145 F1 South-End Herts
348 B5 South End N Linc
224 C1 South End Norfk
140 C4 Southend Oxon
114 C4 Southend W Berk
115 F5 Southend W Berk
122 D3 Southend-on-Sea Sthend
24 D5 Southerly Devon
390 B2 Southerness Cumb
55 G3 Southern Cross Br & H
104 D5 Southerndown V Glam
398 B4 Southerness D & G
170 D3 Southern Green Herts
602 A8 Southerquoy Ork
562 C2 South Erradale Highld
28 A4 Southerton Devon
246 C6 Southery Norfk
173 F3 Southey Green Essex
147 H5 South Fambridge Essex
93 E4 South Farnborough Hants
114 B3 South Fawley W Berk
460 C4 South Feorline N Ayrs
347 E5 South Ferriby N Linc
347 F4 South Field E R Yk
500 D5 Southfield Fife
431 E4 Southfield Nthumb
117 G4 South Field W & M
121 G2 Southfields Essex
119 E5 Southfields Gt Lon
121 G3 Southfields Thurr
121 F5 Southfleet Kent
560 A3 South Flobbets Abers
37 E5 Southford IoW
532 E7 South Garvan Highld
204 D4 Southgate Cerdgn
144 D6 Southgate Gt Lon
255 F3 Southgate Norfk
259 H5 Southgate Norfk
103 G4 Southgate Swans
77 E2 Southgate W Susx
199 H2 Southgate Bridge Suffk
606 D2 South Gluss Shet
95 H5 South Godstone Surrey
49 F2 South Gorley Hants
431 E6 South Gosforth N u Ty
146 D6 South Green Essex
174 D6 South Green Essex
98 C2 South Green Kent
249 E2 South Green Norfk
252 A3 South Green Norfk
225 G5 South Green Suffk
487 G5 South Gyle C Edin
608 D7 South-Haa Shet
119 H3 South Hackney Gt Lon
91 G4 South Ham Hants
147 E5 South Hanningfield Essex
118 B2 South Harefield Gt Lon
118 C2 South Harrow Gt Lon
74 B6 South Harting W Susx
144 B3 South Hatfield Herts
52 C5 South Hayling Hants
142 C4 South Heath Bucks
175 H6 South Heath Essex
56 D4 South Heighton E Susx
406 B6 South Hetton Dur
329 F2 South Hiendley Wakefd
16 D4 South Hill Cnwll
84 B3 South Hill N Som
124 D2 South Hill Pembks
140 B4 South Hinksey Oxon
38 B3 South Hole Devon
372 C4 South Holme N York
94 D6 South Holmwood Surrey
120 D3 South Hornchurch Gt Lon
85 G5 South Horrington Somset
12 B4 South Huish Devon
298 A2 South Hykeham Lincs
406 B3 South Hylton Sundld
169 G1 Southill Beds
81 F1 Southill Dorset
90 D5 Southington Hants
333 E5 South Kelsey Lincs
565 L7 South Kessock Highld
333 G1 South Killingholme N Linc
371 E3 South Kilvington N York
216 D3 South Kilworth Leics
514 D3 South Kingennie Angus
329 H2 South Kirkby Wakefd
556 C3 South Kirkton Abers
461 E4 South Kiscadale N Ayrs
240 D4 South Knighton C Leic
19 H3 South Knighton Devon
299 F5 South Kyme Lincs
119 F4 South Lambeth Gt Lon
55 E4 South Lancing W Susx
32 B4 Southlands Dorset
328 D3 South Lane Barns
28 D4 Southleigh Devon
139 F3 South Leigh Oxon
317 E3 South Leverton Notts
189 G5 South Littleton Worcs
397 H6 South Loftus R & Cl
224 D3 South Lopham Norfk
242 C4 South Luffenham Rutlnd
56 C2 South Malling E Susx
68 B3 Southmarsh Somset
113 E2 South Marston Swindn
109 G4 Southmead Bristl
95 F4 South Merstham Surrey
454 B5 South Middleton Nthumb
344 B3 South Milford N York
12 C4 South Milton Devon
144 B4 South Mimms Herts
148 C5 Southminster Essex
41 E3 South Molton Devon
405 E4 South Moor Dur
139 F5 Southmoor Oxon
115 F2 South Moreton Oxon
527 E4 Southmuir Angus
53 F4 South Mundham W Susx
297 E3 South Muskham Notts
346 D2 South Newbald E R Yk
364 B6 South Newbarns Cumb
165 G3 South Newington Oxon
431 F4 South Newsham Nthumb
70 B3 South Newton Wilts
295 E3 South Normanton Derbys
119 G6 South Norwood Gt Lon
95 G5 South Nutfield Surrey
121 E3 South Ockendon Thurr
195 H2 Southoe Cambs
225 G6 Southolt Suffk
320 C4 South Ormsby Lincs
243 F4 Southorpe C Pete
370 D2 South Otterington N York
30 B5 Southover Dorset
31 E4 Southover Dorset
56 C3 Southover E Susx
79 F4 Southover E Susx
333 F6 South Owersby Lincs
342 B5 Southowram Calder
143 G6 South Oxhey Herts
95 E5 South Park Surrey
501 E4 South Parks Fife
405 G4 South Pelaw Dur
30 B1 South Perrott Dorset
65 E4 South Petherton Somset
16 D2 South Petherwin Cnwll
247 G4 South Pickenham Norfk
10 D2 South Pill Cnwll
12 D4 South Pool Devon
30 C3 South Poorton Dorset
323 E1 Southport Sefton
514 C3 South Powrie C Dund
605 H7 Southpunds Shet
487 F4 South Queensferry C Edin
560 C2 South Quilquox Abers
62 B5 South Radworthy Devon
298 C5 South Rauceby Lincs
254 A3 South Raynham Norfk
312 A1 South Reddish Stockp
256 B2 Southrepps Norfk
320 D3 South Reston Lincs
299 E1 Southrey Lincs
165 F3 Southrop Gloucs
91 H6 Southrope Hants
118 C2 South Ruislip Gt Lon
246 C3 South Runcton Norfk
297 F2 South Scarle Notts
605 G7 South Scousburgh Shet
52 A5 Southsea C Port
288 C4 Southsea Wrexhm
506 F1 South Shian Ag & B
406 B1 South Shields S Tyne
337 E3 South Shore Bpool
394 C4 South Side Dur
603 H6 Southside Ork
335 F6 South Somercotes Lincs
356 C2 South Stainley N York
381 E2 South Stainmore Cumb
405 E4 South Stanley Dur
121 F4 South Stifford Thurr
86 C2 Southstoke BaNES
115 F3 South Stoke Oxon
54 B3 South Stoke W Susx
81 F2 South Stour Kent
514 C5 South Straiton Fife
77 G6 South Street E Susx
96 B3 South Street Gt Lon
97 F2 South Street Kent
98 C2 South Street Kent
99 H3 South Street Kent
100 B2 South Street Kent
25 G4 South Tawton Devon
6 B5 South Tehidy Cnwll
320 D4 South Thoresby Lincs
89 F5 South Tidworth Wilts
27 F6 South Town Devon
73 G2 South Town Hants
251 G3 Southtown Norfk
601 H5 Southtown Ork
44 C4 Southtown Somset
67 F2 Southtown Somset
86 C2 South Twerton BaNES
364 D4 South Ulverston Cumb
91 G4 South View Hants
12 C4 Southville Devon
133 E5 Southville Torfn
400 D6 Southwaite Cumb
250 D2 South Walsham Norfk
92 B5 South Warnborough Hants
76 C4 Southwater W Susx
76 C4 Southwater Street W Susx
11 E1 Southway C Plym
67 E1 Southway Somset
146 B6 South Weald Essex
50 A4 South Weirs Hants
32 B5 Southwell Dorset
296 C4 Southwell Notts
141 E5 South Weston Oxon
23 E4 South Wheatley Cnwll
317 E2 South Wheatley Notts
605 G2 South Whiteness Shet
51 H3 Southwick Hants
219 E1 Southwick Nhants
84 C5 Southwick Somset
406 B3 Southwick Sundld
55 F4 Southwick W Susx
87 F3 Southwick Wilts
85 G3 South Widcombe BaNES
240 C5 South Wigston Leics
81 F1 South Willesborough Kent
319 F3 South Willingham Lincs
119 F5 South Wimbledon Gt Lon
396 B2 South Wingate Donc
294 D3 South Wingfield Derbys
278 C6 South Witham Lincs
227 G4 Southwold Suffk
39 E6 South Wonford Devon
72 C2 South Wonston Hants
275 E5 Southwood Derbys
92 D3 Southwood Hants
250 D3 Southwood Norfk
67 F3 Southwood Somset
187 G2 Southwood Worcs
120 A1 South Woodford Gt Lon
147 G5 South Woodham Ferrers Essex
252 C3 South Wootton Norfk
87 E2 South Wraxall Wilts
213 H3 South Yardley Birm
24 D2 South Yeo Devon
25 G4 South Zeal Devon
341 G5 Sowerby Calder
371 E3 Sowerby N York
341 G5 Sowerby Bridge Calder
390 B1 Sowerby Row Cumb
351 E6 Sower Carr Lancs
42 A3 Sowerhill Somset
199 E4 Sowley Green Suffk
342 A6 Sowood Calder
342 A6 Sowood Green Calder
27 F4 Sowton Devon
26 C5 Sowton Barton Devon
576 C5 Soyal Highld
341 G5 Soyland Town Calder
356 C4 Spacey Houses N York
256 C3 Spa Common Norfk
280 B5 Spalding Lincs
345 H3 Spaldington E R Yk
219 G3 Spaldwick Cambs
317 F6 Spalford Notts
279 F2 Spanby Lincs
482 B5 Spango Inver
92 A3 Spanish Green Hants
255 E4 Sparham Norfk
255 E4 Sparhamhill Norfk
364 D3 Spark Bridge Cumb
213 H3 Sparkbrook Birm
67 G4 Sparkford Somset
213 G3 Sparkhill Birm
18 C6 Sparkwell Devon
2 C5 Sparnon Cnwll
6 C5 Sparnon Gate Cnwll
254 B5 Sparrow Green Norfk
84 D4 Sparrow Hill Somset
313 E3 Sparrowpit Derbys
79 E3 Sparrow's Green E Susx
72 B3 Sparsholt Hants
114 B2 Sparsholt Oxon
403 F5 Spartylea Nthumb
273 G3 Spath Staffs
372 D2 Spaunton N York
64 D4 Spaxton Somset
533 K6 Spean Bridge Highld
71 G4 Spearywell Hants
67 F5 Speckington Somset
97 E1 Speed Gate Kent
110 A5 Speedwell Bristl
142 A4 Speen Bucks
114 D6 Speen W Berk
375 F5 Speeton N York
309 H3 Speke Lpool
78 C1 Speldhurst Kent
171 G6 Spellbrook Herts
165 F5 Spelsbury Oxon
130 D6 Spelter Brdgnd
342 C4 Spen Kirk
92 B1 Spencers Wood Wokham
291 G2 Spen Green Ches
212 B5 Spennells Worcs
369 F2 Spennithorne N York
395 E3 Spennymoor Dur
189 G2 Spernall Warwks
188 C4 Spetchley Worcs
47 G4 Spetisbury Dorset
226 D3 Spexhall Suffk
536 B1 Speybank Highld
568 F3 Spey Bay Moray
551 J4 Speybridge Highld
300 D1 Spilsby Lincs
455 E3 Spindlestone Nthumb
315 F4 Spinkhill Derbys
193 G2 Spinney Hill Nhants
240 C4 Spinney Hills C Leic
576 E6 Spinningdale Highld
295 H1 Spion Kop Notts
112 A4 Spirthill Wilts
117 G4 Spital W & M
308 D3 Spital Wirral
145 E3 Spitalbrook Herts
293 G5 Spitalhill Derbys
330 D6 Spital Hill Donc
318 B1 Spital in the Street Lincs
294 C1 Spitewinter Derbys
56 C1 Spithurst E Susx
416 D5 Spittal D & G
489 F4 Spittal E Loth
359 E4 Spittal E R Yk
588 F6 Spittal Highld
475 F4 Spittal Nthumb
151 G5 Spittal Pembks
483 G2 Spittal Stirlg
512 D1 Spittalfield P & K
538 B3 Spittal of Glenmuick Abers
525 H2 Spittal of Glenshee P & K
25 G4 Spittlegate Lincs
376 B5 Spixworth Norfk
14 C3 Splatt Cnwll
23 E5 Splatt Cnwll
25 E1 Splatt Cnwll
64 D4 Splatt Somset
105 J5 Splayne's Green E Susx
106 C4 Splott Cardif
356 D4 Spofforth N York
275 D4 Spondon C Derb
63 G4 Spon End Covtry
173 E2 Spon Green Flints
249 F5 Spooner Row Norfk
236 B5 Spoonleygate Shrops
247 H2 Sporle Norfk
326 C2 Spotland Bridge Rochdl
490 C4 Spott E Loth
217 F6 Spratton Nhants
74 C1 Spreakley Surrey
25 G3 Spreyton Devon
11 F3 Spriddlestone Devon
318 C3 Spridlington Lincs
141 G5 Sprig's Alley Oxon
389 F5 Spring Bank Cumb
162 D5 Springbank Gloucs
467 F2 Springboig C Glas
34 D2 Springbourne Bmouth
484 C6 Springburn C Glas
239 E1 Spring Cottage Leics
381 H5 Spring End N York
213 G3 Springfield Birm
132 C5 Springfield Caerph
425 G6 Springfield D & G
147 E3 Springfield Essex
501 F2 Springfield Fife
566 B4 Springfield Highld
168 B2 Springfield M Keyn
567 J5 Springfield Sandw
213 E2 Springfield Sandw
324 D3 Springfield Wigan
236 D5 Springfield Wolves
354 B6 Spring Gardens Somset
118 C4 Spring Green Lancs
121 F5 Spring Grove Gt Lon
327 E4 Springhead Oldham
466 D3 Springhill E Rens
51 F5 Springhill IoW
540 A4 Spring Hill Lancs
468 D3 Springhill N Lans
326 D3 Spring Hill Oldham
237 E4 Springhill Staffs
237 G3 Springhill Staffs
236 C5 Spring Hill Wolves
422 D6 Springholm D & G
425 F5 Springkell D & G
95 H1 Spring Park Gt Lon
445 E2 Springside N Ayrs
272 B2 Springthorpe Lincs
171 H1 Springwell Essex
405 G3 Springwell Sundld
406 B3 Springwell Sundld
424 B1 Springwells D & G
348 C3 Sproatley E R Yk
291 E1 Sproston Green Ches
330 B4 Sprotbrough Donc
201 F6 Sproughton Suffk
453 E2 Sprouston Border
250 A2 Sprowston Norfk
278 B5 Sproxton Leics
372 B3 Sproxton N York
400 C5 Sprunston Cumb
269 H3 Spunhill Shrops
142 B5 Spurlands End Bucks
290 A3 Spurstow Ches
210 D6 Spurtree Shrops
30 C4 Spyway Dorset
150 D3 Square and Compass Pembks
337 F3 Squires Gate Bpool
516 B6 Sraid Ruadh Ag & B
595 G6 Srannda W Isls
235 G5 Stableford Shrops
272 B2 Stableford Staffs
314 B1 Stacey Bank Sheff
353 E4 Stackhouse N York
125 G5 Stackpole Pembks
224 D1 Stacksford Norfk
340 C5 Stacksteads Lancs
200 C5 Stackyard Green Suffk
11 F3 Staddiscombe C Plym
346 B4 Staddlethorpe E R Yk
23 H2 Staddon Devon
38 C3 Staddon Devon
313 E5 Staden Derbys
140 D5 Stadhampton Oxon
593 D10 Stadhlaigearraidh W Isls
291 H3 Stadmorslow Staffs
401 F6 Staffield Cumb
543 H3 Staffin Highld
272 D5 Stafford Staffs
235 G2 Stafford Park Wrekin
148 C1 Stafford's Corner Essex
67 G1 Stafford's Green Dorset
186 B3 Stagbatch Herefs
146 C1 Stagden Cross Essex
472 A6 Stagehall Border
194 D5 Stagsden Beds
194 D5 Stagsden West End Beds
40 D2 Stag's Head Devon
388 B4 Stainburn Cumb
356 B5 Stainburn N York
278 C5 Stainby Lincs
342 D5 Staincliffe Kirk
329 E2 Staincross Barns
394 C5 Staindrop Dur
118 A5 Staines Surrey
144 C2 Staines Green Herts
279 F4 Stainfield Lincs
319 E5 Stainfield Lincs
330 D2 Stainforth Donc
353 G1 Stainforth N York
337 G2 Staining Lancs
342 A6 Stainland Calder
387 F3 Stainsacre N York
295 E1 Stainsby Derbys
320 B5 Stainsby Lincs
365 H2 Stainton Cumb
390 D4 Stainton Cumb
400 C3 Stainton Cumb
330 C6 Stainton Donc
396 B6 Stainton Dur
384 D2 Stainton Middsb
382 C5 Stainton N York
318 D4 Stainton by Langworth Lincs
387 G5 Staintondale N York
394 D5 Stainton Grove Dur
334 A6 Stainton le Vale Lincs
364 B5 Stainton with Adgarley Cumb
389 F5 Stair Cumb
445 F5 Stair E Ayrs
329 F3 Stairfoot Barns
415 H6 Stairhaven D & G
386 C1 Staithes N York
431 E2 Stakeford Nthumb
326 C3 Stake Hill Rochdl
212 C4 Stakenbridge Worcs
337 G5 Stake Pool Lancs
68 B6 Stalbridge Dorset
46 D1 Stalbridge Weston Dorset
256 D4 Stalham Norfk
256 D4 Stalham Green Norfk
99 F4 Stalisfield Green Kent
46 B1 Stallen Dorset
334 B2 Stallingborough NE Lin
368 B2 Stalling Busk N York
272 D2 Stallington Staffs
351 E5 Stalmine Lancs
351 E5 Stalmine Moss Side Lancs
327 E5 Stalybridge Tamesd
212 B3 Stambermill Dudley
63 G4 Stamborough Somset
173 E2 Stambourne Essex
173 E2 Stambourne Green Essex
243 E3 Stamford Lincs
309 G6 Stamford Bridge Ches
358 B3 Stamford Bridge E R Yk
430 A5 Stamfordham Nthumb
119 G2 Stamford Hill Gt Lon
467 E3 Stamperland E Rens
52 A4 Stamshaw C Port
351 E6 Stanah Lancs
144 B2 Stanborough Herts
168 D5 Stanbridge Beds
48 C4 Stanbridge Dorset
168 D5 Stanbridgeford Beds
172 C4 Stanbrook Essex
188 B5 Stanbrook Worcs
341 G2 Stanbury Brad
326 A3 Stand Bury
485 F6 Stand N Lans
486 B5 Standburn Falk
236 D3 Standeford Staffs
80 C1 Standen Kent
340 A1 Standen Hall Lancs
80 A3 Standen Street Kent
87 F4 Standerwick Somset
74 C3 Standford Hants
271 G5 Standford Bridge Wrekin
399 H5 Standingstone Cumb
136 B3 Standish Gloucs
324 D2 Standish Wigan
324 D3 Standish Lower Ground Wigan
139 F4 Standlake Oxon
72 B4 Standon Hants
171 E5 Standon Herts
272 B3 Standon Staffs
171 E6 Standon Green End Herts
468 D3 Stane N Lans
444 D2 Stanecastle N Ayrs
291 H4 Stanfield C Stke
254 B3 Stanfield Norfk
169 H1 Stanford Beds
82 B3 Stanford Kent
247 G6 Stanford Norfk
233 F2 Stanford Shrops
187 F2 Stanford Bishop Herefs
187 G1 Stanford Bridge Worcs
115 F5 Stanford Dingley W Berk
92 B2 Stanford End Wokham
276 B5 Stanford Hills Notts
139 E6 Stanford in the Vale Oxon
121 G3 Stanford-le-Hope Thurr
216 C4 Stanford on Avon Nhants
276 B5 Stanford on Soar Notts
187 F1 Stanford on Teme Worcs
146 A4 Stanford Rivers Essex
315 F5 Stanfree Derbys
386 A1 Stanghow R & Cl
244 B5 Stanground C Pete
340 A4 Stanhill Lancs
259 G4 Stanhoe Norfk
449 F4 Stanhope Border
393 G2 Stanhope Dur
81 E1 Stanhope Kent
218 C2 Stanion Nhants
364 B5 Stank Cumb
212 C5 Stanklyn Worcs
343 G2 Stanks Leeds
275 G1 Stanley Derbys
405 F4 Stanley Dur
324 B3 Stanley Lancs
295 F2 Stanley Notts
512 D3 Stanley P & K
211 F3 Stanley Shrops
211 G3 Stanley Shrops
292 B4 Stanley Staffs
343 F5 Stanley Wakefd
111 H5 Stanley Wilts
295 E6 Stanley Common Derbys
394 D2 Stanley Crook Dur
136 B4 Stanley Downton Gloucs
343 G5 Stanley Ferry Wakefd
324 A3 Stanley Gate Lancs
48 C6 Stanley Green Poole
270 C2 Stanley Green Shrops
311 H3 Stanley Green Stockp
187 F6 Stanley Hill Herefs
292 B4 Stanley Moor Staffs
163 E3 Stanley Pontlarge Gloucs
131 G6 Stanleytown Rhondd
309 F4 Stanlow Ches
236 A5 Stanlow Shrops
56 A3 Stanmer Br & H
118 D1 Stanmore Gt Lon
72 C4 Stanmore Hants
211 G1 Stanmore Shrops
114 D4 Stanmore W Berk
185 E3 Stanner Powys
514 C3 Stannergate C Dund
427 H2 Stannersburn Nthumb
93 G2 Stanners Hill Surrey
199 H3 Stanningfield Suffk
430 C4 Stannington Nthumb
314 C2 Stannington Sheff
430 D3 Stannington Station Nthumb
35 E2 Stanpit Dorset
185 F2 Stansbatch Herefs
199 F4 Stansfield Suffk
293 F4 Stanshope Staffs
199 G5 Stanstead Suffk
145 E2 Stanstead Abbots Herts
97 F2 Stansted Kent
171 G4 Stansted Mountfitchet Essex
290 D1 Stanthorne Lodge Ches
274 D6 Stanton Derbys
163 G3 Stanton Gloucs
159 F5 Stanton Mons
430 B2 Stanton Nthumb
293 F5 Stanton Staffs
224 C5 Stanton Suffk
168 A1 Stantonbury M Keyn
275 H2 Stanton by Bridge Derbys
275 H2 Stanton-by-Dale Derbys
224 C5 Stanton Chare Suffk
85 G2 Stanton Drew BaNES
113 E1 Stanton Fitzwarren Swindn
139 G3 Stanton Gate Derbys
139 G3 Stanton Harcourt Oxon
276 D5 Stanton Hill Notts
294 A2 Stanton in Peak Derbys
210 B4 Stanton Lacy Shrops
294 B2 Stanton Lees Derbys
210 D1 Stanton Long Shrops
276 D3 Stanton-on-the-Wolds Notts
86 B2 Stanton Prior BaNES
88 C2 Stanton St Bernard Wilts
140 C3 Stanton St John Oxon
111 G4 Stanton St Quintin Wilts
200 C1 Stanton Street Suffk
239 H2 Stanton under Bardon Leics
270 D5 Stanton upon Hine Heath Shrops
85 H2 Stanton Wick BaNES
135 G2 Stantway Gloucs
269 H5 Stanwardine in the Fields Shrops
269 H4 Stanwardine in the Wood Shrops
174 B5 Stanway Essex
163 G3 Stanway Gloucs
174 C5 Stanway Green Essex
226 A6 Stanway Green Suffk
118 A5 Stanwell Surrey

City, town and village index: Stanwell Moor - Stroud Green 717

118 A5 Stanwell Moor Surrey
218 D5 Stanwick Nhants
383 E2 Stanwick-St-John N York
400 C3 Stanwix Cumb
326 C3 Stanycliffe Rochdl
606 C7 Stanydale Shet
593 C11 Staoinebrig W Isls
386 C6 Stape N York
48 C4 Stapehill Dorset
290 D5 Stapeley Ches
274 D5 Stapenhill Staffs
101 E4 Staple Kent
42 D4 Staple Cross Devon
79 H5 Staplecross E Susx
77 E4 Staplefield W Susx
44 B4 Staple Fitzpaine Somset
197 G4 Stapleford Cambs
144 D1 Stapleford Herts
277 G6 Stapleford Leics
297 G3 Stapleford Lincs
276 A2 Stapleford Notts
70 B2 Stapleford Wilts
145 H5 Stapleford Abbotts Essex
145 H5 Stapleford Tawney Essex
43 H2 Staplegrove Somset
43 H3 Staplehay Somset
110 A4 Staple Hill S Glos
213 E5 Staple Hill Worcs
98 B6 Staplehurst Kent
44 A4 Staple Lawns Somset
37 E3 Staplers IoW
75 G4 Staples Hill W Susx
99 G2 Staplestreet Kent
109 H4 Stapleton Bristl
426 D5 Stapleton Cumb
185 F1 Stapleton Herefs
239 G5 Stapleton Leics
344 C6 Stapleton N York
383 G2 Stapleton N York
234 B4 Stapleton Shrops
66 D5 Stapleton Somset
43 G5 Stapley Somset
195 G2 Staploe Beds
161 F1 Staplow Herefs
501 F4 Star Fife
153 E3 Star Pembks
84 D3 Star Somset
356 C3 Starbeck N York
368 C5 Starbotton N York
20 D1 Starcross Devon
215 E5 Stareton Warwks
405 E2 Stargate Gatesd
134 B4 Star Hill Mons
294 C3 Starkholmes Derbys
325 H2 Starling Bury
171 G3 Starlings Green Essex
58 C4 Starr's Green E Susx
225 H3 Starston Norfk
13 E4 Start Devon
382 B1 Startforth Dur
171 H5 Start Hill Essex
111 G3 Startley Wilts
142 C2 Startop's End Bucks
110 D2 Starveall S Glos
97 F5 Starvecrow Kent
101 E4 Statenborough Kent
310 D2 Statham Warrtn
66 B4 Stathe Somset
277 G3 Stathern Leics
399 G5 Station Hill Cumb
396 B2 Station Town Dur
248 D5 Statland Common Norfk
195 G1 Staughton Green Cambs
195 G2 Staughton Highway Cambs
195 G2 Staughton Moor Cambs
134 D2 Staunton Gloucs
297 F6 Staunton in the Vale Notts
185 G2 Staunton on Arrow Herefs
185 G5 Staunton on Wye Herefs
355 H3 Staupes N York
379 E5 Staveley Cumb
315 E5 Staveley Derbys
356 D2 Staveley N York
365 E2 Staveley-in-Cartmel Cumb
19 G5 Staverton Devon
162 C5 Staverton Gloucs
192 B2 Staverton Nhants
87 F2 Staverton Wilts
65 G4 Stawell Somset
43 E3 Stawley Somset
589 K6 Staxigoe Highld
374 C4 Staxton N York
205 E2 Staylittle Cerdgn
206 D1 Staylittle Powys
351 E6 Staynall Lancs
296 D4 Staythorpe Notts
355 F5 Stead Brad
135 E1 Steam Mills Gloucs
369 E5 Stean N York
67 F2 Steanbow Somset
372 B5 Stearsby N York
65 E2 Steart Somset
67 F4 Steart Somset
172 D5 Stebbing Essex
172 D5 Stebbing Green Essex
214 A2 Stechford Birm
80 C2 Stede Quarter Kent
74 D5 Stedham W Susx
403 G3 Steel Nthumb
428 D3 Steel Nthumb
314 C2 Steel Bank Sheff
78 C3 Steel Cross E Susx
486 D1 Steelend Fife
439 G6 Steele Road Border
439 G6 Steeleroad-End Border
362 D6 Steel Green Cumb
270 C2 Steel Heath Shrops
186 C3 Steen's Bridge Herefs
74 A4 Steep Hants
37 E5 Steephill IoW
341 G5 Steep Lane Calder
33 G3 Steeple Dorset
148 B4 Steeple Essex
87 G3 Steeple Ashton Wilts
166 A4 Steeple Aston Oxon
165 G4 Steeple Barton Oxon
172 D1 Steeple Bumpstead Essex
167 E4 Steeple Claydon Bucks
219 G3 Steeple Gidding Cambs
70 A2 Steeple Langford Wilts
196 C6 Steeple Morden Cambs
74 A4 Steep Marsh Hants
235 F3 Steeraway Wrekin
354 D6 Steeton Brad
542 D5 Stein Highld
599 J8 Steinis W Isls
559 H1 Steinmanhill Abers
405 E2 Stella Gatesd
82 B1 Stelling Minnis Kent
107 E2 Stelvio Newpt
66 C5 Stembridge Somset
102 C3 Stembridge Swans
588 F4 Stemster Highld
8 C2 Stenalees Cnwll
43 E5 Stenhill Devon
487 H5 Stenhouse C Edin
435 F6 Stenhouse D & G
485 H3 Stenhousemuir Falk
319 H3 Stenigot Lincs
4 C1 Stennack Cnwll
600 D2 Stenness Ork
606 B2 Stenness Shet
543 H3 Stenscholl Highld
602 D6 Stenso Ork
275 E4 Stenson Derbys
606 E7 Stenswall Shet
490 B5 Stenton E Loth
501 E5 Stenton Fife
43 F6 Stentwood Devon
278 A2 Stenwith Lincs
599 H8 Steòrnabhagh W Isls
126 C3 Stepaside Pembks
207 H2 Stepaside Powys
119 H3 Stepney Gt Lon
312 B2 Stepping Hill Stockp
169 E2 Steppingley Beds
484 C6 Stepps N Lans
313 F6 Sterndale Moor Derbys
202 D2 Sternfield Suffk
88 B3 Stert Wilts
34 B2 Sterte Poole
198 C3 Stetchworth Cambs
170 B5 Stevenage Herts
53 F4 Steven's Crouch E Susx
444 C1 Stevenston N Ayrs
40 A4 Stevenstone Devon
91 E5 Steventon Hants
114 D1 Steventon Oxon
210 C5 Steventon Shrops
198 C6 Steventon End Essex
194 D4 Stevington Beds
145 F3 Stewards Essex
169 E1 Stewartby Beds
456 D3 Stewarton Ag & B
410 D3 Stewarton D & G
466 B5 Stewarton E Ayrs
168 B4 Stewkley Bucks
168 A4 Stewkley Dean Bucks
44 C4 Stewley Somset
320 C2 Stewton Lincs
37 G3 Steyne Cross IoW
55 E2 Steyning W Susx
125 F3 Steynton Pembks
38 B5 Stibb Cnwll
254 C2 Stibbard Norfk
39 F5 Stibb Cross Devon
89 F2 Stibb Green Wilts
243 F5 Stibbington Cambs
452 D2 Stichill Border
8 B3 Sticker Cnwll
300 C3 Stickford Lincs
96 C6 Stick Hill Kent
25 F4 Sticklepath Devon
60 D5 Sticklepath Devon
44 C5 Sticklepath Somset
63 G4 Sticklepath Somset
67 F2 Sticklinch Somset
171 G3 Stickling Green Essex
300 B3 Stickney Lincs
260 C3 Stiffkey Norfk
187 G5 Stifford's Bridge Herefs
98 D2 Stiff Street Kent
66 D1 Stileway Somset
344 D1 Stillingfleet N York
371 H6 Stillington N York
395 H5 Stillington S on T
219 H2 Stilton Cambs
135 G5 Stinchcombe Gloucs
32 C1 Stinsford Dorset
233 F4 Stiperstones Shrops
213 G3 Stirchley Birm
235 G3 Stirchley Wrekin
561 H1 Stirling Abers
498 C6 Stirling Stirlg
196 A1 Stirtloe Cambs
354 C4 Stirton N York
173 G5 Stisted Essex
113 F6 Stitchcombe Wilts
187 H4 Stitchin's Hill Worcs
4 D1 Stithians Cnwll
566 B2 Stittenham Highld
215 E4 Stivichall Covtry
299 F1 Stixwould Lincs
309 F5 Stoak Ches
430 C3 Stobhill Nthumb
430 D2 Stobhillgate Nthumb
446 C2 Stobieside S Lans
449 G2 Stobo Border
449 G2 Stobo Castle Border
33 G2 Stoborough Dorset
33 G2 Stoborough Green Dorset
439 G3 Stobs Castle Border
443 G6 Stobswood Nthumb
146 D5 Stock Essex
353 H5 Stock Lancs
85 E2 Stock N Som
330 C3 Stockbridge Donc
71 H2 Stockbridge Hants
53 F4 Stockbridge W Susx
323 H6 Stockbridge Village Knows
447 F2 Stockbriggs S Lans
98 C2 Stockbury Kent
114 C6 Stockcross W Berk
400 C6 Stockdalewath Cumb
136 B3 Stockend Gloucs
99 F4 Stocker's Head Kent
241 H5 Stockerston Leics
557 G3 Stockethill C Aber
213 H3 Stockfield Birm
189 E3 Stock Green Worcs
52 C3 Stockheath Hants
224 C6 Stock Hill Suffk
331 G3 Stockholes Turbary N Linc
161 E3 Stocking Herefs
215 E1 Stockingford Warwks
172 B2 Stocking Green Essex
171 F4 Stocking Pelham Herts
28 D2 Stockland Devon
64 D3 Stockland Bristol Somset
213 G1 Stockland Green Birm
97 E6 Stockland Green Kent
26 C1 Stockleigh English Devon
26 D2 Stockleigh Pomeroy Devon
112 B6 Stockley Wilts
44 D4 Stocklinch Somset
312 B1 Stockport Stockp
328 D5 Stocksbridge Sheff
404 C2 Stocksfield Nthumb
97 E5 Stocks Green Kent
173 G5 Stockstreet Essex
186 C2 Stockton Herefs
250 D6 Stockton Norfk
233 E4 Stockton Shrops
235 G5 Stockton Shrops
191 G2 Stockton Warwks
69 G2 Stockton Wilts
235 H1 Stockton Wrekin
292 B4 Stockton Brook Staffs
310 C2 Stockton Heath Warrtn
396 A6 Stockton-on-Tees S on T
187 G1 Stockton on Teme Worcs
358 C3 Stockton on the Forest York
233 E4 Stocktonwood Shrops
27 F2 Stockwell Devon
136 D2 Stockwell Gloucs
119 G4 Stockwell Gt Lon
236 C4 Stockwell End Wolves
273 G5 Stockwell Heath Staffs
67 F5 Stockwitch Cross Somset
110 A6 Stockwood Bristl
30 D1 Stockwood Dorset
189 F3 Stock Wood Worcs
110 A6 Stockwood Vale BaNES
351 G3 Stodday Lancs
100 D3 Stodmarsh Kent
261 E4 Stody Norfk
578 D4 Stoer Highld
45 H5 Stoford Somset
70 B2 Stoford Wilts
43 E6 Stoford Water Devon
64 A4 Stogumber Somset
64 D3 Stogursey Somset
11 E2 Stoke C Plym
215 F4 Stoke Covtry
38 B3 Stoke Devon
52 C4 Stoke Hants
90 C4 Stoke Hants
122 C4 Stoke Medway
201 G6 Stoke Suffk
30 B2 Stoke Abbott Dorset
217 G2 Stoke Albany Nhants
215 F4 Stoke Aldermoor Covtry
225 F5 Stoke Ash Suffk
276 D1 Stoke Bardolph Notts
187 F2 Stoke Bliss Worcs
193 F4 Stoke Bruerne Nhants
199 E6 Stoke by Clare Suffk
174 C2 Stoke-by-Nayland Suffk
27 E3 Stoke Canon Devon
72 C2 Stoke Charity Hants
17 E4 Stoke Climsland Cnwll
72 C5 Stoke Common Hants
187 E4 Stoke Cross Herefs
94 C3 Stoke D'Abernon Surrey
219 E2 Stoke Doyle Nhants
242 B5 Stoke Dry Rutlnd
161 E1 Stoke Edith Herefs
238 B5 Stoke End Warwks
70 A4 Stoke Farthing Wilts
246 D4 Stoke Ferry Norfk
13 F3 Stoke Fleming Devon
33 F2 Stokeford Dorset
13 F1 Stoke Gabriel Devon
109 H3 Stoke Gifford S Glos
239 F5 Stoke Golding Leics
194 A5 Stoke Goldington M Keyn
210 D3 Stokegorse Shrops
117 G3 Stoke Green Bucks
317 E4 Stokeham Notts
168 B4 Stoke Hammond Bucks
215 F3 Stoke Heath Covtry
271 E4 Stoke Heath Shrops
212 D6 Stoke Heath Worcs
27 E4 Stoke Hill Devon
187 E5 Stoke Hill Herefs
250 A4 Stoke Holy Cross Norfk
20 C3 Stokeinteignhead Devon
187 E5 Stoke Lacy Herefs
187 E4 Stoke Lane Herefs
166 C4 Stoke Lyne Oxon
142 A3 Stoke Mandeville Bucks
141 G5 Stokenchurch Bucks
119 G2 Stoke Newington Gt Lon
13 E4 Stokenham Devon
271 E4 Stoke on Tern Shrops
292 B5 Stoke-on-Trent C Stke
162 D4 Stoke Orchard Gloucs
175 F1 Stoke Park Suffk
117 G3 Stoke Poges Bucks
213 E6 Stoke Pound Worcs
186 C3 Stoke Prior Herefs
188 D1 Stoke Prior Worcs
61 F4 Stoke Rivers Devon
278 C4 Stoke Rochford Lincs
115 H3 Stoke Row Oxon
44 C2 Stoke St Gregory Somset
44 B3 Stoke St Mary Somset
86 B5 Stoke St Michael Somset
210 D3 Stoke St Milborough Shrops
209 H3 Stokesay Shrops
251 E2 Stokesby Norfk
385 E3 Stokesley N York
66 D6 Stoke sub Hamdon Somset
141 E5 Stoke Talmage Oxon
68 B4 Stoke Trister Somset
47 E3 Stoke Wake Dorset
30 B2 Stoke Water Dorset
189 E1 Stoke Wharf Worcs
430 A2 Stokoe Nthumb
64 D2 Stolford Somset
146 B4 Stondon Massey Essex
141 G2 Stone Bucks
135 F5 Stone Gloucs
121 E5 Stone Kent
315 H2 Stone Rothm
67 F3 Stone Somset
272 D3 Stone Staffs
212 C5 Stone Worcs
245 G6 Stonea Cambs
234 B6 Stoneacton Shrops
84 D4 Stone Allerton Somset
85 H4 Ston Easton Somset
188 D5 Stonebow Worcs
123 E2 Stonebridge Essex
119 E3 Stonebridge Gt Lon
84 C3 Stonebridge N Som
224 B1 Stonebridge Norfk
214 C3 Stonebridge Solhll
94 D5 Stonebridge Surrey
99 E5 Stonebridge Green Kent
295 E3 Stonebroom Derbys
468 C6 Stonebyres Holdings S Lans
342 B4 Stone Chair Calder
325 H3 Stoneclough Bolton
61 E3 Stonecombe Devon
57 G4 Stone Cross E Susx
78 C4 Stone Cross E Susx
79 E3 Stone Cross E Susx
78 C2 Stone Cross Kent
81 F2 Stone Cross Kent
101 F4 Stone Cross Kent
237 F6 Stone Cross Sandw
79 F3 Stonecrouch Kent
439 H3 Stonedge Border
109 E5 Stone-Edge Batch N Som
348 B3 Stoneferry C KuH
467 G3 Stonefield S Lans
272 C3 Stonefield Staffs
79 F4 Stonegate E Susx
386 C3 Stonegate N York
372 B4 Stonegrave N York
314 D5 Stonegravels Derbys
83 E1 Stonehall Kent
188 C5 Stonehall Worcs
428 B4 Stonehaugh Nthumb
541 G2 Stonehaven Abers
354 B6 Stone Head N York
273 E2 Stone Heath Staffs
331 E3 Stone Hill Donc
81 G2 Stone Hill Kent
99 E5 Stone Hill Kent
110 A5 Stone Hill S Glos
93 G2 Stonehill Surrey
51 E4 Stonehills Hants
11 E3 Stonehouse C Plym
367 F2 Stone House Cumb
136 B3 Stonehouse Gloucs
402 B3 Stonehouse Nthumb
468 B5 Stonehouse S Lans
273 E1 Stonehouses Staffs
80 D4 Stone in Oxney Kent
95 E2 Stoneleigh Surrey
215 E5 Stoneleigh Warwks
290 C4 Stoneley Green Ches
195 G1 Stonely Cambs
189 E3 Stonepits Worcs
77 G2 Stonequarry W Susx
400 C5 Stone Raise Cumb
73 H4 Stoner Hill Hants
277 H5 Stonesby Leics
139 F1 Stonesfield Oxon
176 C4 Stones Green Essex
97 E4 Stone Street Kent
174 C2 Stone Street Suffk
226 D3 Stone Street Suffk
81 F2 Stonestreet Green Kent
377 H2 Stonethwaite Cumb
191 H4 Stoneton Warwks
121 E5 Stonewood Kent
187 G6 Stoneyard Green Herefs
488 C5 Stoneybank E Loth
593 C11 Stoneybridge W Isls
469 F2 Stoneyburn W Loth
20 B4 Stoneycombe Devon
309 E1 Stoneycroft Lpool
49 H2 Stoney Cross Hants
326 C2 Stoneyfield Rochdl
295 E5 Stoneyford Derbys
42 D6 Stoneyford Devon
561 F2 Stoneygate Abers
240 D4 Stoneygate C Leic
213 E5 Stoney Hill Worcs
148 B5 Stoneyhills Essex
340 C3 Stoneyholme Lancs
415 E6 Stoneykirk D & G
210 D4 Stoneylane Shrops
313 H5 Stoney Middleton Derbys
342 A5 Stoney Royd Calder
240 A6 Stoney Stanton Leics
68 B3 Stoney Stoke Somset
67 H2 Stoney Stratton Somset
233 G3 Stoney Stretton Shrops
557 F2 Stoneywood C Aber
485 F3 Stoneywood Falk
609 G4 Stonganess Shet
201 F3 Stonham Aspal Suffk
237 G4 Stonnall Staffs
116 B2 Stonor Oxon
241 F5 Stonton Wyville Leics
71 F4 Stony Batter Hants
604 a3 Stonybreck Shet
39 H2 Stony Cross Devon
186 C1 Stony Cross Herefs
187 G5 Stony Cross Herefs
296 D6 Stony Dale Notts
566 B2 Stonyfield Highld
50 B1 Stonyford Hants
406 A4 Stony Gate Sundld
142 B5 Stony Green Bucks
404 D4 Stony Heap Dur
91 F3 Stony Heath Hants
295 F1 Stony Houghton Derbys
29 G2 Stony Knaps Dorset
40 A2 Stonyland Devon
86 C3 Stony Littleton BaNES
71 G4 Stonymarsh Hants
167 G1 Stony Stratford M Keyn
42 B4 Stoodleigh Devon
151 F2 Stop-and-Call Pembks
314 B2 Stopes Sheff
44 A6 Stopgate Devon
75 G6 Stopham W Susx
353 G5 Stopper Lane Lancs
169 G5 Stopsley Luton
14 C3 Stoptide Cnwll
308 D3 Storeton Wirral
355 E4 Storiths N York
512 D4 Stormontfield P & K
87 E5 Stormore Wilts
599 H8 Stornoway W Isls
187 G5 Storridge Herefs
54 C2 Storrington W Susx
378 C6 Storrs Cumb
314 B2 Storrs Sheff
171 G5 Stortford Park Herts
365 G4 Storth Cumb
358 D6 Storwood E R Yk
568 C1 Stotfield Moray
170 B2 Stotfold Beds
211 F3 Stottesdon Shrops
240 D4 Stoughton Leics
93 G4 Stoughton Surrey
53 E2 Stoughton W Susx
84 D5 Stoughton Cross Somset
188 D5 Stoulton Worcs
212 C3 Stourbridge Dudley
47 G3 Stourpaine Dorset
212 A5 Stourport-on-Severn Worcs
68 C5 Stour Provost Dorset
68 D5 Stour Row Dorset
343 F3 Stourton Leeds
212 C2 Stourton Staffs
164 D2 Stourton Warwks
68 C3 Stourton Wilts
46 D1 Stourton Caundle Dorset
165 E2 Stourton Hill Warwks
66 C3 Stout Somset
603 J4 Stove Ork
605 H6 Stove Shet
609 J2 Stove Shet
227 E3 Stoven Suffk
472 B6 Stow Border
317 G3 Stow Lincs
246 C3 Stow Bardolph Norfk
248 C5 Stow Bedon Norfk
246 B3 Stowbridge Norfk
198 A2 Stow cum Quy Cambs
134 D3 Stowe Gloucs
185 E5 Stowe Herefs
243 G2 Stowe Lincs
209 F5 Stowe Shrops
237 H3 Stowe Staffs
273 F4 Stowe-by-Chartley Staffs
134 D3 Stowe Green Gloucs
137 G2 Stowell Gloucs
68 A5 Stowell Somset
85 G3 Stowey BaNES
134 D1 Stowfield Gloucs
24 B3 Stowford Devon
24 B5 Stowford Devon
28 B5 Stowford Devon
38 C5 Stowford Devon
40 C2 Stowford Devon
61 F3 Stowford Devon
244 A2 Stowgate Lincs
224 C6 Stowlangtoft Suffk
236 D5 Stow Lawn Wolves
219 G5 Stow Longa Cambs
147 G5 Stow Maries Essex
200 D3 Stowmarket Suffk
164 B4 Stow-on-the-Wold Gloucs
107 E2 Stow Park Newpt
81 H1 Stowting Kent
82 B2 Stowting Common Kent
81 H1 Stowting Court Kent
201 E3 Stowupland Suffk
464 A2 Straad Ag & B
540 C1 Strachan Abers
494 B4 Strachur Ag & B
226 A5 Stradbroke Suffk
199 E4 Stradishall Suffk
246 D4 Stradsett Norfk
297 G4 Stragglethorpe Lincs
113 H5 Straight Soley Wilts
471 E1 Straiton Mdloth
433 E4 Straiton S Ayrs
560 C5 Straloch Abers
524 F3 Straloch P & K
273 G2 Stramshall Staffs
135 G2 Strand Gloucs
119 F3 Strand Gt Lon
362 D5 Strands Cumb
322 e7 Strang IoM
326 B5 Strangeways Manch
160 D4 Strangford Herefs
88 D6 Strangways Wilts
557 F5 Stranog Abers
415 E4 Stranraer D & G
182 A1 Strata Florida Cerdgn
116 B6 Stratfield Mortimer W Berk
92 A2 Stratfield Saye Hants
92 A3 Stratfield Turgis Hants
196 A5 Stratford Beds
120 A3 Stratford Gt Lon
162 C2 Stratford Worcs
120 A3 Stratford New Town Gt Lon
202 C2 Stratford St Andrew Suffk
174 D3 Stratford St Mary Suffk
70 C3 Stratford sub Castle Wilts
70 B4 Stratford Tony Wilts
190 C4 Stratford-upon-Avon Warwks
572 F8 Strath Highld
499 E1 Strathallan Castle P & K
532 E4 Strathan Highld
547 G2 Strathan Highld
578 E5 Strathan Highld
586 C4 Strathan Highld
586 D4 Strathan Skerray Highld
467 H6 Strathaven S Lans
484 B4 Strathblane Stirlg
467 E2 Strathbungo C Glas
574 C3 Strathcanaird Highld
547 G1 Strathcarron Highld
505 K4 Strathcoil Ag & B
588 E5 Strathcoul Highld
554 B2 Strathdon Abers
502 D1 Strathkinness Fife
500 D3 Strathmiglo Fife
565 H5 Strathpeffer Highld
564 F2 Strathrannoch Highld
524 C5 Strathtay P & K
461 E2 Strathwhillan N Ayrs
587 H3 Strathy Highld
496 D1 Strathyre Stirlg
23 E1 Stratton Cnwll
31 E4 Stratton Dorset
137 F4 Stratton Gloucs
166 D4 Stratton Audley Oxon
86 B4 Stratton-on-the-Fosse Somset
113 E2 Stratton St Margaret Swindn
249 H6 Stratton St Michael Norfk
255 H3 Stratton Strawless Norfk
503 E2 Stravithie Fife
365 E2 Strawberry Bank Cumb
78 D2 Strawberry Hill E Susx
118 D5 Strawberry Hill Gt Lon
344 A5 Strawberry Hill Wakefd
56 B1 Streat E Susx
119 G5 Streatham Gt Lon
119 G5 Streatham Hill Gt Lon
119 F5 Streatham Park Gt Lon
119 F5 Streatham Vale Gt Lon
169 F4 Streatley Beds
115 F3 Streatley W Berk
380 A3 Street Cumb
28 C5 Street Devon
351 H4 Street Lancs
386 B4 Street N York
29 G1 Street Somset
66 D2 Street Somset
44 B5 Street Ash Somset
215 G3 Street Ashton Warwks
269 F2 Street Dinas Shrops
73 E5 Street End Hants
100 B5 Street End Kent
53 F5 Street End W Susx
405 F3 Street Gate Gatesd
238 A2 Streethay Staffs
343 G5 Streethouse Wakefd
357 G5 Street Houses N York
383 H5 Streetlam N York
294 D5 Street Lane Derbys
237 G5 Streetly Birm
270 A2 Street Lydan Wrexhm
198 C5 Streetly End Cambs
67 G2 Street on the Fosse Somset
210 A2 Strefford Shrops
276 B1 Strelley Notts
358 B3 Strensall York
162 D1 Strensham Worcs
41 G5 Stretch Down Devon
84 A6 Stretcholt Somset
13 E3 Strete Devon
27 G3 Strete Raleigh Devon
186 A3 Stretford Herefs
186 C3 Stretford Herefs
326 A6 Stretford Traffd
171 G2 Strethall Essex
221 H5 Stretham Cambs
53 F3 Strettington W Susx
289 F4 Stretton Ches
294 D2 Stretton Derbys
242 D1 Stretton Rutlnd
236 C2 Stretton Staffs
274 C4 Stretton Staffs
310 C3 Stretton Warrtn
239 E2 Stretton en le Field Leics
187 E6 Stretton Grandison Herefs
233 G2 Stretton Heath Shrops
215 G5 Stretton-on-Dunsmore Warwks
164 C2 Stretton-on-Fosse Warwks
186 B6 Stretton Sugwas Herefs
215 G3 Stretton under Fosse Warwks
234 D5 Stretton Westwood Shrops
571 G4 Strichen Abers
312 C2 Strines Stockp
64 C3 Stringston Somset
194 B2 Strixton Nhants
134 D5 Stroat Gloucs
85 F2 Strode N Som
546 F3 Stromeferry Highld
546 E2 Stromemore Highld
600 C3 Stromness Ork
533 K6 Stronaba Highld
499 H3 Stronachie P & K
496 A2 Stronachlachar Stirlg
520 F1 Stronchreggan Highld
579 H6 Stronchrubie Highld
482 A3 Strone Ag & B
533 H6 Strone Highld
535 K2 Strone Highld
549 J4 Strone Highld
482 C5 Strone Inver
518 D4 Stronganrb Ag & B
507 L4 Stronmilchan Ag & B
417 E4 Stronord D & G
519 K3 Strontian Highld
481 H2 Stronvochlan Ag & B
80 C3 Strood Kent
121 H6 Strood Medway
95 E5 Strood Green Surrey
75 G5 Strood Green W Susx
76 B3 Strood Green W Susx
403 H3 Strothers Dale Nthumb
136 C3 Stroud Gloucs
73 H5 Stroud Hants
75 E3 Stroud Surrey
49 E6 Strouden Bmouth
122 D1 Stroud Green Essex

136 B3 Stroud Green Gloucs
482 B3 Stroul Ag & B
278 C3 Stroxton Lincs
38 D4 Stroxworthy Devon
544 E2 Struan Highld
524 B2 Struan P & K
544 E2 Struanmore Highld
321 E3 Strubby Lincs
187 H1 Structon's Heath Worcs
280 C2 Strugg's Hill Lincs
250 D3 Strumpshaw Norfk
468 B5 Strutherhill S Lans
592 F4 Struth Mòr W Isls
548 F1 Struy Highld
302 B3 Stryd IoA
302 D4 Stryd y Facsen IoA
288 C5 Stryt-Issa Wrexhm
571 H6 Stuartfield Abers
257 E5 Stubb Norfk
52 C3 Stubbermere W Susx
237 F4 Stubber's Green Wsall
116 D3 Stubbings W & M
225 E5 Stubbing's Green Suffk
51 F4 Stubbington Hants
338 D1 Stubbins Lancs
340 B6 Stubbins Lancs
376 D5 Stubble Green Cumb
115 F4 Stubbles W Berk
81 E2 Stubb's Cross Kent
250 D5 Stubbs Green Norfk
340 D5 Stubbylee Park Lancs
47 H2 Stubhampton Dorset
324 D4 Stubshaw Cross Wigan
297 G5 Stubton Lincs
273 G2 Stubwood Staffs
495 G4 Stuckgowan Ag & B
49 F2 Stuckton Hants
101 F6 Studdal Kent
100 C2 Studd Hill Kent
367 G5 Studfold N York
291 E2 Stud Green Ches
117 E4 Stud Green W & M
143 E1 Studham Beds
34 B4 Studland Dorset
189 G2 Studley Warwks
111 H5 Studley Wilts
189 G2 Studley Common Warwks
141 G5 Studley Green Bucks
87 E3 Studley Green Wilts
370 B5 Studley Roger N York
370 B5 Studley Royal N York
163 G3 Stumps Cross Gloucs
222 A4 Stuntney Cambs
57 G2 Stunts Green E Susx
272 B3 Sturbridge Staffs
87 E6 Sturford Wilts
317 G2 Sturgate Lincs
198 D6 Sturmer Essex
47 E2 Sturminster Common Dorset
48 B5 Sturminster Marshall Dorset
47 E2 Sturminster Newton Dorset
100 C3 Sturry Kent
38 B5 Stursdon Cnwll
332 D4 Sturton N Linc
317 G3 Sturton by Stow Lincs
317 E3 Sturton le Steeple Notts
225 F4 Stuston Suffk
344 B1 Stutton N York
175 F3 Stutton Suffk
311 G3 Styal Ches
97 E3 Styants Bottom Kent
271 E2 Styche Hall Shrops
339 G2 Stydd Lancs
316 B1 Styrrup Notts
599 L2 Suainebost W Isls
599 K8 Suardail W Isls
553 J1 Succoth Abers
495 F3 Succoth Ag & B
187 G4 Suckley Worcs
187 G4 Suckley Green Worcs
187 G4 Suckley Knowl Worcs
172 B4 Sucksted Green Essex
218 D3 Sudborough Nhants
203 E4 Sudbourne Suffk
298 B6 Sudbrook Lincs
109 F2 Sudbrook Mons
318 C4 Sudbrooke Lincs
274 B3 Sudbury Derbys
118 D2 Sudbury Gt Lon
173 H1 Sudbury Suffk
326 C2 Sudden Rochdl
136 D3 Sudgrove Gloucs
374 B1 Suffield N York
256 A3 Suffield Norfk
272 A3 Sugnall Staffs
160 A1 Sugwas Pool Herefs
545 K2 Suisnish Highld
545 K6 Suisnish Highld
542 F6 Suladale Highld
599 L7 Sulaisiadar W Isls
322 f3 Sulby IoM
192 C5 Sulgrave Nhants
405 H3 Sulgrave Sundld
115 G5 Sulham W Berk
115 G6 Sulhamstead W Berk
115 G6 Sulhamstead Abbots W Berk
115 G6 Sulhamstead Bannister Upper End W Berk
54 C2 Sullington W Susx
54 C2 Sullington Warren W Susx
606 D3 Sullom Shet
106 C6 Sully V Glam
605 H9 Sumburgh Shet
355 G2 Summerbridge N York
7 G2 Summercourt Cnwll
101 E4 Summerfield Kent
259 E4 Summerfield Norfk
212 B5 Summerfield Worcs
213 F2 Summerfield Park Birm
348 B3 Summergangs C KuH
116 B1 Summer Heath Bucks
557 F3 Summer Hill C Aber
57 F3 Summer Hill E Susx
107 F2 Summerhill Newpt
126 D3 Summerhill Pembks
237 E6 Summer Hill Sandw
237 G3 Summerhill Staffs
212 B4 Summerhill Worcs
271 G6 Summerhill Wrekin
288 D4 Summerhill Wrekin
394 D6 Summerhouse Darltn
365 H2 Summerlands Cumb
45 G4 Summerlands Somset
108 D3 Summerleaze Newpt
314 D4 Summerley Derbys
355 F4 Summerscales N York
53 F3 Summersdale W Susx
326 A2 Summerseat Bury
484 B5 Summerston C Glas
167 E5 Summerstown Bucks
140 B3 Summertown Oxon
326 D3 Summit Oldham
326 B2 Summit Rochdl
341 E6 Summit Rochdl
380 A3 Sunbiggin Cumb
364 C5 Sunbrick Cumb
118 B6 Sunbury Surrey
118 B5 Sunbury Common Surrey
135 F6 Sundayshill S Glos
422 D3 Sundaywell D & G
389 E2 Sunderland Cumb
351 F3 Sunderland Lancs

406 C3 Sunderland Sundld
395 F2 Sunderland Bridge Dur
450 C4 Sundhope Border
169 F4 Sundon Park Luton
120 B5 Sundridge Gt Lon
96 C3 Sundridge Kent
327 E5 Sun Green Tamesd
137 H4 Sunhill Gloucs
122 C3 Sunken Marsh Essex
349 E6 Sunk Island E R Yk
117 G6 Sunningdale W & M
117 F6 Sunninghill W & M
140 A4 Sunningwell Oxon
394 C2 Sunniside Dur
405 E3 Sunniside Gatesd
406 A4 Sunniside Sundld
326 B3 Sunny Bank Bury
339 H3 Sunny Bower Bl w D
394 D3 Sunnybrow Dur
330 B3 Sunnyfields Donc
275 E3 Sunny Hill C Derb
339 G5 Sunnyhurst Bl w D
498 B5 Sunnylaw Stirlg
140 B3 Sunnymead Oxon
117 H4 Sunnymeads W & M
146 D6 Sunnymede Essex
330 A6 Sunnyside Rothm
77 G2 Sunnyside W Susx
185 F3 Sunset Herefs
89 F4 Sunton Wilts
94 D1 Surbiton Gt Lon
280 C4 Surfleet Lincs
280 C4 Surfleet Seas End Lincs
250 C3 Surlingham Norfk
173 H5 Surrex Essex
246 A6 Suspension Bridge Norfk
261 G4 Sustead Norfk
332 A4 Susworth Lincs
38 D5 Sutcombe Devon
38 D5 Sutcombemill Devon
507 G1 Sutherlands Grove Ag & B
249 E5 Sutterby Lincs
566 E3 Sutors of Cromarty Highld
320 C5 Sutterby Lincs
280 C2 Sutterton Lincs
280 C3 Sutterton Dowdyke Lincs
527 G4 Suttieside Angus
196 B5 Sutton Beds
117 H4 Sutton Bucks
243 F5 Sutton C Pete
221 F4 Sutton Cambs
12 C4 Sutton Devon
330 C2 Sutton Donc
56 D5 Sutton E Susx
95 F2 Sutton Gt Lon
101 F6 Sutton Kent
297 G4 Sutton Lincs
344 B4 Sutton N York
256 B5 Sutton Norfk
277 G2 Sutton Notts
139 G3 Sutton Oxon
125 F1 Sutton Pembks
211 G2 Sutton Shrops
234 B2 Sutton Shrops
269 G4 Sutton Shrops
271 F3 Sutton Shrops
67 G3 Sutton Somset
324 C6 Sutton St Hel
271 H5 Sutton Staffs
202 C5 Sutton Suffk
53 H1 Sutton W Susx
94 C5 Sutton Abinger Surrey
120 D5 Sutton at Hone Kent
217 G1 Sutton Bassett Nhants
111 G4 Sutton Benger Wilts
45 G1 Sutton Bingham Somset
276 B4 Sutton Bonington Notts
281 G5 Sutton Bridge Lincs
239 G4 Sutton Cheney Leics
237 G5 Sutton Coldfield Birm
281 F4 Sutton Corner Lincs
140 B6 Sutton Courtenay Oxon
281 F5 Sutton Crosses Lincs
316 C3 Sutton cum Lound Notts
54 A1 Sutton End W Susx
212 B4 Sutton Farm Worcs
295 G3 Sutton Forest Side Notts
221 F4 Sutton Gault Cambs
370 B5 Sutton Grange N York
309 E4 Sutton Green Ches
93 G4 Sutton Green Surrey
289 F5 Sutton Green Wrexhm
235 G4 Sutton Hall Shrops
324 B6 Sutton Heath St Hel
48 C3 Sutton Holms Dorset
370 C4 Sutton Howgrave N York
295 F3 Sutton in Ashfield Notts
354 D6 Sutton-in-Craven N York
348 B3 Sutton Ings C KuH
240 B6 Sutton in the Elms Leics
186 C5 Sutton Lakes Herefs
312 B5 Sutton Lane Ends Ches
310 A1 Sutton Leach St Hel
235 G4 Sutton Maddock Shrops
65 G4 Sutton Mallet Somset
69 G4 Sutton Mandeville Wilts
309 H1 Sutton Manor St Hel
186 C6 Sutton Marsh Herefs
354 D6 Sutton Mill N York
67 G5 Sutton Montis Somset
348 B3 Sutton-on-Hull C KuH
321 F3 Sutton on Sea Lincs
357 H2 Sutton-on-the-Forest N York
274 C3 Sutton on the Hill Derbys
297 E1 Sutton on Trent Notts
32 C3 Sutton Poyntz Dorset
69 G4 Sutton Row Wilts
245 E2 Sutton St Edmund Lincs
281 E6 Sutton St James Lincs
186 C5 Sutton St Michael Herefs
186 C5 Sutton St Nicholas Herefs
315 E6 Sutton Scarsdale Derbys
72 C2 Sutton Scotney Hants
202 C6 Sutton Street Suffk
165 G2 Sutton-under-Brailes Warwks
371 F3 Sutton-under-Whitestonecliffe N York
358 D5 Sutton upon Derwent E R Yk
98 C5 Sutton Valence Kent
69 E1 Sutton Veny Wilts
47 G1 Sutton Waldron Dorset
310 A4 Sutton Weaver Ches
85 G3 Sutton Wick BaNES
140 A6 Sutton Wick Oxon
320 C4 Swaby Lincs
274 D6 Swadlincote Derbys
247 F3 Swaffham Norfk
198 B2 Swaffham Bulbeck Cambs
198 B2 Swaffham Prior Cambs
256 B3 Swafield Norfk
58 C2 Swaile's Green E Susx
384 D4 Swainby N York
342 C2 Swain House Brad
160 B1 Swainshill Herefs
249 H4 Swainsthorpe Norfk
110 C6 Swainswick BaNES
329 F4 Swaithe Barns
165 F2 Swalcliffe Oxon
100 B2 Swalecliffe Kent
330 D1 Swallow Nest
362 C3 Swallowhurst Cumb

333 H4 Swallow Lincs
318 B6 Swallow Beck Lincs
69 G4 Swallowcliffe Wilts
92 B2 Swallowfield Wokham
19 H5 Swallowfields Devon
315 E3 Swallownest Rothm
146 C5 Swallows Cross Essex
405 F2 Swalwell Gatesd
90 C4 Swampton Hants
34 B5 Swanage Dorset
271 F1 Swanbach Ches
600 E3 Swanbister Ork
113 E1 Swanborough Swindn
142 C3 Swan Bottom Bucks
167 H4 Swanbourne Bucks
106 C6 Swanbridge V Glam
311 E5 Swan Green Ches
226 B5 Swan Green Suffk
347 E4 Swanland E R Yk
135 F5 Swanley Gloucs
120 D6 Swanley Kent
120 D6 Swanley Village Kent
51 G1 Swanmore Hants
37 F2 Swanmore IoW
239 G1 Swannington Leics
255 F4 Swannington Norfk
318 A5 Swanpool Lincs
121 F4 Swanscombe Kent
103 G3 Swansea Swans
309 F1 Swanside Knows
488 A6 Swanston C Edin
174 A4 Swan Street Essex
256 B4 Swanton Abbott Norfk
256 B4 Swanton Hill Norfk
254 D4 Swanton Morley Norfk
260 D5 Swanton Novers Norfk
98 D3 Swanton Street Kent
213 E1 Swan Village Sandw
295 E4 Swanwick Derbys
51 F3 Swanwick Hants
279 E1 Swarby Lincs
343 G2 Swarcliffe Leeds
249 G4 Swardeston Norfk
609 G8 Swarister Shet
275 F4 Swarkestone Derbys
443 F4 Swarland Nthumb
73 E2 Swarraton Hants
355 E5 Swartha Brad
364 C4 Swarthmoor Cumb
314 D6 Swathwick Derbys
279 G2 Swaton Lincs
220 D6 Swavesey Cambs
49 H5 Sway Hants
278 D5 Swayfield Lincs
50 D1 Swaythling C Sotn
187 F2 Sweet Green Worcs
26 D3 Sweetham Devon
78 C4 Sweethaws E Susx
43 G3 Sweethay Somset
391 E6 Sweetholme Cumb
22 C3 Sweets Cnwll
8 D1 Sweetshouse Cnwll
202 C2 Swefling Suffk
44 D3 Swell Somset
557 F5 Swellhead Abers
73 G3 Swelling Hill Hants
239 F2 Swepstone Leics
165 F3 Swerford Oxon
291 G1 Swettenham Ches
369 G5 Swetton N York
108 D6 Swffryd Blae G
98 D6 Swift's Green Kent
201 G4 Swilland Suffk
338 C3 Swillbrook Lancs
343 G3 Swillington Leeds
40 C2 Swimbridge Devon
61 F5 Swimbridge Newland Devon
138 D2 Swinbrook Oxon
342 D4 Swincliffe Kirk
356 A3 Swincliffe N York
61 G3 Swincombe Devon
353 H4 Swinden N York
297 G2 Swinderby Lincs
162 D4 Swindon Gloucs
212 C1 Swindon Staffs
112 D2 Swindon Swindn
348 B2 Swine E R Yk
345 H5 Swinefleet E R Yk
110 B6 Swineford S Glos
195 E1 Swineshead Beds
280 B1 Swineshead Lincs
280 B1 Swineshead Bridge Lincs
299 G6 Swineside N York
369 E3 Swinethorpe Lincs
317 G6 Swinethorpe Lincs
583 H2 Swiney Highld
388 C2 Swinford Leics
216 C4 Swinford Leics
139 G3 Swinford Oxon
295 F6 Swingate Notts
221 G2 Swingbrow Cambs
82 D2 Swingfield Minnis Kent
82 D2 Swingfield Street Kent
180 D3 Swingleton Green Suffk
265 E2 Swinhill S Lans
468 B5 Swinhill S Lans
455 G4 Swinhoe Nthumb
334 B5 Swinhope Lincs
607 G4 Swining Shet
606 D1 Swinister Shet
368 D2 Swinithwaite N York
161 F1 Swinmore Common Herefs
440 B1 Swinnie Border
342 B1 Swinnow Moor Leeds
293 F5 Swinscoe Staffs
389 F5 Swinside Cumb
440 D1 Swinside Hall Border
440 D1 Swinside Townfoot Border
279 E5 Swinstead Lincs
474 B5 Swinton Border
467 G2 Swinton C Glas
369 H4 Swinton N York
379 G3 Swinton N York
329 G5 Swinton Rothm
325 H4 Swinton Salfd
329 H3 Swinton Bridge Rothm
474 B5 Swintonmill Border
326 A4 Swinton Park Salfd
128 D4 Swiss Valley Carmth
240 C2 Swithland Leics
565 K3 Swordale Highld
576 D5 Swordale Highld
531 L4 Swordland Highld
586 F4 Swordly Highld
310 D3 Sworton Heath Ches
181 G1 Swyddffynnon Cerdgn
116 A1 Swyncombe Oxon
272 B2 Swynnerton Staffs
30 C5 Swyre Dorset
29 E1 Sycamore Devon
152 B2 Sychnant Powys
288 D3 Sychtyn Powys
136 D2 Syde Gloucs
141 F4 Sydenham Gt Lon
65 F4 Sydenham Oxon
17 F3 Sydenham Damerel Devon
259 G5 Syderstone Norfk
31 E3 Sydling St Nicholas Dorset
90 D3 Sydmonton Hants
291 E3 Sydney Ches
296 D5 Syerston Notts
326 C1 Syke Rochdl
330 D1 Sykehouse Donc
352 C4 Sykes Lancs

225 H4 Syleham Suffk
128 D3 Sylen Carmth
607 H5 Symbister Shet
471 H5 Symington Border
445 E3 Symington S Ayrs
448 C2 Symington S Lans
30 A4 Symondsbury Dorset
134 C1 Symonds Yat Herefs
29 G2 Synderford Dorset
180 B4 Synod Inn Cerdgn
451 F5 Synton Border
451 F5 Synton Mains Border
135 H6 Synwell Gloucs
586 E8 Syre Highld
163 F5 Syreford Gloucs
166 D1 Syresham Nhants
240 D2 Syston Leics
278 C1 Syston Lincs
188 B1 Sytchampton Worcs
212 A1 Sytch Ho Green Shrops
271 E5 Sytch Lane Wrekin
193 H1 Sywell Nhants

T

311 E4 Tabley Hill Ches
230 B3 Tabor Gwynd
597 J4 Tabost W Isls
599 L2 Tabost W Isls
191 E2 Tachbrook Mallory Warwks
12 C4 Tacker Street Somset
165 H5 Tacket Wood Devon
598 C8 Tackley Oxon
249 F6 Tacolneston Norfk
357 F6 Tadcaster N York
48 B4 Tadden Dorset
313 F5 Taddington Derbys
163 G3 Taddington Gloucs
39 G4 Taddiport Devon
86 B5 Tadhill Somset
91 G2 Tadley Hants
115 E2 Tadley Oxon
196 C5 Tadlow Cambs
165 F2 Tadmarton Oxon
32 D2 Tadnoll Dorset
110 C5 Tadwick BaNES
95 E3 Tadworth Surrey
132 B2 Tafarnaubach Blae G
152 B3 Tafarn-y-Bwlch Pembks
288 A2 Tafarn-y-Gelyn Denbgs
132 B5 Taff Merthyr Garden Village Myr Td
106 B3 Taff's Well Rhondd
230 D4 Tafolwern Powys
173 E2 Tagley Essex
104 B2 Taibach Neath
268 B4 Tai-bach Powys
262 D5 Tai-morfa Gwynd
577 G7 Tain Highld
589 G3 Tain Highld
288 C5 Tai-nant Wrexhm
596 F7 Tairbeart W Isls
157 F4 Tai'r Bull Powys
129 H2 Tairgwaith Neath
132 B6 Tai'r-heol Caerph
129 G5 Tai'r-ysgol Swans
172 B5 Takeley Essex
172 A5 Takeley Street Essex
157 H3 Talachddu Powys
307 G3 Talacre Flints
266 D4 Talardd Gwynd
27 H3 Talaton Devon
124 D2 Talbenny Pembks
105 G3 Talbot Green Rhondd
48 D6 Talbot Heath Poole
110 B1 Talbot's End S Glos
48 D6 Talbot Village Bmouth
48 D6 Talbot Woods Bmouth
28 A3 Taleford Devon
231 E4 Talerddig Powys
27 H3 Talewater Devon
180 B4 Talgarreg Cerdgn
158 C3 Talgarth Powys
102 B4 Talgarth's Well Swans
544 E3 Talisker Highld
291 G4 Talke Staffs
291 G4 Talke Pits Staffs
401 F3 Talkin Cumb
563 G2 Talladale Highld
449 F5 Talla Linnfoots Border
9 G3 Talland Cnwll
289 F6 Tallarn Green Wrexhm
388 C2 Tallentire Cumb
155 F3 Talley Carmth
243 F3 Tallington Lincs
586 C4 Talmine Highld
153 G4 Talog Carmth
156 B4 Talsarn Carmth
180 D3 Tal-Sarn Cerdgn
265 E2 Talsarnau Gwynd
14 C5 Talskiddy Cnwll
303 G5 Talwrn IoA
288 C4 Talwrn Wrexhm
288 C5 Talwrn Wrexhm
205 F2 Tal-y-bont Cerdgn
305 G6 Tal-y-bont Gwynd
264 D5 Tal-y-bont Gwynd
304 D5 Tal-y-bont Gwynd
303 F3 Tal -y-Bontan IoA
158 B5 Talybont-on-Usk Powys
305 G5 Tal-y-cafn Conwy
133 H1 Tal-y-coed Mons
229 G3 Tal-y-llyn Gwynd
158 A4 Talyllyn Powys
285 E5 Talysarn Gwynd
285 E5 Tal-y-Waenydd Gwynd
133 E4 Talywain Torfn
230 C4 Tal-y-wern Powys
385 E3 Tame Bridge N York
325 E4 Tamer Lane End Wigan
11 E1 Tamerton Foliot C Plym
327 E3 Tame Water Oldham
485 H4 Tamfourhill Falk
238 C2 Tamworth Staffs
281 E1 Tamworth Green Lincs
357 F3 Tancred N York
80 D2 Tanden Kent
466 A2 Tandlehill Rens
95 H4 Tandridge Surrey
154 B5 Tanerdy Carmth
394 B1 Tanfield Dur
405 E4 Tanfield Lea Dur
356 A3 Tang N York
591 D7 Tangasdal W Isls
358 B4 Tang Hall York
151 G6 Tangiers Pembks
90 A4 Tangley Hants
153 G3 Tanglwst Carmth
53 F3 Tangmere W Susx
606 B2 Tangwick Shet
404 F4 Tan Hills Dur
65 G5 Tan Hinon Powys
206 D2 Tanhouse Lancs
88 A2 Tanis Wilts
601 J3 Tankerness Ork
329 E5 Tankersley Barns
100 B2 Tankerton Kent
285 G2 Tan-Lan Conwy
307 G3 Tanlan Flints
284 D6 Tan-Lan Gwynd

307 G3 Tanlan Banks Flints
589 J7 Tannach Highld
527 G3 Tannadice Angus
213 G5 Tanner's Green Worcs
226 A6 Tannington Suffk
226 A6 Tannington Place Suffk
467 H2 Tannochside N Lans
201 F2 Tan Office Suffk
199 F3 Tan Office Green Suffk
501 E4 Tanshall Fife
294 C3 Tansley Derbys
213 E2 Tansley Hill Dudley
294 C2 Tansley Knoll Derbys
219 F1 Tansor Nhants
338 D3 Tanterton Lancs
405 E4 Tantobie Dur
385 E2 Tanton N York
212 C5 Tanwood Worcs
213 H5 Tanworth-in-Arden Warwks
265 F1 Tan-y-Bwlch Gwynd
286 D2 Tan-y-Fron Conwy
285 E5 Tanyfron Wrexhm
179 F4 Tan-y-Groes Cerdgn
263 K4 Tan-y-Mynydd Gwynd
307 F3 Tan-yr-Allt Derbys
284 D1 Tanygrisiau Gwynd
284 C1 Tanysgafell Gwynd
590 F5 Taobh a' Chaolais W Isls
590 F2 Taobh a Deas Loch Aineort W Isls
597 K4 Taobh a' Ghlinne W Isls
590 F2 Taobh a Tuath Loch Aineort W Isls
596 E7 Taobh Siar W Isls
594 F5 Taobh Tuath W Isls
117 F3 Taplow Bucks
51 F2 Tapnage Hants
314 D5 Tapton Derbys
314 C2 Tapton Hill Sheff
458 C1 Tarbert Ag & B
479 G5 Tarbert Ag & B
480 B6 Tarbert Ag & B
596 F7 Tarbert W Isls
495 G4 Tarbet Ag & B
531 L4 Tarbet Highld
584 C7 Tarbet Highld
309 G2 Tarbock Green Knows
445 F4 Tarbolton S Ayrs
469 G3 Tarbrax S Lans
213 E6 Tardebigge Worcs
338 D4 Tardy Gate Lancs
539 F4 Tarfside Angus
555 E4 Tarland Abers
338 B5 Tarleton Lancs
338 B5 Tarleton Moss Lancs
577 G7 Tarlogie Highld
324 A2 Tarlscough Lancs
137 E5 Tarlton Gloucs
342 C2 Tarn Brad
352 B3 Tarnbrook Lancs
84 C4 Tarnock Somset
399 E5 Tarns Cumb
365 F1 Tarnside Cumb
290 A2 Tarporley Ches
122 B2 Tarpots Essex
64 B5 Tarr Somset
400 D3 Tarraby Cumb
47 H4 Tarrant Crawford Dorset
48 A2 Tarrant Gunville Dorset
47 H2 Tarrant Hinton Dorset
47 H4 Tarrant Keyneston Dorset
48 A3 Tarrant Launceston Dorset
48 A3 Tarrant Monkton Dorset
48 A3 Tarrant Rawston Dorset
48 A3 Tarrant Rushton Dorset
577 J7 Tarrel Highld
56 C4 Tarring Neville E Susx
161 E1 Tarrington Herefs
161 E2 Tarrington Common Herefs
512 D5 Tarsappie P & K
545 K8 Tarskavaig Highld
270 A2 Tarts Hill Wrexhm
560 C3 Tarves Abers
565 G5 Tarvie Highld
524 F3 Tarvie P & K
289 G1 Tarvin Ches
309 G6 Tarvin Sands Ches
249 G6 Tasburgh Norfk
235 F6 Tasley Shrops
165 F5 Taston Oxon
213 E2 Tat Bank Sandw
274 C5 Tatenhill Staffs
274 B5 Tatenhill Common Staffs
193 H5 Tathall End M Keyn
366 C6 Tatham Lancs
320 B3 Tathwell Lincs
117 H2 Tatling End Bucks
96 B3 Tatsfield Surrey
289 G3 Tattenhall Ches
168 A3 Tattenhoe M Keyn
253 H2 Tatterford Norfk
253 G2 Tattersett Norfk
299 G3 Tattershall Lincs
299 G3 Tattershall Bridge Lincs
299 G3 Tattershall Thorpe Lincs
175 F2 Tattingstone Suffk
175 F2 Tattingstone White Horse Suffk
190 B2 Tattle Bank Warwks
311 E3 Tatton Dale Ches
29 F1 Tatworth Somset
44 A3 Taunton Somset
326 D4 Taunton Tamesd
255 G5 Taverham Norfk
172 B6 Taverners Green Essex
126 D2 Tavernspite Pembks
17 G4 Tavistock Devon
25 G3 Taw Green Devon
40 B2 Tawstock Devon
312 D4 Taxal Derbys
462 B5 Tayinloan Ag & B
523 L6 Taymouth Castle P & K
479 J5 Taynish Ag & B
161 G3 Taynton Gloucs
138 C2 Taynton Oxon
507 H3 Taynuilt Ag & B
514 D4 Tayport Fife
479 J4 Tayvallich Ag & B
479 J4 Tayvullin Ag & B
169 G5 Tea Green Herts
319 E1 Tealby Lincs
514 C2 Tealing Angus
405 F2 Teams Gatesd
405 F2 Team Valley Gatesd
273 E1 Teanford Staffs
546 B8 Teangue Highld
592 D5 Teanna Mhachair W Isls
78 C2 Teasley Mead E Susx
379 H4 Tebay Cumb
168 D4 Tebworth Beds
26 C4 Tedburn St Mary Devon
163 E3 Teddington Gloucs
118 D5 Teddington Gt Lon
163 E3 Teddington Hands Gloucs
269 G4 Tedsmore Shrops
187 F3 Tedstone Delamere Herefs
187 F3 Tedstone Wafer Herefs
396 C6 Teesside Park S on T
396 D6 Teesville R & Cl
217 E5 Teeton Nhants
69 G3 Teffont Evias Wilts
69 G3 Teffont Magna Wilts
153 E3 Tegryn Pembks

242 B1 Teigh Rutlnd
20 B3 Teigngrace Devon
20 C3 Teignmouth Devon
20 A1 Teign Village Devon
235 G3 Telford Wrekin
58 C4 Telham E Susx
87 E3 Tellisford Somset
56 C4 Telscombe E Susx
56 B4 Telscombe Cliffs E Susx
424 B2 Templand D & G
484 A6 Temple C Glas
15 G4 Temple Cnwll
471 F3 Temple Mdloth
116 D3 Temple W & M
87 E6 Temple Wilts
214 C4 Temple Balsall Solhll
155 E6 Temple Bar Carmth
180 D4 Temple Bar Cerdgn
53 F3 Temple Bar W Susx
314 D1 Templeborough Rothm
85 H3 Temple Cloud BaNES
68 B5 Templecombe Somset
140 B3 Temple Cowley Oxon
199 G6 Temple End Essex
198 D4 Temple End Suffk
83 E2 Temple Ewell Kent
189 H3 Temple Grafton Warwks
163 G4 Temple Guiting Gloucs
514 D2 Templehall Angus
501 E6 Templehall Fife
513 H4 Templehall P & K
191 F4 Temple Herdewyke Warwks
120 D4 Temple Hill Kent
345 E5 Temple Hirst N York
29 H2 Templeman's Ash Dorset
119 H2 Temple Mills Gt Lon
315 E6 Temple Normanton Derbys
391 G4 Temple Sowerby Cumb
528 D5 Templeton Angus
42 A5 Templeton Devon
126 C2 Templeton Pembks
90 B1 Templeton W Berk
42 A5 Templeton Bridge Devon
404 D4 Templetown Dur
195 H4 Tempsford Beds
213 G3 Ten Acres Birm
524 D3 Tenandry P & K
186 D1 Tenbury Wells Worcs
126 C4 Tenby Pembks
9 G3 Tencreek Cnwll
175 F5 Tendring Essex
175 F4 Tendring Green Essex
175 F4 Tendring Heath Essex
246 B5 Ten Mile Bank Norfk
600 D1 Tenston Ork
80 C3 Tenterden Kent
306 C4 Terfyn Conwy
284 C2 Terfyn Gwynd
64 C5 Terhill Somset
147 F1 Terling Essex
271 E3 Ternhill Shrops
8 A3 Terras Cnwll
423 F4 Terregles D & G
56 D1 Terrible Down E Susx
142 A3 Terrick Bucks
142 B6 Terriers Bucks
372 C5 Terrington N York
252 B4 Terrington St Clement Norfk
252 A5 Terrington St John Norfk
425 H2 Terrona D & G
213 H5 Terry's Green Warwks
74 C5 Terwick Common W Susx
97 G4 Teston Kent
50 C2 Testwood Hants
136 C6 Tetbury Gloucs
136 C5 Tetbury Upton Gloucs
269 G3 Tetchill Shrops
167 E6 Tetchwick Bucks
23 G3 Tetcott Devon
320 B5 Tetford Lincs
331 G2 Tetley N Linc
334 D4 Tetney Lincs
334 D4 Tetney Lock Lincs
141 E4 Tetsworth Oxon
236 C4 Tettenhall Wolves
236 C5 Tettenhall Wood Wolves
196 B4 Tetworth Cambs
561 G2 Teuchan Abers
570 D6 Teuchar Abers
295 F2 Teversal Notts
197 G3 Teversham Cambs
439 E3 Teviothead Border
144 C2 Tewin Herts
144 C1 Tewin Wood Herts
365 H5 Tewitfield Lancs
162 C3 Tewkesbury Gloucs
99 F2 Teynham Kent
99 F2 Teynham Street Kent
342 C2 Thackley Brad
342 C2 Thackley End Brad
388 D5 Thackthwaite Cumb
54 D1 Thakeham W Susx
141 F3 Thame Oxon
94 D1 Thames Ditton Surrey
122 A3 Thames Haven Thurr
137 E5 Thames Head Gloucs
120 C3 Thamesmead Gt Lon
100 B4 Thanington Kent
448 C2 Thankerton S Lans
249 G6 Tharston Norfk
90 D1 Thatcham W Berk
324 B6 Thatto Heath St Hel
172 C3 Thaxted Essex
543 G6 The Aird Highld
370 C2 Theakston N York
346 C6 Thealby N Linc
238 B4 The Alders Staffs
85 E5 Theale Somset
115 G5 Theale W Berk
248 A5 The Arms Norfk
347 G2 Thearne E R Yk
185 E6 The Bage Herefs
511 E6 The Balloch P & K
291 G3 The Bank Ches
312 C2 The Banks Stockp
112 B4 The Banks Wilts
290 D4 The Barony Ches
602 B6 The Barony Ork
112 C4 The Barton Wilts
110 B5 The Batch S Glos
137 F4 The Beeches Gloucs
324 C3 The Bell Wigan
273 F3 The Bents Staffs
203 E1 Theberton Suffk
273 F4 The Blythe Staffs
233 G5 The Bog Shrops
46 D2 The Borough Dorset
119 G4 The Borough Gt Lon
92 D6 The Bourne Surrey
189 E3 The Bourne Worcs
545 J3 The Braes Highld
291 G5 The Brampton Staffs
240 B2 The Brand Leics
236 C6 The Bratch Staffs
600 E4 The Breck Ork
99 G2 The Brents Kent
47 E2 The Bridge Dorset
186 B2 The Broad Herefs
225 E4 The Brook Suffk
314 D4 The Brushes Derbys
133 F3 The Bryn Mons
322 f5 The Bungalow IoM

212 B6 The Burf Worcs
540 B6 The Burn Abers
73 H2 The Butts Hants
136 D3 The Camp Gloucs
143 H3 The Camp Herts
190 D1 The Cape Warwks
96 C4 The Chart Kent
270 B1 The Chequer Wrexhm
237 F5 The Chuckery Wsall
141 G5 The City Bucks
160 C4 The Cleaver Herefs
53 F4 The Close Herefs
165 E2 The Colony Oxon
85 H2 The Common BaNES
167 G3 The Common Bucks
47 E2 The Common Dorset
271 F4 The Common Shrops
102 D3 The Common W Susx
76 C3 The Common W Susx
71 E5 The Common Wilts
87 F2 The Common Wilts
112 B3 The Common Wilts
79 F1 The Corner Kent
162 D5 The Corner Shrops
210 A2 The Cot Mons
134 C5 The Craigs Highld
575 K5 The Crofts E R Yk
375 G5 The Cronk IoM
322 e3 The Cross Hands Leics
239 E4 The Cwm Mons
134 B6 Thedden Grange Hants
73 G2 Theddingworth Leics
216 D2 Theddlethorpe All Saints Lincs
321 E2 Theddlethorpe St Helen Lincs
321 E2 The Delves Wsall
237 F5 The Den N Ayrs
465 G4 The Dene Dur
404 D4 The Dene Hants
90 B4 The Down Kent
79 F2 The Down Shrops
211 F1 The Downs Surrey
75 E2 The Dunks Wrexhm
288 D4 The Eals Nthumb
428 B2 The Eaves Gloucs
135 E3 The Fall Leeds
343 F4 The Fence Gloucs
134 C3 The Flat Gloucs
135 G1 The Flatt Cumb
427 E4 The Flourish Derbys
275 G2 The Folly Herts
143 H2 The Folly S Glos
110 D5 The Fording Herefs
161 E4 The Forge Herefs
185 F3 The Forstal Kent
81 F2 The Forties Derbys
275 E5 The Four Alls Shrops
271 F3 The Fox Wilts
112 C2 The Foxholes Shrops
211 E3 The Frenches Hants
71 F5 The Frythe Herts
144 B2 The Gibb Wilts
111 E4 The Glack Border
449 H2 The Glutt Highld
582 C2 The Gore Shrops
210 D3 The Grange N York
385 F5 The Grange Norfk
255 F3 The Green Barns
328 C4 The Green Beds
169 E6 The Green Cambs
196 C1 The Green Cumb
362 D5 The Green Cumb
365 E4 The Green Essex
173 F6 The Green Hants
71 F4 The Green M Keyn
194 B6 The Green Nhants
193 G6 The Green Norfk
249 E4 The Green Norfk
261 E4 The Green Oxon
165 H4 The Green Shrops
209 F3 The Green Warwks
190 B3 The Green Wilts
69 E3 The Grove Dur
404 C4 The Grove Herts
143 F5 The Grove Shrops
210 A3 The Grove Shrops
233 G3 The Grove Worcs
162 C1 The Gutter Derbys
294 C5 The Gutter Worcs
213 E4 The Hacket S Glos
110 B1 The Hague Tamesd
327 F6 The Hall Shet
609 J5 The Hallands N Linc
347 G5 The Ham Wilts
87 F4 The Handfords Staffs
272 C5 The Harbour Kent
98 C5 The Haven W Susx
76 A3 The Headland Hartpl
396 D3 The Heath Norfk
254 B2 The Heath Norfk
255 G3 The Heath Staffs
273 G3 The Heath Suffk
175 F2 The Hem Shrops
235 H3 The Hendre Mons
134 B2 The Hermitage Cambs
221 F5 The Hermitage Surrey
95 E4 The Highlands E Susx
58 B5 The Hill Cumb
362 D5 The Hobbins Shrops
235 G6 The Hollands Staffs
292 B3 The Hollies Notts
297 F4 The Hollies Wokham
116 C4 The Holt Worcs
162 B1 The Hook Shrops
210 C4 The Hope Cumb
365 G2 The Howe Herefs
186 C2 The Hundred Herefs
119 E2 The Hyde Gt Lon
162 B1 The Hyde Worcs
174 D5 The Hythe Essex
488 B5 The Inch C Edin
103 F4 The Knab Swans
106 A6 The Knap V Glam
187 E4 The Knapp Herefs
110 B1 The Knapp S Glos
213 E2 The Knowle Sandw
236 D3 The Laches Staffs
412 C5 The Lake D & G
211 H4 The Lakes Worcs
406 B1 The Lawe S Tyne
347 F3 The Lawns E R Yk
41 F5 Thelbridge Barton Devon
81 E3 The Leacon Kent
210 D1 The Lee Bucks
142 B4 The Lees Kent
162 C4 The Leigh Gloucs
238 B4 The Leys Staffs
322 f2 The Lhen IoM
250 C5 The Ling Norfk
331 E3 The Lings Donc
248 D3 The Lings Norfk
111 F6 The Linleys Wilts
224 D4 Thelnetham Suffk
237 E5 The Lunt Wolves
225 G3 Thelveton Norfk
310 C2 Thelwall Warrtn
53 E4 The Manor W Susx
291 G2 The Marsh Ches
186 B3 The Marsh Herefs
233 F5 The Marsh Powys
271 F4 The Marsh Shrops
272 B4 The Marsh Staffs

225 E4 The Marsh Suffk
225 F4 The Marsh Suffk
254 D3 Themelthorpe Norfk
405 F4 The Middles Dur
74 B4 The Mint Hants
288 D1 The Moor Flints
79 H4 The Moor Kent
160 C3 The Moors Herefs
30 B3 The Mount Dorset
116 B5 The Mount Readg
114 C4 The Mumbles Swans
103 F4 The Murray S Lans
162 C3 The Mythe Gloucs
288 C4 The Nant Wrexhm
134 C3 The Narth Mons
556 C5 The Neuk Abers
166 B1 Thenford Nhants
170 B5 The Node Herts
270 D3 The Nook Shrops
271 F5 The Nook Shrops
112 B6 Theobald's Green Wilts
86 C2 The Oval BaNES
162 D5 The Park Gloucs
330 D3 The Parks Donc
70 B4 The Pitts Wilts
140 C4 The Platt Cnwll
135 E1 The Pludds Gloucs
20 D1 The Point Devon
550 F8 The Polchar Highld
570 B4 The Pole of Itlaw Abers
177 E3 The Port of Felixstowe Suffk
161 G3 The Pound Gloucs
135 G5 The Quarry Gloucs
234 B2 The Quarry Shrops
80 C3 The Quarter Kent
98 D6 The Quarter Kent
162 B3 The Rampings Worcs
162 D5 The Reddings Gloucs
170 D2 Therfield Herts
125 H2 The Rhos Pembks
160 B3 The Rhydd Herefs
186 B2 The Riddle Herefs
111 F6 The Ridge Wilts
92 D2 The Ridges Wokham
403 G1 The Riding Nthumb
450 C3 The Riggs Border
451 F3 The Rink Border
117 F6 The Rise W & M
235 F3 The Rock Wrekin
97 H3 The Rocks Kent
225 E5 The Rocks S Glos
307 E5 The Roe Denbgs
143 G6 The Rookery Herts
291 H3 The Rookery Staffs
365 G4 The Row Lancs
272 B2 The Rowe Staffs
238 B2 The Sale Staffs
93 E5 The Sands Surrey
161 G4 The Scarr Gloucs
111 E5 The Shoe Wilts
272 D3 The Shruggs Staffs
394 C4 The Slack Dur
115 E5 The Slade W Berk
246 A2 The Smeeth Norfk
235 F5 The Smithies Shrops
87 G2 The Spa Wilts
214 D5 The Spring Warwks
133 E5 The Square Torfn
80 D4 The Stocks Kent
87 G2 The Stocks Wilts
212 D1 The Straits Dudley
74 B2 The Straits Hants
87 G3 The Strand Wilts
143 E5 The Swillett Herts
271 F3 The Sydnall Shrops
243 G2 Thetford Lincs
224 A3 Thetford Norfk
170 D2 The Thrift Herts
272 D6 The Throat Wokham
3 G2 The Towans Cnwll
3 C1 The Town IoS
162 C2 The Twittocks Gloucs
162 D6 The Tynings Gloucs
213 F3 The Vale Birm
290 D3 The Valley Ches
99 F4 The Valley Kent
126 C3 The Valley Pembks
186 C5 The Vauld Herefs
212 C2 The Village Dudley
107 F1 The Village Newpt
117 G5 The Village W & M
212 B5 The Walshes Worcs
99 F6 The Warren Kent
89 F1 The Warren Wilts
233 G4 The Waterwheel Shrops
160 C3 The Weaven Herefs
94 D2 The Wells Surrey
288 C4 The Wern Wrexhm
334 B3 The Willows NE Lin
269 F5 The Wood Shrops
270 B4 The Wood Shrops
240 D5 The Woodlands Leics
175 E1 The Woodlands Suffk
176 C2 The Woodlands Suffk
237 F5 The Woodlands Suffk
58 B5 The Wrangle BaNES
95 F1 The Wrythe Gt Lon
235 G3 The Wyke Shrops
186 C5 The Wymm Herefs
145 F5 Theydon Bois Essex
145 G5 Theydon Mount Essex
210 D3 The Yeld Shrops
86 B3 Thicket Mead BaNES
327 H2 Thick Hollins Kirk
111 E5 Thickwood Wilts
319 G6 Thimbleby Lincs
384 D5 Thimbleby N York
238 A6 Thimble End Birm
395 F3 Thinford Dur
111 F5 Thingley Wilts
308 C3 Thingwall Wirral
464 D5 Thirdpart N Ayrs
371 F3 Thirlby N York
472 D5 Thirlestane Border
369 H2 Thirn N York
371 E3 Thirsk N York
348 C3 Thirtleby E R Yk
338 B2 Thistleton Lancs
242 C1 Thistleton Rutlnd
172 D4 Thistley Green Essex
222 D4 Thistley Green Suffk
359 F2 Thixendale N York
429 E4 Thockrington Nthumb
245 F3 Tholomas Drove Cambs
357 F1 Tholthorpe N York
126 C3 Thomas Chapel Pembks
390 C1 Thomas Close Cumb
558 D2 Thomastown Abers
105 F2 Thomastown Rhondd
248 B5 Thompson Norfk
568 C4 Thomshill Moray
121 G5 Thong Kent
328 B2 Thongsbridge Kirk
368 D2 Thoralby N York
316 B5 Thoresby Notts
321 E4 Thoresthorpe Lincs
333 H5 Thoresway Lincs
334 B5 Thorganby Lincs
345 F1 Thorganby N York
386 B5 Thorgill N York
227 E5 Thorington Suffk

174 D2 Thorington Street Suffk
354 C4 Thorlby N York
171 G6 Thorley Herts
36 B3 Thorley IoW
171 G5 Thorley Houses Herts
36 B3 Thorley Street IoW
371 F5 Thormanby N York
25 G5 Thorn Devon
185 E2 Thorn Powys
384 D1 Thornaby-on-Tees S on T
261 E4 Thornage Norfk
167 F3 Thornborough Bucks
370 B4 Thornborough N York
342 C3 Thornbury Brad
39 F6 Thornbury Devon
187 E3 Thornbury Herefs
109 H2 Thornbury S Glos
400 A4 Thornby Cumb
217 E4 Thornby Nhants
328 C2 Thorncliff Kirk
292 D3 Thorncliffe Staffs
29 G2 Thorncombe Dorset
36 C4 Thorncross IoW
225 F6 Thorndon Suffk
24 D4 Thorndon Cross Devon
23 E2 Thorne Cnwll
331 E2 Thorne Donc
67 E6 Thorne Coffin Somset
59 F4 Thornehillhead Devon
24 A5 Thorne Moor Devon
111 H4 Thornend Wilts
343 G1 Thorner Leeds
237 G4 Thornes Staffs
43 E3 Thorne St Margaret Somset
118 A4 Thorney Bucks
244 C4 Thorney C Pete
317 G5 Thorney Notts
66 C5 Thorney Somset
406 B4 Thorney Close Sundld
201 E2 Thorney Green Suffk
49 F5 Thorney Hill Hants
244 D4 Thorney Toll Cambs
276 C1 Thorneywood Notts
44 B3 Thornfalcon Somset
46 B2 Thornford Dorset
402 D1 Thorngrafton Nthumb
65 G5 Thorngrove Somset
348 D4 Thorngumbald E R Yk
259 E3 Thornham Norfk
326 C3 Thornham Fold Rochdl
225 E5 Thornham Magna Suffk
225 F5 Thornham Parva Suffk
243 F4 Thornhaugh C Pete
51 E2 Thornhill C Sotn
106 B3 Thornhill Caerph
106 C3 Thornhill Cardif
376 C3 Thornhill Derbys
436 A5 Thornhill D & G
313 G3 Thornhill Derbys
343 E6 Thornhill Kirk
329 G6 Thorn Hill Rothm
497 G5 Thornhill Stirlg
133 E5 Thornhill Torfn
112 C4 Thornhill Wilts
342 D6 Thornhill Edge Kirk
51 E2 Thornhill Park C Sotn
361 E2 Thornholme E R Yk
47 G4 Thornicombe Dorset
451 E2 Thornielee Border
394 C2 Thornley Dur
395 H2 Thornley Dur
466 D3 Thornliebank E Rens
466 C2 Thornly Park Rens
560 C3 Thornroan Abers
381 F4 Thorns N York
199 E3 Thorns Suffk
314 A1 Thornseat Sheff
312 D2 Thornsett Derbys
311 F3 Thorns Green Ches
389 F4 Thornthwaite Cumb
355 G3 Thornthwaite N York
527 E5 Thornton Angus
342 A3 Thornton Brad
167 F2 Thornton Bucks
359 E5 Thornton E R Yk
501 E5 Thornton Fife
337 F1 Thornton Lancs
239 H3 Thornton Leics
319 G6 Thornton Lincs
384 D2 Thornton Middsb
474 D5 Thornton Nthumb
125 E3 Thornton Pembks
323 F4 Thornton Sefton
347 G6 Thornton Curtis N Linc
467 E3 Thorntonhall S Lans
119 G6 Thornton Heath Gt Lon
308 D3 Thornton Hough Wirral
354 A5 Thornton-in-Craven N York
366 D5 Thornton in Lonsdale N York
370 D1 Thornton-le-Beans N York
358 C1 Thornton-le-Clay N York
373 F3 Thornton-le-Dale N York
333 E5 Thornton le Moor Lincs
370 D2 Thornton-le-Moor N York
309 F5 Thornton-le-Moors Ches
371 E2 Thornton-le-Street N York
491 E5 Thorntonloch E Loth
368 C2 Thornton Rust N York
369 G2 Thornton Steward N York
370 A2 Thornton Watlass N York
145 G3 Thornwood Common Essex
540 B5 Thornyhill Abers
277 G1 Thoroton Notts
326 D3 Thorp Oldham
357 E5 Thorp Arch Leeds
390 D4 Thorpe Cumb
293 F4 Thorpe Derbys
360 B5 Thorpe E R Yk
321 E3 Thorpe Lincs
354 D2 Thorpe N York
251 E5 Thorpe Norfk
297 E5 Thorpe Notts
117 H6 Thorpe Surrey
225 G4 Thorpe Abbotts Norfk
276 B5 Thorpe Acre Leics
277 G5 Thorpe Arnold Leics
329 H1 Thorpe Audlin Wakefd
373 G5 Thorpe Bassett N York
123 E2 Thorpe Bay Sthend
242 B5 Thorpe by Water Rutlnd
177 E2 Thorpe Common Suffk
238 D3 Thorpe Constantine Staffs
301 E2 Thorpe Culvert Lincs
342 C2 Thorpe Edge Brad
250 B2 Thorpe End Norfk
301 E2 Thorpe Fendykes Lincs
176 C5 Thorpe Green Essex
339 E5 Thorpe Green Lancs
200 B4 Thorpe Green Suffk
117 H6 Thorpe Green Surrey
329 F5 Thorpe Hesley Rothm
330 C2 Thorpe in Balne Donc
217 F1 Thorpe Langton Leics
396 A4 Thorpe Larches S on T
279 G1 Thorpe Latimer Lincs
117 H5 Thorpe Lea Surrey
317 H3 Thorpe le Fallows Lincs
176 D3 Thorpe-le-Soken Essex
359 F6 Thorpe le Street E R Yk
319 F1 Thorpe le Vale Lincs
218 A4 Thorpe Malsor Nhants
192 B5 Thorpe Mandeville Nhants

256 A2 Thorpe Market Norfk
255 G5 Thorpe Marriott Norfk
200 B4 Thorpe Morieux Suffk
203 F3 Thorpeness Suffk
343 F4 Thorpe on the Hill Leeds
297 H2 Thorpe on the Hill Lincs
248 C3 Thorpe Row Norfk
250 B3 Thorpe St Andrew Norfk
301 E2 Thorpe St Peter Lincs
315 G3 Thorpe Salvin Rothm
241 F2 Thorpe Satchville Leics
224 D4 Thorpe Street Suffk
396 A5 Thorpe Thewles S on T
299 E3 Thorpe Tilney Lincs
357 E3 Thorpe Underwood N York
217 G3 Thorpe Underwood Nhants
219 E3 Thorpe Waterville Nhants
344 D3 Thorpe Willoughby N York
344 D3 Thorpe Wood N York
246 C3 Thorpland Norfk
175 E5 Thorrington Essex
27 E2 Thorverton Devon
87 E5 Thoulstone Wilts
218 D4 Thrandeston Suffk
218 D4 Thrapston Nhants
468 B1 Thrashbush N Lans
389 E2 Threapland Cumb
354 C2 Threapland N York
289 F5 Threapwood Ches
292 D6 Threapwood Staffs
432 D3 Threave S Ayrs
91 G2 Three Ashes Hants
160 C5 Three Ashes Herefs
209 G4 Three Ashes Shrops
86 A5 Three Ashes Somset
320 D2 Three Bridges Lincs
77 E2 Three Bridges W Susx
6 D4 Three Burrows Cnwll
80 B2 Three Chimneys Kent
251 E5 Three Cocked Hat Norfk
158 C2 Three Cocks Powys
423 E5 Three Crofts D & G
103 E3 Three Crosses Swans
79 E5 Three Cups Corner E Susx
270 B1 Three Fingers Wrexhm
46 B3 Three Gates Dorset
256 C6 Threehammer Common Norfk
23 E5 Three Hammers Cnwll
245 H4 Three Holes Norfk
15 E4 Three Holes Cross Cnwll
279 F2 Threekingham Lincs
79 F3 Three Leg Cross E Susx
48 D3 Three Legged Cross Dorset
293 E5 Threelows Staffs
213 H4 Three Maypoles Solhll
116 B6 Three Mile Cross Wokham
7 E5 Threemilestone Cnwll
486 D4 Threemiletown W Loth
58 D4 Three Oaks E Susx
472 C6 Threepwood Border
287 F2 Three Sisters Denbgs
15 E5 Threewaters Cnwll
389 H4 Threlkeld Cumb
145 G3 Threshers Bush Essex
354 C2 Threshfield N York
251 F2 Thrigby Norfk
393 F5 Thringarth Dur
275 G6 Thringstone Leics
383 H6 Thrintoft N York
197 F5 Thriplow Cambs
315 G3 Throapham Rothm
463 E5 Throdergay N Ayrs
57 E2 Thrope IoW
122 B2 Thunder's Hill E Susx
140 D1 Thundridge Herts
240 C2 Thurcaston Leics
315 F2 Thurcroft Rothm
38 C5 Thurdon Cnwll
261 G5 Thurgarton Norfk
296 C5 Thurgarton Notts
328 D4 Thurgoland Barns
240 B5 Thurlaston Leics
215 H5 Thurlaston Warwks
44 B3 Thurlbear Somset
243 F1 Thurlby Lincs
297 G2 Thurlby Lincs
321 E4 Thurlby Lincs
195 E3 Thurleigh Beds
12 B4 Thurlestone Devon
65 G5 Thurloxton Somset
328 C4 Thurlstone Barns
251 E5 Thurlton Norfk
251 E5 Thurlton Links Norfk
291 F2 Thurlwood Ches
240 D3 Thurmaston Leics
240 D4 Thurnby Leics
251 E1 Thurne Norfk
98 C3 Thurnham Kent
219 F3 Thurning Nhants
255 E2 Thurning Norfk
329 G3 Thurnscoe Barns
329 H3 Thurnscoe East Barns
400 B4 Thursby Cumb
260 C5 Thursford Norfk
260 C5 Thursford Green Norfk
74 D2 Thursley Surrey
588 D3 Thurso Highld
588 E3 Thurso East Highld
308 B3 Thurstaston Wirral
200 B1 Thurston Suffk
327 E3 Thurston Clough Oldham
199 F4 Thurston End Suffk
400 B3 Thurstonfield Cumb
328 B2 Thurstonland Kirk
250 C4 Thurton Norfk
274 A2 Thurvaston Derbys
274 C2 Thurvaston Derbys
248 D3 Thuxton Norfk
381 F5 Thwaite N York
225 F6 Thwaite Suffk

720 City, town and village index: Thwaite Flat - Tregunna

364 B5 **Thwaite Flat** Cumb
364 D1 **Thwaite Head** Cumb
342 A1 **Thwaites** Brad
250 C6 **Thwaite St Mary** Norfk
374 D5 **Thwing** E R Yk
512 C5 **Tibbermore** P & K
161 H5 **Tibberton** Gloucs
188 C3 **Tibberton** Worcs
271 F5 **Tibberton** Wrekin
225 F2 **Tibenham** Norfk
295 E2 **Tibshelf** Derbys
295 F2 **Tibshelf Wharf** Notts
360 B3 **Tibthorpe** E R Yk
79 F3 **Ticehurst** E Susx
73 E3 **Tichborne** Hants
242 D3 **Tickencote** Rutlnd
108 D5 **Tickenham** N Som
194 B6 **Tickford End** M Keyn
330 C6 **Tickhill** Donc
117 E5 **Tickleback Row** Br For
210 B1 **Ticklerton** Shrops
136 B5 **Tickmorend** Gloucs
275 F5 **Ticknall** Derbys
347 G1 **Tickton** E R Yk
213 H4 **Tidbury Green** Solhll
89 G3 **Tidcombe** Wilts
140 D4 **Tiddington** Oxon
190 C3 **Tiddington** Warwks
79 E4 **Tidebrook** E Susx
10 B2 **Tideford** Cnwll
10 B1 **Tideford Cross** Cnwll
134 D5 **Tidenham** Gloucs
134 C5 **Tidenham Chase** Gloucs
313 G4 **Tideswell** Derbys
115 G5 **Tidmarsh** W Berk
164 D2 **Tidmington** Warwks
160 D2 **Tidnor** Herefs
70 B6 **Tidpit** Hants
89 F5 **Tidworth** Wilts
125 F2 **Tiers Cross** Pembks
193 E4 **Tiffield** Nhants
560 A1 **Tifty** Abers
528 B2 **Tigerton** Angus
592 C3 **Tigh a' Ghearraidh** W Isls
592 C3 **Tigharry** W Isls
498 B1 **Tigh-na-Blair** P & K
480 D5 **Tighnabruaich** Ag & B
573 G6 **Tighnafiline** Highld
495 F4 **Tighness** Ag & B
19 G5 **Tigley** Devon
219 F6 **Tilbrook** Cambs
121 F4 **Tilbury** Thurr
173 E1 **Tilbury Green** Essex
173 F1 **Tilbury Juxta Clare** Essex
214 B2 **Tile Cross** Birm
145 H3 **Tilegate Green** Essex
214 D4 **Tile Hill** Covtry
214 B4 **Tilehouse Green** Solhll
115 H5 **Tilehurst** Readg
171 H5 **Tilekiln Green** Essex
46 C3 **Tiley** Dorset
93 E6 **Tilford** Surrey
93 E6 **Tilford Common** Surrey
93 E6 **Tilford Reeds** Surrey
77 E2 **Tilgate** W Susx
77 E3 **Tilgate Forest Row** W Susx
173 G5 **Tilkey** Essex
10 B1 **Tilland** Cnwll
558 B2 **Tillathrowie** Abers
161 F3 **Tillers' Green** Gloucs
270 C4 **Tilley** Shrops
270 C4 **Tilley Green** Shrops
499 E5 **Tillicoultry** Clacks
468 C5 **Tillietudlem** S Lans
148 C4 **Tillingham** Essex
186 B5 **Tillington** Herefs
272 D5 **Tillington** Staffs
75 F5 **Tillington** W Susx
186 B5 **Tillington Common** Herefs
24 A4 **Tillislow** Devon
29 F2 **Tillworth** Devon
528 B1 **Tillyarblet** Angus
560 D5 **Tillycorthie** Abers
89 H5 **Tilly Down** Hants
555 H5 **Tillydrine** Abers
557 G3 **Tillydrone** C Aber
556 A2 **Tillyfourie** Abers
555 H6 **Tillygarmond** Abers
560 C5 **Tillygreig** Abers
560 B5 **Tillykerrie** Abers
527 E4 **Tillyloss** Angus
101 F5 **Tilmanstone** Kent
252 B4 **Tilney All Saints** Norfk
252 B5 **Tilney cum Islington** Norfk
246 A2 **Tilney Fen End** Norfk
252 B4 **Tilney High End** Norfk
252 A5 **Tilney St Lawrence** Norfk
135 G5 **Tilsdown** Gloucs
88 B5 **Tilshead** Wilts
78 D5 **Tilsmore** E Susx
211 E5 **Tilsop** Shrops
270 C2 **Tilstock** Shrops
289 G4 **Tilston** Ches
290 B3 **Tilstone Bank** Ches
290 B2 **Tilstone Fearnall** Ches
168 D5 **Tilsworth** Beds
241 F3 **Tilton on the Hill** Leics
330 C3 **Tilts** Donc
135 G5 **Tiltups End** Gloucs
172 B4 **Tilty** Essex
96 D2 **Timberden Bottom** Kent
212 D5 **Timberhonger** Worcs
299 E3 **Timberland** Lincs
292 A2 **Timbersbrook** Ches
63 F3 **Timberscombe** Somset
355 G4 **Timble** N York
98 D3 **Timbold Hill** Kent
17 E3 **Timbrelham** Cnwll
311 F2 **Timperley** Traffd
86 B3 **Timsbury** BaNES
71 G5 **Timsbury** Hants
598 A8 **Timsgarry** W Isls
598 A8 **Timsgearraidh** W Isls
223 H6 **Timworth** Suffk
223 H6 **Timworth Green** Suffk
32 D1 **Tincleton** Dorset
401 H3 **Tindale** Cumb
394 D4 **Tindale Crescent** Dur
172 C3 **Tindon End** Essex
166 D3 **Tingewick** Bucks
169 E3 **Tingrith** Beds
602 E7 **Tingwall** Ork
24 A5 **Tinhay** Devon
167 G4 **Tinkers End** Bucks
342 D2 **Tinshill** Leeds
314 D1 **Tinsley** Sheff
77 E2 **Tinsley Green** W Susx
22 A5 **Tintagel** Cnwll
134 C4 **Tintern** Mons
134 C4 **Tintern Parva** Mons
67 E6 **Tintinhull** Somset
327 F5 **Tintwistle** Derbys
423 H3 **Tinwald** D & G
243 E3 **Tinwell** Rutlnd
52 A4 **Tipner** C Port
62 B2 **Tippacott** Devon
214 D2 **Tipper's Hill** Warwks
561 E4 **Tipperty** Abers
23 G5 **Tipple Cross** Devon
245 H5 **Tipps End** Norfk
146 B4 **Tip's Cross** Essex
49 H5 **Tiptoe** Hants
213 E1 **Tipton** Sandw
213 E1 **Tipton Green** Sandw
28 A4 **Tipton St John** Devon
148 A1 **Tiptree** Essex
148 A2 **Tiptree Heath** Essex
156 D1 **Tirabad** Powys
129 G5 **Tircanol** Swans
103 F2 **Tirdeunaw** Swans
524 C2 **Tirinie** P & K
162 B4 **Tirley** Gloucs
162 B4 **Tirley Knowle** Gloucs
132 B4 **Tirphil** Caerph
391 E4 **Tirril** Cumb
580 E7 **Tirryside** Highld
606 E2 **Tirvister** Shet
132 B5 **Tir-y-Berth** Caerph
129 F2 **Tir-y-Dail** Carmth
69 F4 **Tisbury** Wilts
75 H3 **Tisman's Common** W Susx
293 G4 **Tissington** Derbys
38 B2 **Titchberry** Devon
51 F3 **Titchfield** Hants
51 F3 **Titchfield Common** Hants
51 F3 **Titchfield Park** Hants
219 E4 **Titchmarsh** Nhants
259 F3 **Titchwell** Norfk
90 B1 **Titcomb** W Berk
277 F2 **Tithby** Notts
273 G1 **Tithebarn** Staffs
324 D5 **Tithe Barn Hillock** St Hel
185 F2 **Titley** Herefs
443 E1 **Titlington** Nthumb
96 B4 **Titsey** Surrey
23 E2 **Titson** Cnwll
117 F6 **Tittenhurst** W & M
272 C2 **Tittensor** Staffs
210 C3 **Titterhill** Shrops
117 E3 **Tittle Row** W & M
254 A3 **Tittleshall** Norfk
212 B6 **Titton** Worcs
74 D4 **Titty Hill** W Susx
290 B2 **Tiverton** Ches
42 C5 **Tiverton** Devon
225 G2 **Tivetshall St Margaret** Norfk
225 G2 **Tivetshall St Mary** Norfk
213 E1 **Tividale** Sandw
63 E2 **Tivington** Somset
63 E3 **Tivington Knowle** Somset
388 A5 **Tivoli** Cumb
328 D3 **Tivy Dale** Barns
273 E5 **Tixall** Staffs
242 D4 **Tixover** Rutlnd
601 J3 **Toab** Ork
605 G8 **Toab** Shet
294 C4 **Toadmoor** Derbys
227 G2 **Toad Row** Suffk
518 C4 **Tobermory** Ag & B
492 B3 **Toberonochy** Ag & B
593 D10 **Tobha Beag** W Isls
593 D10 **Tobha Mòr** W Isls
598 D8 **Tobhtaral** W Isls
598 C7 **Tobson** W Isls
335 G6 **Toby's Hill** Lincs
559 F3 **Tocher** Abers
112 B4 **Tockenham** Wilts
112 B3 **Tockenham Wick** Wilts
339 G5 **Tockholes** Bl w D
109 H2 **Tockington** S Glos
357 F4 **Tockwith** N York
68 C6 **Todber** Dorset
169 E4 **Toddington** Beds
163 F3 **Toddington** Gloucs
54 B4 **Toddington** W Susx
571 K6 **Toddlehills** Abers
164 C2 **Todenham** Gloucs
514 C2 **Todhills** Angus
400 C2 **Todhills** Cumb
395 E3 **Todhills** Dur
341 E5 **Todmorden** Calder
6 D5 **Todpool** Cnwll
315 F3 **Todwick** Rothm
197 E3 **Toft** Cambs
243 F1 **Toft** Lincs
606 F2 **Toft** Shet
215 H5 **Toft** Warwks
394 D4 **Toft Hill** Dur
299 G2 **Toft Hill** Lincs
251 E6 **Toft Monks** Norfk
318 C2 **Toft next Newton** Lincs
254 A2 **Toftrees** Norfk
342 C4 **Toftshaw** Brad
248 C2 **Toftwood** Norfk
443 G4 **Togston** Nthumb
545 L7 **Tokavaig** Highld
116 B4 **Tokers Green** Oxon
598 D7 **Tolastadh a' Chaolais** W Isls
15 H3 **Tolborough** Cnwll
3 E4 **Tolcarne** Cnwll
4 C2 **Tolcarne** Cnwll
6 C6 **Tolcarne** Cnwll
4 C1 **Tolcarne Wartha** Cnwll
7 H1 **Toldish** Cnwll
6 C5 **Tolgus Mount** Cnwll
79 F3 **Tolhurst** E Susx
188 C3 **Tolladine** Worcs
64 B5 **Tolland** Somset
48 A1 **Tollard Farnham** Dorset
69 F6 **Tollard Royal** Wilts
330 C3 **Toll Bar** Donc
243 E3 **Toll Bar** Rutlnd
324 B6 **Toll Bar** St Hel
215 F4 **Tollbar End** Covtry
237 E6 **Toll End** Sandw
30 D3 **Tollerford** Dorset
30 D3 **Toller Fratrum** Dorset
30 D3 **Toller Porcorum** Dorset
357 G2 **Tollerton** N York
276 D3 **Tollerton** Notts
30 C2 **Toller Whelme** Dorset
148 C2 **Tollesbury** Essex
385 E1 **Tollesby** Middsb
148 B2 **Tolleshunt D'Arcy** Essex
148 B1 **Tolleshunt Knights** Essex
148 B2 **Tolleshunt Major** Essex
561 F3 **Toll of Birness** Abers
599 K8 **Tolm** W Isls
144 C4 **Tolmers** Herts
47 E6 **Tolpuddle** Dorset
6 C5 **Tolskithy** Cnwll
599 L5 **Tolstadh bho Thuath** W Isls
6 C5 **Tolvaddon Downs** Cnwll
536 B3 **Tolvah** Highld
94 D1 **Tolworth** Gt Lon
511 F5 **Tomaknock** P & K
597 K5 **Tom an Fhuadain** W Isls
550 D4 **Tomatin** Highld
550 B3 **Tombreck** Highld
548 C7 **Tomchrasky** Highld
533 J2 **Tomdoun** Highld
548 E4 **Tomich** Highld
566 C2 **Tomich** Highld
537 H4 **Tomintoul** Abers
552 D5 **Tomintoul** Moray
191 G2 **Tomlow** Warwks
553 J2 **Tomnaven** Moray
552 E3 **Tomnavoulin** Moray
7 E5 **Tomperrow** Cnwll
292 B4 **Tompkin** Staffs
77 H3 **Tompset's Bank** E Susx
505 J3 **Tomsleibhe** Ag & B
313 E4 **Tomthorn** Derbys
133 G5 **Ton** Mons
105 F4 **Ton Breigam** V Glam
97 E5 **Tonbridge** Kent
410 D5 **Tonderghie** D & G
104 D3 **Tondu** Brdgnd
43 F3 **Tone** Somset
43 F3 **Tonedale** Somset
43 G3 **Tone Green** Somset
228 D4 **Tonfanau** Gwynd
342 D3 **Tong** Brad
98 C5 **Tong** Kent
236 A3 **Tong** Shrops
275 G5 **Tonge** Leics
99 E1 **Tonge Corner** Kent
325 G3 **Tonge Fold** Bolton
325 G2 **Tonge Moor** Bolton
236 A3 **Tong Forge** Shrops
99 F4 **Tong Green** Kent
93 E5 **Tongham** Surrey
412 C4 **Tongland** D & G
236 A3 **Tong Norton** Shrops
342 C3 **Tong Street** Brad
586 C5 **Tongue** Highld
279 H6 **Tongue End** Lincs
168 B1 **Tongwell** M Keyn
106 B3 **Tongwynlais** Cardif
130 B5 **Tonmawr** Neath
130 B5 **Tonna** Neath
131 F6 **Ton Pentre** Rhondd
106 A2 **Ton-Teg** Rhondd
324 C4 **Tontine** Lancs
144 D1 **Tonwell** Herts
105 F1 **Tonypandy** Rhondd
132 C5 **Ton-y-pistyll** Caerph
105 G2 **Tonyrefail** Rhondd
605 G4 **Toogs** Shet
140 C4 **Toot Baldon** Oxon
342 B5 **Toothill** Calder
145 H4 **Toot Hill** Essex
72 A6 **Toothill** Hants
273 G1 **Toot Hill** Staffs
112 D3 **Toothill** Swindn
119 F5 **Tooting Graveney** Gt Lon
343 E4 **Topcliffe** Leeds
370 D4 **Topcliffe** N York
250 B6 **Topcroft** Norfk
226 B1 **Topcroft Street** Norfk
195 E2 **Top End** Beds
297 E6 **Top Green** Notts
330 D1 **Topham** Donc
75 E6 **Topleigh** W Susx
325 E3 **Top Lock** Wigan
326 C3 **Top of Hebers** Rochdl
339 E5 **Top O'th' Lane** Lancs
327 E3 **Top O' Th' Meadows** Oldham
173 E2 **Toppesfield** Essex
325 G2 **Toppings** Bolton
249 G5 **Toprow** Norfk
27 F5 **Topsham** Devon
295 H5 **Top Valley** C Nott
460 B4 **Torbeg** N Ayrs
468 D3 **Torbothie** N Lans
549 L1 **Torbreck** Highld
485 F1 **Torbrex** Stirlg
19 H4 **Torbryan** Devon
468 C3 **Torbush** N Lans
533 H7 **Torcastle** Highld
13 E4 **Torcross** Devon
565 L6 **Tore** Highld
9 E3 **Torfrey** Cnwll
534 D6 **Torgulbin** Highld
462 D2 **Torinturk** Ag & B
312 B2 **Torkington** Stockp
317 F4 **Torksey** Lincs
593 D7 **Torlum** W Isls
533 H7 **Torlundy** Highld
110 D4 **Tormarton** S Glos
476 B5 **Tormisdale** Ag & B
419 F3 **Tormitchell** S Ayrs
531 H2 **Tormore** Highld
460 B3 **Tormore** N Ayrs
566 D7 **Tornagrain** Highld
554 A3 **Tornahaish** Abers
555 H3 **Tornaveen** Abers
549 K4 **Torness** Highld
394 D3 **Toronto** Dur
389 F2 **Torpenhow** Cumb
486 C5 **Torphichen** W Loth
487 G6 **Torphin** C Edin
555 H4 **Torphins** Abers
10 D3 **Torpoint** Cnwll
20 C5 **Torquay** Torbay
472 A5 **Torquhan** Border
11 G3 **Torr** Devon
18 D5 **Torr** Devon
493 E4 **Torran** Ag & B
543 K7 **Torran** Highld
484 C5 **Torrance** E Duns
504 F5 **Torrans** Ag & B
465 G6 **Torranyard** N Ayrs
63 G3 **Torre** Somset
20 C5 **Torre** Torbay
562 F5 **Torridon** Highld
555 H2 **Torries** Abers
568 B4 **Torrieston** Moray
545 K5 **Torrin** Highld
586 E4 **Torrisdale** Highld
582 C6 **Torrish** Highld
351 G2 **Torrisholme** Lancs
576 C3 **Torroble** Highld
576 B4 **Torroy** Highld
558 A1 **Torry** Abers
557 H3 **Torry** C Aber
486 D2 **Torryburn** Fife
460 D5 **Torrylinn** N Ayrs
472 B6 **Torsonce** Border
472 B6 **Torsonce Mains** Border
571 K6 **Torterston** Abers
34 b4 **Torteval** Guern
423 H4 **Torthorwald** D & G
54 B3 **Tortington** W Susx
212 B5 **Torton** Worcs
135 F6 **Tortworth** S Glos
543 H8 **Torvaig** Highld
378 A6 **Torver** Cumb
485 G3 **Torwood** Falk
451 F2 **Torwoodlee Mains** Border
316 B2 **Torworth** Notts
38 C3 **Tosberry** Devon
546 C2 **Toscaig** Highld
196 B2 **Toseland** Cambs
353 F3 **Tosside** Lancs
517 K6 **Tostary** Ag & B
200 B2 **Tostock** Suffk
542 B6 **Totaig** Highld
544 F2 **Totardor** Highld
543 G7 **Tote** Highld
587 H3 **Totegan** Highld
71 F5 **Tote Hill** Hants
74 D5 **Tote Hill** W Susx
73 E2 **Totford** Hants
147 H2 **Totham Hill** Essex
148 A2 **Totham Plains** Essex
90 D2 **Tot Hill** Hants
320 D3 **Tothill** Lincs
35 H3 **Totland** IoW
314 B3 **Totley** Sheff
314 C3 **Totley Brook** Sheff
314 C3 **Totley Rise** Sheff
273 E2 **Totmonslow** Staffs
46 B3 **Totnell** Dorset
19 H5 **Totnes** Devon
160 D3 **Totnor** Herefs
276 A2 **Toton** Notts
276 B3 **Toton** Notts
516 F4 **Totronald** Ag & B
542 F3 **Totscore** Highld
119 G1 **Tottenham** Gt Lon
119 G2 **Tottenham Hale** Gt Lon
246 C2 **Tottenhill** Norfk
246 C2 **Tottenhill Row** Norfk
142 B6 **Totteridge** Bucks
144 B6 **Totteridge** Gt Lon
168 D5 **Totternhoe** Beds
110 C3 **Totteroak** S Glos
209 G2 **Totterton** Shrops
328 B3 **Totties** Kirk
325 H2 **Tottington** Bury
248 A5 **Tottington** Norfk
364 D3 **Tottlebank** Cumb
340 A3 **Tottleworth** Lancs
50 C2 **Totton** Hants
117 E4 **Touchen-End** W & M
357 E6 **Toulston** N York
64 C5 **Toulton** Somset
577 J7 **Toulvaddie** Highld
573 G7 **Tournaig** Highld
571 H5 **Toux** Abers
98 A4 **Tovil** Kent
14 B4 **Towan** Cnwll
6 D4 **Towan Cross** Cnwll
481 G6 **Toward** Ag & B
193 E5 **Towcester** Nhants
3 E2 **Towednack** Cnwll
141 H6 **Towerage** Bucks
252 D4 **Tower End** Norfk
83 F2 **Tower Hamlets** Kent
84 D3 **Towerhead** N Som
237 G6 **Tower Hill** Birm
312 B4 **Tower Hill** Ches
23 H4 **Tower Hill** Devon
177 E3 **Tower Hill** Essex
143 E4 **Tower Hill** Herts
323 H4 **Tower Hill** Knows
94 D5 **Tower Hill** Surrey
76 C4 **Tower Hill** W Susx
141 F3 **Towersey** Oxon
402 D2 **Tow House** Nthumb
554 D2 **Towie** Abers
568 F6 **Towiemore** Moray
394 C2 **Tow Law** Dur
26 B4 **Town Barton** Devon
235 F3 **Town Centre** Wrekin
141 G5 **Town End** Bucks
245 F5 **Town End** Cambs
365 E2 **Town End** Cumb
365 F3 **Town End** Cumb
366 C3 **Town End** Cumb
378 B3 **Town End** Cumb
378 C4 **Town End** Cumb
378 C5 **Town End** Cumb
391 G4 **Town End** Cumb
313 E3 **Townend** Derbys
313 G4 **Town End** Derbys
358 C4 **Town End** E R Yk
327 G1 **Town End** Kirk
309 G2 **Town End** Knows
273 E2 **Townend** Staffs
483 F4 **Townend** W Duns
403 G5 **Townfield** Dur
290 C2 **Town Fields** Ches
401 F5 **Towngate** Cumb
243 G2 **Towngate** Lincs
323 H3 **Town Green** Lancs
250 D2 **Town Green** Norfk
324 D5 **Town Green** Wigan
464 B2 **Townhead** Ag & B
328 B4 **Townhead** Barns
467 E1 **Townhead** C Glas
378 B2 **Town Head** Cumb
378 D4 **Town Head** Cumb
379 H2 **Town Head** Cumb
380 B2 **Town Head** Cumb
388 C2 **Townhead** Cumb
391 E2 **Townhead** Cumb
391 G3 **Townhead** Cumb
391 G5 **Town Head** Cumb
392 A5 **Town Head** Cumb
412 C5 **Townhead** D & G
313 G4 **Town Head** Derbys
467 H1 **Townhead** N Lans
353 G3 **Town Head** N York
367 F6 **Town Head** N York
441 G6 **Townhead** Nthumb
432 B4 **Townhead** S Ayrs
314 B3 **Townhead** Sheff
292 D5 **Town Head** Staffs
412 D1 **Townhead of Greenlaw** D & G
487 F2 **Townhill** Fife
103 F3 **Townhill** Swans
50 D1 **Townhill Park** C Sotn
395 H2 **Town Kelloe** Dur
17 F4 **Townlake** Devon
80 D3 **Townland Green** Kent
325 F4 **Town Lane** Wigan
77 H6 **Town Littleworth** E Susx
324 D5 **Town of Lowton** St Hel
310 A3 **Town Park** Halton
78 D4 **Town Row** E Susx
85 G3 **Townsend** BaNES
141 F3 **Townsend** Bucks
166 D5 **Town's End** Bucks
40 C2 **Townsend** Devon
30 D1 **Town's End** Dorset
33 H3 **Town's End** Dorset
47 G5 **Town's End** Dorset
91 F3 **Towns End** Hants
143 G3 **Townsend** Herts
114 B2 **Townsend** Oxon
124 C3 **Townsend** Pembks
68 B6 **Towns End** Somset
85 F4 **Townsend** Somset
86 B5 **Town's End** Somset
87 H3 **Townsend** Wilts
88 B3 **Townsend** Wilts
340 C5 **Townsend Fold** Lancs
3 G3 **Townshend** Cnwll
162 B4 **Town Street** Gloucs
110 B1 **Townwell** S Glos
453 F4 **Town Yetholm** Border
359 H2 **Towthorpe** E R Yk
358 B3 **Towthorpe** York
344 B2 **Towton** N York
306 D4 **Towyn** Conwy
309 E2 **Toxteth** Lpool
300 C2 **Toynton All Saints** Lincs
300 C2 **Toynton Fen Side** Lincs
300 C2 **Toynton St Peter** Lincs
96 C4 **Toy's Hill** Kent
445 F5 **Trabboch** E Ayrs
445 G5 **Trabbochburn** E Ayrs
4 D4 **Traboe** Cnwll
472 C5 **Trabrown** Border
43 E3 **Tracebridge** Somset
566 F5 **Tradespark** Highld
601 H3 **Tradespark** Ork
326 A5 **Trafford Park** Traffd
157 F4 **Trallong** Powys
105 H1 **Trallwn** Rhondd
103 G2 **Trallwn** Swans
15 F2 **Tramagenna** Cnwll
160 B3 **Tram Inn** Herefs
133 E4 **Tranch** Torfn
489 E5 **Tranent** E Loth
308 D2 **Tranmere** Wirral
587 J6 **Trantlebeg** Highld
587 J6 **Trantlemore** Highld
430 C3 **Tranwell** Nthumb
155 F6 **Trapp** Carmth
490 A4 **Traprain** E Loth
213 G6 **Trap's Green** Warwks
90 B2 **Trapshill** W Berk
450 C3 **Traquair** Border
115 H6 **Trash Green** W Berk
153 H6 **Travellers' Rest** Carmth
341 E2 **Trawden** Lancs
157 H3 **Trawscoed** Powys
265 F2 **Trawsfynydd** Gwynd
133 G1 **Treadam** Mons
160 C5 **Treaddow** Herefs
4 D5 **Treal** Cnwll
105 G1 **Trealaw** Rhondd
338 B3 **Treales** Lancs
302 C5 **Trearddur** IoA
542 F6 **Treaslane** Highld
5 E3 **Treath** Cnwll
14 B3 **Treator** Cnwll
105 G5 **Tre-Aubrey** V Glam
105 G1 **Trebanog** Rhondd
129 H4 **Trebanos** Neath
7 G1 **Trebarber** Cnwll
16 C3 **Trebartha** Cnwll
22 B5 **Trebarwith** Cnwll
22 A5 **Trebarwith Strand** Cnwll
23 F5 **Trebeath** Cnwll
153 H1 **Trebedw** Cerdgn
105 F6 **Tre-Beferad** V Glam
8 D1 **Trebell Green** Cnwll
158 B4 **Treberfydd** Powys
14 C3 **Trebetherick** Cnwll
8 B1 **Trebilcock** Cnwll
64 B5 **Treble's Holford** Somset
103 F2 **Tre-Boeth** Swans
63 G4 **Treborough** Somset
7 G1 **Trebudannon** Cnwll
16 D3 **Trebullett** Cnwll
15 F3 **Treburgett** Cnwll
16 B6 **Treburgie** Cnwll
16 D3 **Treburley** Cnwll
14 B4 **Treburrick** Cnwll
15 F6 **Trebyan** Cnwll
156 D4 **Trecastle** Powys
106 B2 **Trecenydd** Caerph
25 F2 **Trecott** Devon
151 G3 **Trecwn** Pembks
131 F4 **Trecynon** Rhondd
15 E4 **Tredannick** Cnwll
16 B2 **Tredaule** Cnwll
2 D4 **Tredavoe** Cnwll
132 B3 **Tredegar** Blae G
233 E1 **Trederwen** Powys
268 D5 **Tre-Derwen** Powys
15 F4 **Tredethy** Cnwll
162 D4 **Tredington** Gloucs
190 C6 **Tredington** Warwks
2 D3 **Tredinnick** Cnwll
8 C2 **Tredinnick** Cnwll
9 G2 **Tredinnick** Cnwll
14 C4 **Tredinnick** Cnwll
15 H5 **Tredinnick** Cnwll
105 H6 **Tredogan** V Glam
132 B6 **Tredomen** Caerph
158 B3 **Tredomen** Powys
38 B4 **Tredown** Devon
14 D3 **Tredrizzick** Cnwll
133 G6 **Tredunnock** Mons
158 B3 **Tredustan** Powys
136 B1 **Tredworth** Gloucs
2 C5 **Treen** Cnwll
2 D2 **Treen** Cnwll
8 D2 **Treesmill** Cnwll
315 E2 **Treeton** Rothm
262 D4 **Trefaes** Gwynd
9 G2 **Trefanny Hill** Cnwll
151 E2 **Trefasser** Pembks
282 D1 **Trefdraeth** IoA
158 B3 **Trefeca** Powys
204 D3 **Trefechan** Cerdgn
131 G3 **Trefechan** Myr Td
288 C5 **Trefechan** Wrexhm
207 F1 **Trefeglwys** Powys
158 B3 **Trefeitha** Powys
205 E6 **Trefenter** Cerdgn
175 E6 **Treffgarne** Pembks
150 D4 **Treffynnon** Pembks
151 E4 **Trefgarn Owen** Pembks
132 B2 **Trefil** Blae G
180 D3 **Trefilan** Cerdgn
150 D3 **Trefin** Pembks
269 E4 **Treflach** Shrops
232 C1 **Trefnanney** Powys
307 E5 **Trefnant** Denbgs
269 E3 **Trefonen** Shrops
263 F1 **Trefor** Gwynd
303 E4 **Trefor** IoA
15 F2 **Treforda** Cnwll
105 H2 **Treforest** Rhondd
179 E4 **Treforgan** Cerdgn
130 B3 **Tre-Forgan** Neath
285 G2 **Trefriw** Conwy
16 D3 **Trefrize** Cnwll
16 D2 **Tregada** Cnwll
2 D4 **Tregadgwith** Cnwll
23 F6 **Tregadillett** Cnwll
134 C3 **Tre-Gagle** Mons
303 F5 **Tregaian** IoA
6 C5 **Tregajorran** Cnwll
14 C6 **Tregamere** Cnwll
22 A6 **Tregardock** Cnwll
133 H2 **Tregare** Mons
9 G2 **Tregarland** Cnwll
9 G2 **Tregarlandbridge** Cnwll
5 E4 **Tregarne** Cnwll
181 G3 **Tregaron** Cerdgn
9 G2 **Tregarrick Mill** Cnwll
304 D6 **Tregarth** Gwynd
14 B6 **Tregaswith** Cnwll
14 C6 **Tregatillian** Cnwll
22 B5 **Tregatta** Cnwll
2 D4 **Tregavarah** Cnwll
4 C4 **Tregear** Cnwll
7 G3 **Tregear** Cnwll
23 E5 **Tregeare** Cnwll
268 C3 **Tregeiriog** Wrexhm
303 E2 **Tregele** IoA
15 E3 **Tregellist** Cnwll
2 C3 **Tregeseal** Cnwll
5 F2 **Tregew** Cnwll
131 F3 **Tre-Gibbon** Rhondd
5 E4 **Tregidden** Cnwll
150 B5 **Treginnis** Pembks
150 D4 **Treglemais** Pembks
22 D3 **Tregole** Cnwll
4 D1 **Tregolls** Cnwll
14 B5 **Tregona** Cnwll
14 C4 **Tregonce** Cnwll
14 D6 **Tregonetha** Cnwll
14 C4 **Tregonna** Cnwll
7 G2 **Tregonning** Cnwll
7 H4 **Tregony** Cnwll
22 C6 **Tregoodwell** Cnwll
15 E4 **Tregorden** Cnwll
8 C3 **Tregorrick** Cnwll
8 B1 **Tregoss** Cnwll
158 C2 **Tregoyd** Powys
158 C2 **Tregoyd Mill** Powys
15 F2 **Tregreenwell** Cnwll
8 C3 **Tregrehan Mills** Cnwll
180 B6 **Tregroes** Cerdgn
15 F6 **Tregullon** Cnwll
14 D4 **Tregunna** Cnwll

14 B5 **Tregurrian** Cnwll
3 F3 **Tregurtha Downs** Cnwll
151 E2 **Tregyddulan** Pembks
232 A5 **Tregynon** Powys
154 B6 **Tre-Gynwer** Carmth
105 G1 **Trehafod** Rhondd
208 A1 **Trehafren** Powys
10 C2 **Trehan** Cnwll
132 A5 **Treharris** Myr Td
14 B4 **Trehemborne** Cnwll
131 E5 **Treherbert** Rhondd
106 A5 **Tre-Hill** V Glam
16 D6 **Trehunist** Cnwll
131 F3 **Tre-Ifor** Rhondd
16 B5 **Trekeivesteps** Cnwll
16 D3 **Trekenner** Cnwll
14 B6 **Trekenning** Cnwll
22 B5 **Treknow** Cnwll
4 D5 **Trelan** Cnwll
287 H1 **Tre-Lan** Flints
22 D4 **Trelash** Cnwll
307 F4 **Trelawnyd** Flints
153 F3 **Trelech** Carmth
150 B4 **Treleddyd-fawr** Pembks
6 D5 **Treleigh** Cnwll
5 F1 **Trelew** Cnwll
132 B5 **Trelewis** Myr Td
22 B6 **Treligga** Cnwll
14 D3 **Trelights** Cnwll
15 E3 **Trelill** Cnwll
7 H3 **Trelion** Cnwll
7 F4 **Treliske** Cnwll
7 F6 **Trelissick** Cnwll
14 D5 **Treliver** Cnwll
134 C3 **Trellech** Mons
134 B4 **Trellech Grange** Mons
307 G4 **Trelogan** Flints
4 C3 **Treloquithack** Cnwll
10 A2 **Trelowia** Cnwll
8 B3 **Treloweth** Cnwll
233 E4 **Trelystan** Powys
264 D2 **Tremadog** Gwynd
22 D5 **Tremail** Cnwll
179 E4 **Tremain** Cerdgn
23 E5 **Tremaine** Cnwll
105 E4 **Tremains** Brdgnd
16 C5 **Tremar** Cnwll
10 C2 **Trematon** Cnwll
10 D2 **Trematon Castle** Cnwll
4 B1 **Tremayne** Cnwll
16 C5 **Trembraze** Cnwll
3 E2 **Tremedda** Cnwll
307 F5 **Tremeirchion** Denbgs
2 D3 **Tremethick Cross** Cnwll
154 B3 **Tremle** Carmth
15 E6 **Tremore** Cnwll
14 B6 **Tremorebridge** Cnwll
106 D4 **Tremorfa** Cardif
307 G4 **Tre-Mostyn** Flints
22 B5 **Trenale** Cnwll
14 B5 **Trenance** Cnwll
14 D6 **Trenance** Cnwll
14 D4 **Trenant** Cnwll
16 B5 **Trenant** Cnwll
8 C4 **Trenarren** Cnwll
15 H5 **Trenay** Cnwll
235 F2 **Trench** Wrekin
116 A4 **Trench Green** Oxon
97 E5 **Trench Wood** Kent
7 F1 **Trencreek** Cnwll
22 D3 **Trencreek** Cnwll
3 F2 **Trencrom** Cnwll
7 G3 **Trendeal** Cnwll
4 C2 **Trenear** Cnwll
22 D5 **Treneglos** Cnwll
3 G2 **Trenerth** Cnwll
9 F3 **Trenewan** Cnwll
16 B5 **Trengale** Cnwll
22 D4 **Trengune** Cnwll
16 C3 **Trenhorne** Cnwll
15 E6 **Treningle** Cnwll
7 F1 **Treninnick** Cnwll
4 D5 **Trenoon** Cnwll
4 D2 **Trenoweth** Cnwll
67 F6 **Trent** Dorset
272 C1 **Trentham** C Stke
61 F2 **Trentishoe** Devon
276 A3 **Trentlock** Derbys
4 B2 **Trenwheal** Cnwll
105 E4 **Treoes** V Glam
131 F5 **Treorchy** Rhondd
132 D5 **Treowen** Caerph
208 B1 **Treowen** Powys
105 E5 **Tre-Pit** V Glam
15 E3 **Trequite** Cnwll
205 F1 **Tre'r-ddôl** Cerdgn
105 G4 **Trerhyngyll** V Glam
4 D5 **Trerise** Cnwll
5 E3 **Trerose** Cnwll
10 B2 **Trerulefoot** Cnwll
179 F3 **Tresaith** Cerdgn
6 D6 **Tresamble** Cnwll
15 F4 **Tresarrett** Cnwll
6 D6 **Tresavean** Cnwll
7 G4 **Tresawle** Cnwll
7 E4 **Tresawsen** Cnwll
8 C1 **Trescoll** Cnwll
236 B5 **Trescott** Staffs
3 G3 **Trescowe** Cnwll
7 E2 **Tresean** Cnwll
4 D1 **Tresevern Croft** Cnwll
110 D1 **Tresham** Gloucs
7 G4 **Tresillian** Cnwll
15 G2 **Tresinney** Cnwll
151 F1 **Tresinwen** Pembks
6 D5 **Treskerby** Cnwll
6 C6 **Treskillard** Cnwll
8 C2 **Treskilling** Cnwll
23 E3 **Treskinnick Cross** Cnwll
6 B6 **Treslothan** Cnwll
23 E5 **Tresmeer** Cnwll
3 G4 **Tresowes Green** Cnwll
4 B3 **Tresoweshill** Cnwll
22 C4 **Tresparrett** Cnwll
22 C4 **Tresparrett Posts** Cnwll
576 E3 **Tressady** Highld
524 B3 **Tressait** P & K
606 E7 **Tresta** Shet
609 J6 **Tresta** Shet
317 E4 **Treswell** Notts
6 B5 **Treswithian** Cnwll
6 B5 **Treswithian Downs** Cnwll
205 F1 **Tre Taliesin** Cerdgn
6 D6 **Trethellan Water** Cnwll
22 B5 **Trethevy** Cnwll
5 G1 **Trethewell** Cnwll
2 C5 **Trethewey** Cnwll
14 B3 **Trethillick** Cnwll
106 C2 **Trethomas** Caerph
8 A3 **Trethosa** Cnwll
8 C3 **Trethowel** Cnwll
8 C2 **Trethurgy** Cnwll
150 C4 **Tretio** Cerdgn
160 C5 **Tretire** Herefs
158 C5 **Tretower** Powys
288 B3 **Treuddyn** Flints
16 C3 **Trevadlock** Cnwll
7 E2 **Trevail** Cnwll
22 B4 **Trevalga** Cnwll
3 E1 **Trevalgan** Cnwll
289 E3 **Trevalyn** Wrexhm
14 C4 **Trevance** Cnwll
14 C3 **Trevanger** Cnwll

14 D4 **Trevanson** Cnwll
3 E3 **Trevarrack** Cnwll
7 H1 **Trevarren** Cnwll
14 B5 **Trevarrian** Cnwll
8 B5 **Trevarrick** Cnwll
6 D5 **Trevarth** Cnwll
127 E1 **Trevaughan** Carmth
154 A5 **Trevaughan** Carmth
3 E1 **Treveal** Cnwll
2 C4 **Trevegean** Cnwll
15 F3 **Treveighan** Cnwll
6 D3 **Trevellas** Cnwll
16 B6 **Trevelmond** Cnwll
14 C4 **Trevelver** Cnwll
7 F7 **Trevemper** Cnwll
22 B5 **Treven** Cnwll
22 C4 **Trevena** Cnwll
4 B3 **Trevenen** Cnwll
4 C3 **Trevenen** Cnwll
4 C3 **Trevenen Bal** Cnwll
15 F3 **Trevenning** Cnwll
8 B5 **Treveor** Cnwll
16 A5 **Treverbyn** Cnwll
5 E2 **Treverva** Cnwll
2 C5 **Trevescan** Cnwll
133 E4 **Trevethin** Torfn
22 B6 **Trevia** Cnwll
16 D5 **Trevigro** Cnwll
15 E4 **Trevilder** Cnwll
7 F6 **Trevilla** Cnwll
22 D4 **Trevillian** Cnwll
8 A4 **Trevillick** Cnwll
7 F2 **Trevilson** Cnwll
14 D3 **Trevine** Cnwll
8 A2 **Treviscoe** Cnwll
6 D6 **Treviskey** Cnwll
3 E4 **Trevithal** Cnwll
7 F3 **Trevoll** Cnwll
14 B3 **Trevone** Cnwll
288 C6 **Trevor** Wrexhm
14 C4 **Trevorrick** Cnwll
288 B6 **Trevor Uchaf** Denbgs
7 E2 **Trevowah** Cnwll
2 D2 **Trevowhan** Cnwll
4 B3 **Trew** Cnwll
15 F2 **Trewalder** Cnwll
22 B5 **Trewarmett** Cnwll
3 F2 **Trewartha** Cnwll
7 H6 **Trewartha** Cnwll
7 H5 **Trewarthenick** Cnwll
22 C3 **Trewassa** Cnwll
16 B2 **Treween** Cnwll
2 C3 **Trewellard** Cnwll
22 B6 **Trewen** Cnwll
23 F6 **Trewen** Cnwll
109 E1 **Trewen** Mons
4 C3 **Trewennack** Cnwll
15 F2 **Trewennan** Cnwll
233 E2 **Trewern** Powys
15 E2 **Trewethen** Cnwll
15 E3 **Trewethern** Cnwll
14 D3 **Trewethern** Cnwll
2 D2 **Trewey** Cnwll
9 H2 **Trewidland** Cnwll
15 G6 **Trewindle** Cnwll
16 B2 **Trewint** Cnwll
16 C6 **Trewint** Cnwll
22 D3 **Trewint** Cnwll
5 G1 **Trewithian** Cnwll
23 F5 **Trewithick** Cnwll
8 C5 **Trewollock** Cnwll
16 D4 **Trewoodloe** Cnwll
4 C5 **Trewoon** Cnwll
8 B3 **Trewoon** Cnwll
7 G5 **Treworga** Cnwll
134 A3 **Treworgan Common** Mons
7 G6 **Treworlas** Cnwll
22 C4 **Treworld** Cnwll
14 B4 **Trewornan** Cnwll
16 B5 **Treworrick** Cnwll
16 B5 **Treworthal** Cnwll
23 G2 **Trewyn** Devon
159 F5 **Tre-wyn** Mons
14 B4 **Treyarnon** Cnwll
74 C6 **Treyford** W Susx
8 B2 **Trezaise** Cnwll
3 E3 **Trezelah** Cnwll
341 G5 **Triangle** Calder
134 C4 **Triangle** Gloucs
237 G3 **Triangle** Staffs
8 D5 **Trickett's Cross** Dorset
28 D3 **Tricombe** Devon
151 G5 **Triffleton** Pembks
29 E3 **Trill** Devon
23 F5 **Trillacott** Cnwll
395 H3 **Trimdon** Dur
396 A2 **Trimdon Colliery** Dur
395 H2 **Trimdon Grange** Dur
256 B2 **Trimingham** Norfk
177 E2 **Trimley Lower Street** Suffk
177 E2 **Trimley St Martin** Suffk
177 E2 **Trimley St Mary** Suffk
212 A4 **Trimpley** Worcs
128 C4 **Trimsaran** Carmth
171 G6 **Trims Green** Herts
523 K3 **Trinafour** P & K
132 C4 **Trinant** Caerph
142 C2 **Tring** Herts
142 C2 **Tringford** Herts
142 C2 **Tring Wharf** Herts
528 D2 **Trinity** Angus
488 A4 **Trinity** C Edin
27 F1 **Trinity** Devon
35 I6 **Trinity** Jersey
511 H6 **Trinity Gask** P & K
205 G4 **Trisant** Cerdgn
64 B4 **Triscombe** Somset
533 G8 **Trislaig** Highld
7 F3 **Trispen** Cnwll
430 D1 **Tritlington** Nthumb
7 G2 **Troan** Cnwll
512 A2 **Trochry** P & K
132 C3 **Troearhiwgwair** Blae G
183 F4 **Troedrhiwdalar** Powys
154 B1 **Troedrhiwfenyd** Cerdgn
132 B4 **Troedrhiwfuwch** Caerph
179 G4 **Troedyraur** Cerdgn
131 H4 **Troedyrhiw** Myr Td
306 B5 **Trofarth** Conwy
35 h6 **Trois Bois** Jersey
57 G2 **Trolliloes** E Susx
606 E3 **Trondavoe** Shet
602 B7 **Tronston** Ork
6 C6 **Troon** Cnwll
444 D3 **Troon** S Ayrs
125 G2 **Trooper's Inn** Pembks
423 G4 **Troqueer** D & G
224 B5 **Troston** Suffk
128 D5 **Trostre** Carmth
133 G4 **Trostrey Common** Mons
23 E4 **Troswell** Cnwll
605 H7 **Troswickness** Shet
188 C3 **Trotshill** Worcs
74 C4 **Trotten Marsh** W Susx
514 C3 **Trottick** D & G
74 C5 **Trottiscliffe** Kent
97 F5 **Trotton** W Susx
340 D5 **Trough Gate** Lancs
378 C4 **Troutbeck** Cumb
390 B4 **Troutbeck** Cumb
378 D4 **Troutbeck Bridge** Cumb
28 C5 **Trow** Devon
314 D4 **Troway** Derbys

106 D3 **Trowbridge** Cardif
87 E3 **Trowbridge** Wilts
276 A3 **Trowell** Notts
134 D3 **Trow Green** Gloucs
87 E3 **Trowle Common** Wilts
143 F2 **Trowley Bottom** Herts
452 C3 **Trows** Border
250 B3 **Trowse Newton** Norfk
342 D3 **Troydale** Leeds
96 B5 **Troy Town** Kent
99 H6 **Troy Town** Kent
98 A1 **Troy Town** Medway
22 B5 **Truas** Cnwll
326 C3 **Trub** Rochdl
86 C6 **Trudoxhill** Somset
87 E3 **Trueman's Heath** Worcs
19 H5 **True Street** Devon
43 H3 **Trull** Somset
592 F3 **Trumaisgearraidh** W Isls
330 D2 **Trumfleet** Donc
542 C4 **Trumpan** Highld
161 F2 **Trumpet** Herefs
197 G4 **Trumpington** Cambs
93 G1 **Trumps Green** Surrey
256 D3 **Trunch** Norfk
350 D6 **Trunnah** Lancs
7 E5 **Truro** Cnwll
23 G5 **Truscott** Cnwll
20 B1 **Trusham** Devon
274 D2 **Trusley** Derbys
4 C3 **Trussall** Cnwll
321 F3 **Trusthorpe** Lincs
7 F3 **Truthan** Cnwll
3 F3 **Truthwall** Cnwll
232 C5 **Trwstllewelyn** Powys
303 F4 **Tryfil** IoA
236 C6 **Trysull** Staffs
3 E3 **Trythogga** Cnwll
8 B5 **Tubbs Mill** Cnwll
139 G5 **Tubney** Oxon
79 H3 **Tubslake** Kent
13 E1 **Tuckenhay** Devon
17 F5 **Tuckermarsh** Devon
44 B2 **Tuckerton** Somset
212 A2 **Tuckhill** Shrops
86 D2 **Tucking Mill** BaNES
6 C5 **Tuckingmill** Cnwll
15 F3 **Tuckingmill** Cnwll
23 E4 **Tuckingmill** Cnwll
69 F4 **Tuckingmill** Wilts
34 D2 **Tuckton** Bmouth
223 E5 **Tuddenham** Suffk
201 G5 **Tuddenham St Martin** Suffk
97 F5 **Tudeley** Kent
97 F5 **Tudeley Hale** Kent
29 F2 **Tudhay** Devon
395 F2 **Tudhoe** Dur
395 F3 **Tudhoe Grange** Dur
237 H5 **Tudor Hill** Birm
160 D5 **Tudorville** Herefs
262 C3 **Tudweiliog** Gwynd
325 G6 **Tuebrook** Lpool
16 B5 **Tuelmenna** Cnwll
75 F1 **Tuesley** Surrey
80 D1 **Tuesnoad** Kent
136 B1 **Tuffley** Gloucs
119 F2 **Tufnell Park** Gt Lon
90 D5 **Tufton** Hants
152 A4 **Tufton** Pembks
241 G4 **Tugby** Leics
210 C2 **Tugford** Shrops
455 G4 **Tughall** Nthumb
568 E2 **Tugnet** Moray
606 D8 **Tulkie** Shet
74 C4 **Tullecombe** W Susx
499 E2 **Tullibardine** P & K
498 D6 **Tullibody** Clacks
494 B1 **Tullich** Ag & B
566 C2 **Tullich Muir** Highld
524 E5 **Tulliemet** P & K
541 E5 **Tulloch** Abers
551 H6 **Tulloch** Highld
576 D5 **Tulloch** Highld
512 C4 **Tulloch** P & K
493 G5 **Tullochgorm** Ag & B
528 B5 **Tulloes** Angus
557 G4 **Tullos** C Aber
510 C5 **Tullybannocher** P & K
483 G2 **Tullycross** Stirlg
526 A4 **Tullymurdoch** P & K
558 D6 **Tullynessle** Abers
119 G5 **Tulse Hill** Gt Lon
128 D2 **Tumble** Carmth
173 G4 **Tumbler's Green** Essex
299 H3 **Tumby Woodside** Lincs
523 L4 **Tummel Bridge** P & K
135 G4 **Tumpy Green** Gloucs
186 D5 **Tumpy Lakes** Herefs
122 B5 **Tunbridge Hill** Medway
78 D2 **Tunbridge Wells** Kent
424 D3 **Tundergarth Mains** D & G
599 J7 **Tunga** W Isls
256 B4 **Tungate** Norfk
86 B3 **Tunley** BaNES
136 D4 **Tunley** Gloucs
162 B1 **Tunnel Hill** Worcs
331 F4 **Tunnel Pits** N Linc
326 D2 **Tunshill** Rochdl
291 H4 **Tunstall** C Stke
349 E3 **Tunstall** E R Yk
98 D2 **Tunstall** Kent
366 C5 **Tunstall** Lancs
383 F5 **Tunstall** N York
251 E3 **Tunstall** Norfk
271 H4 **Tunstall** Staffs
202 D3 **Tunstall** Suffk
406 B4 **Tunstall** Sundld
406 B4 **Tunstall Hills** Sundld
313 F5 **Tunstead** Derbys
256 B5 **Tunstead** Norfk
327 F4 **Tunstead** Old Ham
91 H5 **Tunworth** Hants
160 C1 **Tupsley** Herefs
294 D1 **Tupton** Derbys
48 C6 **Turbary Common** Bmouth
15 F5 **Turfdown** Cnwll
570 F6 **Turfhill** Abers
326 D2 **Turf Hill** Rochdl
447 G2 **Turfholm** S Lans
29 E2 **Turfmoor** Devon
269 G6 **Turfmoor** Shrops
92 A3 **Turgis Green** Hants
528 B4 **Turin** Angus
163 H6 **Turkdean** Gloucs
51 G2 **Turkey Island** Hants
74 B6 **Turkey Island** W Susx
160 C4 **Turkey Tump** Herefs
241 F5 **Tur Langton** Leics
87 E2 **Turleigh** Wilts
211 H2 **Turleygreen** Shrops
34 A2 **Turlin Moor** Poole
49 E3 **Turmer** Hants
340 C6 **Turn** Lancs
159 F2 **Turnastone** Herefs
432 A3 **Turnberry** S Ayrs
11 E3 **Turnchapel** C Plym
294 B5 **Turnditch** Derbys
339 F3 **Turner Green** Lancs
79 E3 **Turner's Green** E Susx
79 E6 **Turner's Green** E Susx
115 E6 **Turner's Green** W Berk
214 B6 **Turner's Green** Warwks
77 F2 **Turners Hill** W Susx

47 F6 **Turners Puddle** Dorset
487 G5 **Turnhouse** C Edin
291 H4 **Turnhurst** C Stke
312 D4 **Turnstead Milton** Derbys
570 C6 **Turnworth** Dorset
570 C6 **Turriff** Abers
395 G2 **Tursdale** Dur
325 G1 **Turton Bottoms** Bl w D
244 D5 **Turves** Cambs
213 F4 **Turves Green** Birm
194 C4 **Turvey** Beds
116 B1 **Turville** Bucks
116 B1 **Turville Heath** Bucks
166 D2 **Turweston** Bucks
450 C6 **Tushielaw** Border
274 C4 **Tutbury** Staffs
213 E5 **Tutnall** Worcs
135 E4 **Tutnalls** Gloucs
134 C6 **Tutshill** Gloucs
99 F5 **Tutt Hill** Kent
256 A4 **Tuttington** Norfk
115 F5 **Tutts Clump** W Berk
17 E3 **Tutwell** Cnwll
316 D5 **Tuxford** Notts
602 B7 **Twatt** Ork
606 D7 **Twatt** Shet
485 E4 **Twechar** E Duns
471 E4 **Tweeddaleburn** Mdloth
475 E4 **Tweedmouth** Nthumb
449 E5 **Tweedsmuir** Border
7 E5 **Twelveheads** Cnwll
58 A2 **Twelve Oaks** E Susx
16 A5 **Twelvewoods** Cnwll
311 F6 **Twemlow Green** Ches
101 F2 **Twenties** Kent
279 H5 **Twenty** Lincs
86 C2 **Twerton** BaNES
118 C5 **Twickenham** Gt Lon
162 B5 **Twigworth** Gloucs
77 E6 **Twineham** W Susx
77 E5 **Twineham Green** W Susx
86 C3 **Twinhoe** BaNES
173 H2 **Twinstead** Essex
173 H2 **Twinstead Green** Essex
325 F5 **Twiss Green** Warrtn
29 E2 **Twist** Devon
353 G6 **Twiston** Lancs
62 B5 **Twitchen** Devon
209 G4 **Twitchen** Shrops
62 B5 **Twitchen Mill** Devon
101 E4 **Twitham** Kent
96 D3 **Twitton** Kent
18 D3 **Two Bridges** Devon
135 F3 **Two Bridges** Gloucs
6 D4 **Two Burrows** Cnwll
294 B2 **Two Dales** Derbys
238 C4 **Two Gates** Staffs
167 H2 **Two Mile Ash** M Keyn
76 B4 **Two Mile Ash** W Susx
110 A5 **Two Mile Hill** Bristl
20 A4 **Two Mile Oak Cross** Devon
308 D5 **Two Mills** Ches
60 D3 **Two Pots** Devon
302 B4 **Twr** IoA
239 E4 **Twycross** Leics
98 B1 **Twydall** Medway
167 E4 **Twyford** Bucks
275 E4 **Twyford** Derbys
69 E6 **Twyford** Dorset
72 C4 **Twyford** Hants
241 F2 **Twyford** Leics
254 D3 **Twyford** Norfk
165 H2 **Twyford** Oxon
269 F4 **Twyford** Shrops
116 C4 **Twyford** Wokham
189 F5 **Twyford** Worcs
160 C3 **Twyford Common** Herefs
132 D2 **Twyn-Allws** Mons
412 C4 **Twynholm** D & G
162 C2 **Twyning** Gloucs
162 D2 **Twyning Green** Gloucs
156 A5 **Twynllanan** Carmth
129 G2 **Twynmynydd** Carmth
132 C6 **Twyn Shôn-Ifan** Caerph
131 H3 **Twynyrodyn** Myr Td
106 B5 **Twyn-yr-odyn** V Glam
133 H3 **Twyn-y-Sheriff** Mons
218 D4 **Twywell** Nhants
159 G2 **Tyberton** Herefs
214 A1 **Tyburn** Birm
255 E2 **Tyby** Norfk
103 F3 **Ty-coch** Swans
129 F2 **Tycroes** Carmth
282 B1 **Ty Croes** IoA
268 B6 **Tycrwyn** Powys
281 G6 **Tydd Gote** Lincs
245 F1 **Tydd St Giles** Cambs
281 F6 **Tydd St Mary** Lincs
207 F2 **Tyddyn** Powys
287 F5 **Tyddyn Angharad** Denbgs
303 F2 **Tyddyn Dai** IoA
103 G3 **Ty-draw** Swans
54 C4 **Tye** Hants
146 D6 **Tye Common** Essex
145 F3 **Tye Green** Essex
146 C2 **Tye Green** Essex
146 D5 **Tye Green** Essex
172 A5 **Tye Green** Essex
172 B2 **Tye Green** Essex
173 F5 **Tye Green** Essex
342 C3 **Tyersal** Brad
134 A5 **Ty-fry** Mons
105 G5 **Tyganol** V Glam
262 B4 **Ty-hen** Gwynd
128 D5 **Ty-isaf** Carmth
132 D2 **Tyla** Mons
105 E2 **Tylagwyn** Brdgnd
325 F4 **Tyldesley** Wigan
155 G4 **Tyle** Carmth
105 G3 **Tyle-Garw** Rhondd
100 B3 **Tyler Hill** Kent
144 C3 **Tylers Causeway** Herts
142 B6 **Tylers Green** Bucks
145 H3 **Tyler's Green** Essex
95 G4 **Tyler's Green** Surrey
142 D4 **Tyler's Hill** Bucks
132 C3 **Ty Llwyn** Blae G
131 G5 **Tylorstown** Rhondd
207 F3 **Tylwch** Powys
306 D1 **Ty-mawr** Conwy
286 B5 **Ty Mawr Cwm** Conwy
180 D3 **Ty-nant** Cerdgn
286 D6 **Ty-nant** Gwynd
267 E4 **Ty-nant** Gwynd
105 H3 **Tynant** Rhondd
508 D3 **Tyndrum** Stirlg
406 A1 **Tyne Dock** S Tyne
33 F3 **Tyneham** Dorset
471 G3 **Tynehead** Mdloth
431 G6 **Tynemouth** N Tyne
406 A1 **Tyne Tunnel** S Tyne
179 E4 **Tynewydd** Cerdgn
204 C6 **Ty-Newydd** Cerdgn
130 C3 **Tynewydd** Neath
131 E5 **Tynewydd** Rhondd
86 B3 **Tyning** BaNES
490 A4 **Tyninghame** E Loth
283 E4 **Tyn-lon** Gwynd
435 G6 **Tynron** D & G
109 F5 **Tyntesfield** N Som
131 H5 **Tyntetown** Rhondd
105 F2 **Ty'n-y-bryn** Rhondd
269 E4 **Tyn-y-coed** Shrops

106 C2 **Ty'n-y-coedcae** Caerph
129 H4 **Tyn-y-cwm** Swans
286 D1 **Tynyfedw** Conwy
307 E5 **Ty'n-y-ffordd** Denbgs
268 B3 **Ty-n-y-ffridd** Powys
104 D3 **Ty'n-y-Garn** Brdgnd
304 B3 **Tynygongl** IoA
205 F6 **Tynygraig** Cerdgn
183 G5 **Tyn-y-graig** Powys
305 G5 **Ty'n-y-groes** Conwy
206 D2 **Tynywrwra** Powys
168 D3 **Tyrells End** Beds
94 D3 **Tyrell's Wood** Surrey
286 B2 **Ty'r-felin-isaf** Conwy
106 B3 **Ty Rhiw** Rhondd
152 D1 **Tyrhos** Pembks
571 G3 **Tyrie** Abers
194 B5 **Tyringham** M Keyn
213 H3 **Tyseley** Birm
107 E1 **Ty-Sign** Caerph
39 F4 **Tythecott** Devon
104 D4 **Tythegston** Brdgnd
312 B4 **Tytherington** Ches
110 B2 **Tytherington** S Glos
86 D5 **Tytherington** Somset
69 F1 **Tytherington** Wilts
29 F2 **Tytherleigh** Devon
111 H5 **Tytherton Lucas** Wilts
143 H3 **Tyttenhanger** Herts
8 D3 **Tywardreath** Cnwll
8 D2 **Tywardreath Highway** Cnwll
305 G4 **Tywyn** Conwy
228 D4 **Tywyn** Gwynd

U

592 D6 **Uachdar** W Isls
226 C5 **Ubbeston** Suffk
226 C5 **Ubbeston Green** Suffk
85 F3 **Ubley** BaNES
383 F4 **Uckerby** N York
78 B5 **Uckfield** E Susx
162 C2 **Uckinghall** Worcs
162 D5 **Uckington** Gloucs
234 D3 **Uckington** Shrops
467 G2 **Uddingston** S Lans
447 H3 **Uddington** S Lans
59 E3 **Udimore** E Susx
85 E2 **Udley** N Som
560 C4 **Udny Green** Abers
560 D5 **Udny Station** Abers
467 G3 **Udston** S Lans
467 H5 **Udstonhead** S Lans
112 D4 **Uffcott** Wilts
43 E5 **Uffculme** Devon
243 F3 **Uffington** Lincs
113 H2 **Uffington** Oxon
234 C2 **Uffington** Shrops
243 F4 **Ufford** C Pete
202 B4 **Ufford** Suffk
191 F2 **Ufton** Warwks
115 G6 **Ufton Green** W Berk
91 G1 **Ufton Nervet** W Berk
459 F6 **Ugadale** Ag & B
12 B1 **Ugborough** Devon
70 B3 **Ugford** Wilts
227 E3 **Uggeshall** Suffk
387 E3 **Ugglebarnby** N York
314 B1 **Ughill** Sheff
171 H4 **Ugley** Essex
171 H4 **Ugley Green** Essex
386 C2 **Ugthorpe** N York
591 C8 **Uidh** W Isls
516 F5 **Uig** Ag & B
542 B6 **Uig** Highld
542 B3 **Uig** Highld
598 B8 **Uigen** W Isls
543 G7 **Uigshader** Highld
504 D7 **Uisken** Ag & B
583 K1 **Ulbster** Highld
390 C5 **Ulcat Row** Cumb
320 D5 **Ulceby** Lincs
333 G2 **Ulceby** N Linc
333 G1 **Ulceby Skitter** N Linc
98 C5 **Ulcombe** Kent
389 G2 **Uldale** Cumb
136 A5 **Uley** Gloucs
430 D1 **Ulgham** Nthumb
574 C5 **Ullapool** Highld
43 H6 **Ullcombe** Devon
189 H1 **Ullenhall** Warwks
136 D1 **Ullenwood** Gloucs
344 C2 **Ulleskelf** N York
216 A2 **Ullesthorpe** Leics
315 F2 **Ulley** Rothm
186 D5 **Ullingswick** Herefs
189 H5 **Ullington** Worcs
544 E2 **Ullinish** Highld
388 C5 **Ullock** Cumb
389 F5 **Ullock** Cumb
377 F6 **Ulpha** Cumb
361 F3 **Ulrome** E R Yk
369 F2 **Ulshaw** N York
607 G1 **Ulsta** Shet
214 A3 **Ulverley Green** Solhll
363 F6 **Ulverston** Cumb
34 B4 **Ulwell** Dorset
435 F3 **Ulzieside** D & G
40 B3 **Umberleigh** Devon
28 D3 **Umborne** Devon
579 H3 **Unapool** Highld
328 A3 **Under Bank** Kirk
365 G1 **Underbarrow** Cumb
342 C3 **Undercliffe** Brad
26 D5 **Underdown** Devon
69 E3 **Underhill** Wilts
609 H4 **Underhoull** Shet
98 B5 **Underling Green** Kent
96 D4 **Underriver** Kent
97 E4 **Underriver Ho** Kent
100 D2 **Under the Wood** Kent
314 B2 **Under Tofts** Sheff
211 F1 **Underton** Shrops
11 F2 **Underwood** C Plym
108 C2 **Underwood** Newpt
295 H4 **Underwood** Notts
125 G2 **Underwood** Pembks
222 D3 **Undley** Suffk
108 D2 **Undy** Mons
606 C6 **Unifirth** Shet
322 e7 **Union Mills** IoM
79 G3 **Union Street** E Susx
6 D5 **United Downs** Cnwll
314 D4 **Unstone** Derbys
314 D4 **Unstone Green** Derbys
326 B3 **Unsworth** Bury
390 C2 **Unthank** Cumb
391 G1 **Unthank** Cumb
400 C5 **Unthank** Cumb
314 C4 **Unthank** Derbys
88 D3 **Upavon** Wilts
31 E2 **Up Cerne** Dorset
122 C6 **Upchurch** Kent
38 B4 **Upcott** Devon
40 B5 **Upcott** Devon
40 D6 **Upcott** Devon
60 C4 **Upcott** Devon
185 F4 **Upcott** Herefs
43 G3 **Upcott** Somset
198 D3 **Upend** Cambs

194 C5	Up End M Keyn
27 E2	Up Exe Devon
255 F4	Upgate Norfk
225 E1	Upgate Street Norfk
226 B1	Upgate Street Norfk
92 C2	Up Green Hants
30 D2	Uphall Dorset
487 E5	Uphall W Loth
41 H6	Upham Devon
72 D5	Upham Hants
185 G2	Uphampton Herefs
188 B2	Uphampton Worcs
162 D5	Up Hatherley Gloucs
19 H5	Uphempston Devon
84 B3	Uphill N Som
84 B3	Uphill Manor N Som
324 C4	Up Holland Lancs
136 C3	Uplands Gloucs
103 F3	Uplands Swans
466 B3	Uplawmoor E Rens
161 H4	Upleadon Gloucs
161 H4	Upleadon Court Gloucs
397 F6	Upleatham R & Cl
99 F2	Uplees Kent
30 C4	Uploders Dorset
42 D4	Uplowman Devon
29 F4	Uplyme Devon
52 D2	Up Marden W Susx
121 E2	Upminster Gt Lon
67 F6	Up Mudford Somset
92 B4	Up Nately Hants
43 H6	Upottery Devon
40 A2	Uppacott Devon
577 J3	Uppat Highld
171 G4	Uppend Essex
210 A2	Upper Affcot Shrops
576 D6	Upper Ardchronie Highld
211 H3	Upper Arley Worcs
343 E3	Upper Armley Leeds
140 D1	Upper Arncott Oxon
270 C6	Upper Astley Shrops
236 B6	Upper Aston Shrops
166 B2	Upper Astrop Nhants
578 F1	Upper Badcall Highld
304 C5	Upper Bangor Gwynd
115 F4	Upper Basildon W Berk
270 C6	Upper Battlefield Shrops
55 E2	Upper Beeding W Susx
218 D2	Upper Benefield Nhants
189 E1	Upper Bentley Worcs
587 J5	Upper Bighouse Highld
295 E3	Upper Birchwood Derbys
472 C6	Upper Blainslie Border
106 B2	Upper Boat Rhondd
559 E3	Upper Boddam Abers
192 A4	Upper Boddington Nhants
37 F5	Upper Bonchurch IoW
313 F2	Upper Booth Derbys
204 D2	Upper Borth Cerdgn
571 G3	Upper Boyndlie Abers
164 D2	Upper Brailes Warwks
248 D3	Upper Brandon Parva Norfk
546 B5	Upper Breakish Highld
160 B1	Upper Breinton Herefs
341 H4	Upper Brockholes Calder
277 E4	Upper Broughton Notts
185 G4	Upper Broxwood Herefs
216 D2	Upper Bruntingthorpe Leics
129 H2	Upper Brynamman Carmth
160 D3	Upper Buckenhill Herefs
115 E6	Upper Bucklebury W Berk
72 C1	Upper Bullington Hants
49 E1	Upper Burgate Hants
557 E5	Upper Burnhaugh Abers
97 G1	Upper Bush Medway
400 D4	Upperby Cumb
195 H5	Upper Caldecote Beds
135 H5	Upper Cam Gloucs
583 J1	Upper Camster Highld
84 C3	Upper Canada N Som
49 H2	Upper Canterton Hants
192 B3	Upper Catesby Nhants
213 E5	Upper Catshill Worcs
157 G1	Upper Chapel Powys
44 A2	Upper Cheddon Somset
69 G3	Upper Chicksgrove Wilts
105 H2	Upper Church Village Rhondd
89 G4	Upper Chute Wilts
90 A6	Upper Clatford Hants
137 E1	Upper Coberley Gloucs
270 D3	Upper College Shrops
187 H6	Upper Colwall Herefs
91 G5	Upper Common Hants
293 E5	Upper Cotton Staffs
234 D3	Upper Cound Shrops
85 F6	Upper Croxley Somset
329 F3	Upper Cudworth Barns
328 C3	Upper Cumberworth Kirk
133 E5	Upper Cwmbran Torfn
313 G5	Upperdale Derbys
606 A7	Upperdale Shet
568 F3	Upper Dallachy Moray
436 A3	Upper Dalveen D & G
101 G5	Upper Deal Kent
219 E6	Upper Dean Beds
19 F5	Upper Dean Devon
328 C1	Upper Denby Kirk
328 C3	Upper Denby Kirk
401 H1	Upper Denton Cumb
551 J3	Upper Derraid Highld
562 E4	Upper Diabaig Highld
57 F2	Upper Dicker E Susx
210 A3	Upper Dinchope Shrops
160 D2	Upper Dormington Herefs
588 C3	Upper Dounreay Highld
176 D3	Upper Dovercourt Essex
163 F6	Upper Dowdeswell Gloucs
357 E2	Upper Dunsforth N York
142 C2	Upper Dunsley Herts
93 G6	Upper Eashing Surrey
214 D3	Upper Eastern Green Covtry
566 D4	Upper Eathie Highld
187 E5	Upper Egleton Herefs
293 E3	Upper Elkstone Staffs
293 F6	Upper Ellastone Staffs
95 H1	Upper Elmers End Gt Lon
313 E4	Upper End Derbys
137 F3	Upper End Gloucs
137 H2	Upper End Gloucs
241 F2	Upper End Leics
90 B4	Upper Enham Hants
211 H1	Upper Farmcote Shrops
73 H2	Upper Farringdon Hants
542 D8	Upper Feorlig Highld
44 C3	Upper Fivehead Somset
211 G2	Upper Forge Shrops
135 H2	Upper Framilode Gloucs
92 C6	Upper Froyle Hants
213 E6	Upper Gambolds Worcs
589 J2	Upper Gills Highld
533 L5	Upper Glenfintaig Highld
85 E6	Upper Godney Somset
101 E5	Upper Goldstone Kent
236 D6	Upper Gornal Dudley
169 G2	Upper Gravenhurst Beds
171 F3	Upper Green Essex
343 E4	Upper Green Leeds
159 G6	Upper Green Mons

199 E2	Upper Green Suffk
90 B2	Upper Green W Berk
160 C4	Upper Grove Common Herefs
254 D2	Upper Guist Norfk
294 B2	Upper Hackney Derbys
92 D5	Upper Hale Surrey
542 C5	Upper Halistra Highld
118 B6	Upper Halliford Surrey
97 G2	Upper Halling Medway
162 C2	Upper Ham Worcs
242 C3	Upper Hambleton Rutlnd
186 C3	Upper Hamnish Herefs
527 E6	Upper Handwick Angus
100 B4	Upper Harbledown Kent
100 B5	Upper Hardres Court Kent
185 H3	Upper Hardwick Herefs
78 B3	Upper Hartfield E Susx
294 D4	Upper Hartshay Derbys
163 F1	Upper Haselor Worcs
272 B2	Upper Hatton Staffs
329 G5	Upper Haugh Rothm
97 E6	Upper Hayesden Kent
210 C3	Upper Hayton Shrops
342 C6	Upper Heaton Kirk
249 H2	Upper Hellesdon Norfk
358 C3	Upper Helmsley N York
269 E3	Upper Hengoed Shrops
185 E4	Upper Hergest Herefs
193 E3	Upper Heyford Nhants
166 A4	Upper Heyford Oxon
186 B4	Upper Hill Herefs
135 F5	Upper Hill S Glos
441 E3	Upper Hindhope Border
119 F2	Upper Holloway Gt Lon
226 D4	Upper Holton Suffk
342 D6	Upper Hopton Kirk
57 F2	Upper Horsebridge E Susx
188 A5	Upper Howsell Worcs
292 D2	Upper Hulme Staffs
37 F4	Upper Hyde IoW
75 G3	Upper Ifold Surrey
138 C5	Upper Inglesham Swindn
570 F5	Upper Ironside Abers
503 F2	Upper Kenley Fife
606 F6	Upper Kergord Shet
470 D6	Upper Kidston Border
478 B2	Upper Kilchattan Ag & B
110 D2	Upper Kilcott Gloucs
103 E3	Upper Killay Swans
185 G1	Upper Kinsham Herefs
568 B7	Upper Knockando Moray
113 H3	Upper Lambourn W Berk
237 E3	Upper Landywood Staffs
85 E3	Upper Langford N Som
315 G5	Upper Langwith Derbys
174 D1	Upper Layham Suffk
273 F2	Upper Leigh Staffs
85 G2	Upper Littleton N Som
314 C6	Upper Loads Derbys
556 B5	Upper Lochton Abers
162 C3	Upper Lode Worcs
237 G2	Upper Longdon Staffs
235 E3	Upper Longwood Shrops
236 B5	Upper Ludstone Shrops
583 J2	Upper Lybster Highld
135 E1	Upper Lydbrook Gloucs
186 B6	Upper Lyde Herefs
185 G1	Upper Lye Herefs
159 F2	Upper Maes-Coed Herefs
341 G2	Upper Marsh Brad
328 C5	Upper Midhope Sheff
274 D5	Upper Midway Derbys
327 E3	Uppermill Oldham
542 A7	Upper Milovaig Highld
138 C1	Upper Milton Oxon
85 F5	Upper Milton Somset
112 B1	Upper Minety Wilts
189 E5	Upper Moor Worcs
342 D3	Upper Moor Side Leeds
110 B1	Upper Morton S Glos
125 H4	Upper Nash Pembks
607 H1	Upper Neepaback Shet
211 E1	Upper Netchwood Shrops
314 D5	Upper Newbold Derbys
273 F2	Upper Nobut Staffs
142 A5	Upper North Dean Bucks
119 G6	Upper Norwood Gt Lon
75 E6	Upper Norwood W Susx
106 D2	Upper Ochrwyth Caerph
164 C4	Upper Oddington Gloucs
545 J2	Upper Ollach Highld
314 A4	Upper Padley Derbys
557 F2	Upper Persley C Aber
111 E5	Upper Pickwick Wilts
141 F2	Upper Pollicott Bucks
357 G4	Upper Poppleton York
97 F5	Upper Postern Kent
190 B5	Upper Quinton Warwks
133 E5	Upper Race Torfn
71 G5	Upper Ratley Hants
164 C5	Upper Rissington Gloucs
211 E6	Upper Rochford Worcs
99 E2	Upper Rodmersham Kent
601 J4	Upper Sanday Ork
187 F2	Upper Sapey Herefs
277 E2	Upper Saxondale Notts
111 G3	Upper Seagry Wilts
194 D6	Upper Shelton Beds
261 F3	Upper Sheringham Norfk
50 D2	Upper Shirley C Sotn
137 F5	Upper Siddington Gloucs
482 B6	Upper Skelmorlie N Ayrs
550 B1	Upper Slackbuie Highld
72 A4	Upper Slackstead Hants
164 A5	Upper Slaughter Gloucs
150 C5	Upper Solva Pembks
135 F2	Upper Soudley Gloucs
605 H2	Uppersound Shet
85 H2	Upper Stanton Drew BaNES
195 G2	Upper Staploe Beds
215 F3	Upper Stoke Covtry
250 A4	Upper Stoke Norfk
169 G2	Upper Stondon Beds
192 D3	Upper Stowe Nhants
113 E2	Upper Stratton Swindn
70 D6	Upper Street Hants
225 G4	Upper Street Norfk
250 D1	Upper Street Norfk
256 A2	Upper Street Norfk
256 C5	Upper Street Norfk
175 F3	Upper Street Suffk
199 F4	Upper Street Suffk
201 F4	Upper Street Suffk
162 C2	Upper Strensham Worcs
87 E3	Upper Studley Wilts
169 E4	Upper Sundon Beds
110 C6	Upper Swainswick BaNES
51 G1	Upper Swanmore Hants
164 B4	Upper Swell Gloucs
329 E5	Upper Tankersley Barns
273 F2	Upper Tean Staffs
328 A3	Upperthong Kirk
315 F3	Upperthorpe Derbys
331 G4	Upperthorpe N Linc
289 F5	Upper Threapwood Ches
351 G4	Upper Thurnham Lancs
500 B3	Upper Tillyrie P & K
57 F4	Upperton E Susx
141 E6	Upperton Oxon

75 F5	Upperton W Susx
119 F5	Upper Tooting Gt Lon
543 J5	Upper Tote Highld
294 A4	Upper Town Derbys
294 B3	Upper Town Derbys
294 C2	Uppertown Derbys
394 B2	Uppertown Dur
186 D5	Upper Town Herefs
589 J1	Uppertown Highld
70 C2	Upper Town N Som
428 D5	Uppertown Nthumb
224 B6	Upper Town Suffk
111 H4	Upper Town Wilts
209 E4	Upper Treverward Shrops
566 C2	Upper Tullich Highld
191 E6	Upper Tysoe Warwks
137 F5	Upper Up Gloucs
113 F4	Upper Upham Wilts
122 A5	Upper Upnor Medway
606 D2	Upper Urafirth Shet
86 B5	Upper Vobster Somset
120 A2	Upper Walthamstow Gt Lon
192 A5	Upper Wardington Oxon
74 C4	Upper Wardley W Susx
167 G2	Upper Weald M Keyn
192 D3	Upper Weedon Nhants
162 A1	Upper Welland Worcs
56 C2	Upper Wellingham E Susx
185 E4	Upper Welson Herefs
67 F1	Upper Westholme Somset
86 C1	Upper Weston BaNES
226 A4	Upper Weybread Suffk
315 F2	Upper Whiston Rothm
135 G5	Upper Wick Gloucs
188 B4	Upper Wick Worcs
73 F2	Upper Wield Hants
269 F2	Upper Wigginton Shrops
141 F2	Upper Winchendon Bucks
213 G1	Upper Witton Birm
140 A3	Upper Wolvercote Oxon
188 D4	Upper Wolverton Worcs
294 C3	Upperwood Derbys
559 F6	Upper Woodend Abers
70 C2	Upper Woodford Wilts
115 F6	Upper Woolhampton W Berk
91 F4	Upper Wootton Hants
111 E5	Upper Wraxall Wilts
187 H6	Upper Wyche Worcs
26 D2	Uppincott Devon
242 A5	Uppingham Rutlnd
48 C3	Uppington Dorset
235 E3	Uppington Shrops
371 E2	Upsall N York
200 B6	Upsher Green Suffk
145 F4	Upshire Essex
72 A3	Up Somborne Hants
100 D3	Upstreet Kent
609 J3	Upswall Shet
31 E2	Up Sydling Dorset
135 H4	Upthorpe Gloucs
224 C5	Upthorpe Suffk
141 G2	Upton Bucks
243 G4	Upton C Pete
219 H4	Upton Cambs
309 F6	Upton Ches
16 C4	Upton Cnwll
23 E2	Upton Cnwll
389 H2	Upton Cumb
12 C4	Upton Devon
28 A2	Upton Devon
48 B6	Upton Dorset
361 E4	Upton E R Yk
120 B3	Upton Gt Lon
309 G2	Upton Halton
50 C1	Upton Hants
90 B3	Upton Hants
37 F2	Upton IoW
101 G2	Upton Kent
239 F5	Upton Leics
317 G2	Upton Lincs
193 F2	Upton Nhants
250 D2	Upton Norfk
296 D4	Upton Notts
316 D4	Upton Notts
115 E2	Upton Oxon
138 C2	Upton Oxon
117 G4	Upton Slough
42 C2	Upton Somset
66 D4	Upton Somset
330 A2	Upton Wakefd
189 H3	Upton Warwks
69 E3	Upton Wilts
308 C2	Upton Wirral
161 F4	Upton Bishop Herefs
110 B6	Upton Cheyney S Glos
235 E6	Upton Cressett Shrops
161 E4	Upton Crews Herefs
16 C4	Upton Cross Cnwll
169 G3	Upton End Beds
296 D4	Upton Field Notts
250 D2	Upton Green Norfk
92 A5	Upton Grey Hants
309 F6	Upton Heath Ches
26 C2	Upton Hellions Devon
117 G3	Upton Lea Slough
69 F1	Upton Lovell Wilts
234 C2	Upton Magna Shrops
68 B2	Upton Noble Somset
120 B3	Upton Park Gt Lon
27 E3	Upton Pyne Devon
309 H2	Upton Rocks Halton
136 C2	Upton St Leonards Gloucs
87 F5	Upton Scudamore Wilts
188 D4	Upton Snodsbury Worcs
162 C1	Upton upon Severn Worcs
212 D6	Upton Warren Worcs
53 G2	Upwaltham W Susx
222 A6	Upware Cambs
245 G4	Upwell Norfk
245 H4	Upwell Norfk
31 F6	Upwey Dorset
171 F5	Upwick Green Herts
220 B3	Upwood Cambs
605 H3	Uradale Shet
606 D2	Urafirth Shet
478 B2	Uragaig Ag & B
88 B3	Urchfont Wilts
186 C5	Urdimarsh Herefs
606 B1	Ure Shet
370 C5	Ure Bank N York
67 F5	Urgashay Somset
596 F8	Urgha W Isls
596 F7	Urgha Beag W Isls
384 B2	Urlay Nook S on T
325 H6	Urmston Traffd
405 F4	Urpeth Dur
568 D3	Urquhart Moray
385 F4	Urra N York
565 J6	Urray Highld
529 F4	Usan Angus
395 E1	Ushaw Moor Dur
133 G4	Usk Mons
333 F6	Usselby Lincs
330 C5	Usworth Sundld
405 G3	Utkinton Ches
355 E6	Utley Brad
26 C3	Uton Devon
334 D6	Utterby Lincs
273 G3	Uttoxeter Staffs
262 B5	Uwchmynydd Gwynd

118 B3	Uxbridge Gt Lon
118 A3	Uxbridge Moor Gt Lon
609 M4	Uyeasound Shet
125 G2	Uzmaston Pembks

V

604 b3	Vaasetter Shet
150 C4	Vachelich Pembks
67 E6	Vagg Somset
341 E4	Vale Calder
35 d2	Vale Guern
24 D5	Vale Down Devon
269 G5	Valeswood Shrops
302 C5	Valley IoA
486 D2	Valleyfield Fife
72 B5	Valley Park Hants
22 B6	Valley Truckle Cnwll
609 J2	Valsgarth Shet
543 J4	Valtos Highld
598 B7	Valtos W Isls
106 C2	Van Caerph
207 E2	Van Powys
121 H2	Vange Essex
605 G2	Vanlop Shet
232 D2	Varchoel Powys
3 F3	Varfell Cnwll
133 E3	Varteg Torfn
607 G7	Vassa Shet
112 B3	Vastern Wilts
605 G6	Vatsetter Shet
609 G7	Vatsetter Shet
542 D8	Vatten Highld
84 C2	Vaul Ag & B
213 G2	Vauxhall Birm
119 G4	Vauxhall Gt Lon
308 D1	Vauxhall Lpool
283 F2	Vaynol Hall Gwynd
131 G2	Vaynor Myr Td
34 b3	Vazon Bay Guern
605 H2	Veensgarth Shet
60 C4	Velator Devon
186 D6	Veldo Herefs
158 C2	Velindre Powys
3 F3	Vellanoweth Cnwll
64 A4	Vellow Somset
38 C3	Velly Devon
19 G5	Velwell Devon
606 D6	Vementry Shet
603 H6	Veness Ork
12 C3	Venn Devon
39 E5	Venngreen Devon
233 F3	Vennington Shrops
28 A4	Venn Ottery Devon
186 C5	Venn's Green Herefs
26 C3	Venny Tedburn Devon
16 D4	Venterdon Cnwll
60 C3	Vention Devon
37 F5	Ventnor IoW
11 G2	Venton Devon
25 G4	Venton Devon
7 E3	Ventongimps Cnwll
3 G2	Ventonleague Cnwll
143 E4	Venus Hill Herts
41 F2	Veraby Devon
90 A3	Vernham Bank Hants
90 A3	Vernham Dean Hants
90 A3	Vernham Row Hants
90 B3	Vernham Street Hants
210 B3	Vernolds Common Shrops
48 D3	Verwood Dorset
7 H6	Veryan Cnwll
7 H5	Veryan Green Cnwll
28 D5	Vicarage Devon
289 F1	Vicarscross Ches
364 A6	Vickerstown Cumb
328 B3	Victoria Barns
8 B1	Victoria Cnwll
348 B4	Victoria Dock Village C KuH
142 A2	Victoria Park Bucks
466 D1	Victory Gardens Rens
607 G4	Vidlin Shet
467 H2	Viewpark N Lans
237 F4	Vigo Wsall
97 G2	Vigo Village Kent
35 d3	Village de Putron Guern
35 f5	Ville la Bas Jersey
34 c3	Villiaze Guern
108 D2	Vinegar Hill Mons
58 C2	Vinehall Street E Susx
78 D6	Vines Cross E Susx
135 F3	Viney Hill Gloucs
110 B4	Vinney Green S Glos
117 G6	Virginia Water Surrey
24 A4	Virginstow Devon
86 C5	Vobster Somset
606 D1	Voe Shet
606 F5	Voe Shet
609 J3	Voesgarth Shet
6 D5	Vogue Cnwll
84 C5	Vole Somset
159 G2	Vowchurch Herefs
159 G2	Vowchurch Common Herefs
43 F4	Voxmoor Somset
606 E3	Voxter Shet
600 D1	Voy Ork
233 F3	Vron Gate Shrops
324 D6	Vulcan Village St Hel

W

377 E6	Waberthwaite Cumb
394 D5	Wackerfield Dur
187 E3	Wacton Herefs
225 G1	Wacton Norfk
606 F8	Wadbister Shet
188 C5	Wadborough Worcs
29 F2	Wadbrook Devon
141 F1	Waddesdon Bucks
13 F1	Waddeton Devon
323 G5	Waddicar Sefton
41 H2	Waddicombe Devon
332 D5	Waddingham Lincs
353 E6	Waddington Lancs
298 B2	Waddington Lincs
319 F5	Waddingworth Lincs
20 B2	Waddon Devon
31 E5	Waddon Dorset
95 G2	Waddon Gt Lon
14 D4	Wadebridge Cnwll
44 B5	Wadeford Somset
218 D3	Wadenhoe Nhants
290 D2	Wades Green Ches
170 D6	Wadesmill Herts
58 B4	Wadhurst E Susx
314 C5	Wadshelf Derbys
314 C1	Wadsley Sheff
314 C1	Wadsley Bridge Sheff
111 E6	Wadswick Wilts
90 C4	Wadwick Hants
330 C5	Wadworth Donc
286 D2	Waen Denbgs
287 G1	Waen Denbgs
307 H5	Waen Flints
207 F1	Waen Powys
268 D6	Waen Powys
307 F6	Waen Aberwheeler Denbgs

232 D1	Waen-fâch Powys
284 C1	Waen-pentir Gwynd
304 C6	Waen-wen Gwynd
582 D4	Wag Highld
233 G4	Wagbeach Shrops
66 C4	Wagg Somset
272 C2	Waggersley Staffs
29 F2	Waggs Plot Devon
133 E4	Wainfelin Torfn
301 E3	Wainfleet All Saints Lincs
301 E3	Wainfleet Bank Lincs
301 E3	Wainfleet St Mary Lincs
301 E3	Wainfleet Tofts Lincs
226 C1	Wainford Norfk
295 E5	Waingroves Derbys
22 D3	Wainhouse Corner Cnwll
291 H3	Wain Lee Staffs
122 A5	Wainscott Medway
341 G4	Wainstalls Calder
380 D3	Waitby Cumb
334 C4	Waithe Lincs
343 F5	Wakefield Wakefd
213 G3	Wake Green Birm
369 G5	Wake Hill N York
170 D4	Wakeley Herts
242 D5	Wakerley Nhants
174 A4	Wakes Colne Essex
174 A3	Wakes Colne Green Essex
227 F5	Walberswick Suffk
53 H3	Walberton W Susx
405 E4	Walbottle N u Ty
400 D2	Walby Cumb
85 F5	Walcombe Somset
86 C1	Walcot BaNES
279 F2	Walcot Lincs
346 C5	Walcot N Linc
165 E6	Walcot Oxon
209 F3	Walcot Shrops
113 E3	Walcot Swindn
188 D5	Walcot Worcs
234 D2	Walcot Wrekin
216 C3	Walcote Leics
189 H3	Walcote Warwks
225 F3	Walcot Green Norfk
299 E3	Walcott Lincs
256 D3	Walcott Norfk
368 D3	Walden N York
368 C3	Walden Head N York
330 C1	Walden Stubbs N York
328 C5	Waldershaigh Sheff
98 B2	Waldershare Kent
52 D2	Walderslade Medway
30 B4	Walderton W Susx
30 A4	Walditch Dorset
273 H2	Waldley Derbys
405 G4	Waldridge Dur
202 B6	Waldringfield Suffk
202 B6	Waldringfield Heath Suffk
78 D6	Waldron E Susx
78 C5	Waldron Down E Susx
315 F3	Wales Rothm
67 F5	Wales Somset
315 F3	Wales Bar Rothm
319 E1	Walesby Lincs
316 C5	Walesby Notts
319 E1	Walesby Grange Lincs
199 F5	Wales End Suffk
315 F3	Waleswood Rothm
160 D5	Walford Herefs
209 G5	Walford Herefs
270 A5	Walford Shrops
44 B2	Walford Somset
272 B3	Walford Staffs
270 B6	Walford Heath Shrops
290 D3	Walgherton Ches
217 H5	Walgrave Nhants
162 B5	Walham Gloucs
50 B5	Walhampton Hants
325 G4	Walkden Salfd
405 G2	Walker N u Ty
312 C5	Walker Barn Ches
450 D2	Walkerburn Border
339 G1	Walker Fold Lancs
331 G6	Walkeringham Notts
331 G6	Walkerith Lincs
170 C4	Walkern Herts
186 C5	Walker's Green Herefs
213 G4	Walker's Heath Birm
383 F5	Walkerville N York
49 G6	Walkford Dorset
18 B4	Walkhampton Devon
347 E2	Walkington E R Yk
314 C2	Walkley Sheff
340 D3	Walk Mill Lancs
233 G6	Walkmill Shrops
234 B5	Walkmills Shrops
4 B1	Wall Cnwll
429 E6	Wall Nthumb
237 F3	Wall Staffs
486 B4	Wallacestone Falk
422 D1	Wallaceton D & G
432 C4	Wallacetown S Ayrs
444 D5	Wallacetown S Ayrs
56 C2	Wallands Park E Susx
323 E4	Wallasey Wirral
326 C1	Wallbank Lancs
234 C6	Wall Bank Shrops
236 D6	Wallbrook Dudley
79 F3	Wallcrouch E Susx
363 E5	Wall End Cumb
120 B3	Wall End Gt Lon
100 D3	Wall End Kent
161 F2	Waller's Green Herefs
290 D2	Walley's Green Ches
212 C1	Wall Heath Dudley
327 E3	Wall Hill Oldham
115 H2	Wallingford Oxon
95 F2	Wallington Gt Lon
51 G3	Wallington Hants
170 C3	Wallington Herts
315 H3	Wallingwells Notts
151 H4	Wallis Pembks
48 D6	Wallisdown Poole
76 B2	Walliswood Surrey
86 B3	Wall Mead BaNES
405 F5	Wall Nook Dur
136 B5	Wallow Green Gloucs
429 G4	Wallridge Nthumb
606 B8	Walls Shet
405 G1	Wallsend N Tyne
106 D3	Wallston V Glam
325 F2	Wallsuches Bolton
162 B5	Wallsworth Gloucs
210 C1	Wall under Heywood Shrops
488 D5	Walyford E Loth
101 G5	Walmer Kent
338 C5	Walmer Bridge Lancs
326 A2	Walmersley Bury
358 B4	Walmgate Stray York
238 A6	Walmley Birm
320 C4	Walmsgate Lincs
512 D5	Walnut Grove P & K
168 B2	Walnut Tree M Keyn
171 G5	Walnuttree Green Herts
65 E3	Walpole Somset
226 D5	Walpole Suffk
281 H5	Walpole Cross Keys Norfk
245 H2	Walpole Highway Norfk
281 H6	Walpole Marsh Norfk
281 H6	Walpole St Andrew Norfk
245 H1	Walpole St Peter Norfk
84 B5	Walrow Somset
214 B4	Walsal End Solhll

City, town and village index: Walsall - West Challow 723

237 F5 **Walsall** Wsall
237 F4 **Walsall Wood** Wsall
341 E5 **Walsden** Calder
215 F3 **Walsgrave on Sowe** Covtry
224 D5 **Walsham le Willows** Suffk
325 H2 **Walshaw** Bury
357 E4 **Walshford** N York
245 G2 **Walsoken** Norfk
160 A5 **Walson** Mons
469 G5 **Walston** S Lans
170 A3 **Walsworth** Herts
142 A5 **Walter's Ash** Bucks
78 C1 **Walter's Green** Kent
105 H5 **Walterston** V Glam
159 F4 **Walterstone** Herefs
100 B6 **Waltham** Kent
334 C4 **Waltham** NE Lin
145 E4 **Waltham Abbey** Essex
51 G2 **Waltham Chase** Hants
145 E4 **Waltham Cross** Herts
277 H4 **Waltham on the Wolds** Leics
116 D4 **Waltham St Lawrence** W & M
172 D3 **Waltham's Cross** Essex
119 H2 **Walthamstow** Gt Lon
142 A2 **Walton** Bucks
244 A4 **Walton** C Pete
401 F2 **Walton** Cumb
314 D6 **Walton** Derbys
357 E5 **Walton** Leeds
216 C2 **Walton** Leics
323 G6 **Walton** Lpool
168 B2 **Walton** M Keyn
184 D3 **Walton** Powys
210 B4 **Walton** Shrops
66 D2 **Walton** Somset
272 C3 **Walton** Staffs
272 C4 **Walton** Staffs
177 E2 **Walton** Suffk
329 F1 **Walton** Wakefd
190 D4 **Walton** Warwks
270 D6 **Walton** Wrekin
162 D3 **Walton Cardiff** Gloucs
141 H2 **Walton Court** Bucks
151 H5 **Walton East** Pembks
68 C6 **Walton Elm** Dorset
166 B3 **Walton Grounds** Nhants
51 H3 **Walton Heath** Hants
245 G2 **Walton Highway** Norfk
108 D5 **Walton in Gordano** N Som
339 E4 **Walton-le-Dale** Lancs
140 B3 **Walton Manor** Oxon
94 C1 **Walton-on-Thames** Surrey
273 E5 **Walton-on-the-Hill** Staffs
95 E3 **Walton on the Hill** Surrey
177 E5 **Walton on the Naze** Essex
276 C6 **Walton on the Wolds** Leics
274 C6 **Walton-on-Trent** Derbys
212 D4 **Walton Pool** Worcs
198 B6 **Waltons** Essex
108 D5 **Walton St Mary** N Som
339 E4 **Walton Summit** Lancs
253 E4 **Walton Warren** Norfk
125 E2 **Walton West** Pembks
307 G4 **Walwen** Flints
308 B4 **Walwen** Flints
429 E5 **Walwick** Nthumb
395 E6 **Walworth** Darltn
119 G4 **Walworth** Gt Lon
395 E5 **Walworth Gate** Darltn
125 E2 **Walwyn's Castle** Pembks
44 B6 **Wambrook** Somset
399 G4 **Wampool** Cumb
93 F5 **Wanborough** Surrey
113 F3 **Wanborough** Swindn
448 B4 **Wandel** S Lans
448 C4 **Wandel Dyke** S Lans
95 G1 **Wandle Park** Gt Lon
169 G5 **Wandon End** Herts
119 F5 **Wandsworth** Gt Lon
227 F4 **Wangford** Suffk
240 D2 **Wanlip** Leics
435 H2 **Wanlockhead** D & G
57 F4 **Wannock** E Susx
243 F5 **Wansford** C Pete
360 D3 **Wansford** E R Yk
98 B5 **Wanshurst Green** Kent
22 D2 **Wanson** Cnwll
120 B2 **Wanstead** Gt Lon
68 B1 **Wanstrow** Somset
135 F4 **Wanswell** Gloucs
114 C2 **Wantage** Oxon
187 G3 **Wants Green** Worcs
110 C4 **Wapley** S Glos
215 F6 **Wappenbury** Warwks
192 D5 **Wappenham** Nhants
119 G3 **Wapping** Gt Lon
79 E6 **Warbleton** E Susx
52 C3 **Warblington** Hants
140 C6 **Warborough** Oxon
220 D3 **Warboys** Cambs
337 F2 **Warbreck** Bpool
23 E4 **Warbstow** Cnwll
23 E4 **Warbstow Cross** Cnwll
310 D2 **Warburton** Traffd
311 F3 **Warburton Green** Traffd
380 C1 **Warcop** Cumb
123 G5 **Warden** Kent
403 G1 **Warden** Nthumb
185 E2 **Warden** Powys
213 H2 **Ward End** Birm
162 D5 **Warden Hill** Gloucs
35 H3 **Warden Point** IoW
195 G6 **Warden Street** Beds
329 E4 **Ward Green** Barns
200 D2 **Ward Green** Suffk
339 F2 **Ward Green Cross** Lancs
169 F2 **Wardhedges** Beds
603 J6 **Wardhill** Ork
192 A5 **Wardington** Oxon
438 B1 **Wardlaw** Border
290 C3 **Wardle** Ches
326 D1 **Wardle** Rochdl
290 C3 **Wardle Bank** Ches
405 G2 **Wardley** Gatesd
242 A5 **Wardley** Rutlnd
325 H4 **Wardley** Salfd
74 C4 **Wardley** W Susx
313 G5 **Wardlow** Derbys
69 F4 **Wardour** Wilts
485 F4 **Wardpark** N Lans
141 H4 **Wardrobes** Bucks
312 B3 **Wardsend** Ches
221 G3 **Wardy Hill** Cambs
29 F4 **Ware** Devon
145 E2 **Ware** Herts
101 E3 **Ware** Kent
33 G2 **Wareham** Dorset
81 E3 **Warehorne** Kent
455 E4 **Warenford** Nthumb
455 E3 **Waren Mill** Nthumb
454 D3 **Warenton** Nthumb
145 E1 **Wareside** Herts
196 C4 **Waresley** Cambs
212 B6 **Waresley** Worcs
98 C3 **Ware Street** Kent
117 E5 **Warfield** Br For
13 F2 **Warfleet** Devon
280 B3 **Wargate** Lincs
324 D6 **Wargrave** St Hel
116 C4 **Wargrave** Wokham
160 B2 **Warham** Herefs
260 B3 **Warham** Norfk
327 E5 **Warhill** Tamesd
213 H5 **Waring's Green** Warwks
428 D4 **Wark** Nthumb
453 F2 **Wark** Nthumb
453 F2 **Wark Common** Nthumb
40 C3 **Warkleigh** Devon
218 B3 **Warkton** Nhants
166 A1 **Warkworth** Nhants
443 H3 **Warkworth** Nthumb
370 C1 **Warlaby** N York
341 E5 **Warland** Calder
15 H5 **Warleggan** Cnwll
86 D2 **Warleigh** BaNES
146 B6 **Warley** Essex
341 G4 **Warley Town** Calder
213 F2 **Warley Woods** Sandw
95 G3 **Warlingham** Surrey
294 B4 **Warmbrook** Derbys
343 G5 **Warmfield** Wakefd
290 D2 **Warmingham** Ches
54 D1 **Warminghurst** W Susx
219 F1 **Warmington** Nhants
191 G5 **Warmington** Warwks
87 F5 **Warminster** Wilts
87 F6 **Warminster Common** Wilts
98 C5 **Warmlake** Kent
110 B5 **Warmley** S Glos
110 A5 **Warmley Hill** S Glos
110 B5 **Warmley Tower** S Glos
218 D6 **Warmonds Hill** Nhants
330 B4 **Warmsworth** Donc
32 D2 **Warmwell** Dorset
92 B4 **Warnborough Green** Hants
188 C3 **Warndon** Worcs
143 E3 **Warners End** Herts
73 F5 **Warnford** Hants
76 C3 **Warnham** W Susx
54 B3 **Warningcamp** W Susx
77 E4 **Warninglid** W Susx
140 D5 **Warpsgrove** Oxon
312 A5 **Warren** Ches
33 F1 **Warren** Dorset
125 F5 **Warren** Pembks
329 F5 **Warren** Sheff
397 E5 **Warrenby** R & Cl
74 A4 **Warren Corner** Hants
92 D5 **Warren Corner** Hants
201 H6 **Warren Heath** Suffk
116 D3 **Warren Row** W & M
170 C4 **Warren's Green** Herts
99 E4 **Warren Street** Kent
194 B4 **Warrington** M Keyn
310 C2 **Warrington** Warrtn
488 B4 **Warriston** C Edin
51 E3 **Warsash** Hants
589 J2 **Warse** Highld
355 H1 **Warsill** N York
293 E3 **Warslow** Staffs
315 H6 **Warsop Vale** Notts
213 G4 **Warstock** Birm
237 E3 **Warstone** Staffs
359 G4 **Warter** E R Yk
369 G4 **Warthermarske** N York
358 C3 **Warthill** N York
57 H3 **Wartling** E Susx
277 E5 **Wartnaby** Leics
338 B4 **Warton** Lancs
365 G5 **Warton** Lancs
442 B4 **Warton** Nthumb
238 D4 **Warton** Warwks
337 G4 **Warton Bank** Lancs
190 D1 **Warwick** Warwks
401 E3 **Warwick Bridge** Cumb
401 E3 **Warwick-on-Eden** Cumb
426 B4 **Warwicksland** Cumb
95 G4 **Warwick Wold** Surrey
602 D5 **Wasbister** Ork
377 F3 **Wasdale Head** Cumb
313 E3 **Wash** Derbys
171 F3 **Washall Green** Herts
15 E5 **Washaway** Cnwll
12 D2 **Washbourne** Devon
84 D4 **Washbrook** Somset
175 F1 **Washbrook** Suffk
201 F6 **Washbrook Street** Suffk
90 C2 **Wash Common** W Berk
245 H1 **Wash Dyke** Norfk
292 B5 **Washerwall** Staffs
42 B4 **Washfield** Devon
382 C4 **Washfold** N York
63 H3 **Washford** Somset
189 G1 **Washford** Worcs
41 G5 **Washford Pyne** Devon
318 C5 **Washingborough** Lincs
219 G2 **Washingley** Cambs
405 H3 **Washington** Sundld
54 D2 **Washington** W Susx
405 H3 **Washington Village** Sundld
200 B5 **Washmere Green** Suffk
328 A3 **Washpit** Kirk
90 C2 **Wash Water** W Berk
213 G2 **Washwood Heath** Birm
91 F2 **Wasing** W Berk
404 C5 **Waskerley** Dur
190 D3 **Wasperton** Warwks
95 G5 **Wasp Green** Surrey
298 D2 **Wasps Nest** Lincs
371 G4 **Wass** N York
214 C6 **Waste Green** Warwks
12 A3 **Wastor** Devon
28 D3 **Watchcombe** Devon
63 H3 **Watchet** Somset
113 G1 **Watchfield** Oxon
84 B5 **Watchfield** Somset
379 F5 **Watchgate** Cumb
399 F6 **Watchhill** Cumb
172 D5 **Watch House Green** Essex
399 G1 **Watchill** D & G
20 C4 **Watcombe** Torbay
378 A1 **Watendlath** Cumb
19 G1 **Water** Devon
340 C4 **Water** Lancs
197 G2 **Waterbeach** Cambs
53 F3 **Waterbeach** W Susx
425 E4 **Waterbeck** D & G
143 G4 **Waterdale** Herts
260 A4 **Waterden** Norfk
49 F5 **Waterditch** Hants
168 B3 **Water Eaton** M Keyn
140 B2 **Water Eaton** Oxon
169 F2 **Water End** Beds
195 G5 **Water End** Beds
196 B5 **Water End** Beds
141 G5 **Waterend** Bucks
388 D5 **Waterend** Cumb
346 A2 **Water End** E R Yk
172 B1 **Water End** Essex
135 H2 **Waterend** Gloucs
92 A4 **Water End** Hants
143 E2 **Water End** Herts
144 A2 **Waterend** Herts
144 B4 **Water End** Herts
293 E4 **Waterfall** Staffs
459 G4 **Waterfoot** Ag & B
390 D5 **Waterfoot** Cumb
467 E4 **Waterfoot** E Rens
340 C5 **Waterfoot** Lancs
50 B6 **Waterford** Hants
144 D2 **Waterford** Herts
344 B4 **Water Fryston** Wakefd
364 A6 **Water Garth Nook** Cumb
9 G3 **Watergate** Cnwll
15 G2 **Watergate** Cnwll
45 E4 **Watergore** Somset
146 A5 **Waterhales** Essex
99 H2 **Waterham** Kent
137 G6 **Waterhay** Wilts
378 C4 **Waterhead** Cumb
12 B3 **Waterhead** Devon
470 D4 **Waterheads** Border
251 E6 **Waterheath** Norfk
394 D1 **Waterhouses** Dur
368 A6 **Water Houses** N York
293 E4 **Waterhouses** Staffs
97 G4 **Wateringbury** Kent
136 D4 **Waterlane** Gloucs
86 B6 **Waterlip** Somset
339 G4 **Waterloo** Bl w D
106 C2 **Waterloo** Caerph
15 G4 **Waterloo** Cnwll
295 E2 **Waterloo** Derbys
185 F5 **Waterloo** Herefs
546 B5 **Waterloo** Highld
468 C4 **Waterloo** N Lans
225 F4 **Waterloo** Norfk
251 E6 **Waterloo** Norfk
255 H4 **Waterloo** Norfk
512 C2 **Waterloo** P & K
125 G4 **Waterloo** Pembks
48 C6 **Waterloo** Poole
323 F5 **Waterloo** Sefton
270 C3 **Waterloo** Shrops
326 D4 **Waterloo** Tamesd
323 F5 **Waterloo Park** Sefton
283 E3 **Waterloo Port** Gwynd
52 B3 **Waterlooville** Hants
98 C6 **Waterman Quarter** Kent
136 C1 **Watermead** Gloucs
436 C2 **Watermeetings** S Lans
58 B4 **Watermill** E Susx
390 C5 **Watermillock** Cumb
137 F4 **Watermoor** Gloucs
243 G5 **Water Newton** Cambs
214 B1 **Water Orton** Warwks
140 D3 **Waterperry** Oxon
42 D2 **Waterrow** Somset
54 B1 **Watersfield** W Susx
326 D3 **Watersheddings** Oldham
339 H5 **Waterside** Bl w D
142 D4 **Waterside** Bucks
399 G5 **Waterside** Cumb
312 D3 **Waterside** Derbys
331 E2 **Waterside** Donc
433 F3 **Waterside** E Ayrs
466 C6 **Waterside** E Ayrs
484 D5 **Waterside** E Duns
466 D2 **Waterside** E Rens
96 A5 **Waterside** Surrey
365 G4 **Waterslack** Lancs
325 F3 **Water's Nook** Bolton
542 A7 **Waterstein** Highld
140 D3 **Waterstock** Oxon
125 F3 **Waterston** Pembks
167 E3 **Water Stratford** Bucks
271 E6 **Waters Upton** Wrekin
315 E3 **Waterthorpe** Sheff
561 E3 **Waterton** Abers
105 E4 **Waterton** Brdgnd
364 C2 **Water Yeat** Cumb
143 F5 **Watford** Herts
216 C6 **Watford** Nhants
237 H4 **Watford Gap** Staffs
143 G6 **Watford Heath** Herts
106 B2 **Watford Park** Caerph
380 B3 **Wath** Cumb
369 F6 **Wath** N York
370 C4 **Wath** N York
372 C4 **Wath** N York
370 C2 **Wath Brow** Cumb
472 A5 **Watherston** Border
329 G4 **Wath upon Dearne** Rothm
136 B4 **Watledge** Gloucs
110 B3 **Watley's End** S Glos
246 C2 **Watlington** Norfk
141 E6 **Watlington** Oxon
295 G5 **Watnall** Notts
376 B2 **Watson Hill** Cumb
589 G6 **Watten** Highld
224 D5 **Wattisfield** Suffk
200 D4 **Wattisham** Suffk
200 C4 **Wattisham Stone** Suffk
249 F5 **Wattlefield** Norfk
233 F2 **Wattlesborough Heath** Shrops
30 B4 **Watton** Dorset
360 C4 **Watton** E R Yk
248 B4 **Watton** Norfk
170 D6 **Watton at Stone** Herts
145 H5 **Watton's Green** Essex
485 F6 **Wattston** N Lans
131 G6 **Wattstown** Rhondd
106 D1 **Wattsville** Caerph
528 D5 **Waulkmill** Angus
410 D3 **Waulkmill** D & G
512 D4 **Waulkmill** P & K
528 D6 **Waulkmills** Angus
284 C2 **Waun** Gwynd
103 E3 **Waunarlwydd** Swans
150 C4 **Waun Beddau** Pembks
205 E3 **Waun Fawr** Cerdgn
283 F4 **Waunfawr** Gwynd
153 G2 **Waungilwen** Carmth
129 E4 **Waungron** Swans
132 C3 **Waun-Lwyd** Blae G
128 B4 **Waun y Clyn** Carmth
104 C2 **Waun y Gilfach** Brdgnd
168 C2 **Wavendon** M Keyn
168 C2 **Wavendon Gate** M Keyn
399 G5 **Waverbridge** Cumb
289 G2 **Waverton** Ches
399 G5 **Waverton** Cumb
309 E2 **Wavertree** Lpool
114 B6 **Wawcott** W Berk
347 G2 **Wawne** E R Yk
257 E4 **Waxham** Norfk
349 F4 **Waxholme** E R Yk
101 F2 **Way** Kent
19 G3 **Waye** Devon
161 G2 **Wayend Street** Herefs
98 B2 **Wayfield** Medway
29 G1 **Wayford** Somset
270 D1 **Waymills** Shrops
159 H6 **Wayne Green** Mons
290 C1 **Way's Green** Ches
39 E3 **Waytown** Devon
61 E5 **Waytown** Devon
30 B3 **Waytown** Dorset
42 A5 **Way Village** Devon
84 C2 **Way Wick** N Som
569 L4 **Weachyburn** Abers
64 B3 **Weacombe** Somset
139 E4 **Weald** Oxon
118 D2 **Wealdstone** Gt Lon
10 D2 **Wearde** Cnwll
356 B6 **Weardley** Leeds
84 D4 **Weare** Somset
39 G3 **Weare Giffard** Devon
393 E2 **Wearhead** Dur
66 C4 **Wearne** Somset
380 B4 **Weasdale** Cumb
253 G3 **Weasenham All Saints** Norfk
253 H3 **Weasenham St Peter** Norfk
326 A5 **Weaste** Salfd
95 G6 **Weatherhill** Surrey
213 G5 **Weatheroak Hill** Worcs
310 C5 **Weaverham** Ches
98 B3 **Weavering Street** Kent
274 A6 **Weaverslake** Staffs
374 B5 **Weaverthorpe** N York
84 C3 **Webbington** Somset
189 F1 **Webheath** Worcs
270 B5 **Webscott** Shrops
52 B2 **Wecock** Hants
560 C3 **Wedderlairs** Abers
101 E4 **Weddington** Kent
239 F6 **Weddington** Warwks
88 C3 **Wedhampton** Wilts
84 D5 **Wedmore** Somset
237 E5 **Wednesbury** Sandw
237 E6 **Wednesbury Oak** Sandw
236 D4 **Wednesfield** Wolves
297 F1 **Weecar** Notts
167 H6 **Weedon** Bucks
192 D3 **Weedon** Nhants
192 D3 **Weedon Bec** Nhants
192 D5 **Weedon Lois** Nhants
238 A4 **Weeford** Staffs
17 G2 **Week** Devon
19 G5 **Week** Devon
40 B2 **Week** Devon
41 E4 **Week** Devon
26 B1 **Weeke** Devon
72 C3 **Weeke** Hants
23 E3 **Week Green** Cnwll
218 B3 **Weekley** Nhants
43 F3 **Weekmoor** Somset
37 F2 **Weeks** IoW
23 E3 **Week St Mary** Cnwll
347 G2 **Weel** E R Yk
175 F5 **Weeley** Essex
176 C5 **Weeley Heath** Essex
334 C3 **Weelsby** NE Lin
524 C5 **Weem** P & K
272 D5 **Weeping Cross** Staffs
189 G3 **Weethley** Warwks
189 F4 **Weethley Bank** Warwks
189 G4 **Weethley Bank** Warwks
189 F4 **Weethley Gate** Warwks
223 F2 **Weeting** Norfk
349 G5 **Weeton** E R Yk
337 G3 **Weeton** Lancs
356 B5 **Weeton** N York
343 E2 **Weetwood** Leeds
289 H1 **Weetwood Common** Ches
122 B2 **Weir** Essex
340 D4 **Weir** Lancs
269 F5 **Weirbrook** Shrops
17 F6 **Weir Quay** Devon
606 E7 **Weisdale** Shet
315 H5 **Welbeck Abbey** Notts
249 E3 **Welborne** Norfk
298 B4 **Welbourn** Lincs
249 E3 **Welbourne Common** Norfk
372 C3 **Welburn** N York
372 D6 **Welburn** N York
431 F4 **Welburn** Nthumb
384 B4 **Welbury** N York
278 D2 **Welby** Lincs
221 G2 **Welches Dam** Cambs
38 B4 **Welcombe** Devon
324 D1 **Weld Bank** Lancs
218 C2 **Weldon** Nhants
443 E5 **Weldon** Nthumb
216 D3 **Welford** Nhants
114 B5 **Welford** W Berk
190 A4 **Welford-on-Avon** Warwks
217 G1 **Welham** Leics
316 D3 **Welham** Notts
67 H3 **Welham** Somset
346 A3 **Welhambridge** E R Yk
144 B3 **Welham Green** Herts
92 C5 **Well** Hants
320 D5 **Well** Lincs
370 B3 **Well** N York
162 A2 **Welland** Worcs
162 B2 **Welland Stone** Worcs
514 D2 **Wellbank** Angus
340 B5 **Well Bank** Lancs
47 H1 **Well Bottom** Dorset
78 D4 **Wellbrook** E Susx
399 F1 **Welldale** D & G
117 E2 **Well End** Bucks
144 A5 **Well End** Herts
96 D6 **Weller's Town** Kent
190 D3 **Wellesbourne** Warwks
311 F2 **Well Green** Traffd
168 D5 **Well Head** Beds
342 A3 **Well Heads** Brad
96 C2 **Well Hill** Kent
115 E5 **Wellhouse** W Berk
120 C4 **Welling** Gt Lon
194 B1 **Wellingborough** Nhants
253 H3 **Wellingham** Norfk
298 B3 **Wellingore** Lincs
376 D4 **Wellington** Cumb
186 B5 **Wellington** Herefs
43 F3 **Wellington** Somset
235 E2 **Wellington** Wrekin
161 G1 **Wellington Heath** Herefs
343 G2 **Wellington Hill** Leeds
43 E3 **Wellisford** Somset
86 C3 **Wellow** BaNES
36 B3 **Wellow** IoW
334 C3 **Wellow** NE Lin
296 C1 **Wellow** Notts
71 F5 **Wellow Wood** Hants
115 G2 **Well Place** Oxon
171 F5 **Wellpond Green** Herts
342 D2 **Wellroyd** Leeds
85 G5 **Wells** Somset
239 F4 **Wellsborough** Leics
290 D4 **Wells Green** Ches
260 B3 **Wells-next-the-Sea** Norfk
43 H2 **Wellsprings** Somset
97 G3 **Well Street** Kent
172 C6 **Wellstye Green** Essex
20 C5 **Wellswood** Torbay
15 G5 **Welltown** Cnwll
42 B6 **Well Town** Devon
487 E2 **Wellwood** Fife
245 H6 **Welney** Norfk
38 C3 **Welsford** Devon
270 A3 **Welshampton** Shrops
160 D6 **Welsh Bicknor** Herefs
270 C2 **Welsh End** Shrops
269 G3 **Welsh Frankton** Shrops
119 E2 **Welsh Harp** Gt Lon
151 F4 **Welsh Hook** Pembks
160 B6 **Welsh Newton** Herefs
160 C6 **Welsh Newton Common** Herefs
232 D3 **Welshpool** Powys
105 G4 **Welsh St Donats** V Glam
174 D4 **Welshwood Park** Essex
19 F3 **Welstor** Devon
86 B4 **Welton** BaNES
400 C6 **Welton** Cumb
445 H4 **Welton** E Ayrs
347 E4 **Welton** E R Yk
318 C4 **Welton** Lincs
192 C1 **Welton** Nhants
318 C3 **Welton Hill** Lincs
321 E6 **Welton le Marsh** Lincs
319 H2 **Welton le Wold** Lincs
349 F5 **Welwick** E R Yk
144 B1 **Welwyn** Herts
144 C2 **Welwyn Garden City** Herts
270 C4 **Wem** Shrops
65 E4 **Wembdon** Somset
118 D3 **Wembley** Gt Lon
11 F4 **Wembury** Devon
40 D6 **Wembworthy** Devon
482 A6 **Wemyss Bay** Inver
205 F5 **Wenallt** Cerdgn
229 G1 **Wenallt** Gwynd
267 F1 **Wenallt** Gwynd
171 H2 **Wendens Ambo** Essex
166 C6 **Wendlebury** Oxon
254 B5 **Wendling** Norfk
142 B3 **Wendover** Bucks
142 B3 **Wendover Dean** Bucks
4 C2 **Wendron** Cnwll
196 D5 **Wendy** Cambs
15 F4 **Wenfordbridge** Cnwll
227 E4 **Wenhaston** Suffk
227 E4 **Wenhaston Black Heath** Suffk
220 B4 **Wennington** Cambs
120 D3 **Wennington** Gt Lon
366 C5 **Wennington** Lancs
294 B2 **Wensley** Derbys
369 E1 **Wensley** N York
330 A1 **Wentbridge** Wakefd
209 G1 **Wentnor** Shrops
221 G4 **Wentworth** Cambs
329 F5 **Wentworth** Rothm
106 B5 **Wenvoe** V Glam
185 G4 **Weobley** Herefs
185 H4 **Weobley Marsh** Herefs
213 F3 **Weoley Castle** Birm
54 B3 **Wepham** W Susx
308 C6 **Wepre** Flints
246 D4 **Wereham** Norfk
246 D4 **Wereham Row** Norfk
291 F4 **Wereton** Staffs
236 C4 **Wergs** Wolves
264 C2 **Wern** Gwynd
132 B1 **Wern** Powys
233 E2 **Wern** Powys
269 E5 **Wern** Powys
269 E3 **Wern** Shrops
102 D3 **Wern** Swans
268 D4 **Wern Ddu** Shrops
326 D4 **Werneth** Oldham
312 C1 **Werneth Low** Tamesd
102 D3 **Wernffrwd** Swans
159 F5 **Wern-Gifford** Mons
269 F5 **Wernlas** Shrops
103 E2 **Wern-Olau** Swans
133 G2 **Wernrheolydd** Mons
105 F3 **Wern Tarw** Brdgnd
133 G3 **Wern-y-Cwrt** Mons
308 B6 **Wern-y-Gaer** Flints
243 H4 **Werrington** C Pete
23 G5 **Werrington** Cnwll
292 B5 **Werrington** Staffs
309 F5 **Wervin** Ches
356 B5 **Wescoe Hill** N York
338 B3 **Wesham** Lancs
294 D3 **Wessington** Derbys
105 G6 **West Aberthaw** V Glam
61 E5 **Westacott** Devon
253 F4 **West Acre** Norfk
118 D3 **West Acton** Gt Lon
165 H2 **West Adderbury** Oxon
475 E5 **West Allerdean** Nthumb
431 F5 **West Allotment** N Tyne
12 C4 **West Alvington** Devon
70 C1 **West Amesbury** Wilts
41 G2 **West Anstey** Devon
383 F6 **West Appleton** N York
343 E4 **West Ardsley** Leeds
466 C3 **West Arthurlie** E Rens
319 H5 **West Ashby** Lincs
60 D4 **West Ashford** Devon
53 E3 **West Ashling** W Susx
87 F3 **West Ashton** Wilts
394 D4 **West Auckland** Dur
374 B3 **West Ayton** N York
64 C5 **West Bagborough** Somset
515 F2 **West Balmirmer** Angus
132 D3 **West Bank** Blae G
309 H3 **West Bank** Halton
319 F3 **West Barkwith** Lincs
386 D2 **West Barnby** N York
119 E6 **West Barnes** Gt Lon
490 B4 **West Barns** E Loth
260 A5 **West Barsham** Norfk
30 B4 **West Bay** Dorset
261 F4 **West Beckham** Norfk
118 B5 **West Bedfont** Surrey
468 D2 **West Benhar** N Lans
460 D5 **West Bennan** N Ayrs
100 C3 **Westbere** Kent
174 C4 **West Bergholt** Essex
30 C5 **West Bexington** Dorset
253 E4 **West Bilney** Norfk
393 E2 **West Blackdene** Dur
17 G2 **West Blackdown** Devon
55 G3 **West Blatchington** Br & H
450 D2 **West Bold** Border
406 B2 **West Boldon** S Tyne
297 G6 **Westborough** Lincs
34 C2 **Westbourne** Bmouth
201 F5 **Westbourne** Suffk
52 D3 **Westbourne** W Susx
119 F3 **Westbourne Green** Gt Lon
68 C4 **West Bourton** Dorset
342 C3 **West Bowling** Brad
353 E6 **West Bradford** Lancs
67 F2 **West Bradley** Somset
328 D2 **West Bretton** Wakefd
276 C2 **West Bridgford** Notts
119 F4 **West Brompton** Gt Lon
213 F1 **West Bromwich** Sandw
185 E6 **Westbrook** Herefs
101 F1 **Westbrook** Kent
93 G6 **Westbrook** Surrey
114 C5 **Westbrook** W Berk
310 B2 **Westbrook** Warrtn
87 H1 **Westbrook** Wilts
225 F3 **Westbrook Green** Norfk
143 E3 **Westbrook Hay** Herts
274 A3 **West Broughton** Derbys
61 G5 **West Buckland** Devon
43 G3 **West Buckland** Somset
467 G2 **Westburn** S Lans
540 C5 **West Burnside** Abers
606 C6 **West Burrafirth** Shet
368 D2 **West Burton** N York
54 A2 **West Burton** W Susx
166 D2 **Westbury** Bucks
233 G3 **Westbury** Shrops
87 F4 **Westbury** Wilts
87 F4 **Westbury Leigh** Wilts
135 G2 **Westbury-on-Severn** Gloucs
109 G4 **Westbury on Trym** Bristl
85 F5 **Westbury-sub-Mendip** Somset
404 D6 **West Butsfield** Dur
332 A3 **West Butterwick** N Linc
337 G3 **Westby** Lancs
278 D4 **Westby** Lincs
94 A2 **West Byfleet** Surrey
251 G2 **West Caister** Norfk
469 G2 **West Calder** W Loth
67 F5 **West Camel** Somset
355 H6 **West Carlton** Leeds
347 G3 **West Carr** C KuH
331 F3 **West Carr** N Linc
114 B2 **West Challow** Oxon

12 D4 West Charleton Devon
30 C1 West Chelborough Dorset
443 G5 West Chevington Nthumb
76 A6 West Chiltington W Susx
54 C1 West Chiltington Common W Susx
45 F5 West Chinnock Somset
431 F6 West Chirton N Tyne
88 D4 West Chisenbury Wilts
94 A4 West Clandon Surrey
34 C2 West Cliff Bmouth
387 E2 West Cliff N York
83 F2 West Cliffe Kent
122 D3 Westcliff-on-Sea Sthend
577 J2 West Clyne Highld
45 G5 West Coker Somset
19 G5 Westcombe Devon
66 A4 Westcombe Somset
67 H2 Westcombe Somset
50 D4 West Common Hants
30 D4 West Compton Dorset
67 F1 West Compton Somset
395 G3 West Cornforth Dur
114 A2 Westcot Oxon
240 C4 Westcotes C Leic
141 F1 Westcott Bucks
27 G2 Westcott Devon
233 G4 Westcott Shrops
94 C5 Westcott Surrey
165 G4 Westcott Barton Oxon
89 F2 Westcourt Wilts
345 E5 West Cowick E R Yk
167 H3 Westcroft M Keyn
236 D4 Westcroft Wolves
80 B3 West Cross Kent
103 F4 West Cross Swans
136 D6 West Crudwell Wilts
23 F4 West Curry Cnwll
400 B5 West Curthwaite Cumb
57 E5 Westdean E Susx
53 F2 West Dean W Susx
71 E4 West Dean Wilts
243 G3 West Deeping Lincs
125 F2 West Denant Pembks
55 G3 Westdene Br & H
514 D2 West Denside Angus
405 E1 West Denton N u Ty
323 G6 West Derby Lpool
246 D4 West Dereham Norfk
311 C1 West Didsbury Manch
455 E5 West Ditchburn Nthumb
60 D3 West Down Devon
72 A2 West Down Hants
88 B5 Westdown Camp Wilts
15 E6 West Downs Cnwll
22 A6 Westdowns Cnwll
118 B4 West Drayton Gt Lon
316 D5 West Drayton Notts
589 G2 West Dunnet Highld
118 D3 West Ealing Gt Lon
294 C2 West Edge Derbys
347 F4 West Ella E R Yk
194 D4 West End Beds
195 F2 West End Beds
117 E5 West End Br For
132 D5 West End Caerph
400 B3 West End Cumb
331 E3 West End Donc
47 G4 West End Dorset
346 D3 West End E R Yk
348 C4 West End E R Yk
349 E4 West End E R Yk
360 C2 West End E R Yk
361 F3 West End E R Yk
136 C5 West End Gloucs
263 F4 West End Gwynd
51 E2 West End Hants
51 G3 West End Hants
73 F2 West End Hants
144 C3 West End Herts
99 E3 West End Herts
100 C2 West End Kent
542 C4 West End Kirk
339 H4 West End Lancs
351 F2 West End Lancs
342 D2 West End Leeds
275 G6 West End Leics
300 C5 West End Lincs
335 E5 West End Lincs
134 A5 West End Mons
109 E6 West End N Som
344 C1 West End N York
344 D2 West End N York
355 F3 West End N York
248 B3 West End Norfk
251 G2 West End Norfk
115 F2 West End Oxon
139 G4 West End Oxon
165 E5 Westend Oxon
110 C2 West End S Glos
134 D6 Westend S Glos
469 F5 West End S Lans
68 A3 West End Somset
85 G4 West End Somset
227 F3 West End Suffk
92 D6 West End Surrey
93 G2 West End Surrey
94 C2 West End Surrey
116 D5 West End W & M
55 E1 West End W Susx
69 F5 West End Wilts
69 G5 West End Wilts
111 H4 West End Wilts
163 G2 West End Worcs
91 H2 West End Green Hants
402 D1 Westend Town Nthumb
105 E6 West-End Town V Glam
82 B3 Westenhanger Kent
549 J6 Wester Aberchalder Highld
577 J7 Wester Arboll Highld
484 C5 Wester Auchinloch N Lans
500 C4 Wester Balgedie P & K
490 C4 Wester Broomhouse E Loth
569 L3 Wester Culbeuchly Abers
588 E6 Westerdale Highld
385 H3 Westerdale N York
486 D5 Wester Dechmont W Loth
450 C5 Wester Deloraine Border
526 D6 Wester Denoon Angus
538 D5 Wester Eggie Angus
525 H7 Wester Essendy P & K
451 E5 Wester Essenside Border
606 E7 Westerfield Shet
201 G5 Westerfield Suffk
557 E1 Wester Fintray Abers
551 L5 Wester Fodderletter Moray
527 F5 Wester Foffarty Angus
53 G3 Westergate W Susx
570 D3 Wester Greenskares Abers
575 L5 Wester Gruinards Highld
487 H6 Wester Hailes C Edin
96 B4 Westerham Kent
405 E1 Westerhope N u Ty
451 G2 Wester Housebyres Border
450 D4 Wester Kershope Border
565 L2 Wester Lealty Highld
110 B4 Westerleigh S Glos
110 C4 Westerleigh Hill S Glos
527 G5 Wester Meathie Angus
399 G5 Western Bank Cumb
502 C3 Western Newburn Fife
83 F2 Western Heights Kent
405 G6 Western Hill Dur

240 C4 Western Park C Leic
423 H2 Wester Parkgate D & G
605 H3 Wester Quarff Shet
604 E2 Wester Skeld Shet
529 E4 Westerton Angus
395 E3 Westerton W Susx
53 F3 Westerton W Susx
525 H2 Westerton of Runavey P & K
604 E2 Westerwick Shet
95 E2 West Ewell Surrey
97 H4 West Farleigh Kent
192 B4 West Farndon Nhants
269 F4 West Felton Shrops
514 C3 West Ferry C Dund
527 F5 Westfield BaNES
86 B4 Westfield Cumb
388 A4 Westfield E Susx
58 D3 Westfield Herefs
52 C5 Westfield Highld
187 G5 Westfield Kirk
342 C1 Westfield Leeds
485 E5 Westfield N Lans
348 B6 Westfield Norfk
248 C3 Westfield R & Cl
397 E5 Westfield Sheff
315 E3 Westfield Surrey
93 H3 Westfield Suffk
486 B5 Westfield W Loth
357 H4 Westfield York
46 D3 Westfields Dorset
160 B1 Westfields Herefs
90 D1 West Fields W Berk
526 A5 Westfields of Rattray P & K
98 B2 Westfields Sole Kent
56 D3 West Firle E Susx
455 F4 West Fleetham Nthumb
453 H3 West Flodden Nthumb
565 L3 Westford Highld
43 F3 Westford Somset
343 G3 West Garforth Leeds
401 G6 Westgarth Hill Cumb
393 F2 Westgate Dur
331 G5 Westgate N Linc
260 C3 Westgate Norfk
342 D4 Westgate Hill Brad
101 F1 Westgate on Sea Kent
255 G3 Westgate Street Norfk
114 C2 West Ginge Oxon
326 C5 West Gorton Manch
89 F2 West Grafton Wilts
329 F3 West Green Barns
119 G2 West Green Gt Lon
92 B3 West Green Hants
77 E2 West Green Hants
71 E4 West Grimstead Wilts
76 C5 West Grinstead W Susx
344 D4 West Haddlesey N York
216 D5 West Haddon Nhants
115 E2 West Hagbourne Oxon
212 D4 West Hagley Worcs
559 F4 Westhall Abers
227 E3 Westhall Suffk
275 G1 West Hallam Derbys
138 C2 Westhall Hill Oxon
346 D5 West Halton N Linc
32 B4 Westham Dorset
57 G4 Westham E Susx
120 A3 West Ham Gt Lon
91 G4 West Ham Hants
84 D5 Westham Somset
53 F3 Westhampnett W Susx
119 E2 West Hampstead Gt Lon
314 D4 West Handley Derbys
139 F6 West Hanney Oxon
147 E5 West Hanningfield Essex
343 H6 West Hardwick Wakefd
224 C2 West Harling Norfk
384 C5 West Harlsey N York
85 G3 West Harptree BaNES
118 C2 West Harrow Gt Lon
74 B5 West Harting W Susx
406 B2 West Harton S Tyne
44 B3 West Hatch Somset
69 F4 West Hatch Wilts
66 C1 Westhay Somset
324 A3 Westhead Lancs
246 B3 West Head Norfk
213 F4 West Heath Birm
291 G2 West Heath Ches
120 C4 West Heath Gt Lon
91 F3 West Heath Hants
93 E3 West Heath Hants
582 D6 West Helmsdale Highld
119 E2 West Hendon Gt Lon
114 C2 West Hendred Oxon
606 B2 West Heogaland Shet
406 A4 West Herrington Sundld
373 H4 West Heslerton N York
84 C2 West Hewish N Som
186 D6 Westhide Herefs
557 E3 Westhill Abers
27 H4 West Hill Devon
348 D2 Westhill E R Yk
361 F1 West Hill E R Yk
58 D4 West Hill E Susx
119 E5 West Hill Gt Lon
566 C8 Westhill Highld
109 E4 West Hill N Som
68 B4 West Hill Somset
77 F3 West Hill W Susx
87 F1 West Hill Wilts
528 B6 West Hills Angus
77 G3 West Hoathly W Susx
33 F2 West Holme Dorset
431 F5 West Holywell N Tyne
382 B3 West Hope Dur
186 B4 Westhorpe Herefs
121 F2 West Horndon Essex
192 B4 Westhorp Nhants
280 B3 Westhorpe Lincs
296 C4 Westhorpe Notts
224 D6 Westhorpe Suffk
85 G5 West Horrington Somset
94 B4 West Horsley Surrey
454 C3 West Horton Nthumb
83 E2 West Hougham Kent
325 E3 Westhoughton Bolton
606 C7 West Houlland Shet
32 B5 Westhouse N York
295 E3 Westhouses Derbys
300 B4 West Houses Lincs
48 C5 West Howe Bmouth
63 E4 West Howetown Somset
94 D4 Westhumble Surrey
84 B6 West Huntspill Somset
49 E5 West Hurn Dorset
118 A1 West Hyde Herts
516 B8 West Hynish Ag & B
82 B4 West Hythe Kent
61 H2 West Ilkerton Devon
114 D3 West Ilsley W Berk
609 H3 Westing Shet
164 A2 Westington Gloucs
52 D4 West Itchenor W Susx
405 F1 West Jesmond N u Ty
300 C1 West Keal Lincs
112 D6 West Kennett Wilts
119 E4 West Kensington Gt Lon
465 E5 West Kilbride N Ayrs
97 E2 West Kingsdown Kent

54 C4 West Kingston W Susx
111 E4 West Kington Wilts
111 E4 West Kington Wick Wilts
308 B2 West Kirby Wirral
373 G4 West Knapton N York
32 C2 West Knighton Dorset
69 E3 West Knoyle Wilts
405 E4 West Kyo Dur
11 H3 Westlake Devon
66 C6 West Lambrook Somset
171 F5 Westland Green Herts
291 G6 Westlands Staffs
188 C2 Westlands Worcs
83 F1 West Langdon Kent
576 E2 West Langwell Highld
74 D5 West Lavington W Susx
88 B4 West Lavington Wilts
382 D3 West Layton N York
406 C5 West Lea Dur
430 D3 Westlea Dur
112 D3 Westlea Swindn
276 B4 West Leake Notts
453 F2 West Learmouth Nthumb
25 G1 West Leigh Devon
39 G2 Westleigh Devon
43 E4 West Leigh Devon
52 C3 West Leigh Hants
64 B5 West Leigh Somset
325 E4 Westleigh Wigan
227 E6 Westleton Suffk
253 G4 West Lexham Norfk
233 G3 Westley Shrops
199 G2 Westley Suffk
121 G2 Westley Heights Essex
133 E5 Westley Waterless Cambs
250 B4 West Lilling N York
141 G2 Westlington Bucks
470 C4 West Linton Border
400 C4 Westlinton Cumb
74 B4 West Liss Hants
110 D4 West Littleton S Glos
114 C2 West Lockinge Oxon
9 G3 West Looe Cnwll
63 E2 West Luccombe Somset
33 E3 West Lulworth Dorset
374 A6 West Lutton N York
67 F3 West Lydford Somset
186 D6 West Lydiatt Herefs
182 A2 West Lyn Devon
44 C2 West Lyng Somset
252 C4 West Lynn Norfk
472 D5 West Mains Border
467 F4 West Mains S Lans
469 F5 West Mains S Lans
97 G3 West Malling Kent
187 H5 West Malvern Worcs
162 D2 Westmancote Worcs
52 D2 West Marden W Susx
58 C5 West Marina E Susx
316 D5 West Markham Notts
101 E3 Westmarsh Kent
334 C2 West Marsh NE Lin
354 A4 West Marton N York
69 E5 West Melbury Dorset
329 G4 West Melton Rothm
73 F5 West Meon Hants
73 F4 West Meon Woodlands Hants
148 D2 West Mersea Essex
56 A2 Westmeston E Susx
169 H3 Westmill Herts
171 E4 Westmill Herts
30 C3 West Milton Dorset
119 F4 Westminster Gt Lon
123 E5 West Minster Kent
118 C6 West Molesey Surrey
431 F5 West Monkseaton N Tyne
44 B2 West Monkton Somset
431 E5 West Moor N Tyne
371 F5 West Moor N York
388 D2 Westmoor End Cumb
48 D4 West Moors Dorset
47 H5 West Morden Dorset
355 E6 West Morton Brad
67 F5 West Mudford Somset
527 E4 Westmuir Angus
528 C2 West Muir Angus
372 C4 West Ness N York
602 D6 Westness Ork
399 E6 Westnewton Cumb
348 C2 West Newton E R Yk
252 D2 West Newton Norfk
453 H3 Westnewton Nthumb
44 B2 West Newton Somset
119 G5 West Norwood Gt Lon
25 G3 West Nymph Devon
406 B1 Westoe S Tyne
19 H3 West Ogwell Devon
86 C1 Weston BaNES
50 D3 Weston C Sotn
291 E4 Weston Ches
312 A5 Weston Ches
28 B2 Weston Devon
28 C5 Weston Devon
30 C1 Weston Dorset
32 B5 Weston Dorset
309 H3 Weston Halton
73 H5 Weston Hants
185 G3 Weston Herefs
170 C3 Weston Herts
280 C5 Weston Lincs
355 C5 Weston N York
192 C5 Weston N York
297 E1 Weston Notts
126 A2 Weston Pembks
469 G5 Weston S Lans
209 F5 Weston Shrops
234 D6 Weston Shrops
269 H4 Weston Shrops
270 D4 Weston Shrops
273 E4 Weston Staffs
227 E2 Weston Suffk
114 B5 Weston W Berk
67 G4 Weston Bampfylde Somset
160 D1 Weston Beggard Herefs
111 F2 Westonbirt Gloucs
217 G1 Weston by Welland Nhants
72 D2 Weston Colley Hants
198 C4 Weston Colville Cambs
51 E2 Weston Common N Sotn
270 A4 Westoncommon Shrops
222 D4 Weston Corbett Hants
193 C2 Weston Ditch Suffk
108 C4 Weston Favell Nhants
198 C4 Weston Green Cambs
255 F5 Weston Green Norfk
94 D1 Weston Green Surrey
236 A2 Weston Heath Shrops
280 C5 Weston Hills Lincs
215 F2 Weston in Arden Warwks
169 E3 Westoning Beds
109 E5 Weston in Gordano N Som
271 H5 Weston Jones Staffs
255 F4 Weston Longville Norfk
269 H4 Weston Lullingfields Shrops
35 H3 Weston Manor IoW
190 B4 Weston-on-Avon Warwks
166 B6 Weston-on-the-Green Oxon
275 F4 Weston-on-Trent Derbys
92 A5 Weston Patrick Hants
309 G3 Weston Point Halton
269 E2 Weston Rhyn Shrops

190 B4 Weston Sands Warwks
164 A1 Weston-sub-Edge Gloucs
84 A2 Weston-super-Mare N Som
68 B1 Weston Town Somset
142 B2 Weston Turville Bucks
236 B2 Weston-under-Lizard Staffs
161 E5 Weston under Penyard Herefs
215 F6 Weston under Wetherley Warwks
294 B6 Weston Underwood Derbys
194 B4 Weston Underwood M Keyn
269 H4 Westonwharf Shrops
65 F4 Westonzoyland Somset
47 F1 West Orchard Dorset
112 D6 West Overton Wilts
359 E1 Westow N York
64 B5 Westowe Somset
43 F5 Westown Devon
513 F4 Westown P & K
23 G4 West Panson Devon
347 G4 West Park C Kull
396 C3 West Park Hartpl
343 E2 West Park Leeds
406 B1 West Park S Tyne
324 B5 West Park St Hel
48 D5 West Parley Dorset
393 F5 West Pasture Dur
97 F4 West Peckham Kent
405 F4 West Pelton Dur
67 E2 West Pennard Somset
7 E1 West Pentire Cnwll
195 G1 West Perry Cambs
133 E5 West Pontnewydd Torfn
250 B4 West Poringland Norfk
62 D2 West Porlock Somset
66 B6 Westport Somset
8 A5 West Portholland Cnwll
483 F5 West Porton Rens
46 D3 West Pulham Dorset
39 E4 West Putford Devon
64 B3 West Quantoxhead Somset
486 B4 Westquarter Falk
106 B5 Westra V Glam
405 H5 West Rainton Dur
318 C2 West Rasen Lincs
334 B5 West Ravendale NE Lin
253 H2 West Raynham Norfk
316 C3 West Retford Notts
115 F3 Westridge Green W Berk
469 E1 Westrigg W Loth
408 B2 West Ringuinea D & G
136 B3 Westrip Gloucs
111 F5 Westrop Wilts
115 E5 Westrop Green W Berk
384 C4 West Rounton N York
222 D5 West Row Suffk
253 G2 West Rudham Norfk
118 B2 West Ruislip Gt Lon
333 E3 Westrum Lincs
261 G3 West Runton Norfk
473 E4 Westruther Border
245 F5 Westry Cambs
472 B1 West Saltoun E Loth
26 C2 West Sandford Devon
608 E7 West Sandwick Shet
342 A3 West Scholes Brad
369 E3 West Scrafton N York
85 H6 West Shepton Somset
557 F5 Westside Abers
132 C3 West Side B G
603 G5 West Side Ork
422 D2 West Skelston D & G
431 E2 West Sleekburn Nthumb
257 F6 West Somerton Norfk
34 D2 West Southbourne Bmouth
32 C2 West Stafford Dorset
331 G6 West Stockwith Notts
19 E3 West Stoke Devon
66 D6 West Stoke Somset
53 E3 West Stoke W Susx
381 F4 West Stonesdale N York
84 D5 West Stoughton Somset
68 C5 West Stour Dorset
100 D3 West Stourmouth Kent
223 G5 West Stow Suffk
88 D2 West Stowell Wilts
586 C4 West Strathan Highld
72 D1 West Stratton Hants
98 D4 West Street Kent
101 F5 West Street Kent
121 H4 West Street Medway
224 C5 West Street Suffk
370 B4 West Tanfield N York
15 H6 West Taphouse Cnwll
54 D4 West Tarring W Susx
452 B2 West Third Border
443 F4 West Thirston Nthumb
443 F5 West Thirston Nthumb
52 D4 West Thorney W Susx
315 E4 Westthorpe Derbys
121 E4 West Thurrock Thurr
121 G4 West Tilbury Thurr
73 G4 West Tisted Hants
247 G6 West Tofts Norfk
512 D3 West Tofts P & K
6 C5 West Tolgus Cnwll
319 E3 West Torrington Lincs
85 F2 West Town BaNES
26 D3 West Town Devon
38 D3 West Town Devon
52 C5 West Town Hants
186 A2 West Town Herefs
109 E6 West Town N Som
67 E2 West Town Somset
55 G1 West Town W Susx
71 F3 West Tytherley Hants
342 A5 West Vale Calder
396 C2 West View Hartpl
105 F5 West Village V Glam
12 C4 Westville Devon
296 C5 Westville Notts
245 G2 West Walton Norfk
399 H6 Westward Cumb
39 F2 Westward Ho! Devon
9 F3 West Watergate Cnwll
143 G5 West Watford Herts
24 B4 Westweekmoor Devon
99 F5 Westwell Kent
138 C2 Westwell Oxon
99 F5 Westwell Leacon Kent
71 F6 West Wellow Hants
111 F6 Westwells Wilts
501 F6 West Wemyss Fife
513 E3 West Whitefield P & K
197 F1 Westwick Cambs
382 C1 Westwick Dur
84 C2 West Wick N Som
256 B4 Westwick Norfk
198 C5 West Wickham Cambs
96 A1 West Wickham Gt Lon
126 A3 West Williamston Pembks
298 B6 West Willoughby Lincs
252 C4 West Winch Norfk
71 E3 West Winterslow Wilts
52 D5 West Wittering W Susx
369 E2 West Witton N York
243 H5 Westwood C Pete
20 D1 Westwood Devon
27 G3 Westwood Devon
37 E2 Westwood IoW

100 C6 Westwood Kent
101 G2 Westwood Kent
295 E4 Westwood Notts
467 F4 Westwood S Lans
87 E3 Westwood Wilts
428 D2 West Woodburn Nthumb
90 B2 West Woodhay W Berk
214 D4 Westwood Heath Covtry
86 D6 West Woodlands Somset
174 C3 Westwood Park Essex
325 H5 Westwood Park Salfd
331 F5 Westwoodside N Linc
74 A2 West Worldham Hants
41 F5 West Worlington Devon
54 D4 West Worthing W Susx
198 B4 West Wratting Cambs
141 H6 West Wycombe Bucks
404 D2 West Wylam Nthumb
310 C2 Westy Warrtn
111 E4 West Yatton Wilts
608 F8 West Yell Shet
65 F5 West Yeo Somset
97 E2 West Yoke Kent
38 C4 West Youlstone Cnwll
122 C6 Wetham Green Kent
400 D4 Wetheral Cumb
401 E3 Wetheral Plain Cumb
357 F5 Wetherby Leeds
200 D2 Wetherden Suffk
200 D1 Wetherden Upper Town Suffk
201 F1 Wetheringsett Suffk
173 E3 Wethersfield Essex
606 E4 Wethersta Shet
201 F2 Wetherup Street Suffk
292 C5 Wetley Rocks Staffs
274 D5 Wetmore Staffs
290 C2 Wettenhall Ches
290 C2 Wettenhall Green Ches
210 A2 Wettles Shrops
293 E3 Wetton Staffs
360 A3 Wetwang E R Yk
271 H3 Wetwood Staffs
89 G3 Wexcombe Wilts
117 G3 Wexham Street Bucks
261 F3 Weybourne Norfk
93 E5 Weybourne Surrey
226 A3 Weybread Suffk
94 B1 Weybridge Surrey
29 F2 Weycroft Devon
588 E3 Weydale Highld
89 H5 Weyhill Hants
32 A3 Weymouth Dorset
184 D3 Weythel Powys
167 H3 Whaddon Bucks
197 E5 Whaddon Cambs
136 B2 Whaddon Gloucs
163 E5 Whaddon Gloucs
70 A4 Whaddon Wilts
87 F2 Whaddon Wilts
196 D5 Whaddon Gap Cambs
391 E4 Whale Cumb
315 G5 Whaley Derbys
312 D3 Whaley Bridge Derbys
315 F5 Whaley Thorns Derbys
583 K1 Whaligoe Highld
314 A1 Whalley Lancs
340 A2 Whalley Banks Lancs
324 B6 Whalley Range Manch
324 B3 Whalleys Lancs
430 B3 Whalton Nthumb
353 F2 Wham N York
280 D5 Whaplode Lincs
244 D2 Whaplode Drove Lincs
280 D5 Whaplode St Catherine Lincs
191 G4 Wharf Warwks
367 F6 Wharfe N York
338 B2 Wharles Lancs
194 C6 Wharley End Beds
403 F1 Wharmley Nthumb
328 C6 Wharncliffe Side Sheff
359 G1 Wharram le Street N York
310 C6 Wharton Ches
186 B3 Wharton Herefs
332 A6 Wharton Lincs
310 D6 Wharton Green Ches
383 E3 Washton N York
365 G3 Whasset Cumb
47 F4 Whatcombe Dorset
191 E6 Whatcote Warwks
238 C5 Whateley Warwks
200 D5 Whatfield Suffk
29 G1 Whatley Somset
86 C5 Whatley Somset
58 C3 Whatlington E Susx
82 B2 Whatsole Street Kent
294 C4 Whatstandwell Derbys
277 F2 Whatton Notts
410 D3 Whauphill D & G
382 A4 Whaw N York
3 G2 Wheal Alfred Cnwll
7 E5 Wheal Baddon Cnwll
6 D5 Wheal Busy Cnwll
7 E3 Wheal Frances Cnwll
6 D3 Wheal Kitty Cnwll
6 D5 Wheal Rose Cnwll
251 F6 Wheatacre Norfk
294 D3 Wheatcroft Derbys
135 H3 Wheatenhurst Gloucs
234 B4 Wheathall Shrops
143 H2 Wheathampstead Herts
211 E3 Wheathill Shrops
67 F3 Wheathill Somset
91 E2 Wheat Hold Hants
341 H4 Wheatley Calder
330 C4 Wheatley Donc
74 B1 Wheatley Hants
140 C3 Wheatley Oxon
396 A2 Wheatley Hill Dur
330 C4 Wheatley Hills Donc
340 C2 Wheatley Lane Lancs
330 C3 Wheatley Park Donc
235 B2 Wheaton Aston Staffs
63 E4 Wheddon Cross Somset
558 B4 Wheedlemont Abers
82 C1 Wheelbarrow Town Kent
12 C2 Wheeldon Devon
141 H6 Wheeler End Bucks
75 E1 Wheelerstreet Surrey
291 E3 Wheelock Ches
291 E3 Wheelock Heath Ches
339 F5 Wheelton Lancs
538 D5 Wheen Angus
344 B4 Wheldale Wakefd
358 C5 Wheldrake York
138 B5 Whelford Gloucs
324 D3 Whelley Wigan
156 D5 Whelpley Hill Bucks
389 H2 Whelpo Cumb
200 B4 Whelston Flints
308 B4 Whenby N York
170 D5 Whempstead Herts
372 B6 Whenby N York
199 G3 Whepstead Suffk
3 E4 Wherry Town Cnwll
176 C1 Wherstead Suffk
72 A1 Wherwell Hants
313 F4 Wheston Derbys
30 B2 Whetley Cross Dorset
97 G5 Whetsted Kent
240 B5 Whetstone Leics

210 A3 Whettleton Shrops
362 C5 Whicham Cumb
165 E3 Whichford Warwks
405 E2 Whickham Gatesd
60 D4 Whiddon Devon
25 G4 Whiddon Down Devon
468 A2 Whifflet N Lans
527 G6 Whigstreet Angus
192 D2 Whilton Nhants
192 D2 Whilton Locks Nhants
23 H1 Whimble Devon
27 G3 Whimple Devon
256 D4 Whimpwell Green Norfk
248 C3 Whinburgh Norfk
383 H1 Whinfield Darltn
468 A1 Whinhall N Lans
337 G1 Whin Lane End Lancs
295 G2 Whinney Hill Notts
329 H6 Whinney Hill Rothm
412 D4 Whinnieliggate D & G
561 G3 Whinnyfold Abers
339 G4 Whinny Heights Bl w D
396 A6 Whinny Hill S on T
485 F1 Whins of Milton Stirlg
341 H2 Whins Wood Brad
43 E4 Whipcott Devon
51 F6 Whippingham IoW
14 A6 Whipsiderry Cnwll
169 E6 Whipsnade Beds
27 E4 Whipton Devon
312 A4 Whirley Grove Ches
314 C3 Whirlow Sheff
314 C3 Whirlow Brook Sheff
297 H1 Whisby Lincs
241 H2 Whissendine Rutlnd
254 B3 Whissonsett Norfk
311 G5 Whistlefield Ag & B
495 E6 Whistlefield Ag & B
116 C5 Whistley Green Wokham
165 H4 Whistlow Oxon
194 A2 Whiston Nhants
315 F2 Whiston Rothm
324 B5 Whiston St Hel
236 C2 Whiston Staffs
292 D5 Whiston Staffs
309 G1 Whiston Cross Knows
236 A4 Whiston Cross Shrops
238 C6 Whitacre Heath Warwks
390 C4 Whitbarrow Village Cumb
362 C5 Whitbeck Cumb
187 G3 Whitbourne Herefs
87 E5 Whitbourne Moor Wilts
406 C2 Whitburn S Tyne
469 E2 Whitburn W Loth
309 E4 Whitby Ches
387 E2 Whitby N York
309 E5 Whitbyheath Ches
109 H6 Whitchurch BaNES
167 H5 Whitchurch Bucks
106 B4 Whitchurch Cardif
17 G4 Whitchurch Devon
90 D5 Whitchurch Hants
160 C6 Whitchurch Herefs
150 C4 Whitchurch Pembks
270 C1 Whitchurch Shrops
68 B3 Whitchurch Somset
29 G4 Whitchurch Canonicorum Dorset
115 G4 Whitchurch Hill Oxon
115 G4 Whitchurch-on-Thames Oxon
32 C2 Whitcombe Dorset
67 G5 Whitcombe Somset
209 G1 Whitcot Shrops
209 E3 Whitcott Keysett Shrops
568 D6 Whiteacen Moray
100 B6 Whiteacre Kent
173 F3 Whiteash Green Essex
43 E4 White Ball Somset
339 G4 Whitebirk Bl w D
549 H6 Whitebridge Highld
134 C3 Whitebrook Mons
95 F5 Whitebushes Surrey
560 D6 Whitecairns Abers
339 E1 Whitechapel Lancs
186 D5 Whitchurch Maund Herefs
134 D2 Whitecliff Gloucs
400 D3 Whiteclosegate Cumb
173 H4 White Colne Essex
339 F6 White Coppice Lancs
342 D2 Whitecote Leeds
488 C5 Whitecraig E Loth
466 D3 Whitecraigs E Rens
135 E3 Whitecroft Gloucs
483 H5 Whitecrook D & G
85 G3 White Cross BaNES
85 H3 White Cross BaNES
3 F3 Whitecross Cnwll
4 C4 White Cross Cnwll
7 G2 White Cross Cnwll
9 E3 Whitecross Cnwll
14 D4 Whitecross Cnwll
30 B3 Whitecross Dorset
486 C4 Whitecross Falk
160 B1 White Cross Herefs
66 C5 Whitecross Somset
84 B5 White Cross Somset
272 C5 Whitecross Staffs
68 C3 White Cross Wilts
221 G4 White Cross Hill Cambs
162 A3 White End Worcs
576 E6 Whiteface Highld
460 B1 Whitefarland N Ayrs
432 C3 Whitefaulds S Ayrs
326 B3 Whitefield Bury
47 G6 Whitefield Dorset
43 E2 Whitefield Somset
309 G2 Whitefield Lane End Knows
445 H4 Whiteflat E Ayrs
559 G4 Whiteford Abers
310 C6 Whitegate Ches
326 C4 White Gate Oldham
29 F1 White Gate Somset
233 F5 White Grit Powys
339 G5 Whitehall Bl w D
109 H5 Whitehall Bristl
43 F5 Whitehall Devon
60 D4 Whitehall Devon
92 B4 Whitehall Hants
170 C5 White Hall Herts
170 D3 Whitehall Herts
76 B5 Whitehall W Susx
603 J6 Whitehall Village Ork
439 F1 Whitehaugh Border
388 A6 Whitehaven Cumb
269 E5 Whitehawk Shrops
56 A4 Whitehawk Br & H
213 E2 Whiteheath Gate Sandw
86 C3 White Hill BaNES
341 G1 White Hill Brad
78 C4 Whitehill E Susx
500 D5 Whitehill Fife
99 G3 Whitehill Kent
471 G1 Whitehill Mdloth
569 J5 Whitehill Moray
126 B4 Whitehill Pembks
467 H3 Whitehill S Lans
291 H4 Whitehill Staffs
68 D3 White Hill Wilts
74 C2 Whitehill & Bordon Hants
570 B2 Whitehills Abers
527 G4 Whitehills Angus
405 G2 Whitehills Gatesd

193 F2 White Hills Nhants
467 F4 Whitehills S Lans
337 F1 Whiteholme Bpool
312 D3 Whitehough Derbys
555 H2 Whitehouse Abers
462 D2 Whitehouse Ag & B
201 F5 White House Suffk
238 A5 Whitehouse Common Birm
115 G6 Whitehouse Green W Berk
316 D4 White Houses Notts
466 D1 Whiteinch C Glas
490 A3 Whitekirk E Loth
394 A2 White Kirkley Dur
116 B5 Whiteknights Readg
46 D5 White Lackington Dorset
44 D5 Whitelackington Somset
188 D4 White Ladies Aston Worcs
141 H4 Whiteleaf Bucks
406 B2 Whiteleas S Tyne
161 H2 Whiteleaved Oak Worcs
451 H3 Whitelee Border
440 D3 Whitelee Nthumb
445 E3 Whitelees S Ayrs
405 E4 White-le-Head Dur
37 H4 Whiteley Bank IoW
312 B4 Whiteley Green Ches
94 B2 Whiteley Village Surrey
314 C3 Whiteley Wood Sheff
351 F2 White Lund Lancs
134 C4 Whiteleye Mons
77 E4 Whitemans Green W Susx
154 C5 White Mill Carmth
567 H6 Whitemire Moray
276 B1 Whitemoor C Nott
8 B2 Whitemoor Cnwll
294 D5 White Moor Derbys
214 D5 Whitemoor Warwks
292 A2 Whitemore Staffs
559 G3 Whitemyres Abers
71 H5 Whitenap Hants
605 G2 White Ness Shet
173 F6 White Notley Essex
120 D6 White Oak Kent
139 E2 Whiteoak Green Oxon
86 C3 White Ox Mead BaNES
71 E5 Whiteparish Wilts
320 C4 White Pit Lincs
68 D2 Whitepits Wilts
78 C1 White Post Kent
296 B3 White Post Notts
560 B5 Whiterashes Abers
451 H3 Whiterigg Border
104 D4 Whiterock Brdgnd
160 A5 White Rocks Herefs
146 A2 White Roothing or White Roding Essex
589 K7 Whiterow Highld
75 E4 White's Green W Susx
136 B3 Whiteshill Gloucs
110 A4 Whiteshill S Glos
427 G6 Whiteside Nthumb
469 F1 Whiteside W Loth
57 E2 Whitesmith E Susx
423 F2 Whitespots D & G
338 D4 White Stake Lancs
44 B5 Whitestaunton Somset
26 D4 Whitestone Devon
186 D6 White Stone Herefs
215 F1 Whitestone Warwks
174 C2 Whitestreet Green Suffk
108 D2 Whitewall Common Mons
373 E6 Whitewall Corner N York
117 E4 White Waltham W & M
86 C2 Whiteway BaNES
33 F3 Whiteway Dorset
136 B5 Whiteway Gloucs
136 D2 Whiteway Gloucs
15 F2 Whitewell Cnwll
352 C5 Whitewell Lancs
270 B1 Whitewell Wrexhm
340 C5 Whitewell Bottom Lancs
18 D3 Whiteworks Devon
568 C4 Whitewreath Moray
514 C3 Whitfield C Dund
83 F2 Whitfield Kent
166 D2 Whitfield Nhants
402 D3 Whitfield Nthumb
110 B1 Whitfield S Glos
93 G3 Whitfield Court Surrey
402 D3 Whitfield Hall Nthumb
28 D3 Whitford Devon
307 G4 Whitford Flints
346 B5 Whitgift E R Yk
272 C4 Whitgreave Staffs
426 C2 Whithaugh Border
603 H5 Whithebeir Ork
410 D4 Whithorn D & G
461 E4 Whiting Bay N Ayrs
343 G3 Whitkirk Leeds
126 D1 Whitland Carmth
472 B5 Whitlaw Border
11 E1 Whitleigh C Plym
445 E5 Whitletts S Ayrs
310 C4 Whitley Ches
215 E4 Whitley Covtry
344 D5 Whitley N York
116 B5 Whitley Readg
329 E6 Whitley Sheff
324 D3 Whitley Wigan
87 F1 Whitley Wilts
431 G5 Whitley Bay N Tyne
344 D5 Whitley Bridge N York
403 G3 Whitley Chapel Nthumb
354 D6 Whitley Head Brad
272 B4 Whitley Heath Staffs
342 D6 Whitley Lower Kirk
310 C5 Whitley Reed Ches
431 G5 Whitley Sands N Tyne
344 D5 Whitley Thorpe N York
116 B6 Whitley Wood Readg
213 H4 Whitlock's End Solhll
135 H3 Whitminster Gloucs
43 E5 Whitmoor Dorset
48 D3 Whitmore Dorset
272 B1 Whitmore Staffs
215 E3 Whitmore Park Covtry
42 D4 Whitnage Devon
191 E2 Whitnash Warwks
64 D4 Whitnell Somset
185 E5 Whitney-on-Wye Herefs
389 F2 Whitrigg Cumb
399 G3 Whitrigg Cumb
399 G3 Whitrigglees Cumb
439 H1 Whitriggs Border
70 C6 Whitsbury Hants
472 D6 Whitslaid Border
474 C4 Whitsome Border
474 C5 Whitsomehill Border
142 C2 Whitson Newpt
108 C3 Whitson Newpt
100 B2 Whitstable Kent
23 F3 Whitstone Cnwll
442 D2 Whittingham Nthumb
210 A2 Whittingslow Shrops
314 D5 Whittington Derbys
163 F5 Whittington Gloucs
366 B4 Whittington Lancs
247 E5 Whittington Norfk
269 F3 Whittington Shrops
212 C3 Whittington Staffs
238 B3 Whittington Staffs
272 A3 Whittington Staffs
238 D5 Whittington Warwks

188 C4 Whittington Worcs
314 D5 Whittington Moor Derbys
193 E6 Whittlebury Nhants
339 E5 Whittle-le-Woods Lancs
244 C5 Whittlesey Cambs
197 G5 Whittlesford Cambs
339 H6 Whittlestone Head Bl w D
453 E5 Whitton Border
118 C5 Whitton Gt Lon
209 H5 Whitton Herefs
346 D5 Whitton N Linc
442 D4 Whitton Nthumb
185 E1 Whitton Powys
395 H5 Whitton S on T
210 D5 Whitton Shrops
201 F5 Whitton Suffk
113 G5 Whittonditch Wilts
404 C3 Whittonstall Nthumb
210 A4 Whittytree Shrops
90 D3 Whitway Hants
315 G4 Whitwell Derbys
169 H5 Whitwell Herts
37 E5 Whitwell IoW
383 G5 Whitwell N York
242 C3 Whitwell Rutlnd
358 D1 Whitwell-on-the-Hill N York
255 F3 Whitwell Street Norfk
239 G1 Whitwick Leics
343 H5 Whitwood Wakefd
340 D6 Whitworth Lancs
270 C3 Whixall Shrops
357 E3 Whixley N York
215 E4 Whoberley Covtry
486 B3 Wholeflats Falk
96 D3 Whorne's Place Kent
310 C2 Whorlton Dur
384 D4 Whorlton N York
58 B5 Whydown E Susx
428 B4 Whygate Nthumb
380 B2 Whygill Head Cumb
53 F4 Whyke W Susx
79 G1 Whyle Herefs
95 G3 Whyteleafe Surrey
134 D5 Wibdon Gloucs
342 B3 Wibsey Brad
215 H2 Wibtoft Warwks
188 A2 Wichenford Worcs
99 E3 Wichling Kent
35 E2 Wick Bmouth
28 C2 Wick Devon
589 K6 Wick Highld
110 C5 Wick S Glos
605 H3 Wick Shet
64 D3 Wick Somset
66 C4 Wick Somset
84 B4 Wick Somset
105 E5 Wick V Glam
54 D4 Wick W Susx
70 D5 Wick Wilts
189 E5 Wick Worcs
222 B5 Wicken Cambs
167 F2 Wicken Nhants
171 G3 Wicken Bonhunt Essex
318 D3 Wickenby Lincs
188 B4 Wick Episcopi Worcs
315 F1 Wickersley Rothm
174 C1 Wicker Street Green Suffk
147 E6 Wickford Essex
51 G2 Wickham Hants
114 B5 Wickham W Berk
147 G2 Wickham Bishops Essex
100 D4 Wickhambreaux Kent
199 E4 Wickhambrook Suffk
405 F3 Wickham Fell Gatesd
163 G1 Wickhamford Worcs
225 E6 Wickham Green Suffk
114 B5 Wickham Green W Berk
114 C6 Wickham Heath W Berk
202 B3 Wickham Market Suffk
251 E3 Wickhampton Norfk
173 G2 Wickham St Paul Essex
67 E3 Wickham's Cross Somset
225 E6 Wickham Skeith Suffk
199 F4 Wickham Street Suffk
225 E6 Wickham Street Suffk
117 E5 Wick Hill Br For
80 B1 Wick Hill Kent
92 C2 Wick Hill Wokham
96 D5 Wickhurst Kent
86 B3 Wicklane BaNES
249 E4 Wicklewood Norfk
261 G5 Wickmere Norfk
162 B4 Wickridge Street Gloucs
110 C5 Wick Rocks S Glos
84 C1 Wick St Lawrence N Som
57 E3 Wickstreet E Susx
136 C3 Wick Street Gloucs
110 C2 Wickwar S Glos
87 E3 Widbrook Wilts
86 D2 Widcombe BaNES
171 H3 Widdington Essex
443 G5 Widdrington Nthumb
443 G6 Widdrington Station Nthumb
19 F2 Widecombe in the Moor Devon
10 A2 Widegates Cnwll
160 C1 Widemarsh Herefs
23 E2 Widemouth Bay Cnwll
430 D5 Wideopen N Tyne
601 G6 Widewall Ork
11 E1 Widewell C Plym
146 D3 Widford Essex
145 F1 Widford Herts
198 D3 Widgham Green Cambs
112 C2 Widham Wilts
52 B3 Widley Hants
142 B5 Widmer End Bucks
276 D4 Widmerpool Notts
117 F2 Widmoor Bucks
309 H2 Widnes Halton
38 B5 Widworthy Devon
98 B5 Wierton Kent
208 B2 Wig Powys
324 C3 Wigan Wigan
372 C5 Wigbeth Dorset
48 C3 Wigborough Somset
45 E4 Wig Fach Brdgnd
28 B4 Wiggaton Devon
252 B5 Wiggenhall St Germans Norfk
246 B2 Wiggenhall St Mary Magdalen Norfk
252 B5 Wiggenhall St Mary the Virginl Norfk
252 C5 Wiggenhall St Peter Norfk
172 D1 Wiggens Green Essex
293 E2 Wigginstall Staffs
142 C2 Wigginton Herts
165 F3 Wigginton Oxon
269 F2 Wigginton Shrops
238 B3 Wigginton Staffs
358 A3 Wigginton York
142 C3 Wigginton Bottom Herts
165 F2 Wigginton Heath Oxon
353 G3 Wigglesworth N York
400 A4 Wiggonby Cumb
54 B1 Wiggonholt W Susx
357 F5 Wighill N York
260 B4 Wighton Norfk
314 C5 Wightwick Wolves
275 G4 Wigley Derbys
77 H3 Wigley Hants

269 G4 Wigmarsh Shrops
209 H6 Wigmore Herefs
98 B2 Wigmore Medway
317 G5 Wigsley Notts
219 E3 Wigsthorpe Nhants
240 D5 Wigston Leics
240 D5 Wigston Harcourt Leics
240 D5 Wigston Magna Leics
215 H2 Wigston Parva Leics
316 A3 Wigthorpe Notts
280 C2 Wigtoft Lincs
399 H5 Wigton Cumb
417 E5 Wigtown D & G
328 C5 Wigtwizzle Sheff
356 C6 Wike Leeds
331 E2 Wike Well End Donc
217 H2 Wilbarston Nhants
358 D4 Wilberfoss E R Yk
327 G2 Wilberlee Kirk
221 G5 Wilburton Cambs
194 B1 Wilby Nhants
224 D2 Wilby Norfk
226 A5 Wilby Suffk
88 D2 Wilcot Wilts
269 G6 Wilcott Shrops
269 G6 Wilcott Marsh Shrops
10 D2 Wilcove Cnwll
108 C2 Wilcrick Newpt
314 C5 Wilday Green Derbys
312 C6 Wildboarclough Ches
195 F3 Wilden Beds
212 B5 Wilden Worcs
51 E2 Wildern Hants
96 D3 Wildernesse Kent
310 C2 Wilderspool Warrtn
325 E2 Wilderswood Bolton
222 D4 Wilde Street Suffk
90 B4 Wildhern Hants
144 C5 Wildhill Herts
468 C4 Wildmanbridge S Lans
105 E3 Wild Mill Brdgnd
92 A3 Wildmoor Hants
140 A5 Wildmoor Oxon
212 D4 Wildmoor Worcs
117 E6 Wildridings Br For
331 H5 Wildsworth Lincs
272 D5 Wildwood Staffs
276 C2 Wilford C Nott
99 F3 Wilgate Green Kent
271 E1 Wilkesley Ches
577 K6 Wilkhaven Highld
487 F6 Wilkieston W Loth
67 H5 Wilkinthroop Somset
300 A2 Wilksby Lincs
338 C2 Willacy Lane End Lancs
42 D5 Willand Devon
43 G5 Willand Somset
42 D5 Willand Moor Devon
79 G5 Willard's Hill E Susx
290 D4 Willaston Ches
308 D4 Willaston Ches
270 D2 Willaston Shrops
168 B1 Willen M Keyn
215 F4 Willenhall Covtry
237 E5 Willenhall Wsall
347 F3 Willerby E R Yk
374 B4 Willerby N York
163 G2 Willersey Gloucs
185 F5 Willersley Herefs
81 F1 Willesborough Kent
99 G6 Willesborough Lees Kent
119 E3 Willesden Gt Lon
119 E3 Willesden Green Gt Lon
239 E2 Willesley Leics
111 F2 Willesley Wilts
64 B5 Willett Somset
235 F5 Willey Shrops
216 A3 Willey Warwks
93 F4 Willey Green Surrey
451 E3 Williamhope Border
191 H5 Williamscot Oxon
605 G6 Williamsetter Shet
174 C1 William's Green Suffk
471 F6 Williamslee Border
105 G1 Williamstown Rhondd
295 E1 Williamthorpe Derbys
467 E3 Williamwood E Rens
170 B3 Willian Herts
402 D2 Willimontswick Nthumb
146 B3 Willingale Essex
60 C3 Willingcott Devon
57 F4 Willingdon E Susx
221 F5 Willingham Cambs
227 E3 Willingham Suffk
317 G3 Willingham by Stow Lincs
198 C4 Willingham Green Cambs
195 G5 Willington Beds
275 E4 Willington Derbys
394 D3 Willington Dur
98 B4 Willington Kent
405 H1 Willington N Tyne
164 D2 Willington Warwks
290 A1 Willington Corner Ches
405 H1 Willington Quay N Tyne
201 E4 Willisham Suffk
201 E4 Willisham Tye Suffk
345 G3 Willitoft E R Yk
63 H3 Williton Somset
321 E5 Willoughby Lincs
192 B1 Willoughby Warwks
300 C5 Willoughby Hills Lincs
276 D4 Willoughby-on-the-Wolds Notts
240 C6 Willoughby Waterleys Leics
332 C6 Willoughton Lincs
118 A2 Willowbank Bucks
310 C4 Willow Green Ches
187 H3 Willow Green Worcs
400 C3 Willow Holme Cumb
325 F3 Willows Bolton
173 E6 Willows Green Essex
132 C2 Willowtown Blae G
321 E2 Will Row Lincs
110 B5 Willsbridge S Glos
273 G3 Willslock Staffs
234 B5 Willstone Shrops
190 B3 Wilmcote Warwks
86 B2 Wilmington BaNES
28 D3 Wilmington Devon
57 E3 Wilmington E Susx
120 D5 Wilmington Kent
57 E3 Wilmington Green E Susx
17 G3 Wilminstone Devon
311 G3 Wilmslow Ches
311 H3 Wilmslow Park Ches
238 C4 Wilnecote Staffs
225 E3 Wilney Green Norfk
339 G3 Wilpshire Lancs
342 A2 Wilsden Brad
298 C6 Wilsford Lincs
70 C2 Wilsford Wilts
88 C3 Wilsford Wilts
62 B2 Wilsham Devon
327 H3 Wilshaw Kirk
330 C5 Wilsic Donc
355 G2 Wilsill N York
79 H2 Wilsley Green Kent
80 A2 Wilsley Pound Kent
73 H2 Wilsom Hants
160 D5 Wilson Herefs
240 B5 Wilson Leics
515 E2 Wilsonhall Angus
469 E3 Wilsontown S Lans

195 F6 Wilstead Beds
276 A3 Wilsthorpe Derbys
243 F2 Wilsthorpe Lincs
142 B2 Wilstone Herts
142 C2 Wilstone Green Herts
329 E3 Wilthorpe Barns
439 F1 Wilton Border
376 C2 Wilton Cumb
160 D5 Wilton Herefs
373 G3 Wilton N York
397 E6 Wilton R & Cl
43 H3 Wilton Somset
70 B3 Wilton Wilts
89 G2 Wilton Wilts
390 B4 Wilton Hill Cumb
117 G1 Wilton Park Bucks
43 G4 Wiltown Devon
66 B5 Wiltown Somset
172 B2 Wimbish Essex
172 C3 Wimbish Green Essex
237 F2 Wimblebury Staffs
119 E5 Wimbledon Gt Lon
92 D5 Wimble Hill Hants
221 F1 Wimblington Cambs
309 F5 Wimbolds Trafford Ches
48 C4 Wimborne Minster Dorset
48 C2 Wimborne St Giles Dorset
246 C3 Wimbotsham Norfk
196 D5 Wimpole Cambs
50 C2 Wimpson C Sotn
190 C5 Wimpstone Warwks
68 A4 Wincanton Somset
320 B6 Winceby Lincs
310 D4 Wincham Ches
487 E5 Winchburgh W Loth
163 F4 Winchcombe Gloucs
59 E3 Winchelsea E Susx
59 F3 Winchelsea Beach E Susx
72 B3 Winchester Hants
132 C2 Winchestown Blae G
79 G1 Winchet Hill Kent
92 C4 Winchfield Hants
92 C4 Winchfield Hurst Hants
142 C5 Winchmore Hill Bucks
144 D6 Winchmore Hill Gt Lon
292 C1 Wincle Ches
314 D1 Wincobank Sheff
388 B6 Winder Cumb
378 C5 Windermere Cumb
165 E1 Winderton Warwks
342 C2 Windhill Brad
364 C5 Wind Hill Cumb
330 A4 Windhill Donc
565 J7 Windhill Highld
126 B5 Wind Hill Pembks
608 F6 Windhouse Shet
114 B5 Winding Wood W Berk
308 D4 Windle Hill Ches
312 C2 Windlehurst Stockp
93 F2 Windlesham Surrey
294 C6 Windley Derbys
14 B4 Windmill Cnwll
308 A5 Windmill Flints
109 G5 Windmill Hill Bristl
315 E3 Windmill Hill Derbys
57 H2 Windmill Hill E Susx
310 B3 Windmill Hill Halton
98 C1 Windmill Hill Kent
44 C4 Windmill Hill Somset
188 D5 Windmill Hill Worcs
138 B2 Windrush Gloucs
331 G2 Windsor N Linc
117 G4 Windsor W & M
136 B4 Windsoredge Gloucs
200 A4 Windsor Green Suffk
44 D6 Windwhistle Somset
309 G1 Windy Arbor Knows
214 D5 Windy Arbour Warwks
451 E2 Windydoors Border
557 F6 Windyedge Abers
501 F4 Windygates Fife
311 G5 Windyharbour Ches
288 D4 Windy Hill Wrexhm
486 C6 Windyknowe W Loth
405 G2 Windy Nook Gatesd
568 C2 Windyridge Moray
276 C4 Windyridge Staffs
466 C4 Windy-Yett E Ayrs
76 D6 Wineham W Susx
349 F5 Winestead E R Yk
341 E2 Winewall Lancs
225 E2 Winfarthing Norfk
37 F4 Winford IoW
85 F1 Winford N Som
185 E5 Winforton Herefs
33 E3 Winfrith Newburgh Dorset
168 B5 Wing Bucks
242 B4 Wing Rutlnd
396 B2 Wingate Dur
325 E2 Wingates Bolton
443 E5 Wingates Nthumb
314 D6 Wingerworth Derbys
168 D4 Wingfield Beds
329 G5 Wingfield Rothm
225 H4 Wingfield Suffk
87 E3 Wingfield Wilts
225 H4 Wingfield Green Suffk
294 D4 Wingfield Park Derbys
100 D4 Wingham Kent
100 D4 Wingham Green Kent
100 D4 Wingham Well Kent
82 C1 Wingmore Kent
168 B6 Wingrave Bucks
296 B3 Winkburn Notts
117 F5 Winkfield Br For
117 F5 Winkfield Place Br For
117 F5 Winkfield Row Br For
293 E4 Winkhill Staffs
96 C5 Winkhurst Green Kent
91 G4 Winklebury Hants
40 C6 Winkleigh Devon
370 B5 Winksley N York
49 F5 Winkton Dorset
405 E2 Winlaton Gatesd
405 E2 Winlaton Mill Gatesd
589 J6 Winless Highld
190 C2 Winllan Powys
268 D5 Winmarleigh Lancs
160 A3 Winnal Common Herefs
72 C3 Winnall Hants
188 B1 Winnall Worcs
14 C5 Winnard's Perch Cnwll
116 C5 Winnersh Wokham
310 C5 Winnington Ches
271 G2 Winnington Staffs
233 F2 Winnington Green Shrops
273 F1 Winnothdale Staffs
388 B4 Winscales Cumb
84 D3 Winscombe N Som
26 D3 Winscott Barton Devon
290 C2 Winsford Ches
62 D5 Winsford Somset
60 C4 Winsham Devon
29 G1 Winsham Somset
274 D5 Winshill Staffs
391 F3 Winskill Cumb
39 E4 Winslade Devon
91 H5 Winslade Hants
356 A2 Winsley N York
87 E2 Winsley Wilts

167 G4 Winslow Bucks
161 E2 Winslow Mill Herefs
137 G3 Winson Gloucs
213 F2 Winson Green Birm
50 B2 Winsor Hants
324 C4 Winstanley Wigan
324 D3 Winstanleys Wigan
378 D6 Winster Cumb
294 A2 Winster Derbys
382 G1 Winston Dur
201 G2 Winston Suffk
137 E3 Winstone Gloucs
201 G2 Winston Green Suffk
39 G5 Winswell Devon
32 C2 Winterborne Came Dorset
47 F4 Winterborne Clenston Dorset
32 B2 Winterborne Herringston Dorset
47 F4 Winterborne Houghton Dorset
47 G5 Winterborne Kingston Dorset
31 F5 Winterborne Monkton Dorset
47 G5 Winterborne Muston Dorset
47 F4 Winterborne Stickland Dorset
47 G5 Winterborne Tomson Dorset
47 F4 Winterborne Whitechurch Dorset
47 G5 Winterborne Zelston Dorset
99 H3 Winterbourne Kent
110 A3 Winterbourne S Glos
114 C5 Winterbourne W Berk
31 E4 Winterbourne Abbas Dorset
112 C5 Winterbourne Bassett Wilts
70 D3 Winterbourne Dauntsey Wilts
110 B3 Winterbourne Down S Glos
70 D3 Winterbourne Earls Wilts
70 D3 Winterbourne Gunner Wilts
112 D5 Winterbourne Monkton Wilts
31 E5 Winterbourne Steepleton Dorset
70 B1 Winterbourne Stoke Wilts
115 G2 Winterbrook Oxon
354 B3 Winterburn N York
86 A3 Winterfield BaNES
122 B3 Winter Gardens Essex
44 C4 Winterhay Green Somset
84 D3 Winterhead Somset
346 D5 Winteringham N Linc
291 E3 Winterley Ches
329 F1 Wintersett Wakefd
72 D6 Wintershill Hants
346 D6 Winterton N Linc
257 F6 Winterton-on-Sea Norfk
44 B3 Winter Well Somset
301 G1 Winthorpe Lincs
297 F3 Winthorpe Notts
48 D6 Winton Bmouth
380 D2 Winton Cumb
57 E4 Winton E Susx
384 C5 Winton N York
325 H5 Winton Salfd
373 G5 Wintringham N York
219 G3 Winwick Cambs
216 D5 Winwick Nhants
325 E6 Winwick Warrtn
310 B1 Winwick Quay Warrtn
30 B1 Winyard's Gap Dorset
189 G1 Winyates Worcs
213 G6 Winyates Green Worcs
294 B4 Wirksworth Derbys
294 C4 Wirksworth Moor Derbys
290 A6 Wirswall Ches
245 G3 Wisbech Cambs
245 F3 Wisbech St Mary Cambs
75 G4 Wisborough Green W Susx
316 D2 Wiseton Notts
136 D3 Wishanger Gloucs
468 B3 Wishaw N Lans
238 B6 Wishaw Warwks
94 B3 Wisley Surrey
319 G5 Wispington Lincs
80 C1 Wissenden Kent
226 D4 Wissett Suffk
209 H2 Wistanstow Shrops
271 F4 Wistanswick Shrops
290 D4 Wistaston Ches
290 D4 Wistaston Green Ches
151 H6 Wiston Pembks
448 C3 Wiston S Lans
54 D2 Wiston W Susx
448 B3 Wiston Mains S Lans
220 C3 Wistow Cambs
240 D5 Wistow Leics
344 D2 Wistow N York
340 A2 Wiswell Lancs
221 G4 Witcham Cambs
48 B3 Witchampton Dorset
221 G4 Witchford Cambs
66 D5 Witcombe Somset
39 F4 Witcott Devon
147 F2 Witham Essex
68 B1 Witham Friary Somset
243 E1 Witham on the Hill Lincs
297 G2 Witham St Hughs Lincs
319 H3 Withcall Lincs
55 H3 Withdean Br & H
79 E4 Witherenden Hill E Susx
256 B4 Withergate Norfk
41 G5 Witheridge Devon
116 A3 Witheridge Hill Oxon
239 E5 Witherley Leics
174 D2 Withermarsh Green Suffk
320 D3 Withern Lincs
349 F4 Withernsea E R Yk
348 C1 Withernwick E R Yk
226 B3 Withersdale Street Suffk
99 H5 Withersdane Kent
198 D5 Withersfield Suffk
365 F3 Witherslack Cumb
406 B3 Witherwack Sundld
67 F2 Withial Somset
14 D5 Withiel Cnwll
63 F5 Withiel Florey Somset
15 E5 Withielgoose Cnwll
15 E5 Withielgoose Mills Cnwll
137 F1 Withington Gloucs
186 D6 Withington Herefs
326 B6 Withington Manch
234 D2 Withington Shrops
273 F3 Withington Staffs
186 D6 Withington Green Ches
42 B5 Withington Marsh Herefs
339 F5 Withleigh Devon
339 F5 Withnell Lancs
213 F5 Withnell Fold Lancs
86 B5 Withybed Green Worcs
215 G3 Withybrook Somset
125 G1 Withybrook Warwks
63 G3 Withybush Pembks
21 E1 Withycombe Somset
86 B3 Withycombe Raleigh Devon
78 B2 Withyditch BaNES
86 B3 Withyham E Susx
212 D2 Withy Mills BaNES
62 C4 Withymoor Village Dudley
62 C4 Withypool Somset

292 B5 Withystakes Staffs
109 G6 Withywood Bristl
75 E2 Witley Surrey
212 A3 Witnells End Worcs
201 G4 Witnesham Suffk
139 E2 Witney Oxon
50 A2 Wittensford Hants
243 E4 Wittering C Pete
80 C4 Wittersham Kent
213 G1 Witton Birm
250 C3 Witton Norfk
188 C2 Witton Worcs
256 C3 Witton Bridge Norfk
405 F5 Witton Gilbert Dur
187 H2 Witton Hill Worcs
394 C3 Witton-le-Wear Dur
394 D3 Witton Park Dur
43 E2 Wiveliscombe Somset
73 G2 Wivelrod Hants
77 F5 Wivelsfield E Susx
77 F6 Wivelsfield Green E Susx
174 D5 Wivenhoe Essex
260 D3 Wiveton Norfk
176 C4 Wix Essex
189 G4 Wixford Warwks
270 D4 Wixhill Shrops
199 E6 Wixoe Suffk
168 C3 Woburn Beds
168 C2 Woburn Sands M Keyn
187 F4 Wofferwood Common Herefs
93 H3 Woking Surrey
116 C6 Wokingham Wokham
20 B3 Wolborough Devon
53 F4 Woldhurst W Susx
96 A3 Woldingham Surrey
95 H3 Woldingham Garden Village Surrey
374 C5 Wold Newton E R Yk
334 B5 Wold Newton NE Lin
250 B5 Wolferd Green Norfk
187 F2 Wolferlow Herefs
252 C2 Wolferton Norfk
192 B1 Wolfhampcote Warwks
513 E3 Wolfhill P & K
151 F4 Wolf's Castle Pembks
151 F5 Wolfsdale Pembks
151 F5 Wolfsdale Hill Pembks
451 F5 Woll Border
212 C3 Wollaston Dudley
194 C2 Wollaston Nhants
233 F2 Wollaston Shrops
276 B2 Wollaton C Nott
271 E3 Wollerton Shrops
271 E3 Wollerton Wood Shrops
212 D3 Wollescote Dudley
451 F5 Wollrig Border
394 B2 Wolsingham Dur
291 H5 Wolstanton Staffs
326 B1 Wolstenholme Rochdl
215 G4 Wolston Warwks
398 D4 Wolsty Cumb
261 G5 Wolterton Norfk
140 A3 Wolvercote Oxon
309 F4 Wolverham Ches
236 D5 Wolverhampton Wolves
270 B3 Wolverley Shrops
212 B4 Wolverley Worcs
28 B2 Wolverstone Devon
91 F3 Wolverton Hants
83 E2 Wolverton Kent
167 H1 Wolverton M Keyn
210 B2 Wolverton Shrops
190 C2 Wolverton Warwks
68 C3 Wolverton Wilts
91 E2 Wolverton Common Hants
167 H1 Wolverton Mill M Keyn
134 A5 Wolvesnewton Mons
215 G2 Wolvey Warwks
215 G2 Wolvey Heath Warwks
396 B4 Wolviston S on T
185 E2 Womaston Powys
372 C3 Wombleton N York
236 C6 Wombourne Staffs
235 F2 Wombridge Wrekin
329 F4 Wombwell Barns
100 D5 Womenswold Kent
344 C6 Womersley N York
134 B2 Wonastone Mons
84 B3 Wonderstone N Som
93 H5 Wonersh Surrey
27 E4 Wonford Devon
25 G5 Wonson Devon
46 D3 Wonston Dorset
72 C2 Wonston Hants
117 F2 Wooburn Bucks
117 F2 Wooburn Common Bucks
117 F2 Wooburn Green Bucks
117 F1 Wooburn Moor Bucks
151 E5 Wood Pembks
44 C4 Wood Somset
39 E6 Woodacott Devon
39 E6 Woodacott Cross Devon
368 D4 Woodale N York
309 E5 Woodbank Ches
210 D2 Woodbank Shrops
250 C1 Woodbastwick Norfk
317 E4 Woodbeck Notts
189 G4 Wood Bevington Warwks
296 B5 Woodborough Notts
88 C3 Woodborough Wilts
28 C3 Woodbridge Devon
68 D6 Woodbridge Devon
137 F2 Woodbridge Gloucs
431 E2 Woodbridge Nthumb
454 B3 Woodbridge Suffk
202 B5 Woodbridge Hill Surrey
93 G4 Woodbridge Hill Surrey
202 C5 Woodbridge Walk Suffk
193 E5 Wood Burcote Nhants
27 G5 Woodbury Devon
27 G5 Woodbury Salterton Devon
136 B4 Woodchester Gloucs
80 D3 Woodchurch Kent
308 C2 Woodchurch Wirral
87 F6 Woodcock Wilts
273 F4 Woodcock Heath Staffs
213 F3 Woodcock Hill Birm
118 A1 Woodcock Hill Herts
63 E2 Woodcombe Somset
51 G4 Woodcote Hants
95 F2 Woodcote Gt Lon
115 G3 Woodcote Oxon
95 E3 Woodcote Surrey
235 H1 Woodcote Wrekin
95 F2 Woodcote Green Gt Lon
212 D5 Woodcote Green Worcs
90 C4 Woodcott Hants
134 C5 Woodcroft Gloucs
48 B1 Woodcutts Dorset
255 E2 Wood Dalling Norfk
198 D3 Woodditton Cambs
140 B2 Woodeaton Oxon
272 B6 Wood Eaton Staffs
126 C3 Wooden Pembks
168 D1 Wood End Beds
195 E5 Wood End Beds
195 F1 Wood End Beds
195 F3 Wood End Beds
117 F5 Wood End Br For
167 G3 Wood End Bucks
312 C2 Woodend Ches
215 F3 Wood End Covtry

376 C2 Woodend Cumb
377 F5 Woodend Cumb
388 C5 Woodend Cumb
146 B2 Woodend Essex
500 C5 Woodend Fife
161 E1 Woodend Herefs
170 D4 Wood End Herts
192 D5 Woodend Nhants
295 F3 Woodend Notts
326 D2 Wood End Oldham
274 B4 Woodend Staffs
487 E4 Woodend W Loth
53 E3 Woodend W Susx
213 H5 Wood End Warwks
214 D2 Wood End Warwks
238 C5 Wood End Warwks
236 D4 Wood End Wolves
299 H2 Wood Enderby Lincs
172 B4 Wood End Green Essex
118 B3 Wood End Green Gt Lon
70 D5 Woodfalls Wilts
135 C5 Woodfield Gloucs
166 C5 Woodfield Oxon
444 D5 Woodfield S Ayrs
11 F2 Woodford C Plym
38 B5 Woodford Cnwll
12 D2 Woodford Devon
28 B3 Woodford Devon
135 F5 Woodford Gloucs
120 B1 Woodford Gt Lon
218 D4 Woodford Nhants
63 H4 Woodford Somset
85 F6 Woodford Somset
312 A3 Woodford Stockp
120 B1 Woodford Bridge Gt Lon
120 B1 Woodford Green Gt Lon
192 B4 Woodford Halse Nhants
145 E6 Woodford Wells Gt Lon
213 E3 Woodgate Birm
43 E4 Woodgate Devon
254 D4 Woodgate Norfk
274 A4 Wood Gate Staffs
53 G4 Woodgate W Susx
189 E1 Woodgate Worcs
326 B2 Woodgate Hill Bury
172 B4 Woodgates End Essex
211 E5 Woodgates Green Worcs
213 E3 Woodgate Valley Birm
145 F4 Wood Green Gt Lon
119 G1 Wood Green Gt Lon
70 D6 Woodgreen Hants
225 G4 Wood Green Norfk
139 F2 Woodgreen Oxon
237 E5 Wood Green Sandw
188 B1 Wood Green Worcs
171 G3 Wood Hall Essex
144 B2 Woodhall Herts
482 D5 Woodhall Inver
345 F3 Woodhall N York
368 C1 Woodhall P & K
299 F2 Woodhall Spa Lincs
167 E6 Woodham Bucks
395 F4 Woodham Dur
94 A2 Woodham Surrey
147 F5 Woodham Ferrers Essex
147 G4 Woodham Mortimer Essex
147 G3 Woodham Walter Essex
95 F5 Woodhatch Surrey
514 C4 Woodhaven Fife
236 D4 Wood Hayes Wolves
560 A2 Woodhead Abers
570 D3 Woodhead Abers
423 F5 Woodhead D & G
472 C5 Woodheads Border
326 A1 Woodhey Bury
308 D2 Woodhey Wirral
290 B4 Woodhey Green Ches
147 F4 Woodhill Essex
109 E4 Woodhill N Som
211 G3 Woodhill Shrops
44 D2 Woodhill Somset
431 F2 Woodhorn Nthumb
342 B5 Woodhouse Calder
365 H3 Woodhouse Cumb
376 B1 Woodhouse Cumb
90 B5 Woodhouse Hants
353 E4 Wood House Lancs
343 E2 Woodhouse Leeds
240 B1 Woodhouse Leics
331 G3 Woodhouse N Linc
315 E2 Woodhouse Sheff
343 G5 Woodhouse Wakefd
109 H2 Woodhouse Down S Glos
240 B2 Woodhouse Eaves Leics
292 B2 Woodhouse Green Staffs
470 D2 Woodhouselee Mdloth
311 G2 Woodhouse Park Manch
309 G4 Woodhouses Ches
400 B4 Woodhouses Cumb
326 D4 Woodhouses Oldham
237 G3 Woodhouses Staffs
274 A6 Woodhouses Staffs
311 F1 Woodhouses Traffd
220 D4 Woodhurst Cambs
56 B3 Woodingdean Br & H
71 F5 Woodington Hants
343 E5 Woodkirk Leeds
47 G6 Woodlake Dorset
363 E4 Woodland Cumb
11 H2 Woodland Devon
19 G4 Woodland Devon
394 B4 Woodland Dur
82 B2 Woodland Kent
26 B3 Woodland Head Devon
556 D5 Woodlands Abers
342 A4 Woodlands Calder
424 B4 Woodlands D & G
330 B3 Woodlands Donc
48 C3 Woodlands Dorset
118 C4 Woodlands Gt Lon
50 B2 Woodlands Hants
97 E2 Woodlands Kent
356 C4 Woodlands N York
64 C3 Woodlands Somset
67 E2 Woodlands Somset
327 E5 Woodlands Tamesd
116 C3 Woodlands Wokham
48 D3 Woodlands Common Dorset
116 D4 Woodlands Park W & M
114 A4 Woodlands St Mary W Berk
269 H3 Wood Lane Shrops
274 A5 Wood Lane Staffs
291 G4 Wood Lane Staffs
312 B3 Wood Lanes Ches
12 C5 Woodleigh Devon
343 G4 Woodlesford Leeds
71 H5 Woodley Stockp
326 D6 Woodley Stockp
116 C5 Woodley Wokham
116 C5 Woodley Green Wokham
295 E5 Woodlinkin Derbys
190 D1 Woodloes Park Warwks
135 G5 Woodmancote Gloucs
137 F3 Woodmancote Gloucs
163 E4 Woodmancote Gloucs
52 D3 Woodmancote W Susx
55 F2 Woodmancote W Susx
188 C6 Woodmancote Worcs
73 E1 Woodmancott Hants
347 F2 Woodmansey E R Yk
58 C3 Woodmans Green E Susx

74 D4 Woodmansgreen W Susx
95 F3 Woodmansterne Surrey
27 C5 Woodmanton Devon
274 A5 Woodmill Staffs
69 G5 Woodminton Wilts
101 E4 Woodnesborough Kent
243 E6 Woodnewton Nhants
314 C5 Woodnook Derbys
340 B4 Woodnook Lancs
278 C3 Woodnook Lincs
254 C2 Wood Norton Norfk
189 F5 Wood Norton Worcs
338 D3 Woodplumpton Lancs
43 H4 Woodram Somset
248 C4 Woodrising Norfk
326 A2 Wood Road Bury
142 C5 Woodrow Bucks
399 G5 Woodrow Cumb
46 D2 Woodrow Dorset
343 G4 Wood Row Leeds
189 G1 Woodrow Worcs
79 E3 Woodrow Worcs
237 E5 Woods Bank Wsall
79 H3 Wood's Corner E Susx
327 E6 Woodseats Derbys
329 E5 Wood Seats Sheff
185 F5 Woods Eaves Herefs
271 F3 Woodseaves Shrops
272 A4 Woodseaves Staffs
125 C2 Woodsend Pembks
325 G5 Woods End Traffd
113 F4 Woodsend Wilts
236 D6 Woodsetton Dudley
315 H3 Woodsetts Rothm
188 B5 Woodsfield Worcs
338 C2 Woodsfold Lancs
32 D1 Woodsford Dorset
79 E3 Wood's Green E Susx
195 F4 Woodside Beds
117 F5 Woodside Br For
342 B4 Woodside Brad
557 G3 Woodside C Aber
290 C2 Woodside Ches
309 H5 Woodside Ches
424 A5 Woodside D & G
294 D6 Woodside Derbys
295 E5 Woodside Derbys
212 D2 Woodside Dudley
394 D4 Woodside Dur
145 G4 Woodside Essex
501 E4 Woodside Fife
502 C3 Woodside Fife
95 G1 Woodside Gt Lon
50 B6 Woodside Hants
143 G4 Woodside Herts
144 C3 Woodside Herts
51 F6 Woodside IoW
567 K5 Woodside Moray
331 F4 Woodside N Linc
513 F2 Woodside P & K
126 C3 Woodside Pembks
209 E3 Woodside Shrops
235 F4 Woodside Wrekin
171 H6 Woodside Green Essex
99 E4 Woodside Green Kent
556 C5 Woodside of Arbeadie Abers
144 B6 Woodside Park Gt Lon
312 B6 Woods Moor Stockp
114 C6 Woodspeen W Berk
84 B1 Woodspring Priory N Som
163 G3 Wood Stanway Gloucs
98 D2 Woodstock Kent
139 G1 Woodstock Oxon
152 A4 Woodstock Pembks
244 A5 Woodston C Pete
256 D5 Wood Street Norfk
93 G4 Wood Street Village Surrey
315 E5 Woodthorpe Derbys
240 B1 Woodthorpe Leics
320 D3 Woodthorpe Lincs
296 A6 Woodthorpe Notts
357 H5 Woodthorpe York
250 B6 Woodton Norfk
39 G2 Woodtown Devon
323 F2 Woodvale Sefton
528 D6 Woodville Angus
275 E6 Woodville Derbys
68 D5 Woodville Dorset
528 C6 Woodville Feus Angus
272 A4 Woodwall Green Staffs
220 B3 Wood Walton Cambs
115 E3 Woodway Oxon
215 F3 Woodway Park Covtry
218 D4 Woodwell Nhants
602 D7 Woodwick Ork
290 B3 Woodworth Green Ches
69 H6 Woodyates Dorset
61 G2 Woody Bay Devon
210 C6 Woofferton Shrops
85 F5 Wookey Somset
85 F5 Wookey Hole Somset
33 E2 Wool Dorset
60 B3 Woolacombe Devon
100 D6 Woolage Green Kent
100 D5 Woolage Village Kent
134 D5 Woolaston Gloucs
134 D4 Woolaston Common Gloucs
134 D4 Woolaston Slade Gloucs
134 D4 Woolaston Woodside Gloucs
65 G3 Woolavington Somset
74 D5 Woolbeding W Susx
328 B3 Wooldale Kirk
454 B4 Wooler Nthumb
309 F1 Woolfall Heath Knows
41 G6 Woolfardisworthy Devon
38 D3 Woolfardisworthy or Woolsery Devon
326 A2 Woolfold Bury
469 F3 Woolfords Cottages S Lans
46 C3 Woolford's Water Dorset
34 A4 Woolgarston Dorset
91 F1 Woolhampton W Berk
161 E2 Woolhope Herefs
161 E2 Woolhope Cockshoot Herefs
47 E3 Woolland Dorset
86 A2 Woollard BaNES
39 G5 Woollaton Devon
144 D2 Woollensbrook Herts
110 C6 Woolley BaNES
219 H5 Woolley Cambs
58 C4 Woolley Cnwll
294 D2 Woolley Derbys
329 E2 Woolley Wakefd
87 E2 Woolley Wilts
327 F5 Woolley Bridge Tamesd
117 E3 Woolley Green W & M
87 E2 Woolley Green Wilts
189 E2 Woolmere Green Worcs
170 C6 Woolmer Green Herts
74 D3 Woolmer Hill Surrey
65 E5 Woolmersdon Somset
44 D6 Woolminstone Somset
80 C2 Woolpack Corner Kent
200 C3 Woolpit Suffk
200 C2 Woolpit Green Suffk
200 C3 Woolpit Heath Suffk
162 B5 Woolridge Gloucs
48 D3 Woolsbridge Dorset

216 A6 Woolscott Warwks
26 B2 Woolsgrove Devon
430 C6 Woolsington N u Ty
290 D3 Woolstanwood Ches
234 B5 Woolstaston Shrops
278 A3 Woolsthorpe by Belvoir Lincs
278 C5 Woolsthorpe-by-Colsterworth Lincs
50 D2 Woolston C Sotn
16 C5 Woolston Cnwll
12 C4 Woolston Devon
209 H2 Woolston Shrops
269 F5 Woolston Shrops
64 A4 Woolston Somset
67 G4 Woolston Somset
310 C2 Woolston Warrtn
163 E3 Woolstone Gloucs
168 B2 Woolstone M Keyn
113 G2 Woolstone Oxon
19 G4 Woolston Green Devon
309 F2 Woolton Lpool
90 C2 Woolton Hill Hants
84 C2 Woolvers Hill N Som
176 C2 Woolverstone Suffk
86 D4 Woolverton Somset
18 B5 Woolwell Devon
120 B4 Woolwich Gt Lon
120 B4 Woolwich Ferry Gt Lon
8 C2 Woon Cnwll
185 F4 Woonton Herefs
186 C2 Woonton Herefs
454 C5 Wooperton Nthumb
451 F1 Wooplaw Border
291 E6 Woore Shrops
116 C6 Woose Hill Wokham
30 B3 Wooth Dorset
210 D5 Wooton Shrops
211 H2 Wooton Shrops
226 A5 Wootten Green Suffk
195 E5 Wootton Beds
49 G5 Wootton Hants
160 D2 Wootton Herefs
185 F4 Wootton Herefs
51 F6 Wootton IoW
82 D1 Wootton Kent
333 F1 Wootton N Linc
195 G3 Wootton Nhants
140 A4 Wootton Oxon
165 G5 Wootton Oxon
210 A4 Wootton Shrops
269 F4 Wootton Shrops
272 B4 Wootton Staffs
293 F5 Wootton Staffs
112 C3 Wootton Bassett Wilts
194 D5 Wootton Bourne End Beds
37 E2 Wootton Bridge IoW
195 E6 Wootton Broadmead Beds
37 E2 Wootton Common IoW
63 E3 Wootton Courtenay Somset
29 G3 Wootton Fitzpaine Dorset
194 D6 Wootton Green Beds
214 C4 Wootton Green Solhll
89 E2 Wootton Rivers Wilts
273 G2 Woottons Staffs
91 F4 Wootton St Lawrence Hants
190 A2 Wootton Wawen Warwks
33 F4 Worbarrow Dorset
188 B3 Worcester Worcs
95 E1 Worcester Park Surrey
212 C3 Wordsley Dudley
223 G5 Wordwell Suffk
233 H5 Worfield Shrops
33 G2 Worgret Dorset
601 H2 Work Ork
256 C5 Workhouse Common Norfk
195 G4 Workhouse End Beds
174 B2 Workhouse Green Suffk
174 C3 Workhouse Hill Essex
388 A4 Workington Cumb
315 H4 Worksop Notts
320 B4 Worlaby Lincs
333 E2 Worlaby Lincs
142 A3 World's End Bucks
144 D5 World's End Gt Lon
52 A2 Worlds End Hants
214 A3 Worlds End Solhll
200 C3 World's End Suffk
114 D4 World's End W Berk
77 F4 World's End W Susx
84 B2 Worle N Som
84 B2 Worlebury N Som
290 D3 Worleston Ches
136 B5 Worley Gloucs
227 E2 Worlingham Suffk
60 C5 Worlington Devon
222 D5 Worlington Suffk
225 H6 Worlingworth Suffk
159 H3 Wormbridge Herefs
159 H3 Wormbridge Common Herefs
246 D2 Wormegay Norfk
160 B3 Wormelow Tump Herefs
313 F5 Wormhill Derbys
174 B3 Wormingford Essex
140 B3 Worminghall Bucks
163 F2 Wormington Gloucs
85 G6 Worminster Somset
514 B4 Wormit Fife
191 H2 Wormleighton Warwks
145 E3 Wormley Herts
75 E2 Wormley Surrey
144 D3 Wormleybury Herts
212 D5 Worms Ash Worcs
79 G2 Worms Hill Kent
98 D3 Wormshill Kent
185 H5 Wormsley Herefs
291 G1 Wornish Nook Ches
93 G4 Worplesdon Surrey
314 B1 Worrall Sheff
135 E2 Worrall Hill Gloucs
329 F4 Worsbrough Barns
329 F4 Worsbrough Dale Barns
138 D2 Worsham Oxon
325 G4 Worsley Salfd
324 D4 Worsley Hall Wigan
256 C4 Worstead Norfk
340 D3 Worsthorne Lancs
11 G3 Worston Devon
353 F6 Worston Lancs
99 F6 Worten Kent
101 F4 Worth Kent
85 F5 Worth Somset
77 F2 Worth W Susx
77 F3 Worth Abbey W Susx
225 E4 Wortham Suffk
233 F4 Worthen Shrops
289 F5 Worthenbury Wrexhm
254 D4 Worthing Norfk
55 E4 Worthing W Susx
275 F5 Worthington Leics
34 A5 Worth Matravers Dorset
62 D2 Worthy Somset
134 B2 Worthybrook Mons
91 H4 Worting Hants
328 D5 Wortley Barns
110 D1 Wortley Gloucs
343 E3 Wortley Leeds
368 C1 Worton N York
139 H2 Worton Oxon
87 H3 Worton Wilts
226 B2 Wortwell Norfk

233 E4 **Wotherton** Shrops
243 E3 **Wothorpe** C Pete
18 C5 **Wotter** Devon
162 B6 **Wotton** Gloucs
94 C5 **Wotton** Surrey
19 G4 **Wotton Cross** Devon
135 H6 **Wotton-under-Edge** Gloucs
141 E1 **Wotton Underwood** Bucks
168 B2 **Woughton on the Green** M Keyn
97 H2 **Wouldham** Kent
235 H6 **Woundale** Shrops
176 C3 **Wrabness** Essex
60 C4 **Wrafton** Devon
319 E4 **Wragby** Lincs
335 E5 **Wragholme** Lincs
249 F3 **Wramplingham** Norfk
19 E6 **Wrangaton** Devon
330 A2 **Wrangbrook** Wakefd
559 E3 **Wrangham** Abers
300 D4 **Wrangle** Lincs
300 D4 **Wrangle Bank** Lincs
300 D4 **Wrangle Lowgate** Lincs
300 D4 **Wrangle Low Ground** Lincs
43 F4 **Wrangway** Somset
44 C3 **Wrantage** Somset
333 E3 **Wrawby** N Linc
30 D2 **Wraxall** Dorset
109 E5 **Wraxall** N Som
67 G2 **Wraxall** Somset
366 C6 **Wray** Lancs
95 F4 **Wray Common** Surrey
117 H5 **Wraysbury** W & M
366 C5 **Wrayton** Lancs
338 B3 **Wrea Green** Lancs
363 E4 **Wreaks End** Cumb
44 C6 **Wreath** Somset
527 E6 **Wreaths** Angus
390 C5 **Wreay** Cumb
400 D5 **Wreay** Cumb
92 D5 **Wrecclesham** Surrey
405 G3 **Wrekenton** Gatesd
373 E2 **Wrelton** N York
290 B5 **Wrenbury** Ches
249 G5 **Wreningham** Norfk
227 F3 **Wrentham** Suffk
343 F5 **Wrenthorpe** Wakefd
233 H4 **Wrentnall** Shrops
345 G3 **Wressle** E R Yk
332 D3 **Wressle** N Linc
196 C5 **Wrestlingworth** Beds
224 B2 **Wretham** Norfk
246 D5 **Wretton** Norfk
289 E4 **Wrexham** Wrexhm
19 G1 **Wreyland** Devon
212 A4 **Wribbenhall** Worcs
211 E2 **Wrickton** Shrops
324 C2 **Wrightington Bar** Lancs
145 H1 **Wright's Green** Essex
310 C3 **Wrights Green** Warrtn
291 F5 **Wrinehill** Staffs
23 G5 **Wringsdown** Cnwll
85 E2 **Wrington** N Som
38 D3 **Wrinkleberry** Devon
86 C4 **Writhlington** BaNES
146 D3 **Writtle** Essex
235 E2 **Wrockwardine** Wrekin
331 F4 **Wroot** N Linc
97 E3 **Wrotham** Kent
97 F3 **Wrotham Heath** Kent
144 B5 **Wrotham Park** Herts

113 E3 **Wroughton** Swindn
168 B2 **Wroughton Park** M Keyn
37 F5 **Wroxall** IoW
214 C5 **Wroxall** Warwks
234 D3 **Wroxeter** Shrops
250 C1 **Wroxham** Norfk
165 G1 **Wroxton** Oxon
293 G6 **Wyaston** Derbys
146 C5 **Wyatt's Green** Essex
334 B3 **Wybers Wood** NE Lin
280 D1 **Wyberton** Lincs
195 H3 **Wyboston** Beds
290 D4 **Wybunbury** Ches
188 D1 **Wychbold** Worcs
77 H3 **Wych Cross** E Susx
187 H6 **Wyche** Herefs
238 B1 **Wychnor** Staffs
238 B1 **Wychnor Bridges** Staffs
74 B2 **Wyck** Hants
164 B5 **Wyck Rissington** Gloucs
382 D2 **Wycliffe** Dur
341 E2 **Wycoller** Lancs
277 G5 **Wycomb** Leics
117 E1 **Wycombe Marsh** Bucks
171 E3 **Wyddial** Herts
355 H4 **Wydra** N York
99 H5 **Wye** Kent
99 E4 **Wyebanks** Kent
134 D3 **Wyegate Green** Gloucs
134 C2 **Wyesham** Mons
277 G6 **Wyfordby** Leics
342 C4 **Wyke** Brad
68 C4 **Wyke** Dorset
235 E4 **Wyke** Shrops
93 F4 **Wyke** Surrey
67 H3 **Wyke Champflower** Somset
29 E3 **Wyke Green** Devon
280 C4 **Wykeham** Lincs
373 F4 **Wykeham** N York
374 B3 **Wykeham** N York
215 F3 **Wyken** Covtry
235 H6 **Wyken** Shrops
32 B4 **Wyke Regis** Dorset
269 G4 **Wykey** Shrops
239 F5 **Wykin** Leics
404 D2 **Wylam** Nthumb
210 B6 **Wylde** Herefs
237 H6 **Wylde Green** Birm
132 C6 **Wyllie** Caerph
69 H2 **Wylye** Wilts
162 D5 **Wymans Brook** Gloucs
167 H2 **Wymbush** M Keyn
52 A3 **Wymering** C Port
276 D5 **Wymeswold** Leics
194 D2 **Wymington** Beds
278 B6 **Wymondham** Leics
249 F4 **Wymondham** Norfk
170 B4 **Wymondley Bury** Herts
338 D5 **Wymott** Lancs
105 E1 **Wyndham** Brdgnd
106 A4 **Wyndham Park** V Glam
161 G1 **Wynds Point** Herefs
30 D3 **Wynford Eagle** Dorset
600 E6 **Wyng** Ork
187 E5 **Wynn's Green** Herefs
396 B4 **Wynyard Village** S on T
189 E5 **Wyre Piddle** Worcs
276 D4 **Wysall** Notts
186 C1 **Wyson** Herefs
213 G5 **Wythall** Worcs
139 H3 **Wytham** Oxon

311 G2 **Wythenshawe** Manch
389 E4 **Wythop Mill** Cumb
348 C3 **Wyton** E R Yk
224 D6 **Wyverstone** Suffk
200 D1 **Wyverstone Green** Suffk
224 D6 **Wyverstone Street** Suffk
278 B4 **Wyville** Lincs

Y

332 B3 **Yaddlethorpe** N Linc
36 C4 **Yafford** IoW
384 A6 **Yafforth** N York
451 F3 **Yair** Border
20 B6 **Yalberton** Torbay
97 H4 **Yalding** Kent
109 F6 **Yanley** N Som
391 E4 **Yanwath** Cumb
137 G2 **Yanworth** Gloucs
359 E4 **Yapham** E R Yk
54 A4 **Yapton** W Susx
84 C3 **Yarberry** N Som
334 B3 **Yarborough** NE Lin
37 G3 **Yarbridge** IoW
335 E6 **Yarburgh** Lincs
44 A6 **Yarcombe** Devon
63 H4 **Yarde** Somset
80 D1 **Yardhurst** Kent
213 H2 **Yardley** Birm
193 G6 **Yardley Gobion** Nhants
194 B3 **Yardley Hastings** Nhants
213 H4 **Yardley Wood** Birm
184 D3 **Yardro** Powys
43 H2 **Yarford** Somset
188 A1 **Yarhampton** Worcs
187 H1 **Yarhampton Cross** Worcs
187 E6 **Yarkhill** Herefs
272 D4 **Yarlet** Staffs
85 E5 **Yarley** Somset
67 H4 **Yarlington** Somset
364 B6 **Yarlside** Cumb
384 C2 **Yarm** S on T
36 B3 **Yarmouth** IoW
61 F5 **Yarnacott** Devon
87 F4 **Yarnbrook** Wilts
272 C3 **Yarnfield** Staffs
190 B1 **Yarningale Common** Warwks
40 B3 **Yarnscombe** Devon
140 A2 **Yarnton** Oxon
186 B2 **Yarpole** Herefs
450 D4 **Yarrow** Border
427 H2 **Yarrow** Nthumb
84 C5 **Yarrow** Somset
450 C4 **Yarrow Feus** Border
450 D3 **Yarrowford** Border
185 H5 **Yarsop** Herefs
243 F5 **Yarwell** Nhants
110 C3 **Yate** S Glos
92 D2 **Yateley** Hants
110 C3 **Yate Rocks** S Glos
112 C5 **Yatesbury** Wilts
115 E5 **Yattendon** W Berk
186 A1 **Yatton** Herefs
84 D1 **Yatton** N Som
111 F4 **Yatton Keynell** Wilts
37 G3 **Yaverland** IoW
29 F4 **Yawl** Devon
317 G1 **Yawthorpe** Lincs

248 D2 **Yaxham** Norfk
220 A1 **Yaxley** Cambs
225 F5 **Yaxley** Suffk
185 H5 **Yazor** Herefs
45 E4 **Yeabridge** Somset
118 C3 **Yeading** Gt Lon
342 D1 **Yeadon** Leeds
365 H5 **Yealand Conyers** Lancs
365 G4 **Yealand Redmayne** Lancs
365 G4 **Yealand Storrs** Lancs
11 G3 **Yealmbridge** Devon
11 G3 **Yealmpton** Devon
397 E5 **Yearby** R & Cl
399 E6 **Yearngill** Cumb
372 A5 **Yearsley** N York
270 A6 **Yeaton** Shrops
274 B1 **Yeaveley** Derbys
373 G4 **Yedingham** N York
195 E1 **Yelden** Beds
294 A6 **Yeldersley Hollies** Derbys
139 F4 **Yelford** Oxon
60 C5 **Yelland** Devon
196 C2 **Yelling** Cambs
98 C2 **Yelsted** Kent
216 D4 **Yelvertoft** Nhants
18 B4 **Yelverton** Devon
250 B4 **Yelverton** Norfk
68 B5 **Yenston** Somset
26 B3 **Yeoford** Devon
23 G5 **Yeolmbridge** Cnwll
41 G2 **Yeo Mill** Devon
39 F3 **Yeo Vale** Devon
45 G4 **Yeovil** Somset
67 E6 **Yeovil Marsh** Somset
67 E5 **Yeovilton** Somset
126 B3 **Yerbeston** Pembks
600 C1 **Yesnaby** Ork
442 C3 **Yetlington** Nthumb
46 A2 **Yetminster** Dorset
468 B3 **Yett** N Lans
27 G5 **Yettington** Devon
499 G4 **Yetts O' Muckhart** Clacks
190 C1 **Yew Green** Warwks
99 F3 **Yewhedges** Kent
237 F5 **Yew Tree** Sandw
327 E5 **Yew Tree** Tamesd
82 C2 **Yewtree Cross** Kent
207 E2 **Y Fan** Powys
283 F2 **Y Felinheli** Gwynd
178 D4 **Y Ferwig** Cerdgn
263 F5 **Y Ffôr** Gwynd
307 E3 **Y-Ffrith** Denbgs
205 E4 **Y Gors** Cerdgn
207 E1 **Y Gribyn** Powys
468 D4 **Yieldshields** S Lans
118 B3 **Yiewsley** Gt Lon
601 J2 **Yinstay** Ork
129 F3 **Ynus-Tawelog** Swans
264 D2 **Ynys** Gwynd
131 H5 **Ynysboeth** Rhondd
106 C1 **Ynysddu** Caerph
129 G5 **Ynysforgan** Swans
131 G6 **Ynyshir** Rhondd
130 B2 **Ynys-isaf** Powys
229 E6 **Ynyslas** Cerdgn
130 A5 **Ynysmaerdy** Neath
105 G3 **Ynysmaerdy** Rhondd
129 H3 **Ynysmeudwy** Neath
229 E6 **Ynys Tachwedd** Cerdgn
129 G4 **Ynystawe** Swans
130 C2 **Ynyswen** Powys

131 F5 **Ynyswen** Rhondd
131 G6 **Ynysybwl** Rhondd
104 B1 **Ynysygwas** Neath
368 B4 **Yockenthwaite** N York
233 H3 **Yockleton** Shrops
43 E5 **Yodercott** Devon
346 B5 **Yokefleet** E R Yk
483 H6 **Yoker** C Glas
569 K6 **Yonder Bognie** Abers
18 C6 **Yondertown** Devon
30 B4 **Yondover** Dorset
97 E4 **Yopps Green** Kent
339 H3 **York** Lancs
358 A4 **York** York
467 E1 **Yorkhill** C Glas
100 A3 **Yorkletts** Kent
135 E3 **Yorkley** Gloucs
135 E3 **Yorkley Slade** Gloucs
93 E3 **York Town** Surrey
270 B5 **Yorton** Shrops
270 B5 **Yorton Heath** Shrops
376 C4 **Yottenfews** Cumb
293 G2 **Youlgreave** Derbys
359 E3 **Youlthorpe** E R Yk
357 F2 **Youlton** N York
171 E6 **Youngsbury** Herts
173 E6 **Young's End** Essex
319 E5 **Young Wood** Lincs
274 A6 **Yoxall** Staffs
226 D6 **Yoxford** Suffk
205 G4 **Ysbyty Cynfyn** Cerdgn
286 A5 **Ysbyty Ifan** Conwy
205 G5 **Ysbyty Ystwyth** Cerdgn
307 H5 **Ysceifiog** Flints
287 F3 **Ysgeibion** Denbgs
129 E5 **Yspitty** Carmth
130 A3 **Ystalyfera** Neath
131 F5 **Ystrad** Rhondd
180 D3 **Ystrad Aeron** Cerdgn
131 E2 **Ystradfellte** Powys
182 B5 **Ystradffin** Carmth
130 B2 **Ystradgynlais** Powys
205 G6 **Ystradmeurig** Cerdgn
132 C6 **Ystrad Mynach** Caerph
130 B2 **Ystradowen** Carmth
105 G4 **Ystradowen** V Glam
232 A4 **Ystrad Uchaf** Powys
205 G4 **Ystumtuen** Cerdgn
560 D3 **Ythanbank** Abers
559 E2 **Ythanwells** Abers
560 C3 **Ythsie** Abers

Z

25 H2 **Zeal Monachorum** Devon
68 C3 **Zeals** Wilts
7 F3 **Zelah** Cnwll
3 E2 **Zennor** Cnwll
5 E5 **Zoar** Cnwll
276 B5 **Zouch** Notts

Distances and journey times

The mileage chart shows distances in miles between two towns along AA-recommended routes. Using motorways and other main roads this is normally the fastest route, though not necessarily the shortest.

The journey times, shown in hours and minutes, are average off-peak driving times along AA-recommended routes. These times should be used as a guide only and do not allow for unforeseen traffic delays, rest breaks or fuel stops.

For example, the 378 miles (608 km) journey between Glasgow and Norwich should take approximately 7 hours 28 minutes.

journey times

The chart shows a large triangular mileage and journey-times matrix between the following towns (listed along the diagonal): Aberdeen, Aberystwyth, Barnstaple, Birmingham, Brighton, Bristol, Cambridge, Cardiff, Carlisle, Carmarthen, Dorchester, Dover, Edinburgh, Exeter, Fort William, Glasgow, Gloucester, Guildford, Hereford, Holyhead, Hull, Inverness, Kendal, Leeds, Lincoln, Liverpool, Maidstone, Manchester, Middlesbrough, Newcastle, Northampton, Norwich, Nottingham, Oxford, Penzance, Perth, Peterborough, Plymouth, Portsmouth, Preston, Salisbury, Sheffield, Shrewsbury, Southampton, Stoke-on-Trent, Stranraer, Taunton, Wick, York, LONDON.

distances in miles (one mile equals 1.6093 km)